D1583484
THE UNIVERSITY OF BIRMINGHAM
INFORMATION SERVICES

Seventh Edition

UK & International GAAP

Generally Accepted Accounting Practice in the United Kingdom and under International Accounting Standards

Allister Wilson, Mike Davies,
Matthew Curtis & Gregory Wilkinson-Riddle

© Copyright Ernst & Young LLP 2001.

The United Kingdom firm of Ernst & Young LLP is a membe: of Ernst & Young International.

All rights reserved. No reproduction, copy or transmission of this publication may be made without prior written permission. No paragraph may be reproduced, copied or transmitted save with written permission or in accordance with the provisions of the Copyright and Patents Act 1988, or under the terms of any licence permitting limited copying issued by the Copyright Licensing Agency, 90 Tottenham Court Road, London, W19 9HE.

Any person who does any unauthorised act in relation to this publication may be liable to criminal prosecution and civil claims for damages.

Seventh Edition published 2001 by:

Butterworths Tolley
35 Chancery Lane
London
WC2A 1EL

http://www.gaap.co.uk

ISBN 0 4069 45527

22074570

A catalogue reference for this book is available from the British Library.

This publication has been carefully prepared, but it necessarily contains information in summary form and is therefore intended for general guidance only, and is not intended to be a substitute for detailed research or the exercise of professional judgement. The publishers and Ernst & Young LLP can accept no responsibility for loss occasioned to any person acting or refraining from action as a result of any material in this publication. On any specific matter, reference should be made to the appropriate adviser.

Printed and bound in the UK by William Clowes Limited, Beccles and London.

Foreword to the seventh edition

Stephen A. Zeff
Herbert S. Autrey Professor of Accounting
Rice University
Texas, USA

Following six successful editions of *UK GAAP*, the Financial Reporting Group of Ernst & Young have wisely refocussed their 7th edition on UK and International GAAP. The newly restructured International Accounting Standards Board is working in tandem with the UK Accounting Standards Board, the US Financial Accounting Standards Board, and six other national standard-setting boards to establish high quality International Financial Reporting Standards, constituting International GAAP. It will make every effort to converge these standards with those approved by the eight national boards. In view of the European Commission's decision to require all listed companies in the European Union to adopt International GAAP in their consolidated statements no later than 2005, the emphasis in the UK has shifted from national standards alone to their correspondence with international standards.

UK & International GAAP matches the high standard set in its six previous editions. The authors provide extensive correlations and comparisons between UK GAAP and International GAAP. Unlike most other works of the genre, it is not a mere compilation, description and distillation of standards and practices. In each of the subject area chapters, the authors provide

- a succinct and instructive historical background;
- clear explanations of the UK and international standards and their practical implications for companies, auditors and users; and
- reasoned analyses of the standards and even criticisms where appropriate.

All of this is accompanied by a wealth of numerical examples, diagrams and extracts from actual company financial statements. In my view, no textbook or handbook published in any country is the equal of this volume in clarity, comprehensiveness and incisive commentary.

Chapter 1 should be cited in particular, as it contains an outstanding review and analysis of recent and ongoing financial reporting developments in the UK as well as at the European and international levels.

This handbook continues to be without peer both as an authoritative work for use by experts as well as a textbook for those who seek a grounding in the field.

September 2001

Stephen A. Zeff

Introduction to the seventh edition

Karel Van Hulle*
Head of Unit
Financial Reporting and Company Law
European Commission

Application of IAS within the EU

On 13 February 2001, the European Commission adopted a Proposal for a Regulation which requires all listed EU companies to prepare their consolidated financial statements in conformity with IAS by 2005. This proposal implements the Communication which the Commission published in June 2000 and which sets out the strategy that the Commission believes to be necessary in the accounting field in order to create an integrated capital market in the EU.

Before IAS become part of the EU's legal environment, they must formally be adopted. Adoption will take place by the Commission. The Commission will be assisted in this process by the Accounting Regulatory Committee, composed of representatives of the Member States and chaired by a representative of the Commission. The technical input to this process will come from the private sector through EFRAG (the European Financial Reporting Advisory Group).

It is the Commission's intention that all standards and interpretations issued by the IASC (the predecessor of the IASB) will be adopted as they stand. However, there may be difficulties, particularly with the first time application of the Standards and related Interpretations. In order to facilitate the transition process towards IAS, the Commission has asked the IASB to examine as a matter of priority how companies, which are not applying IAS at present, can move to IAS without having to restate all past transactions. It is expected that the IASB will come forward with a proposal before the end of the year. This proposal will be issued for comment.

* The views expressed in this introduction are only attributable to the author.

As far as future standards are concerned, it is of the utmost importance that the EU be present at the negotiating table from the very start. It is expected that this will happen through EFRAG. Users and preparers of financial statements, the accounting profession, as well as standard setters and regulators in the EU must be closely associated with the international accounting standard setting process. If this is not the case and if standards are adopted without taking account of concerns that exist within the EU, the process of adoption of those standards will be very difficult. In this respect, it is important to underline that the Commission is not in favour of the creation of Euro-IAS. The intention is to adopt IAS without local (EU) variations. If there are major concerns with a standard, the only option available will be to reject it in its entirety. Rejection of a standard would mean, in any event, that something had gone wrong in the process. Indeed, it is to be expected that the IASB would have been made aware of any major concerns raised by the EU, which after all is its major constituency.

If one looks at the Community as a whole, the requirement to apply IAS will apply to some 10,000 companies. Further, to the extent that the companies concerned are parent undertakings of a group, they could well want all members of the group to adapt their accounting systems to IAS in order to facilitate the consolidation process. This means that the number of companies that will be affected directly by IAS will be much larger.

In addition, Member States will be permitted to extend the requirement to apply IAS to other companies. They may also want the application of IAS in individual accounts. In the fields of banking and insurance, it is expected that a number of Member States will want all banks and insurance companies to apply IAS in order to facilitate prudential supervision. Several Member States have also indicated that they will eventually want companies to apply IAS in both individual and consolidated accounts.

IAS as an option under the Accounting Directives

The Accounting Directives do not aim to create uniform accounting rules for limited liability companies throughout the EU. Their objective is to ensure that all limited liability companies produce equivalent and comparable financial information. The emphasis is put more on equivalence than on comparability. Indeed, full comparability is difficult because the Directives contain a whole series of accounting options and because they do not deal with a large number of accounting issues which, as a consequence, are treated individually by Member States.

If the EU wants to move in the direction of an integrated capital market, it is clear that more harmonisation is needed than is presently possible under the Accounting Directives. As early as 1995, the Commission suggested that Member States should allow their global players to prepare their consolidated accounts on the basis of internationally accepted accounting standards, with a clear preference for IAS. That suggestion has been taken up by a number of Member States.

Seven Member States (Austria, Belgium, Finland, France, Germany, Italy and Luxembourg) already allow their companies to depart from national accounting requirements in order to prepare their consolidated financial statements in accordance with IAS (or US GAAP). While Member States may allow a departure from national rules, they clearly cannot allow a departure from EU law. Application of IAS is perfectly possible under the Directives to the extent that no conflicts exist between IAS and the Accounting Directives. In order to help Member States and companies in their assessment of the conformity between IAS and the Accounting Directives, the Commission has set up a Technical Sub-Committee of the Contact Committee on the Accounting Directives which has examined all IAS and interpretations of the SIC for conformity with the Accounting Directives. The results of these examinations have been made public and can be consulted on the Commission's website:

http://europa.eu.int/comm/internal_market/en/company/index.htm

Overall, there are at present only a few conflicts. Indeed, many conflicts can be avoided because both the Directives and IAS contain options, and it is possible for companies to choose those options that avoid a conflict.

If there is a conflict, there is no doubt that companies must give priority to what is required under the Directives. On the other hand, compliance with the Directives in the case of a conflict with an IAS would mean that full compliance with IAS is not possible. This is a problem, because the company can then no longer state that its financial statements are prepared in accordance with IAS. Such a statement is indeed only possible if there is full compliance.

With the adoption on 30 May 2001 of the Directive amending the Fourth and Seventh Directives on annual and consolidated accounts as well as the Bank Accounts Directive concerning the valuation rules, an important conflict between the Accounting Directives and IAS has been removed. Member States are now allowed to permit or require all or certain companies to fair value certain financial assets and liabilities in accordance with the requirements of IAS 39.

IAS as a requirement under the Accounting Directives

When the Commission was preparing its new accounting strategy, it also had to consider the future role of the Accounting Directives under a regime that would require a number of companies to comply with IAS.

The easiest way to deal with this would have been to exclude those companies that apply IAS from the scope of the Accounting Directives. This could have been done in different ways: exemption of listed companies; exemption of companies preparing consolidated financial statements; exemption of those companies applying IAS from most articles in the Directives.

After careful consideration, the Commission has decided to adopt a solution whereby compliance with the Accounting Directives will still be required for all limited liability companies, whether or not they apply IAS. However, at the same time, the conformity requirement is formulated in such a manner that there is no need to amend the Accounting Directives each time a new IAS or SIC interpretation is issued by the IASB.

The Commission has also announced that it will come forward before the end of 2001 with a proposal to modernise the Accounting Directives so as to remove the remaining conflicts with IAS, to introduce new options which are allowed under IAS but not yet allowed under the Accounting Directives, and to make it possible for Member States who so wish to gradually adapt their accounting rules to IAS.

IAS and US GAAP

The Commission's declared intention to require the application of IAS by listed EU companies in 2005 was explicitly endorsed by the Council and by the European Parliament. The objective is to create more comparability within the EU between companies participating in the same capital market, thereby contributing to the development of a more efficient and integrated market.

The objective of comparability requires the application of a single set of accounting standards. These standards will be IAS and not US GAAP. Preference is indeed given to standards that are truly international and which are not linked to any particular national environment.

Of course, the Commission realises that a minority of (important) European companies are listed in the US and that these companies are still required to prepare their financial statements in accordance with US GAAP, or to prepare a reconciliation statement. Rather than to postpone the introduction of the requirement to apply IAS until such time as the Securities and Exchange Commission in the US accepts for listing purposes financial statements prepared on the basis of IAS, the Commission believes that the possible benefits resulting from more comparability within the European environment are such that it would not be right to postpone the introduction of this requirement. However, the Commission will do whatever it can to promote convergence between IAS and US GAAP in the expectation that the situation will have improved considerably by 2005. The IASB has also indicated that convergence is one of its priorities. It has, however, rightly indicated that this convergence should not necessarily exclusively go in the direction of US GAAP.

Enforcement

Requiring the application of IAS does not mean that each company can decide for itself how it intends to comply with IAS. Many companies pretend to apply IAS although they are only applying a "lite" version of IAS. This is not acceptable. The creation of an efficient capital market is not possible if there is no true enforcement of the standards that have to be applied.

The Commission has announced that it regards the proper enforcement of accounting standards as a high priority. This requires not only co-operation from the companies that prepare financial statements, but also from their auditors and from securities regulators. The securities regulators in the EU who are members of CESR (Committee of European Securities Regulators) have decided to set up a special committee that will specifically look into matters of enforcement.

Concluding remarks

The introduction of a requirement for listed EU companies to apply IAS in their consolidated financial statements is quite revolutionary. The Commission attaches great importance to this. It is the only way in which the EU can make real progress towards the creation of an integrated capital market. The ultimate objective must be to lower the cost of capital for companies and to make European industry more competitive.

With the creation of EFRAG, the EU now has an infrastructure that allows it to participate directly in the international accounting standard setting process. This process is now dominated by national accounting standard setting bodies, primarily (if not exclusively) from Anglo-Saxon countries. Accounting standard setting is a complex process. Contributing to this process requires considerable effort. It also implies a change in mentality for many EU countries. Financial reporting will have to move away from conservative, tax-oriented reporting to a system whereby the needs of investors (and other stakeholders) are the primary focus.

September 2001 *Karel Van Hulle*

Preface to the seventh edition

In the Preface to the sixth edition we called for the recognition of International Accounting Standards (IAS) in UK law, on the grounds that this was both a competitive issue for international companies registered in the UK and an issue of pan-European comparability in financial reporting. Since then, two significant events have occurred that will change dramatically the course of European and, ultimately, world accounting:

- First, at the summit of the European Heads of Government held in Lisbon in March 2000, it was agreed that a single European capital market should be developed as a matter of priority. It was acknowledged further that the adoption of a single financial reporting framework for the European Union was a vital element in that process. Consequently, in February 2001, the European Commission published a draft EU Regulation that would require publicly traded EU incorporated companies to prepare, by 2005 at the latest, consolidated accounts under IAS endorsed for application within the EU.
- Second, in April 2001, after twenty-eight years of distinction, the IASC Board was restructured into the International Accounting Standards Board (IASB), under the leadership of Sir David Tweedie. The IASB has now assumed the mantle of global standard-setter.

It is therefore now clear that the notion of global accounting standards, accepted by the international capital markets for cross-border filings, is beginning to emerge as a real possibility. It is clear also that GAAP transcends national boundaries. The IASB has been unambiguous in announcing that it wants to develop International GAAP in partnership with national standard-setters, with global convergence as the goal. And there lies the challenge for David Tweedie and his colleagues: convergence implies people coming together from different directions so as to meet at one place. In accounting standard-setting terms this means the constructive engagement of all constituencies in the quest for harmonised, high quality and transparent financial reporting. It does not mean the dominance of one group over another, or convergence towards one pre-determined solution. The IASB has set itself an ambitious technical agenda, and is planning to tackle some highly controversial issues, such as share-based payments and performance measurement. Its future will depend on how successful it and its national standard-setting partners are in embracing the wider financial reporting community of preparers, users, auditors and regulators.

For these reasons, and in recognition of the international dimension of GAAP and the already substantial influence that international accounting developments are having on European accounting, this seventh edition has been re-named as **UK & International GAAP**. This edition, which has grown by approximately 500 pages, now includes a comprehensive analysis and commentary on the requirements of IAS, illustrated in practice by approximately 130 extracts from the accounts of global companies reporting under International GAAP.

Needless to say, however, we still recognise the importance of UK GAAP, and UK developments are also fully covered A full analysis of all new UK pronouncements, in particular the four new standards published in the last two years, is included. The new UK standards on retirement benefits and deferred tax are particularly complex, and these have been comprehensively explained. In addition, two completely new chapters devoted to hyperinflation and the accounting for employee benefits, including share options, have been added to ensure these matters are specifically dealt with.

As with all previous editions, we are indebted to many of our colleagues in the Financial Reporting Group of Ernst & Young for their help with the publication of this book, most notably Larissa Connor, Tim Denton, Richard Moore, Trevor Pijper and Hedy Richards. We also wish to record our thanks to the many other members of the Financial Reporting Group who contributed both directly and indirectly to the book's creation, especially Denise Brand, Audrey Davis and Gary Hughes. We also received invaluable assistance from colleagues in both the UK and the International firms of Ernst & Young, and our sincere thanks are especially due to John Alton, Tony Clifford, Ken Marshall, Angus McIntyre, Alan Olivey, Paul Rutteman, Leo van der Tas and Mira Tugnait.

The contribution of our colleague Pieter Dekker, both to the content, and to the technical aspects of the book's production, has been particularly important and deserves a special mention.

As authors, however, we take responsibility for all the opinions expressed in the book and the blame for all its faults.

September 2001

Allister Wilson
Mike Davies
Matthew Curtis
Gregory Wilkinson-Riddle

List of chapters

Detailed contents

CHAPTER 3 REVENUE RECOGNITION 169

CHAPTER 7 ASSOCIATES, JOINT VENTURES AND JANES 475

CHAPTER 8 FOREIGN CURRENCIES 555

CHAPTER 9 HYPERINFLATION 675

CHAPTER 10 FINANCIAL INSTRUMENTS 703

CHAPTER 11 INTANGIBLE ASSETS AND GOODWILL 883

CHAPTER 12 TANGIBLE FIXED ASSETS 939

CHAPTER 13 IMPAIRMENT OF FIXED ASSETS AND GOODWILL 1025

CHAPTER 16 STOCKS AND LONG-TERM CONTRACTS 1111

CHAPTER 17 CAPITAL INSTRUMENTS 1151

CHAPTER 18 OFF BALANCE SHEET TRANSACTIONS 1233

CHAPTER 19 LEASES AND HIRE PURCHASE CONTRACTS 1323

CHAPTER 20 GOVERNMENT GRANTS 1399

CHAPTER 21 SEGMENTAL REPORTING 1419

CHAPTER 22 EMPLOYEE BENEFITS 1445

CHAPTER 23 RETIREMENT BENEFITS 1515

CHAPTER 24 TAXATION 1645

CHAPTER 25 REPORTING FINANCIAL PERFORMANCE 1779

CHAPTER 26 EARNINGS PER SHARE 1865

CHAPTER 27 POST BALANCE SHEET EVENTS 1921

CHAPTER 28 PROVISIONS AND CONTINGENCIES 1949

CHAPTER 29 CASH FLOW STATEMENTS 2039

CHAPTER 30 RELATED PARTIES 2077

CHAPTER 31 DIRECTORS' AND OFFICERS' LOANS AND TRANSACTIONS 2129

CHAPTER 33 INTERIM REPORTS AND PRELIMINARY ANNOUNCEMENTS 2243

Abbreviations

The following abbreviations are used in this book:

Professional and regulatory bodies:

AICPA	American Institute of Certified Public Accountants
APB	Accounting Principles Board (of the AICPA, predecessor of the FASB)
	The Auditing Practices Board (in the UK)
ARC	Accounting Regulatory Committee of representatives of EU Member States
ASB	Accounting Standards Board (the standard-setting arm of the FRC)
ASC	Accounting Standards Committee (the predecessor of the ASB)
CCAB	Consultative Committee of Accountancy Bodies
CESR	The Committee of European Securities Regulators
DTI	Department of Trade and Industry
EFRAG	The European Financial Reporting Advisory Group
FASB	Financial Accounting Standards Board (in the US)
FRC	Financial Reporting Council (in the UK, oversees the ASB, FRRP and UITF)
FRRP	The Financial Reporting Review Panel (the policing arm of the FRC)
G4+1	The (now disbanded) group of four plus 1, actually with six members, that comprised an informal 'think tank' of standard setters from Australia, Canada, New Zealand, UK, and USA, plus the IASC
IASB	International Accounting Standards Board
IASC	International Accounting Standards Committee
ICAEW	The Institute of Chartered Accountants in England and Wales
ICAS	The Institute of Chartered Accountants of Scotland
IFRIC	International Financial Reporting Interpretations Committee of the IASB
IOSCO	The International Organisation of Securities Commissions
JWG	Joint Working Group of Standard-setters
SEC	Securities and Exchange Commission (the USA securities regulator)
SIC	The Standing Interpretations Committee of the IASC (to be replaced by IFRIC)
UITF	The Urgent Issues Task Force (a subsidiary committee of the ASB)

Accounting related terms:

CA 85	The Companies Act 1985, as amended by the Companies Act 1989
CCA	Current cost accounting
CIS	Comprehensive income statement, as developed by the G4+1 group of accounting standard-setters, and published in June 1999 in the ASB Discussion Paper *Reporting Financial Performance: Proposals for Change*
E	Exposure Draft (of an IAS)
EBITDA	Earnings Before Interest Taxation Depreciation and Amortisation
ED	Exposure Draft (of a SSAP)
EPS	Earnings per share
FIFO	The first-in, first-out basis of valuation
FRED	Financial Reporting Exposure Draft (of a UK FRS)
FRS	Financial Reporting Standard (issued by the ASB)
GAAP	Generally accepted accounting practice (as it applies to the UK and under IAS), or generally accepted accounting principles (as it applies to the US)
IAS	International Accounting Standard (issued by the IASC)
IFRS	International Financial Reporting Standard (to be issued by the IASB)
LIFO	The last-in, first-out basis of valuation
NRV	Net realisable value
OFR	Operating and financial review
R&D	Research and development
SFAC	Statement of Financial Accounting Concepts (issued by the FASB as part of its conceptual framework project)
SFAS	Statement of Financial Accounting Standards (issued by the FASB)
SoP	The *Statement of Principles for Financial Reporting* issued by the ASB in December 1999
SORP	Statement of Recommended Practice
SSAP	Statement of Standard Accounting Practice (issued by the ASC)
STRGL	Statement of Total Recognised Gains and Losses, the primary financial statement introduced by the ASB in FRS 3.
TR	Technical Release (issued by the ICAEW)

Authoritative literature

The content of this Seventh Edition takes into account all accounting standards and other relevant rules issued up to 24 September 2001. Consequently, it covers all authoritative literature up to and including the following:

- FRS 19 and UITF 30 in the UK, together with all exposure drafts up to FRED 22.
- The ASB's *Statement of Principles*, published in December 1999, and the ASB's Discussion Paper *Revenue Recognition*, published in July 2001.
- The Companies Act 1985, as amended.
- IAS 41 issued by the IASC. It also covers all amendments to pre-existing standards.
- SIC-25 issued by the Standing Interpretations Committee of the IASC, together with Draft Interpretations up to SIC-D32.
- Implementation Guidance to IAS 39 approved in final form at July 2001.
- All extant Position Papers issued by the G4+1 Group of Standard-Setters.
- Joint Working Group of Standard-Setters (JWG) Draft Standard on Financial Instruments and Similar Items.

Chapter 1 The development of UK and International GAAP

1 THE EVOLUTION OF FINANCIAL REPORTING IN THE UK

1.1 Legal background

Prior to 1970, there were no mandatory requirements in the UK outside company law governing the presentation of financial statements of companies, and even the statutory provisions that did exist comprised the basic minimum only.

The Companies Act 1985[1] regulates the constitution and conduct of nearly all British business corporations, that is limited liability and unlimited companies incorporated in Great Britain; unincorporated entities are not subject to the Companies Act. The Limited Liability Partnerships Act 2000 introduced a new form of limited liability vehicle into the UK legislative framework, the limited liability partnership (LLP). LLPs fall within the scope of the Companies Act by virtue of the requirements of the Limited Liability Partnerships Regulations 2001.[2]

This legislation represents almost 150 years of continuous development of British company law and its provisions are extensive, covering, inter alia, company formation, company administration and procedure, the allotment of shares and debentures, the increase, maintenance and reduction of share capital, accounts and audit, and the distribution of profits and assets. Its development has been influenced by the Government, the Courts, changes in the structure and operation of the markets for companies' securities, and membership of the European Union. However, large parts of British companies legislation are archaic and may even be a hindrance to the development of British business. Consequently, as discussed at 1.8 below, British company law is currently undergoing a fundamental review intended to turn the existing Victorian infrastructure into a modern framework.

The Companies Act requires all limited companies to prepare annual accounts that give a 'true and fair view' of the state of the company's affairs at its balance sheet date and of its profit or loss for the year then ended. Where a company has one or more subsidiary undertakings at the balance sheet date, a similar requirement applies to its consolidated accounts also, unless the company is exempt from the requirement to prepare consolidated accounts.

With the exception of certain small companies (as defined in the Companies Act 1985), such annual accounts (individual company as well as consolidated accounts) must be audited in accordance with UK auditing standards. All limited companies are required to deliver annual accounts (individual company as well as consolidated accounts) to the Registrar of Companies, where they are available for public inspection. Concessions are available in the case of small and medium-sized companies (as defined in the Companies Act 1985 – a public company is specifically excluded from being classified as a small or medium-sized company) regarding the content of accounts delivered to the Registrar. The Registrar does not perform a quality control function, but is intended to serve as a depository.

Limited companies may be either public (designated as public limited company or 'p.l.c.') or private. One of the important legal differences between public and private companies is that a public company can offer its securities to the public directly or indirectly, whereas a private company cannot. Public companies whose securities are listed in the Official List of the UK Listing Authority and traded on the London Stock Exchange (LSE) or traded on its Alternative Investment Market (AIM) – the LSE's market for smaller companies – have to comply with stringent rules about the content of prospectuses, issue and quotation procedures and the conduct of their affairs.

Historically, the LSE carried out the twin roles of (i) UK Listing Authority and (ii) recognised investment exchange in admitting securities to trading, and the Official List. During 2000, the role of 'competent authority' or 'UK Listing Authority' was transferred from the LSE to the Financial Services Authority (FSA) and, consequently, these roles are now separated. The FSA acts as the UK Listing Authority that admits securities to the Official List within the framework of the European Directives that are encompassed in its Listing Rules. The LSE admits securities to trading on the exchange.

The Listing Rules require supplementary disclosures in the statutory annual report and accounts. Listed and AIM companies are required also to issue an unaudited statement of their results for the first six months of the financial year and to make a preliminary announcement of their results for the full year in advance of the publication of final annual accounts. It should, however, be noted that in July 2001 the European Commission issued a consultative document proposing that all European Union (EU) companies whose securities are traded on a regulated market should be required to publish quarterly reports and that these reports be subject to limited review by the statutory auditor.[3] It therefore seems likely that quarterly reporting for listed companies will become an EU-wide requirement in the near future.

Foreign companies seeking a listing in the UK (termed 'overseas companies') are subject to the specific requirements in Chapter 17 of the Listing Rules.

1.2 The development of UK accounting standard-setting

1.2.1 The Accounting Standards Committee (ASC)

It was perhaps unavoidable that in a financial reporting environment without codified standards accounting practices were varied, inconsistent and sometimes inappropriate. Inter-firm and inter-period comparisons were difficult as companies altered accounting treatments, and resorted to such practices as 'window-dressing' and 'reserve accounting' to present a favourable picture of profitability and growth. Certain professional accounting bodies such as the Institute of Chartered Accountants in England and Wales (ICAEW) had issued a series of recommendations on accounting principles – but these recommendations were not mandatory.

By 1969, it had become apparent that the basic accounting requirements contained in company law needed the support of more authoritative pronouncements than the recommendations that were being issued. Consequently, the Council of the ICAEW issued a 'Statement of intent on accounting standards in the 1970s',[4] wherein they set out their strategy for the development of accounting standards.

As a result, the ICAEW set up the Accounting Standards Steering Committee in 1970 as the means of implementing this strategy. The Institute of Chartered Accountants of Scotland and the Institute of Chartered Accountants in Ireland became co-sponsors of the Committee almost immediately afterwards; the Chartered Association of Certified Accountants and the Chartered Institute of Management Accountants[5] joined subsequently in 1971 and the Chartered Institute of Public Finance and Accountancy in 1976. With effect from 1 February 1976, the Committee became the Accounting Standards Committee and was reconstituted as a joint committee of these six accountancy bodies who now comprise the Consultative Committee of Accountancy Bodies (CCAB).

The objects of the ASC were 'to define accounting concepts, to narrow differences of financial accounting and reporting treatment, and to codify generally accepted best practice in the public interest'. In order to achieve these objects, the ASC was given the following terms of reference:

(a) to keep under review standards of financial accounting and reporting;

(b) to propose to the Councils of each of the CCAB members statements of standard accounting practice and interpretations of such statements;

(c) to publish consultative documents, discussion papers and exposure drafts and submit to the Councils of each of the CCAB members non-mandatory guidance notes with the object of maintaining and advancing accounting standards;

(d) to consult, as appropriate, with representatives of finance, commerce, industry and government, and other bodies and persons concerned with financial reporting; and

(e) to maintain close links with the International Accounting Standards Committee and the accountancy profession in Europe and throughout the world.[6]

1.2.2 *The Watts Report*

In the light of the eight years' experience gained since its formation, a Review Group was set up in 1978 by the ASC, under the chairmanship of Mr T. R. Watts, to review the standard-setting process and to consider what improvements in that process could be effected. The Review Group submitted a draft consultative document to the ASC in May 1978. The document was adopted by the ASC and published as a basis for public discussion and comment.[7] Following extensive public consultations and debate, the ASC made a number of recommendations in a report to the CCAB, which was published in 1981 (the Watts Report).[8] Many of the recommendations of the Watts Report concern fundamental issues that remained unresolved and were consequently revisited by the Dearing Committee (see below). These included such issues as the need for a conceptual framework; the establishment of a supervisory body to ensure compliance with accounting standards; the application of certain standards only to large companies; a full-time paid ASC Chairman; and the need for more resources.

1.2.3 *The McKinnon Report*

A further review of the standard-setting process was carried out by an ASC working party in 1983. The reasons for the review were:

(a) to develop certain recommendations contained in the Watts Report;

(b) to seek ways by which the standard-setting process could be shortened; and

(c) to consider whether there was a need for alternative or new types of pronouncement.

The findings of this working party were published in a report entitled 'Review of the Standard Setting Process' (the McKinnon Report). However, the report did not address the more fundamental issues raised in the Watts Report, and instead focused on the procedural aspects relating to the development of Statements of Standard Accounting Practice (SSAPs). The report did, nevertheless, recommend that a new category of final pronouncement be introduced, namely the Statement of Recommended Practice (SORP).

1.2.4 *The Dearing Report*

As the complexities of accounting issues and requirements for more sophisticated levels of financial reporting mounted, the increased demands placed on the ASC clearly indicated that it was unable to fulfil satisfactorily the standard-setting role that it was expected to perform. The ASC had to endure mounting criticism for being unable either to respond quickly to changing needs or deal adequately with fundamental issues such as inflation accounting, off balance sheet transactions and goodwill. However, when one considers that the ASC essentially comprised a voluntary part-time committee, it had achieved a great deal. Nevertheless, as companies were required to report in a rapidly changing and increasingly complex environment, it was becoming apparent that the existing standard-setting process was no longer appropriate.

Consequently, in November 1987 the CCAB appointed a Review Committee, under the chairmanship of Sir Ronald Dearing, to review and make recommendations on the standard-setting process.[9]

Probably not surprisingly, the Review Committee addressed many of the issues discussed in the Watts Report, and reached very similar conclusions. The principal recommendations, which were published in a report issued in November 1988 (the Dearing Report), were as follows:[10]

A The need for a conceptual framework

The Committee concluded that the lack of a conceptual framework was a handicap to those setting accounting standards as well as to those applying them. It recommended that further work on a conceptual framework should be undertaken on a modest scale, building on the work already done by the US Financial Accounting Standards Board (FASB) and the International Accounting Standards Committee (IASC) on their respective conceptual framework projects. However, the Committee further recommended that, whether or not a conceptual framework was successfully developed, when accounting standards were issued they should be accompanied by a statement of the principles underlying them and the reasons why alternatives were rejected. (See Chapter 2 for a detailed discussion of the development of a conceptual framework in the UK.)

B Quality of accounting standards versus quantity

The report emphasised that the purpose of accounting standards was to provide authoritative – but not mandatory – guidance on the interpretation of what constituted a true and fair view. Consequently, the Committee recommended that the revised standard-setting framework should concentrate on quality, timeliness, reducing the permitted options and promoting compliance – as opposed to endeavouring to produce a large volume of standards that attempt to cover every option.

C Application of standards to small companies

The Committee was clearly influenced by the approach taken latterly by the ASC in exempting small companies from the requirements of certain standards (see below). Consequently, it recommended that, on the basis of a cost/benefit test, it should be decided whether or not the requirements of a particular standard should apply to small companies.

D Public sector bodies

The report discussed the application of standards to public sector bodies at some length. It concluded that there should be an underlying unity of approach to accounting standards across the public and private sectors, and that, therefore, public sector bodies should come within the framework of the proposals contained in the report, but with support for compliance with standards coming from the responsible Secretary of State.

E The role of the law

The suggestion that accounting standards should be given legal effect is one which had been mooted from time to time, and was considered by the Committee – particularly in the light of developments in other countries where there had been a trend in giving accounting standards increased legal backing.

However, the Committee stated that it did not recommend the incorporation of standards into law 'because this inescapably requires a legalistic approach and a reduction in the ability of the financial community to respond quickly to new developments'.[11] Nevertheless, whilst attempting to avoid a legalistic approach, the Committee made the following recommendations in order to help provide a sound base for the development and implementation of standards:

(a) in the case of all 'large companies', the directors should be required to state in the notes to the financial statements whether or not they had been prepared in accordance with applicable accounting standards, drawing attention to material departures and explaining the reasons for such departures;

(b) there should be a statutory power for certain authorised bodies or the Secretary of State to apply to the courts for an order requiring the revision of accounts which do not give a true and fair view;

(c) if there was a material departure from an accounting standard, then the onus of proof should be on the party who contended that the financial statements did give a true and fair view to show that this was the case. This should similarly apply in the case of auditors who had given an unqualified opinion on financial statements which contained departures; and

(d) there should be a general presumption in any legal proceedings that all accounting standards would have the support of the courts – unless it could be demonstrated that, despite a material departure, the financial statements gave a true and fair view.

F A Financial Reporting Council

The Committee addressed the need for the involvement of a wide constituency of interests in the development of accounting standards. Consequently, it recommended that 'the institutional arrangements for developing accounting standards should reflect the need to involve the whole community of interests in financial reporting at the policy level, while providing for a separate professional capability to translate policy into accounting standards'.[12] Therefore, in order to achieve this, the Committee recommended that a Financial Reporting Council should be created, covering at high level a wide constituency of interests. The Council's chairman would be appointed jointly by the Secretary of State for Trade and Industry and the Governor of the Bank of England. The objectives of the Council would be to guide the standard-setting body on work programmes and issues of public concern; to see that the work on accounting standards is properly financed; and to act as a powerful proactive public influence for securing good accounting practice.[13]

It was recommended that the Council would meet three to four times a year, and have approximately 20 members who would include accountants in practice, as well as in industry, commerce and the public sector. There would be an equal number of members drawn from all other relevant areas of interest, and the UK and Irish Governments would be invited to nominate members or observers.[14]

G An Accounting Standards Board

The Committee recommended that the ASC should be reconstituted into an Accounting Standards Board (ASB) which would be able to issue accounting standards on its own authority, instead of needing the approval of the Councils of all the six accountancy bodies that make up the CCAB. The ASB would have a full-time Chairman and Technical Director and its total membership would not exceed nine. A majority of two-thirds would be required for the approval of an accounting standard. Furthermore, in order to provide an immediate and authoritative response to emerging issues the Committee recommended that the ASB should establish a capability of publishing authoritative, though non-mandatory, guidance on emerging issues.[15]

H A Review Panel

The Committee addressed the difficult question of securing compliance with accounting standards in support of the 'true and fair' requirement. It was therefore recommended that, with the objective of achieving 'good financial reporting',[16] a Review Panel (possibly modelled on the Panel on Take-overs and Mergers) should be established to examine any identified or alleged material departures from accounting standards. The findings of the Review Panel should spell out what revisions to the financial statements, or what additional information it considered should be made available to users, to provide an acceptable set of financial statements giving a true and fair view.[17]

1.2.5 The implementation of the Dearing proposals

The recommendations of the Dearing Committee were greeted favourably, and although there was an initial hiatus during which it was feared that they might suffer the same fate as those of the Watts Committee, the Accounting Standards Board was set up in August 1990, and the Review Panel soon thereafter. The Financial Reporting Council was established initially under the chairmanship of Sir Ronald Dearing himself, with Sir Sydney Lipworth taking over the position from 1 January 1994.

The ASC remained in operation until the ASB was formed, when it was disbanded. During the 20 years of its existence it had published 25 accounting standards, three of which it later withdrew, and a total of 55 exposure drafts, nine of which were issued in the last six months of its life. In retrospect, its achievements were considerable, given the modest resources available to it, and although some of its standards can be criticised, collectively they improved UK GAAP beyond recognition from the state of financial reporting practice in 1970, when the ASC was created.

Two of the more significant changes to company law that had been recommended by the Dearing Committee were taken up in the Companies Act 1989. In particular:

(a) the accounts of large companies have to state whether they have been prepared in accordance with applicable accounting standards and give details of, and the reasons for, any material departures.[18] Small and medium-sized companies and certain small and medium-sized groups are exempt from this disclosure requirement;[19] and

(b) the Act took up the Dearing Committee recommendation that the Secretary of State or other authorised persons should be able to apply to the court for an order requiring the revision of defective accounts.[20] It also enables accounts to be revised without the necessity for court action, by providing procedures both for the voluntary revision of accounts[21] and for the Secretary of State to notify directors of apparent defects in accounts, thus giving them the opportunity to revise the accounts or explain why they believe no revision is required.[22]

The two other proposed changes to the law, described at (c) and (d) of 1.2.4 E above, were not taken up.

1.2.6 *The Accounting Standards Board*

The following diagram illustrates the structure of the present standard-setting regime in the UK:

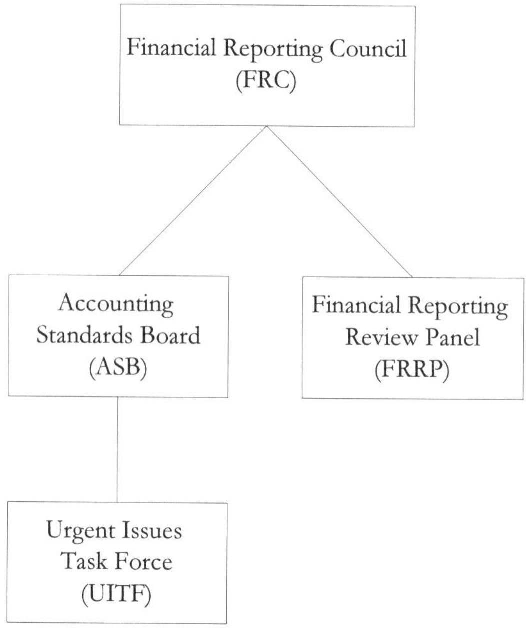

The Accounting Standards Board succeeded the ASC on 1 August 1990, with Sir David Tweedie as its first Chairman, Allan Cook as its Technical Director and seven other members. The total membership of the Board has since been increased to ten. After a highly distinguished period of ten years as Chairman of the ASB, Sir David Tweedie was appointed in January 2001 as the first Chairman of the restructured International Accounting Standards Board (IASB), and was succeeded at the ASB by Mary Keegan.

To date (September 2001), the ASB has published nineteen Financial Reporting Standards (FRSs) in final form, an Interim Statement that preceded one of these standards, amendments to a number of existing standards, various non-mandatory Statements, a finalised Statement of Principles, together with a large number of other exposure drafts and discussion papers.

The Board implemented another part of the Dearing proposals also by establishing the Urgent Issues Task Force. The purpose of this group is to assist the ASB in areas where an accounting standard or a Companies Act provision exists, but where unsatisfactory or conflicting interpretations have developed or seem likely to develop. In such cases, the Task Force will consider the issue put to it, and if it is able to achieve agreement on the appropriate solution, will publish an Abstract setting out its consensus view. Such Abstracts do not constitute 'applicable accounting standards' in terms of the Companies Act, but nonetheless are meant to be observed unless it can be shown that to do so would not give a true and fair view. This view is supported by The Hon Mrs Justice Arden in her Opinion of the true and fair view referred to in more detail below, which states that 'the Court is likely to treat UITF abstracts as of considerable standing even though they are not envisaged by the Companies Acts. This will lead to a readiness on the part of the Court to accept that compliance with abstracts of the UITF is also necessary to meet the true and fair requirement.'[23]

Although it did not do so initially, the UITF now publicises its agenda, and gives interested parties an opportunity to comment on Abstracts that it publishes in draft. This change in policy came about because of public criticism of the Task Force, which was accused of springing Abstracts on the business community without due notice or public debate. In any event, though, the UITF can make a ruling only if a large majority of its members agree to it. The Task Force can have up to 16 members, and it can only publish an Abstract on any issue if no more than two members vote against it. All extant Abstracts are dealt with in this book.

In addition, in accordance with the Dearing proposals, the Financial Reporting Review Panel (FRRP) was set up, initially under the chairmanship of Simon Tuckey QC. The current Chairman of the FRRP is Richard Sykes QC. This body is empowered to consider apparent defects in published accounts, and determine what action to take. To date, the actions of the Panel have been confined to obtaining the agreement of the companies concerned either to issue a statement immediately with the relevant correcting information or to amend the practice complained of in subsequent years. However, in appropriate cases the Panel might ask that the accounts be reissued and, if necessary, institute court proceedings to require the company concerned to do so. As yet, the Panel has not instituted court proceedings against any company, although it seems that they might have come close to doing so on one or two occasions.

No clear pattern can be discerned from the Panel's decisions to date. Many of them have involved relatively minor misdemeanours by companies who are not household names, and this has led some commentators to express the concern that the Panel has yet to establish its credibility in policing the more difficult areas of UK GAAP. However, there have been exceptions, where the Panel has successfully challenged major companies on important matters. A number of the more interesting decisions of the Review Panel are discussed in this book.

1.2.7 *Statements of Recommended Practice (SORPs)*

As stated above, the idea of SORPs was first mooted by the McKinnon Report and adopted by the ASC. SORPs are issued on subjects on which it is not considered appropriate to issue an accounting standard at the time, and usually relate to industry-specific areas of accounting where differences and varieties of accounting treatments exist. SORPs are not issued by the ASB but by industry or sectoral bodies (for example, the British Bankers' Association) recognised for the purpose by the ASB. To secure such recognition, SORP-making bodies are expected to meet criteria laid down by the ASB and to develop their SORP proposals in conformity with the ASB's code of practice for SORPs.[24]

Under the code of practice, SORP-making bodies will not be recognised unless the following conditions are met:

(i) The industry or sector has special accounting or financial reporting problems that require the clarification of accounting standards or interpretation (within the principles of the standards).

(ii) The body represents the whole or a major part of a significant industry or sector for the purposes of financial reporting within the relevant jurisdiction.

(iii) The body shares the ASB's aim of advancing and maintaining standards of financial reporting in the public interest.

(iv) The body agrees to abide by the ASB's code of practice for bodies recognised for issuing SORPs.

(v) Where an industry or sector is regulated or financed by another body, the regulator or financing body is content for the body seeking recognition by the ASB to promulgate SORPs for that industry or sector.

The ASB will, at its discretion, withdraw recognition if it appears that these conditions are no longer met, or if the recognised body fails to comply with the spirit of the code of practice. This would include circumstances in which a SORP-making body publishes a SORP or similar guidance without securing the approval of the ASB.

A SORP is required to carry a statement by the ASB confirming, as appropriate, that the SORP does not appear to contain any fundamental points of principle that are unacceptable in the context of current accounting practice or to conflict with an accounting standard or the ASB's plans for future standards. To assist in dealing with proposals for SORPs the ASB has established two specialist committees to advise it on proposals for SORPs: (i) the Financial Sector and other Special Industries Committee, and (ii) the Public Sector and Not-for-Profit Committee.

A further requirement of the ASB's code of practice for SORPs is that the SORP-making body should keep under review all the SORPs for which it is responsible. In particular, the body should consider:[25]

- any implications for the SORPs of new and proposed accounting standards. In the interests of the SORP-making body and its constituency, any divergences must be notified to the ASB as soon as is practicable;
- any evidence of widespread failure in the relevant industry or sector to follow any part of the guidance in a SORP that has come to the attention of the SORP-making body; and
- any developments in the industry or sector that suggest that further guidance on accounting matters is desirable.

The SORP-making body should report to the ASB, at least annually, the results of such a review. The report should confirm that the body continues to comply with this code of practice and state whether, in the light of the review, it proposes to revise any of the SORPs for which it is responsible.[26]

This review requirement is significant, given the fact that SORPs have now assumed a greater importance via FRS 18 – *Accounting* Policies.[27] FRS 18 introduces into UK GAAP for the first time the requirement for entities to make specific disclosures relating to SORPs.

The standard makes it clear that:

> 'Appropriate accounting policies will result in financial information being presented in such a way that enables users to discern and evaluate similarities in, and differences between, the nature and effects of transactions and other events taking place over time. In selecting accounting policies, an entity will assess whether accepted industry practices are appropriate to its particular circumstances. Such practices will be particularly persuasive if set out in a SORP that has been generally accepted by an industry or sector.'[28]

Put simply, an entity will have a substantial job on its hands to justify not complying with a SORP.

FRS 18 requires that if an entity's financial statements fall within the scope of a SORP, the title of that SORP must be stated and also whether the financial statements have been prepared in accordance with it. In the event of a departure, a brief description of how the financial statements depart from the SORP must be given. This description must include:

(a) the reasons why the treatment adopted is considered more appropriate; and

(b) details of any disclosures recommended by the SORP that have not been provided and the reasons why not.[29]

It should be noted that the provisions of FRS 18 concerning SORPs only become mandatory for accounting periods *beginning* on or after 24 December 2001.[30]

1.3 The concept of true and fair

The requirement that all financial statements that are prepared for the purpose of compliance with the Companies Act should 'give a true and fair view' was first introduced in the Companies Act 1947.[31] This amended the former requirement of 'true and correct', a change considered necessary on the grounds that there was no clear distinction between the two adjectives when used to describe financial statements.

The concept of true and fair was adopted by the EC Council in its Fourth Directive.[32] In terms of the Directive, annual accounts are defined as a 'composite whole' comprising a balance sheet, profit and loss account and notes; the accounts should be drawn up in accordance with the Directive's detailed provisions and 'give a true and fair view of the company's assets, liabilities, financial position and profit or loss'.[33] However, to obviate a potential conflict between its detailed provisions and the achievement of truth and fairness, the Directive declared the obligation to give a true and fair view to be overriding. Consequently, where the application of the provisions of the Directive would not be sufficient to give a true and fair view, additional information must be given; where the application of a provision of the Directive is incompatible with the presentation of a true and fair view, that provision must be departed from (with appropriate disclosure in the notes of the departure).[34]

Interestingly, it is this concept of the overriding requirement to show a true and fair view that has now been adopted in International Accounting Standards in the form of the fair presentation override that is embedded in International Accounting Standards (see below).

The provisions of the Fourth Directive were implemented in the UK through the enactment of the Companies Act 1981. Following the consolidation of the various Companies Acts 1948–1983 into the Companies Act 1985, and the subsequent implementation of the Seventh Directive in the 1989 Act, the detailed requirements of the Directives are contained in Schedules 4 and 4A to the 1985 Act. The requirement that financial statements should give a true and fair view is contained in section 226 for individual companies and section 227 for group financial statements. It is therefore clear that the concept of true and fair is a legal one, and the question as to whether or not a particular company's financial statements comply with sections 226 or 227 can ultimately be decided only by the courts.

1.4 The interaction of accounting standards and the law

The Companies Act 1989 gave, for the first time in the UK, statutory recognition to the existence of accounting standards. This recognition was achieved through the inclusion of a new section (section 256) in the Companies Act 1985 and of a new disclosure requirement in Schedule 4 to that Act. The first two sub-sections of section 256 read as follows:

'(1) In this Part "accounting standards" means statements of standard accounting practice issued by such body or bodies as may be prescribed by regulations.

(2) References in this Part to accounting standards applicable to a company's annual accounts are to such standards as are, in accordance with their terms, relevant to the company's circumstances and to the accounts.'

In addition, the insertion of paragraph 36A of Schedule 4 to the Companies Act 1985 resulted in the new requirement for companies to state by way of note to their accounts whether the accounts have been prepared in accordance with applicable accounting standards and to give the particulars of any material departure from those standards and the reasons therefor. (There is an exemption from this requirement for small and medium-sized companies and for certain small and medium-sized groups.)

As discussed above, for twenty years until 1990 the responsibility for developing accounting standards was discharged by the Accounting Standards Committee (ASC). Since then, that function has been fulfilled by the Accounting Standards Board (ASB), having been prescribed by Statutory Regulation as the standard-setting body for the purposes of section 256(1) of the Companies Act with effect from 20 August 1990.

The ASB's Foreword to Accounting Standards explains the relationship between compliance with the accounting standards and the concept of true and fair. This says that: 'Accounting standards are authoritative statements of how particular types of transaction and other events should be reflected in financial statements and accordingly compliance with accounting standards will normally be necessary for financial statements to give a true and fair view.'[35] It goes on to say that 'because accounting standards are formulated with the objective of ensuring that the information resulting from their application faithfully represents the underlying commercial activity, the Board envisages that only in exceptional circumstances will departure from the requirements of an accounting standard be necessary in order for financial statements to give a true and fair view'.[36]

The meaning of the true and fair requirement, including the legal relationship between accounting standards and the Companies Act, was discussed in two Joint Opinions obtained by the ASC in 1983 and 1984 from Leonard Hoffmann QC (now the Rt. Hon. Lord Justice Hoffmann) and Miss Mary Arden (now The Hon. Mrs Justice Arden). The 1983 opinion states that 'the courts will treat compliance with accepted accounting principles as prima facie evidence that the accounts are true and fair. Equally, deviation from accepted principles will be prima facie evidence that they are not. ... The function of the ASC is to formulate what it considers should be generally accepted accounting principles. Thus the value of a SSAP to a court which has to decide whether accounts are true and fair is two-fold. First, it represents an important statement of professional opinion about the standards which readers may reasonably expect in accounts which are intended to be true and fair. ... Secondly, because accountants are professionally obliged to comply with a SSAP, it creates in the readers an expectation that the accounts will be in conformity with the prescribed standards. This is in itself a reason why accounts which depart from the standard without adequate justification or explanation may be held not to be true and fair.'[37]

This view is supported in the judgement given by Woolf J in *Lloyd Cheyham & Co Ltd v Littlejohn & Co,* in which he stated that 'while they [accounting standards] are not conclusive, ... and they are not as the explanatory foreword makes clear, rigid rules, they are very strong evidence as to what is the proper standard which should be adopted'.[38]

Following statutory recognition of the existence of accounting standards, the ASB requested Miss Mary Arden QC to write a further Opinion that addressed the legal relationship between accounting standards and the true and fair view. The Opinion was issued in April 1993 and published by the ASB as an Appendix to its *Foreword to Accounting Standards*.[39] Whilst this Opinion has been given in the context of the changes in the law discussed above, it is essentially a reiteration of the two previous Joint Opinions. It again explains that 'the immediate effect of the issue of an accounting standard is to create a likelihood that the court will hold that compliance with that standard is necessary to meet the true and fair requirement. That likelihood is strengthened by the degree to which a standard is subsequently accepted in practice. Thus if a particular standard is generally followed, the court is very likely to find that the accounts must comply with it in order to show a true and fair view. The converse of that proposition, that non-acceptance of a standard in practice would almost inevitably lead a court to the conclusion that compliance with it was not necessary to meet the true and fair requirement, is not however the case. Whenever a standard is issued by the Board, then, irrespective of the lack in some quarters of support for it, the court would be bound to give special weight to the opinion of the Board in view of its status as the standard-setting body, the process of investigation, discussion and consultation that it will have undertaken before adopting the standard and the evolving nature of accounting standards.'[40]

Clearly, therefore, although accounting standards have no direct legal authority or effect, it appears highly probable that they will have a very persuasive effect in the courts' interpretation as to whether or not a company's accounts present a true and fair view. This status is further reinforced by the Schedule 4 requirement, described above, that any departures from accounting standards be explained in the financial statements.

1.5 GAAP for small companies

The administrative and legislative burdens that have been imposed on small businesses have been a controversial issue for many years. In particular, issues such as the retention of the small company audit and the application of accounting standards to small companies have been the subject of numerous studies in the UK and around the world.[41] With the increasing number of accounting standards, owners of small companies have complained about the cost and inconvenience of applying accounting requirements that were designed for large public companies. However, expert opinion varies: some hold the view that accounting standards should apply equally to all financial statements which purport to present a true and fair view; others believe that small companies should be exempted from the requirements of certain standards which are unduly burdensome; whilst there is yet a further contention that small companies should have a completely different set of accounting standards altogether.

Whilst it is beyond the scope of this book to discuss all the issues surrounding differential reporting for small companies, it is noteworthy that there has been a general reluctance to pursue the development of two GAAPs. This is reflected, for example, in a Report to the Council of the Institute of Chartered Accountants of

British Columbia, wherein the Task Force on Big GAAP/Little GAAP concluded that 'any attempt to develop two separate sets of generally accepted accounting principles ... raises insurmountable difficulties'.[42] Amongst the reasons offered for these difficulties was that 'defining in a meaningful fashion Big GAAP/Little GAAP principles would appear to be unattainable given that the accounting profession has been unable to adequately define generally accepted accounting principles'.[43]

In a research study carried out in 1985 by Professor B. V. Carsberg *et al.* on small company financial reporting in the UK, the conclusion was reached that 'the burden imposed by accounting standards and other reporting requirements does not seem to be a matter for primary concern among people in small companies'.[44] In attempting to explain this finding, the report suggested that 'perhaps small company managers have little awareness of what is involved in complying with standards because they leave this aspect of their accounting to their professional advisers'.[45]

In 1986, the ASC commissioned a working party to investigate the application of accounting standards to small companies. The findings of the working party, which were set out in Technical Release TR 690,[46] were that 'there is no evidence to suggest that, in general, small companies find compliance with accounting standards unduly burdensome, given that they have to prepare financial statements that give a true and fair view'.[47] TR 690 did, however, indicate that the ASC would consider exempting small companies from certain future standards.[48]

This announcement was later followed up by TR 706, which outlined the basis on which the ASC intended to judge whether exemptions would be appropriate. It defined the class of entities to which any exemption would normally apply and indicated the way in which the exemption would be formulated.[49] In TR 706, the ASC stated that it 'accepts that there is a case, in specific circumstances, for exempting small entities from certain provisions of accounting standards'; however, 'such exemptions are likely to relate more often to disclosure requirements, rather than to recognition or measurement rules'.[50] Where the ASC was satisfied that exemption was merited in a specific instance, it proposed a relaxation for a class of entities which excluded:

(a) public limited companies (plcs),

(b) companies that had a plc as a subsidiary; and

(c) other reporting entities, required to prepare true and fair accounts, which exceeded ten times the qualifying conditions for a company to be treated as a medium-sized company under section 247 of the Companies Act 1985.[51]

The effect of this proposal was that, in terms of the current thresholds (in September 2001) contained in section 247, a company would only be able to take advantage of the exemptions specified in a particular accounting standard if it was neither a plc, nor had a plc as a subsidiary, and it met two or more of the following criteria:

(a) its turnover did not exceed £112m;

(b) its balance sheet total did not exceed £56m;

(c) the average number of persons employed in the year did not exceed 2,500.

Clearly, these criteria can hardly be regarded as relating to 'small companies', and it is apparent that they were designed to apply to companies other than very large ones. It is our view, however, that the ASC introduced an unnecessary complication by including the size criteria in the exemption. It would have been more sensible if the ASC had merely distinguished between public and private companies in its exemption proposals.

This exemption was applied (in slightly modified form) in relation to certain aspects of SSAP 13 (Revised) – *Accounting for research and development* and SSAP 25 – *Segmental reporting*. On the other hand FRS 1 – *Cash flow statements* – contains an exemption for small companies as defined by the Act, which are very much smaller than those exempted under the other two standards.

1.6 The Financial Reporting Standard for Smaller Entities (FRSSE)

1.6.1 Introduction to the FRSSE

In 1994, a working party of the CCAB that had been set up at the ASB's request carried out a consultation exercise on the application of accounting standards to smaller entities,[52] and issued a further paper for comment at the end of 1995.[53] After analysing the responses, the working party passed over the project to the ASB, which published an exposure draft in December 1996. This is known as the *Financial Reporting Standard for Smaller Entities* (or FRSSE), and was originally issued as an FRS in November 1997 and revised versions were issued in December 1998 and December 1999. It comprises a compendium standard for smaller entities, based on a simplified summary of the whole corpus of existing standards. Amendments have been made to these other standards so as to exempt entities that fall under the FRSSE.

The publication of the FRSSE in 1997 introduced a new concept into financial reporting – that of a complete, distinct accounting standard specifically for smaller entities. The FRSSE prescribes the basis, for those entities within its scope that have chosen to adopt it, for preparing and presenting their financial statements. The definitions and accounting treatments are consistent with the requirements of companies legislation and, for the generality of small entities, are the same as those required by other accounting standards or a simplified version of those requirements. The disclosure requirements exclude a number of those stipulated in other accounting standards.

Reporting entities that apply the FRSSE are exempt from complying with other accounting standards (SSAPs and FRSs) and Urgent Issues Task Force (UITF) Abstracts, unless preparing consolidated financial statements, in which case certain other accounting standards apply (namely, FRSs 2, 6 and 7 and, as they apply in respect of consolidated financial statements, FRSs 5, 9, 10 and 11).

Financial statements will generally be prepared using accepted practice. Accordingly, for transactions or events not dealt with in the FRSSE, smaller entities should have regard to other accounting standards and UITF Abstracts, not as mandatory documents, but as a means of establishing current practice.

1.6.2 *Scope of the FRSSE*

The FRSSE may be applied to all financial statements intended to give a true and fair view of the financial position and profit or loss (or income and expenditure) of all entities that are:

(a) companies incorporated under companies legislation and entitled to the exemptions available in the legislation for small companies when filing accounts with the Registrar of Companies; or

(b) entities that would have come into category (a) above had they been companies incorporated under companies legislation, excluding building societies. Such entities should have regard to the accounting principles, presentation and disclosure requirements in companies legislation (or other equivalent legislation) that, taking into account the FRSSE, are necessary to present a true and fair view.[54]

The FRSSE therefore applies to small companies and groups as defined in the Companies Act 1985 and to other entities that meet the same size limits. As at September 2001, this means companies that satisfy at least two of the following criteria:

- Turnover not more than £2.8 million
- Balance sheet total not more than £1.4 million
- No more than 50 employees.

Accordingly, the FRSSE does not apply to:

(i) large or medium-sized companies, groups and other entities;

(ii) public companies;

(iii) banks, building societies or insurance companies;

(iv) authorised persons under the Financial Services Act 1986 (in the UK) or the Investment Intermediaries Act 1995 (in the Republic of Ireland); or

(v) members of groups that contain companies falling under (ii) to (iv) above.

Reporting entities that are entitled to adopt the FRSSE, but choose not to do so, should apply SSAPs, FRSs and UITF Abstracts when preparing financial statements intended to give a true and fair view of the financial position and profit or loss of the entity.

1.6.3 *True and fair view*

Financial statements prepared under the FRSSE should present a true and fair view of the results for the period and of the state of affairs at the end of the period. To achieve such a view, regard should be had to the substance of any arrangement or transaction, or series of such, into which the entity has entered. To determine the substance of a transaction it is necessary to identify whether the transaction has given rise to new assets or liabilities for the reporting entity and whether it has changed the entity's existing assets or liabilities.[55]

Where there is doubt whether applying provisions of the FRSSE would be sufficient to give a true and fair view, adequate explanation should be given in the notes to the accounts of the transaction or arrangement concerned and the treatment adopted.[56]

1.6.4 Accounting principles and policies

FRSSE financial statements should state that they have been prepared in accordance with the Financial Reporting Standard for Smaller Entities (effective March 2000).

If the financial statements are prepared on the basis of assumptions that differ in material respects from any of the fundamental accounting concepts set out in paragraphs 10 to 14 of Schedule 4 to the Companies Act, the facts should be explained.[57] In the absence of a clear statement to the contrary, there is a presumption that the accounting principles have been observed.

The accounting policies followed for dealing with items that are judged material or critical in determining profit or loss for the period and in stating the financial position should be disclosed by way of note to the accounts. The explanations should be clear, fair and as brief as possible.[58]

A change in accounting policy may be made only if it can be justified on the grounds that the new policy is preferable to the one it replaces because it will give a fairer presentation of the result and financial position of a reporting entity.[59] Following a change in accounting policy, the amounts for the current and corresponding periods should be restated on the basis of the new policies. The disclosures necessary when a change of accounting policy is made should include, in addition to those for prior period adjustments, an indication of the effect on the current period's results. In those cases where the effect on the current period is immaterial, or similar to the quantified effect on the prior period, a simple statement saying this suffices. Where it is not practicable to give the effect on the current period, that fact, together with the reasons, should be stated.[60]

1.6.5 Review of the FRSSE as a whole

The ASB established the Committee on Accounting for Smaller Entities (CASE) in 1997 as a standing committee to advise it on accounting for smaller entities. By drawing on the expertise of those appointed to the committee, the ASB hopes to improve financial reporting for smaller entities, through future revisions and modifications of its FRSSE.

The ASB had acknowledged that in the course of the FRSSE's development conflicting views were put forward, ranging from those who believed smaller entities should be exempt from all accounting standards to those who favoured retaining virtually the status quo. Given this divergence of views, the ASB believed that it was particularly important that the FRSSE should be monitored carefully. Therefore, the ASB announced that it intended to review how the FRSSE, as a whole, is working in practice after two full years of effective operation and to propose amendments as necessary.

Consequently, in February 2001 the ASB published for comment a Discussion Paper – *Review of the Financial Reporting Standard for Smaller Entities (FRSSE).* The Paper, which is addressed to preparers, users and auditors of smaller entities' financial statements, seeks views on whether the FRSSE best meets users' needs and whether any fundamental changes should be considered to the way in which it is prepared and presented. The ASB intends in its review to draw on research into the use of the FRSSE carried out by certain accountancy bodies in the UK and the Republic of Ireland. The Discussion Paper asks respondents to comment on a number of issues, including the extent to which the FRSSE should be consistent with the accounting standards and UITF Abstracts on which it is based, in terms both of requirements and of drafting.

1.6.6 *The Company Law Review of provisions relating to small companies*

Changing financial reporting practice, in the form of new FRSs and UITF Abstracts, necessitates periodic revisions to the FRSSE to ensure that it is kept up to date. As a result, in June 2001 the ASB issued an Exposure Draft that proposes amendments to the FRSSE in order to take account of the four new FRSs (FRSs 16 to 19) and eight UITF Abstracts (Abstracts 23 to 30) that had been issued since July 1999, when the last Exposure Draft of amendment to the FRSSE was published.[61] The Exposure Draft contains proposals for amending the FRSSE to take account of these developments in financial reporting, modified and simplified as appropriate for smaller entities.

When the comments on the proposed amendment to the FRSSE have been considered, the ASB envisages that a completely revised FRSSE will be issued, which will supersede the existing FRSSE. The revised FRSSE will thus incorporate the amendments resulting from the proposals in the Exposure Draft but the greater part will be unchanged from the present version at this time. However, before this revision, the ASB will review in detail the responses received to its Discussion Paper referred to above, although it is expected that any developments arising therefrom will be considered over a longer timeframe.

Meanwhile, as part of a wider review of UK Company Law, the Company Law Review Steering Group has made a range of recommendations that will radically change the framework of company law for small firms.[62]

The Steering Group recommends that the current Companies Act should be recast to:

- simplify the statutory requirements for decision-making in private companies;
- make a range of other simplifications to the law to assist the running of small companies;
- reduce the burden of accounting and audit; and
- make legislation on private companies easier to understand.

As part of its measures to reduce the burden of financial reporting and audit, the Steering Group recommends that:[63]

- Thresholds for companies able to use the small company accounting regime should be increased to the maximum possible under European law. Companies would benefit if they met any two of the following criteria (on a two year rolling basis):
  - turnover no more than £4.8 million;
  - balance sheet total no more than £2.4 million;
  - no more than 50 employees.
- Thresholds for exemption from audit should be raised in the same way, although companies in the £1 million to £4.8 million range might be subject to a lesser form of assurance known as the independent professional review (IPR). The UK Government has already raised the audit threshold to £1 million turnover, and has announced its intention to exempt all small companies from the audit requirement once it has been able to consider the Company Law Review Steering Group's recommendations on the IPR. The UK's Auditing Practices Board is carrying out field trials of the IPR, and the Steering Group recommends that, if the DTI determines that the trials demonstrate a sufficient saving over the costs of full audit and positive users' reactions, the IPR should be used for companies in the £1 million to £4.8 million turnover range. If not, the Steering Group recommends a total exemption (i.e. no audit or IPR requirement) for all small companies.
- The format and contents of small company accounts should be simplified, but small companies should no longer be able to file 'abbreviated' accounts, which are considered by the Steering Group to be uninformative.
- The time limit for filing of accounts by private companies should be shortened from 10 months to 7 months after the financial year end, although those companies which retain AGMs will continue to be allowed up to 10 months to hold them.

A major theme of the Review is the delegation to the ASB of authority to make detailed provisions, particularly where the technical content is high and their formulation requires practical experience and knowledge. In line with this, the Steering Group recommends that all requirements governing the form and content of small company accounts (e.g. the present Schedule 8) should become matters for accounting standards underpinned by statute. Consequently, the Steering Group believes that the ASB should be empowered to set different rules for small companies, and envisages that all of the small company requirements will become part of a revised FRSSE, but the precise packaging of the requirements would be for the ASB to determine in due course.[64] Presumably, this will be part of what comes out of the ASB's fundamental review of the FRSSE as a whole.

The Steering Group recommends also that for all companies the directors' report should cease to exist as such. For small companies its disclosures, so far as not incorporated in the notes to the accounts, should be included in a simple cover sheet to the accounts. Such disclosures would largely comprise company standing data (e.g. names of directors, registered office address, directors' share interest details).[65]

1.7 Summary financial statements

1.7.1 The required form of a summary financial statement

In a new departure for UK corporate reporting, the Companies Act 1989 amended the 1985 Act to allow listed companies to send a summary financial statement to shareholders who do not wish to receive the full accounts.[66] The form of the statement is specified by statutory instrument[67] as requiring the following minimum information, extracted from the full accounts:

(a) from the directors' report:
- the whole, or a summary, of the 'fair review of the development of the business of the company and its subsidiary undertakings during the financial year and of their position at the end of it';
- the amount recommended to be paid by way of dividend, if not disclosed in the summary profit and loss account;
- the whole, or a summary, of the details of 'any important events affecting the company or any of its subsidiary undertakings which have occurred since the end of the financial year';
- the whole, or a summary, of the 'indication of future likely developments in the business of the company and of its subsidiary undertakings'; and
- the names of all the directors who served during the financial year;[68]

(b) from the profit and loss account, the information against these headings:
- turnover;
- income from shares in associated undertakings;
- other interest receivable and similar income less interest payable and similar charges;
- profit or loss on ordinary activities before taxation;
- tax on profit or loss on ordinary activities;
- profit or loss on ordinary activities after tax;
- minority interests;
- extraordinary items;
- profit or loss for the financial year;
- dividends paid and proposed; and
- directors' emoluments;[69]

(c) from the balance sheet, the information against these headings:
- fixed assets;
- current assets;
- prepayments and accrued income (if not shown within current assets in the full accounts);
- creditors: amounts falling due within one year;
- net current assets (liabilities);

- total assets less current liabilities;
- creditors: amounts falling due after more than one year;
- provisions for liabilities and charges;
- capital and reserves; and
- minority interests.[70]

Slightly different requirements are specified for banks and insurance companies that do not produce their full accounts under the formats of Schedule 4 to the Companies Act.[71]

As well as including the information specified above, the summary financial statement must include 'any other information necessary to ensure that [it] is consistent with the full accounts'.[72] The interpretation of the word 'consistent' is problematical. At one extreme, it might simply require that the information in the summary is the same as that which is included in the full accounts; at the other, it might be thought to require that the reader of the summary will gain the same impression of the company as he would from reading the full accounts, although if that were possible, the full accounts would be redundant. Probably what is intended is some notion of fairness of summarisation, so that the statement is not unduly selective or biased, but the requirement remains an elusive one.

In addition, the summary financial statement must explain that it is only a summary of the full accounts,[73] remind readers that they are entitled to the full accounts if they want them, and include a warning (in specified form) that it does not contain enough information to allow a full understanding of the results and state of affairs of the company or group concerned.[74] It must also say whether or not the full accounts bore a qualified audit report, and reproduce it if it did,[75] and the auditors must also report whether, in their opinion, the summary is consistent with the full accounts and complies with the legal requirements.[76] Barclays is a company that prepares summary financial statements, giving the above disclosures in its Annual Review and Summary Financial Statement 2000 as follows:

Extract 1.1: Barclays PLC (2000)

Shareholders please note

This annual review and summary financial statement does not contain sufficient information to allow for a full understanding of the results of the Group and state of affairs of the Company or of the Group. For further information consult the Annual Report 2000.

Any shareholder or debenture holder who wishes to be sent the Annual Report 2000 free of charge in addition to this annual review and summary financial statement for this year or future years, should contact the Registrar at the address shown on page 28. The Annual Report 2000 contains the full report of the Directors and the audited accounts.

...

The auditors' report on the full annual accounts of the Group for the year ended 31st December 2000 was unqualified and did not contain a statement under either section 237(2) (accounting records or returns inadequate or accounts not agreeing with records and returns) or 237(3) (failure to obtain necessary information and explanations) of the Companies Act 1985.

1.7.2 Commentary on the summary financial statement regime

It would be encouraging to believe that the Government's initiative in introducing summarised financial statements was motivated by a desire to make financial statements more understandable to the reader. However, the reality is that it was intended as a cost-saving measure, of particular benefit to those companies who, following privatisation, had a large number of small shareholders in respect of whom the preparation of full annual reports is a considerable expense. The form of summary financial statements dictated by the law is not particularly imaginative; it amounts to little more than the primary financial statements without the notes. Although the use of such statements has now become a feature of UK GAAP, it is difficult to see it as either a real advance in the quality of financial reporting or much of a cost saving. Instead, this approach could merely exacerbate the common misunderstanding that the results and financial position of a highly complex organisation can be encapsulated in simple headline measures such as EBITDA, EPS and gearing.

We therefore consider the introduction of summary financial statements to be something of a diversion in relation to the development of better forms of financial reporting. This is because the prime motivation behind their introduction was to save costs for companies and not to provide information in a form that was more readily understood by the small shareholder. We were therefore encouraged that, as part of a wider review of UK Company Law, the Company Law Review Steering Group had proposed in one of its consultation documents that the summary financial should be abolished. However, as explained below, this proposal has not been followed through.

1.7.3 The Review of the summary financial statement by the Company Law Review Steering Group

The Company Law Review Steering Group had originally proposed that the summary financial statement should be abolished, instead converting the preliminary announcement into a statutory statement distributed to all shareholders (electronically and in hard copy). However, the conclusion drawn from the consultation was that this would be impractical; in particular, the market's needs and those of small shareholders would not be served by the same information set. The Steering Group therefore concluded that the summary financial statement should be retained. The Steering Group had asked also in an earlier consultation whether the ASB should have the power to mandate the offer of a summary financial statement by classes of companies where such simpler information was needed. However, this was opposed by the majority of respondents as well, and the Steering Group has recommended the retention of, broadly, the current regime of a summary financial statement offered at the option of the company, subject to the following changes:

- At present, the summary financial statement regime applies to listed companies only. It had been suggested that the facility should be open to all companies (including private companies). This suggestion has been accepted by the Steering Group, on the basis that there is no reason to prohibit the availability of such statements if any company wants to offer them and a properly informed shareholder wants to accept them. The Steering Group has therefore recommend that the regime should be available to all companies, whether public or private.

- The summary financial statement (to be renamed 'summary statement') should include a summary Operating and Financial Review (OFR) for those companies required to prepare one.
- The power to determine the form and content of the statement should be devolved to the ASB.
- The enforcement regime of the Financial Reporting Review Panel should apply to the summary statement as well, on the basis that if there has been a defect in the preparation of the summary statement it is only proper that there should be equivalent enforcement powers as for the full statements.[77]

1.8 The Company Law Review

The Final Report of the Company Law Review was delivered by the Company Law Review Steering Group in June 2001.[78] This is the first fundamental review of British company law for at least 40 years, and arguably the first in the law's 150-year history. For the past four decades, company law reform has been limited to the implementation of European Community Directives and piecemeal re-engineering. As a result, Britain has been left with an archaic, Victorian system that may even be a hindrance to British business. Ironically, former British colonial countries such as Canada, Australia, New Zealand and South Africa – who had in the past based their company law on the British system – have all long since modernised their law, leaving Britain trailing far behind. The Final Report sets out the Steering Group's model for a new company law that is intended to turn the existing Victorian infrastructure into a modern framework. The new framework is designed to provide the necessary safeguards to allow people to deal with and invest in companies with confidence, whilst at the same time to enable British companies to be competitive in a global marketplace where businesses can choose which jurisdiction to adopt for their regulation.

Given that the Final Report proposes a root and branch overhaul of companies legislation, its detailed proposals are beyond the scope of this book. However, there are a number of proposals that relate to financial reporting that are relevant. The Steering Group has made several recommendations aimed at improving the quality, timeliness and accessibility of company reporting, including the following:

- Most public companies and large private companies should be required to publish an operating and financial review (OFR) as part of the annual report. This would provide a review of the business, its performance, plans and prospects, and information the directors judge necessary for an understanding of the business, such as relationships with employees, suppliers and customers, environmental and community impact, corporate governance and management of risk. The OFR would be subject to review by the auditors. The Steering Group states that the thresholds for the mandatory requirement to publish an OFR require empirical research, but suggest in the interim that public companies should be required to prepare an OFR where they satisfy at least two out of the three criteria of turnover in excess of £50 million, balance sheet total in excess of £25 million, and number of employees in excess of 500; and that for private companies the corresponding thresholds should be of the order of £500 million, £250 million and 5,000. The Steering Group emphasises that they regard OFR disclosure as of central importance for the future and consider arguments for exemption for companies of really significant size to be without merit on anything but a transitional basis. Consequently, as the practice of such disclosure becomes widespread and well understood, the Steering Group would expect these thresholds to be reduced.[79] (The present requirements of the OFR are discussed in more detail in Chapter 4 of this book.)

- Where a quoted company publishes a preliminary announcement this should, after release to the market, be immediately published on a website, with electronic notification to those shareholders that want it.[80]
- Quoted companies should make their annual report and accounts (including, where relevant, the OFR) available on a website within four months of the year-end; further time would be allowed for preparing the hard copy, with all public companies being required to lay the accounts in general meeting and file them at Companies House within six months.[81]

One of the main themes of the proposals of the Steering Group relates to the institutional structure of law-making and law enforcement bodies. A modern company law designed to support a competitive economy requires a flexible, expert and responsive institutional structure for rule-making and enforcement, which takes the fullest advantage of all the forms of law which can be deployed. The Steering Group believes that this responsive, responsible and balanced approach can best be achieved by building on the existing model provided by the Financial Reporting Council (FRC), the Accounting Standards Board (ASB) and the Financial Reporting Review Panel (FRRP).

Accordingly, the Steering Group has proposed the following:[82]

- a full exploitation of secondary legislative powers to keep the legislation up-to-date and to complete the more technical aspects in a way which corresponds to changing needs, with the result either incorporated in the Act or in separate subordinate legislation as best suits the needs of users;
- the development of the existing devolved jurisdictions of the FRC, ASB and FRRP to provide rules, standards, guidance and informal sponsorship of best practice developments and specialised enforcement. The remit of these bodies would be expanded to reflect the wider field of company reporting and disclosure which is envisaged under the Act, and this suggests a change in their titles so that they become the Company Law and Reporting Commission (CLRC), the Standards Board and the Reporting Review Panel respectively;

- a new advisory role to be conferred on the CLRC, to keep the whole of company law under review, to report annually to the Secretary of State and to be consulted and report on matters referred to it and on proposals for secondary legislation; and
- a new advisory Private Companies Committee which the CLRC and the Standards Board would be obliged to consult to ensure that their proposals took proper account of the special needs of small and private companies.

Under these proposals, the new Standards Board would have increased devolved powers and be able to set company reporting requirements falling into three broad categories:[83]

- *financial:* the Standards Board would have the power to determine the detailed reporting and accounting requirements (including the implementation of many EC Directive requirements) necessary for the accounts prepared under the Act to achieve the purpose required by the Act, i.e. to give a true and fair view of the performance, position and cash flows of the company and, where the company has any subsidiary undertakings, on a consolidated basis for its group (but subject to any statutory exemptions). This is very similar to the present role of the ASB;
- *qualitative reporting (OFR):* the Standards Board would set the disclosure requirements and reporting standards for the new OFR (within the broad headings set out in primary legislation). These should include: standards for reporting on the 'mandatory' items in the OFR; where the directors judge that other items are material, the standards to be followed in making the required disclosures; general rules about presentation of information in the OFR, such as the presentation of prior year comparatives and treatment of financial matters covered in the accounts; rules permitting companies not to disclose certain information on the grounds that to disclose it would cause serious harm to the company; and rules on the extent to which disclosures may benefit from a 'safe harbour'. While this is a significant widening of the remit as compared with that of the ASB, it is not entirely new (the ASB has for example already issued guidance on broader reporting issues such as its OFR); and
- *governance:* broadly speaking, disclosures of the type required under the Combined Code and information on conflicts of interest and potential conflicts (for example, the disclosures currently required under Schedule 6 of the Act).

The Steering Group has recommended further that the new Standards Board should also have power to make detailed rules on the method of publication of reports and accounts, and related issues, in particular the following:[84]

- detailed rules on what constitutes publication in order to satisfy the new website publication requirement for any preliminary statements and the 120-day requirement for the full annual report for quoted companies;
- rules on what constitutes 'non-statutory accounts' and the disclosure requirements where the accounts or other parts of the annual report are published in circumstances other than in the context of surrounding information reviewed by the company's auditors; and

- the Standards Board would need power to determine both the form and content of the summary statement (the successor to the summary financial statement). The primary legislation would make provision for certain types of company to send shareholders summary statements and stipulate that the summary statement shall be derived from the company's annual accounts (including the OFR), providing the framework within which the Standards Board would then determine the precise form and content.

It is clear that the Steering Group envisages a substantially enhanced and different role for the new Standards Board, with significant additional powers and responsibilities being devolved to it. However, as discussed more fully below, the timing of these changes is such that they will coincide with the adoption throughout the European Union of a new financial reporting regime for publicly traded EU incorporated companies based on International Accounting Standards in place of national standards. Given that it is not yet clear what role national standard setters will play within the new institutional arrangements for financial reporting within the EU, only time will tell whether the Steering Group's proposed new role of the Standards Board will be appropriate.

2 THE EVOLUTION OF INTERNATIONAL GAAP

2.1 The International Accounting Standards Committee

The International Accounting Standards Committee (IASC) was formed as an independent private-sector body in 1973 through an agreement made by professional accountancy bodies from Australia, Canada, France, Germany, Japan, Mexico, the Netherlands, the United Kingdom and Ireland and the United States of America. From 1983, the IASC's members included all the professional accountancy bodies that were members of the International Federation of Accountants (IFAC). At the time when the Board of the IASC was dissolved in 2001, there were 153 members in 112 countries.

The IASC was founded to formulate and publish, in the public interest, International Accounting Standards (IAS) to be observed in the presentation of published financial statements and to promote their worldwide acceptance and observance.[85] It was envisaged that IAS should be capable of worldwide acceptance and contribute to a significant improvement in the quality and comparability of corporate disclosure.[86]

The business of the IASC was conducted by a Board comprising representatives of accountancy bodies in 13 countries (or combinations of countries) appointed by the Council of IFAC, and up to four other organisations with an interest in financial reporting. Each Board Member was permitted to nominate up to two representatives and a technical adviser to attend Board meetings. The IASC encouraged each Board Member to include in its delegation at least one person working in industry and one person who was directly involved in the work of the national standard setting body.[87] In 1999, IASC Board meetings were opened up to public observation.

The IASC Board established an international Consultative Group in 1981 that included representatives of international organisations of preparers and users of financial statements, stock exchanges and securities regulators. The Consultative Group met periodically to discuss the technical issues in IASC projects, IASC's work programme and IASC's strategy. This group played an important part in IASC's due process for the setting of International Accounting Standards and in gaining acceptance for the resulting standards.

In 1995, IASC established a high level international Advisory Council, made up of outstanding individuals in senior positions from the accountancy profession, business and the other users of financial statements. The role of the Advisory Council was to promote generally the acceptability of International Accounting Standards and enhance the credibility of IASC's work.

The IASC Board formed a Standing Interpretations Committee (SIC) in 1997 to consider, on a timely basis, accounting issues that were likely to receive divergent or unacceptable treatment in the absence of authoritative guidance. Its consideration was within the context of existing International Accounting Standards and the IASC Framework. In developing interpretations, the SIC consulted similar national committees that had been nominated for the purpose by Member Bodies. The SIC had up to 12 voting members from various countries, including individuals from the accountancy profession, preparer groups and user groups. The European Commission and the International Organisation of Securities Commissions (IOSCO) had observer seats. In 2000, SIC meetings were opened up to public observation.

The SIC considered the following criteria for taking issues on its agenda:

- the issue should involve an interpretation of an existing Standard within the context of the IASC Framework;
- the issue should have practical and widespread relevance;
- the issue should relate to a specific fact pattern; and
- significantly divergent interpretations must either be emerging or already exist in practice.

SIC interpretations were initially published in draft form for public comment (usually 60 days), and if no more than three of its voting members voted against an interpretation, the SIC asked the Board to approve the final interpretation for issue; as for International Accounting Standards, this required three-quarters of the Board to vote in favour. The SIC dealt with issues of reasonably widespread importance, not issues of concern to only a small number of businesses. The interpretations that were issued covered both mature issues, where there was unsatisfactory practice within the scope of existing International Accounting Standards, and emerging issues relating to topics not considered when the standards were developed.

International Accounting Standards and SIC Interpretations have done a great deal both to improve and harmonise financial reporting around the world. IAS are adopted in some countries as the basis for national accounting standards and are used in other countries as the international benchmark in the development of their own standards. A significant number of Stock Exchanges (including the London

Stock Exchange) allow foreign companies to present financial statements in conformity with IAS in fulfilment of their listing obligations, whilst several EU Member States permit quoted domestic companies to prepare their consolidated accounts in accordance with IAS (with the proviso that they comply also with the EU Accounting Directives).

When International Accounting Standards were first issued, they permitted several alternative accounting treatments. The principal reason for this was that the IASC viewed its initial function as prohibiting undesirable accounting practices, whilst acknowledging that there might be more than one acceptable solution to a specific accounting issue. However, in recent years, international accounting standards have been tightened up considerably.

In 1993, the Board of the IASC completed a major project (known as the comparability/improvements project), which had set out to reduce many of the permitted alternative accounting options. This project took four years and culminated in the publication of a package of ten revised international standards which became operative for accounting periods beginning on or after 1 January 1995. Unfortunately, this project was less successful than everyone had hoped it would be, and although the number of permitted alternative options was reduced, they were not eliminated; this meant that international standards still incorporated 'benchmark' treatments and 'allowed alternative' treatments. However, as discussed more fully below, the new International Accounting Standards Board (IASB) has commenced a new Improvements project and is now making a concerted effort both to reduce the options in current IAS and to effect certain fundamental improvements therein.

2.2 The IASC/IOSCO agreement

An increasingly global marketplace brings with it an increasing interdependence of regulators. There must be strong links between regulators and the capacity to give effect to those links. The International Organisation of Securities Commissions (IOSCO) is the leading international grouping of securities market regulators. Its current membership comprises regulatory bodies from 91 countries who have day-to-day responsibility for securities regulation and the administration of securities laws. The Preamble to IOSCO's By-laws states the following:

'Securities authorities resolve to cooperate together to ensure a better regulation of the markets, on the domestic as well as on the international level, in order to maintain just, efficient and sound markets:

- to exchange information on their respective experiences in order to promote the development of domestic markets;
- to unite their efforts to establish standards and an effective surveillance of international securities transactions;
- to provide mutual assistance to ensure the integrity of the markets by a vigorous application of the standards and by effective enforcement against offences.'

In 1989, IOSCO prepared a report entitled *International Equity Offers*, which noted that cross-border offerings would be facilitated by the development of internationally accepted accounting standards. Rather than attempt to develop those standards itself, IOSCO focused on the efforts of the IASC to provide acceptable international accounting standards for use in multinational securities offerings.

In 1993, IOSCO wrote to the IASC detailing the necessary components of a reasonably complete set of standards to create a comprehensive body of principles for enterprises undertaking cross-border securities offerings. In 1994, IOSCO completed a review of the then-current IASC standards and identified a number of issues that would have to be addressed, as well as standards that the IASC would have to improve, before IOSCO could consider recommending IASC standards for use in cross-border listings and offerings. IOSCO divided the issues into three categories:

- issues that required a solution prior to consideration by IOSCO of an endorsement of the IASC standards;
- issues that would not require resolution before IOSCO could consider endorsement, although individual jurisdictions might specify treatments that they would require if those issues were not addressed satisfactorily in the IASC standards; and
- areas where improvements could be made, but that the IASC did not need to address prior to consideration of the IASC standards by IOSCO.

In July 1995, the Board of the IASC and IOSCO's Technical Committee announced that an important milestone had been reached in the development of IAS. The Board had developed a work plan (to become known as 'the core standards work programme') that the Technical Committee agreed would result, upon successful completion, in IAS comprising a comprehensive core set of standards. Completion of comprehensive core standards that were acceptable to the Technical Committee would allow the Technical Committee to recommend the endorsement of IAS by IOSCO for cross-border capital raising and listing purposes in all global markets. IOSCO had already endorsed IAS 7 – *Cash Flow Statements* – and had indicated to the IASC that fourteen of the existing international standards did not require additional improvement, provided that the other core standards were successfully completed.[88]

Both the IASC and IOSCO agreed that there was a compelling need for high quality, comprehensive IAS. The goal of both bodies in reaching this agreement was that financial statements prepared in accordance with IAS could be used worldwide in cross border offerings and listings as an alternative to the use of national accounting standards.

The IASC Board worked extraordinarily hard over the ensuing four and a half years to fulfil its side of the IOSCO agreement. Board meetings were increased both in terms of frequency and duration, several new Steering Committees were formed and a number of major new projects were placed on the Board's agenda. The Board completed its revised core set of standards at its December 1998 meeting, at which IAS 39 – *Financial Instruments: Recognition and Measurement* – was approved for issue. As a result, the IOSCO review of these core standards began in 1999. In the meantime, IOSCO announced that it wished the issue of accounting for investment properties to be added to the list of core standards, and this matter was dealt with in a new standard, IAS 40 – *Investment Property* – which was approved for issue by the IASC Board at its March 2000 meeting.

So all that remained outstanding was for the IOSCO Technical Committee to announce the result of its assessment of the IASC core standards. However, at the time many observers felt that the US Securities and Exchange Commission (SEC) was unlikely to allow IOSCO to endorse IASC standards unconditionally unless they corresponded closely to existing US standards. A more likely scenario was that some or all of the IASC standards would be accepted by the SEC only on the basis of additional disclosures and other conditions. Such an attitude was likely to have been reinforced by a FASB publication that claimed to have identified 255 differences between US GAAP and IASC standards.[89]

2.3 The SEC Concept Release on International Accounting Standards

Whilst the financial reporting world was waiting for IOSCO's Technical Committee to complete its assessment of the IASC's core standards and to declare its likely attitude towards recognising the new body of IAS without requiring reconciliation to national standards, the US Securities and Exchange Commission (SEC) appeared to pre-empt what was to come by publishing in February 2000 a 'Concept Release' on International Accounting Standards.[90]

The Concept Release set out the hurdles IAS would have to clear if they were to be deemed acceptable for US filing purposes. The document was mainly in the form of a series of questions apparently seeking opinions about, and experiences of using, IAS. However although it claimed to be seeking input to determine under what conditions the SEC 'should accept financial statements of foreign private issuers that are prepared using the standards promulgated by the International Accounting Standards Committee', in reality it discussed a number of other matters related to the financial reporting environment, such as auditing standards, audit quality assurance, regulation and enforcement.

There is little doubt that the SEC would argue that its Release was objective and fair-minded. Indeed, it started out in a noble enough manner: 'the globalisation of the securities markets has challenged securities regulators around the world to adapt to meet the needs of market participants while maintaining the current high levels of investor protection and market integrity'. This sentence contained two main statements; first, the challenge for securities regulators to adapt, and second, an assertion that, in general, levels of investor protection and market integrity are currently high.

However, what followed these encouraging statements was an elaborate exposition on why the SEC should not itself adapt in order to help realise the globalisation aim. Furthermore, it seemed to follow from the SEC's views about the need for changes (i.e. improvements) in what it called 'infrastructure support' that the SEC did not in fact believe that there are high levels of investor protection and market integrity outside the US.

Of course, the central issue at hand was essentially whether the SEC should accept financial statements prepared under IAS. Instead of responding directly to this question and looking for ways of adapting its own approach as a basis for embracing IAS, the SEC's view seemed to be that the world should adopt its philosophy of regulation. However, it made no suggestions as to how this should be done, or by whom. Although the SEC at one point stated that it was not focusing on differences between IAS and US GAAP, elsewhere it made it clear that differences between IAS and US GAAP were less than desirable, and clearly implied that the benchmark that IAS needed to meet was US GAAP.

Unfortunately, this posture led some commentators to the inescapable conclusion that the SEC was in favour of adaptation – but by everyone except the SEC. It seemed that countries that wished to adapt and progress in relation to IAS should do so separately and apart from the SEC.

The phase 'high quality' was a recurring theme throughout the Release. However, on occasion, it seemed to be used to the point of being overdone. This is because no one would disagree with the need for high quality accounting standards in the context of the global financial markets. The problem, though, was that the Release used the phase 'high quality' in a somewhat pejorative manner.

This was achieved by the implicit assumption within the Release that the US model meets the criteria for high quality, and that any other model, being different, by definition does not. The inference inevitably to be drawn by readers of the Release was that US standards are high quality standards; the US system of formulating and explaining standards is best; any standards that are different, or differently formulated and explained, are lesser quality standards; US standards give better investor protection than other standards; and regulation and enforcement of standards and the auditing profession is better in the US than anywhere else.

The SEC position centred on investor protection and the pre-eminence of US GAAP, including its regulatory and enforcement regime, in delivering it. Therefore, the clear message was that companies must use US GAAP if they want to raise capital in the US – at least companies must produce a US GAAP reconciliation, which is tantamount to the same thing – or else investors will be at risk.

However, how much of this is borne out by the facts? Admittedly, there are cultural differences between the way IAS and US GAAP are expressed. IAS are couched in terms of principles not rules, and preparers and auditors exercise professional judgement in their application to particular circumstances, as opposed merely to following detailed rules. This does not seem to have affected investors adversely, though. For example, UK GAAP is similar to IAS, and there is no evidence whatsoever that the UK has a poorer record of investor protection than the US.

The reality is that IAS are as much investor-oriented as US standards. However, the SEC attempted to steal the moral high ground by couching its discussion of IAS in terms of 'issues related to the infrastructure for high quality financial reporting'.

The implied context of the Release is that a FASB-style model meets the criteria for a high quality standard setter, and that any other model does not. This is, of course, simply not true.

First, it should not be presumed that the structure required for a national standard setter is the same as that for a global standard setter. Second, there is no evidence to support the assertion that only a rules-based FASB-style model can produce high quality, internationally acceptable standards. And third, the implied assertion that the FASB itself produces high quality standards on a consistent basis is open to challenge.

Interestingly also, the SEC's attitude towards IAS is in sharp contrast to that of the American investment bank, Morgan Stanley. In their study on global investing, they posed the question 'How close are IAS and U.S. GAAP?'. Perhaps surprisingly to many they gave the following response: 'The answer depends on what benchmark you use; spelling out all the differences would require a textbook. FASB has identified 255 differences, although many investors would find most of them meaningless. For reflecting economic substance in most industries, IAS is easily of comparable quality to U.S. GAAP, if auditors do their jobs.'

This answer highlights a fundamental philosophical difference in approach to accounting harmonisation between the US and Europe. It seems that the SEC views harmonisation as being synonymous with uniform regulatory control. In contrast, the European approach, for example, is based on the notions of equivalence and mutual recognition that are embodied in the EU Accounting and Securities Directives.

Equivalence demands from all sides a willingness to adapt and compromise. This means that, in order to achieve the convergence of the US and European systems of reporting under the IASC umbrella, Europe will have both to compromise on some of its existing practices, and embrace a common system of securities regulation and effective enforcement (discussed at 3.7 below). Similarly, the SEC will have to be persuaded that the accommodation of a different, though equally valid, reporting system is appropriate. This means that the SEC will have to consider a system based on the principle of equivalence instead of uniformity in the light of the practical reality that absolutely identical international reporting based on a uniform system, controlled by a single regulatory authority, is not attainable in the foreseeable future, if indeed ever.

The Concept Release attracted numerous letters of response, many of which expressed views that were unsupportive of the general thrust of the document. To date, though, there has been no follow-up to the Release by the SEC. Nevertheless, as discussed below, it appeared to set the scene for what was to come three months later in IOSCO's Assessment Report on IAS.

2.4 The IOSCO Assessment Report on International Accounting Standards

The IOSCO assessment should be seen in the context of the present situation regarding the acceptance of IAS by the international capital markets. The reality is that many dozens of the world's stock exchanges – including, Amsterdam, London, Sydney, Frankfurt, Tokyo and Zurich – accept IAS financial statements for cross-border listing purposes without reconciliation to national GAAP. The only significant exceptions are the exchanges in Canada and the USA. Consequently, a large part of the IOSCO effort was directed towards gaining the acceptance of the North American securities regulators.

In May 2000, IOSCO announced the completion of its assessment of the IASC's core standards through the publication by IOSCO's Technical Committee of a report that summarised its assessment work.[91] In view of the SEC Concept Release that had been issued three months earlier (see above), the outcome of the Technical Committee's assessment of the IASC's core standards was perhaps not unexpected. Nevertheless, its content was a great disappointment to many observers and those that had been involved in the core standards programme, who believed that the IASC Board had fulfilled all its obligations under the IOSCO agreement.

The report stated that IOSCO had assessed 30 IASC standards, including their related interpretations (termed 'the IASC 2000 standards'), and considered their suitability for use in cross-border offerings and listings. Although the report recommended that IOSCO members permit incoming multinational issuers to use the IASC 2000 standards to prepare their financial statements for cross-border offerings and listings, this recommendation was made subject to a significant proviso. The proviso was that each IOSCO member, in deciding how to implement the IASC 2000 standards in its jurisdiction, could choose to mandate one or more of the following 'supplemental treatments':

- *Reconciliation:* this would require reconciliation of the treatment specified in an IASC 2000 standard to another specified accounting treatment (which may be a host country national accounting treatment). This reconciliation would be expected to be presented in a footnote to the financial statements and would quantify the effect of applying the specified alternative accounting treatment.
- *Supplemental disclosure:* this would require supplemental disclosure, either in the form of:
    - more detailed footnote disclosure than an IASC 2000 standard requires; or
    - additional detail on the face of the primary financial statements (e.g., income statement or balance sheet line items) that would have to be presented.
- *Interpretation:* this would require a specific application of an IASC 2000 standard, either:
    - in cases where an IASC 2000 standard permits different approaches to an issue, generally with one approach identified as a 'benchmark' and another as an 'allowed alternative', specifying which approach (the 'benchmark' or 'allowed alternative') is accepted in a host jurisdiction; or

- to clarify ambiguity or address silence in an IASC 2000 standard, by specifying a particular interpretation of the IASC 2000 standard that should be used in a host jurisdiction.

If the specified treatment is not followed, it is expected that an IOSCO member will require reconciliation to the specified treatment.

In an Appendix running to more than 100 pages, the report identified numerous 'concerns' raised by IOSCO members during the assessment of the IASC 2000 standards. These 'concerns' included an analysis of outstanding substantive issues relating to the standards, specifying supplemental treatments that might be required in a particular jurisdiction to address each of these concerns.

The effect of this report by the Technical Committee of IOSCO was to negate the intention of the IASC/IOSCO agreement. Its impact is to perpetuate the current position whereby a company may have to comply with more than one reporting regime in order to obtain a cross-border listing, thereby doing nothing to remove duplication, complication and expense.

Thus, the long-awaited 'endorsement' from IOSCO was, in fact, only a qualified acceptance of IAS that still allows IOSCO members to request any supplemental treatment that they consider necessary. Whilst one can accept that different regulatory jurisdictions might require additional note disclosures in line with local circumstances, the imposition of any reconciliation requirement requiring different recognition and measurement rules is clearly contrary to any notion of accounting harmonisation. Unfortunately, it seems that any such unconditional endorsement of IAS by IOSCO for cross-border capital raising and listing purposes in all global markets is a long way off, and will require substantial further effort by both sides.

2.5 The restructuring of the IASC

2.5.1 Shaping IASC for the future

Few would disagree that since its formation in 1973, the IASC had achieved a great deal within the limitations of its structure. However, with the globalisation of the world's capital markets, the increasing complexity of business transactions and the growing pressure for a single set of internationally harmonised accounting standards, the IASC Board believed that structural changes were needed for it to anticipate and meet effectively the new challenges that it faced.

Consequently, the IASC Board saw the completion of its core standards programme as an appropriate moment to undertake a review of its strategy. As a result, in 1998 it appointed a Strategy Working Party to conduct a general review of the strategy of the IASC.

The Working Party published its proposals in December 1998 in a Discussion Paper entitled 'Shaping IASC for the future'.[92] The Working Party's proposals were fairly radical, but were framed within the rather nebulous notion of a 'partnership with national standard setters'.[93] The rationale behind this was that the IASC should enter into a partnership with national standard setters enabling the IASC to work with them to accelerate convergence between national standards and International

Accounting Standards. However, in order to form this 'partnership', the Working Party proposed the abolition of the IASC Board structure and the establishment of a bicameral system in its place. Under this system, a disproportionate amount of power would be concentrated in a Standards Development Committee (SDC), comprising a small group of select full-time standard setters. It was also proposed that the SDC would replace the IASC's Steering Committee system, under which Standards had been developed. The Working Party's recommendations covered a number of other areas, including the IASC's system of due process, implementation, education, enforcement and funding.

Perhaps not surprisingly, the Working Party's proposals met with considerable opposition, both from within the IASC Board and outside. The principal criticisms of the proposals centred around the bicameral system, the concept of the SDC and the issue of legitimacy. One general perception was that the Discussion Paper was aimed at further entrenching the position of the group of Anglo-Saxon accounting standard setters known as the G4+1.[94]

However, many saw the biggest single failing of the Working Party's proposals to be that they did not address adequately the key issue of legitimacy among the IASC's constituencies. So whilst there was agreement with the objectives identified by the Working Party, there was less support for the structure that was proposed in order to achieve them, since the proposed structure would not have ensured legitimacy. The Discussion Paper contained little elaboration on the details of the proposed 'partnership with national standard setters' and other key constituencies, with the result that their role under the proposed structure was unclear.

There was particular concern expressed also about the representation of users and preparers of accounts in any new standard setting structure. Ultimately, the long-term credibility of International Accounting Standards would depend on their acceptance by the preparer and user communities as well as the international capital markets. There therefore had to be full participation by all the key players in the marketplace in order to secure the future of IAS.

The IASC Board had a joint meeting on 30 June 1999 with the Strategy Working Party to discuss the comments received on the Discussion Paper. The discussion indicated that the proposed bicameral/SDC system should be abandoned in favour of a single Board structure. There was a general consensus that this single Board should comprise a blend of full and part-time members, although the overall size of the Board and precise proportion of full and part-timers was not agreed. The Strategy Working Party met again during July 1999 in order to develop a new proposal along the lines of its discussions with the IASC Board.

2.5.2 The new IASC structure

In November 1999, the IASC's Strategy Working Party presented its final report – *Recommendations on Shaping IASC for the Future* – to the IASC Board.[95] In fact, the report was delivered somewhat as a *fait accompli*, and it was clear to the members of the IASC Board that there was little room for discussion: they could either take it or leave it. It seemed to many observers that the process had become highly politicised, and that the influence of the US SEC could be detected in ensuring that the IASB would be constituted as closely as possible in the image of the FASB. Thus, although the Strategy Working Party had seemingly dealt with the objections raised concerning its original bi-cameral structure, a number of fundamental difficulties that many observers and commentators had raised had not been resolved.

From a European perspective, these difficulties surrounded the issue of legitimacy and political accountability. This is because many believed that the essential feature of any new model should be that it was seen to be legitimate. This was considered as vital in order to ensure maximum commitment from those constituencies who have to implement, regulate and enforce the system. Legitimacy and enforcement are linked, because broader support from the key constituencies in setting the standards makes it significantly more likely that the standards will be applied and enforced, which in turn gives them credibility. However, there was a clear tension between this 'representative' model that was clearly preferred in Europe and elsewhere on the one hand, and the SEC/FASB 'expert' model on the other.

In any event, the Strategy Working Party's proposal was presented to the IASC Board as a non-negotiable agreement with the SEC. This meant that the Board, left with no room to manoeuvre, adopted unanimously the recommendations of the Strategy Working Party. These were then approved by the member bodies of the International Federation of Accountants, under whose patronage the IASC Board operated. The new structure adopted is outlined below.

The IASC Foundation

The governance of the IASC Organisation[96] is ultimately in the hands of the Trustees of the IASC Foundation. The Trustees were appointed during the second half of 2000 by a Nominating Committee that was set up for that sole purpose under the Chairmanship of the then US SEC Chairman, Mr. Arthur Levitt. There are nineteen Trustees from diverse career backgrounds, under the Chairmanship of Mr. Paul A. Volcker, a Former Chairman of the US Federal Reserve Board. To ensure a broad international representation, there are six Trustees from North America, six from Europe, four from the Asia/Pacific region and three from any area, subject to establishing an overall geographical balance. The appointment of all subsequent Trustees to fill vacancies caused by routine retirement or other reasons is the responsibility of the existing Trustees. The appointment of the Trustees is normally for a term of three years, renewable once. However, to provide continuity, some of the initial Trustees will serve staggered terms so as to retire after four or five years.

The first act of the Board of Trustees was to appoint Sir David Tweedie (who had just completed a highly distinguished period of ten years as the Chairman of the UK's Accounting Standards Board) as the first Chairman of the new International Accounting Standards Board (IASB). Subsequently, in January 2001, the Trustees appointed the thirteen other members of the IASB. The Trustees are responsible also for appointing the members of the Standing Interpretations Committee (SIC) and Standards Advisory Council (SAC). In addition, they are responsible for:[97]

- fundraising;
- establishing or amending operating procedures for the Trustees;

- publishing an annual report on the IASC'S activities, including audited financial statements and priorities for the coming year;
- reviewing annually the strategy of IASB and its effectiveness;
- approving annually the budget of IASC and determining the basis for funding;
- reviewing broad strategic issues affecting accounting standards, promoting the IASC and its work and promoting the objective of rigorous application of IAS (the Trustees are, however, excluded from involvement in technical matters relating to accounting standards);
- establishing and amending operating procedures for the IASB, the SAC and the SIC;
- approving amendments to the Constitution after following a due process, including consultation with the SAC and publication of an Exposure Draft for public comment;
- exercising all powers of IASC except for those expressly reserved to the Board, the SAC and the SIC.

The Trustees are not responsible for setting the Standards. This responsibility rests solely with the IASB.

The IASC Foundation was formed in March 2001 as a not-for-profit corporation and is the parent entity of the IASB. On 1 April 2001, the IASB assumed accounting standard setting responsibilities from the former IASC Board, which was dissolved.

Set out below is a graphical representation of the new IASC Foundation structure:

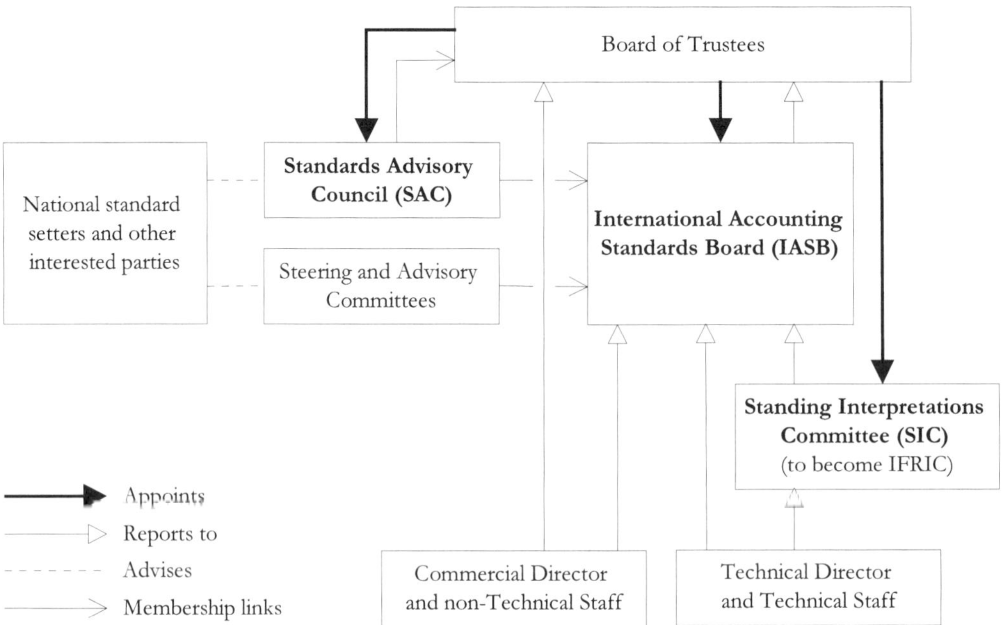

The IASB Constitution

The current text of the Constitution was approved by the Trustees at their meeting of 8 March 2001. The Constitution sets out the basic structural and procedural framework for the various bodies of the IASC Organisation. Article 2 of the Constitution sets the objectives of the IASC as follows:

- to develop, in the public interest, a single set of high quality, understandable and enforceable global accounting standards that require high quality, transparent and comparable information in financial statements and other financial reporting to help participants in the world's capital markets make economic decisions;
- to promote the use and rigorous application of those standards; and
- to bring about convergence of national accounting standards and International Accounting Standards to high quality solutions.

The International Accounting Standards Board (IASB)

As stated above, in accordance with paragraph 23 of the Constitution, the IASC Foundation Trustees have appointed twelve of the IASB Members to full-time positions, including the Chairman and the Vice-Chairman, and two to part-time positions. To encourage cooperation among the new Board and national standard-setters, the Trustees appointed seven of the IASB Members as official liaisons to national bodies. These liaison IASB Members must maintain close contact with their respective national standard-setters and are responsible for coordinating agendas and ensuring that the IASB and national bodies are working toward the goal of convergence on a single set of high quality standards around the world. Countries with formal liaisons are Australia and New Zealand together, Canada, France, Germany, Japan, the United States, and the United Kingdom. In addition, IASB Members will have frequent contacts with the European Commission, financial regulators and central banks, private industry, analysts, and academics throughout the world.

Following the appointment of the members of the IASB, Sir David Tweedie stated the following: 'The mission of the newly-created IASB is simple. In partnership with national standard setters, we will aim to increase the transparency of financial reporting by achieving a single, global method of accounting for transactions – whether in Stuttgart, Sydney, Seattle or Singapore. The potential benefit to the world economy by removing barriers to investment through applying uniform, high-quality standards is enormous.'[98]

The members of the IASB are not selected based on geographical representation. However, the Constitution stipulates that the Trustees shall ensure that the IASB is not dominated by any particular constituency or geographical interest. The foremost qualification for membership of the IASB is technical expertise. The IASB must comprise a group of people representing, within that group, the best available combination of technical skills and background experience of relevant international business and market conditions to contribute to the development of high quality, global accounting standards. No individual can be Trustee and IASB Member at the same time.

To achieve a balance of perspectives and experience, a minimum of five members of the IASB must have a background as practising auditors, a minimum of three a background in the preparation of financial statements, a minimum of three a background as users of financial statements, and at least one an academic background.[99]

The responsibilities of the IASB are listed in paragraph 36 of the Constitution. The primary role of the IASB is to have complete responsibility for all technical matters including the preparation and publication of International Accounting Standards and Exposure Drafts, both of which shall include dissenting opinions, and final approval of Interpretations by the SIC. Decisions by the IASB require only a simple majority (i.e. eight out of fourteen votes) to be adopted. The IASB has full discretion over its technical agenda and over project assignments on technical matters. It must consult the SAC on major projects, agenda decisions and work priorities.

The IASB (whose meetings are open to the public) met in technical session for the first time in April 2001. During this meeting, it approved a resolution to adopt the existing body of International Accounting Standards and Interpretations issued by the former IASC Board and the SIC. The IASB announced also that the IASC Foundation Trustees have agreed that the accounting standards issued by the IASB shall be designated 'International Financial Reporting Standards (IFRS)'. The existing pronouncements shall, however, continue to be designated 'International Accounting Standards (IAS)'.

The Standards Advisory Council (SAC)

The SAC provides a forum for participation by organisations and individuals with an interest in international financial reporting, who have diverse geographic and functional backgrounds, with the objective of (a) giving advice to the IASB on agenda decisions and priorities in the Board's work, (b) informing the IASB of the views of the SAC members on major standard setting projects and (c) giving other advice to the IASB or the Trustees.[100]

The SAC must be consulted by the IASB in advance of Board decisions on major projects and by the Trustees in advance of any proposed changes to the Constitution.[101]

In June 2001, the Trustees of the IASC Foundation announced the appointment of 49 SAC members. The members include chief financial and accounting officers from some of the world's largest corporations and international organisations, leading financial analysts and academics, regulators, accounting standard setters, and partners from leading accounting firms. The members of the SAC are drawn from six continents, 29 countries, and five international organisations. In addition, the European Commission, the US Securities and Exchange Commission, and the Financial Services Agency of Japan will participate as observers.

The SAC (whose meetings are open to the public) will normally meet three times a year under the chairmanship of the IASB Chairman. The SAC met for the first time with the IASB in July 2001, where it:

- discussed the role and operations of the SAC;
- discussed proposals for revisions to the mandate and operating procedures of the SIC (see below);
- discussed a draft of a revised Preface to the IASB standards; and
- discussed the topics and priorities suggested by the IASB for inclusion in its initial technical agenda (see below).

The Standing Interpretations Committee (SIC)

The SIC was formed in 1997 (under the former IASC structure) and for the time being continues to operate under the new IASC structure, in accordance with paragraphs 38 to 41 of the Constitution.

The role of the SIC is to:

- interpret the application of International Accounting Standards, in the context of IASC's framework, and undertake other tasks at the request of the IASB;
- publish draft Interpretations for public comment and consider comments made within a reasonable period before finalising an Interpretation; and
- report to the IASB and obtain Board approval for final Interpretations.[102]

As stated above, at its July 2001 meeting, the SAC discussed with the Board the Board's proposals to amend the mandate and operating procedures of the SIC. The IASB is proposing to rename the committee as the *International Financial Reporting Interpretations Committee (IFRIC)* and to expand its mandate to enable the committee to address issues beyond interpretations of existing standards. IFRIC would be able to provide authoritative guidance on accounting issues that, in the absence of such guidance, would be developed by other parties and perhaps would lead to divergent practices in different jurisdictions. While some members of SAC expressed concern over the status of IFRIC interpretations, it was acknowledged that the committee's proposed due process would provide a suitable degree of review and opportunities for input.

The Board is proposing that the membership of IFRIC will be twelve voting members, with a non-voting chair. The chair will be an IASB member, a senior member of the IASB technical staff or an individual from outside the IASB.

The IFRIC operating procedures will be revised from those used currently to include the use of an agenda committee and to provide for earlier IASB involvement in the process of issuing interpretations. The IASB has proposed that the issuance of *draft* interpretations should be subject to a process of negative clearance by the IASB while preserving the approval of *final* interpretations by way of a positive vote of the IASB in public meeting.

The IASB will present its final proposals, together with the related changes necessary for the IASB Constitution, to the IASC Foundation Trustees in October 2001. The changes to the Constitution will be exposed for public comment. Until such time as the necessary constitutional changes are made, the SIC continues to operate as before, dealing with its current work in progress.

2.6 The IASB's Technical Agenda

2.6.1 An agenda of twenty-five technical projects

After consultation with the SAC, national accounting standard setters, regulators and other interested parties, the IASB has determined an initial agenda of nine technical projects. These are divided into three broad categories:

- Projects intended to provide leadership and promote convergence, which comprise the following:
    - Accounting for insurance contracts
    - Business combinations
    - Reporting financial performance
    - Accounting for share based payments,
- Projects intended to provide for easier application of International Financial Reporting Standards, which comprise the following:
    - Guidance on first-time application of IFRSs
    - Activities of financial institutions: disclosure and presentation; and
- Projects intended to improve existing standards, which comprise the following:
    - Preface to IFRSs
    - Improvements to existing IASs (see 2.6.2 below)
    - Amendments to IAS 39 – *Financial Instruments: Recognition and Measurement.*

In addition to these, sixteen other issues are being worked on by one or more of the IASB's national standard setting partners. The IASB will be working with these partners, or at least monitoring these efforts, in order to ensure that any differences between national standard setters or with the IASB are identified and resolved as quickly as possible. These issues comprise the following:

- Accounting measurement
- Accounting by extractive industries
- Accounting for financial instruments (i.e. the comprehensive full fair value project)
- Accounting for leases
- Accounting by small and medium entities in emerging economies
- Accounting for taxes on income (i.e. dealing with issues of convergence between IAS 12 and certain national standards such as FRS 19)

- Business combinations
- Consolidation policy
- Definitions of elements of financial statements
- Derecognition issues, other than those addressed in IAS 39
- Employee benefits (dealing with issues of convergence between IAS 19 and certain national standards such as FRS 17)
- Impairment of assets
- Intangible assets
- Liabilities and revenue recognition
- Management's Discussion and Analysis (an area not currently dealt with in the IASC literature)
- Revaluation of certain assets.

2.6.2 *The Improvements Project*

The objective of the Improvements Project is to add clarity and consistency to the requirements of existing IASs issued by the former IASC Board. The specific topics that are being addressed come from information already provided to the IASB by sources such as IOSCO, national standard setters, and the SIC. The issues to be addressed are those identified as narrow issues of substance whose resolution could improve the quality of an IAS and/or increase convergence of national and international standards. The Board intends to address these issues immediately, so that companies adopting IAS for the first time will not be faced with significant additional change thereafter.

The IASB has received a report from its Improvements Sub-Committee, which has recommended that separate limited-scope improvement projects should be undertaken on IAS 39/IAS 32 (financial instruments) and first-time application. The IASB has stated further that it is premature to make a decision on the elimination of any specific accounting alternatives. However, the Board has agreed that the following accounting choices present in existing IASs should be discussed with national standard setters:

- Cost formulas (FIFO vs. LIFO) for inventories (IAS 2)
- Treatment of fundamental errors and changes in accounting policy (IAS 8)
- Treatment of initial direct costs by lessors (IAS 17)
- Translation of goodwill and fair value adjustments resulting from an acquisition of a foreign entity (IAS 21)
- Treatment of borrowing costs (IAS 23)
- Measurement of investments and associates in the investor's separate financial statements (IAS 27 and IAS 28)
- Accounting for joint ventures (IAS 31).

These are all controversial issues, as the elimination of currently permitted options (such as LIFO and the capitalisation of borrowing costs) will potentially create conflicts with US GAAP and other national standards.

2.7 Financial reporting in compliance with International Accounting Standards

Although International Accounting Standards, in themselves, do not have the force of law, they have become internationally accepted and are applied by a growing number of companies. More importantly though, an increasing number of countries are beginning to recognise International Accounting Standards in their national legislation as an acceptable financial reporting framework for the purposes of preparing primary financial statements.

The main document setting out the basis on which financial statements should be presented under IAS, and the required contents of those financial statements, is IAS 1 – *Presentation of Financial Statements.*[103] In the remainder of this section, we outline the principal tenets of IAS 1 and provide a general introduction to its requirements.

2.7.1 *Components of financial statements*

A complete set of financial statements under IAS includes the following components:[104]

- balance sheet;
- income statement;
- a statement showing either (1) all changes in equity or (2) changes in equity other than those arising from capital transactions with owners and distributions to owners;
- cash flow statement; and
- accounting policies and explanatory notes.

IAS 1 encourages entities to present, outside the financial statements, a financial review by management that describes and explains the main features of the entity's financial performance and financial position, and the principal uncertainties it faces. Such a report may include a review of:[105]

- the main factors and influences determining performance, including changes in the environment in which the entity operates, the entity's response to those changes and their effect, and the entity's policy for investment to maintain and enhance performance, including its dividend policy;
- the entity's sources of funding, the policy on gearing and its risk management policies; and
- the strengths and resources of the entity whose value is not reflected in the balance sheet under International Accounting Standards.

This 'encouragement' is similar in nature to the framework found in UK GAAP that encourages UK companies to present an Operating and Financial Review (OFR) within their annual reports. The OFR is a framework for the directors to discuss and analyse the business's performance and the factors underlying its results and financial position, in order to assist users to assess for themselves the future potential of the business. In practice, many multinational companies reporting under IAS include in their annual reports a narrative review by management that is at least equivalent to an OFR published by UK companies.

2.7.2 *Fair presentation and compliance with International Accounting Standards*

An entity whose financial statements comply with International Accounting Standards should disclose that fact.[106] IAS compliance involves compliance with all the recognition, measurement and disclosure provisions of the standards. For this reason, IAS 1 now states that 'financial statements should not be described as complying with International Accounting Standards unless they comply with all the requirements of each applicable Standard and each applicable interpretation of the Standing Interpretations Committee.'[107] The IASC has therefore established unambiguously the principle that full application of its standards and related interpretations is a necessary prerequisite for a company to assert that its financial statements comply with International Accounting Standards.

Paragraph 10 of IAS 1 requires that 'financial statements should present fairly the financial position, financial performance and cash flows of an enterprise.' It goes on to state that the appropriate application of International Accounting Standards, with additional disclosure when necessary, results, in virtually all circumstances, in financial statements that achieve a fair presentation, and that inappropriate accounting treatments are not rectified either by disclosure of the accounting policies used or by notes or explanatory material.[108]

Paragraph 13 of IAS 1 provides for those exceptional circumstances where a company's management concludes that compliance with a requirement in an IAS would be misleading. The standard requires that in those circumstances where departure from a requirement is necessary in order to achieve fair presentation, management should depart from a requirement in a standard and explain such departure by giving the following disclosures:[109]

'(a) that management has concluded that the financial statements fairly present the enterprise's financial position, financial performance and cash flows;

(b) that it has complied in all material respects with applicable International Accounting Standards except that it has departed from a Standard in order to achieve a fair presentation;

(c) the Standard from which the enterprise has departed, the nature of the departure, including the treatment that the Standard would require, the reason why that treatment would be misleading in the circumstances and the treatment adopted; and

(d) the financial impact of the departure on the enterprise's net profit or loss, assets, liabilities, equity and cash flows for each period presented.'

These requirements clearly establish the pervasive nature of the fair presentation concept, whilst being a necessary complement to paragraph 10. It is now absolutely clear that accounts that hold themselves out as being drawn up in compliance with IAS must comply with all the requirements of each applicable Standard and SIC Interpretation. At the same time, though, it is also clear that the achievement of fair presentation goes beyond mere compliance with the letter of the standards and interpretations.

It is worth noting that the fair presentation override is a requirement (not an option) of IAS 1 to be applied in the extremely rare circumstances when management concludes that compliance with a requirement in a Standard would be misleading. IAS 1 confirms that 'the existence of conflicting national requirements is not, in itself, sufficient to justify a departure in financial statements prepared using International Accounting Standards.'[110] It goes on to state that it will be the case only if the application of a specific requirement in an International Accounting Standard might result in misleading financial statements 'when the treatment required by the Standard is clearly inappropriate and thus a fair presentation cannot be achieved either by applying the Standard or through additional disclosure alone. Departure is not appropriate simply because another treatment would also give a fair presentation.'[111]

In dealing with the issue of fair presentation and compliance with IAS, the former IASC Board tackled the so-called problem of 'IAS-lite' reporting head on. 'IAS-lite' reporting is the term that has been used to describe situations where accounts purport to have been prepared in accordance with IAS, but which seem to indulge in some notable aspects of non-compliance. In introducing the requirement in paragraph 11 of IAS 1 that financial statements should not be described as complying with International Accounting Standards unless they comply with all the requirements of each applicable Standard and each applicable Interpretation of the SIC, the Board was trying to ensure that users of accounts are not led to infer that accounts are IAS compliant when they are not.

There are several large companies, both European and non-European, that continue to include in their accounts references to IAS of a nature that leave the reader in the dark about what this reference actually means in practice. We have noted instances where companies claim that the accounts, in addition to being in compliance with national requirements, are materially compliant with IAS. However, on closer examination, we have found what appear to be a number of significant examples of non-compliance, such as:

- Formation costs capitalised as an intangible asset on the balance sheet seemingly contrary to the requirements of IAS 38.
- Balance sheets that include large reserves and provisions for risks or reorganisations, which do not appear to comply with the recognition requirements of IAS 37.
- Disclosures that are required by IAS are not given – for example under IAS 19 in respect of pensions and other employee benefits. It is therefore unclear whether or not the recognition and measurement requirements of a given standard have been complied with in full.
- Revaluations of fixed assets that do not appear to comply with the revaluation requirements of IAS 16.
- Lease payments are charged to the income statement, but it is unclear whether any of these leases should be classified as finance lease under IAS 17.
- Income statements that include large extraordinary items, when it is not entirely clear that these items meet the definition of extraordinary under IAS 8.

We hope that, as the adoption of IAS becomes more widespread, greater rigour will be applied by preparers, auditors and regulators in ensuring that paragraph 11 of IAS 1 is properly applied, and that accounts refer to IAS only in those instances where it is appropriate to do so.

2.7.3 *Accounting policies*

A fair presentation requires:[112]

- selecting and applying accounting policies in the way described below;
- presenting information in a manner that provides relevant, reliable, comparable and understandable information. The accounting policies section of the financial statements needs to describe at least the following:[113]
  - the measurement basis used in preparing the financial statements; and
  - each specific accounting policy that is necessary for a proper understanding of the financial statements; and
- providing additional disclosures when the requirements of International Accounting Standards are insufficient to enable users to understand the impact of particular transactions or events on the entity's financial position and financial performance.

Management should select and apply an entity's accounting policies so that the financial statements comply with all requirements under IAS.[114] Where there is no specific requirement under IAS, the entity should develop its accounting policies in such a way as to ensure that the financial statements provide information that is:

- relevant to the decision-making needs of users; and
- reliable in that they:
  - represent faithfully the results and financial position of the entity;
  - reflect the economic substance of events and transactions and not merely the legal form;
  - are neutral, that is free from bias;
  - are prudent; and
  - are complete in all material respects.

In the absence of a specific IAS or SIC Interpretation, management should use its judgement in developing an accounting policy that provides the most useful information for users of the entity's financial statements.[115] In making this judgement, management should consider:

- the requirements and guidance in International Accounting Standards dealing with similar and related issues
- the definitions, recognition and measurement criteria for assets, liabilities, income and expenses set out in the IASC Framework; and
- pronouncements of other standard setting bodies and accepted industry practices to the extent that these are consistent with the guidance as described above.

2.7.4 *Benchmark treatment versus allowed alternative treatment*

In some cases where International Accounting Standards permit two accounting treatments for the same type of transaction or event, one treatment is designated as the *benchmark* treatment and the other as the *allowed alternative* treatment.

The origin of these terms may be traced back to the time when it was thought that a higher degree of comparability might be achieved by identifying a common point of reference in IAS financial reporting. Thus, whilst acknowledging that entities had a free choice between different treatments, it was suggested that all entities reporting under IAS should be required to reconcile their financial statements to this identified point of reference, namely the benchmark treatments in all the standards. However, this proposal received little support, and the idea of reconciliation statements was abandoned. Consequently, although the terms 'benchmark' and 'allowed alternative' were retained, the IASC Board has made it clear that both treatments enjoy equal status. The fact that one approach is labelled 'benchmark' does not mean that it is the Board's preferred approach.

Therefore, in practice, entities can choose freely between applying the benchmark treatment or the allowed alternative treatment on a standard-by-standard basis – taking into account the guidance of SIC-18 *Consistency – Alternative Methods*. SIC-18 requires that if more than one accounting policy is available under an International Accounting Standard or Interpretation, an enterprise should choose and apply consistently one of those policies, unless the Standard or Interpretation specifically requires or permits categorisation of items (transactions, events, balances, amounts, etc.) for which different policies may be appropriate. If a Standard requires or permits categorisation of items, the most appropriate accounting policy should be selected and applied consistently to each category.[116]

2.7.5 *Basis of preparation*

In preparing financial statements under IAS, management should make an assessment of the entity's ability to continue as a going concern.[117] In assessing whether the going concern assumption is appropriate, management should take into account all available information for the foreseeable future, which is not limited to twelve months from the balance sheet date.[118] Material uncertainties relating to events or conditions that may cast significant doubt upon the entity's ability to continue as a going concern should be disclosed.[119]

The financial statements of an entity should not be prepared on a going concern basis if management determines after the balance sheet date either that it intends to liquidate the entity or to cease trading, or that it has no realistic alternative but to do so.[120] If the financial statements are not prepared on a going concern basis, that fact should be disclosed, together with the basis on which the financial statements are prepared and the reason why the entity is not considered to be a going concern.[121]

Financial statements should be prepared, except for cash flow information, under the accrual basis of accounting (i.e., transactions and events are recognised when they occur, and not as cash or its equivalent is received or paid, and they are recorded in the accounting records and reported in the financial statements of the periods to which they relate).[122]

The presentation and classification of items in the financial statements should be retained from one period to the next, unless a significant change in the nature of the operations of the entity, or a review of its financial statement presentation, demonstrates that the change will result in a more appropriate presentation of events or transactions; or unless a change in presentation is required by an IAS or an Interpretation of the SIC.[123]

2.7.6 *Materiality*

Each material item should be presented separately in the financial statements. If a line item is not individually material, it is aggregated with other items either on the face of the financial statements or in the notes. An item that is not sufficiently material to warrant separate presentation on the face of the financial statements may nevertheless be sufficiently material that it should be presented separately in the notes. Information is considered material, based on the size and nature of the item, if its non-disclosure could influence the economic decisions of users taken on the basis of the financial statements. Nevertheless, there is the overriding philosophy that individual IAS are not intended to apply to immaterial items.[124] This fact is stated as a reminder at the start of each IAS.

2.7.7 *Comparative information*

Comparative information should be disclosed in respect of the previous period for all numerical information in the financial statements, unless an IAS permits or requires otherwise. Comparative information should be included in narrative and descriptive information when it is relevant to an understanding of the current period's financial statements. When the presentation or classification of items in the financial statements is amended, comparative amounts should be reclassified to ensure comparability with the current period. The nature, amount of, and reason for, any reclassification should be disclosed. When it is impracticable to reclassify comparative amounts, an entity should disclose the reason for not reclassifying and the nature of the changes that would have been made if amounts were reclassified.[125]

2.7.8 *Distinction between current and non-current*

Each entity should determine, based on the nature of its operations, whether or not to present current and non-current assets and current and non-current liabilities as separate classifications on the face of the balance sheet. When an entity chooses not to make this classification, assets and liabilities should be presented broadly in order of their liquidity. Whether or not an entity presents current and non-current items separately, it should disclose for each asset and liability item that combines amounts expected to be recovered or settled both before and after twelve months from the balance sheet date, the amount expected to be recovered or settled after more than twelve months.[126]

2.7.9 Classification of expenses

An entity should present, either on the face of the income statement or in the notes to the income statement, an analysis of expenses using a classification based on either the nature of expenses or their function within the enterprise. The choice of method depends on both historical and industry factors and the nature of the organisation. Both methods provide an indication of those costs that might be expected to vary, directly or indirectly, with the level of sales or production of the enterprise. Because each method of presentation has merit for different types of entity, IAS 1 requires a choice to be made between classifications based on that which most fairly presents the elements of the entity's performance. However, because information on the nature of expenses is useful in predicting future cash flows, entities classifying expenses by function should disclose additional information on the nature of expenses, including depreciation and amortisation expense and staff costs.[127]

2.7.10 Layout of balance sheet, income statement and statement of changes in equity

IAS do not prescribe standard layouts for the primary financial statements. However, the standard does require that the following information be presented as a minimum:

Balance sheet

The face of the balance sheet should include line items which present the following amounts:[128]

- property, plant and equipment;
- intangible assets;
- financial assets (excluding amounts shown under the headings marked *);
- investments accounted for using the equity method *;
- inventories;
- trade and other receivables *;
- cash and cash equivalents *;
- trade and other payables;
- tax liabilities and assets as required by IAS 12, Income Taxes;
- provisions;
- non-current interest-bearing liabilities;
- minority interest; and
- issued capital and reserves.

Additional line items, headings and sub-totals should be presented on the face of the balance sheet when an IAS requires it, or when such presentation is necessary to present fairly the enterprise's financial position.[129]

An entity should disclose, either on the face of the balance sheet or in the notes to the balance sheet, further sub-classifications of the line items presented, classified in a manner appropriate to the entity's operations. Each item should be sub-classified, when appropriate, by its nature; amounts payable to and receivable from the parent entity, fellow subsidiaries and associates and other related parties should be disclosed separately.[130]

An entity should disclose the following, either on the face of the balance sheet or in the notes:[131]

(a) for each class of share capital:

  (i) the number of shares authorised;

  (ii) the number of shares issued and fully paid, and issued but not fully paid;

  (iii) par value per share, or that the shares have no par value;

  (iv) a reconciliation of the number of shares outstanding at the beginning and at the end of the year;

  (v) the rights, preferences and restrictions attaching to that class including restrictions on the distribution of dividends and the repayment of capital;

  (vi) shares in the entity held by the entity itself or by subsidiaries or associates of the entity; and

  (vii) shares reserved for issuance under options and sales contracts, including the terms and amounts;

(b) a description of the nature and purpose of each reserve within owners' equity;

(c) the amount of dividends that were proposed or declared after the balance sheet date but before the financial statements were authorised for issue; and

(d) the amount of any cumulative preference dividends not recognised.

An entity without share capital, such as a partnership, should disclose information equivalent to that required above, showing movements during the period in each category of equity interest and the rights, preferences and restrictions attaching to each category of equity interest.[132]

Income statement

The face of the income statement should include line items which present the following amounts:[133]

- revenue;
- the results of operating activities;
- finance costs;
- share of profits and losses of associates and joint ventures accounted for using the equity method;
- tax expense;
- profit or loss from ordinary activities;
- extraordinary items;
- minority interest; and
- net profit or loss for the period.

Additional line items, headings and sub-totals should be presented on the face of the income statement when required by an IAS, or when such presentation is necessary to present fairly the enterprise's financial performance.[134]

Statement of changes in equity

The face of the statement of changes in equity should include line items which present the following amounts:[135]

- the net profit or loss for the period;
- each item of income and expense, gain or loss which, as required by other Standards, is recognised directly in equity, and the total of these items; and
- the cumulative effect of changes in accounting policy and the correction of fundamental errors dealt with under the Benchmark treatments in IAS 8.

In addition to the minimum information required on the face of the statement of changes in equity, an entity should present within this statement or in the notes:[136]

- capital transactions with owners and distributions to owners;
- the balance of accumulated profit or loss at the beginning of the period and at the balance sheet date, and the movements for the period; and
- a reconciliation between the carrying amount of each class of equity capital, share premium and each reserve at the beginning and the end of the period, separately disclosing each movement.

The appendix to IAS 1 provides examples of the layout of the balance sheet, income statement and statement of changes in equity.

2.7.11 Offsetting

IAS 1 sets down strict requirements regarding offsetting. It states that assets and liabilities should not be offset except when offsetting is required or permitted by another IAS. Similarly, items of income and expense should be offset only when an International Accounting Standard requires or permits it, or when gains, losses and related expenses arising from the same or similar transactions and events are not material. Immaterial amounts should be aggregated with amounts of a similar nature or function.[137]

2.7.12 First-time application of International Accounting Standards

In the absence of any explicit guidance on how entities should account for the transition from national GAAP to IAS, the SIC was asked to consider the issue of first-time application of IAS. This resulted in the adoption of SIC-8 – *First-time application of IASs as the primary basis of accounting*.

In the period when IAS are applied in full for the first time as the primary accounting basis, SIC-8 requires that the financial statements of an entity should be prepared and presented as if the financial statements had always been prepared in accordance with the IAS and Interpretations effective for the period of first-time application. Therefore, the IAS and Interpretations effective for the period of first-time application should be applied retrospectively, except when:

- individual Standards or Interpretations require or permit a different transitional treatment; or
- the amount of the adjustment relating to prior periods cannot reasonably be determined.

Comparative information should be prepared and presented in accordance with IAS. Any adjustment resulting from the transition to IAS should be treated as an adjustment to the opening balance of retained earnings of the earliest period presented in accordance with IAS. When IAS are applied in full as the primary accounting basis for the first time, an entity should apply the transitional provisions of the effective Standards and Interpretations only for periods ending on the date prescribed in the respective Standards and Interpretations.[138]

Furthermore, in the period when IAS are applied in full for the first time as the primary accounting basis, an entity should disclose:[139]

- where the amount of the adjustment to the opening balance of retained earnings cannot reasonably be determined, that fact;
- where it is impracticable to provide comparative information, that fact; and
- for each IAS that permits a choice of transitional accounting policies, the policy selected.

Entities are encouraged to disclose the fact that IAS are being applied in full for the first time.[140]

Although theoretically sound, SIC-8 can give rise to substantial practical difficulties for entities adopting IAS for the first time. This is because the transitional provisions of individual standards, which were designed to provide a sensible transition from an old standard to a new one, will not normally be available to entities adopting IAS for the first time.

IAS 39 – *Financial instruments: recognition and measurement* – is a case in point. IAS 39 became operative for financial statements covering financial periods beginning on or after 1 January 2001. Earlier application was permitted only as of the beginning of a financial year that ends after 15 March 1999 (the date of issuance of the Standard) and retrospective application was not permitted. IAS 39 includes sensible transitional provisions that are available to companies already reporting under IAS, as well as to those adopting IAS for the first time in 2001. However, in the case of those entities that will adopt IAS for the first time in subsequent years, the use of the transitional provisions is ruled out by SIC-8. As a result, it seems that such entities will be required to adopt IAS 39 retrospectively – which is something that is specifically prohibited under IAS 39's transitional provisions.

Similar difficulties will arise with the implementation for the first time of several other IASs – including IAS 22 on business combinations, which specifically requires retrospective application. Thus, it seems that, at present, entities adopting IAS for the first time face additional burdens that existing IAS reporting entities escape.

However, the European Commission proposal to require all publicly traded EU incorporated companies to prepare, by 2005 at the latest, their consolidated accounts under IAS (see 3.5 below) has placed the spotlight firmly on first-time application of IAS. Conversion to IAS is a major exercise that will be faced by thousands of EU companies using diverse national reporting frameworks. The European Commission has made the IASB aware of the considerable practical difficulties surrounding first-time application. For its part, the IASB has responded positively by agreeing that the issues raised are significant and need to be addressed urgently. Consequently, the IASB has announced that it will undertake a separate project on this subject, and is currently examining how best to respond to the issues raised.

2.7.13 *Audit requirements*

Since International Accounting Standards transcend national boundaries it is understandable that they neither lay down any specific requirements or guidance on the audit of IAS financial statements, nor refer to any comprehensive sets of auditing standards that should be applied in auditing financial statements prepared under IAS. Clearly, though, entities reporting under IAS will be subject to any national auditing requirements set down in their country of domicile.

2.8 The influence of the G4+1 Group of 'standard setters' on international accounting

The G4+1 Group of standard setters was an informal grouping of staff members of the accounting standard-setting bodies of Australia, Canada, New Zealand, the United Kingdom, the United States of America and the IASC. Although not an official standard-setting body in its own right, the G4+1 became influential through the publication of discussion papers that dealt with highly topical and usually controversial accounting issues. Recent examples include: accounting for leases, reporting financial performance and accounting for share-based payments. Although these papers did not reflect the official views of any of the standard-setting bodies represented, the Group was able, through its links with the major Anglo-Saxon standard setters, to set the agenda for the development of new global accounting standards.

Perhaps unfortunately, because of their rather privileged positions and self-referential 'membership' criteria (for example, membership of the Group required acceptance of a conceptual framework similar to that of other members), the Group was somewhat of a closed shop. The result was that much of the output from the Group was predictable, not always of the highest quality and not necessarily informed by practical business considerations.

In any event, at a meeting of the G4+1 held in January 2001, the Group discussed whether its activities should continue given the imminent commencement of activities by the new International Accounting Standards Board (IASB), and agreed to disband and cancel its planned future activities with immediate effect.

3 THE EVOLUTION OF FINANCIAL REPORTING IN THE EUROPEAN UNION

3.1 Generic differences in European accounting

European accounting is the product of disparate social, economic and political factors, which have resulted in a number of deep-rooted differences in financial reporting practice throughout the region. The factors that have caused these differences include a variety of legal and tax systems, the perceived objectives of financial reporting and the significance of different sources of finance.

In contrast to UK GAAP and IAS, there is no broad-based statement of generally accepted theoretical principles that underpins financial reporting in the European Union (EU). Clearly, though, it is not the lack of a conceptual framework that has caused the European differences in financial reporting practices – any more than the recent existence of a conceptual framework in the UK has been responsible for the ethos of financial reporting in the UK. European accounting has evolved over many centuries, and the differences that exist throughout Europe have been shaped by the conditions in each European country.

The principal mechanism employed by the European Union to reduce these differences has been through the adoption of Directives under its company law harmonisation programme. These Directives are not law that apply directly to companies, but instructions to Member States to alter, if necessary, their own national legislation to ensure compliance with the provisions of the Directive. In most cases, the Directives lay down minimum requirements only, so that there is nothing to prevent a Member State having supplementary requirements of a more stringent nature, provided that these are not incompatible with the Directives.

The most significant Directives in the area of financial reporting are the Fourth and Seventh, which were adopted into national legislation by most EU countries during the 1980s.[141] The principal objective of the Fourth Directive was to achieve harmonisation in respect of formats, valuation rules and note disclosure, whilst the Seventh established a requirement for EU companies to prepare consolidated accounts on a common basis.

However, in negotiating the Fourth and Seventh Directives with the EU Member States, the Commission found that the deep-rooted differences in European accounting could be reconciled only through compromise. For example, in the case of the Fourth Directive, this involved a compromise between the German and French desire for certainty and precision in accounts (as reflected in the compulsory charts of accounts in France and the mandatory formats for the balance sheet and profit and loss account in Germany), and the Anglo-Saxon/Dutch desire for a more pragmatic approach requiring the accounts taken as a whole to present a true and fair view; and in the case of the Seventh Directive, a compromise between the economic and legal concepts of a group.

3.2 Harmonisation achieved by the Fourth and Seventh Directives

The objectives of financial reporting vary in different countries, and this fact is reflected in the relative importance given to the various parties who have an interest in accounting information. For example, financial reporting in certain countries has developed on the basis of considering shareholders as being the most important party entitled to receive financial information. This approach arose from the situation where businesses had obtained a substantial proportion of their funds from the public generally and where responsibility for the conduct of the operations of the business was divorced from ownership. Investors required regular reports to assess the performance achieved by management and future prospects, and annual accounts ensured that the stewardship function was being exercised properly.

On the other hand, in other countries financial reporting has evolved from the premise that accounts were provided largely for the tax authorities and other government bodies interested in national economic planning. The assessment of liabilities to tax had to be based on standard rules regarding the recognition of income, deduction of expenses and valuation of assets; in this way, all businesses would be subject to tax on the same basis. In Belgium, France, Germany, Greece, Italy, Luxembourg and Portugal, accounts have been used mainly to measure taxable profits. Although in Germany company law is the principal authority for financial reporting measurement practices, they have historically been based on principles of historical cost and tax-based depreciation.

These contrasting attitudes as to the purposes of financial reporting have adversely affected harmonisation of accounting law and practice in the EU. This being the case, it is probable that the harmonisation programme under the Directives has been only partially successful. This is clearly evidenced by the fact that harmonisation has not been achieved in the areas of recognition and measurement – both of which are fundamental to achieving comparability in financial reporting. Nevertheless, it is clear also that the Fourth and Seventh Directives have provided a base level for harmonisation of financial reporting in the EU, and have undoubtedly led to improvements in the quality and comparability of company accounts throughout the Union over the last twenty years. They have contributed also to improving the conditions for cross-border business and have allowed the mutual recognition of accounts for the purposes of quotation on securities exchanges throughout the EU. Moreover, a further important contribution of the Directives is in the area of creditor protection through the public availability of financial information. In contrast to the US, where only SEC registrant companies are required to publish financial statements, all limited liability companies in the EU are required to produce and publish financial information.

3.3 The European Commission's 1995 Communication on international harmonisation

In 1995, the European Commission issued a Communication (i.e. policy statement)[142] stating that, while EU legislation has considerably improved the quality of financial reporting in the Union, the Directives do not provide answers to all the problems facing preparers and users of accounts and accounting standard setters. In the

Commission's view, the most urgent problem to be addressed concerns European companies with an 'international vocation' (the so-called 'global players') and the need to facilitate the access of such European global players to the international capital markets. The accounts prepared by those companies in accordance with their national legislation (based on the Accounting Directives) are not acceptable for international capital market purposes. These companies are therefore obliged to prepare two sets of accounts, one set which is in conformity with the Accounting Directives and another set required by the international capital markets.

The Commission examined several possible approaches to dealing with the issue of 'upgrading' EU accounting legislation. After careful consideration, the Commission suggested that a closer cooperation between the EU and the IASC, with the objective of ultimately adopting International Accounting Standards at the EU level, was the preferred solution. Referring to the 1995 agreement between IOSCO and the IASC to produce a core set of international accounting standards which would be endorsed by IOSCO (see 2.2. above), the Commission concluded that 'rather than amend the existing Directives, the proposal is to improve the present situation by associating the EU with the efforts undertaken by IASC and IOSCO towards a broader international harmonisation of accounting standards'.

This policy statement of the Commission paved the way to the acceptance of IAS by the EU. Unfortunately, the Commission could not anticipate in 1995 that the ultimate endorsement of IAS by IOSCO in May 2000 would only be a qualified acceptance of the standards. As it turned out, one of the main objectives of the Commission in moving towards IAS (access of European companies to international capital markets) was only partly achieved.

3.4 The European Commission's Financial Services Action Plan

Meanwhile, certain EU Member States set about making it easier for their multinational companies to gain access to the international capital markets. In February 1998, new legislation was enacted in Germany to the effect that International Accounting Standards (or indeed other 'internationally recognised accounting principles' such as US GAAP) may be used in the consolidated financial statements of listed groups instead of German law and accounting principles. There is an added proviso that the financial statements must also be 'consistent with' the EU Accounting Directives.

Similar amended legislation was enacted in France in April 1998, allowing French companies whose securities are traded on a regulated market to use IAS or another body of international standards as the sole basis for their consolidated accounts. A number of other European countries (including Italy, Austria, Luxembourg, Belgium and Spain) have followed suit. At the time, these were revolutionary changes, and demonstrated the influence of Anglo-American accounting philosophies, at least on those companies that wished either to seek access to the international capital markets, or merely achieve greater transparency in their financial reporting. It also raised the stakes for the European Commission, emphasising the need for the Commission to deliver on the strategy set out in its 1995 Communication.

Lufthansa is an example of a company that took advantage of the new legislation in Germany, preparing its consolidated accounts in accordance with IAS for the first time in 1998. The Group's 1998 Annual Report included the following explanation of the impact of adopting IAS:

Extract 1.3: Deutsche Lufthansa AG (1998)

Adoption of IAS enhances transparency

This year the consolidated financial statements have been drawn up for the first time on the basis of the International Accounting Standards (IAS) in accordance with the option provided under the new Section 292a of the German Commercial Code. This obviates the need to compile a separate set of certified consolidated financial statements based on the German Commercial Code.

Lufthansa is also applying many provisions of the IAS standards – the use of which is not yet compulsory in German accounting – in order to improve the comprehensiveness and transparency of the information it publishes. However, a direct comparison of the year-on-year figures is possible only with the specially recompiled consolidated financial statements for 1997 (which are likewise based on IAS) but not with the financial statements of earlier years. The adoption of IAS has effects both on the consolidated balance sheet and the consolidated income statement.

Effects on the balance sheet

The consolidated balance sheet under IAS is affected in particular by the different treatment of leasing agreements and the adjustment of retirement benefit obligations. Thus the capitalisation of leased aircraft, which hitherto were not included in the balance sheet, substantially increases fixed assets. The associated financial obligations are now shown as liabilities. On the other hand, the provisions for anticipated losses in respect of leasing agreements and the inclusion under prepaid expenses of prepaid leasing instalments, which were shown previously in the consolidated balance sheet drawn up in line with German commercial law, are superfluous under IAS.

The use of a more dynamic accounting rule for pension obligations required by IAS has led to a sharp increase in retirement benefit obligations.

IAS adjustments affecting earnings in past years were shown net of offsetting deferred taxes and charged directly against retained earnings. On the other hand, the portion of earnings retained from last year's net profit partly counterbalances this effect.

Impact of IAS on income statement

The use of IAS accounting standards also has an impact on the consolidated income statement. The increase in the profit from operating activities and the concurrent deterioration in the financial result are caused by several factors. Firstly, the transfers to retirement benefit obligations, which in the past were recorded in total as staff costs, are now split into current service costs (under staff costs) and interest expense. Secondly, obligations arising from financial leasing agreements are now included in the balance sheet. Hence the interest component of the leasing instalments, which was formerly included under operating expenses, is now allocated to the financial result. Leasing expenses are no longer included under the cost of materials; however, depreciation and amortisation now also include the depreciation on aircraft acquired under finance leasing agreements.

Revenue increases. This is because under IAS the pro rata revenue earned from partly completed customer orders, including the proportional contribution to earnings, has to be shown, too.

Changes in the Group of consolidated companies

Important changes in the group of companies consolidated compared with the consolidated financial statements published in 1997 according to the German Commercial Code concern the deconsolidation of Condor Flugdienst GmbH and the Delvos companies. By contrast, START was consolidated for the first time.

Lufthansa's statement of accounting policies included the following:

Extract 1.4: Deutsche Lufthansa AG (1998)

Notes to the Consolidated Financial Statements of Deutsche Lufthansa AG 1998

1) Fundamentals and methods

The consolidated financial statements of Deutsche Lufthansa AG and its subsidiaries have been prepared in accordance with the International Accounting Standards (IAS) and the interpretations of the Standing Interpretations Committee (SIC). The provisions set out in SIC-8 concerning the first-time application of IAS have been observed whereby the following new or revised Standards have been voluntarily applied before their effective date: IAS 1 (Presentation of Financial Statements), IAS 14 (Segment Reporting), IAS 17 (Accounting for Leases), IAS 19 (Employee Benefits) and IAS 36 (Impairment of Assets). Standards relevant for the first time in the 1998 financial year have also been applied for 1997.

The following accounting and valuation methods in the present consolidated financial statements deviate from German law:

- Translation of foreign currency receivables and liabilities as at the closing rate
- Accounting for internally generated intangible assets in the balance sheet
- Revenue recognition by reference to the stage of completion of long-term customer orders
- Valuation of long-term provisions and accruals and of high or low interest-bearing liabilities at present value
- No recognition of other provisions if the probability of the outflow of resources is below 50 per cent
- Recognition of deferred tax assets and liabilities in accordance with the balance sheet liability method
- Recognition of assets and of corresponding liabilities resulting from finance lease agreements according to IAS 17
- Valuation of retirement benefit obligations according to the projected unit credit method.

The valuation of some items changed as a result of the transition to IAS at January 1, 1997. The respective changes were treated as adjustments to the opening balance of retained earnings of the earliest period presented.

Capital and Reserves	DM 000
Equity according to HGB as at 31.12.1996 (without minority interest)	5,339,322
Changes in consolidated group	133,848
Valuation using the equity method	11,545
Finance leases on aircraft and buildings	-722,148
Retirement benefit obligations	-1,088,805
Other provisions and accruals	202,413
Other accounting and valuation differences	51,983
Deferred taxes	568,127
Equity according to IAS as at 1.1.1997	4,496,285

The requirements set out in section 292a, German Commercial Code (HGB) are met; thus the consolidated financial statements prepared in accordance with International Accounting Standards have an exempting effect. The assessment as to whether group accounting is consistent with the 7th EU Directive was based on the interpretation of the contact committee for accounting of the European Commission effective at the time of preparation of financial statements.

As part of its strategy to embrace IAS, and in response to its growing use by EU multinational companies, the Commission has since 1995 carried out an ongoing examination of the conformity between the Accounting Directives and IASs and SIC Interpretations.[143] Generally, these comparisons have concluded that (with the exception of IAS 39 – see below) there are few conflicts between the Accounting Directives and IAS. Those minor conflicts that do exist will be addressed by the Commission in the context of the modernisation of the Accounting Directives that is planned to take place within the next two years or so. The Commission's programme of modernising the Accounting Directives not only aims to remove existing conflicts between IAS and the Directives, but also to ensure that all the options currently available under IAS are available to EU companies.

In May 1999, the Commission issued its Financial Services Action Plan.[144] The plan confirmed the Commission's position that comparable, transparent and reliable financial information is fundamental to an efficient and integrated capital market, and that International Accounting Standards seem the most appropriate benchmark for a single set of financial reporting requirements which will enable companies to raise capital on the international markets.

At the summit of the European Heads of Government held in Lisbon in March 2000, it was agreed that a single European capital market should be developed as a matter of priority. It was acknowledged further that the adoption of a single financial reporting framework for the European Union was a vital element in that process. The summit conclusions stressed the need to accelerate completion of the internal market for financial services and set a deadline of 2005 to implement the Commission's Financial Services Action Plan.

Following this lead by the European Heads of Government, the Commission announced in June 2000 that it would present proposals to:

- introduce the requirement that all listed EU companies report in accordance with IAS by 2005; and
- modernise the EU Accounting Directives to reduce potential conflicts with IAS and bring the Directives into line with modern accounting developments.[145]

Meanwhile, EU companies currently reporting under IAS faced an immediate problem with respect to IAS 39 – *Financial instruments: recognition and measurement*. IAS 39 requires that certain financial instruments are valued at fair value and that, in some cases, the changes in fair value are recorded in the profit and loss account. These requirements meant that there was now a significant conflict between an IAS and the Accounting Directives, with the result that EU companies would not be able to continue to apply IAS unless significant amendments were made to the Directives. Consequently, because IAS 39 became operative for financial statements covering financial years beginning on or after 1 January 2001, there arose an urgent need to amend the Directives in order to allow the application of IAS 39 by EU companies.

Accordingly, the Commission put forward a proposal to amend the Fourth and Seventh Directives so as to enable EU companies to comply with IAS 39, and therefore prepare their financial statements in conformity with IAS. This was eventually approved by the Council and by the European Parliament in May 2001 in the form of a Directive that amended the Fourth, Seventh and Bank Accounts Directives.[146]

3.5 The European Commission's proposed Regulation on the application of IAS in the European Union

On 13 February 2001, the European Commission published a draft EU Regulation[147] that would require publicly traded EU incorporated companies[148] to prepare, by 2005 at the latest, consolidated accounts under IAS 'endorsed' (see below) for application within the EU. The proposed Regulation provides an option also for Member States to permit or require the application of endorsed IAS in the preparation of annual (unconsolidated) accounts and to permit or require the application of endorsed IAS by unlisted companies. This means that Member States can require uniform application of endorsed IAS to important sectors such as banking or insurance, regardless of whether or not companies are listed. An EU Regulation has direct effect on companies, without the need for national legislation. The draft is now under negotiation between Member States in the Council and is being debated in the European Parliament.

The proposed Regulation establishes also the basic rules for the creation of an endorsement mechanism that will adopt IAS, the timetable for implementation and a review clause to permit an assessment of the overall approach proposed. The endorsement mechanism is discussed in some detail below.

Internal Market Commissioner, Frits Bolkestein, commented as follows on the proposed Regulation: 'This eagerly awaited proposal signals the beginning of a new era of transparency and the end of the Tower of Babel in financial reporting in Europe. The use of one global accounting language will greatly benefit European companies. It will help them to compete on equal terms for global capital. Investors and other stakeholders will, at last, be in a position to compare company performance against a common standard. Listed companies should start preparing now for this change-over to a single set of financial reporting rules, namely International Accounting Standards. Although some investment will be needed in terms of training, I am confident that it will repay itself many times in the long run, notably through the reduced cost for companies of raising capital.'

There are currently approximately 7,000 companies listed on EU regulated markets, which will be subject to the proposed Regulation. Only about 275 of these companies apply IAS at this time.

3.6 The proposed EU endorsement mechanism

The proposed Regulation includes proposals on an EU endorsement mechanism, which was already foreseen in the Commission's June 2000 Communication. The Commission believes that such an endorsement mechanism is needed to provide the necessary public oversight. The Commission considers that it is not possible, politically or legally, to delegate accounting standard setting unconditionally and irrevocably to a private organisation over which the EU has no influence. In addition, the endorsement mechanism will examine whether the standards adopted by the IASB conform with EU public policy concerns.

The role of the endorsement mechanism is not to reformulate or replace IAS, but to oversee the adoption of new standards and interpretations, intervening only when these contain material deficiencies or have failed to cater for features specific to the EU economic or legal environments. The central task of this mechanism is to confirm that IAS provide a suitable basis for financial reporting by listed EU companies. The mechanism will be based on a two-tier structure, combining a regulatory level with an expert level, to assist the Commission in its endorsement role.

3.6.1 Regulatory level of the endorsement mechanism

An Accounting Regulatory Committee (ARC) will be formed, composed of representatives of the Member States and chaired by a representative of the Commission. The ARC will operate on the basis of appropriate institutional arrangements and under existing comitology rules that will ensure full transparency and accountability towards the Council and the Parliament.

Under these rules, the Commission will present to the ARC a report that will identify the standard, examine its conformity with the Accounting Directives and its suitability as a basis for financial reporting in the EU. The ARC must decide within one month (on the basis of qualified majority voting) to adopt or reject a standard for application in the EU. The same procedure will apply for the adoption of amendments to previously adopted IASs and Interpretations.

Finally, the adoption, or otherwise, of currently existing IASs and SIC Interpretations must follow the same procedure as described above, which should be complete at the latest by 31 December 2002.[149]

3.6.2 *The European Financial Reporting Advisory Group (EFRAG)*

The European Financial Reporting Advisory Group (EFRAG) was established as a private-sector initiative by ten key constituents interested in financial reporting in Europe, including the European Federation of Accountants (FEE), the Union des Confédérations de l'Industrie et des Employeurs d'Europe (UNICE), the European Banking Federation (EBF), and the Comité Européen des Assurances (CEA).

EFRAG is a two-tier organisation, comprising:

- a group of highly qualified experts (the EFRAG Technical Expert Group), to carry out the technical work; and
- a Supervisory Board of European Organisations (the EFRAG Supervisory Board), to guarantee representation of the full European interest and to enhance the legitimacy and credibility of EFRAG.

The principal aim of EFRAG is to provide proactive input into the work of the IASB. EFRAG will advise the Commission on the technical assessment of IASs, IFRSs and Interpretations for application in the EU. The technical work of EFRAG will be carried out by the Technical Expert Group on the basis of a wide consultation process.

The Technical Expert Group was set up by EFRAG on 26 June 2001. It will provide the private sector support and expertise needed to assess the standards and interpretations developed by the IASB on a timely basis.[150] It will also provide input into the IASB standard setting process at all stages of a particular project, and particularly in the early phases. The Technical Expert Group (which only has a consultative role) will ensure that EU users and preparers are involved in the preparatory discussions of the standards at the international level, and in the technical assessment of the standards, before their adoption by the EU.

The Technical Expert Group will initially provide advice to the Commission on the endorsement of existing IAS for their use in the EU. It will advise the Commission also on whether or not an amendment to the Directives is recommended in the light of international accounting developments.

If EFRAG were to recommend the adoption of a standard, but the Commission did not agree with this recommendation, the Commission will provide an explanation for its view, and then ask the Technical Expert Group to examine an alternative solution.

A special sub-committee of EFRAG will be established in close co-operation with the European Insurers Association (CEA) to deal with insurance matters. Insurance has priority in Europe, given the fact that there is no IAS on accounting for insurance contracts yet, whereas listed insurance undertakings will have to apply IAS from the financial year 2005 onwards, in line with other listed companies.

3.7 Building an integrated European capital market

The European Commission has set an ambitious agenda for the European Union to become the world's most competitive economy by 2010. However, progress with European capital market integration – a vital ingredient of this agenda – so far has been slow. Nevertheless, the economic gains to be derived from an integrated pan-European financial and capital market are considerable. European companies will have greater access to a deep and liquid market at lower costs of capital; European consumers will enjoy wider investment choice and increasing net returns on their investments. The macroeconomic benefits could be substantial also: increased investment implies stronger job creation and GDP growth. A deep, accessible and liquid capital market in Europe is important for the development of new businesses in Europe. The growth and entrepreneurial culture essential to development will thrive better with a clear route to market for equity. This is particularly important to an enlarged community, as new businesses will grow more strongly with the help of equity capital.

So why does it matter? It matters because Europe's future economic growth and prosperity depend on it. Without an integrated capital market these potential macro-economic benefits will not be realised, economic growth will be lower and the opportunity of achieving competitive advantage in the global capital markets will be lost.

Yet despite the economic imperatives, the basic structures needed for an integrated market are far from being in place. In Europe, trans-national companies have to report to regulators in fifteen member states. They face a wide variety of different rules and regulations. Investors have to negotiate fragmented markets; for example, the equity markets throughout Europe all have different listing rules, accounting standards, trading platforms and securities' clearing and settlement systems. These problems are likely to have played a significant part in the failed London/Frankfurt stock exchange merger of 1999. They certainly frustrate cross-border trading and the merger of exchanges. Taken together with the differences in regulation, enforcement, taxation, legal systems and bankruptcy laws, this gives a situation that Baron Alexandre Lamfalussy describes as 'a remarkable cocktail of Kafkaesque inefficiency that serves no-one – neither consumers, nor investors, nor SMEs, nor large companies, nor governments.'[151]

Nevertheless, a deep and liquid European bond market has already developed. The euro-denominated issuance overtook US dollar issuance in the first quarter of 2001. This clearly reflects the relatively simple nature of the bond instrument, which makes it easier to switch between different issues and issuers and develop a deep market with cross-border trade.

However, no such simplicity exists in the equity markets, which remain highly fragmented. Again, the US provides a benchmark. In US chemicals for example, Monsanto and Dow Chemical issue comparable financial statements under US GAAP and their valuations can be compared directly. Switching trades can be executed simultaneously with the same exchange, virtually eliminating timing and settlement risk. Electronic integration of different exchanges through Electronic Communications Networks (ECNs) is highly efficient. This kind of arbitrage process tends to reduce valuation anomalies and effectively unifies and deepens sectors like chemicals. Investors have reasonably reliable valuation benchmarks, which helps confidence and boosts demand for stock.

None of this is happening in Europe. Financial reporting is a mosaic of largely divergent national systems. It is simply not realistic to compare BASF with Rhodia or ICI. It is rarely profitable to switch between them to try to take advantage of valuation differences. Valuations simply remain divergent. With the exception of the UK, the demand for stock is weak and valuations remain low. This is reflected in a high cost of equity capital and low issuance, with market spreads adding significantly to cost as well. All of these factors help to maintain the traditional reliance of many European companies – large and small – on less efficient debt financing systems.

The US capital markets provide clear evidence that efficiencies are forced upon businesses once their performances are easily comparable; without these pressures inefficiency can go unnoticed. Globalisation of competition will punish less efficient businesses that cannot be price-competitive, and their revenues will reduce. Businesses enjoying semi-protected markets for their services, under less than transparent financing arrangements, will not be able to enjoy that shelter indefinitely.

Consequently, in introducing its proposed Regulation, the European Commission has stated that one of its key actions will be the development of an enforcement infrastructure that will ensure the rigorous application of IAS by listed companies in the EU. The main focus will be on disseminating implementation guidance, encouraging high quality auditing, and reinforcing coordinated regulatory oversight.

The European Commission's proposal has given significant impetus to the objective of building a fully integrated, globally competitive European capital market and financial services industry. In this instance, it is fair to say that the commercial and electronic communication imperatives that are driving the amalgamation of the major European stock exchanges are being matched by a far-sighted policy.

However, the greatest challenge facing Europe in delivering an efficient single capital market is the task of efficient regulation and enforcement. The absence of an effective and coordinated enforcement mechanism severely limits the credibility of any financial reporting regime. Clearly, the adoption of IAS in Europe will improve the functioning of the securities markets only when it is properly and rigorously enforced. This means that the supervisors of the European capital markets have a crucial role to play in ensuring that companies comply with financial reporting requirements. In the view of the authors, this can be achieved only through the establishment of an efficient and lean Europe-wide regulatory system. This implies the co-operative development and implementation of a common EU approach to regulation that would establish a level playing field for EU financial reporting, maintained by rigorous enforcement that will prevent regulatory arbitrage.

4 WHAT CONSTITUTES GAAP?

4.1 UK GAAP

4.1.1 Principles or practice?

Although a familiar term in other countries, the expression 'GAAP' first became commonplace in the UK only after the publication of the first edition of this book in 1989. In the UK the term 'GAAP' is used more loosely than in most other countries, probably because GAAP in the UK does not have any statutory definition or regulatory authority, in the way that it does, for example, in the US.[152] Consequently, references to GAAP are rarely found in regulatory or statutory pronouncements in the UK, and where the expression is used, it is not adequately explained or defined.

There are two instances where the term is used in the Companies Act. In order for a business combination to be treated as a merger, one of the qualifying criteria is that the method 'accords with generally accepted accounting principles or practice'.[153] This is usually taken to mean that the transaction qualifies to be so treated under the relevant accounting standard, but the use of the alternative words 'principles or practice' suggests some doubt on the part of the legislators as to which phrase has general currency. The other arises in the context of realised profits and losses; the Act states that they are 'such profits or losses of the company as fall to be treated as realised in accordance with principles generally accepted, at the time when the accounts are prepared, with respect to the determination for accounting purposes of realised profits or losses'.[154]

In one of their Joint Opinions referred to earlier in this Chapter, Hoffmann and Arden cited the decision in *Odeon Associated Theatres Ltd v Jones (Inspector of Taxes)*[155] as an illustration of the relationship between 'generally accepted accounting principles' and the legal concept of true and fair, and in so doing reached the conclusion that 'the function of the ASC is to formulate what it considers should be generally accepted accounting principles'.[156] Nevertheless, whilst most would agree that the accounting standards represent 'generally accepted accounting principles', what about those areas of accounting which are not addressed in the standards? Furthermore, what about the accounting and disclosure requirements of the Companies Act and Stock Exchange – do they constitute 'generally accepted accounting principles'?

Our view is that GAAP is a dynamic concept that requires constant review, adaptation and reaction to changing circumstances. UK GAAP changes in response to changing business and economic needs and developments. As circumstances alter, accounting practices are modified or developed accordingly. The UK's Accounting Standards Board recognises this in its *Statement of Aims*, which discusses the Board's ongoing need to issue new accounting standards, or amend existing ones, 'in response to evolving business practices, new economic developments and deficiencies being identified in current practice'.[157] Thus, UK GAAP goes far beyond mere rules and principles, and encompasses contemporary permissible accounting *practice*.

Nevertheless, companies do not have *carte blanche* to select whatever accounting policies they see fit, even if a particular policy is regarded as being permissible. This is because (as discussed more fully in Chapter 2 at section 7) FRS 18 – *Accounting policies* – makes it clear that a business must select accounting policies that are judged by it to be most appropriate to its particular circumstances for the purpose of giving a true and fair view.[158] This notion of 'appropriateness' is undefined and, as with most other contexts in which it is used contemporarily, is really a method of conveying a general sense that entities are expected to 'play the game' without actually defining precisely what that game is.

All the same, even if appropriateness is not defined, the standard does provide guidance on how the appropriateness of accounting policies is to be judged. It lists four objectives of financial statements:

- relevance;
- reliability;
- comparability; and
- understandability,

and two constraints:

- the need to balance the four objectives, and
- the cost/benefit balance of providing information.[159]

The standard makes it clear that these objectives and constraints must be considered together in judging the appropriateness of accounting policies to an entity's particular circumstances. The standard goes on to assert that appropriate accounting policies will result in information that is relevant, and that where more than one accounting policy would achieve this result, an entity will consider which of those policies presents the most relevant financial information.[160] This assertion seems to reflect a growing tendency amongst standard setters to place relevance in order of importance above the other qualitative characteristics of financial reporting. This is all very well, but it is still the case that users of financial statements find information relevant only if they consider it to be reliable. Therefore, in our view, reliability (and indeed the other objectives) needs to be given equal consideration in determining the appropriateness of accounting policies.

4.1.2 'Normal accounting practice'

The term 'normal accounting practice' has recently started appearing in UK tax legislation, which is unfortunate. What is 'normal' is shrouded in legal fog, particularly when more than one approach can be regarded as acceptable. Furthermore, where transactions are unique or novel, the lack of directly comparable cases may make it impossible to say, strictly, that any accounting treatment is 'normal', but perfectly possible to determine the principles that should be followed under UK GAAP. Moreover, given the emphasis now in FRS 18 on the selection of accounting policies that are judged by the reporting entity to be most appropriate to its particular circumstances for the purpose of giving a true and fair view,[161] it seems unnecessary for the legislation to introduce the concept of 'normal accounting practice', which is not understood by anyone. Consequently, we believe that it would be more satisfactory to replace this term with 'UK Generally Accepted Accounting Practice' wherever it occurs in UK corporation tax legislation.

4.2 International GAAP

International Accounting Standards (IAS) are just beginning to be used widely by large businesses, and consequently no substantial body of custom, practice or generally accepted ways of employing IAS has had an opportunity to develop. Indeed, one of the challenges for the European Commission and EFRAG is to put in place a regime under which 'International GAAP', understood and commonly applied throughout the EU, can develop. Paradoxically, it may be that this situation best illustrates the real meaning of GAAP in an IAS context.

A comprehensive set of International Accounting Standards exists, but no GAAP as yet. So what else has to happen before 'International GAAP' can be said to have emerged? The extra element, which only time, practical application, and the inevitable disputes and compromises can supply, is generally accepted practice. It will only be after a number of years of full implementation by a representative cross-section of businesses, in a number of countries, that a consensus will emerge over the way that, in practice, in the context of real commercial transactions, IAS is actually to be applied.

The term 'generally accepted' does not necessarily imply that there must exist a large number of actual applications of a particular accounting practice. For example, new areas of accounting that have not yet been generally applied may be accepted as part of GAAP. Similarly, alternative accounting treatments for similar items may both be generally accepted.

It is our view that in the developing context of IAS, 'generally accepted' will refer to accounting practices that are regarded as permissible by the accounting profession and regulators internationally – which means a broad consensus will come to exist between users, preparers, auditors, regulators and the markets, across what are currently regarded as national boundaries. If this happens, the process of establishing 'International GAAP' will mirror the way UK GAAP emerged.

In general, any accounting practice which is legitimate in the circumstances under which it has been applied has come to be regarded as GAAP. The decision as to whether or not a particular practice is permissible or legitimate is normally governed by one or more of the following factors, which may therefore be expected to apply to the emergence of 'International GAAP':

- Is the practice addressed in accounting standards or other official pronouncements?
- Is the practice addressed in accounting standards that deal with similar and related issues?
- If the practice is not addressed in accounting standards, is it dealt with in the standards of another country that could reasonably be considered to offer authoritative guidance?

- Is the practice consistent with the needs of users and the objectives of financial reporting?
- Does the practice have authoritative support in the accounting literature?
- Is the practice consistent with the underlying conceptual framework document?
- Are other companies in similar situations generally applying the practice?
- Is the practice consistent with the fundamental concept of 'true and fair'?

In an IAS context, these factors build on the requirements set out in paragraph 22 of IAS 1, which states that 'In the absence of a specific International Accounting Standard and an interpretation of the Standing Interpretations Committee, management uses its judgement in developing an accounting policy that provides the most useful information to users of the enterprise's financial statements. In making this judgement, management considers:

(a) the requirements and guidance in International Accounting Standards dealing with similar and related issues;

(b) the definitions, recognition and measurement criteria for assets, liabilities, income and expenses set out in the IASC Framework; and

(c) pronouncements of other standard setting bodies and accepted industry practices to the extent, but only to the extent, that these are consistent with (a) and (b) of this paragraph.'[162]

Relatively speaking, IAS financial reporting is still in its infancy. All those involved with the development of IAS into a global financial reporting framework bear a considerable responsibility to ensure that the development is evolutionary and not revolutionary. For the EU in particular, the need to ensure cross-border consistency in application, regulation and enforcement is paramount if this bold initiative is to succeed. Consequently, one of the interesting aspects of financial reporting during the next decade will be to observe how the process of acceptance and implementation of IAS across the world generally, and the EU in particular, develops. Put simply, it will be interesting to watch the emergence of 'International GAAP'.

4.3 Who 'owns' International GAAP?

International GAAP is, relatively speaking, still in its infancy. However, the adoption of IAS in the European Union as the single financial reporting framework for listed companies will mean that it will soon become a major force in world accounting. Its adoption by thousands of EU companies, including some of the largest companies in the world, will inevitably ensure its prominence. It will therefore not be long before the question of the 'ownership' of International GAAP arises, and who, therefore, is the ultimate authority when the inevitable differences of opinion and disputes occur.

This issue has a number of practical implications for EU companies, for example:

- What happens in cases where different (and potentially conflicting) interpretations of the same standard are given by different regulators?

- There is uncertainty surrounding the legal issue of who has jurisdiction in cases of conflict between two parties on the question of the conformity of a specific set of financial statements with IAS. For example, what are the roles of the national courts, the European Court of Justice, the Financial Reporting Review Panel, the IASB, IFRIC etc.?

However there is a possibility of an even greater level of uncertainty being created as the custom and practice that are an essential part of any GAAP, begin to accrue. Hitherto all standard setting bodies have been given their legitimacy by, and have operated within, national legislative frameworks; by contrast the IASB is a private sector body, with no political accountability. In theory at least, all it does is set the standards; issues of compliance and enforcement are outside its frame of reference. As International GAAP develops, there will no longer be a supreme legislative body that can decide, for all concerned with applying International GAAP, what does and does not constitute conformity with it. Moreover, pronouncements, rulings, and interpretations issued by others outside the IASB setup, may become part of International GAAP.

Therefore, it seems that it is only a matter of time before the ultimate ownership and authority of International GAAP is tested. Paradoxically it may be that the more successful International GAAP becomes as a global financial reporting system, the more its interpretation, integrity and meaning will become subject to dispute.

5 CONCLUSION

The European Commission's proposal that all EU companies listed on a regulated market should prepare their consolidated accounts in accordance with International Accounting Standards means that the much talked about notion of harmonised financial reporting under a single set of accounting standards is now set to become a practical reality. For European companies the time for speculation and debate is over. The minds of company management should now focus on 2005 as an immediate issue requiring action. The requirement to adopt IAS is not merely a technical exercise involving the reordering of information and rearrangement of the financial statements. Conversion to IAS will often challenge fundamentally a company's existing business model. It will provide a unique opportunity for the company to re-examine and re-engineer the way it looks at itself through its internal management reporting. It will affect the way the company presents itself to investors and other users of its financial statements.

It is vital that company managements recognise the far-reaching impact that IAS will have on their businesses. Failure to do so now could risk placing their companies at a competitive disadvantage. The adoption of IAS is not about choosing different accounting policies; it involves the adoption of an entirely different system of performance measurement and communication with the markets. There will be substantially increased levels of transparency for many companies – for example, through expanded segmental disclosures and the recognition of derivatives on balance sheets at fair value. In addition, IAS conversion presents management with an opportunity to re-shape the business, for example:

- how key performance indicators are determined and used in the business;
- how company performance is communicated to, and evaluated by, the markets and how the market evaluates the company against its competitors;
- how financial data is made more accessible to the markets more frequently, but in a secure environment;
- how the company's finance function is organised;
- how executives are compensated; and
- how performance-related remuneration for employees is determined.

Changing accounting standards may not sound strategic, but it will change fundamentally the way that businesses are run, the way that success is measured and the information and records that companies need to maintain. For many European companies, this change is huge. This is because, by embracing International GAAP, Europe is embracing also a vision for financial reporting that is not necessarily particularly widely known or understood. It is a vision that considers fair value measurement to be paramount, rejecting historical costs, accruals and the realisation principle as irrelevant. A vision that regards the determination of taxable income or realised profits as having no place in financial reporting.

This vision is based on an approach to company financial reporting that has been developed over the past several years by a group of Anglo-Saxon accounting standard setters, and has now been adopted by the International Accounting Standards Board. This approach is based on a balance sheet oriented, fair value model, where the emphasis is on measuring the fair values of companies' assets and liabilities. This means that the accounting process will in future be focused extensively on the recognition, derecognition and measurement at fair value of companies' assets and liabilities. The measurement of income will rely heavily on changes in the fair value of net assets. Income will be reported in a single statement of financial performance that aggregates all accrual-based income with all value changes, whether realised or unrealised. The implications of this fair value approach for reported earnings are enormous; for example, will it any longer be possible to maintain any form of linkage between financial reporting and the determination of tax liabilities?

For many companies, the impact of IAS on investor relations will be considerable. Not only will the increased transparency provide the markets with substantially more insight into European companies, but companies will also have to rethink the ways in which they measure performance and communicate with the markets. This is because the adoption of IAS will have a fundamental impact on a number of important areas of financial reporting, for example:

- structured financial products are often entered into on the basis of a specific accounting treatment. If that treatment is no longer permitted, material liabilities not currently shown on the balance sheet might have to be included;
- IAS will necessitate the redefinition of the scope of the group consolidation so as to include material subsidiaries or special purpose entities currently not consolidated;

- moves are afoot to require the capitalisation on balance sheet at fair value of leases currently held off balance sheet. Again this could have a significant impact on both the balance sheet and income statement;
- the requirement under IAS to include on the balance sheet the company's net pension liability or asset at fair value may have a material impact on the equity of companies with under-funded pension obligations. Companies will be required to have annual actuarial valuations of their pension liabilities according to the requirements of IAS, and many will face the likelihood of large amounts of equity being wiped off their balance sheets on adoption of the employee benefits standard alone. Even for those companies that have adequately funded pension liabilities, the adoption of the fair value approach to employee benefit accounting is likely to cause significant volatility in reported earnings;
- proposals are being developed to require companies to record a charge in the income statement for the value of share options granted to employees, calculated on the basis of the market value of the options on the date that they vest; and
- the IASB is proceeding with its plans to require companies to record all financial assets and financial liabilities in the balance sheet at current market value, with all changes in market value being recorded in earnings.

Clearly, therefore, company management will have to learn how to deal with volatility in reported performance. The examples listed above show that the adoption of the IASB's fair value financial reporting regime will inevitably introduce significant volatility in the balance sheet and, more importantly, in earnings. This increases substantially the challenge for company management of providing to the markets a coherent articulation of their company's performance. The challenge will be compounded if the current proposal by the European Commission to require quarterly financial reporting is adopted.

Analysts will, perhaps for the first time, have truly transparent and comparable data about all companies within a particular industry on a pan-European basis. Companies will be benchmarked against their cross-border competitors and key performance indicators will be compared. As a result, companies presently operating in less than transparent and semi-protected financial reporting environments will soon have no place to hide.

References

1 Equivalent legislation exists in Northern Ireland in the Companies (Northern Ireland) Order 1986 for companies incorporated there.
2 *The Limited Liability Partnerships Regulations 2001* (SI 2001/1090).
3 European Commission, Internal Market Directorate General, *Towards an EU Regime on Transparency Obligations of Issuers Whose Securities Are Admitted to Trading on a Regulated Market*, Consultation Document of The Services of The Internal Market Directorate General, MARKT/11.07.2001.
4 The Institute of Chartered Accountants in England and Wales, Occasional Council and Other Pronouncements, *Statement of intent on accounting standards in the 1970s*.
5 At that stage, the Association of Certified Accountants and the Institute of Cost and Management Accountants respectively.
6 ICAEW, *Statement of intent on accounting standards in the 1970s*, p. 1.4.
7 Accounting Standards Committee, *Setting Accounting Standards: A consultative document*.
8 Accounting Standards Committee, *Setting Accounting Standards.*
9 Report of the Review Committee under the chairmanship of Sir Ronald Dearing, *The Making of Accounting Standards*, September 1988, p. ix.
10 This summary of the recommendations has been extracted from the Dearing Report, *ibid.*, pp. 17–45, *passim.*
11 *Ibid.*, para. 10.2.
12 *Ibid.*, para. 11.1.
13 *Ibid.*, p. 44.
14 *Ibid.*, para. 11.3.
15 *Ibid.*, pp. 27–29.
16 *Ibid.*, p. 31.
17 *Ibid.*, p. 33.
18 CA 85, Sch. 4, para. 36A.
19 *Ibid.*, s 246(1)(a).
20 *Ibid.*, s 245B.
21 *Ibid.*, s 245.
22 *Ibid.*, s 245A.
23 Miss Mary Arden QC, *Accounting Standards Board, The True and Fair Requirement, Opinion,* 21 April 1993, para. 12.
24 ASB, *SORPs: Policy and Code of Practice*, 27 July 2000.
25 *Ibid.,* para. 16.
26 *Ibid.,* para. 17.
27 FRS 18, *Accounting Policies*, ASB, December 2000.
28 *Ibid.*, para. 40.
29 *Ibid.*, para. 58.
30 *Ibid.*, para. 67.
31 CA 47, s 13(1), re-enacted as CA 48, s 149(1).
32 EC Fourth Directive, Article 2.
33 *Ibid.*, paras. 1 to 3.
34 *Ibid.*, paras. 4 and 5.
35 *Foreword to Accounting Standards*, ASB, 1993, para. 16.
36 *Ibid.*, para. 18.
37 Leonard Hoffmann QC and Mary H. Arden, *op. cit.*, paras. 9 and 10.
38 *Lloyd Cheyham & Co Ltd v Littlejohn & Co* [1987] BCLC 303 at 313.
39 Miss Mary Arden QC, *Accounting Standards Board, The True and Fair Requirement, Opinion,* 21 April 1993.
40 *Ibid.*, para. 10.
41 See, for example: Department of Trade and Industry, *Accounting and Audit Requirements for Small Firms*, London: DTI, 1985; Department of Trade and Industry, *Burdens on Business, Report of a Scrutiny of Administrative and Legislative Requirements*, London: HMSO, March 1985; B. V. Carsberg *et al.*, *Small Company Financial Reporting*, London: Prentice-Hall International, 1985; AICPA, Accounting Standards Division, Committee on Generally Accepted Accounting Principles for Smaller and/or Closely Held Businesses, *Report of the Committee on Generally Accepted Accounting Principles for Smaller and/or Closely Held Businesses*, New York: AICPA, August 1976; Institute of Chartered Accountants of British Columbia, *Task Force on Big GAAP/Little GAAP*, Report to Council, Submitted 30 July 1981.
42 Institute of Chartered Accountants of British Columbia, *op. cit.*, p. 3.
43 *Ibid.*, p. 4.
44 B. V. Carsberg *et al.*, *op. cit.*, p. 83.
45 *Ibid.*, pp. 83–84.
46 TR 690*: Statement by the Accounting Standards Committee on the application of accounting standards to small companies*, February 1988.
47 *Ibid.*, para. 5.
48 *Ibid.*, para. 17.
49 TR 706: *Statement by the Accounting Standards Committee on the definition of 'small company' for the purpose of applying accounting standards,* July 1988, para. 1.1.
50 *Ibid.*, para. 5.1.
51 *Ibid.*, para. 5.2.
52 Consultative Document, *Exemptions from Standards on Grounds of Size or Public Interest*, CCAB, November 1994.

53 *Designed to fit – A Financial Reporting Standard for Smaller Entities*, CCAB, December 1995.
54 *Financial Reporting Standard for Smaller Entities (Effective March 2000)*, ASB, December 1999, para. 1.1.
55 *Ibid.*, para. 2.1.
56 *Ibid.*, para. 2.2.
57 *Ibid.*, paras. 2.3 and 2.4. Schedule 4 sets out the following five accounting principles: going concern, consistency, prudence, accruals/matching and non-aggregation.
58 *Ibid.*, para. 2.5.
59 *Ibid.*, para. 2.6.
60 *Ibid.*, para. 2.8.
61 Exposure Draft, *Amendment to Financial Reporting Standard for Smaller Entities*, ASB, June 2001.
62 The Company Law Review Steering Group, Final Report, *Modern Company Law for a Competitive Economy*, DTI, June 2001, Chapters 2 and 4.
63 *Ibid.*, Chapter 2, paras. 2.32 and 2.33.
64 *Ibid.*, Chapter 4, paras. 4.34 and 4.35.
65 *Ibid.*, Chapter 8, para. 8.68.
66 CA 85, s 251.
67 *The Companies (Summary Financial Statement) Regulations 1995* (SI 1995/2092).
68 *Ibid.*, Sch. 1, para. 2.
69 *Ibid.*, Sch. 1, para. 3.
70 *Ibid.*, Sch. 1, para. 4.
71 *Ibid.*, Schedules 2 and 3.
72 *Ibid.*, Sch. 1, para. 1(1).
73 CA 85, s 251(4) (a).
74 *The Companies (Summary Financial Statement) Regulations 1995* (SI 1995/2092), para. 7(3) and (4).
75 CA 85, s 251(4) (c) and (d).
76 *Ibid.*, s 251(4) (b).
77 The Company Law Review Steering Group, Final Report, *Modern Company Law for a Competitive Economy*, Chapter 8, paras. 8.72 to 8.79.
78 The Company Law Review Steering Group, Final Report, *Modern Company Law for a Competitive Economy*, DTI, June 2001.
79 *Ibid.*, Chapter 3, paras. 3.33 to 3.45. See also Chapter 8, paras. 8.29 to 8.71.
80 *Ibid.*, Chapter 3, para. 3.47.
81 *Ibid.*
82 *Ibid.*, Chapter 3, paras. 3.56 to 3.66.
83 *Ibid.*, Chapter 5, para. 5.47.
84 *Ibid.*,. Chapter 5, para. 5.48.
85 IASC, *Preface to Statements of International Accounting Standards*, para. 2.
86 IASC, *Shaping IASC for the future: A Discussion Paper issued for comment by the Strategy Working Party of the International Accounting Standards Committee*, IASC, 7 December 1998, para. 2.
87 At the time of its dissolution on 1 April 2001, the IASC Board members were: Australia, Canada, France, Germany, India, Japan, Malaysia, Mexico, Netherlands, Nordic Federation of Public Accountants, South Africa, United Kingdom, United States of America and representatives of the International Council of Investment Associations (ICIA), the Federation of Swiss Industrial Holding Companies and the International Association of Financial Executives Institutes (IAFEI). The Indian delegation included a representative from Sri Lanka and the South African delegation included a representative from Zimbabwe. Representatives of the European Commission, the United States Financial Accounting Standards Board (FASB), the International Organisation of Securities Commissions (IOSCO), and the People's Republic of China attended Board meetings as observers.
88 IASC Board and IOSCO Technical Committee, *Joint Press Release*, Paris, July 9, 1995.
89 *The IASC-U.S. Comparison Project: A Report on the Similarities and Differences between IASC Standards and U.S. GAAP*, FASB, November 1996.
90 U.S. Securities And Exchange Commission, *SEC Concept Release: International Accounting Standards*, Release Nos. 33-7801, 34-42430; International Series No. 1215 Washington, 18 February 2000.
91 IOSCO, Report of the Technical Committee of the International Organisation of Securities Commissions, *IASC Standards – Assessment Report,* May 2000.
92 IASC, *Shaping IASC for the future: A Discussion Paper issued for comment by the Strategy Working Party of the International Accounting Standards Committee*, IASC, 7 December 1998, para. 2.
93 *Ibid.*, para. 115 *et seq.*
94 The G4+1 was an informal grouping of staff members of the standard-setting bodies of Australia, Canada, New Zealand, the United Kingdom, the United States of America and the IASC. From time to time, the G4+1 published position papers on accounting topics of current interest. These papers did not necessarily reflect the official views of any of the standard-setting bodies represented. At a meeting of the G4+1 held in January 2001, the Group discussed whether its activities should continue given the imminent commencement of activities by the new International Accounting Standards Board (IASB) and agreed to disband and cancel its planned future activities.

95 Report of the IASC's Strategy Working Party, *Recommendations on shaping IASC for the future*, November 1999.
96 The IASB Constitution refers to the 'IASC' as the overall 'Organisation'.
97 IASB Constitution, paras. 18 and 20.
98 IASC Foundation Press Release, 25 January 2001.
99 IASB Constitution, para. 26.
100 *Ibid.*, para. 42.
101 *Ibid.*, para. 44.
102 *Ibid.*, para. 41.
103 IAS 1, *Presentation of financial statements*, IASC, Revised August 1997.
104 *Ibid.*, para. 7.
105 *Ibid.*, para. 8.
106 *Ibid.*, para. 11.
107 *Ibid.*
108 *Ibid.*, paras. 10 and 12.
109 *Ibid.*, para. 13.
110 *Ibid.*, para. 14.
111 *Ibid.*, para. 16.
112 *Ibid.*, para. 15.
113 *Ibid.*, para. 97.
114 *Ibid.*, para. 20.
115 *Ibid.*, para. 22.
116 SIC–18, *Consistency – Alternative Methods*, SIC, May 1999, para. 3.
117 IAS 1, para. 23.
118 *Ibid.*, para. 24.
119 *Ibid.*, para. 23.
120 IAS 10, *Events after the balance sheet date*, IASC, Revised May 1999 para. 13.
121 IAS 1, para. 23.
122 *Ibid.*, para. 25.
123 *Ibid.*, para. 27.
124 *Ibid.*, paras. 29 to 31.
125 *Ibid.*, paras. 38 and 40.
126 *Ibid.*, paras. 53 to 54.
127 *Ibid.*, paras. 77 to 84.
128 *Ibid.*, para. 66.
129 *Ibid.*, para. 67.
130 *Ibid.*, para. 72.
131 *Ibid.*, para. 74.
132 *Ibid.*
133 *Ibid.*, para. 75.
134 *Ibid.*
135 *Ibid.*, para. 86.
136 *Ibid.*
137 *Ibid.*, paras. 33 to 37.
138 SIC–8, *First-time application of IASs as the primary basis of accounting*, SIC, January 1998, paras. 3 to 6.
139 *Ibid.*, para. 7.
140 *Ibid.*, para. 8.
141 Fourth Council Directive 78/660/EEC of 25 July 1978 based on Article 54 (3) (g) of the Treaty on the annual accounts of certain types of companies; Seventh Council Directive 83/349/EEC of 13 June 1983 based on the Article 54 (3) (g) of the Treaty on consolidated accounts.
142 Communication from the European Commission, *Accounting harmonisation: a new strategy vis-à-vis international harmonisation,* 1995.
143 See for example, European Commission, *Examination of the conformity between International Accounting Standards applicable to accounting periods beginning before 1 July 1999 and the European Accounting Directives*, February 2000; European Commission, *Examination of the Conformity between SIC-1 to SIC-25 and the European Accounting Directives*, February 2001. The full set of these comparisons may be found on the EC website: http://europa.eu.int/comm/internal_market/en/company/account/index.htm
144 European Commission, COM(1999) 232 final of 11.05.1999, *Financial Services: Implementing the Framework for Financial Markets : Action Plan*, May 1999.
145 European Commission, *EU Financial Reporting Strategy: the way forward*, June 2000.
146 European Union, *Directive of the European Parliament and of the Council amending Directives 78/660/EEC, 83/349/EEC and 86/635/EEC as regards the valuation rules for the annual accounts and consolidated accounts of certain types of companies as well as of banks and other financial institutions*, PE-CONS 3624/01, Brussels, 22 May 2001.
147 European Commission, *Proposal for a Regulation of the Parliament and of the Council on the Application of International Accounting Standards*, COM(2001) 80, February 2001.
148 This means those with their securities admitted to trading on a regulated market within the meaning of Article 1(13) of Council Directive 93/22/EEC (on investment services in the securities field) or those offered to the public in view of their admission to such trading under Council Directive 80/390/EEC (co-ordinating the requirements for the drawing up, scrutiny and distribution of the listing particulars to be published for the admission of securities to official stock exchange listing).
149 An annex to the proposed Regulation lists the IASs and SIC Interpretations that will need to be adopted by 31 December 2002. The list includes all current IASs and SIC Interpretations, except IAS 41, *Agriculture*.
150 Although EFRAG is a private sector body, the European Commission and CESR (The Committee of European Securities Regulators) have been granted observer status.
151 The Chairman of the Committee of Wise Men, Baron Alexandre Lamfalussy's, opening comments to the Press on Thursday 15 February

2001 on the release of the Committee's final report on the regulation of European securities markets. The Lamfalussy Report, *Final Report of the Committee of Wise Men on The Regulation of European Securities Markets,* Brussels, 15 February 2001, sets out the regulatory reforms that the Committee believes are required in order to build an integrated European financial and securities market.

152 It is worth noting that there is not even general agreement internationally as to what 'GAAP' stands for. In the UK, GAAP stands for Generally Accepted Accounting Practice, whilst in North America it means Generally Accepted Accounting Principles. This difference perhaps reflects the fact that in the UK (and indeed under IAS), compliance with GAAP goes beyond mere compliance with a rules-based system.

153 CA 85, Sch. 4A, para. 10(1)(d).

154 *Ibid.*, s 262(3).

155 *Odeon Associated Theatres Ltd v Jones (Inspector of Taxes)* [1971] 1 WLR 442.

156 Leonard Hoffmann QC and Mary H. Arden, The Accounting Standards Committee Joint Opinion, *Legal Opinion on 'True and Fair'*, paras. 9 and 10.

157 *Statement of Aims*, ASB, 1993, para. 2.

158 FRS 18, para. 17.

159 *Ibid.,* paras. 30 and 31.

160 *Ibid.*, para. 34.

161 *Ibid.*, para. 17.

162 IAS 1, *Presentation of financial statements,* IASC, Revised August 1997, para. 22.

Chapter 2 The quest for a conceptual framework

1 INTRODUCTION

1.1 What is a conceptual framework?

In general terms, a conceptual framework is a statement of generally accepted theoretical principles which form the frame of reference for a particular field of enquiry. In terms of financial reporting, these theoretical principles provide the basis for both the development of new reporting practices and the evaluation of existing ones. Since the financial reporting process is concerned with the provision of information that is useful in making business and economic decisions, a conceptual framework will form the theoretical basis for determining which events should be accounted for, how they should be measured and how they should be communicated to the user. Therefore, although it is theoretical in nature, a conceptual framework for financial reporting has a highly practical end in view.

1.2 Why is a conceptual framework necessary?

A conceptual framework for financial reporting should therefore be a theory of accounting against which practical problems can be tested objectively, the utility of which is decided by the adequacy of the practical solutions it provides. However, the various standard-setting bodies around the world initially often attempted to resolve practical accounting and reporting problems through the development of accounting standards, without such an accepted theoretical frame of reference. The end result was that standard-setters determined the form and content of external financial reports, without resolving such fundamental issues as:

- what are the objectives of these reports?
- who are the users of these reports?
- what are the informational needs of these users?
- what types of report will best satisfy their needs?

Consequently, standards were often produced on a haphazard and 'fire-fighting' approach; evidence of this in the UK was provided by the way in which the (now defunct) ASC attempted to deal with issues such as off balance sheet finance and the capitalisation of brand names. On the other hand, if an agreed framework were to exist, the role of the standard-setters would be changed from that of fireman to that of architect, by being able to design external financial reports on the basis of the needs of the user.

Perhaps the word 'agreed' is the key qualification in this argument. Over the last decade the ASB and the IASC have developed conceptual frameworks that have many elements in common. Both of these are derived from work undertaken by the FASB, which started much earlier, and the underlying similarity between the conceptual frameworks is explained within this chapter. However, whilst there is now a degree of fundamental similarity between the conceptual frameworks of the main global standard setting bodies, the way these principles are translated into detailed rules within the accounting standards issued by each can result in very different financial reports.

The existence of a conceptual framework can also be a lever to move the basis of financial reporting towards a type of measurement base, the full implications of which may not be fully understood by accountants generally. For example the current apparent keenness of the IASB and the ASB to use fair values, rather than cost-based measurements, for assets and liabilities, provides an instance of this possibility.

Equally, experience of the last thirty years shows that in the absence of an agreed conceptual framework, the same theoretical issues are revisited on numerous occasions by different standard-setting working parties. This inevitably sometimes resulted in the development of standards which were inconsistent with each other, or which were founded on incompatible concepts. For example, inconsistencies and conflicts have existed between substance versus form; matching versus prudence; and whether earnings should be determined through balance sheet measurements or by matching costs and revenue. Some UK standards have permitted two or more methods of accounting for the same set of circumstances, whilst others permitted certain accounting practices to be followed on an arbitrary and unspecified basis. These ambiguities perhaps illustrate the difficulty involved in determining what is 'true and fair'.

There are also differences in the tactics adopted by standard setters concerning how the tenets of a conceptual framework become practically realised in actual financial reports. There are significant differences between the tactics adopted by the FASB on the one hand, and the ASB and IASC on the other. In the US the FASB, in spite of its pioneering work on a conceptual framework, has also produced a large number of highly detailed accounting rules. Clearly, the proliferation of accounting standards in the US stems from many factors; however, a more satisfactory conceptual framework might reduce the need for such a large number of highly detailed standards, since more emphasis could be placed on general principles rather than specific rules. It is also true that the more 'general principles' based ASB and IASC approach to standard setting does not imply their frameworks are more satisfactory than the FASB's; rather that the legal and statutory context within which European businesses habitually work is quite different from that of the USA.

However, standard-setters around the world must also contend with the politicisation of accounting caused by the conflicting interests of the various groups of users, preparers and auditors. Where proposed accounting standards are thought likely to affect the economic interests of a particular interested party, it is possible that the quality of the accounting standard will suffer. There are instances where this is evident in the UK. For example, lobbying by the property industry led to the temporary exemption for investment properties from the requirements of SSAP 12 to depreciate fixed assets. This temporary exemption was originally intended to last for one year, but was extended first for a further year and subsequently for a further 18 months before SSAP 19 became effective, and SSAP 12 was then amended to make the exemption for investment properties permanent. Even in its recently published standard FRS 15 – *Tangible Fixed Assets* – on the measurement of tangible fixed assets, the ASB has specifically exempted investment properties[1] – despite the fact that the Board had conceded in its preceding discussion paper that there was no conceptual justification for such an exemption.[2]

The only defence that standard-setters can have against such political interference in the standard-setting process is to be able to demonstrate that a proposed accounting practice is derived from a sound theoretical foundation. Otherwise, how does one persuade, for example, an industry lobby that a particular accounting treatment which they perceive as adversely affecting their economic interests is better than one which does not?[3]

An agreed framework is not the panacea for all accounting problems. Nor does it obviate the need for judgement to be exercised in the process of resolving accounting issues. What it can provide is a framework within which those judgements can be made. Indeed there is evidence of this beginning to happen, as the principles expressed in the ASB's *Statement of Principles* and the IASC's *Framework for the Preparation and Presentation of Financial Statements* become more obvious within their later accounting standards. Nevertheless, there is clear evidence also of the ASB and the IASB issuing standards that contravene their own conceptual frameworks. For example FRS 10 and IAS 38 require the capitalisation of goodwill as an asset, despite the fact that goodwill does not meet the definition of an asset in either standard setter's conceptual framework. Similarly FRS 19 and IAS 12 require recognition of deferred tax liabilities that do not meet the liability definition under either framework.

2 THE AICPA'S EARLY INITIATIVES IN THE UNITED STATES

2.1 Accounting Research Studies

The Accounting Principles Board (APB) of the American Institute of Certified Public Accountants (AICPA) was formed in 1959 to replace the former Committee on Accounting Procedure and the Committee on Terminology. During its existence, the Committee on Accounting Procedure had issued a series of Accounting Research Bulletins (ARBs). In 1953, the first 42 ARBs (eight of which dealt solely with terminology) were revised and restated as a consolidated ARB No. 43 and Accounting Terminology Bulletin No. 1; thereafter, a further eight ARBs were issued. The ARBs were supposedly aimed at the development of generally accepted accounting principles; however, the Committee met with considerable criticism over its failure to deal with contemporary accounting issues (such as leasing and business combinations), which could not be solved from precedents and required the development of accounting principles through pure accounting research.

As a direct response to this, the President of the AICPA set up the Special Committee on Research Program in 1957; in 1958 the Committee recommended the formation of the APB, and the appointment of a director of research with a permanent research staff. The Special Committee also recommended that 'an immediate project of the accounting research staff should be a study of the basic postulates underlying accounting principles generally, and the preparation of a brief statement thereof. There should be also a study of the broad principles of accounting. ... The results of these, as adopted by the [Accounting Principles] Board, should serve as the foundation for the entire body of future pronouncements by the Institute on accounting matters, to which each new release should be related.'[4]

This, therefore, was probably the first mandate given by a professional body for the development of a conceptual framework. The AICPA appointed Maurice Moonitz as its first Director of Accounting Research; Moonitz started work on the postulates study, and appointed Robert Sprouse to work with him on the study of broad accounting principles. The products of the research were contained in Accounting Research Study No. 1 – *The Basic Postulates of Accounting*[5] – and Accounting Research Study No. 3 – *A Tentative Set of Broad Accounting Principles for Business Enterprises* – which were published in 1961 and 1962 respectively.[6]

These studies, however, caused a storm of controversy. Instead of establishing a sound foundation of accounting theory through rigorous argument based on deductive reasoning, Moonitz and Sprouse attempted to persuade the accounting profession to accept a new system of financial reporting based on current values. Furthermore, the realisation principle was discarded on the basis of the assertion that 'profit is attributable to the whole process of business activity, not just to the moment of sale'.[7] This was reflected, for example, in the statement that 'inventories which are readily saleable at known prices with negligible costs of disposal, or with known or readily predictable costs of disposal, should be measured at net realizable value'.[8]

However, the criticism which was levelled at these studies appeared to be based more on the fear of the unknown, rather than on any intellectual shortcomings. Consequently, they were viewed as being too radically different from contemporary generally accepted accounting practice to be accepted, and were rejected by the APB. This resulted in the commissioning of Grady's Accounting Research Study No. 7 – *Inventory of Generally Accepted Accounting Principles for Business Enterprises* – which was published in 1965 and which catalogued the various accounting methods which had been approved by ARBs, APB Opinions or some other precedent.

In all, 15 Accounting Research Studies were published during the life of the APB. However, following the rejection of ARS Nos. 1 and 3, the studies tended to be carried out on an ad hoc basis and without the support of a common foundation. Furthermore, the recommendations contained in the research studies appeared to have been largely ignored in the drafting of the 31 Opinions which the APB issued between 1962 and 1973. Consequently, generally accepted accounting principles in the US were continuing to be formulated without the benefit of research or the foundation of an agreed theoretical framework and, for all intents and purposes, the APB slowly resorted to the position of its predecessor, the Committee on Accounting Procedure.

2.2 APB Statement No. 4

In 1965 the APB made a further attempt to provide a basis for guiding the future development of accounting by establishing a committee to carry out a study which could be used as a basis for understanding the broad fundamentals of accounting. In 1970, the APB approved Statement No. 4 – *Basic Concepts and Accounting Principles Underlying Financial Statements of Business Enterprises.*[9] The statement contained a description of (1) the environment of financial accounting, (2) the objectives of financial statements, (3) the basic features and basic elements of financial accounting and (4) a summary of existing generally accepted accounting principles.

Therefore, it was (on its own admission)[10] a descriptive statement, not prescriptive. For example, assets and liabilities were defined as economic resources and obligations 'that are recognised and measured in conformity with generally accepted accounting principles',[11] which meant that the definitions failed to provide a theoretical basis for the development of generally accepted principles. As a result APB No. 4 was deficient as a theory of accounting and did not respond to the problems which were facing the profession at the time and which had been brought about by the inconsistencies and inadequacies of financial reporting practice.

2.3 The Wheat and Trueblood Committees

In 1971, in response to continued criticism from both within the profession and from the SEC about its inability to establish sound accounting principles, the AICPA announced the formation of two study groups: the *Study Group on Establishment of Accounting Principles*, to be chaired by Francis Wheat, and the *Study Group on Objectives of Financial Statements*, to be chaired by Robert

Trueblood. The Wheat Committee published its report in 1972, resulting in the establishment of the Financial Accounting Standards Board (FASB) in 1973 as the successor to the APB. This had the effect of taking the responsibility for setting accounting standards away from the accounting profession and placing it in the hands of an independent body in the private sector. The FASB comprises seven members appointed by the Financial Accounting Foundation (FAF), and is funded by the sale of publications and from contributions made to the FAF. The Board of Trustees of the FAF is appointed by its eight sponsoring organisations, which include, inter alia, the American Accounting Association, the AICPA and two organisations which represent government.

The study carried out by the Trueblood Committee represents the next significant step in the attempt to develop a conceptual framework. In setting the terms of reference of the study group, the Board of Directors of the AICPA stated that the main purpose of the study was 'to refine the objectives of financial statements'.[12] They went on to suggest that APB Statement No. 4 would be a logical starting point for the study, whilst at the same time noting that APB 4 'contains objectives in terms of what is considered acceptable today rather than in terms of what is needed and what is attainable to meet these needs'.[13] The study group was asked to consider at least the following questions:

- Who needs financial statements?
- What information do they need?
- How much of the needed information can be provided by accounting?
- What framework is required to provide the needed information?[14]

The Trueblood Report[15] was published in October 1973 and developed twelve objectives of financial statements. The principal objective was stated in the following terms: 'the basic objective of financial statements is to provide information useful for making economic decisions'.[16] Having established its twelve objectives of financial statements, the report then discussed seven qualitative characteristics which information contained in financial statements should possess in order to satisfy the needs of users.[17] As will be seen below, the Trueblood Report's objectives of financial statements formed the basis for the development of the FASB's first concepts statement, whilst the qualitative characteristics identified were amongst those discussed in the second concepts statement.

3 THE FASB CONCEPTUAL FRAMEWORK

3.1 Introduction

The Trueblood Committee was at work on its report when the FASB came into existence. Consequently, the Trueblood Report was effectively passed on to the FASB for consideration, thus signalling the beginnings of the FASB's Conceptual Framework Project. The FASB duly considered the report and in June 1974 published a Discussion Memorandum – *Conceptual Framework for Accounting and Reporting: Consideration of the Report of the Study Group on the Objectives of Financial Statements* – which asked for comments on the issues raised.[18] A public hearing was held during September 1974, and in December 1976 the FASB published its *Tentative Conclusions on Objectives of Financial Statements of Business Enterprises*. In December 1976 the FASB also published a paper – *Scope and Implications of the Conceptual Framework Project* – which summarised its aims for the project, the expected benefits to be derived and the main areas which were expected to be covered.[19]

Following the criticism and eventual replacement of first the Committee on Accounting Procedure, followed by the APB, the FASB was seen by many commentators to be the last opportunity of keeping accounting standard-setting in the private sector. The FASB was clearly aware that accounting standards had to regain the credibility of public opinion which had been lost as a result of the many perceived abuses of financial reporting during the 1960s. The FASB referred to this lack of public confidence, and the possible consequences thereof, as follows: 'skepticism about financial reporting has adverse effects on businesses, on business leaders, and on the public at large. One of these effects is the risk of imposition of government reporting and other regulatory requirements that are not justified – requirements that are not in the public interest because the perceived benefits do not exist or are more than offset by costly interference with the orderly operation of the economy. Skepticism creates adverse public opinion, which may be the antecedent of unjustified government regulation. Every company, every industry stands to suffer because of skepticism about financial reporting.'[20] The FASB, therefore, saw its conceptual framework project as the means of enhancing the credibility of financial statements in the eyes of the public.

The FASB also recognised that although there had been many attempts by individuals and organisations (such as the American Accounting Association) to develop a theory of accounting, none of these individual theories had become universally accepted or relied on in practice. They therefore expressed a need for a '*constitution*, a coherent system of interrelated objectives and fundamentals that can lead to consistent standards and that prescribes the nature, function, and limits of financial accounting and financial statements'.[21] The conceptual framework was expected to:

(a) guide the body responsible for establishing standards;

(b) provide a frame of reference for resolving accounting questions in the absence of a specific promulgated standard;

(c) determine bounds for judgement in preparing financial statements;
(d) increase financial statement users' understanding of and confidence in financial statements; and
(e) enhance comparability.[22]

To date the FASB has issued seven concepts statements, of which one (SFAC No. 4) deals with the objectives of financial reporting by non-business organisations and is beyond the scope of this book, whilst another (SFAC No. 3) dealt with elements of financial statements by business enterprises, and was superseded by SFAC No. 6, which expanded the scope of SFAC No. 3 to encompass not-for-profit organisations. The remaining five are discussed in the sections which follow.

3.2 The objectives of financial reporting

The first phase of the FASB's conceptual framework project was to develop a statement of the objectives of financial reporting. Clearly, some pioneering work in this area had been done by the Trueblood Committee (see 2.3 above), and this formed the basis of the FASB's first concepts statement. Nevertheless, it was not until 1978 that the FASB finally published this statement.

SFAC No. 1 – *Objectives of Financial Reporting by Business Enterprises* – starts off by making the point that financial reporting includes not only financial statements, but also incorporates other means of communicating financial and non-financial information; this may be achieved, for example, through the medium of stock exchange documents, news releases, management forecasts etc.[23] Having said this, the statement stresses that 'financial reporting is not an end in itself but is intended to provide information that is useful in making business and economic decisions'.[24] This, however, is no new revelation; it is the type of broad generalisation that has characterised numerous previous attempts at establishing a conceptual framework. On the other hand, what it does do is raise all the same issues which the Trueblood Committee had been asked to consider seven years previously, such as: For whom is this information intended? What types of 'business and economic decisions' do they make? What information do they need to enable them to make these decisions? What framework is required to provide this needed information?

The statement details an extensive list of potential users, distinguishing between those with a direct interest and those with an indirect interest in the information provided by financial reporting.[25] The groups of user which have a direct interest include owners, management, creditors and employees; whilst user groups such as financial analysts and advisers, journalists, regulatory authorities and trade unions are deemed to have an indirect interest, since they advise or represent those who have a direct interest. However, having identified this wide range of users, the statement focuses on the information needs of investors and creditors. These are encompassed in the first of three primary objectives identified in the statement: 'financial reporting should provide information that is useful to present and potential investors and creditors and other users in making rational investment, credit, and similar decisions'.[26]

This objective leads to the first of the two most significant and far-reaching conclusions in the statement, namely that 'financial reporting should provide information to help investors, creditors, and others assess the amounts, timing, and uncertainty of prospective net cash inflows to the related enterprise'.[27] The statement articulated its reasoning behind this conclusion as follows: 'Potential users of financial information most directly concerned with a particular business enterprise are generally interested in its ability to generate favourable cash flows, because their decisions relate to amounts, timing, and uncertainties of expected cash flows. To investors, lenders, suppliers, and employees, a business enterprise is a source of cash in the form of dividends or interest and perhaps appreciated market prices, repayment of borrowing, payment for goods or services, or salaries and wages. They invest cash, goods, or services in an enterprise and expect to obtain sufficient cash in return to make the investment worthwhile. They are directly concerned with the ability of the enterprise to generate favourable cash flows and may also be concerned with how the market's perception of that ability affects the relative prices of its securities. To customers, a business enterprise is a source of goods or services, but only by obtaining sufficient cash to pay for the resources it uses and to meet its other obligations can the enterprise provide those goods or services. To managers, the cash flows of a business enterprise are a significant part of their management responsibilities, including their accountability to directors and owners. Many, if not most, of their decisions have cash flow consequences for the enterprise. Thus, investors, creditors, employees, customers, and managers significantly share a common interest in an enterprise's ability to generate favourable cash flows. Other potential users of financial information share the same interest, derived from investors, creditors, employees, customers, or managers whom they advise or represent or derived from an interest in how those groups (and especially stockholders) are faring.'[28]

In reaching this conclusion, the FASB was aware of the fact that it might precipitate an adverse reaction leading to the possible rejection of the statement through what might have been seen as an objective which would ultimately result in companies being required to present cash flow, management forecast or current value information. The FASB pre-empted this potential adverse reaction by stating that 'the objective focuses on the purpose for which information provided should be useful ... rather than the kinds of information that may be useful for that purpose. The objective neither requires nor prohibits "cash flow information", "current value information", "management forecast information", or any other specific information. Conclusions about "current value information" and "management forecast information" are beyond the scope of this Statement. Paragraphs 42-44 [of SFAC No. 1] note that information about cash receipts and disbursements is not usually considered to be the most useful information for the purposes described in this objective.'[29]

However, in examining this objective, it is important to take cognisance of empirical research which has been conducted in this area. In 1979, Chang and Most investigated the views of individual investors, institutional investors and financial analysts in the USA, UK and New Zealand as part of a study into the importance of financial statements for investment decisions.[30] Their study included an investigation into the investment objectives of individual and institutional investors, and reached the conclusion that 'the most important investment objective for both individual and institutional investors is long-term capital gains. This, and a combination of dividend income and capital gains, are considerably more important than short-term capital gains. It would appear that prediction of short-term cash flows would not be one of the more important investor uses of financial statements, and this calls in question the conventional assumption that a principal objective of financial statements is to assist users to predict future cash flows in terms of timing, as distinct from amount and relative uncertainty.'[31] On the other hand, it is, of course, possible that institutional investors are much more influenced by short-term expectations today than they were over twenty years ago; consequently, the findings of Chang and Most may no longer be valid.

The second fundamental conclusion reached in SFAC No. 1 which has far-reaching implications for the future development of accounting standards is concerned with the primary focus of financial reporting. During the early stages of the development of accounting rules in the first half of this century, the primary focus of financial statements was based on the principle of 'stewardship'. This arose from the fact that the management of an enterprise were primarily seen to be accountable to the owners for safeguarding the assets which had been entrusted to them, leading to a balance sheet emphasis in financial reporting. However, the focus has gradually shifted away from the notion of the balance sheet reporting on the custodianship of assets, to an earnings emphasis based on the principle that the income statement should present 'decision-useful' information. This is encapsulated in the statement in SFAC No. 1 that 'the primary focus of financial reporting is information about an enterprise's performance provided by measures of earnings and its components. Investors, creditors, and others who are concerned with assessing the prospects for enterprise net cash inflows are especially interested in that information.'[32]

SFAC No. 1 still recognises the fact that financial reporting should provide information about how the management of an enterprise has discharged its stewardship responsibility.[33] However, it goes on to say that 'earnings information is commonly the focus for assessing management's stewardship or accountability. Management, owners, and others emphasize enterprise performance or profitability in describing how management has discharged its stewardship accountability.'[34]

In other words, the statement is asserting that the measurement of earnings in the income statement should take precedence over the measurement of assets and liabilities in the balance sheet. This is an important principle which should have had an important impact on the principles laid down in the development of future accounting standards. However, as will be seen below, the FASB's subsequent concepts statements have essentially avoided the issue of how to determine net income. Furthermore, more recent statements issued by the FASB tend to suggest an uncertainty as to whether an earnings or balance sheet approach should be followed (for example, SFAS 109 – *Accounting for Income Taxes* – would appear to view the balance sheet as the primary statement).

This tension between income statement or balance sheet primacy has swayed towards the balance sheet, at least as far as recent IASC and ASB standards indicate. As is more fully described at 5 and 6 below, both the IASC's and the ASB's conceptual frameworks adopt a balance sheet approach to recognition, whereby all the elements of financial statements are defined in terms of assets and liabilities, and income recognition is a function of increases and decreases in net assets rather than the completion of acts of performance.

Consequently, despite the focus of the capital markets on performance measurement, the conceptual underpinning for financial reporting adopted by the FASB, the ASB and the IASC appears to be focusing principally on the recognition and derecognition of assets and liabilities.

3.3 The qualitative characteristics of accounting information

The FASB's second Concepts Statement – *Qualitative Characteristics of Accounting Information* – examines the characteristics that make accounting information useful to the users of that information. The statement views these characteristics as 'a hierarchy of accounting qualities', which then form the basis for selecting and evaluating information for inclusion in financial reports. The hierarchy is represented in Figure 1 below:[35]

Figure 1

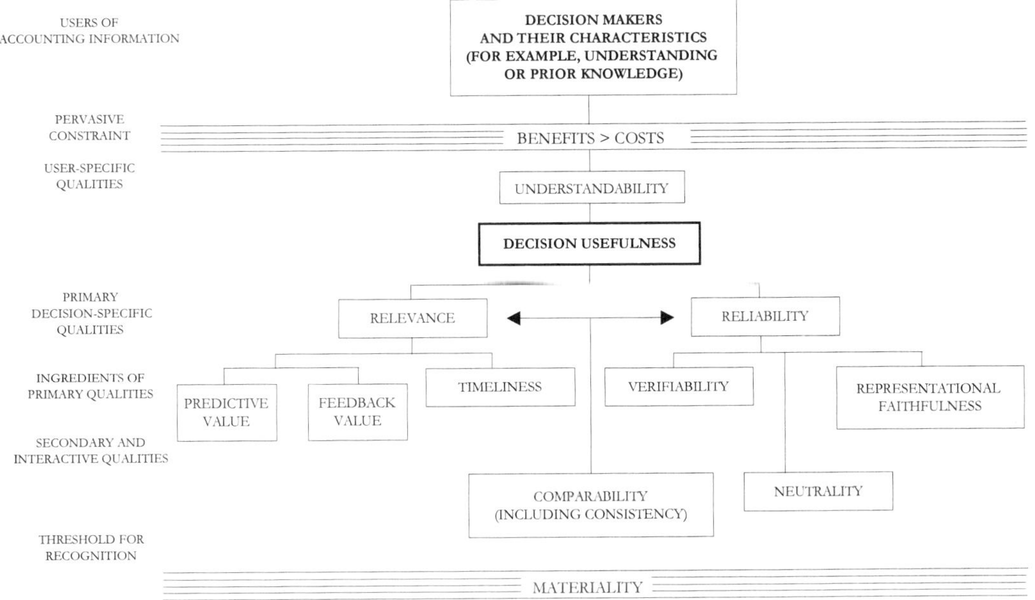

3.3.1 *The decision-makers*

The decision-makers (users) appear at the top of the hierarchy against the background of their own specific characteristics. Whilst usefulness for decision-making is the most important quality that accounting information should possess, each decision-maker has to judge what information is useful for a specific decision. This judgement would be based on such factors as the nature of the decision to be made, the information already in the individual's possession or available from other sources, the decision-making process employed and the decision maker's capacity to process all the information obtained.

3.3.2 *The cost/benefit constraint*

Since information should be provided only if the benefits to be derived from that information outweigh the costs of providing it, the cost/benefit constraint pervades the hierarchy. However, the application of this constraint may cause a certain amount of difficulty, since the costs of providing financial information are normally borne by the enterprise (and ultimately passed on to its customers), whilst the benefits are reaped by the users. For this reason, the normal forces of demand and supply will not prevail in the market of financial information, since the external user will almost always view the benefits of additional information as outweighing the costs.

3.3.3 *Understandability*

The hierarchy depicts understandability as being the key quality for accounting information to achieve 'decision usefulness'. SFAC No. 1 stated that the information provided by financial reporting 'should be comprehensible to those who have a reasonable understanding of business and economic activities and are willing to study the information with reasonable diligence'.[36] Information, whilst it may be relevant, will be wasted if it is provided in a form which cannot be understood by the users for whom it was intended. SFAC No. 1 elaborated on the relationship between useful information and understandability as follows: 'financial information is a tool and, like most tools, cannot be of much direct help to those who are unable or unwilling to use it or who misuse it. Its use can be learned, however, and financial reporting should provide information that can be used by all – nonprofessionals as well as professionals – who are willing to learn to use it properly. Efforts may be needed to increase the understandability of financial information. Cost-benefit considerations may indicate that information understood or used by only a few should not be provided. Conversely, financial reporting should not exclude relevant information merely because it is difficult for some to understand or because some investors or creditors choose not to use it.'[37]

3.3.4 *Relevance and reliability*

The qualities that distinguish 'better' (more useful) information from 'inferior' (less useful) information are primarily the qualities of relevance and reliability, with some other characteristics that those qualities imply. SFAC No. 2 identifies relevance and reliability as 'the two primary qualities that make accounting information useful for decision making. Subject to constraints imposed by cost and materiality, increased relevance and increased reliability are the characteristics that make information a more desirable commodity – that is, one useful in making decisions.'[38] However, this was not new – the qualitative characteristics of relevance and reliability have been discussed in several preceding studies (such as the Trueblood and Corporate Reports). What was new (and probably the most significant aspect of SFAC No. 2), was the explicit recognition of the fact that 'reliability and relevance often impinge on each other'.[39] Consequently, whenever accounting standards are set, decisions have to be made concerning the relative importance of these two characteristics, often resulting in trade-offs being made between them.

In today's context, where standard-setting bodies seem intent on replacing the historical cost system by an income and measurement system based on fair values (discussed below at 5 and 6) deciding the relative weight to be attributed to relevance and to reliability, when presenting information is of increasingly pertinent. However, one matter that is easily overlooked in the debate is that reliability is, in our view, a necessary precondition for relevance. If markets and users generally consider information is not reliable, it will certainly not be considered relevant. Consequently, fair values attributed to assets that do not have readily available market prices, may be subjective to a degree that negates any claim to relevance.

A Relevance

The statement defines relevant accounting information as being information which is 'capable of making a difference in a decision by helping users to form predictions about the outcomes of past, present, and future events or to confirm or correct prior expectations'.[40] The statement further describes 'timeliness' as an 'ancillary aspect of relevance. If information is not available when it is needed or becomes available only so long after the reported events that it has no value for future action, it lacks relevance and is of little or no use.'[41] Therefore, in the context of financial reporting, the characteristic of timeliness means that information must be made available to users before it loses its capacity to influence their decisions. However, timeliness alone cannot make information relevant, but a lack of timeliness can result in information losing a degree of relevance which it once had.[42] On the other hand, in many instances there also has to be a trade-off between timeliness and reliability, since generally the more timely the information the less reliable it is.

The hierarchy identifies 'predictive value' and 'feedback value' as the other components of relevance on the basis that 'information can make a difference to decisions by improving decision makers' capacities to predict or by confirming or correcting their earlier expectations'.[43] Predictive value is defined as 'the quality of information that helps users to increase the likelihood of correctly forecasting the outcome of past or present events',[44] whilst feedback value is defined as 'the quality of information that enables users to confirm or correct prior expectations'.[45] Clearly, however, in saying that accounting information has predictive value, it is not suggesting that it is itself a prediction.

B Reliability

Reliability is the second of the primary qualities, and is ascribed three attributes in the hierarchy. The statement asserts that the 'reliability of a measure rests on the faithfulness with which it represents what it purports to represent, coupled with an assurance for the user, which comes through verification, that it has that representational quality'.[46] This definition gives rise to the three subsidiary qualities of 'representational faithfulness', 'verifiability', and 'neutrality'. Representational faithfulness is an unnecessary piece of jargon introduced into accounting terminology by SFAC No. 2; what it essentially means is that information included in financial reports should represent what it purports to represent. In other words, financial reporting should be truthful. For example, if a group's consolidated balance sheet discloses cash and bank balances, users would be justified in assuming that, in the absence of any statement to the contrary, the financial statements were truthful, and that these represented cash resources freely available to the group; however, if the reality of the situation was that the cash resources were situated in countries which had severe exchange control restrictions, and were, therefore, not available to the group, some might hold the view that the financial statements were not entirely 'representationally faithful'.

It should be noted, however, that there are degrees of representational faithfulness. Because the financial reporting process involves allocations, estimations and subjective judgements, it cannot produce an 'exact' result; consequently, the trade-off between relevance and reliability will often apply, resulting in the presentation of information which is assigned a high degree of relevance, but which sacrifices representational faithfulness. An example of where this might apply is in fair value accounting for an acquisition, where fair values have to be assigned to the separable net assets acquired.

Reliable information should also be verifiable and neutral so that neither measurement nor measurer bias results in the information being presented in such a way that it influences the particular decision being made. Verifiability is a quality of representational faithfulness in that it excludes the possibility of measurement bias, whilst neutrality implies the provision of all relevant and reliable information – irrespective of the effects that the information will have on the entity or a particular user group.

3.3.5 Comparability

The hierarchy lists comparability as an additional quality that financial information should possess in order to achieve relevance and reliability. The quality of comparability includes the fundamental accounting concept of consistency, since the usefulness of information is greatly enhanced if it is prepared on a consistent basis from one period to the next, and can be compared with corresponding information of the same enterprise for some other period, or with similar information about some other enterprise.

3.3.6 *Materiality*

All the qualitative criteria discussed in SFAC No. 2 are subject to a materiality threshold, since only material information will have an impact on the decision-making process. However, the statement provides no quantitative guidelines for materiality, and it will be a matter of judgement for the providers of information to determine whether or not an item of information has crossed the materiality threshold for recognition. Materiality is closely related to the characteristic of relevance, since both are defined in terms of what influences or makes a difference to an investor or other decision-maker. On the other hand, the two concepts can be distinguished; a decision by management not to disclose certain information may be made because users have no interest in that kind of information (i.e. it is not relevant to their specific needs), or because the amounts involved are too small to make a difference to the users' decisions (i.e. they are not material).

However, if the preparers of financial statements are to decide on what to include in their reporting package, they must have a clear understanding of the users of their reports and their specific information and decision-making needs. In so doing, they should be aware of the types of information likely to influence their decisions (i.e. relevance) as well as the associated magnitude of this information (i.e. materiality). Consequently, financial reporting will focus generally on information which is regarded as relevant, and specifically on that which is material. The principal difficulty with this, however, is that the materiality decisions of users vary from class to class and amongst individual users in the same class.

There is an element of rationalisation of practice, rather than revelation of principle, about the entire relevance-reliability-materiality discussion, which has also pervaded many subsequent conceptual framework attempts. It is becoming increasingly noticeable that new accounting standards are seemingly heavily biased towards relevance at the expense of reliability. For example, in introducing fair value accounting for most financial assets in IAS 39 – *Financial Instruments: Recognition and Measurement*, the IASC has effectively codified the assumption that 'fair value can be reliably determined for most financial assets classified as available for sale or held for trading'.[47] Under the standard, the reliability of measurement presumption can only be rebutted under very limited circumstances, with the result that the fair value measurement attribute has to be applied even in circumstances where it might be deemed to produce relatively unreliable results.

The standard setters rationalise this by asserting (perhaps rather pejoratively) that it is better to have financial statements that are approximately right rather than precisely wrong. By this they imply that historical cost information is *ipso facto* irrelevant, and it is preferable to have financial statements that are prepared on a fair value basis that are, in the view of the standard setters, considerably more relevant, if not as reliable. Consequently, as the use of fair values is introduced more and more into the measurement of assets and liabilities, the context of the trade-off between relevance and reliability has changed considerably. This is particularly evident in much of the thinking behind, and content in, the Joint Working Group discussion paper – *Financial Instruments and Similar Items* – which is discussed in detail in Chapter 10 at 1.1.

3.3.7 *Conservatism*

SFAC No. 2 includes an interesting discussion on the convention of 'conservatism' (i.e. prudence).[48] In so doing, it draws a distinction between the 'deliberate, consistent understatement of net assets and profits',[49] and the practice of ensuring that 'uncertainties and risks inherent in business situations are adequately considered'.[50] The statement recognised the fact that, in the eyes of bankers and other lenders, deliberate understatement of assets was desirable, since it increased their margin of safety on assets pledged as security for debts. On the other hand, it was also recognised that consistent understatement was difficult to maintain over a period of any length, and that understated assets would clearly lead to overstated income in later periods when the assets were ultimately realised. Consequently, unwarranted and deliberate conservatism in financial reporting would lead to a contravention of certain of the qualitative characteristics, such as neutrality and representational faithfulness.

3.4 The elements of financial statements

SFAC No. 6 – *Elements of Financial Statements* – was issued in 1985 as a replacement to SFAC No. 3 – *Elements of Financial Statements of Business Enterprises* – having expanded its scope to encompass non-profit organisations. The statement defines ten 'elements' of financial statements that are directly related to the measurement of performance and financial status of an entity. However, the elements are very much interrelated, as six of them are arithmetically derived from the definitions of assets and liabilities.

3.4.1 *Assets*

Assets are defined as being 'probable future economic benefits obtained or controlled by a particular entity as a result of past transactions or events'.[51] However, the statement then goes on to say that the kinds of items that qualify as assets under this definition are also commonly called 'economic resources'. They are the scarce means that are useful for carrying out economic activities, such as consumption, production and exchange.[52] The common characteristic possessed by all assets is 'service potential' or 'future economic benefit' which eventually results in net cash inflows to the enterprise.[53]

The adequacy of this definition, which is used almost unchanged in the IASC's and the ASB's own conceptual frameworks, is discussed in more detail at 5 below. It does however represent a major shift from the implied definition of an asset under historical cost accounting. Under historical cost accounting a non-monetary asset is no more than a deferred cost; a cost which has been incurred before the balance sheet date and, in terms of the accruals concept, relates to future periods beyond the balance sheet date, thereby justifying it being carried forward as an asset. This applies to all non-monetary assets which are recognised in a historical cost balance sheet – whether they be tangible fixed assets, stock, prepayments or deferred development expenditure. Consequently, there are certain occasions when items will be recognised as assets under the traditional historical cost system, but which will not fit the SFAC No. 6 definition of an asset.

Practical problems continue to arise as a consequence of this definition. For example FRS 17, the new UK pensions standard, no longer allows the spreading of certain pension-related expenses over the service lives of the employees concerned. This is because the unexpensed portion carried forward in the balance sheet would fail to conform to the 'economic resource with future benefits' definition of an asset.

The selection of this definition has also embedded a deep-rooted problem within the FASB's conceptual framework project. First, as far as SFAC No. 6 is concerned, since most of the elements defined in the statement are derived from the definition of an asset, any inadequacy in this definition inevitably affects the validity of the definitions of other elements. Second, in identifying the elements of financial statements before addressing the fundamental issues of how they are to be measured and on what basis of capital maintenance profit is to be determined, the FASB seriously limited its ability to address the issues of recognition and measurement properly. The result of this is that SFAC No. 5 – *Recognition and Measurement in Financial Statements of Business Enterprises* – has serious shortcomings (see 3.5 below).

3.4.2 *Liabilities*

Liabilities are defined as 'probable future sacrifices of economic benefits arising from present obligations of a particular entity to transfer assets or provide services to other entities in the future as a result of past transactions or events'.[54] The statement goes on to say that a liability has three essential characteristics:

(a) it embodies a present duty or responsibility to one or more other entities that entails settlement by probable future transfer or use of assets at a specified or determinable date, on occurrence of a specified event, or on demand;

(b) the duty or responsibility obligates the entity, leaving it little or no discretion to avoid the future sacrifice; and

(c) the transaction or other event obligating the entity has already happened.[55]

Thus, in terms of this definition, liabilities represent the amounts of obligations – giving rise to a problem similar to that outlined above in respect of the definition of assets. There are certain items which have traditionally been recognised as liabilities, but which do not meet the statement's definition. This is because they are deferred credits awaiting recognition in the profit and loss account, or are 'voluntary' liabilities such as provisions for refurbishing components of assets, rather than obligations to other entities. This has led to quite tortuous methods of accounting for what are straightforward matters under traditional historic cost accounting. Examples of items for which the definition has caused difficulties might include deferred government grants, and the methods of accounting for decommissioning costs under FRS 12.

3.4.3 *Equity*

Equity is defined as 'the residual interest in the assets of an entity that remains after deducting its liabilities'.[56] This is a somewhat tautological definition arising from the accounting equation that assets minus liabilities equals equity. Equity is, in fact, the sum of the equity investments made by the entity's owners, and the entity's earnings retained from its profit-making activities. Because of the way in which the definitions of the various elements are interrelated, it might appear to some that the FASB have taken the easy route in defining equity as net assets, rather than in terms of capital contributions plus retained earnings; a possible explanation for this might be that it enabled the FASB to define income in terms of changes in equity. Interestingly, and underlining the fundamental similarity of many of the framework attempts, the ASB's *Statement of Principles* document (see section 5 below) has taken exactly this route to defining equity.

3.4.4 Investments by owners

Investments by owners are defined as being 'increases in equity of a particular business enterprise resulting from transfers to it from other entities of something valuable to obtain or increase ownership interests (or equity) in it'.[57] The statement goes on to say that although investments by owners are most commonly made in the form of assets, the investments can also be represented by services, or the settlement or conversion of liabilities of the enterprise.[58]

3.4.5 Distributions to owners

Distributions to owners are defined as 'decreases in equity of a particular business enterprise resulting from transferring assets, rendering services, or incurring liabilities by the enterprise to owners'.[59] Distributions to owners, therefore, incorporate all forms of capital distributions which result in a decrease in net assets.

3.4.6 Comprehensive income

Comprehensive income is defined as 'the change in equity of a business enterprise during a period from transactions and other events and circumstances from nonowner sources. It includes all changes in equity during a period except those resulting from investments by owners and distributions to owners.'[60] On its own, the term 'comprehensive income' is somewhat meaningless; for example, how does it tie in with the statement in SFAC No. 1[61] that 'the primary focus of financial reporting is information about an enterprise's performance provided by measures of earnings and its components'? Clearly, the FASB was keeping its options open by not defining earnings; in fact, it explained (in a footnote to SFAC No. 6) that whilst 'comprehensive income' is the term used in the statement for the concept that was called 'earnings' in SFAC No. 1, SFAC No. 5 had described earnings for a period as excluding certain cumulative accounting adjustments and other non-owner changes in equity that are included in comprehensive income for a period.[62]

The FASB issued a standard on this topic in June 1997, SFAS 130 – *Reporting Comprehensive Income.*

3.4.7 *Revenues, expenses, gains and losses*

SFAC No. 6 identifies the remaining four elements as those which constitute the basic components of 'comprehensive income':

Revenues, which are 'inflows or other enhancements of assets of an entity or settlements of its liabilities (or a combination of both) from delivering or producing goods, rendering services, or other activities that constitute the entity's ongoing major central operations'.[63]

Expenses, which are 'outflows or other using up of assets or incurrences of liabilities (or a combination of both) from delivering or producing goods, rendering services, or carrying out other activities that constitute the entity's ongoing major or central operations'.[64]

Gains, which are 'increases in equity (net assets) from peripheral or incidental transactions of an entity and from all other transactions and other events and circumstances affecting the entity except those that result from revenues or investments by owners'.[65]

Losses, which are 'decreases in equity (net assets) from peripheral or incidental transactions of an entity and from all other transactions and other events and circumstances affecting the entity except those that result from expenses or distributions to owners'.[66]

Therefore, comprehensive income equals revenues minus expenses plus gains minus losses; however, although the statement states that revenues, expenses, gains and losses can be combined in various ways to obtain various measures of enterprise performance,[67] it fails to define net income.

The difficulty surrounding the FASB's definitions of the ten elements is that they are so interrelated, that in attempting to piece them together into a meaningful accounting framework, one gets caught up in a tautology of terms which all lead back to the definitions of assets and liabilities. Essentially, what the FASB is saying is that assets minus liabilities equals equity and comprehensive income equals changes in equity (excluding transactions with owners), therefore comprehensive income equals the change in net assets. Consequently, the definition of comprehensive income would incorporate items such as capital contributions from non-owners, government grants for capital expenditure and unrealised holding gains. This is all very well, provided that the issues of measurement and capital maintenance have already been settled. However, this is clearly not the case, with the result that the FASB is either restricting itself in the future development of different accounting models for different purposes, or it might have to develop different definitions of the elements of financial statements as different models are developed.

In fact it now seems that the major accounting standard setters, including the FASB, ASB and IASB, have concluded that the definitions of the elements of financial statements are, indeed, deficient and require reconsideration. This view is confirmed by the IASB announcement in July 2001 that it has placed the definitions of the elements of financial statements on its agenda of technical projects.

3.5 Recognition and measurement

Throughout the framework project, the FASB had avoided dealing with certain fundamental issues on the basis that they were the 'subject of another project'.[68] The result was the publication in December 1984 of SFAC No. 5 – *Recognition and Measurement in Financial Statements of Business Enterprises* – which attempted to deal with all the previously unresolved issues. However, the statement was somewhat inconclusive – possibly as a consequence of both its self-imposed restrictions discussed above, and the need to reach compromises in order to complete this phase of the project. The statement tends to describe practices current at the time, rather than indicate preferences or propose improvements; for example, in dealing with the issue of measurement attributes, the statement merely states that 'items currently reported in financial statements are measured by different attributes, depending on the nature of the item and the relevance and reliability of the attribute measured'.[69] Then, instead of either prescribing a particular measurement attribute, or discussing the circumstances under which particular attributes should apply, the statement discusses five different attributes which 'are used in present practice' – historical cost, current cost, current market value, net realisable value and present value of future cash flows – and concludes that 'the use of different attributes will continue'.[70] Furthermore, the statement fails to prescribe a particular concept of capital maintenance that should be adopted by an entity, although the FASB bases its discussions on the concept of financial capital maintenance.[71]

The statement defines recognition as 'the process of formally recording or incorporating an item into the financial statements of an entity as an asset, liability, revenue, expense, or the like'.[72] It goes on to discuss four 'fundamental recognition criteria' which any item should meet in order for it to be recognised in the financial statements of an entity. These criteria, which are subject to a cost-benefit constraint and a materiality threshold, are described as follows:

Definitions – the item meets the definition of an element of financial statements.

Measurability – the item has a relevant attribute measurable with sufficient reliability.

Relevance – the information about the item is capable of making a difference in user decisions.

Reliability – the information is representationally faithful, verifiable and neutral.[73]

Although it was probably worth setting out these criteria, they are no more than an encapsulation of certain criteria contained in Concepts Statements 2 and 6.

SFAC No. 5 does make some progress in distinguishing between comprehensive income, earnings and net income. It states that the concept of earnings is similar to net income in present practice, and that a statement of earnings will be much like a present income statement, although 'earnings' does not include the cumulative effect of certain accounting adjustments of earlier periods that are recognised in the current period.[74] However, the statement goes on to say that the FASB 'expects the concept of earnings to be subject to the process of gradual change or evolution that has characterised the development of net income'.[75] Whilst many would agree with the principle that gradual change is the best approach towards gaining general acceptance, one of the problems with SFAC No. 5 is that the FASB does not indicate what it considers to be the desirable direction for this gradual change to follow. Furthermore, the FASB seems to be saying that concepts will evolve as accounting standards are developed – instead of the other way around.

In an evaluation of the FASB's conceptual framework, Professor David Solomons (who, incidentally, was the principal author of SFAC No. 2) took a distinctly critical view of this 'evolutionary' view of the emergence of concepts, stating the following: 'These appeals to evolution should be seen as what they are – a cop-out. If all that is needed to improve our accounting model is reliance on evolution … why was an expensive and protracted conceptual framework project necessary in the first place? … And, for that matter, if progress is simply a matter of waiting for evolution, who needs the FASB?'[76] Professor Solomons came to the following conclusions about SFAC No. 5: 'Under a rigorous grading system I would give Concepts Statement No. 5 an F and require the board to take the course over again – that is, to scrap the statement and start afresh.'[77] This led Solomons to conclude ultimately that 'my judgment of the project as a whole must be that it has failed'.[78]

Interestingly, the FASB's own special report on its conceptual framework (see 3.6 below) makes the point that although SFAC No. 5's name implies that it gives conceptual guidance on recognition and measurement, its conceptual contributions to financial reporting are not really in those areas.[79] The report goes on to say that 'as a result of compromises necessary to issue it, much of Concepts Statement 5 merely describes present practice and some of the reasons that have been used to support or explain it but provides little or no conceptual basis for analyzing and attempting to resolve the controversial issues of recognition and measurement about which accountants have disagreed for years.'[80] The concluding sentence of the FASB's report sums up elegantly the views that have long been expressed by critics of SFAC No. 5: 'Concepts Statement 5 does make some noteworthy conceptual contributions—they are just not on recognition and measurement.'[81]

3.6 The FASB's Special Report

In January 1998 the FASB published a Special Report entitled *The Framework of Financial Accounting Concepts and Standards*, written by Reed K. Storey and Sylvia Storey. By its own admission this book is 'more of a generous introduction to the FASB's conceptual framework than a comprehensive description or analysis of it'.[82] The main content of the book was first written in 1990 and has been variously updated since that time; but it does not deal with the most recent concepts statement SFAC 7 – *Using cash flow information and present value in accounting measurements* – discussed in section 3.7 below.

It does contain a useful historical overview of the subject, including a critique of some of the earlier (pre-conceptual framework project) attempts to define such terms as assets and liabilities. In the main, such early attempts are characterised as unsatisfactory for reasons of either their circularity or their inability to filter out unwanted asset categories, or both. For example, concerning the definitions within

APB Statement 4, the authors note: 'Those definitions were circular and open ended'[83] and 'Definitions of that type provide no effective limits or restraints on the matching of costs and revenues'.[84] The report makes explicit that a main aim of the concepts project was to ensure definitions of assets and liabilities were found that would bolster 'the conceptual and practical superiority of definitions of assets and liabilities based on resources and obligations that exist in the real world rather than on deferred charges and credits that result only from bookkeeping entries'.[85] The authors indicate that the circular definitions of APB 4 were of 'little help to the Board in deciding whether results of research and development expenditures qualified as assets'.[86]

Whether it is fair to characterise (for instance) the intellectual property gained from research and development as resulting only from bookkeeping entries is not discussed. However, the circularity of a definition is, quite correctly, characterised as fatal to its acceptance, and this is discussed at 5.5.1 below in the context of the assets definition adopted by the ASB.

The special report contains an interesting section discussing the 'conceptual primacy' of either the asset and liability view or the revenue and expense view of income measurement – already outlined in section 3.4 above. This discussion, like much of the debate concerning this topic, contains a number of assertions for which no evidence is offered. The reluctance of the majority of practitioners to endorse the FASB's balance sheet view is referred to in terms that seem condescending when describing professional accountants who have serious reservations about the practical implications of the FASB's pronouncements. For example, 'The revenue and expense view is still deeply ingrained in many accountants' minds and their first reaction to an accounting problem is to think about "proper matching of costs and revenues". Time will be needed for them to become accustomed to thinking first about effects of transactions … on assets or liabilities … and then about how [this] has affected revenues, expenses, gains or losses. Many will be able to make the adjustment only with difficulty'.[87]

In our view the main utility of the Special Report is that it provides a clear summary of the FASB's position and reasons for its adoption of the balance sheet view. While the report does refer to dissenting views, these are mainly in the form of short quotations from the dissenters, in contrast to the main body of the text, where the authors' own opinions clearly coincide with those of the FASB.

3.7 Using cash flow information in accounting measurements (discounting)

In February 2000 the FASB issued a new Statement of Financial Accounting Concepts, SFAC 7 – *Using cash flow information and present value in accounting measurements*. The finalised statement resulted from drafts published in 1999 and 1997. The purpose of statement is to provide a framework for using future cash flows as the basis for accounting measurement. It aims to provide general principles governing the use of present value, especially when the amounts of future cash flows and/or their timing are uncertain. The proposals are limited to issues of measurement and do not address recognition questions.

Present values are used to incorporate the time value of money in a measurement. In their simplest form, present value techniques capture the amount that an entity demands (or that others demand from it) for money that it will receive (or pay) in the future.[88] The FASB's objective of using present value in an accounting measurement is to capture, to the extent that it is possible, the economic difference between sets of estimated future cash flows, taking into account their uncertainty as well as their timing differences. Normal discounting distinguishes between a cash flow of £1,000 due in one day and a cash flow of £1,000 due in ten years, although both have an undiscounted measurement of £1,000. SFAC 7 seeks to distinguish additionally between cash flows based upon their different risks. For example to distinguish between two identical inflows due in (say) five years time, but which have different risks attached to them because of the relative uncertainties of their being received. Consequently, SFAC 7 postulates that a present value measurement which incorporates the uncertainty in estimated future cash flows always provides more relevant information than a measurement based on the undiscounted sum of those cash flows or a discounted measurement that ignores uncertainty.[89]

Any combination of cash flows and interest rates could be used to compute a present value, at least in the broadest sense of the term. However, present value is not an end in itself. Simply applying an arbitrary interest rate to a series of cash flows provides limited information to financial statement users, and may mislead rather than assist. To provide relevant information in financial reporting, present value must represent some observable measurement attribute of assets or liabilities. The statement identifies the following characteristics of a present value measurement which would capture fully the economic differences between various future cash flows:

- An estimate of the future cash flow;
- Expectations about possible variations in amount or timing of those cash flows;
- The time value of money, represented by the risk free rate of interest;
- The price for bearing the uncertainty inherent in the asset or liability;
- Other, sometimes unidentifiable, factors including illiquidity and market imperfections.[90]

SFAC 7 selects fair value as the sole measurement attribute that incorporates all the above aspects, and rejects the possible alternatives of value in use, effective settlement and cost-accumulation as being less satisfactory. The FASB holds that each of the rejected measurement attributes (a) adds factors that are not contemplated in the price of a market transaction for the asset or liability in question, (b) inserts assumptions made by the entity's management in the place of those the market would make, and/or (c) excludes factors that would be contemplated in the price of a market transaction. Consequently fair value represents a price and, as such, provides an unambiguous objective for the development of the cash flows and interest rates used in present value measurement.[91]

The statement sets out the following four general principles that, it considers, govern any application of present value techniques in measuring assets:

- To the extent possible, estimated cash flows and interest rates should reflect assumptions about all future events and uncertainties that would be considered in deciding whether to acquire an asset or group of assets in an arm's-length transaction for cash.
- Interest rates used to discount cash flows should reflect assumptions that are consistent with those inherent in the estimated cash flows. Otherwise, the effect of some assumptions will be double counted or ignored. For example, an interest rate of 12 per cent might be applied to contractual cash flows of a loan. That rate reflects expectations about future defaults from loans with particular characteristics. That same 12 per cent rate should not be used to discount expected cash flows because those cash flows already reflect assumptions about future defaults.
- Estimated cash flows and interest rates should be free from both bias and factors unrelated to the asset or group of assets in question. For example, deliberately understating estimated net cash flows to enhance the apparent future profitability of an asset introduces a bias into the measurement.
- Estimated cash flows or interest rates should reflect the range of possible outcomes rather than a single most likely, minimum, or maximum possible amount.[92]

The stance adopted by SFAC 7 on the measurement of liabilities is consistent with its conclusion on assets. Thus fair value is the single measurement objective when present value is to be used in measuring liabilities, although the statement is not particularly specific as to how fair value is to be determined, stating that the measurement of liabilities 'may require different techniques in arriving at fair value'. However it does state that the objective of using present value techniques to estimate the fair value of a liability is to estimate the value of assets required currently to (a) settle the liability or (b) transfer the liability to an entity of comparable credit standing.[93]

The most significant element of SFAC 7 as concerns liabilities centres around the incorporation into the measurement of the entity's own credit standing. Fair value in settlement as described above implies that the credit standing of the entity must be taken into account in arriving at the fair value of its liabilities. Accordingly, the fair value in settlement of an entity's liability should assume settlement with an entity of comparable, rather than superior, credit standing. Consequently, as the entity's credit standing affects the interest rate at which it borrows in the market place, it therefore affects the fair value of its liabilities.

This view entails the FASB adopting a quite complex form of discounting in its draft, to facilitate which it has defined for its purposes a number of terms that are not necessarily used in their normal everyday sense. Instead of discounting the best estimate of any future cash flow (i.e. the most likely amount), the statement insists that the 'expected' cash flows should be discounted. The 'expected' cash flow to be used is defined as the sum of probability-weighted amounts in a range of possible estimated amounts.[94] Therefore, SFAC 7 requires the estimation of the likelihood of a range of outcomes (for example, for the repayment of a debt); the probability weighting of each; the calculation of each probability weighted amount; their summation and finally the calculation of the present value of that derived total. The statement does not define the rate to be used in any discounting but appears to indicate that a risk free rate is often the appropriate rate to use.

The statement implies a number of practical results, which many will find odd. For instance the fair valuation of warranty obligations, if not calculated on a cost accumulation (incremental) basis, could result in the liability being overstated. It is probable that the market's rate for performing warranty work would involve overhead costs not incurred by the entity itself, which would incur only incremental costs. This could result in the understatement of current profits and the overstatement of subsequent ones, as the extra cost factored into the (market price based) fair value warranty obligations and charged as an expense at the time of sale, was subsequently written back (usually referred to as 'unwound').

The inclusion of the credit standing of entities in the calculations can produce unwanted results. The lower the credit rating of a business, the higher the interest rate it will have to pay. Therefore, after discounting, the obligation of a low credit rated firm (using the higher discount rate its higher borrowing rate implies) will produce a lower net present value than that of a firm with an identical obligation and a better credit rating. This produces the extraordinary result whereby a poorer credit rated, less safe firm, shows a significantly lower liability than a higher rated, safer firm; in spite of the fact that both have an identical settlement payment to make. Nevertheless, as discussed more fully in Chapter 10 at 1.1, this is precisely the position that the Joint Working Group of standard setters has adopted in its draft standard on the recognition and measurement of financial instruments. The draft standard proposes that, in determining the fair value of its liabilities, an entity should take account of its own credit risk.[95]

All in all, SFAC 7 comes across as no more than an overview of the issues surrounding the use of present values in accounting measurement. In spite of choosing fair values as the sole allowable measurement base, it leaves the door open to a fairly wide range of discounting practices, which can be applied as and when the FASB so decides. It is unfortunate that the statement contains no explanation in plain English of what its practical ramifications are and where, if it were to be adopted, financial reporting would be heading. It is therefore possible that the FASB has deliberately adopted a SFAC that will seemingly provide conceptual support for the introduction of an ever widening variety of discounting practices into US financial reporting, and further extend the notion of fair value. In view of the manner in which the ASB and the IASC have followed the FASB's lead throughout their own conceptual framework projects (see 5 and 6 below) SFAC 7 may have wide ranging implications for financial reporting in the EU in the future.

3.8 Concluding remarks on the FASB conceptual framework

In order to be able to assess the success or failure of the FASB's conceptual framework project, one must refer back to the originally perceived benefits of the project and evaluate whether or not any of them has been achieved (see 3.1 above). Perhaps the acid test may be found in analysing the extent to which the FASB has used the framework in the development of accounting standards. Possibly the best example of where the framework has been used as the basis for an accounting standard is in the development of SFAS 95 – *Statement of Cash Flows*; however, this is clearly the exception. An analysis of the Appendices headed 'Basis for Conclusions' in the more recently issued SFASs, reveals few references to the fact that the members of the FASB have used the concepts statements to guide their thinking – and where reference is made it is generally to broad objectives or qualitative characteristics. On the other hand, it might be argued that the concepts statements have guided the thinking of FASB members without it being expressly stated. However, if this were the case, why is it that the FASB has, for example, issued a statement on reporting comprehensive income (SFAS 130) which seemingly lacks any conceptual integrity and is in conflict with the framework? The same might be said of the standard on deferred tax (SFAS 109) which similarly lacks any discernible conceptual underpinning.

The weakness of the FASB's conceptual framework project may be attributed to a number of factors; however, the most significant reason will probably be shown to be the Board's failure to deal with the fundamental issues of recognition and measurement. To a certain extent, the FASB has fallen into the same trap as the AICPA did in APB Statement No. 4, in that SFAC No. 5 is a descriptive rather than a prescriptive statement; a statement of accounting concepts should provide a frame of reference for the formulation of financial reporting practice, and not be a description of what current reporting practices are. In the words of Professor Stephen Zeff, 'the FASB's conceptual framework failed to fulfil expectations that it might constitute a powerful intellectual force for improving financial reporting'.[96]

Underlying the entire issue of developing a conceptual framework is the unspoken yet pervasive view of the project's authors that the logical structure for the framework should be a highly deductive one whereby the entire schema follows from a number of definitional assertions. To the practically minded accountant it seems the problem of (for instance) ensuring worthless research and development expenditure is not carried forward, is one of determining whether the expenditure in question is likely to result in profitable sales in the future. By contrast, this precise problem is cited in the FASB special report as a prime reason for adopting a definition that excludes all deferred charges. This desire for an entirely deductive system amounts to a view of what accounting is that may not coincide with reality. Accounting is an activity born out of the needs of society (principally the needs of industrialised nations) that responds to those needs as and when conditions alter. The fact that the framework project has not obviously impinged upon the thinking behind a number of standards seems to be evidence for this view. It may not be a fault that accounting lacks a set of principles that accurately and inescapably predict the future in the way that scientific laws do; rather it may be a necessary attribute of accounting continuing to be useful to society.

This is not to say that the FASB's project should be rejected out of hand; it contains some outstanding work, particularly in the area of qualitative characteristics. However, a way must be found to address the fundamental issues, which does not involve both attempting to maintain the truth of the framework's definitions while quietly compromising them when events require it. What is undeniable is the huge influence that the FASB's project has had on the IASC and the ASB. As will be discussed later in this chapter, the definitions adopted by the conceptual frameworks of the IASC, the ASB and other national standard setters, are taken essentially unchanged from the FASB's concept statements. Thus, intentionally or otherwise, the FASB's framework project has created a global language and definitional structure used by all the major standard setting bodies.

4 THE DEVELOPMENT OF A CONCEPTUAL FRAMEWORK IN THE UK

4.1 SSAP 2 Disclosure of accounting policies

SSAP 2[97] – *Disclosure of accounting policies* – was one of the earliest standards ever issued in the UK. It has also been one of the most durable, only having been superseded by FRS 18 – *Accounting Policies* – in June 2001. SSAP 2 did not really set out to form part of a conceptual framework, but its content covers some of the same ground. It was issued in 1971, its principles pervaded financial reporting practice in the UK until quite recently, and they continue to have great influence. The overall objectives of SSAP 2 were to assist the understanding and interpretation of financial statements by promoting improvement in the quality of information disclosed. It sought to achieve this by establishing as generally accepted accounting practice, for the first time in the UK, the disclosure of clear explanations of the accounting policies followed in the preparation of the financial statements, in so far as these are significant for the purpose of giving a true and fair view.

SSAP 2 developed the standard accounting practice for the disclosure of accounting policies in three stages: first, it described the four fundamental accounting concepts, it then related these to the development of accounting bases, and finally it dealt with the selection of accounting policies.

4.1.1 SSAP 2's fundamental accounting concepts

SSAP 2 set out four fundamental accounting concepts, as follows.

A The going concern concept

This concept is applied on the basis that the reporting entity will continue in operational existence for the foreseeable future.

B The accruals (or matching) concept

Revenues, profits, costs and expenses are accrued, and matched with one another in so far as their relationship can be established or justifiably assumed, and dealt with in the profit and loss account for the period to which they relate.

Where the accruals concept is inconsistent with the prudence concept (described below), the latter prevails.[98]

C The consistency concept

There should be consistency of accounting treatment of like items within each accounting period and from one period to the next.

D The prudence concept

Under the prudence concept, revenue and profits are not anticipated but are recognised by inclusion in the profit and loss account only when realised in the form of cash or of other assets the ultimate cash realisation of which can be assessed with reasonable certainty. On the other hand, provision is made for all known liabilities whether the amount of these is known with certainty or is a best estimate in the light of the information available.

These four fundamental accounting concepts, together with a fifth concept, have broadly been adopted by the Companies Act 1985 as the accounting principles which should be used in the determination of all items shown in a company's financial statements, although the terms in which they are described are not identical.[99] The fifth principle introduced by the Companies Act is that of 'non-aggregation'. This principle states that 'in determining the aggregate amount of any item the amount of each individual asset or liability that falls to be taken into account shall be determined separately'.[100] For example, compensating inaccuracies in individual amounts should not be lost in one large total, and a group of assets should be valued on an individual asset basis, as opposed to a portfolio basis.

While the fundamental accounting concepts are, in theory, firmly entrenched in the Companies Act, they have been changed by the various ASB initiatives over the last decade. For example, FRS 12 – *Provisions, Contingent Liabilities and Contingent Assets* – specifically prohibits businesses from making a provision in certain circumstances: for instance where a company's Board has made a decision to close a division but has not communicated this to the outside world. A similar line is taken by the IASC in its standard IAS 37 – *Provisions, Contingent Liabilities and Contingent Assets.* The contents of the ASB's *Statement of Principles* and the replacement of SSAP 2 by FRS 18, are further examples of how UK accounting regulation has moved away from the old SSAP 2 based concepts. Indeed it may be that accounting regulation is now ahead of the legislative base it rests upon, as arguably Article 31.1(c)(bb) of the EU's Fourth Directive is contradicted by IAS 37 and IAS 12. This is because the Directive's concept of prudence will, in some instances, require companies to record a provision in circumstances where both IAS 37 and FRS 12 prohibit it.[101]

Perhaps more fundamentally, the realisation principle enshrined in SSAP 2, which remains within the Companies Act and the EU Fourth Directive is clearly at variance with the stance adopted to the recognition of gains put forward in the ASB's *Statement of Principles*. Although the realisation principle has been included in FRS 18, the ASB may soon seek to remove it, particularly in view of the publication of FRED 22 – *Revision of FRS 3 Reporting financial performance* – which envisages a single statement of financial performance that makes no distinction between realised and unrealised gains.

4.1.2 Accounting bases and accounting policies under SSAP 2

Accounting bases were defined in SSAP 2 as 'the methods developed for applying fundamental concepts to financial transactions and items, for the purpose of financial accounts, and in particular:

(a) for determining the accounting periods in which revenue and costs should be recognised in the profit and loss account; and

(b) for determining the amounts at which material items should be stated in the balance sheet'.[102]

Accounting bases, therefore, under SSAP 2 were accounting treatments which had evolved in response to the necessity of having to apply the fundamental concepts to areas of practice. Under SSAP 2 there could exist more than one legitimate accounting base for dealing with a particular item; for example, there could be several acceptable accounting bases for the depreciation of fixed assets.

The bases which were judged by management to be most appropriate for their own particular circumstances then became the entity's accounting policies under SSAP 2. Thereafter, the accounting policies selected for dealing with items which are judged material in determining financial position and profit or loss for the year had to be disclosed by way of note to the financial statements.[103]

4.1.3 The replacement of SSAP 2 by FRS 18

As discussed at 5 below, the ASB's *Statement of Principles* has advanced a theoretical framework that is very different from that implied by SSAP 2. The matching of costs and revenues, and the reporting of realised profits only, as set out in SSAP 2, has been fundamentally challenged by the ASB's conceptual framework, and this alternative view is manifest in FRS 18 – *Accounting policies*. FRS 18 superseded SSAP 2 in June 2001, and is fully discussed at 7 below. It clearly paves the way for a balance sheet-based approach to the reporting of gains and losses, and places considerably less emphasis on the importance of reporting realised profits only. The magnitude of this change is illustrated by the fact that prudence is no longer a fundamental concept under FRS 18. The balance sheet based approach to the definition of gains and losses, and much of the language used in FRS 18 and the ASB's *Statement of Principles*, has its roots back in the FASB's own conceptual framework documents, discussed at 3 above. The adoption of FRS 18 amounts to a fundamental reinterpretation of the prudence concept which has for many decades been at the heart of UK financial reporting.

4.2 The Corporate Report

The first real attempt by the accounting profession in the UK to develop a conceptual framework is to be found in a discussion paper which was issued in 1975 by the then-styled Accounting Standards Steering Committee (later the ASC) and entitled *The Corporate Report*.[104]

The discussion paper dealt with 'the fundamental aims of published financial reports and the means by which these aims can be achieved'[105] and used the term 'corporate report' to mean 'the comprehensive package of information of all kinds which most completely describes an organisation's economic activity'.[106] It was suggested that this 'comprehensive package' should include more than the 'basic financial statements' (i.e. the balance sheet, profit and loss account and funds statement), and should incorporate additional narrative and descriptive statements.[107] The discussion paper centred around three main elements: 'the types of organisation which should be expected to publish regular financial information; the main users of such information and their needs; and the form of report which will best meet those needs'.[108]

The discussion paper followed the basic approach that corporate reports should seek to satisfy, as far as possible, the information needs of users.[109] The Committee argued that every economic entity of significant size has an implicit responsibility to report publicly, and concluded that general purpose reports designed for general purpose use are the primary means by which this public accountability is fulfilled. Users were defined 'as those having a reasonable right to information concerning the reporting entity',[110] a right which arises from the entity's public accountability.

The paper identified seven user groups[111] as having a reasonable right to information, and discussed the basis of the rights of each group and their information needs. Not surprisingly, the Committee identified a considerable overlap of interest between each of the user groups, including items such as 'evaluating the performance of the entity', 'estimating the future prospects of the entity', 'evaluating managerial performance', 'assessing the liquidity of the entity, its present or future requirements for additional fixed or working capital, and its ability to raise long and short term finance'.[112]

On this basis the Committee concluded that 'the fundamental objective of corporate reports is to communicate economic measurements of and information about the resources and performance of the reporting entity useful to those having reasonable rights to such information'.[113] They went on to say that in order to fulfil this objective and be useful, corporate reports should be relevant, understandable, reliable, complete, objective, timely and comparable[114] (these qualitative characteristics identified were similar to those discussed in the Trueblood Report).

The discussion paper then reviewed the conventional thinking on the aim of published reports together with the then-existing features of published financial statements of UK companies. The Committee also conducted a survey of corporate objectives amongst the chairmen of 300 of the largest UK listed companies, and concluded that 'distributable profit can no longer be regarded as the sole or premier indicator of performance'.[115] Consequently, it was suggested that there was a need for additional indicators of performance in the corporate reports of all entities.[116]

Part II of the study considered the 'measurement and method' of achieving the above aims. Since the Committee had concluded that current reporting practices did not fully satisfy the needs of users, it was suggested that the following additional statements should be published in the corporate report: a statement of value added, an employment report, a statement of money exchanges with government, a statement of transactions in foreign currency, a statement of future prospects and a statement of corporate objectives.[117] In addition, the Committee recommended further study into methods of social accounting as well as the disaggregation of certain financial information.[118]

Finally, the Committee discussed the concepts and measurements employed in the 'basic financial statements'. In considering the purpose of profit measurement, it concluded that income statements 'should be concerned with the measurement of performance although they may also be used in the measurement of capital maintenance and income distributability'.[119] It was, however, recognised that this dual purpose of income statements often gave rise to conflict in the application of accounting concepts – particularly the fundamental concepts of prudence and matching. Various measurement bases were then discussed in the context of the inadequacies of the historical cost system. The Committee stated that 'the usefulness of financial statements in fulfilling user needs is restricted at the present time because of the defects of the basis of measurement generally used. Historical cost accounting fails, in times of rapidly changing prices and values, to ensure that sufficient provision is made for capital maintenance.'[120]

The committee then briefly surveyed several bases of measurement, including historical cost, current purchasing power (CPP) and various current value bases such as replacement cost and net realisable value. The conclusion reached was that no one system of measurement is capable of satisfying the user needs identified in the study, and that, therefore, research should be undertaken into the feasibility of multi-column reporting, as well as into the development of a standardised system of current value accounting.[121]

The publication of the Corporate Report, however, closely coincided with the release of the Sandilands Report on inflation accounting,[122] (discussed at 4.3 below) which overshadowed the Corporate Report. This was probably to the relief of the business community who were concerned about the possibility of their reporting responsibility being extended beyond that of the existing requirements, through the development of the Committee's concept of public accountability. Although this aspect of the Corporate Report has largely been absent from all further conceptual framework documents, arguably it was a far-sighted approach. The rise of public interest in and of academic research into alternative reports such as environmental reports by businesses, may indicate that the public accountability aspect of corporate reporting will have to become more formally recognised as integral to company financial reporting. Indeed, this is the case already with the reports on corporate governance that the UK Listing Authority requires listed UK companies to provide.

4.3 The Sandilands Report

Through most of the 1970s and early 1980s, inflation was an intractable problem in the UK, with rates of inflation well above 10% common, and on occasion over 20%. Consequently, it was within this context that, on 21 January 1974, the announcement of the membership and terms of reference of the government's Inflation Accounting Committee was made to the House of Commons by the Secretary of State for Trade and Industry. The Sandilands Committee's principal term of reference was 'to consider whether, and if so how, company accounts should allow for changes (including relative changes) in costs and prices'.[123] The Sandilands Report followed a similar approach to that of the Corporate Report to the extent that it focused on the information needs of users. The report stated that 'the requirements of users of accounts should be the fundamental consideration in deciding the information to be disclosed in company accounts'.[124]

The report proposed that the development of accounting for inflation should be an evolutionary process towards a system of current cost accounting, the essential features of which are:

(a) money is the unit of measurement (as opposed to the 'current purchasing power' basis of expressing financial information in terms of a unit of measurement of constant value when prices change);

(b) assets and liabilities should be shown in the balance sheet at their 'value to the business'; and

(c) operating profit (to be known as 'current cost profit') is calculated after charging the 'value to the business' of the assets consumed during the period, thereby excluding holding gains and showing them separately.[125]

4.3.1 *Current Purchasing Power accounting*

In formulating its system of current cost accounting, the Committee examined three alternative accounting systems which had been developed in an attempt to overcome the deficiencies of historical cost accounting. The first of these systems studied was the 'current purchasing power' (CPP) method of inflation accounting recommended in the Provisional SSAP, PSSAP 7, which was published in May 1974.[126] Under PSSAP 7, companies were expected to supplement their conventional historical cost financial statements with a statement which illustrated the effects of changes in the purchasing power of money on these statements. The main features of PSSAP 7 were set out in the standard as follows:

'(a) companies will continue to keep their records and present their basic annual accounts in historical pounds, ie in terms of the value of the pound at the time of each transaction or revaluation;

(b) in addition, all listed companies should present to their shareholders a supplementary statement in terms of the value of the pound at the end of the period to which the accounts relate;

(c) the conversion of the figures in the basic accounts into the figures in the supplementary statement should be by means of a general index of the purchasing power of the pound;[127] and

(d) the standard requires the directors to provide in a note to the supplementary statement an explanation of the basis on which it has been prepared and it is desirable that directors should comment on the significance of the figures.'[128]

The Committee concluded that the CPP method 'does not remedy the main deficiencies of historic cost accounting during a time of changing costs and prices and we do not recommend it as the best long-term solution to the problem of accounting for inflation'.[129] Numerous arguments were put forward to support this conclusion, for example:

- since, during a period of changing prices, historical cost figures expressed in terms of monetary units do not show the 'value to the business' of assets, a CPP supplementary statement will show the historic cost figures restated in units of current purchasing power, not the 'value to the business' of assets.[130] Thus, a major deficiency of historical cost accounts would not be overcome;
- since companies were required to express their CPP supplementary statements in terms of the current purchasing power of the pound at the closing balance sheet date, the unit of measurement in the supplementary statement would change from year to year. This was likely to cause confusion, compounded by the fact that companies which had different accounting dates would be preparing supplementary statements in terms of different units, resulting in a lack of comparability;[131] and
- since a unit of measurement with an absolute value through time is unattainable, there is no advantage in preparing financial statements in CPP units rather than in units of money.[132]

4.3.2 *Value accounting*

The Committee then examined three forms of 'value accounting' – a term used to describe a wide range of different accounting systems which measure net assets by reference to their 'value' rather than their cost. The three value accounting systems examined were replacement cost accounting, present value accounting and continuously contemporary accounting.

A Replacement cost accounting based on current entry values

'Replacement cost' is the price which will have to be paid to replace an asset used or given up in exchange for another asset. Consequently, the basic principle underlying replacement cost accounting is that, since a business has to replace its assets over time in order to continue in operational existence, charges for the consumption or exchange of an asset should be based on the cost of replacing it. Consequently, assets are valued at the balance sheet date by reference to the price which would have to be paid at that date to purchase a similar asset in a similar condition – i.e. the replacement cost of the assets. This system, therefore, adopts a method of income determination which reflects changes in capital both at the point of realisation of assets and, before realisation, while holding assets.

The pioneers of an income and value model based on replacement costs (entry values) were Edwards and Bell,[133] who attempted to interpret accounting concepts in terms of economic concepts. Their theory abandoned both the realisation principle and the idea of the 'unitary income statement' which does not separate operating profit from holding gains. They introduced a new concept of 'business profit', which was made up of current operating profit of the current period, realised holding gains of the same period and unrealised holding gains.

A major disadvantage of the replacement cost model is difficulty and subjectivity in assigning replacement costs; for example, are replacement costs based on identical or equivalent replacement, and how is technological obsolescence dealt with? However, this disadvantage is far outweighed by the usefulness of the information provided by the system in the form of meaningful balance sheet values and a segregated business profit figure. The Sandilands Committee concluded that the replacement cost accounting system 'comes close to meeting the dominant requirements of users of accounts and the Committee's own proposals have many similarities with certain forms of this system of accounting'.[134]

B Present value accounting

Present value accounting is based on the economic concept of income, and values an asset on the basis of the present value of the cash flows which are expected to be derived from that asset. In order to maintain the capital of the entity, an amount at least equal to the original investment should be reinvested, whilst the remaining cash flows are treated as realised. For example, if the discounted net present value of all expected future cash flows of an entity are £100,000 at the beginning of the year and £115,000 at the end of the year, and if the net cash flows arising during the year were £10,000, then the profit for the year will be £25,000, since this amount could be distributed whilst maintaining the original capital base of £100,000.

Whilst this approach might have some degree of theoretical soundness, the Sandilands Committee considered it to be totally impracticable. The Committee believed that issues such as risk, the determination of discount rates, changes in interest rates and the uncertainty of future cash flows presented virtually insurmountable problems. The Sandilands Committee therefore rejected present value accounting on the grounds that use of economic value as the basis of valuation of an asset would not meet the needs of users, as it would only be in comparatively few cases that this would represent the value of an asset to a business.[135]

C *Continuously Contemporary Accounting (CoCoA)*

The current value income model based on exit prices or realisable market values was first advocated by MacNeal in a book published by him in 1939 which dealt, inter alia, with the ethical issue of 'truth' in accounting.[136] MacNeal maintained that financial statements could only present the 'truth' if assets were stated at their current value and the profit and losses accruing from the changes in these values are included in income, and classified as either realised or unrealised. MacNeal did, however, concede that under certain circumstances the use of net realisable values was not appropriate, and that in such cases current replacement costs should be used.

The system known as continuously contemporary accounting (CoCoA) was formally introduced by Chambers in a book which he published in 1966,[137] and the case for exit value accounting was further developed by Sterling.[138] Chambers' theory is based on the premise that entities must be able to choose between alternative courses of action and, because resources are limited, they need to know what resources are available to enable them to engage in exchanges. Consequently, Chambers asserts that this capacity to engage in exchanges is measured by the opportunity cost of holding assets in their existing form, and that this opportunity cost is represented by the current cash equivalent of assets – which Chambers defines as being their current sales value. Initially, Chambers did not apply this principle rigorously and proposed that stocks should be valued at current replacement cost. However, he subsequently amended his view and advocated that exit values should be applied to the valuation of all assets. A difference in the theories of Chambers and Sterling is, for example, that Chambers believes that net realisable values should be based on the assumption that assets are realised in an orderly manner based on sensible adaptations to changing circumstances; Sterling, on the other hand, believes that net realisable values should be based on immediate liquidation prices.

The capital maintenance concept adopted by CoCoA is based on the preservation of the purchasing power of shareholders' equity (using the monetary unit as the unit of measurement, and not the current purchasing power unit used in CPP accounting). Consequently, since all assets (both monetary and non-monetary) are measured at net realisable value, income is defined as the difference between opening and closing equity after maintaining the purchasing power or cash equivalent of such equity. Income for the year, therefore, will comprise (1) the net profit/loss on business operations, (2) the accrued profit/loss arising from the change in the current cash equivalent of assets and (3) the effect on the capital of the entity brought about by the change in the purchasing power of money.

However, despite the widespread publication of his theories, Chambers failed to gain any measure of support for CoCoA outside academic circles. Chambers believed that one of the reasons for this was the lack of empirical evidence that the users of financial statements needed financial information based on net realisable values. Consequently, he set about obtaining this evidence through an empirical survey which he published in 1980.[139] Through carefully designed (but somewhat simplistic) questions, Chambers was able to conclude that his empirical evidence justified the use of net realisable values as the primary basis of measurement.

Chambers' principal survey did, however, produce some anomalous and inconsistent answers, resulting in his having to conduct a supplementary survey of four questions. This highlighted several weaknesses in the formulation of his questions, and cast doubt about the validity of the survey as a whole. These doubts are expressed, for example, in an article by Edward Stamp[140] who stated that 'his questionnaire was inadequate and failed to include necessary questions on valuation, performance measures, and liabilities, that would not have been difficult to frame, even with the constraints imposed by Chambers'.[141] Consequently, these omissions and the style of his research undermine Chambers' claim that his empirical evidence demonstrates that CoCoA provides the best basis for financial reporting.

There is no doubt that there are some compelling theoretical arguments for the presentation of financial statements based on net realisable values; for example, they provide useful information in the assessment of liquidity and financial flexibility. However, net realisable value is unlikely to reflect an asset's 'value to the business', since, for instance, an item of plant might have negligible net realisable value but substantial use value. Therefore, whilst the disclosure of net realisable values might provide useful supplementary information, the arguments in favour of CoCoA as the primary basis of accounting are unconvincing. CoCoA was rejected by the Sandilands Committee on the basis that, as a whole, it did not satisfy the information needs of users which they had identified.[142] It is, however, noteworthy that in its discussion document – *Making Corporate Reports Valuable* – the Research Committee of the ICAS advocated a reporting system based on net realisable values[143] (see 4.6 below).

4.3.3 *Cash flow accounting*

The principal proponents of cash flow reporting are Lee[144] and Lawson,[145] although there are several other advocates of various approaches to cash flow reporting. Lee's system of cash flow reporting relies heavily on exit value theory and aims to report both actual and potential cash flows. Assets are classified according to their realisability, based on Chambers' principle of orderly liquidation. If a sale price does not exist, assets are to be accounted for as having a zero cash equivalent.[146] Lee has suggested the following four asset classifications for his statement of financial position:

1. realised assets (e.g. bank balances);
2. readily-realisable assets (i.e. assets which have a ready market and sale price, such as listed securities, debtors and stocks of finished goods);
3. non-readily-realisable assets (i.e. assets which do have a market and sale price, but which would not be quickly realised because of the limited nature of the market, such as certain items of plant and work-in-progress); and
4. not-realisable assets (i.e. assets which have no known sales price and no market, and would therefore be ascribed a zero value, such as highly specialised or obsolete plant).[147]

Liabilities are classified according to maturity, in line with conventional accounting practice.

Lee proposes that, in addition to a 'statement of financial position', the cash flow reporting system should present a 'statement of realised cash flow', a 'statement of realisable earnings' and a 'statement of changes in financial position'.[148] The statement of realised cash flow reports an entity's actual cash inflows and outflows during a particular period; it is noteworthy that the information contained in this statement would be broadly equivalent to that which would be presented in a statement of cash flows under FRS 1 (see Chapter 28). The statement of realisable earnings reports periodic profit similar to that provided by a net realisable value accounting system, except that it is described in terms of realised and realisable cash flows. The statement provides an analysis of realised earnings (derived from the entity's operating cash flow), and unrealised earnings (which represent potential cash flows that have accrued during the period as a result of changes in the realisable values of assets, net of the changes in liabilities). The statement of changes in financial position is effectively a conventional funds statement presented on an exit value basis.

Although there are a number of practical accounting and disclosure problems in cash flow reporting, it does have considerable merit. Furthermore, a number of the problems are not unique to cash flow reporting, with equivalent issues remaining unsolved in historical cost accounting. However, one difficulty which does exist is caused by the artificial 12 month reporting period and the necessity to measure 'profitability' over that period and from one period to the next. The principal reason for the development of the accrual basis of accounting was that financial statements prepared on a cash basis (which was probably the oldest form of presentation) provided distorted profit figures from one period to the next. Although the Sandilands Committee stated that there was 'much of value in the cash flow accounting principle',[149] it was felt that cash flow accounting would rekindle all the 'old difficulties of assessing the profit or loss for the year when the accounting system does not match revenues against costs incurred in their generation'.[150] The Committee therefore concluded that the abandonment of the existing concept of the profit and loss account in favour of a cash flow statement would result in the information needs of users not being met. Clearly, however, the Committee had not considered the possibility of the presentation of a 'statement of realisable earnings' as advocated by Lee, which would provide a more stable basis for reporting profit than the statement of receipts and payments envisaged by the Committee. Lee, however, recognised the problems created by the traditional 12 month reporting period, and suggested that a solution might be found in the use of multi-period aggregates for analysis purposes.

4.3.4 *Current cost accounting (CCA)*

The Sandilands Committee recommended the development of a system of current cost accounting which used the monetary unit as the unit of measurement and dealt with the effects of specific price changes (as opposed to changes in the general purchasing power of money) on individual businesses. The Committee recommended that the balance sheet should present the 'value to the business' of the company's assets, which was equated with the amount of the loss which would be suffered by an entity if the asset were to be lost or destroyed. Whilst it was stated that the 'value to the business' of an asset might, under certain circumstances, be its net realisable value or economic value, it would normally be based on its replacement cost. Because the Committee recommended that financial statements be drawn up in terms of the monetary unit, no adjustment would be made for monetary items.[151] However, it is arguable that current cost accounting does not produce a balance sheet which seeks to be a statement of values of the resources of the company; it simply updates the costs at which they are recorded. This distinction can be illustrated by looking at the financial statements of an oil and gas exploration company. Even on a current cost basis, the carrying value of its principal assets is still based on the (backward-looking) cost of exploration expenditure incurred, not the (forward-looking) value of the oil and gas it has found.

Under the Sandilands system, an entity's 'current cost profit' for a period would be calculated by charging against income 'the value to the business' of assets consumed during the year. In simple terms, therefore, the current cost profit could be derived from the historical cost profit by means of an adjustment to depreciation and a cost of sales adjustment. The Committee also recommended the presentation of a summary statement of total gains or losses for the period, which would present the entity's total gains/losses in terms of three classifications: operating gains/losses (i.e. current cost profit/loss), extraordinary gains/losses and holding gains/losses. An interesting observation regarding these two statements recommended by the Committee is that each is based on different capital maintenance concepts. The calculation of current cost profit was based on the concept of physical capital maintenance, whilst the summary statement of total gains was concerned with the maintenance of financial capital. However, because the calculation of current cost profit subsequently received greater prominence than the summary of total gains, it is generally thought that the Sandilands proposals were based on the concept of physical capital maintenance.[152]

The Committee recommended that current cost accounting should replace historical cost accounting, and that its proposals should be incorporated in an accounting standard. Consequently, the ASC established the Inflation Accounting Steering Group, giving them the task of preparing a proposal for an exposure draft based on the Sandilands proposals, resulting in the publication in November 1976 of ED 18 – *Current cost accounting*. ED 18, however, met with little support, as did the Sandilands recommendations. The ASC attributed this to the fact that there was considerable objection to the replacement of historical cost accounting by a new untested system; the proposals were considered too complicated; and the profit figure was considered misleading without adjustment for monetary items.[153]

Nevertheless, the ASC perceived an urgent need for companies to disclose how their historical cost financial statements were affected by changing prices. Therefore, in order to find an immediate solution to this problem, the ASC published an interim recommendation in November 1977 which outlined a simplified version of current cost accounting (known as the 'Hyde Guidelines').[154] These guidelines recommended that the published financial statements of companies listed on the Stock Exchange should include a prominent separate statement which showed the profit/loss calculated on a current cost basis.[155] The Hyde Guidelines recommended that three adjustments should be made to the historical cost results: in addition to the depreciation and cost of sales adjustments proposed by Sandilands, it was recommended that a 'gearing adjustment' be made as an interim solution to dealing with monetary items in inflation-adjusted financial statements. Since no account of the existence of borrowings was taken in calculating current cost operating profit, the implication was that operating capability had to be maintained entirely out of the generation of revenues. However, the reality is clearly that this could be financed partly by borrowings; consequently, the gearing adjustment was designed to take account of the extent to which fixed assets and working capital were financed by borrowings.

In April 1979 the ASC issued ED 24 – *Current Cost Accounting* – which was developed from the Hyde Guidelines, taking into account comments received on both the Guidelines and ED 18. ED 24 followed the Hyde proposal that a separate statement be presented which disclosed the current cost adjustments made to the historical cost profit in respect of depreciation, cost of sales and gearing. However, the ED went further than the guidelines by:

(a) introducing a further adjustment, called the 'monetary working capital adjustment', which effectively extended the cost of sales adjustment (which allowed for increases in the investment needed to maintain stocks when prices were increasing) to the other working capital items. Consequently, the monetary working capital adjustment represented an estimate of the extra investment in debtors, creditors and liquid resources required to maintain operations when prices were increasing;

(b) proposing the presentation of a current cost balance sheet, in which fixed assets and stock would be measured on a current cost basis; and

(c) proposing that listed companies disclose current cost earnings per share.[156]

ED 24 subsequently became SSAP 16,[157] which was issued in March 1980. SSAP 16 gave companies the choice as to how they could present their current cost information. They could present historical cost accounts as their main accounts with supplementary current cost accounts, or they could present current cost accounts as the main accounts with supplementary historical cost accounts, or they could present current cost accounts as the only accounts 'accompanied by adequate historical cost information'.[158]

SSAP 16 perpetuated the concept of current cost operating profit based on the maintenance of physical capital, which had been extended to monetary working capital through the monetary working capital adjustment. The associated gearing adjustment probably arose as a result of the ASC's need to compromise with its critics in order to find an acceptable solution – as opposed to having any theoretically sound justification.

At the time that SSAP 16 was issued, the ASC stated that it was its intention, as far as possible, 'to make no change to SSAP 16 for three years so as to enable producers and users to gain experience in dealing with practical problems and interpreting the information'. However, this statement probably contributed to the eventual demise of the standard, because it was taken as an intention that it would inevitably be revised at the end of the three year period and allowed SSAP 16 to be characterised as 'experimental' or 'provisional'.[159] Over the next few years, there was a continuing decline in the level of compliance with the standard.

In July 1984, the ASC issued a further exposure draft ED 35 – *Accounting for the effects of changing prices.* This restricted the scope of the proposals to public companies which were neither value-based enterprises nor wholly owned subsidiaries, but in respect of these it sought to make CCA a mandatory feature of the primary financial statements (rather than in supplementary statements), declaring that the inclusion of this information was essential to a true and fair view. However, it soon became clear that these proposals could not command general acceptance, and the exposure draft was withdrawn in early 1985. Soon afterwards, in the face of increasing opposition to the standard, the CCAB bodies voted to make SSAP 16 non-mandatory, and it was later completely withdrawn.

It might be argued that activities described in this section provide evidence for the view that accounting standard setting is a process of establishing convention in response to the needs of the times. The high inflation rates of the late 1970s and early 1980s drove both practitioners and academics to undertake various studies and produce a number of recommendations. Since inflation has ceased to be a concern, interest in this problem has noticeably waned.

4.4 The Macve Report

As a consequence of the written submissions received in response to its consultative document 'Setting Accounting Standards' (see 1.3 above), the ASC commissioned Professor Richard Macve to 'review critically current literature and opinion in the UK, US and elsewhere with a view to forming preliminary conclusions as to the possibilities of developing an agreed conceptual framework for setting accounting standards and the nature of such a framework; and to identify areas for further research'.[160]

Macve's report – *A Conceptual Framework for Financial Accounting and Reporting: the possibilities for an agreed structure* – was published in August 1981. As would be expected from his terms of reference, Macve concentrated his efforts on evaluating selected conceptual framework projects and studies, focusing in particular on the Corporate Report and the FASB's conceptual framework project. His discussions centred around the problems that arise in determining profit and net assets, and these he related to the difficulties involved in establishing what constitutes useful accounting information. He further highlighted the fact that the variety of user needs and conflicts of interest between different parties were likely to cause disagreement as to what information financial statements should provide.[161] On this issue, he came to the conclusion that 'recognition of the variety of user needs and of conflicts between different interests and different rights leads to the view that reaching agreement on the form and content of financial statements is as much a "political" process, a search for compromise between different parties, as it is a search for the methods which are "technically" best'.[162]

As far as the FASB's conceptual project was concerned, Macve concluded his review by saying that 'given the difficulties experienced in arriving at "useful" definitions of the elements of profit and loss accounts and balance sheets, it seems to me likely that the continuing attempts to develop "recognition criteria" and "measurement rules", that can both command general acceptance and have an impact on individual accounting disputes in relation to profit and net asset calculation, will be similarly unsuccessful'.[163] Macve concluded his study by putting forward several suggestions for further research.

The ASC did not demonstrate any apparent inclination to pursue Macve's proposals for further research with noticeable fervour, and allowed his report to fade slowly into the background. It was not until the publication in January 1989 of the Solomons Report[164] that the ASC displayed any evidence that they were actively seeking conceptual guidelines to assist them in the standard-setting process (see 4.7 below).

4.5 The Stamp Report

In 1980, Professor Edward Stamp produced a research study primarily for the Canadian Institute of Chartered Accountants which was 'intended to provide a Canadian solution to the problem of improving the quality of corporate financial reporting standards'.[165] Stamp adopted a similar approach to that of other studies (such as the Corporate Report and Trueblood) by looking at users, their needs, their rights to information and the qualitative characteristics of that information. Stamp identified a more detailed list of users (15 in all) than did, for example, the Corporate or Sandilands Reports.

Stamp developed a set of 20 qualitative criteria which could be used as yardsticks whereby standard-setters, as well as the preparers and users of published financial statements, can decide whether or not the financial statements are meeting the objectives of financial reporting and the needs of users. An interesting rider to this aspect of Stamp's study was that he subsequently used his list of qualitative criteria as the basis of an empirical study of the ASC members' assessment of the relative importance of each of the criteria.[166] Stamp supplied each member of the ASC with a copy of chapter 7 of his CICA research study in which the significance and meaning of each of the 20 criteria were discussed. He also gave them each a questionnaire in which they were asked to rank the 20 criteria in order of importance.[167] Although the ranking revealed 'relevance' as the most important criterion and 'conservatism' as the least important this, in itself, was not the most significant aspect of Stamp's study. The real significance was that he demonstrated it would be possible to establish rankings of characteristics of accounting information for each category of user.

In his CICA research study, Stamp also devoted a considerable amount of effort towards discussing certain fundamental conceptual issues such as problems of allocation, income measurement, capital maintenance, the proprietary versus the entity theory, and the question of which attribute accounting should measure.[168] These issues are all fundamental to the development of a conceptual framework for financial reporting; yet have not been unequivocally resolved by any of the conceptual framework projects currently extant.

4.6 The ICAS discussion document: 'Making Corporate Reports Valuable'

4.6.1 *Background to the study*

This discussion document, which was issued in 1988, was the product of a major research project undertaken by the Research Committee of the Institute of Chartered Accountants of Scotland. However, it is vital that it is seen and evaluated taking into account the spirit in which it had been prepared; namely, for the purpose of stimulating discussion and experimentation.[169] The reason why this paper was so refreshing revolved principally around the fact that the research committee started from the basis of a 'clean sheet'. In other words, the members were able to ignore existing laws, accounting rules, terminology and all other constraints in order to try and achieve what they believed to be the best result. Clearly, this approach had widespread practical implications for the ultimate implementation of any proposals made. This was recognised by the committee, and the document noted some of the implications of its suggestions.[170]

The Committee started off by explaining what motivated it to reconsider the nature of corporate reporting. The reasons which were given included the following basic conclusions:

- all financial reports ought to reflect economic reality;
- the information which investors need is the same in kind, but not in volume, as the information which managements need to run their entities;
- some of the information that management has but does not normally communicate comes out into the open when management wants something – such as additional capital or to be able to defend a hostile take-over bid;
- present-day financial reports are deficient in that they are based on legal form rather than economic substance, on cost rather than value, on the past rather than the future, and on 'profit' rather than 'wealth';
- there is no consistent conceptual basis underlying the production of either the profit and loss account or the balance sheet, and some of the concepts used appear to defy normal understanding of financial affairs;
- corporate reports are not made public sufficiently speedily; and
- the audit report is insufficiently informative and is often incomprehensible to non-auditors.[171]

4.6.2 *Users and their needs*

The committee then considered who are the users of financial reports and what are their informational needs. In so doing, it referred to the Corporate Report, concluding that corporate reporting should aim to communicate directly to only four of the groups identified in that report. These were identified as:

(a) the equity investor group;

(b) the loan creditor group;

(c) the employee group; and

(d) the business contact group (which includes ordinary creditors).[172]

Having identified these four groups of users, the committee listed the following five fundamental information needs of these groups which external corporate reports should be able to contribute to meeting:

(a) knowledge of the corporate objectives of the entity, and information which would enable users to evaluate the entity's performance against these objectives;

(b) a comparison of the total wealth of the entity now as against what it was at the time of the last corporate report, together with an explanation of the reasons for change;

(c) the ability to judge where the entity is going in the future and whether it has the necessary financial and other resources to do so;

(d) adequate information about the economic environment within which the entity has been and will be operating; and

(e) knowledge of the ownership and control of the entity and the experience and background of its directors and officials.[173]

As the Committee pointed out, these proposals were a digest of the information needs of the equity investor group identified in the Corporate Report.[174] The Committee suggested further that, in order to enable users to judge the reliability of management's planning based on past period performance, they should also be given information on:

(a) the entity's actual performance for the accounting period just past as compared with its previously published plan for that period;

(b) management's explanations of any significant variances between the two; and

(c) management's financial plan for the current and future accounting periods, together with explanations of the major assumptions used in preparing it.[175]

Clearly, these additional proposals were designed to provide information on how management of an entity had discharged its stewardship responsibility to owners and, as the Committee suggested, this assessment should be based on earnings information and entity performance.

4.6.3 *Valuation of assets and liabilities*

The Committee then discussed various bases for applying values to assets, focusing on historical cost, current replacement cost, current net realisable values and economic values. It is necessary to read the full text of the discussion document in order to appreciate properly the basis for the Committee's conclusions; however, having discussed what it saw as the deficiencies of historical cost and economic value, the Committee noted that current replacement cost and net realisable value both met its criteria of economic reality and 'additivity' (i.e. the total number in a statement should not mean something different in kind from its constituent numbers). Nevertheless, the Committee expressed a preference for net realisable value as the basis for applying values to assets, 'principally because it is value-based whereas replacement cost is cost-based',[176] and it was felt that 'value rather than cost is important in assessing financial wealth'.[177]

It is in this area that the paper is most open to criticism and debate. For example, the Committee dismissed replacement cost accounting by citing the problems associated with it, without giving equal consideration to the problems associated with net realisable value accounting. The problems attributed to the use of replacement costs were as follows:

'(a) there is an assumption that assets will be replaced, which is frequently not the case;

(b) there are significant practical problems in assessing replacement values if there have been improvements in technology; and

(c) arbitrary depreciation allocations are still required.'[178]

Whilst there can be no dispute that these are valid points, there are equally several practical and theoretical problems surrounding net realisable value accounting (see 4.3.2 above for a more detailed discussion of both models). For example, should net realisable values be based on the assumption that assets are realised in an orderly manner, or should they be based on immediate liquidation prices? Furthermore, there is the whole question of whether or not net realisable values do, in fact, necessarily measure the financial wealth of a going concern; for example, what about the case of plant which has negligible realisable value but significant use value? This also raises the further issue of how compatible are net realisable values with the qualitative characteristics of accounting information – particularly with respect to the primary quality of relevance.

In addition, it is noteworthy that the literature surveys,[179] which were commissioned by the ICAS Research Committee in order to identify key issues for consideration in the production of the discussion paper, reached the following conclusion on using net realisable values (NRVs) as the main basis for financial accounting: 'generally, the literature suggests that there is a strong case for the publication of NRV based figures as supplementary accounting information, as important information on liquidity, and on the adaptability of entities, is given which is not provided by the competing valuation bases. ... However, the arguments for the adoption of NRVs as the main valuation base of financial reports are uncompelling. The arguments against this, and in particular the lack of relevance of NRVs for many assets in most situations, are substantial. The income statement is likely to be misleading. One development which may be worthy of consideration is the publication of, possible supplementary, balance sheets based on net realisable values and income statements based on replacement costs or some other valuation base.'[180]

4.6.4 *The proposed new information package*

Despite the conclusions reached in the literature surveys, the Committee proposed an entirely new information package, using net realisable values as the basis of valuation. In order to present the financial wealth of an entity, the Committee proposed that the following four basic statements should replace the existing financial statements:

(a) *Assets and Liabilities Statement*, which would present the assets and liabilities of the entity at the reporting date, each stated at its net realisable value. Net realisable values would normally be determined according to the principle of orderly disposal, unless the entity is in financial trouble, in which case 'a more appropriate method' (such as break-up values) should be used;[181]

(b) *Operations Statement*, which calculates the financial wealth added to the entity by trading and by its operations generally. It differs from the present form of profit and loss account in that:

  (i) there would be no depreciation charge,

  (ii) the stock would be accounted for at net realisable value, and

  (iii) the only exceptional or extraordinary items would be those arising out of unusual events of a revenue nature; exceptional or extraordinary gains or losses on fixed assets would be dealt with in the Statement of Changes in Financial Wealth outlined at (c) below;[182]

(c) *Statement of Changes in Financial Wealth*, which shows the change in the worth of the business for the period under consideration, such change being split into its main components with an indication of how each of these arose. The Committee proposed that the change in wealth would be measured in terms of year-end pounds, although 'in times of significant inflation it may be helpful if investors can be given an indication of the real change in financial wealth over the period concerned by applying the retail price index';[183] and

(d) *Distributions Statement*, which reflects the distributable change in financial wealth for the period plus any surpluses retained from previous periods, less dividends paid and proposed. In times of rising prices the 'real value' of capital should be maintained by an inflation adjustment which should be shown in the distributions statement and might be computed by applying the retail price index to the value of shareholders' contributed capital as at the start of the period. The paper went on to say that entities wishing to maintain their operating capability in physical terms could make a further appropriation to maintain the asset portfolio or to provide for the replacement of the services which these assets have been supplying.[184]

4.6.5 *Additional information*

In addition to the four basic statements and the information relating to corporate objectives and future financial plans discussed under 4.6.2 above, the Committee suggested the inclusion of the following additional information in the reporting package:

(a) a Cash Flow Statement showing the inflow and outflow of cash broken down into its main components, dealing with the current period and going three years forward.[185] This proposal was, for obvious reasons, somewhat controversial – particularly in the light of the recommendation that management should explain forecast variances (see 4.6.2 above);

(b) segmental information split by product, by manufacturing location, geographically and by currency;[186]

(c) information on related parties;

(d) information on accounting areas subject to uncertainty, for example management's view on the margin of error in accounting estimates;

(e) a statement on relative innovation which would illustrate the stance that the company is adopting in relation to innovation. In other words, the statement will show the proportion of production that is new and conceived internally or self-generated, and will compare this with that of its competitors;

(f) information on effectiveness and lead-time of research and development;

(g) information on the economic environment within which the entity operates, including an analysis of facts such as market share, market strength, market size, the activities of competitors etc.;

(h) comparative operational statistics 'culled from similar statements by its competitors or other entities in similar markets';[187]

(i) information on staff resources; and

(j) information on ownership, management and their responsibilities.

The Committee also made the interesting suggestion that reports should be arranged on the basis of 'layering'.[188] In other words, each statement would start with the simplest possible presentation of the main factors, and as the user works through the information, it can be called down in layers of increasing complexity and detail.

4.6.6 *Conclusion*

This was one of the boldest, most innovative and refreshing discussion documents to be published by a professional body for a long time, exposing the several weaknesses of present day financial reporting practice. Of course it has flaws and can be criticised for either failing to address or inadequately addressing certain issues; however, it should be seen for what it was – a document designed to stimulate discussion, experimentation and further research. Nevertheless, there was always the danger that the document would be regarded as too revolutionary in its approach, and be dismissed as being an amusing intellectual exercise.

More importantly, though, it is now clear that the ASB's agenda of accounting reform and development as manifest throughout the 1990s drew heavily on MCRV for its inspiration and guidance. The list of supplementary information in 4.6.5 above no longer looks innovative – solely because so much of its suggested contents now appears in the financial reports of companies.

4.7 The Solomons Report

In May 1987, the Research Board of the ICAEW announced that it had decided to sponsor a project to address the need for guidelines for decisions in financial reporting; the project had been originally inspired by Professor Bryan Carsberg when he was the ICAEW's Director of Research, and Professor David Solomons, a recently retired academic, agreed to carry out the study.

Solomons followed what has become an almost traditional approach to a study of this nature; perhaps not surprisingly considering that he acted as consultant to the FASB on its conceptual framework project and was principal author of SFAC No. 2. He started by examining the purposes of financial reporting, identifying users and how their needs were at present being met. His report then discussed the elements of financial statements and decided upon the asset and liability rather than the revenue and expense approach to financial accounting. The report stated that although 'there is no prospect of proving that one of these views is right and the other wrong, it is possible to find reasons for preferring one view to the other, and these Guidelines will be uncompromisingly based on the asset and liability view'.[189]

Solomons' principal argument against the revenue and expense view of income determination was that it 'opens the door to all kinds of income smoothing'[190] and that it 'threatens the integrity of the balance sheet and its value as a useful financial statement. Its value is maximized if it can be seen as a statement of financial position; but it can only be that if all the items in it are truly assets, liabilities, and equity, and not other bits left over from the profit and loss account, and if all such items that are capable of being recognised are included in it.'[191] This attitude of Solomons has obviously been influential in the thinking of the ASB and the IASC subsequently.

Having established that he would be following an asset and liability approach, Solomons then set about defining the elements of financial statements on much the same basis as was done in SFAC No. 6 (see 3.4 above). Assets are defined as 'resources or rights incontestably controlled by an entity at the accounting date that are expected to yield it future economic benefits',[192] whilst liabilities are defined as 'obligations of an entity at the accounting date to make future transfers of assets or services (sometimes uncertain as to timing and amount) to other entities'.[193] All the other elements are then derived from these basic definitions; for example, owners' equity comprises net assets and income is the change in net assets.[194]

The Report then ran quickly through the qualitative characteristics of accounting information, giving what might be viewed as a summarised version of SFAC No. 2 (see 3.3 above). Thereafter he focused his attention on the issues of recognition and measurement and the choice of an accounting model for use in preparing general purpose financial statements. In view of the fact that Solomons' guidelines are based on the asset and liability view, it is not surprising that his recognition criteria concentrate on these two elements. Consequently, under Solomons' approach, an item should only be recognised in financial statements if:

'(a) it conforms to the definition of an asset or liability or of one of the sub-elements derived therefrom; and

(b) its magnitude as specified by the accounting model being used can be measured and verified with reasonable certainty; and

(c) the magnitude so arrived at is material in amount'.[195]

Solomons then examined the historical cost accounting model which was generally accepted in the UK at the time, listing its deficiencies and pointing out that it is not a true historical cost model (as a result, for example, of asset revaluations and the translation of monetary assets and liabilities designated in foreign currencies at closing rates). Thereafter, he set about devising an improved model for general purpose financial reporting, and listed the following five criteria that such an improved model should possess:

(a) the balance sheet should be a true and fair statement of an entity's financial condition, showing all its assets and liabilities that satisfy the above recognition criteria and conform with the asset and liability definitions;

(b) the entity's assets and liabilities should be carried in the balance sheet at their value to a going concern at the balance sheet date;

(c) profits or losses should mean increases or decreases of real financial capital as compared with the amount at the beginning of the year;

(d) the results shown by the financial statements should be measured consistently and should therefore be comparable from year to year, both in periods of fluctuating prices and stable prices; and

(e) all the information given by the financial statements should be verifiable and cost-effective.[196]

(In a subsequent posthumous publication entitled *Commentary: criteria for choosing an accounting model*[197] the number of criteria is expanded to seven, the extra two being essentially clarifications of the meanings of the original five.)

Solomons then attempted to prove that the model which best satisfies these requirements rests on two concepts: value to the business (as espoused by the Corporate Report and Sandilands Committee) and the maintenance of real financial capital. Although these may have some intellectual appeal, it is difficult to see whether either of them has any practical meaning. Solomons sees an asset's value to the business as being the loss that the business would suffer if it were deprived of the asset; since, if deprived of an asset, the business would normally seek to replace it, replacement cost would determine value to the business. However, Solomons recognises that circumstances exist where an asset's value to the business might be less than its replacement cost; for example, in the case of a plant asset which is technologically inferior to an equivalent new asset, the current cost of replacing the services rendered by the existing asset should be used. Furthermore, where an asset would not be replaced by a business if it were lost, its value to the business would be its recoverable amount, which is the higher of the asset's present value and its net realisable value. Therefore, Solomons' final formula for value to the business is that it is equal to 'current cost or recoverable amount, if that is lower'.[198]

In the case of liabilities, the equivalent to an asset's deprival value is a liability's relief value. In other words, liabilities would be valued at the amount that the entity 'could currently raise by the issue of a precisely similar debt security or the cost of discharging the liability by the most economical means, whichever is the higher'.[199] This view is very similar to that advanced by the G4+1 discussed at 6.2 below.

Solomons ended his discussion on 'value to the business' by referring to the ICAS discussion document – *Making Corporate Reports Valuable* – and explains why he believes net realisable values to be irrelevant, resulting in net realisable value accounting being unsuitable for general purpose financial statements.

As mentioned above, Solomons' model is based on the maintenance of real financial capital, with income being defined in terms of the change in net worth. He took the view that because of the uncertainty surrounding the measurement and verification of intangible assets, the changes in such assets cannot be recognised in financial statements; consequently, income will only include changes in recognised tangible assets minus changes in recognised liabilities.[200] This view seems untenable today in view of the important role intangibles play in business and commerce.

Solomons describes his income model as a 'current-cost-constant-purchasing-power model', differing in a number of respects from the SSAP 16 model. First, it recognises both changes in the general level of prices and changes in specific prices and, second, it is based on the maintenance of real financial capital, not operating capacity.[201] It therefore does not require SSAP 16's unpopular gearing and monetary working capital adjustments. The following pro forma profit and loss account illustrates how Solomons' version of real income is derived:[202]

Pro forma profit and loss account as proposed by Solomons

		£
Sales revenue		xxx
Current cost (or lower recoverable amount) of goods sold		xxx
		xxx
Depreciation at current cost	xxx	
Other expenses	xxx	
		xxx
Current operating profit		xxx
Add:		
Holding gains less losses on non-monetary assets (net of inflation)	xxx	
Purchasing power gains on monetary liabilities less purchasing power losses on monetary assets	xxx	
		xxx
Real income		xxx

The views expressed by Solomons on pensions seem extraordinarily prescient and influential to the present day reader. For example he recommended if all or most of the assets of a pension plan can be freely moved back to the employer from the plan by a vote of the trustees, then the affairs of the plan should be consolidated with those of the employer. This approach is based on the view that a pension fund is, in effect, an off balance sheet vehicle set up to meet a company's future obligations. Solomons' proposal is close to what has recently been adopted by the IASC in IAS 19 (Revised) – *Employee Benefits*, and by the ASB in FRS 17 – *Retirement benefits* – both of which are discussed in Chapter 22.

On the subject of goodwill, Solomons states that non-purchased goodwill should not be recognised; his reason for this being that 'determining the value of goodwill where it is not the subject of a purchase and sale transaction and in the presence of a highly imperfect market is too subjective to yield a reliable measure for the purpose of recognition'.[203] What he is saying, is that since non-purchased goodwill does not have an historical cost, it is not possible to update an unknown cost in order to determine its current cost. The same argument applies to all internally generated intangibles, such as brand names. This remains a considerable problem for standard setters, in view of the commercial importance of intangible assets, and is a major stumbling block to the adoption of a full fair-value based system of accounting, which the IASB and the ASB are clearly moving towards, as discussed in 5 and 6 below.

The Research Board of the ICAEW thereafter worked along with its ICAS counterpart to see what practical initiatives might be developed on the basis of both the Guidelines and the ICAS project 'Making Corporate Reports Valuable' (see 4.6 above), and this resulted in the publication of a joint paper, *The Future Shape of Financial Reports* which is discussed below.

4.8 The Future Shape of Financial Reports

In 1991, the ICAS Research Committee and the ICAEW Research Board jointly published a discussion paper with the above title. This was essentially an amalgam of the ideas in MCRV and the Solomons Report which they had previously published separately and which are discussed at 4.6 and 4.7 above. The main points covered in *The Future Shape of Financial Reports* are summarised below.

The authors of the paper start by identifying two purposes of financial reporting: (a) to provide information to shareholders, lenders and others to appraise past performance in order to form expectations about an organisation's future performance and hence, to inform their decisions concerning their relationships with the organisation; and (b) to enable the enforcement of contracts, the terms of which include reference to accounting information. The paper identified the first of these as their primary concern.[204]

Next, the paper identified what it considered to be five main defects of existing reporting practice:

- the predominant use of historical costs;
- excessive emphasis on earnings per share;
- insufficient emphasis on cash and liquidity;
- too much focus on the past rather than the future; and
- too much emphasis on legal form rather than economic substance.[205]

The paper went on to suggest that an improved reporting package would comprise the following elements:

- a statement of objectives and related strategic plan;
- a statement of assets and liabilities;
- an income statement;
- a gains statement;
- a cash flow statement; and
- information on future prospects.

The paper could not settle upon an agreed valuation approach and thus compromised on allowing a number of different ones, as long as they were not historical-cost based. The paper added little to the debate apart from providing a perhaps useful summary of the improvements to the contents of the reporting package – which to contemporary eyes looks unexceptionable.

The University of Birmingham
Issue receipt

24/07/06
11:38 am

UK & international GAAP : generally accepted accounting practice in the Unit
22074570
Due Date: 25/07/2006 10:00

** Please retain this receipt
in case of query **

5 THE ASB'S STATEMENT OF PRINCIPLES

5.1 Introduction

In contrast to its predecessor, the ASB made it clear from the outset that it intended to pursue the idea of a conceptual framework to underpin its standards, although it avoided the use of the term, preferring the less daunting phrase 'Statement of Principles'. In its *Foreword to Accounting Standards*, the ASB stated that 'FRSs are based on the Statement of Principles for Financial Reporting currently in issue, which addresses the concepts underlying the information presented in financial statements. The objective of this *Statement of Principles* is to provide a framework for the consistent and logical formulation of individual accounting standards. The framework also provides a basis on which others can exercise judgement in resolving accounting issues.'[206]

The ASB issued its *Statement of Principles for Financial Reporting* in exposure draft form in November 1995[207] and then effectively withdrew it in July 1996 following overwhelming criticism from commentators, stating that 'the Board has concluded that it would not be appropriate to proceed directly to the development of a final document'.[208] A revised exposure draft in 1997 was promised, but was actually published in March 1999.[209] The finalised version of the ASB's *Statement of Principles for Financial Reporting* was published in December 1999 and the abbreviation 'SoP' is used in this part of the chapter.[210] The *Statement of Principles* is dealt with in some detail because of the influence it has on UK GAAP.

The SoP comprises a compendium of eight chapters, many of which had previously been issued by the ASB in draft form on a piecemeal basis. The chapters are as follows, and are discussed below:

1. The objective of financial statements
2. The reporting entity
3. The qualitative characteristics of financial information
4. The elements of financial statements
5. Recognition in financial statements
6. Measurement in financial statements
7. Presentation of financial information
8. Accounting for interests in other entities.

Each chapter is in two sections, 'Principles' and 'Explanation'. The principles are in effect short statements of the ASB's beliefs concerning that chapter's accounting topic, and the explanation section a discussion and justification of those views.

5.2 Chapter 1: The Objective of Financial Statements

The principles set out in this chapter are that:

- 'The objective of financial statements is to provide information about the reporting entity's financial performance and financial position that is useful to a wide range of users for assessing the stewardship of the entity's management and for making economic decisions.
- That objective can usually be met by focusing exclusively on the information needs of present and potential investors, the defining class of user.
- Present and potential investors need information about the reporting entity's financial performance and financial position that is useful to them in evaluating the entity's ability to generate cash (including the timing and certainty of its generation) and in assessing the entity's financial adaptability.'[211]

The ASB acknowledged that, in drafting the *Statement of Principles*, it was drawing heavily on the work of previous projects in other countries, notably the FASB concept statements discussed at 3 above and the IASC Framework discussed at 7 below. This is particularly true of the early chapters of the ASB's work. Chapter 1's principle that the objective of financial statements is to provide information about the financial position and performance useful to a wide range of users for assessing the stewardship of management and for making economic decisions, is therefore quite familiar.[212]

The term 'financial adaptability' is one which is used by a number of standard-setters in this context. It is described by the ASB as being an entity's 'ability to take effective action to alter the amount and timing of its cash flows so that it can respond to unexpected events and opportunities.'[213] As an objective of financial reporting, it seems both desirable and commendable that enterprises should strive to provide the information necessary for users to assess 'financial adaptability'. However, the question is whether it is really feasible for enterprises to do so in practice and, if it is, what this information would comprise. The chapter goes on to state that:

'Financial adaptability comes from several sources, including the ability to:

(a) Raise new capital, perhaps by issuing debt securities, at short notice;

(b) Repay capital or debt at short notice;

(c) Obtain cash by selling assets without disrupting continuing operations; and

(d) Achieve a rapid improvement in the net cash inflows generated by operations'.[214]

Thus, financial adaptability refers to the fact that it is desirable to have plenty of cash, readily realisable assets and a good credit rating.

A familiar list of possible users is also identified, comprising investors, employees, lenders, suppliers and other creditors, customers, government and their agencies and the public.[215] However, the chapter then narrows down the focus by saying that: 'in preparing financial statements, the rebuttable assumption is made that financial statements that focus on the interest that investors have in the reporting entity's financial performance and financial position will, in effect, also be focusing on the common interest that all users have in that entity's financial performance and financial position.'[216] In essence, therefore, the investor's perspective is chosen as the one most likely to be useful in the preparation of what will remain general purpose financial statements.

Having established this generalisation, the chapter then goes on to assert that investors need information about the generation and use of cash in order to assess the entity's: liquidity and solvency; the relationship between profits and cash flows; the implications that financial performance has for future cash flows; and other aspects of financial adaptability.[217]

5.3 Chapter 2: The Reporting Entity

This chapter sets out the following principles:

- An entity should prepare and publish financial statements if there is a legitimate demand for the information that its financial statements would provide and it is a cohesive economic unit.
- The boundary of the reporting entity is determined by the scope of its control. For this purpose, first direct control and, secondly, direct plus indirect control are taken into account.[218]

The first principle raises so many definitional problems that it seems valueless; for instance 'legitimate demand' is not a clear idea and neither is 'cohesive economic unit'. However, the second principle clearly rests upon the meaning of 'control' which the explanation section attempts to clarify. Control has two aspects: 'the ability to deploy the economic resources involved and to benefit (or suffer) from their deployment'.[219] This is further sub-divided into direct control and indirect control in a way that does not sit easily with the above and other definitions. Direct control seems to mean the business owns the asset while indirect control seems to mean the business owns, or has some sort of interest in, another business which owns the asset.

This direct/indirect control distinction is actually the familiar legal one of ownership and it makes no sense without that background understanding. What these explanations of control really amount to is the truism that businesses are in charge of the things they own and are indirectly in charge of things belonging to other businesses they own. Essentially the chapter is saying that, if one business owns or has a significant financial or economic exposure to another it should prepare consolidated accounts.

5.4 Chapter 3: The Qualitative Characteristics of Financial Information

A large number of principles are stated at the beginning of this chapter that centre around and adhere closely to the work of earlier framework projects, which in turn were heavily influenced by the FASB's SFAC No. 2. Like the FASB, the ASB has presented the inter-relationship of its qualitative characteristics in diagrammatic form, which is reproduced below.

Figure 2

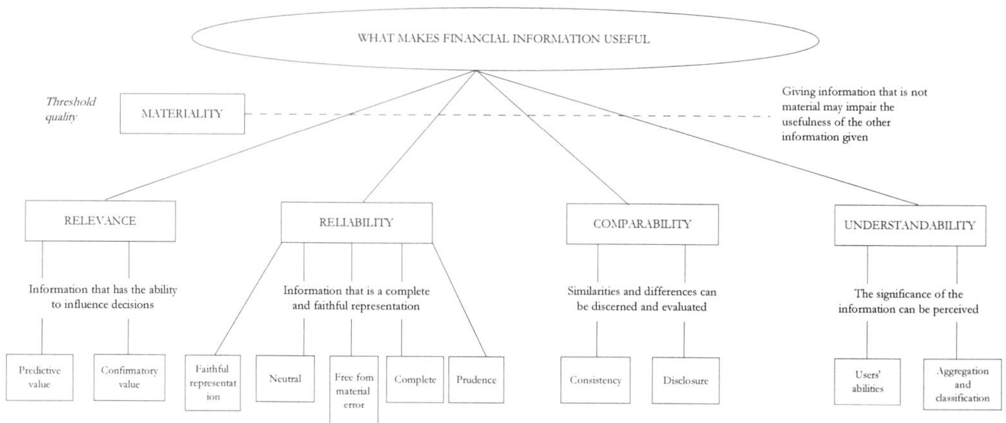

The ASB confirms relevance and reliability as the two primary characteristics of accounting information, and again recognises that they are sometimes in conflict, so as to require a trade-off between them. In this case the principles state that:

> 'if a choice exists between relevant and reliable approaches that are mutually exclusive, the approach chosen needs to be the one that results in the relevance of the information provided being maximised.'[220]

Therefore, the SoP takes the view that relevance takes priority over reliability and states that relevant information has the ability to 'influence the economic decisions of users and is provided in time to influence those decisions'.[221]. This assertion of the priority of relevance over reliability is a substantial departure from the traditional view of prudence, as further explained at 6 below in the context of FRS 18. However it is a departure that is not altogether surprising, given the move towards fair value accounting that is predicated on the view, held by standard setters, that fair values are more relevant than cost even if they are somewhat unreliable. However, users find information relevant only if it is reliable, and it is therefore questionable whether the needs of users are being properly served by sacrificing reliability in the name of relevance.

Information is reliable if:

'(a) it can be depended upon by users to represent faithfully what it either purports to represent or could reasonably be expected to represent;

(b) it is free from deliberate or systematic bias (ie it is neutral);

(c) it is free from material error;

(d) it is complete within the bounds of materiality; and

(e) in its preparation under conditions of uncertainty, a degree of caution (ie prudence) has been applied in exercising judgement and making the necessary estimates.'[222]

This list is useful, but it does assume satisfactory answers exist to fundamental questions. In particular, answers about what a given item in a set of financial statements might 'purport to represent'. Fundamentally this is taking as solved and understood the entire set of difficulties that the accounting profession and the many framework attempts have, and are still, grappling with.

The primary characteristics are supported by what are in effect secondary characteristics of comparability, understandability and materiality. Comparability embraces notions of consistent application of accounting methods throughout an enterprise and through time, as well as the ability to compare one enterprise with another, which implies adequate disclosure of accounting policies.[223] Understandability requires that users are able to perceive the significance of the information provided.[224]

The chapter also refers to materiality as a 'threshold quality', i.e. one that needs to be considered first, because if information is immaterial, the other characteristics do not matter. Material information is information whose omission or misstatement might reasonably be expected to influence the economic decisions of users.[225] The important question, however, is against which yardstick information should be judged to be material or immaterial. The difficulty which arises is that the many different users of financial statements cannot be consulted by the preparer to discover what is material to them; the preparer must make that assessment on their behalf.

According to the ASB, aspects of the nature of the item that affect a judgement about its materiality include

'(a) The item's size is judged in the context both of the financial statements as a whole and of the other information available to users that would affect their evaluation of the financial statements. This includes, for example, considering how the item affects the evaluation of trends and similar considerations.

(b) Consideration is given to the item's nature in relation to:

  (i) the transactions or other events giving rise to it;

  (ii) the legality, sensitivity, normality and potential consequences of the event or transaction;

  (iii) the identity of the parties involved; and

  (iv) the particular headings and disclosures that are affected.'

Where there are two or more similar items, the materiality of the aggregate as well as the individual items needs to be considered.'[226]

One of the factors that all framework attempts have paid lip-service to is understandability. This chapter advances as a principle the notion that 'information provided by financial statements needs to be understandable';[227] however, this is significantly different from actually being understood. In the explanation section relating to understandability, when identifying the required capabilities of users, the Board asserts: 'Those preparing financial statements are entitled to assume that users have a reasonable knowledge of business and economic activities and accounting and a willingness to study with reasonable diligence the information provided'.[228] This assertion, whilst similar to those in other frameworks, similarly avoids the understandability problem in two ways.

First the phrase 'reasonable knowledge … of accounting' is entirely open-ended. It is highly *unlikely* that this could possibly be interpreted to mean 'a complete technical understanding of all the nuances involved with the intricacies of the many accounting rules and regulations', for example. In which case it is clear that much of what the ASB promulgates is not, in this sense, understandable.

Second, the required capabilities would probably reduce the 'allowable' users to a small set of professional analysts, accountants, academics, and the odd graduate of the subject. When this constituency is contrasted with the many types of people who actually own shares, it becomes apparent that the issue of understandability is considerable and cannot comfortably be defined away. This point is, perhaps inadvertently, reinforced by the SoP itself in view of the final paragraph of this chapter, which warns that 'it may not always be possible … to present information in a way that can be understood by all users with the capabilities described in paragraph 3.27(b)'.[229]

5.5 Chapter 4: The Elements of Financial Statements

The following seven elements are defined in the chapter: Assets, Liabilities, Ownership Interest, Gains, Losses, Contributions from Owners, Distributions to Owners.

5.5.1 Assets

Assets are defined as 'rights or other access to future economic benefits controlled by an entity as a result of past transactions or events'.[230] This is obviously based on the equivalent definition in SFAC 6 (see 3.4.1 above), except that the US statement refers to *probable* future economic benefits rather than *rights or other access to* future economic benefits. By using the phrase 'rights or other access', the ASB is emphasising that what constitutes an asset is not a particular item of property itself, but rather the rights deriving from ownership or other rights of occupation and use.[231] This definition, seeking as it does to alter the natural meaning of the word 'asset' (which does indeed refer to the item itself) presents serious logical difficulties. There is another difference between the FASB and ASB definition also, under SFAC 6 the discussion is in the context of benefits 'obtained or controlled', while the SoP definition is refers solely to benefits 'controlled' by the entity. This is a fundamental difference – for example goodwill is an asset under the US definition, but not under the SoP or the IASC's framework, as it fails to meet the 'controlled' requirement.

It is the attempts made in the SoP to explain and make sense of the definition that highlight its unsatisfactory nature. By insisting that an asset is actually 'not the item of property itself'[232] the Board is saying that, for example, an item of stock or a vehicle is not an asset. It holds that an asset actually is 'the rights or other access to some or all of the future economic benefits derived from that item of property'.[233] Further, even cash and cash flows are not assets:

> 'Future economic benefits eventually result in net cash inflows to the entity. Assets are not, however, always direct representations of the cash flows: they are rights and other access to the future economic benefits that can generate or be used to generate future cash flows.
>
> (a) Cash (including bank deposits) can be exchanged for virtually any good or service that is available or it can be saved and exchanged for them in the future. The command that cash gives over resources is the basis of its future economic benefits'.[234]

It is in trying to make sense of these startlingly counter-intuitive claims that the Board's difficulties become apparent; indeed these are difficulties inherent in the FASB's and other similar framework attempts that adopt similar definitions.

The SoP also has to deal with the problem that future economic benefits may not materialise. Consequently it allows that 'this future economic benefit need not, however, be certain'.[235] Thus, the Board maintains that cash is not an asset, fixed and current assets are not assets, but the uncertain future economic benefits they may bring are. However, the question may legitimately be asked: what is a future economic benefit? It cannot be a car or a machine or cash in the bank. If it were, the definition would be self-contradictory, as it expressly states an asset is *not* an item of property or cash. What then is a future economic benefit, if not an item of property or cash? Similarly what is the 'good' referred to above that cash can be exchanged for, if it is not an asset?

In fact, it is an inescapable logical consequence of this definition of assets that 'future economic benefits' cannot be items of property or cash – which they obviously are. This logical bind, and the absence of any other meaning being given to the phrase 'future economic benefits' has the inescapable consequence that the ASB has a flawed definition at the heart of the *Statement of Principles*. If the definition of assets is flawed the entire logical structure derived from it is too, including all the remaining definitions of the elements of financial statements the SoP contains.

Nevertheless, what the ASB seems to be driving at in its definition is that an asset is not the physical property, but the rights that the property bestows on the entity. In other words, if a retailer owns a shop, it is not the shop that is the asset, it is the right to use the shop in order to derive cash inflows that is the asset. This approach is inextricably linked to the concept of value in use. The value in use of an asset is the present value of the cash flows that will be derived from the asset through its use in the business. Thus the ASB seems to be saying that an asset is the right to these cash flows.

That is why it is necessary to include the notion of control within the definition of an asset. The SoP states that 'the definition of an asset requires that … the future economic benefits are controlled by the reporting entity'.[236] How the future can be controlled is not dealt with; however, the SoP seems to be saying that in order to recognise a right on the balance sheet as an asset, it is necessary to control the right so that future cash inflows that are going to be derived from those rights are also controlled.

The notion of control also avoids an unwanted side-effect of the Board's asset definition. There are various expenditures, such as those incurred in staff training or developing market share, that the Board does not want to allow into the balance sheet, even though they bring future benefits. Therefore a further definitional refinement is added, namely that for a future economic benefit to be an asset it must also be 'controlled independently of the business as a whole'.[237] This new concept of independence from the business as a whole is only illustrated, not defined. However, to take the Board's own example, it asserts that 'market share, superior management or good labour relations … cannot be controlled independently of the business as a whole'.[238] In this way, the ASB believes that it is able to prevent expenditure that is being deferred in order to smooth profits from being carried forward in the balance sheet as an asset.

5.5.2 *Liabilities*

Liabilities are defined as 'obligations of an entity to transfer economic benefits as a result of past transactions or events'.[239] Here, the wording is much shorter than the US equivalent (see 3.4.2 above) but the main features of the definition appear to be the same. Again, it is the application of this definition which has had a fundamental impact on UK GAAP. For example, FRS 12 – *Provisions, Contingent Liabilities and Contingent Assets* – published in September 1998 relies heavily on this definition to severely restrict the circumstances under which provisions can be recognised. This is because provisions are not seen as a separate element of financial statements and, instead, are defined as being a subset of liabilities (see Chapter 27). Similarly, FRS 7's strict criteria for the recognition of provisions, as part of the determination of the fair values of the assets and liabilities in an acquisition, stem from this definition.

The concept of the 'constructive obligation'[240] familiar from FRS 12, is included in the SoP as another definitional refinement, this time to prevent the directors of a company creating a liability unless certain other conditions are fulfilled. In particular, 'where the event that gave rise to the obligation was the communication of the decision to transfer economic benefits – the liability will have existed at the balance sheet date only if the communication took place before that date'.[241]

It seems untenable that the existence of a liability really does rest upon whether the directors have told anyone about it. We believe that the ASB is wrong to exclude the effect of management decisions in portraying the financial performance and financial position of an entity, particularly as this view is not being applied consistently. For instance, while a business is precluded by FRS 12 from recognising the direct costs of a large scale restructuring announced just after the balance sheet date, FRS 11 – *Impairment of Fixed Assets and Goodwill* – requires that business to make provision for any impairment to the carrying value of the fixed assets involved.

Assets and liabilities are therefore characterised as rights and obligations – rights to receive future economic benefits in the form of cash inflows and obligations to transfer out economic benefits in the form of cash outflows. The remaining definitions are derived from these definitions of assets and liabilities.

5.5.3 *Ownership interest*

Ownership interest is defined as being 'the residual amount found by deducting all the entity's liabilities from all the entity's assets'.[242] Again the wording is similar to that used in SFAC 6. The logic of the definition is identical, and follows from the equation that assets minus liabilities equals equity.

5.5.4 *Gains*

Gains are defined as 'increases in ownership interest, not resulting from contributions from owners'.[243] Here the ASB has adopted a simpler approach than the FASB, because it uses a single element to cover what SFAC 6 describes separately as revenues and gains (see 3.4.7 above). The distinction is that the US definitions differentiate between gains arising from central operations and those which do not, whereas the ASB uses a single definition for both.

5.5.5 *Losses*

Losses are defined as 'decreases in ownership interest, not resulting from distributions to owners'.[244] Again, this embraces both expenses and losses as the terms are used in SFAC 6 (see 3.4.7 above).

5.5.6 *Contributions from owners*

These are defined as 'increases in ownership interest resulting from transfers from owners in their capacity as owners'.[245] This is a straightforward definition, and is needed in order to exclude capital injections from being included within the definition of gains.

5.5.7 *Distributions to owners*

These are defined as the mirror image: 'decreases in ownership interest resulting from transfers to owners in their capacity as owners'.[246] Again, this prevents dividends and capital repayments being categorised as losses.

5.5.8 *The overall approach*

The approach taken by Chapter 4 is therefore very similar to that used by SFAC No. 6. It employs only seven elements, rather than the US statement's ten, having combined two pairs of the American terms into two single elements, and not sought to use the further term 'comprehensive income' (which would equate to gains minus losses as the terms are used by the ASB).

This approach is also, therefore, open to some of the same challenges as its American counterpart, because all the other elements are dependent on the definitions of the first two: those of assets and liabilities. This might be acceptable providing the definitions are meaningful and as long as workable recognition and measurement rules for assets and liabilities can be devised. However, as discussed above, there is room for serious doubt on both counts. It will be recalled from 3.5 above that it was over recognition and measurement that the US Framework project also ran into difficulty.

5.6 Chapter 5: Recognition in Financial Statements

The principles adopted in this chapter set out the conditions for recognition, rather than define what recognition is, which is discussed in the explanation section. The chapter gives these conditions for the recognition of assets and liabilities:

'If a transaction or other event has created a new asset or liability or added to an existing asset or liability, that event will be recognised if:

> Sufficient evidence exists that the new asset or liability has been created or that there has been an addition to an existing asset or liability; and
>
> The new asset or liability or the addition to the existing asset or liability can be measured at a monetary amount with sufficient reliability.'[247]

Revenue recognition (which is not characterised as such) is referred to in the principles section of chapter 5 as follows:

> 'In a transaction involving the provision of services or goods for a net gain, the recognition criteria described above [i.e. the asset/liability criteria above] will be met on the occurrence of the critical event in the operating cycle involved'.[248]

By including this paragraph, the ASB seems to be fending off any potential criticism of its asset/liability approach to revenue recognition. In defending the approach that gains and losses are merely increases and decreases in net assets, other than those resulting from transactions with shareholders, the ASB is attempting to assert that both an asset/liability approach and a critical event approach to revenue recognition end up with the same answer. What the above paragraph is saying is that a net gain that is recognised on the basis of the critical event approach will necessarily result in an increase in net assets, with the result that the asset/liability recognition criteria will also be met.

However, while this is so, the converse is not. The ASB is trying to assert that irrespective of whether one follows a balance sheet approach to income recognition or a transactions-based income statement approach, one will always get to the same end-result. This is patently not true. Just because all revenue recognised under an income statement based transactions system will satisfy the asset/liability recognition criteria, it does not follow that the reverse will apply. Revenue recognition criteria are more demanding than those for recognising assets and liabilities, since they should embody the concept of the revenue having been earned, based on performance by the reporting company. The issue of revenue recognition in the context of the SoP is discussed in detail in section 4.1 of Chapter 3 of this book.

'Recognition' is described as involving 'depiction of the element both in words and by monetary amounts and the inclusion of those amounts in the primary financial statement totals'. The chapter describes the recognition and derecognition of assets and liabilities' as falling into three stages: initial recognition, subsequent remeasurement and derecognition.[249]

Recognition may be subject to delay because of uncertainty of two types:

(a) element uncertainty, which involves uncertainty whether an item exists and meets the definitions of the elements of financial statements; and

(b) measurement uncertainty, which concerns the appropriate monetary amount at which to recognise the item.[250]

Prudence is largely discussed in the mechanical context of whether there is sufficient evidence for an asset to be recognised; rather than whether it is prudent to recognise it at all, a subtle downgrading of the concept.[251]

An asset or liability should cease to be recognised (derecognised) if the item concerned has been eliminated, or if there is no longer sufficient evidence that the item concerned exists, or when it cannot be measured with sufficient reliability – which is stated to be a rare event.[252] This means that whenever a change in an entity's total assets is not offset by an equal change in total liabilities or ownership interest, a gain or loss will arise. Subsequent remeasurement is not discussed further.

The chapter identifies two broad classes of past events that may involve a measurable change in assets or liabilities and hence that may trigger recognition: 'transactions' and 'events other than transactions'. The subsequent discussion of the recognition process under these two broad headings reveals that it would radically alter conventional financial reporting practices if applied rigorously. In particular it becomes clear that the rules would require assets and liabilities under certain contracts for future performance to be recognised immediately unless it was possible to cancel the contract without incurring a significant penalty. An example of the practical application of this principle, now being actively canvassed in the leasing discussion paper issued by the G4+1 in 2000, is that assets obtained under operating leases would appear on the balance sheet of the lessee, as well as those obtained under finance leases.

The ASB's proposals for the recognition of gains and losses are very similar to those in the ICAS study Making Corporate Reports Valuable (see 4.6 above). The idea that gains and losses arise whenever there is a change in net assets which is not offset by a transaction with owners reflects MCRV's notion of changes in financial wealth. Thus the ASB's model does not make, or wish to make, a fundamental distinction between realised and unrealised gains and losses. All changes in balance sheet assets and liabilities (excluding transactions with shareholders) are recognised as gains and losses – irrespective of whether or not they are realised.

The section of chapter 5 concerning unperformed contracts seems to imply the recognition of a sale, and hence profit, where a contract has been agreed, but nothing else has happened. Certainly rights to future benefits exist at this point. This represents a fundamental change of emphasis in accounting recognition of revenue under UK GAAP and most others.

This difficulty is glossed over by the statement that 'if the historical cost basis of measurement is being used, the carrying amount will be the cost of entering into the agreement, which is usually nil. In effect, therefore, the contract is recognised at nil.'[253] However, assuming a profitable sale has been contracted, this cannot be the case. The very inclusion of the notion in the SoP seems to envisage the possibility that in the future unperformed contracts might generally be recognised. In our view this would be a grave mistake, the possibility of which the Board should specifically renounce. The matter does provide a further example of the manner in which the inadequate definitions chosen by the ASB lead to unworkable results in practice.

5.7 Chapter 6: Measurement in Financial Statements

This chapter sets out clearly the three realistic alternatives the historical cost/current value measurement options provide:

> 'all assets and liabilities could be measured at historical cost. This is known as the historical cost system.
>
> all assets and liabilities could be measured at current value. This is known as the current value system.
>
> some categories of assets or liabilities could be measured on a historical cost basis and some on a current value basis. This is known as the mixed measurement system.'[254]

The chapter goes on to say that 'the Statement envisages that the mixed measurement system will be used'.[255] The chapter then proceeds to discuss the alternatives and how they apply to initial measurement and subsequent remeasurement. Although curiously it states that the purpose under modified historical cost of remeasurement is to 'ensure that assets are not reported at greater than their recoverable amount'[256] when in practice under this system, revaluations are mainly to ensure users appreciate the true market value of a company's property assets; that is, to ensure property assets are not reported at substantially *less* than their recoverable amount.

There is a section which discusses the relative reliability of current value and historical cost systems claiming, somewhat disingenuously, that current values are not that much less reliable than historical cost. For instance, that under historical cost 'adjustments made to the carrying value of debtors … for bad and doubtful debts involve a degree of estimation that is not dissimilar to that involved in estimating current values not derived from an active market'.[257] In our view, this is an enormous oversimplification of the issue that seems to ignore the fact that bad debt estimations are frequently made on the basis of both historical bad debt collection experience and actual post balance sheet date collections. There is a vast difference between, for example, a retailer estimating a provision for doubtful debts on trade receivables and a bank determining the fair value of a portfolio of loans and advances for which there is no observable market value. It should also be borne in mind that doubtful debt provisions can only involve losses, whereas fair valuations can result in reporting unrealised gains.

The chapter contains a discussion of how current values should be determined, which centres round the concept of 'value in use' now rejected by the FASB (see section 3.7 above). Discounting and capital maintenance are briefly alluded to; but overall the chapter sensibly acknowledges the modified historical cost approach to measurement will continue. Whether this represents a true ASB conviction, or whether it has just been included as a tactical ploy in order to forestall criticism is a moot point. The ASB actively participated in the international project on the accounting for financial instruments known as the Joint Working Group on Financial Instruments (see Chapter 10 of this book). This group published a discussion paper in 2000 that envisages a comprehensive system of fair value accounting for all financial assets and liabilities, which if adopted would not leave much of the mixed model left.

What is not in doubt, is the fact that the ASB (and the IASB) is advancing rapidly down the road of fair value accounting. FRS 18 clearly envisages this development, which is explained further at 6 below. Whilst being semantically attractive, on examination, the notion of fair value is far from clear and this presents a difficulty that remains unresolved. The various documents published by the major standard setters imply very different methods of how fair value it is to be determined. The JWG document, referred to above, prefers the market price-based exit value approach – showing FASB influence – whereas much of IAS literature implies an entity specific, value in use approach. Even the market based approach to fair value as applied in IAS 39 and IAS 40, is couched in terms of transaction prices between 'knowledgeable and willing parties', which is a far broader concept than that being promulgated by the JWG.

5.8 Chapter 7: Presentation of Financial Information

Three primary financial statements are envisaged:

'(a) financial performance …

(b) financial position (the balance sheet); and

(c) cash inflows and outflows (the cash flow statement)'.[258]

The Board has decided that, after all, there is no need for a statement of total recognised gains and losses (STRGL) as a separate statement; but this is because the Board is in favour of merging the profit and loss account and STRGL into a single statement of comprehensive income, as envisaged by FRED 22 (discussed below at 6.2). There is no attempt in this chapter to discuss the wisdom of edging the performance statement away from the realisation principle.

Otherwise the chapter contains a rather anodyne discussion of the value of clear communication and presentation, and makes no concrete proposals for the improvement of either.

5.9 Chapter 8: Accounting for Interests in other Entities

This chapter mentions rather than clarifies some of the issues surrounding consolidation and accounting for business combinations. The chapter identifies: 'Control, Joint control, Significant influence and Lesser or no influence',[259] as the principle cases covering when consolidation accounting should be used and the form it should take.

The chapter essentially rationalises the treatment adopted by FRS 9 – *Associates and joint ventures* – which involves consolidating the investor's share of the results and net assets of the investee. FRS 9 is discussed in Chapter 7 of this book.

One of the difficulties the Board has is that its definition of assets excludes goodwill, which poses a particular problem for the presentation of consolidated accounts. Chapter 8 acknowledges this difficulty and seeks to justify the departure from the ASB's principles as follows:

> 'Purchased goodwill … is not an asset in itself … [but] if the parent's investment is to be fully reflected in the group's financial statements and the parent is to be held accountable for its investment … purchased goodwill needs to be recognised as if it were an asset'.[260]

Perhaps this admission puts the ASB's entire conceptual framework project into perspective. The point of the exercise is to make decisions based on principle, rather than on an ad hoc basis. The rational conclusion when principles do not fit reality is to find ones that do, and acknowledge the principles' inadequacies. The fundamental purpose of a conceptual framework is to avoid inconsistencies of the 'goodwill is not an asset but let's pretend it is' type.

5.10 Overall assessment of the ASB's Statement of Principles

The *Statement of Principles* seeks to build accounting around its FASB-derived definitions of assets and liabilities and the proposed criteria for recognising them in the balance sheet. This approach inherent in FRS 18 and many of the ASB's more recent publications, replaces the long-established accounting process in use throughout the world, whereby transactions are allocated to accounting periods by reference to the matching and prudence concepts.

The *Statement of Principles* views the accounting process differently from how it has been viewed traditionally. Traditionally assets and liabilities have not formed the natural starting point for devising recognition rules. Traditionally the building blocks of accounting practice are transactions, to which are applied criteria for revenue and expense recognition, the balance sheet being a result of this process, not the starting point – the balance sheet was never intended to capture all the aspects of a company's value.

A general concern about the *Statement of Principles* and the approach that it has taken, is that it does not adequately acknowledge the legal and business context in which accounting is practised and the constraints thereby placed on it. The objective of financial statements is said to be to provide information about the financial position, performance and financial adaptability of an enterprise that is useful to a wide range of users for assessing the stewardship of management and for making economic decisions. But this definition is then gradually narrowed. Assessing the stewardship of management as an objective is quickly defined out of existence, because it too is apparently only done to make economic decisions; the wide range of users is collapsed down to the providers of risk capital – shareholders; and the economic decisions to be taken are based on an evaluation of cash generation. The objective of financial statements, therefore, becomes to predict future cash flows.

This tenet is the fundamental assumption in an established branch of academic thought. As an aid to academic thought and research it is a helpful simplification. As the basis for regulatory endeavour, however, it is not appropriate. Accounts do not, in fact, exist primarily to predict cash flows for investment decisions; they form a report by the stewards of an enterprise to its owners, and they sit within a legal and social context that cannot simply be ignored. They also fulfil a variety of other roles, including the identification of profits available for dividend; a starting point for the assessment of taxation (particularly in the light of recent tax cases that have enhanced the importance of accounting rules); a reference point that can be used for conditions in contracts with lenders and other parties; the calculation of executive directors' performance bonuses, and so on.

Undoubtedly how accounting is actually done in the world is, in fact, transactions based. Arguably even though equivalent frameworks elsewhere in the world also suggest a balance sheet approach, these documents do not correspond to the reality of the accounting process in those countries either. If the (equivalent) approach in the FASB's concepts were actually applied in the US, for example, the extensive literature on revenue recognition in that country would be redundant. The question therefore arises why the ASB has adopted a set of criteria that do not fit the practice of accounting they attempt to govern.

An answer to this question might be that the standard setters want to fundamentally change the basis of financial reporting, and the SoP is a step in that direction. A full balance sheet oriented, fair-value based system of reporting is inherent in many of the recent publications of the G4+1 (in effect the standard setters' think-tank) and this approach appears to have wide support in the ASB and the IASB. The adoption of FRS 18, in place of SSAP 2, appears to be a decisive step in this direction for UK GAAP, and is discussed further at 7.10 below.

6 OTHER ASB FINANCIAL REPORTING INITIATIVES

6.1 Discounting in Financial Reporting

In April 1997 the ASB issued a 'Working Paper' on discounting in financial reporting. The ASB pointed out that the Working Paper was not a prelude to a future FRS on the topic, and that the decision on whether discounting will be prescribed in any particular circumstance will form part of the development of the relevant Standard. As a result, the Working Paper is described as being 'for the Board's own reference as the Board considers discounting within various projects'.[261]

The ASB states that, in preparing the paper, it has drawn extensively on the research of the FASB in this area. However, since the publication of the ASB's working paper the FASB has issued SFAC 7 on this subject which contains significant changes from the draft which influenced the ASB's paper. SFAC 7 (see 3.7 above) contains substantial extra complication which may end up being recommended by the ASB, in view of the commonality that exists between their framework projects.

The Board has not examined the issue of discounting at a fundamental level in this paper;. for example, where do finance costs fit into the overall framework of financial reporting? This affects matters such as the capitalisation of finance costs and imputed interest, dividends and the distinction between different stakeholders.

Instead, the paper starts with no particular objectives, meanders around the subject of discounting and comes to its conclusions rather abruptly. In fact, the only real conclusion that the paper reaches is that it 'has shown that discounting future cash flows to reflect the time value of money and the effect of the variability of the cash flows is consistent with both historical cost and current value bases of accounting'.[262] However, this comes to the reader of the paper as a bolt from the blue, since there has been no real indication that this was where the paper was leading. This is because the paper was really just a rationalisation of what the ASB wanted to do on some of its current projects, such as impairment, provisions and pension liabilities. As a result, the paper includes statements such as: 'discounting is, therefore, a useful tool in accounting measurements'.[263] The paper does devote some time to discussing the issue of risk, but it does so in the context of specific projects such as pensions and provisions.

Moreover, what the paper does not adequately consider is that discounting is not just a balance sheet issue, it affects profit and loss measurement and classification as well whenever cash flows are separated from accruals of income or expenses – for example, the measurement of profit where assets are sold on deferred terms. Furthermore, even in addressing discounting in the context of accounting for environmental liabilities, the paper does not deal with issues such as accounting for abandonment costs, or explain why the balance sheet approach of recognising a discounted liability is preferable to the generally accepted unit of production approach. It is therefore not clear why the ASB believes that entities should be required to record interest on the accretion of a liability in circumstances where no cash is borrowed.

All in all, the ASB's paper adds little to existing knowledge and seems more of a rationalisation of the ASB's current agenda.

6.2 Reporting Financial Performance

6.2.1 *Introduction*

The ASB published FRED 22 – *Revision of FRS 3 Reporting Financial Performance* – in December 2000. It proposes significant amendments to FRS 3 (FRS 3 is discussed in Chapter 25) and has been greatly influenced by a paper developed by the G4+1 'think-tank' which itself reflected 'an agreed approach to reporting financial performance that each body … intends to develop in its own constituency'.[264] The G4+1 is made up from the staff of the standard setters from the USA, UK, Canada, Australia, New Zealand and the IASC.

The G4+1 paper took the view that there should be only one statement of performance in which should be reported all recognised gains and losses, this single statement usually being called a 'comprehensive income statement' (CIS). It further regarded realisation as an unnecessary characteristic for the recognition of a gain. The paper therefore suggests that there should be one single statement of financial performance, divided into three major components, and it is this precise approach has been adopted by FRED 22.

6.2.2 *FRED 22 – Revision of FRS 3: Reporting Financial Performance*

The main conclusion to be drawn from FRED 22, taken together with the ASB's *Statement of Principles* and FRS 18 (see 5 above and 7 below respectively) is that the ASB is moving UK financial reporting decisively towards a balance sheet oriented, fair value based, model. FRED 22 adopts a single statement of financial performance in which realisation plays no significant part, other than as an inconvenient legal restriction that has to be accommodated in the letter rather than the substance of the concept.

The exposure draft defines financial performance as:

> 'The financial performance of an entity comprises the return it obtains on the resources it controls, the components of that return and the characteristics of those components, insofar as they can be captured by the accounting model.
>
> Financial performance of an entity for a period encompasses all recognised gains and losses. As such, in mathematical terms it is the change in net assets of the reporting entity from the end of the previous period to the end of the present period, excluding distributions to and contributions from owners.'[265]

This is a key passage which formally installs the recognition of all gains and losses as the definition of financial performance. Thus the reporting structure of financial performance will not in future have the earned profits focus it has had previously. More importantly the definition, with its complete absence of any realisation criteria, needs no further adjustment when a full fair value model is introduced. Once all gains are accepted into the performance statement, the regular restatement of the balance sheet to fair values can be accommodated seamlessly.

FRED 22 advocates a single statement of financial performance, in place of a profit and loss account followed by a statement of recognised gains and losses. Following the G4+1 paper referred to at 6.1.1 above, FRED 22 adopts a three section approach:

> 'An entity should divide its performance statement into the following three sections:
>
> (a) operating;
>
> (b) financing and treasury; and
>
> (c) other gains and losses.
>
> All gains and losses recognised in the financial statements for the period should be included in a section of the single performance statement.'[266]

Dividends paid or declared account will no longer appear in the profit and loss, but be given in memorandum form at the foot of the statement, together with earnings per share figures and cumulative adjustments recognised in the period that arise from prior period adjustments.

The FRED also advocates the addition of a new primary statement, the 'Reconciliation of ownership interests'. This statement is required because the single performance statement is limited solely to gains and losses which therefore exclude dealings with the owners. It will contain a reconciliation of the opening and closing totals of ownership interests of the period. The FRED mandates that certain reconciling items namely, the results of the period as reported in the performance statement; dividends for the period (broken down into equity and non-equity dividends as required by FRS 4 – *Capital Instruments*) and the cumulative effect of prior period adjustments; should be disclosed separately in the reconciliation.[267]

However it is the single performance statement that is the most far-reaching alteration proposed by FRED 22. Appendix 1 gives two illustrative examples, the second of which is reproduced below.

Figure 3

STATEMENT OF FINANCIAL PERFORMANCE (Example 2)

	Continuing operations 2001 £m	Acquisitions 2001 £m	Discontinued operations 2001 £m	Total 2001 £m	Total 2000 Restated £m
Operating					
Turnover	600	50	175	825	690
Cost of sales	(445)	(40)	(165)	(650)	(555)
Gross profit	155	10	10	175	135
Other expenses	(95)	(4)	(25)	(124)	(83)
Operating income/profit	**60**	**6**	**(15)**	**51**	**52**
Financing and treasury					
Interest on debt				(26)	(15)
Financing relating to pension provision				20	11
Financing and treasury income/profit				**(6)**	**(4)**
Operating and financing income before taxation				**45**	**48**
Taxation on operating and financing income				(5)	(10)
Operating and financing income after taxation				40	38
Minority interests				(5)	(4)
Income from operating and financing activities for the period*				**35**	**34**
Other gains and losses					
Revaluation gain on disposal of properties in continuing operations				6	4
Revaluation of fixed assets				4	3
Actuarial gain on defined benefit pension scheme				276	91
Profit on disposal of discontinued operations				3	–
Exchange translation differences on foreign currency net investments				(2)	5
Other gains and losses before taxation				**287**	**103**
Taxation on other gains and losses				(87)	(33)
Other gains and losses after taxation				200	70
Minority interests				(30)	(10)
Other gains and losses of the period				**170**	**60**
Total gains and losses of the period				**205**	**94**
MEMORANDUM ITEMS					
Earnings per share				39p	41p
Adjustments [to be itemised and described]				Xp	Xp
Adjusted earnings per share				Yp	Yp
Diluted earnings per share				Zp	Zp
Dividend per share: equity				3.0p	1.8p
Dividend per share: preference				0.6p	0.6p
Total dividend for the period: equity				£6.7m	£0.7m
Total dividend for the period: preference				£1.3m	£1.3m
Prior period adjustment recognised during the period (see note X)				(£10m)	-

*Any extraordinary items would be shown after this line, with a subsequent subtotal for the statutory 'profit for the financial year' after extraordinary activities.

FRED 22 is discussed in more detail in Chapter 25 of this book. Suffice it to say here that if and when FRED 22 is converted to a standard, the ASB will have all the necessary pieces in place to move UK GAAP towards a full fair value basis of financial reporting, with comprehensive income (i.e. all changes in net assets) being reflected in a single statement of financial performance.

7 FRS 18 ACCOUNTING POLICIES

7.1 Introduction

FRS 18 is a paradigm case of the influence that the ASB's conceptual framework document, the *Statement of Principles*, has had on UK GAAP. The standard's requirements are set out below, but to understand the underlying theory that led to FRS 18, it is essential to study the *Statement of Principles*, which is discussed at 5 above. The new standard makes explicit the changes that have been implicit in many of the ASB's recent standards, and clearly opens up the way to a full fair value-based, balance sheet oriented approach to the compilation of financial reports under UK GAAP. This would not have been possible under the more rigorously prudence-orientated concepts of SSAP 2.

FRS 18 – *Accounting policies* – was published in December 2000 and superseded SSAP 2. It came into effect for periods ending on or after 22 June 2001, with early adoption being encouraged but not required. However those parts of the standard governing compliance with Statements of Recommended Practice (SORPs) need not be applied for accounting periods beginning on or before 23 December 2001. That is, for most companies, the SORP requirements of FRS 18 do not have to be complied with until December 2002 year ends, or later.[268]

The standard provides definitions of accounting policies, estimation techniques and measurement bases. The accounting treatment it requires for an item depends upon which of the definitions the item falls under. The definition of accounting policies in the new standard is relatively familiar, however the criteria for selecting them are changed radically from those used in SSAP 2. Somewhat paradoxically this does not result, for the time being at least, in changes to the policies themselves. The purpose of the criteria change from those in SSAP 2 is to ensure that, if and when fundamental changes to the basis on which accounts are prepared are promulgated, there will be no impediment to their adoption.

7.2 Definitions in FRS 18

The new standard seeks to make a distinction between accounting policies, estimation techniques and measurement bases. Accounting policies are defined as:

> 'Those principles, bases, conventions, rules and practices applied by an entity that specify how the effects of transactions and other events are to be reflected in its financial statements through
>
> (i) recognising,
>
> (ii) selecting measurement bases for, and
>
> (iii) presenting
>
> assets, liabilities, gains, losses and changes to shareholders' funds. Accounting policies do not include estimation techniques.'[269]

The standard goes on to amplify this definition further:

> 'Accounting policies define the process whereby transactions and other events are reflected in financial statements. For example an accounting policy for a particular type of expenditure may specify whether an asset or loss is to be recognised; the basis on which it is to be measured; and where in the profit and loss account or balance sheet it is to be presented.'

It should be noted that estimation techniques are specifically excluded from the definition. As is discussed below, normally only changes in accounting policies may be accounted for by utilising prior period adjustments, thus the FRS specifically prohibits changes in estimation techniques being accounted for in this manner.

Estimation techniques are defined as:

> 'The methods adopted by an entity to arrive at estimated monetary amounts, corresponding to the measurement bases selected, for assets, liabilities, gains, losses and changes to shareholders' funds.
>
> 'Estimation techniques implement the measurement aspects of accounting policies. An accounting policy will specify the basis on which an item is to be measured; where there is uncertainty over the monetary amount corresponding to that basis, the amount will be arrived at by using an estimation technique.'[270]

In short, estimation techniques are such things as depreciation methods (e.g. straight line, reducing balance), or methods used to estimate bad debts, or warranty claim liabilities.

The standard then seeks to explain and define a third category, 'measurement bases' for which the exposition is rather less clear. In fact the definition of measurement bases seems to explain the term 'monetary attributes' – merely stating at the end of two paragraphs of description, rather than definition, that:

> 'A monetary attribute, or combination of attributes, that may be reflected in financial statements is called a measurement basis.'[271]

It is a far from clear concept, but it would seem that the term actually refers to the two main alternative systems under which the financial statements can be compiled: historical cost or current value.

These definitions do have importance when a business is considering changing a policy, estimation technique, or measurement base, in as much as FRS 18 is definite on how a change in each should be reported. These aspects are further discussed below.

7.3 Selecting accounting policies under FRS 18

The standard lays down specific new criteria for choosing accounting policies, requires their regular review, and sets out how changes to accounting policies must be accounted for. In addition, the standard states that all changes to presentation are to be treated as a change in accounting policy. FRS 18 is unequivocal in its overall requirement that:

> 'An entity should adopt accounting policies that enable its financial statements to give a true and fair view. Those accounting policies should be consistent with the requirements of accounting standards, Urgent Issues Task Force (UITF) Abstracts and companies legislation.'[272]

Further it refers to the 'exceptional circumstances' where compliance with a standard may be inconsistent with the need to present a true and fair view.[273] In these circumstances a departure is allowed, but the disclosures previously set out in UITF 7, now incorporated into FRS 18, have to be given. A disclosure summary is included below at 6.9.

The standard goes on to make it clear that, subject to the above overall requirement, a business must select those policies that 'are judged by the entity to be most appropriate to its particular circumstances for the purpose of giving a true and fair view'.[274] This notion of 'appropriateness' is undefined and, as with most other contexts in which it is used contemporarily, is really a method of conveying a general sense that entities are expected to 'play the game' without actually defining precisely what that game is. However the requirement to select the most appropriate policy is arguably a more strict requirement than at present. A merely adequate policy is presumably not sufficient.

Even if appropriateness is not defined, the standard does provide guidance on how the appropriateness of accounting policies is to be judged. It lists four objectives of financial statements, which are derived directly from the ASB's *Statement of Principles*:

- relevance, reliability, comparability, and understandability,

and two constraints:

- the need to balance the four objectives, and the cost/benefit balance of providing information.[275]

These objectives give a very clear example of the indebtedness of the ASB's conceptual framework to the work done by the FASB. For example, 3.3.4 above mentions how SFAC 2 sets out the characteristics of relevance and reliability as important qualities for financial reports. FRS 18 makes it clear that these objectives and constraints must be 'considered together in judging the appropriateness of accounting policies to an entity's particular circumstances'. Some of the explanation of the meaning of the objectives is a little circular, for example:

> 'appropriate accounting policies will result in financial information being presented that is relevant. Where more than one accounting policy would achieve this result, an entity will consider which of those policies presents the most relevant financial information ...'.[276]

However some of it is definitely helpful, most particularly the section dealing with reliability, which states:

> 'Financial information is reliable if:
>
> (a) it can be depended upon by users to represent faithfully what it either purports to represent or could reasonably be expected to represent, and therefore reflects the substance of the transactions and other events that have taken place;
>
> (b) it is free from deliberate or systematic bias (i.e. it is neutral);
>
> (c) it is free from material error;
>
> (d) it is complete within the bounds of materiality; and
>
> (e) under conditions of uncertainty, it has been prudently prepared (i.e. a degree of caution has been applied in exercising judgement and making the necessary estimates).'[277]

The discussion of reliability in the standard includes a warning against exercising prudence where there is no uncertainty. This discussion specifically states that prudence is not a reason to over-provide, as that would mean the financial statements are not free from deliberate bias, i.e. are not neutral. Paragraph 36 contains the assertion that 'appropriate accounting policies will result in information being presented that is reliable'. Clearly this cannot be inevitably the case. It is quite possible to envisage circumstances where fair value measurement could be mandated by an accounting standard, which resulted in financial statements that turned out to be highly unreliable, owing to the absence of observable market prices.

Comparability is rightly stressed as important if financial statements are to be useful, and comparability with prior years and with other entities is mentioned in this context. However the statement that 'comparability can usually be achieved through a combination of consistency and disclosure'[278] is unsupported by evidence – at least as far as comparability between entities is concerned. It may be that the encouragement given in the standard that industry practices should be followed, particularly in the form of SORPs, may play a part in subsequently providing evidence for this claim.

Finally understandability is mentioned, albeit briefly. As in previous ASB documents, understandability is cited as a major objective of financial statements; indeed it would be indefensible to hold a contrary view. Nevertheless the manner in which understandability is explained somewhat reduces the laudable headline impact of the objective. Understandability turns out to mean:

> 'capable of being understood by users having a reasonable knowledge of business and economic activities and accounting and a willingness to study with reasonable diligence the information provided'.[279]

It would seem that this reduces understandability to a very much smaller sub-set than that represented by shareholders and others with an interest in the progress and prospects of a business. This may or may not be inevitable, but it remains true that understandability is a Cinderella objective in both FRS 18 and the ASB's *Statement of Principles*.

Importantly FRS 18 makes it clear that additional disclosures do not either justify or remedy the selection of an accounting policy other than the 'most appropriate' one. Moreover the standard specifies that this judgement must be made by reference to the four objectives and two constraints set out above.[280]

In practice the four objectives can be in conflict, which the standard acknowledges in paragraphs 42 and 43. These parts of the standard discuss the circumstances where the most relevant policy might not be the most reliable, or where the most reliable might not be the most relevant. The guidance given is that the most appropriate accounting policy will usually be that which is the most relevant of those that are reliable.

Paragraph 43 discusses the conflict between neutrality and prudence. To some extent the ASB in various of its publications, including the exposure draft preceding FRS 18, has tended to characterise prudence as unnecessary profit smoothing. Paragraph 43 of FRS 18 characterises prudence as:

> 'a potentially biased concept that seeks to ensure that, under conditions of uncertainty, gains and assets are not overstated and losses and liabilities are not understated.'

Paragraph 43 indicates that it is part of the accounting policy selection process to reconcile the competing demands of neutrality and prudence by finding a balance between them that does not systematically understate assets and gains, or overstate liabilities and losses. The general implication in the standard, as set out in the discussion on reliability in paragraphs 35 to 38, is that 'it is not necessary to exercise prudence where there is no uncertainty'.[281]

This part of FRS 18 also owes much to the work of the FASB published in SFAC 2 (see 3.3.4 and 3.3.7 above). The FASB concepts statement contains discussions about the balance between reliability and neutrality, and about the distinction between conservatism (prudence) and the deliberate understatement of profits, with which those in FRS 18 are essentially identical.

7.4 Reviewing and changing accounting policies under FRS 18

FRS 18 prescribes definite rules for the accounting treatment of changes in accounting policies and an explicit requirement that policies must be regularly reviewed in order to ensure they remain the 'most appropriate'.

'An entity's accounting policies should be regularly reviewed to ensure that they remain the most appropriate to its particular circumstances for the purpose of giving a true and fair view'. This sentence in paragraph 45 of the standard is somewhat ameliorated by the sentence following it:

> 'However in judging whether a new policy is more appropriate than the existing policy, an entity will give due weight to the impact on comparability, as explained in paragraph 49.'

While paragraph 49 goes on to state:

> 'Frequent changes in accounting policies will not enhance comparability…'

Thus it seems that regular review is important, as long as it does not lead to too frequent actual alterations in the policies concerned. In truth 'appropriate' is a seemingly intentionally vague concept, and the guidance given in the standard about how to choose accounting policies is also rather vague. The real import of this requirement is to ensure an entity does not have an excuse for retaining a policy that is unsuitable, while trying to ensure entities do not alter their policies with unseemly frequency.

Paragraphs 46 to 48 of the standard indicate that entities may wish to take into account recently issued FRSs that have not yet become mandatory when reviewing the appropriateness of their accounting policies, with paragraph 46 clearly stating that:

> 'where it is necessary either to implement a new accounting policy or to change an existing accounting policy, an entity will ensure wherever possible that the new accounting policy is in accordance with recently issued FRSs.'

Although an entity may take account of Financial Reporting Exposure Drafts (FREDs) in choosing and reviewing accounting policies, policies based on FREDs may only be adopted if they are consistent with the requirements of existing accounting standards and UITF abstracts.

7.4.1 Treatment of changes in policies and presentation under FRS 18

In accordance with FRS 3 all material adjustments resulting from changes in accounting policy should be treated as prior period adjustments. FRS 18 regards changes in presentation as being changes in accounting policy, and therefore requires all changes in presentation to be accounted for as changes in accounting policy:

> 'Where an entity changes the way it presents a particular item in the balance sheet or the profit and loss account, that is a change in accounting policy'.[282]

However paragraph 12 goes on the state that providing additional information is not a change in accounting policy. Thus where a more detailed analysis is provided, or when information is disclosed for the first time, that would not constitute a change in presentation and would not be a change in policy. Furthermore a change may involve both a change in presentation on the one hand, and in estimation technique on the other. In these circumstances, paragraph 13 of FRS 18 draws attention to the fact that care is required, since the change in presentation is treated as a change of accounting policy, but the change in estimation technique is not.

The ASB clearly recognises that changes in accounting policies and changes in estimation techniques can be hard to distinguish. In order to assist in this matter, Appendix 1 to the standard gives examples. These analyse typical change scenarios and classify them according to whether they represent a change to all or any of the following:

- recognition,
- presentation, and
- measurement basis.

Anything that involves an alteration to presentation, or to a measurement basis, is to be accounted for as a change in policy, as set out in FRS 3. In Appendix 1, the presentation change is illustrated by a depreciation charge example. A change to the location within the profit & loss account of the depreciation charge, from being within cost of sales to being within overheads, would be a change in presentation, and so would be accounted for as a change in policy.

A change of measurement basis is illustrated by a deferred tax example. If an entity altered its deferred tax provision to a discounted basis from an undiscounted one, this would be a change in a measurement basis, and thus a change in policy,[283] as would a change from using the closing rate to the average rate under SSAP 20 – Foreign currency translation.

However the consequences of making a change in recognition are rather less clearly explained in the standard. The standard is explicit that where an accounting standard allows a choice over what is to be recognised, that choice is a matter of accounting policy, and consequently any change is a change in policy.[284] However FRS 18 is not clear whether it is possible to have a change in recognition that is not a change in policy. A disclosure summary is provided below, which includes the disclosures required if an accounting policy is changed.

7.5 Selecting and changing estimation techniques under FRS 18

FRS 18 requires entities to select estimation techniques that enable its financial statements to give a true and fair view and which are consistent with the requirements of accounting standards, UITF abstracts and companies legislation.[285] If it is necessary to choose between estimation techniques, an entity should choose the 'most appropriate to its particular circumstances for the purpose of giving a true and fair view'.[286]

Paragraphs 52 and 53 of the standard further discuss the matters to be considered when choosing estimation techniques. They state that it is important for estimation techniques to be reliable, but point out that estimation techniques are only used in circumstances where an amount is unknown. Cost/benefit and materiality considerations play a part in the selection of estimation techniques, and great accuracy may not be justified.

Put into a practical context, it would appear that this means (for example) that if a machine has a ten year life, it may be impossible to be certain about the exact extent to which its useful life dissipates each year. In this case straight line is normally acceptable, rather than going to great lengths to establish the exact pattern of consumption.

The standard also mentions other factors that may be taken into account in the selection of estimation techniques. In particular comparability with financial statements of other entities, and understandability are mentioned.[287]

FRS 18 makes it explicit that a change to an estimation technique should not be accounted for as a prior period adjustment, unless it represents a correction of a fundamental error or another authority (standard, UITF abstract or legislation) requires it.[288] Appendix 1 to the standard gives examples of changes to estimation techniques, to assist in distinguishing them from changes in policies or presentation. Making these distinctions can be less than obvious, as shown by example 6b, which deals with a change in reporting an FRS 12 provision from an undiscounted basis to a discounted basis, because the effect of discounting has now become material. The appendix states that this would not be a change in either presentation or measurement basis, and thus would not be accounted for as a change in policy. This is because the change in measurement basis has occurred only because the item has become material; it is not a change of policy, in the sense that had the item been material previously, it would have been discounted previously.

Although not a change in policy, where a change in an estimation technique is material, an entity is required to disclose a description of the change, and where practicable, the effect of the change on the results for the current period.[289] FRS 18 does not contain any explicit guidance on accounting for changes in estimation techniques other than to state that they should not be accounted for as prior period adjustments. This implies that the impact of any change is recognised in the period in which the estimation technique is altered, unless a standard or other authority states otherwise.

7.6 Going concern, accruals and realisation under FRS 18

FRS 18 slightly ambiguously states that two concepts – going concern and accruals – 'play a pervasive role in financial statements, and hence in the selection of accounting policies'.[290] The standard noticeably increases and more precisely specifies the responsibilities of directors in the area of going concern. In particular the standard requires directors to assess whether there are any significant doubts about the entity's ability to continue as a going concern, and to disclose any material uncertainties that may cast doubt on the entity's ability to continue as one.

The requirement to report only realised profits is acknowledged, but it is made clear paragraph 18 of Appendix IV to the standard – *The development of the FRS*

– that 'the Board does not believe that it is useful to link prudence and realisation'. This represents a considerable change in thinking between FRS 18 and SSAP 2, and fundamentally amends the concept of prudence as it was defined in SSAP 2. In paragraph 14(d) of SSAP 2 prudence was defined by reference to realisation of profits with the specific requirement that profit should not be anticipated. The ASB's view inherent in FRS 18, and set out in Appendix IV, is that realisation is a less effective way to deliver reliability than focusing on reasonable certainty that a gain exists.

No discussion or definition of what is meant by reasonable certainty is contained within the standard; nor is it clear what thresholds are to be applied on order to determine whether or not an unrealised gain 'exists'. One clear implication of these matters is that the ASB has in mind a new and different definition of prudence, and is using the term in this new sense in the standard. However there is no explicit definition or elaboration of this 'new prudence', leaving preparers and auditors in the dark as to its application, and implying that the ASB is now paying little more than lip service to the once fundamental concept of prudence.

7.6.1 Basis on which financial statements are to be prepared

Instead of the four fundamental accounting concepts familiar from SSAP 2, FRS 18 requires the application of two bases of accounting in the preparation of financial statements: going concern and accruals. Going concern is to be used unless the entity concerned is being liquidated or has ceased trading, or there is no realistic alternative but to liquidate it or to cease trading, in which case the entity may, if appropriate, use a basis other than going concern.[291]

It is important to note that the requirement under FRS 18 for an entity to prepare its financial statements (except for cash flow information) on the accruals basis[292], will give different results from the application of the matching concept under SSAP 2. In the *Statement of Principles* matching does not form part of the rules on the recognition of assets and liabilities; consequently FRS 18 adopts the same stance:

> 'The accruals basis of accounting requires the non-cash effects of transactions and other events to be reflected, as far as is possible, in the financial statements for the accounting period in which they occur, and not, for example, in the period in which any cash involved is received or paid.'[293]

This definition of accruals does not include matching as part of the concept. For instance, in a situation where costs are incurred but revenue is delayed, the accruals basis of accounting embodied in FRS 18 does not imply that recognition of the costs should be postponed to match the revenue timing. That would be a matter for the recognition criteria embodied in various standards and, in particular, paragraph 27 of FRS 18 cites the definitions of assets and liabilities in FRS 5 – *Reporting the substance of transactions* – as having the accruals concept at their heart.

The subtlety of this assertion is to make it clear that the deferral of costs under the accruals concept will no longer be permitted if the resultant debit on the balance sheet does not meet the definition of an asset under FRS 5. The distinction between accruals and matching, therefore, is that the normal application of the matching concept resulted in the recognition of deferred costs that did not necessarily represent assets under FRS 5, whilst now, the application of the new accruals concept allows deferral only if there is an FRS 5 asset. Thus the recognition criteria embodied in the Statement of Principles are now at the centre of the accruals concept, rather than matching.

Finally, as a result of what the ASB seems to regard as a somewhat inconvenient Companies Act provision, paragraph 28 of FRS 18 requires that:

> 'an entity will have regard to requirements in companies legislation that only profits realised at the balance sheet date should be included in the profit and loss account'.

However paragraph 29 cannot quite resist pointing out that:

> 'The requirements in paragraph 28 relating to realised profits and the profit and loss account apply unless there are special reasons for departing from them.'

This appears to be a welcome and necessary clarification of wording when compared with the exposure draft which preceded FRS 18. Many commentators considered that FRED 21 actively encouraged businesses to ignore the realisation requirement embodied within company law.

The fair value based, balance sheet approach to reporting gains and losses that is being embraced by the ASB runs counter to the requirement to report only realised profits. Consequently we consider it is only a matter of time before the ASB seeks to remove the requirement to report only realised profits in the profit & loss account. A view has been confirmed by the publication in December 2000 of FRED 22 – *Revision of FRS 3 Reporting Financial Performance* – (see 6.2 above) which envisages a single performance statement making no distinction between realised and unrealised profits.

7.7 Disclosure of material going concern uncertainties under FRS 18

The ASB is to be congratulated on the important safeguards for investors it has incorporated into FRS 18 in the area of going concern. First the new standard makes it an explicit requirement that directors should assess whether there are 'significant doubts about an entity's ability to continue as a going concern'.[294] This is followed by an explicit requirement that any material uncertainties that may cast significant doubt on an entity's ability to continue as a going concern must be disclosed. Thus even if a decision is made to present financial statements on a going concern basis, if these are subject to material uncertainties, those uncertainties must be disclosed.[295]

Furthermore, there is a specific requirement that in making their assessment of going concern, directors should 'take into account all available information about the foreseeable future'. This disclosure is further refined by the necessity of stating, if the foreseeable future is less than one year, the fact that this is so.[296]

The effect of these provisions is (a) to strengthen the requirement for UK listed companies contained within paragraph D.13. of the combined code that 'the directors should report that the business is a going concern, with supporting assumptions or qualifications as necessary' and (b) to extend the requirement to all companies.

However it also has considerable implications for the audit of any company that has to make disclosures under these provisions of FRS 18. For example the term 'material uncertainty' used in the standard must be associated with the term 'fundamental uncertainty' used in auditing standards. Quite whether the terms are identical is unclear. However there is sufficient similarity to make it possible that an FRS 18 going concern material uncertainty disclosure might trigger a fundamental uncertainty disclosure under SAS 600.

7.8 Compliance with 'SORP's

FRS 18 introduces into UK GAAP for the first time the requirement for entities to make specific disclosures relating to Statements of Recommended Practice (SORPs). SORPs recommend accounting practices for specialised industries or sectors. They supplement accounting standards and other legal or regulatory requirements in the light of the special factors prevailing in a particular industry or sector.

The standard makes it clear that:

> 'Appropriate accounting policies will result in financial information being presented in such a way that enables users to discern and evaluate similarities in, and differences between, the nature and effects of transactions and other events taking place over time. In selecting accounting policies, an entity will assess whether accepted industry practices are appropriate to its particular circumstances. Such practices will be particularly persuasive if set out in a SORP that has been generally accepted by an industry or sector.'[297]

Put simply, an entity will have a substantial job on its hands to justify not complying with a SORP.

FRS 18 requires that if an entity's financial statements fall within the scope of a SORP, the title of that SORP must be stated and also whether the financial statements have been prepared in accordance with it. In the event of a departure, a brief description of how the financial statements depart from the SORP must be given. This description must include:

(a) the reasons why the treatment adopted is considered more appropriate; and

(b) details of any disclosures recommended by the SORP that have not been provided and the reasons why not.[298]

It should be noted that the provisions of FRS 18 concerning SORPs only become mandatory for accounting periods *beginning* on or after 24 December 2001.[299]

7.9 Required disclosures under FRS 18

Accounting policies and estimation techniques

The following should be disclosed:

- a description of each material policy;
- details of any changes to accounting policies, including:
  - a brief explanation of why the new policy is thought to be more appropriate;
  - where practicable the effect of the change on the results of the prior period in accordance with FRS 3;
  - where practicable the effect of the change on the results for the current period; and
  - if it is not practicable to give the effects of the changes, that fact should be stated with the reasons why it is not;
- a description of the significant estimation techniques;
  - where the effect of a change in estimation technique is material, a description of the change and, where practicable, the effect on the results for the current period.

Statements of recommended practice (SORPs)

The following should be disclosed where an entity's financial statements fall within the scope of a SORP:

- the title of that SORP and whether the financial statements have been prepared in accordance with it;
- in the event of a departure, a brief description of how the financial statements depart from the SORP, this description should include:
  - the reasons why the treatment adopted is considered more appropriate; and
  - details of any disclosures recommended by the SORP that have not been provided and the reasons why not.

Going concern

The following should be disclosed in relation to the going concern assessment required by FRS 18:

- any material uncertainties of which the directors are aware in making their assessment;
- where the foreseeable future considered by the directors is a period of less than one year from the date of approval of the financial statements, that fact; and
- where the financial statements are not prepared on a going concern basis, that fact, the reasons why the entity is not a going concern, together with a statement of the basis on which the financial statements have been prepared.

True and fair override

If there has been any material departure from an accounting standard, UITF abstract, or companies legislation, the following should be disclosed:

- particulars of the departure, the reasons for it and its effect;
- a 'clear and unambiguous' statement that there has been a departure, and from what, and that this is necessary to give a true and fair view;
- a statement of the treatment normally required and a description of the treatment actually adopted;
- a statement of why the prescribed treatment would not give a true and fair view; and
- a description of how the position shown in the financial statements is different as a result of the departure, normally with quantification, unless
  - quantification is already evident in the financial statements, or
  - the effect cannot be reasonably quantified, in which case the circumstances should be explained.

Where a departure continues in subsequent periods these disclosures should be made in all subsequent financial statements. If a departure concerns only the comparative figures, the disclosures for those comparative figures should be given. Where companies legislation requires an entity to state whether its financial statements have been prepared in accordance with applicable accounting standards, that statement must be cross referenced to, or include, the above true and fair override disclosures. Where companies legislation requires disclosure of particulars of a departure from a specific statutory requirement, disclosure equivalent to those set out above should be given.[300]

7.10 The strategic importance of FRS 18 to fair value based accounting

FRS 18 is necessary to provide the required conceptual underpinning for, and to remove conceptual impediments to, the establishment of a system of financial reporting in the UK that is not necessarily that widely known or understood. It is a system that considers fair value measurement to be paramount, and which rejects historical costs, matching and the realisation principle as irrelevant. This view of financial reporting does not regard the determination of taxable income or realised profits as the primary function of the process.

This idea is based on an approach to company financial reporting which the ASB have moved towards over the past decade. This idea is also embraced by an informal group that was known as the G4+1 group of accounting standard setters. This group has recently disbanded itself as a result of the formation of the restructured IASC and, in particular, the formation of the IASB. The G4+1 was not itself an official body, but was made up of members of staff from various official standard setting bodies. It nevertheless became influential through the publication of often controversial discussion papers that dealt with a variety of highly topical accounting issues. Recent examples have included: accounting for leases, reporting financial performance, and accounting for share-based payments. Though it ceased to exist in

February 2001, the G4+1 has effectively set the agenda for the development of new global accounting standards based on a balance sheet oriented, fair value model; and it seems certain that the IASB, and the ASB, will continue to follow it.

Under traditional accounting, profits are measured on the basis of transactions-based historical costs, through the application of such concepts as matching and SSAP 2 prudence. Generally, the balance sheet has limited significance in that it gives little indication of the value of the reporting entity. By contrast, under the fair value model the emphasis is on measuring the fair values of companies' assets and liabilities. The approach is reasonably easy to explain: it encompasses three stages of the recognition process, all of which are focused on assets and liabilities. These are:

- *initial recognition and measurement* (which is where an item is included in the primary financial statements for the first time, measured at its fair value),
- *subsequent re-measurement* (which involves changing the amount at which an already recognised asset or liability is stated in the primary financial statements) and
- *derecognition* (which is where an item that was until then recognised ceases to be recognised).

Under this model, *defining* income is relatively uncomplicated: assets minus liabilities equal ownership interest; gains and losses are increases and decreases in ownership interest (other than those relating to contributions from and distributions to owners). However, *ascertaining* income, which has to rely heavily on measuring the changes in fair value of assets and liabilities, is far from straightforward.

One consequence of this is that income will almost certainly be reported in a single statement of financial performance that aggregates all accrual-based trading income with fair value changes, whether realised or unrealised. Indeed, this is already envisaged in the UK through the publication of FRED 22 in December 2000. The impact of these changes for financial reporting will be far-reaching, and the pace of change from the traditional model to the fair value model will undoubtedly gather speed with the advent of the IASB, and the adoption of IAS throughout the European Union.

8 THE IASC'S INITIATIVES

8.1 The IASC conceptual framework

In May 1988, the Board of the IASC (before it was reconstituted as the IASB) issued an exposure draft – *Framework for the Preparation and Presentation of Financial Statements* – which set out its understanding of 'the conceptual framework that underlies the preparation and presentation of financial statements'.[301] This was converted without major change into a final statement in September 1989, although it is stressed within the statement that it will be revised from time to time in the light of the Board's experience in working with it.[302] The statement is not an accounting standard and does not override any specific IAS;[303] it therefore has much the same status as the FASB's concepts statements, and the ASB's *Statement of Principles.*

8.1.1 *The contents of the IASC's Framework*

The IASC's *Framework* is divided into seven major sections:

- The objective of financial statements
- Underlying assumptions
- Qualitative characteristics of financial statements
- The elements of financial statements
- Recognition of the elements of financial statements
- Measurement of the elements of financial statements
- Concepts of capital maintenance

The *Framework* is a relatively short document, just over 100 numbered paragraphs, and clearly is derived from the FASB's first six concepts statements. It is therefore open to the same criticisms and contains the same flaws as the FASB's framework, which are discussed at 3 above. The status quo seems to be taken as read by the *Framework*; as evidenced, for example, by the statement in the introduction to the effect that financial statements normally include a balance sheet, a profit and loss statement, a statement of changes in financial position and notes.[304] The statement is then devoted to applying its discussion to this traditional financial reporting package, without, for example, following the ICAS approach of considering the possibility of an entirely new package.

The objective of financial statements is quite familiar to readers of either the FASB or the ASB equivalents:

> 'to provide information about the financial position, performance and changes in financial position of an enterprise that is useful to a wide range of users in making economic decisions.'[305]

The remainder of the section contains a quite unexceptionable discussion of how users need to know about profitability and financial position, cash generation and so forth.

The underlying assumptions are, significantly, the accruals basis of accounting and the going concern basis. Prudence is not an underlying assumption, and accruals is defined, as in FRS 18, so as to omit matching from the concept. The statement specifically says that 'the application of the matching concept under this framework does not allow the recognition of items in the balance sheet which do not meet the definition of assets and liabilities'.[306]

The qualitative characteristics advanced in the document are also taken directly from the FASB conceptual framework project. The familiar list of understandability, relevance, reliability and comparability is advanced, and has clearly influenced the subsequent ASB conceptual framework document, the *Statement of Principles.* This similarity can be illustrated by the paragraph on understandability, which exactly like its ASB equivalent in both the *Statement of Principles* and FRS 18 (see 5.4. and 7.3 above) is defined as understandable by users with:

> '... a reasonable knowledge of business and economic activities and accounting and a willingness to study the information with reasonable diligence.[307]

This part of the Framework also contains similarly equivalent paragraphs dealing with neutrality, prudence (which is similarly characterised as caution rather than as an SSAP 2 fundamental concept governing profit recognition) and substance over form.

The section of the Framework that deals with the elements of financial statements is also derived from its FASB equivalent. Assets, liabilities and equity are defined as:

'(a) An asset is a resource controlled by the enterprise as a result of past events and from which future economic benefits are expected to flow to the enterprise.

(b) A liability is a present obligation of the enterprise arising from past events, the settlement of which is expected to result in an outflow from the enterprise of resources embodying economic benefits.

(c) Equity is the residual interest in the assets of the enterprise after deducting all its liabilities.'[308]

Thus the future economic benefit definition of assets, complete with its logical failing described in 5.1.1 above, is adopted wholesale from the FASB conceptual framework project. Similarly the 'present obligation arising from a past event' definition of a liability is adopted with the same consequences for recognising provisions which, if based solely on the basis of a management decision, will not qualify under this definition. Income and expenses are defined in terms of balance sheet recognition criteria, in the same manner as the UK and US frameworks. Realisation is not mentioned at all in the IASC's *Framework.*

The recognition criteria adopted in the Framework are also entirely familiar from other conceptual framework projects. Thus an asset will be recognised if 'it is probable that the future economic benefits will flow to the enterprise and the asset has a cost or value that can be measured reliably'.[309] A liability is recognised when

'when it is probable that an outflow of resources embodying economic benefits will result from the settlement of a present obligation and the amount at which the settlement will take place can be measured reliably.'[310] Just as with its UK and US equivalents, the recognition criteria for income and expenses are derived by deduction from these definitions.

Measurement is dealt with in an extremely cursory and entirely descriptive manner, in three paragraphs, ending with the statement that historical cost is most commonly adopted. No recommendations are made about which measurement base is considered the most satisfactory. Finally, there is a short discussion of the concepts of capital maintenance. This describes physical and financial capital maintenance concepts, and ends rather unconvincingly with the assertion that the *Framework* is:

> 'applicable to a range of accounting models and provides guidance on preparing and presenting the financial statements constructed under the [any] chosen model.'[311]

8.1.2 Assessment of the IASC's Framework

There is essentially no difference between the IASC's *Framework* and the ASB's *Statement of Principles* (see 5 above), which was published more than ten years later. They both rest upon the original FASB work embodied in its concepts statements (see 3 above). In effect the IASC's *Framework* is little more than a synopsis of the FASB conceptual framework. It is perhaps unfortunate, and certainly a lost opportunity, that a major body has not taken the chance presented by the publication of a conceptual framework document to explore more fundamentally the questions posed by such an endeavour. A conceptual framework should be more than an ex post facto justification of an already chosen approach, in our view. Alternatively, it is also true that the wholesale adoption of the FASB approach by the IASC does at least mean that harmonisation of global accounting becomes more, rather than less likely, even if on a basis that has theoretical and practical drawbacks.

9 CONCLUSION

This chapter provides an outline of the immense amount of energy that has been expended (both on the part of individuals and on the part of specifically constituted committees) in attempting to establish an agreed conceptual framework for financial reporting. It has also highlighted the irreconcilable differences and logical difficulties that exist in the various accounting theories that have developed over the years.

The emergence of the IASC's and the ASB's conceptual framework documents, both heavily indebted to the FASB's work from the 1970s, might have raised the prospect of a degree of rigour and consistency being applied to accounting standards issued by all those bodies. In practice, these framework documents have been used to prevent practices disliked by the standard setters, but have been conveniently ignored when a standard is required that conflicts with them. Inconsistencies of this nature are probably inevitable whilst matters that are fundamental to their resolution remain unresolved. Since Edwards and Bell and

Maurice Moonitz (see 4.3.2 and 2.2 above respectively) published their work in the early 1960s, there has been controversy over, and disagreement about, the valuation basis to be used in financial reporting. These disagreements have been over whether current values should to be used in place of historical costs at all, and if so what type of current value system is to be used. Further disagreement surrounds the way current values are to be determined even if a given system is selected.

What has emerged is the adoption of a particular balance sheet orientated model by the major global standard setters, the IASB, the FASB and the ASB. It seems likely that this model has been adopted because it supports the fair value model, described at 7.10 above and elsewhere, which appears to be the goal towards which the IASB and the ASB wish to move financial reporting. We can understand the attraction of stating all assets and liabilities at 'fair value' but there are important issues about what this means in practice to resolve. Most obviously, the enduring underlying difficulties and disagreements, referred to above, have not been removed by the common adoption of the words 'fair value' if each standard setter means something different by the term.

It is clearly the view of the authors of the JWG draft standard – *Financial Instruments and Similar Items* – (discussed in Chapter 10 at 1.1) that determining fair values should be a matter of market price based exit values. By contrast, a great deal of the extant IASC literature takes an entity specific, value in use approach, and where prices are referred to, such as in IAS 40 – *Investment properties* – determining fair value is couched in much broader terms than that used by the JWG document. We consider, therefore, that the current appearance of unanimity between standard setters in their adoption of fair values, disguises the continued existence of the same unresolved fundamental difficulties that have existed for many decades.

We agree that financial reports should be relevant and reliable, but these terms as used in the current literature seem in danger of being confused. Much of what is published by the standard setters and their think tanks seems to carry a presumption that a fair value, however determined, will always be relevant. This is not obviously the case, particularly where fair values are not based upon observable market prices, or where markets do not exist for the item concerned. It is an open question whether a 'fair value' that is not based upon a proper market for the item in question, is in fact more relevant than some other measure. Therefore we are concerned that the importance of reliability is in danger of being overshadowed by a presumption of relevance attaching to fair values, however arrived at, with the consequent subjectivity and volatility having a detrimental effect on financial reporting. Our view is that reliability is a necessary condition for information to be relevant, and that information needs to pass a reliability threshold before it will be considered relevant at all. Hence we consider it is important that reliability is given due weight under a fair value system in cases where observable market prices are not available.

At the global level, the demand for harmonisation is being led by the EU, who intend to require all listed EU companies to apply IAS in the preparation of their consolidated accounts. This is an important development in European accounting that we strongly support, and that we hope will contribute to the development of an eventual global GAAP. To be successful, the IASB needs to help this initiative remain recognisably within the accepted basis of European financial reporting, and to be careful not to push European companies towards unnecessary change which confuses unrealised unreliable fair value changes with real revenue and earnings generated by commercial activity.

References

1 FRS 15, *Tangible Fixed Assets*, ASB, February 1999, para. 4.
2 Discussion Paper, *Measurement of tangible fixed assets*, ASB, October 1996, para. 6.6.
3 For a full discussion on the politicisation of accounting see: David Solomons, 'The Politicization of Accounting', *Journal of Accountancy*, November 1978, p. 71.
4 Maurice Moonitz, *The Basic Postulates of Accounting*, Accounting Research Study No. 1, AICPA, 1961, Preface.
5 *Ibid.*
6 Robert T. Sprouse and Maurice Moonitz, *A Tentative Set of Broad Accounting Principles for Business Enterprises*, Accounting Research Study No. 3, AICPA, 1962.
7 *Ibid.*, p. 14.
8 *Ibid.*, p. 27.
9 APB Statement No. 4, *Basic Concepts and Accounting Principles Underlying Financial Statements of Business Enterprises*, AICPA, October 1970.
10 *Ibid.*, para. 3.
11 *Ibid.*, para. 132.
12 Report of the Study Group on the Objectives of Financial Statements, *Objectives of Financial Statements*, AICPA, October 1973, p. 65.
13 *Ibid.*
14 *Ibid.*
15 Report of the Study Group on the Objectives of Financial Statements, *Objectives of Financial Statements*, AICPA, October 1973.
16 *Ibid.*, p. 13.
17 *Ibid.*, pp. 57–60.
18 FASB Discussion Memorandum, *Conceptual Framework for Accounting and Reporting: Consideration of the Report of the Study Group on the Objectives of Financial Statements*, FASB, June 6, 1974.
19 FASB, *Scope and Implications of the Conceptual Framework Project*, FASB, December 2, 1976.
20 *Ibid.*, p. 5.
21 *Ibid.*, p. 2.
22 *Ibid.*, pp. 5 and 6.
23 SFAC No. 1, *Objectives of Financial Reporting by Business Enterprises*, FASB, November 1978, para. 7.
24 *Ibid.*, para. 9.
25 *Ibid.*, para. 24.
26 *Ibid.*, para. 34.
27 *Ibid.*, para. 37.
28 *Ibid.*, para. 24.
29 *Ibid.*, footnote 6.
30 Lucia S. Chang and Kenneth S. Most, *Financial Statements and Investment Decisions*, Miami: Florida International University, 1979.
31 *Ibid.*, p. 33.
32 SFAC 1, para. 43.
33 *Ibid.*, para. 50.
34 *Ibid.*, para. 51.
35 SFAC No. 2, *Qualitative Characteristics of Accounting Information*, FASB, May 1980, Figure 1.
36 SFAC 1, para. 34.
37 SFAC 2, para. 36.
38 *Ibid.*, p. x.
39 *Ibid.*, para. 90.
40 *Ibid.*, p. xi.
41 *Ibid.*, para. 56.
42 *Ibid.*
43 *Ibid.*, para. 51.
44 *Ibid.*, p. xvi.
45 *Ibid.*
46 *Ibid.*, para. 59.
47 IAS 39, *Financial Instruments: Recognition and Measurement*, IASC, December 1998, para. 70.
48 SFAC 2, paras. 91–97.
49 *Ibid.*, para. 93.
50 *Ibid.*, para. 95.

51 SFAC No. 6, *Elements of Financial Statements*, a replacement of FASB Concepts Statement No. 3, FASB, December 1985, para. 25.
52 *Ibid.*, para. 27.
53 *Ibid.*, para. 28.
54 *Ibid.*, para. 35.
55 *Ibid.*, para. 36.
56 *Ibid.*, para. 49.
57 *Ibid.*, para. 66.
58 *Ibid.*
59 *Ibid.*, para. 67.
60 *Ibid.*, para. 70.
61 SFAC 1, para. 43.
62 SFAC 6, p. 1, footnote 1.
63 *Ibid.*, para. 78.
64 *Ibid.*, para. 80.
65 *Ibid.*, para. 82.
66 *Ibid.*, para. 83.
67 *Ibid.*, para. 77.
68 See, for example, SFAC No. 3, *Elements of Financial Statements of Business Enterprises*, FASB, December 1980, para. 58.
69 SFAC No. 5, *Recognition and Measurement in Financial Statements of Business Enterprises*, FASB, December 1984, para. 66.
70 *Ibid.*, paras. 66–70.
71 *Ibid.*, paras. 45–48.
72 *Ibid.*, para. 58.
73 *Ibid.*, para. 63.
74 *Ibid.*, paras. 33 and 34.
75 *Ibid.*, para. 35.
76 David Solomons, 'The FASB's Conceptual Framework: An evaluation', *Journal of Accountancy*, June 1986, pp. 114–124, at p. 122.
77 *Ibid.*, p. 124.
78 *Ibid.*
79 Reed K. Storey and Sylvia Storey, *Special Report: The Framework of Financial Accounting Concepts and Standards*, FASB, January 1998, p. 158.
80 *Ibid.*
81 *Ibid.*, p. 160.
82 *Ibid.*, p. 161.
83 *Ibid.*, p. 74.
84 *Ibid.*, p. 75.
85 *Ibid.*, p. 74.
86 *Ibid.*, p. 74.
87 *Ibid.*, p. 83.
88 Statement of Financial Accounting Concepts 7, *Using Cash Flow Information and Present Value in Accounting Measurements*, FASB, February 2000, para. 19.
89 *Ibid.*, para. 21.
90 *Ibid.*, para. 23.
91 *Ibid.*, paras. 31 and 37
92 *Ibid.*, para. 41.
93 *Ibid.*, para. 75
94 *Ibid.*, Glossary of terms.
95 Draft standard *Financial Instruments and similar items*, , JWG, December 2000, paras. 118 to 121.
96 Stephen A. Zeff, *Accounting Horizons*, 'A Perspective on the U.S. Public/Private-Sector Approach to the Regulation of Financial Reporting', Vol. 9 No. 1, March 1995, p. 60.
97 SSAP 2, *Disclosure of accounting policies*, ASC, November 1971.
98 *Ibid.*
99 CA 85, Sch. 4. paras. 9–13.
100 *Ibid.*, para. 14.
101 This is a recognised conflict between IAS 37 and the EU Fourth Directive that the European Commission plans to eliminate during its programme to modernise the accounting directives – see chapter 1 at 3.4
102 SSAP 2, para. 15.
103 *Ibid.*, para. 18.
104 *The Corporate Report*, A discussion paper published for comment by the Accounting Standards Steering Committee, London, 1975.
105 *Ibid.*, para. 0.1.
106 *Ibid.*, para. 0.2.
107 The committee's recommended package of information which should be contained in the annual corporate reports of business enterprises is listed in Appendix 2 of the discussion paper.
108 *The Corporate Report*, para. 0.3.
109 *Ibid.*, para. 1.1.
110 *Ibid.*, para. 1.8.
111 *Ibid.*, para. 1.9. The seven user groups identified were: (a) the equity investor group, (b) the loan creditor group, (c) the employee group, (d) the analyst-adviser group, (e) the business contact group, (f) the government and (g) the public.
112 *Ibid.*, paras. 2.1–2.40.
113 *Ibid.*, para. 3.2.
114 *Ibid.*, para. 3.3.
115 *Ibid.*, para. 4.30.
116 *Ibid.*, para. 4.40.
117 *Ibid.*, para. 6.56.
118 *Ibid.*, paras. 6.56 and 6.57.
119 *Ibid.*, para. 7.4.
120 *Ibid.*, para. 7.15.
121 *Ibid.*, paras. 7.40 and 7.43.
122 Report of the Inflation Accounting Committee, *Inflation Accounting*, Cmnd. 6225, London: HMSO, 1975, (the Sandilands Report).
123 *Ibid.*, p. iv.
124 *Ibid.*, para. 144.
125 *Ibid.*, Chapter 12.
126 SSAP 7 (Provisional), *Accounting for changes in the purchasing power of money*, May 1974.
127 SSAP 7 recommended that the RPI should be used for this purpose.
128 SSAP 7, para. 12.
129 The Sandilands Report, para. 20.

130 *Ibid.*, para. 422.

131 *Ibid.*, paras. 411 and 412.

132 *Ibid.*, para. 415.

133 Edwards and Bell have made significant contributions in the areas of income determination and value measurement — however, it is beyond the scope of this book to provide a detailed analysis of their theories. Their case for income and value measurement based on replacement costs may be found in their classic work: E. O. Edwards and P. W. Bell, *The Theory and Measurement of Business Income*, University of California Press, 1961.

134 The Sandilands Report, para. 453.

135 *Ibid.*, para. 499.

136 Kenneth MacNeal, *Truth in Accounting*, Philadelphia: University of Pennsylvania Press, 1939.

137 R. J. Chambers, *Accounting, Evaluation and Economic Behaviour*, Prentice-Hall, 1966.

138 R. R. Sterling, *Theory of the Measurement of Enterprise Income*, University of Kansas Press, 1970.

139 R. J. Chambers, *The Design of Accounting Standards*, University of Sydney Accounting Research Centre, Monograph No. 1, 1980.

140 Edward Stamp, 'Does the Chambers' Evidence Support the CoCoA System', *Accounting and Business Research*, Spring 1983, pp. 119–127.

141 *Ibid.*, p. 127.

142 The Sandilands Report, para. 510.

143 The Institute of Chartered Accountants of Scotland, *Making Corporate Reports Valuable*, London: Kogan Page, 1988, paras. 6.20–6.23.

144 Lee has published numerous papers on the subject of cash flow accounting, the ideas of which have been drawn together in his book: Tom Lee, *Cash Flow Accounting*, Wokingham, Van Nostrand Reinhold (UK), 1984.

145 Lawson has published widely on the subject of cash flow accounting — see, for example: G. H. Lawson, 'Cash-flow Accounting', *The Accountant*, October 28th, 1971, pp. 586–589; G. H. Lawson, 'The Measurement of Corporate Profitability on a Cash-flow Basis', *The International Journal of Accounting Education and Research*, Vol. 16, No. 1, pp. 11–46.

146 Tom Lee, *op. cit.*, p. 51.

147 *Ibid.*, pp. 51–52.

148 Lee presents a quantified example of his proposed cash flow reporting system, *Ibid.*, pp. 57–72.

149 The Sandilands Report, para. 518.

150 *Ibid.*, para. 517.

151 *Ibid.*, para. 537.

152 For a detailed discussion of the capital maintenance concepts which apply in the Sandilands proposals, see: H. C. Edey, 'Sandilands and the Logic of Current Cost', *Accounting and Business Research*, Volume 9, No. 35, Summer 1979, pp. 191–200.

153 ASC, ED 24, *Current cost accounting*, para. 6.

154 ASC, *Inflation accounting — an interim recommendation by the Accounting Standards Committee*, November 1977.

155 *Ibid.*, para. 4.

156 *Ibid.*, para. 9.

157 SSAP 16, *Current cost accounting*, March 1980.

158 *Ibid.*, para. 48.

159 In January 1983, the Research Board of the ICAEW initiated a research project into the usefulness of current cost accounting. The research was divided into a number of studies designed to investigate the uses made by different interest groups, the benefits and the costs of current cost accounting; the whole project was undertaken under the control of the ICAEW's then Director of Research, Professor Bryan Carsberg. The project was completed in September 1983 and the results were made available to the ASC to assist with its review of SSAP 16. See: Bryan Carsberg and Michael Page (Joint Editors), *Current Cost Accounting: The Benefits and the Costs*, ICAEW, 1984.

160 Richard Macve, *A Conceptual Framework for Financial Accounting and Reporting: the possibilities for an agreed structure*, A report prepared at the request of the Accounting Standards Committee, ICAEW, 1981, Preface, p. 3.

161 *Ibid.*, Chapter 6, *passim.*

162 *Ibid.*, p. 52.

163 *Ibid.*, p. 64.

164 David Solomons, *Guidelines for Financial Reporting Standards*, A Paper Prepared for The Research Board of the Institute of Chartered Accountants in England and Wales and addressed to the Accounting Standards Committee, ICAEW, 1989, (the Solomons Report).

165 Edward Stamp, *Corporate Reporting: Its Future Evolution*, a research study published by the Canadian Institute of Chartered Accountants, 1980, (the Stamp Report), Ch. 1, para. 3.

166 Edward Stamp, 'First steps towards a British conceptual framework', *Accountancy*, March 1982, pp. 123-130.

167 Stamp's qualitative criteria were ranked (from most important to least important) by the ASC members as follows (*Ibid.*, Figure 2, p. 126): relevance, clarity, substance over form, timeliness, comparability, materiality, freedom from bias, objectivity, rationality, full disclosure, consistency, isomorphism, verifiability, cost/benefit effectiveness, non-arbitrariness, data availability, flexibility, uniformity, precision, conservatism.

168 The Stamp Report, Chapter 2.
169 ICAS, *Making Corporate Reports Valuable*, para. 0.2.
170 *Ibid.*, Chapter 8.
171 *Ibid.*, paras. 1.1–1.20, *passim.*
172 *Ibid.*, para. 3.6.
173 *Ibid.*, para. 3.11.
174 The Corporate Report, paras. 2.2–2.8.
175 ICAS, *Making Corporate Reports Valuable*, para. 3.12.
176 *Ibid.*, para. 6.36.
177 *Ibid.*
178 *Ibid.*, para. 6.24.
179 The Institute of Chartered Accountants of Scotland, *Making Corporate Reports Valuable — The Literature Surveys*, ICAS, 1988.
180 *Ibid.*, p. 301.
181 ICAS, *Making Corporate Reports Valuable*, paras. 7.12–7.20, *passim.*
182 *Ibid.*, para. 7.21.
183 *Ibid.*, paras. 7.23–7.26, *passim.*
184 *Ibid.*, paras. 7.27–7.32, *passim.*
185 *Ibid.*, para. 7.35.
186 *Ibid.*, para. 7.39.
187 *Ibid.*, para. 5.44.
188 *Ibid.*, para. 7.54.
189 David Solomons, *Guidelines for Financial Reporting Standards*, p. 17.
190 *Ibid.*, p. 18.
191 *Ibid.*
192 *Ibid.*, p. 20.
193 *Ibid.*, p. 21.
194 *Ibid.*, pp. 23–28.
195 *Ibid.*, p. 43.
196 *Ibid.*, pp. 51–52.
197 Accounting Horizons, vol. 9 no.1, pages 42-51
198 David Solomons, *Guidelines for Financial Reporting Standards*, p. 53.
199 *Ibid.*
200 *Ibid.*, p. 54.
201 *Ibid.*, p. 55.
202 *Ibid.*, p. 56.
203 *Ibid.*, p. 69.
204 *The Future Shape of Financial Reports*, ICAEW/ICAS, 1991, para. 1-2.
205 *Ibid.*, paras. 3-1 to 3-5.
206 *Foreword to Accounting Standards*, ASB, June 1993, para. 4.
207 Statement of Principles Exposure Draft, *Statement of Principles for Financial Reporting*, ASB, November 1995.
208 *Statement of Principles for Financial Reporting – the way ahead, progress paper on the exposure draft*, ASB, July 1996.
209 Statement of Principles Revised Exposure Draft, *Statement of Principles for Financial Reporting*, ASB, March 1999.
210 Statement of Principles for Financial Reporting, ASB, December 1999.
211 *Ibid.*, Chapter 1, Principles.
212 *Ibid.*, Chapter 1, Principles
213 *Ibid.*, para. 1.19.
214 *Ibid.*, Chapter 1, para. 1.19.
215 *Ibid.*, para. 1.3
216 *Ibid.*, para. 1.11.
217 *Ibid.*, para. 1.18
218 *Ibid.*, Chapter 2, Principles.
219 *Ibid.*, Chapter 2, para. 2.8.
220 *Ibid.*, Chapter 3, Principles.
221 *Ibid.*, Chapter 3, Principles.
222 *Ibid.*, para. 3.8 .
223 *Ibid.*, paras. 3.21-3.22.
224 *Ibid.*, para. 3.26 .
225 *Ibid.*, Chapter 3 Principles.
226 *Ibid.*, para. 3.31-3.32.
227 *Ibid.*, Chapter 3, Principles.
228 *Ibid.*, para. 3.25(b).
229 *Ibid.*, para. 3.37.
230 *Ibid.*, Chapter 4 Principles.
231 *Ibid.*, para. 4.8
232 *Ibid.*, para. 4.8.
233 *Ibid.*, para. 4.9.
234 *Ibid.*, para. 4.14.
235 *Ibid.*, para. 4.15.
236 *Ibid.*, para. 4.17.
237 *Ibid.*, para. 4.21.
238 *Ibid.*, para..4.21.
239 *Ibid.*, para. 4.23.
240 *Ibid.*, para. 4.26.
241 *Ibid.*, Chapter 4, para. 4.31.
242 *Ibid.*, para. 4.37.
243 *Ibid.*, para. 4.39.
244 *Ibid.*, para. 4.39
245 *Ibid.*, Chapter 4, Principles.
246 *Ibid.*
247 *Ibid.*, Chapter 5, Principles.
248 *Ibid.*, Chapter 5, Principles.
249 *Ibid.*, para. 5.1.
250 *Ibid.*, para. 5.12.
251 *Ibid.*, para. 5.18.
252 *Ibid.*, paras. 5.22-5.25.
253 *Ibid.*, para. 5.21.
254 *Ibid.*, para. 6.2.
255 *Ibid.*, para. 6.4.
256 *Ibid.*, para. 6.18.
257 *Ibid.*, para. 6.28.
258 *Ibid.*, Chapter 7, Principles.
259 *Ibid.*, para. 8.4.
260 *Ibid.*, para. 8.13.
261 Accounting Standards Board Working Paper, *Discounting in Financial Reporting*, ASB, April 1997, p. 3.
262 *Ibid.*, para. 9.1.
263 *Ibid.*, para 1.6.

264 Discussion paper, *Reporting Financial Performance; Proposals for Change*, ASB, June 1999, p. 1.
265 Exposure draft, *Revision of FRS 3: Reporting Financial Performance,* ASB, December, Definitions.
266 *Ibid.,* paras. 14, 15.
267 *Ibid.,* para. 91.
268 FRS 18 Accounting policies, ASB December 2000, paras. 66, 67.
269 *Ibid.*, para. 4.
270 *Ibid.*, para. 4.
271 *Ibid.*, para. 4.
272 *Ibid.*, para. 14.
273 *Ibid.*, para. 15.
274 *Ibid.*, para. 17.
275 *Ibid.*, paras. 30, 31.
276 *Ibid.*, para. 34.
277 *Ibid.*, para. 35.
278 *Ibid.*, para. 39.
279 *Ibid.*, para. 41.
280 *Ibid.*, para. 18.
281 *Ibid.*, para. 38
282 *Ibid.*, paras. 12.
283 *Ibid.*, Appendix 1, examples 3, 4(a), 6(a).
284 *Ibid.*, Para. 9.
285 *Ibid.*, para. 50.
286 *Ibid.*, para. 51.
287 *Ibid.*, para. 53.
288 *Ibid.*, para. 54.
289 *Ibid.*, para. 58(d).
290 *Ibid.*, para. 20.
291 *Ibid.*, para. 21.
292 *Ibid.*, para. 25.
293 *Ibid.*, para. 27.
294 *Ibid.*, para. 23.
295 *Ibid.*, para. 61.
296 *Ibid.*, para. 61.
297 *Ibid.*, para. 40.
298 *Ibid.*, para. 58.
299 *Ibid.*, para. 67.
300 *Ibid.*, paras. 55 to 65.
301 Exposure Draft, *Framework for the Preparation and Presentation of Financial Statements*, IASC, May 1988.
302 *Framework for the Preparation and Presentation of Financial Statements*, IASC, September 1989, para. 4.
303 *Ibid.*, para. 2.
304 *Ibid.*, para. 12.
305 *Ibid.*, paras. 22, 23.
306 *Ibid.*, para. 95.
307 *Ibid.*, para. 49.
308 *Ibid.*, para. 25.
309 *Ibid.*, para. 88.
310 *Ibid.*, para. 91.
311 *Ibid.*, para. 110.

Chapter 3 Revenue recognition

1 THE NATURE OF REVENUE

Revenue is generally discussed in accounting literature in terms of inflows of assets to an enterprise which occur as a result of outflows of goods and services from the enterprise. For this reason, the concept of revenue has normally been associated with specific accounting procedures which were primarily directed towards determining the timing and measurement of revenue and the debate has taken place in the context of the historical cost double-entry system. For example, APB Statement No. 4 defined revenue as the "gross increases in assets or gross decreases in liabilities recognized and measured in conformity with generally accepted accounting principles that result from those types of profit-directed activities of an enterprise that can change owners' equity".[1] The accounting principles which evolved focused on determining when transactions should be recognised in the financial statements, what amounts were involved in each transaction, how these amounts should be classified and how they should be allocated between accounting periods.

Historical cost accounting in its pure form avoids having to take a valuation approach to financial reporting by virtue of the fact that it is transactions-based; in other words, it relies on transactions to determine the recognition and measurement of assets, liabilities, revenues and expenses. Over the life of an enterprise, its total income will be represented by net cash flows generated; however, because of the requirement to prepare periodic financial statements, it is necessary to break up the enterprise's operating cycle into artificial periods. The effect of this is that at each reporting date the enterprise will have entered into a number of transactions which are incomplete; for example, it might have delivered a product or service to a customer for which payment has not been received, or it might have received payment in respect of a product or service yet to be delivered. Alternatively, it might have expended cash on costs which relate to future sales transactions, or it might have received goods and services which it has not yet paid for in cash. Consequently, the most important accounting questions which have to be answered revolve around how to allocate the effects of these incomplete transactions between periods for reporting purposes, as opposed to simply letting them fall into the periods in which cash is either received or paid. Under historical cost accounting this allocation process is based on two, sometimes conflicting, fundamental accounting concepts: accruals (or matching), which attempts to move the costs associated with earning revenues to the periods in which the related revenues will be reported; and prudence, under which revenue and profits are not anticipated, whilst anticipated losses are provided for as soon as they are foreseen, with the result that costs are not deferred to the future if there is doubt as to their recoverability.

As a result, the pure historical cost balance sheet contains items of two types: cash (and similar monetary items), and debits and credits which arise as a result of shifting the effects of transactions between reporting periods by applying the accruals and prudence concepts; in other words, the balance sheet simply reflects the balances which result from the enterprise preparing an accruals-based profit and loss account rather than a receipts and payments account. A non-monetary asset under the historical cost system is purely a deferred cost which has been incurred before the balance sheet date and, by applying the accruals concept, is expected (provided it passes the prudence test) to benefit periods beyond the balance sheet date, so as to justify its being carried forward. Similarly, the balance sheet incorporates non-monetary credit balances which are awaiting recognition in the profit and loss account but, as a result of the application of the prudence concept, have been deferred to future reporting periods.

It is the aim of this chapter to suggest broad principles under the existing historical cost accounting system for the recognition of revenues earned from operations. At the same time, though, we are mindful of the fact that the ASB's *Statement of Principles* and the IASC's *Framework* (see Chapter 2 at 5 and 8) have introduced a strong balance sheet focus to income recognition that will change, over time, the basis on which gains and losses are recognised. Nevertheless, the traditional approach to revenue recognition remains in place for most practical purposes.

Meanwhile, the IASC has already embraced an accounting model based on fair values, meaning that gains and losses are determined by reference to the change in fair value that has occurred over the financial reporting period. This approach is set out in IAS 39 – *Financial Instruments: Recognition and Measurement* (see Chapter 10 at 4), IAS 40 – *Investment Property* (see Chapter 12 at 5.3) and IAS 41 – *Agriculture* (see 3.2.3 below).

Because, extraordinarily, there is rather limited literature on revenue recognition under UK GAAP, and no accounting standard on the topic, this chapter discusses the subject drawing on both IASC and US pronouncements. IAS 18 – *Revenue* – provides the main source of guidance on revenue recognition, but several other standards also address revenue recognition issues. However, the US particularly has a substantial body of literature on revenue recognition which can prove useful when there is no UK or IAS guidance available.

2 REALISED PROFITS

The term 'realised profits' was introduced into UK company legislation in the Companies Act 1980 as a result of the implementation of the Second EC Directive on company law, which provided the basic framework for the co-ordination of national provisions dealing with the maintenance, increase and reduction of the capital of public limited companies.[2] The Directive stated that the amount of a distribution to shareholders may not exceed the amount of the profits at the end of the last financial year plus any profits brought forward and sums drawn from reserves available for this purpose, less any losses brought forward and sums placed to reserve in accordance with the law or the statutes.[3]

As a result, the 1980 Act restricted a company's profits available for distribution to its accumulated realised profits less accumulated realised losses, and in so doing reversed the principle which had been laid down in a number of legal cases which permitted companies to make distributions out of current profits without making good past losses. Nevertheless, it is clear that profit for this purpose is discussed in the context of individual companies and not of groups, and that intra-group transactions are sometimes capable of generating realised and, therefore, distributable profits.

The 1980 Act did not define 'realised profits', although a definition was subsequently provided as a result of the implementation of the Fourth EC Directive in the Companies Act 1981. This definition, which was later incorporated into Schedule 4 to the Companies Act 1985, has been amended by the Companies Act 1989, and is now contained in section 262(3) of the Act. It reads as follows: 'References in this Part to "realised profits" and "realised losses", in relation to a company's accounts, are to such profits or losses of the company as fall to be treated as realised in accordance with principles generally accepted, at the time when the accounts are prepared, with respect to the determination for accounting purposes of realised profits or losses.

'This is without prejudice to—

(a) the construction of any other expression (where appropriate) by reference to accepted accounting principles or practice, or

(b) any specific provision for the treatment of profits or losses of any description as realised.'

Whilst the Part of the Act referred to in the above definition is Part VII – Accounts and Audit – the definition is given a slightly wider application through section 742(2) which states that 'references in this Act to "realised profits" and "realised losses", in relation to a company's accounts, shall be construed in accordance with section 262(3)'.

This definition is clearly not concerned with GAAP in its broad sense, but with generally accepted accounting principles for determining realised profits for accounting purposes only. In any event, it might be argued that such principles do not necessarily exist, since UK accounting principles are directed towards the recognition and disclosure of items in the financial statements of entities in order to present a true and fair view, and not towards the determination of realised profits.

Nevertheless, in its technical release on the subject (TR 481), the CCAB indicated that the term 'principles generally accepted' incorporates the legal principles laid down in Schedule 4 of the Companies Act 1985 and the requirements of the SSAPs.[4] TR 481 concluded that 'a profit which is required by statements of standard accounting practice to be recognised in the profit and loss account should normally be treated as a realised profit, unless the SSAP specifically indicates that it should be treated as unrealised'.[5]

The difficulty that arises from this interpretation is that there are a number of areas of profit recognition which are not, as yet, dealt with in accounting standards; furthermore, certain areas which are covered by accounting standards incorporate inconsistencies in approach. For this reason, it is necessary to establish broad principles for determining 'realised profit'. Some might hold the view that SSAP 2's definition of the prudence concept does, in fact, provide a basis for recognising realised profits in that it states that 'revenue and profits are not anticipated, but are recognised by inclusion in the profit and loss account when realised in the form either of cash or of other assets the ultimate cash realisation of which can be assessed with reasonable certainty'.[6] Though others hold the view that this definition may be flawed, since the emphasis on 'cash' and 'ultimate cash realisation' would appear to rule out the recognition of barter transactions or even the accrual of investment income on a time basis. In any event, in December 2000 the ASB published FRS 18 – *Accounting Policies* – which eliminates SSAP 2's definition of 'prudence' for accounting periods ending after 22 June 2001 (see Chapter 2 at 7.1).

Both the ASB and the IASB wish to eliminate realisation as a criterion for profit, and therefore revenue recognition. The ASB's *Statement of Principles* does not set out realisation as a criterion for the recognition of revenue; rather it replaces it with reliability of measurement and reasonable certainty of a gain. This same thinking underlies FRS 18, though, in deference to the Companies Act, FRS 18 continues to require companies to report only realised profits – for now.

2.1 Draft guidance on realised and distributable profits

In August 2000 the Company Law Committee of the Institute of Chartered Accountants in England and Wales (ICAEW) and the Institute of Chartered Accountants of Scotland (ICAS) published a revised draft statement of guidance on the determination of realised profits and distributable profits. The aim is for this document ultimately to replace Technical Releases 481 and 482 that were issued in 1982. This draft replaced a previous draft issued more than a year before in June 1999.

The draft guidance makes the point that the concept of what is a realised profit or loss may change over time. This is recognised in the requirement in section 262(3) that realised profits or losses should be determined in accordance with principles generally accepted at the time when the accounts are prepared. It goes on to explain that SSAP 2's requirements on prudence are not now the only basis for the recognition of realised profits. The statement recognises that there have been 'changes in the financial and economic environment, as well as principles generally accepted for accounting purposes, since the issue of SSAP 2 and therefore extends the concept of realisation to include, in particular, marked to market gains as realised profits in certain circumstances'.[7]

The draft Technical Release is not, however, an attempt to redefine realised profits in the context of mark to market (i.e. fair value) accounting. Neither does it define the term 'generally accepted accounting principles'. Instead it describes principles based on SSAP 2 that it considers are generally accepted as giving rise to realised profits and losses; these are based on historical cost accounting rules and the SSAP 2 principles of prudence and realisation. Although SSAP 2 has now been superseded by FRS 18, only the exposure draft FRED 21 – *Accounting Policies* – had been published by the time the draft Technical Release was issued.[8] FRED 21 did not attempt to update the concept of realisation in SSAP 2 but instead reflected the ASB's view that realisation is a less effective way to deliver reliability than focusing on whether it is reasonable certain that a gain exists. This is unchanged in FRS 18, where, for example, in paragraph 18 of Appendix IV to the standard (the development of the standard) it states that 'the Board does not believe that it is useful to link prudence and realisation'.

The draft technical release uses the language of the ASB's balance sheet approach to income recognition in defining 'profits'. Profits are, primarily, 'gains' as defined in the *Statement of Principles*,[9] although they also include legal profits such as contributions from owners, reserves such as merger reserves and reserves arising from the cancellation of share capital and share premium accounts.[10] 'Realised profits' are a subset of profits and are based on two important concepts. The first is that the entity reporting a profit has received 'qualifying consideration', the second is that only certain transactions are capable of giving rise to realised profits.

'Qualifying consideration' is defined as:

'(a) cash, or

(b) a current asset for which there is a liquid market, or

(c) the release of all or part of a liability of the company, or

(d) the settlement or assumption by a third party of all or part of a liability of the company, or

(e) an amount receivable in any of the above forms of consideration where the amount is capable of reliable measurement and the debtor is capable of settling the receivable within a reasonable period of time and will be capable of settling when called upon to do so, unless there is an intention or expectation that the receivable will not be settled.'[11]

A current asset for which there is a liquid market is defined as being one for which there is an active market, where the asset can be readily disposed of without negotiation at a readily ascertainable price and where the disposal will not have a significant effect on the asset's price.[12]

A profit is realised *only* where it arises from:

'(a) a transaction where the consideration received by the company is "qualifying consideration", or

(b) an event (for example, a so-called "capital contribution") which results in "qualifying consideration" being received by the company, or

(c) previous consideration received by the company becoming "qualifying consideration", or

(d) the use of the marking to market method of accounting for current assets and liabilities, or

(e) the translation of a monetary asset or liability denominated in a foreign currency, or

(f) the reversal of a loss previously regarded as unrealised (for example, the writing back of a charge for impairment or for a specific loss), or

(g) a profit previously regarded as unrealised (for example, a revaluation reserve, merger reserve or other similar reserve) becoming realised as a result of:

    (i) the related asset being disposed of in a transaction where the consideration received by the company is "qualifying consideration", or

    (ii) a realised loss being recognised on the scrapping or disposal of the related asset, or

    (iii) a realised loss being recognised on the write-down for depreciation, amortisation, diminution in value or impairment of the related asset, in which case the appropriate proportion of the related unrealised profit becomes a realised profit, or

(h) a reduction or cancellation of capital (ie, share capital, the share premium account or capital redemption reserve) which is credited to reserves where the reduction or cancellation is confirmed by the court, except for as long as the company has undertaken that it will not treat the reserve arising as a realised profit, or where the court has directed that it shall not be treated as a realised profit.'[13]

Perhaps the most controversial of these is (h) above, which completely disregards the concept of 'qualifying consideration', although it is easy to see why the Company Law Committees may have seen this as a pragmatic solution to a particular problem.

Therefore, whilst the ASB is content to report realised and unrealised profits alongside each other in a single performance statement,[14] the ICAEW and ICAS do not believe that what is reported in the profit and loss account is the basis on which a company may make distributions.

This point is evident from the draft guidance making it clear that a realised profit only arises through the use of mark to market accounting for *current* assets and liabilities (see condition (d) above). This means, for example, that according to the draft guidance the recognition of fixed assets at fair value does not give rise to a realised profit. Conversely, because the ASB has adopted the stance that the distinction between realised and unrealised profits is irrelevant, it avoids the issue.

It is hard to see how the ASB's vision of a single statement of performance showing all gains and losses as discussed Chapter 25 can be reconciled with the draft Technical Release's proposed realisation principles, which in turn reflect the ASB's understanding of the law, without there being in fact two separate statements.

2.2 Influence of the ASB

In conclusion, therefore, it is not altogether clear whether or not there exists at present a set of principles generally accepted with respect to the determination for accounting purposes of realised profits or losses, as is suggested by the Companies Act. The ASB is having an influence of its own on this matter through Chapter 5 (Recognition in financial statements) of its *Statement of Principles*, by creating a direct link between revenue recognition and changes in balance sheet assets and liabilities.[15] This approach is discussed at 4.1 below although, as noted above, the ASB views the realisation principle as 'irrelevant', with the result that it aims to recognise, as envisaged by FRED 22, all gains and losses in a performance statement without any distinction between realised and unrealised profits.[16] As set out in the *Statement of Principles*, the ASB aims to recognise a gain and report a profit if there is reasonable certainty that it exists and if it can be measured reliably.[17] Consequently, the effect of the ASB's approach is to establish a system of revenue recognition that is based on the initial recognition, subsequent measurement and derecognition of assets and liabilities – rather than on transactions.

With the adoption of FRS 18 in December 2000 (see Chapter 2 at 7), the ASB has replaced SSAP 2, which was a bastion of prudence and matching, and represented a bulwark against the fair value-based balance sheet approach to accounting. The adoption of FRS 18 will make the advent of a full fair-value based approach to reporting gains and losses, without distinguishing between realised and unrealised profits, considerably easier to arrange.

As discussed more fully at 4.2 below, this approach is directly linked with FRS 5's rules on asset recognition and derecognition. FRS 5's rules have a direct impact on the timing of revenue recognition in respect of sales of assets (fixed or current) that are recognised in the balance sheet. Again, these rules are not based on any principles of 'convertibility to cash', but instead are dependent on the transferral of all the significant benefits and risks relating to an asset disposed of, and the reliability of the measurement of the monetary amount of the asset received in exchange.

3 THE TIMING OF REVENUE RECOGNITION

Under the historical cost system revenues are the inflows of assets to an enterprise as a result of the transfer of products and services by the enterprise to its customers during a period of time, and are recorded at the cash amount received or expected to be received (or, in the case of non-monetary exchanges, at their cash equivalent) as the result of these exchange transactions. However, because of the system of periodic financial reporting, it is necessary to determine the point (or points) in time when revenue should be measured and reported. This is governed by what is known as the 'realisation principle', which acknowledges the fact that for revenue to be recognised it is not sufficient merely for a sale to have been made – there has to be a certain degree of performance by the vendor as well. In the US, this principle was formally codified in 1970 in APB Statement No. 4 as follows: 'revenue is generally recognised when both of the following conditions are met: (1) the earning process is complete or virtually complete, and (2) an exchange has taken place'.[18]

The accounting practice which had developed under this principle was essentially as follows:

(a) revenue from the sale of goods was recognised at the date of delivery to customers;

(b) revenue from services was recognised when the services had been performed and were billable;

(c) revenue derived from permitting others to use enterprise resources (e.g., rental, interest and royalty income) was recognised either on a time basis or as the resources were used; and

(d) revenue from the sale of assets other than products of the enterprise was recognised at the date of sale.[19]

As stated above, revenue is recognised at the amount received or expected to be received as a consequence of the exchange transaction.

Although APB Statement No. 4 did acknowledge that there were certain exceptions to the sales basis of revenue recognition established under the realisation principle (for example, in the case of long-term construction contracts),[20] many more exceptions have developed in recent years. As a result, no common basis of revenue recognition exists in contemporary financial accounting for all types of exchange transaction; different (and sometimes inconsistent) rules exist for different circumstances. Nevertheless, these rules have been derived from three broad approaches to the recognition of revenue: the critical event, accretion and revenue allocation approaches, each of which is appropriate under particular circumstances. Each of the three approaches is discussed in turn below.

3.1 The critical event approach

In general terms, the operating cycle of an enterprise involves the acquisition of merchandise or raw materials, the production of goods, the sale of goods or services to customers, the delivery of the goods or performance of the services and the ultimate collection of cash; in some cases it might even extend beyond the cash collection stage, for example, if there are on-going after-sales service obligations. The critical event approach is based on the belief that revenue is earned at the point in the operating cycle when the most critical decision is made or the most critical act is performed.[21] It is therefore necessary to identify the event which is considered to be critical to the revenue earning process. In theory, the critical event could occur at various stages during the operating cycle; for example, at the completion of production, at the time of sale, at the time of delivery or at the time of cash collection.

Revenue recognition is subject to a number of uncertainties; these include the estimation of the production cost of the asset, the selling price, the additional selling costs and the ultimate cash collection. However, since these uncertainties fall away at various stages throughout the operating cycle, it is necessary to identify a point in the cycle at which the remaining uncertainties can be estimated with sufficient accuracy to enable revenue to be recognised. In other words, the critical event should not be judged to occur at a point when the prudence concept would preclude recognition by virtue of the uncertainties which still remain.

3.1.1 The recognition of revenue at the completion of production

Clearly, the uncertainty surrounding the cost of production is removed when the product is completed; it is therefore necessary to evaluate the remaining uncertainties in order to determine whether or not the completion of production can be used as the critical event for revenue recognition. Where the enterprise has entered into a firm contract for the production and delivery of a product, the sales price will have been determined and the selling costs will have already been incurred. Consequently, provided that both the delivery expenses and the bad debt risk can be satisfactorily assessed, it may be appropriate to report revenue on this basis. An application of this practice is the completed contract method of recognising revenue on construction contracts, in terms of which revenue is recognised only when the contract is completed or substantially completed.

It has also become accepted practice in certain industries to recognise revenue at the completion of production, even though a sales contract may not have been entered into. Normally, this practice would only be adopted in the case of the production of certain precious metals and agricultural commodities, provided that the following criteria are met:

(a) there should be a ready market for the commodity;

(b) the market price should be determinable;

(c) the market price should be stable; and

(d) selling should not be a major activity of the enterprise and there should be no substantial cost of marketing.

FASB's Statement of Financial Accounting Concepts No. 5 – *Recognition and Measurement in Financial Statements of Business Enterprises* – refers to such assets as being 'readily realisable' (since they are saleable at readily determinable prices without significant effort), and acknowledges that revenue may be recognised on the completion of production of such assets, provided that they consist of interchangeable units and quoted prices are available in an active market that can rapidly absorb the quantity held by the enterprise without significantly affecting the price.[22] The accounting treatment for this basis would be to value closing stock at net realisable value (i.e., sales price less estimated selling costs), and write off the related production costs.

An extension of this approach is to be found in the generally accepted accounting practice adopted by many UK securities dealers and commodity traders of including commodities, futures and options in their financial statements at market value.

This has now been taken a step further by both the IASC (in IAS 39[23]) and the FASB (in SFAS 115[24] and SFAS 133[25]), in terms of which all derivative financial instruments and financial assets held for trading are remeasured at fair value at each balance sheet date, with the changes in fair value being recognised in net profit or loss for the period. IAS 39 goes further than SFAS 115 and SFAS 133 in that it requires unquoted equity securities that are not held for trading to be carried at fair value, although the standard gives companies the choice of showing the changes in fair value either in net profit or loss for the period or in the statement of changes in equity.[26] Under US GAAP, all unquoted equity instruments are reported at cost, even if fair value can be measured reliably by means other than a quotation in an active market.[27]

The important point to note is that IAS 39's fair value model for certain financial assets is predicated on the assumption that 'fair value can be reliably determined for most financial assets classified as available for sale or held for trading'.[28] The standard goes on to state that the presumption of reliability of measurement can be overcome for an investment in an equity instrument that does not have a quoted market price in an active market and for which other methods of reasonably estimating fair value are clearly inappropriate or unworkable.[29] This means that the reliability of measurement presumption can only be rebutted under very limited circumstances, with the result that for virtually all trading financial assets, revenue is recognised in the income statement on the basis of changes in fair value. By decreeing that the fair value of all trading assets are measurable reliably (apart from unquoted equity instruments, and only then in very specific circumstances) the IASC is effectively designating the assets to be 'readily realisable'—whether or not they in fact are.

A major point of departure between the FASB on the one hand and the ASB on the other is on the issue of realisation. The FASB still does regard the distinction between realised and unrealised profits as being important, and this is evidenced by the FASB approach to 'reclassification adjustments' (otherwise known as recycling) when reporting comprehensive income. Under this approach certain unrealised gains are reported in comprehensive income, and later recycled through the income statement when realised. Under UK GAAP, recycling is prohibited and, as stated above, the ASB regards the realisation principle as being irrelevant.

The European Commission's declared policy is to keep the European Accounting Directives in line with International Accounting Standards. In May 2001 the European Parliament and the Council adopted the amendment of the Accounting Directives, the main objective of which is 'to enable companies to fully apply International Accounting Standards (IAS), including IAS 39 on the valuation of financial instruments that is mandatory as of financial year 2001, within the framework of the Accounting Directives'.[30] The amendment, once implemented by Member States, will permit EU companies to recognise certain financial assets and liabilities in their balance sheets at fair value, with the corresponding unrealised gains and losses being shown in the profit and loss account.

3.1.2 The recognition of revenue at the time of sale

The time of sale is probably the most widely used basis of recognising revenue from transactions involving the sale of goods. The reason is that, in most cases, the sale is the critical point in the earning process when most of the significant uncertainties are eliminated; the only uncertainties which are likely to remain are those of possible return of the goods (where the customer has the right to do so, thereby cancelling the sale), the failure to collect the sales price (in the case of a credit sale), and any future liabilities in terms of any express or implied customer warranties. However, under normal circumstances, these uncertainties will be both minimal and estimable to a reasonable degree of accuracy, based, inter alia, on past experience.

Nevertheless, the time of sale basis of revenue recognition is not always straightforward. In a large number of cases, a contract for the sale of goods would be entered into after the goods have been acquired or produced by the seller, and delivery takes place either at the same time as the contract, or soon thereafter. However, should revenues be recognised at the time of sale if the sale takes place before production, or if delivery only takes place at some significantly distant time in the future?

From a legal point of view in the UK, delivery does not necessarily have to have occurred for a sale to take place. Under the Sale of Goods Act 1979, 'a contract of sale of goods is a contract by which the seller transfers or agrees to transfer the property in goods to the buyer for a money consideration, called the price'.[31] Where, under a contract of sale, title to the goods is transferred from the seller to the buyer the contract is called a sale;[32] where the contract specifies that title to the goods will be transferred at some future date or transfer of title is subject to conditions to be fulfilled in the future, the contract is called an agreement to sell.[33] Consequently, the 'critical event' which determines whether a contract of sale is a 'sale' or only an 'agreement to sell' is the passing of title.

Where the contract of sale contains no conditions as to the passing of title, and the goods are physically capable of immediate delivery to the purchaser, title will pass as soon as the contract is entered into (i.e., at the time of sale), regardless of the time fixed for payment or delivery.[34] However, where the seller is bound to do something to the goods before the purchaser is obliged to take delivery, title will pass as soon as that thing is done and the purchaser has been notified.[35] The passing of title, therefore, is a legal issue (and may be of crucial importance to the parties in certain circumstances, such as liquidation), which is governed by the terms of the contract and can occur at various stages along the earning process. As a result, for revenue recognition purposes, the time of sale is generally taken to be the point of delivery. This, in fact, would appear to be the principle implicit in the conditions for recognition set out in APB Statement No. 4 (see 3 above), where it is stated that revenue from the sales of products is recognised 'at the date of sale, usually interpreted to mean the date of delivery to customers'.[36]

This principle was reinforced by SFAC No. 5 as follows: 'Revenues are not recognized until earned. An entity's revenue-earning activities involve delivering or producing goods, rendering services, or other activities that constitute its ongoing major or central operations, and revenues are considered to have been earned when the entity has substantially accomplished what it must do to be entitled to the benefits represented by the revenues. … If sale or cash receipt (or both) precedes production and delivery (for example, magazine subscriptions), revenues may be recognised as earned by production and delivery.'[37]

However, the use of the words 'substantially accomplished' in SFAC No. 5 suggests that delivery does not necessarily have to have taken place for revenue to be recognised. Where, for example, delivery is a relatively insignificant part of the earning process, the goods are on hand and available for delivery and there is every expectation that delivery will be made, it may be appropriate to recognise the sale as revenue before delivery takes place. (See 4.5.2 below for discussion of the principles laid down by the IASC in IAS 18 – *Revenue* – for determining when to recognise revenue from a transaction involving the sale of goods.)

3.1.3 *The recognition of revenue subsequent to delivery*

Under certain circumstances, the uncertainties which exist after delivery are of such significance that recognition should be delayed beyond the normal recognition point. Where the principal uncertainty concerns collectibility, a possible approach would be to record the sale and defer recognition of the profit until cash is received; alternatively, it might be appropriate to defer recognition of the whole sale (and not just the profit) until collection is reasonably assured.

A further example of where it might be appropriate to defer the recognition of revenue beyond the date of delivery is where the enterprise sells its product but gives the customer the right to return the goods (for example, in the case of a mail order business where the customer is given an approval period of, say, 14 days). In such circumstances, revenue may be recognised on delivery if future returns can be reasonably predicted; if this is not possible, then revenue should be recognised on receipt of payment for the goods, or on customer acceptance of the goods and express or implied acknowledgement of the liability for payment, or after the 14 days have elapsed – whichever is considered to be the most appropriate under the circumstances.

This area of uncertainty is dealt with in the US under SFAS 48 – *Revenue Recognition When Right of Return Exists* – which states that if an enterprise sells its product but gives the buyer the right to return the product, revenue from the sales transaction is recognised at time of sale only if *all* of the following conditions are met:

(a) the seller's price to the buyer is substantially fixed or determinable at the date of sale;

(b) the buyer has paid the seller, or the buyer is obligated to pay the seller and the obligation is not contingent on resale of the product;

(c) the buyer's obligation to the seller would not be changed in the event of theft or physical destruction or damage of the product;

(d) the buyer acquiring the product for resale has economic substance apart from that provided by the seller (i.e., the buyer does not merely exist 'on paper' with little or no physical facilities, having been established by the seller primarily for the purpose of recognising revenue);

(e) the seller does not have significant obligations for future performance to directly bring about resale of the product by the buyer; and

(f) the amount of future returns can be reasonably estimated.[38]

Revenue which was not recognised at the time of sale because the above conditions were not met, should be recognised either when the return privilege has 'substantially expired', or when all the above conditions are met, whichever occurs first.[39]

The ability to make a reasonable estimate of future returns depends on many factors and will vary from one case to the next. Furthermore, SFAS 48 lists the following factors as being those which might impair a seller's ability to make such an estimate:

(a) the susceptibility of the product to significant external factors, such as technological obsolescence or changes in demand;

(b) relatively long periods in which a particular product may be returned;

(c) absence of historical experience with similar types of sales of similar products, or inability to apply such experience because of changing circumstances; for example, changes in the selling enterprise's marketing policies or its relationships with its customers; and

(d) absence of a large volume of relatively homogeneous transactions.[40]

These rules should be seen against the background of APB Statement No. 4's requirement that revenue should generally be recognised only when the 'earning process is complete or virtually complete'.[41] The right of return is, therefore, viewed as a significant uncertainty which would preclude recognition under certain circumstances.

3.1.4 The critical event approach and the ASB's Statement of Principles

As discussed above, the ASB's *Statement of Principles* is attempting to create a direct link between revenue recognition and changes in balance sheet assets and liabilities.[42] Under the ASB's approach, gains and losses are defined as being increases and decreases in net assets, other than those resulting from transactions with owners.[43] However, the ASB has attempted to relate its revenue recognition proposals back to critical event theory. It does so by asserting that in a transaction involving the provision of services or goods for a net gain, the general asset/liability recognition principles will be met on the occurrence of the critical event in the operating cycle involved.[44] The ASB then goes on to suggest that 'Sometimes it is easier to identify the appropriate point at which to recognise gains arising from the provision of services or goods – and therefore changes to the entity's assets and liabilities – by focusing on the operating cycle of the reporting entity and, in particular, on the critical event in that cycle.'[45]

This is explained further as follows: 'The critical event is the point in an operating cycle at which there will usually be sufficient evidence that the gain exists and it will usually be possible to measure that gain with sufficient reliability. In other words, it is the point at which the recognition criteria will be met and the gain and related change to assets and liabilities will be recognised.

'For many types of transaction, the critical event in the operating cycle is synonymous with full performance. In such cases a gain will be recognised when the entity providing the service or goods has fully performed. That need not, however, be the case: the critical event could occur at other times in the cycle and there could be more than one critical event in the cycle.'[46]

The ASB goes on to suggest that 'the identity of the critical event or events of an operating cycle will depend on the particular circumstances involved. For example:

(a) if the reporting entity has carried out all its obligations under an agreement except for a few minor acts of performance, the critical event will have occurred.

(b) if a sale is contingent upon acceptance by the buyer, whether the critical event has occurred will depend on whether the act of acceptance creates substantial uncertainty as to whether the contractual obligations will be met. The critical event will not have occurred if the likelihood of the goods or services not being accepted is significant.

(c) the operating cycle might involve a contract that is performed in stages, for each of which there is a critical event. (Contracts to build large buildings are usually an example of such an operating cycle.) In such circumstances, the gain that is expected to be earned on the contract as a whole will need to be allocated among the critical events.'[47]

Whilst we understand the ASB's motives for attempting to link its approach to the recognition of gains and losses with the critical event approach, we do not think that the two approaches sit together very easily. This is because, in our view, the critical event approach is closely aligned with the realisation principle, which the ASB views as being irrelevant. At the draft stage, the ASB admitted that probably the most significant inconsistency between its proposals of what is now set out in its *Statement of Principles* and the Companies Act relates to the recognition of gains.[48] We therefore do not see how the ASB can imply that its proposed system of reporting realised and unrealised profits alongside each other in the income statement is consistent with the critical event approach which is based upon title passing to the buyers, not the remeasuring of assets not necessarily for sale. In our view, any alignment of the two approaches will occur purely by chance.

3.2 The accretion approach

The accretion approach involves the recognition of revenue during the process of 'production', rather than at the end of a contract or when production is complete. There are three broad areas of enterprise activity where the application of the accretion approach might be appropriate.

3.2.1 *The use by others of enterprise resources*

The traditional accrual basis of accounting recognises revenue as enterprise resources are used by others; this approach is followed, for example, in the case of recognising rental, royalty or interest income. However, the question of uncertainty of collection should always be considered (for example, accrual of interest on third world debt), in which case it might be appropriate to delay recognition until cash is received or where ultimate collection is assured beyond all reasonable doubt.

3.2.2 *Long-term contracts*

The second accepted application of the accretion approach to revenue reporting may be found in the accounting practice for long-term construction contracts. For example under IAS 11 (and SSAP 9), the amount of revenue to be recognised on construction contracts is determined according to the 'percentage-of-completion method', whereby revenue is estimated by reference to the stage of completion of the contract at the end of each accounting period. Normally, the main uncertainty in the application of this approach are the estimation of the total costs and the degree of completion attained at the balance sheet date, particularly in the early stages of the contract. However, the selling price is sometimes uncertain as well, owing to contract modifications which give rise to revenue from 'extras'. (Accounting for long-term contacts is dealt with in detail in Chapter 16.)

3.2.3 *Natural growth and 'biological transformation'*

Where an enterprise's activity involves production through natural growth or ageing, the accretion approach would suggest that revenue should be recognised at identifiable stages during this process. For example, in the case of livestock, there could be market prices available at the various stages of growth; revenue could, therefore, be recognised throughout the production process by making comparative stock valuations and reporting the accretions at each accounting date.

In fact, this is dealt with in IAS 41 – *Agriculture* – which was adopted by the IASC in December 2000 and is effective for financial periods starting on or after 1 January 2003. The standard requires application of fair value accounting to all 'biological assets' throughout their period of growth, which the Board refers to as 'biological transformation'.

IAS 41 defines agricultural activity as 'the management by an enterprise of the biological transformation of biological assets for sale, into agricultural produce, or into additional biological assets', whilst a biological asset is 'a living animal or plant'. Biological transformation 'comprises the processes of growth, degeneration, production, and procreation that cause qualitative or quantitative changes in a biological asset'.[49]

IAS 41 requires enterprises that undertake agricultural activity to measure all biological assets at fair value less estimated point-of-sale costs,[50] whilst all agricultural produce should be measured at fair value less estimated point-of-sale costs at the point of harvest, and thereafter inventory accounting (IAS 2) should be applied.[51] Fair value is defined as 'the amount for which an asset could be exchanged or a liability settled between knowledgeable, willing parties in an arm's length transaction',[52] which, in practical terms, means that it is the highest price obtainable in any available market.

The change in fair value of biological assets during a period is to be reported in net profit or loss for the period.[53] The standard acknowledges that the change in fair value of biological assets is part physical change (growth, etc.) and part unit price change. However, separate disclosure of the two components is only encouraged but not required.[54] As stated above, fair value measurement stops at harvest, and IAS 2 – *Inventories* – applies after harvest. IAS 41 also draws a distinction between biological assets and agricultural land, requiring agricultural land to be accounted for under IAS 16 – *Property, Plant and Equipment*.[55]

In taking this approach in IAS 41, it seems that the IASC has formulated its ideas on a number of assumptions that do not appear to be necessarily true. These are that:

- it is assumed that efficient markets exist for all biological assets;
- it is assumed that there exist active and liquid markets for all biological assets, at all stages of growth;
- it is assumed that biological transformation can be measured with a degree of reliability which is sufficient for recognition in the accounts; and
- it is assumed that all sectors of agriculture are sufficiently similar as to be accounted for on the same basis.

We consider it unlikely that these assumptions are universally valid. For instance, it seems unlikely that there exist active liquid markets for all intermediate agricultural products, such as forests and unripened fruit. Even if active and liquid markets do exist, it is doubtful that the risks and volatilities of the markets justify recognising revenue on the basis required by the standard. Though fair value information concerning biological assets could conceivably be relevant and useful, it seems unlikely that many enterprises will be able to measure the fair value sufficiently reliably to make it so.

In any event, implementation of IAS 41 will put a significant burden on the preparers of accounts to the extent that the costs (including audit costs) may outweigh the benefits. Users of financial statements should be aware that accounting for agricultural activities under IAS is the most advanced outpost of fair value accounting to date whereby the chicks are literally counted before they are hatched.

3.3 The revenue allocation approach

The revenue allocation approach is essentially a combination of the critical event and accretion approaches. One of the difficulties in adopting, for example, the time of sale as the critical event for revenue recognition, is the existence of the uncertainty surrounding after-sale costs (such as customer support service and warranty costs). One way of dealing with these costs could be to make a provision for the future costs to be incurred on the basis of best estimate; alternatively, an approach could be followed whereby revenue is apportioned on the basis of two or more critical events. Consequently, part of the sale price could be treated as revenue at the point of sale, and the balance could either be recognised on an accretion basis over a warranty period or on the expiration of the warranty. The recognition of profit by manufacturer/dealer lessors is an example of such an application (see Chapter 19 at 7.6 and 8.5.3).

4 ASB, IASC AND FASB PRONOUNCEMENTS ON REVENUE RECOGNITION

It is a requirement of the Companies Act 1985 that 'only profits realised at the balance sheet date shall be included in the profit and loss account';[56] as indicated at 2 above, in establishing whether or not profits of a company should be treated as 'realised profits', reference should be made to 'principles generally accepted, at the time when the accounts are prepared, with respect to the determination for accounting purposes of realised profits or losses'.[57] It is unclear as to whether or not generally accepted accounting principles exist for the purposes of determining realised profits for accounting purposes. The only direct reference to realisation in a UK accounting standard could be found in SSAP 2's definition of prudence; which is now superseded by FRS 18, which merely requires compliance with the Act and does not further explain the term.[58] For this reason, revenue recognition issues tend to be dealt with on an ad hoc basis, without either a clear definition of the concept of realisation or generally accepted recognition criteria.

The ASB has attempted to address revenue recognition, though not realisation, in Chapter 5 of its Statement of Principles, which was issued in December 1999. Regrettably, that document offers only limited practical guidance. It has also recently published a Discussion Paper on the subject, see 4.4 below. However, until the ASB has established clear recognition principles in final form the authoritative literature which exists internationally is both helpful and relevant. Although this literature has no authority to dictate accounting practice in the UK, it may provide a basis for achieving some consistency in approach towards dealing with practical revenue recognition issues.

4.1 ASB Statement of Principles for Financial Reporting, Chapter 5: Recognition in financial statements[59]

Chapter 5 of the ASB's *Statement of Principles* sets out three stages of the recognition process, all of which are focused on assets and liabilities. These are: initial recognition (which is where an item is depicted in the primary financial statements for the first time), subsequent remeasurement (which involves changing the amount at which an already recognised asset or liability is stated in the primary financial statements) and derecognition (which is where an item that was until then recognised ceases to be recognised).[60]

The 'subsequent remeasurement' stage in the recognition process provides the first hint of the ASB's balance sheet-focused approach to current value income recognition. This is because the recognition process requires that all events that may have an effect on elements of the financial statements are, as far as is possible, identified and reflected in an appropriate manner in the financial statements. Thus, whilst existing accounting practice is to record gains and losses that occur as a result of transactions and other events (such as an adverse court judgement or damage to property as a result of a fire), it is now clear that the ASB envisages that changes in the fair value of assets and liabilities will also be recorded as gains and losses in the statement of financial performance.

Since gains and losses are defined as being increases and decreases in net assets, other than those resulting from transactions with owners, the ASB developed its approach to revenue recognition by first establishing the following general recognition principles for assets and liabilities:

- If a transaction or other event has created a new asset or liability or added to an existing asset or liability, that effect will be recognised if:
  - (a) sufficient evidence exists that the new asset or liability has been created or that there has been an addition to an existing asset or liability; and
  - (b) the new asset or liability or the addition to the existing asset or liability can be measured at a monetary amount with sufficient reliability.
- In a transaction involving the provision of services or goods for a net gain, the recognition criteria described above will be met on the occurrence of the critical event in the operating cycle involved. (This aspect is discussed in more detail at 3.1.4 above.)
- An asset or liability will be wholly or partly derecognised if:
  - (a) sufficient evidence exists that a transaction or other past event has eliminated a previously recognised asset or liability; or
  - (b) although the item continues to be an asset or a liability, the criteria for recognition are no longer met.[61]

By applying these principles to the process of revenue recognition, it means that if the effect of the transaction or other event is to increase the entity's recognised net assets, a gain will be recognised. A loss will be recognised if, and to the extent that, previously recognised assets have been reduced or eliminated or cease to qualify for recognition as assets without a commensurate increase in other assets or reduction in liabilities. Similarly, a loss will be recognised when and to the extent that a liability is incurred or increased without a commensurate increase in recognised assets or a reduction in other liabilities.[62] In other words, whenever a change in an entity's total assets is not offset by an equal change in total liabilities or ownership interest, a gain or loss will arise.

The ASB's approach to recognition implies that a gain should be recognised if there is sufficient evidence that the gain exists and it is possible to measure the gain with sufficient reliability. In other words, when the asset/liability recognition criteria are met, the related change to assets and liabilities will be recognised together with the resultant gain. The implications of this are highly significant when combined with the ASB's vision of a current value measurement system: all increases in net assets (including those brought about by increases in current values) should be recognised as gains (provided that there is sufficient evidence that the change has occurred and it can be measured reliably). This thinking is clear in much of FRS 18's description of relevance and reliability (see Chapter 2 at 7.3).

In our view, revenue recognition criteria are more demanding than those for recognising assets and liabilities, since they should embody the concept of the revenue having been earned, based on performance by the reporting company. Although, the rules promulgated in the *Statement of Principles* for accounting based on what assets and liabilities materialise from the transaction may be conceptually 'clean' in practice, in anything but the most straightforward cases, it simply does not provide the concepts with which to address practical situations. Business activity is, in the main, directed towards accomplishing sales transactions, not measuring asset values so we consider rules reflecting this reality of commercial life would have been more obviously appropriate. Accounting in real life is essentially an allocative process in which transactions are allocated to appropriate accounting periods, pretending this is not the case is unlikely to provide durable helpful guidance to users or preparers.

4.2 FRS 5: Reporting the substance of transactions

FRS 5 – *Reporting the substance of transactions* – is a manifestation of the balance sheet approach adopted in the *Statement of Principles.* Since FRS 5 is concerned with the recognition and derecognition of assets and liabilities, it will necessarily have an impact on the recognition of gains and losses. However, it is unclear as to whether the ASB intended that FRS 5 should alter existing accounting practice in the area of revenue recognition.

FRS 5's rules on asset derecognition deal with the issue of when to remove from the balance sheet assets which have previously been recognised. The rules are designed to determine one of three possible outcomes, and essentially involve a process of determining whether or not a transaction transfers to another party all the significant benefits and risks relating to an asset. FRS 5 anticipates that in the case of most transactions affecting items recognised as assets the situation will be that either (a) the benefits and risks will not be transferred – in which case the asset will continue to be recognised and no sale or disposal will be recorded – or (b) the benefits and risks will be transferred – in which case the asset will cease to be recognised (i.e., a sale or disposal together with the resulting gain or loss will be recorded).

The third possible outcome envisaged by FRS 5 occurs where, although not all of the benefits and risks have been transferred, the transaction is more than a mere financing and has transferred enough of both the benefits and risks to warrant at least some derecognition of the asset. These cases arise where the transaction takes one or more of the following forms:

(a) where the asset has been subdivided and part of it transferred;

(b) where the asset is sold for less than its full life; and

(c) where an asset is transferred for all of its life but some risk or benefit is retained.

FRS 5 states that in these special cases, where the amount of any resulting gain or loss is uncertain, full provision should be made for any probable loss but recognition of any gain, to the extent that it is in doubt, should be deferred.

However, the transfer of the risks and rewards of ownership associated with an asset is not in itself sufficient for revenue to be recognised. It is also necessary to complete the other side of the transaction – namely the recognition of the asset received in exchange for the asset disposed of. The principal rule for recognition of an item as an asset under FRS 5 is that the item can be measured at a monetary amount with sufficient reliability – seemingly irrespective of whether or not the item is readily convertible into known amounts of cash or cash equivalents.

4.3 FRS 12: Provisions, contingent liabilities and contingent assets

The ASB published its original Discussion Paper on accounting for provisions on the same day as it published the first version of its Draft *Statement of Principles.* There was therefore no doubt about the ASB's intention to link the definition and recognition of provisions with its balance sheet approach generally, and with the definition and recognition of liabilities specifically. As it turned out, FRS 12 defines a provision as 'a liability of uncertain timing or amount',[63] which means that an entity may only recognise a provision if it has a present obligation that arose as a result of a past event (i.e. a liability) and it is probable that a transfer of economic benefits will be required to settle the obligation'.[64]

The question that arises, therefore, is whether FRS 12 has any impact on generally accepted accounting practice concerning revenue recognition, given that the UK does not have an accounting standard that deals specifically with the subject. It is clear that the basic accrual-based requirement to account for transactions when they occur, rather than when cash passes, together with the realisation principle, will mean that on occasion it will be appropriate for entities to recognise an item of deferred income in the balance sheet. This will arise for example, in the case of income received but not yet earned or realised, and which is deferred and matched against future expenditure incurred to earn the income, or until significant acts of performance are completed.

However, the ASB's *Statement of Principles* does not recognise deferred income as an element of financial statements. Thus, deferred income can be recognised in the balance sheet under the ASB's *Statement of Principles* only as a liability. A strict interpretation might mean that if an entity receives income in advance that is non-refundable, even though it is still to be earned, the entity has no alternative but to recognise the advance as revenue immediately and in full. It seems that to defer recognition of the income until it is earned would be in conflict with FRS 12, since the deferred income does not represent a present obligation for which it is probable that a transfer of economic benefits will be required to settle the obligation.

However, all that having been said, common sense has prevailed in practice and we do not believe that this approach is generally applied by UK companies in these situations. It is our view that, despite murmurings from the ASB to the contrary, the principles of matching, prudence and realisation still prevail in practice and that revenue should be recognised only once it is earned and realised.

4.4 ASB Discussion Paper – Revenue Recognition

In July 2001 the ASB published its Discussion Paper – *Revenue Recognition* –which it sees as a first step towards the development of an accounting standard.[65] In the paper the ASB recognises that revenue recognition is currently based on notions 'such as 'earning', realisation, accrual/matching and prudence' that sometimes point in opposite directions.[66] The ASB also acknowledges that 'different companies have found different answers, and practices have developed that are in some respects inconsistent from one industry to another and with a single industry'.[67]

4.4.1 *Definition and recognition*

The paper looks at basic revenue recognition and measurement questions such as: 'what should revenue represent?' and 'how should revenue recognition relate to contractual performance?'[68] However, curiously it makes proposals 'only in respect of revenue, and not for profit recognition in itself'[69] to prevent the project becoming unmanageable. Given that revenue recognition is normally inextricably linked with profit recognition, the piecemeal approach taken by the ASB may not be the most effective one to adopt.

The paper states that 'in the context of a business operating cycle, revenue is the class of gains, before deduction of associated costs, arising as a result of benefit being transferred to a customer in an exchange transaction (i.e. under a contract)'.[70] The operating cycle is 'a sequence of business activities, carried out with a view to profit, which involves the transfer of benefit to customers in exchange for consideration (i.e. payment)'.[71] The definition of revenue provided is remarkably impracticable as it is defined in terms that need to be defined themselves, such as 'performance', 'operating cycle' and 'benefit'. The success of the ASB's efforts will depend on its ability to move from an abstract description of revenue to a practical definition that can be applied to actual transactions across a range of industries.

Revenue is thought to arise only as a result of 'benefit being transferred to a customer through the seller's performance under a contract'.[72] One of the positions taken in the paper is that gains arise over a business's operating cycle as the enterprise 'takes and eliminates necessary risks'.[73] It then asserts that differences of opinion on profit recognition in essence centre on the question of how 'unexpired' risk should affect recognition of profit:

- the belief that no profit should be recognised until the risks in the operating cycle have been substantially eliminated is equated to gain recognition under historical cost principles; and
- profit recognition rateably with the reduction of risk over the various stages of a business's operating cycle is thought to correspond with recognition under current value principles.[74]

Though the paper links revenue and profit recognition to unexpired risk, it does not actually contain a definition of 'risk' itself. The paper mentions an assortment of risks (e.g. credit risk, performance risk, obsolescence risk, slow movement risk and risks related to customer return options), but it does not even begin to address problems related to risk measurement. Without a real framework for determining and measuring risk many of the paper's proposals are in fact impracticable.

The paper states that for the purposes of revenue recognition 'it may be argued that for businesses in general the earliest point at which risks in the operating cycle have been substantially eliminated is after performance by the seller in a contractual exchange with a third party'.[75] This is in effect a wordy restatement of the transfer of title-based critical event reality of most sales transactions. However, the paper goes on to propose that in situations 'where contractual performance is incomplete, revenue should be recognised to the extent that the seller has performed and that performance has resulted in benefit accruing to the customer'.[76] In summary the paper argues strongly in favour of an accretion approach towards revenue recognition that takes into account partial performance, rather than a critical event approach that requires full performance. Despite the strong preference expressed in the paper, it acknowledges that 'dealing with incomplete performance is likely to be the biggest single difficulty arising in practice'.[77]

It is clear that in arguing for the recognition of partial performance the ASB is attempting to set revenue recognition criteria that will not conflict with the Board's stated desire to recognise unrealised valuation gains. Obviously, a critical event approach would preclude recognising unrealised gains in asset values. As discussed in Chapter 2, one of the biggest problems with the ASB's balance sheet approach is the valuation of unsold goods and the recognition of unperformed contracts. It is thus to be expected that care will have been taken to adopt recognition criteria that are capable of subsequent interpretation to include unperformed contracts, rather than selecting recognition criteria that are not capable of that subsequent interpretation.

The paper suggests two approaches to accounting for right of return and post-performance options. The 'expected sale approach' under which goods that are transferred along with a right of return 'should be recognised on the transfer of benefit, with an appropriate adjustment to reflect the risk of returns'.[78] Whereas the 'accounting policy approach' is one under which 'an entity should select and consistently apply whichever of the following accounting policies is most appropriate to its circumstances',[79] which means that:

- '*either* revenue should be recognised on the transfer of benefit, with an appropriate adjustment to reflect the risk of returns
- *or* revenue should be recognised on the expiry of the right to return'.[80]

4.4.2 *Measurement*

Chapter 5 of the paper addresses measurement principles and includes the following proposal that 'Revenue should be measured as the change in fair value, arising from the seller's performance, of (i) assets representing rights or other access to consideration and (ii) liabilities in respect of consideration received in advance of performance'.[81] This proposal is an interesting twist on the *Statement of Principles*' definition of an asset as 'rights or other access to future economic benefits'[82], itself a logically flawed definition as explained in Chapter 2 at 5.5.1. By stating that revenue is access to *consideration*, i.e. selling price, the ASB is smuggling profit recognition into the concept.

The paper states that it 'favours the view that revenue reflects the *amount to which a seller becomes entitled* under a contract as a result of performance, rather than the *fair value of that performance*'.[83] Consequently, when revenue and payment do not coincide the following accounting is required:

- when performance by the enterprise precedes payment by the customer, revenue is equal to the discounted value of the consideration received. The difference between the discounted and nominal value of the consideration is not part of revenue but should be recognised as a gain;[84] and
- when payment by the customer precedes performance by the enterprise, it is possible that the fair value of performance will change. Such changes in fair value are to be ignored under the proposals in the paper. However, the liability in respect of consideration received should be remeasured to reflect the time value of money.[85]

  Assuming a customer paying 100 in respect of services that are to be performed after a year, and a time value of money of 8% per annum, the paper proposes that the enterprise would accrete interest of 8 – which is presumably recognised as an expense – and recognise revenue of 108 upon performance of the services.

The paper also addresses measurement of revenue in situations where the consideration is determinable but dependent upon uncertain factors. The document identifies three types of situations:[86]

- when the determining factors are outside the control of the seller and customer, the paper concludes that 'the consideration asset should be measured on recognition at fair value';[87]
- when the determining factors are within the control of the seller, the paper prefers the 'fair estimate' approach under which 'the amount of consideration to be recognised should be arrived at by reviewing the various possible outcomes, assessing the most likely and adjusting it for the risk of variations from it';[88]
- when the determining factors are within the control of the customer, the paper favours use of either the 'expected sale approach' or the 'accounting policy approach' as discussed above.[89]

The paper addresses several other questions in connection with revenue recognition:

- bartering transactions may give rise to revenue depending on the circumstances. To cite the paper 'A transaction is with a customer – and hence gives rise to revenue – if, on its completion, the entity has been rewarded for eliminating the risks previously outstanding in the relevant operating cycle';[90]
- in cases where the customer pays for a pre-performance option 'to require future performance from a seller, that payment gives rise to a liability, which should be released as revenue only when the future performance to which it relates occurs';[91]
- contracts should be only combined if 'either legally or economically, one is conditional or dependent on the other'; and[92]

- when a principal acts through a disclosed agent 'the principal's revenue should reflect the full consideration payable by the customer in the transaction.'[93] Undisclosed agents 'should account for revenue in the same way as a principal' whereas disclosed agents should only recognise their commission or other income receivable as revenue.[94]

In summary, the Discussion Paper on Revenue Recognition is filled with dense prose that does not uncover valuable new insights and predictably the ASB proposes a fair value based approach for many revenue recognition issues. In addition, many of the paper's proposals rely on a rigid definition of 'risk' which the paper itself does not provide. We doubt whether the paper will do much to advance the work on a UK revenue recognition standard as it omits, perhaps deliberately, an overt a discussion of profit recognition and industry specific revenue recognition issues.

4.5 IAS 18: Revenue

The original version of IAS 18 – *Revenue Recognition* – was issued in 1982 and defined revenue as the 'gross inflow of cash, receivables or other consideration arising in the course of the ordinary activities of an enterprise from the sale of goods, from the rendering of services, and from the use by others of enterprise resources yielding interest, royalties and dividends'.[95] In revising IAS 18 in 1993, the IASC attempted to retain the approach of the original standard, whilst at the same time create a link between the revised standard and the IASC's conceptual framework.

Consequently, the revised IAS 18 – *Revenue* – now includes the definition of income from the IASC's conceptual framework and states that revenue is income that arises in the course of ordinary activities of an enterprise and is referred to by a variety of different names including sales, fees, interest, dividends and royalties.[96] It goes on to explain that the objective of the revised standard is to prescribe the accounting treatment of revenue arising from the following types of transactions and events:

(a) the sale of goods;

(b) the rendering of services; and

(c) the use by others of enterprise assets yielding interest, royalties and dividends.[97]

However, there are a number of matters which the standard expressly states that it does not deal with. These are[98]:

(a) lease agreements;

(b) dividends arising from investments which are accounted for under the equity method;

(c) insurance contracts of insurance enterprises;

(d) changes in the fair value of financial assets and financial liabilities or their disposal;

(e) changes in the value of other current assets;

(f) natural increases in herds, and agricultural and forest products; and

(g) the extraction of mineral ores.

The standard then defines 'revenue' as 'the gross inflow of economic benefits during the period arising in the course of the ordinary activities of an enterprise when those inflows result in increases in ownership interest, other than increases relating to contributions from equity participants'.[99] This, in fact, is not too dissimilar from the ASB's *Statement of Principles* which defines 'gains' and 'losses' as increases and decreases in ownership interest other than those resulting from contributions from and distributions to owners.[100] However, in distinguishing between 'gains' and 'revenue' in its definition of income, the IASC is able to exclude 'gains' from the scope of IAS 18, thereby avoiding the issue of the recognition of gains that are earned but unrealised.

In any event, though, having established the link between the *Framework* and IAS 18, the IASC then abandons the *Framework* and reverts to the transactions-based critical event approach for the recognition of revenues derived from the sale of goods and the rendering of services, and an accretion approach in respect of revenues derived from the use by others of enterprise resources.

It should be noted that IAS 18 and IAS generally do not address the issue of realisation. Whether or not income and gains recognised in accordance with International Accounting Standards are distributable to shareholders of the enterprise will depend entirely on the national laws and regulations with which the enterprise needs to comply. Thus a gain reported in accordance with IAS does not necessarily imply that gain would be either realised or distributable under UK or other applicable national legislation.

4.5.1 Measurement of revenue

IAS 18 states that the amount of revenue arising on a transaction is usually determined by agreement between the enterprise and the buyer or user of the asset. This means that it is measured at the fair value of the consideration received or receivable taking into account the amount of any trade discounts and volume rebates allowed by the enterprise.[101] The standard defines fair value as 'the amount for which an asset could be exchanged, or a liability settled, between knowledgeable, willing parties in an arm's length transaction'.[102]

Usually, this will present little difficulty as the consideration will normally be in the form of cash or cash equivalents and the amount of revenue will be the amount of cash or cash equivalents received or receivable. However, an issue does arise when the inflow is deferred, since the fair value of the consideration will then be less than the nominal amount of cash received or receivable. IAS 18 attempts to deal with this by introducing a discounting requirement under these circumstances. Consequently, when an arrangement effectively constitutes a financing transaction, the fair value of the consideration is determined by discounting all future receipts using an imputed rate of interest. The difference between the fair value and the nominal amount of the consideration is recognised as interest revenue.[103]

Under IAS 18 an exchange of assets or services of a similar nature and value does not give rise to revenue. However, when goods are sold or services are rendered in exchange for dissimilar goods or services, the exchange is regarded as a transaction which generates revenue. The revenue is measured at the fair value of the goods or services received, adjusted by the amount of any cash or cash equivalents transferred. When the fair value of the goods or services received cannot be measured reliably, the revenue is measured at the fair value of the goods or services given up, adjusted by the amount of any cash or cash equivalents transferred.[104]

IAS 18 requires transactions to be combined or segmented where this is necessary in order to reflect the substance of the transactions,[105] as does IAS 11 – *Construction Contracts*.[106] Combining a series of transactions for the purpose of revenue recognition is required when two or more transactions 'are linked in such a way that the commercial effect cannot be understood without reference to the series of transactions as a whole', for example when those transactions were negotiated as a single package. Conversely, the revenue recognition criteria need to be applied to separately identifiable components of a transaction when the components are essentially unrelated (for example, when the customer had the option to reject individual components of the transaction). IAS 18 does not establish criteria for segmenting and combining transactions, but we recommend that enterprises take the criteria mentioned in IAS 11 into account (IAS 11 is dealt with in Chapter 16).[107]

4.5.2 *The sale of goods*

IAS 18 lays down the following five criteria which must be satisfied in order to recognise revenue from the sale of goods:

(a) the enterprise has transferred to the buyer the significant risks and rewards of ownership of the goods;

(b) the enterprise retains neither continuing managerial involvement to the degree usually associated with ownership nor effective control over the goods sold;

(c) the amount of revenue can be measured reliably;

(d) it is probable that the economic benefits associated with the transaction will flow to the enterprise; and

(e) the costs incurred or to be incurred in respect of the transaction can be measured reliably.[108]

If the costs incurred cannot be measured reliably, the standard requires that 'any consideration already received for the sale of the goods is recognised as a liability.'[109]

It is clear that IAS 18 views the passing of risks and rewards as the most crucial of the five criteria, giving the following four examples of situations in which an enterprise may retain the significant risks and rewards of ownership:

(a) when the enterprise retains an obligation for unsatisfactory performance not covered by normal warranty provisions;

(b) when the receipt of the revenue from a particular sale is contingent on the derivation of revenue by the buyer from its sale of the goods;

(c) when the goods are shipped subject to installation and the installation is a significant part of the contract which has not yet been completed by the enterprise; and

(d) when the buyer has the right to rescind the purchase for a reason specified in the sales contract and the enterprise is uncertain about the probability of return.[110]

On closer examination of these examples, though, it is clear that the standard still advocates a critical event approach – despite its attempt to create a link with the IASC's *Framework*. This is further borne out by the statement in IAS 18 that 'in most cases, the transfer of risks and rewards of ownership coincides with the transfer of legal title or the passing of possession to the buyer'.[111]

It is, therefore, necessary to establish at which point in the earnings process both the significant risks and rewards of ownership are transferred from the seller to the buyer and any significant uncertainties (which would otherwise delay recognition) are removed. For example, the responsibilities of each party during the period between sale and delivery should be established, possibly by examination of the customer agreements. If the goods have merely to be uplifted by the buyer, and the seller has performed all his associated responsibilities, then the sale may be recognised immediately. However, if the substance of the sale is merely that an order has been placed, and the stock has still to be acquired by the seller, then the sale should not be recognised.

IAS 18 also recognises that under certain circumstances goods are sold subject to reservation of title in order to protect the collectibility of the amount due; in such circumstances, provided that the seller has transferred the significant risks and rewards of ownership, the transaction can be treated as a sale and revenue can be recognised.[112] This issue is discussed more fully at 5.2 below.

Examples of accounting policies for the recognition of revenues from the sale of goods are illustrated below:

Extract 3.1: Melexis NV (2000)

6.5.2. Summary of Significant Accounting Policies [extract]

Revenue recognition The company recognizes revenue from sales of product upon shipment or delivery, depending on when title and risk of loss are transferred under the specific contractual terms of each sale, which may vary from customer to customer.

Revenue from research projects is recognized upon meeting all contractual conditions.

Extract 3.2: H. Lundbeck A/S (2000)

Accounting policies [extract]
Revenue

Revenue comprises invoiced sales for the year less returned goods and sales taxes consisting mainly of value added taxes and foreign drug taxes.

Sales subject to a price adjustment clause are recognised as income at the time of delivery at the guaranteed minimum price. The balance of the invoiced price is recorded in the balance sheet as prepayment and recognised as income when the price has finally been determined.

Moreover, revenue includes licence income and royalties from outlicensed products as well as non-refundable down-payments and payments relating to research cooperation from research partners.

4.5.3 *The rendering of services*

IAS 18 requires that when the outcome of a transaction involving the rendering of services can be estimated reliably, revenue is recognised 'by reference to the stage of completion of the transaction at the balance sheet date'[113] (in other words, using the percentage-of-completion method). In applying the percentage-of-completion method, the requirements of IAS 11 – *Construction Contracts* – are 'generally applicable to the recognition of revenue and the associated expenses for a transaction involving the rendering of services.'[114] When the outcome cannot be estimated reliably, revenue is recognised only to the extent of the expenses recognised that are recoverable.[115]

According to IAS 18, the outcome of a transaction can be estimated reliably when all the following conditions are satisfied:

(a) the amount of revenue can be measured reliably;

(b) it is probable that the economic benefits associated with the transaction will flow to the enterprise;

(c) the stage of completion of the transaction at the balance sheet date can be measured reliably; and

(d) the costs incurred for the transaction and the costs to complete the transaction can be measured reliably.[116]

However, whilst the IASC is to be commended for attempting to relate these criteria back to its Framework's fundamental recognition criterion of reliability of measurement, it is clear that they provide little practical guidance. This is borne out by the illustrative examples in the Appendix to IAS 18 which show that, in the case of a transaction involving the rendering of services, the performance of the service is the critical event for revenue recognition.

When it comes to determining the stage of completion of a transaction, IAS 18 suggests three methods that may be used:

(a) surveys of work performed;

(b) services performed to date as a percentage of total services to be performed; or

(c) the proportion that costs incurred to date bear to the estimated total costs of the transaction. Only costs that reflect services performed to date are included in costs incurred to date. Only costs that reflect services performed or to be performed are included in the estimated total costs of the transaction.[117]

For practical purposes, though, when services are performed by an indeterminate number of acts over a specified period, the standard permits revenue to be recognised on a straight-line basis over the specified period unless there is evidence that some other method better represents the stage of completion. However, when a specific act is much more significant than any other acts, the standard again reverts to critical event theory requiring that the recognition of revenue be postponed until the significant act is executed.[118]

Examples of accounting policies for the recognition of revenues from services are illustrated below:

Extract 3.3: Libertel NV (2000)

Notes to the Consolidated Financial Statements [extract]
Recognition of revenue and expenses

Revenue, net of sales taxes and discounts, and expenses are recorded on an accrual basis regardless of the timing of receipt or payment.

Revenue from telecommunication services, net of sales taxes and discounts, is recognised when earned. Unbilled revenue from the billing cycle dating to the end of each month is determined based on traffic and is accrued at the end of the month. Revenue from the sale of equipment including handsets and related accessories, net of sales taxes, and discounts, is recognised upon shipment (in case of sales to dealers) or at point-of-sale (in the case of sales through the Libertel-Vodafone 's retail outlets). Revenue from the sale of prepaid airtime cards and the prepaid airtime, net of discounts, is recognised based on usage. …

Nokia recognises revenue from rendering services using the percentage of completion method:

Extract 3.4: Nokia Corporation (2000)

Accounting policies [extract]
Revenue recognition

The Group recognizes sales when persuasive evidence of an arrangement exists, delivery has occurred, the fee is fixed and determinable, and collectibility is probable. For Nokia networks, substantially all sales are derived from contracts for products and services which involve solutions achieved through significant customization and modification. The percentage of completion method is used for all such contracts, provided that the outcome of the contract can be assessed with reasonable certainty. Sales are recognized over the contract period based on the progress to completion as determined by relevant input measures or milestone activities. When it is probable that contract costs will exceed total contract revenue, the expected loss is expensed immediately.

4.5.4 *Interest, royalties and dividends*

When it is probable that the economic benefits associated with the transaction will flow to the enterprise and that the amount of revenue can be measured reliably, IAS 18 requires that the revenue arising from the use by others of enterprise assets yielding interest, royalties and dividends should be recognised as follows:

(a) *interest:* on a time proportion basis that takes into account the effective yield on the asset;

(b) *royalties:* on an accrual basis in accordance with the substance of the relevant agreement; and

(c) *dividends:* when the shareholder's right to receive payment is established.[119]

An example of an accounting policy for interest and dividends of a company that applies IAS is illustrated below:

Extract 3.5: AngloGold Limited (2000)

Accounting policies [extract]
Revenue recognition

Revenue is recognised to the extent that it is probable that the economic benefits will flow to the group and the revenue can be reliably measured. The following criteria must also be met before revenue is recognised:

...

- Dividends are recognised when the right to receive payment is established;
- Interest is recognised on a time proportion basis, taking account of the principal outstanding and the effective rate over the period to maturity, when it is determined that such income will accrue to the group.

4.5.5 *Disclosure*

IAS 18 requires a greater level of disclosure about revenue than is generally found in the accounts of UK companies. The disclosures relate to both revenue recognition policies and amounts included in the accounts under the different categories of revenue. The principal disclosures required by the standard are as follows:

(a) the accounting policies adopted for the recognition of revenue including the methods adopted to determine the stage of completion of transactions involving the rendering of services;

(b) the amount of each significant category of revenue recognised during the period including revenue arising from:

  (i) the sale of goods;

  (ii) the rendering of services;

  (iii) interest;

  (iv) royalties;

  (v) dividends; and

(c) the amount of revenue arising from exchanges of goods or services included in each significant category of revenue.[120]

4.6 Revenue recognition initiatives in the United States

4.6.1 *'The general rule'*

Chapter 1 of Accounting Research Bulletin No. 43 (issued in 1953) reprinted the six rules which had been adopted by the membership of the AICPA in 1934. The first of these rules stated that 'profit is deemed to be realized when a sale in the ordinary course of business is effected, unless the circumstances are such that the collection of the sale price is not reasonably assured'.[121] The rule then goes on to state that 'an exception to the general rule may be made in respect of inventories in industries (such as the packing-house industry) in which owing to the impossibility of determining costs it is a trade custom to take inventories at net selling prices, which may exceed cost'.[122] However, it is not entirely clear as to what the 'general rule' actually is. Does the term 'effected' mean that profit is realised when the sale takes place, when delivery takes place, or when title passes?

In addition, a number of further exceptions are created by other authoritative pronouncements. For example, Chapter 11 of ARB 43 (which deals with cost-plus-fixed-fee government contracts) states that 'delivery of goods sold under contract is normally regarded as the test of realization of profit or loss'.[123] Nevertheless, it then goes on to say that 'it is, however, a generally accepted accounting procedure to accrue revenues under certain types of contracts and thereby recognize profits, on the basis of partial performance, where the circumstances are such that total profit can be estimated with reasonable accuracy and ultimate realization is reasonably assured'.[124]

The percentage-of-completion method of recognising revenue on long-term construction contracts is another example of 'an exception to the general rule'. ARB 45 – *Long-Term Construction-Type Contracts* – recognises both the percentage-of-completion and completed contract methods of accounting for long-term contracts. The Bulletin states that: 'in general when estimates of costs to complete and extent of progress toward completion of long-term contracts are reasonably dependable, the percentage-of-completion method is preferable. When lack of dependable estimates or inherent hazards cause forecasts to be doubtful, the completed-contract method is preferable'.[125] It would appear that the criteria to be applied in the selection of method are only broadly similar to those which should be applied in the case of cost-plus-fixed-fee contracts.

APB Statement No. 4 views these practices as exceptions to the realisation principle's exchange rule (see 3 above). However, as will be seen below, there exists a number of other variations to both the general rule laid down in ARB 43 and the realisation principle.

4.6.2 *SFAC No. 5*

As discussed in Chapter 2 at 3, the FASB's Concepts Statement No. 5 – *Recognition and Measurement in Financial Statements of Business Enterprises* – has primarily dealt with recognition issues from the angle of providing reliability of measurement. However, the broad principle for revenue recognition laid down by SFAC No. 5 is that revenues are not recognised until they are (a) realised or realisable and (b) earned.[126] According to the Statement, revenues are realised 'when products (goods or services), merchandise, or other assets are exchanged for cash or claims to cash', and are realisable 'when related assets received or held are readily convertible to known amounts of cash or claims to cash'.[127] The characteristics of 'readily convertible assets' are that they have '(i) interchangeable (fungible) units and (ii) quoted prices available in an active market that can rapidly absorb the quantity held by the entity without significantly affecting the price'.[128] Revenues are considered to have been 'earned' when the entity 'has substantially accomplished what it must do to be entitled to the benefits represented by the revenues'.[129]

The most significant difference between the recognition principles laid down in SFAC No. 5 as opposed to APB Statement No. 4 is that whilst the APB interpreted recognition and realisation as being broadly synonymous, SFAC No. 5 uses the terms 'realized' and 'realizability' to focus on conversion and convertibility of non-cash assets into cash or claims to cash. However, it is doubtful whether SFAC No. 5's revised interpretation of the realisation principle has made any significant progress towards providing a rigorous theory of recognition and measurement. This is highlighted by the fact that SFAC No. 5 provides guidance for applying its recognition criteria and, in so doing, goes on to condone certain existing revenue practices (for example, the percentage-of-completion method and the accrual of certain revenues on a time basis) which clearly are not in accordance with the basic principles laid down in the Statement, since an exchange for cash or claims to cash may not necessarily have occurred.

Interestingly, the FASB's own special report on its conceptual framework makes the point that although SFAC No. 5's name implies that it gives conceptual guidance on recognition and measurement, its conceptual contributions to financial reporting are not really in those areas.[130] The report goes on to say that 'as a result of compromises necessary to issue it, much of Concepts Statement 5 merely describes present practice and some of the reasons that have been used to support or explain it but provides little or no conceptual basis for analyzing and attempting to resolve the controversial issues of recognition and measurement about which accountants have disagreed for years.'[131] The concluding sentence of the FASB's report sums up elegantly the views that have long been expressed by critics of SFAC No. 5: 'Concepts Statement 5 does make some noteworthy conceptual contributions—they are just not on recognition and measurement.'[132]

4.6.3 FASB Statements and AICPA Statements of Position

There exist a number of FASB Statements and AICPA Statements of Position which deal with either the recognition of certain forms of revenue, or the recognition of revenue in certain specific industries. These are dealt with under 5 below.

4.6.4 SEC Staff Accounting Bulletin 101

In December 1999, the SEC staff issued Staff Accounting Bulletin No. 101 (SAB 101) – *Revenue Recognition in Financial Statements* – which summarises certain of their views in applying generally accepted accounting principles to revenue recognition in financial statements. Though the SEC staff believed that SAB 101 did not change any of the existing rules on revenue recognition, a Frequently Asked Questions document[133] was issued in October 2000 to clarify issues raised on how the guidance in SAB 101 and the authoritative accounting literature on revenue recognition would apply to certain transactions.

SAB 101 spells out four basic criteria – based on the FASB's Concepts Statements– that all must be met before enterprises can record revenue. These are:

- persuasive evidence that an arrangement exists;
- delivery has occurred or services have been rendered;
- the seller's price to the buyer is fixed or determinable; and
- collectibility is reasonably assured.[134]

SAB 101 and the Frequently Asked Questions document contain many examples that illustrate how revenue recognition criteria should be applied to specific problem areas. The most important areas covered by SAB 101 are discussed below.

A Consignment sales

Consignment sales should not be recognised in revenue upon delivery, because the seller retains the risks and rewards of ownership and usually title to the product.[135] In addition, the following characteristics preclude revenue recognition even if title to the product has passed to the buyer:

- 'the buyer has the right to return the product'[136] and the seller retains significant obligations related to the resale of the product, or the buyer has no obligation to pay the seller at any specified date, or the buyer acquiring the product for resale has no economic substance apart from that provided by the seller;
- 'the seller is required to repurchase the product … at specified prices that are not subject to change except for fluctuations due to finance and holding costs, and the amounts to be paid by the seller will be adjusted … to cover substantially all fluctuations in costs incurred by the buyer in purchasing and holding the product (including interest)';[137]
- 'the transaction possesses the characteristics set forth in EITF Issue No. 95-1, Revenue Recognition on Sales with a Guaranteed Minimum Resale Value, and does not qualify for sales-type lease accounting.';[138] or
- 'the product is delivered for demonstration purposes'.[139]

B Bill and hold transactions

Under SAB 101 'delivery generally is not considered to have occurred unless the customer has taken title and assumed the risks and rewards of ownership of the products specified in the customer's purchase order or sales agreement'.[140] However, revenue should be recognised before delivery has occurred when the following criteria have been met:

'1. The risks of ownership must have passed to the buyer;

2. The customer must have made a fixed commitment to purchase the goods, preferably in written documentation;

3. The buyer, not the seller, must request that the transaction be on a bill and hold basis. The buyer must have a substantial business purpose for ordering the goods on a bill and hold basis;

4. There must be a fixed schedule for delivery of the goods. The date for delivery must be reasonable and must be consistent with the buyer's business purpose (e.g., storage periods are customary in the industry);
5. The seller must not have retained any specific performance obligations such that the earning process is not complete;
6. The ordered goods must have been segregated from the seller's inventory and not be subject to being used to fill other orders; and
7. The equipment [product] must be complete and ready for shipment.'

C *Layaway sales*

Layaway sales for which the customer has made a substantive forfeitable deposit should only be recognised as revenue when all criteria for revenue recognition have been met, which effectively means that revenue should be recognised upon delivery. Until that time, any deposit should be accounted for as a liability.[141]

D *Non-refundable payments*

Enterprises should consider all the facts and circumstances in determining whether a non-refundable payment represents the culmination of a separate earnings process.' If that is not the case then deferral of revenue is considered appropriate.[142]

E *Initial set-up fees*

An enterprise may receive a prepayment for all services at the inception of a service arrangement and the company performs set-up procedures to facilitate delivery of services to its customers. Under SAB 101, the revenue should be recognised on a straight-line basis over (1) the term of the arrangement or (2) the expected period during which those specified services will be performed, whichever is longer, if all other revenue recognition criteria are met.[143]

F *Refundable fees for services*

When the customer has the right to cancel an arrangement and receive a cash refund, the amount of the sale is not considered fixed or determinable under SAB 101 until those cancellation rights lapse. If the cancellation rights expire at the end of the arrangement then:

- the refundable fees, net of estimate refunds, may be recognised ratably if there is a sufficiently large pool of homogeneous transactions and several additional criteria have been met; or
- revenue should be recognised upon expiration of the cancellation rights in all other cases.[144]

G *Rights of return*

SFAS 48 – *Revenue Recognition When Right of Return Exists* – requires recognition of revenue when in addition to the normal revenue recognition criteria the amount of future returns can be reasonably estimated. In determining whether this is the case, SAB 101 requires enterprises to consider, among others, the following factors:

- significant increases in or excess levels of inventory in a distribution channel;
- the inability to determine or observe the levels of inventory in a distribution channel and the current level of sales to end users;
- expected introductions of new products that may result in the technological obsolescence of and larger than expected returns of current products;
- the significance of a particular distributor to the registrant's business, sales and marketing;
- the newness of a product;
- the introduction of competitors' products with superior technology or greater expected market acceptance; and
- other factors that affect market demand and changing trends in that demand for the registrant's products.[145]

4.7 Summary of broad approaches to revenue recognition

Although, FRS 5 and the *Statement of Principles* are clearly trying to introduce a balance sheet approach to revenue recognition, to date we see no evidence that this has had any significant effect on the general principles of revenue recognition which are currently enshrined in UK GAAP: namely that the buyer must assume from the seller the significant risks and rewards of ownership of the assets sold and that the amount of revenue must be reliably measurable and certain. It is clear that the ASB's Discussion Paper has fundamental implications for revenue recognition and it remains to be seen how the suggestions it contains are developed.

However, at the time of writing the following table summarises the broad approaches to revenue reporting that would appear to have achieved general acceptance through existing reporting practice. The table indicates the circumstances under which it might be appropriate to apply each of the approaches; nevertheless, it is essential that each situation is considered on its individual merits, with particular attention being paid to the risks and uncertainties that remain at each stage of the earning process and the extent to which the amount of revenue can be measured reliably.

The timing of recognition	*Criteria*	*Examples of practical application*
During production (accretion)	Revenues accrue over time, and no significant uncertainty exists as to measurability or collectibility. A contract of sale has been entered into and future costs can be estimated with reasonable accuracy.	The accrual of interest, royalty and dividend income. Accounting for long-term construction contracts using the percentage-of-completion method.
At the completion of production	There should exist a ready market for the commodity which could rapidly absorb the quantity held by the entity; the commodity should comprise interchangeable units; the market price should be determinable and stable; there should be insignificant marketing costs involved.	Certain precious metals and commodities.
At the time of sale (but before delivery)	Goods must have already been acquired or manufactured; goods must be capable of immediate delivery to the customer; selling price has been established; all material related expenses (including delivery) have been ascertained; no significant uncertainties remain (e.g., ultimate cash collection, returns).	Certain sales of goods (e.g., 'bill and hold' sales). Property sales where there is an irrevocable contract.
On delivery	Criteria for recognition before delivery were not satisfied and no significant uncertainties remain.	Most sales of goods and services. Property sales where there is doubt that the sale will be completed.
Subsequent to delivery	Significant uncertainty regarding collectibility existed at the time of delivery; at the time of sale it was not possible to value the consideration with sufficient accuracy.	Certain sales of goods and services (e.g., where the right of return exists). Goods shipped subject to conditions (e.g., installation and inspection/performance).
On an apportionment basis (the revenue allocation approach)	Where revenue represents the supply of initial and subsequent goods/services.	Franchise fees. Sale of goods with after sales service.

5 PRACTICAL ISSUES

Because of the lack of established generally accepted principles for revenue recognition, coupled with the fact that minimal specific guidance is given in UK accounting standards as to the timing of revenue reporting, it is necessary to examine specific areas in practice which might be open to inconsistent, controversial or varied accounting practices. Many of the issues discussed below relate to specific industries which pose their own particular revenue recognition problems; in fact, much of the accounting literature on the subject has been developed (predominantly in the US) in the context of these industries.

5.1 Receipt of initial fees

The practice which has developed in certain industries of charging an initial fee at the inception of a service, followed by subsequent service fees, can present revenue allocation problems. The reason for this is that it is not always altogether clear what the initial fee represents; consequently, it is necessary to determine what proportion (if any) of the initial fee has been earned on receipt, and how much relates to the provision of future services. In some cases, large initial fees are paid for the provision of a service, whilst continuing fees are relatively small in relation to future services to be provided; if it is probable that the continuing fees will not cover the cost of the continuing services to be provided, then a portion of the initial fee should be deferred over the period of the service contract such that a reasonable profit is earned throughout the service period.

5.1.1 Franchise fees

The franchise agreements which form the basis of the relationships between franchisors and franchisees can vary widely both in their complexity and in the extent to which various rights, duties and obligations are dealt with in the agreements. For this reason, no standard form franchise agreement exists which would dictate standard accounting practice for the recognition of all franchise fee revenue. Consequently, only a full understanding of the franchise agreement will reveal the substance of a particular arrangement so that the most appropriate accounting treatment can be determined; nevertheless, the following are the more common areas which are likely to be addressed in any franchise agreement and which would be relevant to franchise fee revenue reporting:[146]

(a) *rights transferred by the franchisor:* the agreement would give the franchisee the right to use the trade name, processes, know-how of the franchisor for a specified period of time or in perpetuity.

(b) *the amount and terms of payment of initial fees:* payment of initial fees (where applicable) may be fully or partially due in cash, and may be payable immediately, over a specified period or on the fulfilment of certain obligations by the franchisor.

(c) *amount and terms of payment of continuing franchise fees:* the franchisee will normally be required to pay a continuing fee to the franchisor – usually on the basis of a percentage of gross revenues.

(d) *services to be provided by the franchisor initially and on a continuing basis:* the franchisor will usually agree to provide a variety of services and advice to the franchisee, such as:

- site selection;
- the procurement of fixed assets and equipment – these may be either purchased by the franchisee, leased from the franchisor or leased from a third party (possibly with the franchisor guaranteeing the lease payments);
- advertising;
- training of franchisee's personnel;
- inspecting, testing and other quality control programmes; and
- bookkeeping services.

(e) *acquisition of equipment, stock, supplies etc.:* the franchisee may be required to purchase these items either from the franchisor or from designated suppliers. Some franchisors manufacture products for sale to their franchisees, whilst others act as wholesalers.

In the US, SFAS 45 – *Accounting for Franchise Fee Revenue* – states that franchise fee revenue should be recognised 'when all material services or conditions relating to the sale have been substantially performed or satisfied by the franchisor'.[147] Substantial performance for the franchisor means that:

(a) the franchisor has no remaining obligation or intent (in terms of the franchise agreement, the law or trade practice) to refund any cash received or waive any debts receivable;

(b) substantially all of the initial services of the franchisor required by the franchise agreement have been performed; and

(c) no other material conditions or obligations related to the determination of substantial performance exist.[148]

SFAS 45 also deals with the issue of mixed revenue – i.e. where the initial franchise fee incorporates not only the consideration for the franchise rights and the initial services to be provided by the franchisor, but also tangible assets such as equipment, signs etc. In such cases, the portion of the initial fee which is 'applicable to the tangible assets shall be based on the fair value of the assets and may be recognized before or after recognizing the portion applicable to the initial services. For example, when the portion of the fee relating to the sale of specific tangible assets is objectively determinable, it would be appropriate to recognize that portion when their titles pass, even though the balance of the fee relating to services is recognized when the remaining services or conditions in the franchise agreement have been substantially performed or satisfied.'[149]

The Appendix to IAS 18 includes a broad discussion of the receipt of franchise fees, where it is stated that they 'are recognised as revenue on a basis that reflects the purpose for which the fees were charged'.[150] The standard states that the following methods of franchise fee recognition are appropriate:[151]

(a) the fees, based on the fair value of the assets sold, are recognised as revenue when the items are delivered or title passes;

(b) franchise fees for the provision of initial and subsequent services, whether part of the initial fee or a separate fee, are recognised as revenue as the services are rendered. When the separate fee does not cover the cost of continuing services together with a reasonable profit, part of the initial fee, sufficient to cover the costs of continuing services and to provide a reasonable profit on those services, is deferred and recognised as revenue as the services are rendered;

(c) fees charged for the use of continuing rights granted by the franchise agreement or other services are recognised as revenue as the services are provided or the rights used; and

(d) the franchisor should not recognise revenue on a gross basis when it acts as an agent for the franchisee.

In summary, therefore, we suggest that the following basic principles may be applied for the recognition of initial franchise fees:

(a) first, it is necessary to break down the fee into its various components; for example, fee for franchise rights, fee for initial services to be performed by the franchisor, fair value of tangible assets sold etc. The reason for this is that the individual components may be recognised at different stages; the portion that relates to the franchise rights may be recognised in full immediately, or part of it may have to be deferred (see (b) below); the fee for initial services to be performed should only be recognised when the services have been 'substantially performed' (it is unlikely that substantial performance will have been completed before the franchisee opens for business); and the portion of the fee which relates to tangible assets may be recognised when title passes;

(b) next, it should be considered whether or not the continuing fee will cover the cost of continuing services to be provided by the franchisor. If not, then a portion of the initial fee should be deferred and amortised over the life of the franchise;

(c) if the collection period for the initial fees is extended and there is doubt as to the ultimate collectibility, revenue should be recognised on a cash received basis; and

(d) in the event of the franchisor having the option to buy out the franchisee, and there is considered to be a significant probability that he will do so, initial franchise fee revenue should be deferred in full and credited against the cost of the investment when the buy-out occurs.

5.1.2 *Advance royalty/licence receipts*

Under normal circumstances, the accounting treatment of advance royalty/licence receipts is straightforward; under the accruals concept the advance should be treated as deferred income when received, and released to the profit and loss account when earned under the royalty/licence agreement. However, there are certain industries where the forms of agreement entered into are such that advance receipts comprise a number of components, each requiring different accounting treatments.

For example, in the record and music industry, a record company will normally enter into a contractual arrangement with either a recording artist or a production company to deliver finished recording masters over a specified period of time. The albums are then manufactured and shipped to retailers for ultimate sale to the customer. The recording artist will normally be compensated through participating in the record company's sales and licence fee income (i.e., a royalty), although he may receive a non-refundable fixed fee on delivery of the master to the record company.

Example 3.1 Revenue recognition for licensors in the record and music industry

For each recording master delivered by a pop group, THRAG, the group (which operates through a service company) receives a payment of £1,000,000. This amount comprises a non-returnable, non-recoupable payment of £200,000, a non-returnable but recoupable advance of £600,000 and a returnable, recoupable advance of £200,000. The recoupable advances can be recouped against royalties on net sales earned both on the album concerned and on earlier and subsequent albums. This is achieved by computing the total royalties on net sales on all albums delivered under THRAG's service company's agreement with its recording company, and applying against this total the advances and royalties previously paid on those albums.

It is clear that the non-recoupable advance should be recognised in income when received, since it is not related to any future performance; at the other end of the spectrum, recognition of the refundable advance should be deferred and recognised only when recouped. However, the question arises as to whether the non-refundable but recoupable advance on royalties should be recognised immediately or deferred. If one accepts that revenue may be recognised when it is absolutely assured, there is an argument to justify the immediate recognition of the recoupable advance, since it is non-refundable; furthermore, it might be argued that, as far as THRAG is concerned, the earning process is complete, since the group does not have any further performance obligations. Conversely, some might argue that although the advance is non-refundable, it is not earned until it is recouped; furthermore, immediate recognition of royalty advances is likely to lead to a significant distortion of reported income, resulting in there being little correlation between reported income and album sales.

Clearly, therefore, there is no clear-cut answer, and it is our view that either approach is acceptable – i.e. the non-refundable but recoupable advance may be recognised in full as soon as the master is delivered to the recording company or, alternatively, it may be treated as deferred income when received and matched to subsequent album sales, being released to the profit and loss account in the period in which the sales are made. The most important point is that, whichever method is adopted, it is applied consistently. Of course, if the ASB's *Statement of Principles* was to be used as the sole source of guidance for determining the revenue recognition policy, the asset/liability approach to the recognition of gains would dictate that all non-returnable advances – whether recoupable or not – would be recognised in income immediately. This is because the ASB's conceptual framework, like the IASC's Framework, does not recognise deferred income as an element of financial statements. Indeed, it is even arguable that under FRS 12 – *Provisions, Contingent Liabilities and Contingent Assets* – it is no longer permitted to recognise deferred income on the balance sheet if it does not meet the definition of a 'liability', i.e. an obligation to transfer economic benefits as a result of past transactions or events. Consequently, since there is no obligation to repay the non-refundable advance, it may be argued that there is no alternative but to recognise it as revenue as soon as it becomes payable (see 4.3 above).

It is, perhaps, noteworthy that the deferral approach is supported by the US accounting requirement contained in SFAS 50 – *Financial Reporting in the Record and Music Industry* – which states that where an amount is paid in advance by a licensee to a licensor for the right to sell or distribute records or music, 'the licensor shall report such a minimum guarantee as a liability initially and recognize the guarantee as revenue as the license fee is earned under the agreement. If the licensor cannot otherwise determine the amount of the license fee earned, the guarantee shall be recognized as revenue equally over the remaining performance period, which is generally the period covered by the license agreement.'[152]

Chrysalis is an example of a company that has adopted this approach of deferring the recognition of non-returnable advances against royalties, as illustrated by the following extract:

Extract 3.6: Chrysalis Group PLC (2000)

NOTES TO THE ACCOUNTS
For the year ended 31st August 2000

1 Accounting policies
Record royalties (excluding record producer services and music publishing royalties)

Royalty income is included on a receivable basis calculated on sales of records arising during each accounting period as reported by licensees. …

Advances received in respect of individual albums are carried forward and recognised as income over the expected life of each individual license.

Similar recognition principles should be applied in the case of advance fees paid on the sale of film/TV rights. Receipts that are non-refundable and non-recoupable should be recognised immediately, whilst any non-refundable but recoupable royalty advances may either be recognised immediately, or be deferred and recognised as earned; again, the accounting policy selected should be applied consistently.

5.1.3 *Loan arrangement fees*

The practice of recognising loan arrangement fees as income in the year that the loans are arranged was outlawed in the US through the publication of SFAS 91 – *Accounting for Nonrefundable Fees and Costs Associated with Originating or Acquiring Loans and Initial Direct Costs of Leases* – which requires loan origination fees to be deferred and recognised over the life of the related loan as an adjustment of interest income.[153] Similarly, direct loan origination costs should be deferred and recognised as a reduction in the yield of the loan.[154]

Since there is no corresponding requirement in the UK, the recognition of arrangement fees on receipt may be regarded as acceptable, providing that these fees really are for setting up the arrangement, rather than for providing continuing services thereafter, this being the view taken by the SORP on Advances published by the British Bankers Association.[155] Our preferred approach, however, is that the principles contained in SFAS 91 should be applied in the UK. Nevertheless, situations may exist where the lending institution is providing other financial services which are, in themselves, valuable to the borrower and which are covered by the arrangement fee. If this is the case, then it may be argued that the portion of the initial fee that relates to those services should be recognised as income immediately, provided that the interest rate to be charged on the loan is fair and reasonable in relation to the risk involved and that the arrangement fee is not merely an interest prepayment.

The Appendix to IAS 18 includes a series of illustrative examples which relate to financial service fees, pointing out that the recognition of revenue for financial service fees depends on the purposes for which the fees are assessed and the basis of accounting for any associated financial instrument. The examples in the Appendix divide up the types of fees which arise into three categories, distinguishing between:

(a) those which are an integral part of the effective yield of a financial instrument – in which case the fees are generally treated as an adjustment to the effective yield;

(b) those which are earned as services are provided – in which case the fees are recognised as revenue either as the services are provided or on a time proportion basis; and

(c) those which are earned on the execution of a significant act – in which case the fees are recognised as revenue when the significant act has been completed.[156]

Consequently, provided that the arrangement fee is not an integral part of the effective yield of a loan, the fee can be recognised as revenue when the loan has been arranged.

5.1.4 *Commitment fees*

Commitment fees are fees paid by potential borrowers for a commitment to originate or purchase a loan or group of loans within a particular period of time. According to the ICAEW Industry Accounting and Auditing Guide on banks, 'Where a bank charges an arrangement fee that reflects the administrative costs of setting up a transaction, it will generally be recognised immediately.'[157] This contrasts with the accounting treatment prescribed by SFAS 91, namely that the fee should be deferred until either the commitment is exercised or it expires. If the commitment is exercised, it should normally be recognised over the life of the loan as an adjustment to interest income, and if it expires unexercised it should be recognised in income on expiration.[158]

SFAS 91 does, however, allow the following two exceptions to this general rule:

(a) if the enterprise's experience with similar arrangements indicates that the likelihood that the commitment will be exercised is remote (i.e., the likelihood is slight that a loan commitment will be exercised prior to its expiration), the commitment fee should be recognised over the commitment period on a straight-line basis as service fee income. If the commitment is subsequently exercised during the commitment period, the remaining unamortised commitment fee at the time of exercise should be recognised over the life of the loan as an adjustment to interest income;[159]

(b) if the amount of the commitment fee is determined retrospectively as a percentage of the line of credit available but unused in a previous period, then the fee should be recognised as service fee income as of the determination date, provided that:

(i) the percentage applied is nominal in relation to the stated interest rate on any related borrowing; and

(ii) the borrowing will bear a market interest rate at the date the loan is made.[160]

Applying the criteria set out in the Appendix to IAS 18[161] (see 5.1.3 above), if it is unlikely that a specific lending arrangement will be entered into, the commitment fee will be recognised as revenue on a time proportion basis over the commitment period.

5.1.5 *Credit card fees*

It is common practice in the UK for credit card companies to levy a charge, payable in advance, on its cardholders. Although such charges may be seen as commitment fees for the credit facilities offered by the card, they clearly cover the many other services available to cardholders as well. Accordingly, we would suggest that the fees which are periodically charged to cardholders should be deferred and recognised on a straight-line basis over the period the fee entitles the cardholder to use the card.[162]

5.2 Goods sold subject to reservation of title

The Romalpa case,[163] which was decided in 1976, focused attention on the terms of a particular form of sale whereby the seller retains title to the goods sold and, in some cases, the right to other goods produced from them and the ultimate sale proceeds. The appropriate accounting treatment of such sales will depend on the commercial substance of the transaction, rather than its legal form. For example, it may be that the reservation of title is of no economic relevance to either party, except in the event of the insolvency of the purchaser; in other words, the goods are supplied and payment is due on an identical basis to other goods which are sold without reservation of title. In such circumstances, provided there is no significant uncertainty regarding the collectibility of the amount due, the sale should be recognised as revenue.

However, the circumstances surrounding the sale might be such that the parties view it as a consignment sale; for example, the purchaser may retain the right to return unsold goods to the seller, and the obligation to pay for the goods might be deferred until such time as the goods are sold to a third party. In such a case it would be inappropriate for the seller to recognise the sale until such time as the purchaser sells the goods and is liable for payment. However, situations of this nature fall within the scope of FRS 5 generally and Application Note A thereof in particular – the details of which are discussed in Chapter 18 at 3.1.

The accounting treatment of goods sold subject to reservation of title is discussed in a statement of guidance issued by the ICAEW in July 1976 and, although rather out of date, it has never been superseded by a more authoritative document.[164]

IAS 18 includes guidance that is similar to the requirements in the UK. The standard assumes that in most cases transfer of the legal title will coincide with the transfer of the risks and rewards of ownership, but acknowledges that this may not always be the case. In fact, transfer of legal title is not a condition for revenue recognition under IAS.[165] A seller should account, therefore, for a sale when it only retains 'the legal title to the goods solely to protect the collectability of the amount due.'[166] On the other hand, a sale to an intermediate party acting, in substance, as an agent is treated as a consignment sale.[167]

5.3 Subscriptions to publications

Publication subscriptions are generally paid in advance and are non-refundable. Nevertheless, since the publications will still have to be produced and delivered to the subscriber, the subscription revenue cannot be regarded as having been earned until production and delivery takes place. Consequently, we recommend the IAS 18 approach under which revenue should be deferred and recognised either on a straight-line basis over the subscription period or, where the publications vary in value, revenue should be based on the proportion of the sales value that each publication bears to the total sales value of all publications covered by the subscription.[168] Metal Bulletin is an example of a company which follows such an approach:

Extract 3.7: Metal Bulletin plc (2000)

Statement of Accounting Policies
A) TURNOVER [extract]

Turnover comprises the value of goods and services supplied during the year, excluding value added tax and intra group sales, in particular:

(i) Subscription revenue is allocated to accounting periods in proportion to the number of issues covered by the subscription published before and after the accounting date. Unappropriated subscription revenue is included within current liabilities.

This accounting policy is a perfect illustration of the difference between the balance sheet approach to the recognition of gains (as supported in the ASB's *Statement of Principles*), and conventional transactions-based accounting. Metal Bulletin is, quite appropriately, applying the accruals and prudence concepts to allocate the subscription revenue to its profit and loss account as it is earned. Subscriptions received in advance of being earned are carried in the balance sheet as deferred income.

However, the ASB's *Statement of Principles* implicitly denies that such a separate category exists, since it is not acknowledged as one of the elements of financial statements. The ASB, in its original draft *Statement of Principles*, tried to reconcile this anomaly by using the example of a magazine subscription that had been received in advance by a publisher, asserting that what is in reality deferred income can be embraced satisfactorily within the definition of a liability.[169]

It does not take much to show that this argument does not stand up. If one was to accept that a balance sheet approach should be followed in accounting for this situation, it would be necessary to consider the nature of the 'liability' involved and measure it appropriately. The publisher's contractual obligation is to provide the magazine, and it would be appropriate to measure such liability at the cost of doing so, not the amount of advance subscriptions received. This would therefore mean recording the profit in the year in which the cash happened to be received, not when the sale was performed, which would be quite inappropriate. It would also mean, for example, that the publisher could boost its immediate reported profits by inducing customers to take out subscriptions for longer periods in advance, such as a five-year subscription at a reduced rate.

It is therefore perhaps not surprising that, in the *Statement of Principles*, the ASB has deleted the magazine subscription example referred to above, and instead has made the general (and unsubstantiated) assertion that 'although the starting point for the recognition process may be the effect on assets and liabilities, the notions of matching and the critical event in the operating cycle will often help in identifying these effects'.[170] As explained immediately above, this too is complete nonsense, since by applying matching and the critical event approach you would end up with an entirely different outcome to that which would result from applying the ASB's asset/liability approach.

5.4 Advertising revenue

The examples in the Appendix to IAS 18 adopt the performance of the service as the critical event for the recognition of revenue derived from the rendering of services. Consequently, media commissions are recognised when the related advertisement or commercial appears before the public. Production commissions are recognised by reference to the stage of completion of the project.[171] We concur with this broad approach which, as illustrated by the following extracts, appears to have been enshrined in UK GAAP:

Extract 3.8: Metal Bulletin plc (2000)

Statement of Accounting Policies

A) TURNOVER [extract]

Turnover comprises the value of goods and services supplied during the year, excluding value added tax and intra group sales, in particular:

. . .

(ii) Advertisement revenue is recognised on publication date. All publication expenses are written off at that date.

Extending this principle to media commissions would mean that such revenue should be recognised when the related advertisement or commercial appears before the public. Similarly, production commissions should generally be recognised by reference to stage of completion of the project. This is, in fact, the approach adopted by media group Aegis:

Extract 3.9: Aegis Group plc (2000)

1. Principal accounting policies
Turnover [extract]

... Turnover is recognised when charges are made to clients, principally when advertisements appear in the media. Fees are recognised over the period of the relevant assignments or agreements.

5.5 Software revenue recognition

There are a number of issues relating to the timing of revenue recognition in the software services industry. The issues that arise surround the question of when to recognise revenue from contracts to develop software, software licensing fees, customer support services and data services. However, few of these issues have been addressed in the authoritative literature and, because of the nature of the products and services involved, applying the general revenue recognition principles to software transactions can sometimes be difficult. The result of this has been that in practice software companies have used a variety of methods to recognise revenue, often producing significantly different financial results for similar transactions.

This problem was recognised in the US by the FASB and SEC who encouraged the AICPA to provide guidance on software revenue recognition methods. This culminated in AICPA Statement of Position (SOP) 91–1, which was issued in December 1991. The SOP applied to all entities that earned revenue from licensing, selling, leasing or otherwise marketing computer software, although it did not apply to revenue from the sale or licensing of a product containing software that is incidental to the product as a whole, such as software sold as part of a telephone system.

However, it was found that certain provisions of SOP 91–1 were being applied inconsistently, thereby leading to diversity in practice. As a result, in October 1997 the AICPA issued SOP 97–2,[172] entitled *Software Revenue Recognition,* which superseded SOP 91–1. In 1998 two further SOPs were issued amending SOP 97–2: SOP 98–4 (which merely deferred the effective date of a provision of SOP 97–2), and SOP 98–9 (which modified SOP 97-2 with respect to certain transactions, adding a further example of revenue recognition in the case of the sale of software product which included post-contract customer support).

Whilst SOP 97–2 has no direct bearing on companies reporting under UK GAAP, many such companies tend to adopt the US requirements in the absence of a comparable UK pronouncement, particularly if they have long-term ambitions of a NASDAQ listing. We therefore encourage companies to adopt the provisions of the SOP in all appropriate circumstances, as we consider that at present it probably represents best practice.

5.5.1 *The basic principles of SOP 97–2*

Software arrangements range from those that simply provide a licence for a single software product, to those that require significant production, modification or customisation of the software. Arrangements also may include multiple products or services. SOP 97–2 states that if the arrangement does not require significant production, modification or customisation of existing software (i.e., contract accounting does not apply – see 5.5.2 below), revenue should be recognised when all of the following criteria are met:[173]

- persuasive evidence of an arrangement exists (e.g. signed contract, purchase authorisation, on-line authorisation);
- delivery has occurred (and no future elements to be delivered are essential to the functionality of the delivered element);
- the vendor's fee is fixed or determinable (for arrangements with multiple elements, the threshold for meeting the 'determinable' criterion is 'vendor-specific objective evidence of fair value'); and
- collectibility is probable (fee is not subject to forfeiture, refund or other concessions if the undelivered elements are not delivered).

These criteria are similar in many respects to those previously required by SOP 91-1, but SOP 91–1 also required that there be no remaining significant vendor obligations (such as installation, testing and data conversion) in order to recognise revenue. Under SOP 97–2, it is no longer necessary or appropriate to differentiate between significant and insignificant vendor obligations. The licence fee under an arrangement with multiple elements should be allocated to the elements according to the 'vendor-specific objective evidence of fair value'.

In addition, SOP 97–2 requires a company to allocate a portion of the licence fee from a software arrangement to elements that are deliverable on a when-and-if-available basis, whereby a vendor agrees to deliver software only when or if it becomes deliverable while the agreement is in effect. Furthermore, SOP 97–2 requires that if a vendor has a customary practice of obtaining written contracts, revenues should not be recognised until the contract is signed by both parties. Therefore, in the absence of a signed contract, revenue should not be recognised even if the software has been delivered and payment made.

5.5.2 *Accounting for arrangements which require significant production, modification or customisation of software*

Where companies are running well-established computer installations with systems and configurations which they do not wish to change, off-the-shelf software packages are generally not suitable for their purposes. For this reason, some software companies will enter into a customer contract whereby they agree to customise a generalised software product to meet the customer's specific processing needs. A simple form of customisation would be to modify the system's output reports so that they integrate with the customer's existing management reporting system. However, customisation will often entail more involved obligations; for example, having to translate the software so that it is able to run on the customer's specific hardware configuration, data conversion, system integration, installation and testing.

The question that arises, therefore, is on what basis should a software company be recognising revenue where it enters into this type of contract which involves significant contractual obligations? It is our view that the principles laid down in SSAP 9 – *Stocks and long-term contracts* – should be applied in this situation.[174] SSAP 9 defines a long-term contract as 'a contract entered into for the design, manufacture or construction of a single substantial asset or the provision of a service (or of a combination of assets or services which together constitute a single product) where the time taken substantially to complete the contract is such that the contract activity falls into different accounting periods'.[175] The standard requires that 'long-term contracts should be assessed on a contract by contract basis and reflected in the profit and loss account by recording turnover and related costs as contract activity progresses. Turnover is ascertained in a manner appropriate to the stage of completion of the contract, the business and the industry in which it operates. Where it is considered that the outcome of a long-term contract can be assessed with reasonable certainty before its conclusion, the prudently calculated attributable profit should be recognised in the profit and loss account as the difference between the reported turnover and related costs for that contract.'[176]

Consequently, where the software company is able to make reliable estimates as to the extent of progress toward completion of a contract, related revenues and related costs, and where the outcome of the contract can be assessed with reasonable certainty, the percentage-of-completion method of profit recognition should be applied. One company which follows this approach is Logica, a company whose principal activities include the marketing, design, production, integration and maintenance of custom built software and associated hardware systems:

Extract 3.10: Logica plc (2000)

Accounting policies

4 Recognition of profits [extract]

Profit is taken on fixed price contracts while the contract is in progress, having regard to the proportion of the total contract which has been completed at the balance sheet date. Provision is made for all foreseeable future losses.

5 Amounts recoverable on contracts

Amounts recoverable on contracts represent turnover which has not yet been invoiced to clients. Such amounts are separately disclosed within debtors.

The valuation of amounts recoverable on fixed price contracts is adjusted to take up profit to date or foreseeable losses in accordance with the accounting policy for recognition of profits.

Other amounts recoverable on contracts are valued at the lower of cost or estimated net realisable value.

Cost comprises:

- professional amounts recoverable valued at the cost of salaries and associated payroll expenses of employees engaged on assignments and a proportion of attributable overheads
- unbilled expenses incurred and equipment purchased for clients in connection with specific contracts.

On the other hand, where the uncertainties are such that prudence would preclude the accrual of profit, or where the contracts are of a relatively short duration, the completed contract method of accounting should be applied.

Under SOP 97-2, if an arrangement to deliver software or a software system, either alone or together with other products or services, requires significant production, modification or customisation of software, the entire arrangement should be accounted for in accordance with Accounting Research Bulletin (ARB) No. 45 – *Long-Term Construction-Type Contracts* – and SOP 81–1 – *Accounting for Performance of Construction-Type and Certain Production-Type Contracts.*[177]

Similarly, the Appendix to IAS 18 suggests that fees from the development of customised software are recognised as revenue by reference to the stage of completion of the development, including completion of services provided for post delivery service support.[178]

5.5.3 *Accounting for arrangements with multiple elements*

Software arrangements may provide licences for multiple software products or for multiple software products and services (referred to in SOP 97–2 as 'multiple elements') such as: additional software products, upgrades/enhancements, rights to exchange or return software, post-contract customer support (PCS) or other services including elements deliverable only on a when-and-if-available basis. The SOP states that if contract accounting does not apply (because significant customisation is not needed), revenue recognition should be based on an allocation of the total fee to the individual elements based on 'vendor-specific objective evidence of fair value' of each of the elements. This requirement (explained at 5.5.4 below) could have a significant impact on income if elements are recognised as revenue in different periods. If sufficient vendor-specific objective evidence of fair value does not exist for each element, revenue from the arrangement should be deferred until such sufficient evidence exists, or until all elements have been delivered.[179]

If a discount is offered in a multiple element arrangement, a proportionate amount of that discount should be applied to each element included in the arrangement based on each element's fair value without regard to the discount.[180]

5.5.4 *Determining fair value based on vendor-specific objective evidence*

SOP 97–2 states that if an arrangement includes multiple elements, the fee should be allocated to the various elements based on vendor-specific objective evidence of fair value, regardless of any separate prices stated within the contract for each element.[181] Under the SOP, vendor-specific objective evidence of fair value is limited to the following:

- the price charged when the same element is sold separately; and
- for an element not yet being sold separately, the price established by management having the relevant authority; it must be probable that the price, once established, will not change before the separate introduction of the element into the marketplace.[182]

With the exception of changes in the estimated percentage of customers not expected to exercise an upgrade right, the amount allocated to undelivered elements is not subject to later adjustment.[183] However, if it becomes probable that the amount allocated to an undelivered element will result in a loss on that element of the arrangement, the loss should be recognised.[184]

If a multiple-element arrangement includes an upgrade right, the fee should be allocated between the elements based on vendor-specific objective evidence of fair value. The fee allocated to the upgrade right is the price for the upgrade/ enhancement that would be charged to existing users of the software product being updated. If the upgrade right is included in a multiple-element arrangement on which a discount has been offered, no portion of the discount should be allocated to the upgrade right. If sufficient vendor-specific evidence exists to reasonably estimate the percentage of customers that are not expected to exercise the upgrade right, the fee allocated to the upgrade right should be reduced to reflect that percentage. SOP 97–2 goes on to state that this estimated percentage should be reviewed periodically, and that the effect of any change in that percentage should be accounted for as a change in accounting estimate.[185]

As stated above, if sufficient vendor-specific objective evidence does not exist for the allocation of revenue to the various elements of the arrangement, the SOP provides that all revenue from the arrangement should be deferred until the earlier of the dates at which:

(a) such sufficient vendor-specific objective evidence does exist; or

(b) all elements of the arrangement have been delivered.[186]

However, the SOP provides for the following exceptions to this principle:

- if the only undelivered element is post-contract customer support (PCS), the entire fee is recognised on a pro-rata basis;[187]
- if the only undelivered element is services that do not involve significant production, modification or customisation of software, the entire fee should be recognised over the period during which the services are expected to be performed;[188]
- if the arrangement is in substance a subscription, the entire fee should be recognised on a pro-rata basis;[189] and
- if the fee is based on the number of copies, the revenue should be accounted for on an allocation basis, as specified in the SOP.[190] For example, some fixed fee licence arrangements provide customers with the right to reproduce or obtain copies at a specified price per copy of two or more software products up to the total amount of the fixed fee. A number of the products covered by the arrangement may not be deliverable or specified at the inception of the arrangement. In such cases, the revenue allocated to the delivered products should be recognised when the product master or first copy is delivered. If during the term of the arrangement, the customer reproduces or receives enough copies of these delivered products so that revenue allocable to the delivered products exceeds the revenue previously recognised, such

additional revenue should be recognised as the copies are reproduced or delivered. The revenue allocated to the undeliverable product(s) should be reduced by a corresponding amount.[191]

5.5.5 *Upgrades, enhancements and post-contract customer support (PCS)*

Under SOP 97–2, the right to receive specified upgrades or enhancements (even on a when-and-if-available basis) under a PCS arrangement is considered a separate element of licensing arrangement. However, rights to receive unspecified upgrades/enhancements on a when-and-if-available basis are PCS services and generally should be recognised as revenue on a pro rata basis over the term of the PCS arrangement. SOP 97–2 defines PCS to exclude rights to specific upgrades/enhancements. For a specific upgrade, a portion of the total licensing fee should be allocated to the elements using the 'vendor-specific objective evidence of fair value' criteria. The fee allocated to the upgrade right is the price for the upgrade/enhancement that would be charged to existing users of the software product being updated.[192]

If a multiple-element software arrangement includes explicit or implicit rights to PCS, the total fees from the arrangement should be allocated among the elements based on vendor-specific objective evidence of fair value. The fair value of the PCS should be determined by reference to the price the customer will be required to pay when it is sold separately (that is, the renewal rate). The portion of the fee allocated to PCS should be recognised as revenue on a pro rata basis over the term of the PCS arrangement, because PCS services are assumed to be provided on a pro rata basis. However, revenue should be recognised over the period of the PCS arrangement in proportion to the amounts expected to be charged to expense for the PCS services rendered during the period if:

- sufficient vendor-specific historical evidence exists demonstrating that costs to provide PCS are incurred on other than a straight-line basis; and
- the vendor believes that it is probable that the costs incurred in performing under the current arrangement will follow a similar pattern.[193]

The following extract illustrates what we consider to be an appropriate policy:

Extract 3.11: Total Systems plc (2001)

1. Accounting policies
Software maintenance

For own software covered by maintenance contracts income is credited to the profit and loss account over the period to which the contract relates. Costs associated with these contracts are expensed as incurred.

5.5.6 *Evaluation of whether a fee is fixed or determinable and arrangements that include extended payment terms*

One of the SOP's basic criteria for software revenue recognition is determining whether the fee under the arrangement is fixed or determinable. The SOP states that any extended payment terms in a software licensing arrangement may indicate that the fee is not fixed or determinable.[194] Furthermore, it goes on to state that a software licensing fee should be presumed not to be fixed if payment of a significant portion of the fee is not due until after expiration of the licence or more than twelve months after delivery of the software. However, this presumption may be overcome by evidence that the vendor has a standard business practice of using long-term or instalment contracts and a history of successfully collecting under the original payment terms without making concessions.[195]

If it cannot be concluded that the fee is fixed or determinable at the outset of the arrangement, revenue should be recognised as payments from customers become due (assuming, of course, that the other revenue recognition criteria have been met).[196]

5.5.7 *Rights to return or exchange software*

As part of a software licensing arrangement, a software vendor may provide a customer with the right to return or exchange software. Depending on the circumstances, the customer might exchange software for a product with minimal or more than minimal differences in price, functionality and features. Consistent with SFAS 48 – *Revenue Recognition When Right of Return Exists*, SOP 97–2 requires a software vendor to establish a reserve for estimated returns; however, no amounts should be reserved for the right to exchange because exchange rights do not affect revenue recognition, although any estimated costs for such exchanges should be accrued. SOP 97–2 also provides that exchanges of software products for different software products or for similar software products with more than minimal differences in price, functionality or features are considered returns and are accounted for in conformity with SFAS 48.[197]

5.5.8 *Services*

Many software arrangements include both software and service elements (services). Services may include training, installation or consulting (but do not include PCS-related services). Consulting services often include implementation support, software design or development or the customisation or modification of the licensed software.[198]

According to the SOP, if an arrangement includes such services, a determination must be made as to whether the service element can be accounted for separately as the services are performed.[199] The SOP lays down the following criteria that must be met in order to account separately for the service element of an arrangement that includes both software and services:

- sufficient vendor-specific objective evidence of fair value must exist to permit allocation of the revenue to the various elements of the arrangements (see 5.5.4 above);

- the services must not be essential to the functionality of any other element of the transaction; and
- the services must be described in the contract such that the total price of the arrangement would be expected to vary as the result of the inclusion or exclusion of the services.[200]

If these criteria are met, revenue should be allocated between the service and software elements of the contract. This allocation should be based on vendor-specific objective evidence of fair value. Revenue from the service element should be recognised as the services are performed or on a straight-line basis over the service period if no pattern of performance is discernible.[201]

A number of UK software companies have recently amended their revenue recognition policies to fall in line with the requirements of SOP 97-2. Cedar Group provides an example as shown below.

Extract 3.12: Cedar Group plc (2001)

Accounting policies
Turnover

Turnover comprises amounts derived from the provision of software and services and is stated net of Value Added Tax and trade discounts. If services are essential to the functionality of the software, or the payment terms are linked, the revenue for both software and services is recognised rateably over the implementation period. Where services are not essential to the functionality, and the payment terms are not linked, revenue from the grant of a perpetual license to use Cedar's software is recognised when the following conditions are met: a signed contract exists; delivery has occurred; the sales price is fixed or determinable; collectability is probable; and no significant obligations remain. Revenue from sales to resellers is recognised where these conditions are met and there is also either an identified end user or an irrevocable commitment to pay within twelve months. Software rentals are recognised over the term of the agreement. Service revenue is recognised as the services are performed. Maintenance revenue is recognised over the life of the contract.

5.5.9 *Disclosures in practice*

The following extracts illustrate other software revenue recognition policies that are to be found in practice in the UK and which, in our view, provide examples of good practice:

Extract 3.13: Misys plc (2000)

ACCOUNTING POLICIES
REVENUE RECOGNITION

Turnover represents amounts invoiced to customers net of sales taxes for goods and services. Revenue from system sales are recognised upon delivery to a customer, when there are no significant vendor obligations remaining and the collection of the resulting receivable is considered probable. In instances where a significant vendor obligation exists, revenue recognition is delayed until the obligation has been satisfied. Recurring license fees are recognised rateably over the period of the contract. Electronic data interchange and remote processing services (transaction processing) are recognised as the work is performed. Professional services, such as implementation, training and consultancy, are recognised when the services are performed.

Extract 3.14: Northgate Information Solutions plc (2000)

1. ACCOUNTING POLICIES
Recognition of revenue

Revenue on the outright sale of equipment and standard software, where no significant vendor obligations exist, is recognised on despatch. Revenue on non-standard software or where significant vendor obligations exist, is recognised on customer acceptance.

Revenue from professional services (project management, implementation and training) is recognised as the services are performed. Revenue from software support and hardware maintenance agreements is recognised rateably over the term of the agreement.

On contracts involving a combination of products and services, revenue is recognised separately on each deliverable in accordance with the above policy, unless all deliverables are considered to be interdependent when revenue is recognised on final acceptance.

On major contracts extending over more than one period, revenue is taken based on the stage of completion when the outcome of the contract can be foreseen with reasonable certainty and after allowing for costs to completion.

Where equipment is leased or software is licensed under certain long term contracts for the greater part of their economic life, the contracts are classified as sales-type (finance) leases and the present value of future lease rentals, after calculating a deduction for maintenance, is recognised as revenue at the inception of the lease. Interest is included in turnover over the period of the contract so as to produce a constant rate of return on the net investment in the lease.

Where equipment in an equipment lease or the interest in a software licence is sold to a finance company which then leases the equipment or licences the software to a customer, revenue is taken on the sales value after deferral of income for future maintenance, where applicable.

Provision for maintenance on equipment or software licences sold to finance companies as described above is released to revenue over the period of the contract. The related interest is charged to profit over the same period and represents a constant proportion of the balance outstanding.

Where the Group leases equipment or licences software under contracts which do not have the characteristics of a sales-type lease, the rentals are taken to revenue on an accruals basis.

5.6 Film exhibition rights

Revenue received from the licensing of films for exhibition at cinemas and on television should be recognised in accordance with the general recognition principles discussed in this chapter. Contracts for the television broadcast rights of films normally allow for multiple showings within a specific period; these contracts usually expire either on the date of the last authorised telecast, or on a specified date, whichever occurs first. It is our view that the revenue from the sale of broadcast or exhibition rights may be recognised in full (irrespective of when the licence period begins), provided the following conditions are met:

(a) a contract has been entered into;

(b) the film is complete and available for delivery;

(c) there are no outstanding performance obligations, other than having to make a copy of the film and deliver it to the licensee; and

(d) collectibility is reasonably assured.

Rights for the exhibition of films at cinemas are generally sold either on the basis of a percentage of the box office receipts or for a flat fee. In the case of the percentage basis, revenue should be recognised as it accrues through the showing of the film. Where a non-refundable flat fee is received, we suggest that revenue be recognised on the same basis as described above for television broadcast rights.

The Appendix to IAS 18 states that 'An assignment of rights for a fixed fee or non refundable guarantee under a non cancellable contract which permits the licensee to exploit those rights freely and the licensor has no remaining obligations to perform is, in substance, a sale.'[202] When a licensor grants rights to exhibit a motion picture film in markets where it has no control over the distributor and expects to receive no further revenues from the box office receipts, revenue is recognised at the time of sale.[203]

In the US, under SFAS 53 – *Financial Reporting by Producers and Distributors of Motion Picture Films* – revenue from a television broadcast contract should be recognised in full only when the licence period begins, and all of the following conditions have been met:

(a) the licence fee for each film is known;

(b) the cost of each film is known or reasonably determinable;

(c) collectibility of the full licence fee is reasonably assured;

(d) the film has been accepted by the licensee in accordance with the conditions of the licence agreement; and

(e) the film is available for its first telecast.[204]

5.7 The disposal of land and buildings

Unlike the US, there are no laid down rules in the UK for the recognition of the proceeds on disposal of land and buildings. Consequently, the general principles of revenue recognition should be applied in order to determine the point in time at which property sales should be recognised in the profit and loss account. There are two significant points in the earning process which could, depending on the circumstances of the sale, be considered to be the critical event for recognition. The first point is on exchange of contracts, at which time the vendor and purchaser are both bound by a legally enforceable contract of sale; whilst the second possible point of recognition is on completion of the contract. The following extracts illustrate the fact that both approaches are followed in practice:

Extract 3.15: Crest Nicholson Plc (2000)

Accounting policies
REVENUE RECOGNITION [extract]
(d) Income recognition
Profit is recognised on houses when contracts are exchanged and building is substantially complete. Profit is recognised on commercial property developments or units of development when they are substantially complete and subject to binding and unconditional contracts of sale and where legal completion has occurred shortly thereafter. Where the sale price is conditional upon letting, profit is restricted by reference to the space unlet. Profit in respect of construction is recognised when the contract is complete.

In the case of contracts that are regarded as long term, profit is recognised during execution provided a binding contract for sale exists and the outcome can be foreseen with reasonable certainty.

Extract 3.16: Hammerson plc (2000)

1. **ACCOUNTING POLICIES**
Profits on Sale of Properties [extract]
Profits on sale of properties are taken into account on the completion of contract and receipt of cash.

Extract 3.17: Countryside Properties PLC (2000)

1 Accounting policies

Profit Profit is taken on legal completion of sale of each property, except in the case of long-term building contracts where attributable profit is taken having regard to the proportion of the contract completed at the Balance Sheet date.

Although legal title and beneficial ownership do not pass until the contract is completed and the transfer is registered, it is likely that the earnings process is sufficiently complete to permit recognition to take place on exchange of contracts. The reason for this is that the selling price would have been established, all material related expenses would have been ascertained and, usually, no significant uncertainties would remain. If, however, on exchange of contracts there exists doubt that the sale will be ultimately completed, recognition should take place on the receipt of sales proceeds at legal completion.

Since both approaches appear to be widely used in practice, they should both be regarded as being acceptable accounting practice. Nevertheless, it is important to ensure that, whichever policy is adopted, it is applied consistently, although recognition should always be delayed until completion if significant uncertainties still exist on exchange of contracts. The income recognition policy of Crest Nicholson reproduced above is a good example of the application of this principle.

The prudence-based view that no significant uncertainties should remain was reinforced by the Financial Reporting Review Panel's ruling on the 1999 accounts of Wiggins Group.[205] The Review Panel ruled that recognition of revenue 'on the strength of non-binding Heads of Agreement which were not turned into contracts'[206] until well after the year-end was unacceptable. The Panel also concluded that it was inappropriate to recognise revenue in respect of a contract that 'was conditional upon the company's subsequent fulfilment of a material condition: namely, that planning permission had been obtained on terms satisfactory to the purchaser and without which the purchaser had certain rights not to proceed'.[207]

The illustrative example in the Appendix to IAS 18 states that revenue is normally recognised when legal title passes to the buyer; however, at the same time, it acknowledges that recognition might take place before legal title passes, provided that the seller has no further substantial acts to complete under the contract.[208]

In the US, SFAS 66 – *Accounting for Sales of Real Estate* – lays down rigid rules for the recognition of profit on real estate transactions, and distinguishes between retail land sales (i.e., sales under a property development project) and other sales of real estate. The statement contains extensive provisions which have been developed to deal with complex transactions which are beyond the scope of this book. However, the general requirements for recognising all of the profit on a non-retail land sale are as follows:

Profit should not be recognised in full until all of the following criteria are met:

(a) the sale is consummated;

(b) the purchaser's initial and continuing investments are adequate to demonstrate a commitment to pay for the property;

(c) the vendor's receivable is not subject to future subordination; and

(d) the vendor has transferred to the purchaser the usual risks and rewards of ownership in a transaction that is in substance a sale and does not have a substantial continuing involvement with the property.[209]

A sale is not considered to be consummated until:

(a) the parties are bound by the terms of the contract;

(b) all consideration has been exchanged (i.e., either all monies have been received, or all necessary contractual arrangements have been entered into for the ultimate payment of monies – such as notes supported by irrevocable letters of credit from an independent lending institution);

(c) any permanent financing for which the vendor is responsible has been arranged; and

(d) all conditions precedent to closing the contract have been performed.[210]

SFAS 66 states that these four conditions are usually met 'at the time of closing or after closing, not when an agreement to sell is signed or at a preclosing'.[211]

5.8 Sale and leaseback transactions

A sale and leaseback transaction takes place when an owner sells an asset and immediately reacquires the right to use the asset by entering into a lease with the purchaser. The accounting treatment of any apparent profit arising on the sale of the asset will depend on whether the leaseback is an operating or finance lease. In general terms, if the leaseback is an operating lease, the seller-lessee has disposed of substantially all the risks and rewards of ownership of the asset, and so has realised a profit on disposal. Conversely, if the leaseback is a finance lease, the seller-lessee is, in effect, reacquiring substantially all the risks and rewards of ownership of the asset; consequently, it would be inappropriate to recognise a profit on an asset which, in substance, was never disposed of.[212]

The accounting treatment of the profit arising on sale and leaseback transactions is discussed in Chapter 19 at 7.4 and 8.6.

5.9 Non-monetary/barter transactions

In November 2000, UITF 26 – *Barter transactions for advertising* – was issued which prescribes 'that turnover and costs in respect of barter transactions for advertising should not be recognised unless there is persuasive evidence of the value at which, if the advertising had not been exchanged, it would have been sold for cash in a similar transaction. In these circumstances, that value should be included in turnover and costs'.[213] Such persuasive evidence is deemed only to exist when 'where it can be demonstrated that similar advertising has been sold for cash. This will be the case only where the entity has a history of selling similar advertising for cash, and where substantially all of the turnover from advertising within the accounting period is represented by cash sales'.[214] The Abstract only applies to barter transactions for advertising, but its principles may be relevant to other types of barter transactions.[215] However, there is currently no authoritative guidance in the UK that comprehensively deals with accounting for non-monetary transactions.

The IASC issued a draft interpretation, SIC-D31 – *Revenue - Barter transactions involving advertising services* – in September 2001. The draft consensus was that the revenue from a barter transaction involving advertising services received should be recognised at fair value unless it is impracticable to measure it reliably; in which case the fair value of the advertising services provided should be used, again unless it is impracticable to measure it reliably. The draft interpretation suggests that reliable measurement can only be made if there are frequently occurring similar transactions that are expected to continue, that represent the predominant source of revenue of the type being bartered, that involve cash or other forms of consideration that have a reliably measurable fair value, and that do not involve the barter-counterparty.

Under IAS 18, when goods or services are exchanged for goods or services that are of a similar nature and value, the exchange is not regarded as a transaction that generates revenue.[216] This is often the case, for example, with exchanges of licence interests in the oil and gas industry.

However, when goods or services are exchanged for dissimilar goods or services, the exchange is regarded as a transaction which generates revenue. The revenue is measured at the fair value of the goods or services received, adjusted by the amount of any cash or cash equivalents transferred. When the fair value of the goods or services received cannot be measured reliably, the revenue is measured at the fair value of the goods or services given up, adjusted by the amount of any cash or cash equivalents transferred.[217]

IAS 16 deals also with exchanges of fixed assets. An item of property, plant and equipment may be acquired in exchange for a similar asset that has a similar use in the same line of business and which has a similar fair value. An item of property, plant and equipment may also be sold in exchange for an equity interest in a similar asset. IAS 16 states that in both cases, since the earnings process is incomplete, no gain or loss is recognised on the transaction. Instead, the cost of the new asset is the carrying amount of the asset given up.[218] However, the fair value of the asset received may provide evidence of an impairment in the asset given up. Under these circumstances the asset given up is written down and this written down value assigned to the new asset.[219]

Where an item of property, plant and equipment is acquired in exchange or part exchange for a dissimilar item of property, plant and equipment or other asset, IAS 16 states that the cost of the item received is measured at its fair value, which is equivalent to the fair value of the asset given up adjusted by the amount of any cash or cash equivalents transferred.[220] IAS 16 is silent on the matter of whether the difference between the book value and the fair value of the asset given up represents a gain, although it would seem to imply that it does. For example, if an enterprise owns a machine with a book value of 100 and a fair value of 120 and it exchanges it for a vehicle, then the cost of the vehicle acquired is measured at 120, resulting in a gain of 20 on the disposal of the machine. This may, therefore, result in the recognition of gains as well as losses in the income statement (see Chapter 12 at 5.2.4). However, in our view, this does not constitute a realised profit under UK GAAP and the 20 would be included in the STRGL and held in an unrealised reserve until such time as the vehicle acquired is, itself, realised. The draft Technical Release on realised profits, see 2.1 above, deals extensively with the determination of realised profits under UK GAAP.

IAS 38 deals with exchanges of intangible assets.[221] Exchanges of intangible assets should be accounted for in the same way as exchanges of property, plant and equipment, though the wording of that standard is slightly different (see Chapter 11 at 5.3.1).

The general principles under US GAAP are similar to IAS 18 and are addressed in APB Opinion No. 29 – *Accounting for Nonmonetary Transactions*. APB 29 states that the basis of accounting for non-monetary transactions is the same as for monetary transactions – i.e. fair values – and a gain or loss is recognised when the book value of the asset given up differs from the fair value recorded for the asset received.[222] However, APB 29 recognises that when neither the fair value of the non-monetary asset received nor the fair value of the non-monetary asset given up can be determined within reasonable limits, the recorded amount of the asset transferred from the enterprise may be the only available measure of the transaction.[223] Furthermore, where the exchange involves 'similar productive assets' – i.e. assets that are of the same general type, that perform the same function or that are in the same line of business – a gain is not recognised.[224]

APB 29 also recognises that the exchange of non-monetary assets may include an amount of monetary consideration. In such cases, the recipient of the monetary consideration has realised a gain on the exchange to the extent that the amount of the monetary receipt exceeds a proportionate share of the recorded amount of the asset surrendered. The portion of the cost applicable to the realised amount should be based on the ratio of the monetary consideration to the total consideration received (i.e., monetary consideration plus the estimated fair value of the non-monetary asset received) or, if more clearly evident, the fair value of the non-monetary asset transferred.

The UITF published in May 2001 a draft abstract on exchanges of businesses or other non-monetary assets for equity in a subsidiary, joint venture or associate. This deals with, among other matters, the recognition of gains on the transfer of non-monetary assets by the investor into subsidiaries, joint ventures and associates, and is discussed in Chapters 6 and 7. The Standing Interpretations committee of the IASC issued SIC-13 – *Jointly Controlled Entities - Non-Monetary Contributions by Venturers* – in June 1998 that also deals with this topic under IAS. This guidance is discussed in Chapter 7.

Finally it must be emphasised that under UK GAAP currently, where non-monetary consideration is received for the provision of goods and services, that such consideration can only be included in the profit and loss account if it represents a realised profit. The draft Technical Release dealing with the determination of realised profits, dealt with at 2.1 above discusses this aspect in detail.

6 CONCLUSION

The growing complexity and diversity of business activity have given birth to a variety of forms of revenue-earning transactions which were never contemplated when the point of sale was established several decades ago as the general rule for revenue recognition. Added to this, the gradual move away from strict adherence to the realisation concept has resulted in contemporary generally accepted practice for the recognition of revenue becoming haphazard. Whilst there appears to be a growing practice of recognising revenue during the course of productive activity, it is generally done on the basis of exception, rather than in terms of an established principle.

At the current time, the ASB and the IASB are pushing forward a balance sheet based fair-value approach to revenue recognition. This approach, if implemented, would replace the long-established accounting process in use throughout the world, whereby transactions are allocated to accounting periods by reference to the matching and prudence concepts. The ASB's discussion paper (dealt with at 4.4 above) fundamentally contrasts two approaches to revenue recognition:

- the belief that no profit should be recognised until the risks in the operating cycle have been substantially eliminated, which the discussion paper equates to the historical cost model; and
- profit recognition rateably with the reduction of risk over the various stages of a business's operating cycle.

It is clearly the second approach which the ASB favours, as it sits more comfortably with the Board's fair-value based balance sheet approach to the recognition of gains and losses. However, it remains unclear in the absence of a definite statement to the contrary, whether the Board plans to allow revenue recognition before there is any contractual right to receive it, which would be in contradiction to the most basic tenet of common law. The adoption of such an approach would imply the valuation of unsold stock at selling price (i.e. its fair value) with the consequent recognition of profit on unsold goods. Such a development is not ruled out by the conceptual frameworks of either the ASB or the IASB, indeed it is implied by them as explained in Chapter 2 at 5.6. In our view, making the sale is *the* crucial prerequisite to recognising revenue and making a profit, and we hope that the standard-setters will clarify their attitude to this matter quickly and unambiguously.

These developments and uncertainties are further brought into prominence by the plans of the ASB and the IASB for a single statement of financial performance, which in our view, if adopted, will confuse two very different aspects of commercial activity. The operating performance of a business, resulting from its success or otherwise in selling its products, is at the heart of the current profit and loss account. In our view, users need to have this aspect of company performance – real commercial success at the operating level – clearly distinguished from holding gains. We are concerned that the current revenue recognition and performance statement proposals of the ASB and the IASB do not sufficiently reflect this important distinction.

References

1 APB Statement No. 4, *Basic Concepts and Accounting Principles Underlying Financial Statements of Business Enterprises*, AICPA, October 1970, para. 134.

2 The Council of the European Communities, *The Second Council Directive on Company Law*, 77/91/EEC.

3 *Ibid.*, Article 15.1(c).

4 CCAB, *The determination of realised profits and disclosure of distributable profits in the context of the Companies Acts 1948 to 1981 (TR 481)*, September 1982, paras. 4–6, passim.

5 *Ibid.*, para. 10.

6 SSAP 2, *Disclosure of accounting policies*, ASC, November 1971, para. 14.

7 Draft Technical Release (TECH 25/00), *The determination of realised profits and distributable profits in the context of the Companies Act 1985*, ICAEW and ICAS, 10 August 2000, para. 11.

8 FRED 21 *Accounting Policies*, ASB, January 1999, now replaced by FRS 18, *Accounting Policies*, ASB, December 2000.

9 Gains are defined as being increases on balance sheet net assets other than those resulting from contributions from owners. *Statement of Principles for Financial Reporting*, ASB, December 1999, para. 4.39.

10 TECH 25/00, para. 20.
11 *Ibid.*, para. 21.
12 *Ibid.*, para. 22.
13 *Ibid.*, para. 16.
14 *Statement of Principles for Financial Reporting*, Appendix III, para. 40.
15 *Statement of Principles for Financial Reporting*, para. 5.26.
16 *Ibid.*, Appendix III, paras. 40–50.
17 *Ibid.*, para. 50.
18 APB Statement No. 4, para. 150.
19 *Ibid.*, para. 151.
20 *Ibid.*, para. 152.
21 John H. Myers, 'The Critical Event and Recognition of Net Profit', *Accounting Review 34*, October 1959, pp. 528–532.
22 SFAC No. 5, *Recognition and Measurement in Financial Statements of Business Enterprises*, FASB, December 1984, paras. 83 and 84.
23 IAS 39, *Financial Instruments: Recognition and Measurement*, IASC, December 1998, paras. 69 and 103.
24 SFAS 115, *Accounting for Certain Investments in Debt and Equity Securities*, FASB, May 1993, paras. 12–13.
25 SFAS 133, *Accounting for Derivative Instruments and Hedging Activities*, FASB, June 1998, paras. 17–18.
26 IAS 39, para. 103.
27 US GAAP requires fair value measurement for all derivatives, including those linked to unquoted equity instruments if they are to be settled in cash but not those to be settled by delivery, which are outside the scope of SFAS 133.
28 IAS 39, para. 70.
29 *Ibid.*
30 European Commission, Directorate General – Internal Market, *Financial reporting: Commission welcomes adoption of fair value accounting Directive*, press release, Brussels, 31 May 2001.
31 Sale of Goods Act 1979, s 2(1).
32 *Ibid.*, s 2(4).
33 *Ibid.*, s 2(5).
34 *Ibid.*, s 18, Rule 1.
35 *Ibid.*, s 18, Rule 2.
36 APB Statement No. 4, para. 151.
37 SFAC No. 5, paras. 83 and 84.
38 SFAS 48, *Revenue Recognition When Right of Return Exists*, FASB, June 1981, para. 6.
39 *Ibid.*, para. 6.
40 *Ibid.*, para. 8.
41 APB Statement No. 4, para. 150.
42 *Statement of Principles for Financial Reporting*, para. 5.26.
43 *Ibid.*, para. 4.39.
44 *Ibid.*, Chapter 5, Principles.
45 *Ibid.*, para. 5.33.
46 *Ibid.*, paras. 5.34 and 5.35.
47 *Ibid.*, para. 5.36.
48 *Ibid.*, Appendix I, para. 14.
49 IAS 41, *Agriculture*, IASC, December 2000, para. 5.
50 *Ibid.*, para. 12.
51 *Ibid.*, para. 13.
52 *Ibid.*, para. 8.
53 *Ibid.*, para. 26.
54 *Ibid.*, para. 51.
55 *Ibid.*, para. 2.
56 CA 85, Sch. 4, para. 12(a).
57 *Ibid.*, s 262(3).
58 FRS 18, Appendix IV, para. 15.
59 For a full analysis of the ASB's *Statement of Principles for Financial Reporting* (conceptual framework), see Section 5 of Chapter 2.
60 *Ibid.*, para. 5.1.
61 *Ibid.*, Chapter 5, Principles.
62 *Ibid.*, para. 5.26.
63 FRS 12, *Provisions, Contingent Liabilities and Contingent Assets*, ASB, September 1998, para. 2.
64 *Ibid.*, para. 14.
65 Discussion Paper, *Revenue Recognition*, ASB, July 2001.
66 *Ibid.*, Preface.
67 ASB PN 189, 5 July 2001.
68 *Ibid.*
69 *Revenue Recognition*, Preface.
70 *Ibid.*, para. 1.2.
71 *Ibid.*, para. 1.2.
72 *Ibid.*, para. 2.15.
73 *Ibid.*, para. 1.18.
74 *Ibid.*, para. 1.30.
75 *Ibid.*, para. 2.20.
76 *Ibid.*, para. 3.3.
77 *Ibid.*, para. 3.43.
78 *Ibid.*, para. 4.2.
79 *Ibid.*, para. 4.2.
80 *Ibid.*, para. 4.2.
81 *Ibid.*, para. 5.2.
82 *Statement of Principles for Financial Reporting*, para. 4.6.
83 *Revenue Recognition*, para. 5.8.
84 *Ibid.*, para. 5.16.
85 *Ibid.*, para. 5.18.
86 *Ibid.*, para. 5.23.
87 *Ibid.*, paras. 5.23 and 5.39.
88 *Ibid.*, paras. 5.43 and 5.47.
89 *Ibid.*, para. 5.51.
90 *Ibid.*, para. 5.62.
91 *Ibid.*, para. 6.20.
92 *Ibid.*, para. 6.48.
93 *Ibid.*, para. 7.5.
94 *Ibid.*, paras. 7.5 and 7.10.
95 IAS 18 (Original), *Revenue Recognition*, IASC, December 1982, para. 4.
96 IAS 18, *Revenue*, IASC, December 1993, Objective.

97 *Ibid.*, para. 1.
98 *Ibid.*, para. 6.
99 *Ibid.*, para. 7.
100 *Statement of Principles for Financial Reporting*, para. 4.39.
101 IAS 18, para. 10.
102 *Ibid.*, para. 7.
103 *Ibid.*, para. 11.
104 *Ibid.*, para. 12.
105 *Ibid.*, para. 13.
106 IAS 11, *Construction Contracts*, IASC, December 1993, paras. 7–10.
107 *Ibid.*
108 IAS 18, para. 14.
109 *Ibid.*, para. 19.
110 *Ibid.*, para. 16.
111 *Ibid.*, para. 15.
112 *Ibid.*, para. 17.
113 *Ibid.*, para. 20.
114 *Ibid.*, para. 21.
115 *Ibid.*, para. 26.
116 *Ibid.*, para. 20.
117 *Ibid.*, para. 24.
118 *Ibid.*, para. 25.
119 *Ibid.*, paras. 29–30.
120 *Ibid.*, para. 35.
121 ARB 43, *Restatement and Revision of Accounting Research Bulletins*, AICPA, June 1953, Chapter 1, Section A, para. 1.
122 *Ibid.*, para. 1.
123 *Ibid.*, para. 11.
124 *Ibid.*, para. 13.
125 ARB 45, *Long-Term Construction-Type Contracts*, AICPA, October 1955, para. 15.
126 SFAC No. 5, para. 83.
127 *Ibid.*
128 *Ibid.*
129 *Ibid.*
130 Reed K. Storey and Sylvia Storey, *Special Report: The Framework of Financial Accounting Concepts and Standards*, FASB, January 1998, p. 158.
131 *Ibid.*
132 *Ibid.*, p. 160.
133 Securities and Exchange Commission, *Office of the Chief Accountant: Staff Accounting Bulletin No. 101: Revenue Recognition in Financial Statements – Frequently Asked Questions and Answers*, October 2000.
134 Securities and Exchange Commission, *Staff Accounting Bulletin: No. 101 – Revenue Recognition in Financial Statements*, 3 December 1999, Topic 13A.
135 *Ibid.*, question 2.
136 *Ibid.*, question 2.
137 *Ibid.*, question 2.
138 *Ibid.*, question 2.
139 *Ibid.*, question 2.
140 *Ibid.*, question 3.
141 *Ibid.*, question 4.
142 *Ibid.*, question 5.
143 *Ibid.*, question 6.
144 *Ibid.*, question 7.
145 *Ibid.*, question 9.
146 Based on the AICPA Industry Accounting Guide, *Accounting for Franchise Fee Revenue*, AICPA, 1973.
147 SFAS 45, *Accounting for Franchise Fee Revenue*, FASB, March 1981, para. 5.
148 *Ibid.*, para. 5.
149 *Ibid.*, para 12.
150 IAS 18, Appendix, para. 18.
151 *Ibid.*
152 SFAS 50, *Financial Reporting in the Record and Music Industry*, FASB, November 1981, para. 8.
153 SFAS 91, *Accounting for Nonrefundable Fees and Costs Associated with Originating or Acquiring Loans and Initial Direct Costs of Leases*, FASB, December 1986, para. 5.
154 *Ibid.*
155 SORP on Advances, British Bankers Association and Irish Bankers Association, November 1997, para. 41
156 IAS 18, Appendix, para. 14.
157 J.Hitchens, M.Hogg, D.Mallett, *Banking: An Industry Accounting and Auditing Guide*, published by the ICAEW, 1996, para. 10.9.3.
158 SFAS 91, para. 8.
159 *Ibid.*, para. 8a.
160 *Ibid.*, para. 8b.
161 IAS 18, Appendix, para. 14(b)(ii).
162 This is also the view taken in the US; see SFAS 91 at para. 10.
163 Aluminium Industrie Vaassen B.V. v Romalpa Aluminium Limited [1976] WLR 676.
164 Accounting Recommendation 2.207, *Accounting for goods sold subject to reservation of title*, ICAEW, July 1976.
165 IAS 18, para. 14.
166 *Ibid.*, para. 17.
167 *Ibid.*, Appendix, para. 6.
168 *Ibid.*, para. 7.
169 Exposure Draft, *Statement of Principles for Financial Reporting*, ASB, November 1995, para. 4.30.
170 Revised Exposure Draft, *Statement of Principles for Financial Reporting*, ASB, March 1999, para. 5.27.
171 *Ibid.*, Appendix, para. 12.
172 Statement of Position 97–2, *Software Revenue Recognition*, Accounting Standards Executive Committee, American Institute of Certified Public Accountants, October 27, 1997.
173 *Ibid.*, para. 8.
174 Companies reporting under US GAAP would apply Accounting Research Bulletin (ARB)

No. 45, *Long-Term Construction-Type Contracts*, and SOP 81–1, *Accounting for Performance of Construction-Type and Certain Production-Type Contracts*.
175 SSAP 9, *Stocks and long-term contracts*, ASC, Revised September 1988, para. 22.
176 *Ibid.*, paras. 28 and 29.
177 SOP 97–2, para. 7.
178 IAS 18, Appendix, para. 19.
179 SOP 97–2, para. 12.
180 *Ibid.*, para. 11.
181 *Ibid.*, para. 10.
182 *Ibid.*
183 *Ibid.*
184 *Ibid.* Companies reporting under UK GAAP would recognise the loss in accordance with FRS 12, *Provisions, Contingent Liabilities and Contingent Assets*, whilst companies reporting under US GAAP would apply SFAS 5, *Accounting for Contingencies.*
185 SOP 97–2, para. 37.
186 *Ibid.*, para. 12.
187 *Ibid.*, paras. 56–62.
188 *Ibid.*, paras. 63–71.
189 *Ibid.*, paras. 48 and 49.
190 *Ibid.*, paras. 43–47.
191 *Ibid.*, paras. 43 and 47.
192 *Ibid.*, para. 37.
193 *Ibid.*, para. 57.
194 *Ibid.*, para. 28.
195 *Ibid.*
196 *Ibid.*, para. 29.
197 *Ibid.*, para. 51.
198 *Ibid.*, para. 63.
199 *Ibid.*, para. 64.
200 *Ibid.*, para. 65.
201 *Ibid.*, para. 66.
202 IAS 18, Appendix, para. 20.
203 *Ibid.*
204 SFAS 53, *Financial Reporting by Producers and Distributors of Motion Picture Films*, FASB, December 1981, para. 6.
205 FRRP PN65, 8 March 2001.
206 *Ibid.*
207 *Ibid.*
208 IAS 18, Appendix, para. 9.
209 SFAS 66, *Accounting for Sales of Real Estate*, FASB, October 1982, para. 5.
210 *Ibid.*, para. 6.
211 *Ibid.*
212 ASC, *Guidance Notes on SSAP 21, Accounting for Leases and Hire Purchase Contracts*, August 1984, paras. 150–156, passim.
213 UITF 26, *Barter transactions for advertising*, UITF, November 2000, para. 10.
214 *Ibid.*, para. 10.
215 *Ibid.*, para. 8.
216 IAS 18, para. 12.
217 *Ibid.*
218 IAS 16, *Property, Plant and Equipment*, IASC, Revised 1998, para. 22.
219 *Ibid.*, para. 22.
220 *Ibid.*, para. 21.
221 IAS 38, *Intangible Assets*, IASC, July 1998, paras. 34 and 35.
222 APB Opinion No. 29, *Accounting for Nonmonetary Transactions*, Accounting Principles Board, May 1973, para. 18.
223 *Ibid.*, para. 26.
224 *Ibid.*, paras. 3e and 21b.

Chapter 4 Corporate governance

1 THE NEED FOR CORPORATE GOVERNANCE REFORM

A series of spectacular corporate failures and financial scandals in the late 1980s, including BCCI, Polly Peck and Maxwell, heightened concerns about the standard of financial reporting and accountability. These concerns centred around an apparent low level of confidence both in financial reporting and in the ability of auditors to provide the safeguards which the users of company annual reports sought and expected. The factors underlying these were seen as the looseness of accounting standards, the absence of a clear framework for ensuring that directors kept under review the controls in their businesses, and competitive pressures both on companies and on auditors which made it difficult for auditors to stand up to demanding boards.[1] These concerns were heightened by criticisms of the seeming lack of effective board accountability for such matters as directors' remuneration – particularly in the light of an increasing trend in directors being appointed on lucrative rolling contracts, as well as certain well-publicised large compensation payments for loss of office.

1.1 The Cadbury Committee

In response to these concerns, the Committee on the Financial Aspects of Corporate Governance (the Cadbury Committee) was set up in May 1991 by the Financial Reporting Council, the London Stock Exchange and the accountancy profession, under the chairmanship of Sir Adrian Cadbury. The terms of reference of the Committee were to consider the following issues in relation to financial reporting and accountability and to make recommendations on good practice:[2]

(a) the responsibilities of executive and non-executive directors for reviewing and reporting on performance to shareholders and other financially interested parties; and the frequency, clarity and form in which information should be provided;

(b) the case for audit committees of the board, including their composition and role;

(c) the principal responsibilities of auditors and the extent and value of the audit;
(d) the links between shareholders, boards and auditors; and
(e) any other relevant matters.

The Committee's approach was to provide a framework for establishing good corporate governance and accountability. This was done through its Code of Best Practice (the Cadbury Code), which it put forward as a benchmark against which companies could be assessed. The Code embodied underlying principles of openness, integrity and accountability which, according to the Committee, went together.

Although compliance with the Code was recommended, the Committee stressed that it was voluntary and directed at establishing best practice. The Committee was also of the view that companies should be allowed some flexibility in implementing the Code; this was necessary in order to encourage companies to comply with the spirit of the recommendations. The Code provided a target to which companies could aspire, rather than a straitjacket of rules and regulations.

In response to the Committee's recommendations, the London Stock Exchange adopted as part of its Listing Rules the requirement for UK incorporated listed companies to include in their annual report and accounts a statement as to whether or not they had complied throughout the accounting period with the Code. This was supplemented by the requirement to report details of, and reasons for, any non-compliance during the period and to have the directors' statement reviewed by the auditors insofar as it related to objectively verifiable matters in the Code.[3]

Two aspects of the Code could not initially be complied with as they were the subject of continuing debate. These were the requirements for directors to report on the effectiveness of internal control and that the business was a going concern. The Committee noted that companies would not be able to comply with these points until the necessary guidance had been developed. It recommended that such guidance be developed by the accountancy profession together with representatives of preparers of accounts. Two working parties were set up under the auspices of the Hundred Group of Finance Directors, the ICAEW and the ICAS: the Going Concern Working Group, under the chairmanship of Mr Rodney Baker-Bates and the Internal Control Working Group, under the chairmanship of Mr Paul Rutteman. However, the development of the guidance proved to be a difficult task and it was to be about two years after the issue of the Cadbury Report before the working parties produced the necessary guidance to enable the Cadbury jigsaw to be completed.

1.2 The Greenbury Committee

The remit of the Cadbury Committee had been corporate governance as a whole, of which executive remuneration was only a part. The comprehensive review of directors' pay as a single issue fell to the Study Group on Directors' Remuneration, commonly known as the Greenbury Committee after its chairman Sir Richard Greenbury, chairman of Marks and Spencer. This Committee was established in January 1995 at the initiative of (but independent from) the CBI, with the remit of identifying good practice in determining directors' remuneration and preparing a Code of such practice for use by UK PLCs.

The Greenbury Committee issued its report in July 1995,[4] which contained a Code of Best Practice. In October 1995 and June 1996 the London Stock Exchange gave effect to certain of these recommendations by amending its *Listing Rules*.

1.3 The Hampel Committee

In the Cadbury Report, the Committee stated that it would 'remain responsible for reviewing the implementation of the proposals until a successor body is appointed in two years' time, to examine the progress and to continue the ongoing governance review. It will be for our sponsors to agree the remit of the new body and to establish the basis of its support. In the meantime, a programme of research will be undertaken to assist the future monitoring of the Code.'[5]

In fulfilling that latter responsibility the Cadbury Committee:

(a) set up a Monitoring Sub-Committee;

(b) encouraged research into a number of projects related to corporate governance; and

(c) collaborated with the Association of British Insurers in a project to monitor best practice.

In the event, it was to be almost three years before a successor body was formed, in November 1995, under the chairmanship of Sir Ronald Hampel, Chairman of ICI. The remit of this Committee was to seek to promote high standards of corporate governance in the interests of investor protection and in order to preserve and enhance the standing of companies listed on the Stock Exchange. The Committee's remit was to extend to listed companies only. Against this background the Committee was to:

(a) conduct a review of the Cadbury Code and its implementation to ensure that the original purpose was being achieved, proposing amendments to and deletions from the Code as necessary;

(b) keep under review the role of directors, executive and non-executive, recognising the need for board cohesion and the common legal responsibilities of all directors;

(c) be prepared to pursue any relevant matters arising from the report of the Study Group on Directors' Remuneration chaired by Sir Richard Greenbury;

(d) address as necessary the role of shareholders in corporate governance issues;

(e) address as necessary the role of auditors in corporate governance issues; and

(f) deal with any other relevant matters.

Without impairing investor protection the Committee was always to keep in mind the need to restrict the regulatory burden on companies, e.g. by substituting principles for detail wherever possible.[6]

The Hampel Committee began its work early in 1996, and published a preliminary report in August 1997. In January 1998 it published its final report, taking into account comments on the earlier document.

As can be seen from its remit, the work of the Hampel Committee was in large part one of review of the findings of earlier committees, the overwhelming majority of which it endorsed in its final report.[7]

The Hampel Report accepted the Cadbury Committee's definition of corporate governance[8] being 'the system by which companies are directed and controlled'.[9] Hampel then notes that this 'puts the directors of a company at the centre of any discussion on corporate governance, linked to the role of shareholders, since they appoint the directors.'[10] The report emphasises that how companies are run cannot be prescribed, saying: 'Good corporate governance is not just a matter of prescribing particular corporate structures and complying with a number of hard and fast rules. There is a need for broad principles. All concerned should then apply these flexibly and with common sense to the varying circumstances of individual companies.'[11] More generally still, it states that 'The true safeguard for good corporate governance lies in the application of informed and independent judgement by experienced and qualified individuals - executive and non-executive directors, shareholders and auditors.'[12] Having reached broad conclusions on the nature and purpose of corporate governance, the Committee identified some broad principles which it hoped would command general support.[13] These were supplemented with a number of detailed Code provisions. The objective of the principles and Code, like those of the Cadbury and Greenbury Codes, is not to prescribe corporate behaviour in detail but to secure sufficient disclosure so that investors and others can assess companies' performance and governance practice and respond in an informed way.[14] In a sensible evolution from Cadbury and Greenbury, Hampel recommends that companies describe how they have applied these general principles as well as stating whether or not they have complied with the detailed provisions.[15]

The final task of the Hampel Committee was to pass on this set of principles and Code of good corporate governance practice embracing Cadbury, Greenbury and its own work to the London Stock Exchange with the intention that it would be incorporated into the listing rules.[16] In June 1998, the London Stock Exchange published the final version of the Principles of Good Governance and Code of Best Practice (the 'Combined Code'), together with revisions to the *Listing Rules*. The content of the Combined Code is discussed at 2 below.

In this chapter we review the recommendations of the Hampel Committee in so far as they impact on the company annual report and accounts.

2 REPORTING UNDER THE COMBINED CODE

The Combined Code is presented in two sections. Section 1 relates to companies whereas Section 2 relates to institutional investors and is outside the scope of this book. As stated above, we are primarily concerned in this chapter with the impact that the Combined Code has on the company annual report and accounts. This is governed by the rules of the Financial Services Authority as follows:

'In the case of a company incorporated in the United Kingdom, the following additional items must be included in its report and accounts:

(a) a narrative statement of how it has applied the principles set out in Section 1 of the Combined Code, providing explanation which enables its shareholders to evaluate how the principles have been applied;

(b) a statement as to whether or not it has complied throughout the accounting period with the Code provisions set out in Section 1 of the Combined Code. A company that has not complied with the Code provisions, or complied with only some of the Code provisions or (in the case of provisions whose requirements are of a continuing nature) complied for only part of an accounting period, must specify the Code provisions with which it has not complied, and (where relevant) for what part of the period such non-compliance continued, and give reasons for any non-compliance;'[17]

The most significant change from the previous regime is part (a) above. Rather than making a simple statement of compliance, or otherwise, with the detailed provisions of a code, boards must now also describe, in their own words, how they apply the general principles of corporate governance. We believe this to be a much more meaningful requirement, although to give a reasoned and considered description of their governance procedures represents a significant challenge for boards. The detailed Combined Code provisions set out some basic elements of the governance process, and it is perhaps not surprising that some are reproduced by companies in these discussions. It is to be hoped, however, that this be kept to a minimum to prevent the disclosures degenerating into general boilerplate.

Section 1 of the Combined Code is divided into four parts as follows:

A Directors;

B Directors' remuneration;

C Relations with shareholders; and

D Accountability and audit.

Set out below is a discussion of the points under A, C and D. Some of the detailed provisions are of a factual nature and hence self explanatory. The principles are shown in bold text, followed by the related Code provisions. The provisions which must be covered by the auditors' review are marked with an asterisk, although auditors' review procedures are not discussed. The requirements of part B are discussed at 3.1 in Chapter 32. It should be noted that the Hampel Report did not seek to reproduce all the discussions of Cadbury and Greenbury with which it agreed, and accordingly much of these earlier reports remains relevant. For this reason many of the footnote references that follow are to the Cadbury Report as well as the Hampel Report.

Some examples of corporate governance disclosures from company accounts are shown in the Appendix at the end of this chapter.

2.1 Directors

A.1 The Board

Every listed company should be headed by an effective board which should lead and control the company.

A.1.1 The board should meet regularly.

A.1.2* The board should have a formal schedule of matters specifically reserved to it for decision.

A.1.3* There should be a procedure agreed by the board for directors in the furtherance of their duties to take independent professional advice if necessary, at the company's expense.

A.1.4 All directors should have access to the advice and services of the company secretary, who is responsible to the board for ensuring that board procedures are followed and that applicable rules and regulations are complied with. Any question of the removal of the company secretary should be a matter for the board as a whole.

A.1.5 All directors should bring an independent judgement to bear on issues of strategy, performance, resources, (including key appointments) and standards of conduct.

A.1.6 Every director should receive appropriate training on the first occasion that he or she is appointed to the board of a listed company, and subsequently as necessary.

Every public company should be headed by an effective board which can both lead and control the business. Within the context of the UK unitary board system, this means a board made up of a combination of executive directors, with their intimate knowledge of the business, and of non-executive directors, who can bring a broader view to the company's activities, under a chairman who accepts the duties and responsibilities which the position entails.[18]

The arrangements whereby boards ensure effective leadership and control will differ greatly between companies. The level of direct involvement with management below board level will depend on the extent of empowerment of executive management, and the amount of monitoring required will vary accordingly.

Provision A.1.1

The prime responsibility of the board of directors is to determine the broad strategy of the company and to ensure its implementation. To do this successfully requires high quality leadership. It also requires that the directors have sufficient freedom of action to exercise their leadership. The board can only fulfil its responsibilities if it meets regularly and reasonably often.[19]

The frequency of board meetings may also vary considerably between companies, depending, inter alia, on the role of its sub-committees and executive management.

Provision A.1.2

Some companies have policies and procedures manuals which specifically cover this point, while others have prepared a list of items to be considered, if appropriate, at each board meeting. Irrespective of the form of such a schedule, it is important that it is formally adopted by the board, that it is circulated to directors and, at least, to executive management and that it is kept up to date.

The schedule might include:

- approval of material acquisitions, disposals, investments, capital projects and other significant transactions;
- authority levels, including the definition of transactions which require multiple board signatures;
- procedures to be followed when decisions are required between board meetings;
- corporate business plan and strategy;
- treasury and risk management policy;
- selection and appointment of non-executive directors and company secretary;
- selection and appointment of senior executives;
- approval of accounts and other reports to shareholders; and
- the establishment of codes of conduct regarding compliance with laws and ethical standards of behaviour.

The existence of a formal schedule will meet the basic requirement of the Combined Code provision. However, as part of effective leadership and control, the directors should consider the procedures to ensure that all relevant matters are referred to the board together with adequate information on which to base decisions, and the sanctions available to them where, for example, authority levels are exceeded.

Provision A.1.3

This requirement is in addition to any procedures that enable the directors to consult the company's advisers, and recognises that there may be situations in which a director might wish to take independent advice.

The procedures should be formalised, for example, by board resolution, in the company's articles or in a director's letter of appointment.[20]

Provision A.1.4

The company secretary has a key role to play in ensuring that board procedures are both followed and regularly reviewed. The chairman and the board will look to the company secretary for guidance on what their responsibilities are under the rules and regulations to which they are subject and on how those responsibilities should be discharged. All directors should have access to the advice and services of the company secretary and should recognise that the chairman is entitled to the strong and positive support of the company secretary in ensuring the effective functioning of the board.[21] Although the procedures allowing such access may be clearly understood, they should be acknowledged by the board by way of minute or in the letter of appointment for each director.

Provision A.1.5

The basic legal duties of directors are to act in good faith in the interests of the company and for a proper purpose; and to exercise care and skill. These are derived from common law and are common to all directors. The duties are owed to the company, meaning generally the shareholders collectively, both present and future, not the shareholders at a given point in time.[22] The Cadbury Committee clearly saw independence of judgement as the essential quality which non-executive directors should bring to the board's deliberations,[23] the Combined Code makes clear that this is a duty of all directors. Hampel also notes that there is a view that non-executive directors should face less onerous duties than executive directors. However, it supports the retention of common duties in the interests of the unity and cohesion of the board.[24]

A.2 Chairman and CEO

There are two key tasks at the top of every public company - the running of the board and the executive responsibility for the running of the company's business. There should be a clear division of responsibilities at the head of the company which will ensure a balance of power and authority, such that no one individual has unfettered powers of decision.

A.2.1 A decision to combine the posts of chairman and chief executive officer in one person should be publicly justified. Whether the posts are held by different people or by the same person, there should be a strong and independent non-executive element on the board, with a recognised senior member other than the chairman to whom concerns can be conveyed. The chairman, chief executive and senior independent director should be identified in the annual report.

Cadbury saw the chairman's role in securing good corporate governance as being crucial and described it as follows: 'Chairmen are primarily responsible for the working of the board, for the balance of its membership subject to board and shareholders' approval, and for ensuring that all directors, executive and non-executive alike, are enabled to play their full part in its activities'.[25] Hampel endorsed this description, subject to its view on the role of the nomination committee (see later), and added: 'The chief executive officer's task is to run the business and to implement the policies and strategies adopted by the board. There are thus two distinct roles.'[26]

Accordingly, both committees came to the view that the roles of chairman and chief executive should in principle be separate. Hampel further noted that a number of companies have combined the two roles successfully, either permanently or for a time.[27] Where the roles are combined the board should explain and justify the fact.

Whether or not the roles are combined, the Combined Code now requires a senior non-executive director to be identified, to cater for occasions when there is a need to convey concerns to the board other than through the chairman or chief executive.[28] The Cadbury Code only required this when these two posts were held by the same individual.

A.3 Board Balance

The board should include a balance of executive and non-executive directors (including independent non-executives) such that no individual or small group of individuals can dominate the board's decision taking.

A.3.1 The board should include non-executive directors of sufficient calibre and number for their views to carry significant weight in the board's decisions. Non-executive directors should comprise not less than one third of the board.

A.3.2 The majority of non-executive directors should be independent of management and free from any business or other relationship which could materially interfere with the exercise of their independent judgement. Non-executive directors considered by the board to be independent in this sense should be identified in the annual report.

As a consequence of its remit, precipitated largely by corporate failures, Cadbury emphasised the control function of non-executive directors. Hampel sought to rebalance the debate by stressing that non-executives should have a strategic as well as a monitoring function.[29]

Provision A.3.1

Non-executive directors can bring to boards both breadth of experience and specialist knowledge and contribute to business prosperity, as well as independently monitoring the governance of the company. For non-executives to be effective, Hampel considered that they should comprise at least one third of the board.

Provision A.3.2

Cadbury recommended that a majority of non-executive directors should be independent, and defined this as 'independent of management and free from any business or other relationship which could materially interfere with the exercise of their independent judgement'.[30] Hampel agreed with this definition, and did not consider it practicable to lay down more precise criteria for independence.[31] The Committee made it clear that it is for the board to decide in particular cases whether this definition of independence is met. The corollary is that boards should disclose in the annual report which of the directors are considered to be independent and be prepared to justify their view if challenged.[32] Hampel recognised, however, that non-executive directors who are not in this sense 'independent' may nonetheless make a useful contribution to the board.[33]

A.4 Supply of information

The board should be supplied in a timely manner with information in a form and of a quality appropriate to enable it to discharge its duties.

A.4.1 Management has an obligation to provide the board with appropriate and timely information, but information volunteered by management is unlikely to be enough in all circumstances and directors should make further enquiries where necessary. The chairman should ensure that all directors are properly briefed on issues arising at board meetings.

Hampel endorsed the view of the Cadbury Committee that the effectiveness of non-executive directors (indeed, of all directors) turns, to a considerable extent, on the quality of the information they receive.[34]

A.5 Appointments to the Board

There should be a formal and transparent procedure for the appointment of new directors to the board.

A.5.1 Unless the board is small, a nomination committee should be established to make recommendations to the board on all new board appointments. A majority of the members of this committee should be non-executive directors and the chairman should be either the chairman of the board or a non-executive director. The chairman and members of the nomination committee should be identified in the annual report.

Appointment to the board should be a transparent process, with decisions taken, in reality as well as in form, by the whole board. To assist in this process Hampel recommends that the use of a nomination committee should be accepted as best practice, with the proviso that smaller boards may prefer to fulfil the function themselves.[35]

Hampel also considered the practice of appointment of directors to represent outside interests, for example a major creditor or a major shareholder. It concluded that this practice is, other than in exceptional cases, incompatible with board cohesion.[36]

A.6 Re-election

All directors should be required to submit themselves for re-election at regular intervals and at least every three years.

A.6.1* Non-executive directors should be appointed for specified terms subject to re-election and to Companies Act provisions relating to the removal of a director, and reappointment should not be automatic.

A.6.2* All directors should be subject to election by shareholders at the first opportunity after their appointment, and to re-election thereafter at intervals of no more than three years. The names of directors submitted for election or re-election should be accompanied by sufficient biographical details to enable shareholders to take an informed decision on their election.

Directors of listed companies are required by the Listing Rules to submit themselves for election at the first AGM after their appointment. The National Association of Pension Funds (NAPF) and the Association of British Insurers (ABI) expect all directors to submit themselves for re-election at intervals of no more than three years. Hampel endorsed this latter view and recommended that those companies who do not as yet conform with it should make the necessary changes in their Articles of Association as soon as possible. Hampel also recommended that all names submitted for election or re-election as directors should be accompanied by biographical details indicating their relevant qualifications and experience. As a result of this provision the previous Stock Exchange requirement for the annual report to give a short biographical note on each of the independent non-executive directors has been repealed.

2.2 Relations with shareholders

C.1 Dialogue with Institutional Shareholders

Companies should be ready, where practicable, to enter into dialogue with institutional shareholders based on the mutual understanding of objectives.

C.2 Constructive use of the AGM

Boards should use the AGM to communicate with private investors and encourage their participation.

C.2.1 Companies should count all proxy votes and, except where a poll is called, should indicate the level of proxies lodged on each resolution, and the balance for and against the resolution, after it has been dealt with on a show of hands.

C.2.2 Companies should propose a separate resolution at the AGM on each substantially separate issue and should in particular propose a resolution at the AGM relating to the report and accounts.

> C.2.3 The chairman of the board should arrange for the chairmen of the audit, remuneration and nomination committees to be available to answer questions at the AGM.
>
> C.2.4 Companies should arrange for the Notice of the AGM and related papers to be sent to shareholders at least 20 working days before the meeting.

The recommendation of Cadbury, reiterated by Hampel, was that 'Institutional investors should encourage regular, systematic contact at senior executive level to exchange views and information on strategy, performance, board membership and quality of management'.[37] The idea of greater contact between companies and institutions was developed in 1995 in the report of a joint City/Industry working group chaired by Mr Paul Myners and titled Developing a Winning Partnership. The main recommendations of this report included:

- investors to articulate their investment objectives to management;
- investors to be more open with managements in giving feedback on companies' strategies and performance;
- improved training for fund managers on industrial and commercial awareness;
- improved training for company managers involved in investor relations;
- meetings between companies and institutional investors to be properly prepared, with a clear and agreed agenda.[38]

Principle C.1 now requires boards to describe how they conduct such dialogue with their institutional investors.

Provision C.2.1

Hampel considered recommending that companies should put all resolutions to a postal vote, and announce the results of the ballot at the beginning of the meeting. However, it concluded that this might be seen as a move to stifle debate, and that the time was not ripe for a radical change of this kind.[39]

Provision C.2.2

The practice of 'bundling' different proposals in a single resolution has been widely criticised. Hampel considered that shareholders should have an opportunity to vote separately on each substantially separate proposal.[40] The directors must lay before the AGM the annual accounts and the directors' report.[41] Whilst many boards propose a resolution relating to the report and accounts, this is not a legal requirement. Hampel recommended this as best practice, to allow a general discussion of the performance and prospects of the business, and provide an opportunity for the shareholders in effect to give – or withhold – approval of the directors' policies and conduct of the company.[42]

Provision C.2.3

Cadbury had recommended that the chairman of the audit committee should be available to answer questions about its work at the AGM,[43] and Greenbury had made a similar recommendation relating to the chairman of the remuneration committee. Hampel extended this requirement to the chairman of the nomination committee, although noted that it should be for the chairman of the meeting to decide which questions to answer himself and which to refer to a colleague.[44]

As well as allowing reasonable time for discussion at the meeting, Hampel also recommended that the chairman should, if appropriate, also undertake to provide the questioner with a written answer to any significant question which cannot be answered on the spot.[45]

Provision C.2.4

The requirement to give 20 working days (i.e. excluding weekends and Bank Holidays) notice of the AGM is a lengthening of the notice currently required by law of 21 days.[46] The reason given by Hampel is that this longer period will help institutions to consult their clients before deciding how to vote.

2.3 Accountability and audit

D.1 Financial reporting

The board should present a balanced and understandable assessment of the company's position and prospects.

D.1.1* The directors should explain their responsibility for preparing the accounts and there should be a statement by the auditors about their reporting responsibilities.

D.1.2 The board's responsibility to present a balanced and understandable assessment extends to interim and other price-sensitive public reports and reports to regulators as well as to information required to be presented by statutory requirements.

D.1.3 The directors should report that the business is a going concern, with supporting assumptions or qualifications as necessary.

It is well known that both the flexibility allowed to directors through the selection of accounting policies, and the degree of judgement and estimation which underlies the financial reporting process, are significant elements of the expectation gap. The fact that different accounting treatments could be applied to essentially the same facts, means that a company could theoretically report several materially different results of operations and financial positions, each of which could comply with the overriding requirement to show a true and fair view.

Consequently, in order to obviate as far as possible the effects of alternative accounting treatments and presentational techniques, Cadbury placed considerable emphasis on the need for shareholders to receive a coherent narrative, supported by figures, of a company's performance and prospects. The Cadbury Committee recommended that boards should pay particular attention to their duty to present a balanced and understandable assessment of their companies' position, stressing that balance requires that setbacks should be dealt with as well as successes.[47]

With this in mind, and with a view to providing a framework within which directors can discuss the main factors underlying their companies' financial performance and position, the ASB issued in July 1993 a statement of best practice entitled *Operating and Financial Review*. The Operating and Financial Review (OFR) is discussed in detail at 5 below.

Provision D.1.1

(a) Directors' responsibilities

The requirement for such an explanation of responsibilities is included in the auditing standard *Auditors' Reports on Financial Statements* (SAS 600), which requires auditors to provide such an explanation in their audit report if directors have not done so in the accounts. SAS 600 provides example wording for the statement of directors' responsibilities in respect of the accounts as set out below. As it is phrased in terms of a single company a group will need to amend it accordingly.[48]

> Company law requires the directors to prepare financial statements for each financial year which give a true and fair view of the state of affairs of the company and of the profit or loss of the company for that period. In preparing those financial statements, the directors are required to
>
> – select suitable accounting policies and then apply them consistently;
>
> – make judgements and estimates that are reasonable and prudent;
>
> – state whether applicable accounting standards have been followed, subject to any material departures disclosed and explained in the financial statements;[6]
>
> – prepare the financial statements on the going concern basis unless it is inappropriate to presume that the company will continue in business.[7]
>
> The directors are responsible for keeping proper accounting records which disclose with reasonable accuracy at any time the financial position of the company and to enable them to ensure that the financial statements comply with the Companies Act 1985. They are also responsible for safeguarding the assets of the company and hence for taking reasonable steps for the prevention and detection of fraud and other irregularities.
>
> [6] Large companies only.
>
> [7] If no separate statement on going concern is made by the directors.

It is no longer necessary for the final bullet point to be included since listed companies are required to make a specific statement about going concern (discussed under provision D.1.3 below).

An article on directors' responsibilities statements appeared in the 3 November 1993 issue of the Law Society *Gazette*.[49] The article (which emanated from the Law Society's Committee on Company Law) expressed concern that companies could, if they did not take legal advice on the contents of the statement of responsibilities, run the risk of extending the legal liability of directors 'unnecessarily'. It is, however, difficult to understand how the example statement in SAS 600 could give rise to an extension of directors' liability as it merely summarises the responsibilities imposed on directors by the Companies Act together with their fiduciary duty to safeguard the company's assets.

The article implied that there is some element of shared responsibility between the directors and auditors for the preparation of financial statements, whereas the legal position is that the directors have sole responsibility in this regard. Further, it was implied that the directors are responsible for instructing the auditors to take whatever steps and undertake whatever inspections they consider necessary. In fact, the auditors' responsibilities in company law already require them to perform whatever work they consider necessary; this legal responsibility may neither be added to nor diminished by the directors.

The Cadbury Committee recommended the inclusion in the report and accounts of a statement of directors' responsibilities 'so that shareholders are clear where the boundaries between the duties of directors and auditors lie'.[50] Unfortunately, the wording suggested in the *Gazette* appeared to confuse rather than clarify in this regard.

It is probably for this reason that a further article on the matter appeared in the 17 December 1993 issue of the *Gazette* which, following discussions between the Auditing Practices Board and the Law Society's Committee on Company Law, took a more measured view of the issue, concluding that 'the directors' responsibility statement and the wording describing the auditors' responsibilities and the basis of their opinion should, in all cases, be considered together so as to avoid inconsistency and yet correctly reflect the legal and factual position'.[51]

(b) Auditors' responsibilities

The requirement for such an explanation of responsibilities was also included in SAS 600. Following the publication of the Combined Code, and the resultant changes in the *Listing Rules*, the APB considered it appropriate to revisit auditors' responsibilities in relation to corporate governance and to reconsider the way in which these, and the broader responsibilities of auditors, are communicated to users of the annual report.[52] As a result of this exercise the APB published Bulletin 1998/10, *Corporate Governance Reporting and Auditors' Responsibilities Statements*. Following the publication of the Turnbull Guidance in September 1999 (discussed under provision D.2.1 below) the APB again revised its guidance to auditors by publishing, in November 1999, Bulletin 1999/5, *The Combined Code: Requirements of Auditors Under the Listing Rules of the London Stock Exchange.* This bulletin provides example wording for the statement of auditors' responsibilities as follows:

> **Respective responsibilities of directors and auditors**
>
> The directors are responsible for preparing the Annual Report, including as described on page … the financial statements. Our responsibilities, as independent auditors, are established by statute, the Auditing Practices Board, the Listing Rules of the London Stock Exchange and by our profession's ethical guidance.
>
> We report to you our opinion as to whether the financial statements give a true and fair view and are properly prepared in accordance with the Companies Act. We also report to you if, in our opinion, the directors' report is not consistent with the financial statements, if the company has not kept proper accounting records, if we have not received all the information and explanations we require for our audit, or if the information specified by law or the Listing Rules regarding directors' remuneration and transactions with the [company] [group] is not disclosed.
>
> We review whether the corporate governance statement on page … reflects the company's compliance with the seven provisions of the Combined Code specified for our review by the Stock Exchange, and we report if it does not. We are not required to consider whether the board's statements on internal control cover all risks and controls, or form an opinion on the effectiveness of the [company's] [group's] corporate governance procedures or its risk and control procedures.
>
> We read the other information contained in the Annual Report, including the corporate governance statement, and consider whether it is consistent with the audited financial statements. We consider the implications for our report if we become aware of any apparent misstatements or material inconsistencies with the financial statements.

On 1 May 2000 the Financial Services Authority (FSA) took over the role of UK Listing Authority from the Stock Exchange. Accordingly, references in the statement of auditors' responsibilities above to the Stock Exchange are now to the FSA.

The directors' review of internal controls is discussed under Provision D.1.4 below, while the auditors' review of corporate governance disclosures is discussed at 3 below.

Provision D.1.3

As noted at 1.1 above, this was one of the aspects of the Cadbury Code that companies could not initially comply with until guidance became available. A working party comprising representatives of the Hundred Group of Finance Directors, the ICAEW and the ICAS finally issued its guidance in November 1994.[53] At the same time, the APB issued guidance for auditors reviewing directors' statements on going concern[54] and also issued an auditing standard, SAS 130,[55] which provides guidance to auditors considering, as part of their work in forming their audit opinion, the appropriateness of the going concern basis.

Since the necessary guidance was now available, in August 1995 the Stock Exchange introduced a separate requirement for listed companies to include in their annual report a statement by the directors that the business is a going concern with supporting assumptions or qualifications as necessary, as interpreted by the guidance for directors. Such a statement was to be reviewed by the auditors before publication.[56] The Hampel report did not recommend changing the current practice, saying 'We understand that directors in preparing 'going concern' statements and auditors in reporting on them have found the guidance satisfactory, and we see no need for legislation.'[57]

The guidance for directors recommends a number of procedures relevant to considering going concern under the following categories:[58]

- forecasts and budgets
- borrowing requirements
- liability management
- contingent liabilities
- products and markets
- financial risk management
- other factors
- financial adaptability.

An appendix suggests more detailed procedures under these categories.

When the directors have weighed up the results of the procedures that they have undertaken in order to establish the appropriateness of the going concern basis, there are three basic conclusions that they can reach:

- they have a reasonable expectation that the company will continue in operational existence for the foreseeable future and have therefore used the going concern basis in preparing the financial statements;
- they have identified factors which cast some doubt on the ability of the company to continue in operational existence in the foreseeable future but they have used the going concern basis in preparing the financial statements; or
- they consider that the company is unlikely to continue in operational existence in the foreseeable future and therefore the going concern concept is not an appropriate basis on which to draw up the financial statements.[59]

The guidance envisages that in normal circumstances where the going concern presumption is appropriate the following statement should be made:[60]

> After making enquiries, the directors have a reasonable expectation that the company has adequate resources to continue in operational existence for the foreseeable future. For this reason, they continue to adopt the going concern basis in preparing the accounts.

The guidance recommends that the statement on going concern should be included in the company's Operating and Financial Review (see 5 below). However, some companies include the statement with the rest of the corporate governance disclosures.

For accounting periods ending on or after 22 June 2001 UK companies will have to comply with FRS 18 – *Accounting Policies*. This standard introduces a requirement, in certain circumstances, to discuss going concern within the accounts. FRS 18 is discussed in detail at 7 in Chapter 2.

The guidance also illustrates the form of statement where the going concern basis is used despite doubts about going concern as follows:[61]

> The company is in breach of certain loan covenants at its balance sheet date and so the company's bankers could recall their loans at any time. The directors continue to be involved in negotiations with the company's bankers and as yet no demands for repayments have been received. The negotiations are at an early stage and, although the directors are optimistic about the outcome, it is as yet too early to make predictions with any certainty.
>
> In light of the actions described elsewhere in the Operating and Financial Review, the directors consider it appropriate to adopt the going concern basis in preparing the accounts.

The Cadbury Report emphasised that the directors are not expected to give a guarantee about their company's prospects because there can never be complete certainty about future trading. Therefore the directors are required to state only that they have a 'reasonable expectation' that the company will continue in operation for the foreseeable future. However, the principal area of controversy concerned the meaning of the phrase 'foreseeable future'.

The draft guidance issued by the working party had proposed that the directors should consider at least the period to the next balance sheet date. However, the guidance then went on to state that 'the foreseeable future should extend beyond the next balance sheet date to the extent that the directors are aware of circumstances which could affect the validity of the going concern basis for the company'.[62]

It seems that this guidance was drafted on the basis that most companies would prepare detailed budgets covering the 12 months after the balance sheet date. An alternative would have been to require the directors to look at a period of at least one year from the date that the accounts are signed, but this approach would have been more difficult for some companies as detailed budgets will not always be available. This was the approach taken by the APB when drafting a new auditing standard on the subject. It was clear that a compromise position had to be found.

The final guidance produced for directors by the working party discusses 'foreseeable future' and now concludes that it is not possible to specify a minimum period to which directors should pay particular attention in assessing going concern. Stipulating a minimum period would, the working party believes, be artificial and arbitrary. Instead of inventing a 'cut-off point' after which there would be a sudden change in the approach adopted, the working party believes that directors should take account of all information of which they are aware at the time.

However, the working party goes on to state that 'where the period considered by the directors has been limited, for example, to a period of less than one year from the date of approval of the financial statements, the directors should determine whether, in their opinion, the financial statements require any additional disclosure to explain adequately the assumptions that underlie the adoption of the going concern basis'.[63]

In its guidance to auditors reporting on whether the financial statements give a true and fair view, SAS 130 requires that 'if the period to which the directors have paid particular attention in assessing going concern is less than one year from the date of approval of the financial statements, and the directors have not disclosed that fact, the auditors should do so within the section of their report setting out the basis of their opinion, unless the fact is clear from any other references in their report'.[64]

It would therefore appear that one year from the date of approval of financial statements is a reasonable working definition of 'foreseeable future', although information beyond that period cannot be ignored. However, this does not necessarily mean that cash flow forecasts and budgets are needed for the whole of this period – SAS 130 says that it will depend on the circumstances.[65]

D.2 Internal control

The board should maintain a sound system of internal control to safeguard shareholders' investment and the company's assets.

D.2.1* The directors should, at least annually, conduct a review of the effectiveness of the group's system of internal control and should report to shareholders that they have done so. The review should cover all controls, including financial, operational and compliance controls and risk management.

D.2.2 Companies which do not have an internal audit function should from time to time review the need for one.

Provision D.2.1

This provision stems from the earlier Cadbury recommendation that 'The directors should report on the effectiveness of the company's system of internal control.'[66] Of all the suggestions in the Cadbury Code, this proved the most problematic and it was the one that took the longest time to bring into force. The trouble is that it is much harder than it sounds. Superficially, it seems entirely sensible that the directors of a company should be able to comment on how good their control systems are. But on reflection, it soon becomes apparent that this is fraught with difficulty, because there can be no objective yardstick against which to judge the adequacy of internal controls. For one thing, the need for controls depends upon perceived risks, and accordingly their adequacy can only be judged in that context; there is no all-purpose standard of controls that is accepted as necessary in all circumstances. For another, there is a cost/benefit judgement to be made in relation to any system of controls, which means that some managements will legitimately decide to spend more than others on control mechanisms. And since the people who are being asked to report on the adequacy of controls are also those who have had the responsibility of installing them, the requirement is always in danger of becoming a self-fulfilling one – it seems implausible that any board would ever determine that the system they themselves had established was in fact ineffective, unless it had demonstrably broken down to a material degree. Thus the undoubtedly well-intentioned requirement in the Cadbury Code proved difficult to deliver in practice.

Initially, the requirement was inoperative pending the issue of guidance for directors on how to implement it, and a working party was established to prepare such guidance. This guidance was finalised in December 1994, and took effect for financial years beginning on or after 1 January 1995.[67]

As a matter of fact, it did not contain much guidance at all; rather, it watered down the requirements of the Cadbury Code. Whereas that Code unequivocally called upon the directors to report on the effectiveness of the company's system of internal control, the Guidance demoted this to an optional extra and required instead that the directors make a statement covering these four points:

- acknowledgement by the directors that they are responsible for the company's system of internal financial control;
- explanation that such a system can provide only reasonable and not absolute assurance against material misstatement or loss;
- description of the key procedures that the directors have established and which are designed to provide effective internal financial control; and
- confirmation that the directors (or a board committee) have reviewed the effectiveness of the system of internal financial control.[68]

Thus, when Hampel came to review this area, the original Cadbury proposal that directors report on the effectiveness of internal controls had been attenuated in two ways. First, the requirement to report on the effectiveness of controls was replaced by a requirement to say that the effectiveness of the controls had been reviewed, without the need to say what that review had revealed. Second, the internal controls in question were restricted from all internal controls to only internal financial controls.

Regarding the first of these restrictions, Hampel concurred by saying 'It has been suggested that point 4.5 of the Cadbury Code should be amended to read 'The directors should report on the company's system of internal control' – i.e dropping the word 'effectiveness'. This would not require any change to the minimum requirements of the working group's guidance – the directors would still need to review the system's effectiveness. This would recognise what is happening in practice and seems eminently sensible.'[69]

As regards the second dilution of the original Cadbury recommendations, Hampel did not agree, saying 'We are not concerned only with the financial aspects of corporate governance and we fully endorse the Cadbury comment that internal control is a key aspect of efficient management. Directors should therefore maintain and review controls addressing all relevant control objectives. These should include business risk assessment and response, financial management, compliance with laws and regulations and the safeguarding of assets, including minimising the risk of fraud.[70]

Following publication of the Combined Code, the Institute of Chartered Accountants in England and Wales (ICAEW) agreed with the Stock Exchange to convene a working party, under the chairmanship of Mr Nigel Turnbull, to produce guidance for directors on the scope, extent, nature and review of internal controls to which Code principle D.2 and provision D.2.1 refer.

The Turnbull Guidance

The ICAEW Internal Control Working Party published its final report, *Internal Control Guidance for Directors on the Combined Code* (The Turnbull report) in September 1999. Much of the guidance addresses the aim of internal control and the principle characteristics of, and processes for reviewing, a sound system of internal control, which is outside the scope of this book. The guidance also covers the content of the statement on internal control required by the Listing Rules as follows.

'The board's statement on internal control

35. In its narrative statement of how the company has applied Code principle D.2, the board should, as a minimum, disclose that there is an ongoing process for identifying, evaluating and managing the significant risks faced by the company, that it has been in place for the year under review and up to the date of approval of the annual report and accounts, that it is regularly reviewed by the board and accords with the guidance in this document.
36. The board may wish to provide additional information in the annual report and accounts to assist understanding of the company's risk management processes and system of internal control.
37. The disclosures relating to the application of principle D.2 should include an acknowledgement by the board that its responsible for the company's system of internal control and for reviewing its effectiveness. It should also explain that such a system is designed to manage rather than eliminate the risk of failure to achieve business objectives, and can only provide reasonable and not absolute assurance against material misstatement or loss.
38. In relation to Code provision D.2.1, the board should summarise the process it (where applicable, through its committees) has applied in reviewing the effectiveness of the system of internal control. It should also disclose the process it has applied to deal with material internal control aspects of any significant problems disclosed in the annual report and accounts.
39. Where a board cannot make one or more of the disclosures in paragraphs 35 and 38, it should state this fact and provide an explanation. The Listing Rules require the board to disclose if it has failed to conduct a review of the effectiveness of the company's system of internal control.
40. The board should ensure that its disclosures provide meaningful, high-level information and do not give a misleading impression.
41. Where material joint ventures and associates have not been dealt with as part of the group for the purposes of applying this guidance, this should be disclosed.'[71]

It is interesting to note that the these recommendations on what companies should say in their annual report actually *extend* the requirements of the Listing Rules in two ways. Firstly, the Listing Rules simply require a narrative statement of how the principles have been applied, whereas paragraphs 35 and 37 above seek to prescribe the content of this description. Secondly, the Listing Rules only require a statement as to whether or not the code provisions have been complied with, and an explanation of any non-compliance. Paragraph 38 above extends this requirement to include a discussion of the review process and how the company has dealt with any problems - but only those problems it has disclosed.

Notwithstanding this apparent extension of the Listing Rule requirement, the Stock Exchange contributed a foreword to the Turnbull report, in which it noted 'The Working Party's guidance is consistent with both the requirements of the Combined Code and of the related Listing Rule disclosure requirements, and clarifies to boards of directors of listed companies what is expected of them. We consider that compliance with the guidance will constitute compliance with the Combined Code provisions D.2.1 and D.2.2 and provide appropriate narrative disclosure of how Code principle D.2 has been applied.' So it would seem that compliance with the Turnbull disclosure requirements above is now necessary under the Listing Rules.

At the same time as the publication of the final Turnbull guidance, the Stock Exchange sent a letter to all listed companies dealing with its implementation. Whilst it noted that full compliance with the disclosure requirements regarding internal control was possible, it only required this disclosure for accounting periods ending on or after 23 December 2000. For earlier periods it set out the following transitional provisions.

'To allow all companies to take the steps necessary to adopt the new guidance, a company will have satisfied its disclosure requirements in respect of internal controls, if it either:

(a) complies in full with those requirements (see paragraph 12.43A(a) and (b) of the Listing Rules); or

(b) adopts the following approach to disclosure for accounting periods ending on or after 23 December 1999 and up to 22 December 2000:

Paragraph 12.43A(a) of the Listing Rules

(i) as a minimum, in respect of the application of Code principle D.2, state in their annual report and accounts that they have established the procedures necessary to implement the guidance (Internal Control: Guidance for Directors on the Combined Code) or provide an explanation of when they expect to have those procedures in place; and

Paragraph 12.43A(b) of the Listing Rules

(ii) in respect of Code provision D.2.1, report on their internal financial controls pursuant to 'Internal Control and Financial Reporting - Guidance for directors of listed companies registered in the UK' (the Rutteman Guidance).

A company which adopts this transitional approach should indicate within its corporate governance disclosures that it has done so.'

The majority of companies took advantage of these transitional provision in their December 1999 accounts.

Whatever the merits of public reporting in relation to internal control, we believe that the debate initiated by Cadbury has achieved a useful objective; that of raising the profile of internal controls on board agendas, and providing a framework in which they can be discussed, which has provided a mechanism through which companies' systems can be assessed and improved. However, no controls are, or are intended to be, foolproof and failures will occur. The inevitable outcome is that really meaningful disclosure is probably always going to come only after a control failure, as illustrated by Powerscreen:

Extract 4.1: Powerscreen International PLC (1998)

Internal financial control [extract]

The directors have overall responsibility for the group's system of internal financial control and had established a framework designed to provide reasonable but not absolute assurance against material mis-statement or loss. Over a period of time, the control system was over-ridden and there were no compensating mechanisms in place to detect, report on, control and eliminate this abuse. Eventually, the group's systems, primarily based on cash forecasting, detected the Matbro losses.

Any framework supporting internal financial controls is designed to provide reasonable but not absolute assurance against material misstatement or loss. This framework has been fundamentally reviewed since 31 March 1998. The key procedures are being critically assessed and strengthened.

Unlike under the previous structure, the group financial function is now completely independent of operations. It will also have its own full time, permanent staff under the newly appointed Group Finance Director, Mr JFW Kennerley. The appointment of other group financial staff will follow shortly.

Provision D.2.2

The Turnbull report also provides guidance on how to interpret the Code provision that companies not having an internal audit function should from time to time review the need for one. It observes that the need for an internal audit function will vary depending on company-specific factors,[72] and that in the absence of an internal audit function companies will need other monitoring processes to provide assurance that the system of internal control is functioning as intended. In these circumstances, the board will need to assess whether such processes provide sufficient and objective assurance.[73] The Turnbull report also seeks to interpret the meaning of 'from time to time' as it states that the need for an internal audit function should be assessed (by those companies which don't have one) annually.[74]

D.3 Audit Committee and Auditors

The board should establish formal and transparent arrangements for considering how they should apply the financial reporting and internal control principles and for maintaining an appropriate relationship with the company's auditors.

D.3.1*The board should establish an audit committee of at least three directors, all non-executive, with written terms of reference which deal clearly with its authority and duties. The members of the committee, a majority of whom should be independent non-executive directors, should be named in the report and accounts.

> D.3.2 The duties of the audit committee should include keeping under review the scope and results of the audit and its cost effectiveness and the independence and objectivity of the auditors. Where the auditors also supply a substantial volume of non-audit services to the company, the committee should keep the nature and extent of such services under review, seeking to balance the maintenance of objectivity and value for money.

Provision D.3.1

Cadbury recommended that 'The Board should establish an audit committee of at least three non-executive directors with written terms of reference which deal clearly with its authority and duties'.[75] The notes to the Code further recommended that a majority of the non-executive directors on the committee should be independent of management. Both recommendations were endorsed by Hampel, saying 'Larger companies have implemented the recommendations almost universally, and we believe that the results have been beneficial. Audit committees have strengthened the independence of the auditors by giving them an effective link to the board; and the explicit remit of the audit committee has strengthened its members in questioning the executive directors.'[76]

The original Cadbury paragraph was supported by detailed recommendations in the notes to the Code on the working of audit committees. These remain relevant and should be considered by directors when describing the application of principle D.3. These recommendations are outlined below.

The audit committee should be a formally constituted sub-committee reporting to the board and should meet at least twice a year. It should have written terms of reference dealing with membership, authority and duties. It should have full support to carry out its duties both from within the company and, if necessary, from external advisers. Membership of the committee should be confined to non-executive directors, the majority of whom should be independent. The internal and external auditors and finance director should normally attend audit committee meetings, whilst other members of the board should have the right to attend. The Cadbury Report also included specimen terms of reference for an audit committee including such matters as constitution, membership, frequency of meetings, authority, duties and reporting procedures.

This was the main area of the Cadbury Code where companies, particularly smaller companies, reported non-compliance. Whilst this was noted by Hampel, it saw no justification for relaxing the rules, saying: 'We recognise that smaller companies may find it difficult to recruit a sufficient number of non-executive directors to meet Cadbury's preferred composition of the audit committee. We recommend shareholders to examine such cases carefully on their merits. But we do not favour relaxing the guidelines on this point by size of company.'[77]

Provision D.3.2

Cadbury identified the central issue with regard to the audit as being how to ensure its objectivity and effectiveness. The responsibility for maintaining an appropriate relationship rests with both the board and the auditors. Hampel added that 'The audit committee is an essential safeguard of auditor independence and objectivity; we suggest that it should keep under review the overall financial relationship between the company and the auditors.' An audit committee can play an important part in maintaining such a relationship by providing a forum dedicated to the review of matters within the purview of audit, such as financial statements and internal control.

An audit committee gives the non-executive directors the opportunity to consider, in more detail than is generally possible at board meetings, the important financial aspects of the approach to, and system of, corporate governance. A specific step in the process is for the audit committee to hold a separate meeting with the auditors at least once a year, without executive board members present. This allows discussion to ensure that there are no unresolved issues of concern. Cadbury included this process in its recommendations on audit committees in the notes to the Cadbury Code.

3 THE ROLE OF AUDITORS IN CORPORATE GOVERNANCE

The *Listing Rules* require the directors' statement on compliance with the provisions of the Combined Code to be reviewed by the auditors insofar as it relates to seven of the forty five provisions.[78] The *Listing Rules* are silent on whether the auditors should report on their review and whether any report should be made public. Cadbury recommended that auditors should not be required formally to report a satisfactory review, but rather mention any non-disclosed non-compliance in their report on the accounts; and this was not changed by Hampel.

Before the publication of the Turnbull guidance, guidance for auditors in this area was contained in APB Bulletin 1995/1, as supplemented by APB Bulletin 1996/3, and APB Bulletin 1998/10. The last of these was published in response to the Combined Code and related *Listing Rules* changes, and significantly amended, but did not supersede the earlier Bulletins. One of the most notable changes introduced by Bulletin 1998/10 related to the issue and publication of a formal report on the review of corporate governance disclosures. Notwithstanding the Cadbury recommendation mentioned above, Bulletin 1995/1 originally stated that auditors should always issue a report to the company and that the APB 'strongly recommends that such reports be included in the annual report'.[79] In light of the changes brought about by the Combined Code the APB reassessed this recommendation, and concluded as follows: 'The APB is of the view that a description of the auditors' responsibilities in relation to the whole annual report would be helpful to users of annual reports. Since such a description will encompass the auditors' review of the company's compliance with the specified provisions of the Combined Code it will remove the need for a separate auditors' report on this aspect. In view of the narrow scope of the auditors' review and the introduction of a statement of auditors' responsibilities, the APB believes that it is no longer appropriate for auditors' reports on the directors' compliance statement to be published in the annual report. For listed companies this supersedes the APB's recommendation in paragraph 46 of Bulletin 1995/1 and is expected to result in the discontinuance of published auditors' reports on corporate governance matters in the annual reports of listed companies.'[80]

Following the publication of the Turnbull guidance the APB published, in November 1999, Bulletin 1999/5, *The Combined Code: Requirements of Auditors Under the Listing Rules of the London Stock Exchange*. The main reason for the Bulletin was to provide guidance to auditors in reviewing directors' statements regarding internal control. However it also took the opportunity to consolidate (without changing) all of the APBs extant guidance on corporate governance matters.

The statement of auditors' responsibilities is discussed under Provision D.1.1 at 2.3 above.

The possibility of a wider role for auditors regarding internal control is a subject of ongoing debate. On 16 July 2001, the APB published a Briefing Paper *Providing assurance on the effectiveness of internal control*. It describes a framework for forming an opinion on the effectiveness of internal control which illustrates:

- the separate elements of such an engagement (risk identification and assessment, design, and operation of internal controls);
- the considerations that apply to each process; and
- the inherent complexity of engagements to provide assurance about internal control effectiveness.

The APB believes a narrative rather than a standardised short-form report would be necessary to communicate effectively the judgements made by practitioners, the reasoning underpinning those judgements and context in which the opinion is given. Such reports are likely to be lengthy and therefore it seems that reports providing assurance on the effectiveness of internal control will usually be provided by practitioners to those that instructed them and not be published. The briefing paper includes an example of a narrative report based on an imaginary engagement examining the effectiveness of the system of internal control over the recording of revenue.

The Briefing Paper is intended to raise debate and communicate the APB's views, and does not set out mandatory requirements. It follows two earlier discussion papers on the subject of providing assurance on internal controls, the responses to which indicated that there was not yet a consensus on how such engagements should be performed or its conclusions reported.

4 SMALLER QUOTED COMPANIES

Cadbury made no distinction in its recommendations between larger and smaller listed companies. Hampel considered whether such a distinction should be drawn, and concluded that it should not, saying: 'For the most part, the larger listed companies have implemented both codes fully. Smaller companies have also implemented most provisions, but there are some aspects with which they find it harder to comply. We considered carefully whether we should distinguish between the governance standards expected of larger and smaller companies. We concluded that this would be a mistake. Any distinction by size would be arbitrary; more importantly, we consider that high standards of governance are as important for smaller listed companies as for larger ones. But we would urge those considering the governance arrangements of smaller listed companies to do so with flexibility and a proper regard to individual circumstances.'[81]

In our view this is sensible; it is for the board to determine its corporate governance procedures in the best interests of the company. Whilst the provisions of the Combined Code form a basic framework in which to do this they are not, and should not be, prescriptive. If the board determines that a particular provision is not appropriate to them it is perfectly proper for them to disapply it, as long as they can clearly communicate the fact and the reasons for it to shareholders. Shareholders can then consider the decisions and performance of the board in an informed way, based on the individual circumstances of the company.

In considering any Combined Code provisions that the board has not complied with, shareholders may want to consider the guidance prepared by the Quoted Companies Alliance (QCA), formerly called The City Group for Smaller Companies (CISCO).

Early in 1994, in response to Cadbury, CISCO published guidance for smaller quoted companies which was aimed at identifying those areas of the Cadbury Code which may, initially, prove difficult for smaller companies to implement and, wherever possible, suggesting alternative recommendations which are believed feasible and appropriate.[82] The idea behind this was to provide a guide to the measures that all companies (without exception) could reasonably be expected to implement, which is preferable to the option of companies doing nothing. In response to the publication of the Combined Code, CISCO published revised guidance in March 1999.[83] In April 2001 the QCA again revised its guidance[84], this is discussed below.

The areas where alternative recommendations are given mainly relate to the number of non-executive directors and the constitution of audit committees. However, it should be noted that these recommendations do not represent an alternative code, and therefore a listed company that has complied with the QCA's recommendations but not the full Combined Code is still required to report such non-compliance (with reasons) in its annual report.

The QCA's principal alternative recommendations and other refinements are as follows:

- provision A.3.1 of the Combined Code requires companies to appoint non-executives of sufficient calibre and number for their views to carry significant weight in the board's decisions, and that they should comprise not less than one third of the board. To meet the recommendation on the composition of the audit committee, boards will require a minimum of three non-executives, a majority of whom should be independent. The QCA has recommended that there should be at least two independent non-executives, to enable them to liaise with each other and not feel isolated. The appointment of more that two may, in the QCA's view, be excessive in some companies and may impose a disproportionate financial burden. Where companies have only two non-executives the QCA considers it sufficient for those directors to constitute the audit committee;
- in line with the Combined Code requirement that boards should meet regularly, and effectively lead and control the company, the QCA suggests that boards should normally meet monthly, and not less than six times a year and that the agenda of regular board meetings should always include a report of management accounts from the finance director. It also suggests that whilst it is accepted that any system of corporate governance should not fetter entrepreneurial talent, systems can nevertheless be established where, in relation to certain areas of management, the director must always consult the board as a whole before implementing a decision taken in principle. An appendix to the QCA's guidance sets out a suggested list of matters which should always be addressed by the board before a decision is taken;
- the QCA recommends that companies should seek to define the role each non-executive director is expected to fulfil, and the specific objectives of that role, as they should for any other senior appointment, in order to ensure that they receive optimum benefit from the appointment. This should be done before starting the selection or reselection procedure;
- provision A.2.1 of the Combined Code recommends that all boards recognise a senior independent non-executive, who is identified in the annual report. The QCA disagreed and, seemingly going beyond its remit of small companies, said 'This requirement is possibly excessive (particularly in companies which have only two non-executive directors) and may be divisive. It is the QCA's view that the undefined role of a senior non-executive director may lead to matters being brought to him which ought properly to be referred to the chairman in the first instance.' The guidance does, however, reiterate that companies not identifying a senior non-executive will need to explain why in their annual reports;
- provision A.5.1 requires that unless the board is small, a nomination committee should be established to make recommendations to the board on all new board appointments. The QCA considers a board to be small for these purposes if it comprises six or fewer members.

It must again be emphasised that the QCA's refined code is not, for Listing Rules reporting purposes, to be seen as an alternative option to the Combined Code. All UK incorporated quoted companies (irrespective of size) are required by the Listing Rules to include in their annual report and accounts a statement as to whether or not they have complied throughout the accounting period with the Combined Code, and to report details of, and reasons for, any non-compliance.

5 THE OPERATING AND FINANCIAL REVIEW (OFR)

In considering the responsibility of boards with respect to financial reports, the Cadbury Committee concluded that what shareholders need from the report and accounts is a coherent narrative, supported by figures, of the company's performance and prospects. As a result, the Committee recommended that boards should pay particular attention to their duty to present a balanced and understandable assessment of their company's position. It went on to say that balance requires that setbacks should be dealt with as well as successes, while the need for the report to be readily understood emphasises that words are as important as figures.[85] The Committee further recognised the advantage to users of accounts of being provided with some explanation of the factors likely to influence their company's future progress, and concluded that the inclusion of an essentially forward-looking Operating and Financial Review (OFR), along the lines of that which was being developed by the ASB, would serve this purpose.[86] The Hampel Committee did not add further guidance on this topic, but incorporated the Cadbury recommendation as follows: 'The board should present a balanced and understandable assessment of the company's position and prospects.'[87] The report makes clear that this principle is not limited to annual reports to shareholders, but also covers interim and other price-sensitive public reports and reports to regulators.[88]

The ASB document to which the Cadbury Committee referred was ultimately published in July 1993 as a Statement of best practice. It has persuasive rather than mandatory force and is not an accounting standard. It is intended that the OFR should be a discussion of the business as a whole and should give insights into the facts which underlie the figures in the accounts; it should not just repeat these figures in narrative form with no amplification. It should discuss individual aspects of the business in the context of explaining the performance of the business as a whole. The statement requires a consideration of the factors that will affect future performance as well as the year under review. Consequently, although the OFR is a report on the year under review, not a forecast of future results, it should nevertheless draw out those aspects of the year under review that are relevant to an assessment of future prospects.

The essential features of an OFR are as follows:[89]

- it should be written in a clear style and as succinctly as possible, to be readily understandable by the general reader of annual reports, and should include only matters that are likely to be significant to investors;
- it should be balanced and objective, dealing even-handedly with both good and bad aspects;

- it should refer to comments made in previous statements where these have not been borne out by events;
- it should contain analytical discussion rather than merely numerical analysis;
- it should follow a 'top-down' structure, discussing individual aspects of the business in the context of a discussion of the business as a whole;
- it should explain the reason for, and effect of, any changes in accounting policies;
- it should make it clear how any ratios or other numerical information given relate to the financial statements; and
- it should include discussion of:
  - trends and factors underlying the business that have affected the results but are not expected to continue in the future; and
  - known events, trends and uncertainties that are expected to have an impact on the business in the future.

In discussing trends and uncertainties, the OFR should explain their significance to the business, but it is not intended that the OFR should necessarily include a forecast of the outcome of such uncertainties; nor is it suggested that the OFR should contain anything of the nature of a profit forecast.[90] Furthermore, the directors may conclude that, in some cases, a proper discussion of some aspects of the business would require disclosure of confidential or commercially sensitive information. Where the directors decide not to disclose such information, the OFR should ensure that the user is not misled by a discussion that is no longer complete and balanced.[91]

As its title suggests, the OFR consists of two sections: the operating review and the financial review. These are discussed below.

5.1 The operating review

The principal aim of the operating review is to enable the user to understand the dynamics of the various lines of business undertaken – that is, the main influences on the overall results, and how these inter-relate. Thus the OFR needs to identify and explain the main factors that underlie the business, and in particular those which either have varied in the past or are expected to change in the future.[92] It should include a discussion of:[93]

- the significant features of the operating performance for the period. This should cover changes in the industry or the environment in which the business operates, developments within the business, and their effect on results. Examples of such changes given by the Statement are as follows:
  - changes in market conditions;
  - new products and services introduced or announced;
  - changes in market share or position;
  - changes in turnover and margins;

  - changes in exchange rates and inflation rates; and
  - new activities, discontinued activities and other acquisitions and disposals;
- the dynamics of the business, discussing the main factors and influences that may have a major effect on future results, whether or not they were significant in the period under review; for example, dependence on major suppliers or customers. The Statement lists the following additional examples of matters that may be relevant:
  - scarcity of raw materials;
  - skill shortages and expertise of uncertain supply;
  - patents, licences or franchises;
  - product liability;
  - health and safety;
  - environmental protection costs and potential environmental liabilities;
  - self insurance;
  - exchange rate fluctuations; and
  - rates of inflation differing between costs and revenues, or between different markets;
- the extent to which the directors have sought to maintain and enhance future income or profits by investment in, for example, capital expenditure, marketing and advertising campaigns and pure and applied research. The Statement lists the following additional examples of activities and expenditure for the enhancement of future profits that may be relevant:
  - training programmes;
  - refurbishment and maintenance programmes;
  - development of new products and services; and
  - technical support to customers;
- the overall return attributable to shareholders, in terms of dividends and increases in shareholders' funds, commenting on the contributions from the operating performance of the various business units and on other items reported as part of total recognised gains and losses;
- a comparison between profit for the financial year and dividends, both in total and per share terms, indicating the directors' overall dividend policy. Other measures of earnings per share reported should also be discussed; and
- any subjective judgements to which the financial statements are particularly sensitive.

5.2 The financial review

The principal aim of the financial review is to explain the capital structure of the business, its treasury policy and the dynamics of its financial position – i.e. its sources of liquidity and their application, including the implications of the financing requirements arising from its capital expenditure plans.[94] It should include a discussion of:[95]

- the capital structure of the business, in terms of maturity profile of debt, type of capital instruments used, currency and interest rate structure. This should include comments on relevant ratios such as interest cover and debt/equity ratios;
- the capital funding and treasury policies and objectives. These will cover the management of interest rate risk, the maturity profile of borrowings and the management of exchange rate risk. The Statement suggests that the OFR should also discuss the implementation of these policies in the period under review in terms of:
  - the manner in which treasury activities are controlled;
  - the currencies in which borrowings are made and in which cash and cash equivalents are held;
  - the extent to which borrowings are at fixed interest rates;
  - the use of financial instruments for hedging purposes; and
  - the extent to which foreign currency net investments are hedged by currency borrowings and other hedging instruments;
- the main components of the reconciliation between the actual and standard tax charges where the overall tax charge is different from the standard charge (i.e. the normal UK tax rate applied to the profit before taxation);
- the cash generated from operations and other cash inflows during the period, commenting on any special factors that influenced these. Where segmental cash flows are significantly out of line with segmental profits, this should be indicated and explained;
- the business's liquidity at the end of the period, including comment on the level of borrowings at the end of the period, the seasonality of borrowing requirements and the maturity profile of both borrowings and committed borrowing facilities;
- any restrictions on the ability to transfer funds from one part of the group to meet the obligations of another part of the group where they represent, or might foreseeably come to represent, a significant constraint on the group;
- debt covenants which could have the effect of restricting the use of credit facilities, and where a breach of a covenant has occurred or is expected to occur, the OFR should give details of the measures taken or proposed to remedy the situation;
- the business's ability to remain a going concern as recommended by the Cadbury Committee [now superseded by the Combined Code as discussed under provision D.1.3 at 2.3 above]; and
- the strengths and resources of the business whose value is not fully reflected in the balance sheet – for example, as is the case with intangible assets which have not been capitalised.

Much of the information in the first two points above is now mandatory for listed companies as it is required by FRS 13, which is discussed in Chapter 10. Under FRS 19 – *Deferred Tax* – the reconciliation recommended in the third point above will be required to be disclosed in accounts for periods ending on or after 23 January 2002. This is discussed at 5.11.3 in Chapter 24.

5.3 Statement of compliance

As the OFR Statement represents voluntary best practice, directors are not expected to include in the annual report any formal confirmation that they have complied with the principles set out in the Statement – although, clearly, the inclusion of some comment on the extent to which the Statement has been followed may be helpful to the user. However, the Statement suggests that where it is implied, through the use of the words 'operating and financial review' or otherwise, that the directors have endeavoured to follow the principles laid down in the Statement, they should signal any fundamental departure therefrom.[96]

5.4 Future developments

The Final Report of the Company Law Review was delivered by the Company Law Review Steering Group in June 2001.[97] This is the first fundamental review of British company law for at least 40 years, and arguably the first in the law's 150-year history. The Final Report sets out the Steering Group's model for a new company law that is intended to turn the existing Victorian infrastructure into a modern framework. The new framework is designed to provide the necessary safeguards to allow people to deal with and invest in companies with confidence, whilst at the same time enable British companies to be competitive in a global marketplace where businesses can choose which jurisdiction to adopt for their regulation.

One of the proposals put forward is that most public companies and large private companies should be required by law to publish an operating and financial review (OFR) as part of the annual report.[98] The objective of the statutory OFR would be 'to provide a discussion and analysis of the performance of the business and the main trends and factors underlying the results and financial position and likely to affect performance in the future, so as to enable users to assess the strategies adopted by the business and the potential for successfully achieving them.'[99]

The Steering Group suggests that the statutory content of the OFR should take two forms: first, matters always required to be included; and second, those to be included whenever the directors regard them as material to achieving the objective of the OFR. The areas to be covered are summarised in the table below. Only the italic text is intended to form the basis of legislation; the plain type sets out additional detail which the Steering Group envisage will be delegated to a newly formed Standards Board (discussed at 1.8 in Chapter 1).[100]

		Always required	Required to the extent material
(i)	*The company's business and business objectives, strategy and principle drivers of performance.* the criteria by reference to which its success is evaluated and the source from which that success is derived, including development of each part of the business against objectives, and competitive positioning.	Yes	
(ii)	*A fair review of the development of the company's and/or group's business over the year and position at the end of it, including material post year-end events, operating performance and material changes:* including: market changes, new product and service introductions, changes in market positioning, turnover and margins, new and discontinued products and services, acquisitions and disposals.	Yes	
(iii)	*Dynamics of the business – i.e. known events, trends, uncertainties and other factors which may substantially affect future performance, including investment programmes:* risks, opportunities and related responses in connection with: competition and other changes in market conditions, customer/supplier dependencies, technological change, financial risks, health and safety, environmental costs and liabilities; and projects and programmes to maintain and enhance: tangible and itellectual capital, brands, research and development, training.	Yes	
(iv)	*Corporate governance – values and structures:* an account of the company's and/or group's systems and structures for controlling and focusing the powers of management and securing an effective working relationship between members, directors and senior management, including the names, roles and qualifications of directors.		Yes
(v)	*An account of the company's key relationships, with employees, customers, suppliers and others on which its success depends:* including employment policies and practices (including disability and non-discrimination policies); policies and practices on employee involvement and compliance with international labour conventions and anti-discrimination laws; policies and practices on creditor payment.		Yes
(vi)	*Policies and performance on environmental, community, social, ethical and reputational issues including compliance with relevant laws and regulations:* including any social or community programmes, policies for the business on ethical and environmental issues and their impact for the business, policies on international trade and human rights issues and any political and charitable contributions.		Yes
(vii)	*Receipts from, and returns to, shareholders:* including distribution policy, distributions, share repurchases and capital issues.		Yes

6 CONCLUSION

We believe that great strides have been made in Corporate Governance over recent years and welcome the development of the Combined Code. In our view such matters are better dealt with in this relatively informal manner, rather than, as is sometimes suggested, by way of statute which would be necessarily more detailed and would be open to all the difficulties of statutory interpretation. Furthermore a code of practice is much better able to respond quickly to the changing market place and the changing expectations of shareholders and other interested parties. The latest changes to the Listing Rules now require boards to describe in their own words how they apply the general principles of corporate governance as well as making a statement of compliance, or otherwise, with the detailed provisions of the Combined Code. We believe this to be a much more meaningful requirement, although to give a reasoned and considered description of their governance procedures represents a significant challenge for boards. The detailed Code provisions set out some basic elements of the governance process, and it is perhaps not surprising that some are reproduced by companies in these discussions. However, we hope that this be kept to a minimum to prevent the disclosures degenerating into general boilerplate.

We think that the OFR should be regarded as one of the ASB's most successful innovations. By providing a well-considered framework but allowing scope for experimentation, the Board has encouraged companies to approach the task imaginatively and constructively. Inevitably, some have carried it out better than others, but as the capital markets become more demanding and directors become more aware of their corporate governance responsibilities, balanced, objective and understandable OFRs are increasingly becoming a standard feature of UK GAAP.

APPENDIX: EXAMPLES OF CORPORATE GOVERNANCE DISCLOSURES

The following extracts reproduce the corporate governance disclosures of two different companies. The first extract (ICI) illustrates a company disclosing full compliance with all the provisions of the Combined Code. The second extract (Huntingdon Life Sciences) is an example of a company identifying and discussing certain provisions with which it has not complied.

Extract 4.2: Imperial Chemical Industries PLC (2000)

Corporate governance [extract]

Corporate governance

The Group is committed to high standards of corporate governance. The Board is accountable to the Company's shareholders for good governance and this statement describes how the relevant principles of governance are applied to the Company. Throughout the year the Company has been in compliance with the provisions set out in the Combined Code for Corporate Governance appended to the Listing Rules of the UK Listing Authority.

The ICI Board currently comprises the Chairman, the Chief Executive, four other Executive Directors and five Non-Executive Directors. Their biographies appear on page 32. These demonstrate a range of business, financial and global experience, which is vital to the successful direction of a multi-national company. All the Non-Executive Directors are independent of management. The Board is balanced both numerically and in experience.

All Directors are equally accountable under the law for the proper stewardship of the Company's affairs. The Non-Executive Directors have a particular responsibility to ensure that the strategies proposed by Executive Directors are fully discussed and critically examined, not only against the best long-term interests of shareholders, but also to ensure that they take proper account of the interests of employees, customers, suppliers and the many communities within which ICI is represented. The Non-Executive Directors also test fully the operational performance of the whole Group. The Board has prescribed reserved powers which reinforce its control of the Company. There is a procedure for Directors to obtain independent professional advice at the Company's expense in the performance of their duties as Directors.

To enable them to do this all Directors have full and timely access to all relevant information. The Board meets at least eight times a year and there is frequent contact between meetings to progress the Company's business.

The Non-Executive Directors fulfil a vital role in corporate accountability. The remits and memberships of the three relevant Board Committees are set out on page 35. The Remuneration and Nomination Committee and the Audit Committee comprise solely Non-Executive Directors and report regularly to the Board.

Remuneration and Nomination Committee

The Chairman and Chief Executive are in attendance at the Remuneration and Nomination Committee for appropriate items but are always excluded when their own performance and remuneration are under review. The Chairman is not a member of the Remuneration and Nomination Committee except when it meets as the Nomination Committee. He attends all remuneration discussions except when his own position is being discussed. The Chairman from time to time promotes discussion with the Executive Directors about Non-Executive Directors' remuneration based on full external comparisons. Any recommendations are tabled to the full Board. Non-Executive Directors have the option of taking part of their remuneration in the Company's shares.

The Remuneration report, on pages 37 to 43, includes details on remuneration policy and practices, and on the remuneration of Directors.

The Chairman of the Remuneration and Nomination Committee, currently Sir Roger Hurn, acts as the Company's lead Non-Executive Director. In this position he promotes discussion at appropriate times about the Company's chairmanship and succession to it.

The Non-Executive Directors normally meet twice a year with the Chairman and Chief Executive to discuss Board and individual Directors' performance and succession plans. At appropriate times the Chief Executive and then the Chairman absent themselves so their performance can be assessed. The final discussion is led by the Chairman of the Remuneration and Nomination Committee and there is feedback to individuals.

Appointments to Executive Director are fully discussed by the Chairman and Chief Executive with the Remuneration and Nomination Committee before a proposal is formally made to the Board by the Chairman of that Committee. Possible new Non-Executive Directors are suggested by all members of the Board against the requirements of the Company's business and the need to have a balanced Board. In appropriate cases recruitment consultants are used to assist the process. Possible candidates are discussed with all Directors before any approach is made to them. All Directors are subject to re-election at least every three years.

Audit and internal control

Following publication of guidance for directors on internal control (The Turnbull Guidance), the Board confirm that there is a process for identifying, evaluating and managing the significant risks to the achievement of the Group's strategic objectives. The process has been in place throughout 2000 and up to the date of approval of the Annual Report and Accounts and Form 20-F, and accords with The Turnbull Guidance. The effectiveness of this process has been reviewed regularly by the Audit Committee who report their findings for consideration by the Board. The processes used by the Audit Committee to review the effectiveness of the system of internal control include:

- Discussions with management on risk areas identified by management and/or the audit process;
- The review of internal and external audit plans;
- The review of significant issues arising from internal and external audits; and
- The review of significant Group risks reported by the Group Risk Committee.

The Audit Committee reports to the Board the results of their review of the risk assessment process. The Board then draws its collective conclusion as to the effectiveness of the system of internal control.

The Group Risk Committee (GRC) was established during the year to consolidate and prioritise for the Board the inputs received from management of the businesses and corporate functions. The GRC is chaired by the Executive Vice President, Strategy and Group Control, and comprises the heads of major corporate functions, the Chief Internal Auditor and General Counsel. The GRC meets on a regular basis to review updated input from businesses and corporate management and to report its conclusions to the Audit Committee.

The internal audit function reviews internal controls in all key activities of the ICI Group, typically over a three year cycle. It acts as a service to the Businesses by assisting with continuous improvement of controls and procedures. Actions are agreed in response to its recommendations and these are followed up to ensure that satisfactory control is maintained. Quarterly reviews are also conducted between internal audit management and the senior management of the Businesses and major functions to assess their current control status and to identify and address any areas of concern.

The Board is responsible for the effectiveness of the Group's system of internal controls. The internal control systems are designed to meet the Group's particular needs and the risks to which it is exposed, and by their nature can only provide reasonable but not absolute assurance against misstatement or loss.

The Group's strategic direction is regularly reviewed by the Board, and the Executive Management Team considers the strategy for the individual Businesses through an integrated disciplined process on a biannual basis. Annual plans and performance targets for each Business are set by the Chief Executive and are reviewed in total by the Board in the light of the Group's overall objectives.

The processes to identify and manage the key risks to the success of the Group are an integral part of the internal control environment. Such processes, which are reviewed and improved as necessary, include strategic planning, the appointment of senior managers, the regular monitoring of performance, control over capital expenditure and investments and the setting of high standards and targets for safety, health and environmental performance.

Within the financial and overall objectives for the Group, agreed by the Board, the management of the Group as a whole is delegated to the Chief Executive and the Executive Directors. The conduct of ICI's individual businesses is delegated to the Executive Management Team. They are accountable for the conduct and performance of their businesses within the agreed business strategy. They have full authority to act subject to the reserved powers and sanctioning limits laid down by the Board and to Group policies and guidelines.

Businesses are responsible for meeting the defined reporting timetables and compliance with Group accounting manuals which set out accounting policies, controls and definitions.

The Executive Management Team receives a monthly summary of financial results from each Business, and the Group's published quarterly financial information is based on a standardised and timely reporting process.

On completion of all major investments, post event reviews are carried out by the relevant businesses and reviewed by the Executive Management Team. This process helps improve the quality of business judgements through the understanding and experience gained.

Responsibility for ensuring compliance with selected Group policies and guidelines has been delegated by the Board to nominated senior functional managers. These nominated managers receive annual compliance reports from Executive Vice Presidents, Chief Executive Officers of Businesses and from other senior managers. In turn, there is an annual report to the Audit Committee, on behalf of the Board, on the degree of compliance with Group policies and guidelines. Corrections to any weaknesses found are monitored and controls are developed to match changing circumstances.

Principles of business conduct

As a leading international company, ICI's reputation for high ethical standards is central to its business success. A new Code of Business Conduct has been developed to replace the previous Business Ethics Statement and is now being communicated throughout the Group.

Communications

Communications with shareholders are given a high priority. There is a succinct Annual Review which is sent to shareholders; a full Annual Report and Accounts and Form 20-F is available on request. At the half year, an interim report is published and the quarterly results are published via the Stock Exchange and by press release. The company also has a website (www.ici.com) which contains up to date information on Group activities and published financial results. There is a regular dialogue with individual institutional shareholders as well as presentations to analysts after the quarterly results. There is also an opportunity for individual shareholders to question the Chairman at the AGM. As an alternative, shareholders can leave written questions for response by the Company. Directors meet informally with shareholders after the meeting. The Company responds throughout the year to numerous letters from individual shareholders on a wide range of issues.

...

Directors' report [extract]
Going concern

The operation of the Group's control procedures gives the Directors a reasonable expectation that the Group has adequate resources to continue in operation for the foreseeable future. Accordingly they continue to adopt the going concern basis in preparing the Group accounts.

Extract 4.3: Huntingdon Life Sciences Group plc (2000)

CORPORATE GOVERNANCE REPORT

In June 1998 the Hampel Committee and the London Stock Exchange published the Combined Code on corporate governance. This combines the Cadbury Code on corporate governance, the Greenbury Code on directors' remuneration and requirements arising from the findings of the Hampel Committee.

Statement about applying the Principles of Good Governance

The Company has applied the Principles of Good Governance set out in section 1 of the Combined Code by complying with the Code of Best Practice as reported below. Further explanation of how the Principles have been applied is set out in this Annual Report and, in connection with directors' remuneration, in the Directors' Report.

Statement of compliance with the Code of Best Practice

The Company has complied throughout the year with the Provisions of the Code of Best Practice set out in section 1 of the Combined Code except for the following matters:

Although the Non-Executive Directors do not have fixed term appointments as required by Code Provision A.6.1, their service contracts require only three months' notice of termination and they are subject to the requirement contained in the Articles of Association that at every Annual General Meeting one-third of the Directors for the time being or, if their number is not three or a multiple of three, the number nearest to but not exceeding one-third, shall retire from office and submit themselves, if they so wish, for re-election. Every Director must submit himself for re-election at every third Annual General Meeting as a minimum.

The remuneration Committee has followed the provisions of Schedule A of the Combined Code as required by Code Provision B.1.6 with the exception of paragraph 5 which deals with the grant of share options. This matter is discussed in the Directors' Report.

Mr Cass, Managing Director, has a service contract which provides for a notice period in excess of one year as required by Code Provision B.1.8. This matter is referred to in the Directors' Report; there are no plans to reduce such period in accordance with Code Provision B.1.7.

Mr Balthazar, who is chairman of the Audit and Remuneration Committees was unable to attend the Annual General Meeting as required by Code Provision C.2.3.

From the period up to the appointment of Mr Balthazar and after the resignation of Mr J Dowling, the Company only had two non-executive directors, and therefore less that one-third of the Board comprised non-executive directors as required by Code Provision A.3.1.

The Company considers that the size of the Board is too small to require a Nominations Committee.

Going Concern

As a result of the refinancing of the Group's bank debt on January 20, 2001 bank loans totalling £22,586,000 currently shown as current liabilities are now repayable in June 2006.

As part of the refinancing additional working capital was made available to the Group to meet its immediate trading requirements. This, together with other financing options still available to the Group, are expected to provide adequate finance for the foreseeable future.

In the light of the above the Directors have formed a judgement that it is appropriate to adopt the going concern basis in preparing the accounts.

Directors' Statement on Internal Control

The Directors are responsible for the Group's system of internal controls, including financial, operational and compliance controls and risk management. They are also responsible for reviewing the system's effectiveness which they have undertaken for the year. Such a system is designed to manage rather than eliminate the risk of failure to achieve the business objectives and can only provide reasonable and not absolute assurance against material reinstatement or loss. Key procedures are described under the headings set out below.

An embedded ongoing process for identifying, evaluating and managing the significant risks faced by the Group was in place for the period from May 1, 2000 to the date of approval of the annual report and accounts. That process is regularly reviewed by the Board and accords with the Internal Control Guidance for Directors on the Combined Code produced by the Turnbull working party. During the preceding part of the financial year procedures were being established to meet the requirements for the system of internal control determined by the Board.

Risk management

A risk management workshop was held during the year which was attended by senior management. Major risks of the Group have been identified. The necessary change issues have been prioritised, and a control strategy for each of the significant risks established. The Board has prepared a risk management policy document which sets out the Board's attitude to risk to the achievement of the business objectives. This is reviewed by the Board on a regular basis.

Control environment

The Directors are responsible for reviewing key aspects of strategic, financial, organisational and compliance risk to which the company is exposed. Controls such as segregation of duties and physical controls are utilised where they are deemed appropriate to maintain the security of assets for which the Directors are responsible.

Huntingdon operates an organisational structure which has clearly defined and communicated responsibilities. This is supported by established procedures and policies including delegation of authorities and completion periodically of an internal control questionnaire by management which is used to identify any remedial action which may be needed.

Monitoring

The Board of Directors have delegated to Executive Directors and senior management the implementation of the system of internal controls. A cyclical review of the internal control environment is performed with an emphasis towards key aspects of the business and the results are reported direct to the Audit Committee.

Financial information

The Group has a comprehensive system for reporting financial results to the Board; each operating unit prepares monthly results with a comparison against budget. The Board reviews these for the Group as a whole and determines appropriate action.

Computer systems

The group has established controls and procedures over the security of data held on computer systems.

Dialogue with institutional shareholders

The Directors seek to build a mutual understanding of objectives between the Company and its institutional investors through a combination of formal and informal communications. Specifically the company regularly meets all its large shareholders, both institutional and private, to discuss long-term issues and obtain feedback, communicates proactively throughout the year orally, via its quarterly trading statements and press releases and responds to investor enquiries through a senior employee experienced in providing appropriate and responsive investor relations support.

Directors' report [extract]

...

Mr Cass has a service contract providing for a minimum notice of termination by the Company of two years. The contract provides for liquidated damages amounting to two years' basic salary and an amount equal to twice the annual average of bonuses, if any, received during the two financial years of the company immediately preceding a change in control of the company (as defined in the contract) or in the event of termination in certain circumstances. The Committee has determined that both the period of notice required for termination of Mr Cass' contract and the change of control provisions are warranted by Mr Cass' value to the Company.

...

Options, other than founder options, were granted to key employees who joined the group after December 31, 1998. Although it was necessary to award these employees a significant number of options in order to recruit them, the performance conditions to which they are subject are such that their exercise will be phased.

References

1 The Committee on the Financial Aspects of Corporate Governance, *The Financial Aspects of Corporate Governance*, (The Cadbury Report), December 1992, para. 2.1.
2 The Cadbury Report, Appendix 1.
3 *The Listing Rules*, London Stock Exchange, Chapter 12, para. 12.43(j).
4 The Study Group on Directors' Remuneration, *Directors' Remuneration: Report of a Study Group chaired by Sir Richard Greenbury*, (The Greenbury Report), July 1995.
5 The Cadbury Report, para. 1.4.
6 Committee on Corporate Governance: *Final Report* (Hampel Report), January 1998, annex B.
7 *Ibid.,*, para. 1.7.
8 *Ibid.*, para. 1.15.
9 The Cadbury Report, para. 2.5.
10 Hampel Report, para. 1.15.
11 *Ibid.*, para. 1.11.
12 *Ibid.*, para. 1.14.
13 *Ibid.*, para. 1.20.
14 *Ibid.*, para. 1.25.
15 *Ibid.*, para. 1.24.
16 *Ibid.*, para. 1.25.
17 *The Listing Rules*, Financial Services Authority, Chapter 12, para. 12.43A.
18 The Cadbury Report, para. 4.1.
19 Hampel Report, para. 3.11.
20 The Cadbury Report, para. 4.18.
21 *Ibid.*, para. 4.25.
22 Hampel Report, para. 3.2.
23 The Cadbury Report, para. 4.12.
24 Hampel Report, para. 3.3.
25 The Cadbury Report, para. 4.7.
26 Hampel Report, para. 3.16.
27 *Ibid.*, para. 3.17.
28 *Ibid.*, para. 3.18.
29 *Ibid.*, para. 3.8.
30 The Cadbury Report, para. 4.12.
31 Hampel Report, para. 3.9.
32 *Ibid.*, para. 3.9.
33 *Ibid.*, para. 3.9.
34 *Ibid.*, para. 2.6.
35 *Ibid.*, para. 3.19.
36 *Ibid.*, para. 3.20.
37 The Cadbury Report, para. 6.11.
38 Hampel Report, para. 5.10.
39 *Ibid.*, para. 5.14.
40 *Ibid.*, para. 5.17.
41 Companies Act 1985, s.241.
42 Hampel Report, para. 5.20.
43 The Cadbury Report, Appendix 4, para. 6(f).
44 Hampel Report, para. 5.19
45 *Ibid.*, para. 5.18
46 Companies Act 1985, s.369.
47 The Cadbury Report, para. 4.50.
48 SAS 600, *Auditors' reports on financial statements*, APB, May 1993, Appendix 3.
49 *Gazette*, 'Directors Responsibilities', Gazette 90/40, 3 November 1993.
50 The Cadbury Report, para. 4.28.
51 *Gazette*, 'Directors responsibilities for financial statements', Gazette 90/46, 17 December 1993.

52 Bulletin 1998/10, *Corporate Governance Reporting and Auditors' Responsibilities Statements*, APB, December 1998.
53 Going Concern Working Group, *Going Concern and Financial Reporting: Guidance for directors of listed companies registered in the UK*, November 1994.
54 Bulletin 1994/1, *Disclosures relating to corporate governance (revised)*, APB, November 1994.
55 SAS 130, *The going concern basis in financial statements*, APB, November 1994.
56 *The Listing Rules*, London Stock Exchange, Chapter 12, para. 12.43(v).
57 Hampel Report, para. 6.17.
58 Going Concern Working Group, *Going Concern and Financial Reporting: Guidance for directors of listed companies registered in the UK*, paras. 24–40.
59 *Ibid.*, para. 47.
60 *Ibid.*, para. 49.
61 *Ibid.*, paras. 51 and 52.
62 Going Concern Working Group, *Going Concern and Financial Reporting: Draft guidance for directors of listed companies developed in response to the recommendations of the Cadbury Committee*, May 1993, para. 2.14.
63 Going Concern Working Group, *Going Concern and Financial Reporting: Guidance for directors of listed companies registered in the UK*, para. 20.
64 SAS 130, para. 45.
65 SAS 130, para. 47.
66 The Cadbury Code, para. 4.5.
67 Internal Control Working Group, *Internal Control and Financial Reporting: Guidance for directors of listed companies registered in the UK*, December 1994.
68 *Ibid.*, para. 8.
69 Hampel Report, para. 6.12.
70 *Ibid.*, para. 6.13.
71 ICAEW, *Internal Control: Guidance for directors on the Combined Code*, September 1999, paras. 35 and 41.
72 *Ibid.*, para. 43.
73 *Ibid.*, para. 44.
74 *Ibid.*, para. 46.
75 The Cadbury code, para. 4.3.
76 Hampel Report, para. 6.3.
77 *Ibid.*, para. 6.4.
78 *The Listing Rules*, London Stock Exchange, Chapter 12, para. 12.43A.
79 Bulletin 1995/1, *Disclosures relating to corporate governance (revised)*, APB, February 1995, para. 46.
80 Bulletin 1998/10, *Corporate Governance Reporting and Auditors' Responsibilities Statements*, APB, December 1998, paras. 16 and 17.
81 Hampel Report, para. 1.10.
82 The City Group for Smaller Companies, *The Financial Aspects of Corporate Governance: Guidance for Smaller Companies*, CISCO, London, 1994.
83 The City Group for Smaller Companies, *The Committee on Corporate Governance Report and The Combined Code: Guidance for Smaller Quoted Companies*, CISCO, 1999.
84 *Guidance for Smaller Companies, The Committee on Corporate Governance Report and The Combined Code*, QCA, 2001.
85 The Cadbury Report, para. 4.50.
86 *Ibid.*, para. 4.53.
87 Hampel Report, para. 2. D. I.
88 *Ibid.*, para. 2.19
89 ASB Statement, *Operating and Financial Review*, ASB, July 1993, para. 3.
90 *Ibid.*, para. 4.
91 *Ibid.*, para. 5.
92 *Ibid.*, para. 8.
93 *Ibid.*, paras. 9–22.
94 *Ibid.*, para. 23.
95 *Ibid.*, paras. 25–37.
96 *Ibid.*, para. 38.
97 The Company Law Review Steering Group, Final Report, *Modern Company Law for a Competitive Economy*, DTI, June 2001.
98 *Ibid.*, Chapter 3, paras. 3.33 to 3.45.
99 *Ibid.*, Chapter 8, para. 8.32.
100 *Ibid.*, para. 8.40.

Chapter 5 Consolidated accounts

1 THE CONCEPT OF A GROUP

1.1 The objectives of group accounts

Group accounts are designed to extend the reporting entity to embrace other entities which are subject to its control. They involve treating the net assets and activities of subsidiaries held by the holding company as if they were part of the holding company's own net assets and activities; the overall aim is to present the results and state of affairs of the group as if they were those of a single entity.

The basic legal framework for group accounts in the UK is to be found in the Companies Act 1985, as amended by the Companies Act 1989. This requires that group accounts are to be in the form of consolidated accounts which 'give a true and fair view of the state of affairs as at the end of the financial year, and the profit or loss for the financial year, of the undertakings included in the consolidation as a whole, so far as concerns members of the company',[1] and that they should comply with the provisions of Schedule 4A with respect to their form and content.[2]

The relevant accounting standard in the UK on the subject is FRS 2 – *Accounting for subsidiary undertakings*. This explains that the purpose of consolidated financial statements is to present financial information about a parent undertaking and its subsidiary undertakings as a single economic entity to show the economic resources controlled by the group, the obligations of the group and the results it achieves with those resources.[3] FRS 2 is drafted in terms of the Companies Act, but it applies to all parent undertakings that prepare consolidated financial statements intended to give a true and fair view of the group.[4]

The principal international accounting standard dealing with this topic is IAS 27 – *Consolidated Financial Statements and Accounting for Investments in Subsidiaries.* This requires a parent to present consolidated financial statements in which virtually all foreign and domestic subsidiaries are consolidated.[5]

1.2 What is a subsidiary?

The question of the definition of a subsidiary is fundamental to any discussion of group accounts because otherwise it is impossible to say what constitutes the entity which is the subject of the report. The question is also related to the subject of off balance sheet financing, because frequently this hinges on whether the group balance sheet should embrace the accounts of an entity which holds certain assets and liabilities which management may not wish to include in the group accounts (see Chapter 18).

The term used in the UK legislation is 'subsidiary undertaking'. The definition of this (see 2.2 below) is based on the EC Seventh Directive and the same definition has also been adopted by FRS 2. The definitions are mainly based on the concept of control which is defined in FRS 2 as 'the ability of an undertaking to direct the financial and operating policies of another undertaking with a view to gaining economic benefits from its activities'.[6]

IAS 27 also defines a subsidiary in terms of control which is defined in similar terms to that in FRS 2.[7]

1.3 Consolidating partly owned subsidiaries

Various alternative ways of looking at a group become relevant when there are subsidiary companies which are not wholly owned by the holding company; the particular matters which are affected are the elimination of the effects of inter-company transactions, the calculation of minority interests and the treatment of changes in stake in the subsidiary. There are two widely accepted concepts, referred to respectively as the entity concept and the proprietary concept, but the latter has a number of further variants. These are described in turn below.

1.3.1 The entity concept

The entity concept focuses on the existence of the group as an economic unit, rather than looking at it only through the eyes of the dominant shareholder group. It concentrates on the resources controlled by the entity, and regards the identity of owners with claims on these resources as being of secondary importance. It therefore makes no distinction between the treatment given to different classes of shareholders, whether majority or minority, and transactions between the shareholders are regarded as internal to the group.

1.3.2 The proprietary concept

The proprietary concept emphasises ownership through a controlling shareholding interest, and regards the purpose of the production of the consolidated financial statements as being primarily for the information of the shareholders of the holding company. Correspondingly, it makes no attempt to present financial statements which are relevant to the minority shareholders. This is achieved either by treating the minority shareholders as 'outsiders' and reflecting their interests as quasi-liabilities or by leaving them out of the group financial statements entirely, thereby only consolidating the parent's percentage interest in the assets and liabilities of the subsidiary (the 'proportional consolidation' method). The proprietary concept is sometimes referred to as the 'parent company' concept, and there is a variant of it known as the 'parent company extension' concept, which leans more towards the entity concept described above.

1.3.3 *Comparison between the different concepts of a group*

The distinction between the different methods in practice can best be illustrated by an example:

Example 5.1: Comparison between the different concepts of a group

Assume that company A buys 75% of company B for £1,200 when company B has total net assets with a fair value of £1,000 and a book value of £800. Under the concepts described above, the consolidated balance sheet of company A would incorporate the effects of the acquisition calculated as follows:

	Entity concept	Proprietary concept	Parent coy. extension concept
	£	£	£
Net assets of B	1,000	950	1,000
Goodwill	600	450	450
	1,600	1,400	1,450
Minority interest	400	200	250
Investor interest	1,200	1,200	1,200

Under the entity concept, both the tangible net assets and goodwill are reported in the balance sheet at the full amount of their fair value as determined by the transaction involving the majority shareholder. These amounts are then apportioned between the majority and minority shareholders. By way of contrast, the proprietary concept leaves the minority interest unaffected by the transaction of the majority shareholder; it is shown simply as their proportionate share of the book values of the assets of the company. This means that the goodwill is stated at a figure which represents the difference between the cost of the 75% investment (£1,200) and 75% of the fair value of the assets (£750). Perhaps more disturbingly, the assets are carried on a mixed basis which represents 75% of their fair value and 25% of their book value. This feature is eliminated if proportional consolidation is adopted; the minority interest is disregarded altogether, being set against the assets and liabilities of the subsidiary on a line by line basis, so that only the majority investor's share of the subsidiary's assets are consolidated. This would result in consolidation of assets of £750 and goodwill of £450, representing the total of the investment of £1,200. However, neither UK GAAP nor IAS allow the proportional consolidation approach to be adopted for subsidiary undertakings. The feature is also avoided in the parent company extension concept, which includes the assets at the whole amount of their fair value and apportions that between the majority and minority interests, but includes goodwill only as it relates to the majority investor.

The rules contained in the UK legislation do not permit the use of the entity concept as set out above, because they require that goodwill be calculated by comparing the acquisition cost with the investor's proportionate share of the investee's capital and reserves (after adjusting for fair values); by requiring the assets and liabilities to be included at their fair values, they would also appear to rule out the proprietary concept (although the rules on minority interests do not refer to *adjusted* capital and reserves).[8] FRS 2 uses a variant of the parent company extension concept (see 3.4 below). The entity method is also ruled out by the international standard on business combinations, IAS 22. However, this permits either of the other two methods, with the proprietary concept being the preferred approach and the parent company extension method a permitted alternative.[9]

The different concepts are also relevant to the calculation of the adjustments made to eliminate the effects of inter-company transactions. If company A in the above example sold an item of stock to company B for a profit of £100, and company B still held the asset in stock at the year end, it would be necessary to make an adjustment on consolidation to eliminate what was an unrealised profit from the group point of view. Under the proprietary concept, the minority shareholders are regarded as outsiders, and therefore there is a case for saying that 25% of the profit *has* been realised; this would be done by limiting the write-down of stock to £75, all of which is taken off the balance on the group profit and loss account. Under the proportional consolidation method, only 75% of the stock would appear in the consolidated balance sheet in the first place, so the adjustment would simply be to deduct £75 from both the group profit and loss account and from the stock. If the entity concept is followed, as it is the parent which has made the sale, the whole write down of stock of £100 would be charged against the group profit and loss account; no amount would be attributed to the minority interest. Under another approach, the separate entities approach,[10] the adjustment would be effected by apportioning the £100 between the group profit and loss account and the minority interest in the ratio 75:25. In this case the Companies Act rules in the UK permit inter-company profit eliminations to be made either at their gross amounts or in proportion to the investor's stake in the investee.[11] However, FRS 2 uses its variant of the parent company extension concept, whereby all of the profit is eliminated, but the adjustment is apportioned between the majority and minority interests in proportion to their holdings in the selling company (see 3.5 below). In this example, this gives the same answer as the entity concept which is effectively that used in IAS 27 (see 6.2 below).

A further practical situation where differences between the concepts emerge is when the partly owned subsidiary makes losses which put it into overall deficit. Under the entity concept, the consolidated financial statements would continue to account for these losses and apportion them between the majority and minority interests in proportion to their holdings, even if these created a debit balance for the minority interest in the balance sheet. A proprietary viewpoint would not normally permit the minority interest to be shown as a debit balance, because it could not usually be regarded as a recoverable asset from the point of view of the majority interest, which is the orientation of the financial statements under the proprietary concept. This is the position taken by IAS 27 which requires that the excess should be charged against the majority interest except to the extent that the minority has a binding obligation to, and is able to, make good the losses.[12] FRS 2, on the other hand, has effectively adopted an entity perspective and requires that losses are attributable to the minority interests according to their holdings in loss making subsidiaries, regardless of whether or not this leads to a debit balance or not. Such a debit balance is not regarded as an asset, but the minority share of net liabilities. However, the standard does require the group to make provision to the extent that it has 'any commercial or legal obligation (whether formal or implied) to provide finance that may not be recoverable in respect of the accumulated losses attributable to the minority interest'.[13]

It is clear from the discussion above that these different concepts are not followed on a consistent basis by either FRS 2 or by IAS.

FRS 2 does not contain a detailed discussion of the concepts described above, supposedly leaving the conceptual basis of consolidated accounts to be dealt with in the ASB's *Statement of Principles*. However, as can be seen from the discussion in 5.9 of Chapter 2, this really now discusses how interests in other entities should be dealt with in consolidated accounts. However, apart from the treatment of debit balances relating to minority interests as discussed above, FRS 2 adopts an approach in respect of minority interests similar to that proposed by ED 50, the forerunner of FRS 2, which did discuss these conceptual issues.

ED 50 developed a new concept, called the 'control/ownership concept', which is effectively a variant of the parent company extension concept described above. Under this concept, it is argued that the shareholders of the holding company need information not only on the group as a whole but also on the distinction between what they own and what others own.[14] In deciding how to deal with the particular matters which are affected by the existence of the minority shareholders, the concept looks at whether 'control' or 'ownership' is the most relevant issue. In respect of questions where control is the most relevant issue, minorities are considered to be within the group, similar in nature to equity, because they are part of the controlled entity. Where ownership is considered to be most important, the minorities are treated as external to the group and regarded as being a liability.[15]

1.4 Other issues

Although the general requirements of FRS 2 and IAS 27 are for subsidiaries to be consolidated within the group accounts, both standards set out situations where certain subsidiaries should not be consolidated, but dealt with in a different way in the group accounts. These requirements are discussed at 5 and 6.5 respectively.

The composition of what constitutes a group may also change, either through entities joining or leaving the group, or by the parent's increasing or decreasing its stake in existing subsidiaries. These issues are dealt with in Chapter 6.

The concept of a group discussed above, focuses on those entities over which the parent has control. Many groups conduct part of their activities by taking substantial minority stakes in other entities, over which they either exercise joint control with another party or exercise significant influence which falls short of control. The accounting for such entities is dealt with in Chapter 7.

One final issue is that there may be some situations where it is considered unnecessary for a parent to prepare consolidated accounts in respect of the group, particularly where it itself is a subsidiary of another entity. The exemptions given by FRS 2 and IAS 27 are dealt with at 4 and 6.4 respectively.

2 THE UK DEFINITION OF A SUBSIDIARY UNDERTAKING

As indicated at 1.2 above, the question of the definition of a subsidiary is fundamental to any discussion of group accounts. The question is also related to the subject of off balance sheet financing, because frequently this hinges on whether the group balance sheet should embrace the accounts of an entity which holds certain assets and liabilities which management may not wish to include in the group accounts (see Chapter 18).

The term used in the UK legislation is 'subsidiary undertaking'. The definition of this (see 2.2 below) is based on the EC Seventh Directive and the same definition has also been adopted by FRS 2.

2.1 The EC Seventh Directive

Article 1 of the EC Seventh Directive on Company Law sets out six sets of circumstances under which a parent/subsidiary relationship will be regarded as existing, so as to require the parent to present consolidated accounts, and one further situation requiring consolidation even though such a relationship does not exist. Five of the six sets of circumstances have been incorporated in the UK legislation through the enactment of the Companies Act 1989 and these are discussed at 2.2 below. The other two situations contained in the Directive, which were optional and have not been incorporated, are as follows:

(a) De facto control over appointment of the board

The parent shall consolidate its subsidiary if it is a shareholder or member of it and a majority of the members of the board who have held office throughout the year, the previous year, and up to the time of the issue of the consolidated accounts have *in fact* been appointed solely as a result of the exercise of the parent's voting rights.[16] This is to cater for the situation where, due to the fact that the majority of the shares are widely dispersed, a minority shareholder can exercise de facto control. The Directive allows member states not to implement this part of the definition, or to make it conditional on the holding of at least 20% of the voting rights; the UK government was opposed to this part of the definition at the time of the negotiation of the terms of the directive, and they decided to take advantage of the first of these exemptions.

(b) Horizontal groups

Consolidated accounts must be prepared for companies which have no shareholding relationship in either of two sets of circumstances. The first is if they are managed on a unified basis under the terms of a contract or provisions in their memorandum or articles of association; the second is if the same people form the majority of the members of the board of both companies during the year and for the period up to the preparation of the accounts.[17] Although the thinking behind the second set of circumstances is easy to understand, it would appear to result occasionally in the consolidation of separate enterprises which were associated with each other only by coincidence and whose combined accounts would have neither meaning nor relevance to anyone. Neither of these provisions has been incorporated in the Companies Act.

2.2 The Companies Act

In implementing the Directive, the Companies Act 1989 introduced the term 'subsidiary undertaking' and moved the definition from one based strictly on the form of the shareholding relationship between the companies, nearer to one which reflects the substance of the commercial relationship and in particular who exercises de facto control. The use of the term 'undertaking' also extended the types of entity which may have to be consolidated, in that it not only includes companies or bodies corporate, but also unincorporated associations and partnerships.[18]

Under the Act, a subsidiary undertaking is one in which the parent:

(a) has a majority of the voting rights; or

(b) is a member and can appoint or remove a majority of the board; or

(c) is a member and controls alone a majority of the voting rights by agreement with other members; or

(d) has the right to exercise a dominant influence through the Memorandum and Articles or a control contract; or

(e) has a participating interest and either

 (i) actually exercises a dominant influence over it, or

 (ii) both are managed on a unified basis.[19]

These are discussed further below.

2.2.1 *Majority of voting rights*

This is the main definition based on the power of one entity to control another through the exercise of shareholder voting control. Unlike the old definition of a subsidiary,[20] it concentrates on those shares which can exercise voting power rather than those which are defined in terms of their rights to participate beyond a specified amount in a distribution.

'Voting rights' are defined as 'rights conferred on shareholders in respect of their shares or, in the case of an undertaking not having a share capital, on members, to vote at general meetings of the undertaking on all (or substantially all) matters'.[21]

There are a number of detailed provisions for determining whether or not certain rights are to be taken into account.[22] Paragraph 21 of ED 50, the forerunner of FRS 2, summarised these as follows:

'One example is where rights are only exercisable under certain circumstances; in this case those rights should be taken into account for as long as the particular circumstances continue, or the circumstances are within the control of the holder of the rights. Rights which are normally exercisable but which are temporarily interrupted should continue to be taken into account. Rights should be treated as held by the enterprise on whose behalf a nominee holds them or whose instruction, consent or concurrence is required for their exercise. Fiduciary interests are not taken into account and rights given as security remain the rights of the provider of the security, if the rights are mainly exercisable only in accordance with his instructions or in his interests. Rights of any of its subsidiaries are to be treated as the rights of the parent but rights of a parent should not be attributed to its subsidiaries. The voting rights in an enterprise are to be reduced by any rights held by the enterprise itself.'

2.2.2 *Control of the board of directors*

Essentially this is an anti-avoidance measure, which extends the control concept from control of the company in general meeting to control of the board, to cover situations where the latter exists but not the former.

Whereas previously the right to control the composition of the board only meant the right to appoint or remove a majority in number of the directors, the Companies Act 1989 extended it to mean the right to appoint or remove members of the board entitled to a majority of the voting rights on all (or substantially all) matters at board meetings.[23] This was a further anti-avoidance measure, to cope with the situation where control of the board's decisions is achieved either through the exercise of differential voting rights or a casting vote without having a majority in number of the membership of the board.

However, this criterion could have implications for 'true' 50:50 joint ventures. Where the shareholders in such a joint venture, in order to prevent a deadlock, take it in turns each year to appoint the chairman (with the casting vote), this will mean that the joint venture will be a subsidiary undertaking of each shareholder company every second year. The question then arises, should the undertaking be consolidated, then equity accounted, in alternate years? (Depending on the timing, this could actually mean the undertaking is consolidated for the first part of the shareholding company's year and equity accounted for the remainder, and vice versa in alternate years!) In our view this would clearly be a nonsense and we believe that the appropriate treatment would be not to consolidate on the grounds that there are long-term restrictions which hinder control (see 5.3 below), but to equity account throughout in accordance with FRS 9 – *Associates and Joint Ventures* (see Chapter 7).

One company which discloses the fact that it has a subsidiary by virtue of board control is Rio Tinto, as shown below:

Extract 5.1: Rio Tinto plc and Rio Tinto Limited (2000)

28 PRINCIPAL SUBSIDIARIES [extract]

Company and country of incorporation	Principal activities	Class of shares held	Proportion of class held %	Group interest %
Namibia				
Rössing Uranium Limited (note c)	Uranium mining	'B'N$1	71.16	68.58
		'C'N10c	70.59	

(c) The Group holding of shares in Rössing Uranium Limited carries 35.54 per cent of the total voting rights. Rössing is consolidated by virtue of Board control.

Another company which has had a subsidiary due to board control is Sema Group, as shown below:

Extract 5.2: Sema Group plc (1996)

11. GROUP UNDERTAKINGS [extract]

The principal Group undertakings at 31 December 1996, all of which are engaged in the provision of information technology services, were as follows (all holdings were in ordinary shares):

	Immediate holding company (%)	County of registration and operation
DIRECT GROUP UNDERTAKINGS		
BAeSEMA Limited	50	England
Sema Group SA	99.8	France
OWNED BY BAeSEMA LIMITED		
Aerosystems International Limited	50	England
OWNED BY SEMA GROUP SA		
TS FM Holdings	40	France

BAeSEMA Limited and TS FM Holdings have been fully consolidated as Group undertakings as defined by the Companies Act 1985. BAeSEMA is consolidated on the basis of a shareholders' agreement which gives the Group control of the Board of directors. TS FM Holdings is consolidated on the basis that it is managed on a unified basis with Sema Group SA.

BAeSEMA's 50% holding in Aerosystems International Limited has been fully consolidated from 1 January 1996 since it is managed on a unified basis with BAeSEMA.

2.2.3 *Control by contract*

Such a contract, which is a feature of German business organisations, is not usually possible under general principles of UK company law, because it would conflict with the directors' fiduciary duty to conduct the affairs of the company in accordance with its own best interests, and is allowed only where the Memorandum and Articles specifically permit it. The Directive provides that this part of the definition applies only where it is consistent with the company law of the country concerned, and for this reason it has been enacted in the UK in a fairly restricted way; it will apply only in cases where the parent company has the right to give directions with respect to the operating and financial policies of the other undertaking which its directors are obliged to comply with whether or not they are for the benefit of that other undertaking, where the undertaking's domestic law and its Memorandum and Articles permit a dominant influence to be exerted through such a contract, and where the contract in question is in writing.[24] This criterion is therefore likely to be of relevance only where a company has a business operation in Germany or another country which adopts the German model.

One company which has disclosed the fact that it had a subsidiary by virtue of a control contract is Sema Group, as shown below:

> *Extract 5.3: Sema Group plc (1993)*
>
> **11. GROUP UNDERTAKINGS** [extract]
>
> The Group's 50% holding in BAeSEMA Limited, its 50% holding in Sema Group Télécom SA and its 49% holding in Tibet SA have been fully consolidated as Group undertakings as defined by the Companies Act 1989.
>
> BAeSEMA is consolidated on the basis of a shareholders' agreement which gives the Group control of the board of directors. Tibet SA is consolidated on the basis of actual dominant influence exercised by the Group by virtue of a control contract.

2.2.4 *Control by agreement*

This is a more stringent application of the concept of de facto control by a minority investor (see 2.1 (a) above), requiring agreement with other shareholders rather than merely their tacit acceptance that control can be exercised. The Directive provides that the member states may introduce more particular requirements for the form and content of such agreements, and the Department of Trade and Industry announced that it intended to draft the legislation so that the agreement must be legally binding but need not be in writing, and that it should include agreements *not* to exercise voting rights as well as those to exercise them in a particular way.[25] Neither of these issues is, in fact, specifically dealt with in the Act; it may, therefore, be that in their absence, oral agreements and agreements not to exercise voting rights are intended to come within the scope of the legislation.

2.2.5 *Participating interest with dominant influence or unified management*

This criterion is one of the member state options contained in the Directive which has been introduced into the legislation in addition to the mandatory definitions set out in 2.2.1 to 2.2.4 above. This part of the Directive has been introduced in a very broad form which is based on a wide definition of 'participating interest', with the clear intention of preventing artificial structures designed to achieve the purposes of off balance sheet finance schemes.

A participating interest in an undertaking is deemed to mean an interest in the shares of the undertaking which is held for the long term for the purpose of securing a contribution to the activities of the investing company by the exercise of control or influence arising from that interest.[26] This is similar to the definition of a related company previously contained in the Companies Act 1985, but is wider in that it includes interests in partnerships and unincorporated associations; it also includes interests which are convertible into interests in shares, such as convertible loan stock, and options to acquire an interest in shares.[27] There is a rebuttable presumption that a holding of 20% or more is a participating interest.[28] FRS 2 regards an interest held on a long term basis as one which is held other than 'exclusively with a view to subsequent resale' (see 5.4 below).[29]

Although 'participating interest' is defined in the Act, there is no further definition of the concept of either 'actually exercises a dominant influence' or 'managed on a unified basis' (both are concepts derived from German law); the reason being that the DTI did not want to elaborate on these definitions, since it regarded this as an area to be more appropriately dealt with by means of accounting standards, although ultimately it is a matter of law to be interpreted by the courts. The Act does state, however, that although 'a right to exercise a dominant influence' over another undertaking is defined as 'a right to give directions with respect to the operating and financial policies of that other undertaking which its directors are obliged to comply with whether or not they are for the benefit of that other undertaking' (see 2.2.3 above), this is not to be read as affecting the construction of 'actually exercises a dominant influence'.[30]

In FRS 2, 'dominant influence' is defined as 'influence that can be exercised to achieve the operating and financial policies desired by the holder of the influence, notwithstanding the rights or influence of any other party' and the 'actual exercise of dominant influence' is defined as being 'the exercise of an influence that achieves the result that the operating and financial policies of the undertaking influenced are set in accordance with the wishes of the holder of the influence and for the holder's benefit whether or not those wishes are explicit. The actual exercise of dominant influence is identified by its effect in practice rather than by the way in which it is exercised.'[31]

As explained in FRS 2, 'the effect of the exercise of dominant influence is that the undertaking under influence implements the operating and financial policies that the holder of the influence desires. Thus a power of veto or any other reserve power that has the necessary effect in practice can form the basis whereby one undertaking actually exercises a dominant influence over another. However, such powers are likely to lead to the holder actually exercising a dominant influence over an undertaking only if they are held in conjunction with other rights or powers or if they relate to the day-to-day activities of that undertaking and no similar veto is held by other parties unconnected to the holder.'[32]

Clearly, it will be a matter of judgement and interpretation as to whether these definitions apply to any particular set of circumstances. As FRS 2 explains, 'the full circumstances of each case should be considered, including the effect of any formal or informal agreements between the undertakings, to decide whether or not one undertaking actually exercises a dominant influence over another. Commercial relationships such as that of supplier, customer or lender do not of themselves constitute dominant influence.'[33]

The standard also states that dominant influence can be exercised 'in an interventionist or non-interventionist way. For example, a parent undertaking may set directly and in detail the operating and financial policies of its subsidiary undertaking or it may prefer to influence these by setting out in outline the kind of results it wants achieved without being involved regularly or on a day-to-day basis. Because of the variety of ways that dominant influence may be exercised evidence of continuous intervention is not necessary to support the view that dominant influence is actually exercised. Sufficient evidence might be provided by a rare intervention on a critical matter. Once there has been evidence that one undertaking has exercised a dominant influence over another, then the dominant undertaking should be assumed to continue to exercise its influence until there is evidence to the contrary.'[34]

Where a subsidiary undertaking is so only by virtue of this criterion then FRS 2 requires disclosure of the basis of the parent company's dominant influence.[35] One company which consolidates a subsidiary undertaking which qualifies under this criterion is Rentokil Initial as shown in the following extract:

Extract 5.4: Rentokil Initial plc (2000)

PRINCIPAL OPERATING SUBSIDIARY AND ASSOCIATED UNDERTAKINGS [extract]
South Korea
Yu Yu Calmic Co Ltd (50%)

The group's 50% interest in Yu Yu Calmic Co Ltd is consolidated as a subsidiary to reflect the group's dominant influence exercised over this company because of its shareholding and its involvement in the management and because the business is conducted under licence from the group.

One interesting example is that of Booker which in its 1995 accounts consolidated a subsidiary under this criterion, as indicated below:

Extract 5.5: Booker plc (1995)

Subsidiary and associated undertakings [extract]
Recheio Distribuição SA (40%)[5]

5 Recheio Distribuição SA is treated as a subsidiary on the grounds of Booker plc exercising a dominant influence over the operating and financial policies of that company.

However in the following year the position would appear to have changed:

Extract 5.6: Booker plc (1996)

13. Fixed asset investments [extract]

Recheio Distribuição SA, in which the group holds a 40% equity interest and which has been consolidated hitherto on the basis of the group exercising dominant control, has been deconsolidated and treated as an associated undertaking effective from 28 December 1996. The change in the status of the investment in Recheio reflects the group's loss of dominant control over the operating and financial policies of that company.

One difficulty which this definition can give rise to is the apportionment of the results and net assets of the subsidiary undertaking between the parent and the minority interests, particularly where the participating interest is in the form of convertible loan stock or options to acquire an interest in shares. This is discussed at 3.4 below.

The ASB has defined 'managed on a unified basis' in FRS 2 as being where 'two or more undertakings are managed on a unified basis if the whole of the operations of the undertakings are integrated and they are managed as a single unit. Unified management does not arise solely because one undertaking manages another.'[36]

One company which consolidates subsidiary undertakings which qualify under this criterion is Unilever, as indicated below:

Extract 5.7: Unilever PLC (2000)

Unilever [extract]

The two parent companies, NV and PLC, operate as nearly as is practicable as a single entity (the Unilever Group, also referred to as Unilever or the Group). NV and PLC have the same directors and are linked by a series of agreements, including an Equalisation Agreement, which is designed so that the position of the shareholders of both companies is as nearly as possible the same as if they held shares in a single company.

Basis of consolidation [extract]

By reason of the operational and contractual arrangements referred to above and the internal participating interests ..., NV and PLC and their group companies constitute a single group under Netherlands and United Kingdom legislation for the purposes of presenting consolidated accounts. Accordingly, the accounts of the Unilever Group are presented by both NV and PLC as their respective consolidated accounts.

Another example can be seen in Extract 5.2 at 2.2.2 above.

Questions which have arisen include that of whether more than one party can exercise dominant influence over a single undertaking. We believe that logically, there can only be one *dominant* influence, but there is a more general question of whether an undertaking can be the subsidiary of more than one parent, given that there are five alternative definitions of a subsidiary undertaking relationship, and if it is possible for an undertaking to have two parent companies, should both companies consolidate the undertaking?

On this question, FRS 2 states that 'where more than one undertaking is ... identified as a parent of one subsidiary undertaking, not more than one of those parents can have control as defined in paragraph 6 [of the standard]'.[37] It then suggests that such anomalies might be resolved by taking into account:

(a) the existence of a quasi subsidiary (see Chapter 18);

(b) the existence of severe long-term restrictions on the rights of the parent undertaking (see 5.3 below); or

(c) the existence of a joint venture agreement, whether formal or informal.[38]

In relation to the last of these, the standard states that 'where the tests of the Act identify more than one undertaking as the parent of one subsidiary undertaking it is likely that they have shared control and, therefore, their interests in the subsidiary undertaking are in effect interests in a joint venture and should be treated accordingly (see Chapter 7). Alternatively, one or more of the undertakings identified under the Act as a parent undertaking may exercise a non-controlling but significant influence over its subsidiary undertaking, in which case it would be more appropriate to treat that subsidiary undertaking in the same way as an associated undertaking rather than to include it in the consolidation.'[39]

3 UK REQUIREMENTS FOR CONSOLIDATION OF SUBSIDIARIES

3.1 Basic principles

It is beyond the scope of this chapter to discuss the detailed mechanics of the consolidation process; there are a number of basic texts which give a full exposition of this subject. The Companies Act 1989 introduced into the legislation some rules relating to the consolidation of subsidiaries,[40] but until then there were no authoritative rules on the subject at a detailed level; the previous standard on group accounts, SSAP 14, merely stated that 'the method of preparation of consolidated financial statements on an item-by-item basis, eliminating intra-group balances and transactions and unrealised intra-group profit, is well understood ...'.[41]

FRS 2 now defines consolidation as 'the process of adjusting and combining financial information from the individual financial statements of a parent undertaking and its subsidiary undertakings to prepare consolidated financial statements that present financial information for the group as a single economic entity'.[42] This is not as explicit as the definition contained in ED 50 which stated that consolidation was 'a method of accounting under which the information contained in the separate financial statements of a parent and its subsidiaries is presented as though for a single entity. Investments in subsidiaries are eliminated against the subsidiaries' share capital and reserves in accordance with the method of accounting adopted for the business combination. After any necessary consolidation adjustments for such matters as minority interests, intra-group transactions and to obtain consistency of accounting policies, the amounts for assets and liabilities, revenue and expenses in the individual financial statements are added together on a line-by-line basis to form the consolidated accounts.'[43] (Arguably, this was more of a description rather than a definition of a consolidation.) FRS 2 introduces authoritative rules relating to some of these consolidation adjustments and these are referred to below.

One interesting example is that of Photo-Me International which in its 1997 accounts did not eliminate intra-group sales by invoking the true and fair override as shown below.

Extract 5.8: Photo-Me International Plc (1997)

1 **Accounting policies** [extract]

(k) Turnover

Turnover comprises the net invoiced value of sales and the revenue arising from cash takings in operating companies, stated net of value added tax. Turnover includes sales, by the Group's manufacturing divisions to Group undertakings, of equipment which is then capitalised within the accounts of the Group's undertakings. It is the opinion of the directors that excluding sales from turnover would understate the Group's activities and as such would fail to give a true and fair view. Inter-company profit arising on such sales is excluded from the Group's profit.

2 Turnover [extract]				
Turnover was contributed as follows:				
	1997		1996	
Area of activity	£'000	%	£'000	%
Manufacturing:				
Sales to Group undertakings	10,788	6.3	15,552	7.8
Sales to third parties	35,307	20.8	43,327	21.8
	46,095	27.1	58,879	29.6
Operating	123,864	72.9	139,813	70.4
	169,959	100.0	198,692	100.0

This highly unusual treatment attracted the attention of the Review Panel who were not persuaded by the company's arguments for departing from the basic principles contained in the Companies Act as regards intra-group sales.[44] Accordingly, Photo-Me International changed its policy in this regard in the following year as shown below.

Extract 5.9: Photo-Me International Plc (1998)

1 **Accounting policies** [extract]

(b) Changes in accounting policy

(i) Following discussion with the Financial Reporting Review Panel the Group has this year decided to change the method of accounting for sales of operating equipment, manufactured by Group undertakings, sold to other Group undertakings, and then capitalised. The Group now shows the removal of these from turnover (Note 2) and reflects a corresponding reduction in cost of sales (Note 3) by inclusion of the same value (which excludes intra-group profit) as "own work capitalised". The turnover shown in the profit and loss account now excludes any intra-group turnover.

The comparative figures for the year to 30 April 1997 have been adjusted to reflect the new policy.

The effect of this change is shown in Notes 1(l), 2 and 3.

3.2 Uniform accounting policies

It is axiomatic that the figures being aggregated in the consolidation process must have been compiled on a consistent basis and therefore that uniform accounting policies should have been adopted by all the members of the group. Of course, local reporting requirements for each subsidiary might dictate that different policies must be used for domestic purposes; the only necessity where this occurs is that appropriate adjustments are made in the course of the consolidation process to eliminate the effects of such differences. FRS 2 endorses this general principle.[45]

The Companies Act does not refer to accounting policies as such in this context, but says that 'where assets and liabilities ... have been valued or otherwise determined by undertakings according to accounting rules differing from those used for the group accounts, the values or amounts shall be adjusted so as to accord with the rules used for the group accounts'.[46] However, this need not be done if the effect is immaterial,[47] or if there are 'special reasons' for leaving them unchanged (in which case disclosure of particulars of the departure, the reasons for it and its effect are to be given).[48] FRS 2 also acknowledges that this may be appropriate in exceptional cases.[49]

Notwithstanding these apparent loopholes in FRS 2 and the Act, the accounts must still give a true and fair view of the group as a whole and it is difficult to imagine that this could be achieved by adding together material figures which have been compiled using profoundly different policies. In practice, however, the relaxation allowed does not seem to be relied on in many cases and groups generally do exert themselves to achieve consistency of policies unless the effect is insignificant.

Although there is no requirement to do so, some companies disclose the fact that adjustments are made to achieve uniform accounting policies, as illustrated below:

> *Extract 5.10: British Telecommunications plc (2001)*
>
> **I Basis of preparation of the financial statements** [extract]
>
> Where the financial statements of subsidiary undertakings, associates and joint ventures do not conform with the group's accounting policies, appropriate adjustments are made on consolidation in order to present the group financial statements on a consistent basis.

3.3 Coterminous accounting periods

Since the group is seen as an extension of the parent company in UK law, it is necessary that the period covered by the group accounts corresponds to the accounting reference period of the parent, both in terms of duration and balance sheet date.[50] Once again, this requirement is implicit in the objective that the group accounts should be prepared as if the group were a single entity.

The Companies Act places an onus on the directors of the parent company to ensure that the financial year of each subsidiary is the same as the parent. However, it does acknowledge that there can be good reasons why the individual subsidiaries' own accounts might be drawn up to a different date;[51] for example, in certain countries their year end might be dictated by law, they might choose to adopt a particular accounting period for tax purposes or their trade may be seasonal and have a natural cycle which makes it appropriate to choose a particular reporting date. Another reason could be that they deliberately prepare their accounts to a date shortly before that of the parent (as a materially accurate approximation to the period of the parent) so as to facilitate speedy reporting by the parent of the group results.

Where the period covered by the accounts of an individual member of the group does not correspond to that of the parent, two solutions are possible. The first is for the subsidiary to prepare special accounts solely for the purpose of the consolidation for a period which does match that of the parent. Under the provisions of the Act, such special statements (termed interim accounts) *must* be used if the subsidiary's year end is more than three months before that of the parent; their use is only optional if the year end is no more than three months before that of the parent.[52] One company which has had to use interim accounts is HSBC Holdings, as shown below:

Extract 5.11: HSBC Holdings plc (2000)

1 **Basis of preparation** [extract]

(c) The consolidated financial statements of HSBC comprise the financial statements of HSBC Holdings and its subsidiary undertakings. Financial statements of subsidiary undertakings are made up to 31 December. For HSBC Bank Canada, which until 1998 had a 31 October year-end, financial statements for a period of 14 months were used in the 1998 consolidated financial statements. In the case of the principal banking and insurance subsidiaries of HSBC Bank Argentina, whose financial statements are made up to 30 June annually to comply with local regulations, HSBC uses audited interim financial statements, drawn up to 31 December annually.

Although, under the Companies Act, the use of interim accounts is only optional if the year end is no more than three months before that of the parent, FRS 2 requires interim accounts to be used in such circumstances unless it is impracticable to do so, in which case the second solution should be adopted.[53] This solution is to use the statutory accounts of the subsidiary for the period last ending before that of the parent. As indicated above such an approach is only possible where the subsidiary's year end is no more than three months before that of the parent. FRS 2 then requires that any changes that have taken place in the intervening period that materially affect the view given by the group's accounts should be taken into account by adjustments in the preparation of the consolidated accounts.[54] In effect, therefore, this means that the group accounts must present (within limits of materiality) the same position as if coterminous year ends had been adopted.

One company which has used interim accounts when statutory accounts made up to within three months of the parent's year end were available is Johnson Fry Holdings, as shown below:

Extract 5.12: Johnson Fry Holdings plc (1996)

Basis of preparation [extract]

The financial statements include the financial statements of the Company and all its subsidiary undertakings made up to 31 December 1996, with the exception of the Pinnacle businesses which changed their year end to 31 October so that audited figures would be available prior to the anticipated sale which was completed on 15 January 1997. In respect of these subsidiary undertakings, audited financial statements to 31 October, together with management accounts covering the remaining two months have been used to draw up these financial statements.

Notwithstanding the preference in FRS 2 for interim accounts to be used, some companies appear to regard the use of such accounts as impracticable as they use the accounts of some of their subsidiaries made up to earlier dates in order to avoid undue delay in the presentation of the group's accounts, as illustrated in the extracts below:

Extract 5.13: Imperial Chemical Industries PLC (2000)

1 **Basis of presentation of financial information** [extract]

Non co-terminous year ends

Owing to local conditions and to avoid undue delay in the presentation of the Group financial statements, five subsidiaries made up their financial statements to dates earlier than 31 December, but not earlier than 30 September; additionally five subsidiaries made up their financial statements prior to 30 September but interim financial statements to 31 December were drawn up for consolidation purposes.

Extract 5.14: The Royal Bank of Scotland Group plc (2000)

1 **Accounting convention and bases of consolidation** [extract]

To avoid undue delay in the presentation of the Group's accounts, the accounts of certain subsidiary undertakings have been made up to 30 November. There have been no changes in respect of these subsidiary undertakings, in the period from their balance sheet dates to 31 December, that materially affect the view given by the Group's accounts.

FRS 2 requires that, where coterminous year ends are *not* used in respect of any of the group's subsidiaries, there should be disclosure of the name of the subsidiaries involved, the year ends used (and duration of accounting periods, if different from that of the parent) and the reasons for the use of the different dates.[55] The Act contains similar requirements.[56] Given that, as discussed above, the accounts must in any event present materially the same picture as if coterminous years had been used, these requirements seem irrelevant.

The use of the accounts of foreign subsidiaries with non-coterminous year ends also raises the question of what exchange rate should be used for translation purposes. This point is covered in 3.4.1 of Chapter 8.

3.4 Minority interests in partly owned subsidiaries

The minority interest in a subsidiary is the interest in that subsidiary which is included in the consolidation that is attributable to the shares held by or on behalf of persons other than the parent and its subsidiary undertakings.[57]

The aggregate share of net assets or liabilities of the subsidiary included in the consolidation that is attributable to the minority interests should be shown separately in the consolidated balance sheet under a heading of 'minority interests'. For companies adopting Format 1 for the balance sheet, this will be either after all liabilities or after shareholders' funds. For companies adopting Format 2, it will be under the general heading of liabilities, but immediately after shareholders' funds.[58]

The aggregate of the profit or loss for the period attributable to the minority interests should be shown separately in the consolidated profit and loss account under a heading of 'minority interests'. Any extraordinary profit or loss should be shown separately.[59]

Where a company becomes a parent of another entity, then as it controls that entity as a whole, all of the net assets of the subsidiary should be restated at fair values and included in the consolidated accounts, not just the proportion owned. Consequently, a minority interest should be recognised at the date of the acquisition based on those fair values, not on the book values in the accounts of the subsidiary. The amount for the minority should not include any share of goodwill arising on the acquisition.[60] In Example 5.1 at 1.3.3 above, this would result in the same treatment as shown under the parent company extension concept. Thereafter, any profits or losses of the subsidiary are consolidated in full, with an allocation made to the minority interest based on the proportion held by the minority shareholders. As indicated at 1.3.3 above, losses continue to be allocated to minority interests even if this leads to a debit balance, although provision should be made to the extent that the parent has any commercial or legal obligation to provide finance that may not be recoverable.[61]

FRS 2 emphasises that despite the title 'minority interests', there is in principle no upper limit to the proportion of shares in a subsidiary undertaking which may be held as a minority interest while the parent undertaking still qualifies as such under the Companies Act (and the standard).[62] This is due to the fact that the parent/subsidiary relationship is based on the parent having a 'controlling interest', whereas the apportionment of the results and net assets of the subsidiary between the parent and the minority interests is effectively based on their respective equity interests. This will be particularly relevant where the parent/subsidiary relationship is due to the parent having a participating interest in and exercising a dominant influence over the subsidiary (see 2.2.5 above). For example, a company may only have a 45% interest in the ordinary shares of another company but be in a position to exercise dominant influence over it, in which case 55% of the results and net assets of the subsidiary would be attributable to the minority interests.

One area which the standard does not deal with is are those unusual situations which can arise because control and ownership are divorced. There may be difficulties in determining the relevant apportionment particularly where the parent's participating interest is in the form of convertible loan stock or an option to acquire an interest in the shares of the subsidiary. An extreme example of this would be 'the 0% subsidiary' where the participating interest is in the form of an option over all the shares. In our view the apportionment to the minority interests will depend on the particular circumstances. On the one hand, it may be that the minority interests should be attributed 100%; for example, where the option price is yet to be determined or it is based on future results/net assets of the subsidiary, or where it has been agreed between the parties that prior to the exercise of the option all retained profits of the subsidiary are to be distributed to the existing shareholders. On the other hand, it may be that there is a put and call option over the shares, the option price is fixed and it is agreed between the parties that no dividends will be paid to the existing shareholders, in which case no amounts should be attributed to the minority interests; the minority interests should be included at an amount equivalent to the exercise price under the option.

Where dealings in the shares of the subsidiary subsequently take place between the parent company and the minority interests, then as these are ownership issues, FRS 2 considers these to be external to the group and therefore requires them to be accounted for as such. Where the parent is increasing its stake in the subsidiary, then any difference between the consideration paid and the appropriate proportion of the net assets (based on fair values if necessary), i.e. the amount of the minority interest therein, should be treated as goodwill.[63] Where the parent reduces its stake in the subsidiary then a profit or loss should be recorded.[64] These issues are discussed further at 2.5 and 3.4 in Chapter 6 respectively.

The other main area of potential difficulty is where there have been inter-company transactions involving a group company in which a minority interest has a stake. This is discussed below.

3.5 Elimination of unrealised profits/losses on inter-company transactions

The reasons for making such an elimination are straightforward; 'no man can make a profit by trading with himself', and when a group is trying to present its results as if it were a single entity, it clearly must not regard internal transactions as giving rise to a realised profit.

In most cases the treatment is uncontentious and entails writing down the value of items of stock (if that is what is involved) held by one group company at the year end which have been purchased from another group company which has made a profit on the deal; the adjusting entry is simply to remove the profit element from the stock valuation and from the balance on the group profit and loss account (net of a deferred tax adjustment if appropriate; the elimination of this profit is regarded as giving rise to a timing difference, because the group will still be taxed on the profit which is eliminated – see Chapter 24). This will result in the assets being stated at their cost to the group. Similar adjustments should normally be made where a loss arises on the transfer. However, as indicated in ED 50, where a loss arises on the transfer, this may be indicative of an impairment in value of the asset (or a reduction to net realisable value) and therefore no adjustment should be made. The cost (or written down value) of the asset to the group is then used in calculating the profit or loss with anyone outside the group, so that the full profit or loss to the group is reflected at the point at which the asset is sold to the outside party.[65]

Complications can arise when either the selling or the purchasing company (or both) is not a wholly owned subsidiary, or when one of the parties to the transaction is a subsidiary which is not consolidated. There are essentially two questions: (a) what proportion of the profit in the stock is to be eliminated, and (b) whether, and if so how, to make the elimination against minority interests as well as group shareholders' funds (which has already been discussed to some extent at 1.3.3 above). FRS 2 requires that the whole amount of the profit be eliminated, and that the adjustment be apportioned between the majority and minority interests in proportion to their holdings in the selling company.[66] The reason for this treatment is that it is regarded as a control issue, as transactions between two companies under common control may be arranged without reference to any external party. The minority is, therefore, internal to the group for the calculation of these adjustments and it is not sufficient to adjust only for that part of the transaction which relates to the parent's interest; adjustment for the whole transaction and thus the full amount of any unrealised profit or loss must be made, with a suitable allocation made between the parent and the minority.[67] In Example 5.1 at 1.3.3 above, the parent company was the selling company and therefore *no* amount would be attributed to the minority shareholders; if, on the other hand, the subsidiary had made the profit on selling to the parent, 25% would have been attributed to the minority shareholders.

The Companies Act also contains provisions requiring intra-group profits (and losses) included in the book value of assets to be eliminated in preparing the consolidated accounts. However, where a partly owned subsidiary is involved the Act allows the elimination to be either the whole of the profit (or loss) or the group's interest thereof. These rules do not extend to transactions with subsidiaries which are equity accounted in the group accounts; for example, subsidiaries excluded from consolidation on grounds of different activities.[68] Nevertheless, as indicated above, FRS 2 requires the whole of the profit (or loss) to be eliminated and clarifies that this also applies to transactions with subsidiaries excluded from consolidation on grounds of different activities.[69] It also says that profits and losses arising on transactions with subsidiaries which are excluded for other reasons need not be eliminated except to the extent appropriate if they are equity accounted because significant influence is retained.[70]

The foreign currency complications which can arise from inter-company transactions are dealt with in 3.7.2 of Chapter 8.

4 EXEMPTIONS IN THE UK FROM PREPARING GROUP ACCOUNTS

As well as various rules on exclusion of particular subsidiaries (see 5 below), there are a number of provisions which exempt parent companies from having to present consolidated accounts at all. Previously both SSAP 14[71] and the Companies Act[72] contained provisions that group accounts need not be produced if the reporting company was itself a wholly owned subsidiary, although the Companies Act exemption applied only if it was owned by another British company. This exemption in the legislation was extended by the Companies Act 1989 to companies owned by parents incorporated elsewhere in the EEC, and is not limited to subsidiaries which are wholly owned, although there are provisions which allow minority shareholders to demand the preparation of consolidated accounts.[73] As a result of the creation of the European Economic Area with effect from 1994, the exemption was further extended.[74] The Companies Act also contains provisions to exempt parent companies from having to prepare consolidated accounts if the group falls within certain size limits.[75] FRS 2 repeats the exemptions contained in the legislation.[76] These exemptions are discussed below.

4.1 Intermediate holding companies

As indicated above, intermediate holding companies whose immediate parent undertaking is established in a member state of the European Economic Area (EEA) are exempt from preparing group accounts. The exemption is not confined to wholly owned subsidiaries, but is available where the immediate parent holds more than 50% of the shares in a company. However, minority shareholders have the right to request the preparation of consolidated accounts for a financial year by serving a notice on the company within six months of the end of the previous financial year. The minority in question must hold more than half of the shares in the company not held by the immediate parent or more than 5% of the total shares of the company.[77] The exemption does not apply to companies having shares or debentures listed on a stock exchange in a member state[78] and is subject to the following conditions:

(a) the company must be included in audited consolidated accounts of a parent undertaking established under the law of a member state of the EEA and which comply with the Seventh Directive. The consolidated accounts must be drawn up to the same date as the company's accounts or an earlier date during the same financial year;[79]

(b) the following disclosures must be given in the accounts of the company:

 (i) the fact that the company is exempt from preparing group accounts;[80] and

 (ii) the name of the parent undertaking which drew up the accounts referred to in (a) above; and

 - its country of incorporation, if incorporated outside Great Britain; or
 - if it is unincorporated, the address of its principal place of business;[81] and

(c) the accounts referred to in (a) above must be delivered by the company to the registrar together with (if they are not in English) a certified English translation.[82]

This exemption can result in the same set of group accounts being filed by a number of different companies and an example will show that it has some rather surprising effects.

Example 5.2: Exemption for intermediate parents

The Company A group has the following structure:

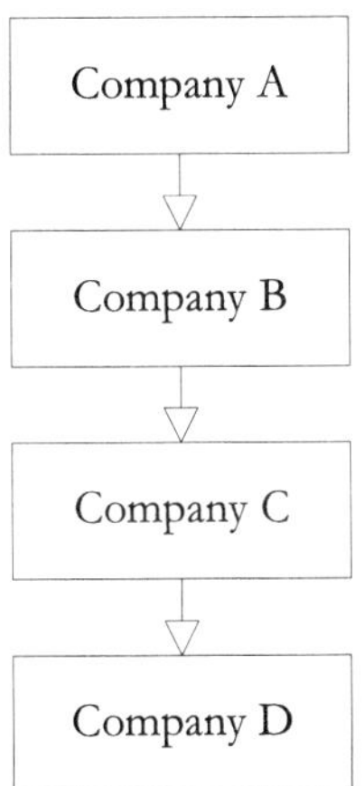

All the subsidiary undertakings of Company A are 100% owned and all companies prepare their accounts up to the same year end. The effect of the exemption on several different sets of circumstances will be considered as shown by the columns in the following table:

	Incorporated in		
	(a)	(b)	(c)
Company A	Great Britain	Netherlands	Netherlands
Company B	United States of America	France	Great Britain
Company C	Great Britain	Great Britain	Great Britain
Company D	Great Britain	Great Britain	Great Britain

(a) Company A and Company C must both prepare group accounts. In the case of Company C, this is because its immediate parent is not incorporated in a member state of the EEA. This structure is, however, unlikely to arise frequently in practice as Company A would not be in the same UK tax group as Company C and Company D.

It would make no difference to the above if Company B were incorporated in the Channel Islands or the Isle of Man as these are not member states of the EEA. Northern Ireland is part of a member state so if Company B were incorporated there, only Company A would have to prepare group accounts.

(b) Company C is exempt from preparing group accounts. If Company B as well as Company A chose to prepare consolidated accounts complying with the Seventh Directive, then Company C could choose to file an English translation of either Company A or Company B's group accounts.

(c) Company B and Company C are exempt from preparing group accounts but both companies must file an English translation of Company A's group accounts. If the Company B (or Company C) group were small or medium-sized (see 4.2 below), it could claim exemption on grounds of size without having to file Company A's accounts. However, this would not be of any assistance if the Company B (or Company C) group contained a public company, a bank or an insurance or financial services company. There is also the drawback that the disclosure requirements are more onerous where the exemption is claimed on grounds of size rather than as an intermediate parent company.

One situation where the exemption may not be available is in the accounting period when a holding company becomes a subsidiary of another EEA company. Under the legislation, the exemption will not be available if the company has not been included in a set of consolidated accounts of the new parent made up to a date which is coterminous or earlier than its own year end. It should be noted that the requirement is not that the *particular accounts* of the company will be included in a set of consolidated accounts of the parent, but that the *company* is included in accounts made up to a date which is coterminous or *earlier* than its own year end.

One other problem with the particular requirements is that other member states may not have actually implemented the Seventh Directive, in which case the UK intermediate holding company will not be able to avail itself of the exemption. Most of the major countries in the EEA have now implemented the Seventh Directive so this will now be less of a problem. However, if the EEA is expanded to encompass other European countries, then it may become more of an issue. It will be necessary, therefore, to check whether a particular member state has embodied the Seventh Directive into its local legislation and, if so, whether there are any transitional provisions delaying the application of the provisions.

Even where the year ends of the UK intermediate holding company and the parent company are the same, problems can arise. The directors of the intermediate holding company have to state in the company's accounts that they are exempt from the obligation to prepare group accounts. However, some of the conditions which have to be met may not have taken place by the time the directors approve their accounts. For example, the consolidated accounts, in which the company is to be included, may not have been prepared and audited; this will be the case if the parent company has a timetable which requires audited accounts of the company to be submitted prior to the audit report on the consolidated accounts being signed. Certainly, the company will still have to file with the registrar the consolidated accounts of the parent. In order to get round these logistical problems, it may be possible for the directors to anticipate these conditions in preparing their accounts, in which case they should only release one set of their audited accounts to the parent company and only file those accounts once they have received the consolidated accounts of the parent. Another possibility would be to submit only an audited consolidation package to the parent company and only prepare their statutory accounts once they have received the consolidated accounts of the parent.

4.2 Small and medium-sized groups

The Companies Act contains provisions such that small and medium-sized groups are exempt from the requirement to prepare consolidated accounts. Where advantage is taken of this exemption, certain disclosures are required in the parent company's accounts concerning its subsidiary undertakings.[83]

To qualify as small or medium-sized, a group must satisfy certain criteria based on the statutory accounts of companies within the group and on the number of employees of the group. The provisions actually include criteria for both small and medium-sized groups although those relating to small groups are redundant for the purposes of the exemption, since any group satisfying them will also satisfy the medium-sized group criteria.

Certain groups may not claim exemption even if they satisfy the criteria. These are groups which contain:

(a) a public company or a body corporate other than a company (this would include foreign companies) whose constitution allows it to offer its shares or debentures to the public;

(b) an authorised institution under the Banking Act 1987;

(c) an insurance company to which Part II of the Insurance Companies Act 1982 applies; or

(d) an authorised person under the Financial Services Act 1986.[84]

A group qualifies for this exemption if it satisfies at least two of the following three tests:

(a) its aggregate turnover is not more than £11.2 million net (or £13.44 million gross);

(b) its aggregate balance sheet total is not more than £5.6 million net (or £6.72 million gross);

(c) its aggregate number of employees is not more than 250.[85]

It can be seen that there are two sets of financial limits for small or medium-sized groups, one based on aggregate figures from the accounts of group companies before making consolidation set-offs ('gross') and the other on aggregate figures after consolidation set-offs ('net'). If a group satisfies the criteria on either basis, it is exempt from preparing consolidated accounts. The bases can be mixed, i.e. one limit satisfied on a net basis, the other on a gross basis.[86] These financial limits are subject to periodic revision.

The use of the gross basis allows groups to claim exemption from preparing group accounts without having to perform a consolidation exercise to prove their entitlement. Some groups with a significant amount of intra-group trading are likely to have to use the net basis as they may not meet the gross limits.

Unlike the provisions for individual companies filing abbreviated accounts, there is no requirement to adjust the turnover limit in respect of a financial year which is less than or more than 12 months in length.

The Act explains how the aggregate figures should be determined and defines 'balance sheet total' as the total of items A to D if Format 1 is used and the total under the heading 'Assets' if Format 2 is used.[87] All the figures must be taken from statutory accounts.[88] Management accounts are not allowed to be used for this purpose but are permitted, and in some cases required, as a basis for consolidated accounts (see 3.3 above). Some groups may find that, because of the different periods the accounts may cover, consolidated accounts prepared using management accounts give the impression that the group qualifies for the new exemption when this is not in fact the case. In deciding whether the criteria are satisfied, all subsidiary undertakings must be taken into account even if the group is entitled to exclude some of them from consolidation.

The rules for changing an existing status as a small, medium-sized or large group are the same as those for individual companies. This means that an existing status will only change in the second consecutive year in which a group fails to meet (or meets) two out of the three criteria.[89] In the first accounting reference period of the parent company, the group qualifies if it satisfies two out of the three criteria in that year.[90]

4.3 Exemptions contained in FRS 2

As indicated above, FRS 2 repeats the exemptions contained in the Act. Where these exemptions are taken the standard requires that certain disclosures are made in addition to those required by the Act. It requires that the parent's accounts should contain a statement that they present information about it as an individual undertaking and not about its group. The statement should also include or refer to a note giving the grounds on which the parent is exempt from preparing consolidated financial information.[91]

5 EXCLUSION OF SUBSIDIARIES FROM GROUP ACCOUNTS IN THE UK

5.1 Sources of rules on exclusion of particular subsidiaries

Where group accounts are required, there are various circumstances under which it is considered appropriate not to consolidate particular subsidiaries, but instead either to deal with them in some other manner or to exclude them from the group accounts altogether.

Under the Companies Act subsidiaries may be excluded from the consolidated accounts where:

(a) their activities are sufficiently different from those of the rest of the group;

(b) there are severe long-term restrictions over the parent's rights;

(c) they are held with a view to subsequent resale;

(d) obtaining the information needed would involve disproportionate expense or undue delay; or

(e) they are immaterial (in aggregate).[92]

FRS 2 only permits subsidiaries to be excluded from consolidation on grounds of criteria (a) to (c) above,[93] although as the standard does not apply to immaterial items exclusion under criterion (e) is also permissible. The ASB took the view that criterion (d) was not an appropriate reason for excluding material subsidiaries.[94] The circumstances under which the three permissible criteria might be applied are discussed in turn below.

5.2 Different activities

The specific rules on this in the Companies Act read as follows:

'Where the activities of one or more subsidiary undertakings are so different from those of other undertakings to be included in the consolidation that their inclusion would be incompatible with the obligation to give a true and fair view, those undertakings shall be excluded from consolidation.

'This ... does not apply merely because some of the undertakings are industrial, some commercial and some provide services, or because they carry on industrial or commercial activities involving different products or provide different services.'[95] In the case of banking and insurance groups, undertakings may not be excluded under the Companies Act on these grounds if their activities are a direct extension of, or ancillary to, the banking or insurance business.[96]

FRS 2 adopts the same approach, stressing that the exclusion is to be applied only in very exceptional cases. It explains that 'the key feature of this exclusion is that it refers only to a subsidiary undertaking whose activities are so different from those of other undertakings included in the consolidation that to include that subsidiary undertaking in the consolidation would be incompatible with the obligation to give a true and fair view. Cases of this sort are so exceptional that it would be misleading to link them in general to any particular contrast of activities. For example, the contrast between Schedule 9 and 9A companies (banking and insurance companies and groups) and other companies or between profit and not-for-profit undertakings is not sufficient of itself to justify non-consolidation. The different activities of undertakings included in the consolidation can better be shown by presenting segmental information rather than by excluding from consolidation the subsidiary undertakings with different activities.'[97]

Where a subsidiary is excluded from consolidation on these grounds, both the Act[98] and FRS 2 require it to be equity accounted.[99] Unlike some of the other exclusions, therefore, this is in essence a different manner of incorporating the company concerned in the group accounts, rather than excluding it altogether.

FRS 2 and the Companies Act require various general disclosures in respect of subsidiaries excluded from consolidation, which are discussed at 5.6 below. In addition to these general disclosures, the standard requires that, where subsidiaries have been excluded from consolidation because of different activities, their separate accounts should be included in the consolidated accounts. These can be presented in summary form unless the excluded undertakings account for more than 20% of any of the following: the group's operating profits; or its turnover; or its net assets. These amounts should be measured by including the excluded subsidiary undertakings.[100]

Where an excluded subsidiary undertaking is either:

(a) a body corporate incorporated outside Great Britain which does not have an established place of business in Great Britain; or

(b) an unincorporated undertaking,

the Act requires its latest accounts (or group accounts) to be appended to the accounts delivered to the registrar. However, this does not require the preparation of accounts which would otherwise not be prepared; neither does it require the publication of accounts which would not otherwise be required to be published, but the reason for such accounts not being appended must be explained.[101] For example, a partnership excluded on these grounds might prepare accounts for its own purposes; however, these would not need to be appended provided the accounts delivered to the registrar contained a note to the effect that the partnership accounts were not appended as they were not required to be published. In the case of foreign companies, this means that, for example, the accounts of a Canadian company would have to be appended but not those of most US companies (since US companies, other than those with a SEC listing, are not required to publish their accounts).

5.3 Operating under severe restrictions

The provisions of the Companies Act which deal with this exclusion state that 'a subsidiary undertaking may be excluded from consolidation where … severe long-term restrictions substantially hinder the exercise of the rights of the parent company over the assets or management of that undertaking'.[102] The Act specifies that the rights which are restricted must be rights in the absence of which the company would not be the parent company.

FRS 2 goes further and *requires* subsidiaries to be excluded from consolidation when these circumstances apply. The standard explains that this ground for exclusion ties in with its underlying concept of control as the basis for consolidation. Thus, where the restrictions amount to a loss of control, it would be misleading to continue to include the subsidiary in the consolidation. However, it emphasises that the exclusion should not be applied where only the prospect of restrictions exists, or if the restrictions are minor. The standard refers to the need for them to have 'a severe and restricting effect in practice in the long-term on the rights of the parent undertaking'. It quotes the case of a subsidiary undertaking which is subject to an insolvency procedure in the UK such that control over that undertaking may have passed to a designated official, e.g. an administrator, administrative receiver or liquidator, with the effect that severe long-term restrictions are in force. However, it states that a company voluntary arrangement does not necessarily lead to loss of control. Similarly, in some overseas jurisdictions even formal insolvency procedures may not amount to loss of control.[103]

Two companies which have not consolidated subsidiaries due to insolvency proceedings are Huntingdon Life Sciences and Creston Land and Estates, as shown below:

Extract 5.15: Huntingdon Life Sciences Group plc (2000)

Basis of consolidation [extract]

The consolidated accounts incorporate the accounts of the Company and each of its subsidiaries for the 12 months ended December 31, 2000. The Travers Morgan Group of Companies has not traded since February 1995 and although these companies are 100% owned by the Group, their assets and liabilities have not been included since control of these companies is exercised by an administrator.

Extract 5.16: Creston Land and Estates plc (1996)

BASIS OF CONSOLIDATION [extract]

The group accounts consolidate the accounts of the company and all of its subsidiaries except those where severe long term restrictions substantially hinder the exercise of rights over the assets or management of the subsidiary undertaking. Where such restrictions exist a subsidiary undertaking is treated as a fixed asset investment in accordance with Financial Reporting Standard 2.

9 INVESTMENTS HELD AS FIXED ASSETS [extract]

During the year Co-ordinated Land and Estates Limited ("CLE") and its subsidiaries were put into creditors' voluntary liquidation. In addition, British Patent Glazing Limited was put, during the year, into administrative receivership.

Two companies which have invoked this rule in circumstances where insolvency procedures would not appear to have been in progress are shown in the following extracts:

Extract 5.17: London and Metropolitan plc (1997)

b) BASIS OF CONSOLIDATION [extract]

The Company and other Group companies have been released from any financial liability in respect of certain subsidiaries' liabilities and borrowings. As a result of this, the Group has ceased to have any financial interest in the losses of these subsidiaries. As the prospect of the relevant subsidiaries ever making profits is extremely remote and as there are severe long term restrictions on the Group's interest in these subsidiaries, their results have not been consolidated.

34. GROUP COMPANIES [extract]

During the year the Group disposed of its 99% subsidiary undertaking, Pont Royal SA, a company incorporated in France, with net liabilities of £19,300,000 for nil consideration.

For the reasons detailed in the Accounting Policies (Note 2b), the results of The Bicester Park Development Company Limited and Bettertrade Limited are not consolidated in the Group financial statements. For the same reasons, the results of Pont Royal SA had not been consolidated.

Summary financial information in respect of subsidiary undertakings not consolidated in the Group accounts is set out below.

	Capital and reserves as at 31 December 1977 £'000	Profit/(loss) for the year ended 31 December 1997 £'000
The Bicester Park Development Company Limited	(15,984)	312
Bettertrade Limited	–	–

During the year ended 31 December 1997 the Group received £120,000 from The Bicester Park Development Company Limited for the provision of development and project management services to that company. As at 31 December 1997 there were no balances outstanding between the Group and either of the above companies.

Extract 5.18: Regal Hotel Group PLC (1996)

BASIS OF CONSOLIDATION [extract]

The consolidated financial statements incorporate the financial statements of the Company and all of its subsidiaries, with the exception of Bramhope Limited.

11. INVESTMENTS IN SUBSIDIARIES [extract]

Bramhope Limited ceased to be treated as a consolidated subsidiary undertaking on 25th March 1993 in accordance with Financial Reporting Standard 2.

This was as a result of the severe long term restrictions placed on the Company's control over Bramhope Limited in having to accommodate the wishes of Bramhope's bankers.

Other circumstances which may justify non-consolidation on these grounds involve political unrest in the country in which the subsidiary is based. An example of this was to be found in the 1991 accounts of Booker set out below:

Extract 5.19: Booker plc (1991)

11 FIXED ASSET INVESTMENTS [extract]

	1991 **£m**	1990 £m
Attributable net asset value of subsidiary companies not consolidated at 31 December 1991	**3.7**	3.2
Reduction required under stated accounting policy	**1.1**	0.9
Balance sheet value 31 December 1991	**2.6**	2.3
Profit on order activities before taxation attributable to parent company	**1.6**	1.7
Attributable profit after extraordinary items	**1.4**	1.2

Consolidation [extract]

Certain subsidiary undertakings operate in countries overseas where the amount of profit that may be remitted is restricted or where freedom of action may be limited. In the opinion of the directors, it would be misleading to consolidate these subsidiaries and the group share of their results is therefore included in profit only to the extent of remittances received. The group's total investment in these subsidiaries is shown as an asset at attributable net asset value either at the date from which this accounting policy was adopted for such companies adjusted for capital subsequently invested or withdrawn, or attributable net asset value at the balance sheet date, whichever is the lower amount.

The reduction to net asset value at the balance sheet date was presumably to recognise an impairment in value.

Another example was in the 1991 accounts of Low & Bonar in respect of its African subsidiaries shown below:

Extract 5.20: Low & Bonar PLC (1991)

(ii) Basis of consolidation [extract]

(b) The accounts of Group companies in Africa are not consolidated as the Directors consider the control of those companies by Low & Bonar PLC significantly impaired by severe long term restrictions.

6. Income from Fixed Asset Investments

	1991	1990
	£000	£000
Income from shares in group companies not consolidated	**1,355**	683

13. Fixed Asset Investments [extract]

	£000
African interests:	
At 30 November 1990 and 30 November 1991	
– Directors' valuation	**2,230**

29. Subsidiaries and Associates not Consolidated

	Accounting period	% owned	1991 Profit after tax	1991 Net assets	1990 Profit after tax	1990 Net assets
Subsidiaries			**£000**	**£000**	£000	£000
Bonar Industries (Pty) Ltd	12 months to 30/11/91	100	332	1,769	483	2,253
Bonar (EA) Ltd	12 months to 31/08/91	75	(142)	439	(235)	570
Bonar Colwyn Ltd	12 months to 30/09/91	90	172	1,390	471	1,052
Bonar Plastics Ltd	12 months to 30/09/91	72	41	183	97	169
Bonar Industries (Pty) Ltd	12 months to 31/08/91	100	203	969	285	1,551
Associate Tarpaulin Industries (WA) Ltd	12 months to 30/11/91	40	(9)	254	(13)	274

The required accounting treatment under FRS 2 in these circumstances is to 'freeze' the carrying value of the subsidiary at its equity amount at the time the restrictions came into force, and to carry it as a fixed asset investment. It should not accrue for any trading results thereafter as long as the restrictions remain, unless it is still able to exercise significant influence, in which case it should equity account for the subsidiary as if it were an associate. A provision for impairment in the value of the investment and any inter-company balances may also be needed.[104]

If the restrictions are subsequently removed, the trading results of the subsidiary which accrued during the period when the investment was carried at a frozen amount will need to be accounted for. FRS 2 requires that they be dealt with as a separately disclosed item in the profit and loss account in the year in which control is resumed, along with the release of any previous provision for impairment.[105]

The disclosures required in respect of subsidiaries excluded from consolidation on these grounds are discussed at 5.6 below.

5.4 Held for subsequent resale

The Companies Act allows a subsidiary undertaking to be excluded from the consolidated accounts when 'the interest of the parent company is held exclusively with a view to subsequent resale and the undertaking has not previously been included in consolidated group accounts of the parent company'.[106] This reason cannot be used to justify exclusion of a subsidiary which the parent company has previously consolidated and decides to sell some years after its acquisition; it should be used only for those cases where a group acquires a subsidiary with the intention of selling it on soon thereafter. The Act, however, does not define what is meant by 'held exclusively for subsequent resale'.

FRS 2 supplies such a definition, saying that it is

(a) an interest for which a purchaser has been identified or is being sought, and which is reasonably expected to be disposed of within approximately one year of its date of acquisition; or

(b) an interest that was acquired as a result of the enforcement of a security, unless the interest has become part of the continuing activities of the group or the holder acts as if it intends the interest to become so.[107]

As with subsidiaries subject to severe restrictions, FRS 2 goes further than the Act by *requiring* subsidiaries to be excluded when these circumstances apply.[108] Instead, the standard requires that the investment should be carried in the group balance sheet as a current asset, at the lower of cost and net realisable value.[109]

Examples of situations where subsidiaries have been excluded from consolidation as they are held for subsequent resale are shown in the following extracts:

Extract 5.21: Fine Art Developments p.l.c. (1996)

13 INVESTMENTS HELD FOR RESALE

The group owns the whole of the issued share capital of Greeting Card House Limited (formerly Flaxcase Limited), a holding company which in turn owns the whole of the issued share capital of Flaxcase Limited (formerly Macsel Greetings Limited), a greeting card wholesaler. Greeting Card House Limited and Flaxcase are both registered in England and Wales.

The group assumed management control of Greeting Card House and Flaxcase on 7 March 1996. Those companies have been excluded from consolidation as the group's interest is held exclusively with a view to subsequent resale and accordingly the investment has been accounted for as a current asset, at cost. No material trading transactions with other group companies took place during the period from acquisition to 31 March 1996.

Flaxcase and Greeting Card House prepare accounts to 31 January although audited accounts to 31 January 1996 are not yet available. The unaudited management accounts of Flaxcase show a deficit on capital and reserves of £1.4m at 31 January 1996 and a loss for the year then ended of £0.7m. The unaudited management accounts of Greeting Card House show capital and reserves of £0.2m at 31 January 1996 and a loss for the year then ended of £nil.

Extract 5.22: Barclays PLC (1997)

46 Principal subsidiary undertakings [extract]

In 1992, the Group acquired a 100% interest in Imry Holdings Limited (Imry), a company registered in England, as a result of enforcing security against a loan to Chester Holdings (UK) Limited, the parent company of Imry. The interest was held exclusively with a view to subsequent resale and therefore was not consolidated. The assets of Imry Holdings have been sold in two parts. The first resulted in a provision release of £25m in March 1997, which was reported in the first half results. A second sale was agreed in December 1997 and is due to be completed in February 1998. This transfers Imry's remaining significant assets to a joint venture in which the Group has a 50% interest. This transaction resulted in a provision release of £19m in December 1997. The companies which own the assets were still within the ownership of the Group at 31st December 1997 but have not been consolidated pending disposal or liquidation. Had Imry been consolidated in 1996 or 1997, there would have been no material effect on total assets, shareholders' funds or profit before tax of the Group.

Imry's accounts are made up to 31st March. At 31st December 1997, the unaudited consolidated capital and reserves of Imry (including the Imry Jersey Limited preference shares held by the Group) amounted to £71m (1996 £81m) and its total assets amounted to £74m (1996 £326m). The unaudited loss before taxation of Imry for the 12 months ended 31st December was £15m (1996 loss £8m, 1995 profit £8m). There were outstandings of £nil (1996 £94m) due to the Group, secured by a fixed and floating charge on the assets of Imry. Interest payments by Imry to the Bank in the year amounted to £3m (1996 £7m). Except as noted above, there were no other material transactions between Imry and the Group during the year.

One question which can be significant in some circumstances is how to account for the interest cost of financing a temporary investment in a subsidiary; if no profits are consolidated during the period of ownership then the financing cost will result in the group reporting a loss. Where the subsidiary to be sold has been acquired as part of a group then this should not cause a problem because FRS 7 requires that the fair value to be attributed to the subsidiary should be based on the estimated sales proceeds, discounted to obtain the net present value at date of acquisition, if material (see 2.4.3 G of Chapter 6). This does not offend the requirement of FRS 2 to carry such investments at cost, because in this case cost is derived from an allocation of the total purchase price on the basis of their fair value to the acquiring company. The subsequent unwinding of the discount will be credited to the profit and loss account thereby offsetting any interest cost of financing such a temporary investment.

An example of this can be seen in the 1996 accounts of De La Rue:

Extract 5.23: De La Rue plc (1996)

Basis of consolidation [extract]

A number of subsidiaries which were acquired as part of the acquisition of Portals Group plc in the year ended 31 March 1995 were excluded from consolidation because they were held exclusively with a view to subsequent resale. These subsidiaries were recorded as assets held for disposal within current assets. In the year, the Group has disposed of virtually all of its investments in these businesses.

13 Assets held for disposal [extract]

Group	£m
At 1 April 1995	**160.0**
Unwinding of discounted value of expected proceeds of assets held for disposal	**4.0**
Cash inflow from disposals	**(141.7)**
Cash payments to businesses held for resale	**15.4**
Retained interests in businesses sold	**(6.6)**
Further goodwill arising on the acquisition of Portals Group plc	**(21.3)**
At 31 March 1996	**9.8**

Assets held for disposal at 1 April 1995 included the Group's investment in businesses and properties, all of which were owned by Portals Group plc or its subsidiaries when the Group acquired Portals Group plc, and were held exclusively with a view to resale. In the year, the Group has disposed of its investment in these businesses and certain properties. Assets held for disposal at 31 March 1996 include properties, which following consultation with professional advisers, are held at the directors' valuation of anticipated sales proceeds.

5.5 Immateriality

As indicated above, the Companies Act allows subsidiaries to be excluded from consolidation where they are immaterial in aggregate. FRS 2 does not contain a specific ground for exclusion on this basis because the standard only deals with material items.[110]

One company which had excluded a subsidiary for this reason was Alliance Trust in its 1994 accounts, as shown below:

Extract 5.24: The Alliance Trust PLC (1994)

1. **ACCOUNTING POLICIES** [extract]

f. The accounts of Alliance Trust (Finance) Limited have not been consolidated with those of the Company as the directors consider that the amounts involved are not material and that their inclusion would detract from the clarity of the accounts in respect of the principal activity of the Company as an authorised investment trust. A separate statement of affairs of Alliance Trust (Finance) Limited is on page 23.

The value attributable to the subsidiary amounted to £23,028m out of total investments of £1,042,252m and this was presumably why the directors considered the subsidiary not to be material (although it seems odd that a summarised profit and loss account and summarised balance sheet should be given for something that is considered to be not material). However, this treatment attracted the attention of the Review Panel following the company's approach to the Stock Exchange for guidance on the question of consolidation. Although not explicitly stated by the Review Panel it would appear that it was of the view that the subsidiary was material and therefore should have been consolidated. The Review Panel ruling does not state why it thought it was material but it may have been because of the impact on the revenue account or on particular assets and liabilities. Accordingly, the 1995 accounts were prepared on this basis, as shown below:

Extract 5.25: The Alliance Trust PLC (1995)

REPORT OF THE DIRECTORS [extract]

The consolidated accounts, which are provided for the first time this year, include the results of our banking and savings subsidiary, Alliance Trust (Finance) Limited. These have been produced in the light of developing accounting standards, which will lead shortly to adoption of a Statement of Recommended Practice for investment trusts, and after discussion with the Financial Reporting Review Panel, the Company having raised the issue of consolidation with the Stock Exchange. Full information on the subsidiary had previously been included separately within the accounts. Relevant information continues to be given in note 12.

Clearly whether a subsidiary is material or not is a matter of judgement and companies should therefore consider carefully whether a subsidiary is immaterial or not before excluding it from the consolidated accounts.

5.6 General disclosure requirements in respect of excluded subsidiaries

The Companies Act requires the following information to be given in respect of each subsidiary excluded from the consolidated accounts:

(a) its name;[111]

(b) the reasons for excluding it;[112] and

(c) the aggregate amount of its share capital and reserves as at the end of its financial year and of its profit or loss for that year.[113]

The information described in (c) above is not required if the subsidiary is equity accounted or if less than 50% of its nominal value of shares is held and it does not publish its balance sheet anywhere in the world.[114]

FRS 2 requires that in addition to the information required by the Companies Act the following information should be disclosed:

(a) particulars of the balances between the excluded subsidiary undertakings and the rest of the group;

(b) the nature and extent of transactions of the excluded subsidiary undertakings with the rest of the group; and

(c) unless the excluded subsidiary is equity accounted, any amounts included in the consolidated accounts in respect of:

 (i) dividends received and receivable from that undertaking;

 (ii) any write-down in the period in respect of the investment in that undertaking or amounts due from that undertaking.[115]

These disclosures should be given for each excluded subsidiary. However, the standard states that 'if the information about excluded subsidiary undertakings is more appropriately presented for a sub-unit of the group comprising more than one excluded subsidiary undertaking, the disclosures may be made on an aggregate basis. Any individual sub-unit for these disclosures is to include only subsidiary undertakings excluded under the same sub-section of section 229 [of the Act]. Individual disclosures should be made for any excluded subsidiary undertaking, including its sub-group where relevant, that alone accounts for more than 20% of any one or more of operating profits, turnover or net assets of the group. The group amounts should be measured by including all excluded subsidiary undertakings.'[116]

6 IAS REQUIREMENTS

The principal international accounting standard dealing with this topic is IAS 27 – *Consolidated Financial Statements and Accounting for Investments in Subsidiaries.* This requires a parent to present consolidated financial statements in which all foreign and domestic subsidiaries are consolidated.[117] As its title suggests, IAS 27 also deals with the accounting for the investment in subsidiaries in the parent's separate financial statements. This aspect of the standard is dealt with at 3 in Chapter 14.

6.1 What is a subsidiary?

IAS 27 simply defines a subsidiary as 'an enterprise which is controlled by another enterprise (known as the parent)'. Control is defined as 'the power to govern the financial and operating policies of an enterprise so as to obtain benefits from its activities'.[118]

Control is presumed to exist if the parent owns, directly or indirectly, a majority of the voting rights in the enterprise unless, in exceptional circumstances, it can be clearly demonstrated that such ownership does not constitute control. Control is also considered to exist even when the parent does not own a majority of the voting rights when there is:

(a) power over more than one half of the voting rights by virtue of an agreement with other investors;

(b) power to govern the financial and operating policies of the enterprise under a statute or an agreement;

(c) power to appoint or remove the majority of the members of the board of directors or equivalent governing body; or

(d) power to cast the majority of votes at meetings of the board of directors or equivalent governing body.[119]

The use of the terms 'enterprise' and 'equivalent governing body' means that subsidiaries do not have to be companies or bodies corporate, but will encompass partnerships and unincorporated bodies which are controlled by the parent.

The situations described above are similar to those in the UK discussed at 2.2.1 to 2.2.4 above. IAS 27 does not deal with the specific situation where a parent has a participating interest with dominant influence or unified management (see 2.2.5 above), but such circumstances are likely to mean that the enterprise is controlled by the parent so it will be a subsidiary under IAS 27.

An enterprise may own share warrants, share call options, debt or equity instruments that are convertible into ordinary shares, or other similar instruments that have the potential, if exercised or converted, to either give the enterprise additional voting power or reduce another party's voting power over the financial and operating policies of another enterprise. To what extent should such potential voting rights be taken into account in determining whether an enterprise controls another enterprise? In September 2001, the SIC issued a draft interpretation which proposes that the existence and effect of potential voting rights that are presently exercisable or convertible should be considered when assessing whether an enterprise controls another enterprise. All potential voting rights should be considered, including potential voting rights held by other enterprises.[120] An appendix to the draft interpretation provides illustrations as to how the interpretation is to be applied.

It should also be recognised that both IAS and UK GAAP contain requirements for the consolidation of various special purpose vehicles that do not meet the definition of a subsidiary, but where the substance of the relationship between the enterprise and special purpose vehicle is that the vehicle is controlled by that enterprise. Under IAS, this is dealt with in SIC-12 *Consolidation – Special Purpose Entities* (see Chapter 18 at 4.4) and in the UK it is dealt with through the concept of a quasi subsidiary in FRS 5 – *Reporting the substance of transactions* (see Chapter 18 at 2.8.1).

6.2 Consolidation of subsidiaries

IAS 27 describes the mechanics of the consolidation process as follows:

'In preparing consolidated financial statements, the financial statements of the parent and its subsidiaries are combined on a line-by-line basis by adding together like items of assets, liabilities, equity, income and expenses. In order that the consolidated financial statements present financial information about the group as that of a single enterprise, the following steps are then taken:

(a) the carrying amount of the parent's investment in each subsidiary and the parent's portion of equity of each subsidiary are eliminated (see IAS 22 (revised 1998), Business Combinations, which also describes the treatment of any resultant goodwill);

(b) minority interests in the net income of consolidated subsidiaries for the reporting period are identified and adjusted against the income of the group in order to arrive at the net income attributable to the owners of the parent; and

(c) minority interests in the net assets of consolidated subsidiaries are identified and presented in the consolidated balance sheet separately from liabilities and the parent shareholders' equity. Minority interests in the net assets consist of:

   (i) the amount at the date of the original combination calculated in accordance with IAS 22 (revised 1998), Business Combinations; and

   (ii) the minority's share of movements in equity since the date of the combination.'[121]

The consolidated financial statements should be prepared using uniform accounting policies for like transactions and other events in similar circumstances. Where a subsidiary uses different accounting policies in preparing its own financial statements, appropriate adjustments should be made to those statements when they are used in preparing the consolidated financial statements. If it is not practicable to use uniform accounting policies in preparing the consolidated financial statements, that fact should be disclosed together with the proportions of the items in the consolidated financial statements to which the different accounting policies have been applied.[122]

When the financial statements used in the consolidation are drawn up to different reporting dates, adjustments should be made for the effects of significant transactions or other events that occur between those dates and the date of the parent's financial statements. In any case the difference between reporting dates should be no more than three months.[123] The standard emphasises that the consistency principle dictates that the length of the reporting periods and any difference in the reporting dates should be the same for period to period.[124] Unlike FRS 2, IAS 27 does not require any disclosure where coterminous year ends are not used.

Intragroup balances and intragroup transactions (including sales, expenses and dividends) and resulting unrealised profits should be eliminated in full. Unrealised losses resulting from intragroup transactions that are deducted in arriving at the carrying amount of assets should also be eliminated unless the cost of the assets cannot be recovered.[125]

The above consolidation procedures required by IAS 27 are principally similar to those required in the UK (discussed at 3 above).

Although not required by IAS 27, some companies include an accounting policy summarising these consolidation procedures as illustrated below.

Extract 5.26: Danisco A/S (2000)

Basis of consolidation [extract]

The consolidated accounts included Danisco A/S (parent company) and all undertakings (subsidiary undertakings) in which the parent company, directly or indirectly, holds more than 50 per cent of the voting rights or otherwise has a controlling interest.

...

The Group accounts comprise the consolidated audited accounts of the parent company and the individual subsidiary undertakings, which have all been prepared in accordance with the Group's accounting policies. Inter-company income and expenditure, shareholdings, balances and dividends as well as unrealised internal profits and losses have been eliminated.

...

Newly acquired subsidiary undertakings ... are included in the consolidated accounts as from the date of acquisition.

On the winding up or disposal of subsidiary undertakings an undertaking's profit is consolidated in the profit and loss account on a line-by-line basis until the date of disposal. ...

6.3 Minority interests in partly-owned subsidiaries

Minority interests should be presented in the consolidated balance sheet separately from liabilities and the parent shareholders' equity. Minority interests in the income of the group should also be separately presented.[126] If a subsidiary has outstanding cumulative preference shares which are held outside the group, the parent computes its share of profits or losses after adjusting for the subsidiary's preferred dividends, whether or not dividends have been declared.[127] Although UK GAAP requires separate presentation of minority interests on the balance sheet (see 3.4 above), the presentation in the balance sheet differs from that under IAS. An example of the presentation under IAS is illustrated below.

Extract 5.27: Serono International S.A. (2000)

Consolidated balance sheets [extract]
As of December 31

	2000	1999
	US$	US$
Total liabilities	**787,621**	763,939
Minority interests	**740**	574
SHAREHOLDERS' EQUITY		
Share capital	**252,992**	236,978
Share premium	**968,581**	33,965
Retained earnings	**845,124**	621,615
Cumulative foreign currency translation adjustments	**(60,281)**	(65,773)
Total shareholders' equity	**2,006,416**	826,785
Total liabilities, minority interests and shareholders' equity	**2,794,777**	1,591,298

Where there are losses applicable to the minority interest in a subsidiary and these exceed the minority interest in the equity of the subsidiary, IAS 27 requires that the excess should be charged against the majority interest except to the extent that the minority has a binding obligation to, and is able to, make good the losses.[128] This differs from the position in the UK as discussed at 3.4 above. FRS 2 requires the minority interest in the net liabilities to be recognised as a minority interest, but that the group should make provision to the extent that it has any commercial or legal obligation (whether formal or implied) to provide finance that may not be recoverable in respect of the accumulated losses attributable to the minority interest.

As indicated above, the amount for the minority interest in the balance sheet is dependent upon the amount at the date of the original combination calculated in accordance with IAS 22. That standard adopts as its benchmark treatment that any minority interest arising on an acquisition should be calculated based on the pre-acquisition carrying amounts of the net assets of the subsidiary, although it does allow the use of fair values as an alternative.[129] As discussed at 3.4 above, FRS 2 requires the minority interest to be based on the fair values attributed to the net assets of the subsidiary.

As indicated at 6.1 above, the SIC issued a draft interpretation in September 2001 which considers the extent to which potential voting rights should be taken into account in determining whether an enterprise has control of another enterprise.

The draft interpretation also considers whether the proportion allocated to the parent and minority interest in preparing consolidated accounts should be determined based on the present ownership interests or ownership interests that would be held if the potential voting rights were exercised or converted, and has concluded that the proportion should be determined solely based on present ownership interests.[130]

6.4 Exemption from preparing consolidated financial statements

The only exemption in IAS 27 from producing consolidated financial statements is for intermediate holding companies. A parent that is a wholly owned subsidiary need not produce consolidated financial statements. The exemption is also available to a parent which is virtually wholly owned (it is suggested in the standard that this will often mean that the parent owns 90% or more of the voting power) provided that it obtains the approval of the owners of the minority interest.[131] A parent which uses this exemption should disclose the reasons why consolidated financial statements have not been presented together with the bases on which subsidiaries are accounted for in its separate financial statements. The name and registered office of its parent that publishes consolidates financial statements should also be disclosed.[132]

This exemption differs from the UK equivalent discussed at 4.1 above in a number of respects. The UK exemption is not available to companies having shares or debentures listed on a stock exchange and it is subject to a number of conditions, principally that the company's immediate parent must be in the EEA and it must be included in a set of consolidated accounts of an EEA parent which comply with the EC Seventh Directive. On the other hand, the UK exemption is available where the immediate parent merely holds more than 50% of the shares in the company. Approval of the minority shareholders is not required, but certain minority shareholders have the right to request the preparation of consolidated accounts within six months of the previous year end.

IAS 27 has no equivalent exemption to that in the UK for small or medium sized enterprises. (see 4.2 above)

6.5 Subsidiaries excluded from consolidation

Under IAS 27, a subsidiary should be excluded for consolidation when:

(a) control is intended to be temporary because the subsidiary is acquired and held exclusively with a view to its subsequent disposal in the near future; or

(b) it operates under severe long-term restrictions which significantly impair its ability to transfer funds to the parent.[133]

These grounds for non-consolidation of subsidiaries are similar to those in the UK. However, in the former case, as discussed at 5.4 above, FRS 2 imposes a time limit of 'approximately one year from [the] date of acquisition', whereas IAS 27 is somewhat less restrictive requiring only 'subsequent disposal in the near future'.

Under IAS 27 it is not possible to exclude from consolidation those subsidiaries which undertake dissimilar activities.[134] In the UK, FRS 2 requires non-consolidation where the subsidiary's activities are so different from those of the rest of the group that its inclusion would be incompatible with the obligation to give a true fair view. However, FRS 2 also stresses that this exclusion is to be applied only in very exceptional circumstances.

IAS 27 requires that subsidiaries excluded from consolidation should be accounted for in accordance with IAS 39 – *Financial Instruments: Recognition and Measurement*,[135] which will result in the unconsolidated subsidiaries being classified as either available for sale or held for trading – both of which require measurement at fair value. On the other hand, UK GAAP prescribes various methods of accounting for excluded subsidiaries, depending on the reason for the exclusion (see 5.2 to 5.4 above).

In the UK, a subsidiary excluded because it is held for subsequent resale should be accounted for as a current asset investment. On acquisition, the fair value of the excluded subsidiary should be based on the net proceeds of the sale (either actual, if the sale has taken place by the time the accounts are prepared, or estimated if not), adjusted for any assets or liabilities transferred into or out of the business, unless such adjusted net proceeds are demonstrably different from the fair value at the date of acquisition as a result of a post-acquisition event. Under IAS the net cash flows from operations of a business held for resale between the date of acquisition and the date of sale should not be taken into consideration in the allocation of the purchase price to the assets and liabilities. This means that, unlike UK GAAP, the fair value on acquisition is likely to be different from the disposal proceeds of the excluded subsidiary.

Where severe long-term restrictions exist, UK GAAP requires the excluded subsidiary to be treated as a fixed asset investment, frozen at its equity amount at the time the restrictions came into force. However, where the parent is still in a position to exercise significant influence over it, it should be treated as an associated undertaking using the equity method. FRS 2 also deals with the situation where the restrictions are removed (see 5.3 above), but IAS 27 is silent on this issue.

In the UK, where in exceptional circumstances a subsidiary is excluded on grounds of dissimilar activities, it is required to be equity accounted and its separate accounts (which in certain circumstances may be in summary form) included in the consolidated accounts.

Like FRS 2, IAS 27 does not contain a specific ground for exclusion on the basis of immateriality. However, since IASs are not intended to apply to immaterial items some companies do not consolidate their immaterial subsidiaries. An example of a company adopting such an approach is Deutsche Lufhansa as shown below.

Extract 5.28: Deutsche Lufthansa AG (2000)

4 **Group of consolidated companies** [extract]

... Lufthansa Technik Immobilien-und Verwaltungsgesellschaft mbH, LSG Lufthansa Service Catering-und Dienstleistungsgesellschaft mbH, Top Flight Catering AB including its four subsidiaries, and LSG Lufthansa Service Cape Town (Pty) Ltd. have for the first time been included in the group of consolidated companies. ...

The inclusion of other subsidiaries has been unnecessary because their combined influence on the Group's net assets, financial position and results of operations is insignificant. All in all, these non-consolidated companies account for approximately five per cent of revenue, results, capital and reserves, debts and balance sheet total.

Clearly, whether the non-consolidation of such subsidiaries is immaterial is a matter of judgment, but it can be seen that where any of the subsidiaries do become material it will be necessary to consolidate them.

6.6 Disclosures

In addition to the specific disclosures mentioned earlier above, IAS 27 requires the following disclosures to be made in consolidated financial statements:[136]

(a) a listing of significant subsidiaries including the name, country of incorporation or residence, proportion of ownership interest and, if different, proportion of voting power held;

(b) where applicable:

   (i) the reasons for not consolidating a subsidiary;

   (ii) the nature of the relationship between the parent and any subsidiary of which the parent does not own, directly or indirectly through subsidiaries, more than one half of the voting power;

   (iii) the name of any enterprise in which more than one half of the voting power is owned, directly or indirectly through subsidiaries, but which, because of the absence of control, is not a subsidiary; and

   (iv) the effect of the acquisition and disposal of subsidiaries on the financial position at the reporting date, the results for the reporting period and on the corresponding amounts for the preceding period.

Examples of disclosures given by companies in satisfying the above final requirement are given in Chapter 6 at 5.6.5.

References

1 CA 85, s 227(2)–(3).
2 *Ibid.*, s 227(4).
3 FRS 2, *Accounting for subsidiary undertakings*, ASB, July 1992, para. 1.
4 *Ibid.*, para. 18.
5 IAS 27, *Consolidated Financial Statements and Accounting for Investments in Subsidiaries*, IASC, Reformatted November 1994, paras. 7 and 11.
6 FRS 2, para.6.
7 IAS 27, para. 6.
8 CA 85, Sch. 4A, paras. 9(2) and 17(2).
9 IAS 22, *Business Combinations*, IASC, September 1998, paras. 32–35.
10 R. M. Wilkins, *Group Accounts*, Second edition, London: ICAEW, 1979, p.170.
11 CA 85, Sch. 4A, para. 6(3).
12 IAS 27, para. 27.
13 FRS 2, para. 37.
14 ED 50, *Consolidated accounts*, ASC, June 1990, para. 28.
15 *Ibid.*, para. 33.
16 EC Seventh Directive, Article 1(1)(d)(aa).
17 *Ibid.*, Article 12.
18 CA 85, s 259(1).
19 *Ibid.*, s 258(1)–(2).
20 CA 85 (original), s 736(1).
21 CA 85, Sch. 10A, para. 2(1).
22 *Ibid.*, paras. 5–8.
23 *Ibid.*, para. 3(1).
24 *Ibid.*, para. 4(1)–(2).
25 Companies Bill, Clause 19, s 258(2).
26 CA 85, s 260(1).
27 *Ibid.*, s 260(3).
28 *Ibid.*, s 260(2).
29 FRS 2, para. 10.
30 CA 85, Sch. 10A, para. 4(1), (3).
31 FRS 2, para. 7.
32 *Ibid.*, paras. 69–73.
33 *Ibid.*, para. 72.
34 *Ibid.*, para. 73.
35 *Ibid.*, para. 34.
36 *Ibid.*, para. 12.
37 *Ibid.*, para. 62.
38 *Ibid.*, para. 63.
39 *Ibid.*, para. 67.
40 CA 85, Sch. 4A.
41 SSAP 14, *Group accounts*, ASC, September 1978, para. 3.
42 FRS 2, para. 5.
43 ED 50, para. 85.
44 FRRP PN 54, 2 September 1998.
45 FRS 2, para. 40.
46 CA 85, Sch. 4A, para. 3(1).
47 *Ibid.*, para. 3(3).
48 *Ibid.*, para. 3(2).
49 FRS 2, para. 41.
50 *Ibid.*, para. 42.
51 CA 85, s 223(5).
52 *Ibid.*, Sch. 4A, para. 2(2).
53 FRS 2, para. 43.
54 *Ibid.*
55 *Ibid.*, para. 44.
56 CA 85, Sch. 5, para. 19.
57 *Ibid.*, Sch. 4A, para. 17; FRS 2, para. 13.
58 CA 85, Sch. 4A, para. 17; FRS 2, para. 35.
59 CA 85, Sch. 4A, para. 17; FRS 2, para. 36.
60 FRS 2, paras. 38 and 82.
61 *Ibid.*, paras. 37 and 81.
62 *Ibid.*, para. 80.
63 *Ibid.*, paras. 51 and 90.
64 *Ibid.*, paras. 52 and 91.
65 ED 50, para. 36.
66 FRS 2, para. 39.
67 *Ibid.*, paras. 39 and 83.
68 CA 85, Sch. 4A, para. 6
69 FRS 2, para. 39.
70 *Ibid.*, para. 83.
71 SSAP 14, para. 19.
72 CA 85 (original), s 229(2).
73 CA 85, s 228.
74 European Economic Area Act 1993, s 2, states that references to the European Economic Community in earlier legislation, such as the Companies Act 1985, is to be interpreted as being to a reference to the European Economic Area.
75 CA 85, ss. 248–249.
76 FRS 2, para. 21.
77 CA 85, s 228(1).
78 *Ibid.*, s 228(3).
79 *Ibid.*, s 228(2)(a).
80 *Ibid.*, s 228(2)(c).
81 *Ibid.*, s 228(2)(d).
82 *Ibid.*, s 228(2)(e)–(f).
83 *Ibid.*, Sch. 5, paras. (1)–(6).
84 CA 85, s 248(2).
85 *Ibid.*, s 249(3).
86 *Ibid.*, s 249(4).
87 *Ibid.*, s 247(5).
88 *Ibid.*, s 249(5).
89 *Ibid.*, s 249(1)–(2).
90 *Ibid.*, s 249(1)(a).
91 FRS 2, para. 22.
92 CA 85, s 229(2)–(4).
93 FRS 2, para. 25.
94 *Ibid.*, paras. 24 and 78(b).
95 CA 85, s 229(4).
96 *Ibid.*, Sch. 9, Part II, para. 1.

97 FRS 2, paras. 25(c) and 78(e).
98 CA 85, Sch. 4A, para. 18.
99 FRS 2, para. 30.
100 *Ibid.*, para. 31(d).
101 CA 85, s 243.
102 *Ibid.*, s 229(3)(a).
103 FRS 2, para. 78(c).
104 *Ibid.*, para. 27.
105 *Ibid.*, para. 28.
106 CA 85 s 229(3)(c).
107 FRS 2, para. 11.
108 *Ibid.*, para. 25(b).
109 *Ibid.*, para. 29.
110 *Ibid.*, para. 78(a).
111 CA 85, Sch. 5, para. 15(2).
112 *Ibid.*, para. 15(4).
113 *Ibid.*, para. 17.
114 *Ibid.*, para. 17(2).
115 FRS 2, para. 31.
116 *Ibid.*, para. 32.
117 IAS 27, paras. 7 and 11.
118 *Ibid.*, para. 6.
119 *Ibid.*, para. 12.
120 Draft Interpretation SIC-D33, *Consolidation and Equity Method– Potential Voting Rights*, SIC, September 2001, paras. 1–3.
121 IAS 27, para. 15.
122 *Ibid.*, paras. 21 and 22.
123 *Ibid.*, para. 19.
124 *Ibid.*, para. 20.
125 *Ibid.*, paras. 17 and 18.
126 *Ibid.*, para. 26.
127 *Ibid.*, para. 28.
128 *Ibid.*, para. 27.
129 IAS 22, paras. 32–35.
130 Draft Interpretation SIC-D33, paras. 2 and 4.
131 IAS 27, paras. 8 and 10.
132 *Ibid.*, para. 8.
133 *Ibid.*, para. 13.
134 *Ibid.*, para. 14.
135 *Ibid.*, para. 13.
136 *Ibid.*, para. 32.

Chapter 6 Business combinations and disposals

1 INTRODUCTION

Chapter 5 deals with the preparation of consolidated accounts by a parent undertaking, but is restricted to issues such as when such accounts should be prepared, what entities should be considered to be part of the group for the purposes of inclusion therein, and how such entities should be dealt with in the consolidated accounts. This chapter deals with those situations where the group structure changes, through entities either joining or leaving the group.

A 'business combination' is defined in the UK in FRS 6 as 'the bringing together of separate entities into one economic entity as a result of one entity uniting with, or obtaining control over the net assets and operations of, another'.[1] This applies not only when an entity becomes a subsidiary undertaking of a parent company but also where an individual company or other reporting entity combines with a business other than a subsidiary undertaking.[2] The relevant international standard, IAS 22, defines a business combination in similar terms to that in FRS 6 and applies irrespective of the particular structure adopted for the combination.[3]

In accounting terms there are two distinctly different forms of reporting the effects of a business combination, referred to in the UK as acquisition accounting and merger accounting respectively and in IAS as the purchase method of accounting and pooling of interests method respectively.

The two methods of accounting look at business combinations through quite different eyes. An acquisition is seen as the absorption of the target into the clutches of the predator; there is continuity only of the holding company, in the sense that only the post-acquisition results of the target are reported as earnings of the group, and the comparative figures remain those of the holding company (and any previously held subsidiaries). In contrast, a merger is seen as the uniting of the interests of two formerly distinct shareholder groups, and in order to present continuity of both entities there is retrospective restatement to show the group as if the companies had always been together, by combining the results of both companies pre- and post-combination and also by restatement of the comparatives. The difficulty for accountants, however, has been how to translate this difference in philosophy into criteria which permit particular transactions to be categorised as being of one type or the other.

In the UK there have been several successive attempts to distinguish between the circumstances when each of these methods is appropriate, culminating in the issue of FRS 6 – *Acquisitions and mergers* – in September 1994. In addition, the Companies Act, which incorporates the requirements of the EC Seventh Directive, also sets forth qualifying conditions for merger accounting. FRS 2 – *Accounting for subsidiary undertakings* – which is the general accounting standard on consolidated accounts in the UK, has some requirements which are relevant to business combinations, and there are currently two further accounting standards which deal in detail with business combinations. FRS 7 – *Fair values in acquisition accounting* – was published in September 1994 and FRS 10 – *Goodwill and intangible assets* – was issued in December 1997. This latter standard is dealt with in Chapter 11 at 2.3. The other standards are all explained in this chapter at 2 below.

The relevant international standard is IAS 22 – *Business Combinations*. The original standard was issued in November 1983, but has been revised and amended on a number of occasions since then. This covers not only those areas dealt with in FRSs 6 and 7 but also the accounting for goodwill. The requirements of IAS 22 (apart from those dealing with goodwill) are discussed at 5 below.

In December 1998 the ASB published for public comment a Discussion Paper – *Business Combinations*. This paper was not developed by the ASB but merely reprinted a Position Paper prepared by G4+1, the international group of representatives of the standard-setting bodies of Australia, Canada, New Zealand, the UK and the USA, together with the IASC. This paper proposed that there should only be one method of accounting for business combinations, acquisition accounting, and that merger accounting should be banned. Although the ASB has acknowledged that there is no general demand in the UK for a revision of FRS 6, it has indicated that it shares the concerns of the G4+1 about the application of merger accounting in cases where it is not appropriate. It has said that it will examine FRS 6 to see whether changes are required and will watch international developments with a view to possible further changes. We disagree with the proposals in the paper and think it would be a retrograde step if the adoption of merger accounting were to be prohibited.

The other possible change in the composition of a group involves the disposal of a business. There is no specific accounting standard in the UK dealing with this issue. It is generally covered in FRS 2 in relation to the disposal of subsidiaries, and FRS 3 – *Reporting financial performance* – and FRS 10 will also be of some relevance. The issues relating to disposals are dealt with at 3 below. As in the UK, there is no international standard dealing with this issue, although IAS 27 – *Consolidated Financial Statements and Accounting for Investments in Subsidiaries*

– deals with disposals of subsidiaries and IAS 35 – *Discontinued Operations* – may also be relevant.

The chapter also deals with some issues in the UK relating to group reorganisations at 4 below. These involve the restructuring of the relationships between companies in a group by, for example, setting up a new holding company, changing the direct ownership of a subsidiary within the group, or transferring businesses from one company to another because of a process of divisionalisation. In principle, most of such changes should have no impact on the consolidated financial statements (provided there are no minority interests affected), because they are purely internal and cannot affect the group when it is being portrayed as a single entity. However, all such transactions can have a significant impact on the financial statements of the individual companies in the group.

2 BUSINESS COMBINATIONS

2.1 Criteria for mergers and acquisitions

2.1.1 FRS 6

As indicated at 1 above, there have been several successive attempts to distinguish between the circumstances when business combinations should be accounted for as mergers or acquisitions, culminating in the issue of FRS 6 – *Acquisitions and mergers* – in September 1994.[4] The accounting practices set out in FRS 6 were to be adopted in respect of business combinations first accounted for in accounts relating to periods beginning on or after 23 December 1994.[5] Since it would clearly be impracticable to restate accounts for previous business combinations that had taken place in earlier years, the standard did not require retrospective application for previous periods.

The overall approach of FRS 6 is that merger accounting should only be applied to those rare business combinations that can properly be regarded as mergers in substance, and that, except for such rare cases, business combinations are more appropriately accounted for as acquisitions.

A 'business combination' is defined in FRS 6 as 'the bringing together of separate entities into one economic entity as a result of one entity uniting with, or obtaining control over the net assets and operations of, another'.[6] The standard applies not only when an entity becomes a subsidiary undertaking of a parent company but also where an individual company or other reporting entity combines with a business other than a subsidiary undertaking.[7]

FRS 6 defines a merger as 'a business combination that results in the creation of a new reporting entity formed from the combining parties, in which the shareholders of the combining entities come together in a partnership for the mutual sharing of the risks and benefits of the combined entity, and in which no party to the combination in substance obtains control over any other, or is otherwise seen to be dominant, whether by virtue of the proportion of its shareholders' rights in the combined entity, the influence of its directors or otherwise'.[8] It is thus regarded not as the augmentation of one entity by the addition of another, but as the creation of a new reporting entity from the parties to the combination. An acquisition is defined as any other business combination that is not a merger.

The standard sets out the following five criteria that a business combination must meet for it to be accounted for as a merger, at the same time emphasising that merger accounting must also be allowed by companies legislation (see 2.1.2 below). In aggregate, these criteria are very restrictive and in interpreting them the parties to the merger are considered to be not just the business of each entity that is combining but also the management of the entity and the body of its shareholders. Merger accounting is considered by the ASB not to be appropriate where any of the parties does not have an established independent track record as a result of it being a recent divestment from a larger entity.[9] It is unclear why this should be the case.

(a) No party to the combination is portrayed as either acquirer or acquired, either by its own board or management or by that of another party to the combination.[10]

If the terms of a share for share exchange indicate that one party has paid a premium over the market value of the shares acquired, this is evidence that that party has taken the role of acquirer unless there is a clear explanation for this apparent premium other than its being a premium paid to acquire control.[11]

It is necessary to consider all the circumstances surrounding the transaction in interpreting the nature of the combination.[12]

(b) All parties to the combination, as represented by the boards of directors or their appointees, participate in establishing the management structure for the combined entity and in selecting the management personnel, and such decisions are made on the basis of a consensus between the parties to the combination rather than purely by exercise of voting rights.[13]

It is necessary to consider not only the formal management structure of the combined entity but also the identity of all persons involved in the main financial and operating decisions and the way in which the decision making process operates in practice within the combined entity.[14]

Also, although it is only necessary to consider the decisions made in the period of initial integration and restructuring at the time of the combination, both the short term and long term consequences of decisions made in this period need to be considered.[15]

(c) The relative sizes of the combining entities are not so disparate that one party dominates the combined entity by virtue of its relative size.[16]

A party would be presumed to dominate if its ownership interest in the combined entity is more than 50% larger than that of each of the other parties to the combination (although this presumption is rebuttable).[17] This means that if any party obtains a 60% interest in the combined entity, the combination probably cannot be accounted for as a merger.

(d) Under the terms of the combination or related arrangements, the consideration received by equity shareholders of each party to the combination, in relation to their equity shareholding, comprises primarily equity shares in the combined entity, and any non-equity consideration, or equity shares carrying substantially reduced voting or distribution rights, represents an immaterial proportion of the fair value of the consideration received by the shareholders of that party. Where one of the combining entities has, within the period of two years before the combination, acquired equity shares in another of the combining entities, the consideration for this acquisition should be taken into account in determining whether this criterion has been met.[18]

For the purpose of this criterion, the consideration should not be taken to include the distribution to shareholders of:

(i) an interest in a peripheral part of the business of the entity in which they were shareholders and which does not form part of the combined entity; or

(ii) the proceeds of the sale of such a business, or loan stock representing such proceeds.

A peripheral part of the business is one that can be disposed of without having a material effect on the nature and focus of the entity's operations.[19] However, interpretation of what is a peripheral part of an entity would necessarily be a fairly subjective judgement.

(e) No equity shareholders of any of the combining entities retain any material interest in the future performance of only part of the combined entity.[20] In particular, therefore, any earn-out arrangements or similar performance related schemes would mean the combination could not be interpreted as a merger.[21]

For the purposes of these criteria, any convertible shares or loan stock should be regarded as equity to the extent that they are converted into equity as a result of the business combination.[22] Equity and non-equity shares are defined in identical terms to those set out in FRS 4 (see 2.2.2 A of Chapter 17).

FRS 6 states that in applying these criteria, it is necessary to consider the substance and not just the form of the arrangements, and to take account of all relevant information related to the combination.[23] It also discusses each of the criteria in more detail, providing examples of situations which might indicate whether or not the particular criterion is met.[24] Failure to meet any of the five criteria is to be regarded as meaning that the definition of a merger has not been met and thus merger accounting is not to be used for the business combination. Conversely, where a business combination meets these criteria, acquisition accounting is not permitted. In reality, however, merger accounting remains voluntary in the sense that it would be very easy for any company not wishing to use the method to 'fail' one of the very restrictive criteria.

Since the issue of FRS 6, merger accounting has become a much rarer occurrence as most business combinations have to be regarded as acquisitions. When it issued FRED 6 (the exposure draft which led to FRS 6), the ASB also suggested an alternative approach of prohibiting the use of merger accounting entirely other than for certain group reconstructions, but did not, in the event, take this more extreme step. It may be just as well that they did not do so because since the standard was issued there have been a number of instances where merger accounting has been applied.[25] The main use of merger accounting nowadays, however, is for combinations made within a group, i.e. group reconstructions (see 4 below).

2.1.2 *Companies Act requirements*

The Companies Act requirements result from the implementation of the EC Seventh Directive on Company Law.

The conditions laid down in the Act which have to be met before merger accounting can be applied are as follows:

'(a) that at least 90% of the nominal value of the relevant shares in the undertaking acquired is held by or on behalf of the parent company and its subsidiary undertakings,

(b) that the proportion referred to in (a) was attained pursuant to an arrangement providing for the issue of equity shares by the parent company or one or more of its subsidiary undertakings,

(c) that the fair value of any consideration other than the issue of equity shares given pursuant to the arrangement by the parent company and its subsidiary undertakings did not exceed 10% of the nominal value of the equity shares issued, and

(d) that adoption of the merger method of accounting accords with generally accepted accounting principles or practice.'[26]

'Relevant shares' are defined as being those carrying unrestricted rights to participate both in distributions and in surplus assets on a winding up.[27]

In satisfying condition (c), it should be noted that it refers to the *nominal* value of the shares issued, rather than their *fair* value in setting the 10% limit, and therefore could be quite restrictive. It should also be noted that as the limit applies to any consideration other than the issue of equity shares, it does not just apply to cash consideration, but also to other forms such as loan stock or the assumption of debt. (This differs from Article 20 of the Directive which disqualifies transactions where the consideration includes a cash payment exceeding 10% of the nominal value of the shares issued to effect the business combination. However, in drafting the Companies Act, the DTI extended the restriction on cash to cover any form of consideration other than equity.)

Given the restrictive criteria contained in FRS 6, these requirements are really only of relevance in the context of group reconstructions (see 4 below). However, even then it should be noted that the conditions in the Act only apply where an undertaking becomes a subsidiary undertaking of the parent company;[28] they do not apply to group reconstructions involving a business which is not a subsidiary undertaking.

2.1.3 *Merger relief*

The mechanics of merger accounting require the shares issued by the holding company as consideration for the shares of the subsidiary to be recorded at their nominal value rather than their fair value, In order to be able to do this, and record the cost of an investment in the subsidiary acquired in exchange for these shares at the same amount, it is necessary to satisfy the requirements of section 131 of the Companies Act 1985.

The section broadly relieves companies from the basic requirement to set up a share premium account (described as 'merger relief') in respect of equity shares issued in exchange for shares in another company in the course of a transaction which results in the issuing company securing at least a 90% holding in the equity shares of the other company. (This paraphrases the words in the Act, and the precise wording should be referred to in order to ensure that any particular transaction falls within its terms.) In addition there are further provisions with a similar purpose which apply to shares issued in the course of a group reconstruction.

The rules on merger relief and those on merger accounting are frequently confused with each other. However, not only are they based on the satisfaction of different criteria, they in fact have quite distinct purposes. Merger accounting is a form of financial reporting which applies to business combinations, but although the merger relief provisions were brought in to facilitate it, merger relief is purely a legal matter to do with the maintenance of capital for the protection of creditors and has very little to do with accounting per se. Moreover, merger relief may be available under transactions which are accounted for as acquisitions, rather than mergers, and the two are not interdependent in that sense.

There are some differences of legal opinion as to whether merger relief is in fact *compulsory* when the conditions of section 131 are met, or whether it is optional. The Act says that where the conditions are met, then section 130 does not apply to the premiums on the shares issued. Section 130 is the basic requirement to set up a share premium account where shares are issued at a premium and therefore some people argue that the effect of this relief is simply to make section 130 optional rather than mandatory, but others take the view that it makes it illegal to set up a share premium account. The most common treatment adopted by those who qualify for merger relief but account for the transaction as an acquisition has in fact been to regard the issue as having taken place at fair value, but to record a 'merger reserve' rather than a share premium account.

On the other hand, some companies record the transaction in their individual company financial statements based on the nominal value of the shares issued, the merger reserve only arising in the consolidated financial statements where it is used for writing off the goodwill on the acquisition. One company which adopts such a treatment is Aga Foodservice Group, as indicated below:

Extract 6.1: Aga Foodservice Group plc (2000)

1. Accounting policies
Acquisitions [extract]

In the company accounts, where advantage can be taken of the merger relief rules, shares issued as consideration for acquisitions are accounted for at nominal value.

On the face of it, such a treatment is not allowed since paragraphs 11 and 45 of FRS 4 – *Capital instruments* – require the net proceeds received on the issue of shares to be credited to shareholders' funds, based on the fair value of the consideration. This appears to remove the 'nominal value' option except where the shares have been issued as part of a business combination that is accounted for as a merger, although paragraph 3 of Appendix I to the standard which deals with legal requirements might suggest otherwise as it states that nothing in the standard affects the availability of merger relief under section 131 of the Act. Similarly, Appendix I to FRS 6 states that the requirements of that standard do 'not deal with the form of accounting to be used in the acquiring or issuing company's own accounts and in particular does not restrict the reliefs available under sections 131-133 of the Companies Act'.[29] We therefore do not consider that the ASB can have intended to ban this practice, and in our view it remains acceptable.

2.2 Acquisitions: basic principles

When Company A acquires Company B, it has to consolidate B's trading results from the effective date of acquisition onwards. Similarly, it thereafter includes B's assets and liabilities in its consolidated balance sheet, eliminating the share capital and reserves of B at the acquisition date against the cost of A's investment in B's shares. In contrast to merger accounting, the pre-acquisition results and reserves of B are completely eliminated from the consolidated financial statements, rather than brought in retrospectively. These principles are enshrined within the Companies Act.[30]

FRS 2 defines the date of acquisition in terms of when control passes; it states that 'the date for accounting for an undertaking becoming a subsidiary undertaking is the date on which control of that undertaking passes to its new parent undertaking'.[31] This is a matter of fact and cannot be artificially backdated or otherwise altered. It then explains when such a date might be under various circumstances: 'Where control is transferred by a public offer, the date control is transferred is the date the offer becomes unconditional, usually as a result of a sufficient number of acceptances being received. For private treaties, the date control is transferred is generally the date an unconditional offer is accepted. Where an undertaking becomes ... a subsidiary undertaking as a result of the issue or cancellation of shares, the date control is transferred is the date of issue or cancellation. The date that control passes may be indicated by the acquiring party commencing its direction of the operating and financial policies of the acquired undertaking or by changes in the flow of economic benefits.' It also states that 'the date on which the consideration for the transfer of control is paid is often an important indication of the date on which a subsidiary undertaking is acquired or disposed of. However, the date the consideration passes is not conclusive evidence of the date of the transfer of control because this date can be set to fall on a date other than that on which control is transferred, with compensation for any lead or lag included in the consideration. Consideration may also be paid in instalments.'[32]

Although the definition and explanation in FRS 2 are expressed in terms of an acquisition of a subsidiary undertaking, these also apply to the acquisition of businesses which are not subsidiary undertakings since FRS 7 contains a definition in similar terms. It states that the date of acquisition is 'the date on which control of the acquired entity passes to the acquirer. This is the date from which the acquired entity is accounted for by the acquirer as a subsidiary undertaking under FRS 2 'Accounting for Subsidiary Undertakings''.[33]

In order to account for the acquisition, the acquiring company must first measure the cost of what it is accounting for, which will normally represent both the cost of the investment in its own balance sheet and the amount to be allocated between the identifiable net assets of the subsidiary and goodwill in the consolidated financial statements. This issue is considered at 2.3 below.

Secondly, in allocating the cost of the acquisition, the acquiring company then needs to identify the assets and liabilities of the subsidiary and attribute fair values to them, rather then merely relying on the book values in the subsidiary's accounts. This is discussed at 2.4 below.

Once the fair values of both the consideration given and the net assets acquired have been measured, the difference between the two represents purchased goodwill which remains to be accounted for. How to account for it is a subject on which widely differing opinions are held, and this is evidenced both by the time which it originally took the ASC to develop a standard on the subject and by the fact that the eventual standard, SSAP 22, permitted a choice between two alternative methods: amortisation through the profit and loss account and immediate write-off direct to reserves. Most companies adopted the latter approach. This standard was superseded when the ASB issued FRS 10 in December 1997 which radically changed the way companies account for goodwill. No longer can companies write off goodwill immediately to reserves but they must now capitalise it as an asset. The subsequent accounting for goodwill is dealt with in Chapter 11 at 2.3.

2.3 Acquisitions: measuring the fair value of the consideration

Although the Companies Act specifies that the cost is to be based on the fair value of the consideration given if acquisition accounting is used, it wasn't until the publication of FRS 7 in September 1994 that there was a standard which elaborated on how this was to be determined.

Although FRS 7 is framed in terms of the acquisition of a subsidiary undertaking, it also applies where an individual company or other reporting entity acquires a business other than a subsidiary undertaking.[34]

The basic requirement of FRS 7 is that 'the cost of acquisition is the amount of cash paid and the fair value of other purchase consideration given by the acquirer, together with the expenses of the acquisition .... Where a subsidiary undertaking is acquired in stages, the cost of acquisition is the total of the costs of the interests acquired, determined as at the date of each transaction.'[35] This latter aspect of acquiring a subsidiary in stages is discussed further at 2.5 below. Issues relating to the first part of the requirement are discussed at 2.3.1 to 2.3.7 below.

2.3.1 *Cash and other monetary consideration*

The purchase consideration may comprise cash or other monetary items, including the assumption of liabilities by the acquirer. FRS 7 states that the fair value of such items 'is normally readily determinable as the amount paid or payable in respect of the item'.[36] However, when settlement is deferred, fair values are to be obtained by discounting to their present value the amounts expected to be payable in the future, using an appropriate discount rate (see 2.3.4 below).

The effect of discounting future obligations is to reduce the amount of goodwill recognised on the acquisition (or increase the amount of any negative goodwill). This is because the amount of consideration given is deemed smaller. It is then augmented by notional interest charges in the post-acquisition profit and loss account to bring the carrying value of the obligation up to the settlement value by the due date.

2.3.2 *Capital instruments*

The purchase consideration may comprise capital instruments issued by the acquirer, including shares, debentures, loans and debt instruments, share warrants and other options relating to the securities of the acquirer.

Where such instruments are quoted on a ready market, FRS 7 states that 'the market price on the date of acquisition would normally provide the most reliable measure of fair value'. Where the acquisition arises out of a public offer, 'the relevant date is the date on which the offer or, where there is a series of revised offers, the successful offer becomes unconditional, usually as a result of a sufficient number of acceptances being received'. However, 'where, owing to unusual fluctuations, the market price on one particular date is an unreliable measure of fair value, market prices for a reasonable period before the date of acquisition, during which acceptances could be made, would need to be considered'.[37] Unfortunately, FRS 7 gives no guidance as to what a reasonable period might be. ED 53, an exposure draft issued by the ASC, observed that the period chosen would depend on both specific conditions and also general market conditions.[38] However, it advised that usually a period of 10 dealing days prior to the date of acquisition would be appropriate. It may be that in the absence of anything more specific in FRS 7, this could be taken as a guide, although obviously the specific circumstances would have to be taken into account. The purpose of this is to take some sort of average price so that the value of the consideration given is not distorted by a transient fluctuation.

For other securities, a suitable market price might not exist; this might be due to the fact that the securities are not quoted, or if they are quoted, the market price is unreliable owing, for example, to the lack of an active market in the quantities involved. Where this is the case, the fair value should be estimated by taking into account items such as:

(a) the value of similar securities that are quoted;

(b) the present value of the future cash flows of the instrument issued;

(c) any cash alternative to the issue of securities; and

(d) the value of any underlying security into which there is an option to convert.[39]

Where it is not possible to value the consideration given by any of the above methods, the best estimate of its value may be given by valuing the entity acquired.[40]

One company which explicitly says that it uses the price ruling at the date at which the offer becomes unconditional is Travis Perkins, as shown in Extract 6.2.

Extract 6.2: Travis Perkins plc (2000)

Accounting Policies

(b) BASIS OF PREPARATION [extract]

The cost of acquisition represents the cash value of the consideration and/or the market value of the shares issued on the date the offer became unconditional, plus expenses.

One company which did not use the market price of its shares at the date of acquisition was Harveys Furnishing (then named Cantors) in respect of its acquisition of Harveys Holdings. The company took the view that its market price at that date (£1.65) was unreliable so instead adopted the share valuation (£1) ruling at the date four months earlier when the transaction had been negotiated. This treatment was challenged by the Review Panel[41] and as a result the company issued a supplementary note in respect of its 1997 accounts (as part of its 1998 Annual Report) which contained the following explanation of the issue.

Extract 6.3: Harveys Furnishings plc (1998)

SUPPLEMENTARY NOTE TO THE FINANCIAL STATEMENTS

for the 52 weeks ended 26 April 1997 [extract]

The company has held discussions with the Financial Reporting Review Panel ("the Panel") regarding the value of the consideration given by Cantors for Harveys following the acquisition by Cantors, as stated in the financial statements for the 52 weeks ended 26 April 1997 and as to the way that certain other financial information has been presented in those financial statements. As a result of these discussions, the directors have decided to revise the financial statements in accordance with Statutory Instrument 2570(1990), which permits revision by way of Supplementary Note.

The issue concerning the valuation of Harveys relates to a complex accounting matter. At the point at which the acquisition of Harveys was negotiated in March 1996, the Cantors' share price was in the region of £1. This formed the basis for the valuation of Harveys by both parties and the basis of the share exchange ratio. At the date of the shareholder approval for the transaction in July 1996, the price had moved to £1.65. As this was a reverse take-over the directors considered that the Cantors' share price had reacted in a similar way as a target in a bid would normally react; anticipating the benefits that an acquisition would bring to the existing Cantors' shareholders. The situation was exacerbated by the existence of a thin market in which a small transaction could move the price dramatically. Trading in Cantors' shares was suspended in June 1996 and the dealings in this period were the subject of a Stock Exchange enquiry

Both the Directors and Coopers & Lybrand were concerned that if a price of £1.65 were used to determine the carrying value of the investment in Harveys the carrying value would be approximately £55 million, which in the context of expected after tax profits for the year ended 31 August 1996 of approximately £2.3 million imputed an inflated earnings multiple. After considering the above factors and taking into account the abnormal circumstances of a reverse takeover, the Directors and Coopers & Lybrand deemed the share price of £1.65 to be unreliable for the purposes of attributing a value to Harveys as at the date of the merger. We consequently adopted an alternative valuation of £1, since this had formed the basis of the negotiations for the merger. However, the Panel considered that the price of £1.65 formed the appropriate basis for the fair value of the consideration as required by FRS 7, which the directors have decided to accept.

Interestingly, the auditors in their report on the revised accounts still maintained that valuing the cost of the acquisition on the basis of £1 per share was acceptable, but conceded in the circumstances that the revised basis now adopted by the directors was also acceptable.

Perhaps mindful of this Review Panel ruling, Brown & Jackson, who had similarly negotiated a deal based on the company's share price at the date of the acquisition agreement, used the market price at the date the acquisition became unconditional following shareholder approval as shown below.

Extract 6.4: Brown & Jackson plc (1998)

18 Notes to the cash flow statement [extract]

(d) Acquisitions of Your More Store Ltd and WEW Group Plc (see note 19)

On 27 September 1997 two new wholly owned subsidiaries, Your More Store Ltd (YMS) and WEW Group Plc (WEW) were acquired. WEW was acquired for £6.543 million in cash plus expenses of £539,000.

The agreement for the purchase of the shares in YMS dated 27 August 1997 provided for a consideration of £7.651 million to be settled by the issue of 34,242,424 10p ordinary shares at 16.5p (which was the closing mid-market share price on the date of the agreement) and the payment of £2 million in cash. The agreement was conditional upon the subsequent approval in General Meeting by the independent shareholders and this approval was obtained on 27 September 1997

Financial Reporting Standard 7 'Fair values in acquisition accounting' requires the fair value of the share consideration for accounting purposes to be determined at the date that the acquisition became unconditional. At 27 September 1997, the date the agreement became unconditional, the mid-market price of the shares in the Company was 21.5p. Accordingly the fair value of the share consideration for these purposes was £7.363 million as shown below.

The fair values of the identifiable assets and liabilities of the new subsidiaries at the date of acquisition are provisional subject to the agreement of certain tax computations and were as follows:

Net assets acquired	Book value at acquisition YMS £'000	Fair value adjustments YMS £'000	Fair value YMS £'000	Book value at acquisition WEW £'000	Accounting policy alignment WEW £'000	Fair value WEW £'000
Fixed assets	8,614	–	8,614	21,983	–	21,983
Stocks	7,725	–	7,725	16,717	–	16,717
Debtors	1,977	–	1,977	6,874	–	6,874
Cash at bank and in hand	78	–	78	812	–	812
Creditors and provisions	(6,618)	13	(6,605)	(19,444)	(793)	(20,237)
Reorganisation provision previously created in the accounts to 2 August 1997				(3,117)	–	(3,117)
Bank overdrafts	(2,771)	–	(2,771)	(8,506)	–	(8,506)
Loans and finance leases	(2,500)	–	(2,500)	(2,424)	–	(2,424)
Less minority interests	–	–	–	(2,178)	–	(2,178)
	6,505	13	6,518	10,717	(793)	9,924
Goodwill/(negative goodwill)			3,229			(2,842)
			9,747			7,082
Satisfied by						
34,242,424 shares at 16.5p per agreement			5,651			–
Increase in share price between 27 August and 27 September 1997			1,712			–
Fair value of share consideration for these purposes			7,363			–
Cash to ordinary shareholders			2,000			6,543
Expenses of acquisition			384			539
			9,747			7,082

Sometimes, shares are issued by the acquirer which rank fully for dividends which are to be paid in respect of a period before the acquisition took place. In these circumstances, some companies apportion the subsequent dividend into two components when it is paid, with a 'pre-acquisition' element added to the cost of the investment in the subsidiary (and therefore increasing the goodwill) and leaving only the post-acquisition element to be taken out of the profit and loss account. FRS 7 does not deal with this specific issue. In our view such a treatment is inappropriate where the cost of the investment in the acquired subsidiary is recorded at the (cum div) fair value of the securities issued as consideration; this is because the fair value of the securities will already reflect the fact that the shareholders are entitled to the dividend and therefore the dividend cost is double-counted. This is not the case where merger relief has been taken (see 2.1.3 above) and the cost of the investment is recorded at the nominal value of the shares issued as consideration. One example of this is to be found in the 1989 financial statements of BICC, as shown in the following extract:

Extract 6.5: BICC plc (1989)

11 ORDINARY DIVIDENDS

	1989		1988	
	Per share p	**Amount £m**	**Per share p**	**Amount £m**
Interim payable	**5.75**	**15.1**	4.75	11.2
Final proposed	**13.25**	**36.0**	11.25	26.7
	19.00	**51.1**	16.00	37.9
Pre-acquisition proportion relating to shares issued for acquisitions		**(2.2)**		(0.9)
		48.9		37.0

15 INVESTMENTS [extract]

BICC plc issued 7.6m ordinary shares in 1988 and 2.6m ordinary shares in 1989 for the share capital of Ceat Cavi Industrie Srl. 22.1m were also issued in 1989 to acquire Manshine Ltd, a company formed in connection with the acquisition of BRIntic Corporation, and 0.7m ordinary shares were issued for the share capital of Syntek Ltd and Cruickshank and Partners Ltd.

...

Having taken advantage of the merger relief provisions under s 131, Companies Act 1985, the investment in these companies is recorded at the nominal value of the shares issued as consideration, plus costs, including the pre-acquisition proportion of dividend and related advance corporation tax in respect of the shares issued in the year.

2.3.3 *Non-monetary assets*

The purchase consideration may comprise non-monetary assets, including securities of another entity. FRS 7 states that for such consideration 'fair values would be determined by reference to market prices, estimated realisable values, independent valuations, or other available evidence'.[42] This is not as specific as the proposal in ED 53 which focused on the value of the sacrifice made by the acquirer by giving up such assets, and invoked a concept similar to that of 'deprival value' which was used as the basis of valuations in current cost accounting. The loss suffered by the acquirer was the alternative proceeds he could have received for the asset, unless he could make good his loss by replacing the asset, in which case it was the cost of such replacement. In the absence of anything more specific in FRS 7, the deprival value principle seems a sensible one to adopt.

One common situation where such non-monetary consideration is given is where a company exchanges a business in return for an interest in a subsidiary or other business. Two companies which had to address this issue were George Wimpey and Tarmac when they swapped their respective construction and housing businesses in 1996. George Wimpey regarded the consideration given as being the equivalent of the book values of the net assets of the construction business, as seen below:

Extract 6.6: George Wimpey PLC (1996)

26 Asset Exchange with Tarmac plc

On 1 March 1996, George Wimpey PLC acquired Tarmac's Housing division, McLean Homes, by exchange of Wimpey's Construction and Minerals divisions. The Group has used acquisition accounting to account for the acquisition. Goodwill arising on consolidation has been written off direct to reserves. The impact of this acquisition on the consolidated net assets was as follows:

	Book Cost of Assets Acquired £m	Revaluation £m	Provisions £m	Reassessment of Fair Values of Net Current Assets £m	Fair Value of Assets Acquired £m
Net assets acquired from Tarmac:					
Tangible assets and fixed asset investments	6.1	0.3	–	–	6.4
Net current assets	316.7	–	–	(14.1)	302.6
Provisions	–	–	(1.2)	–	(1.2)
Cash at bank and in hand	2.2	–	–	–	2.2
Borrowings and inter-company debt	(51.1)	–	–	–	(51.1)
Total net assets	273.9	0.3	(1.2)	(14.1)	258.9
Consideration:					
Net assets of Construction and Minerals divisions					
Tangible assets and fixed asset investments					335.7
Net current assets					(7.1)
Cash at bank and in hand					43.9
Borrowings and inter-company debt					(35.3)
Provisions					(27.0)
Minority interests					(13.6)
Total net assets					296.6
Professional fees and other costs of the transaction					4.2
Goodwill arising on asset exchange					41.9

Provisions acquired from Tarmac relate mainly to rental provisions for void property which existed at the date of acquisition. Of this provision, £0.2 million had been utilised at 31 December 1996. The fair value adjustment to net current assets mainly results from a reassessment of the net realisable value of work in progress and land.

This can be contrasted with Tarmac which regarded the consideration given for the Wimpey business acquired as being an estimate of the fair value of the housing division given in return as shown below:

Extract 6.7: Tarmac plc (1996)

29 Acquisitions and Divestments [extract]
Exchange of businesses with George Wimpey PLC

On 1st March 1996 the Group's UK and US private sector housing business ('the Housing Division') was exchanged for the world-wide minerals and construction businesses of George Wimpey PLC ('Wimpey'). The effects of this exchange on the net assets of the Group are summarised below:

	Wimpey businesses acquired				
		Fair value adjustments in respect of:			
	Book value £m	Revaluation of assets acquired £m	Accounting policy alignment £m	Fair value £m	Housing Division divested £m
Tangible assets	334.6	13.3	–	347.9	6.1
Associated undertakings	1.1	(1.1)	–	–	–
Stocks	30.9	(0.4)	–	30.5	397.4
Debtors	183.2	(38.6)	–	144.6	58.8
Cash, less overdrafts	36.5	–	–	36.5	(53.5)
Creditors, deferred liabilities and provisions	(249.2)	(18.8)	(9.5)	(277.5)	(130.1)
Inter-group loans	(29.2)	–	–	(29.2)	4.5
Equity minority interests	(13.6)	(5.3)	–	(18.9)	–
Net assets	294.3	(50.9)	(9.5)		
Fair value of assets exchanged				233.9	283.2
Professional fees and other costs of transaction				(7.5)	7.1
				226.4	290.3
Directors' estimate of fair value of Housing Division, as divested				291.0	291.0
Goodwill arising on acquisition of Wimpey businesses, written off directly to reserves				64.6	
Unrealised profit on disposal of Housing Division					0.7

The £9.5 million accounting policy alignment adjustment represents additional environmental and restoration provisions, which remain substantially unutilised at the year end.

The revaluation of assets acquired within the above table incorporates the adjustment of book values to those achieved on subsequent divestments of US businesses, an independent valuation of mineral reserves (note 12) and a reassessment of the realisable values of amounts recoverable on contracts and other net current assets.

It is interesting to note from the above extracts that both parties to the transaction considered that the fair value of the assets acquired was less than the corresponding book value. Indeed, they also disagreed as to what the book values were.

Another company which acquired a subsidiary in return for non-monetary consideration is Kingfisher as shown below:

Extract 6.8: Kingfisher plc (1999)

37 Acquisitions [extract]
(a) Merger of B&Q and Castorama

On 18 December 1998, the effective date of acquisition, the Group completed the combination of B&Q plc with Castorama Dubois Investissements S.C.A. (Castorama). The transaction has been treated as an acquisition and was effected by the transfer by the Group of its 100% interest in B&Q in exchange for a 57.9% interest (54.6% on a fully diluted basis) in the consequently enlarged Castorama group. The transaction was effected by an exchange of shares, being new shares in Castorama for the Group's shares in B&Q and the book value of the 42.1% of the assets of B&Q at the date of acquisition has been treated as the cost of that investment. The difference between the consideration and the fair value of the Castorama net assets received has been treated as a non-distributable reserve.

The details of the transaction adjustments are set out below. The fair value adjustments are of a provisional nature, because the timing of the acquisition has meant that it has not been possible to complete the investigation for determining fair values. The exercise will be completed in 1999 and any further fair value adjustments will be made in next year's accounts.

		Fair value adjustments:		
£ millions	Book value	Revaluations	Accounting policy alignments	Fair value to the Group
Tangible fixed assets	614.3	–	84.8	699.1
Investments	1.6	–	–	1.6
Stocks	400.6	–	–	400.6
Other current assets	312.7	–	1.2	313.9
Creditors	(862.8)	–	(23.5)	(886.3)
Castorama net assets	466.4	–	62.5	528.9
B&Q net assets on completion				325.5

£ millions	Reserve arising
Share of Castorama net assets acquired (57.9% of £528.9m)	306.2
Share of B&Q net assets given up (42.1% of £325.5m)	(137.0)
Transaction expenses	(22.9)
Non-distributable reserve arising	146.3

Accounting policy alignments have been made to the books of Castorama as at 31 December 1998 principally comprising the reversal of depreciation on freehold buildings and the restatement of deferred tax from a full provision basis to a partial provision basis. Deferred tax assets arising on unutilised tax losses and charges to the consolidated profit and loss account on which tax relief will be available in future years have been eliminated.

As the Castorama merger was completed very close to the Group's year end, an exercise to revalue land and buildings has not been undertaken. A full valuation exercise will be undertaken during 1999 for reflection next year. Land and buildings are shown at cost in the above provisional fair value table

The book values of the assets and liabilities have been translated at the actual exchange rate as at 31 December 1998 of £1:FF 9.241.

It can be seen that, like Wimpey, Kingfisher has regarded the consideration as being the equivalent of its share of the book value of the B&Q net assets given up. However, rather than treating the difference of £146.3m between this consideration and the fair value of the assets (after allowing for the transaction expenses) as negative goodwill under FRS 10, it has taken it to a non-distributable reserve. This seems to treat the transaction more like a disposal, but regarding the gain as unrealised.

It is clear from the above discussion that such exchange transactions raise a number of issues and there has been an inconsistent approach to the accounting treatment. The topic has recently been considered by the UITF and in May 2001 it issued a draft Abstract on exchanges of businesses and other non-monetary assets for equity in a subsidiary, joint venture or associate. This is discussed further at 3.6 below and in Chapter 7 at 4.2.3.

One company which was recently taken to task by the Review Panel was Avesco in respect of the value attributed to non-monetary assets given as consideration for an acquisition in its 2000 accounts. In this case the acquisition was of an associate, not a subsidiary, but the provisions of FRS 7 are still applicable. The Review Panel noted that the accounts stated that the cost of the investment had been determined by the net book value of equipment transferred, together with the associated acquisition costs. In the light of their discussion with the Review Panel, the directors included a note in the 2001 accounts clarifying that, in their opinion, the book value of the assets transferred approximated their fair value.[43]

2.3.4 *Deferred consideration*

The term 'deferred consideration' is not used in FRS 7 but was stated in the ASB's earlier Discussion Paper to denote consideration, payable in cash, shares or other securities, which is determined precisely at the time of the acquisition either in value or as a number of shares, but where the payment is delayed for a defined period.[44]

The standard only discusses the situation where settlement of cash consideration is deferred, in which case 'fair values are obtained by discounting to their present value the amounts expected to be payable in the future. The appropriate discount rate is the rate at which the acquirer could obtain a similar borrowing, taking into account its credit standing and any security given.'[45]

Deferred consideration in a form other than cash is not discussed in FRS 7; it is unclear why this should be the case. However, it may be that where such consideration is payable in shares, or other securities, then the acquirer is regarded as having issued a capital instrument as part of the consideration at the time of the acquisition and therefore the fair value should be determined following the principles set out for capital instruments discussed at 2.3.2 above. The standard also does not deal with how deferred consideration payable in shares should be dealt with, but in our view it should be dealt with in a similar manner to contingent consideration which is to be satisfied by shares (see 2.3.5 below).

Although many companies refer to deferred consideration in their accounts, such consideration usually is in reality contingent consideration under FRS 7.

2.3.5 *Contingent consideration*

The terms of an acquisition may provide that the value of the purchase consideration, which may be payable in cash, shares or other securities at a future date, depends on uncertain future events, such as the future performance of the acquired company. FRS 7 quotes the example of an 'earn out', 'where consideration payable to the vendor takes the form of an initial payment, together with further payments based on a multiple of future profits of the acquired company. By its nature, the fair value of such contingent consideration cannot be determined precisely at the date of acquisition.'[46]

The standard requires that 'where the amount of purchase consideration is contingent on one or more future events, the cost of acquisition should include a reasonable estimate of the fair value of amounts expected to be payable in the future. The cost of acquisition should be adjusted when revised estimates are made, with consequential corresponding adjustments continuing to be made to goodwill until the ultimate outcome is known.'[47]

For this calculation, therefore, goodwill can remain open for several periods after the acquisition. This is in contrast to the normal rule that fair values and thus goodwill should not be adjusted after the first full period following the one in which the acquisition took place (see 2.4.2 below).

Although the ASB's Discussion Paper proposed that if such amounts were to be payable in cash or by the issue of a debt instrument, they were to be discounted to their present value,[48] FRS 7 does not specifically state this to be the case. However, it is arguable that such amounts by their nature are 'deferred' and therefore any amount payable in cash should be discounted, and if payable by the issue of a loan instrument, the fair value of such an instrument would reflect a discounted value. Similarly, the ASB Discussion Paper proposed that if such amounts were payable in shares, then the fair value of contingent consideration should be based on its expected value.[49] Again, FRS 7 is silent on this issue.

Although, as the standard comments, by its nature the fair value of contingent consideration cannot be determined precisely at the date of acquisition, acquiring companies should provide for a reasonable estimate of the outcome. Usually, an indication of the likely amounts payable should be available since in drawing up the terms of the agreement the parties will have had to consider closely the likely outcomes.

In some cases it will be clear that at least a certain amount is very likely to be payable, and in these circumstances it would seem appropriate to provide for that amount. This is more likely to be the case in those situations where the contingent consideration is based on the target company maintaining a level of profits which it is currently earning (either for a particular period or as an average over a set period) or achieving profits which it is currently budgeting.

One company which made full provision for contingent consideration in respect of an acquisition was Logica as shown below:

Extract 6.9: Logica plc (1998)

26 Acquisitions [extract]
Aldiscon Limited

The acquisition of Aldiscon Limited, a company registered in Ireland, was completed on 1 August 1997.

The consideration paid or payable is as follows:

(i) a fixed amount of IR£52.4 million (£47.0 million) excluding costs of the acquisition.

(ii) an amount contingent upon Logica Aldiscon achieving certain performance criteria in the period to 30 June 1998, the maximum amount payable being IR£4.5 million (£3.8 million). This is expected to be paid subject only to the continued employment of certain of the vendors.

The provisional fair value to the group of net assets acquired is shown below:

	Book value of assets acquired £'000	Revaluation adjustments £'000	Accounting policy adjustments £'000	Provisional fair value £'000
Intangible fixed assets	35	–	(35)	–
Tangible fixed assets	2,074	–	422	2,496
Debtors/work in progress	12,939	(937)	1,365	13,367
Cash at bank and in hand	2,712	–	–	2,712
Creditors	(8,748)	(886)	–	(9,634)
Taxation	(334)	(622)	–	(956)
Borrowings	(853)	–	–	(853)
Net assets acquired	7,825	(2,445)	1,752	7,132
Goodwill				44,065
				51,197
Satisfied by:				
Cash (including costs of the acquisition of £831,000)				47,831
Contingent consideration (discounted)				3,366
				51,197

The main adjustments are:

Intangible fixed assets

Capitalised patents of £35,000 have been written off to bring Aldiscon into line with Logica's accounting policy on intangible assets.

Tangible fixed assets

The net book value of fixed assets was adjusted to realign Aldiscon fixed asset depreciation policies with those of Logica.

Debtors/work in progress

Reversal of general work in progress provision of £90,000 to confirm with Logica accounting policy. Logica revenue recognition policy was applied against Aldiscon's open projects as at 1 August 1997 resulting in an acceleration of revenue recognition compared to Aldiscon's existing policy. The impact was an increase in debtors of £2.9 million and an increase in accrued costs associated with those revenues of £1.4 million. Specific provisions of £937,000 were made for all debts more than 12 months old at the date of acquisition. There has been no movement in this provision to 30 June 1998.

Creditors

Provisions were established in respect of a planned US office relocation entered into prior to the acquisition date (£246,000) and identified social security expenditure (£640,000).

Taxation

Provisions were established to cover specific tax exposures identified.

Movements on fair value provisions

An amount of £123,000 of the provision for the US office relocation has been utilised in the period since acquisition to cover the rent on the property for the period since it was vacated and other costs of relocation.

It can be seen from the above extract that Logica has discounted the contingent consideration. Another company that does likewise and has an accounting policy on the matter is Daily Mail and General Trust as illustrated below:

Extract 6.10: Daily Mail and General Trust plc (2000)

Accounting Policies [extract]
Goodwill and Other Intangible Assets [extract]

(c) In calculating the goodwill, the total consideration, both actual and deferred, is taken into account. Where the deferred consideration is payable in cash, the liability is discounted to its present value. Where the deferred consideration is contingent and dependent upon future trading performance, an estimate of the present value of the likely consideration payable is made. This contingent deferred consideration is re-assessed annually and a corresponding adjustment is made to the goodwill arising on acquisition. The difference between the present value and the total amount payable at a future date gives rise to a finance charge which is charged to the profit and loss account and credited to the liability over the period in which the consideration is deferred. The discount used approximates to market rates.

Notes to the Profit and Loss Account [extract]
9 Other Finance Charges (Net)

	2000 £m	1999 £m
Premium on repurchase of Exchangeable Bonds	**(4.9)**	(2.3)
Premium on repurchase of other borrowings	**(1.2)**	–
	(6.1)	(2.3)
Finance credit on discounting of deferred proceeds	**0.9**	–
Finance charge on discounting of deferred consideration	**(3.1)**	(3.0)
	(8.3)	(5.3)

The premium on repurchase of Exchange Bonds (Note 25 iii) and of other borrowings (Note 30 iv) arose as a result of their being acquired for a price in excess of their par value. The premium on repurchase of Exchangeable Bonds has been treated as exceptional in calculating adjusted earnings per share (Note 15).

The finance charge on the discounting of deferred consideration arises from the requirement under FRS 7 to discount consideration, deferred in respect of acquisitions, back to current values. The finance credit arises from the adoption of the same treatment in respect of proceeds, deferred in respect of the disposal of 60% of Soccernet in 1999.

Notes to the Balance Sheet [extract]
35 Summary of the Effects of Acquisitions [extract]

The principal acquisitions completed during the year and their dates of acquisition were:

Riddell Exhibitions Promotions	October 1999
Bristol United Press (BUP) (76%)	February 2000
Mayhill Publications	May 2000
Expositions	May 2000
GD Ventures	May 2000
Australian Trade Exhibitions	July 2000
Forum Verlagsgruppe	July 2000

The aggregate consideration for these and other businesses was £260.8 million, of which £236.0 million was paid during the year, £7.6 million issued in the form of loan notes and an estimated amount of £17.2 million payable in the form of deferred consideration, dependent upon trading results. This deferred consideration has been discounted back to current values in accordance with FRS 7. A further £5.0 million of loans were taken on in the form of debt.

As there is an element of uncertainty about the ultimate amount payable occasionally it will be necessary to revise the liability originally recognised. One company which has had to reverse out its provision was Cobham as shown below.

Extract 6.11: Cobham plc (1998)

21 Reserves [extract]

	Profit and Loss Account £m
Group	
At 1 January 1998	**76.2**
Goodwill written back on sale of a subsidiary (note 3)	**2.6**
Contingent consideration provision, no longer required (note below)	**3.9**
Profit retained for the year	**28.5**
Foreign exchange	**(0.1)**
At 31 December 1998	**111.1**

£3.9m has been added to reserves as a result of the release from provisions of this sum which was deferred consideration potentially due to certain vendors of Westwind which is now no longer payable.

The cumulative goodwill written off on acquisition net of disposals totals £182.0m from 1954 to 31 December 1998 (1997 – £188.5m) after writing back £6.5m in 1998 (1997 – nil).

It can be seen from the above that in line with FRS 7 the corresponding adjustment has been made against goodwill. (In this case the adjustment was in respect of pre-FRS 10 goodwill, hence the credit to reserves. If the adjustment had been in respect of FRS 10 goodwill it would have been credited against the goodwill recognised as an intangible asset).

Occasionally the terms of the agreement may be such that it is impossible to say whether, and if so how much, additional consideration will be paid, and in that case companies may have no option but to deal with the matter by disclosure, rather than by provision. Where consideration is only payable on profits which are in excess of those currently being earned or budgeted for by the target company, then it may be more appropriate to disclose only the contingent consideration. FRS 7 is clear, however, that even 'where it is not possible to estimate the total amounts payable with any degree of certainty, at least those amounts that are reasonably expected to be payable would be recognised'.[50]

A number of companies have not made any provision for contingent consideration but merely give disclosure of its existence, an example of which is shown below.

Extract 6.12: Carclo plc (2000)

29 Acquisition [extract]

On 4 December 2000 Finespark (Horsham) Limited (trading as the Alan Group) was acquired for the sum of £6.924 million including costs.

Deferred cash consideration of up to a maximum £1.100 million is payable contingent upon the business achieving minimum operating profit targets in the two years ended 31 March 2003. The deferred consideration has not been provided.

Where contingent consideration is to be satisfied by the issue of shares, then as FRS 7 explains 'there is no obligation to transfer economic benefits and, accordingly, amounts recognised would be reported as part of shareholders' funds, for example as a separate caption representing shares to be issued. In the analysis of shareholders' funds, amounts would be attributed to equity and non-equity interests depending on the nature of the shares to be issued, in accordance with FRS 4 "Capital Instruments". When the shares are issued, appropriate transfers would be necessary between any amounts then held in shareholders' funds in respect of their issue and called up share capital and share premium.'[51]

In some situations the acquirer has an option to issue either shares or cash; because there is no obligation to transfer economic benefits then this future consideration is not a liability. Accordingly, the standard states that the expected future consideration should be accounted for as a credit to shareholders' funds (as explained above) until an irrevocable decision regarding the form of consideration has been taken. Where the vendor has the choice, then the expected future consideration represents an obligation to the vendor and should be accounted for as a liability until the shares are issued or the cash is paid.[52] One company which includes contingent consideration within shareholders' funds is Vodafone as shown below:

Extract 6.13: Vodafone Group Plc (2001)

CONSOLIDATED BALANCE SHEET at 31 March 2001 [extract]

	Note	2001 £m	2000 £m
Capital and reserves			
Called-up share capital	19	**4,054**	3,797
Share premium account	20	**48,292**	39,577
Merger reserve	20	**96,914**	96,914
Other reserve	20	**1,024**	1,120
Profit and loss account	20	**(5,869)**	(575)
Shares to be issued	19	**978**	–
Total equity shareholders' funds		**145,393**	142,833

NOTES TO THE CONSOLIDATED FINANCIAL STATEMENTS [extract]

19 Called up share capital [extract]

Following the receipt of regulatory approvals and the agreement of Swisscom AG's shareholders, the acquisition of a 25% equity interest in Swisscom Mobile SA was completed. The Company satisfied the first tranche of consideration by the issue of 422,869,008 ordinary shares and the payment of CHF 25 million in cash. The second tranche will be satisfied in ordinary shares or cash, or a combination of both, at the Company's discretion and is payable by March 2002. The deferred consideration of approximately £978m has been disclosed as 'Shares to be issued' within equity shareholders' funds.

22 Acquisitions and disposals [extract]

The Group completed the acquisition of a 25% interest in Swisscom Mobile SA for a total consideration of £1,828m. The consideration will be settled in two tranches. The first tranche was settled with the issue of new ordinary shares with a value of £840m and £10m in cash. The second tranche or approximately £978m will be satisfied in ordinary shares or cash, or a combination of both, at the Group's discretion and is payable by March 2002. The share of net assets acquired is provisionally calculated as £57m, resulting in goodwill of £1,771m, and no significant fair value adjustments have been made.

2.3.6 *Purchase consideration or payment for employee services?*

FRS 7 discusses the situation where acquisition agreements may require payments to be made in various forms, for example as non-competition payments or as bonuses to the vendors who continue to work for the acquired company. The standard states that 'in such circumstances, it is necessary to determine whether the substance of the agreement is payment for the business acquired, or an expense such as compensation for services or profit sharing. In the first case the expected payments would be accounted for as contingent purchase consideration; in the other case the payments would be treated as expenses of the period to which they relate.'[53]

In making an acquisition, an acquirer may have to make loyalty bonuses or other payments to secure the services of key (or all) employees of the target company. It is sometimes argued that such costs should be considered as part of the cost of the acquisition. However, despite FRS 7 being silent on this issue, it is clear from the discussion above that these are compensation for employee services and not part of the cost of the business acquired. It would be incongruous for payments made to non-vendor employees to be treated as a cost of the acquisition but not payments to vendor employees. Similarly, if in such circumstances the acquirer grants options to the employees, then these again should not be considered as part of the cost of the acquisition, but as compensation for future services of the employees. If such options are granted at an exercise price below the market price of the company's shares at the date of grant (or the book value of any shares purchased by an ESOP), UITF 17 will require a charge to be made in the profit and loss account. The requirements of UITF 17 are discussed more fully at 2.5.4 of Chapter 22.

Another issue is where the target company has outstanding share options granted to its employees under various employee share schemes. In some cases, such schemes will contain a 'change of control' clause which will allow the employees to exercise their options and accept the offer made by the acquiring company for the target's shares. Clearly, in that situation any consideration paid by the acquiring company will be treated as part of the cost of the acquisition, with any proceeds received by the target company increasing its net assets at the date of acquisition.

As an alternative to the above, the acquiring company may make a cash payment to the employees equivalent to the intrinsic value of the options based on the offer price for the shares in return for the employees giving up their rights under the option schemes. Although in this case the employees have not become shareholders, and therefore it could be argued that this is not a transaction with the shareholders, the overall effect is the same as if they had exercised their options and therefore we believe that such payments can be regarded as part of the cost of the acquisition.

Another alternative would be for the acquiring company to grant fresh options over its own shares to replace those already held by the employees over the shares of the target company. This is likely to happen in those situations where the employees are unable to exercise their options due to the fact that at the date of acquisition they have not satisfied all the performance criteria relating to the options. Arguably, since the employees do not yet have any vested rights in the shares then any intrinsic value in the replacement options is in respect of their service from the date of acquisition and therefore should be recognised as an expense in the profit and loss account over the remainder of the performance period. Another view would be that to the extent that the intrinsic value relates to past services up to the date of the acquisition then that portion should be expensed immediately at the date of acquisition, with the balance recognised over the remainder of the performance period. One company which has adopted a different approach and included a value for unvested options as part of the cost of an acquisition is Vodafone as shown in the following extract:

Extract 6.14: Vodafone AirTouch Plc (2000)

Notes to the Consolidated Financial Statements [extract]

21 Acquisitions and disposals [extract]

Merger with AirTouch Communications, Inc.

	£m
Consideration satisfied by:	
Vodafone AirTouch ordinary shares	38,467
Cash consideration	3,477
Unvested options	1,165
Tax on unvested options	(449)
Other	36
	42,696

Although there is no indication in the above extract as to how the value of the unvested options has been determined, it has been suggested by other commentators that the intrinsic value of such unvested options which relate to services up to the date of acquisition should be regarded as part of the cost of acquisition, rather than reflected as a post-acquisition expense. This issue is discussed further in 2.5.4 F in Chapter 22.

2.3.7 *Acquisition expenses*

FRS 7 takes a deliberately restrictive view as to what acquisition expenses should be treated as part of the cost of the acquisition in order to avoid the danger of overstating the cost of acquisition. The standard requires that only 'fees and similar incremental costs incurred directly in making an acquisition should, except for the issue costs of shares and other securities that are required by FRS 4 "Capital Instruments" to be accounted for as a reduction in the proceeds of a capital instrument, be included in the cost of acquisition. Internal costs and other expenses that cannot be directly attributed to the acquisition should be charged to the profit and loss account.'[54] Issue costs in respect of capital instruments are discussed in Chapter 17 at 2.2.5 A. Costs which may be capitalised as part of the cost of an acquisition include 'incremental costs such as professional fees paid to merchant banks, accountants, legal advisers, valuers and other consultants'; they do not include 'any allocation of costs that would still have been incurred had the acquisition not been entered into – for example, the costs of maintaining an acquisitions department or management remuneration'.[55]

One issue that the UITF was asked to consider was whether costs such as arrangement fees for bridging finance facilities, participation fees and costs of researching alternative financing arrangements for a takeover could properly be included in the cost of an acquisition (and thus in effect in goodwill). The UITF having discussed the issue took the view that the requirements of FRSs 4 and 7 were sufficiently clear and that there was consequently no need to issue an abstract. Incidental financing costs that do not themselves fall to be accounted for under FRS 4 are not incremental costs incurred directly in making an acquisition and therefore should not be included as part of the cost of the acquisition, but should be written off immediately.[56]

Despite the UITF's assertion that the requirements of FRSs 4 and 7 are sufficiently clear there may well be an overlap in the nature of costs incurred and therefore it is likely to be necessary for some allocation to be made.

The Companies Act also allows 'such amount (if any) in respect of fees and other expenses of the acquisition as the company may determine' to be included in arriving at the cost of the acquisition.[57]

2.3.8 *Pre-acquisition dividends*

Although it has no bearing on the determination of the fair value of the consideration given under FRS 7, one question which sometimes arises is how the acquiring company should account for dividends received from the subsidiary out of its pre-acquisition profits. The rules on this are less than clear. The traditional view was that this was, in effect, a return of the capital paid to acquire the company and was not in any sense a profit, and that accordingly it should be applied to reduce the cost of the investment in the acquiring company's balance sheet. This view was supported by some rather arcane wording that used to be in paragraph 15(5) of Schedule 8 to the Companies Act 1948, but this was changed in the Companies Act 1981.[58] This was also the conclusion favoured by Accountants Digest No. 189 on SSAP 23.[59]

Appendix I to FRS 6 does address the topic but does not come out with a firm conclusion. It states that 'where a dividend is paid to the acquiring or issuing company out of pre-combination profits, it would appear that it need not necessarily be applied as a reduction in the carrying value of the investment in the subsidiary undertaking. Such a dividend received should be applied to reduce the carrying value of the investment to the extent necessary to provide for a diminution in value of the investment in the subsidiary undertaking as stated in the accounts of the parent company. To the extent that this is not necessary, it appears that the amount received will be realised profit in the hands of the parent company.'[60]

The more widely accepted view of the law is now that the question of whether or not pre-acquisition dividends have to be written off against the cost of the investment has to be subdivided into two sub-questions:

(a) does the receipt of the dividend constitute a realised profit in the financial statements of the holding company? and

(b) does provision for impairment have to be made against the cost of the investment?

This approach has been confirmed in the draft Technical Release – *The determination of realised profits and distributable profits in the context of the Companies Act 1985*, which takes the view that such dividends should be treated in the same way as any other dividend which it receives from a subsidiary.[61]

For dividends received or receivable from a subsidiary to be treated as a realised profit, the consideration must be in the form of 'qualifying consideration'.[62] This term is discussed further at 2.1 in Chapter 3. The paper goes on to say that it will also be necessary to consider the effect any dividend has on the value of the investment in the subsidiary and, where its recoverable amount has fallen below book value, to take account of the effect of any such impairment.[63] It is this latter issue which really needs to be considered.

The Companies Act requires provision to be made only for *permanent* diminution in the value of a fixed asset. The view is sometimes advanced that, provided the investment will eventually recover the value which has been removed from it by making the distribution (by earning further profits, say) then it is unnecessary to write it down and hence the dividend to the holding company can be passed on to its own shareholders. Following this approach would allow an acquiring company to distribute immediately all the pre-acquisition profits shown in the subsidiary's balance sheet provided that it could foresee that the subsidiary would earn an equivalent amount of profits in the future. Even if this is good law, it is questionable whether it is good accounting. In our view any assessment of impairment should be based on FRS 11 – *Impairment of Fixed Assets and Goodwill* (see 2.2 of Chapter 13). That standard requires companies to carry out an impairment review of fixed assets, including investments in subsidiaries, if events or circumstances indicate that the carrying amount of the asset may not be recoverable. Although FRS 11 includes a list of examples of such indicators of impairment, the receipt of a pre-acquisition dividend from a subsidiary is not one of them. However, FRS 11 indicates that these are only examples and there have to be no other indications that an investment in a subsidiary has become impaired. It could be argued that if the subsidiary has paid a significant dividend out of pre-acquisition profits then the investment in the subsidiary *may* have become impaired, so an impairment test should be carried out. As such a test involves discounting future cash flows it may well be that an impairment loss needs to be recognised.

It should of course be pointed out that the above discussion is based on the premise that the cost of the investment in the holding company's books does represent the fair value of the subsidiary. There may be circumstances where it does not, such as when merger relief has been taken or if the subsidiary was not purchased in an arm's-length transaction, and obviously this could require a different view to be taken. In such a case there would seem to be no reason to write down the value of the investment unless the effect of the dividend was to reduce the underlying value of the subsidiary below its carrying amount in the financial statements of the holding company.

2.4 Acquisitions: measuring the fair value of the net assets acquired

2.4.1 *Basic principles*

The central requirement to bring in the assets of the subsidiary in the group accounts at their fair value rather than their book value in the subsidiary's accounts has been laid down in accounting standards for many years. However, until FRS 7, no standard elaborated in much detail on how this should be done.

The Companies Act takes a similar approach; it states that 'the identifiable assets and liabilities of the undertaking acquired shall be included in the consolidated balance sheet at their fair values at the date of the acquisition'.[64] The Act defines such assets and liabilities as those which are capable of being disposed of or discharged separately without necessarily disposing of a business of the undertaking.

The purpose of the fair value allocation is simply to establish a realistic starting point for the consolidation of the subsidiary's assets and results. The book values in the subsidiary's own financial statements are of no direct relevance for this purpose, because they do not stem from transactions of the reporting entity (the acquiring group), and in effect they are based on the original cost of what are second-hand assets from the group's point of view. The fair value exercise is an attempt to account fairly for the acquisition transaction by asking what the acquiring group has spent, and what it has got for its money.

Of course, the purchase price for most acquisitions is not settled on the basis of an analysis of the individual assets and liabilities of the target company; it is based instead on factors such as the earnings and cash flows which can be brought to the acquiring group. In that sense the purchase allocation exercise is an artificial one rather than portraying the results of a real analysis which has formed part of a business decision. Nevertheless such an allocation has to take place if the group is to be able to present consolidated financial statements, and the hypothetical nature of the allocation does not render it invalid.

The two basic questions which need to be answered in carrying out such an exercise are:

(a) what assets and liabilities have been acquired? and

(b) what values should be placed on them?

The answers to these questions depend on whether the exercise should be carried out based on the perspective of the acquiring company or not. An acquirer's perspective would mean that the acquirer's intentions regarding the future use of assets or the incurring of future costs would be allowed to be taken into account. On the basis of this perspective provision could be made in the fair value exercise for, for example, reorganisation costs. However, FRS 7 does not adopt such an approach, but adopts a 'neutral perspective.

The key to the approach adopted by the ASB in FRS 7 is that 'the identifiable assets and liabilities to be recognised should be those of the acquired entity that existed at the date of the acquisition'.[65] The standard defines identifiable assets and liabilities as those 'that are capable of being disposed of or settled separately, without disposing of a business of the entity'.[66] It indicates that these may include items that were not previously recognised in the accounts of the acquired company, such as pension surpluses or deficiencies and contingent assets.[67] It also indicates that identifiable liabilities include items such as onerous contracts or commitments that existed at the time of acquisition, whether or not the corresponding obligations were recognised as liabilities in the accounts of the acquired company.[68] Although these items were not recognised in the accounts of the acquired company, the ASB would nevertheless see them as assets and liabilities. The key point is that they existed at the date of the acquisition; they merely had not been recognised.

However, items such as provisions for reorganisation costs expected to be incurred as a result of the acquisition are not permitted; this is because they are not liabilities of the acquired company at the date of acquisition.[69] The perspective of the acquirer, the acquiring company management's intention to undertake a programme of reorganisation, is not relevant. In the acquired company at the time of acquisition there is no such programme contemplated which would justify provision – only if the acquired entity was already committed to the reorganisation, and unable realistically to withdraw from it, would it be regarded as pre-acquisition.

In Appendix III to FRS 7, the ASB explains that it takes the view that 'under its …Statement of Principles, management intent is not a sufficient basis for recognising changes to an entity's assets or liabilities. It is events, not intentions for future actions, that increase or decrease an entity's assets and liabilities. When intentions are translated into actions that commit the entity to particular courses of action, the accounting should then reflect any obligations or changes in assets that arise from those actions. In relation to acquisition accounting, the Board concluded that events of a post-acquisition period that resulted in the recognition of additional liabilities or the impairment of existing assets of an acquired entity should be reported as events of that period rather than of the pre-acquisition period.'[70]

FRS 7 says that its general principles will result in the following being treated as post-acquisition items:

(a) changes resulting from the acquirer's intentions or future actions;

(b) impairments, or other changes, resulting from events subsequent to the acquisition; and

(c) provisions or accruals for future operating losses or for reorganisation and integration costs expected to be incurred as a result of the acquisition, whether they relate to the acquired entity or to the acquirer.[71]

The recognised assets and liabilities are to be measured at fair values that reflect the conditions at the date of the acquisition.[72]

The requirements of FRS 7 for attributing fair values to particular categories of assets and liabilities are discussed at 2.4.3 below. FRS 7 defines 'fair value' as 'the amount at which an asset or liability could be exchanged in a transaction in an arm's length transaction between informed and willing parties, other than in a forced or liquidation sale'.[73]

Although most of the detailed rules are based on the perspective outlined above, there are occasions (for example, deferred tax) where they do not seem to be in accordance with the principle that they should not be affected by the acquirer's intentions.

One area where the judgement of the acquirer is still specifically important is in the choice of accounting policies to be used in recognising and measuring the assets and liabilities which have been acquired. Although FRS 7 sets out the general principles already discussed and sets out further specific rules which are discussed below, it allows that subject to these, fair values should be determined in accordance with the acquirer's accounting policies for similar assets and liabilities. One particular area where this will be important is in the discretion allowed to reporting entities in the calculation of cost. For example, a property development company which does not capitalise interest into the cost of its developments may acquire a company which does. (Rather surprisingly, the standard appears to imply that the fair value of development stocks should be calculated with reference to cost rather than market value.) In that case, the fair value of the acquired company's developments should be calculated according to the acquirer's policies i.e. excluding interest. The post-acquisition profit shown on disposal of the developments will therefore be higher in the hands of the acquirer than it would have been in the hands of the acquired company. Fair values are thus not independent of the acquirer's choices.

2.4.2 *The use of hindsight*

The fact that the fair value process is inevitably, to some degree, a rationalisation of the price paid after the event means that an accounting issue arises: how much hindsight can the acquirer impute into the values assigned, or must the allocation be based solely on the information which he had at the time when he was making his bid? There is a theoretical argument for the latter, which is that if he was unaware of a particular matter, such as the fact that there was a deficiency in the pension fund of the target, then it cannot have influenced the acquisition price and thus should not feature in any allocation of that price.

Whatever the merits of that view in theory, however, it cannot be used in practice. If the acquirer was only able to assign values to items that he knew about at the time of the acquisition, the exercise would in many cases be completely impossible, because, as noted above, most acquisitions are not primarily based on an assessment of the value of the assets and liabilities of the target company. It is therefore necessary to allow the acquirer a reasonable period of time in which to investigate the assets and liabilities which have been acquired and make a reasoned allocation of values to them. The remaining question is, how much time should be allowed?

FRS 7 requires that adjustments to the fair values of assets and liabilities should be fixed, if possible, by the date at which the accounts for the first full financial year following the acquisition are approved by the directors. If that is not possible, however, provisional valuations should be made (and disclosed as such). These should be amended, if necessary, in the next financial statements for the first full financial year following the acquisition, with a corresponding adjustment to goodwill.[74]

Thereafter, adjustments should be recognised as profits or losses when identified. The only circumstances in which a retrospective adjustment to the goodwill calculation could be regarded as appropriate would be if the original allocation was regarded as a fundamental error which required to be dealt with as a prior year adjustment under FRS 3.[75] This would probably be the case only if the original allocation was based on a complete misinterpretation of the facts which were available at the time; it would not apply simply because new information had come to light which changed the acquiring management's view of the value of the item in question.

As indicated at 2.4.1 above, the recognised assets and liabilities are to be measured at fair values that reflect the conditions at the date of the acquisition. So whatever period of hindsight is used, therefore, it is important that the allocation reflects conditions as they existed at the date of the acquisition, rather than being affected by subsequent events. There is a parallel to be drawn here with the accounting treatment of post-balance sheet events; only those events which provide further evidence of conditions as they existed at the acquisition date should be taken into account.

A number of extracts in this chapter make it clear that the fair value assessment is provisional and therefore it may be that further adjustments will be required in the following year. One company which made further adjustments was Reckitt & Colman as illustrated in Extracts 6.42 to 6.44 at 2.8.2 below.

2.4.3 *Requirements for individual assets and liabilities*

The requirements of FRS 7 for each class of asset or liability are set out below.

A Non-monetary assets

FRS 7 states that, 'where similar assets are bought and sold on a readily accessible market, the market price will represent the fair value. Where quoted market prices are not available, market prices can often be estimated, either by independent valuations, or valuation techniques such as discounting estimated future cash flows to their present values. In some cases, where quoted market prices are not available, subsequent sales of acquired assets may provide the most reliable evidence of fair value at the time of the acquisition.'[76]

An important factor which this fails to address is whether the market price is intended to be a buying price or a selling price, and this confusion pervades much of the standard. Also, although the passage cited above might suggest that market values, if available, are to be used for all non-monetary assets, it is clear that this is not always to be the case. For example, it is not envisaged that stocks of finished goods are included at their sales value, but on the other hand, the discussion of investments implies that a sales price is being discussed. In contrast, FRED 7 (the exposure draft which immediately preceded FRS 7) contained a more understandable general rule, which was not carried through to the standard, that non-monetary assets were to be measured at the lower of replacement cost and recoverable amount.[77] It is not clear what the ASB intended by making that change, particularly since some of the more detailed discussion continues to reflect the terms of the exposure draft.

Where the value of an asset is impaired due, for example, to lack of profitability, underutilisation or obsolescence, such that the replacement cost is not recoverable in full, the fair value is the estimated recoverable amount.[78] 'Recoverable amount' is described as 'the greater of the net realisable value of an asset and, where appropriate, the value in use', which is in turn defined as 'the present value of the future cash flows obtainable as a result of an asset's continued use, including those resulting from the ultimate disposal of the asset'.[79] This is similar to the 'value to the business' rule for valuing assets advocated in the ASB's *Statement of Principles* (see 5.7 of Chapter 2) and now incorporated within FRS 11 (see 2.2 of Chapter 13).

The recoverable amount should reflect the condition of the asset on acquisition but not any impairments resulting from subsequent events.[80] FRS 7 emphasises that where acquired assets that had not been impaired before acquisition are subsequently disposed of for a reduced price (for example, as part of a post-acquisition reorganisation of the enlarged group), any losses resulting from their disposal are to be treated as post-acquisition losses, not as adjustments to the fair values as at the acquisition date.[81]

FRS 7 contains more detailed provisions for particular types of non-monetary asset as follows:

I Tangible fixed assets

'The fair value of a tangible fixed asset should be based on:

(a) market value, if assets similar in type and condition are bought and sold on an open market; or

(b) depreciated replacement cost, reflecting the acquired business's normal buying process and the sources of supply and prices available to it.'

The fair value should not exceed the recoverable amount of the asset.[82]

The standard also suggests that in some circumstances, the historical cost of an asset updated by the use of price indices may be the most reliable means of estimating replacement cost. Where prices have not changed materially, or where no relevant price indices are available, it would be acceptable to use a carrying value based on historical cost as a reasonable proxy for fair value.[83]

Examples of fair value adjustments in respect of tangible fixed assets are illustrated in the following extracts:

Extract 6.15: The Royal Bank of Scotland Group plc (2000)

41 Acquisitions [extract]

The acquisitions made by the Group during the 15 months ended 31 December 2000 are set out below. All acquisitions have been accounted for using acquisition accounting principles.

(a) National Westminster Bank plc and its Subsidiaries

On 6 March 2000, the Group's offer for the entire issued ordinary share capital of NatWest was declared unconditional in all respects.

The fair values of the assets and liabilities of NatWest and its subsidiaries at the date of acquisition, and the consideration paid, were as follows:

	Book value of net assets acquired £m	Revaluations (note i) £m	Accounting policy alignments (note ii) £m	Other adjustments (note iii) £m	Fair value to the Group £m
Cash and balances at central banks and items in the course of collection	3,680	–	–	–	3,680
Treasury and other eligible bills	2,736	–	–	–	2,736
Loans and advances to banks	32,952	(25)	–	–	32,927
Loans and advances to customers	89,235	(22)	–	–	89,213
Debt securities	37,857	48	–	–	37,905
Equity shares	301	149	–	–	450
Intangible fixed assets	533	(533)	–	–	–
Tangible fixed assets	3,574	(130)	100	–	3,544
Other assets	22,473	(186)	–	1,139	23,426
Subsidiaries held for resale	106	1,137	–		1,243
Deposits by banks and items in the course of transmission	(26,612)	5	–	–	(26,607)
Customer accounts	(97,959)	(28)	–	–	(97,987)
Debt securities in issue	(10,309)	–	–	–	(10,309)
Other liabilities	(42,105)	(429)	(78)	(637)	(43,249)
Subordinated liabilities	(6,763)	(137)	–	–	(6,900)
Preference shares	(488)	13	–	–	(475)
Net assets	9,211	(138)	22	502	9,597
Goodwill					11,390
Consideration paid					20,987
Satisfied by:					
Issue of 1,563.5 million new RBSG 25 pence ordinary shares to NatWest ordinary shareholders (note iv)					13,462
Payment of cash to NatWest ordinary shareholders (note v)					7,110
Issue of loan notes to NatWest ordinary shareholders (note v)					239
Fees and expenses relating to the acquisition					176
					20,987

Notes

(i) Revaluations reflect the restatement of assets and liabilities of NatWest to their estimated fair values at the date of acquisition, and the related tax effect, as follows:
- financial instruments at market value, or, where market values are not available, discounted estimated future cash flows less provisions for irrecoverable amounts where appropriate;
- freehold and leasehold properties at existing use value, or, where properties were not occupied by NatWest, either open market value or, in the case of development properties, replacement cost; in the case of leasehold properties, an asset or liability is recognised to reflect rents payable below, or above, current market rents;
- other fixed assets at estimated depreciated replacement cost or net recoverable amount if lower;
- other assets at lower of cost and net realisable amount;
- business subsequently sold, at the net sales proceeds.

(ii) Accounting policy alignments reflect the adoption of Group accounting policies in respect of capitalisation of certain software costs, hedge accounting, and recognition of mortgage incentives and insurance commission, together with the related tax effects.

(iii) Other adjustments reflect the recognition, together with the related tax effects, of the deferred contingent consideration arising from NatWest's disposal of Bancorp in 1996; the actuarial surplus on the NatWest pension funds, to the extent that it is expected to be recoverable; and additional provisions relating to costs crystallised on the change of control, together with other provisions including litigation, reassessed by the Group management at the date of acquisition.

(iv) The 'Consideration paid' information above is based on the closing price on the London Stock Exchange on 3 March 2000, the trading day immediately prior to the offer for NatWest being declared unconditional in all respects, of 861 pence per RBSG ordinary share of 25 pence.

(v) NatWest ordinary shareholders had the right to receive, for each NatWest share held, 0.968 new RBSG 25 pence ordinary shares plus 400 pence in cash or loan notes. A 'Partial cash alternative' was also offered, which, for each NatWest share held, consisted of 0.92 new RBSG 25 pence ordinary shares plus 450 pence in cash or loan notes.

(vi) The goodwill arising on acquisition is being amortised over its estimated economic life of 20 years, resulting in a charge of £570 million per annum.

It can be seen from the above extract that the Royal Bank of Scotland has incorporated valuation adjustments for tangible fixed assets other than properties. It is fair to say that although most companies will make adjustments to include properties at a valuation, very few companies appear to make similar adjustments for plant and machinery. However, that is not to say that no fair value adjustments are made in respect of such assets. It can be seen from Extract 6.9 at 2.3.5 above that Logica has an adjustment to align the depreciation policy in line with that of the group.

Arguably such adjustments to reflect the acquirer's depreciation methods or lives are not necessary to align the accounting policies of the two companies as they both had policies to depreciate the assets over their useful service lives. If the target company were to change its depreciation methods or asset lives to those adopted by its new parent, then FRS 15 would not allow these to be dealt with by way of prior year adjustment as a change in accounting policy (see Chapter 12 at 2.3.3 B and 2.3.4).

Other companies which have made adjustments to reflect their own accounting policies are Oxford Instruments and Kingfisher, as shown below:

Extract 6.16: Oxford Instruments plc (1999)

17 Acquisitions [extract]

Vickers Medical Neurology Business

As reported last year on 18 December 1997 the Group acquired the entire share capital of all the companies comprising the neurology business of Vickers PLC Medical Division. The total cash consideration previously indicated as £12.9 million has now been finalised and settled at £11.0 million, including costs of acquisition.

The fair values attributed to the business at the date of the acquisition have now been finalised and were:

	Book value £000	Accounting policy alignment £000	Fair value adjustments £000	Fair value to the Group £000
Tangible fixed assets	3,434	(64)	(206)	3,164
Stocks	6,854	(463)	(1,133)	5,258
Debtors	11,715	–	(668)	11,047
Cash at bank and in hand	4,106			4,106
Bank overdrafts and loans	(2,349)	–	–	(2,349)
Creditors	(17,197)	(182)	(863)	(18,242)
Taxation	466	286	(293)	459
Net assets	7,029	(423)	(3,163)	3,443
Negative goodwill				(2,057)
Cash consideration				1,386
Cash at bank and in hand acquired				(4,106)
Bank overdrafts and loans acquired				13,725
Net outflow of cash in respect of the purchase				11,005

The fair value adjustments for the alignment of accounting policies reflect the adoption of Group accounting policies in respect of fixed asset capitalisation, stock provisioning including accelerated depreciation of demonstration stocks, stock overhead absorption, warranty and holiday pay entitlements.

The revaluation adjustments in respect of tangible fixed assets include the write off of obsolete plant, machinery and computers. The revaluation of stocks reflect the write down to estimated realisable value. The revaluation of debtors relates wholly to bad debt provisioning to reflect the estimated recoverable value. The revaluation of creditors relates to liabilities which were not fully reflected in the balance sheet on acquisition. These include provisions for reorganisation which relate to the following areas:

	£000
Provision for the transfer of needle manufacturing operation from the US to UK	183
Provision for the reduction in the headcount in Northern Europe	275
Provision for the reorganisation of manufacturing in the UK	170

All the reorganisation provisions relate to commitments made prior to the date of acquisition. Net deferred tax assets have not been recognised.

Extract 6.17: Kingfisher plc (1999)

37 Acquisitions [extract]

(c) Acquisition of Wegert

On 29 June 1998 the Group acquired a 60% interest in Wegert-Verwaltungs GmbH & Co Beteiligungs-KG (Wegert), a German electrical retailer. Simultaneously, Wegert purchased the entire share capital of the German electrical ProMarkt Holding GmbH (ProMarkt) using cash from its own resources for the equivalent of £14.5m. These transactions have been accounted for using acquisition accounting.

Details of these transactions showing fair value adjustments are set out in the table below:

£ millions	Book value	Fair value adjustments: Revaluations	Accounting policy alignments	Fair value to the Group
Intangible fixed assets	8.6	–	(8.6)	–
Tangible fixed assets	17.7	–	7.4	25.1
Investments	3.5	–	–	3.5
Stocks	67.5	(2.6)	–	64.9
Other current assets	24.0	–	(0.7)	23.3
Creditors	(101.9)	–	(8.3)	(110.2)
	19.4	(2.6)	(10.2)	6.6

£ millions	Goodwill arising
Consideration	54.7
Net assets acquired (60% of £6.6m)	(4.1)
Goodwill	50.6
Consideration satisfied by:	
Cash (Including £2.7m acquisition expenses)	54.7

The fair value revaluation adjustment was made in the books of Wegert at acquisition in respect of unprovided risks relating to slow moving stocks and stocks with decreasing sales prices.

Accounting policy alignments have been made in the books of Wegert to eliminate internally generated goodwill, to eliminate historical acquisition goodwill, to apply UK finance lease accounting to a property asset, to write off pre-opening expenses capitalised on loss making stores and to apply UK pension accounting.

The book values of the assets and liabilities have been translated using the exchange rate at the date of acquisition of £1: DM 2.910.

It can be seen that in these situations the difference in accounting policy for fixed assets was not in respect of differences in depreciation policy but, in the case of Oxford Instruments, whether or not the policy was to capitalise the particular type of asset and, in the case of Kingfisher, to align the policy with UK GAAP. It can be seen from Extract 6.15 above, that the Royal Bank of Scotland also made an adjustment with respect to its policy of capitalising certain software costs.

II Intangible assets

FRS 7 does not define or explain what it means when it refers to intangible assets; it merely says that, 'where an intangible asset is recognised, its fair value should be based on its replacement cost, which is normally its estimated market value'.[84] In other words, FRS 7 does not mandate the recognition of intangible assets, it only requires them to be accounted for in a certain way *if* the decision is made to recognise them.

However, FRS 10 requires that intangible assets within the scope of that standard which are acquired as part of the acquisition of a business should be recognised separately as long as a reliable value can be placed on such assets. The option of not recognising such intangible assets is no longer available under FRS 10. The intangible assets must be recognised if they meet the 'measured reliably' criterion of FRS 10. However, this may be somewhat illusory since it would still be possible for the acquiror to take the view that some acquired intangible assets could not be measured reliably. This is discussed further in Chapter 11 at 2.3.3.

One other change that FRS 10 has made is that any value that is attributed to such intangible assets is to be limited to such an amount that neither creates nor increases negative goodwill arising on the acquisition.[85]

The main issue is to what extent assets such as brand names or newspaper titles can be regarded as part of the identifiable assets as defined.

One company which recognises such intangible assets (and makes fair value adjustments to the items already recognised) is Johnson Press as shown below.

Extract 6.18: Johnston Press plc (2000)

14. Fixed Asset Investments [extract]

Acquisition of subsidiary undertakings

On 13 June 2000 the Company through its wholly owned subsidiary, Johnston Publishing Ltd, acquired the entire issued shared capital of Four Counties Newspapers Ltd and Lincolnshire Standard Group Ltd. The total consideration amounted to £16,387,030 and was paid for wholly in cash. The fair value of net assets acquired are outlined below:

	Book value	Adjustments	Fair value to Group
	£'000	£'000	£'000
Fixed assets			
Tangible	964	(261) a	703
Intangible	100	15,817 d	15,917
Current assets			
Stock	17	(17) e	–
Debtors	793	(92) b	701
Cash in bank	74	–	74
Total assets	**1,948**	**15,447**	**17,395**
Creditors			
Finance leases	9	–	9
Other creditors	237	–	237
Taxes and social security costs	254	–	254
Accruals	361	147 c	508
Total liabilities	861	147	1,008
Net assets	**1,087**	**15,300**	**16,387**

The fair value accounting adjustments are:

a Additional depreciation in respect of plant and machinery to align to Group policy.
b Addition provision for bad debts.
c Additional accruals.
d Value of publishing titles.
e Amount to write down stocks to align to Group policy.

	£'000
Summary of fair value of publishing titles capitalised on acquisition of:	
Portsmouth & Sunderland Newspapers plc	126
Four Counties Newspapers/Lincolnshire Standard Group	15,917
Total (note 12)	16,043

The adjustment of £126,000 represents an additional fair value adjustment to the value of the Portsmouth & Sunderland Newspapers plc titles acquired in 1999.

Other examples are shown in Chapter 11 at 2.2.1 and 2.3.3.

An example of a company which has made a fair value adjustment on the basis of aligning accounting policies, to eliminate intangible assets previously recognised by the target company, is Vodafone, as shown below:

Extract 6.19: Vodafone Group Plc (1999)

20 Acquisitions and disposals [extract]
Acquisition of subsidiary undertakings
Vodafone New Zealand

	Balance sheet acquisition £m	Fair value adjustments (2), (3) £m	Accounting policy conformity (4) £m	Fair value balance sheet £m
Tangible fixed assets	94.8	–	–	94.8
Intangible fixed assets	136.5	–	(134.8)	1.7
Other net current assets/(liabilities)	1.0	(0.8)	(1.7)	(1.5)
	232.3	(0.8)	(136.5)	95.0
Goodwill				139.6
Cash consideration paid				234.6

Notes

1. The table above sets out details of the acquisition of the New Zealand GSM cellular network and related assets, radio communication rights and licences.
   The transaction was completed on 30 October 1998.
2. Adjustments to net current assets primarily comprise stock provisions and other accruals.
3. Due to the proximity of the acquisition to the year end, fair value adjustments are provisional.
4. Under UK GAAP, the intangible fixed assets acquired have been included within goodwill on consolidation. Deferred payments for licences have been accrued and capitalised in accordance with Group policy.

It is not entirely clear from the above extract what the intangible assets actually were, but it would appear from Note 1 that they may have been radio communications rights and licences. If that is the case it seems strange that under UK GAAP they have been included within goodwill rather than being recognised separately.

These rules introduced by FRS 10 only apply to those intangibles within its scope. They therefore do not apply to:

(a) oil and gas exploration and development costs; and

(b) research and development costs.

This raises one further area of interest which is the interplay between the acquiring company's own accounting policy for development costs and the requirements of FRS 7. For example, a computer software development company may base its own accounting policy on the treatments permitted by SFAS 86 (the US standard on the topic). This is very much more prescriptive, and restrictive, about the capitalisation of software development costs than the more general rules in SSAP 13 (see Chapter 11 at 2.4). In particular, all expenditures are written off until technological feasibility, strictly evidenced by a working model, has been established. If such a company buys another software company, the target may have several valuable products on the brink of commercial realisation – this may indeed be the reason for the acquisition. However, despite the value of such products, there would appear to be no requirement for the acquiring company to attempt to ascribe a fair value to them. FRS 7 refers only to situations where an intangible is recognised – if the accounting policies of the acquirer do not call for recognition, there is no need to include any amount in respect of the software products in the fair value exercise. This is likely to enhance post-acquisition profits since the amortisation, if any, of the enhanced figure for goodwill may be over a longer period than any amortisation of the development costs if they had been recognised separately.

III Stocks and work in progress

FRS 7 requires that 'stocks including commodity stocks, that the acquired entity trades on a market in which it participates as both a buyer and a seller should be valued at current market prices'.[86]

However, 'other stocks, and work-in-progress, should be valued at the lower of replacement cost and net realisable value. Replacement cost is for this purpose the cost at which the stocks would have been replaced by the acquired entity, reflecting its normal buying process and the sources of supply and prices available to it – that is, the current cost of bringing the stocks to their present location and condition.'[87] For example, for a business purchasing in wholesale markets the replacement cost would be the wholesale price.

On the other hand, the replacement cost of manufactured stocks and work-in-progress would normally be the current cost of manufacturing based, for example, on current standard costs where these are employed. The standard does indicate that in practice, where there is a short manufacturing cycle, replacement cost may not be materially different from historical cost.[88]

For long-term maturing stocks, replacement cost would be based on market values if stocks at similar stages are regularly traded in the market. In other situations, a surrogate for replacement cost may be the historical cost of bringing such stock to its present location and condition, including an amount representing an interest cost in respect of holding the stock.[89] For long-term contracts, the standard envisages that no fair value adjustments will be made, other than those that would normally result from assessing the outcome of the contract under SSAP 9, or reflecting the changeover to the acquirer's accounting policies.[90]

Another issue which FRS 7 addresses is the effect of incorporating stocks at their net realisable value. The standard states that where an acquirer reaches a judgement about the value of slow-moving or redundant stocks that differs from that of the management of the acquired company, any material write-down of the carrying value of stocks in the acquired company's books before or at the time of the acquisition needs to be justified by the circumstances of the acquired company before acquisition. If exceptional profits appear to have been earned on the realisation of stocks after the date of the acquisition, the fair values should be re-examined and, if necessary, an adjustment made to these values and a corresponding adjustment to goodwill.[91] This is clearly aimed at ensuring that acquirers do not make excessive provisions against the carrying value of stock, but then sell the stock at prices which give rise to a profit.

Although the standard appears to be very strict about write-downs, it is nevertheless the case that the acquirer can genuinely have a view about the value of slow moving or redundant stocks that differs from that of the management of the acquired entity. Existing management, particularly if the company has been going through a hard time with poor profitability, may have actively resisted write-downs in the value of the stock. The acquiring management may feel less accountable for the levels of such stock and feel able to take a much more critical look at its value.

One company which would appear to have had a significantly different view of the value of stock compared to that of the existing management is Kingfisher in relation to its acquisition of part of Norweb Retail in 1996, as indicated below:

Extract 6.20: Kingfisher plc (1997)

28 Acquisitions [extract]

On 24 November 1996, Comet Group PLC completed the purchase of a substantial part of Norweb Retail, a division of Norweb plc. Details of the net assets acquired are given in the following table:

£ millions	Book value at acquisition	Revaluation adjustments	Fair value to the Group
Tangible fixed assets	23.2	(3.2)	20.0
Stocks	55.2	(25.2)	30.0
Provision for reorganisation	(22.0)	–	(22.0)
Warranty provision	(4.2)	–	(4.2)
	52.2	(28.4)	23.8
Goodwill written off to reserves			1.2
Net cost of acquisition satisfied wholly in cash			25.0

The revaluation adjustments are made to reflect the fair value of the net assets acquired.

The provision for reorganisation of £22.0m relates to the closure of the Norweb high street stores which had been a commitment prior to acquisition. A further post acquisition provision has been charged in this year's profit and loss account of £8.7m relating to the reorganisation of the combined portfolio of out of town stores.

Although there are other examples of companies making fair value write-downs in respect of the net realisable values of stocks acquired the impact is not as great as that in the extract above. It is also fair to say that there do not appear to be many examples whereby adjustments are made to increase book values of stocks, although this may be due to the fact that replacement cost is not materially different from book values given the current low levels of inflation.

Where adjustments have been made to reduce the carrying value of stocks, an interesting question which then arises is where the new management turns the company around and generates a profit on the now written-down stock. Such a profit would be disclosable (see 2.8.2 below) but as discussed, FRS 7 also entertains the idea that the profit should not be taken, but that the fair values should be re-opened and the goodwill figure adjusted instead. It appears necessary, therefore, to assess what would have been the value of the stock in the target company, with the old management and prospects. The acquiring management may feel that the value of the stock was low, justifying its fair value exercise write-down. If the profits on the disposal of the stock have then been generated because of the new management's efforts in finding new outlets or uses for that stock then it is consistent with the philosophy of FRS 7 that those profits should be taken post-acquisition.

A further issue which arises in the context of the fair value of stocks is the calculation of cost. The accounting policy adopted for the identification of stock cost can legitimately differ as between the acquirer and the acquired company. Mention has already been made of the choice as to whether interest is capitalised into cost. In the context of stocks, issues such as the level of overheads to be costed into stocks are legitimate bases of difference as between companies. Application of the costing basis adopted by the acquiring company may result in quite legitimately lower stock carrying values being adopted by the acquiring company, and thus higher post-acquisition profits being reported. Thus, although the standard quite rightly directs attention to unusual post-acquisition profits being made on acquired stock, there can be acceptable reasons why such profits are not inappropriate.

One company which made fair value adjustments due to different policies in respect of determining the cost of stocks is Persimmon as shown in the following extract:

Extract 6.21: Persimmon plc (1996)

15 Acquisitions [extract]

On 26 February 1996 the company acquired the whole of the issued share capital of Ideal Homes Holdings Limited for a total consideration of £177,572,000. The consideration was satisfied by cash and the acquisition expenses amounted to £2,373,000. The acquisition has been accounted for by the acquisition method of accounting.

The consolidated assets and liabilities of Ideal Homes Holdings Limited acquired are set out below:

	Book value £'000	Revaluations £'000	Other adjustments £'000	Accounting policy alignment £'000	Fair value £'000
Tangible fixed assets	1,627	(480)	(336)	–	811
Investments	9,546	–	(1,000)	–	8,546
Stock	173,380	–	(3,917)	(3,437)	166,026
Debtors	13,217	–	(510)	–	12,707
Deferred tax	–	–	7,000	–	7,000
Total assets	197,770	(480)	1,237	(3,437)	195,090
Creditors	(41,733)	–	(1,307)	–	(43,040)
Net assets	156,037	(480)	(70)	(3,437)	152,050
Goodwill					27,895
Total cost of assets acquired					179,945

The book value of the assets and liabilities shown above have been taken from the management accounts of the acquired business at the date of acquisition.

The fair value adjustments above principally arise for the following reasons:

a. Revaluations representing the restatement of certain of the long leasehold properties acquired to their estimated market values.

b Other adjustments principally representing the:
- write down of fixed assets following a physical verification exercise and assessment of the realisable value of certain assets
- write down of investments following a review of the underlying net assets and assessment of their realisable value
- write down of stock following an assessment of the realisable value of work in progress and strategic land
- write down of debtors following an assessment of the estimated recoverable value
- recognition of unprovided amounts in respect of onerous contracts and other liabilities
- recognition of a deferred tax asset in respect of trading losses acquired

c. Accounting policy realignments, which align the accounting policies of the acquired group with those adopted by Persimmon. being principally the write-off of capitalised selling costs and ground rents which were both carried in stocks.

Another example, but in respect of work in progress, is Logica as shown in Extract 6.9 at 2.3.5 above.

One interesting fair value adjustment made in respect of stocks was that made by FKI in respect of its acquisition of Bridon. As shown in Extract 6.24 at 2.4.3 B below, an adjustment has been made to eliminate intercompany profit in stocks for the element which existed in Bridon in relation to stocks sold by other FKI companies prior to acquisition, amounting to £523,000. This would appear to have been made so that the stocks are reflected at 'cost' to the group. However, we do not believe this to be appropriate because FRS 7 regards replacement cost to be the cost at which the stocks would have been replaced by the acquired entity, rather than reflecting their value to the acquiring company.

IV Investments

FRS 7 says that 'quoted investments should be valued at market price, adjusted if necessary for unusual price fluctuations or for the size of the holding'.[92]

Little guidance is given as to how these values, or adjustments to them, are to be determined. As noted above, it is not clear whether the market price is that for a purchase or a sale and thus whether the adjustment for an unmarketable size of holding is intended to be made upwards or downwards. Rather confusingly, the standard comments that the adjustments for large holdings may be to reflect either a lower realisable value representing the difficulties of disposal or a higher value for a holding representing a substantial voting block.[93]

No specific guidance is given on the treatment of unquoted investments which therefore fall to be valued at the amount they could be exchanged at in an arm's length transaction between informed and willing parties. The standard does briefly discuss the valuation of unquoted instruments in the context of valuing capital instruments given as part of the consideration (see 2.3.2 above). Similar considerations would apply in the valuation of unquoted investments acquired.

One company which made a significant adjustment in respect of investments was Granada Group:

Extract 6.22: Granada Group PLC (1996)

25 Acquisition of Businesses [extract]

	Book value £m	Fair value adjustment £m	Fair value to Group £m
a Summary of the effect of the acquisition of Forte			
Tangible fixed assets	3,908.3	4.7	3,913.0
Investments	177.9	117.2	295.1
Stocks	29.6	(1.4)	28.2
Debtors	182.7	(8.1)	174.6
Creditors	(439.3)	(173.2)	(612.5)
Cash and cash equivalents	228.0	–	228.0
Corporation tax	(61.5)	–	(61.5)
Deferred taxation	(49.7)	–	(49.7)
Finance lease obligations	(517.6)	–	(517.6)
Borrowings	(981.8)	–	(981.8)
Minority interests	(63.5)	–	(63.5)
Net assets acquired	2,413.1	(60.8)	2,352.3
Shares issued			1,911.9
Cash paid (excluding share issue costs)			2,084.0
Fair value of consideration			3,995.9
Goodwill			(1,643.6)
			2,352.3

No indication is given in the accounts as to what the fair value adjustment was. However, the major investments held by Forte were its associates, The Savoy Hotel and ALPHA Airports Group, both of which were quoted.

An example of a company making adjustments in respect of unquoted investments is United Utilities, as shown below:

Extract 6.23: United Utilities PLC (1996)

Financial review [extract]
Acquisition of Norweb [extract]

The consideration was offset by the realisation of £300 million in cash on the disposal of Norweb's investments in the National Grid and the Pumped Storage Business. These proceeds exceeded our expectations at the time of the acquisition.

The investments in the National Grid and Pumped Storage Business were revalued upward by £199.6 million, net of £48 million tax provisions, reflecting the net proceeds received on disposal.

It can be seen that the investments have been valued at amounts subsequently realised, rather than the values which were expected to be realised at the time of the acquisition. This is consistent with the guidance in the standard in respect of businesses held for resale (see 2.4.3 G below).

B Monetary assets and liabilities

The standard states that 'the fair value of monetary assets and liabilities, including accruals and provisions, should take into account the amounts expected to be received or paid and their timing. Fair value should be determined by reference to market prices, where available, by reference to the current price at which the business could acquire similar assets or enter into similar obligations, or by discounting to present value.'[94]

Short-term monetary items, such as trade debtors and creditors, will be recognised at the amount expected to be received or paid on settlement or redemption. It is unlikely that these will require to be discounted. However, the fair values of certain long-term monetary items may be materially different from their book values. This is designed to deal with the situation, say, where the acquired company has long-term debt with a fixed rate of interest that no longer reflects current rates. Another example is a material long-term debtor where the delay in settlement is not compensated for by an interest charge reflecting current rates.

FRS 7 does not specify a discount rate which is appropriate for all situations. It states that 'the choice of interest rate to be applied to long-term borrowings would be affected by current lending rates for an equivalent term, the credit standing of the issuer and the nature of any security'. (The reference to the issuer suggests that the interest rate is to be specific to the acquired company, not that of the acquirer, which is consistent with the standard's general approach.) 'For long-term debtors (after any necessary provisions had been made) the interest rate would be based on current lending rates.'[95]

The differences between fair values arrived at by discounting and the total amounts receivable or payable in respect of the relevant items represent discounts or premiums on acquisition and are dealt with as interest income or expense by allocation to accounting periods over the term of the monetary amounts at a constant rate based on their carrying amounts, along the lines of FRS 4.[96]

Example 6.1: Effect of discounting long-term loans

A company, X plc, acquires another, Y plc on 1 January 1999. Y has a fixed rate bank loan of £10,000 taken out when interest rates were higher. It is committed to a rate of 10% pa on this borrowing which is due for repayment in two years. Interest is payable annually in one year and two years' time and the principal is to be repaid with the final interest payment. If it took a two year loan out at the time of the acquisition, it would be able to obtain a rate of only 6%.

Under FRS 7 the fair value of the loan is :

$$[£1{,}000 \div 1.06] + [£11{,}000 \div (1.06^2)]$$
$$= £10{,}733$$

The acquired loan would therefore be recorded at this figure.

The accounting should therefore be as follows. The profit and loss account charge for the first period will be £1,000, the coupon, reduced by a debit to the carrying value of the loan of £356. This gives a 'correct' charge of £644 for the period being £10,733 x 6%. The carrying value of the loan is then £10,377.

The charge for the second period will be £1,000, the coupon, reduced by a debit to the carrying value of the loan of £377. This gives a 'correct' charge of £623 for the period, being £10,377 x 6%. The carrying value of the loan is then the amount repayable.

	Cash flows	Interest charge	Carrying value in the balance sheet
	£	£	£
At 1 January 1999			10,733
At 31 December 1999	(1,000)	644	10,377
At 31 December 2000	(11,000)	623	0

Where debt instruments are quoted, market values at the date of acquisition will be used instead of present values. However, the standard states that where a reduced pre-acquisition market value on an acquired company's debt reflected the market's perception that it was at risk of being unable to fulfil its repayment obligations, the reduction would not be recognised in the fair value allocation if the debt was expected to be repaid at its full amount[97] (presumably as a result of having been acquired). In contrast to the choice of interest rate discussed above in this case it seems that the credit rating of the *acquiring* company is to be reflected in the value attached to such items, which seems to depart from the standard's general approach on this occasion.

One possible difficulty with this requirement is the extent to which the principle of discounting should be applied to some of the other requirements for attributing fair values of particular assets or liabilities. For example, if provisions are to be made in respect of deferred taxation or for environmental liabilities should these be discounted? Clearly, any provision, such as one for environmental liabilities, which is now covered by FRS 12 – *Provisions, Contingent Liabilities and Contingent*

Assets – should be discounted where the effect is material. Although there may be a theoretical argument for doing the same for any provision for deferred tax, we do not believe that this was intended by the ASB. It would clearly be anomalous for the deferred tax relating to the acquired company to be discounted, but the rest of the group's deferred tax not to be discounted. However, where under FRS 19 it is the group's policy to discount deferred tax (see 5.10 at Chapter 24), then clearly any deferred tax relating to the acquired company should be discounted.

Examples of companies making fair value adjustments for monetary assets or liabilities based on market values or by discounting amounts receivable or payable are few and far between. This could be due to the fact that companies have floating rate debt and therefore the existing book value will be equivalent to the fair value, or any adjustments may not be material. However, FKI has made a fair value adjustment in respect of loan capital, as shown in the following extract.

Extract 6.24: FKI plc (1998)

28 Acquisitions during the year [extract]

During the year the Group made the following acquisitions, to which were applied the acquisition method of accounting:
Bridon plc on 1 August 1997 and
CMP Corporation on 1 October 1997.
The acquisition of Bridon plc represents a substantial acquisition and the following table sets out the book values of the identifiable assets and liabilities acquired as a result of the acquisition and their fair value to the Group.

	Book value £'000	Accounting policy alignments £'000	Fair value adjustments £'000	Fair value to Group £'000
Fixed assets				
Tangible assets	75,565	–	(7,064)	68,501
Investments	590	–	–	590
Current assets				
Assets held for resale	8,599	–	1,649	10,248
Stocks	57,313	–	(523)	56,790
Debtors	72,539	–	–	72,539
Short-term deposits	1,285	–	–	1,285
Cash	13,524	–	–	13,524
Total assets	229,415	–	(5,938)	223,477
Liabilities				
Loans, overdrafts and finance leases	(63,482)	–	(1,250)	(64,732)
Other creditors	(63,902)	(1,500)	(2,147)	(67,549)
Deferred tax	(577)	(3,763)	–	(4,340)
Minority interest	(1,156)	–	–	(1,156)
Net assets acquired	100,298	(5,263)	(9,335)	85,700
Total consideration				137,488
Goodwill				51,788

> The accounting policy alignments were to:
> a) provide for known environmental obligations amounting to £1,500,000 and
> b) provide for deferred taxation in accordance with the Group's accounting policy for deferred taxation whereby provision is made for deferred taxation using the liability method to take account of timing differences between the incidence of income and expenditure for taxation and accounting purposes.
>
> The principal fair value adjustments were made to:
> a) Revalue land and buildings based upon valuations prepared by independent professionally qualified valuers. The effect of these valuations was to reduce the value of land and buildings by £6,193,000.
> b) Adjust the book value of business assets acquired which were disposed of shortly after acquisition to their net realisable value. The effect of these adjustments was to increase the value of assets held for resale by £1,649,000.
> c) Eliminate intercompany profit in stocks for the element which existed in Bridon in relation to stocks sold by other FKI companies prior to acquisition, amounting to £523,000.
> d) Provide for the loss on sale of businesses and assets acquired which are planned to be disposed of amounting to £3,018,000.
> e) Adjust the fair value of the US dollar fixed rate guaranteed senior notes which existed in Bridon plc to reflect the market rate of interest prevailing at the date of acquisition by FKI plc. The effect of this was to increase the value of the obligation by £1,250,000.

Another example is shown in Extract 6.28 at 2.4.3 D I below.

Most fair value adjustments relating to monetary assets, such as debtors, are due to reassessments of their recoverable amount or to align accounting policies for bad debt provisions; for example, see Extract 6.16 at 2.4.3 A I above.

C Contingencies

Both contingent assets and contingent liabilities should be measured at fair values where these can be determined. For this purpose reasonable estimates of the expected outcome may be used.[98] The treatment of contingent assets is an example of the situation whereby assets are recognised as part of the fair value exercise when they are not normally recognised in accounts when no acquisition is involved; FRS 12 does not allow any contingent assets to be recognised as this could give rise to recognition of a profit that may never be realised. However, where the realisation is virtually certain, then the related asset is not contingent and should therefore be recognised as an asset.[99] The level of probability under FRS 7 is lower than in FRS 12, and although the treatment in FRS 7 seems imprudent at first sight, it is in fact designed to *exclude* from post-acquisition profits any windfall gains from transactions or events which took place before the acquisition was made. In effect, the acquirer has made an investment in a speculative asset.

On a practical note, acquiring managements will often be reluctant to recognise contingent assets. The details surrounding them will often be hazy and managements will be reluctant to threaten post-acquisition profits with the possibility of a write down of the contingent asset if the gain does not in the event materialise – from their point of view there is downside but no upside. An example of a contingent asset, however, would be the need to reflect expected receipts under an 'earn-out' arrangement in respect of a company previously disposed of from the acquired group.

Certain contingent assets and liabilities that crystallise as a result of the acquisition are also to be recognised as part of the fair value exercise, provided that the underlying contingency was in existence before the acquisition. An example is where the acquired company has previously entered into a contract that contains a clause under which obligations are triggered in the event of a change in ownership.[100]

One company which made a fair value adjustment in respect of a contingent asset was GKN in its 1994 accounts, as shown below:

Extract 6.25: GKN plc (1994)

23 ACQUISITIONS [extract]

The fair value adjustments made include:

(c) a debtor for the net cash received in June 1994 amounting to £112 million arising from an arbitration award against the Arab Organisation for Industrialisation (AOI) following the termination of a joint venture between AOI and Westland Helicopters Limited to manufacture Lynx helicopters under licence. This receipt was secured as a result of actions initiated by Westland prior to acquisition and has accordingly been referred back to 31st March 1994. A further final net receipt of £51 million was negotiated in August 1994 and has been treated as a post acquisition exceptional profit (see note 4). These items, taken together with the net £15 million received by Westland in December 1993, give a total net receipt of £178 million from the award.

An example of a company providing for contingent liabilities is TI Group in Extract 6.28 at 2.4.3 D I below.

D Pensions and other post-retirement benefits

As discussed in Chapter 23, in November 2000 the ASB published FRS 17 – *Retirement Benefits* – which represents a radical change to the current requirements contained in SSAP 24 and UITF 6. As a result, the ASB has made some consequential changes to the requirements of FRS 7 so that it is consistent with FRS 17. The requirements of FRS 7 in the context of SSAP 24 and UITF 6 are discussed immediately below and the revised requirements in relation to FRS 17 are discussed thereafter.

I SSAP 24 and UITF 6

FRS 7 requires that the fair value of a deficiency in a funded pension or other post-retirement benefits scheme, or accrued obligations in an unfunded scheme, should be recognised as a liability of the acquiring group. To the extent that it is reasonably expected to be realised, a surplus in a funded scheme should be recognised as an asset.[101] The assets or liabilities which are recognised are in substitution for any existing prepayments or provisions that have accumulated in the accounts of the acquired company under the requirements of SSAP 24 or UITF 6.

This is another example where assets or liabilities are to be recognised as part of the fair value exercise which would otherwise not be allowed in the absence of an acquisition; in most situations SSAP 24 does not allow the immediate recognition of surpluses or deficiencies of pension schemes, but requires them to be recognised systematically over the average remaining service lives of the employees. Essentially this requirement is based on the fact that a pension fund represents an off balance sheet resource (which may be positive or negative, depending on the solvency of the fund), and that post-acquisition results will be distorted unless recognition is given to the existence of this asset or liability at the time of the acquisition.

A change from the exposure draft which preceded FRS 7 was the introduction of the proviso regarding the recognition of assets through use of the phrase 'to the extent that it is reasonably expected to be realised'. As was indicated when FRED 7 was published, this was an area which the ASB could not agree upon. A minority of the members disagreed with giving instant recognition to a pension surplus and would have preferred to spread it forward over the average service lives of the employees.[102] The wording above appears to have been the compromise reached, but like many compromises it is far from satisfactory, because it is unclear what it means.

The explanation section of FRS 7 states that 'the fair value attributed to a surplus in a funded scheme would be determined taking into account not only the actuarial surplus of the fund, but also the extent to which the surplus could be realised in cash terms, by way of reduction of future contributions or otherwise, and the time-scale of such potential realisations',[103] but this still does not clarify the issue, because it introduces a vague test of recoverability that has no equivalent in SSAP 24 itself. It further states that 'a pension asset ... would be recognised only insofar as the acquired entity or the acquirer was able to benefit from the existing surplus',[104] but it remains unclear in what circumstances the acquired entity or acquirer will not benefit from such a surplus.

FRS 7 says that changes in pension or other post-retirement arrangements following an acquisition should be accounted for as post-acquisition items.[105] An example is the cost of improvements to benefits granted to members of an acquired scheme as part of harmonising remuneration packages in the enlarged group. This is consistent with accounting for any changes affecting the pension arrangements of the acquirer's own workforce. The cost of these changes should therefore be dealt with in accordance with SSAP 24 or UITF 6 by being spread forward over average service lives.

BICC made an adjustment to incorporate a pension surplus in its 1996 accounts, as shown below:

Extract 6.26: BICC plc (1996)

19 Acquisitions [extract]

	Consideration and costs £m	Fair value of assets acquired £m	Goodwill £m
British Rail Infrastructure companies	53	30	23
BTCC Phillips Inc minority interest	7	1	6
	60	31	29

On 3 April 1996 the Group acquired three British Rail Infrastructure companies. The total consideration including expenses was £33m of which £32m was paid on completion. On 29 March 1996 the Group acquired the outstanding minority interest in its Canadian subsidiary BICC Phillips Inc for £7m. The Group has used acquisition accounting to account for these purchases. Adjustments have been made to reflect the fair value of assets of the British Rail Infrastructure companies acquired as follows:

	Net tangible assets acquired £m	Fair value adjustments £m	Fair value of assets acquired £m
Fixed assets	16	–	16
Stocks	8	–	8
Debtors	79	31	110
Creditors	(70)	–	(70)
Provisions, including deferred taxation	(2)	(20)	(22)
Net borrowings	(12)	–	(12)
	19	11	30

Fair value adjustments, which include, principally, recognition of the pension fund surplus, related deferred taxation and provisions for known liabilities, are provisional estimates which will be revised if necessary in 1997.

Another example is shown in Extract 6.15 at 2.4.3 A I above.

One company which did not appear to have made any fair value adjustment in respect of a pension surplus was United Utilities in its 1996 accounts. No reference is made to pensions in the discussion of fair value adjustments yet the pensions note disclosed the following:

Extract 6.27: United Utilities PLC (1996)

23 Pensions [extract]

Most employees of NORWEB plc who joined prior to 1 October 1991 are members of the ESPS, a defined benefit scheme. This scheme is now closed to new employees.

The latest full actuarial valuation of NORWEB's section of the ESPS was carried out by Bacon & Woodrow, consulting actuaries, as at 31 March 1995. The attained age method was used for the valuation and the principal actuarial assumptions adopted for average annual growth rates were investment returns 9 per cent, salary increases (exclusive of merit awards) 6.5 per cent and pensions increases 5 per cent.

The total market value of NORWEB's share of the net assets of the ESPS at 31 March 1995 was £662.3 million.

The valuation showed that the actuarial value of the assets of NORWEB's section of the ESPS as at 31 March 1995 represented 112.8 per cent of the actuarial value of the accrued benefits. This is within the statutory maximum. The accrued benefits include all benefits for pensioners and other former members as well as benefits based on service completed to date for active members, allowing for future salary rises. In deriving the pension cost, the surplus remaining after benefit improvements is being spread over the future working lifetime of the members.

It would seem from the above that there may have been a pension surplus at the date of acquisition. Although the fair values in respect of Norweb were reassessed in the following year, pensions was not one of the areas adjusted.[106]

TI Group made an adjustment to reflect a pension deficit in respect of its acquisition of EIS Group, as shown below.

Extract 6.28: TI Group plc (1998)

23. ACQUISITIONS AND DISPOSALS [extract]
Provisional fair value of net assets – EIS Group

		Provisional fair value adjustments				
	Book values prior to acquisition	Transfer to assets held for disposal	Conformity with TI accounting policies	Pensions & other liabilities	Onerous contracts	**Provisional fair values to TI Group**
	£m	£m	£m	£m	£m	**£m**
Fixed tangible assets	93.7	(16.8)	(3.4)	–	(1.9)	**71.6**
Investments	0.7	–	–	–	–	**0.7**
Stocks	113.5	(45.1)	(3.1)	–	(0.2)	**65.1**
Assets held for disposal	–	35.6	–	–	–	**35.6**
Debtors	130.0	(31.5)	(3.0)	–	–	**95.5**
Creditors	(110.5)	25.1	(0.3)	–	(1.2)	**(86.9)**
Pensions and other post-retirement obligations	(6.4)	0.6	–	(20.7)	–	**(26.5)**
Other provisions	(4.3)	–		(14.5)	(9.0)	**(27.8)**
Deferred taxation	6.5	(0.1)	(6.5)	6.0	–	**5.9**
Minority interests	(1.3)	–	–	–	–	**(1.3)**
Net debt	(63.4)	–	–	–	–	**(63.4)**
Net assets	158.5	(32.2)	(16.3)	(29.2)	(12.3)	**68.5**

> Provisional fair value adjustments comprise the following:
>
> Transfers to assets held for disposal: Businesses identified at acquisition as being held for disposal in the short term were valued at their actual or estimated disposal proceeds, discounted to their present values as at the date of the transaction of EIS Group.
>
> Conformity with TI accounting policies: Adjustments were made to align accounting policies principally affecting tooling capitalisation, and stock, debtor and deferred taxation provisions.
>
> Pensions and other liabilities: As anticipated at the time of acquisition an adjustment of £21.0m was made to recognise the initial estimate of a deficit in the principal EIS Group UK pension schemes, which will be the subject of a full actuarial valuation during 1999. Provisions of £14.5m were made for the estimated costs of disputes and claims, actual and potential, principally related to businesses discontinued by EIS Group prior to its acquisition by TI Group.
>
> Onerous contracts: Provisions of £9.0m and asset write downs of £2.1m were made for expected future losses on specific customer contracts. Fixed rate borrowings were revalued to their fair values, based on market rates at the date of acquisition, resulting in an increase in creditors of £1.2m.
>
> All fair value adjustments will be reviewed during 1999; any revisions made will be adjustments to goodwill.
>
> The carrying value of land and buildings at acquisition was reviewed and no material adjustment was required to restate to open market existing use value.

II FRS 17

Following the consequential amendments made by FRS 17, FRS 7 still requires that the fair value of a deficiency in a funded pension or other post-retirement benefits scheme, or accrued obligations in an unfunded scheme, should be recognised as a liability of the acquiring group. However, a surplus in a funded scheme should be recognised as an asset, to the extent that it can be recovered through reduced contributions or refunds from the scheme.[107]

The explanation section of FRS 7 now states that 'the fair value of the deficiency or surplus should be measured in accordance with the requirements of FRS 17 'Retirement Benefits'. The extent to which a surplus can be recovered should also be determined in accordance with the requirements of FRS 17'.[108] These requirements of FRS 17 are discussed at 3.7.5 A of Chapter 23.

Accordingly, although the vague test of recoverability in FRS 7 which had no equivalent in SSAP 24 has disappeared, the recoverability is still based on an assessment of how much can be recovered through reduced contributions or refunds from the scheme.

FRS 7 still requires that changes in pension or other post-retirement arrangements following an acquisition should be accounted for as post-acquisition items.[109] An example is the cost of improvements to benefits granted to members of an acquired scheme as part of harmonising remuneration packages in the enlarged group. This is consistent with accounting for any changes affecting the pension arrangements of the acquirer's own workforce. However, the cost of these changes now be dealt with in accordance with FRS 17. Thus to the extent that any improvements relate to past service, this could result in a significant one-off charge in the profit and loss account in the period the benefit improvement is awarded (which will be post-acquisition), unless there is an unrecognised surplus in the scheme. This is discussed at 3.8.2 B of Chapter 23.

One further issue which has been considered by FRS 17 is where the method of arriving at the fair value of the deficit or surplus under FRS 17 differs from that adopted in an earlier acquisition under FRS 7. The position taken by FRS 17 is that any difference is to be treated as a post acquisition actuarial gain or loss, and hence recorded in the statement of total recognised gains and losses in the year of implementing FRS 17 in full. The goodwill arising on such acquisitions are not to be restated.[110]

E Taxation

As discussed in Chapter 24 at 5, in December 2000 the ASB published FRS 19 – *Deferred Tax* – which adopts a full provision approach to deferred tax (subject to some exceptions) rather than the partial provision approach contained in SSAP 15. As a result, the ASB has made some consequential changes to the requirements of FRS 7 so that it is consistent with FRS 19. The requirements of FRS 7 in the context of SSAP 15 are discussed immediately below and the revised requirements in relation to FRS 19 are discussed thereafter.

I SSAP 15

FRS 7 says that deferred tax assets and liabilities recognised in the fair value exercise should be determined by considering the enlarged group as a whole.[111]

No specific guidance is given by the standard as to how this is to be achieved. The explanation section in the standard merely confirms that deferred tax has to be determined on a group basis, and indicates that this should be based on assumptions applicable to the group as a whole, rather than using assumptions applicable to the acquired company at the date of the acquisition.[112]

The equivalent explanation section in FRED 7 had indicated that the recognition of deferred tax in the context of a fair value exercise falls into two areas. First of all there will be existing timing differences within the acquired company which will give rise to a potential liability to deferred tax which will need to be considered. In addition, the adjustments made as a result of the fair value exercise may lead to quasi-timing differences which will also need to be considered in determining the provision for deferred tax. The difference between the fair values assigned and the tax base values of the assets and liabilities acquired are in fact not strictly timing differences within the SSAP 15 definition; however, differences between accounting profits and taxable profits will arise in subsequent periods as items pass through the profit and loss account and therefore it is necessary to treat them as such in order to avoid distorting post-acquisition earnings. Arguably, however, not all fair value adjustments are to be regarded as timing differences; as FRED 7 proposed, it is only those that would be timing differences under SSAP 15 if reflected in the accounts of the acquired company.[113]

Although not specifically addressed by FRS 7, where assets or liabilities are recognised in respect of pension schemes and post-retirement benefits, then the deferred tax implications should be accounted for in accordance with SSAP 15 (as amended in December 1992) – see Chapter 21 at 1.2.8. This should obviously be based on the accounting policy of the acquirer for such differences. One company which made full provision in respect of the tax implications of incorporating a pension surplus as part of a fair value exercise was Premier Farnell in its 1996 accounts, as shown below.

Extract 6.29: Premier Farnell plc (1996)

23. ACQUISITIONS AND DISPOSALS [extract]
(i) Acquisition of Premier

On 11th April 1996 the Group acquired Premier Industrial Corporation ("Premier") for a consideration of £1,877.2 million. Details of the acquisition, including the fair value adjustments made to the assets and liabilities acquired are set out below:

		Book value at acquisition £m	Accounting policy alignment £m	Other £m	Fair value £m
Tangible fixed assets		43.2	(2.0)	4.9 [a]	46.1
Intangible assets		8.5	(8.5) [1]	–	–
Investments		2.0	–	(2.0)	–
Stock		127.3	(20.8) [2]	–	106.5
Debtors	– due within one year	92.5	(3.4)	(1.2)	87.9
	– due after one year	13.7	–	40.4 [b]	54.1
Creditors		(57.7)	(2.1)	(2.7)	(62.5)
Corporate and deferred taxes		(7.1)	(3.7) [3]	(18.0) [b]	(28.8)
Provisions		–	–	(4.6) [c]	(4.6)
Net cash		82.0	–	–	82.0
		304.4	(40.5)	16.8	280.7
Consideration					
Shares					923.7
Cash including costs					953.5
					1,877.2
Goodwill written off (note 21)					1,596.5

Accounting policy alignment
[1]write-off of goodwill.
[2]adjustments required to reflect UK GAAP eliminate overheads from stock valuation and adopt stock provisioning in accordance with Group accounting practice.
[3]write-off of deferred tax assets in accordance with UK GAAP.
Accounting policy alignments also reflect the adoption of Group policies in respect of fixed asset capitalisation, catalogue costs, sales returns and holiday pay.

Other
[a] revaluation of land and buildings.
[b] actuarial valuation of pension surplus in accordance with FRS7 and SSAP24 and recognition of corresponding deferred tax provision.
[c] actuarial valuation of post-retirement obligation.
Other adjustments also reflect the write-down of investments to net realisable value and the recognition of liabilities existing at the acquisition date.

The standard also requires that the benefit to the group of any tax losses attributable to an acquired entity at the date of acquisition should be recognised in accordance with the requirements of SSAP 15.[114] Again, application of this principle may result in deferred tax assets being recognised on acquisition that were previously unrecognised in the acquired company's accounts because SSAP 15 did not allow it. One company which has made a fair value adjustment to reflect a deferred tax asset in respect of losses is Persimmon, as shown in Extract 6.21 at 2.4.3 A III above. However, it would appear that such an approach has not always been adopted in practice.[115]

It can be seen that FRS 7 requires that the deferred tax to be recognised should be determined on an overall group basis; similarly, losses can be recognised if they benefit the group. This seems to be at odds with the standard's general approach that assets and liabilities recognised as part of the fair value exercise should not reflect increases or decreases resulting from the acquirer's intentions or future actions. However, the ASB has taken the view that the partial provision approach of SSAP 15 has to be based on future intentions and these can only be those of the reporting entity, therefore it has to be done on an overall group basis.

II FRS 19

Following the consequential amendments made by FRS 19, FRS 7 now states that 'deferred tax on adjustments to record assets and liabilities at their fair values should be recognised in accordance with the requirements of FRS 19'.[116] Interestingly, this makes no reference to existing deferred tax balances in the accounts of the acquired entity. We presume that this is a drafting error and it is intended that any such balances are to be adjusted to an FRS 19 basis if they are not already on such a basis. This is likely to be the case where the entity acquired does not produce its accounts under UK GAAP.

Taken on its own, the requirement would imply that deferred tax should not be recognised on fair value adjustments, since they are not timing differences as defined in FRS 19. However, the revised explanation section states that such adjustments are to be 'treated in the same way as they would be if they were timing differences arising in the [acquired] entity's own accounts'.[117]

FRS 19 also amends FRS 7 to clarify the accounting treatment for previously unrecognised tax assets (typically unrelieved tax losses). Under the revised requirements of FRS 7, deferred tax assets that were not recognised before the acquisition may, as a consequence of the acquisition, satisfy the recognition criteria of FRS 19. To the extent that these relate to the acquired entity, then they should be recognised in the fair value exercise, as they are regarded as contingent assets that have crystallised as a result of the acquisition (see 2.4.3 C above). However, those of the acquirer, or other entities within the acquiring group, which are now recoverable as a result of the acquisition are to be recognised as a credit to the tax charge in the post-acquisition period.[118] The existing requirements of FRS 7 could be construed as requiring this already, but as amended it is much clearer.

The above revised requirements of FRS 7 are discussed more fully in Chapter 24 at 5.6.

F Provisions

The most significant impact of FRS 7 has been on the area of provisions, particularly reorganisation or rationalisation provisions and provisions for future trading losses of the acquired companies.

I Reorganisation or rationalisation provisions

As indicated at 2.4.1 above, FRS 7 states that the assets and liabilities that are to be fair valued are to be those of the acquired company and should not include 'provisions or accruals … for reorganisation and integration costs expected to be incurred as a result of the acquisition, whether they relate to the acquired entity or to the acquirer'.[119] Only if the acquired entity was already committed to the course of action in question, and unable realistically to withdraw from it would it be regarded as pre-acquisition.

In practice this had been one of the areas of fair value accounting which prior to FRS 7 had given rise to a great deal of controversy, and alleged abuse. The ability to provide for costs of reorganisation programmes without having to charge these costs in the profit and loss account was a very attractive opportunity, and one which understandably tempted some companies to be enthusiastic in their estimation of these provisions.

The ASB adopted a restrictive approach, with the costs of any such reorganisations or rationalisation being treated as post-acquisition costs. By doing this the ASB really only moved the goalposts so far, because although provisions for such costs could no longer bypass the profit and loss account as part of the goodwill calculation, such one-off provisions were still being made but highlighted in the profit and loss account as exceptional items. The ASB has now taken this a stage further by issuing FRS 12 which restricts the ability of companies to create such big bath provisions (see Chapter 28 at 5.1).

It might be thought that it is possible to get around the FRS 7 rules by getting the vendor to commit itself, prior to the formal acquisition date, to a particular course of action to reorganise or restructure the business so that the costs can be regarded as being pre-acquisition costs. However, the standard emphasises that where provisions for future costs were made by the acquired company shortly before the acquisition took place, particular attention has to be paid to the circumstances in order to determine whether obligations were incurred by the acquired company before the acquisition. Only if the acquired company was demonstrably committed to the expenditure whether or not the acquisition was completed would it have a liability at the date of acquisition. If obligations were incurred as a result of the influence of the acquirer, it would be necessary to consider whether control had passed to the acquirer at an earlier date and, consequently, whether the date of acquisition pre-dated such commitments.[120] One company which disregarded these rules in FRS 7 by invoking the true and fair override was Aim Group as shown below.

Extract 6.30: Aim Group plc (1998)

24 Purchase of undertaking

On 16th February 1998 the Group acquired the assets and business of Hunting Aviation Interiors Division from Hunting plc.

Details of the acquisition are as follows:

Net assets acquired	£'000
Tangible fixed assets	137
Stocks and work in progress	2,482
Provisions for onerous contracts	(410)
Provisions for closure costs	(951)
	1,258
Goodwill arising on acquisition	2,189
	3,447
Analysis of consideration:	
Cash (including expenses of acquisition)	2,847
Deferred consideration	600
	3,447

The deferred consideration is payable over three years commencing in May 1999 and is based on sales of the division.

True and fair override on determination of goodwill arising on acquisition

The net assets acquired include a provision for the costs associated with the closure of the operational facility at Biggin Hill. Financial Reporting Standard 7 only allows these costs to be included in the fair value adjustment to goodwill where the vendor was already committed to the closure. Although the closure decision was taken by the Group, the Directors consider that these closure costs were an integral part of the overall decision to purchase the business, and their inclusion is necessary to give a true and fair view of the goodwill on acquisition. The effect on the Group's financial statements of this departure from the requirements of Financial Reporting Standard 7 is to increase the goodwill capitalised on acquisition by £951,000. These costs would otherwise have been charged to the profit and loss account as an exceptional item increasing the loss for the year by £951,000.

This treatment was challenged by the Review Panel which did not accept the directors' justification for invoking the true and fair override and argued that since Aim Group had taken the closure decision, it was therefore a post-acquisition event.[121] As a result, the company revised its 1998 accounts by way of supplementary note published the same day as the ruling by the Review Panel. The directors also amended the accounts to give more disclosures in respect of the fair value table to meet the requirements of FRS 6 and the Companies Act (see 2.8 below).

An example of a company that has reflected a pre-acquisition reorganisation provision as part of the book values of the net assets acquired without making any adjustment thereto is Kingfisher as shown in Extract 6.20 at 2.4.3 A III above. In that example, the note discloses that a further post-acquisition provision has been charged to the profit and loss account. Oxford Instruments in Extract 6.16 at 2.4.3 A I above provides an example of a company making a fair value adjustment for a reorganisation provision which was not fully reflected in the book values. Rentokil Initial at Extract 6.33 at 2.4.3 F III below is another example of a company making a fair value adjustment to an existing pre-acquisition reorganisation provision.

However, there were also further reorganisation costs in respect of the acquisition charged to the profit and loss account.

II Provisions for future operating losses

For the same reasons as for reorganisation provisions, FRS 7 requires that the assets and liabilities that are to be fair valued are to be those of the acquired company and should not include provisions for future operating losses.[122] The future trading results of the subsidiary do not represent one of its identifiable assets or liabilities, and they must be consolidated with those of the rest of the group from the date of acquisition. Thus the effect on the acquisition price of whatever future results were anticipated will fall to be dealt with as part of goodwill, positive or negative.

III Other provisions

Although FRS 7 takes a restrictive view in setting up provisions for reorganisation costs or for future losses, this does not mean that it does not allow any provisions to be set up as part of the fair value exercise. An acquired company may have certain commitments which are not reflected as liabilities in its own accounts which nevertheless should form part of the identifiable liabilities to be recognised as part of the acquisition. Paragraph 38 of the standard states that 'identifiable liabilities include items such as onerous contracts and commitments that existed at the time of acquisition, whether or not the corresponding obligations were recognised as liabilities in the financial statements of the acquired entity'.

It is clear that the possibility under the FRS of recognising as liabilities of the acquired entity such items as onerous contracts and commitments, and thus bringing them into the fair value exercise, will provide some scope for reflecting the affairs of an acquired company more fully than if the fair value exercise were limited to items just recognised by the acquired company. FRS 7 does not define what it regards as an onerous contract, nor does it give any examples. Although FRS 12 defines an onerous contract as 'a contract in which the unavoidable costs of meeting the obligations exceed the economic benefits expected to be received under it',[123] i.e. a loss-making contract, in our view this is not necessarily the same as an onerous contract for the purposes of FRS 7. The only example of an onerous contract quoted in FRS 12 is vacant leasehold property.

Some might argue that examples of onerous contracts could include leases at an unfavourable rental or for an excessive amount of space; and contracts to provide services in an area of business which is uneconomic. It has been argued by some commentators that provision for leases, the rentals for which at the date of acquisition are above present market rents, should not be made as part of the fair value exercise. This is because under SSAP 21 such operating leases are not reflected as liabilities.[124] However, the counter argument to this is that FRS 7 requires fair value adjustments to be made for other items such as contingencies and pensions which would not otherwise be allowed by the relevant accounting standards in these areas (see 2.4.3 C and 2.4.3 D above). Also, much of the guidance in other areas in the standard require fair values to be based on market conditions at the acquisition date. In our view such leases can be regarded as onerous leases under FRS 7 and provision made for the excess over market rates. However, where this is done, all leases should be considered and an asset recognised for any leases where the rentals at the date of acquisition are below market rents. This view is shared by other commentators.[125] One company which has adopted this approach is The Royal Bank of Scotland as can be seen from Extract 6.15 at 2.4.3 A I above.

Other examples of companies making provisions for onerous contracts are Scottish Power and Arriva as shown below:

Extract 6.31: Scottish Power plc (2001)

29 Acquisition

In March 2001, the group acquired the business and assets of Rye House power station for a total consideration of £227.7 million. The acquisition method of accounting has been adopted and the goodwill on the purchase has been capitalised and is being amortised over 20 years. The directors have estimated the useful economic life of the goodwill acquired after assessment of the earnings generating life of the plant. The details of the transaction are shown below.

Fair value of Rye House consideration	Provisional fair values £m
Tangible fixed assets	300.0
Stocks	2.1
Debtors	1.8
Creditors: amounts falling due within one year	(1.8)
Provisions for liabilities and changes	(171.5)
Net assets	130.6
Goodwill arising on acquisition of Rye House	97.1
Purchase consideration	227.7
Satisfied by:	
Cash paid	217.2
Acquisition expenses	10.5
	227.7

The net assets of the Rye House power station did not form part of a separate legal entity acquired and therefore no information on book values is available. The tangible fixed assets acquired have been provisionally fair valued at net depreciated replacement cost and a provision for an onerous gas contract has been established by reference to market prices prevailing at the time of the acquisition.

The post-acquisition results and cash flows of the Rye House business are not material to the group's results and cash flows for the year ended 31 March 2001.

The fair values attributed to the acquisition are provisional due to the proximity of the date of acquisition to the financial year end.

Extract 6.32: Arriva plc (2000)

23 **Acquisitions and disposal** [extract]
(b) Fair value of businesses acquired:

	MTL Services plc			Other acquisitions			Total
	Acquired book value £m	Fair value adjustments £m	Net cost £m	Acquired book value £m	Fair value adjustments £m	Net cost £m	Net cost £m
Intangible assets	42.9	(42.9)	–	0.5	(0.5)	–	–
Tangible fixed assets	47.6	(3.7)	43.9	8.6	(1.2)	7.4	51.3
Stocks	3.0	(0.5)	2.5	–	–	–	2.5
Debtors	57.3	4.2	61.5	2.1	–	2.1	63.6
Net overdrafts	(33.5)	–	(33.5)	0.6	–	0.6	(32.9)
Finance leases	(19.7)	–	(19.7)	–	–	–	(19.7)
Creditors	(71.8)	1.5	(70.3)	(5.8)	(2.4)	(8.2)	(78.5)
Loans	(5.2)	–	(5.2)	–	–	–	(5.2)
Provisions	–	(34.0)	(34.0)	–	–	–	(34.0)
	20.6	(75.4)	(54.8)	6.0	(4.1)	1.9	(52.9)
Goodwill			91.8			14.3	106.1
Satisfied by cash			37.0			16.2	53.2

The value of the intangible fixed assets has been adjusted to eliminate goodwill created by MTL Services plc on a group reconstruction. The value of tangible fixed assets has been adjusted to comply with the Group's depreciation policy for buses and coaches. The value of debtors has been increased in order to recognise the fair value of the pension prepayment acquired on the acquisition of MTL Services plc. The creation of provisions of £34 million on acquisition represents a contract loss provision of £30 million, representing the losses incurred from acquisition until 18 February 2001 on the Northern Spirit and Merseyrail Electrics rail franchises of MTL Services plc, and a provision of £4 million for deferred tax. Certain of the fair value adjustments are provisional, pending the final determination of the value of the related assets and liabilities.

Further details of the principal acquisitions made during the year are provided in the Directors' Report on page 23.

Directors' Report [extract]
Acquisitions [extract]
As reported last year the Company completed the acquisition of the entire issued capital of MTL Services plc on 18 February 2000 for a consideration of £34.7 million plus expenses.

It can be seen from the above extract that the onerous contract related to rail franchises which in fact represented the whole operations of the company acquired. The provision of £30m reflects the operating losses of the business for the final year of the remaining franchise. As a result of this 'contract', Arriva has been able to make provision for the future operating losses of the business, which would ordinarily not be allowed under FRS 7.

Another example of a company making provisions for onerous contracts is TI Group as shown in Extract 6.28 at 2.4.3 D I above.

One company which made significant fair value adjustments to reflect various provisions was Rentokil Initial in respect of its acquisition of BET in 1996, as can be seen from the following extract.

Extract 6.33: Rentokil Initial plc (1996)

29 Acquisitions [extract]

The group purchased 15 companies and businesses during the year as set out on page 63 for a total consideration of £2,230.3m of which £2,221.7m was in respect of the acquisition on 29th April 1996 of BET Public Limited Company. The total adjustments required to the balance sheet figures of companies and businesses acquired in order to present the net assets of those companies and businesses at fair values in accordance with group accounting principles were £260.8m, of which £259.7m related to BET, details of which are set out on pages 58 and 59 together with the matching adjustment to goodwill. All of these businesses have been accounted for as acquisitions.

BET acquisition

	Book value £m	Revaluations £m	Consistency of accounting policy £m	Other £m	Fair value £m
Tangible fixed assets	609.2	(24.1)	(22.9)	–	562.2
Investments	33.0	(3.4)	(18.3)	(1.0)	10.3
Stock	35.0	(3.3)	–	–	31.7
Debtors	372.5	12.4	(0.6)	–	384.3
Creditors	(472.1)	(61.4)	(6.0)	–	(539.5)
Provisions					
– Vacant property	(20.7)	–	–	(47.5)	(68.2)
– Environmental	(4.4)	–	–	(49.9)	(54.3)
– Subsidiary	–	–	–	(33.0)	(33.0)
– Pre-acquisition restructuring	(1.8)	–	–	(5.0)	(6.8)
Taxation	(108.2)	3.5	–	–	(104.7)
Net debt	(130.5)	–	–	–	(130.5)
	312.0	(76.3)	(47.8)	(136.4)	51.5
Minority interests	(1.7)	0.8	–	–	(0.9)
Net assets acquired	310.3	(75.5)	(47.8)	(136.4)	50.6
Special dividend to BET shareholders					38.2
Adjusted assets					88.8
Goodwill					2,132.9
Consideration					2,221.7
Satisfied by					
Shares issued					1,653.2
Cash (including special dividend paid of £38.2m and deducting cash received from exercise of share options of £18.0m)					568.5
					2,221.7

The book values of the assets and liabilities shown on page 58 have been taken from the management accounts of BET at the date of acquisition (at actual exchange rates at that date). The fair value adjustments set out on page 58 are provisional figures which will be finalised in the 1997 financial statements following professional property valuations as at the date of acquisition and on final review of judgemental areas.

Revaluation adjustments in respect of tangible fixed assets comprise the revaluation of certain freehold properties and the write-off of obsolete or impaired plant and machinery and fixtures and fittings.

Revaluations of investments and stock reflect the write-down to estimated realisable value. The adjustment to debtors includes establishing an asset (£16.9m) to reflect the pension fund surplus arising from actuarial valuations, offset by various write-downs to reflect estimated realisable value.

> The revaluations of creditors relate to liabilities which were not fully reflected in the balance sheet of BET's business on acquisition. These include adjustments to provisions for insurance claims, liabilities under onerous contracts and the reassessment of legal claims. An adjustment of £5.6m has been made in order to reflect a market coupon on the BET US $ bond.
>
> A net deferred tax asset of £10.7m for expected tax relief on fair value adjustments has been recognised partially offset by tax liabilities of £7.2m.
>
> The book values acquired included provisions for reorganisation and restructuring costs amounting to £1.8m. These provisions related to reorganisations established by BET in the year prior to acquisition, which were reviewed and increased by £5.0m. This increase relates to irrevocable reorganisations commenced by BET management before the acquisition.
>
> The fair value adjustments for alignment of accounting policies reflect the restatement of assets and liabilities in accordance with the policies of the group including the removal of capitalised security alarm installation costs (£14.3m), the write-off of capitalised container and vehicle refurbishment costs in distribution companies, provision for the group's share of deferred consideration payable by an associated company for the acquisition of a business (£18.3m), provision for outstanding holiday pay entitlements of employees and the alignment of general bad debt provisioning policy.
>
> Additional provision has also been made for vacant property costs relating to future net rental outgoings of the substantial number of vacant and sub-let properties owned and leased by BET. Environmental provisions were also made for the estimated costs of remediation on BET sites. Provision has also been made for major regulatory and taxation problems in a subsidiary.

It can be seen from the above that most of the adjustments made by Rentokil Initial are not to reflect new liabilities, but are reassessments of provisions and creditors which were already recorded within the books of BET. In the fifth edition of this book we stated that it would be 'interesting to see when these provisional fair values are reviewed in 1997 as to whether the company has been over-enthusiastic in making these provisions'. As it turned out the company had to increase the amounts of creditors and provisions as shown below.

Extract 6.34: Rentokil Initial plc (1997)

30 Acquisitions and disposals [extract]

As indicated in the 1996 financial statements the provisional fair value adjustments recorded in relation to the acquisition of BET PLC have been finalised during the year, following professional property valuations and final reviews of judgemental areas. As a result, further adjustments of £41.5m were made in 1997. Details of these adjustments are set out below.

BET PLC fair value adjustments

	Fair value as stated in the 1996 financial statements	Adjustments			Fair value as now restated
		Revaluations	Consistency of accounting policy	Other	
	£m	£m	£m	£m	£m
Tangible fixed assets	562.2	(1.5)			560.7
Investments	10.3				10.3
Stock	31.7				31.7
Debtors	384.3				384.3
Creditors	(539.5)	(12.0)	(0.4)		(551.9)
Provisions					
– Vacant property	(68.2)			(17.3)	85.5
– Environmental	(54.3)			(6.2)	(60.5)
– Subsidiary	(33.0)				(33.0)
– Pre-acquisition restructuring	(6.8)				(6.8)
Taxation	(104.7)	(4.1)			(108.8)
Net debt	(130.5)				(130.5)
	51.5	(17.6)	(0.4)	(23.5)	10.0
Minority interests	(0.9)				(0.9)
Net assets acquired	50.6	(17.6)	(0.4)	(23.5)	9.1

The further adjustments above comprise the following items:

Professional property valuations performed in the year as at the date of acquisitions resulted in £1.5m reduction in value.

The increase in creditors principally relates to the reassessment of legal claims as a result of additional information being obtained subsequent to the original fair value exercise concerning the circumstances relating to the claims made against BET PLC and its subsidiaries.

The increase in taxation provisions principally arises from a further review of the taxation affairs of the BET PLC group both in the UK and overseas. The taxation liabilities of a number of group companies had not been agreed with the appropriate revenue authorities for many years and the adjustment made arises from detailed reviews of certain tax computations since the original fair value exercise, including some for companies which BET PLC had sold prior to the date of acquisition, with indemnities relating to taxation liabilities.

Additional provisions of £17.3m have been made for future net rental and outgoings on a sublet property leased by BET to reflect contractual arrangements separate from the sub-lease agreement which enabled the sub-tenant to terminate the sub-lease. These arrangements had not been identified at the time of the original fair value exercise.

The additional environmental provision (£6.2m) in respect of cost of remediation arises from further knowledge gained on one of the former BET PLC operational sites in the US as a result of further reports by environmental and legal specialists provided during the course of the year.

G Businesses held exclusively with a view to subsequent resale

This is another area where the detailed rules of the standard seem to be at odds with its general approach that the fair value exercise should not reflect the acquirer's intentions for future actions. It requires that 'where an interest in a separate business of the acquired entity is sold as a single unit within approximately one year of the date of acquisition, the investment in that business should be treated as a single asset for the purposes of determining fair values. Its fair value should be based on the net proceeds of the sale, adjusted for the fair value of any assets or liabilities transferred into or out of the business, unless such adjusted net proceeds are demonstrably different from the fair value at the date of acquisition as a result of a post-acquisition event. This treatment should be applied to any business operation, whether a separate subsidiary undertaking or not, provided that its assets, liabilities, results of operations and activities are clearly distinguishable, physically, operationally and for financial reporting purposes, from the other assets, liabilities, results of operations and activities of the acquired entity.'[126]

Where the business has not yet been sold by the time of approval of the first set of accounts after the date of acquisition, the fair value of the interest in the business is based on the estimated net proceeds of sale and carried as a current asset, provided that:

'(a) a purchaser has been identified or is being sought; and

(b) the disposal is reasonably expected to occur within approximately one year of the date of acquisition.'[127]

This is based on the requirement of FRS 2, that a subsidiary which is reasonably expected to be disposed of with approximately one year of acquisition is to be included in the consolidated balance sheet as a current asset at the lower of cost and net realisable value; its results and assets and liabilities should not be consolidated (see 5.4 of Chapter 5). However, the principle has been extended to other business operations that are not subsidiaries.

The fair value to be attributed will normally be the actual realised amount as this is considered to be the most reliable evidence of fair value at the date of acquisition (or if the sale has not yet been completed, at the estimated sales proceeds). The net proceeds, which should take into account any costs of disposal (including incremental costs such as professional fees), should be discounted to obtain the net present value at date of acquisition, if material.[128]

This appears inconsistent with the general approach of FRS 7, as it depends on the acquirer's intentions for the business operation. However, in an appendix to FRED 7 the ASB said that it 'rejects that interpretation because it believes that the resale value of a business in an arm's length transaction would normally provide the most reliable evidence of its fair value, and should be used unless specific post-acquisition events occur during the holding period that require a profit or loss on disposal to be recorded'.[129]

The overall objective is therefore to produce a neutral impact on the group's results (apart from any interest effect, if discounting is applied). Accordingly, any initial estimate of fair value should normally be adjusted to actual net realised value within the period allowed for completing the investigation of fair values (see 2.4.4 below). However, it will be appropriate for a post-acquisition profit or loss on disposal to be recognised and for the fair values at acquisition to be different from the net realised value where:

(a) the acquirer has made a material change to the acquired business before disposal;

(b) specific post-acquisition events occur during the holding period that materially change the fair value of the business from the fair value estimated at the date of acquisition; or

(c) the disposal is completed at a reduced price for a quick sale.[130]

Examples of companies making fair value adjustments to reflect businesses held for resale at their actual or estimated net sale proceeds are The Royal Bank of Scotland, FKI and TI Group as shown in Extracts 6.15, 6.24 and 6.28 above.

One company which included businesses held for resale as part of the net assets acquired (and having provisionally revalued them upwards in the year of acquisition reduced the values the following year) was Reckitt & Colman, as illustrated in Extracts 6.42, 6.43 and 6.44 at 2.8.2 below.

2.4.4 *Subsequent amendments to fair value*

FRS 7 says that the fair value exercise should be completed, if possible, by the date on which the first post-acquisition accounts of the acquirer are approved by the directors, although if this is not possible, a provisional allocation of fair values is allowed which must be finalised in the next year (see 2.4.2 above). Otherwise, the only circumstances in which a retrospective adjustment to the goodwill calculation could be regarded as appropriate would be if the original allocation was regarded as a fundamental error which required to be dealt with as a prior year adjustment under FRS 3. This would probably be the case only if the original allocation was based on a complete misinterpretation of the facts which were available at the time; it would not apply simply because new information had come to light which changed the acquiring management's view of the value of the item in question.

2.4.5 *'Push-down accounting'*

The term 'push-down accounting' relates to the practice of incorporating, or 'pushing-down', the fair value adjustments which have been made by the acquiring company into the financial statements of the acquired subsidiary, including the goodwill arising on the acquisition. Such a practice is used in the US, where it has been required in certain situations by the Securities and Exchange Commission.[131] It is argued that the acquisition, being an independently bargained transaction, provides better evidence of the values of the assets and liabilities of the subsidiary than those previously contained within its financial statements, and therefore represents an improved basis of accounting.

There are, however, contrary views, which hold that the transaction in question was one to which the reporting entity was not a party, and there is no reason why it should intrude into the entity's own accounting records.

Whatever the theoretical arguments, it is certainly true that push-down accounting could be an expedient practice, because it obviates the need to make extensive consolidation adjustments in each subsequent year, based on parallel accounting records. But in fact most of the adjustments which push-down accounting would entail would fall foul of the Companies Act valuation rules or of other UK accounting standards and could not be made directly in the subsidiary's financial statements. It would be possible, by using the alternative valuation rules, to revalue fixed assets directly in the subsidiary's financial statements; however, this will create differences going forward since under FRS 15 the subsidiary would have to keep these valuations up to date, whereas the group is unlikely to have chosen that option when implementing FRS 15. The requirements of FRS 15 are discussed in Chapter 12.

2.5 Step-by-step acquisitions

2.5.1 *Background*

So far, this chapter has discussed acquisitions which result from a single purchase transaction, or at least a series of related transactions which occur over a relatively short period of time. However, in practice some subsidiaries are acquired in a series of steps which take place over an extended period, during which the underlying value of the subsidiary is likely to change, both because of the trading profits (or losses) which it retains and because of other movements in the fair values of its assets and liabilities. The accounting problems which this creates are therefore how to establish the fair values of the net assets acquired, and how to measure its pre-acquisition reserves.

2.5.2 *Example*

The problem can be illustrated by the following example, which is based on one included in an ASC Discussion Paper on fair value accounting.[132]

Example 6.2: Step-by-step acquisitions

Company A acquires an 80% holding in Company B as a result of four separate transactions over a number of years, as set out in the table below. At the time of these transactions, the fair values of the net assets of B are reflected in B's accounts at the values shown, and for the purpose of this illustration, the consideration paid was exactly proportionate to the share of the net assets, at fair value, which was thereby being acquired.

Transaction number	Holding acquired %	Total value of investee £m	Price paid £m	Cumulative holding %	Cumulative price paid £m
1	10	10	1.00	10	1.00
2	20	13	2.60	30	3.60
3	21	15	3.15	51	6.75
4	29	20	5.80	80	12.55
	80		12.55		

As the above table shows, Company B was merely an unconsolidated investment after transaction 1, became an associate as a result of transaction 2 and a subsidiary as a result of transaction 3, while transaction 4 resulted in the minority interest being reduced from 49% to 20%.

The accounting choices which are available are of two sorts; when to make the initial calculation of fair values for the purposes of determining goodwill, and whether to make a revised calculation when each successive change in the size of the holding takes place. As stated at 4.1 of Chapter 7, FRS 9 requires that the investment in an associate should be analysed at the time of acquisition between the investor's share of the underlying separable net assets (at fair value, if possible) and goodwill, so the answer to the first question above is that this calculation should be made after transaction 2; however, if Company A is unable to get the information on fair values which is required for that exercise, it may be possible to carry it out only after transaction 3. The more significant question is whether each further purchase of shares thereafter should lead to a recalculation of the goodwill equation.

If the exercise were first carried out after transaction 2, and reperformed after each subsequent increase in the shareholding, the calculations would be as follows:

After transaction 2	£m
Cost of investment	3.60
Share of assets at fair value (30% of £13m)	3.90
Negative goodwill on consolidation	0.30

Note that, in this particular example (because all purchases take place at the underlying asset value), the negative goodwill in fact represents the increase in reserves attributable to the 10% stake held by Company A during the period when its value grew from £10m to £13m. However, it has been beyond the scope of normal consolidation accounting entries to treat this as part of the group's post-acquisition reserves. For the purposes of illustration, the negative goodwill is not being released thereafter (as would be required by FRS 10 – see Chapter 11 at 2.3.5)

After transaction 3	£m
Cost of investment	6.75
Share of assets at fair value (51% of £15m)	7.65
	0.90
Less: post-acquisition share of reserves of associate (30% of (£15m – £13m))	0.60
Negative goodwill on consolidation	0.30

After transaction 4	£m	£m
Cost of investment		12.55
Share of assets at fair value (80% of £20m)		16.00
		3.45
Less: post-acquisition share of reserves		
of associate (30% of (£15m – £13m))	0.60	
of subsidiary (51% of (£20m – £15m))	2.55	
		3.15
Negative goodwill on consolidation		0.30

Although the accounting set out above may be appropriate in principle, it can give ise to difficulties in practice. One of these is that, once the shareholding crosses the 50% threshold, the assets of the investee will be consolidated on a line-by-line basis and it is thereafter difficult (and arguably inappropriate) to ascribe new fair values to them when further shares have been acquired, so as to reduce the size of the minority interest. If, in the above example, Company B owned a single investment property (and nothing else) which was appreciating in value throughout the period during which Company A's stake was changing, the accounting consequences would be as follows:

Example 6.3: Step-by-step acquisitions: consolidating the assets concerned

After transaction 2	£m
Cost of investment as before	3.60
Represented by:	
Share of associate's assets at fair value (30% of £13m)	3.90
Negative goodwill on consolidation	(0.30)
	3.60

After transaction 3	£m
Cost of investment as before	6.75
Represented by:	
Investment property	15.00
Minority interest (49% of £15m)	(7.35)
	7.65
Negative goodwill on consolidation	(0.30)
Post-acquisition reserves (as before)	(0.60)
	6.75

The post-acquisition reserves would in fact represent Company A's 30% share of the revaluation reserve arising from the uplift in the value of the property from £13m to £15m.

After transaction 4	£m
Cost of investment as before	12.55
Represented by:	
Investment property	20.00
Minority interest (20% of £20m)	(4.00)
	16.00
Negative goodwill on consolidation	(0.30)
Post-acquisition reserves (as before)	(3.15)
	12.55

In order to achieve this accounting, it is necessary to revalue the investment property in the consolidated accounts following transaction 4. (This would happen under SSAP 19 since it is an investment property (see Chapter 12 at 2.4), but wouldn't necessarily happen if it was another type of asset.) (This revaluation also takes place implicitly following transaction 3, but is not obvious because an investment property, less the minority interest, appears in the consolidated balance sheet in substitution for an investment in an associate which already reflected that value.) The ASC Discussion Paper on fair value had mentioned two other possibilities when increasing stakes in existing subsidiaries, which are discussed below:

The first of these is that the asset remains at £15m, in which case the consolidated financial statements after transaction 4 will show the following:

	£m
Cost of investment as before	12.55
Represented by:	
Investment property	15.00
Minority interest (20% of £15m)	(3.00)
	12.00
Goodwill on consolidation*	1.15
Post-acquisition reserves (as after transaction 3)	(0.60)
	12.55
*This can be analysed as follows:	
Cost of 29% acquired	5.80
Minority interest: 29% of £15m	(4.35)
Goodwill on acquisition of minority interest	1.45
Negative goodwill existing after transaction 3	(0.30)
	1.15

The defect with this treatment is that it overstates goodwill by attributing to it an amount which is in reality attributable to the property. Conversely, the cost of the property to the group is understated and gains on any subsequent valuation or on disposal which are measured by reference to that cost will be overstated.

The ASC Discussion Paper therefore offered a further alternative which involved accounting for the property on a 'mixed' basis that takes account of the cost of the different transactions. Applying this approach to transaction 4 would give the following result:

	£m
Cost of investment as before	12.55
Represented by:	16.45
Property	
Minority interest (20% of £15m)	(3.00)
	13.45
Negative goodwill on consolidation	(0.30)
Post-acquisition reserves (as after transaction 3)	(0.60)
	12.55

This is achieved by applying the cost of the transaction 4 investment of £5.8m to increase the asset by 29% of £5m (the increase in the stake of the uplift in value since the previous transaction) and applying the remainder to reduce the minority interest. Whatever the theoretical case for this treatment, it seems to produce figures which have little meaning or usefulness.

2.5.3 *FRS 2 requirements*

There is no ideal solution to this problem of accounting for step-by-step acquisitions; each of the approaches shown in the above example would appear to have some defects.

The ASB reconsidered this issue in FRS 2 and effectively adopted the treatment recommended by the ASC Discussion Paper, although there are some differences due to the implications of the Companies Act provisions on acquisition accounting.

A Investment becoming a subsidiary

The standard states that the Companies Act requires that 'the identifiable assets and liabilities of a subsidiary undertaking should be included in the consolidation at fair value at the date of its acquisition, that is the date it becomes a subsidiary undertaking. This requirement is also applicable where the group's interest in the undertaking that becomes a subsidiary undertaking is acquired in stages.'[133] As explained by the standard, 'the effect of the Schedule 4A paragraph 9 method of acquisition accounting is to treat as goodwill, or negative goodwill, the whole of the difference between, on the one hand, the fair value, at the date an undertaking becomes a subsidiary undertaking, of the group's share of its identifiable assets and liabilities and, on the other hand, the total acquisition cost of the interests held by the group in that subsidiary undertaking. This applies even where part of the acquisition cost arises from purchases of interests at earlier dates.'[134]

The effect of this on Example 6.3 above would appear to be as follows:

Example 6.4: Step-by-step acquisitions: consolidating the assets concerned

After transaction 3

In consolidating the subsidiary there is a difference between the fair value of the net assets at the date of becoming a subsidiary and the aggregate cost of the investment, being:

	£m
Investment property	15.00
Minority interest (49% of £15m)	(7.35)
	7.65
Cost of investment	6.75
Difference	0.90

FRS 2 indicates that this difference is negative goodwill in terms of the Companies Act. However, as the consideration paid was exactly proportionate to the share of net assets, at fair value, which was thereby being acquired, there was in fact no goodwill. This difference is equivalent to:

	£m
Post-acquisition reserves of associate (as before)	0.60
Negative goodwill on consolidation (as before)	0.30
	0.90

The post-acquisition reserves represent Company A's 30% share of the revaluation reserve arising from the uplift in the value of the property from £13m to £15m which will be reflected in the group's reserves. However, in other situations these post-acquisition reserves may have been reflected in the group retained profits. Such reserves have now effectively become part of goodwill, in this case negative goodwill (which under FRS 10 is treated as a negative asset).

However, FRS 2 indicates that, in special circumstances (such as an associate becoming a subsidiary), 'not using fair values at the dates of earlier purchases, while using an acquisition cost part of which relates to earlier purchases, may result in accounting that is inconsistent with the way the investment has been treated previously and, for that reason, may fail to give a true and fair view. ... In the rare cases where the Schedule 4A paragraph 9 calculation of goodwill would be misleading, goodwill should be calculated as the sum of the goodwill arising from each purchase of an interest in the relevant undertaking adjusted as necessary for any subsequent diminution in value. Goodwill arising on each purchase should be calculated as the difference between the cost of that purchase and the fair value at the date of that purchase of the identifiable assets and liabilities attributable to the interest purchased. The difference between the goodwill calculated on this method and that calculated on the method provided by the Act is shown in reserves.'[135] The amount in reserves will generally represent the share of the associate's reserves which had already been reflected in the group accounts, together with an additional amount being the associate's share of any fair value adjustments made when it becomes a subsidiary. When such a 'true and fair override' is used, it will be necessary to disclose the particulars of the departure, the reasons for it and its effect as required by the Act.[136]

Although the extract from FRS 2 quoted above suggests that such a treatment will only happen in 'rare' cases, it is in fact used in most situations where an associate becomes a subsidiary. An example of a company using the 'true and fair override' is Cable and Wireless, as shown below:

Extract 6.35: Cable and Wireless plc (1999)

31 Acquisitions [extract]

On 24 November 1998, Cable & Wireless Optus was listed on the Australian Stock Exchange. The listing involved the issue by Cable & Wireless Optus of 1,402 shares for a cash consideration of Aus$2,917m including 556.4 shares to Cable and Wireless plc for a cash consideration of Aus$1,105m, the exercise by Cable and Wireless plc of its option to subscribe for 332.9 shares for a cash consideration of Aus$583m and the conversion of loan notes held by third parties for 130m shares. In addition, Aus$209m was paid up on the outstanding partly paid shares. Of this amount Aus$105m was paid by Cable and Wireless plc. Following the listing, Cable and Wireless plc's interest in Cable & Wireless Optus increased from 49.1% to 52.8%.

Prior to becoming a subsidiary undertaking, Cable & Wireless Optus was accounted for as an associated undertaking. In accordance with FRS 2 – 'Accounting for Subsidiary Undertakings', and in order to give a true and fair view, purchased goodwill has been calculated as the sum of the goodwill arising on each purchase of shares in Cable & Wireless Optus, being the difference at the date of each purchase between the fair value of the consideration paid and the fair value of the identifiable assets and liabilities attributable to the interest purchased. This represents a departure from the statutory method, under which goodwill is calculated as the difference between cost and fair value on the date that Cable & Wireless Optus became a subsidiary undertaking.

FRS 2 recognises that, where an investment in an associated undertaking is increased and it becomes a subsidiary undertaking, in order to show a true and fair view goodwill should be calculated on each purchase as the difference between the cost of that purchase and the fair value at the date of that purchase. The statutory method would not give a true and fair view because it would result in the Group's share of Cable & Wireless Optus' retained reserves, during the period that it was an associated undertaking, being recharacterised as goodwill. The effect of this departure is to increase retained profits by £80m, and to increase purchased goodwill by £80m.

A number of other companies have adopted a similar method to calculate goodwill but have not given the 'true and fair override' disclosures, presumably on the basis that the effect was not material.

B Increased investment in existing subsidiary

Where a group increases its holding in the equity of a subsidiary undertaking, the standard requires that the net identifiable assets and liabilities of that subsidiary undertaking should be revalued to fair value and goodwill arising on the increase in interest should be calculated by reference to those fair values. This revaluation is not required if the difference between net fair values and carrying amounts of the assets and liabilities is not material.[137] The required treatment is that recommended in the ASC Discussion Paper as illustrated in Example 6.3 above.

Although the legislation contains certain detailed acquisition accounting rules which refer to fair values,[138] it only states that they apply 'where an undertaking becomes a subsidiary undertaking of the parent company';[139] they would, therefore, appear not to apply to acquisitions of shares in a company after it has become a subsidiary.

An example of a company making fair value adjustments in these circumstances was Glaxo Wellcome in its 1996 accounts, as shown in the following extract:

Extract 6.36: Glaxo Wellcome plc (1996)

23 Acquisitions and Disposals [extract]
Acquisitions

Nippon Glaxo Limited

In December 1996 the Group redeemed the 50 per cent equity interest in Nippon Glaxo Limited previously held by its joint venture partner, Shin Nihon Jitsugyo Co. Ltd. ("SNJ"), thereby increasing the Group's interest to 100 per cent. SNJ is the family company of the then president and vice-president of Nippon Glaxo Limited, who relinquished these positions on the redemption. The cost of the redemption was Yen 68 billion (£343 million) comprising consideration of Yen 67 billion (£339 million) and redemption expenses of Yen 1 billion (£4 million). The consideration was paid in cash, Yen 54 billion on 25th December 1996 and Yen 13 billion on 10th January 1997.

Previously Nippon Glaxo Limited had been consolidated as a subsidiary undertaking in accordance with Section 258(4)(a) of the Companies Act 1985 and a minority interest of 50 per cent had been accounted for. The redemption eliminates the minority interest.

The fair value of the net assets of Nippon Glaxo Limited at the date of redemption exceeded the book value by £39 million, comprising adjustments of £42 million in respect of the value of land and £3 million for additional liabilities. Consolidated Group net assets have therefore been increased by £39 million, with the 50 per cent attributable to the Group's pre-existing interest added to reserves and 50 per cent added to minority interests. Goodwill on consolidation is calculated as the difference between the cost of redemption and the adjusted value of the minority interest.

Burroughs Wellcome (India) Limited

In February 1996 the Group purchased an additional 19 per cent equity interest in Burroughs Wellcome (India) Limited, increasing its holding to 51 per cent. From that point Burroughs Wellcome (India) Limited has been consolidated as a subsidiary undertaking, having previously been accounted for as an associated undertaking.

Goodwill arising on acquisitions in the year

	Book values £m	Fair value adjustments £m	Net assets acquired £m	Cost of acquisition £m	Goodwill £m
Nippon Glaxo Limited	85	20	105	343	238
Burroughs Wellcome (India) Limited	7	–	7	15	8
	92	20	112	358	246

It is unclear why there should have been a fair value adjustment to reflect additional liabilities, because as the company was an existing subsidiary all liabilities would normally already have been provided. However, we believe that there are significant difficulties with this requirement of FRS 2, which effectively make it inoperable. A number of the fair value adjustments required by FRS 7 discussed at 2.4.3 above would fall foul of the Companies Act valuation rules or of other accounting standards. For example, one fair value adjustment might be to incorporate a pension scheme surplus, but this would not be allowed by SSAP 24. Another might be an increase in the value of an intangible asset recognised at the date of original acquisition of the subsidiary, but which under FRS 10 cannot be revalued. So clearly there are limitations as to the fair value adjustments which can be made in this sort of situation. Also although it would be possible, by using the alternative valuation rules, to revalue tangible fixed assets of the subsidiary, this would mean that the group would have to keep these valuations up to date, and it may also mean that the group would also have to value other tangible fixed assets within the same class in order to comply with FRS 15 (see Chapter 12 at 2.5.2), which it would otherwise not want to do.

We believe that companies should use the materiality let-out where they can and just compare the consideration paid with the carrying value of the minority interest acquired and regard the difference as goodwill.

2.6 Reverse acquisitions

A reverse acquisition, or reverse takeover, occurs when the owners of a company being 'acquired' (Company B) receive as consideration sufficient voting shares of the 'acquiring company' (Company A) so as to obtain control over the new combined entity. The acquisition is 'reverse' because from an economic point of view the acquiror (Company A) is, in economic terms, being taken over by the acquiree (Company B). This could arise, for example, in the case where a smaller listed company takes over a larger unlisted company in exchange for voting shares and, as a result, the owners of the unlisted company gain control over the majority of the voting shares of the new combined entity.

The Companies Act 1985, however, regards Company A as being the parent undertaking of Company B and therefore it is Company A which is required to prepare consolidated accounts. In preparing those accounts, Company A is required by the Act to acquisition account for the acquisition of its subsidiary undertaking, Company B.[140] FRS 6 is framed in terms of an entity becoming a subsidiary of a parent company and does not address reverse acquisitions.

As noted at 5.4.2 F below, in these circumstances IAS 22 requires that the entity issuing the shares is deemed to be acquired by the other, i.e. Company A in preparing its consolidated accounts should regard itself as having been acquired by Company B. Fair values would be attributed to the net assets of Company A rather than those of Company B. However, IAS 22 is then silent as to how its requirements should be applied in practice in such situations. As indicated earlier FRS 6 does not address reverse acquisitions. However, Appendix II notes that the accounting in IAS 22 is incompatible with companies legislation in the UK and the Republic of Ireland.[141] It had been suggested, that in the light of this reference in FRS 6, it was not possible to apply reverse acquisition accounting by invoking the true and fair override in such cases.

This issue was considered by the UITF and in its Information Sheet no 17 issued in July 1996 it was stated that the UITF 'concluded that, whilst each case should be considered on its merits, there are some instances where it would be right and proper to invoke the true and fair override and apply reverse acquisition accounting. It also agreed that, as this is simply an application of the general requirement that the true and fair override may be invoked in the circumstances prescribed by companies legislation, and the point could be clarified by this announcement, no useful purpose would be served by issuing an Abstract on this issue.'

It is fair to say that reverse acquisition accounting is very rarely seen in the UK. However, one company that has adopted this treatment is Redbus Interhouse as can be seen from the following extract.

Extract 6.37: Redbus Interhouse plc (2000)

Basis of consolidation

On 5th April, 2000 the Company, then named Horace Small Apparel plc, became the legal parent company of Redbus Interhouse Limited in a share-for-share transaction. Due to the relative values of the companies, the former Redbus Interhouse Limited shareholders became the majority shareholders with 69% of the enlarged share capital. Further, the Company's continuing operations and executive management were those of Redbus Interhouse Limited. Accordingly, the substance of the combination was that Redbus Interhouse Limited acquired Horace Small Apparel plc in a reverse acquisition. As part of the business combination Horace Small Apparel plc changed its name to Redbus Interhouse plc and changed its year end to 31st December.

Under the requirements of the Companies Act 1985 it would normally be necessary for the Company's consolidated accounts to follow the legal form of the business combination. In that case the pre-combination results would be those of Horace Small Apparel plc and its subsidiary undertakings, which would exclude Redbus Interhouse Limited. Redbus Interhouse Limited would then be brought into the Group from 5th April, 2000. However, this would portray the combination as an acquisition of Redbus Interhouse Limited by Horace Small Apparel plc and would, in the opinion of the directors, fail to give a true and fair view of the substance of the business combination. Accordingly, the directors have adopted reverse acquisition accounting as the basis of consolidation in order to give a true and fair view.

In invoking the true and fair override the directors note that reverse acquisition accounting is endorsed under International Accounting Standard 22 and that the Urgent Issues Task Force of the UK's Accounting Standards Board considered the subject and concluded that there are instances where it is right and proper to invoke the true and fair override in such a way.

As a consequence of applying reverse acquisition accounting, the results for the year ended 31st December, 2000 comprise the results of Redbus Interhouse Limited for its year ended 31st December, 2000 plus those of Horace Small Apparel plc from 5th April, 2000, the date of reverse acquisition, to 31st December, 2000. The comparative figures are those of Redbus Interhouse Limited for the 17 months ended 31st December, 1999. As set out in note 23, goodwill amounting to £47,231,000 arose on the difference between the fair value of Horace Small Apparel plc's share capital and the fair value of its net assets at the reverse acquisition date. The goodwill has been written off in the year ended 31st December, 2000 because Horace Small Apparel plc had no continuing business and therefore the goodwill has no intrinsic value.

The effect on the consolidated financial statements of adopting reverse acquisition accounting, rather than following the legal form, are widespread. However, the following table indicates the principal effect on the composition of the reserves.

	Reverse acquisition accounting (as disclosed) £000	Normal Acquisition accounting £000	Impact of reverse acquisition accounting £000
Called up share capital	1,508	1,508	–
Capital redemption reserve	46	46	–
Share premium account	102,147	102,147	–
Merger reserve	–	111,433	(111,433)
Other reserves	14,306	–	14,306
Profit and loss account	(5,652)	8,809	(14,461)
	112,355	223,943	111,588

2.7 Mergers

2.7.1 *Basic principles*

In contrast to acquisition accounting, merger accounting involves retrospective restatement of the consolidated financial statements to show the reporting entity as if the combining companies had always been members of the group.[142] This means that the effective date of the combination has no significance other than for the purposes of various disclosures; both pre- and post-combination results of the subsidiary are combined with those of the holding company in showing the results for the period of the combination, and it is therefore of little significance whether it took place at the beginning or the end of the year. Similarly, the comparative figures and any historical summaries should be restated to consolidate the results of the new subsidiary retrospectively, which will usually mean that the earnings trend will be significantly different from what it would have been had acquisition accounting been applied.

In the balance sheet, the assets and liabilities of both companies are combined on the basis of their book values, with adjustments made only to eliminate any differences in accounting policies between the two.[143] Thus, there is no equivalent of the requirement under acquisition accounting to attribute fair values to the net assets of the subsidiary so as to reflect their cost to the group; merger accounting seeks to portray continuity of both of the combining entities, not that of the holding company, and therefore makes no amendment to the values at which the assets of either are included other than to harmonise accounting policies.

These basic principles are also embodied in the Companies Act.[144]

Although no goodwill arises as a result of a merger (see 2.7.2 below), any existing goodwill relating to the businesses of the combining companies which formerly has been treated as an asset under FRS 10 (see 2.3.3 of Chapter 11) will be reflected on the balance sheet. Although it might be argued that since goodwill does not meet the definition of an asset under the ASB's *Statement of Principles* (see Chapter 2 at 5.5.1) it cannot therefore be part of the assets and liabilities to be combined in the balance sheet, FRS 10 is quite clear that purchased goodwill is to be treated as if it were. Such treatment is evident from the accounts of Kidde following its demerger from Williams PLC during 2000 as shown below.

Extract 6.38: Kidde plc (2000)

1 ACCOUNTING POLICIES
Basis of preparation [extract]

Kidde plc acquired its investments at the date of demerger under a scheme of arrangement in exchange for the issue of 828,534,733 ordinary shares. Prior to this date, these companies were subsidiaries of Williams PLC. Certain of the companies transferred to Kidde also had investments in non-Kidde businesses. These companies, which do not form part of the continuing Kidde Group, have been shown in demerger and discontinued activities in the results. Merger accounting principles have been adopted in the preparation of the results to reflect the position as if the Group had legally existed for the past two financial years.

Goodwill [extract]

Goodwill arising in 1997 or earlier has been offset against reserves. Goodwill arising on businesses acquired on or after 1 January 1998 has been capitalised in intangible fixed assets and amortised over expected useful economic lives depending upon the type of business acquired, subject to impairment reviews.

Demergers are discussed further at 4.5 below.

2.7.2 *Equity eliminations*

The cost of the investment will normally be carried at the nominal value of the shares of the holding company which have been issued to effect the combination, together with the fair value of any other consideration given. (The ability to record these shares at nominal rather than fair values on issue depends on qualifying for merger relief under section 131 of the Companies Act 1985, which is discussed under 2.1.3 above.)

As well as combining the assets and liabilities of the companies concerned, it will be necessary to eliminate the share capital of the subsidiary against the cost of the investment as stated in the balance sheet of the holding company. This is in principle a straightforward exercise, but when the two amounts do not equate to each other, the question arises of what to do with the difference, positive or negative.

FRS 6 requires the difference to be shown as a movement on other reserves in the consolidated accounts and also to be shown in the reconciliation of shareholders' funds.[145] It also emphasises that such a difference is not goodwill.[146] The Companies Act also requires such difference to be shown as a movement in consolidated reserves.[147] However, neither the standard nor the legislation specify any particular reserve.

Where the cost of the investment is less than the nominal value of the share capital of the subsidiary, the elimination of these two amounts will leave a residual credit in shareholders' funds in the consolidated balance sheet; this is generally classified as some form of capital reserve.

Where the reverse situation applies, the net debit has to be eliminated against consolidated reserves in some way and choices have to be made as to the order in which the group's reserves should be applied for this purpose. There are no particular rules on the matter in any authoritative document, but the normal practice is to apply these first against the most restricted categories of reserves,[148] and subsequently if any excess remains, against the group's retained earnings. Where the reserves are in the subsidiary concerned then, in effect, this is equivalent to the partial capitalisation of the reserves of the subsidiary; if they had had a bonus issue out of their own reserves prior to the merger, to make their share capital equal to the consideration shares offered by the new holding company, no consolidation difference would have emerged.

Apart from the effects of dealing with any imbalance as discussed above, there is no other elimination of the reserves of the subsidiary, which are combined with those of the holding company, in contrast to the treatment under acquisition accounting. However, some of the subsidiary's reserves may need to be reclassified in order to make sense in the context of the group financial statements.

FRS 6 requires that any existing balance on the share premium account or capital redemption reserve of the new subsidiary undertaking should be brought in by being shown as a movement on other reserves.[149] This is because they do not relate to the share capital of the reporting entity. Again, this difference should be shown in the reconciliation of movements in shareholders' funds.[150] Such a difference should probably be taken to the same reserve as that on the elimination of the share capital of the subsidiary, because in reality the distinction between share capital and share premium can be seen to be arbitrary in this context.

2.7.3 *Expenses of the merger*

One other question which sometimes arises in this context is how to account for the expenses of the merger. Although in the past there may have been good arguments for various treatments, FRS 6 requires that *all* merger costs should be charged through the profit and loss account at the effective date of the merger as costs of a fundamental reorganisation or restructuring under FRS 3 (see Chapter 25 at 2.6.3).[151]

However, some of these costs may be regarded as share issue expenses and therefore qualify to be written off against the share premium account of the holding company (if such an account exists). FRS 6 does not prohibit the subsequent charging of such costs to the share premium account by means of a transfer between reserves.[152]

2.7.4 *Non-coterminous accounting periods*

Particular practical problems in accounting for the merger can arise in the frequent circumstances that the accounting periods of the combining companies do not match each other. Although this can also create problems when acquisition accounting is used, the requirement in merger accounting to restate the consolidated financial statements retrospectively makes the difficulties particularly severe.

Company law dictates that the financial statements of the group must give a true and fair view in respect of the accounting period of the holding company, so this will require the period used by the subsidiary to be made to conform to that of its parent rather than the other way round. Naturally, the parent can change its own accounting reference date, but this can only be done for the future, not retrospectively. It will therefore be necessary to try to draw up financial statements for the subsidiary at each of the relevant balance sheet dates of the holding company.

The easiest part of the process will be to make sure that the subsidiary prepares a balance sheet at the next balance sheet date of the holding company, to allow a consolidated balance sheet at that date to be prepared. The difficult part will be to recreate balance sheets at the dates previously used by the parent, which will be necessary not only for the purposes of comparative figures for the balance sheet but also in order to allow the profit and loss account and cash flow statement of the current and comparative periods (together with any historical periods disclosed) to be drawn up.

Quite often it might prove impossible to draw up financial statements at these earlier dates with the same degree of accuracy that would be attainable in normal circumstances, because it is not possible after the event to institute normal year-end procedures such as stock counts and so on. It may therefore be necessary to make estimates of what such financial statements would have shown if they had been drawn up at that time, by relying on management information or by extrapolation between the reporting dates which were used (with allowance for seasonal or other relevant factors).

Another treatment which may be found appropriate would be to use non-coterminous years for the comparative figures, with the result that there will be the need to deal with the effects of either a 'gap' or an overlapping period as an adjustment to reserves. This was the solution chosen by Belhaven when it merger accounted for its acquisition of Garfunkels Restaurants, as explained in the following extract:

Extract 6.39: Belhaven plc (1987)

BASIS OF CONSOLIDATION [extract]

The accounting year end of Belhaven plc has been changed and the results are therefore presented for a nine-month period to December 31, 1987. The comparative figures combine the results of Belhaven plc for the year to March 31, 1987 and the audited results of Garfunkels Restaurants plc for the year to December 28, 1986, and the Balance Sheets of the two Groups as at these dates. The results for Garfunkels for the three months to March 31, 1987 are dealt with as a movement in reserves (Note 21).

The use of such non-coterminous accounts is only appropriate if the consolidated accounts present materially the same picture as if coterminous years had been used (see 3.3 of Chapter 5).

A particular problem can arise when a company is incorporated specially for the purpose of acting as the new holding company of a merging group. Because, as noted above, the accounting reference period of the group must by law be that of the holding company, this may result in the inadvertent creation of an accounting period which is not the one which the group would have preferred. Moreover, unless the company has been in existence for two years, arguably its statutory accounts should not be able to deal with the results of the group for the current and comparative periods, because strictly they should only go as far back as the date of incorporation of the holding company. One solution to this might be to present the information for the more relevant chosen period in supplementary pro-forma form. However, it appears that in practice, particularly in situations where a new holding company is set up as part of a group reconstruction, some companies do not go to such trouble and just produce accounts for the period they wish, as if the company had always been in existence. This was the approach adopted in the 1996 accounts of Securicor Group.

The best solution to the problem, however, would be to ensure that the new holding company has an accounting reference date which suits that of the group, and has been in existence long enough to allow a full set of group accounts for the chosen period to be presented. This was the approach adopted by PIC (see Extract 6.53 at 4.2 below).

2.7.5 *Dividends of the subsidiary*

Since the profit and loss accounts of both the combining companies will be aggregated retrospectively, it will be necessary to consider how to deal with the dividends of the subsidiary paid before the date of the combination. Essentially, the pre-merger dividends of both the parent and the subsidiary will be combined and shown as distributions in the consolidated profit and loss account, although it would be helpful to distinguish them either on the face of the profit and loss account or in a note. However, after the date of the merger, the only dividends shown will be those of the parent (those of the subsidiary will by then be inter-company payments and will thus be eliminated on consolidation).

2.8 Disclosure requirements relating to business combinations

Most disclosures relating to business combinations in group accounts arise from the requirements of FRS 6. These are considered at 2.8.1 to 2.8.3 below.

The Companies Act contains a number of detailed disclosure requirements. Many of these duplicate those contained in the standards, but there are a few additional matters in the legislation and these are considered at 2.8.4 below.

2.8.1 *All business combinations*

The following information should be disclosed in respect of all business combinations occurring in the financial year, whether they be acquisitions or mergers:

(a) the names of the combining entities (other than the reporting entity);

(b) whether the combination has been accounted for as an acquisition or a merger;

(c) the date of the combination.[153]

Taking both the requirements of the Companies Act (see 2.8.4 below) and the standard together, details must be given for all combinations, even small ones. There is no explicit materiality limitation – all entities must be named and the date of acquisition given.

FRS 2 requires that where an undertaking becomes a subsidiary undertaking other than as a result of a purchase or exchange of shares then the circumstances should be disclosed.[154]

2.8.2 *Acquisitions*

FRS 6 requires the disclosures set out below in (a) to (k) to be given for each material acquisition, and in aggregate for other acquisitions that are material in total but not individually.[155]

(a) the composition and fair value of the consideration given by the acquiring company and its subsidiary undertakings should be disclosed. The nature of any deferred or contingent consideration should be stated. For contingent consideration, the range of possible outcomes and principal factors affecting the outcome should be given.[156]

Examples of disclosures in respect of contingent consideration are given at 2.3.5 above.

(b) a table should be provided showing, for each class of assets and liabilities of the acquired entity:

   (i) the book values recorded in the acquired entity's books immediately before the acquisition and before any fair value adjustments;

   (ii) the fair value adjustments, analysed into

   - revaluations,
   - adjustments to harmonise accounting policies, and
   - any other significant adjustments.

   The reasons for the adjustments must be given; and

   (iii) the fair values at date of acquisition.

   The table should include a statement of the amount of goodwill (positive or negative) arising on the acquisition.[157]

It may be necessary to modify the disclosures given in the fair value table where a business is acquired, rather than a company, because the acquiring company may be unable to give all the required information as it may not have access to the book values of the assets and liabilities recorded by the previous owner. However, we would recommend that where a business is acquired a full fair value table should be provided if at all possible. Extract 6.20 at 2.4.3 A III above shows an example of a company giving a full fair value table in respect of a business acquired.

Stratagem Group gave the following disclosures about an acquisition in its 1996 accounts.

Extract 6.40: Stratagem Group plc (1996)

2. Companies consolidated for the first time during the year [extract]

On 3rd January 1996 the Group purchased the whole of the issued share capital of NRC Refrigeration Ltd (formerly Northampton Refrigeration Co Limited) for an initial consideration of £4,000,000, plus acquisition costs of £353,000.

NRC Refrigeration Ltd has been accounted for under the acquisition method of accounting. The assets and liabilities of NRC Refrigeration Ltd which were acquired are set out below:

	Book Value £'000	Adjustments £'000	Fair Value £'000
Fixed assets	11,098	(1,883)	9,215
Current assets			
Stock	8,480	(1,405)	7,075
Debtors	8,933	(338)	8,595
Cash	922	–	922
	18,335	(1,743)	16,592
Current liabilities			
Creditors	(19,031)	(1,256)	(20,287)
Bank overdrafts	(5,828)	–	(5,828)
	(24,859)	(1,256)	(26,115)
Due to Stratagem Group PLC	(3,400)	–	(3,400)
Creditors due > 1 year	(2,426)	–	(2,426)
	(5,826)	–	(5,826)
Net liabilities	(1,252)	(4,882)	(6,134)
Goodwill			10,487
Consideration (including acquisition costs)			4,353

However, this disclosure was considered inadequate by the Review Panel as it did not analyse the fair value adjustments into revaluations, adjustments to achieve consistency of accounting policies, and other significant adjustments, and the table did not include an explanation for the adjustments.[158] As a result the company had to include the following note in its 1997 accounts.

Extract 6.41: Stratagem Group plc (1997)

35. Companies consolidated in the financial year ended 31st August 1996

Last year a table was provided of the fair value adjustments made to the assets and liabilities of NRC Refrigeration Ltd at the time of its acquisition on 3rd January 1996. The Financial Reporting Review Panel considered that certain additional analysis and information should be provided to explain those adjustments. This is provided below:

NRC Refrigeration Ltd has been accounted for under the acquisition method of accounting. The assets and liabilities of NRC Refrigeration Ltd which were acquired are set out below:–

		Revaluations	Accounting policy alignment	Increase in provisions	Total
	£'000	**£'000**	**£'000**	**£'000**	**£'000**
Fixed assets	11,098	(253)	(1,630)	–	9,215
Stock	8,480	(1,405)	–	–	7,075
Debtors	8,933	–	–	(338)	8,595
Cash	922	–	–	–	922
Creditors and provisions	(19,031)	–	–	(1,256)	(20,287)
Bank overdrafts	(5,828)	–	–	–	(5,828)
Stratagem Group PLC	(3,400)	–	–	–	(3,400)
Creditors due after one year	(2,426)	–	–	–	(2,426)
Net liabilities	(1,252)	(1,658)	(1,630)	(1,594)	(6,134)
Goodwill					10,487
Consideration (including acquisition costs)					4,353

Explanatory notes:

Fixed assets

The figure for revaluations reflects a third party valuation of freehold properties. The accounting policy alignment reflects the application of the depreciation policies of Stratagem Group PLC.

Stock

The adjustment to stock reflects the result of a review of the net realisable values of the stock.

Debtors

Bad debt provisions have been reviewed and adjusted as appropriate.

Creditors and provisions

Of the total figure of £1,256,000, £600,000 relates to increases in the provision for disposal of surplus properties. The balance reflects the outcome of an examination of the accounts on acquisition which identified a number of items that had not been adequately provided.

Stratagem Group is not alone in having incurred the wrath of the Review Panel in this area. The Panel has also issued a ruling on the 1997 accounts of Concentric which did not include any fair value table in its accounts, yet the Chairman's statement had referred to an acquisition.[159] As indicated at 2.4.3 F I above, it also required Aim Group to give extra disclosures in this area.

(c) also in the table above, there must be separately identified any provisions for reorganisation and restructuring costs included in the liabilities of the acquired entity (and any related asset write downs) made in the twelve months up to the date of acquisition.[160]

As already discussed at 2.4.3 F I above, the creation of reorganisation provisions has been made much more difficult by FRS 7. However, there may still be circumstances where they can be made and will feature in the liabilities recognised for the acquired entity. Although, strictly speaking, this requirement does not call for separate disclosure of reorganisation and similar provisions set up in the context of the fair value exercise rather than by the management of the acquired entity within the twelve months prior to the date of acquisition, there appears to be no reason why the disclosure of the two elements of any provisions should be different. It may be best therefore to disclose all such provisions in the fair value table required, whenever made. Extracts 6.20 and 6.33 show examples of companies giving disclosure of pre-acquisition reorganisation provisions.

(d) where fair values are determined on a provisional basis only, that fact has to be stated and the reasons given. Subsequent material adjustments to these provisional fair values (and corresponding adjustments to goodwill) should be disclosed and explained.[161]

Many of the extracts at 2.4.3 above show examples of companies giving disclosure in respect of provisional fair values. One company which made subsequent adjustments to provisional fair values was Reckitt & Colman. In its 1994 accounts Reckitt & Colman gave the following disclosures in respect of its acquisition of the L&F household products business:

Extract 6.42: Reckitt & Colman plc (1994)

27 ACQUISITION OF BUSINESSES [extract]

On 31 December 1994 the group purchased the L&F household products business ('L&F Household') of Eastman Kodak Company ('Kodak'). The purchase consideration, including fees and costs of £8.40m associated with the acquisition, amounted to £1,001.90m, payable in cash, of which £1.25m was paid in 1994 and $989.50m on 3 January 1995. The remaining cost of acquisition has been or will be paid during 1994. The value of these assets and the consequent adjustment to the consideration is subject to agreement with Kodak. The net assets of all acquisitions were:

	Book value	Revaluation of assets/ (liabilities)	Other	Fair value of assets/ (liabilities) acquired
	£m	£m	£m	£m
L&F Household:				
Intangible fixed assets	–	635.99	–	635.99
Tangible fixed assets	59.45	44.04	–	103.49
Current assets/(liabilities)				
Stocks	31.99	–	–	31.99
Debtors	40.20	–	13.00	53.20
Business and brands held for disposal	11.60	77.10	(8.80)	79.90
Creditors	(44.39)	–	(2.46)	(46.85)
Provisions for liabilities and charges/liabilities due after more than one year	(41.86)	(4.40)	(4.01)	(50.27)
	56.99	752.73	(2.27)	807.45
Other businesses acquired	1.09	–	–	1.09
All acquisitions	58.08	752.73	(2.27)	808.54

Subsequent adjustments were made the following year and the 1995 accounts contained the following disclosure in respect of these adjustments:

Extract 6.43: Reckitt & Colman plc (1995)

25 ACQUISITION OF BUSINESSES [extract]

On 31 December 1994 the group purchased the L&F household products business (L&F Products) which was provisionally valued in the 1994 accounts. In accordance with FRS 7, an adjustment has been made in the 1995 accounts for amendments to that provisional fair value, now that the investigation for determining such a value has been completed. The difference has been taken as an adjustment to goodwill on acquisition. Amended and provisional values of net assets acquired are as follows:

	Amended value 1995 £m	Provisional value 1994 £m
L&F Products		
Intangible fixed assets	**636.0**	636.0
Tangible fixed assets	**72.6**	103.5
Current assets/(liabilities)		
Stocks	**29.4**	32.0
Debtors	**53.2**	53.2
Businesses and brands held for disposal	**31.9**	79.9
Creditors	**(49.8)**	(46.9)
Provisions for liabilities and charges/liabilities due after more than one year	**(47.1)**	(50.3)
	726.2	807.4
Goodwill	**279.9**	194.5
Cost of acquisition	**1,006.1**	1,001.9
L&F Products : amount paid in year	**1,004.8**	1.3
Other businesses acquired : amounts paid relating to prior year acquisitions	**1.6**	10.8
Effect on cash flow	**1,006.4**	12.1

The company obviously felt that this gave adequate disclosure and explanation of the adjustments that were made. However, the matter was brought to the attention of the Financial Reporting Review Panel and it concluded that the disclosure was insufficient. In the Panel's view this second stage of disclosure requires a similar level of disclosure and explanation as is given in the year of acquisition under (b) above and should include an analysis of the adjustments and an explanation of the reasons for them. Accordingly, Reckitt & Colman included the following disclosure in its 1996 accounts:

Extract 6.44: Reckitt & Colman plc (1996)

24. Acquisition of Businesses

a) Fair value adjustments in 1995 Annual Accounts (see Note *25* of the 1995 Annual Accounts)

As a result of an enquiry by the Financial Reporting Review Panel, the note on the fair value adjustments that were made in the 1995 accounts has been reissued in order to give full disclosure and reason for these adjustments. The figures themselves are unchanged.

On 31 December 1994 the group purchased the L&F household products business (L&F Products) which was provisionally valued in the 1994 accounts. In the initial period post acquisition communications between the acquired L&F business and Reckitt & Colman were specifically prohibited by a "hold separate" decree issued by the Federal Trade Commission (FTC). This gave rise to one of the issues referred to in Note i). The acquisition was also conditional on the disposal of certain businesses in the US as required by the FTC.

In accordance with FRS 7 an adjustment was made in the 1995 accounts for amendments to that provisional fair value.

The difference was taken as an adjustment to goodwill on acquisition. Amended and provisional values of net assets acquired were as follows and the explanations for those changes are given in the notes below:

	Amended value 1995 £m	Adjustments Total	Adjustments revaluation	Adjustments Other	Provisional value 1994 £m
L&F Products					
Intangible fixed assets	636.0				636.0
Tangible fixed assets	72.6	(30.9)	(30.9) i		103.5
Current assets/(liabilities)					
Stocks	29.4	(2.6)		(2.6) ii	32.0
Debtors	53.2				53.2
Businesses and brands held for disposal	31.9	(48.0)	(48.0) iii		79.9
Creditors	(49.8)	(2.9)		(2.9) ii	(46.9)
Provisions for liabilities and charges due after more than one year	(47.1)	3.2		3.2 ii	(50.3)
	726.2	(81.2)	(78.9)	(2.3)	807.4
Goodwill	279.9 iv	85.4			194.5
Cost of Acquisition	1,006.1	4.2			1,001.9

Note i) – The adjustments to the provisional fair values of the tangible assets arose because the initial calculations, carried out by external appraisal consultants, were based on US fair value accounting and included inappropriate elements of future cash flow as a basis of their valuation. As some of these cash flows were brand-related the plant was inappropriately overvalued. This anomaly was not identified until later in 1995 when full control and access to the business was gained (see introductory paragraph for an explanation of this).

Note ii) – Small adjustments in drawing up the definitive disposal balance sheet.

Note iii) – A more detailed investigation into the businesses held for disposal was completed subsequent to the date of signing the annual accounts. The businesses and brands held for disposal comprised parts of the acquired operation in both the US and Germany, and these were immediately placed for sale following the acquisition. As a result of the tight timetable for the completion of the 1994 accounts, the value of the businesses held for disposal had not been fully evaluated when the 1994 accounts were completed and this meant that the provisional fair value of the businesses held for disposal had been overstated by some £48m in the 1994 accounts against their estimated worth as at the end of 1995.

Note iv) – The goodwill adjustment is a reflection of the amended fair values mentioned above.

It can be seen that not only does this give more explanation about the adjustments, it also gives more detailed explanation as to why the fair value adjustments were provisional in the first place.

(e) any exceptional post-acquisition profit or loss that is determined using the fair values recognised on acquisition should be disclosed in accordance with FRS 3, and identified as relating to the acquisition.[162] The explanatory note in the standard gives three examples:

 (i) profits or losses on the disposal of acquired stocks where the fair values of stocks sold lead to abnormal trading margins after the acquisition;

 (ii) the release of provisions in respect of an acquired loss making long-term contract that the acquirer makes profitable; and

 (iii) the realisation of contingent assets or liabilities at amounts materially different from their attributed fair values.[163]

This is potentially a rather onerous disclosure requirement but it is not clear what it was intended to achieve or that it adds much of use to the existing FRS 3 disclosures about exceptional items. It would seem that it is necessary to ascertain whether any exceptional items arising in the period are calculated using fair values that were ascribed in a fair value exercise (regardless of how far in the past those fair values were ascribed). If so, the identification of the exceptional items must be given, as for the rest of these disclosures, separately for each material acquisition and in aggregate for the rest. It is fair to say that such disclosure is rarely seen.

(f) movements on provisions or accruals for costs related to acquisitions should be disclosed and analysed between the amounts used for the specific purpose for which they were created and amounts released unused.[164]

The ASB probably intended this to mean that provisions should not be used for anything other than the purpose for which they were established (although this is not actually stated). It is again worth stressing that this disclosure must be given for each material acquisition separately. It is therefore necessary that any provisions maintained must be analysed by acquisition, so that any individually material movement relating to an acquisition provision established in a material acquisition can be disclosed separately.

(g) as required by FRS 3, in the period of acquisition the post-acquisition results of the acquired entity should be shown as a component of continuing operations in the profit and loss account (other than those which are also discontinued in the same period). Where an acquisition has a material impact on a major business segment, this should be disclosed and explained.[165]

(h) where it is not practicable to determine the post-acquisition results of an operation, an indication of its contribution to turnover and operating profit should be given, or, if even that is not possible, that fact and the reasons for it should be explained.[166]

Although (g) and (h) appear to duplicate FRS 3 requirements, the information is now required for each material acquisition separately and only in aggregate for others. The requirements of FRS 3 are discussed further at 2.5 of Chapter 25.

One way of giving this disclosure is for the material acquisition to be identified on the face of the profit and loss account, as shown below:

Extract 6.45: WPP plc (2000)

Consolidated profit and loss account (UK sterling) [extract]
For the year ended 31 December 2000

	Notes	2000 Continuing operations* £m	2000 Acquisition (Young & Rubicam only) £m	2000 Total £m	1999 £m	1998 £m
Turnover (gross billings)	1	**12,212.7**	**1,736.7**	**13,949.4**	9,345.9	8,000.1
Cost of sales		**(9,591.4)**	**(1,377.3)**	**(10,968.7)**	(7,173.3)	(6,081.7)
Revenue	1	**2,621.3**	**359.4**	**2,980.7**	2,172.6	1,918.4
Direct costs		**(244.6)**	**–**	**(244.6)**	(317.3)	(285.9)
Gross profit		**2,376.7**	**359.4**	**2,736.1**	1,855.3	1,632.5
Operating costs	2	**(2,046.3)**	**(311.8)**	**(2,358.1)**	(1,591.8)	(1,403.4)
Operating profit		**330.4**	**47.6**	**378.0**	263.5	229.1
Income from associates		**35.4**	**2.6**	**38.0**	27.3	16.1
Profit on ordinary activities before interest and taxation	1	**365.8**	**50.2**	**416.0**	290.8	245.2
Net interest payable and similar charges	4	**(47.8)**	**(2.5)**	**(50.3)**	(35.4)	(32.4)
Profit on ordinary activities before taxation		**318.0**	**47.7**	**365.7**	255.4	212.8
Taxation on profit on ordinary activities	5			**(109.7)**	(76.6)	(67.0)
Profit on ordinary activities after taxation				**256.0**	178.8	145.8

* The figures presented for continuing operations include 2000 acquisitions, other than Young and Rubicam Inc. Aggregated figures for acquisitions were revenue of £438.9 million, operating profit of £61.5 million and PBIT of £66.4 million.

Alternatively the information can be disclosed by way of note, as shown below:

Extract 6.46: BTP plc (1999)

28 Purchase of businesses and subsidiary undertakings [extract]

Archimica

During the year, the Archimica businesses contributed turnover of £47.1 million and operating profit of £12.9 million to the results of the Fine Chemicals Division. The net assets of the Archimica businesses at 31 March 1999 were £30.5 million.

Hexachimie

During the year, Hexachimie contributed turnover of £21.3 million and operating profit of £4.4 million to the results of the Fine Chemicals Division. The net assets of Hexachimie at 31 March 1999 were £31.9 million.

One company which failed to give this (and other) information for a material (and substantial) acquisition was Photobition in its 1998 accounts in respect of its acquisition of Novo Group during that period. Following an investigation by the Review Panel,[167] the company had to provide additional disclosures in its 1999 accounts about the acquisition, including the following split of the impact on the 1998 profit and loss account:

Extract 6.47: Photobition Group plc (1999)

32. Acquisitions [extract]

Profit and loss account effect of acquired operations for the fifteen months ended 30th June 1998:

	Novo Group £'000	Other £'000	Total £'000
Turnover	12,641	7,161	19,802
Cost of sales	(6,372)	(4,090)	(10,462)
Gross profit	6,269	3,071	9,340
Operating expenses	(3,452)	(1,596)	(5,048)
Other operating income	72	–	72
Operating profit	2,889	1,475	4,364

(i) in accordance with FRS 1, the cash flow statement should show the amount of cash paid in respect of the consideration, showing separately any balances of cash and overdrafts acquired. In addition, a note to the cash flow statement should show a summary of the effects of acquisitions indicating how much of the consideration comprised cash.[168]

(j) in accordance with FRS 1, material effects on amounts reported under each of the standard headings reflecting the cash flows of the acquired entity in the period should be disclosed, as far as is practicable.[169]

Although (i) and (j) appear to duplicate FRS 1 requirements, the disclosures must be given for each material acquisition and in aggregate for the remainder. The requirements of FRS 1 are discussed further at 2.4.7 and 2.7.1 of Chapter 29.

(k) in financial statements following the acquisition, the costs incurred in the period in reorganising, restructuring and integrating the acquisition should be shown. Such costs are those that:

  (i) would not have been incurred had the acquisition not taken place; and

  (ii) relate to a project identified and controlled by management as part of a reorganisation or integration programme set up at the time of acquisition or as a direct consequence of an immediate post-acquisition review.[170]

These costs, whether relating to a fundamental restructuring or not, are to be disclosed separately from other exceptional items.[171] The point of this disclosure requirement appears to be to ensure that the costs of reorganisation are still disclosed even though they do not feature any longer in the fair value exercise. The disclosure, however, appears to be voluntary since it will be easy for managements who feel burdened by the disclosure requirements to 'fail' the test of having set up the programme of reorganisation at the time of acquisition or in an immediate post-acquisition review. Nevertheless, where reorganisation or restructuring costs are incurred most companies are giving disclosure (see for example Extract 6.20 at 2.4.3 A III above).

As these costs may extend over more than one period, it is suggested in the explanation section of the standard that 'for major acquisitions, therefore, management may wish to state in the notes to the financial statements the nature and amount of such costs expected to be incurred in relation to the acquisition (including asset write-downs), indicating the extent to which they have been charged to the profit and loss account'.[172] An illustrative example of how such information might be shown is included in Appendix IV to the standard. As this is not a requirement of the standard, companies do not appear to be bothering with such disclosure other than giving disclosure under (k) above.

It should be emphasised again that the disclosures discussed in (a) to (k) above are to be given for each material acquisition, and in aggregate for other acquisitions that are material in total but not individually. Most of the extracts to which reference has been made generally have been in situations when there has been only one material acquisition. Where a company is acquisitive, then it may be that separate disclosures will need to be given for a number of acquisitions in the year.

The disclosure requirements discussed at (d), (e), (f) and (k) above do not necessarily apply to the period in which the acquisition is made, but in future accounting periods following the acquisition.

FRS 6 clarified and extended the disclosures to be given in respect of pre-acquisition performance (which used to be required under paragraph 13(4) of Schedule 4A to the Companies Act 1985). For each material acquisition the profit after taxation and minority interests of the acquired entity should be given for:

(a) the period from the beginning of the acquired entity's financial year to the date of acquisition, giving the date on which this period began; and

(b) its previous period.

There is no requirement to give this information in aggregate for other acquisitions.[173] The information is not only required when a material subsidiary is acquired but also if a material unincorporated business has been acquired.

The standard also extended the pre-acquisition information to be given in the context of substantial acquisitions, i.e. those where:

(a) for listed companies, the combination is a Class I or Super Class I transaction under the *Listing Rules*; or

(b) for other entities, either

   (i) the net assets or operating profits of the acquired entity exceed 15 per cent of those of the acquiring entity, or

   (ii) the fair value of the consideration given exceeds 15 per cent of the net assets of the acquiring entity;

and in any other exceptional cases where disclosure is necessary to give a true and fair view. For the purposes of (b) above, net assets and profits should be those shown in the accounts for the last financial year before the date of the acquisition; and the net assets should be augmented by any purchased goodwill eliminated against reserves as a matter of accounting policy and not charged to the profit and loss account.[174] About a year after the standard was issued the *Listing Rules* were amended deleting all reference to Class 1 transactions. In order to maintain the status quo, the UITF issued Abstract 15 – *Disclosure of substantial acquisitions.* In February 1999, the UITF had to revise its abstract because the *Listing Rules* were again amended so that they no longer refer to Super Class 1 transactions but Class 1 transactions. The revised abstract again maintains the status quo. Accordingly, for the purposes of (a) above, the reference to Class 1 transactions should be interpreted as meaning those business combinations in which any of the ratios set out in the Stock Exchange Listing Rules for the classification of transactions exceeds 15%.[175] The required information is:

(a) the summarised profit and loss account and statement of total recognised gains and losses of the acquired entity for the period from the beginning of its financial year to the effective date of acquisition, giving the date on which this period began. The summarised profit and loss account should show, as a minimum, the analysis of turnover, operating profit and those exceptional items falling under paragraph 20 of FRS 3; profit before taxation; taxation and minority interests; and extraordinary items; and

(b) the profit after tax and minority interests for the acquired entity's previous financial year.

This information should be shown on the basis of the acquired entity's accounting policies prior to the acquisition.[176] An example of such disclosure is shown below:

Extract 6.48: Scottish Power plc (2000)

30 Acquisition [extract]

The results and total recognised gains and losses of PacifiCorp, based on PacifiCorp's accounting policies under US GAAP prior to acquisition and excluding fair value adjustments arising from the acquisition for the year to 31 December 1998 and for the pre-acquisition period from 1 January 1999 to 28 November 1999, are shown below expressed in US dollars:

Results	Period from 1 Jan 1999 to 28 Nov 1999 $m	Year to 31 Dec 1998 $m
Turnover	3,626.2	5,580.4
Operating profit	653.8	680.8
Profit on ordinary activities before taxation	251.9	196.9
Taxation	(146.7)	(59.1)
Profit in ordinary activities after taxation	105.2	137.8
Income/(loss) from discontinued operations net of tax benefit	1.1	(146.7)
Minority interests	(26.0)	(27.2)
Profit/(loss) for the financial year	80.3	(36.1)
Preferred dividends	(17.6)	(19.3)
Profit/(loss) attributable to shareholders	62.7	(55.4)

Profit on ordinary activities before taxation for the year to 31 December 1998 included \$123 million in special charges, \$13 million in merger costs, \$80 million relating to the write down of investments and \$73 million net costs of the aborted bid for The Energy Group plc. Profit on ordinary activities before taxation for the period from 1 January 1999 to 28 November 1999 included \$23 million for the write down of projects under construction and \$157 million in merger costs.

Statement of total recognised gains and losses	Period from 1 Jan 1999 to 28 Nov 1999 \$m	Year to 31 Dec 1998 \$m
Profit/(loss) attributable to shareholders	62.7	(55.4)
Exchange movements	9.5	(7.3)
Unrealised gain on available for sale securities	1.1	6.2
Total recognised gains and losses	73.3	(56.5)

As noted above, this disclosure requirement is effectively an extension of the now repealed Companies Act requirement to disclose information about the pre-acquisition results of acquired subsidiaries. It seems of questionable relevance, as it is to be based on pre-acquisition accounting policies and values which do not reflect the terms of the acquisition transaction. Nevertheless the information should be disclosed. This was one of the areas which the Review Panel found to be deficient in Photobition's 1998 accounts and required the information to be given the following year.[177]

2.8.3 *Mergers*

FRS 6 requires that for each business combination accounted for as a merger (other than group reconstructions), the following information should be disclosed:[178]

(a) an analysis of the principal components of the current year's profit and loss account and statement of total recognised gains and losses into:

  (i) amounts relating to the merged entity for the period after the effective date of the merger, and

  (ii) for each party to the merger, amounts relating to that party for the period up to the date of the merger;

(b) an analysis similar to (a) (ii) for the previous year;

(c) the composition and fair value of the consideration given by the issuing company and its subsidiary undertakings;

(d) the aggregate book value of the net assets of each party to the merger at the date of the merger; and

(e) the nature and amount of significant accounting adjustments made to the net assets of any party to the merger to achieve consistency of accounting policies, and an explanation of any other significant adjustments made to the net assets of any party to the merger as a consequence of the merger; and

(f) a statement of the adjustments to consolidated reserves.

The analysis of the profit and loss account in (a) and (b) above should show as a minimum the turnover, operating profit and exceptional items, split between continuing operations, discontinued operations and acquisitions; taxation and minority interests; and extraordinary items.

An example of these disclosures is shown below:

Extract 6.49: United News & Media plc (1996)

29. Business merger As explained in the accounting policies, on 8 February 1996, United and MAI announced plans for the merging of their respective businesses. The merger was to be effected by way of offers made by United for the whole of the issued share capital of MAI, being 332,718,123 ordinary shares of 5 pence each and 120,956,330 preference shares of 5 pence each, for a consideration of 242,090,550 ordinary shares of 25 pence each, the fair value of which amounted to £1,560.3 million. These offers became unconditional on 2 April 1996. The merger has been accounted for using the merger accounting principles set out in Financial Reporting Standard 6. Accordingly the financial information for the current period has been presented, and that for the prior periods restated, as if MAI had been owned by United throughout the current and prior accounting periods.

The book value of net assets at the time of the merger together with adjustments arising from the alignment of accounting policies were

	£m
United	
Book value of net assets at time of merger	238.0
Merger adjustment (note 24)	(73.0)
Restated net assets at time of merger	165.0
MAI	
Book value of net assets at time of merger	224.6
Merger adjustment (note 24)	(27.7)
Restated net assets at time of merger	196.9

An analysis of contribution to the profit attributable to shareholders made by the combining groups in the period prior to the merger date on 2 April 1996, the principal components of the profit and loss accounts and statements or total recognised gains and losses is as follows:

Profit and loss account	United pre merger £m	MAI pre merger £m	Combined post merger £m	Total £m
Turnover				
Continuing operations	268.8	196.9	1,451.8	1,917.5
Acquisitions	2.7	–	18.3	21.0
Discontinued operations	6.8	14.6	30.8	52.2
	278.3	211.5	1,500.9	1,990.7
Operating profit				
Continuing operations	21.4	23.5	129.6	174.5
Acquisitions	0.7	–	(18.1)	(17.4)
Discontinued operations	0.2	4.0	6.9	11.1
	22.3	27.5	118.4	168.2
Income from interests in associated undertakings	1.9	3.9	(47.1)	(41.3)
Income from other fixed asset investments	0.6	–	1.6	2.2
Total operating profit	24.8	31.4	72.9	129.1
Merger expenses	–	–	(31.0)	(31.0)
Profit on the disposal of fixed asset investments	–	11.6	–	11.6
Profit on sales and closure of businesses	–	–	138.0	138.0
Profit on ordinary activities before interest	24.8	43.0	179.9	247.7
Net interest expense	(4.0)	(1.0)	(8.9)	(13.9)
Profit before tax	20.8	42.0	171.0	233.8

Tax	(6.8)	(14.0)	(55.1)	(75.9)
Profit after tax	14.0	28.0	115.9	157.9
Minority interest	–	(0.2)	(5.3)	(5.5)
Profit for the year	14.0	27.8	110.6	152.4
Total recognised gains and losses				
Profit for the year	14.0	27.8	110.6	152.4
Exchange gains	–	–	1.4	1.4
	14.0	27.8	112.0	153.8

The equivalent analysis for the year ended 31 December 1995 is as follows

Profit and loss account	United £m	MAI £m	Total £m
Turnover			
Continuing operations	1,032.9	768.2	1,801.1
Discontinued operations	37.7	52.6	90.3
	1,070.6	820.8	1,891.4
Operating profit			
Continuing operations	111.2	89.1	200.3
Discontinued operations	3.9	12.8	16.7
	115.1	101.9	217.0
Income from interests in associated undertakings	0.9	12.9	13.8
Income from other fixed asset investments	3.3	–	3.3
Total operating profit	119.3	114.8	234.1
Loss on sales and closure of businesses	(2.9)	–	(2.9)
Profit on ordinary activities before interest	116.4	114.8	231.2
Net interest expense	(11.9)	(4.0)	(15.9)
Profit before tax	104.5	110.8	215.3
Tax	(34.3)	(36.0)	(70.3)
Profit after tax	70.2	74.8	145.0
Minority interest	(1.5)	1.4	(0.1)
Profit for the year	68.7	76.2	144.9
Total recognised gains and losses			
Profit for the year	68.7	76.2	144.9
Exchange losses	(0.5)	–	(0.5)
	68.2	76.2	144.4

24. Merger adjustments The merger adjustments reflect the alignment of accounting policies following the merger:

(a) Intangible assets – in previous periods publishing rights and titles had been stated at directors' valuation. These are now stated at fair value on acquisition and are not revalued. The effect of this restatement is a debit adjustment to the revaluation reserve of £73 million. The comparative figures for 1995 have been restated

(b) Consolidation – on acquisition of subsidiary undertakings, businesses or associated undertakings the purchase consideration is allocated between underlying assets on a fair value basis. Any goodwill arising is written off direct to reserves. Previously in MAI the goodwill relating to certain associates was amortised over its expected economic life. The effect of this restatement is a debit adjustment to goodwill of £27.7 million. The comparative figures for 1995 have been restated.

23. Share premium account and reserves [extract]

Group	Share premium account £m	Merger reserve £m	Revaluation reserve £m	Other reserves £m	Goodwill reserve £m	Profit and loss account £m	Total £m
At 1 January 1996							
As previously reported:							
United	205.6	–	80.2	467.3	(826.5)	236.3	162.9
MAI	60.7	–	–	30.2	(237.4)	340.2	193.7
Consolidation adjustment	–	(37.1)	–	–	–	–	(37.1)
Merger adjustment	(60.7)	60.7	(73.0)	–	(27.7)	–	(100.7)
As restated	205.6	23.6	7.2	497.5	(1,091.6)	576.5	218.8

The consolidation adjustment represents the difference between the nominal value of 25 pence of the shares issued to former MAI shareholders and the nominal value of 5 pence of the MAI shares acquired.

Many of these disclosures have their origin in the previous disclosure requirements of the earlier standard on acquisitions and mergers, SSAP 23, updated for the impact of FRS 3. In our view, these original disclosure requirements were needed to compensate for the fact that merger accounting was very easily available under SSAP 23 for business combinations which, in substance, were acquisitions. This information would seem to be irrelevant in the context of a true merger.

Group reconstructions that are accounted for by using merger accounting are exempted from the disclosure requirements in the FRS, but must still give the information required by companies legislation.

2.8.4 Companies Act

As indicated at 2.8.1 above, some of the above disclosure requirements which are contained in FRS 6 are duplicated in the Companies Act,[179] but in many cases the standard has extended the information required by the legislation.

However, the Act requires the names of subsidiaries acquired, and whether they have been accounted for as acquisitions or mergers, even if they do not significantly affect the figures shown in the group accounts.[180] This was an issue noted by the Financial Reporting Review Panel in its findings in respect of the 1990 financial statements of Williams Holdings.[181]

Any information required by the Companies Act need not be given in respect of an undertaking established under the law of a country outside the UK or an undertaking which carries on business outside the UK if the directors consider it would be prejudicial to the business of the undertaking or any other group member. However, this is subject to the agreement of the Secretary of State.[182]

As indicated at 2.8.3 above, group reconstructions that are accounted for by using merger accounting are exempted from the disclosure requirements in FRS 6, but must still give (in addition to the information outlined at 2.8.1 above) the following information which is required by companies legislation:

(a) the composition and fair value of the consideration given by the issuing company and its subsidiary undertakings;[183] and

(b) an explanation of any significant adjustments made to the assets and liabilities of the undertaking acquired, together with a statement of any resulting adjustment to the consolidated reserves (including the re-statement of the opening consolidated reserves).[184]

3 DISPOSALS

3.1 Basic principles

The other possible change in the composition of a group involves the disposal of a group company. In principle the results of the company being disposed of should continue to be consolidated as part of the group results until the effective date of disposal, and the gain or loss on disposal should be determined by comparing the carrying value of the subsidiary's net assets at that date with the sales proceeds obtained. There are, however, a number of aspects which need to be considered, which are discussed more fully below.

3.2 Effective date of disposal

FRS 2 defines the date of disposal in terms of when control passes; it states that 'the date for accounting for an undertaking ceasing to be a subsidiary undertaking is the date on which its former parent undertaking relinquishes its control over that undertaking'.[185] These provisions are discussed further at 2.2 above.

One complication which can arise is when a decision has been taken before a year-end to dispose of a subsidiary after the year-end and a loss is expected to emerge. Under FRS 3, if a decision has been made to sell an operation, any consequential provision should reflect the extent to which obligations have been incurred that are not expected to be covered by the future profits of the operation. Such a provision can only be made in respect of a proposed sale if the company is demonstrably committed to the sale; this should be evidenced by a binding sale agreement. In these circumstances, provision should be made for the loss which is anticipated, and this should also take account of the trading results which are expected to arise up to the date of disposal, which will either be trading losses which increase the amount of the loss on disposal or trading profits which go to mitigate it. The effective date of 'deconsolidation' will be the balance sheet date in the sense that the group financial statements for the following period will not be impacted by the results of the subsidiary being disposed of, except to the extent of any difference between the amount provided and the actual results until the date of disposal.

This then gives rise to questions of presentation of the 'deconsolidated' subsidiary, both in the balance sheet and in the profit and loss account. In the balance sheet, the treatment is to continue to consolidate the company on a line-by-line basis as normal. This treatment is the one required by the Companies Act; at the balance sheet date it is still a subsidiary which must be consolidated (none of the grounds for non-consolidation applies) and the Act requires line-by-line consolidation. This is also reinforced by the fact that FRS 2 requires consolidation up to the date of disposal.

In the profit and loss account, the treatment is to continue to consolidate the results of the subsidiary in question as normal. Again, this is what is required by the Companies Act. Where a provision for losses up to the date of actual disposal has been made at the balance sheet date, the question arises of whether, and if so how, to show the actual results in the consolidated financial statements of the following year. Frequently companies used to show only the net effect of any over or under provision. However, a strict application of the rules on the effective date of disposal would require the results to continue to be consolidated until that date as normal, and to show an offsetting release of the provision made at the previous year-end.

FRS 2 requires that the consolidated profit and loss account should include the results of a subsidiary undertaking up to the date of its disposal.[186] In addition, FRS 3 indicates that the results of discontinued operations should be shown under the statutory format headings with the utilisation of the provision analysed as necessary between the operating loss and the loss on sale.[187] It would seem therefore that the strict application of the rules is required and the alternative treatment is no longer possible.

3.3 Goodwill of subsidiaries disposed of

Where a subsidiary has been acquired and then disposed of it is necessary to keep sight of what has happened to any goodwill, positive or negative, which arose on the acquisition. If it has been taken to reserves (which was by far the predominant practice before FRS 10) and has not been re-instated as an asset on implementation of that standard, then there is a danger that it will bypass the profit and loss account altogether and result in a mis-statement of the gain or loss on disposal because the goodwill has not been taken into account.

This matter was first considered by the UITF when in December 1991 it issued Abstract 3 – *Treatment of Goodwill on Disposal of a Business.* Although UITF 3 has since been superseded, FRS 10 retains the regime, which is that the goodwill should be taken into account in the calculation of the gain or loss on disposal. This treatment is also reinforced by FRS 2 which requires that where a subsidiary undertaking is disposed of, the gain or loss should be calculated 'by comparing the carrying amount of the net assets of that subsidiary undertaking attributable to the group's interest before the cessation with any remaining carrying amount attributable to the group's interest after the cessation together with any proceeds received. The net assets compared should include any related goodwill not previously written off through the profit and loss account or attributed to prior period amortisation or impairment on applying paragraph 70 of FRS 10.'[188]

3.4 Partial disposals

When part of the investment in a subsidiary is sold, but a sufficient number of the shares are held for it to retain subsidiary or associate status, it is necessary to consider how to account for the disposal in the consolidated financial statements. When more than 50% of the shares are retained, all the assets and liabilities remain consolidated on a line-by-line basis, so the accounting entries affect only the consolidated reserves and the minority interest. The calculation of the gain or loss on sale will be achieved by comparing the sale proceeds with the consolidated net asset value (including any related goodwill) attributable to the shares sold at the date of the disposal, as in the following example:

Example 6.5: Partial disposal of shares in a subsidiary

Company A has a 100% investment in Company B, based on an original investment of £4,000. No goodwill arose on this transaction. Company B has subsequently earned profits of £6,000 which it has retained. The balance sheets of the companies and of the group show the following immediately before the sale:

	Company A	Company B	Consolidated
	£000	£000	£000
Investment in B	4		
Other net assets	20	10	30
	24	10	30
Share capital	10	4	10
Reserves	14	6	20
	24	10	30

Company A sells 40% of its shares in Company B to a third party for £7,000. It will compute its gain on this transaction (ignoring any taxation payable on the gain), in its own profit and loss account and in that of the group, thus:

	Own accounts	Group accounts
	£000	£000
Sale proceeds	7.0	7.0
40% of investment/net assets	1.6	4.0
Gain on sale	5.4	3.0

The balance sheets will now show the following:

	Company A	Company B	Consolidated
	£000	£000	£000
Investment in B	2.4		
Other net assets	27.0	10.0	37.0
	29.4	10.0	37.0
Minority interest			4.0
Share capital	10.0	4.0	10.0
Reserves	19.4	6.0	23.0
	29.4	10.0	37.0

The same basic principles apply where only an associate holding is retained, the only difference being that the balance sheet will carry the underlying assets of Company B on one line. If Company A had sold 60% of its holding for £11,000, the effect on the profit and loss accounts and balance sheets (again ignoring the effects of any taxation payable) would have been as follows:

	Own accounts	Group accounts
	£000	£000
Sale proceeds	11.0	11.0
60% of investment/net assets	2.4	6.0
Gain on sale	8.6	5.0

The balance sheets would now show the following:

	Company A	Company B	Consolidated
	£000	£000	£000
Investment in B	1.6		4.0
Other net assets	31.0	10.0	31.0
	32.6	10.0	35.0
Share capital	10.0	4.0	10.0
Reserves	22.6	6.0	25.0
	32.6	10.0	35.0

The above approach is that which is required by FRS 2.[189] It might be thought that such an approach is inconsistent with the treatment of intra-group transactions under the standard (see 3.4 of Chapter 5). However, as explained by the ASB, 'where the group disposes of part of its interest in a subsidiary undertaking it transacts directly with third parties and a profit or loss for the group is reported in the consolidated financial statements. This can be contrasted with the treatment of intra-group transactions where no profit or loss arises for the group as a whole because the transaction involves only undertakings included in the consolidation and under common control and does not directly involve any third party.'[190]

3.5 Deemed disposals

An undertaking may cease to be a subsidiary undertaking, or the group may reduce its proportional interest in that undertaking, other than by actual disposal. These deemed disposals may arise for a number of reasons:

(a) the group does not take up its full allocation in a rights issue;

(b) the subsidiary undertaking declares special scrip dividends which are not taken up by the parent so that its proportional interest is diminished;

(c) another party exercises its options or warrants; or

(d) the subsidiary undertaking issues shares to third parties.

FRS 2 says that the accounting for deemed disposals and direct disposals should be the same; in respect of both, the profit or loss should be calculated as described in 3.3 above.[191]

Example 6.6: Dilution in the holding of an investment in a subsidiary undertaking

Company H owns 800,000 £1 shares in Company S which has a share capital of £1,000,000 and net assets of £2,500,000, the balance of £1,500,000 being retained profits. Company H has owned its investment since the formation of Company S, and therefore has consolidated 80% of its profits (£1,200,000). Its share of Company S's net assets is therefore £2,000,000.

Company S issues 1,000,000 shares to third parties for cash of £3,000,000 thereby increasing its net assets to £5,500,000. The share capital and reserves of Company S and the amounts attributable to Company H (40%) are now as follows:

	Company S	Attributable to Company H
	£	£
Share capital	2,000,000	800,000
Share premium account	2,000,000	800,000
Profit and loss account	1,500,000	600,000
Total	5,500,000	2,200,000

Company H has increased its share of net assets from £2,000,000 to £2,200,000. On the face of it, FRS 2 would seem to require this gain of £200,000 to be included in Company H's consolidated profit and loss account. However, it could be argued that this does not represent a realised profit and therefore under the Companies Act it should be included not in the profit and loss account,[192] but in the statement of total recognised gains and losses. Also, Company H's share of Company S's distributable reserves has actually declined from £1,200,000 to £600,000. It could also be argued that Company H should reclassify its group reserves by making a transfer of £800,000 from retained profits to some other reserve, reflecting the fact that these profits have been replaced by a share of Company S's share premium account, which is not distributable. This may be the preferable route particularly if Company S is now to be treated as an associate of Company H. However, FRS 2 does not give any guidance on this issue.

An example of a company recognising a profit through the profit and loss account in respect of a deemed disposal is shown in the following extract from the 2000 accounts of Courts:

Extract 6.50: Courts Plc (2000)

4. Exceptional Credit

	2000	1999
	£'000	£'000
Profit on deemed disposal of interest in Courts (Mauritius) Limited (see note 11)	**3,600**	

11. Principal subsidiaries and associated undertaking [extract]

On 31 October 1999 Courts (Mauritius) Ltd issued new shares by way of a rights issue underwritten by Profurn Ltd which resulted in the acquisition by them of a 33.3% stake in Courts (Mauritius) Ltd and the dilution of the group's shareholding from 76.9% to 51.3%. The issue of the 39 million shares by Courts (Mauritius) Ltd realised £13.9 million resulting in an exceptional group profit of £3.6 million (see note 4).

South African Breweries has reflected the gain on a deemed disposal through its statement of total recognised gains and losses, as illustrated in Extract 6.51.

Extract 6.51: South African Breweries plc (1999)

29. Acquisitions [extract]

The Suncrush business was purchased through the Group's subsidiary undertaking, ABI, which issued shares to Suncrush Limited as part of the purchase consideration. The immediate effect of this was to dilute the Group's holding in ABI from 68 per cent to 53 per cent. At the same time, the Group repurchased from Suncrush Limited a portion of the shares issued by ABI issuing shares of SAB Limited as consideration. This resulted in the Group's holding in ABI being increased to 65 per cent. On consolidation, the reduction in the Group's holding in ABI from 68 per cent to 65 per cent has resulted in a deemed disposal of 3 per cent of ABI. The profit of US$52 million (R290 million) arising on this deemed disposal has not been realised and has been accounted for as a movement through the consolidated statement of total recognised gains and losses.

In this case it can be seen that the subsidiary was not issuing shares for cash, but to acquire a business, and the company considered that the gain did not represent a realised profit.

One company which has adopted both treatments is Reuters as shown below.

Extract 6.52: Reuters Group PLC (2000)

31. ACQUISITIONS AND DISPOSALS [extract]

Deemed disposals	TSI £M	OTHERS £M	TOTAL £M
Increase in net assets	195	9	204
Consideration	1	(2)	(1)
Gains	196	7	203

Of the above gains £164 million are shown in the profit and loss account, reflecting principally the profit of £157 million generated by the follow-on offering in March 2000 of 4.8 million TSI shares and the exercise of share options. Unrealised gains of £39 million arose from a share-based acquisition by TSI.

3.6 Disposals or swap transactions?

As noted at 3.3 above, FRS 2 requires that where a subsidiary undertaking is disposed of, the gain or loss should be calculated 'by comparing the carrying amount of the net assets of that subsidiary undertaking attributable to the group's interest before the cessation with any remaining carrying amount attributable to the group's interest after the cessation together with any proceeds received. The net assets compared should include any related goodwill that has not previously been written-off through the profit and loss account or attributed to prior period amortisation or impairment on applying paragraph 70 of FRS 10.'[193]

However, a parent may sell a subsidiary, or a business, in return for receiving shares in an entity whereby that entity becomes either an associate or a joint venture or even a subsidiary. The issue then is whether such a transaction should be accounted for as a disposal of a subsidiary (with a gain or loss being recognised) together with an acquisition of an associate, joint venture or subsidiary (with fair values being attributed to the net assets acquired and goodwill being recognised on the acquisition) or whether it should be accounted for in some other way. UK literature on this subject is lacking.

3.6.1 Draft UITF Abstract

As discussed at 4.2.3 of Chapter 7, many commentators, including ourselves, have criticised this lack of clear guidance for some time, since it has become increasingly common for two or more companies to set up a joint venture by a contribution of assets or a business. This has led to the matter being put on the agenda of the UITF, which in May 2001 issued a draft Abstract – *Exchanges of businesses or other non-monetary assets for equity in a subsidiary, joint venture or associate.* At the time of writing it appears likely that this Abstract will be issued in final form later in 2001 without substantial change. For this reason, we have used its proposals as the basis for the following discussion.

The scope of the draft Abstract is quite wide applying to all 'transactions in which an entity (a) exchanges a business or other non-monetary assets for equity in another entity (b) which thereby becomes A's subsidiary or which is or thereby becomes A's joint venture or associate'.[194] The most common of these situations in practice is the contribution of a business for equity in a joint venture or associate, and this situation is discussed in Example 7.7 at 4.2.3 in Chapter 7. However, the draft Abstract will also apply to the situation where a parent exchanges a subsidiary, or a business, in return for receiving shares in an entity which becomes a subsidiary. This type of situation forms the basis of the following discussion, which assumes the circumstances set out in Example 6.7 below. This example uses essentially the same facts as in Example 7.7 at 4.2.3 in Chapter 7, but looks at the position of company B who for the purposes of this example will be the 60% parent of the new company being formed.

Example 6.7: Creation of larger subsidiary by contribution of existing subsidiary

A and B are two major pharmaceutical companies, which agree to form a new company (Newco) in respect of a particular part of each of their businesses. B will own 60% of Newco, and A 40%. The parties agree that the total value of the new business is £250m.

B's contribution to the venture is one of its subsidiaries, the net assets of which are included in B's consolidated balance sheet at £85m (including goodwill capitalised under FRS 10 of £15m). The fair value of the separable net assets of the subsidiary contributed by B is considered to be £120m. The implicit fair value of the business contributed is £150m (60% of total fair value £250m).

The separable net assets of the business to be contributed by A have a carrying amount of £50m, but their fair value is considered to be £80m. A also has goodwill capitalised under FRS 10 of £10m. The implicit fair value of the business contributed is £100m (40% of total fair value £250m).

The book and fair values of the businesses contributed by A and B can therefore be summarised as follows:

	A		B	
(in £m)	Book value	Fair value	Book value	Fair value
Separable net assets	50	80	70	120
Goodwill	10	20	15	30
Total	60	100	85	150

How should B account for this transaction?

A UITF Information Sheet accompanying the draft Abstract discusses three potential approaches:[195]

- the swap approach;
- the sale and repurchase approach; and
- the UITF's proposed approach which is given no particular name in the draft Abstract, but which amounts to a partial sale/partial acquisition approach.

A The swap approach

Under the swap approach, all the items that are the subject of the exchange are kept at their pre-exchange book values. Accordingly, the carrying value of B's 60% interest in Newco would be based on its share of book values of the underlying net assets. The accounting entries for the transaction in Example 6.7 under this approach would be:

	£m	£m
Net assets of Newco[1]	145	
Minority interest in Newco[2]		58
Net assets contributed to Newco[3]		85
Other reserves[4]		2

1 Book value of B's net assets (including goodwill) + book value of A's net assets (including goodwill) i.e. £85m+£60m = £145m. In reality there would be a number of entries to consolidate these on a line-by-line basis.

2 40% of (book value of B's net assets + book value of A's net assets) i.e. 40% x (£85m+£60m) = £58m.

3 Previous carrying amount of net assets contributed by B. In reality there would be a number of entries to deconsolidate these on a line-by-line basis.

4 This represents 60% of book value of A's net assets received by B in return for 40% of book value of B's net assets i.e. 60% x £60m less 40% x £85m = £2m.

Under this approach the £2 million credit to other reserves does not represent a gain or loss but an accounting difference, similar to that arising from an equity elimination under merger accounting (see 2.7.2 above).

The draft Abstract states that this approach would be favoured by those who believe it is not appropriate to recognise a gain or loss on the transaction because of the close relationship between A and B. In fact, however, the 'swap approach' as set out in the Information Sheet differs somewhat from what would normally be understood by an asset swap method, under which the cost of B's 60% investment in Newco would be treated as the £85m carrying value of the assets contributed, but fair value would then be attributed to the net assets acquired. This was effectively the approach adopted by George Wimpey when it exchanged its housing business for Tarmac's construction and minerals businesses in 1996, although as can be seen in Extract 6.6 at 2.3.3 above, Wimpey treated the difference as goodwill. Similarly, as noted at 2.3.3 above, Kingfisher treated its combination of B&Q with Castorama as if it were exchanging a 42.1% interest in B&Q for a 57.9% interest in Castorama, but treating the difference as an unrealised gain through the statement of total recognised gains and losses.

In fact, however, the swap approach is arguably not actually permitted by the general requirements of FRS 7 that, where a business is acquired, the consideration and net assets acquired should be recorded at fair value (see 2.3 and 2.4 above). This requirement for non-monetary consideration to be at fair value has been reinforced by the ruling of the Financial Reporting Review Panel in the case of Avesco plc (see 2.3.3 above).

B The sale and repurchase approach

This approach takes the view that B has sold its existing business (including goodwill) in full, giving rise to a gain or loss, and then acquired a 60% interest in a new entity, which should be reflected in B's accounts at fair value, giving rise to goodwill or negative goodwill. The basic accounting entries for the transaction in Example 6.7 under this approach would be:

	£m	£m
Net assets of Newco[1]	200	
Minority interest in Newco[2]		80
Goodwill[3]	30	
Net assets contributed to Newco[4]		85
Gain on disposal[5]		65

1 Fair value of B's separable net assets + fair value of A's separable net assets i.e. £120m+£80m = £200m. In reality there would be a number of entries to consolidate these on a line-by-line basis.

2 40% of (fair value of B's separable net assets + fair value of A's separable net assets) i.e. 40% x (£120m+£80m) = £80m.

3 Fair value of business contributed by B less 60% of fair value of separable net assets of new business acquired, i.e. £150m-£120m (1 less 2 above) = £30m.

4 Previous carrying amount of net assets contributed by B. In reality there would be a number of entries to deconsolidate these on a line-by-line basis.

5 Fair value of new business received less book value of business disposed of, i.e. 60% of £250m less £85m = £65m. This would be recognised in the statement of total recognised gains and losses, but probably not in the profit and loss account, as it is unrealised (see further discussion at C II below).

The question then arises as to whether any or all of the gain should be eliminated. The Information Sheet suggests that some would argue that no elimination is required, on the grounds that two separate arm's length transactions have taken place. Others, it is stated, would argue for elimination, either in full or of B's 60% share. Although FRS 2 does not deal with such a situation, an analogy can be drawn with FRS 9 whereby consolidation adjustments are made not only in respect of transactions with associates and joint ventures but also on setting up such entities (see 4.2.3 of Chapter 7). However, under FRS 2 as B is the selling entity then all of the gain should be eliminated even although the business has been sold to a 60% subsidiary.

If a full elimination approach were adopted, the accounting entries would be:

	£m	£m
Gain on disposal (as above)	65	
Net assets of Newco[1]		50
Goodwill[2]		15

1 Difference between fair value and book value of B's separable net assets contributed to Newco, i.e. £120m-£70m.

2 Difference between inherent fair value and book value of B's goodwill contributed to Newco, i.e. (£150m-£120m)-£15m = £15m.

This results in the net assets of Newco being included at £150m, which can be analysed as:

	£m
Book value of B's former net assets	70
Fair value of A's former net assets	80
	150

The minority interest of £80m, however, is based on fair values.

Goodwill is now included at £15m, which is effectively:

	£m
60% of inherent fair value of B's goodwill (60% x £30m) less gain eliminated of £15m	3
60% of goodwill relating to A (60% x [£100m-£80m])	12
	15

If a partial elimination approach were adopted, the accounting entries would be:

	£m	£m
Gain on disposal[1]	39	
Net assets of Newco[2]		30
Goodwill[3]		9

1 60% x £65m = £39m.

2 60% of difference between fair value and book value of B's separable net assets contributed to Newco, i.e. 60% x (£120m-£70m).

3 60% of difference between inherent fair value and book value of B's goodwill contributed to Newco, i.e. 60% x (£30m-£15m).

This results in the net assets of Newco attributable to B being included at £90m (net assets of £170m less minority interest of £80m), which can be analysed as:

	£m
Attributable net assets	
60% of book value of B's former net assets (60% x £70m)	42
60% of fair value of A's former net assets (60% x £80m)	48
	90

Goodwill is now included at £21m, which can be analysed as follows:

	£m
60% of book value of B's goodwill (60% x £15m)	9
60% of goodwill relating to A (60% x [£100m-£80m])	12
	21

It is, in our view, hard to reconcile elimination of only B's 60% share with the requirements of FRS 2 and FRS 9. However, it gives the same result as the UITF's preferred approach for the calculation of goodwill and the gain on sale, as discussed in C below, although net assets and minority interest are different.

C *The proposed 'partial sale/partial acquisition' approach*

This approach takes the view that B effectively retains 60%, and sells 40%, of its existing business. It should therefore continue to record the 60% retained at book value, and recognise a gain or loss on the disposal of the 40%, calculated as the difference between the book value of the assets and the fair value of the business transferred. The difference between the fair value of the business given up and the new net assets acquired (i.e. the 60% of A's former net assets) represents goodwill or negative goodwill.[196]

The basic accounting entries for the transaction in Example 6.7 under this approach would be:

	£m	£m
Net assets of Newco[1]	150	
Minority interest in Newco[2]		60
Goodwill[3]	21	
Net assets contributed to Newco[4]		85
Gain on disposal[5]		26

1 Book value of B's separable net assets + fair value of A's separable net assets) i.e. (£70m+£80m) = £150m. In reality there would be a number of entries to consolidate these on a line-by-line basis.

2 40% of (book value of B's separable net assets + fair value of A's separable net assets) i.e. 40% x (£70m+£80m) = £60m.

3 Fair value of business given up by B less fair value of separable net assets of A's business acquired, i.e. 40% of £150m less 60% of £80m = £12m, plus 60% of B's original goodwill of £15m retained (£9m) = £21m. See further discussion at I below.

4 Previous carrying amount of net assets contributed by B, now deconsolidated. In reality there would be a number of entries to deconsolidate these on a line-by-line basis.

5 Fair value of business given up, less book value of assets disposed of, 40% of £150m - 40% of £85m = £26m. See further discussion under II below.

I *Treatment of goodwill*

The accounting treatment above deals with the goodwill recognised by B before the transaction in the same way as the other net assets of B. This is specifically required by the draft Abstract, not only for goodwill recognised as an asset, but also for goodwill that was set off against reserves under SSAP 22 and the transitional rules in FRS 10.[197]

If in Example 6.7 above, the carrying value of assets transferred by B had been £70m, with the £15m goodwill set off against reserves, the required accounting entries would have been:

	£m	£m
Net assets of Newco[1]	150	
Minority interest in Newco[2]		60
Goodwill[3]	12	
Net assets contributed to Newco[4]		70
Goodwill reinstated[5]		6
Gain on disposal[6]		26

1 Book value of B's separable net assets + fair value of A's separable net assets) i.e. (£70m+£80m) = £150m. In reality there would be a number of entries to consolidate these on a line-by-line basis.

2 40% of (book value of B's separable net assets + fair value of A's separable net assets) i.e. 40% x (£70m+£80m) = £60m.

3 Fair value of business given up by B less fair value of separable net assets of A's business acquired, i.e. 40% of £150m less 60% of £80m = £12m.

4 Previous carrying amount of net assets (excluding goodwill not included in the balance sheet as an asset) contributed by B, now deconsolidated. In reality there would be a number of entries to deconsolidate these on a line-by-line basis.

5 40% of goodwill of £15m set off against reserves. This would appear in the reconciliation of movements in shareholders' funds (but not the profit and loss account or statement of total recognised gains and losses).

6 Fair value of business given up less book value of assets disposed of, 40% of £150m - 40% of [£70m 'on balance sheet' net assets plus £15m goodwill in reserves] = £26m. See further discussion under II below.

II Treatment of any gain arising

The draft Abstract requires that any gain arising that is not realised should be reported in the statement of total recognised and losses (i.e. not the profit and loss account),[198] without, however, giving any guidance on determining whether or not a gain is realised.

In our view, it is very doubtful that transactions of the type illustrated in Example 6.7 can be regarded as realising a profit, in either the entity or the group accounts of B, since the gain is realised not in the form of cash or near-cash, but of a 60% stake in an unquoted investment. This would also be the analysis under the draft Technical Release on the determination of realised profits (see Chapter 3 at 2.1). Interestingly, the Financial Reporting Review Panel took the same view in its adverse ruling on the accounts of Butte Mining PLC in 1996.[199]

A different conclusion might be possible where A received cash as part of the overall transaction (see III below).

III Transactions with a cash element

Suppose for example that the transaction in Example 6.7 above had been that B was to receive only a 50% stake in Newco (but still have control), and that A had paid cash of £25 million direct to B in compensation. Following the approach set out in the Abstract might be thought to give rise to the following accounting entries:

	£m	£m
Net assets of Newco[1]	150.0	
Minority interest in Newco[2]		75.0
Cash	25.0	
Goodwill[3]	47.5	
Net assets contributed to Newco[4]		85.0
Gain on disposal[5]		57.5

1 Book value of B's separable net assets + fair value of A's separable net assets) i.e. (£70m+£80m) = £150m. In reality there would be a number of entries to consolidate these on a line-by-line basis.

2 50% of (book value of B's separable net assets + fair value of A's separable net assets) i.e. 50% x (£70m+£80m) = £75m.

3 Fair value of business given up by B less fair value of separable net assets of A's business acquired, i.e. 50% of £150m less 50% of £80m = £40.0m, plus 50% of B's goodwill of £15m retained (£7.5m) = £47.5m.

4 Previous carrying amount of net assets (excluding goodwill) contributed by B, now deconsolidated. In reality there would be a number of entries to deconsolidate these on a line-by-line basis.

5 Fair value of business given up less book value of assets disposed of, 50% of £150m - 50% of 85m = £32.5m plus cash of £25m = £57.5m.

However, this is clearly incorrect. B had a business with a book value of £85 million which was worth £150 million. If it sold the entire business the gain would have been £65 million. As B has effectively sold 50% of the business, then only that proportion of the gain should be recognised, i.e. £32.5 million. Also as explained below, the carrying value of the net assets and goodwill attributable to B is overstated.

In this case, the transaction should be accounted for on the basis that B has exchanged a 50% interest in its business worth £75 million (with a book value of £42.5 million) in return for a 50% interest in A's business worth £50 million plus cash of £25 million.

Accordingly, in calculating the goodwill and the gain on sale, the fair value of the part of the business given as consideration should be net of an amount equivalent to the cash of £25 million, as shown below.

	£m	£m
Net assets of Newco[1]	150.0	
Minority interest in Newco[2]		75.0
Cash	25.0	
Goodwill[3]	17.5	
Net assets contributed to Newco[4]		85.0
Gain on disposal[5]		32.5

1 Book value of B's separable net assets + fair value of A's separable net assets) i.e. (£70m+£80m) = £150m. In reality there would be a number of entries to consolidate these on a line-by-line basis.

2 50% of (book value of B's separable net assets + fair value of A's separable net assets) i.e. 50% x (£70m+£80m) = £75m.

3 Fair value of business given up by B (net of amount given up for cash of £25m received from A) less fair value of separable net assets of A's business acquired, i.e. 50% of £150m, less £25m, less 50% of £80m = £10.0m, plus 50% of B's goodwill of £15m retained (£7.5m) = £17.5m.

4 Previous carrying amount of net assets (excluding goodwill) contributed by B, now deconsolidated. In reality there would be a number of entries to deconsolidate these on a line-by-line basis.

5 Fair value of business given up (net of amount given up for cash of £25m received from A) less book value of assets disposed of, i.e. (50% of £150m, less £25m) - 50% of £85m = £7.5m, plus cash received of £25m. (This could alternatively be calculated under the draft Abstract as the fair value of business given up less book value of assets disposed of, i.e. 50% of £150m - 50% of £85m = £32.5m, thereby just treating the cash received as negative consideration for the purposes of calculating goodwill under 3 above.)

Although this treatment may seem counter-intuitive, it can be proved that it is the correct approach by analysing the resulting net assets and goodwill attributable to B, as follows:

	£m	£m
Attributable net assets		
50% of book value of B's former net assets (50% x £70m)	35.0	
50% of fair value of A's former net assets (50% x £80m)	40.0	
		75.0
Goodwill		
50% of book value of B's former goodwill (50% x £15m)	7.5	
50% of goodwill relating to A (50% x [£100m-£80m])	10.0	
		17.5
		92.5

The total amount relating to A in the above is £50m (share of net assets £40.0m plus share of goodwill £10.0). This represents 50% of the total fair value of A of £100m, as would be expected. If an amount equivalent to the cash had not been deducted from the fair value of the business given up as consideration (giving rise to a gain of £57.5m and goodwill of £42.5m), the total carrying amounts of the net assets and goodwill attributable to B would have been greater than B's underlying share of its own former business at book value and A's former business at fair value.

In this example, £25 million has been realised in cash, raising the question of how much of the gain on disposal can be recognised in the profit and loss account. In our view there are a number of possible approaches:

- a 'top slicing' approach, whereby as much of the total gain as is backed by cash is treated as realised (i.e. £25 million).
- a 'proportionate' approach, whereby the gain is treated as realised to the extent that the cash forms part of the total consideration of £75 million. This would allow 25/75 x £32.5 million = £10.8 million of the gain to be treated as realised.
- an approach which reflects the fact that the calculation of the gain does not depend on the amount of cash received and that the cash is effectively negative consideration in acquiring 60% of A's business. This would regard none of the gain as having been realised.

In our view, the 'top slicing' approach is perfectly acceptable, and is moreover supported by the draft Technical Release on the determination of realised profits (see Chapter 3 at 2.1).[200]

IV Artificial transactions

The draft Abstract proposes that no gain or loss should be recognised on a transaction of this type 'in those rare cases where the artificiality or lack of substance of the transaction is such that any gain or loss on the exchange could not be justified'. Where no gain or loss is recognised on these grounds, the circumstances should be explained.[201]

Unfortunately, there is no elaboration as to the circumstances where this might be applicable. One concern may have been that in transactions such as this, it is the relative, rather than the absolute, value of the transaction that is of concern to the parties. In other words, in Example 6.7 above, it is clear that A and B have agreed that the relative values of the businesses they have each contributed is 40:60, rather than that the business as a whole is worth £250 million. Thus it might be open to A and B, without altering the substance of the transaction, to assert that the value of the combined operations is £500 million (with a view to inflating their balance sheets) or £200 million, (with a view to reducing future goodwill amortisation).

Another way in which the valuation of the transaction might be distorted is through disaggregation of the consideration. Suppose that the £85 million net assets contributed by B in Example 6.7 above comprised:

	£m
Cash	15
Other net current assets	30
Fixed assets and stock	25
Goodwill	15
	85

Further suppose that, for tax reasons, the transaction was structured such that A was issued with 5% of the shares of Newco in exchange for the cash and 55% in exchange for the remaining assets. This could lead to the suggestion that, as there can be no doubt as to the fair value of the cash, B's entire investment must be worth £180 million (i.e. £15 million x 60/5). In our view, it is important in such cases to focus on the fair value of the transaction as a whole and not to follow the strict legal form.

V Comparison with deemed disposals

An alternative way that the combination in Example 6.7 could have been undertaken would have been for B's subsidiary to acquire A's business by issuing shares for a value of £100m. In this situation, A would have to account for the transaction under the draft Abstract. However, B would not, since it has not exchanged a business or non-monetary asset for equity in A. B's subsidiary has made an acquisition of A by issuing shares. As a result B's proportional interest in its subsidiary has reduced and therefore it should be accounted for as a deemed disposal under FRS 2 (see 3.5 above). The impact on the B's group accounts would therefore be as follows:

	Existing subsidiary	Acquisition of A's business[1]	Enlarged subsidiary
	£m	£m	£m
Goodwill	15	20	35
Net assets	70	80	150
	85	100	185
Minority interest[2]			74
Attributable net assets to B	85		111
Gain on deemed disposal[3]			26

1 The net assets of A's business are incorporated at their fair value and the excess of the fair value of the consideration given, i.e. £100m, over the net assets is recorded as goodwill.

2 40% of net assets including goodwill of the enlarged subsidiary, i.e. 40% x £185m.

3 The net assets including goodwill of the subsidiary attributable to B have increased from £85m (100% x £85m) to £111m (60% x £185m) giving rise to a gain on the deemed disposal of £26m.

It can be seen that the gain on the deemed disposal is the same as that under the proposed approach in C above. However, the amounts for goodwill and the minority interest are different.

3.7 Disclosure requirements relating to disposals

FRS 10 requires disclosure of the profit or loss on each material disposal of a previously acquired business or business segment.[202] Any amount of goodwill which remained eliminated against reserves on implementation of that standard which is included within the calculation of the profit or loss should also be disclosed.[203]

For businesses which were acquired before 1 January 1989, if it is impossible or impracticable to ascertain the attributable goodwill, then this fact should be stated and the reason for non-disclosure given.[204]

In addition, the Companies Act requires that where there has been a disposal of a material subsidiary during the financial year, disclosure should be made of the name of the subsidiary and of its results up to the date of disposal.[205] However, a similar exemption to that in respect of business combinations indicated at 2.8.4 above applies if disclosure is thought to be prejudicial.

FRS 2 has repeated the requirements of the Act, but has extended them such that the name of each material undertaking which ceases to be a subsidiary undertaking, together with any ownership interest retained, should be disclosed. Where this arises other than by way of disposal of at least part of the interest held by the group, the circumstances in which the undertaking ceased to be a subsidiary undertaking should be explained.[206]

In addition, FRS 1 requires disclosure of the effects of disposals of subsidiaries on the cash flow statement and FRS 3 requires separate disclosure of the aggregate results of discontinued operations during the period. These are discussed at 2.7.1 of Chapter 29 and 2.3 of Chapter 25 respectively.

4 GROUP REORGANISATIONS

4.1 Introduction

Group reorganisations involve the restructuring of the relationships between companies in a group by, for example, setting up a new holding company, changing the direct ownership of a subsidiary within the group, or transferring businesses from one company to another because of a process of divisionalisation. In principle, most such changes should have no impact on the consolidated financial statements (provided there are no minority interests affected), because they are purely internal and cannot affect the group when it is being portrayed as a single entity. However, all such transactions can have a significant impact on the financial statements of the individual companies in the group, and this is described for each of the main types of transaction in the sections which follow. All the examples given assume that all the subsidiaries are owned 100% by the parent company.

4.2 Setting up a new top holding company

Reorganisations of this type may take place, for example, to introduce a public company over the top of an existing group as a vehicle for flotation, or to improve the co-ordination of diverse businesses. It involves H becoming the new holding company of A, as shown in the diagram below, and this may be achieved either by the shareholders subscribing for shares in H and then H paying cash for A or, more usually, by H issuing its own shares to the shareholders of A in exchange for the shares in A.

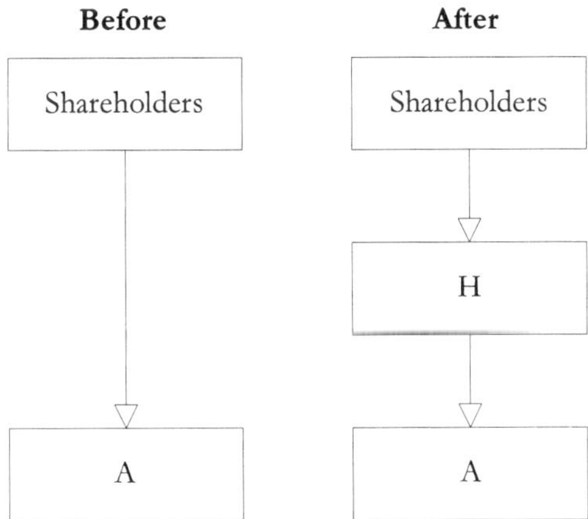

This type of reorganisation will qualify as a 'group reconstruction' under FRS 6 which is defined as any of the following arrangements:

(a) the transfer of a shareholding in a subsidiary undertaking from one group company to another;

(b) the addition of a new parent company to a group;

(c) the transfer of shares in one or more subsidiary undertakings of a group to a new company that is not a group company but whose shareholders are the same as those of the group's parent; and

(d) the combination into a group of two or more companies that before the combination had the same shareholders.[207]

FRS 6 has not exempted group reconstructions from its provisions but states that merger accounting may be used for group reconstructions, even though there is no business combination meeting the definition of a merger, provided:

(a) the requirements of the Companies Act for merger accounting are met (see 2.1.2 above);

(b) the ultimate shareholders remain the same, and the rights of each such shareholder, relative to the others, are unchanged; and

(c) no minority's interest in the net assets of the group is altered by the transfer.[208]

It can be seen that under FRS 6 the use of merger accounting for group reconstructions is to be optional. However, because of condition (a) above, if the new holding company pays cash for the subsidiary, then merger accounting will not be possible as the Companies Act provisions will not be met. Merger accounting is only permitted under the legislation where the shares are acquired by means of a share for share exchange and the fair value of any consideration other than equity shares does not exceed 10% of the nominal value of the equity shares issued.[209]

Therefore if H pays cash for A, it should (in theory at least) account for the transaction as an acquisition, which involves attributing fair values to A's assets, consolidating only the post-acquisition results of A and possibly freezing A's pre-acquisition reserves from being distributed to H's shareholders in the future (see 2.3.8 above for a discussion of the treatment of pre-acquisition dividends). All these consequences are usually undesirable when the sole intention is to insert a new holding company at the top of the group, and it is relatively unlikely that this means of effecting the transaction will be chosen. In any event, H could have difficulty in financing such a transaction, and A could not provide the necessary finance (e.g. by any kind of loan or guarantee) because UK company law does not permit a company to provide financial assistance for the purchase of its own shares.[210]

It is therefore more likely that the transaction will be effected by the exchange of shares. In this case the transaction will qualify for merger accounting (subject to all the provisos in FRS 6 set out above) and hence the consolidated financial statements may continue to carry the assets and liabilities of A at their previous book values and all profits before and after the merger can continue to be consolidated (although there are possible problems if H does not have the same accounting period and has not been in existence long enough – see 2.7.4 above). Also, the transaction will qualify for merger relief under section 131 of the Companies Act, so the investment in A can be recorded by H at the nominal value of the shares issued by H (although as indicated at 2.1.3 above, this may only be possible under FRS 4 if merger accounting is adopted); the reserves of A will potentially be 'frozen' as a result of the transaction, but only to the extent that the nominal value of H's shares exceeds that of A's shares.

Where the option of using merger accounting is not taken, or cannot be taken because cash is involved, it would seem that acquisition accounting needs to be used, although as FRS 6 states 'acquisition accounting would require the restatement at fair value of the assets and liabilities of the company transferred, and the recognising of goodwill, which is likely to be inappropriate in the case of a transaction that does not alter the relative rights of the ultimate shareholders'.[211]

In recent years a number of companies have created a new holding company as part of an arrangement to return capital to the shareholders. This generally involves the new company issuing shares to the members of the existing company together with cash and/or loan notes in exchange for their existing shares. However, the value of the non-share element generally exceeds 10% of the nominal value of the share element of the consideration which means that not all of the requirements of the Companies Act are met. Nevertheless, such companies have adopted merger accounting by invoking the true and fair override,[212] as illustrated in the extract below.

Extract 6.53: PIC International Group PLC (1998)

1 ACCOUNTING POLICIES [extract]
a) Basis of preparation

The accounts are prepared on historical cost accounting principles modified to incorporate the revaluation of certain tangible fixed assets. The accounts are prepared in accordance with applicable UK accounting standards except for the adoption of merger accounting referred to below.

The consolidated profit and loss account, balance sheet and cash flow statement include the Company and its subsidiaries, together with the Group's share of the profits and retained post acquisition reserves of joint ventures and associates, which have been accounted for under the gross equity method and equity method of consolidation respectively. Except as noted below, the profits or losses of subsidiaries, joint ventures and associates acquired or sold during the year are included as from or up to their respective dates of acquisition or disposal.

The Company was incorporated on 24 June 1996 as Joyce Café Limited, changed its name to PIC International Group PLC and re-registered as a public limited company on 3 April 1998. Up to 3 April 1998, the Company's assets and paid up capital amounted to only £2, and it did not trade or declare or pay any dividends or make any other distributions.

Effective from 22 June 1998, the Company acquired 100% of the issued share capital of Dalgety Limited (formerly Dalgety PLC) following implementation of a Scheme of Arrangement under section 425 of the Companies Act 1985.

The Scheme of Arrangement involved the cancellation of the issued share capital of Dalgety Limited amounting to £292,015,716; the issuance of £292,015,716 of share capital of Dalgety Limited to the Company; and for each share cancelled the issuance of the following consideration by the Company to the former shareholders of Dalgety Limited:

- one 10 pence ordinary share in the Company;
- one convertible loan note redeemed for 138.0 pence;
- cash of 94.5 pence.

The Scheme of Arrangement has been accounted for in accordance with the principles of merger accounting, although it does not satisfy all the conditions required (see below). The consolidated accounts are presented as if the Scheme of Arrangement had been effected on 24 June 1996, except for the effect of the issue of the redeemable convertible loan notes which took place on 22 June 1998 and the redemption payment under the loan notes and the return of cash to shareholders which took place on 26 June 1998. The consolidated profit and loss account combines the results of the Company with those of the Dalgety Limited Group for the year ended 30 June 1998. The comparative figures combine the results of the

Company from incorporation to 30 June 1997 with those of the Dalgety Limited Group for the year ended 30 June 1997. The comparative consolidated balance sheet as at 30 June 1997 combines the balance sheet of the Company and that of the Dalgety Limited Group as at that date.

Schedule 4A to the Companies Act 1985 and FRS 6 "Acquisitions and Mergers" require acquisition accounting to be adopted where all the conditions laid down for merger accounting are not satisfied. The Scheme of Arrangement does not satisfy the condition that the fair value of the non-share element of the consideration given by the Company for the shares in Dalgety Limited should not exceed 10% of the nominal value of the share element of the consideration.

However, in the opinion of the directors, the Scheme of Arrangement is a Group reconstruction rather than an acquisition, since the shareholders of the Company are the same as the former shareholders in Dalgety Limited and the rights of each shareholder, relative to the others, are unchanged and no minority interest in the net assets of the Group is altered. Hence the shareholders have a continuing interest in the businesses of Dalgety Limited, both before and after the Scheme of Arrangement. Consequently, the directors consider that to record the Scheme of Arrangement as an acquisition by the Company, to attribute fair values to the assets and liabilities of the Group and to reflect only the post-Scheme of Arrangement results within these accounts would fail to give a true and fair view of the Group's results and financial position.

Accordingly, having regard to the overriding requirement under section 227(6) of the Companies Act 1985 for the accounts to give a true and fair view of the Group's results and financial position, the directors have adopted merger accounting principles in drawing up these accounts. The directors consider that it is not practicable to quantify the effect of this departure from the Companies Act 1985 requirements.

4.3 Changing direct ownership of a company within a group

4.3.1 Subsidiary moved 'up'

This involves a 'grandson' subsidiary being moved up to become a 'son', as shown in the diagram below. Such a change might be made say, to allow B to be disposed of while C is retained, or because B and C are in different businesses and the group wishes to restructure itself so that the different businesses are conducted through directly owned subsidiaries.

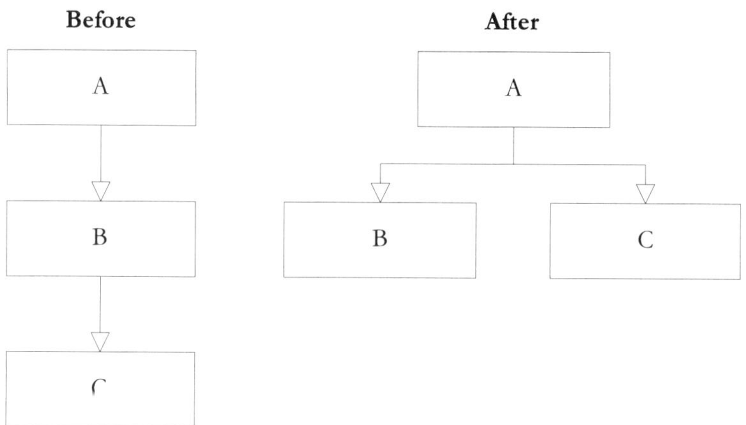

This result could be achieved either by B transferring its investment in C to A as a dividend in specie, or by A paying cash (or a cash equivalent) to B for the investment in C. It is not possible to effect this transaction by a share for share exchange, because an allotment by a holding company (A) to its subsidiary (B) is void.[213]

If the mechanism used is to be a dividend in specie then B must have sufficient distributable profits. If B has previously revalued its investment in C then the amount of that revaluation may be treated as a realised profit in deciding whether the dividend is legal and in accounting for the dividend; for example, if B's balance sheet is as follows:

	£
Investment in C (cost £100)	900
Other net assets	100
	1,000
Share capital	100
Revaluation reserve	800
Profit and loss account	100
	1,000

On the face of it, B cannot make a distribution of more than £100. However, if it makes a distribution in kind of its investment in C, the revaluation reserve can be treated as realised.[214]

Where the transaction is effected as a dividend in specie then the problem of how A accounts for it also arises. It will need to reflect its new investment in C at a value, but two questions then arise; what value to place on it, and whether the transaction gives rise to a realised profit. The legal position on both of these points is unclear. On the first question, a range of possible values would appear to be possible – the value might for example be agreed between the parties, it could be at current fair value, it could be the carrying value previously recorded in B's financial statements or it might even be nil. In practice, it might be convenient to use B's carrying value, but it cannot be said with certainty that this is the right answer. On the second issue, it may appear that A has made a profit by being given a valuable asset (subject to the need to write down its investment in B), but it might be contended with some justification that this is not realised, since in substance nothing has changed – A still owns the same two subsidiaries as it did before. This is the position taken in the draft Technical Release – *The determination of realised profits and distributable profits in the context of the Companies Act 1985*, which states that 'a dividend in specie from a subsidiary is an unrealised profit in the hands of the parent (even where there is a cash alternative) unless the asset distributed meets the definition of qualifying consideration.[215] Where it is sufficiently significant (e.g. in relation to a proposed distribution), it may be advisable to seek legal advice on these points.

If A pays cash to B in exchange for its investment in C, the transaction is on the face of it straightforward. B will have to record a gain or loss on sale if the purchase price differs from the value at which it carried its investment in C, although frequently the transfer may be made on such terms that no gain or loss is recorded. However, there is a danger that a transfer at a price which does not fully reflect the true value of C (i.e. made at less than an arm's-length price) will be regarded as having given rise to a distribution, and if the transaction is made to facilitate B's leaving the group, it could also be regarded as financial assistance which may be illegal – there are therefore various possible legal pitfalls which must be borne in mind.

Regardless of the value at which these transactions take place, there should be no effect on the group financial statements, because the group as a whole is in no different position from before; it has made neither an acquisition nor a disposal.

4.3.2 *Subsidiary moved 'down'*

This involves a 'son' becoming a 'grandson' as shown in the diagram below. Such a change might be made, say, if A is a foreign holding company but B and C are UK companies who will form a UK tax group as a result of the reorganisation.

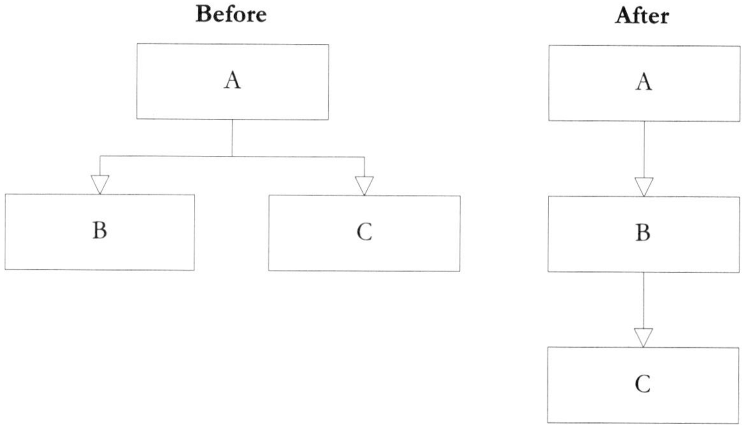

This reorganisation could be achieved either by B paying cash to A or by B issuing its shares to A in exchange for the shares in C. As in the previous two examples, there should be no effect on the group financial statements as a result of the reorganisation.

The accounting in the case of a cash transaction is relatively straightforward, following the principles described above in 4.3.1. However, if C is sold at an amount greater or smaller than its carrying value, the issue of whether A should recognise a gain or loss will again arise; as with the question discussed in 4.3.1 above, the law on this is unclear. The question of whether B has effectively made a distribution is again unlikely to arise; in the context of this transaction it could arise only if the transfer were made at a price which was in excess of the fair value of C, which is in practice unlikely.

In the case of a share-for-share exchange, the provisions of section 132 of the Companies Act 1985 become relevant. This section is designed to give partial relief from the requirement to set up a share premium account in the circumstances of a group reconstruction involving the issue of shares. It requires a share premium account of the 'minimum premium value' to be established; this is the amount by which the book value of the investment (or cost, if lower) exceeds the nominal value of the shares issued. The effect of this is to preserve the book value of the investment (any amount by which the investment had been revalued would effectively be reversed, but the investment could also be revalued again). The operation of the section is illustrated in the following example:

Example 6.8

The balance sheets of A and its direct subsidiaries B and C are as follows:

	A	B	C	Group
	£	£	£	£
Investment in B	200			
Investment in C	100			
Other net assets	300	275	300	875
	600	275	300	875
Share capital	500	200	100	500
Profit and loss account	100	75	200	375
	600	275	300	875

B then issues 50 £1 shares to A in exchange for A's investment in C, which is shown in A's balance sheet at a cost of £100. The minimum premium value is therefore £50. The resultant balance sheets would be:

	A	B	C	Group
	£	£	£	£
Investment in B	300			
Investment in C		100		
Other net assets	300	275	300	875
	600	375	300	875
Share capital	500	250	100	500
Share premium		50		
Profit and loss account	100	75	200	375
	600	375	300	875

Care must be taken in this situation to avoid issuing shares at a discount; this means that it must be possible to demonstrate that C is worth at least the nominal value of the shares issued by B.

If B were to prepare group accounts then the accounting considerations are similar to those discussed at 4.2 above.

4.3.3 *Subsidiary moved 'along'*

This involves a 'grandson' subsidiary being moved along to become another 'grandson' but under a different 'son', as shown in the diagram below. It would be achieved by C paying cash or other assets to B rather than issuing shares, because otherwise the resulting holding of B in C would probably negate the desired effect of the transaction.

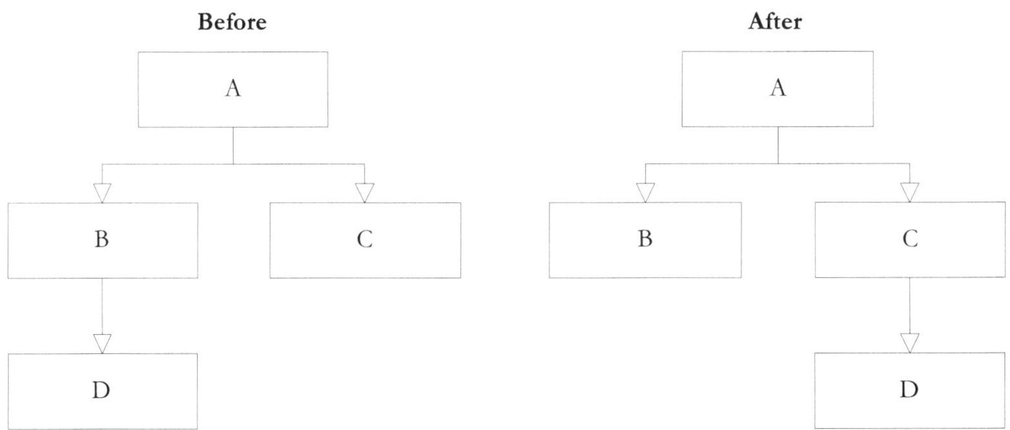

The accounting considerations are similar to those under 4.3.1 above, and once again there can be no effect on the group financial statements, because when the group is looked upon as a single entity there has been no change. The question of an effective distribution is unlikely to arise because the purchaser is not the holding company. As above, if the transaction is a prelude to B leaving the group, or is intended to facilitate it, and C pays less than fair value then problems of financial assistance can arise. If C were to prepare group accounts then the accounting considerations are similar to those discussed at 4.2 above where the new holding company pays cash.

Although C cannot issue shares directly to B as it might negate the desired effect of the transaction, it may, however, be possible to achieve the same effect by utilising a combination of the reorganisations outlined at 4.3.1 and 4.3.2 above.

4.4 Divisionalisation of an existing group

The term 'divisionalisation' in this context is used to signify the transfer of the assets and trades of a number of subsidiaries into one company so that the businesses are brought together. It is a means of rationalising and simplifying the group and can result in a saving of administration costs. Transactions of this type are usually effected for a cash consideration, which is often left outstanding on inter-company account as the shell company has no requirement for cash.

In principle the accounting treatment is straightforward. However, one complication which can arise is that there might be an apparent need to write down the investment in the shell company to reflect an impairment in its value, depending on the price at which the assets were transferred. This will typically arise where the shell company was originally purchased at a price which included goodwill, but the business is then transferred to another company at a price which reflects only the value of the net tangible assets; this will mean that, although the goodwill still exists, the business to which it relates is now in another company, and although the group as a whole is unaffected, the value of the investment in the shell company now falls short of its cost. This issue is discussed in Chapter 14 at 2.2.1 C.

4.5 Demergers

In this context, this refers to splitting up an existing group of companies into two or more separate groups of companies, in order to separate their different trades, possibly as a prelude, say, to floating off one of the businesses.

This could be achieved in a number of ways:

(a) Company A transfers its shareholdings in a subsidiary, B, to its shareholders as a dividend in specie.

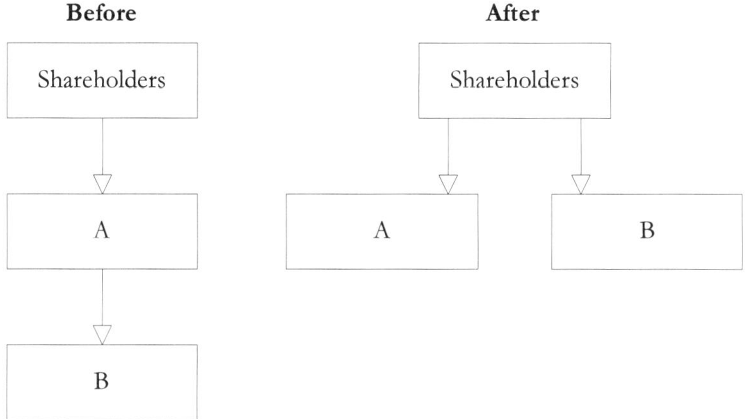

(b) Company A transfers a trade to another company, C (usually formed for the purposes of the demerger) and in exchange C issues shares to the shareholders of A.

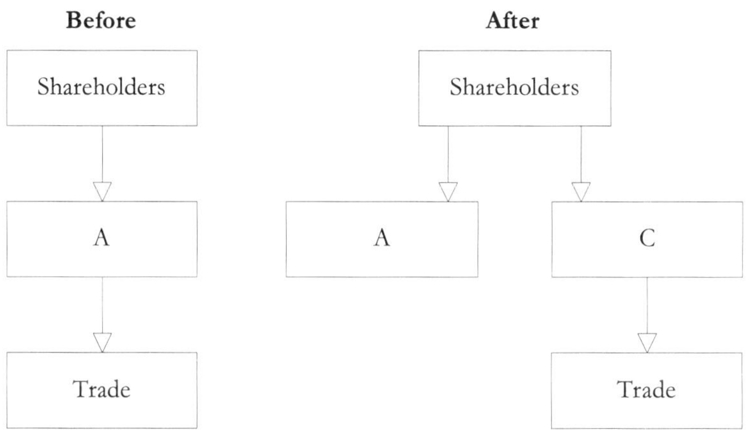

(c) Company A transfers its shareholding in a subsidiary, B, to another company, C; in return, shares in C are issued to some or all of the shareholders in A.

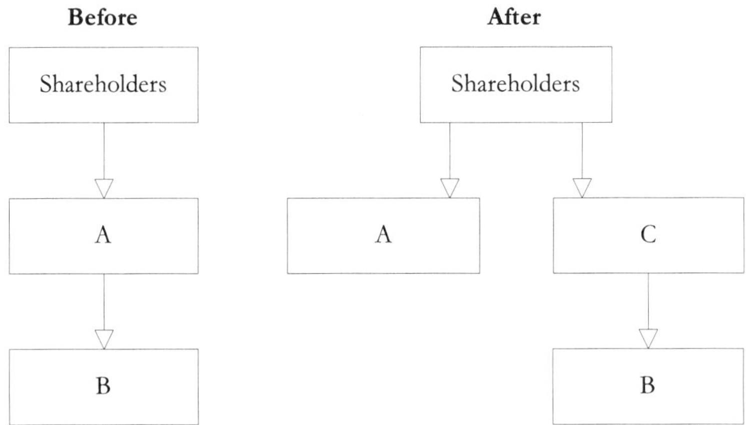

Whichever route is adopted, the transaction involves a distribution by A to its shareholders. This is less obvious in the second and third examples outlined above, but it is as though A had distributed the assets or shares in question to its own shareholders, which they then exchange for shares in C. Similar accounting issues arise in each case; for the purposes of illustration, an example is shown below of a transaction of type (c) above.

Example 6.9

B is a subsidiary of A and is to be demerged from the group. The form of the transaction is that a new company, C, is to be formed which will issue shares to the shareholders of A in exchange for A's investment in B. The balance sheets before the demerger are as follows:

	A	B	A group
	£	£	£
Investment in B	500		
Other net assets	1,200	800	2,000
	1,700	800	2,000
Share capital	1,000	500	1,000
Profit and loss account	700	300	1,000
	1,700	800	2,000

C is to issue 500 £1 ordinary shares to the shareholders of A in exchange for the shares in B held by A. In effect this amounts to a distribution of £500 by A to its shareholders so that, in the A group financial statements the company's net assets are reduced by £500 and the group's net assets by £800 (i.e. the net asset value of B). In the financial statements, the usual treatment is to disclose these amounts as movements on retained earnings, along the following lines:

Profit and loss account	Group	Company
	£	£
Balance at 1 January 1999	1,000	700
Demerger of B	(800)	(500)
Profit for the year	350	350
Balance at 31 December 1999	550	550

From C's point of view, the questions which arise are whether its shares are being issued at a premium and if so whether share premium relief should be taken. As this part of the transaction amounts to a merger of C with B, the answers to both questions are yes. However, if the demerger was of an unincorporated business, then merger relief would not be available, since it applies only to share exchanges and not to issues of shares in exchange for assets; this contrasts with group reconstruction relief, which is available for both – see 4.3.2 above. The same point applies to a transaction of type (b) above.

It also seems logical to use merger accounting for this kind of transaction and it is likely to be a 'group reconstruction' under FRS 6; merger accounting can therefore be adopted provided all the conditions are met. Although this is likely to be the case for the demerger transaction itself, in many cases it is likely to have been preceded by a number of other internal transactions involving transfers of subsidiaries or businesses around the group some of which may have been for shares and others for cash or on inter-company account.

One example of a demerger was that of ICI's bioscience interests to Zeneca in 1993. However, as disclosed in Zeneca's 1993 accounts merger accounting was applied even though all the conditions laid down for merger accounting were not met, the 'true and fair override' being used:

Extract 6.54: Zeneca Group PLC (1993)

2 BASIS OF CONSOLIDATION AND PRESENTATION OF FINANCIAL INFORMATION [extract]

The transfer of ZENECA Limited to the Company has been accounted for in accordance with the principles of merger accounting set out in Statement of Standard Accounting Practice No. 23 (SSAP 23) and Schedule 4(A) to the Companies Act 1985. The financial statements are therefore presented as if ZENECA Limited and its subsidiaries had been owned and controlled by the Company throughout.

ZENECA Limited was created through an internal reorganisation within ICI which resulted in the transfer to it of ICI's bioscience activities with effect from 1 January 1993. The bioscience interests included both subsidiaries, some of which were themselves subject to reorganisation prior to transfer, and certain unincorporated business activities of ICI. These transactions have been accounted for in these group accounts using the principles of merger accounting as if ZENECA Limited had been in existence throughout. This is not in accordance with SSAP 23 and Schedule 4(A) to the Companies Act 1985 as the transfer of the unincorporated business activities and the reorganisation of certain subsidiaries prior to transfer to ZENECA Limited do not meet all the conditions laid down for merger accounting.

The directors consider that to apply acquisition accounting to any part of the reorganisation of the Zeneca businesses, with consequent adjustments to the fair values of the related assets and liabilities and the reflection of post reorganisation results only within ZENECA Group PLC's accounts, would fail to give a true and fair view of the Group's state of affairs and results for the shareholders since they have had a continuing interest in the Zeneca businesses both before and after the demerger. Due to the number and complexity of transactions involved, it is not practicable to quantify the effect of this departure.

Although this demerger preceded FRS 6, such preliminary transactions would also not have met the conditions laid down in FRS 6 (given that one of the conditions for group reconstructions is that it is allowed by the Companies Act).

As far as ICI's accounts are concerned, the businesses transferred to Zeneca were consolidated up to the date of demerger and shown as discontinued operations. As indicated above, a demerger involves a distribution to the shareholders. ICI dealt with this as follows:

Extract 6.55: Imperial Chemical Industries PLC (1993)

10 DIVIDENDS

	1993	1992	**1993**	1992
	pence per £1 share		**£m**	£m
Interim, paid 4 October 1993	**10.5p**	21p	**76**	150
Second interim, to be confirmed as final, payable 28 April 1994	**17.0p**	34p	**123**	243
	27.5p	55p	**199**	393
Demerger dividend – This comprises the net assets of Zeneca at date of demerger. The resolution to give effect to the demerger, which was passed at the Extraordinary General Meeting of the Company on 28 May 1993, approved a dividend of £464,566,941 on the Ordinary Shares of £1 each in the Company: this was the holding value of Zeneca Limited by the Company.			**363**	
			562	393

23 RESERVES [extract]

The cumulative amount of goodwill resulting from acquisitions during 1993 and prior years, net of goodwill attributable to subsidiary undertakings or businesses demerged or disposed of prior to 31 December 1993, amounted to £609m (1992 £1,700m, reduced by £69m following a detailed review to identify all such goodwill). Goodwill in respect of Zeneca businesses which were demerged totalled £1,011m.

It can be seen that ICI has charged as the demerger dividend in the consolidated profit and loss account the amount of the net assets of businesses demerged, although noting the dividend approved by the shareholders which was based on the carrying amount of the investment in the parent's books. Although not a disposal or closure of a business, it is arguable that the demerger dividend should also have included the goodwill attributable to the businesses demerged based on the then requirements of UITF 3 (see 3.3 above). Such an approach was adopted by Fine Art Developments in respect of its demerger of Creative Publishing in 1998, as shown below:

Extract 6.56: Fine Art Developments p.l.c. (1998)

8 DEMERGER DIVIDEND

	Group	
The demerger dividend represents the net assets and attributable goodwill of the Creative Publishing business and is calculated as follows:	1998	1997
	£'000	£'000
Tangible fixed assets	30,901	–
Investments	562	–
Stocks	68,550	–
Debtors	74,233	–
Net borrowings	(68,961)	–
Creditors and provisions	(44,509)	–
Net assets on demerger	60,776	–
Goodwill previously written off	14,070	–
Demerger dividend	74,846	–

4.6 Capital contributions

One form of transaction which is sometimes made within a group is a 'capital contribution', where one company injects funds in another (usually its subsidiary) in the form of a non-returnable gift. Whenever capital contributions are made, complex tax considerations can arise and should be addressed.

Capital contributions have no legal status in the UK – certainly the term is not used anywhere in the Companies Acts. This has led to uncertainty over the appropriate accounting treatment in the financial statements of both the giver and the receiver of the capital contribution.

The only reference to capital contributions in accounting standards is in the Application Notes in FRS 4 – *Capital instruments*. However, this just deals with the treatment from the standpoint of a subsidiary receiving the contribution.

4.6.1 *Treatment in the financial statements of the paying company*

In the most common situation, where the contribution is made by a company to one of its subsidiaries, the treatment is relatively straightforward; the amount of the contribution should be added to the cost of the investment in the subsidiary. However, it will not be possible to regard it as part of the purchase price of shares in the subsidiary, so it should be classified as a separate item when the cost of the investment is analysed. As with any fixed asset, it will be necessary to write down the investment whenever it is recognised that its value has been impaired; this should be considered when subsequent dividends are received from the subsidiary which could be regarded as having been met out of the capital contribution and hence representing a return of it.

Where the contribution is made to a fellow-subsidiary, it will not be possible to regard it as an asset of any kind; it is neither an investment in the other company, nor can it be treated as a monetary receivable, since by definition there is no obligation on the part of the recipient to return it. Accordingly, the only available treatment to the paying company in these circumstances will be to write it off in the profit and loss account of the period in which the payment is made.

4.6.2 *Treatment in the financial statements of the receiving company*

The Application Notes in FRS 4 state that a subsidiary should include capital contributions received from its parent within shareholders' funds, and in the year in which a contribution is received, it should be reported in the reconciliation of movements in shareholders' funds. No indication is given as to where in shareholders' funds it is to be included, but the most common treatment would appear to be to credit the amount received to a separate reserve with a suitable title, such as 'capital contribution', or 'capital reserve'.

Notwithstanding this, it is generally considered that the contribution can be regarded for distribution purposes as a realised profit, and accordingly is available to be paid out by way of dividend. However, where the contribution received is in the form of a non-monetary asset it is doubtful whether this should be the case. This is the position taken in the draft Technical Release – *The determination of realised profits and distributable profits in the context of the Companies Act 1985*, which regards the contribution of assets from owners in their capacity as such as giving rise to a 'profit', but whether it is a realised profit will depend on the assets contributed meeting the definition of qualifying consideration.[216] Where a contribution is regarded for distribution purposes as a realised profit, it may be appropriate to reclassify the reserve to which the contribution was originally taken as part of the profit and loss account balance.

Where the contribution is received from a fellow-subsidiary, then it could be argued the contribution should be credited to the profit and loss account in the year of receipt as it is not a transaction with the company's shareholder.

There is no compelling reason why there need be symmetry of treatment between the accounting used by the giving and receiving companies, although this will usually be the case; it would, for example, be theoretically possible for the giving company to charge the contribution made to the profit and loss account, while the recipient credited the contribution directly to shareholders' funds. Whatever treatment is adopted, the whole effect of the transaction will be eliminated from the consolidated financial statements.

5 IAS REQUIREMENTS

The relevant international standard is IAS 22 – *Business Combinations*. The original standard was issued in November 1983, but has been revised and amended on a number of occasions since then. This covers not only those areas dealt with in FRSs 6 and 7 but also the accounting for goodwill.

The requirements of IAS 22 relating to goodwill are dealt with at 5.2 of Chapter 11. The other requirements and the main differences between them and those in the UK are dealt with below.

5.1 Scope

As its title suggests, IAS 22 should be applied in accounting for business combinations.[217] As in the UK, a business combination is defined as 'the bringing together of separate enterprises into one economic entity as a result of one enterprise uniting with or obtaining control over the net assets and operations of another enterprise'.[218]

IAS 22 notes that a business combination may be structured in a variety of ways which are determined for legal, taxation or other reasons. It may involve the purchase by an enterprise of the equity of another enterprise or the purchase of the net assets of a business enterprise; it therefore doesn't need to be the purchase of a legal entity for the standard to be applicable. It may be effected by the issue of shares or by the transfer of cash, cash equivalents or other assets. The transaction may be between the shareholders of the combining enterprises or between one enterprise and the shareholders of the other enterprise. The business combination may involve the establishment of a new enterprise to have control over the combining enterprises, the transfer of the net assets of one or more of the combining enterprises to another enterprise or the dissolution of one or more of the combining enterprises. When the substance of the transaction is consistent with the definition of a business combination in the standard, the accounting and disclosure requirements of IAS 22 are appropriate irrespective of the particular structure adopted for the combination.[219]

As indicated above, a business combination may involve the purchase of the net assets, including any goodwill, of another entity rather than the purchase of the shares in the other entity. In such circumstances, the acquirer applies the standard in its separate financial statements and consequently in its consolidated financial statements.[220]

The standard excludes from its scope:[221]

(a) transactions among entities under common control: and

(b) interests in joint ventures and the financial statements of joint ventures.

Although IAS 22 specifically excludes business combinations between entities under common control from its scope, the standard does not define such transactions and therefore, it is at best unclear which transactions the scope exemption applies to. This is an issue which had been under discussion by the SIC. However, while the discussions were at an advanced stage, the topic has now been removed from the agenda of the SIC as it is expected that the Board might consider this matter in its project on IAS 22. Nevertheless, if it is determined that a common control transaction exists, no guidance exists in IAS as to how the transaction should be accounted for. As a result, such transactions may be accounted for by analogy under the purchase method of accounting (see 5.4 below), or the uniting of interests method (see 5.3 below), or indeed by any other method deemed to be appropriate. In our view this is a significant area where wide and varied practice is developing and should be addressed by the IASB as a matter of priority. However, although the topic of business combinations is regarded as first priority for the IASB, this particular aspect is to be dealt with in phase 2 of the project.

Under UK GAAP allowance is made for group reconstructions. As indicated at 4.2 above, FRS 6 specifically defines a group reconstruction as an arrangement involving:

(a) the transfer of a shareholding in a subsidiary undertaking from one group company to another;

(b) the addition of a new parent company to a group;

(c) the transfer of shares in one or more subsidiary undertakings of a group to a new company that is not a group company but whose shareholders are the same as those of the group's parent;

(d) the combination into a group of two or more companies that before the combination had the same shareholders.

FRS 6 permits but does not require such transactions to be accounted for using merger accounting. Any business combinations between related parties not meeting the definition of a group reconstruction fall within the general scope of FRS 6, and should be accounted for under the guidance in that standard.

As a result of the uncertainty under IAS 22 as to which business combinations are included within its scope, and the lack of guidance on how to account for those transactions which are not, it is likely that GAAP differences in this area will arise in practice.

5.2 General approach

IAS 22 requires business combinations to be classified as either an acquisition or a uniting of interests (merger) and contains both general definitions and additional guidance for each classification. A uniting of interests is a business combination in which it is not possible to identify an acquirer. Instead of a dominant party emerging, the shareholder groups of the combining entities join in a substantially equal arrangement to share control over effectively the whole of their net assets and operations and share mutually in the risks and benefits of the combined entity. Furthermore, the managements of the combining entities participate in the management of the combined entity. Under those circumstances, a business combination is accounted for as a uniting of interests.[222]

Nevertheless, the standard is clear that it will be possible to identify an acquirer in virtually all cases and hence uniting of interests are expected to occur in exceptional circumstances. However, it is recognised that the standard does not provide explicit guidance on the interaction between the definitions and the additional guidance.[223] Accordingly, the SIC considered this issue as well as whether a business combination might be classified as neither and in January 2000 issued an interpretation, SIC-9 – *Business Combinations – Classification either as Acquisitions or Unitings of Interests.*

SIC-9 confirms that all business combinations under IAS 22 are either an acquisition or a uniting of interests.[224] It also states that a business combination should be accounted for as an acquisition, unless an acquirer cannot be identified. In virtually all business combinations an acquirer can be identified, i.e. the shareholders of one of the combining enterprises obtain control over the combined enterprise.[225]

The classification of a business combination should be based on an overall evaluation of all relevant facts and circumstances of the particular transaction. The guidance given in IAS 22 (see 5.3 and 5.4 below) provides examples of important factors to be considered, not a comprehensive set of conditions to be met. Single characteristics of a combined enterprise such as voting power or relative fair values of the combining enterprises should not be considered in isolation in order to determine how a business combination should be accounted for.[226]

IAS 22 also emphasises that 'legal mergers' (the requirements for which may differ among countries) are dealt with as acquisitions or uniting of interests under the requirements of the standard, unless they are exempt from the standard due to being transactions among enterprises under common control.[227]

5.3 Uniting of interests

A uniting of interests is defined as 'a business combination in which the shareholders of the combining enterprises combine control over the whole, or effectively the whole, of their net assets and operations to achieve a continuing mutual sharing in the risks and benefits attaching to the combined entity such that neither party can be identified as the acquirer'.[228]

5.3.1 *Conditions for uniting of interests*

IAS 22 states that in order to achieve a mutual sharing of the risks and benefits of the combined entity:[229]

(a) the substantial majority, if not all, of the voting common shares of the combining enterprises must be exchanged or pooled;

(b) the fair value of one enterprise is not significantly different from that of the other enterprise; and

(c) the shareholders of each enterprise maintain substantially the same voting rights and interest in the combined entity, relative to each other, after the combination as before.

SIC-9 states that an enterprise should classify a business combination as an acquisition, unless *all* of these three characteristics are present. However, even if all of the three characteristics are present, an enterprise should classify a business combination as a uniting of interests only if the enterprise can demonstrate that an acquirer cannot be identified.[230]

IAS 22 also comments that the likelihood of a mutual sharing of the risks and benefits of the combined entity diminishes and the likelihood that an acquirer can be identified increases when:[231]

(a) the relative equality in fair values of the combining enterprises is reduced and the percentage of voting common shares exchanged decreases;

(b) financial arrangements provide a relative advantage to one group of shareholders over the other shareholders; and

(c) one party's share of the equity in the combined entity depends on how the business which it previously controlled performs subsequent to the business combination.

As indicated at 5.2 above, the classification of a business combination should be based on an overall evaluation of all relevant facts and circumstances of the particular transaction.

The criteria to be satisfied before a combination can be accounted for as a uniting of interests under IAS 22 are similar to the criteria in FRS 6, although they are not phrased quite as prescriptively. However, under both standards, it is clear that mergers or uniting of interests will occur infrequently. Nevertheless, while the general definitions and overall philosophy are similar, the detail supporting them differs between the respective standards, with the result that in certain circumstances it may be possible to have a business combination that is accounted for as uniting of interests under IAS but which must be accounted for as an acquisition under UK GAAP, or vice versa.

5.3.2 *Accounting for uniting of interests*

A uniting of interests should be accounted for using the pooling of interests accounting method. This method requires that the financial statement items of the combining entities for the period on which the combination occurs and for any comparative periods presented should be included as if they had been combined from the beginning of the earliest period presented. Thus the pre- and post-combination results of both entities are included in the income statements. Also, the existing carrying values of the assets and liabilities of the separate entities are combined in the balance sheets; no fair value adjustments are made.[232]

The combined entity should apply a single uniform set of accounting policies. The carrying amount of assets, liabilities and equity of the combining entities may only be adjusted to reflect the effect of conforming to the combined entity's accounting policies to all periods presented. There is no recognition of any new goodwill or negative goodwill.[233]

Similarly, transactions between the combining entities occurring before or after the uniting of interests must be eliminated in preparing the financial statements of the combined entity.[234]

Any difference between (1) the amount recorded as share capital issued plus any additional consideration in the form of cash or other assets and (2) the amount recorded for the share capital acquired should be adjusted against equity.[235] However, the standard does not specify the reserves against which the adjustment should be made or whether it should be shown as a separate component within equity.

Expenses related to effecting the uniting of interests should be recognised as expenses in the period in which they are incurred.[236] These include registration fees, costs of furnishing information to shareholders, finders' and consultants' fees, and salaries and other expenses related to services of employees involved in achieving the business combination. They also include any costs or losses incurred in combining operations of the previous separate businesses.[237]

The financial statements of an entity must not incorporate a uniting of interests to which the entity is a party if the date of the uniting of interests is after the date of the most recent balance sheet included in the financial statements.[238] IAS 22 does not contain a clear definition of 'the date of the uniting of interests', although it is likely to be the date of legal completion.

The method of accounting for a uniting of interests under IAS 22 is similar to that for accounting for a merger under FRS 6. Similar issues to those discussed at 2.7 above therefore arise. One difference, however, is in the treatment of expenses relating to the uniting of interests. As noted above, under IAS 22, such expenses are recognised as incurred. Under FRS 6 in the UK, the expenses are recognised 'at the effective date of the merger'.

5.4 Acquisitions

An acquisition is defined as 'a business combination in which one of the enterprises, the acquirer, obtains control over the net assets and operations of another enterprise, the acquiree, in exchange for the transfer of assets, incurrence of a liability or issue of equity'. Control is 'the power to govern the financial and operating policies of an enterprise so as to obtain benefits from its activities'.[239]

5.4.1 *Conditions for acquisitions*

IAS 22 recognises that in virtually all business combinations one of the combining entities obtains control over the other, thereby enabling an acquirer to be identified. Control is presumed to be obtained when one of the combining entities acquires more than one half of the voting rights of the other entity unless, in exceptional circumstances, it can be clearly demonstrated that such ownership does not constitute control. Even when one of the combining entities does not acquire more than one half of the voting rights of the other entity, it may still be possible to identify an acquirer when one of the combining entities, as a result of the business combination, acquires:

(a) power over more than one half of the voting rights of the other entity by virtue of an agreement with other investors;

(b) power to govern the financial and operating policies of the other entity under a statute or an agreement;

(c) power to appoint or remove the majority of the members of the board of directors or equivalent governing body of the other entity; or

(d) power to cast the majority of votes at meetings of the board of directors or equivalent governing body of the other entity.[240]

These provisions about 'control' are equivalent to those in IAS 27 with respect to the identification of subsidiaries for the purposes of consolidation. (See Chapter 5 at 6.1)

The standard notes that although it may sometimes be difficult to identify an acquirer, there are usually indications that one exists. For example:

(a) the fair value of one entity is significantly greater than that of the other. In such cases, the larger entity is the acquirer;

(b) the business combination is effected through an exchange of voting common shares for cash. In such cases, the entity giving up cash is the acquirer; or

(c) the business combination results in the management of one entity being able to dominate the selection of the management team of the resulting combined entity. In such cases the dominant entity is the acquirer.[241]

As indicated at 5.2 above, the classification of a business combination should be based on an overall evaluation of all relevant facts and circumstances of the particular transaction. As also referred to in 5.2 above, however, SIC-9 states that a business combination should be accounted for as an acquisition, unless an acquirer cannot be identified. In virtually all business combinations an acquirer can be identified, i.e. the shareholders of one of the combining enterprises obtain control over the combined enterprise.

5.4.2 *Accounting for acquisitions*

If a business combination does not meet the uniting of interests criteria, it must be accounted for as an acquisition by applying the purchase method of accounting.[242]

The purchase method follows principles normally applicable under historical cost accounting when recording acquisitions of assets for cash, by exchanging other assets, or by issuing shares.[243] Acquiring assets in a group requires ascertaining the cost of those assets as a group and then allocating the cost to the individual assets that comprise the group. IAS 22 provides guidance on determining the cost of business acquired and on assigning a portion of the total cost to each individual asset and liability acquired based on fair values. A difference between the sum of the assigned costs of the tangible and identifiable intangible assets acquired less liabilities assumed, and the cost of the acquisition, is evidence of unspecified intangible values, i.e. goodwill.[244] As noted earlier, the requirements of IAS 22 relating to goodwill are dealt with at 5.2 of Chapter 11.

A *Date of acquisition*

The application of the purchase method commences from the date of acquisition when the acquirer must:

(a) incorporate the results of operations of the acquiree in its own income statement; and

(b) recognise in its own balance sheet the identifiable assets and liabilities of the acquiree and any goodwill or negative goodwill on the acquisition.[245]

The date of acquisition is the date on which the control of the net assets and operations of the acquiree is effectively transferred to the acquirer. Control is not deemed to have been transferred to the acquirer until all conditions necessary to protect the interests of the parties involved have been satisfied. However, the standard notes that it is not necessary for a transaction to be closed or finalised at law before control may effectively pass to the acquirer.[246]

B *The cost of the acquired entity*

An acquisition must be accounted for at cost, which is the amount of cash or cash equivalents, or the fair value of the other purchase consideration given, as determined at the 'date of exchange', plus any costs directly attributable to the acquisition.[247] Although IAS 22 is silent on the issue, if any of such costs are deductible for tax, then we believe that they should be accounted for on a gross basis. Though accounting for the acquisition commences as of the date of acquisition, the value of the consideration is determined at the date of each exchange transaction.

I *Date of exchange*

IAS 22 is not entirely clear as to the meaning of 'date of exchange'. In theory, there are several possibilities, including date of exchange of binding contracts, date of exchange of control over the net assets, date of legal closure and date of exchange of consideration. However, in July 2001 the SIC issued a draft interpretation which states that when an acquisition is achieved in one exchange transaction, the date of exchange 'should be the date of acquisition; that is, the date when the acquirer obtains control over the net assets and operations of the acquiree'.[248]

II Monetary consideration

As indicated above, consideration other than cash, or cash equivalents, is to be recorded at its fair value which is defined as 'the amount for which an asset could be exchanged or a liability settled between knowledgeable, willing parties in an arm's length transaction'.[249] The standard gives no guidance as to how such fair values might be arrived at, other than in respect of deferred consideration and securities issued by the acquirer.

When settlement of the purchase consideration is deferred, the cost of the acquisition is the present value of the consideration, taking into account any premium or discount likely to be incurred in settlement, and not the nominal value of the payable.[250]

III Marketable securities issued as consideration

IAS 22 states that marketable securities issued by the acquirer must be measured at their fair value, which is normally their market value. When the market price on one particular day is not a reliable indicator of the fair value, price movements for a reasonable period before and after the announcement of the terms of the acquisition need be considered.[251] Extract 6.60 at 5.5.3 below shows that Syngenta used the average trading price over the first 5 days of trading in accounting for its acquisition of the AstraZeneca agrochemicals business.

However, IAS 22 states further that when the market is unreliable or no quotation exists, the fair value of the securities issued by the acquirer is estimated by reference to their proportional interest in the fair value of the acquirer's enterprise or by reference to the proportional interest in the fair value of the enterprise acquired, whichever is the more clearly evident. Purchase consideration which is paid in cash to shareholders of the acquiree as an alternative to securities may also provide evidence of the total fair value given. All aspects of the acquisition, including significant factors influencing the negotiations, need to be considered, and independent valuations may be used as an aid in determining the fair value of securities issued.[252]

However, as noted above the SIC has now issued a draft interpretation which states that the date of exchange 'should be the date of acquisition' and that the fair value of shares issued should be the published price in an active market at that date. Another price should be used only if it can be demonstrated that a price fluctuation is undue, and the other price provides a more reliable measure of the share's fair value.[253]

IV Costs of acquisition

Direct costs incurred by the acquirer in connection with the acquisition, e.g. cost of registering and issuing securities, and professional fees paid, are part of the cost of the acquired entity. General administrative costs, the costs of maintaining an acquisitions department and other costs which cannot be directly attributable to the particular acquisition being accounted for must be expensed as incurred.[254]

V Contingent consideration

IAS 22 recognises that the acquisition agreement may provide for adjustments to the purchase consideration contingent on one or more future events, such as specified levels of earnings being maintained or achieved in future periods or on the market price of the securities issued as part of the purchase consideration being maintained.[255] At the date of acquisition, any contingent purchase consideration that is probable and can be measured reliably should be recognised in the cost of the acquisition.[256] The standard suggests that it will usually be possible to estimate the amount of any adjustment, even although some uncertainty exists.[257] GN Great Nordic provides an example of a company that has made provision in respect of two acquisitions on this basis. However, it can also be seen that it has not made any provision in respect of another acquisition since it is unlikely that the amount will be paid, merely noting the contingent liability.

Extract 6.57: GN Great Nordic (2000)

Note 21: Other Provisions [extract]

The total conditional acquisition payment of DKK 47 million (FRF 41 million) in connection with the acquisition of Optran is included in other provisions. The total conditional payment of DKK 24 million (USD 3 million) in connection with the acquisition of AGC is also included. The acquisition payments have been included since it is considered most likely that the acquisition conditions will be met. The provisions are expected to be spent within one to four years.

Note 26: Contingent Liabilities [extract]

Conditional payments in connection with acquisitions
According to concluded acquisition agreements the Group is under an obligation to pay a further DKK 950 million in acquisition payment in addition to the amounts concerning company acquisitions included in the balance sheet. The amount is not included in the balance sheet as it is not considered likely that the amount will fall due for payment.

FINANCIAL REPORT [extract]
Acquisitions/Sales of Companies [extract]

On November 10, 2000, NetTest acquired French company Photonetics S.A., and that company is now a part of NetTest. The acquisition price was DKK 9.1 billion. The parties also agreed a potential additional payment of up to USD 100 million to be paid with NetTest shares depending on NetTest's market capitalization on an IPO. The additional payments is not included in debt at December 31, 2000, as it is not considered likely that the amount will fall due for payment given the current stock market price levels.

Photonetics S.A. is a provider of equipment and systems for testing and monitoring optical communications networks. Goodwill amounts to DKK 8,254 million and other intangibles amount to DKK 1,234 million, equal to an annual impact on income of DKK 413 million in the amortization of goodwill and of DKK 136 million in the amortization of other intangibles.

Any contingent purchase consideration that only becomes probable and reliably measurable subsequent to the date of the acquisition should be recorded as an adjustment to the cost of the acquisition.[258] Similarly, the cost of acquisition is adjusted for the difference between the actual outcome and the estimate on which the accounting was based.[259] These adjustments will therefore have a consequential effect on the amount of goodwill, or negative goodwill, as the case may be. However, where an acquirer is required to make subsequent payment to the seller as compensation for a reduction in the value of the purchase consideration, e.g. the acquirer has guaranteed the market price of securities or debt issued and has to make a further issue of securities or debt for the purpose of restoring the originally determined cost of acquisition, the cost of acquisition and goodwill should not be adjusted. The subsequent payment should be accounted for as a reduction in the premium or an increase in the discount on the initial issue.[260]

VI Comparison with UK GAAP

These prescribed treatments under IAS 22 are in general very similar to those specified by FRS 7 which are discussed at 2.3 above, however there are some differences. As noted above, IAS 22 uses the 'date of exchange' (which presently is open to interpretation) to measure the fair value of non-cash consideration, including marketable securities issued by the acquirer. As discussed at 2.3.2 above, for shares or other capital instruments issued by an acquirer, under UK GAAP, the market price on the date of acquisition (i.e. the date on which control passes, or for a public offer, the date on which the offer becomes unconditional) would normally provide the most reliable measure of fair value.

Another difference between the UK and the international standard is in the treatment of contingent consideration. The requirement in IAS 22 described above is less prescriptive than the requirements of FRS 7 discussed at 2.3.5 above.

The cost of an acquisition under IAS includes all direct costs relating to that acquisition, which will include the costs of registering and issuing equity securities. Under UK GAAP, issue costs of shares or other securities should be accounted for as a reduction in the proceeds of the related capital instruments and should not be included in the cost of acquisition as discussed at 2.3.7 above.

C Determining fair values of identifiable assets and liabilities assumed

I General approach

The identifiable assets and liabilities of the acquiree that existed at the date of acquisition, together with any liabilities recognised under paragraph 31 of IAS 22 (see J below) should be recognised separately at the date of acquisition if, and only if:

(a) it is probable that any associated future economic benefits will flow to, or resources embodying economic benefits will flow from, the acquirer; and

(b) a reliable measure is available of their cost or fair value.[261]

Identifiable assets and liabilities over which the acquirer obtains control may not necessarily have been recognised in the financial statements of the acquiree. For example, an asset may not have been recognised by the acquiree in respect of tax losses but which may qualify for recognition as a result of the acquirer earning sufficient taxable income.[262]

The liabilities to be recognised at the date of acquisition should not include any which result from the acquirer's intentions or actions, except for reorganisation provisions which satisfy specific criteria (see X below). Liabilities should also not be recognised for future losses or other costs expected to be incurred as a result of the acquisition, whether they relate to the acquirer or the acquiree.[263]

Under IAS, where the acquirer purchases less than 100% of the acquiree so that a minority interest has a stake in the identifiable assets and liabilities, two different methods of allocating the cost of an acquisition to the assets and liabilities acquired are permitted:

(a) the benchmark treatment requires identifiable assets and liabilities to be recognised at the sum of:

  (i) the aggregate of the acquirer's share in their fair values plus

  (ii) the minority's proportion of their pre-acquisition carrying amounts, i.e. book values.[264]

  The valuation of the newly acquired identifiable assets and liabilities will be based on a combination of fair values and pre-acquisition carrying amounts. The minority interest will be equal to the minority's proportion of the pre-acquisition carrying amounts of the identifiable assets and liabilities.[265]

(b) the allowed alternative treatment requires the identifiable assets and liabilities to be valued at their respective fair values as at the date of acquisition.[266]

  The minority interest will be equal to the minority's proportion of the fair values of the identifiable assets and liabilities.[267]

Accounting for minority interests in general is discussed in Chapter 5 at 6.3.

Identifiable assets and liabilities must be valued at fair value, taking into account the guidance below.

II Tangible fixed assets

Land and buildings should be valued at their market value. Plant and equipment should similarly be at market value, normally determined by appraisal. Where there is no market value available for items of plant and equipment because of their specialised nature or absence of a market for them, they are valued at their depreciated replacement cost.[268] In our view, the same must also be true for certain types of specialised property.

III Intangible assets

Intangible assets, not including goodwill, should be valued by reference to an active market as defined in IAS 38 –*Intangible Assets* (see Chapter 11 at 5.3.1 E).[269] IAS 38 notes that the appropriate market price is usually the current bid price and adds that if such prices are unavailable then the price of the most recent similar transaction may provide a basis for estimating fair value, provided there has not been a significant change in economic circumstances in the meantime.[270]

If no active market exists for an intangible asset, it should be valued at the amount that the entity would have paid for the asset in an arm's length transaction between knowledgeable willing parties, based on the best information available.[271] For additional guidance, see Chapter 11 at 5.3.1 C.

If the fair value cannot be measured by reference to an active market, the amount recognised for the intangible asset should be limited to an amount that does not give rise to, or increase, negative goodwill on the transaction.[272]

IV Inventories

Finished goods and merchandise are valued at selling prices less the cost of disposal and a reasonable profit margin for the selling effort of the acquirer. Work in progress is valued at selling prices less the sum of the costs to complete, the cost of disposal and a reasonable profit margin for the selling effort of the acquirer. Raw materials should be valued at current replacement costs.[273]

V Marketable and non-marketable securities

Marketable securities are valued at their current market values.[274] Non-marketable securities are recognised at estimated values that take into consideration the characteristics of the securities, e.g. price earnings ratios, dividend yields and expected growth rates of comparable securities of entities with similar characteristics.[275]

VI Monetary assets and liabilities

Receivables are valued at the present values of the amounts to be received – determined using an appropriate discount rate – less allowances for uncollectability and collection costs.[276] Accounts and notes payable, long-term debt, liabilities, accruals and other claims payable are valued at the present values of amounts to be disbursed.[277] Discounting is not required for short-term items for which the difference between the nominal and discounted amounts is not material.[278]

VII Pensions and post retirement/employment benefits

Net employee benefit assets or liabilities for defined benefits plans must be valued at the present value of the defined benefit obligation less the fair value of any plan assets. An asset is only recognised to the extent that it is probable that it will be available to the entity in the form of refunds from the plan or a reduction in future contributions.[279] In computing the present value of the obligation, IAS 19 – *Employee Benefits* – states that any items such as actuarial gains and losses (whether or not within the 10% corridor allowed by IAS 19), past service costs and amounts not yet recognised by the acquiree under the transitional provisions of IAS 19 at the date of the acquisition should be included.[280]

VIII Tax assets and liabilities

Tax assets and liabilities are valued at the amount of tax benefit arising from tax losses or the taxes payable in respect of the net profit or loss, assessed from the perspective of the group resulting from the acquisition. Deferred tax assets and liabilities should be recognised on an undiscounted basis for temporary differences resulting from a difference between the tax bases and the fair values attributed to identifiable assets and liabilities as part of the fair value exercise. The tax assets include any deferred tax asset of the *acquirer* that now satisfy the recognition criteria in IAS 12 – *Income Taxes* – because of the business combination.[281] However, under IAS 12 an entity should not recognise deferred tax assets or liabilities arising from non-deductible goodwill or non-taxable negative goodwill.[282] The deferred tax consequences of business combinations are discussed further in Chapter 24 at 7.2.2 and 7.2.7.

IX Onerous contracts and other identifiable liabilities

Onerous contracts and other identifiable liabilities of the acquiree should be valued at the present values of the amounts to be disbursed in meeting the obligation determined at appropriate current interest rates.[283]

X Provisions for reorganisations and future losses

As indicated earlier, the liabilities to be recognised at the date of acquisition should not include any which result from the acquirer's intentions or actions, except for reorganisation provisions which satisfy specific criteria. Liabilities should also not be recognised for future losses or other costs expected to be incurred as a result of the acquisition, whether they relate to the acquirer or the acquiree.[284]

The exception to this general rule concerns reorganisation plans that are an integral part of the acquirer's plan of acquisition, that relate the acquiree's business only, that come into existence as a direct consequence of the acquisition. In that instance, IAS 22 requires that, at the date of acquisition, the acquirer should recognise a provision that was not a liability of the acquiree at that date if, and only if, the acquirer has:

(a) at, or before, the date of acquisition, developed the main features of a plan that involves terminating or reducing the activities of the acquiree and that relates to:
   (i) compensating employees of the acquiree for termination of their employment;
   (ii) closing facilities of the acquiree;
   (iii) eliminating product lines of the acquiree; or
   (iv) terminating contracts of the acquiree that have become onerous because the acquirer has communicated to the other party at, or before, the date of acquisition that the contract will be terminated;

(b) by announcing the main features of the plan at, or before, the date of acquisition, raised a valid expectation in those affected by the plan that it will implement the plan; and

(c) by the earlier of three months after the date of acquisition and the date when the annual financial statements are authorised for issue, developed those main features into a detailed formal plan identifying at least:
   (i) the business or part of a business concerned;
   (ii) the principal locations affected;
   (iii) the location, function, and approximate number of employees who will be compensated for terminating their services;
   (iv) the expenditures that will be undertaken; and
   (v) when the plan will be implemented.

Any provision recognised under this paragraph should cover only the costs of the items listed in (a)(i) to (iv) above.[285]

Danisco and GN Great Nordic indicate in their accounting policies the treatment of restructuring costs, both in respect of the acquired company and the acquiring company, as shown below.

Extract 6.58: Danisco A/S (2000)

Basis of consolidation [extract]

On the acquisition of new undertakings the purchase method is applied, according to which assets and liabilities of newly-acquired undertakings are restated at their fair value at the date of acquisition. Provision is made for obligations concerning declared restructuring in the acquired undertaking in connection with the acquisition. The related tax effect is taken into account. Any excess cost of acquisition over the fair value of the net assets acquired is capitalised as goodwill or consolidated goodwill in the acquisition year and amortised systemically in the profit and loss account after an individual assessment of the estimated life of the asset up to a maximum of 20 years.

Where the real value of acquired assets or liabilities subsequently proves to differ from the computed values at the time of acquisition, goodwill is adjusted until the end of the financial year following the year of acquisition if the new higher value does not exceed anticipated future income. All other adjustments are charged to the profit and loss account.

Newly-acquired subsidiary undertakings and associated undertakings are included in the consolidated accounts as from the date of acquisition.

Restructuring in acquiring undertaking

Restructuring costs incurred in conjunction with acquisitions and related to the acquiring undertaking are provided for and recorded in the profit and loss account. In contrast, restructuring costs related to the acquired undertaking are included in the acquisition price.

Other provisions

Other provisions primarily relate to obligations concerning acquisitions and restructuring. Provision is made where an obligation rests on the Group as a result of events in the financial year or previous years, and where it is probable that meeting the obligation will involve use of the company's financial resources.

Other provisions in connection with acquisitions include provisions related to the acquired company which had been resolved at the time of acquisition at the latest and which are included in the computation of the cost of acquisition and of goodwill or consolidated goodwill.

Other provisions for restructuring comprise provisions concerning the acquiring undertaking in connection with acquisitions, as well as provisions concerning resolutions on restructuring of existing business units. Such provisions are charged to the profit and loss account.

Extract 6.59: GN Great Nordic (2000)

Consolidation [extract]

The acquisition method is applied when new companies are acquired: i.e. the identifiable assets and liabilities acquired are measured in the balance sheet at their fair value on the date of acquisition. Provisions are recognized for obligations associated with restructuring the acquired company when the decision is made and announced on the date of acquisition. The impact of tax on any revaluations and provisions made is recognized.

When the acquisition price exceeds the fair value of the net assets acquired, including provisions for restructuring the acquired companies, a positive differential is capitalized as goodwill. Goodwill is amortized systematically in the income statement in accordance with an individual assessment of the asset's expected useful life, which may not, however, exceed 20 years. In the year of acquisition, amortization is pro rata. If the differential is negative (negative goodwill), the amount is presented under provisions and booked as income systematically over the useful life of the depreciable assets. However, negative goodwill that exceeds the value of non-monetary assets is booked as income in the year of acquisition.

The acquisition value of goodwill is adjusted for any changes to the purchase price after the acquisition. Reversal of provisions for restructuring stated in the goodwill calculation reduces the carrying value of the goodwill. Furthermore, if it becomes apparent that the fair value of assets and liabilities acquired on the date of acquisition differs from the values given in the statement of goodwill, it is to be adjusted before the end of the fiscal year following the year of acquisition. All other subsequent adjustments are recognized in the income statement.

Many of the guidelines contained in IAS 22 for determining the fair values of particular assets and liabilities are similar to those in FRS 7 (see 2.4.3 above), however, there are a few differences. The principal difference relates to the fact the reorganisation provisions discussed above. In the UK, FRS 7 does not permit provisions to be recognised at the date of acquisition if they result from the acquirer's intentions or actions (see 2.4.3 F I above).

Another difference relates to inventory. The guidance in IAS 22 is based on the equivalent rules in the US. However, in the UK, FRS 7 requires stocks and work in progress to be fair values at the lower of replacement cost and net realisable value (see 2.4.3 A III above).

There are also differences relating to deferred taxation, although these are mainly due to the difference in approach in the relevant standards on that topic. This is discussed in Chapter 24. However, one difference is in respect of deferred tax assets which may as a consequence of the acquisition satisfy the relevant recognition criteria. Under IAS 12, such assets are recognised as part of the fair value exercise, regardless of whether they arise in the acquiree or the acquirer. Under UK GAAP, although assets of the acquired entity would be recognised in the fair value exercise, if they arose in the acquirer then they should be recognised as a post-acquisition credit not as part of the fair value exercise.

One area which is covered by FRS 7 in the UK, but not by IAS 22, is businesses sold or held exclusively with a view to subsequent resale. Under UK GAAP, the fair value of a business which is purchased and held for subsequent resale should be based on the net proceeds of the sale (either actual, if the sale has taken place by the time the accounts are prepared, or estimated if not). However, the fair value can be different from the net realised value in certain circumstances. This is discussed more fully at 2.4.3 G above.

By contrast, IAS 27 – *Consolidated Financial Statements and Accounting for Investments in Subsidiaries* – requires that the net cash flows from operations of a business held for resale between the date of acquisition and the date of sale, should not be taken into consideration under IAS in the allocation of the purchase price to the assets and liabilities i.e. the fair value on acquisition may well be different from the disposal proceeds of the excluded subsidiary.

It should also be noted that FRS 7 imposes a time limit of 'approximately one year from the date of acquisition', whereas IAS 27 is somewhat less restrictive requiring only 'subsequent disposal in the near future'.

Another area which is covered by FRS 7 in the UK, but not by IAS 22 is pre-acquisition contingencies. Under UK GAAP, both contingent assets and liabilities should be measured at fair values where these can be determined. For this purpose reasonable estimates of the expected outcome may be used. As discussed more fully at 2.4.3 C above, the level of probability for recognising deferred tax assets under FRS 7 is lower than that in FRS 12 – *Provisions, Contingent Liabilities and Contingent Assets.* Also, certain contingent assets and liabilities that crystallise as a result of the acquisition are also to be recognised as part of the fair value exercise, provided that the underlying contingency was in existence before the date of acquisition.

D *Subsequent amendments to fair value*

After the date of acquisition, additional information may become available about the identifiable assets and liabilities acquired. The additional evidence may necessitate either recognition of a previously unrecognised asset or liability or an adjustment to the fair values assigned at the date of acquisition. The amount assigned to goodwill or negative goodwill should also be adjusted to the extent that:

(a) the adjustment does not increase the carrying amount of goodwill above its recoverable amount; and

(b) such adjustment is made by the end of the first annual accounting period commencing after acquisition.

If these conditions are not met the adjustments to the identifiable assets and liabilities should be recognised as income or expense.[286] The time limit in (b) above does not apply to any reorganisation provisions. For such liabilities, the time limit in paragraph 31(c) of the standard applies. (See 5.4.2 C X above)

Extracts 6.58 and 6.59 at 5.4.2 C X above provide examples of companies that explicitly state this treatment in their accounting policies.

In June 2000, the SIC issued an interpretation of these requirements, SIC-22 – *Business Combinations – Subsequent Adjustment of Fair Values and Goodwill Initially Reported* – which considered the following issues:[287]

(a) whether an adjustment to the initial fair values of identifiable assets and liabilities acquired should include the effects of depreciation and other changes which would have resulted if the adjusted fair values had been applied from the date of acquisition;

(b) whether a related adjustment of goodwill or negative goodwill should include the effect of amortisation of the adjusted amount assigned to goodwill or negative goodwill from the date of acquisition; and

(c) how the adjustments to identifiable assets and liabilities acquired, and to goodwill or negative goodwill, should be presented.

The SIC concluded that such adjustments to the identifiable assets and liabilities should be calculated as if the adjusted fair values had been applied from the date of acquisition. They should include both the effect of the change to the fair values initially assigned, and the effect of depreciation and other changes which would have resulted if the adjusted fair values had been applied from the date of acquisition.[288] The carrying amount of goodwill or negative goodwill should also be calculated as if the adjusted fair values had been applied from the date of acquisition, with goodwill amortisation or recognition of negative goodwill also being adjusted from the date of acquisition. However, the adjustment to goodwill should not increase the carrying amount above its recoverable amount.[289] The adjustments to depreciation and amortisation, impairment charges and other amounts should be included in the net profit or loss in the respective classification of income or expense.[290] The disclosure requirements of SIC-22 are given at 5.5.3 below.

These requirements are illustrated in Examples 6.10 and 6.11 below, which are based on the examples in the Appendix to SIC-22. The deferred tax implications are ignored.

Example 6.10: Increase in identifiable assets leading to decrease in goodwill

Company A reports financial statements for annual periods ending 31 December and does not report interim financial information. Company A made an acquisition on 30 September 2001. In its financial statements for the annual period ending 31 December 2001, Company A initially recognised goodwill of £100,000 to be amortised over 20 years. The carrying amount of goodwill at 31 December 2001 was £98,750 (the initial amount of £100,000 less amortisation of £1,250).

During 2002, Company A receives the results of a valuation study and concludes that £20,000 of the £100,000 initially allocated to goodwill should be allocated to property, plant and equipment assets having a remaining useful life of 5 years at the date of acquisition.

The adjustment to the carrying amount of property, plant and equipment assets is measured at the adjusted fair value at the date of the acquisition of £20,000, less the amount which would have been recognised as depreciation of the adjusted fair value (£1,000 at 31 December 2001).

As the adjustment is made by Company A prior to the end of the first annual accounting period commencing after acquisition, the carrying amount of goodwill is also adjusted for the reduction in value at the date of the acquisition of £20,000, and a reduction in amortisation (£250 at 31 December 2001).

The £1,000 increase in the depreciation of property, plant and equipment and the reduction in goodwill amortisation of £250 have the net effect of reducing net profit for the year ended 31 December 2002 by £750 relating to the comparative year ended 31 December 2001.

Example 6.11: Decrease in identifiable assets leading to increase in goodwill

This example assumes an adjustment which is in the reverse direction of Example 6.10 above. The adjustment to identifiable assets and liabilities is instead a £20,000 decrease to the amount initially allocated to property, plant and equipment assets having a remaining useful life of 5 years at 30 September 2001, the date of acquisition. Assume also that Company A determines that the recoverable amount of additional goodwill is only £17,000 at 31 December 2001.

The carrying amount of property, plant and equipment assets is reduced by £19,000, representing the decrease in fair value of the £20,000 and a reduction of £1,000 in the depreciation expense recognised through 31 December 2001.

Company A initially determines the adjusted carrying amount of goodwill relating to the £20,000 increase would be £19,750, after taking into consideration £250 in amortisation from the date of the acquisition through 31 December 2001. However, Company A recognises only £17,000 in goodwill as that is the maximum amount of the £19,750 increase that is recoverable.

The £1,000 decrease in the depreciation expense relating to property, plant and equipment and an increase in goodwill amortisation of £250 have the net effect of increasing net profit for the year ended 31 December 2002 by £750 relating to the prior comparative period. However, net profit for this period is also decreased by an impairment loss of £2,750 (£19,750 less £17,000). Accordingly, the difference of £2,000 between the decrease in the fixed assets of £19,000 and the increase in goodwill of £17,000 is recognised as an expense in the year ended 31 December 2002.

However, there are two exceptions to the above requirements.

First, the potential benefit of income tax loss carry forwards, or other deferred tax assets of an acquired enterprise, which were not recognised as an identifiable asset by the acquirer at the date of acquisition, may subsequently be realised. When this occurs, the acquirer recognises the benefit as income under IAS 12, and the acquirer:

(a) adjusts the gross carrying amount of the goodwill and the related accumulated amortisation to the amounts that would have been recorded if the deferred tax asset had been recognised as an identifiable asset at the date of the business combination; and

(b) recognises the reduction in the net carrying amount of the goodwill as an expense.

However, this procedure does not create negative goodwill, nor does it increase the carrying amount of negative goodwill.[291]

Second, provisions for terminating or reducing activities, when recognised under paragraph 31 of IAS 22 (see 5.4.2 C X above), should be reversed if, and only if:

(a) the outflow of economic benefits is no longer probable; or

(b) the detailed formal plan is not implemented:

 (i) in the manner set out in the detailed formal plan; or

 (ii) within the time established in the detailed formal plan.

In these situations, the reversal of such a provision should be reflected as an adjustment to goodwill or negative goodwill (and minority interests, if appropriate).[292] Extract 6.59 at 5.4.2 C X above shows an example of a company which explicitly states this treatment in its accounting policies. However, no income (in respect of the release of the provision) or expense (in respect of any amortisation of goodwill which would have been charged) is recognised in respect of such reversal. The adjusted goodwill amount should be amortised prospectively, while adjustments to negative goodwill should be accounted for in accordance with paragraph 62 of IAS 22 (See Chapter 11 at 5.2.2).[293]

FRS 7 in the UK uses the same time limit as IAS 22 for finalising fair values, but only requires that there should be a 'corresponding adjustment to goodwill'. (See 2.4.2 and 2.4.4 above for a discussion of the UK requirements.)

E Step-by-step acquisitions

A step-by-step acquisition involves more than one exchange transaction. When this occurs, IAS 22 requires that each significant transaction is treated separately for the purpose of determining the fair values of the identifiable assets and liabilities acquired and for determining the amount of any goodwill or negative goodwill on that transaction. The acquirer should compare the costs of the individual investments with the fair values of the identifiable assets and liabilities acquired at each significant step.[294]

Prior to qualifying as an acquisition, an investment may have qualified as an associate and been accounted for under the equity method under IAS 28 (see Chapter 7 at 6.1). If that is the case, then IAS 22 notes that a notional determination of the fair values of the identifiable assets and liabilities acquired and the amount of any goodwill or negative goodwill would have occurred at the date when the equity method was first applied. When the investment did not qualify previously as an associate, the fair values of the identifiable assets and liabilities are determined as at the date of each significant step and goodwill or negative goodwill is recognised from the date of acquisition.[295]

When an acquisition is achieved by successive purchases, the fair values of the identifiable assets and liabilities may vary at the date of each exchange transaction. If all the identifiable assets and liabilities relating to an acquisition are restated to fair values at the time of successive purchases, any adjustment relating to the previously held interest of the acquirer is a revaluation and is accounted for as such.[296]

These requirements of IAS 22 are effectively the same as those contained in FRS 2 in the UK (see 2.5.3 above), although FRS 2 explicitly requires such a calculation of goodwill to be carried out for increased investments in existing subsidiaries, not just when a controlling interest in the subsidiary is acquired.

F Reverse acquisitions

As indicated at 5.1 above, IAS 22 defines an acquisition as 'a business combination in which one of the enterprises, the acquirer, obtains control over the net assets and operations of another enterprise, the acquiree, in exchange for the transfer of assets, incurrence of a liability or issue of equity'.[297] The standard recognises that occasionally an enterprise obtains ownership of the shares of another enterprise but as part of the exchange transaction issues enough voting shares, as consideration, such that control of the combined enterprise passes to the owners of the enterprise whose shares have been acquired. This situation is described as a reverse acquisition. Although legally the enterprise issuing the shares may be regarded as the parent or continuing enterprise, the enterprise whose shareholders now control the combined enterprise is the acquirer for the purposes of IAS 22. The enterprise issuing the shares is deemed to have been acquired by the other enterprise; the latter enterprise is deemed to be the acquirer and applies the purchase method to the assets and liabilities of the enterprise issuing the shares.[298] However, the standard is then silent as to how its requirements should be applied in practice in such situations.

As discussed more fully at 2.6 above, in the UK, FRS 6 makes no reference to reverse acquisitions, other than to state that the provision in the previous version of IAS 22 is incompatible with companies legislation in the UK and the Republic of Ireland.[299]

5.5 Disclosure requirements relating to business combinations

The disclosure requirements of IAS 22 (apart from those that relate to goodwill which are dealt with in Chapter 11 at 5.2) together with those of related SIC interpretations are dealt with below.

5.5.1 *All business combinations*

The following disclosures should be made in the financial statements for the period during which the combination has taken place:

(a) the names and descriptions of the combining entities;

(b) the method of accounting for the combination, i.e. uniting of interests or purchase method;

(c) the effective date of the combination for accounting purposes; and

(d) any operations resulting from the business combination which the enterprise has decided to dispose of.[300]

These are similar to the requirements of FRS 6 in the UK discussed at 2.8.1 above, although FRS 6 does not require the descriptions of the combining entities to be disclosed nor does it require the information under (d) above.

5.5.2 *Uniting of interests*

For a business combination which is a uniting of interests, the following additional disclosures should be made in the financial statements for the period during which the uniting of interests has taken place:

(a) description and number of shares issued, together with the percentage of each entity's voting shares exchanged to effect the uniting of interests;

(b) amounts of assets and liabilities contributed by each entity; and

(c) sales revenue, other operating revenues, extraordinary items and the net profit or loss of each entity prior to the date of the combination that are included in the net profit or loss shown by the combined entity's financial statements.[301]

These disclosure requirements are essentially similar to those contained in FRS 6 in the UK, (see 2.8.3 above) however, there are some differences. The main differences being that FRS 6 requires more detailed information about each entity's contribution to the results as well as information about any necessary adjustments to net assets and reserves.

5.5.3 *Acquisitions*

For a business combination which is an acquisition, the following additional disclosures should be made in the financial statements for the period during which the acquisition has taken place:

(a) the percentage of voting shares acquired; and

(b) the cost of acquisition and a description of the purchase consideration paid or contingently payable.[302]

Examples of disclosures in respect of these requirements (and those outlined at 5.5.1 above) are illustrated below.

Extract 6.60: Syngenta AG (2000)

3 Changes in the scope of consolidation [extract]
Acquisitions 2000

With effect from 13 November 2000, Novartis agribusiness and Zeneca agrochemicals business were separated from their previous parent companies and merged to form Syngenta. The separations were treated as a spin-off transaction with the shareholders of Novartis and AstraZeneca receiving a proportional interest in Syngenta (61% and 39%) respectively). Novartis shareholders and AstraZeneca shareholders received 69 million and 44 million shares of Syngenta, respectively.

The merger of Novartis agribusiness and Zeneca agrochemicals business has been accounted for as a purchase business combination with Novartis agribusiness considered to be the acquirer of Zeneca agrochemicals business for accounting purposes. The purchase price is determined as the number of Syngenta shares issued to AstraZeneca shareholders multiplied by the average trading price of those shares over the first five days of trading. Goodwill arising in the merger will be amortized over 20 years using the straight line method. The assets acquired and liabilities assumed from AstraZeneca for Zeneca agrochemicals business have been included at their estimated fair value on 13 November 2000. The acquired business contributed revenues of US$301 million and an operating loss before merger and restructuring costs, net of divestment gains, of US$14 million during the period from 13 November 2000 to 31 December 2000.

Details of the net assets acquired and goodwill are follows:
(US$ million)

Purchase consideration:	
– fair value of purchase consideration	1,975
– capital contribution received from AstraZeneca	(210)
Net purchase consideration	**1,765**
Less: fair value of net assets required	(1,166)
Goodwill (Note 11)	**599**

Extract 6.61: Nokia Corporation (2000)

6. Acquisitions [extract]

In October 2000, Nokia increased its ownership of the Brazilian handset manufacturing joint venture NG Industrial (NGI) from 51% to 100% by acquiring all the shares of NGI held by Gradiente Telecom S.A. for EUR 492 million in cash. The fair value of net assets acquired was EUR 43 million giving rise to a goodwill of EUR 449 million.

In August 2000, Nokia acquired DiscoveryCom, a company which provides solutions that enable communications service providers to rapidly install and maintain Broadband Digital Subscriber Line (DSL) services for fast Internet access. The acquisition price was EUR 223 million, which was paid in Nokia stock and Nokia stock options. The fair value of net assets acquired was EUR -4 million giving rise to a goodwill of EUR 227 million.

In March 2000, Nokia acquired Network Alchemy, a provider of IP Clustering solutions for EUR 336 million, which was paid in Nokia stock and Nokia stock options. The fair value of net assets acquired was EUR -2 million giving rise to a goodwill of EUR 338 million.

In October 1999, Nokia acquired Telekol Corporation, a company specializing in intelligent corporate communications solutions, for EUR 45 million in cash. The fair value of net assets acquired was EUR 2 million giving rise to a goodwill of EUR 43 million.

In September 1999, Nokia strengthened its capabilities in IP wireless bypass technology with an agreement to acquire Rooftop Communications Corporation for EUR 48 million, of which EUR 42 million was paid in Nokia stock and EUR 6 million in cash. The fair value of net assets acquired was EUR 0.2 million giving rise to a goodwill of EUR 48 million.

In February 1999, Nokia acquired Diamond Lane Communications for EUR 112 million in cash. The fair value of net assets acquired was EUR 5 million giving rise to a goodwill of EUR 107 million.

If the fair values of the identifiable assets and liabilities or the purchase consideration can only be determined on a provisional basis at the end of the period in which the acquisition took place, this should be stated and reasons given. When there are subsequent adjustments to such provisional fair values, those adjustments should be disclosed and explained in the financial statements of the period concerned.[303] SIC-22 expands on this by requiring adjustments to the carrying amounts of identifiable assets or liabilities or goodwill or negative goodwill should be disclosed and explained in the financial statements of the period in which the adjustment is made. The amount of an adjustment which relates to prior and comparative periods should also be disclosed.[304]

Any provisions recognised for terminating or reducing the activities of an acquiree (see 5.4.2 C X above) should be treated as a separate class of provisions for the purpose of disclosure under IAS 37. (See Chapter 28 at 7.5.1) In addition, the aggregate carrying amount of these provisions should be disclosed for each individual business combination.[305]

Examples of disclosures relating to provisions for restructuring acquired companies are illustrated below.

Extract 6.62: Danisco A/S (2000)

DKK million — Group

18. Other provisions [extract]

	Acquisitions	Restructuring	Other	Other Provisions Total
Other provisions at 1 May 1999	195	331	214	740
Exchange adjustment of opening value	17	–	14	31
Provisions for the year	411	26	132	569
Provisions spent during the year	–105	–44	–30	–179
Reversed provisions concerning previous periods	–38	–15	–24	–77
Other provisions at 30 April 2000	**480**	**298**	**306**	**1,084**

Provisions in connection with acquisitions primarily relate to Cultor, acquired in the financial year ended, and Sidlaw, acquired at the end of the 1998/99 financial year. The provisions are to cover costs for restructuring of acquired undertakings.

Extract 6.63: Deutsche Bank AG (2000)

[46] Provisions [extract]

Restructuring provision

The restructuring provision – broken down by programme – developed as follows during the 2000 financial year:

in € m.	Strategic Group Restructuring	Bankers Trust Integration	Other restructuring programmes	Total
as at 1.1.2000	**294**	**479***	**234**	**1,007**
Addition in the reporting year	–	–	38	38
Designated for				
staff measures	139	232	74	445
infrastructure measures	33	105	29	167
Release	71	142	27	240
as at 31.12 2000	**51**	**0**	**142**	**193**

*after adjustment of €33 million effect of exchange rate changes

Bankers Trust Integration

Owing to the first-time consolidation of Bankers Trust in 1999 the restructuring provisions rose by €630 million, which were included in goodwill. Furthermore, €531 million were charged to the Income Statement in 1999 for restructuring measures in connection with the acquisition of Bankers Trust. Of the total of €1.2 billion, €0.9 billion were provided for staff measures and €0.3 billion for infrastructure measures.

The implementation of the measures was already begun in the second half of 1999, and €715 million were designated for specific use.

After that, taking into account €33 million for exchange rate changes, €479 million were still available for the measures to be implemented by the end of 2000. In the 2000 financial year, €337 million were designated for specific use.

The restructuring plan was scheduled to be implemented by the end of 2000. Certain measures were not implemented, as a result of which €142 million have been released, thereof €64 million to the credit of P&L and €78 million as an adjustment to goodwill.

It would appear from the above extract that not all of the restructuring costs relating to Bankers Trust met the criteria to be included as part of a restructuring provision in attributing fair values, since €531m had to be charged to the income statement in 1999. Accordingly, when the provision has been released, some has been credited to the income statement and the rest against goodwill as required by IAS 22.

The above disclosures are also required to be given for any business combinations effected after the balance sheet date. However, if it is impracticable to disclose any this information, this fact should be disclosed.[306]

IAS 27 also requires disclosure of the effect of the acquisition of subsidiaries on the financial position at the reporting date and on the results for the reporting period.[307]

A number of companies in meeting this requirement appear only to disclose the impact on the financial position (see, for example Nokia at Extract 6.61 above). However, other companies do provide information about the impact on the results as shown below.

Extract 6.64: Libertel NV (2000)

Note 22 Acquisitions

Libertel acquired the mobile telecom activities of SB Telecom B.V. on 11 January 2000. No assets or liabilities were acquired. Libertel paid NLG 1.9 million for the acquired telecom activities. The acquired activities have contributed NLG 30 thousand to revenue and resulted in an operating loss of NLG 15 thousand since 11 January 2000.

Novartis indicates the amount of goodwill arising and the period of amortisation, but notes that none of the acquisitions have a material impact on the results, cash flows or financial position, as can be seen from the following extract.

Extract 6.65: Novartis AG (2000)

2. Changes in the scope of consolidation [extract]

The following significant changes were made during 2000 and 1999.

Acquisitions 2000

Generics
On April 10, 2000, the generics sector acquired 72% of Grandis Biotech GmbH, Freiburg, Germany for CHF 26 million in cash. The acquisition was accounted for under the purchase method of accounting and the related goodwill was CHF 32 million which is being amortized over 15 years.

CIBA Vision
On October 2, 2000 the sector acquired 100% of Wesley Jessen VisionCare Inc., Des Plaines, Illinois, USA for CHF 1.3 billion (USD 0.8 billion) in cash.

The net assets acquired consisted of tangible fixed assets (CHF 177 million), inventories (CHF 182 million), trade accounts receivable (CHF 93 million), deferred tax assets (CHF 56 million), other assets (CHF 118 million); deferred tax liabilities (CHF 241 million), short term financial debts (CHF 155 million) and other liabilities (CHF 330 million). The acquisition was accounted for under the purchase method of accounting and the related goodwill was CHF 1.4 billion which is being amortized on a straight-line basis over 20 years.

Animal Health
In January 2000, Novartis Animal Health completed the 100% acquisition of Vericore Ltd., a UK-based company focused on vaccines, parasiticides and other products for farm animals, pharmaceuticals for companion animals, and aquaculture. The acquisition price amounted to CHF 96 million and was paid in cash.

In June 2000, Novartis Animal Health increased the 40% stake in the Canadian-based aquaculture company Cobequid Life Sciences Inc., which had been obtained in the Vericore acquisition, to 100% for CHF 38 million in cash.

These acquisitions were accounted for under the purchase method of accounting and the related goodwill was CHF 163 million which is being amortized on a straight-line basis over 15 years.

Acquisitions 1999

Generics
On December 9, 1999, the sector company Geneva Pharmaceuticals Inc., USA acquired the assets of Invamed Inc., New Jersey, USA for CHF 149 million. The acquisition was accounted for under the purchase method of accounting and the related goodwill was CHF 127 million which is being amortized on a straight-line basis over 15 years.

CIBA Vision
On July 2, 1999, the sector acquired the assets of the interocular lens business of Mentor Corporation, California for CHF 60 million. The acquisition was accounted for under the purchase method of accounting and the related goodwill was CHF 26 million which is being amortized on a straight-line basis over 15 years.

The above mentioned 2000 and 1999 acquisitions did not have a material pro forma impact on the Group's results of operations, cash flows or financial position.

Divestments 2000

Agribusiness
On December 1, 1999. the Board of Novartis approved the divestment of the Agribusiness sector by merging it with the Agrochemicals business of AstraZeneca Plc.

Novartis spun-off its Agribusiness sector on November 6, 2000 to its shareholders as part of the transactions necessary to form Syngenta AG. On the same day AstraZeneca Plc. also spun-off its Crop Protection activities which were then merged with Novartis Agribusiness. On spin-off, Novartis AG shareholders owned 61% of the new company and AstraZeneca shareholders 39%. Syngenta AG was listed on the Swiss, New York, London and Stockholm exchanges on November 13, 2000.

The sales and operating income recorded by Novartis Agribusiness up to the spin-off date were CHF 6.7 billion and CHF 1.2 billion, respectively. This transaction involved the Novartis Group transfering CHF 3.3 billion of debt to Syngenta. The Novartis Group's equity has been reduced by a net CHF 3.8 billion (after taking into account a receipt from Novartis shareholders of CHF 687 million in connection with this transaction) due to this spin-off to its shareholders. Novartis incurred costs in relation to this transaction of CHF 69 million.

Divestments 1999

Consumer Health
The Group's 51% interest in OLW Snacks AB, Sweden and 49% interest in Chips OLW AB, Sweden were sold on January 25, 1999. The Group's 100% stake in the German Eden Group was sold on May 11, 1999 and the 100% interest in Wasa operations in Sweden, Germany, Denmark, Norway and Poland were sold on June 30, 1999.

The sales price for these divestments totalled CHF 625 million and resulted in a pre-tax gain of CHF 352 million which has been recorded in operating income in the consolidated income statement. 1999 sales of the various divested activities up to their respective date of divestment amounted to CHF 182 million.

Sales relating to these businesses generated an operating income in 1999 of CHF 23 million.

One interesting form of disclosure in meeting this requirement is that given by Deutsche Lufthansa as illustrated below.

Extract 6.66: Deutsche Lufthansa AG (2000)

4 Group of consolidated companies [extract]

Compared with the prior year, the group of consolidated companies was expanded in 2000 by the newly acquired companies Globe Services Sweden AB and Hamburger Gesellschaft für Flughafenanlagen mbH. A total amount of €115.8m was spent on the acquisition. The financial and operating control of both companies was transferred to the Group effective 1 April 2000. In addition to that, Lufthansa Technik Immobilien- und Verwaltungsgesellschaft mbH, LSG Lufthansa Service Catering- und Dienstleistungsgesellschaft mbH, Top Flight Catering AB including its four subsidiaries, and LSG Lufthansa Service Cape Town (Pty) Ltd. have for the first time been included in the group of consolidated companies.

The effects of the changes in the changes in the group of consolidated companies and the group of companies carried at equity are shown in the following tables.

Except for the effects on the minority shares in capital, which have increased by 20 per cent due to the first inclusion of Top Flight Catering AB and its four subsidiaries, the effects on the balance sheet total and the other balance sheet items account for less than 5 per cent each.

Balance sheet	Group 31.12.2000 €m	of which from changes in group of consolidated companies €m
Fixed assets	10,733.1	+257.3
Current assets	3,666.0	–185.5
Balance sheet total	14,810.4	+72.5
Capital and reserves	4,113.5	–18.9
Minority shares in capital	51.3	+8.6
Provisions and accruals	5,942.8	–6.3
Liabilities	4,461.4	+77.0

Income Statement	Group 31.12.2000 €m	of which from changes in group of consolidated companies €m
Revenue	15,200.4	+43.2
Operating income	16,885.9	+46.6
Operating expenses	15,403.9	+31.5
Profit from operating activities	+1,482.0	+15.1
Financial result	–266.7	–7.6
Profit from ordinary activities	+1,215.3	+7.5
Taxes	529.3	+1.8
Net profit for the period	+689.0	+5.0

Effects concerning the income statement are explained in more detail in the Notes to individual items.

7 Other revenue [extract]

The expansion of the group of consolidated companies caused revenue from catering services to rise by €21.1m and other services by €22.1m.

10 Cost of materials [extract]

Cost of materials rose by €20.1m as a result of the expansion of the group of consolidated companies. The increase nearly exclusively relates to expense for purchased merchandise in the amount of €19.8m as a result of the initial consolidation of the new catering companies.

It can be seen that in additional to disclosing the impact on the main balance sheet and income statement headings, the company has also disclosed the impact in each of the detailed notes (notes 7 and 10 of which are illustrated above).

In addition, IAS 7 – *Cash Flow Statements* – requires disclosures in respect of acquisitions of subsidiaries or other business units. These are discussed in Chapter 29 at 4.1.6.

The disclosures required for an acquisition under IAS are generally less onerous than those under UK GAAP (see 2.8.2 above); The major items required by UK GAAP which are not required by IAS are:

(a) a fair value table, including details about any fair value adjustments which have been made; and

(b) in the year of acquisition, separate presentation of results of the acquired entity in the profit and loss account for all headings before interest – as a minimum the analysis of turnover and operating profit must be given on the face of the statement.

5.6 Disposals

5.6.1 *Basic requirements*

IAS 27 requires that the results of operations of a subsidiary disposed of are included in the consolidated income statement until the disposal which is the date on which the parent ceases to have control of the subsidiary.[308] This is similar to the requirement of FRS 2 in the UK (see 3.2 above).

The difference between the proceeds from the disposal of the subsidiary and the carrying amount of its assets less liabilities as at the date of disposal is recognised in the consolidated income statement as the profit or loss on disposal of the subsidiary.[309] Again, this is similar to the requirement of FRS 2 in the UK (see 3.1 above).

It should also be borne in mind that IAS 35 – *Discontinued Operations* – may also be applicable to disposals of subsidiaries or businesses. The requirements of that standard are not addressed here but are discussed in Chapter 25 at 3.8.

5.6.2 *Goodwill of subsidiaries disposed of*

Although IAS 27 makes no reference to goodwill, we believe that the calculation of the gain or loss on disposal should include any unamortised goodwill relating to the subsidiary which is carried as an asset in the balance sheet at the date of disposal. One company which explicitly states that it takes into account unamortised goodwill is Danisco as shown by the following extract.

> *Extract 6.67: Danisco A/S (2000)*
>
> **Basis of consolidation** [extract]
>
> On the winding up or disposal of subsidiary undertakings an undertaking's profit is consolidated in the profit and loss account on a line-by-line basis until the date of disposal. Any profit or loss is computed as the difference between the sales sum and the carrying amount of the net asset at the time of disposal, including non-amortised goodwill and expected costs of disposal, and is stated in the profit and loss account.

It may also be the case that under the transitional provisions of IAS 22, any goodwill that arose on acquisitions in a period before 1 January 1995 and was written off against reserves was not reinstated in the balance sheet. Again, IAS 27 is silent as to whether or not such goodwill should be taken into account in computing the gain or loss on disposal. Accordingly, we believe that either treatment is acceptable. This contrasts with the position in the UK where such goodwill must be taken into account (see 3.3 above).

5.6.3 *Partial disposals*

It may be that an entity only disposes of part of its interest in a subsidiary. IAS 27 does not discuss the situation where the subsidiary remains a subsidiary following the partial disposal of some of the shares held by the parent entity. In such a case, the subsidiary will continue to be consolidated and we believe that the requirements discussed above for the calculation of the gain or loss should be interpreted as applying to the percentage interest sold in the net assets of the subsidiary. This is the treatment which is required in the UK (see 3.4 above).

An example of a company that adopts such a treatment is Roche as can be seen from the first paragraph of the following extract.

> *Extract 6.68: Roche Holding Ltd (2000)*
>
> 3. **Group organisation** [extract]
>
> Genentech
>
> On 23 July 1999 and 21 October 1999 the Group sold a total of 34% of the Common Stock of Genentech through public offerings yielding total proceeds of 4.9 billion US dollars (7.4 billion Swiss francs). The total resulting pre-tax gain of 4.5 billion Swiss francs is calculated as the difference between the proceeds of the sales, net of incidental costs, and the proportion of net assets.
>
> On 29 March 2000 the Group sold 17.3 million shares of Genentech through a public offering yielding proceeds of 2,771 million US dollars (4,599 million Swiss francs). The resulting pre-tax gain after incidental costs was 3,949 million Swiss francs. Roche's ownership interest in Genentech at 31 December 2000 was 58%.

(Although the second paragraph makes no reference to the proportion of net assets being taken into account, it is evident from the movement in the minority interest shown elsewhere in the accounts that the gain reflects such an amount.)

If the partial disposal of the subsidiary results in it ceasing to be a subsidiary of the parent entity, then IAS 27 requires the investment to be accounted for in accordance with IAS 39 from the date it ceases to be a subsidiary (see Chapter 10 at 4), unless it becomes an associate under IAS 28 (see Chapter 7 at 6.1).[310] The carrying amount of the investment at the date that it ceases to be a subsidiary is regarded as cost thereafter.[311] Again, we believe that a gain or loss should be calculated for the percentage interest sold, and that the carrying amount of the investment means the percentage interest in the net assets retained. This is the treatment which is required in the UK.

5.6.4 *Deemed disposals*

An entity may cease to be a subsidiary, or the group may reduce its proportionate share in that entity, other than by actual disposal. This may be due to the subsidiary issuing shares to a third party. IAS 27 makes no reference to such deemed disposals. This is an issue which has been addressed in the UK where the requirement is to treat such deemed disposals in the same way as actual disposals (see 3.5 above).

5.6.5 *Disclosures*

IAS 27 requires disclosure of the effect of disposal of subsidiaries on the financial position at the reporting date, the results for the reporting period and on the corresponding amounts for the preceding period.[312]

An example of such disclosure is given by Melexis as shown below.

Extract 6.69: Melexis NV (2000)

6.5.3. Changes in Group's Organisation

Melexis NV disposed Melexis AG on December 31, 2000 to Elex NV, the parent company. The gain on the sale amounted to EUR 240.540. In 2000 Melexis AG generated sales of EUR 758.221 and generated a net income of EUR 55.676. In 1999, sales and net income amounted to EUR 2,585.331 and EUR 184.864 respectively.

Another example is that of Novartis as shown in Extract 6.65 at 5.5.3 above.

In addition, IAS 7 requires disclosures in respect of disposals of subsidiaries or other business units and IAS 35 requires disclosures about discontinuing operations. These are discussed in Chapter 29 at 4.1.6 and Chapter 25 at 3.8 respectively.

6 CONCLUSION

By issuing FRSs 6 and 7, the ASB narrowed down some of the contentious issues relating to business combinations in the UK. Merger accounting is now rare, and therefore all the attention is now focused on acquisition accounting. Although the ASB has acknowledged that there is no general demand for a revision of FRS 6, it has indicated that if other countries ban merger accounting, then the subject would be very likely to come under review. As noted at 1 above, we disagree with the proposals put forward in the G4+1 paper and think it would be a retrograde step if the adoption of merger accounting were to be prohibited.

FRS 7 has certainly reduced some of the more significant abuses in fair value accounting, but it has to be said that it is not a very convincing standard at a conceptual level and shows signs of the haste with which it was finalised. Although the general approach within the standard that fair values should not reflect increases or decreases from the acquirer's intentions or future actions effectively removed the opportunity for including reorganisation provisions as part of the fair value exercise, the guidance within the standard on areas such as taxation (although less so under FRS 19) and businesses held for resale seem to be at odds with that approach.

It also has to be said that there still seems to be a tendency for fair value adjustments to reduce the book values of the net assets acquired, generally on the basis of alignment of accounting policies; adjustments reflecting increased values of tangible fixed assets, other than land and buildings, or pension scheme surpluses, are rarely seen.

Internationally, the IASB clearly sees business combinations as an area of considerable divergence across jurisdictions and considers it to be of first priority. The project is to be split into two phases. The first phase of the project is intended to converge existing standards on the definition of a business combination, the appropriate method(s) of accounting for a business combination (purchase or pooling/merger accounting), and the accounting for goodwill and intangible assets acquired in a business combination.

The second phase of the project would be to develop a single standard to converge the approaches in various existing standards on the accounting procedures for business combinations including issues such as purchase price allocation, liability and asset recognition at date of combination, contingent consideration, planned restructurings, transactions involving entities under common control (including joint ventures), step acquisitions, and new-basis issues.

Clearly, this project is likely to result in either an amendment of IAS 22 or the issuance of a new IFRS with guidance to supplement IAS 22.

References

1 FRS 6, *Acquisitions and Mergers*, ASB, September 1994, para. 2.
2 *Ibid.*, para. 4.
3 IAS 22, *Business Combinations*, IASC, Revised 1998, para. 8.
4 See Appendix III to FRS 6 and Chapter 6 at 2.1 of the Sixth Edition of this book for a discussion of the historical development of the rules on the criteria for mergers and acquisitions.
5 FRS 6, para. 38.
6 *Ibid.*, para. 2.
7 *Ibid.*, para. 4.
8 *Ibid.*, para. 2.
9 *Ibid.*, para. 58.
10 *Ibid.*, para. 6.
11 *Ibid.*, para. 61.
12 *Ibid.*, para. 62.
13 *Ibid.*, para. 7.
14 *Ibid.*, para. 64.
15 *Ibid.*, para. 66.
16 *Ibid.*, para. 8.
17 *Ibid.*, para. 68.
18 *Ibid.*, para. 9.
19 *Ibid.*, para. 10.
20 *Ibid.*, para. 11.
21 *Ibid.*, para. 76.
22 *Ibid.*, para. 12.
23 *Ibid.*, para. 56.
24 *Ibid.*, paras. 60–77.
25 For example, BP Amoco, Diageo and GlaxoSmithKline.
26 CA 85, Sch. 4A, para. 10.
27 *Ibid.*, para. 10(2).
28 *Ibid.*, para. 7(1).
29 FRS 6, Appendix I, para. 15.
30 CA 85, Sch. 4A, para. 9.

31 FRS 2, *Accounting for subsidiary undertakings*, ASB, July 1992, para. 45.
32 *Ibid.*, para. 85.
33 FRS 7, *Fair Values in Acquisition Accounting*, ASB, September 1994, para. 2.
34 *Ibid.*, para. 4.
35 *Ibid.*, para. 26.
36 *Ibid.*, para. 77.
37 *Ibid.*, para. 78.
38 ED 53, *Fair value in the context of acquisition accounting*, ASC, July 1992, para. 58.
39 FRS 7, para. 79.
40 *Ibid.*
41 FRRP PN 53, 7 August 1998.
42 FRS 7, para. 80.
43 FRRP PN 68, 18 July 2001.
44 ASB Discussion Paper, *Fair values in acquisition accounting*, ASB, April 1993, para. 12.2.
45 FRS 7, para. 77.
46 *Ibid.*, para. 81.
47 *Ibid.*, para. 27.
48 ASB Discussion Paper, *Fair values in acquisition accounting*, para. 12.4.
49 *Ibid.*
50 FRS 7, para. 81.
51 *Ibid.*, para. 82.
52 *Ibid.*, para. 83.
53 *Ibid.*, para. 84.
54 *Ibid.*, para. 28.
55 *Ibid.*, para. 85.
56 Information Sheet 35, UITF, 24 February 2000.
57 CA 85, Sch. 4A, para. 9(4).
58 CA 81, s 40(3).
59 Accountants Digest No. 189, *A Guide to Accounting Standards – SSAP 23 Accounting for acquisitions and mergers*, Summer 1986.
60 FRS 6, Appendix I, para. 16.
61 Draft Technical Release (TECH 25/00), *The determination of realised profits and distributable profits in the context of the Companies Act 1985*, ICAEW, 10 August 2000, Appendix A, A7.
62 *Ibid.*, A4.
63 *Ibid.*, A5.
64 CA 85, Sch. 4A, para. 9(2).
65 FRS 7, para. 5.
66 *Ibid.*, para. 2.
67 *Ibid.*, para. 35.
68 *Ibid.*, para. 38.
69 *Ibid.*, para. 39.
70 *Ibid.*, Appendix III, para. 14.
71 FRS 7, para. 7.
72 *Ibid.*, para. 6.
73 *Ibid.*, para. 2.
74 *Ibid.*, paras. 23–24.
75 *Ibid.*, para. 25.
76 *Ibid.*, para. 43.
77 FRED 7, *Fair values in acquisition accounting*, ASB, December 1993, para. 13.
78 FRS 7, para. 47.
79 *Ibid.*, para. 2.
80 *Ibid.*, para. 47.
81 *Ibid.*, para. 48.
82 *Ibid.*, para. 9.
83 *Ibid.*, para. 51.
84 *Ibid.*, para. 10.
85 FRS 10, *Goodwill and Intangible Fixed Assets*, ASB, December 1997, para. 10.
86 FRS 7, para. 11.
87 *Ibid.*, para. 12.
88 *Ibid.*, paras. 53 and 54.
89 *Ibid.*, para. 55.
90 *Ibid.*, para. 56.
91 *Ibid.*, para. 57.
92 *Ibid.*, para. 13.
93 *Ibid.*, para. 58.
94 *Ibid.*, para. 14.
95 *Ibid.*, para. 61.
96 *Ibid.*, para. 62.
97 *Ibid.*, para. 63.
98 *Ibid.*, para. 15.
99 FRS 12, *Provisions, Contingent Liabilities and Contingent Assets*, ASB, September 1998, paras. 31–33.
100 FRS 7, para. 37.
101 *Ibid.*, para. 19.
102 FRED 7, Appendix III, para. 35.
103 FRS 7, para. 71.
104 *Ibid.*, para. 72.
105 *Ibid.*, para. 20.
106 United Utilities PLC, Annual Report & Accounts 1997, p. 48.
107 FRS 7, para. 19 as amended by FRS 17, *Retirement Benefits*, ASB, November 2000, para. 101.
108 *Ibid.*, para. 71 as amended by FRS 17, para. 101.
109 *Ibid.*, para. 20.
110 FRS 17, para. 97.
111 FRS 7, para. 21.
112 *Ibid.*, para. 74.
113 FRED 7, paras. 74-76.
114 FRS 7, para. 22.
115 FRS 19, *Deferred Tax*, ASB, December 2000, para. 141.
116 FRS 7, para. 21 as amended by FRS 19, para. 71(a).
117 *Ibid.*, para. 74 as amended by FRS 19, para. 71(b).
118 *Ibid.*, paras. 22 and 75 as amended by FRS 19, para. 71.
119 *Ibid.*, para. 7.
120 *Ibid.*, para. 40.
121 FRRP PN 56, 24 February 1999.
122 FRS 7, para. 7.
123 FRS 12, para. 2.
124 A. Lennard and S. Peerless, Accountancy, January 1995, p.129.

125 Accounting Solutions, Accountancy, June 2001, p. 107.
126 FRS 7, para. 16.
127 *Ibid.*, para. 17.
128 *Ibid.*, paras. 65 and 66.
129 FRED 7, Appendix III, para. 33.
130 FRS 7, para. 69.
131 Staff Accounting Bulletin No. 54, SEC, Washington, 1983.
132 ASC Discussion Paper, *Fair value in the context of acquisition accounting*, ASC, June 1998, Chapter 12.
133 FRS 2, para. 50.
134 *Ibid.*, para. 89.
135 *Ibid.*
136 CA 85, s 228(6).
137 FRS 2, para. 51.
138 CA 85, Sch. 4A, para. 9.
139 *Ibid.*, para. 7(1).
140 *Ibid.*, paras. 7–9.
141 FRS 6, Appendix II.
142 FRS 6, paras. 16 and 17.
143 *Ibid.*, para. 17.
144 CA 85, Sch. 4A, para. 11.
145 FRS 6, para. 18.
146 *Ibid.*, para. 41.
147 CA 85, Sch. 4A, paras. 11(5)–(6).
148 However, it is probably not permissible to use reserve categories which would not have been available as a destination for goodwill if acquisition accounting had been applied; see the discussion on this topic at 2.5.2 in the previous edition of this book.
149 FRS 6, para.18.
150 *Ibid.*
151 *Ibid.*, para. 19.
152 *Ibid.*, para. 51.
153 *Ibid.*, para. 21.
154 FRS 2, para. 49.
155 FRS 6, para. 23.
156 *Ibid.*, para. 24.
157 *Ibid.*, para. 25.
158 FRRP PN 48, 10 November 1997.
159 FRRP PN 55, 20 October 1998.
160 FRS 6, para. 26.
161 *Ibid.*, para. 27.
162 *Ibid.*, para. 30.
163 *Ibid.*, para. 85.
164 *Ibid.*, para. 32.
165 *Ibid.*, para. 28.
166 *Ibid.*, para. 29.
167 FRRP, PN 57, 28 October 1999.
168 FRS 6, para. 33. The requirement of FRS 6 is based on the original FRS 1 and has been interpreted in a way which is consistent with FRS 1 (Revised 1996).
169 *Ibid.*, para. 34. Again, the requirement of FRS 6 is based on the original FRS 1 and has been interpreted in a way which is consistent with FRS 1 (Revised 1996).
170 *Ibid.*, para. 31.
171 *Ibid.*, para. 86.
172 *Ibid.*, para. 87.
173 *Ibid.*, para. 35.
174 *Ibid.*, para. 37.
175 UITF 15 (revised 1999), para. 5.
176 FRS 6, para. 36.
177 FRRP, PN 57, 28 October 1999.
178 FRS 6, para. 22.
179 CA 85, Sch. 4A, para. 13.
180 *Ibid.*, para. 13(2).
181 FRRP PN 5, 28 January 1992.
182 CA 85, Sch. 4A, para. 16.
183 *Ibid.*, para. 13(3).
184 *Ibid.*, para. 13(6).
185 FRS 2, para. 45.
186 *Ibid.*, para. xxii.
187 FRS 3, *Reporting financial performance*, ASB, October 1992, para. 18.
188 FRS 2, para. 47.
189 *Ibid.*, para. 52.
190 *Ibid.*, para. 91.
191 *Ibid.*, para. 87.
192 CA 1985, Schedule 4, para. 12(a).
193 FRS 2, para. 47.
194 Draft Abstract *Exchanges of businesses or other non-monetary assets for equity in a subsidiary, joint venture or associate*, UITF, May 2001, para. 2.
195 Information Sheet 47, UITF, May 2001.
196 Draft Abstract *Exchanges of businesses or other non-monetary assets for equity in a subsidiary, joint venture or associate*, para. 12.
197 *Ibid.*
198 *Ibid.*
199 FRRP PN 43, October 1996.
200 TECH 25/00, para. 28.
201 Draft Abstract *Exchanges of businesses or other non-monetary assets for equity in a subsidiary, joint venture or associate*, para. 13.
202 FRS 10, para. 54.
203 *Ibid.*, para. 71(c).
204 *Ibid.*
205 CA 85, Sch. 4A, para. 15.
206 FRS 2, para. 48. Para. 49 appears to contain a similar requirement.
207 FRS 6, para. 2.
208 *Ibid.*, para. 13.
209 CA 85, Sch. 4A, para. 10(c).
210 *Ibid.*, s 151 et seq.
211 FRS 6, para. 78.
212 See also Reuters Group PLC, Report and Accounts 1998, p. 51 and Viridian Group PLC, Report and Accounts 1998, p.27.
213 CA 85, s 23.
214 *Ibid.*, s 276.

215 TECH 25/00, Appendix A, A11.
216 *Ibid.*, para. 20 and Appendix A, A12.
217 IAS 22, para. 1.
218 *Ibid.*, para. 8.
219 *Ibid.*, para. 2.
220 *Ibid.*, para. 4.
221 *Ibid.*, para. 7.
222 *Ibid.*, para. 13.
223 SIC-9, *Business Combinations – Classification either as Acquisitions or Unitings of Interests*, SIC, January 2000, para. 1.
224 *Ibid.*, para. 7.
225 *Ibid.*, para. 4.
226 *Ibid.*, para. 5.
227 IAS 22, para. 5.
228 *Ibid.*, para. 8.
229 *Ibid.*, para. 15.
230 SIC-9, para. 6.
231 IAS 22, para. 16.
232 *Ibid.*, paras. 77 and 78.
233 *Ibid.*, para. 81.
234 *Ibid.*
235 *Ibid.*, para. 79.
236 *Ibid.*, para. 82.
237 *Ibid.*, para. 83.
238 *Ibid.*, para. 78.
239 *Ibid.*, para. 8.
240 *Ibid.*, para. 10.
241 *Ibid.*, para. 11.
242 *Ibid.*, para. 17.
243 *Ibid.*, para. 18.
244 *Ibid.*, para. 41.
245 *Ibid.*, para. 19.
246 *Ibid.*, para. 20.
247 *Ibid.*, para. 21.
248 Draft Interpretation SIC-D28, *Business Combinations – Measurement of Shares Issued as Purchase Consideration*, SIC, para. 4.
249 IAS 22, para. 8.
250 *Ibid.*, para. 23.
251 *Ibid.*, para. 24.
252 *Ibid.*
253 Draft Interpretation SIC-D28, *Business Combinations – Measurement of Shares Issued as Purchase Consideration*, para. 5.
254 IAS 22, para. 25.
255 *Ibid.*, para. 66.
256 *Ibid.*, para. 65.
257 *Ibid.*, para. 67.
258 *Ibid.*, para. 68.
259 *Ibid.*, para. 67.
260 *Ibid.*, para. 70.
261 *Ibid.*, para. 26.
262 *Ibid.*, para. 28.
263 *Ibid.*, para. 29.
264 *Ibid.*, para. 32.
265 *Ibid.*, para. 33.
266 *Ibid.*, para. 34.
267 *Ibid.*, para. 35.
268 *Ibid.*, para. 39(e) and (f).
269 *Ibid.*, para. 39(g).
270 IAS 38, *Intangible Assets*, IASC, Revised 1998, para. 28.
271 *Ibid.*, para. 39(g).
272 *Ibid.*, para. 40.
273 *Ibid.*, para. 39(d).
274 *Ibid.*, para. 39(a).
275 *Ibid.*, para. 39(b).
276 *Ibid.*, para. 39(c).
277 *Ibid.*, para. 39(j).
278 *Ibid.*, para. 39(c) and (j).
279 *Ibid.*, para. 39(h).
280 IAS 19, *Employee Benefits*, IASC, Revised 2000, para. 108.
281 IAS 38, para. 39(i).
282 IAS 12, *Income Taxes*, IASC, Revised 2000, paras. 15 and 66.
283 IAS 22, para. 39(k).
284 *Ibid.*, para. 29.
285 *Ibid.*, para. 31.
286 *Ibid.*, para. 71.
287 SIC-22, *Business Combinations – Subsequent Adjustment of Fair Values and Goodwill Initially Reported*, SIC, June 2000, para. 3.
288 *Ibid.*, para. 5.
289 *Ibid.*, para. 6.
290 *Ibid.*, para. 7.
291 IAS 22, para. 85.
292 *Ibid.*, para. 75.
293 *Ibid.*
294 *Ibid.*, para. 36.
295 *Ibid.*, para. 38.
296 *Ibid.*, para. 37.
297 *Ibid.*, para. 8.
298 *Ibid.*, para. 12.
299 FRS 6, Appendix II.
300 IAS 22, para. 86.
301 *Ibid.*, para. 94.
302 *Ibid.*, para. 87.
303 *Ibid.*, para. 93.
304 SIC-22, para. 8.
305 IAS 22, para. 92.
306 *Ibid.*, para. 96.
307 IAS 27, para. 32(b).
308 *Ibid.*para. 23.
309 *Ibid.*
310 *Ibid.*, para. 24.
311 *Ibid.*, para. 25.
312 *Ibid.*, para. 32.

Chapter 7 Associates, joint ventures and JANEs

1 INTRODUCTION

Traditionally, investments in companies which did not satisfy the criteria for classification as subsidiaries were carried at cost, and the revenue from them was recognised only on the basis of dividends received. However, during the 1960s it was recognised that there was a case for an intermediate form of accounting, since there was a growing tendency for groups to conduct part of their activities by taking substantial minority stakes in other companies and exercising a degree of influence over their business which fell short of complete control. Mere recognition of dividends was seen to be an inadequate measure of the results of this activity (and one which could be manipulated by the investor, where it could influence the investee's distribution policy). Moreover, since it was unlikely that the investee would fully distribute its earnings, the cost of the investment would give an increasingly unrealistic indication of its underlying value.

This intermediate form of accounting, equity accounting, was first used by the Royal Dutch Shell group in 1964. It involves a modified form of consolidation of the results and assets of investees in the investor's financial statements when the investor exercises 'significant influence', but not control, over the management of the investee. The essence of equity accounting is that, rather than full scale consolidation on a line by line basis, it requires incorporation of the investor's share of net assets of the investee in one line in the investor's consolidated balance sheet and the share of its results at only some levels of the profit and loss account.

Another form of 'intermediate consolidation' used by some entities, particularly in certain industries, was proportional consolidation. As its name implies, this involves bringing in the results and assets and liabilities of an investment on a line-by-line basis, but only to the extent of the investor's share, rather than, as under normal consolidation, in full with credit given for any minority interest.

1.1 UK position

Equity accounting was first formally recognised in UK accounting literature by the issue of SSAP 1 – *Accounting for associated companies* – by the ASC in 1971. SSAP 1 was revised a number of times without fundamental change, until being finally superseded by FRS 9 – *Associates and joint ventures*, issued by the ASB in November 1997. Whilst this made changes more far-reaching than the previous revisions to SSAP 1, the fundamentals of equity accounting remain much the same as when it first appeared in the 1960s.

The main changes made by FRS 9 were to restrict the circumstances in which equity accounting can be applied and to provide, for the first time in UK GAAP, detailed rules on accounting for joint ventures. Given that these changes were hardly radical, FRS 9 took a surprisingly long time to develop.

The initial impetus for change came in 1989 with the incorporation into UK law of the EU Seventh Accounting Law Directive on consolidated accounts. This changed the law so as to require associated undertakings (see 2.1.2 below) to be equity accounted (previously the Companies Act only permitted such treatment),[1] and to permit unincorporated joint ventures to be proportionally consolidated (see 2.2.2 below). In June 1990 the ASC issued ED 50 *Consolidated accounts*, which proposed changing the definition of associate in SSAP 1 to bring it more in line with the then new legislation. With the winding up of the ASC, this document was not formally progressed further, although many of its ideas can be seen in the ASB's later work.

The ASB's work on this area was dominated by two issues in particular. The first was a concern that equity accounting was being applied in situations where it may not have been appropriate, such as where the reporting entity held a significant stake in another company as the result of a failed take-over bid, but was unable to exercise any real influence over it.[2] In our view, however, such abuse as there had been of equity accounting under SSAP 1 tended to be at the other end of the spectrum; in other words, where a company *failed* to equity account for an investment (usually loss-making!) on the assertion that it did not have significant influence over it. There must be a concern that FRS 9 may have made such abuse rather easier, although we have not seen any evidence of this in practice.

The second major issue was the treatment of joint ventures, for which proportional consolidation had become the normal method of accounting in certain sectors, particularly the extractive, property and construction industries. However, the ASB was concerned it was in many cases difficult to distinguish between such entities as were then being proportionally consolidated and associated undertakings accounted for under the equity method.[3] In addition, the Companies Act 1989 had amended the Companies Act 1985 so as to prohibit proportional consolidation of incorporated joint ventures,[4] leading to the potential for inconsistent treatment between corporate and non-corporate joint ventures.

For these reasons FRS 9 ostensibly prohibits proportional consolidation, but effectively allows it in certain cases (generally corresponding to those where it was already being applied in the UK), by introducing the concept of the 'joint arrangement that is not an entity' (or 'JANE'). This requires the reporting entity to account for certain activities carried on through another entity to be accounted for as if the reporting entity carried them out directly. Whilst this is not technically 'proportional consolidation', it is often arithmetically identical (see 2.3 below).

FRS 9 is discussed in detail in 2 to 5 below.

1.2 IAS position

Under IAS accounting for associates is dealt with by IAS 28 – *Accounting for Investments in Associates*, and IAS 31 – *Financial Reporting of Interests in Joint Ventures*, originally issued in November 1988 and November 1990 respectively. Both standards have been subject to several minor amendments since first being issued, most recently in 2000. In broad terms, the main difference between IAS and UK GAAP is the treatment of joint ventures. In many cases where UK GAAP requires equity accounting to be used, IAS requires proportional consolidation (although reluctantly allowing equity accounting). At a more detailed level, however, there are quite significant differences in the treatment of both associates and joint ventures. The requirements of IAS and the main differences from UK GAAP are discussed in section 6 below.

2 THE SCOPE OF FRS 9

Despite its title *Associates and Joint Ventures*, FRS 9 in fact deals with four types of vehicle:

- associates;
- joint ventures;
- joint arrangements that are not entities, which the UK accounting profession was quick to reduce to the acronym 'JANE', the term now in such common use that, although it is not used in FRS 9, we shall adopt it in the remainder of this chapter; and
- structures with the form but not the substance of a joint venture.

The last two of these strictly cuckoos in the nest of FRS 9, being neither associates nor joint ventures. The definitions of each of these types of vehicle in FRS 9 are set out and discussed below, together, where relevant, with the requirements of the Companies Act 1985. FRS 9 does not make it clear what is to be done when an investment falls within more than one definition – for example, almost any 'joint venture' as defined will also be an 'associate' (but not vice-versa). We presume that in such cases the more exclusive definition (i.e. joint venture) is intended to apply.

2.1 Definition of associate

2.1.1 *FRS 9*

An associate is defined as 'an entity (other than a subsidiary[5]) in which another entity (the investor) has a *participating interest* and over whose operating and financial policies the investor *exercises a significant influence*'.[6] The phrases in italics are further defined, and are discussed below.

There is something of an ambiguity in the phrase '(other than a subsidiary)' since it begs the question 'A subsidiary of what?'. We believe that it means a subsidiary in the reporting group. In other words the phrase is simply for the avoidance of doubt, since any subsidiary will also meet the definition of associate. This is because a subsidiary is an investment subject to the 'control' of the group; any investment under the 'control' of the group must inevitably be subject to its 'significant influence' as well. However, a respectable case could be made that the phrase in fact means a subsidiary of anything, such that no investment could be both a subsidiary of one entity and an associate of another. This latter interpretation is supported by the overall thrust of FRS 9 (that the burden of proof is on the investor to show that it has significant influence over any purported associate).

The wording of the equivalent definition of 'associated undertaking' in the Companies Act states unambiguously that an associate cannot be a subsidiary 'of the parent company'.[7] The omission of these words in FRS 9 could be argued to be deliberate so as to admit a wider interpretation. More plausibly, it could be said that the Companies Act definition was clearly the inspiration for that in FRS 9 and the two should, therefore, be construed in the same way.

A Participating interest

A 'participating interest' is an interest in the shares (or equivalent ownership rights) of an entity held on a long term basis for the purpose of securing a contribution to the investor's activities by the exercise of control or influence arising from or related to that interest.[8] This definition is essentially the same as that in section 260 of the Companies Act and, as in the Act, there is a presumption that a holding of 20% or more is a participating interest.[9]

An interest 'held on a long-term basis' is one held other than exclusively with a view to subsequent resale. An interest is held with a view to subsequent resale if either:

(a) a purchaser is being actively sought and disposal of the interest is reasonably expected to occur within approximately one year of its acquisition; or

(b) the interest was acquired as the result of enforcement of a security, and has not subsequently become part of the continuing activities of the group.[10]

FRS 9 clarifies that the issue of whether an investment is held for the long-term is to be determined by reference to the time at which the investment is first acquired, rather than at each balance sheet date. Thus, once an investment has been treated as held on a long-term basis, it should continue to be so treated, even if the investor intends to dispose of it.[11]

FRS 9 contains a reminder that, as is the case under the Companies Act, a 'participating interest' includes an interest convertible into shares or an option to acquire shares.[12] This means that entities (such as start-up ventures) in which the reporting entity currently has only a small, or no, equity stake, but has an option to increase it later, may still qualify as associates if the other necessary conditions are met.

B Exercise of significant influence

FRS 9's definition of 'exercise of significant influence' was intended to restrict the number of entities that qualified as associates compared to those so treated by SSAP 1. SSAP 1 defined an associate as an investee over which the investor was 'in a position to exercise significant influence'.[13] By contrast, FRS 9 requires the investor actually to exercise influence.

The introduction of FRS 9 did indeed result in some companies ceasing to regard as associates certain investments which had been so treated under SSAP 1.[14]

An investor 'exercises significant influence' when it 'is actively involved and is influential in the direction of the investee through its participation in policy decisions covering aspects of policy relevant to the investor, including decisions on strategic issues such as:

(a) the expansion or contraction of the business, participation in other entities or changes in products, markets and activities of its investee; and

(b) determining the balance between dividend and reinvestment.'[15]

FRS 9 notes that in the Companies Act there is a presumption that control of 20% or more of the voting rights of an investee gives rise to significant influence over it,[16] but gives a strong hint that rebuttal of this presumption will be quite frequent. As FRS 9 puts it, a holding of 20% or more 'suggests but does not ensure' that the investor exercises significant influence.[17] An example of a company which rebuts the presumed exercise of significant influence over an investment of more than 20% is RMC Group.

Extract 7.1: RMC Group p.l.c. (2000)

13d) Other investments [extract]

At 31st December 2000, RMC Group p.l.c. held 22.17% of the issued Ordinary share capital of Alexander Russell PLC, a company registered and principally operating in Scotland as listed in the United Kingdom. The latest date to which accounts have been published is 31st December 1999. These disclosed a profit for the year of £4.2 million, and capital and reserves of £36.7 million. This company is not regarded as an associated undertaking as RMC Group p.l.c. is not in a position to exercise significant influence in management.

The converse situation of a holding of less than 20% being regarded as an associate is still to be found. For example, Daily Mail and General Trust disclosed an 18.9% interest in GWR Group plc being accounted for as an associate in its accounts for the year ended 3 October 1999, although this was increased to a 26.8% interest in the following period.[18]

What principally distinguishes an associate from an ordinary fixed asset investment, in the ASB's view, is that in the case of an ordinary fixed asset investment the investor takes a relatively passive role, whereas an associate is a medium through which the investor conducts part of its business. An associate is therefore expected to implement policies that are consistent with, or complementary to, those of the investor.[19]

FRS 9 also suggests that the investor's attitude towards the investee's dividend policy may indicate the status of the investment. In the case of an ordinary fixed asset investment, the investor may often press for the highest dividend possible. In the case of an associate, however, 'the investor's long-term interest in the future cash flows of its investee is compatible with a policy of reinvestment', so that the investor will tend not to be so concerned with a high dividend.[20] In practical terms, FRS 9 indicates that associate status is 'usually achieved' when the investor has board representation (or other active participation in the decision-making process) combined with at least 20% of the voting rights.[21]

The somewhat surprising implication of this is that the ASB envisages 'significant influence' over an investee as requiring more active involvement by the investor than 'control' may entail. 'Control' is defined in FRS 9 as the 'ability' to direct the operating and financial policies of the investee;[22] the same definition is also used in FRS 2 – *Accounting for subsidiary undertakings*, FRS 5 – *Reporting the substance of transactions* and FRS 8 – *Related party disclosures*. By contrast, the mere 'ability' to exercise significant influence is not enough; the investor must actively exercise it. Rather confusingly, however, in FRS 8 the mere ability to exercise influence may be enough to create a related party relationship – see Chapter 30 at 2.2.1 B.[23]

As noted in 1 above, FRS 9's emphasis on the actual exercise of influence might provide a loop-hole for those seeking to avoid equity accounting for an investment, particularly when it is making losses, as may be the case in a start-up company. The ASB clearly shares this concern. FRS 9 emphasises that, once an investee has qualified as an associate or joint venture, this relationship is not disturbed by minor or temporary changes in it. In particular, whether the investment is profitable or loss-making does not, in itself, alter the relationship.

Accordingly, FRS 9 provides that, once an investor has exercised significant influence over an entity, it should be presumed to continue to do so until some specific event or transaction occurs that removes the investor's ability to exercise such influence.[24] The most common such event in practice is likely to be the loss of representation on the board. An example of a company ceasing to treat an investment as an associate on these grounds was Hanson.

Extract 7.2: Hanson PLC (1998)

12 Investments [extract]

The group's investment in Westralian Sands Limited (formerly RGC Limited) was previously treated as an associate. The group's investment does not now meet the definition of an associate since the group has not exercised significant influence since January 1, 1998 because Hanson no longer has appropriate board representation. The investment is now treated as a fixed asset investment. As the investment was no longer regarded as being an associate the carrying amount was restated by adjusting for goodwill of £184.0m previously written off to reserves on acquisition. The directors consider that the resultant investment was permanently impaired and therefore the investment was written down based on market value and the charge of £155.8m taken through the profit and loss account as an exceptional item.

Whilst we understand the need for such a provision as an anti-avoidance measure, it does rather stand the underlying rationale of FRS 9 on its head, in that, whilst *actual* exercise of significant influence is necessary to create an associate relationship, to maintain that relationship requires merely the *ability* to exercise significant influence. This opens up at least the possibility that an investor may at the balance sheet date have two similar investments over which it could (but does not) exercise significant influence, of which one is equity accounted for because of an actual exercise of influence five years ago, but the other treated as a fixed asset investment because influence has yet to be positively exercised.

On the whole, we do not regard FRS 9 as an improvement on SSAP 1 in this respect. Any instances of companies equity accounting for investments over which they had no real influence in our view indicated a failure to comply with, rather than an inherent deficiency in, SSAP 1.

2.1.2 *Companies Act 1985*

The Act defines associated undertakings in similar terms to FRS 9, as an undertaking in which a participating interest is held and over which significant influence is exercised.[25] A participating interest in an undertaking is an interest in the shares of the undertaking which is held for the long term for the purpose of securing a contribution to the activities of the investing company by the exercise of control or influence arising from that interest.[26] This includes interests in partnerships and unincorporated associations; it also includes interests which are convertible into interests in shares, such as convertible loan stock, and options to acquire an interest in shares.[27] The Act also asserts that a holding of 20% of the shareholders' or members' voting rights is presumed to confer significant influence.

2.2 Definition of joint venture

2.2.1 *FRS 9*

A joint venture is 'an entity in which the reporting entity holds an interest on a long-term basis and is jointly controlled by the reporting entity and one or more other venturers under a contractual arrangement.' A reporting entity jointly controls a venture with one or more other entities when 'none of the [investing] entities alone can control that entity but all together can do so and decisions on financial and operating policy essential to the activities, economic performance and financial position of that venture require each venturer's consent'.[28]

Key to this definition is the fact that a 'joint *venture*' must be an 'entity', whereas a 'joint *arrangement*', or JANE, (discussed in 2.3 below) is not. FRS 9 defines an entity as a 'body corporate, partnership or incorporated association carrying on a trade or business with or without a view to profit',[29] which is essentially the same as the definition of 'undertaking' in the Companies Act.[30] FRS 9, however, goes on to clarify that the reference to the entity's 'carrying on a trade or business' means a trade or business of its own, and not just part of the trades or businesses of the entities that have interests in it (as is the case with a JANE).[31] FRS 9 does not envisage a formal agreement between the venturers as necessary to create joint control, provided that in practice each venturer's consent is required for high-level strategic decisions.[32]

This seems straightforward enough, but it raises a number of issues. Most importantly, this definition has the effect that all 50/50 companies are joint ventures rather than associates as, in the nature of things, mutual consent of the shareholders is required for all major decisions. The significance of this is that FRS 9 imposes slightly more extensive accounting, presentational and disclosure requirements on joint ventures than on associates (see 3.2 and 5 below).

It could be argued that because the definition refers to joint control 'under a contractual arrangement', a 50/50 shareholding structure does not, of itself, create a joint venture in the absence of a separate shareholders' agreement. It is our view, however, that in a 50/50 company there is inevitably de facto joint control and it seems perverse that the accounting treatment should depend on whether or not there is a shareholders' agreement. In practice, the norm for such companies, particularly where they are specific vehicles for a single venture, is to have shareholders' agreements, in which case it is beyond doubt that they are joint ventures under FRS 9.

In other shareholding structures (assuming that all shares have equal rights), a shareholders' agreement will clearly be needed to assure joint control. FRS 9 allows for control by some but not all shareholders, as the following example shows.

Example 7.1: Joint control of joint venture by some, but not all, shareholders

A company has three shareholders holding shares in the proportions 45/45/10 and there is an agreement between the two 45% shareholders requiring their agreement on all major issues. They clearly control the company between them, even though the minority shareholder is not party to the agreement. This is quite common in companies which have a 'sleeping' minority shareholder, perhaps for tax or local regulatory reasons. In this case the 45% shareholders would account for their interests as a joint venture, but the 10% shareholder would account for its interest as an ordinary investment.[33]

Somewhat controversially, in our view, FRS 9 provides that a partly-owned subsidiary of the reporting entity should not be consolidated, but treated as a joint venture, where there is a contractual arrangement with the minority shareholder(s) that has the effect of giving the reporting entity joint, rather than sole, control. FRS 9 argues that such an arrangement amounts to 'severe long term restrictions' within the meaning of paragraph 25 of FRS 2 and, by implication, section 229 of the Companies Act.[34]

This is, in our view, a rather free interpretation of FRS 2 and the law, both of which make it clear that the 'severe long-term restrictions' referred to are restrictions only over those rights 'by reason of which the parent undertaking is defined as such … and in the absence of which it would not be the parent undertaking'.[35] To put this in plainer English, the most usual reason why an undertaking is a subsidiary of its parent is that the parent has the majority of the voting rights (i.e. as a shareholder at general meetings) in the subsidiary. The law and FRS 2 therefore require non-consolidation only where there are real restrictions over the parent's rights as a member, and these may well be unaffected by shareholders' agreements (see Chapter 5 at 5.3).

Suppose, for example, that a parent company enters into a shareholders' agreement with a minority shareholder of a subsidiary that the subsidiary, absent mutual consent for change, must not operate outside the UK, diversify its product range, spend more than £1 million on new plant, or declare a dividend beyond a certain level. Whilst such an agreement clearly puts significant commercial restrictions on the parent's freedom of action with respect to the subsidiary, it does not affect its voting rights in a shareholders' meeting (i.e. the rights by virtue of which it is the parent). It should also be borne in mind that any restrictions imposed by a shareholders' agreement are presumably entered into voluntarily by the parent.

It is therefore, in our view, questionable whether such an agreement amounts to 'significant long-term restrictions' as defined in the law and FRS 2. If, however, the shareholders' agreement required mutual consent on matters normally decided by the shareholders in general meeting (e.g. appointment of directors and auditors), then it would impose significant restrictions as defined by FRS 2 and the Companies Act. We presume that the ASB has had the benefit of legal advice that its wider interpretation is sustainable.

Apart from these admittedly rather technical concerns on this aspect of FRS 9, the more real risk is that it may have created an unintended opportunity for off-balance sheet financing. Suppose, for example, that a company sets up a 99%-owned subsidiary with the 1% held by a 'friendly' third party. It then puts in place a shareholders' agreement requiring unanimity on all issues, which the parent is certain will in practice be obtained. On the face of it FRS 9 requires that, as the parent has only joint, rather than sole, control in these circumstances, the subsidiary should not be consolidated, so that its borrowings (for example) do not appear as such on the consolidated balance sheet!

We realise that in practice companies are unlikely to establish, or their auditors to accept, as blatant a scheme as this. The provisions of the Companies Act relating to nominee shareholdings might also be relevant. However, there are bound to be cases that are more on the borderline, where FRS 9 may have readmitted at least the possibility of some of the abuses that the Companies Act 1989, and FRSs 2 and 5, were aimed at eradicating.

2.2.2 *Companies Act 1985*

Although FRS 9 prohibits proportional consolidation, the Companies Act 1985 contains provisions which permit proportional consolidation in group accounts for certain joint ventures[36] and the following points are worth noting:

(a) the Act restricts proportional consolidation to unincorporated joint ventures. Incorporated joint ventures will therefore generally be equity accounted;

(b) the Act requires that the joint venture should be managed 'jointly with one or more undertakings not included in the consolidation' but otherwise places no restriction on the type of non-corporate joint venture which may be proportionally consolidated; and

(c) the Act contains no detailed description of the proportional consolidation method, stating merely that 'the provisions of this Part relating to the preparation of consolidated accounts apply, with any necessary modifications, to proportional consolidation under this paragraph'.

A number of companies availed themselves of these provisions before FRS 9 came into force. Now such companies must demonstrate that an investee for which it wishes to 'proportionally consolidate' is in fact a JANE (see 2.3 below).

2.3 Definition of JANE and 'structure with the form but not the substance of a joint venture'

A JANE ('joint arrangement that is not an entity') is defined by FRS 9 as 'a contractual arrangement under which the participants engage in joint activities that do not create an entity because it would not be carrying on a trade or business of its own. A contractual arrangement where all significant matters of operating and financial policy are predetermined does not create an entity because the policies are those of its participants, not of a separate entity.'[37] This is one of the more difficult aspects of FRS 9, which can be understood only by considering the background to it.

As noted in 1 above, it had been a long-standing practice in certain industries (in particular oil exploration, engineering and property) to account for certain types of joint venture using proportional consolidation, and it is no secret that during the development of FRS 9 those industries vigorously lobbied the ASB not to change this practice. However, the ASB is strongly opposed to proportional consolidation. The grounds for this, set out in Appendix III to FRS 9, are that proportional consolidation misleadingly presents the reporting entity's shares of the assets and liabilities, profits and losses and cash flows of jointly controlled entities as equivalent to the completely controlled assets and liabilities, profits and losses and cash flows of subsidiaries.[38]

The ASB attempted a creative solution to this problem by, in effect, challenging whether the practice in these industries really was 'proportional consolidation'. In the oil industry, for example, several companies may agree to explore a particular site. Whilst the detail of such arrangements may vary quite considerably, typical features are that all the companies contribute to the cost of exploration and take an agreed share of the output (which is sold separately by each of them), but one of the companies actually operates the site, earning a fee from the other partners for doing so.

While such arrangements can create the illusion of a separate entity, closer examination may reveal this not to be the case. The test of whether or not a business arrangement is a separate entity or a JANE is whether it is carrying on a trade of its own or is merely an extension of the individual businesses of the participants in the arrangement. FRS 9 states that the following are indicators that a joint arrangement is not an entity:

(a) the participants derive their benefit from product or services taken in kind rather than by receiving a share in the results of trading; or

(b) each participant's share of the output or result of the joint activity is determined by its supply of key inputs to the process producing that output or result.[39]

It seems that under FRS 9 a JANE is an arrangement involving full control of a part of an operation, whereas proportional consolidation of the sort criticised in Appendix III to FRS 9 implies partial control of the whole operation.

Unfortunately, matters are complicated by the fact that sometimes these joint arrangements may actually be conducted through separate legal entities. FRS 9 notes that in some cases there may be 'structures with the form but not the substance of a joint venture', which should be accounted for in exactly the same way as JANEs.[40] Examples of such structures might include agency or distribution companies. Similarly, joint interests in pipelines and other plant may, for regulatory or other legal reasons, actually be held through a legal entity rather than directly by the participants.

Appendix I to FRS 9 (which discusses the interaction of FRS 9 with the provisions of the Companies Act) makes it clear that there will be cases where a JANE will be 'contained' within a legal entity, such as a company or partnership.[41] In such cases, FRS 9 argues (in effect) that the *form* of the arrangement is that each participant in the venture has an investment in another entity, but the *substance* is that each is carrying on its own business through that entity, and that the accounting should be driven by the substance, not the form.

FRS 9 adds to the confusion by noting that sometimes the nature of a JANE changes over time and it may begin to trade as an entity in its own right. In such circumstances the accounting treatment must be modified accordingly (i.e. it should be treated as a joint venture, associate or ordinary investment as appropriate).[42]

What all this may mean in practice can be illustrated with the following simple example.

Example 7.2: Distinction between joint venture and JANE

Property X and Property Y are identical blocks containing 50 high quality residential flats. Legal title to the properties is held by two management companies, X Limited and Y Limited, in both of which two property companies, A plc and B plc, each own 50% of the shares. However, in the case of property Y there is a shareholders' agreement to the effect that A plc is entitled to the net income relating to Flats 1 to 25 and B plc to the net income relating to Flats 26 to 50.

Under FRS 9, A plc and B plc would account for their interests in X Limited as a joint venture, but their interests in Y Limited as a JANE. This is because in the case of Property X, A plc and B plc bear all risks and rewards of the whole block of flats equally. Thus, if the rent for, say, Flat 10 falls into arrears, A plc and B plc both suffer 50% of the bad debt. In Property Y, however, the effect of the shareholders' agreement is such that the bad debt risk on Flat 10 would fall entirely on A plc, rather than on A plc and B plc equally.

Examples of companies that conduct business through both joint ventures and JANEs, and distinguish between the two in their accounting policies are BP Amoco and Rolls Royce.

Extract 7.3: BP Amoco p.l.c. (2000)

Accounting policies [extract]

A joint venture is an entity in which the group has a long-term interest and shares control with one or more co-venturers. The consolidated financial statements include the group proportion of turnover, operating profit or loss, exceptional items, stock holding gains or losses, interest expense, taxation, gross assets and gross liabilities of the joint venture (the gross equity method).

Certain of the group's activities are conducted through joint arrangements and are included in the consolidated financial statements in proportion to the group's interest in the income, expenses, assets and liabilities of these joint arrangements.

Extract 7.4: Rolls-Royce plc (2000)

Basis of consolidation [extract]

The Group financial statements include the financial statements of the Company and all of its subsidiary undertakings made up to December 31, together with the Group's share of the results up to December 31 of:

i) joint ventures

A joint venture is an entity in which the Group holds a long-term interest and which is jointly controlled by the Group and one or more other venturers under a contractual arrangement. The results of joint ventures are accounted for using the gross equity method of accounting.

ii) joint arrangements that are not entities

The Group has certain contractual arrangements with other participants to engage in joint activities that do not create an entity carrying on a trade or business of its own. The Group includes its share of assets, liabilities and cash flows in such joint arrangements, measured in accordance with the terms of each arrangement, which is usually pro-rata to the Group's risk interest in the joint arrangement.

Interestingly, both these extracts refer to 'interests in' or 'share of' the joint arrangements, which could imply that the arrangements concerned are entities and therefore not JANEs. It is our view that the arrangements as described are JANEs as defined in FRS 9, but that the wording used to describe the accounting treatment reveals the tension (referred to above) between the companies' perception that this is a form of proportional consolidation and the view in FRS 9 that they are in fact accounting directly for 'their own' activities that happen to be carried on through an arrangement involving other parties.

Examples of interests in JANEs held through a separate legal entity is given by Hammerson.

Extract 7.5: Hammerson plc (2000)

11. Land and Buildings [extract]

Certain property and corporate interests with a total book value of £728.5m (1999: £620.8m) have been accounted for as joint arrangements. These are set out in the following table:

	Group share %	Partner(s)
Investment portfolio		
B5 Designer Outlet Center	50	Morrison GmbH, Demex Systembau GmbH
Brent Cross Shopping Centre	41.2	The Standard Life Assurance Company
Essen Shopping Center BV	22	Algemeen Burgerlijk Pensioenfonds
The Martineau Galleries Limited Partnership	33.33	Henderson Investors Ltd, Land Securities PLC
The Oracle Limited Partnership	50	Akaria Investments Limited
West Quay Shopping Centre Limited	50	Barclays Bank plc
Development portfolio		
The Bull Ring Limited Partnership	33.33	Henderson Global Investors Ltd, Land Securities PLC
The London Wall Limited Partnership	50	Kajima London Wall Limited
The Martineau Limited Partnership	33.33	Henderson Global Investors Ltd, Land Securities PLC
Spitalfields Development Group	66.66	Balfour Beatty Property Investments Limited

All in all, we consider the JANE concept as one of the weaker aspects of FRS 9. It appears to have been developed in order to avoid disturbing established practice in specific industries. Significantly, much of FRS 9's discussion of JANEs refers to, or uses examples specific to, the oil, property and engineering industries,[43] which have also provided all of the extracts relating to JANEs included above. The problem, in our view, is that in attempting to rationalise practice in those industries, FRS 9 introduced a definition of a JANE which could include certain entities which (we assume) were never meant to be accounted for as JANEs.

For example, many groups have companies whose sole function is to act as a distributor, hold properties, raise finance or perform some other function on behalf of the group, such that it is not 'carrying on a trade or business of its own'. It seems clear to us that the ASB had no intention that such companies should be regarded as JANEs.

At the other end of the spectrum, one sees arrangements with many characteristics of JANEs which do not fall within the definition in FRS 9. This is because the discussion of the JANE in FRS 9 relies on a clearly-defined distinction (that often does not exist in the real world) between an entity carrying on a business of its own and one that is simply a conduit for the businesses of the participants. In the pharmaceutical industry, for example, two drug companies may set up a company to market two products (or groups of products), one from each company. Often, there is some sharing of results up to, (or beyond) a certain threshold, but with each company receiving only the profits from its own product before (or after) the threshold point. It is our view that, whilst such 'hybrid' arrangements have many of the characteristics of JANEs, FRS 9 requires them to be accounted for as associates or joint ventures as appropriate.

In addition there are situations which could, and perhaps should, be accounted for as JANEs (or structures with the form but not the substance of a joint venture), but which are so far removed from the types of operation discussed in FRS 9 as to leave room for genuine doubt, as shown by the following example.

Example 7.3: Is it a JANE? – protected cell company

Some overseas jurisdictions permit the formation of so called 'protected cell' companies. Essentially these are entities which have a number of 'cells', with the assets and liabilities of each cell being completely ring-fenced – in other words the creditors of a particular cell have recourse only to the assets of that cell. In addition to the cells, each one of which has its own capital, there is a so-called 'core', whose shareholders may manage the activities of the cells on behalf of their owners. Diagramatically, the structure can be portrayed as follows:

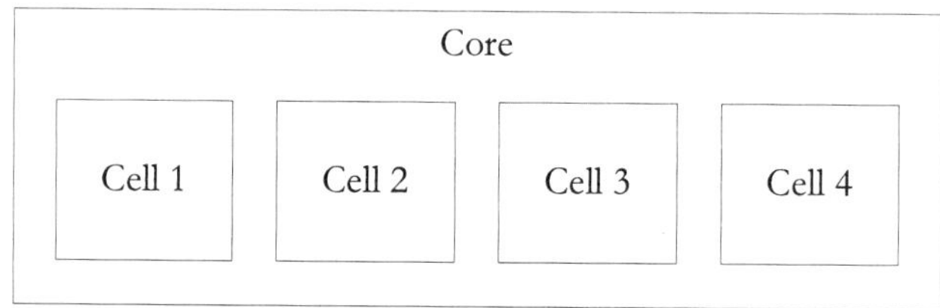

An original intention of this structure was to allow a fund-manager (who would hold the core shares) to run a number of independent funds (whose investors would hold the shares in the particular cell(s) concerned), with the incorporation of a single legal entity, as compared to the position in the UK where each managed fund, and the management company, would be a separate legal entity.

However, protected cell companies are now used for a number of different purposes. For example, a UK company rather than conducting its offshore captive insurance arrangements through a separate company may do so through one or more cells in a protected cell company. The issue then arises as to how the UK company should account for its cells.

There is no one answer to this question since the treatment will depend, *inter alia*, on whether the UK company holds the core shares, the cell shares, both or neither, and, if there is no legal ownership, the nature of the relationship between the legal owner and the company. However, in our view, it is extremely unlikely to be appropriate for the company to regard an investment in a cell as an associate or joint venture. This is because the 'ring-fencing' of the assets and liabilities of each cell means that there is a direct linkage between the UK company and one particular cell, rather than that the UK company has some share of the profits or losses of the company as a whole.

The most likely conclusion is that each cell is a JANE (or structure with the form but not the substance of a joint venture), and accordingly that the UK company should directly account for the transactions, assets and liabilities of 'its' cell(s). Other possible analyses might be that the cell is a subsidiary undertaking (if the UK company's cell shares give it voting control over the activities of the cell) or a quasi-subsidiary under FRS 5 (see, respectively, Chapter 5 at 2.2 and Chapter 18 at 2.8).

Another unsatisfactory consequence of the concepts of a JANE and a structure with the form but not the substance of a joint venture is the requirement to account for it not only on consolidation, but also in the individual accounts of the member of the group with the interest in the JANE (see 3.4 below). It seems bizarre that a company should be forbidden to account directly for transactions undertaken through a wholly-owned subsidiary (over which it has complete control) but required to account directly for those undertaken through a JANE (over which it will have at best some form of joint control).

We suggest that the confusion surrounding the JANE concept illustrates that it is generally unwise to promote as a general accounting principle what is in reality a solution to a specific problem (i.e. in this case, the fact that influential sectors of British industry would not have accepted a prohibition on proportional consolidation without a strong fight). An earlier example of this was the 'linked presentation' in FRS 5 (see Chapter 18 at 2.6).

3 ACCOUNTING TREATMENT UNDER FRS 9

As discussed in 2 above, the ASB distinguishes in FRS 9 between associates, joint ventures, joint arrangements that are not entities and structures with the form but not the substance of a joint venture. Not surprisingly, therefore, FRS 9 requires different accounting treatments for each, which are discussed in detail below. In practice, however, the accounting for associates and joint ventures differs only in detail, whereas that for JANEs (and structures with the form but not the substance of a joint venture) is substantially different. The discussion below concentrates on only the basic treatments required. More complicated aspects of equity accounting are dealt with in 4 below.

3.1 Accounting for associates

3.1.1 Consolidated accounts

In the investor's consolidated accounts associates are to be accounted for using the equity method, which FRS 9 defines (or more correctly describes) as follows:

'A method of accounting that brings an investment into its investor's financial statements initially at its cost, identifying any goodwill arising. The carrying amount of the investment is adjusted in each period by the investor's share of the results of its investee less any amortisation or write-off for goodwill, the investor's share of any relevant gains or losses, and any other changes in the investee's net assets including distributions to its owners, for example by dividend. The investor's share of its investee's results is recognised in its profit and loss account. The investor's cash flow statement includes the cash flows between the investor and its investee, for example relating to dividends and loans.'[44]

FRS 9 then deals with the requirements for each of the primary statements in more detail, as set out below.

A Consolidated profit and loss account

In spite of the fact that FRS 9 ostensibly prohibits proportional consolidation, it requires the share of associates' results to be shown at more levels of the group profit and loss account than was the case under SSAP 1 (and remains the case under international practice generally). Indeed, what is required is in reality proportional consolidation at every level except turnover and operating costs. A comprehensive example of the presentation required by FRS 9 is given by Cable and Wireless (see Extract 7.6 below).

At the turnover level, the share of associates' sales is not included. However, FRS 9 goes on to provide that, where it is helpful to give an indication of the size of the business as a whole, the total of group turnover plus the share of associates' turnover may be included as a memorandum item on the face of the profit and loss account. The share of associates' turnover must be clearly distinguished from group turnover, and it is the latter that must form the starting point for the group profit and loss account. This effectively sanctioned what had, before the issue of FRS 9, been a long-standing practice by a number of companies, and is the approach adopted by Cable and Wireless in Extract 7.6. Where segmental analysis of turnover is given, any amounts relating to associates also should be clearly distinguished from those relating to the group.[45]

The share of associates' operating results should be included after the group operating result and, where applicable, after and separately from the share of the operating results of joint ventures[46] (see Extract 7.6). We presume that this approach is to be followed at each level of the profit and loss account where the share of associates' and joint ventures' results is to be included. This is implied by the illustrative examples in Appendix IV to FRS 9, but not explicitly stated.

Extract 7.6: Cable and Wireless plc (2001)

CONSOLIDATED PROFIT AND LOSS ACCOUNT [extract]†

FOR THE YEAR ENDED 31 MARCH

	Continuing operations £m	Discontinued operations £m	2001 £m
Turnover of the Group including its share of joint ventures and associates	7,498	995	**8,493**
Share of turnover of			
– joint ventures	(333)	–	**(333)**
– associates	(60)	(1)	**(61)**
Group turnover	7,105	994	**8,099**
Operating costs before depreciation, amortisation and exceptional items	(5,737)	(580)	**(6,317)**
Exceptional operating costs	–	–	**–**
Operating costs before depreciation and amortisation	(5,737)	(580)	**(6,317)**
EBITDA	1,368	414	**1,782**
Depreciation before exceptional items	(1,006)	(129)	**(1,135)**
Exceptional depreciation	(444)	–	**(444)**
Depreciation	(1,450)	(129)	**(1,579)**
Amortisation of capitalised goodwill	(466)	(3)	**(469)**
Group operating (loss)/profit	(548)	282	**(266)**
Share of operating profits in joint ventures	97	–	**97**
Share of operating profits in associates	17	–	**17**
Total operating (loss)/ profit	(434)	282	**(152)**

Exceptional profits less (losses) on sale and termination of operations	5	4,067	**4,072**
Exceptional costs of fundamental reorganisation	(530)	–	**(530)**
Profits less (losses on disposal of fixed assets before exceptional items)	4	–	**4**
Exceptional items	42	–	**42**
Profits less (losses) on disposal of fixed assets	46	–	**46**
Exceptional write down of investments	(43)	–	**(43)**
(Loss)/profit on ordinary activities before interest	(956)	4,349	**3,393**
Net interest and other similar income/(charges)			
– Group (including exceptional finance charges of £110m, 2000 - £nil)			**–**
– joint ventures and associates			**–**
Total net interest and other similar income/(charges)			**–**
Profit on ordinary activities before taxation			**3,393**
Tax on profit on ordinary activities			**(503)**
Profit on ordinary activities after taxation			**2,890**
Equity minority interests			**(258)**
Profit for the financial year			**2,632**
Dividends – interim			**(138)**
– final (proposed)			**(324)**
Profit for the year retained			**2,170**

† This extract is also relevant to the discussion of accounting for joint ventures in 3.2 below.

Any amortisation or write-off of goodwill relating to associates must be 'charged at this point and disclosed'.[47] This implies (but without specifically requiring or permitting it) that the amount shown on the face of the profit and loss account can be the aggregate of the share of profit and the amortisation of goodwill, provided that these are shown separately in the notes. We consider that this is the most appropriate treatment given the requirement of FRS 10, reinforced by various rulings of the Financial Reporting Review Panel, that amortisation of goodwill is an integral part of operating profit (see Chapter 11 at 2.3.4). Accounting for such goodwill is considered in more detail at 4.5 below.

It is not clear how FRS 9 interacts with the provision of FRS 3 that, whilst income from associates and other participating interests does not normally form part of operating profit, it may do so in certain cases.[48] FRS 9 is explicit that the share of associates' operating profit must never be included in group operating profit. It also provides that any segmental analysis of operating profit should clearly distinguish amounts relating to associates from those relating to the group.[49] This implies that the group's share of its associates' operating profit (like that of turnover) is not to be considered as part of the true group result. Moreover, FRS 9 amended or deleted those paragraphs of FRS 1 (Revised) that referred to the investor's share of the operating results of associates being included in operating profit.[50] All this leads us to conclude that the lack of a consequential amendment to FRS 3 was an oversight.

That said, however, the requirement to exclude the operating results of associates from those of the group seems inconsistent with the definition of associate in FRS 9, which, with its emphasis on the active exercise of influence, should arguably mean associates are likely to form part of the reporting entity's main operations. Example 2 in Appendix IV to FRS 9 gives the name 'Total operating profit' to profit including the results of associates and joint ventures, a pragmatic description that has been adopted by many companies, including Cable and Wireless in Extract 7.6 above, even when using the more normal presentation in Example 1 in the same Appendix.

The group's share of its associates' post-operating exceptional items and interest must be separately given. At the levels of profit before tax and below, the associates' share of each item should be aggregated with that of the group, but must be separately disclosed.[51] The requirement to give the share of associates' interest is somewhat curious, since the related borrowings are not included within liabilities in the consolidated balance sheet. This means that, where associates have material borrowings, the effective interest rate shown in the accounts (i.e. total interest charge in the profit and loss account divided by borrowings in the balance sheet) will be seriously overstated. We do not regard this as a satisfactory result.

Equally unsatisfactorily, there is a lack of clarity in FRS 9 as to whether the group's share of its associates' post-operating exceptional items and interest is to be given on the face of the profit and loss account or in a note. The (somewhat loose) wording of paragraph 27 of the standard is that:

(a) the share of operating results must be 'included' in the profit and loss account. We take this to mean that it must be presented on the face of the profit and loss account;

(b) the share of post-operating exceptional items and interest should be '*shown* separately from the amounts for the group'. We believe that this means that the portion of such items relating to associates can be aggregated with the amounts for the group on the face of the accounts and shown separately in the notes. However, the wording here could also suggest that these amounts must be given on the face of the profit and loss account. This view is supported both by the examples in Appendix IV to FRS 9 and by the contrasting wording ('should be *disclosed*') in respect of profit before tax and items below it (see following). This is the interpretation adopted by Cable and Wireless in Extract 7.6 above;

(c) the share of profit before tax and items below it 'should be included within the amounts for the group, although for items below this level, such as taxation, the amounts relating to associates should be disclosed.' This clearly envisages aggregation on the face of the accounts and analysis in the notes. An example of the disclosure of the share of tax of associates and joint ventures is given in Extracts 24.7 and 24.8 in Chapter 24 at 3.1.6. Bizarrely, if FRS 9 is read literally, it seems:

    (i) not to require the group's share of its associates' profit before tax to be disclosed, since this applies only to items 'below' that point; and

    (ii) to prohibit companies from presenting the shares of these items on the face of the profit and loss account if they so wish.

    We do not believe that either of these consequences was intended.

All in all, FRS 9's precise requirements on these straightforward issues could, and should, have been much clearer. Our analysis above is not intended as some form of pedantic point-scoring; rather it is made against the background of a number of adverse findings by the Financial Reporting Review Panel against companies for failure to comply with the detailed presentational requirements of standards. It is surely not unreasonable to expect the ASB to draft standards with the same attention to detail applied by the Panel in enforcing them.

B *Consolidated statement of total recognised gains and losses*

In the statement of total recognised gains and losses (STRGL), the amount relating to associates should be 'shown separately under each heading' where material, although there are no 'headings' in the STRGL specified as such by FRS 3. FRS 9 is apparently indifferent as to whether this is done on the face of the STRGL or in an accompanying note, which must be cross-referred to in the STRGL.[52]

In practice, this requirement, at least if interpreted strictly, is more honoured in the breach than in the observance. The one component of the STRGL of a group with associates in which there will always be an amount relating to associates is the profit or loss for the period, but companies do not normally disclose this. We presume that the real intention is that where an item in the STRGL other than profit or loss for the year (e.g. foreign exchange movements, revaluation gains) contains a material amount relating to associates, that amount should be shown separately. A comprehensive example is given by BOC.

Extract 7.7: The BOC Group plc (2000)

Total recognised gains and losses [extract]
Years ended 30 September

	2000	1999	1998
	£ million	£ million	£ million
Parent	**139.2**	63.2	482.8
Subsidiary undertakings	**173.3**	176.3	(171.3)
Joint ventures	**12.6**	11.5	2.4
Associates	**1.3**	1.6	0.7
Goodwill written off on disposal of subsidiary undertakings	**–**	(2.5)	(100.0)
Goodwill written off on impairment	**–**	–	(51.8)
Profit for the financial year	**326.4**	250.1	162.8
Unrealised surplus on revaluations	**–**	1.9	1.0
Exchange translation effect on:			
– results for the year of subsidiaries	**(0.9)**	(1.3)	(5.0)
– results for the year of joint ventures	**1.1**	(0.4)	(1.3)
– results for the year of associates	**0.2**	(0.1)	–
– foreign currency net investments in subsidiaries	**76.5**	18.1	(130.8)
– foreign currency net investments in joint ventures	**8.1**	2.9	(17.5)
– foreign currency net investments in associates	**6.8**	2.7	(4.8)
Total recognised gains and losses for the financial year	**418.2**	273.9	4.4

A rare example of a STRGL where the only item relating to associates and joint ventures is profit for the year that gives the full disclosure strictly required by FRS 9 is that of Severn Trent.

Extract 7.8: Severn Trent Plc (2000)

Statement of total recognised gains and losses [extract]
year ended 31 March 2000

		2000	1999
		£m	£m
Profit for the financial year	- group	**250.0**	301.7
	- joint ventures	**0.8**	0.6
	- associates	**1.1**	1.5
Total profit for the financial year		**251.9**	303.8
Currency translation differences		**(0.7)**	3.9
Total recognised gains and losses for the year		**251.2**	307.7

C Consolidated balance sheet

The consolidated balance sheet should include the reporting entity's share of the net assets (or liabilities) of associates and the amount of goodwill arising on acquisition, less any amounts amortised or written off. The investment in associates must be shown separately on the face of the balance sheet. It cannot be aggregated with other investments on the face and disclosed separately in the notes (as would be permitted under the Companies Act 1985). The amount of goodwill included in the carrying amount must be separately disclosed.[53] Presumably this disclosure can be made in the notes rather than on the face of the balance sheet, although FRS 9 does not contain explicit guidance on this.

D Consolidated cash flow statement

FRS 9 amended FRS 1 so as to require dividends received from associates and joint ventures to be included in the cash flow statement under a separate main heading 'Dividends from joint ventures and associates' immediately after cash flow from operating activities. Further discussion of this will be found in Chapter 29 at 2.4.3.

3.1.2 *Single entity accounts*

In the investor's single entity accounts, associates are treated as fixed asset investments and carried at cost (less any amounts written off) or valuation. FRS 9 gives no specific guidance on the treatment in the other primary statements (i.e. to include only transactions between the investor and the associate), presumably because these are assumed to be sufficiently well understood as not to warrant guidance.

A company which has no subsidiaries, but which has an investment in an associate, has a particular problem because of the requirement of the Companies Act that only realised profits can be included in the profit and loss account.[54] Since it does not produce group financial statements, its profit and loss account will be a company profit and loss account, and the only income 'realised' from the associate in that context will be dividends received and receivable.

FRS 9 therefore requires investors that do not prepare consolidated accounts (other than those that are exempt from preparing them, or would be exempt if they had subsidiaries) to give the amounts for associates that would be given in the consolidated financial statements. This can be done either by preparing pro-forma 'consolidated' accounts including the associates' results and net assets, or by simply disclosing the relevant amounts for associates and the effect of including them.[55]

There is a certain amount of confusion as to the treatment of associates in the cash flow statements of the single entity, since FRS 9, if read literally, amended FRS 1 so as to require the caption 'Dividends from joint ventures and associates' in both consolidated and single entity cash flow statements. However, this would mean that, whilst dividends from subsidiaries are simply included in the main heading 'Returns on investments and servicing of finance', those from associates and joint ventures are given under a separate heading. We do not believe that this can have been the ASB's intention. In practice, fortunately, the company with investments in associates that is required to prepare a single entity cash flow statement is so rare that this does not cause any real difficulty.

3.2 Accounting for joint ventures

The accounting treatment for joint ventures is the same as that for associates as set out in 3.1 above, except that in the consolidated profit and loss account and balance sheet the reporting entity must apply the 'gross equity method', a term introduced by FRS 9 and defined as follows:

'A form of equity method under which the investor's share of the aggregate gross assets and liabilities underlying the net amount included for the investment is shown on the face of the balance sheet and, in the profit and loss account, the investor's share of the investee's turnover is noted.'[56]

The effect of this treatment in practice is discussed in more detail below.

3.2.1 *The gross equity method*

A Consolidated profit and loss account

Under the gross equity method, the reporting entity must present its share of the turnover of joint ventures on the face of the profit and loss account and in the segmental analysis of turnover, whereas under the equity method applicable to associates this presentation is optional. However, as under the equity method, this does not form part of the group turnover, and must be clearly distinguished from it.[57] An example of this can be seen in the accounts of Cable and Wireless (see Extract 7.6 at 3.1.1 A above).

For most companies, which prepare their accounts in accordance with Schedule 4 to the Companies Act 1985, this disclosure is relatively straightforward, since turnover is the first item in the profit and loss account formats. However, it poses something of a practical difficulty for banking and insurance companies, which prepare their accounts under Schedule 9 and Schedule 9A, respectively, of the Act. The issue is partly that those formats do not contain an item 'turnover', but more substantially that the amount that is generally agreed within each of those industries to comprise the equivalent of 'turnover' is in fact the aggregate of a number of items required by the Companies Act to be shown under separate headings.

B Consolidated balance sheet

In the consolidated balance sheet, the gross equity method requires the share of net assets shown under the equity method to be analysed into the share of total assets and total liabilities on the face of the balance sheet. The analysis is to be given in the form of a linked presentation[58] (rather than by including the shares of assets and liabilities separately in the relevant sections of the balance sheet), which the ASB believes 'emphasises the special nature of joint control'.[59] FRS 9 in fact avoids using the phrase 'linked presentation', possibly because the amounts shown linked under the gross equity method would not meet the criteria for linked presentation in FRS 5 (see Chapter 18 at 2.6).

Although FRS 9 is not explicit on this point, the share of total assets must include any unamortised acquisition goodwill relating to a joint venture; otherwise, the analysis would not total to the carrying value of the joint venture. For the same reason, the share of total liabilities must include provisions.

A complication not explicitly anticipated by FRS 9 is that the carrying amount of a group's total investment in a joint venture is very often not in fact the share of the underlying assets and liabilities, such that the disclosure required by FRS 9 is not actually possible. For example, there could be loans between the reporting entity and the joint venture, or provisions against the joint venture in the reporting entity's accounts that are not included in the underlying accounts of the venture. An example of a company that has had to address this issue is Billiton, which has distinguished between the share of net assets of, and loans to, joint ventures on the face of the group balance sheet.

Extract 7.9: Billiton Plc (2000)

Group Balance Sheet [extract]
as at 30 June 2000

		2000 US$m	1999 US$m
Fixed assets			
...			
Investments	– joint ventures	**140**	130
	– share of gross assets	**756**	750
	– share of gross liabilities	**(616)**	(620)
	– loans to joint ventures and other investments	**334**	313
...			

Cable and Wireless has also had to address this issue, but with the additional complication that its total net investment in joint ventures comprised a mixture of investments in net assets, shown within fixed assets, and investments in net liabilities, shown within liabilities. (The accounting treatment of an interest in net liabilities is discussed in more detail in 4.7 below). Its solution is to provide a short narrative footnote on the face of the balance sheet and a more detailed analysis in the notes to the accounts.

The 'Share of net assets' in note 16 in Extract 7.10 below reconciles to the net of the two figures shown in the balance sheet (e.g. for 2000, interest in net assets of £273m less interest in net liabilities £5m gives £268m, the figure in note 16). We presume that Cable and Wireless included the narrative footnote at the bottom of the balance sheet so as comply with the requirement of FRS 9 that the share of gross assets and liabilities be shown 'on the face' of the balance sheet.

Extract 7.10: Cable and Wireless plc (2001)

[GROUP] BALANCE SHEET [extract]

		2001 £m	2000 £m
Fixed assets			
...			
Interest in net assets of joint ventures	16	363	273
...			
Interest in net liabilities of joint ventures	16	–	5
...			

[Footnote to balance sheet]

Interests in the net assets and net liabilities of joint ventures include the Group's share of gross assets of joint ventures of £806m (2000 – £615m) and the Group's share of gross liabilities of joint ventures of £491m (2000 – £366m) – see note 16.

16 Fixed asset investments [extract]

Group share of net assets of joint ventures ...

	2001 £m	2000 £m
Fixed assets	518	420
Current assets	288	195
Share of gross assets	806	615
Current borrowings	(41)	(145)
Other current liabilities	(159)	(171)
Long term borrowings	(261)	(41)
Other long term liabilities	(30)	(9)
Group share of gross liabilities	(491)	(366)
Less: Loans from Group companies	48	19
	(443)	(347)
Share of net assets	363	268

3.2.2 *Voluntary additional disclosure of amounts relating to joint ventures*

FRS 9 permits (and indeed encourages through an example in Appendix IV) separate disclosure on the face of the consolidated profit and loss account and balance sheet of amounts relating to the group's investments in joint ventures where these represent a significant part of the business of the reporting entity.[60]

Where this is done, however, all amounts relating to joint ventures (other than those included in profit and loss account captions below profit before tax) must be clearly distinguished from amounts relating to the group.[61] The exemption for items below profit before tax is presumably because the equity method requires the share of these items applicable to joint ventures to be aggregated with the corresponding group figures and disclosed separately (see 3.1.1 A above).

The presentation suggested in Appendix IV to FRS 9 is to give two additional columns: one for the reporting entity's share of its joint ventures' results, assets and liabilities and another for the total of group and joint ventures. The total column thus represents proportional consolidation of the reporting group's share of its interests in joint ventures. It seems inconsistent that FRS 9, while rejecting proportional consolidation as a method of accounting because it 'can be misleading',[62] states that as a method of disclosure it may be appropriate 'because an investor's joint control of a joint venture is a more direct form of influence than the significant influence exercised over associates'.[63]

An example of a company that has adopted this approach is Henlys Group.

Extract 7.11: Henlys Group plc (2000)

Group Profit and Loss Account [extract]

	Group 2000 £000	Interest in Joint Ventures 2000 £000	Total 2000 £000
Turnover			
...			
Total turnover	679,982	202,781	882,763
Cost of sales	(566,346)	(167,298)	(733,644)
Gross Profit	113,636	35,483	149,119
Other operating expenses (net)	(55,788)	(25,386)	(81,174)
Operating Profit			
Existing operations	70,938	11,203	82,141
Discontinued operations	5,099	—	5,099
Amortisation of goodwill	(18,189)	(1,106)	(19,295)
	57,848	10,097	67,945
Share of operating profit in joint ventures	10,097		
Total Operating Profit	67,945		
...			

It will be seen that the share of the £10,097,000 operating profit of joint ventures is carried across into the total operating profit, and the rest of the group profit and loss account is presented as a single column. Whilst this form of presentation works well enough in the relatively straightforward circumstances of the example above, we have some reservations as to whether it would add clarity to the accounts of most large groups. When it is combined with the requirement of FRS 3 to distinguish the results of continuing, acquired and discontinued operations[64] (not to mention the so-called 'railway timetable' multi-columnar profit and loss accounts used by many companies as a method of excluding various items from what they consider their 'true' results), the overall result could be a bewildering matrix of figures.

What happens in such a case if, for example, the joint ventures themselves have acquired or discontinued operations or exceptional items? In fact, in 1998 a joint venture of Henlys made a significant acquisition. In the notes to the accounts for that year Henlys gave an analysis of the components of the operating profit of the joint venture between acquisitions and other continuing operations. However, the analysis given was of the total results of the joint venture, rather than of Henlys' share of them.

Henlys also gives a full memorandum analysis of the group balance sheet as shown below.

Extract 7.12: Henlys Group plc (2000)

Balance sheets [extract]

	Group 2000 £000	Interest in Joint Ventures 2000 £000	Total 2000 £000
Fixed Assets			
Intangible assets	352,347	19,465	371,812
Tangible assets	58,368	21,657	80,025
Investments	62,304	(57,074)	5,230
	473,019	(15,952)	457,067
Current Assets			
Stocks	121,658	68,370	190,028
Debtors	40,216	33,696	73,912
Cash at bank and in hand	26,371	4,746	31,117
	188,245	106,812	295,057
Creditors			
Amounts falling due within one year	113,625	78,613	192,238
Net Current Assets	74,620	28,119	102,819
Total Assets less Current Liabilities	547,639	12,247	559,886
Creditors: Amounts falling due after more than one year	265,931	1,853	267,784
Provisions for Liabilities and Charges	34,198	10,394	44,592
	247,510	–	247,510

3.3 Investment funds

Investment funds, such as investment trusts or venture capitalists, are not required to equity account for associates or joint ventures that are held as part of their investment portfolios. For this purpose, investments are held as part of an investment portfolio if their value to the investor is through their marketable value as part of a basket of investments rather than as media through which the investor carries out its business.[65] This effectively sanctions long-standing practice in at least some sections of the investment trust and venture capital industries.

The grounds given for what amounts almost to an exemption from FRS 9 are that it is important for all portfolio investments to be accounted for consistently whether or not the investor has significant influence or joint control.[66] However, it is perhaps more realistic to see the prescribed treatment as a concession to established industry practice. One consequence of FRS 9 is an inconsistency between the treatment of subsidiaries held as portfolio investments, which both the law and FRS 2 still require to be fully consolidated, and that of associates or joint ventures similarly held, which are to be accounted for as ordinary investments.

3.4 Accounting for JANEs (and structures with the form but not the substance of a joint venture)

The accounting treatment for JANEs (including structures with the form but not the, substance of a joint venture) is relatively straightforward. As indicated in the discussion in 2.3 above, the distinguishing feature of a JANE is that it has no activity of its own and is simply a conduit through which the participants conduct their own business. On this basis, the participants are simply required to account for their own 'assets, liabilities and cash flows' (and presumably results as well!) within the arrangement, measured according to the terms of the agreement governing the arrangement.[67]

As noted in 2.3 above, in many cases this will generate the same numbers in the accounts that would have been obtained using proportional consolidation, particularly where the arrangement is structured as a legal entity. However, it is important to be clear that, according to FRS 9, this is *not* proportional consolidation, but the reporting entity recording its own transactions. Therefore FRS 9 requires JANEs to be accounted for at the individual entity level as well as on consolidation. Examples of companies accounting for JANEs are given in Extracts 7.3 to 7.5 at 2.3 above, the wording of which indicates that, to some extent at least, the companies concerned regard accounting for a JANE as little more than proportional consolidation under another name.

4 APPLYING THE EQUITY AND GROSS EQUITY METHODS

FRS 9 provides some detailed guidance on a number of aspects of the application of the equity and gross equity methods, which are discussed below.

In four of these, FRS 9 can be seen as conforming the consolidation requirements for associates and joint ventures to those for subsidiaries in FRS 2:

- fair values and goodwill;
- transactions between associates and joint ventures and the reporting entity;
- accounting policies; and
- non-coterminous accounting periods.

Other issues covered by FRS 9 are:

- goodwill (in periods after the acquisition);
- calculation of the share of net assets to be accounted for;
- non-corporate associates and joint ventures;
- losses and deficiencies of assets; and
- commencement or cessation of a joint venture or associate relationship.

We discuss all these issues in turn below.

4.1 Fair values and goodwill

When an associate or joint venture is first acquired, the share of its underlying net assets included in the reporting entity's consolidated balance sheet should be stated at fair value using the reporting entity's accounting policies.[68] Presumably, such fair values are to be calculated in accordance with FRS 7 – *Fair values in acquisition accounting*, although neither FRS 9 nor FRS 7 is explicit on the matter. The consideration and any goodwill arising are to be accounted for 'in the same way as on the acquisition of a subsidiary'. This again presumably means that the consideration must be recorded at fair value, determined in accordance with FRS 7.

The following example illustrates why such fair value adjustments are necessary:

Example 7.4: Attributing fair values to the assets of associates

Company A buys a 40% stake in Company B for £2,000,000. Company B is an investment company and its only asset is a portfolio of investments with a book value of £3,000,000 but a fair value of £5,000,000.

If Company A did not apply fair value accounting to the analysis of its stake in Company B, it would record its share of the net assets of B at £1,200,000 and goodwill of £800,000. The proper treatment in this particular case would be to attribute all of its investment in B to the underlying portfolio of investments and to recognise no goodwill. (Tax effects have been ignored in this example for the sake of simplicity.)

If one year later, Company B sells its portfolio for £6,000,000, it will report a pre-tax profit of £3,000,000, of which Company A's share will be £1,200,000. However, A must make an adjustment to this figure to eliminate the £800,000 fair value adjustment which reflected the pre-acquisition gain made by B, but not recorded in its own books at that time, and therefore record a profit of only £400,000. That this is the appropriate answer is easily proved as follows:

	£
A's share of net assets of B (40% of £6,000,000)	2,400,000
Cost of investment in B	2,000,000
Gain	400,000

The attribution of fair values can be problematical in practice because the investor has only influence, not control, over the investee and therefore cannot insist on receiving the same degree of information that could be demanded from a subsidiary. It may therefore be that the fair value exercise will have to be confined to the most significant items, such as the revaluation of major property assets, and this will often be acceptable on grounds of materiality.

FRS 9 provides that, where access by the investor to information on fair values (or on other items necessary in order to apply the equity or gross equity methods) is 'limited', estimates may be used instead. Where information is 'extremely limited', however, this may call into question whether the investor in fact exercises the significant influence, or joint control, necessary for the investment to be treated as an associate or joint venture.[69]

The investor's share of depreciation of fixed assets held by the associate or joint venture at acquisition should be based on their fair value rather than their cost to the associate or joint venture.[70] Similar adjustments apply to the profit and loss account treatment of all other assets and liabilities whose fair value differs from their carrying amount in the associate's own accounts.

Any goodwill included in the accounts of an associate or joint venture at the date of acquisition by the investor is ignored in calculating the investor's share of its net assets.[71] The arithmetical effect of this is to increase the portion of the reporting entity's carrying value for its investment represented by goodwill. It also has the questionable result that, in effect, the investor's share of any existing goodwill of an associate or joint venture will be written off over the period appropriate to the premium paid by the investor rather than the period applicable to the underlying goodwill of the associate or joint venture.

Somewhat inconsistently, this appears to apply only to any goodwill recognised by the associate or joint venture at the date of acquisition. Any goodwill arising on a post-acquisition transaction of the associate or joint venture will apparently fall to be included in the share of net assets. Conversely, if the associate or joint venture converts goodwill recognised at the date of acquisition into cash through disposal, the reporting entity must, on the face of it, continue to account for its share of this cash as 'goodwill'. In practice, however, we believe that, where the effect is material, it will be appropriate to adjust the allocation of the carrying value of the investee as between share of net assets and goodwill.

Where an associate or joint venture is itself a parent undertaking, FRS 9 provides that the share of net assets included in the reporting entity's balance sheet should be based on the associate's or joint venture's consolidated balance sheet.[72] FRS 9 is silent on what is to be done where such an associate or joint venture does not prepare group accounts. Presumably, the share of net assets should still be based on notional group accounts. Otherwise the overall carrying value of the investment could include a huge amount for 'goodwill' that is in reality a share of the investee group's underlying net assets, particularly if the investee is a thinly capitalised holding company.

4.2 Transactions between associates and joint ventures and the reporting entity

4.2.1 *General requirements*

Where an investor transacts with an associate or joint venture, the investor's share of any profit arising should be eliminated in the consolidated accounts.[73] FRS 9 requires that 'where profits and losses resulting from transactions between the investor and its associate or joint venture are included in the carrying amount of assets in either entity, the part relating to the investor's share should be eliminated'.

This treatment should be contrasted with that required when an inter-company transaction takes place involving a company which is not a wholly owned subsidiary. In such a situation, FRS 2 requires elimination of *all* of the profit or loss.[74] Therefore, if a parent sells an asset to a 51% subsidiary all of the profit will be eliminated and no amount would be attributed to the minority shareholders. However, if the parent sold the asset to a 50% associate or joint venture, under FRS 9 only 50% has to be eliminated.

It is, to put it mildly, extremely unfortunate that FRS 9 provides no further guidance as to what precisely is intended by this requirement, since the elimination of such profits sounds much more straightforward than it actually is. We believe that what is intended is the treatment originally proposed, and more clearly explained, by the ASC in ED 50 *Consolidated Accounts*, i.e.:

- In the consolidated profit and loss account the adjustment should be taken against either the group profit or the share of the associate's (or joint venture's) profit, according to whether the group or the associate (or joint venture) recorded the profit on the transaction.
- In the consolidated balance sheet the adjustment should be made against the asset which was the subject of the transaction if it is held by the group or against the carrying amount for the associate (or joint venture) if the asset is held by the associate (or joint venture).[75]

Our interpretation of this treatment is illustrated by Examples 7.5 and 7.6 below. Both examples deal with H plc and its 50% joint venture JV Limited. The journal entries are based on the premise that the consolidation is initially prepared as a simple aggregation of each member of the group and the relevant share of its associates and joint ventures. The entries below would then be applied to the numbers at that stage of the process.

Example 7.5: Elimination of profit on sale by group to joint venture

On 1 December 2001 H plc sells goods costing £750,000 to JV Limited for £1 million. On 10 January 2002, JV sells the goods to a third party for £1.2 million. What adjustments are made in the group accounts of H plc at 31 December 2001 and 31 December 2002?

In the year to 31 December 2001, the group has recorded turnover of £1m and cost of sales of £0.75m. However, at the balance sheet date, since the stock is still held by JV Limited, only half this transaction is regarded by FRS 9 as having taken place (in effect with the other 50% shareholder of JV Limited). This is reflected by the consolidation entry:

	£	£
Turnover	500,000	
Cost of sales		375,000
Investment in JV Limited		125,000

This effectively defers recognition of half the sale and offsets the deferred profit against the carrying amount of JV Limited.

During 2002, when the stock is sold by the joint venture, this deferred profit can be released to the group profit and loss account, reflected by the following accounting entry.

	£	£
Opening reserves	125,000	
Cost of sales	375,000	
Turnover		500,000

Opening reserves are adjusted because the consolidation runners (if prepared as assumed above) will already include this profit in opening reserves, since it forms part of H plc's opening reserves.

Example 7.6: Elimination of profit on sale by joint venture to group

This is the mirror image of the transaction in Example 7.4 above. On 1 December 2001 JV Limited sells goods costing £750,000 to H plc for £1 million. On 10 January 2002, H plc sells the goods to a third party for £1.2 million. What adjustments are made in the group accounts of H plc at 31 December 2001 and 31 December 2002?

H plc's share of the profit of JV Limited as included on the consolidation runners at 31 December 2001 will include a profit of £125,000, being 50% of (£1,000,000 – £750,000), which is regarded by FRS 9 as unrealised by the group, and is therefore deferred and offset against closing stock of the group:

	£	£
Share of profit of JV (P&L)	125,000	
Stock		125,000

In the following period when the stock is sold H plc's single entity accounts will record a profit of £200,000, which must be increased on consolidation by the £125,000 deferred from the previous period. The entry is:

	£	£
Opening reserves	125,000	
Share of profit of JV (P&L)		125,000

Again, opening reserves are adjusted because the consolidation runners (if prepared as assumed above) will already include this profit in opening reserves, this time, however, as part of H plc's share of the opening reserves of JV Limited.

A slightly counter-intuitive consequence of this treatment is that at the end of 2001 the investment in JV Limited in the balance sheet has increased by £125,000 more than the share of profit of joint ventures as reported in the group profit and loss account (and in 2002 by £125,000 less). This is because the balance sheet adjustment at the end of 2001 is made against stock rather than carrying value of the investment in JV Limited. It might therefore be necessary to indicate in the fixed asset note that part of the profit made by JV Limited is regarded as unrealised by the group in 2001 and has therefore been deferred until 2002 by offsetting it against stock.

An example of a company that has consistently adopted this treatment (even before FRS 9 was issued) is Tesco, as shown in this extract from its 1998 accounts.

Extract 7.13: Tesco PLC (1998)

Note 12 Fixed asset investments [extract]

		Group
	Associated Undertakings (b) £m	Other Investments £m
At 22 February 1997	21	2
Additions	179	–
Share of loss of associated undertakings	(15)	–
Disposals	–	(2)
At 28 February 1998	185	–

b) ...

An amount of £3m representing the unrealised 50% element of the profit on sale of properties to the Tesco British Land Property Partnership has been offset against the cost of the investment of £179m shown above.

A *Loans etc. between reporting entity and associates or joint ventures*

The requirement to eliminate partially unrealised profits or losses on transactions with associates or joint ventures applies only to transactions involving such profits, such as trading transactions or asset disposals. It does not apply in the case of items such as interest paid on loans between associates or joint ventures and the reporting entity. This is consistent with the view that loans to and from joint ventures are not part of the investor's share of the net assets of the joint venture, but separate transactions (see discussion of Extract 7.11 at 3.2.1 B above).

B *Consolidated cash flow statement*

In the consolidated cash flow statement no adjustment is made in respect of the cash flows relating to transactions with associates and joint ventures (whereas cash flows between members of the group are eliminated in the same way as intra-group profits).

4.2.2 *Turnover disclosed under the 'gross equity' method*

An issue related to Examples 7.5 and 7.6 above is whether similar adjustments should be made to the amount required by FRS 9 to be disclosed as the group's share of the turnover of associates or joint ventures (see 3.1.1A and 3.2.1A above). If, in the circumstances of those examples, H plc were to show both its own turnover as stated in its individual accounts and 50% of the turnover of JV Limited as stated in that entity's accounts, there would clearly be an element of double counting. Whilst FRS 9 does not address this directly, we believe that some adjustment should be made to compensate for this. Rolls-Royce deals with the issue by disclosing what appears to be the full amount of sales to joint ventures and the group's share of sales by joint ventures.

Extract 7.14: Rolls-Royce plc (2000)

Group profit and loss account [extract]

	Continuing operations before exceptional items £m	Total 2000 £m	Restated Total 1999 £m
Turnover: Group and share of joint ventures	**5,955**	**5,955**	4,697
Sales to joint ventures	**893**	**893**	799
Less share of joint ventures' turnover	**(984)**	**(984)**	(862)
Group turnover	**5,864**	**5,864**	4,634

...

Oxford Instruments adopts a slightly different approach.

Extract 7.15: Oxford Instruments plc (2000)

Group Profit and Loss Account [extract]

	Notes	Continuing operations £000	Discontinuing operations £000	2000 £000
Turnover	2,3			
Group and share of joint venture turnover		200,479	589	201,068
Less share of joint venture's turnover	5	(40,378)	–	(40,378)
Group turnover *(including acquisitions of £1,596,000)*		160,101	589	160,690

5 JOINT VENTURE [extract]

The Group share of the joint venture's turnover as shown in the Group Profit and Loss Account on pages 26 and 27 has been derived after adjusting for trading between the Group and OMT as follows:

	2000 £000	1999 £000
49% of joint venture turnover	49,304	59,275
Less 49% of sales of materials and services by OMT to group	(4,396)	(4,895)
Less 49% of sales of materials and services by group to OMT	(4,530)	(5,160)
Group share of joint venture's turnover	40,378	49,220

As can be seen, Oxford Instruments discloses the group's share of the joint venture turnover adjusted by sales both to and from the joint venture. The objective appears to be to ensure that the 'grossed-up' turnover figure (i.e. £200.5 million) represents only sales by the group to third parties and the group's share of joint venture's sales to third parties.

4.2.3 *Transactions to create an associate or joint venture*

The requirement to eliminate unrealised profits applies not only to transactions with an existing associate or joint venture, but also to those undertaken in order to set up an associate or joint venture.[76] Again, however, what this actually means in terms of accounting entries is not at all clear. Many commentators, including ourselves, have criticised this lack of clear guidance in FRS 9 for some time, since it has become increasingly common for two or more companies to set up a joint venture by a contribution of assets or a business. This has led to the matter being put on the agenda of the UITF, which in May 2001 issued a draft Abstract *Exchanges of businesses or other non-monetary assets for equity in a subsidiary, joint venture or associate*. At the time of writing it appears likely that this Abstract will be issued in final form later in 2001 without substantial change, since to a large extent it codifies what has emerged as best practice. For this reason, we have used its proposals as the basis for the following discussion.

The scope of the draft Abstract is quite wide applying to all 'transactions in which an entity (A) exchanges a business or other non-monetary assets for equity in another entity (B) which thereby becomes A's subsidiary or which is or thereby becomes A's joint venture or associate'.[77] The most common of these situations in practice is the contribution of a business for equity in a joint venture or associate, and therefore forms the basis of the following discussion, which assumes the circumstances set out in Example 7.7 below. This uses the same facts as Example 6.7 at 3.6.1 in Chapter 6, but looks at the position from the perspective of company A, which ends up with a 40% stake in a joint venture.

Example 7.7: Creation of joint venture by contribution of non-cash assets

A and B are two major pharmaceutical companies, which agree to form a joint venture (JV Co) in respect of a particular part of each of their businesses. A will own 40% of the joint venture, and B 60%. The parties agree that the total value of the new business is £250m.

A's contribution to the venture is one of its subsidiaries, the net assets of which are included in A's consolidated balance sheet at £60m (including goodwill capitalised under FRS 10 of £10m). The fair value of the separable net assets of the subsidiary contributed by A is considered to be £80m. The implicit fair value of the business contributed is £100m (40% of total fair value £250m).

B also contributes a subsidiary, the net assets of which have a carrying amount of £85m (including goodwill capitalised under FRS 10 of £15m). The fair value of the separable net assets is considered to be £120m. The implicit fair value of the business contributed £150m (60% of total fair value £250m).

The book and fair values of the businesses contributed by A and B can therefore be summarised as follows:

	A		B	
(in £m)	Book value	Fair value	Book value	Fair value
Separable net assets	50	80	70	120
Goodwill	10	20	15	30
Total	60	100	85	150

How should A account for the set-up of the joint venture?

A UITF Information Sheet accompanying the draft Abstract discusses three potential approaches:

- the swap approach;
- the sale and repurchase approach; and
- the UITF's proposed approach which is given no particular name in the draft Abstract, but which amounts to a partial sale/partial acquisition approach.

A The swap approach

Under the swap approach, all the items that are the subject of the exchange are kept at their pre-exchange book values. Accordingly, the carrying value of A's 40% interest in JV Co would be based on its share of book values of the underlying net assets. The accounting entry for the transaction in Example 7.7 under this approach would be:

	£m	£m
Investment in JV Co[1]	58	
Other reserves	2	
Net assets contributed to JV Co[2]		60

1 40% of (book value of A's net assets + book value of B's net assets), including goodwill in both cases, i.e. 40% x (£60m+£85m) = £58m.

2 Previous carrying amount of net assets contributed by A, now deconsolidated. In reality there would be a number of entries to deconsolidate these on a line-by-line basis.

Under this approach the £2 million debit to other reserves does not represent a gain but an accounting difference, similar to that arising from an equity elimination under merger accounting (see Chapter 6 at 2.7.2).

The draft Abstract states that this approach would be favoured by those who believe it is not appropriate to recognise a gain or loss on the transaction because of the close relationship between A and B. In fact, however, the 'swap approach' as set out in the Information Sheet differs somewhat from what would normally be understood by an asset swap method, under which the cost of A's 40% investment would be treated as the £60m carrying value of the assets contributed, but fair value would then be attributed to the net assets acquired.

In fact, however, the swap approach is not actually permitted by the general requirement of FRS 9 that, where an associate is acquired, the consideration and net assets acquired should be recorded at fair value (see 4.1 above). This has been reinforced by the ruling of the Financial Reporting Review Panel in the case of Avesco plc. The Panel had made enquiries into the company's accounts for the year ended 31 March 2000 because it had acquired a stake in an associate for the transfer of assets, and recorded the cost of its investment at the book value of those assets. It subsequently transpired, however, that the book and fair values of the assets transferred were in fact the same, as was clarified by the company in its accounts for the following year.[78]

B The sale and repurchase approach

This approach takes the view that A has sold its existing business (including goodwill) in full, giving rise to a gain or loss, and then acquired a 40% interest in a new entity, which should be reflected in A's accounts at fair value, giving rise to goodwill or negative goodwill. The basic accounting entry for the transaction in Example 7.7 under this approach would be:

	£m	£m
Share of net assets of JV Co[1]	80	
Goodwill[2]	20	
Net assets contributed to JV Co[3]		60
Gain on disposal[4]		40

1 40% of (fair value of A's separable net assets + fair value of B's separable net assets), i.e. 40% x (£80m+£120m) = £80m.

2 Fair value of business contributed by A less fair value of separable net assets of new business acquired, i.e. £100-£80m (as calculated in 1 above) = £20m. This goodwill would be included as part of the carrying value of the investment in JV Co.

3 Previous carrying amount of net assets contributed by A, now deconsolidated. In reality there would be a number of entries to deconsolidate these on a line-by-line basis.

4 Fair value of new business received less book value of business disposed of, i.e. 40% of £250m = £100m less £60m = £40m. This would be recognised in the statement of total recognised gains and losses, but probably not in the profit and loss account, as it is unrealised (see further discussion at C II below).

The question then arises as to whether any or all of the gain should be eliminated. The Information Sheet suggests that some would argue that no elimination is required, on the grounds that two separate arm's length transactions have taken place. Others, it is stated, would argue for elimination, either in full or of A's 40% share. It is, in our view, hard to reconcile full elimination with the requirements of FRS 2 and FRS 9. These require full elimination only where the net assets that are the subject of the transaction remain within A's consolidated group However, where, the assets are transferred to an entity over which A has joint control (as here) or significant influence, FRS 9 (as noted above), the general requirements of FRS 9 summarised at 4.2.2 above require only A's 40% share of the profit to be eliminated.

If a partial elimination approach were adopted, the accounting entries would be:

	£m	£m
Gain on disposal[1]	16	
Goodwill (included in carrying amount of JV Co)[2]		4
Share of net assets of JV Co[3]		12

1 40% x £40m = £16m.

2 40% of difference between inherent fair value and book value of A's goodwill contributed to JV Co, i.e. 40% x (£20m-£10m).

3 40% of difference between fair value and book value of A's separable net assets contributed to JV Co, i.e. 40% x (£80m-£50m).

The total carrying value of A's investment in JV Co is now £84m, which can be analysed as:

	£m	
Share of net assets		
40% of book value of A's former net assets (40% x £50m)	20	
40% of fair value of B's former net assets (40% x £120m)	48	
		68
Goodwill		
40% of book value of A's former goodwill (40% x £10m)	4	
40% of fair value of goodwill relating to B (40% x £30m)	12	
		16
Total carrying value		84

In our view, this is the approach that is actually envisaged by FRS 9. However, it gives the same result as the UITF's preferred approach, as discussed in C below.

An example of a company that accounted for a transaction of this type in a manner similar to this was EMI, in its accounts for 1998. In March 1998 it sold its investment in HMV to the newly-floated HMV Media Group, in which it immediately acquired a 45.2% equity interest. As explained in the extract below, EMI did not recognise 45.2% of the profit on disposal as a profit, but credited it to reserves.

Extract 7.16: EMI Group plc (1998)

29. Disposal of business [extract]

The only disposal in the current year is HMV, which was substantially disposed of on 28 March 1998. …

In order to determine the profit on disposal recognised in the profit and loss account for the year, in accordance with UK GAAP, the disposal of HMV to HMV Media Group plc has been considered in conjunction with the Group's subsequent acquisition of an initial 45.2% equity investment in HMV Media Group plc. Looking at both of these transactions together results in 45.2% of the gross profit on disposal being deemed intercompany. This intercompany element of the profit, together with the associated taxation charge, has been eliminated on consolidation and treated as a reserves movement netting against the goodwill on acquisition of the investment in HMV Media Group plc. The estimated goodwill arising on the acquisition of the associated undertaking HMV Media Group plc is £184.7m, £278.1m on acquisition (based on estimated net liabilities: see Note 13(ii)) less a net £93.4m intercompany elimination (gross profit: £120.5m less taxation charge £27.1m).

C *The proposed 'partial sale/partial acquisition' approach*

This approach takes the view that A effectively retains 40%, and sells 60%, of its existing business. It should therefore continue to record the 40% retained at book value, and recognise a gain or loss on the disposal of the 60%, calculated as the difference between the book value of the assets and the fair value of the business transferred. The difference between the fair value of the business given up and the new net assets acquired (i.e. the 40% of B's former net assets) represents goodwill or negative goodwill.[79]

The basic accounting entry for the transaction in Example 7.7 under this approach would be:

	£m	£m
Share of net assets of JV Co[1]	68	
Goodwill[2]	16	
Net assets contributed to JV Co[3]		60
Gain on disposal[4]		24

1 40% of (book value of A's separable net assets + fair value of B's separable net assets), i.e. 40% x (£50m+£120m) = £68m.

2 Fair value of business given up by A less fair value of separable net assets of B's business acquired, i.e. 60% of £100m less 40% of £120m = £12m, plus 40% of A's original goodwill of £10m retained (£4m) = £16m. This goodwill will be included in the total carrying value of JV Co. See further discussion at I below.

3 Previous carrying amount of net assets contributed by A, now deconsolidated. In reality there would be a number of entries to deconsolidate these on a line-by-line basis.

4 Fair value of business given up, less book value of assets disposed of, 60% of £100m - 60% of £60m = £24m. See further discussion under II below.

I *Treatment of goodwill*

The accounting treatment above deals with the goodwill recognised by A before the transaction in the same way as the other net assets of A. This is specifically required by the draft Abstract, not only for goodwill recognised as an asset, but also for goodwill that was set off against reserves under SSAP 22 and the transitional rules in FRS 10.[80]

If in Example 7.7 above, the carrying value of assets transferred by A had been £50m, with the £10m goodwill set off against reserves, the required accounting entry would have been:

	£m	£m
Share of net assets of JV Co[1]	68	
Goodwill[2]	12	
Net assets contributed to JV Co[3]		50
Goodwill reinstated[4]		6
Gain on disposal[5]		24

1 40% of (book value of A's separable net assets + fair value of B's separable net assets) i.e. 40% x (£50m+£120m) = £68m.

2 Fair value of business given up by A less fair value of separable net assets of B's business acquired, i.e. 60% of £100m less 40% of £120m = £12m. This goodwill would be included in the total carrying value of JV Co.

3 Previous carrying amount of net assets (excluding goodwill not included in the balance sheet as an asset) contributed by A, now deconsolidated. In reality there would be a number of entries to deconsolidate these on a line-by-line basis.

4 60% of goodwill of £10m set off against reserves. This would appear in the reconciliation of movements in shareholders' funds (not the profit and loss account or statement of total recognised gains and losses).

5 Fair value of business given up less book value of assets disposed of, 60% of £100m - 60% of [£50m 'on balance sheet' net assets plus £10m goodwill in reserves] = £24m. See further discussion under II below.

II Treatment of any gain arising

The draft Abstract requires that any gain arising that is not realised should be reported in the statement of total recognised and losses (i.e. not the profit and loss account),[81] without, however, entering into the potential minefield of giving guidance on determining whether or not a gain is realised.

In our view, it is very doubtful that transactions of the type illustrated in Example 7.7 can be regarded as realising a profit, in either the entity or the group accounts of A, since the gain is realised not in the form of cash or near-cash, but of a 40% stake in an unquoted investment. This would also be the analysis under the ICAEW's draft Technical Release on the determination of realised profits (see Chapter 3 at 2.1). Interestingly, the Financial Reporting Review Panel took the same view in its adverse ruling on the accounts of Butte Mining PLC in 1996.[82]

A different conclusion might be possible where A received cash as part of the overall transaction (see III below).

III Transactions with a cash element

Suppose for example that the transaction in Example 7.7 above had been that A was to receive only a 36% stake in JV Co, and that B had paid cash of £10 million direct to A in compensation. The approach set out in the Abstract might be thought to give rise to the following accounting entries:

	£m	£m
Share of net assets of JV Co[1]	61.2	
Cash	10.0	
Goodwill[2]	24.4	
Net assets contributed to JV Co[3]		60.0
Gain on disposal[4]		35.6

1 36% of (book value of A's separable net assets + fair value of B's separable net assets) i.e. 36% x (£50m+£120m) = £61.2m.

2 Fair value of business given up by A less fair value of separable net assets of B's business acquired, i.e. 64% of £100m less 36% of £120m = £20.8m, plus 36% of A's goodwill of £10m retained (£3.6m) = £24.4m.

3 Previous carrying amount of net assets (excluding goodwill) contributed by A, now deconsolidated. In reality there would be a number of entries to deconsolidate these on a line-by-line basis.

4 Fair value of business given up less book value of assets disposed of, 64% of £100m - 64% of 60m = £25.6m, plus cash of £10m = £35.6m.

However, this is clearly incorrect. A had a business with a book value of £60 million which was worth £100 million. If it had sold the whole of this it would have realised a gain of £40 million. As it has sold only 64% of its holding, the expected gain should be 64% of £40 million, i.e. £25.6 million.

In this case the transaction should be accounted for on the basis that A has exchanged a 64% interest in its business, worth £64 million (with a book value of £38.4 million) for a 36% interest in B's business, worth £54m plus cash of £10 million. Accordingly, in calculating the goodwill and the gain on sale, the fair value of the part of the business given as consideration should be net of an amount equivalent to the cash received of £10 million, as shown below.

	£m	£m
Share of net assets of JV Co[1]	61.2	
Cash	10.0	
Goodwill[2]	14.4	
Net assets contributed to JV Co[3]		60.0
Gain on disposal[4]		25.6

1 36% of (book value of A's separable net assets + fair value of B's separable net assets) i.e. 36% x (£50m+£120m) = £61.2m.

2 Fair value of business given up by A (net of amount given up for £10m cash received from B) less fair value of separable net assets of B's business acquired, i.e. 64% of £100m (£64m) less £10m = £54m less 36% of £120m = £10.8m, plus 36% of A's goodwill of £10m retained (£3.6m) = £14.4m.

3 Previous carrying amount of net assets (excluding goodwill) contributed by A, now deconsolidated. In reality there would be a number of entries to deconsolidate these on a line-by-line basis.

4 Fair value of business given up (net of amount given up for £10m cash received from B) less book value of assets disposed of, 64% of £100m = £64m less £10m = £54m - 64% of 60m = £15.6m, plus cash received £10m = £25.6m. (This could alternatively have been calculated under the draft Abstract as simply the difference between the fair value of the business given up and the book value of assets disposed of, thereby simply treating the cash as negative consideration in calculating goodwill under 2 above.)

Although this approach may seem counter-intuitive, it can be proved that it is correct by analysing the resulting carrying value of the investment as follows:

	£m	£m
Share of net assets		
36% of book value of A's former net assets (36% x £50m)	18.0	
36% of fair value of B's former net assets (36% x £120m)	43.2	
		61.2
Goodwill		
36% of book value of A's former goodwill (36% x £10m)	3.6	
36% of goodwill relating to B (36% x £30m)	10.8	
		14.4
Total carrying value		75.6

The total amount relating to B in the above is £54m (share of net assets £43.2m plus share of goodwill £10.8). This represents 36% of the total fair value of B of £150m, as would be expected. If the cash had been treated as gross proceeds (giving rise to a gain of £35.6m and goodwill of £24.4m), the total carrying amount of the investment in JV Co would have been greater than A's underlying share of its own former business at book value and B's former business at fair value.

In this example £10 million has been realised in cash, raising the question of how much of the total gain can be recognised in the profit and loss account. In our view there are a number of possible approaches:

- a 'top slicing' approach, whereby as much of the total gain as is backed by cash is treated as realised (i.e. £10 million).
- a 'proportionate' approach, whereby the gain is treated as realised to the extent that the cash forms part of the total consideration of £64 million. This would allow 10/64 x £25.6 million = £4.0 million of the gain to be treated as realised.

- an approach which reflects the fact that the calculation of the gain does not depend on the amount of cash received and that the cash is effectively negative consideration paid for the acquisition of a 36% share of B's business. This would regard none of the gain as having been realised.

In our view, the 'top slicing' approach is perfectly acceptable, and is moreover supported by the ICAEW's draft Technical Release on the determination of realised profits (see Chapter 3 at 2.1).

IV Accounts of JV Co

In the accounts of the JV Co itself (assuming that these are subject to UK GAAP), the acquisition of the former businesses of both A and B will be accounted for at fair value if JV Co adopts acquisition accounting, and at former book value if it adopts merger accounting. This means that the amounts taken up in the accounts of A and B may bear little relation to its share of the underlying financial statements of the investee, and it may be necessary for both A and B to keep a 'memorandum' set of books for consolidation purposes reflecting their own assets at book value those of the other party at fair value. In practice, however, this may be easier said than done, and a fairly broad brush approach may be needed.

V Artificial transactions

The draft Abstract proposes that no gain or loss should be recognised on a transaction of this type 'in those rare cases where the artificiality or lack of substance of the transaction is such that any gain or loss on the exchange could not be justified'. Where no gain or loss is recognised on these grounds, the circumstances should be explained.[83]

Unfortunately, there is no elaboration as to the circumstances where this might be applicable. One concern may have been that in transactions such as this, it is the relative, rather than the absolute, value of the transaction that is of concern to the parties. In other words, in Example 7.7 above, it is clear that A and B have agreed that the relative values of the businesses they have each contributed is 40:60, rather than that the business as a whole is worth £250 million. Thus it might be open to A and B, without altering the substance of the transaction, to assert that the value of the combined operations is £500 million (with a view to inflating their balance sheets) or £200 million, (with a view to reducing future goodwill amortisation).

Another way in which the valuation of the transaction might be distorted is through disaggregation of the consideration. Suppose that the £60 million net assets contributed by A in Example 7.7 above comprised:

	£m
Cash	12
Other net current assets	13
Fixed assets and stock	25
Goodwill	10
	60

Further suppose that, for tax reasons, the transaction was structured such that A was issued with 4% of the shares of JV Co in exchange for the cash and 36% in exchange for the remaining assets. This could lead to the suggestion that, as there can be no doubt as to the fair value of the cash, A's entire investment must be worth £120 million (i.e. £12 million x 40/4). In our view, it is important in such cases to focus on the fair value of the transaction as a whole and not to follow the strict legal form.

The draft Abstract notes the requirement of SIC-13 (see 6.2.5 A below) that a gain or loss should not be recognised on a transaction of this type where the non-monetary assets contributed by each party are 'similar', but emphasises that 'similar' is tightly defined as to mean assets of a similar nature, a similar use in the same line of business and a similar fair value. It is not entirely clear what point the UITF intended to make by this, but it may have been to clarify that it will not generally be possible to avoid the requirements of the Abstract by appealing to SIC-13 to argue that that assets exchanged are similar.

VI Impairment highlighted by contribution of assets to a new entity

FRS 9 provides that, where a transaction between an investor and its associate or joint venture provides evidence of the impairment of the asset transferred, 'this should be taken into account'.[84] What is envisaged here is not clear, but the suggestion seems to be that, where a transaction between the investor and an associate or joint venture generates a loss, the loss should be reflected in the accounts of the contributing entity before accounting for the contribution of assets. However, the approach proposed in the draft Abstract implies that any such losses should be dealt with as part of the overall gain or loss on the exchange.

4.3 Conformity of accounting policies

FRS 9 requires the investor to account for its share of the results and net assets of an associate or joint venture, by adjusting them where necessary so as to conform them to its own accounting policies. Similar considerations in respect of the availability of information apply to such adjustments as to fair value adjustments (see 4.1 above).[85] This may mean that, in more complex cases, such as the arrangements assumed in Example 7.7 above, the amounts taken up in the accounts of the investor may bear little relation to its share of the underlying financial statements of the investee, and it may be necessary to keep a 'memorandum' set of books for consolidation purposes. An example of a company disclosing that consolidation adjustments have been made in respect of equity accounted investments is United Business Media.

Extract 7.17: United Business Media plc (2000)

Group accounting policies [extract]

INVESTMENTS

...

Where the accounting policies of associates and/or joint ventures do not conform in all material respects to those of the group, adjustments are made on consolidation.

4.4 Non-coterminous accounting periods

Where possible, FRS 9 requires the investor's share of an associate or joint venture to be included on the basis of financial statements prepared to the investor's period end. Where this is not practicable, the investor may use financial statements prepared to a date preceding its own period end by not more than three months.[86]

This period can be extended up to six months if use of financial statements for an earlier period would entail publication of restricted, price-sensitive information.[87] In amplifying this requirement, FRS 9 emphasises the need to have regard to any relevant 'regulations' on the dissemination of price-sensitive information.[88] The implication seems to be that the exemption for 'price-sensitive' information applies only in respect of information that is treated as such by applicable regulations rather than to any information considered as such by the investor or investee. This is consistent with the requirements of the law and FRS 2 in respect of the consolidation of subsidiaries with non-coterminous year ends.[89]

FRS 9 requires that, where the investor's equity accounting is based on the accounts of an associate or joint venture for a period ending before its own, adjustments should be made in respect of any material event that has occurred in the interim.[90]

FRS 9 recognises that it can be difficult to ensure that the associate provides up-to-date information. A holding company can usually secure that a subsidiary has a coterminous year end, but the various investors in an associate or joint venture may all have different year ends. None of them has the control needed in order to dictate the year end of the investee, nor can they necessarily demand the production of interim accounts for their own purposes (although this can sometimes give an indication of whether or not they do, in fact, exercise significant influence or joint control).[91]

An example of a company disclosing that interim accounts of associates have been used for consolidation purposes is Pearson, even though this is technically no longer required, as it was under SSAP 1.

Extract 7.18: Pearson plc (2000)

B) BASIS OF CONSOLIDATION [extract]

The profit of the Group includes the Group's share of the results of associated undertakings, and the consolidated balance sheet includes the Group's interest in associated undertakings at the book value of attributable net assets and attributable goodwill. The figures included in the financial statements have been based on unaudited management accounts for the period to 31 December.

4.5 Goodwill

FRS 9 provides that the element of the carrying value of an investment in an associate or joint venture represented by goodwill must be accounted for in accordance with FRS 10,[92] the detailed requirements of which are discussed in Chapter 11 at 2.3. This means that, for any associate or joint venture acquired in a period to which FRS 10 applied, any goodwill arising on acquisition must be included in the carrying value of the investment and either:

(a) amortised over twenty years (or less); or

(b) amortised over more than twenty years or not amortised, subject in either case to an annual impairment review.

Neither FRS 9 nor FRS 10 gives any guidance as to how to undertake an annual impairment review of an investment in an associate or joint venture. The basic principle is to compare the carrying value of the investment with the higher of its net realisable value (if known) or value in use (effectively, discounted future cash flows from the investment).

Unless the associate or joint venture is a listed company it may be difficult to estimate a net realisable value for it. So far as estimating a value in use is concerned, however, this is a difficult enough exercise at the best of times as we discuss more fully in Chapter 13.

At least where the investment concerned is a subsidiary, the parent can usually ensure full distribution of profits if it so wishes. This means that the future profits of that investment form a starting point for estimating future cash flows from it. In the case of an investment in an associate or joint venture, however, the only cash flows are normally dividends received together with the proceeds of any eventual realisation of the investment. Both the amount and the timing of such cash flows will in many cases be very difficult to determine.

The difficulties of assessing either net realisable value or value in use for investments in associates and joint ventures are such that we doubt whether any goodwill in the carrying value of such investments is, except in very rare circumstances, 'capable of continued measurement' within the terms of FRS 10.[93] This means that it must be amortised over twenty years or less, and a longer (or indefinite) life cannot be used.

There may, however, be cases where the cash flows are sufficiently predictable to enable an impairment review to be undertaken. This might be the case, for example, where cash flows from the associate or joint venture are expected to be generated through sales to it by the reporting entity, or where the investee has been set up for a specific, and relatively short-term, project. There are companies that have taken the view that goodwill relating to associates is capable of continued measurement, an example being Cadbury Schweppes (see Extract 11.8 at 2.3.4 A in Chapter 11).

There may also be a more general argument that, in the case of a joint venture, the investor's joint control gives it more power to convert profits into cash flows than is the case with an associate. On this basis, the forecast future profits of a joint venture may form a more valid basis than those of an associate for predicting future cash flows.

Where an impairment review identifies any impairment in the value of goodwill arising on acquisition of an associate or joint venture, FRS 9 requires the goodwill to be written down and the amount written off to be disclosed.[94] FRS 9 notes that any impairment in the assets of the associate or joint venture will 'normally' be reflected in its own accounts with the result that further adjustments should not 'usually' be necessary in the investor's financial statements.[95]

The use of the words 'normally' and 'usually', combined with the requirement to adjust the underlying accounts of an associate or joint venture to reflect the investor's accounting policies (see above), implies that, where an investee does not make adjustments for impairment of assets in its own accounts (e.g. because it is not subject to UK GAAP), the investor should do so on consolidation. However, we simply do not see how this can be practicable. If, as we suggest above, the investor would be hard-pressed to undertake an impairment review of its entire investment in an associate or joint venture, it could hardly do so in respect of the underlying assets of the associate or joint venture.

4.6 Calculation of the share of an associate or joint venture to be accounted for

FRS 9 provides some guidance on the calculation of the share of net assets to be accounted for under the equity and gross equity methods. It first clarifies that the group's effective interest in an associate or joint venture is the aggregate of the interests held by the parent and its subsidiaries, and that any interests held by its associates or joint ventures are to be ignored.[96] No specific guidance is provided in respect of cross-holdings (i.e. where the reporting entity and an associate (or joint venture) have shares in each other). However, the requirement (discussed above) partially to eliminate profits of transactions between the group and its associates and joint ventures clearly suggests that cross-holdings should be adjusted for.

FRS 9 notes that in most cases the investor's effective interest will be determined by the proportion of equity shares held.[97] However, matters may be complicated when the investee has two or more classes of share, with differing rights, in issue, or where the investor holds non-equity shares, convertibles or options in the investee. FRS 9 states that in some cases the rights attaching to options, convertibles, or non-equity shares are such that the investor should take them into account.[98]

FRS 9 does not elaborate on the circumstances in which such rights should be adjusted for. The implication is that where an investor has a contingent right to acquire equity shares in an associate or joint venture (e.g. through an option or convertible security), and that right is likely to be exercised, the investor should equity account for the share of its investment that it would have if those rights were exercised. Where this is done, however, the costs of exercising such rights should be taken into account, and care must be taken not to double count such interests. For example, an investor should not increase its equity accounted interest in an investment on the basis that some contingent right will be exercised whilst simultaneously marking that right to market.[99] It would also be necessary to have regard to the dividend rights of other shareholders, since it would clearly be wrong to equity account for profits that were in reality more likely to be paid as dividend to other shareholders than to the reporting entity.

This aspect of FRS 9 is slightly curious in that it has no parallel in the requirements of FRS 2 for the consolidation of subsidiaries, although there might well be situations in which it would be appropriate to adopt a similar approach to accounting for subsidiaries. This is discussed further in Chapter 5 at 3.4.

FRS 9 deals only with rights held by the reporting entity. It is of course quite possible that other investors in an associate or joint venture may have a contingent right to acquire shares in it which, if exercised, would dilute the effective interest of the reporting entity. We believe that, in assessing the interest of the reporting entity, regard should be had to such rights and interests of other investors.

FRS 9 also notes that the arrangements for sharing dividends and other distributions may be more complicated and may depend on the type of distribution or the nature of the underlying cash flows of the investee. In such cases, it is necessary for the substance of the arrangements to be taken into account in establishing the most appropriate measure of the investor's share.[100]

4.7 Losses and deficiencies of assets

FRS 9 requires an investor to account for the appropriate share of a loss-making associate or joint venture, even where this results in the investor showing a share of net liabilities rather than net assets. Where this occurs, the resulting balance is shown as a provision or liability rather than as a negative fixed asset. The only exception is where there is sufficient evidence that there has been an irrevocable change in the relationship between the parties marking the 'irreversible withdrawal' of the investor. FRS 9 implies that in such cases it is necessary that either:

(a) the investor makes a public statement of its intention to walk away from its investment combined with a demonstrable commitment to the process of withdrawal; or

(b) there is evidence that the operating and financing policies of the investee are to become the responsibility of its creditors rather than the shareholders (e.g. the appointment of a receiver).[101]

Examples of companies disclosing such a deficit are Cable and Wireless (see Extract 7.11 above), and Cordiant Communications Group (see Extract 7.19 below). Both companies present it as a separate balance sheet format heading, after 'Provisions for liabilities and charges' in the case of Cable and Wireless, but before it in the case of Cordiant, which also analyses the deficit between the underlying share of gross assets and gross liabilities. It is noteworthy that neither Cable and Wireless nor Cordiant strictly includes the share of net deficit *within* provisions, as suggested by FRS 9. It may be that the companies share our view that FRS 9's required treatment is not altogether appropriate since the investor's share of such deficits does not meet the definition either of 'provision' in FRS 12 (see Chapter 28), or of 'liability' in the ASB's *Statement of Principles* (see Chapter 2).

Extract 7.19: Cordiant Communications Group plc (2000)

CONSOLIDATED BALANCE SHEET [extract]

	2000	1999
	£m	£m
...		
Total asset less current liabilities	**654.9**	139.2
Creditors – Due after one year	**(130.7)**	(123.2)
Provision for joint venture deficit		
Share of gross assets	**130.6**	86.1
Share of gross liabilities	**(142.7)**	(100.5)
	(12.1)	(14.4)
Provisions for liabilities and charges	**(40.0)**	(41.8)
Net liabilities	**472.1**	(40.2)
...		

An example of an entity that does not provide for its share of net liabilities of joint ventures and associates, on the grounds that there is no obligation to make good such deficits, is the BBC. Whilst this may well fairly represent the substance of the arrangements, it is not clear that FRS 9's very demanding conditions for this treatment (as set out in (a) and (b) above) have strictly been satisfied.

Extract 7.20: British Broadcasting Corporation (2001)

12d Interests in joint ventures [extract]

The Group, through its subsidiary BBC Worldwide Limited, has major partnership deals with Flextech plc ('Flextech') for the production and marketing of subscription channels in the UK, and with Discovery Communications Inc. ('Discovery') for incorporating and operating new channels around the world and providing new co-production funding for programmes.

...

Under the terms of the agreements with Flextech and Discovery, the Group has no obligation to fund losses incurred by the entities nor to make good their net liabilities. As a result, the Group does not share in the losses of the relevant entities and accordingly no share of losses is included in the financial statements for the year ended 31 March 2001 (2000 nil). The Group is entitled to its share of any profits or net assets once the ventures' cumulative profits exceed cumulative losses since incorporation.

4.8 Non-corporate associates and joint ventures

The issue here is related to that discussed in 4.7 above. Where the investor has an interest in an unincorporated associate or joint venture it may have liabilities greater than the amount that results from taking into account only its share of net assets. This may be the case, for example, where the investors in the entity concerned have joint and several liability for its debts and one of the other investors gets into financial difficulties. In such cases, FRS 9 requires the reporting investor to disclose any such additional obligation as a contingent liability or, in more extreme cases, to recognise it in the financial statements.[102]

Whilst this provision of FRS 9 appears under the heading 'Non-corporate associates and joint ventures' the same principles will apply to an investment in an incorporated entity where the shareholders have joint and several liability (e.g. where the shareholders of a company jointly guarantee a bank loan).

4.9 Commencement or cessation of an associate or joint venture relationship

An investment becomes an associate on the date that the investor first holds a participating interest in it *and* exercises significant influence over it. It therefore ceases to be one when the investor ceases *either* to hold a participating interest *or* exercise significant influence.[103]

As noted in the discussion in 2.1.1 B above, there is a presumption in FRS 9 that once an investor has exercised significant influence over an investment, it carries on doing so until some transaction or event occurs to remove this influence. Moreover, once an investment is considered to be long-term (one of the key elements of a 'participating interest'), FRS 9 requires that it continue to be treated as such until disposal. Taken together, this all means that, in practice, it will be relatively rare that an investment ceases to be an associate, other than by disposal or dilution of the reporting entity's interest, or loss of board representation.

An investment becomes a joint venture on the day on which the investor first exercises joint control over it, and ceases to be one when the investor ceases to exercise joint control.[104] These dates may not be as clear-cut as might appear at first sight, given that FRS 9 provides that joint control can be established through habitual behaviour as well as through a formal agreement.

Where an associate or joint venture is disposed of, in whole or in part, the profit or loss should be calculated as the sales proceeds less:

(a) share of net assets (i.e. the amount at which the investment would have been stated under the equity method on the date on which it ceased to qualify as an associate or joint venture); and

(b) any goodwill that arose on acquisition (to the extent not already charged to the profit and loss account, or charged as a prior year adjustment under the transitional rules in FRS 10).[105]

If an investment ceases to be an associate or joint venture other than through disposal, it should be carried in the consolidated balance sheet at an amount comprising the share of net assets plus goodwill (calculated as in (a) and (b) above).[106] This carrying amount should be reviewed for impairment and adjusted, if necessary, to reflect dividend payments and other distributions to shareholders.

It has to said that FRS 9 could be clearer as to whether unamortised goodwill is to be included in the carrying amount, but it is our view that this is the intention of paragraphs 40-43 of the standard when read as a whole. It is also not clear, if goodwill is included in the carrying value of a former associate or joint venture in this way, whether it is meant to be separately identified and treated as such, or simply added to the cost of investment.

We believe FRS 9 intends the latter treatment, because it refers to the resulting figure as a 'surrogate cost'.[107] On this view, the 'cost' of a former associate or joint venture is the amount originally paid (i.e. including goodwill) plus the share of profits 'foregone' as a result of the loss of influence (or joint control). If this interpretation is correct, it has the effect that, where an associate or joint venture loses its status as such, any goodwill that arose on acquisition and was eliminated against reserves under SSAP 22 must under FRS 9 be added to the carrying value. This was the treatment adopted by Hanson in these circumstances (see Extract 7.2 at 2.1.1 B above).

In fact, this treatment of former associates and joint ventures may be relatively short-lived, since they will be carried at market value if the proposals in the ASB's 1996 discussion paper *Derivatives and other financial instruments*, and more recently in the consultation paper on financial instruments issued by the Joint Working Group of Standard-Setters in December 2000, are given effect in a future standard.[108] These proposals are discussed in Chapter 10.

Where an associate or joint venture is acquired or disposed of piecemeal, processes similar to those required by FRS 2 for piecemeal acquisition or disposals of subsidiaries should be applied.[109] These are discussed more fully in sections 2.5, 3.4 and 3.5 of Chapter 6.

5 DISCLOSURE REQUIREMENTS FOR ASSOCIATES AND JOINT VENTURES

In addition to the disclosures that directly amplify the primary statements (discussed in 3 above), FRS 9 requires further disclosures in respect of associates and joint ventures. Most of these are duplicated by the requirements of the Companies Act, but there are a few additional ones in the legislation. Where a company has acquired or disposed of an associate during the year, certain disclosures may also be required by FRS 10 – *Goodwill and intangible assets*.

There are, broadly, two tiers of disclosure in FRS 9. Some items, mostly of a narrative nature, are required in respect of all associates and joint ventures, irrespective of size. Where, however, associates and joint ventures form a particularly large part of the reporting entity's business, additional financial information must be given.

5.1 Scope of disclosures

There is some lack of clarity in FRS 9 as to exactly what entities are required to give these disclosures. Because paragraph 51 of FRS 9 states that they should be given 'in addition to the amounts required on the face of the primary financial statements under the equity or the gross equity method', it is our view that:

They are required in consolidated accounts (because these include equity accounted amounts on the face of the profit and loss account and balance sheet).

They are not required in single entity accounts of investors that are not required to give supplementary information on associates or joint ventures (see 3.1.2 above).

This is because disclosure is required only 'in addition' to equity accounted amounts, and no such information appears on the face of the primary statements. Moreover, most of the disclosures would be of no relevance to the accounts of such a company. However, it must be remembered that some information, similar to that which would otherwise be required by FRS 9, is required under the Companies Act (see 5.3 below and Chapter 30 at 3.1.3).

They are probably required in (and are certainly relevant to) single entity accounts of investors that are required to give supplementary information on associates or joint ventures (see 3.1.2 above). There is room for debate here, however, as to whether the supplementary equity accounted information given by such companies appears 'on the face of the primary statements' (a necessary condition for triggering the disclosure requirement). The information does not, obviously, appear on the face of the primary financial statements of the *company*, but it does appear on the face of the *supplementary* primary financial statements. The position is even less clear when the supplementary information is given by way of note, rather than in pro-forma accounts.

If this is the intended position, however, it is slightly confusing that the disclosures required by paragraph 52 (but no other paragraph) are specifically restricted to the group accounts. If our interpretation of paragraph 51 is correct, it is not necessary to restrict the scope of paragraph 52 in this way.

5.2 Disclosures required for all associates and joint ventures

5.2.1 *Name, shareholding, accounting date etc.*

In group accounts only, an investor should give for each principal associate and joint venture:

(a) its name;

(b) the proportion of shares held, together with any special rights or restrictions attaching to the shares;

(c) the accounting period or date of the financial statements used, if different from that of the reporting group; and

(d) an indication of the nature of its business.[110]

5.2.2 *Matters material to understanding the effect of associates and joint ventures*

FRS 9 requires an investor to disclose matters that are disclosed in the accounts of its associates or joint ventures (or would have been noted had the associate or joint venture applied the investor's accounting policies), and which are material to understanding the effect on the investor of its investments. FRS 9 particularly highlights the investor's share of contingent liabilities and capital commitments as being relevant to this requirement.[111]

5.2.3 *Restrictions on distribution*

The investor should indicate the extent of any significant statutory, contractual or exchange restrictions on the distribution of the reserves of an associate or joint venture (other than those shown as non-distributable).[112] This corresponds to the similar requirement in respect of investments in subsidiaries in FRS 2.[113]

5.2.4 *Balances with associates and joint ventures*

FRS 9 requires balances between the investor and its associates or joint ventures to be analysed between loans and trading balances,[114] as do the balance sheet formats in the Companies Act 1985.[115] FRS 9 notes that these disclosures overlap somewhat with those required by FRS 8 – *Related party disclosures* – which are discussed in Chapter 30, and permits the disclosures made under the two standards to be combined.[116]

5.2.5 *Rebuttal of presumptions relating to interests of 20% or more*

FRS 9 requires the reporting entity to disclose why the facts in any particular case rebut the presumption that control of 20% or more of the voting rights in an investment gives rise to significant influence over it. It also requires similar disclosure where the presumption that a 20% (or greater) shareholding gives rise to a participating interest has been rebutted.[117] See Extract 7.1 at 2.1.1 B above for an example of disclosure under this requirement.

5.3 Disclosures required for material associates or joint ventures

FRS 9 requires disclosure of supplementary financial information in respect of associates and joint ventures where these represent a material part of the group's activities. Broadly speaking, this information must be given in respect of:

(a) total associates (and/or joint ventures) where these comprise more than 15% of the group; and

(b) each individual associate (or joint venture) that represents more than 25% of the group.

The precise rules for calculating whether these thresholds have been reached are slightly complicated.

5.3.1 *Determining whether disclosure is required*

In order to determine whether the additional disclosures are required, the reporting group must first calculate its own:

(a) turnover;

(b) average operating profit for the current and previous two periods;

(c) gross assets; and

(d) gross liabilities.

Somewhat inconsistently, whilst profit is calculated using a rolling three-year average, turnover is simply the figure for the year. Each of these adjusted group figures is then compared with the corresponding figures for the group's share of:

(a) associates in total;

(b) joint ventures in total; and

(c) each individual associate or joint venture.

The disclosure thresholds are reached when any one of the figures for total associates or total joint ventures is more than 15%, or any of the figures for an individual associate or joint venture is more than 25%, of the corresponding adjusted group figure.[118] The disclosures required are set out in 5.3.2 and 5.3.3 below.

In undertaking the calculations in each case the reporting entity must exclude from the 'group' numbers (for reasons that are not entirely clear) any amounts arising from equity accounting for associates or joint ventures. This raises the issue of how to treat goodwill included in the carrying amount of associates or joint ventures. We consider that, because it represents part of the group's equity accounted interest in associates or joint ventures, it should be treated as a gross asset of the associate or joint venture rather than of the group. However, it could be argued that, at least to the extent that it represents a premium paid on acquisition rather than underlying goodwill of the associate or joint venture, it should be treated as an asset of the group.

5.3.2 *The '15%' disclosures*

A Associates

Where the 15% threshold is reached in respect of total associates, the group should disclose its share, in total, of its associates':

(a) turnover (unless shown already as a memorandum item);

(b) fixed assets;

(c) current assets;

(d) liabilities due within one year; and

(e) liabilities due after one year or more.[119]

B Joint ventures

Where the 15% threshold is reached in respect of total joint ventures, the group should disclose its share, in total, of its joint ventures':

(a) fixed assets;

(b) current assets;

(c) liabilities due within one year; and

(d) liabilities due after one year or more.[120]

5.3.3 *The '25%' disclosures*

Where the 25% threshold is reached in respect of any individual associate or joint venture, the accounts should name the entity concerned and disclose the group's share of its:

(a) turnover;

(b) profit before tax;

(c) taxation;

(d) profit after tax;

(e) fixed assets;

(f) current assets;

(g) liabilities due within one year; and

(h) liabilities due after one year or more.[121]

If a single associate or joint venture falling within the 25% threshold represents nearly all the total amount included for associates or joint ventures respectively, these disclosures may be given in respect of total associates (and/or joint ventures) rather than for the individual investment concerned. The accounts must disclose that this approach has been adopted, and name the main associate or joint venture concerned.[122]

Further analysis of any amounts disclosed under these requirements should be given where this is necessary to understand the total amount involved. FRS 9 suggests that it may be important to give more information on the size and maturity profile of liabilities.[123]

5.4 Companies Act 1985

5.4.1 *Associated undertakings*

The following information must be given in group accounts in respect of each associated undertaking:

(a) its name;

(b) its country of incorporation (if outside Great Britain);

(c) if it is unincorporated, the address of its principal place of business; and

(d) the identity of each class of shares held and the proportion of the nominal value of the shares of that class represented by those shares. If applicable, the holdings should be split between those held directly by the parent company, and those held indirectly via other group companies.[124]

Equivalent disclosures must be given in respect of joint ventures accounted for under the gross equity method, by virtue of the fact that they will typically fall within the Companies Act definitions of 'associated undertaking' and/or 'significant holding'.[125]

5.4.2 *Proportionally consolidated joint ventures*

As noted above, FRS 9 no longer permits proportional consolidation of joint ventures. However, as noted in 2.2.2 above, the Companies Act permits proportional consolidation of unincorporated joint ventures and, where this is done, requires certain disclosures to be made in respect of each such venture, as follows:

(a) its name;

(b) its principal place of business;

(c) the factors on which joint management is based;

(d) the proportion of the capital of the joint venture held by the group; and

(e) where the financial year end of the joint venture did not coincide with that of the parent company of the reporting group, the date of its last year end (ending before the financial year end of the parent company).[126]

At present these requirements are of no practical effect and we include them only for the sake of completeness.

5.5 The disclosures in practice

A comprehensive example of most of the disclosures required by FRS 9 and the Companies Act is that given by Pilkington as shown below.

Extract 7.21: Pilkington plc (2001)

		2001 Group £m	2000 Group £m
18	Investments – joint ventures		
	Cost		
	At beginning of the year	**45**	46
	Exchange rate adjustments	**(4)**	(1)
	Additions	**16**	–
		57	45
	Share of post-acquisition profits less losses		
	At beginning of the year	**40**	38
	Exchange rate adjustments	**(3)**	1
	Retained (Losses)/profits	**(1)**	1
		36	40
	At the end of the year	**93**	85

The Group's principal joint ventures are as follows:

	Proportion of issued shares held	Accounting date	Activity	Country of operation and incorporation
Cebrace Cristal Plano Limitada (Cebrace)	50%	31.3.2001	Glass manufacturing	Brazil
Pilkington Glass France SAS	51%	31.3.2001	Glass manufacturing	France
Interpane Glass Casting France SAS	49%	31.3.2001	Glass processing	France
Flovetro SpA	50%	31.12.2000	Glass manufacturing	Italy

In addition, there are a further three joint ventures at 31st March 2001.

Pilkington Glass France SAS and Interpane Glass Casting France SAS, in which Pilkington respectively owns 51% and 49% of the shares, are treated as Joint Ventures under FRS 9 as both companies are jointly controlled with the other shareholder.

No significant additional taxation would be payable if the joint ventures were sold at the carrying value.

At 31st March 2001 the share of profits less losses retained by joint ventures included within the Group's profit and loss account balance amounted to £36 million (2000 £40 million) of which £11 million (2000 £8 million) is considered to be distributable, the remainder being subject to restriction within the countries in which the joint ventures operate.

The Group's share of net assets of joint ventures comprises:

	2001 **£m**	2000 £m
Fixed assets	**88**	93
Current assets	**31**	20
Liabilities due within one year	**(11)**	(12)
Liabilities due after more than one year	**(15)**	(16)
	93	85

19 **Investments - associates**	**2001 Group £m**	2000 Group £m
Cost or valuation		
At beginning of the year	**116**	82
Exchange rate adjustments	**3**	14
Additions	**5**	12
Transfer from trade investments	**–**	8
	124	116
Share of post-acquisition profits less losses		
At beginning of the year	**17**	2
Exchange rate adjustments	**1**	–
Retained (losses)/profits	**(1)**	15
	17	17
Goodwill (note 15)		
At beginning of the year	**(8)**	–
Additions	**–**	(8)
Amortisation for the year	**1**	–
	(7)	(8)
At end of the year	**134**	125

The Group's principal associates are as follows:

	Proportion of issued shares held	Accounting date	Activity	Country of operation and incorporation
Vitro Plan SA de CV+	35%	31.12.2000	Glass manufacturing And processing	Mexico
Shanghai Yaohua Pilkington Glass Co Limited	19%	31.12.2000	Glass manufacturing	China
Shanghai Yaohua Pilkington Autoglass Co. Limited+	25%	31.12.2000	Glass processing	China
Wuhan Yaohua Pilkington Safety Glass Limited+	46%	31.12.2000	Glass processing	China
Holding Concorde SA+	45%	31.12.2000	Glass manufacturing	Colombia

+Audited by a firm other than PriceWaterhouseCoopers.

Pilkington acquired an additional 2% holding in Shanghai Yaohua Pilkington Glass Co Limited (SYP) between 27th November 2000 and 19th February 2001. The acquisition gave rise to positive goodwill (note 15).

SYP is quoted on the Shanghai Stock Exchange. The market value of the Group's 19% holding amounts to £60 million (2000 £10 million).

Pilkington acquired 51% of Shanghai Yaohua Pilkington Autoglass Co Limited (formerly Shanghai FuHua Glass Company) on 5th September 2000 and immediately disposed of 26% to Shanghai Yaohua Pilkington Glass Co Limited leaving Pilkington with a direct holding of 25%. Shanghai Yaohua Pilkington Glass Co Limited owns 40% of Shanghai Yaohua Pilkington Autoglass Co Limited, leaving Pilkington with a direct and indirect holding of 33%. The acquisition by Pilkington of the 25% direct shareholding gave rise to negative goodwill (note 15) and in accordance with FRS 9 this is offset against the carrying value of associates.

No significant additional taxation would be payable if the associates were sold at the carrying value.

At 31st March 2001, the share of profits less losses retained by associates included within the Group's profit and loss account balance amounted to £17 million (2000 £17 million) of which £20 million of the profits (2000 £21 million) are considered to be distributable.

The Group's share of net assets of associates comprises:

	2001	2000
	£m	£m
Fixed assets	**165**	150
Current assets	**112**	68
Liabilities due within one year	**(80)**	(44)
Liabilities due after more than one year	**(63)**	(49)
	134	125

Additional disclosures are given in respect of the Group's share of Vitro Plan SA de CV which exceeds certain thresholds under FRS 9, as follows:

	2001	2000
	£m	£m
Turnover	**239**	195
Profit before taxation	**24**	33
Taxation	**(9)**	(10)
Profit after taxation	**15**	23
Fixed assets	**142**	128
Current assets	**96**	62
Liabilities due within one year	**(67)**	(43)
Liabilities due after more than one year	**(63)**	(49)
Net assets	**108**	98

6 IAS REQUIREMENTS

One of the more striking features of FRS 9 at the time of its issue was that it took the UK further away from international accounting practice than had been the case under SSAP 1. This seemed particularly ironic given the ASB's strong support for, and involvement in, the IASC's harmonisation project (see Chapter 1). In contrast to UK GAAP, IAS addresses the accounting treatment of associates and joint ventures in different pronouncements, IAS 28 and IAS 31 respectively.

6.1 Accounting for associates

As noted above, the relevant standard is IAS 28 – *Accounting for Investments in Associates*, which has been the subject of two SIC Interpretations:

- SIC-3 – *Elimination of Unrealised Profits and Losses on Transactions with Associates*; and
- SIC-20 – *Equity Accounting Method – Recognition of Losses*.

6.1.1 *Definition of associate and related terms*

IAS 28 defines an associate as 'an enterprise in which the investor has significant influence and which is neither a subsidiary nor a joint venture of the investor.' Certain of the terms embedded within this definition are defined as follows:

- 'significant' influence is 'the power to participate in the financial and operating policy decisions of the investee but is not control over those policies', with control being defined, for the purposes of IAS 28, as 'the power to govern the financial and operating policies of an enterprise so as to obtain benefit from its activities' (see 6.1.2 below);
- a 'subsidiary' is 'an enterprise that is controlled by another enterprise (known as the parent)'.[127]

IAS 28 does not define 'joint venture' for the purposes of the definition of associate, but the definition in IAS 31 (see 6.2.1 below) should presumably be applied.

6.1.2 *Presumption of significant influence*

Under IAS 28, a holding of 20% or more of the voting power of the investee is presumed to give rise to significant influence, unless it can be clearly demonstrated that this is not the case. Conversely, a holding of less than 20% of the voting power is presumed not to give rise to significant influence, unless it can be clearly demonstrated that this is not the case. The existence of a substantial or majority interest of another investor does not necessarily preclude the investor from having significant influence. In calculating the interest of a group, account should be taken of shares held directly by the parent and those held indirectly through subsidiaries.[128]

IAS 28 states that the exercise of significant influence will usually be evidenced in one or more of the following ways:

- representation on the board of directors or equivalent governing body of the investee;

- participation in policy-making processes;
- material transactions between the investor and the investee;
- interchange of managerial personnel; or
- provision of essential technical information.[129]

A Potential voting rights

In September 2001, the SIC issued a draft interpretation SIC–D33 *Consolidation and Equity Method – Potential Voting Rights.* This proposes that the effect of potential voting rights (such as those arising from share warrants, share call options, and convertible debt, including those held by other investors) should be taken into account in assessing whether an enterprise exercises significant influence over another. However, the investor should account for its share of an investment by reference only to its present ownership interests.[130] If approved, this interpretation would create a difference between IAS and UK GAAP, which appears to suggests that in certain circumstances an investment in an associate should be accounted for by reference to potential ownership rights (see 4.7 above).

6.1.3 *Accounting requirements*

A Consolidated financial statements

An investment in an associate should be accounted for in consolidated financial statements under the equity method except when:

(a) the investment is acquired and held exclusively with a view to its subsequent disposal in the near future; or

(b) it operates under severe long-term restrictions that significantly impair its ability to transfer funds to the investor.

Such investments should be accounted for in accordance with IAS 39 – *Financial Instruments: Recognition and Measurement* (see Chapter 10 at 4.6).[131]

The equity method is defined as 'a method of accounting whereby the investment is initially recorded at cost and adjusted thereafter for the post acquisition change in the investor's share of net assets of the investee. The income statement reflects the investor's share of the results of operations of the investee.'[132] The application of this method is discussed in more detail at 6.1.4 below.

An investor should discontinue the use of the equity method from the date that:

(a) it ceases to have significant influence in an associate but retains, either in whole or in part, its investment; or

(b) the use of the equity method is no longer appropriate because the associate operates under severe long-term restrictions that significantly impair its ability to transfer funds to the investor.

The carrying amount of the investment at that date should be regarded as cost.[133] Thereafter, the investment should be accounted for in accordance with IAS 39.[134]

B Individual entity financial statements

I Entity preparing consolidated accounts

Where the investor issues consolidated accounts, an investment in an associate that is not held exclusively with a view to its disposal in the near future should be either:

(a) carried at cost; or

(b) accounted for using the equity method; or

(c) accounted for as an available-for-sale financial asset as described in IAS 39 (see Chapter 10 at 4.6.4).[135]

Method (b) would not normally be a possible method in jurisdictions subject to the EC Fourth Directive, such as the United Kingdom, owing to the Directive's prohibition on the recognition of unrealised profits.

There is a slight, and we presume unintentional, inconsistency in the drafting of this requirement and the rules for the consolidated accounts. The rules for consolidated accounts provide that an investment subject to long-term restrictions should not be accounted for using the equity method (see A above), whereas there is no comparable restriction in the rules for the entity accounts. It would, however, be inappropriate in our view to use the equity method in such circumstances.

IAS 28 adds that the preparation of consolidated financial statements does not obviate the need for separate financial statements.[136] This comment seems rather out of place in a standard on associates rather than one on subsidiaries or consolidated accounts.

II Entity not preparing consolidated accounts

Where the investor does not issue consolidated accounts, an investment in an associate that is not held exclusively with a view to its disposal in the near future should be either:

- carried at cost; or
- accounted for using the equity method, provided that this method would be appropriate for the associate if the issuer were to issue consolidated financial statements; or
- accounted for as an available-for-sale financial asset as described in IAS 39 (see Chapter 10 at 4.6.4).[137]

IAS 28 goes on to observe that 'an investor that has investments in associates may not issue consolidated financial statements because it does not have subsidiaries. It is appropriate that such an investor provides the same information about its investments in associates as those enterprises that issue consolidated financial statements.'[138] This seems rather strange, since the requirements above effectively allow a company not preparing group accounts to give far less information about its associates that one that does, since there is no need to account for them using the equity method.

6.1.4 *Application of the equity method*

A *Basic principles*

IAS 28 summarises the equity method as follows. The investment is initially recorded at cost and the carrying amount is increased or decreased to recognise the investor's share of the profits or losses of the investee after the date of acquisition. Distributions received from an investee reduce the carrying amount of the investment. Adjustments to the carrying amount may also be necessary for alterations in the investor's proportionate interest in the investee arising from changes in the investee's equity that have not been included in the income statement. Such changes include those arising from the revaluation of property, plant, equipment and investments, from foreign exchange translation differences and from the adjustment of differences arising on business combinations.[139]

B *Elimination of profits on transactions with associates*

IAS 28 notes that the general principles regarding consolidation of subsidiaries are equally applicable to associates.[140] An interpretation of the application of these principles to transactions between an investor and its associate is given in SIC-3 *Elimination of Unrealised Profits and Losses on Transactions with Associates*. SIC-3 distinguishes between 'upstream' transactions (i.e. sales from the associate to the investor) and 'downstream' transactions (i.e. sales from the investor to the associate), for reasons that are not entirely apparent, since there is no difference in the prescribed accounting treatment, which is to eliminate any unrealised profit on such transactions to the extent of the investor's interest in the associate. However, unrealised losses should not be eliminated when they provide evidence of an impairment of the asset transferred.[141]

SIC-3 does not define what it means by an 'unrealised' profit, but the context makes it plain that it is referring to profits that have not been fully crystallised by onward sale to a third party by the investor or the associate as the case may be. SIC-3 also does not specify what balance sheet items should be adjusted on elimination of such profits, although it would, it our view, be reasonable to use the approach in ED 50, as discussed at 4.4.2 above. In other words, the adjustment should be made against the asset which was the subject of the transaction if it is held by the group or against the carrying amount for the associate if the asset is held by the associate.

The overall effect of SIC-3 is to ensure that unrealised profits and losses arising between investors and associates are treated consistently with those arising between investors and joint ventures (see 6.2.5 below).[142]

There is no guidance under IAS on the accounting treatment of transactions involving the contribution of non-monetary assets to associates (see 4.2.2 above for discussion of the treatment of UK GAAP). However, it would in our view be reasonable to adopt the treatment for contributions of assets to joint ventures set out in SIC-13 (see 6.2.5 A below).

C Goodwill on acquisition

On acquisition of the investment any difference (whether positive or negative) between the cost of acquisition and the investor's share of the fair values of the net identifiable assets of the associate is accounted for in accordance with IAS 22 – *Business Combinations* (see Chapter 6 at 5.4 and following). Appropriate adjustments are made to the investor's share of the post-acquisition results to account for:

- depreciation of the depreciable assets, based on their fair values; and
- amortisation of the difference between the cost of the investment and the investor's share of the fair values of the net identifiable assets.[143]

Neither IAS 28 nor IAS 22 specify whether the goodwill arising on acquisition of an associate should be accounted for separately or as part of the carrying amount of the investment in the associate (as would be the case under FRS 9). However, IAS 28's general description of the equity method (see A above) implies that the carrying amount must include goodwill. This is the treatment adopted by AngloGold, which contrasts it with its treatment of the goodwill arising on acquisition of subsidiaries and joint ventures.

Extract 7.22: AngloGold Limited (2000)

Notes to the group financial statements [extract]

Acquisition and goodwill arising thereon [extract]

...

Goodwill in respect of subsidiaries and proportionately consolidated joint ventures is disclosed as goodwill. Goodwill relating to associates is included within the carrying value of the investment in associates.

D Non-coterminous year-ends

Where the investor's year-end is different from that of the associate, the investor should normally use financial statements of the associate drawn up to the investor's reporting date. Where this is not practicable, however, financial statements drawn up to a different date may be used. IAS 28 does not place any restrictions on the latest date to which these must be drawn up, nor does it require accounts for an earlier date to be used. In the interests of consistency, the length of the reporting period of the financial statements of an associate used for consolidation purposes, and any difference between the reporting date of those statements and that of the investor, must be the same from period to period.[144]

It is not entirely clear, as a matter of drafting, whether IAS 28 intends the rules on the use of consistent periods to apply only in those cases when special accounts are prepared for consolidation purposes, or in all cases. We presume that the latter is intended.

Where non-coterminous accounts of associates are used for consolidation purposes, adjustments should be made for any significant events between the associate's balance sheet date and that of the investor.[145]

E Consistency of accounting policies

Where the investor's accounting policies are different from those of its associate, it should base the equity accounting for its associates on the associate's financial statements as adjusted to reflect the investor's accounting policies. IAS 28 states that, where it is not practicable to make such adjustments, 'that fact is generally disclosed', which curiously falls short of requiring companies to make such disclosure.[146] An example of a company disclosing that an associate's accounting policies may be different from its own is Nestlé.

> *Extract 7.23: Nestlé S.A. (2000)*
>
> **Accounting policies** [extract]
>
> **Associated companies**
>
> Companies where the Group has a participation of 20% or more and a significant influence but does not exercise management control are accounted for by the equity method. The net assets and results are recognised on the basis of the associates' own accounting policies, which may differ from those of the Group.

F Cumulative preference shares issued by associates

Where an associate has cumulative preference shares in issue, the investor's share of profits or losses should be calculated after adjusting for the preference dividends, whether these have been declared or not.[147]

G Losses of associates

An investor should generally account for its share of losses of an associate only to the extent that it reduces the carrying amount of its investment to zero. Additional losses should be provided for to the extent that the investor has incurred obligations or made payments on behalf of the associate to satisfy obligations of the associate that the investor has guaranteed or otherwise committed. If the associate subsequently reports profits, the investor resumes including its share of those profits only after its share of the profits equals the share of net losses not recognised[148] (i.e. in most cases, when its share of net assets becomes positive again). This treatment is commonly referred to as 'waterline' accounting (since movements in the carrying value below nil are ignored).

SIC-20 – *Equity Accounting Method – Recognition of Losses*, provides some clarification of these requirements, as follows.

The 'carrying amount' of its investment comprises only the carrying amount of instruments which provide unlimited rights of participation in earnings or losses and a residual equity interest in the investee.[149] Examples of financial interests in an associate falling outside this category might be preferred shares, loans, advances, debt securities, options to acquire ordinary shares and trade receivables. Such interests should be accounted for in accordance with other applicable standards, in particular IAS 39 (see Chapter 10 at 4.6).[150]

SIC-20 states that continuing losses of an associate should be considered as objective evidence of the impairment of all the investor's interests in the associate, not just of its residual equity interest.[151] Where the investor has guaranteed or is otherwise committed to obligations of the investee or to satisfying obligations of the investee, it may be necessary for it to provide not only for its share of the losses of the associate, but also for any additional losses that may result from its guarantees or other commitments.[152]

Where, in accordance with IAS 28, an investor has ceased to recognise its share of the losses of an investee, it should disclose its share of the unrecognised losses both for the period and cumulatively.[153]

H Impairment of associates

If there is an indication that an investment in an associate may be impaired, an enterprise should apply IAS 36 – *Impairment of Assets*, which is discussed in more detail in Chapter 13 at 4. In determining the value in use of the investment, an enterprise estimates:

- its share of the present value of the estimated future cash flows expected to be generated by the investee as a whole, including the cash flows from the operations of the investee and the proceeds on the ultimate disposal of the investment; or
- the present value of the estimated future cash flows expected to arise from dividends to be received from the investment and from its ultimate disposal.

IAS 28 states that both methods give the same result 'under appropriate assumptions', whereas it could be argued that they should be the same as a matter of fact. Any resulting impairment loss for the investment is allocated in accordance with IAS 36, and therefore allocated first to any remaining goodwill.[154]

The recoverable amount of each associate should be assessed individually, unless an individual associate does not generate cash inflows from continuing use that are largely independent of those from other assets of the reporting enterprise.[155]

I Income Taxes

Income taxes arising from investments in associates are accounted for in accordance with IAS 12.[156] This will often lead to full provision for deferred tax on the investor's share of the retained reserves of associates (see Chapter 24 at 7.2.8).

J Contingencies

The investor should disclose:

- its share of the contingent liabilities and capital commitments of an associate for which it is also contingently liable; and
- those contingent liabilities that arise because the investor is severally liable for all the liabilities of the associate.[157]

IAS 28 comments that this is in accordance with IAS 37 – *Provisions, Contingent Liabilities and Contingent Assets*, which is discussed in Chapter 28 at 7.

6.1.5 Disclosure

In addition to the various other disclosures mentioned above, an investor should disclose:

- an appropriate listing and description of significant associates including the proportion of ownership interest and, if different, the proportion of voting power held; and
- the methods used to account for such investments.[158]

Investments in associates accounted for using the equity method should be classified as long-term assets and disclosed as a separate item in the balance sheet. The investor's share of the profits or losses of such investments should be disclosed as a separate item in the income statement. The investor's share of any extraordinary or prior period items should also be separately disclosed.[159]

An example of some of these disclosures is given in the accounts of AngloGold.

Extract 7.24: AngloGold Limited (2000)

Group income statement [extract]
Figures in million

1999	**2000**		Notes	**2000**	1999
US Dollars				**SA Rands**	
2,324	**2,299**	**Revenue**	3	**15,972**	14,197
2,205	**2,208**	Gold sales	3	**15,338**	13,473
(1,700)	**(1,740)**	Cost of sales	4	**(12,065)**	(10,385)
505	**468**	**Operating profit**		**3,273**	3,088
(29)	**(25)**	Corporate administration and other expenses		**(175)**	(179)
(15)	**(12)**	Market development costs		**(82)**	(91)
(7)	**(8)**	Research and development costs		**(54)**	(43)
(47)	**(44)**	Exploration costs	5	**(309)**	(287)
407	**379**	**Profit from operations**		**2,653**	2,488
4	**10**	Other net income	6	**73**	25
84	**45**	Investment income	7	**302**	511
(53)	**(69)**	Finance costs	8	**(481)**	(321)
407	**379**	**Profit from operations**		**2,653**	2,488

Accounting policies [extract]

Associates

The equity method of accounting is used for an investment over which the group exercises significant influence and normally owns between 20 per cent and 50 per cent of the voting equity. Associates are equity accounted from the effective dates of acquisition, to the effective dates of disposal.

Results of associates are equity accounted from their most recent audited financial statements or unaudited interim financial statements. Any losses of associates are brought to account in the consolidated financial statements until the investment in such associates is written down to a nominal amount. Thereafter, losses are accounted for only insofar as the group is committed to providing financial support to such associates.

The carrying values of the investments in associates represent the cost of each investment, including unamortised goodwill, the share of post-acquisition retained earnings and any other movements in reserves. The carrying value of associates is reviewed on a regular basis and if any impairment in value has occurred, it is written off in the period in which these circumstances are identified.

7 Investment income

1999	2000		2000	1999
US Dollars			SA Rands	
		Investment income consists of the following principal categories:		
72	**37**	Interest receivable (note 3)	**250**	437
7	**4**	Income from associates before taxation	**27**	43
4	**4**	Growth in AngloGold Environment Rehabilitation Trust (note 19)	**25**	26
1	**–**	Dividends received from other investments (note 3)	**–**	5
84	**45**		**302**	511

16 Investment in associates

1999	2000		2000	1999
US Dollars			SA Rands	
		The group has the following associated undertakings:		
		A 42.73% (1999: 42.73%) interest in Rand Refinery Limited, which is involved in the refining of bullion and by-products which are sourced inter alia from South Africa and foreign gold producing mining companies. The year end of Rand Refinery Limited is 30 September.		
		A 25% (1999: Nil) interest in Oro Group (Proprietary) Limited which is involved in the manufacture and wholesale of jewellery. The year end of Oro Group (Proprietary) Limited is March. Equity accounting is based on the results for the six months ended 30 September 2000.		
		Carrying value of associates consists of:		
1	**1**	Unlisted shares at cost	**9**	9
12	**9**	Share of retained earnings	**71**	71
–	**4**	Profit after taxation	**26**	–
–	**7**	Acquisitions	**55**	–
–	**(2)**	Dividends	**(12)**	–
–	**–**	Disposals	**(1)**	–
–	**1**	Translation adjustment	**–**	–
13	**20**	Carrying value	**148**	80
13	**20**	Directors' valuation of unlisted associates	**148**	80
		The group's effective share of certain balance sheet items of its associates are as follows:		
11	**11**	Non-current assets	**79**	65
10	**12**	Current assets	**94**	62
21	**23**	Total assets	**173**	127
1	**4**	Non-current liabilities	**34**	6
7	**5**	Current liabilities	**37**	41
8	**9**	Total equity and liabilities	**71**	47
13	**14**	Net assets	**102**	80
		Reconciliation of the carrying value of investments in associates with net assets:		
13	**14**	Net assets	**102**	80
–	**6**	Goodwill	**46**	–
13	**20**	Carrying value of investments in associates	**148**	80

A *Profit and loss account*

IAS 28 requires that the results of associates included in the income statement should be separately disclosed, but does not specify the 'level' of the income statement at which they should be included. As can be seen from Extract 7.24 above, AngloGold includes the pre-tax results of its associates as part of investment income, below operating profit.

Nokia includes the results of associates at a similar level, but discloses them on the face of the profit and loss account.

Extract 7.25: Nokia Corporation (2000)

Consolidated profit and loss account, IAS [extract]

Financial year ended December 31	**2000 EURm**	1999 EURm
Net sales	**30 376**	19 772
Cost of goods sold	**-19 072**	-12 227
Research and development expenses	**-2 584**	-1 755
Selling, general and administrative expenses	**-2 804**	-1 811
Amortization of goodwill	**-140**	-71
Operating profit	**5 776**	3 908
Share of results of associated companies	**-16**	-5
Financial income and expenses	**102**	-58
Profit before tax and minority interests	**5 862**	3 845

...

Although Nokia, unlike AngloGold, does not specify whether these amounts are its share of the pre- or post-tax results of its associates, it appears from the notes to the accounts almost certain that they are the post-tax results.

Nestlé, however, includes the post-tax results of its associates as the last item in its group profit and loss account.

Extract 7.26: Nestlé S.A. (2000)

Consolidated income statement [extract]

In millions of CHF	Notes	**2000**	1999
Profit before taxes		**8,341**	6,859
Taxes		**(2,761)**	(2,314)
Net profit of consolidated companies		**5,580**	4,545
Share of profit attributable to minority interests		**(212)**	(160)
Share of results of associated companies	6	**395**	339
Net profit for the year		**5,763**	4,724

6. Share of results of associated companies

In millions of CHF	**2000**	1999
Share of profit before taxes	**605**	521
Less share of taxes	**(210)**	(182)
Share of profit after taxes	**395**	339

12. Investments in associated companies

This item primarily includes the Group's indirect (26,3%) participation in the equity of L'Oréal, Paris for CHF 1986 million (1999: CHF. 1683 million). Its market value at 31st December 2000 amounts to CHF 24 689 million (1999: CHF. 22 814 million).

B Cash flow statement

The treatment of cash flows between an investor and its associates is addressed in IAS 7 – *Cash Flow Statements*, and is discussed in Chapter 29 at 4.1.4.

6.1.6 *Comparison with UK GAAP*

There are a number of differences between the accounting treatment of associates under FRS 9 and IAS 28, which FRS 9 seeks, not altogether convincingly, to portray as 'minor',[160] as follows:

A Exercise of significant influence

Under FRS 9, an investor has actually to exercise significant influence over an investment for it to be treated as an associate. Under IAS 28, it is sufficient to be in a position to exercise such influence. FRS 9 seeks to play down this important difference of emphasis with the argument that 'the best evidence of an entity's ability to exercise significant influence is the fact that it is exercising such influence'.[161] Under IAS 28, a holding of 20% or more of the voting rights is presumed to give rise to significant influence. Whilst this is also true under FRS 9, it suggests that this presumption may be rebutted relatively frequently.

B Exclusions from equity accounting

IAS 28 excludes from equity accounting any investment that is acquired and held exclusively for subsequent disposal in the near future. FRS 9 does not have a specific exclusion for such investments, although it notes that the definition of 'participating interest' (see 2.1.1 A above) will produce much the same result.[162]

IAS 28 also excludes from equity accounting any investment that operates under severe long-term restrictions that significantly impair its ability to transfer funds to the investor. FRS 9 has no such specific exclusion. However, Appendix II to FRS 9 states that the definition of 'exercise of significant influence' (see 2.1.1 B above) is unlikely to be fulfilled in respect of such an investment, such that the overall effect is the same. It is not entirely clear how this statement can be reconciled to FRS 9's requirement to disclose details of 'significant' restrictions on the ability of an associate or joint venture to distribute its profits (see 5.1.3 above). The implication seems to be that an investor can exercise significant influence over an investee subject to 'significant', but not 'severe', restrictions.

C Single entity accounts

Where an investor does not have any subsidiaries, IAS 28 permits associates either to be equity accounted for or to be carried at cost (or valuation). FRS 9 (and the Companies Act) requires them to be carried at cost (or valuation).

D Application of the equity method

IAS 28 simply requires that 'the income statement reflects the share of the results of the operations of the investee'. FRS 9 is much more specific, requiring the investing group's share of the results to be included at every main level of the profit and loss account except turnover and other components of operating profit. However, IAS 28 requires that the net investment in associates should be included as a separate item in the balance sheet and the share of profits should be separately disclosed in the income statement, with disclosure of the investor's share of any extraordinary or prior period items.

Under FRS 9, losses of associates must continue to be accounted for until some event occurs that marks the investor's irreversible withdrawal. Under IAS 28, the treatment is to account for losses only until the investment is reduced to zero unless the investor has an obligation to make good those losses.

E Disclosures

There is no equivalent in IAS 28 for the additional disclosures required by FRS 9 where total associates represent more than 15% (or an individual associate represents more than 25%) of the group.

6.2 Accounting for joint ventures

The relevant international standard is IAS 31 – *Financial Reporting of Interests in Joint Ventures*, which has been the subject of an SIC Interpretation, SIC–13 – *Jointly Controlled Entities – Non-Monetary Contributions by Venturers.*

6.2.1 *Definitions*

The standard defines a joint venture as 'a contractual arrangement whereby two or more parties ('venturers') undertake an economic activity which is subject to joint control'. A 'venturer' is a party to a joint venture and has joint control over it, as opposed to an 'investor', which is a party to a joint venture and does have not joint control over it. Joint control is the 'contractually agreed sharing of control over an economic activity', control being defined as 'the power to govern the financial and operating policies of an economic activity so as to obtain benefits from it'.[163]

A Forms of Joint Venture

IAS 31 identifies three broad types of joint venture:

- jointly controlled operations (see 6.2.2 below);
- jointly controlled assets (see 6.2.3 below); or
- jointly controlled entities (see 6.2.4 below).

Whatever their form, however, all joint ventures share the common characteristics that two or more venturers are bound by a contractual arrangement which establishes joint control.[164]

B Contractual arrangement

It is the existence of a contractual arrangement that distinguishes interests which involve joint control from investments in associates in which the investor has significant influence. Activities which have no contractual arrangement to establish joint control are not joint ventures for the purposes of IAS 31.[165]

The contractual arrangement may be evidenced in a number of ways, for example by a contract between the venturers or minutes of discussions between the venturers. In some cases, the arrangement is incorporated in the articles or other by-laws of the joint venture. Whatever its form, the contractual arrangement is usually in writing and deals with such matters as:

- the activity, duration and reporting obligations of the joint venture;
- the appointment of the board of directors or equivalent governing body of the joint venture and the voting rights of the venturers;
- capital contributions by the venturers; and
- the sharing by the venturers of the output, income, expenses or results of the joint venture.[166]

The effect of a contractual arrangement is to establish joint control over the joint venture, so that no single venturer is in a position to exercise unilateral control over the activity. The arrangement identifies those decisions in areas essential to the goals of the joint venture which require the consent of all the venturers and those decisions which may require the consent of a specified majority of the venturers.[167]

C *Investors without joint control*

An investor in a joint venture that does not participate in joint control of the venture should account for its investment in accordance with IAS 39 – *Financial Instruments: Recognition and Measurement* (see Chapter 10), or, if it has significant influence over the venture, in accordance with IAS 28 – *Accounting for Associates* (see 6.1 above). An investor that issues consolidated financial statement may report its investment at cost in its individual financial statements.[168]

D *Operators or managers of a joint venture*

The contractual arrangement may identify one venturer as the operator or manager of the joint venture. However, the operator does not control the joint venture but acts within the financial and operating policies which have been agreed by the venturers in accordance with the contractual arrangement and delegated to the operator. If the operator does have the power to govern the financial and operating policies of the economic activity, it controls the venture and the venture is a subsidiary of the operator rather than a joint venture of all the parties.[169]

Where a venturer acts as operator or manager, it will usually receive a management fee, which it should account for in accordance with IAS 18 – *Revenue* (see Chapter 3). Such fees are accounted for by the joint venture itself as an expense.[170]

6.2.2 *Jointly controlled operations*

A jointly controlled operation is one which involves the use of assets and other resources of the venturers, rather than the establishment of an entity or financial structure separate from the venturers themselves. Each venturer uses its own property, plant and equipment and carries its own inventories. It also incurs its own expenses and liabilities and raises its own finance, which represent its own obligations. The joint venture activities may be carried out by the venturer's employees alongside similar activities of the venturer. The joint venture agreement usually provides the basis for sharing among the venturers the revenue sales of the joint product and any common expenses incurred.[171]

An example of a jointly controlled operation might be that two or more venturers combine their operations, resources and expertise in order jointly to manufacture, market and distribute a particular product, such as an aircraft, with each venturer undertaking different parts of the manufacturing process. Each venturer bears its own costs and takes a share of the revenue from the sale of the aircraft, such share being determined in accordance with the contractual arrangement.[172]

In respect of its interest in a jointly controlled operation, IAS 31 requires a venturer to recognise in both its own and its consolidated financial statements:

- the assets that it controls and the liabilities that it incurs; and
- the expenses that it incurs and its share of the income that it earns from the sale of goods or services by the joint venture.[173]

Because the assets, liabilities, income and expenses are already recognised in the financial statements of the venturer, no adjustments or other consolidation procedures are required in respect of these items when the venturer presents consolidated financial statements. Separate accounting records may not be required for the joint venture itself and financial statements may not be prepared for the joint venture, although the venturers may prepare management accounts so that they may assess the performance of the joint venture.[174]

6.2.3 *Jointly controlled assets*

Some joint ventures involve the joint control and/or ownership of one or more assets contributed to, or acquired for, the joint venture and dedicated to the purposes of the joint venture. The assets are used to obtain benefits for the venturers, who may each take a share of the output from the assets and bear an agreed share of the expenses incurred. Such ventures do not involve the establishment of an entity or financial structure separate from the venturers themselves, so that each venturer has control over its share of future economic benefits through its share in the jointly controlled asset.[175]

IAS 31 notes that joint ventures of this type are particularly common in extractive industries. For example, a number of oil companies may jointly control and operate an oil pipeline. Each venturer uses the pipeline to transport its own product in return for which it bears an agreed proportion of the expenses of operating the pipeline. Another example of a jointly controlled asset could be that two enterprises jointly control a property, each taking a share of the rents received and bearing a share of the expenses.[176]

In respect of its interest in jointly controlled assets, IAS 31 requires a venturer to recognise in both its own and its consolidated financial statements:

- its share of the jointly controlled assets, classified according to the nature of the assets (e.g. a share in a jointly controlled pipeline should be shown within plant, property and equipment rather than as an investment);
- any liabilities which it has incurred;
- its share of any liabilities incurred jointly with the other venturers;
- any income from the sale or use of its share of the output of the joint venture, together with its share of any expenses incurred by the joint venture; and
- any expenses which it has incurred in respect of its interest in the joint venture (e.g. those relating to financing the venturer's interest in the assets and selling its share of the output).[177]

The IASC believes that this treatment reflects the substance and economic reality and, usually, the legal form of the joint venture. Because the assets, liabilities, income and expenses are already recognised in the financial statements of the venturer, no adjustments or other consolidation procedures are required in respect of these items when the venturer presents consolidated financial statements. Separate accounting records may not be required for the joint venture itself and financial statements may not be prepared for the joint venture, although the venturers may prepare management accounts so that they may assess the performance of the joint venture.[178]

6.2.4 *Jointly controlled entities*

A jointly controlled entity is a joint venture which involves the establishment of a corporation, partnership or other entity in which each venturer has an interest. The entity operates in the same way as other enterprises, except that a contractual arrangement between the venturers establishes joint control over the economic activity of the entity.[179]

A jointly controlled entity controls the assets of the joint venture, incurs liabilities and expenses and earns income. It may enter into contracts in its own name and raise finance for the purposes of the joint venture activity. Each venturer is entitled to a share of the results of the jointly controlled entity, although some jointly controlled entities also involve a sharing of output.[180]

A common example of a jointly controlled entity is that two enterprises combine their activities in a particular line of business by transferring the relevant assets and liabilities into a jointly controlled entity. Another example might be that an enterprise, in order to commence a business in a foreign country in conjunction with the government or other agency in that country, establishes a separate entity which is jointly controlled by the enterprise and the government or agency.[181]

IAS 31 notes that many jointly controlled entities are similar in substance to those joint ventures referred to as jointly controlled operations or jointly controlled assets (see 6.4.2 and 6.4.3 above). For example, the venturers may transfer a jointly controlled asset, such as an oil pipeline, into a jointly controlled entity, for tax or other reasons. Similarly, the venturers may contribute into a jointly controlled entity assets which will be operated jointly. Some jointly controlled operations also involve the establishment of a jointly controlled entity to deal with particular aspects of the activity, for example, the design, marketing, distribution or after-sales service of the product.[182]

Another feature of a jointly controlled entity is that it maintains its own accounting records and prepares and presents financial statements in the same way as other enterprises in conformity with the appropriate national requirements and IAS. Each venturer usually contributes cash or other resources to the jointly controlled entity. These contributions are included in the accounting records of the venturer and recognised in its separate financial statements as an investment in the jointly controlled entity.[183]

A Benchmark Treatment – Proportionate consolidation

In its consolidated financial statements, a venturer should include its interest in a joint venture entity by means of proportionate consolidation (subject to the allowed alternative treatment of equity accounting – see B below) .[184] IAS 31 notes that the procedures for consolidation of subsidiaries set out in IAS 27 – *Consolidated Financial Statements and Accounting for Investments in Subsidiaries* – will generally be appropriate for the proportionate consolidation of joint ventures.[185] IAS 27 is discussed in Chapter 5 at 6.

Proportionate consolidation should be carried out either:

- on an aggregated line-by-line basis (i.e. the venturer includes its share of the assets, liabilities, income and expenditure of the entity within the corresponding items in its own consolidated accounts); or
- as separate items (i.e. the venturer includes separate line items for its share of the total assets, liabilities, income and expenditure of the entity in its own consolidated accounts. Thus for example the item 'debtors' in the group accounts would include a sub-heading 'share of debtors of joint ventures').[186]

IAS 31 states that, whatever format is used to give effect to proportionate consolidation, it is inappropriate to offset any assets or liabilities by the deduction of other liabilities or assets or any income or expenses by the deduction of other expenses or income, unless a legal right of set-off exists and the offsetting represents the expectation as to the realisation of the asset or the settlement of the liability.[187]

Proportionate consolidation of a jointly controlled entity should cease on the date that the venturer ceases to have joint control over the entity. IAS 31 adds somewhat unnecessarily that this may occur either when the venturer disposes of its investment or when external restrictions are placed on the entity.[188]

B Allowed alternative treatment – Equity accounting

IAS 31 also permits equity accounting for jointly controlled entities in consolidated financial statements in accordance with IAS 28 (see 6.1 above). However, this treatment is not recommended since, in the IASC's view, proportionate consolidation better reflects the substance and economic reality of an venturer's interest in a jointly controlled entity.[189] To some extent, the IASC was probably compelled to permit equity accounting as an allowed alternative treatment by the fact that proportionate consolidation is not permitted for all joint ventures in all jurisdictions. In the UK for example, the Companies Act 1985 prohibits the proportional consolidation of corporate joint ventures (see 2.2.2 above).

Where equity accounting is used, it should be discontinued from the date on which it ceases to have joint control over, or significant influence in, the jointly controlled entity.[190]

C Interests held for resale or subject to long-term restrictions

An interest in a jointly controlled entity that is either acquired and held exclusively for resale in the near future, or operates under severe long-term restrictions that significantly impair its ability to transfer funds to the venturer, should be accounted for as an investment in accordance with IAS 39 – *Financial Instruments: Recognition and Measurement* (see Chapter 10 at 4.6).[191]

D Jointly controlled entity becoming a subsidiary

IAS 31 feels it necessary to state that where a jointly controlled entity becomes a subsidiary it should, from that date, be accounted for as a subsidiary in accordance with IAS 27 – *Consolidated Financial Statements and Accounting for Investments in Subsidiaries* (see Chapter 5 at 6).[192]

E Individual financial statements of venturer

IAS 31 expresses no preference for the treatment of jointly controlled entities in a venturer's individual financial statements, on the grounds that in many countries separate financial statements are presented by a venturer in order to meet a variety of needs, with the result that different reporting practices are in use in different countries.[193] It seems rather curious that this consideration did not prevent the IASC from prescribing accounting treatments for subsidiaries and associates in the individual financial statements of investors in IAS 27 (see Chapter 5 at 6) and IAS 28 (see 6.1 above).

6.2.5 *Transactions between a venturer and a joint venture*

When a venturer contributes or sells assets to a joint venture, the recognition of any gain or loss should reflect the substance of the transaction. While the assets are retained by the joint venture, and provided that the venturer has transferred the significant risks and rewards of ownership, the venturer should recognise only that portion of the gain or loss which is attributable to the interests of the other venturers. The venturer should recognise the full amount of any loss when the contribution or sale provides evidence of a reduction in the net realisable value of current assets or an impairment loss.[194]

When a venturer purchases assets from a joint venture, the venturer should not recognise its share of the profits of the joint venture from the transaction until it resells the assets to an independent party. A venturer should recognise its share of the losses resulting from these transactions in the same way as profits except that losses should be recognised immediately when they represent a reduction in the net realisable value of current assets or an impairment loss.[195]

The venturer should assess whether a transaction between itself and a joint venture provides evidence of impairment of any asset transferred in accordance with IAS 36 – *Impairment of Assets*,[196] which is discussed in Chapter 13 at 4.

A Transfer of non-monetary assets in exchange for equity in jointly controlled entities

SIC-13 – *Jointly Controlled Entities – Non-Monetary Contributions by Venturers* provides guidance on the application of these general principles to the specific situation of a transfer of non-monetary assets to a jointly controlled entity in exchange for equity. This states that the venturer should recognise in its income statement the portion of any gain or loss arising on the transfer attributable to the other venturers unless:

- significant risks and rewards of ownership of the contributed non-monetary asset(s) have not been transferred to the jointly controlled entity;
- the gain or loss on the non-monetary contribution cannot be measured reliably; or
- the non-monetary assets contributed are similar to those contributed by the other venturers. Non-monetary assets are similar to those contributed by other venturers when they have a similar nature, a similar use in the same line of business and a similar fair value. A contribution is 'similar' for this purpose only if all of the significant component assets are similar to those contributed by the other venturers.[197]

If any of the above conditions applies, the gain or loss arising would be considered unrealised (and therefore not recognised in the income statements), unless in addition to receiving an equity interest in the entity, a venturer receives monetary or non-monetary assets dissimilar to those it contributed, in which case an 'appropriate portion' of the gain or loss on the transaction should be recognised by the venturer. SIC-13 does not elaborate on what would constitute an appropriate portion of the gain or loss in such circumstances (see the discussion on this issue under UK GAAP at 4.2.3 C II above).[198]

Where the venturer accounts for the jointly controlled entity using proportionate consolidation, any unrealised gains or losses should be eliminated against the venturer's share of the underlying assets of the entity. Where equity accounting is used, the elimination should be against the carrying value of the investment in the entity. Unrealised gains or losses should not be accounted for as deferred income or expenditure.[199]

6.2.6 Disclosure

The following disclosures should be made in the consolidated accounts of a venturer, and in the single entity accounts of a venturer that does not present consolidated accounts because it does not have subsidiaries.[200]

A Interests in joint ventures

A venturer should disclose a listing and description of interests in significant joint ventures and the proportion of ownership interest held in jointly controlled entities. A venturer which reports its interests in jointly controlled entities using the line-by-line reporting format for proportionate consolidation or the equity method should disclose the aggregate amounts of each of current assets, long-term assets, current liabilities, long-term liabilities, income and expenses related to its interests in joint ventures.[201]

B Contingencies and commitments

A venturer should disclose the aggregate amount of the following contingent liabilities, unless the probability of loss is remote, separately from the amount of other contingent liabilities:

- any contingent liabilities that the venturer has incurred in relation to its interests in joint ventures and its share in each of the contingent liabilities which have been incurred jointly with other venturers;
- its share of the contingent liabilities of the joint ventures themselves for which it is contingently liable; and;
- those contingent liabilities that arise because the venturer is contingently liable for the liabilities of the other venturers of a joint venture.[202]

A venturer should also disclose the aggregate amount of the following commitments in respect of its interests in joint ventures separately from other commitments:

- any capital commitments of the venturer in relation to its interests in joint ventures and its share in the capital commitments that have been incurred jointly with other venturers; and
- its share of the capital commitments of the joint ventures themselves.[203]

Examples of some of these disclosures are given by AngloGold, which accounts for its joint ventures using the line-by-line format for proportionate consolidation.

Extract 7.27: AngloGold Limited (2000)

1 Accounting policies [extract]

Joint ventures

A joint venture is an entity which the group holds a long-term interest and which is jointly controlled by the group and one or more other venturers under a contractual arrangement. The group's interest in a jointly controlled entity is accounted for by proportionate consolidation.

18 Interest in joint ventures

1999	**2000**			**2000**	1999
US Dollars				SA Rands	
		18	Interest in joint ventures		
			The group's effective share of income, expenses, assets, liabilities and cash flows of joint ventures, which are included in the consolidated financial statements, are as follows:		
			Income statement		
108	**133**		Gold sales	**902**	661
70	**80**		Cost of sales	**544**	428
38	**53**		Operating profit	**358**	233
5	**(1)**		Other net income	**(7)**	32
2	**3**		Investment income	**21**	12
(14)	**(16)**		Finance costs	**(106)**	(87)
31	**39**		Profit on ordinary activities before taxation	**266**	190
			Balance sheet		
65	**573**		Non-current assets	**4,344**	403
55	**110**		Current assets	**836**	338
120	**683**		Total assets	**5,180**	741
3	**425**		Shareholders' equity	**3,223**	22
3	**3**		Minority interests	**23**	21
			Non-current liabilities		
74	**172**		Interest-bearing borrowings	**1,304**	453
1	**2**		Provisions	**18**	7
			Current liabilities		
28	**47**		Interest-bearing borrowings	**354**	171
11	**34**		Other	**258**	67
120	**683**		Total equity and liabilities	**5,180**	741
			Cash flow statement		
42	**172**		Cash flows from operating activities	**1,167**	256
(3)	**(150)**		Cash flows from investing activities	**(1,017)**	(18)
(29)	**(33)**		Cash flows from financing activities	**(224)**	(177)
10	**(11)**		Net (decrease) increase in cash and cash equivalents	**(74)**	61

6.2.7 Comparison with UK GAAP

Of the three types of joint venture in IAS 31 'jointly controlled operations' and 'jointly controlled assets' will generally be equivalent to a JANE (or a structure with the form but not the substance of a joint venture) under FRS 9, and accounted for in the same way. While a 'jointly controlled entity' under IAS 31 is broadly equivalent to a 'joint venture' under FRS 9, the accounting treatment is quite different, since FRS 9 requires joint ventures to be equity accounted, whereas under IAS 31, the benchmark treatment is proportional consolidation, with equity accounting being merely an allowed (and strongly discouraged) alternative.

There is no equivalent in IAS 31 for the additional disclosures required by FRS 9 where total joint ventures represent more than 15% (or an individual joint venture represents more than 25%) of the group.

7 POSSIBLE FUTURE DEVELOPMENTS

About three years ago, the whole question of accounting for associates and joint ventures became the subject of some debate by the G4+1 group. At a meeting in March 1999, the G4+1 discussed a preliminary paper on the underlying rationale for equity accounting. As a result of those discussions it was agreed to explore limiting the use of equity accounting to jointly controlled entities, with full consolidation being used for controlled entities and other investments being marked to market.[204]

Building on these proposals, in October 1999 the G4+1 group issued a paper on accounting for joint ventures, which proposed the abolition of the proportional consolidation method, with equity accounting being used instead.[205] The IASC did not progress either of these projects significantly further, and the new IASB has so far shown little interest in them.

We are far from convinced that there is any need for a radical change from current practice in either of these areas. Indeed we think that the proposed abolition of equity accounting for associates would be a retrograde step. With all its faults, equity accounting for associates has generally served its purpose very well for nearly thirty years. It would, in our view, be a mistake to abandon it in the pursuit of what many will see as a somewhat esoteric conceptual purity, particularly when the proposed alternative will be generally perceived as a less robust method of accounting, given the absence of reliable market values for large holdings of unquoted securities, which currently comprise the great majority of equity accounted investments.

References

1 CA 85, Sch. 4A, para. 22.
2 FRS 9, *Associates and Joint Ventures*, ASB, November 1997, Appendix III, para. 3.
3 *Ibid.*, para. 2.11.
4 CA 85, Sch. 4A, para. 19(1)(a).
5 Throughout FRS 9 and this Chapter, 'subsidiary' means 'subsidiary undertaking' as defined in FRS 2 and the Companies Act 1985 (see Chapter 5).
6 FRS 9, para. 4.
7 CA 85, Schedule 4A, para. 20(1)(a).
8 FRS 9, para. 4.
9 *Ibid.*
10 *Ibid.*
11 *Ibid.*, para. 43.
12 *Ibid.*, para. 13.
13 SSAP 1, *Accounting for associated companies*, ASC, 1971, amended 1982 and 1990, para. 13.
14 Examples included Norcros p.l.c. (see annual report for year ended 31 March 1998) and William Baird PLC (see annual report for year ended 31 December 1998). Norcros restated its former associate at cost, whereas William Baird revalued it to net asset value under the alternative accounting rules (with the result that the carrying amount of the investment remained unchanged, but the previously equity accounted profits were transferred to the revaluation reserve).
15 FRS 9, para. 4.
16 *Ibid.*
17 *Ibid.*, para. 16.
18 Daily Mail and General Trust plc, Annual Report and Accounts 1999, note 23.
19 FRS 9, para. 14.
20 *Ibid.*, para. 15.
21 *Ibid.*, para. 16.
22 *Ibid.*, para. 4.
23 FRS 8, *Related party disclosures*, ASB, October 1995, para. 2.5(a)(iii).
24 FRS 9, para. 17.
25 CA 85, Sch. 4A, para. 20.
26 *Ibid.*, s 260(1).
27 *Ibid.*, s 260(3).
28 FRS 9, para. 4.
29 *Ibid.*
30 CA 85, s 258.
31 FRS 9, para. 4.
32 *Ibid.*, para. 12.
33 *Ibid.*, para. 10.
34 *Ibid.*, para. 11.
35 CA 85 s 229(3); FRS 2, *Accounting for subsidiary undertakings*, ASB, July 1992, para. 25a.
36 CA 85, Sch. 4A, para. 19.
37 FRS 9, para. 4
38 *Ibid.*, Appendix III, para. 13
39 FRS 9, para. 8.
40 *Ibid.*, paras. 24 and 25.
41 *Ibid.*, Appendix I, para. 6.
42 FRS 9, para. 9.
43 *Ibid.*, paras. 8 and 9.
44 *Ibid.*, para. 4
45 *Ibid.*, para. 27
46 *Ibid.*
47 *Ibid.*
48 FRS 3, *Reporting financial performance*, ASB, October 1992, para. 39.
49 FRS 9, para. 27.
50 *Ibid.*, para. 61.
51 *Ibid.*, para. 27.
52 *Ibid.*, para. 28.
53 *Ibid.*, para. 29.
54 CA 85, Sch. 4, para. 12(a).
55 FRS 9, para. 26.
56 *Ibid.*, para. 4.
57 *Ibid.*, para. 21.
58 *Ibid.*
59 *Ibid.*, Appendix III, para. 7(b).
60 FRS 9, para. 23.
61 *Ibid.*, para. 22.
62 *Ibid.*, Appendix III, para. 13.
63 FRS 9, para. 23.
64 FRS 3, para. 14.
65 FRS 9, para 49.
66 *Ibid.*
67 *Ibid.*, paras. 18 and 24.
68 *Ibid.*, para. 31(a).
69 *Ibid.*, para. 35.
70 *Ibid.*, para. 31(a).
71 *Ibid.*
72 *Ibid.*, para. 32.
73 *Ibid.*, para. 31(b).
74 FRS 2, para. 39.
75 ED 50, *Consolidated accounts*, ASC, June 1990, para. 115.
76 FRS 9, para. 36.
77 Draft Abstract *Exchanges of businesses or other non-monetary assets for equity in a subsidiary, joint venture or associate*, UITF, May 2001, para. 2.
78 FRRP PN 68, July 2001.
79 Draft Abstract *Exchanges of businesses or other non-monetary assets for equity in a subsidiary, joint venture or associate*, para. 12.
80 *Ibid.*
81 *Ibid.*
82 FRRP PN 43, October 1996.

83 Draft Abstract *Exchanges of businesses or other non-monetary assets for equity in a subsidiary, joint venture or associate*, para. 13.
84 FRS 9, para. 31(b).
85 *Ibid.*, paras. 31(c) and 35.
86 *Ibid.*, para. 31(d).
87 *Ibid.*
88 *Ibid.*, para. 37.
89 CA 85, Schedule 4A, para. 2(2); FRS 2, para. 43
90 FRS 9, para. 31(d).
91 *Ibid*, para. 35.
92 *Ibid.*, paras. 31(a).
93 FRS 10, *Goodwill and Intangible Assets*, ASB, December 1997, para. 19(b).
94 FRS 9, para. 38.
95 *Ibid.*, para. 39.
96 *Ibid.*, para. 32.
97 *Ibid.*, para. 34.
98 *Ibid.*, para. 33.
99 *Ibid.*
100 *Ibid.*, para. 34.
101 *Ibid.*, paras. 44-45.
102 *Ibid.*, paras. 46-47.
103 *Ibid.*, para. 40.
104 *Ibid.*
105 *Ibid.*
106 *Ibid.*, para. 42.
107 *Ibid.*, para. 43.
108 Discussion paper, *Derivatives and other financial instruments*, ASB, July 1996, paras. 1.4.1 and 2.5.1. Consultation paper *Financial Instruments and Similar Items*, JWG, December 2000, draft standard, para. 1(a).
109 FRS 9, para. 41.
110 *Ibid.*, para. 52.
111 *Ibid.*, para. 53.
112 *Ibid.*, para. 54.
113 FRS 2, para. 53.
114 FRS 9, para. 55.
115 CA 85, Schs. 4, 9 and 9A, Balance sheet formats, Sch. 4A para. 21, Sch. 9, Pt. II, para. 3, Sch. 9A Pt. II, paras. 3 and 4.
116 FRS 9, para. 55.
117 *Ibid.*, para. 56.
118 FRS 9, para. 57.
119 *Ibid.*, para. 58(a).
120 *Ibid.*, para. 58(b).
121 *Ibid.*, para. 58(c).
122 *Ibid.*
123 *Ibid.*, para. 58.
124 CA 85, Sch. 5, Part II, para. 22.
125 *Ibid.*, Sch. 4A, para. 21; Sch. 5, Part II, para. 23
126 *Ibid.*, Sch. 5, Part II, para. 21.
127 IAS 28, *Accounting for investments in associates*, IASC, revised October 2000, para. 3.
128 *Ibid.*, para. 4.
129 *Ibid.*, para. 5.
130 SIC–D33 *Consolidation and Equity Method – Potential Voting Rights*, SIC, September 2001.
131 IAS 28, para. 8.
132 *Ibid.*, para. 3.
133 *Ibid.*, para. 11.
134 *Ibid.*, para. 8 and IAS 39 (revised 2000) *Financial Instruments: Recognition and Measurement*, IASC, March 1999 and October 2000, para. 1(a).
135 IAS 28, para. 12.
136 *Ibid.*, para. 13.
137 *Ibid.*, para 14.
138 *Ibid.*, para. 15.
139 *Ibid.*, para. 6.
140 *Ibid.*, para. 16.
141 SIC-3, *Elimination of Unrealised Profits and Losses on Transactions with Associates*, SIC, July 1997, paras. 1-4.
142 *Ibid.*, paras. 5-7.
143 IAS 28., para. 17.
144 *Ibid.*, para. 18.
145 *Ibid.*, para. 19.
146 *Ibid.*, para. 20.
147 IAS 28, para. 21.
148 *Ibid.*, para. 22.
149 SIC-20 – *Equity Accounting Method – Recognition of Losses*, SIC, August 1999, paras. 5 and 12.
150 *Ibid.*, paras. 1, 7 and 12.
151 *Ibid.*, paras. 8 and 14.
152 *Ibid.*, para. 9 and 15.
153 *Ibid.*, para. 10.
154 IAS 28, para. 23.
155 *Ibid.*, para. 24.
156 *Ibid.*, para. 25.
157 *Ibid.*, para. 26.
158 *Ibid.*, para. 27.
159 *Ibid.*, para. 28.
160 FRS 9, Appendix II, para. 2.
161 *Ibid.*
162 *Ibid.*.
163 IAS 31, *Financial Reporting of Interests in Joint Ventures*, IASC, November 1990, revised October 2000 para. 2.
164 *Ibid.*, para. 3.
165 *Ibid.*, para. 4.
166 *Ibid.*, para. 5.
167 *Ibid.*, para. 6.
168 *Ibid.*, para. 42.
169 *Ibid.*, paras. 7.
170 *Ibid.*, para. 43-44.
171 *Ibid.*, para. 8.
172 *Ibid.*, para. 9.
173 *Ibid.*, para. 10.
174 *Ibid.*, paras. 11-12.
175 *Ibid.*, paras. 13-14.
176 *Ibid.*, para. 15.
177 *Ibid.*, paras. 16-17.
178 *Ibid.*, paras. 17-18.

179 *Ibid.*, para. 19.
180 *Ibid.*, para. 20.
181 *Ibid.*, para. 21.
182 *Ibid.*, para. 22.
183 *Ibid.*, paras. 23-24.
184 *Ibid.*, paras. 25-26.
185 *Ibid.*, para. 27
186 *Ibid.*, para. 28.
187 *Ibid.*, para. 29.
188 *Ibid.*, paras. 30-31.
189 *Ibid.*, paras. 32-33.
190 *Ibid.*, para. 34.
191 *Ibid.*, paras. 35-36.
192 *Ibid.*, para. 37.
193 *Ibid.*, para. 38.
194 *Ibid.*, para. 39.
195 *Ibid.*, para. 40.
196 *Ibid.*, para. 41.
197 SIC-13, paras. 5-6.
198 *Ibid.*, para. 6.
199 *Ibid.*, para. 7.
200 IAS 31, para. 48.
201 *Ibid.*, para. 47.
202 *Ibid.*, para. 45.
203 *Ibid.*, para. 46.
204 ASB PN 136, April 1999.
205 *Reporting Interests in Joint Ventures and Similar Arrangements*, G4+1 group, October 1999.

Chapter 8 Foreign currencies

1 INTRODUCTION

1.1 Background

A company can engage in foreign currency operations in two ways. It may enter directly into transactions which are denominated in foreign currencies, the results of which need to be translated into the currency in which the company reports. Alternatively, it may conduct foreign operations through a foreign enterprise, normally a subsidiary or associated company, which keeps its accounting records in a foreign currency and, in order to prepare consolidated financial statements, will need to translate the financial statements of the foreign enterprise into its own reporting currency.[1]

Before the present UK and international standards were developed, there were four distinct methods which could be used in the translation process:

(a) *current rate method* – all assets and liabilities are translated at the current rate of exchange, i.e. the exchange rate at the balance sheet date;

(b) *temporal method* – assets and liabilities carried at current prices are translated at the current rate of exchange, e.g. cash, debtors, creditors, investments at market value. Assets and liabilities carried at past prices, e.g. property, investments at cost, prepayments, are translated at the rate of exchange in effect at the dates to which the prices pertain;

(c) *current/non-current method* – all current assets and current liabilities are translated at the current rate of exchange. Non-current assets and liabilities are translated at historical rates, i.e. the exchange rate in effect at the time the asset was acquired or the liability incurred; and

(d) *monetary/non-monetary method* – monetary assets and liabilities, i.e. items which represent the right to receive or the obligation to pay a fixed amount of money, are translated at the current rate of exchange. Non-monetary assets and liabilities are translated at the historical rate.

There was no consensus either in the UK or internationally on the best theoretical approach to adopt. In essence, the arguments surround the choice of exchange rates to be used in the translation process and the subsequent treatment of the exchange differences which arise.

1.2 UK Position

1.2.1 SSAP 20

Following a number of proposals, stemming from the mid 1970s, the relevant standard in the UK, SSAP 20, was eventually issued in April 1983. The reason for the long gestation period was that following the implementation of SFAS 8 in the USA it gradually became evident that when consolidated accounts are drawn up in a relatively weak currency, the temporal method produces results which do not seem to make commercial and economic sense. As a result the FASB decided to review SFAS 8.[2] In Canada, the Canadian Institute of Chartered Accountants (CICA), which had published its standard on foreign currencies in 1978,[3] advocating the use of the temporal method, suspended it in 1979 pending further study. Conscious of the need for international harmonisation in this field, there then followed a long period of consultation between the ASC, the FASB and the CICA.

So it was that the ASC issued SSAP 20 in April 1983. This, like its US counterpart, SFAS 52, is based on the closing rate/net investment concept and an approach to translation which is related to the cash flow consequences of exchange movements. Exchange differences which give rise to cash flows, i.e. those resulting from business transactions, are reported as part of the profit or loss for the period. Other exchange differences which do not give rise to cash flows, because they result from retranslations of the holding company's long-term investment in the foreign subsidiary, are reported as reserve movements. However, deviation from this approach can be made where a foreign currency loan has been used to finance the purchase of an investment in a foreign subsidiary (the 'cover method').

The standard therefore requires that the procedures to be adopted when accounting for foreign operations should be considered in two stages, namely the preparation of the financial statements of the individual company and the preparation of the consolidated financial statements.

1.2.2 UITF Abstracts

Over the years the UITF has issued a number of abstracts dealing with aspects relating to foreign currencies.

In June 1993 it issued Abstract 9 – *Accounting for Operations in Hyper-inflationary Economies* – which became effective for accounting periods ending on or after 23 August 1993. This is discussed in Chapter 9 at 2.2.

Following the introduction of a new tax regime for foreign exchange differences in 1995 whereby exchange gains and losses on foreign currency borrowings can now be taxable, the UITF considered how the tax effect on such borrowings should be reported and also whether taxation should be taken into account in applying the cover method under SSAP 20. Accordingly, in February 1998 the UITF issued Abstract 19 – *Tax on gains and losses on foreign currency borrowings that hedge an investment in a foreign enterprise,* which became effective for accounting periods ending on or after 23 March 1998. The requirements of this abstract are dealt with at 2.5.2 and 3.5 below.

In addition, as a result of some concerns over the advent of the introduction of the euro, in March 1998 the UITF issued Abstract 21 – *Accounting issues arising from the proposed introduction of the euro,* again effective for accounting periods ending on or after 23 March 1998. This was supplemented in August 1998 by an Appendix to the abstract dealing with some further accounting issues. These are discussed at 3.8 below.

1.2.3 *Financial instruments project*

The financial instruments project impinges on many of the areas covered by this chapter, particularly in relation to forward currency contracts, currency swaps and currency options as well as extending the disclosures in respect of foreign currencies. In September 1998 the ASB issued the first instalment of its rules on financial instruments, FRS 13 – *Derivatives and Other Financial Instruments: Disclosures.* The requirements of FRS 13 and a discussion of the ASB's other proposals for financial instruments are covered in Chapter 10.

The exposure draft which preceded FRS 13 had proposed currency disclosures which were aimed at showing the currency exposures which gave rise to exchange differences taken directly to reserves under SSAP 20 (see 2.3.7 below). It tried to do this by suggesting disclosure of a currency analysis of net assets compared to borrowings.[4] This proposed requirement was dropped from the final standard for non-financial entities, although a variant of the requirement was retained for banks. In February 1999 the ASB resurrected this idea by issuing an exposure draft to amend SSAP 20 calling for such disclosures. However, many commentators raised other concerns about SSAP 20 and proposed further amendments or even a full-scale review of SSAP 20. In the light of these comments in May 1999 the ASB withdrew this proposal but indicated that it plans to review SSAP 20 in its entirety and that an exposure draft will be developed as soon as the project on financial instruments has settled some key issues that are fundamental to foreign currency translation.

1.3 International position

The principal international standard dealing with this topic is IAS 21 – *The Effects of Changes in Foreign Exchange Rates.* The original standard was issued in July 1983, but a revised version was published in December 1993. Although the revised standard follows the same general approach as SSAP 20, nevertheless there are a number of differences.

However, the main difference from the UK is that international standards are further developed in respect of financial instruments. Derivative instruments such as forward currency contracts, swaps and options are covered by IAS 39 –

Financial Instruments: Recognition and Measurement – which has detailed rules on hedging (see Chapter 10 at 4.9).

The SIC has issued three interpretations of IAS 21; SIC-7 – *Introduction of the Euro*, SIC-11 – *Foreign Exchange - Capitalisation of Losses Resulting from Severe Currency Devaluations* and SIC-19 – *Reporting Currency – Measurement and Presentation of Financial Statements under IAS 21 and IAS 29*. This last Interpretation is effective for annual financial periods beginning on or after 1 January 2001.

2 REQUIREMENTS OF SSAP 20

2.1 Objectives of translation

SSAP 20 states that 'the translation of foreign currency transactions and financial statements should produce results which are generally compatible with the effects of rate changes on a company's cash flows and its equity and should ensure that the financial statements present a true and fair view of the results of management actions. Consolidated statements should reflect the financial results and relationships as measured in the foreign currency financial statements prior to translation.'[5] It will be seen when looking at the requirements of the standard that in certain situations these objectives conflict.

2.2 Definitions of terms

The main definitions of terms which are contained in SSAP 20 are as follows:[6]

A *foreign enterprise* is a subsidiary, associated company or branch whose operations are based in a country other than that of the investing company or whose assets and liabilities are denominated mainly in a foreign currency.

A *foreign branch* is either a legally constituted enterprise located overseas or a group of assets and liabilities which are accounted for in foreign currencies.

Translation is the process whereby financial data denominated in one currency are expressed in terms of another currency. It includes both the expression of individual transactions in terms of another currency and the expression of a complete set of financial statements prepared in one currency in terms of another currency.

A company's *local currency* is the currency of the primary economic environment in which it operates and generates net cash flows.

An *exchange rate* is a rate at which two currencies may be exchanged for each other at a particular point in time; different rates apply for spot and forward transactions.

The *closing rate* is the exchange rate for spot transactions ruling at the balance sheet date and is the mean of the buying and selling rates at the close of business on the day for which the rate is to be ascertained.

A *forward contract* is an agreement to exchange different currencies at a specified rate. The difference between the specified rate and the spot rate ruling on the date the contract was entered into is the discount or premium on the forward contract.

The *net investment* which a company has in a foreign enterprise is its effective equity stake and comprises its proportion of such foreign enterprise's net assets; in appropriate circumstances, intra-group loans and other deferred balances may be regarded as part of the effective equity stake.

Monetary items are money held and amounts to be received or paid in money and, where a company is not an exempt company, should be categorised as either short-term or long-term. Short-term monetary items are those which fall due within one year of the balance sheet date. (An exempt company is essentially a bank or an insurance company.)

2.3 Individual companies

As indicated in 1.1 above, a company can either enter directly into foreign currency transactions or it may conduct foreign operations through a foreign enterprise. The standard therefore requires that the procedures to be adopted when accounting for foreign operations should be considered in two stages, namely the preparation of the financial statements of the individual company and the preparation of the consolidated financial statements.

The first stage to be considered is the preparation of the financial statements of an individual company. The procedures to be followed should be applied to each company within a group prior to the preparation of the consolidated accounts. The general requirements of SSAP 20 are as follows.

2.3.1 Recording of transactions

Generally, all foreign currency transactions entered into by a company should be translated into its local currency at the exchange rate ruling on the date the transaction occurs. An average rate for a period is acceptable if rates do not fluctuate significantly during the relevant period. Where the transaction is to be settled at a contracted rate then that rate should be used.[7]

2.3.2 Retranslation of monetary/non-monetary assets and liabilities at balance sheet date

At the balance sheet date, monetary assets and liabilities denominated in foreign currencies resulting from unsettled transactions should be translated using the closing rate. Again, where the transaction is to be settled at a contracted rate then that rate should be used.[8]

Non-monetary assets should not be retranslated but should remain translated at the rate ruling when they were originally recorded.[9]

2.3.3 *Treatment of exchange differences*

Exchange differences will arise when transactions are settled at exchange rates which are different from those used when the transactions were previously recorded. They will also arise on any unsettled transactions at the balance sheet date if the closing rate differs from those used previously.[10] All exchange differences should be included as part of the profit or loss for the period from ordinary activities, unless they arise as a result of events which themselves are treated as extraordinary, in which case they should be included as part of such items. This treatment should be adopted for all monetary items irrespective of whether they are short-term or long-term and irrespective of whether the exchange differences are gains or losses.[11]

The rationale for the above treatment is that the exchange differences have already been reflected in cash flows, in the case of settled transactions, or will be in the future in the case of unsettled transactions.[12] This is consistent with the accruals concept; it results in reporting the effect of a rate change that will have cash flow effects when the event causing the effect takes place. As paragraph 10 of SSAP 20 explains, 'exchange gains on unsettled transactions can be determined at the balance sheet date no less objectively than exchange losses; deferring the gains whilst recognising the losses would not only be illogical by denying in effect that any favourable movement had occurred but would also inhibit fair measurement of the performance of the enterprise in the year. In particular, this symmetry of treatment recognises that there will probably be some interaction between currency movements and interest rates and reflects more accurately in the profit and loss account the true results of currency involvement.'

2.3.4 *Worked examples*

The above general requirements can be illustrated in the following examples:

Example 8.1

A UK company purchases plant and machinery on credit from a US company for US$328,000 in January 1999 when the exchange rate is £1=US$1.64. The company records the asset at a cost of £200,000. At the UK company's year end at 31 March 1999 the account has not yet been settled. The closing rate is £1=US$1.61. The creditor would be retranslated at £203,727 in the balance sheet and an exchange loss of £3,727 would be reported as part of the profit or loss for the period from ordinary operations. The cost of the asset would remain as £200,000.

Example 8.2

A UK company sells goods to a German company for €87,000 on 28 February 1999 when the exchange rate is £1=€1.45. It receives payment on 31 March 1999 when the exchange rate is £1=€1.50. On 28 February the company will record a sale and corresponding debtor of £60,000. When payment is received on 31 March the actual amount received is only £58,000. The loss on exchange of £2,000 would be reported as part of the profit or loss for the period from ordinary operations.

2.3.5 *Examples of accounting policies*

Extract 8.1: United Biscuits (Holdings) plc (1998)

Foreign currency translation [extract]

Company: Monetary assets and liabilities denominated in foreign currencies are translated at the rate of exchange ruling at the balance sheet date. Transactions in foreign currencies are recorded at the rate ruling at the date of the transaction, all differences being taken to the profit and loss account.

Extract 8.2: Safeway plc (2001)

Foreign currency [extract]

Transactions in foreign currencies are translated into sterling at the rates of exchange current at the dates of the transactions. Foreign currency monetary assets and liabilities in the balance sheet are translated into sterling at the rates of exchange ruling at the end of the year. Resulting exchange gains and losses are taken to the profit and loss account.

2.3.6 *Exchange gains where there are doubts as to convertibility or marketability*

As indicated in 2.3.3 above SSAP 20 requires both exchange gains and losses on long-term monetary items to be recognised in the profit and loss account. However, paragraphs 11 and 50 of the standard indicate that where there are doubts as to the convertibility or marketability of the currency in question then it may be necessary to consider on the grounds of prudence whether the amount of any exchange gain, or the amount by which exchange gains exceed past exchange losses on the same items, to be recognised in the profit and loss account should be restricted.

2.3.7 *Foreign equity investments financed by borrowings*

One exception to the rule that non-monetary items are not retranslated is where foreign equity investments have been financed by foreign currency borrowings, or where the borrowings have been taken out to hedge the exchange risks associated with existing equity investments. Application of the procedures set out in 2.3.1 to 2.3.3 above would cause exchange differences on loans to pass through the profit and loss account while no exchange differences would arise on the equity investments. The standard recognises that in such situations a company may be covered in economic terms against any movement in exchange rates and states that it would be inappropriate in such cases to record an accounting profit or loss when exchange rates change.[13]

Paragraph 51 of the standard therefore allows companies in such situations, subject to the conditions set out below, to treat the cost of the investments as being denominated in the appropriate foreign currencies and retranslating them at the closing rates each year. Where this is done the resulting exchange differences should be taken to reserves. The exchange differences arising on the related foreign currency borrowings should also be taken to reserves and should not be reported as part of the profit or loss for the period.

The conditions to be fulfilled are:

(a) exchange gains or losses arising on the borrowings may be offset only to the extent of exchange differences arising on the equity investments in that particular period;

(b) the foreign currency borrowings should not exceed the total amount of cash that the investments are expected to generate, whether from profits or otherwise; and

(c) the accounting treatment should be applied consistently from period to period.

Example 8.3

A UK company purchases equity shares in a Canadian company for C$1,200,000 on 31 January 1999 when the exchange rate is £1=C$2.48. It partially finances the investment by borrowing C$1,000,000 on the same date. The investment would therefore be recorded as £483,871 and the loan as £403,226. At the UK company's year end of 30 April 1999 the closing rate is £1=C$2.34. The loan would be retranslated as £427,350 resulting in an exchange loss of £24,124. The investment would be translated as £512,821 resulting in an exchange gain of £28,950. Both the exchange gain and the exchange loss would be taken to reserves.

If the UK company did not wish to adopt the treatment contained in paragraph 51 of the standard then the exchange loss of £24,124 would have to be reported as part of the profit or loss for the period and the investment would have been retained at its original cost of £483,871 with no exchange gain being recognised.

Examples of accounting policies of companies which have adopted such a treatment are illustrated below:

Extract 8.3: Hilton Group plc (2000)

Foreign currencies [extract]
Gains or losses arising on the translation of the net assets of overseas subsidiaries and associates are taken to reserves, net of exchange differences arising on related foreign currency borrowings, as are differences arising on equity investments denominated in foreign currencies in the holding company's accounts.

Extract 8.4: Imperial Chemical Industries PLC (2000)

Foreign currencies [extract]

In the Group accounts, exchange differences arising on consolidation of the net investments in overseas subsidiary undertakings and associates are taken to reserves, as are differences arising on equity investments denominated in foreign currencies in the Company accounts. Differences on relevant foreign currency loans are taken to reserves and offset against the differences on net investments in both Group and Company accounts.

2.3.8 *Forward contracts*

The standard recognises that where a company has covered a foreign currency transaction by entering into a related or matching forward contract it may not be appropriate to record the transaction using the spot rate ruling at the date of the transaction or to retranslate the monetary asset or liability at the closing rate. Accordingly, paragraphs 46 and 48 allow companies to use the rate of exchange specified in the related or matching forward contract instead.

Example 8.4

A UK company sells goods to a Swiss company for SFr100,000 on 30 April 1999 at which date the exchange rate is £1=SFr2.45. As payment is not due until 31 July 1999, the company decides to hedge its exposure to exchange risk by entering into a forward contract to sell SFr100,000 in three months time at a rate of £1=SFr2.425. As a result the company has fixed the amount of sterling it will realise from the sale at £41,237. The standard allows the company to record the sale and corresponding debtor at that amount and not at £40,816 using the rate ruling at the date of the transaction. If at its year end of 30 June 1999 the exchange rate is £1=SFr2.50 there is no need for the company to retranslate the debtor at £40,000 and record a loss on exchange, but it retains it at £41,237. This treatment recognises the fact that as a result of entering into the forward contract the company is no longer susceptible to exchange rate movements and therefore there should be no effect on its profit or loss if exchange rates do change.

An example of an accounting policy of a company which adopts such a treatment is illustrated below:

Extract 8.5: Reckitt Benckiser plc (2000)

Foreign currency translation [extract]

Transactions denominated in foreign currencies are translated at the rate of exchange on the day the transaction occurs or at the contracted rate if the transaction is covered by a forward exchange contract.

Assets and liabilities denominated in a foreign currency are translated at the exchange rate ruling on the balance sheet date or, if appropriate, at a forward contract.

2.4 Consolidated accounts

The second stage to be considered is the preparation of consolidated financial statements.

2.4.1 *Scope*

The procedures to be adopted apply not only to the inclusion of subsidiaries but also to the incorporation of the results of associated companies and joint ventures. They also apply when the results of a foreign branch are to be incorporated into the accounts of an individual company.[14]

2.4.2 *Choice of method*

The standard requires that the method to be used for translating the financial statements of a foreign enterprise should reflect the financial and other operational relationship which exists between the holding company and its foreign enterprise.[15] It recognises that in most cases this means that the consolidated accounts will be prepared using the closing rate/net investment method as described in 2.4.3 below. However, as explained in 2.4.4 below, in certain circumstances the standard requires the temporal method to be used.

The method used for translating the financial statements of a foreign enterprise should only be changed when the financial and other operational relationship changes and renders the method used inappropriate.[16]

2.4.3 *Closing rate/net investment method*

For most investing companies in the UK where foreign operations are carried out by foreign enterprises it is normally the case that the foreign enterprises operate as separate or quasi-independent entities.[17] The day to day operations of the foreign enterprise will be based in its local currency, are likely to be financed wholly or partly in its own currency, and will not be dependent on the reporting currency of the holding company. The foreign enterprise will be managed so as to maximise the local currency profits attributable to the holding company. Consequently, the financial statements of the foreign enterprise expressed in its local currency will be the best available indicator of its performance and value to the group. In order to preserve the inherent relationships included in these local currency financial statements it is therefore necessary to use a single rate of exchange when translating the financial statements in the preparation of the consolidated financial statements.[18]

A Balance sheet

The standard therefore requires that under the closing rate/net investment method the balance sheet of the foreign enterprise should be translated into the reporting currency of the investing company using the rate of exchange at the balance sheet date, i.e. the closing rate.[19]

B Profit and loss account

The profit and loss account of the foreign enterprise under this method should be translated at the closing rate or at an average rate for the period.[20] Conceptually, the use of the closing rate is preferable as this will achieve the objective of translation of reflecting the financial results and relationships as measured in the foreign currency financial statements prior to translation.[21] The use of an average rate is justified by SSAP 20 on the grounds that it reflects more fairly the profits or losses and cash flows as they arise to the group throughout an accounting period.[22] Most major companies use the average rate method. Although the standard allows a choice as to which rate is used it does require that the one selected is applied consistently from period to period.[23]

C Treatment of exchange differences

Exchange differences will arise under the closing rate/net investment method if the exchange rate used for translating the balance sheet differs from that ruling at the previous balance sheet date or at the date of any subsequent capital injection or reduction.[24] Exchange differences will also arise where an average rate is used for translating the profit and loss account and this differs from the closing rate.[25] The standard requires that both such exchange differences should be recorded as a movement on reserves.[26] As paragraph 19 of SSAP 20 explains: 'If exchange differences arising from the retranslation of a company's net investment in its foreign enterprise were introduced into the profit and loss account, the results from trading operations, as shown in the local currency financial statements would be distorted. Such differences may result from many factors unrelated to the trading performance or financing operations of the foreign enterprise; in particular, they do not represent or measure changes in actual or prospective cash flows. It is therefore inappropriate to regard them as profits or losses and they should be dealt with as adjustments to reserves.'

Example 8.5

A UK company owns 100% of the share capital of a foreign company which was set up a number of years ago when the exchange rate was £1=FC4. It uses the closing rate method for incorporating the accounts of the subsidiary in its consolidated accounts for the year ended 31 December 2000. The exchange rate at the year end is £1=FC2 (1999: £1=FC3). The profit and loss account of the subsidiary for that year and its balance sheet at the beginning and end of the year in local currency and translated into sterling are as follows:

Profit and loss account

	FC	£
Sales	35,000	17,500
Cost of sales	(33,190)	(16,595)
Depreciation	(500)	(250)
Interest	(350)	(175)
Profit before taxation	960	480
Taxation	(460)	(230)
Profit after taxation	500	250

Balance sheets	1999 FC	2000 FC	1999 £	2000 £
Fixed assets	6,000	5,500	2,000	2,750
Current assets				
Stocks	2,700	3,000	900	1,500
Debtors	4,800	4,000	1,600	2,000
Cash	200	600	67	300
	7,700	7,600	2,567	3,800
Current liabilities				
Creditors	4,530	3,840	1,510	1,920
Taxation	870	460	290	230
	5,400	4,300	1,800	2,150
Net current assets	2,300	3,300	767	1,650
	8,300	8,800	2,767	4,400
Long-term loans	3,600	3,600	1,200	1,800
	4,700	5,200	1,567	2,600
Share capital	1,000	1,000	250	250
Retained profits	3,700	4,200	1,317	2,350
	4,700	5,200	1,567	2,600

The movement in retained profits is as follows:

	£
Balance brought forward	1,317
Profit for year	250
Exchange difference	783
	2,350

The exchange difference of £783 is the exchange difference on the opening net investment in the subsidiary and is calculated as follows:

Opening net assets at opening rate	– FC4,700 at FC3=£1 =	£1,567
Opening net assets at closing rate	– FC4,700 at FC2=£1 =	£2,350
Exchange gain on net investment		£ 783

This exchange gain should be shown as a movement on reserves and should not be reflected in the profit and loss account.

If the company were to have adopted a policy of translating the profit and loss account at an average rate of exchange and the appropriate weighted average rate was FC2.5=£1 then the profit and loss account would have been as follows:

	FC	£
Sales	35,000	14,000
Cost of sales	(33,190)	(13,276)
Depreciation	(500)	(200)
Interest	(350)	(140)
Profit before taxation	960	384
Taxation	(460)	(184)
Profit after taxation	500	200

The difference between the profit and loss account translated at an average rate, i.e. £200, and at the closing rate, i.e. £250, would be recorded as a movement in reserves.

Examples of accounting policies of companies using this method of translation are illustrated below:

Extract 8.6: Racal Electronics Plc (1999)

4 **Foreign currencies** [extract]

The accounts of overseas subsidiary companies, associated companies and joint ventures, and assets and liabilities denominated in foreign currencies held by United Kingdom companies, have been translated at the rates ruling on 31 March 1999. Exchange differences arising on the retranslation of these accounts at the beginning of the year, and differences on long term foreign currency loans which relate to investments in overseas companies, are dealt with as a movement in reserves.

Extract 8.7: BP Amoco p.l.c. (2000)

Foreign currencies [extract]

On consolidation, assets and liabilities of subsidiaries are translated into US dollars at closing rates of exchange. Income and cash flow statements are translated at average rates of exchange. Exchange differences resulting from the retranslation of net investments in subsidiaries and associates at closing rates, together with differences between income statements translated at average rates and at closing rates, are dealt with in reserves.

2.4.4 Temporal method

As already indicated in 2.4.2 above, the standard recognises that in certain circumstances it would be inappropriate to use the closing rate/net investment method for translating the financial statements of a foreign enterprise and requires the temporal method to be used.

Such a method is to be used where the trade of the foreign enterprise is more dependent on the economic environment of the investing company's currency than that of its own reporting currency. By using the temporal method the consolidated accounts reflect the transactions of the foreign enterprise as if they had been carried out by the investing company itself.[27]

A Determination of dominant currency

It is impossible to specify any one factor which would indicate when the temporal method should be used. The standard indicates that the following factors should be taken into account:[28]

(a) 'the extent to which the cash flows of the enterprise have a direct impact upon those of the investing company' (e.g. whether there is a regular and frequent movement of cash between the holding company and the foreign enterprise or whether there are only occasional remittances of, for example, dividends);

(b) 'the extent to which the functioning of the enterprise is dependent directly upon the investing company' (e.g. whether management is based locally or at head office and whether pricing decisions are based on local competition and costs or are part of a worldwide decision process);

(c) 'the currency in which the majority of the trading transactions are denominated' (e.g. whether the foreign currency is used for both invoicing goods and paying expenses, or whether the majority of such items are denominated in the currency of the investing company);

(d) 'the major currency to which the operation is exposed in its financing structure' (e.g. whether the company is dependent on local financing or whether the majority of the financing is in the currency of the investing company and possibly obtained through, or guaranteed by, that company).[29]

B Example of situations

Situations where the temporal method may be appropriate are where the foreign enterprise:

(a) 'acts as a selling agency receiving stocks of goods from the investing company and remitting the proceeds back to the company';

(b) 'produces a raw material or manufactures parts or sub-assemblies which are then shipped to the investing company for inclusion in its own products';

(c) 'is located overseas for tax, exchange control or similar reasons to act as a means of raising finance for other companies in the group'.[30]

C Method

The mechanics of the temporal method are essentially the same as those procedures used in preparing the accounts of an individual company[31] discussed in 2.3 above. In theory, this means translating each transaction of the foreign enterprise at the rates ruling at the date of each transaction. In order to simplify the translation process, however, average rates may be used as an approximation.

Example 8.6

Using the same basic facts as Example 8.5 above, i.e. a UK company owns 100% of the share capital of a foreign company which was set up a number of years ago when the exchange rate was £1=FC4. It uses the temporal method for incorporating the accounts of the subsidiary in its consolidated accounts for the year ended 31 December 2000. The exchange rate at the year end is £1=FC2 (1999: £1=FC3) and the average exchange rate for the year is £1=FC2.5.

Details of fixed assets are as follows:

Date of acquisition	1 January 1996	1 July 1997
	FC	FC
Cost	2,500	5,000
Aggregate depreciation – 31/12/99	668	832
Depreciation charge for year	167	333
Aggregate depreciation – 31/12/00	835	1,165
Net book value – 31/12/99	1,832	4,168
Net book value – 31/12/00	1,665	3,835

The relevant exchange rates at the dates of acquisition are £1=FC3.8 and £1=FC3.4 respectively. The average rates of exchange relating to opening and closing stocks are £1=FC3.3 and £1=FC2.4.

The profit and loss account of the subsidiary for that year and its balance sheet at the beginning and end of the year in local currency and translated into sterling using the temporal method are as follows:

Profit and loss account

	FC	Exchange rate	£
Sales	35,000	Average – FC2.5	14,000
Opening stock	2,700	Historical – FC3.3	818
Purchases	33,490	Average – FC2.5	13,396
Closing stock	(3,000)	Historical – FC2.4	(1,250)
Cost of sales	(33,190)		(12,964)
Gross profit	1,810		1,036
Depreciation	(500)	Historical – FC3.8/3.4	(142)
Interest	(350)	Average – FC2.5	(140)
Translation loss		Balance	(596)
Profit before taxation	960		158
Taxation	(460)	Average – FC2.5	(185)
Profit after taxation	500		(27)

Balance sheets	1999 FC	Exchange rate	1999 £	2000 FC	Exchange rate	2000 £
Fixed assets	6,000	FC3.8/3.4	1,708	5,500	FC3.8/3.4	1,566
Current assets						
Stocks	2,700	FC3.3	818	3,000	FC2.4	1,250
Debtors	4,800	FC3	1,600	4,000	FC2	2,000
Cash	200	FC3	67	600	FC2	300
	7,700		2,485	7,600		3,550
Current liabilities						
Creditors	4,530	FC3	1,510	3,840	FC2	1,920
Taxation	870	FC3	290	460	FC2	230
	5,400		1,800	4,300		2,150
Net current assets	2,300		685	3,300		1,400
	8,300		2,393	8,800		2,966
Long-term loans	3,600	FC3	1,200	3,600	FC2	1,800
	4,700		1,193	5,200		1,166
Share capital	1,000	FC4	250	1,000	FC4	250
Retained profits	3,700	Balance	943	4,200	Balance	916
	4,700		1,193	5,200		1,166

The translation loss of £596 which is shown in the profit and loss account represents the exchange loss on monetary items during the year and is calculated as follows:

	Opening monetary items FC	Closing monetary items FC
Debtors	4,800	4,000
Cash	200	600
Creditors	(4,530)	(3,840)
Taxation	(870)	(460)
Long-term loans	(3,600)	(3,600)
	(4,000)	(3,300)

			£	£
Opening monetary items at opening rate	– FC(4,000) at FC3	=	(1,334)	
Opening monetary items at closing rate	– FC(4,000) at FC2	=	(2,000)	
				(666)
Change in monetary items at average rate	– FC700 at FC2.5	=	280	
Change in monetary items at closing rate	– FC700 at FC2	=	350	
				70
Total exchange loss				(596)

Examples of accounting policies of companies using this method of translation are illustrated below:

Extract 8.8: Reuters Group PLC (2000)

Foreign currency translation [extract]

Where it is considered that the functional currency of an operation is sterling the financial statements are expressed in sterling on the following basis:

a. Fixed assets are translated into sterling at the rates ruling on the date of acquisition as adjusted for any profits or losses from related financial instruments.
b. Monetary assets and liabilities denominated in a foreign currency are translated into sterling at the foreign exchange rates ruling at the balance sheet date.
c. Revenue and expenses in foreign currencies are recorded in sterling at the rates ruling for the month of the transactions.
d. Any gains or losses arising on translation are reported as part of profit.

Extract 8.9: Babcock International Group PLC (2000)

Foreign currencies [extract]

Where it is considered that the results of an overseas undertaking are more dependent on sterling than its own reporting currency the Financial Statements of the undertaking are consolidated using the temporal method, thereby treating all transactions as though they had been entered into by the undertaking itself in sterling.

2.4.5 *Foreign equity investments financed by borrowings*

We have already seen in 2.3.7 above that where a company has used foreign currency borrowings to finance, or provide a hedge against, its foreign equity investments the standard allows the exchange differences on the borrowings to be taken to reserves rather than the profit and loss account.

A similar provision for consolidated accounts is contained in paragraph 57 of the standard. This is because under the closing rate method exchange differences on the net investment in foreign enterprises are taken to reserves and not reflected in the profit for the year. It would therefore be inappropriate for exchange differences on group borrowings which have been used to finance the investments or provide a hedge against the exchange risk associated with the investments to be taken to the profit and loss account. As the group is covered in economic terms against any movement in exchange rates then the exchange differences on the borrowings should be taken to reserves to offset the exchange differences on the net investments in the foreign enterprises.[32]

Where foreign currency borrowings of the group, therefore, have been used to finance, or provide a hedge against group equity investments then, subject to the conditions set out below, the exchange differences arising on the related foreign currency borrowings may be offset against the exchange differences arising on the retranslation of the net investments as a movement on reserves so that they are not reported as part of the profit or loss for the period.[33]

The conditions to be fulfilled are:

(a) the relationships between the investing company and the foreign enterprises concerned justify the use of the closing rate method for consolidation purposes;

(b) exchange gains or losses arising on foreign currency borrowings are offset only to the extent of the exchange differences arising on the net investments in foreign enterprises in that particular period;

(c) the foreign currency borrowings should not exceed the total amount of cash that the net investments are expected to generate, whether from profits or otherwise; and

(d) the accounting treatment should be applied consistently from period to period.[34]

The last three conditions are similar to those contained in paragraph 51 of the standard relating to the offset procedures for individual companies. The first condition is necessary as it is only when the closing rate method is used that the financial statements would not otherwise reflect the fact that the group is covered in economic terms against movements in exchange differences. Where a foreign enterprise is consolidated using the temporal method then, as all exchange differences are taken to the profit and loss account, any exchange differences on related borrowings should also be taken to the profit and loss account.

Although the general principles of paragraph 57 of the standard are the same as those used in the offset procedures for individual companies there are a number of differences in detail. These will normally require the calculations used in the individual companies' financial statements to be reversed on consolidation and the amount recalculated for the purposes of the consolidated financial statements:

(a) in the individual companies' financial statements *all* equity investments are included in the calculation, whereas for the consolidated financial statements investments which are consolidated using the temporal method are excluded;

(b) in the individual companies' financial statements it is the exchange difference on the carrying value of the investment which is included in the calculation, whereas for the consolidated financial statements it is the exchange difference on the underlying net assets which is included; and

(c) in the individual companies' financial statements only borrowings of the company can be included in the calculation, whereas in the consolidated financial statements borrowings of any group company can be included.

The only situation in which there will be no need to recalculate the amount of the offset is where the provisions of paragraph 51 of the standard have been applied in the investing company's financial statements to a foreign equity investment which is neither a subsidiary nor an associated company. This is because paragraph 58 of the standard allows the amount of the offset in the individual company's financial statements to be carried forward to the consolidated financial statements, since the exchange risk is hedged in both the company and the group. It should be borne in mind, however, that this does not mean that all such equity investments throughout the group can be retranslated at closing rates and the resulting exchange differences used in the offset process.

Example 8.7

A UK company is preparing its financial statements for the year ended 31 December 1998. It has two wholly owned subsidiaries:

(i) A Japanese company which it acquired a number of years ago at a cost of ¥500m. It incorporates the financial statements of the subsidiary in its consolidated financial statements using the closing rate method. During 1997 the company borrowed ¥1,000m repayable in ten years' time in 2007, to provide a hedge against the investment, which was then considered to be worth in excess of ¥1,500m. The net assets of the subsidiary at 31 December 1997 were ¥1,200m.

(ii) A Canadian company which it set up on 1 February 1998 at a cost of C$5m. It is going to incorporate this subsidiary in its consolidated financial statements using the temporal method. The exchange loss for the period is £38,925. It partially financed the acquisition of the shares by borrowing C$4m repayable in 2003.

In addition, the UK company has a 10% investment in a US company which it acquired in 1997 at a cost of US$2m, financed by means of a US dollar loan of the same amount. At 31 December 1998 none of the loan has been repaid.

The relevant exchange rates are:

	£1=¥	£1=C$	£1=US$
31/12/97	207		1.64
1/2/98		2.39	
31/12/98	188	2.56	1.66

Using the provisions of paragraphs 51, 57 and 58 of the standard the treatment in the company and consolidated financial statements would be as follows:

Company financial statements			Profit/loss for year	Reserves
			£	£
Investment in Japanese company				
31/12/97 – ¥500m	@ 207	= £2,415,459		
31/12/98 – ¥500m	@ 188	= £2,659,574		
Exchange gain		£ 244,115		244,115
¥1,000m Loan				
31/12/97 – ¥1,000m	@ 207	= £4,830,918		
31/12/98 – ¥1,000m	@ 188	= £5,319,149		
Exchange loss		£ (488,231)	(244,116)	(244,115)
Investment in Canadian company				
1/2/98 – C$5m	@ 2.39	= £2,092,050		
31/12/98 – C$5m	@ 2.56	= £1,953,125		
Exchange loss		£ (138,925)		(138,925)
C$4m Loan				
1/2/98 – C$4m	@ 2.39	= £1,673,640		
31/12/98 – C$4m	@ 2.56	= £1,562,500		
Exchange gain		£ 111,140		111,140
Investment in US company				
31/12/97 – US$2m	@ 1.64	= £1,219,512		
31/12/98 – US$2m	@ 1.66	= £1,201,819		
Exchange loss		£ (14,693)		(14,693)
US$2m Loan				
31/12/97 – US$2m	@ 1.64	= £1,219,512		
31/12/98 – US$2m	@ 1.66	= £1,204,819		
Exchange gain		£ 14,693		14,693
Net exchange loss			(244,116)	(27,785)

The exchange loss on the ¥1,000m loan taken to reserves has had to be restricted as a result of condition (a) of paragraph 51 of the standard.

It can be seen that where an exchange gain arises on a foreign loan and it is taken to reserves under paragraph 51 then it is possible to have a net exchange loss being taken to reserves as the exchange loss on the investment can exceed the exchange gain on the related loan.

Consolidated financial statements			Profit/loss for year	Reserves
			£	£
Net investment in Japanese company				
31/12/97 – ¥1,200m	@ 207	= £5,797,101		
31/12/98 – ¥1,200m	@ 188	= £6,382,979		
Exchange gain		£ 585,878		585,878
¥1,000m Loan				
31/12/97 – ¥1,000m	@ 207	= £4,830,918		
31/12/98 – ¥1,000m	@ 188	= £5,319,149		
Exchange loss		£ (488,231)		(488,231)
Investment in Canadian company				
Exchange loss (as given)			(38,925)	
C$4m Loan				
1/2/98 – C$4m	@ 2.39	= £1,673,640		
31/12/98 – C$4m	@ 2.56	= £1,562,500		
Exchange gain		£ 111,140	111,140	
Investment in US company				
31/12/97 – US$2m	@ 1.64	= £1,219,512		
31/12/98 – US$2m	@ 1.66	= £1,204,819		
Exchange loss		£ (14,693)		(14,693)
US$2m Loan				
31/12/97 – US$2m	@ 1.64	= £1,219,512		
31/12/98 – US$2m	@ 1.66	= £1,204,819		
Exchange gain		£ 14,693		14,693
Net exchange gain			72,215	97,647

In the consolidated financial statements all of the exchange loss on the ¥1,000m loan can be taken to reserves as it is less than the exchange gain on the net investment in the Japanese subsidiary. The exchange gain on the C$4m loan has to be taken to the profit/loss for the year as the temporal method is used and therefore condition (a) of paragraph 57 of the standard is not met. It can be seen that the same treatment is adopted for the US$ investment and loan as in the company financial statements as a result of paragraph 58.

2.4.6 *Associates and joint ventures*

As indicated in 2.4.1 above, the provisions of the standard relating to consolidated financial statements apply to the incorporation of the results of all foreign enterprises, including associates and joint ventures. The definition of associates and joint ventures and the required accounting treatment are dealt with in FRS 9[35] and are discussed in Chapter 7.

When incorporating the results of foreign associates or joint ventures, therefore, the closing rate/net investment method should normally be used. In view of the fact that the investing company only has significant influence over an associate and does not control it, and only has joint control over a joint venture, it is unlikely that the affairs of such entities are so closely linked with those of the investing company that the use of the temporal method will be appropriate. The requirements of the closing rate/net investment method have been explained in 2.4.3 above.

2.4.7 *Foreign branches*

The provisions of the standard relating to consolidated financial statements also apply to the incorporation of the results of foreign branches, not only in the consolidated financial statements but also in the financial statements of an individual company.[36] The definition of a foreign branch contained in the standard is such that it includes not just a legally constituted enterprise located overseas but also a group of assets and liabilities which are accounted for in foreign currencies.[37]

The reason for this wide definition was to cater for the situation where a company had international assets such as ships or aircraft which earn revenues in a foreign currency, normally US dollars, financed by borrowings in the same currency and to allow the use of the closing rate/net investment method. If this had not been done, then under the provisions of the standard it would have been necessary for such assets to be translated at historical rates, the borrowings to be translated at closing rates and any exchange difference thereon taken to the profit or loss for the year. The cover method contained in paragraphs 51 and 57 of the standard would not have applied as these provisions only deal with borrowings which finance equity investments and not other types of non-monetary assets.

A Possible situations

In addition to the situation referred to above, the statement issued by the ASC on the publication of the standard also quoted the following as being examples of situations where a group of assets and liabilities should be accounted for under the closing rate/net investment method:

(a) a hotel in France financed by borrowings in French francs;

(b) a foreign currency insurance operation where the liabilities are substantially covered by the holding of foreign currency assets.[38]

B Treatment

The results of a foreign branch should be incorporated in the financial statements in the same way as foreign subsidiaries are included in the consolidated financial statements, i.e. the closing rate/net investment method should normally be used.[39] The use of this method is explained in 2.4.3 above.

However, in many cases the operations of a branch are a direct extension of the trade of the investing company and its cash flows have a direct impact upon those of the investing company in which case the temporal method is required to be used. It should not automatically be assumed, therefore, that the closing rate/net investment method is the correct method to use and careful consideration should be given to the factors referred to in 2.4.4 above.

British Airways effectively regards its aircraft and related financing as a foreign branch as illustrated in its accounting policy below:

Extract 8.10: British Airways Plc (2001)

Foreign currency translation

Foreign currency balances are translated into sterling at the rates ruling at the balance sheet date, except for certain loan repayment instalments which are translated at the forward contract rates where instalments have been covered forward at the balance sheet date. Aircraft which are financed in US dollars either by loans, finance leases or hire purchase arrangements are regarded together with the related assets and liabilities as a separate group of assets and liabilities and accounted for in US dollars. The amounts in US dollars are translated into sterling at rates ruling at the balance sheet date and the net differences arising from the translation of aircraft costs and related US dollar loans are taken to reserves. Exchange differences arising on the translation of net assets of overseas subsidiary undertakings and associated undertakings are taken to reserves. Profits and losses of such undertakings are translated into sterling at average rates of exchange during the year. All other profits or losses arising on translation are dealt with through the profit and loss account.

2.5 Disclosures

2.5.1 Requirements of SSAP 20

The standard requires the following disclosures to be made in the financial statements:

(a) the methods used in the translation of the financial statements of foreign enterprises, i.e. closing rate method or temporal method. Where the closing rate method is used it should also be stated whether the closing rate or an average rate has been used to translate the profit and loss account;[40]

(b) the net amount of exchange gains and losses on foreign currency borrowings less deposits charged or credited to the profit and loss account.[41] It should be noted that exchange differences on deposits have to be taken into account; it is not just the exchange differences on borrowings;

(c) the net amount of exchange gains and losses on foreign currency borrowings less deposits offset in reserves under the provisions of paragraphs 51, 57 and 58 of the standard;[42]

(d) the net movement on reserves arising from exchange differences.[43] This will normally be the exchange differences on the net investments of those subsidiaries translated using the closing rate method.

There is no requirement for exchange differences taken to the profit and loss account, other than those referred to in (b) above, to be disclosed. This is because the ASC considered 'that such disclosure is not necessarily helpful since it is influenced by the extent to which the company's trade is conducted in foreign currencies and the extent to which the company covers its exchange risk by entering into forward exchange contracts. Moreover, an agreement to settle a transaction in a foreign currency reflects only one aspect of the pricing or purchasing decision involved in normal trading. In any case a small difference may disguise a significant gain and significant loss and disclosure of the net figure will not indicate the risks inherent in trading in foreign currencies.'[44]

2.5.2 *Examples of disclosures*

Examples of disclosures of the methods used have been illustrated earlier in the chapter in giving extracts of accounting policies used. A good example of an accounting policy for foreign currencies which covers most of the various aspects is that of Reckitt Benckiser:

Extract 8.11: Reckitt Benckiser plc (2000)

Foreign currency translation

Transactions denominated in foreign currencies are translated at the rate of exchange on the day the transaction occurs or at the contracted rate if the transaction is covered by a forward exchange contract.

Assets and liabilities denominated in a foreign currency are translated at the exchange rate ruling on the balance sheet date or, if appropriate, at a forward contract rate. Exchange differences arising in the accounts of individual undertakings are included in the profit and loss account except that, where foreign currency borrowing has been used to finance equity investments in foreign currencies, exchange differences arising on the borrowing are dealt with through reserves to the extent that they are covered by exchange differences arising on the net assets represented by the equity investments.

The accounts of overseas subsidiary undertakings are translated into Sterling on the following basis:

Assets and liabilities are at the rate of exchange ruling at the year-end date.

Profit and loss account items at the average rate of exchange for the year.

Exchange differences arising on the translation of accounts into Sterling are recorded as movements on reserves.

The accounts of subsidiaries operating in hyper-inflationary environments are adjusted where possible to reflect current price levels before being translated into Sterling.

(The particular problem of hyperinflation is discussed in Chapter 9 at 2.1.)

The requirements to disclose those exchange differences taken to reserves are usually met in one of two ways:

(a) Show both types of exchange difference separately.

Extract 8.12: Reckitt Benckiser plc (2000)

22 Reserves [extract]

	Group Profit and loss £m
Net exchange loss on foreign currency borrowings	**(47)**
Exchange differences arising on the translation of net investments in overseas subsidiary undertakings	**68**

(b) Show a net figure but disclose that relating to borrowings by way of a note.

Extract 8.13: Bunzl plc (2000)

20 Movements on reserves [extract]	Share premium account £m	Revaluation reserve £m	Profit and loss account £m
Consolidated:			
Currency translation movement		–	(2.3)

Currency (losses)/gains of £(3.0)m (1999: £0.8m) relating to foreign currency exchange contracts and borrowings to finance investment overseas have been included within the currency translation movement in the profit and loss account.

Such exchange differences have to be reported in the statement of total recognised gains and losses and UITF 19 requires that the amount of any tax charges and credits that are also taken to that statement should be disclosed, in addition to the gross amount of the exchange differences on the borrowings (see 6.3 of Chapter 24).[45]

2.5.3 *FRS 13*

As mentioned earlier, in September 1998 the ASB issued FRS 13 which requires disclosures relating to the foreign currency aspects of a company's financial instruments (see 2 of Chapter 10).

3 PRACTICAL ISSUES

3.1 Individual companies

3.1.1 Date of transaction

The basic requirement of paragraph 46 of SSAP 20 is that transactions should be recorded at the rate ruling at the date the transaction occurred. No guidance is given in the standard as to what that date should be. SFAS 52 gives some help by defining the transaction date as being the date at which a transaction is recorded in accounting records in conformity with generally accepted accounting principles.[46] The following example illustrates the difficulty in determining the transaction date:

Example 8.8: Establishing the transaction date

A UK company buys an item of stock from a German company. The dates relating to the transaction, and the relevant exchange rates, are as follows:

Date	Event	£1–€
14 April 1999	Goods are ordered	1.50
5 May 1999	Goods are shipped from Germany and invoice dated that day	1.53
7 May 1999	Invoice is received	1.52
10 May 1999	Goods are received	1.51
14 May 1999	Invoice is recorded	1.52
28 May 1999	Invoice is paid	1.53

In our view the date of the transaction should be when the company should recognise an asset and liability as a result of the transaction. This will normally be when the risks and rewards of ownership of the goods have passed to the UK company.

It is unlikely at the date the goods are ordered that all the risks and rewards of ownership of the goods have passed to the UK company and therefore this date should not be used as the date of the transaction.

If the goods are shipped free on board (f.o.b.) then as the risks and rewards of ownership pass on shipment then this date should be used.

If, however, the goods are not shipped f.o.b. then the risks and rewards of ownership normally pass on delivery and therefore the date the goods are received should be treated as the date of the transaction.

The dates on which the invoice is received and is recorded are irrelevant to when the risks and rewards of ownership pass and therefore should not be considered to be the date of the transaction. In practice, it may be acceptable that as a matter of administrative convenience that the exchange rate at the date the invoice is recorded is used, particularly if there is no undue delay in processing the invoice. If this is done then care should be taken to ensure that the exchange rate used is not significantly different from that ruling on the 'true' date of the transaction.

It is clear from SSAP 20 that the date the invoice is paid is not the date of the transaction because if it were then no exchange differences would arise on unsettled transactions.

Most companies do not indicate in their accounting policies what is meant by the date of transaction. One company which did do so was Racal Electronics:

Extract 8.14: Racal Electronics Plc (1999)

4 **Foreign currencies** [extract]

United Kingdom exports in foreign currencies are converted at the rates relative to the period of shipment.

3.1.2 *Use of average rate*

As indicated in 2.3.1 above, rather than using the actual rate ruling at the date of the transaction 'if the rates do not fluctuate significantly, an average rate for the period may be used as an approximation'.[47] For companies which engage in a large number of foreign currency transactions it will be more convenient for them to use an average rate rather than using the exact rate for each transaction. If an average rate is to be used, what guidance can be given in choosing and using such a rate?

(a) Length of period

As an average rate should only be used as an approximation of actual rates then care has to be taken that significant fluctuations in the day to day exchange rates do not arise in the period selected. For this reason the period chosen should not be too long. We believe that the maximum length of period should be one month and where there is volatility of exchange rates it will be better to set rates on a more frequent basis, say, a weekly basis, especially where the value of transactions is significant.

(b) Estimate of average rate

The estimation of the appropriate average rate will depend on whether the rate is to be applied to transactions which have already occurred or to transactions which will occur after setting the rate. Obviously, if the transactions have already occurred then the average rate used should relate to the period during which those transactions occurred; e.g. purchase transactions for the previous week should be translated using the average rate for that week, not an average rate for the week the invoices are being recorded.

If there is no time delay between the date of the transaction and the date of recording and the rate is therefore being set for the following period then the rate selected should be a reasonable estimate of the expected exchange rate during that period. This could be done by using the closing rate at the end of the previous period or by using the actual average rate for the previous period. We would suggest that the former be used. Although a forward rate could be used, it should be remembered that forward rates are not estimates of future exchange rates but are a function of the spot rate adjusted by reference to interest differentials (see 3.3.1 A below). Whatever means is used to estimate the average rate, the actual rates during the period should be monitored and if there is a significant move in the exchange rate away from the average rate then the rate being applied should be revised.

(c) Application of average rate

We believe that average rates should only be used as a matter of convenience where there are a large number of transactions. Even where an average rate is used we would recommend that for large one-off transactions the actual rate should be used; e.g. purchase of a fixed asset or an overseas investment or taking out a foreign loan. Where the number of foreign currency transactions is small it will probably not be worthwhile setting and monitoring average rates and therefore actual rates should be used.

3.1.3 *Dual rates or suspension of rates*

One practical difficulty in translating foreign currency amounts is where there is more than one exchange rate for that particular currency depending on the nature of the transaction. In some cases the difference between the exchange rates can be small and therefore it probably does not matter which rate is actually used. However, in other situations, such as was the case with the South African rand, the difference can be quite significant. In these circumstances, what rate should be used? SSAP 20 is silent on this matter, but some guidance can be found in SFAS 52. It states that 'the applicable rate at which a particular transaction could be settled at the transaction date shall be used to translate and record the transaction. At a subsequent balance sheet date, the current rate (closing rate) is that rate at which the related receivable or payable could be settled at that date.'[48] Companies should therefore look at the nature of the transaction and apply the appropriate exchange rate. If there are doubts as to whether funds will be receivable at the more favourable rate then it may be necessary on the grounds of prudence to use the less favourable rate.

Another practical difficulty which could arise is where for some reason exchangeability between two currencies is temporarily lacking at the transaction date or at the subsequent balance sheet date. Again SSAP 20 makes no comment on this matter but SFAS 52 requires that the first subsequent rate at which exchanges could be made shall be used.[49]

3.1.4 *Monetary or non-monetary*

As discussed in 2.3.2 above, SSAP 20 generally requires that monetary items denominated in foreign currencies be retranslated using closing rates at each balance sheet date and non-monetary items should not be retranslated. Monetary items are defined as 'money held and amounts to be received or paid in money'.[50] The only examples of such items given in the standard are the obvious ones such as 'cash and bank balances, loans and amounts receivable and payable'.[51] Examples of non-monetary items given are equally obvious: 'plant, machinery and equity investments'.[52] Further examples of non-monetary items are those items listed in SFAS 52 as accounts to be remeasured using historical exchange rates when the temporal method is being applied.[53] Even with this guidance there are a number of particular items where the distinction may not be that clear.

A Deposits or progress payments paid against fixed assets or stocks

Companies may be required to pay deposits or progress payments when acquiring fixed assets or stocks from overseas. The question then arises as to whether such payments should be retranslated as monetary items or not.

Example 8.9

A UK company contracts to purchase an item of plant and machinery for C$10,000 on the following terms:

Payable on signing contract (1 April 1999) – 10%
Payable on delivery (19 April 1999) – 40%
Payable on installation (3 May 1999) – 50%

At 30 April 1999 the company has paid the first two amounts on the due dates when the respective exchange rates were £1=C$2.46 and £1=C$2.41. The closing rate at its balance sheet date, 30 April 1999, is £1=C$2.34.

		(i) £	(ii) £
First payment	– C$1,000	407	427
Second payment	– C$4,000	1,660	1,709
		2,067	2,136

(i) If the payments made are regarded as progress payments then the amounts should be treated as non-monetary items and included in the balance sheet at £2,067. This would appear to be consistent with SFAS 52 which in defining 'transaction date' states: 'A long-term commitment may have more than one transaction date (for example, the due date of each progress payment under a construction contract is an anticipated transaction date).'[54]

(ii) If the payments made are regarded as deposits, and are refundable, then the amounts should probably be treated as monetary items and included in the balance sheet at £2,136 and an exchange gain of £69 recorded in the profit and loss account.

In practice, it will often be necessary to consider the terms of the contract to ascertain the nature of the payments made in order to determine the appropriate accounting treatment.

B Debt securities held as investments

Companies may acquire or invest in overseas debt securities which have a fixed term of redemption, e.g. a US treasury bond or loan stock of an American company.

Example 8.10

A UK company invests in US$1m 6% Treasury bonds at a cost of US$950,000 on 30 September 1998 when the exchange rate was £1=US$1.70. The bonds are redeemable at par on 30 September 2003. At the company's year end, 31 March 1999, the closing rate of exchange is US$1.61.

In our view whether the investment is regarded as a monetary item or not depends on how the company is accounting for the investment.

(i) At lower of cost or market value

If the company is accounting for the investment at lower of cost or market value, then the investment should be regarded as a non-monetary item and recorded at a cost of £558,824 and no exchange difference taken to profit and loss account. If the investment is written down because the market value at the year end is lower than cost, then the investment should be translated using the rate of £1=US$1.61 as this is the rate relevant to the measurement date of the item.

(ii) At amortised cost

If the company intends holding the investment to the redemption date and is amortising the difference between cost and redemption value over the period to redemption we believe that the carrying amount is in the nature of a monetary item and therefore should be retranslated at the closing rate:

Cost	$950,000		
Amortisation – $50,000 ÷ 10	5,000		
	$955,000	@ £1=US$1.61	= £593,168

(For the purposes of illustration, amortisation has been calculated on a straight-line basis, rather than to give a constant rate of return over the life of the bonds.)

(iii) Marking to market

If the company is accounting for the investment by marking it to market then the investment should be translated using the rate of £1=US$1.61 as this is the rate relevant to the measurement date of the item.

C Foreign currency loans convertible into equity shares

Occasionally companies in the UK have issued bonds (or debentures), expressed in a foreign currency (usually US dollars), which are convertible into a fixed number of ordinary shares of the UK company at the holder's option. The terms of the bonds normally require the company to redeem the bonds at a fixed amount (expressed in the foreign currency) at the end of their term. The holders and/or the company may also have the option of redeeming the bonds at an agreed amount (expressed in the foreign currency). The question then arises – do the bonds represent a monetary liability to be translated at closing rates or, because they may never be repaid in cash if they are converted for shares, do they represent a non-monetary item which should not be retranslated at closing rates?

Example 8.11

A UK company issues US$100m 6% convertible bonds on 31 March 1997 when the exchange rate was £1=US$1.64. The share price at that date was £2.75 per share and the conversion terms are based on a share price of £3.05. The bonds are expressed as being convertible into shares at a share price of £3.05 per share and at a fixed exchange rate of £1=US$1.64. Assuming full conversion, therefore, the maximum number of shares which would be issued would be 19,999,200. (The conversion terms could have been expressed as 'convertible into shares at a fixed price of US$5.00' or as 'convertible into 1,000 shares for each US$5,000 of bonds held'; the number of shares to be issued would effectively be the same.) The bonds are only redeemable in 20 years' time on 31 March 2017.

How should the company account for these bonds in its accounts for the year ended 30 September 1997 and the year ended 30 September 1998? The exchange rates at the balance sheet dates are £1=US$1.61 and £1=US$1.70 respectively. No bonds have been converted by 30 September 1998.

	Option 1	Option 2	Option 3	Option 4
	£m	£m	£m	£m
Accounts for 30 September 1997				
Issue price	61.0	61.0	61.0	61.0
Exchange loss taken to p/l account	1.1	–	1.1	1.1
Balance sheet liability	62.1	61.0	62.1	62.1
Accounts for 30 September 1998				
Exchange gain taken to p/l account	(3.3)	–	(1.1)	(1.1)
Exchange gain deferred	–	–	–	(2.2)
Balance sheet liability	58.8	61.0	61.0	58.8

The rationale for each of these theoretical options are as follows:

Option 1

It could be argued that until such time as the bonds have been converted they are monetary liabilities of the company and therefore should be retranslated at the closing rate of exchange at each year end. The fact that the company may never actually pay any cash if all the bondholders exercise their right of conversion is irrelevant. At the time of conversion the bondholder will assess whether it is beneficial to convert his holding into shares with regard to the then sterling amount of the bond using the exchange rate at that time. It is therefore this value which the company should treat as having received in return for the issue of shares.

Option 2

It could be argued that as the terms are likely to be set so that it is probable that conversion will take place during the term of the bond then as no cash will actually be paid by the company the bonds should not be treated as a monetary liability. They should, therefore, not be retranslated at closing rates of exchange at each balance sheet date but should be translated at the historical rate of US$1.64. The company should treat the amount received on the issue of the bonds as being the amount received on the issue of the shares.

Option 3

This is a variation of option 2 above. The difference is that until conversion has taken place some recognition should be given to the fact that the bonds may be redeemed and if the bonds translated at closing rate gives a greater liability than that using the historical rate then, on the grounds of prudence, a loss should be recognised. Gains would only be recognised to the extent that they matched losses previously taken to profit and loss account.

Option 4

This is a variation of option 1 above. The difference is that as the bonds may be converted into shares and not repaid in cash it is considered that they may not ultimately be a monetary item and therefore some recognition of this fact should be given. This is done by not recognising any gains in the profit and loss account except to the extent that they offset previously recognised losses. On the grounds of prudence any excess gains would be treated as a deferred credit as they may not ultimately be realised if the bonds are converted.

Under FRS 4, convertible bonds should be accounted for by reference to their current form, i.e. as liabilities; the finance cost should be calculated on the assumption that the debt will never be converted (see Chapter 17 at 2.2.2 C). Accordingly, it would be inconsistent, if for translation purposes, any allowance were made for the possible conversion of the bond. In our view, convertible bonds should now be treated no differently from normal borrowings for translation purposes and therefore option 1 should be adopted.

It would appear that such bonds are commonly treated as monetary items as they are retranslated at closing rates of exchange. However, frequently the cover method (see 2.3.7 and 2.4.5 above) is applied and the exchange differences on the bonds are taken to reserves and not reflected in the profit or loss for the year.

3.1.5 *Treatment of exchange differences*

The general rule of SSAP 20 is that all exchange differences on monetary items should be recognised as part of the profit or loss for the year.[55] Apart from the possible treatment of gains on long-term monetary items (see 2.3.6 above) and the treatment of exchange differences on borrowings financing, or hedging against, foreign equity investments (see 2.3.7 above), are there any other circumstances where it is possible for exchange differences not to be taken as part of the profit or loss for the year?

A *Capitalisation of exchange differences*

On many occasions where a UK company is acquiring an asset (other than an equity investment) from overseas it finances the acquisition by means of a foreign loan. The general rules of SSAP 20 require the asset to be translated at historical rates and for the loan to be translated at closing rates.[56] Consequently, exchange differences on the loan are taken to profit and loss account with no offsetting exchange difference on the asset. One means of avoiding this situation is if the asset and liability can be regarded as a foreign branch, as discussed in 2.4.7 above. However, it will not always be possible to regard them as such and therefore consideration has to be given to any other way in which the exchange differences on the loan need not be taken to the profit or loss for the year.

In our view the only other possible circumstance is where the asset is still in the course of production. The Companies Act 1985 requires assets to be included at their purchase price or production cost.[57] Under the Act, production cost can include indirect overheads attributable to the production of the asset to the extent that they relate to the period of production[58] One of the overheads that the Companies Act 1985 specifically allows to be included is interest on borrowings.[59]

However, FRS 15 – *Tangible Fixed Assets* – only allows directly attributable costs to be capitalised as part of the cost of an asset (see 2.3 of Chapter 12 for a fuller discussion of these requirements). This might suggest that exchange differences can no longer be included. Nevertheless, it is often argued that exchange differences on foreign borrowings are really part of the interest cost of the foreign borrowing. A UK company may take out a borrowing in a 'hard' currency, e.g. Swiss francs, rather than in sterling so as to benefit from the low interest rate. However, as this lower interest charge is likely to be offset by exchange losses on the borrowing then these losses should be treated as part of the interest cost of the borrowing. Indeed, paragraph 68 of SSAP 20 suggests that exchange differences on borrowings should be disclosed as part of 'other interest receivable/payable and similar income/expense' in the profit and loss account.

FRS 15 allows companies to adopt a policy of capitalising finance costs that are directly attributable to the construction of a fixed asset as part of the cost of the asset. The standard is silent on whether exchange differences are 'finance costs'; however, IAS 23, the international standard on the capitalisation of borrowing costs, specifically allows exchange differences to be included within borrowing costs. We therefore believe that exchange differences on foreign currency loans can be capitalised as part of the cost of the asset when interest costs on the same borrowings are being capitalised. Capitalisation of borrowing costs is discussed more fully in Chapter 15. Where such a treatment is being adopted then similar disclosure to that of the interest costs shown in 5.1.2 of that chapter should be given for the exchange differences on the borrowings.

B Hedging transactions – deferment of exchange differences

The only specific reference which SSAP 20 makes to hedging is in respect of foreign currency borrowings providing a hedge against its foreign currency equity investments.[60] It also allows transactions to be recorded at the rate specified in a related forward contract,[61] which is another way of hedging. A further method by which companies may hedge against a foreign currency exposure is by matching foreign currency debtors in one currency with creditors in the same currency. By requiring the exchange differences on both these items to be taken to profit and loss account then SSAP 20 recognises this matching. However, what happens if one of the items is only a commitment (e.g. an agreement to purchase a fixed asset) and is still to be recognised in the accounts?

Example 8.12

A UK company has a debtor of US$1m resulting from a sale on 1 March 1999 and expects to receive payment on 31 March 1999. On 15 March 1999 the company signs a contract for the purchase of a fixed asset for US$1m from a US company. The asset is due to be delivered on 15 April 1999 with payment due on 31 May 1999. Rather than entering into a forward contract for the purchase of the US$1m to fix the sterling cost of the asset the company decides on 15 March 1999 that it will retain the US$1m once it is received from the debtor in a US$ bank account as a hedge against the cost of the fixed asset. Is it possible for the company to freeze the debtor at the rate ruling on 15 March 1999 and record the asset at the same amount? If not, can the exchange differences on the debtor and the bank balance be deferred and included in recording the cost of the asset?

It would appear that under SSAP 20 the answer to both questions is no. The debtor and bank balance are monetary items requiring to be translated at closing rates and the exchange differences on the settlement of the debtor and the bank balance taken to profit and loss account. The fixed asset should be recorded at the rate ruling at the date of the transaction, i.e. the date of delivery. It could be argued that this is illogical as the company could have entered into two forward contracts on 15 March 1999, one to buy US$1m to fix the cost of the fixed asset and one to sell US$1m to fix the amount to be received, and therefore have achieved what it wished.

SFAS 52 recognised this illogicality by requiring not only exchange gains and losses on a forward contract that is intended to hedge an identifiable foreign currency commitment to be deferred and included in the cost of the related foreign currency transaction, but also those which arise on other foreign currency transactions, e.g. cash balances, which are intended to hedge an identifiable foreign currency commitment.[62] This was because the accounting for the transaction should reflect the economic hedge of the foreign currency commitment.[63] Losses could not be deferred, however, if it was estimated that deferral would lead to recognising losses in later periods.[64]

3.1.6 *Foreign currency share capital*

The share capital of UK companies is generally denominated in sterling, but there is no requirement for this to be the case, except that a public company must have a minimum share capital of £50,000.[65] However, occasionally companies in the UK may issue share capital expressed in a foreign currency (usually US dollars). Neither SSAP 20 nor FRS 4 – *Accounting for Capital instruments* – addresses the treatment of translation of share capital denominated in a currency other than the reporting currency. In theory two treatments are possible: the foreign currency share capital (and any related share premium) could be maintained at a fixed sterling amount by being translated at a historical rate of exchange, or it could be retranslated annually at the closing rate as if it were a monetary amount. In the latter case a second question would arise: whether to take the difference arising on translation to the profit and loss account or deal with it within reserves.

Where the shares denominated in a foreign currency are ordinary shares, or are otherwise irredeemable, it might be more appropriate to use a historical exchange rate. This is because the effect of rate changes are not expected to have an impact on the company's cash flows. Such capital items are included within the examples of non-monetary items listed in SFAS 52 as accounts to be remeasured using historical exchange rates when the temporal method is being applied.[66] One company which has adopted this approach in respect of preference shares which are redeemable only at the company's option is Enterprise Oil as can be seen from the following extract from its 1999 accounts:

Extract 8.15: Enterprise Oil plc (1999)

21. Called-up Share Capital [extract]

The share capital of the company at 31 December was as follows:	**1999 £m**	1998 £m
Authorised:		
666,000,000 (1998: 666,000,000) ordinary shares of 25p each	**166.5**	166.5
24,000,000 (1998: 24,000.000) Cumulative Dollar Preference Shares of US$25 each (total: $600 million)	**367.5**	358.3
	534.0	524.8
Allotted, called-up and fully paid:		
498,326,126 (1998: 497,861,676) ordinary shares of 25p each	**124.6**	124.5
5,100,000 (1998: 5,100,000) Cumulative Dollar Preference Shares of US$25 each, Series B	**74.3**	74.3
	198.9	198.8

The Series B Cumulative Dollar Preference Shares are redeemable at the option of the company only, in whole or in part, at US$25.75 per share prior to 30 September 2000 and at decreasing prices thereafter declining to US$25 per share on 30 September 2002 and thereafter. Dividends are payable on the Series B Cumulative Dollar Preference Shares, in US dollars, quarterly in arrears at the rate of 9.84 per cent inclusive of tax credits.

Although, the allotted share capital is translated at a historical rate, the authorised share capital is translated at closing rates. Interestingly, Enterprise Oil redeemed the Dollar Preference Shares the following year as shown below.

Extract 8.16: Enterprise Oil plc (2000)

21. CALLED-UP SHARE CAPITAL [extract]

The share capital of the company at 31 December was as follows:	**2000 £m**	1999 £m
Authorised:		
666,000,000 (1999: 666,000,000) ordinary shares of 25p each	**166.5**	166.5
24,000,000 (1999: 24,000,000) Cumulative Dollar Preference Shares of US$25 each (total $600 million)	**401.7**	367.5
	568.2	534.0
Allotted, called up and fully paid:		
498,908,994 (1999: 498,326,126) ordinary shares of 25p each	**124.7**	124.6
Nil (1999: 5,100,000) Cumulative Dollar Preference Shares of US$25 each, Series B	**–**	74.3
	124.7	198.9

On 10 October 2000 all of the 5,100,000 Series B Cumulative Dollar Preference Shares were redeemed at a premium of US$0.50 per share, resulting in an appropriation of £1.8 million. The Preference Shares were recorded at historical cost exchange rates within called-up share capital and the foreign exchange difference of £13.6 million which arose on redemption has been charged to reserves since the shares provided a partial hedge against currency movements of the group's overseas investments. In accordance with UK legal requirements an amount equal to the nominal value of the redeemed shares has been credited to a Capital Redemption Reserve.

One company which has translated its foreign currency ordinary shares (and related share premium account) at closing rate is Lonmin.

Extract 8.17: Lonmin plc (2000)

24 Called up share capital and share premium account [extract]

2000 £m	1999 £m			**2000 $m**	1999 $m
		Authorised			
301	301	300,875,000	Ordinary shares of £1 each	**439**	494
		Issued			
178	160	177,872,464	Ordinary shares of £1 each, fully paid	**259**	262
Paid up amount £m	Share premium £m	Issued		Paid up amount $m	Share premium $m
160	189	159,610,804	At 30 September 1999	262	310
			(i) The exercise of options under:		
1	4	1,472,273	The Lonmin Executive Share Option Schemes (at prices ranging from 241p to 767.8p per share)	2	6
		50,523	The Lonmin Savings Related Share Option Schemes (at prices ranging from 193p to 383.1p per share)		
17	91	16,738,864	(ii) Conversion of 6% and 8% Guaranteed Convertible Bonds	25	138
			Exchange differences	(30)	(40)
178	**284**	**177,872,464**	**At 30 September 2000**	**259**	**414**

26 Reserves

Group	Revaluation reserve $m	Other reserves $m	Profit and loss account $m
At 30 September 1999	19	(70)	212
Profit for the financial year			229
Dividends			(90)
Negative goodwill realised on disposal of Duiker		(13)	
Transfers	(1)		1
Exchange differences		70	
Other items		1	
At 30 September 2000	**18**	**(12)**	**352**

Interestingly, in this case the foreign currency share capital is actually denominated in sterling. This is because Lonmin regards its functional currency (local currency) and reporting currency to be in US dollars (see Extract 8.32 at 3.9 below). It can be seen that in this case the exchange differences on the share capital and share premium have been taken to reserves and not to the profit and loss account. Where such share capital is retranslated, we believe that this is the most appropriate treatment for the exchange differences since they do not affect the cash flows of the company. Whether such share capital is maintained at a historical rate, or is dealt with in this way, has no impact on the overall equity of the company.

The annual retranslation of share capital (and related share premium) at closing rate is probably the most appropriate treatment for forms of share capital which are closely akin to debt, such as redeemable preference shares. Again, the question then arises as to whether to take the difference arising on translation to the profit and loss account or deal with it within reserves. In this case, if the shares are expected to be redeemed then clearly the exchange difference will have an impact on the company's cash flows. Therefore it would seem appropriate for the exchange difference to be taken to the profit and loss account as an appropriation of profit along with the dividends on the shares. However, if such shares were issued to finance or provide a hedge against foreign equity investments then the exchange difference could be taken to reserves under the cover method (see 2.3.7 above).

3.2 Exchange gains on long-term monetary items

Paragraphs 11 and 50 of SSAP 20 indicate that where there are doubts as to the convertibility or marketability of the currency in question then it may be necessary to consider on the grounds of prudence whether the amount of any exchange gain, or the amount by which exchange gains exceed past exchange losses on the same items, to be recognised in the profit and loss account should be restricted.

3.2.1 *In what circumstances do 'doubts as to convertibility or marketability' arise?*

Such circumstances do not include normal currency fluctuations after the year end or even devaluations of a foreign currency after the year end.[67] It is thought that such circumstances will be rare and would only arise when there is political upheaval or very stringent exchange control regulations in the country whose currency is being considered.[68]

Such events will probably only arise in those countries whose currencies are weakest and therefore UK companies are unlikely to have liabilities expressed in the foreign currency on which exchange gains would arise. Even if a UK company did have a liability expressed in such a currency why should it not recognise the gain? It is unlikely that the UK company would have to pay more than the foreign currency amount at the closing rate and if anything is likely to pay less as the foreign currency will probably continue to weaken.

It is more likely that UK companies will have amounts receivable in these foreign currencies and therefore exchange losses are likely to arise. If for some reason such a currency were to strengthen against sterling so that exchange gains did arise on the amounts receivable the restriction of exchange gains suggested by SSAP 20 is irrelevant in these circumstances. If these circumstances did apply then it will probably be necessary for a UK company to make provision against all amounts receivable in that currency, whether short-term or long-term, to reduce them to their expected recoverable amounts.

If it is considered that the restriction of exchange gains contained in SSAP 20 is sufficient to deal with the situation, there are a number of problem areas relating to the accounting for the restriction.

3.2.2 *Past exchange losses*

Paragraph 50 of the standard states that 'the amount of the gain, or the amount by which exchange gains exceed past exchange losses on the same items to be recognised in the profit and loss account should be restricted'. It is unclear whether this means that where there have been past exchange losses on the same item a company has the option of restricting either the whole amount of the gain arising in the year or only the excess over the past losses. In our view the proper interpretation of this paragraph is that past losses are to be taken into account in determining the amount to be restricted.

3.2.3 *Settled or unsettled transactions*

The part of paragraph 50 quoted above refers to past exchange losses on the 'same items'. This is clearly meant to stop companies taking into account past exchange losses on unrelated items. However, what if part of a transaction has been settled and only part of it remains unsettled? If a realised loss arose on the part that was settled can this be taken into account in determining the amount of the gain on the unsettled portion to be restricted? In our view as the gain only relates to the unsettled portion then only past exchange losses on that portion should be taken into account in determining the amount to be restricted.

3.2.4 *Current portion of long-term item*

Paragraph 50 of the standard only relates to long-term items. What happens, therefore, where a company has an amount receivable part of which is due within one year of the balance sheet date and part which does not? It could be argued that all of the item should be regarded as a long-term item and therefore all of the exchange gain is to be restricted. However, this would mean that the current portion would be treated differently from any other amount receivable in that same currency within one year. It could therefore be argued that the current portion should be excluded and it is only the non-current portion which is the long-term item. It is only the exchange gain on that part which is restricted and the exchange gain on the current portion has to be taken to the profit or loss for the year. In our view it is illogical to treat the gains differently and, if it is necessary in the circumstances envisaged by the standard for exchange gains on long-term items expressed in one currency to be excluded from the profit and loss account on the grounds of prudence, then a similar treatment should be adopted for short-term items in the same currency.

3.2.5 *Restriction of gain*

It is not clear from the standard how gains in these circumstances should be restricted. Three possible treatments would be:

(a) subtract the gain from the monetary item, i.e. effectively translate it at the historical rate; or

(b) credit the gain to a deferral account; or

(c) credit the gain directly to reserves.

In our opinion, treatment (b) is to be preferred as it treats the item as a monetary amount and excludes the gain from the net equity of the company. However, we consider that the other treatments are acceptable as they achieve the objective of paragraph 50 of the standard by excluding gains which ultimately may not be realised from the profit or loss for the year.

3.3 Forward contracts, currency swaps and currency options

In view of the volatility of exchange rates nowadays many companies are entering into such transactions to protect themselves from the potentially adverse effects of foreign currency rate movements. As indicated in 2.3.8 above, SSAP 20 only mentions forward contracts very briefly and does not say anything about currency swaps or currency options. The accounting for such items could be affected in the future as a result of the proposals on financial instruments (see Chapter 10), particularly in relation to whether any form of hedge accounting is allowed. In the meantime, however, how should companies account for such items?

Much of the guidance given below is based on the rules contained in SFAS 52. It should be borne in mind that in the US, SFAS 133 has introduced new requirements which supersede these provisions. However, as the hedging rules in SFAS 133 are based on measuring the financial instruments within its scope at fair values, then we believe that until such time as there is an applicable standard in the UK for financial instruments, SFAS 52 is still appropriate as an aid to the interpretation of SSAP 20.

3.3.1 *Forward contracts*

A What are forward contracts?

A forward contract is an agreement to exchange different currencies at a specified future date and at a specified rate.[69] A contract will normally be for a fixed period; e.g. one month, three months, six months, from the date of entering the contract. The rate under the contract is not an estimate of what the exchange rate will be at the end of the contract but is essentially a function of:

(a) the spot rate at the date the contract is taken out; and

(b) the interest rate differential between the two countries.

This is illustrated in the following example:

Example 8.13

On 31 March 1999 a UK company wishes to enter into a forward contract to buy €1m in six months' time. Ignoring any profit which the bank would take on the transaction the rate under contract would be calculated as if the bank had on 31 March 1999:

(i) sold the company an amount of euros at the spot rate on that date, which would yield a total of €1m in six months' time;

(ii) placed the amount of euros in (i) above on deposit for the company; and

(iii) lent the company the amount of sterling in (i) above repayable, with interest, in six months' time.

At 31 March 1999 the spot rate is £1=€1.50 and the euro and sterling interest rates are 2.5% p.a. and 5.25% p.a. respectively.

The amount of euros which the bank would 'sell' to the company would be €987,654. Interest on the 'deposit' at 2.5% p.a. for six months would be €12,346 which would mean that the company would be entitled to €1m in six months' time.

The amount of sterling 'lent' to the company would be £658,436 (i.e. €987,654 @ €1.50=£1). Interest on this loan at 5.25% p.a. for the six months would be £17,284 and therefore the company would have to pay £675,720 at the end of the six months.

This cost of £675,720 for the €1m gives an exchange rate of £1=€1.48.

Sometimes forward contract rates are not quoted as single figures but are quoted as being either at a discount or premium on the spot rate. To arrive at the contract rate a discount is *added* to the spot rate and a premium is *deducted* from the spot rate.

B Reasons for companies taking out forward contracts

In most situations companies enter into a forward contract to protect themselves from the risks of exchange rate variations. This will normally be done to hedge:

(a) a future commitment or an expected transaction which will require the purchase or sale of foreign currency; or

(b) an existing foreign currency monetary asset or liability; or

(c) an investment in a foreign enterprise, such as an overseas subsidiary; or

(d) the results of a foreign enterprise.

In the first two situations a company is hedging the transaction to fix the amount of cash in sterling terms which will be required, whereas in the other two situations a company is hedging to offset the effect of translating the investment or results of the foreign enterprise.

In addition, companies may also enter into a forward contract by way of speculation in the hope that they can make a profit out of doing so.

In our view the accounting for forward contracts should be based on the economic rationale for the company entering into the contract in the first place and therefore will be different in each of these situations. We will now look at how this can be done by considering examples of each of these situations.

C Forward contracts taken out to hedge future commitments or transactions

Example 8.14

On 30 September 1998 a UK company contracts to buy an item of plant and machinery from a US company for US$500,000, with delivery on 31 January 1999 and payment due on 31 March 1999. In order to hedge against the movements in exchange rates it enters into a forward contract on 30 September 1998 to buy US$500,000 in six months' time. The premium on such a contract is US$0.02 and based on the spot rate of £1=US$1.70 gives a contracted rate of £1=US$1.68.

The relevant spot rates are:

	£1=US$
31 December 1998	1.66
31 January 1999	1.64
31 March 1999	1.61

How should the company account for these transactions in its financial statements for the years ended 31 December 1998 and 31 December 1999?

There are two basic methods:

(i) Record the asset and the liability at 31 January 1999 at £297,619 being US$500,000 translated at the contracted rate of £1=US$1.68. No exchange loss would be recognised on the forward contract in either year and no exchange gain on the liability to the supplier would be recognised in the year ended 31 December 1999. This treatment is straightforward and reflects the fact that the company has eliminated all currency risks by entering into the forward contract.

It could however be argued that such a treatment is not allowed by SSAP 20. Paragraph 46 of the standard only refers to *trading* transactions being translated at rates specified in related forward contracts. Trading transactions are not defined in SSAP 20 and a narrow interpretation would preclude capital transactions, such as the purchase of fixed assets, from being so treated. However, it would appear that some companies adopt a wider interpretation, as indicated in 3.3.1 D below. We concur with such an interpretation.

(ii) The forward contract and the acquisition of the asset are accounted for as two separate transactions. The asset and the liability to the supplier are initially recorded at 31 January 1999 at £304,878 (US$500,000 @ 1.64). An exchange loss on the amount due to the supplier up to the date of payment of £5,681, being £310,559 (US$500,000 @ 1.61) less £304,878, is recognised in the profit and loss account for the year ended 31 December 1999.

The exchange difference on the forward contract up to the transaction date is not recognised in the profit and loss account but is deferred and included in the recorded amount of the asset. Thereafter, any exchange difference on the contract is matched against the exchange difference on the liability to the supplier. Accordingly, although there is an exchange gain on the contract at 31 December 1998 of £7,087, being £301,205 (US$500,000 @ 1.66) less £294,118 (US$500,000 @ 1.70) this is not recognised in the profit and loss account but is deferred. In 1999 there is an exchange gain on the contract up to the date of the transaction on 31 January 1999 of £3,673, being £304,878 (US$500,000 @ 1.64) less £301,205. Again, this is not recognised in the profit and loss account. This gain together with the gain previously deferred is included in recording the asset. Accordingly, the asset is recorded at £294,118 (£304,878 – £7,087 – £3,673). This is equivalent to the asset being recorded at the spot rate ruling when the forward contract was entered into.

Following the transaction date there is an exchange gain on the forward contract of £5,681 which should be taken to the profit and loss account. It can be seen that this will offset the exchange loss on the amount due to the supplier in the same period and therefore reflects the fact that the company had hedged its exposure to exchange differences.

In addition to the exchange difference on the forward contract, recognition has to be given to the premium on the contract, i.e. the difference between the contracted amount translated at the contracted rate and translated at the spot rate when the contract was taken out. In this case the premium is £3,501 being £297,619 (US$500,000 @ 1.68) less £294,118 (US$500,000 @ 1.70). As this premium essentially represents an interest cost (see Example 8.13 above) over the period of the contract then this should be amortised over that period as a finance charge. Accordingly, £1,750 would be charged to the profit and loss account in the year ended 31 December 1999 and £1,751 in the following year. This second method was that suggested by SFAS 52.[70]

We believe that both of these methods are acceptable but would recommend that companies adopt the approach suggested in SFAS 52 as outlined in (ii) above. However, it should be borne in mind that where an exchange loss on the forward contract arises it should not be deferred if it would lead to recognising losses in later periods.[71] An alternative treatment allowed by SFAS 52 for the premium or discount on a contract which hedges a future commitment or transaction was to include that proportion of the premium or discount which relates to the commitment period, i.e. up to the date of the transaction, as part of the transaction.[72]

It should be noted that the treatment discussed in the second method in the above example was only allowed by SFAS 52 if the contract is designated as a hedge and the foreign currency commitment is firm.[73] Accordingly, if in the above example the company had not contracted for the plant and machinery at 30 September 1999 but it was only their intention at that date to enter into such contract then the US standard would not have allowed deferral of any of the exchange differences on the forward contract prior to contracting for the plant. We believe that in the UK it is unnecessary for such a stringent test to be applied and the treatment can be applied where a company has a reasonable expectation of entering into the transaction.

One company which refers to forward contracts taken out to hedge future transactions is Diageo, as shown in the extract below:

> *Extract 8.18: Diageo plc (2000)*
>
> **Financial instruments** [extract]
>
> Gains and losses on contracts hedging forecast transactional cash flows, and on option instruments hedging the sterling value of foreign currency denominated income, are recognised in the hedged periods.

D *Forward contracts taken out to hedge an existing foreign currency monetary asset or liability*

Example 8.15

Suppose the UK company in the previous example enters into the same forward contract. However, this time it does so because it has an existing loan of US$500,000 which is due for repayment on 31 March 1999 and wishes to hedge against any further exchange risk.

How should the forward contract and the loan be treated in the financial statements for the years ended 31 December 1998 and 31 December 1999?

There are three basic methods:

(i) Translate the loan at the contracted rate of £1=US$1.68, i.e. £297,619. The difference between this amount and the recorded amount at 30 September 1998 based on the spot rate at that date, i.e. £294,118, is written off in the profit and loss account for the year ended 31 December 1998 along with the previous exchange differences on the loan. No amounts are recorded in the profit and loss account for the year ended 31 December 1999.

(ii) Again, translate the loan at the contracted rate. However, as the difference of £3,501 (£297,619 less £294,118) represents the premium on the contract then it is deferred and amortised over the period of the contract. Accordingly, £1,750 is charged in the profit and loss account for the year ended 31 December 1998 and £1,751 in the following year.

It has been suggested that the treatment of the loans in each of these methods is not allowed by SSAP 20 as loans are not trading transactions.[74] However, we believe this to be a narrow interpretation of the standard and it would appear that companies do translate loans at rates specified in forward contracts (see Extract 8.19 below).

(iii) Treat the loan and the forward contract as two separate transactions. The loan is translated at the closing rate at 31 December 1998 and the exchange difference thereon is taken to profit and loss account. This exchange difference will include an exchange loss of £7,087 for the period from 30 September 1998 to 31 December 1998, being £301,205 (US$500,000 @ 1.66) less £294,118 (US$500,000 @ 1.70). The forward contract should also be regarded as a foreign currency transaction on which an exchange difference arises. SSAP 20 does not make this clear. However, it was clear from SFAS 52 that a forward contract is a foreign currency transaction.[75] Accordingly, an exchange gain of £7,087 on the contract should be recognised in the profit and loss account for the year ended 31 December 1998. This will offset the loss on the loan and therefore the results will not be affected by exchange differences from 30 September 1998, which was the purpose of taking out the contract. In the profit and loss account for the year ended 31 December 1999 a further exchange loss of £9,354, being £310,559 (US$500,000 @ 1.61) less £301,205 will be recognised on the loan offset by an equivalent exchange gain on the forward contract. As in method (ii) the premium on the contract would be amortised over the period of the contract. This method is that was required by SFAS 52.[76]

We believe that all three methods are acceptable but would recommend that companies adopt method (iii). However, it would appear that at least some companies are translating loans at contracted rates, as the following extract shows:

Extract 8.19: British Airways Plc (2001)

Foreign currency translation [extract]

Foreign currency balances are translated into sterling at the rates ruling at the balance sheet date, except for certain loan repayment instalments which are translated at the forward contract rates where instalments have been covered forward at the balance sheet date.

E *Forward contracts taken out to hedge a foreign currency investment*

Example 8.16

A UK company has a US subsidiary which had net assets of US$1m at 31 December 1997. On that date the UK company enters into a forward contract to sell US$400,000 in six months' time as a means of partially hedging against the investment in the subsidiary. The premium on such a contract is US$0.02 and based on the spot rate of £1=US$1.65 gives a contracted rate of £1=US$1.63. On maturity of the contract the company buys US$400,000 at the spot rate in order to fulfil the contract. At that time it decides not to enter into another forward contract.

The relevant spot rates are:

	£1=US$
30 June 1998	1.67
31 December 1998	1.66

The exchange difference on the net investment in the subsidiary taken to reserves in the consolidated financial statements for the year ended 31 December 1998 will be a loss of £3,651, being £606,061 (US$1m @ 1.65) less £602,410 (US$1m @ 1.66), of which £7,259 relates to the six months to 30 June 1998.

The overall gain which the company has made on the contract is £5,878 being £245,399 (US$400,000 @ 1.63) less £239,521 (US$400,000 @ 1.67). This gain represents the exchange gain on the contract of £2,903, being £242,424 (US$400,000 @ 1.65) less £239,521, and the premium of £2,975 (£245,399 less £242,424).

How should the forward contract be accounted for in the consolidated financial statements for the year ended 31 December 1998?

(i) It could be argued that all of the gain of £5,878 should be reflected in the profit and loss account. This is based on the fact that SSAP 20 only refers to forward contracts in the context of recording related transactions or monetary items. In this case there is no corresponding transaction or monetary item. However, this fails to recognise the rationale for entering into the contract which was to hedge against exchange rate movements on the investment in the subsidiary.

(ii) In order to recognise the rationale for entering into the contract, the exchange gain of £2,903 should be taken to reserves to be offset against the exchange loss on the investment. This will reflect the fact that the exchange loss on the investment for the six months to 30 June 1998 of £7,259 was hedged to the extent of 40%. The premium of £2,975 should be reflected in the profit and loss account.

The effect of such a treatment is similar to that which would have arisen if the company had decided to hedge the investment by borrowing US$400,000 for six months and investing the proceeds in a sterling deposit for the same period.

This second method is essentially that which was required by SFAS 52.[77] An alternative treatment for the premium would be to take it to reserves in addition to the exchange gain on the contract which was an option allowed by SFAS 52.[78]

In the absence of specific requirements in SSAP 20, we believe that both methods are acceptable although we would recommend that companies adopt the method (ii) as it more fairly recognises the rationale for entering into the contract.

Where at its year end a company has an open forward contract which is intended as a hedge against a foreign currency investment, similar principles should be applied. We recommend that this is achieved by translating the assets and liabilities of the foreign enterprise at the relevant closing rate and by recording an exchange difference on the related forward contract.

An alternative approach may be to translate the assets and liabilities at the contracted rate, although it could be argued that this method is not allowed by SSAP 20 as it is only *transactions* of individual companies which can be translated at rates specified in forward contracts and the translation of the net assets of foreign investments for the purposes of consolidation is not a transaction. Another argument for not adopting such an approach is that the contract may not necessarily be for the same amount of currency as the net assets represent.

F Forward contracts taken out to hedge the results of a foreign currency investment

Example 8.17

Suppose in the previous example the company took out the forward contract not as a hedge against the net investment in the subsidiary but against the expected profits of the subsidiary for the year ended 31 December 1998. The company normally translates the results of the subsidiary at closing rates. The actual profits of the subsidiary were US$500,000, all of which were retained by the subsidiary.

How should the company account for the results of the subsidiary and the forward contract?

(i) The profits of the subsidiary should be translated at the closing rate and, therefore, included as £301,205 (US$500,000 @ 1.66). The total gain on the contract of £5,878 should also be included in the profit and loss account. This will, therefore, reflect the fact that the company hedged against the effects of movements in the exchange rate up to 30 June 1998 on the results but not for exchange rate movements after that date.

(ii) That part of the profits covered by the forward contract should be translated at the contracted rate and the balance translated at the closing rate. This would mean that the profits included would be as follows:

	£
US$400,000 @ 1.63 =	245,399
US$100,000 @ 1.66 =	60,241
	305,640

It can be seen that this is lower than the total profits arrived at under (i) above by £1,443. It will therefore be necessary to credit a gain of a similar amount as a movement in reserves. This amount represents the gain on exchange on the US$400,000, which has been translated at the contracted rate, as a result of retaining those profits in the subsidiary from 30 June 1998 until 31 December 1998, being £240,964 (US$400,000 @ 1.66) less £239,521 (US$400,000 @ 1.67).

It could be argued that this method is not allowed by SSAP 20 as it is only *transactions* of individual companies which can be translated at rates specified in forward contracts and the translation of the results of subsidiaries for the purposes of consolidation is not a transaction. Another argument against this method is that it is effectively translating some of the results at an 'average' rate and some at the closing rate, further distorting the underlying ratios.

For these reasons we believe method (i) to be more appropriate, particularly where companies normally translate results of foreign subsidiaries at closing rates and the forward contract only covers part of the period. We also consider it preferable that the exchange difference on the forward contract is treated as a finance cost within the profit and loss account, rather than being absorbed within the operating results.

Where companies translate the results of subsidiaries at an average rate or the contract covers the full period of the results then using method (ii) will be acceptable. If in the above example the contract had been for the full year then the overall gain on the contract would have been £4,435, being £245,399 less £240,964 (US$400,000 @ 1.66). Accordingly, both methods would have yielded the same overall profit of £305,640, although as noted above the classification within the profit and loss account would be different.

Where a forward contract is taken out towards a year end with the intention of hedging the remainder of a subsidiary's results for the current year and its expected results for the following year then that part of the exchange difference on the contract which relates to the current year's results should be taken to the profit and loss account and the remainder deferred until the following year. The premium should preferably be amortised over the period of the contract.

It can be seen from Examples 8.16 and 8.17 above that different treatments for the contract arise depending on what the contract is supposed to be hedging; the net investment or the results of the investment. For this reason it is particularly important that the company recognises at the time of taking out the contract the reason for doing so.

One company which translates the results of subsidiaries at contracted rates is Rolls-Royce, as the following extract from its accounting policy indicates:

Extract 8.20: Rolls-Royce plc (2000)

Foreign currencies [extract]

The trading results of overseas undertakings are translated at the average exchange rates for the year or, where applicable, at the estimated sterling equivalent, taking account of future foreign exchange and similar contracts.

G *Speculative forward contracts*

Example 8.18

A UK company enters into a forward contract on 30 September 1998 to sell US$500,000 in six months' time in the hope that it will make a profit out of doing so. It has no monetary liabilities in US dollars and is not planning to enter into any transaction which requires US dollars.

The relevant spot rates are:

	£1=US$
30 September 1998	1.70
31 December 1998	1.66

The premium on the contract is US$0.02, giving a contracted rate of £1=US$1.68. At 31 December 1998 the company still has the contract. The premium on three month contracts at that date is US$0.01 giving a contract rate of £=US$1.65.

How should the company account for the contract in its financial statements for the year ended 31 December 1998?

There are three possible methods:

(i) Record an exchange loss of £7,087, being £301,205 (US$500,000 @1.66) less £294,118 (US$500,000 @ 1.70). In addition, recognise the proportion of the premium of £3,501, being £297,619 (US$500,000 @ 1.68) less £294,118 which relates to the period up to December, 1998, i.e. £1,750. This is the same treatment which has been recommended if the contract had been taken out to hedge an amount of US$500,000 receivable on 30 March 1999. However, as in this case the reason for taking out the contract was speculative then it is likely that a company will 'close' such a contract at such time either when it considers that it has made the maximum profit it will make or to cut its losses. Rather than deferring the premium to a period where the contract may be closed out, an alternative approach is not to give any separate recognition to the premium but to recognise the gain or loss on the contract based on its 'realisable value'.

(ii) One method of doing this would be to record a loss of £3,586 being £301,205 less £297,619 (US$500,000 @1.68). This represents the difference between the sterling amount receivable under the contract and the dollar amount translated at the spot rate. This effectively assumes that the company could buy the required amount of foreign currency at the spot rate on the balance sheet date and therefore fix the loss at that amount. However, this ignores the cost of holding the currency until the contract matures.

(iii) The method which overcomes the deficiencies in the other two methods is to record a loss of £5,411, being £303,030 (US$500,000 @ 1.65) less £297,619. This effectively represents the difference between the sterling amount receivable under the contract less the amount it would cost to take out an equal and opposite forward contract to buy US$500,000 on the date the existing contract matures. This method is that which was required by SFAS 52.[79]

In the absence of detailed requirements in SSAP 20 we believe that all three methods are acceptable although we would recommend that companies adopt method (iii) above.

H Conclusion

It can be seen from the above examples that different treatments of a forward contract are possible depending on the reason for entering into the contract in the first place. It is therefore important that companies should establish the reason for so doing prior to or at the same time as entering into the contract. As mentioned previously, the accounting for such items could be affected in the future as a result of the proposals on financial instruments (see Chapter 10), particularly in relation to whether any form of hedge accounting is allowed.

The methods recommended, and the other suggested possibilities, in each of the above examples follow the general principle in SSAP 20 that there should be symmetry of treatment of exchange gains and losses and should meet the objectives of translation contained in the standard. However, as there are no specific requirements relating to forward contracts in the standard then it may be possible that other treatments such as recognising losses but not profits on such contracts or treating them as 'commitments' are acceptable. Where such alternative treatments are adopted then the policy adopted should be disclosed and details of the financial commitments under the contracts will probably be required to meet the requirements of the Companies Act.[80]

3.3.2 *Currency swaps*

Another way in which companies can hedge against the risk of exchange rate movements is by entering into currency swaps. SSAP 20 makes no reference to such agreements and therefore the question arises as to how these should be accounted for. As currency swaps are essentially similar in nature to forward contracts then we believe that they should be accounted for in the same way as we have suggested for forward contracts above. Indeed, SFAS 52 stated that 'agreements that are, in substance, essentially the same as forward contracts, for example, currency swaps, shall be accounted for in a manner similar to the accounting for forward contracts'.[81]

Most companies who have entered into currency swaps appear to do so to hedge against foreign currency borrowings and translate their borrowings at the swap rate. For example:

Extract 8.21: BP Amoco p.l.c. (2000)

24 Finance debt [extract]

Where a borrowing is swapped into another currency, the borrowing is accounted in the swap currency and not in the original currency of denomination.

One company which uses currency swaps to hedge its foreign currency investments is Boots, as shown below:

> *Extract 8.22: The Boots Company PLC (2001)*
>
> **Foreign currencies** [extract]
>
> Exchange differences arising from the translation of the results and net assets of overseas subsidiaries, less offsetting exchange differences on foreign currency borrowings and currency swaps hedging those assets (net of any related tax effects) are dealt with through reserves.

3.3.3 *Currency options*

Where companies use forward contracts and currency swaps to hedge against exchange risks they eliminate not only the risk of exchange losses but also the possibility of exchange gains. One way that companies can eliminate the 'downside' of exchange losses but still participate in the 'upside' of exchange gains is to enter into currency options. As the name suggests these give companies the *right* to buy or sell foreign currency on or by a certain date in the future at a specified rate, but they are not *obliged* to do so. A company which purchases an option will have to pay a premium at the outset. The amount of the premium will depend on:

(a) the current spot rate;

(b) the specified rate (generally referred to as the strike price);

(c) the period to the expiry of the option; and

(d) the volatility of the exchange rate.

How should companies account for currency options?

SSAP 20 makes no reference to currency options at all. Due to the nature of currency options it is not really possible to translate transactions or monetary items in foreign currencies at the rates ruling under related currency options as they may never be exercised. Accordingly, it will be more appropriate to account for the currency option and any related transaction, asset or liability separately.

In accounting for the currency option it must be remembered that the maximum loss that the company can make is the cost of the premium. There are essentially two ways of calculating the gain or loss on a currency option:

(i) The premium paid for the option should initially be recorded as an asset. At a subsequent balance sheet date this should be revalued to the current premium for the currency option, known as 'marking to market'. If the exchange rate has moved such that it is likely that the currency option will be exercised then the premium will have increased. This increase will represent the gain that the company can make by closing out the option. If the exchange rate has moved such that it is unlikely that the currency option will be exercised then the premium will have decreased. If the time remaining to the expiry date is short then the premium is likely to be a nominal sum. This decrease will represent the loss on the option.

(ii) Again the premium is initially recorded as an asset. At a subsequent balance sheet date the currency amount under the option is translated at the current rate. If this shows an exchange gain when compared to the rate under the option then this gain is recognised. However, it will then be necessary to offset against this gain the cost of the option. If the comparison with the spot rate shows a loss exceeding the amount of the premium then the premium paid should be written off. If the loss is less than the premium paid then the premium should be written off to the extent of the loss.

These methods can be illustrated in the following example:

Example 8.19

On 30 April 1999 a UK company records a creditor of US$503,125 which it is due to pay on 31 July 1999. The exchange rate at 30 April 1999 is £1=US$1.61 and the creditor is recorded at £312,500. The company decides to take out some July put option contracts at a strike price of US$1.60 in order to provide a hedge against the creditor. Accordingly, it takes out 10 contracts of £31,250 on the Philadelphia Stock Exchange at a premium of US$0.0171 per £1. The total premium paid is £3,319 (being 10 x £31,250 x US$0.0171 = US$5,344 @ £1=US$1.61).

At 30 June 1999, the company's balance sheet date, the creditor is translated at the exchange rate ruling on that date of £1=US$1.576 at £319,242, thereby recording an exchange loss of £6,742.

At 30 June 1999 the premium on July put option contracts at a strike price of US$1.60 is now US$0.0241 per £1. Accordingly, under method (i) above, the gain on the option contracts is as follows:

Premium at 30 June 1999 – 10 x £31,250 x US$0.0241 = US$7,531 @ 1.576 =	£4,779
Less premium paid	3,319
Gain on option contracts	£1,460

Under method (ii) above the gain is as follows:

Currency amount of contracts = 10 x £31,250 x US$1.60 =		US$500,000
Amount payable at option rate –	US$500,000 @ 1.60 =	£312,500
Amount payable at current rate –	US$500,000 @ 1.576 =	£317,259
Exchange gain on option contracts		£ 4,759
Less premium paid		3,319
Gain on option contracts		£ 1,440

In the absence of detailed guidance in SSAP 20, we believe either method of calculation is acceptable, although we would recommend that the first method be adopted if possible as the gain or loss recognises the 'time value' contained in the premium.

The accounting for such gains or losses on the currency options should essentially follow the same principles as those outlined for forward contracts in 3.3.1 above and will again depend on the reason for taking out the currency option.

As mentioned previously, the accounting for such items could be affected in the future as a result of the proposals on financial instruments (see Chapter 10), particularly in relation to whether any form of hedge accounting is allowed.

3.4 Consolidated accounts – closing rate/net investment method

3.4.1 Subsidiary with non-coterminous year end

It is sometimes the case that UK companies consolidate the financial statements of foreign subsidiaries made up to a date which is not coterminous with the year end of the parent company. Where the results of the subsidiary are consolidated using the closing rate/net investment method the question then arises – which closing rate is to be used? The rate applying to the subsidiary's balance sheet date or the one applying to the parent company's balance sheet date?

SSAP 20 makes no reference to which one it should be. However, guidance can be drawn from SFAS 52 which states that the rate to be used is the one in effect at the date of the subsidiary's balance sheet.[82] The reason for this is that this presents the functional currency performance of the subsidiary during the subsidiary's financial year and its position at the end of that period in terms of the parent company's reporting currency.[83] The subsidiary may have entered into transactions in other currencies, including sterling, and monetary items in these currencies will have been translated using rates ruling at the subsidiary's balance sheet date. The profit and loss account of the subsidiary will reflect the economic consequences of carrying out these transactions during the period ended on that date. In order that the effects of these transactions in the subsidiary's financial statements are not distorted, the financial statements should be translated using the closing rate at the subsidiary's balance sheet date.

An alternative argument can be advanced for using the closing rate ruling at the parent company's balance sheet date. All subsidiaries within a group should normally prepare financial statements up to the same date as the parent company so that the parent company can prepare consolidated accounts which show a true and fair view of the state of affairs of the group at the parent company's balance sheet date and of the results of the group for the period then ended. The use of financial statements of a subsidiary made up to a date earlier than that of the parent is only an administrative convenience and must be recognised as being a surrogate for financial statements made up to the proper date. In view of this the closing rate which should be used is that which would have been used if the financial statements were made up to the proper date, i.e. that ruling at the date of the balance sheet date of the parent company. Another reason for using this rate is that there may be subsidiaries who have the same functional currency who make up their financial statements to the same date as the parent company and therefore in order to be consistent it is necessary for the same rate to be used.

We believe that both treatments are acceptable. In many cases where companies have such subsidiaries it is unclear from their accounting policies which treatment is adopted as they just refer to the financial statements being translated at the 'closing rate'. However, it would appear that where companies do make it clear which treatment is adopted, the use of the rate ruling at the parent company's balance sheet date is favoured. Two companies which have subsidiaries with non-coterminous year ends and would appear to use such a rate are Blue Circle and ICI. Extracts from their accounting policies are illustrated below:

Extract 8.23: Blue Circle Industries PLC (2000)

4 **Foreign currency** [extract]

Profit and loss accounts of foreign entities in foreign currencies are translated into sterling at average rates for the year. Assets and liabilities denominated in foreign currencies are translated into sterling at the rates of exchange ruling at 31 December.

Extract 8.24: Imperial Chemical Industries PLC (2000)

Foreign currencies [extract]

Profit and loss accounts in foreign currencies are translated into sterling at average rates for the relevant accounting periods. Assets and liabilities are translated at exchange rates ruling at the date of the Group balance sheet.

3.4.2 *Dual rates or suspension of rates*

The problems of dual rates and suspension of rates in relation to the accounts of an individual company have already been discussed in 3.1.3 above and many of the points made in that section apply equally to the consolidated accounts.

SSAP 20 makes no reference to what should happen when applying the closing rate/net investment method when there is more than one exchange rate for a particular currency. Again, guidance can be sought from SFAS 52 which states that the rate to be used to translate foreign statements should be, in the absence of unusual circumstances, the rate applicable to dividend remittances.[84] The reason for this is that the use of that rate is more meaningful than any other rate because cash flows to the parent company from the foreign enterprise can be converted only at that rate, and realisation of a net investment in the foreign enterprise will ultimately be in the form of cash flows from that enterprise.[85]

As mentioned in 3.1.3 above one currency where there used to be dual rates was the South African rand. It would appear that companies generally used the commercial rand, which was applicable to dividend remittances, for translating the financial statements of their South African subsidiaries.

3.4.3 *Calculation of average rate*

Paragraph 54 of SSAP 20 allows the profit and loss account of foreign enterprises to be translated at an average rate for the period. No definitive method of calculating the average rate has been prescribed and all the standard says is that 'the average rate used should be calculated by the method considered most appropriate for the circumstances of the foreign enterprise'. It does, however, give some guidance on the factors to be taken into account in determining what is most appropriate 'Factors that will need to be considered include the company's internal accounting procedures and the extent of seasonal trade variations; the use of a weighting procedure will in most cases be desirable.'[86] What methods are, therefore, available to companies to use? Possible methods might be:

(a) mid-year rate;

(b) average of opening and closing rates;

(c) average of month end/quarter end rates;
(d) average of monthly average rates;
(e) monthly/quarterly results at month end/quarter end rates; or
(f) monthly/quarterly results at monthly/quarterly averages.

Example 8.20

A UK company has a US subsidiary and is preparing its consolidated accounts for the year ended 30 April 1999. It intends to use an average rate for translating the results of the subsidiary. The relevant exchange rates for £1=US$ (rounded to two decimal places) are as follows:

Month	Month end	Average for month	Average for quarter	Average for year
April 1998	1.67			
May 1998	1.63	1.67		
June 1998	1.67	1.64		
July 1998	1.64	1.65	1.65	
August 1998	1.67	1.64		
September 1998	1.70	1.63		
October 1998	1.67	1.68	1.65	
November 1998	1.65	1.70		
December 1998	1.66	1.66		
January 1999	1.64	1.67	1.68	
February 1999	1.60	1.65		
March 1999	1.61	1.63		
April 1999	1.61	1.62	1.63	1.65

Average of month end rates – 1.65
Average of quarter end rates – 1.64

The results of the subsidiary for each of the 12 months to 30 April 1999 and the translation thereof under each of the above methods (using monthly figures where appropriate) are shown below:

		(e) quarterly	(e) monthly	(f) quarterly	(f) monthly
Month	US$	£	£	£	£
May 1998	1,000		613		599
June 1998	1,100		659		671
July 1998	1,200	2,012	732	2,000	727
August 1998	1,300		778		793
September 1998	1,300		765		798
October 1998	1,350	2,365	808	2,394	804
November 1998	1,400		848		824
December 1998	1,400		843		843
January 1999	2,000	2,927	1,220	2,857	1,198
February 1999	5,000		3,125		3,030
March 1999	10,000		6,211		6,135
April 1999	4,000	11,801	2,484	11,656	2,469
Total	31,050	19,105	19,086	18,907	18,891

Method (a)	US$31,050 @ 1.67= £18,593
Method (b)	US$31,050 @ 1.64= £18,933
Method (c) – monthly	US$31,050 @ 1.65= £18,818
Method (c) – quarterly	US$31,050 @ 1.64= £18,933
Method (d)	US$31,050 @ 1.65= £18,818

It can be seen that by far the simplest methods to use are the methods (a) to (d).

In our view methods (a) and (b) should not be used as it is unlikely in times of volatile exchange rates that they give appropriate weighting to the exchange rates which have been in existence throughout the period in question. They are only likely to give an acceptable answer if the exchange rate has been static or steadily increasing or decreasing throughout the period.

Method (c) based on quarter end rates has similar drawbacks and therefore should not normally be used.

Method (c) based on month end rates and method (d) are better than the previous methods as they do take into account more exchange rates which have applied throughout the year with method (d) being preferable as this will have taken account of daily exchange rates. Average monthly rates for most major currencies are likely to be given in publications issued by the government, banks and other sources and therefore it is unnecessary for companies to calculate their own. The work involved in calculating an average for the year, therefore, is not very onerous. Method (d) will normally give reasonable and acceptable results when there are no seasonal variations in items of income and expenditure.

Where there are seasonal variations in items of income and expenditure then this may not be the case. In these situations appropriate exchange rates should be applied to the appropriate items. This can be done by using either of methods (e) or (f) preferably using figures and rates for each month. Where such a method is being used care should be taken to ensure that the periodic accounts are accurate and that cut-off procedures have been adequate, otherwise significant items may be translated at the wrong average rate.

Where there are significant one-off transactions then it is likely that actual rates at the date of the transaction should be used to give a more accurate weighting. Indeed, SFAS 52 requires that for revenues, expenses, gains, and losses the exchange rate at the date on which these elements are recognised should be used or an appropriately weighted average.[87]

Most companies do not indicate how they have applied an average rate, but merely state that the results are translated at average rates or weighted average rates. Two companies which are more specific in their accounting policies on the use of average rates are Allied Domecq and Boots, as illustrated below:

Extract 8.25: Allied Domecq PLC (2000)

Foreign currencies [extract]

The results of undertakings outside the UK are translated at weighted average exchange rates each month.

Extract 8.26: The Boots Company PLC (2001)

Foreign currencies [extract]

The results and cash flows of overseas subsidiaries and the results of joint ventures are translated into sterling on an average exchange rate basis, weighted by the actual results of each month.

3.4.4 *Change from closing rate to average rate or vice versa*

By allowing companies the choice of using either the closing rate or an average rate for the period in translating the results of foreign enterprises, the question then arises – can a company change the method used by switching from closing rate to an average rate or vice versa?

Paragraph 17 of the standard states that the use of either method is permitted 'provided that the one selected is applied consistently from period to period'. It could be argued that this means that once a company has chosen a particular method no change should be made on the grounds of consistency. However, in view of the arguments expressed in paragraph 17 about the use of each of the methods it would seem possible that a company could justify changing from one method to the other on the grounds that it was adopting a better method.

If a change is made, it could be argued either that it is a change in accounting policy needing a prior year adjustment under FRS 3[88] and therefore the previous year's profit and loss account changed to the new basis, or that it is only a refinement of the existing policy which would not require a prior year adjustment. A refinement of an accounting policy is normally one that seeks to give a more accurate estimation in pursuit of the same basis of measurement; for example, a provision for stock obsolescence. This is not the case here, and in view of the conceptual differences of each method discussed in paragraph 17 of SSAP 20 we believe that this suggests a change in accounting policy. This would also appear to be required by paragraph 17 when it says that the method should be applied consistently from period to period.

A number of companies did change from the closing rate method to the average rate method in 1985/86. This was probably due to the dramatic weakening of the US dollar from January/February 1985 to the autumn of that year. In particular, the exchange rate moved from £1=US$1.08 at the end of February to £1=US$1.24 at the end of March. Companies were finding that, in addition to depressing their reported results, they were having to reassess their expected results due to the change in the exchange rate. They were also finding that figures previously reported in their interim announcements could be remarkably different when the annual figures were being translated at the closing rate. This particular problem is discussed in 3.4.11 below.

Since then more companies have changed to using average rates. Most major companies now use the average rate method.

3.4.5 *To which reserve should exchange differences be taken?*

SSAP 20 requires that exchange differences arising from the retranslation of the net investment at the closing rate should be recorded as a movement on reserves; however, it does not specify the category of reserves to which they should be taken. A number of companies take them to retained profits. Many companies in addition to showing such exchange differences as movements on retained profits also show them as movements on other reserves such as revaluation reserves and capital reserves. However, this is likely to be as a result of items dealt with in 3.4.6 below.

One company which has taken the exchange differences to a separate currency translation reserve is Low & Bonar, as shown below:

Extract 8.27: Low & Bonar PLC (2000)

21 Reserves [extract]	**Group £000**
Exchange reserve	
At 30 November 1999	**(14,542)**
Adjustment on translation of currency loans to fund overseas investments	**1,756**
Adjustment on translation of net assets and results of overseas subsidiaries	**458**
Transfer on repayment of currency loans to fund overseas investments	**1,921**
At 30 November 2000	**(10,407)**

3.4.6 *Post-acquisition capital or revaluation reserves*

As indicated above, SSAP 20 does not specify the reserve to which the exchange difference arising from the retranslation of the net investment at the closing rate should be taken. Normally, they should be taken to only one category of reserve. However, the foreign enterprise may have a non-distributable capital reserve which arose after the company was acquired by the investing company. Alternatively, it may have revalued some assets since it was acquired and therefore has a revaluation reserve. As these reserves will not be reported as part of retained profits in the consolidated financial statements the question then arises – if exchange differences are normally taken to retained profits, should part of the exchange difference be taken to these other categories of reserves so that they are effectively translated at the closing rate?

Example 8.21

A UK company has a German subsidiary which was set up on 1 January 1997 with a share capital of DM500,000. In the year to 31 December 1997 the subsidiary made a post-tax profit of DM100,000 and at its year end transferred 5% thereof to a non-distributable legal reserve. In the following year the subsidiary made no profit or loss and therefore made no further transfer to the legal reserve. In the consolidated financial statements at 31 December 1997 the legal reserve was treated as a capital reserve and the exchange difference on the net investment was taken to retained profits. How should the capital reserve and the current year's exchange difference be treated in the consolidated financial statements at 31 December 1998?

The relevant exchange rates are:

	£1=DM
1 January 1997	2.64
31 December 1997	2.96
31 December 1998	2.77

	31 December 1998 DM	31 December 1997 £	(i) 31 December 1998 £	(ii) 31 December 1998 £
Net assets	600,000	202,703	216,606	216,606
Share capital	500,000	189,394	189,394	189,394
Opening retained profits	90,000	–	9,931	9,931
Profit for year	–	33,784	–	–
Transfer to capital reserve	–	(3,378)	–	–
Exchange difference	–	(20,475)	13,903	13,671
Closing retained profits	90,000	9,931	23,834	23,602
Opening capital reserve	10,000	–	3,378	3,378
Transfer from retained profits	–	3,378	–	–
Exchange difference	–	–	–	232
Closing capital reserve	10,000	3,378	3,378	3,610
	600,000	202,703	216,606	216,606

(i) This method has continued to take the exchange difference on the opening net investment to retained profits. The capital reserve has been retained at the rate ruling at which the reserve was created.

(ii) This method has taken that part of the exchange difference which relates to the net investment which is not distributable to the capital reserve so that the reserve represents the amount which is non-distributable at the closing rate. It should be borne in mind, however, that the split of consolidated reserves between distributable and non-distributable amounts are really irrelevant as it is the parent company's reserves which are important in determining whether a company can legally make a distribution. In any case, the figure for retained profits does not represent the amount that the subsidiary could distribute translated at the closing rate.

In our view either of these treatments is acceptable.

Example 8.22

A UK company has a Swiss subsidiary which was set up on 1 August 1997 with a share capital of SFr1m. The main asset of the subsidiary is an investment property which it acquired on the same day that the company was set up at a cost of SFr800,000. The subsidiary made a profit after tax of SFr50,000 for the six months to 31 January 1998 and a profit after tax of SFr100,000 in the following year. The property was revalued at 31 January 1998 at SFr950,000 which was incorporated in its financial statements. The valuation was updated at 31 January 1999 to SFr1.2m. The exchange difference on the net investment was taken to a separate exchange reserve in the 1998 financial statements. How should the revaluation reserve and the current year's exchange difference be treated in the consolidated financial statements at 31 January 1999?

The relevant exchange rates are:

	£1=SFr
1 August 1997	2.48
31 January 1998	2.41
31 January 1999	2.33

	31/1/98 SFr	31/1/98 £	31/1/99 SFr	(i) 31/1/99 £	(ii) 31/1/99 £
Investment property	950,000	394,191	1,200,000	515,021	515,021
Other assets	250,000	103,734	350,000	150,215	150,215
	1,200,000	497,925	1,550,000	665,236	665,236
Share capital	1,000,000	403,226	1,000,000	403,226	403,226
Opening retained profits			50,000	20,747	20,747
Profit for year	50,000	20,747	100,000	42,919	42,919
Closing retained profits	50,000	20,747	150,000	63,666	63,666
Opening revaluation reserve			150,000	62,241	62,241
Surplus for year	150,000	62,241	250,000	107,296	107,296
Exchange difference					2,137
Closing revaluation reserve	150,000	62,241	400,000	169,537	171,674
Opening exchange reserve				11,711	11,711
Exchange difference		11,711		17,096	14,959
Closing exchange reserve		11,711		28,807	26,670
Total capital and reserves	1,200,000	497,925	1,550,000	665,236	665,236

(i) This method has continued to take the exchange difference on the opening net investment to the separate exchange reserve. Surpluses credited to the revaluation reserve are retained at the rates ruling at the date the surpluses arise.

(ii) This method has taken that part of the exchange difference on the opening net investment which arises only because of the fact that the investment property has been revalued to the revaluation reserve. If the property had been retained at cost then that exchange difference would not have arisen in the consolidated financial statements. This treatment means that the revaluation reserve in the consolidated financial statements represents the revaluation reserve expressed in the foreign currency translated at the closing rate. It also represents the difference between the carrying amount of the asset in the consolidated financial statements and the historical cost of the asset translated at the closing rate which should be included in the historical cost information required by the Companies Act 1985 in respect of assets affected by revaluations[89] (see 3.2.3 of Chapter 12); i.e.

	£
Carrying value at 31 January 1999	515,021
Historical cost at 31 January 1999 SFr800,000 @ £1=SFr2.33 =	343,347
	171,674

Although we believe both methods to be acceptable, in our view method (ii) is preferable for the reasons stated above. It would appear that this is the method adopted by a number of companies, as indicated in 3.4.5 above.

3.4.7 *Treatment of exchange differences on disposal of subsidiary*

The issues relating to the calculation of the gain/loss on disposal of subsidiaries are discussed at 3 in Chapter 6. In relation to foreign subsidiaries there is one further issue – what should happen to the cumulative exchange differences on the net investment in a foreign subsidiary when all or part of it is sold? SSAP 20 does not specifically deal with this.

Example 8.23

A UK company has a US subsidiary which was set up on 1 January 1996 with a share capital of US$200,000 when the exchange rate was £1=US$1.55. The subsidiary is included at its original cost of £129,032. The profits of the subsidiary, all of which have been retained by the subsidiary, for each of the three years ended 31 December 1998 were US$40,000, US$50,000 and US$60,000 respectively. In the consolidated financial statements the results of the subsidiary have been translated at the respective closing rates of £1=US$1.71, £1=US$1.65 and £1=US$1.66. All exchange differences have been taken to a separate exchange reserve. The consolidated reserves have therefore included the following amounts in respect of the subsidiary:

	Retained profit	Exchange reserve
	£	£
1 January 1996	–	–
Movement during 1996	23,392	(12,073)
31 December 1996	23,392	(12,073)
Movement during 1997	30,303	(5,104)
31 December 1997	53,695	(6,969)
Movement during 1998	36,144	(1,059)
31 December 1998	89,839	(8,028)

The net assets at 31 December 1998 of US$350,000 are included in the consolidated financial statements at £210,843.

On 1 January 1999 the subsidiary is sold for US$400,000 (£240,964), thus resulting in a gain on sale in the parent company's books of £111,932, i.e. £240,964 less £129,032. On consolidation the gain on sale is reduced to £30,121, being the difference between the proceeds of £240,964 and net asset value of £210,843. How should the cumulative exchange difference of £(8,028) be treated in the consolidated financial statements for 1999?

Option (i) – Leave it as a negative exchange reserve.

In our view this is illogical as the consolidated financial statements will include in retained profits a different amount in respect of the subsidiary than has actually been realised by the parent company and included in its own retained profits. In addition, a consolidation entry will be required forever more in respect of the former subsidiary.

Option (ii) – Transfer it to retained profits as a reserve movement.

This is based on the view that the consolidated retained profits should reflect the same amount of retained profits that the parent company has realised and recorded in its own financial statements. This treatment, therefore, overcomes the criticism made above in respect of the previous option. It also means that the retained profits position is now the same as it would have been if the company had adopted the policy of taking the exchange differences to retained profits as they arose rather than taking them to a separate reserve.

Option (iii) – Transfer it to the profit and loss account for the year and treat it in a similar way as the gain on sale.

This is based on the view that one of the objectives of SSAP 20 is to produce results which are compatible with the effects of rate changes on a company's cash flow; that is why exchange differences on monetary items are normally recognised as part of the profit or loss for the year. Exchange rate changes in this instance have ultimately caused the company to receive less cash and therefore should be reflected at some time in arriving at the profit or loss for the year. It could also be argued in this particular case that not to do so would mean that the company has reported more profits in the consolidated profit and loss account than has actually been realised, contrary to the requirements of the Companies Act 1985.[90]

The treatment suggested in option (iii) above is that which is required by SFAS 52 upon the sale or upon complete or substantially complete liquidation of an investment in a foreign entity.[91] Indeed, under US GAAP if a partial sale takes place then the relevant proportion of the accumulated exchange difference should be included in the gain/loss on sale.[92] Similar requirements are contained in the international standard, IAS 21.[93] In the above example if 25% of the shares in the subsidiary had been sold then £(2,007) would have been included in the calculation of the gain/loss on sale.

However, under FRS 3, as the original exchange differences would have been reflected in the statement of total recognised gains and losses when they arose then they should not be recognised again in the year of disposal in either the profit and loss account or the statement of recognised gains and losses (see Chapter 25 at 2.9.1). Accordingly, option (iii) is unacceptable and in our view option (ii) is preferable to option (i).

3.4.8 *Change from closing rate/net investment method to temporal method or vice versa*

As indicated in 2.4.2 above, the method used for translating the financial statements of a foreign enterprise should normally only be changed when the financial and other operational relationship changes and renders the method used inappropriate. Where this is the case, therefore, it must be remembered that, as it is a change in the circumstances which has given rise to the change in method, this is not a change in accounting policy and therefore a prior year adjustment under FRS 3 is inappropriate. How should the change, therefore, be accounted for?

SSAP 20 does not deal with this situation; however, guidance can be sought from SFAS 52 and IAS 21.

A Change from closing rate/net investment method to temporal method

SFAS 52 states that the translated amounts of non-monetary assets at the end of the period prior to the change should become the accounting basis for those assets for the current and future periods.[94] There is therefore no need to translate these assets at the historical rates that applied when the assets were acquired. The cumulative exchange differences that have been taken to reserves in prior periods should not be taken to the profit and loss account in the year of change but should remain in reserves. SFAS 52 actually requires these exchange differences to remain in equity.[95] IAS 21 has similar requirements.[96]

B Change from temporal method to closing rate/net investment method

SFAS 52 states that the adjustment attributable to restating non-monetary assets, previously translated at historical rates, at closing rates should be reported in the cumulative translation adjustments component of equity.[97] This adjustment should, therefore, be treated as a reserve movement. Again, IAS 21 has similar requirements.[98]

3.4.9 *Hyperinflation*

One particular problem with the use of the closing rate/net investment method is when it is applied to a foreign enterprise which operates in a country where a very high rate of inflation exists. This issue is discussed in Chapter 9.

3.4.10 *Goodwill on consolidation*

FRS 10 – *Goodwill and Intangible Assets* – now requires goodwill on consolidation to be capitalised and classified as an asset on the balance sheet.[99] (This was also one of the options allowed by SSAP 22 – *Accounting for goodwill*.)[100] Where goodwill is capitalised on the purchase of a foreign enterprise, the question then arises as to whether or not such goodwill should be retranslated at closing rates.

Example 8.24

A UK company acquires all of the share capital of an Australian company on 31 January 1999 at a cost of A$3m. The fair value of the net assets of the Australian company at that date was A$2.1m. In the consolidated financial statements at 30 April 1999 the goodwill is capitalised as an intangible asset and amortised over its useful economic life. (For the purposes of this example, amortisation for the three months to 30 April 1999 is ignored.) The relevant exchange rates at 31 January 1999 and 30 April 1999 are £1=A$2.61 and £1=A$2.43 respectively. At what amount should the goodwill on consolidation be included in the balance sheet?

		(i)	(ii)
	A$	£	£
Goodwill	900,000	344,828	370,370

(i) This method regards goodwill as being the excess of (a) the sterling price paid over (b) the fair value of the net assets of the subsidiary expressed in the foreign currency translated into sterling at the date of acquisition; i.e. a sterling asset which does not fluctuate with changes in the exchange rate. Although not specifically covered by SSAP 20 this would appear to be the method adopted by the standard.

Paragraph 53 of the standard only refers to the exchange difference on the net investment being taken to reserves and the definition of the net investment contained in the standard refers to the net assets of the foreign enterprise.[101] As the goodwill only arises on consolidation and is not included in the balance sheet of the foreign enterprise then it could be argued that the goodwill is not part of the net assets of the foreign enterprise. This view is supported by the statement issued by the ASC on the publication of SSAP 20 which indicated that any goodwill element contained in the carrying amount of the investment in the investing company's financial statements would not be available for offset on consolidation when applying the cover method provisions of paragraph 57 of the standard.[102]

(ii) This method regards goodwill as being the excess of (a) the foreign currency price paid or the sterling price paid translated into the foreign currency at the date of acquisition over (b) the fair value of the net assets of the subsidiary expressed in the foreign currency, i.e. a currency asset which is retranslated at closing rates.

This treatment is required by SFAS 52[103] and is, in our view, more logical as the value of the foreign company as a whole is likely to be based on the expected future earnings stream expressed in the foreign currency and the goodwill relates to a business which operates in the economic environment of that currency.

For these reasons we believe method (ii) to be preferable and many companies adopt this approach, although both treatments are seen in practice.

3.4.11 *Inter-period comparisons*

As indicated in 2.4.3 above the use of the closing rate/net investment method is intended to reflect in the consolidated financial statements the financial results and relationships as measured in the foreign currency financial statements of the foreign enterprise prior to translation. This is likely to be the case for amounts within the profit and loss account for the year; amounts within the balance sheet; and the relationship of the profit or loss for the year to the balance sheet, particularly where the closing rate is used for translating the results of the foreign enterprise. However, this will not be the case when a comparison is made between figures for the current year and figures for the previous year or, alternatively, figures for the first half of the year and figures for the second half. This is normally more important when looking at a comparison of the results for the respective periods.

Example 8.25

A UK company has a wholly owned Canadian subsidiary. In preparing its consolidated financial statements the company translates the results of the subsidiary using the closing rate. The profits of the subsidiary for the four six-month periods ended 31 December 1998 and the rate of exchange at the end of each period are as follows:

Six-month period ended	C$	£1=C$
30 June 1997	100,000	2.30
31 December 1997	110,000	2.35
30 June 1998	121,000	2.45
31 December 1998	133,100	2.56

The two interim financial statements ended 30 June and the two annual financial statements ended 31 December for the group therefore include the profits of the subsidiary as follows:

	C$	£1=C$	£
Six months ended 30 June 1997	100,000	2.30	43,478
Six months ended 31 December 1997	110,000	Balance	45,884
Year ended 31 December 1997	210,000	2.35	89,362
Six months ended 30 June 1998	121,000	2.45	49,388
Six months ended 31 December 1998	133,100	Balance	48,870
Year ended 31 December 1998	254,100	2.56	99,258

It can be seen from the above that the reported sterling figures do not show the 10% increase each period that the Canadian dollar figures show. In 1998, the annual profit shows an increase of approximately 11% compared to the 1997 profit whereas in Canadian dollar terms the profit has increased by 21% and the second half results appear to show a decrease of approximately 1% compared to the results of the first half instead of the 10% increase. This latter effect is caused by the second half results effectively including the exchange adjustment resulting from restating the first half's results at the year-end exchange rate. The results of the first half translated at the year-end rate are £47,266 and therefore a loss of £2,122 is effectively included in the second half's results. This restatement of previously reported figures is one of the reasons why some companies have changed to using average rates when translating profit and loss accounts. Even where this is done this problem will still arise if each period's results are not translated at the average rate for that period, i.e. if the annual results are translated at an average rate for the year, although the effect is unlikely to be particularly significant.

If average rates had been used in the above example the figures would have been as follows:

Example 8.26

		Method (i)		Method (ii)	
	C$	£1=C$	£	£1=C$	£
Six months ended 30 June 1977	100,000	2.24	44,643	2.24	44,643
Six months ended 31 December 1977	110,000	Balance	47,868	2.30	47,826
Year ended 31 December 1977	210,000	2.27	92,511	Balance	92,469
Six months ended 30 June 1998	121,000	2.37	51,055	2.37	51,055
Six months ended 31 December 1998	133,100	Balance	50,993	2.54	52,402
Year ended 31 December 1998	254,100	2.49	102,048	Balance	103,457

Method (i) translates the results for the year at the average rate for the year and method (ii) translates each six-month period at the average rate for the respective period. It can be seen that under method (i) the second half results for 1998 still show a decrease compared to the first half. Method (ii) shows an increase but nothing like the 10% shown by the Canadian dollar figures.

In order to try to overcome this, some companies have disclosed the effect of using different exchange rates. For example, Fisons in its 1993 accounts disclosed the following:

Extract 8.28: Fisons plc (1993)

1 **Analysis of results** [extract]

Group turnover – continuing operations	**1993** **£m**	1992 £m
At 1992 average exchange rates	**1,143.8**	1,139.7
Translation effect of exchange rate movements	**118.3**	–
At average exchange rates for the year	**1,262.1**	1,139.7

An alternative treatment is to express the figures for the comparative year in terms of the current exchange rates, as illustrated below:

Extract 8.29: Guinness PLC (1996)

1. **SEGMENTAL ANALYSIS OF TURNOVER AND PROFIT**

(F) Exchange rates [extract]

If the trading results of overseas companies for 1995 had been translated at the average exchange rates ruling during 1996 and if the rates achieved in 1995 for transaction receipts under hedging arrangements had been the same as those achieved in 1996, turnover for 1995 would have been £33m lower and profit before interest and taxation (excluding MH) for 1995 would have been £13m higher.

Some companies go further than Guinness in that they, in giving their segmental disclosures, restate all the comparative figures based on the current year's exchange rates.[104]

Although this extra disclosure can only help a user of financial statements it must be remembered that this mathematical effect of different exchange rates ignores the economic effect of the changes in the exchange rates on the actual trading results of the foreign enterprises. SFAS 52 states that the Financial Accounting Standards

Board when preparing the standard 'considered a proposal for financial statement disclosure that would describe and possibly quantify the effects of rate changes on reported revenue and earnings. This type of disclosure might have included the mathematical effect of translating revenue and expenses at rates that are different from those used in a preceding period as well as the economic effects of rate changes, such as the effects on selling prices, sales volume, and cost structures.' The Board rejected requiring such disclosures 'primarily because of the wide variety of potential effects, the perceived difficulties of developing the information, and the impracticality of providing meaningful guidelines'. However, the Board encouraged management to give extra disclosure of 'an analysis and discussion of the effects of rate changes on the reported results of operations. The purpose is to assist financial report users in understanding the broader economic implications of rate changes and to compare recent results with those of prior periods.'[105]

3.4.12 *Branches*

We have discussed previously the application of the provisions of SSAP 20 in relation to branches and we have seen that the definition of a foreign branch is a very wide one in that it includes a group of assets and liabilities which are accounted for in foreign currencies. This was mainly to cater for international assets which are financed by foreign borrowings, since the cover method could not be used as it is only applicable to equity investments. In many cases, therefore, the reason for regarding assets and liabilities as a foreign branch will be to allow exchange differences on the related borrowing to be taken to reserves rather than to the profit and loss account.

Once a company has decided that a particular category of assets and liabilities should be regarded as a foreign branch consideration should be given as to which assets and liabilities should be included. In our view the minimum which can be included is the international asset itself, e.g. aircraft, ship or oil and gas interest, and the related borrowing. However, we recommend that, in addition, any trading balances, e.g. debtors and creditors, should also be included. In particular, as the branch should not be an integral part of the company's business and its cash flows should not have an impact upon those of the rest of the company in order to justify the use of the closing rate/net investment method, the bank account through which most of the cash flows of the branch will flow should be considered to be part of the branch assets and liabilities.

It should be borne in mind that the exchange difference which is taken to reserves is on the net investment in the branch. As such this amount can be a net exchange gain or loss and the exchange difference on the borrowings included in the branch can exceed the corresponding exchange difference on the branch assets. There is, therefore, no restriction on the exchange differences on the borrowings taken to reserves as there would be if the provisions of the cover method applied.

3.5 Cover method

We have looked at the basic requirements of the cover method in 2.3.7 above and 2.4.5 above as it is applied in individual companies' financial statements and consolidated financial statements respectively. There are, however, a number of problem areas resulting from the provisions of the standard which we believe have to be addressed. Many of these problem areas are relevant to both sets of financial statements. Until recently, the main focus of attention in this area has generally been in relation to the external financial reporting aspects of the consolidated financial statements. However, due to the introduction of a new tax regime for foreign exchange differences in 1995 the focus has shifted to the position in individual companies since taxation is assessed on individual companies not groups. All of the examples used in the rest of this section to illustrate these problem areas assume that a matching election has been made and therefore no taxation arises on any of the exchange differences. Where taxation does arise then UITF 19 requires that the provisions of the cover method should be applied after taking into account any tax charge or credit directly or solely attributable to the borrowings. It also requires that in considering the amount of cash that the investment is expected to generate, consideration should be in after-tax terms.[106]

3.5.1 What are 'foreign currency borrowings'?

By adopting the cover method companies can take some, if not all, of the exchange differences arising on the foreign currency borrowings to reserves. Borrowings are not defined in the standard, so what should be regarded as borrowings?

The statement issued by the ASC on the publication of the standard in commenting on these provisions referred to 'loans'[107] but even then we do not believe that this term should be interpreted too literally.

The Stock Exchange used to require disclosure of 'indebtedness' in listing particulars of listed companies Included within this category was loan capital, term loans, bank overdrafts, liabilities under acceptances (other than normal trade bills), acceptance credits, hire purchase commitments and obligations under finance leases.[108] In our view all of these items can be regarded as borrowings for the purpose of the standard although it is unlikely that liabilities under hire purchase contracts, or finance leases, will have been taken out with a view to providing a hedge against foreign equity investments. Normal trade creditors and trade bills should not be regarded as borrowings, although it has been suggested that extended credit from a supplier could be included as the economic effects are the same as for a straightforward loan.[109]

3.5.2 Borrowings taken out before or after the investment

The provisions of the standard apply to borrowings which have been used to finance, or provide a hedge against, its foreign equity investments. Accordingly, the provisions not only apply to borrowings taken out at the same time as the investment is made but also to borrowings which have been taken out before the investment is made and to borrowings which are taken out after the investment is made. How should the provisions be applied, therefore, in the first accounting period when the investment holding period has been different from the period for which the borrowing has been in place?

A *Borrowings taken out before the investment*

Example 8.27

A UK company is intending to invest in a US company so on 1 December 1998 it borrows US$500,000, repayable in five years' time, which it places in a US$ deposit account in the meantime. On 31 December 1998 it purchases all of the shares of the US company at a cost of US$800,000 using the US$500,000 in the deposit account and the balance paid out of its sterling bank account. How should the company apply the cover method in its financial statements for the period to 30 April 1999?

The relevant exchange rates are:

	£1=US$
1 December 1998	1.69
31 December 1998	1.66
30 April 1999	1.61

			Option (i)		Option (ii)	
			P/L account	Reserves	P/L account	Reserves
Exchange differences			£	£	£	£
Investment						
US$800,000	@ 1.66 =	£481,928				
	@ 1.61 =	£496,894				
				14,966		14,966
Deposit						
US$500,000	@ 1.69 =	£295,858				
	@ 1.66 =	£301,205				
			5,347		5,347	
Borrowing						
US$500,000	@ 1.69 =	£295,858				
	@ 1.66 =	£301,205				
				(5,347)	(5,347)	
	@ 1.61 =	£310,559		(9,354)		(9,354)
			5,347	265	nil	5,612

Option (i) is based on the view that as the borrowings were used to finance the purchase of the investment all of the exchange difference on the borrowings can be offset against the exchange differences as long as the criteria of the standard are met. However, in our view this ignores the fact that for the period prior to purchasing the investment the borrowing was effectively matched against the deposit. Therefore our preference would be for the exchange difference on the borrowing for the period up to purchasing the investment to be taken to profit and loss to offset the exchange difference on the deposit as shown in option (ii).

We also believe that such a treatment should be adopted if the proceeds of the borrowings had been placed in a sterling deposit account as the company would have been uncovered during that period. The effect of exchange differences would have impacted on the cash flow of the company as it would have been required to pay an extra £5,347 out of its sterling bank account to purchase the investment. Accordingly, the exchange difference should be taken to profit and loss account.

Problems also arise when borrowings are taken out as a hedge against existing foreign investments.

B *Borrowings taken out after the investment*

Example 8.28

A UK company has an equity investment in a Swiss company which it acquired a number of years ago at a cost of SFr500,000 when the exchange rate was £1=SFr5.00. Up until 1998 the UK company has had no foreign borrowings so the investment has been carried in the company's financial statements at its historical sterling cost of £100,000. On 30 June 1998 the company considered the investment to be worth SFr1,000,000 and in order to provide a hedge against the investment borrowed SFr1,000,000, repayable in three years' time, and used the proceeds to reduce its sterling overdraft. How should the company apply the cover method in its financial statements for the year ended 31 December 1988?

The relevant exchange rates are:

	£1=SFr
31 December 1997	2.40
30 June 1998	2.53
31 December 1998	2.29

			P/L account	Reserves
			£	£
Option (i)				
Exchange differences				
Investment – SFr500,000	@ 5.00 =	£100,000		
	@ 2.29 =	£218,341		
				118,341
Borrowing – SFr1,000,000	@ 2.53 =	£395,257		
	@ 2.29 =	£436,681		
				(41,424)
				76,917
Option (ii)				
Exchange differences				
Investment – SFr500,000	@ 5.00 =	£100,000		
	@ 2.40 =	£208,333		
				108,333
	@ 2.29 =	£218,341		10,008
Borrowing – SFr1,000,000	@ 2.53 =	£395,297		
	@ 2.29 =	£436,681		
			(31,416)	(10,008)
			(31,416)	108,333
Option (iii)				
Exchange differences				
Investment – SFr500,000	@ 5.00 =	£100,000		
	@ 2.53 =	£197,629		
				97,629
	@ 2.29 =	£218,341		20,712
Borrowing – SFr1,000,000	@ 2.53 =	£395,257		
	@ 2.29 =	£436,681		
			(20,712)	(20,712)
			(20,712)	97,629

Option (i) regards all of the exchange gain on the investment which is recognised in this accounting period as being available for offset against the exchange loss on the total borrowing. This would appear to meet the conditions laid down in paragraphs 51 and 57 of the standard.

Option (ii) regards only the exchange difference arising on the investment during the year as being available for offset. As there is only a gain of £10,008, then under the conditions of the above paragraphs the exchange loss on the borrowings taken to reserves is restricted to £10,008, with the balance of £20,712 being taken to profit and loss for the year.

Neither of these options, although acceptable under the standard, reflects the rationale for taking out the borrowings in the first place which was to hedge the exchange risk on the investment from the date it was decided to do so, i.e. 30 June 1998. To achieve this, the exchange differences on the investment available for offset should be those which arise during the same period as the borrowing has been in existence.

Option (iii) is done on this basis and it can be seen that only half of the exchange loss on the borrowings can be offset against the exchange difference on the investment. This is due to the fact that the investment is recorded at the original cost of SFr500,000 whereas the borrowing is twice that amount. In order for the company to reflect fully the rationale behind their decision they should incorporate the investment at its valuation of SFr1,000,000. If this were done, then all of the exchange loss on the borrowing could be taken to reserves.

It can be seen from option (iii) in the above example that the carrying amount of the investment can have implications for the amount of exchange differences on the borrowings which can be taken to reserves under the cover method. Under the tax regime introduced in 1995, individual companies may make an election to match a foreign currency borrowing against shares in a foreign currency subsidiary, so that no taxable loss or gain on the borrowing results. However, to achieve such a result it is necessary that the translation of the carrying amount of the subsidiary gives rise to exchange differences which at least equal those on the borrowings. Thus in the above example, the UK company would need to incorporate the investment at its valuation at 30 June 1998 to ensure such a result on an ongoing basis (assuming all the conditions of paragraph 51 of SSAP 20 are met). If under its hedging strategy the company were to increase the amount of foreign currency borrowings because the underlying value of the subsidiary had increased, then it would be necessary to incorporate further valuations at the time the borrowings were increased in order to ensure that no exchange differences on the borrowings have to be taken to the profit and loss account.

3.5.3 *Repayment of borrowings*

Similar problems also arise when a company repays a foreign currency borrowing which has provided a hedge against a foreign equity investment.

A Treatment of exchange differences

Example 8.29

A UK company has an equity investment in a Canadian company which it acquired for a cost of C$3m when the exchange rate was £1=C$2.00. It financed the acquisition by borrowing C$3m. In the financial statements up to 31 December 1997 the cover method has been applied. On 30 August 1998 the company took advantage of the strong pound and decided to repay the borrowings in full. The company has no other foreign borrowings. How should the company apply the cover method in its financial statements for the year ended 31 December 1998?

The relevant exchange rates are:

	£1=C$
31 December 1997	2.35
30 August 1998	2.62
31 December 1998	2.56

			Option (i) P/L account	Option (i) Reserves	Option (ii) P/L account	Option (ii) Reserves
			£	£	£	£
Exchange differences						
Investment						
C$3,000,000	@ 2.35 =	£1,276,596				
	@ 2.62 =	£1,145,038				
				(131,558)		(131,558)
Borrowing						
C$3,000,000	@ 2.35 =	£1,276,596				
	@ 2.62 =	£1,145,038				
			131,558			131,558
			131,558	(131,558)	nil	nil

Option (i) is based on the view that as there are no borrowings at the year end then the cover method does not apply and the matching should be considered as having ceased at the beginning of the accounting period. As the exchange gain on the loan has arisen on a settled transaction it should be reported as part of the profit or loss for the year. However, it could be argued that this does not comply with condition (c) of paragraph 51 of the standard which requires the accounting treatment adopted to be applied consistently. Again, such a treatment does not reflect the fact that the company had hedged its investment up to 30 August 1998 and it is only after that date that it has not been covered. Accordingly, we believe that option (ii) should be followed.

Another problem which arises when such borrowings are repaid is – how should the related investment which is no longer hedged subsequently be accounted for in the financial statements of the investing company?

B Subsequent treatment of investment

Example 8.30

In the above example, how should the investment be included in the balance sheet at 31 December 1998 and at subsequent year ends?

Option (i) – The investment should be retained at the exchange rate ruling at the final date of repaying the loan, i.e. £1,145,038 (£1=C$2.62). No further retranslation should take place until another borrowing is taken out to provide a hedge. This method regards the investment as being a currency asset only during the period there are related currency borrowings. This would appear to be the method suggested by other commentators.[110] It does mean, however, that the figure for the investment in future periods is rather meaningless as it represents neither the historical cost in sterling terms nor the currency amount at closing rates. It does not even necessarily represent the actual sterling cost of the investment, as not all of the investment may have been financed by borrowings and the borrowings may have been repaid at different dates.

Option (ii) – The investment is translated at the closing rate of £1=C$2.56 and included at £1,171,875 and is retranslated each year at closing rates. This is based on the view that the company *has* used foreign currency borrowings to finance the investment and therefore the provisions of paragraph 51 can still be applied. It also means that the accounting treatment for this investment is being applied consistently from period to period. Even if it were considered that such a policy was not in accordance with the standard then it would be possible for the company to adopt such a treatment by retaining a nominal borrowing in the foreign currency!

Option (iii) – The investment is retained at the rate ruling at the beginning of the period, i.e. £1,276,596 (£1=C$2.35). This is based on the same premise as option (i) in the previous example.

Option (iv) – The investment should be restated at the historical rate ruling at the date of purchase, i.e. £1,500,000 (£1=C$2.00). This is based on the view that the company no longer has a hedge against its investment and should account for it as if this had always been the case. The financial statements will, therefore, reflect the effect on net equity of choosing to finance the investment for the period it was so financed only by including the net exchange difference on the borrowing in reserves.

In our view all of the above options are acceptable, but the one chosen should be consistently applied.

3.5.4 *Goodwill on consolidation*

We have already discussed in 3.4.10 above the question of whether or not goodwill on consolidation, which arises on the acquisition of a foreign enterprise and is capitalised and amortised, is a currency asset. We indicated that our preference was to treat it as such. Where the investment is financed by foreign currency borrowings the question then arises, can the exchange differences arising on the goodwill be used in the offset process under the provisions of paragraph 57 of the standard? Indeed, where the company has chosen to write off goodwill on consolidation immediately to reserves under SSAP 22 (and under FRS 10 has not reinstated such goodwill as an asset), can any of the exchange differences on the related borrowing be taken to reserves in the consolidated financial statements?

Example 8.31

A UK company acquired all the equity share capital of an Australian company for A$3m on 31 January 1999. The acquisition was financed by taking out a loan of A$3m which is repayable over ten years commencing 31 March 1999. As the net assets of the Australian company are negligible, all of the purchase price is represented by goodwill. The company has applied the cover method in its own financial statements for the period ended 30 April 1999. The relevant exchange rates at 31 January 1999 and 30 April 1999 are £1=A$2.61 and £1=A$2.43 respectively.

Accordingly, the investment and the loan are both included in the company's financial statements at £1,234,568 and an exchange gain on the investment of £85,143 and a corresponding exchange loss on the loan are taken to reserves.

The company capitalises the goodwill on consolidation and treats it as a currency asset and translates it at closing rate then, ignoring any amortisation of the goodwill for the three months to 30 April 1999, an exchange gain of £85,143 on the goodwill will arise and be taken to reserves in the consolidated financial statements. Can the company apply the cover method under paragraph 57 of the standard and take the exchange loss on the loan to reserves?

Paragraph 57 of the standard only allows the exchange difference on the borrowing to be taken to reserves to the extent that it is offset by the exchange difference on the net investment which is taken to reserves and the definition of the net investment contained in the standard refers to the net assets of the foreign enterprise.[111] As the goodwill only arises on consolidation and is not included in the balance sheet of the foreign enterprise then it could be argued that the goodwill is not part of the net assets of the foreign enterprise. (However, the same could also be said about any fair value adjustments made in respect of the net assets.) This view is supported by the statement issued by the ASC on the publication of SSAP 20 which indicated that any goodwill element contained in the carrying amount of the investment in the investing company's financial statements would not be available for offset on consolidation when applying the cover method provisions of paragraph 57 of the standard.[112] Based on these arguments it would appear that the answer to this question is no.

However, we believe that in such circumstances the company should be able to apply the cover method provided that condition (c) of paragraph 57 is met.

The goodwill is being regarded as a currency asset which is retranslated at closing rates. This treatment is required by SFAS 52[113] and, in our view, more logical as the value of the foreign company as a whole is likely to be based on the expected future earnings stream expressed in the foreign currency and the goodwill relates to a business which operates in the economic environment of that currency. Not to take into account the exchange differences arising on the goodwill in applying the cover method ignores the economic reality that the group is covered against movements in exchange rates.

What if the acquisition in the above example had taken place in an earlier year when SSAP 22 applied and under that standard the company had chosen to write off the goodwill to reserves immediately?

Again, it could be argued that the cover method cannot be applied. No asset is being recognised in the financial statements and therefore there can be no exchange differences arising thereon against which the exchange difference on the loan can be offset. However, most companies who chose a policy of writing off goodwill immediately did so as a matter of policy, not because of the fact that the goodwill had suddenly become worthless and it could be argued that the treatment of exchange differences on borrowings should not be affected by the choice of accounting policy for goodwill. We believe, therefore, there is a case to say that such goodwill, which would have been included in the consolidated balance sheet had a policy of capitalisation and amortisation been followed, can be taken into account when applying the cover method.

An example of a company which takes goodwill into account when applying the cover method is United Business Media, as illustrated below:

Extract 8.30: United Business Media plc (2000)

FOREIGN CURRENCIES [extract]

Differences arising on the retranslation of investments, including goodwill, in foreign subsidiary undertakings and related net foreign currency borrowings, and from the translation of the results of those companies at average rate, are taken to reserves, and are reported in the statement of total recognised gains and losses.

3.5.5 *All investments/borrowings?*

Companies may have more than one foreign currency investment which have been financed, or are hedged by, more than one foreign currency borrowing. The question may then arise, can a company apply the cover method for some investments/borrowings and not apply it for others?

Example 8.32

On 31 January 1999 a UK company acquires all the equity share capital of two foreign companies as follows:

(i) A US company at a cost of US$1,640,000 financed by a loan of US$1,640,000 repayable in five years' time.

(ii) A German company at a cost of €1,450,000 financed by a loan of €1,450,000 repayable in five years' time.

The company wishes to apply the cover method to the US investment and related loan but not to apply it to the German investment and related loan in its financial statements for the year ended 30 April 1999. Is such a treatment possible under SSAP 20?

The relevant exchange rates are:

	£1= €	£1=US$
31 January 1999	1.45	1.64
30 April 1999	1.52	1.61

The effect of such a treatment is as follows:

			P/L account	Reserves
Exchange differences			£	£
Investments				
– US$1,640,000	@ US$1.64 =	£1,000,000		
	@ US$1.61 =	£1,018,634		
				18,634
– €1,450,000	@ €1.45 =	£1,000,000		
	@ €1.45 =	£1,000,000		
				–
Loans				
– US$1,640,000	@ US$1.63 =	£1,000,000		
	@ US$1.61 =	£1,018,634		
				(18,634)
– €1,450,000	@ €1.45 =	£1,000,000		
	@ €1.52 =	£ 953,947		
			46,053	
			46,053	–

It can be seen that by applying the cover method to the US investment/loan only the exchange gain on the Euro loan has been taken to profit and loss account whereas the exchange loss on the US$ loan has been taken to reserves offset by a corresponding exchange gain on the net investment. It would appear that this is allowed by SSAP 20, as paragraph 51 states that the equity investments *may* be denominated in foreign currencies. It must be emphasised, however, that where exchange losses on the investments are arising but are not being recognised consideration has to be given as to whether a provision for impairment is necessary. Paragraph 57 in dealing with the consolidated financial statements is equally permissive as it states that the exchange differences on the borrowings *may* be offset as reserve movements. If in the above example the net assets of the German company at the date of acquisition were equivalent to the price paid then although an exchange loss of £46,053 would be taken to group reserves, the company could continue to take the exchange gain on the loan to the profit and loss account.

It has been suggested that the final condition of paragraphs 51 and 57 requires companies to apply the cover method to all matched investments.[114] The final condition requires companies to apply the same accounting policy from *period to period* and therefore this suggestion seems to be a rather broad interpretation of the provisions. Nevertheless, we believe it is preferable for companies to adopt the same policy for all matched investments.

3.5.6 *Must currencies be the same?*

All of the previous examples which we have considered have been based on situations where the investment and the related borrowing have been expressed in the same foreign currency. The provisions of the standard actually make no reference to the currencies of the borrowings or the investments, and consequently it is not necessary for this to be the case. ED 27, the forerunner to SSAP 20, included such a restriction but this was removed 'since a number of commentators considered it to be unacceptably rigid, particularly having regard to the wide variety of loan arrangements available and to the multi-currency nature of many of them. Since the alternative of a complete offset of currencies would allow too much freedom and carry the risk of imprudent accounting, a compromise solution has been adopted. The offset is now permitted only to the extent that the underlying foreign currency borrowings do not exceed the amount of cash expected to be generated by the net investments, either from profits or otherwise. ASC considers that this restriction should ensure that offset is permitted only when there is genuine cover for the related exchange gains and losses, whilst at the same time recognising the realities of treasury management.'[115] Specific problems relating to this compromise solution are addressed at 3.5.8 and 3.5.9 below.

An illustration of the cover method provisions where the currencies are not the same can be seen in the following example:

Example 8.33

On 1 January 1993 a UK company acquires an equity investment in a Swiss company at a cost of SFr2,270,000 and finances the acquisition by borrowing DM2,470,000 repayable in seven years' time. Based on the exchange rates at that date both amounts are equivalent to £1,000,000. By applying the cover method in SSAP 20 the amounts of the investment and the borrowing in the financial statements for each of the years ended 31 December up until 1998 would be as follows:

	Investment		Borrowing	
	£1=SFr	£	£1=DM	£
31 December 1993	2.20	1,031,818	2.57	961,089
31 December 1994	2.05	1,107,317	2.45	1,008,163
31 December 1995	1.79	1,268,156	2.22	1,112,613
31 December 1996	2.30	986,957	2.64	935,606
31 December 1997	2.40	945,833	2.96	834,459
31 December 1998	2.29	991,266	2.77	891,697

The treatment of exchange differences under the cover method would be as follows:

	Investment Reserves	Borrowing Reserves	P/L account
	£	£	£
31 December 1993	31,818	–	38,911
31 December 1994	75,499	(47,074)	–
31 December 1995	160,839	(104,450)	–
31 December 1996	(281,199)	177,007	–
31 December 1997	(41,124)	41,124	60,023
31 December 1998	45,433	(45,433)	(11,805)
	(8,734)	21,174	87,129

In 1993 as both the investment and the borrowing are showing exchange gains then none of the exchange gain in the borrowing can be offset in reserves and therefore all of the gain must be taken to the profit and loss account.

In 1994 and 1995 all of the exchange loss on the borrowing can be offset in reserves. Similarly, in 1996 all of the exchange gain on the borrowing can be offset in reserves.

In 1997 although there is a total exchange gain on the borrowing of £101,147, only £41,124 can be offset in reserves as that is the extent of the exchange loss on the investment. The balance of £60,023 has to be taken to the profit and loss account. No account can be taken of the previous exchange losses on the investment which are sitting in reserves. It is only the exchange difference arising in the year which can be used in the offset process.

Similarly, in 1998 the exchange loss which is capable of being offset is limited. It can be seen from the figures for 1997 and 1998 that this applies whether or not the exchange difference on the borrowing is a gain or a loss.

It can be seen from the above example that when the cover method contained in SSAP 20 is used in circumstances where the investment and borrowings are in different currencies it can lead to inconsistent treatment of the exchange differences on the borrowing. In the above example in two of the years part of the exchange difference is taken to reserves and part to the profit and loss account. In three of the years all of the difference is taken to reserves and in the other year all of the difference is taken to profit and loss account. In our view this makes a nonsense of the consistency concept.

Another weakness of the cover method when different currencies are involved can be illustrated by the following example:

Example 8.34

A UK company has a Canadian subsidiary. At 30 April 1998 the net assets of the subsidiary are C$2,390,000. On 1 May 1998 the company decides to double its investment in the Canadian company by investing a further C$2,390,000 and borrows US$1,670,000 repayable in five years' time.

The relevant exchange rates are as follows:

	£1=C$	£1=US$
30 April 1998 and 1 May 1998	2.39	1.67
30 April 1999	2.34	1.61

Using the cover method, the financial statements would reflect the following treatment for the resulting exchange differences:

Exchange gain on investment			
C$4,780,000	@ 2.39 =	£2,000,000	
	@ 2.34 =	£2,042,735	
			£42,735
Exchange loss on borrowing			
US$1,670,000	@ 1.67 =	£1,000,000	
	@ 1.61 =	£1,037,267	
			(37,267)
Net gain taken to reserves			£ 5,468

The cover method allows all of the exchange difference on the investment to be used in the offset process. However, the result of the decision to finance the extra investment by the US$ loan has been:

Gain on increased investment of C$2,390,000	£21,367
Loss on US$ loan	(37,267)
	£(15,900)

Although a net loss has arisen as a result of the decision no loss is reflected in the profit and loss account.

The above examples demonstrate that the cover method of SSAP 20 does not produce sensible results which reflect the economic substance of the transactions when different currencies are involved.

In our view proper cover can only exist if the risk of exposure to currency movements is removed. This can only happen if the borrowings, which are providing the hedge, are in the same currency as the investment. One of the arguments put forward by the ASC for removing the restriction of having the same currency was that it was too rigid 'particularly having regard to the wide variety of loan arrangements available and to the multi-currency nature of many of them'.[116] We consider the fact that companies can borrow in most of the major foreign currencies means that having a requirement for the same currency would not be too rigid because they can arrange to have the borrowings in the currency they want in order to provide effective cover against their investments.

Another criticism of the cover method in SSAP 20 is that 'the position taken by the ASC is that if there is a gain on a net investment and a loss on borrowings, then ex-post facto there has been cover; if there has been a gain on both or a loss on both, then there has been no cover. The basic flaw here is that cover by its very nature – to remove the risk – is a matter of premeditated intent. Evidence of this intent is a key feature of SFAS 52's approach to cover.'[117]

SFAS 52 requires that exchange gains and losses on transactions that are designated as, and are effective as, economic hedges of a net investment in a foreign entity shall not be included in the profit and loss account but shall be reported in the same manner as the translation adjustments relating to the net investment.[118] Ordinarily, a transaction that hedges a net investment should be denominated in the same currency as the net investment. SFAS 52 recognises that it may not be practical or feasible for this to be the case and, therefore, in these situations allows the hedging transaction to be in a currency which generally moves in tandem with the currency of the net investment.[119]

3.5.7 *Pooled basis?*

Where companies have a number of investments financed by a number of borrowings, how should the cover method be applied? Should it be applied on a pooled basis, i.e. by aggregating all the investments and all the borrowings and comparing the net exchange difference on each; or should it be done on an individual basis if specific borrowings can be identified or on a currency by currency basis?

Depending on how it is done different treatments are likely to arise. We can see this from the following example:

Example 8.35

A UK company has two wholly owned foreign subsidiaries, a Norwegian company and a Danish company. The net investments in these subsidiaries at 30 April 1998 are NKr50m and DKr15m respectively. The original investments in these companies were financed by borrowings of NKr45m and DKr18m respectively. How should the company apply the cover method in its consolidated financial statements for the year ended 31 April 1999?

The relevant exchange rates are:

	£1=NKr	£1=DKr
30 April 1998	12.47	11.44
30 April 1999	12.54	11.30

		P/L account	(i) Reserves	(ii) Reserves
		£	£	£
Exchange difference on investments				
Norwegian company				
– NKr50m @ 12.47 =	£4,009,623			
@ 12.54 =	£3,987,241			
			(22,382)	(22,382)
Danish company				
– DKr15m @ 11.44 =	£1,311,189			
@ 11.30 =	£1,327,434			
			16,245	16,245
				(6,137)
Exchange difference on borrowings				
Norwegian kroner loan				
– NKr45m @ 12.47 =	£3,608,661			
@ 12.54 =	£3,588,517			
			20,144	20,144
Danish kroner loan				
– DKr18m @ 11.44 =	£1,573,426			
@ 11.30 =	£1,592,920			
		(3,249)	(16,245)	(19,494)
				650
		(3,249)	(2,238)	(5,487)

Method (i) has applied the cover method by regarding the investments/borrowings as being in two separate pools of currencies. As a result, that part of the loss on the DKr loan which has not been covered by exchange gain on the DKr investment has been taken to the profit and loss account.

Method (ii) has taken a global approach and as there are sufficient net losses on the investments to offset the net gains on the borrowings then all of the exchange differences can be offset to reserves.

It has been suggested that SSAP 20 requires an aggregate basis as illustrated in method (ii). The reason is that companies usually manage their treasuries on a pool basis and finance groups of investments with the basket of loans, often in different currencies.[120] In our view companies are permitted to apply the cover method on an individual basis or a currency by currency pool basis, as illustrated in method (i) above. We believe that such a basis is preferable as it is only when the currencies are the same that proper cover exists.

The global approach will have the same effect where all the investments in each particular currency exceed the amount of the borrowings in each particular currency. However, where there may be a shortfall of investments in any particular currency when compared to borrowings in the same currency, the global approach has the effect of regarding the excess borrowings as providing a hedge against investments in different currencies.

Whichever method is used it should be applied consistently from period to period.

3.5.8 *What is meant by condition (b) of paragraph 51 and condition (c) of paragraph 57?*

These conditions require that the foreign currency borrowings used in the offset process should not exceed the total amount of cash that the investments are expected to be able to generate, whether from profits or otherwise. As explained in 3.5.6 above the reason for this condition was to allow the cover method to be used when different currencies were involved. No guidance is given in the standard as to how such amount of cash should be determined. UITF 19, however, requires that the comparison with the total amount of cash that the investments are expected to be able to generate and the exposure created by the borrowings should be considered in after-tax terms.[121]

How should these conditions therefore be applied? For the purposes of illustration, the examples below assume that there is no taxation relating to the borrowings and the cash expected to be generated is in after-tax terms.

Example 8.36

A UK company acquires an equity investment in a Japanese company at a cost of ¥225m on 1 May 1998. During 1997 the company had taken out a loan of US$2m repayable in five years' time with a view to investing in a US company. However, this investment was never made and the company was left with the loan. In preparing its financial statements for the year ended 30 April 1999 the company wishes to regard the US$ loan as providing a hedge against the Japanese investment and apply the cover method. How should this be done?

The relevant exchange rates are:

	£1=¥	£1=US$
30 April 1998		1.67
1 May 1998	221	
30 April 1999	192	1.61

Exchange differences			
Investment – ¥225m	@ 221 =	£1,018,100	
	@ 192 =	£1,171,875	
Exchange gain			£153,775
Loan – US$2m	@ 1.67 =	£1,197,605	
	@ 1.61 =	£1,242,236	
Exchange loss			£(44,631)

By just applying condition (a) of paragraph 51 of the standard it would seem that all of the exchange loss on the loan can be taken to reserves as there are sufficient exchange gains on the investment available for offset.

However, what about condition (b)? How should the amount of cash which the investment is expected to generate be determined?

(i) It could be argued that it should be calculated as being the amount that would be raised if the investment were sold immediately.

If this is equivalent to its book value at the year end, i.e. £1,171,875, then as the loan exceeds this amount it could be argued that the cover method cannot be applied and therefore all of the exchange loss on the loan of £44,631 should be taken to the profit and loss account and the investment should be recorded at the historical rate; i.e. £1,018,100. Alternatively, it could be argued that a proportion of the loan can be used in the offset process to the extent that it is covered by the value of the investment. This means that US$1,886,719 (£1,171,875 @ £1=US$1.61) can be used in the process. The exchange loss on this amount is £42,103 and it is this amount which can be taken to reserves. The remainder of the exchange loss on the loan of £2,528 would be taken to the profit and loss account. We believe the latter approach is the more appropriate treatment.

What if the amount at which the investment could be sold is in excess of its book value? It may be that the investment is now worth ¥250m which is equivalent to £1,302,083. It would appear that in these circumstances all of the exchange loss on the borrowing can be offset in reserves, even although the financial statements do not reflect the fact that the borrowings are covered. On the grounds of prudence, we believe it would be preferable to use the carrying value of the investment.

(ii) It could be argued that it is not necessary to consider an immediate sale of the investment, particularly as it is unlikely that such a course of action is the intention of the investing company, but that regard should be given to future profits which will result in further dividends being received or an increase in the amount ultimately received when the investment is sold. No guidance is given at all in the standard as to the period over which profits are to be taken into account. In view of the impracticalities of forecasting future dividend streams and ultimate sale proceeds, we believe that companies in applying these provisions should consider the cash proceeds which would be received from the immediate sale of the investment as in (i) above. If a future sale and future dividends have to be taken into account then consideration should also be given to the future interest expense which will be incurred on the borrowing.

Where the currencies are the same, in most situations condition (b) of paragraph 51 and condition (c) of paragraph 57 are irrelevant. This is because of the requirement that exchange differences on the borrowings can only be offset in reserves to the extent that there are corresponding exchange differences on the related investment. This ensures that full cover will only arise if the carrying value of the investment is at least equivalent to the amount of the borrowings. If the investment will not generate cash equivalent to the amount of the borrowings then provision should be made against the carrying value of the investment. This means that the amount of exchange differences on the net investment will correspondingly be less and therefore the exchange differences on the borrowings which exceed that amount will have to be taken to the profit and loss account.

However, even where the currencies are the same, problems can arise in the year the conditions are not met.

3.5.9 *What should happen in the year of change of the above conditions not being met?*

A *Investment making losses*

Example 8.37

A UK company has a wholly owned Japanese subsidiary which it set up several years ago at a cost of ¥1,000m. Up until 1996 the subsidiary was profitable and on 1 January 1977 the company borrowed ¥1,000m repayable in four years' time to provide a hedge against its investment. During 1997 the subsidiary began to make losses such that at 31 December 1997 the net assets of the subsidiary had been reduced to ¥1,000m. In its financial statements for the year ended 31 December 1997 the company applied the cover method and exchange gains of £455,308 were offset in reserves. At that date, exchange gains on the investment included in the company and consolidated reserves were £1,175,000 and £1,500,000 respectively. In the year to 31 December 1998 the subsidiary has made further losses of ¥400m but it is now considered that the losses have been stemmed and that the subsidiary will break even in the next three years. The results of the subsidiary are translated using closing rates. Assuming that the net asset value at 31 December 1998 is considered to be the cash expected to be generated by the investment, how should the cover method be applied in the financial statements for the year ended 31 December 1998?

The relevant exchange rates are:

	£1=¥
31 December 1997	214
31 December 1998	188

Exchange differences			
Investment – ¥1,000m	@ 214 =	£4,672,897	
	@ 188 =	£5,319,149	
			£646,252
Loan – ¥1,000m	@ 214 =	£4,672,897	
	@ 188 =	£5,319,149	
			£(646,252)

As the exchange loss on the loan is matched by the exchange gain on the investment it would appear that none of the exchange loss on the loan need be taken to profit and loss account. However, as the cash expected to be generated from the investment is only ¥600m then this condition has to be considered. The possible effects of this on the cover method are as follows:

(a) Abandon the cover method with retrospective effect.

It could be argued that as the amount of the loan exceeds the cash expected to be generated then the cover method cannot be applied and therefore this year's exchange loss on the loan should be reflected in the profit and loss account for the year. The previous exchange gains on the loan cannot be taken through the profit or loss account for the year as a result of FRS 3, but if necessary should be transferred to retained profits. In the company financial statements the investment should be translated at historical rates and the exchange gains of £1,175,000 on the investment reversed. This reflects the position which would have been shown if the cover method had not been applied. A prior year adjustment is inappropriate as it is a change in circumstances which has given rise to the cover method not being used.

(b) Abandon the cover method for the current year and thereafter.

As in (a), this year's exchange loss on the loan should be reflected in the profit and loss account. However, as the company was hedged last year, the company's financial statements should still reflect that fact. The investment would not be restated at historical rates but a provision of £1,481,408 would be made against last year's carrying value for the investment to reduce it to ¥600m @ £1=188, i.e. £3,191,489.

(c) Apply the cover method for the current year but abandon it thereafter.

The calculation of exchange differences is based on opening figures for the investment and the loan. At that time the cash expected from the investment was sufficient to meet the loan, and accordingly the cover method can still be applied and therefore all of the exchange loss on the loan can be taken to reserves. However, provision would have to made in the company's financial statements to reduce the retranslated cost of investment of £5,319,149 to its recoverable amount of £3,191,489.

(d) Apply the cover method to the amount recoverable.

This treatment considers that in applying the cash restriction the loan is effectively split into two parts: (i) an amount equivalent to the cash expected to be generated and (ii) the excess over this amount. The first part is still considered to hedge the investment and the cover method can still be applied to that part. The second part is no longer providing a hedge against any investment and therefore any exchange differences relating to this part must be taken to profit and loss account. In this example, therefore, the treatment would be as follows:

Exchange gain on investment (as above)		£646,252	
Exchange loss on restricted loan			
¥600m	@ 214 =	£2,803,738	
	@ 188 =	£3,191,489	
			(387,751)
Net exchange gain taken to reserves			£258,501

The exchange loss on the remainder of the loan, of £258,501, would be taken to the profit and loss account. In the company's financial statements a provision of £2,127,660 would be made to reduce the retranslated cost of investment to its recoverable amount as in (c) above.

In our view all of these treatments are acceptable under the standard but we believe that method (d) is preferable as this recognises that the company is still hedged to a certain extent.

B Respective currency movements

We indicated earlier that the reason for condition (b) of paragraph 51 and condition (c) of paragraph 57 of the standard was to allow the cover method to be used when different currencies were involved. Although companies may decide to invest in one currency and borrow in another with the expectation or hope that they will generally move in tandem in relation to sterling, this will not always be the case. In any period some currencies will strengthen in relation to sterling and others will weaken and of those that move in the same direction the extent to which they strengthen or weaken can be markedly different. As a result, the cash restriction conditions may become relevant where they have not been before.

Example 8.38

On 1 May 1998 a UK company invests in an Australian company at a cost of A$2,560,000. How should the company apply the cover method in its financial statements for the year ended 30 April 1999 if it financed the investment with (a) a loan of 1,670,000 US dollars or (b) a loan of 2,510,000 Swiss francs ?

The relevant exchange rates are:

	£1=A$	£1=US$	£1=SFr
1 May 1998	2.56	1.67	2.51
30 April 1999	2.43	1.61	2.45

			(a) £	(b) £
Exchange gain on investment				
A$2,560,000	@ 2.56 =	£1,000,000		
	@ 2.43 =	£1,053,498		
			53,498	53,498
Exchange loss on loan				
(a) US$1,670,000	@ 1.67 =	£1,000,000		
	@ 1.61 =	£1,037,267		
			(37,267)	
(b) SFr2,510,000	@ 2.51 =	£1,000,000		
	@ 2.45 =	£1,024,490		
				(24,490)
			16,231	29,008

It can be seen that in both cases the hedging has been successful and the cover method can be applied.

We now look at the position in the financial statements for the following year, 30 April 2000. Assuming the relevant exchange rates at the year end are £1=A$2.50=US$1.62=SFr2.40.

			(a) £	(b) £
Exchange loss on investment				
A$2,560,000	@ 2.43 =	£1,053,498		
	@ 2.50 =	£1,024,000		
			(29,498)	(29,498)
Exchange difference on loan				
(a) US$1,670,000	@ 1.61 =	£1,037,267		
	@ 1.62 =	£1,030,864		
			6,403	
(b) SFr2,510,000	@ 2.45 =	£1,024,490		
	@ 2.40 =	£1,045,833		
				(21,343)

It can be seen that in the case of the US$ loan condition (a) of paragraph 51 of the standard is met and therefore it would appear that the cover method can be applied. However, if the book value of the investment is considered to be the recoverable amount of the investment then condition (b) has to be considered as the book value of £1,024,000 is less than the amount of the loan which is £1,030,864.

This is due to the fact that although both currencies have weakened in relation to sterling the Australian dollar has weakened more than the US dollar.

In the case of the Swiss franc loan the cover method cannot be applied as there are exchange losses on both the investment and the loan. This is because the currencies have moved in opposite directions in relation to sterling with the Swiss franc continuing to strengthen. Again, consideration has to be given to the effect of condition (b) as this loan is even more clearly not covered by the amount of the investment.

The possible treatments of condition (b) are those which were considered in the previous example. In the case of the US$ loan in this example, adopting either of methods (a), (b) or (d) will have the curious effect of actually improving the results shown in the profit and loss account as all or part of the exchange gain on the loan will be reflected therein.

3.6 Intra-group long-term loans and deferred trading balances

3.6.1 *General requirement*

SSAP 20 requires that all monetary items are translated at closing rates[122] and the resulting exchange differences are taken to profit and loss account.[123] This requirement is equally valid for amounts due to or from other companies within the group.[124] Any exchange differences on these inter-company accounts would be reflected, initially, in the profit and loss account of the group company which was exposed to the currency risk. On consolidation, such exchange differences would normally remain in the profit and loss account in the same way as exchange differences on monetary items resulting from transactions with third parties.

In certain circumstances, however, a holding company may decide to finance a subsidiary with loan capital rather than equity share capital with the intention of providing long-term capital for the subsidiary. This may be done for a variety of reasons: there may be tax advantages in so doing; the subsidiary may be restricted in paying dividends but not interest payments; or it may be easier to recover loans rather than equity in the event of nationalisation of the subsidiary.

Whatever the reason, the substance of the transaction is to provide long-term finance for the subsidiary and therefore the question arises of why the financial statements should show a different result by including exchange differences on the loan in the profit and loss account when exchange differences relating to the equity finance would be taken to reserves.

3.6.2 *Paragraphs 20 and 43*

Paragraph 20 of SSAP 20 recognises this and the fact that companies may finance subsidiaries by deferring trading balances as follows: 'Although equity investments in foreign enterprises will normally be made by the purchase of shares, investments may also be made by means of long-term loans and inter-company deferred trading balances. Where financing by such means is intended to be, for all practical purposes, as permanent as equity, such loans and inter-company balances should be treated as part of the investing company's net investment in the foreign enterprise; hence exchange differences arising on such loans and inter-company balances should be dealt with as adjustments to reserves.'

The definition of 'net investment' in paragraph 43 of the standard states that 'in appropriate circumstances, intra-group loans and other deferred balances may be regarded as part of the effective equity stake'.

3.6.3 *How permanent is permanent?*

It can be seen from the above that this treatment for the exchange differences should be applied where such inter-company accounts are intended to be, for all practical purposes, as permanent as equity. How should this be interpreted?

It could be argued that if it is planned or intended to repay the inter-company amount at any time while the company is a subsidiary then it is not as permanent as equity and the exchange differences should be taken to the profit and loss account. The amount should be considered as permanent as equity only if it will be repaid when the holding company disinvests entirely from the subsidiary. This would mean that even if a company had financed a subsidiary by providing it with a loan which was due to be repaid in twenty or thirty years' time and the intention was that this would be repaid at that time then the exchange differences on the loan during that period should be recorded in the profit and loss account. This is because the exchange differences will ultimately be reflected in cash flows.

However, it is recognised that in such circumstances this would be unrealistic and therefore a shorter timespan should be considered. It has been suggested by other writers that if there is no intention to repay the amount within the foreseeable future then the inter-company account can be regarded as permanent as equity.[125]

The term 'foreseeable future' is used in paragraph 12 of SSAP 15 – *Accounting for deferred taxation* – and, although not defined, is often taken to mean a period of approximately three to five years.[126] It has been suggested that this same criterion is used in considering whether an inter-company account is as permanent as equity.[127]

It is probably easier to regard a long-term loan which is not repayable until twenty or thirty years as being as permanent as equity. What if the loan is a short-term one which is continually rolled over? In our view, if the intention is that the loan will continue to be rolled over so that it is effectively a long-term one which is not repayable in the foreseeable future, then the loan can be regarded as permanent as equity. However, we believe that if the intention is that the loan will only be rolled over until such time as the subsidiary can repay the loan, then the loan should not be regarded as permanent as equity.

The standard also allows deferred trading balances to be regarded as permanent as equity.[128] As well as including balances arising from purchase and sale of goods and services these could also include interest payments and dividend payments which have not been paid for in cash but are accumulated in the inter-company account.

In our view, such balances should only be regarded as permanent if cash settlement is not made or planned to be made in the foreseeable future. If a subsidiary makes payment for purchases from its parent company, but is continually indebted to the parent company as a result of new purchases, then in these circumstances, as individual transactions are settled, no part of the inter-company balance should be regarded as permanent. Accordingly, such exchange differences should be taken to profit and loss account.

3.6.4 *What happens in year of change?*

It may happen that a company will decide that its subsidiary requires to be refinanced and instead of investing more equity capital in the subsidiary decides that an existing inter-company account, which has previously been regarded as a normal monetary item, should become a long-term deferred trading balance and no repayment of such amount will be requested within the foreseeable future. How should the company treat the exchange differences relating to the inter-company account in the consolidated financial statements in the year it was so designated?

Example 8.39

A UK company has a wholly owned Canadian subsidiary whose net assets at 31 December 1997 were C$2,000,000. These net assets were arrived at after taking account of a liability to the UK parent of £250,000. Using the closing exchange rate of £1=C$2.35 this liability was included in the Canadian company's balance sheet at that date at C$587,500. On 30 June 1998 the company decided that in order to refinance the Canadian subsidiary it would regard the liability of £250,000 as a long-term liability which would not be called for repayment in the foreseeable future. Consequently, the company thereafter regarded such loan as being part of its net investment in the subsidiary. In the year ended 31 December 1998 the Canadian company made no profit or loss other than any exchange difference to be recognised on its liability to its parent company. The relevant exchange rate at that date was £1=C$2.56.

The financial statements of the subsidiary in C$ and translated using the closing rate are as follows:

Balance sheet	31 December 1998		31 December 1997	
	C$	£	C$	£
Assets	2,587,500	1,010,742	2,587,500	1,101,064
Amount due to parent	640,000	250,000	587,500	250,000
Net assets	1,947,500	760,742	2,000,000	851,064
Profit and loss account				
Exchange difference	(52,500)			

The normal treatment would be for this exchange loss to be translated at the closing rate and included in the consolidated profit and loss account as £20,508. As the net investment was C$2,000,000 then there would have been an exchange loss taken to reserves of £69,814, i.e. £851,064 less £781,250 (C$2,000,000 @ £1=C$2.56).

However, as the company now regards the amount due as being as permanent as equity it has to be included in the net investment. The question then arises as to when this should be regarded as having happened and how the exchange difference on it should be calculated. The only guidance given in SSAP 20 is in paragraph 16 which states that when applying the closing rate/net investment method, exchange differences arise if the rate ruling at the balance sheet date differs from the rate ruling at the date of subsequent capital injection. In this case there has been no capital injection as such, merely a 'redesignation' of a previous inter-company balance.

One treatment would be to regard the 'capital injection' as having taken place at the beginning of the accounting period and, therefore, the net investment increased at that date to C$2,587,500. The exchange loss on this amount is £90,322, i.e. £1,101,064 less £1,010,742, and this amount should be taken to reserves. Accordingly, all of the exchange loss included in the subsidiary's profit and loss account would be taken to reserves on consolidation. This has the merit of treating all of the exchange loss for this year consistently in the same way and it could be argued that this treatment is necessary as none of the exchange loss has any impact on the prospective cash flows of the group.

An alternative treatment would be to regard the 'capital injection' as having occurred when it was decided to redesignate the inter-company account and to take the exchange difference arising on the account up to that date to the profit and loss account. Only the exchange difference arising thereafter would be taken to reserves. At 30 June 1998 the subsidiary would have translated the inter-company account as C$612,500 (£250,000 @ £1=C$2.45) and therefore the exchange loss up to that date was C$25,000. Translated at the closing rate this amount would be included in the consolidated profit and loss account as £9,766. Accordingly, £10,742 (£20,508 less £9,766) would be taken to reserves.

This amount represents the exchange loss on the 'capital injection' of C$612,500. Translated at the closing rate this amounts to £239,258 which is £10,742 less than the original £250,000. This treatment has the merit of treating the inter-company account up to the date of redesignation consistently with previous years and taking the same exchange difference to reserves which would have been taken if a capital injection had taken place at 30 June 1988. For these reasons we believe that this treatment is preferable to the former treatment although both treatments are acceptable.

Suppose, instead of the inter-company account being £250,000, it was denominated in dollars at C$587,500. In this case the parent company would be exposed to the exchange risk; what would be the position?

The subsidiary's net assets at both 31 December 1997 and 1998 would be:

Assets	US$2,587,500
Amount due to parent company	587,500
Net assets	US$2,000,000

As the inter-company account is expressed in Canadian dollars, there will be no exchange difference thereon in the subsidiary's profit and loss account.

There will, however, be an exchange loss in the parent company as follows:

C$587,500	@ 2.35 =	£250,000
	@ 2.56 =	£229,492
		£20,508

Again, in the consolidated financial statements as the inter-company account is now regarded as part of the equity investment some or all of this amount can be taken to reserves. If the treatment of regarding this as happening at the beginning of the period is adopted then all of the exchange loss would be taken to reserves. This gives the same result as when the account was expressed in sterling.

If the alternative treatment is adopted then the position would be:

C$587,500	@ 2.35 =	£250,000	
	@ 2.45 =	£239,796	
			£10,204
	@ 2.45 =	£239,796	
	@ 2.56 =	£229,492	
			£10,304

The exchange loss up to 30 June 1998 of £10,204 would be taken to the profit and loss account and the exchange loss thereafter of £10,304 would be taken to reserves. This is different from when the account was expressed in sterling because the 'capital injection' in this case is C$587,500 whereas before it was effectively C$612,500.

3.6.5 *Is such a treatment allowed in the company financial statements?*

We saw in the above example that when the inter-company account was expressed in Canadian dollars an exchange difference arose in the parent company and how this would be treated in the consolidated financial statements. What about the parent company financial statements? Is a similar approach allowed?

Some people take the view that SSAP 20 does not permit exchange differences on loans and deferred trading balances which are considered to be as permanent as equity to be taken to reserves in the parent company's own financial statements.[129] This is because the standard only refers to such treatment when discussing the closing rate/net investment method and in defining the net investment in the foreign enterprise.[130] As a result, it is only relevant to consolidated financial statements. No allowance is made in the provisions of SSAP 20 dealing with the financial statements of individual companies for such a treatment. These provisions require all exchange differences on monetary items to be taken to the profit and loss account (except in circumstances which are not relevant here).[131] The parent company's financial statements should therefore reflect in the results the effect of the parent company being exposed to exchange risk on its inter-company account as it is a monetary item.

Another view is that the parent company's financial statements should reflect the fact that in substance the inter-company account is not a monetary item. If the account is intended to be as permanent as equity then the financial statements of the parent company should effectively show the same results and financial position as if it were an equity investment. One of the objectives of SSAP 20 is to produce results which are compatible with the effects of exchange rate changes on a company's cash flows.[132] As there is no intention for the inter-company account to be repaid until disinvestment or at least in the foreseeable future then there will be no effect on the company's cash flows as no repayments are being made. Accordingly, no exchange differences relating to the inter-company account should be reflected in the profit and loss account. We believe that this is the approach which companies should be adopting.

3.6.6 *If so, how should loans be translated?*

Example 8.40

Suppose in the previous example the inter-company account of C$587,500 initially arose when the exchange rate was £1=C$2.00. The possible treatments would be:

(a) Translate at closing rate

The reason for this treatment is to reflect the fact that the inter-company account is a monetary item and as such should be retranslated at closing rate. However, as the exchange differences will not impact on cash flows they should not all be taken to the profit and loss account for the year but some or all of them should be taken to reserves as explained in 3.6.1 above. It could be argued that as paragraph 20 of the standard refers to exchange differences being taken to reserves that this is the treatment required by the standard.

(b) Translate at historical rate ruling when account originally arose

As the account is considered to be as permanent as equity then it should be translated as such. Equity investments should be included at the historical rate of exchange (unless they have been financed or hedged by foreign borrowings). The account would therefore be included in the parent company balance sheet at £293,750, i.e. C$587,500 @ £1=C$2.00. The difference between this and the previously recorded amount of £250,000, or the amount when it was regarded as permanent, of £239,796, should be treated as a reserve movement.

(c) Retain at the rate ruling when the account was considered to be permanent

The reason for this treatment is that the decision during the year is a change in circumstance. Accordingly, the nature of the account only changed on 30 June 1998 and it is this date which is relevant for determining the historical rate of exchange. The account would therefore be translated as £239,796 and no further exchange difference would be recorded. (If the former treatment referred to in 3.6.4 above is adopted on consolidation then a consistent treatment in the parent company's financial statements would be to retain the account at the amount included in the previous balance sheet, i.e. £250,000.)

All previous exchange differences relating to the account should not be reversed as they arose when the inter-company account was considered to be a monetary amount.

In our view method (c) is preferable as this would be the amount included if it were an equity investment; however, all three methods are probably acceptable.

3.6.7 *UK subsidiary with loan from overseas parent company*

The previous sections have dealt with a UK parent considering that an amount due by a foreign subsidiary is as permanent as equity. What about the opposite situation where an amount is owed by a UK company to its overseas parent company, expressed in the foreign currency? Can similar treatments be adopted where the overseas parent company considers the amount due by the UK company as permanent as equity so that exchange differences on the inter-company account do not need to be reflected in the UK company's profit or loss for the year in its own financial statements?

SSAP 20 does not deal with this specific point. It could be argued that if there is no intention that such an amount will be repaid then any exchange differences will have no effect on the cash flows of the UK company and, therefore, they should not be reflected in the profit and loss account. To adopt similar treatments to those referred to above would reflect the substance of the transaction.

We believe, however, that the UK company has to translate the inter-company account at closing rate and take the exchange differences arising thereon to the profit and loss account. This is because under FRS 4 the amount will be shown as a liability in the balance sheet and cannot be shown as equity until such time as shares are issued to the parent company or the parent company writes off the inter-company account as a capital contribution.

3.7 Other intra-group transactions

As indicated in 3.6.1 above, exchange differences on intra-group transactions should normally be treated in the same way as if they arose on transactions with third parties. However, there are two further problem areas which arise when preparing the consolidated financial statements.

3.7.1 *Dividends*

The first area relates to dividends payable by a foreign subsidiary to its UK parent company.

If a subsidiary pays a dividend to the parent company during the year the UK company should record the dividend at the rate ruling when the dividend was declared. An exchange difference will arise in the parent company's own financial statements if the exchange rate moves between the declaration date and the date the dividend is actually received. This exchange difference requires to be taken to profit and loss account and will remain there on consolidation. However, on consolidation another exchange difference is likely to arise as the dividend paid by the subsidiary will be translated at closing rate (or average rate) and this is likely to be different from the dividend received recorded by the parent company.

Example 8.41

A UK company has a wholly owned US subsidiary. On 30 September 1998 the subsidiary declares a dividend of US$0.10 per share and is due to pay a dividend of US$100,000 to the UK parent company. In preparing the consolidated financial statements for the year ended 31 March 1999 the UK company uses the closing rate/net investment method and translates the results of the US subsidiary at the closing rate. The relevant exchange rates at 30 September 1998 and 31 March 1999 are £1=US$1.70 and £1=US$1.61 respectively. Accordingly, the dividend received is recorded at £58,824 and the dividend paid in the translated profit and loss account is £62,112. What should happen to the difference of £3,288 when the inter-company dividends are eliminated on consolidation?

One treatment would be to take it to the profit and loss account as an adjustment of the subsidiary's profit or loss, as suggested by Westwick.[153] This has the effect of including in the consolidated profit and loss account the profits of the subsidiary which were distributed at the sterling amount received and the profits retained by the subsidiary translated at the closing rate.

An alternative treatment would be to treat it as a movement on reserves as the consolidated profit and loss account should reflect the profits of the subsidiary translated at the closing rate. This method will therefore retain the same financial relationships shown in the subsidiary's own financial statements in the consolidated financial statements. Consequently, we consider this treatment to be preferable.

We believe that such a treatment should also be adopted even if the dividend was unpaid at the year end. In the above example, if this had been the case, by the year end the parent company would have recorded an exchange gain of £3,288 on the dividend receivable in its own profit and loss account. We consider that this gain should remain in the profit and loss account and the difference on consolidation taken to reserves even although it is a loss of the same amount.

Another situation concerning intra-group dividends is when a dividend is proposed by the subsidiary company and this is recorded at the year end in both companies' financial statements. There is no problem in that year as both the intercompany accounts and the dividends will eliminate on consolidation with no exchange differences arising. However, as the dividend will not be received until the following year an exchange difference will arise in the parent company's financial statements in that year.

Example 8.42

A UK company has a wholly owned French subsidiary. When preparing the financial statements for the year ended 31 December 1998 it was decided that the French company would propose a dividend of FFr0.20 per share for the year then ended payable on 30 April 1999, resulting in a dividend due to the parent company of FFr200,000. The parent company, therefore, recorded in its financial statements for the year ended 31 December 1998 a dividend receivable of FFr200,000, which translated at the exchange rate ruling on that date of £1=FFr9.29, amounted to £21,529. As the subsidiary was consolidated using the closing rate/net investment method then the dividend receivable and the dividend payable cancelled each other out on consolidation. On 30 April 1999 the dividend was paid and as the exchange rate was then £1=€1.52=FFr9.98 the amount actually received was £20,040 and, therefore, the parent company recorded an exchange loss of £1,489. How should this exchange difference be dealt with in the consolidated financial statements for the year ended 31 December 1999?

This exchange difference should remain in the profit and loss account as it is no different from any other exchange difference arising on inter-company accounts resulting from other types of inter-company transactions. It should not be taken to reserves.

It may seem odd that the consolidated results can be affected by exchange differences on inter-company dividends. In order to minimise the effect of exchange rate movements companies should, therefore, arrange for inter-company dividends to be paid on the same day the dividend is declared, or as soon after the dividend is declared as possible. In addition, they should consider not booking proposed dividends in the year to which they relate but when they are actually declared unless there are commercial reasons for doing so, e.g. in order to maximise the distributable profits of the parent company shown in the year end financial statements.

One company which discloses the fact that exchange differences on payment of inter-company dividends impact on the group's results is British American Tobacco:

Extract 8.31: British American Tobacco p.l.c. (2000)

4 **Foreign currencies** [extract]

The differences between retained profits of overseas subsidiaries and associated undertakings translated at average and closing rates of exchange are taken to reserves, as are differences arising on the retranslation to sterling (using closing rates of exchange) of overseas net assets at the beginning of the year, after taking into account related foreign currency borrowings. Other exchange differences, including those on remittances, are reflected in profit.

3.7.2 *Unrealised profits on inter-company transactions*

The other problem area is the elimination of unrealised profits resulting from inter-company transactions when one of the parties to the transaction is a foreign subsidiary whose results are incorporated into the consolidated financial statements using the closing rate/net investment method.

Example 8.43

A UK company has a wholly owned German subsidiary. On 28 February 1999 the subsidiary sold goods to the parent company for €1,000. The cost of the goods to the subsidiary was €700. The goods were recorded by the parent company at £685 based on the exchange rate ruling on 28 February 1999 of £1=€1.46. All of the goods are unsold by the year end, 30 April 1999. The exchange rate at that date was £1=€1.52. How should the inter-company profit be eliminated?

SSAP 20 contains no guidance on this matter and it has been suggested that it would be logical to use the rate ruling at the date of the transaction.[134]

The profit shown by the subsidiary is €300 which translated at the rate ruling on the transaction of £1=€1.46 equals £205. Consequently, the goods will be included in the balance sheet at:

Per parent company balance sheet	£685
Less unrealised profit eliminated	205
	£480

It can be seen that the resulting figure for stock is equivalent to the original euro cost translated at the rate ruling on the date of the transaction. This is the treatment required by SFAS 52.[135] However, it should be remembered that SFAS 52 requires the results of foreign enterprises to be translated using actual or weighted average rates[136] and, therefore, is to be recommended when a weighted average is being used. Where the closing rate is being used then such an approach does not eliminate the profit from the profit and loss account. In this example, the profit of the subsidiary includes €300 which translated at €1.52 equals £197 and the amount eliminated is £205. We believe it is the former amount which should be eliminated even though this will not result in a balance sheet figure for the goods equivalent to the original cost of the goods to the group.

Consequently, where the closing rate is used to translate the results of foreign subsidiaries then we would recommend that any adjustment made to eliminate any of those profits which are unrealised as far as the group is concerned should be calculated using that closing rate. If a weighted average rate is used then the rate ruling on the date of the transaction should be used.

If in the above example the goods had been sold by the UK company to the US subsidiary then we believe the amount to be eliminated is the amount of profit shown in the UK company's financial statements. Again, this will not necessarily result in the goods being carried in the consolidated financial statements at their original cost to the group.

3.8 Introduction of the euro

The advent of the introduction of the euro raised a number of concerns and in June 1997 the European Commission published a paper – *Accounting for the introduction of the euro.* Most of the areas addressed in that paper were really of relevance to those countries who were going to participate in the first phase of Economic and Monetary Union from 1 January 1999. Nevertheless, there were some issues which were relevant in the UK and in March 1998 the UITF issued Abstract 21 – *Accounting issues arising from the proposed introduction of the euro,* effective for accounting periods ending on or after 23 March 1998. This was supplemented in August 1998 by an Appendix to the abstract dealing with some further accounting issues.

3.8.1 UITF 21

UITF 21 deals with, firstly, the treatment of costs incurred in connection with the introduction of the euro and, secondly, potential accounting implications.

A Treatment and disclosure of costs incurred

The expenditures that may be incurred in preparation for the euro not only relate to modifications to computer software; UITF 21 also cites such examples as staff training, providing information to customers and the modification of cash handling equipment such as vending machines or cash registers.[137] The impact of the euro will clearly be greatest for companies that operate in those EU member states that have joined the system (which may include subsidiaries of UK companies), but there may be some effect on UK domestic companies as well.

Most of the expenditure mentioned above is of a revenue nature and will be expensed as incurred. However, the Abstract indicates that capitalisation of expenditure necessary to modify assets will be allowed where an entity already has an accounting policy to capitalise assets of the relevant type, but only to the extent that the expenditure clearly results in an enhancement of an asset beyond that originally assessed rather than merely maintaining its service potential.[138]

The Abstract requires that any expenditure incurred in preparing for the changeover to the euro and regarded as exceptional should be disclosed in accordance with FRS 3. Particulars of commitments at the balance sheet date in respect of costs to be incurred (whether to be treated as capital or revenue) should be disclosed where they are regarded as relevant to assessing the entity's state of affairs. However, it takes a much softer line on narrative disclosures than UITF 20 did on Year 2000 disclosures, imposing no mandatory requirement but simply recommending that some discussion should be made of the impact of the euro where it is expected to be significant, including an indication of the total costs likely to be incurred. Such disclosure may be more appropriately located in the directors' report or any operating and financial review or other statement included in the annual report published by the entity.[139]

B Foreign currency translation effects

The foreign currency issues dealt with are likely to be relevant only to those companies that account in a currency that has become linked to the euro. The first deals with those companies that have taken exchange differences in respect of their investment in foreign subsidiaries to reserves under SSAP 20, and now find that the two currencies are irrevocably locked to the euro (and therefore to each other), so that no future exchange differences can arise. The question is whether the cumulative exchange difference in reserves should now be regarded as 'realised' and recycled through the profit and loss account. However, there is no such concept of recycling in SSAP 20, and UITF 21 makes it clear that it would be contrary to FRS 3; so the answer is that such differences should remain in reserves.[140]

The second foreign currency issue concerns anticipatory hedges of future transactions (see 3.3.1 C above). Where a company has taken out a hedge against a future transaction in a foreign currency, and once again the two currencies become linked by joining the euro, so that there will be no further exchange movements between them and no need for any hedge to be continued, should any deferred gain or loss on the hedge now be recognised in the profit and loss account? Again, UITF 21 says that the answer is no: the deferred gain or loss should continue to be carried forward and matched with the income or expense that it was originally designed to hedge.[141]

These foreign currency issues discussed are unlikely to be relevant to UK companies until sterling is linked to the euro, and by that time some of the guidance given in UITF 21, notably on hedging, may have been superseded by any eventual standard on financial instruments.

3.8.2 *UITF 21 – Appendix*

The Appendix to UITF 21 deals primarily with issues arising for companies whose functional currency is participating in monetary union. The document itself makes clear that it is not presenting any new concepts, but rather setting out how the existing rules in SSAP 20 should be applied to some of the issues raised by the euro. The issues addressed and answers given by the UITF are summarised below:[142]

(a) What translation rate should be used where an entity chooses to provide a convenience translation of its financial statements, including comparative amounts in respect of accounting periods before the introduction of the euro?

The original reporting currency amounts should be translated at that currency's conversion rate to the euro established at 1 January 1999. It is not appropriate to rework the translations underlying the preparation of the original financial statements in the relevant national currency of the Member State.

(b) What exchange rate should be used for financial statements with year-ends other than 31 December (for example, should the fixed conversion rates be anticipated in respect of balances at dates earlier than the date of introduction of the euro)?

The normal rules in SSAPs 17 and 20 should apply. If, for example, a company with a September 1998 year-end includes in its assets and liabilities foreign currency amounts with participating Member States (amounts that may not be settled until after 1 January 1999) it would not be appropriate to record the balances at other than the closing rate at the end of September 1998.

(c) Is any special treatment needed for apparent differences arising from the use of the temporal method as, for example, the same asset may be reported at a different euro figure in a subsidiary's own accounts and in the group accounts?

The temporal method is described in paragraphs 21-24 of SSAP 20 (see 2.1.1 above). It is possible that there could be a different euro figure for the same asset (acquired before 1 January 1999) in a subsidiary's own accounts and in the group accounts, but this is a natural consequence of the temporal method, which preserves in group accounts the historical rates of exchange at which transactions were undertaken.

(d) Does the introduction of the euro and the fixing of exchange rates mean that exchange gains on unsettled items (in respect of currencies of countries in participating Member States) become realised?

The UITF notes that the European Commission's paper concludes that such gains should be treated as realised. However, SSAP 20 requires continuous recognition of gains and losses on all monetary items, even long-term ones, whether realised or not. There is no cause to recognise any further gain or loss when realisation takes place.

3.9 Reporting currency, measurement currency and presentation currency

As noted at 2.2 above, SSAP 20 defines a company's local currency as 'the currency of the primary economic environment in which it operates and generates net cash flows'. The translation procedures embodied within SSAP 20 are then intended to measure transactions and financial statements expressed in other currencies against that currency. SSAP 20 does not explicitly say what currency should be used for reporting or presenting the accounts, but paragraph 1 of the standard refers to foreign transactions and operations as having to be translated into the currency in which the company reports, so it seems to presume that companies will report and present its accounts in terms of its local currency. Although SSAP 20 uses the term 'local currency', the definition is similar to that of 'functional currency' which is the term used in the US in SFAS 52. Incidentally, FRS 13 uses the term 'functional currency', with an identical definition to that of 'local currency' in SSAP 20.

SSAP 20 effectively assumes that the local currency of a UK reporting company is sterling and only discusses the determination of local currency in the context of the translation of foreign enterprises which should be translated using the temporal method (see 2.4.4 above).

For most UK companies the local currency (or functional currency) is regarded as sterling and the accounts are prepared and presented in sterling. However, in the light of increasing globalisation of business in recent years, some UK companies have determined that this is no longer the case and they now regard the US dollar to be their functional currency and use that currency for the purpose of financial reporting. One such company is Lonmin which changed its reporting currency for the purposes of its 1999 accounts as shown in the following extract.

Extract 8.32: Lonmin plc (1999)

Statement on accounting policies [extract]

Basis of accounting [extract]

Following the disposal of most of the non-mining businesses, the Group's earnings stream is primarily US dollars. The Group's principal functional currency is now the US dollar. The Group has also adopted the US dollar as its reporting currency with effect from 1 October 1998. Sterling equivalent figures are also shown to provide additional assistance to shareholders.

Foreign currencies [extract]

The Group's functional currency is primarily the US dollar. The reporting currency of the Group is also the US dollar.

Subsidiaries that keep their accounts in currencies other than their functional currency translate them into the functional currency by the temporal method prior to consolidation. This results in non-monetary assets and liabilities being recorded at their historical cost expressed in the functional currency whilst monetary assets and liabilities are stated at the closing exchange rate. Differences on translation are included in the profit and loss account.

Where the functional currency is not the US dollar, the results and assets and liabilities are consolidated by the net investment method. In such cases, profit and loss items are translated into US dollars at weighted average exchange rates, except material exceptional items which are translated at the exchange rate at the date of the transaction.

The use of weighted average exchange rates to translate results is a change in accounting policy from the previous method of using closing exchange rates and is considered to give a fairer and more meaningful reflection of the results of Group businesses.

This change in accounting policy has increased 1998 profit before taxation and profit for the year by $5 million (£3 million) and $2 million (£1 million) respectively.

Sterling equivalents are presented to provide information to shareholders and are derived from the US dollar amounts by translating profit and loss items at average exchange rates and balance sheet items at closing exchange rates.

Statement of total consolidated recognised gains and losses
For the year ended 30 September

1999	1998 Restated			**1999**	1998 Restated
£m	£m			**$m**	$m
64	30	Profit for the year	– Group	**104**	46
16	10		– Associates	**26**	17
(4)		Dilution of the Group's interest in Ashanti		**(6)**	
9	1	Group share of equity issued by Ashanti		**15**	2
9	(117)	Exchange adjustments	– Group		(119)
4	(8)		– Associates		(14)
98	(84)	Total recognised gains/(losses) relating to the year		**139**	(68)

There are no exchange adjustments in the US dollar figures for 1999 as the figures are prepared utilising the US dollar as the functional currency. The equivalent sterling figures for 1999 include the translation adjustment from US dollars to sterling on the opening equity figure at 1 October 1998.

The comparative figures for 1998 are not prepared on a comparable basis as the US dollar was not used as the functional currency in this period. The sterling figures represent those exchange adjustments reported last year restated for the utilisation of average exchange rates. The US dollar figures for 1998 include the exchange adjustments originally reported in sterling, the translation adjustment of the sterling equity figures at 1 October 1997 into US dollars, and the differences between the average and closing exchange rates on the profits for the year.

It can be seen from the extract that the reason for the change in functional currency was due to the disposal of the non-mining businesses. As this represents a change in circumstances, the prior year figures for 1998, although now reported in US dollars, have not been remeasured using US dollars as the functional currency for that period since this was not the case. This is consistent with the guidance discussed at 3.4.8 A above where the method used for translating a foreign enterprise is changed from the closing rate/net investment method to the temporal method.

Where a UK company does regard a currency other than sterling as its functional currency, one issue which it will need to consider is how to translate its share capital as it has now effectively become denominated in a foreign currency (assuming it remains as sterling share capital). This is discussed at 3.1.6 above.

It can be seen from Extract 8.32 above, that although Lonmin now reports in US dollars, it has also provided sterling equivalents which have been derived from the US dollar amounts by translating profit and loss items at average exchange rates and balance sheet items at closing exchange rates. Again, SSAP 20 does not discuss such 'convenience translations' but the treatment adopted by Lonmin is that which is normally adopted by other companies when providing such supplementary information. Arguably, the same exchange rate should be used throughout so as to preserve the inherent relationships included in the main accounts. However, the approach adopted by Lonmin and other companies in preparing the convenience translations is consistent with the closing rate method used in preparing the main accounts.

This distinction between reporting currency, measurement currency and presentation currency is something which has been considered internationally by the SIC (see 5.2.3 below).

4 RELATED COMPANIES ACT REQUIREMENTS

There are a number of requirements of the Companies Act 1985 which have to be considered when accounting for foreign exchange transactions. The main implications are considered below.

4.1 Realised profits

Most companies in the UK when preparing their financial statements have to comply with the accounting requirements of Schedule 4 to the Companies Act 1985.

4.1.1 *Schedule 4, paragraph 12*

Paragraph 12 of Schedule 4 requires that items in a company's financial statements shall be determined on a prudent basis and only profits which are realised at the balance sheet date can be included in the profit and loss account. However, what is meant by realised profits?

4.1.2 Section 262(3)

Section 262(3) of the Companies Act 1985 states that realised profits should be interpreted as 'such profits of the company as fall to be treated as realised profits for the purposes of those accounts in accordance with principles generally accepted with respect to the determination for accounting purposes of realised profits at the time when those accounts are prepared'.

The normal requirement for exchange differences in the financial statements of a company is that they are taken to the profit and loss account. As a result the ASC in considering this treatment for exchange differences had to give some guidance as to whether exchange gains were to be regarded as realised or not and whether the treatment of such gains required by the standard was consistent with the provisions of paragraph 12.

SSAP 20 identifies three categories of exchange gains which have to be considered.

4.1.3 Settled transactions

First, those arising on settled transactions. As such exchange gains have already impacted on the cash flows of the company then they are clearly realised in cash terms and, therefore, their inclusion in the profit and loss account does not conflict with paragraph 12.

4.1.4 Short-term monetary items

Second, those arising on short-term monetary items. A short-term monetary item is defined in SSAP 20 as one which falls due within one year of the balance sheet date.[143] The statement issued by the ASC at the time the standard was issued said that such exchange gains could be regarded as realised. Accordingly, their inclusion in the profit and loss account is not considered to be in conflict with paragraph 12.[144]

4.1.5 Long-term monetary items

Third, those arising on long-term monetary items. At the time SSAP 20 was issued, it was generally considered that such gains were probably unrealised. The ASC recognised this potential conflict with paragraph 12 but still decided that exchange gains on such items should be taken to the profit and loss account. It considered that a symmetrical treatment of exchange gains and losses was necessary to show a true and fair view of the results of a company involved in foreign currency operations. This treatment acknowledges that exchange gains can be determined no less objectively than exchange losses and it would be illogical to deny that favourable movements in exchange rates had occurred whilst accounting for adverse movements. As there will probably be some interaction between currency movements and interest rates then the profit and loss account will reflect the full impact of the currency involvement.[145] So how was the conflict resolved?

One way would have been to invoke the true and fair view override allowed by what is now section 226 of the Companies Act 1985. However, as the problem was with one of the accounting principles contained in Schedule 4 it was decided to invoke paragraph 15 of that schedule.[146]

This paragraph specifically permits a departure from the accounting principles where there are special reasons and it is considered that the need for a symmetrical treatment constitutes a special reason. As a result, companies which have taken exchange gains (which are considered to be unrealised) on long-term monetary items to the profit and loss account need to disclose the particulars of the departure, the reasons for it and its effect in a note to the financial statements. An example of such disclosure is as follows:

The profit and loss account includes gains on translation of long-term monetary items. The inclusion of these gains represents a departure from the statutory requirement that only realised profit may be included in the profit and loss account. The directors consider that this accounting treatment, which is in accordance with SSAP 20, is necessary in order to give a true and fair view. The unrealised gains included for the year amounted to £10,000 (1998–£5,000) and the cumulative amount included at 31 December 1999 is £15,000.

A *Problem areas*

In 3.2 above we considered a number of problem areas in relation to exchange gains on long-term monetary items which will also be relevant in deciding whether it is necessary to invoke paragraph 15 and give the necessary disclosures, in particular the amount of the exchange gains which are involved.

(a) Past exchange losses

It could be argued that past exchange losses on a long-term monetary item should be ignored and that all of the exchange gain in the current year is unrealised and therefore disclosure is required of the full amount. This would appear to be an ultra cautious view.[147]

Our view is that past exchange losses should be taken into account and that disclosure is only required to the extent that the exchange gain exceeds the net losses previously recognised. Any exchange gain up to the amount of the past losses is effectively a reversal of a provision for losses no longer required. This would appear to be the approach taken by other writers.[148]

Accordingly, if the exchange gain is less than the past exchange losses no disclosure is required under paragraph 15.

(b) Settled or unsettled transactions

As the exchange gain in question relates to an unsettled long-term monetary item then in considering the effect of past exchange losses we believe that it is only the past exchange losses which relate to the proportion that is still outstanding which should be taken into account. Past exchange losses and any current year's exchange losses which relate to amounts that have already been settled should be ignored.

(c) Current portion of long-term monetary items

As any current portion at the end of the financial year will be reflected in cash flows within one year then any exchange gains relating thereto should be regarded as realised. Accordingly, if a long-term item at the end of the previous period has all become due within one year at the end of the current period then no disclosure is required under paragraph 15.

In view of these problem areas we would recommend that companies keep a detailed record of the exchange differences which have arisen on all long-term monetary items since origination.

4.1.6 *Draft Technical Release on realised and distributable profits*

As discussed more fully in Chapter 3 at 2.1, in August 2000 a draft Technical Release – *The determination of realised profits and distributable profits in the context of the Companies Act 1985* – was issued by the ICAEW and ICAS. This takes the view that gains on the translation of a monetary asset or liability denominated in a foreign currency are realised profits.[149] It also discusses the particular issue of exchange gains on unsettled long-term monetary items being taken to the profit and loss account (see 4.1.5 above). It states that, since the issue of SSAP 20, 'the currency markets have significantly become more sophisticated and companies have significantly more flexibility to crystallise exchange profits on long-term monetary items. Consequently, unless there are doubts as to the convertibility or marketability of the currency in question, foreign exchange profits arising on the retranslation of monetary items are realised, irrespective of the maturity date of the monetary item'.[150]

4.2 Distributable profits

4.2.1 *Section 263(3)*

Under section 263(3) of the Companies Act 1985, dividends can only be paid by a company out of cumulative realised profits less realised losses and, therefore, the question of whether exchange gains are realised or not, or indeed whether exchange losses are realised or not, has an important bearing on the distributable profits of a company. The distributable profits of a public company are further restricted to the extent that unrealised losses exceed unrealised profits.[151]

The statement issued by the ASC at the time the standard was published made it clear that the statement only set out the standard accounting practice for foreign currency translation and was not intended to deal with the determination of distributable profits. It emphasised that the question of distributability depends upon the interpretation of company legislation and should be resolved by individual companies, with legal advice where necessary.[152] It did, however, comment on two possible problem areas – long-term monetary items (see 4.2.2 below) and the cover method (see 4.2.4 below).

The draft Technical Release mentioned at 4.1.6 above should also be taken into account in considering the impact of exchange differences on distributable profits.

4.2.2 *Long-term monetary items*

The first area mentioned by the ASC was in relation to exchange gains on long-term monetary items. In 4.1.5 above we considered whether such gains were realised or not. Where the exchange gains are unrealised, then even although they can be taken to the profit and loss account, they cannot be included in arriving at the distributable profits of a company.[153] This makes it even more important for companies to keep a detailed record of exchange differences on such items.

As noted at 4.1.6 above, the draft Technical Release takes the view that gains on the translation of a monetary asset or liability denominated in a foreign currency are realised profits,[154] and this also applies to gains on long-term monetary items, unless there are doubts as to the convertibility or marketability of the currency in question.[155]

4.2.3 *Section 275 and Schedule 4, paragraph 89*

So much for exchange gains, what about exchange losses?

Section 275 of the Companies Act 1985 requires that for the purposes of determining distributable profits a provision of any kind mentioned in paragraph 89 of Schedule 4 is to be treated as a realised loss.

Paragraph 89 states that 'references to provisions for liabilities or charges are to any amount retained as reasonably necessary for the purpose of providing for any liability or loss which is either likely to be incurred, or certain to be incurred but uncertain as to amount or as to the date on which it will arise'.

It is generally recognised that exchange losses on settled transactions and on unsettled short-term monetary items should be regarded as realised losses. It is also considered, on the grounds of prudence, that exchange losses on long-term monetary items should also be regarded as realised.

The draft Technical Release takes the view that losses should be regarded as realised losses except to the extent that the law, accounting standards or the statement provide otherwise.[156] Although not specifically covered in the statement, since gains on the translation of a monetary asset or liability denominated in a foreign currency are realised profits, then it would seem that losses on translation of a monetary asset or liability denominated in a foreign currency are to be treated as realised losses.

However, this brings us to the second possible problem area mentioned by the ASC – the cover method.

4.2.4 *Cover method*

As the cover method can be applied in individual companies' financial statements, this will result in exchange gains and losses on borrowings being taken to reserves to be offset against exchange differences on related equity investments. If exchange losses have arisen on the borrowings should these be regarded as realised?

A Technical Release 504 – paragraph 33(b)

It could be argued that any exchange loss on a borrowing should be regarded as a provision under paragraph 89 of Schedule 4 and therefore a realised loss which would have to be deducted before arriving at distributable profits, whereas the compensating exchange gain on the investment would be unrealised and not available for distribution. However, as stated by the ASC 'this does not reflect the economic realities of hedging which is designed to avoid the creation of any loss' and it can therefore be argued that the exchange 'loss' on the borrowing is not a provision (nor a realised loss) 'either likely to be incurred, or certain to be incurred but uncertain as to amount or as to the date on which it will arise'.

The draft Technical Release issued by the ICAEW and ICAS makes no reference to such losses.

B Problem of timing – income required before payment of loan

We believe that one possible approach to this problem is to consider the timing of the cash flows relating to the investment and the borrowings. The statement by the ASC makes no reference to the fact that some of the exchange losses which have been offset in reserves may relate to borrowings which have already been repaid. We believe that such losses should be regarded as realised as they have been reflected in the cash flows of the company. If the company has regarded the borrowing as a hedge against its investment it is likely to have received dividends from the investment to enable it to repay the borrowings. As the dividends will be recorded at the rate ruling when the dividends were due these will reflect an element of exchange difference since the investment was made. The inherent exchange gain will offset the realised exchange loss on the borrowings which have been repaid.

In considering whether any exchange losses on the borrowings which are still outstanding should be regarded as realised or not, regard should be had to the timing of the income to be received from the investment. If sufficient dividends will be received from the investment prior to each instalment on the borrowings being repaid then it could be argued that there will be no loss on the borrowings. Although any exchange loss will become realised at the time the instalment is paid this will be offset by the inherent exchange gain in the dividend. Accordingly, any exchange losses on the borrowings do not represent a provision for a loss and therefore do not have to be regarded as a realised loss under section 275. We believe that this approach recognises the economic reality that the company is hedged.

If insufficient dividends will be received prior to an instalment of the borrowing being repaid then to the extent that the borrowing is uncovered the exchange loss relating to that portion should be regarded as a realised loss.

Although we believe such an approach to be a sensible one it is unclear as to whether the courts would take a similar view. Accordingly it is important to emphasise the advice given by the ASC in its statement that where the existence of an economic hedge would have to be taken into account in order to make a distribution, it may be appropriate for the directors of the company to seek legal advice.[157]

4.2.5 *Branch accounting*

Another area, which the ASC did not deal with in its statement and is also not covered in the draft Technical Release issued by the ICAEW and ICAS, is where an individual company has a foreign branch. As we have already seen the definition of a foreign branch is a wide one and can include a group of assets and liabilities which are accounted for in foreign currencies.[158] The standard requires the exchange difference on the net investment in the foreign branch to be taken to reserves.[159] The question then arises, is this one net exchange difference which has to be regarded as a realised or unrealised item, or is it an amalgamation of a number of exchange differences some of which may be realised and some of which may be not?

It could be argued that the former treatment is the more correct, particularly as the closing rate/net investment method should only be used if there is no cash flow impact on the rest of the company. If all of the net cash flows of the branch are retained in the foreign currency and not converted into sterling then why should any of the exchange difference be regarded as realised?

In our view it is likely that this former treatment can only be applied where the branch is a legally constituted branch overseas. Where the branch is a group of assets and liabilities then it is likely that the latter approach will have to be applied as the legal entity is the company. This, therefore, gives rise to a couple of problems.

A Similar to cover method

First, the main asset is likely to be a non-monetary item and the main liability is likely to be a long-term monetary item. This gives rise to a similar problem as that discussed in relation to the cover method above in that the exchange differences on the asset will be unrealised and the exchange differences on the borrowing could be regarded as realised. We believe, however, that it would be sensible to adopt a similar approach to that suggested in relation to borrowings under the cover method at 4.2.4 B above.

B Short-term monetary items

Second, it is likely that part of the branch will be represented by trading balances i.e. debtors, creditors, and bank balances. As these are all short-term monetary items then any exchange gains or losses should be regarded as realised.

As a result of the above it is recommended that detailed records are kept of the breakdown of exchange differences on the net investment in the foreign branch. The cumulative exchange difference at each year end should be split into:

(a) the cumulative exchange difference on the non-monetary assets.

This will be the difference between the net book value in currency terms translated at closing rate and translated at historical rates applying at the date of purchase. This difference should be regarded as an unrealised difference;

(b) the cumulative exchange difference on the borrowings.

This will be the difference between the amount outstanding in currency terms translated at closing rate and translated at historical rate when the borrowing originated. This difference should then be determined to be realised or unrealised as recommended above, i.e. consider whether sufficient net income will be received from the asset prior to paying each instalment of the borrowing;

(c) the remainder.

This should represent the exchange differences on assets which have been depreciated or sold, borrowings which have been repaid, and on the monetary trading balances. All of this amount should be regarded as realised.

We would emphasise that although we believe such an approach to be a sensible one the courts may take a different view. Therefore, if it is necessary in order to make a distribution to regard some of the exchange differences on the borrowings as unrealised because they are covered by foreign currency assets, then it may be appropriate for the directors of the company to seek legal advice.

4.3 Disclosure

There are a number of provisions of the Companies Act which have to be considered in relation to disclosure within a company's financial statements.

4.3.1 *Basis of translation*

Paragraph 58(1) of Schedule 4 requires that 'where sums originally denominated in foreign currencies have been brought into account under any items shown in the balance sheet or profit or loss account, the basis on which those sums have been translated into sterling shall be stated'. This effectively extends the requirement of paragraph 59 of the standard so that disclosure of the method of translating monetary and non-monetary items by individual companies is given. Paragraph 59 only requires the method used in translating the financial statements of foreign enterprises to be disclosed.

4.3.2 *Treatment of exchange differences in profit and loss account*

A Formats

The profit and loss formats contained in Schedule 4 set out the headings of income and expenditure which a company should use in preparing its profit and loss account. It will therefore be necessary for companies to consider under which heading exchange differences reported as part of the profit or loss for the year should be included. Distinction is effectively made in the formats between operating income and expenditure and other income and expenditure. Accordingly, the nature of each exchange difference will have to be considered.

B SSAP 20, paragraph 68

Guidance is given in paragraph 68 of the standard. Gains or losses arising from trading transactions should normally be shown as 'other operating income or expense' while those arising from arrangements which may be considered as financing should be disclosed separately as part of 'other interest receivable/payable and similar income/expense'. The amounts included do not have to be separately disclosed; however, it should be borne in mind that the standard requires the net exchange difference on foreign currency borrowings less deposits to be disclosed.

4.3.3 *Reserve movements*

Paragraph 46 of Schedule 4 requires the following information to be disclosed about movements on any reserve:

(a) the amount of the reserve at the date of the beginning of the financial year and as at the balance sheet date respectively;

(b) any amounts transferred to or from the reserve during that year; and

(c) the source and application respectively of any amounts so transferred.

These requirements are unlikely to have any major impact as paragraph 60 of the standard requires the net movement on reserves arising from exchange differences to be disclosed.

4.3.4 *Movements on provisions for liabilities and charges*

The requirements referred to above in respect of reserve movements apply equally to movements on provisions for liabilities and charges, e.g. a provision for deferred tax. FRS 12 – *Provisions, Contingent Liabilities and Contingent Assets* –also requires disclosure of the movements on provisions (see 6.1.2 of Chapter 28). Accordingly, it will be necessary to disclose separately the net movement on the provision which arises from exchange differences.

4.3.5 *Movements on fixed assets*

Paragraph 42 of Schedule 4 requires, inter alia, disclosure of movements on fixed assets resulting from:

(a) acquisitions of any assets during the year;

(b) disposals of any assets during the year; and

(c) any transfer of assets of the company to and from another category of asset during the year.

Similarly, movements on provisions for depreciation or diminution in value have to be shown. FRS 15 – *Tangible Fixed Assets* – also requires disclosure of the movements on fixed assets (see 3.5.2 of Chapter 12).

As a result of these requirements, where fixed assets are translated at closing rates it will be necessary to disclose separately the net movements arising on the cost or valuation of the fixed assets and on any related provision resulting from exchange differences.

4.4 Alternative accounting rules

4.4.1 *Schedule 4, Part II, section C*

Section C of Part II of Schedule 4 allows companies to include assets in the balance sheet at amounts based on valuations or current costs rather than being included at amounts based on historical costs. Where this is done there are a number of requirements which have to be followed, e.g. disclosure of comparable figures based on historical costs.

The question then arises – does the process of translating assets at closing rates constitute a departure from the normal historical cost rules and the requirements of Section C apply?

It could be argued, particularly where the cover method is being used and investments are translated at closing rates or where a tangible asset is regarded as part of a branch and translated at closing rates, that items do have a sterling historical cost and if they are included at an amount other than that cost then it must be a departure.

4.4.2 *SSAP 20, paragraph 66*

Paragraph 66 of SSAP 20, however, makes it clear that this is not the view taken by the standard. The translation process by itself merely translates the historical cost expressed in foreign currency at a closing rate of exchange. It does not result in a valuation of the asset or express it at its current cost. Accordingly, if it is thought that the provisions of SSAP 20 do result in a departure from the historical cost rules then it would appear that the provisions of the Companies Act are being breached. This is because the alternative accounting rules only allow assets to be included at a valuation, normally a market value, or at current cost.

5 IAS REQUIREMENTS

5.1 General comment

The principal international standard dealing with this topic is IAS 21 – *The Effects of Changes in Foreign Exchange Rates.* The original standard was issued in July 1983, but a revised version was published in December 1993. Although the revised standard follows the same general approach as SSAP 20, nevertheless there are a number of differences, of which the main ones are outlined in the discussion below.

In addition, derivative instruments such as forward currency contracts, swaps and options are covered by IAS 39 – *Financial Instruments: Recognition and Measurement* – which has detailed rules on hedging (see Chapter 10 at 4.9).

The SIC has issued three interpretations of IAS 21: SIC-7 – *Introduction of the Euro*, SIC-11 – *Foreign Exchange – Capitalisation of Losses Resulting from Severe Currency Devaluations* and SIC-19 – *Reporting Currency – Measurement and Presentation of Financial Statements under IAS 21 and IAS 29.* This last Interpretation is effective for annual financial periods beginning on or after 1 January 2001.

5.2 Requirements of IAS 21

5.2.1 *Scope*

Like SSAP 20, IAS 21 should be applied:[160]

(a) in accounting for transactions in foreign currencies; and

(b) in translating the financial statements of foreign operations that are included in the financial statements of the enterprise by consolidation, proportionate consolidation or by the equity method.

However, there are a number of matters which the standard expressly states that it does not deal with. These are:[161]

(a) hedge accounting for foreign currency items (other than the treatment of exchange differences on a foreign currency liability hedging a net investment in a foreign entity);

(b) the reporting currency to be used by an entity in presenting its financial statements;

(c) the restatement of the reporting entity's financial statements from its reporting currency into another currency (convenience translations); and

(d) the presentation in a cash flow statement of cash flows arising from transactions in a foreign currency and the translation of cash flows of a foreign operation.

Item (a) is dealt with in IAS 39 which has detailed rules on hedging (see Chapter 10 at 4.9) and item (d) is dealt with in IAS 7 – *Cash Flow Statements* (see Chapter 29 at 4.1.11).

Item (b) is now covered by SIC-19 and the SIC has issued a draft interpretation dealing with the issues raised by item (c). These are discussed at 5.2.3 below.

5.2.2 *Definitions of terms*

The main definitions of terms which are contained in IAS 21 are as follows:[162]

A *foreign operation* is a subsidiary, associate, joint venture or branch of the reporting enterprise, the activities of which are based or conducted in a country other than the country of the reporting enterprise.

A *foreign entity* is a foreign operation, the activities of which are not an integral part of those of the reporting enterprise.

The *reporting currency* is the currency used in presenting the financial statements.

A *foreign currency* is a currency other than the reporting currency of an enterprise.

An *exchange rate* is the ratio for exchange of two currencies.

An *exchange difference* is the difference resulting from reporting the same number of units of a foreign currency in the reporting currency at different exchange rates.

The *closing rate* is the spot exchange rate at the balance sheet date.

The *net investment in a foreign entity* is the reporting enterprise's share in the net assets of that entity.

Monetary items are money held and assets and liabilities to be received or paid in fixed or determinable amounts of money.

Fair value is the amount for which an asset could be exchanged, or a liability settled, between knowledgeable, willing parties in an arm's length transaction.

Many of these terms are also used in SSAP 20 in the UK, and although not identical in wording, are effectively the same.

5.2.3 Reporting currency, measurement currency and presentation currency

The objective of foreign currency translation under IAS 21 is to express foreign currency transactions and the financial statements of foreign operations in the entity's reporting currency. As indicated at 5.2.2 above, the reporting currency is the currency used in presenting the financial statements of the entity. The standard does not specify the currency in which an entity presents its financial statements, although it notes that an entity would normally use the currency in which it is domiciled.[163] However, the choice of reporting currency establishes that all other currencies are treated as foreign currencies for the purposes of IAS 21 and therefore will affect the financial statements.

This has now been considered by the SIC in SIC-19 which deals with:[164]

(a) how an enterprise determines a currency for measuring items in its financial statements (the measurement currency);

(b) whether an enterprise may use a currency other than the measurement currency for presenting its financial statements (the presentation currency); and

(c) if the presentation currency may be different from the measurement currency, then how the financial statements should be translated from the measurement currency to the presentation currency.

SIC-19 states that the measurement currency should provide information about the entity that is useful and reflects the economic substance of the underlying events and circumstances relevant to that entity. If a particular currency is used to a significant extent in, or has a significant impact on, the entity, that currency may be an appropriate currency to be used as the measurement currency.[165] Although the use of the word 'may' in the second sentence seems to suggest an element of choice, such as continuing to use the currency of the country in which the entity is domiciled, this would not comply with the first part of the requirement. Appendix A to SIC 19 provides the following guidance on identifying the appropriate measurement currency:

'Circumstances where a particular currency (e.g. Japanese Yen) is used to a significant extent in, or has a significant impact on, the enterprise (including an enterprise that is a foreign operation), and may be an appropriate currency to be used in measuring items in the financial statements, include:

1. Purchases are financed mainly from Japanese Yen generated by financing activities (e.g. borrowings and issuance of equity instruments);
2. Receipts from operating activities are usually retained in (or converted by choice or otherwise to) Japanese Yen;
3. Sales prices for goods and services are:
   (a) denominated and settled in Japanese Yen (or in a currency other than Japanese Yen but the price is sensitive to movements in the foreign exchange rate with the Japanese Yen); and
   (b) established mainly by reference to competitive forces and government regulations of Japan; and
4. Labour, materials, and other costs of providing goods or services are denominated and settled in Japanese Yen.'

The appendix emphasises that this is not intended to be a comprchensive checklist of circumstances and that the purpose is to illustrate examples of circumstances, amongst others, that collectively may indicate a currency to be used in measuring items in the financial statements. Clearly, where only some of such circumstances apply it will be a matter of judgment as to whether they 'collectively' indicate the currency to be used.

Once the measurement currency has been selected, it should not be changed unless there is a change in the underlying events and circumstances relevant to determining the measurement currency of the entity.[166]

An example of a company which, for the purposes of its consolidated accounts, reports in a currency other than that of the country in which it is domiciled, is Serono as can be seen from note 1 below.

Extract 8.33: Serono International S.A. (2000)

1. General [extract]

Serono S.A. is a leading global biotechnology company, with executive headquarters in Geneva, Switzerland. Biotechnology companies use human genetic information to discover and manufacture therapeutic products for the treatment of human diseases. We currently focus on the niche markets of reproductive health, neurology, growth and metabolism, and have a global presence with operations in 45 countries, production facilities in eight countries and sales in over 100 countries.

The bearer shares of Serono S.A., the holding company of the group, incorporated in Coinsins (Vaud), Switzerland, are listed on the Swiss stock exchange and, in the form of American depositary shares, on the New York Stock Exchange.

The consolidated financial statements have been prepared in accordance with and comply with the accounting and reporting requirements of International Accounting Standards (IAS) as issued by the International Accounting Standards Committee. In view of the international nature of the company's activities and due to the fact that more of the company's revenues are denominated in US dollars than in any other single currency, the consolidated financial statements are reported in that currency.

1.4 Foreign currencies [extract]

Assets and liabilities of the holding company, its subsidiaries and equity investments are translated into US dollars at year-end exchange rates. Income and expense items are translated at average rates of exchange prevailing during the year. The translation adjustments resulting from exchange rate movements are accumulated in shareholder's equity.

It would appear, however, from note 1.4 that the parent company itself does not use the US dollar as its measurement currency but presumably uses the Swiss franc.

One company which explicitly uses a measurement and reporting currency different from that of its country of domicile is TMM as can be seen from the following extract.

Extract 8.34: Transportación Maritima Mexicana, S.A. de C.V. (1999)

a) Basis of preparation of financial statements [extract]

The consolidated financial statements of TMM and subsidiaries (hereinafter identified, at times, as "the Company") have been prepared in conformity with international accounting standards on an historical-cost basis and in U.S. dollars, the currency in which most transactions and a significant portion of their assets and liabilities arose and/or are denominated. This method was approved by the National Banking and Securities Commission.

Since 1985, TMM and its subsidiaries have translated and recorded their transactions and balances in U.S. dollars, as authorized by the National Banking and Securities Commission. For this purpose monetary assets and liabilities in currencies other than the U.S. dollar are remeasured and recorded in U.S. dollars at the prevailing exchange rate on the day of the related transaction, its settlement or valuation at the balance sheet date.

Non-monetary assets, liabilities and equity accounts are recorded in U.S. dollars using the prevailing exchange rate on the day of the transaction or when earnings were generated.

The statement of operations is translated using the prevailing exchange rate on the day of the related transaction. Depreciation and amortization are translated at the historical exchange rate.

In the first year in which this procedure was applied, a translation loss of $63,250 was determined, which was presented in the balance sheet in the stockholders' equity caption as "Accumulated translation loss".

Although an entity will normally present its financial statements in the same (as the measurement currency, SIC-19 confirms that it may choose to pr(financial statements in a different currency. The method of translating the financial statements of a reporting entity from the measurement currency to a different currency for presenting its financial statements (the presentation currency) is not specified under IAS, but the translation method applied by an entity should not lead to reporting in a manner that is inconsistent with the measurement of items in the financial statements.[167] No further guidance is given in SIC-19 as to how this should be done, but it could be interpreted as meaning that the same rate should be used for the translation of all amounts, including comparative figures. However, in July 2001 the SIC has issued a draft interpretation which proposes that:

(a) assets and liabilities should be translated at the closing rate existing at the date of each balance sheet presented;

(b) income and expense items should be translated at the exchange rates existing at the dates of the transactions or a rate that approximates the actual exchange rates; and

(c) all resulting exchange differences should be classified as equity.

However, where an enterprise's measurement currency is the currency of a hyperinflationary economy, then all items should be translated at the closing rate existing at the date of the most recent balance sheet or period presented.[168]

It is also proposed that when additional information not required by International Accounting Standards is displayed in a currency, other than the currency used in presenting its financial statements, as a convenience to certain users, an enterprise should:

(a) clearly identify the information as supplementary information to distinguish it from the main financial statements; and

(b) disclose the method of translation used as a basis for presenting the information.[169]

One company which provides convenience translations of its primary statements is AngloGold as can be seen from the following extract.

Extract 8.35: AngloGold Limited (2000)

Translation into US dollars

To assist international investors, a translation of convenience into the currency of the United States of America is provided. These translations are based on the average rates of exchange for income statement items and at those ruling at the year end for the balance sheet. The cash flow statement has been translated at average rates to give effect to transaction based conversion.

The disclosures required by SIC-19 are dealt with at 5.2.6 below.

5.2.4 *Individual companies*

A Recording of transactions

Foreign currency transactions should be translated into the reporting currency using the exchange rate between the foreign currency and the reporting currency on the date of the transaction. For convenience, an average rate for a week or month may be used for all foreign currency transactions occurring during that period, if the exchange rate does not fluctuate significantly.[170]

This is similar to the requirements in the UK, although SSAP 20 allows, but does not require, companies to record transactions and monetary assets and liabilities using the forward rate specified in any related or matching forward contract.[171]

IAS 21 regards an unperformed foreign exchange contract as being like any other type of foreign currency transaction.[172] However, it does not deal with forward contracts in any detail as they are now covered by IAS 39 (see Chapter 10 at 4). On the other hand, SSAP 20 contains very little guidance on accounting for forward exchange contracts.

Some of the practical issues in applying SSAP 20 also apply to IAS 21 and therefore the discussion at 3.1.1 to 3.1.3 above will be relevant.

B Retranslation at subsequent balance sheet dates

At each balance sheet date:[173]

(a) foreign currency monetary items should be reported using closing rate;

(b) non-monetary items which are carried at historical cost denominated in a foreign currency should be translated using the historical exchange rate; and

(c) non-monetary items that are carried at fair value should be translated at the exchange rate that existed at the date the fair value was determined.

Again, this is similar to the requirements in the UK, although as noted in A above, SSAP 20 allows, but does not require, companies to use contracted rates.

Some of the practical issues in applying SSAP 20 may also apply to IAS 21 and therefore the discussion at 3.1.4 above will be relevant.

C Treatment of exchange differences

Exchange differences on the settlement or retranslation of monetary items to be recognised as income or as expenses in the period in which they arise, with the exception of:

(a) those arising on a monetary item that, in substance, forms part of an enterprise's net investment in a foreign entity; and

(b) those arising on a foreign currency liability accounted for as a hedge of an enterprise's net investment in a foreign entity.

In these situations the exchange differences should be classified as equity until the disposal of the investment (see 5.2.5 A below).[174]

These are similar to the requirements in SSAP 20. However, because the requirements and explanations relating to the exceptions differ between the two standards there could be differences in practice.

IAS 21 explains that exception (a) above should apply when settlement of the monetary item is neither planned nor likely to occur in the foreseeable future since this is, in substance, an extension to, or deduction from, the entity's net investment. Examples of such monetary items include long-term receivables or loans, but do not include trade receivables or trade payables. As can be seen from the discussion at 3.6 above, the corresponding requirement of SSAP 20 is that the financing should be 'as permanent as equity' (which might be interpreted differently from that in IAS 21) and that such financing can include 'deferred trading balances'. Also, SSAP 20 is silent on whether an exception can be made in individual company financial statements, and therefore where an exception is made, it may be done in such a way that is different from the treatment required by IAS 21. (See Example 8.40 at 3.6.6 above)

As far as exception (b) is concerned, whether a foreign currency liability can be accounted for as a hedge of the net investment in the foreign entity will depend on whether the criteria in IAS 39 for using hedge accounting are met (see Chapter 10 at 4.9). Under IAS 39, hedges of a net investment in a foreign entity should be accounted for similarly to cash flow hedges, i.e.:[175]

(a) the portion of the gain or loss on the hedging instrument that is determined to be an effective hedge should be recognised directly in equity through the statement of changes in equity;

(b) the ineffective portion should be reported:
   - immediately in income if the hedging instrument is a derivative; or
   - in accordance with paragraph 19 of IAS 21 (i.e. in equity until disposal of the investment), in the limited circumstances in which the hedging instrument is not a derivative.

The gain or loss on the hedging instrument relating to the effective portion of the hedge should be classified in the same manner as the foreign currency translation gain or loss.[176]

Thus, where an entity has, say, a foreign currency borrowing which it is accounting for as a hedge of a net investment in a foreign entity, all exchange differences are taken to equity until disposal of the investment, even if a portion of the hedge is ineffective. Also, this treatment is irrespective as to whether there are corresponding exchange differences being recognised on the related investment. Under the requirements of IAS 21 discussed at B above, investments in foreign entities carried at historical cost are not retranslated.

This is in contrast to the corresponding requirements of SSAP 20 discussed at 2.3.7, 2.4.5 and 3.5 above, which restrict the amount of exchange differences on foreign currency borrowings to be excluded from the income statement to those recognised on the related foreign currency investments. When the 'cover method' is applied under SSAP 20, such investments are translated at closing rates in the investing company's individual financial statements.

In addition to these two exceptions, IAS 21 also allows an alternative treatment for exchange differences which result from a severe devaluation or depreciation of a currency against which there is no practical means of hedging and that affects liabilities which cannot be settled and which arise directly on the recent acquisition of an asset invoiced in a foreign currency. Such exchange differences can be included in the carrying amount of the related asset, provided that the adjusted carrying amount does not exceed the lower of the replacement cost and the amount recoverable from the sale or use of the asset.[177] This treatment requires several conditions to be met cumulatively before an enterprise can include exchange losses on foreign currency liabilities in the carrying amount of related assets. SIC-11 deals with how the conditions should be interpreted that the liability 'cannot be settled' and that there is 'no practical means of hedging' against the foreign currency exchange risk and that the liability should arise on the 'recent acquisition' of an asset.[178] The SIC agreed that foreign exchange losses on liabilities that result from the recent acquisition of assets should only be included in the carrying amount of the assets if those liabilities could not have been settled or if it was not practically feasible to hedge the foreign currency exposure before the severe devaluation or depreciation occurred.[179] Only in these cases foreign exchange losses are unavoidable and therefore part of the asset's acquisition costs. Recent acquisitions of assets are acquisitions within twelve months prior to the severe devaluation or depreciation of the reporting currency.[180] SSAP 20 has no similar rules.

Although the rules in IAS 21 suggest that all exchange differences should be taken to the income statement (other than the specific exclusions discussed above), IAS 23 – *Borrowing Costs* – allows exchange differences arising from foreign currency borrowings to be capitalised to the extent that they are regarded as an adjustment to interest costs.[181] Netia is an example of a company which capitalises exchange differences as shown below.

Extract 8.36: Netia Holdings S.A. (1999)

2. Summary of Significant Accounting Policies [extract]

Foreign Exchange Gains and Losses

Foreign currency transactions are accounted for at the exchange rates prevailing at the date of the transactions. Gains and losses resulting from the settlement of such transactions and from the translations of monetary assets and liabilities denominated in foreign currencies, are recognized in the income statement or capitalized as part of network under construction in accordance with the Company's fixed assets capitalization policy when the exchange differences arise from foreign currency borrowings used to finance self constructed assets.

5.2.5 *Consolidated financial statements*

The method used to translate the financial statements of a foreign operation for inclusion in consolidated accounts depends on the way in which it is financed and operates in relation to the reporting entity. For this purpose, foreign operations are classified as either 'foreign entities' or 'foreign operations that are integral to the operations of the reporting enterprise'.[182] IAS 21 notes that in some cases, the classification may not be clear, and judgement is necessary to determine the appropriate classification.[183]

A Foreign entities

Based on the definitions in IAS 21, a foreign entity is a subsidiary, associate, joint venture or branch of the reporting entity, the activities of which are:

(a) based or conducted in a country other than the country of the reporting entity; and

(b) not an integral part of those of the reporting entity.

IAS 21 regards the following as indicating that a foreign operation is a foreign entity rather than a foreign operation that is integral to the operations of the reporting entity:[184]

(a) while the reporting entity may control the foreign operation, the activities of the foreign operation are carried out with a significant degree of autonomy from those of the reporting entity;

(b) transactions with the reporting entity are not a high proportion of the foreign operation's activities;

(c) the activities of the foreign operation are financed mainly from its own operations or local borrowings rather than from the reporting entity;

(d) costs of labour, material and other components of the foreign operation's products or services are primarily paid or settled in the local currency rather than in the reporting currency;

(e) the foreign operation's sales are mainly in currencies other than the reporting currency; and

(f) cash flows of the reporting entity are insulated from the day-to-day activities of the foreign operation rather than being directly affected by the activities of the foreign operation.

By setting out indicators as to when it is appropriate to classify an operation as a foreign entity, IAS 21 could be regarded as giving the impression that this is the exception to the norm but we do not believe that this is intended to be the case. This can be contrasted with the position in SSAP 20 in the UK where it is recognised that most foreign operations will be 'foreign entities' and it is only in certain circumstances that foreign operations would be accounted for as if they were an integral to those of the reporting entity (see 2.4.4 above).

The following procedures should be followed by the reporting entity in translating the financial statements of a foreign entity:[185]

(a) the assets and liabilities, both monetary and non-monetary, of the foreign entity should be translated at the closing rate;

(b) income and expense items of the foreign entity should be translated at exchange rates at the dates of the transactions (except when the foreign entity reports in the currency of a hyperinflationary economy, in which case income and expenses should be translated at the closing rate – see Chapter 9 at 3); and

(c) all resulting exchange differences should be classified as equity until the disposal of the net investment.

For convenience reasons, the reporting entity may use a rate that approximates to the actual exchange rate, e.g. an average exchange rate for the period, to translate income and expense items.[186]

Danisco is an example of a company that treats all its foreign subsidiaries and associates on this basis as shown below.

Extract 8.37: Danisco A/S (2000)

Foreign currency translation

Transactions in foreign currencies (e.g. purchase/sales) are translated into the local currency at monthly average rates of exchange or at forward rates. The monthly average rates of exchange are used for practical reasons, as these reflect approximately the rates of exchange at the date of transaction.

Any differences in exchange rates arising between the average monthly rate and the rate at the date of payment are stated in the profit and loss account as a financial item.

Debtors and creditors in foreign currencies are translated into the local currency at the exchange rates ruling at the balance sheet date or at forward rates. The difference between the rate of exchange at the balance sheet date or the forward rate and the rate of exchange at the time when the debtor or the creditor was incurred is included in the profit and loss account as a financial item.

Tangible fixed assets purchased in foreign currencies are translated into the local currency at the rates of exchange at the date of transaction or at forward rates.

The profit and loss accounts of independent foreign subsidiary undertakings and foreign associated undertakings are translated into Danish kroner at monthly average rates of exchange, and the balance sheets are translated at the exchange rates ruling at the balance sheet date. Exchange rate differences occurring on the translation of opening net investments of foreign subsidiary undertakings at the rates of exchange ruling at the balance sheet date are stated under capital and reserves. The same applies to the exchange rate differences following the translation of results from a monthly average rate of exchange to the exchange rate at the balance sheet date.

All present subsidiary undertakings are considered independent.

In the case of accounts with foreign subsidiary undertakings which in reality are an addition to or deduction from the capital and reserves of subsidiary undertakings, exchange adjustments are taken to reserves. The same applies to exchange differences concerning the hedging of capital and reserves of foreign subsidiary undertakings.

Another example is GN Great Nordic as can be seen from Extract 8.39 below.

These procedures are similar to the closing rate/net investment method which is required by SSAP 20 in the UK (see 2.4.3 above), except that SSAP 20 allows a choice of translating the results of the foreign enterprise either at the closing rate of exchange or at an average rate for the period.[187]

As with SSAP 20, there are a number of issues in applying these procedures which IAS 21 does not address and, accordingly, the following discussions in 3.4 above may be relevant:

(a) dual rates and suspension of rates (see 3.4.2 above);

(b) calculation of average rate (see 3.4.3 above);

(c) inter-period comparisons (see 3.4.11 above);

However, IAS 21 does address some other areas.

It explains that when a foreign entity is consolidated but is not wholly owned, accumulated exchange differences arising from translation and attributable to minority interests are allocated to, and reported as part of, the minority interest in the consolidated balance sheet.[188] Although this is not addressed in SSAP 20, this would be the treatment adopted under UK GAAP.

Under IAS 21, goodwill and any fair value adjustments arising on the acquisition of a foreign entity are treated as either:[189]

(a) assets and liabilities of the foreign entity and translated at the closing rate; or

(b) assets and liabilities of the reporting entity that are reported at their historical costs expressed in the reporting currency, i.e., no exchange differences will be recorded in connection with these items after the date of acquisition.

Roche is an example of a company that adopts the former treatment, as can be seen below.

Extract 8.38: Roche Holding Ltd (2000)

'Intangible assets' and 'Business combinations'. Goodwill is recorded as an intangible asset and is the surplus of the cost of acquisition over the fair value of identifiable assets acquired. Any goodwill and fair value adjustments are treated as assets and liabilities of the acquired company and are recorded in the local currency of that company.

GN Great Nordic, on the other hand, adopts the latter approach.

Extract 8.39: GN Great Nordic (2000)

Translation of Foreign Currencies

Foreign currency transactions (e.g. purchases/sales) are translated into local currencies at transaction date exchange rates or at hedged rates based on forward contracts.

Exchange rate differences arising between the date of transaction and the date of payment are recognized in the income statement as financial items.

Receivables and payables in foreign currencies and hedging contracts are included at the year-end exchange rate. Exchange rate gains or losses are recognized in the income statement under financial items.

In the consolidated financial statements, the income statements of foreign entities are translated into Danish kroner at average rates of exchange for the year, and assets and liabilities are translated at year-end exchange rates. Goodwill arising from the acquisition of a company and possible market value adjustments in the book value of assets and liabilities arising from the acquisition of this foreign entity are included in the acquiring company's accounts using the exchange rate for the date of acquisition.

Exchange differences arising from adjusting foreign entities' start-of-year equity and from adjusting foreign entities' income statements expressed using the year's average exchange rates to year-end rates are recognized as an adjustment to equity.

Exchange differences of outstanding or hedging contracts that hedge the equity investment in foreign subsidiaries are taken directly to equity.

Transactions made by foreign entities which have been integrated into the operations of the parent company are translated into Danish kroner as if the transactions had been made by the parent company.

The translation of goodwill on consolidation is not specifically covered in SSAP 20 and therefore both of the above options are adopted and seen in practice in the UK (see 3.4.10 and 3.5.4 above). However, although not specifically covered in SSAP 20, fair value adjustments are not regarded as separate from the assets or liabilities to which they relate, so where the closing rate/net investment method is being used to translate the foreign entity, the relevant assets and liabilities will be translated at closing rates.

In preparing consolidated financial statements it may be that a foreign entity is consolidated on the basis of financial statements made up to a different date from that of the parent. In such a case, IAS 21 initially states that the assets and liabilities of the foreign entity are to be translated at the exchange rate applying at the balance sheet date of the foreign entity rather than that at the date of the consolidated accounts. However, it then goes on to say that adjustments are made when appropriate for significant movements in exchange rates up to the balance sheet date of the reporting entity.[190] Thus, it seems that if the exchange effect of using the more up-to-date rate is material then that rate should be used, otherwise the rate at the foreign entity's year end should be used. As indicated at 3.4.1 above, SSAP 20 in the UK makes no reference to what rate should be used.

IAS 21 notes that the incorporation of the financial statements of a foreign entity in the consolidated financial statements should follow normal consolidation procedures, such as the elimination of intra-group balances and intra-group transactions. However, it merely indicates that exchange differences on an intra-group monetary item should not be eliminated, but should be recognised as income or an expense in the consolidated financial statements, unless it arises from circumstances which come under exceptions (a) or (b) discussed at 5.2.4 C above.[191] As with SSAP 20, IAS 21 does not address problem areas relating to intra-group dividends or unrealised profits and, accordingly, the discussions in 3.7 above may be relevant. The problems will not be as great in the UK since actual or average rates will be used under IAS for translation of the foreign entity's income and expenditure.

IAS 21 requires that on the disposal of a foreign entity, the cumulative amount of the deferred exchange differences recorded in equity and which relate to that foreign entity are to be included as income or expenses in the same period in which the gain or loss on disposal is recognised.[192] (This is equivalent to option (iii) in Example 8.23 set out in 3.4.7 above.) As indicated at 5.2.4 C above, these will include exchange differences on intra-group long-term loans considered to extensions or deductions from the net investment in the foreign entity and foreign currency liabilities accounted for as hedges of the net investment in the foreign entity.

This treatment is to be adopted not only when an entity sells an interest in a foreign entity, but also when it disposes of its interest through liquidation, repayment of share capital, or abandonment of that entity. It also applies for partial disposals, in which case, only the proportionate share of the related accumulated exchange differences is included in the gain or loss. A write-down of the carrying amount of a foreign entity does not constitute a partial disposal, therefore no deferred exchange difference should be recognised in income at the time of the write-down.[193]

In the UK, SSAP 20 contains no provisions as to what should happen to the cumulative exchange differences when the investment is sold or liquidated. However, under FRS 3, as the original exchange differences would have been reflected in the statement of total recognised gains and losses when they arose, then they should not be recognised again in the year of disposal in either the profit and loss account or the statement of recognised gains and losses (see Chapter 25 at 2.9.1).

B *Foreign operations integral to the operations of the reporting entity*

A foreign operation that is integral to the operations of the reporting entity carries on its business as if it were an extension of the reporting entity's operations. IAS 21 gives an example of a foreign operation which only sells goods imported from the reporting entity and remits the proceeds to the reporting entity.[194]

Transactions, assets and liabilities of foreign operations that are integral to the operations of the reporting entity should be translated as if they had been those of the reporting entity itself, i.e. using the procedures as discussed at 5.2.4 above.[195] Accordingly, the cost and depreciation of property, plant and equipment is translated using the exchange rate at the date of purchase of the asset or, if the asset is carried at fair value, using the rate that existed on the date of the valuation. The cost of inventories is translated at the exchange rates that existed when those costs were incurred. The recoverable amount or realisable value of an asset is translated using the exchange rate that existed when the recoverable amount or net realisable value was determined. For example, when the net realisable value of an item of inventory is determined in a foreign currency, that value is translated using the exchange rate at the date at which the net realisable value is determined. The rate used is therefore usually the closing rate. The standard goes on to explain that an adjustment may be required to reduce the carrying amount of an asset to its recoverable amount or net realisable value in the financial statements of the reporting entity even when no such adjustment is necessary in the financial statements of the foreign operation. Alternatively, an adjustment in the financial statements of the foreign operation may need to be reversed in the financial statements of the reporting entity.[196]

For practical reasons, a rate that approximates the actual rate at the date of the transaction may be used for all transactions in each foreign currency occurring during that period, unless the exchange rates fluctuate significantly which makes the use of the average rate for a period unreliable.[197]

H. Lundbeck treats all of its foreign subsidiaries on this basis as shown below.

Extract 8.40: H. Lundbeck A/S (2000)

Foreign currencies [extract]

Transactions denominated in foreign currencies are translated by using standard rates which essentially reflect the exchange rates at the transaction date. Exchange differences arising between the rate at the transaction date and the rate at the date of payment are included in the income statement as financial items.

Balances denominated in foreign currencies are translated at the exchange rates at the balance sheet date.

Non-monetary assets acquired in foreign currencies, including goodwill, are translated at the exchange rates at the time of acquisition.

All foreign subsidiaries are regarded as integral entities, which means that the transactions are dealt with as if they had been executed in the parent. For consolidation purposes, the financial statements of foreign subsidiaries are translated according to an adapted temporal method.

Income statements are translated at the average exchange rates during the year because these essentially reflect the exchange rates at the transaction date. Exchange differences arising from the translation of both the balance sheets and the income statements of the foreign entities are included in the Group's income statement as financial items.

As can be seen from Extract 8.39 at 5.2.5 A above, GN Great Nordic also treats some of its foreign operations on this basis.

This procedure is similar to the temporal method discussed at 2.4.4 C above.

C Change in classification of a foreign operation

As indicated earlier, IAS 21 notes that in some cases, the classification may not be clear, and judgement is necessary to determine the appropriate classification A change in the way in which a foreign operation is financed and operates may lead to a change in the classification of that foreign operation. When this is the case, IAS 21 requires that the translation procedures applicable to the revised classification should be applied from the date of the change in the classification.[198] When a foreign operation that is integral to the operations of the reporting enterprise is reclassified as a foreign entity, exchange differences arising on the translation of non-monetary assets at the date of the reclassification are classified as equity. When a foreign entity is reclassified as a foreign operation that is integral to the operation of the reporting enterprise, the translated amounts for non-monetary items at the date of the change are treated as the historical cost for those items in the period of change and subsequent periods. Exchange differences which have been deferred are not recognised as income or expenses until the disposal of the operation.[199] As discussed at 3.4.8 above, SSAP 20 does not deal with such situations.

5.2.6 *Disclosure*

IAS 21 requires the amount of exchange differences taken to profit and loss account to be disclosed. It also requires the exchange adjustments, which result from translating the financial statements of foreign entities, classified as equity to be disclosed as a separate component of equity, and for a reconciliation of the amount of such exchange differences at the beginning and end of the period to be given. Accordingly, the cumulative exchange differences will be disclosed.[200]

An illustration of the profit and loss account disclosures is given in the following extract, although it should be noted that it is not necessary to split the differences between realised and unrealised amounts.

Extract 8.41: Danisco A/S (2000)

	Group	
DKK million	1998/99	**1999/00**
7. Interest receivable and similar income		
Financial accounts with subsidiary undertakings	–	–
Bank deposits	70	106
Other receivables	30	35
Unrealised gain on financial instruments	5	1
Realised gain on financial instruments	–	–
Unrealised exchange gain	11	40
Realised exchange gain	18	132
Total	**134**	**314**
8. Interest payable and similar charges		
Financial accounts with subsidiary undertakings	–	–
Mortgage debt	37	31
Bank debt and similar capital procurement	240	760
Unrealised loss on financial instruments	12	10
Realised loss on financial instruments	48	124
Unrealised exchange loss	12	4
Realised exchange loss	30	–
Total	**379**	**929**

Roche discloses its cumulative exchange differences as follows.

Extract 8.42: Roche Holding Ltd (2000)

Consolidated statement of changes in equity in millions of CHF [extract]

	Year ended 31 December	
	2000	**1999**
Other reserves		
– Equity conversion options		
Conversion option embedded in 'Sumo' bonds [24]	24	–
– Currency translation differences		
Balance at 1 January	125	(149)
Gains (losses) recognised during the year	(374)	274
Balance at 31 December	(249)	125
Balance other reserves at 31 December	(225)	125

Other companies merely include a column for 'translation differences' within their statement of changes in equity.

These disclosures can be contrasted with those in the UK where SSAP 20 does not require the net exchange gain or loss included in net profit to be disclosed. It does, however, require the net exchange gain or loss on borrowings less deposits included in net profit to be disclosed.[201] Also, SSAP 20 only requires the translation adjustments which result from translating the financial statements of foreign entities to be taken to reserves and for the movement in reserves during the period to be disclosed.[202] They do not have to be taken to a separate reserve and therefore the cumulative exchange differences will not be apparent from the financial statements.

IAS 21 also requires disclosure of the following:

(a) the amount of exchange differences arising during the period which is included in the carrying amount of an asset in accordance with the allowed alternative treatment for exchange differences which result from severe devaluation or depreciation of a currency discussed at 5.2.4 C above;[203]

(b) when the reporting currency is different from that of the country in which the enterprise is domiciled the reason for using that different currency. The reason for any change in reporting currency should also be disclosed;[204]

(c) When there is a change in the classification of a significant foreign operation :

  (i) the nature of the change in classification;

  (ii) the reason for the change;

  (iii) the impact of the change in classification on shareholders' equity; and

  (iv) the impact on net profit or loss for each prior period had the change in classification occurred at the beginning of the earliest period presented;[205] and

(d) the method selected to translate goodwill and fair value adjustments arising on the acquisition of a foreign entity.[206]

SIC-19 also requires the following disclosures:

(a) when the measurement currency is different from the currency of the country in which the enterprise is domiciled, the reason for using a different currency;

(b) the reason for any change in the measurement currency or presentation currency; and.

(c) when the financial statements are presented in a currency different from the enterprise's measurement currency, the measurement currency, the reason for using a different presentation currency, and a description of the method used in the translation process.

In consolidated financial statements, the references to measurement currency for the purpose of these disclosure requirements are to the measurement currency of the parent.

6 CONCLUSION

Ever since the first edition of this book in 1989 we have criticised SSAP 20 and suggested improvements in relation to forward contracts and similar hedging contracts and the cover method. We continue to believe that the reporting of foreign currency transactions in the UK would be significantly improved if SSAP 20 were amended:

(a) to deal with the topic of forward contracts and similar agreements, such as currency swaps, in a similar way to SFAS 52 as suggested in 3.3 above, except that companies should be able to account for forward contracts which are designated as a hedge against anticipated future transactions rather than just those which are the subject of a firm commitment; and

(b) the cover method should be amended along similar lines to that contained in SFAS 52, whereby the hedging instrument would have to be designated, and effective, as a hedge and to be in the same currency (or a tandem currency) as the hedged investment.[207]

As these suggestions are compatible with the existing provisions of SSAP 20 we would recommend that companies adopt such treatments presently.

We therefore welcome the ASB's announcement that it plans to review SSAP 20 in its entirety and that an exposure draft is to be developed. However, this is tempered by the fact that this is only to be as soon as the project on financial instruments has settled some key issues that are fundamental to foreign currency translation and, as indicated in our conclusion to Chapter 10, we have significant concerns about the way that project is heading. We are therefore not confident that any improvements to SSAP 20 will be achieved in the near term.

References

1 SSAP 20, *Foreign currency translation*, ASC, April 1983, para. 1.
2 SFAS 8, *Accounting for the translation of foreign currency transactions and foreign currency financial statements*, FASB, October 1975.
3 CICA Handbook, Section 1650, *Translation of foreign currency transactions and foreign currency financial statements.*
4 FRED 13, *Derivatives and other financial instruments: Disclosures*, ASB, April 1997, para. 15.
5 SSAP 20, para. 2.
6 *Ibid.*, paras. 36–44.
7 *Ibid.*, para. 46.
8 *Ibid.*, para. 48.
9 *Ibid.*, para. 47.
10 *Ibid.*, para. 7.
11 *Ibid.*, paras. 49 and 50.
12 *Ibid.*, para. 8.
13 *Ibid.*, para. 28.
14 *Ibid.*, para. 52.
15 *Ibid.*, para. 13.
16 *Ibid.*, para. 14.
17 *Ibid.*, para. 21.
18 ED 27, para. 98.
19 SSAP 20, para. 16.
20 *Ibid.*, para. 54.
21 *Ibid.*, para. 2.
22 *Ibid.*, para. 17.
23 *Ibid.*
24 *Ibid.*, para. 16.
25 *Ibid.*, para. 54.
26 *Ibid.*, paras. 53 and 54.
27 *Ibid.*, para. 22.
28 *Ibid.*, para. 23.
29 Accountants Digest No. 150, *A guide to accounting standards – foreign currency translation*, Winter 1983/84, p. 9.
30 SSAP 20, para. 24.
31 *Ibid.*, para. 22.
32 *Ibid.*, para. 30.
33 *Ibid.*, para. 51.
34 *Ibid.*
35 FRS 9, *Associates and Joint Ventures*, ASB, November 1997.
36 SSAP 20, para. 52.
37 *Ibid.*, para. 37.
38 Technical Release 504, *Statement by the Accounting Standards Committee on the publication of SSAP 20: Foreign currency translation*, April 1983, para. 24.
39 SSAP 20, para. 52.
40 *Ibid.*, para. 59.
41 *Ibid.*, para. 60.
42 *Ibid.*
43 *Ibid.*
44 TR 504, para. 28.
45 UITF 19, *Tax on gains and losses on foreign currency borrowings that hedge an investment in a foreign enterprise*, UITF, February 1998, para. 9.
46 SFAS 52, *Foreign currency translation*, FASB, December 1981, para. 162.
47 SSAP 20, para. 46.
48 SFAS 52, para. 27.
49 *Ibid.*, para. 26.
50 SSAP 20, para. 44.
51 *Ibid.*, para. 6.
52 *Ibid.*, para. 5.
53 SFAS 52, para. 48.
54 *Ibid.*, para. 162.
55 SSAP 20, para. 49.
56 *Ibid.*, paras. 46 and 47.
57 CA 85, Sch. 4, paras. 17 and 22.
58 *Ibid.*, para. 26(3).
59 *Ibid.*, para. 26(3).
60 SSAP 20, para. 51.
61 *Ibid.*, para. 46.
62 SFAS 52, paras. 21 and 132.
63 *Ibid.*, para. 133.
64 *Ibid.*, para. 21.
65 CA 85, ss. 117 and 118.
66 SFAS 52, para. 48.
67 Accountants Digest No. 150, p. 6.
68 C. A. Westwick, *Accounting for Overseas Operations*, Aldershot: Gower, 1986, p. 18.
69 SSAP 20, para. 42.
70 SFAS 52, paras. 17, 18 and 21.
71 *Ibid.*, para. 21.
72 *Ibid.*, para. 18.
73 *Ibid.*, para. 21.
74 Accountants Digest No. 150, p. 5.
75 SFAS 52, para. 17.
76 *Ibid.*, paras. 17 and 18.
77 *Ibid.*, paras. 18 and 20.
78 *Ibid.*, para. 20.
79 *Ibid.*, para. 19.
80 CA 85, Sch. 4, para. 50(5).
81 SFAS 52, para. 17.
82 *Ibid.*, para. 28.
83 *Ibid.*, para. 139.
84 *Ibid.*, para. 27.
85 *Ibid.*, para. 138.
86 SSAP 20, para. 18.
87 SFAS 52, para. 12.
88 FRS 3, *Reporting financial performance*, ASB, October 1992, paras. 29 and 62.
89 CA 85, Sch. 4, para. 33.
90 *Ibid.*, para. 12.
91 SFAS 52, para. 14.

92 FASB Interpretation No. 37, *Accounting for Translation Adjustments upon Sale of Part of an Investment in a Foreign Entity*, FASB, July 1983, para. 2.
93 IAS 21, *The Effects of Changes in Foreign Exchange Rates*, IASC, Revised 1993, para. 37.
94 SFAS 52, para. 46.
95 *Ibid.*
96 IAS 21, paras. 39 and 40.
97 SFAS 52, para. 46.
98 IAS 21, paras. 39 and 40.
99 FRS 10, *Goodwill and Intangible Assets*, ASB, December 1997, para. 7.
100 SSAP 22, *Accounting for goodwill*, ASC, Revised July 1989, para. 41.
101 SSAP 20, para. 43.
102 TR 504, para. 21.
103 SFAS 52, para. 101.
104 See, for example, The Weir Group PLC, Report & Accounts 2000, p. 36.
105 SFAS 52, para. 144.
106 UITF 19, para. 9.
107 TR 504, paras. 18 and 19.
108 The London Stock Exchange, *The Listing Rules*, Chapter 6, para. 6.E.15(a).
109 Westwick, *op. cit.*, p. 22.
110 N. Spinney, *The Accountant's Magazine*, May 1983, p. 178.
111 SSAP 20, para. 43.
112 TR 504, para. 21.
113 SFAS 52, para. 101.
114 Accountants Digest No. 150, p. 7.
115 TR 504, para. 18.
116 *Ibid.*
117 D. Hegarty, *Accountancy*, November 1983, p. 147.
118 SFAS 52, para. 20.
119 *Ibid.*, para. 130.
120 Accountants Digest No. 150, p. 7.
121 UITF 19, para. 8.
122 SSAP 20, para. 48.
123 *Ibid.*, para. 49.
124 *Ibid.*, para. 12.
125 See Westwick, *op. cit.*, p. 99 and J. Carty, *Foreign Currency Accounting – A practical guide for 1982 financial statements*, pp. 21 and 22.
126 SSAP 15, *Accounting for deferred tax*, ASC, Amended December 1992, appendix, para. 4.
127 Carty, *op. cit.*, pp. 21 and 22.
128 SSAP 20, para. 20.
129 See Accountants Digest No. 150, p. 16 and Westwick, *op. cit.*, p. 99.
130 SSAP 20, paras. 20 and 43.
131 *Ibid.*, paras. 46–51.
132 SSAP 20, para. 2.
133 Westwick, *op. cit.*, p. 101.
134 Accountants Digest No. 150, p. 15.
135 SFAS 52, para. 25.
136 *Ibid.*, para. 12.
137 UITF 21, *Accounting issues arising from the proposed introduction of the euro*, UITF, March 1998, para. 2.
138 *Ibid.*, para. 17.
139 *Ibid.*, para. 18.
140 *Ibid.*, para. 19.
141 *Ibid.*, para. 20.
142 *Ibid.*, Appendix.
143 SSAP 20, para. 44.
144 TR 504, para. 10.
145 *Ibid.*, para. 11.
146 *Ibid.*, para. 12.
147 Westwick, *op. cit.*, p. 77.
148 *Ibid.* and Accountants Digest No. 150, p. 32.
149 Draft Technical Release (TECH 25/00), *The determination of realised profits and distributable profits in the context of the Companies Act 1985*, ICAEW, 10 August 2000, para. 16.
150 *Ibid.*, para. 30.
151 CA 85, s 264.
152 TR 504, para. 32.
153 *Ibid.*, para. 33(a).
154 TECH 25/00, para. 16.
155 *Ibid.*, para. 30.
156 *Ibid.*, para. 17.
157 TR 504, para. 32.
158 SSAP 20, para. 36.
159 *Ibid.*, para. 53.
160 IAS 21, para. 1.
161 *Ibid.*, paras. 2–6.
162 *Ibid.*, para. 7.
163 *Ibid.*, para. 4.
164 SIC-19, *Reporting Currency – Measurement and Presentation of Financial Statements under IAS 21 and IAS 29*, SIC, November 2000, para. 3.
165 *Ibid.*, para. 5.
166 *Ibid.*, para. 6.
167 *Ibid.*, para. 9.
168 Draft Interpretation SIC-D30, *Reporting Currency – Translation from Measurement Currency to Presentation Currency*, SIC, July 2001, para. 5.
169 *Ibid.*, para. 7.
170 IAS 21, paras. 9 and 10
171 SSAP 20, paras. 46 and 48.
172 IAS 21, para. 8(c).
173 *Ibid.*, para. 11.
174 *Ibid.*, paras. 15–19.
175 IAS 39, *Financial Instruments: Recognition and Measurement*, IASC, Revised October 2000, para. 164.
176 *Ibid.*
177 IAS 21, para. 21.
178 SIC-11, *Foreign Exchange – Capitalisation of Losses Resulting from Severe Currency Devaluations*, SIC, July 1998, para. 2.
179 *Ibid.*, para. 3.

180 *Ibid.*, para. 6.
181 IAS 23, *Borrowing Costs*, IASC, Revised 1993, para. 5.
182 IAS 21, para. 23.
183 *Ibid.*, para. 26.
184 *Ibid.*
185 *Ibid.*, para. 30.
186 *Ibid.*, para. 31.
187 SSAP 20, para. 54.
188 IAS 21, para. 32.
189 *Ibid.*, para. 33.
190 *Ibid.*, para. 35.
191 *Ibid.*, para. 34.
192 *Ibid.*, para. 37.
193 *Ibid.*, para. 38.
194 *Ibid.*, para. 24.
195 *Ibid.*, para. 27.
196 *Ibid.*, para. 28.
197 *Ibid.*, para. 29.
198 *Ibid.*, para. 39.
199 *Ibid.*, para. 40.
200 *Ibid*, para. 42(a) and (b).
201 SSAP 20, para. 60(a).
202 *Ibid*, paras. 54 and 60(b).
203 IAS 21, para. 42(c).
204 *Ibid*, para. 43.
205 *Ibid*, para. 44.
206 *Ibid*, para. 45.
207 SFAS 52, paras. 20, 128 and 130.

Chapter 9 Hyperinflation

1 INTRODUCTION

Accounting standards generally and the historical cost basis of accounting, assume that the value of money – the unit of measurement – is constant over time, which normally is an acceptable practical assumption. However, when the effect of inflation on the value of money is no longer negligible, the usefulness of historical cost based financial reporting is often significantly reduced. High rates of inflation give rise to a number of problems in financial reporting, for example:

- historical cost figures expressed in terms of monetary units do not show the 'value to the business' of assets;
- holding gains on non-monetary assets that are reported as operating profits do not represent real economic gains;
- financial information presented for the current period is not comparable with that presented for the prior periods; and
- 'real' capital can be reduced because profits reported do not take account of the higher replacement costs of resources used in the period. Therefore, if in calculating profit 'return on capital' is not distinguished properly from 'return of capital', the erosion of 'real' capital may go unnoticed in the financial statements. This is the underlying point in the concept of capital maintenance.

As described in Chapter 2 at 4.3, rates of inflation well in excess of 10% during most of the 1970s and early 1980s in the UK brought these and other shortcomings of historical cost based financial reporting in an inflationary environment to prominence. Though methods of inflation accounting were extensively debated, interest in the subject dissipated quickly in the late 1980s when inflation all but disappeared in the UK. Moreover, the discussions about inflation accounting and concepts of capital maintenance, undeservingly, have left little traces in modern accounting standards. The ASB's *Statement of Principles* and the IASC's *Framework* both pay lip service to the existence of different concepts of capital maintenance but ultimately are based on the financial capital maintenance concept (see Chapter 2 at 5.7 and 8.1.1, respectively). Under this concept 'the capital of the entity will be maintained if the amount of gains during a period is at least equal to the amount of losses in that period'.[1] Unlike the ASB's *Statement of Principles*, the IASC's *Framework* describes the concept of physical capital maintenance under which 'a profit is earned only if the physical productive capacity (or operating capability) of the enterprise (or the resources or funds needed to achieve that capacity) at the end of the period exceeds the physical productive capacity at the beginning of the period, after excluding any distributions to, and contributions from, owners during the period'.[2] However, the IASC does not really develop the physical capital maintenance concept in its Framework or any of its standards. As the ASB acknowledges, the financial capital maintenance concept on which UK GAAP and International Accounting Standards are based is only satisfactory under conditions of stable prices.[3] Neither the ASB nor the IASC defines a concept of capital maintenance that is more appropriate when accounting in a highly inflationary currency.

From a Western European perspective it is easy to overlook that there are many countries where inflation is still a major economic concern. In some of these countries, inflation has reached such levels – hyperinflation – that (1) the local currency is no longer a useful measure of value in the economy and (2) the general population may no longer prefer to hold its wealth in the local currency. Instead, they hold their wealth in a stable foreign currency or non-monetary assets. For financial reporting purposes hyperinflation is deemed to exist under UK[4], International[5] and US[6] accounting standards when the cumulative rate of inflation over a three-year period approaches or exceeds 100%.[7] Countries that are generally considered hyperinflationary under that definition, because they have recently had three-year cumulative inflation of 100% or more, include:[8]

Afghanistan	Ghana	Myanmar	Ukraine
Angola	Guinea-Bissau	Romania	Venezuela
Azerbaijan	Indonesia	Russia	Zambia
Belarus	Lao People's D.R.	Sierra Leone	Zimbabwe
Bulgaria	Malawi	Sudan	
Congo, D.R. of	Moldova	Suriname	
Ecuador	Mozambique	Turkey	

Information on inflation rates in various countries is available in *International Financial Statistics*, published monthly by the International Monetary Fund.

The historical cost based financial reporting problems reach such magnitude under hyperinflationary circumstances that financial reporting in the hyperinflationary currency is all but meaningless. Therefore, a solution is needed to allow meaningful financial reporting by enterprises and subsidiaries that operate in hyperinflationary economies. Two solutions to accounting for hyperinflation, which have gained broad acceptance, are discussed is this chapter and can be summarised as follows:

- *Restatement approach* – Financial information recorded in the hyperinflationary currency is adjusted by applying a general price index and expressed in the measuring unit (the hyperinflationary currency) current at the balance sheet date; and

- *Stable foreign currency* – The enterprise uses a relatively stable currency, for example the reporting currency of its parent, as the functional currency of the foreign operations. If the transactions of the operation are not recorded initially in that stable currency, then they must be remeasured into the stable currency by applying the temporal method (see Chapter 8 at 2.4.4). Under IAS, SIC-19 prohibits the use of this method.

This Chapter deals with accounting for hyperinflation under UK GAAP in section 2. Section 3 on accounting for hyperinflation under IAS comprises a discussion on how the standards on foreign currency translation and hyperinflation interrelate and the effect of the changes as a result of the adoption of SIC-19. This section also includes a detailed description of the requirements of IAS 29 – *Financial Reporting in Hyperinflationary Economies* – and the problems that enterprises may experience when applying that standard.

2 ACCOUNTING FOR HYPERINFLATION UNDER UK GAAP

2.1 SSAP 20

In the UK extreme levels of inflation have ceased to be a major concern since the early 1980s, hence it is not surprising that there is no standard that deals with financial reporting under hyperinflationary conditions. However, via their foreign subsidiaries, UK companies are sometimes indirectly confronted with hyperinflation. The closing rate/net investment method of foreign currency translation (see Chapter 8 at 1.2.1) gives rise to one particular problem when it is applied to a foreign enterprise which operates in a country where a very high rate of inflation exists. Consider the following example:

Example 9.1: Disappearing assets

On 30 June 1991 a UK company sets up a subsidiary overseas. On that date the subsidiary acquires property for HC100,000. Ignoring depreciation on the property, this asset would be included in the group financial statements at 30 June 1991 and 30 June 2001, as follows:

	HC	Exchange rate	£
30 June 1991	100,000	£1=HC1	100,000
30 June 2001	100,000	£1=HC200	500

This example illustrates the 'disappearing assets' problem and it is for this reason that SSAP 20 – *Foreign currency translation* – says that in these circumstances 'it may not be possible to present fairly in historical cost accounts the financial position of a foreign enterprise simply by a translation process'.[9] The other impact is that profits may be inflated (either from high interest income on deposits in a rapidly depreciating currency or from trading operations at unrealistic levels of profitability) whilst a significant exchange loss is reflected in the statement of total recognised gains and losses. The standard suggests, therefore, that the local currency financial statements should be adjusted where possible to reflect current price levels before the translation process is undertaken. No indication is given as to whether this restatement should be done based on specific price changes (current cost principles) or general price changes (current purchasing power principles), so either would appear to be acceptable.

SSAP 20 does not define what 'a very high rate of inflation' is; in addition, it does not provide clear guidance about how this aspect of the standard should be applied in practice.

2.2 UITF 9

As a result of this uncertainty the UITF considered the matter and in June 1993 issued Abstract 9 – *Accounting for Operations in Hyperinflationary Economies* – which became effective for accounting periods ending on or after 23 August 1993.

The UITF agreed that adjustments are required where the cumulative inflation rate over three years is approaching, or exceeds, 100% and the operations in the hyperinflationary economies are material.[10] Although this sounds high, this is equivalent to an annual inflation rate of 26% compounded over that period. Under US GAAP, SFAS 52 – *Foreign Currency Translation* – adopts a similar approach to identify a highly inflationary economy.[11]

Although SSAP 20 suggests that the local currency financial statements should be adjusted to reflect current price levels, the UITF recognised that a lack of reliable and timely inflation indices can pose a major practical problem. Accordingly, the UITF regards two methods as being acceptable to eliminate the distortion caused by hyperinflation:

(a) adjust the local currency financial statements to reflect current price levels before the translation process (as suggested by SSAP 20). This includes taking any gain or loss on the net monetary position through the profit and loss account. This is the same treatment as required by IAS 29 – *Financial Reporting in Hyperinflationary Economies* which is discussed at 3.2 below; or

(b) use a relatively stable currency (not necessarily sterling) as the functional currency of the foreign operations. If the transactions of the operation are not recorded initially in that stable currency, then they must be remeasured into the stable currency by applying the temporal method (see Chapter 8 at 2.4.4). These remeasured financial statements are then translated into sterling using the closing rate method.[12] This is effectively the same treatment as required under US GAAP by SFAS 52 which regards the reporting currency of the investing company (the US dollar) as if it were the functional currency of the foreign enterprise.[13]

We can see the effect of using these two methods on the 'disappearing assets' problem illustrated above in the following example:

Example 9.2

(a) Adjusting for current price levels

The relevant consumer price indices at 30 June 1991 and 30 June 2001 are 100 and 23,000 respectively. The asset would therefore be included in the group financial statements at 30 June 2001 as follows:

HC100,000 x 23,000/100 = HC23,000,000 @ (£1=HC200) = £115,000.

(b) Remeasuring using a stable currency

The US dollar is regarded as the relevant stable currency. The asset is remeasured using a historical rate of exchange for US dollars at 30 June 1990 of US$1=HC0.60. This produces a cost for the asset of US$166,667. This is then translated into sterling at the US dollar exchange rate at 30 June 2001 of £1=US$1.58 which gives an amount of £105,485.

Unilever follows the former method, as illustrated in the following extract:

> *Extract 9.1: Unilever PLC (2000)*
>
> **Foreign currencies** [extract]
>
> In preparing the consolidated accounts, the profit and loss account, the cash flow statement and all movements in assets and liabilities are translated at annual average rates of exchange. The balance sheet, other than the ordinary share capital of NV and PLC, is translated at year-end rates of exchange. In the case of hyper-inflationary economies, the accounts are adjusted to remove the influences of inflation before being translated.

On the other hand, Diageo adopted the latter method, as shown below:

> *Extract 9.2: Diageo plc (2000)*
>
> **Foreign currencies** [extract]
>
> The results, assets and liabilities of operations in hyper-inflationary economies are determined using an appropriate relatively stable currency as the functional currency. The exchange differences arising from this process are taken to the profit and loss account.

Although UITF 9 allows either of its two methods to be used in dealing with this problem of hyperinflation, it does state that if neither of them is appropriate, then the reasons should be stated and alternative methods to eliminate the distortions should be adopted.[14]

The Abstract also requires that where group operations in areas of hyperinflation are material, the accounting policy adopted to eliminate the distortions of such inflation should be disclosed.[15]

3 IAS REQUIREMENTS

3.1 Introduction

IAS 21 is the international standard on foreign currency translation, while IAS 29 is the international standard on hyperinflation. Before the adoption of SIC-19 – *Reporting Currency – Measurement and Presentation of Financial Statements under IAS 21 and IAS 29* – enterprises could choose between the IAS 21 and IAS 29 method of accounting for hyperinflation. SIC-19 prescribes how enterprises should select a measurement currency. A detailed discussion on the selection of a measurement currency and the definition of reporting currency and presentation currency can be found in Chapter 8 at 5.2.3.

3.1.1 IAS 21

IAS 21 – *The Effects of Changes in Foreign Exchange Rates* – deals with foreign currency translation but does not prescribe how an enterprise should select its reporting and/or measurement currency (see Chapter 8 at 5.2.3). As a result, it is possible for enterprises operating in hyperinflationary environments to change their measurement currency to a stable foreign currency or the reporting currency of their parent. IAS 21 not only allows enterprises to change their measurement currency,[16] but to make matters worse it does not prescribe a method, neither does it give any guidance as to how enterprises should effect such a change.

Enterprises changing their measurement currency in the light of hyperinflation, therefore, could restate their financial statements to the new currency as they saw fit, as shown in Example 9.3:

Example 9.3: Accounting for hyperinflation under IAS 21

Possible options:

a. restate its financial statements by going back to the past and using the historical exchange rate between the hyperinflationary currency and the new stable measurement currency;
b. convert the year-end balances in the hyperinflationary currency of the most recent financial period at the year-end exchange rate to amounts expressed in the stable foreign currency; or
c. any other method that meets the criteria set out in IAS 1 – *Presentation of Financial Statements.*[17]

The table below illustrates how Enterprise A would restate to Sterling using Methods (a) and (b) above:

Enterprise A	Hyper-inflationary currency amount (HC)	Method (a) Historical rate	Method (a) £	Method (b) Year-end rate	Method (b) £
Fixed assets	1,200	1.00	1,200	2.50	480
Inventory	300	1.50	200	2.50	120
Cash	200	2.50	80	2.50	80
Total assets	1,700		1,480		680
Accounts payable	600	2.50	240	2.50	240
Long-term debt	900	2.50	360	2.50	360
Equity	200		880	2.50	80
	1,700		1480		680

Method (a) has the disadvantage that, though it was possible to find the historical exchange rates for assets and liabilities, the restatement of equity would be a balancing figure that results after the restatement of all other items in the balance sheet. The restatement in equity reflects the gain or loss on the net monetary position held at the beginning of the hyperinflationary period.

Method (b) though easy to apply would have the disadvantage that the starting figures in the stable currency already contain the effects of a significant amount inflation, the effect of which is especially noticeable in the new carrying amount of the fixed assets.

In the above example, the question of restatement of comparative periods has not been addressed. Each of the methods shown could theoretically be applied at any of the following dates:

a. beginning of the first comparative period shown;
b. end of the most recent financial period shown;
c. a date before the first comparative period, when inflation was still unimportant;
d. any other date.

Clearly, accounting for hyperinflation under IAS 21 by changing the measurement currency to a stable foreign currency leaves much to be desired in terms of consistency of application between enterprises and disclosure of the effects of the restatement. IAS 21 only requires disclosure of the 'reason for any change in the reporting currency',[18] therefore, disclosure of a change in measurement currency would not even be required under a disingenuous interpretation of the standard.

3.1.2 IAS 29

IAS 29 – *Financial Reporting in Hyperinflationary Economies* – which was adopted in 1989 by the IASC deals specifically with the preparation of financial statements of any enterprise that reports in the currency of a hyperinflationary economy. The underlying premise of this standard is that 'reporting of operating results and financial position in the local [hyperinflationary] currency without restatement is not useful'.[19] The standard's approach is therefore to require that all items in the financial statements be restated in terms of the measuring unit current at the balance sheet date, by applying a general price index. Any gain or loss from such restatement is to be included in the net income for the period. The example below gives an outline of how this would apply to the balance sheet of an enterprise (for a detailed discussion of IAS 29 and restatement process see 3.2 below):

Example 9.4: Accounting for hyperinflation under IAS 29

Assuming Enterprise B operates in a hyperinflationary economy, it would be required under IAS 29 to restate all non-monetary items in its balance sheet to the measuring unit at balance sheet date by applying a general price index.

Enterprise B	Before restatement (HC)	Historical general price index	Year-end general price index	After restatement (HC)
Fixed assets	225	150	600	900
Inventory	250	500	600	300
Cash	100			100
Total assets	575			1,300
Accounts payable	180			180
Long-term debt	250			250
Equity	145			870
	575			1300

The simplified example above already raises a number of questions, such as:

- which balance sheet items are monetary and which are non-monetary?
- how does the enterprise select the appropriate general price index?
- what was the general price index when specific assets were acquired?

These difficulties and other aspects of the practical application of the IAS 29 method of accounting for hyperinflation are discussed at 3.2 below. Apart from the more technical reservations that one might have in respect of IAS 29, the concept of restating financial information to the measuring unit at balance sheet date is rather weak itself. The IASC Framework lists 'understandability' as one of the four principal qualitative characteristics of financial statements; i.e. information should be readily understandable by users.[20] The table below illustrates the problem that users have with the IAS 29 method:

Enterprise C	Equity (HC)	Date	General price index
Equity:			
– Year-end	1,200	31 December 2001	450
– Publication financial statements	1,560	8 April 2002	585
– User reading the financial statements	1,872	20 June 2002	702

Equity reported by Enterprise C – which is stated in the measurement unit at balance sheet date – in accordance with IAS 29 would be 1,200. However, as a result of the ravages of hyperinflation the general price index increased 30% by the time the financial statements are published and a further 20% by the time the user reads the financial statements. The IAS 29 equity figure is meaningful on 31 December 2001; however, in mere months the IAS 29 information becomes increasingly difficult to interpret and ultimately irrelevant. In a similar vein, the comparability of financial statements of enterprises with different year-ends appears to be limited.

Given the choice between (1) restating financial information for hyperinflation after the balance sheet date or (2) financial statements expressed in a stable foreign currency, many users would probably prefer the latter. Nevertheless, even when translated to a stable foreign currency the above difficulty remains in reality – in as much as if re-translated at the publication date the equity figure produced in the stable currency might be very different.

3.1.3 SIC-19

The IASC's Standing Interpretations Committee arguably went far beyond its original remit when it issued SIC-19 as that Interpretation effectively introduced the functional currency concept into IAS literature. SIC-19, which is effective for financial years starting on or after 1 January 2001, requires that the measurement currency of an enterprise 'should provide information about the enterprise that is useful and reflects the economic substance of the underlying events and circumstances relevant to that enterprise'.[21] The criteria in Appendix A of the Interpretation make clear that SIC-19 requires enterprises to use their functional currency as their measurement currency (see Chapter 8 at 5.2.3). If the measurement currency determined in accordance with SIC-19 is the currency of a hyperinflationary economy then:

'(a) the enterprise's own financial statements should be restated under IAS 29, and

(b) when the enterprise is a foreign entity as defined in IAS 21 and is included in the financial statements of another reporting enterprise, its financial statements should be restated under IAS 29 before being translated into the reporting currency of the other reporting enterprise.'[22]

Under SIC-19, it is therefore no longer possible to adopt any random stable foreign currency as the measurement currency of the enterprise. Enterprises operating in most hyperinflationary economies will therefore be subject to the accounting regime of IAS 29. Even after the adoption of SIC-19 there are situations where application of IAS 29 is not required:

a. some hyperinflationary economies have adopted a stable foreign currency, such as the US Dollar, in a process called dollarisation as the preferred currency to do business in;

b. subsidiaries are sometimes integral to the operations of their foreign parent; and

c. some subsidiaries in hyperinflationary economies can legitimately argue that the local hyperinflationary currency is not their functional currency as defined by SIC-19.

Consequently, there may still be situations in which the IAS 21 method of accounting for hyperinflation is still possible and appropriate under IAS.

3.1.4 SIC-D30

The objective of foreign currency translation under IAS 21 is to express foreign currency transactions and the financial statements of foreign operations in the entity's reporting currency (see Chapter 8 at 5.2.3). When SIC-19 introduced the concept of a measurement currency into IAS, it identified the potential problem that 'the method of translating the financial statements of a reporting enterprise from the measurement currency to a different currency for presentation is not specified under International Accounting Standards'.[23]

The Draft Interpretation SIC-D30 – *Reporting Currency – Translation from Measurement Currency to Presentation Currency* – states that where an enterprise's measurement currency is the currency of a hyperinflationary economy, then all items should be translated to the presentation currency at the closing rate existing at the date of the most recent balance sheet or period presented.[24] Whilst at the time of writing the draft SIC has not been adopted, it does provide a useful guide to the way this problem might be resolved. Translation from the measurement currency to a different presentation currency is discussed in detail in Chapter 8 at 5.2.3.

3.2 IAS 29

The IASC adopted IAS 29 in April 1989 and has not addressed the subject of hyperinflation since. This is not very surprising as memories of high inflation rapidly receded from the collective memory of most of the IASC's more influential constituents in the 1990s. The standard takes as fact that in a hyperinflationary economy financial statements are only useful when they are expressed in terms of the measuring unit at the balance sheet date, irrespective of whether they are based on a historical cost or a current cost approach.[25]

The main requirements of IAS 29 can be summarised as follows:

a. 'the financial statements of an enterprise that reports in the currency of a hyperinflationary economy, whether they are based on a historical cost approach or a current cost approach, should be stated in terms of the measuring unit current at the balance sheet date';[26]

b. 'the corresponding figures for the previous period required by IAS 1, Presentation of Financial Statements, and any information in respect of earlier periods should also be stated in terms of the measuring unit current at the balance sheet date';[27] and

c. 'the gain or loss on the net monetary position should be included in net income and separately disclosed'.[28]

The standard provides guidance on the restatement to the measuring unit current at the balance sheet date, but concedes that its approach is more an art than a science when it states that 'the consistent application of these [inflation accounting] procedures and judgements from period to period is more important than the precise accuracy of the resulting amounts included in the restated financial statements'.[29] The requirements of the standard look deceptively straightforward but actually represent a considerable challenge to enterprises.

3.2.1 *Scope*

IAS 29 should be applied by all enterprises that report in the currency of a hyperinflationary economy because 'money loses purchasing power at such a rate that comparison of amounts from transactions and other events that have occurred at different times, even within the same accounting period, is misleading'.[30] The standard should be applied both by enterprises in their stand-alone reporting as well as by enterprises that report to their parent under IAS.[31]

Determining whether an economy is hyperinflationary in accordance with IAS 29 requires exercise of judgement. However, the standard itself considers the following characteristics of the economic environment of a country to be strong indicators of the existence of hyperinflation:

'(a) the general population prefers to keep its wealth in non-monetary assets or in a relatively stable foreign currency. Amounts of local currency held are immediately invested to maintain purchasing power;

(b) the general population regards monetary amounts not in terms of the local currency but in terms of a relatively stable foreign currency. Prices may be quoted in that currency;

(c) sales and purchases on credit take place at prices that compensate for the expected loss of purchasing power during the credit period, even if the period is short;

(d) interest rates, wages and prices are linked to a price index; and

(e) the cumulative inflation rate over three years is approaching, or exceeds, 100%.'[32]

In determining whether an economy is hyperinflationary, only condition (e) is practicable while the other indicators often will not be reliably determinable and would require undue reliance on anecdotal evidence. For the purposes of testing condition (e), reference should be made to authoritative sources such as the IMF report referred to in 1 above, though we advise against too mechanical an application of the 100% criterion. Despite the fact that IAS 29 expresses a preference 'that all enterprises that report in the currency of the same hyperinflationary economy apply this Standard from the same date',[33] that is at best an unrealistic wish given its woolly definition of hyperinflation. In any event, once an enterprise has identified the existence of hyperinflation, it should apply IAS 29 from the beginning of the reporting period in which it identified the existence of hyperinflation.[34]

The identification of when a currency becomes hyperinflationary, and even more so when it ceases to be so, is not easy in practice. The consideration of trends, and the application of common sense, is important in this judgement, as are considerations of consistency of measurement and of presentation.

3.2.2 *The restatement process*

Restatement of financial statements in accordance with IAS 29 can be seen as a process comprising the following steps:

a. selection of a general price index (see 3.2.3 below);
b. analysis and restatement of assets and liabilities (see 3.2.4 below);
c. restatement of the income statement (see 3.2.5 below);
d. calculation of the gain or loss on the net monetary position (see 3.2.6 below);
e. restatement of the cash flow statement (see 3.2.7 below); and
f. restatement of the corresponding figures (see 3.2.8 below).

These steps are discussed below.

3.2.3 *Selection of a general price index*

The standard requires enterprises to use 'a general price index that reflects changes in general purchasing power',[35] preferably the same price index should be used by all enterprises in the same hyperinflationary currency. National statistical offices in most countries issue several price indices that potentially could be used for the purposes of IAS 29. Important characteristics of a good general price index include the following:

- a wide range of goods and services should be included in the price index;
- continuity and consistency of measurement techniques and underlying assumptions;
- free from bias;
- frequently updated; and
- available for a long period.

The enterprise should use the above criteria to choose the most reliable and most readily available general price index and use that index consistently. It is important that the index selected is representative of the real position of the hyperinflationary currency concerned. There are frequently in practice a number of different indices available, not all of which may be designed to provide an unbiased view.

Sometimes the general price index chosen by the enterprise is not available for all periods for which the restatement of long-lived assets is required. In that case, the enterprise will need to make an estimate of the price index based, for example, on 'the movements in the exchange rate between the reporting currency and a relatively stable foreign currency'.[36] It should be noted that this method is not acceptable unless the currency of the hyperinflationary economy is freely exchangeable, i.e. not subject to currency controls and 'official' exchange rates. Enterprises could use a similar approach when they cannot find a general price index that meets its minimum criteria for reliability (e.g. because the national statistical office in the hyperinflationary economy is subject to significant political bias). However, this would only be acceptable if all available general price indices are fatally flawed.

3.2.4 *Analysis and restatement of balance sheet items*

A broad outline of the process to restate assets and liabilities in accordance with the requirements of IAS 29 is shown in the diagram below:

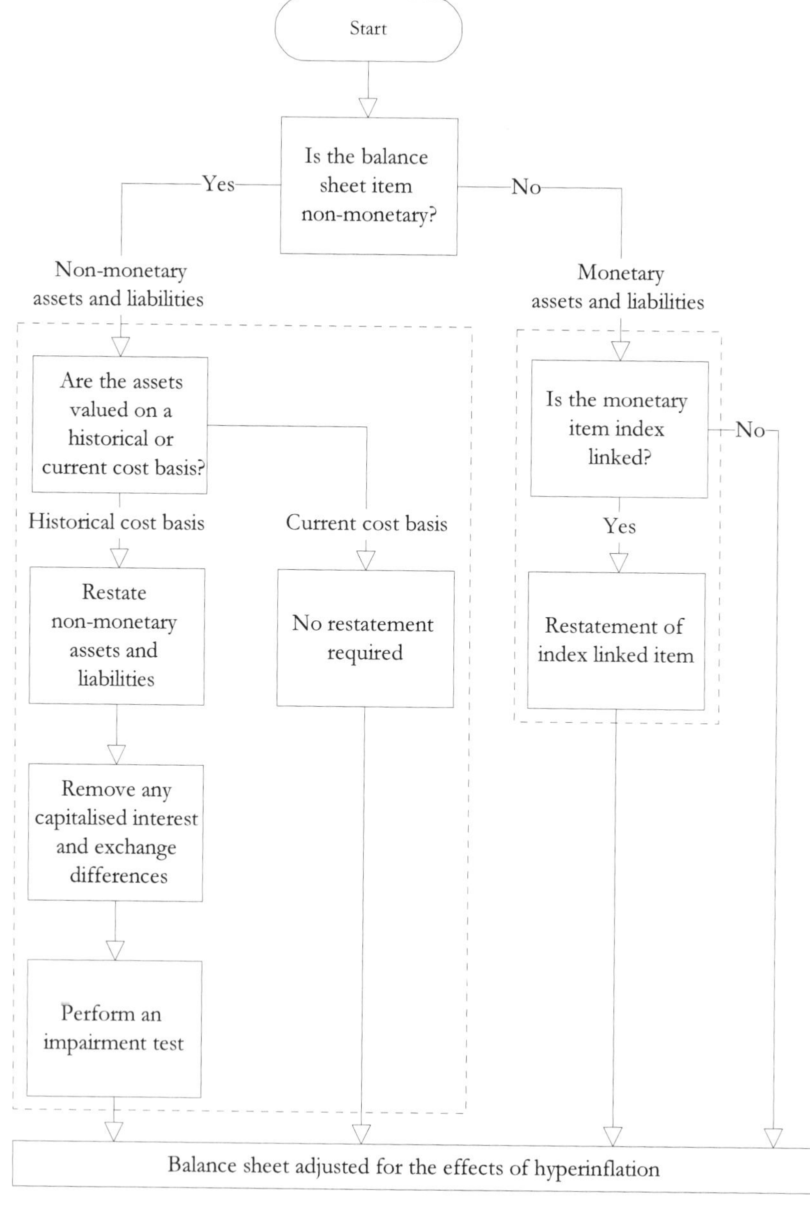

In many hyperinflationary economies, national legislation may require enterprises to adjust historical cost based financial information in a way that not in accordance with IAS 29 (for example, national legislation may require enterprises to adjust the carrying amount of tangible fixed assets by applying a multiplier). Though financial information adjusted in accordance with national legislation is sometimes described as 'current cost' information, it will often not meet the definition of current cost in accordance with the IASC's *Framework* (see 3.2.4 C below).[37] Where this is the case, enterprises must first determine the real historical cost basis of assets and liabilities before applying the requirements of IAS 29.

The above flowchart does not show the restatement of investees and subsidiaries (see E below), deferred taxation (see F below) and equity (see G below).

A Monetary or non-monetary

The first question to be addressed in the restatement of the balance sheet is which items are monetary and which are not. This is because monetary items normally need not be restated as they are already expressed in the measurement unit current at the balance sheet date. Monetary items are defined in IAS 29 as 'money held and items to be received or paid in money'.[38] However, IAS 21 expands somewhat on this definition by defining monetary items as 'money held and assets and liabilities to be received or paid in fixed or determinable amounts of money'.[39]

Most balance sheet items are readily classified as either monetary or non-monetary as is shown in the table below:

Monetary items	*Non-monetary items*
Assets	**Assets**
Cash and cash equivalents	Property, plant and equipment
Investment securities	Intangible assets
Trade and other receivables	Assets held for sale
Other receivables	Inventories
	Construction contract work-in-progress
	Prepaid costs
Liabilities	**Liabilities**
Trade and other payables	Warranty provision
Interest-bearing loans and borrowings	
Other liabilities	
Tax payable	

However, certain assets and liabilities require careful analysis before they can be classified, and even then their classification is not entirely satisfactory. Examples of items that are not easily classified as either monetary or non-monetary include:

a. *provisions for liabilities*: these can be either monetary, non-monetary or partly monetary. For example, a warranty provision would be:
   i. entirely monetary when customers only have a right to return the product and obtain a cash refund equal to the amount they originally paid;
   ii. non-monetary when customers have the right to get a replacement of any defect product; and

   iii. partly monetary, or inflation linked, if customers can choose between a refund and a replacement of the defect product.

   Obviously, classification as either monetary or non-monetary is not very satisfactory in iii. above. In the spirit of the IAS 29 requirements, part of the provision should be treated as a non-monetary item and the remainder as a monetary item;

b. *deferred tax assets and liabilities*: characterising these as monetary or non-monetary is fraught with difficulties, which are explained in F below;

c. *associates and joint ventures*: these are most likely to be at least partly monetary, depending on the degree to which they themselves hold monetary items or non-monetary items. Whatever the case may be, IAS 29 provides separate rules on restatement of investees that do not rely on the distinction between monetary and non-monetary (see E below); and

d. *deposits or progress payments paid against fixed assets or stocks*: these are not obviously either monetary or non-monetary and require careful analysis.

In summary, the practical application of the monetary/non-monetary distinction is beset with difficulties, and once one is past the classification of the more obvious items requires judgement on the part of preparers of financial statements. Further examples of problem areas in the application of the monetary/non-monetary distinction are discussed in Chapter 8 at 3.1.4.

B Monetary items

Generally, monetary items need not be restated to reflect the effect of inflation. However, monetary assets and liabilities linked by agreement to changes in prices – such as index linked bonds and loans – should be adjusted in accordance with the underlying agreement to show the repayment obligation in accordance with the terms of the agreement at the balance sheet date.[40] This type of restatement is in fact not an inflation accounting adjustment, but rather a gain or loss on a financial instrument. Accounting for inflation linked bonds and loans under IAS 39 may well lead to incomprehensible financial reporting. Depending on the specific wording of the inflation adjustment clause, such contracts may give rise to embedded derivatives and gains or losses are recorded either in income or equity depending on how the instrument qualifies for IAS 39 purposes.

C Non-monetary items carried at current cost

Non-monetary items carried at current cost 'are not restated because they are already expressed in term of the measuring unit current at the balance sheet date'.[41] Current cost is not defined by the standard, but the Framework provides the following definition:

> 'Assets are carried at the amount of cash or cash equivalents that would have to be paid if the same or an equivalent asset was acquired currently. Liabilities are carried at the undiscounted amount of cash or cash equivalents that would be required to settle the obligation currently.'[42]

For the purposes of restating historical cost financial statements, IAS 29 expands this definition by including net realisable value and market value into the concept of 'amounts current at the balance sheet date'.[43] In the same way, non-monetary items valued at fair value are included in IAS 29's current cost concept.

It is important to note that revalued amounts, at which some non-monetary items are measured, are not necessarily equal to current cost and need to be restated from the date of their revaluation.[44]

D Non-monetary items carried at historical cost

Non-monetary items carried at historical cost, or cost less depreciation, are stated at amounts that were current at the date of their acquisition. The restated cost, or cost less depreciation, of those items is calculated as follows:

$$\text{provisional restated cost} = \text{historical cost x} \frac{\text{general price index at the balance sheet date}}{\text{general price index at the date of acquisition}}$$

Application of this formula to 'property, plant and equipment, investments, inventories of raw materials and merchandise, goodwill, patents, trademarks and similar assets'[45] appears to be straightforward, but does require detailed records of their acquisition dates. Where such information is not available, IAS 29 requires 'an independent professional assessment of the value of the items as the basis for their restatement'[46] in the first period of application of the standard.

Inventories of finished and partly finished goods should be restated from the dates on which the costs of purchase and of conversion were incurred.[47] This means that the individual components of finished goods should be restated from their respective purchase dates. Similarly, if assembly takes place in several distinct phases, the cost of each of those phases should be restated from the date that the cost was incurred.

When an enterprise purchases an asset and payment is deferred beyond normal credit terms, it would normally recognise the present value of the cash payment as its cost.[48] IAS 29 provides relief by allowing that when it is impracticable to determine the amount of interest, such assets are restated from the payment date and not the date of purchase.[49]

In order to arrive at the restated cost of the non-monetary items, the provisional restated cost needs to be adjusted as follows:

restated cost = provisional restated costs - finance costs capitalised under IAS 23
- exchange losses capitalised under IAS 21
- any impairment

Capitalisation of finance costs (see Chapter 15 at 5.1) is not considered appropriate under IAS 29 because of the risk of double counting because the enterprise would both 'restate the capital expenditure financed by borrowing and … capitalise that part of the borrowing costs that compensates for the inflation during the same period'.[50] In effect, application of the allowed alternative treatment under IAS 23, which requires capitalisation of borrowing costs, is prohibited when an enterprise falls within the scope of IAS 29.

The standard also prohibits capitalisation of foreign exchange differences resulting from a severe and recent devaluation in accordance with the allowed alternative treatment of IAS 21 (see Chapter 8 at 5.2.4 C), which it deems inappropriate 'for an enterprise reporting in the currency of a hyperinflationary economy when the carrying amount of the asset is restated from the date of its acquisition'.[51]

Finally, IAS 29 requires that 'the restated amount of a non-monetary item is reduced, in accordance with appropriate International Accounting Standards, when it exceeds the amount recoverable from the item's future use (including sale or other disposal)'.[52] This requirement should be taken to mean impairment should be calculated in accordance with IAS 36 – *Impairment of Assets.*

Example 9.5: Restatement of property, plant and equipment

The table below illustrates how the restatement of a non-monetary item (for example, property, plant and equipment) would be calculated in accordance with the requirements of IAS 29.

Property, plant and equipment	Historical movements	Conversion factor	Restated for hyperinflation	
Opening balance, 1 January	510	2.40	1,224	(a)
– Additions (May)	360	1.80	648	(b)
– Disposals (March)	(120)	2.10	(252)	(c)
– Depreciation	(200)	1.70	(340)	(d)
IAS 29 restatement			304	(e)
Closing balance, 31 December	550	2.88	1,584	(f)

(a) The opening balance is restated by adjusting the historical balance for the increase in the price index during the period;

(b) The additions are restated from using the increase in the price index from May to December;

(c) The disposals are restated for the increase in the price index between March and December;

(d) Depreciation is restated on a monthly basis, e.g. the depreciation charge for July is restated for the increase in the price index between July and December. Alternatively, restatement of depreciation can be based on a comparison of the accumulated depreciation at the end of the period with that at the beginning, both expressed in the measuring unit current at balance sheet date;

(e) The IAS 29 restatement is calculated as the residual after restatement of all other items in the schedule;

(f) The closing balance is restated by determining the acquisition date of the individual assets and restating that amount for the change in the price index.

The calculations described under (a)-(d) and (f) all require estimates regarding the general price index at given dates and are sometimes based on averages or best estimates of the actual date of the transaction.

E Restatement of investees and subsidiaries

IAS 29 provides separate rules for the restatement of investees that are accounted for under the equity method, which may include both associates and joint ventures. If the investee itself operates in the currency of a hyperinflationary economy, the enterprise should restate the balance sheet and income statement of the investee in accordance with the requirements of IAS 29 in order to calculate its share of the investee's net assets and results of operations. If the financial statements of the investee are expressed in a foreign currency, they should be translated at the closing rate.[53]

If a parent that reports in the currency of a hyperinflationary economy has subsidiaries that also report in the currency of hyperinflationary economies, then the financial statements of those subsidiaries must first be 'restated by applying a general price index of the country in whose currency it reports before they are included in the consolidated financial statements issued by its parent'.[54] We take this to mean that the subsidiary itself should apply the requirements of IAS 29 as well. Where such a subsidiary is a foreign subsidiary the standard requires that its restated financial statements be translated at closing rates. The financial statements of subsidiaries that do not report in the currencies of hyperinflationary economies should be translated in accordance with IAS 21.[55]

Finally, IAS 29 requires that when 'financial statements with different reporting dates are consolidated, all items, whether non-monetary or monetary, ... be restated into the measuring unit current at the date of the consolidated financial statements'.[56]

F Calculation of deferred taxation

Determining whether deferred tax assets and liabilities are monetary or non-monetary is extremely difficult because:

- deferred taxation could be seen as a valuation adjustment which is either monetary or non-monetary depending on the asset or liability it relates to;
- on the other hand one could also argue that any deferred taxation payable or receivable in the very near future is almost identical to current tax payable and receivable. Therefore, at least the short-term portion of deferred taxation, if payable or receivable, could be treated as if it were monetary; and
- deferred taxation often relates to items that are not valued on a consistent basis. Some of the assets and liabilities it relates to are valued at historical costs, while others are valued at net realisable value, value in use, fair value or appraised values.

In any event, the debate as to whether deferred taxation is monetary or non-monetary is for practical purposes settled by the requirement of IAS 12 – *Income Taxes* – to calculate deferred taxation based on the difference between the carrying amount and the tax base of assets and liabilities at balance sheet date. Therefore, irrespective of the monetary/non-monetary distinction, deferred taxation needs to be recalculated at balance sheet date.

IAS 29 refers to IAS 12 for guidance on the calculation of deferred taxation by enterprises operating in hyperinflationary economies.[57] IAS 12 recognises that IAS 29 restatements of assets and liabilities may give rise to temporary differences when equivalent adjustments are not allowed for tax purposes.[58] Where IAS 29 adjustments give rise to temporary differences, IAS 12 requires the following accounting treatment:

'(1) the deferred taxation is charged in the income statement; and

(2) if, in addition to the restatement, the non-monetary assets are also revalued, the deferred tax relating to the revaluation is charged to equity and the deferred tax relating to the restatement is charged in the income statement.'[59]

For example, deferred taxation arising on *revaluation* of property, plant and equipment should be recognised in equity, just as it would be if the enterprise were not operating in a hyperinflationary economy. On the other hand, *restatement* in accordance with IAS 29 of property, plant and equipment that is measured at historical cost should be recognised in the income statement. Thus the treatment of deferred taxation related to non-monetary assets valued at historical cost and those that are revalued, is consistent with the general requirements of IAS 12.

G Restatement of equity and first-time application of IAS 29

At the beginning of the first period where an enterprise applies IAS 29, because the economy in which it is operating has become hyperinflationary, it should restate the components of owners' equity as follows:

- 'the components of owners' equity, except retained earnings and any revaluation surplus, are restated by applying a general price index from the dates the components were contributed or otherwise arose';[60]
- 'any revaluation surplus that arose in previous periods is eliminated';[61] and
- 'restated retained earnings are derived from all the other amounts in the restated balance sheet'.[62]

'At the end of the first period and in subsequent periods, all components of owners' equity are restated by applying a general price index from the beginning of the period or the date of contribution, if later.'[63] It seems anomalous that the restatement of an historical cost balance sheet for hyperinflationary conditions may possibly result in an increase in retained, and therefore distributable, earnings. However, this may well be the effect of the transfer of revaluation reserve to retained earnings implicit in the third bullet point above.

Though IAS 29 provides guidance on the restatement of assets, liabilities and individual components of shareholders' equity, it should be noted that national laws and regulations with which the enterprise needs to comply typically do not permit such revaluations. This can mean that IAS 29 may require restatement of distributable reserves, but that from a legal point of view those same reserves remain unchanged.

Example 9.6: Restatement of equity

The table below shows the effect of a hypothetical IAS 29 restatement on individual components of equity. Issued share capital and share premium increase by applying the general price index, the revaluation reserve is eliminated as required, and retained earnings is the balancing figure derived from all other amounts in the restated balance sheet.

	Amounts before restatement	Amounts after IAS 29 restatement	Components of equity under national law
Issued share capital	1,500	3,150	1,500
Revaluation reserve	800	–	800
Retained earnings	350	1,600	350
Total equity	2,650	4,750	2,650

A user of the financial statements of the enterprise might get the impression, based on the information restated in accordance with IAS 29, that distributable reserves have increased from 350 to 1,600. However, if national law does not permit revaluation of assets, liabilities and components of equity then distributable reserves remain unchanged.

Users of financial statements restated under IAS 29 are for that reason easily misled about the extent to which components of equity are distributable. Enterprises reporting under IAS 29 should therefore disclose the extent to which components of equity are distributable where this is not obvious from the financial statements. An example of an enterprise disclosing the difference between reported equity and distributable reserves is Rostelecom (see Extract 9.3 at 3.2.10). In our view it is important for entities to give supplementary information in the circumstances where the IAS 29 adjustments have produced large apparently distributable reserves, that are in fact not distributable.

Because of the IASB's constituency, its standards cannot deal with all specific national legal requirements relating to a legal entity's equity. Therefore, instead of prescribing an accounting treatment for individual components of equity, we consider that the IASB would be better advised to recognise the wide variety in national legislation, and prescribe disclosure requirements that ensure users of financial statements are not misled.

3.2.5 *Restatement of the income statement*

IAS 29 requires that all items in historical cost based income statements be expressed in terms of the measuring unit current at the balance sheet date.[64] The standard contains a similar requirement for current cost based income statements, because the underlying transactions or events are recorded at current cost at the time they occurred rather than in the measuring unit current at the balance sheet date.[65] Therefore, all amounts in the income statement need to be restated as follows:

$$\text{restated amount} = \text{amount before restatement} \times \frac{\text{general price index at the balance sheet date}}{\text{general price index when the underlying income or expenses were initially recorded}}$$

Actually performing the above calculation on a real set of financial statements is often difficult for the following reasons:

a. enterprises would need to keep a very detailed record of when they entered into transactions and when they incurred expenses; and

b. it is not realistic to assume that the rate of inflation was relatively constant throughout the period. Therefore, it is often necessary to have monthly information on the general price index since interpolations or averages do not approximate reality.

Example 9.7 illustrates how an enterprise might, for example, restate its revenue to the measuring unit current at the balance sheet date. A similar calculation would work well for other items in the income statement, with the exception of:

a. depreciation and amortisation charges which are often easier restated using the restated asset or liability as a starting point for the calculation;

b. deferred taxation which should be based on the temporary differences between the carrying amount and tax base of assets and liabilities, the restated carrying amount of balance sheet items, and the underlying tax base of those items; and

c. the net monetary gain or loss which results from the IAS 29 restatements (see 3.2.6 below).

Example 9.7: Restatement of historical cost income statement

An enterprise would restate its revenue for the period ending 31 December 2001 using a calculation as shown in the table below.

	General price index	Conversion factor	Revenue before restatement	Restated revenue
31 January 2001	1,315	(2,880/1,315) = 2.19	40	87.6
28 February 2001	1,345	(2,880/1,345) = 2.14	35	74.9
31 March 2001	1,371	etc. = 2.10	45	94.5
30 April 2001	1,490	1.93	45	87.0
31 May 2001	1,600	1.80	65	117.0
30 June 2001	1,846	1.56	70	109.2
31 July 2001	1,923	1.50	70	104.8
31 August 2001	2,071	1.39	65	90.4
30 September 2001	2,163	1.33	75	99.9
31 October 2001	2,511	1.15	75	86.0
30 November 2001	2,599	1.11	80	88.6
31 December 2001	2,880	1.00	80	80.0
			745	1,119.9

A similar calculation can be made for other items in the income statement. Inevitably, in practice there is some approximation because of the assumptions that the enterprise is required to make, for example:

a. the use of weighted averages rather than more detailed calculations; and

b. the calculation above assumes are revenues for the month are earned on the final day of the month, which is not realistic.

3.2.6 *Calculation of the gain or loss on the net monetary position*

In theory, hyperinflation only affects the value of money and monetary items and does not affect the value of non-monetary items. Therefore, any gain or loss because of hyperinflation will be the gain or loss on the net monetary position of the enterprise. By arranging the items in an ordinary balance sheet, it can be shown that the monetary position minus the non-monetary position is always equal to zero:

	Monetary items	Non-monetary items	Total
Monetary assets	280		280
Non-monetary assets		170	170
Monetary liabilities	(200)		(200)
Non-monetary liabilities		(110)	(110)
Assets minus liabilities			140
Shareholders' equity		(140)	(140)
Net position	80	(80)	0

Theoretically, the gain or loss on the net monetary position can be calculated by applying the general price index to the enterprise's monetary assets and liabilities. This would require the enterprise to determine its net monetary position on a daily basis, which would be entirely impracticable given the difficulties in making the monetary/non-monetary distinction (see 3.2.4 A above). The standard therefore allows the gain or loss on the net monetary position to 'be estimated by applying the change in a general price index to the weighted average for the period of the difference between monetary assets and monetary liabilities'.[66] A calculation based on averages for the period (or monthly averages) can be very unreliable when the pattern of hyperinflation and the net monetary position are very volatile.

However, as shown in the above table, any restatement of the non-monetary items must be met by an equal restatement of the monetary items. Therefore, in preparing financial statements it is more practical to assume that the gain or loss on the net monetary position is exactly the reverse of the restatement of the non-monetary items. A stand-alone calculation of the net gain or loss can serve, however, as a crude check on the reasonableness of the restatement of the non-monetary items.

The gain or loss on the net monetary position should be included in net income and disclosed separately. It may be helpful to present it together with items that are also associated with the net monetary position such as 'interest income and expense, and foreign exchange differences related to invested or borrowed funds'.[67]

3.2.7 *Restatement of the cash flow statement*

The standard in also requires that all items in the cash flow statement are expressed in terms of the measuring unit current at the balance sheet date.[68] This is a most difficult requirement to fulfil in practice.

To see why preparation of a cash flow statement under IAS 29 can be very complicated, one needs to look at the information that is presented in the cash flow statement and how that information is restated under the standard. The following information is presented in a cash flow statement prepared under IAS 7 – *Cash Flow Statements*:[69]

a. cash flows from operating activities, which are the principal revenue-producing activities of the enterprise and other activities that are not investing or financing activities;

b. cash flows from investing activities, which include the acquisition and disposal of long-term assets and other investments not included in cash equivalents; and

c. cash flows from financing activities, which are activities that result in changes in the size and composition of the equity capital and borrowings of the enterprise.

Effectively, IAS 29 requires restatement of most items in the cash flow statement, i.e. the actual cash flows at the time of the transactions will be different from the number presented in the cash flow statement. However, not all items are restated using the same method and many of the restatements are based on estimates. For example, items in the income statement are to be restated using an estimate of the general price index at the time that the revenues were earned and the costs incurred. Unavoidably this will give rise to some inconsistencies. Similarly, the restatement of balance sheet items will give rise to discrepancies because some items are not easily classified as either monetary or non-monetary and slightly different rules apply to investees and deferred taxation. The result of all this is inevitably a balancing figure in the cash flow under the heading 'IAS 29 monetary gain' which actually contains the undifferentiated sum of all the restatements outlined above. This is illustrated in the table below:

Long-term borrowings	Historical movements	Conversion factor	Restated for hyperinflation
Opening balance, 1 January	1,020	2.40	2,448
– Additional borrowings	720	1.80	1,296
– Repayments	(240)	2.10	(504)
– Accrued interest	400	1.70	680
IAS 29 monetary gain			(2,020)
Closing balance, 31 December	1,900	1.00	1,900

It is not clear from IAS 29 where the monetary gain item in the table above should be presented:

a. as a separate item classified as a financing cash flow; or

b. presented in the same line item as the financing flow to which it relates; or

c. presented together with all IAS 29 restatements as a separate item in the cash flow statement.

Method (a) seems reasonable because cash flows relating to long-term borrowings are presented as cash flows from financing activities. Reconciling items related to other balance sheet items could be classified in a similar manner, with the occasional problems when individual balance sheet items (e.g. current taxation) are split across categories.

Method (b) would require the IAS 29 monetary gain item to be grossed-up and allocated to 'additional borrowings' and 'repayments'. Such allocation inevitably is arbitrary and does not appear to improve the understandability of the cash flow statement, which makes this approach less desirable.

Method (c) is probably the most frequently used in practice and has the merit of not attempting to classify what is, in reality, a mixed bag of adjustments as anything else but that.

However, ultimately one has to wonder what the value is of a cash flow statement that contains items that are not cash flows (contrary to the requirements of IAS 7)[70] and which cannot be readily understood.

3.2.8 *Restatement of the corresponding figures*

The standard requires that all financial information be presented in terms of the measurement unit current at the balance sheet date, therefore:

- 'corresponding figures for the previous reporting period, whether they were based on a historical cost approach or a current cost approach, are restated by applying a general price index';[71] and
- 'information that is disclosed in respect of earlier periods is also expressed in terms of the measuring unit current at the end of the reporting period'.[72]

3.2.9 *Economies ceasing to be hyperinflationary*

When an economy ceases to be hyperinflationary, enterprises should discontinue preparation and presentation of financial statements in accordance with IAS 29. The amounts expressed in the measuring unit current at the end of the previous reporting period will be treated as the deemed cost of the items in the balance sheet.[73]

It is possible or even likely that an economy becomes hyperinflationary sometime during an enterprise's financial year. Therefore, it would be reasonable and sensible that as soon as an enterprise determines that it is operating in hyperinflation it starts preparing its interim reports using the principles underlying IAS 29. The standard should be applied from the beginning of the reporting period in which the existence of hyperinflation is identified.[74] Conversely, it is possible that an economy ceases to be hyperinflationary during the year. The standard is silent on the question whether an enterprise can stop applying the requirements of IAS 29 during one of its interim periods. In practice an amalgamation of interim periods during which IAS 29 was applied with those where it was not, may result in financial statements that are extremely difficult to interpret. Therefore, we believe that enterprises should only stop applying the standard at the end of their financial year.

Determining when a currency stops becoming hyperinflationary is not easy in practice. It is important to review trends, not just at the balance sheet date but subsequently. In addition, consistency demands that the financial statements do not unnecessarily 'yo-yo' in and out of a hyperinflationary presentation, where a more careful judgement would have avoided it.

3.2.10 *Disclosures*

IAS 29 requires that enterprises should disclose the following information when they apply the provisions of the standard:

'(a) the fact that the financial statements and the corresponding figures for previous periods have been restated for the changes in the general purchasing power of the reporting currency and, as a result, are stated in terms of the measuring unit current at the balance sheet date;

(b) whether the financial statements are based on a historical cost approach or a current cost approach; and

(c) the identity and level of the price index at the balance sheet date and the movement in the index during the current and the previous reporting period.'[75]

Rostelecom and Koç Holding disclose that they operate in a hyperinflationary economy and make the appropriate disclosures:

Extract 9.4: OAO Rostelecom (2000)

NOTES TO THE CONSOLIDATED FINANCIAL STATEMENTS [extract]
(In millions of Russian Roubles in terms of purchasing power of the Rouble at December 31, 2000)

2. BASIS OF PRESENTATION [extract]

...

The consolidated financial statements have been prepared using the historical cost convention, restated for the effects of inflation and modified by the initial valuation of property, plant and equipment as further disclosed in Notes 4 and 5 to these financial statements. The functional currency of the Group and the reporting currency for these financial statements is the Russian Rouble.

4. ACCOUNTING FOR THE EFFECTS OF INFLATION

IAS 29 "Financial Reporting in Hyperinflationary Economies", requires that financial statements prepared on a historic cost basis be adjusted to take account of the effects of inflation, for entities reporting in hyperinflationary economies. The consolidated financial statements have been restated in terms of the measuring unit current at the latest presented balance sheet date and the net gains or losses arising on the net monetary position of assets and liabilities expressed in Roubles during the periods presented have been included in the statement of operations and disclosed separately.

During the years ending December 31, 2000, 1999 and 1998, the general price index issued by Goskomstat, the official Russian Government Statistical Bureau, indicates that the domestic rate of inflation has been 20.13%, 36.6% and 84.5% respectively. The Group has utilized the general price index issued by Goskomstat in the application of IAS 29.

The application of IAS 29 to specific categories of transactions and balances within the consolidated financial statements is set out as follows:

a) Corresponding figures

Corresponding figures for the previous reporting periods have been restated by applying to the amounts included in the previous years' financial statements the change in the general price index. Comparative financial information is therefore presented in terms of the measuring unit current as of December 31, 2000, being the latest date for which financial statements are presented.

b) Monetary assets and liabilities

Cash and cash equivalents, marketable securities, receivables, payables, interest bearing loans, current taxation and dividends have not been restated as they are monetary assets and liabilities and are stated in Roubles current at the balance sheet date.

Gains or losses on the net monetary position of assets and liabilities expressed in Roubles which arise as a result of inflation, are computed by applying the change in the general price index to the monetary assets and monetary liabilities, during the period.

c) Non monetary assets and liabilities

Non monetary assets and liabilities are restated from their historic cost or valuation by applying the change in the general price index from the date of recognition to the balance sheet date.

d) Consolidated statement of operations

Items included in the consolidated statement of operations are restated by applying the change in the general price index from the dates when the items were initially recorded to the balance sheet date. The depreciation expense for the year is based on the restated property, plant and equipment balances at each year end.

12. SHAREHOLDERS EQUITY [extract]

...

The statutory accounting reports of the Company are the basis of profit distribution and other appropriations. Russian legislation identifies the basis of distribution as the current year's statutory net profit. For 2000, the statutory profit after taxation for the Company as reported in the published annual statutory reporting forms was 1,022. However, this legislation and other statutes and regulations dealing with the distribution rights are open to legal interpretation and accordingly Management believes that, at present, it would not be appropriate to disclose an amount for the distributable reserves in the financial statements.

Extract 9.5: Koç Holding A.Ş. (2000)

NOTES TO THE CONSOLIDATED FINANCIAL STATEMENTS
31 DECEMBER 2000
(Amounts expressed in billions of Turkish lira (TL) in terms of the purchasing power of TL at 31 December 2000 unless otherwise indicated)

NOTE 2 - BASIS OF PREPARATION OF FINANCIAL STATEMENTS

a) Turkish lira financial statements [extract]

...

These consolidated financial statements are based on the statutory records, which are maintained under the historical cost convention (except for the revaluation of property, plant and equipment as discussed in Note 17), with adjustments and reclassifications including restatement for changes in the general purchasing power of the Turkish lira, for the purpose of fair presentation in accordance with IAS, issued by the International Accounting Standards Committee.

The restatement for the changes in the general purchasing power of the Turkish lira as of 31 December 2000 is based on IAS 29 ("Financial Reporting in Hyperinflationary Economies"). IAS 29 requires that financial statements prepared in the currency of a hyperinflationary economy be stated in terms of the measuring unit current at the balance sheet date, and that corresponding figures for the previous periods be restated in the same terms. One characteristic that necessitates application of IAS 29 is a cumulative three-year inflation rate approaching or exceeding 100%. The restatement was calculated by means of conversion factors derived from the Turkish nationwide wholesale price index ("WPI") published by the State Institute of Statistics ("SIS"). Such indices and conversion factors used to restate the accompanying financial statements at 31 December are given below:

Dates	Index	Conversion factors
31 December 2000	2,626.0	1.000
31 December 1999	1,979.5	1.327
31 December 1998	1,215.1	2.161

The main procedures for the above mentioned restatement are as follows:

– Financial statements prepared in the currency of a hyperinflationary economy are stated in terms of the measuring unit current at the balance sheet date, and corresponding figures for previous periods are restated in the same terms.

Monetary assets and liabilities that are carried at amounts current at the balance sheet date are not restated because they are already expressed in terms of the monetary unit current at the balance sheet date.

– Non-monetary assets and liabilities that are not carried at amounts current at the balance sheet sate and components of shareholders' equity are restated by applying the relevant monthly conversion factors.

– Comparative financial statements are restated using general inflation indices at the currency purchasing power at the latest balance sheet date.

– All items in the statements of income are restated by applying the relevant (monthly, yearly average, year-end) conversion factors.

– The effect of inflation on the net monetary asset position of Koç Holding, the Subsidiaries and Joint Ventures is included in the statement of income as loss on net monetary position.

Serono discloses that it restates the local currency financial statements of its subsidiaries operating in hyperinflationary economies before translating their financial statements into the parent reporting currency:

Extract 9.6: Serono International S.A. (2000)

1.4 Foreign currencies [extract]

...

The local currency financial statements of foreign entities operating in highly inflationary economies are restated using appropriate indices to current values at the balance sheet date before translation into the company's reporting currency.

Serono does not disclose the identity of the indices used to restate the financial statements of its hyperinflationary subsidiaries. IAS 29 does not specifically require this and so far this disclosure has not developed into an accepted practice common among companies reporting under IAS.

4 CONCLUSION

The ASB's *Statement of Principles* and the IASC's *Framework* are based on the financial capital maintenance concept which, as the ASB acknowledges, is only satisfactory under conditions of stable prices. Accounting for hyperinflation under UK GAAP and IAS therefore lacks a solid theoretical and conceptual basis.

UK GAAP takes a practical approach and allows enterprises operating in hyperinflationary economies to use either a restatement approach or to use a stable foreign currency as their measurement currency. Though flexible, this means that there is little consistency between enterprises accounting for activities in hyperinflationary economies. However, in the absence of significant inflation in the UK and other parts of the world in which UK companies do most of their business, the ASB will have little incentive to provide guidance beyond that provided in UITF 9.

With the adoption of SIC-19, IAS only allows enterprises to use a restatement approach to accounting for activities in hyperinflationary economies. However, the restatement approach prescribed by IAS 29 is cumbersome in its application and, to make matters worse for preparers of financial statements, the standard only provides loosely worded guidance that is open to interpretation. In addition, the application of IAS 29 presents users with financial statements that are difficult to interpret. Hyperinflation has received little attention from the IASB, probably because the major economies are not afflicted by it at the moment. However, the issue deserves more attention because:

- a significant number of countries with hyperinflationary economies have adopted IAS as their national standards or basis thereof; and
- IAS 29, perhaps inevitably, leaves significant room for interpretation while the guidance it offers is not comprehensive. As a consequence, it would seem entirely possible for two identical enterprises to report significantly different numbers under IAS 29.

There is no persuasive evidence to indicate that the IAS 29 approach, which is somewhat complex and perhaps cumbersome, is superior to an approach that requires use of a stable foreign currency as the measurement currency. However, an obvious drawback of the stable foreign currency approach is that it might inadvertently give the impression that the company was in fact trading in a stable currency and holding its liquid resources in it. This points up the importance for users of financial statement of companies in hyperinflationary economies of having information about, for example:

- the steps management are taking to reduce the company's exposure to the local hyperinflationary currency;
- how the management is structuring its purchasing and sales contracts to protect its real capital; and
- how any steps being taken by the national government to address the hyperinflation are expected to affect the business.

This type of information is important for users regardless of the approach taken towards accounting for hyperinflation. While it is not, perhaps, the role of accounting standards to require it, clearly the inclusion of such supplementary information in any management review would greatly enhance the utility of the financial statements.

Financial reporting in hyperinflationary economies is not part of the IASB's improvements project at the time of writing and IAS 29, flawed as it may be, remains mandatory for many enterprises operating in hyperinflationary economies. We consider that a simplified and improved standard would be of great utility to enterprises accounting for hyperinflation under IAS.

References

1 *Statement of Principles for Financial Reporting*, ASB, December 1999, para. 6.41.

2 *Framework for the Preparation and Presentation of Financial Statements* (Framework), IASC, September 1989, para. 104.

3 *Statement of Principles for Financial Reporting*, para. 6.42.

4 UITF 9, *Accounting for Operations in Hyper-inflationary Economies*, UITF, June 1993, para. 5.

5 IAS 29, *Financial Reporting in Hyperinflationary Economies*, IASC, July 1989, para. 3.

6 SFAS 8, *Accounting for the translation of foreign currency transactions and foreign currency financial statements*, FASB, October 1975, para. 11.

7 It should be noted that the definition of hyperinflation used in financial reporting does not have a solid theoretical basis. In fact, economists

researching hyperinflation often use Cagan's definition which defines hyperinflation as consumer price increases of more than 50% per month. International Monetary Fund, *World Economic Outlook – Fiscal Policy and Macroeconomic Stability*, May 2001. Cagan, Phillip. *op. cit.*, "The Monetary Dynamics of Hyperinflation." In Studies in the Quantity Theory of Money, ed. by Milton Friedman, pp. 25-117. Chicago: University of Chicago Press.

8 Based on information published by the International Monetary Fund, *International Financial Statistics*, Volume LIV, Number 3, March 2001. Countries which are close to the highly inflationary criteria are Burundi, Haiti, Iran, Kyrgyz Republic and Mongolia. There may be additional countries with cumulative inflation of 100% or more, because the cited source does not include data for some 95 countries that have not reported data for 2000.

9 SSAP 20, *Foreign currency translation*, ASC, April 1983, para. 26.

10 UITF 9, *Accounting for Operations in Hyper-inflationary Economies*, June 1993, para. 5.

11 SFAS 52, *Foreign currency translation*, FASB, December 1981, para. 11.

12 UITF 9, para. 6.

13 SFAS 52, para. 11.

14 UITF 9, para. 7.

15 *Ibid.*, para. 8.

16 IAS 21, *The Effects of Changes in Foreign Exchange Rates*, IASC, Revised 1993, para. 4.

17 IAS 1, *Presentation of financial statements*, IASC, Revised 1997, para. 20.

18 IAS 21, para. 43.

19 IAS 29, para. 2.

20 Framework, paras. 24-25.

21 SIC-19, *Reporting Currency – Measurement and Presentation of Financial Statements under IAS 21 and IAS 29*, SIC, February 2000, para. 5.

22 *Ibid.*, para. 7.

23 *Ibid.*, para. 9.

24 Draft Interpretation SIC-D30, *Reporting Currency – Translation from Measurement Currency to Presentation Currency*, SIC, May 2001, para. 5.

25 IAS 29, para. 7.

26 *Ibid.*, para. 8.

27 *Ibid.*

28 *Ibid.*, para. 9.

29 *Ibid.*, para. 10.

30 *Ibid.*, paras. 1-2.

31 SIC-19, para. 7.

32 IAS 29, para. 3

33 *Ibid.*, para. 4.

34 *Ibid.*

35 *Ibid.*, para. 37.

36 *Ibid.*, para. 17.

37 Framework, para. 100(b).

38 IAS 29, para. 12.

39 IAS 21, para. 7.

40 IAS 29, para. 13.

41 *Ibid.*, paras. 14 and 29.

42 Framework, para. 100(b).

43 IAS 29, para. 14.

44 *Ibid.*, para. 18.

45 *Ibid.*, para. 15.

46 *Ibid.*, para. 16.

47 *Ibid.*

48 IAS 16, para. 16.

49 IAS 29, para. 22.

50 *Ibid.*, para. 21.

51 *Ibid.*, para. 23.

52 *Ibid.*, para. 19.

53 *Ibid.*, para. 20.

54 *Ibid.*, para. 35.

55 *Ibid.*

56 *Ibid.*, para. 36.

57 *Ibid.*, para. 32.

58 IAS 12, Appendix A, para. A.18.

59 *Ibid.*

60 IAS 29, para. 24.

61 *Ibid.*

62 *Ibid.*

63 *Ibid.*, para. 25.

64 *Ibid.*, para. 26.

65 *Ibid.*, para. 30.

66 *Ibid.*, paras. 27 and 31.

67 *Ibid.*, para. 28.

68 *Ibid.*, para. 33.

69 IAS 7, *Cash Flow Statements*, IASC, December 1992, para. 6.

70 *Ibid.*, para. 43.

71 IAS 29, para. 34.

72 *Ibid.*

73 *Ibid.*, para. 38.

74 *Ibid.*, para. 4.

75 *Ibid.*, para. 39.

Chapter 10 Financial instruments

1 INTRODUCTION

1.1 Background

The development of sophisticated financial markets, which permit companies to trade in newly invented contracts and thereby transform their risk profile, is perhaps the new factor in business life that poses the most searching challenge to traditional financial reporting practices. The IASC, in its newsletter of December 1996, commented on the issue in these terms:

'At the roots of the need for change in accounting for financial instruments are fundamental changes in international financial markets. … An enterprise can substantially change its financial risk profile instantaneously, requiring careful and continuous monitoring. … Alternatively, an enterprise may use derivatives as speculative tools to multiply the effects of changes in interest, foreign exchange or security or commodity prices, thus multiplying the gains if prices move advantageously or, alternatively, multiplying the losses if they move adversely. … Accounting for financial instruments has not kept pace with information needs of financial market participants.

'Existing accounting practices are founded on principles developed when the primary focus of accounting was on manufacturing companies that combine inputs (materials, labour, plant and equipment, and various types of overheads) and transform them into outputs (goods or services) for sale. Accounting for these revenue-generating processes is concerned primarily with accruing costs to be matched with revenues. A key point in this process is the point of revenue realisation – the point at which a company is considered to have transformed its inputs into cash or claims to cash (i.e., financial instruments).

'These traditional realisation and cost-based measurement concepts are not adequate for the recognition and measurement of financial instruments. Recognising this, many countries have moved part way to embrace fair value accounting for some financial instruments. …'[1]

This was the forerunner of the IASC Discussion Paper published in March 1997 referred to below and it lays down the challenge very cogently. Do we need a new approach to accounting if we are to cope with the particular characteristics of financial instruments? And indeed, does this approach in turn imply that we should now abandon traditional accounting methods for other areas of business activity as well? The IASC authors felt able to distinguish the two issues, but in the UK some of the thinking behind the financial instruments proposals has had a profound effect on the ASB's work in other areas. However, putting these broader ramifications to one side, the subject matter of this chapter is the improvement of the recognition, measurement and disclosure of financial instruments themselves.

The ASB is addressing the subject in two stages, by developing first a disclosure standard and then a standard that deals with recognition and measurement issues. It published a comprehensive Discussion Paper[2] on the topic in July 1996, which set out its long-term aims for both stages of the project, and in April 1997 it issued FRED 13, a proposed standard on disclosure.[3] This was later modified, in July 1997, by a further exposure draft proposing a different regime for banks and similar institutions.[4] The Discussion Paper envisaged that although the recognition and measurement rules would apply only to listed companies and other public interest entities, most of the disclosure requirements would apply to all entities. However, by the time FRED 13 had been developed the scope of the proposed disclosure requirements had been limited to publicly traded companies, banks and insurance companies. The final standard, FRS 13,[5] was published in September 1998 and represents the culmination of the ASB's efforts as far as the disclosure aspects of financial instruments are concerned. Although most of the disclosures proposed in FRED 13 remain in FRS 13, the scope was amended again to exclude insurance companies. The Board's rules on disclosure are covered in 2 and 3 below.

The ASB's Discussion Paper proposed much greater use of current values for measuring financial instruments, the main exception being that changes in the value of an entity's own debt resulting from changes in its own creditworthiness would be ignored. Most gains or losses arising on remeasurement would have been reported in the profit and loss account, the main exceptions being realised and unrealised gains and losses on the following, which would be reported in the STRGL:

- strategic holdings of shares;
- changes in fixed rate borrowings, match-funding investments and related interest rate derivatives arising from movements in interest rates; and
- currency borrowings and derivatives used to hedge investments in foreign net investments.

It was also proposed that the use of hedge accounting should be limited, although the Board was divided on the extent of any restrictions.

The IASC was conducting a project on financial instruments for several years, initially in conjunction with the Canadian Institute of Chartered Accountants. Two attempts were made to deal comprehensively with the issue, in two successive exposure drafts (E40 in 1991 and E48 in 1994). However, the IASC then decided to lower its sights in the same way as other standard setters and converted E48 into a standard dealing with classification, presentation and disclosure issues alone; IAS 32[6] was published in March 1995, and is covered in 5 below.

Two years later, the IASC/CICA Steering Committee published the Discussion Paper referred to above dealing extensively with the measurement and recognition issues and making proposals for a comprehensive standard on financial assets and liabilities. In concept, its main proposals were very simple: all financial assets and liabilities should be recognised as soon as the reporting entity becomes a party to the contractual provisions that they entail;[7] thereafter they should be stated at fair value in the balance sheet;[8] and all movements in fair value thereafter should be reported in income.[9] The Discussion Paper also took a very restrictive view of hedge accounting. With two minor exceptions, it proposed that no special treatment should be accorded to financial instruments that are designated as hedges of other exposures; they should all still be carried at fair value and gains or losses reported in income.

However, later in 1997 the IASC recognised that completion of such a comprehensive standard to meet the IOSCO deadline (see Chapter 1 at 2.2) was not a realistic possibility and therefore committed to completing an interim international standard on recognition and measurement in 1998. Consequently in May 1998 the IASC issued an exposure draft, E62,[10] and in December 1998 approved IAS 39[11] for publication. This standard is covered in 4 below.

Also in 1997, both the ASB and IASC decided that they should join with other national standard setters to develop an integrated and harmonised standard on financial instruments, building on their own Discussion Papers, existing and emerging national standards, and the best thinking and research on the subject world-wide. The Joint Working Group of standard setters (JWG), comprising representatives from the ASB, IASC, the US FASB and seven other international bodies, was charged with carrying out this project. December 2000 saw the culmination of the their work with the publication by each constituent member of its proposals in the form of a Draft Standard.[12] According to the ASB this 'contains the most comprehensive consideration yet of the issues that would arise if a 'full fair value' model were to be implemented for financial instruments'.[13]

Perhaps not surprisingly the JWG proposals build on the theoretical approach of the discussion papers. With only very minor exceptions, all financial instruments would be recorded at fair value with corresponding gains and losses reported in income. This means that the fair value of an entity's own debt would take account of changes in the entity's credit risk and even changes in the value of debt and other instruments used to hedge foreign currency net investments would be reported in income. A corollary of this is that hedge accounting would no longer be allowed.

1.2 What is a financial instrument?

1.2.1 *Definition*

The ASB and IASC have adopted substantially the same definitions in their standards. The main terms used are defined as follows:

A *financial instrument* is any contract that gives rise to both a financial asset of one entity and a financial liability or equity instrument of another entity.

A *financial asset* is any asset that is:

(a) cash;

(b) a contractual right to receive cash or another financial asset from another entity;

(c) a contractual right to exchange financial instruments with another entity under conditions that are potentially favourable; or

(d) an equity instrument of another entity.

A *financial liability* is any liability that is a contractual obligation:

(a) to deliver cash or another financial asset to another entity; or

(b) to exchange financial instruments with another entity under conditions that are potentially unfavourable.

An *equity instrument* is any contract that evidences an ownership interest in an entity, i.e. a residual interest in the assets of the entity after deducting all of its liabilities.[14]

The terms 'contract', 'contractual right' and 'contractual obligation' are fundamental to the above definitions.[15] The reference to a contract is 'to an agreement between two or more parties that has clear economic consequences and which the parties have little, if any, discretion to avoid, usually because the agreement is enforceable at law.' Such contracts need not be in writing.[16]

Contractual rights and contractual obligations are rights and obligations that arise out of a contract. It is also noted that most contracts give rise to a variety of rights and obligations and these will change as the contract is performed. The Appendix to FRS 13 goes on to say 'some of these rights and obligations may fall within the definition of a financial instrument and some may not. For example, an unperformed contract for the purchase or sale of a tangible asset usually gives rise to rights and obligations to exchange a physical asset for a financial asset (although it is possible that, if the contract is breached, the exchange will involve the payment of compensation). These rights and obligations do not represent a financial instrument. Under the same contract, once the physical asset has been delivered, a debtor or creditor will usually arise and this will be a financial instrument.' Contractual rights and contractual obligations encompass rights and obligations that are contingent on the occurrence of a future event, e.g. those arising under a financial guarantee.

Assets and liabilities which are not contractual in nature are not financial assets or financial liabilities. It is for this reason that tax liabilities are not financial liabilities, as such liabilities arise from statutory requirements, not from a contract.

'Equity instruments' has a wider meaning than 'equity shares' (as defined in FRS 4) because it includes some non-equity shares, as well as warrants and options to subscribe for or purchase equity shares in the issuing entity. Conversely, some non-equity shares (as defined in FRS 4) are 'financial liabilities'. The distinction between equity instruments and financial liabilities is, perhaps, more important under IAS because these definitions determine whether an instrument is recorded as debt or within shareholders' equity – this is covered in more detail in Chapter 17 at 5.3.

The JWG has used slightly different definitions in its Draft Standard. However, this is primarily to clarify aspects of the earlier definitions and is not intended to involve a fundamental change of meaning.[17]

1.2.2 *Examples of financial instruments*

Appendix II to FRS 13 cites the following as examples of financial instruments:[18]

(a) deposits, debtors, creditors, notes, loans, bonds, and debentures to be settled in cash;

(b) unconditional lease obligations;

(c) shares including ordinary shares, preference shares and deferred shares;

(d) warrants or options to subscribe for shares of, or purchase shares from, the issuing entity;

(e) obligations of an entity to issue or deliver its own shares, such as a share option or warrant;

(f) derivative instruments such as forward contracts, futures, swaps and options that will be settled in cash or another financial instrument. An example of the latter is an option to purchase shares; and

(g) contingent liabilities that arise from contracts and, if they crystallise, will be settled in cash – an example is a financial guarantee.

In fact, in terms of the definitions quoted at 1.2.1 above, many of these are actually examples of financial *assets* or *liabilities*, not financial *instruments*; for example, debtors cannot be described as contracts, which is an essential element of the definition, although they may arise from such contracts. The ASB had originally asserted in the Discussion Paper that even 'cash' was a financial instrument but Appendix II now says that 'cash, including foreign currency, is a financial asset because it represents the medium of exchange and is the basis on which all transactions are measured and reported in financial statements'. FRS 13 tends to use the terms loosely rather than strictly as they are defined, which sometimes makes its requirements difficult to interpret.

Appendix II to FRS 13 does make it clear that the following are *not* financial instruments:[19]

(a) physical assets, such as stock, property, plant and equipment;

(b) intangible assets, such as patents and trademarks;

(c) prepayments for goods or services, since these will not be settled in cash or another financial instrument;

(d) obligations to be settled by the delivery of goods or the rendering of services, such as most warranty obligations;

(e) income taxes (including deferred tax), since these are statutory rather than contractual obligations;

(f) forwards, swaps and options to be settled by the delivery of goods or the rendering of services;

(g) contingent items that do not arise from contracts, for example a contingent liability for a tort judgement; and

(h) the minority interest that arises on consolidating a subsidiary that is not wholly-owned.

The overall scope of the financial instruments project therefore seems to embrace the following:

- cash;
- other monetary assets and liabilities, insofar as they have arisen as a result of a contract rather than by some other means;
- derivatives to be settled by the exchange of monetary assets or liabilities, but not those to be settled by the delivery of commodities or other physical assets;[20] and
- shares, both in the reporting entity and in other entities, and derivatives giving rights over such shares.

2 THE ASB'S DISCLOSURE REQUIREMENTS

2.1 Introduction

As noted earlier in this chapter, although the ASB's long term objective is to resolve the measurement issues that arise on financial instruments, its more immediate aim has been to improve their disclosure. Their Discussion Paper contained a number of recommended disclosures which were to be regarded as best practice pending the development of a standard on the subject. This was superseded in April 1997 by the publication of FRED 13, and then in September 1998 the final standard, FRS 13, was published, the requirements of which are set out below.

The disclosures required by FRS 13 fall into two categories: narrative disclosures, which may be either included in the accounts or relegated, with an appropriate cross reference, to the Operating and Financial Review (or equivalent statement); and numerical disclosures to be included in the notes to the accounts. In the ASB's earlier Discussion Paper, the narrative disclosures were to be separate from the accounts and non-mandatory, but FRED 13 proposed to make them compulsory. Notwithstanding concerns raised about this proposal, FRS 13 makes the narrative disclosures mandatory. Accordingly, they are subject to audit. These narrative disclosures apply to all entities included within the scope of FRS 13 and are discussed at 2.3 below.

As mentioned at 1.1 above, FRED 13 was modified in relation to banks and similar institutions by the publication in July 1997 of a further exposure draft. This disapplied most of the numerical disclosure requirements in the original exposure draft so far as banks were concerned and substituted a different set of proposals. Most significantly, it acknowledged the need for different disclosures as between banks' trading and non-trading activities – a distinction that had until then been largely rejected.

It was to be expected that other financial institutions which were not banks would argue that a similar distinction was appropriate to them and this proved to be the case. However, given the wide range of different types of financial institution and the difficulty of deciding which disclosures were most relevant to which type of financial institution, FRS 13 effectively allows such entities to decide (with a couple of exceptions) which body of numerical disclosures best suits their circumstances.

Accordingly, FRS 13 has different numerical disclosure requirements for:

- entities other than financial institutions (Part A);
- banks and similar institutions (Part B);
- other financial institutions (Part C).

For the purposes of FRS 13, a bank or similar institution is defined in such a way as to include building societies and credit unions. The definition of 'financial institution' is very broad and encompasses entities such as leasing companies, stockbrokers and money brokers, investment dealing companies, investment managers, corporate finance companies and investment vehicles, such as investment trusts and unit trusts.

Although FRS 13 is structured in such a way that all of the requirements (and related definitions) for each of these three types of entity are set out in separate parts of the standard, it is only the numerical disclosures which are different. The numerical disclosures required by entities other than financial institutions are discussed in this section below. Although there is a different regime for banks and similar institutions, some of the disclosures are the same as for other entities. Those disclosures which are specific to banks and similar institutions are discussed at 3.1 below. The disclosures by other financial institutions are discussed at 3.2 below.

2.2 Scope

2.2.1 *Entities required to comply*

For non-financial institutions, the disclosure requirements in FRS 13 only apply to those entities with capital instruments listed or publicly traded on a stock exchange or market.[21] This refers to both domestic and foreign exchanges and primary and secondary markets and therefore includes the London Stock Exchange, EASDAQ, NASDAQ and the Alternative Investment Market.[22]

This requirement applies equally for listed or publicly traded debt instruments as to equities and there are no exemptions for subsidiaries. However the disclosures are not required for a parent's own financial statements if those statements are presented together with the parent's consolidated financial statements.[23] The financial statements of insurance companies and groups are also excluded.[24]

Example 10.1: Subsidiaries with listed debt

An unlisted manufacturing company, S Ltd, owns a single purpose finance subsidiary, F plc, that has made a public debt issue. This debt is listed on the Luxembourg Stock Exchange. The financial statements requiring FRS 13 disclosures are the consolidated, but not solus, accounts of S Ltd and the individual accounts of F plc. S Ltd would make the disclosures required by Part A of FRS 13 and F plc those required by Part C of FRS 13 (see 2.3 to 2.4 and 3.2 below).

If S Ltd was the parent of an insurance group, neither its consolidated nor solus financial statements would have to include FRS 13 disclosures, although F plc's would.

It appears that a number of companies have failed to appreciate the scope of the standard and this has resulted in a series of pronouncements by the Review Panel over the past year. Three companies, Artisan, Wiggins Group and Princedale Group, received adverse rulings highlighting that they had failed to provide any of the disclosures required by FRS 13[25] and in April 2001 the Panel issued a press notice containing a general reminder as to its scope.[26]

2.2.2 *Instruments to be included in the disclosures*

In view of the wide-ranging nature of the definition of a financial instrument, steps are taken within the standard to exclude certain items which fall within the definition from the disclosure requirements. The first category of items which are excluded are those which are the subject of other standards or statutory rules that the ASB does not wish to disturb at this stage. These are:

(a) interests in subsidiary and quasi-subsidiary undertakings which are consolidated under FRS 2 and FRS 5 respectively;

(b) interests in associated undertakings, partnerships and joint ventures accounted for under FRS 9;

(c) obligations to employees under employee share option and employee share schemes, and any shares held in order to fulfil these obligations;

(d) assets and liabilities relating to pensions and other post-retirement benefits that fall within SSAP 24, UITF Abstract 6 and, when applied in full, FRS 17;

(e) rights and obligations arising under operating leases, as defined by SSAP 21. (This makes it clear that assets and liabilities under finance leases are to be so included.);

(f) equity shares of the reporting entity, and warrants and options over such shares, other than those that are held exclusively with a view to a subsequent resale;

(g) financial assets, financial liabilities and cash-settled commodity contracts of an insurance company or group.

The above items are to be excluded from all of the disclosure requirements, except for the currency risk disclosures set out in 2.7 and 3.1.2 below.[27] Interests in subsidiary, quasi-subsidiary and associated undertakings, partnerships and joint ventures which are held exclusively with a view to subsequent resale do fall within the disclosure requirements because they are really like any other current asset investment. The same would also appear to apply to interests held by a reporting entity in its own equity shares (including warrants and options) which are held exclusively with a view to a subsequent resale.

Non-equity shares are financial instruments, but only some of them are financial liabilities of the reporting entity; the rest are equity instruments. However, FRS 13 requires that they should all be dealt with in the disclosures in the same way as financial liabilities, except that they should be disclosed separately. The ASB sees this as a pragmatic approach to save entities from categorising such shares into equity instruments and financial liabilities.[28]

Equity minority interests in subsidiaries and quasi-subsidiaries are not financial instruments and therefore do not need to be dealt with in the disclosures.[29] By analogy with non-equity shares, and because there is no specific exemption as there is for equity minority interests, we believe the intention was for non-equity minority interests to be similarly included within the disclosures.

The next category of items which *may* be excluded from the disclosures (except for the currency risk disclosures set out in 2.7 and 3.1.2 below) are short-term debtors and creditors.[30] These are defined in the standard as being:

'Financial assets and financial liabilities that meet all of the following criteria:

(a) they would be included in the balance sheet under one of the following headings if the entity was preparing its financial statements in accordance with Schedule 4 to the Companies Act 1985:
   (i) debtors;
   (ii) prepayments and accrued income;
   (iii) creditors: amounts falling due within one year, other than items that would be included under the 'debenture loans' and 'bank loans and overdrafts' sub-headings;
   (iv) provisions for liabilities and charges; and
   (v) accruals and deferred income;

(b) they mature or become payable within 12 months of the balance sheet date; and

(c) they are not a derivative financial instrument.'[31]

The reason why such items can be excluded is that they are not regarded by the ASB as being the main focus of the standard. We agree that such items should be excluded, because in our view they do not give rise to significant financial risks of the nature which the standard is trying to address. However, as a result of (b) above, any debtors which are not due within 12 months have to be included within the disclosures as would any provisions (if they meet the definition of a financial liability) which are expected to be payable after more than one year. Similarly, all creditors due after more than one year are also to be included within the disclosures. We would also have excluded such items from the disclosures.

We would recommend that reporting entities take advantage of this optional exemption for short-term debtors and creditors. If the exemption is not taken, then *all* such debtors and creditors need to be included in *all* of the disclosures.

The term 'short-term debtors and creditors' is restricted for banks and other financial institutions as indicated in 3.1 and 3.2 below.

In summary, the standard effectively requires the following items to be included within the disclosures:

- fixed asset investments (other than associated undertakings, partnerships and joint ventures accounted for under FRS 9 and investments in own shares held in respect of employee share schemes);
- current asset investments (including interests in subsidiary, quasi-subsidiary and associated undertakings, partnerships and joint ventures held exclusively with a view to subsequent resale);
- debtors which are receivable after one year (other than non-contractual debtors such as tax recoverable);
- cash and bank deposits;
- bank overdrafts;
- bank loans and debenture loans;
- other loans, creditors and provisions which are payable after one year (other than non-contractual items such as tax liabilities or provisions that are not financial liabilities);
- non-equity shares issued by the reporting entity and, seemingly, non-equity minority interests; and
- derivative instruments.

In addition, although commodity contracts requiring settlement by physical delivery are not financial instruments, the standard requires cash-settled commodity contracts (including those for the delivery of gold) nevertheless to be included within certain of the disclosures (see 2.12 below).

Banks and other financial institutions also have to treat all other contracts for the delivery of gold as if they were financial instruments (see 3.1 and 3.2 below).

2.3 Narrative disclosures

FRS 13 requires entities to include narrative disclosures which discuss their objectives, policies and strategies in using financial instruments. The intention of these disclosures is to put in context the numerical disclosures required by the standard. It is emphasised that the primary focus of the narrative disclosures is the risks that arise in connection with financial instruments and how they have been managed. These risks, which are discussed in more detail in Appendix I to FRS 13, include credit risk, liquidity risk, cash flow risk, interest rate risk, currency risk and other types of market price risk.[32]

It is envisaged that the information provided in respect of these risks will be presented in the context of a discussion of the entity's activities, structure and financing and that the discussion will consider the financial risk profile of the entity as a whole, before focusing specifically on financial instruments.[33]

First of all, an explanation should be provided of the role that financial instruments have had during the period in creating or changing the risks that an entity faces in its activities. This should include an explanation of the objectives and policies for holding or issuing financial instruments and similar contracts, and the strategies for achieving those objectives that have been followed during the period.[34]

This disclosure is intended to include a discussion of the nature of the main types of financial instruments and similar contracts and the purposes for which they are held or issued, with separate disclosure of instruments used for financing, risk management or hedging, and trading or speculation.[35]

The disclosure would also normally include a description of the financial risk management and treasury policies agreed by the board of directors, including its main policies, with quantification where appropriate, on:

(a) the fixed/floating split, maturity profile and currency profile of financial assets and liabilities;

(b) the extent to which foreign currency debtors and creditors are hedged to the functional currency of the business unit concerned;

(c) the extent to which foreign currency borrowings and other instruments are used to hedge foreign currency net investments; and

(d) any other hedging.[36]

As far as hedging is concerned, the standard also calls for specific disclosure of a description of:

(a) the transactions and risks that have been hedged, including the period of time until they are expected to occur; and

(b) the instruments used for hedging purposes, distinguishing between those that have been accounted for using hedge accounting and those that have not.[37]

In this context, a 'hedge' is 'an instrument that individually, or with other instruments, has a value or cash flow that is expected, wholly or partly, to move inversely with changes in the value or cash flows of the position being hedged'.[38]

The above explanation of the role of financial instruments is intended to put in context the numerical disclosures required by the standard. Accordingly, an explanation of how the year end figures reflect the agreed objectives, policies and strategies is also required. If the year end position is unrepresentative of the position during the year or of the agreed objectives, policies and strategies, an explanation of the extent to which it is regarded as unrepresentative should be provided.[39]

If the explanation about the role of financial instruments reflects a significant change from that stated in the previous year, that fact should be disclosed and the reasons for the change explained. This is intended to encompass both changes in the risks faced by the entity and changes in the way the exposures to such risks are managed.[40]

The standard also says that if by the date of approving the accounts, the directors have agreed to make a significant change in the role of financial instruments, then that change should be explained.[41]

As indicated at 2.1 above, these narrative disclosures are to be either included in the accounts or relegated, with an appropriate cross reference, to the Operating and Financial Review (or equivalent statement).[42]

Appendix III to FRS 13 provides illustrations of the disclosures required by the standard. The first two illustrations include examples of those narrative disclosures which would be relevant for companies which are not financial institutions. Examples of the sort of disclosures which companies are giving in practice are shown in the following extracts:

Extract 10.1: Cable and Wireless plc (2001)

24 Operating and Financial Review [extract]

Treasury activities and policies

The Group's principal treasury and funding operations are carried out by the London-based central treasury on the basis of objectives, policies and authorities approved by the Board. The central treasury function is responsible for managing liquidity risk, credit risk, interest rate risk and currency risk. The Group's treasury policies and strategies are regularly reviewed. Other subsidiaries that operate treasury and funding operations have their policies and authorities adopted by their respective boards. These are consistent with the Group's objectives, policies and strategies. The Group uses financial instruments including forward foreign exchange contracts, interest rate swaps and cross currency swaps in its management of exchange rate and interest rate exposures. The Group does not speculate in derivative financial instruments. Counterparty credit risk is closely monitored and derivatives activity is tightly controlled. Both UK and overseas treasury activities are subject to close supervision and regular review.

Funding

The Group continues to maintain a broad portfolio of debt, diversified by source and maturity and reflecting the long-term nature of its worldwide business and asset base.

Group gearing at 31 March 2000 was 16%. At 31 March 2001 the Group had net cash (including treasury instruments held as current asset investments) of £3,096 million primarily due to the disposal of Cable & Wireless HKT and the sale to ntl Inc (ntl) of ConsumerCo during the year.

Cable and Wireless plc's debt ratings remained stable during the year. At 31 March 2001, the long-term ratings stood at A from Standard & Poor's and A2 from Moody's Investors Service.

At 31 March 2001, the Group's net cash comprised cash and equivalent assets of £6,027 million and gross debt of £2,931 million. Included within gross debt is £1,167 million in Cable & Wireless Optus. The Group's debt has an average maturity of 5.9 years.

Borrowing facilities

The total amount of the Group's undrawn committed facilities available as at 31 March 2001 was £1,551 million. Of this total, the Cable & Wireless central treasury has access to £680 million in available facilities and Cable & Wireless Optus has £871 million. As at 31 March 2001, Cable and Wireless plc had undrawn committed medium-term bank facilities of £395 million with maturities ranging from 2001 through to 2002. None of the Group's covenants relating to loans and other financing is expected to restrict normal business activities.

Cash management and credit risk

Cash deposits and other financial instruments give rise to credit risk which represents the loss that would be recognised if a counterparty failed to perform as contracted. The counterparties to the Group's financial instruments are major international institutions. It is the Group's policy to monitor the financial standing of these counterparties on an ongoing basis. During the year, the Board approved a new policy for investing surplus funds, consistent with the significant increase in the amount of cash invested during the year.

Group treasury has been managing investments averaging £4,587 million during the year to 31 March 2001. At the year end, the weighted average maturity of the cash and equivalent investments was 1.5 months.

Interest rate risk management

The Group's policy is to maximise the after-tax return on cash deposits and minimise interest expense. The Group assesses the exposure of its overall financial position on a net basis, after considering the extent to which variable rate liabilities can be offset with variable rate assets.

In order to secure the return on cash deposits, Cable and Wireless plc has hedged approximately 50% of cash under management at 31 March 2001 using forward rate agreements and short dated interest rate swaps for the next financial year.

To minimise interest expense, the Group maintains an appropriate level of fixed rate debt to ensure it is not significantly affected by adverse interest rate movements. To maintain this ratio in a cost efficient manner, the Group mainly uses interest rate swaps that have the effect of converting specific debt obligations from fixed to variable rates, or vice versa, as required. Approximately 68% of the Group's medium and long-term borrowings is currently at fixed rates of interest.

Exchange rate risk management

The Group carries out foreign exchange hedging operations, mainly using forward foreign exchange contracts to manage its exposures in respect of material transactions. Although the Group trades in over 50 countries, much of its revenue is from international traffic flows and is settled in major currencies on a regular basis. For this reason, the Group is not unreasonably exposed to localised currency fluctuations or exchange controls.

At 31 March 2001 approximately 85% of Group cash and cash equivalents was invested in Sterling and approximately 9% was invested in US dollars. The balance was invested in the national currencies of the Group's foreign subsidiaries.

Approximately 25% of Group debt is denominated in Sterling while a proportion of the overseas asset base is matched by foreign currency borrowings. Of these, approximately 40% are in Australian dollars, 27% in US dollars and 8% in other currencies.

Extract 10.2: Volex Group p.l.c. (2001)

Treasury

The Group has a central treasury function, which monitors and updates treasury controls throughout the Group in line with Board policies. Subject to these controls, day to day foreign exchange transactions are dealt with at the operating unit level with the Group's foreign exchange policy being generally to hedge transaction exposures. Foreign currency borrowings are used to hedge the balance sheet translation exposure to major foreign currency net assets and as at the year end the Group considered that it had a satisfactory position against this exposure other than in the case of its Irish punt denominated assets against which it is not hedged. The principal currencies in which the Group has both trading and translational risk are US dollars, Canadian dollars, Singapore dollars, Brazilian Reais and Irish punts, with UK sterling being a risk only in respect of trading.

The Group regularly reviews its asset risk management strategy and through internal financial controls and the use of appropriate risk limitation instruments, principally insurance policies, considers it has adequate financial protection against potentially significant operating risks.

The Group holds or issues financial instruments for three main purposes – to finance its operations, to manage the interest rate and currency risks arising from its operations and from its sources of finance and for trading purposes. In addition, various financial instruments – for example, trade debtors, trade creditors, accruals and prepayments – arise directly from the Group's operations.

The Group finances its operations by a mixture of retained profits, bank current borrowings and bank medium term loans. The Group borrows in the major global debt markets in a range of currencies at fixed and floating rates of interest, using derivatives where appropriate to generate the desired effective currency profile and interest rate basis. The derivatives used for this purpose are principally interest rate contracts and forward foreign currency contracts.

The main risks arising from the Group's financial instruments are interest rate risk, liquidity risk and foreign currency risk. The Board reviews and agrees policies for managing each of these risks and they are summarised below. These policies have remained unchanged during the year.

Interest rate risk

The Group borrows in the desired currencies at both fixed and floating rates of interest so as to generate the desired interest profile and to manage the Group's exposure to interest rate fluctuations. The Group's policy is to keep its medium term borrowings at rates of interest fixed for between 6 to 12 month periods.

Liquidity risk

The Group's objective is to maintain a balance between continuity of funding and flexibility through the use of borrowings with a range of maturities. In addition, to preserve continuity of funding, the majority of borrowings matures in more than two years. As detailed in Note 21, 20% of the Group's total borrowings at the year-end will mature in the next twelve months, with the balance maturing between two and five years.

Currency risk

Although the Group is based in the UK, it has a significant investment in overseas operations in the USA, Singapore, China, Canada, Ireland, Brazil and Sweden. As a result, the Group's sterling balance sheet can be significantly affected by movements in exchange rates between £ sterling and the currencies of these countries. The Group seeks to mitigate the effect of these structural currency exposures by borrowing in the same currencies as the operating (or "functional") currencies of its main operating units and to match the currency of some of its other borrowing to its various functional currencies. With the exception of Irish Punt and Brazilian Real, exposures between 50 per cent and 100 per cent of the Group's principal investments in non-sterling operations at the year end were hedged back into sterling in this way, with the exact percentage varying depending on the Group's transactional currency exposures (which are described below). In managing its structural currency exposures, the Group's objectives are to maintain a low cost of borrowings and to retain some potential for currency-related appreciation while partially hedging against currency depreciation.

The Group also has certain transactional currency exposures. Such exposures arise from sales or purchases by an operating unit in currencies other than the unit's functional currency. The Group's policy is that all its operating units use forward currency contracts to eliminate the currency exposure on any significant balances on its debtor and creditor ledgers.

The disclosures are intended to be a summary of the facts specific to the reporting company, and not either subjective statements or a forecast of what might happen in the future. The ASB expects that the disclosures will be drawn from documented policies and decisions and be about transactions and exposures that have occurred.[43] Some companies may need to determine what their objectives, policies and strategies in respect of financial instruments actually are, before considering the disclosures to be made in the accounts.

The illustrations of these narrative disclosures in Appendix III and the above extracts are relevant to companies which are not financial institutions. Banking companies and other financial institutions also have to give narrative disclosures, but although the requirements of the standard are the same, their discussion needs to reflect the nature of their business. This is likely to involve more discussion on credit risk and other market price risk, particularly in relation to their financial assets.

Aside from those that failed to include any FRS 13 disclosures at all in their accounts, Ensor Holdings is the only company to have amended its disclosures as a result of a Review Panel investigation.[44] Because of the implied endorsement by the Panel, the extracts below, which show Ensor's main financial instrument disclosures before and after amendment, go some way towards establishing a minimum benchmark level of disclosure for non-complex companies.

Extract 10.3: Ensor Holdings plc (1999)

25. Financial instruments

The Group's treasury activities are designed to provide suitable, flexible funding arrangements to satisfy the Group's requirements. The Group uses financial instruments comprising borrowings, cash, liquid resources and items such as trade debtors and creditors that arise directly from its operations.

The Group finances its operations through a combination of retained profits, cash resources, finance leases and bank borrowings. Exposure to interest rate fluctuations on its borrowings is managed by the use of both fixed and floating facilities. The Group also mixes the duration of its deposits and borrowings to reduce the impact of interest rate fluctuations. At 31 March 1999, sterling bank loans of £325,000, representing 62% of borrowings, were at an interest rate of 1.5% above base rate.

The Group aims to achieve a balance between continuity and flexibility of funding by maintaining a range of maturities on its borrowings. These are analysed in notes 15 and 16. Short term flexibility is satisfied by overdraft facilities. At 31 March 1999 the Group had undrawn committed borrowing facilities of £1,000,000.

Under the transitional rules of FRS13, "Derivatives and Other Financial Instruments", prior year comparatives have not been stated.

Extract 10.4: Ensor Holdings plc (2000)

18. Financial instruments

The Group's treasury activities are designed to provide suitable, flexible funding arrangements to satisfy the Group's requirements. The Group uses financial instruments comprising borrowings, cash, liquid resources and items such as trade debtors and creditors that arise directly from its operations. The main risks arising from the Group financial instruments are interest rate, liquidity and foreign currency risks. The Board reviews policies for managing each of these risks and they are summarised below. These policies have remained unchanged from previous years.

The Group finances its operations through a combination of retained profits, cash resources, finance leases and bank borrowings. Exposure to interest rate fluctuations on its borrowings is managed by the use of both fixed and floating facilities. The Group also mixes the duration of its deposits and borrowings to reduce the impact of interest rate fluctuations. At 31 March 2000, sterling bank loans of £225,000 (1999 – £325,000), repayable by instalments, representing 25% (1999 – 62%) of borrowings, were at an interest rate of 1.5% above base rate.

The Group aims to achieve a balance between continuity and flexibility of funding by maintaining a range of maturities on its borrowings which are analysed in notes 16 and 17. Short term flexibility is satisfied by overdraft facilities which are repayable on demand and due for review in November 2000. At 31 March 2000 the Group had undrawn committed borrowing facilities of £626,000 (1999 – £1,000,000).

The Group has fixed interest finance leases of £308,000 (1999 – £200,000) with a weighted average interest rate of 7.2% (1999 – 7.9%). These leases are secured on the assets to which they relate. The weighted average period for which the rates are fixed is 3.7 years (1999 – 1.8 years). These amounts represent 34% (1999 – 38%) of total borrowings.

The Group has net foreign currency monetary liabilities of £105,000 (1999 – £50,000) denominated in Spanish pesetas. No forward foreign currency contracts were used during the financial year.

There is no material difference between the fair values and book values of the Group's financial instruments.

Short term debtors and creditors have been excluded from the above disclosures other than the currency risk disclosures.

2.4 Disclosure of accounting policies

FRS 13 also includes a reminder that SSAP 2 (and now FRS 18) require disclosure of all significant accounting policies, and suggests this extensive list of matters that might require to be disclosed in relation to financial instruments:

(a) the methods used to account for derivative financial instruments, the types of derivative financial instruments accounted for under each method and the criteria that determine the method used;

(b) the basis for recognising, measuring (both on initial recognition and subsequently), and ceasing to recognise financial assets and liabilities;

(c) how income and expenses (and other gains and losses) are recognised and measured;

(d) the treatment of financial assets and financial liabilities not recognised, including an explanation of how provisions for losses on such items are recognised; and

(e) policies on offsetting.[45]

It is also suggested that these further policies may be relevant where financial instruments are carried on a historical cost basis:

(a) the treatment of premiums and discounts on financial assets;

(b) the treatment of changes in the estimated amount of determinable future cash flows associated with a financial instrument, such as a debenture indexed to a commodity price;

(c) the treatment of a fall in the fair value of a financial asset below its carrying amount; and

(d) the treatment of restructured financial liabilities.[46]

Where hedge accounting has been applied, yet more detailed policies are suggested:

(a) the circumstances in which a financial instrument is accounted for as a hedge;

(b) the recognition and measurement treatment applied to the instrument;

(c) the method used to account for an instrument that ceases to be accounted for as a hedge;

(d) the method used to account for the hedge when the underlying item or position matures, is sold, extinguished or terminated; and

(e) the method used to account for the hedge of a future transaction when that transaction is no longer likely to occur.[47]

The above list goes far beyond the level of detail which had in the past been disclosed by most companies, although it should be emphasised that the standard is only suggesting that they should be included where the choice of policy has had a material impact on the accounts. Indeed many companies have not had an accounting policy note devoted to financial instruments or derivatives at all. Examples of the sort of accounting policies which companies are now disclosing in this area are shown in the following extracts:

Extract 10.5: Johnson Matthey plc (2001)

Accounting Policies [extract]

Financial Instruments: The group uses financial instruments, in particular forward currency contracts and currency swaps, to manage the financial risks associated with the group's underlying business activities and the financing of those activities. The group does not undertake any trading activity in financial instruments.

A discussion of how the group manages its financial risks is included in the Financial Review on page 10. Financial instruments are accounted for as follows:

- Forward exchange contracts are used to hedge foreign exchange exposures arising on forecast receipts and payments in foreign currencies. These forward contracts are revalued to the rates of exchange at the balance sheet date and any aggregate unrealised gains and losses arising on revaluation are included in other debtors / other creditors. At maturity, or when the contract ceases to be a hedge, gains and losses are taken to the profit and loss account.
- Currency options are occasionally used to hedge foreign exchange exposures, usually when the forecast receipt or payment amounts are uncertain. Option premia are recognised at their historic cost in the group balance sheet as prepayments. At maturity, or upon exercise, the option premia net of any realised gains on exercise are taken to the profit and loss accounts.
- Interest rate swaps are occasionally used to hedge the group's exposure to movements on interest rates. The interest payable or receivable on such swaps is accrued in the same way as interest arising on deposits or borrowings. Interest rate swaps are not revalued to fair value prior to maturity.
- Currency swaps are used as balance sheet hedging instruments to hedge foreign currency assets and borrowings. Currency swaps are used to reduce costs and credit exposure where the group would otherwise have cash deposits and borrowings in different currencies. The difference between spot and forward rate for these contracts is recognised as part of the net interest payable over the period of the contract. These swaps are revalued to the rates of exchange at the balance sheet date and any aggregate unrealised gains or losses arising on revaluation are included in other debtors / other creditors. Realised gains and losses on these currency swaps are taken to reserves in the same way as for the foreign investments and borrowings to which the swaps relate.

The aggregate fair values at the balance sheet date of the hedging instruments described above are disclosed as a note on the accounts.

The group has taken advantage of the exemption available for short term debtors and creditors.

Extract 10.6: Cable and Wireless plc (2001)

Statement of accounting policies [extract]
Derivatives

Swaps and forward rate agreements

The net interest paid or received under interest rate and cross currency swaps and forward rate agreements (FRAs) is recorded on an accruals basis and included within net interest in the profit and loss account.

The notional amounts of interest rate swaps and FRAs are recorded off balance sheet. Cross currency swaps are used to hedge the initial draw down and final repayment of currency denominated debt, as well as the currency interest flows.

Forward exchange contracts

Forward exchange contracts are carried on balance sheet at the difference between the amounts of the payable and receivable currency revalued at the closing exchange rate. The interest differential, being the difference between the contract rate and the spot rate on the date of entering into the forward exchange contract, is charged to the profit and loss account as interest over the life of the contract.

Exchange gains and losses

Exchange gains and losses on revaluation and maturity of forward exchange contracts are treated differently depending on the underlying exposure they hedge:

- for contracts which hedge firm third party commitments the exchange gains and losses are recognised in the profit and loss account in the same period as the underlying transaction;
- for contracts over underlying currency assets or liabilities exchange gains and losses are off-set against the equal and opposite exchange gains or losses arising on the retranslation of the underlying assets or liabilities;
- for contracts taken out to hedge overseas equity investments the exchange gains and losses are taken to reserves to off-set against the exchange differences arising on the retranslation of the net assets of the investments on consolidation;
- for contracts which hedge general trading flows the exchange gains or losses are taken to the profit and loss account in the period they arise.

Where the underlying exposure changes, or ceases to exist, the contract would be terminated and the exchange gain or loss arising taken to the profit and loss account.

Extract 10.7: British Telecommunications plc (2001)

Accounting policies [extract]

XV Financial instruments

(a) Debt instruments

Debt instruments are stated at the amount of net proceeds adjusted to amortise any discount evenly over the term of the debt, and further adjusted for the effect of currency swaps acting as hedges.

(b) Derivative financial instruments

The group uses derivative financial instruments to reduce exposure to foreign exchange risks and interest rate movements. The group does not hold or issue derivative financial instruments for financial trading purposes.

Criteria to qualify for hedge accounting

The group considers its derivative financial instruments to be hedges when certain criteria are met. For foreign currency derivatives, the instrument must be related to actual foreign currency assets or liabilities or a probable commitment and whose characteristics have been identified. It must involve the same currency or similar currencies as the hedged item and must also reduce the risk of foreign currency exchange movements on the group's operations. For interest rate derivatives, the instrument must be related to assets or liabilities or a probable commitment, such as a future bond issue, and must also change the interest rate or the nature of the interest rate by converting a fixed rate to a variable rate or vice versa.

Accounting for derivative financial instruments

Principal amounts underlying currency swaps are revalued at exchange rates ruling at the date of the group balance sheet and, to the extent that they are not related to debt instruments, are included in debtors or creditors.

Interest differentials, under interest rate swap agreements used to vary the amounts and periods for which interest rates on borrowings are fixed, are recognised by adjustment of interest payable.

The forward exchange contracts used to change the currency mix of net debt are revalued to balance sheet rates with net unrealised gains and losses being shown as part of debtors, creditors, or as part of net debt. The difference between spot and forward rate for these contracts is recognised as part of net interest payable over the term of the contract.

The forward exchange contracts hedging transaction exposures are revalued at the prevailing forward rate on the balance sheet date with net unrealised gains and losses being shown as debtors and creditors.

Instruments that form hedges against future fixed-rate bond issues are marked to market. Gains or losses are deferred until the bond is issued when they are recognised evenly over the term of the bond.

2.5 Numerical disclosures by entities that are not financial institutions

FRS 13 requires various numerical disclosures which are to be given in the accounts. These disclosures are intended to be highly summarised. One effect of this is that it may not be possible for the components to be traced back to their respective balance sheet captions. Where this is the case, the standard encourages provision of additional detail to enable the figures to be traced back unless it would unduly complicate the disclosure.[48]

The following are the main numerical disclosures required by the standard:

- interest rate risk disclosures;
- currency risk disclosures;
- liquidity disclosures; and
- fair value disclosures.

There are also further numerical disclosures for particular types of financial instruments:

- those used as hedges;
- those held or used for trading; and
- commodity contracts treated as financial instruments.

Each of these requirements is discussed below.

2.6 Interest rate risk disclosures

The standard requires information on interest rate risks for both financial liabilities (not just borrowings) and financial assets. Information is only required for the latter where an entity has a significant holding of financial assets.[49] For most companies, information will only be necessary for their financial liabilities. The specific information which is called for is as follows:

(a) An analysis of the aggregate carrying amount of financial liabilities by principal currency, further subdivided between:

   (i) those at fixed interest rates,

   (ii) those at floating interest rates, and

   (iii) those on which no interest is paid.[50]

   For the purpose of this analysis, floating rate financial liabilities are those that attract an interest charge and have their interest reset at least once a year.[51] Those that are reset less frequently are to be treated as fixed rate financial liabilities. It is unclear how the third category is to be interpreted. Is it to include items which involve no interest payments, but into which interest is imputed for accounting purposes? The standard states that finance lease obligations, and deep discounted bonds and similar liabilities whose finance costs are allocated in accordance with FRS 4, do not fall within this category.[52] However, it is silent on other items such as deferred consideration or long-term monetary provisions wherever they are discounted. One interpretation is that where the financial liability stems from a transaction that will implicitly have considered the time value of money (such as deferred consideration) the liability should be classified as fixed rate, along with deep discounted bonds and finance lease obligations. But in other cases, such as a provision for the onerous rentals on a vacant property where there is no implicit interest in the rentals, the provision should be treated as one on which no interest is paid.

This analysis is after taking account of interest rate swaps, currency swaps, forward contracts and other derivatives whose effect is to 'alter' the interest basis or currency of the financial liabilities (it is noteworthy that the ASB has chosen to avoid the word 'hedge' in this context).[53] For example, if a company has taken out a currency swap in respect of US$ borrowings to effectively convert the liability into sterling, then for the purposes of this analysis the borrowing should be treated as a sterling liability.

The analysis is to be shown on a gross basis (i.e. without netting off cash and liquid resources or similar items). However, if entities wish to provide the information on a net basis they can do so as long as the gross position is also shown.[54]

(b) The above analysis should exclude the effect of financial liabilities and other derivative instruments that cannot be adequately reflected in it. These are likely to include interest rate caps, collars and floors and instruments that incorporate an option to exercise. Instead, a summary should be provided of the main effects of such instruments. This might include such elements as the notional principal amounts involved, the rates of interest, the period for which the instrument is operative and the terms of any options contained within the instrument.[55]

(c) For the fixed rate liabilities, the weighted average interest rate and weighted average period for which rates are fixed are both to be disclosed, again analysed by principal currency.

(d) For the floating rate liabilities, the benchmark rate (such as LIBOR) for determining interest payments is to be given, again by principal currency. Although the standard does not require disclosure of the particular margin over that rate that is payable, it emphasises that it may need to be given in order to comply with companies legislation.

(e) For the liabilities on which no interest is paid, the weighted average period until maturity, again analysed by currency.[56]

The first two illustrations within Appendix III to the standard provide examples of these disclosures. Examples of how companies are presenting the required information are given in the extracts below:

Extract 10.8: Johnson Matthey plc (2001)

19 Financial risk management [extract]

19a Interest rate risk

Financial liabilities	2001 At fixed interest rates £ million	2001 At floating interest rates £ million	2001 Total £ million	2000 At fixed interest rates £ million	2000 At floating interest rates £ million	2000 Total £ million
Sterling	–	–	–	–	2.1	2.1
US dollar	71.0	7.3	78.3	62.7	39.6	102.3
Japanese yen	–	17.9	17.9	–	9.2	9.2
Euro	–	4.9	4.9	–	6.0	6.0
Malaysian ringgit	–	8.1	8.1	–	6.0	6.0
Australian dollar	–	4.0	4.0	–	5.5	5.5
Other currencies	–	3.2	3.2	–	1.2	1.2
	71.0	45.4	116.4	62.7	69.6	132.3

Fixed rate financial liabilities	2001 Weighted average interest rates %	2001 Weighted average period for which rates are fixed Years	2000 Weighted average interest rates %	2000 Weighted average period for which rates are fixed Years
US dollar	6.38	5	6.36	6

The financial liabilities of the group comprised:	2001 £ million	2000 £ million
Total borrowings and finance leases	97.5	116.2
Borrowings generated by swaps	17.9	15.9
Other creditors falling due after more than one year	1.0	0.2
	116.4	132.3

Floating rate financial liabilities comprise bank borrowings and overdrafts bearing interest at commercial rates.

Financial assets	2001 At floating interest rates £ million	2001 Interest free £ million	2001 Total £ million	2000 At floating Interest rates £ million	2000 Interest free £ million	2000 Total £ million
Sterling	205.0	–	205.0	251.7	–	251.7
US dollar	8.1	–	8.1	–	–	–
Japanese yen	–	–	–	2.1	–	2.1
Euro	17.1	–	17.1	10.2	–	10.2
Malaysian ringgit	1.3	–	1.3	0.8	–	0.8
Australian dollar	1.1	–	1.1	–	–	–
Hong Kong dollar	14.5	–	14.5	24.2	–	24.2
Other currencies	8.2	2.4	10.6	9.1	2.8	11.9
	255.3	2.4	257.7	298.1	2.8	300.9

The financial assets of the group comprised:	2001 £ million	2000 £ million
Cash and deposits	237.4	282.0
Deposits generated by swaps	17.9	15.9
Debtors due after more than one year (excluding prepaid pensions)	–	0.2
Investments listed on overseas stock exchanges	2.4	2.8
	257.7	300.9

Floating rate financial assets comprise bank deposits bearing interest at commercial rates. Interest free financial assets are shares held in two publicly quoted companies, Ballard Power Systems, Inc. and AnorMED Inc.

Extract 10.9: British Telecommunications plc (2001)

35. Financial instruments and risk management [extract]
Financial liabilities

After taking into account the various interest rate swaps and forward foreign currency contracts entered into by the group, the interest rate profile of the group's financial liabilities at 31 March was:

				2001
	Fixed rate financial liabilities £m	**Floating rate financial liabilities £m**	**Financial liabilities on which no interest is paid £m**	**Total £m**
Currency:				
Sterling	**13,501**	**10,528**	**357**	**24,386**
US dollar	**806**	**145**	**293**	**1,244**
Euro	**4,759**	**664**	**72**	**5,495**
Yen	**508**	**–**	**–**	**508**
Other	**–**	**–**	**–**	**–**
Total	**19,574**	**11,337**	**722**	**31,633**

				2000
	Fixed rate financial liabilities £m	Floating rate financial liabilities £m	Financial liabilities on which no interest is paid £m	Total £m
Currency:				
Sterling	2,429	6,686	376	9,491
US dollar	353	83	7	443
Euro	424	389	30	843
Yen	508	–	1	509
Other	–	111	4	115
Total	3,714	7,269	418	11,401

For the fixed rate financial liabilities, the average interest rates and the average periods for which the rates are fixed are:

	2001		2000	
	Weighted average interest rate %	**Weighted average period for which rate is fixed Years**	Weighted average interest rate %	Weighted average period for which rate is fixed Years
Currency:				
Sterling	**7.5**	**16**	9.1	15
US dollar	**8.5**	**7**	8.7	8
Euro	**6.3**	**6**	5.8	8
Yen	**1.2**	**4**	1.2	4
Total	**7.1**	**13**	7.6	12

The floating rate financial liabilities bear interest at rates fixed in advance for periods ranging from one day to one year by reference to LIBOR. The financial liabilities on which no interest is paid are due to mature within one year of the balance sheet date.

The maturity profile of financial liabilities is as given in note 23.

Financial assets

After taking into account the various interest rate swaps and forward foreign currency contracts entered into by the group, the interest rate profile of the group's financial assets at 31 March was:

				2001
	Fixed rate financial assets £m	**Floating rate financial assets £m**	**Financial assets on which no interest is paid £m**	**Total £m**
Currency:				
Sterling	**56**	**2,935**	**306**	**3,297**
US dollar	**–**	**293**	**–**	**293**
Euro	**19**	**315**	**–**	**334**
Other	**–**	**27**	**–**	**27**
Total	**75**	**3,570**	**306**	**3,951**

				2000
	Fixed rate financial assets £m	Floating rate financial assets £m	Financial assets on which no interest is paid £m	Total £m
Currency:				
Sterling	395	2,869	265	3,529
US dollar	–	31	–	31
Euro	–	53	–	53
Other	–	29	–	29
Total	395	2,982	265	3,642

The sterling fixed rate financial assets yield interest at a weighted average of 6.3% (2000 – 6.6%) for a weighted average period of 30 months (2000 – 18 months).

The floating rate financial assets bear interest at rates fixed in advance for periods up to one year by reference to LIBOR.

Extract 10.10: Pilkington plc (2001)

27 Analysis of financial liabilities and assets [extract]

(a) Financial liabilities

An analysis of interest bearing financial liabilities is set out below. This analysis excludes non-interest bearing creditors of £2 million (2000 £4 million) and non-interest bearing provisions of a contractual nature totalling £44 million (2000 £45 million):

2001

	Total	**Floating rate financial liabilities**	**Fixed rate financial liabilities**	**Fixed rate financial liabilities-weighted average interest rate**	**Weighted average period for which rate is fixed**
	£m	**£m**	**£m**	**%**	**Months**
Currency					
Sterling	**38**	**38**	**–**	**–**	**–**
US dollar	**96**	**(96)**	**192**	**9.14**	**76**
Euro	**390**	**205**	**185**	**4.86**	**35**
Australian dollar	**46**	**44**	**2**	**6.73**	**42**
Swedish kroner	**82**	**53**	**29**	**4.90**	**57**
Polish zloty	**36**	**8**	**28**	**12.75**	**57**
Argentinian peso	**39**	**39**	**–**	**–**	**–**
Other currencies	**16**	**16**	**–**	**–**	**–**
Financial liabilities excluding non-equity shares	**743**	**307**	**436**	**7.26**	**56**
Non-equity minority shares	**240**	**218**	**22**	**3.54**	
	983	**525**	**458**	**7.08**	**56**

2000

	Total	Floating rate financial liabilities	Fixed rate financial liabilities	Fixed rate financial liabilities-weighted average interest rate	Weighted average period for which rate is fixed
	£m	£m	£m	%	Months
Currency					
Sterling	121	121	–	–	–
US dollar	90	(42)	132	9.26	88
Euro	281	55	226	4.70	34
Australian dollar	26	23	3	6.73	54
Swedish kroner	78	78	–	–	–
Polish zloty	25	25	–	–	–
Argentinian peso	15	15	–	–	–
Other currencies	26	26	–	–	–
Financial liabilities excluding non-equity shares	662	301	361	6.39	54
Non-equity minority shares	219	197	22	3.54	
	881	498	383	6.23	54

The disclosures made in notes 27 and 28 should be read in conjunction with the finance and liquidity, treasury and hedging policies and currency and interest rate risk sections of the Financial Review on pages 16 and 17.

Floating rates are based on LIBOR and EURIBOR.

The financial liabilities include non-equity minority interests of £218 million, which relate to the preference shareholders in Pilkington Channel Islands Limited, who have a right to a fixed dividend of 6.55% per annum, fixed for 23 months. This fixed dividend has been swapped into floating rate using financial instruments. These preference shares can be redeemed after 4th March 2003. The remaining non-equity minority shares of £22 million relate to Pilkington Deutschland AG and Dahlbusch AG with rights to a dividend of 3.65% and 3.09% respectively. These rates remain fixed in perpetuity and, in consequence, the average periods for which the rates are fixed are excluded from the figures noted in the above table.

As indicated earlier, if an entity has significant holdings of financial assets it should give similar analyses to those described above in relation to financial liabilities. Included within such financial assets may be investments in equity shares and other instruments that neither pay interest nor have a maturity rate. The standard therefore indicates that the disclosures will typically be limited to information about the currency exposures involved.[57] Although this is of some relevance, the major risks of equity shares and similar investments are more likely to be attributable to the businesses they are in than their currency exposure.

2.7 Currency risk disclosures

The next analysis required by FRS 13 is an analysis of the net monetary assets and liabilities at the balance sheet date, by reference to the principal functional currency of operations, showing the amount denominated in each principal currency.[58] The purpose of this analysis is to explain the currency exposures that give rise to exchange gains or losses which are taken to the profit and loss account under SSAP 20.[59] Accordingly, assets and liabilities denominated in the same currency as the functional currency of operations are excluded from the analysis, as are any foreign currency borrowings that are treated as a hedge against foreign net investments under SSAP 20.[60]

Like the interest rate risk disclosures discussed above, this analysis is also after taking account of currency swaps, forward contracts and other derivative financial instruments that contribute to the matching of the foreign currency exposures (again, it is noteworthy that the ASB has chosen to avoid the word 'hedge' in this context).[61] For example, if a company has taken out a forward contract in respect of DM debtors to effectively convert the amounts receivable into sterling, then for the purposes of this analysis the debtors should be treated as a sterling asset.

Although not specifically mentioned in the standard, it would seem that derivatives such as currency options should be excluded from the analysis. This is because the standard also requires disclosure of a summary of the main effect of any derivative financial instruments that are not so included.

Clearly, in order to meet this disclosure requirement reporting entities have to collate the underlying information, which may be no easy task. This is the sort of information which prior to FRS 13 companies had not usually disclosed.

Illustration 2 in Appendix III to the standard provides an example of this disclosure. Some examples of what companies are reporting in practice are given in the extracts below:

Extract 10.11: Volex Group p.l.c. (2001)

22 Derivatives and other financial instruments [extract]

b. Currency exposures

As explained on page 17 of the Financial Review, the Group's objectives in managing its structural currency exposures arising from its net investment overseas are to maintain a low cost of borrowings whilst partially hedging against currency depreciation. Gains and losses arising from these structural currency exposures are recognised in the statement of total recognised gains and losses. The Group does not hedge directly the translation exposure of the profit and loss account whether by use of options or other derivatives.

The table below shows the Group's currency exposures, in other words, those transactional exposures that give rise to the net currency gains and losses recognised in the profit and loss account. Such exposures comprise the monetary assets and monetary liabilities of the Group that are not denominated in the operating currency of the operating unit involved, other than certain non-sterling borrowings treated as hedges of net investment in overseas operations. As at 31 March 2001 these exposures were as follows:

Functional currency of Group operation	Net foreign currency monetary assets (liabilities)*						
	Sterling £'000	US dollar £'000	Irish Punt £'000	Euro £'000	HK dollar £'000	CH Rmb £'000	Total £'000
Sterling	–	1,250	241	35	–	–	1,526
Irish punt	(11)	(251)	–	3,703	–	–	3,441
Singapore dollar	(226)	5,055	–	–	(314)	3,995	8,510
Total	(237)	6,054	241	3,738	(314)	3,995	13,477

* comprising net trade debtors and creditors.

The exposures at 31 March 2000 for comparison purposes were as follows:-

Functional currency of Group operation	Net foreign currency monetary assets (liabilities)*					
	Sterling £'000	US dollar £'000	Euro £'000	HK dollar £'000	CH Rmb £'000	Total £'000
Sterling	–	1,811	46	–	–	1,857
Irish punt	(1,692)	930	2,335	–	–	1,573
Singapore dollar	(711)	(629)	–	(427)	2,754	987
Total	(2,403)	2,112	2,381	(427)	2,754	4,417

* comprising net trade debtors and creditors.

The amounts shown in the tables above take into account the effect of any derivatives (including forward contracts) entered into to [illegible] [illegible] currency [illegible]

Extract 10.12: Cable and Wireless plc (2001)

25 Financial instruments [extract]
Exchange risk management

The following table shows the Group's currency exposures at 31 March on currency transactions that give rise to the net currency gains and losses recognised in the profit and loss account. Such exposures comprise the monetary assets and liabilities of the Group that are not denominated in the functional currency of the operating company involved, other than certain non-sterling borrowings treated as hedges of net investments in overseas companies.

	Net foreign currency monetary assets/(liabilities) in £m							
	2001				2000			
Functional currency of the operating company	US$	Sterling	Other	Total	US$	HK$	Other	Total
Sterling	131	–	(14)	**117**	(8)	7	(4)	(5)
US$	–	(41)	2	**(39)**	–	–	–	–
Yen	13	–	(20)	**(7)**	(8)	–	(11)	(19)
HK$	–	–	–	**–**	1,333	–	31	1,364
Other	(387)	–	(5)	**(392)**	(147)	1	(80)	(226)
	(243)	(41)	(37)	**(321)**	1,170	8	(64)	1,114

The amounts shown in the table above take into account the effect of any cross currency swaps, forward exchange contracts and other derivatives entered into to manage these currency exposures.

FRED 13 originally proposed further currency disclosures which were aimed at showing the currency exposures which gave rise to exchange differences taken directly to reserves under SSAP 20. It tried to do this by suggesting disclosure of a currency analysis of net assets compared to borrowings. This proposed requirement was dropped in the standard for non-financial entities, although a variant of the requirement was retained for banks (see 3.1.2 below). In February 1999 the ASB released an Exposure Draft[62] which was intended to introduce the disclosure as a modification to SSAP 20. However, in May 1999 it announced that it would not be proceeding with the amendment in advance of a review of SSAP 20 as a whole.[63]

2.8 Liquidity disclosures

The next category of numerical disclosures relates to liquidity risk. First, the standard requires entities to disclose a maturity profile of the carrying amount of financial liabilities, showing the amounts falling due:

- in 1 year or less, or on demand;
- in more than 1 year but not more than 2 years;
- in more than 2 years but not more than 5 years; and
- in more than 5 years.

This maturity profile is to be determined by reference to the earliest date on which payment can be required or on which the liability falls due.[64] This is the same as the equivalent rule within FRS 4 and the companies legislation in relation to loans.

This disclosure is similar to the existing requirement of FRS 4 to give a maturity analysis of debt and that of SSAP 21 in relation to finance lease obligations, but it is not quite the same.

The time bands are slightly different from those originally in FRS 4, therefore a corresponding amendment was made to that standard.[65] The effect of this amendment is that any amount which is due exactly 5 years after the balance sheet date now falls within the third band rather than the fourth band. Also, amounts due exactly 2 years after the balance sheet date now fall within the second band, whereas previously it was possible for such an amount to be included in the third band.

It is noted in FRS 13 that in order to provide the disclosures required, the maturity analyses already provided in FRS 4 and SSAP 21 could be brought together. However, if this is done the information needs to be extended to provide further analysis of finance lease obligations showing the split between the second and third bands. Also it will be necessary for the disclosures to include any financial liabilities, other than debt and finance lease obligations; this would include any creditors due after more than one year and any monetary provisions which are expected to be paid after more than one year.[66]

The standard also notes that the analysis of debt and finance lease obligations for this purpose needs to be based on the carrying amount, not on the amounts to be paid on maturity.[67] Accordingly, if companies have traditionally given the maturity analysis of their finance lease obligations by showing the rentals payable in each of the relevant periods and then deducting the aggregate finance charges to reconcile to the carrying amounts of the obligations in the balance sheet, they will need to revise their treatment if they wish to combine all of the disclosures within one table.

In addition, FRS 13 asks for disclosure of a maturity analysis of any material committed but undrawn borrowing facilities. This is similar to the maturity analysis described above, but only requires a distinction between those expiring:

- in 1 year or less;
- in more than 1 year but not more than 2 years; and
- in more than 2 years.

Facilities should only be included in the above analysis if all conditions precedent attached to the facility were satisfied at the balance sheet date.[68]

The standard suggests that this disclosure might also go on to explain the purpose and period for which the facilities are committed and whether they are subject to annual review.[69]

Paragraph 41 of the standard indicates that where the maturity analysis of debt under FRS 4 takes into account committed borrowing facilities, then to avoid double-counting, such facilities should not be included within this disclosure. This could be interpreted as meaning none of the facilities are to be disclosed. However, we believe the excess of the facilities over the amount taken into account should be disclosed.

The Review Panel has made it clear that the standard provides no exemption from disclosure of this information on the grounds of commercial sensitivity.[70]

An example of the disclosure is given in the extract below:

Extract 10.13: Pilkington plc (2001)

28 Financial instrument disclosures [extract]

(b) Borrowing facilities

The Group has various available borrowing facilities. The undrawn committed facilities available in respect of which all conditions precedent had been met at 31st March 2001, were as follows:

	2001	2000
	£m	£m
Expiring in one year or less	**–**	31
Expiring in more than two years	**186**	338
	186	369

The standard also suggests that some companies might wish to produce a maturity analysis of financial assets 'in order to show the maturity analyses of financial liabilities and borrowing facilities in their proper context'.[71]

2.9 Fair values

As with some of the other disclosure requirements of FRS 13, this requirement reflects the ASB's views as to the eventual measurement rules for financial instruments. Although those who do not necessarily agree that it is appropriate to carry all instruments at fair value may not be persuaded about the relevance of disclosing such values, nevertheless such information must now be given.

The requirement is for an entity to group its financial assets and liabilities, including amounts not recognised in the balance sheet, into appropriate categories and for each category to disclose either:

- the aggregate fair value at the balance sheet date compared to the aggregate book value; or
- the aggregate fair value of those financial instruments at the balance sheet date with a positive fair value and, separately, those with a negative fair value, compared to the book amounts.[72]

FRED 13 only proposed the former type of disclosure, but a number of commentators suggested the latter form of disclosure and as the ASB believed that the arguments involved were evenly balanced, the standard permits a choice. However, the standard warns that if a subsequent FRS requires most or all financial instruments to be carried on the balance sheet at fair value, systems capable of producing the latter type of disclosure would then be required.[73]

The exposure draft had also proposed that those financial assets and liabilities that are not traded on organised markets in a standard form were to be shown separately, but this has been dropped from the standard.

The first stage in giving these disclosures is to determine the appropriate categories. The standard is not prescriptive about how this should be done, but suggests that the classification should take account of the nature of the item and the purpose for which it is held. This should tie in with the discussion of the use of these instruments given in the narrative disclosures (see 2.2 above). One categorisation might be between items used for financing, risk management or hedging, and trading or speculation. However, the standard then suggests that these categories should be analysed in more detail; for example, with interest rate swaps shown separately from currency swaps, and separate disclosure of optional derivatives, such as currency options and interest collars and caps. It is also suggested that financial assets would not be included in the same sub-category as financial liabilities.[74] (This would be necessary if entities wished the components to be traced back to the respective balance sheet captions as discussed at 2.5 above.) It may be that for this purpose similar derivative financial instruments held or issued for the same purpose would be grouped together, regardless of whether their fair value was positive or negative, although clearly this could only be done if the former method of disclosure was being followed.

The next stage in the process is to determine the fair values to be disclosed. Fair value is defined in the usual manner as 'the amount at which an asset or liability could be exchanged in an arm's length transaction between informed and willing parties, other than in a forced or liquidation sale'.[75] Guidance on procedures for estimating the fair value of financial assets and financial liabilities is set out in Appendix IV to the standard. Where quoted market prices are available, these should generally be used. Where quoted market prices are not available or may not be indicative of the fair value due to infrequent activity in a market, then fair values might be estimated by using discounted cash flow techniques or option-pricing models.

For some financial assets and liabilities the estimated difference between the carrying amount and its fair value may not be material, in which case the carrying amount may be used as the fair value for the purposes of the disclosure.[76] This is likely to be the case with any floating rate debt and could also apply to cash on short-term deposit. Where an entity decides to include short-term debtors and creditors within its disclosures, then this is also likely to be appropriate for such items.

The methods and any significant assumptions used in determining the fair values have to be disclosed.[77] This applies in all cases, not just in those situations where fair values have had to be estimated in the absence of quoted market prices, or such prices were not considered indicative of fair value.

If it is not practicable to estimate with sufficient reliability the fair values of items that are not traded on an organised market in a standard form, it is permissible instead to disclose a description of such items, their book values, the reasons why estimating their value is impracticable, and information about the main characteristics that affect their value and the market for such instruments. If the directors consider the disclosure of this last item would be seriously prejudicial, then it can be omitted but that fact and the reasons for doing so need to be stated. However, disclosure of all of this information is not meant to be an easy loophole to avoid disclosure of the fair value – FRS 13 makes it clear that this alternative is only available in rather extreme circumstances and that the entity should have exhausted all viable methods of estimating and disclosing the information, e.g. by disclosing a range of values.[78]

Some examples of the disclosures companies are giving in practice are set out below:

Extract 10.14: National Grid Group plc (2001)

19 Financial instruments [extract]
Fair values of financial instruments at 31 March

	2001		2000	
	Book value £m	Fair value £m	Book value £m	Fair value £m
6% mandatorily exchangeable bonds 2003	**(242.6)**	**(196.7)**	(242.6)	(391.6)
Other short term debt	**(766.1)**	**(768.7)**	(426.4)	(413.5)
Exchangeable bonds 2008	**(480.3)**	**(627.7)**	(469.0)	(654.6)
Other long term debt	**(2,700.4)**	**(2,704.8)**	(2,537.2)	(2,533.4)
Total borrowings	**(4,189.4)**	**(4,297.9)**	(3,675.2)	(3,993.1)
Cash and deposits	**271.2**	**271.2**	1,011.6	1,011.6
Net borrowings	**(3,918.2)**	**(4,026.7)**	(2,663.6)	(2,981.5)
Other financial liabilities(i)	**(519.9)**	**(516.3)**	(428.0)	(426.3)
Net investment in finance lease	**48.9**	**56.0**	52.3	60.6
Assets held for exchange	**16.6**	**205.1**	16.6	429.7
Other financial assets (ii)	**43.5**	**44.8**	149.7	149.7
Net financial liabilities (i),(ii)	**(4,329.1)**	**(4,237.1)**	(2,873.0)	(2,767.8)
Financial instruments held to manage interest rate and currency profile:				
Interest rate swaps	**(2.9)**	**(40.4)**	(2.4)	6.1
Forward foreign currency contracts and cross currency swaps	**(169.8)**	**(250.1)**	21.0	(1.2)
Cross currency option	**–**	**–**	(11.1)	(10.1)

(i) Excluding interest rate swaps £2.9m (2000: £2.4m), forward currency contracts £3.4m (2000: £0.2m), cross currency swaps £166.4m (2000: £nil) and cross currency option £nil (2000: £11.1m).

(ii) Excluding cross currency swaps £nil (2000: £21.2m).

Market values, where available, have been used to determine fair values. Where market values are not available, fair values have been calculated by discounting cash flows at prevailing interest rates.

Extract 10.15: Cable and Wireless plc (2001)

25 Financial instruments [extract]

Fair value

The estimated fair value of the Group's financial instruments are summarised below:

		2001		2000	
		Carrying amount £m	Estimated fair value £m	Carrying amount £m	Estimated fair value £m
Primary financial instruments held or issued to finance the Group's operations					
Trade investments (excluding ESOP shares)		**90**	**90**	112	112
Cash		**285**	**285**	421	421
Short term deposits		**4,938**	**4,938**	4,567	4,567
Current asset investments		**2,344**	**2,344**	9	9
Net investment in finance lease receivables		**25**	**25**	66	66
Loans and obligations under finance leases due within one year		**(567)**	**(567)**	(761)	(761)
Convertible bonds		**–**	**–**	(37)	(204)
Other loans and obligations under finance leases due after more than one year		**(2,364)**	**(2,570)**	(5,447)	(5,828)
Derivative financial instruments held to manage interest rate and currency exposure					
Forward rate agreement, interest rate swaps	– assets	–	**7**	–	25
	– (liabilities)	–	**(15)**	–	(6)
Cross currency swaps	– assets	–	**239**	–	11
	– (liabilities)	–	**(51)**	–	(134)
Forward exchange contracts		**10**	**10**	(17)	(17)

Trade investments
Trade investments above are detailed in note 16 but exclude ESOP shares carried at £27m (2000 – £14m). The fair value is based on year end quoted prices for listed investments and estimates of likely sales proceeds for other investments.

Current asset investments
The fair value is based on market value or estimates of likely sales proceeds.

Cash at bank and in hand, short term deposits and short term borrowings
The carrying value approximates to fair value either because of the short maturity of the instruments or because the interest rate on investments is reset after periods not greater than six months.

Convertible bonds and other long term debt
The fair value is based on quoted market prices or, where these are not available, on the quoted market prices of comparable debt issued by other companies.

Forward agreements, interest rate and cross currency swaps
The fair value of forward rate agreements, interest rate and cross currency swaps is the estimated amount which the Group would expect to pay or receive were it to terminate the swaps at the balance sheet date. This is based on quotations from counterparties and takes into consideration current interest rates, current exchange rates and the current creditworthiness of the counterparties. The nominal value of swaps at 31 March 2001 was £7,226m (2000 – £6,906m).

Forward exchange contracts
The value of these contracts is the estimated amount which the Group would expect to pay or receive on the termination of the contracts. At 31 March 2001 the Group had £193m of such contracts outstanding (2000 – £746m).

Extract 10.16: The British Land Company PLC (2001)

16 Net debt [extract]

Comparison of market values and book values at 31 March 2001

	Market Value £m	Book Value £m	**Difference £m**
Fixed rate debt:			
Securitised debt	1,658.0	1,579.2	**78.8**
Unsecured bonds (2016 and 2023)	407.1	401.5	**5.6**
Other fixed rate debt	698.4	576.1	**122.3**
Convertible debt	492.5	463.9	**28.6**
Bank debt (net)	800.0	800.0	
Derivatives	(23.6)	(20.3)	**(3.3)**
Total*	4,032.4	3,800.4	**232.0**

*This includes the accrual of £83.6m for the premium payable (net of the profit on the close out of associated derivatives of £20.3m) on the repurchase of the unsecured bonds (£150m 12.5% Bonds 2016 and the £150m 8.875% Bonds 2023) which has been included in the accounts for the year to 31 March 2001. (See note 5).

The Market Value and Difference are shown before any tax relief. The difference between book value and market value on the convertibles arises principally from the British Land share price.

In accordance with Accounting Standards the book value of debt is par value net of amortised issue costs. Short term debtors and creditors have been excluded from the disclosures (other than the currency disclosures). The valuations of the Broadgate Notes have been undertaken by Morgan Stanley. The valuations of 135 Bishopsgate Securitisations 2018 have been undertaken by The Royal Bank of Scotland. The valuations of other fixed rate debt and convertible debt have been undertaken by UBS Warburg. The bank debt has been valued assuming it could be renegotiated at contracted margins. The derivatives have been valued by the independent treasury advisor Record Treasury Management.

2.10 Hedges

Many entities use financial assets and liabilities as hedges to manage their risk profile. A 'hedge' is not defined in FRS 13, but in the discussion of the narrative disclosures within the standard it regards a 'hedge' as 'an instrument that individually, or with other instruments, has a value or cash flow that is expected, wholly or partly, to move inversely with changes in the value or cash flows of the position being hedged'.[79] As explained in paragraph 58 of FRS 13, when instruments are used for hedging purposes, they are usually accounted for using hedge accounting whereby 'changes in fair values of the hedge (referred to hereafter as "the gain or loss on the hedge") are not recognised in the profit and loss account immediately they arise. Instead, they either are not recognised at all or are recognised and carried forward in the balance sheet; then, when the hedged transaction occurs, the gain or loss on the hedge is usually either used to adjust the amount at which the hedged item is dealt with in the financial statements or recognised in the profit and loss account at the same time as the hedged item.'

The ASB's distrust of hedge accounting is evident from the extent of the required disclosures where instruments have been accounted for as hedges. FRED 13 had proposed that these disclosures should only be in respect of hedges of future transactions, but they have now been extended to all hedges. However, the proposal in FRED 13 for separate disclosure of hedges of firm contracts and other hedges has been dropped.

The standard calls for disclosure of the following information about gains and losses on financial assets and financial liabilities for which hedge accounting has been used:

(a) the cumulative aggregate gains and cumulative aggregate losses that are unrecognised at the balance sheet date. If an item's fair value is not disclosed under the standard (see 2.9 above), any gain or loss on the item need not be included within this disclosure;

(b) the cumulative aggregate gains and losses carried forward in the balance sheet pending their recognition in the profit and loss account;

(c) the extent to which the gains and losses disclosed under (a) and (b) above are expected to be recognised in the profit and loss account of the following year; and

(d) the amount of gains and losses included in the current year's profit and loss account that arose in previous years but were brought forward to the current year as a hedge.[80]

The amounts disclosed under (b), (c) and (d) above should exclude any amounts which have been accounted for by adjusting the carrying amount of a fixed asset recognised in the balance sheet.[81] This exception has been allowed as a pragmatic response to the practical difficulties of keeping track of such gains and losses and their recognition in the profit and loss account as part of the depreciation charge on those assets.[82] However, the exception does not seem to apply to instruments taken out to hedge future purchases of fixed assets as these assets are not yet 'recognised on the balance sheet'. Thus, any 'gain or loss' on the instrument which is carried forward in the balance sheet should be included in the disclosures under (b). Any 'gain or loss' which is unrecognised at the balance sheet will need to be included under (a) since no exemption is given in respect of the disclosures under that sub-paragraph. As far as disclosure under (c) is concerned, arguably the impact of any such 'gains or losses' on the following year's depreciation charge should be included. We do not think that is appropriate because once the asset is purchased and included in the balance sheet, the 'gain or loss' is not to be included within the disclosures. However, we do not believe that is the only problem. If the 'gain or loss' is excluded from the disclosure under (c), users of the accounts might infer that the excess of the amounts disclosed under (a) and (b) over the amount shown under (c) are to be recognised in the profit and loss in later years. This problem will be exacerbated if entities follow the illustrations of these disclosures contained in Appendix III to the standard, which include a line for the gains and losses to be recognised in later years. We would therefore suggest that entities should indicate how much of the gains and losses disclosed under (a) and (b) relate to future fixed asset purchases.

As the exception is only made in respect of fixed assets, it would seem that where gains and losses have been recognised and have been accounted for as part of the cost of stock, then such gains and losses need to be included within the disclosures, even although there may be similar practical difficulties.

These requirements are worded in language that reflects the ASB's views on hedge accounting; in particular, they ask for the disclosure of 'gains' and 'losses' on financial assets and financial liabilities for which hedge accounting has been used. From the point of view of the companies who use them, however, these are not gains and losses at all, but simply constitute an element of the cost of the item being hedged, and there is a significant risk that the disclosures will be misinterpreted as a result.

The wording of the standard is also unclear as to whether what is required to be disclosed is the gains and losses on both hedging instrument and hedged item (where both are financial assets or financial liabilities for which hedge accounting has been used) or just those gains and losses on the hedging instrument. The UITF has subsequently clarified that it is just the gains and losses on the hedging instrument which have to be disclosed.[83]

Occasionally an entity may reclassify an instrument previously accounted for as a hedge. Where, as a consequence of such a reclassification during the year, gains or losses that arose in previous years and were deferred in the balance sheet or not recognised are now recognised in the current year's profit and loss account, then the amount of such gains and losses should be disclosed.[84] This should not be taken to mean that this is the most appropriate way that gains or losses should be dealt with. As the standard says, such reclassifications can be accounted for in different ways. We believe that in most circumstances the gains or losses up to the point of reclassification should continue to be deferred or not recognised, and recognised when the transaction it was originally intended to hedge takes place (see Chapter 17 at 2.2.6 A). Although the standard does not call for any specific disclosure where such gains and losses continue to be deferred or not recognised, we believe that they should continue to be incorporated within the disclosures set out above.

Examples of disclosures in respect of hedges are illustrated below:

Extract 10.17: Scottish Power plc (2001)

21 Loans and other borrowings [extract]

(h) Hedges

Gains and losses on instruments used for hedging are not recognised until the exposure that is being hedged is itself recognised. Unrecognised gains and losses on instruments used for hedging, and the movements therein, are as follows:

	Notes	Gains £m	Losses £m	Total net gains/ losses £m
Unrecognised gains and (losses) on hedges at 1 April 1999		10.7	(91.7)	(81.0)
Transfer from gains to losses	(i)	(4.6)	4.6	–
Transfer from losses to gains	(i)	(5.3)	5.3	–
Losses arising in previous years that were recognised in 1999-00		4.8	40.9	45.7
Gains and (losses) arising before 1 April 1999 that were not recognised in 1999-00		5.6	(40.9)	(35.3)
Gains and (losses) arising in 1999-00 that were not recognised in 1999-00		46.3	(43.2)	3.1
Unrecognised gains and (losses) on hedges at 31 March 2000		51.9	(84.1)	(32.2)

Gains and (losses) expected to be recognised in 2000-01		(3.5)	(21.8)	(25.3)
Gains and (losses) expected to be recognised in 2001-02 or later		55.4	(62.3)	(6.9)

(i) Figures in the table above are calculated by reference to the 31 March 2000 fair value of the derivative concerned.

	Notes	Gains £m	Losses £m	Total net gains/ losses £m
Unrecognised gains and (losses) on hedges at 1 April 2000		51.9	(84.1)	(32.2)
Transfer from gains to losses	(ii)	(5.8)	5.8	–
Transfer from losses to gains	(ii)	(4.5)	4.5	–
(Gains) and losses arising in previous years that were recognised in 2000-01		(20.6)	22.3	1.7
Gains and (losses) arising before 1 April 2000 that were not recognised in 2000-01		21.0	(51.5)	(30.5)
Gains and (losses) arising in 2000-01 that were not recognised in 2000-01		59.4	(64.1)	(4.7)
Unrecognised gains and (losses) on hedges at 31 March 2001		80.4	(115.6)	(35.2)
Gains and (losses) expected to be recognised in 2001-02		(1.6)	(14.1)	(15.7)
Gains and (losses) expected to be recognised in 2002-03 or later		82.0	(101.5)	(19.5)

(ii) Figures in the table above are calculated by reference to the 31 March 2001 fair value of the derivative concerned.

Extract 10.18: Cable and Wireless plc (2001)

25 Financial Instruments [extract]

Hedges

Gains and losses on instruments used for hedging are not recognised until the exposure that is being hedged is itself recognised. Unrecognised gains and losses on instruments used for hedging (excluding hedges that have been accounted for by adjusting the carrying value of a fixed asset recognised on the balance sheet), and on the underlying asset or liability, are as follows:

	Gains £m	(Losses) £m	Net gains/ (losses) £m
Unrecognised gains and losses on hedges			
At 1 April 2000	69	(386)	(317)
Recognised during the year	(44)	189	145
Arising in the year that were not recognised during the year	222	(84)	138
At 31 March 2001	**247**	**(281)**	**(34)**
Of which:			
Expected to be recognised in less than one year	242	(163)	79
Expected to be recognised after more than one year	5	(118)	(113)

As highlighted in the interest rate management table on page 67, 68% of the Group's financial liabilities have fixed interest rates. The above net unrecognised loss is a reflection of different market interest rates ruling at 31 March 2001.

It can be seen that Cable and Wireless has not disclosed comparative information for its hedging disclosures. This practice has been followed by a number of major companies[85], presumably because they do not believe the information is relevant, however there is no exemption from making such disclosures.

It should be noted that the illustration of these disclosures in Appendix III to the standard goes beyond that which is required. In the table below, which is taken from Illustration 2, it is only the lines which are shaded which are required to be disclosed, although the amounts in the first line would be disclosed as part of the comparatives.

	Gains	Losses	Total net gains/(losses)
	£ millions	£ millions	£ millions
Unrecognised gains and losses on hedges at 1.1.X1	53	28	25
Gains and losses arising in previous years that were recognised in 19X1	22	21	1
Gains and losses arising before 1.1.X1 that were not recognised in 19X1	31	7	24
Gains and losses arising in 19X1 that were not recognised in 19X1	66	41	25
Unrecognised gains and losses on hedges at 31.12.X1	97	48	49
Of which:			
Gains and losses expected to be recognised in 19X2	71	40	31
Gains and losses expected to be recognised in 19X3 or later	26	8	18

The following examples set out what may be included in the hedging disclosures (and how this relates to the fair value disclosures) for two common situations, an interest rate swap used to convert fixed rate debt into floating rate and a forward currency contract used to hedge the foreign currency exposure on the acquisition of stock from an overseas supplier.

Example 10.2: Hedging disclosures: interest rate swap

On 1 April 2002 XYZ plc issues £10,000 of debt paying interest fixed at 7%, the prevailing rate at the time. It is repayable in five years time (i.e. on 31 March 2007) and interest is payable half yearly in arrears (i.e. on 30 September and 31 March). At the same time it enters into a pay floating-receive fixed interest rate swap whereby for five years XYZ receives 7% and pays a variable rate on a notional principal of £10,000. The swap is also settled net half yearly in arrears (i.e. on 30 September and 31 March) and the variable rate paid corresponds to the prevailing rate at the start of the six months preceding settlement date (i.e. on 1 April and 1 October).

What XYZ has effectively done is to use the swap to convert the fixed rate loan into a floating rate loan. Indeed the interest rate risk disclosures (see 2.6 above) would describe this arrangement as a floating rate loan.

The prevailing rate falls to 5% at the end of June 2002 and remains at this level until the accounts for the year ended 31 December 2002 are drawn up in March 2003. The prevailing interest rate falls again at the end of June 2003 to 4% and remains at this level until the subsequent accounts are drawn up in March 2004. Therefore the first four net settlements received under the swap are:

	£
30 September 2002 – pay 7% (based on 1 April 2002 rate) receive 7%	–
31 March 2003 – pay 5% (based on 1 October 2002 rate) receive 7%	100
30 September 2003 – pay 5% (based on 1 April 2003 rate) receive 7%	100
31 March 2004 – pay 4% (based on 1 October 2003 rate) receive 7%	150

Accounting entries

Using traditional hedge accounting principles, XYZ accounts for the swap by accruing the interest rate differential and recording this in the profit and loss account as an adjustment to interest payable.

2002

Issue of loan:

	£	£
Cash	10,000	
Loan		10,000

Interest on loan paid and accrued at 7% for 9 months:

	£	£
Interest payable (P&L)	525	
Cash		350
Accrued interest – loan		175

Interest differential on swap paid and accrued for 9 months to 31 December 2002:

	£	£
Accrued interest – swap	50	
Interest payable (P&L)		50

The accrued interest balance is calculated as £100 x 3/6, i.e. time apportioning the payment to be received on 31 March 2003.

2003

Interest on loan paid and accrued at 7% for 12 months:

	£	£
Interest payable (P&L)	700	
Cash		700

Interest differential on swap paid and accrued for 12 months to 31 December 2003:

	£	£
Cash	200	
Accrued interest – swap	25	
Interest payable (P&L)		225

The cash was received on 31 March and 30 September; the balance on the accrued income is now £75 (£50+£25) and represents the time apportioned element of the payment to be received on 31 March 2004, i.e. £150 x 3/6.

Fair value disclosures

Discounting expected future cash flows at the prevailing rates of 4% (2002: 5%), the fair values of the loan and the swap are £11,093 (2002: £10,956) negative, and £981 (2002: £808) positive, respectively (calculations not illustrated here). Assuming the accrued interest is included in the carrying amount of the loan, the associated fair value information could be presented as follows:

	2003		2002	
	Book value	Fair value	Book value	Fair value
	£	£	£	£
Loan	(10,075)	(11,093)	(10,075)	(10,956)
Swap	75	981	50	808

Hedging disclosures

The unrecognised gain on the swap at the year end is £906 (2002: £758) being the difference between its fair value and book value – paragraph 59(a) of FRS 13 requires this to be disclosed.

In the following year the swap will give rise to a profit or loss equal to the accrued interest differential. Based on the prevailing rates at the year end, XYZ would expect this to be £300 (2002: £200). However, it is not the *total* expected profit or loss for the following year that paragraph 59(c) of FRS 13 requires but *the extent to which the unrecognised gain or loss* (calculated above) is expected to be recognised. As the total unrecognised amount is a discounted figure it appears that, in theory at least, the expected amount should be too. In practice the effect of discounting over a period of up to one year is unlikely to be material – in this case the amounts would change to approximately £291 (2002: £192).

Paragraph 59(d) of the standard requires disclosure of the amount of gains and losses included in the current period's profit and loss account that arose in previous years and were unrecognised at the start of the period. It is tempting to assume this means the actual profit or loss recognised in the period, provided the hedging instrument was in existence at the start of the period. In this example this would be £225 for 2003. Using the format suggested in the standard the disclosures could then be presented as follows (the shading shows the mandatory information):

	2003	2002
	£	£
Unrecognised gains on hedges at 1 January	758	–
Gains arising in previous years that were recognised in year	(225)	–
Gains arising in previous years that were not recognised in year	533	–
Gains arising in year that were not recognised in year	373	758
Unrecognised gains on hedges at 31 December	906	758
Of which, gains expected to be recognised:		
– next year	291	192
– in subsequent years	615	566

However, strictly, not all of the £225 recognised in the current year arose in the previous year – aside from the £8 effect of the discounting, £25 of this gain arose only because interest rates fell during the year, i.e. it arose during the current year. Therefore it would appear that the following table shows a more technically correct presentation:

	2003	2002
	£	£
Unrecognised gains on hedges at 1 January	758	–
Gains arising in previous years that were recognised in year	(192)	–
Gains arising in previous years that were not recognised in year	566	–
Gains arising in year that were not recognised in year	340	758
Unrecognised gains on hedges at 31 December	906	758
Of which, gains expected to be recognised:		
– next year	291	192
– in subsequent years	615	566

Example 10.3: Hedging disclosures – forward currency contract

On 1 September 2002, PQR plc enters into a contract with a US supplier to purchase 1,000 units of stock on 1 December 2002. The price of the stock, US$90,000, is denominated in US dollars and is payable to the supplier on 31 January 2003.

In order to fix its cost in sterling terms, on 1 September 2002, PQR also takes out a forward currency contract to buy US$90,000 on 31 January 2003 at the forward rate of £1:US$1.50.

Following delivery, PQR sells 50 units during its year ended 31 December 2002, 700 units during 2003 (although 900 were originally expected to be sold in total before the end of 2003) and the remaining 250 units are sold in 2004.

The relevant spot rates are as follows:

1 December 2002	£1:US$1.48
31 December 2002	£1:US$1.47
31 January 2003	£1:US$1.43

Accounting entries

PQR's accounting policy in respect of such hedges is to translate its foreign currency assets and liabilities at the forward rate, as permitted by paragraph 46 of SSAP 20, and not to record the forward contract until it matures. Consequently the calculations below do not separately identify the forward premium inherent in the currency contract, being the difference between the forward rate and the spot rate at 1 December 2002.

Conceptually, rolling the forward premium into the cost of the stock in this way is unsatisfactory as it is akin to interest. An alternative treatment would be to amortise it to P&L over the life of the contract and to record the stock at the spot rate at 1 September 2002, the date of inception of the forward currency contract. This is discussed further in Chapter 8 at 3.3.1.

2002

Purchase of 1,000 units at stock on 1 December, recorded at forward rate (£1:US$1.50):

	£	£
Stock	60,000	
Creditor		60,000

Sale of 50 units of stock:

	£	£
Cost of sales	3,000	
Stock		3,000

2003

Settlement of forward contract, recorded at spot rate (£1:US$1.43):

	£	£
Cash (US$90,000)	62,937	
Cash		60,000
Exchange gain		2,937

Settlement of creditor, recorded at spot rate (£1:US$1.43):

	£	£
Creditor	60,000	
Exchange loss	2,937	
Cash (US$90,000)		62,937

Sale of 700 units of stock:

	£	£
Cost of sales	42,000	
Stock		42,000

2004

Sale of 250 units of stock:

	£	£
Cost of sales	15,000	
Stock		15,000

Fair value disclosures

Using year end exchange rates and ignoring the time value of money for the two months until settlement on the grounds of materiality, the forward contract has a positive fair value at 31 December 2002 of approximately £1,224 ([US$90,000 ÷ 1.47] – [US$90,000 ÷ 1.50]) and the creditor a negative fair value of £61,224 (US$90,000 ÷ 1.47). The associated fair value information could be presented as follows:

	2003		2002	
	Book value	Fair value	Book value	Fair value
Forward contract	–	–	0	1,224
Creditor	–	–	(60,000)	(61,224)

If advantage is taken of the exemption from disclosing short term debtors and creditors, only the information relating to the forward contract need be given.

Hedging disclosures

There are a number of ways of viewing this arrangement for the purpose of the hedging disclosures. It might be thought that there is an unrecognised gain or loss on the forward contract (the hedging instrument) from inception date to settlement date together with an opposite offsetting unrecognised loss or gain on the creditor from delivery date to settlement date and each unrecognised gain and loss would be recognised when the forward contract and creditor are settled. Under this analysis the hedging disclosures could be presented as follows (only the shaded information is mandatory):

	2003	2002
Unrecognised gains on hedges at 1 January	1,224	–
Gains arising in previous years that were recognised in year	(1,224)	–
Gains arising in previous years that were not recognised in year	–	–
Gains arising in year that were not recognised in year	–	1,224
Unrecognised gains on hedges at 31 December	–	1,224
Of which, gains expected to be recognised:		
– next year	–	1,224
– in subsequent years	–	–

However, by recording the transaction at the rate specified in the forward contract rather than the spot rate, the stock has been recorded at a different amount as a result of the use of hedge accounting and therefore gains or losses are being deferred in the balance sheet. Consequently it seems reasonably clear this analysis does not accord with the standard.

On 1 December 2002 there is a gain on the forward contract attributable solely to foreign currency movements, i.e. ignoring the time value of money for the two months until settlement, of £811 (US$90,000 ÷ 1.48 – US$90,000 ÷ 1.50). Further, the stock is recorded at £811 less than it would otherwise have been. Therefore it appears that the gain arising on the forward contract to this date has been deferred within the carrying amount of the stock. Of this deferred gain, £41 is realised in the profit and loss account during December as the first 50 units of stock are sold (by way of a reduced cost of sales).

Therefore, of the £1,224 gain on the forward contract at 31 December 2002, £41 has been realised in the profit and loss account, £770 remains deferred in the balance sheet and the remainder, £413, is apparently unrecognised. Of the deferred gain, £689 is expected to be realised in 2003 by selling a further 850 units of stock. The unrecognised gain is expected to be realised on settlement of the forward contract and creditor on 31 January 2003.

During 2003 just £567 of the deferred gain is recognised in the profit and loss account as only 700 units of stock are sold. Unrecognised gains on the forward contract are realised on 31 January. At the end of the year, therefore, a gain of £203 remains deferred in the balance sheet which will be recognised on sale of the stock during 2004.

The hedging disclosures could be presented as follows (only the shaded information is mandatory):

Gains on hedging instruments:	2004	2003		2002	
	Defer'd	Unrec'd	Defer'd	Unrec'd	Defer'd
– on hedges at 1 January	203	413	770	–	–
– arising in previous years, recognised in current year	(203)	(413)	(567)	–	–
– arising in previous years that were not recognised in year	–	–	–	–	–
– arising in current year that were not recognised in current year	–	–	–	413	770
– on hedges at 31 December	–	–	203	413	770
Of which expected to be recognised:					
– next year	–	–	203	413	689
– in subsequent years	–	–	–	–	81

Alternatively, it could be argued that the gain on the forward contract that arises between the date of delivery and 31 December 2003 (£413) has effectively been recognised in the profit and loss account together with an equivalent loss on the creditor – under this analysis only the deferred gains shown in the table above would be disclosed. This views the creditor balance as representing both the liability to pay the supplier and the forward contract, whereas the former treatment viewed it representing only the liability, with the forward contract being an unrecognised instrument.

2.11 Instruments held or issued for trading

It might be thought that this requirement would only be applicable to banks and other financial institutions. However, for the purposes of the standard, trading in financial assets and financial liabilities is defined as 'buying, selling, issuing or holding financial assets and financial liabilities in order to take advantage of short-term changes in market prices or rates …'[86] Arguably, this could embrace financial instruments taken out for hedging purposes, so the standard clarifies that items taken out to hedge the risks associated with another transaction or position are deemed to be trading only if that other transaction or position involves such trading.

It would seem therefore that these disclosures would embrace current asset investments, derivatives which are not regarded as hedges, and any derivatives which hedge such items.

Where an entity trades in financial assets and financial liabilities, the following information should be disclosed:

- The net gain or loss included in the profit and loss account from trading such assets and liabilities during the period. This is to be analysed by type of financial instrument, business activity, risk or 'in such other way as is consistent with the entity's management of this activity'. If the analysis provided is other than by type of financial instrument, then a description of the types of financial instruments involved should be given for each item in the analysis. However, there is no need to quantify the net gain or loss for each type of instrument involved.

- The fair values at the balance sheet date of financial assets and, separately, financial liabilities that are held or issued for trading. This information may already be disclosed as part of the fair value disclosures discussed in 2.9 above. However, since information has to be given for financial assets and financial liabilities separately, then it may be necessary to give additional disclosure to meet this requirement. This is likely to be the case where derivative financial instruments have been grouped together for the purposes of the fair value disclosures regardless of whether the fair values were positive or negative. If the year-end position is considered to be materially unrepresentative of the entity's use of such instruments during the year, then average amounts for the year are also to be disclosed. Ideally, these average amounts should be calculated using daily figures, but if this is not the case, then the entity should use the most frequent interval that its systems generate for management, regulatory or other reasons.[87]

2.12 Commodity contracts treated as financial instruments

As noted earlier at 2.1 above, although commodity contracts requiring settlement by physical delivery are not financial instruments, the standard requires some such contracts nevertheless to be included within certain of the disclosures. The contracts to be included are cash-settled commodity contracts which are commodity contracts (including contracts for the delivery of gold) which, though having contract terms that require settlement by physical delivery only, are of a type that is normally extinguished other than by physical delivery in accordance with general market practice.[88]

Such contracts are to be included within the following disclosures:

- the narrative disclosures (see 2.3 above);
- the fair value disclosures (see 2.9 above);
- the disclosures about hedges (see 2.10 above); and
- the disclosures about instruments held or issued for trading (see 2.11 above).[89]

However there is a 'commercially prejudicial' exemption which allows some or all of the numerical disclosures to be omitted in exceptional cases. This applies where the market in the commodity is illiquid and dominated by very few participants, and if disclosure of the information at the time the financial statements become publicly available would be likely to move the market significantly and, in the directors' opinion, would be seriously prejudicial to the reporting entity's interests. If this exemption is taken, this fact must be disclosed, with an explanation of the reasons.[90]

2.13 Market price risk

The standard's final set of disclosures is non-mandatory, to encourage experimentation in an admittedly difficult area. It calls for additional numerical disclosures to explain the magnitude of market price risk for all financial instruments, cash-settled commodity contracts and, if significant, all other items that carry market price risk. The manner in which this is done should reflect the way (or ways) in which the entity manages its risk exposures.[91] This disclosure should be accompanied by narrative explanation that puts the figures in context.

This disclosure should also be supplemented by:

(a) an explanation of the method used and the main parameters and assumptions underlying the data provided;

(b) an explanation of the objective of the method used and of the limitations that may result in the information not fully reflecting the market price risk; and

(c) reasons for any material changes in the amount of reported market price risk when compared with that reported for the previous period.[92]

If material changes are made to the method, or main assumptions and parameters, used in providing this disclosure, the reasons for the change should be given and the comparative information restated using the basis adopted in the current year.[93]

Paragraph 68 of FRS 13 gives a number of suggestions as to how market price risk might be evaluated and presented, but notes that each has its shortcomings and thus a combination of approaches might be more helpful.

This seems a very ambitious suggestion given the already far-reaching nature of the mandatory disclosures, and it seems unlikely that many companies will respond to this particular challenge. Nevertheless some companies have been providing some sensitivity analysis information as illustrated below:

Extract 10.19: Johnson Matthey plc (2001)

19 **Financial risk management** [extract]
19g **Market price risk**

The group monitors its interest rate and currency risks and other market price risks to which it is exposed primarily through a process known as 'sensitivity analysis'. This involves estimating the effect on profit before tax over various periods of possible changes in interest rates and exchange rates.

Most of the group's borrowings and deposits are at floating rates. A 1% change on all interest rates would have a 1.2% impact on group profit before tax. This is well within the range the group regards as acceptable.

The main impact of movements in exchange rates on the group's results arises on translation of overseas subsidiaries' profits into sterling. The group's largest exposure is to the US dollar since Johnson Matthey's largest single overseas investment is in the US. A 5 cent (3.4%) movement in the average exchange rate for the US dollar against sterling has a 1.7% impact on group profit before tax. This exposure is part of the group's economic risk of operating globally which is essential to remain competitive in the markets in which the group operates.

One company which gives value at risk disclosures is Reuters, as shown below:

Extract 10.20: Reuters Group PLC (2000)

Operating and Financial Review [extract]

Reuters has adopted value at risk (VAR) analysis as a means of quantifying the potential impact of exchange rate volatility on reported earnings. VAR is a measure of the potential loss on a portfolio within a specified time horizon, at a specified confidence interval. Loss is defined, in this instance, as the diminution in value of rolling 12-month forecast group profits denominated in sterling. Due to the approximations used in determining VAR, the theory provides order of magnitude estimates only but these are useful for comparison purposes.

Reuters estimates that at 31 December 2000 there is a 5% chance that profits forecast for the coming 12 months will deteriorate by more than £77 million as a result of currency fluctuations before hedging and £42 million after hedging (actual 1999: £52 million before hedging and £27 million after hedging). These figures represent the value at risk.

During 2000 the average value at risk on forecast profits for the coming 12 months was as follows:

VALUE AT RISK		BEFORE HEDGING £M	AFTER HEDGING £M
2000	Average	64	32
	High	78	42
	Low	49	27
1999	Average	60	33

2.14 Comparatives

Comparatives are required for all of the numerical disclosures, however the standard states that this may not be practicable in all circumstances for the first accounting period in which the standard comes into effect and, accordingly, such disclosure is not required for that period, although it is encouraged.[94]

The first accounting period in which FRS 13 comes into effect for a particular entity will not necessarily be its first accounting period ending after 23 March 1999 if it was not publicly quoted at that time. It therefore appears that this limited transitional relief continues to be available for companies entering the capital markets at a later date. However, it would certainly be best practice to include full comparatives in such cases and the question would effectively be moot if comparatives were included in the associated listing circular or equivalent document.

3 UK DISCLOSURE REQUIREMENTS FOR FINANCIAL INSTITUTIONS

3.1 Banks and similar institutions

The requirements for banks and similar institutions are contained within Part B of FRS 13. Additional disclosure requirements are included within relevant legislation and industry SORPs, but these are outside the scope of this publication. FRS 13 defines a bank or similar institution as 'an entity that:

(a) is authorised under the Banking Act 1987 (in the UK) or the Central Bank Acts 1942-1989 (in the Republic of Ireland); or

(b) whose business is to receive deposits or other repayable funds from the public and to grant credits for its own account.'[95]

As a result of paragraph (b) above, entities such as building societies and credit unions are brought within the scope of this alternative regime. This regime is also to be followed by banking or similar groups, i.e. groups where:

(a) the parent company is a bank or similar institution; or

(b) the parent company:

  (i) does not carry on any material business apart from the acquisition, management and disposal of interests in subsidiary undertakings; and

  (ii) its principal subsidiary undertakings are wholly or mainly entities that are banks or similar institutions.[96]

Unlike non-financial institutions the standard applies to all banks and similar institutions, whether or not they have capital instruments that are listed or publicly traded.[97]

The instruments to be included within the disclosures by banks and similar institutions are effectively the same as for non-financial institutions. However, it should be noted that banks and similar institutions cannot exclude financial assets and financial liabilities arising from traditional lending activities and deposit-making activities from the disclosures, since they cannot be treated as falling within the term 'short-term debtors and creditors' (see 2.1 above).[98] Also, for the purposes of the disclosures in respect of commodity contracts, all contracts for the delivery of gold are to be treated as if they were financial instruments (see 3.1.5 below).[99]

Like non-financial institutions, banks and similar financial institutions have to provide narrative disclosures of objectives, policies and strategies (see 2.3 above).[100] This discussion will need to reflect the nature of their business and is likely to involve more discussion on credit risk and market price risk, particularly in relation to financial assets. The recommendations in FRS 13 for disclosures in respect of accounting policies also apply to banks and financial institutions (see 2.4 above).[101]

As mentioned at 2.1 above, the main impact of the different regime in FRS 13 is in respect of the numerical disclosures to be given by banks and similar institutions.

The requirements for banks and similar institutions reflect the fact that financial instruments play an integral part in generating such an entity's net income, which arises from the management of the mismatches in the exposures arising from such instruments and the margins earned thereon. Also, a distinction is made between the trading and non-trading activities of such entities by requiring different disclosures in respect of the 'trading book' and the 'non-trading book'.

The trading book comprise those assets and liabilities arising from the trading activity of the entity which includes:

- providing financial instruments to clients (other than through traditional lending and deposit-taking activities or by granting finance leases) – i.e. customer facilitation;
- providing liquidity to the market – i.e. market making;
- acting as a connecting link between different markets – i.e. arbitrage;
- taking proprietary positions; and
- related hedges.

The non-trading book comprises all the entity's other assets and liabilities which arise from non-trading activities which include:

- traditional lending and deposit-taking;
- granting of finance leases;
- asset/liability and liquidity management;
- investment activity, including activity of a strategic nature; and
- related hedges.

The standard indicates that this categorisation is not exactly the same as for capital adequacy purposes.[102] However, in practice, there is likely to be little difference and it will be in the bank's interest for it to be the same.

3.1.1 *Interest rate risk disclosures*

The interest rate risk disclosures reflect the fact that the net income of banks and similar institutions is generated by mismatches in the exposures arising from such instruments and the margins earned thereon. Accordingly, an interest rate sensitivity gap analysis (sometimes referred to as an 'interest rate repricing table') is to be provided showing the aggregate carrying amounts of assets and liabilities in the non-trading book, analysed by major category of asset and liability and, within those categories, into time bands. In preparing this analysis:

(a) items should be allocated to time bands by reference to whichever is the earlier of the period to the next interest rate repricing date and the maturity date;

(b) the time bands used should include at least the following:

  (i) not more than the next three months;

  (ii) more than three months but not more than six months;

  (iii) more than six months but not more than one year;

(iv) more than one year but not more than five years; and

(v) more than five years; and

(c) the analysis should show the net position for each time band.[103]

The analysis is also to be after taking account of derivatives whose effect is to alter the interest basis of the assets and liabilities. Where any derivatives have not been included within the analysis, a summary should be provided of the main effects of such instruments.[104] This might include such elements as the notional principal amounts involved, the period for which the instruments are operative, the main potential effect of the instruments on information provided in the analysis and the terms of any options contained within the instrument. The aim of this information should be to ensure that the risks associated with such instruments are adequately disclosed.[105]

One aspect of interest rate risk is the currency in which the assets and liabilities are denominated. It may be that a bank has a financial asset in one currency funded by a liability in another currency, both repricing within the same time band. The analysis would therefore suggest there is no interest rate risk exposure. However, it may be that the asset is in a currency of a country with high and volatile interest rates whereas the liability is in a currency of a country with low and stable interest rates, giving rise to potentially significant interest rate risk in the future. Nevertheless, the standard only encourages, but does not require, incorporation of the currency in which assets and liabilities within the table are denominated where this is of significance.[106]

The third illustration in Appendix III to the standard provides an example of the disclosures required. This example includes all assets and liabilities including shareholders' funds and non-financial assets, whether interest bearing or not. Arguably this is not strictly necessary but it does provide a reconciliation to the balance sheet. One company which gives such disclosures is Northern Rock as shown in the following extract:

Extract 10.21: Northern Rock plc (2000)

35. Derivatives and other financial instruments [extract]

The following table gives an analysis of the re pricing periods of assets and liabilities on the Group balance sheet at 31 December:

2000	Within 3 months	After 3 months but within 6 months	After 6 months but within 1 year	After 1 year but within 5 years	After 5 years	Non-interest bearing funds	Total
	£m	£m	£m	£m	£m	£m	£m
Assets							
Loans and advances to banks	684.4	–	7.0	97.0	–	–	788.4
Loans and advances to customers	11,424.3	423.0	1,515.1	4,041.8	686.6	–	18,090.8
Investment securities	1,663.7	234.7	119.7	848.9	188.9	–	3,055.9
Interest earning assets	13,772.4	657.7	1,641.8	4,987.7	875.5	–	21,935.1
Non-interest earning assets	–	–	–	–	–	609.1	609.1
Total assets	13,772.4	657.7	1,641.8	4,987.7	875.5	609.1	22,544.2

Liabilities							
Deposits by banks	794.8	32.7	47.0	–	–	–	874.5
Customer accounts	9,024.5	1,008.8	1,931.7	1,976.1	–	–	13,941.1
Debt securities in issue	5,130.8	283.5	–	–	–	–	5,414.3
Subordinated liabilities	90.5	266.5	–	–	168.4	–	525.4
Interest bearing liabilities	15,040.6	1,591.5	1,978.7	1,976.1	168.4	–	20,755.3
Reserve capital instruments	200.0	–	–	–	–	–	200.0
Interest free liabilities	–	–	–	–	–	673.4	673.4
Shareholders' equity	–	–	–	–	–	915.5	915.5
Total liabilities	15,240.6	1,591.5	1,978.7	1,976.1	168.4	1,588.9	22,544.2
Off balance sheet items affecting interest rate sensitivity	(648.9)	(671.6)	(518.9)	1,789.0	50.4	–	–
	14,591.7	919.9	1,459.8	3,765.1	218.8	1,588.9	22,544.2
Interest rate sensitivity gap	(819.3)	(262.2)	182.0	1,222.6	656.7	(979.8)	–
Cumulative interest rate sensitivity gap	(819.3)	(1,081.5)	(899.5)	323.1	979.8	–	–
Cumulative interest rate sensitivity gap as a percentage of interest earning assets	(3.7%)	(4.9%)	(4.1%)	1.5%	4.5%	–	–

The comparative information provided by Northern Rock has not been included in the above extract.

As discussed at 3.1.4 below, similar interest rate risk disclosures may be provided in respect of the trading book, but such disclosures should be shown separately from those for the non-trading book.

3.1.2 *Currency risk disclosures*

FRS 13 states that the currency risk exposure of banks and similar institutions comprises three elements:

(a) the structural currency exposures that arise from the entity's foreign equity investments as mitigated by the foreign currency borrowings taken out to finance or hedge such investments;

(b) the currency exposures arising on the monetary assets and liabilities in the non-trading book; and

(c) the currency exposures that arise on the monetary assets and liabilities in the trading book.[107]

The disclosures required by the standard in respect of the trading book are dealt with in 3.1.4 below. The other disclosures are intended to be constructed to reflect the entity's application of SSAP 20.[108]

First, the entity's foreign net investments should be analysed according to its main functional currencies and these amounts compared with the currencies of its borrowings which qualify as a hedge under the cover method of SSAP 20.[109]

In preparing this analysis, account should be taken of the effect of currency swaps, forward contracts and other derivatives that contribute to the matching or hedging. Derivatives whose effect is variable or conditional (e.g. options) should be excluded from the analysis and disclosed separately.[110]

The second analysis which is required is one that shows the currency exposures on the non-trading book by principal functional currencies of the operations involved. Again, account should be taken of the effect of currency swaps, etc. that contribute to the matching or hedging of the foreign currency exposures, with separate disclosure of derivatives whose effect is variable or conditional.[111] This is similar to the currency risk disclosures required by non-financial institutions (see 2.7 above).

The standard recognises that many banks and similar institutions transfer all their currency risk arising from the commercial banking/lending activities to their trading book. If, as a result, there are no remaining currency exposures in the non-trading book, or if any remaining exposures are not material, the standard suggests that it would be helpful to explain why no disclosures have been provided.[112]

Barclays provides the following currency risk disclosures:

Extract 10.22: Barclays PLC (2000)

46 Derivatives and other financial instruments [extract]

Non-trading currency risk

Non-trading currency risk exposure arises principally from the Group's investments in overseas branches and subsidiary and associated undertakings, principally in the United States, Japan and Europe.

The Group's structural currency exposures at 31st December 2000 were as follows:

	Net investments in overseas operations		Borrowings which hedge the net investments		Remaining structural currency exposures	
	2000	1999	2000	1999	2000	1999
Functional currency of the operation involved	£m	£m	£m	£m	£m	£m
US dollar	**628**	627	**619**	620	**9**	7
Yen	**109**	87	**–**	56	**109**	31
Euro	**3,090**	2,752	**2,671**	2,264	**419**	488
Other non-sterling	**480**	394	**129**	48	**351**	346
Total	**4,307**	3,860	**3,419**	2,988	**888**	872

In accordance with Group policy, as at 31st December 2000 and 31st December 1999 there were no material net currency exposures in the non-trading book relating to transactional (or non-structural) positions that would give rise to net currency gains and losses recognised in the profit and loss account.

As discussed at 3.1.4 below, similar currency risk disclosures may be provided in respect of the trading book, but such disclosures should be shown separately from those for the non-trading book.

3.1.3 *Fair value disclosures*

FRS 13 requires banks and similar institutions to provide fair value disclosures in respect of certain of their financial assets and financial liabilities. The items to be included are:

(a) all financial assets and financial liabilities held in the trading book; and

(b) the following financial assets and liabilities held in the non-trading book:

   (i) all derivatives;

   (ii) all listed and/or publicly traded securities; and

   (iii) any other financial asset or financial liability for which a liquid and active market exists for the asset or liability or for its component parts.

These items are included regardless of whether they are recognised or unrecognised.[113]

A market is liquid and active if all of the following apply:

- Assets (or liabilities) of the same type are regularly traded on the market.
- The price determined from the market (by reference to, for example, quoted prices or last traded prices) is a reliable indicator of the price that would be obtained if some or all of the asset (or liability) was actually sold in the market at the time in normal market conditions.
- There are willing buyers and sellers in the market at all times during normal business hours at the price determined from the market.[114]

Although there may be markets for certain types of financial assets (or liabilities), such as unlisted bonds, commercial debt, distressed debt and trade finance paper, determining whether they fall within this definition of a liquid and active market is a matter of judgement and will depend on the particular circumstances.

The standard indicates that because markets are evolving rapidly, the fact that a liquid and active market does not exist at present does not mean that such a market will not exist in the future.[115] Banks will therefore need to keep the status of markets under frequent review.

The requirement is for an entity to group the relevant financial assets and liabilities, including amounts not recognised in the balance sheet, into appropriate categories of trading book and non-trading book items and for each category to disclose either:

- the aggregate fair value at the balance sheet date compared to the aggregate book value; or
- the aggregate fair value of those financial instruments with a positive fair value and, separately, those with a negative fair value, compared to the book amounts.[116]

This requirement is similar to that for other entities (see 2.9 above).

As with other entities, for some financial assets and liabilities the estimated difference between the carrying amount and its fair value may not be material, in which case the carrying amount may be used as the fair value for the purposes of the disclosure.

Similarly, the methods and any significant assumptions used in determining the fair values have to be disclosed.

3.1.4 *Trading book disclosures*

Banks and similar institutions have to provide the same disclosures as that given by other entities in respect of financial assets and financial liabilities held or issued for trading (see 2.11 above).[117] However, the standard also requires them to provide additional disclosures relating to the risks arising on the trading book but, in recognition of the fact that different entities manage their trading book in different ways, allows some flexibility in how this information is provided.

The entity should disclose the highest, lowest and average exposure of its trading book to market price risk during the reporting period together with the exposure at the balance sheet date, using at least one of the following methods:

(a) The value at risk of the trading book as a whole.

(b) Sensitivity analysis showing the potential effect on earnings or net assets of selected hypothetical changes in market prices and rates on the trading book. In this analysis:

  (i) separate disclosures should be provided for each type of market price risk; and

  (ii) the hypothetical changes used should be reasonably possible during the twelve months following the date of approval of the financial statements. One of the hypothetical changes should be an adverse change of at least 10% in the period-end market prices or rates unless such a fall can be shown to be not reasonably possible.

(c) Some other market price risk measure, but only if it is used by the management for the purpose of managing the market price risk of the trading book, and the model used has been approved by the entity's regulator for the purpose of providing that regulator with capital adequacy returns.[118]

Paragraph (c) has been included to allow for the possibility of more sophisticated risk management being developed.

If an entity does not use one of the above methodologies for managing the market price risk of its trading book, then instead of providing one of the disclosures above, it can provide the interest rate risk disclosures and currency risk disclosures discussed at 3.1.1and 3.1.2 above in respect of its trading book.[119]

The above disclosure should also be accompanied by:

(a) an explanation of the method used and the key parameters and assumptions underlying the data provided;

(b) an explanation of the objective of the method used and of the limitations that may result in the information not fully reflecting the market price risk;

(c) the frequency with which the figures were calculated when determining the highest, lowest and average figures for the period. This should, as a minimum, be the frequency at which the figures are calculated for risk management purposes. However, if figures are calculated more frequently than daily, then it will be sufficient to use daily figures for the purposes of the disclosure; and

(d) reasons for any material changes in the amount of reported market price risk when compared with that reported for the previous period.[120]

An example of the disclosure is given in the following extract from the financial statements of Standard Chartered:

Extract 10.23: Standard Chartered PLC (2000)

Operating and Financial Review [extract]
Financial information [extract]
Value at Risk

The Group measures the risk of losses arising as a result of potential adverse movements in interest and exchange rates, prices and volatilities using a Value at Risk (VAR) system, which is described in more detail in Note 53 to the accounts.

The total VAR for the market risks in the Group's Trading Book as at 31 December 2000 was estimated at £3.9 million of which £2.4 million arose from interest rate risk and £1.6 million from exchange rate risk. The Group has no significant trading exposure to equity or commodity price risk. No offsets are allowed between exchange rate and interest rate exposures when VAR limits are set. The year end figures are higher than 1999 year end, which reflected unusually low levels of position taking as a precaution against year 2000 market disturbances. The average VAR for the Group during the year was £3.1 million with the highest exposure reaching £5.6 million.

In addition to the close supervision of trading activities by senior management, there are limits on the size of positions and concentrations of instruments as well as stress testing of certain product groups and currencies. The Group regularly stress tests its main portfolios to identify any exposure to low-probability events that may not be highlighted by VAR measures.

53. Market Risk for the Trading Book

	12 months to 31.12.00			**31.12.00**	12 months to 31.12.99			31.12.99
	Average £million	**High £million**	**Low £million**	**Actual £million**	Average £million	High £million	Low £million	Actual £million
Daily value at risk:								
Interest rate risk	**1.8**	**4.4**	**1.2**	**2.4**	2.9	5.1	1.6	1.6
Foreign exchange risk	**1.3**	**2.1**	**0.7**	**1.6**	1.3	2.0	0.8	0.8
Total	**3.1**	**5.6**	**2.0**	**3.9**	4.2	6.0	2.4	2.4

This note should be read in conjunction with the Financial Information section of the Operating & Financial Review on pages 25 to 27 which explains the Group's risk management, including Value at Risk (VAR) and derivatives.

The Group measures the risk of losses arising from future potential adverse movements in interest and exchange rates, prices and volatilities using VAR methodology. This methodology measures on a daily basis the estimated potential change in the market value or realisable value of the portfolio during a specified period.

The total Group exposure shown in the table above is not a sum of the interest rate and exchange rate risks. The highest and lowest VAR, are independent, and could have occurred on different days.

The Group uses a combination of variance-covariance methodology and historical simulation to measure VAR on its trading positions. In 2000, most of the trading book was measured using the historical simulation with the remainder using the variance-covariance approach.

> VAR is calculated for expected movements over a minimum of one business day and to a confidence level of approximately 97.5 per cent. This confidence level suggests that potential daily losses, i.e. in excess of the VAR measure, are only likely to be experienced six times per year.
>
> For derivative products and FX products the historic simulation method is used with an observation period of 250 days. The historical simulation approach involves the complete revaluation of all unmatured contracts to reflect the effect of historically observed changes in market risk factors on the valuation of the current portfolio. This entails building a set of valuations of the portfolio and a set of changes in value relative to the current market valuation, from which VAR can be derived.
>
> The variance-covariance method used is based on statistical analysis of past interest and exchange rate movements over the past 2 to 3 years with greater weight given to more recent data.
>
> Offsetting between exchange rate and interest rate exposures is not allowed. This approach is conservative, as the diversification effects that would be implied if such offsetting were allowed, are likely to have the impact of reducing the overall VAR.
>
> The Group recognises that there are limitations to the VAR methodology. These include the fact that the risk factors may not fall within the assumption of a Normal distribution, i.e. that a greater than expected number of observations may fall outside the stated confidence level. Also the historical data may not be the best proxy for future price movements, either because the observation period does not include extreme price movements or, in some cases, because data is not available. Losses beyond the confidence interval are not captured by a VAR calculation, which therefore gives no indication of the size of unexpected losses in these situations. This is particularly relevant in the case of extreme market movements, which may arise in periods of low liquidity and thus making the assumption, that positions can be closed in a liquid market, invalid.
>
> To manage the risks arising from events which the VAR methodology does not capture the Group regularly back-tests and stress tests its main risk exposures. In back testing actual profits and losses are compared with VAR estimates to track the accuracy of the predictions. Stress testing involves valuing portfolios at prices which assume extreme changes in risk factors beyond the range of normal experience. Positions that would give rise to potentially significant losses under a low probability stress event are reviewed by senior management.

If an entity makes material changes to the method used, or to the main assumptions and parameters used, in providing these market price risk disclosures, then the reasons for the change should be given and the previous period's balance sheet date information should be restated using the basis adopted for the current period. In addition, entities are encouraged to restate the highest, lowest and average information.[121]

3.1.5 *Other numerical disclosures*

In addition to the disclosures discussed in 3.1.1 to 3.1.4 above, as mentioned earlier, banks and similar institutions are required to give the numerical disclosures discussed in 2.10 to 2.13 above. However, for the purposes of the disclosures in respect of commodity contracts which are to be treated as financial instruments (see 2.12 above), banks and similar institutions are required to include all contracts for the delivery of gold held or issued within the disclosures. The fair value disclosures in respect of commodity contracts which are to be treated as financial instruments are those outlined in 3.1.3 above rather than those in 2.9 above.

3.2 Other financial institutions

The requirements for financial institutions, other than banks and similar institutions, are contained within Part C of FRS 13.

As noted earlier the definition of 'financial institution'[122] is very broad and encompasses entities such as leasing companies, stockbrokers and money brokers, investment dealing companies, investment managers, corporate finance companies and investment vehicles, such as investment trusts and unit trusts.

Like non-financial institutions, the standard only applies to financial institutions that are not banks or similar institutions if they have capital instruments that are listed or publicly traded.[123]

The instruments to be included within the disclosures by such institutions are the same as for banks and similar institutions. Therefore, they cannot exclude financial assets and financial liabilities arising from traditional lending activities and deposit-making activities from the disclosures as they cannot be treated as falling within the term 'short-term debtors and creditors' (see 2.1 above).[124] Also, for the purposes of the disclosures in respect of commodity contracts, all contracts for the delivery of gold are to treated as if they were financial instruments.[125]

Like other entities, such financial institutions have to provide narrative disclosures of objectives, policies and strategies (see 2.2 above).[126] This discussion will need to reflect the nature of their business and is likely to involve more discussion on credit risk and other market price risk, particularly in relation to financial assets. The recommendations in FRS 13 for disclosures in respect of accounting policies also apply to such financial institutions (see 2.4 above).[127]

The main impact of this different regime for such financial institutions is in respect of the numerical disclosures. As mentioned in 2.1 above, financial institutions (other than banks or similar institutions) effectively have a choice as to which requirements to follow in respect of their numerical disclosures. They can give the disclosures required by those entities that are not financial institutions discussed in 2 above. Alternatively, they can omit the interest rate risk and currency risk disclosures for such entities (2.6 and 2.7 above) and give the corresponding disclosures for banks and similar institutions together with the trading book disclosures required by such entities (3.1.1, 3.1.2 and 3.1.4 above).[128]

In view of the wide range of entities which fall within this category it is impossible to suggest a rule of thumb for deciding which types of entity should follow which route. It may be that leasing companies and investment dealing companies see the bank-type disclosures as more relevant to their business, but on the other hand such disclosures are more onerous. For the other types of financial institutions, it may be that the non-bank regime is more appropriate, although for investment vehicles the emphasis is more likely to be in respect of their financial assets rather than their financial liabilities.

4 IAS REQUIREMENTS FOR THE RECOGNITION AND MEASUREMENT OF FINANCIAL INSTRUMENTS

4.1 Introduction

As indicated at 1.1 above, in December 1998 the IASC approved for publication IAS 39, its interim standard dealing with recognition and measurement of financial instruments, including rules on hedging; it was actually published in March 1999. In October 2000 the board approved five limited revisions to IAS 39 and related standards, which are effective on initial implementation.[129]

By dealing with most aspects of virtually all financial instruments, it is the longest, and by far the most complex, standard issued by the IASC. Because of this the IASC instructed its staff to monitor implementation issues, consider how best to respond to these and thereby help preparers, auditors and users to understand IAS 39, particularly those preparing to apply it for the first time. In March 2000, the Board approved an approach to publishing implementation guidance in the form of Questions and Answers (Q&A) and appointed an IAS 39 Implementation Guidance Committee (IGC) to review and approve draft Q&A and to seek public comment before approval of final Q&A.[130]

The implementation guidance has been developed to be consistent with the requirements and guidance in the standard and should be considered when selecting and applying accounting policies. It does not actually have the status of a standard or SIC interpretation[131] although the new Board may elevate its status in due course, perhaps by making it an appendix to IAS 39.

To date the IGC has issued over 200 final Q&A, based on five batches of draft Q&A, and has one batch outstanding. The new Board appears to have little appetite for making the IGC a permanent part of its new structure in its current form, although it is allowing it to convert the outstanding draft into final Q&A.

The origins of IAS 39 can be found in US GAAP and at a high level there are only limited differences between the two. Consequently, the main ideas embodied in the standard are:

- derivatives are measured at fair value;
- many financial assets are also measured at fair value;
- non-derivative liabilities are measured at amortised cost;
- hedging rules are established such that:
  - the methods of hedge accounting are defined;
  - hedges are tested for effectiveness; and
  - ineffectiveness is reported in income; and
- certain fair value gains and losses may be reported initially in equity before being recycled into income at a later date.

This is not all that IAS 39 shares with US GAAP – together with its attendant implementation guidance, it is much more of a rule-based standard than one based on principles like UK, and previous IASC, standards.

At present IAS 39 appears incompatible with European law, which in general does not allow unrealised gains to be reported in the profit and loss account. However, in May 2001, the EU's Council of Ministers and the European Parliament paved the way for IAS 39's widespread implementation with the adoption of a directive amending the EU Fourth and Seventh Directives, to be implemented by member states before 2004.[132]

4.2 Scope

IAS 39 is effective for periods beginning on or after 1 January 2001. It applies to all entities and all financial instruments except that certain financial instruments are then excluded from its scope.[133] Certain commodity contracts that behave in a similar way to financial instruments, but do not actually fall within the definition, are also included.

4.2.1 *Subsidiaries, associates, joint ventures and similar investments*

Most interests in subsidiaries, associates, and joint ventures that are consolidated, proportionately consolidated or equity accounted in consolidated accounts are outside the scope of IAS 39. However, if they are not consolidated, proportionately consolidated or equity accounted because they are acquired and held exclusively with a view to their subsequent disposal in the near future, or operate under severe long-term restrictions that significantly impair their ability to transfer funds to the parent or investor, IAS 39 does apply.[134]

Accounting for these investments in investors' separate financial statements is dealt with in IASs 27, 28 and 31 (see Chapter 14 at 3) and these requirements are largely unchanged by IAS 39.[135]

Sometimes strategic equity investments are made with the intent of establishing or maintaining a long-term operating relationship with the investee. Unless these are equity accounted as associates or proportionately consolidated or equity accounted as joint ventures, they are covered by IAS 39.[136]

4.2.2 *Other unique instruments dealt with by other standards*

The following instruments, which are dealt with by other international accounting standards, are also largely outside the scope of IAS 39:

- rights and obligations under leases to which IAS 17 applies (see Chapter 19 at 8.2);[137]
- employers' assets and liabilities under employee benefit plans, to which IAS 19 applies (see Chapter 22 at 3.4 and Chapter 23 at 6.2);[138]
- contracts for contingent consideration in a business combination accounted for under IAS 22 (see Chapter 6 at 5.4.2 B V);[139] and
- equity instruments issued by the reporting entity including options, warrants, and other financial instruments that are classified as shareholders' equity in accordance with IAS 32 (see Chapter 17 at 5.2 and 5.3).[140]

However, lease receivables are subject to IAS 39's derecognition provisions (see Chapter 18 at 4.2) and IAS 39 does apply to derivatives embedded within lease contracts[141] (see 4.3.3 below). The standard also applies to the holders, as opposed to issuers, of equity instruments.[142]

4.2.3 *Financial guarantee contracts*

Financial guarantee contracts, including letters of credit, that provide for payments to be made if the debtor fails to make payment when due are generally excluded from IAS 39 – they are dealt with by IAS 37 (see Chapter 28 at 7.1).

Such contracts are, however, within the scope of IAS 39 if they provide for payments to be made in response to changes in a specified interest rate, security price, commodity price, credit rating, foreign exchange rate, index of prices or rates, or other underlying variable.[143] They are also subject to IAS 39, in the hands of both the issuer and the holder, if they provide for payments to be made if a debtor fails to make payment to a third party (as opposed to the holder) when due.[144]

Example 10.4: Credit derivative within the scope of IAS 39

Company ABC owns £100 million of bonds issued by Company XYZ that mature in 20 years. XYZ is rated 'BBB' by the rating agencies and ABC is concerned that XYZ may be downgraded and hence that the value of the bonds may decline. To protect against this, ABC enters into a contract with a bank that will pay ABC for any decline in the fair value of the XYZ bonds related to a credit downgrade to 'B' or below during a specified period. ABC pays a fee to the bank for entering into the contract.

Because the contract pays ABC in the event of a downgrade and is not tied to any failure by XYZ to pay, it is a derivative instrument within the scope of IAS 39.[145]

Example 10.5: Credit derivative outside the scope of IAS 39

Bank A has total outstanding loans of £100 million to its largest customer, Company C. Bank A is concerned about concentration risk and enters into a credit default swap with Bank B to diversify its exposure without actually selling the loans. Under the terms of the swap, Bank A pays a fee to Bank B at an annual rate of 50 basis points (0.5%) on amounts outstanding. In the event that Company C defaults on any principal or interest payments, Bank B pays Bank A for any loss.

The credit default swap provides for payments to a creditor (Bank A) in the event of failure of a debtor (Company C) to pay when due and it has no characteristic that distinguishes it from a financial guarantee contract that would be excluded from IAS 39. Therefore it is outside the scope of IAS 39.[146]

In addition, IAS 39 requires recognition of financial guarantees incurred or retained as a result of its derecognition provisions (see Chapter 18 at 4.2).[147]

4.2.4 *Insurance and similar contracts*

An insurance contract is defined as one that exposes the insurer to identified risks of loss from events or circumstances occurring or discovered within a specified period, including death (in the case of an annuity, the survival of the annuitant), sickness, disability, property damage, injury to others and business interruption.[148] A separate project on accounting for insurance contracts is currently under way and accordingly rights and obligations arising from these contracts are generally excluded from IAS 39.[149]

However, IAS 39 does apply to contracts that take the form of insurance or reinsurance contracts but principally involve the transfer of financial risks including currency risk, interest rate risk, market risk, credit risk, liquidity risk and cash flow risk (see 5.2 below) as illustrated in the following example:[150]

Example 10.6: Insurance contract within the scope of IAS 39

An insurance company sells a policy to a customer for £1,000. In five years time the insurance company will pay the policyholder £1,000 multiplied by the change in a stock market index in that period.

The amount of payment is not a reimbursement for a cost or loss incurred as a result of events or circumstances noted above. Accordingly the contract is a financial instrument that is included within the scope of IAS 39, both from the point of view of the insurance company and the customer.[151]

Contracts that require a payment based on climatic, geological, or other physical variables are commonly used as insurance policies. It was recognised that, unlike most insurance contracts, the payout under some of these instruments is unrelated to the amount of an entity's loss and while leaving such derivatives within IAS 39's scope was considered, the IASC concluded that further study was needed to develop operational definitions distinguishing between 'insurance-type' and 'derivative type' contracts. Therefore these contracts are excluded from IAS 39.[152]

IAS 39 does apply to derivatives that are embedded either in insurance contracts or in weather derivatives[153] (see 4.3.3 below) and to other financial instruments held by insurance companies.[154]

Example 10.7: Combined interest rate swap and weather derivative

An interest rate swap for which payment is contingent on heating degree days (a climatic variable) is a contract that has more than one underlying variable including a climatic, geological, or other physical variable and accordingly falls within the scope of IAS 39. The climatic derivative is a host contract that is excluded from the scope of the standard but it contains an embedded derivative (an interest rate swap – see 4.3.3 below) that should be separated from the host unless it cannot be separately measured, in which case the combined contract is accounted for a financial instrument.[155]

4.2.5 *Commodity based contracts*

The provisions of IAS 39 should be applied to commodity-based contracts that give either party the right to settle in cash or some other financial instrument, with the exception of commodity contracts that:

- were entered into and continue to meet expected purchase, sale, or usage requirements;
- were designated for that purpose at inception; and
- are expected to be settled by delivery.[156]

If a pattern of entering into offsetting contracts is followed that effectively accomplishes settlement on a net basis, those contracts should be accounted for as if they were financial instruments as they are deemed not to be entered into to meet expected purchase, sale, or usage requirement.[157] Seemingly this is the case even if, legally, the contracts *require* settlement by delivery – this is covered in more detail at 4.3.2 D below in the context of derivative commodity contracts.

The implementation guidance emphasises that whilst highly liquid, gold bullion gives no contractual right to receive cash or another financial asset and is therefore a commodity. Consequently gold bullion contracts are not always accounted for as financial instruments.[158]

4.3 Classification of financial instruments

Subsequent to initial recognition the accounting for a particular financial instrument depends on how it is classified. The main classes of instrument defined in IAS 39 are set out below.

4.3.1 *Financial assets and liabilities*

Four types of financial assets and, effectively, two types of financial liabilities are defined as follows:

- *Financial assets or liabilities held for trading* – these are acquired or incurred principally for the purpose of generating a profit from short-term fluctuations in price or dealer's margin. A financial asset should be classified as held for trading if, regardless of why it was acquired, it is part of a portfolio for which there is evidence of a recent actual pattern of short-term profit-taking. Derivative financial instruments (see 4.3.2 and 4.3.3 below) are always deemed held for trading unless they are designated and effective hedging instruments.
- *Held-to-maturity investments* – financial assets with fixed or determinable payments and fixed maturity, other than originated loans and receivables, for which there is a positive intent and ability to hold to maturity.
- *Loans and receivables originated by the enterprise* – financial assets that are created by providing money, goods, or services directly to a debtor, other than those that are originated with the intent to be sold immediately or in the short term, which should be classified as held for trading. Originated loans and receivables are not classified as held-to-maturity investments.
- *Available-for-sale financial assets* – financial assets that are not originated loans and receivables, held-to-maturity investments or trading assets.[159]
- *Other financial liabilities* are not explicitly defined but are those that are not held for trading.

These definitions are covered in more detail below.

A *Assets and liabilities held for trading*

A financial asset is classified as held for trading, rather than available for sale, if it is part of a portfolio of similar assets for which there is a pattern of trading for the purpose of generating a profit from short-term fluctuations in price or dealer's margin.[160]

Entities should adopt their own definition of short-term and apply it consistently. Whilst there must be an intent to profit from short-term price fluctuations, there is no limit on the time period in which a trading instrument can be held and a single instrument in a portfolio may in fact be held for a longer period of time, e.g. a year. However, a non-derivative asset that is intended to be held for a long period, irrespective of short-term fluctuations in price, cannot be classified as trading.[161]

Evidence of 'a recent actual pattern of short-term profit taking' should be based on the frequency of buying and selling, the turnover rate, or average holding period of a group of identifiable, similar financial assets that are managed as part of a group.[162] A portfolio is a group of financial assets that are managed as part of that group. For example, assets that are managed separately from an entity's other financial instruments by a trading desk might constitute a portfolio.[163]

Example 10.8: Portfolio balancing

Company A has an investment portfolio of debt and equity securities. The documented portfolio management guidelines specify that the equity exposure of the portfolio should be limited to between 30% and 50% of total portfolio value. The investment manager of the portfolio is authorised to balance the portfolio within the designated guidelines by buying and selling equity and debt securities. The securities should be classified as trading or available-for-sale depending on A's intent and past practice.

If the portfolio manager is authorised to buy and sell securities to balance the risks in a portfolio, but there is no intention to trade and there is no past practice of trading for short-term profit, the securities are classified as available-for-sale. If securities are bought and sold to generate short-term profits, the financial instruments in the portfolio are classified as held for trading. Financial assets should be reclassified into the trading category only if there is evidence of a recent actual pattern of short-term profit taking that justifies such reclassification, not just because some assets have been sold.[164]

Liabilities held for trading include derivative liabilities that are not hedging instruments and the obligation to deliver securities and other assets borrowed by a short seller (short selling involves selling assets that an entity does not own – see Example 10. 9 below). The fact that a liability is used to fund trading activities does not make that liability one held for trading, even if the entity has a policy of actively issuing and repurchasing debt instruments. Further, where hybrid instruments contain embedded derivatives that require separation (see 4.3.3 above) and can be reliably measured, as well as a host liability, the host is not considered a trading instrument.[165]

Example 10.9: Accounting for short selling

Company A borrows a financial asset under a securities borrowing agreement which it does not record as an asset (see 4.4.3 above). It subsequently 'short sells' that borrowed asset for cash.

The short sale is accounted for by recording the cash as an asset and the obligation to deliver the financial asset as a trading liability.[166]

It is apparent that there are much tighter restrictions on classifying non-derivative liabilities as held for trading than there are on non-derivative assets. Because trading instruments, as defined, are marked to market under IAS 39 (see 4.6.1 below) and most others are not, this can lead to accounting mismatches where financial institutions hold what they *consider* to be trading liabilities.

B Held to maturity investments

The held-to-maturity category is viewed as an exception to be used only in limited circumstances.[167] Consequently its use is restricted by a number of detailed conditions, largely designed to test whether there is a genuine intent and ability to hold such investments to maturity. This assessment is not only made when those financial assets are initially acquired but at each balance sheet date too.[168]

To further restrict the use of this category, special hedge accounting cannot be used if interest rate risk associated with held-to-maturity investments is hedged (see 4.9.1 A below).[169]

I Instruments that may be classified as held-to-maturity

A debt security with a variable interest rate can satisfy the criteria for a held-to-maturity investment. Most equity securities cannot be held-to-maturity investments either because they have an indefinite life (such as ordinary shares) or because the amounts the holder may receive can vary in a manner that is not predetermined (such as share options, warrants, and rights).[170]

A perpetual debt instrument on which interest payments are made for an indefinite period cannot be classified as a held-to-maturity investment because there is no maturity date. However, a perpetual debt instrument with fixed or determinable payments for a limited period can be classified as held-to-maturity – the amount invested is recovered through fixed or determinable payments and the rights in liquidation have no fair value (see Example 10.48 at 4.6.3 B).[171]

A financial asset that is callable by the issuer satisfies the criteria for a held-to-maturity investment if the holder intends and is able to hold it until it is called, or until maturity, and if the holder would recover substantially all of its carrying amount. The call option, if exercised, simply accelerates the investment's maturity. However, if the investment is callable in a manner such that the holder would not recover substantially all of its carrying amount, it is not classified as held-to-maturity. Any premium paid and capitalised transaction costs should be considered in determining whether the carrying amount would be substantially recovered.[172]

The standard states that a financial asset that is puttable (the holder has the right to require the issuer to repay or redeem the instrument before maturity) is classified as a held-to-maturity investment only if the holder has the positive intent and ability to hold it until maturity and not to exercise the put feature.[173] However, the implementation guidance explains that the use of the held-to-maturity classification for such assets requires great care as it seems inconsistent with the likely intent of purchasing a puttable debt instrument – it would seem counterintuitive that an investor would be willing to do this and represent that the option will not be exercised.[174]

The reference to 'fixed or determinable payments and fixed maturity' in the definition means a contractual arrangement that defines the amounts and dates of payments to the holder, such as interest and principal payments on debt.[175] The likelihood of default is not a consideration in qualifying for this category provided there is an intent and ability, considering the credit condition existing at the acquisition date, to hold the investment to maturity. Even if there is a significant risk of non-payment of interest and principal, for example a bond with a very low credit rating, the contractual payments on the bond may well be fixed or determinable.[176]

Where a combined instrument contains a host contract and an embedded derivative (see 4.3.3 below), the host may be classified as held-to-maturity if it has fixed or determinable payments and no other conditions are breached. This is illustrated in the following examples.

Example 10.10: Note with index-linked principal

Company A purchases a five year interest free equity-index-linked note, with an original issue price of £10, for its market price of £12. At maturity, the note requires payment of the original issue price of £10 plus a supplemental redemption amount that depends on whether a specified stock price index exceeds a predetermined level at the maturity date. If the stock index does not exceed the predetermined level, no supplemental redemption amount is paid. If it does, the supplemental redemption amount equals the product of 1.15 and the difference between the level of the stock index at maturity and original issuance divided by the level at original issuance. A has the positive intent and ability to hold the note to maturity.

The note can be classified as a held-to-maturity investment because it has a fixed payment of £10 and fixed maturity and there is the positive intent and ability to hold it to maturity. However, the equity index feature is a call option not closely related to the debt host which must be separated as an embedded derivative (see 4.3.3 below). The purchase price of £12 is allocated between the host debt instrument and the embedded derivative, e.g. if the fair value of the embedded option at acquisition is £4, the host debt instrument is measured at £8 on initial recognition.[177]

Example 10.11: Note with index-linked interest

Subsequently A purchases a note with a fixed payment at a fixed maturity date and interest payments that are indexed to the price of a commodity or equity. There is an intention and ability to hold the note to maturity.

Again the note can be classified as a held-to-maturity investment because it has a fixed payment and fixed maturity. However the commodity-indexed or equity-indexed interest payments result in an embedded derivative that is separated and accounted for as a derivative. In practice it should be straightforward to separate the host debt investment (the fixed payment at maturity) from the embedded derivative (the index-linked interest payments).[178]

II Positive intent and ability to hold to maturity

If any one of the following criteria is met, a positive intent to hold an investment to maturity is deemed not to exist (and the asset cannot be classified as such):

- the intent to hold the investment is for only an undefined period;
- the holder stands ready to sell the financial asset in response to changes in market interest rates or risks, liquidity needs, changes in the availability of and the yield on alternative investments, changes in financing sources and terms, or changes in foreign currency risk – this does not apply to situations that are non-recurring and could not have been reasonably anticipated; or
- the issuer has a right to settle the financial asset at an amount significantly below its amortised cost.[179]

Further, an investor is deemed not to have a demonstrated ability to hold an investment to maturity if either of the following conditions is met:

- it does not have the financial resources available to continue to finance the investment until maturity; or
- it is subject to an existing legal or other constraint that could frustrate its intention to hold the financial asset to maturity, although as noted above an issuer's call option does not necessarily frustrate this intention.[180]

The intent and ability to hold debt securities to maturity is not necessarily constrained if those securities have been pledged as collateral or are subject to a repurchase or securities lending agreements. However, an entity would not have the positive intent and ability to hold the debt securities until maturity if it did not expect to be able to maintain or recover access to the securities.[181]

The standard also suggest that circumstances other than those described above can indicate that an entity does not have a positive intent or ability to hold an investment to maturity.[182]

III The tainting provisions

When an entity's actions have cast doubt on its intent or ability to hold such investments to maturity, the use of amortised cost for held-to-maturity assets is precluded for 'a reasonable period of time'.[183] Consequently no investment should be classified as held-to-maturity if, during either the current financial year or the two preceding financial years, the reporting entity has sold, transferred, or exercised a put option on more than an insignificant amount (in relation to the total held-to-maturity portfolio) of such investments before maturity other than by those effected:

(a) close enough to maturity or exercised call date so that changes in the market rate of interest did not have a significant effect on the investment's fair value;

(b) after substantially all of the investment's original principal had been collected through scheduled payments or prepayments; or

(c) due to an isolated non-recurring event that is beyond the holder's control and could not have been reasonably anticipated by the holder.[184]

Therefore if an entity makes any 'not insignificant' sale or similar transfer of a held-to-maturity investment that does not fall within (a) to (c) above, the entire remaining portfolio of such investments will have to be reclassified – normally as available-for-sale, but possibly trading, assets (see 4.6.6 below) – and will be remeasured to fair value for the following two financial years. The nature of this 'punishment' is unique within accounting standards and has become known as the 'tainting' or, by rugby followers, the 'sin-bin' provisions.

The term 'transfer' comprises any reclassification out of the held-to-maturity category. Thus, the transfer of more than an insignificant portion of held-to-maturity investments into the available-for-sale or trading category would not be consistent with an intent to hold other held-to-maturity investments to maturity.[185]

Conditions (a) and (b) relate to situations in which an entity is expected to be indifferent whether to hold or sell a financial asset because movements in interest rates after substantially all of the original principal has been collected or when the instrument is close to maturity will not have a significant impact on its fair value. Accordingly, such a sale should not affect reported income and no price volatility would be expected during the remaining period to maturity. Condition (a) addresses the extent to which interest rate risk is substantially eliminated as a pricing factor and condition (b) provides guidance as to when a sale is for not more than an insignificant amount.

If a financial asset is sold less than three months prior to maturity, that would generally qualify for this exception because the impact on the instrument's fair value of a difference between the stated interest rate and the market rate would generally be small for an instrument that matures in three months relative to an instrument that matures in several years. If sold after 90% or more of its original principal has been collected through scheduled payments or prepayments, that would generally qualify for this exception. However if only, say, 10% of the original principal has been collected, then that condition is clearly not met.[186]

The guidance makes it clear that condition (c) does not extend to an unsolicited tender offer on economically favourable terms.[187]

The conditions must be applied to all held-to-maturity investments in aggregate and not to separate sub-categories of such assets.[188] In consolidated accounts they must be applied to all investments classified as held-to-maturity in those accounts, even if they are held by different companies within the group, in different countries or in different economic environments.[189]

A 'disaster scenario' that is extremely remote, such as a run on a bank or a similar situation affecting an insurance company, is not anticipated in deciding whether there is positive intent and ability to hold an investment to maturity.[190] The standard also explains that sales before maturity may satisfy condition (c) above – and therefore not trigger the tainting provisions – if they are due to:

- a significant deterioration in the issuer's creditworthiness;
- a change in tax law that eliminates or significantly reduces the tax-exempt status of interest on the held-to-maturity investment, but not a change in tax law that revises the marginal tax rates applicable to interest income;
- a major business combination or major disposition, such as the sale of a segment, that necessitates the sale or transfer of held-to-maturity investments to maintain the holder's existing interest rate risk position or credit risk policy – although the business combination itself is an event within the holder's control, the changes to its investment portfolio to maintain interest rate risk position or credit risk policy may be consequential rather than anticipated;
- a change in statutory or regulatory requirements significantly modifying either what constitutes a permissible investment or the maximum level of certain kinds of investments, thereby causing disposal of a held-to-maturity investment;
- a significant increase by the regulator in the industry's capital requirements that causes a downsizing by selling held-to-maturity investments; or

- a significant increase in the risk weights of held-to-maturity investments used for regulatory risk-based capital purposes.[191]

A sale of a held-to-maturity investment following a downgrade of the issuer's credit rating, either by a rating agency or an internal rating process, might raise a question about the holder's intent to hold other investments to maturity. A downgrade may well indicate a decline in the issuer's creditworthiness, however that deterioration must be significant and be judged by reference to the credit rating on initial recognition. Also, the rating downgrade must not have been reasonably anticipated when the investment was classified as held-to-maturity. A credit downgrade of a notch within a class or from one rating class to the immediately lower one could often be considered reasonably anticipated. However if the rating downgrade, in combination with other information, provides evidence of impairment (see 4.7 below), this would often be considered significant.[192]

Sales of held-to-maturity investments in response to an unanticipated significant increase by the regulator in the *industry's* capital requirements may not necessarily raise a question about the intention to hold other investments to maturity. However in some countries, regulators may set capital requirements on an *entity-specific basis* based on an assessment of the risk in that particular entity. Therefore sales that are due to a significant increase in entity-specific capital requirements imposed by regulators *will* raise doubt over the intent to hold other financial assets to maturity unless it can be demonstrated that the sales fulfil condition (c) above, in other words that they result from an increase in capital requirements which is an isolated non-recurring event that is beyond the entity's control and could not have been reasonably anticipated.[193]

A change in management is not identified as an exception and the guidance explains that sales in response to such a change would call into question the intent to hold investments to maturity.[194]

Example 10.12: Change of management

A company has a portfolio of financial assets that is classified as held-to-maturity. In the current period, at the direction of the board of directors, the senior management team has been replaced. The new management wishes to sell a portion of the held-to-maturity financial assets in order to carry out an expansion strategy designated and approved by the board.

Although the previous management team had been in place since the company's formation and had never before undergone a major restructuring, the sale nevertheless calls into question the company's intent to hold remaining held-to-maturity financial assets to maturity.[195]

C Originated loans and receivables

This category will mainly comprise trade receivables and other debtors, however for banks and similar financial institutions they will constitute a significant amount of their non-trading assets, in particular loans and advances to customers.

A loan acquired by way of a participation in a loan from another lender is considered to be originated provided it is funded by the reporting entity on the date that the loan is originated by the other lender. Similarly, a loan acquired through a syndication is an originated loan because each lender shares in the origination of the loan and provides money directly to the debtor.

However, the acquisition of an interest in a pool of loans or receivables, for example in connection with a securitisation, is a purchase, not an origination, because money, goods, or services were not provided directly to the underlying debtors nor was the interest acquired through a participation with another lender on the date the underlying loans or receivables were originated. A transaction that is, in substance, a purchase of a loan that was previously originated – for example, a loan to an unconsolidated special purpose entity to provide funding for its purchases of loans originated by others – is not an originated loan.[196] Purchased, as opposed to originated, loans or receivables are classified as held to maturity, available for sale, or held for trading, as appropriate.[197]

Provided there is no intention to sell the instrument immediately or in the short term, a term deposit with a bank is classified as an originated loan even if the proof of deposit is negotiable, i.e. the deposit is capable of being sold. If there was such an intention to sell, the deposit would be a trading asset.[198] Similarly debt securities, such as bonds or sovereign debt that are purchased at original issuance are classified as originated if the funds are transferred directly to the issuer.[199]

Securities that have the legal form of equities, such as preference shares, but which under IAS 32 would be classified as liabilities in the accounts of the issuer because they have fixed or determinable payments and fixed maturity (see Chapter 17 at 5.3.3) will potentially be classified as originated loans if funds are transferred directly to the issuer. However if, under IAS 32, the security would be classified as an equity instrument in the accounts of the issuer, it could not be classified as an originated loan.[200]

A loan acquired in a business combination is considered to be originated by the acquiror provided that it was similarly classified by the acquired entity. The loan is measured at its fair value at acquisition.[201]

D Available-for-sale assets

A financial asset is classified as available for sale if it does not properly belong in one of the three other categories of financial assets – held for trading, held to maturity and originated loans and receivables.[202] This is therefore the default classification.

4.3.2 Derivatives

A *derivative* is defined as a financial instrument:

(a) whose value changes in response to the change in a specified interest rate, security price, commodity price, foreign exchange rate, index of prices or rates, a credit rating or credit index, or similar underlying;

(b) that requires no, or little, initial net investment relative to other types of contracts that have a similar response to changes in market conditions; and

(c) that is settled at a future date.[203]

The following table provides examples of contracts that normally qualify as derivatives. The list is not exhaustive – any contract that has an underlying may be a derivative. Moreover, even if an instrument meets the definition of a derivative, it may not fall within the scope of IAS 39.

Type of contract	*Main pricing-settlement underlying variable*
Interest rate swap	Interest rates
Currency swap (foreign exchange swap)	Currency rates
Commodity swap	Commodity prices
Equity swap	Equity prices (equity of another entity)
Credit swap	Credit rating, credit index, or credit price
Total return swap	Total fair value of the reference asset and interest rates
Purchased or written treasury bond option (call or put)	Interest rates
Purchased or written currency option (call or put)	Currency rates
Purchased or written commodity option (call or put)	Commodity prices
Purchased or written stock option (call or put)	Equity prices (equity of another entity)
Interest rate futures linked to government debt (treasury futures)	Interest rates
Currency futures	Currency rates
Commodity futures	Commodity prices
Interest rate forward linked to government debt (treasury forward)	Interest rates
Currency forward	Currency rates
Commodity forward	Commodity prices
Equity forward	Equity prices (equity of another entity)[204]

A Changes in value in response to changes in underlying

A derivative usually has a notional amount, such as an amount of currency, number of shares or units of weight or volume but does not require the holder or writer to invest or receive the notional amount at inception. Alternatively, a derivative could require a fixed payment as a result of some future event that is unrelated to a notional amount. For example, a contract that requires a fixed payment of £1,000 if six-month LIBOR increases by 100 basis points is a derivative but does not have a specified notional amount.[205]

Example 10.13: Derivative containing no notional amount

XYZ enters into a contract that requires payment of £1,000 if ABC's share price increases by £5 or more during a six month period; XYZ will receive £1,000 if the share price decreases by £5 or more during the same six month period; no payment will be made if the price swing is less than £5 up or down.

The settlement amount changes with an underlying, ABC's share price, although there is no notional amount to determine the settlement amount. Instead there is a payment provision that is based on changes in the underlying. Provided all the other characteristics of a derivative are present, which they are in this case, such an instrument is a derivative.[206]

A contract to pay a royalty in exchange for the use of certain property that is not exchange traded and where the payment is based on the volume of related sales or service revenues, is not accounted for as a derivative. Guidance on accounting for royalty agreements is included in IAS 18 (see Chapter 3 at 4.5.4).[207] However, derivatives that are based on sales volume are not excluded from the scope of IAS 39.[208]

Example 10.14: Derivative containing two underlyings

Company XYZ, whose reporting currency is the US dollar, sells products in France denominated in French francs. XYZ enters into a contract with an investment bank to convert French francs to US dollars at a fixed exchange rate. The contract requires XYZ to remit French francs based on its sales volume in France in exchange for US dollars at a fixed exchange rate of 6.00.

The contract has two underlying variables, the foreign exchange rate and the volume of sales, no initial net investment, and a payment provision. Therefore it is a derivative.[209]

B Little initial net investment

The phrase 'little initial net investment' is not defined in the standard and the implementation guidance explains that it should be interpreted on a relative basis and that judgement is generally required. It goes on to say it is less than that needed to acquire a primary financial instrument with a similar response to market changes which reflects the inherent leverage features typical of derivative agreements compared to the underlying instruments.[210]

An option contract generally meets this criterion because the premium is significantly less than the investment that would be required to obtain the underlying item to which the option is linked.[211] However a significant premium would be paid to acquire a 'deep in the money' call option which, if equal or close to the amount required to invest in the underlying, would fail criterion (b).[212]

The following examples illustrate how the phrase 'little initial net investment' is interpreted by the guidance:

Example 10.15: Little initial net investment – prepaid interest rate swap (prepaid fixed leg)

Company S enters into a £1,000 notional amount five year pay-fixed, receive-variable interest rate swap. The interest rate of the variable part of the swap resets on a quarterly basis to three month LIBOR. The interest rate of the fixed part of the swap is 10% per annum. At inception of the swap S prepays its fixed obligation of £500 (£1,000 x 10% x 5 years), discounted using market interest rates, while retaining the right to receive the LIBOR based interest payments on the £1,000 over the life of the swap.

The initial net investment in the swap is significantly less than the notional amount on which the variable payments under the variable leg will be calculated and requires little initial net investment relative to other types of contracts that have a similar response to changes in market conditions, such as a variable rate bond. It therefore fulfils criterion (b) above. Even though S has no future performance obligation, the ultimate settlement of the contract is at a future date and its value changes in response to changes in LIBOR. Accordingly, it is a derivative.[213]

Example 10.16: Little initial net investment – prepaid interest rate swap (prepaid floating leg)

Continuing the previous example, S subsequently enters into a £1,000 notional amount five year pay-variable, receive-fixed interest rate swap. The variable leg of the swap resets on a quarterly basis to three month LIBOR. The fixed interest payments under the swap are calculated as 10% of the notional amount, i.e. £100 per year. By agreement with the counterparty, S prepays and discharges its obligation under the variable leg of the swap at inception by paying a fixed amount determined according to current market rates, while retaining the right to receive the fixed interest payments of £100 per year.

The cash inflows under the contract are equivalent to those of a financial instrument with a fixed annuity stream since S knows it will receive £100 per year over the life of the swap. Therefore, all else being equal, the initial investment in the contract should equal that of other financial instruments consisting of fixed annuities. Thus, the initial net investment in the pay-variable, receive-fixed interest rate swap is equal to the investment required in a non-derivative contract that has a similar response to changes in market conditions. For this reason, the instrument fails criterion (b) above and is not a derivative.[214]

Not only is this an extremely unlikely transaction but the analysis appears straightforward – quite why it is the subject of an implementation guidance Q&A is not clear.

Example 10.17: Little initial net investment – prepaid forward purchase of shares

Company XYZ enters into a forward contract to purchase 100 shares in T in one year. The current share price is £50 per share and the one year forward price £55. XYZ is required to prepay the forward contract at inception with a £5,000 payment.

The initial investment in the forward contract of £5,000 is less than the notional amount applied to the underlying, 100 shares at the forward price of £55 per share, i.e. £5,500. However, the initial net investment approximates the investment that would be required for other types of contracts that would be expected to have a similar response to changes in market factors because T's shares could be purchased at inception for the same price of £50. Accordingly, the prepaid forward does not meet the little initial net investment criteria of a derivative.[215]

A currency swap that requires an exchange of different currencies of equal value at inception does not result in an initial net investment in the contract. Rather, it is simply an exchange of one form of cash for another of equal value.[216]

Example 10.18: Currency swap – initial exchange of principal

Company A and Company B enter into a five year fixed-for-fixed currency swap on euros and US dollars. The current spot exchange rate is €1 per US$. The five-year interest rate in the US is 8%, while the five-year interest rate in Europe is 6%. On initiation of the swap, A pays €2,000 to B, which in return pays US$2,000 to A. During the swap's life, A and B make periodic interest payments to each other without netting. B pays 6% per year on the €2,000 it has received (€120 per year), while A pays 8% per year on the US$2,000 it has received (US$160 per year). On termination of the swap, the two parties again exchange the original principal amounts.

The currency swap is a derivative financial instrument since the contract involves no initial net investment (only an exchange of one currency for another of equal fair values), it has an underlying, and it will be settled at a future date.[217]

C Future settlement

The third criterion requires that settlement takes place at a future date. For the purposes of determining whether, say, an interest rate swap is a derivative, it makes no difference whether the parties make the interest payments to each other (gross settlement) or settle on a net basis.[218]

Example 10.19: Interest rate swap – gross or net settlement

Company ABC is considering entering into an interest rate swap with a counterparty, XYZ. The proposed terms are that ABC pays a fixed rate of 8% and receives a variable amount based on three month LIBOR, reset on a quarterly basis; the fixed and variable amounts are determined based on a £1,000 notional amount; ABC and XYZ do not exchange the notional amount and ABC pays or receives a net cash amount each quarter based on the difference between 8% and three month LIBOR. Alternatively, settlement may be on a gross basis.

The contract meets the definition of a derivative regardless of whether there is net or gross settlement because its value changes in response to changes in an underlying variable (LIBOR), there is no initial net investment and settlements (gross or net) occur at future dates.[219]

Expiration of an option at its maturity is a form of settlement even though there is no additional exchange of consideration. Therefore even if an option is not expected to be exercised, e.g. because it is significantly 'out of the money', it can still be a derivative.[220]

D Derivatives involving non-financial assets (including commodities)

As noted in 4.2.5 above, commitments to buy or sell non-financial assets and liabilities that are intended to be settled by making or taking delivery in the normal course of business, and for which there is no practice of settling net (either with the counterparty or by entering into offsetting contracts), are not accounted for as derivatives but as executory contracts. Settling net means making a cash payment based on the change in fair value.[221] The following examples illustrate how the concept of net settlement should be interpreted.

Example 10.20: Copper forward

Company XYZ enters into a fixed-price forward contract to purchase 1,000kg of copper. The contract permits XYZ to take physical delivery of the copper at the end of twelve months or to pay or receive a net settlement in cash, based on the change in fair value of copper.

The contract is a derivative instrument because there is no initial net investment, the contract is based on the price of copper, and it is to be settled at a future date. However, if XYZ intends to settle the contract by taking delivery and has no history of settling in cash, the contract is accounted for as an executory contract rather than as a derivative.[222]

Example 10.21: Commodity contract settled net

Company A enters into a forward contract to purchase a commodity or other non-financial asset that, contractually, is to be settled by taking delivery. A has an established pattern of settling such contracts prior to delivery by contracting with a third party to settle any market value difference for the contract price directly with them.

Because A does not expect to take delivery and has a pattern of entering into offsetting contracts that effectively accomplishes net settlement, the contract does not qualify for the exemption for delivery in the normal course of business and is accounted for as a derivative.

The contract would not be accounted for as a derivative if A intended to take delivery and taking delivery was consistent with its past practice.[223]

Example 10.22: Put option on office building

Company XYZ owns an office building. It enters into a put option with an investor, which expires in five years, that permits it to put the building to the investor for £150 million. The current value of the building is £175 million. The option, if exercised, may be settled through physical delivery or net cash, at XYZ's option.

XYZ's accounting depends on its intent and past practice for settlement. Although the contract meets the definition of a derivative, XYZ does not account for it as a derivative if it intends to settle the contract by delivering the building in the event of exercise and there is no past practice of settling net.

The investor, however, cannot conclude that the option was entered into to meet its expected purchase, sale, or usage requirements because it does not have the ability to require delivery – the holder has the choice of physical delivery or net cash settlement. Regardless of past practices, its intention does not affect whether settlement is by delivery or in cash. If the contract *required* physical delivery and the investor had no past practice of settling net in cash, the contract would not be accounted for as a derivative.[224]

E In-substance derivatives

The implementation guidance explains that the accounting should follow the substance of arrangements, in particular non-derivative transactions should be aggregated and treated as a derivative when, in substance, the transactions result in a derivative. Indicators of this would include:

- they are entered into at the same time and in contemplation of one another;
- they have the same counterparty;
- they relate to the same risk; and
- there is no apparent economic need or substantive business purpose for structuring the transactions separately that could not also have been accomplished in a single transaction.[225]

Example 10.23: In-substance derivative – offsetting loans

Company A makes a five-year fixed rate loan to Company B, while at the same time B makes a five-year variable rate loan for the same amount to A. There are no transfers of principal at inception of the two loans, since A and B have a netting agreement.

The combined contractual effect of the loans is the equivalent of an interest rate swap arrangement with no initial net investment, i.e. there is an underlying variable, no initial net investment, and future settlement. This meets the definition of a derivative. This would be the case even if there was no netting agreement, because the definition of a derivative instrument does not require net settlement (see Example 10.19 above).[226]

F Margin payments

Many derivative instruments, such as futures contracts and exchange traded written options, require margin payments. The margin payment is not part of the initial net investment in a derivative, but is a form of collateral for the counterparty or clearing house and may take the form of cash, securities, or other specified assets, typically liquid assets. They are separate assets that are accounted for separately.[227]

G Regular way contracts

If an entity contracts to buy a financial asset, e.g. a fixed rate debt instrument, on terms that require delivery of the asset within the time frame established generally by regulation or convention in the market place concerned (sometimes called a 'regular way contract'), the fixed price commitment between trade date and settlement date is a forward contract that meets the definition of a derivative. However there are special accounting rules for such contracts, which are discussed in 4.4.2 below.[228]

4.3.3 Embedded derivatives

Sometimes, a derivative may be a component of a hybrid or combined financial instrument that includes both the derivative and a host contract with the effect that some of the cash flows of the combined instrument vary in a similar way to a stand-alone derivative. Such derivatives are sometimes known as 'embedded derivatives'. An embedded derivative causes some or all of the cash flows that otherwise would be required by the contract to be modified based on a specified underlying.[229]

Embedded derivatives should be separated from the host contract and accounted for as a derivative if, and only if, all of the following conditions are met:

(a) the economic characteristics and risks of the embedded derivative are not closely related to those of the host contract;

(b) a separate instrument with the same terms as the embedded derivative would meet the definition of a derivative; and

(c) the hybrid (combined) instrument is not measured at fair value with changes in fair value reported in income.[230]

If any of these conditions are not met, the embedded derivative should not be accounted for separately.[231] The process is similar, although not identical, to that applied when separating the equity element of a hybrid contract under IAS 32 (see Chapter 17 at 5.3.5).

A Identifying embedded derivatives

When separating an embedded derivative, the stated or implied substantive terms of the hybrid instrument should determine those of the host. In the absence of implied or stated terms, judgement will be necessary, however this must not result in a separate embedded derivative that is not already clearly present in the hybrid, i.e. a cash flow that does not exist cannot be created. For example, if a five year debt instrument has fixed annual interest payments of £40 and a principal payment at maturity of £1,000 multiplied by the change in an equity price index, it would be inappropriate to identify a floating rate host and an embedded equity swap that has an offsetting floating rate leg – the host should be a fixed rate debt instrument that pays £40 annually because there are no floating interest rate cash flows in the hybrid instrument.[232] However, the nature of the host is not always apparent from the terms of the hybrid as shown in the following example taken from the draft implementation guidance:

Example 10.24: Equity linked debt

Company A purchases a five year 'debt' instrument issued by Company B with a principal of £1,000, indexed to Company C's share price. At maturity, A will receive the principal plus or minus the change in the fair value of 100 of C's shares and no interest payments are made before maturity. On the date of acquisition, the purchase price is £1,000 and C's share price is £10. A classifies the instrument as available for sale and has a policy of reporting gains and losses on available-for-sale assets in equity.

The instrument is a hybrid instrument with an embedded derivative because of the equity-indexed principal. Perhaps surprisingly the host contract is a debt instrument because the hybrid has a stated maturity – it does not meet the definition of an equity instrument – and is accounted for as a zero coupon debt as there are no interest payments.[233]

A hybrid instrument can have more than one embedded derivative requiring separation, but only if they are clearly present, as evidenced by the hybrid's contractual terms and if its economic substance relates to different risk exposures that are readily separable and independent of each other. In addition, as noted earlier, any embedded non-option derivative must be determined so as to have an initial fair value of zero. Otherwise a single hybrid could be decomposed into an infinite number of combinations of embedded derivatives and it would be possible to separate embedded derivative features that can only be valued in combination with other embedded derivative features, e.g. because they are mutually exclusive or otherwise interdependent.

In many cases, embedded derivative features should not be separated. For example, if a debt instrument has a principal amount related to an equity index and that amount doubles if the equity index exceeds a certain level, it is not appropriate to separate both a forward and an option on the equity index because those derivative features relate to the same risk exposure. Instead the forward and option elements are treated as a single compound embedded derivative. For the same reason, an embedded floor or cap on interest rates should not be separated into a series of 'floorlets' or 'caplets'.

In addition, if a single hybrid contains both a put option and a written call option on the hybrid instrument that require separation, e.g. callable debt with a put to the holder, those options are treated as a single embedded derivative because they are not independent of each other. Furthermore, if an investor holds callable convertible debt for which separation of the call option is required, it is not appropriate to separate an equity conversion option and a written call option on the debt instrument separately because the two embedded derivative features should not be valued independently of each other.

On the other hand, if a hybrid debt instrument contains, for example, two options that give the holder a right to choose both the interest rate index on which interest payments are determined and the currency in which the principal is repaid, those two options may qualify for separation as two separate embedded derivatives since they relate to different risk exposures and are readily separable and independent of each other.[234] The application of this principle where one of the options is an equity instrument of the issuer is illustrated in the following example taken from the draft guidance:

Example 10.25: Issued puttable convertible debt

Company Q issues puttable convertible bonds at their total par value of £2,000. Each bond pays fixed interest and is convertible at any time up to maturity into Company Q shares. Each bond also contains an embedded put option that gives the holder the right to redeem the bond at its par value at any time.

The conversion option is an equity instrument and, therefore, is outside the scope of IAS 39. First, in accordance with IAS 32, Q separates the equity element of the proceeds, which gives an initial carrying amount of, say, £200.

As a second step, Q determines whether there is an embedded derivative, a written put option, requiring separation in addition to the equity conversion option. Since the conversion and embedded put options are mutually exclusive, i.e. if one is exercised the other is extinguished, the assessment of whether the put option is closely related to the host is made before separating the equity component.

If the debt was not issued at a significant premium or discount before separating out the embedded equity conversion option, the put is considered closely related to the host debt instrument (see below).[235]

B Synthetic instruments

A non-derivative instrument with an attached derivative that is capable of being transferred independently to another party is not a hybrid instrument, but two standalone instruments, which should always be accounted for separately.[236] A derivative added to a non-derivative financial instrument by a third party contemporaneously with, or subsequent to, the issuance of the non-derivative instrument is similarly treated as a stand-alone derivative because it is not part of the original contract at issuance.[237]

Example 10.26: Bond issued and marketed with an attached put option

Company A issues a 15 year bond to Investment Bank B for £102. B attaches a call option to the bond and sells the bond with the attached call option to Investor C for £100. The call option is a written option from the perspective of C and a purchased option from the perspective of B. The call option is sold from B to A.

Since the option was attached to the bond by a third party, it is treated as a stand-alone derivative.[238]

This is also the case where a synthetic instrument is created by using derivatives to 'alter' the nature of a non-derivative instrument, as illustrated in the following example:

Example 10.27: Investment in synthetic fixed-rate debt

Company A acquires a five year floating rate debt instrument issued by Company B. At the same time, it enters into a five year pay-variable receive-fixed interest rate swap with Bank C. A considers the combination of the two instruments to be a synthetic fixed rate bond and, since it has the positive intent and ability to hold them to maturity, wants to classify them as a held-to-maturity investment.

Embedded derivatives are terms and conditions that are *included in* non-derivative host contracts and it is generally inappropriate to treat two or more separate financial instruments as a single combined, or synthetic, instrument. Each of the financial instruments has its own terms and conditions and may be transferred or settled separately. Therefore, the debt instrument and the swap must be classified separately.[239]

C *The meaning of 'closely related'*

The standard does not define what 'closely related' means but provides a series of situations where the embedded derivative is, or is not, considered to be closely related to the host contract. In the following examples the economic characteristics and risks of the embedded derivative are not considered to be closely related to the host contract. Therefore, assuming conditions (b) and (c) above are also met, the embedded derivative is accounted for separately from the host:

- a put option on an equity instrument is not closely related to the host equity instrument;
- a call option embedded in an equity instrument is not closely related to the host equity instrument from the perspective of the holder;
- an option or automatic provision to extend the term or maturity date of debt is not closely related to the host debt unless there is a concurrent adjustment to the market rate of interest at the time of extension;
- similarly a call or put option on debt that is issued at a significant discount or premium is not closely related to the debt unless it is callable or puttable at its accreted amount, e.g. certain zero coupon bonds;
- equity-indexed interest or principal payments are not closely related to the host debt instrument (or insurance contract) because the risks inherent in the host and the embedded derivative are dissimilar;
- commodity-indexed interest or principal payments are not closely related to the host debt instrument (or insurance contract) because, as above, the risks inherent in the host and the embedded derivative are dissimilar;
- an equity conversion feature embedded in a debt instrument is not closely related to the host debt instrument; and
- arrangements known as credit derivatives that are embedded in a host debt instrument and that allow one party (the 'beneficiary') to transfer the credit risk of an asset, which it may or may not actually own, to another party (the 'guarantor') are not closely related to the host debt instrument. Such credit derivatives allow the guarantor to assume the credit risk associated with a reference asset without directly purchasing it.[240]

On the other hand, in the following examples the economic characteristics and risks of the embedded derivative are considered to be closely related to those of the host contract and therefore the hybrid contract is accounted for as a single instrument:

- the embedded derivative is linked to an interest rate or interest rate index that can change the amount of interest that would otherwise be paid or received on the host debt contract, i.e. floating rate debt cannot be treated as fixed rate debt with an embedded derivative;
- an embedded floor or cap on interest rates is considered to be closely related to the interest rate on a debt instrument if the cap is at or above the market interest rate or the floor is at or below the market interest rate when the instrument is issued, and the cap or floor is not leveraged in relation to the host instrument;[241]

  Similar provisions apply in sale and purchase contracts that establish a higher and lower limit on the price of the asset subject to the contract (see Example 10.33 below).[242]
- the embedded derivative is a stream of principal or interest payments that are denominated in a foreign currency. Such a derivative is not separated from the host contract because IAS 21 requires that foreign currency translation gains and losses on the entire host monetary item be recognised in income (see Chapter 8 at 5.2.4);
- the host contract is not a financial instrument and it requires payments denominated in:

  (i) the currency of the primary economic environment in which any substantial party to that contract operates; or

  (ii) the currency in which the price of the related good or service that is acquired or delivered is routinely denominated in international commerce, e.g. the US dollar for crude oil transactions.

  Such a contract is not regarded as a host contract with an embedded foreign currency derivative;[243]

  For the purposes of (i), the relevant currencies are the measurement currencies of any substantial party to the contract or those of the countries in which any substantial party to the contract is domiciled.[244] Companies based in countries with significant inflation often negotiate sale and purchase contracts in a hard currency such as the US dollar – unless the dollar is one of the parties' measurement currency (or (ii) applies) the embedded derivative is not closely related to the sale and purchase contract.[245]

  In (ii), the currency must be used for similar transactions all around the world, not just in one local area. For example, if cross border transactions in natural gas in North America are routinely denominated in US dollars and such transactions are routinely denominated in euros in Europe, neither the US dollar nor the euro is a currency in which the good or service is routinely denominated in international commerce.[246]
- the embedded derivative is a prepayment option with an exercise price that would not result in a significant gain or loss;

- the embedded derivative is a prepayment option that is embedded in an interest-only or principal-only strip that:
  - (i) initially resulted from separating the right to receive contractual cash flows of a financial instrument that, in and of itself, did not contain an embedded derivative; and
  - (ii) does not contain any terms not present in the original host debt;
- with regard to a host contract that is a lease, the embedded derivative is:
  - (i) an inflation-related index such as an index of lease payments to a consumer price index (provided that the lease is not leveraged and the index relates to inflation in the entity's own economic environment);
  - (ii) contingent rentals based on related sales; and
  - (iii) contingent rentals based on variable interest rates; or
- the embedded derivative is an interest rate or interest rate index that does not alter the net interest payments that otherwise would be paid on the host contract in such a way that the holder would not recover substantially all of its recorded investment or (in the case of a derivative that is a liability) the issuer would pay a rate more than twice the market rate at inception.[247]

  If a holder is permitted, but not required, to settle the combined instrument in a manner such that it does not recover substantially all of its recorded investment, for example puttable debt, this condition is not satisfied and the embedded derivative need not be separated.[248]

D Initial measurement of embedded derivatives

Where an embedded non-option derivative, such as a forward or swap, is separated, its terms should be evaluated so that its initial fair value is nil based on the conditions existing at that time. Otherwise, a single hybrid instrument could be decomposed into an infinite variety of combinations of host debt instruments and embedded derivatives, e.g. by separating embedded derivatives with terms that create leverage, asymmetry, or some other risk exposure not already present in the hybrid instrument.[249]

The same is not true of an embedded option-based derivative – such a derivative would have to be infinitely out of the money, i.e. have a zero probability of being exercised, to have a fair value of nil – nor should it be determined to have a nil strike price. The separation of such a derivative (including any embedded put, call, cap, floor, 'caption', 'floortion', or 'swaption' feature in a hybrid instrument) should be based on the stated terms of the option feature documented in the hybrid instrument.[250]

E Accounting for host contracts

Where an embedded derivative is separated, the host should be accounted for under IAS 39 if it is itself a financial instrument; otherwise it should be accounted for in accordance with other appropriate standards.[251] This doesn't necessarily mean that the host and the embedded derivative should be shown separately in the balance sheet, however as discussed at 5.1 below, financial instruments carried at cost should be disclosed separately from those carried at fair value.[252]

If an embedded derivative is required to be separated from its host contract but the reporting entity is unable to separately measure the embedded derivative either at acquisition or at a susequent financial reporting date, it should treat the entire combined contract as a financial instrument held for trading.[253] However if the fair values of both the hybrid and host instruments can be reliably measured, the difference between the two provides reliable evidence of the fair value of the embedded derivative and it should be separated.[254]

Example 10.28: Accounting for investment in convertible bond

Company A makes an investment in a bond that is convertible either into shares of the issuing company, or of another specified company, at any time prior to maturity.

The guidance states that an investment in such a bond generally cannot be classified as held-to-maturity as that would be inconsistent with paying for a conversion feature exercisable before maturity. (This seems a slightly more onerous test than for a bond with an embedded put option, which the standard allows to be classified as held-to-maturity if the holder has the positive intent and ability not to exercise the put, although the implementation guidance did attempt to backtrack somewhat from this position – see 4.3.1 B I).

The bond may be classified as available-for-sale, provided it is not purchased for trading purposes, and the equity conversion option would be considered an embedded derivative. If fair value changes on available-for-sale assets were initially reported in equity rather than income (see 4.6.4 B below), the option would generally be separated.

If the bond is carried at fair value with changes in fair value reported in income, i.e. it is a trading asset or an available-for-sale asset with fair value changes reported in income, separating the embedded derivative from the host bond is not permitted.[255]

F Examples of embedded derivatives

The following examples illustrate how the implementation guidance, final and draft, interprets whether or not a contract contains an embedded derivative that requires separation:

Example 10.29: Gold indexed debt

Company A issues a debt instrument on which it pays interest indexed to the price of gold.

As set out above commodity-indexed interest is not considered closely related to a host debt instrument and A should therefore separate the embedded derivative, a forward contract indexed to the price of gold, from the host debt instrument.[256]

Example 10.30: Oil contract denominated in Swiss francs

A Norwegian company agrees to sell oil to a company in France. The oil contract is denominated in Swiss francs, although oil contracts are routinely denominated in US dollars in international commerce. Neither company carries out any significant activities in Swiss francs.

In the unlikely event that such a transaction were to take place, the Norwegian company should regard the supply contract as a host contract with an embedded foreign currency forward (to purchase Swiss francs) and the French company should regard it as a host contract with an embedded foreign currency forward (to sell Swiss francs).[257]

Example 10.31: Dual currency bond

Company A purchases a dual currency bond with principal denominated in its domestic currency and interest payment obligations denominated in a foreign currency and classifies the bond as a held-to-maturity investment (carried at amortised cost).

No embedded derivative is separated because the embedded derivative is a stream of principal or interest payments that are denominated in a foreign currency; principal and interest payments do not necessarily have to be in the same currency. Therefore the foreign currency component of the carrying amount is reported using the closing rate under IAS 21.[258]

Example 10.32: Oil contract, denominated in US dollars and containing a leveraged foreign exchange payment

Company A, whose measurement currency is the euro, enters into a contract with Company B, whose measurement currency is the Norwegian krone, to purchase oil in six months for US$1,000. The host oil contract will be settled by making and taking delivery in the normal course of business and is not accounted for as a financial instrument. The oil contract includes a leveraged foreign exchange provision whereby the parties, in addition to the provision of, and payment for, oil will exchange an amount equal to the fluctuation in the exchange rate of the US dollar and Norwegian krone applied to a notional amount of US$100,000.

The payment of US$1,000 under the host oil contract can be viewed as a foreign currency derivative because the dollar is neither Company A nor B's measurement currency. However it would not be separated as the US dollar is the currency in which crude oil transactions are routinely denominated in international commerce.

The leveraged foreign exchange provision is in addition to the required payment for the oil transaction. It is unrelated to the host oil contract and is therefore separated and accounted for as an embedded derivative.[259]

Example 10.33: Long term supply contract with embedded cap and floor

A manufacturer enters into a long-term contract to purchase a specified quantity of a commodity from a supplier. The current market price at the inception of the contract is £110 per unit and in future periods the supplier will provide the commodity at the current market price subject to the price not exceeding £120 per unit or falling below £100 per unit. The commodity-based contract is not within the scope of IAS 39 because it will be settled by making and taking delivery in the normal course of business.

From the manufacturer's perspective, the price limits specified in the purchase contract can be viewed as a purchased call on the commodity with a strike price of £120 per unit (a cap) and a written put on the commodity with a strike price of £100 per unit (a floor). At inception, both the cap and floor on the purchase price are out of the money. Therefore, they are considered closely related to the host purchase contract and are not separately recognised as embedded derivatives.[260]

Example 10.34: Equity kicker

A Venture Capital Company, V, provides a subordinated loan to Company A and agrees that, in addition to interest and repayment of principal, if A lists its shares on a stock exchange, V will be entitled to receive shares in A for free or at a very low price (an 'equity kicker'). As a result of this feature, interest on the loan is lower than it would otherwise be. The loan is not measured at fair value with changes in fair value reported in income.

The economic characteristics and risks of an equity return are not closely related to those of a host debt instrument. The equity kicker meets the definition of a derivative because it has a value that changes in response to the change in the price of A's shares, it requires little initial net investment, and it is settled at a future date – it does not matter that the right to receive shares is contingent upon the borrower's future listing.[261]

Jardine Matheson is an example of a company that, prior to the implementation of IAS 39, had an accounting policy of separating certain embedded derivatives – in this case the embedded option within a debt instrument that is exchangeable into shares of an unrelated entity.

Extract 10.24: Jardine Matheson Holdings Limited (2000)

Principal Accounting Policies [extract]
Borrowings and borrowing costs [extract]

Borrowings are recognised initially at the proceeds received, net of transaction costs incurred. In subsequent periods, borrowings are stated at amortised costs using the effective yield method.

On issue of convertible bonds, the fair value of the liability portion is determined using a market interest rate for an equivalent non-convertible bond; this amount is included in long-term borrowings on the amortised cost basis until extinguished on conversion or maturity of the bond. The remainder of the proceeds is allocated to the conversion option which is recognised and included in shareholders' funds or non-current liabilities, as appropriate.

20 Borrowings [extract]

In September 2000, JMH Finance Limited, a wholly-owned subsidiary undertaking, issued US$550 million 4.75% guaranteed bonds due 2007. The bonds are guaranteed by the Company. Proceeds of the bonds were used to finance the repurchase of the Company's shares. The bonds are exchangeable, at the option of the holders, into shares of common stock of J.P. Morgan Chase & Co. on the basis of 15.83 shares for each US$1,000 principal amount of the bonds from 6th September 2001 until 30th August 2007. The bonds will mature on 6th September 2007. The fair values of the liability component and option component are determined on issue of the bond. The fair value of the liability component, included in long-term borrowings, is calculated using a market interest rate for an equivalent non-convertible bond. The residual amount, representing the value of the conversion option component, is included in other non-current liabilities (*refer note 22*).

22 Other Non-current Liabilities

	2000 US$m	1999 US$m
Motor vehicle repurchase commitments	**10.3**	7.6
Conversion option component of guaranteed bonds (*refer note 20*)	**67.6**	–
Other creditors due after more than one year	**2.7**	1.9
	80.6	9.5

4.4 Recognition and derecognition

4.4.1 *Recognition*

With the exception of the special case of 'regular way' purchases (see 4.4.2 below) all financial assets and liabilities are to be recognised on the balance sheet of the reporting entity as soon as it becomes a party to the contractual provisions of the instrument.[262] Consequently all contractual rights or obligations under derivatives are recognised on the balance sheet as assets or liabilities.[263]

The following are examples of applying this principle:

- unconditional receivables and payables are recognised as assets or liabilities when the entity becomes a party to the contract and, as a consequence, has a legal right to receive, or a legal obligation to pay, cash;
- assets to be acquired and liabilities to be incurred as a result of a firm commitment to purchase or sell goods or services are not recognised under present accounting practice until at least one of the parties has performed under the agreement such that it either is entitled to receive an asset or is obligated to disburse an asset. For example, an entity that receives a firm order does not recognise an asset (and the entity that places the order does not recognise a liability) at the time of the commitment but, rather, delays recognition until the ordered goods or services have been shipped, delivered, or rendered;
- in contrast, however, a commitment to purchase or sell a specified financial instrument or commodity subject to IAS 39 on a future date at a specified price (a forward contract) is recognised as an asset or a liability on the commitment date, rather than waiting until the closing date on which the exchange actually takes place. When an entity becomes party to a forward, the fair values of the right and obligation are often equal, so that the forward's net fair value is zero, and only any net fair value of the right and obligation is recognised as an asset or liability. However, each party is exposed to the associated price risk from that date. Such a contract satisfies the recognition principle above from the perspectives of both the buyer and the seller, at the time the entities become parties to the contract, even though it may have a zero value at that date. The fair value of the contract may become a net asset or liability in the future depending on, among other things, the time value of money and the value of the underlying instrument or commodity that is the subject of the forward;
- financial options are recognised as assets or liabilities when the holder or writer becomes a party to the contract;
- planned future transactions, no matter how likely, are not assets and liabilities since the reporting entity has not become a party to a contract requiring future receipt or delivery of assets arising out of the future transactions;[264] and
- the economic benefits of cash received as collateral for, say, a securities borrowing transaction that is not legally segregated from an entity's other assets should be recognised as an asset together with a related obligation to repay the cash.[265]

4.4.2 *Regular way transactions*

Contracts for the purchase or sale of a financial asset that require delivery of the asset within the time frame generally established by regulation or convention in the market place concerned ('regular way' contracts) are financial instruments. In fact the fixed price commitment between execution and settlement is a derivative – a forward contract – however, because of its short duration, it is not accounted for as a derivative under IAS 39.[266]

In this context, the term 'market place' is not limited to a formal stock exchange or organised over-the-counter market. Rather, it means the environment in which the financial asset is customarily exchanged. An acceptable time frame would be the period reasonably and customarily required for the parties to complete the transaction and prepare and execute closing documents. For example, a market for private issue securities can be a market place for this purpose.[267]

A contract under which neither party is required to deliver the asset because it allows for, or requires, net cash settlement cannot be accounted for as a regular way contract. Instead such a contract is accounted for as a derivative in the period between trade date and settlement date.[268]

If a security is traded in more than one active market, and the settlement provisions differ in these markets, the provisions in the one in which the purchase actually takes place apply when assessing whether a contract to purchase those securities is a regular way contract.[269]

These principles are illustrated in the following examples:

Example 10.35: Purchase of shares through broker

Company XYZ purchases 100 shares of Company ABC on a US stock exchange through a broker. The settlement date of the contract is six business days later. Trades for equity securities on US exchanges customarily settle in three business days.

Because the trade settles in six business days, it does not meet the exemption as a regular-way security trade. However, if XYZ did the same transaction on a foreign exchange that has a customary settlement period of six business days, the contract would meet the exemption.[270]

Example 10.36: Purchase of shares with extended settlement terms

Company ABC enters into a forward contract to purchase one million shares of M in two months for £10 per share. The contract is with an individual, is not exchange-traded and requires ABC to take physical delivery of the shares in return for paying the counterparty £10 million in cash. M's shares trade in an active market at an average of 100,000 shares a day. Regular-way delivery is three days.

The contract must be accounted for as a derivative because it is not settled in the way established by regulation or convention in the market place concerned.[271]

Example 10.37: Regular way settlement of call option

Company A purchases a call option in a public market permitting it to purchase 100 shares of XYZ at any time over the next three months at a price of £100 per share. If the option is exercised, A has 14 days to settle the transaction according to regulation or convention in the options market. XYZ shares are traded in an active public market that requires three-day settlement.

The purchase of shares by exercising the option is a regular way purchase of shares because the settlement of an option by delivery of the shares within 14 days is governed by regulation or convention in the market place for options and therefore is a regular way transaction. Consequently, upon exercise of the option it is no longer accounted for as a derivative.[272]

Regular way purchases and sales of financial assets should be recognised using either *trade date accounting* or *settlement date accounting*. The method used should be applied consistently for all purchases and sales of assets that belong to the same category set out in 4.3.1 above.[273] The *trade date* is when an entity commits to purchase or sell an asset and the *settlement date* when the asset is delivered. Trade date and settlement date accounting refer to:

- recognition of an asset to be received, and a liability to pay for it; and
- derecognition of an asset that is sold, and the recognition of a receivable from the buyer;

on the trade date or settlement date respectively. Generally, interest does not start to accrue on the asset and corresponding liability until the settlement date when title passes.[274]

When settlement date accounting is applied to the purchase of trading or available-for-sale assets, any change in the fair value of the asset to be received between the trade and settlement dates is recognised on the balance sheet, seemingly as a payable or receivable; the reporting of this gain or loss follows the treatment for the asset to be received – see 4.6.1 B and 4.6.4 B below respectively. If the asset to be acquired will be carried at cost or amortised cost, changes in its fair value between trade date and settlement date are not recognised.[275]

These two methods of accounting are illustrated in the following examples:

Example 10.38: Regular way asset purchases – comparison of trade and settlement date accounting

On 29 December 2001, Company A commits to purchase a financial asset for £1,000, its then fair value. On 31 December 2001, A's year end, and on 4 January 2002, settlement date, the asset's fair value is £1,002 and £1,003 respectively. This is a regular way transaction.

The accounting will depend on how the asset will be classified and whether trade or settlement date accounting is used as illustrated below (all amounts are cumulative balances):[276]

Settlement date accounting

	Held-to-maturity asset, recorded at amortised cost	Available-for-sale asset with fair value changes reported in equity	Trading or available-for-sale assets with fair value changes reported in income
	£	£	£
29 December 2001			
Asset	–	–	–
Liability	–	–	–
31 December 2001			
Receivable	–	2	2
Asset	–	–	–
Liability	–	–	–
Equity	–	(2)	–
Income	–	–	(2)
4 January 2002			
Receivable	–	–	–
Asset	1,000	1,003	1,003
Liability	–	–	–
Equity	–	(3)	–
Income	–	–	(3)

Trade date accounting

	Held-to-maturity asset, recorded at amortised cost	Available-for-sale asset with fair value changes reported in equity	Trading or available-for-sale assets with fair value changes reported in income
	£	£	£
29 December 2001			
Asset	1,000	1,000	1,000
Liability	(1,000)	(1,000)	(1,000)
31 December 2001			
Receivable	–	–	–
Asset	1,000	1,002	1,002
Liability	(1,000)	(1,000)	(1,000)
Equity	–	(2)	
Income	–	–	(2)
4 January 2002			
Receivable	–	–	–
Asset	1,000	1,003	1,003
Liability	–	–	–
Equity	–	(3)	–
Income	–	–	(3)

Example 10.39: Regular way asset sales – comparison of trade and settlement date accounting

Continuing the previous example, on 29 December 2002, A enters into a contract to sell the financial asset for its current fair value of £1,010. Its amortised cost is £1,000 and interest during 2001 is ignored. On 31 December 2002, the asset's fair value is £1,012 and on 4 January 2003, the settlement date, £1,013. The accounting is illustrated below (again all amounts are cumulative).[277]

Settlement date accounting

	Held-to-maturity asset, recorded at amortised cost	Available-for-sale asset with fair value changes reported in equity	Trading or available-for-sale assets with fair value changes reported in income
	£	£	£
29 December 2002			
Receivable	–	–	–
Asset	1,000	1,010	1,010
Equity	–	(10)	–
Income	–	–	(10)
31 December 2002			
Receivable	–	–	–
Asset	1,000	1,010	1,010
Equity	–	(10)	–
Income	–	–	(10)
4 January 2003			
Equity	–	–	–
Income	–	(10)	(10)

Trade date accounting

	Held-to-maturity asset, recorded at amortised cost	Available-for-sale asset with fair value changes reported in equity	Trading or available-for-sale assets with fair value changes reported in income
	£	£	£
29 December 2002			
Receivable	1,010	1,010	1,010
Asset	–	–	–
Equity	–	–	–
Income	(10)	(10)	(10)
31 December 2002			
Receivable	1,010	1,010	1,010
Asset	–	–	–
Equity	–	–	–
Income	(10)	(10)	(10)
4 January 2003			
Equity	–	–	–
Income	(10)	(10)	(10)

Although not a purchase in the conventional sense, the implementation guidance states that commitments to originate loans or receivables may, in certain circumstances, be treated as regular way contracts. For example a bank might make a loan commitment based on representations of the borrower and preliminary underwriting activities – the commitment period is then allows the bank to complete its underwriting and the borrower to schedule and execute an associated transaction. These are considered to be a regular way transaction when they are:

- entered into with the intent to settle by execution of a loan;
- there is no past practice of settling the commitment based on changes in interest rates; and
- the commitment period does not extend beyond the period expected to be necessary to perform appropriate underwriting, effect orderly closing and facilitate the scheduling and execution of the associated transaction.[278]

These special provisions do not apply to the recognition or derecognition of financial liabilities, such as deposit liabilities and trading liabilities. Instead these should be treated under the normal recognition and derecognition rules (see 4.4.1 above and 4.4.3 below).[279]

4.4.3 *Derecognition*

There are extensive rules as to when assets and liabilities (or part thereof) should be derecognised and these are covered in Chapter 18 at 4.2.

4.5 Initial measurement

On initial recognition all financial assets and liabilities are recorded at cost, which is the fair value of the consideration given (in the case of an asset) or received (in the case of a liability). Initial transaction costs are included in this initial measurement and no account is taken of such costs that would arise on disposal or settlement of the financial instrument.[280]

Transaction costs are defined as incremental costs that are directly attributable to the acquisition or disposal of a financial asset or liability.[281] They include fees and commissions paid to agents, advisers, brokers, and dealers; levies by regulatory agencies and securities exchanges; and transfer taxes and duties. They do not include debt premium or discount, financing costs, or allocations of internal administrative or holding costs.[282]

Example 10.40: Transaction costs – initial measurement

Company A acquires an equity security at a price of £100 and pays a purchase commission of £2. If the asset was sold, a sales commission of £3 would be payable.

The initial measurement of the asset is £102, i.e. the sum of the purchase price and the purchase commission – the commission payable on sale is not considered for this purpose.[283]

In certain circumstances not all of what appears to be the consideration given or received actually relates to the financial instrument in question as illustrated in the following example.

Example 10.41: Interest-free loan to supplier

Company A lends £1,000 to Company B for five years and classifies the asset as an originated loan. The loan carries no interest and instead, A expects other future economic benefits, such as an implicit right to receive goods or services at favourable prices or influence over the activities of B. On initial recognition, the market rate of interest for a similar five-year loan with payment of interest at maturity is 10% per year.

The consideration of £1,000 is for two assets. On initial recognition, the carrying amount of the loan is the fair value of the consideration given to obtain the right to a payment of £1,000 in five years. The fair value of that right is the present value of the future payment of £1,000 discounted using the market rate of interest for a similar loan of 10% for five years, £621.

A also obtains other future economic benefits that have a fair value of £379 (the difference between the total consideration given of £1,000 and the consideration given for the loan of £621). The difference is not a financial asset, since it is paid to obtain expected future economic benefits other than the right to receive payment on the loan asset. A recognises that amount as an expense unless it qualifies for recognition as an asset under other applicable standards.[284]

For non-cash transactions, the fair value of the consideration is often determinable by reference to the transaction price or other market prices. If these are not reliably determinable, an estimate is made taking account of all future cash payments or receipts, discounted where material, using the prevailing market rate(s) of interest for a similar instrument. The one exception to this general rule is for assets or liabilities that are subject to cash flow hedges, where certain hedging gains or losses are included as part of the initial cost – this is discussed in more detail at 4.9.5 below.[285]

The initial carrying amounts of a separated embedded derivative and associated host should be determined so that the derivative is initially recorded at its fair value and the host as the balance. This is to prevent the recording of an immediate gain or loss on the derivative's subsequent remeasurement to fair value. As discussed in Chapter 17 at 5.6, IAS 32 suggests that when separating the liability and equity components contained in a compound capital instrument, the aggregate carrying amount could be allocated based on the relative fair values of the liability and equity components. However, this is not applicable to the separation of a derivative from a hybrid instrument.[286]

4.6 The treatment of specific classes of instrument

4.6.1 Assets and liabilities held for trading

A Subsequent measurement

Trading assets and liabilities should be measured at fair value, with no deduction for sale or disposal costs, except for:

- equity instruments that do not have a quoted market price in an active market and whose fair value cannot be reliably measured;[287] and
- derivative liabilities that are linked to, and must be settled by, delivery of an unquoted equity instrument whose fair value cannot be reliably measured.[288]

These should be measured at cost.[289]

Fair value is defined as the amount for which an asset could be exchanged, or a liability settled, between knowledgeable, willing parties in an arm's length transaction.[290] Methods of estimating fair value are covered at 4.8 below. If an asset's fair value is below zero, it is accounted for as a liability.[291]

There is a presumption that fair value can be reliably determined for most trading assets. However, that presumption can be overcome for an investment in an equity instrument (including an in-substance equity instrument) that does not have a quoted market price in an active market and for which other methods of reasonably estimating fair value are clearly inappropriate or unworkable. The presumption can also be overcome for a derivative asset or liability that is linked to, and that must be settled by, delivery of such an unquoted equity instrument.[292] An example of an in-substance equity instrument is special participation rights without a specified maturity whose return is linked to an entity's performance.[293]

Example 10.42: Complex stand-alone derivative – no unquoted equity underlying

Company A acquires a complex stand-alone derivative that is based on several underlying variables, including commodity prices, interest rates, and credit indices. There is no active market or other price quotation for the derivative and no active markets for some of its underlying variables.

The presumption that the derivative's fair value can be reliably determined cannot be overcome because it is not linked to, and need not be settled by delivery of, an unquoted equity instrument. It cannot, therefore, be carried at cost.[294]

Example 10.43: Embedded derivative cannot be reliably measured

A company enters into a contract containing an embedded derivative that requires separation. However, the derivative cannot be reliably measured because it will be settled by an unquoted equity instrument whose fair value cannot be reliably measured.

The entire combined contract is treated as a financial instrument held for trading (see 4.3.3 E above) and if the fair value of the combined instrument can be reliably measured, the combined contract is measured at fair value. However, the equity component of the combined instrument may be sufficiently significant to preclude the reliable estimation of the hybrid's fair value. In this case, it is measured at cost less impairment.[295]

If a reliable measure of fair value subsequently becomes available, the trading instrument should be remeasured at that fair value.[296] If a reliable measure ceases to be available, it should thereafter be measured at cost based on the fair value carrying amount at that time.[297]

Trading assets, in particular in those rare cases when they are carried at cost, are subject to review for impairment (see 4.7 below).[298]

B Gains and losses

All gains and losses arising on trading assets and liabilities should be included in income when they arise.[299]

Where regular way purchases of trading assets are recognised using settlement date accounting (see 4.4.2 above), any change in the fair value of the asset to be received between the trade and settlement dates is also recognised in income.[300] For regular way sales, the fair value of the asset subsequent to trade date will generally be determined by reference to the amount expected to be received in the sale (see 4.8 below) and not by market price movements, even though the asset is not derecognised. The only likely exception is where there is a risk the transaction will not be settled, for example because the counterparty defaults, in which case an impairment may have arisen.[301]

4.6.2 *Held-to-maturity investments*

A *Subsequent measurement*

Subsequent to initial recognition, held-to-maturity investments should be measured at amortised cost using the effective interest rate method.[302]

The amortised cost of a financial instrument is defined as the amount at which it was measured at initial recognition minus principal repayments, plus or minus the cumulative amortisation of any difference between that initial amount and the maturity amount, and minus any write-down (directly or through the use of an allowance account) for impairment or uncollectability.

The effective interest method calculates amortisation using the effective interest rate of a financial asset. The effective interest rate is the rate that exactly discounts the expected stream of future cash payments, including all fees and points paid or received, over the period to maturity or to the next market-based repricing date, to the instrument's current net carrying amount, i.e. a constant rate on the carrying amount. The effective interest rate is sometimes termed the level yield to maturity or to the next repricing date, and is the internal rate of return of the financial asset or financial liability for that period.[303]

The following examples illustrate the use of the effective interest method.

Example 10.44: Effective interest method – amortisation of premium or discount on acquisition

At the end of 2001 a company purchases a debt instrument with five years remaining to maturity for its fair value of US$1,000 (including transaction costs). The instrument has a principal amount of US$1,250 and carries fixed interest of 4.7% payable annually (US$1,250 x 4.7% = US$59 per year). In order to allocate interest receipts and the initial discount over the term of the instrument at a constant rate on the carrying amount, it can be shown that interest needs to be accrued at the rate of 10% annually. The table below provides information about the amortised cost, interest income, and cash flows of the debt instrument in each reporting period.[304]

Year	*(a)* Amortised cost at start of year (US$)	*(b = a x 10%)* Interest income (US$)	*(c)* Cash flows (US$)	*(d = a + b – c)* Amortised cost at end of year (US$)
2002	1,000	100	59	1,041
2003	1,041	104	59	1,086
2004	1,086	109	59	1,136
2005	1,136	113	59	1,190
2006	1,190	119	1,250 + 59	–

Example 10.45: Effective interest method – stepped interest rates

On 1 January 2002, Company A acquires a debt instrument for its fair value of £1,250 (including transaction costs). The principal amount is £1,250 which is repayable on 31 December 2006. The rate of interest is specified in the debt agreement as a percentage of the principal amount as follows: 6% in 2002 (£75), 8% in 2003 (£100), 10% in 2004 (£125), 12% in 2005 (£150) and 16.4% in 2006 (£205). It can be shown that the interest rate that exactly discounts the stream of future cash payments to maturity is 10%. In each period, the amortised cost at the beginning of the period is multiplied by the effective interest rate of 10% and added to the amortised cost. Any cash payments in the period are deducted from the resulting balance. Accordingly, the amortised cost in each period is as follows:[305]

	(a)	*(b = a x 10%)*	*(c)*	*(d = a + b – c)*
	Amortised cost at start of year	Interest income	Cash flows	Amortised cost at end of year
Year	(£)	(£)	(£)	(£)
2002	1,250	125	75	1,300
2003	1,300	130	100	1,330
2004	1,330	133	125	1,338
2005	1,338	134	150	1,322
2006	1,322	133	1,250 + 205	–

For floating rate instruments, periodic re-estimation of cash flows to reflect movements in market interest rates changes the effective yield. Such changes in cash flows are recognised over the remaining term of the asset, or to the next repricing date if the asset reprices at market. In the case of a floating rate financial asset initially recognised at an amount equal to the principal repayable on maturity, re-estimating the future interest payments normally has no significant effect on the carrying amount of the asset.[306]

Determining whether to recognise such changes over the remaining term of the asset or to the next repricing date generally depends on whether, at the next repricing date, the fair value of the financial asset will be its par value. Two potential reasons for the discount or premium are:

- the timing of interest payments, e.g. because interest payments are in arrears or have otherwise accrued since the most recent interest payment date or market interest rates have changed since the debt instrument was most recently repriced to par; or
- the market's required yield differs from the stated variable rate, e.g. because the credit spread required by the market for the specific instrument is higher or lower than the credit spread that is implicit in the variable rate.

A discount or premium that reflects interest that has accrued on the instrument since interest was last paid or changes in market interest rates since the debt instrument was most recently repriced to par, is amortised to the date that the accrued interest will be paid and the variable interest rate reset to market. To the extent that the discount or premium results from a change in the credit spread over the variable rate specified in the instrument, this element is amortised over the remaining term to maturity of the instrument. In this case, the date the interest rate is next reset is not a market-based repricing date of the entire instrument, since the variable rate is not adjusted for changes in the credit spread for the specific issue.[307]

Example 10.46: Effective interest method – amortisation of discount arising from credit downgrade

A twenty-year bond is issued at £100, has a principal amount of £100, and requires quarterly interest payments equal to current three-month LIBOR plus 1% over the life of the instrument. The interest rate reflects the market-based required rate of return associated with the bond issue at issuance. Subsequent to issuance, the credit quality of the bond deteriorates resulting in a rating downgrade and therefore it trades at a significant discount. Company A purchases the bond for £95 and classifies it as held-to-maturity.

The discount of £5 is amortised to income over the period to the maturity of the bond and not to the next date interest rate payments are reset as it results from a change in credit spreads.[308]

If, due to a change of intent or ability, or because the tainting or sin-bin provisions have now expired, it becomes appropriate to carry a financial asset at amortised cost rather than at fair value, the fair value carrying amount of the financial asset on that date becomes its new amortised cost. Any previous gain or loss on that asset that has been recognised in equity should be amortised over the remaining life of the investment; any difference between the new amortised cost and maturity amount should be amortised over the remaining life of the financial asset as an adjustment of yield, similar to the amortisation of a premium or discount.[309]

Held-to-maturity investments are subject to review for impairment (see 4.7 below)[310] and those that are designated as hedged items are subject to measurement under the hedge accounting provisions (see 4.9 below).[311]

B Gains and losses

A gain or loss is recognised in income when the investment is derecognised or impaired, as well as through the amortisation process.

Where a held-to maturity investment is part of a hedging relationship subject to the hedge accounting provisions, associated gains and losses will be recognised according to those provisions (see 4.9 below).[312]

4.6.3 *Originated loans and receivables*

A Subsequent measurement

Subsequent to initial recognition, originated loans and receivables should be measured at amortised cost using the effective interest rate method (see 4.6.2 A above).[313]

The effective interest rate is defined as the rate that exactly discounts the *expected* stream of future cash payments through maturity or the next market-based repricing date to the net carrying amount. Accordingly the effective interest rate of a portfolio of originated loans that contain embedded prepayment options should reflect the expected timing and amount of those prepayments.[314]

Example 10.47: Effective interest rate – embedded prepayment options

Bank ABC originates 1,000 ten-year loans of £10,000 with 10% stated interest. Prepayments are probable and it is possible to reasonably estimate the timing and amount of prepayments. ABC determines that the effective interest rate considering loan origination fees is 10.2% based on the contractual payment terms of the loans since the fees received reduce the initial carrying amount. However, if the expected prepayments were considered, the effective interest rate would be 10.4% since the difference between the initial amount and maturity amount is amortised over a shorter period.

The effective interest rate that should be used by ABC for this portfolio is 10.4%.[315]

Where perpetual debt instruments are originated and interest is paid either at a fixed or variable rate, the amortised cost (the present value of the stream of future cash payments discounted at the effective interest rate) equals the principal amount in each period and the difference between the initial consideration and zero ('the maturity amount') is not amortised.[316]

However, where the stated rate of interest on perpetual debt decreases over time, some or all of the interest payments are, from an economic perspective, repayments of the principal amount as illustrated in the following example.[317]

Example 10.48: Amortised cost – perpetual debt with decreasing interest rate

On 1 January 2001 Company A subscribes £1,000 for a debt instrument which yields 25% interest for the first five years and 0% in subsequent periods. The funds are transferred directly to the issuer and it is classified as an originated loan. It can be determined that the effective yield is 7.9% and the amortised cost is shown in the table below.[318]

Year	*(a)* Amortised cost at start of year (£)	*(b = a x 7.9%)* Interest income (£)	*(c)* Cash flows (£)	*(d = a + b – c)* Amortised cost at end of year (£)
2001	1,000	79	250	829
2002	829	66	250	645
2003	645	51	250	446
2004	446	36	250	232
2005	232	18	250	–
2006	–	–	–	–

Other effective interest rate calculations are shown in Examples 10.44 and 10.45 at 4.6.2 A above and Example 10.49 at 4.6.4 B below.

Provided they are not held for trading, originated loans and receivables are measured at amortised cost without regard to any intent to hold them to maturity.[319]

Short-duration receivables with no stated interest rate are normally measured at original invoice amount unless the effect of imputing interest would be significant.[320]

Originated loans and receivables are subject to review for impairment (see 4.7 below)[321] and those that are designated as hedged items are subject to measurement under the hedge accounting provisions (see 4.9 below).[322]

B Gains and losses

A gain or loss is recognised in income when the loan or receivable is derecognised or impaired, as well as through the amortisation process.

However where originated loans or receivables are part of a hedging relationship subject to the hedge accounting provisions, associated gains and losses will be recognised according to those provisions (see 4.9 below).[323]

4.6.4 *Available-for-sale financial assets*

A Subsequent measurement

Available-for-sale assets should be measured at fair value except for those whose fair value cannot be reliably measured, which should be measured at cost.[324] The presumption as to the reliable determination of fair values applies equally to available-for-sale assets as it does to trading assets (see 4.6.1 A above) and therefore only certain unquoted equity instruments will be measured at cost.

If a reliable measure of fair value subsequently becomes available, the asset should be remeasured at that fair value and the gain or loss reported according to the accounting policy adopted (see B below).[325] If a reliable measure ceases to be available, it should thereafter be measured at cost based on the fair value carrying amount on that date.[326]

Available-for-sale assets, in particular in those rare cases when they are carried at cost, are subject to review for impairment (see 4.7 below)[327] and those that are designated as hedged items are subject to measurement under the hedge accounting provisions (see 4.9 below).[328]

B Gains and losses

Recognised gains or losses arising from changes in the fair value of available-for-sale financial assets that are not part of a hedging relationship should be either:

(i) included in income when they arise; or

(ii) recognised directly in equity, through the statement of changes in equity, until the financial asset is sold, collected, or otherwise disposed of, or until it is determined to be impaired (see 4.7 below), at which time the cumulative gain or loss previously recognised in equity should be recycled into income.[329]

Either (i) or (ii) should be chosen as an accounting policy and (except for hedges – see 4.9 below) this policy should be applied to all available-for-sale financial assets.[330] Under IAS 8 a voluntary change in accounting policy should be made only if the change will result in a more appropriate presentation in the financial statements of events or transactions. This is highly unlikely to be the case for a change from (i) to (ii).[331]

As set out in 4.7.2 and 4.7.3 below, where option (ii) is adopted, impairment losses and reversals thereof are recognised in income rather than in equity.

If an investment in bonds is classified as available-for-sale, and a policy of reporting fair value changes in equity is adopted, the amortisation of any premium or discount should be reported in income as part of interest income.[332]

Example 10.49: Available-for-sale asset – determination of interest

A company acquires a zero coupon bond at the end of 2000 for £760, its fair value, which matures at the beginning of 2004 at £1,000. It is classified as an available-for-sale asset, fair value gains and losses on which are reported in equity. Its fair value at the end of 2001, 2002 and 2003 is £850, £950 and £1,000 respectively and it can be determined that the effective interest rate is 9.6%.

The accounts would therefore show the information in the following table (amortised cost is memorandum information used to determine interest).

Year	Amortised cost at start of year (£)		Interest – net P&L (£)		Gains and losses – equity (£)		Cash flow (£)	Fair value B/S (£)
2000	–		–		–		–	760
2001	760		73	*[=760 x 9.6%]*	17	*[=850 – {760 + 73}]*	–	850
2002	833	*[=760 + 73]*	80	*[=833 x 9.6%]*	20	*[=950 – {850 + 80}]*	–	950
2003	913	*[=833 + 80]*	87	*[=913 x 9.6%]*	(37)	*[=1,000 – {950+87}]*	–	1,000
2004	1,000	*[=913 + 87]*	–		–		1,000	–

Other effective interest rate calculations are shown in Examples 10.44 and 10.45 at 4.6.2 A above and in Example 10.48 at 4.6.3 A above.

The standard does not address the recognition of other types of revenue arising from financial instruments, for example dividends arising on equity instruments, which are covered by IAS 18 (see Chapter 3 at 4.5.4).

Gains or losses initially reported in equity should be reported in income if a transaction results in the available-for-sale asset being derecognised.[333]

Example 10.50: Gain or loss on available-for-sale shares in takeover target

Company A holds a small number of shares in Company B. The shares are classified as available for sale, gains and losses on which A reports in equity. On 20 December 2001, the fair value of the shares is £120 and the cumulative gain included in equity is £20. On the same day, B is acquired by Company C, a large public company. As a result, A receives shares in C in exchange for those it had in B of equal fair value.

The transaction qualifies for derecognition because A gave up control of B's shares in exchange for C's shares (see Chapter 18 at 4.2). The cumulative gain of £20 that has been included in equity should therefore be included in income.[334]

If a reliable measure ceases to be available and, consequently, an asset is recorded at cost, any gains or losses previously recognised in equity should be left there until the asset has been sold or otherwise disposed of, at which time it should be recycled into income.[335]

Where regular way purchases of available-for-sale financial assets are recognised using settlement date accounting (see 4.4.2 above), any change in the fair value of the asset to be received during the period between trade date and settlement date should be recognised in income or in equity, as appropriate, under (i) or (ii) above.[336] For regular way sales, the fair value of the asset subsequent to trade date will generally be determined by reference to the amount expected to be received in the sale (see 4.8 below) and not by market price movements, even though the asset is not derecognised. The only likely exception is where there is a risk the transaction will not be settled, for example because the counterparty defaults, in which case an impairment may have arisen.[337]

4.6.5 *Other liabilities*

Financial liabilities that are not held for trading and are not derivatives should be measured at amortised cost using the effective interest method (see 4.6.1 A above).[338] Those liabilities that are designated as hedged items are subject to measurement under the hedge accounting provisions (see 4.9 below).[339] Measurement of financial liabilities is covered in more detail in Chapter 17 at 5.4.1 and 5.4.2.

4.6.6 *Reclassifications*

If, due to a change of intent or ability, it is no longer appropriate to carry a held-to-maturity investment at amortised cost, it would be classified as available-for-sale unless, as set out below, there was evidence that justified a trading reclassification. In either case the asset would be remeasured to fair value and gains or losses would be reported in accordance with the accounting policy for the new asset classification.[340]

Because of a change of intent or ability it may sometimes be appropriate to reclassify available-for-sale assets as held-to-maturity; this may also occur as a result of the tainting period expiring (see 4.3.1 B III above). The fair value carrying amount of the financial asset on that date becomes its new amortised cost and any previous gain or loss on that asset recognised in equity should be amortised over the remaining life of the investment. Any difference between the new amortised cost and maturity amount should be amortised over the remaining life of the asset as an adjustment of yield, similar to the amortisation of a premium or discount.[341]

A financial asset should only be reclassified into the trading category if there is evidence of a recent actual pattern of short-term profit taking that justifies such reclassification[342] – a decision to sell a non-trading asset does not make it a financial asset held for trading. On the other hand if the asset is part of a portfolio of similar assets, for example a portfolio of treasury notes classified as available-for-sale, for which there is a recent pattern of trading, they would all be reclassified into the trading category.[343]

If gains or losses on equity instruments reclassified from available-to-sale to trading had previously been recognised in equity, those gains and losses should be left in equity until the asset has been sold or otherwise disposed of, and only then would they be recycled into income.[344] It is not made clear how similar gains and losses on other instruments, e.g. debt securities, should be dealt with, although we believe a similar approach should be taken.

The standard explains that because the designation of a financial asset as held for trading is based on the objective for initially acquiring it, financial assets that are being remeasured to fair value should not be reclassified out of the trading category while they are held.[345] Presumably those rare trading assets carried at cost should not be transferred from the trading category either, although this is not explicitly stated.

Other than for originated loans and receivables (see 4.3.1 C above) the standard contains no explicit guidance on whether financial instruments acquired as part of a business combination can be reclassified on acquisition based on the acquirer's intent. If the rules set out above were meant to apply, an asset classified by the acquired entity as held for trading, for example, could not be reclassified by the acquiring entity in its group accounts, no matter what its intention was towards holding or selling that asset. We therefore doubt the IASC meant these rules to be followed in this situation.

4.6.7 *Foreign currency instruments and foreign entities*

A Foreign currency instruments

The provisions in IAS 21 and IAS 39 partly overlap each other, e.g. for the purposes of determining gains and losses that should be reported in income or equity. Therefore the order in which those standards are applied can affect the measurement of assets, liabilities and income.

Generally, the balance sheet measurement of a foreign currency financial instrument is determined as follows:

- firstly, it is recorded and measured in the foreign currency in which it is denominated, whether it is carried at fair value, cost, or amortised cost;
- secondly, that amount is retranslated to the measurement currency using:
  - closing rate, for non-monetary items (e.g. an equity share) carried at fair value and all monetary items (e.g. a debt security); or
  - an historical rate, for non-monetary items carried at cost or amortised cost.

As an exception, if the financial instrument is designated as a hedged item in a fair value hedge of foreign currency exposure, it is remeasured for changes in foreign currency rates even if it would otherwise have been reported using a historical rate, i.e. the foreign currency amount is reported using the closing rate (see 4.9.5 below).

The reporting of changes in a financial instruments' carrying amount in income or equity depends on a number of factors, including whether it is an exchange difference or other change in carrying amount, whether the instrument is a monetary or non-monetary item and whether it is designated as part of a foreign currency cash flow hedge.

Exchange differences arising on retranslating monetary items are reported in income. All other fair value changes are reported in income or equity depending on the nature of the asset and the accounting policy chosen (see 4.6.1 B and 4.6.4 B above). Special hedge accounting rules apply for instruments designated as hedges of future foreign currency transactions (see 4.9.5 below) or net investments in foreign entities (see 4.9.6 below).

In cases where some portion of the change in carrying amount is reported in income and in equity, e.g. if the fair value of a bond has increased in foreign currency and decreased in the measurement currency, those two components cannot be offset for the purposes of determining gains or losses that should be recognised in income and equity.[346]

These principles are illustrated in the following example:

Example 10.51: Available-for-sale foreign currency debt security

On 31 December 2001 Company A, whose measurement currency is the euro, acquires a US dollar bond for its fair value of US$1,000. The bond is the same as the one in Example 10.44 at 4.6.2 A above, i.e. it has five years to maturity and a US$1,250 principal, carries fixed interest of 4.7% paid annually (US$1,250 x 4.7% = US$59 per year), and has an effective interest rate of 10%.

A classifies the bond as available for sale and has a policy of reporting gains and losses on such assets in equity. The exchange rate is US$1 to €1.50 and the carrying amount of the bond is €1,500 (= US$1,000 x 1.50).

	€	€
Bond	1,500	
Cash		1,500

On 31 December 2002, the US dollar has appreciated and the exchange rate is US$1 to €2.00. The fair value of the bond is US$1,060 and therefore its carrying amount is €2,120 (= US$1,060 x 2.00). Its amortised cost is US$1,041 (= €2,082) and the cumulative gain or loss to be included in equity is the difference between its fair value and amortised cost, i.e. a gain of €38 (= €2,120 – €2,082).

Interest received on the bond on 31 December 2002 is US$59 (= €118); interest income determined in accordance with the effective interest method is US$100 (= US$1,000 x 10%). It is assumed that the average exchange rate during the year is US$1 to €1.75 and that the use of an average exchange rate provides a reliable approximation of the spot rates applicable to the accrual of interest during the year. Therefore, reported interest income is €175 (= US$100 x 1.75) including accretion of the initial discount of €72 (= [US$100 – US$59] x 1.75).

Accordingly, the exchange difference reported in income is €510 (= €2,082 – €1,500 – €72); there is also an exchange gain on the interest receivable of €15 (= US$59 x [2.00 – 1.75]).

	€	€
Bond	620	
Cash	118	
Interest income (P&L)		175
Exchange gain (P&L)		525
Fair value change (equity)		38

On 31 December 2003, the US dollar has appreciated further and the exchange rate is US$1 to €2.50. The fair value of the bond is US$1,070 and therefore its carrying amount is €2,675 (= US$1,070 x 2.50). Its amortised cost is US$1,086 (= €2,715) and the cumulative gain or loss to be included in equity is the difference between its fair value and the amortised cost, i.e. a loss of €40 (= €2,675 – €2,715). Therefore, there is a debit to equity equal to the change in the difference during 2003 of €78 (= €40 + €38).

Interest received on the bond on 31 December 2003 is US$59 (= €148); interest income determined in accordance with the effective interest method is US$104 (= US$1,041 x 10%). Using the same assumptions as in the previous year reported, interest income is €234 (= US$104 x 2.25) including accretion of the initial discount of €101 (= [US$104 – US$59] x 2.25).

Accordingly, the exchange difference reported in income is €532 (= €2,715 – €2,082 – €101); there is also an exchange gain on the interest receivable of €15 (= US$59 x [2.50 – 2.25]).[347]

	€	€
Bond	555	
Cash	148	
Fair value change (equity)	78	
Interest income (P&L)		234
Exchange gain (P&L)		547

It is worth noting that the treatment would be slightly different for equity instruments, which under IAS 21 are not considered monetary items – exchange differences would not automatically be reported in income, but would form part of the change in the instrument's fair value, which could be reported in equity if it was classified as available for sale and the holder had chosen to report fair value gains and losses on such assets in equity.

B Foreign entities

IAS 39 did not amend IAS 21 and therefore did not change the application of the net investment method of accounting for foreign entities (see Chapter 8 at 5.2.5 A) even for assets marked to market through income. Consequently the treatment of gains and losses on trading assets held by a foreign entity should follow the treatment in the example below:

Example 10.52: Interaction of IAS 21 and IAS 39 – foreign currency debt investment

Company A is domiciled in the US and has a UK subsidiary, B which is classified as a foreign entity. B is the owner of a debt instrument held for trading and which is therefore carried at fair value.

In B's financial statements for 2002, the fair value and carrying amount of the debt instrument is £100. In A's consolidated financial statements, the asset is translated into US dollars at the spot exchange rate applicable at the balance sheet date, say 2.0, and the carrying amount is US$200 = £100 x 2.0.

At the end of 2003, the fair value of the debt instrument has increased to £110. B reports the trading asset at £110 in its balance sheet and recognises a fair value gain of £10 in income. During the year, the spot exchange rate has increased from 2.0 to 3.0 resulting in an increase in the fair value of the instrument from US$200 to US$330 = £110 x 3.0. Therefore, A reports the trading asset at US$330 in its consolidated financial statements.

Since B is classified as a foreign entity, A translates B's income statement 'at the exchange rates at the dates of the transactions'. Since the fair value gain has accrued through the year, A uses the average rate of 2.5 (= [3.0 + 2.0] ÷ 2) as a practical approximation. Therefore, while the fair value of the trading asset has increased by US$130 = US$330 – US$200, A recognises only US$25 = £10 x 2.5 of this increase in income. The resulting exchange difference, i.e. the remaining increase in the fair value of the debt instrument of US$105 = US$130 – US$25, is classified as equity until the disposal of the net investment in the foreign entity.[348]

4.7 Impairment

4.7.1 Impairment reviews

All financial assets are subject to review for impairment.[349] A financial asset is impaired if its carrying amount is greater than its estimated recoverable amount. An assessment should be made at each balance sheet date as to whether there is any objective evidence that a financial asset or group of assets may be impaired. If any such evidence exists, the recoverable amount of that asset or group of assets should be estimated and any impairment loss should be recognised according to the nature of the asset – see 4.7.2 and 4.7.3 below.[350]

Objective evidence that a financial asset or group of assets is impaired or uncollectable includes information that comes to the attention of the holder about:

- significant financial difficulty of the issuer;
- an actual breach of contract, such as a default or delinquency in interest or principal payments;
- the granting of a concession for reasons relating to the borrower's financial difficulty that would not otherwise be considered;
- a high probability of bankruptcy or other financial reorganisation of the issuer;
- recognition of an impairment loss on that asset in an earlier reporting period;
- the disappearance of an active market for that asset due to financial difficulties; or
- an historical pattern of collections that indicates the entire face amount of a portfolio of accounts receivable will not be collected.[351]

It is not necessary to identify a single, distinct past causative event to conclude that it is probable that not all amounts due will be collected. For example a credit rating downgrade is not, of itself, evidence of impairment; nor, necessarily, is the value of an equity security, or an entire portfolio of such items, falling below cost. However, when considered with other available evidence, such combined information may provide objective evidence of an impairment.[352]

Other factors that might be considered are the debtor's or issuer's liquidity, solvency, and business and financial risk exposures, levels of and trends in delinquencies for similar financial assets, national and local economic trends and conditions, and the fair value of collateral and guarantees. The disappearance of an active market because an issuer's securities are no longer publicly traded is not evidence of impairment.[353]

4.7.2 Financial assets carried at amortised cost

If it is probable that not all amounts due (principal and interest) will be collected according to the contractual terms of loans, receivables, or held-to-maturity investments carried at amortised cost, an impairment or bad debt loss has occurred.[354]

The amount of the loss is the difference between the asset's carrying amount and the present value of expected future cash flows discounted at the instrument's original effective interest rate ('recoverable amount'), although cash flows relating to short-term receivables generally are not discounted. The carrying amount of the asset should be reduced to its estimated recoverable amount either directly or by using an allowance or provision account. As noted in 4.6.2 B and 4.6.3 B above, the amount of the loss should be included in income.[355]

Example 10.53: Impairment – changes in amount or timing of payments

A bank is concerned that, because of financial difficulties, five customers, Companies A to E, will not be able to make all principal and interest payments due on originated loans in a timely manner. It negotiates a restructuring of the loans and expects the customers will meet their restructured obligations. The restructured terms are as follows:

- Company A will pay the full principal amount of the original loan five years after the original due date, but none of the interest due under the original terms.
- Company B will pay the full principal amount of the original loan on the original due date, but none of the interest due under the original terms.
- Company C will pay the full principal amount on the original due date with interest only at a lower interest rate than the interest rate inherent in the original loan.
- Company D will pay the full principal amount five years after the original due date and all interest accrued during the original loan term, but no interest for the extended term.
- Company E will pay the full principal amount five years after the original due date and all interest, including interest on all outstanding amounts for both the original term of the loan and the extended term.

The amount and timing of payments has changed for each of Company A to E above, therefore impairment must be assessed based on current expectations regarding collection of principal and interest. For Companies A to D, the present value of the future principal and interest payments discounted at the loan's original effective interest rate (the recoverable amount) will be lower than the carrying amount of the loan. Therefore an impairment loss is recognised in those cases.

For Company E, even though the timing of payments has changed, the bank will receive interest on interest, so that the present value of the future principal and interest payments discounted at the loan's original effective interest rate will equal the carrying amount of the loan. Therefore, there is no impairment loss. However, this fact pattern is unlikely given Company E's financial difficulties.[356]

Impairment and uncollectability should be measured and recognised individually for financial assets that are individually significant, but may be measured and recognised on a portfolio basis for a group of similar financial assets that are not individually identified as impaired.[357] A portfolio basis can only be used when impairment cannot be identified for individual assets in the group. Therefore if it is known that one asset in a group is impaired but the fair value of another exceeds its amortised cost, an impairment loss must be recognised on the first asset in isolation.[358]

Similarly, if an individual asset is separately assessed for impairment evaluation, it cannot be included in a group of similar financial assets for which impairment is recognised and measured on a portfolio basis.[359] In other words general bad debt provisions should only be assessed on populations that exclude debts on which a specific provision is assessed.

Impairment of a financial asset carried at amortised cost is measured using the instrument's original effective interest rate because discounting at the current market interest rate would, in effect, impose fair-value measurement on assets that would otherwise be measured at amortised cost. If a loan, receivable, or held-to-maturity investment has a variable interest rate, the discount rate for measuring the recoverable amount is the current effective interest rate(s) determined under the contract – as a surrogate, a creditor may measure impairment based on an instrument's fair value using an observable market price.[360] This is not allowed for fixed rate assets, although an observable market price may provide evidence of credit deterioration and impairment if interest rates have not increased subsequent to initial recognition.[361]

If an asset is collateralised and foreclosure is probable, then impairment should be measured based on the fair value of the collateral less any costs of obtaining it.[362] However collateral does not generally meet the recognition criteria until it is transferred to the lender and should not be recognised as an asset, separately from the impaired asset, prior to foreclosure. Similarly, the recoverable amount should take account of any guarantee securing the asset.[363]

The recognition of impairment losses in excess of those that are determined based on objective evidence is not permitted.[364]

It is common practice for companies to determine bad debt provisions using a provisioning matrix or similar formula based on the number of days a loan or debt is overdue, e.g. 0% if less than 90 days, 20% if 90 to 180 days, 50% if 180 to 365 days and 100% if more than 365 days overdue. Unless such a formula can be demonstrated to produce an estimate sufficiently close to the above methodology, this will not satisfy the requirements of IAS 39.[365]

A financial asset should initially be measured at the fair value of the consideration given which, for a loan asset, is generally the amount of cash lent, adjusted for any fees and costs. Therefore the recognition of an impairment loss at the time a loan is made, through the establishment of an allowance for future losses, is not permitted. The implementation guidance feels the need to illustrate this by way of the following example:[366]

Example 10.54: Immediate recognition of impairment

Bank A lends £1,000 to Customer B and based on historical experience, expects that 1% of the principal amount of loans given will not be collected.

A cannot recognise an immediate impairment loss of £10.[367]

Where an asset with fixed interest rate payments is hedged against the exposure to interest rate risk by a receive-variable pay-fixed interest rate swap, the carrying amount will include an adjustment for fair value changes attributable to movements in interest rates (see 4.9.4 below) and the original effective interest rate, prior to the hedge, becomes irrelevant. Therefore, the original effective interest rate and amortised cost of the loan are adjusted to take into account these recognised fair value changes and the adjusted effective interest rate is calculated using the adjusted carrying amount of the loan. An impairment loss on the hedged loan is calculated as the difference between its carrying amount after adjustment for fair value changes attributable to the risk being hedged and the expected future cash flows of the loan discounted at the adjusted effective interest rate.[368]

If, in a subsequent period, the amount of the impairment or bad debt loss decreases and the decrease can be objectively related to an event occurring after the write-down (such as an improvement in the debtor's credit rating), the write-down of the financial asset should be reversed either directly or by adjusting an allowance account. The reversal should not result in a carrying amount of the asset that exceeds what its amortised cost would have been at the date of reversal, had the impairment not been recognised. As set out in 4.6.2 B and 4.6.3 B above, the amount of the reversal should be included in income.[369]

The carrying amount of any financial asset that is not carried at fair value because its fair value cannot be reliably measured should be reviewed for an indication of impairment at each balance sheet date based on an analysis of expected net cash inflows. If there is an indication of impairment, the amount of the impairment loss of such a financial asset is the difference between its carrying amount and the present value of expected future cash flows discounted at the current market rate of interest for a similar financial asset ('recoverable amount').[370] Such losses should be reversed if the reversal can be objectively related to an event occurring after the write down.[371]

4.7.3 *Impairment of assets carried at fair value*

If a fair value loss on an available-for-sale asset has been recognised in equity and there is objective evidence (see 4.7.1 above) that the asset is impaired, the cumulative loss in equity should be recycled into income even though the asset has not been derecognised.[372]

The amount of the loss that should be recycled into income is the difference between its acquisition cost, net of any principal repayment and amortisation, and current fair value (for equity instruments) or recoverable amount (for debt instruments), less any impairment loss on that asset previously recognised in income.[373] For non-monetary assets, such as equity instruments, the cumulative net loss included in equity, including any portion attributable to foreign currency changes, should be recognised in income.[374]

The recoverable amount of a debt instrument remeasured to fair value is the present value of expected future cash flows discounted at the current market interest rate for a similar financial asset.[375] Such a rate is not defined and care must be taken not to include expected defaults in both the discount rate and expected future cash flows – the discount rate must be consistent with the assumptions made about expected defaults in the expected future cash flows. The current market interest rate for an otherwise comparable financial asset is its effective yield which reflects the impairment loss the marketplace expects.[376]

If, in a subsequent period, the fair value or recoverable amount of a financial asset carried at fair value increases and the increase can be objectively related to an event occurring after the loss was recognised in income, the loss should be reversed and included in income.[377]

4.7.4 *Interest income after impairment recognition*

Once a financial asset has been written down to its estimated recoverable amount, interest income is thereafter recognised based on the rate of interest that was used to discount the future cash flows for the purpose of measuring the recoverable amount. Additionally, after initially recognising an impairment loss, the asset should be reviewed for further impairment at subsequent financial reporting dates (see 4.7.1 above). Guidance for recognising interest income on unimpaired financial assets is included in IAS 18 – see Chapter 3 at 4.5.4.[378]

4.8 Fair value measurement considerations

The question of how fair values should be determined seem to receive a good deal of attention in IAS 39 and the implementation guidance. However, on closer examination, much of this is little more than an attempt at providing reassurance that fair values can actually be determined reliably. It explains that the fair value of a financial instrument is deemed to be reliably measurable if:

- the variability in the range of reasonable fair value estimates is not significant for that instrument; or
- the probabilities of the various estimates within the range can be reasonably assessed and used in estimating fair value.

Often an estimate of the fair value of a financial instrument that is sufficiently reliable to use in financial statements can be made. Only occasionally will the variability in the range of reasonable estimates be so great, and the probabilities of the various outcomes so difficult to assess, that the usefulness of a single estimate of fair value is negated.[379]

The implementation guidance states that in rare cases estimates of fair value of an unquoted equity instrument may exist for which there is no appropriate or workable method to select a single estimate of fair value because the range of reasonable fair value estimates is significant and the probabilities of the various estimates cannot be reasonably assessed. In such circumstances the equity instrument cannot be recorded at 'fair value', e.g. by judgementally picking an estimate within the range.[380] In quite what circumstances this guidance would prove useful is not entirely clear.

Situations in which fair value is reliably measurable include financial instruments with a published price quotation in an active market, debt instruments that have been rated by an independent rating agency and whose cash flows can be reasonably estimated, and financial instruments for which there is an appropriate valuation model and for which the data inputs to that model can be measured reliably because the data come from active markets.[381]

The fair value of an instrument may be determined by one of several generally accepted methods. Valuation techniques should incorporate the assumptions that market participants would use in their estimates of fair values, including assumptions about prepayment rates, rates of estimated credit losses and interest or discount rates. As set out in 5.2 below, disclosure is required of the methods and significant assumptions applied in estimating fair values.[382]

Underlying the definition of fair value is a presumption that an entity is a going concern without any intention or need to liquidate, curtail materially the scale of operations, or undertake a transaction on adverse terms. Fair value is not, therefore, the amount that would be received or paid in a forced transaction, involuntary liquidation, or distress sale. However, an entity's current circumstances are taken into account in determining the fair values of its financial instruments. For example, the fair value of a financial asset that an entity has decided to sell for cash in the immediate future is determined by the amount that it expects to receive from such a sale. The amount of cash to be realised from an immediate sale will be affected by factors such as the current liquidity and depth of the market for the asset.[383]

The existence of published price quotations in an active market is normally the best evidence of fair value. The appropriate quoted market price for an asset held, or liability to be issued, is usually the current bid price; for an asset to be acquired or liability held, the current offer or asking price. When current bid and offer prices are unavailable, the price of the most recent transaction may provide evidence of the current fair value provided that there has not been a significant change in economic circumstances between the transaction date and the reporting date. Only when matching asset and liability positions are held, is it appropriate to use mid-market prices as a basis for establishing fair values.[384]

Rules applicable to some investment funds require net asset values to be reported to investors based on mid-market prices. However, the existence of such regulations does not justify a departure from the general requirement to use the current bid price in the absence of a matching liability position. In its financial statements, an investment fund should measure its assets at current bid prices and, in reporting its net asset value to investors, it may wish to provide a reconciliation between the fair values reported on its balance sheet and the prices used for the net asset value calculation.[385]

If the market for a financial instrument is not active, published prices may have to be adjusted to arrive at a reliable measure. If there is infrequent activity, the market is not well established (for example, some 'over the counter' markets) or relatively small volumes are traded, quoted prices may not be indicative of fair value. In some cases where the volume traded is relatively small, a price quotation for a larger block may be available from market makers. In other circumstances, as well as when a quoted market price is not available, estimation techniques may be used to determine fair value with sufficient reliability. However, the implementation guidance implies these 'other circumstances' are tightly restricted – see Example 10.55 below.

Techniques that are well established in financial markets include reference to the current market value of another substantially similar instrument, discounted cash flow analysis and option pricing models. In applying discounted cash flow analysis, the discount rate(s) used should equal the prevailing rate of return for instruments having substantially the same terms and characteristics, including the creditworthiness of the debtor, the remaining term over which the contractual interest rate is fixed, the remaining term to repayment of the principal, and the currency in which payments are to be made.[386]

Example 10.55: Valuing publicly quoted shares at other than market price

Company A holds 15% of the share capital in Company B. The shares are publicly traded in an active market, the currently quoted price is £100 and daily trading volume is 0.1% of outstanding shares. Because A believes that the fair value of the shares it owns, if sold as a block, is greater than the quoted market price, it obtains several independent estimates of the price it would obtain if it sells its holding. These estimates indicate that it would be able to obtain a price of £105, a 5% premium above the quoted price.

There is a presumption that a published price quotation in an active market is the best estimate of fair value. Therefore, the published price quotation (£100) should be used. A cannot depart from the quoted market price solely because independent estimates indicate that it would obtain a higher (or lower) price by selling the holding as a block. However, if A could present objective, reliable evidence validating a higher (or lower) amount, an adjustment may be made to the quoted price. For example, if it had entered into a contract with a third party to sell the shares at a fixed price in the immediate future, that might justify an adjustment to the quoted price.[387]

If a market price does not exist for a financial instrument in its entirety but markets exist for its component parts, fair value is constructed on the basis of the relevant market prices. If a market exists for a similar financial instrument, fair value can be constructed on the basis of the market price of the similar financial instrument.[388]

There are many other situations in which the variability in the range of reasonable fair value estimates is likely not to be significant and the standard states that it is normally possible to estimate the fair value of a financial asset. Further, it (somewhat ambitiously) asserts that an entity is unlikely to purchase a financial instrument for which it does not expect to be able to obtain a reliable measure of fair value after acquisition and refers to the IASC Framework which states: 'In many cases, cost or value must be estimated; the use of reasonable estimates is an essential part of the preparation of financial statements and does not undermine their reliability.'[389]

4.9 Hedge Accounting

One of the main reasons businesses use financial instruments, in particular derivatives, is for hedging risk exposures. Historically, entities have developed various ways of accounting for hedges and standard setters have long been suspicious of what they term 'special hedge accounting', which in practice means very different things to different people. For this reason IAS 39 attempts to narrow the choices available for hedge accounting which it describes as 'recognising symmetrically the offsetting effects on net profit or loss of changes in the fair values of hedging instruments and related items being hedged'. In fact this topic accounts for some of the most complex aspects of IAS 39.[390]

As noted in 4.1 above, legal restrictions are in the process of being lifted to allow the use of IAS 39 throughout Europe. However it is unlikely that a standard based on IAS 39 will be adopted in the UK before Europe's move to IAS in 2005, not least because the hedging rules are incompatible with FRS 3 – *Reporting Financial Performance*. As discussed in 4.9.5 below, hedges of future transactions are accounted for under IAS 39 by initially recognising fair value gains and losses on hedging instruments in equity (reserves). They are subsequently recycled into income to match recognised gains and losses from the hedged future transactions.

If hedges of future transactions were recorded at fair value in the UK, FRS 3 would require the hedging gains and losses to be reported immediately, possibly in the STRGL, and subsequent recycling would be prohibited.

4.9.1 Hedge accounting definitions

Some of the more commonly used definitions within the IAS 39 hedging rules are set out below.

Hedging, for accounting purposes, means designating one or more hedging instruments so that their change in fair value is an offset, in whole or in part, to the change in fair value or cash flows of a hedged item.[391]

A *hedged item* is an asset, liability, firm commitment, or forecasted future transaction with exposure to the risk of changes in fair value or future cash flows, which is designated as being hedged.[392] A *firm commitment* is a binding agreement for the exchange of a specified quantity of resources at a specified price on a specified future date or dates.[393] A *forecasted transaction* is an uncommitted but highly probable anticipated transaction.[394]

A *hedging instrument* is a designated derivative or, in limited circumstances, another financial asset or liability whose fair value or cash flows are expected to offset changes in the fair value or cash flows of a designated hedged item – a non-derivative financial instrument may only be designated as a hedging instrument if it hedges the risk of changes in foreign currency exchange rates[395] notwithstanding the fact that, in economic terms, non-derivatives certainly can be effective hedges.

A Hedged items

Hedged items can be single assets, liabilities, firm commitments or forecasted transactions or groups of such items with similar risk characteristics.[396] However, except where a written option hedges a purchased option (see B below), a derivative cannot be a hedged item.[397]

Held-to-maturity investments cannot be hedged items with respect to interest rate risk because 'designation of an investment as held-to-maturity involves not accounting for associated changes in interest rates'.[398] Not only is this statement patently untrue (for a held-to-maturity bond paying variable rate interest, changes in interest rates will certainly be accounted for), but it applies equally to originated loans and receivables for which there is no equivalent restriction. In fact this statement could be interpreted as allowing hedge accounting of variable rate held-to-maturity investments and guidance was published to clarify that this was not the intention.[399] In reality this seems to be just another restriction on the use of the held-to-maturity classification.

This restriction also applies to prepayment risk, say on a held-to-maturity mortgage-backed pass-through security, because prepayment risk is largely a function of interest rate changes.[400] However, held-to-maturity investments or related cash flows can be part of a hedging relationship in the following circumstances:

- the investment may be a hedged item with respect to risks from changes in foreign currency exchange rates and credit risk;[401]
- the forecast purchase of such an investment may be a hedged item, say to lock in current interest rates, as an investment is not given an IAS 39 classification until it is actually purchased;[402] and
- the forecasted reinvestment of interest receipts can be hedged items with respect to the risk of interest rate changes.[403]

Financial instruments may be hedged items with respect to the risks associated with only a portion of their cash flows or fair value, for example risk free interest rates, credit spreads or even a proportion, say 75%, of the total exposure, provided effectiveness can be measured.[404]

An intra-group monetary balance may be designated as a hedged item if it gives rise to exchange differences in the income statement that cannot be eliminated on consolidation. This can occur, for example, where there is an outstanding balance between two group companies that are foreign entities, they have different measurement currencies and the balance is denominated in one of those measurement currencies.[405] Similarly, a forecasted intra-group transaction that will give rise to exchange differences in income may also be a hedged item.[406]

With the possible exception of foreign currency risk, changes in the price of an ingredient or component of a non-financial asset or liability generally do not have a predictable, separately measurable effect on the price of the item that is comparable to the effect, say, of a change in market interest rates on the price of a bond. Therefore, such items may only be hedged either for foreign currency risk or in their entirety for all risks.[407] Consequently a firm commitment to acquire a business in a business combination cannot be a hedged item except with respect to foreign exchange risk because the other risks being hedged cannot be specifically identified and measured – it is a hedge of a general business risk.[408]

In fact in most cases it will be difficult to identify a separately measurable effect on non-financial assets, even for foreign currency risk, as illustrated in the following example from the implementation guidance:

Example 10.56: Foreign currency borrowings hedging a ship

A Danish shipping company, D, has a US subsidiary that is integral to the operations of the company, i.e. it is not a 'foreign entity'. Accordingly in D's consolidated accounts, ships owned by the subsidiary, which are carried at depreciated historical cost, are reported in Danish kronor using historical exchange rates. To hedge the potential currency risk on the disposal of the ships for dollars, purchases of ships are normally financed with loans denominated in dollars.

US dollar borrowings cannot be classified as fair value hedges of a ship as ships do not contain any separately measurable foreign currency risk even if their purchase was, and sale is likely to be, denominated in US dollars. The proceeds from the anticipated sale of the ship may, however, be designated in a cash flow hedge, provided all the hedging criteria are met (see 4.9.3 below). Those conditions require that the sale is highly probable, which is only likely if the sale is expected to occur in the immediate future.[409]

To aggregate and hedge similar assets or liabilities as a group, the individual items need to share the risk exposure for which they are hedged. Further, the standard requires that fair value changes attributable to the hedged risk for each individual item should be approximately proportional to the equivalent fair value change of the entire group.[410] For example, the risk characteristics of the individual shares in a portfolio designed to replicate a share index will be different from each other and from the portfolio as a whole – therefore the portfolio could not be hedged with respect to movements in the index[411] even though, in economic terms, the portfolio of shares may well be perfectly hedged.

As discussed in 4.9.3 C below, hedge effectiveness is assessed by comparing the change in value or cash flow of hedging instruments and of hedged items. Therefore, comparing a hedging instrument to an overall net position rather than to a specific hedged item cannot qualify for hedge accounting. However, approximately the same effect in the income statement can be achieved by designating part of the underlying items as the hedged position. For example, a UK company with firm commitments to make purchases and sales of US$100 and US$90 respectively could hedge the net exposure by acquiring a derivative and designating it as a hedging instrument associated with purchases of US$10. Similarly, a bank with £100 of assets and £90 of liabilities with risks and terms of a similar nature could hedge the net exposure by designating £10 of those assets as the hedged item.[412] The issue of macro-hedging is considered further in 4.9.8 below.

B Hedging instruments

Except for certain written options (see below), the circumstances in which a derivative may be designated as a hedging instrument are not restricted, provided the criteria for hedge accounting set out in 4.9.3 below are met.[413] In fact two or more derivatives, or proportions thereof, whether entered into concurrently or not, may be viewed in combination and jointly designated as the hedging instrument, provided the combination is not a net written option.[414]

Non-derivative instruments, including held-to-maturity investments, may only be designated as hedging instruments in foreign currency hedges. The reason given for this limitation is that derivatives and non-derivatives are measured on different bases: derivatives are nearly always remeasured to fair value, with associated gains and losses in income, or equity for cash flow hedges; non-derivatives are sometimes measured at fair value with associated gains and losses either in income or in equity, sometimes at amortised cost; consequently 'to allow non-derivatives to be designated as hedging instruments in more than limited circumstances creates measurement inconsistencies'.[415] Given the many measurement inconsistencies that already exist, this argument appears to lack credibility, although this fact does not change the rule.

An entity's own equity securities are not financial assets or liabilities of the entity and, therefore, cannot be hedging instruments.[416] IAS 32 states that minority interests are not financial liabilities of a group (see Chapter 17 at 5.3.6) and, consequently, it appears that they cannot be treated as hedging instruments.

In general, potential losses on written options can be significantly greater than potential gains on related hedged items and are not effective in reducing profit and loss exposure. Therefore, a written option cannot be a hedging instrument unless designated as an offset to a purchased option. In contrast, purchased options have potential gains equal to or greater than losses and therefore have the potential to reduce profit or loss exposure. Accordingly, they can qualify as hedging instruments.[417]

This does not necessarily preclude the use of an interest rate collar or similar combined instrument as a hedging instrument, provided it is not a net written option. The following factors, taken together, indicate that an instrument is not a net written option:

- no net premium is received, either at inception or over the life of the instrument – the distinguishing feature of a written option is the receipt of a premium to compensate for the risk incurred;
- except for the strike prices, the critical terms and conditions of the written and purchased option components are the same, including underlying variable(s), currency denomination and maturity date; and
- the notional amount of the written option component is not greater than that of the purchased option component.[418]

A derivative instrument that is expected to be settled gross by delivery of the underlying asset in exchange for the payment of a fixed price may be designated as a hedge of that gross settlement (this would be a cash flow hedge of the variability of the purchase or sale price without the derivative – see 4.9.2 below). It doesn't matter that the derivative is the contract under which the asset will be transferred.[419]

A hedging instrument normally has a single fair value measure with co-dependent factors causing fair value changes, hence hedging instruments should normally be designated in their entirety.[420] Therefore an instrument, such as an interest rate collar, that contains both a written and a purchased option, cannot be split such that only the purchased option component is designated as a hedging instrument.[421] The standard does, however, allow the following two exceptions to this rule:

- splitting an option's intrinsic and time value, designating only the change in intrinsic value as the hedging instrument and excluding its time value; and
- splitting the interest element and the spot price on a forward.

These exceptions recognise that the intrinsic value of the option and the premium on the forward can generally be measured separately. They are not mandatory and a dynamic hedging strategy that assesses both the intrinsic and time value of an option, say, can qualify for hedge accounting.[422]

A single hedging instrument may be designated as a hedge of more than one type of risk provided that those risks can be clearly identified, hedge effectiveness can be demonstrated and the different risk positions are specifically designated.[423]

A financial instrument whose fair value cannot be reliably measured cannot be a hedging instrument except when a foreign currency denominated non-derivative instrument, whose foreign currency component is reliably measurable, is designated as a foreign currency hedge.[424]

A proportion of the entire hedging instrument, such as 50% of the notional amount, may be designated in a hedging relationship. However, a hedging relationship may not be designated for only a portion of the time period in which the hedging instrument is outstanding.[425] It follows that:

- the hedging instrument need not be acquired at the inception of the hedge and a derivative contract may be designated as a hedge subsequent to entering into it;[426]
- the first three years cash flows associated with, say, a ten year foreign currency borrowing could not qualify as a hedging instrument;[427] and
- a derivative may be designated as a hedge for a proportion of the time to maturity of the hedged item provided this period is the entire remaining period of the hedging instrument.[428]

Example 10.57: Partial term hedging

Company A acquires a 10% fixed rate government bond with a remaining term to maturity of ten years and classifies it as available-for-sale. To hedge against the fair value exposure on the bond associated with the first five years' interest payments, it acquires a five year pay-fixed receive-floating swap.

The swap may be designated as hedging the fair value exposure of the interest rate payments on the government bond until year five and the change in value of the principal payment due at maturity to the extent affected by changes in the yield curve relating to the five years of the swap.[429]

Exposure should be assessed on a transaction basis and therefore a hedging instrument need not reduce risk at an entity-wide level. For example if a company has a fixed rate asset and a fixed rate liability, each with the same principal terms, it may enter into a pay-fixed receive-variable interest rate swap to hedge the fair value of the asset even though the effect of the swap is to create an interest rate exposure that previously did not exist.[430]

In a group of companies, it is not necessary for the hedging instrument to be held by the same company as the one that has the exposure being hedged. For example, a Swiss parent with an Australian subsidiary that has a Japanese yen exposure may, itself, purchase a derivative that offsets the yen exposure in the subsidiary.[431]

For hedge accounting purposes, only derivatives that involve an external party can be designated as hedging instruments. The stated reason is that although individual companies or divisions within a group may enter into hedging transactions with other group companies, any gains and losses on such transactions are eliminated on consolidation; therefore, such arrangements do not qualify for hedge accounting treatment on consolidation.[432] This is not strictly true – as noted in A above, foreign currency intra-group balances may well give rise gains or losses in the income statement that are not eliminated on consolidation – but again this fact does not change the rules. The issue of macro-hedging is considered further in 4.9.8 below.

4.9.2 Hedging relationships

There are three types of hedging relationship defined in IAS 39:

- *fair value hedge:* a hedge of the exposure to changes in the fair value of a recognised asset or liability, or an identified portion of such an asset or liability, that is attributable to a particular risk and that will affect reported net profit or loss;
- *cash flow hedge:* a hedge of the exposure to variability in cash flows that (i) is attributable to a particular risk associated with a recognised asset or liability (such as future interest payments on variable rate debt) or a forecasted transaction (such as an anticipated purchase or sale) and that (ii) will affect reported net profit or loss; and
- *hedge of a net investment in a foreign entity:* which has the same meaning as in IAS 21 (see Chapter 8 at 5.2.2).[433]

A Fair value hedges

An example of a fair value hedge is a hedge of the exposure to changes in the fair value of fixed rate debt as a result of changes in interest rates – if interest rates increase the fair value of the debt decreases and vice versa. Such a hedge could be entered into either by the issuer or by the holder.[434] However this could not be a cash flow hedge because changes in interest rates will not affect cash flows.[435]

A variable rate debt may be the subject of a fair value hedge – its fair value will change if the issuer's credit risk changes; it may also have some fair value exposure, albeit minor, to interest rate changes in the periods between which the variable rate is reset.[436]

On the face of it, if an originated fixed rate loan is held to maturity, changes in its fair value will not affect reported net income. However the implementation guidance explains that such assets may still be the subject of fair value hedges because the loan *could* be sold, in which case fair value changes *would* affect net income.[437]

The exposure to changes in the price of inventories that are carried at the lower of cost and net realisable value may also be the subject of a fair value hedge because their fair value will affect income when they are sold or written down. Alternatively the same hedging instrument may qualify as a cash flow hedge of the future sale of the inventory.[438]

A hedge of a foreign currency asset or liability using a forward exchange contract may be treated as a fair value hedge – its fair value will change as foreign exchange rates change or alternatively it may be treated as a cash flow hedge (see B below).[439]

B Cash flow hedges

Examples of cash flow hedges are:

- a hedge of the future foreign currency risk in an unrecognised contractual commitment by an airline to purchase an aircraft for a fixed amount of a foreign currency;
- a hedge of the change in fuel price relating to an unrecognised contractual commitment by an electric utility to purchase fuel at a fixed price, with payment in its domestic currency;
- use of a swap to, in effect, change floating rate debt to fixed rate debt (this is a hedge of future transactions, i.e. the future variable interest payments);[440]

A hedge of a firm commitment in an entity's own reporting currency, e.g. a contract to purchase a quantity of stocks, is not a hedge of a cash flow exposure but rather of an exposure to a change in fair value. Nonetheless, such a hedge is accounted for as a cash flow hedge, rather than as a fair value hedge – this is to avoid recognising a commitment that would not otherwise be recognised as an asset or liability under current accounting practice (see 4.9.4 below which covers the accounting for fair value hedges).[441]

Forecasted issues of equity shares or forecasted distributions on such shares cannot be hedged items in a cash flow hedge because the transactions will not affect reported income. However, if a foreign currency distribution has been declared and a liability established in accordance with IAS 10, the foreign currency liability may be the subject of a hedge.[442]

A hedge of a foreign currency asset or liability using a forward exchange contract may be treated as a cash flow hedge as changes in exchange rates will affect the amount of cash required to settle the item. Alternatively, as noted under A above, it may also be treated as a fair value hedge.[443]

C Hedges of net investments in foreign entities

A foreign entity is defined in IAS 21 as a foreign operation, the activities of which are not an integral part of the reporting entity and will be subsidiaries, associates or joint ventures. Under IAS 21, all foreign exchange differences that result from translating the financial statements of the foreign entity into the parent's reporting currency are classified as equity until disposal of the net investment.[444]

An equity method investment cannot be the subject of a fair value hedge and IAS 39 explains this as follows: The investor recognises its share of, say, the associate's results in income, rather than fair value changes – if it were a hedged item, it would be adjusted for both fair value changes and profit and loss accruals, which would result in double counting because the fair value changes include the profit and loss accruals. For a similar reason, an investment in a consolidated subsidiary cannot be a hedged item in a fair value hedge because consolidation recognises the parent's share of the subsidiary's accrued income, rather than fair value changes, in the income statement. A hedge of a net investment in a foreign subsidiary is different – there is no double counting because it is a hedge of the foreign currency exposure, not a fair value hedge of the change in the value of the investment.[445]

4.9.3 *Criteria for using special hedge accounting*

A hedging relationship qualifies for special hedge accounting as set out in 4.9.4 to 4.9.6 below if, and only if, all of the following conditions are met:

(a) at the inception of the hedge there is formal documentation of both the hedging relationship and the risk management objective and strategy for undertaking the hedge which should include identification of:
- the hedging instrument;
- the related hedged item or transaction;
- the nature of the risk being hedged; and
- how the hedging instrument's effectiveness in offsetting the exposure to changes in the hedged item's fair value or the hedged transaction's cash flows, attributable to the hedged risk, will be assessed;

(b) the hedge is expected to be highly effective (see C below) in achieving offsetting changes in fair value or cash flows attributable to the hedged risk, consistent with the originally documented risk management strategy for that particular hedging relationship;

(c) a forecasted transaction that is the subject of a cash flow hedge must be highly probable (see B below) and must present an exposure to variations in cash flows that could ultimately affect reported income;

(d) the effectiveness of the hedge can be reliably measured, i.e. the fair value or cash flows of the hedged item and the fair value of the hedging instrument can be reliably measured (see 4.8 above); and

(e) the hedge was assessed on an ongoing basis and determined actually to have been highly effective throughout the financial reporting period (see C below).[446]

Even where borrowings are used to hedge net investments in foreign entities, these criteria must be met in order to use the special hedge accounting described in 4.9.6 below.[447]

If a hedge does not qualify for special hedge accounting because it fails to meet the criteria above, the hedged item and hedging instrument should be accounted for as if they were not part of a hedging relationship. For example if the hedging instrument was a derivative it would be classified as a trading item and be remeasured to fair value with changes being recognised in income.[448]

A Designation and documentation

Designation takes effect, prospectively, from the date all of the above criteria are met. Therefore retroactive designation is not permitted as hedge accounting can only be applied, at the earliest, from the date all of the necessary documentation is completed.[449]

The documentation need not identify the exact date a forecasted transaction is expected to occur. However, the time period in which the forecasted transaction is expected to occur should be identified and documented within a reasonably specific and generally narrow range of time from a most probable date. This will be required as a basis for assessing hedge effectiveness – to determine that the hedge will be highly effective it may be necessary to ensure that changes in the fair value of the expected cash flows are offset by changes in the fair value of the hedging instrument and this test may be met only if the timing of the cash flows occur within close proximity to each other.[450]

Hedged forecasted transactions must be identified and documented with sufficient specificity so that when the transaction occurs, it is clear whether the transaction is, or is not, the hedged transaction. Therefore, a forecasted transaction may be identified as the sale of the first 15,000 units of a specific product during a specified three-month period, but it could not be identified as the last 15,000 units of that product sold because they cannot be identified when they occur. For the same reason, a forecasted transaction cannot be specified solely as a percentage of sales or purchases during a period.[451]

The standard explains that dynamic hedging strategies under which the quantity of the hedging instrument is constantly adjusted in order to maintain a desired hedge ratio, for example to achieve a delta-neutral position insensitive to changes in the fair value of the hedged item may qualify for hedge accounting. Further, the documentation must specify how the hedge will be monitored and updated, how effectiveness will be measured and must be able to properly track all terminations and redesignations of the hedging instrument in addition to demonstrating that all other criteria are met. Also, it must be demonstrated that the hedge is expected to be highly effective for a specified short period of time during which adjustment of the hedge is not expected.[452]

The standard does not address whether, once designated, a hedge may be 'undesignated' although other commentators have suggested management may simply choose to undesignate a hedge.[453] An equivalent effect may, in fact, be achieved by choosing not to assess effectiveness which, because of criterion (e), would preclude the use of hedge accounting.

B *Probability of forecasted transactions*

The implementation guidance explains, somewhat unhelpfully, that the term 'highly probable', indicates a significantly greater likelihood of occurrence than the term 'more likely than not' although it does add some slightly more practical pointers. It states that probability should be supported by observable facts and attendant circumstance – it should not be based solely on management intent because that is not verifiable. In making this assessment consideration should be given to the following circumstances:

- the frequency of similar past transactions;
- the financial and operational ability to carry out the transaction;
- substantial commitments of resources to a particular activity, e.g. a manufacturing facility that can be used in the short run only to process a particular type of commodity;

- the extent of loss or disruption of operations that could result if the transaction does not occur;
- the likelihood that transactions with substantially different characteristics might be used to achieve the same business purpose, e.g. there are several ways of raising cash ranging from a short-term bank loan to a public share offering; and
- the entity's business plan.

The length of time until a forecasted transaction is projected to occur is also a consideration in determining probability. Other factors being equal, the more distant a forecasted transaction is, the less likely it is to be considered highly probable and the stronger the evidence that would be needed to support an assertion that it is highly probable. For example, a transaction forecasted to occur in five years may be less likely to occur than a transaction forecasted to occur in one year. However, forecasted interest payments for the next 20 years on variable-rate debt would typically be highly probable if supported by an existing contractual obligation.

In addition, other factors being equal, the greater the physical quantity or future value of a forecasted transaction in proportion to transactions of the same nature, the less likely it is that the transaction would be considered highly probable and the stronger the evidence that would be required to support such an assertion. For example, less evidence would generally be needed to support forecasted sales of 100 units in the next month than 950 units when recent sales have averaged 950 units for each of the past three months.[454]

The implementation guidance uses the following example to elaborate on this:

Example 10.58: Hedge of foreign currency revenues

An airline operator uses sophisticated models based on past experience and economic data to project its revenues in various currencies. If it can demonstrate that forecasted revenues for a period of time into the future in a particular currency are 'highly probable', it may designate a currency borrowing as a cash flow hedge of the future revenue stream.

However it is unlikely that 100% of revenues for a future year could be reliably predicted. On the other hand, it is possible that a portion of predicted revenues, normally those expected in the short-term, will meet the 'highly probable' criterion.[455]

The standard asserts that a history of having designated hedges of forecasted transactions and then determining that the forecasted transactions are no longer expected to occur should call into question both the ability to accurately predict forecasted transactions and the propriety of using hedge accounting in the future for similar forecasted transactions.[456] Fortunately, however, there are no tainting provisions equivalent to those applied to held-to-maturity investments.

Cash flows arising after the prepayment date on an instrument that is prepayable at the issuer's option may be highly probable for a group or pool of similar assets for which prepayments can be estimated with a high degree of accuracy, e.g. mortgage loans, or if the prepayment option is significantly out of the money.[457]

C Assessing hedge effectiveness

A hedge is normally regarded as highly effective if, at inception and throughout its life:

- changes in the fair value or cash flows of the hedged item can be expected to be almost fully offset by changes in the fair value or cash flows of the hedging instrument; and
- actual results are within a range of 80% to 125%.

For example, if the loss on the hedging instrument is £120 and the gain on the cash instrument is £100, offset can be measured by £120 ÷ £100, which is 120%, or by £100 ÷ £120, which is 83%, and therefore the hedge is highly effective.[458] It is not permitted to purposely hedge, say, 85% of the total exposure and designate this as a hedge of 100% of the exposure. As noted in 4.9.1 A above, 85% of the total exposure *could* be hedged, but the expectation that the hedging instrument will 'almost fully offset' the exposure to losses on the hedged item, i.e. 100%, will almost certainly not be achieved. In this case the 85% portion would become the entire hedged exposure and the basis for assessing hedge effectiveness; therefore the 80% to 125% range would apply to the 85% portion.[459]

No single method for assessing hedge effectiveness is specified by IAS 39 – the method used will depend on the risk management strategy adopted. The appropriateness of a given method will depend on the nature of the risk being hedged and the type of instrument used. The method must be reasonable and consistent with other similar hedges unless different methods are explicitly justified. In some cases, different methods will be adopted for different types of hedges.[460]

In the case of interest rate risk, it is suggested that hedge effectiveness may be assessed by preparing a maturity schedule that shows a reduction of all or part of the rate exposure, for each strip of maturity schedule, resulting from the aggregation of elements, the net position of which is hedged, providing such net exposure can be associated with an asset or liability giving rise to such net exposure and correlation can be assessed against that asset or liability.[461] Macro-hedging is covered further in 4.9.8 below.

Several mathematical techniques can be used including ratio analysis, i.e. a comparison of hedging gains and losses to the corresponding gains and losses on the hedged item at a point in time, and statistical measurement techniques such as regression analysis. If regression analysis is used, the hedge documentation must specify how the results of the regression will be assessed.[462]

A swap's fair value comes from its net settlements and the fixed and variable rates on a swap can be changed without affecting the net settlement if both are changed by the same amount – in other words, a 'pay 7%-receive LIBOR' swap should have the same fair value as a 'pay 6%-receive LIBOR minus 1%' swap. Consequently, the fixed rate on a hedged item need not exactly match the fixed rate on a swap designated as a fair value hedge, nor does the variable rate on an interest-bearing asset or liability need to be the same as the variable rate on a swap designated as a cash flow hedge. However, the time value of money will generally need to be considered in assessing the effectiveness of a hedge.[463]

At inception the method for assessing effectiveness should be documented and that method applied on a consistent basis throughout the hedge. The documentation should state whether the assessment will include all of the gain or loss on a hedging instrument or whether the instrument's time value will be excluded.[464] Effectiveness should be assessed, at a minimum, at the time annual or interim financial reports are prepared.[465]

If a forecasted transaction such as a commodity sale is properly designated in a hedge and, subsequently, its expected timing changes to, say, an earlier period, this does not affect the validity of the original designation. However, this may well affect the assessment of the hedge's effectiveness, especially as the hedging instrument will be designated for the remaining period of its existence, which will exceed the period to the sale.[466]

Expected hedge effectiveness may be assessed on a cumulative basis if that is how the hedge is designated and is reflected in the hedging documentation. Therefore, even if a hedge is not expected to be highly effective in a particular period, hedge accounting is not precluded if effectiveness is expected to remain sufficiently high over the life of the hedging relationship.[467]

Example 10.59: Cumulative hedge effectiveness

A company designates a LIBOR based interest rate swap as a hedge of a borrowing whose interest is a UK base rate plus a margin. The UK base rate changes, perhaps, once each quarter or less, in increments of 25 to 50 basis points, while LIBOR changes daily. Over a one to two year period, the hedge is expected to be almost perfect, however there will be quarters when the UK base rate does not change at all while LIBOR has changed significantly. This would not necessarily preclude hedge accounting.

However, as set out in 4.9.4 and 4.9.5 below, any ineffectiveness will be recognised in earnings as it occurs.[468]

Hedge effectiveness may be assessed on a pre-tax or after-tax basis. If it is to be assessed on an after tax basis this should be designated at inception as part of the formal documentation of the hedging strategy.[469]

If the principal terms of the hedging instrument and of the entire hedged item are the same, the associated changes in fair value and cash flows normally offset fully, both when the hedge is entered into and thereafter until completion. For example, an interest rate swap is likely to be an effective hedge if the notional and principal amounts, term, repricing dates, dates of interest and principal receipts and payments, and basis for measuring interest rates are the same.[470] Similarly a hedge of a forecasted commodity purchase with a forward contract is likely to be highly effective if:

- the forward contract is for the purchase of the same quantity of the same commodity at the same time and location as the hedged forecasted purchase;
- the fair value of the forward contract at inception is zero; and

- either the change in the discount or premium on the forward contract is excluded from the assessment of effectiveness and included directly in income or the change in expected cash flows on the forecasted transaction is based on the forward price for the commodity.[471]

On the other hand, sometimes offset will only be partial. For example, if the hedging instrument and hedged item are denominated in different currencies that do not move in tandem, the hedge would not be fully effective.[472]

However, even if the principal terms of the hedging instrument and hedged item are the same, hedge effectiveness cannot be assumed throughout the life of the hedge. This is because ineffectiveness may arise because of other attributes such as the liquidity of the instruments or their credit risk.[473] Therefore when assessing effectiveness, both at inception and thereafter, the risk of counterparty default should be considered. In a cash flow hedge, if default becomes probable the hedging relationship is unlikely to achieve offsetting cash flows and hedge accounting would be discontinued. In a fair value hedge, if there is a change in the counterparty's creditworthiness, the hedging instrument's fair value will change which affects its effectiveness and hence whether it qualifies for continued hedge accounting.[474]

To improve hedge effectiveness, it may be possible to designate only certain risks as being hedged. For example, if an interest rate swap issued by a counterparty with a AA credit rating is used to hedge the fair value of a debt instrument, designating only the exposure related to AA rated interest rate movements will reduce the effect of market changes in credit spreads (although not the risk of changes in the counterparty's credit risk).[475]

The foreign currency risk associated with a holding of shares may be hedged if there is a clear and identifiable exposure to changes in foreign exchange rates. It is suggested in the implementation guidance that this will be the case if:

- the shares are not traded on an exchange, or other established market, in which trades are denominated in the same currency as the holder's measurement currency; and
- dividends on the shares are not denominated in that currency.

Consequently, if the share trades in multiple currencies, one of which is the holder's measurement currency, hedge accounting would not be permitted.[476] However this assertion does not stand up to close scrutiny as illustrated in the following example:

Example 10.60: Foreign currency risk associated with equity shareholding

ABC plc, a UK company whose measurement currency is sterling, acquires a small shareholding in IJK Limited. IJK is a South African company whose operations are based solely in that country and whose income, expenditure and dividends are all denominated in South African rand. IJK's shares are listed on the Johannesburg Stock Exchange where trades are denominated in rand.

The guidance suggests that, potentially, ABC could hedge the foreign currency risk arising from the sterling/rand exchange rate on its IJK holding which appears quite sensible. If, on day 1, the shares trade at R50 and the exchange rate is R10 to £1, the shares would have a sterling value of £5.00 (= R50 ÷ 10). If, on day 2, the exchange rate moves to R8 to £1, all other things being equal, the rand value of IJK should not change, but its sterling value would be £6.25 (= R50 ÷ 8), exactly mirroring the exchange rate movement.

If IJK had a secondary listing on the London Stock Exchange where trades were denominated in sterling, but its business fundamentals were unchanged, in the scenario outlined above ABC's foreign exchange exposure would be exactly the same – in fact the operation of the markets should ensure that share price in London on days 1 and 2 are £5.00 and £6.25 respectively. However the guidance suggests that because of the secondary listing, ABC no longer has a clear and identifiable exposure to changes in foreign exchange rates on the IJK shares.

In practice, given the international nature of many groups of companies, it is extremely difficult to identify and assess the effectiveness of a single foreign currency exchange rate risk associated with an equity shareholding for all but the most geographically concentrated entities.

The risk of a physical asset's obsolescence, of expropriation of property by a government, or the risk that a transaction does not occur are not reliably measurable. Hence effectiveness cannot be measured and the risk cannot be the subject of a hedge under IAS 39. To qualify for special hedge accounting, the hedge must relate to a specific identified and designated risk, and not merely to overall business risks.[477]

4.9.4 Accounting for fair value hedges

If a fair value hedge meets the conditions set out in 4.9.3 above during the reporting period, it should be accounted for as follows:

- the gain or loss from remeasuring the hedging instrument at fair value should be recognised immediately in income.[478]

  In the case of non-derivative instruments used to hedge foreign currency risk, this only refers to fair value changes in respect of foreign exchange rate movements, recognised in accordance with IAS 21, and does not mean such items should necessarily be remeasured to fair value in their entirety;[479] and

- the carrying amount of the hedged item should be adjusted to recognise fair value changes attributable to the hedged risk and the associated gain or loss is recognised immediately in income. This applies even if a hedged item is an available-for-sale asset measured at fair value with changes in fair value recognised directly in equity as set out in 4.6.4 B above or is otherwise measured at cost.[480]

The following simple example illustrates how this would apply to a fair value hedge of interest rate exposure on an investment in fixed rate debt.

Example 10.61: Fair value hedge

During Year 1 an investor purchases a debt security for £100 and classifies it as available-for-sale, gains and losses on which it has chosen to report in equity. At the end of Year 1, the fair value of the asset is £110. To protect this value, the investor enters into a hedge by acquiring a derivative with a nil fair value. By the end of Year 2, the derivative has a fair value of £5 and the debt security has a corresponding decline in fair value.

The investor would record the following accounting entries:

Year 1

	£	£
Debt security	100	
Cash		100

To reflect the acquisition of the security.

	£	£
Debt security	10	
Equity		10

To reflect the increase in the security's fair value.

Year 2

	£	£
Derivative	–	
Cash		–

To record the acquisition of the derivative at its cost of nil.

	£	£
Derivative	5	
Income		5

To record the increase in the derivative's fair value.

	£	£
Income	5	
Debt security		5

To record the decrease in the security's fair value.[481]

If only certain risks attributable to an available-for-sale asset whose changes in fair value are otherwise recognised in equity, have been hedged, changes in the fair value of the asset that are unrelated to the hedge continue to be reported in equity.[482]

Example 10.62: Hedging foreign currency risk of publicly traded shares

ABC Ltd, a UK company whose measurement currency is sterling, acquires 100 shares in a listed US corporation for US$1,000. The shares are classified as available-for-sale, gains and losses on which ABC has chosen to report in equity. It is assumed the shares gives rise to a clear and identifiable exposure to changes in the US$/sterling exchange rate and to protect itself from changes in this exchange rate, ABC enters into a forward contract to sell US$750 which it intends to roll over for as long as the shares are held.

A portion of an exposure may be designated as a hedged item, and so the forward contract may be designated as a hedge of part of the shareholding. It could be a fair value hedge of the foreign exchange exposure of US$750 associated with the shares (alternatively it could be a cash flow hedge of a forecasted sale of the shares but only if the timing of the sale is identified with sufficient certainty). Any variability in the fair value of the shares in US dollars would not affect the assessment of hedge effectiveness unless their fair value fell below US$750.

Gains and losses on the forward contract would be reported in income. Gains and losses arising from remeasuring the dollar value of the hedged proportion of the shares to sterling would also be reported in income; the remainder would be reported in equity.[483]

The implementation guidance explains that where two offsetting derivatives are acquired, it is generally not permitted to designate one of them as a hedging instrument in a fair value hedge unless:

- the second swap was not entered into in contemplation of the first; or
- there is a 'substantive business purpose' for structuring the transactions separately.

It emphasises that judgement should be applied in determining what is a substantive business purpose. A centralised treasury company may enter into third party derivative contracts on behalf of other subsidiaries to hedge their interest rate exposures and, to track those exposures within the group, enter into internal derivative transactions with those subsidiaries. It may also enter into a derivative contract with the same counterparty during the same business day with substantially the same terms as a contract entered into as a hedging instrument on behalf of another subsidiary as part of its trading operations, or because it wishes to rebalance its overall portfolio risk. In this case, there is a valid business purpose for entering into each contract. However, a desire to achieve fair value accounting for the hedged item is not a substantive business purpose.[484]

The special hedge accounting specified above should be discontinued prospectively if any one of the following occurs:

- the hedging instrument expires or is sold, terminated, or exercised (for this purpose, the replacement or a rollover of a hedging instrument into another is not considered an expiration or termination if that is part of the documented hedging strategy); or
- the hedge no longer meets the criteria for qualification for hedge accounting in 4.9.3 above.[485]

An adjustment to the carrying amount of a hedged interest-bearing financial instrument should be amortised to income although IAS 39 specifies no amortisation method. It does state that amortisation should begin no later than when the hedged item ceases to be adjusted for changes in its fair value attributable to the hedged risk and should be fully amortised by maturity.[486] This does not preclude amortisation starting earlier than when hedge accounting ceases, although that may be administratively more burdensome. Whatever method is adopted, it should be applied consistently for all such adjustments.[487]

4.9.5 *Accounting for cash flow hedges*

If a cash flow hedge meets the conditions in 4.9.3 above during the reporting period and the hedging instrument is a derivative, it should be accounted for as follows:

- the effective portion of the gain or loss from remeasuring the derivative to fair value should be recognised in equity; and
- the ineffective portion should be reported immediately in income.

In the limited circumstances in which the hedging instrument is a non-derivative, i.e. for hedges of foreign currency risk, a similar treatment should be adopted for those changes in fair value attributable to foreign currency changes unless both the hedging instrument and the hedged items are monetary items, in which case the associated gains and losses are reported in income in accordance with IAS 21.[488]

More specifically, the accounting is as follows:

- the separate component of equity associated with the hedged item is adjusted to the lesser of the following (in absolute amounts):
  (i) the cumulative gain or loss on the hedging instrument necessary to offset the cumulative change in expected future cash flows on the hedged item from inception of the hedge excluding the ineffective component; and
  (ii) the fair value of the cumulative change in expected future cash flows on the hedged item from inception of the hedge;
- any remaining gain or loss on the hedging instrument (which is not an effective hedge) is included in income or directly in equity as appropriate according to its nature and the entity's accounting policy as set out in 4.6.1 B and 4.6.4 B above; and
- if the documented risk management strategy for a particular hedging relationship excludes a specific component of the gain or loss or related cash flows on the hedging instrument from the assessment of hedge effectiveness, that excluded component of gain or loss is recognised according to its nature and the entity's accounting policy as set out in 4.6.1 B and 4.6.4 B above.[489]

Therefore even if the hedge is considered to be highly effective because the actual risk offset is within the 80% to 125% range from full offset, a gain or loss may still be recognised in income representing ineffectiveness.[490]

The following examples illustrate these principles:

Example 10.63: Cash flow hedge of anticipated commodity sale

On 30 September 2001, Company A hedges the anticipated sale of 24 tonnes of pulp on 1 March 2002 by entering into a short forward contract. The contract requires net settlement in cash determined as the difference between the future spot price of 24 tonnes of pulp on a specified commodity exchange and £1,000. A expects to sell the pulp in a different, local market.

A determines that the forward contract is an effective hedge of the anticipated sale and that the other conditions for hedge accounting are met. It assesses hedge effectiveness by comparing the entire change in the fair value of the forward contract with the change in the fair value of the expected cash inflows. On 31 December 2001, the spot price of pulp has increased both in the local market and on the exchange although the increase in the local market exceeds the increase on the exchange. As a result, the present value of the expected cash inflow from the sale on the local market is £1,100 and the fair value of the forward is £80 negative. The hedge is determined to be still highly effective.

The cumulative change in the fair value of the forward contract is £80, while the fair value of the cumulative change in expected future cash flows on the hedged item is £100. Ineffectiveness is not recognised in the financial statements because the cumulative change in the fair value of the hedged cash flows exceeds the cumulative change in the value of the hedging instrument. The whole of the fair value change in the forward would be recognised in equity.

However if A concluded that the hedge was no longer highly effective, it would discontinue hedge accounting prospectively as from the date the hedge ceased to be highly effective.[491]

Example 10.64: Cash flow hedge of a floating rate liability

Company A has a floating rate liability of £1,000 with five years remaining to maturity. It enters into a five year pay-fixed, receive-floating interest rate swap with the same principal terms to hedge the exposure to variable cash flow payments on the floating rate liability attributable to interest rate risk.

At inception, the swap's fair value is £nil. Subsequently, there is an increase of £49 which consists of a change of £50 resulting from an increase in market interest rates and a change of minus £1 resulting from an increase in the credit risk of the swap counterparty. There is no change in the fair value of the floating rate liability, but the present value of the future cash flows needed to offset the exposure to variable interest cash flows on the liability increases by £50.

A hedge of interest rate risk is not fully effective if part of the change in the fair value of the derivative is due to the counterparty's credit risk (see 4.9.3 C above). However, if the hedge relationship is still highly effective, A credits the effective portion of the swap's fair value change, £49, to equity. There is no debit to income for the change in fair value of the swap attributable to the deterioration in the credit quality of the swap counterparty because the cumulative change in the present value of the future cash flows needed to offset the exposure to variable interest cash flows on the hedged item, £50, exceeds the cumulative change in value of the hedging instrument, £49 (see Example 10.63 above). If A concluded that the hedge was no longer highly effective, it would discontinue hedge accounting prospectively as from the date the hedge ceased to be highly effective.

Alternatively if the fair value of the swap increased to £51 of which £50 results from the increase in market interest rates and £1 from a decrease in the counterparty's credit risk, there would be a credit to income of £1 for the change in the swap's fair value attributable to the improvement in the counterparty's credit quality. This is because the cumulative change in the value of the hedging instrument, £51, exceeds the cumulative change in the present value of the future cash flows needed to offset the exposure to variable interest cash flows on the hedged item, £50. The difference of £1 represents the excess ineffectiveness attributable to the swap, and is reported in income.[492]

In 4.9.2 A and 4.9.2 B above, it was stated that using a forward exchange contract to hedge a foreign currency payable or receivable could be treated either as a fair value or a cash flow hedge under IAS 39. The effect on income should be very similar:

Example 10.65: Cash flow hedge of foreign currency asset or liability

In a fair value hedge, the gain or loss on remeasurement of the forward contract and the hedged item are recognised immediately in income. In a cash flow hedge the gain or loss on remeasuring the forward contract is initially recognised in equity and recycled into income when the payable or receivable affects income. This will be when it is remeasured for changes in foreign exchange rates.

Therefore, assuming the hedge is effective, the gain or loss on the forward contract is released to income in the same periods during which the liability is remeasured, not when the payment occurs, which should be very similar, if not identical, to the fair value hedge treatment.[493]

If the hedged firm commitment or forecasted transaction results in the recognition of an asset or liability, the associated gains or losses recognised in equity should be removed and enter into the asset or liability's initial measurement (a so-called 'basis adjustment').[494] A gain or loss included in the initial carrying amount of an asset or liability will be recognised in income when the asset or liability itself affects income (such as in the periods that depreciation, interest or cost of sales is recognised). The provisions of other International Accounting Standards with respect to impairment of assets and net realisable values of inventories apply to assets arising from hedges of forecasted transactions.[495]

The application of a basis adjustment is illustrated in the following example which is based on the implementation guidance:

Example 10.66: Forecasted issuance of debt in foreign currency

Company A has the euro as its measurement currency. On 1 November 2001, it expects to borrow US$1,000 on 1 April 2002. To offset the exposure to changes in foreign exchange rates, it takes out a forward exchange contract to buy €1,100 and sell US$1,000 on 1 April 2002. The forward exchange contract is designated as a cash flow hedge of the forecasted borrowing and the relationship meets the criteria for hedge accounting. On 1 April 2002 the dollar has depreciated and the forward exchange contract has a cumulative gain that has been reported in equity that is the equivalent of US$100; A borrows US$1,000 and settles the forward exchange contract.

The initial carrying amount of the US dollar borrowing is adjusted for this cumulative gain, i.e. US$1,100. The effective interest rate on the US dollar borrowing should reflect the adjustment to its initial carrying amount and is expressed as a US dollar interest rate. Accordingly, for the purpose of applying the effective interest method the adjustment is expressed in US dollars rather than in euros.[496]

Like a number of the Q&As, this example appears to be based on an unlikely series of facts – one simply has to assume that a company planning to issue foreign currency denominated debt has a good reason for hedging only the foreign currency exposure for the five months until the date of issue rather than the unspecified period for which the debt will be outstanding.

For all cash flow hedges other than those resulting in a basis adjustment to an asset or liability, amounts that had been recognised directly in equity should be included in income in the same period or periods during which the hedged firm commitment or forecasted transaction affects income, e.g. when a forecasted sale actually occurs.[497]

Special hedge accounting should be discontinued prospectively if any one of the following occurs:

(a) the hedging instrument expires or is sold, terminated, or exercised;

For this purpose, the replacement or a rollover of a hedging instrument into another hedging instrument is not considered an expiration or termination if such replacement or rollover is part of the documented hedging strategy.

The cumulative gain or loss recognised in equity should remain there until the forecasted transaction occurs. Thereafter it is treated as a basis adjustment of the associated asset or liability, where applicable, or else it is recognised in income at the time the transaction affects income;

(b) the hedge no longer meets the criteria for qualification for hedge accounting in 4.9.3 above – the accounting for the cumulative gain or loss recognised in equity is that same as in (a) above; or

(c) the committed or forecasted transaction is no longer expected to occur, in which case any related net cumulative gain or loss that has been reported directly in equity should be reported in income for the period.[498]

Where a forecasted transaction is no longer 'highly probable' (see 4.9.3 C above) this does not necessarily mean that it is no longer expected to occur. If the transaction is still expected to occur, hedge accounting should be discontinued and gains or losses treated in accordance with (b); otherwise they would be treated in accordance with (c).[499]

4.9.6 *Accounting for hedges of a net investment in a foreign entity*

Hedges of a net investment in a foreign entity should be accounted for in a similar way to cash flow hedges:

- the portion of the gain or loss on the hedging instrument that is determined to be an effective hedge should be recognised directly in equity through the statement of changes in equity; and
- the ineffective portion should be reported:
  - (i) immediately in income if the hedging instrument is a derivative; or
  - (ii) in equity in the limited circumstances in which the hedging instrument is not a derivative, consistent with IAS 21, (see Chapter 8 at 5.2.4 C).

The gain or loss on the hedging instrument relating to the effective portion of the hedge should be classified in the same manner as the foreign currency translation gain or loss.[500]

The main impact for companies using borrowings to finance net investments will be to restrict the amount of borrowings that qualify for hedge accounting. Under IAS 21, at least since its revision in 1993, there was no explicit prohibition on a company using, say, a loan of US$100 to hedge a net investment of US$40 and reporting exchange differences on the entire US$100 in equity; however this relationship would almost certainly not be highly effective within the terms established in IAS 39 and only a proportion of the loan, perhaps US$40, could be designated in an effective hedge.

If the hedging instrument is a forward exchange contract, the discount or premium in the contract cannot be amortised to income over the contract term, even if this was the treatment prior to the adoption of IAS 39, because derivatives are always measured at fair value. The effective portion of the associated gain or loss should initially be included in equity pending recycling into income on disposal of the net investment. The interest element (time value) of the fair value of a forward may be excluded from the designated hedge relationship, however in this case changes in the interest element portion of the fair value of the forward exchange contract, would be included in interest – this could produce very different results to amortising the net premium or discount.[501]

4.9.7 *Further examples of applying the hedging rules*

The rules covered in 4.9.1 to 4.9.6 above are the building blocks for hedge accounting under IAS 39 and it will often be necessary to combine these to achieve hedge accounting in any particular scenario. For example, although fair value and cash flow hedges are discussed completely separately, a single instrument may in fact be simultaneously designated as a hedging instrument in both a fair value and a cash flow hedge – a combined interest rate and currency swap could be used to convert a variable rate position in a foreign currency to a fixed rate position in the reporting currency.[502] The following examples are based on those included in the implementation guidance, both final and draft, and illustrate the practical application of the hedging rules.

The first example, which is based on the draft implementation guidance, deals comprehensively with a type of hedge that is very common in practice, the hedging of foreign currency risk associated with future sales using a forward currency contract. In 4.9.1 B above, it was explained that the spot and interest elements of a forward contract could be treated separately for the purposes of hedge designation and the example deals with both possibilities – the whole forward is designated as the hedging instrument in part (a) whilst in part (b) only the spot element is.

In each case the hedge is perfectly effective because of the way effectiveness is measured, but there is a significant difference on the income statement – all gains and losses on the forward are initially deferred in equity in part (a) whereas in part (b) changes in the fair value of the interest element of the forward are immediately recognised in income. The example also sets out how such a hedge is initially a cash flow hedge of the future sale and then become a fair value hedge of the associated receivable.

Example 10.67: Cash flow hedge of forecasted sale and resulting receivable

Company A has the Reporting Currency (RC) as its measurement currency. On 30 June 2001, it enters into a forward exchange contract to receive Foreign Currency (FC) 100,000 and deliver RC 109,600 on 30 June 2002 at an initial cost and fair value of zero. It designates the forward exchange contract as a hedging instrument in a cash flow hedge of a firm commitment to purchase a certain quantity of paper for FC 100,000 on 31 March 2002 and, subsequently, as a fair value hedge of the resulting payable of FC 100,000, which is to be paid on 30 June 2002. All hedge accounting conditions in IAS 39 are met.

On 30 June 2001, the spot exchange rate is RC 1.072 to 1 FC, while the twelve-month forward exchange rate is 1.096. On 31 December 2001, the spot exchange rate is 1.080, while the six-month forward exchange rate is 1.092. On 31 March 2002, the spot exchange rate is 1.074, while the three-month forward rate is 1.076. On 30 June 2002, the spot exchange rate is 1.072. The applicable yield curve in the reporting currency is flat at 6% per annum throughout the period. The fair value of the forward exchange contract is negative RC 388 on 31 December 2001 ({[1.092 x 100,000] – 109,600} ÷ $1.06^{(6/12)}$), negative RC 1,971 on 31 March 2002 ({[1.076 x 100,000] – 109,600} ÷ $1.06^{(3/12)}$), and negative RC 2,400 on 30 June 2002 (1.072 x 100,000 – 109,600).

(a) Changes in the fair value of the forward contract are designated in the hedge

The hedge is expected to be fully effective because the critical terms of the forward exchange contract and the purchase contract and the assessment of hedge effectiveness are based on the forward price.

The accounting entries are as follows.

30 June 2001

	RC	RC
Forward	–	
Cash		–

To record the forward exchange contract at its initial cost, zero.

31 December 2001

	RC	RC
Equity	388	
Forward – liability		388

To record the change in the forward's fair value between 30 June 2001 and 31 December 2001, i.e. 388 – 0 = 388, in equity. The hedge is fully effective because the loss on the forward exchange contract, RC 388, exactly offsets the change in cash flows associated with the purchase based on the forward price {([1.092 x 100,000] – 109,600) ÷ $1.06^{(6/12)}$} – {([1.096 x 100,000] – 109,600) ÷ 1.06} = –388.

31 March 2002

	RC	RC
Equity	1,583	
Forward – liability		1,583

To record the change in the forward's fair value between 1 January 2002 and 31 March 2002, i.e. 1,971 – 388 = 1,583, in equity. The hedge is fully effective because the loss on the forward exchange contract, RC 1,583, exactly offsets the change in cash flows associated with the purchase based on the forward price {([1.076 x 100,000] – 109,600) ÷ $1.06^{(3/12)}$} – {([1.092 x 100,000] – 109,600) ÷ $1.06^{(6/12)}$} = –1,583.

	RC	RC
Paper (purchase price)	107,400	
Paper (hedging loss)	1,971	
Equity		1,971
Payable		107,400

To record the purchase of the paper at the spot rate (1.074 x 100,000) and remove the cumulative loss on the forward reported in equity, RC 1,971, and include it in the initial measurement of the purchased paper. Accordingly, the initial measurement of the purchased paper is RC 109,371 consisting of a purchase consideration of RC 107,400 and a hedging loss of RC 1,971.

30 June 2002

	RC	RC
Payable	107,400	
Cash		107,200
Income		200

To record the settlement of the payable at the spot rate (100,000 x 1.072 = 107,200) and the associated exchange gain of 200 = 107,400 – 107,200.

	RC	RC
Income	429	
Forward – liability		429

To record the loss on the forward exchange contract between 1 April 2002 and 30 June 2002, i.e. 2,400 – 1,971 = 429) in income. The hedge is considered to be fully effective because the loss on the forward exchange contract, RC 429, exactly offsets the change in the fair value of the payable based on the forward price [1.072 x 100,000] – 109,600 – {([1.076 x 100,000] – 109,600) ÷ $1.06^{(3/12)}$} = –429.

	RC	RC
Forward – liability	2,400	
Cash		2,400

To record the net settlement of the forward exchange contract.

Although this arrangement has been set up to be a 'perfect hedge', the loss on the forward in the last three months is significantly different from the gain recorded on retranslating the hedged payable. The principal reason for this is that the change in the fair value of the swap includes changes in its interest element, as well as its currency element, and economically it is largely the currency element that is hedging the payable.

(b) Changes in the spot element of the forward contract only are designated in the hedge

The hedge is expected to be fully effective because the critical terms of the forward exchange contract and the purchase contract are the same and the change in the premium or discount on the forward contract is excluded from the assessment of effectiveness.

30 June 2001

	RC	RC
Forward	–	
Cash		–

To record the forward exchange contract at its initial cost, zero.

31 December 2001

	RC	RC
Income (interest element of forward)	1,165	
Equity (spot element)		777
Forward – liability		388

To record the change in the forward's fair value between 30 June 2001 and 31 December 2001, i.e. 388 – 0 = 388. The change in the present value of spot settlement of the forward exchange contract is a gain of 777 = {([1.080 x 100,000] – 107,200) ÷ $1.06^{(6/12)}$} – {([1.072 x 100,000] – 107,200) ÷ 1.06}), which is recognised directly in equity. The change in the interest element of the forward exchange contract (the residual change in fair value) is a loss of 1,165 = 388 + 777, which is recognised in income. The hedge is fully effective because the gain in the spot element of the forward contract, RC 777, exactly offsets the change in the purchase price at spot rates {([1.080 x 100,000] – 107,200) ÷ $1.06^{(6/12)}$} – {([1.072 x 100,000] – 107,200) ÷ 1.06} = –777.

31 March 2002

	RC	RC
Equity (spot element)	580	
Income (interest element)	1,003	
Forward – liability		1,583

To record the change in the forward's fair value between 1 January 2002 and 31 March 2002, i.e. 1,971 – 388 = 1,583. The change in the present value of spot settlement of the forward exchange contract is a loss of 580 ={([1.074 x 100,000] – 107,200) ÷ $1.06^{(3/12)}$} – {([1.080 x 100,000] – 107,200) ÷ $1.06^{(6/12)}$}, which is recognised in equity. The change in the interest element of the forward contract (the residual change in fair value) is a loss of 1,003 = 1,583 – 580), which is recognised in income. The hedge is fully effective because the loss in the spot element of the forward contract, RC 580, exactly offsets the change in the purchase price at spot rates {([1.074 x 100,000] – 107,200) ÷ 1. $06^{(3/12)}$} – {([1.080 x 100,000] – 107,200) ÷ $1.06^{(6/12)}$} = –580.

	RC	RC
Paper (purchase price)	107,400	
Equity	197	
Paper (hedging gain)		197
Payable		107,400

To recognise the purchase of the paper at the spot rate (= 1.074 x 100,000) and remove the cumulative gain on the spot element of the forward contract that has been recognised in equity (777 – 580 = 197) and include it in the initial measurement of the purchased paper. Accordingly, the initial measurement of the purchased paper is RC 107,203 consisting of a purchase consideration of RC 107,400 and a hedging gain of RC 197.

30 June 2002

	RC	RC
Payable	107,400	
Cash		107,200
Income		200

To record the settlement of the payable at the spot rate (100,000 x 1.072 = 107,200) and the associated exchange gain of 200 (= – [1.072 – 1.074] x 100,000).

	RC	RC
Income (spot element)	197	
Income (interest element)	232	
Forward – liability		429

To record the change in the forward's fair value between 1 April 2002 and 30 June 2002, i.e. 2,400 – 1,971 = 429). The change in the present value of spot settlement of the forward exchange contract is a loss of 197 = {[1.072 x 100,000] – 107,200 – {([1.074 x 100,000] – 107,200) ÷ $1.06^{(3/12)}$}, which is recognised in income. The change in the interest element of the forward contract (the residual change in fair value) is a loss of 232 = 429 –197, which is recognised in income. The hedge is fully effective because the loss in the spot element of the forward contract, RC 197, exactly offsets the gain on the payable reported using spot rates = {[1.072 x 100,000] – 107,200 – {([1.074 x 100,000] – 107,200) ÷ $1.06^{(3/12)}$} = –197.

	RC	RC
Forward – liability	2,400	
Cash		2,400

To record the net settlement of the forward exchange contract.[503]

The use of hedge accounting is sometimes unnecessary when foreign currency exposures on recognised instruments are being hedged:

Example 10.68: Fair value hedge of foreign currency bond

Company J, whose measurement currency is the Japanese yen, has issued US$5,000 five year fixed rate debt. Also, J owns a US$5,000 five year fixed rate bond, which is classified as available for sale, gains and losses on which J has chosen to report in equity.

J's bond has a fair value exposure to foreign currency rate changes, interest rate changes and credit risk and a cash flow exposure to foreign currency changes. A non-derivative can be used as a hedging instrument only for a hedge of a foreign currency risk. Therefore the US dollar liability can be designated as a fair value hedge or cash flow hedge of the bond's foreign currency component.

However, hedge accounting is unnecessary because the amortised cost of the hedging instrument and the hedged item are both remeasured using closing rates with differences reported in income as required by IAS 21.[504]

Hedge accounting is necessary when the hedged foreign currency exposure arises from an unrecognised derivative:

Example 10.69: Foreign currency debt hedging firm sales commitment

Continuing the previous example, J has also issued US$5,000 of fixed rate debt maturing in two years at face value and has entered into a US$5,000 fixed price sales commitment maturing in two years. The commitment is not accounted for as a derivative because it meets the exemption for normal sales (see 4.2.5 above).

Because the sales contract is not accounted for as a derivative it cannot be a hedging instrument. The debt is a non-derivative and can therefore only be designated as a hedge of the currency exposure on the sales commitment. This could not be a fair value hedge because the sales contract is not a *recognised* asset or liability – it would be a cash flow hedge.[505]

A derivative that is denominated only in currencies other than an entity's reporting currency may be used as a hedge if it is hedging positions in those currencies. The following two examples illustrate this:

Example 10.70: Foreign currency forward hedging positions in two foreign currencies

Company J now issues five year floating rate US dollar debt and acquires a ten year fixed rate sterling bond. The principal amounts of the asset and liability, when converted into the Japanese yen, are the same. J enters into a single foreign currency forward contract to hedge its foreign currency exposure on both instruments under which it receives US dollars and pays sterling at the end of five years.

Designating a single hedging instrument as a hedge of multiple types of risk is permitted if three conditions are met:

- the hedged risks can be clearly identified;

  In this case the risks are exposures to changes in the US dollar/yen and yen/sterling exchange rates respectively.

- the effectiveness of the hedge can be demonstrated;

  For the sterling loan, effectiveness can be measured as the degree of offset between the fair value of the principal repayment in sterling and the fair value of the sterling payment on the forward exchange contract.

For the US dollar liability, effectiveness can be measured as the degree of offset between the fair value of the principal repayment in US dollars and the US dollar receipt on the forward exchange contract.

Even though the receivable has a ten year life and the forward only protects it for the first five years, hedge accounting is permitted for only a portion of the exposure; and

- it is possible to ensure that there is a specific designation of the hedging instrument and the different risk positions.

  The hedged exposures are identified as the principal amounts of the liability and the note receivable in their respective currency of denomination.

The hedging instrument satisfies all of these conditions and J can designate the forward as a hedging instrument in a cash flow hedge against the foreign currency exposure on the principal repayments of both instruments and qualify for hedge accounting.[506]

Example 10.71: Cross-currency interest rate swap hedging two foreign currency rate exposures and fair value interest rate exposure

Finally J issues five year floating rate US dollar debt and acquires a ten year fixed rate sterling bond and wishes to hedge the foreign currency exposure on both the bond and the debt as well as the fair value interest rate exposure on the bond. To do this it enters into a matching cross-currency interest rate swap to receive floating rate US dollars, pay fixed rate sterling and exchange the US dollars for sterling at the end of five years.

Hedge accounting is permitted for components of risk, provided effectiveness can be measured, and a single hedging instrument may be designated as a hedge of more than one type of risk if the risks can be clearly identified, effectiveness demonstrated, and specific designation of the hedging instrument and the risk positions can be ensured.

The swap can be designated as a hedging instrument in a fair value hedge against both foreign currency risk and interest rate risk, even though both sterling and US dollars are foreign currencies. Therefore, the swap may be designated as a hedging instrument in a fair value hedge of the sterling receivable against exposure to changes in its fair value associated with changes in UK interest rates for the initial partial term of five years and the sterling US dollar exchange rate.

The swap is measured at fair value with changes in fair value reported in income. The carrying amount of the receivable is adjusted for changes in its fair value caused by changes in UK interest rates for the first five year portion of the yield curve. Both the receivable and payable are remeasured using spot exchange rates under IAS 21 and the changes to their carrying amounts included in income.[507]

In 4.9.1 B above it was stated that the intrinsic and time values of an option could be split for the purpose of hedge designation. The following example, based on the draft implementation guidance, illustrates how this may be applied in practice – in this case a put option hedges an equity shareholding, but the broad principles may be applied to other hedges, such as the use of commodity options.

Example 10.72: Using an out of the money put option to hedge an equity share

Company ABC has an investment in one share of Company XYZ. The share is classified as available-for-sale, gains and losses on which ABC has chosen to report in equity. The share has a quoted price of £100 and to partially protect itself against decreases in the share price, ABC acquires a put option, which gives it the right to sell one XYZ share for £90.

ABC is permitted to designate changes in the option's intrinsic value as the hedging instrument and designates changes in the put's intrinsic value as a hedging instrument in a fair value hedge of its XYZ share. Price changes above £90 are not hedged. Since the put gives ABC the right to dispose of the share at £90, it should normally be fully effective in offsetting price declines of below £90 on an intrinsic value basis.

Accordingly, gains and losses on one XYZ share for prices above £90 are not attributable to the hedged risk for the purpose of assessing hedge effectiveness and reporting gains and losses on the hedged item.

Therefore, ABC reports changes in the fair value of the XYZ share above £90 in equity; changes below £90 form part of the designated fair value hedge and are reported in income. Assuming the hedge is effective, those changes are offset by changes in the intrinsic value of the put, which are also reported in income. Changes in the time value of the put are excluded from the designated hedging relationship and recognised in income.[508]

The following example from the implementation guidance explains how a company might hedge the anticipated issuance of fixed rate debt, i.e. to lock in current interest rates, and suggests how hedge effectiveness could be measured.

Example 10.73: Hedge of anticipated issuance of fixed rate debt

Company R periodically issues new bonds to refinance maturing bonds, provide working capital, and for various other purposes. When R decides it will be issuing bonds, it sometimes hedges the risk of changes in long-term interest rates to the date the bonds are issued. If long-term interest rates go up (down), the bond will be issued either at a higher (lower) rate, with a higher (smaller) discount or with a smaller (higher) premium than was originally expected. The higher (lower) rate being paid or decrease (increase) in proceeds is normally offset by the gain on the hedge.

In August 2001 R decides it will issue £2,000 seven-year bonds in January 2002. Historical correlation studies suggest that a seven-year treasury bond adequately correlates to the bonds R expects to issue, assuming a hedge ratio of 0.93 futures contracts to one debt unit. Therefore, it hedges the anticipated issuance of the bonds by selling (shorting) £1,860 worth of futures on seven-year treasury bonds.

From August 2001 to January 2002 interest rates increase and the short futures positions are closed on the date the bonds are issued. This results in a £12 gain, which offsets the increased interest payments on the bonds and, therefore, will affect income over the life of the bonds. The hedge qualifies as a cash flow hedge of the interest rate risk on the forecasted debt issuance.[509]

4.9.8 Macro-hedging

At first glance, IAS 39 appears to prohibit or severely restrict the use of hedge accounting for entities that manage risk on a net basis, especially when internal derivatives are used to collect and offset exposures within a group. The main problem is that only gross exposures and derivatives that *involve* a third party may be designated in a hedging relationship (see 4.9.1 A and 4.9.1 B above respectively). Intra-group derivatives may well qualify for hedge accounting in the individual accounts of group companies, however they would normally be eliminated on consolidation. Similarly, intra-company derivatives, e.g. between an operating and a treasury division, should normally be eliminated when preparing that company's individual accounts.[510]

This is not the whole picture and there are a number of ways of overcoming these restrictions, at least partially. In particular the implementation guidance emphasises that an entity may continue to *manage* its exposures on a net basis provided that hedge *designation* is on a gross basis.[511] It also implies that a flexible approach should be adopted when interpreting the word 'involve' in the context of third party hedges and goes some way towards dismissing some of its own anti-avoidance rules, although we are not entirely convinced that some of this guidance complies with the standard.

In any event, most companies will still need to amend their risk management and hedging strategies and associated procedures, at least to some extent, to allow the use of hedge accounting under IAS 39.

The initial position the guidance takes is relatively uncontroversial and explains that if the exposure on an internal derivative is offset with a third party, say by the treasury operation entering into an offsetting external derivative, hedge accounting is permitted. Therefore internal derivatives may be used for risk management purposes, e.g. by accumulating exposures in the treasury operation so that risk can be managed on a group-wide basis. The underlying exposure in the operating division will be the hedged item, the external derivative the hedging instrument and the internal derivative contract will form part of the hedging documentation.[512]

The next stage involves determining the extent to which these internal derivatives may be aggregated, or offset, before being laid off to a third party. The initial guidance suggested that several internal derivatives could be aggregated, before being offset with a single external derivative, but only if they were not of themselves offsetting.[513] Again this was relatively uncontroversial because this effectively means the external derivative is the hedging instrument and the exposures hedged by the internal derivatives the hedged items.

Subsequently it was suggested that the exposure on internal derivatives *could* be netted prior to laying off the risk. This was provided the external derivative exactly offset the net exposure and designation was on a gross basis, i.e. so that the external derivative was designated as a hedge of only part of the underlying exposures hedged by the internal derivatives.[514] The inclusion of these conditions suggests this also complies with the standard.

The guidance then explains that if each internal derivative is laid off with a single external counterparty under a netting agreement, i.e. all external derivatives subject to the arrangement are settled net, they may be treated as individual hedges. The fact that each external leg offsets an internal exposure is considered a valid business purpose for determining whether or not the gross elements of the external arrangement have substance (see 4.9.4 above).[515]

An extension to this arrangement is then considered:

> 'Treasury observes that by entering into the external offsetting contracts and including them in the centralised portfolio, it is no longer able to evaluate the exposures on a net basis. Treasury wishes to manage the portfolio of offsetting external derivatives separately from other exposures of the enterprise. Therefore, it enters into an additional, single derivative to offset the risk of the portfolio.'[516]

The guidance explains that the purpose of structuring the external derivatives like this is consistent with the entity's risk management policies and strategies and, generally, hedge accounting may still be used. This is the case even if this final external derivative is effected with the same counterparty under the same netting arrangement and notwithstanding the fact that all exposures with that counterparty will, as a result, net to zero.[517]

The arguments used by Treasury in this scenario appear to have little, if any, substance and consequently the guidance appears to allow the use of internal derivatives for hedge accounting, provided that an agreement is reached with a third party to give the appearance of laying off the exposure even though the risk is immediately taken back again. This seems a long way from what the standard requires and, in fact, begs the question of why an entity should even go to the trouble of creating such an artificial external agreement. It remains to be seen to what extent this becomes accepted practice.

The guidance referred to above was given in the context of using interest rate swaps to manage interest rate risk, although there appears to be no reason why it should not apply to hedges of other exposures.

In fact hedge accounting using internal foreign currency derivatives is somewhat easier to achieve. If the underlying exposures are recognised foreign currency non-derivative assets or liabilities, those instruments may be designated as hedging instruments in foreign currency hedges whereas the same is not true for other exposures. Care should be taken to determine whether adjustments to assets based on the internal derivative, e.g. a basis adjustment in a cash flow hedge, would also arise in the macro-hedging relationship or whether reversal is required as a consolidation adjustment.[518] This process is illustrated in the following example, which is based on the draft implementation guidance:

Example 10.74: Using internal derivatives to hedge foreign currency risk

In each of the following cases, 'FC' represents a foreign currency, 'RC' the group's reporting currency and TC the group's treasury centre.

Case 1: Offset of fair value hedges

Subsidiary A has trade receivables of FC 100, due in 60 days, which it hedges using a forward contract with TC. Subsidiary B has payables of FC 50, also due in 60 days, which it hedges using a forward contact with TC. TC nets the two internal derivatives and enters into a net external forward contract to pay FC 50 and receive RC in 60 days.

At the end of month 1, FC weakens against RC. A incurs a foreign exchange loss of RC 10 on its receivables, offset by a gain of RC 10 on its forward. B makes a foreign exchange gain of RC 5 on its payables offset by a loss of RC 5 on its forward. TC makes a loss of RC 10 on its internal forward with A, a gain of RC 5 on its internal forward with B and a gain of RC 5 on its external forward.

Both A and B could claim hedge accounting in their separate IAS financial statements. However, because gains and losses on the internal derivatives and the offsetting losses and gains on the hedged receivables and payables are recognised immediately in the income statement without hedge accounting no hedge accounting is necessary.

At the group level, the internal derivatives are eliminated. In economic terms, B's payable hedges FC 50 of A's receivables. The external forward in TC hedges the remaining FC 50 of A's receivable.

Case 2: Offset of cash flow hedges

To extend the example, A also has highly probable future revenues of FC 200 on which it expects to receive cash in 90 days' time. B has a contract to purchase advertising space for FC 500, also to be paid for in 90 days' time. Both A and B enter into separate forward contracts with TC to hedge these exposures and TC enters into an external forward contract to receive FC 300 in 90 days.

As before, FC weakens at the end of month 1. A incurs a 'loss' of RC 20 on its anticipated revenues because the RC value of these revenues decreases and this is offset by a gain of RC 20 on its forward. Similarly B incurs a 'gain' of RC 50 on its anticipated advertising cost and this is offset by a loss of RC 50 on its forward.

TC incurs a gain of RC 50 on its forward with B, a loss of RC 20 on its forward with A and a loss of RC 30 on its external forward.

Both A and B complete the necessary documentation, the hedges are effective and qualify for hedge accounting in A and B's standalone financial statements. A defers the gain of RC 20 on its internal derivative transaction in a hedging reserve in equity and B does the same with its loss of RC 50. TC does not claim hedge accounting, but measures both its internal and external derivative positions at fair value, which net to zero.

At the group level, there is no need to make consolidation adjustments to reverse hedge accounting and then to separately designate the hedge for group reporting purposes. The impact is the same – a net RC 30 is deferred in equity.

Case 3: Offset of fair value and cash flow hedges

The example is extended further and it is assumed that the exposures and the internal derivative transactions are the same as in Cases 1 and 2. However, instead of entering into two external derivatives to separately hedge the fair value and cash flow exposures, TC enters into a single net external derivative to receive FC 250 in exchange for RC in 90 days.

TC has four internal derivatives, two maturing in 60 days and two maturing in 90 days. These are offset by a net external derivative maturing in 90 days. The interest rate differential between FC and RC is minimal, and therefore the ineffectiveness resulting from the mismatch in maturities is expected to have a minimal effect on income in TC.

As in Cases 1 and 2, A and B claim hedge accounting for their cash flow hedges and TC measures its derivatives at fair value. A defers a gain of RC 20 on its internal derivative transaction in equity and B does the same with its loss of RC 50 as follows:

	A	B	Total
Income (fair value hedges)	10	(5)	5
Equity (cash flow hedges)	20	(50)	(30)
Total	30	(55)	(25)

On consolidation, the external forward contract for FC 250, which has a loss of 25, can be used to offset the net of the internal derivatives of 5 and (30) even though one is a hedging instrument in a cash flow hedge and the other in a fair value hedge. This is permitted because the hedging instruments in the fair value hedges in A and B are foreign currency receivables and payables and they can first be applied against the cash flow exposures of each other. Thus, the loss on A's receivables of 10 offsets the 'gain' on B's anticipated transaction of 50 leaving a remaining cash flow exposure (gain) of 40 in B. The gain on B's payables of 5 offsets the 'loss' on A's forecasted transaction of 20 leaving a remaining cash flow exposure (loss) of 15 in A. Then the two cash flow exposures of 40 and 15 are netted, which results in a net exposure of 25 at the consolidated level which equals the net exposure of 25 hedged by the external derivative. Therefore, there is no need to unwind the hedging relationships in A and B for group reporting purposes.

The combined exposure is as follows after applying hedge accounting for the foreign currency receivables and payables:

	A	B	Total
Income (fair value hedges)	–	–	–
Equity (cash flow hedges)	15	(40)	(25)
Total	15	(40)	(25)

Case 4: Offset of fair value hedges with adjustment to carrying amount of inventory

Similar transactions to those in Case 3 are assumed except that the anticipated cash outflow of FC 500 in B relates to the purchase of inventory that is delivered after 60 days. At the end of month 2, there are no further changes in exchange rates or fair values. At that date, the inventory is delivered and the loss of RC 50 on B's internal derivative, deferred in equity in month 1, is adjusted against the carrying amount of inventory in B. The gain of RC 20 on A's internal derivative is deferred in equity as before.

At the group level, there is now a mismatch compared to the result that would have been achieved by unwinding and redesignating the hedges. The external derivative (FC 250) and the receivable (FC 50) hedge FC 300 of the anticipated inventory purchase. There is a natural hedge between the remaining FC 200 of anticipated cash outflow in B and the anticipated cash inflow of FC 200 in A. This relationship does not qualify for hedge accounting under IAS 39 and this time there is only a partial offset between gains and losses on the internal derivatives that hedge these amounts:

	A	B	Total
Income (fair value hedges)	10	(5)	5
Equity (cash flow hedges)	20	–	20
Basis adjustment	–	(50)	(50)
Total	30	(55)	(25)

Again, the fair value hedges for A and B are foreign currency receivables and payables and they can first be applied against the cash flow exposures of each other. The loss on A's receivables of 10 offsets the 'gain' on B's purchase of inventory of 50 leaving a remaining cash flow exposure (gain) of 40 in B. The gain on B's payables of 5 offsets the 'loss' on A's forecasted transaction of 20, leaving a remaining cash flow exposure (loss) of 15 in A. The loss on the external derivative of 25 offsets the cash flow exposure in B of 40 leaving 15 for which there is no external offset. At the group level, therefore, RC 15 of the loss on B's internal derivative that is deferred in inventory should be reclassified to equity to offset the corresponding gain from the hedge of anticipated revenues in A.

The combined exposure is as follows after applying hedge accounting for the foreign currency receivables and payables and reclassifying a portion of the basis adjustment to equity:[519]

	A	B	Total
Income (fair value hedges)	–	–	–
Equity (cash flow hedges)	15	(15)	–
Basis adjustment	–	(25)	(25)
Total	15	(40)	(25)

The implementation guidance provides further detailed guidance explaining how financial institutions may adapt their existing risk management strategies and systems to achieve hedge accounting under IAS 39.[520] This is extremely specialised and beyond the scope of this publication.

4.10 Effective date and transitional provisions

4.10.1 Effective date

Adoption of IAS 39 is mandatory for periods beginning on or after 1 January 2001; earlier application was permitted only as of the beginning of a financial year ending after 15 March 1999, the date the standard was issued. Retrospective application was not permitted.[521] In practice early adoption has been extremely rare.

4.10.2 Comparative periods

The standard's approach to first time implementation is inconsistent with both the benchmark and allowed alternative treatments in IAS 8 (refer Chapter 25 at 3.5.2). It is, however, pragmatic as recognition, derecognition, measurement, and hedge accounting policies followed in periods prior to the effective date should not be reversed and, therefore, those financial statements should not be restated.[522]

The implementation requirements for companies adopting IAS for the first time after 2001, say in 2003, are less clear. Draft guidance was published suggesting that IAS 39 transitional provisions would be adopted, i.e. it should be applied with effect from the beginning of, say, 2003 without restating comparative information.[523] However, this ignored the more difficult question of what accounting policies should be used in deriving the comparatives, given that only local GAAP would have been used in that year. That guidance has not been converted into a final Q&A and this question is now likely to be dealt with in the new Board's project dealing with first time application of international standards (see Chapter 1 at 2.7.12).

4.10.3 Transition – financial assets, liabilities and equity instruments

From the start of the first period IAS 39 is applied, all financial instruments should be included within the appropriate financial asset, liability and/or equity classification. Assets and liabilities held for trading and available-for-sale assets should be remeasured at fair value; other assets and liabilities should be remeasured at cost or amortised cost. Any adjustment to the previous carrying amount should be recognised as an adjustment of the balance of retained earnings at the beginning of that first period.[524]

This applies to derivatives too which should be remeasured at fair value (except for a derivative that is linked to and that must be settled by delivery of an unquoted equity instrument whose fair value cannot be measured reliably). Other than derivatives that are designated hedging instruments in a cash flow hedge, the difference between their previous carrying amount (which may have been zero) and fair value should be recognised as an adjustment of the balance of retained earnings at the beginning of that first period.[525]

If an entity chooses to recognise changes in the fair value of available-for-sale assets in equity, rather than income, the adjustment should still be recognised in retained earnings rather than as a separate component of equity. This appears to have been an oversight in the original drafting and the implementation guidance states that this adjustment should continue to be tracked and recognised in income if the asset is sold or impaired.[526] In practice it would not be surprising if many companies ignored this strict requirement and recognised the adjustment as a separate component of equity.

If an asset had previously been revalued with changes in value reported in a separate component of equity, the treatment of the pre-IAS 39 gain depends on the new classification of the asset and, for available-for-sale assets, the accounting policy adopted for reporting gains. If the asset is now held for trading or is available-for-sale and a policy of recognising fair value changes in income has been adopted, the gain will be reclassified to retained earnings. Otherwise it should remain as a separate component of equity.[527]

If the impairment of assets carried at amortised cost was previously measured on an undiscounted basis, the effect of using discounting should be recognised as an adjustment to retained earnings. However, a reassessment of the expected cash flows or other relevant measure is a change in accounting estimate, the effect of which should be recognised in income.[528]

If 'held-to-maturity' investments have been sold or transferred in the previous two financial years, this does preclude the use of this category on transition.[529]

4.10.4 Transition - hedging relationships

Transactions entered into before the start of the first period IAS 39 is applied should not be retrospectively designated as hedges, even if this is the first year of adopting IAS in their entirety.[530] The designation and documentation of hedge relationships must be completed on or before the first day of that period for the hedge relationship to qualify for hedge accounting. Hedge accounting can only be applied prospectively from the date that the hedge is fully designated and documented, therefore hedges cannot be retroactively designated 'as of' the beginning of the year.[531]

The recognition, derecognition, and measurement provisions of IAS 39 should be applied prospectively for transactions that were previously designated as hedges; accounting in prior periods should not be retrospectively changed. Therefore, if the hedge does not qualify for hedge accounting (see 4.9.3 above) and the hedging instrument is still held, hedge accounting will no longer be appropriate from the beginning of this first period. Hedge accounting is discontinued in the manner set out in 4.9.4 and 4.9.5 above.[532] This applies equally for hedges using internal derivatives that no longer qualify for hedge accounting.[533]

In a fair value hedge that, on initial application, does not qualify for hedge accounting, the treatment of any previous fair value adjustments to the carrying amount of the hedged item depends on whether it is a debt or equity instrument and, if the former, whether it is now carried at fair value or at amortised cost:

- for interest bearing financial instruments now carried at amortised cost, e.g. fixed rate held-to-maturity debt securities, any previous adjustment to the carrying amount should be amortised to income; the adjustment should be fully amortised by maturity of the debt instrument;

- for interest bearing financial instruments now carried at fair value, no transition adjustment is necessary unless the carrying amount was only partially adjusted to fair value in which case the adjustment to full fair value is recognised in equity (retained earnings) as set out in 10.4.3 above;
- for equity securities, no transition adjustment is required if it was already carried at fair value in previous financial statements since equity securities continue to be measured at fair value; otherwise a transition adjustment should be made to record it at fair value which should be recognised in equity (retained earnings) as set out in 10.4.3 above.[534]

Any balance sheet positions in fair value hedges of existing assets and liabilities should be accounted for by adjusting their carrying amounts to reflect the fair value of the hedging instrument.[535]

If gains or losses on cash flow hedges were previously deferred as assets and liabilities, those deferred gains and losses should be reclassified as a separate component of equity to the extent that those transactions qualify for hedge accounting (see 4.9.3 above). Thereafter they should be removed from equity and either enter into the initial measurement of an associated asset or liability as a basis adjustment, or be reported in income when the hedged item also affects income, as appropriate.[536] The implementation guidance suggests the same treatment should be adopted for hedges that, on adoption of IAS 39, do not meet the hedge accounting criteria solely because the forecasted transaction is not highly probable – hedge accounting would be discontinued prospectively from the beginning of that first period.[537] It would appear sensible to account for unrecognised gains and losses on cash flow hedges in a similar way.

4.10.5 Prior period derecognition transactions

If securitisations, transfers, or other derecognition transactions entered into in prior years would not have resulted in derecognition under the new rules, they should not be retrospectively or prospectively changed to conform to the new requirements.[538] However, any further transfers of financial assets as part of an existing scheme, e.g. to maintain a specified balance of mortgage or credit card receivables under a securitisation, would have to meet the IAS 39 criteria to be derecognised.[539]

5 IAS DISCLOSURE REQUIREMENTS

As noted earlier in the chapter the IASC issued IAS 32, dealing with disclosure of financial instruments, in March 1995 in advance of developing its interim measurement standard, IAS 39. It was subject to minor revision in December 1998 and again in October 2000 to make it more consistent with IAS 39 – these amendments are effective on adoption of IAS 39. The disclosure requirements within IAS 39 are also dealt with in this section.

IAS 32 also deals with certain presentational matters, in particular the classification of instruments between debt and equity and the offsetting of financial assets and liabilities. These topics are dealt with in Chapter 17 at 5.3 and Chapter 18 at 4.3.2.

5.1 Introduction and scope

IAS 32 came into force for accounting periods beginning on or after 1 January 1996. It is intended to be applied by all companies, whereas FRS 13 is mandatory only for companies that have capital instruments which are listed or publicly traded (other than insurance companies) and for banks and similar institutions. Its main definitions are the same as those subsequently used by the ASB (see 1.2.1 above).

The basic disclosure requirements in IAS 32 are no different for banks or other financial institutions, although a number of different approaches are allowed to suit an entity's circumstances. In addition IAS 30 – *Disclosures in the Financial Statements of Banks and Similar Financial Institutions* – contains additional disclosure requirements which complement, and sometime overlap with, those in IASs 32 and 39.

Unlike FRS 13, IAS 32 does not prescribe either the format of the disclosures or their location within the accounts. For on-balance sheet instruments information presented on the face of the balance sheet need not be repeated in the notes. However, for unrecognised instruments (i.e. those not recorded on the balance sheet), supplementary information will be the primary means of disclosure. The disclosures may include a combination of narrative descriptions and specific quantified data, as appropriate to the nature of the instruments and their relative significance.[540]

The standard emphasises that judgment should be exercised in determining the level of detail to be disclosed, taking into account the relative significance of the particular instruments concerned. A balance should be maintained between providing excessive detail and obscuring significant information in aggregated disclosures. Summarised information by reference to particular classes of instrument will be appropriate when dealing with large homogeneous groups whilst specific information about an individual instrument may be important when, for example, that instrument represents a significant element in an entity's capital structure.[541]

Financial instruments should therefore be grouped into classes that are appropriate to the nature of the information to be disclosed, taking into account matters such as the characteristics of the instruments, whether they are recognised or unrecognised and, if they are recognised, the measurement basis (e.g. cost or fair value) that has been applied. In general, classes should be determined on a basis that distinguishes items carried at cost from items carried at fair value. When disclosures relate to recognised assets and liabilities, there should be sufficient information to permit a reconciliation to relevant balance sheet line items.[542]

Like FRS 13, IAS 32 does not apply to interests in subsidiaries, associates or joint ventures, or to obligations arising under post-employment benefits, employee stock option or purchase plans. However, all interests in subsidiaries, associates or joint ventures are excluded by IAS 32, whereas FRS 13 still includes any such interests that are held exclusively with a view to subsequent resale. IAS 32 has no similar exemptions to those in FRS 13 in respect of certain equity shares (and warrants and options over such shares) of the reporting company. It also does not permit short-term debtors and creditors to be excluded from its provisions. Unlike FRS 13, IAS 32 originally did not require certain types of commodity contracts to be dealt with in the disclosures. However, following adoption of IAS 39 those commodity contracts falling within the scope of that standard (see 4.2.5 above) will also fall within the scope of IAS 32.[543]

5.2 Narrative disclosures

The standard explains that transactions in financial instruments may result in the assumption or transfer of one or more of the following types of financial risk:

(a) *Price risk*, of which there are three types: currency risk, interest rate risk and market risk.

  (i) *Currency risk* is the risk that the value of a financial instrument will fluctuate due to changes in foreign exchange rates.

  (ii) *Interest rate risk* is the risk that the value of a financial instrument will fluctuate due to changes in market interest rates.

  (iii) *Market risk* is the risk that the value of a financial instrument will fluctuate as a result of changes in market prices whether those changes are caused by factors specific to the individual security or its issuer or factors affecting all securities traded in the market.

  The term 'price risk' embodies not only the potential for loss but also the potential for gain.

(b) *Credit risk* is the risk that one party to a financial instrument will fail to discharge an obligation and cause the other party to incur a financial loss.

(c) *Liquidity risk*, also referred to as funding risk, is the risk of encountering difficulty in raising funds to meet commitments associated with financial instruments. Liquidity risk may result from an inability to sell a financial asset quickly at close to its fair value.

(d) *Cash flow risk* is the risk that future cash flows associated with a monetary financial instrument will fluctuate in amount. In the case of a floating rate debt instrument, for example, such fluctuations result in a change in the effective interest rate of the financial instrument, usually without a corresponding change in its fair value.[544]

IAS 32 explains that disclosing management's policies for controlling these risks, including policies on hedging, avoiding undue risk concentrations and collateral requirements to mitigate credit risk, provides a valuable additional perspective, independent of the specific instruments outstanding at a particular time. Accordingly it encourages entities to include a discussion of the extent to which financial instruments are used, the associated risks and the business purposes served, within the financial statements, although this is not required.[545]

The following extracts from the financial statements of Novartis and Roche illustrate examples of voluntary narrative disclosures:

Extract 10.25: Novartis AG (2000)

10. Marketable securities and derivative financial instruments [extract]

Market risk The Group is exposed to market risk, primarily related to foreign exchange, interest rates and market value of the investment of liquid funds. Management actively monitors these exposures. To manage the volatility relating to these exposures, the Group enters into a variety of derivative financial investments. The Group's objective is to reduce, where it is deemed appropriate to do so, fluctuations in earnings and cash flows associated with changes in interest rates, foreign currency rates and market rates of investment of liquid funds and of the currency exposure of certain net investments in foreign subsidiaries. It is the Group's policy and practice to use derivative financial instruments to manage exposures and to enhance the yield on the investment of liquid funds. The Group does not enter any financial transaction containing a risk that cannot be quantified at the time the transaction is concluded; i.e. it does not sell short assets it does not have or does not know it will have in the future. The Group only sells existing assets or transactions and future transactions (in the case of anticipatory hedges) it knows it will have in the future based on past experience. In the case of liquid funds, it writes options on assets it has or on positions it wants to acquire and has the liquidity to acquire.

The Group therefore expects that any loss in value for those instruments generally would be offset by increases in the value of those hedged transactions.

(a) Foreign exchange rates

The Group uses the CHF as its reporting currency and is therefore exposed to foreign exchange movements, primarily in USD, European, Japanese, other Asian and Latin American currencies. Consequently, it enters into various contracts, which change in value as foreign exchange rates change, to preserve the value of assets, commitments and anticipated transactions. The Group uses forward contracts and foreign currency option contracts to hedge certain anticipated foreign currency revenues and the net investment in certain foreign subsidiaries. At December 31, 2000, the Group had long and short forward exchange/option contracts with equivalent values of CHF 8.2 billion and CHF 13.8 billion, respectively. At December 31, 1999, the Group had long and short forward exchange/option contracts with equivalent values of CHF 4.3 billion and CHF 19.1 billion, respectively.

(b) Commodities

The Group has only a very limited exposure to price risk related to anticipated purchases of certain commodities used as raw materials by the Group's businesses. A change in those prices may alter the gross margin of a specific business, but generally by not more than 10% of that margin and is thus below materiality levels. Accordingly, the Group does not enter into commodity future, forward and option contracts to manage fluctuations in prices of anticipated purchases.

(c) Interest rates

The Group manages its exposure to interest rate risk through the proportion of fixed rate debt and variable rate debt in its total debt portfolio. To manage this mix, the Group may enter into interest rate swap agreements, in which it exchanges the periodic payments, based on a notional amount and agreed upon fixed and variable interest rates. The Group's percentage of fixed rate debt to total financial debt was 34% and 28% at December 31, 2000 and 1999, respectively.

Use of the above-mentioned derivative financial instruments has not had a material impact on the Group's financial position at December 31, 2000 and 1999 or the Group's results of operations for the years ended December 31, 2000 and 1999.

Counterparty risk Counterparty risk encompasses issuer risk on marketable securities, settlement risk on derivative and money market contacts and credit risk on cash and time deposits. Issuer risk is minimized by only buying securities which are at least AA rated. Settlement and credit risk is reduced by the policy of entering into transactions with counterparties that are usually at least AA rated banks or financial institutions. Exposure to these risks is closely monitored and kept within predetermined parameters.

The group does not expect any losses from non-performance by these counterparties and does not have any significant grouping of exposures to financial sector or country risk.

Extract 10.26: Roche Holding Ltd (2000)

2. Financial risk management

Financial risk management within the Group is governed by policies approved by senior management. These policies cover foreign exchange risk, interest rate risk, market risk, credit risk and liquidity risk. Group policies also cover areas such as cash management, investment of excess funds and the raising of short- and long-term debt.

When deemed appropriate, certain of the above risks are altered through the use of financial instruments. Group management believes that, in order to create the optimum value for the Group, it is not desirable to eliminate or mitigate all possible market fluctuations. Financial instruments are selectively used to create and optimise value. Group companies report details of the financial instruments outstanding and financial liquidity position to Group Treasury on at least a monthly basis.

Foreign exchange risk

The Group operates across the world and is exposed to movements in foreign currencies affecting its net income and financial position, as expressed in Swiss francs.

Transaction exposure arises because the amount of local currency paid or received for transactions denominated in foreign currencies may vary due to changes in exchange rates. For many Group companies income will be primarily in the local currency. A significant amount of expenditure, especially for purchase of goods for resale and interest on and repayment of loans will be in foreign currencies. Similarly, transaction exposure arises on net balances of monetary assets held in foreign currencies. Group companies manage this exposure at a local level, if necessary by means of financial instruments such as options and forward contracts. In addition, Group Treasury monitors total worldwide exposure with the help of comprehensive data received on a monthly basis.

Translation exposure arises from the consolidation of the foreign currency denominated financial statements of the Group's foreign subsidiaries. The effect on the Group's consolidated equity is shown as a currency translation movement. The Group hedges significant net investments in foreign currencies by taking foreign currency loans or issuing foreign currency denominated debt instruments. Major translation exposures are monitored on a regular basis.

A significant part of the Group's cash outflows for research, development, production and administration is denominated in Swiss francs, while a much smaller proportion of the Group's cash inflows are Swiss franc denominated. As a result, an increase in the value of the Swiss franc relative to other currencies has an adverse impact on consolidated net income. Similarly, a relative fall in the value of the Swiss franc has a favourable effect on results published in Swiss francs.

Interest rate risk

Interest rate risk arises from movements in interest rates which could have adverse effects on the Group's net income or financial position. Changes in interest rates cause variations in interest income and expenses on interest-bearing assets and liabilities. In addition, they can affect the market value of certain financial assets, liabilities and instruments as described in the following section on market risk.

The interest rates on the Group's major debt instruments are fixed, as described in Note 24, which reduces the Group's exposure to changes in interest rates. Group companies manage their short-term interest rate risk at a local level, if necessary using financial instruments such as interest rate forward contracts, swaps and options.

Market risk

Changes in the market value of certain financial assets, liabilities and instruments can affect the net income or financial position of the Group. The Group's long-term investments are held for strategic purposes, and changes in market value do not affect the carrying value, unless a permanent loss in value is indicated. The Group's marketable securities are held for fund management purposes. The risk of loss in value is reduced by a very careful review prior to investing, concentration of investments and continuous monitoring of the performance of investments and changes in their risk configuration.

Credit risk

Credit risk arises from the possibility that the counter-party to a transaction may be unable or unwilling to meet their obligations causing a financial loss to the Group.

Trade receivables are subject to a policy of active risk management focussing on the assessment of country risk, credit availability, ongoing credit evaluation and account monitoring procedures. There are no significant concentrations within trade receivables of counter-party credit risk, due to the Group's large number of customers and their wide geographical spread. Country risk limits and exposures are continuously monitored.

The exposure of other financial assets and liabilities to credit risk is controlled by setting a policy of limiting credit exposure to high-quality counter-parties, continuously reviewing credit ratings, and limiting individual aggregate credit exposure accordingly.

Liquidity risk

Group companies need to have sufficient availability of cash to meet their obligations. Individual companies are responsible for their own cash management, including the short-term investment of cash surpluses and the raising of loans to cover cash deficits, subject to guidance by the Group and, in certain cases, to approval at Group level.

The Group maintains sufficient reserves of cash and readily realisable marketable securities to meet its liquidity requirements at all times. In addition, the strong international creditworthiness of the Group allows it to make efficient use of international capital markets for financing purposes.

On adoption of IAS 39 certain narrative disclosures become mandatory. Entities will be required to describe their financial risk management objectives and policies including their policies for hedging each major type of forecasted transaction for which hedge accounting is used. The hedging policies should indicate the nature of the risks being hedged, for each type of future transaction how long, and what proportion of, those transactions are hedged, e.g. approximately how many months or years of expected future sales, and the approximate percentage of sales in those future months.[546]

5.3 Accounting policies

IAS 32 contains an explicit requirement to disclose, for each class of financial asset, financial liability and equity instrument, whether recognised or unrecognised, the accounting policies adopted and methods used to apply those policies.[547] This compares to the reminder in FRS 13 of the requirements of SSAP 2 and FRS 18. Adoption of IAS 39 is likely to go a long way towards harmonising the accounting policies adopted and disclosed by most entities and may even make some of IAS 32 redundant.

This disclosure should include:

- the criteria applied in determining when to recognise and derecognise financial asset and liabilities;
- the measurement basis applied on initial recognition and subsequently; and
- the basis on which associated income and expenses are recognised and measured.[548]

Where IAS 39 has been adopted this should also include, for each of the four categories of financial assets (see 4.3.1 above), an explanation of whether regular way purchases and sales are accounted for at trade date or settlement date.[549]

The types of transactions for which it may be necessary to disclose the relevant accounting policies include:

- transfers of financial assets when a continuing interest in, or involvement with, the assets is retained, e.g. securitisations, repurchase agreements or reverse repurchase agreements;
- transfers of financial assets to a trust, such as an in-substance defeasance trust, for the purpose of satisfying liabilities when they mature without the transferor's obligation being discharged (this is extremely unlikely to be relevant once IAS 39 comes into force – see Chapter 17 at 5.4.3);
- acquisition or issuance of separate financial instruments as part of a series of transactions designed to synthesise the effect of acquiring or issuing a single instrument;
- acquisition or issuance of financial instruments as hedges of risk exposures[550] – in such cases the accounting policies should indicate the circumstances in which financial instruments are accounted for as hedges and the nature of the special recognition and measurement treatment applied to the instrument.[551]
- acquisition or issuance of monetary financial instruments bearing a stated interest rate that differs from the prevailing market rate at the date of issue.[552]

The disclosures should indicate how the method of applying a measurement basis has been applied to a specific class of asset or liability. For instruments carried at cost, disclosure of how the following are accounted for may be required:

- acquisition or issue costs;
- premiums and discounts on monetary financial assets and financial liabilities;

- changes in the estimated amount of determinable future cash flows associated with a monetary financial instrument such as a bond indexed to a commodity price;
- changes in circumstances that result in significant uncertainty about the timely collection of all contractual amounts due from monetary financial assets;
- declines in the fair value of financial assets below their carrying amount; and
- restructured financial liabilities.[553]

For instruments carried at fair value, the disclosures should include an indication as to whether fair value is determined from quoted market prices, independent appraisals, discounted cash flow analysis or other appropriate methods, together with any significant assumptions made in applying those methods.[554] Where IAS 39 has been adopted, this information should be given separately for significant classes of financial assets and include, where appropriate, prepayment rates, rates of estimated credit losses, and interest or discount rates used.[555]

The basis for reporting realised and unrealised gains and losses, interest and other associated items of income and expense within income should be disclosed, including information on hedging instruments. When income and expense items are presented on a net basis even though the corresponding financial assets and liabilities have not been offset, the reason for that presentation should be disclosed if the effect is significant.[556] Where IAS 39 has been adopted, the disclosure will explain whether gains and losses arising from changes in the fair value of available-for-sale financial assets are included in income or in equity.[557]

The following extracts from the financial statements of Nestlé and Novartis show the type of accounting policies disclosed prior to the adoption of IAS 39:

Extract 10.27: Nestlé S.A. (2000)

Accounting policies [extract]
Hedging

Derivative financial instruments are used to manage operational exposures to foreign exchange, interest rate and commodity price risks. They are entered into with high credit quality financial institutions, consistent with specific approval, limit and monitoring procedures. The instruments used to hedge foreign currency flows and positions mainly include forward foreign exchange contracts, options and currency swaps. Foreign exchange gains and losses on hedging instruments are matched with foreign exchange gains and losses on the underlying asset or liability. When an anticipated future transaction has been hedged and the underlying position has not been recognised in the financial statements any change in the fair value of the hedging instrument is not recognised in the income statement for the period.

Where derivatives are held for the long term and are used to manage interest rate risks, they are accounted for on the cost basis (where the underlying asset or liability is accounted for on the cost basis) and payments and receipts relating to the instruments are recognised under net financing cost as they accrue. In other cases the instruments are carried at fair value and changes in the market value are taken to income. The instruments used consist of interest rate swaps, interest rate options and futures.

Commodity instruments are used to ensure the Group's access to raw materials at an appropriate price. Outright purchase transactions are recorded at the contracted rates. Changes in the fair value of open commodity instruments are not recognised until the actual purchase transactions are recognised in the financial statements.

Extract 10.28: Novartis AG (2000)

1. **Accounting Policies** [extract]

Derivative financial instruments The Group uses the concept of portfolio basis valuation. For each portfolio the net unrealized gain or loss is determined by combining all unrealized gains and losses per instrument.

Realized and unrealized gains and losses on contracts designated as specific hedges are recognized in the same period that the foreign currency exposure is realized. The result on instruments which hedge risk positions in future years (forecasted transactions including foreign currency hedges of anticipated transactions, cash flows and earnings) is deferred to the period when gains and losses on the corresponding positions materialize. Option premiums, realized and unrealized gains and losses are included in the currency result component of financial income.

Unrealized gains and losses on contracts designated as a hedge of available-for-sale securities are deferred until the underlying security is disposed of when they are included in the related capital gain or loss component of financial income.

Realized and unrealized gains and losses on contracts designated as a hedge of a net investment in foreign subsidiaries are recognized through the statement of changes in equity and are included in cumulative translation differences.

Non-hedging currency instruments are valued at the lower of cost on inception and fair value on a portfolio basis. A net unrealized loss is included in the current year's result. A net unrealized gain is not recorded. Option premiums, realized gains and losses and changes in net unrealized losses are recorded in the income or expense on options and forward contracts component of financial income.

Financial instruments which are intended to be held for the long-term or to maturity, principally interest rate swaps and Forward Rate Agreements (FRAs), are valued on a portfolio basis at the lower of cost, which is usually zero, and a valuation taking into account market values and anticipated cash flows through to the maturity of the instruments. A net unrealized loss is recorded in the current year's result in the income or expense on options and forward contracts component of financial income. A net unrealized gain is not recorded. FRA settlement sums and interest paid and received are recorded as interest income and expense.

Forward Rate Agreements (FRAs) not included above are valued on a portfolio basis with a net loss recognized in the income statement, in the income or expense on options and forward contracts component of financial income, together with the settlement sums. A net unrealized gain is not recorded.

Options on securities are accounted for at the lower of cost and fair value. Net unrealized losses on written options and the underlying assets as well as option premiums are recorded in the income statement, in the income or expense on options and forward contracts component of financial income. Net unrealized gains are not recorded.

Option premiums are recognized immediately on payment or receipt.

...

Financial assets Associated companies and joint ventures are accounted for by the equity method. All other minority investments are reported at their acquisition cost and loans at their nominal value. Adjustments are made for any permanent impairment in value.

...

Trade accounts receivable The reported values represent the invoiced amounts, less adjustments for doubtful receivables.

Cash and cash equivalents Cash and cash equivalents include highly liquid investments with original maturities of three months or less. This position is readily convertible to known amounts of cash.

> **Marketable securities** Marketable securities consist of equity and debt securities which are traded in liquidity markets and are classified as available-for-sale or as bonds held-to-maturity. Marketable securities available-for-sale are stated at the lower of cost or market value on an individual basis. Gross unrealized losses are included as financial expense in the income statement. Unrealized gains are not recorded.
>
> Up to January 1, 2000, the portfolio of bonds intended to be held-to-maturity was valued at amortized cost, whereby the discount or premium was amortized into the income statement on a pro rata basis until maturity and included in the financial result. Except for permanent diminutions in value, if any, changes in market value were not recorded for this portfolio of bonds. The majority of this portfolio was disposed of in 2000 and any remaining bonds were reclassified to available-for-sale marketable securities.
>
> **Repurchase agreements** The underlying securities are contained within marketable securities. The repurchase agreements for the securities sold and agreed to be repurchased under the agreement, are recognized gross and included in cash and cash equivalents and short-term financial debts. Income and expenses are recorded in interest income and expense, respectively.

Munich Re has adopted IAS 39 and discloses the following policies for its financial assets:

> *Extract 10.29: Münchener Rückversicherungs-Gesellschaft AG (2000)*
>
> **ACCOUNTING AND VALUATION OF ASSETS** [extract]
> **B. Investments** [extract]
>
> LOANS are stated at amortized cost. Writedowns for impairments are made in cases where the repayment of a loan can no longer be expected.
>
> FIXED-INTEREST SECURITIES HELD TO MATURITY are – like loans – stated at amortized cost. The main investments shown here are registered bonds and promissory notes.
>
> SECURITIES AVAILABLE FOR SALE are stated at market value. Unrealized gains or losses are not included in the income statement; rather, after deduction of deferred taxes and the amounts apportionable to policy-holders by the life and health insurers on realization, they are reflected in shareholders' equity. This item also includes registered bonds and promissory notes.
>
> SECURITIES HELD FOR TRADING comprise all fixed-interest and non-fixed-interest securities that we have acquired for trading purposes to earn short-term profits from price changes and differences; in addition, they include all derivative financial instruments that we have not acquired for hedging purposes. Securities held for trading are stated at the market value at the balance sheet date; all unrealized gains or losses from this valuation are included in the investment result.
>
> Writedowns are made on all securities that are not investments held for trading if they suffer an impairment in value that is not temporary. These writedowns are recognized in the income statement.

5.4 Interest rate risk disclosures

Changes in interest rates can have a direct effect on the cash flows associated with some financial instruments and on the fair value of others. Therefore IAS 32 requires disclosure of information concerning interest rate exposure.[558] Whilst similar in concept, the disclosures under IAS 32 could be presented somewhat differently from those required by FRS 13.

This information should include, for each class of instrument, both recognised and unrecognised:

- contractual repricing or maturity dates, whichever dates are earlier; and
- effective interest rates, when applicable.[559]

Maturity dates, or repricing dates when earlier, indicate for how long interest rates are fixed; effective interest rates indicate the levels at which they are fixed. This provides a basis for evaluating the exposure to interest rate price risk and the associated potential for gain or loss. For instruments that reprice to a market rate before maturity, the period until the next repricing is more important than the period to maturity.[560]

To supplement this, information about *expected* repricing or maturity dates may be given when those dates differ significantly from the contractual dates. Such information may be particularly relevant when, for example, it is possible to predict with reasonable reliability the amount of fixed rate mortgage loans that will be repaid prior to maturity and this data is used as the basis for managing interest rate risk exposure. Such information should explain that it is based on management's expectations and explain the assumptions used and how they differ from the contractual dates.[561]

An indication should be given of which instruments are:

- exposed to interest rate price risk, such as fixed rate instruments;
- exposed to interest rate cash flow risk, such as floating rate instruments that reset as market rates change; and
- not exposed to interest rate risk, such as equity securities.[562]

The effective interest rate (effective yield) of an instrument is the rate that, when applied to the stream of future cash receipts or payments to the next repricing (maturity) date and to the expected carrying amount (principal amount) at that date in a present value calculation, results in the carrying amount of the instrument. The rate is a historical one for fixed rate instruments carried at amortised cost and a current market rate for a floating rate instrument or an instrument carried at fair value. The effective interest rate is sometimes termed the level yield to maturity or to the next repricing date, and is the internal rate of return of the instrument for that period.[563]

Effective interest rates should be disclosed for bonds, notes and similar instruments that create a return and a cost reflecting the time value of money. This requirement does not apply to those instruments that do not bear a determinable effective interest rate – whilst interest rate swaps, forward rate agreements and options are exposed to price or cash flow risk from changes in interest rates, disclosure of an effective interest rate is not relevant. When providing such information, the effect of hedging or 'conversion' transactions such as interest rate swaps should be disclosed.[564]

Interest rate risk can arise from derecognised financial assets and from transactions in which no financial instrument is recognised, such as a commitment to lend funds at a fixed interest rate. Accordingly, information should be provided to explain the nature and extent of these exposures. In the case of a securitisation or similar transfer where interest rate risk is retained, this information would normally include the nature of the assets transferred, their stated principal, interest rate and term to maturity, and the terms of the transaction giving rise to the retained exposure. In the case of a commitment to lend funds, it will normally include the stated

principal, interest rate and term to maturity of the amount to be lent and any other significant terms of the transaction.[565]

The nature of an entity's business and the extent of its activity in financial instruments will determine whether interest rate risk information is presented in narrative form, in tables, or by using a combination of the two. The standard suggests that one or more of the following approaches may be used:

- Tables showing the carrying amounts of instruments exposed to interest rate price risk, grouped by those that will mature or be repriced:
  - within one year of the balance sheet date;
  - more than one year and less than five years from the balance sheet date; and
  - five years or more from the balance sheet date.
- When performance is significantly affected by interest rate exposure, more detailed information is desirable, for example banks may use the following additional groupings:
  - within one month of the balance sheet date;
  - more than one and less than three months from the balance sheet date; and
  - more than three and less than twelve months from the balance sheet date.
- Similarly, tables aggregating the carrying amount of floating rate instruments maturing within various future time periods give an indication of interest rate cash flow exposure.
- Information may be disclosed for individual instruments or weighted average rates or a range of rates may be presented for each class. Instruments denominated in different currencies or having substantially different credit risks should be grouped into separate classes when these factors result in substantially different effective interest rates.[566]

The standard suggests that indicating the effect of a hypothetical change in market rates on the fair value of financial instruments and future earnings and cash flows may provide useful information. Such information may be based on an assumed 1% change in rates occurring at the balance sheet date. The effects should include changes in interest income and expense relating to floating rate financial instruments and gains or losses resulting from changes in the fair value of fixed rate instruments, but may be restricted to the direct effects on interest-bearing instruments on hand at the reporting date since the indirect effects of a rate change on financial markets and individual entities cannot normally be predicted reliably. When disclosing interest rate sensitivity information, the basis on which the information has been prepared should be indicated, including any significant assumptions.[567]

Jardine Matheson provides an analysis of fixed and floating rate borrowings by currency, together with weighted average interest rates and maturities for fixed rate debt, a similar approach to that required by FRS 13:

Extract 10.30: Jardine Matheson Holdings Limited (2000)

20 Borrowings [extract]

	Fixed rate borrowings				
	Weighted average interest rates %	Weighted average period outstanding Years	US$m	Floating rate borrowings US$m	Total US$m
Currency:					
2000					
Australian Dollar	6.9	1.3	77.6	199.5	277.1
Hong Kong Dollar	7.1	2.3	378.2	468.0	846.2
Malaysian Ringgit	6.6	–	–	32.2	32.2
New Taiwan Dollar	5.8	0.2	9.1	63.1	72.2
New Zealand Dollar	7.0	1.0	26.4	30.8	57.2
Singapore Dollar	3.6	–	–	28.1	28.1
United Kingdom Sterling	6.4	0.1	56.1	272.3	328.4
United States Dollar	7.5	8.4	519.0	917.5	1,436.5
Other	6.3	5.6	34.1	14.1	48.2
			1,100.5	**2,025.6**	**3,126.1**
1999					
Australian Dollar	6.1	0.9	101.1	150.6	251.7
Hong Kong Dollar	7.4	1.4	258.8	542.0	800.8
Malaysian Ringgit	7.6	–	–	26.3	26.3
New Taiwan Dollar	5.8	1.1	11.1	78.8	89.9
New Zealand Dollar	6.3	1.6	46.8	36.4	83.2
Singapore Dollar	3.3	–	–	36.6	36.6
United Kingdom Sterling	6.3	0.1	47.5	367.2	414.7
United States Dollar	6.8	1.6	20.2	343.1	363.3
Other	9.8	2.0	26.4	16.4	42.8
			511.9	1,597.4	2,109.3

All borrowings were within subsidiary undertakings.

In September 2000, JMH Finance Limited, a wholly-owned subsidiary undertaking, issued US$550 million 4.75% guaranteed bonds due 2007. The bonds are guaranteed by the Company. Proceeds of the bonds were used to finance the repurchase of the Company's shares. The bonds are exchangeable, at the option of the holders, into shares of common stock of J P Morgan Chase & Co on the basis of 15.83 shares for each US$1,000 principal amount of the bonds from 6th September 2001 until 30th August 2007. The bonds will mature on 6th September 2007. The fair values of the liability component and option component are determined on issue of the bond. The fair value of the liability component, included in long-term borrowings, is calculated using a market interest rate for an equivalent non-convertible bond. The residual amount, representing the value of the conversion option component, is included in other non-current liabilities (*refer note 22*).

In March 2000, Mandarin Oriental issued US$75.8 million 6.75% convertible bonds due 2005. Proceeds of the bonds were used to finance the acquisition of The Rafael Group. The bonds are convertible up to and including 23rd February 2005 into fully paid ordinary shares of Mandarin Oriental at a conversion price of US$0.671 per ordinary share. At 31st December 2000, US$60.7 million of the bonds were held by Jardine Strategic and were netted off the carrying amount of the bonds.

Secured borrowings at 31st December 2000 included US$354.0 million (*1999: US$309.4 million*) which were secured against Mandarin Oriental's tangible fixed assets. The net book value of these assets at 31st December 2000 was US$951.2 million (*1999: US$837.5 million*).

The weighted average interest rates and period of fixed rate borrowings are stated after taking account of hedging transactions.

Roche, on the other hand, provides 'economic' interest rates (presumably the same as effective rates) for each of its borrowings together with other supplementary information:

Extract 10.31: Roche Holding Ltd (2000)

24. Debt in millions of CHF [extract]

Debt instruments

The carrying value of the Group's debt instruments is given in the table below. Supplementary information about the Group's debt instruments, including redemption and conversion terms, if any, is given on pages 99 to 101.

	Economic interest rate if held to maturity	2000	1999
Swiss franc bonds			
'Bullet' 2% due 2003, principal 1.25 billion Swiss francs	1.78%	1,245	1,242
'Rodeo' 1.75% due 2008, principal 1 billion Swiss francs	2.66%	923	912
US dollar bonds			
'Knock Out' 2.75% due 2000, principal 1 billion US dollars	6.20%	–	1,586
'Bull Spread' 3.5% due 2001, principal 1 billion US dollars	8.60%	1,610	1,506
'Chameleon' 6.75% due 2009, principal 1 billion US dollars	6.75%	1,622	1,584
Japanese yen bonds			
'Samurai' 1% due 2002, principal 100 billion Japanese yen	5.19%	1,051	1,011
Swiss franc convertible bonds			
'Helveticus' dividend-linked convertible bonds, due 2003, principal 1 billion Swiss francs	–	215	990
Zero coupon US dollar exchangeable notes			
'LYONs II' due 2010, principal 2.15 billion US dollars	7.00%	1,785	1,618
'LYONs III' due 2012, principal 3 billion US dollars	6.375%	2,301	2,098
'LYONs IV' due 2015, principal 1.506 billion US dollars	2.75%	1,363	–
Japanese yen exchangeable bonds			
'Sumo' 0.25% due 2005, principal 104.6 billion Japanese yen	1.00%	1,388	–
Limited conversion preferred stock	–	7	6
Total debt instruments		13,510	12,553

The economic interest rate if held to maturity is the market rate of interest at the date of issuance for a similar debt instrument, but with no conversion rights or discount upon issuance.

Issue of 'LYONs IV' US dollar notes exchangeable into Genentech shares

On 19 January 2000 the Group issued zero coupon US dollar exchangeable notes due 19 January 2015 with a principal amount of 1,506 million US dollars. The notes are exchangeable into shares of the Group's subsidiary, Genentech, at any time prior to maturity. If all of the notes were exchanged into Genentech shares, the Group's percentage of ownership of Genentech would decrease by 2.5%.

Net proceeds from the issue were 980 million US dollars (1,562 million Swiss francs). These were initially allocated as 2,369 million Swiss francs of debt, 1,094 million Swiss francs of unamortised discount, 172 million Swiss francs of minority interest (in respect of the conversion option embedded in the notes) and 115 million Swiss francs of deferred tax liability.

Issue of 'Sumo' Japanese yen bonds exchangeable into non-voting equity securities

On 26 April 2000 the Group issued 0.25% Japanese yen exchangeable bonds due 25 March 2005 with a principal amount of 104.6 billion Japanese yen. The bonds are exchangeable into non-voting equity securities until 17 March 2005.

Net proceeds from the issue were 98.76 billion Japanese yen (1,599 million Swiss francs). These were initially allocated as 1,694 million Swiss francs of debt, 132 million Swiss francs of unamortised discount, 24 million Swiss francs of equity (in respect of the conversion option embedded in the bonds) and 13 million Swiss francs of deferred tax liability.

Repayment of 'Knock Out' US dollar bonds

On the due date of 14 April 2000 the Group repaid the principal amount of 1 billion US dollars of the 2.75% US dollar bonds originally issued in 1993. The resulting cash outflow was 1,648 million Swiss francs.

Exercise of 'Helveticus' Swiss franc convertible bonds

During May 2000 'Helveticus' dividend-linked Swiss franc convertible bonds due 2003 with a principal amount of 698 million Swiss francs were exercised. The resulting cash outflow was 659 million Swiss francs. Other smaller amounts were exercised during the year.

Swiss franc convertible bonds

An annual payment distribution amount is paid on 31 July for each bond of CHF 9,530 par value in the place of a fixed rate of interest. This annual payment distribution amount equals two times the ordinary and/or extraordinary dividend declared on one non-voting equity security of Roche Holding Ltd for the business year ended on 31 December which was nineteen months prior to 31 July for the relevant year.

Emirates Bank is an example of a company providing an 'interest rate gap' analysis, similar to the FRS 13 requirement for banks:

Extract 10.32: Emirates Bank International PJSC (2000)

32 Interest rate repricing analysis

	Less than 1 month	Over 1 month to 3 months	Over 3 months to 6 months	Over 6 months to 1 year	Over 1 year	Non interest bearing	Total
	AED 000	AED 000	AED 000	AED 000	AED 000	AED 000	AED 000
Assets							
Cash and deposits with Central Banks	110,498	135,000	–	–	–	983,882	1,229,380
Due from banks	3,167,308	557,552	334,518	42,240	17,183	223	4,119,024
Trading securities	–	–	–	–	–	43,302	43,302
Property development receivables	–	–	–	–	–	133,559	133,559
Loans and advances	6,046,675	1,382,998	1,958,584	484,730	1,375,217	–	11,248,204
Investment securities	240,737	417,904	118,476	45,084	68,249	267,402	1,157,852
Investment properties	–	–	–	–	–	941,679	941,679
Fixed assets	–	–	–	–	–	187,605	187,605
Other assets	–	–	–	–	–	531,938	531,938
Total assets	**9,565,218**	**2,493,454**	**2,411,578**	**572,054**	**1,460,649**	**3,089,590**	**19,592,543**

Liabilities and shareholders' equity							
Customer deposits	7,215,941	1,865,659	657,826	608,849	44,224	1,674,250	12,066,749
Due to banks	1,013,033	250,993	141,561	9,182		1,028	1,415,797
Medium term borrowing	–	1,414,105	–	–	–	–	1,414,105
Minority interests	–	–	–	–	–	448,582	448,582
Other liabilities	–	–	–	–	–	496,827	496,827
Shareholders' funds	–	–	–	–	–	3,750,483	3,750,483
Total liabilities and shareholders' funds	**8,228,974**	**3,530,757**	**799,387**	**618,031**	**44,224**	**6,371,170**	**19,592,543**
Off balance sheet							
Letters of Credit, Acceptances and Guarantees	–	–	–	–	–	3,582,492	3,582,492
Foreign Exchange Contracts	1,930,551	349,031	150,743	124,944	20,794	696,226	3,272,289
Total	**1,930,551**	**349,031**	**150,743**	**124,944**	**20,794**	**4,278,718**	**6,854,781**
On balance sheet gap	1,336,244	(1,037,303)	1,612,191	(45,977)	1,416,425	(3,281,580)	–
Off balance sheet gap	(1,990,883)	202,335	104,057	(26,127)	1,710,618	–	–
Interest rate sensitivity gap – 2000	(654,639)	(834,968)	1,716,248	(72,104)	3,127,043	(3,281,580)	–
Cumulative interest rate sensitivity gap – 2000	(654,639)	(1,489,607)	226,641	154,537	3,281,580	–	–
Cumulative interest rate sensitivity gap – 1999	957,289	(13,099)	662,811	(78,027)	3,300,849	–	–

Maturity of assets and liabilities has been determined on the basis of contractual pricing or maturity dates, whichever dates are earlier.

The off balance sheet gap represents the net notional amounts of off balance sheet financial instruments such as interest rate swaps which are used to manage interest rate risk.

Interest rate swaps that have been used for asset and liability management purposes to hedge overall exposure to interest rate risk are included separately as off balance sheet gaps.

The general provision for loan losses is deducted from less than one month assets.

5.5 Credit risk

A failure by counterparties to discharge their obligations could reduce the amount of future cash inflows from financial assets on hand at the balance sheet date and give rise to a recognised loss. Consequently, to allow an assessment of the extent of such failures, IAS 32 requires disclosure of information relating to credit risk[568] – there are no equivalent disclosures within FRS 13.

For each class of financial asset, both recognised and unrecognised, information about credit risk exposure should be disclosed, including:

- the amount that best represents the maximum credit risk exposure at the balance sheet date in the event other parties fail to perform their obligations, without taking account of the fair value of any collateral; and
- significant concentrations of credit risk.[569]

The reasons given for ignoring potential recoveries from the realisation of collateral are to provide a consistent measure of credit risk exposure for both recognised and unrecognised financial assets and to take into account the possibility that the maximum exposure may differ from an asset's carrying amount.[570]

A recognised financial asset's carrying amount, net of any applicable provisions, usually represents the credit risk exposure at a particular point in time. For example, the maximum exposure to loss for an interest rate swap carried at fair value is normally its carrying amount as this represents its current replacement cost in the event of default. In these circumstances, no additional disclosure beyond that provided on the balance sheet is necessary; otherwise additional disclosure is required.[571]

Financial assets subject to legally enforceable rights of set-off against financial liabilities are not presented net unless settlement is intended to take place net or simultaneously (refer Chapter 18 at 4.3.2). However, where a legal right of set-off exists, a loss can be avoided in the event of default if the receivable is due before a payable of equal or greater amount. When a liability is due to be settled before an asset, credit risk exposure may also be mitigated if default is known about before the liability is settled. On the other hand, if the likely response to default is the extension of the asset's term, an exposure would exist if collection is deferred beyond the date the liability is due. Therefore the existence of legal rights of set-off should normally be disclosed to explain the maximum potential loss, but only when the relevant asset is expected to be collected in accordance with its terms.[572]

Master netting arrangements can mitigate credit risk but do not always meet the offset criteria. When such arrangements significantly reduce credit risk, additional information about the arrangement should be provided, indicating that:

- credit risk is eliminated only to the extent that amounts due to the same counterparty will be settled after the assets are realised; and
- the extent to which overall credit risk is reduced may change substantially within a short period because the exposure is affected by each transaction subject to the arrangement.

The standard states it is also desirable to disclose the terms of master netting arrangements that determine the extent of the reduction in credit risk.[573]

When no credit risk arises on unrecognised financial assets, or the maximum exposure of recognised financial assets is equal to the disclosed principal, stated, face or other similar contractual amount (refer 5.6 below) or to their fair value, no additional disclosure is required. However, with some unrecognised financial assets, the maximum default loss may be substantially different, e.g. a legal right to offset unrecognised instruments may mitigate losses. In such circumstances, additional disclosure is required.[574]

Financial guarantees expose the guarantor to credit risk and are covered by IAS 32 even though they are largely excluded from the scope of IAS 39. They should therefore be taken into account in making the credit risk disclosures; in fact similar disclosures are likely to be necessary under IAS 37 (refer Chapter 28 at 7.5.1 and 7.5.2). Credit risk can arise in securitisation transactions, even though the financial assets have been derecognised, e.g. where there is an obligation to indemnify the purchaser of the assets for credit losses. In such cases the nature of the derecognised assets, the amount and timing of the associated future cash flows, the terms of the recourse obligation and the maximum loss that could arise under that obligation should be disclosed.[575]

Significant credit risk concentrations should be disclosed when they are not otherwise apparent. They may arise from exposures to a single debtor or to groups of debtors whose ability to meet their obligations is expected to be affected by similar changes in economic or other conditions.[576] This should include a description of the shared characteristic that identifies each concentration and the amount of the maximum credit risk exposure associated with all recognised and unrecognised financial assets sharing that characteristic.[577]

Characteristics that may give rise to a concentration of risk include the nature of the debtors' activities, such as the industry in which they operate, the geographic area in which activities are undertaken and the level of creditworthiness of groups of borrowers. For example, a manufacturer of equipment for oil and gas producers will normally have debtors for which the risk of non-payment is affected by economic changes in the energy industry. A bank that lends internationally may have significant loans outstanding to less developed nations, which may be adversely affected by local economic conditions.[578]

The standard acknowledges that identification of significant concentrations is a matter of judgement and suggests using the guidance in IAS 14 – *Segment Reporting* – to identify industry and geographic segments within which concentrations may arise (see Chapter 21 at 4.1.2).[579]

Bayer provides the following disclosure in respect of its maximum credit risk:

Extract 10.33: Bayer AG (2000)

[37] Financial instruments [extract]
Primary financial instruments [extract]

Credit risk
Credit risk arises from the possibility of asset impairment occurring because counterparties cannot meet their obligations in transactions involving financial instruments.

Since we do not conclude master netting arrangements with our customers, the total of the amounts recognized in assets represents the maximum exposure to credit risk.

Derivative financial instruments [extract]

Credit risk
Credit risk exposure is €227 million (1999: €30 million), this amount being the total of the positive fair values of derivatives that give rise to claims against the other parties to the instruments. It represents the losses that could result from non-performance of contractual obligations by these parties. We minimize this risk by imposing a limit on the volume of business in derivative financial instruments transacted with individual parties.

Emirates Bank identifies the 'credit risk' from its derivatives – whilst not strictly in line with the suggestions in the standard, the 'potential future exposure' loading is likely to be used in managing day-to-day credit risk exposures and is presumably considered more relevant to a user than simple fair values amounts. It also analyses this amount by type of counterparty, bank or customer, the credit risk of which will be very different.

Extract 10.34: Emirates Bank International PJSC (2000)

29 Hedging and foreign exchange instruments

The Bank utilises hedging and foreign exchange instruments to meet the needs of its customers, to generate trading revenues and as part of its asset and liability management activity to hedge its own exposure to interest rate and currency risk.

In the case of hedging transactions the notional principal typically does not change hands. It is simply a quantity which is used to calculate payments. While notional principal is a volume measure used in the hedging and foreign exchange markets, it is neither a measure of market nor credit risk.

The credit risk on these instruments is calculated by marking individual contracts to market and adding a factor to reflect the potential future exposure over the remaining life of the contract. The add-on factors are those recommended by the Central Bank of the UAE.

	Notional Amount		Credit Risk	
	2000	1999	2000	1999
	AED 000	AED 000	AED 000	AED 000
Unmatured spot and forward contracts	**3,272,289**	2,563,575	**6,388**	12,826
Interest rate swaps	**2,717,383**	3,424,753	**4,915**	24,265
	5,989,672	5,988,328	**11,303**	37,091

Counterparty analysis of credit risk amounts is as follows:

	2000		**1999**	
	Banks	Customers	Banks	Customers
	AED 000	AED 000	AED 000	AED 000
Credit risks	**9,561**	**1,742**	26,943	10,148

Munich Re adopts an unusual approach to disclosing the credit risk associated with its fixed interest securities, analysing their market values by reference to their credit rating:

Extract 10.35: Münchener Rückversicherungs-Gesellschaft AG (2000)

(6) Other securities, held to maturity [extract]
Rating on market-value basis

All figures in €m	**31.12.2000**
AAA	347
AA	381
A	30
BBB and lower	–
No rating	455
Total	1,213

The rating categories are based on the gradings of the leading international rating agencies.

(7) Other securities, available for sale [extract]
Rating of fixed-interest securities on market-value basis

All figures in €m	**31.12.2000**
AAA	47,684
AA	14,178
A	5,400
BBB	627
Lower	160
No rating	4,000
Total	72,049

5.6 Terms and conditions of financial instruments

For each class of financial asset and liability, both recognised and unrecognised, information should be disclosed about the extent and nature of those instruments, including significant terms and conditions that may affect the amount, timing and certainty of future cash flows. Unlike the other numerical disclosures, this requirement of IAS 32 also applies to each class of equity instrument issued by an entity.[580] These are the closest equivalents to the currency and liquidity risk disclosures required by FRS 13 and FRS 4's disclosure requirements for capital instruments.

The contractual terms and conditions of an instrument affect the amount, timing and certainty of associated cash receipts and payments. When recognised and unrecognised instruments are important to the financial position or future operating results, either individually or as a class, their terms and conditions should be disclosed. If no single instrument is individually significant, the essential characteristics of the instruments should be described by reference to appropriate groupings of like instruments.[581]

When financial instruments held or issued, either individually or as a class, create a potentially significant exposure to the risks described in 5.2 above, terms and conditions that may warrant disclosure include:

(a) the principal, stated, face or other similar amount, which for some derivatives may be the notional amount;

(b) the date of maturity, expiry or execution;

(c) early settlement options held by either party to the instrument, including the period in which, or date at which, the options may be exercised and the exercise price or range of prices;

(d) options held by either party to convert the instrument into, or exchange it for, another financial instrument or some other asset or liability, including the period in which, or date at which, the options may be exercised and the conversion or exchange ratio(s);

(e) the amount and timing of principal repayments, including instalment repayments and any sinking fund or similar requirements;

(f) the stated rate or amount of interest, dividend or other periodic return on principal and the timing of payments;

(g) any collateral held or pledged;

(h) the currency in which cash flows are denominated, where this is not the entity's measurement currency;

(i) in the case of an instrument that provides for an exchange, information described in (a) to (h) for the instrument to be acquired in the exchange; and

(j) any condition or associated covenant that, if contravened, would significantly alter any of the other terms (for example, a maximum debt-to-equity ratio in a bond covenant that, if contravened, would make the full principal amount of the bond due and payable immediately).[582]

When the balance sheet presentation of a financial instrument differs from its legal form, the nature of the instrument should be explained.[583] This would be the case for preference shares that are classified as liabilities.

The standard states that the usefulness of this information is enhanced when it highlights any relationships between individual instruments that may affect the amount, timing or certainty of the future cash flows. For example, it is important to disclose hedging relationships such as might exist when an investment in shares is held for which a put option has been purchased. Similarly, it is important to disclose relationships between the components of 'synthetic instruments' such as fixed rate debt created by borrowing at a floating rate and entering into a floating to fixed interest rate swap. In each case the individual financial assets and liabilities should be presented in the balance sheet according to their nature, either separately or in the class of asset or liability to which they belong. The extent to which a risk exposure is altered by the relationships among the assets and liabilities may be apparent to financial statement users from information of the type described in (a) to (j) above but in some circumstances further disclosure is necessary.[584]

In practice, the type of disclosure seen identifying the terms and conditions of an entity's financial instruments is extremely varied – some of the information in each of Extracts 10.24 at 4.3.3, 10.30 to 10.32 at 5.4 and 10.34 at 5.5 above and 10.39 to 10.41 at 5.7 and 10.42 at 5.8 below identifies the terms and conditions of the associated financial instruments. In addition to the information shown in

Extract 10.31 at 5.4, Roche provides further information on each of its significant debt instruments along the following lines:

Extract 10.36: Roche Holding Ltd (2000)

Outstanding bonds [extract]

Summarised bond terms	**Exchange terms and warrants**
'LYONs' 1995 to 20 April 2010 Face value: USD 2,150,000,000 Coupon: Zero Issuer: Roche Holdings, Inc. Keep well: Roche Holding Ltd Exchange right: Roche ADSs	The notes are exchangeable for American Depositary Shares (ADSs) at an adjusted exchange ratio of 4.84495 exchange ADSs per USD 1,000 principal amount at maturity of the Notes. The exchange ratio was changed in accordance with the indenture agreement, dated 20 April 1995, with an effective date of 8 June 2000. The Group will purchase any Note for cash, at the option of the holder, on 20 April 2003 for a purchase price per USD 1,000 principal amount of the Notes of USD 617.78. In addition, the Notes will be redeemable at the option of the Group in whole or in part at any time after 20 April 2003 at the issue price plus accrued original issue discount (OID).

Novartis also provides information on its significant debt instruments in the following extract:

Extract 10.37: Novartis AG (2000)

18. Long-term financial debts

	2000 CHF millions	**1999** CHF millions
Convertible bonds	1 110	1 088
Straight bonds	961	1 574
Liabilities to banks and other financial institutions[1]	278	563
Finance lease obligations	8	12
Total (including current portion of long-term debt)	**2 357**	**3 237**
Less current portion of long-term debt	-74	-793
Total	**2 283**	**2 444**
Convertible bonds		
USD USD 750 million 2.00% conversation bonds 1995/2002 of Novartis Capital Ltd., British Virgin Islands[2]	1 085	1 026
CHF CHF 750 million 1.25% convertible bonds 1995/2002 of Novartis Capital Ltd., British Virgin Islands[3]	25	62
Total convertible bonds	**1 110**	**1 088**
Straight bonds		
USD USD 300 million 6.375% bonds 1993/2000 of Novartis Overseas Finance Ltd., British Virgin Islands	–	478
USD USD 100 million 5.88% Euro Medium Term Note 1993/2000 of Novartis Corporation, Summit, New Jersey, USA	–	160
USD USD 300 million 6.625% bonds 1995/2005 of Novartis Corporation, Summit, New Jersey, USA	492	478
USD USD 250 million 6.625% Euro Medium Term Note 1995/2005 of Novartis Corporation, Summit, New Jersey, USA and subsidiaries	410	398
USD USD 36 million 9.0% bonds 2006 of Gerber Products, Fremont	59	60
Total straight bonds	**961**	**1 574**

[1] Average interest rate 3.7% (1999: 3.6%)

[2] Bonds of USD 10 000 par value are convertible up to September 30, 2002 into approx. 9.60 issued and outstanding, fully paid registered shares of Novartis AG. Novartis Capital Ltd. has acquired options from the non-consolidated employee share participation and employee benefit foundations to cover partly its obligation to deliver shares under the conversion terms of the bonds. It also has options to cover the balance of its obligations from entities, which are consolidated. At December 31, 2000 the outstanding hedge with the non-consolidated entities represented 595 816 shares. An appropriate number of treasury shares are reserved for the balance. At December 31, 2000 bonds totaling USD 32.2 million had been converted. The difference between the nominal value of USD 717.8 million and the balance sheet value of USD 662.3 million is due to the accrual from the original debt value to the maturity value of 100%.

[3] Bonds of CHF 5 000 par value are convertible up to October 9, 2002 into 5 issued and outstanding, fully paid shares of Novartis AG and 5 issued and outstanding fully paid shares of Syngenta AG with each converting bondholder receiving an amount of CHF 239.95 per bond in cash. Novartis Capital Ltd. has acquired options from consolidated entities to cover its obligation to deliver shares under the conversion terms of the bonds. An appropriate number of treasury shares and Syngenta AG shares are reserved. At December 31, 2000 bonds totaling CHF 725.5 million had been converted.

		2000 CHF millions	1999 CHF millions
Breakdown by maturity	2000		793
	2001	74	121
	2002	1 204	1 184
	2003	21	36
	2004	40	81
	2005	907	
	Thereafter	111	1 022
Total		**2 357**	**3 237**
Breakdown by currency	USD	2 068	2 712
	CHF	26	63
	JPY	59	209
	Others	204	253
Total		**2 357**	**3 237**

Fair value comparison

	2000 Balance Sheet CHF millions	2000 Fair Values CHF millions	1999 Balance Sheet CHF millions	1999 Fair Values CHF millions
Convertible bonds	1 110	2 079	1 088	1 782
Straight bonds	961	984	1 574	1 551
Others	286	286	575	575
Total	**2 357**	**3 349**	**3 237**	**3 908**

Collateralized long-term debts and pledged assets	2000 CHF millions	1999 CHF millions
Total amount of collateralized long-term financial debts	263	245
Total net book value of tangible fixed assets pledged as collateral for long-term financial debts	168	415

The financial debts including short-term financial debts, contain only general default covenants. The Group is in compliance with these covenants.

In addition to the disclosures regarding its convertible instruments in Extracts 10.31 and 10.36 above, Roche makes the following disclosures about its equity instruments:

Extract 10.38: Roche Holding Ltd (2000)

21. Equity
Share capital

At 31 December 2000 and 1999, the authorised and called-up share capital was 1,600,000 shares with a nominal value of CHF 100 each.

Based on information supplied to Roche by a shareholders' group with pooled voting rights, comprising the Hoffmann and Oeri-Hoffmann families, that group holds 800,200 shares as in the preceding year. (This figure does not include any shares without pooled voting rights that are held outside this group by individual members of the group.) There were no transactions with these individuals other than those in the ordinary course of business.

Non-voting equity securities *(Genussscheine)*

As of 31 December 2000 and 1999, 7,025,627 non-voting equity securities had been issued. Under Swiss company law these non-voting equity securities have no nominal value, are not part of the share capital and cannot be issued against a contribution which would be shown as an asset in the balance sheet of Roche Holding Ltd. Each non-voting equity security confers the same rights as any of the shares to participate in the net profit and any remaining proceeds from liquidation following repayment of the nominal value of the shares and, if any, participation certificates. In accordance with the law and the Articles of Incorporation of Roche Holding Ltd, the company is entitled at all times to exchange all or some of the non-voting equity securities into shares or participation certificates.

Own equity instruments

As at 31 December 2000 the Group held 284,566 (1999; 251,589) of its own non-voting equity securities and financial instruments to acquire these securities. These have been acquired primarily to meet the obligations that may arise in respect of certain of the Group's debt instruments. For 2000 the Group's holdings in its own equity instruments are recorded as a deduction from equity.

Dividends

On 9 May 2000 the shareholders approved the distribution of a dividend of CHF 100 per share and non-voting equity security (1999: CHF 87) in respect of the 1999 business year. The distribution to holders of outstanding shares and non-voting equity securities totalled 835 million Swiss francs and has been charged to retained earnings in 2000. The shareholders also approved the special dividend in respect of the Givaudan spin-off. The accounting effect of this distribution, which primarily includes the carrying value in the Group's financial statements of the assets and liabilities of Givaudan, totalled 2,642 million Swiss francs and has been included with the special dividend as a movement in retained earnings in 2000.

5.7 Fair values

The fair value disclosure requirements under IAS are similar, but not identical, to those required by FRS 13. The basic requirement is that information about fair value should be disclosed for each class of financial asset and financial liability, both recognised and unrecognised.[585] Once IAS 39 has been adopted, however, the disclosures described in this section are not applicable to those financial assets and liabilities carried at fair value.[586]

The information should be provided in a way that permits comparison between carrying amounts and fair values. Accordingly, the fair values of recognised financial assets and financial liabilities should be grouped into classes and offset only to the extent that their related carrying amounts are offset. Fair values of unrecognised instruments should be presented in a class or classes separate from recognised items and should only be offset to the extent that they meet the offset criteria for recognised instruments.[587]

Guidance on determining fair values is provided in IAS 32 and is virtually identical to that in IAS 39 (see 4.8 above). The one significant difference is that prior to the adoption of IAS 39, these fair values should have taken into account transaction costs to be incurred on disposal or settlement of the instrument; subsequently, and consistent with the measurement requirements of IAS 39, they should not take account of such costs.[588]

For an instrument not traded in an organised financial market, it may not be appropriate to determine and disclose a single amount that represents an estimate of fair value. Instead, it may be more useful to disclose a range of amounts within which the fair value of a financial instrument is reasonably believed to lie.[589]

In extreme cases it may not be practicable, within constraints of timeliness or cost, to determine the fair value of a financial asset or liability with sufficient reliability. If so, that fact should be stated, together with information about its principal characteristics that are pertinent to its fair value, including information about the market for such instruments – in some cases the terms and conditions (see 5.6 above) may prove sufficient. An indication of management's opinion as to the relationship between fair value and carrying amount may be given when there is a reasonable basis for doing so.[590]

Because the fair value of an instrument may be determined by one of several generally accepted methods, where indications of fair value are given, the method adopted and any significant assumptions made should be disclosed.[591]

The following extracts are typical of fair value disclosures seen in practice:

Extract 10.39: Novartis AG (2000)

10. Marketable securities and derivative financial instruments [extract]

Derivative financial instruments The tables below show the contract or underlying principal amounts and fair values of derivative financial instruments analyzed by type of contract at December 31, 2000 and 1999. Contract or underlying principal amounts indicate the volume of business outstanding at the balance sheet date and do not represent amounts at risk. The fair values represent the gain or loss a contract would realize when exchanged or settled using values determined by the markets or standard pricing models at December 31, 2000 and 1999.

	Contract or underlying principal amount CHF millions		Positive fair values CHF millions		Negative fair values CHF millions	
	2000	1999	2000	1999	2000	1999
Currency related hedging instruments						
Forward foreign exchange rate contracts	7 617	1 632	334	25	-5	-49
Over the counter currency options	3 684	4 911	106	10	-4	-59
Total of currency related hedging instruments	**11 301**	**6 543**	**440**	**35**	**-9**	**-108**

Currency related non-hedging instruments						
Forward foreign exchange rate contracts	574	2 638	21	19	–	-54
Over the counter currency options	10 131	14 169	13	4	-151	-22
Cross currency swaps	–	354	–	3	–	-29
Total of currency related non-hedging instruments	**10 705**	**17 161**	**34**	**26**	**-151**	**-105**
Interest related instruments						
Interest rate swaps	2 854	3 945	21	44	-30	-39
Forward rate agreements	2 950	11 310	1	8	-6	-22
Caps and floors	300	960	–	3	-2	-11
Total of interest related instruments	**6 104**	**16 215**	**22**	**55**	**-38**	**-72**
Options on securities	**10 386**	**2 050**	**503**	**46**	**-528**	**-122**
Total derivative financial instruments	**38 496**	**41 969**	**999**	**162**	**-726**	**-407**

All of the currency related hedging instruments mature within twelve months. Out of the total currency related hedging instruments included above, CHF 3 083 million (1999: CHF 1 659 million) was contracted with the intention of hedging anticipated transactions which are expected to occur in 2001.

The amount of deferred hedging gains and losses at December 31, 2000 are as follows:

	CHF millions
Anticipated transactions	138
Available-for-sale securities	-281
Net investment in foreign subsidiaries	128

Net losses per portfolio on non-hedging currency contracts and on interest related instruments are recognized in the income statement. Net unrealized gains are not recorded.

The majority of interest related instruments are utilized for managing the returns on the Group's liquidity.

The contract or underlying principal amount of currency and interest related derivative financial instruments at December 31, 2000 and 1999 are set forth by currency in the table below.

	Forward Foreign Exchange CHF millions	Forward rate agreements CHF millions	Options, Caps and Floors CHF millions	Total 2000 CHF millions	Total 1999 CHF millions
CHF		2 950	300	3 250	11 860
USD	574		1 967	2 541	6 850
EUR			6 697	6 697	8 771
DEM					410
GBP			1 467	1 467	1 186
Total	**574**	**2 950**	**10 431**	**13 955**	**29 077**
Currency related hedging instruments				11 301	6 543
Cross currency swaps					354
Interest rate swaps				2 854	3 945
Equity options				10 386	2 050
Total derivative financial instruments				**38 496**	**41 969**

Marketable securities

	Balance sheet value CHF millions		Unrealized gains/losses CHF millions		Market value CHF millions	
	2000	1999	2000	1999	2000	1999
Bonds held-to-maturity						
Debt securities issued or backed by foreign governments		1 134		-17		1 117
Corporate debt securities		5 373		-113		5 260
Other debt securities		1 104		-21		1 083
Total bonds held-to-maturity[1]	**–**	**7 611**	**–**	**-151**	**–**	**7 460**
Available-for-sale						
Equities	3 364	2 141	1 157	319	4 521	2 460
Debt securities	6 118	5 998	185	139	6 303	6 137
Total available-for-sale securities	**9 482**	**8 139**	**1 342**	**458**	**10 824**	**8 597**
Time deposits longer than 90 days	**2 238**	**570**			**2 238**	**570**
Total at December 31	**11 720**	**16 320**	**1 342**	**307**	**13 062**	**16 627**

[1] During 2000, the Group disposed of the majority of its holding of bonds designated as being held-to-maturity. Any remaining bonds in this category have been reclassified to the available-for-sale category of marketable securities.

Extract 10.40: Roche Holding Ltd (2000)

25. Financial instruments in millions of CHF [extract]

The notional principal values, fair values and carrying values of derivative financial instruments held by the Group are shown in the table on page 87. The notional amounts do not represent the amounts actually exchanged by the parties, and therefore are not a measure of the Group's exposure. Fair value is determined by reference to quoted market prices and the use of established estimation techniques. The carrying values are those included in the consolidated balance sheet as either other current assets or accrued liabilities.

	Notional principal amount	Fair value	Carrying value
2000			
Foreign currency derivatives			
– forward exchange contracts and swaps	8,223	156	84
– options	1,391	18	17
Interest rate derivatives			
– swaps	4,289	(34)	5
– other	114	–	1
Other derivatives	1,512	97	99
Total derivative financial instruments	15,529	237	206
1999			
Foreign currency derivatives			
– forward exchange contracts and swaps	7,933	(5)	(49)
– options	6,088	4	101
Interest rate derivatives			
– swaps	4,482	(48)	1
– other	633	(6)	–
Other derivatives	1,807	210	189
Total derivative financial instruments	20,943	155	242

The net unrecognised gains on open contracts which hedge future anticipated foreign currency sales amounted to 75 million Swiss francs (1999: 44 million Swiss francs). These gains will be recognised in the income statement when these open contracts mature at various dates up to one year from the balance sheet date.

Extract 10.41: Jardine Matheson Holdings Limited (2000)

32 Financial Instruments [extract]

Derivative financial instruments	**2000** Contract amount US$m	Fair value asset US$m	Fair value liability US$m	1999 Contract amount US$m	Fair value asset US$m	Fair value liability US$m
Forward foreign exchange contracts	**793.1**	**4.3**	**3.8**	457.1	2.8	3.2
Currency options	**–**	**–**	**–**	5.1	–	0.1
Forward rate agreements	**7.5**	**0.1**	**–**	27.4	–	0.2
Interest rate options	**5.0**	**–**	**0.1**	121.0	0.4	0.1
Interest rate swaps	**542.2**	**0.2**	**11.7**	519.1	2.1	0.5
Interest rate caps	**192.0**	**–**	**0.2**	172.5	–	–

The fair value of derivative financial instruments represents the unrealised gains or losses of open contracts of which a net loss of US$0.9 million *(1999: net gain of US$1.6 million)* arising from the hedge of assets and liabilities in the balance sheet is recognised in the financial statements.

Forward foreign exchange contracts	**2000** Forward purchase US$m	Forward sale US$m	1999 Forward purchase US$m	Forward sale US$m
Contract amount:				
Deutschemark	**–**	**–**	12.5	–
Euro	**90.2**	**29.0**	46.3	2.0
French Franc	**0.2**	**1.3**	–	56.1
Hong Kong Dollar	**2.8**	**546.3**	20.3	228.4
Japanese Yen	**2.8**	**5.8**	4.2	20.5
United Kingdom Sterling	**39.6**	**56.8**	14.7	26.5
Other	**6.2**	**12.1**	5.1	20.5
	141.8	**651.3**	103.1	354.0

Forward foreign exchange contracts which relate to hedges of firm and anticipated commitments mature at various dates over the following two years.

Interest rate swaps	**2000** US$m	1999 US$m
Due dates:		
– within one year	**87.9**	358.4
– between one and five years	**444.2**	160.7
– beyond five years	**10.1**	–
	542.2	519.1

At 31st December 2000, the fixed interest rates relating to interest rate swaps vary from 4.2% to 8.5% (*1999: 4.1% to 8.5%*).

Financial assets that are carried above their fair value are viewed with particular suspicion and singled out for further disclosure. This is to provide a basis for understanding management's exercise of judgment and assessing the possibility of future write-downs.[592]

In addition to the carrying amount and fair value of such assets the reasons for not reducing the carrying amount, including the nature of the evidence supporting management's belief that the carrying amount will be recovered, should be stated.

These disclosures should be provided for either individual assets, or appropriate groupings of such assets, that reflect the reasons for not reducing the carrying amount and should be specific to the asset(s) in question.[593]

For example, the fair value of a fixed rate loan intended to be held to maturity may have declined below its carrying amount as a result of an increase in interest rates. In such circumstances, the lender may not have reduced the carrying amount because there is no evidence to suggest that the borrower is likely to default.[594]

5.8 Hedges

Prior to adopting IAS 39, IAS 32 required disclosure about financial instruments accounted for as hedges of anticipated future transactions, in particular:

- a description of the anticipated transactions, including the period of time until they are expected to occur;
- a description of the hedging instruments; and
- the amount of any deferred or unrecognised gain or loss and the expected timing of their recognition as income or expense.[595]

As discussed in 2.10 above, FRS 13 requires disclosures relating to hedging instruments whenever hedge accounting has been used, not just for hedges of anticipated future transactions.

The information required by IAS 32 may be provided on an aggregate basis when a hedged position comprises several anticipated transactions or has been hedged by several financial instruments.[596]

The amount of deferred or unrecognised gains or losses disclosed should include all gains and losses on those instruments designated as hedges of anticipated future transactions that have not been recognised in the income statement pending completion of the hedged transaction. This is without regard to whether they have somehow been recognised in the financial statements, e.g. they may:

- be unrealised but recorded in the balance sheet as a result of carrying the hedging instrument at fair value,
- be unrecognised if the hedging instrument is carried on the cost basis; or
- have been realised if the hedging instrument has been sold or settled.[597]

In addition to Extracts 10.39 to 10.41 at 5.7 above, Nestlé provides a comprehensive example of pre-IAS 39 hedging disclosures:

Extract 10.42: Nestlé S.A. (2000)

29. Foreign exchange hedge instruments

Forward foreign currency sales

In millions of CHF	**2000**			1999		
	Contractual or notional amounts	Unrealised gains	Unrealised losses	Contractual or notional amounts	Unrealised gains	Unrealised losses
Recognised transactions						
Forward contracts and swaps	**7 926**	**169**	**1**	7 869	–	292
Options purchased	**–**	**–**	**–**	1 675	–	6
Options written	**1 674**	**3**	**–**	1 610	–	2
Anticipated future transactions						
Forward contracts	**615**	**3**	**7**	647	5	13
Options purchased	**37**	**1**	**–**	–	–	–
Options written	**–**	**–**	**–**	80	–	–

Recognised transactions relate to balance sheet positions resulting from liquid assets in foreign currencies and, to a lesser extent, from export receivables, while anticipated future transactions refer to expected export sales.

Due to the nature of the Group's operations, most of the transactions have maturities of less than one year. They are denominated mainly in USD, in GBP and in EUR.

Forward foreign currency purchases

In millions of CHF	**2000**			1999		
	Contractual or notional amounts	Unrealised gains	Unrealised losses	Contractual or notional amounts	Unrealised gains	Unrealised losses
Recognised transactions						
Forward contracts and swaps	**2 988**	**6**	**84**	2 564	51	7
Options purchased	**1 712**	**–**	**6**	–	–	–
Options written	**1 548**	**–**	**8**	65	–	–
Anticipated future transactions						
Forward contracts	**1 101**	**28**	**7**	1 026	–	20
Options purchased	**225**	**1**	**1**	127	2	1
Options written	**285**	**1**	**1**	372	1	–

Recognised transactions are related to balance sheet positions such as suppliers and financial liabilities, while anticipated future transactions refer to commitments for commodity and machinery imports.

Due to the nature of the Group's operations, most of the transactions have maturities of less than one year. They are denominated mainly in USD, in EUR and in JPY.

30. Commodity hedge instruments

In millions of CHF	**2000**			1999		
	Contractual or notional amounts	Unrealised gains	Unrealised losses	Contractual or notional amounts	Unrealised gains	Unrealised losses
Futures	**312**	**3**	**13**	245	9	24
Options purchased	**19**	**1**	**–**	38	–	1
Options written	**21**	**–**	**1**	26	–	1

Commodity hedge instruments are designed to hedge the price risks on the anticipated purchases of coffee, cocoa and other commodities used for the manufacture of finished goods.

31. Interest rate instruments

Liquid assets

Interest exposures on liquid assets are hedged by using instruments which have the effect of altering the average maturities and the interest rates on the underlying positions. The notional amounts of these instruments and the unrealised gains and losses on revaluation at market rates are given below:

In millions of CHF	2000			1999		
	Contractual or notional amounts	Unrealised gains	Unrealised losses	Contractual or notional amounts	Unrealised gains	Unrealised losses
Interest rate swaps	**4 193**	**5**	**117**	5 116	2	188
Interest rate futures	**558**	**–**	**1**	–	–	–

These instruments have maturity dates of three months to five years. The instruments are denominated in CHF, in EUR and in USD with annual interest rates ranging from 2.5% on CHF to 5.6% on USD.

Financial liabilities

The majority of interest rate swaps and interest rate and currency swaps modify the maturities and the interest rates of long term bonds thus creating obligations in the reporting currency of the issuer (see note 18), while other interest rate and currency swaps, forward rate agreements and options hedge interest rate exposures of the affiliated companies. The notional amounts of these instruments and the unrealised gains and losses on revaluation at market rates are given below:

In millions of CHF	2000			1999		
	Contractual or notional amounts	Unrealised gains	Unrealised losses	Contractual or notional amounts	Unrealised gains	Unrealised losses
Interest rate swaps [(a)]	**2 820**	**75**	**6**	2 510	110	15
Interest rate and currency swaps	**3 374**	**157**	**228**	3 527	36	300
Forward rate agreements	**1 211**	**–**	**1**	1 892	57	41
Options purchased	**272**	**1**	**1**	341	–	–
Options written	**402**	**–**	**2**	1 003	1	1

[a)] Include equity swaps.

These instruments have maturity dates of one month to six years. They are denominated mainly in USD, CAD, AUD, EUR, GBP and JPY. Their annual interest rates range from 0.5% on JPY to 6.3% on AUD.

Following the adoption of IAS 39, which includes detailed rules on hedge accounting, this requirement is deleted and replaced by more relevant disclosures. The following should be disclosed separately for designated fair value hedges, cash flow hedges and hedges of a net investment in a foreign entity:

- a description of the hedge;
- a description of the designated hedging instruments and their fair values;
- the nature of the risks being hedged; and
- for hedges of forecasted transactions:
  - the periods in which the forecasted transactions are expected to occur;
  - when they are expected to impact net profit or loss; and
  - a description of any forecasted transaction for which hedge accounting had previously been used but that is no longer expected to occur.[598]

As explained in 4.9.7 above single hedging instruments may be simultaneously designated in a cash flow and a fair value hedge. In such cases the instrument in question would be at least partially included in the disclosures for both cash flow hedges and fair value hedges.[599]

In addition, for cash flow hedges, where gains or losses on designated hedging instruments have been recognised in equity, the following should be disclosed:

- the amount recognised in equity during the period;
- the amount removed from equity during the period and reported in income; and
- the amount that was removed from equity during the period and added to the initial measurement of hedged assets or liabilities.[600]

5.9 Voluntary disclosures

The following additional disclosures are encouraged by the standard, although they are not mandatory:

- the total amount of the change in fair value of financial assets and financial liabilities that have been recognised as income or expense for the period;
- until IAS 39 is adopted, the total amount of deferred or unrecognised gains or losses on hedging instruments other than those relating to hedges of anticipated future transactions; and
- the average aggregate during the year of:
  - carrying amounts of recognised financial assets and liabilities;
  - principal, stated, notional or other similar amounts of unrecognised financial assets and liabilities; and
  - fair values of all financial assets and liabilities, particularly when the amounts on hand at the year end are unrepresentative of the position during the year.[601]

5.10 Other disclosures for entities applying IAS 39

Following adoption of IAS 39, the following disclosures are required to illustrate the application of that standard's measurement rules:

- where gains or losses from remeasuring available-for-sale financial assets to fair value (other than assets relating to hedges) have been recognised in equity:
  - the amount so recognised during the current period; and
  - the amount removed from equity during the period and reported in income;
- where the presumption that the fair value of all trading and available-for-sale assets can be reliably measured has been rebutted and such assets are measured at cost, that fact should be disclosed together with a description of the financial assets, their carrying amount, an explanation of why fair value cannot be reliably measured, and, if possible, the range of estimates within which fair value is highly likely to lie.

Further, where such assets are sold, that fact should also be disclosed together with their carrying amount at the time of sale and the amount of gain or loss recognised;

- significant items of income, expense, gains and losses resulting from financial assets and financial liabilities, whether included in income or equity. For this purpose the following should be disclosed separately:
    - total interest income and expense (both on an historical cost basis);[602]

      Interest income should be shown for trading assets as well as other classes of asset, although it could be shown in the notes if the face of the income statement shows the total change in fair value.[603]
    - total gains and losses recognised in income from the derecognition of available-for-sale assets carried at fair value, separately from equivalent 'unrealised' gains and losses reported in income (a similar split for trading instruments is not required);
    - interest accrued on impaired loans, but not yet received in cash.[604]

  Therefore disclosure should be provided of significant fair value changes, distinguishing between those that are reported in income and in equity. Additionally, breakdowns of those changes that relate to available-for-sale assets, trading instruments, and hedging instruments is also necessary.

  Disclosure of components of the change in fair value by the way items are classified for internal purposes is neither required nor prohibited. A bank, for example, may choose to disclose separately the change in fair value of those derivatives that IAS 39 classifies as held for trading but that the company classifies as part of risk management activities outside the trading portfolio;[605]
- for securitisation or repurchase agreements:
    - the nature and extent of such transactions, including a description of any collateral and quantitative information about the key assumptions used in calculating the fair values of new and retained interests; and
    - whether the financial assets have been derecognised.

  This should be provided separately for transactions occurring in the current period and for remaining interests retained from prior period transactions;
- the reason for any reclassification of a financial asset as one required to be reported at cost or amortised cost rather than at fair value, e.g. because it can no longer be measured reliably or because the two year tainting period for held-to-maturity investments is over (see 4.3.1 and 4.6.6 above);
- the nature and amount of any recognised impairment loss or reversal thereof, separately for each significant class of financial asset;
- for borrowers, the carrying amount of financial assets pledged as collateral for liabilities and any significant terms and conditions relating to these assets; and

- for lenders:
  - the fair value of collateral (both financial and non-financial assets) that has been accepted and can be sold or repledged in the absence of default;
  - the fair value of collateral sold or repledged; and
  - any significant terms and conditions associated with the use of collateral.[606]

Originally IAS 39 required lenders to recognise collateral they could sell or repledge without constraint, together with a liability representing the obligation to return those securities; it also required the borrower to disclose those assets separately.[607] These requirements were deleted by the October 2000 revisions and the final points above dealing with disclosure of collateral were added.

5.11 Comparatives

If comparative information for prior periods is not available when IAS 32 is first adopted, such information need not be presented.[608] This relief will also apply when an entity prepares its accounts under IAS for the first time. There is no equivalent exemption within IAS 39 even though the transitional provisions render comparatives for many of the numerical disclosures irrelevant.

6 CONCLUSION

It is clear that the subject of accounting for financial instruments is likely to remain one of the most difficult regulatory challenges for a number of years. Perhaps surprisingly, there seems to be a high degree of consensus among the major standard-setters and their representatives on the Joint Working Group that fair valuing all financial instruments can be the only ultimate solution (although there is less agreement on what fair value actually means). This is a controversial view that is meeting with considerable resistance. Standard setters in this area appear to have moved considerably ahead of current practice since the proposed solution has not yet commanded acceptance in any country. This is a bold step since the traditional role of accounting regulators has been to codify accepted best practice rather than, as now, to invent new practice.

The arguments for fair value accounting seem cogent, and they have been assembled very persuasively in the IASC Discussion Paper and JWG Draft Standard. But they are nonetheless revolutionary; by the IASC's own admission, they require the adoption of a new capital maintenance concept ('current-market-rate-of-return') for measuring financial instruments.[609] And this will simply introduce a new inconsistency, unless it is applied to the measurement of other items in the accounts as well, which would be an even more radical proposal. Although elegant, the proposals do not sit well with widespread perceptions of the role and meaning of accounts.

Recently the ASB admitted that even if the JWG's measurement proposals were widely supported (which they are certainly not) it seems unlikely that a standard could be put in place within the next five years,[610] i.e. before Europe's wholesale move to IAS by 2005. Therefore the major issue for UK companies will be the implementation of IAS 39's half-way house approach, which is more of an unknown quantity. Many companies are experiencing difficulty in applying the standard for the first time in 2001, especially its hedging provisions, and it has become apparent that a degree of quality and due process was sacrificed to meet the IOSCO deadline. Fortunately the new Board seems to have acknowledged this and have already established a distinct project aimed at improving the standard.[611] In the meantime the disclosure requirements in FRS 13 are somewhat less controversial, and do in some respects make companies' treasury activity more transparent.

References

1 *IASC Update*, IASC, December 1996.
2 Discussion Paper, *Derivatives and other financial instruments*, ASB, July 1996.
3 FRED 13, *Derivatives and other financial instruments: Disclosures*, ASB, April 1997.
4 FRED 13 Supplement – *Derivatives and other financial instruments: Disclosures by banks and similar institutions*, ASB, July 1997.
5 FRS 13, *Derivatives and other financial instruments: Disclosures*, ASB, September 1998
6 IAS 32, *Financial Instruments: Disclosure and Presentation*, IASC, March 1995.
7 Discussion Paper, *Accounting for Financial Assets and Financial Liabilities*, Chapter 3, para. 3.1.
8 *Ibid.,* Chapter 4, para. 2.1 and Chapter 5, para. 3.1.
9 *Ibid.*, Chapter 6, para. 5.1.
10 E62, *Financial Instruments: Recognition and Measurement*, IASC, June 1998.
11 IAS 39, *Financial Instruments: Recognition and Measurement*, IASC, December 1998.
12 Draft Standard, *Financial Instruments and Similar Items*, JWG, December 2000.
13 Forward to the JWG Draft Standard, ASB, December 2000.
14 FRS 13, para. 2, IAS 32, para. 5, IAS 39, para. 8.
15 *Ibid.*, Appendix II, para. 5.
16 *Ibid.*, Appendix II, para. 6, IAS 32, para. 6.
17 JWG Basis for Conclusions, para. 2.14.
18 FRS 13, Appendix II, para. 3.
19 *Ibid.*, Appendix II, para. 4.
20 *Ibid.*, paras. 2, 10 and 64.
21 *Ibid.*, para. 4.
22 *Ibid.*, para. 5.
23 *Ibid.*, para. 4.
24 *Ibid.*, para. 3.
25 FRRP PN 64, 23 February 2001, PN 65, 8 March 2001 and PN 69, 28 August 2001.
26 FRRP PN 66, 11 April 2001.
27 FRS 13, para. 5.
28 *Ibid.*, paras. 8 and 9.
29 *Ibid.*, footnote to para. 5.
30 *Ibid.*, para. 6.
31 *Ibid.*, para. 2.
32 *Ibid.*, para. 11.
33 *Ibid.*, para. 12.
34 *Ibid.*, para. 13.
35 *Ibid.*, para. 14.
36 *Ibid.*, para. 15.
37 *Ibid.*, para. 21.
38 *Ibid.*, para. 22.
39 *Ibid.*, para. 20.
40 *Ibid.*, paras. 16 and 17.
41 *Ibid.*, para. 18.
42 *Ibid.*, para. 23.
43 *Ibid.*, Appendix VII, para. 26.
44 FRRP PN 61, 11 July 2000.
45 FRS 13, para. 74.
46 *Ibid.*, para. 75.
47 *Ibid.*, para. 76.
48 *Ibid.*, paras. 24 and 25.
49 *Ibid.*, para. 32.
50 *Ibid.*, para. 26.
51 *Ibid.*, para. 2.
52 *Ibid.*, para. 27.
53 *Ibid.*, para. 26(a).
54 *Ibid.*, para. 31.
55 *Ibid.*, paras. 26(b) and 29.
56 *Ibid.*, para. 30.

57 *Ibid.*, para. 33.
58 *Ibid.*, para. 34.
59 *Ibid.*, para. 35.
60 *Ibid.*, para. 34(b) and (c).
61 *Ibid.*, para. 34(d).
62 ASB Exposure Draft, *Amendment to SSAP 20 'Foreign Currency Translation': Disclosure.*
63 ASB Press Notice number 138.
64 FRS 13, para. 38.
65 *Ibid.*, para. 77.
66 *Ibid.*, para. 39.
67 *Ibid.*
68 *Ibid.*, para. 40.
69 *Ibid.*, para. 42.
70 FRRP PN 66, 11 April 2001
71 FRS 13, para. 43
72 *Ibid.*, para. 44.
73 *Ibid.*, para. 45.
74 *Ibid.*, para. 46.
75 *Ibid.*, para. 2.
76 *Ibid.*, para. 48.
77 *Ibid.*, para. 51.
78 *Ibid.*, paras. 53 and 54.
79 *Ibid.*, para. 22.
80 *Ibid.*, para. 59.
81 *Ibid.*, para. 60.
82 *Ibid.*, para. 61.
83 UITF Information Sheet No. 33.
84 FRS 13, para. 62.
85 For example, see Vodafone Group Plc, *Annual Report & Accounts For the year ended 31 March 2001*, page 43 or BHP Billiton Plc, *Annual Report 2001*, pages 126 and 127.
86 *Ibid.*, para. 2.
87 *Ibid.*, para. 57.
88 *Ibid.*, para. 2.
89 *Ibid.*, para. 64.
90 *Ibid.*, para. 65.
91 *Ibid.*, para. 66.
92 *Ibid.*, para. 69.
93 *Ibid.*, para. 71.
94 *Ibid.*, para. 80.
95 *Ibid.*, para. 81.
96 *Ibid.*
97 *Ibid.*. para. 82.
98 *Ibid.*, para. 83(c).
99 *Ibid.*, para. 113.
100 *Ibid.*, para. 84.
101 *Ibid.*, para. 116.
102 *Ibid.*, para. 81.
103 *Ibid.*, para. 87.
104 *Ibid.*
105 *Ibid.*, para. 89.
106 *Ibid.*, para. 88.
107 *Ibid.*, para. 90.
108 *Ibid.*, para. 91.
109 *Ibid.*, para. 92.
110 *Ibid.*, para. 97.
111 *Ibid.*, para. 95.
112 *Ibid.*, para. 96.
113 *Ibid.*, para. 98.
114 *Ibid.*, para. 99.
115 *Ibid.*, para. 100.
116 *Ibid.*, para. 101.
117 *Ibid.*, para. 103.
118 *Ibid.*, para. 104.
119 *Ibid.*, para. 111.
120 *Ibid.*, para. 107.
121 *Ibid.*, paras. 108 and 109.
122 *Ibid.*, para. 119.
123 *Ibid.*, para. 120.
124 *Ibid.*, para. 121.
125 *Ibid.*, para. 130.
126 *Ibid.*, para. 122.
127 *Ibid.*, para. 133.
128 *Ibid.*, para. 124.
129 IAS 39 (revised 2000), *Financial Instruments: Recognition and Measurement*, IASC, October 2000
130 IAS 39 Implementation Guidance, Introduction
131 *Ibid.*
132 Directive of the European Parliament and of the Council amending Directives 78/660/EEC, 83/349/EEC and 86/635/EEC as regards the valuation rules for the annual and consolidated accounts of certain types of companies as well as of banks and other financial institutions, European Commission, May 2001.
133 IAS 39, para. 1.
134 *Ibid.*, para. 1(a), Q&A 1-4.
135 *Ibid.*, para. 3.
136 *Ibid.*, para..4.
137 *Ibid.*, para. 1(b).
138 *Ibid.*, para. 1(c).
139 *Ibid.*, para. 1(g).
140 *Ibid.*, para. 1(e).
141 *Ibid.*, para. 1(b).
142 *Ibid.*, para. 1(e).
143 *Ibid.*, para. 1(f).
144 *Ibid.*, Q&A 1-5-a and 1-5-b.
145 *Ibid.*, Q&A 1-1
146 *Ibid.*, Q&A 1-2
147 *Ibid.*, para. 1(f).
148 IAS 32, para. 3.
149 IAS 39, para. 5.
150 *Ibid.*, Q&A 1-3-a and 1-3-b; IAS 32, paras. 3 and 43.
151 IAS 39, Q&A 1-3-b.
152 *Ibid.*, paras. 1(h) and 2.
153 *Ibid.*, para. 1(d) and (h).
154 *Ibid.*, para. 5.
155 *Ibid.*, Q&A 1-6.
156 *Ibid.*, para. 6.
157 *Ibid.*, para. 7.
158 *Ibid.*, Q&A 8-1.
159 *Ibid.*, para. 10.

160 *Ibid.*, para. 21.
161 *Ibid.*, Q&A 10-15.
162 *Ibid.*, Draft Q&A 10-22.
163 *Ibid.*, Draft Q&A 10-21.
164 *Ibid.*, Q&A 10-9.
165 *Ibid.*, para. 18, Q&A 18-2, Draft Q&A 18-3.
166 *Ibid.*, Q&A 18-1.
167 *Ibid.*, para. 84.
168 *Ibid.*, para. 89.
169 *Ibid.*, para. 127.
170 *Ibid.*, para. 80.
171 *Ibid.*, Q&A 10-17.
172 *Ibid.*, para. 81.
173 *Ibid.*, para. 82.
174 *Ibid.*, Q&A 83-3.
175 *Ibid.*, para. 80.
176 *Ibid.*, Q&A 10-16.
177 *Ibid.*, Q&A 80-1.
178 *Ibid.*, Q&A 80-2.
179 *Ibid.*, para. 79.
180 *Ibid.*, para. 87.
181 *Ibid.*, Q&A 87-1.
182 *Ibid.*, para. 88.
183 *Ibid.*, para. 84.
184 *Ibid.*, para. 83.
185 *Ibid.*, Q&A 83-2.
186 *Ibid.*, Q&A 83-1.
187 *Ibid.*, Q&A 83-4.
188 *Ibid.*, Q&A 83-5.
189 *Ibid.*, Q&A 83-6.
190 *Ibid.*, para. 85.
191 *Ibid.*, para. 86.
192 *Ibid.*, Q&A 83-7, Draft Q&A 83-8.
193 *Ibid.*, Q&A 86-2.
194 *Ibid.*, Q&A 86-1.
195 *Ibid.*
196 *Ibid.*, para. 19.
197 *Ibid.*, para. 20.
198 *Ibid.*, Q&A 10-7.
199 *Ibid.*, Q&A 10-11-a, Draft Q&A 10-20.
200 *Ibid.*, Q&A 10-11-b.
201 *Ibid.*, para. 19.
202 *Ibid.*, para. 21.
203 *Ibid.*, para. 10.
204 *Ibid.*, Q&A 10-1.
205 *Ibid.*, para. 13.
206 *Ibid.*, Q&A 10-6.
207 *Ibid.*, Q&A 13-1.
208 *Ibid.*, Q&A 13-2.
209 *Ibid.*, Q&A 13-2.
210 *Ibid.*, Q&A 10-10.
211 *Ibid.*, para. 15.
212 *Ibid.*, Q&A 10-10.
213 *Ibid.*, Q&A 10-4-a.
214 *Ibid.*, Q&A 10-4-b.
215 *Ibid.*, Q&A 15-1.
216 *Ibid.*, Q&A 10-3.
217 *Ibid.*
218 *Ibid.*, Q&A 10-2.
219 *Ibid.*
220 *Ibid.*, Q&A 10-18.
221 *Ibid.*, para. 14.
222 *Ibid.*, Q&A 14-1.
223 *Ibid.*, Q&A 14-2.
224 *Ibid.*, Q&A 14-3.
225 *Ibid.*, Q&A 10-8.
226 *Ibid.*
227 *Ibid.*, Q&A 15-2.
228 *Ibid.*, para. 16, Q&A 10-5.
229 *Ibid.*, para. 22.
230 *Ibid.*, para. 23.
231 *Ibid.*, Q&A 23-4.
232 *Ibid.*, Q&A 22-1.
233 *Ibid.*, Draft Q&A 23-12.
234 *Ibid.*, Q&A 23-8.
235 *Ibid.*, Draft Q&A 23-11.
236 *Ibid.*, Q&A 23-6.
237 *Ibid.*, Q&A 23-7.
238 *Ibid.*
239 *Ibid.*, Q&A 25-1.
240 *Ibid.*, para. 24.
241 *Ibid.*, para. 25.
242 *Ibid.*, Q&A 25-8.
243 *Ibid.*, para. 25.
244 *Ibid.*, Q&A 25-6.
245 *Ibid.*, Draft Q&A 25-9.
246 *Ibid.*, Q&A 25-5.
247 *Ibid.*, para. 25.
248 *Ibid.*, Q&A 25-7.
249 *Ibid.*, Q&A 22-1.
250 *Ibid.*, Draft Q&A 22-2.
251 *Ibid.*, para. 23.
252 *Ibid.*, Q&A 23-1.
253 *Ibid.*, para. 26.
254 *Ibid.*, Draft Q&A 23-10.
255 *Ibid.*, Q&A 23-2.
256 *Ibid.*, Q&A 23-5.
257 *Ibid.*, Q&A 25-2.
258 *Ibid.*, Q&A 25-3.
259 *Ibid.*, Q&A 25-4.
260 *Ibid.*, Q&A 25-8.
261 *Ibid.*, Draft Q&A 23-9.
262 *Ibid.*, para. 27.
263 *Ibid.*, para. 28.
264 *Ibid.*, para. 29.
265 *Ibid.*, Q&A 27-2.
266 *Ibid.*, para. 31.
267 *Ibid.*, Q&A 16-1.
268 *Ibid.*, Q&A 30-2.
269 *Ibid.*, Q&A 16-3.
270 *Ibid.*
271 *Ibid.*, Q&A 16-2.
272 *Ibid.*, Q&A 16-4.
273 *Ibid.*, para. 30.
274 *Ibid.*, paras. 32 and 33.
275 *Ibid.*, para. 33.

276 *Ibid.*, para. 34.
277 *Ibid.*, Q&A 34-1.
278 *Ibid.*, Q&A 30-1.
279 *Ibid.*, Q&A 27-1.
280 *Ibid.*, para. 66, Q&A 66-1 and 66-2.
281 *Ibid.*, para. 10.
282 *Ibid.*, para. 17.
283 *Ibid.*, Q&A 66-2.
284 *Ibid.*, Q&A 66-3.
285 *Ibid.*, para. 67.
286 *Ibid.*, Q&A 23-3.
287 *Ibid.*, para. 69.
288 *Ibid.*, para. 93 and Q&A 93-1.
289 *Ibid.*, para. 73.
290 *Ibid.*, para. 8.
291 *Ibid.*, para. 72.
292 *Ibid.*, para. 70.
293 *Ibid.*, para. 71.
294 *Ibid.*, Q&A 70-1.
295 *Ibid.*, Q&A 70-3.
296 *Ibid.*, para. 91.
297 *Ibid.*, para. 92.
298 *Ibid.*, para. 73.
299 *Ibid.*, para. 103.
300 *Ibid.*, para. 106.
301 *Ibid.*, Q&A 106-1.
302 *Ibid.*, para. 73.
303 *Ibid.*, para. 10, Q&A 10-12. The implementation guidance actually discusses this instrument in the context of the issuer, rather than the holder, but the principles are the same.
304 *Ibid.*, Q&A 73-1.
305 *Ibid.*, Q&A 10-12.
306 *Ibid.*, para. 76.
307 *Ibid.*, Q&A 76-1.
308 *Ibid.*
309 *Ibid.*, para. 91.
310 *Ibid.*, para. 73.
311 *Ibid.*, para. 69.
312 *Ibid.*, para. 108.
313 *Ibid.*, para. 73.
314 *Ibid.*, Q&A 10-19.
315 *Ibid.*
316 *Ibid.*, Q&A 10-13.
317 *Ibid.*, Q&A 10-14.
318 *Ibid.*
319 *Ibid.*, para. 75.
320 *Ibid.*, para. 74.
321 *Ibid.*, para. 73.
322 *Ibid.*, para. 69.
323 *Ibid.*, para. 108.
324 *Ibid.*, paras. 69 and 73.
325 *Ibid.*, para. 91.
326 *Ibid.*, para. 92.
327 *Ibid.*, para. 73.
328 *Ibid.*, para. 69.
329 *Ibid.*, para. 103.
330 *Ibid.*, para. 104.
331 *Ibid.*, para. 105.
332 *Ibid.*, Q&A 103-1.
333 *Ibid.*, Q&A 103-2.
334 *Ibid.*
335 *Ibid.*, para. 92.
336 *Ibid.*, para. 106.
337 *Ibid.*, Q&A 106-1.
338 *Ibid.*, para. 93 and Q&A 93-1.
339 *Ibid.*, para. 69.
340 *Ibid.*, para. 90.
341 *Ibid.*, para. 92.
342 *Ibid.*, para. 107.
343 *Ibid.*, Q&A 107-2.
344 *Ibid.*, Q&A 107-1.
345 *Ibid.*, para. 107.
346 *Ibid.*, paras. 78 and 94, Q&A Other-5.
347 *Ibid.*, Q&A Other-6.
348 *Ibid.*, Q&A Other-3.
349 *Ibid.*, para. 73.
350 *Ibid.*, para. 109.
351 *Ibid.*, para. 110.
352 *Ibid.*, para. 110, Q&A 109-1 and 117-1, Draft Q&A 117-3.
353 *Ibid.*, para. 110, Q&A 109-1.
354 *Ibid.*, para. 111.
355 *Ibid.*
356 *Ibid.*, Q&A 111-1.
357 *Ibid.*, para. 112.
358 *Ibid.*, Q&A 112-1.
359 *Ibid.*, Q&A 112-2, Draft Q&A 112-3.
360 *Ibid.*, para. 113.
361 *Ibid.*, Q&A 113-3.
362 *Ibid.*, para. 113, Q&A 113-1.
363 *Ibid.*, Q&A 113-2.
364 *Ibid.*, Q&A 111-4.
365 *Ibid.*, Q&A 111-3.
366 *Ibid.*, Q&A 110-1.
367 *Ibid.*
368 *Ibid.*, Q&A 111-2.
369 *Ibid.*, para. 114.
370 *Ibid.*, para. 115.
371 *Ibid.*, Draft Q&A 115-1.
372 *Ibid.*, para. 117.
373 *Ibid.*, para. 118.
374 *Ibid.*, Q&A 117-2.
375 *Ibid.*, para. 118.
376 *Ibid.*, Q&A 118-1.
377 *Ibid.*, para. 119.
378 *Ibid.*, para. 116.
379 *Ibid.*, para. 95.
380 *Ibid.*, Q&A 70-2.
381 *Ibid.*, para. 96.
382 *Ibid.*, para. 97.
383 *Ibid.*, para. 98, IAS 32, para. 80.
384 *Ibid.*, para. 99, IAS 32, para. 81.
385 *Ibid.*, Q&A 99-1.
386 *Ibid.*, para. 100, IAS 32 para. 82.
387 *Ibid.*, Q&A 100-1.

388 *Ibid.*, para. 101.
389 *Ibid.*, para. 102; Framework for the Preparation and Presentation of Financial Statements, IASC, September 1989, para. 86.
390 IAS 39, para. 136.
391 *Ibid.*, para. 10.
392 *Ibid.*
393 *Ibid.*
394 *Ibid.*, para. 127.
395 *Ibid.*, para. 10.
396 *Ibid.*, para. 127.
397 *Ibid.*, Q&A 127-5.
398 *Ibid.*, para. 127.
399 *Ibid.*, Q&A 127-2.
400 *Ibid.*, Q&A 127-6.
401 *Ibid.*, para. 127.
402 *Ibid.*, Q&A 127-3.
403 *Ibid.*, Q&A 127-4.
404 *Ibid.*, para. 128, Q&A 128-3.
405 *Ibid.*, Q&A 137-13.
406 *Ibid.*, Q&A 137-14.
407 *Ibid.*, paras. 129 and 130.
408 *Ibid.*, para. 135.
409 *Ibid.*, Q&A Other-4.
410 *Ibid.*, para. 132.
411 *Ibid.*, Q&A 132-1.
412 *Ibid.*, para. 133.
413 *Ibid.*, para. 122.
414 *Ibid.*, Q&A 122-1.
415 *Ibid.*, para. 122 and 125.
416 *Ibid.*, para. 123.
417 *Ibid.*, para. 124.
418 *Ibid.*, Q&A 124-1.
419 *Ibid.*, Q&A 137-5.
420 *Ibid.*, para. 144.
421 *Ibid.*, Q&A 144-1.
422 *Ibid.*, para. 144.
423 *Ibid.*, para. 131.
424 *Ibid.*, para. 126.
425 *Ibid.*, para. 145.
426 *Ibid.*, Q&A 142-7.
427 *Ibid.*, Draft Q&A 145-1.
428 *Ibid.*, Q&A 128-2.
429 *Ibid.*
430 *Ibid.*, Q&A 137-6.
431 *Ibid.*, Q&A 134-4.
432 *Ibid.*, para. 134.
433 *Ibid.*, para. 137.
434 *Ibid.*, para. 138.
435 *Ibid.*, Q&A 137-7.
436 *Ibid.*, Q&A 137-11.
437 *Ibid.*, Q&A 137-1.
438 *Ibid.*, Q&A 137-12.
439 *Ibid.*, Q&A 137-9 and 137-10.
440 *Ibid.*, para. 139.
441 *Ibid.*, para. 140.
442 *Ibid.*, Q&A 137-16.
443 *Ibid.*, Q&A 137-9 and 137-10.
444 *Ibid.*, para. 141.
445 *Ibid.*, para. 150.
446 *Ibid.*, para. 142.
447 *Ibid.*, Q&A Other-2.
448 *Ibid.*, para. 165.
449 *Ibid.*, Q&A 142-4.
450 *Ibid.*, Q&A 142-8.
451 *Ibid.*, Q&A 142-5.
452 *Ibid.*, Q&A 144-2.
453 *Understanding IAS 39*, PricewaterhouseCoopers, 2000, Chapter 8.
454 IAS 39, Q&A 142-1.
455 *Ibid.*, Q&A 137-4.
456 *Ibid.*, Q&A 142-1.
457 *Ibid.*, Q&A 128-1.
458 *Ibid.*, para. 146.
459 *Ibid.*, Q&A 146-3.
460 *Ibid.*, paras. 147 and 151, Q&A 146-1.
461 *Ibid.*, para. 143.
462 *Ibid.*, Q&A 146-1.
463 *Ibid.*, para. 152.
464 *Ibid.*, para. 151, Q&A 146-1.
465 *Ibid.*, para. 151.
466 *Ibid.*, Draft Q&A 158-3.
467 *Ibid.*, Q&A 142-3.
468 *Ibid.*
469 *Ibid.*, Q&A 142-2.
470 *Ibid.*, para. 147.
471 *Ibid.*, para. 151.
472 *Ibid.*, para. 148.
473 *Ibid.*, para. 148, Q&A 147-1.
474 *Ibid.*, Q&A 142-6.
475 *Ibid.*, Q&A 147-1.
476 *Ibid.*, Q&A 128-4.
477 *Ibid.*, para. 149, Q&A 149-1.
478 *Ibid.*, para. 153.
479 *Ibid.*, Q&A 153-1.
480 *Ibid.*, para. 153.
481 *Ibid.*, para. 154.
482 *Ibid.*, para. 155.
483 *Ibid.*, Q&A 128-4.
484 *Ibid.*, Q&A 137-15.
485 *Ibid.*, para. 156.
486 *Ibid.*, para. 157.
487 *Ibid.*, Q&A 157-1.
488 *Ibid.*, paras. 78, 94 and 158, Q&A 78-1.
489 *Ibid.*, para. 159.
490 *Ibid.*, Q&A 146-2.
491 *Ibid.*, Q&A 158-2.
492 *Ibid.*, Q&A 158-1.
493 *Ibid.*, Q&A 137-9 and 137-10.
494 *Ibid.*, para. 160.
495 *Ibid.*, para. 161.
496 *Ibid.*, Q&A 160-1.
497 *Ibid.*, para. 162.
498 *Ibid.*, para. 163.
499 *Ibid.*, Q&A 163-1.
500 *Ibid.*, para. 164.

501 *Ibid.*, Q&A 164-1.
502 *Ibid.*, Q&A 131-1.
503 *Ibid.*, Draft Q&A 158-5.
504 *Ibid.*, Q&A 122-2.
505 *Ibid.*, Q&A 122-3.
506 *Ibid.*, Q&A 131-3.
507 *Ibid.*, Q&A 131-2.
508 *Ibid.*, Draft Q&A 144-3.
509 *Ibid.*, Q&A 137-2.
510 *Ibid.*, Q&A 134-1.
511 *Ibid.*, Q&A 127-1.
512 *Ibid.*, Q&A 134-1.
513 *Ibid.*
514 *Ibid.*, Q&A 134-3.
515 *Ibid.*, Q&A 134-4.
516 *Ibid.*, Q&A 134-4.
517 *Ibid.*
518 *Ibid.*, Q&A 134-1-a and b.
519 *Ibid.*, Draft Annex to Q&A 134-1-b.
520 *Ibid.*, Q&A 121-1, 121-2, Draft Annexe to Q&A 121-2.
521 *Ibid.*, para. 171.
522 *Ibid.*, para. 172(a).
523 Fifth Batch of Proposed Implementation Guidance, Draft Q&A 172-10, IGC, December 2000.
524 IAS 39, para. 172(d) and (i).
525 *Ibid.*, para. 172(c).
526 *Ibid.*, Q&A 172-1.
527 *Ibid.*, Q&A 172-3.
528 *Ibid.*, Draft Q&A 172-10.
529 *Ibid.*, Q&A 172-7.
530 *Ibid.*, para. 172(g), Q&A 172-5.
531 *Ibid.*, Q&A 172-8.
532 *Ibid.*, para. 172(b).
533 *Ibid.*, Q&A 172-9.
534 *Ibid.*, Q&A 172-6.
535 *Ibid.*, para. 172(e).
536 *Ibid.*, para. 172(f).
537 *Ibid.*, Q&A 172-2.
538 *Ibid.*, para. 172(h).
539 *Ibid.*, Q&A 172-4.
540 IAS 32, para. 44.
541 *Ibid.*, para. 45.
542 *Ibid.*, para. 46.
543 *Ibid.*, para. 1.
544 *Ibid.*, para. 42.
545 *Ibid.*, para. 42.
546 *Ibid.*, para. 43A; IAS 39, para. 169(a).
547 IAS 32, para. 47.
548 *Ibid.*, para. 52.
549 IAS 39, para. 167(c).
550 IAS 32, para. 53.
551 *Ibid.*, para. 92.
552 *Ibid.*, para. 53.
553 *Ibid.*, para. 54.
554 *Ibid.*
555 IAS 39, paras. 167(a) and 168.
556 IAS 32, para. 55.
557 IAS 39, para. 167(c).
558 IAS 32, para. 57.
559 *Ibid.*, para. 56.
560 *Ibid.*, para. 58.
561 *Ibid.*, para. 59.
562 *Ibid.*, para. 60.
563 *Ibid.*, para. 61.
564 *Ibid.*, para. 62.
565 *Ibid.*, para. 63.
566 *Ibid.*, para. 64.
567 *Ibid.*, para. 65.
568 *Ibid.*, para. 67.
569 *Ibid.*, para. 66.
570 *Ibid.*, para. 68.
571 *Ibid.*, para. 69.
572 *Ibid.*, para. 70.
573 *Ibid.*, para. 71.
574 *Ibid.*, para. 72.
575 *Ibid.*, para. 73.
576 *Ibid.*, paras. 74 and 75.
577 *Ibid.*, para. 76.
578 *Ibid.*, para. 75.
579 *Ibid.*, para. 74.
580 *Ibid.*, para. 47.
581 *Ibid.*, para. 48.
582 *Ibid.*, para. 49.
583 *Ibid.*, para. 50.
584 *Ibid.*, para. 51.
585 *Ibid.*, para. 77.
586 IAS 39, para. 166.
587 IAS 32, para. 87.
588 *Ibid.*, para. 83.
589 *Ibid.*, para. 84.
590 *Ibid.*, paras. 77 and 85.
591 *Ibid.*, para. 77.
592 *Ibid.*, para. 90.
593 *Ibid.*, paras. 88, 89 and 90.
594 *Ibid.*, para. 90.
595 *Ibid.*, para. 91.
596 *Ibid.*, para. 92.
597 *Ibid.*, para. 93.
598 IAS 39, para.169(b).
599 *Ibid.*, Q&A 131-1.
600 *Ibid.*, para. 169(c).
601 IAS 32, para. 94.
602 IAS 39, para. 170.
603 *Ibid.*, Q&A 170-2.
604 *Ibid.*, para. 170.
605 *Ibid.*, Q&A 170-1.
606 *Ibid.*, para. 170.
607 *Ibid.*, paras. 44 to 46 (now deleted).
608 IAS 32, para. 95.
609 Discussion Paper, *Accounting for Financial Assets and Financial Liabilities*, Chapter 6, para. 2.4.
610 *Inside Track*, ASB, July 2001.
611 *Press Release*, IASB, 31 July 2001.

Chapter 11 Intangible assets and goodwill

1 INTRODUCTION

1.1 The incidence of intangible assets

Economic, commercial and marketing imperatives in the more developed world economies, particularly over the last twenty years, have driven many businesses to invest substantial sums in ways that were not previously commonplace. For example, it is no longer unusual for the premium paid to acquire a business to be greater than the balance sheet value of net assets acquired. The commercial importance of brands that are attractive to consumers, and the cost and uncertainty of attempting to develop them from scratch, has partly fuelled this trend. Equally, businesses that own successful brands spend large sums in maintaining consumer awareness of, and loyalty to them.

There has also emerged over the last five years or so the requirement to reflect in financial statements expenditure on a relatively new type of asset, based on software and related expenditure for computerised sales and marketing systems and website development. As with goodwill and brands, this type of expenditure was not unknown before. It is the commercial imperative brought about by much higher levels of spending on these items, and larger numbers of businesses incurring it, that has forced the topic into prominence.

These relatively high levels of expenditure on intangible aspects of commerce inevitably resulted in companies wanting to account for it in various different ways. As the incidence and magnitude of such expenditure increased, it became necessary for the ASB, and the accounting profession generally, to develop common rules for its recognition and treatment in financial statements. For example Extract 11.1 illustrates the substantial sums that may be invested in intangibles, in this case Reckitt Benckiser's intangibles at £1.6 billion total approximately 146% of shareholders funds. Of this intangible figure, all but £54 million is described as brands in the accompanying note, shown in Extract 11.2.

Extract 11.1: Reckitt Benckiser plc (2000)

Group Balance Sheet as at 31 December 2000 [extract]

		Group	
	Notes	**2000 £m**	1999 £m
Fixed assets			
Intangible assets	9	**1,638**	1,537
Tangible assets	10	**535**	514
Investments	11	**–**	–
		2,173	2,051
Capital and reserves			
Called up share capital (including non-equity capital of £5m)	21	**71**	70
Shares to be issued	21	**7**	8
Share premium account	22	**165**	145
Merger reserve	22	**142**	148
Profit and loss account	22	**731**	574
Total shareholders' funds (including non-equity shareholders' funds of £5m)		**1,116**	945

1.2 Background to accounting for intangible assets

The main debate surrounding the accounting treatment of expenditure on intangibles has centred on whether such expenditure should be written off immediately as incurred, or whether it should be capitalised in the balance sheet as a type of asset. A secondary consideration, if the decision to write off the expenditure was taken, was the manner of any write-off. For example was goodwill to be written off directly to reserves, rather than through the profit and loss account? If expenditure on intangibles was to be capitalised, there were a number of matters to be considered further. For example, could expenditure on creating a new brand from scratch (i.e. an internally developed intangible) be capitalised? Over what period would such expenditure be written off, if at all? Could such assets be revalued and if so on how would they be valued?

The situation by the early 1990s was that there were well established ways of accounting for goodwill (SSAP 22 – *Accounting for goodwill)* and for research and development costs (SSAP 13 – *Accounting for research and development*). At that time there was relatively little incidence of other 'traditional' intangibles such as patents and licenses, though 'new' intangibles such as brands were appearing on an increasing number of company balance sheets. There were no specific rules governing expenditure on intangibles such as brands, and the most common method of accounting for goodwill (writing it off directly against reserves) began to seem inappropriate for the large goodwill figures being generated by acquisitions.

This unsatisfactory situation was resolved by the ASB standardising the basis on which goodwill arising on acquisitions, and any other types of intangible asset, were to be treated by UK companies, and the manner in which such assets were to be amortised. There are now, under UK GAAP as well as under IAS, definite criteria that must be met before any expenditure may be considered to have given rise to an intangible asset. Similarly there are definite requirements governing the amortisation and revaluation of such assets. The ASB and the IASC have adopted a similar stance on the treatment of intangible assets, indeed the IASC's standard is clearly based upon that adopted by the ASB. In the UK, FRS 10 is the ASB's main pronouncement dealing with intangible assets and goodwill, while IAS 38 – *Intangible assets* – is the IASC's equivalent. However in the UK, SSAP 13 deals separately with intangible assets that arise from research and development expenditure, while IAS 38 includes them.

FRS 10 came into force for accounting periods ending on or after 23 December 1998, while IAS 38 is mandatory for financial statements for periods beginning on or after 1 July 1999. SSAP 13 was issued originally in 1977 and in revised form in January 1989.

The accounting treatment of software related expenditure is not quite so definitive, either in the UK or under IAS. There is an inherent difficulty in deciding if such expenditures should be recognised as tangible assets, intangible assets or expenses. This is particularly so in relation to the costs of developing web-based marketing and information provision systems. The late 1990s saw very large sums spent on the operation and development of websites and this led to the issue of UITF Abstract 29 – *Website development costs* – which is discussed mainly in Chapter 12 at 4.1.

2 UK REQUIREMENTS

2.1 Introduction

In the UK the Companies Act 1985 lays down broad principles and requirements for the accounting treatment for all types of fixed assets, including intangible assets, and their depreciation or amortisation. In general these provisions are also contained, explicitly or implicitly, within the various ASB pronouncements such as FRS 10 and SSAP 13.

Therefore the UK requirements section of the chapter will outline the Companies Act provisions followed by those of the other regulatory pronouncements, principally those of the relevant accounting standards. The detailed disclosures in financial statements required under UK GAAP for all types of intangible asset are dealt with separately at 3 below, that contains the requirements of the Companies Act, accounting standards and any other relevant pronouncements.

2.2 The requirements of the Companies Act 1985

2.2.1 *Definition and classification*

The Companies Act 1985 defines fixed assets as those which are intended for use on a continuing basis in the company's activities and any assets which are not intended for such use are taken to be current assets.[1] The Companies Act allows for the existence of three major classes of fixed asset:

I Intangible assets

II Tangible assets

III Investments [2]

Intangible assets, which by their nature will obviously be intended for continuing use within the business, may be disclosed under one of four headings:

1 development costs,

2 concessions, patents, licenses, trademarks, and similar rights and assets

3 goodwill

4 payments on account [3]

As is permitted by the Act, the format categories with Arabic numerals, shown above for intangible assets, may be modified to suit the circumstances of the business. For example Reckitt Benckiser use the term 'brands' in the note accompanying their balance sheet total of intangible assets, as shown in Extract 11.2.

Extract 11.2: Reckitt Benckiser plc (2000)

Notes to the Accounts
9 Fixed assets – intangible assets

Group	Brands £m	Goodwill £m	Total £m
Cost			
At 1 January 2000	1,503	52	1,555
Additions during the year	3	7	10
Exchange adjustments	94	2	96
At 31 December 2000	1,600	61	1,661
Accumulated write offs and amortisation			
At 1 January 2000	(14)	(4)	(18)
Written off/amortised during the year	(2)	(3)	(5)
At 31 December 2000	(16)	(7)	(23)
Net book amounts			
At 1 January 2000	1,489	48	1,537
At 31 December 2000	1,584	54	1,638

The amount or originally stated for brands represents the fair value at the date of acquisition of brands acquired since 1985. A brand is only recognised where it is supported by a registered trade mark, is established in the marketplace and holds significant brand share.

While the Act permits a company's balance sheet or profit and loss account to include items not otherwise covered by any of the items listed in the formats set out in Schedule 4 to the Act, it specifically prohibits the treatment of costs of *research* as an asset.[4]

Paragraph 20(1) of Schedule 4 states that development costs that are included under fixed assets in the balance sheet formats may only be included in a company's balance sheet in 'special circumstances', which are discussed further at 2.2.4 below.

2.2.2 *Measurement of the cost of intangible assets*

The Companies Act requires that, subject to any provision for depreciation or diminution in value, the amount to be included in respect of any fixed asset shall be its purchase price or production cost.[5] The Companies Act also allows revaluations of intangible assets except goodwill. In addition to historical cost, intangibles, except goodwill, may be included at current cost.[6]

The Companies Act further defines purchase price as any consideration, whether in cash or otherwise, given by the company in respect of that asset.[7] In addition, according to the Act, 'the purchase price of an asset shall be determined by adding to the actual price paid any expenses incidental to its acquisition'.[8]

'Expenses incidental to its acquisition' are those costs which have been incurred as a direct consequence of the purchase of the asset and are necessary in order to make it available for use.

The production cost of any asset (fixed or current, tangible or intangible) 'shall be determined by adding to the purchase price of the raw materials and consumables used the amount of the costs incurred by the company which are directly attributable to the production of that asset.

In addition there may be included in the production cost of an asset –

(a) a reasonable proportion of the costs incurred by the company which are only indirectly attributable to the production of that asset, but only to the extent that they relate to the period of production; and

(b) interest on capital borrowed to finance the production of that asset, to the extent that it accrues in respect of the period of production.'[9]

Under very specific and restrictive circumstances only, which are discussed below, FRS 10 allows intangible assets with a 'readily ascertainable market value' to be capitalised and/or revalued to their market value. However examples of this type of intangible assets are rare. For most intangible assets therefore, the normal requirement of the Companies Act is followed and intangible assets are included at purchase price, subject to any provision for depreciation or diminution in value. The issues relating to internally generated intangibles are discussed further at 4 below. Capitalisation of finance costs is discussed in Chapter 15.

2.2.3 *Depreciation of intangible assets*

The Companies Act requires any fixed asset, whether tangible or intangible, that has a limited useful economic life to be depreciated over that life, on a systematic basis, down to its residual value (if any).[10] Depreciation is to be based on the carrying value; on the purchase price or production cost under the historical cost rules,[11] and on the revalued amount if the alternative accounting rules are being followed.[12] Depreciation and other amounts written off tangible and intangible fixed assets must be shown, either on the face of the profit and loss account or in the notes, as further set out at 3 below.

The Act does not permit goodwill to be accorded an indefinite life.[13] This provision of the Companies Act is specifically rejected by the ASB in FRS 10, the provisions of which are discussed 2.3.4 below. FRS 10 allows for the possibility of goodwill having an indefinite life, in which case the true and fair override provisions of the Companies Act have to be invoked.

The Act also requires provisions for diminution in value to be made in respect of any fixed asset, even after depreciation, if the reduction in value is expected to be permanent.[14] This impairment aspect of accounting for fixed assets is covered in Chapter 13.

2.2.4 *Distributable profits*

The possible existence of development expenditure as an intangible asset in the balance sheet of a company has consequences for the amount of distributable profit available. This is because the Companies Act only allows distributions to be made out of net realised profits.[15] The Act also specifically provides that in determining such net realised profits, any amount which is included as an asset in the balance sheet as development costs, is to be treated as a realised loss,[16] unless:

(a) there are special circumstances in the company's case justifying the directors in deciding that the amount shown in respect of development costs is not to be treated as a realised loss; and

(b) the note to the accounts required by paragraph 20 of Schedule 4 to the Companies Act (reasons for showing development costs as an asset) states that the amount is not to be so treated and explains the circumstances relied upon to justify the decision of the directors to that effect.[17]

The 'special circumstances' referred to in (a) have been taken to mean circumstances where the development expenditure qualifies for deferral under SSAP 13. Thus providing the condition in (b) is also met, deferred development expenditure does not have to be treated as a realised loss for distributable profit purposes.

In September 1982 the CCAB issued a technical release on distributable profits which states that development costs carried forward in accordance with SSAP 13 will not normally affect distributable profits. It emphasised that such justification must be included in the note on capitalised development costs required under (b) above.[18] This provision has been repeated in substance in a more recent draft technical release on the same topic issued in August 2000 by the ICAEW.[19]

2.3 The requirements of FRS 10

2.3.1 *Introduction*

The commercial developments, briefly outlined at the start of the chapter, that caused large goodwill and brands valuation figures to be generated, highlighted the unsatisfactory nature of the allowable treatment of goodwill under SSAP 22 – *Accounting for goodwill.* One of the allowed treatments under SSAP 22 was to write off all the goodwill generated on an acquisition in total, directly against reserves, immediately, rather than through the profit and loss account. At least one consequence of this development was to remove from the post-acquisition financial statements any clear information about the acquiring group's post acquisition performance.

In addition to this aspect there was, in the early 1990s, no reference in UK GAAP to the intangible asset of brands, but brands were increasingly being recognised. One consequence of this was that a number of companies classified a large element of the premium on acquisition as brands, which were then treated as fixed assets with an indefinite life and not depreciated.

It was against this background of uncertainty that the ASB published FRS 10 – *Goodwill and intangible assets* – which came into force for accounting periods ending on or after 23 December 1998 and replaced SSAP 22. FRS 10 has the following clear objectives:

> 'The objective of this FRS is to ensure that:
>
> (a) capitalised goodwill and intangible assets are charged in the profit and loss account in the periods in which they are depleted; and
>
> (b) sufficient information is disclosed in the financial statements to enable users to determine the impact of goodwill and intangible assets on the financial position and performance of the reporting entity.'[20]

2.3.2 *Definition of intangible assets and goodwill*

FRS 10 – *Goodwill and intangible assets* – applies to all intangible assets with the exception of oil and gas exploration and development costs, research and development costs (which are discussed separately in this chapter) and any other intangible assets that are specifically addressed by another accounting standard.[21]

FRS 10 defines intangible fixed assets as:

> 'Non-financial fixed assets that do not have physical substance but are identifiable and are controlled by the entity through custody or legal rights.'[22]

'Identifiable' assets are further defined as those 'that can be disposed of separately without disposing of a business of the entity'.[23] This, therefore, really means 'separable' rather than 'identifiable'.

This definition has a number of important features. 'Control' is quite central to the ASB's notion of an asset, and central to the definition of an asset in the *Statement of Principles.* The notion of maintaining custody over something that has no physical substance may seem rather strange, but FRS 10 explains that it means such things as keeping technical or intellectual knowledge secret.[24]

The requirement for this to be through custody or legal rights means that pseudo-assets such as portfolios of clients or a team of skilled staff could not be recognised as assets as there is insufficient control. They therefore fall short of this requirement and are specifically excluded.[25]

The definition does not cover prepayments because they are not fixed assets.'[26]

Software costs to bring computer systems into working condition are deemed to be part of the related hardware, i.e. part of the related tangible fixed asset.[27] Thus FRS 10 solves by decree one problem of how to account for software expenditure; but there remains commercial pressure to recognise other types of software expenditure as an intangible asset. These are discussed further in 4.2 below.

Goodwill itself is defined by FRS 10 as:

> 'The difference between the cost of an acquired entity and the aggregate of the fair values of that entity's identifiable assets and liabilities. Positive goodwill arises when the acquisition cost exceeds the aggregate fair values of the identifiable assets and liabilities. Negative goodwill arises when the aggregate fair values of the identifiable assets and liabilities of the entity exceed the acquisition cost.'[28]

2.3.3 *Recognition of positive goodwill and intangible assets*

FRS 10 states that positive goodwill should be capitalised and recognised as an asset on the balance sheet, but that internally generated goodwill should not be capitalised.[29] The standard uses a three part approach to set different rules for the various circumstances in which intangible assets, other than goodwill, can be included in the balance sheet:

(a) Intangible assets bought separately should be capitalised at cost;[30]

(b) Intangible assets obtained in the course of acquiring a business should be recognised separately from goodwill if their value can be measured reliably on initial recognition;[31]

(c) Internally developed intangible assets should be recognised only if they have a readily ascertainable market value.[32]

The rule in (a) is quite straightforward, and is illustrated by Extract 11.3:

Extract 11.3: Manchester United plc

Notes to the Accounts
1 Accounting policies [extract]

Intangible fixed assets
The costs associated with the acquisition of players' registrations are capitalised as intangible fixed assets. These costs are fully amortised, in equal annual instalments, over the period of the players' initial contract.

11 Intangible fixed assets [extract]

Group	£'000
Cost of players' registrations	
At 1 August 1999	54,608
Additions	19,697
Disposals	(6,013)
At 31 July 2000	68,292
Amortisation of players' registrations	
At 1 August 1999	24,483
Charge for the year	13,092
Disposals	(1,598)
At 31 July 2000	35,977
Net Book Value of players' registrations	
At 31 July 2000	32,315
At 31 July 1999	30,125

In the application of (b), intangible assets obtained in the course of acquiring a business, the standard explains that the reliable measurement of value does not necessarily have to be a market value. FRS 10 also allows the use of valuation methods based on factors such as notional royalties or multiples of turnover to establish a reliable value on initial recognition.[33] The standard restricts the amount that can be attributed to intangible assets on the acquisition of a business, stating that the fair value attributed to any intangible must be limited to an amount that does not create or increase any negative goodwill that arises on the acquisition.[34] The requirement for reliable measurement is important, as otherwise FRS 10 requires that 'an intangible asset purchased as part of the acquisition of a business should be subsumed within the amount of the purchase price attributed to goodwill'.[35] However, the requirement that intangible assets must be capable of being measured reliably is not meant to be a major obstacle. The test is often likely to be met by such assets as brands, publishing rights and titles, concessions, patents, licences, trade marks and similar rights and assets.

UITF Information sheet 24 (January 2000) clarifies that certain non-separable licences, such as those that are necessary for a business to operate, may also be treated as intangible assets under FRS 10.

Diageo provides a typical example of the recognition of acquired intangibles in Extract 11.4:

Extract 11.4: Diageo plc (2000)

Accounting policies [extract]

Acquired brands and other intangible assets which are controlled through custody or legal rights and could be sold separately from the rest of the business are capitalised, where fair value can be reliably measured.

Notes

12 Fixed assets – intangible assets [extract]

Brands are stated at fair value on acquisition, denominated in the currencies of their principal markets. An annual review is carried out by the directors to consider whether any brand has suffered an impairment in value. The principal acquired brands included above are Johnnie Walker, Smirnoff, Pillsbury, Old El Paso, Progresso and Burger King.

It is with (c) internally developed intangible assets, that the position is more difficult and in this area the standard is quite restrictive. FRS 10 requires there to be a readily ascertainable market value before any internally generated intangible asset may be recognised.[36] FRS 10 defines a readily ascertainable market value as:

> 'The value of an intangible asset that is established by reference to a market where:
>
> (a) the asset belongs to a homogeneous population of assets that are equivalent in all material respects; and
>
> (b) an active market, evidenced by frequent transactions, exists for that population of assets.
>
> Intangible assets that meet those conditions might include certain operating licences, franchises and quotas. Other intangible assets are by their nature unique: although there may be similar assets, they are not equivalent in all material respects and so do not have readily ascertainable market values. Examples of such assets include brands, publishing titles, patented drugs and engineering design patents.'[37]

This definition explicitly rules out the possibility of recognising unique intangibles such as brands, publishing titles, and patented inventions if they are home-grown rather than acquired. The restrictive attitude of FRS 10 to internally generated intangibles is discussed further at 4.2 below.

2.3.4 *Amortisation of positive goodwill and intangible assets*

Depreciation is the term usually applied to tangible assets while 'amortisation' is the equivalent term for intangible assets. The standard adopts a combination of amortisation and impairment review in attempting to ensure that its objective 'that capitalised goodwill and intangible assets are charged in the profit and loss account in the periods in which they are depleted'[38] is achieved. A flowchart which depicts how the combination of amortisation and impairment review applies to different circumstances is shown below. Note that the impairment review aspects of FRS 10 are dealt with in Chapter 13 Impairment.

FRS 10 Amortisation and impairment review flowchart

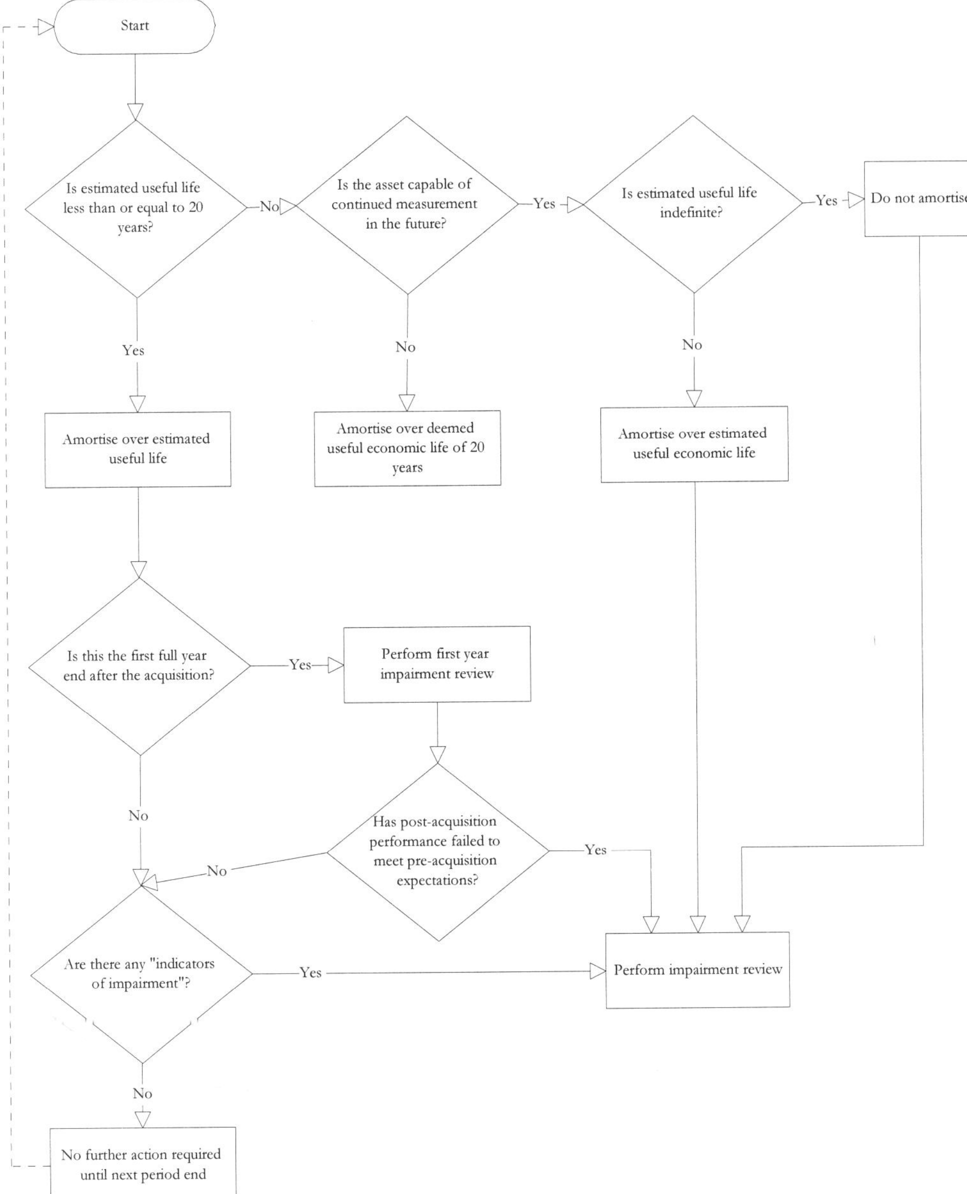

FRS 10 states that where goodwill and intangible assets are regarded as having limited useful economic lives, they should be amortised on a systematic basis over those lives but that where goodwill and intangible assets are regarded as having indefinite useful economic lives, they should not be amortised.[39]

FRS 10 makes it clear that amortisation of goodwill and intangible assets should be charged to the profit and loss account but it does not explicitly state that it should be charged in arriving at operating profit. However a number of Financial

Reporting Review Panel cases have confirmed that goodwill amortisation should be charged before operating profit is struck and that it should be included within the appropriate Companies Act format heading. For example PWS Holdings (see extracts 11.5 and 11.6) reissued their accounts at the request of the Financial Reporting Review Panel in order to clarify that goodwill amortisation is charged before arriving at operating profit.

Extract 11.5: PWS Holdings plc (1998)

Consolidated Profit and Loss Account for the Year Ended [extract]

	Note	30 September 1998 **£000**	30 September 1997 £000
Turnover	2and3	**10,976**	10,860
Other operating income	4	**2,307**	2,318
		13,283	13,178
Trading expenses	5 to 7	**(12,022)**	(12,054)
Operating profit before exceptional operating items		**1,261**	1,124
Net exceptional operating items	8	**(45)**	(16)
Operating profit after exceptional operating items		**1,216**	1,108

In the Panel's view, the £45,000 net exceptional operating item, which represented the amortisation of goodwill, should not have been classified as an exceptional item, as it failed to meet the FRS 3 definition by virtue of either size or incidence. Furthermore the Panel held that it was not appropriate that a new line item 'Operating profit before exceptional operating items' be introduced in circumstances where an there is an amortisation charge to be reported, as operating profit includes such an item.

Therefore the accounts of PWS Holdings were adjusted, as shown in the comparative figures in Extract 11.6, where the goodwill amortisation is included in the non-exceptional trading expenses figure for 1998.

Extract 11.6: PWS Holdings plc (1998)

Consolidated Profit and Loss Account for the Year Ended [extract]

		Note	**30 September 1999 £000**	30 September 1998 £000
Turnover		2 and 3	**12,443**	10,976
Other operating income		4	**2,378**	2,307
			14,821	13,283
Trading expenses	– non-exceptional	5 to 7	**(13,482)**	(12,067)
	– exceptional (pensions mis-selling provision)		**(153)**	–
Profit on ordinary activities before taxation			**1,186**	1,216

A Useful economic life

The standard defines useful economic lives of intangible assets and purchased goodwill differently as follows:

> 'The useful economic life of an intangible asset is the period over which the entity expects to derive economic benefit from that asset. The useful economic life of purchased goodwill is the period over which the value of the underlying business acquired is expected to exceed the values of its identifiable net assets.'[40]

An intangible asset's useful life is defined in terms of the periods expected to benefit, while that of goodwill is defined in terms of the length of time the underlying business will be worth more than its net assets. An apparent implication of this definition of goodwill is that it might normally have an indefinite life – an acquiring company is unlikely to consider that the value of the target will be lower under the its future management than at the time it is bought. However the standard also sets out to influence the length of useful life an entity will ascribe to an intangible asset.

> 'There is a rebuttable presumption that the useful economic lives of purchased goodwill and intangible assets are limited to periods of 20 years or less. This presumption may be rebutted and a useful economic life regarded as a longer period or indefinite only if:
>
> (a) the durability of the acquired business or intangible asset can be demonstrated and justifies estimating the useful economic life to exceed 20 years; and
>
> (b) the goodwill or intangible asset is capable of continued measurement (so that annual impairment reviews will be feasible).'[41]

If a life in excess of 20 years, or an indefinite life, is selected, an annual impairment review is required.

In practice, most preparers seem to have ignored the implication of the definition of the useful economic life of goodwill, and to have used an amortisation approach, perhaps because of the onerous consequences of doing otherwise. Tesco provides a typical example of a goodwill policy where a life of up to a maximum of 20 years has been chosen.

Extract 11.7: Tesco PLC (2001)

Accounting policies

Goodwill

Goodwill arising from transactions entered into after 1 March 1998 is capitalised and amortised on a straight line basis over its useful economic life, up to a maximum of 20 years. All goodwill from transactions entered into prior to 1 March 1998 has been written off to reserves.

There are, however, a number of companies who have chosen to ascribe indefinite useful lives to goodwill and therefore have to utilise the true and fair override to do so, for instance Cadbury Schweppes as illustrated in Extract 11.8.

Extract 11.8: Cadbury Schweppes plc (2000)

Since 1998, acquired goodwill has been capitalised and its subsequent measurement (via annual impairment review or an annual amortisation charge) determined based on the individual circumstances of each business acquired. Goodwill written off to reserves prior to 1998 has not been recorded on the balance sheet.

The Group has concluded that goodwill arising on its associate, Dr Pepper/Seven Up Bottling Group ("DPSUBG"), should not be amortised as it has an indefinite useful economic life. This investment is considered to have indefinite durability that can be demonstrated, and the value of the investment can be readily measured. Additionally, no amortisation was charged in 1999 or 1998 on goodwill arising on Amalgamated Beverages Industries Ltd ("ABI"). ABI was disposed of in 2000.

DPSUBG operates in a longstanding and profitable market sector; the US soft drinks bottling industry has over 100 years of history. The sector has high market entry barriers due to the nature of licence agreements with soft drink concentrate owners (including the Group's subsidiary Dr Pepper/Seven Up, Inc. ("DPSU")) and the capital required to operate as a bottler and distributor. As an associate, the company is managed separately from the Group and can be valued on a discounted cash flow basis.

The Group has not amortised this goodwill, a departure from the Companies Act 1985 Paragraph 21 of Schedule 4, for the over-riding purpose of giving a true and fair view of the Group's results, for the reasons outlined above. If the goodwill arising on DPSUBG and ABI had been amortised over a period of 20 years, operating profit and investment in associates would have decreased by £15m in 2000 (1999: 1998: £5m).

The standard stresses that where the economic benefits are achieved through legal rights that have been granted for a finite period, the economic life of the intangible asset may only be assessed as longer than that period if the legal rights are renewable and renewal is assured.[42]

The presumption that the useful life of both goodwill and intangible assets will not exceed 20 years can be rebutted only where:

(a) the durability of the acquired business or intangible asset can be demonstrated and justifies estimating the useful economic life to exceed 20 years; and

(b) the goodwill or intangible asset is capable of continued measurement (so that the annual impairment reviews will be feasible).[43]

Durability depends on a number of factors such as:

- the nature of the business;
- the stability of the industry in which the acquired business operates;
- typical lifespans of the products to which the goodwill attaches;
- the extent to which the acquisition overcomes market entry barriers that will continue to exist;
- the anticipated future impact of competition on the business.[44]

Several companies regard their intangible assets as having an indefinite life and do not amortise them. An example is Reckitt Benckiser, as shown below.

Extract 11.9: Reckitt Benckiser plc (2000)

Accounting Policies

Intangible fixed assets [extract]

Acquired brands are only recognised on the balance sheet as intangible assets where title is clear, brand earnings are separately identifiable, the brand could be sold separately from the rest of the business and where the brand achieves earnings in excess of those achieved by unbranded products. The value of an acquired brand is determined by allocating the purchase consideration of an acquired business between the underlying fair values of the tangible assets, goodwill and brands acquired.

Brands are not amortised, as it is considered that their useful lives are not limited. Their carrying values are reviewed annually by the Directors to determine whether there has been any permanent impairment in value and any such reductions in their values are taken to the profit and loss account.

There may be instances where goodwill or intangible assets have an estimated useful economic life of more than 20 years, or the useful economic life is indefinite, but the goodwill or intangibles are not expected to be capable of continued measurement. By definition, it is not possible to perform an annual impairment review under these conditions. The standard implies that in such circumstances, the goodwill or intangible asset should be amortised over a deemed useful life of 20 years.

It is not entirely obvious what 'capable of continued measurement' means. The standard states that 'Goodwill and intangible assets will not be capable of continued measurement if the cost of such measurement is considered to be unjustifiably high. This may be the case when, for example:

- acquired businesses are merged with existing businesses to such an extent that the goodwill associated with the acquired business cannot readily be tracked thereafter; or
- the management information systems used by the entity cannot identify and allocate cash flows at a detailed income-generating unit level; or
- the amounts involved are not sufficiently material to justify undertaking the detailed procedures of annual impairment reviews.'[45]

The first bullet point has a bearing on the rules for the impairment review where an acquired business is merged with an existing business. This circumstance is the subject of detailed procedures, as set out in FRS 11, and discussed in Chapter 13 at 2.2.8. The second bullet point appears to raise the possibility of companies with poorer management information being able to avoid undertaking an impairment test. However, such companies would then have to apply a maximum economic life of 20 years to their goodwill and intangible assets.

One scenario where goodwill may not be capable of continued measurement is where it arises on the acquisition of an associate. Most investors are unlikely to be able to obtain detailed cash flows of their associates in order to perform an impairment review. Accordingly, in most cases, goodwill on associates will be written off over a maximum of 20 years.

Although the useful economic life of goodwill and intangibles is often uncertain, the standard makes it clear that this uncertainty should not bc grounds for adopting a 20 year period by default.[46] Nor should the life be unrealistically short or goodwill or an intangible asset written off as impaired, unless that impairment can be justified by reference to an impairment test.[47]

FRS 10 requires the review of the estimated useful lives of goodwill and intangible assets at the end of each reporting period and their revision if necessary.[48] If the useful economic life is revised (either extended or shortened), then the carrying value of the goodwill or intangible assets at the date of revision should be amortised over the remaining useful life of that asset.

In December 2000 the UITF published Abstract 27 – *Revision to estimates of the useful economic life of goodwill and intangible assets* – which clarified the way in which a change from a useful life of over twenty years to twenty years or fewer, should be treated. If an entity that has previously rebutted the twenty year life presumption, subsequently decides it is now unable or unwilling to do so; the consequence is that amortisation over a period of up to 20 years from the date of acquisition becomes necessary. UITF 27 clarifies that the change should be treated as a change of useful economic life (and thus accounted for prospectively in accordance with paragraph 33 of FRS 10) rather than as a change of accounting policy (with a consequential prior period adjustment). The UITF concluded that:

'(a) where estimates of the useful economic lives of goodwill or intangible assets are revised, the carrying value should be amortised over the revised remaining useful economic life, as required by paragraph 33 of FRS 10; and

(b) this requirement applies equally where the presumption of a 20-year life has previously been rebutted, as it does to other revisions of estimates of the useful economic lives of goodwill and intangible assets.[49]

If the review results in the estimated useful economic life being extended to more than 20 years *from the date of acquisition*, the additional requirements of the standard applying to goodwill and intangible assets that are amortised over periods of more than 20 years become applicable.

B Amortisation methods and residual values

In amortising goodwill, no residual value may be attributed to it.[50] This corresponds to the requirements of the Companies Act 1985. In contrast, a residual value may be assigned to an intangible asset, but only if such residual value can be 'measured reliably'.[51] FRS 10 suggests that, in most cases, the residual value of an intangible asset may be insignificant and will be capable of being measured reliably only when:

(a) there is a legal or contractual right to receive a certain sum at the end of the period of use of the intangible asset; or

(b) there is a readily ascertainable market value for the residual asset.[52]

Having established the original carrying value of the goodwill or intangible asset, its estimated useful economic life and the amount of its residual value (if applicable), the only remaining question concerning amortisation is how to spread the amount to be amortised over the estimated useful economic life. FRS 10 states that 'the method of amortisation should be chosen to reflect the expected pattern of depletion of the goodwill or intangible asset. A straight line method should be chosen unless another method can be demonstrated to be more appropriate'.[53] If an intangible asset relates to an entitlement to produce a given quantity of a product, an acceptable method of amortisation could be on a unit-of-production basis.[54] In addition the standard does specifically prohibit methods of amortisation of goodwill which aim to produce a constant rate of return on the carrying value of an investment.[55] Hence an annuity approach (briefly explained in Chapter 12 at 2.3.4 (c)) is ruled out.

2.3.5 *Negative goodwill*

Negative goodwill arises in accounting for an acquisition where the amount paid for a business is less than the fair value of the net assets acquired. FRS 10 requires that it should be shown as a negative asset in the balance sheet, immediately after any positive goodwill, with a sub-total of the net amount of positive and negative goodwill also shown.[56] The ASB's view was that the requirement to include negative goodwill within the assets section of the balance sheet ensured consistency with the treatment of positive goodwill. Some standards of other bodies require negative goodwill to be offset against the fair value of fixed assets acquired. The ASB rejected this possibility because it would mean that these assets would be valued at something other than their fair value, contrary to the requirements of FRS 7. It might seem more obvious for negative goodwill be included as a deferred credit in the balance sheet. Unfortunately it does not fit the definition of a liability under the Board's *Statement of principles*, which may be why that option was rejected by the Board, but neither does the *Statement of principles* justify the appearance of a negative asset.

FRS 10 requires that negative goodwill is subsequently released to the profit and loss account on one of the two bases. The primary basis on which negative goodwill is to be released to the profit and loss account is over the periods in which the non-monetary assets acquired when the negative goodwill was generated are recovered, whether through depreciation or sale.[57] The reference to 'non-monetary assets', which includes items such as stocks, may not actually postpone recognition of negative goodwill for very long. Since stocks are usually turned over relatively quickly, any negative goodwill up to the fair value of the stocks may be released to the profit and loss account over a short period following the acquisition.

The secondary basis on which negative goodwill should be released to the profit and loss account involves that element, if any, of negative goodwill in excess of the fair values of non-monetary assets acquired. This element should be released 'in the periods expected to be benefited'.[58] The exact meaning of this wording is not completely clear, but any reasonable interpretation is likely to be acceptable. It is unusual for negative goodwill to exceed the non-monetary assets acquired. Where it does apply, the amount of negative goodwill that is released in this way should be disclosed, together with an explanation of where it came from and the period over which it is being released.[59]

Although the positioning of any negative goodwill released to the profit and loss account is not specifically dealt with in the standard, we believe that releases of negative goodwill should be credited in arriving at operating profit, mirroring the way positive goodwill is charged.

Babcock has a significant amount of negative goodwill (which until 1999 actually exceeded its positive goodwill) as shown in this extract.

Extract 11.10: Babcock International Group PLC (2001)

Accounting policies

Goodwill When the fair value of the consideration for an acquired undertaking exceeds the fair value of its separable net assets the difference is treated as purchased goodwill and is capitalised and amortised through the profit and loss account over its estimated economic life. The estimated economic life of goodwill is between ten and twenty years.

Where the fair value of the separable net assets exceeds the fair value of the consideration for an acquired undertaking the difference is treated as negative goodwill and is capitalised and amortised through the profit and loss account in the period in which the non-monetary assets acquired are recovered. In the case of fixed assets this is the period over which they are depreciated, and in the case of current assets, the period over which they are sold or otherwise realised.

12 Fixed assets – intangible assets

Group

	Goodwill £'000	Negative goodwill £'000	Development costs £'000	**Total £'000**
Cost				
At 1 April 2000	38,715	(34,406)	6,731	**11,040**
On acquisition of subsidiaries (note 29)	63,778	–	-	**63,778**
Adjustment in the year (note 29)	(986)	–	-	**(986)**
At 31 March 2001	**101,507**	**(34,406)**	**6,731**	**73,832**
Accumulated amortisation				
At 1 April 2000	(10,914)	15,703	(4,960)	**(171)**
(Charge)/credit for the year	(2,314)	3,787	(264)	**1,209**
As at 31 March 2001	(10,914)	15,703	(4,960)	**(171)**
Net book value at 31 March 2001	**88,279**	**(14,916)**	**1,507**	**74,870**
Net book value at 31 March 2000	27,801	(18,703)	1,771	10,869

The standard states quite clearly that purchased goodwill arising on a single transaction should not be divided into positive and negative components.[60] It is not clear whether this should also apply if an entity acquires a number of separate businesses as part of a single transaction. To apply the standard literally could lead to anomalous results, not least if one of the businesses were subsequently sold.

2.3.6 *Goodwill arising before FRS 10*

FRS 10 does not have to be applied to goodwill that arose in periods before the standard came into force. Although it is permitted to bring this old goodwill on to the same basis as the new goodwill, the ASB acknowledged that this might be impracticable. Consequently, old goodwill may continue to be accounted for under the previously existing standard SSAP 22. By far the predominant practice under SSAP 22 was to write goodwill off directly to reserves and leave it there. FRS 2 requires that any goodwill previously directly written off must be included in the gain or loss on sale reported in the profit and loss account, if the business it related to is subsequently sold. Also included in FRS 10 paragraph 71 was the requirement that the amount of 'old' goodwill that remained written off against reserves must be disclosed.

For companies that elected not to resurrect old goodwill from reserves on implementing FRS 10, this remains the regime. Goodwill remains in reserves, offset against a suitable reserve, unless and until the business concerned is disposed of, at which point it is recycled through the profit and loss account. De Vere Group is one example of many companies who decided not to reinstate 'old' goodwill on adopting FRS 10

Extract 11.11: De Vere Group plc (2000)

Accounting policies
Basis of Consolidation [extract]

For acquisitions prior to September 1998, the difference between the cost of investment in subsidiary and associated undertakings and businesses acquired and the fair value of relevant net assets at the date of acquisition was dealt with as a movement on reserves. On subsequent disposal of such businesses such goodwill is taken into account in determining the profit or loss on sale or closure.

2.3.7 *Impairment of goodwill and intangible assets*

In addition to its provisions concerning the amortisation of goodwill and intangible assets, FRS 10 also requires that the carrying value of any intangible asset should be reviewed for impairment as follows.

Goodwill and intangible assets that are amortised over a period of 20 years or less from the date of acquisition should be reviewed for impairment at the end of the first full financial year following the acquisition and in other periods if there are indicators of impairment.[61]

If the amortisation period exceeds 20 years from the date of acquisition or the assets are not amortised, they should be reviewed for impairment at the end of each reporting period.[62]

Reference should be made to Chapter 13 for a full discussion and explanation of impairment, including FRS 11 – *Impairment of fixed assets and goodwill* – and the special provisions contained within FRS 10 concerning the recognition and accounting treatment of impairment of goodwill.

2.4 The requirements of SSAP 13

2.4.1 *Introduction*

SSAP 13 – *Accounting for research and development* – was published by the Accounting Standards Committee (the forerunner of the ASB) in December 1977, with a revised standard being issued in 1989. Prior to this companies adopted a variety of approaches to accounting for this type of expenditure, particularly in manufacturing industries that required high levels of research expenditure. In at least one case this led to a largely unforeseen and spectacular collapse, so the commercial and political imperative to standardise the accounting for research and development expenditure was considerable at the time SSAP 13 was originally published. It is important to note that research and development expenditure that falls to be capitalised is an intangible fixed asset.

Some of the terminology within SSAP 13 is rather different from that currently used. For example SSAP 13 describes the capitalisation of development expenditure in terms of deferred expenditure being matched against future revenue:

> 'The development of new products or services is, however, distinguishable from pure and applied research. Expenditure on such development is normally undertaken with a reasonable expectation of specific commercial success and of future benefits arising from the work, either from increased revenue and related profits or from reduced costs. On these grounds it may be argued that such expenditure, to the extent that it is recoverable, should be deferred to be matched against the future revenue.'[63]

The ASB's *Statement of principles* does not generally describe or discuss items included in the balance sheet as assets in terms of deferred expenditure awaiting matching revenue. Expenditure is now only recognised as an asset if it fits the definition of 'rights or other access to future economic benefits controlled by an entity as a result of past transactions or events.'[64] Presumably the justification for the inclusion of development expenditure as an asset at all is that it represents access to future economic benefits controlled by the entity.

2.4.2 *Definitions*

Research and development expenditure is defined in SSAP 13 as expenditure falling into one or more of the following broad categories:

(a) *pure (or basic) research:* experimental or theoretical work undertaken primarily to acquire new scientific or technical knowledge for its own sake rather than directed towards any specific aim or application;

(b) *applied research:* original or critical investigation undertaken in order to gain new scientific or technical knowledge and directed towards a specific practical aim or objective;

(c) *development:* use of scientific or technical knowledge in order to produce new or substantially improved materials, devices, products or services, to install new processes or systems prior to the commencement of commercial production or commercial applications, or to improving substantially those already produced or installed.'[65]

The definitions of the different types of research and development used in the standard were based on those used by the Organisation for Economic Co-operation and Development (OECD).[66] However, as paragraph 4 of the standard states, 'the dividing line between these categories is often indistinct and particular expenditure may have characteristics of more than one category. This is especially so when new products or services are developed through research and development to production, when the activities may have characteristics of both development and production.' For example, a project may start out as basic research, the results of which may lead to the development of new products or systems, particularly in, say, the pharmaceutical industry.

The standard specifically excludes from the definition:

(a) expenditure incurred in locating and exploiting oil, gas and mineral deposits. However, development of new surveying methods and techniques as an integral part of research on geographical phenomena should be included in research and development;[67] and

(b) research and development expenditure which is reimbursed by a third party. Any such expenditure which has not been reimbursed at the balance sheet date should be dealt with as contract work in progress.[68]

2.4.3 *Recognition*

A Fixed assets used in the activity

The cost of fixed assets acquired or constructed in order to provide facilities for research and development activities over a number of accounting periods should be capitalised and written off over their useful life through the profit and loss account.[69] The depreciation so written off should be included as part of the expenditure on research and development.[70] Where an asset is used in the course of the development activities, however, the depreciation thereon can be regarded as part of the overhead costs to be included as part of development costs, if such costs are to be deferred (i.e. capitalised as an asset and depreciated).

B Pure and applied research expenditure

Expenditure on pure and applied research (except for fixed assets used for research purposes) should be written off in the year of expenditure through the profit and loss account.[71] SSAP 13 justifies this by explaining that such expenditure is required to maintain a company's business and competitive position generally; no one particular period will be expected to benefit and so these costs should be written off as they are incurred.[72] In any event, the Companies Act does not allow pure or applied research expenditure to be treated as an asset (see 2.2.1 above).

C Development expenditure

Under certain prescribed circumstances only, SSAP 13 allows development expenditure to be capitalised, but this is strictly to be considered on a project-by-project basis, not as a pool. The standard distinguishes between the development of new products or services, and pure or applied research. Development expenditure is normally undertaken with a view to commercial success and to future profits arising from the work, whether from reduced costs or increased revenues. On these grounds the standard holds that such expenditure, to the extent that it is recoverable, may be deferred (i.e. capitalised as an intangible asset) to be matched against future revenue.[73]

It is important to emphasise that SSAP 13 requires development expenditure to be written off in the year of expenditure except in the following circumstances when it *may* be deferred to future periods:

(a) there is a clearly defined project; and

(b) the related expenditure is separately identifiable; and

(c) the outcome of such a project has been assessed with reasonable certainty as to:
   (i) its technical feasibility, and
   (ii) its ultimate commercial viability considered in the light of factors such as likely market conditions (including competing products), public opinion, consumer and environmental legislation; and

(d) the aggregate of the deferred development costs, any further development costs, and related production, selling and administration costs is reasonably expected to be exceeded by related future sales or other revenues; and

(e) adequate resources exist, or are reasonably expected to be available, to enable the project to be completed and to provide any consequential increases in working capital.[74]

Where these circumstances exist, the standard permits (but does not require) development expenditure to be deferred to the extent that its recovery can reasonably be regarded as assured.[75] However, if a policy of deferral is adopted, it should be consistently applied to all development projects that meet the above criteria.[76]

2.4.4 *Amortisation and impairment*

SSAP 13 requires that any deferred (i.e. capitalised) development expenditure must be amortised, starting at the time the application being developed starts being commercially exploited:

> 'If development costs are deferred to future periods, they should be amortised. The amortisation should commence with the commercial production or application of the product, service, process or system and should be allocated on a systematic basis to each accounting period, by reference to either the sale or use of the product, service, process or system or the period over which these are expected to be sold or used.'[77]

There is also, in effect, an impairment review requirement in SSAP 13, although it is not characterised as such. Regular reviews of any deferred expenditure are required at the end of each accounting period to ensure the expenditure still qualifies for deferral under the provisions of the standard:

> 'Deferred development expenditure for each project should be reviewed at the end of each accounting period and where the circumstances which have justified the deferral of the expenditure (paragraph 25) no longer apply, or are considered doubtful, the expenditure, to the extent to which it is considered to be irrecoverable, should be written off immediately project by project.'[78]

In addition, FRS 11 – *Impairment of fixed assets and goodwill* – applies to development expenditure capitalised under the provisions of SSAP 13. Impairment is discussed in detail as a separate topic in Chapter 13.

3 REQUIRED UK DISCLOSURES

3.1 Introduction

This section sets out the principal disclosures required in financial statements compiled under UK GAAP for intangible assets and goodwill, followed separately by those required additionally for development expenditure. Within each part, the disclosures required by each authoritative source are separately shown.

3.2 Intangible assets and goodwill:

3.2.1 *Companies Act 1985*

A Balance sheet and profit and loss account

The statutory formats require that intangible fixed assets are disclosed under the headings shown below.

I Intangible assets

1 development costs,

2 concessions, patents, licenses, trademarks, and similar rights and assets

3 goodwill

4 payments on account[79]

Company accounts usually include only the net book amounts of any category of fixed asset on the face of the balance sheet, with the information required by the Arabic numerals relegated to the notes. The Act permits the format categories with Arabic numerals to be modified to suit the circumstances of the business.

If profit and loss account Formats 2 or 4 are chosen, then 'depreciation and other amounts written off tangible and intangible fixed assets' must be shown, either on the face of the profit and loss account or in the notes.[80] If Formats 1 or 3 are chosen, the equivalent information must be given in the notes to the accounts.[81]

If a provision for permanent diminution in value of any fixed asset has been made then it must be disclosed in the notes to the accounts if it is not shown in the profit and loss account.[82]

As discussed in Chapter 25, under FRS 3 the gain or loss on sale of fixed assets, including intangible fixed assets, is one of the three specified exceptional items which is required to be shown after operating profit in the profit and loss account.[83]

B Notes to the accounts

The note disclosures required by the Companies Act about the cost and depreciation of all fixed assets, including intangible fixed assets, are duplicated to some extent by accounting standards. The Act sets out the following required disclosures for each category of intangible fixed asset shown in the statutory formats (see above):

(a) the appropriate amounts at the beginning of the financial year and as at the balance sheet date, based either on historical cost (purchase price or production cost) or alternative accounting rules;[84]

(b) all movements during the year, including revaluation surpluses and deficits, acquisitions, disposals and transfers.[85] Other movements that might also be reflected in the carrying value of the asset, such as exchange differences, will also be disclosed in the note; and

(c) the cumulative amount of depreciation as at the beginning and end of the financial year on the appropriate basis of cost or valuation, the depreciation charge for the period and adjustments in respect of disposals or for other reasons.[86]

C Non-depreciation of goodwill

In the event that a company chooses to carry goodwill as a permanent asset and not amortise it, the company has to invoke the 'true and fair override' to justify departing from the statutory requirement to amortise goodwill. Under these circumstances the Companies Act requires disclosure of 'particulars of the departure, the reasons for it and its effect' in a note to the accounts.[87]

3.2.2 FRS 10

A Accounting policies

FRS 10 requires disclosure of the method used to 'value' intangible assets.[88] This disclosure comes under the heading 'Recognition and measurement' and therefore is not intended to cover the rare case of intangible assets that are being revalued, for which there are separate requirements. Instead, the word 'valued' refers to the initial measurement of the intangible asset when it is first recognised in the financial statements.

The following disclosures are required about the policies adopted for amortisation of positive goodwill and intangible assets:

(a) the methods and periods of amortisation of goodwill and intangible assets and the reasons for choosing those periods;[89]

(b) where an amortisation period is shortened or extended following a review of the remaining useful lives of goodwill and intangible assets, the reason and the effect, if material, should be disclosed in the year of change;[90]

(c) where there has been a change in the amortisation method used, the reason and the effect, if material, should be disclosed in the year of change;[91]

(d) where goodwill or an intangible asset is amortised over a period that exceeds 20 years from the date of acquisition or is not amortised, the grounds for rebutting the 20 year presumption should be given. This should be a reasoned explanation based on the specific factors contributing to the durability of the acquired business or intangible asset.[92]

If a business carries goodwill as an unamortised intangible asset, as noted above it will have to invoke the true and fair override to justify not complying with the Companies Act requirement to amortise goodwill. In this event FRS 10 paragraphs 59 and 60 require certain extra disclosures. Paragraph 59 of FRS 10 states that:

> 'Particulars of the departure, the reasons for it and its effect should be given in sufficient detail to convey to the reader of the financial statements the circumstances justifying the use of the true and fair override. The reasons for the departure should incorporate the explanation of the specific factors contributing to the durability of the acquired business or intangible asset…'

Paragraph 60 requires that the disclosures concerning the use of the true and fair override set out in FRS 18 – *Accounting policies* – are given. These supersede those of UITF Abstract 7. FRS 18 requires a 'clear and unambiguous' statement:

- that there has been a departure;
- that this is necessary to give a true and fair view;
- of the treatment normally required and of the treatment actually adopted;
- of why the prescribed treatment would not give a true and fair view.

Additionally, there should be a description of how the position shown in the financial statements is different as a result of the departure, normally with quantification of the difference. In the case of unamortised goodwill where a statement quantifying the effect of the departure is not reasonably practicable owing to the indefinite life ascribed to the asset, the FRS 18 statement should explain the circumstances.[93] FRS 18 is discussed in Chapter 2 at 7.

The disclosure required by FRS 18 should either be included, or cross-referenced, in the note stating compliance with accounting standards (as required by the Companies Act).[94]

B Notes to the accounts

FRS 10 requires the following information to be disclosed separately for positive goodwill, negative goodwill and each class of capitalised intangible asset. These requirements largely duplicate the Companies Act requirements described above:

(a) the cost or revalued amount at the beginning of the financial period and at the balance sheet date;

(b) the cumulative amount of provisions for amortisation or impairment at the beginning of the financial period and at the balance sheet date;

(c) a reconciliation of the movements, separately disclosing additions, disposals, revaluations, transfers, amortisation, impairment losses, reversals of past impairment losses and amounts of negative goodwill written back in the financial period; and

(d) the net carrying amount at the balance sheet date.[95]

For negative goodwill, these further disclosures are required:

(a) the period in which it is being written back in the profit and loss account;[96] and

(b) where the negative goodwill exceeds the fair values of the non-monetary assets, an explanation of the amount and source of this excess and the period in which it is being written back.[97]

C Revaluation

Even though the revaluation of intangible assets is most unusual in practice, paragraphs 61 and 62 of FRS 10 sets out the disclosures that are required in this eventuality.

D Pre-FRS 10 goodwill

Paragraph 71 of FRS 10 provides that if goodwill remains eliminated against reserves the financial statements should state:

(i) the previous accounting policy ;

(ii) the cumulative amounts of goodwill taken to reserves, net of any goodwill attributable to businesses disposed of before the balance sheet date; and

(iii) the fact that this goodwill had been eliminated as a matter of accounting policy and would be charged or credited in the profit and loss account when the business to which it related is disposed of.

3.3 Research and development expenditure disclosures

3.3.1 Additional Companies Act 1985 disclosures

A Financial statements

As deferred development expenditure is to be treated as a fixed asset, all the Companies Act requirements for fixed assets disclosure (as set out in 3.2.1 above) apply to it.

In addition, where an amount is included in a company's balance sheet in respect of development costs the following information must be given in a note to the accounts:

(a) the period over which the amount of those costs originally capitalised is being written off; and

(b) the reasons for capitalising the development costs in question.[98]

B Directors' report

The Companies Act also requires that the directors' report should contain an indication of the activities (if any) of the company and its subsidiary undertakings in the field of research and development.[99] In practice this frequently results in a fairly minimal statement on the subject being given, for example:

Extract 11.12: British American Tobacco p.l.c. (2000)

Directors' Report [extract]
Research and development

The Group's research and development activities are concentrated on the development of new products, new processes, quality improvement of existing products and cost reduction programmes.

Research is also undertaken into various aspects of the science and behavioural science related to smoking, and the Group continues to provide significant funding for independent studies.

A much more comprehensive example of this disclosure is that of GlaxoSmithKline which being a research based pharmaceutical business, has a much greater than usual level of research and development activity.

Extract 11.13: GlaxoSmithKline plc (2000)

Directors' Report [extract]
Research and development – Pharmaceuticals [extract]

The global biological and pharmaceutical Research and Development (R&D) function in GlaxoSmithKline is responsible for the generation of information and the acquisition of knowledge required to discover, develop, register, commercialise and effectively market innovative prescription medicines, vaccines and delivery systems for the treatment and prevention of human disease.

Fundamental to this goal is a thorough understanding of the diseases under investigation, increasingly through original work in genetics and predictive medicine research. In addition to the work to create new medicines and vaccines, extensive efforts are made to gain a clear understanding of the unmet needs of patients and healthcare providers as a contribution to the overall direction of R&D.

In 2000 Glaxo Wellcome and SmithKline Beecham together invested over £2.4 billion in pharmaceuticals R&D.

Approximately 16,000 staff are involved in biological and pharmaceutical R&D activities, at more than 20 sites worldwide.

These sites include:

– UK:	Beckenham, Cambridge, Dartford, Greenford, Harlow, Stevenage, Tonbridge, Ware, Welwyn Garden City
– USA:	Research Triangle Park, North Carolina; Philadelphia, Upper Merion and Upper Providence, Pennsylvania; Santa Clara and Palo Alto, California
– Belgium:	Rixensart
– Canada:	Mississauga
– France:	Les Ulis, Rennes
– Italy:	Verona, Milan
– Japan:	Tsukuba Science City and Takasaki
– Spain:	Madrid
– Switzerland:	Geneva

During 2000 a significant amount of work in R&D went into preparing plans and procedures for the optimal integration of key Glaxo Wellcome and SmithKline Beecham R&D processes, so that GlaxoSmithKline would be able to operate effectively and efficiently from day one of the merger. Despite the resources devoted to these activities, several significant new medicines were delivered on schedule to the markets

3.3.2 *SSAP 13*

The disclosure requirements of SSAP 13 are as follows:

(a) the accounting policy on research and development expenditure should be stated and explained;[100]

(b) the total amount of research and development expenditure charged in the profit and loss account should be disclosed, analysed between the current year's expenditure and amounts amortised from deferred expenditure.[101] It is emphasised that the amounts disclosed should include any amortisation of fixed assets used in the research and development activity;

(c) movements on deferred development expenditure and the amount carried forward at the beginning and the end of the period should be disclosed;[102] and

(d) deferred development expenditure should be disclosed under intangible fixed assets in the balance sheet.[103]

However, the information contained in (b) above need only be given by:[104]

(a) public companies (as defined in section 1 of the Companies Act 1985) or holding companies that have one or more public companies as a subsidiary;

(b) banking and insurance companies (as defined in section 744 of the Companies Act), and preparing accounts in accordance with Schedules 9 or 9A thereto, or holding companies that have one or more banking and insurance companies as a subsidiary; and

(c) private companies (and other enterprises) which do not satisfy the criteria, multiplied in each case by ten, for defining a medium-sized company under section 247 of the Companies Act.

    At present, this means that enterprises with any two of the following fall outside the exemption and will have to give the additional disclosures:

    (i) turnover exceeding £112m,

    (ii) total assets exceeding £56m,

    (iii) average number of employees exceeding 2,500.[105]

4 UK PRACTICAL ISSUES

4.1 The definition and cost of intangible assets

Critics of FRS 10 have questioned why the same intangible asset should sensibly pass or fail tests for inclusion on the balance sheet solely according to the manner in which it was acquired or created. However, by their nature, intangible assets have certain characteristics which cause unusual accounting difficulty, and this is what has led to these apparent inconsistencies. Some of these characteristics are described below.

A Identifiable and Separable

One element of the definition of intangible assets in FRS 10 is that they must be identifiable, meaning that they must be capable of separate disposal without disposing of the business to which they relate. The Companies Act[106] contains a similar concept and similar wording to FRS 10.

However, the characteristic of 'separability' is not generally seen as a criterion for recognition of an asset. There are many examples of tangible fixed assets which are not separable from the business which owns them, in the sense that the business could continue without them. Equally it can be convincingly argued that the brand of a one-brand company was not separable because without it there would be no business left. Whereas if it belonged to a company with a hundred brands then it would be separable, in spite of the fact that the same asset is involved in each case.

Possibly underlying the definition is the view that the intangible asset must be distinguishable from goodwill. The definition may have simply sought to disqualify assets which are too much like goodwill, by setting a test which goodwill itself could not satisfy. If this was so, an unfortunate side effect has been to introduce the above noted inconsistencies.

There is also a broader aspect of identifiability which may be relevant to the debate; this is the question of whether the intangible asset is a discrete asset, in the sense that the boundaries between it and other assets can be clearly and unequivocally drawn. In the case of intangible assets, discreteness is particularly hard to establish because of their essential intangibility. In some obvious cases it is possible to establish it, for example a right to an income stream which is independent of any other asset; such as a copyright giving royalty income.

However where the intangible is used in combination with other assets, then it is may be very hard to say where the boundaries of the asset lie. An example would be a set of brands that are used in combination with both the tangible assets of the business and other intangible assets, such as a skilled workforce, an established distribution network, active customer lists and an effective advertising campaign. It may be very difficult, if not impossible, to put an individual value on any of these intangible elements in a meaningful way.

B Maintenance or substitution?

A related difficulty in accounting for intangible assets is that it is often difficult to determine whether the asset originally recorded is being maintained or whether a new asset is being gradually substituted for it. This widens the question to include how best to account for the intangible asset in subsequent years. Should the original asset be written down as it erodes, even if a very similar asset grows up to replace it at the same time, as a result of management's efforts in nurturing the valuable aspects of the business? The question of whether the asset is the same one or a different one can take on a metaphysical air. For example, if a customer list is bought, does it have to be written off if the customers on the list change, even if the new ones are as valuable as the old ones? That is a relatively concrete example; it may be even more difficult to determine whether a brand remains the same asset over time as it is subtly reshaped to meet new market opportunities.

In FRS 10 and FRS 11 the ASB has taken a sensibly pragmatic view, that substitution does not matter so long as overall value is maintained, and thus it countenances indefinite lives for intangible assets. The Board has, though, dismissed the same argument in relation to tangible assets; FRS 15 rejects the notion that increases in value or regular maintenance obviate the need for depreciation, as discussed in Chapter 12 at 2.3.3.

C Uncertainty of cost of creation

A third difficulty, again on the same theme, is that when intangible assets are created, it is generally not as the result of specific expenditure on that particular asset but as the by-product of expenditures made in the general conduct of the business. The value of a brand is made not only by inventing a desirable product with a copyrightable name, but also by building market share in a whole host of ways. Thus determining the cost of an internally generated brand poses very considerable difficulties. Joint or by-product costing is not a new technique for accountants, but it would be tested beyond the limit if it had to address how to determine the cost of intangible assets developed as a result of the general operations of the business.

4.2 Internally generated intangible assets

FRS 10 does not allow the capitalisation of internally-generated intangible assets. The ASB acknowledged that there are some intangible assets that would be more appropriately treated in the same way as tangible fixed assets but claimed that it would be very difficult to define the difference between these and those intangibles that are essentially goodwill. Rather than run the risk of allowing internally-generated goodwill to be capitalised, the ASB has banned the capitalisation of all internally-generated intangibles.[107]

In spite of the ban some companics, cspccially thosc whosc cxisting intangiblcs did not meet the FRS 10 definition, have tried to find routes to avoid an inappropriate outcome. Great Universal Stores has invoked SSAP 13 as the relevant standard, as shown in Extract 11.14

Extract 11.14: The Great Universal Stores plc (2001)

1. Accounting policies

Other intangible fixed assets

Intangible fixed assets other than goodwill comprise the data purchase and data capture costs of internally developed databases and are capitalised under SSAP 13 to recognise these costs over the period of their commercial use. Depreciation is provided by equal annual instalments on the cost of the assets over three to five years.

13 Other intangible assets

Group	
Cost	
At 1 April 2000	292.5
Differences on exchange	29.2
Additions	86.3
Sales	(1.9)
At 31 March 2001	**406.1**
Amortisation	
At 1 April 2000	153.4
Differences on exchange	15.4
Charge for year	58.9
Sales	(0.5)
At 31 March 2001	**227.2**
Net Book Value at 31 March 2000	139.1
Net Book Value at 31 March 2001	**178.9**

We agree that such costs should be capitalised and amortised over the period that they benefit, but whether they properly fall under SSAP 13 is more questionable. That standard addresses only a narrow class of expenditure that relates to scientific or technical knowledge and does not really embrace costs of this kind. On the other hand, since this expenditure would not qualify to be capitalised under FRS 10, we entirely understand why it is desirable to assert that SSAP 13 is the more relevant standard.

So far the ASB has tended to address the problem of capitalisation of intangible assets by deeming some of them to be tangible fixed assets. Under FRS 10 the software content of making computer system or other computer-operated machinery into working condition for its intended use is to be treated as part of the tangible fixed asset.[108] Note that this only refers to software necessary to bring *new* hardware into use. The ASB has now also applied this solution to website development costs, stating in UITF Abstract 29 – *Website development costs* – that if they meet the recognition criteria they are to be treated as tangible fixed assets. This is discussed in Chapter 12 at 4.1.1.

This solves the immediate problem for the standard setter. However the real problem is not solved. There are new sorts of assets being developed by businesses, and the arbitrary ban on recognising internally generated intangible assets in FRS 10 seems increasingly unsuitable and unrepresentative of the underlying commercial reality. If anything, the decision in UITF 29 to call an intangible asset a tangible one indicates that both the distinction between tangible and intangible fixed assets, and the FRS 10 ban on recognising internally generated intangibles, are becoming increasingly unsustainable.

4.3 Practical issues with SSAP 13

4.3.1 *Types of activity and costs to be included in development expenditure*

Although the definition of research and development is very broad, there may be difficulties in determining what types of activity constitute 'research and development'. SSAP 13 states that research and development activity is distinguished from non-research based activity by the presence or absence of an element of innovation. If the activity departs from routine and breaks new ground it should normally be included; if it follows an established pattern it should normally be excluded.[109]

SSAP 13 gives illustrative examples of activities that would normally be included in research and development as follows:[110]

(a) experimental, theoretical or other work aimed at the discovery of new knowledge, or the advancement of existing knowledge;

(b) searching for applications of that knowledge;

(c) formulation and design of possible applications for such work;

(d) testing in search for, or evaluation of, product, service or process alternatives;

(e) design, construction and testing of pre-production prototypes and models and development batches;

(f) design of products, services, processes or systems involving new technology or substantially improving those already produced or installed; and
(g) construction and operation of pilot plants.

SSAP 13 also gives illustrative examples of activities which should not be included as follows:[111]

(a) testing and analysis either of equipment or product for purposes of quality or quantity control;
(b) periodic alterations to existing products, services or processes even though these may represent some improvement;
(c) operational research not tied to a specific research and development activity;
(d) cost of corrective action in connection with break-downs during commercial production;
(e) legal and administrative work in connection with patent applications, records and litigation and the sale or licensing of patents;
(f) activity, including design and construction engineering, relating to the construction, relocation, rearrangement or start-up of facilities or equipment other than facilities or equipment whose sole use is for a particular research and development project; and
(g) market research.

SSAP 13 does not contain guidance on the types of costs that *should* be allocated to the activities to be included as development expenditure. IAS 38, which is discussed at 5.3 below, does contain guidance on this issue. As is accepted practice, in the absence of authoritative guidance, it is acceptable to refer to other authoritative sources. We therefore suggest that in the event of difficulty, IAS 38 is taken as guidance in this matter.

4.3.2 *Changes in the treatment of development expenditure*

A Changes in accounting policy

Under SSAP 13 a company may choose a policy of either writing off, or deferring and amortising, development expenditure which fulfils all the conditions laid down in paragraph 25. In view of this initial choice, is it possible for a company to change from a policy of writing off such expenditure to one of deferring and amortising or vice versa? We believe that a change of policy will normally be acceptable; but it will be necessary to restate comparative figures to reflect the new policy in accordance with FRS 3 (see Chapter 25). Importantly, where a change of policy to deferring and amortising is contemplated, care should be taken to ensure that all the conditions required to allow deferral were fulfilled at the time the expenditure was incurred. If the conditions were not met at that time, then the costs should not be capitalised under the new policy but should remain written off. This is because such costs would not have been capitalised if the new policy had been in force at the time the expenditure was incurred.

In addition the requirements of FRS 18 – *Accounting policies* – concerning changes in accounting policies will have to be complied with before a change in policy towards deferral of development expenditure would allowable under UK GAAP. FRS 18 is discussed in Chapter 2 at 7.

B Expenditure not previously capitalised

A variation on the theme of changing the way development expenditure is treated arises when the recoverability of expenditure that was not capitalised originally because of uncertainty, subsequently becomes certain. The original SSAP 13 made it clear that such expenditure could not be reinstated as an asset; while the revised SSAP 13 does not mention it. We believe that such expenditure should not be reinstated as an asset.

C Expenditure previously capitalised and subsequently written down

Paragraph 29 of SSAP 13 requires deferred development expenditure to be reviewed annually and to be written down to its recoverable amount. What happens if at a later date the uncertainties that gave rise to the write-down no longer apply? Again, SSAP 13 is silent on this issue; however, consideration in this instance has to be given to the requirements of the Companies Act relating to provisions for diminutions in value of fixed assets. These require that where the reasons for which any provision was made have ceased to apply to any extent, then the provision shall be written back to the extent that it is no longer necessary.[112] These requirements of the Companies Act do not apply to the situation discussed above as no asset was recorded in the first instance.

In addition the requirements of FRS 11 concerning the reversal of impairment losses will have to be considered in these circumstances. Depending upon exactly what the reasons for the original write down were, FRS 11 contains strict rules governing whether impairments my be reversed. Chapter 13 deals with impairment as a separate topic.

4.3.3 *Current reporting practice*

Most major companies which incur research and development costs adopt a policy of writing off the expenditure as it is incurred.[113] One company which adopts such a policy is SmithKline Beecham, as illustrated below:

Extract 11.15: GlaxoSmithKline plc (2000)

Accounting policies [extract]
Research and development

Research and development expenditure is charged to the profit and loss account in the period in which is it incurred. Tangible fixed assets used for research and development are depreciated in accordance with the Group's policy.

Consolidated Profit and Loss Account [extract]

			2000
	Business performance £m	**Merger – restructuring and disposal of subsidiaries £m**	**Total £m**
Turnover	18,079	–	18,079
Cost of sales	(3,811)	(151)	(3,962)
Gross profit	14,268	(151)	14,117
Selling, general and administrative expenditure	(6,732)	(404)	(7,136)
Research and development expenditure	(2,510)	(16)	(2,526)
Trading profit	5,026	(571)	4,455

It is noteworthy that SmithKline Beecham has disclosed the research and development charge for the year as a separate item in the body of its profit and loss account, as opposed to disclosing the amount in the notes, which is the route which most companies have taken. Furthermore, in compliance with SSAP 13, the company treats its fixed assets which are used in research and development activities in the same way as any other fixed asset.

5 IAS REQUIREMENTS

5.1 Introduction

Unlike UK practice, IAS 1 – *Presentation of financial statements* – does not use the term fixed assets, instead drawing a distinction between current and non-current assets. However alternative terms are not prohibited:

> 'This Standard uses the term 'non-current' to include tangible, intangible, operating and financial assets of a long-term nature. It does not prohibit the use of alternative descriptions as long as the meaning is clear.'[114]

Nor under IAS is an entity required to separate its balance sheet into current and non-current assets, though it may do so. The classification of current assets used in FRS 1 is based upon realisation within 12 months of the balance sheet date, while all other assets are termed non-current.[115] If this distinction is not made, assets are to be presented broadly in order of their liquidity.[116] Paragraph 66 of IAS 1 makes it clear that intangible assets should be shown as a separate category of asset on the face of the balance sheet. Therefore under IAS, intangible assets, will normally appear as a separate category of asset in the balance sheet at a suitable point within non-current assets, or at a point in an undifferentiated balance sheet that reflects their relative liquidity – that is the time over which they are to be amortised. While the balance sheet figure for intangible assets may include goodwill, the relevant standards require more detailed disclosures of the constituent elements of the balance sheet figure to be included in the notes to the financial statements.

Negative goodwill should be presented as a deduction from the assets of the reporting enterprise, in the same balance sheet classification as goodwill.[117]

Of necessity IAS must apply to a large number of different statutory reporting regimes. For example with the imminent adoption of IAS for all listed companies in the European Union, IAS will be applied under at least 15 different member states' statutes. Consequently the requirements of IAS for intangible assets as dealt with below, are in addition to, not instead of the statutory requirements applicable to the entity.

There are two IASC standards currently in force that are relevant: IAS 22 - *Business Combinations (revised 1998)* – and IAS 38 – *Intangible assets*. IAS 22 deals with all aspects of business combinations, but its treatment of goodwill and negative goodwill concern this chapter. IAS 38 scopes out any intangible assets that are dealt with in other international accounting standards, as well as financial assets, mineral rights and those arising from insurance contracts. The Standing Interpretations Committee of the IASC, which has a similar role to that of the UITF in the UK, has also published SIC-22 – *Business Combinations - Subsequent Adjustment of Fair Values and Goodwill Initially Reported* – which is relevant to this chapter.

5.2 The requirements of IAS 22 – Business Combinations – concerning goodwill

5.2.1 *Goodwill: definition recognition and measurement*

IAS 22 is laid out in sections that deal with various aspects of business combinations and it deals separately with goodwill (by which it means positive goodwill) and negative goodwill. IAS 22 does not formally define goodwill, but it does incorporate a description within paragraph 41:

> 'Any excess of the cost of the acquisition over the acquirer's interest in the fair value of the identifiable assets and liabilities acquired as at the date of the exchange transaction should be described as goodwill and recognised as an asset.'

The standard requires goodwill to be carried at cost less any accumulated amortisation and any accumulated impairment losses.[118] Because a separate standard – IAS 38 – deals with intangible assets other than goodwill arising on an acquisition, IAS 22 assumes the distinction between goodwill and other types of intangible asset, such as brands, has been satisfactorily made. For the same reason IAS 22 has no references to internally generated goodwill, as this cannot arise from an acquisition.

IAS 22 envisages circumstances where either assets or liabilities that could not be separately recognised at the time of the acquisition may subsequently become so, or their fair values may need to be adjusted as additional evidence becomes available.

Consequently, goodwill will be adjusted as long as this change is made by the end of the first annual accounting period beginning after the acquisition, and the carrying amount of the goodwill does not increase beyond its recoverable amount as defined in IAS 36[119] (refer to Chapter 13 at 4.2 for a discussion of IAS 36 – *Impairment of assets*). SIC-22 clarified the way these adjustments should be dealt with, in brief requiring that they should be:

> 'calculated as if the adjusted fair values had been applied from the date of acquisition. As a result, the adjustment should include both the effect of the change to the fair values initially assigned and the effect of depreciation and other changes which would have resulted if the adjusted fair values had been applied from the date of acquisition.'[120]

In addition SIC-22 makes it clear that:

> 'the carrying amount of goodwill or negative goodwill should also be adjusted, when necessary, to the amount which would have been determined if the adjusted fair values had been available at the date of acquisition. As a result, goodwill amortisation or recognition of negative goodwill is also adjusted from the date of acquisition.'[121]

SIC-22 requires all such adjustments to go through the income statement.[122]

IAS 38 expands on the treatment of goodwill which is found to be impaired by the end of the first annual accounting period after acquisition.[123] Normally any adjustment to the fair values of the assets will affect the carrying value of goodwill. If, however, there is evidence that goodwill itself has become impaired then the loss should be expensed as part of the results for the year.[124]

Adjustments made after the first annual accounting period beginning after the acquisition must be dealt with through the income statement[125], as must impairments to goodwill that have arisen as a result of specific events or changes in circumstances that have arisen since the date of acquisition.[126]

The reversals of provisions made by the acquirer to reduce or terminate the activities of the acquired company are treated differently. They are reflected as adjustments to goodwill or negative goodwill and the adjusted amount of goodwill is be amortised prospectively over its remaining useful life.[127]

5.2.2 *Negative goodwill: definition recognition and measurement*

IAS 22 incorporates a description of negative goodwill into paragraph 59, which states:

> 'Any excess, as at the date of the exchange transaction, of the acquirer's interest in the fair values of the identifiable assets and liabilities acquired over the cost of the acquisition, should be recognised as negative goodwill.'

The standard cautions against the possibility of recognising phantom goodwill, by stating that:

> 'The existence of negative goodwill may indicate that identifiable assets have been overstated and identifiable liabilities have been omitted or understated.

It is important to ensure that this is not the case before negative goodwill is recognised.'[128]

The standard draws a distinction between various types of negative goodwill, according to what it 'relates to', and on this basis lays down how it should be recognised in the profit and loss account.

Negative goodwill may relate to expected future losses and expenses that have been identified by the acquirer in its plan for the acquisition. These may be measured reliably, but do not represent identifiable liabilities at the date of acquisition. The appropriate portion of negative goodwill will be recognised as income when the losses and expenses are recognised.[129]

If the negative goodwill does not relate to identifiable expected future losses and expenses in this way, it is a gain that should be recognised as income as follows:

(a) on a systematic basis over the remaining weighted average useful life of the identifiable acquired depreciable/amortisable assets; and

(b) to the extent that it exceeds the fair values of acquired identifiable non-monetary assets, it should be recognised as income immediately.[130]

In the case of monetary assets, a gain should be recognised as income immediately.[131]

5.2.3 *Amortisation of goodwill under IAS 22*

In direct contrast to the UK position under FRS 10, IAS 22 does not allow goodwill to be ascribed an indefinite life. The standard points out that the acquirer is prepared to pay for goodwill in anticipation of future economic benefits, whether from synergy between identifiable assets (presumably acquired and existing assets) or from assets that individually do not qualify for recognition.[132] This also means that it is difficult to estimate the useful life of goodwill and, it is argued, makes such estimates inherently more unreliable the longer the estimated life. Hence, there is a presumption in the standard that the life will not exceed twenty years.[133]

The standard, like the UK equivalent, expresses a strong preference for a maximum life of twenty years for goodwill, but will allow under certain specific conditions only, a longer life. In the words of the standard, there exists a 'rebuttable presumption that the useful life of goodwill will not exceed twenty years from initial recognition'.[134] Extract 11.16 shows a typical goodwill accounting policy under IAS.

Extract 11.16: GN Great Nordic (2000)

Accounting policies [extract]
Consolidation [extract]

When the acquisition price exceeds the fair value of the net assets acquired, including provisions for restructuring the acquired companies, a positive differential is capitalized as goodwill. Goodwill is amortized systematically in the income statement in accordance with an individual assessment of the asset's expected useful life, which may not, however, exceed 20 years. In the year of acquisition, amortization is pro rata.

IAS 22 requires goodwill to be amortised on a systematic basis over its useful life. The period chosen should reflect the best estimate of the period in which future benefits from the acquisition are expected to accrue. While stating that the amortisation method should reflect 'the pattern in which the benefits arising from the goodwill are expected to be consumed', the Standard expresses a strong preference for the straight-line method. This should be adopted unless there is persuasive evidence that another method is more appropriate in the circumstances.[135] Enterprises are especially dissuaded from applying methods that result in a lower amount of accumulated depreciation than the straight line method.[136]The amortisation for each period should be recognised as an expense in the income statement[137]

The standard contains quite comprehensive guidance in paragraphs 47 to 53 setting out the IASC's view of goodwill and the circumstances in which it may have a useful life in excess of twenty years. As time passes, if goodwill remains valuable, that is because it is being replaced by internally generated goodwill – which is prohibited by IAS 38 from being recognised. Therefore, the reasoning goes, goodwill arising on acquisition always has a finite life. Thus the IASC has rejected the principle that underpinned FRS 10, that internally generated goodwill could replace purchased goodwill so as to justify an indefinite life.[138] The standard also includes a list of the factors to be taken into account in deciding the useful life of goodwill:

(a) the nature of the acquired business and its foreseeable life;

(b) the stability of the industry to which the goodwill relates;

(c) information regarding similar businesses or industries, their lifecycles and the effect this has on goodwill;

(d) product obsolescence, changes in demand and other economic factors that may affect the life of goodwill;

(e) the expected service lives of key individuals or groups of employees and whether the acquired business could be efficiently managed by another management team;

(f) the company's ability and intent to reach the level of maintenance expenditure or of funding required to obtain the expected future economic benefits from the acquired business

(g) the existence of competitors or potential competitors; and

(h) the and legal, regulatory, contractual or other means by which the acquiror controls the acquired business and the extent to which these affect its useful life.[139]

Although the enterprise should use a prudent basis in estimating the useful life of goodwill, it is not acceptable to write it off over an unrealistically short period.[140]

IAS 22 allows that in rare cases there may be persuasive evidence that goodwill has a useful life of over twenty years, although it states that examples are hard to find. Presumably this is because most examples of enduring goodwill are in fact examples of internally generated goodwill seamlessly replacing that originally purchased. The only circumstances in which a life of longer than twenty years might occur is: 'when the goodwill is so clearly related to an identifiable asset or a group of identifiable assets that it can reasonably be expected to benefit the acquirer over the useful life of the identifiable asset or group of assets.'[141]

Thus the standard effectively restricts the possibility of a useful life of over twenty years for goodwill to those circumstances where the related fixed assets also last longer. However, if these conditions are met, the presumption that the useful life of goodwill will not exceed twenty years is rebutted, and the enterprise should then:

(a) amortise the goodwill over the best estimate of its useful life;

(b) estimate the recoverable amount of the goodwill at least annually to identify any impairment loss; and

(c) disclose the reasons why the presumption is rebutted and the factor(s) that played a significant role in determining the useful life of the goodwill.[142]

The most onerous of these provisions is the requirement for an annual estimate of the recoverable amount. By this, the standard means that an annual impairment test in accordance with IAS 36 must be performed, even if there are no indications that the goodwill is impaired. The test must also be performed if the useful life of goodwill, while originally less than twenty years, has been extended so as to exceed twenty years in total.[143] Impairment is dealt with separately in Chapter 13.

An impairment review may also be required when accounting for an acquisition if it appears that the goodwill is not capable of being supported by the future economic benefits that the entity expects to obtain. For example there may have been a decline in the expected cash flows.[144]

IAS 22 requires a review of the amortisation period and method, at the end of each accounting period at least, of all goodwill. If this reveals lives or consumption of benefits that are significantly different from previous estimates, the amortisation period or method should be changed. These changes are to be accounted for as changes in accounting estimates under IAS 8, and the adjustments reflected prospectively by altering the amortisation charge for the current and future periods, not as prior year adjustments.[145]

5.3 The requirements of IAS 38 – Intangible assets

5.3.1 Definition recognition and measurement

IAS 38 applies to all intangible assets except for:

- those that are covered by other International Accounting Standards;
- financial assets as defined by IAS 32;
- mineral rights and exploration expenditure; and
- intangible assets arising in insurance companies from contracts with policyholders.[146]

Specific intangible assets that are beyond the scope of IAS 38 include:

- intangible assets held for sale in the ordinary course of business, to which IAS 2 – *Inventories* – or IAS 11 – *Construction Contracts* – apply (see Chapter 16);
- deferred tax assets (see Chapter 24);
- goodwill arising on a business combination, covered by IAS 22 – *Business Combinations* – and dealt with above;

- assets arising from employee benefits that are dealt with in IAS 19 – *Employee benefits* – (see Chapter 22); and
- financial assets as defined by IAS 32 – *Financial Instruments, Disclosure and Presentation*.[147] These are dealt with in Chapter 10.

Leases are not covered to the extent that they fall within IAS 17 (see Chapter 19). However, if the rights under a licensing agreement relate to intangible assets such as films or videos, copyrights or patents, they are outside the scope of IAS 17 and fall within IAS 38.[148] The issues relating to intangible assets that arise in extractive industries and insurance businesses have been excluded on the grounds that they are so specialised that they may need to be dealt with in other ways.[149]

The standard explicitly prohibits the recognition of internally generated goodwill[150] and the recognition of 'goodwill lookalikes' such as brands, mastheads and customer lists.[151] However, it does not actually prohibit the recognition of internally generated intangible assets, principally because it also deals with research and development expenditure. It also *requires* the capitalisation of intangible assets that meet its stringent criteria, unlike SSAP 13, which merely allows it.

A Tangible and intangible assets

The standard acknowledges that the distinction between intangible and tangible assets is not always clear-cut:

> 'In determining whether an asset that incorporates both intangible and tangible elements should be treated under IAS 16, Property, Plant and Equipment, or as an intangible asset under this Standard, judgement is required to assess which element is more significant.'[152]

The IAS contains a certain amount of guidance to assist making the judgement, using computer software as an example. Software without which the hardware cannot operate is part of the hardware and is accounted for as property, plant and equipment. If the software is not integral it is treated as an intangible asset.[153]

Paragraph 4 of IAS 38 makes it clear that it applies to, among other things, expenditure on advertising, training, start-up and research and development activities. It uses the example of research and development expenditure that results in a prototype as another example of the difference between tangible and intangible assets, explaining that the significant element is the intangible component, the knowledge that the prototype embodies.

B Identification and control of intangible assets

IAS 38 defines an asset as 'a resource controlled by an enterprise as a result of past events; and from which future economic benefits are expected to flow to the enterprise'. Intangible assets form a sub-section of this group and are further defined as 'identifiable non-monetary assets without physical substance held for use in the production or supply of goods or services, for rental to others, or for administrative purposes.'[154] Businesses frequently incur expenditure on all sorts of intangible resources such as scientific or technical knowledge, design of new processes or systems, licences, intellectual property, market knowledge, trademarks, brand names and publishing titles. Examples that fall under these headings are computer software, patents, copyrights, motion picture films, customer lists, and many others.[155]

However, although these items are covered by the standard, not all of them will meet the standard's definition of an intangible asset, which requires identifiability, control and the existence of future economic benefits. If they do not meet the definition they will be expensed when incurred, unless they have arisen in the context of an acquisition, where they will form part of the calculation of goodwill.[156]

IAS 38 contains three paragraphs which attempt to clarify and explain the concept of identifiability. If an asset can be sold without effectively selling also the business it was part of, it is automatically identifiable. However, a non-separable asset may also be identifiable; 'if an asset generates future economic benefits only in combination with other assets, the asset is identifiable if the enterprise can identify the future economic benefits that will flow from the asset.' Such identifiable assets may be acquired with a group of assets or internally generated.[157]

IAS 38 does not contain a blanket prohibition on the recognition of internally generated intangible assets. The principal reason for which is the incorporation within the standard of research and development expenditure, which is discussed further below. However IAS 38 is so worded that it is very hard to conceive of an internally generated intangible asset, other than development expenditure, that it would permit. As mentioned above, internally generated goodwill is specifically prohibited from being recognised as an asset.[158] Similarly IAS 38 states that 'internally generated brands, mastheads, publishing titles, customer lists and items similar in substance should not be recognised as intangible assets' as these items cannot be distinguished from the cost of developing the business as a whole.[159]

Control is defined as the ability to obtain the future economic benefits generated by the resource and the ability to deny access to those benefits to others. While these are normally legal rights, control may also be demonstrated in the absence of legal enforceability by factors such as market and technical knowledge.[160] However, skilled staff, customer portfolios or market share are unlikely to be controlled in such a way as to meet the definition of intangible assets.[161]

Future economic benefits include not only future revenues from the sale of products or services but also cost savings.[162]

C *Recognition and initial measurement*

The standard requires that intangible assets must meet the same general definition of assets as contained within IAS 16 for property, plant and equipment:

'(a) it is probable that the future economic benefits that are attributable to the asset will flow to the enterprise; and

(b) the cost of the asset can be measured reliably.'[163]

IAS 38 also requires that 'an enterprise should assess the probability of future economic benefits using reasonable and supportable assumptions that represent management's best estimate of the set of economic conditions that will exist over the useful life of the asset.'[164]

An intangible asset should be measured initially at cost.[165] Its carrying value should be determined as follows:

- if the intangible asset is acquired separately the cost is the sum of the purchase consideration plus any direct costs associated with the purchase. If the payment terms are extended beyond 'normal' credit terms, the cost to be recognised must be the cash price equivalent and the difference must be treated as an interest expense. If the asset is acquired in exchange for equity instruments, the cost – and fair value - of the intangible asset is the fair value of the equity instruments issued;[166]
- if the intangible asset is acquired in a business combination it is valued at its fair value at the date of acquisition in accordance with IAS 22 – *Business Combinations* – (see Chapter 6). An intangible should be recognised at its fair value, which in substance is its market value, or in the absence of a market value, a derived value analogous to it. The most reliable market values would be the current bid price but recent similar transactions may be used to estimate the fair value in their absence. If there is no active market the enterprise will estimate the amount that it would have paid in an arm's length transaction. Other techniques have been developed by enterprises within various sectors. Multiples are applied to indicators such as revenue or market share or discounted net cash flows calculated.[167] However, the value that may be placed upon an intangible asset acquired as part of a business combination for which there is no active market is limited to a sum which does not create or increase any negative goodwill;[168]
- an intangible asset acquired by way of government grants may be valued at either fair value or nominal value in accordance with IAS 20 – *Government Grants* – (see Chapter 20);[169] and
- an intangible asset acquired in exchange for a similar asset, that is one that has a similar use in the same line of business and has a similar fair value, will be recorded at the carrying value of the asset given up and no gain or loss will be recorded on the exchange. If the asset received has a lower fair value, this probably indicates that the asset given up had been impaired in value and the new asset will be recorded at the written down value. If there are any cash payments or receipts the subsequent carrying value of the new asset will be adjusted accordingly. If the asset received is dissimilar, its cost is measured at the fair value of the asset received. This is the same as the *fair value* of the asset given up, as adjusted for any cash received or paid. This may, therefore, result in the recognition of gains as well as losses in the income statement.[170]

D Research and development

If a business is involved in research and development, the development part of the expenditure should be treated as an intangible asset if certain conditions are met. There is a specific prohibition on the recognition of any research expenditure as an asset, and the Standard requires it to be expensed. If the enterprise cannot distinguish between the research and development phases of a project, all of the expenditure must be treated as research.[171]

The standard contains considerable, helpful, guidance and discussion of the distinction between the two. Research is 'original and planned investigation undertaken with the prospect of gaining new scientific or technical knowledge and understanding'. Development is defined as 'the application of research findings or other knowledge to a plan or design for the production of new or substantially improved materials, devices, products, processes, systems or services prior to the commencement of commercial production or use.'[172]

Development costs may be recognised as an internally generated intangible 'if, and only if, all the following can be demonstrated by the business:

'(a) the technical feasibility of completing the intangible asset so that it will be available for use or sale;

(b) its intention to complete the intangible asset and use or sell it;

(c) its ability to use or sell the intangible asset;

(d) how the intangible asset will generate probable future economic benefits. Among other things, the enterprise should demonstrate the existence of a market for the output of the intangible asset or the intangible asset itself or, if it is to be used internally, the usefulness of the intangible asset;

(e) the availability of adequate technical, financial and other resources to complete the development and to use or sell the intangible asset; and

(f) its ability to measure the expenditure attributable to the intangible asset during its development reliably.'[173]

Condition (d) above is more restrictive than is immediately apparent because the enterprise needs to assess the probable future economic benefits using the principles in IAS 36 – *Impairment of Assets* – i.e. using discounted cash flows. If the asset will generate economic benefits only in conjunction with other assets, the enterprise applies the concept of cash-generating units. The requirements of the IAS 36 are discussed in Chapter 13 at 4.2.

Examples of development expenditure include the design, construction and testing of prototypes, tools, pilot plants and alternatives for new or improved materials, processes, systems or services.[174] The cost of an internally generated intangible is the sum of expenditure incurred from the date the recognition criteria are first met, and comprises 'all expenditure that can be directly attributed, or allocated on a reasonable and consistent basis, to creating, producing and preparing the asset for its intended use.' Allowable costs are such items as materials and services, salaries and wages, directly attributable expenses, and overheads that can be reasonably allocated to the generation of the intangible asset.[175] Overheads are to be allocated on a similar basis to the allocation allowed for inventories, which is discussed in Chapter 16 at 4. Capitalised overheads do not include general overhead costs, nor selling or administrative costs unless these are directly attributable. Neither may capitalised overheads include inefficiencies and initial operating losses before an asset reaches its planned level of performance, or staff training costs.[176] Extract 11.17 below shows a typical accounting policy for research and development under IAS:

Extract 11.17: Danisco A/S (2000)

Accounting policies [extract]
Research and development costs

Research and development costs include costs, salaries and depreciation directly or indirectly attributable to the research and development activities of the Group. Research costs are charged to the profit and loss account in the year in which they are incurred.

The main part of the Group's development costs is similarly charged to the profit and loss account in the year in which it is incurred, as it has been defrayed to sustain earnings on a continuous basis.

Clearly defined and identifiable development projects in which the technical degree of exploitation, adequate resources and potential market or development possibility in the undertaking are recognisable, and where it is the intention to produce, market or execute the project, are capitalised when a correlation exists between the costs incurred and future benefits.

Unless expenditure is in connection with an intangible item that the standard requires to be recognised, it should be expensed. The only exception is in connection with an acquisition, where the costs associated with an intangible that cannot be recognised will form part of the carrying amount of goodwill.[177] An example would be the costs of research written off by the acquired enterprise.

The following types of expenditure do not form part of the cost of an intangible and so are to be expensed:

- certain start-up costs, unless they are allowed as part of the cost of the asset under IAS 16 (see Chapter 12);
- training costs;
- advertising and promotional activities; and
- relocation and reorganisation costs.[178]

Any expenditure recognised as an expense may not be subsequently written back to be part of an intangible asset.[179]

Subsequent expenditure on an intangible asset after its purchase should be recognised as an expense unless the expenditure will produce benefits in excess of those originally assessed, and then only if the expenditure can be measured and attributed reliably to the intangible asset.[180]

E *Measurement after initial recognition*

IAS 38, in common with a number of other international standards, provides for a benchmark and an allowed alternative treatment. They are set out in paragraphs 63 and 64 and may be summarised as follows:

(a) benchmark treatment: cost less any accumulated amortisation and any accumulated impairment losses; or

(b) allowed alternative treatment: revalued amount less any subsequent accumulated amortisation and any subsequent accumulated impairment losses. The revalued amount should be the fair value of the asset. However, this treatment is permitted if, and only if, fair value can be determined by reference to an active market for the intangible asset.

An active market is defined as one where 'all the following conditions exist:

(a) the items traded within the market are homogeneous;

(b) willing buyers and sellers can normally be found at any time; and

(c) prices are available to the public.'[181]

The allowed alternative treatment is therefore very restricted in its possible application, and it is limited still further. If an intangible asset is revalued, all other assets in that class of assets must be revalued, unless there is no active market.[182] Any asset that cannot be revalued must be carried at cost less accumulated depreciation and impairment. If an active market disappears, the asset should be carried at its last revalued amount and the benchmark treatment applied to that valuation from then on.[183] Increases in valuations are to be credited directly to equity under a revaluation surplus heading, while decreases (on an asset by asset, not a pool basis) may be charged directly against a revaluation surplus. However any write down in excess of an existing revaluation surplus must be recognised as an expense in the income statement. If these downward valuations recognised as expenses are subsequently reversed, they may, on an asset by asset basis, be recognised as income to the extent that they reverse the amount previously charged.[184]

Generally, revaluation of intangible assets will not be permitted because there is no active market and the remainder of this section deals with the benchmark treatment.

5.3.2 *Amortisation of intangible assets under IAS 38*

The treatment of intangible assets under IAS 38 subsequent to initial recognition is systematic amortisation, impairment if required, with a rebuttable presumption that the useful life will not exceed twenty years.[185] The useful life must always be finite.[186]

The standard identifies a number of factors that may affect the useful life of an intangible asset. The factors relate to the potential useful life of development costs and other intangible assets and include:

- the asset's expected usage;
- its typical product life cycles;
- technical and technological obsolescence. This will particularly affect the useful life of computer software and many other intangible assets;
- the stability of the industry and changes in market demand
- the actions of competitors, both existing and potential;
- the ability and intention of the entity to maintain the asset; and
- whether the useful life depends on the useful life of other assets of the business.[187]

If the enterprise controls the intangible through legal rights, the useful life should not exceed the period of those rights unless renewal of the rights is virtually certain. Other evidence of the certainty of renewal would be given if, for example, the fair value reduces by no more than the costs of renewal as the initial expiry date approaches.[188]

Amortisation of all intangible assets including development costs should reflect the pattern of consumption of the economic benefits that the intangible provides, or if that cannot be reliably determined, a straight line basis should be used.[189] This does not appear to rule out absolutely the amortisation of development costs in line with the sale or use of the product, service, process or system over the period in which these are expected to be sold or used, the policy required by SSAP 13. However, it may not be easy to demonstrate such a pattern of use with sufficient reliability for it to be allowable under IAS 38. All amortisation costs must be recognised as an expense in the income statement.

In common with the UK standard, IAS 38 allows that in 'rare cases there may be persuasive evidence' that an intangible has a useful life of over twenty years. In these rare cases, an enterprise should:

(a) amortise the intangible asset over the best estimate of its useful life;

(b) estimate the recoverable amount of the intangible asset at least annually in order to identify any impairment loss; and

(c) disclose the reasons why the presumption is rebutted and the factor(s) that played a significant role in determining the useful life of the asset.[190]

If the useful life is uncertain, an enterprise may use a prudent estimate but it must not use an unrealistically short life.[191]

The residual value of an intangible must be assumed to be zero unless there is a commitment by a third party to purchase the asset at the end of its useful life or there is an active market for the asset from which to determine its residual value. A residual value other than zero implies that the enterprise intends to dispose of the asset before the end of its useful life.[192]

The residual value of an intangible asset held at cost is estimated using prices prevailing at the date of acquisition and is not restated for changes in price or value. In the unlikely event that the asset is held at a valuation, the residual value is recalculated every time the asset is revalued.[193]

The amortisation period of all intangible assets must be reviewed at the end of each financial year. Subsequent expenditure may extend the life, while an impairment loss may also indicate that the life is shorter than previously estimated. The standard also suggests that experience may indicate that a different method of depreciation, such as reducing balance, is more appropriate than straight line. Any significant differences in the estimated useful life, or the pattern of consumption of the intangible, must be reflected in the amortisation period or method. All such changes must be accounted for prospectively, that is by adjusting the amortisation charge for the current and future periods only.[194]

All intangible assets recognised under IAS 38 are subject to the provisions of IAS 36 – *Impairment of assets.*[195] This subject is dealt with in Chapter 13 at 4.

There are two circumstances referred to in IAS 38 where an annual impairment test and calculation of the recoverable amount in accordance with IAS 36 is required, whether or not there are any indications of impairment:

(a) intangible assets are not yet available for use, where the standard suggests that it may be very difficult to estimate with sufficient reliability the future economic benefits; and

(b) intangible assets that have a useful life of over twenty years, as it may otherwise be difficult to identify impairment factors such as obsolescence.[196]

If an asset's life is extended through subsequent expenditure so that its useful life will, in total, exceed twenty years from when it first came into use, an annual impairment review will have to be performed under (b) above.[197]

Derecognition should take place on the disposal or retirement of an intangible asset, and all gains or losses (i.e. the difference between the carrying amount and any disposal proceeds) should be recognised in the income statement.[198] Asset exchanges for assets of similar fair value will result in no gains or losses as the new asset will be recorded at the carrying amount of the asset disposed of.[199] Assets held for disposal rather than use must be tested for impairment in accordance with IAS 36 at least at each financial year end.[200]

6 REQUIRED IAS DISCLOSURES

6.1 Introduction

This section sets out the principal disclosures required in financial statements compiled under IAS for intangible assets and goodwill, as contained within IAS 22 and IAS 38. The disclosures relevant to this topic required by each standard are separately shown. However any disclosures required by other authorities such as national statutes are not included. The disclosure requirements of UK companies legislation are shown above at 3.

6.2 IAS 22 goodwill disclosures

IAS 22 has an extremely comprehensive and clearly laid out disclosure section, which principally deals with disclosure matters concerning business combinations, which are dealt with in Chapter 6. The specific goodwill disclosures required are set out below.

A Goodwill

'For goodwill, the financial statements should disclose:

(a) the amortisation period(s) adopted;

(b) if goodwill is amortised over more than twenty years, the reasons why the presumption that the useful life of goodwill will not exceed twenty years from initial recognition is rebutted. In giving these reasons, the enterprise should describe the factor(s) that played a significant role in determining the useful life of the goodwill;

(c) if goodwill is not amortised on the straight-line basis, the basis used and reason why that basis is more appropriate than the straight-line basis;

(d) the line item(s) of the income statement in which the amortisation of goodwill is included; and

(e) a reconciliation, of the carrying amount of goodwill, at the beginning and end of the period showing:

   (i) the gross amount and the accumulated amortisation (aggregated with accumulated impairment losses), at the beginning of the period;

   (ii) any additional goodwill recognised during the period;

   (iii) any adjustments resulting from subsequent identification or changes in value of identifiable assets and liabilities;

   (iv) any goodwill derecognised on the disposal of all or part of the business to which it relates during the period;

   (v) amortisation recognised during the period;

   (vi) impairment losses recognised during the period under IAS 36, Impairment of Assets (if any);

   (vii) impairment losses reversed during the period under IAS 36 (if any);

   (viii) other changes in the carrying amount during the period (if any); and

   (ix) the gross amount and the accumulated amortisation (aggregated with accumulated impairment losses), at the end of the period.

Comparative information is not required.'[201]

It is noteworthy that in the event of goodwill being amortised over a longer period than 20 years the factors that played a significant role in the decision, the disclosure of which is referred to in (b) above, are listed in paragraph 48 of IAS 22 which is reproduced in 5.2.3 above.

B Negative goodwill

There are separate disclosures for negative goodwill, in which case 'the financial statements should disclose:

(a) to the extent that negative goodwill is treated under paragraph 61, a description, the amount and the timing of the expected future losses and expenses;

(b) the period(s) over which negative goodwill is recognised as income;

(c) the line item(s) of the income statement in which negative goodwill is recognised as income; and

(d) a reconciliation of the carrying amount of negative goodwill at the beginning and end of the period showing:

   (i) the gross amount of negative goodwill and the accumulated amount of negative goodwill already recognised as income, at the beginning of the period;

   (ii) any additional negative goodwill recognised during the period;

(iii) any adjustments resulting from subsequent identification or changes in value of identifiable assets and liabilities;

(iv) any negative goodwill derecognised on the disposal of all or part of the business to which it relates during the period;

(v) negative goodwill recognised as income during the period, showing separately the portion of negative goodwill recognised as income under paragraph 61 (if any);

(vi) other changes in the carrying amount during the period (if any); and

(vii) the gross amount of negative goodwill and the accumulated amount of negative goodwill already recognised as income, at the end of the period.

Comparative information is not required.'[202]

C Post balance sheet date combinations

In the event of a business combination happening after the balance sheet date but before the date of approval of the financial statements, the information required for goodwill and negative goodwill should be disclosed, or if it is impracticable to do so, that fact must be disclosed.[203]

6.3 IAS 38

A General disclosures

In common with all of the more recent international standards, IAS 38 is laid out with a comprehensive and clear disclosure section. The general disclosures required by IAS 38 are as follows.

'The financial statements should disclose the following for each class of intangible assets, distinguishing between internally generated intangible assets and other intangible assets:

(a) the useful lives or the amortisation rates used;

(b) the amortisation methods used;

(c) the gross carrying amount and the accumulated amortisation (aggregated with accumulated impairment losses) at the beginning and end of the period;

(d) the line item(s) of the income statement in which the amortisation of intangible assets is included;

(e) a reconciliation of the carrying amount at the beginning and end of the period showing:

  (i) additions, indicating separately those from internal development and through business combinations;

  (ii) retirements and disposals;

  (iii) increases or decreases during the period resulting from revaluations under paragraphs 64, 76 and 77 and from impairment losses recognised or reversed directly in equity under IAS 36, Impairment of Assets (if any);

(iv) impairment losses recognised in the income statement during the period under IAS 36 (if any);

(v) impairment losses reversed in the income statement during the period under IAS 36 (if any);

(vi) amortisation recognised during the period;

(vii) net exchange differences arising on the translation of the financial statements of a foreign entity; and

(viii) other changes in the carrying amount during the period.

Comparative information is not required.'[204]

The standard states that a class of intangible assets is a grouping of assets of a similar nature, and gives examples such as brands, publishing titles, software, and rights like copyrights and patents.[205]

Any impairment of intangibles is to be disclosed in accordance with IAS 36, which is discussed in Chapter 13 at 4, while any changes in amortisation or residual value estimates should be disclosed in accordance with the provisions of IAS 8.

There are a number of additional disclosure requirements, some of which only apply in certain circumstances, such as when assets are amortised over a life greater than twenty years. Unusually, and of potential benefit to users of financial statements, there is a requirement to single out information about any single intangible assets that is material to the financial statements as a whole. The additional disclosures that are required if the circumstances apply are:

'(a) if an intangible asset is amortised over more than twenty years, the reasons why the presumption that the useful life of an intangible asset will not exceed twenty years from the date when the asset is available for use is rebutted. In giving these reasons, the enterprise should describe the factor(s) that played a significant role in determining the useful life of the asset;

(b) a description, the carrying amount and remaining amortisation period of any individual intangible asset that is material to the financial statements of the enterprise as a whole;

(c) for intangible assets acquired by way of a government grant and initially recognised at fair value (see paragraph 33):

(i) the fair value initially recognised for these assets;

(ii) their carrying amount; and

(iii) whether they are carried under the benchmark or the allowed alternative treatment for subsequent measurement;

(d) the existence and carrying amounts of intangible assets whose title is restricted and the carrying amounts of intangible assets pledged as security for liabilities; and

(e) the amount of commitments for the acquisition of intangible assets.'[206]

The factors to be taken into account in determining the useful life of an asset that is amortised over longer than twenty years that are required to be described in (a) above are listed in paragraph 80 of IAS 38.

B Extra disclosures under the allowed alternative treatment

A class of intangible assets may not contain assets that are recognised under the benchmark treatment and under the allowed alternative treatment. If intangible assets are carried under the allowed alternative treatment 'at revalued amounts the following should be disclosed:

(a) by class of intangible assets:
   (i) the effective date of the revaluation;
   (ii) the carrying amount of revalued intangible assets; and
   (iii) the carrying amount that would have been included in the financial statements had the revalued intangible assets been carried under the benchmark treatment in paragraph 63; and

(b) the amount of the revaluation surplus that relates to intangible assets at the beginning and end of the period, indicating the changes during the period and any restrictions on the distribution of the balance to shareholders.'[207]

C Extra disclosure for research and development expenditure

The aggregate total amount of research and development expenditure recognised as an expense should be disclosed.

D 'Encouraged' disclosures under IAS 38

Finally IAS 38 encourages businesses to provide a description of any fully amortised intangible that is still in use, and also to describe any significant intangible not recognised as an asset.

Extract 11.18 provides a typical example of goodwill and intangible assets disclosures under IAS

Extract 11.18: Bayer AG (2000)

Notes to the Balance Sheets [extracts]

17 Intangible assets

Acquired intangible assets other than goodwill are recognized at cost and amortized over a period of 4 to 15 years, depending on their estimated useful lives. Write-downs are made for any declines in value that are expected to be permanent. Assets are written back if the reasons for previous years' write-downs no longer apply. Goodwill, including that resulting from capital consolidation, is capitalized in accordance with IAS 22 and amortized on a straight-line basis over a maximum estimated useful life of 20 years. The value of goodwill is reassessed regularly and written down if necessary.

Self-created intangible assets are not capitalized.

Changes in intangible assets in 2000 were as follows:

	Acquired concessions, industrial property rights, similar rights and assets, and licences thereunder	Acquired goodwill	Advance payments	Total
Gross carrying amounts, Dec. 31, 1999	1,903	944	84	2,931
Exchange differences	126	22	6	154
Changes in companies consolidated	5	36	–	41
Acquisitions	2,268	301	–	2,569
Capital expenditures	293	5	56	354
Retirements	(95)	(28)	–	(123)
Transfers	66	9	(75)	–
Gross carrying amounts, Dec. 31, 2000	**4,566**	**1,289**	**71**	**5,926**
Accumulated amortization and write-downs, Dec. 31, 1999	479	239	–	718
Exchange differences	39	5	–	44
Changes in companies consolidated	1	(3)	–	(2)
Amortization and write-downs in 2000	345	99	–	444
– Of which write-downs	[–]	[1]	[–]	[1]
Write-backs	(1)	(1)	–	(2)
Retirements	(91)	(28)	–	(119)
Transfers	–	–	–	–
Accumulated amortization and write downs, Dec. 31, 2000	**772**	**311**	**–**	**1,083**
Net carrying amounts, Dec. 31, 2000	**3,794**	**978**	**71**	**4,843**
Net carrying amounts, Dec. 31, 1999	1,424	705	84	2,213

The exchange differences are the differences between the carrying amounts at the beginning and the end of the year that result from translating foreign companies' figures at the respective different exchange rates and changes in their assets during the year at the average rate for the year.

7 IAS PRACTICAL ISSUES

A number of practical issues are discussed in a UK context at 4 above, that are also relevant to the international standards dealing with this topic. Although by no means identical, the provisions under both IAS and UK GAAP are such that the practical matters they raise are similar in nature. However one welcome advance in the way that international standards on this topic are written is the inclusion within them of substantial amounts of guidance to preparers on how to go about making the judgements the standards require.

Having said that, it is true that IAS 38 is almost as harsh in prohibiting the recognition of internally generated intangibles as its UK equivalent FRS 10. We consider that while this attitude is understandable, it may not be sustainable in the future if businesses continue to develop intellectual property and information-related assets that have value commercially, and that ought to be recognised if accounts are to be useful. Nevertheless the inconsistency embodied within IAS 38 that the intangible you buy may be recognised as an asset, while the identical one you make may not be, will inevitably require resolution if the importance of intangibles continues to grow, and if the move towards fair value accounting also continues.

The other, perhaps related, matter is that of determining useful lives of more than twenty years. There is a clear difficulty here, particularly in the matter of brand valuation. A strong brand may be reasonably considered by the most prudent manager to have a life well in excess of twenty years. Thus the attitude to intangibles that only exceptionally will they have a life in excess of twenty years cannot be expected to have much influence upon those who make major brand acquisitions. In these cases the entire justification of the expenditure rests upon the long-term advantage of a strong brand.

It may also be argued that although IAS 38 and IAS 22 forbid indefinite lives being ascribed to intangible assets and goodwill, there may be a loophole in that the intangible assets may have such long lives (and perhaps, in some cases, such high residual values) that the effect is immaterial. Such a situation would not necessarily contravene the spirit of the standard or be anything other than in accordance with the genuine commercial judgement of the management of the business concerned. Coca-Cola appears to have lasted longer than Communism, for example. These matters are ultimately not solvable by decree, rather the underlying reality of the importance of intangibles will have to be assimilated into financial statements, and reported by them, in a manner which aids the utility of the report. It seems that so far matters are at an interim stage, workable but not without inconsistencies.

It is possible therefore to view the impairment requirement for intangibles ascribed a life in excess of twenty years (discussed in Chapter 13) as potentially the most important component in the development of the valuation of intangible assets. However, as discussed in Chapter 13, the impairment test is not a straightforward concept to apply in practice.

8 CONCLUSION

Throughout the last decade there has been a gradual shift in the emphasis of what financial statements are meant to portray, from a transactions-based, performance-orientated model in which the profit and loss account is the most important statement towards a balance sheet-orientated model based on fair values. As embodied in the ASB's *Statement of principles*, and the IASC's *Framework* document, performance has come to be defined primarily in terms of changes in assets and liabilities that effectively define the contents of the income statement.

This approach has not made the treatment of intangible assets in the balance sheet at the conceptual level any easier. The IASC and the ASB have promulgated standards that have greatly reduced the scope for creative accounting as far as intangibles are concerned, as well as producing standards that are as unambiguously drafted as may reasonably be expected. It is also true that, in spite of the considerable effort put into their conceptual frameworks, neither the IASC nor the ASB have come up with a conceptually integrated or logically consistent treatment of intangible assets.

Paragraph 47 of IAS 22 sets out the arguments for maintaining an unamortised intangible valuation when the intangible is being constantly 'topped up' by continuing business activity, promotion, marketing and so on. The fact that another standard (IAS 38) chooses to ignore this argument and prohibit such an approach, neither invalidates it nor removes the commercial reality it may reflect. Similarly the blanket prohibition on the recognition of almost all internally generated intangibles, is a tacit admission of the limits of our ability to deal with such items, rather than a deductive consequence of the reasons offered in the standards themselves. Thus it appears accounting for intangibles is at the stage of having a workable but imperfect set of rules which falls well short of consistency.

If the move towards an accounting model based on recording the entire balance sheet at fair values continues, the challenge will be to find an acceptable, logically consistent method that can value all intangibles that have worth, without arbitrarily scoping out those that present too many difficulties.

References

1 CA 85, s 262(1).
2 *Ibid.*, Sch. 4, para. 8, balance sheet formats.
3 *Ibid.*
4 *Ibid.*, Sch. 4, para. 3(2).
5 *Ibid.*, Sch. 4, para. 17
6 *Ibid.*, para. 31(1).
7 *Ibid.*, s 262(1).
8 *Ibid.*, Sch. 4, para. 26(1).
9 *Ibid.*, Sch. 4, paras. 26(2) and 26(3).
10 *Ibid.*, Sch. 4, para. 18.
11 *Ibid.*
12 *Ibid.*, Sch. 4, para. 32.
13 *Ibid.*, Sch. 4, para. 21.
14 *Ibid.*, Sch. 4, para. 19(2).
15 *Ibid.*, s 263.
16 *Ibid.*, s 269(1).
17 *Ibid.*, s 269(2).
18 CCAB, *The determination of distributable profits in the context of the Companies Act (TR 482)*, September 1982, para. 23.
19 Draft technical release 25/00 *The Determination of Realised Profits and Distributable Profits in the*

Context of the Companies Act 1985. ICAEW, August 2000, para. B28.
20 FRS 10, *Goodwill and intangible fixed assets,* ASB, December 1997, para. 1.
21 *Ibid.*, paras. 4-6.
22 *Ibid.*, para. 2.
23 *Ibid.*
24 *Ibid.*
25 *Ibid.*
26 *Ibid.*
27 *Ibid.*
28 *Ibid.*
29 *Ibid.*, paras. 7-8.
30 *Ibid.*, para. 9.
31 *Ibid.*, para. 10.
32 *Ibid.*, para. 14.
33 *Ibid.*, para. 12.
34 *Ibid.*, para. 10.
35 *Ibid.*, para. 13.
36 *Ibid.*, para. 14.
37 *Ibid.*, para. 2.
38 *Ibid.*, para. 1.
39 *Ibid.*, paras. 15 and 17.
40 *Ibid.*, para. 2.
41 *Ibid.*, para. 19.
42 *Ibid.*, para. 24.
43 *Ibid.*, para. 19.
44 *Ibid.*, para. 20.
45 *Ibid.*, para. 23.
46 *Ibid.*, para. 21.
47 *Ibid.*, paras. 22 and 36.
48 *Ibid.*, para. 33.
49 UITF Abstract 27, *Revision to estimates of the useful economic life of goodwill and intangible assets*, ASB December 2000, para. 5
50 FRS 10, para. 28.
51 *Ibid.*
52 *Ibid.*, para. 29.
53 *Ibid.*, para. 30.
54 *Ibid.*, para. 31.
55 *Ibid.*, para. 32.
56 *Ibid.*, para. 48.
57 *Ibid.*, para. 49.
58 *Ibid.*, para. 50.
59 *Ibid.*, para. 64.
60 *Ibid.*, para. 51.
61 *Ibid.*, para. 34.
62 *Ibid.*, para. 37.
63 SSAP 13, *Accounting for research and development*, ASC issued December 1977, revised January, para. 9.
64 *Statement of principles for financial reporting*, ASB, December 1999, Chapter 4, para. 4.6.
65 SSAP 13, para. 21.
66 *Ibid.*, para. 2.
67 *Ibid.*, para. 18.
68 *Ibid.*, para. 17.
69 *Ibid.*, para. 23.
70 *Ibid.*, para. 16.
71 *Ibid.*, para. 24.
72 *Ibid.*, para. 8.
73 *Ibid.*, para. 9.
74 *Ibid.*, para. 25.
75 *Ibid.*, para. 26.
76 *Ibid.*, para. 27.
77 *Ibid.*, para. 28.
78 *Ibid.*, para. 29.
79 CA 85, Sch. 4, para. 8, balance sheet formats.
80 *Ibid.*, Sch. 4, para. 8, profit and loss account formats.
81 *Ibid.*, note (17) on the profit and loss account formats.
82 *Ibid.*, paras. 19(1) and 19(2).
83 FRS 3, para. 20.
84 CA 85, Sch. 4, paras. 42(1)(a) and 42(2).
85 *Ibid.*, para. 42(1)(b).
86 *Ibid.*, para. 42(3).
87 CA 85, s 227(6).
88 FRS 10, para. 52.
89 *Ibid.*, para. 55.
90 *Ibid.*, para. 56.
91 *Ibid.*, para. 57.
92 *Ibid.*, para. 58.
93 FRS 18, *Accounting policies*, ASB, December 2000, Para. 62.
94 *Ibid.*, para. 64.
95 FRS 10, para. 53.
96 *Ibid.*, para. 63.
97 *Ibid.*, para.64.
98 CA 85, Sch. 4, para. 20(2).
99 *Ibid.*, Sch. 7, para. 6(c).
100 SSAP 13, para. 30.
101 *Ibid.*, para. 31.
102 *Ibid.*, para. 32.
103 *Ibid.*
104 *Ibid.*, para. 22.
105 In March 1999, the DTI issued a Consultative Document, *Raising the Threshold Levels for SMEs*, outlining proposals to raise the financial limits up to the level permitted by EC law. There is also a proposal that the limits under the EC Accounting Directives should be increased by 25%. If that is adopted the new UK financial limits would be increased to those higher levels. This would mean that the limits under SSAP 13 would be £192m for turnover and £96m for total assets.
106 CA 85, Sch. 4A, para. 9(2).
107 FRS 10, Appendix III para. 27.
108 *Ibid.*, para 2.
109 SSAP 13, para. 5.
110 *Ibid.*, para. 6.
111 *Ibid.*, para. 7.
112 CA 85, Sch. 4, para. 19(3).
113 It was reported in *Company Reporting No. 104*, Company Reporting Limited, February 1999,

p. 10 that its database shows that, of companies with evidence of research and development spend, 73% write it off as incurred.
114 IAS 1, *Presentation of financial statements*, IASC, August 1997, para. 58.
115 *Ibid.,* paras. 53-54
116 *Ibid.*, para. 53.
117 IAS 22, *Business combinations*, IASC, September 1998, para. 64.
118 *Ibid.*, para. 43.
119 *Ibid.*, para. 71.
120 SIC-22, SIC, October 1999, para. 5.
121 *Ibid.*, para. 6
122 *Ibid.*, para. 7.
123 IAS 22 para. 71.
124 IAS 38 para. 98
125 IAS 22, para. 73.
126 *Ibid.*, para. 75.
127 *Ibid.*
128 *Ibid.*, para. 60.
129 *Ibid.*, para. 61.
130 *Ibid.*, para. 62.
131 *Ibid.*, para. 63.
132 *Ibid.*, para. 42.
133 *Ibid.*, paras. 44 and 49.
134 *Ibid.*, para. 44.
135 *Ibid.*, para. 45.
136 *Ibid.*, para. 52.
137 *Ibid.*, para. 46.
138 *Ibid.*, para. 47.
139 *Ibid.*, para. 48.
140 *Ibid.*, para. 51.
141 *Ibid.*, para. 50.
142 *Ibid.*, para. 50.
143 *Ibid.*, paras. 55-58.
144 *Ibid.*, para. 53.
145 *Ibid.*, para. 54
146 IAS 38, para. 1.
147 *Ibid.*, para. 2.
148 *Ibid.*, para. 5.
149 *Ibid.*, para. 6.
150 *Ibid.*, para. 36.
151 *Ibid.*, para. 51.
152 *Ibid.*, para. 3.
153 *Ibid.*, para. 3.
154 *Ibid.*, para. 7.
155 *Ibid.*, para. 8.
156 *Ibid.*, para. 9.
157 *Ibid.*, paras. 10-12.
158 *Ibid.*, para. 36.
159 *Ibid.*, para. 51.
160 *Ibid.*, paras. 13-14.
161 *Ibid.*, paras. 15-16.
162 *Ibid.*, para. 17.
163 *Ibid.*, para. 19.
164 *Ibid.*, para. 20.
165 *Ibid.*, para. 22.
166 *Ibid.*, para. 23-26.
167 *Ibid.*, paras. 27-30.
168 *Ibid.*, para. 32.
169 *Ibid.*, para. 33.
170 *Ibid.*, paras. 34-35.
171 *Ibid.*, paras. 41-42.
172 *Ibid.*, para. 7.
173 *Ibid.*, para. 45.
174 *Ibid.*, para. 44.
175 *Ibid.*, para. 54.
176 *Ibid.*, para. 55.
177 *Ibid.*, para. 56.
178 *Ibid.*, para. 57.
179 *Ibid.*, para. 59.
180 *Ibid.*, para. 60.
181 *Ibid.*, para. 7.
182 *Ibid.*, para. 70.
183 *Ibid.*, paras. 72-73.
184 *Ibid.*, paras. 76-77.
185 *Ibid.*, para. 79.
186 *Ibid.*, para. 84
187 *Ibid.*, paras. 80-81.
188 *Ibid.*, paras. 80, 85-87.
189 *Ibid.*, para. 88.
190 *Ibid.*, para. 83.
191 *Ibid.*, para. 84.
192 *Ibid.*, paras. 91-92.
193 *Ibid.*, para. 93.
194 *Ibid.*, paras. 94-96.
195 *Ibid.*, para. 97.
196 *Ibid.*, paras. 99-101.
197 *Ibid.*, para. 102
198 *Ibid.*, paras. 103-104.
199 *Ibid.*, para. 105.
200 *Ibid.*, para. 106.
201 IAS 22., para. 88.
202 IAS 38., para. 91.
203 *Ibid.*, para. 96.
204 *Ibid.*, para. 107.
205 *Ibid.*, para. 108.
206 *Ibid.*, para. 111.
207 *Ibid.*, para. 113.

Chapter 12 Tangible fixed assets

1 INTRODUCTION

The broad principles for accounting for tangible fixed assets are generally well understood. The cost is capitalised when they are acquired, subsequently depreciated through the profit and loss account over their working lives, and written down if at any time the carrying value is seen not to be fully recoverable. When a tangible fixed asset is sold or scrapped, the difference between the written down value and any proceeds is recorded as the gain or loss on disposal.

There are inevitably some detailed rules required to apply these principles in practice, such as precisely when should a tangible fixed asset initially be recognised, and how should its cost be measured? If a policy of revaluation is adopted, how should the asset be accounted for? In the UK the Companies Act sets out the basic rules to be followed, but as in most other areas of financial reporting, the development of more detailed requirements has been left to accounting standards.

The principal accounting standard on tangible fixed assets in the UK is FRS 15 – *Tangible fixed assets* – and under IAS the main standard is IAS 16 – *Property plant and equipment*. Impairment of tangible fixed assets is a major consideration in accounting for them, and is covered by separate standards under both IAS and UK GAAP. The UK standard is FRS 11 – *Impairment of fixed assets and goodwill* – which as its name implies deals with intangible and tangible fixed assets, as does its international equivalent, IAS 36 – *Impairment of assets*. Impairment is covered as a separate topic in Chapter 13.

In addition, under both IAS and UK GAAP there is a separate standard dealing with one particular class of tangible fixed assets, investment properties. The UK standard is SSAP 19 – *Accounting for investment properties* – while its international equivalent is IAS 40 – *Investment property*. In the UK the measurement and classification of a disposal of a tangible fixed asset is addressed by FRS 3 – *Reporting financial performance* – which is discussed in Chapter 25.

FRS 15 became mandatory for periods ending on or after 23 March 2000; IAS 16 was revised in 1998 and became operative for annual financial statements covering periods *beginning* on or after 1 July 1999. IAS 40 became operative for annual financial statements covering periods beginning on or after 1 January 2001, while SSAP 19 was adopted in 1981 with a minor amendment in 1994.

2 UK ACCOUNTING REQUIREMENTS

2.1 Introduction

In the UK the Companies Act 1985 lays down broad principles and requirements for the accounting treatment all types of fixed assets, including tangible fixed assets and their depreciation. These provisions are also largely contained, explicitly or implicitly, within the main ASB pronouncement FRS 15. This part of the chapter outlines the Companies Act provisions followed by those of the other regulatory pronouncements, principally those of the relevant accounting standards, FRS 15 and SSAP 19. The principal disclosures in financial statements required under UK GAAP for all types of tangible fixed assets are dealt with separately at 3 below.

2.2 Companies Act requirements

2.2.1 *Definition and classification*

The Companies Act 1985 defines fixed assets as those which are intended for use on a continuing basis in the company's activities and any assets which are not intended for such use are taken to be current assets.[1] The Companies Act allows for the existence of three major classes of fixed asset:

I Intangible assets

II Tangible assets

III Investments [2]

Within the heading 'tangible assets' the following headings are set out in the Act, though the Act permits categories with Arabic numerals to be modified to suit the circumstances of an individual business.

1. Land and buildings
2. Plant and machinery
3. Fixtures, fittings, tools and equipment
4. Payments on account and assets in course of construction

The distinction between fixed and current assets is usually clear and the statutory definition is not normally interpreted to mean that individual assets are transferred to current assets when a decision to dispose of them has been made. Nevertheless, some companies do make such transfers. This is discussed further in 2.3.2 below.

2.2.2 *Measurement of the cost of tangible fixed assets*

The Companies Act requires that, subject to any provision for depreciation or diminution in value, the amount to be included in respect of any fixed asset shall be its purchase price or production cost.[3] The Companies Act also allows tangible fixed assets to be carried at a valuation, the rules that specify what basis of valuation can be used in company accounts are to be found in the Alternative Accounting Rules in Part C of Schedule 4 of the Companies Act 1985. In addition to historical cost, this schedule of the Act enables tangible fixed assets to be included at market value or current cost;[4] The entire subject of carrying tangible fixed assets at a valuation is separately discussed at 2.5 below.

Most tangible fixed assets are included at purchase price or production cost, subject to any provision for depreciation or diminution in value. The Companies Act defines purchase price as any consideration, whether in cash or otherwise, given by the company in respect of that asset.[5] In addition, according to the Act, 'the purchase price of an asset shall be determined by adding to the actual price paid any expenses incidental to its acquisition'.[6]

'Expenses incidental to its acquisition' are those costs which have been incurred as a direct consequence of the purchase of the asset and are necessary in order to make it available for use.

The definition in the Act of the production cost of any asset (fixed or current, tangible or intangible) says that it:

> 'shall be determined by adding to the purchase price of the raw materials and consumables used the amount of the costs incurred by the company which are directly attributable to the production of that asset.
>
> In addition there may be included in the production cost of an asset –
>
> (a) a reasonable proportion of the costs incurred by the company which are only indirectly attributable to the production of that asset, but only to the extent that they relate to the period of production; and
>
> (b) interest on capital borrowed to finance the production of that asset, to the extent that it accrues in respect of the period of production.'[7]

Some of the elements of these definitions require further interpretation, notably the meanings of 'indirectly attributable costs' and 'period of production', and these are addressed by FRS 15 which is discussed below at 2.3. Capitalisation of interest costs is dealt with separately in Chapter 15.

2.2.3 *Depreciation of tangible fixed assets*

The Companies Act requires any fixed asset, whether tangible or intangible, that has a limited useful economic life to be depreciated over that life, on a systematic basis, down to its residual value (if any).[8] Depreciation is to be based on the carrying value; on the purchase price or production cost under the historical cost rules,[9] and on the revalued amount if the alternative accounting rules are being followed.[10] Depreciation and other amounts written off tangible and intangible fixed assets must be shown, either on the face of the profit and loss account or in the notes, as further set at 3 below. The entire subject of carrying tangible fixed assets at a valuation is separately discussed at 2.5 below.

The Act also requires provisions for diminution in value to be made in respect of any fixed asset, even after depreciation, if the reduction in value is expected to be permanent.[11] This impairment aspect of accounting for fixed assets is covered in Chapter 13.

2.3 The requirements of FRS 15

2.3.1 *Introduction*

FRS 15 – *Tangible fixed assets* – is a comparatively recent standard, that came into force in March 2000. It contains a number of changes to, and clarifications about, how tangible fixed assets are to be accounted for. One of the most important was a new approach to the recognition and depreciation of substantial tangible fixed assets such as buildings. These types of fixed asset may now have to be recognised using a 'components approach' whereby each major sub-assembly of the whole (e.g. elevators in buildings) is allocated a separate life and depreciated separately. Other aspects of the treatment of tangible fixed assets have been clarified by FRS 15, for example indirectly attributable costs may not be capitalised and the period of production during which costs may be capitalised is also specifically defined.

With the exception of the components approach it requires, FRS 15 is less an innovative standard than one which has clarified current practice, while at the same time firmly removing a number of ambiguities in it. The standard applies to all tangible fixed assets, with the exception of investment properties as defined in SSAP 19.[12]

2.3.2 *Definition and recognition*

FRS 15 defines tangible fixed assets as:

> 'Assets that have physical substance and are held for use in the production or supply of goods and services, for rental to others, or for administrative purposes on a continuing basis in the reporting entity's activities.'[13]

This builds upon the Companies Act definition but is much more specific. Its use of the wording 'held for use' is somewhat stronger than the statutory 'intended for use', and could again encourage the view that it would be appropriate to reclassify fixed assets held for sale as current assets. While this is an acceptable practice, as an asset being held for resale is no longer held for use in the business, in our view it is not necessary for companies to make such reclassifications.

Hilton Group provides an example of assets held for sale being reclassified as current assets in the extract below.

Extract 12.1: Hilton Group plc (2000)

Consolidated balance sheet [extract]

	Note	**2000**	1999
		£m	£m
Current assets			
Assets held for resale	14	**2.8**	5.9
Stocks	15	**22.7**	22.2
Debtors			
– amounts falling due within one year	16	**324.7**	324.4
– amounts falling due after more than one year	16	**29.6**	44.6
Cash at bank and in hand		**86.2**	107.0

Notes [extract]
14 Assets held for resale

Assets held for resale in 2000 comprise properties with a carrying value of £2.8m (1999: £5.9m).

The standard requires that tangible fixed assets should be measured initially at cost[14] and this should include 'costs, but only those costs, that are directly attributable to bringing the asset into working condition for its intended use'.[15] The standard does allow tangible fixed assets to be carried at a valuation, after initial recognition at cost, as follows:

> 'Tangible fixed assets should be revalued only where the entity adopts a policy of revaluation. Where such a policy is adopted then it should be applied to individual classes of tangible fixed assets (in accordance with paragraph 61), but need not be applied to all classes of tangible fixed assets held by the entity.
>
> Where a tangible fixed asset is subject to a policy of revaluation its carrying amount should be its current value as at the balance sheet date.'[16]

The entire subject of carrying tangible fixed assets at a valuation is separately discussed at 2.5 below.

A Attributable cost

As FRS 15 now only permits *directly* attributable costs to be included in tangible fixed assets, the standard has removed the possibility of including indirectly attributable ones. Directly attributable costs are defined as:

'(a) the labour costs of own employees (eg site workers, in-house architects and surveyors) arising directly from the construction, or acquisition, of the specific tangible fixed asset; and

(b) the incremental costs to the entity that would have been avoided only if the tangible fixed asset had not been constructed or acquired.'[17]

The standard includes the following examples of directly attributable costs:

- acquisition costs such as stamp duty, import duties and non-refundable purchase taxes;
- the costs of site preparation and clearance;
- initial delivery and handling costs;
- installation costs;
- professional fees such as legal, architects' and engineers' fees; and
- the estimated cost of dismantling and removing the asset and restoring the site, to the extent that it is recognised as a provision under FRS 12 'Provisions, Contingent Liabilities and Contingent Assets'. The fact that the prospect of such expenditures emerges only some time after the original capitalisation of the asset (eg because of legislative changes) does not preclude their capitalisation.[18]

FRS 15 makes it clear that administration and other general overheads fall outside the definition. It also stresses that employee costs not related to a specific asset, such as site selection activities, do not qualify for capitalisation.[19] The capitalisation of management time is thus unlikely to be permitted under FRS 15.

The standard also states that any 'abnormal costs' are not directly attributable either. Examples of these are 'those relating to design errors, industrial disputes, idle capacity, wasted materials, labour or other resources and other production delays', and 'costs such as operating losses that occur because a revenue activity has been suspended during the construction of a tangible fixed asset'.[20]

Taken together, the rules on what may be capitalised are therefore quite restrictive. They are much narrower than the equivalent rules on what may be carried forward in the cost of stock. SSAP 9 excludes from stock neither abnormal costs that arise from inefficiencies nor costs that are not incremental, and it requires an appropriate allocation of relevant overheads. FRS 15 essentially restricts the costs that may be included to those that are essential to the creation of the asset and that would not otherwise have been incurred. Extract 12.2 from Williams shows an example of such indirectly attributable costs being removed from asset carrying values on the adoption of FRS 15.

Extract 12.2: Williams plc (1999)

1 Accounting policies [extract]

FRS 15: Tangible fixed assets. The group has adopted the option within the transitional arrangements to retain the book values of fixed assets at their previously revalued amounts. No further revaluations will be undertaken. FRS 15 only permits directly attributable costs to be included in fixed assets. Previously indirect overhead costs associated with the acquisition of certain fixed assets have been capitalised. Adopting FRS 15 has resulted in a prior year adjustment of £17.3m to net assets and has reduced 1999 and 1998 operating profit by £5.8m and £2.7m and increased the exceptional profit on disposal of subsidiaries by £0.8m and £2.9m respectively.

Restatement summary [extract[

				Restatement analysed between		
	1998 As published	**Restatement**	**1998 Restated**	**FRS 15**	**deferred costs**	**exchange on goodwill**
Profit and loss account	**£m**	**£m**	**£m**	**£m**	**£m**	**£m**
Operating profit	347.5	(6.8)	340.7	(2.7)	(4.1)	–
Share of operating profit of associated companies	9.8	–	9.8	–	–	–
Exceptional items	175.9	7.0	182.9	2.9	–	4.1
Profit before interest and taxation	533.2	0.2	533.4	0.2	(4.1)	4.1
Interest (net)	(70.7)	–	(70.7)	–	–	–
Profit before tax	462.5	0.2	462.7	0.2	(4.1)	4.1
Tax	(117.6)	2.2	(115.4)	1.0	1.2	–
Profit after tax	344.9	2.4	347.3	1.2	(2.9)	4.1
Balance sheet						
Fixed assets	618.3	(25.9)	592.4	(25.9)	–	–

The inclusion of the last example of attributable costs – the estimated cost of dismantling and removing the asset and restoring the site – is definitely odd. FRS 12 – *Provisions, Contingent Liabilities and Contingent Assets* – has had some curious knock-on effects, of which this is one. This example of an attributable cost obviously contradicts the rule that only those costs directly attributable to bringing the asset *into* working condition should be included. However FRS 12 requires obligations arising from past events existing independently of an entity's future actions (i.e. the future conduct of its business) to be recognised as provisions, essentially in full immediately the obligation arises (see Chapter 28 for a full discussion of FRS 12). The ASB has attempted to neutralise the profit and loss account effect of this FRS 12 requirement by allowing the debit associated with the provision entry to be capitalised as an asset and subsequently depreciated, rather than expensed immediately. This therefore explains the inclusion within FRS 15 of the estimated costs of site restoration as directly attributable costs – hence allowing their capitalisation.

A common instance of this treatment is dilapidation obligations in lease agreements, where, arguably, a provision is required whenever the 'damage' is incurred. Therefore, if a retailer rents two adjoining premises and knocks them into one, it probably has an obligation to make good the party wall at the end of the lease term and should immediately provide for the costs of so doing. Under FRS 12 the 'other side' of the provision entry is an asset that will be amortised over the lease term – notwithstanding that some of the costs of modifying the premises may also have been capitalised as assets.

Finally FRS 15 lays down a specific rule for the recognition of tangible fixed assets donated to charities, the initial carrying amount of which should be the current value of the assets at the date they are received.[21]

B Period of production

As explained above, the Companies Act allows certain costs to be included in production cost to the extent that they relate to the period of production. However, there is no guidance in the Act to help determine when the period of production either starts or finishes.

FRS 15 requires capitalisation of directly attributable costs to cease when substantially all the activities that are necessary to get the tangible fixed asset ready for use are complete (i.e. its physical construction), even if it has not yet been brought into use.[22] It therefore prohibits the practice of extending the production period beyond the date of practical completion of the physical asset. This applies particularly to sectors where this period may be prolonged, such as property investment. The argument in the past has been that the asset being constructed is not simply the physical structure of the building but a fully tenanted investment property, and the production period correspondingly includes not simply the construction period but also the letting period. The accounting policies of investment property companies frequently took this line, but Hammerson has changed its policy to accord with the requirement of FRS 15 as shown in the extract below.

Extract 12.3: Hammerson plc (2000)

1 ACCOUNTING POLICIES [extract]
Cost of properties

An amount equivalent to the net development outgoings, including interest gross of taxation, attributable to properties held for development or resale is added to the cost of such properties. In accordance with Financial Reporting Standard 15, a property is regarded as being in the course of development until ready for its intended use. For buildings that are pre-let this will be when construction and the fitting out period are complete. In the case of unlet buildings this will be at the end of the construction period. Comparative figures have not been restated as any adjustment would not be material to the financial statements.

FRS 15 prohibits extending the production period beyond the date of practical completion of the physical asset. Although FRS 15 exempts investment properties from its scope, the definition of investment properties includes the requirement that any construction work and development has been completed. Accordingly, properties which are in the course of construction or development fall within the scope of FRS 15.

FRS 15 endorses the practice of continuing to capitalise costs during an initial commissioning period, but only where 'the asset is available for use but incapable of operating at normal levels without such a start-up or commissioning period'.[23] This would allow capitalisation of, for example, the costs of a commissioning period that is necessary for running in machinery or testing equipment. It distinguishes this from the case where the asset is fully operational but is not yet achieving its targeted profitability because demand is still building up, for example in a new hotel or bookstore. In this case, the production period has finished and no further costs should be capitalised. Any further costs will not meet the definition of 'directly attributable' because they will have been incurred after physical completion and they are not necessary in order to use the asset.[24]

While FRS 15 precludes start-up costs being capitalised as fixed assets, UITF 24 was published in June 2000 to deal directly with the practice in certain sectors of deferring start-up costs as prepayments.

UITF 24 defines start-up costs very broadly: 'one-time activities related to opening a new facility, introducing a new product or service, conducting business in a new territory, conducting business with a new class of customer, initiating a new process in an existing facility, starting some new operation and similar items. They include costs of relocating or reorganising part or all of an entity, costs related to organising a new entity, and expenses and losses incurred both before and after opening.'[25]

The UITF reached a consensus that start-up costs should be accounted for in the same way as similar costs incurred as part of the entity's on-going activities. Therefore, for example, if the entity normally expenses marketing and training costs it should continue to do so if the costs are incurred as part of a start-up. Costs specific to a start up may be capitalised only if they meet the criteria for recognition as assets under FRS 15, FRS 10 or SSAP 13. Otherwise, they should be recognised as an expense when they are incurred.[26]

Thus the capitalisation or deferral of any start up costs, other than those allowed under FRS 15, is considerably restricted. FRS 10 prohibits the capitalisation of internally-generated intangible assets except in the most unusual of cases (see Chapter 11 at 2.3.3). Attempts to use SSAP 13 had already been successfully challenged by the Financial Reporting Review Panel.

In its accounts for the year ended 31 December 1999, Sinclair Montrose Healthcare capitalised as development costs all costs other than marketing and advertising incurred on its Medicentre project. These were carried forward as 'development expenditure' in accordance with the following policy:

Extract 12.4: Sinclair Montrose Healthcare (1998)

Development expenditure

Since its inception in 1996, Medicentre has been following a phased development plan with an end date of March 1999, at which point the directors concluded that there would be a reasonable certainty as to it commercial viability. Consequently, the development phase has been recognised by capitalising development expenditure incurred for the year, net of revenue earned, to the end of the development period. Marketing, advertising and other expenditure incurred in order to establish the Medicentre brand, which was previously capitalised, has now been written off. The impact on the 1997 results is set out in note 11.

The Financial Reporting Review Panel was of the view that these costs were not 'development costs' as defined by SSAP 13 (whose requirements for capitalisation are given in Chapter 11 at 2.4.3). The costs had not been incurred prior to the commencement of commercial application as the business was trading, albeit making start-up losses. Some of the costs capitalised would have related to the running of the commercial business.[27] In other words, the Panel had concluded that the 'development costs' were start-up costs that could not be capitalised under SSAP 13. The company replaced its accounts for the year, writing off the development costs and removing the policy on deferred development expenditure.

C Subsequent expenditure and the 'components approach'

It is often difficult to decide whether expenditure on improvements and repairs is capital or revenue in nature and, if it is capital, whether it should be treated as part of the original asset or as a new tangible fixed asset. To aid this decision the standard differentiates between revenue and capital expenditure in the following manner.

Subsequent expenditure is *revenue* and should be expensed as incurred, if it is for repairs and maintenance that maintains the asset's previously assessed standard of performance, or is necessary in order to prevent the useful life or residual value of the asset from decreasing.[28] Examples include the costs of servicing or overhauling plant or repainting buildings.

Subsequent expenditure is *capital* and should be included in the carrying value of the assets, only if it falls within one of the following three circumstances:

(a) where the subsequent expenditure provides an enhancement of the economic benefits of the tangible fixed asset in excess of the previously assessed standard of performance; or

(b) where a component of the tangible fixed asset that has been treated separately for depreciation purposes and depreciated over its individual useful economic life, is replaced or restored; or

(c) where the subsequent expenditure relates to a major inspection or overhaul of a tangible fixed asset that restores the economic benefits of the asset that have been consumed by the entity and have already been reflected in depreciation.[29]

Examples of the enhancement of benefits given by the standard include:

- an extension in the estimated useful life or an increase in capacity; or
- a substantial improvement in the quality of output. [30]

Criterion (b) has been added to prevent the capitalisation criteria being unnecessarily restrictive. Repairs would otherwise almost always have been excluded from being capitalised as they rarely extend the life of the asset beyond that previously assessed (and indeed expenditure on replacing components would almost undoubtedly have been taken into account in the previous assessment, whether this was made at the point of purchase or occasioned by subsequent capital expenditure)

The principle is straightforward. If, for example, a property's roof or lift system has been separately identified and depreciated, its replacement can be capitalised, subject, of course, to writing off the remaining carrying amount of the old asset. This is simply straightforward asset accounting but with the existing asset reclassified as a series of separate assets with separate lives. However, by no means all organisations have records that would allow suitable asset components to be identified and it would not necessarily be to their advantage to do so; the costs could well outweigh the benefits.

This would appear to mean that expenditure that does not enhance the benefits and has not been separately identified and depreciated will be deemed to be repairs and maintenance expenditure and expensed when incurred, unless it falls within criterion (c).

Criterion (c) is a consequence of FRS 12. One of the examples in the application notes to that standard deals with those entities that make major periodic repairs to large assets and have accounted for these by setting up provisions to meet the costs. This has been a common practice in the airline and oil refining industries, although it has never been universally applied in either sector; some companies accounted for the expenditure when incurred, others capitalised the cost and depreciated it over the period until the next major overhaul. Similar policies have been followed by utilities that apply 'asset maintenance plans' (the treatment of infrastructure assets is discussed further at 2.3.3H below).

FRS 12 explicitly disallows setting up provisions for such periodic overhauls on the basis that there is no obligation to carry out the expenditure independently of the entity's future actions. However, FRS 12 suggests that the entity's results can be largely insulated from the effects of any change in the policy of providing for repair costs over time by adjusting the asset's carrying value and depreciation charge.[31]

FRS 15 argues that this is similar to treating a major component of an asset as a separate asset and depreciating it over its useful life, i.e. as a variation of category (b) above. Under (b), a company may choose to account separately for major components such as furnace linings; these linings would be capitalised and depreciated over the period until they are replaced, whereupon the replacement lining is capitalised in its place. Major inspections and overhauls could be treated in the same way. The depreciation of the asset could reflect an amount equivalent to the expected overhaul costs over the period until the next overhaul, when those costs would be capitalised and the cycle repeated.[32]

There are a number of shortcomings in these rules. The costs themselves are not necessarily tangible – they may comprise inspection costs rather than tangible assets like a furnace lining. Nothing is being made or added at the periodic overhaul; it is not the same as replacing a tangible part of the asset whose cost could be established and written off over its useful life. The depreciation over the period until the first overhaul would have to be an estimate. It would be neither an allocation of the asset's cost over its life, nor an allocation of value consumed.

As this treatment only applies where there is no separately identifiable asset being depreciated and replaced, this could result in some rather odd depreciation charges. An asset that is not otherwise distinguished into separate parts would be regarded as having more than one life and be depreciated at different rates, as can be seen in the following example:

Example 12.1: Subsequent Expenditure and Cyclical Repairs

Cost 100
Life 10 years

Cost of cyclical repair:
Year 3 3
Year 6 5

Year	*1*	*2*	*3*	*4*	*5*	*6*	*7*	*8*	*9*	*10*
Cost	100	100	100	103	103	103	108	108	108	108
Additions			3			5				
	100	100	103	103	103	108	108	108	108	108
Depreciation										
Brought forward		10.7	21.4	32.1	42.8	53.5	64.2	75.15	96.1	97.05
Depreciation	10.7	10.7	10.7	10.7	10.7	10.7	10.95	10.95	10.95	10.95
	10.7	21.4	32.1	42.8	53.5	64.2	75.15	96.1	97.05	108
Net Book Value	89.3	78.6	70.9	60.2	49.5	43.8	32.85	21.9	10.95	0

Years 1 – 3
The depreciation charge is 97/10 + 3/3, ie, the estimated cost of the cyclical maintenance in year 3 is added to the depreciation charge. The cost of the cyclical maintenance (£3) is added to the asset.

Years 4 – 6
The asset continues to be depreciated at £9.7 per annum and the first cyclical repair of £3 is depreciated over the period to the next cyclical repair.

Year 6
The cost of the cyclical maintenance (£5) is added to the asset.

Years 7 – 10
As there is no more planned maintenance spend, the remaining NBV of the asset of £43.8 is written off over the remaining life.

At first sight it is surprising that the depreciation for years 1 to 3 is based on the cost of the first cyclical repair, while in year 4 to 6 the additional depreciation is based on the cost of £3 and not the estimated cost of the next overhaul of £5. This is because the cost of the economic benefits consumed in years 1 to 3 is estimated to be the cost of that first overhaul. Its cost of £3, when incurred in year 3, is now a separate component of the asset with a life of 3 years.

The ASB does not appear to take a rigorous view of categories (b) or (c). It suggests that the decision to identify separate components or overhauls for depreciation over a shorter economic life would depend on a number of factors, including:

- whether the useful economic lives of the components or the period until the next overhaul is substantially different from the useful economic life of the rest of the asset;
- the degree of irregularity in the levels of expenditure required to restate the component or asset in different accounting periods; and
- their materiality.[33]

Ultimately, therefore, the ASB appears to accept that it may often be preferable to expense subsequent expenditure that does not enhance the economic benefits in excess of the previously assessed standard of performance. It may be neither practicable nor desirable to record each individual asset as several different assets nor to depreciate part of the asset over a different timescale to the rest of the asset.

2.3.3 *Depreciation of tangible fixed assets under FRS 15*

A Definitions and general requirement

FRS 15 includes the following definitions relating to depreciation.

Depreciation is the measure of the cost or revalued amount of the economic benefits of the tangible fixed asset that have been consumed during the period.

Depreciable amount is the cost of a tangible fixed asset (or, where an asset is revalued, the revalued amount) less its residual value.

Residual value is the net realisable value of an asset at the end of its useful economic life. Residual values are based on prices prevailing at the date of acquisition (or revaluation) of the asset and do not take account of expected future price changes.

The *useful economic life* of a tangible fixed asset is the period over which the entity expects to derive economic benefits from that asset.[34]

FRS 15's basic requirement is that the depreciable amount of a tangible fixed asset is to be allocated on a systematic basis over its useful economic life, using a method that reflects as fairly as possible the pattern in which its economic benefits are consumed.[35] It is emphasised that this is done in order to charge operating profits with the consumption of the asset. In other words the treatment has a profit and loss account objective not a balance sheet one.[36] Unless the asset's residual value at the end of its useful economic life is at least going to equal its present book value in real terms, then depreciation is required. FRS 15 is specific that assets carried at a valuation (which are separately dealt with in 2.5 below) are still subject to the requirement to be depreciated:

> 'The fundamental objective of depreciation is to reflect in operating profit the cost of use of the tangible fixed assets (ie amount of economic benefits consumed) in the period. This requires a charge to operating profit even if the asset has risen in value or been revalued.'[37]

B Useful economic life and residual values

One of the critical assumptions on which the depreciation charge depends is the useful economic life of the asset. The useful economic life is the period over which the present owner will benefit and not the total potential life of the asset; the two will often not be the same. For example, a company may have a policy of replacing all of its cars after three years, so this will be their estimated useful life for depreciation purposes.

FRS 15 says that the following factors should be considered in assessing the useful life, residual value and depreciation method to be used for an asset:

- the expected usage of the asset by the entity, assessed by reference to the asset's expected capacity or physical output;

- the expected physical deterioration of the asset through use or effluxion of time; this will depend upon the repair and maintenance programme of the entity both when the asset is in use and when it is idle;
- economic or technological obsolescence, for example arising from changes or improvements in production, or a change in the market demand for the product or service output of that asset;
- legal or similar limits on the use of the asset, such as the expiry dates of related leases.[38]

The effects of technological change are often underestimated. It affects many assets, not only high technology plant and equipment such as computer systems. Many offices that have been purpose-built in the post-war period have become obsolete long before their fabric has physically deteriorated, for reasons such as the difficulty of introducing computer network infrastructures, or air conditioning.

The standard requires asset lives to be estimated on a realistic basis and reviewed at the end of each reporting period.[39] The effects of changes in estimated life are to be recognised prospectively, over the remaining life of the asset.[40]

In practice, many companies tend to use quite a 'broad brush' approach to estimating asset lives, often based on perceived norms (for example, 50 years for freehold buildings) rather than a close analysis of their own expectations. As a result, companies often have a material proportion of assets still in use but fully depreciated.

Disclosure of this figure is not required under UK GAAP, though it is encouraged under IAS. One company that discloses the amount of its fully depreciated assets is Corus Group, shown below:

Extract 12.5: Corus Group plc (2000)

Notes [extract]

Tangible fixed assets [extract]

(i) Included above are fully depreciated assets with an original cost of £1,450m (2 Oct 1999: £1,492m; 3 Apr 1999: £1,332m) which are still in use. In addition, there are fully depreciated assets with an original cost of £163m (2 Oct 1999: £124m; 3 Apr 1999: £139m) which are permanently out of use and pending disposal, demolition or reapplication elsewhere in the business.

An example of a company that explicitly states that it regularly reviews asset lives is ICI. As a result the accounting policy note cannot give the period over which the assets are depreciated, except as global averages, as illustrated below:

Extract 12.6: Imperial Chemical Industries PLC (2000)

Accounting policies [extract]

Depreciation

The Group's policy is to write-off the book value of each tangible fixed assets to its residual value evenly over its estimated remaining life. Reviews are made annually of the estimated remaining lives of individual productive assets, taking account of commercial and technological obsolescence as well as normal wear and tear. Under this policy it becomes impracticable to calculate average asset lives exactly; however, the total lives approximate to 34 years for buildings and 16 years for plant and equipment. Depreciation of assets qualifying for grants is calculated on their full cost.

C Residual values

Both FRS 15 and the Act require residual values to be taken into account when calculating depreciation on an asset. Prior to the implementation of FRS 15, residual values were rarely considered a major issue. However now that property assets must be separated into land and building elements, and buildings have to be depreciated, the residual values of buildings may have begin to have a material effect on financial statements.

The residual value must be based on prices prevailing at the time of purchase or subsequent revaluation.[41] For example, if an asset has an estimated useful life of six years, the company should look at the net realisable value of a six year old equivalent asset as at the date of purchase, rather than considering how much the asset can be sold for in six years' time. Other factors to be taken into account will include location (in the case of property), the risk of obsolescence, and the planned maintenance policy. This obviously makes an accurate assessment of residual value difficult and entities with large portfolios normally use surveyors to assist in the estimation.

Basing residual values on prices prevailing at the time of purchase means that it is not permitted to anticipate inflationary holding gains. FRS 15 requires material residual values to be reassessed at the end of each reporting period to take account of the effects of technological changes (if possible, still at price levels consistent with the date of acquisition or revaluation). Changes to the residual value should result in a prospective write off over the remaining useful life unless they indicate that the asset has been impaired at the balance sheet date.[42]

FRS 15 accepts that some assets may have such high residual values, or such long useful lives, that depreciation becomes immaterial and on these grounds allows depreciation not to be charged. Assets may also have useful lives in excess of fifty years. In either of these cases an annual impairment test must be performed (impairment is discussed in Chapter 13). The standard also suggests that it will only be plausible to assume a high residual value where all of the following apply:

- the entity has a policy of regular repair to keep its assets to their previously assessed standard of performance;
- the asset is not prone to obsolescence;
- the entity habitually sells such assets well before the end of their economic lives; and
- such sales do not give rise to material losses (after excluding the effects of price changes).[43]

D Depreciation of property assets

The emphasis in FRS 15 on the purpose of depreciation is designed to negate the arguments that some companies have made in the past in order to justify non-depreciation of certain properties. This has been a source of continual argument ever since SSAP 12 was originally published in 1977. The charging of depreciation to the profit and loss account when the property asset concerned was increasing in value seemed counter-intuitive to many businesses, including retailers and banks as well as hotel and pub chains.

Usually, non-depreciation was justified on the grounds that the buildings were maintained to such a high standard that any depreciation charge would be immaterial. The ASB does not accept this argument. The standard explicitly states that maintenance expenditure of itself does not negate the need to charge depreciation and should not be assumed to extend an asset's life indefinitely.[44] In addition, subsequent spend to maintain the previously assessed standard of performance is already assumed when calculating an asset's useful economic life (see 2.3.2C above).

Marks and Spencer is an example of a company that changed its accounting policy when it implemented FRS 15 in 1999. Under its original policy freehold and long leasehold properties were not depreciated on the basis that they were maintained to such a standard that deprecation was immaterial, as shown below.

Extract 12.7: Marks and Spencer p.l.c. (1998)

Accounting Policies [extract]
Fixed assets
B Depreciation

(iii) Given that the lives of the Group's freehold and long leasehold properties are so long and that they are maintained to such a high standard, it is the opinion of the directors that in most instances the residual values would be sufficiently high to make any depreciation charge immaterial. The directors have based their estimates of residual values on prices prevailing at the time of acquisition or revaluation. Where residual values are lower than cost or valuation, depreciation is charged to the profit and loss account. Any permanent diminution in value in also charged to the revaluation reserve or the profit and loss account as appropriate

FRS 15 requires changes to asset lives or residual values to be changes in estimates to be recognised prospectively over the remaining useful economic life.[45] The transitional requirements of FRS 15 state that, unless the revisions to the useful economic lives and residual values have resulted from the separation, for the first time, of assets into separate components for depreciation purposes, they are not to be treated as a change in accounting policy.[46] These transitional rules were clarified by UITF Abstract 23 – *Application of the transitional rules in FRS 15* – according to which the building is not a separate component and so any depreciation of the buildings component arising from the introduction of FRS 15 should be dealt with prospectively.[47]

Marks and Spencer is explicit in its change in policy note following adoption of FRS 15, shown below, that buildings were previously subject to depreciation but that this depreciation was immaterial. The changed treatment accords with the interpretation of FRS 15's transitional rules by UITF 23, and the properties are now being depreciated prospectively over their remaining useful lives.

Extract 12.8: Marks and Spencer p.l.c. (1999)

Accounting Policies [extract]
Fixed assets
B Depreciation [extract]

Depreciation is provided to write off the cost or valuation of tangible fixed assets, less residual value, by equal annual instalments as follows:

Land: not depreciated;

Freehold and leasehold buildings over 50 years: depreciated to their estimated residual value over their estimated remaining economic lives (see also c below);

11. Tangible fixed assets (extract)
B Change of Accounting Policy (extract)

(ii) In previous years the Group has stated that the useful economic lives of its freehold and long leasehold properties are so long and the residual values are so high that any depreciation charge was immaterial. The Group agrees with the theory of 'consumption' and has charged depreciation against the book value of its properties this year amounting to £10.8m. There is no corresponding prior year adjustment since the previous policy was to depreciate properties at 1% or nil.

As stated above, FRS 15 allows that there will be some assets with such long lives and/or residual values that are so high, that depreciation would genuinely be immaterial, in which case it need not be charged, though under these circumstances an annual impairment review is required. An example of a company that is not depreciating its freehold and long leasehold properties but instead performing an annual impairment review is Wyevale Garden Centres.

Extract 12.9: Wyevale Garden Centres plc (2000)

Depreciation [extract]

On adoption of FRS15, the Group has following the transitional provisions to retain the book value of land and buildings certain of which have been revalued in years 1989 to 1996.

Depreciation is not charged on freehold on long leasehold properties. In accordance with FRS15 an impairment review under FRS11 is performed on those properties. The results of this review showed that the recoverable amount is in excess of the carrying amount supporting the policy.

E *Separation into components*

FRS 15 makes the point that an asset may actually comprise several different assets that may have substantially different useful economic lives (some of which may not be depreciated at all) that should be disaggregated for the purposes of charging depreciation. The most obvious example is land and buildings. The element of the carrying value that relates to the land should not be depreciated but the buildings have a finite useful life and should be depreciated over that life. Particular reference is made to the fact that increases in land values do not affect the residual value of the building or its useful economic life.[48]

However, it has become apparent that many entities had included within the category of land and buildings substantial amount relating to fixtures and fittings that in fact had a shorter life than the fabric of the building itself. On implementing the standard these assets had to be reclassified. This usually led to their being depreciated for the first time as they had previously been subsumed within a property asset that was not being depreciated. Hence the standard allowed the backlog depreciation to be charged by way of prior year adjustment.[49] In some cases the effect has been very significant.

Marks and Spencer used to have an explicit policy that certain fixtures were capitalised on acquisition but that replacement expenditure was expensed:

Extract 12.10: Marks and Spencer p.l.c. (1998)

Accounting Policies [extract]
Fixed assets
d Repairs and renewals

Certain major items of fixed plant and structure are incorporated within the cost of the buildings when purchased. When replaced, these are fully expensed as repairs and renewals in the profit and loss account.

In 1999, when the group implemented FRS 15, this policy was changed to one under which these assets, now called 'fit out', were to be capitalised and amortised over their useful economic life of between 10 and 25 years. The effects of the change in policy can be seen in the following extract from the accounts:

Extract 12.11: Marks and Spencer p.l.c. (1999)

Notes to the Financial Statements
11. Tangible fixed assets [extract]
A Tangible fixed assets

	The Group				The Company			
	Land & Buildings	Fit out, fixtures, fittings & equipment	Assets in the course of construction	**Total**	Land & Buildings	Fit out, fixtures, fittings & equipment	Assets in the course of construction	**Total**
	£m	£m	£m	**£m**	£m	£m	£m	**£m**
Cost or valuation								
As previously reported	3,627.0	1,189.7	123.4	**4,940.1**	3,254.6	908.4	54.3	**4,217.3**
Reclassification of fit out (see 11B)	(808.0)	808.0	–	**–**	(671.4)	671.4	–	**–**
Prior year adjustment (11B)	–	53.2	–	**53.2**	–	53.2	–	**53.2**
At 1 April 1998 as restated	2,819.0	2,050.9	123.4	**4,993.3**	2,583.2	1,633.0	54.3	**4,270.5**
Additions	74.2	311.5	297.4	**683.1**	59.8	263.6	230.3	**553.7**
Transfers	115.7	194.6	(310.3)	**–**	33.7	145.4	(179.1)	**–**
Disposals	(13.7)	(28.7)	–	**(42.4)**	(10.6)	(7.1)	–	**(17.7)**
Revaluation surplus	32.7	–	–	**32.7**	32.7	–	–	**32.7**
Differences on exchange	10.0	17.4	5.0	**32.4**	–	–	–	**–**
At 31 March 1999	**3,037.9**	**2,545.7**	**115.5**	**5,699.1**	**2,698.8**	**2,034.9**	**105.5**	**4,839.2**
Accumulated depreciation								
As previously reported	103.6	660.8	–	**764.4**	52.3	518.9	–	**571.2**
Reclassification of fit out (see 11B)	(40.0)	40.0	–	**–**	–	–	–	**–**
Prior year adjustment (see 11B)	–	264.1	–	**264.1**	–	254.0	–	**254.0**
At 1 April 1998 as restated	63.6	964.9	–	**1,028.5**	52.3	772.9	–	**825.2**
Depreciation for the year	20.4	280.0		**300.4**	18.4	173.0	–	**191.4**
Disposals	(1.1)	(22.1)	–	**(23.2)**	(1.2)	(5.6)	–	**(6.8)**
Differences on exchanges	0.6	5.3	–	**5.9**	–	–	–	**–**
At 31 March 1999	**83.5**	**1,228.1**	**–**	**1,311.6**	**69.5**	**940.3**	**–**	**1,009.8**
Net book value								
At 31 March 1999	**2,954.4**	**1,317.6**	**115.5**	**4,387.5**	**2,629.3**	**1,094.6**	**105.5**	**3,829.4**
At 31 March 1998 as restated	2,755.4	1,086.0	123.4	3,964.8	2,530.9	860.1	54.3	3,445.3

> **B Change of Accounting Policy**
> The Group has adopted FRS 15, 'Tangible Fixed Assets' and has followed the transitional provisions to retain the book value of land and buildings, certain of which were revalued in 1988 (see 11D below)
> Adoption has resulted in two key changes
> (i) The FRS encourages the separation of assets into components where they have very different useful economic lives and states that these changes should be dealt with as prior year adjustments. The cost of fitting out properties, which has up to now been included within the cost of buildings, has been separately identified and disclosed together with fixtures, fittings and equipment. Fit out has previously been accounted for on a replacement basis but under this policy will be depreciated evenly over periods ranging from 10-25 years depending on its nature. As a result, £53.2 of fit out which had been expensed in previous years has now been capitalised as at 31 March 1998. In addition, £264.1m of accumulated depreciation has also been recognised as at that date, being the depreciation on fit out which would have been recognised had the new policy been in place in previous years. As a consequence of the prior year adjustment, the net book value of Group tangible fixed assets as at 31 March 1998 has been reduced by £210.9m with a corresponding reduction in the profit and loss account reserve. The effect of this on reported profits has been an additional Group depreciation charge in the current year of £28.6m (last year £23.5m) and a reduction in the charge for repairs and renewals of £18.3m (last year £10.5m).

Some £808 million of fit out has been reclassified as fixtures and fittings and £264.1 million backlog depreciation provided by way of prior year adjustment, in accordance with paragraph 108 of the transitional rules in FRS 15. In addition, £52.3 million of fit out previously charged to reserves as repairs and maintenance has been reinstated.

FRS 15 makes it clear that the land component of a freehold property does not normally have to be depreciated:

> 'Land and buildings are separable components and are dealt with separately for accounting purposes, even when they are acquired together. With certain exceptions, such as sites used for extractive purposes or landfill, land has an unlimited life and therefore is not depreciated'.[50]

The guidance available to businesses in making an apportionment between the land and building elements of a freehold property is discussed further in 4.2 below.

F *Commencing to charge depreciation*

In principle, depreciation should be charged from the date the asset is brought into use. Companies often charge a full year's depreciation in the year of acquisition, regardless of when the assets were acquired, but many instead depreciate their assets on a monthly basis for management accounts purposes and carry the same figures into their annual accounts. At the opposite extreme, one or two commence depreciation only in the year following acquisition, but charge a full year's depreciation in the year of disposal; GKN is an example, as shown in the following extract:

Extract 12.12: GKN plc (2000)

Notes on the accounts [extract]

3 Operating profit [extract]

Depreciation is not provided on freehold land. In the case of buildings and computers, depreciation is provided on valuation or original cost. For all other categories of asset, depreciation is provided on the written down value at the beginning of the financial year. Except in special cases, depreciation is not charged on fixed assets capitalised during the year and available for use but a full year's depreciation is charged on fixed assets sold or scrapped during the year.

However, Wyevale Garden Centres were challenged by the Financial Reporting Review Panel for applying a similar policy:

Extract 12.13: Wyevale Garden Centres plc (2000)

Depreciation [extract]

Depreciation is provided on plant and equipment in the accounting year following that in which the assets were acquired, this basis is considered more appropriate to the nature of the Group's business..

The Panel argued that depreciation needed to be charged throughout the useful life of the asset.[51] The group has changed its policy in the interim accounts for the 26 weeks ended 1 July 2001 and now charges depreciation from the date that the assets are brought into use.[52]

In fact, charging a full year's depreciation in the year of disposal only affects the classification of the profit and loss account, because it changes the gain or loss reported on sale by an equal and opposite amount. GKN's practice of providing no depreciation in the first year is probably convenient, and is unlikely to create a material distortion in practice. Policies need only be disclosed for items that have a material effect on the accounts.

G *Depreciating assets for part only of their lives*

There have been examples of companies only depreciating assets, such as mineral reserves, in the last ten or twenty years of the reserves lives, presumably on the grounds that their value does not fall significantly until that stage. We consider that this practice has been prevented by the general requirement of FRS 15 that the depreciation method 'should result in a depreciation charge throughout the asset's useful economic life and not just towards the end of its useful economic life or when the asset is falling in value.'[53] The accounts of Hanson, below, show a policy for depreciating mineral reserves that is in line with this FRS 15 requirement.

Extract 12.14: Hanson PLC (2000)

Accounting policies [extract]

Tangible fixed assets [extract]

No depreciation is provided on freehold land except for mineral reserves which are depleted on the basis of tonnage extracted.

Wyevale Garden Centres were only depreciating their leasehold properties over the last ten years of the lease.

> *Extract 12.15: Wyevale Garden Centres plc (2000)*
>
> **Depreciation** [extract]
>
> Depreciation is not provided on land and short leasehold properties are not depreciated until the last 10 years of the lease. At this time depreciation is then provided to write the properties off systematically over the remaining period.

It was held by the Financial Reporting Review Panel in September 2001 that this policy did not comply with the requirements of FRS 15 as it did not result in a depreciation charge throughout the asset's life. The company has amended its policy and is now depreciating the leasehold properties on a straight-line basis over the lease term.[54]

It has also sometimes been argued that assets not currently in use, for example ships that have been laid up, do not need to be depreciated. However, depreciation is viewed as an allocation of the cost of an asset over its useful life, so it should normally continue to be charged while the asset is not used. The lack of use may affect the asset's estimated useful life or be symptomatic of circumstances that affect its residual value (for example, it may be caused by a major slump in the world shipping markets), either of which may affect the amount of depreciation being charged. It might be argued that where an asset has not been used in a particular year its useful economic life has effectively been extended; but in that case depreciation will still need to be charged, albeit at a reduced rate.

H *Depreciation of infrastructure assets*

The infrastructure assets of public utilities were generally not depreciated prior to FRS 15. The standard acknowledges that assets of this kind may need special consideration, and once again the issue arises as a consequence of FRS 12. Provisions for rolling programmes for the maintenance of infrastructure assets would not fit the definition of an obligation under FRS 12, being 'voluntary' in nature rather then obligatory. Thus FRS 15 contains separate requirements for the depreciation of infrastructure assets.

> 'Definable major assets or components within an infrastructure system or network with determinable finite lives should be treated separately and depreciated over their useful economic lives. For the remaining tangible fixed assets within the system or network ('the infrastructure asset'), renewals accounting … may be used as a method of estimating depreciation in the following circumstances:
>
> (a) the infrastructure asset is a system or network that as a whole is intended to be maintained at a specified level of service potential by the continuing replacement and refurbishment of its components;
>
> (b) the level of annual expenditure required to maintain the operating capacity (or service capability) of the infrastructure asset is calculated

from an asset management plan that is certified by a person who is appropriately qualified and independent; and

(c) the system or network is in a mature or steady state.'[55]

The most exacting of these criteria to meet is (c) as any entity that is intending to expand its infrastructure may find it difficult to satisfy this condition. In a mature economy such as the UK this condition is likely to be fulfilled for the major traditional utilities, though not, for example by the newer mobile telephone and cable infrastructure providers.

Renewals accounting means 'the level of annual expenditure required to maintain the operating capacity of the infrastructure asset is treated as the depreciation charged for the period and is deducted from the carrying amount of the asset (as part of accumulated depreciation). Actual expenditure is capitalised (as part of the cost of the asset) as incurred'.[56] Anglian Water provides an example of a company that has such assets, as shown below.

Extract 12.16: Anglian Water plc (2000)

Notes [extract]

1 Accounting policies [extract]

(e) **Tangible fixed assets and depreciation** [extract]
Tangible fixed assets comprise:
Infrastructure assets (being mains and sewers, impounding and pumped raw water storage reservoirs, dams, sludge pipelines and sea outfalls) comprise a network of systems. Investment expenditure on infrastructure assets, relating to increases in capacity or enhancements of the network and on maintaining the operating capability of the network in accordance with defined standards of service, is treated as an addition and included at cost after deducting grants and contributions. The depreciation charge for infrastructure assets is the estimated level of annual expenditure required to maintain the operating capability of the network, which is based on the company's independently-certified asset management plan.

2.3.4 *Depreciation methods*

There is little discussion of depreciation methods in FRS 15, which simply says that 'the depreciation method should reflect as fairly as possible the pattern in which the asset's economic benefits are consumed'.[57] The standard describes only two depreciation methods, straight line and reducing balance. A change from one method of providing depreciation to another is permitted only if the new method will more fairly present the enterprise's results and financial position. A change of method is not a change in accounting policy, and should accordingly be accounted for prospectively.[58]

The straight line and reducing balance methods are well known and understood. It may be appropriate to use other methods with particular assets, and for reference purposes, some are illustrated below.

A Double declining balance

This method is sometimes applied in the US, where it has corresponded to tax allowances on assets. The method involves determining the asset's depreciation on a straight line basis over its useful life. This annual amount is multiplied by an appropriate factor (it does not have to be doubled) to give the first year's charge and depreciation at the same percentage rate is charged on the reducing balance in subsequent years.

Example 12.2: Double declining balance depreciation

An asset costs £6,000 and has a life of ten years, which means that, calculated on the straight line basis, the annual depreciation charge would be £600. On the double declining balance method (assuming a factor of two), the depreciation charge for the first year would be £1,200 and depreciation would continue to be charged at 20% on the reducing balance thereafter.

B Sum of the digits

This is another form of reducing balance method, but one that is based on the estimated life of the asset and which can therefore easily be applied if the asset has a residual value. If an asset has an estimated useful life of four years then the digits 1, 2, 3, and 4 are added together, giving a total of 10. Depreciation of four-tenths, three-tenths and so on, of the cost of the asset, less any residual value, will be charged in the respective years. The method is sometimes called the 'rule of 78', 78 being the sum of the digits 1 to 12.

Example 12.3: Sum of the digits depreciation

An asset costs £10,000 and is expected to be sold for £2,000 after four years. Depreciation is to be provided over four years using the sum of the digits method.

		£
Year 1	Cost	10,000
	Depreciation at 4/10 of £8,000	3,200
	Net book value	6,800
Year 2	Depreciation at 3/10 of £8,000	2,400
	Net book value	4,400
Year 3	Depreciation at 2/10 of £8,000	1,600
	Net book value	2,800
Year 4	Depreciation at 1/10 of £8,000	800
	Net book value	2,000

C Annuity method

This is a method where account is taken of the cost of capital notionally invested in the asset. Notional interest and depreciation combined will give an approximately constant charge to revenue: depreciation is therefore low in the early years when the capital invested is high. What really differentiates the annuity method from other approaches is that it takes account of the cost of capital invested in the fixed asset. Whilst FRS 15 does not specifically prohibit this method, in June 2000 the ASB published an exposure draft of an amendment to FRS 15 that would do so in all but very exceptional cases.

D Unit of production method

Under this method, the asset is written off in line with its estimated total output. By relating depreciation to proportion of productive capacity utilised to date, it reflects the fact that the useful economic life of certain assets, principally machinery, is more closely linked to its usage and output than to time. This method is normally used in extractive industries, for example, to amortise the costs of development of productive oil and gas facilities,[59] as shown by BP Amoco below:

> *Extract 12.17: BP Amoco p.l.c. (2000)*
>
> **Accounting policies** [extract]
>
> **Depreciation** [extract]
>
> Oil and gas production assets are depreciated using a unit-of-production method based upon estimated proved reserves.

The essence of choosing a fair depreciation method is to reflect the consumption of economic benefits provided by the asset concerned. In most cases straight line will give perfectly acceptable results, and the vast majority of companies use this method. Where there are instances, such as the extraction of a known proportion of a mineral resource, or the use of a certain amount of the total available number of working hours of a machine, it may be that a unit of production method will give fairer results.

2.3.5 *Treatment of minor items*

Some types of business may have a very large number of minor fixed assets such as tools, cutlery, small containers, sheets and towels. There are practical problems in recording them on an asset-by-asset basis in an asset register; they are difficult to control and frequently lost. The main consequence is that it becomes very difficult to provide depreciation on them.

There are a number of ways in which companies attempt to deal with the problems of depreciating minor assets. The items may be written off to the profit and loss account (the company will probably have a minimum value for capitalising assets), they may be capitalised at a fixed amount, a treatment which is permitted in the Act, or the company may have some other form of policy that writes them off when they are used up but without having to identify them individually.

Some companies capitalise their minor items at a fixed amount when they are originally provided, as a form of capital 'base stock'; additions are not capitalised and depreciation is not charged. This is permitted under the accounting rules in the Companies Act, which state that tangible fixed assets may be included at a fixed amount provided that their overall value is not material to assessing the company's state of affairs and their quantity, value and composition are not subject to material variation.[60]

Although this is a recognised accounting practice, it does not strictly conform to the requirement of FRS 15 that all assets be depreciated. Therefore it is only acceptable as an accounting policy provided that the amounts involved are not material. Companies that apply such a policy do so on the basis that the continual loss and replacement of stock items does actually result in a base amount that does not materially vary.

2.4 The requirements of SSAP 19

SSAP 19 – *Accounting for investment properties* – is a rare example of the particular commercial characteristics of an industry resulting in special treatment of certain of its tangible fixed assets (investment properties), even though the assets themselves are not intrinsically different. Investment properties are defined under SSAP 19 as 'an interest in land and/or buildings:

(a) in respect of which construction work and development have been completed; and

(b) which is held for its investment potential, any rental income being negotiated at arm's length'.[61]

It is important to note that SSAP 19 is not optional. If a property fits the definition of an investment property, it must be accounted for under the standard. The arguments to support the special treatment accorded to investment properties at the time of the advent of SSAP 19 in 1980 were as follows:

'(a) the financial statements of enterprises holding investments are more helpful to users of financial statements if the investments are accounted for at current values rather than on the basis of a cost or valuation established some time in the past; and

(b) depreciation is only one element which enters into the annual change in the value of a property and as the use of a current value places the prime emphasis on the values of the assets, it is not generally useful to attempt to distinguish, estimate and account separately for the element of depreciation; and

(c) depreciation, although not separately identified, will be taken into account in dealing with changes in current values.'[62]

SSAP 19, which was published in 1981, requires freehold investment properties to be carried at the current market valuation without provision for depreciation. Leasehold investment property must also be carried at current market valuation and may be depreciated over the life of the lease, or not be depreciated until the lease has twenty years or fewer remaining, when it must be depreciated. Specifically excluded from SSAP 19 are properties owned and occupied by a company for its own purposes and properties let to and occupied by other companies in the same group[63] which fall under FRS 15.

The other main provisions of SSAP 19 are as follows. Investment properties should be included in the balance sheet at their open market value ('OMV' is defined by the Royal Institute of Chartered Surveyors and is further explained at 2.5.3 below). With the exception of insurance companies, pension funds and certain investment companies which may have separate rules, changes in the market value of investment properties should not be taken to the profit and loss account but should be taken to the statement of total recognised gains and losses. However, if a deficit (or its reversal) on an individual investment property is expected to be permanent, it should be charged (or credited) in the profit and loss account of the period.[64] 'Deficit' in this case is taken to mean a valuation deficit below cost. All other valuation movements in investment properties are to be shown in the statement of total recognised gains and losses (as movements on the investment revaluation reserve)[65] even if this results in a temporary revaluation deficit. SSAP 19 requires companies to consider their properties individually.

The standard does not require the valuations to be carried out by qualified or independent valuers, but recommends that 'where investment properties represent a substantial proportion of the total assets of a major enterprise (e.g. a listed company) the valuation thereof would normally be carried out:

(a) annually by persons holding a recognised professional qualification and having recent post-qualification experience in the location and category of the properties concerned; and

(b) at least every five years by an external valuer'.[66]

It is not unusual to have annual external valuations and some property companies have included a copy of the valuer's report in their annual report and accounts.[67]

As further detailed at 3.2 and 3.3 below, the non-depreciation of investment properties under SSAP 19 is in contravention of the Companies Act requirement that all tangible fixed assets with a limited useful economic life should be depreciated over that life on a systematic basis. Therefore compliance with SSAP 19 requires the use of the true and fair override provisions of the Companies Act.

The existence of SSAP 19 is probably viewed as an anomaly by the ASB. The underlying reasons for the non-depreciation of investment properties are equally applicable to hotels and pubs where the argument has been rejected. The difference between an investment property earning rent and a hotel earning profits, does not seem to be sufficiently distinct to justify different treatments.

The value of SSAP 19 to property companies is considerable. Office buildings can easily become obsolete in thirty or forty years, and are frequently redeveloped within these periods; yet the value of the property as a whole may not have diminished. It is the land element of the freehold property (or the 'land-use' element of the leasehold property) in these cases that increases in value, and which counteracts the depreciation of the building element. However the building element's depreciation has not been charged against profits. This is directly contrary to the provisions of FRS 15 (see 2.3.3 above) that these elements should be separately accounted for.[68].

2.5 Revaluations of tangible fixed assets

2.5.1 *Background*

The legal rules that specify what basis of valuation can be used in company accounts, as stated above are set out in Companies Act 1985 in the Alternative Accounting Rules in Part C of Schedule 4. In addition to historical cost, the Act recognises the following bases of valuation for the various classes of fixed asset:

(a) tangible fixed assets may be included at market value or current cost;[69]

(b) intangibles, except goodwill, may be included at current cost;[70]

(c) investments may be included at market value or at directors' valuation.[71]

In each case 'market value' is at the date of the asset's last valuation; in other words, the Act does not require the value to be as of the date of the accounts. Current cost, however, implies a value as at the balance sheet date.

The three bases listed above (current cost, market value and directors' valuation) are not explained further in the Act, but they are discussed further below. It is important to appreciate, however, that these are not three distinct and mutually exclusive valuation bases: on the contrary, they overlap with each other.

Current cost as used in the Act is really a broader valuation *concept* developed in relation to current cost accounting, and is generally defined as shown in this diagram:[72]

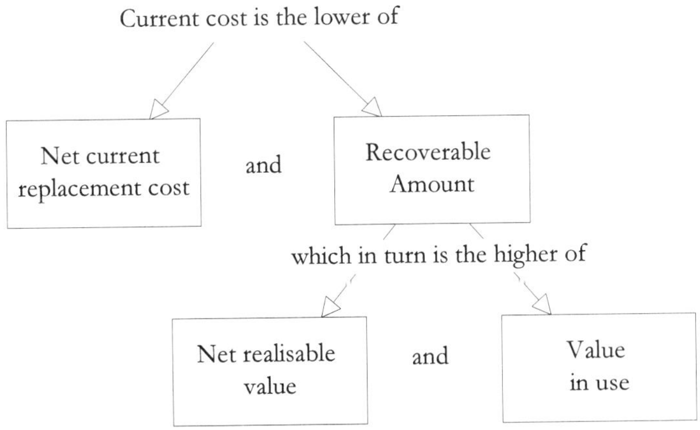

Each of these three elements still requires a *method* of valuation to measure what the relevant amount is. 'Market value' may be appropriate in determining replacement cost or net realisable value, depending on the manner in which the enterprise would replace or dispose of the asset in question, and there are a number of different valuation methods which are designed to arrive at some form of market value. Similarly, 'directors' valuation' is not a basis as such, but simply permits the directors to adopt whatever basis seems to them appropriate in the circumstances of the company, subject to disclosure of the basis used and the reasons for choosing it. Accordingly, in exercising that judgement, they may be trying to assess the replacement cost of the asset in question and consequently may be aiming to estimate its market value for that purpose. It can therefore be seen that the three apparently different 'bases' are in fact pitched at different levels of description and the application of all three is substantially intertwined.

FRS 15 uses the model shown in the above diagram as its conceptual basis for valuation, although calling the resulting amount 'current value to the business' rather than 'current cost'. In fact, it can be argued that *neither* term properly describes the model. 'Current cost' really only refers to the net current replacement cost leg of the diagram. Whereas 'current value to the business', in any normal meaning of the words, would mean the amount the entity expected to recoup from its existing asset; that is, its recoverable amount. The true significance of the model is that it reflects the greatest loss the entity could suffer if, hypothetically, it were to be deprived of the asset. This 'deprival value' is the foundation of current cost accounting, in which its function is to measure the cost of replacing resources as they are consumed in the profit and loss account, not the value of those that remain in the balance sheet.

This is a fundamental distinction: measuring consumption in the profit and loss account is a backwards-looking exercise designed to match costs (albeit current costs, in this context) against revenues. Replacement cost is an entry value, and movements in it are not gains and losses but rather adjustments to the (physical) capital that must be maintained before any profit can be achieved. To measure value in the balance sheet it is necessary to concentrate on forward-looking measures – exit values – and forget about cost-based measures. Modified historical cost accounting, the ad hoc mixture of costs and valuations that has grown up in the UK, is an amalgam of the two approaches.

At a practical level, from time to time there have been concerns about the reliability of valuations in company accounts, fuelled most notably in 1993 by the publication of a succession of valuations of the hotels operated by Queens Moat Houses. The *Financial Times* summarised the salient facts in an article in November of that year:

'The two firms of chartered surveyors under scrutiny for valuing Queens Moat Houses' assets at figures that differed by nearly £500m used the same basis to prepare their figures, the company said yesterday. Both Weatherall Green and Smith and Jones Lang Wootton compiled their valuations on an open market, willing seller basis … Weatherall produced a final valuation of £1.35bn for the 1992 accounts. Within four months, Jones had submitted an alternative figure of £861m based on the same financial information.'

The article also went on to describe earlier valuations: 'QMH … said Weatherall had prepared a 1991 valuation of £2bn and a draft valuation for 1992 of £1.86bn. The latter was presented to banks in April this year and did not take into account the changed circumstances of the group. At the board's request, Weatherall supplied a revised figure in May of £1.35bn, qualified because it was based on unaudited financial information.'

When the accounts were eventually issued, the properties were included at a valuation of £732 million, which meant that £1,342 million had to be written off the previous year's valuation. The fixed assets note contained the following footnote:

Extract 12.18: Queens Moat Houses plc (1992)

12 Tangible fixed assets [extract]

The group's properties were valued as at 31st December 1992 by Jones Lang Wootton, Chartered Surveyors, on an open market existing use basis as fully operational business units. The valuations were carried out in accordance with the Statements of Asset Valuation Practice and Guidance Notes published by the Royal Institution of Chartered Surveyors. The group has revalued its property assets as at 31 December 1992 on the basis of these independent professional valuations.

As explained in the directors' report, the current directors consider that they do not have a sufficient understanding of the 1991 property valuation to enable them to provide a full explanation for the decline in the property values from 31 December 1991 to 31 December 1992 of £1,341.5 million, of which £537.6 million has been charged to evaluation reserve (note 21) and £803.9 million charged as an exceptional item in the profit and loss account (note 6).

In March 1994, the Royal Institution of Chartered Surveyors (RICS) published the report of a working party (the Mallinson Report) responding to recent criticisms of its profession. This said that 'valuers need to be able to demonstrate to clients that, although there are many valuers who will make different judgements, all work within a common body of knowledge, application and expression. Differences will therefore be as narrow as possible, and where they occur they will be reasonable and explicable, not perverse or chaotic.'[73] The report went on to make 43 detailed recommendations aimed at improving the practices of the valuation profession, which have also contributed to its present guidance. The RICS guidance now forms the basis of the valuation rules and requirements that FRS 15 contains.

2.5.2 *Revaluations under FRS 15*

FRS 15 neither prohibits valuations nor makes them compulsory, rather it codifies existing practice and imposes a requirement for consistency of policy. The standard gives no reasons for its pragmatic approach, containing no arguments for or against incorporating valuations in financial statements.

The standard prohibits piecemeal valuations by requiring a consistent policy to be applied to all assets within a class Thus a decision must be for each class about whether it is to be carried at historical cost or at a valuation.[74] The definition of a 'class' is not over-prescriptive, being 'a category of tangible fixed assets having a similar nature, function or use in the business of the entity'.[75]

The standard implies that identification of classes of assets should start from the broad classifications in the Companies Act 1985, reproduced above at 2.2. Entities are 'within reason' permitted to adopt other, narrower classes that meet the definition and are appropriate to their business. This is expanded: land and buildings may be split between specialised and non-specialised categories, or analysed by business segment.[76] There is no indication that 'business segments' must be those disclosed in the entity's segmental information. The only limitation is that detailed disclosures have to be made for each class of revalued asset. The disclosure requirements for tangible fixed assets are dealt with in 3 below.

Under FRS 15, valuations must be kept up to date. Where a tangible fixed asset is revalued its carrying amount should be its current value at the balance sheet date.[77] The standard does not require valuations to be carried out annually but has detailed rules on frequency and nature of the valuations that are needed to meet its requirements, as discussed below. FRS 15 allows that charities and other not-for-profit and public sector organisations may adopt other more appropriate approaches, for cost/benefit reasons, than the normal FRS 15 detailed revaluation requirements set out below.[78]

The FRS requires properties to have a full valuation at least every five years and an interim valuation in the third year. Interim valuations should also be carried out in the remaining years 'where it is likely that there has been a material change in value'.[79] This is defined as meaning a change in value that would reasonably influence the decisions of a user of the accounts.[80]

There are detailed requirements for full and interim valuations. Full valuations must either be performed by qualified external valuers or by suitably qualified employees. If it is an internal valuation it must be reviewed by an external valuer, who is required to value a sample of the entity's properties for comparison purposes and express an opinion on the overall accuracy of the valuation based on this sample. The external valuer must be satisfied that the sample is representative of the entity's portfolio.[81]

Interim valuations are to be performed by qualified external or internal valuers.

A full valuation is to include the following procedures:

(a) detailed inspection of the interior and exterior of the property (on an initial valuation this will involve detailed measurement of floor space etc, but this would need to be reperformed in future full valuations only if there was evidence of a physical change to the buildings);
(b) inspection of the locality;
(c) enquiries of the local planning and similar authorities;
(d) enquiries of the entity or its solicitors; and
(e) research into market transactions in similar properties, identification of market trends, and the application of these to determine the value of the property under consideration.[82]

Interim valuations include the same processes as in (e) above but, in addition, the valuer is required to confirm that there have been no significant changes to the physical buildings, the legal rights or local planning considerations. The property need only be physically inspected to the extent that this is considered professionally necessary.[83]

The standard explicitly allows rolling valuations of portfolios of non-specialised properties. Entities will be required to carry out a full valuation over a five-year cycle with interim valuations of the remaining four fifths of the portfolio if it is likely that there has been a material change in value. Rolling valuations will only be appropriate where either all properties are of broadly similar types or they can be stratified so that each year's revalued properties form a reasonable cross-section of the total portfolio.[84] However the practical drawback with rolling valuations is that if (say) 20% of the portfolio is valued and a material revaluation up or down is required, this will trigger a requirement for a valuation of the entire portfolio, somewhat negating the purpose of a rolling programme.

Assets other than properties are not subject to the same revaluation regime of full and interim valuations described above, where either:

- there is an active second-hand market (e.g. company cars); or
- there are appropriate indices on which the company's directors may rely.[85]

The indices must not only be appropriate to the asset's class, location and condition but also take technological change into account. They must also have a proven record of regular publication and use that is expected to continue for the foreseeable future.[86]

In such cases the directors will be required to update the assets' values annually. If this information is not available, revaluations will need to be made by valuers and full and interim valuations performed using the same rules as those for properties outlined above.

A First implementation of FRS 15

If an entity had previously revalued any of its fixed assets, it had to decide what its future policy would be when it first implemented FRS 15. If it did not wish to tie itself into a consistent revaluation policy for all assets of a certain class, it had the following options:

(a) restate the assets at depreciated historical cost, as a change in accounting policy; or

(b) continue to carry the assets at the revalued book amounts, subject to any indications of impairment that require the carrying value to be reviewed in accordance with FRS 11. If this option was chosen the entity had to disclose:

    (i) the fact that the transitional arrangements are being followed and that the valuation has not been updated; and

    (ii) the date of the last revaluation.

Option (b) was only available when the standard was first introduced. The standard does not specify whether these disclosures need to be made in subsequent years, although (b.ii) is in any case required by the Companies Act.[87] By far the most common decision by companies on first adopting FRS 15 was to choose option (b), freezing assets at their previously revalued amounts. An example of this policy is shown by De Vere Group below. A few companies chose option (a) to revert to historical cost and rather interestingly, it remains an option under FRS 15 to revert to historical cost at any time.

> *Extract 12.19: De Vere Group plc (2000)*
>
> **Accounting policies** [extract]
>
> **Basis of Accounts**
>
> The Accounts have been prepared in accordance with applicable Accounting Standards under the historical cost convention with the exception of properties which, under the transitional provisions of FRS15 – Tangible Fixed Assets, are included at their 1999 valuations. From 1999/2000 it is the Group's policy not to revalue fixed assets.

Thus the majority of UK companies now include some property assets at a frozen revalued amount in the financial statements. It is on this value that subsequent depreciation and impairment are based. However, if an asset at a frozen revalued amount is impaired, there appears to be no impediment to making a transfer from the revaluation reserve to profit and loss reserves of an amount of the revaluation surplus equivalent to the impairment adjustment, always providing that the revaluation surplus pertaining to the impaired asset can be identified.

2.5.3 *FRS 15's rules on the bases of valuation*

A Valuation of land and buildings

FRS 15 requires the following bases for the valuation of properties:

(a) non-specialised properties should be valued on the basis of existing use value (EUV), with the addition of notional directly attributable acquisition costs where material;

(b) specialised properties should be valued on the basis of depreciated replacement cost; and

(c) properties surplus to an entity's requirements should be valued on the basis of open market value (OMV), with expected directly attributable selling costs deducted where material.[88]

For the purpose of the standard, specialised properties have the same meaning as given by the Royal Institute of Chartered Surveyors (RICS) in its Appraisal and Valuation Manual (and quoted in Appendix 1 of the standard), as follows:

'Specialised properties [are] those which, due to their specialised nature, are rarely, if ever, sold on the open market for single occupation for a continuation of their existing use, except as part of a sale of the business in occupation. Their specialised nature may arise from the construction, arrangement, size or location of the property, or a combination of these factors, or may be due to the nature of the plant and machinery and items of equipment which the buildings are designed to house, or the function, or the purpose for which the buildings are provided.'

Examples given by the RICS are shown in D below. All other properties are non-specialised. They are those for which there is a general demand and for which there is an open market in their existing or similar use. The RICS's examples of properties to which this definition applies include residential properties, shops, offices, standard industrial and warehouse buildings, public houses and petrol filling stations.

Although many specialised buildings are built for their specific purpose, what really distinguishes them is the lack of market. A building that might be specialised by virtue of its size and location, e.g. a large administrative centre put up in a remote location because of the nature of the entity's business, could be non-specialised if it had been built in a town centre. A number of non-specialised buildings (public houses, petrol filling stations) are usually sold with regard to their trading potential, i.e. as businesses, but unlike the specialised properties they are frequently bought and sold on the open market.

Notional directly attributable acquisition costs include professional fees and non-recoverable taxes and duties (e.g. stamp duty) but exclude any conversion or enhancement costs. The standard accepts that these, and directly attributable selling costs, may well not be material and can thus be ignored.[89]

B Valuation bases for non-specialised properties

The valuation bases Open Market Value (OMV) and Existing Use Value (EUV) have been developed by the RICS in conjunction with the accounting profession for use in company accounts.

OMV is 'an opinion of the best price at which the sale of an interest in property would have been completed unconditionally for cash consideration on the date of valuation, assuming:

(a) a willing seller;

(b) that, prior to the date of valuation, there had been a reasonable period (having regard to the nature of the property and the state of the market) for the proper marketing of the interest, for the agreement of the price and terms and for the completion of the sale;

(c) that the state of the market, level of values and other circumstances were, on any earlier assumed date of exchange of contracts, the same as on the date of valuation;

(d) that no account is taken of any additional bid by a prospective purchaser with a special interest; and

(e) that both parties to the transaction had acted knowledgeably, prudently and without compulsion.'[90]

EUV is open market value with two extra conditions:

(f) the property can be used for the foreseeable future only for the existing use; and

(g) that vacant possession is provided on completion of the sale of all parts of the property occupied by the business.[91]

The RICS Manual explains that, where a property is fully developed for its most beneficial use, its EUV is likely to be the same as its OMV with vacant possession.[92] However, there will be occasions where the two diverge. On the one hand, OMV may exceed EUV because the latter does not admit the possibility of putting a higher value on a property because it could be redeployed to a more valuable use.

Less usually, OMV may fall short of EUV, for example because the present owner enjoys some benefits that could not be passed on in a sale, such as planning consents that are personal to the present occupier. Where the OMV is materially different from EUV, the OMV and the reasons for the difference should be disclosed in the notes to the accounts.[93]

Tottenham Hotspur, below, provides an example of properties being carried at EUV and OMV.

> *Extract 12.20: Tottenham Hotspur plc (2000)*
>
> **Note 12 Tangible Fixed Assets** [extract]
>
> The Group's property interests were valued as at 31st July 1998 by Drivers Jonas who acted as independent valuers. The valuations were prepared in accordance with the Royal Institution of Chartered Surveyors' Appraisal and Valuation Manual. The Stadium was valued on the basis of Depreciated Replacement Cost; Existing Use Value was adopted for properties occupied for the purpose of the business and other properties were valued on the basis of Open Market Value.
>
> The Directors are not aware of any material change in value and therefore the valuations have not been updated.
>
> Freehold land totalling £5,636,000 (1999 - £5,636,000) has not been depreciated.

The RICS manual also explains that EUV has been developed specifically for financial reporting purposes. The concept behind it is that of net current replacement cost, i.e. 'the cost of purchasing, at the least cost, the remaining service potential of the asset at the balance sheet date'.[94]

There is one particular variant of EUV that is customarily applied to certain types of property – valuations that include trading potential. This approach is based upon the earning capacity of the properties, essentially valuing them more as businesses than physical assets. Such properties, which can include hotels, pubs, cinemas, theatres, petrol stations, betting shops or specialised leisure and sporting facilities, are sold on the open market as fully operational business units at prices based directly on trading potential. The valuation will therefore include all of the assets of the business as a going concern, including fixtures and fittings and the value of the trading potential. The report may not distinguish between the various elements that make up the valuation.

FRS 15 allows such valuations but requires specific disclosures, at set out at 3.5 below. It comments on this method as follows:

> 'The EUV of a property valued as an operational entity is determined by having regard to trading potential, but excludes personal goodwill that has been created in the business by the present owner or management and is not expected to remain with the business in the event of the property being sold.'[95]

Trading potential is an entirely different basis of valuation from a straightforward EUV, as it is a value of a business and not a property. These units are valued according to the business they can generate by examining the 'fair maintainable level of trade'[96] and the valuer is concerned with factors such as hotel occupancy rates or sales of alcoholic drinks. It is not actually possible to disaggregate such an overall valuation into separate parts representing the physical assets involved without being left with a balancing figure. The implication in the FRS is that the 'trading potential' is a balancing figure, the difference between the value of the unit taken as a whole and the value of the underlying assets. Exactly what the difference is between this and internally generated goodwill is less than obvious.

It is arguable that the intangible asset inherent in the trading potential valuation *should* be split out from the tangible fixed assets' valuation and accounted for separately. Even if it is not capable of being disposed of separately from the land and buildings it may well have a different useful life from the bricks and mortar and hence justify a different period of amortisation from the life attributed to the building for depreciation purposes. After all, the trading potential would appear to comprise at least part of the 'goodwill' that would have been accounted for under a fair value exercise if the separate assets were valued. It may even include other separate intangibles, such as the value of the licence.

FRS 15 does not accept this argument or allow such a distinction to be made. It states that it would not be appropriate to treat the trading potential associated with a property as a separate component (i.e. as a separate asset) because the value and life of any such trading potential is inherently inseparable from that of the property.[97]

Trading potential valuations can also cause problems in respect of fixtures and fittings. The trading potential valuation will include those fixtures and fittings that are necessary for the business to function. For example, a hotel's valuation would have to include beds, bed linen and other necessary furnishings. A valuation may also be performed on the hotel in its current condition, i.e. including fixtures and fittings that have been added by the existing owner over and above this basic level. However, part or all of either category of fixtures and fittings may have been purchased by the current owner and included in the accounts, probably at cost, as a separate category of fixed asset.

C *Valuation basis for specialised properties*

Some specialised buildings do not have a readily obtainable market value because they are usually sold only as part of the businesses in which they are used. If they are to be revalued it will be necessary for them to be incorporated on the basis of their depreciated replacement cost (DRC).

The RICS Manual gives the following examples of specialised properties:

- oil refineries and chemical works where, usually, the buildings are no more than housings or cladding for highly specialised plant;
- power stations and dock installations where the building and site engineering works are related directly to the business of the owner, it being highly unlikely that they would have a value to anyone other than a company acquiring the undertaking;
- properties of such construction, arrangement, size or specification that there would be no market (for a sale to a single owner occupier for the continuation of existing use) for those buildings;

- standard properties in particular geographical areas and remote from main business centres, located there for operational or business reasons, which are of such an abnormal size for that district that there would be no market for such buildings there;
- schools, colleges, universities and research establishments where there is no competing market demand from other organisations using these types of property in the locality;
- hospitals, other specialised health care premises and leisure centres where there is no competing market demand from other organisations wishing to use these types of property in the locality; and
- museums, libraries, and other similar premises provided by the public sector.[98]

DRC is defined as 'the aggregate amount of the value of the land for the existing use or a notional replacement site in the same locality, and the gross replacement cost of the buildings and other site works, from which appropriate deductions may then be made to allow for the age, condition, economic or functional obsolescence and environmental factors etc; all of these might result in the existing property being worth less to the undertaking in occupation than would a new replacement.'[99]

FRS 15 suggests that the objective of DRC is to 'make a realistic estimate of the current cost of constructing an asset that has the same service potential as the existing asset'.[100] DRC is inevitably a rather unsatisfactory valuation basis at the theoretical level. It is represented as a valuation of property, but in circumstances where, by definition, the asset has no market value. As a consequence increases in the cost of replacing assets will be reported as gains (possibly being considered as relevant in measuring the company's performance) in the statement of total recognised gains and losses.

Moreover, a DRC valuation is often likely to give a higher valuation than one done on an open market basis. For this reason, it is necessary to ensure that the property really is so specialised that an open market value cannot be obtained. The RICS also points out that it is necessary to be satisfied that the potential profitability of the business is adequate to support the value derived on a DRC basis, failing which a lower figure should be adopted.[101]

Tottenham Hotspur in Extract 12.20 above, provides an example of a property (its football stadium) being carried at a DRC valuation. Another example is Henlys:

Extract 12.21: Henlys Group plc (2000)

Notes to the Accounts [extract]

11 Tangible Fixed Assets [extract]

The Group's freehold properties in the United Kingdom were valued by Lambert Smith Hampton, Chartered Surveyors, on an existing use open market basis as at 31 December 1996 except for two properties which were valued at depreciated replacement cost as at 31 December 1996

D Adaptation works

The standard notes that structural changes or special fittings may comprise adaptation works that have a low or nil market value owing to their specialised nature. The standard suggests that the adaptation works and shell of the building should be separately valued, the former using DRC and the latter at EUV.[102]

E Valuations of other assets

Assets other than properties are rarely revalued. However, should it be the entity's policy to revalue such assets, FRS 15 requires them to be valued using market value where possible. As discussed above at 2.5.1 in some cases market values could be established by the directors, perhaps using indices as guides. If market value is not obtainable, assets should be valued on the basis of depreciated replacement cost. The FRS states that such assets should be valued in accordance with the RICS guidance and refers to the RICS's definition of the value of plant and machinery to the business:[103.]

'An opinion of the price at which an interest in the plant and machinery utilised in a business would have been transferred at the date of valuation assuming:

(a) that the plant and machinery will continue in its present use in the business;

(b) adequate potential profitability of the business, or continuing viability of the undertaking, both having due regard to the value of the total assets employed and the nature of the operation; and

(c) that the transfer is part of an arm's length sale of the business wherein both parties acted knowledgeably, prudently and without compulsion.'[104]

This is similar to the definition of EUV for properties.

2.5.4 Accounting for revaluations

A Basic provisions of the Companies Act 1985

When an asset is revalued the Companies Act states that the 'profit or loss' on revaluation must go to a separate reserve, the revaluation reserve.[105] Under FRS 3 and FRS 15, this also means that the revaluation surplus or deficit is reported in the statement of total recognised gains and losses.[106] The Companies Act requires permanent deficits below historical cost on individual properties to be charged to profit and loss account but permits temporary valuation deficits to be included in revaluation reserve even if this results in a negative reserve.[107]

Under the Act, the revaluation reserve has to be reduced if amounts standing to its credit are, in the opinion of the directors, 'no longer necessary for the purposes of the valuation method used'.[108] Amounts may be released to the profit and loss account only if they were previously charged to that account or if they represent realised profits.[109] This permits transfers from revaluation reserve to retained profits of any depreciation which has been charged through the profit and loss account on the revaluation surplus. It permits any surplus realised on the sale of a revalued asset to be transferred to retained profits. It also allows a company to change its policy from one where assets are revalued and to write back the reduction in the carrying value against any credit balance in the revaluation reserve.

The Act also states that the revaluation reserve can be capitalised in a bonus issue, and it may also be increased or decreased by the tax effect of the gains and losses taken to the reserve. The revaluation reserve is not to be reduced for any other purpose. Although the word 'reduced' is ambiguous in the context of a reserve that may contain either debit or credit balances, the intention is to prevent companies from charging costs (eg, valuation fees) directly to the reserve, or from releasing credits to the profit and loss account, except in ways permitted by the Act.

B Accounting for revaluation gains

The accounting treatment of a gain arising on the revaluation of a fixed asset is uncontroversial. The whole of the revaluation surplus is credited to the revaluation reserve. There is no adjustment to the profit and loss account balance, even though any depreciation that was originally charged there has now been reversed.

The treatment is based on the view that the revaluation establishes a new base 'cost' of a used asset and, accordingly, the surplus to be taken to the revaluation reserve is the difference between the valuation and the net book value at the date of the valuation. This is consistent with the Companies Act, which states that the amount of the profit to be credited to the revaluation reserve is to be 'after allowing, where appropriate, for any provisions for depreciation or diminution in value made otherwise than by reference to the value so determined'.[110]

C Accounting for revaluation losses

The rules become more complex when there are revaluation losses and subsequent reversals thereof. The main question is whether these movements belong in the profit and loss account or the statement of total recognised gains and losses, or some combination of the two. In addressing this, FRS 15 sets out three overlapping rules:

(a) First of all, FRS 15 says that a revaluation loss is to be recognised wholly in the profit and loss account if it is caused by 'a clear consumption of economic benefits'.[111] The standard cites as examples physical damage or a deterioration in the quality of the service provided by the asset. This is equated to an impairment, and accordingly the whole deficit should be charged in the profit and loss account as an operating charge analogous to depreciation.[112] This applies even if the asset was previously valued upwards and is still worth more than its depreciated historical cost. If the deficit against carrying value is charged to the profit and loss account any corresponding credit balance in the revaluation reserve relating to that asset will be transferred to the profit and loss account as a reserve movement.

(b) In the absence of evidence of a clear consumption of economic benefits, the loss will be recognised in the statement of total recognised gains and losses until the carrying amount reaches the asset's depreciated historical cost. Thus, if the asset had previously been revalued upwards, any downward valuation adjustment is first set against the previous surplus. The standard then imposes a rule that any falls in value below depreciated historical cost are presumed to be due to a 'consumption of economic value' and must be taken through the profit and loss account.[113]

(c) As an exception to (b), if it can be demonstrated that the asset's recoverable amount is greater than its revalued amount, the loss can be recognised in the statement of total recognised gains and losses and taken to the revaluation reserve. This means that even if the value of the asset now falls below depreciated cost, the deficit does not have to be charged in the profit and loss account.[114]

Recoverable amount is calculated in accordance with FRS 11 (see Chapter 13) and is the higher of net realisable value and value in use. Usually companies will have to demonstrate that the asset's value in use is higher than the revalued amount. In some cases, however, the asset may have a net realisable value that exceeds its EUV, for example the value of a property in alternative use. While in principle the asset may continue to be carried at EUV, with the deficit being carried forward in the revaluation reserve, it will be necessary to consider whether the asset is still part of the class of assets being revalued. EUV may not be the appropriate basis of valuation if the asset is being held for resale.

The operation of these rules is illustrated by this example, which is partly based on an example in the standard:

Example 12.4: Reporting revaluation gains and losses

A non-specialised property costs £1 million and has a useful life of 10 years and no residual value. It is depreciated on a straight-line basis and revalued annually. The entity has a policy of calculating depreciation based on the opening book amount. At the end of years 1 and 2 the asset has an EUV of £1,080,000 and £700,000 respectively. At the end of year 2, the recoverable amount of the asset is £760,000 and its depreciated historical cost is £800,000. There is no obvious consumption of economic benefits in year 2, other than that accounted for through the depreciation charge.

Accounting treatment under modified historical cost

	Year 1	Year 2
	£000	£000
Opening book amount	1,000	1,080
Depreciation	(100)	(120)
Depreciated book amount	900	960
Revaluation gain (loss)		
– recognised in the STRGL	180	(220)
– recognised in the profit and loss account	–	(40)
Closing book amount	1,080	700

In year 1, after depreciation of £100,000, a revaluation gain of £180,000 is recognised in the statement of total recognised gains and losses.

In year 2, depreciation of £120,000 is charged. At the beginning of year 2, as the remaining useful economic life of the asset is nine years, the depreciation charge in year 2 is 1/9th of the opening book amount. The book value of the building at the end of year 2, before taking account of the year end valuation, is £960,000. The EUV of the property at the end of the year is £700,000 so the asset has to be written down by £260,000. If there is not a clear consumption of economic benefits, revaluation losses should be recognised in the statement of total recognised gains and losses until the carrying amount reaches its depreciated historical cost. Therefore, the fall in value from the adjusted book amount (£960,000) to depreciated historical cost (£800,000) of £160,000 is recognised in the statement of total recognised gains and losses.

The rest of the revaluation loss, £100,000 (i.e. the fall in value from depreciated historical cost (£800,000) to the revalued amount (£700,000)), should be recognised in the profit and loss account, unless it can be demonstrated that recoverable amount is greater than the revalued amount. In this case, recoverable amount of £760,000 is greater than the revalued amount of £700,000 by £60,000. Therefore £60,000 of the revaluation loss is recognised in the statement of total recognised gains and losses, rather than the profit and loss account – giving rise to a total revaluation loss of £220,000 (£60,000+£160,000) that is recognised in the statement of total recognised gains and losses. The remaining loss (representing the fall in value from depreciated historical cost of £800,000 to recoverable amount of £760,000) of £40,000 is recognised in the profit and loss account.

The entity would reflect these transactions in its accounts as follows:

	Year 1 £000	Year 2 £000
Profit and loss account (extract)		
Depreciation	100	120
Impairment in value		40
Statement of total recognised gains and losses		
Surplus/deficit on revaluation of properties	180	(220)
Fixed assets		
Cost or valuation		
At beginning of year	1,000	1,080
Surplus/deficit on revaluation	80	(380)
At end of year	1,080	700
Depreciation		
Charge for the year	(100)	(120)
Depreciation written back on revaluation	100	120
At end of year	–	–
Net book value	1,080	700
Revaluation reserve		
At beginning of year	–	180
Surplus/deficit on revaluation	180	(220)
At end of year	180	(40)

In practice, it seems likely that a clear consumption of economic benefits of the assets concerned will seldom be evident, so in most cases any remaining valuation surplus will be reversed before making any charge to the profit and loss account.

The Companies Act also requires that any permanent diminution in value of a revalued asset should be measured by reference to the asset's revalued amount rather than its historical cost.[115] However, this again depends on a determination that a provision for permanent diminution has been made, rather than a downward revaluation, which should be debited to the revaluation reserve in terms of the Act.

The complexity is increased if revaluation deficits are themselves later reversed. FRS 15 says that revaluation gains are only taken to the profit and loss account if they are the reversal of losses previously recognised there.[116] It also states that if the revalued asset is being depreciated, the credit to the profit and loss account must take account of the depreciation that would have been charged on the previously higher book value.[117] The latter requirement is not easy to follow, but the credit must be split between the profit and loss account and the statement of total recognised gains and losses, and the following example demonstrates a way in which the requirements may be interpreted:

Example 12.5: Reversal of downward valuations

An asset has a cost of £1,000,000 and a life of 10 years. At the end of year 3, when the asset's NBV is £700,000, it is written down to £350,000. This write down below historical cost is taken through the profit and loss account.

The entity will now depreciate its asset by £50,000 per annum, so as to write off the carrying value of £350,000 over the remaining 7 years.

At the end of year 6, the asset is revalued to £500,000. The effect on the entity's fixed asset is as follows:

Fixed assets	
Valuation	£000
At beginning of year	350
Surplus on revaluation	150
At end of year	500
Depreciation at beginning of year*	100
Charge for the year	50
Depreciation written back on revaluation	(150)
At end of year	–
Net book value at the end of the year	500
Net book value at the beginning of the year	250

* Two year's depreciation (years 4 and 5) at £50,000 per annum. The asset will be written off over the remaining four years at £125,000 per annum.

The total credit is £300,000. The standard says that only £200,000 may be taken to the profit and loss account as £100,000 represents depreciation that would otherwise have been charged to the profit and loss account in years 4 and 5. This will be taken to the revaluation reserve via the statement of total recognised gains and losses.

In the example the amount of the revaluation that is credited to the revaluation reserve represents the difference between the net book value on a historical cost basis (£400,000) and on a revalued basis (£500,000).

The standard says that the charge to the profit and loss account is restricted in order to achieve the same overall effect that would have been reached had the original downward revaluation reflected in the profit and loss account not occurred.[118] There may be major practical difficulties for any entity that finds itself in the position of reversing revaluation deficits on depreciating assets, although whether in practice this eventuality actually occurs is open to doubt. If it were to occur though, the business would need to continue to maintain asset registers on the original, pre-write down basis.

2.5.5 *Depreciation of revalued assets*

FRS 15 unambiguously requires depreciation even if an asset has risen in value or been revalued.[119] Depreciation is based on the revalued amount and the remaining life of the asset at the time of the valuation. The estimated residual value to be taken into account should be based on prices prevailing at the date of the valuation.

If the asset has been revalued the standard suggests that ideally the depreciation charge should be based on the average carrying value during the year, or else on the opening or closing balance.[120] In practice the depreciation charge is generally based on the opening value and the written down asset is revalued as at the end of the accounting period.

FRS 15 requires the whole of the depreciation charge to be passed through the profit and loss account. This requirement is included (as it was in the standard FRS 15 replaced) specifically to outlaw 'split depreciation'. Under this practice, the depreciation provision in the balance sheet was based on the asset's carrying amount, but only that portion relating to historical cost was charged to the profit and loss account, the balance being charged directly to the revaluation reserve.

The accounting treatment for a depreciable asset that is revalued is shown in the following example:

Example 12.6: Effect of depreciation on revaluation reserve

On 1 January 1997 a company acquires an asset for £1,000. The asset has an economic life of ten years and is depreciated on a straight line basis. The residual value is assumed to be £nil. At 31 December 2000 the asset is valued at £1,200. The company accounts for the revaluation by crediting £600 to the revaluation reserve. At 31 December 2000 the economic life of the asset is considered to be the remainder of its original life, i.e. six years, and its residual value is still considered to be £nil. In the year ended 31 December 2001 and later years, depreciation charged to the profit and loss account is £200 p.a.

The usual treatment thereafter is to transfer £100 p.a. from the revaluation reserve to retained profits within the reserves note. This avoids the revaluation reserve being maintained indefinitely even after the asset ceases to exist, which does not seem sensible. The transfer is to retained earnings and not to the profit and loss account for the year; the latter treatment would be tantamount to allowing split depreciation and would also fall foul of FRS 3, which does not permit amounts which have previously been reported in the statement of total recognised gains and losses to pass subsequently through the profit and loss account.[121] The treatment is also sanctioned by paragraph 34(3) of Schedule 4 to the Companies Act which allows amounts to be transferred to the profit and loss account if the amount has previously been charged there or is a realised profit. A transfer is possible because the amount of £100 is a realised profit in terms of s 275(2) of the Companies Act.

Where the revaluation reserve has been capitalised by making a bonus issue, further allocation issues arise. If all of the revaluation reserve has been capitalised then obviously no allowable transfers from, or write-offs to it, can be made. However if only some of the reserve has been capitalised it will be necessary to consider in what way the balance has been utilised. The options appear to be to:

(a) decide that specific revaluation surpluses have been capitalised and, therefore, no transfers or write-offs can be made in respect of the assets to which the surpluses related. However, transfers and write-offs in respect of other assets can continue; or

(b) decide that a proportion of each revaluation surplus has been capitalised and, therefore, a proportion still remains. Accordingly, a proportion of the amount of the transfers or write-offs which would have been made can be made; or

(c) continue to make the transfers or write-offs until the remaining surplus has been extinguished.

All three methods are probably acceptable, and arguably (c) is the most straightforward.

2.5.6 *Accounting for the disposal of revalued assets*

FRS 15 endorses the treatment of profits and losses on sale of fixed assets required by FRS 3. The profit or loss is the difference between the net sale proceeds and the carrying value of the asset, whether carried at historical cost or at valuation. This is disclosed in accordance with the requirements of FRS 3 (see Chapter 25) which means that the profit or loss, or provision for loss on disposal, should be shown as an exceptional item below operating profit. However, losses or provisions for losses are *prima facie* evidence that the asset had been impaired in value before sale, so care will have to be taken with the requirements of FRS 11 as, under that standard, impairment write downs are to be reflected in operating profit.[122]

2.5.7 *Transfers of properties between current assets and fixed assets*

A *Reclassifications from investment property to trading property*

Property companies sometimes transfer properties from their investment portfolio to their trading portfolio. The question then arises about what should happen to the revaluation surplus or deficit recognised when the property was regarded as an investment property. If the transfer is between two distinct companies (i.e. an investment and a trading company) the profit may be realised in the transferor company. However, it is difficult to reconcile treating gains as realised in the group accounts, as opposed to an individual company's accounts, with the notion that consolidation is intended to represent the group as a single economic entity. Nevertheless, such profits at least do not distort the profit and loss account in the year of transfer since they are dealt with as a realisation of the revaluation reserve by a transfer between reserves.

An alternative treatment is to leave the property at its valuation on transfer but not to treat the accumulated valuation surplus as realised. If this treatment is adopted, interest capitalised on any subsequent development should be based on cost.

Another approach is to reverse any revaluation surplus/deficit relating to a property transferred and include it in trading property at the lower of cost and net realisable value; this will ensure consistency in the accounting treatment of all trading properties.

If the transfer takes place within an individual company, the property may be left at valuation (in which case the accumulated valuation surplus should not be treated as realised) or the property should be restated at historical cost.

B *Reclassifications from trading property to investment property*

On a reclassification from trading property to investment property, the basis of valuation in the accounts will change from the lower of cost and net realisable value to open market value. Although such transfers are often between two separate companies, any intra-group profit should be eliminated from the profit and loss account on consolidation.

In July 1992 UITF Abstract 5 – *Transfers from Current Assets to Fixed Assets* – was issued. The UITF was concerned, particularly in the economic climate of the time, that there was a 'possibility that companies could avoid charging the profit and loss account with write-downs to net realisable value arising on unsold trading assets. This could be done by transferring the relevant assets from current assets to fixed assets at above net realisable value, as a result of which any later write down might be debited to revaluation reserve.'[123]

The UITF agreed that in respect of such transfers, the current asset accounting rules should be applied up to the effective date of transfer, which is the date of management's change of intent. Consequently, the transfer from current to fixed assets should be made at the lower of cost and net realisable value, and accordingly an assessment should be made of the net realisable value at the date of transfer. If this is less than its previous carrying value the diminution should be charged in the profit and loss account, reflecting the loss to the company while the asset was held as a current asset.[124]

2.5.8 *Distributable profits and revaluations of fixed assets*

The Companies Act states that a revaluation surplus is not a realised profit and may only be transferred to the profit and loss account on realisation.[125] It is not available for distribution.[126]

Provisions made against fixed assets normally are to be treated as realised losses.[127] These are defined in paragraph 88 of Schedule 4 to the Companies Act. The definition includes provisions for depreciation, except to the extent that the charge has been increased because of a previous upward revaluation of the asset, in which case the surplus over depreciation based on historical cost is a realised profit[128] and should be transferred from the revaluation reserve.

Amounts provided for 'diminution in value of assets' are also to be treated as realised losses. Although the wording is rather obscure, the effects may be mitigated as, to the extent that the diminution reverses a previous revaluation of the asset in question, that valuation surplus may now be treated as a realised profit. Therefore, only net diminutions in value on individual assets below depreciated historical cost need be considered as realised losses.

An exception to the rule that provisions for diminution in value are regarded as realised losses is made for such a provision if it appears on a revaluation of *all* of the fixed assets other than goodwill of the company, under the following circumstances. The directors do not have to formally revalue all fixed assets and incorporate these revaluations into the accounts in order to take advantage of the exception; the value only has to be 'considered', and this does not imply that the book amount of the asset has to be altered. The Act states that fixed assets that have not actually been revalued are to be treated as if they had, if the directors are satisfied that the aggregate value of all fixed assets is not less than the amount at which they are currently stated in the company's accounts.[129] Thus a downward valuation of a particular fixed asset need not be treated as a realised loss if the directors are satisfied that the company's fixed assets are worth, in total, not less than their net book value.

This exception can only be taken if the following note disclosure is made:[130]

(a) that the directors have considered the value of some of the fixed assets of the company, without actually revaluing those assets;

(b) that they are satisfied that the aggregate value of those assets at the time in question is or was not less than the aggregate amount at which they are being stated in the company's accounts; and

(c) that the relevant items are accordingly stated in the relevant accounts on the basis that a revaluation of all of the company's fixed assets which was deemed to have taken place included the assets that have suffered a diminution in value.

An example of this basis is shown in the accounts of Enodis below:

Extract 12.22: Enodis plc (2000)

Notes [extract]

21 Reserves [extract]

a) The Directors, up to 30 September 1999, had valued the Company's investments in subsidiary entities at cost plus post-acquisition retained profits, unless there was evidence of an impairment in value in which case the lower value was adopted. The valuations have not been updated since 30 September 1999. The Directors have considered the value of the remaining fixed assets and are satisfied that these are worth, in total, not less than the aggregate amount at which they are stated in the Company's accounts. Accordingly, in accordance with Section 275 of the Companies Act 1985 the aggregate provision does not fall to be classified as a realised loss and therefore distributable reserves of the Company are £36.5m (1999: £109.8m) as analysed below:

	2000 £m	1999 £m
Profit and loss account	(48.8)	24.5
Provisions against investments in subsidiary entities	85.3	85.3
Excess of provisions over surpluses on revaluation of investments in subsidiary entities	–	–
Distributable reserves	36.5	109.8

The note must be repeated in subsequent accounts for as long as advantage is to be taken of the exemption as these may become 'relevant accounts', i.e. those on which a distribution is to be based.[131]

However, it has also been argued by the ICAEW and ICAS in their draft technical release *The Determination Of Realised Profits And Distributable Profits In The Context Of The Companies Act 1985*, that a downward valuation that results in a deficit on the revaluation reserve is not a realised loss. FRS 15 only allows an overall revaluation deficit on an individual asset if its value in use is higher than its market value. Paragraph 65 of FRS 15 requires the loss below recoverable amount to be reflected in the Statement of Total Recognised Gains and Losses (rather than the profit and loss account for the year). The exposure draft argues that the inference to be drawn from this is that this loss would be regarded as unrealised under FRS 15 (and hence, presumably, unrealised in law as well).[132] This would further suggest that the downward valuation, being unrealised, is not a provision as defined in paragraph 88.

If this view were taken, then any revaluation deficit would be an unrealised loss and only affect distributions by public limited companies, whose distributable profits are reduced to the extent that they have net unrealised losses.

3 UK DISCLOSURE REQUIREMENTS

3.1 Introduction

This section sets out the principal disclosures required in financial statements compiled under UK GAAP for tangible fixed assets, followed separately by those required additionally for investment properties. Within each part, the disclosures required by each authoritative source are separately shown.

3.2 Companies Act disclosures

3.2.1 *Balance sheet and profit and loss account*

The statutory formats require that tangible fixed assets are disclosed under the headings shown below.

II Tangible assets

1. Land and buildings
2. Plant and machinery
3. Fixtures, fittings, tools and equipment
4. Payments on account and assets in course of construction[133]

Company accounts usually include only the net book amounts of any category of fixed asset on the face of the balance sheet, with the information required by the Arabic numerals relegated to the notes. The Act permits the format categories with Arabic numerals to be modified to suit the circumstances of the business. A common example would be the separate classification of investment properties.

If profit and loss account Formats 2 or 4 are chosen, then 'depreciation and other amounts written off tangible and intangible fixed assets' must be shown, either on the face of the profit and loss account or in the notes.[134] If Formats 1 or 3 are chosen, the equivalent information must be given in the notes to the accounts.[135]

If a provision for permanent diminution in value of any fixed asset has been made then it must be disclosed in the notes to the accounts if it is not shown in the profit and loss account.[136]

3.2.2 *Notes to the accounts*

The note disclosures required by the Companies Act about the cost and depreciation of all fixed assets, including tangible fixed assets, are duplicated to some extent by accounting standards. The Act sets out the following required disclosures for each category of tangible fixed asset shown in the statutory formats (see 3.2.1 above):

(a) the appropriate amounts at the beginning of the financial year and as at the balance sheet date, based either on historical cost (purchase price or production cost) or alternative accounting rules;[137]

(b) all movements during the year, including revaluation surpluses and deficits, acquisitions, disposals and transfers.[138] Other movements that might also be reflected in the carrying value of the asset, such as exchange differences, will also be disclosed in the note; and

(c) the cumulative amount of depreciation as at the beginning and end of the financial year on the appropriate basis of cost or valuation, the depreciation charge for the period and adjustments in respect of disposals or for other reasons.[139]

3.2.3 *Additional disclosures for tangible fixed assets carried at a valuation*

The Companies Act requires that where assets have been included in the accounts at amounts based on a valuation then the items affected and the basis of valuation adopted should be disclosed in a note to the accounts.[140] The revaluation reserve itself should be included as a separate sub-heading in the position shown in the formats, but need not be so called.[141] The treatment for tax purposes of amounts credited or debited to the revaluation reserve must be disclosed in a note to the accounts.[142]

In the case of each balance sheet item affected, disclosure should be made of either:

(a) the comparable amounts based on historical costs; or

(b) the differences between the amounts in (a) above and the amounts actually included in the balance sheet.[143]

The comparable amounts are the gross amounts and cumulative provisions for depreciation or diminution in values and should relate to *all* of the assets covered by the balance sheet item.[144] Note that these disclosures still have to be made by companies that have opted for 'frozen' valuations under the transitional provisions of FRS 15.

Most major companies would appear to adopt the former method of disclosure, as shown by Cadbury Schweppes below:

Extract 12.23: Cadbury Schweppes plc (2000)

Notes [extract]

11 Tangible Fixed Assets

	Group		
	Land and buildings £m	**Plant and equipment £m**	**Assets in course of construction £m**
Net book value at beginning of year	365	651	75
Net book value at end of year	381	626	99

The Group properties were professionally revalued at 30 September 1995. If the revalued assets were stated on a historical cost basis, the amounts would be as follows:

	Group		Company	
	2000 £m	1999 £m	2000 £m	1999 £m
Land and buildings at cost	**242**	245	**6**	6
Accumulated depreciation thereon	**(73)**	(68)	**(1)**	(1)
	169	177	**5**	5
Depreciation charge for the year	**5**	3	**–**	–

These disclosures may be included as part of a fixed asset table; or be given by footnote.

Although the Act requires the amounts to be disclosed to deal with all the assets included in the balance sheet item affected by valuations, some companies disclose the comparable historical cost information for only the assets which have been revalued. Where such an approach is taken then it is necessary to disclose the gross amount and accumulated depreciation for the revalued assets which are included in the balance sheet so that the total figures, in historical cost terms, can be deduced. For all items (other than listed investments) that are carried at valuation, the Companies Act also requires the years in which the assets were valued and the amounts at which they were valued to be disclosed.[145] An example of this disclosure is given by the following extract from the notes to Delta's accounts:

Extract 12.24: Delta plc (2000)

Notes [extract]

Tangible assets [extract]

Analysis of cost or valuation of land and buildings at professional valuation in:

1998 and earlier years	27.4
1999	10.2
2000	–
At cost	71.7
At 30 December 2000	**109.3**

The information in this extract is often the only information given by companies in respect of past valuations, despite the fact that, as mentioned earlier, the Companies Act also strictly requires the basis of valuation to be disclosed.[146] Where fixed assets (other than investments) have been revalued during the year, then the Companies Act also requires disclosure of the names or qualifications of the persons making the valuation and the bases used by them.[147]

3.2.4 *True and fair override disclosures for investment properties*

The use of the 'true and fair override' was referred to above at 2.4 in relation to compliance with SSAP 19. Consequently the true and fair override disclosures required by the Act must be given by companies that hold investment properties that (in compliance with SSAP 19, but in contravention of the Act's requirements) are not depreciated. The Act requires that 'particulars of the departure, the reasons for it and its effect' must be given in a note to the accounts.[148]

An example of such disclosures is illustrated by Hammerson below:

Extract 12.25: Hammerson plc (2000)

1. Accounting policies [extract]

Basis of Accounting

The financial statements are prepared under the historical cost convention as modified by the revaluation of investment properties and in accordance with all applicable accounting standards. The financial statements are in compliance with the Companies Act 1985 except that, as explained below, investment properties are not depreciated.

Depreciation [extract]

In accordance with Statement of Standard Accounting Practice No. 19, no depreciation is provided in respect of freehold properties or leasehold properties with over 20 years to expiry. This is a departure from the requirements of the Companies Act 1985 which requires all properties to be depreciated. Such properties are not held for consumption but for investment and the directors consider that to depreciate them would not give a true and fair view. Depreciation is only one of many factors reflected in the annual valuation of properties and accordingly the amount of depreciation which might otherwise have been charged cannot be separately identified or quantified. The directors consider that this policy results in the accounts giving a true and fair view.

Additional disclosures are required by FRS 18 – *Accounting policies* – and are detailed below at 3.3.

Directors report

The market value of 'interests in land' (taken to mean land and buildings)[149] should be disclosed if it differs substantially from the amount at which the assets are carried in the balance sheet and if, in the directors' opinion, the difference is of such significance that it should be brought to the attention of the members or debenture holders. The difference should be quantified 'with such degree of precision as is practicable'.[150] This requirement was originally instigated in 1967 as a result of shareholders not realising the true market value of the property assets of their companies. This state of affairs sometimes resulted in businesses being taken over for sums considerably lower than their break-up value by 'asset strippers'.

This disclosure has often been seen but rarely quantified in the last twenty years. However, with the advent of FRS 15, under which most companies have chosen to 'freeze' their property asset valuations rather than revalue them annually, it is possible that this disclosure may become more common if market values move significantly away from FRS 15 'frozen' values.

3.3 Disclosures required by FRS 18 in relation to SSAP 19 compliance

If a business carries investment property that is not depreciated, as noted above at 2.4, it will have to invoke the true and fair override to justify not complying with the Companies Act requirement to depreciate. In this event FRS 18 paragraphs 62 and 63 require certain extra disclosures. Paragraph 62 of FRS 18 requires a 'clear and unambiguous' statement:

- giving particulars of the departure, the reasons for it, and its effect;
- that there has been a departure;
- that this is necessary to give a true and fair view;
- of the treatment normally required and of the treatment actually adopted;
- of why the prescribed treatment would not give a true and fair view.

In addition, if the effect of the departure cannot reasonably be quantified, which is the view normally taken in practice with investment properties, the circumstances should be explained.

3.4 Disclosures required by SSAP 19

The following details concerning the valuation should also be given:

(a) the basis of the valuation;

(b) the names or qualifications of the valuers; and

(c) if the valuation was made by an officer or employee of the company or group owning the property, the financial statements should disclose this fact.[151]

SSAP 19 requires that the carrying value of investment properties and the investment revaluation reserve be 'displayed prominently in the accounts'.[152] This means that if assets other than investment properties are revalued, the revaluation reserve should be split to show the amount relating to investment properties as opposed to other revalued assets. In practice, such splits are seldom seen.

SSAP 19 refers to an 'investment revaluation reserve'[153] but in practice this description is seldom used in property company accounts. Most companies just use the term 'revaluation reserve', although some take advantage of the freedom allowed by the Companies Act to change this particular heading[154] with headings such as 'property revaluation reserve' and 'unrealised capital account'.

3.5 Disclosures required by FRS 15

Note that the disclosures required by FRS 15 in relation to the capitalisation of finance costs are dealt with in Chapter 15 at 3.2.

3.5.1 *Accounting policies*

FRS 15 requires that disclosure be made for each class of tangible fixed asset of the depreciation methods used and the useful economic lives or the depreciation rates used.[155] This information is usually given in the accounting policies note. Certain categories of asset, for example plant and machinery, will probably include items depreciated at a variety of rates. It is usual to disclose a range of lives and/or rates in order to satisfy the disclosure requirements.

Bass gives a comprehensive description of its accounting policies on fixed assets and depreciation, as shown below:

Extract 12.26: Bass PLC (2000)

Accounting policies [extract]

Fixed Assets and Depreciation [extract]

iii Tangible assets Freehold and leasehold land and buildings are stated at cost, or valuation, less depreciation. All other fixed assets are stated at cost less depreciation.

iv Revaluation Surpluses arising from the professional valuations of properties are taken direct to the revaluation reserve. Deficits are eliminated against any revaluation reserve in respect of that income generating unit with any excess, to the extent that it represents an impairment, being charged to the profit and loss account. Surpluses or deficits realised on the disposal of an asset are transferred from the revaluation reserve to the profit and loss account reserve.

v Impairment Any impairment arising on an income generating unit, other than an impairment which represents a consumption of economic benefits, is eliminated against any revaluation reserve in respect of that income generating unit with any excess being charged to the profit and loss account.

vi Depreciation and amortisation Goodwill and other intangible assets are amortised over their estimated useful lives, generally 20 years.

Freehold land is not depreciated. All other tangible fixed assets are depreciated to a residual value over their estimated useful lives, namely:

Freehold buildings	50 years
Leasehold buildings	lesser of unexpired term of lease and 50 years
Fixtures, fittings and equipments	3-25 years
Plant and machinery	4-20 years

All depreciation and amortisation is charged on a straight line basis

3.5.2 *Notes to the accounts*

For the most part, FRS 15's disclosure requirements for tangible fixed assets repeat those of the Act. It requires that, for each major class of depreciable asset, the following is disclosed:

- total depreciation charged for the period;
- where material, the financial effect of a change during the period in either the estimate of useful economic lives or the estimate of residual values;

- the cost or revalued amount at the beginning of the financial period and at the balance sheet date;
- the cumulative amount of provisions for depreciation or impairment at the beginning of the financial period and at the balance sheet date;
- a reconciliation of the movements, separately disclosing additions, disposals, revaluations, transfers, depreciation, impairment losses, and reversals of past impairment losses written back in the financial period; and
- the net carrying amount at the beginning of the financial period and at the balance sheet date.[156]

In addition, where there has been a change in depreciation method any material effect and the reason for the change should be disclosed in the year of change.[157]

3.5.3 *Extra disclosures for tangible fixed assets that have been revalued*

FRS 15 requires the following disclosures for every class of tangible fixed assets that has been revalued. The information is required in each reporting period:[158]

(a) the valuer's name and qualifications or the valuer's organisation and a description of its nature;

(b) the basis or bases of valuation. This should include whether the valuation has reflected notional directly attributable acquisition costs or expected selling costs;

(c) the date and amounts of the valuations;

(d) the carrying amount that would have been included in the accounts if the assets had been carried at historical cost less depreciation. This is only required where historical cost records are available;

(e) whether the valuer is internal or external to the entity;

(f) a statement by the directors if the valuations have not been updated because they are not aware of any material change in value; and

(g) the date of the last full valuation where it is an interim valuation or the valuation has not been updated.

In addition, the standard requires the following additional disclosure for revalued properties:[159]

(a) a statement where properties have been valued having regard to their trading potential and the amount of such properties; and

(b) the total amount of notional directly attributable acquisition costs or expected selling costs reflected in the carrying amount, where material.

Where the open market value is materially different from existing use value, the open market value and the reasons for the difference should be disclosed in the notes to the accounts.[160]

If it has not proved possible to obtain a reliable valuation of an asset held outside the UK or the Republic of Ireland, the carrying amount of that tangible fixed asset and the fact that it has not been revalued must be stated.[161]

4 UK PRACTICAL ISSUES

4.1 Tangible or intangible assets – the issue of new technology costs?

FRS 10's prohibition on capitalising internally-generated intangible assets has focused attention on the treatment of many internal costs. During 2000, this was particularly the case with internet-related costs such as website development costs.

In spite of FRS 10's general prohibition on the recognition of internally generated intangible assets, it includes an exception for certain software development costs:

> Software development costs that are directly attributable to bringing a computer system or other computer-operated machinery into working condition for its intended use within the business are treated as part of the cost of the related hardware rather than as a separate intangible asset.[162]

In other words, software may be capitalised in certain circumstances (if it is necessary to bring new hardware into use) but only if it is capitalised as a tangible asset. This exception did nothing to alleviate the problem of how to treat website development costs, which the UITF therefore considered. The UITF's response to the problem was UITF Abstract 29 – *Website development costs* – which was issued in February 2001. Even though 'dotcom fever' has abated, the treatment of such costs remains an important issue.

Websites are used for many business purposes, and companies incur significant costs in getting them up and running, as well as in keeping them functioning and attractive to users. UITF 29 sets out four types of activity involved in creating a website:

> *Planning costs*: such things as feasibility studies, researching hardware and software availability, 'exploring' (i.e. researching) functionality and how to achieve it, selecting suppliers and consultants.
>
> *Application and infrastructure development costs*: including items such as acquiring the domain name, buying the hardware and software required, integrating it into the IT structure of the entity.
>
> *Design costs*: the expenditure to develop the appearance of the website, including any graphics, page layout and similar design matters.
>
> *Content costs*: expenditure incurred on preparing and loading the content onto the website.[163]

The Abstract further emphasised 'the substantial uncertainty regarding the viability, useful economic life and value of a website'.[164] The task force consequently tried to identify criteria that would ensure costs will only be capitalised if they create an enduring asset that will also generate future economic benefits in excess of the amounts capitalised.[165]

Of the four categories of expenditure identified, the Abstract held that planning costs may not be capitalised and should be expensed when incurred.[166] The remaining three categories are capable of being recognised as assets, so as a result the UITF decided that application and infrastructure development costs, design, and content costs may be capitalised to the extent that:

(a) the expenditure is separately identifiable;

(b) the technical and commercial feasibility is reasonable certain;

(c) the website will generate revenue directly and the expenditure makes an enduring contribution to the website's revenue generating capabilities;

(d) there is a reasonable expectation that the present value of the future cash flows from the site will at least equal the amounts capitalised; and

(e) adequate resources exist, or will be available, to enable the project to be completed.

Points (c) and (d) above are expanded: if the site is used only for advertising or promoting the entity's products or services, it is unlikely to be possible to demonstrate that it generates income directly.[167] Insufficient evidence means that the expenditure should be expensed.

These criteria are based on those used in SSAP 13 in identifying development expenditure that may be capitalised. By contrast, FRS 15 does not require an entity to demonstrate that it will generate sufficient revenue to cover the cost of a fixed asset prior to capitalising it. Although under FRS 11 an entity may have to demonstrate that revenues are sufficient to do so in discounted terms, if there are indications of impairment. Impairment is dealt with in Chapter 13.

As in the case with computer software development costs dealt with in FRS 10, the UITF has decided that website development costs should be capitalised as *tangible,* rather than *intangible,* assets.

Capitalised website development costs should be depreciated over their estimated useful economic life. The Abstract points out that the useful economic life of a website is likely to be short. In addition, if the design or content of a website has to be replaced more often than the site as a whole, it may have to be depreciated over a period that is shorter than the depreciation period selected for the remainder of the asset.

4.2 Separation of assets

FRS 15 requires the separation of certain fixed assets into component parts, most notably the separation of the land and building elements of a freehold property. This will inevitably be a matter of some judgement. FRS 15 states that an asset may need to be analysed for depreciation purposes into any subcomponents that have substantially different useful economic lives.[168] Some subcomponents may have indefinite lives and will not need to be depreciated at all, for example freehold land should not be depreciated. FRS 15 stresses that increases in land values do not offset the depreciation of the building or its useful economic life.[169] For most companies then, the FRS 15 'frozen' values of property are required to be separated into land and building elements.

The Royal Institution of Chartered Surveyors (RICS) gives guidance to its members on how to apportion the cost or valuation of a property between the depreciable amount and the land element.[170] This, it argues, may be done in either of the following ways:

(a) by valuing the land in its existing use and deducting this from the total. It is argued that this may be appropriate where there is suitable evidence of land values; or

(b) by assessing the net current replacement cost of the asset, in which case the value of the land is the balancing figure.[171]

This is relatively straightforward where the analysis is only between land and buildings, and when assets are recorded on the basis of cost, although even then the apportionments may be somewhat arbitrary. However, the issue quickly becomes more complicated if additional subcomponents are identified, or if the asset is revalued, because the property as a whole may be valued on a basis that is not readily disaggregated into component parts in any meaningful way.

More complexity is added if the property was valued on the basis of its earning potential, e.g. as a pub or hotel. This basis is described in more detail at 2.5 above. One major problem is what to do with the 'trading potential', which reflects the goodwill attaching to the business and represents the difference between the underlying separable fixed assets and the total valuation. Should it should be added to the land value (which does not depreciate) or carried with the buildings? FRS 15 states that it would be inappropriate to treat the trading potential as a separate component, where the value and life of any such trading potential is inseparable from that of the property.[172]

In practice, companies that are affected by this issue have assessed the net current replacement cost of the buildings and fixtures and fittings and have included the trading potential with the land so that it is not depreciated. The brewers, for example, have argued that the licence goes with the site and not with the building, so it would be inappropriate to depreciate it in line with the building's physical fabric.

Although these components have to be accounted for separately, companies are not required to disclose separately the land and building elements of their freehold property under UK GAAP, which are normally shown in aggregate, as illustrated by Bass below.

Extract 12.27: Bass PLC (2000)

Notes [extract]

Tangible Fixed Assets [extract]

	Land and buildings* £m
Cost of valuation	
At 30 September 1999	4,138
Exchange and other adjustments	18
Acquisitions	887
Additions	362
Disposals	(178)
At 30 September 2000	**5,227**
Depreciation:	
At 30 September 1999	59
Exchange and other adjustments	(1)
Provided	25
On disposals	(41)
At 30 September 2000	**42**
Net book value	
At 30 September 2000	**5,185**
At 30 September 1999	4,079

* Restated. On implementation of FRS15, properties were disaggregated into their separate components being land and buildings and fixtures, fittings and equipment. As a result, £560m has been reclassified as fixtures, fittings and equipment.

		2000			1999	**2000**	1999
Land and buildings		**Cost or valuation £m**	**Depreciation £m**	**Group total £m**	Group total £m	**Company total £m**	Company total £m
Freehold		4,643	(19)	4,624	3,642	6	6
Leasehold:	unexpired term of more than 50 years	336	(2)	334	266	1	1
	unexpired term of 50 years or less	248	(21)	227	171	1	2
		5,227	**(42)**	**5,185**	4,079	**8**	9

5 IAS REQUIREMENTS

5.1 Introduction

Unlike UK practice, IAS 1 *Presentation of financial statements* does not use the term 'fixed assets', although it does distinguish between tangible and intangible assets. Instead it draws a distinction between current and non-current assets. However, alternative terms are not prohibited:

> 'This Standard uses the term 'non-current' to include tangible, intangible, operating and financial assets of a long-term nature. It does not prohibit the use of alternative descriptions as long as the meaning is clear.'[173]

Therefore a UK company that reported under IAS would not be prohibited from using the term 'tangible fixed assets' in its financial statements. Under IAS an entity is not required to separate its balance sheet into current and non-current assets, though it may do so. The classification of current assets used in IAS 1 is based upon realisation within 12 months of the balance sheet date, while all other assets are termed non-current.[174] If this distinction is not made, assets are to be presented broadly in order of their liquidity.[175] Paragraph 66 of IAS 1 makes it clear that property plant and equipment should be shown as a separate category of asset on the face of the balance sheet.

Therefore under IAS, property, plant and equipment will normally appear as a separate category of asset in the balance sheet at a suitable point within non-current assets, or at a point in an undifferentiated balance sheet that reflects its relative liquidity – that is the time over which the property, plant and equipment will be depreciated. While the balance sheet figure for property, plant and equipment may be a single net carrying amount, the relevant standards require more detailed disclosures of the constituent elements of the balance sheet figure to be included in the notes to the financial statements.

An example of this aspect of balance sheet layout under IAS is provided below by Bossard, where the term 'Long-term assets' is used.

Extract 12.28: Bossard Holding AG Zug (2000)

Consolidation Balance Sheet [extract]

Amounts in CHF 1,000	**2000**	1999
Long-term assets		
Long-term loans and deposits	**2,777**	18,245
Investments in associated companies	**504**	4,281
Intangible assets	**77,386**	40,591
Property, plant and equipment	**84,517**	73,118
	165,184	136,235

Of necessity IAS must apply to a large number of different statutory reporting regimes. With the imminent adoption of IAS for all listed companies in the European Union, IAS will be applied under at least 15 different member states' statutes. Consequently the requirements of IAS for property, plant and equipment as dealt with below are in addition to, not instead of any statutory requirements applicable to the entity.

There are two IASC standards currently in force that are relevant: IAS 16 – *Property, plant and equipment (revised 1998)* – and IAS 40 – *Investment property*. IAS 16 deals with all aspects of property, plant and equipment, except for investment property, mineral rights and biological assets. Biological assets, e.g. crops, herds and so forth, are dealt with in IAS 41 and beyond the scope of this book. The Standing Interpretations Committee of the IASC, which has a similar role to that of the UITF in the UK, has also published SIC-14 – *Property, plant and equipment - Compensation for the impairment or loss of items* – and SIC-23 – *Property, plant and equipment - major inspection or overhaul costs* – which are relevant to this chapter.

5.2 The requirements of IAS 16

5.2.1 Definition recognition and measurement

IAS 16 came into force for periods beginning on or after 1 January 1999 and defines property, plant and equipment as 'tangible assets that :

(a) are held by an enterprise for use in the production or supply of goods or services, for rental to others, or for administrative purposes; and

(b) are expected to be used during more than one period.'[176]

An item of property, plant and equipment should be recognised as an asset when it is probable that future economic benefits will flow to the enterprise and the cost of the asset can be measured reliably.[177]

This is expanded in paragraph 9 of IAS 16. Until the risks and rewards of ownership have passed to the enterprise, which will usually mean that the future economic benefits no longer belong to another enterprise, the acquisition of the asset can usually be cancelled without 'significant penalty' and it should not be recognised.

Useful advice and guidance is contained in the recognition section of IAS 16. Major spare parts, for example, qualify as property, plant and equipment, while smaller spares would be carried as inventory. However if a set of spares can only be used on one item of property, plant and equipment and the use of the spares is 'irregular' then this set of spares should be depreciated over the useful life of the assets to which it relates.[178]

IAS 16 allows the 'components approach' to the recognition of certain items of property. It states that expenditure should be allocated to component parts of property, plant and equipment if these components require to be depreciated at different rates or using different methods. The standard's example is of an aircraft, where the airframe and engines have different useful lives.[179]

IAS 16 also addresses the issue of expenditure for safety and environmental reasons. Such expenditure, of course, does not give rise on its own account to future economic benefits for the enterprise. The standard argues that it can be recognised as an asset as long as it enables benefits to be derived from related assets in excess of those that could have obtained had the expenditure not been made. In other words, had the enterprise not been able to use the asset without the additional spend (for example, the hotel would have been closed down without the fire doors and escape routes), then safety or environmental enhancements may be recognised as an asset. The combined carrying value must not exceed the recoverable amount.[180]

A Initial measurement

All property, plant and equipment that is recognised as an asset should be recognised initially at cost.[181] Cost is defined by the standard as 'the amount of cash or cash equivalents paid or the fair value of the other consideration given to acquire an asset at the time of its acquisition or construction.'[182] Paragraph 15 sets out the following helpful guidance.

> 'The cost of an item of property, plant and equipment comprises its purchase price, including import duties and non-refundable purchase taxes, and any directly attributable costs of bringing the asset to working condition for its intended use; any trade discounts and rebates are deducted in arriving at the purchase price. Examples of directly attributable costs are:
>
> (a) the cost of site preparation;
>
> (b) initial delivery and handling costs;
>
> (c) installation costs;
>
> (d) professional fees such as for architects and engineers; and
>
> (e) the estimated cost of dismantling and removing the assets, restoring the site, to the extent that it is recognised as a provision under IAS 37 Provisions, contingent liabilities and contingent assets.'

Directly attributable costs are the key issue here in the measurement of cost. The standard goes on to make it plain that administrative and other general overheads are not a component of cost, unless they can be directly attributed to the asset's acquisition or installation. Start up costs, unless necessary to bring the asset into working condition, may not be capitalised as part of the cost of an asset either. Similarly any initial operating losses, for example while demand builds up, are to be recognised as an expense.[183]

IAS 16 is unclear about the extent to which an asset's carrying amount should be affected by subsequent changes in the estimated amount of dismantling and site restoration costs that occur subsequently to initial measurement. It is our view that the carrying amount should be adjusted for such changes as well as the provision. As this is a change in estimate so IAS 8 paragraph 26(b) applies. The consequence of this is that the depreciation of the dismantling costs will also be adjusted prospectively.

In the event of any revenue being earned during the start up period (for example by selling some of the output from commissioning a machine) such revenue should in our view be credited to turnover, not be deducted from the start up costs written off or capitalised.

The standard specifically eliminates the capitalisation of 'hidden' credit charges as part of the cost of an item of property, plant and equipment. Thus if the payment terms are extended beyond 'normal' credit terms, the cost to be recognised must be the cash price equivalent; the difference must be treated as an interest expense.[184] There are certain circumstances where IAS allows interest costs to be capitalised, and these are discussed in Chapter 15 at 5.

If an asset is self-built by the enterprise, the same general principles apply. If the same type of asset is made for resale by the business, it should be recognised at cost of production, without including the profit element, on the same basis as set out for valuing inventory held for sale under IAS 23, see Chapter 16 at 4.2. Abnormal amounts of wasted resources, whether labour, materials or other resources are not to be included in the cost of self-built assets.[185]

Assets partly paid for by government grants, and those held under finance leases are discussed in chapters 20 and 19 respectively.

B Subsequent expenditure and SIC-23

Apart from the separate recognition of major components and their replacement, discussed above, the recognition of subsequent expenditure is a matter for judgement. The decision depends upon whether or not the performance of an asset is enhanced beyond that originally assessed. If the 'economic benefits' expected to flow from using the asset are higher as a result of the subsequent expenditure, then it can be capitalised, if not it must be expensed.[186] Once again the guidance provided in IAS 16 is helpful as paragraph 24 gives examples of improvements which result in increased future economic benefits:

'(a) modification of an item of plant to extend its useful life, including an increase in its capacity;

(b) upgrading machine parts to achieve a substantial improvement in the quality of output; and

(c) adoption of new production processes enabling a substantial reduction in previously assessed operating costs.'

Expenditure on repairs and maintenance is usually recognised as an expense when incurred. However, in certain circumstances this may not be the case. In particular, if an item of property, plant and equipment has had its carrying value reduced as part of an impairment adjustment, subsequent repair expenditure to restore its performance may be capitalised, providing the carrying amount thus recognised is recoverable. This also applies if an asset is acquired that needs expenditure to bring it into working condition.[187] Impairment is separately discussed in Chapter 13. Subsequent expenditure may also be in respect of a component previously recognised as a separate asset, in which case the replaced asset will be written off and the expenditure capitalised as a separate asset.[188]

Capitalisation of expenditure on repairs and maintenance was dealt with further in SIC-23 – *Property, plant and equipment - major inspection and overhaul costs* – published in October 1999. It covers the situation where a business has an asset such as an aircraft that requires periodic major inspections or overhauls. As these overhauls may not result in the replacement of any particular component, the problem was that IAS 37 – *Provisions, contingent liabilities and contingent assets* – like FRS 12, would not permit an entity to provide for their costs (see Chapter 28).

The consensus was that major inspection and overhaul costs must be expensed when incurred unless:

(a) the enterprise has identified an 'amount representing major inspection or overhaul' as a separate component of the asset. It must have already depreciated that component to reflect the amount that will be replaced or restored by the subsequent major inspection or overhaul (whether the asset is carried at historical cost or revalued);

(b) it is probable that future economic benefits associated with the asset will flow to the enterprise; and

(c) the cost of the major inspection or overhaul to the enterprise can be measured reliably.

If these criteria are met, the cost should be capitalised and accounted for as a component of the asset.[189]

It appears that these requirements will have the same effect as the equivalent rules in FRS 15, described in 2.3.2 above, i.e. that the amount identified does not have to represent a separate physical component. In other words, as long as the entity identifies an amount that represents the 'benefit' of the future overhaul and depreciates this on an appropriate basis up to the point of the overhaul, it may then capitalise the overhaul cost. Example 12.1 above outlines the equivalent treatment under FRS 15.

C SIC-14 and SIC-6

SIC-14 – *Property, plant and equipment - compensation for the impairment or loss of items* – was issued in June 1988 and deals with the accounting treatment of monetary and non-monetary compensation received by companies from such things as:

(a) reimbursement by insurance companies, for example, due to natural disasters, theft or mishandling of items of property plant and equipment;

(b) indemnities by the government for items of property, plant and equipment that were expropriated;

(c) compensation related to the involuntary conversion of items of property, plant and equipment, for example land and buildings that have been subject to compulsory purchase; or

(d) physical replacement in whole or in part of an impaired or lost asset.

The SIC considered that the central issue was how a business should account for the three identifiable stages involved:

(a) the impairments or losses of items of property, plant and equipment;

(b) the related compensation from third parties; and

(c) the subsequent restoration, purchase or construction of assets.

Its consensus was that each stage should be accounted for separately. Impairments should be recognised under IAS 36, and retirements or disposals under IAS 16. Whatever monetary or non-monetary compensation received should be included in the income statement when recognised. Finally the cost of repairing or restoring existing assets, buying or constructing their replacements, or receiving an asset as compensation should be determined and recognised under IAS 16.[190]

SIC-6 – *Costs of modifying existing software* – became effective in July1999 and makes it clear that costs of modifying software so as to maintain its original performance, must be expensed, the reason being this would not be an enhancement. An example would be modifying software to be able to cope with the introduction of the Euro unit of currency

5.2.2 *Revaluations*

IAS 16, in common with a number of international standards, allows alternative treatments to be selected by a business. The 'benchmark treatment' of property, plant and equipment, once initially recognised, is to carry the asset at cost less depreciation and any impairment losses.[191] Impairment is separately discussed in Chapter 13. However IAS 16 contains an allowed alternative treatment which permits property, plant and equipment to be carried at a valuation, after initial recognition at cost:

> 'Subsequent to initial recognition as an asset, an item of property, plant and equipment should be carried at a revalued amount, being its fair value at the date of the revaluation less any subsequent accumulated depreciation and subsequent accumulated impairment losses. Revaluations should be made with sufficient regularity such that the carrying amount does not differ materially from that which would be determined using fair value at the balance sheet date.'[192]

If the allowed alternative treatment is adopted, land and buildings are to be carried at fair value, which is normally to be determined by professional valuers, though there is no requirement for a professional external valuation. 'Fair value' will usually be the market value of the asset. Although market value is not discussed further, fair value is defined as the amount at which an asset could be exchanged between knowledgeable, willing parties in an arm's length transaction.[193] It would therefore appear to be more like open market value (OMV) which is described in 2.5 above, rather than existing use value (EUV), which is the valuation basis required by FRS 15.

EUV differs from OMV in that it is an attempt to estimate net current replacement cost, whereas OMV is an estimate of net realisable value as at a particular point in time. The EUV valuation assumptions therefore include two extra conditions: (i) the asset can be used for the foreseeable future only for the existing use, and (ii) vacant possession is forthcoming on completion. In addition and consistent with EUV being an entry value rather than an exit value – purchasers' costs are added.

lant and equipment is normally to be carried at market value determined 'by aisal'. Thus, IAS 16 does not require any valuations to be performed by l valuers. If there is no market value because of the specialised nature of the epreciated replacement cost is to be used.[194]

Valuation frequency is not laid down precisely by IAS 16, which states that the required frequency depends upon the 'movements in the fair values of the items of property, plant and equipment being revalued. When the fair value of a revalued asset differs materially from its carrying amount, a further revaluation is necessary.' However 'significant and volatile movements in fair value' necessitate annual revaluations, while insignificant movements require valuations only at three or five year intervals.[195] Quite how this is to be known without a valuation exercise being done first is not explained, but if it refers to the materiality of the valuation differences, then the timing is not a condition at all.

If the revaluation allowed alternative treatment is adopted, the standard requires that an entire class of assets must be revalued. This requirement is to preclude selective revaluation of individual assets. The following are examples of separate classes of asset given in IAS 16:

(i) land;
(ii) land and buildings;
(iii) machinery
(iv) ships;
(v) aircraft;
(vi) motor vehicles;
(vii) furniture and fixtures; and
(viii) office equipment.[196]

A rolling valuation of a class of assets, whereby the class is revalued over an (undefined) short period of time is permitted, 'provided the valuations are kept up to date'.[197] This final condition makes it difficult to see how rolling valuations can be performed unless the value of the assets changes very little.

Extract 12.29 below shows the accounting policy, and other related disclosures of Mandarin Oriental International towards revaluations.

Extract 12.29: Mandarin Oriental International Limited (2000)

Accounting policies [extract]

E Tangible Assets and Depreciation [extract]
Other freehold properties and properties held on leases with an expected remaining life of more than 20 years are stated at valuation. Independent valuations are performed at intervals not exceeding three years on an open market basis. In the intervening years the Directors review the carrying value of properties and adjustment is made where there has been a material change. Revaluation surpluses and deficits are dealt with in capital reserves except for movements on individual properties below cost which are dealt with in the consolidation profit and loss account. Other tangible assets are stated at cost less amounts provided for depreciation.

Notes [extract]

9 Tangible Assets [extract]
Land and building were revalued at 31st December 1998 by independent valuers on an open market basis. The Directors have reviewed the carrying values of all properties at 31st December 1999 and 2000 in consultation with the Group's independent valuers. The Group's share of the resulting surplus of US$81.1 million has been dealt with in capital reserves and US$0.2 million dealt with in the profit and loss account (1999: surplus of US$135.0 million dealt with in capital reserves).

If the land and buildings had been included in the financial statements are cost, the carrying value would have been US$592.2 million (1999: US$520.2 million).

A Realisation of valuation surpluses

IAS 16 specifies that a revaluation surplus is not a realised profit. Increases in a valuation should be credited to a revaluation surplus within equity. If a revaluation increase reverses a decrease that was recognised as an expense, it may be credited to income. Decreases in valuation should be charged to the income statement, except to the extent that they reverse an existing revaluation surplus on the same asset.[198]

The revaluation surplus included in equity may be transferred directly to retained earnings when the surplus is realised. All of it may be realised when the asset is disposed of. However, the difference between depreciation based on the revalued carrying amount of the asset and depreciation based on its original cost may be realised as the asset is used by the enterprise. This is illustrated in Example 12.6 above. This provision recognises that any depreciation on the revalued part of an asset's carrying value has been realised by being charged to income. Thus a transfer can be made of an equivalent amount from the revaluation surplus in equity to retained profits. However any transfers is made directly from revaluation surplus to retained earnings and not through the income statement.[199] The effect on taxation, both current and deferred, of a policy of revaluing assets is dealt with in Chapter 24.

B Adopting a policy of revaluation

Although the initial adoption of a policy of revaluation is a change in accounting policy it is not dealt with as a prior year adjustment in accordance with IAS 8, instead being treated as a revaluation during the year.[200]

5.2.3 *Depreciation*

IAS 16 requires the depreciable amount of an asset, that is the difference between the 'cost of an asset, or other amount substituted for cost in the financial statements, less its residual value'[201] to be allocated on a systematic basis over its useful life. The 'amount substituted for cost' may reflect an impairment; alternatively the asset may have been revalued or included at fair value on acquisition. The depreciation method should reflect the pattern in which the asset's benefits are used by the enterprise, and the charge should be recognised as an expense in the income statement.[202] Depreciation may be included in the carrying amount of another asset, so, for example, depreciation included within stock will end up within costs of sales of manufactured items.[203]

The standard requires a depreciation charge to be made even if the asset is worth more than its carrying amount.[204] It provides the following guidance about the factors to be considered when estimating the useful life of an asset:

(a) the asset's expected usage, assessed by reference to its expected capacity or physical output;

(b) physical wear and tear;

(c) technical obsolescence either from changes or improvements in production, or from a change in the market demand; and

(d) legal or similar limits on the use of the asset, such as the expiry dates of related leases.'[205]

The useful life of an asset is defined in terms of its use to the business, not its economic life, so it is quite possible that an asset's useful life will be shorter than its economic life.[206] This is common with property but less usual for plant and machinery.

The standard requires the land and the building element of property to be accounted for as separate components. Land, which usually has an unlimited life, is not depreciated, while buildings are depreciable assets. The useful life of a building is not affected by an increase in the value of the land on which it stands.[207] The standard also explicitly states that, while the repairs and maintenance policy may extend an asset's useful life or increase its residual value, it does not negate the need to charge depreciation.[208]

IAS 16 does not specifically say that depreciation does not have to be charged if the depreciable amount of an asset is so high that the charge would not be material. As shown below, Mandarin Oriental International indicates that the level of maintenance is such that the value of its properties is not diminished, and so implies that depreciation is not necessary. Although this is in apparent contravention of IAS 16 paragraphs 42 and 51, as international standards only apply to material items, it may be that this aspect of interpreting IAS requirements was in mind when the company decided upon its policy.

Extract 12.30: Mandarin Oriental International Limited (2000)

Accounting policies [extract]

E Tangible Assets and Depreciation [extract]

It is the Group's practice to maintain freehold properties, leasehold properties with an expected remaining life of more than 20 years and integral fixed plant in a continual state of sound repair, such that their value is not diminished by the passage to time. Accordingly, the Directors consider that the useful economic lives of these assets are sufficiently long and their residual values, based on prices prevailing at the time of valuation, are sufficiently high that their depreciation is insignificant. The cost of maintenance and repairs of the properties is charged to the consolidation profit and loss account as incurred and the cost of significant improvements is capitalised.

Note that there is no requirement in IAS 16 for an impairment review if no depreciation is charged.

A Depreciation methods

The standard is not prescriptive about methods of depreciation, mentioning straight line, reducing balance and sum of the units as possibilities. The overriding requirement is that the depreciation charge reflects the pattern of usage of the benefits the asset brings over its useful life.[209] If there has been a change in the pattern of use of an asset's benefits, the depreciation method should be changed to reflect it. The consequent depreciation adjustment should be made prospectively, that is the asset's depreciable amount should be written off over current and future periods.

The standard requires periodic reviews of an asset's useful life, and if significant differences are found, the depreciation charge should be adjusted prospectively.[210]

B Residual value

Although the depreciable amount of an asset is determined after deducting its residual value, IAS 16 offers no guidance on calculating residuals. Indeed, it states that the residual is often insignificant and may therefore be disregarded.

For those assets where this is not the case (and this will particularly apply to property, of course), the residual value is to be estimated at the date of acquisition or date of valuation. It is to be based on the present day residual values of similar assets. If the asset is carried at historical cost the residual will not be adjusted for subsequent price changes.[211]

C Disposal or retirement

The standard requires that an item of property, plant and equipment should be removed from the balance sheet when the asset is no longer in use and there are no expected 'benefits from its disposal' that is, it has no resale or trade-in value. Gains or losses on disposal or retirement must be recognised in the income statement as the difference between the asset's carrying value and the sale proceeds if any.[212]

The question has been raised as to whether entities that revalue their assets are either permitted or required to revalue an item of property, plant and equipment immediately prior to its disposal. This issue is not addressed by IAS 16 and in our opinion such revaluations are neither required nor prohibited. However, whatever approach is followed should be applied consistently and in accordance with the entity's stated accounting policy.

Any property, plant and equipment held for disposal that is not being actively used should be included at its carrying value at the date active use ceased. In this case, annual impairment reviews are required.[213]

5.2.4 Exchanges of assets

An item of property, plant and equipment may be acquired in exchange for a similar asset, that is one that has a similar use in the same line of business and has a similar fair value. It may also be sold for an equity stake in a similar asset. As 'the earnings process is incomplete' (a phrase which is not further explained), no gain or loss will be recorded on the exchange and the new asset will be recorded at the carrying value of the asset given up. However, the assets may not have similar fair values. If the asset received has a lower fair value, this probably indicates that the asset given up had been impaired in value. The new asset will be recorded at the written down value and a loss recognised in the income statement. The carrying value of the new asset will be adjusted if the transaction includes a cash payment or receipt.

If the asset received is dissimilar, its cost is measured at the fair value of the asset received. This is the same as the fair value of the asset given up, as adjusted for any cash received. The gain or loss on the transaction will be taken to the income statement.[214]

IAS 16 does not directly address the exchange of an asset for an equity instrument, as distinct from an equity stake in a similar asset. Our view is that under these circumstances the cost of the tangible asset given up should be the fair value of the equity instrument issued in exchange for it, though the fair value of the asset itself may be a more practical measure of the cost.

5.3 The requirements of IAS 40

5.3.1 *Introduction*

IAS 40 – *Investment property* – came into force for all accounting periods beginning on or after 1 January 2001. The standard represents a major conceptual shift, as it is the first international standard to introduce the possibility of applying a full fair value model when accounting for non-financial assets. Under this option the asset is not depreciated, and all valuation changes (i.e. fair value changes) from one period to the next are treated as gains and losses and reported in the income statement. Consequently the fair value option of IAS 40 entails that the income statement will contain a mixture of realised gains and losses (for example rental income and maintenance costs) and unrealised ones, as the fair value gains and losses are not separately presented in a special part of the income statement. This contrasts with the revaluation approach allowed under IAS 16 (see 5.2.2 above) where increases above cost, and their reversals, are recognised as revaluation surpluses and deficits directly in reserves.

IAS 40 also allows investment property to be accounted for more conventionally, by being carried at cost less depreciation, under the benchmark treatment set out in IAS 16.

The exposure draft that preceded IAS 40 allowed only a fair value approach to the treatment of investment property and the Board appears to have relaxed its proposals in allowing the alternative treatment solely for pragmatic reasons. In Appendix B, when discussing the background to the standard, it states:

> '…the Board believes that it is impracticable, at this stage, to require a fair value model for all investment property. At the same time, the Board believes that it is desirable to permit a fair value model. This evolutionary step forward will allow preparers and users to gain greater experience working with a fair value model and will allow time for certain property markets to achieve greater maturity'.[215]

The treatment under the fair value model is in stark contrast to the treatment of properties held as inventory, even though the latter are more liquid assets. However, it is argued that this is entirely reasonable and that it is more important to use fair value accounting for investment properties than for assets that are held for a short time. This, it is proposed, is because cost-based measurements become increasingly irrelevant and the aggregation of costs incurred over a long period is of 'questionable relevance'.[216]

There is one aspect of IAS 40 that, even under the cost model, will have considerable consequences for the UK property investment industry, if the standard is adopted in the UK unchanged. As explained below, certain leasehold properties do not qualify for treatment as fixed assets at all under IAS 40. Rather leasehold interests are considered to be examples of operating leases and are to be treated as such. The up-front premium is a prepayment of operating lease rental payments. Only if the property in question is acquired under a finance lease (which will not be possible in the UK unless the lessee already owns the land), can it qualify as an investment property under IAS 40. The finance lease criteria as set out in IAS 17 – *Leases* – must of course also be met. These are discussed in Chapter 19.

5.3.2 *Definition, recognition and initial measurement*

An investment property is defined in IAS 40 as a:

> 'property (land or a building - or part of a building - or both) held (by the owner or by the lessee under a finance lease) to earn rentals or for capital appreciation or both, rather than for:
>
> (a) use in the production or supply of goods or services or for administrative purposes; or
>
> (b) sale in the ordinary course of business.'[217]

The standard gives guidance to help determine whether an asset is an investment property or not.

Land may be an investment property if it is either held for long-term capital appreciation or for a currently undetermined future use. This is by contrast with land that is held for sale in the short term in the ordinary course of business. If the enterprise has not concluded that it will use the land for its own purposes as occupied property or for short-term sale in the ordinary course of business, it is deemed to be held for capital appreciation.[218]

Buildings leased out under one or more operating leases are investment properties, whether they are owned by the reporting enterprise or held under finance leases. This will also apply if the building is currently vacant while tenants are being sought.[219]

Specific examples of items that are not investment properties and that are to be dealt with under other accounting standards are also given:

(a) property held for sale in the ordinary course of business, including property in the process of construction or development. This includes property acquired exclusively for sale in the near future or for development and resale. These are accounted for as inventory under IAS 2 *Inventories* (see Chapter 16);

(b) property being built or redeveloped under a construction contract for third parties. These are covered by IAS 11 *Construction Contracts*; which is discussed in Chapter 16;

(c) Owner-occupied property is specifically excluded from being treated as investment property, and is subject to the provisions of IAS 16. This includes:

  (i) property that is going to be owner-occupied in future (whether or not it has first to be redeveloped);

  (ii) property occupied by employees, whether or not they pay rent at market rates; and

  (iii) owner-occupied property awaiting disposal[220].

However, property held by one group company for occupation by another group company is an investment property in the accounts of the individual enterprise that owns it, even if the rental is not arm's length. It will be an owner-occupied property from the perspective of the group as a whole.[221]

(d) property that is being constructed or developed for future use as investment property. IAS 16 applies to such property until construction or development is complete, at which time the property becomes investment property.

However, IAS 40 continues to apply to existing investment property that is being redeveloped for continued future use as investment property.[222] While this means that enterprises will not have to reclassify investment properties when they are being redeveloped, they will still have to revalue them.

If a property has both investment property and non-investment property uses, providing the parts of the property could be sold separately (or leased under a finance lease separately) they should be accounted for separately. In the event that no separation is possible, only if an insignificant proportion is used for non-investment property purposes may the property be treated as an investment property.[223] Similarly if ancillary services are supplied by the owner to the user of the investment property, the value of these services must be insignificant component of the arrangement as a whole if the property is to qualify as investment property. An owner-managed hotel, for example, would be precluded from being an investment property as the services provided to guests are a significant component of the commercial arrangements. At the other extreme the owner may be effectively a passive investor who has transferred all responsibilities under a management contract. The crucial issue is the extent to which the owner retains significant exposure to the risks of running a hotel business.[224] The standard admits that this distinction can require judgements to be made, and specifies that businesses should develop consistent criteria for use in such instances that reflect the spirit of the provisions described above. These criteria must be disclosed in cases where classification is difficult.[225]

A Leaseholds

Paragraph 13 of IAS 40 states that:

> 'Under IAS 17 *Leases*, a lessee does not capitalise property held under an operating lease. Therefore, the lessee does not treat its interest in such property as investment property.'

In turn paragraph 11 of IAS 17 states:

> 'Leases of land and buildings are classified as operating or finance leases in the same way as leases of other assets. However, a characteristic of land is that it normally has an indefinite economic life and, if title is not expected to pass to the lessee by the end of the lease term, the lessee does not receive substantially all of the risks and rewards incident to ownership. A premium paid for such a leasehold represents pre-paid lease payments which are amortised over the lease term in accordance with the pattern of benefits provided.'[226]

This is of great significance to the UK property industry, where long leasehold interests in property are common, and to other jurisdictions such as Hong Kong where there are no freehold interests. However, the IASC considered that there was no conceptual difference between leasehold interests that should be accounted for under the fair value model under IAS 40, as against those that should be treated as operating leases under IAS 17. Accordingly, it decided not to amend IAS 17.[227] The asset will not qualify as an investment property, or be eligible for revaluation to current market value. The enterprise will have to treat it as prepaid rent and amortise it over the lease term, although in such circumstances it would be appropriate to treat the premium as a discounted sum and unwind the discount over the period for which rent has been paid.

This would radically alter the balance sheets of many UK property investment companies. It would reduce their assets as leasehold interests would no longer be carried at valuation and reduce profits (both on an ongoing basis and retained reserves) as amortising the prepayment would effectively force the companies to depreciate assets that, until now, have not been depreciated.

B *Recognition*

An investment property should be recognised as an asset when it is probable that the future economic benefits that are associated with the investment property will flow to the enterprise and the cost of the investment property can be measured reliably.[228]

The standard goes on to state that 'In determining whether an item satisfies the first criterion for recognition, an enterprise needs to assess the degree of certainty attaching to the flow of future economic benefits on the basis of the available evidence at the time of initial recognition.'[229] This could provide a problem for companies completing investment property and holding it unlet in times of property surplus. The property would, in any event, have to be carried at no more than its recoverable amount and written down if necessary.

C *Initial measurement and subsequent expenditure*

IAS 40 requires that an investment property should be measured initially at cost including transaction costs.[230] If a property is purchased, cost means purchase price and any directly attributable expenditure such as professional fees, and taxes such as stamp duty.[231] Self-constructed investment property during construction is subject to IAS 16. Only upon completion does it become investment property to which IAS 40 applies.[232]

Start up costs (unless necessary to bring the property into working condition), operating losses before the investment property is fully occupied, and abnormal wastage of resources in constructing it, are not part of the cost of an investment property. If payment for the property is deferred the cost to be recognised is the cash price. Any difference between the cash price and the total payments to be made is recognised as interest over the credit period.[233]

The treatment of any subsequent expenditure on an investment property depends upon the circumstances. If the expenditure adds to the 'originally assessed standard of performance' so that enhanced economic benefits will flow to the owner, the subsequent expenditure should be capitalised. Thus if, for instance, an elevator was renewed, the standard points out that such expenditure is often treated as an integral part of a building and not capitalised separately.[234] It is in any event arguable whether such expenditure enhances the originally assessed standard of performance. If the 'additional benefits' criterion is not met, then the subsequent expenditure should be expensed. On the other hand, if a property was purchased requiring renovation, so that the renovation is necessary to bring the asset into its working condition, the expenditure should be capitalised.[235] However IAS 40 does not specifically envisage a 'components approach', in which respect it is unlike FRS 15 or IAS 16.

5.3.3 *Treatment after initial recognition: fair value or cost model*

Once recognised, IAS 40 allows one of two methods of accounting for investment property to be chosen: the 'fair value model' or the 'cost model'. Unusually the standard does not identify a benchmark treatment and an allowed alternative. As explained above, IAS 40 is the first time that a full fair value model has been introduced for non-monetary assets.

A business has to choose to use one model or the other, and to use it for all its investment property.[236] The standard discourages changes from the fair value model to the cost model, stating that it is highly unlikely that this will result in a more appropriate presentation, as required by IAS 8 for any change in accounting policy.[237] The requirements of each model are described below.

A The fair value model

Under this model all investment property is included in the balance sheet at its fair value at the balance sheet date, and all changes in the fair value from one balance sheet to the next are included in the profit and loss account for the period. Fair value will usually be market value.[238] The standard defines fair value as 'the amount for which an asset could be exchanged between knowledgeable, willing parties in an arm's length transaction'.[239]

Fair value is not the same as value in use as defined in IAS 36. In particular, it does not take account of additional value derived from holding a portfolio of assets, synergies between the investment properties and other assets or legal rights or tax benefits or burdens pertaining to the current owner.[240] However, fair value is also not the same as net realisable value. It is a valuation as a specific point in time rather than at a time at which the entity may realistically have expected to sell the property. It assumes simultaneous exchange and completion.[241] Transaction costs are not deducted.[242]

Paragraphs 29 to 46 contain a substantial amount of guidance on the methodology of revaluations in practice, necessitated by the number of jurisdictions to which the standard may apply. Fair value assumes a valuation as at a specific moment in time at arm's length between a willing buyer and willing seller. It is further assumed that buyer and seller are reasonably informed about the property and the market at the date of the transaction and neither is under any compulsion to buy or sell.[243] There is to be a reasonable time to market the property properly and the seller will endeavour to sell the asset for the best price obtainable in the open market. The transaction is presumed to be at arm's length between unrelated parties.[244] These criteria are similar to those taken into account in determining open market value under FRS 15 (see 2.5 above). The standard states that the best evidence of fair value will be given by actual transactions in similar property in a similar location and condition.[245] However, it allows the fair value to be estimated by using other information when market values are not available. This means that gains and losses may be recorded in the income statement where there is no market value for the property and its fair value has been constructed from a variety of other sources.

The other information that an entity may draw on includes:

(a) transactions in an active market for dissimilar property (e.g. property of a different nature, condition or location, or subject to a different type of lease), as adjusted to reflect the differences;

(b) transactions on less active markets if they have been adjusted to take account of subsequent changes in economic conditions; or

(c) discounted cash flow projections based on estimated future cash flows (as long as these are reliable). These should be supported by existing leases and current market rents for similar properties in the same location and condition. The discount rate should reflect current market assessments of the uncertainty and timing of the cash flows.[246]

The technique suggested in (c) above is not dissimilar to a valuation in the UK using property yields (a basis on which properties are bought and sold) except that yields already assume rental growth that would have to be separately factored into a discounted cash flow calculation. Future capital expenditure that will enhance the benefits may not be taken into account in determining the fair value, nor may the income that will arise from the expenditure.[247]

As these various bases may result in a range of valuations, the enterprise must consider the underlying reasons for the variation in order to arrive at the most reliable estimate, within a 'relatively narrow' range of estimates of fair value.[248]

An enterprise must also take care not to double count assets and liabilities. The standard states that fixtures and fittings such as lifts or air conditioning are usually subsumed within the investment property rather than being accounted for separately. In other cases, additional assets may be necessary in order that the property can be used for its specific purposes. The standard refers to furniture within a property that is being let as furnished offices, and argues that this should not be recognised as a separate asset.[249] This presumably means that any replacement expenditure will have to be expensed as no part of the investment property will be depreciated. It is probably assumed that the revaluation would take account of the state of the fixtures and the property's value would increase once they have been replaced.

Prepaid or accrued operating lease income should be treated as separate assets and liabilities and not subsumed within the carrying value of the asset.[250]

The standard stresses that it is only in exceptional cases that the entity will be unable, on first recognition of a particular investment property, to determine a fair value.

Entities are strongly discouraged from arguing that there is no fair value. It would only be an acceptable argument if there were infrequent market transactions and either that the entity was unable to construct a fair value using the alternative measures in the standard or that the range of fair value estimates was too great to establish a reliable value. In such cases, property should be treated under the benchmark treatment of IAS 16 and assumed to have a nil residual value.[251] This means that it has to be carried at cost and depreciated over its useful life, as IAS 16's allowed alternative treatment under which assets may be revalued to fair value, is specifically ruled out in these circumstances. It should continue to be so treated until disposal. Even if an entity is 'compelled' to carry an individual property at cost, all other investment property must be carried at fair value.[252]

In addition, once a property is initially recognised at its fair value, it must always be so recognised until disposed of, even if market prices become less easily available.[253] No doubt this clause is to prevent a switch to the cost model if the fair value becomes uncomfortably low.

Any entity that chooses the fair value model will be taking through its income statement gains and losses that are often tentative and uncertain and that would, under a historical cost accounting system, be considered unrealised.

B The cost model

The cost model requires that all investment property is measured after initial recognition under the benchmark treatment of IAS 16 as explained above in 5.2.1. This means that the asset must be recognised at cost. and depreciated systematically over its useful life.[254] The alternative treatment whereby the asset may be revalued is not available. Such assets are also subject to the impairment provisions of IAS 36. Impairment is separately discussed in Chapter 13.

5.3.4 *Transfer of assets into or from investment property*

The standard specifies the circumstances in which a property becomes, or ceases to be, an investment property. There must be a change in use, evidenced by:

(a) the commencement or end of owner-occupation;

(b) the commencement of development with a view to sale, at which point an investment property would be transferred to inventories. The standard allows a transfer to inventory only when there is a change of use evidenced by the start of a development with a view to subsequent sale;

(c) entering into an operating lease to another party; or

(d) the end of construction or development, when a property in the course of construction or development is transferred to investment property.[255] IAS 16 covers properties in the course of construction.

However, some changes in status do not result in transfers:

(a) If an entity decides to dispose of an investment property, rather than develop it, it may not be transferred to inventory but remains as an investment property until disposal.

(b) An existing investment property that is being redeveloped for continued future use as an investment property by the entity also must remain classified as an investment property. [256]

The transfers to and from the status of investment property are accounted for as follows.

- *Transfers to inventory or owner occupation*: the cost for subsequent accounting under IAS 16 or IAS 2 should be its fair value at the date the use changed;[257]
- *Transfers from owner occupation*: IAS 16 will be applied up to time the use changed. At that date any difference between the IAS 16 carrying amount and the fair value is to be treated in the same way as a revaluation under IAS 16 (as described above at 5.2.2);[258]

  Up until the time that an owner occupied property becomes an investment property carried at fair value, depreciation under IAS 16 continues and any impairment losses up to that date of change of use must be recognised in accordance with IAS 36.[259]
- *Transfers from inventory*: the difference between the inventory carrying amount and the fair value at the date of change of use is to be recognised in the profit and loss account for the period. The standard points out that the treatment of transfers is consistent with the treatment of sales of inventories.[260]
- *Transfers from self constructed property*: the difference between the previous carrying amount and the fair value at the date of change of use must be recognised in the profit and loss account for the period.[261]

When the business uses the cost model for investment property, transfers between investment property, inventory and owner occupation do not change the carrying amount of the property transferred.[262]

5.3.5 Disposal of investment property

IAS 40 requires that an asset should be removed from the balance sheet ('derecognised') under the following circumstances:

- When it is sold;
- When it becomes the subject of a finance lease (the owner becoming the lessor);
- When it becomes the subject of a sale and leaseback deal (the original owner becoming the lessee); or
- When it is withdrawn from use and no further economic benefits are expected to arise.[263]

IAS 18 – *Revenue* – applies on a sale. That standard recognises that while revenue would normally be recognised when legal title passes, in some jurisdictions the risks and rewards of ownership may pass to the buyer before legal title is passed. This would allow the UK practice of recognising revenue on exchange but only if the vendor does not have to perform any further substantial acts; an example in IAS 18 is the completion of construction.[264] Another common UK example of a 'substantial act' that might be required before recognition of a sale was permitted would be if shareholder approval were required.

IAS 17 – *Leases* – applies on disposal by a finance lease or by sale and leaseback.[265] Gains and losses on disposal by finance lease are the difference between the carrying amount and the net proceeds, which are computed as the present value of the minimum lease payments discounted using a commercial rate of interest.[266] IAS 17 only allows the immediate recognition of profits and losses on a sale and operating leaseback if the transaction is established at fair value; no gains would be recognised if the transaction resulted in a finance leaseback. Refer to Chapter 19 for a discussion of sale and leaseback under IAS 17.

If the sale proceeds are deferred, which we interpret as being beyond normal credit terms, the consideration recognised on the disposal will be the cash price equivalent. Any difference between the total payments received and the cash equivalent will be treated as interest receivable under IAS 18 and accounted for on a time-proportionate basis that also takes account of the effective yield on the outstanding amount.[267]

5.3.6 *Transitional provisions on adoption of IAS 40*

The standard came into force for accounting periods beginning on or after 1 January 2001.

The transitional arrangements for the fair value model differ from both the benchmark and allowed alternative treatment under IAS 8. The entity should adjust the opening balance of retained earnings for the period in which the standard is first adopted.[268] This will include the transfer of any amount held in revaluation surplus for investment property to retained profits (though these may not necessarily be *distributable* profits, as discussed at 5.4 below).[269]

If, however, the business has previously published fair value information about its investment property, and the fair value has been calculated in accordance with the standard's definition and guidance, it is encouraged but not required to adjust any comparative figures for earlier periods.[270] Presumably this is on the basis that the information is available, so it would enhance the financial statements to use it throughout. If the entity has not previously disclosed such information about the fair value of its investment property, comparative information should not be restated and that fact disclosed.[271]

If an enterprise chooses to adopt the cost model for its investment properties it may have to reclassify any existing revaluation surplus. IAS 8 would apply and the reclassification be effected by way of prior year adjustment.[272]

5.4 IAS 40 practical issues – the fair value model and realised profits

Although IAS 40 only came into force from 1 January 2001, it raises a number of practical issues, some of which have a more general application. It includes nearly twenty substantial paragraphs dealing with fair value, what it means, how to arrive at it, and similar guidance

Possibly the most remarkable thing about IAS 40 is that it exists at all. There is considerable disagreement over whether investment property is in fact any different in principle from any other building that is accounted for as property plant and equipment. Appendix B paragraphs B5 and 6 to the standard, discusses this point of view, but takes the view that the fair value information is paramount. Of course this information could be given, even if the cost model is chosen, and even if IAS 16 were to be adopted for investment property. It is possible that the IASC's wish to try out fair value accounting through the income statement influenced the decision.

However, as well as the practical difficulties in obtaining investment properties' fair values, there is a legal difficulty associated with using any fair value model, as currently in the EU only realised profits may be included in the income statement. In a press release issued on 31 May 2001 in which the adoption of the fair value accounting Directive was welcomed, the European Commission pointed out that historic cost has not yet been replaced as the basis of accounting valuation. It went on to say 'fair value accounting will therefore not be permitted for balance sheet items such as fixed assets (for example land and buildings or plant and equipment)'.

Moreover, it will not be permitted to use a true and fair override to apply the fair value model in IAS 40. The Commission considers that an override cannot be used except by individual enterprises to meet their individual circumstances, and that it should not be applied to an entire class or category by an accounting standard. However, it is noteworthy that this consideration has not stopped the UK applying the true and fair override to negate the depreciation requirement in both FRS 10 (for non-depreciation of goodwill with an indefinite life, see Chapter 11) and SSAP 19 (for non-depreciation of investment properties, see 2.4 above).

Until the legislative background is amended, it is hard to see how the fair value model in IAS 40 can be applied in the EU. However, as the IASB has a project to develop a single statement of financial performance, it must be assumed that some groundwork is already being done by the standard setters to lobby for an amendment to the EU realised profit requirement.

6 IAS DISCLOSURE REQUIREMENTS

6.1 Introduction

This section sets out the principal disclosures required in financial statements complied under IAS for property plant and equipment, and investment property, as contained within IAS 16 and IAS 40. The disclosures relevant to this topic required by each standard are separately shown. However any disclosures required by other authorities such as national statutes are not included.

6.2 IAS 16 disclosures

IAS 16 contains a clear and well laid out disclosure section which is easy to use and understand. The main requirements are set out below, but note that the requirements of IAS 36 are discussed in Chapter 13.

6.2.1 *General disclosures*

For each class of property plant and equipment the following should be disclosed in the financial statements:

(a) the measurement bases used for determining the gross carrying amount (for example, cost, revaluation to market prices). When more than one basis has been used, the gross carrying amount for that basis in each category should be disclosed (however the standard requires that if revaluation is adopted the entire class of assets must be revalued);

(b) the depreciation methods used;

(c) the useful lives or the depreciation rates used;

(d) the gross carrying amount and the accumulated depreciation (aggregated with accumulated impairment losses) at the beginning and end of the period;

(e) a reconciliation of the carrying amount at the beginning and end of the period showing:

  (i) additions;

  (ii) disposals;

  (iii) acquisitions through business combinations;

  (iv) increases or decreases during the period resulting from revaluations and from impairment losses recognised or reversed directly in equity under IAS 36, Impairment of Assets (if any);

  (v) impairment losses recognised in the income statement during the period under IAS 36 (if any);

  (vi) impairment losses reversed in the income statement during the period under IAS 36 (if any);

  (vii) depreciation for the period;

  (viii) the net exchange differences arising on the translation of the financial statements of a foreign entity; and

  (ix) other movements.

Comparative information is not required for the reconciliation in (e) above.[273]

IAS 16 also requires the disclosure of the following information which is useful to gain a fuller understanding of the entire position of the business' holdings of and commitments to purchase, property plant and equipment.

(a) the existence and amounts of restrictions on title, and property, plant and equipment pledged as security for liabilities;

(b) the accounting policy for the estimated costs of restoring the site of items of property, plant or equipment;

(c) the amount of expenditures on account of property, plant and equipment in the course of construction; and

(d) the amount of commitments for the acquisition of property, plant and equipment.[274]

In addition there is a reminder in the standard that, in accordance with IAS 8, any changes in accounting estimate (e.g. depreciation methods, useful lives, residual values) that have a material effect on the current or future periods must be disclosed.[275]

6.2.2 *Extra disclosures for revalued assets*

The IASC has gone to some lengths in IAS 16 to ensure that if the allowed alternative treatment, revaluation, is adopted, users of the financial statements should have enough information to clearly see its effects. The extra requirements if the revaluation basis is adopted are:

(a) the basis used to revalue the assets;

(b) the effective date of the revaluation;

(c) whether an independent valuer was involved;

(d) the nature of any indices used to determine replacement cost;

(e) the carrying amount of each class of property, plant and equipment that would have been included in the financial statements had the assets been carried under the benchmark treatment (cost less depreciation); and

(f) the revaluation surplus, indicating the movement for the period and any restrictions on the distribution of the balance to shareholders.[276]

In particular the requirement under (e) is quite onerous for companies, as it entails their keeping asset register information in some detail in order to meet it.

The standard encourages but does not require companies to disclose other additional information such as the carrying amount of any idle assets, the gross amount of any fully depreciated assets in use, and any held for disposal. For any property plant and equipment held at cost less depreciation, the disclosure of its fair value is also encouraged if it is materially different from the carrying amount.[277]

The extract below from Bayer provides a comprehensive illustration of the disclosure requirements of IAS concerning property plant and equipment.

Extract 12.31: Bayer AG (2000)

Notes [extract]

18 Property, plant and equipment

Property, plant and equipment is carried at the cost of acquisition or construction. Assets subject to depletion are depreciated over their estimated useful lives. Write-downs are made for any declines in value that are expected to be permanent, aside from those reflected in depreciation. Assets are written back if the reasons for previous years' write-downs no longer apply.

The cost of construction of self-constructed property, plant and equipment comprises the direct cost of materials, direct manufacturing expenses, appropriate allocations of material and manufacturing overheads, and an appropriate share of the depreciation and write-downs of assets used in construction. It includes the shares of expenses for company pension plans and discretionary employee benefits that are attributable to construction.

If the construction phase of property, plant or equipment extends over a long period, the interest incurred on borrowed capital up to the date of completion is capitalized as part of the cost of acquisition or construction.

Expenses for the repair of property, plant and equipment are normally charged against income, but they are capitalized if they result in an enlargement or substantial improvement of the respective assets.

Property, plant and equipment is depreciated by the straight-line method, except where the declining-balance method is more appropriate in light of the actual utilization period

The following depreciation periods, based on the estimated useful lives of the respective assets, are applied throughout the Group:

Buildings	20 to 50 years
Outdoor infrastructure	10 to 20 years
Plant installations	6 to 20 years
Machinery and apparatus	6 to 12 years
Laboratory and research facilities	3 to 5 years
Storage tanks and pipelines	10 to 20 years
Vehicles	4 to 8 years
Computer equipment	3 to 5 years
Furniture and fixtures	4 to 10 years

Changes in property, plant and equipment in 2000 were as follows:

€ million	Land and buildings	Machinery and technical equipment	Furniture, fixtures and other equipment	Construction in progress and advance payments to vendors and contractors	Total
Gross carrying amounts, Dec. 31, 1999	7,529	17,860	2,360	1,458	29,207
Exchange differences	129	399	28	49	605
Changes in companies consolidated	(32)	98	1	–	67
Acquisitions	57	207	10	317	591
Capital expenditures	115	522	295	1,361	2,293
Retirements	(142)	(589)	(276)	(17)	(1,024)
Transfers	322	1,489	95	(1,906)	–
Gross carrying amounts, Dec. 31, 2000	**7,978**	**19,986**	**2,513**	**1,262**	**31,739**

Accumulated depreciation and write-downs, Dec. 31, 1999	3,867	11,742	1,605	7	17,221
Exchange differences	42	122	17	–	181
Changes in companies consolidated	(18)	77	1	–	60
Depreciation and write-downs in 2000	238	1,174	283	–	1,695
** of which write-downs*	*[5]*	*[11]*	*[–]*	*[–]*	*[16]*
Write-backs	–	(2)	–	–	(2)
Retirements	(37)	(530)	(194)	–	(761)
Transfers	–	–	–	–	–
Accumulated depreciation and write-downs, Dec 31, 2000	**4,092**	**12,583**	**1,712**	**7**	**18,394**
Net carrying amounts, Dec. 31, 2000	**3,886**	**7,403**	**801**	**1,255**	**13,345**
Net carrying amounts, Dec. 31, 1999	3,622	6,118	755	1,451	11,986

Capitalized property, plant and equipment includes assets with a total net value of €199 million (1999: €188 million) held under finance leases. The gross carrying amounts of these assets total €277 million (1999: €245 million). These assets are mainly furniture and fixtures where the present value of the minimum lease payments cover substantially all of the cost of acquisition, or buildings where title passes to the lessee on expiration of the lease.

Also included are products leased to other parties, except where the lessee is to be regarded as the economic owner and the relevant agreements therefore constitute finance leases as defined in IAS 17 (Leases); in this case a receivable is recognized in the balance sheet in the amount of the discounted future lease payments.

6.3 The disclosure requirements of IAS 40

6.3.1 Introduction

As discussed earlier in the chapter, IAS 40 heralds a major practical step towards what we consider to be the long term aim of the IASB, namely full fair value based financial statements. If revaluation of investment property under IAS 40 is adopted, all revaluation changes go through the income statement (i.e. the profit and loss account). Thus businesses with investment property reporting under IAS will show profits that include realised and unrealised profits, trading transactions and revaluations.

For businesses that adopt the revaluation option in IAS 40, it will be a major change in the way such items are reported. It will focus attention on the judgmental and subjective aspects of property revaluations, because they will be reported in the income statement rather than directly to equity. If a counter-intuitive failure were to occur (for instance a company that had reported large profits soon afterwards ran out of cash) this type of income statement easily could be discredited. Possibly as a consequence of these considerations, the disclosures under IAS 40 require significant amounts of information to be disclosed about the judgements involved and the cash-related performance of the investment property, as set out below.

6.3.2 *Disclosures under both fair value and cost models*

Whatever model is chosen, fair value or cost, IAS 40 requires all companies to disclose the fair value of their investment property. Therefore the following disclosures are required in both instances.

(a) when classification is difficult, the criteria developed by the enterprise to distinguish investment property from owner-occupied property and from property held for sale in the ordinary course of business;

(b) the methods and significant assumptions applied in determining the fair value of investment property, including a statement whether the determination of fair value was supported by market evidence or was more heavily based on other factors (which the enterprise should disclose) because of the nature of the property and lack of comparable market data;

(c) the extent to which the fair value of investment property (as measured or disclosed in the financial statements) is based on a valuation by an independent valuer who holds a recognised and relevant professional qualification and who has recent experience in the location and category of the investment property being valued. If there has been no such valuation, that fact should be disclosed;

(d) the amounts included in the income statement for:

   (i) rental income from investment property;

   (ii) direct operating expenses (including repairs and maintenance) arising from investment property that generated rental income during the period; and

   (iii) direct operating expenses (including repairs and maintenance) arising from investment property that did not generate rental income during the period;

(e) the existence and amounts of restrictions on the realisability of investment property or the remittance of income and proceeds of disposal; and

(f) material contractual obligations to purchase, construct or develop investment property or for repairs, maintenance or enhancements.[278]

6.3.3 *Additional disclosures for the fair value model*

A reconciliation of the carrying amounts of investment property at the start and finish of the period must be given showing the following:

(a) additions, disclosing separately those additions resulting from acquisitions and those resulting from capitalised subsequent expenditure;

(b) additions resulting from acquisitions through business combinations;

(c) disposals;

(d) net gains or losses from fair value adjustments;

(e) the net exchange differences arising on the translation of the financial statements of a foreign entity;

(f) transfers to and from inventories and owner-occupied property; and
(g) other movements.

Comparative information is not required.[279]

A Extra disclosures where fair value cannot be reliably determined

The standard envisages an exception to the rule that all property must be valued either under one model or the other, where fair value cannot be reliably measured. In this case the asset is accounted for under the provisions of the benchmark treatment of IAS 16 and the reconciliations noted in this section should separately disclose the amounts for such investment property. In addition to this the following should be disclosed:

(a) a description of the investment property;
(b) an explanation of why fair value cannot be reliably measured;
(c) if possible, the range of estimates within which fair value is highly likely to lie; and
(d) on disposal of investment property not carried at fair value:
    (i) the fact that the enterprise has disposed of investment property not carried at fair value;
    (ii) the carrying amount of that investment property at the time of sale; and
    (iii) the amount of gain or loss recognised.[280]

6.3.4 *Additional disclosures for the cost model*

In the event that investment property is carried at cost less depreciation, the following disclosures are required by IAS 40.

(a) the depreciation methods used;
(b) the useful lives or the depreciation rates used;
(c) the gross carrying amount and the accumulated depreciation (aggregated with accumulated impairment losses) at the beginning and end of the period;
(d) a reconciliation of the carrying amount of investment property at the beginning and end of the period showing the following (comparative information is not required):
    (i) additions, disclosing separately those additions resulting from acquisitions and those resulting from capitalised subsequent expenditure;
    (ii) additions resulting from acquisitions through business combinations;
    (iii) disposals;
    (iv) depreciation;
    (v) the amount of impairment losses recognised, and the amount of impairment losses reversed, during the period under IAS 36, Impairment of Assets;
    (vi) the net exchange differences arising on the translation of the financial statements of a foreign entity;
    (vii) transfers to and from inventories and owner-occupied property; and
    (viii) other movements; and

(e) the fair value of investment property. In the exceptional cases when an enterprise cannot determine the fair value of the investment property reliably, the enterprise should disclose:
   (i) a description of the investment property;
   (ii) an explanation of why fair value cannot be determined reliably; and
   (iii) if possible, the range of estimates within which fair value is highly likely to lie.[281]

7 CONCLUSION

The current state of accounting for tangible fixed assets combines conventional treatments – as exemplified by IAS 16 and FRS 15 – with a quite radical new approach to the income statement being given a field test by the fair value model of IAS 40. In principle, accounting for fixed assets is straightforward, the essential purpose is to allocate expenditure which provides enduring benefits against the revenues of the periods use them. This objective is increasingly difficult to achieve for a number of reasons.

First the meaning of 'tangible fixed asset' is deeply rooted in the manufacturing tradition and the conventional model still works well for machinery assets that wear out reasonably predictably. However the position is complicated by two factors: the first is the appearance of new types of asset, such as customer lists, brands, websites, and their generally ephemeral nature. The second has been a complicating factor for decades – the way to account for revaluations of assets.

As discussed above and in Chapter 11, it may be that the distinction between tangible and intangible assets is not sustainable indefinitely, and the main focus should be on whether future benefits exist. This would reduce the current anomalous position whereby a self-constructed tangible asset may be capitalised, while an intangible one may not. Revaluations pose a number of accounting questions; for example, how to treat the revaluation surplus, whether depreciation is necessary if assets are carried at a valuation and more fundamentally, what a balance sheet is meant to be.

It is almost certain that fair value based accounting, with all valuation changes going through a single income statement, is the ultimate aim of the IASB and consequently the ASB. This would reduce a number of the inconsistencies that currently exist in the group of standards issued by each of them. For example, in addition to the one mentioned above, FRS 10 accepts that maintenance of value can justify non-amortisation of intangibles, which seems to imply acceptance of the principle that maintenance can negate the need to depreciate. However, the ASB in FRS 15 has specifically rejected this approach for tangible fixed assets.

If IAS 40 is the harbinger of a wholesale shift to fair values in the balance sheet, and of an undifferentiated income statement in which realised profits and unrealised gains are not distinguished, this may reduce the logical inconsistencies. It will not, however, reduce the uncertainties inherent in predicting the future, which are an inescapable part of accruals accounting for fixed assets, tangible or intangible. What it will do is exacerbate and extend the valuation difficulties present in the current situation that are extensively discussed in this chapter. This and other related problems, most importantly the education of users into what the cash implications of a fair value based 'profit' actually are, will have to be solved.

References

1 CA 85, s 262(1).
2 *Ibid.*, Sch. 4, para. 8, balance sheet formats.
3 *Ibid.*, Sch. 4, para. 17.
4 *Ibid.*, Sch. 4, para. 31(2).
5 *Ibid.*, 262(1).
6 *Ibid.*, Sch. 4, para. 26(1).
7 *Ibid.*, Sch. 4, paras. 26(2) and 26(3).
8 *Ibid.*, Sch. 4, para. 18.
9 *Ibid.*, Sch. 4, para. 18.
10 *Ibid.*, para. 32.
11 *Ibid.*, Sch. 4, para. 19(2).
12 FRS 15, paras. 3-4.
13 FRS 15, para. 2.
14 *Ibid.*, para. 6.
15 *Ibid.*, para. 7.
16 *Ibid.*, paras. 42-43.
17 *Ibid.*, para. 9.
18 *Ibid.*, para. 10.
19 *Ibid.*, para. 9.
20 *Ibid.*, para. 11.
21 *Ibid.*, para. 17.
22 *Ibid.*, paras. 12-13.
23 *Ibid.*, para. 14.
24 *Ibid.*, paras. 15-16.
25 UITF Abstract 24, *Accounting for start-up costs*, UITF, June 2000, para. 4.
26 *Ibid.*, para. 9.
27 Financial Reporting Review Panel, FRRP PN 60, 25 February 2000
28 FRS 15, paras. 34-35.
29 *Ibid.*, para. 36.
30 *Ibid.*, para. 37.
31 FRS 12, Appendix III. Examples 11A and 11B.
32 FRS 15, paras. 38-39.
33 FRS 15, para. 40.
34 *Ibid.*, para. 2.
35 *Ibid.*, para. 77.
36 *Ibid.*, para. 78.
37 *Ibid.*, para. 78.
38 *Ibid.*, para. 80.
39 *Ibid.*, para. 93.
40 *Ibid.*
41 *Ibid.*, para. 2.
42 *Ibid.*, paras. 95-96.
43 *Ibid.*, para. 91.
44 *Ibid.*, paras. 86-88
45 *Ibid.*, paras. 93-96
46 *Ibid.*, paras. 106 and 108
47 UITF Abstract 23, *Application of the transitional rules in FRS 15*, UITF, May 2000, para. 5.
48 *Ibid.*, para. 84.
49 *Ibid.*, paras. 38-39.
50 *Ibid.*, para. 84.
51 Financial Reporting Review Panel, FRRP PN 70, 13 September 2001.
52 Wyevale Garden Centres PLC, interim accounts for the 26 weeks ended 1 July 2000, Chairman's Statement
53 *Ibid.*, para. 81.
54 Wyevale Garden Centres PLC, interim accounts for the 26 weeks ended 1 July 2000, Chairman's Statement.
55 *Ibid.*, para. 97.
56 *Ibid.*, para. 98.
57 *Ibid.*, para. 77.
58 *Ibid.*, paras. 81, 82.
59 See the SORP on *Accounting for oil and gas exploration and development activities*, Oil Industry Accounting Committee, December 1987, paras. 62–65 and 84–87.
60 CA 85, Sch. 4, para. 25.
61 SSAP 19, para. 7.
62 *Statement by the Accounting Standards Committee on the publication of ED 26 'Accounting for investment properties'*, paras. 7 and 8.
63 SSAP 19, para. 8.
64 *Ibid.*, paras. 11-14.
65 *Ibid.*, . para. 13.
66 *Ibid.*, para. 6.
67 See for example Land Securities PLC, Report and Financial Statements 2001, p. 47,
68 FRS 15, para. 84
69 CA 85, Sch. 4, para. 31(2).
70 *Ibid.*, Sch. 4, para. 31(1).
71 *Ibid.*, Sch. 4, para. 31(3).
72 In fact, the same diagram is often used to describe the alternative term 'value to the business' – see, for example, *Ibid.*, Appendix IV para. 19.

73 *Report of the President's Working Party on Commercial Property Valuations*, Foreword.
74 FRS 15, para. 42.
75 *Ibid.*, para. 2.
76 *Ibid.*, para. 62.
77 *Ibid.*, para. 43.
78 *Ibid.*, para. 44.
79 *Ibid.*, para. 45.
80 *Ibid.*, para. 52.
81 *Ibid.*, para. 48.
82 *Ibid.*, para. 47.
83 *Ibid.*, para. 49.
84 *Ibid.*, para. 46.
85 *Ibid.*, para. 50.
86 *Ibid.*, para. 51.
87 *Ibid.*, paras. 104 and 105.
88 *Ibid.*, para. 53.
89 *Ibid.*, para. 55.
90 RICS Appraisal and Valuations Manual Practice Statement 4, para. 4.2.
91 *Ibid.*, para. 4.3.1.
92 *Ibid.*, para. 4.3.10.
93 FRS 15, para. 53(a).
94 RICS Appraisal and Valuations Manual Practice Statement 4, para. 4.3.2.
95 FRS 15 para. 56.
96 RICS Guidance Note 7, para. 7.2.8.
97 FRS 15 para. 85.
98 RICS, Definitions.
99 *Ibid.*, Practice Statement 4, para. 4.8.1.
100 FRS 15, para. 58.
101 RICS, Practice Statement 4, para. 4.8.5.
102 FRS 15, para. 57.
103 *Ibid.*, para. 60 and RICS Practice Statement 4, para. 4.17.
104 RICS Practice Statement 4, para. 4.17.
105 CA 85, Sch. 4, para. 34(1).
106 FRS 3, para. 13, and FRS 15, para. 63.
107 CA 85, Sch. 4, paras. 19 and 34.
108 *Ibid.*, Sch. 4, para. 34(3). Until amended by the CA 89, this read '... for the purpose of the accounting policies adopted by the company', which was capable of wider interpretation.
109 *Ibid.*, para. 34(3)(a).
110 *Ibid.*, para. 34(1).
111 FRS 15, para.65.
112 *Ibid.*, para. 68.
113 *Ibid.*, para. 65 and 69.
114 *Ibid.*, para. 65 and 70.
115 CA 85, Sch. 4, para. 32.
116 FRS 15., para. 63.
117 *Ibid.*, para. 64.
118 *Ibid.*
119 *Ibid.*, para. 78.
120 *Ibid.*, para. 79.
121 FRS 3, para. 56.
122 FRS 11, para. 67.
123 UITF 5, *Transfers from Current Assets to Fixed Assets*, UITF, July 1992, para. 2.
124 *Ibid.*, para. 5.
125 CA 85, Sch. 4, para. 34(3).
126 *Ibid.*, s263(3).
127 *Ibid.*, s275(1).
128 *Ibid.*, s275(2).
129 *Ibid.*, s275(5).
130 *Ibid.*, s275(6).
131 'Relevant accounts' are defined in *Ibid.*, ss. 270-273.
132 Draft Technical Release, *The determination of realised profits and distributable profits in the context of the companies act 1985*, ICAEW and ICAS, 10 August 2000, para. 18.
133 CA 85, Sch. 4, para. 8, balance sheet formats.
134 *Ibid.*, Sch. 4, para. 8, profit and loss account formats.
135 *Ibid.*, Sch. 4, note (17) on the profit and loss account formats.
136 *Ibid.*, Sch. 4, paras. 19(1) and 19(2).
137 CA 85, Sch. 4, paras. 42(1)(a) and 42(2).
138 *Ibid.*, para. 42(1)(b).
139 *Ibid.*, para. 42(3).
140 *Ibid.*, paras. 33(1) and (2).
141 *Ibid.*, Sch. 4, para. 34(2).
142 *Ibid.*, Sch. 4, para. 34(4).
143 *Ibid.*, Sch. 4, para. 33(3).
144 *Ibid.*, Sch. 4, para. 33(4).
145 *Ibid.*, Sch. 4, para. 43(a).
146 *Ibid.*, Sch. 4, para. 33(2).
147 *Ibid.*, Sch. 4, para. 43(b).
148 *Ibid.*, s 277(6).
149 Interpretation Act 1978, Sch. 1.
150 CA 85, Sch. 7, para. 1(2).
151 SSAP 19, para. 12.
152 SSAP 19, para. 15.
153 *Ibid.,* para. 13.
154 CA 85, Sch. 4, para. 34(2).
155 FRS 15, para. 100.
156 *Ibid.,* para. 100.
157 *Ibid.*, para. 102.
158 *Ibid.*, para. 74.
159 *Ibid.*
160 *Ibid.*, para. 53(a).
161 *Ibid.*, para. 61.
162 *Ibid.*, Definitions.
163 UITF Abstract 29, *Website development costs*, UITF, February 2001, para. 3.
164 *Ibid.*, para. 6.
165 *Ibid.*, para. 6.
166 *Ibid.*, para. 4.
167 Ibid., para 14.
168 FRS 15, para. 83.
169 *Ibid.*, para. 84.
170 RICS Guidance Note 5, para. 5.3.4.
171 *Ibid.*, para. 5.3.5.
172 FRS 15, para. 85.

173 IAS 1, *Presentation of financial statements*, IASC, August 1997, paras. 58.
174 *Ibid.*, paras. 53-54.
175 *Ibid.*, para. 53.
176 IAS 16, *Property plant and equipment*, IASC, Revised 1998, para. 6.
177 *Ibid.*, para. 7.
178 *Ibid.*, para. 11.
179 *Ibid.*, para. 12.
180 *Ibid.*, para. 13.
181 *Ibid.*, para. 14.
182 *Ibid.*, para. 6.
183 *Ibid.*, para. 17.
184 *Ibid.*, para. 16.
185 *Ibid.*, para. 18.
186 *Ibid.*, para. 23.
187 *Ibid.*, para. 26.
188 *Ibid.*, para. 27.
189 SIC-23, *Property plant and equipment – major inspection and overhaul costs*, SIC, October 1999.
190 SIC-14, *Property plant and equipment – compensation for the impairment or loss of items*, SIC, June 1998.
191 IAS 16, para. 28.
192 *Ibid.*, para. 29.
193 *Ibid.*, para. 6.
194 *Ibid.*, para. 31.
195 *Ibid.*, para. 32.
196 *Ibid.*, para. 35.
197 *Ibid.*, para. 36.
198 *Ibid.*, paras. 37-38.
199 *Ibid.*, para. 39.
200 IAS 8, para. 44.
201 IAS 16, para. 6.
202 *Ibid.*, para. 41.
203 *Ibid.*, para. 48.
204 *Ibid.*, para. 42.
205 *Ibid.*, para. 43.
206 *Ibid.*, para. 44.
207 *Ibid.*, para. 45.
208 *Ibid.*, para. 51.
209 *Ibid.*, para. 47.
210 *Ibid.*, paras. 49 and 52.
211 *Ibid.*, para. 46.
212 *Ibid.*, paras. 55-56.
213 *Ibid.*, para. 59.
214 *Ibid.*, paras. 21-22.
215 IAS 40, *Investment property*, IASC, March 2000, Appendix B para. B4.
216 *Ibid.*, Appendix B, para. B31.
217 *Ibid.*, para. 4.
218 *Ibid.*, para. 6(b).
219 *Ibid.*, para. 6.
220 *Ibid.*, para. 7.
221 *Ibid.*, para. 14.
222 *Ibid.*, para. 7.
223 *Ibid.*, para. 8.
224 *Ibid.*, paras. 9-11.
225 *Ibid.*, para. 12.
226 IAS 17, *Leases* para. 11.
227 IAS 40, Appendix B, paras. B10 to B15.
228 *Ibid.*, para. 15.
229 *Ibid.*, para. 16.
230 *Ibid.*, para. 17.
231 *Ibid.*, para. 18.
232 *Ibid.*, para. 19.
233 *Ibid.*, paras. 20-21.
234 *Ibid.*, para. 44.
235 *Ibid.*, paras. 22-23.
236 *Ibid.*, para. 24.
237 *Ibid.*, para. 25.
238 *Ibid.*, paras. 27-28 and 31.
239 *Ibid.*, para. 4.
240 *Ibid.*, para. 43.
241 *Ibid.*, para. 32.
242 *Ibid.*, para. 30.
243 *Ibid.*, paras. 32-35.
244 *Ibid.*, paras. 36-38.
245 *Ibid.*, para. 40.
246 *Ibid.*
247 *Ibid.*, para. 45.
248 *Ibid.*, para. 41.
249 *Ibid.*, para. 44.
250 *Ibid.*, para. 44.
251 *Ibid.*, para. 47.
252 *Ibid.*, para. 48.
253 *Ibid.*, para. 49.
254 *Ibid.*, para. 50.
255 *Ibid.*, para. 51.
256 *Ibid.*, para. 52.
257 *Ibid.*, para. 54.
258 *Ibid.*, para. 55.
259 *Ibid.*, para. 56.
260 *Ibid.*, paras. 57-58.
261 *Ibid.*, para. 59.
262 *Ibid.*, para. 53.
263 *Ibid.*, paras. 60-61.
264 IAS 18, *Revenue*, Appendix para. 9.
265 IAS 40, para. 6.
266 IAS 17, *Leases*, para 34.
267 IAS 16, para. 63, IAS 18 para. 30.
268 IAS 40, para 70.
269 *Ibid.*, para 72.
270 *Ibid.*, para 70.
271 *Ibid.*, para. 70.
272 *Ibid.*, para. 73.
273 IAS 16, para 60.
274 *Ibid.*, para. 61.
275 *Ibid.*, para. 63.
276 *Ibid.*, para. 64.
277 *Ibid.*, para. 66.
278 IAS 40, para. 66.
279 *Ibid.*, para. 67.
280 *Ibid.*, para. 68.
281 *Ibid.*, para. 69.

Chapter 13 Impairment of fixed assets and goodwill

1 INTRODUCTION

1.1 Background

In principle an asset is impaired when the business will not be able to recover its balance sheet carrying value, either through using it or selling it. Both the IASC and the ASB introduced impairment standards in the late 1990s. FRS 11 – *Impairment of fixed assets and goodwill* – took effect for periods *ending* on or after 23 December 1998, while the IAS 36 – *Impairment of assets* – covers periods *beginning* on or after 1 July 1999. The ASB at the time their standard was introduced made the point that writing down impaired assets was not, in principle, a new requirement. In the UK there is a legal requirement to write down fixed assets with carrying values, after depreciation, that cannot be justified. The Companies Act states that provisions for diminution in value are to be made for any fixed asset if the reduction in value is expected to be permanent.[1]

However, prior to FRS 11 there was little detailed guidance in the UK to support this broad principle; an absence that has been remedied by FRS 11's extensive and complex rules on how impairment is to be determined. Under the IASC's rules the position prior to IAS 36 was either explicit or implicit in a number of standards. The position now is that the thrust of the impairment provisions of both standard setters is similar, unsurprisingly as they were developed in parallel, though their detailed provisions are not the same.

A broad summary of both standards is that, if circumstances arise which indicate assets might be impaired, a review should be undertaken of their cash generating abilities either through use or sale. This review will produce an amount which should be compared with the assets' carrying value, and if the carrying value is higher, the difference must be written off as an impairment adjustment in the income statement. The provisions within each standard setting out exactly how this is to be done, and how the figures involved are to be calculated, are detailed and quite complex. However, in view of the underlying similarity of principle between the IASC and ASB standards, the following section explains the common theory underlying the type of impairment review adopted by the two.

1.2 The theory behind the impairment review

Because this section seeks to explain the underlying theory, its description of some terms used may not be identical to those used in a particular standard, though the underlying principle should not be different.

The purpose of the review is to ensure that intangible and tangible fixed assets, and goodwill are not carried at a figure greater than their *recoverable amount*. This recoverable amount is compared with the carrying value of the asset to detect if the asset is impaired. The definition of recoverable amount, therefore, is key. It is defined as the higher of *net realisable value* (NRV) and *value in use* (VIU), the underlying concept is that an asset should not be carried at more than the amount it will raise, either from selling it now or from using it in future.

Net realisable value essentially means what the asset could be sold for, after selling costs. *Value in use* is defined in terms of discounted future cash flows, as the present value of the cash flows expected from the future use and sale of the asset. As the recoverable amount is to be expressed as a present value, not in actual terms, discounting is a central technical feature of the impairment test.

Diagrammatically, this comparison between carrying value and recoverable amount, and the definition of recoverable amount, can be portrayed as follows:

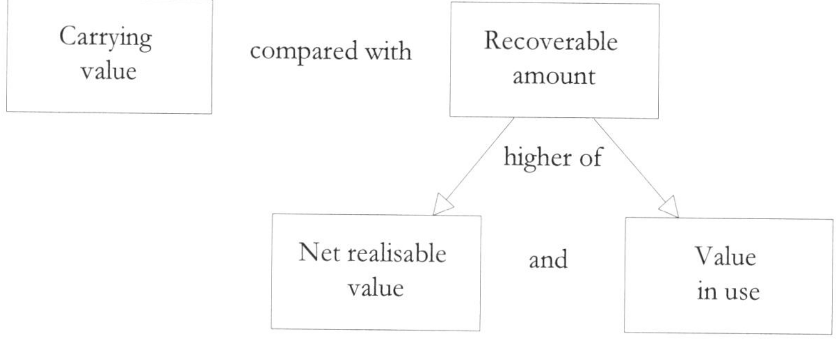

It may not always be necessary to identify both VIU and NRV. If either VIU or NRV is higher than the carrying amount then there is no impairment and no write-down is necessary. Thus, if NRV is greater than the carrying amount then no further consideration need be given to VIU, or to the need for an impairment write down. The more complex issues arise when the NRV is not greater than the carrying value, and so a VIU calculation is necessary. Typically for tangible assets used in manufacturing, this will be the case.

Although an impairment review might theoretically be conducted by looking only at individual fixed assets, this is likely to be a rare occurrence for a number of reasons. It may not be possible to obtain reliable NRV estimates for all fixed assets and some, such as goodwill or certain intangible assets, may not have an NRV at all. Even if NRVs can be obtained for individual fixed assets, estimates of VIUs usually cannot be. This is because the cash flows necessary for the VIU calculation are not usually generated by single assets, but by groups of assets being used together.

Often, therefore, the impairment review cannot be done at the level of the individual asset and it must be done at what might be termed an operating unit level. FRS 11 uses the term *income-generating unit* (IGU), while IAS 36 uses the term *cash generating unit.* Both basically mean a part of the business that generates income and which is largely independent other parts of the business. This focus on the IGU is fundamental, as it has the effect of making the review a business value test, in as much as the assets of a business unit cannot usually be carried at an amount greater than the value of that business unit.

As it would be unduly onerous for all fixed assets and goodwill to be reviewed for impairment every year, FRS 11 and IAS 38 in the main require fixed assets and goodwill to be reviewed only if there is some indication that impairment may have occurred. If events or changes in circumstances indicate that the carrying amount of the fixed asset may not be recoverable, a review for impairment should be carried out. These events or changes in circumstances may affect either the fixed assets themselves or the economic environment in which they are operated. Both standards give examples of circumstances that would be indicators of impairment, and these are discussed at 2.2.2 for FRS 11, and 4.2.2 for IAS 36, below.

The discussion of each individual standard goes further into the precise nature of the terms used by each, and their individual provisions which are frequently detailed and complex.

2 UK ACCOUNTING REQUIREMENTS

2.1 Companies Act 1985 requirements

The Act requires provisions for diminution in value to be made in respect of any fixed asset if the reduction in value is expected to be permanent.[2]

The provisions are to be made through the profit and loss account.[3] Provisions no longer required are to be written back, again through the profit and loss account.[4] In either case, amounts not shown in the profit and loss account must be disclosed in the notes to the accounts.[5] It should also be noted that, except in the circumstances of a revaluation of all assets, as discussed in Chapter 12, the Act requires any provision to be treated as a realised loss for distribution purposes whether it is considered to be permanent or temporary.[6]

2.2 FRS 11 requirements

2.2.1 *Objectives, scope and definitions*

On 2 July 1998 the ASB published FRS 11, to become mandatory in respect of financial statements relating to accounting periods ending on or after 23 December 1998.[7]

The objectives of the standard are to ensure that:

(a) fixed assets and goodwill are recorded in the financial statements at no more than their recoverable amount;

(b) any resulting impairment loss is measured and recognised on a consistent basis; and

(c) sufficient information is disclosed in the financial statements to enable users to understand the impact of the impairment on the financial position and performance of the reporting entity.[8]

A Scope

FRS 11 is a general impairment standard, designed to be applied to all fixed assets as well as to purchased goodwill recognised in the balance sheet. However, there are some exceptions to this general rule[9] and in particular the standard does not apply to the following:

(a) fixed assets within the scope of FRS 13, the standard on financial instrument disclosures.[10]

The definition of financial instruments in FRS 13 is very broad and encompasses things such as investments and loans. There are, however, some financial assets that are excluded from its scope and therefore do fall within the scope of FRS 11. This includes interests in subsidiaries, associates, partnerships and joint ventures (unless those interests are held exclusively for resale). The effect of this standard on parent company accounts is therefore very significant. If goodwill on consolidation has been subject to an impairment review which revealed an impairment loss, the investment in the subsidiary, as recorded in the parent's accounts, should also be reviewed for impairment. This matter must be considered even if there has been no impairment of group assets. It can be a serious issue, because any write-down of an investment in the parent will directly affect its retained profits, and hence the group's ability to pay dividends.

(b) investment properties

The exemption for investment properties is unlikely to have much effect as investment properties are carried at market value under SSAP 19 anyway.

(c) an entity's own shares held by an ESOP and shown as a fixed asset in the entity's balance sheet under UITF Abstract 13 – *Accounting for ESOP Trusts.*

(d) costs capitalised pending determination (i.e. while a field is still being appraised) under the Oil Industry Accounting Committee SORP, *Accounting for oil and gas exploration and development activities.*

This exemption is for oil companies in respect of exploration and development costs carried forward before the viability of the field has been determined. This is clearly a necessary exemption as the standard could otherwise require forecasts of the cash flows to be generated from the field (among other things) and by definition these will not be available. However, the standard does apply to such costs after the viability of the field has been established.

The standard also makes it clear that it does not apply to goodwill already written off to reserves (under SSAP 22) and not subsequently resurrected on the implementation of FRS 10.[11] As a consequence, such goodwill still has to be passed through the profit and loss account when the related business is sold or terminated.

B Definitions

FRS 11 contains a comprehensive definitions section. The key definitions coined specifically in the standard, and necessary to understand its detailed provisions are:

- Income-generating unit (IGU):

  A group of assets, liabilities and associated goodwill that generates income that is largely independent of the reporting entity's other income streams. The assets and liabilities include those directly involved in generating the income and an appropriate portion of those used to generate more than one income stream.

- Net realisable value (NRV):

  The amount at which an asset could be disposed of, less any direct selling costs.

- Readily ascertainable market value:

  In relation to an intangible asset, the value that is established by reference to a market where:

  (a) the asset belongs to a homogeneous population of assets that are equivalent in all material respects; and

  (b) an active market, evidenced by frequent transactions, exists for that population of assets.

- Recoverable amount:

  The higher of net realisable value and value in use.

- Value in use (VIU):

  The present value of the future cash flows obtainable as a result of an asset's continued use, including those resulting from its ultimate disposal.[12]

2.2.2 *Indications of impairment*

An impairment review is only required when there are indications that assets might be impaired. It does not have to be carried out if there are no such indications. FRS 11 states that:

> 'A review for impairment of a fixed asset or goodwill should be carried out if events or changes in circumstances indicate that the carrying amount of the fixed asset or goodwill may not be recoverable.'[13]

The standard lists examples of indications, but they are examples, not an exhaustive list. Failure to carry out an impairment review would not be justified if an indicator was ignored because it was not among the examples given. The standard states that:

> 'The requirements of this FRS are such that if no such events or changes in circumstances are identified, and there are no other indications that a tangible fixed asset or investment in a subsidiary, associate or joint venture has become impaired, there is no requirement for an impairment review.'[14]

It is clear that the phrase 'and there are no other indications' requires a proper assessment to be made of any indications of impairment. However the examples given in the standard are important ones, and are discussed below.[15] The first example of an indicator of impairment is:

> A current period operating loss in the business in which the fixed asset or goodwill is involved or net cash outflow from the operating activities of that business, combined with either past operating losses or net cash outflows from such operating activities or an expectation of continuing operating losses or net cash outflows from such operating activities.

A single period's operating loss or net cash outflow from operations would not by itself be enough to trigger an impairment review. However, if this is combined with past losses then the review is triggered. The standard does not discuss when these past losses need have happened, but it would be unreasonable to count them if they were in the distant past. Recent losses, such as those of the previous year, would however trigger the review.

If there are expectations of continuing future losses alongside the current losses or outflows, the review is also triggered. The question arises of what the standard means by 'continuing' losses – however, we suggest that if losses are expected in the next period (as reflected in the latest budgets) that should trigger the review.

If losses (or net cash outflows) have not yet occurred but are expected to do so in the future, then as drafted the standard would require the review to be triggered only when they do materialise. However, it may be prudent to address the matter in advance if the losses are reasonably certain.

This indicator of impairment is primarily concerned with impairment at a higher level than that of the individual fixed asset. It is concerned with losses or net cash outflows at the business or IGU level. If the losses or outflows are occurring only in one part of the business then only that part needs to be reviewed for impairment. The rest of the business has not experienced an indication of impairment and thus no review is required.

Two further example indicators of impairment given in the standard are:

- A significant decline in a fixed asset's market value during the period
- Evidence of obsolescence or physical damage to the fixed asset.

These two examples appear to be aimed primarily at individual fixed assets (rather than IGUs). However, they may also spill over into a wider review of the business or IGU. For example, if there is a property slump, and the value of the entity's new head office falls below its cost this would constitute an indicator of impairment and trigger a review. At the level of the individual asset, NRV is below carrying amount and this might indicate that a write-down is necessary. However, the standard is clear that if NRV is lower than the carrying amount of the fixed asset, it is necessary, before writing down the asset to net realisable value, to establish whether VIU is higher than NRV. If it is, the recoverable amount will be based on VIU, not NRV.[16]

Accordingly, the option of just writing fixed assets down to their market value is not available, although some reporting entities may well be tempted to do this as a simpler way of giving effect to an apparent impairment than carrying out a full review. In practice much depends upon the size of the amounts involved, and whether there is going to be a material difference between the two. Strictly, however, FRS 11 allows no fast track option to recognising an impairment loss just because NRV is lower than the carrying amount.

FRS 11 states that indicators of impairment will trigger an impairment review only if they are relevant to the assessment of the asset in question.[17] A decline in the market value of, say, the head office may not be relevant if the enterprise remains as profitable as it was before. Therefore such a decline will not necessarily trigger an impairment review.

The remaining examples of indicators of impairment given in FRS 11 are:

- A significant adverse change in:
  - either the business or the market in which the fixed asset or goodwill is involved, such as the entrance of a major competitor
  - the statutory or other regulatory environment in which the business operates
  - any 'indicator of value' (for example turnover) used to measure the fair value of a fixed asset on acquisition
- A commitment by management to undertake a significant reorganisation (an intention to do so is apparently not enough)
- A major loss of key employees
- A significant increase in market interest rates or other market rates of return that are likely to affect materially the fixed asset's recoverable amount[18]

Powergen in Extract 13.1 provides an example of an external event, in this case wholesale gas and electricity prices, triggering an impairment of their combined heat and power assets.

Extract 13.1: Powergen plc (2000)

Notes to the Accounts
3 Exceptional Items [extract]
Exceptional items comprise:

	Year ended 31 December 2000 £m	Year ended 2 January 2000 £m	Nine months ended 3 January 1999 £m
Asset impairment – UK Operations	(79)	–	–
US acquisition related costs	(18)	–	–
Re-negotiation of gas contract portfolio	–	(197)	(535)
Reorganisation and restructuring costs	–	(96)	–
Charged against operating profit	**(97)**	**(293)**	**(535)**

Charged Against Operating Profit
An impairment provision of £79 million has been made in respect of the Group's CHP plant portfolio in the light of changes in wholesale electricity and gas prices. The cash flows used in this impairment review were discounted at Powergen's cost of capital for CHP Operations.

Trinity Mirror impaired the value of some its press equipment as a result of an assessment of the group's press policy, as shown in extract 13.2. This may well be an internal reorganisation indicating the carrying amounts were not recoverable.

Extract 13.2: Trinity Mirror plc (2000)

Notes to the Financial Statements

5 Exceptional items [extract]	2000 £m	1999 £m
Operating exceptional items		
Restructuring costs (a)	13.3	8.3
Accelerated depreciation in respect of press impairment (b)	7.5	–
Total exceptional items charged against operating profit	20.8	8.3
(Profit)/loss on sale/termination of operations (c)	(164.5)	4.6
Share of exceptional item of associated undertaking (d)	(17.5)	(0.6)
Net exceptional items before taxation	(161.2)	12.3

(b) Following an assessment of the Group's future press policy undertaken during the year, accelerated depreciation of £7.5 million has been applied to certain press facilities reflecting their impairment.

Clearly there is an important judgement to be made in deciding whether an impairment review is needed. As discussed below, once triggered, an impairment review can become a complicated process with serious implications for the financial statements of an entity. Many will therefore wish to avoid performing such a process and thus may wish to argue that there has not been an indication of impairment of sufficient consequence. Much might turn on whether there has been a *significant* adverse change in the market or just an adverse change, or whether any loss of key employees constitutes a *major* one.

The last of the indicators is particularly noteworthy, because it highlights how radically FRS 11 could be interpreted. Assets could be judged to be impaired if they are no longer expected to earn a current market rate of return. A rise in general interest rates would then cause a write-down in fixed assets even though they would generate the same cash flows as before. Similarly, a corresponding decline in interest rates would lead to the reversal of any such write-down. The standard asserts that short-term market rates may increase without affecting the rate of return that the market would require on long-term assets.[19] The period since the standard came into force has been marked, broadly, by falling interest rates which may help to explain why there has been no evidence of companies adjusting asset values to reflect market rates of return.

Note that for certain assets, FRS 10 and FRS 15 contain extra rules on when an impairment review must be carried out, and these are discussed below at 2.3 and 2.4 respectively.

2.2.3 *Recognition of impairment losses*

FRS 11 requires that 'The impairment review should comprise a comparison of the carrying amount of the fixed asset or goodwill with its recoverable amount (the higher of net realisable value and value in use). To the extent that the carrying amount exceeds the recoverable amount, the fixed asset or goodwill is impaired and should be written down.'[20] Any impairment loss should be recognised in the profit and loss account, except for those involving revalued assets, where the loss may be set against the revaluation surplus until the carrying value of the asset is reduced to its historical cost. Only thereafter must impairment losses on revalued assets be recognised in the profit and loss account.[21]

FRS 11 requires the deferred tax aspects of the situation to be taken into account. It clearly states this and gives an illustration:

> 'In determining whether recoverable amount should be based on value in use or net realisable value, the deferred tax balances that would arise in each case need to be taken into account. For example, if net realisable value is £100 and would give rise to a deferred tax liability of £30 and value in use is £110 and would give rise to a deferred tax liability of £45, recoverable amount is based on net realisable value.'[22]

This requirement is almost impossible to apply under a system of partial provision for deferred tax. However, it may become relevant under FRS 19 which requires full provision for deferred tax. FRS 19 is discussed in Chapter 24.

The standard also specifies that after an impairment loss has been recognised the residual value and the useful life of the assets concerned must be reviewed and revised if necessary, and the new carrying amount written off over the revised remaining useful life. No retrospective adjustment to goodwill is allowed.[23]

2.2.4 *Determining net realisable value (NRV)*

Potentially, both the NRV and the VIU must be determined. In most cases finding the NRV, if it can be found all, will be straightforward and the definition itself (see above at 2.2.1B) is uncontroversial. The standard makes it plain though, that direct selling costs do not include reorganisation or redundancy costs and the like, that might be associated with the selling of a factory, for example. If an NRV is unavailable, the review must be done on the basis of the VIU alone.[24]

2.2.5 *Identifying the IGU and calculating its value in use (VIU)*

If an impairment review has to be carried out then it will frequently be necessary to calculate the VIU of the impaired asset or, more likely, IGU. This is because:

- if a single asset appears to be impaired because NRV is below carrying value, it will be necessary to calculate its VIU (assuming the cash flows arising from it can be separately identified) to ensure that the VIU is not higher.[25]
- where an IGU is being reviewed for impairment, this will involve calculation of the VIU of the IGU as a whole unless a reliable estimate of the IGU's NRV can be made. If no such NRV is identifiable, or if it is below the total of the IGU's net assets, VIU will have to be calculated.

  VIU calculations at the level of the IGU will thus crop up when:

  - goodwill is suspected of being impaired;
  - an IGU itself is suspected of being impaired (and no satisfactory NRV is available); or
  - intangible assets or other fixed assets are suspected of being impaired, individual future cash flows cannot be identified for them, and either no reliable NRV is available or the NRV is below carrying amount.

Much of the complexity of the impairment review is associated with the VIU concept. The process of carrying out an impairment review, and the role of the VIU concept in it, is portrayed below.

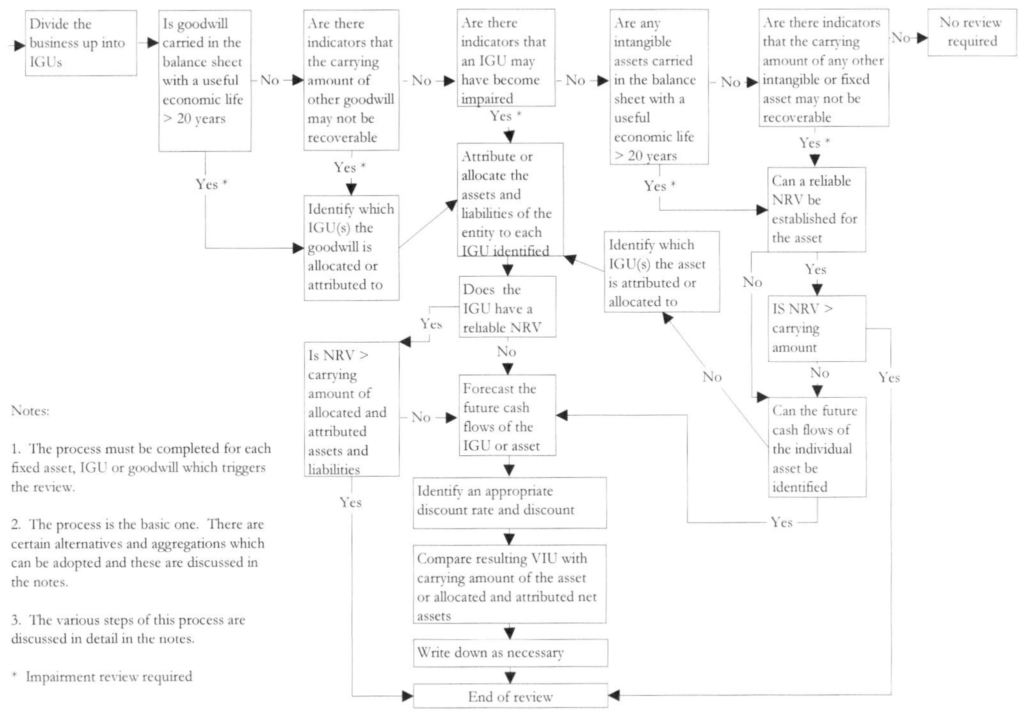

The method falls into five steps, described below. The first two discuss how to identify an IGU and its carrying value, the remainder how to determine the VIU of the IGU so identified.

Step 1 Dividing the enterprise into income-generating units (IGUs)

If an impairment review is called for, one of the early tasks will be to divide the entity into IGUs. The group of assets and liabilities that are considered together should be as small as is reasonably practicable, i.e. the entity should be divided into as many IGUs as possible.[26] That said, the division should not go beyond the level at which each income stream is capable of being separately monitored and not beyond the point at which it would become necessary to start allocating direct costs between IGUs.

Nevertheless, the degree of flexibility over what constitutes an IGU is obvious. The key guidance which the standard offers is that 'the income streams identified are likely to follow the way in which management monitors and makes decisions about continuing or closing the different lines of business of the entity'.[27] In the same way that the reporting of segmental information ultimately has to be left to the discretion of the directors, so too does the division of the entity into IGUs. The standard does, however, further discuss the issue, saying for example that unique intangible assets will often have their own income stream and associated IGU. It also gives four examples[28] which are intended to assist the process of identifying other income streams by reference to major products or services. These examples deal with the following scenarios :

- Supporting routes operated by a transport company are to be treated as part of the income stream represented by the trunk routes (as these onward routes are operated to contribute to the trunk routes rather than being maintained for their own sake). The key justifications for this are: (i) that the decision to continue or close the supporting routes is made with reference to the contribution they make to the trunk routes; and (ii) the income from the supporting routes is not deemed to be independent from the trunk routes. Accordingly, the two are deemed to be part of one income stream.
- If a product can be manufactured at one of several manufacturing sites and in total those sites are utilised at less than 100%, the sites should all be considered one IGU. The logic is that the cash inflows of each site are not independent from each other since they depend on an allocation of the production.
- In a restaurant chain each restaurant should be considered an IGU if its cash flows can be monitored and sensible allocations of costs made to it. However, the standard allows a grouping of restaurants to be treated as the IGU if they are affected by the 'same economic factors', which presumably means that they tend to either rise or fall in value together.
- In a sequential production process (growing and felling of trees, creating parts of wooden furniture and assembling the parts into finished goods) the IGUs are determined by whether there is an external market for the output of each stage. Thus, since there is an external market for timber this creates an IGU of the first stage, but the second and third stages are to be considered together as one IGU. In any impairment review, the deemed cash flows of the two IGUs are to be based on the market price of the timber (rather than the internal transfer price) to give their notional cash inflows from sales and cash outflows for purchases respectively.

In practice different entities will inevitably have varying approaches to determining their IGUs. There is judgement to be exercised in determining an income stream and in determining whether it is largely independent of other streams. The retail sector is likely to be able to identify separate cash flows for its trading outlets more readily than, say, a manufacturing concern could for its factories and warehouses, and there is still likely to be a reasonable degree of flexibility in most organisations. Given this, therefore, entities may tend towards larger rather than smaller IGUs, to keep the complexity of the process within reasonable bounds. One incidental effect of this may be to reduce the incidence of write-downs, as the larger the IGU, the more likely that an impairment loss can be avoided, because poor cash flows from some assets may be offset by better ones from others in the IGU. However J. Sainsbury wrote down its entire Egyptian operation by £111 million, as shown in Extract 13.3.

Extract 13.3: J Sainsbury plc (2001)

Group Profit and Loss Account for the year ended 31 March 2001 [extract]

	Note	2001 Before exceptional items	Exceptional items	Total
Disposal of Homebase operations	4	–	**21**	**21**
Impairment of Egyptian business	5	–	**(111)**	**(111)**
Disposal of operations – discontinued		–	**(90)**	**(90)**

Notes to the financial statements

5 Impairment of Egyptian business [extract]

The net assets of Egyptian Distribution Group SAE (EDGE) have been written down to reflect the estimated net realisable value. This resulted in a write off of £111 million, including £54 million of goodwill previously capitalised.

13 Intangible fixed assets [extract]

	Goodwill £m	Pharmacy licences £m	Total £m
Amortisation			
At 2 April 2000	11	2	13
Impairment of Egyptian business	51	–	51
Charge for the year	16	1	17
At 31 March 2001	**78**	**3**	**81**

14 Tangible fixed assets [extract]

	Group Properties £m	Fixtures, equipment and vehicles £m	Total £m	Company Properties £m
Accumulated depreciation				
At 2 April 2000	904	2,165	3,069	5
Charge for the year	92	317	409	4
Disposals	(68)	(332)	(400)	–
Disposal of subsidiary	(96)	(316)	(412)	–
Impairment of Egyptian business	37	13	50	–
Exchange adjustments	26	22	48	–
At 31 March 2001	**895**	**1,869**	**2,764**	**9**

An inevitable result of the IGU-based approach to impairment is that the impairment of assets is usually going to be assessed on some sort of portfolio basis. It is debatable whether this in fact complies with company law, which strictly requires impairment to be assessed on an individual asset by asset basis. Of course, there are circumstances where the standard appears to require the entity to move from the IGU to focus on the individual asset, e.g. where the indicator of impairment is obsolescence or physical damage. In these circumstances, the entity should provide for impairment of individual assets, notwithstanding that they are part of a larger IGU. In addition, assets held for resale are no longer part of a larger IGU and their impairment or otherwise should be judged solely by the cash flows expected to be generated by sale.

Step 2 Allocating the assets and liabilities of the enterprise to the IGUs

Once the IGUs have been determined, FRS 11 requires that all the assets and liabilities of the entity be allocated to them.[29] This is done either by attributing them to an IGU that they are directly involved with, or apportioning them over several IGUs. The only things not to be allocated in this way are financing and tax items. Other than these, the IGUs should be complete and non-overlapping, so that the sum of the net carrying amounts of the IGUs equals the carrying amount of the net assets of the entity as a whole. There are, however, some exceptions to this basic rule which are discussed below.

Financing items are likely to include interest-bearing debt, interest payable, dividends payable, finance lease obligations and interest-bearing deposits. The reason for not allocating them is explained by the future cash flows that are to be identified and discounted. The cash flows that will be forecast are the cash flows before interest and dividends (i.e. the cash flows which will be available to service the debt and share capital of the entity). The higher levels of cash flow (i.e. before interest deduction) should therefore be related to the higher level of net assets of the IGU (i.e. before deduction of debt and other financing items).

Tax items are also to be excluded. Accordingly, the allocation of assets and liabilities should exclude tax assets and liabilities as well. In fact, the standard does not explicitly say this, referring only to the exclusion of *deferred* tax balances. However, the logic would appear to require that all tax balances be excluded from the allocation.

Central assets also have to be allocated. The allocation of central assets to the various IGUs is often referred to as the 'head office issue' – the head office being the prime example of an asset that relates to more than one IGU. The standard requires that such central assets should be allocated on a 'logical and systematic basis' across the units.[30] This obviously affords some flexibility; any reasonable basis of allocation would appear to be acceptable.

However FRS 11 says that if it is not possible to apportion central assets such as the head office, then a two tier approach may be adopted.[31] This first requires the calculation of any impairment without allocation of the central assets. Next, it is necessary to compare the VIU of all the IGUs to which the central assets contribute against the carrying amounts of those IGUs (after any initial write-down) plus the central assets. Any impairment revealed at this stage goes against the central assets.

Similarly, capitalised goodwill is also to be attributed to or apportioned between IGUs in the same way as are other assets and liabilities of the entity.[32] However, where similar IGUs were acquired together in one investment, these units may be combined to assess the recoverability of the associated goodwill.

Example 13.1: Two-tier impairment test

A company acquires a business comprising three IGUs, X, Y and Z. Each IGU contains an intangible asset which is not being amortised. After five years the carrying amount of the net assets in the three IGUs and the purchased goodwill compares with the VIU as follows:

Income generating unit	X	Y	Z	Goodwill	Total
Carrying amount	£120m	£180m	£210m	£75m	£585m
Value in use	£150m	£210m	£180m		£540m

An impairment loss of £30m is recognised in respect of IGU Z, reducing its carrying value to £180m and the total carrying value to £555m. A further impairment loss of £15m is then recognised in respect of the goodwill.

FRS 11 says that 'if there is any working capital in the balance sheet that will generate cash flows equal to its carrying amount, the carrying amount of the working capital may be excluded from the income-generating units and the cash flows arising from its realisation/settlement excluded from the value in use calculation.'[33] It is not entirely clear why this extra twist was thought necessary. Obviously, it will make no net difference to the calculation, but since cash flow forecasts are unlikely to distinguish the settlement of existing working capital items separately, it seems an unnecessary elaboration.

The steps above lead to the identification of the IGUs of the reporting entity and the allocation of the net assets to them. This is the 'carrying value' half of the exercise. The other half of the exercise is to compute the VIU. This is dealt with below.

Step 3 Estimating the future pre-tax cash flows of the IGU under review

This step need be performed only for those IGUs that are actually being reviewed for impairment. The expected future cash flows of the IGU which is being assessed for impairment should be estimated, based on reasonable and supportable assumptions.[34]

These cash flows should be those that relate to the net assets attributed to the IGU, and accordingly should exclude flows relating to financing and tax. Additionally, depending on the treatment of central assets and working capital items as discussed above, they may also exclude the cash flows associated with such items. More usually, however, they are likely to include a share of central overheads. As with the allocation of central assets, there may be some flexibility in how overhead cash flows are allocated to the various IGUs, although obviously the two should be consistent.

Cash flows should be consistent with the most up-to-date budgets and plans that have been formally approved by management. Cash flows for the period beyond that covered by formal budgets and plans should normally assume a steady or declining growth rate that does not exceed the long-term average for the country or countries in which the business operates. (The standard explains that the UK average post-war growth in gross domestic product, expressed in real terms, is 2.25% per annum).

Only in exceptional circumstances should a higher growth rate be used, or should the period before a steady or declining growth rate is assumed extend to more than five years.[35] The reason for this five year rule is based on general economic theory that postulates above-average growth rates will only be achievable in the short-term, because such above-average growth will lead to competitors entering the market. This increased competition will, over a period of time, lead to a reduction of the growth rate, towards the average for the economy as a whole.

This stage of the impairment review really illustrates the point that it is not only fixed assets that are being assessed. The future cash flow to be forecast is *all* cash flows – receipts from sales, purchases, administrative expenses, etc. It is akin to a free cash flow valuation of a business with the resulting valuation then being compared to the carrying value of the assets in the IGU. It is not at all straightforward in practice.

A further complication is that the future cash flows should be forecast for IGUs or assets in their *current* condition, and should not take account of either:

(a) future cash outflows or related cost savings (for example reductions in staff costs) or benefits that are expected to arise from a future reorganisation for which provision has not yet been made; or

(b) future capital expenditure that will improve or enhance the income-generating units or assets in excess of their originally assessed standard of performance or the related future benefits of this future expenditure.[36]

While this may be understandable on the basis of common prudence, it adds an element of unreality to the process which is hard to reconcile with other assumptions made in the VIU process. For example, the formally approved budgets that the standard makes the foundation of the cash flow forecast will obviously be based on the business as it is actually expected to develop in the future, growth, improvements and all. Producing a special forecast based on unrealistic assumptions, even for this limited purpose, may be difficult. It will probably be logically impossible to check it against actual future cash flows, as the standard requires, because the actual figures will not emanate from the theoretical scenario (post-impairment monitoring of cash flows is discussed below at 2.2.6).

The restriction may stop optimistic forecasts, but an assumption of new capital investment is actually intrinsic to the VIU test. What has to be assessed is the future cash flows of a productive unit, such as a factory. The cash flows, out into the far future, will include the sales of product, cost of sales, administrative expenses, etc. They must necessarily include capital expenditure as well, at least to the extent required to keep the IGU functioning as forecast. Accordingly, *some* capital expenditure cash flows must be built into the forecast cash flows. Whilst improving capital expenditure may not be recognised, routine or replacement capital expenditure has to be. This distinction may not be easy to draw in practice.

There is one exception to this restriction, although it is hard to see the conceptual distinction. Where a new income-generating unit is acquired and the purchaser has planned certain reorganisation or investment expenditure in order to obtain the benefits from its investment, these planned actions and their benefits can be included in the forecast.[37]

Finally, although probably inherent in their identification, the forecast cash flows of the IGU have to be allocated to different periods for the purpose of the discounting step, discussed next.

Step 4 Identifying an appropriate discount rate and discounting the future cash flows

When the future cash flows have been estimated and allocated to different periods, the present value of these cash flows should then be calculated by discounting them. The discount rate to be applied should be an estimate of the rate that the market would expect on an equally risky investment, and should be calculated on a pre-tax basis.[38]

These discounting provisions introduced a new aspect into fixed asset accounting in the UK. Under FRS 11, assets are judged to be impaired if they are no longer expected to earn a current market rate of return. This also means in principle, though the practical application may not quite follow the theory, that an upward movement in general interest rates may give rise to a write-down in assets even though they may generate the same cash flows as before. Correspondingly, a decline in interest rates may lead to the reversal of any such write-down. The standard emphasises, however, that there may be less volatility of this sort than one might think; as even though short term interest rates may fluctuate, the discount rates that are relevant for assessing impairment are longer term rates which are likely to be more stable.[39]

The 'discount rate that the market would expect on an equally risky investment' may be estimated in a variety of ways and in particular by reference to:

- the rate implicit in market transactions of similar assets; or
- the current weighted average cost of capital (WACC) of a listed company whose cash flows have similar risk profiles to those of the IGU; or
- the WACC for the entity as a whole but only if adjusted for the particular risks associated with the IGU.[40]

In the case of the last bullet point, the standard makes two caveats. The first is that where the cash flows assume a growth rate that exceeds the long-term average for more than five years, it is likely that the discount rate used will be increased to reflect a higher risk. The second is that the discount rates applied to individual IGUs must always be such that, if they were to be calculated for every unit, the weighted average rate would equal the entity's overall WACC.[41]

It is likely that an estimate of the appropriate discount rate will have to be made using the concept of the WACC underlying the second and third bullet points. The first bullet point is really applicable to traded assets (such as properties) rather than to IGUs. Since most VIU calculations are done in the context of an IGU, and only rarely is there likely to be a market in similar IGUs, it will not usually be possible to calculate the discount rate in this way.

The second and third bullet points both refer to the WACC; one for a listed company with 'similar risk profiles' to the IGU, and the other for the IGU directly (albeit arrived at by adjusting the entity's WACC for the particular risks of the IGU).

The appropriate discount rate to use is an extremely technical subject, and one about which there is much academic literature and no general agreement. At a more practical level, the standard provides no guidance on how to calculate the required rate. The selection of the rate is obviously a crucial part of the impairment testing process and in practice it will probably not be possible to obtain a rate which is theoretically perfect – the task is just too intractable for that. The objective, therefore, must be to obtain a rate which is sensible and justifiable.

There are probably a number of acceptable methods of arriving at the appropriate rate and one method is set out below. While this illustration may appear to be quite complex, it has been written at a fairly general level. In practice, the calculation of the appropriate discount rate will be extremely complex and specialist advice may be needed.[42]

Example 13.2: Calculating a discount rate

This example is based on determining the WACC for a listed company with a similar risk profile to the IGU in question. Because it is highly unlikely that such a company will exist, it will usually have to be simulated by looking at a hypothetical company with a similar risk profile.

The following three elements need to be estimated for the hypothetical listed company with a similar risk profile:

- gearing, i.e., the ratio of market value of debt to market value of equity
- cost of debt; and
- cost of equity.

Gearing can best be obtained by reviewing quoted companies operating predominantly in the same industry as the IGU and identifying an average level of gearing for such companies. The companies need to be quoted so that the market value of equity can be readily determined.

Where companies in the sector typically have quoted debt, the cost of such debt can be determined directly. In order to calculate the cost of debt for bank loans and borrowings more generally, one method is to take the rate implicit in gilt-edged bonds – with a period to maturity similar to the expected life of the assets being reviewed for impairment – and to add to this rate a bank's margin, i.e., the commercial premium that would be added to the bond rate by a bank lending to the hypothetical listed company. In some cases, the margin being charged on existing borrowings to the company in question will provide evidence to help with establishing the bank's margin. Obviously, the appropriateness of this will depend upon the extent to which the risks facing the IGU being tested are similar to the risks facing the company or group as a whole.

If goodwill or fixed assets being reviewed for impairment were expected to have an indefinitely long life, the appropriate gilt-edged bond rate to use would be that for irredeemable bonds. The additional bank's margin to add would be a matter for judgement but would vary according to the ease with which the sector under review was generally able to obtain bank finance and, as noted above, there might be evidence from the borrowings actually in place of the likely margin that would be chargeable. Sectors that invest significantly in tangible assets such as properties that are readily available as security for borrowings, would require a lower margin than other sectors where such security could not be found so easily. Some sectors typically have no bank finance, for instance the biotechnology sector where bank financing is hardly ever seen.

Cost of equity is the hardest component of the cost of capital to determine. One technique frequently used in practice and written up in numerous textbooks is the 'Capital asset pricing model' (CAPM). The theory underlying this model is that the cost of equity is equal to the risk-free rate plus a multiple, known as the beta, of the market risk premium. The risk-free rate is the same as that used to determine the nominal cost of debt and described above as being obtainable from gilt-edged bond yields with an appropriate period to redemption. The market risk premium is the premium that investors require for investing in equities rather than government bonds. There are also reasons why this rate may be loaded in certain cases, for instance to take account of specific risks in the IGU in question that are not reflected in its market sector generally. Loadings are typically made when determining the cost of equity for a small company. The beta for a quoted company is a number that is greater or less than one according to whether market movements generally are reflected in a proportionately greater (beta more than one) or smaller (beta less than one) movement in the particular stock in question. Most betas fall into the range 0.4 to 1.5.

Various bodies, such as The London Business School, publish betas on a regular basis both for individual stocks and for industry sectors in general. Published betas are levered, i.e., they reflect the level of gearing in the company or sector concerned.

The cost of equity for the hypothetical company having a similar risk profile to the IGU is:

Cost of equity = risk-free rate + (levered beta x market risk premium)

Having determined the component costs of debt and equity and the appropriate level of gearing, the WACC for the hypothetical company having a similar risk profile to the IGU in question is:

$$\text{WACC} = (1 - t) \times D \times \frac{g}{(1 + g)} + E \times \left[1 - \frac{g}{(1 + g)}\right]$$

where:

D is the cost of debt;
E is the cost of equity
g is the gearing level (i.e. the ratio of debt to equity) for the sector; and
t is the rate of tax relief available on the debt servicing payments.

The standard requires that the forecast cash flows be before tax and finance costs. It is more common in discounted cash flow valuations to use cash flows after tax. However, as pre-tax cash flows are being used, the standard requires a pre-tax discount rate to be used.[43] This will involve discounting higher future cash flows (before deduction of tax) with a higher discount rate. In principle, this is the rate of return that, after deduction of tax, gives the required post-tax rate of return.

The standard is difficult to interpret on this subject, but for most purposes we suggest that a simple grossing-up calculation will suffice. Once the WACC has been calculated, the pre-tax WACC can be calculated by applying the fraction 1/(1-t). Thus, if the WACC comes out at, say, 12% the pre-tax WACC will be 12% divided by 0.7 (given a corporation tax rate of 30% and assuming it is the appropriate rate in the context of the reporting entity) which would give a rate of 17.1%. (Note, however, that Appendix I to the standard[44] warns that this simple grossing-up method may not be sufficiently accurate where the various cash flows involve disparate tax consequences, although we believe that this will seldom make a material difference.)

Finally, on the subject of discount rates, the standard gives two variants which can be chosen. Firstly, the standard allows the cash flows to be forecast in terms of either current or expected future prices (with a real or nominal discount rate as appropriate).[45] Secondly, although the risk associated with the cash flows is usually reflected in the chosen discount rate, the standard introduces the possibility of adjusting the cash flows for risk and then discounting them using a risk free rate (such as the return on a government bond).[46] This no doubt can be made (mathematically) to give the same answer but no guidance is contained in the standard suggesting how to adjust the cash flows for risk.

In theory, risk in the context of investment capital is a highly technical issue that is measured against the yardstick of other alternative investments. The forecast cash flows should strictly be adjusted for their riskiness in that sense. This is a difficult concept in the standard and guidance about it would improve the pronouncement.

The selection of discount rates leaves considerable room for judgement in the absence of clearer guidance, and it is likely that many very different approaches have been applied in practice, even though this may not always be evident from the accounts. A number of companies have, however, given good disclosure of their methodology and assumptions. Cable and Wireless reported an impairment loss in relation to its switched circuit voice business, using a 9.5% discount rate, as shown in Extract 13.4.

Extract 13.4: Cable and Wireless plc (2000)

Notes

5 Operating costs [extract]

	Continuing operations before exceptional items £m	Exceptional items (note 10) £m	Discontinued operations £m	2001 £m
Depreciation of owned tangible fixed assets	994	444	129	**1,567**
Depreciation of tangible fixed assets held under finance leases	12	–	–	**12**

10 Exceptional items [extract]

(i) Implementation of the Group's strategy based on IP has affected the useful life and carrying value of certain network assets employed in its switched circuit voice business. An assessment of the value in use of this business, based on a discount rate of 9.5%, has resulted in an impairment charge to these assets of £444m which is disclosed separately as an exceptional item within depreciation. Their residual book value is being depreciated over their remaining estimated useful life of three years.

One company that has been very explicit about its problems in this area is Eurotunnel, which is in an unusual position both because of the nature of its activities and the difficult economic position it has found itself in. As described in the Extract 13.5, it has not felt able to use a market-based discount rate and has made no write-down as a result.

Extract 13:5: Eurotunnel plc (2000)

Notes [extract]

1. Accounting Policies [extract]

Tangible Fixed Assets and Depreciation [extract]

During 1998, Financial Reporting Standard 11 "Impairment of fixed assets and goodwill" (FRS 11) was issued. FRS 11 requires that any impairment be identified and measured by comparing the carrying value of fixed assets to the present value of projected cash flows using a market based discount rate.

Eurotunnel PLC is currently in a "stabilisation period" after the Financial Restructuring in 1998. During this period Eurotunnel does not have access to capital markets in the usual way and interest which cannot be paid in cash may be settled by issuing Stabilisation Notes, which do not bear interest until 2006. In addition, Eurotunnel, being a single service concession company with highly dedicated fixed assets, is not able to reinvest its existing capital in alternative assets or services in order to improve stakeholder returns. In these circumstances, the Directors consider that identifying and applying a market-based discount rate is inappropriate and would not give a true and fair view of the state of affairs of the Eurotunnel PLC Group. Instead, the Directors think that the discount rate to be applied in any year should be the internal rate of return for that year implicit in the lower case financial projections used in the Financial Restructuring and published in the May 1997 prospectus.

> During 2000 Financial Reporting Standard 15 "Tangible Fixed Assets" (FRS 15) was issued. FRS 15 requires that an FRS 11 impairment review is undertaken annually where the estimated remaining useful economic life of the tangible fixed asset exceeds 50 years. Therefore an impairment review was carried out at 31 December 2000, using a discount rate (determined as referred to above) of 7.8% on the basis of which there was no impairment. Application of a discount rate of 9.2% to this projection would have yielded a present value approximately equal to book value. Increasing the discount rate by a further 1% from this level would have given an impairment of £1.2 billion. Because it was not practicable to identify a market-based discount rate, it was not otherwise possible to quantify the effect of this departure from FRS 11.

Once the discount rate has been chosen, and the other decisions about which calculation options to use have been made, the future cash flows are discounted in order to produce a figure representing the FRS 11 defined VIU of the IGU. The final step in the impairment review can now be taken.

Step 5 Compare the carrying value of the IGU with its VIU and allocate the impairment loss (if any)

Where the carrying value of the IGU is less than (or equal to) its calculated VIU, there is no impairment. Where, on the other hand, the carrying value of the IGU is greater than its VIU, an impairment write-down should be recognised.

Unless there is an obvious impairment of specific assets within an IGU, the impairment should be allocated as follows:

- firstly, to any capitalised goodwill in the unit;
- secondly, to any capitalised intangible in the unit; and
- finally, to the tangible assets in the unit on a pro rata or more appropriate basis.[47]

The clear intention of this hierarchy of allocation is to write down the assets with the less reliable measures before those with more reliable measures.

There are a couple of qualifications to this allocation process. Firstly, no *intangible* asset which has a 'readily ascertainable market value' should be written down below its net realisable value.[48] 'Readily ascertainable market value' is defined as 'the value of an intangible asset that is established by reference to a market where (a) the asset belongs to a homogeneous population of assets that are equivalent in all material respects; and (b) an active market, evidenced by frequent transactions, exists for that population of assets'.[49] Secondly, no *tangible* asset with a net realisable value that can be measured reliably should be written down below that value.[50] These qualifications act as a restraint on an arbitrary allocation process that could lead to anomalous results.

This process, then, writes down the fixed assets and goodwill attributed or allocated to an IGU until the carrying value of the net assets is not more than the computed VIU. It is logically possible, even if all fixed assets and goodwill are either written off or down to their NRV, the carrying value of the assets may still be higher than the computed VIU. There is no suggestion that the net assets should be reduced any further because at this point the NRV would be the relevant impairment figure.

If an impairment is indicated for an IGU, the write-down will eat into both the assets directly attributed to it and the share of central assets allocated to it. Accordingly, for the latter it may be worthwhile just writing down the specific assets and then doing the two-stage test (as discussed above) to see if the central assets do need to be written down.

Once the impairment write-down has been made, henceforth the entity will theoretically be able to make the rate of return on its assets which the providers of its capital are looking to see on their funds invested. This is the rate implicit in the calculation that forms the basis of the discount rate chosen for the impairment calculations. An implication of the standard, therefore, but not one that we have seen much evidence of in practice, is that no UK companies need to report materially sub-standard returns on an ongoing basis – at least not those in which an impairment review has been triggered by an 'indicator of impairment'.

If the profitability of such a company was below the return on capital that investors would require to invest in it now; the currently required rate would be reflected in the discount rate chosen for the impairment test. If an impairment is found, this in turn would result in the assets being written down, with shareholders funds being reduced equally. Given the same absolute profits, the rate of return on capital employed must rise. However it must be remembered that the appearance of an 'indicator of impairment' is required before an impairment review is required at all.

2.2.6 *Subsequent monitoring of cash flows*

Where an impairment review has been performed, and the recoverable amount has been based on VIU, the standard requires that the future cash flows incorporated in the review be monitored, regardless of whether the original VIU-based test resulted in a write-down or not. This is to be done for five years following the original review, by comparing the forecast cash flows with the actual out-turn.[51] Where the actual cash flows are 'so much less' than those forecast that the use of the actual cash flows could have resulted in an impairment loss being recognised in previous periods, the original impairment calculations should be re-performed, this time using the actual cash flows. Any impairment identified as a result of this later calculation should be recognised in the current period and not as a prior year adjustment.

This subsequent monitoring of cash flows is necessary even where a 'new' impairment review is not required to be performed for the current period. In theory, therefore, once an IGU undergoes a VIU test, it will need to be reassessed in each of the next five years. This appears a quite onerous task, although in practice it is likely to be achieved by the process of updating previous forecasts. In any event, a recalculation is only triggered when the actual cash flows are 'so much less' than forecast that an impairment might have been triggered.

In re-performing the original impairment review, all the actual cash flows for the intervening period (of up to five years) have to be incorporated, but the cash flows which are still in the future have to be the ones forecast in the original test. The test is thus just a straight re-performance, using the same assumptions (e.g. about what constitutes the various IGUs) but adjusted for actual events. The only changes that can be made to the future cash flows are ones that result directly from the actual cash flows.[52] For example, if the re-performance is being done after three years and cash flows originally expected in the fourth year have already been received, they should not be double counted.

If an impairment is revealed by the re-performance, it will have to be recognised in the current period unless the impairment has reversed (and this reversal is permitted to be recognised as discussed below). In order to test whether it has reversed, however, a new impairment review, as at the current date, with revised forecasts will now have to be performed.

2.2.7 *Restoration of past impairment losses*

The restoration of past impairment losses is another part of FRS 11 which can prove problematic in practice. If an impairment loss has been recognised and that loss has now reversed, whether or not the reversal can be recognised depends on the nature of both the asset and the reversing event. Tangible fixed assets and investments are subject to one regime; goodwill and intangible assets to another.

A Tangible fixed assets and investments

If an impairment has been recognised for a tangible fixed asset or investment, and a change in economic conditions or in the expected use of an asset reverses that loss, the carrying value of the relevant asset can be written back up. The credit is taken through the profit and loss account. However, the reversal should not be recognised in full, but only enough to write the asset back up to the amount it would now be carried at if the original impairment had not been recognised. For example, if the asset was being depreciated when the impairment took place it will only be reinstated to its original value minus the depreciation appropriate to the intervening period.[53]

However, there are a number of conditions before a reversal can be recognised. The reversal must take place as a consequence of a change in economic conditions or in the expected use of the asset, which can include the occurrence of the capital expenditure that the entity was previously required to exclude.[54] Indicators of the increase in value will tend to be the reverse of those indicators of impairment discussed above at 2.2.2. If recoverable amount is based on VIU and this increases for reasons other than a change in economic conditions, the rise in recoverable amount cannot be recognised. The standard gives two examples of such increases – the passage of time (the present value of future cash flows increases as they come closer) and the occurrence of forecast cash outflows.[55] This means that tangible assets are not written back up as the discount reverses.

However, this inability to recognise the rise in value can give rise to some illogical results, as shown in Example 13.3:

Example 13.3: Double counted losses

At the end of 2000, a company with a single IGU is carrying out an impairment review. The discounted forecast cash flows for years 2002 and onwards are just enough to support the carrying value of the firm's assets. However, 2001 is forecast to produce a loss and net cash outflow. The discounted value of this amount is accordingly written off the carrying value of the fixed assets in 2000 as an exceptional impairment loss. It is then suffered again in 2001 (at a slightly higher amount being now undiscounted) as the actual loss. Once that loss is past, the future cash flows are sufficient to support the original unimpaired value of the fixed assets. Nevertheless, the assets cannot be written back up through the profit and loss account to counter the double counting effect as the increase in value does not derive from a change in economic conditions or in the expected use of an asset. The entity will only 'benefit' as the assets are amortised.

The treatment above is tantamount to providing for certain costs in advance but then charging the ensuing costs to the profit and loss account without releasing the provision, which would be absurd. In fact, a number of the aspects of FRS 11 raise the suspicion that its logic is not entirely consistent with that of FRS 12. The ASB took great pains in that other standard to stamp out provisions for future losses. However, as can be seen, FRS 11 requires equivalent provisions against the carrying value of fixed assets, and indeed goes beyond mere losses so that provision is made for inadequate profits as well.

B Goodwill and intangible assets

An impairment review may identify that an impairment loss recognised in an earlier accounting period appears to have been reversed in the current period. However, the standard does not allow such reversals to be recognised for goodwill and intangibles unless 'an external event caused the recognition of the impairment loss in previous periods and subsequent external events clearly and demonstrably reverse the effects of that event in a way that was not foreseen in the original impairment calculations'.[56] This is illustrated in example 13.4 below.

There is also the possibility of recognising reversals of write-downs in the carrying value of intangibles with readily ascertainable market values when their net realisable values rise, but as such assets are rare, such reversals will seldom be recognised.[57]

Example 13.4: Impairment of goodwill

Company A has an income-generating unit which has a carrying value of £2,000,000 at 31 December 2001. This carrying value comprises £500,000 relating to goodwill and £1,500,000 relating to net tangible assets. The goodwill is not being amortised as its useful life is believed to be indefinite.

In 2002, as a result of losses, net tangible assets have decreased to £1,400,000 reducing the total carrying value of the unit to £1,900,000. Changes in the regulatory framework surrounding its business mean that the income-generating unit has a VIU of £1,600,000 and has thus suffered an impairment loss of £300,000. This is charged to the profit and loss account. The carrying value of goodwill is reduced to £200,000.

In 2003 the company develops a new product with the result that the VIU of the income-generating unit rises to £1,700,000. Net tangible assets have remained at £1,400,000. Despite the VIU of the business unit now being £1,700,000 compared to its carrying value of £1,600,000, it is not possible to reverse £100,000 of the prior year's impairment loss of £300,000 since the reason for the increase in value of the business unit (the launch of the new product) is not the same as the reason for the original impairment loss (the change in the regulatory environment in which the business operates).

The logic of this rule within the standard is quite clear. If the reason for the recovery in value is not the same as the reason for the original loss, then recognising a reversal of the impairment loss would be tantamount to giving credit for internally generated goodwill. However, this ignores two points. Firstly, the existence of sufficient internally generated goodwill can be used, implicitly, to justify the belief that no impairment write-down is required in the first place. Secondly, while the above example seems clear-cut, in practice the 'reasons' quoted may be much wider than those used in that example. For instance, if a company argues that the reason for its impairment loss is the economic recession within the country in which the business operates, it would be reasonably easy to argue that the reason for the recovery in value of the business is the improvement in the general economy. While this may be an extreme example, there may be a number of variations such as 'a lack of demand for our products' or 'a lack of confidence in the market place'. The reason for an impairment loss and its reversal would need to be credible however, because disclosure of the reason for the reversal of a past impairment loss is required by the standard.[58]

The reversal of the impairment loss should be recognised to the extent that it increases the carrying amount of the goodwill or intangible asset up to the amount that it would have been had the original impairment not occurred.[59] This theoretically means having to make some assumptions about what the amortisation of the goodwill or intangible asset would have been if the impairment had not occurred. In practice the sensible assumption is that the previous amortisation policy which existed prior to the impairment loss being recognised would have continued.

2.2.8 *Allocation of impairment when an acquired business is merged with an existing business*

One particularly convoluted aspect of the standard is the discussion of how an impairment is to be recognised where an acquired business has been merged with an existing business to form a larger IGU.[60] This unit will include both purchased and internally generated goodwill and the problem to be guarded against is that the internally generated goodwill of the existing unit can be used to shield the assets of an underperforming acquired business.

In these circumstances it is necessary to value the goodwill of the existing business (which will be internally generated goodwill or any purchased goodwill previously written off to reserves under SSAP 22) at the date of the merging of the businesses.[61] The standard explains that the goodwill is estimated by deducting the fair values of the assets and the carrying value of any purchased goodwill within the existing IGU from its estimated VIU (on a pre-merger basis). The calculation of this notional internally generated goodwill does not mean that it will be recognised as an asset. It is merely a notional figure to be used in determining how an impairment loss in respect of assets which *are* recognised on the balance sheet should be accounted for. The effect of this exercise means that any previous impairment in the goodwill relating to the existing business will be notionally recognised for this purpose before the acquisition takes place.

The notional goodwill on the existing business is then added to the actual carrying amount of the new enlarged IGU, purely for the purposes of the impairment review.

Once the merger of operations does take place, the VIU test may or may not give rise to an impairment loss in the new enlarged business. If an impairment arises on the merging of the businesses, this must be attributable to the newly acquired business (since the existing business has already been 'tested' for impairment). Accordingly, the purchased goodwill within the newly acquired business (and, if necessary, any intangible assets and tangible assets) would be written down by the amount of the impairment loss.

If a VIU test is performed in a subsequent period, it will not be possible to attribute the impairment directly to either the newly acquired business or the existing business. Therefore, in these circumstances, the impairment is allocated, on a pro rata basis, between the recognised goodwill on the acquisition of the acquired business and the notional internally generated goodwill relating to the 'old' business. The impairment loss attributed to the recognised goodwill should be recognised in the profit and loss account. The impairment loss attributed to the notional goodwill is not recognised in the financial statements since it is a loss in value of notional goodwill which itself is not recognised in the accounts.[62]

The notional goodwill is to be amortised on the same basis as the recognised goodwill.[63]

Rather counter-intuitively, therefore, a VIU impairment review can result in a write-down even when the VIU is greater than the carrying value of the net assets. This is because the net assets are to be inflated by the notional internally generated goodwill.

2.2.9 *Impairment of goodwill written off directly to reserves pre-FRS 10*

As explained in Chapter 11 at 2.3.6, goodwill written off directly to reserves did not have to be reinstated on adoption of FRS 10; the rule in FRS 10 being that when the subsidiary is sold, such 'old' goodwill must be recycled through the income statement as part of the calculation of the gain or loss on disposal. However, the circumstance can arise where 'old' goodwill, previously written off directly to reserves, becomes impaired but the subsidiary is not disposed of. Both FRS 10 and FRS 11 are silent on the matter, so the question arises how this impairment should be accounted for.

In our view it is important for companies to adopt a policy on this matter and to apply it consistently. We consider that the most appropriate treatment, that is clearly within the spirit of both FRS 10 and FRS 11 as well as being consistent with the required treatment for post-FRS 10 goodwill, is for the impaired old goodwill to be recycled and the impairment to be recognised in the profit and loss account, as an operating exceptional item if sufficiently material. Andrews Sykes provide a clear example of this treatment, which is shown below.

Extract 13.6: Andrews Sykes Group plc (2000)

Accounting Policies

Goodwill [extract]

The profit or loss on the sale or closure of a previously acquired business is calculated after charging the amount of any related goodwill not previously written off through the profit and loss account, including amounts previously taken directly to reserves.

Goodwill either written off directly to reserves or capitalised in previous financial periods is written off through the profit and loss account to the extent that it is considered to have suffered permanent diminution in value or an impairment.

Notes to the Financial Statements

3 Goodwill [extract]

	52 weeks ended 30 December 2000 *£000*	53 weeks ended 1 January 2000 *£000*
Other pre FRS 10 goodwill:		
Provision against goodwill previously written off to reserves	**(2,971)**	–

The directors consider that the goodwill arising on the acquisition of Refrigeration Compressor Remanufacturers Limited has suffered a permanent diminution in value and the value of the total goodwill arising on acquisition of £2,971,000, which was previously charged directly to reserves in accordance with SSAP 22: Accounting for Goodwill, can no longer be supported. The full amount has been credited back to reserves and charged to the current period profit and loss account in accordance with the Group's stated accounting policy.

2.3 The requirements of FRS 10

FRS 10 contains additional provisions governing the circumstances in which goodwill and intangible assets must be subject to an impairment revue, not all of which require indicators of impairment to be present. The circumstances are:

- at the end of the first full year following an acquisition;
- in other periods if events or changes in circumstances indicate that the carrying values may not be recoverable;
- when a business has ascribed an indefinite economic life, or one greater than 20 years, to the goodwill or intangible asset concerned; in which case FRS 10 requires that an annual impairment review has to be carried out.[64]

Apart from the circumstance described below where a post-acquisition review is carried out, all impairment revues required by FRS 10 must be performed in accordance with the requirements of FRS 11.[65]

At the end of the first full year following an acquisition, the review must compare the post-acquisition performance of the acquired business with the pre-acquisition forecasts used to support its purchase price.[66] If the performance falls short of that expected, this triggers a full impairment review. This is to make sure that goodwill and intangibles are not carried in the balance sheet at amounts which reflect a bad purchase, even where the goodwill and intangible assets are being amortised over a fairly short period.

The standard states that if an impairment is identified at the time of the first year impairment review, this impairment reflects:

(a) an overpayment,

(b) an event that occurred between the acquisition and the first year review; or

(c) depletion of the acquired goodwill or intangible asset between the acquisition and the first year review that exceeds the amount recognised through amortisation.[67]

It is necessary to interpret the requirement that a comparison should be made of the post-acquisition performance with the pre-acquisition forecasts used to support the purchase price. The standard does not set out what this might or should involve. It could be a simple comparison of post-acquisition profit with pre-acquisition forecast profit; but it also appears open to preparers to consider the whole gamut of performance measures that they apply to the business. For example, a poorer than expected profit may be offset by a better than expected market share. Perhaps order books, product development and many other performance measures can be taken into account. Judgement will have to be used in weighing the various over and under-achievements that the acquired business may have experienced since its acquisition. It is likely that, in practice, it will only be in those cases where it is inescapably evident that the purchase has been a 'bad' one that the preparers of the reporting entity's accounts will feel it necessary to perform a full impairment review. However, if the post-acquisition review does indicate an impairment, then a full impairment revue in accordance with FRS 11 must be carried out.[68]

FRS 10 requires that if an impairment loss is recognised, the revised carrying value, if being amortised, should be amortised over the current estimate of the remaining useful economic life.[69]

Importantly, FRS 10 specifically states that:

> 'If goodwill arising on consolidation is found to be impaired, the carrying amount of the investment held in the accounts of the parent undertaking should also be reviewed for impairment.'[70]

This requirement may have implications for the dividend-paying abilities of a group, as any impairment of the holding company's investment will result in a reduction of retained profits available for dividends.

2.4 The requirements of FRS 15

FRS 15 contains a general requirement that assets should not be carried at more than their recoverable amount, and that any impairment should be conducted in accordance with FRS 11.

There is one further rule in FRS 15 that requires certain tangible assets to be annually tested for impairment, even in the absence of any indicator of impairment. Any tangible asset (other than non-depreciable land) that is not being depreciated on grounds of immateriality under FRS 15, or has a remaining useful economic life that is estimated for depreciation purposes to exceed 50 years, must be subject to an annual impairment review.[71]

3 UK DISCLOSURE REQUIREMENTS

3.1 Introduction

This section summarises disclosures required in financial statements compiled under UK GAAP for impairment losses and reversals of losses. The disclosures required by each authoritative source are separately shown.

3.2 Companies Act 1985 disclosures

As noted in 3.3 below, FRS 11 requires impairment losses that are recognised in the profit and loss account to be included within operating profit under the appropriate statutory heading, and disclosed as an exceptional item if appropriate.[72] For tangible and intangible assets, the choice of 'appropriate statutory heading' will depend on which of the Companies Act profit and loss account formats is being used. Under Format 2 of Schedule 4, it will be 'depreciation and other amounts written off tangible and intangible fixed assets', but under Format 1 it may have to be analysed among cost of sales, distribution costs and administrative expenses, according to the nature of the assets being written down. For investments, the two formats contain the same heading – 'amounts written off investments' – which incidentally means that such an impairment will be shown after operating profit, despite FRS 11's requirement that it be included within operating profit. The Companies Act formats used by banks and insurance companies are different again.

3.3 FRS 11 disclosures

FRS 11 requires impairment losses that are recognised in the profit and loss account to be included within operating profit under the appropriate statutory heading, and disclosed as an exceptional item if appropriate.[73]

Impairment losses that are recognised in the statement of total recognised gains and losses (those that are the reversal of revaluation gains and that do not represent the consumption of economic benefits) should be disclosed separately on the face of that statement.[74]

FRS 11 addresses whether amounts written off a fixed asset should be regarded as a reduction of the gross amount (cost or valuation) of the asset in question or as an increase in the cumulative depreciation charged against it. This will affect the presentation of the amounts in the fixed assets note. The standard concludes that the answer to this question depends on how the amount at which the asset is carried is determined.[75] Thus:

- if the asset is carried on a historical cost basis, the impairment loss should be included within cumulative depreciation;
- if the asset is carried at market value, the impairment loss should be included within the revalued carrying amount;
- if the asset is carried at a valuation based on depreciated replacement cost, the classification of the impairment for this purpose depends on where the write-down has been charged. If the impairment has been charged in the profit and loss account, it should be added to cumulative depreciation, but if it has been charged to the statement of total recognised gains and losses, it should be deducted from the gross amount of the asset.

FRS 11 requires certain additional disclosures to be made in respect of impairment reviews as follows:

(a) Where an impairment loss has been recognised following a VIU calculation has been made, the discount rate should be disclosed. If a risk-free discount rate was used, some indication of the risk adjustments made to the cash flows should be given.[76]

    As drafted this seems to require disclosure only in cases where a loss has actually been recognised. However, it would arguably be much more significant in those cases where a calculation was undertaken, but it was concluded that no impairment need be recognised.

(b) Where an impairment loss recognised in a previous period is reversed in the current period, the financial statements should disclose the reason for the reversal, including any changes in the assumptions upon which the calculation of recoverable amount is based.[77]

(c) Where an impairment loss would have been recognised in previous period had the forecasts of future cash flows been more accurate but the impairment has reversed and the reversal of the loss is permitted to be recognised (see 2.2.7 above), the impairment now identified and its reversal should be disclosed.[78]

(d) Where, in the measurement of VIU, the period before a steady or declining long-term growth rate has been assumed extends to more than five years, the financial statements should disclose the length of the longer period and the circumstances justifying it.[79]

(e) Where, in the measurement of VIU, the long-term growth rate used has exceeded the long-term average growth rate for the country or countries in which the business operates, the financial statements should disclose the growth rate assumed and the circumstances justifying it.[80]

It appears that the disclosures under (d) and (e) above are required in respect of all VIU calculations, not just those (as in (a) above) resulting in an actual impairment write-down in the financial statements.

The disclosure requirements concerning the amounts by which assets have been adjusted are included in the disclosure requirements of the relevant standards.

3.4 FRS 10 disclosures

The disclosures required by FRS 10 about impairment of goodwill and intangible assets are included in the Chapter 11 at 3.2.2, which deals with the principal disclosures required by that standard.

3.5 FRS 15 disclosures

The disclosures required by FRS 15 about impairment of tangible fixed assets are included in Chapter 12 at 3.2.4, which deals with the principal disclosures required by that standard.

4 IAS REQUIREMENTS

4.1 Introduction

The theory and basic method that underlies both the IASC's and the ASB's approach to impairment is set out in section 1.2 above.

IAS 36 – *Impairment of assets* – is similar in principle to the UK standard FRS 11, but there are important differences in its detailed provisions. IAS 36 was published in April 1998 and became effective for all periods beginning on or after 1 July 1999. The standard is a general impairment standard and its provisions are referred to in other standards, for example IAS 16 and IAS 22, where impairment is to be considered.

4.2 The requirements of IAS 36

4.2.1 Objective, scope, and definitions

The objective of the standard is to ensure that assets are not carried at more than their recoverable amount (recoverable amount and other terms are explained in 1.2 above). If the carrying amount is higher than the amount to be recovered by use or sale of the asset, then the business should recognise an impairment loss.[81]

The standard has a general application to all assets, but the following are outside its scope: inventories, assets arising from construction contracts, deferred tax assets, assets arising from employee benefits, financial assets that are included in the scope of IAS 32, investment property that is measured at fair value and biological assets under IAS 41.[82] The effect of these exclusions is to reduce the scope of IAS 36 considerably, however, it does not exempt investment properties not carried at fair value, oil exploration costs or an entity's own shares held by an ESOP. Investments in subsidiaries, joint ventures and associates are within the scope of IAS 36.[83]

The key definitions used in IAS 36 are similar in effect to their UK equivalents, but not identical. The key definition in IAS 36 are:

> 'Recoverable amount is the higher of an asset's net selling price and its value in use.
>
> Value in use is the present value of estimated future cash flows expected to arise from the continuing use of an asset and from its disposal at the end of its useful life.
>
> A cash-generating unit is the smallest identifiable group of assets that generates cash inflows from continuing use that are largely independent of the cash inflows from other assets or groups of assets.'[84]

4.2.2 *Indications of impairment*

The standard, in common with its UK equivalent, only requires an impairment test to be carried out if there is an indication of impairment. There is no general requirement to carry out impairment tests after a certain time has passed. The business is required by IAS 36 to assess at each balance sheet date whether there are any indications of impairment. If there are, a formal estimate of the asset's recoverable amount, as set out in the standard, must be undertaken.[85] However, it is pointed out that there may be no need to estimate the asset's recoverable amount if there was sufficient headroom in previous calculations that would not have been eroded by subsequent events.[86]

IAS 36 lists examples of indications of impairment. The standard states that the examples represent the minimum indications that should be considered by the entity, and that the list is not exhaustive.[87] They are divided into external and internal indications as follows:[88]

External sources of information

(a) a significant decline in an asset's market value, exceeding that which would be expected as a result of the passage of time or normal use;

(b) significant adverse changes in the technological, market, economic or legal environment in which the enterprise operates or the market for which an asset is used;

(c) increases in market interest rates or other market rates of return on investments to the extent that they will affect the discount rate and thereby decrease an asset's VIU;

(d) the carrying amount of the net assets of the reporting enterprise is more than its market capitalisation;

Internal sources of information

(e) evidence of obsolescence or physical damage of an asset;

(f) significant changes with an adverse effect on the enterprise either have taken place during the period, or are expected to take place in the near future. These will affect the way in which, an asset is used or is expected to be used. These include plans to discontinue or restructure the operation to which an asset belongs or to dispose of an asset before the previously expected date; and

(g) there is internal evidence that indicates that the economic performance of an asset is, or will be, worse than expected. Internal evidence may include:
   (i) either acquisition or operating and maintenance costs are significantly higher than originally budgeted;
   (ii) actual net cash flows and operating profits are significantly worse than budgeted;
   (iii) the performance of the asset has declined significantly when measured against budgeted cash flows or operating profits; or
   (iv) current period results, when aggregated with budgeted future performance, indicate the there are operating losses or net cash outflows.[89]

There are two significant departures compared with FRS 11's indicators. The first is the inclusion of market capitalisation as an 'external' indication of impairment. Market capitalisation is, analytically, a powerful indicator as, if it shows a lower figure than the book value of shareholders' funds, it inescapably suggests the market considers the assets are overvalued. The second departure is an explicit reference to internal evidence that future performance *will be* worse than expected. FRS 11 refers only to an expectation of continuing losses or net cash outflows.

The inclusion of interest rates as an indicator of impairment implies that an upward movement in general interest rates may give rise to a write-down in assets even though they may generate the same cash flows as before. The standard does however give a limited exemption from the full force of this indicator. If the discount rate used in the impairment test is unlikely to be affected by short term changes in rates, or the VIU (i.e. profitability) of the product is not likely to be affected, then the enterprise is not required to make a formal estimate of the recoverable amount.[90]

If there are indications that the asset is impaired, it may also be necessary to examine the remaining useful life of the asset, its residual value and the depreciation method as these may also need to be adjusted.[91]

4.2.3 *The impairment test*

The standard (like its UK equivalent) requires the carrying amount to be compared with the recoverable amount. The recoverable amount is the higher of VIU (the discounted expected future cash flows) and net selling price. If either the net selling price or the VIU is higher than the carrying amount, no further action is necessary as the asset is not impaired.[92] It may be possible to estimate the net selling price even in the absence of an active market but if it cannot be estimated satisfactorily then the value of an asset must be based on its VIU.[93]

There is however, an important practical clause in IAS 36 that may save businesses a great deal of administrative work, even if not saving any admission of impairment losses. Paragraph 18 of IAS 36 states that 'if there is no reason to believe that an asset's value in use materially exceeds its net selling price, the asset's recoverable amount may be taken to be its net selling price.' Paragraph 20 allows the use of estimates, averages and computational shortcuts to provide a reasonable approximation of net selling price or VIU. We consider that these are sensible practical points that may well prevent unnecessary work.

The standard goes into detail regarding the estimation of an asset's net selling price. It should be the net realisable value in a binding sale agreement negotiated at arm's length.[94] If there is a market, net realisable value may be estimated from current or recent bid prices.[95] In the absence of an active market or a binding sale agreement the enterprise may still be able to estimate the market price of the asset in an arm's length transaction.[96]

In all cases, net selling price should take account of estimated disposal costs. These include legal costs, stamp duty and other transaction costs, costs of moving the asset and direct incremental costs. Business reorganisation costs and employee termination costs (as defined in IAS 19 *Employee benefits* – see Chapter 22) may not be treated as costs of disposal.[97]

A The value in use (VIU) calculation – future cash flows

The detailed requirements concerning the data to be assembled to calculate VIU are similar to those set out and explained in detail in steps 1 to 5 for the UK standard in 2.2.5 above. Reference should be made to this section for a detailed analysis of the practicalities and difficulties in determining the VIU of an asset. The parameters set by IAS 36 for the data to be used in the calculation are also similar to the UK standard, and are outlined below.

Cash flow projections must be based on reasonable and supportable assumptions, and on the most recent budgets approved by management.[98] These projections should cover a maximum of five years unless management is confident that its longer projections are reliable and can demonstrate this from past experience.[99] It should extrapolate the budgets or forecasts for subsequent periods, using a steady state or declining growth rate after five years, unless a higher one can be justified from objective information about patterns over a product or industry lifecycle.[100] A growth rate not exceeding the 'long-term average growth rate for the products, industries, or country or countries in which the enterprise operates, or for the market in which the asset is used' must be chosen unless a higher one can be justified.[101]

Cash flow projections will include:

(a) cash inflows from continuing use of the asset;

(b) cash outflows necessary to generate the cash inflows from continuing use, including any costs to complete the asset and the estimated costs of directly attributable and allocated overheads; and

(c) net cash flows from the disposal of the asset at the end of its useful life.[102] This is an estimate of the arm's length selling price, taking account of the costs of disposal.[103]

The projected cash flows must be for the asset in its present condition and may not include the effects of a restructuring to which the entity is not yet committed, or that of future capital expenditure that will improve the asset's standard of performance. However, once the organisation is committed to a restructuring (as defined and governed by IAS 37) estimates of future cash inflows and outflows that reflect the cost savings and other benefits of the restructuring should be used in determining VIU.[104] Treatment of such a future restructuring is illustrated in Appendix A Example 5. In the case of capital expenditure to enhance the performance of an asset, future cash flow estimates may not include the benefits of this expenditure until is actually incurred.[105] The purpose of this provision is clearly to prevent the construction of imaginary cash flows. The treatment is illustrated in Appendix A Example 6.

Cash flows should exclude the effects of financing activities and taxes.[106] The projections may include general price increases or not, but in either case the discount rate must be selected accordingly.[107] They should be determined in the currency in which they will be generated and discounted using a rate appropriate for that currency. Foreign currency cash flows are translated into the reporting currency of the entity using the period end exchange rate.[108]

B The value in use (VIU) calculation – the discount rate

There is little guidance in IAS 36 about the selection of a suitable discount rate, other than that it should be a pre-tax rate that reflects current market assessments of the time value of money and the risks specific to the asset.[109] The underlying intention is that the rate should reflect the return that investors would require if they were to invest in the asset being tested at the time the impairment test is being conducted.[110] Thus the implicit effect of the impairment test, as explained above in the UK context, is that businesses must earn market rates of return on their assets.

'As a starting point, the enterprise may take into account the following rates:

(a) the enterprise's weighted average cost of capital determined using techniques such as the Capital Asset Pricing Model;

(b) the enterprise's incremental borrowing rate; and

(c) other market borrowing rates.'[111]

The standard gives a few more guidelines for selecting the appropriate discount rate:

- it should be adjusted to reflect the specific risks associated with the projected cash flows (such as country, currency, price and cash flow risks) and to exclude risks that are not relevant;[112]
- to avoid double counting, the discount rate does not reflect risks for which future cash flow estimates have been adjusted;[113]
- the discount rate is independent of the entity's capital structure and the way it financed the purchase of the asset.[114]
- if the basis for the rate is post-tax (such as a weighted average cost of capital), it is adjusted to reflect a pre-tax rate[115]; and
- the entity should use separate discount rates for different future periods if the VIU is sensitive to different risks or the terms structure of interest rates.[116]

Therefore the standard is even less specific than FRS 11 as it allows (see (b) above) that the marginal borrowing rate of the business is relevant to the selection of a discount rate. This may sit a bit uncomfortably with the statement (see the third bullet point above) that the discount rate should be independent of the entity's capital structure or the way in which it financed the purchase of the asset.

The selection of discount rates is crucial to the result of the VIU calculation. The ambiguity and lack of detailed guidance on rate selection in both the UK and international impairment standards is unfortunate and may easily give rise to genuine differences over VIU calculations under similar conditions.

C Identification of cash-generating units (CGUs)

The recoverable amount is normally measured for an individual asset, except for cases where the cash flows are interdependent with those from other assets or groups of assets and the VIU cannot be estimated to be close to the net selling price. In such cases, the recoverable amount should be measured at the level of the CGU to which the asset belongs.[117]

Identifying CGUs requires judgement. They should be defined consistently from period to period; if assets are reallocated and there is a material impairment or restatement, there are additional disclosure requirements (see 5 below). A CGU is presumed to exist where there is an active market for the output of an asset or group of assets, even if some or all of the output is used internally. If this is the case, management's best estimate of future market prices for the output should be used in determining the VIU of this CGU.[118] The Standard includes in Appendix A Example 1 a number of illustrations of identification of CGUs.

The carrying amount of a CGU, which should include only directly attributable or allocated assets, must be determined on a basis this is consistent with the unit's recoverable amount.[119]However, the standard notes that for practical reasons the carrying amount of the CGU may include financial assets (such as receivables) or various liabilities, such as payables, pensions or other provisions. Presumably, this is where the entity has been unable to exclude the cash flows relating to these items, which the standard suggests should normally be done.[120]

IAS 36 specifies how goodwill and corporate assets that cannot be directly identified with a given CGU are to be treated. It refers to the normal allocation of assets including goodwill and corporate assets to CGUs as the 'bottom up' test.

If the entity cannot allocate goodwill the 'top down' method is required, that is, 'the enterprise should:

(i) identify the smallest cash-generating unit that includes the cash-generating unit under review and to which the carrying amount of goodwill can be allocated on a reasonable and consistent basis (the 'larger' cash-generating unit); and

(ii) then, compare the recoverable amount of the larger cash-generating unit to its carrying amount (including the carrying amount of allocated goodwill)'[121]

This same method applies to corporate assets. The exact nature of these depends upon the circumstances, but research centres, head offices, computer and data systems in general use would be typical examples.[122]

The standard includes illustrative examples of the 'bottom-up' and 'top-down' tests of goodwill and the allocation of corporate assets in Appendix A Examples 7 and 8.

4.2.4 *The recognition of impairment losses*

Impairment losses under IAS 36 should be recognised in the income statement as an expense immediately.[123] The standard does not indicate where in the statement such losses should be shown. After an impairment loss is recognised, the depreciation charge should be adjusted to allocate the asset's revised carrying amount, less any residual value, systematically over its remaining useful life.[124]

If an impairment loss is recognised, any related deferred tax items are to be determined using the revised carrying amounts in accordance with IAS 12.[125] Appendix A Example 3 illustrates the possible effects. This is also discussed in Chapter 24 at 5.3.2A.

The allocation of impairment losses to the assets within a CGU is different under IAS 36 than under FRS 11. Both IAS 36 and FRS 11 require impairment losses first to reduce the value of any goodwill. Thereafter IAS 36 requires losses to be set pro-rata against all the remaining assets within the CGU, a process that it admits is arbitrary.[126] FRS 11 by contrast requires any remaining intangible assets to be reduced before the tangible assets (see 2 above). Under IAS 36, no individual asset may be reduced below the highest of its net selling price, VIU and zero. However, if the recoverable amount of an individual asset cannot be determined, because it is part of a CGU, no impairment loss will be recognised if the related CGU is not impaired. This is the case even if the asset's carrying value is above its net selling price.[127]

IAS 36 includes at Appendix A Example 2 an example of the calculation, recognition and allocation of an impairment loss across CGUs and the goodwill attributed to them.

If the amount estimated as the impairment loss is greater than the carrying amount of the asset to which it relates, an enterprise may recognise a liability only if it would be required by another standard.[128] This is to prevent the recognition of future operating losses.

If an entity will be compensated by third parties for the impairment of property, plant and equipment, the impairment of the assets, receipt of compensation and purchase of replacement assets should each be accounted for separately. The entity should disclose separately any monetary or non-monetary compensation recognised for the impairment or loss of tangible assets.[129]

FRS 11 contains extremely complex rules on how goodwill should be treated when an existing business has been combined with a purchased one, and an indicator of impairment is recognised. IAS 36 does not contain any specific guidance, which presumably means that an entity can, in effect, take internally-generated goodwill in the existing business into account in assessing goodwill – as well, of course, as goodwill generated by both parts of the business since acquisition. IAS 36 does not include a requirement for a five year post-impairment cash flow monitoring period, in contrast to FRS 11 that does.

4.2.5 *The reversal of impairment losses*

Under IAS 36 businesses should assess at each balance sheet date whether there are any indications that an impairment recognised in a previous period has reversed. If any such indications exist, the VIU test must be done to quantify the reversal.[130] The standard sets out examples of what are in effect 'reverse indications' of impairment. These are the reverse of those set out in paragraph 9 of the standard as indications of impairment (see 4.2.2 above) and are:

> 'External sources of information
>
> (a) the asset's market value has increased significantly during the period;
>
> (b) significant changes with a favourable effect on the enterprise have taken place during the period, or will take place in the near future, in the technological, market, economic or legal environment in which the enterprise operates or in the market to which the asset is dedicated;
>
> (c) market interest rates or other market rates of return on investments have decreased during the period, and those decreases are likely to affect the discount rate used in calculating the asset's value in use and increase the asset's recoverable amount materially;
>
> Internal sources of information
>
> (d) significant changes with a favourable effect on the enterprise have taken place during the period, or are expected to take place in the near future, in the extent to which, or manner in which, the asset is used or is expected to be used. These changes include capital expenditure that has been incurred during the period to improve or enhance an asset in excess of its originally assessed standard of performance or a commitment to discontinue or restructure the operation to which the asset belongs; and
>
> (e) evidence is available from internal reporting that indicates that the economic performance of the asset is, or will be, better than expected.'[131]

However there are two notable omissions from this list of 'reverse indicators'. One important external indication not included, is one that reverses 'the carrying amount of the net assets of the reporting enterprise is more than its market capitalisation'. No explanation is provided about why, if a market capitalisation below shareholders' funds is an indication of impairment, its reversal should not be an indication of a reversal. The second omission from the list of 'reverse indicators' is that evidence of obsolescence or physical deterioration has been reversed, presumably because there would have to be further expenditure on the asset. This would be subject to the capitalisation rules described in Chapter 12, which include a requirement that the asset's carrying value does not exceed its recoverable amount.

Reversal, like impairment, is evidence that depreciation method or residual value should be reviewed and may need to be adjusted.[132]

Impairment losses should only be reversed only if there has been a change in the estimates used to determine the impairment loss, e.g. a change in cash flows or discount rate (for VIU) or a change in net selling price. IAS 36 like its UK counterpart does not allow the mere passage of time, (the unwinding of the discount) to trigger the reversal of an impairment. In other words the 'service potential' of the asset must genuinely improve if a reversal is to be recognised.[133]

In the event of an asset's impairment being reversed, the reversal may not raise the carrying value above the figure it would have stood at taking into account depreciation, if no impairment had originally been recognised.[134] All reversals are to be recognised in the income statement immediately, except for revalued assets which are dealt with below.[135]

The Standard includes an example of the reversal of an impairment loss in Appendix A Example 4.

A Reversals of impairments - revalued assets

If an asset is recognised at a revalued amount under another IAS any reversal of an impairment loss should be treated as a revaluation increase under that other international standard. Thus a reversal of an impairment loss on a revalued asset is credited directly to equity under the heading revaluation surplus. However, to the extent that an impairment loss on the same revalued asset was previously recognised as an expense in the income statement, a reversal of that impairment loss is recognised as income in the income statement.[136]

As with assets carried at cost, after a reversal of an impairment loss is recognised on a revalued asset, the depreciation charge should be adjusted in future periods to allocate the asset's revised carrying amount, less any residual value, on a systematic basis over its remaining useful life.[137]

B Reversals of impairments – cash-generating units

Where an entity recognises a reversal of an impairment loss on a CGU, the increase in the carrying amount of the assets of the unit should be allocated by increasing the carrying amount of the assets other than goodwill in the unit on a pro-rata basis. However, the carrying amount of an individual asset should not be increased above the lower of its recoverable amount and the carrying amount that would have resulted had no impairment loss been recognised in prior years.[138]

Normally the carrying amount of goodwill is not reversed, unless the impairment loss was caused by a specific external event of an exceptional nature that is outside the control of the entity, that is not expected to recur, and subsequent external events have occurred that reverse the effect of that event.[139]

4.3 The impairment requirements of IAS 16

IAS 16 has a general requirement that all assets recognised under that standard are subject to the impairment requirements of IAS 36.[140]

It makes an exception for an impairment loss recognised before the end of the first annual accounting period commencing after a business combination that is an acquisition. In this case the impairment should be recognised in accordance with the special rules contained within IAS 22, explained below.

In addition IAS 16 specifies that any assets that are retired from active use and held for resale must be tested for impairment at least at each period end.[141]

4.4 The impairment requirements of IAS 22

IAS 22 also contains a general requirement that any goodwill arising on acquisitions is subject to the impairment rules of IAS 36. In addition it recognises the possibility of a deal being recognised as less advantageous than was thought during the early stages after finalisation. In this case the goodwill recognised becomes immediately subject to an impairment test in accordance with the requirements of IAS 36.[142]

IAS 22 also contains, in paragraph 56, a stipulation that any goodwill being ascribed a useful life of more than 20 years must be reviewed annually for impairment, whether or not indications of impairment exist.

There are circumstances envisaged in IAS 22 where the carrying amount of goodwill can be adjusted to compensate for an impairment loss recognised in the first annual accounting period beginning after acquisition. If this is in connection with an identifiable asset and liability acquired, and the impairment loss does not relate to specific events or changes in circumstances occurring after the date of acquisition, then the goodwill arising on the acquisition can be adjusted accordingly (see Chapter 11 at 5.2.1).[143] However the goodwill so adjusted must not be at a figure higher than its recoverable amount as determined by IAS 36.[144]

4.5 The impairment requirements of IAS 38

Like the standards described above, IAS 38 – *Intangible assets* – has a general requirement for all intangible assets to be subject to the requirements of IAS 36.[145] It also recognises a similar exception to that described above for goodwill under IAS 22, for other intangible assets:

> 'if an impairment loss occurs before the end of the first annual accounting period commencing after acquisition for an intangible asset acquired in a business combination that was an acquisition, the impairment loss is recognised as an adjustment to both the amount assigned to the intangible asset and the goodwill (negative goodwill) recognised at the date of acquisition.'[146]

However, if the impairment loss was caused by specific events or changes in circumstances occurring *after* the date of acquisition, the impairment loss is recognised under IAS 36 and not as an adjustment to the amount assigned to the goodwill recognised at the date of acquisition. IAS 38 also requires that any intangible assets being amortised over more than twenty years, or any intangible assets not available for use, are subject to an impairment test at each period end regardless of whether or not indications of impairment are present.[147] The requirements of IAS 38 are described in detail in Chapter 11 at 5.3.

In addition IAS 38, like IAS 16, specifies that any intangible assets that are retired from active use and held for resale must be tested for impairment at least at each period end.[148]

4.6 The impairment requirements of IAS 40

If the fair value model is chosen under IAS 40 then IAS 36 does not apply, in effect because investment property in this situation should always be carried at its realisable value.

If the cost model is chosen, then the investment property is subject to the requirements of IAS 16, including its impairment requirements, dealt with above.

5 REQUIRED IAS DISCLOSURES

5.1 Introduction

This section sets out the principal disclosures required in financial statements complied under IAS for impairment as set out in IAS 36 – *Impairment of assets*. The disclosures relevant to this topic required by IAS 22 and IAS 38 are set out in Chapter 11 at 6.2 and 6.3 respectively, while those relevant to impairment in IAS 16 are included in Chapter 12 at 6.2. However any disclosures required by other authorities such as national statutes are not included.

5.2 IAS 36 disclosures

For each class of assets, the financial statements should disclose:

‘(a) the amount of impairment losses recognised in the income statement during the period and the line item(s) of the income statement in which those impairment losses are included;

(b) the amount of reversals of impairment losses recognised in the income statement during the period and the line item(s) of the income statement in which those impairment losses are reversed;

(c) the amount of impairment losses recognised directly in equity during the period; and

(d) the amount of reversals of impairment losses recognised directly in equity during the period.’[149]

A class of assets is defined as a grouping of assets of a similar nature or use.[150]

These disclosures can be made as an integral part of the other disclosures, for example the property plant and equipment note reconciling the opening and closing values (as set out in Chapter 12 at 6.2) may contain the required information.[151]

Segmental disclosures

The most interesting disclosure requirement in IAS 36 is the linking of any impairment with the segment disclosures. If a business is subject to IAS 14 – *Segment reporting* – then any impairments or reversals must be disclosed by reportable segment.[152]

Material impairments

If an impairment loss for an *individual* asset or an *individual* cash-generating unit is recognised or reversed during the period and is material to the financial statements of the reporting enterprise as a whole, an enterprise should disclose:

(a) the events and circumstances that led to the recognition or reversal of the impairment loss;

(b) the amount of the impairment loss recognised or reversed;

(c) for an individual asset:

  (i) the nature of the asset; and

  (ii) the reportable segment to which the asset belongs, based on the enterprise's primary format;

(d) for a cash-generating unit:

  (i) a description of the cash-generating unit (such as whether it is a product line, a plant, a business operation, a geographical area, a reportable segment or other);

  (ii) the amount of the impairment loss recognised or reversed by class of assets and by reportable segment based on the enterprise's primary format; and

  (iii) if the aggregation of assets for identifying the cash-generating unit has changed since the previous estimate of the cash-generating unit's recoverable amount (if any), the enterprise should describe the current and former way of aggregating assets and the reasons for changing the way the cash-generating unit is identified;

(e) whether the recoverable amount of the asset or cash-generating unit is its net selling price or its VIU;

(f) if recoverable amount is net selling price, the basis used to determine net selling price (such as whether selling price was determined by reference to an active market or in some other way); and

(g) if recoverable amount is VIU, the discount rate used in the current estimate and previous estimate (if any) of VIU.[153]

If the impairment adjustments *in aggregate* are material to the financial statements of the business, and the main classes of assets affected by these impairment losses or reversals are not disclosed any other way, these main classes affected must be disclosed. Finally the main events and circumstances that led to the recognition or reversal of any material impairment losses, for which no information is disclosed on an individual basis, must be disclosed.[154]

IAS 36 encourages the disclosure of key assumptions made in the recoverable amount calculations used to determine any impairments recognised in the period.[155]

Novartis in Extract 13.7 gives an illustration of impairment policy under IAS; it is interesting that the company makes the point that the projections associated with the exercise can vary significantly from the actual outcomes.

Extract 13.7: Novartis AG (2000)

Accounting Policies

Tangible Fixed Assets [extract]

Long lived assets, including identifiable intangibles and goodwill, are reviewed for impairment whenever events or changes in circumstances indicate that the carrying amount of the asset may not be recoverable. When such events or changes in circumstances indicate the asset may not be recoverable, the Group estimates the future cash flows expected to result from the use of the asset and its eventual disposition. If the sum of such expected discounted future cash flows is less than the carrying amount of the asset, an impairment loss is recognised for the amount by which the asset's net book value exceeds its fair market value. For purposes of assessing impairment, assets are grouped at the lowest level for which there are separately identifiable cash flows. Fair value can be based on sale of similar assets, or other estimates of fair value such as discounting estimated future cash flows. Considerable management judgment is necessary to estimate discounted future cash flows. Accordingly, actual outcomes could vary significantly from such estimates.

Extract 13.8 shows the impairment write down disclosure given by Dansico. This extract shows the income statement disclosure note, and the fixed asset disclosure for one of the categories of asset that was impaired.

Extract 13.8: Danisco A/S (2000)

Notes [extract]

Parent company			Group	
1998/99	**1999/00**	DKK million	1998/99	**1999/00**
		3 Depreciation writedown [extract]		
		Writedowns for the year included in the costs below:		
–	–	Other operating expenses	3	**–**
–	–	Writedown of fixed assets	–	**1,495**
–	–	**Total**	–	**1,495**

Group

11. Intangible fixed assets [extract]

DKK million	Goodwill	Soft-ware	Patents and licences	Product develop-ment	Other	Total
Depreciation and writedowns at 1 May 1999	1,401	3	31	5	–	**1,440**
Exchange adj. of opening value, etc.	51	–	4	–	2	**57**
Disposals due to sale of activities	-223	–	–	–	-1	**-224**
Depreciation for disposals of the year	-8	–	–	–	–	**-8**
Depreciation for the year	539	25	48	5	25	**642**
Writedowns for the year etc.	831	–	–	–	28	**859**
Total	**2,591**	**28**	**83**	**10**	**54**	**2,766**

6 CONCLUSION

The two impairment standards FRS 11 and IAS 36 both rest upon the same underlying concept and both tackle the impairment test in the same manner. FRS 11 is a complicated standard, both in terms of its provisions and in terms of how it is to be implemented in practice. The selection of a suitable discount rate is a case in point: as a small alteration in the discount rate used can have an enormous effect on the VIU, there is inevitably scope for genuine differences of opinion to occur in practice. In fact, there is so little guidance in the standards on selection of a suitable discount rate, that it raises the possibility that an impairment provision could, to some extent at least, be regarded as optional.

The international standard is slightly less complex than its UK equivalent, particularly as it omits in its entirety the part of FRS 11 surrounding the treatment of goodwill in an IGU made up of acquired and internal businesses. However IAS 36 is inevitably open to the same criticisms as FRS 11 because of its conceptual similarity. IAS 36 is even more vague than FRS 11 when it comes to the selection of discount rates. For example the advice it gives on the selection of a discount rate when an asset-specific rate is not available from the market, taken from paragraph 51, is a masterpiece of deliberate fence-sitting

'As a starting point, the enterprise may take into account the following rates:

(a) the enterprise's weighted average cost of capital determined using techniques such as the Capital Asset Pricing Model;

(b) the enterprise's incremental borrowing rate; and

(c) other market borrowing rates.'

Such a spread of rates is implied here that the comparability requirement that underlies the entire framework of the IASC's standards is obviously in danger of being lost. Accounting is straying into economics with the way the impairment standards have been drafted. It is possible that by not specifying more definitely how the discount rate is to be chosen, the standard setters have avoided academic economic criticism that might otherwise attend the specification of a definite rate, or method of choosing one. Whatever the reason is, the practitioner and the preparer, who have more immediate concerns, are entitled to a standard which gives more definite guidance.

An important achievement of the standard has been to bring a necessary prominence to the general Companies Act requirements to recognise impairments in value. So it is ironic that having introduced an impairment standard which brings into focus the possible overvaluation of assets, the ASB has subsequently downgraded prudence as a fundamental accounting concept with the replacement of SSAP 2 by FRS 18. We are of course in favour of a prudent approach to asset valuation, indeed we consider this will become a serious issue under the fair value based accounting the ASB and the IASB appear intent upon introducing. Whether the manner in which the standard goes about the task is too complicated, too detailed in some areas and too open in others, thus rendering it therefore less helpful, is the question.

The adoption of fair value based accounting, which we consider to be on the agenda of both the ASB and the IASB, will place further strains on the part to be played by an impairment standard in the future. When there is an income statement that contains a mix of both realised and unrealised gains and losses, resulting from the recognition at fair value of all types of assets and liabilities both financial and non-financial, huge reliance will rest on the identification of impairment.

The impairment test will become more important as time passes, for two reasons. First, the blanket prohibition on the recognition of most internally generated intangible assets is not sustainable indefinitely in a world that places ever greater value on information. Arguably it is not justified under present conditions except on the grounds of common prudence. Certainly there is no theoretical soundness to the recognition of an intangible you bought, but not an equivalent you made, any more than if the same attitude were taken to a self-constructed tangible fixed asset. Therefore impairment becomes a key issue, in effect the modern prudence principle, in the recognition of internally generated intangible assets.

Second, the advent of fair value accounting itself places a premium on impairment because once an asset is stated at a valuation, a test is going to be required to ensure that the value is fair. Most assets used by manufacturing businesses, which still remain the core of the world economy, do not have observable market prices in the stock market sense. If they are to be placed on company balance sheets at valuations that directly affect the income statement, then a useable, comparable, unambiguous impairment test becomes a necessity rather than a priority.

References

1 CA 85, Sch. 4, para. 19(2).
2 *Ibid.*, Sch. 4, para. 19(2).
3 *Ibid.*, Sch. 4, para. 19(2).
4 *Ibid.*, Sch. 4, para. 19(3).
5 *Ibid.*, Sch. 4, paras. 19(1) and (2). The use of the word 'shown' makes the wording ambiguous, but it is generally considered to mean that the provisions must be made through the profit and loss account and either disclosed on the face of the profit and loss account or in the notes to the accounts.
6 *Ibid.,* s275(1).
7 FRS 11, *Impairment of fixed assets and goodwill*, ASB, July 1998, para. 74.
8 *Ibid.*, para. 1.
9 *Ibid.*, para. 5.
10 FRS 13, *Derivatives and Other Financial Instruments: Disclosures*, ASB, September 1998, para. 5.
11 FRS 11, para. 7.
12 *Ibid.*, para. 2.
13 *Ibid.*, para. 8.
14 *Ibid.*, para. 13.
15 *Ibid.*, para. 10.
16 *Ibid.*, para. 17.
17 *Ibid.*, para. 11.
18 *Ibid.*, para. 10.
19 *Ibid.*, para. 11.
20 *Ibid.*, para. 14.
21 *Ibid.*, para. 14 and 63
22 *Ibid.*, para. 19.
23 *Ibid.*, para. 21.
24 *Ibid.*, paras. 16 and 23.
25 *Ibid.*, para. 17.
26 *Ibid.*, para. 27.
27 *Ibid.*, para. 29.
28 *Ibid.*, Examples 1-4.
29 *Ibid.*, para. 30.
30 *Ibid.*, para. 30.
31 *Ibid.*, para. 32.
32 *Ibid.*, para. 34.
33 *Ibid.*, para. 33.
34 *Ibid.* para. 36.
35 *Ibid.* para. 37.
36 *Ibid.* para. 38.
37 *Ibid.* para. 39.
38 *Ibid.* para. 41.
39 *Ibid.* para. 11.
40 *Ibid.* para. 42.
41 *Ibid.* para. 43.
42 One source of reference which may prove useful is a Digest issued by the Corporate Finance Faculty of the ICAEW – *The Cost of Capital*, Simon Pallett, ICAEW, 1999.
43 FRS 11, para. 44.
44 *Ibid.*, Appendix I.
45 *Ibid.*, para. 46.
46 *Ibid.*, para. 45.
47 *Ibid.*, para. 48.
48 *Ibid.*, para. 49.
49 *Ibid.*, para. 2.
50 *Ibid.*, para. 49.
51 *Ibid.*, para. 54
52 *Ibid.*, para. 55.
53 *Ibid.*, para. 56.
54 *Ibid.*, para. 57.
55 *Ibid.*, para. 58.
56 *Ibid.*, para. 60.
57 *Ibid.*, para. 60.
58 *Ibid.*, para. 70.
59 *Ibid.*, para. 61.
60 *Ibid.*, para. 50.
61 *Ibid.*, para. 52.
62 *Ibid.*, para. 50.
63 *Ibid.*, para. 52.
64 FRS 10, para. 34.
65 *Ibid.*, para. 39.
66 *Ibid.*, para. 34(a).
67 *Ibid.*, para. 35.
68 *Ibid.*, para. 40(b).

69 *Ibid.*, para. 41(b).
70 *Ibid.*, para. 42.
71 FRS 15, para. 89.
72 FRS 11, para. 67.
73 *Ibid.*
74 *Ibid.*
75 *Ibid.*, para. 68.
76 *Ibid.*, para. 69.
77 *Ibid.*, para. 70.
78 *Ibid.*, para. 71.
79 *Ibid.*, para. 72.
80 *Ibid.*, para. 73.
81 IAS 36, *Impairment of assets*, IASC, April 1998, Objective.
82 *Ibid.*, para. 1.
83 *Ibid.*, para. 3.
84 *Ibid.*, para. 5.
85 *Ibid.*, para. 8.
86 *Ibid.*, para. 12.
87 *Ibid.*, para. 10.
88 *Ibid.*, para. 9.
89 *Ibid.*, para. 11.
90 *Ibid.*, para. 13.
91 *Ibid.*, para. 14.
92 *Ibid.*, para. 16.
93 *Ibid.*, para. 17.
94 *Ibid.*, para. 21.
95 *Ibid.*, para. 22.
96 *Ibid.*, para. 23.
97 *Ibid.*, para. 24.
98 *Ibid.*, para. 27.
99 *Ibid.*, paras. 27 and 28.
100 *Ibid.*, para. 27.
101 *Ibid.*, para. 27.
102 *Ibid.*, para. 32, 34 and 35.
103 *Ibid.*, paras. 45 and 46.
104 *Ibid.*, paras. 37-40.
105 *Ibid.*, para. 41.
106 *Ibid.*, paras. 43 and 44.
107 *Ibid.*, para. 33.
108 *Ibid.*, para. 47.
109 *Ibid.*, para. 48.
110 *Ibid.*, para. 49.
111 *Ibid.*, para. 51.
112 *Ibid.*, para. 52.
113 *Ibid.*, para. 53.
114 *Ibid.*, para. 54.
115 *Ibid.*, para. 55.
116 *Ibid.*, para. 56.
117 *Ibid.*, paras. 65 and 66.
118 *Ibid.*, paras. 67-72.
119 *Ibid.*, paras. 74 and 75.
120 *Ibid.*, paras. 36 and 78.
121 *Ibid.*, paras. 80-83.
122 *Ibid.*, paras. 84-86.
123 *Ibid.*, paras. 59 and 60.
124 *Ibid.*, para. 62.
125 *Ibid.*, para. 63
126 *Ibid.*, para. 88
127 *Ibid.*, paras.89 and 92.
128 *Ibid.*, paras. 61 and 93.
129 SIC-14, paras. 4-5.
130 IAS 36, para. 95.
131 *Ibid.*, para. 96.
132 *Ibid.*, para. 98.
133 *Ibid.*, paras. 99-101.
134 *Ibid.*, para. 102.
135 *Ibid.*, para. 104.
136 *Ibid.*, paras. 103 and 105.
137 *Ibid.*, para. 106.
138 *Ibid.*, paras.107 and 108.
139 *Ibid.*, para. 109-112.
140 IAS 16, para. 53.
141 *Ibid.*, para. 59.
142 IAS 22, para. 53.
143 *Ibid.*, para. 71.
144 *Ibid.*, para. 74.
145 IAS 38, para. 97.
146 *Ibid.*, para. 98.
147 *Ibid.*, para. 99.
148 *Ibid.*, para. 106.
149 IAS 36, para. 113.
150 *Ibid.*, para. 114.
151 *Ibid.*, para. 115.
152 *Ibid.*, para. 116.
153 *Ibid.*, para. 117.
154 *Ibid.*, para. 118.
155 *Ibid.*, para. 119.

Chapter 14 Investments

1 INTRODUCTION

Investments come in so many different forms, and may be held for such different purposes, that it can be difficult to formulate a precise definition of them. Although not directly relevant to financial reporting, the Financial Services Act 1986 includes the following in its definition of an investment:

- shares and stock in the share capital of a company;
- debentures, including debenture stock, loan stock, bonds, certificates of deposit and other instruments creating or acknowledging indebtedness including those issued by public bodies;
- warrants or other instruments entitling the holder to subscribe for any of the above;
- certificates or other instruments which confer property rights in respect of the above, rights to acquire, dispose of, underwrite or convert an investment, and rights (other than options) to acquire investments other than by subscription;
- units in collective investment schemes including shares in or securities of an open-ended investment company;
- options to acquire or dispose of currency, gold or silver, or any investment as defined in the Act, including other options;
- futures;
- contracts for differences and similar instruments;
- long-term insurance contracts; and
- rights and interests in any of the above.[1]

Each of these is further described in some detail by the Act.

In 1990, the ASC published an exposure draft on the subject, ED 55 – *Accounting for investments*, but it has never been progressed further. Its definition of investments was at the other end of the spectrum; whereas the Financial Services Act is highly specific, ED 55's definition was very general. It defined an investment simply as 'an asset that is characterised by its ability to generate economic benefits in the form of distributions and/or appreciation in value'.[2] This was a slight variant of the equivalent in the then international accounting standard on the subject, which said that 'an investment is an asset held by an enterprise for the accretion of wealth through distribution (such as interest, royalties, dividends and rentals), for capital appreciation or for other benefits to the investing enterprise such as those obtained through trading relationships'.[3]

Although they would otherwise fall within the above definition, investment properties were excluded from the scope of ED 55 because they are dealt with in a separate accounting standard, SSAP 19. They are similarly excluded from the scope of this chapter, but are discussed in Chapter 12.

As mentioned above, enterprises may hold investments for a variety of different purposes. For example, an investment may be held:

- as a short-term store of wealth, perhaps by a seasonal business during the part of the year when its stocks are low, or by any enterprise for a period pending investment in operational assets;
- as a trading asset, by an enterprise whose business entails dealing in investments for profit;
- as a means of exercising control or influence over another enterprise which becomes its subsidiary or associated undertaking as a result;
- as a trade investment, to form a long-term but less influential relationship with another enterprise in a similar line of business;
- as a means of building up resources to meet long-term obligations, as in the case of a pension fund or an insurance company;
- as a means of hedging against some obligation of the enterprise, where the investment and the obligation have certain risk-related characteristics in common;
- as part of a managed portfolio of investments, in order to allow members of the enterprise to spread their risk without having to invest directly in the underlying components of the portfolio, as in the case of investment trusts and unit trusts.

Schedule 4 to the Companies Act addresses accounting for investments at a general level, but does not apply to banking and insurance companies, which are governed by separate schedules of their own. There are also some particular provisions for investment companies in Schedule 4 itself.[4] It is beyond the scope of this book to discuss detailed requirements for companies in specialised industries, and accordingly this chapter will confine itself to the general requirements for accounting for investments.[5]

In the absence of any accounting standard,[6] the Companies Act remains the only source of rules on accounting for investments in the UK. As indicated above, the ASB never progressed ED 55; however, the current international project on financial instruments, in which both the ASB and IASC are participating, is broad enough to embrace almost all investments within its scope and this is likely to form the basis of accounting for investments in the future. This project, and some of the background to it, is covered in Chapter 10 at 1.1; the IASC's interim standard on accounting for financial instruments, IAS 39, is covered briefly in 3 below and in detail in Chapter 10 at 4. The present UK statutory requirements are discussed in 2 below.

2 REQUIREMENTS FOR ACCOUNTING FOR INVESTMENTS

2.1 Classification

The formats in Schedule 4 to the Companies Act 1985 indicate that investments may be classified as either fixed asset investments or current asset investments. The available categories within each are shown opposite:[7]

B	**Fixed assets**
III	Investments
	1. Shares in group undertakings
	2. Loans to group undertakings
	3. Participating interests
	4. Loans to undertakings in which the group has a participating interest
	5. Other investments other than loans
	6. Other loans
	7. Own shares
C	**Current assets**
III	Investments
	1. Shares in group undertakings
	2. Own shares
	3. Other investments

The Act does not have a particular rule for distinguishing between fixed and current asset *investments*. It is necessary to apply the general rule that a fixed asset is one which is intended for use on a continuing basis in the company's activities and a current asset is one not intended for such use.[8] However, this is an unhelpful distinction for investments which, by their nature, are not intended for *use* in a company's activities at all, whether on a continuing basis or otherwise.

2.2 Accounting rules

2.2.1 *Fixed asset investments*

The general statutory rule for the valuation of a fixed asset applies, namely that it should be included at its purchase price (production cost is an irrelevant alternative for an investment).[9] Purchase price includes any expenses incidental to its acquisition,[10] which will normally only include relatively minor dealing costs and stamp duty, but in the context of a contested takeover of a public company, the incidental costs may be very significant indeed.

A Revaluations

Where the alternative accounting rules are invoked, fixed asset investments may be carried either at their market value determined at the date of their last valuation or at a directors' valuation.[11] The latter may be on any basis which appears to the directors to be appropriate in the circumstances of the company, so long as details of the basis and the reasons for adopting it are disclosed in a note to the accounts. One common practice is to include investments in subsidiary and/or associated undertakings in the balance sheet of the parent company at their net asset value, as shown in this extract:

Extract 14.1: Royal & Sun Alliance Insurance Group plc (2000)

Accounting Policies
Investments [extract]

Investments in subsidiaries are included in the Parent Company balance sheet at net asset value and unrealised gains and losses are dealt with in the revaluation reserve.

Where a revalued investment is subsequently sold, FRS 3 requires the profit or loss to be measured by reference to its revalued amount rather than its book value.[12] Any net surplus previously credited to and retained in the revaluation reserve may normally be released to the profit and loss account as a reserve transfer. The treatment is slightly different for investment companies as defined in the Companies Act.[13] Their articles prohibit them from distributing gains on disposal of investments and accordingly they are required to deal with capital gains and losses, both realised and unrealised, in the STRGL.[14]

B Amortisation of premiums and discounts on acquisition

Investments are not excluded from the depreciation rules of the Act (although they are outside the scope of FRS 15, which deals only with tangible fixed assets), but these usually do not apply because most investments have an indefinite life. However, for investments such as dated gilts, bonds or redeemable preference shares that are to be held to maturity it is common to amortise the premium or discount to redemption over their term.

The Post Office discloses such a policy, as shown in this extract:

Extract 14.2: The Post Office (2001)

Accounting policies and general notes
H Investments [extract]

(ii) Financial investments held as fixed assets are stated in the balance sheet on the basis of cost adjusted so as to amortise to redemption value over the period to maturity. If sold before maturity, the difference between the proceeds and the amortised value is taken to the profit and loss account in the year of realisation.

GlaxoSmithKline discloses a policy of recognising income on this basis for such investments if they are to be held to redemption, although it is not entirely clear why such a condition should apply to investments held as current assets, as shown in this policy:

Extract 14.3: GlaxoSmithKline plc (2000)

3 Accounting policies
Current asset investments [extract]

… In the case of securities acquired at a significant premium or discount to maturity value, and intended to be held to redemption, cost is adjusted to amortise the premium or discount over the life to maturity of the security. …

A policy of amortising premiums or discounts is most frequently applied to gilts, but is equally relevant to other types of redeemable security, such as deep discounted bonds. The application of this policy is considered further at 2.2.4 A below.

C Diminutions in value and impairments

Fixed asset investments are also subject to the statutory requirement to write them down to reflect any permanent diminution in their value. Such a provision is to be charged in the profit and loss account, except to the extent it reverses a revaluation gain reported in the STRGL, and is to be released if it is subsequently found to be unnecessary, with disclosure of the amounts in each case.[15] As well as these requirements, which apply to all fixed assets, the Act specifically allows provision to be made against the value of fixed asset investments even where their fall in value is not expected to be permanent.[16]

FRS 11 – *Impairment of Fixed Assets and Goodwill* – contains further rules on the impairment of fixed assets and states that where an impairment 'is caused by a clear consumption of economic benefits' the entire loss should be recognised in the profit and loss account,[17] even if it reverses a previous revaluation gain. However it scopes out most investments, essentially those that are covered by the ASB's project on financial instruments,[18] which means that it addresses only investments in subsidiaries, associates and the like in the accounts of the parent, whose unconsolidated profit and loss account is seldom published.

One particular issue which frequently arises is how a holding company should deal with investments in subsidiaries whose value has been impaired, either as a result of trading losses or following a group reconstruction.

If a subsidiary company has made losses then the amount at which the investment is stated in the parent company's balance sheet may exceed its 'recoverable amount' as defined in FRS 11 (see Chapter 13), in which case the parent must recognise a loss in its own accounts. As described above, it is quite common for holding companies to carry investments in subsidiaries at their consolidated net asset value, taking movements to revaluation reserve. Any fall in net asset value as a result of losses does not necessarily mean that the investment is not recoverable in terms of FRS 11 – the test is still whether the carrying amount of the investment can be recouped, whether through future dividend streams or proceeds of sale, albeit using a discounting methodology. However, where an impairment of this kind is identified, then it should be charged to the profit and loss account.

In 2001 QXL ricardo recognised an impairment in the carrying value of a number of its subsidiaries at the same time as it recognised a goodwill impairment as shown in the extract below. Unusually each subsidiary written down was identified, although the statutory requirement to separately show information relating to both cost and provisions for diminution in value (see 2.3 below) does not appear to have been complied with.

Extract 14.4: QXL ricardo plc

3 Exceptional items [extract]
(i) Goodwill impairment provision

UK GAAP prescribes that the carrying value of goodwill should be no more than the higher of the stand alone value of the assts in use and their net realisable value.

Most of the goodwill arising during the year was attributable to the market value of the Company's shares when they were issued as consideration for acquisitions. Subsequent falls in the value of the Company's shares have been considered in assessing net realisable value. Stand alone valuations have been calculated using the present value of discounted projected cash flows.

Having considered these tests, the initial carrying value of goodwill has been impaired primarily due to the decrease in the market valuation of the Company's shares between the date of acquisition and the balance sheet date.

15 Investments [extract]

Company	**31 March 2001 £'000**	31 March 2000 £'000
At 1 April 2000	**356**	24
Additions in the year	**125,283**	13,299
Impairment provision	**(101,711)**	(12,967)
At 31 March 2001	**23,928**	356

Name of undertaking	Country of incorporation	Ordinary shares held 31 March 2001	Book value 31 March 2000 £'000	Acquisitions £'000	Capital contribution £'000	Impairment provision £'000	**Book value 31 March 2001 £'000**
QXL Sarl	France	100%	6	–	–	–	**6**
QXL GmbH	Germany	73%	18	36,080	–	(28,819)	**7,279**
QXL Srl	Italy	95%	3	–	–	–	**3**
QXL BV	Netherlands	100%	–	–	–	–	**–**
QXL SL	Spain	100%	2	–	–	–	**2**
QXL Finland OY	Finland	100%	5	–	–	–	**5**
QXL Sweden AB	Sweden	100%	7	–	–	–	**7**
QXL Marketing e Projectors Lda	Portugal	100%	–	–	–	–	**–**
Quixell Ltd	UK	100%	–	–	–	–	**–**
Quixell Ltd	Eire	100%	–	–	–	–	**–**
QXL Auksjon Norge AS	Norway	100%	263	–	–	(68)	**195**
QXL Denmark ApS	Denmark	100%	2	–	400	–	**402**
QXL Sp zoo	Poland	100%	48	–	–	(10)	**38**
(Under incorporation)	Greece	–	2	–	–	–	**2**
Idefi SA	Luxembourg	100%	–	2,525	–	(2,525)	**–**
ibidlive NV	Netherlands	62%	–	6,780	–	(6,780)	**–**
Bidlet AB	Sweden	99.6%	–	62,152	8,607	(63,509)	**7,250**
ricardo.de AG	Germany	66%	–	8,739	–	–	**8.739**
At 31 March 2001			**356**	**116,276**	**9,007**	**(101,711)**	**23,928**

D Impairments and group reconstructions

A common form of group reconstruction involves the transfer to another group company of the tangible assets and trade of a subsidiary. If the original purchase price included an element of goodwill, the remaining shell may have a carrying value in the parent company's balance sheet in excess of its net worth. It could be argued that as the subsidiary is now a shell company a provision should be made against the carrying value to reduce it to its net worth. However, in such a reorganisation there has been no real loss either to the holding company or to the group, and as a result companies frequently conclude that it would be inappropriate to make a provision. Nevertheless, the impairment in carrying value should always be recognised if the assets and/or the trade transferred are themselves sold outside the group. It is only possible to argue that the loss need not be recognised as long as there is a matching gain elsewhere in the group which has also not been recognised.

Most companies adopting this treatment do not make any specific disclosures in their accounts, although Atlantic Telecom is one company that has done, as shown in the following extract:

Extract 14.5: Atlantic Telecom Group PLC (2001)

9 Fixed Asset Investments [extract]

Additions to investment in Group undertakings for the year ended 31 March 2001 relate to the acquisition of First Telecom Group plc and as a result of capitalisation of inter-company debts with subsidiary undertakings the investment in Atlantic Telecommunications Limited has increased.

During the year ended 31 March 2001, the entire trade and assets of the subsidiary undertakings of First Telecom Group plc were transferred to Atlantic Telecommunications Limited at their book value. Both companies are ultimately wholly owned subsidiary undertakings of Atlantic Telecom Group PLC. No adjustment has been made to the carrying value of the Company's investment in individual subsidiary companies. This represents a departure from accounting principles, which require assets to be written down to the lower of cost and net realisable value. If an adjustment had been made, it would require a write-off in relation to First Telecom Group plc through the Company profit and loss account. As there has been no overall loss to the Group because the trade and assets are retained in another subsidiary that is wholly owned by the Company, the directors consider that this policy is necessary in order that the financial statements may give a true and fair view.

For many years Signet took a different approach to this problem, applying a true and fair override and transferring the excess amount to goodwill, as shown in this extract:

Extract 14.6: Signet Group plc (1999)

31 Company balance sheet
(I) Intangible assets and investments (held as fixed assets) [extract]

True and fair override on divisionalisation of subsidiary undertakings As part of a rationalisation of the Group in previous years, the trade and net assets of a subsidiary undertaking were transferred to the Company at their book value. The cost of the Company's investment in that subsidiary undertaking reflected the underlying fair value of its net assets and goodwill at the time of its acquisition. As a result of this transfer, the value of the Company's investment in that subsidiary undertaking fell below the amount at which it was stated in the Company's accounting records. Schedule 4 to the Companies Act 1985 requires that the investment be written down accordingly and that the amount be charged as a loss in the Company's profit and loss account. However, the directors consider that, as there had been no overall loss to the Group, it would fail to give a true and fair view to charge the diminution to the Company's profit and loss account and it should instead be re-allocated to goodwill and the identifiable net assets transferred, so as to recognise in the Company's individual balance sheet the effective cost to the Company of those net assets and goodwill. The effect on the Company's balance sheet of this departure is to recognise goodwill of £60,320,000 (1998: £62,205,000), net of amortisation of £15,080,000 (1998: £13,195,000).

Given that the business concerned operates in a generally stable market, the directors have concluded that the estimated economic life of the resulting intangible asset was 40 years at the date the transfer took place.

The asset is reviewed annually for impairment. The review at 30 January 1999 indicated that no such impairment had arisen.

2.2.2 *Current asset investments*

The valuation rules for current asset investments in the Companies Act again dictate that the investment should initially be recorded at its purchase price, including any incidental expenses.[19] A current asset investment must be written down to its net realisable value if it is less than its purchase price, but that write-down should again be reversed if the reasons for it cease to apply.[20] If the alternative accounting rules are adopted, a current asset investment may be revalued to its current cost.[21]

'Current cost' is not defined in the Act and the fact that the alternative accounting rules for *fixed* asset investments refer to 'market value' implies it does not mean market value. A sensible construction of the term suggests the amount it would currently cost to acquire the investment, i.e. for quoted securities the offer price plus acquisition costs. However, for readily marketable current asset investments, ED 55 saw no legal problem in simply using market values, whether they were based on bid, offer or mid-market prices.[22] In fact for highly liquid securities the difference between these various measures is unlikely to be material.

'Marking to market' is a variation on the alternative accounting rules whereby all revaluation gains and losses are reported in the profit and loss account, rather than being taken to reserves. This is commonly applied by companies whose business involves dealing in investments, but is not generally used by most other companies. The Post Office discloses such a policy in relation to gilts, as shown in this extract:

Extract 14.7: The Post Office (2001)

Accounting policies and general notes

H Investments [extract]

(iv) Investments held as current assets are stated at market value at the balance sheet date and the difference between cost and market value is taken to the profit and loss account. This treatment is a departure from UK accounting rules which stipulate that unrealised profits be credited to a revaluation reserve. In the opinion of the Board Members, the treatment adopted is necessary to present a true and fair view. All such investments are readily marketable Government securities. The accounting treatment adopted represents a fairer reflection of the investment return.

As illustrated in the above extract, marking to market involves a departure from the requirements of the Companies Act. The difficulty is not so much that any appreciation in value does not represent a realised profit – recent guidance on the subject states that marking to market current assets does give rise to a realised profit[23] (see Chapter 3 at 2.1). Rather, the balance sheet valuation rules in Schedule 4 do not allow valuations unless the other side of the entry is taken to a revaluation reserve under the alternative accounting rules.

ED 55 proposed such a treatment for readily marketable investments and sought to justify this departure from the rules on the basis that it was necessary in order to give a true and fair view. This was a controversial proposition, because the true and fair override can only be invoked in 'special circumstances' and it may be argued that the mere decision to hold such investments as a current asset does not give rise to circumstances which are sufficiently special to warrant the departure. This legal difficulty was probably one of the factors that prevented the ASB from picking up the project and turning ED 55 into a standard. However, in May 2001, the EU's Council of Ministers and the European Parliament paved the way for mark-to-market accounting with the adoption of a directive amending the EU Fourth and Seventh Directives.[24]

Companies which are not required to prepare their accounts under Schedule 4 to the Act are not subject to this legal obstacle. This category includes banks, which are also among those most likely to be engaging in investment dealing activities where marking to market is most appropriate. Schedule 9 to the Companies Act explicitly recognises the practice.[25]

Coats Viyella discloses accounting policies for fixed and current asset investments which follow the orthodox measurement rules described above:

Extract 14.8: Coats Viyella Plc (2000)

Statement of accounting policies

Investments

Fixed asset investments are stated at cost unless, in the opinion of the Directors, there has been an impairment, in which case an appropriate adjustment is made.

Listed current asset investments are stated at the lower of cost or market value, and other current asset investments are stated at the lower of cost and estimated net realisable value.

2.2.3 Other matters relevant to all investments

One issue which sometimes arises is the treatment of reclassifications of investments from current assets to fixed assets or vice versa, since the rules governing their measurement are not the same. Under UITF 5, current assets which are transferred to fixed assets should continue to be accounted for under the appropriate rules for current assets up to the date of transfer, and therefore transferred at the amount that is appropriate under these rules.[26] This rule was devised to prevent companies avoiding a write-down of current assets to net realisable value by redesignating them as fixed assets. The Abstract does not deal with transfers in the opposite direction, from fixed to current assets.

Where a company has an investment holding that results from a number of purchases and sales at different prices, it is not necessary for the actual purchase price to be assigned to the specific securities acquired in each transaction; instead it is permissible to use one of the methods suggested by the Act for 'fungible assets' (which are most commonly used for valuing stock – see Chapter 16 at 1.2). These allow costs to be assigned on the basis of FIFO, LIFO, weighted average or any other similar method rather than using the actual cost, but with the proviso that the replacement cost or most recent purchase price of the holding should be disclosed if it is materially different from the balance sheet amount.[27] However each investment within a category should be accounted for separately, rather than on a portfolio basis.[28]

ED 55 proposed that an investment transaction should be accounted for as of the date on which the risks and rewards of ownership pass from the seller to the purchaser.[29] This will generally be the date on which the trade was made, rather than the subsequent settlement date, a view supported by UK banking industry practice,[30] whereas IAS 39 allows either approach.[31] ED 55 also said that if an investment was acquired with an accrued entitlement to interest or a fixed dividend, its cost should be based on its purchase price excluding the amount of the accrued interest or dividend.[32] There is no equivalent discussion in the law.

2.2.4 Income recognition

A Interest and similar income

ED 55 proposed that all income from investments should be recognised in the profit and loss account when it became receivable.[33] This implies a normal accruals basis for interest and fixed rate dividends and is consistent with amortising premiums and discounts on the acquisition of such securities as discussed at 2.2.1 B above.

Some have questioned whether, in the context of a long term instrument, the accrual of a redemption premium, or discount on acquisition, represents a realised profit. Consider, for example, the acquisition of a government bond for £800 that pays £40 interest per year and is redeemable in 25 years at £1,000. Amortising the discount over the term on a straight line basis would result in recognising income of £48 per year (£40 interest plus amortisation of £8=[1,000–800]÷25) of which only £40 would be received in cash immediately. Recent guidance on the subject (see Chapter 3 at 2.1) states that a realised profit arises from a transaction where the consideration received is an amount receivable in cash where:

- the amount is capable of reliable measurement;
- the debtor is capable of settling within a reasonable period of time;
- the debtor will be capable of settling when called upon to do so; and
- there is no intention or expectation that the receivable will not be settled.[34]

In our view it is important that a 'reasonable period of time' is viewed in the context of the terms of the instrument. Therefore provided the issuer (in this case the government) is expected to make payments within a reasonable period of time from when they are contractually due, the fact that the security has a remaining term of 25 years should not prevent the accrual of the discount being treated as a realised profit.

In the case of more complex securities which have a number of redemption options at different dates and different prices it has become fairly common practice for entities to account on a 'mirror-image' basis, i.e. to recognise income to match the finance costs recognised by the issuer under FRS 4. However this will not always be appropriate and prudence should be exercised in determining the amount of income to be recognised in order to avoid the danger of reporting income which is not subsequently received. This is illustrated in the following example:

Example 14.1: Convertible discounted bond

At the start of 2001, ABC Ltd issues a convertible discounted bond to PQR plc for £100. No interest is paid on the bond and at the end of 2003, PQR has the option of redeeming it for £130 or converting it into 50 ABC shares. Under FRS 4, ABC is not allowed to anticipate conversion and charges finance costs of £30=£130–£100 over the term of the bond at a constant rate (approximately 9.1%) on its carrying amount, i.e. £9 in 2001, £10 in 2002 and £11 in 2003 (see Chapter 17 at 2.2.5).

Using mirror-image accounting, PQR would recognise income of £9, £10 and £11 in 2001, 2002 and 2003 respectively. However if the bond is converted, rather than redeemed, PQR will receive shares in a private company which is not 'qualifying consideration' (see Chapter 3 at 2.1) and it would be inappropriate to regard it as a realised profit.

Unfortunately, until the end of 2003, the outcome is uncertain and PQR's assessment of whether to recognise income prior to maturity would have to take into account the likelihood of the bond being redeemed – this may be justified if conversion is very unlikely, e.g. because the conversion option is significantly out of the money; otherwise caution should be exercised.

B *Equity dividends*

In the case of dividends on equity securities ED 55's general approach implies that the amount due should be recognised when declared or, in the case of quoted securities, on the ex-dividend date; in practice, a cash basis of accounting for such income may produce materially the same results. However, it suggested an exception for the case of intra-group dividends, where frequently decisions on such dividends are made after the year end but before the accounts are finalised; it said that the parent company could recognise such dividends from subsidiary undertakings provided they were declared before the date of approval of its own financial statements.[35]

This approach is common, and is symmetrical with the present accepted practice of accruing outgoing dividends that are proposed after the year end and before the date of approval of the accounts. However, the ASB has voiced its doubts as to the appropriateness of such accruals on the basis that they do not reflect liabilities that existed at the balance sheet date, and the IASC banned the practice in its revision to IAS 10 in 1999.[36] It is therefore possible that accruing incoming dividends from subsidiaries may be similarly challenged at some time in the future.

2.3 Disclosure requirements

The Act requires various disclosures to be made in relation to investments. In respect of fixed asset investments, the following must be shown:

(a) the appropriate amounts at the beginning of the financial year and as at the balance sheet date, based either on historical cost or alternative accounting rules.[37] Where investments are carried at valuation, equivalent historical cost information must be disclosed;[38]

(b) all movements during the year, including revaluation surpluses and deficits, acquisitions, disposals and transfers.[39] Such movements would also include exchange differences; and

(c) the cumulative amount of provisions for depreciation or diminution in value as at the beginning and end of the financial year on the appropriate basis of cost or valuation, the provision for the period and adjustments in respect of disposals or for other reasons.[40] Systematic depreciation will not apply to most investments since they will not have a finite life and hence will not be depreciated; however, it will apply to dated securities where they are being amortised to their eventual redemption price. The need to provide for permanent diminution in value can of course apply to any investment.

This information has to be disclosed in respect of each type of investment included in the balance sheet formats (see 2.1 above). The following extract shows the investments note relating to the consolidated accounts of Tate & Lyle.

Extract 14.9: Tate & Lyle Public Limited Company (2001)

14 Fixed Asset Investments [extract]	**2001 £million**	2000 £million
Group		
Own shares [1]	**2**	–
Joint ventures – unlisted	**151**	123
Associates – unlisted	**11**	11
Other fixed asset investments:		
Listed – at cost [2]	**9**	9
Unlisted – at cost less amounts provided of £5 million (2000 – £5 million) [3]	**11**	11
Loans	**19**	21
Total	**203**	175

1 Market value £2 million.
2 Market value £14 million (2000 – £12 million).
3 Directors' valuation £11 million (2000 – £11 million).

Movement in book value	Joint Ventures £ million	Associates £ million	Other equity investments £ million	Loans £ million	**Group £ million**
At 25 March 2000	123	11	20	21	**175**
Differences on exchange	13	1	1	1	**16**
Additions	8	–	2	–	**10**
Business sold	(2)	–	–	(3)	**(5)**
Disposals	(2)	(2)	–	–	**(4)**
Reduction in loans to Group undertakings	–	–	–	–	**–**
Retained profits of joint ventures and associates	11	1	–	–	**12**
Movement in provisions	–	–	(1)	–	**(1)**
At 25 March 2001	**151**	**11**	**22**	**19**	**203**

The Act also requires these disclosures in respect of both fixed and current asset investments:

(a) the amount relating to listed investments;[41]

(b) the aggregate market value of listed investments, if different from the book value, and the stock exchange value if it is less than the market value thus disclosed;[42]

(c) various details where the investment is 'significant', i.e. where it is either 20% or more of the nominal value of the shares of that class in the investee, or it represents more than 20% of the investor's own assets. The details to be disclosed are:

   (i) the name of the investee;

   (ii) its country of incorporation (if outside Great Britain). For unincorporated investees the address of the principal place of business has to be disclosed; and

   (iii) a description and the proportion of each class of shares held.[43]

Two examples of balance sheet notes are shown below: on fixed asset investments in an extract from the accounts of Cookson, and on current asset investments in an extract from the accounts of Pearson:

Extract 14.10: Cookson Group plc (2000)

12 Fixed asset investments

	Group		Company	
	2000 £m	1999 £m	**2000 £m**	1999 £m
Investments in joint ventures	**42.0**	50.6	**13.4**	8.2
Investments in subsidiaries	**–**	–	**2,256.2**	1,921.9
Own shares held for Employee Share Ownership Plan	**8.7**	9.0	**8.7**	9.0
Other investments	**42.3**	35.9	**–**	–
Other fixed assets investments	**51.0**	44.9	**8.7**	9.0
Total fixed assets investments	**93.0**	95.5	**2,278.3**	1,939.1

Other investments include an investment of £30.8m (1999: £28.0m) made by the Group in a revenue-sharing arrangement with Electric Lightwave, Inc. related to a fibre optic cable network in the USA.

(i) Own shares held for Employee Share Ownership Plan

	Number of shares m	Cost £m
At 1 January 2000	4.8	9.0
Movements	(0.3)	(0.3)
At 31 December 2000	**4.5**	**8.7**

The shares included in the table above are ordinary shares of the Company and are held by Cookson Investments (Jersey) Limited as Trustee of the Cookson Group Employee Share Ownership Plan. The purchase of these shares was financed by Cookson Group plc out of borrowings included in the Group and Company balance sheets as at 31 December 2000. The market value of these shares at 31 December 2000 was £7.9m (1999: £12.0m). Dividends receivable of £0.2m have been waived by the Trustee.

(ii) Company investments in subsidiaries

	Cost £m	Loans £m	Provisions £m	Net book value £m
At 1 January 2000	453.7	1,514.6	(46.4)	1,921.9
Exchange adjustments	–	75.4	–	75.4
Additions	–	265.5	–	265.5
Disposals	(10.7)	(8.6)	8.2	(11.1)
Written-back during the year	–	–	4.5	4.5
At 31 December 2000	**443.0**	**1,846.9**	**(33.7)**	**2,256.2**

(iii) Principal subsidiaries and joint ventures

The principal subsidaries and joint ventures of Cookson Group plc and the countries in which they are incorporated are as follows:

* Cookson America, Inc., USA
* Cookson Ceramics Ltd, England and Wales
* Cookson Fukuda Ltd, England and Wales (50%)
* Cookson Investments, Inc., USA
* Cookson Investments Ltd, England and Wales
Cookson Overseas Ltd, England and Wales
* Ebara-Udylite Co. Ltd, Japan (45%)
* Electroplating Engineers of Japan Ltd, Japan (50%)
* Polyclad Laminates, Inc., USA
* Speedline Technologies, Inc., USA
* Vesuvius Crucible Company, USA
* Vesuvius USA Corporation, USA
* Wilkes Lucas Ltd, England and Wales

Where marked with an asterisk(*), the ordinary capital of the above companies was owned by a Cookson Group plc subsidiary at 31 December 2000. All of the above are wholly-owned, unless otherwise stated. A full list of Group companies will be included in the Company's Annual Return.

Extract 14.11: Pearson plc (2000)

19 CURRENT ASSET INVESTMENTS [extract]

	2000		**1999**	
all figures in £ millions	valuation	book value	valuation	book value
Listed	8	8	–	–
Unlisted	4	4	4	4
	12	**12**	4	4

note The valuations of unlisted investments are directors' valuations as at 31 December 2000. If all investments were realised at valuation there would be no liability for taxation.

In addition, the statutory formats for the profit and loss account contain separate headings for the following:

- Income from shares in group undertakings
- Income from participating interests
- Income from other fixed asset investments
- Other interest receivable and similar income
- Amounts written off investments.

There are also various statutory disclosure requirements concerning investments in subsidiary and associated undertakings when group accounts are not prepared, which are beyond the scope of this chapter but are listed in Chapter 30 at 3.1.3.

Insofar as marking to market invokes the 'true and fair override' (see 2.2.2 above), it will also be necessary to disclose particulars of the departure from the valuation rules of Schedule 4 to the Companies Act, the reasons for the departure and its effect on the financial statements.[44]

3 COMPARISON WITH IASC PRONOUNCEMENTS

The international standard IAS 25 – *Accounting for Investments* – was issued in 1986 and was fairly accommodating in its requirements. However, it has now been superseded by IAS 39, *Financial Instruments: Recognition and Measurement*, and IAS 40, *Investment Property*. As noted earlier, the IASC was a participant in the international project on financial instruments which is likely to form the basis of accounting for investments in the future – this project is covered in Chapter 10 at 1.1.

IAS 39 was finalised in December 1998, issued in March 1999 and came into force for periods beginning on or after 1 January 2001. In summary it requires investments (which are a subset of financial assets) to be analysed into the following categories:

- fixed maturity investments that the enterprise both intends and is able to keep to maturity. (There are obsessively detailed rules that set conditions to constrain that apparently straightforward definition). These are to be measured at amortised cost;[45]
- originated loans and receivables that are not intended to be disposed of in the short term. These are also to be measured at amortised cost;[46]
- investments held for trading purposes. Apart from some minor exceptions, these are to be marked to market, with the differences going to the profit and loss account;[47]
- investments that are available for sale (the rest). These are also to be carried at market value, but the enterprise must decide, as a matter of policy, whether movements in value also go to the profit and loss account or whether they are taken to equity initially and only recycled into the profit and loss account when the investment is subsequently disposed of or judged to be impaired.[48]

This standard is covered in more detail in Chapter 10 at 4.

Accounting for investments in subsidiaries, associates and joint ventures in the separate accounts of parents or investors is not dealt with by IAS 39. In those accounts, subsidiaries and associates should be either:

- carried at cost;
- accounted for using the equity method; or
- accounted for as available-for-sale financial assets under IAS 39.[49]

No accounting treatments are prescribed, or indeed proscribed, for investments in joint ventures in the separate accounts of venturers.[50]

4 CONCLUSION

ED 55 was never progressed, largely because of the legal obstacles that appear to rule out mark-to-market accounting for most UK companies, however there is now a clear trend among standard setters internationally towards the increased use of this treatment. Indeed under IAS 39 many investments are being carried at fair value, sometimes with associated gains being reported in income, and there has now been some relaxation of the legal prohibitions to allow the use of this standard in Europe. The issue then becomes how far to take the approach and it is clear both the ASB and the IASB wish to move towards a more comprehensive fair value model for all financial instruments. This remains controversial, not least when it involves reporting in the profit and loss account unrealised gains on the revaluation of unmarketable securities that are held for the long term. The future direction of this subject, therefore, is likely to depend on the degree to which such an approach commands international acceptance.

References

1 Financial Services Act 1986, Sch. 1, Part 1.
2 ED 55, *Accounting for investments*, ASC, July 1990, para. 54.
3 IAS 25, *Accounting for Investments*, IASC, March 1986, para. 3.
4 CA 85, Sch. 4, Part V.
5 For recommendations on accounting by Investment Trusts, see the SORP on *Financial Statements of Investment Trust Companies*, The Association of Investment Trust Companies, December 1995. For recommendations on accounting for securities in the financial statements of banks, see the SORP on *Securities*, British Bankers Association and Irish Bankers' Federation, September 1990. For recommendations on accounting for investments in the financial statements of insurers, see the SORP on *Accounting for Insurance Business*, Association of British Insurers, December 1998.
6 Other than FRS 9, which deals with associates, joint ventures and JANEs: see Chapter 7.
7 CA 85, Sch. 4, para. 8, balance sheet formats.
8 *Ibid.*, s 262(1).
9 CA 85, Sch. 4, para. 17.
10 *Ibid.*, para. 26(1).
11 *Ibid.*, para. 31(3).
12 FRS 3, *Reporting financial performance*, ASB, December 1992, para. 21.
13 CA 85, s 266 and Sch. 4, para. 73.
14 FRS 3, para. 31.
15 CA 85, Sch 4, paras. 19(2) and (3).
16 *Ibid.*, para. 19(1).
17 FRS 11, *Impairment of Fixed Assets and Goodwill*, ASB, July 1998, para. 63.
18 *Ibid.*, para. 5(a).
19 CA 85, Sch 4, para. 22.
20 *Ibid.*, para. 23.
21 *Ibid.*, para. 31(5).
22 ED 55, paras. 1.17 and 28.
23 TECH 25/00, *The determination of realised profits and distributable profits in the context of the Companies Act 1985* (a draft technical release), ICAEW, 10 August 2000, para. 16(d).
24 Press Release, European Commission (Internal Market), 31 May 2001.
25 CA 85, Sch. 9, Part 1, paras. 33 and 34.
26 UITF 5, *Transfers from current assets to fixed assets*, UITF, July 1992, para. 5.
27 CA 85, Sch. 4, para. 27.
28 *Ibid.*, para. 14.
29 ED 55, para. 76.
30 SORP on Securities paras. 39 and 66.
31 IAS 39, *Financial Instruments: Recognition and Measurement*, IASC, Revised October 2000, para. 30.
32 ED 55, para. 64.
33 *Ibid.*, para. 73.
34 TECH 25/00, paras. 16 and 21.
35 *Ibid.*, para. 41.

36 IAS 10, *Events After the Balance Sheet Date*, IASC, Revised May 1999, para. 11.
37 CA 85, Sch. 4, paras. 42(1)(a) and 42(2).
38 *Ibid.*, para. 33(3).
39 *Ibid.*, para. 42(1)(b).
40 *Ibid.*, para. 42(3).
41 *Ibid.*, para. 45(1).
42 *Ibid.*, para. 45(2).
43 *Ibid.*, Sch. 5, paras. 7 and 8.
44 CA 85, ss 226(5) and 227(6).
45 IAS 39, para. 73.
46 *Ibid.*
47 *Ibid.*, para. 103(a).
48 *Ibid.*, para. 103(b).
49 IAS 27, *Consolidated Financial Statements and Accounting for Investments in Subsidiaries*, IASC, Reformatted November 1994, paras. 29 and 30, and IAS 28, *Accounting for Investments in Associates*, IASC, Reformatted November 1994, paras. 12 and 14.
50 IAS 31, *Financial Reporting of Interests in Joint Ventures*, IASC, Reformatted November 1994, para. 38.

Chapter 15 Capitalisation of finance costs

1 INTRODUCTION

A point of contention in determining the initial measurement of an asset is whether or not finance costs incurred during the period of its construction should be capitalised. This issue was referred to in company law for the first time in 1981, with the Companies Act 1981 permitting the inclusion of interest in the production cost of an asset.[1]

Since then, the practice of capitalising finance costs has become increasingly common in the UK in industries that have major fixed asset developments, such as property, retail and hotels. However, the issue had not been dealt with in any UK accounting standard until the ASB published FRS 15 – *Tangible Fixed Assets* – in February 1999, and only then on the basis that the capitalisation of finance costs is optional.

In March 1984, the IASC published IAS 23 – *Capitalisation of Borrowing Costs.* Under this original version of IAS 23, capitalisation was optional, but certain rules were laid down if a policy of capitalisation was adopted.[2] A revised version of IAS 23 – *Borrowing Costs* – was issued in 1993 with an entirely different approach. Under the revised IAS 23 the 'benchmark treatment' for borrowing costs is that they should be recognised as an expense in the period in which they are incurred regardless of how the borrowings are applied.[3] However, the IASC did not go so far as to ban the capitalisation of borrowing costs altogether, and the revised IAS 23 incorporates capitalisation as an 'allowed alternative treatment'. Thus, there is currently a similar approach between the UK and IAS on the issue. In the UK, capitalisation is permitted under the Companies Act and FRS 15 but is entirely optional, whilst IAS 23 prefers interest to be expensed but allows capitalisation within a framework of rules.

In the Discussion Paper that preceded FRS 15, the ASB stated that it believed that the capitalisation of interest should be either mandatory or prohibited, and that the position it finally adopted in the standard, where it is optional, could not be regarded as satisfactory.[4] In the Appendix on the development of FRS 15, the ASB acknowledges that it would have preferred either to prohibit or to require the capitalisation of finance costs.[5] It states that the Board believes that, conceptually, there are strong arguments in favour of the capitalisation of directly attributable finance costs. However, it was influenced by the argument that if capitalisation is to become mandatory, in theory notional interest should also be capitalised.[6] Otherwise, capitalisation of finance costs results in the same type of asset having a different carrying amount, depending on the method of financing adopted by the enterprise.

2 THE POSITION UNDER UK GAAP

2.1 The Companies Act

The Companies Act 1985 permits the inclusion in the production cost of an asset of:

> '(a) a reasonable proportion of the costs incurred by the company which are only indirectly attributable to the production of that asset; and
>
> (b) interest on capital borrowed to finance the production of that asset, to the extent that it accrues in respect of the period of production;
>
> provided, however, in a case within paragraph (b) above, that the inclusion of the interest in determining the cost of that asset and the amount of the interest so included is disclosed in a note to the accounts'.[7]

The Companies Act does not restrict the inclusion of interest into the cost of an asset to fixed assets. In principle under the Companies Act, current assets may also have interest costs included in their cost.

The words 'interest on capital borrowed ...' in the Companies Act clearly indicate that actual borrowings must have been incurred before capitalisation can take place. This rules out the capitalisation of 'notional interest', a point reinforced by FRS 15.[8]

2.2 SSAP 9

In the case of long-term contracts, interest is referred to in Appendix 1 to SSAP 9 – *Stocks and long-term contracts* – in the following terms:

'In ascertaining costs of long-term contracts it is not normally appropriate to include interest payable on borrowed money. However, in circumstances where sums borrowed can be identified as financing specific long-term contracts, it may be appropriate to include such related interest in cost, in which circumstances the inclusion of interest and the amount of interest so included should be disclosed in a note to the financial statements.'[9]

Whilst this paragraph would appear to discourage rather than encourage capitalisation, it is nevertheless clear that, provided that the Companies Act criteria for capitalisation of interest costs are met, it is perfectly acceptable to do so. This is, in fact, the position adopted by IAS 11 – *Construction Contracts* – which states that costs that may be attributable to contract activity in general and can be allocated to specific contracts also include borrowing costs when the contractor adopts the allowed alternative treatment in IAS 23.[10] SSAP 9 and IAS 11 are discussed in detail in Chapter 16.

2.3 FRS 15

2.3.1 *Introduction*

FRS 15 – *Tangible fixed assets* – came into force in 2000 and deals with the entire subject of accounting for tangible fixed assets (see Chapter 12) with the result that it devotes relatively little attention to the issue of the capitalisation of finance costs. Its provisions on the capitalisation of finance costs appear to have been based on IAS 23 – *Borrowing Costs (revised 1993)* – and the two will have similar results in practice.

2.3.2 *Definition of finance costs*

FRS 15 defines finance costs as being 'the difference between the net proceeds of an instrument and the total amount of payments (or other transfers of economic benefits) that the issuer may be required to make in respect of the instrument.'[11] This definition is taken from FRS 4 – *Capital Instruments* – and means that all finance costs may be capitalised, including:

(a) interest on bank overdrafts and short-term and long-term debt;

(b) amortisation of discounts or premiums relating to debt; and

(c) amortisation of ancillary costs incurred in connection with the arrangement of debt.[12]

Consequently, the scope for capitalisation extends beyond interest alone.

2.3.3 *Accounting policy*

As already mentioned, under FRS 15 – *Tangible Fixed Assets* – capitalisation of finance costs is neither required nor prohibited, but is a matter of accounting policy for companies. However, if a policy of capitalisation is adopted it must be applied consistently to all finance costs directly attributable to the construction of tangible fixed assets.[13] Kingfisher in Extract 15.1 shows a policy of interest capitalisation.

Extract 15.1: Kingfisher plc (2001)

Accounting Policies [extract]
Capitalisation of Interest

Interest on borrowings to finance property development is capitalised. Interest is capitalised from the date work starts on the development to practical completion.

Interest on borrowings to finance the construction of properties held as tangible fixed assets is capitalised. Interest is capitalised from the date work starts on the property to the date when substantially all the activities that are necessary to get the property ready for use are complete. Where construction is completed in parts, each part is considered separately when capitalising interest.

Interest is capitalised before any allowances for tax relief.

FRS 15 requires further that the total amount of finance costs capitalised during a period should not exceed the total amount of finance costs incurred during that period,[14] which means that notional interest may not be capitalised. Furthermore, only finance costs that are directly attributable to the construction of a tangible fixed asset, or the financing of progress payments in respect of the construction of a tangible fixed asset by others for the entity, should be capitalised. Directly attributable finance costs are those that would have been avoided (for example by avoiding additional borrowings or by using the funds expended for the asset to repay existing borrowings) if there had been no expenditure on the asset. Finance costs are to be capitalised on a gross basis, that is, before the deduction of any attributable tax relief.[15] As 'directly attributable' finance costs are those that would have been avoided if the expenditure had not taken place, this means that the company must be able to identify avoidable borrowings.

2.3.4 *Capitalisation rate*

If an entity has borrowed funds specifically to construct the asset, the costs capitalised are to be the actual finance costs during the period.[16] If a project has been financed from the entity's general borrowings, the standard imposes a detailed calculation method, applying a capitalisation rate calculated as follows:

(a) the expenditure is the weighted average carrying amount of the asset during the period, including finance costs previously capitalised;

(b) the capitalisation rate is the weighted average of rates applicable to general borrowings outstanding in the period; and

(c) general borrowings exclude loans for other specific purposes including constructing other fixed assets, finance leases and loans held to hedge foreign investments.[17]

The standard acknowledges that determining general borrowings will not always be straightforward. It will be necessary to exercise judgement to meet the main objective – a reasonable measure of the directly attributable finance costs. The particular problem of groups is alluded to; the standard suggests that sometimes all group borrowings will have to be taken into account while in other cases only the individual subsidiaries' borrowings will be applicable.[18] Presumably this will be largely determined by the extent to which borrowings are made centrally (and, perhaps, expenses met in the same way) and passed through to individual group companies via intercompany accounts. An illustrative example of the calculation of a capitalisation rate is included at 4.2.1 below.

While the standard lays down that interest capitalised should not exceed the total interest incurred in the period,[19] practice in relation to other aspects of the calculation has probably varied quite widely. Few companies disclose their method of calculating interest to be capitalised, although an exception to this is Safeway, as shown in Extract 15.2:

Extract 15.2: Safeway plc (2000)

Notes to the Accounts [extract]
5.0 Net interest payable and similar charges

Interest costs relating to the financing of freehold and long leasehold developments are capitalised at the weighted average cost of the related borrowings up to the date of completion of the project.

The standard makes no recommendations regarding the treatment of interest income where borrowed funds are invested until they are needed to meet expenditure. We consider that in this specific situation the investment income earned should be deducted from the finance costs eligible to be capitalised. However, the more general point as to whether the amount of borrowing costs which may be capitalised is the gross amount of borrowing costs incurred, or whether this amount should be reduced by interest income earned, is discussed more fully at 4.2.2 below.

2.3.5 *Capitalisation period*

FRS 15 stipulates that where finance costs are capitalised, capitalisation should begin when all three of the following conditions are fulfilled:

(a) finance costs are being incurred; and

(b) expenditures for the asset are being incurred; and

(c) activities that are necessary to get the asset ready for use are in progress.[20]

These conditions are identical to those to be found in IAS 23.[21] Necessary activities can start before the physical construction of the asset, for example technical and administrative work such as obtaining permits.[22]

FRS 15 requires that capitalisation of borrowing costs should cease during 'extended periods in which active development is interrupted'; such costs are costs of holding partially completed assets and do not qualify for capitalisation under the standard.[23]

Land awaiting development is specifically dealt with by FRS 15. Given that there must be a period of production, the standard states that finance costs incurred while land acquired for building purposes is held without any associated development activity do not qualify for capitalisation.[24]

The rule regarding the end of the capitalisation period in FRS 15 is that capitalisation of finance costs should cease when substantially all the activities that are necessary to get the asset ready for use are complete. Furthermore, when construction of a tangible fixed asset is completed in parts and each part is capable of being used while construction continues on other parts, capitalisation of finance costs relating to a part should cease when substantially all the activities that are necessary to get that part ready for use are completed. A business park comprising several buildings, each of which can be used individually, is an example of an asset of which parts are usable while construction continues on other parts.[25]

In the context of a development consisting of a number of individual buildings, our view is that capitalisation will have to cease when an individual building is physically complete, not at the later date when the development as a whole is deemed to be complete, or the building is let. The policy of Kingfisher in Extract 15.1 reflects this view.

3 UK DISCLOSURE REQUIREMENTS

3.1 Disclosures required by the Companies Act and the Listing Rules

The disclosures required by FRS 15 are more extensive than those required by the Companies Act, and complying with them will satisfy the disclosure requirements of the Companies Act. However, as FRS 15 applies to fixed assets only, companies that capitalise finance costs in respect of current assets will need to comply only with the related disclosure requirements in the Companies Act. These are that the company should disclose that its accounting policy is to include interest in determining the cost of the asset, identifying the asset(s) to which the policy applies and the amount of interest so included.[26]

Where interest is being capitalised on tangible fixed assets (which must by definition be in a period of production) strictly the assets to which it relates will have to be disclosed separately from other tangible fixed assets. This is because the balance sheet formats require 'payments on account and assets in course of construction' to be disclosed separately.[27]

Companies listed on The Stock Exchange must also disclose the amount of interest capitalised during the year and give an indication of the amount and treatment of any related tax relief.[28]

3.2 Disclosures required by FRS 15

FRS 15 requires that where an enterprise adopts a policy of capitalisation of finance costs, the financial statements should disclose:

(a) the accounting policy adopted;

(b) the aggregate amount of finance costs included in the cost of tangible fixed assets;

(c) the amount of finance costs capitalised during the period;

(d) the amount of finance costs recognised in the profit and loss account during the period; and

(e) the capitalisation rate used to determine the amount of finance costs capitalised during the period.

These requirements are illustrated by Canary Wharf in Extract 15.3:

Extract 15.3: Canary Wharf Group plc (2000)

Principal Accounting Policies [extract]
4 Property interests [extract]
Properties under construction and properties held for development [extract]
Additions to properties under construction or held for development include all expenses of development, including attributable interest. Interest capitalised is calculated by reference to the rate of interest payable on the borrowings drawn down to finance the development.

6 Debt [extract]
Finance costs are charged to the profit and loss account, except in the case of development financings where interest and related financing costs are capitalised as part of the cost of development.

Notes to the Accounts [extract]
4 Interest Payable

	Year ended 30 June 2000 £m	**Year ended 30 June 1999 £m**
Notes and debentures	44.4	65.8
Bank loans and overdrafts	7.3	9.2
Finance lease charges	44.7	35.0
	96.4	110.0
Less:		
Interest at 6/7% (year ended 30 June 1999 6/7%) on development financings transferred to development properties	(11.7)	(6.8)
	84.7	103.2

Interest payable of £11.7 million (year ended 30 June 1999 - £6.8 million) has been transferred to development properties (Note 10). The amount transferred in respect of the year ended 30 June 2000 includes £2.7 million attributable to funds borrowed specifically for the purpose of financing the construction of development properties. In addition, following the adoption of FRS15 (Tangible Fixed Assets), the amount transferred includes £9.0 million attributable to the cost of funds forming part of the group's general borrowings which were utilised in financing construction. Of this amount £5.1 million relates to the six months ended 30 June 2000 and £3.9 million to the six months ended 31 December 1999. This latter amount was exposed for the purposes of the group's interim statement. The additional amount of interest attributable to the group's general borrowings which would have fallen to be capitalised under the terms of FRS15 in respect of periods prior to 30 June 1999 is not material.

4 UK ISSUES ARISING IN PRACTICE

As already stated, FRS 15 deals with the entire subject of accounting for tangible fixed assets and is mainly dealt with in Chapter 12. As a consequence the standard devotes relatively little attention to capitalisation of finance costs, leaving a number of practical issues that need to be considered.

4.1 Qualifying assets

In the UK, the range of assets on which companies have capitalised interest covers both fixed assets and stock. Although FRS 15 is confined to tangible fixed assets, the Companies Act permits capitalisation across a broader spectrum of assets (see 2.1 above). Specific examples of the types of assets included are property developments, ships, aircraft, maturing whisky stocks and tobacco, allowing the policy of capitalising interest to be fairly widespread in the UK – particularly in the case of the property industry.

The Companies Act is drawn sufficiently widely to permit interest to be included in the production cost of any fixed or current asset,[29] but in practice capitalisation only takes place where the production period is sufficiently long for borrowing costs to be significant in relation to the total production cost. Extract 15.4 shows an example of the capitalisation of interest on the payments towards the construction costs of ships.

Extract 15.4: The Peninsular and Oriental Steam Navigation Company (2000)

Notes to the Accounts
4 Net Interest and Similar Items [extract]

	2000 £m	1999 £m
Interest payable on:		
bank loans on overdrafts	(74.1)	(56.2)
other loans	(62.2)	(85.1)
finance leases	(5.8)	(5.0)
	(142.1)	(146.3)
Interest capitalised	15.0	9.6
Interest receivable and similar items	27.9	26.5
	(99.2)	(110.2)
Joint ventures	(14.9)	(31.1)
Associates	(2.2)	(2.0)
	(116.3)	(143.3)

Interest capitalised in the year comprises £14.4m (1999 £9.0m) in respect of ships and other fixed assets and £0.6m (1999 £0.6m) in respect of overseas development properties. At the year end the aggregate interest capitalised was £3.5m (1999 £79.2m) on ships and other fixed assets and £15.7m (1999 £19.2m) on overseas development properties in the Group and £nil (1999 £21.2m) on ships and other fixed assets in the Company.

4.2 Determination of amount to be capitalised

4.2.1 *Borrowings and capitalisation rate*

FRS 15 requires that the interest costs capitalised are to be the actual finance costs during the period. If a project has been financed from the entity's general borrowings, the standard imposes a detailed calculation method as indicated at 2.3.4 above.

The standard acknowledges that determining general borrowings will not always be straightforward. It will be necessary to exercise judgement to meet the main objective – a reasonable measure of the directly attributable finance costs.[30]

The following example illustrates the practical application of FRS 15's method of calculating the amount of finance costs to be capitalised:

Example 13.1: Calculation of capitalisation rate

On 1 April 2001 a company engages in the development of a property which is expected to take five years to complete, at a cost of £6,000,000. The balance sheets at 31 December 2000 and 31 December 2001, prior to capitalisation of interest, are as follows:

	31 December 2000	31 December 2001
	£	£
Development property	–	1,200,000
Other assets	6,000,000	6,800,000
	6,000,000	8,000,000
Loans		
8% debenture stock	2,500,000	2,500,000
Bank loan at 10% p.a.	–	2,000,000
Bank loan at 12% p.a.	1,000,000	1,000,000
	3,500,000	5,500,000
Shareholders' equity	2,500,000	2,500,000

The bank loan at 10% was taken out on 31 March 2001 and the total interest charge for the year ended 31 December 2001 was as follows:

	£
£2,500,000 x 8%	200,000
£2,000,000 x 10% x 9/12	150,000
£1,000,000 x 12%	120,000
	470,000

Expenditure was incurred on the development as follows:

	£
1 April 2001	600,000
1 July 2001	400,000
1 October 2001	200,000
	1,200,000

(a) If the bank loan at 10% p.a. is a new borrowing taken out specifically to finance the development, then the amount of interest to be capitalised is:

	£
£600,000 x 10% x 9/12	45,000
£400,000 x 10% x 6/12	20,000
£200,000 x 10% x 3/12	5,000
	70,000

(b) If all the borrowings would have been avoided but for the development then the amount of interest to be capitalised is:

$$\frac{\text{Total interest expense for period}}{\text{Weighted average total borrowings}} \text{ x Development expenditure}$$

i.e.

$$\frac{470{,}000}{3{,}500{,}000 + (2{,}000{,}000 \text{ x } 9/12)} = 9.4\%$$

	£
£600,000 x 9.4% x 9/12	42,300
£400,000 x 9.4% x 6/12	18,800
£200,000 x 9.4% x 3/12	4,700
	65,800

If the 8% debenture stock was irredeemable then as the borrowings could not have been avoided the above calculation would be done using the figures for the bank loans and their related interest costs only.

4.2.2 *Limitation on interest capitalised*

As already stated at 2.3.4 above, FRS 15 requires that the amount of borrowing costs capitalised during a period should not exceed the total amount of borrowing costs incurred by the enterprise in that period. However, the standard makes no recommendations concerning the treatment of interest income where funds borrowed specifically for the project are invested until they are needed to meet expenditure. The same issue arises when specific borrowings are not involved, i.e. finance costs incurred in respect of an entity's general borrowings are capitalised. In these circumstances, in our view, companies should adopt the following approach if capitalising interest costs under FRS 15:

(a) in cases where specific borrowed funds are invested until they are needed to meet expenditure on a specific asset, the investment income earned should be deducted from the finance costs eligible to be capitalised; and

(b) in cases where funds are borrowed generally, the amount of borrowing costs which may be capitalised is limited to the gross amount of borrowing costs incurred, and this amount is not reduced by interest income earned.

This would be consistent with IAS 23, as discussed at 5.1.2 below.

4.2.3 *Accrued costs*

In principle, costs of a qualifying asset which have only been accrued but have not yet been paid in cash should be excluded from the amount on which interest is capitalised, as by definition no interest can have been incurred on an accrued payment. It should be noted that the effect of applying this principle is often merely to delay the capitalisation of interest since the costs will be included once they have been paid in cash. In most cases it is unlikely that the effect will be material as the time between accrual and payment of the cost will not be that great. However, the effect is potentially material where a significant part of the amount capitalised relates to costs which have been financed interest-free by third parties for a long period. An example of this is retention money which is not generally payable until the asset is completed.

4.2.4 *Asset carried in the balance sheet below cost*

An asset may be recognised in the financial statements during the period of production on a basis other than cost, i.e. it may have been written down below cost as a result of being impaired. The question then arises whether the calculation of interest to be capitalised should be based on cost or book value. In this case, cost should be used as this is the amount that the company or group has had to finance. This is consistent with IAS 23 and SIC-2 (see 7 below).

4.3 Group financial statements

4.3.1 *Borrowings in one company and development in another*

A question which often arises in practice is whether it is appropriate to capitalise interest in the group financial statements on borrowings that appear in the financial statements of a different group company from that carrying out the development. Based on the underlying philosophy of FRS 15, capitalisation in such circumstances would only be appropriate if the amount capitalised fairly reflected the interest cost of the group on borrowings from third parties which could theoretically have been avoided if the expenditure on the qualifying asset were not made.

Although it may be appropriate to capitalise interest in the group financial statements, the company carrying out the development should not capitalise any interest in its own financial statements as it has no borrowings. If, however, the company has intra-group borrowings then interest on such borrowings may be capitalised.

4.3.2 *Qualifying assets held by joint ventures*

In the UK, property developments are often carried out through the medium of joint ventures. In such cases, the joint venture may be financed principally by equity and the joint venture partners may have financed their participating interests by borrowings. It is not appropriate to capitalise interest in the joint venture on the borrowings of the partners as the interest charge is not a cost of the joint venture. Neither would it be appropriate to capitalise interest in the individual (as opposed to group) financial statements of the investing companies because the qualifying asset does not belong to them. The asset which the investing companies have is a participating interest, which is not in the course of production. However, the question does arise whether an adjustment may be made in the investor's group financial statements to capitalise interest on the borrowings financing the participating interest when the joint venture is equity accounted.

Example 13.2: Capitalisation of interest on borrowings to finance investment in joint venture

A company has a 50% investment in a joint venture whose balance sheet is as follows:

	£'000		£'000
Expenditure on development	1,600		
Capitalised interest	100	*	
			1,700
Cash			300
			2,000
Share capital			100
Share premium			900
			1,000
Borrowings: 10% loan			1,000
			2,000

* £1,600,000 x 10% restricted to actual interest incurred of £100,000.

The cost of the investment was £500,000 which was financed by a borrowing at 9% p.a. The investing company could, therefore, capitalise additional interest of £27,000 (being (1,600,000 – 1,000,000) x 50% x 9%) in its group financial statements (recognising that only 50% of the development expenditure not funded by borrowings is funded by the investing company).

Capitalisation in these circumstances appears to be justified on the basis that the borrowings are effectively financing the company's share of the development. It would have been possible for a similar result to be shown if the investing companies had decided to finance the joint venture with borrowings and only a nominal amount of equity. However, under IAS 23, the IASC decided that investments in enterprises should not be qualifying assets.

Where the qualifying assets are held by an investment which is not effectively an interest in a joint venture it is unlikely that an adjustment should be made in the group financial statements. This is because the interest in the investing company would probably not have been avoided if the investee had not incurred the costs on the qualifying asset.

4.4 Other issues

4.4.1 Change of policy

When interest is capitalised for the first time, FRS 3 requires that a prior year adjustment be made as this is a change of accounting policy. In theory, the adjustment should be made in respect of all assets still held which would, during their period of production, have satisfied the criteria adopted for capitalisation. However, this can create considerable difficulty in the case of fixed assets that were produced many years ago; accordingly, some compromises may have to be made in calculating the prior year adjustment; nevertheless it should be possible to produce a materially accurate figure.

Under FRS 18 accounting policies should be regularly reviewed and a change in policy may only be made where the Directors consider the new policy to be more 'appropriate' for the purpose of giving a true and fair view.[31] Thus a business which has previously not capitalised interest, if it wishes to do so subsequently, must presumably have good reasons which explain why the new policy of capitalisation is more 'appropriate'. However, in deciding upon a new policy the requirement for comparability must be given due weight.[32] IAS 18 is discussed in Chapter 2 at 7.

4.4.2 *Exchange differences as a borrowing cost*

Borrowings in one currency may have been used to finance a development the costs of which are incurred primarily in another currency, e.g. a Swiss franc loan financing a sterling development. This may have been done on the basis that, over the period of the development, the interest cost, after allowing for exchange differences, was expected to be less than the interest cost of an equivalent sterling loan. In these circumstances, there is a good argument for capitalising the interest cost and the exchange difference. In fact, SSAP 20 – *Foreign currency translation* – suggests that gains or losses arising from arrangements which may be considered as financing should be disclosed separately as part of 'Other interest receivable/payable and similar income/expense'.[33] This approach would also be consistent with IAS 23, which defines borrowing costs as including exchange differences arising from foreign currency borrowings to the extent that they are regarded as an adjustment to interest costs.[34]

4.4.3 *Assets produced by others*

According to the Companies Act 1985, the production cost of an asset 'shall be determined by adding to the purchase price of the raw materials and consumables used the amount of the costs incurred by the company which are directly attributable to the production of that asset'.[35] Similarly, under FRS 15, the cost of a fixed asset comprises those costs that are directly attributable to bringing the asset into working condition for its intended use. Consequently, although finance costs may of course be included in cost, this could be interpreted as meaning that finance costs may only be capitalised on assets produced by the company itself rather than assets produced by others for the company. This is because, if the assets are produced entirely by others, the production costs are not incurred by the company.

However, this interpretation would rule out capitalisation on most development and construction projects, which hardly seems logical given that the rationale for capitalising interest is strongly dependent on the view that it is an integral part of cost. Not surprisingly, therefore, a wider interpretation of the Companies Act is currently used in practice, and we do not consider that FRS 15 changes such practice. Extract 15.5 illustrates the application of this approach:

> *Extract 15.5: The Peninsular and Oriental Steam Navigation Company (2000)*
>
> **Accounting Policies**
> **Ships and Other Fixed Assets** [extract]
>
> Interest incurred in respect of payments on account of assets under construction is capitalised to the cost of the asset concerned.

FRS 15 mentions capitalising finance costs 'in respect of expenditures to date on the tangible fixed asset',[36] which would seem to imply that finance costs that relate to deposits and progress payments can be capitalised.

5 IAS REQUIREMENTS

5.1 The requirements of IAS 23

The revised IAS 23 – *Borrowing Costs (revised 1993)* – was issued in December 1993 with the 'benchmark treatment' that borrowing costs should be recognised as an expense in the period in which they are incurred regardless of how the borrowings are applied.[37] However, the IASB did not go so far as to prohibit the capitalisation of borrowing costs altogether, and the revised standard incorporates capitalisation as an 'allowed alternative treatment'.[38] Under the allowed treatment, borrowing costs that are directly attributable to the acquisition, construction or production of a qualifying asset are included in the cost of that asset. Such borrowing costs are capitalised when it is probable that they will result in future economic benefits to the enterprise and the costs can be measured reliably.[39] In the case of enterprises which follow this allowed alternative treatment, the requirements of IAS 23 are as follows.

5.1.1 Qualifying assets under IAS 23

IAS 23 defines a qualifying asset as 'an asset that necessarily takes a substantial period of time to get ready for its intended use or sale'.[40] Examples of qualifying assets are stocks that require a substantial period of time to bring them to a saleable condition, manufacturing plants, power generation facilities and investment properties. Stocks that are routinely manufactured, or otherwise produced in large quantities on a repetitive basis over a short period of time, and assets that are ready for their intended use or sale when acquired are not qualifying assets. In the case of equity accounted investments, the IASC considered whether or not the investor should look through to the investee's activities when applying the proposed revised Standard. However, it decided that this could involve an element of double-counting, since the investee itself would apply the Standard.[41] Accordingly, IAS 23 states that 'other investments' should not be qualifying assets.[42]

5.1.2 *Borrowing costs eligible for capitalisation*

The fundamental requirement for capitalisation under IAS 23 is that the borrowing costs must be 'directly attributable to the acquisition, construction or production of a qualifying asset'.[43] Borrowing costs themselves are interest and other costs incurred by an enterprise in connection with the borrowing of funds.[44] These may include:

(a) interest on bank overdrafts and short-term and long-term borrowings;

(b) amortisation of discounts or premiums relating to borrowings;

(c) amortisation of ancillary costs incurred in connection with the arrangement of borrowings;

(d) finance charges in respect of finance leases; and

(e) exchange differences arising from foreign currency borrowings to the extent that they are regarded as an adjustment to interest costs.[45]

In determining which borrowing costs satisfy the 'directly attributable' criterion, the standard starts from the premise that directly attributable borrowing costs are those that would have been avoided if the expenditure on the qualifying asset had not been made[46] – which is very much in line with the strict interpretation of the requirements in the UK as laid down in the Companies Act and FRS 15. Nevertheless, IAS 23 concedes that practical difficulties arise in identifying a direct relationship between particular borrowings and a qualifying asset and in determining the borrowings which could otherwise have been avoided; for example, in the case of an enterprise with a group treasury function that uses a range of debt instruments to borrow funds at varying rates of interest and lends those funds on various bases to other enterprises in the group. (Some might argue that it is for this very reason that capitalisation of borrowing costs should always be recognised as an expense when incurred.)

In any event, though, the standard makes allowance for the difficulties that arise in practice and concedes that the exercise of judgement is required[47]. Consequently, to the extent that funds are borrowed specifically for the purpose of obtaining a qualifying asset, the amount of borrowing costs eligible for capitalisation on that asset should be determined as the actual borrowing costs incurred on that borrowing during the period, less any investment income on the temporary investment of those borrowings.[48] The UK equivalent standard, FRS 15 is silent on this issue, though it is our opinion that under UK GAAP, interest received on the temporary investment of specific borrowings should be treated as laid down in IAS 23.

On the other hand, to the extent that funds are borrowed generally and used for the purpose of obtaining a qualifying asset, the amount of borrowing costs eligible for capitalisation should be determined by applying a capitalisation rate to the expenditures on that asset. The capitalisation rate should be the weighted average of the borrowing costs applicable to the borrowings of the enterprise that are outstanding during the period, other than borrowings made specifically for the purpose of obtaining a qualifying asset. The amount of borrowing costs capitalised during a period should not exceed the amount of borrowing costs incurred during that period.[49]

It is noteworthy that, where funds are borrowed generally, the amount of borrowing costs which may be capitalised is limited to the gross amount of borrowing costs incurred, and that this amount is *not* reduced by interest income earned. In our view this is the correct approach to the treatment of interest on general borrowings, since to deduct interest income in determining the amount to be capitalised would, in these circumstances, produce odd results. For example, retail groups are likely to have substantial amounts of excess cash available for short-term investment, and to attempt to establish a relationship between the interest earned on these funds and the interest paid on project finance would seem to be a misapplication of the principles of interest capitalisation.

The exchange difference that may be capitalised under IAS 23 (see IAS 23 paragraph 5(e) above) in our view refers only the exchange difference between interest on local currency borrowing and interest on foreign currency borrowing, not the whole of the exchange difference on the principal sum borrowed.

In the event that the carrying amount or the expected ultimate cost of the qualifying asset exceeds its recoverable amount or net realisable value, the asset must be written down in accordance with the relevant international standard.[50] In most cases IAS 36 – *Impairment of assets* – will apply; impairment is fully discussed in Chapter 13.

5.1.3 SIC-2: Consistency

An area of apparent uncertainty surrounding IAS 23 was whether an enterprise that has chosen a policy of capitalising borrowing costs should apply this policy to all qualifying assets or whether the enterprise could choose to capitalise borrowing costs for certain qualifying assets and not for others. In other words, is a policy of 'selective' capitalisation permitted under IAS? This issue was referred to the IASC's Standing Interpretations Committee (SIC), who issued the following consensus in interpretation SIC-2 entitled *Consistency - Capitalisation of Borrowing Costs*:

'Where an enterprise adopts the Allowed Alternative Treatment, that treatment should be applied consistently to all borrowing costs that are directly attributable to the acquisition, construction or production of all qualifying assets of the enterprise. If all the conditions laid down in IAS 23.11 are met, an enterprise should continue to capitalise such borrowing costs even if the carrying amount of the asset exceeds its recoverable amount. However, IAS 23.19 explains that the carrying amount of the asset should be written down to recognise impairment losses in such cases.'[51]

This interpretation is consistent with FRS 15's requirement that if an entity adopts a policy of capitalisation of finance costs, then it should be applied consistently to all tangible fixed assets where finance costs fall to be capitalised.[52]

5.1.4 Commencement, suspension and cessation of capitalisation

A Commencement of capitalisation

IAS 23 requires that capitalisation should commence when:

(a) expenditures for the asset are being incurred;

(b) borrowing costs are being incurred; and

(c) activities that are necessary to prepare the asset for its intended use or sale are in progress.[53]

The standard makes it explicit that only those expenditures on a qualifying asset that have resulted in payments of cash, transfers of other assets or the assumption of interest-bearing liabilities, may be included in determining borrowing costs. Such expenditures must be reduced by any progress payments received and grants received in connection with the asset. The standard allows that the average carrying amount of the asset during a period, including borrowing costs previously capitalised, is normally a reasonable approximation of the expenditures to which the capitalisation rate is applied in that period.[54]

IAS 23 acknowledges that the activities necessary to prepare an asset for its intended use or sale encompass more than the physical construction of the asset. They also include technical and administrative work (such as activities associated with obtaining permits) prior to the commencement of physical construction. However, such activities exclude the holding of an asset when no production or development that changes the asset's condition is taking place. For example, borrowing costs incurred while land is under development are capitalised during the period in which activities related to the development are being undertaken. However, borrowing costs incurred while land acquired for building purposes is held without any associated development activity do not qualify for capitalisation.[55]

B Suspension of capitalisation

IAS 23 states that capitalisation should be suspended during extended periods in which active development is interrupted. However, the standard distinguishes between extended periods of interruption (when capitalisation would be suspended) and periods of temporary delay that are a necessary part of preparing the asset for its intended purpose (when capitalisation is not normally suspended). Additionally capitalisation continues during periods when stock is undergoing slow transformation – the example is given of stocks taking an extended time to mature (presumably such as scotch whisky or cognac). A bridge construction delayed by temporary adverse weather conditions, where such conditions are common in the region, would also not be a cause for suspension of capitalisation.[56]

C Cessation of capitalisation

The standard requires that capitalisation should cease when substantially all the activities necessary to prepare the qualifying asset for its intended use or sale are complete.[57] An asset is normally ready for its intended use or sale when the physical construction of the asset is complete even though routine administrative work might still continue. If minor modifications, such as the decoration of a property to the purchaser's specification, are all that are outstanding, this indicates that substantially all the activities are complete.[58]

Furthermore, when the construction of a qualifying asset is completed in parts and each part is capable of being used while construction continues on other parts, capitalisation should cease when substantially all the activities necessary to prepare that part for its intended use or sale are completed.[59] An example of this might be a business park comprising several buildings, each of which is capable of being fully utilised while construction continues on other parts.[60]

The question could theoretically arise that an entire building itself was not complete, yet floors of if were complete and ready for use. This might be unlikely, as usually if some floors are incomplete and contractors are still working on substantial matters, it means that common services such as lifts, air conditioning and so forth are not working either, so that none of the floors are complete. However if individual floors of a large building are substantially complete and ready for their intended use, then paragraph 27 of IAS 23 clearly implies that capitalisation on those parts should cease.

5.2 Disclosure requirements of IAS 23

Under IAS 23 the following disclosures are required to be made:

Under the benchmark treatment:

The financial statements should disclose that the entity expenses all borrowing costs immediately.[61]

Under the allowed alternative treatment:

(a) that the entity capitalises borrowing costs in accordance with the allowed alternative treatment;

(b) the amount of borrowing costs capitalised during the period; and

(c) the capitalisation rate used to determine the amount of borrowing costs eligible for capitalisation.[62]

The accounts of Bayer provide an example of disclosure under IAS for interest capitalised, as shown in Extract 15.6.

Extract 15.6: Bayer AG (2000)

Notes to the Accounts

[8] Interest Expense – Net [extract]

Interest expense incurred to finance the construction phase of major investment projects is not included here. Such interest expenses, amounting in 2000 to €28 million (1999: €32 million), is capitalized as part of the cost of acquisition or construction of the property, plant or equipment concerned, based on an average capitalization rate of 5 per cent.

[18] Property, plant and equipment [extract]

If the construction phase of property, plant or equipment extends over a long period, the interest incurred on borrowed capital up to the date of completion is capitalized as part of the cost of acquisition or construction.

6 CONCLUSION

The ASB and the IASC have in effect adopted a holding position on the issue of capitalisation of borrowing costs, by neither banning it nor making it compulsory. The capitalisation of finance costs is an important part of the wider issue of accounting for interest effects, about which there is no international consensus. The decision on whether or not to capitalise interest requires a discussion of the nature of finance costs and how they fit within the structure of financial reporting by a company to its stakeholders – in short, whether or not the capitalisation of finance costs is a conceptually sound basis of accounting. Given the enthusiasm with which the ASB has introduced discounting into aspects of UK GAAP, it is surprising that it has taken such an equivocal stance on the capitalisation of finance costs.

At the conceptual level, there is a valid argument for measuring the cost of financing the acquisition of qualifying assets on the basis of the entity's cost of capital, including imputed interest on equity capital as well as interest on borrowings. At the same time it must be recognised that the capitalisation of the cost of equity capital does not conform to the historical cost accounting framework, under which the cost of a resource is measured by reference to historical exchange prices. Neither may such an approach conform to the definition of assets adopted by the ASB and the IASB in their conceptual frameworks (see Chapter 2 at 5.5.1 and 8.1.1). Nevertheless, to permit the capitalisation of interest only on borrowed capital is an incomplete approach.

Conversely, it may be argued that the capitalisation of borrowing costs into most types of property development is an entirely logical and appropriate policy. Interest is a development cost and is no different in this respect to the concrete and bricks. The IASB and the ASB will, therefore, need to decide whether or not the arguments in favour of capitalisation of borrowing costs outweigh the disadvantages of allowing an accounting practice which is essentially arbitrary. The only way to do this is to conduct a proper debate on the issue of accounting for interest effects, which would encompass both the capitalisation of all types of finance costs as well as discounting.

References

1 CA 85, Sch. 4, para. 26(3)(b).
2 IAS 23 (Original), *Capitalisation of Borrowing Costs*, IASC, March 1984, paras. 21–27.
3 IAS 23, *Borrowing Costs*, IASC, Revised December 1993, para. 8.
4 ASB Discussion Paper, *Measurement of tangible fixed assets*, para. 1.13.
5 FRS 15, *Tangible Fixed Assets*, Appendix IV, para. 10.
6 *Ibid.*, para. 11.
7 CA 85, Sch. 4, para. 26(3).
8 FRS 15, para. 19.
9 SSAP 9, *Stocks and long-term contracts*, Issued May 1975, Revised September 1988, Appendix 1, para. 21.
10 IAS 11, *Construction Contracts*, IASC, Revised December 1993, para. 18.
11 FRS 15, para. 2.
12 *Ibid.*
13 *Ibid.*, paras. 19 and 20.
14 *Ibid.*, para. 19.
15 *Ibid.*, para. 21.
16 *Ibid.*, para. 22.
17 *Ibid.*, para. 23.
18 *Ibid.*, para. 24.
19 *Ibid.*, para. 19.
20 *Ibid.*, para. 25.
21 IAS 23, para. 20.
22 FRS 15, para. 26.
23 *Ibid.*, paras. 27 and 28.
24 *Ibid.*
25 *Ibid.*, paras. 29 and 30.
26 CA 85, Sch. 4, para. 26(3).
27 *Ibid.*, para. 8.
28 *The Listing Rules*, Financial Services Authority, Chapter 12, para. 12.43(c).
29 CA 85, Sch. 4, paras. 17, 22 and 26(3).
30 FRS 15, paras. 23 and 24.
31 FRS 18, para. 45.
32 *Ibid.*
33 SSAP 20, *Foreign currency translation*, ASC, April 1983, para. 68.
34 IAS 23, para. 5(e).
35 CA 85, Sch. 4, para. 26(2).
36 FRS 15, para. 21.
37 IAS 23, Revised 1993, paras. 7 and 8.
38 *Ibid.*, paras. 10.
39 *Ibid.*, paras. 11 and 12.
40 *Ibid.*, para. 4.
41 IASC, *Insight*, October 1991, p. 10.
42 IAS 23, para. 6.
43 *Ibid.*, para. 11.
44 *Ibid.*, para. 4.
45 *Ibid.*, para. 5.
46 *Ibid.*, para. 13.
47 *Ibid.*, para. 14.
48 *Ibid.*, para. 15.
49 *Ibid.*, para. 17.
50 *Ibid.*, para. 19.
51 SIC-2, *Consistency - Capitalisation of Borrowing Costs*, SIC, July 1997, para. 3.
52 FRS 15, para. 20.
53 *Ibid.*, para. 20.
54 *Ibid.*, para. 21.
55 *Ibid.*, para. 22.
56 *Ibid.*, paras. 23 and 24.
57 *Ibid.*, para. 25.
58 *Ibid.*, para. 26.
59 *Ibid.*, para. 27.
60 *Ibid.*, para. 28.
61 *Ibid.*, para. 9.
62 *Ibid.*, para. 29.

Chapter 16 Stocks and long-term contracts

1 INTRODUCTION

SSAP 9 (revised) – *Stocks and long-term contracts* – is the principal pronouncement under UK GAAP dealing with the topic. Under IAS two standards are relevant: IAS 2 – *Inventories* – (inventory being the equivalent term to stocks) and IAS 11 – *Construction contracts*. The term 'stocks' includes raw materials, work-in-progress, finished goods, and goods for resale. A long-term contract (a construction contract under IAS) is specifically defined in the relevant standard, the essence of the definition being that the contract is started and completed in a different accounting period. Clearly the distinctions between goods bought in for resale, work-in-progress associated with manufactured goods, and the costs involved with the partial completion of long-term contracts, really represent useful reference points on a continuum. Although this means there can be somewhat arbitrary categorisations, particularly whether a contract is or is not treated as long-term, the distinctions seem to work reasonably satisfactorily in practice.

Long-term contracts are effectively a special category of stocks, with special rules governing how the costs incurred will be accounted for. Consequently this chapter discusses long-term contracts ('construction contracts' under IAS) separately. In the text the terms 'stocks' and 'inventories' are used to include manufactured work-in-progress. The original SSAP 9 was issued in 1975 and then revised in 1988; throughout this chapter SSAP 9 is used to refer to the revised standard.

1.1 Objectives of stock measurement

For many years the principal objective of stock measurement remained unchallenged within the historical cost accounting system as being the proper determination of income through the process of matching costs with related revenues.[1] In order to match costs and revenue, 'costs' of stocks should comprise that expenditure which has been incurred in the normal course of business in bringing the product or service to its present location and condition.[2] Under this system all costs incurred in respect of stocks should be charged as period costs, except for those which relate to those unconsumed stocks which are expected to be of future benefit to the entity. These should be carried forward to be matched with the revenues that they will generate in the future. Therefore, in measuring income under the historical cost system, stocks in the balance sheet have characteristics similar to those of prepaid expenses or fixed assets such as plant and equipment.

If, however, there is expected to be no future benefit, or if the future benefit is expected to be less than the associated costs, then the prudence is applied, and the carrying value of those stocks must be reduced to the value of their future benefit. This gives rise to the basic rule for the balance sheet valuation of stocks, i.e. that they should be stated at the lower of cost and net realisable value.[3] Clearly, however, the application of this rule can result in stocks being reported at amounts which neither reflect the historical costs which have been incurred in bringing them to their present location or condition, nor the replacement cost of such stocks.

Although the IASB and the ASB have both published conceptual frameworks that clearly are moving in the direction of stating all assets and liabilities at fair value, at least for the present stocks continue to be stated in the balance sheet and the profit and loss account on a recognisably historical cost basis. However, the second objective of stock measurement – which is to present a value of stock in the balance sheet – heightens the relevance of the current conceptual framework debate. Considering this objective, and indeed whether it is more important than the first income-related objective, implies a view of the purpose of the balance sheet which, as discussed extensively in Chapter 2, is far from settled.

Stocks could be reported in the balance sheet on a number of different bases, for example realisable value or current replacement cost. The decision about what valuation basis to adopt for assets and liabilities generally in financial reporting is the subject of considerable debate currently within the IASB and the ASB, which will not be resolved in the context of stocks alone.

1.2 Cost flow assumptions

In many industries, particularly those dealing in fast moving consumer goods or non-deteriorating raw material stocks, stock movements are not tracked individually by the accounting system. Rather some sort of aggregation takes place and the cost of stock sold, or used, or transferred to work-in-progress, is calculated based on the number or quantity used up multiplied by the price paid for that item. However, as prices for stocks acquired often change, it has been necessary to develop systematic bases for the recognition of the cost of sales, founded on certain cost flow assumptions. The principal methods used are outlined below. The explanatory note to SSAP 9 states that 'the methods used in allocating costs to stocks need to be selected with a view to providing the fairest possible approximation to the expenditure actually incurred in bringing the product to its present location and condition'.[4] Consequently, SSAP 9 sees the allocation of actual costs on the basis of the physical flow of goods as the ideal.

1.2.1 *Specific identification/actual cost*

Where it is both possible and practicable to attach a specific cost to each item of stock, the costs of goods sold are specifically identified and matched with the goods physically sold. In practice this is a relatively unusual method of valuation as the clerical effort required does not make it feasible unless there are relatively few high value items being bought or produced. Consequently, it would normally be used where the stock comprised items such as antiques, jewellery and cars in the hands of dealers.

1.2.2 *FIFO (first-in, first-out)*

In the vast majority of businesses it will not be practicable to keep track of stock cost on an individual unit basis; nevertheless, the objective of stock measurement is still to match costs and revenues. The FIFO method probably gives the closest approximation to actual cost flows, since it is assumed that when stocks are sold or used in a production process, the oldest are sold or used first and that, therefore, the balance of stock on hand at any point represents the most recent purchases or production. This can best be illustrated in the context of a business which deals in perishable goods, since clearly such a business will use the earliest goods received first. Therefore, by allocating the earliest costs incurred against revenue, actual cost flows are being matched with the physical flow of goods with reasonable accuracy. In any event, even in the case of businesses which do not deal in perishable goods, this would reflect what would probably be a sound management policy. Consequently, in practice where it is not possible to value stock on an actual cost basis, the FIFO method is generally used since it is most likely to approximate the physical flow of goods sold, resulting in the most accurate measurement of cost flows. For example, GlaxoSmithKline discloses a FIFO stock policy as shown in Extract 16.1.

Extract 16.1: GlaxoSmithKline plc (2000)

Stocks

Stocks are included in the accounts at the lower of cost (including manufacturing overheads, where appropriate) and net realisable value. Cost is generally determined on a first in, first out basis.

1.2.3 *Weighted average*

This method, which is suitable where stock units are identical or near identical, involves the computation of an average unit cost by dividing the total cost of units by the number of units. The average unit cost then has to be revised with every receipt of stock, or alternatively at the end of predetermined periods. In practice, weighted average would appear to be less widely used than FIFO as it involves more clerical effort, and its results are not very different from FIFO in times of relatively low inflation, or where stock turnover is relatively quick.

Nevertheless, there are certain businesses which hold large quantities of relatively homogeneous stock for which the weighted average method of stock valuation is the most appropriate, as shown in Extract 16.2 by Unilever.

> *Extract 16.2: Unilever PLC (2000)*
>
> **Current assets**
>
> Stocks are valued at the lower of cost and estimated net realisable value. Cost is mainly average cost, and comprises direct costs and, where appropriate, a proportion of production overheads.

1.2.4 LIFO (last-in, first-out)

This method is, as its name suggests, the opposite to FIFO and assumes that the most recent purchases or production are used first; in certain cases this could represent the physical flow of stock (e.g. if a store is filled and emptied from the top). LIFO is an attempt to match current costs with current revenues so that the profit and loss account excludes the effects of holding gains. Essentially, therefore, LIFO is an attempt to achieve something closer to replacement cost accounting for the profit and loss account, whilst disregarding the balance sheet. Consequently, the period-end balance of stock on hand represents the earliest purchases of the item, resulting in stocks being stated in the balance sheet at amounts which may bear little relationship to recent cost levels. For this reason, LIFO is ordinarily not permitted to be used under SSAP 9[5] despite the fact that it is allowed by the Companies Act.[6]

While there may be no conceptual difficulty in using LIFO in a pure historical cost accounting system which is profit and loss oriented, there are difficulties with the balance sheet orientated approach favoured by the IASB and ASB, as well as severe practical drawbacks. LIFO distorts the calculation of working capital ratios and makes inter-firm comparisons difficult, and in the UK the Inland Revenue has never permitted its use for tax purposes.

The revision in 1993 of IAS 2 had the effect of setting down the FIFO and weighted average cost formulas as the 'benchmark treatments' for determining the cost of inventories,[7] although LIFO is retained as an 'allowed alternative treatment'[8] (see 4.2.2 below).

2 UK REQUIREMENTS

2.1 The requirements of the Companies Act 1985

The legal requirements governing accounting for stocks within a company's financial statements are included along with most other legal accounting requirements in Schedule 4 to the Companies Act 1985. There is no specific mention made in the legislation of long-term contracts, this is because the legislation treats all current assets in the same way. The Companies Act requires stocks to be classified into the categories in the standard balance sheet formats contained in Schedule 4 to the Companies Act 1985. These sub-headings are as follows:

- raw materials and consumables
- work in progress
- finished goods and goods for resale
- payments on account.[9]

In practice, most companies follow these classifications strictly and present stock as a note to the financial statements, as illustrated in Extract 16.3.

Extract 16.3: Smiths Industries plc (2000)

Notes to Accounts [extract]

	Consolidated	
	2000	1999
17 Stocks	**£m**	£m
Stocks comprise:		
Raw materials and consumables	**89.5**	66.2
Work in progress	**79.2**	67.5
Finished goods	**93.0**	83.5
	261.7	217.2
Less: Payments on account	**(14.0)**	(13.3)
	247.7	203.9

The application of these classifications should, however, be done in conjunction with the requirements of Schedule 4, paragraph 3(3), which states that 'in preparing a company's balance sheet or profit and loss account the directors of the company shall adapt the arrangement and headings and sub-headings ... in any case where the special nature of the company's business requires such adaptation'.[10]

2.1.1 *Valuation in the balance sheet*

Paragraphs 22 and 23 of Schedule 4, which apply to all current assets and not just stocks, are very similar to paragraph 26 of SSAP 9 and provide that current assets should be stated at the lower of their purchase price or production cost, and net realisable value.

Paragraph 25 of Schedule 4 provides that stocks of raw materials and consumables which are constantly being replaced may be included at a fixed quantity and value provided that the overall value of such stocks is not material to the company's balance sheet and that their quantity, value and composition are not subject to material variation.

2.1.2 *Determination of purchase price or production cost*

The rules that apply in determining the cost of an asset (including current assets and therefore stocks) are set out in paragraph 26 of Schedule 4, as follows:

(a) the purchase price of an asset should include any expenses incidental to the acquisition of that asset, e.g. customs duties;

(b) the production cost of an asset should include, in addition to the cost of the raw materials and consumables, any other directly attributable production costs, e.g. direct labour costs;

(c) in the case of current assets, distribution costs may not be included in production costs;

(d) in addition to the costs at (b) above there may be included some costs 'which are only indirectly attributable to the production of that asset'. Most commonly these would be costs that vary with time rather than production, e.g. rent, rates and insurance; and

(e) 'Interest on capital borrowed to finance the production' may also be included in stock. Capitalisation of interest is discussed in Chapter 15.

Any costs that fall to be included under (d) and (e) above can only be included to the extent that they accrue during the period of production, and the amount of any interest included must be separately disclosed.

2.1.3 *Costing method and replacement cost*

Paragraph 27 of Schedule 4 provides that stocks may be stated using FIFO, LIFO, weighted average or any other method similar to any of those, but whichever method is chosen, it must be appropriate to the circumstances of the company. However, where any item of stock is valued by one of these methods rather than at actual cost, the difference between the amount at which it is included in the financial statements and its replacement cost or most recent actual purchase price or production cost is required to be disclosed if that difference is material. A strict interpretation of the paragraph could require some meaningless disclosures to be given. However, in practice, if an amount is disclosed it is usually the total replacement cost of stocks, as shown by BP Amoco in Extract 16.4.

Extract 16.4: BP Amoco p.l.c. (2000)

		$ million
21 Stocks	**2000**	1999
Petroleum	**6,933**	3,517
Chemicals	**1,046**	828
Other	**504**	202
	8,483	4,547
Stores	**751**	577
	9,234	5,124
Replacement cost	**9,392**	5,165

It should be noted that paragraph 27(5) of Schedule 4 permits the use of the most recent actual purchase price or production cost rather than replacement cost if the former appears more appropriate to the directors of the company – although such disclosure is likely to have most relevance in the cases of companies that value their stocks on bases other than FIFO and is, therefore, rarely seen in practice.

2.1.4 *Current cost*

Paragraph 31 of Schedule 4 allows stocks to be included at their current cost. However, this treatment is rarely seen in practice, as almost all companies prepare their statutory financial statements under the historical cost convention.

2.2 The accounting and disclosure requirements of SSAP 9 for stocks

SSAP 9 (revised) – *Stocks and long-term contracts* – was issued in 1988 and contained minor revisions from the original 1975 version. The revisions it contained related to the presentation of long-term contract balances, which for technical reasons required alteration to comply with the requirements of the Companies Act 1985. Thus SSAP 9 is one of the oldest accounting standards still extant, as SSAP 2 has now been superseded by FRS 18. This part of the chapter includes all the general requirements of SSAP 9 concerning stocks, but the provisions of the standard that apply solely to long-term contracts are separately dealt with at 2.3 below.

2.2.1 *Definitions*

SSAP 9 states that stocks fall into the following categories:

‘(a) goods or other assets purchased for resale;

(b) consumable stores;

(c) raw materials and components purchased for incorporation into products for sale;

(d) products and services in intermediate stages of completion;

(e) long-term contract balances; and

(f) finished goods.’[11]

SSAP 9 defines cost in relation to stock as ‘that expenditure which has been incurred in the normal course of business in bringing the product or service to its present location and condition’.[12] There should be included in the expenditure both cost of purchase and such costs of conversion ‘as are appropriate to that location and condition’.[13] Cost of purchase comprises ‘purchase price including import duties, transport and handling costs and any other directly attributable costs, less trade discounts, rebates and subsidies’;[14] whilst cost of conversion comprises:

‘(a) costs which are specifically attributable to units of production, eg, direct labour, direct expenses and sub-contracted work;

(b) production overheads (as defined in paragraph 20 [of SSAP 9]);

(c) other overheads, if any, attributable in the particular circumstances of the business to bringing the product or service to its present location and condition’.[15]

See 2.2.3 below for the valuation basis prescribed for stocks by SSAP 9 and definition given in the standard of net realisable value.

2.2.2 *Accounting policies*

SSAP 9 requires that the accounting policies that have been applied to stocks should be stated and applied consistently within the business from year to year.[16] In practice, the degree of detail given varies quite considerably, with some policies being particularly comprehensive and informative, for example Corus Group as shown in Extract 16.5.

> *Extract 16.5: Corus Group plc (2000)*
>
> **IX Stocks**
>
> Stocks of raw materials are valued at cost or, if they are to be realised without processing, the lower of cost and net realisable value. Cost is determined using the 'first in first out' method. Stocks of partly processed materials, finished products and stores and individually valued at the lower of cost and net realisable value. Cost of partly processed and finished products comprises cost of production including works overheads. Net realisable value is the price at which the stocks can be realised in the normal course of business after allowing for the cost of conversion from their existing state to a finished condition and cost of disposal. Provisions are made to cover slow moving and obsolescent items.

We believe that the accounting policy for stock should at least provide the following level of detail of information (where applicable):

Stocks

Stocks are stated at the lower of cost and net realisable value. Cost includes all costs incurred in bringing each product to its present location and condition, as follows:

Raw materials, consumables and goods for resale	–	purchase cost on a first-in, first-out basis.
Work in progress and finished goods	–	cost of direct materials and labour plus attributable overheads based on a normal level of activity.

Net realisable value is based on estimated selling price less any further costs expected to be incurred to completion and disposal.

2.2.3 *Valuation basis*

Stocks should be stated in financial statements at 'the total of the lower of cost and net realisable value of the separate items of stock or of groups of similar items'.[17] SSAP 9 defines net realisable value as:

> 'the actual or estimated selling price (net of trade but before settlement discounts) less:
>
> (a) all further costs to completion; and
>
> (b) all costs to be incurred in marketing, selling and distributing.'[18]

Appendix 1 to SSAP 9 identifies the following situations where net realisable value might be less than cost:

> '(a) an increase in costs or a fall in selling price;
>
> (b) physical deterioration of stocks;
>
> (c) obsolescence of products;

(d) a decision as part of a company's marketing strategy to manufacture and sell products at a loss;

(e) errors in production or purchasing'.[19]

In addition it points out that when a company has excess stocks on hand the risk of situations (a) to (c) above occurring increases and must be considered in assessing net realisable value. A provision will also be required for losses on commitments made for both the future purchases and sales of stocks. SSAP 9 requires that the comparison of cost and net realisable value should be done on an item by item basis or by groups of similar items.[20]

The practical considerations in determining the constituents of cost are discussed at 3.1.1 below.

2.2.4 *Disclosure of the analysis of stocks*

SSAP 9 requires that stocks should be sub-classified on the face of the balance sheet or in the notes thereto, so as to indicate the amounts held in each of the main categories in the standard balance sheet formats contained in Schedule 4 to the Companies Act 1985.[21] These sub-headings are as follows:

- raw materials and consumables
- work in progress
- finished goods and goods for resale
- payments on account.[22]

In practice, most companies follow these classifications strictly and present stock as a note to the financial statements, as shown in Extract 16.3 at 2.1 above. Directors are permitted by the Companies Act[23] to adjust these categories if the nature of the business requires such adaptation, as explained at 2.1 above. It is therefore the responsibility of the directors to ensure that the classifications used are appropriate to the nature of the company's business. Although variations are rarely found in practice, Bellway, see Extract 16.6, is a company that has taken advantage of this provision to describe its stock categories in more detail.

Extract 16.6: Bellway plc (2000)

9 Stocks	**2000**	1999
	£000	£000
Group		
Work in progress and stocks	**506,437**	483,230
Grants	**(7,383)**	(8,265)
Payments on account	**(16,164)**	(7,979)
	482,890	466,986
Showhomes	**16,799**	14,730
Part exchange properties	**8,825**	8,448
	508,514	490,164

Another example is BP Amoco as shown in Extract 16.4 at 2.1.3 above.

2.3 The accounting and disclosure requirements of SSAP 9 concerning long-term contracts

Typically, long-term contracts cover large civil engineering and construction schemes, such as motorway, skyscraper or bridge building, that take a considerable time to complete and are in progress during more than one accounting period, although there are many smaller types of long-term contract that are subject to the standard. A different treatment is required for long-term contracts because if the basic rule of accounting for stocks was applied to them, it would result in an annual profit and loss account reflecting only the outcome of contracts completed during the year. In a contracting company this might bear no relation to the company's actual level of activity for that year, so turnover and attributable profit has to be recognised on uncompleted contracts in order to present a consistent view of the results of the company's activities during the period.

2.3.1 *Definition*

SSAP 9 defines a long term contract as:

> 'a contract entered into for the design, manufacture or construction of a single substantial asset or the provision of a service (or of a combination of assets or services which together constitute a single project) where the time taken substantially to complete the contract is such that the contract activity falls into different accounting periods. A contract that is required to be accounted for as long-term by this accounting standard will usually extend for a period exceeding one year. However, a duration exceeding one year is not an essential feature of a long-term contract. Some contracts with a shorter duration than one year should be accounted for as long-term contracts if they are sufficiently material to the activity of the period that not to record turnover and attributable profit would lead to a distortion of the period's turnover and results such that the financial statements would not give a true and fair view, provided that the policy is applied consistently within the reporting entity and from year to year.'[24]

The practical impact of this definition is that short-term contracting businesses will probably be able to account for all their contracts as short term (even if some contracts extend for more than a year), and long-term contracting businesses will be able to account for all their contracts as long term (even if some are for less than a year). However, if a business is clearly in both the short-term and long-term contracting businesses, criteria must be established for distinguishing between such contracts, and appropriate accounting policies must be established and applied consistently.

However, it should be noted that there is an area of potential controversy over the accrual of profit on short-term contracts. This is discussed at 3.2.4 below.

2.3.2 *Turnover, related costs and attributable profit*

Long-term contracts should be:

(a) assessed on a contract by contract basis; and

(b) reflected in the profit and loss account by recording turnover and related costs as contract activity progresses.[25]

The standard does not lay down a method for determining turnover, stating that 'turnover is ascertained in a manner appropriate to the stage of completion of the contract, the business and the industry in which it operates'.[26] SSAP 9 then states that 'where it is considered that the outcome of a long-term contract can be assessed with reasonable certainty before its conclusion, the prudently calculated attributable profit should be recognised in the profit and loss account as the difference between the reported turnover and related costs for that contract'.[27] Based on this requirement, it would appear that the attributable profit is the balancing figure once 'turnover' and 'related costs' have been determined. One would therefore have expected SSAP 9 to define 'related costs' and require companies to disclose an accounting policy for the determination of 'related costs'. Instead it defines 'attributable profit' and requires an accounting policy which sets out how it has been ascertained. As a result, either turnover or related costs will be the balancing figure.

'Attributable profit' is defined as 'that part of the total profit currently estimated to arise over the duration of the contract, after allowing for estimated remedial and maintenance costs and increases in costs so far as not recoverable under the terms of the contract, that fairly reflects the profit attributable to that part of the work performed at the accounting date. (There can be no attributable profit until the profitable outcome of the contract can be assessed with reasonable certainty.)'[28]

This definition arguably leaves open whether or not a company is required to book a loss in the early years of a contract that is profitable overall, merely because the high-cost work of the contract is being carried out in the earlier years. In our view, this was clearly not the intention of SSAP 9, always provided that the overall profitability of the contract can be assessed with reasonable certainty.

See 3.2 below for further discussion of the problems associated with determining profit and turnover.

2.3.3 *Accounting policies*

SSAP 9 requires that companies must disclose their accounting policies in respect of long-term contracts; in particular the method of ascertaining both turnover and attributable profit. These policies must be applied consistently within the business and from year to year.[29]

Current reporting practice reflects a wide variety in the amount of detail given by companies in their accounting policies for turnover and profit recognition. Balfour Beatty discloses fairly comprehensive policies, as shown in Extract 16.7:

Extract 16.7: Balfour Beatty plc (2000)

Principal accounting policies [extract]
6 Profit recognition on contracting activities`

Profit on individual contracts is taken only when their outcome can be foreseen with reasonable certainty, based on the lower of the percentage margin earned to date and that prudently forecast at completion, taking account of agreed claims. Full provision is made for all known or expected losses on individual contracts, taking a prudent view of future claims income, immediately such losses are foreseen. Profit for the year includes the benefit of claims settled on contracts completed in prior years..

2.3.4 *The financial statement presentation of long-term contracts*

SSAP 9 requires that long-term contracts should be disclosed in the financial statements as follows:

'(a) the amount by which recorded turnover is in excess of payments on account should be classified as "amounts recoverable on contracts" and separately disclosed within debtors;

(b) the balance of payments on account (in excess of amounts (i) matched with turnover; and (ii) offset against long-term contract balances) should be classified as payments on account and separately disclosed within creditors;

(c) the amount of long-term contracts, at costs incurred, net of amounts transferred to cost of sales, after deducting foreseeable losses and payments on account not matched with turnover, should be classified as "long-term contract balances" and separately disclosed within the balance sheet heading "Stocks". The balance sheet note should disclose separately the balances of:

 (i) net cost less foreseeable losses; and

 (ii) applicable payments on account;

(d) the amount by which the provision or accrual for foreseeable losses exceeds the costs incurred (after transfers to cost of sales) should be included within either provisions for liabilities and charges or creditors as appropriate.'[30]

The 'amounts recoverable on contracts' figure in debtors represents the excess of the value of work carried out at the balance sheet date (which has been recorded as turnover) over cumulative payments on account. The amount and realisability of this balance therefore depends on the value of work carried out being ascertained appropriately. As the standard explains 'the balance arises as a derivative of this process of contract revenue recognition and is directly linked to turnover. In substance, it represents accrued revenue receivable and has the attributes of a debtor.'[31]

GKN in Extract 16.8 provides a comprehensive example of the type of disclosures of accounting policy, stocks, debtors and creditors associated with long-term contracts.

Extract 16.8: GKN plc (2000)

13 Stocks [extract]	**2000**	1999
	£m	£m
Raw materials and consumables	**169**	140
Work in progress	**246**	190
Long-term work in progress	**75**	108
Finished goods and goods for resale	**112**	89
	602	527

Stocks, other than long-term work in progress, are valued at the lower of cost and estimated net realisable value, due allowance being made for obsolete or slow-moving items. Costs includes the relevant proportion of works overheads assuming normal levels of activity.

Long-term work in progress consists of net costs, after deducting foreseeable losses, of £631 million (1999 - £629 million) less payments on account £556 million (1999 - £521 million). Payments received from customers are deducted from stock and work in progress to the extent of the cost of the work carried out and any excess is shown as customer advances. Profit on long-term contracts is taken when sales are recognised based on estimated overall profitability. On aerospace contracts where volumes are not contractually fixed, net non-recurring initial costs consisting of design, development and tooling, are amortised on a straight line basis over five years from the start of serial production subject to the programme remaining in existence. On major commercial programmes where a component is integral to the aircraft the amortisation period may be extended up to a maximum of ten years. Work in progress includes £71 million (1999 - £41 million) in respect of net non-recurring costs.

The replacement cost of stocks is not materially different from the historical cost value.

14 Debtors [extract]	**2000**	1999
	£m	£m
Due within one year:		
Amounts recoverable on contracts	**37**	7

17 Creditors [extract]	**2000**	1999
	£m	£m
Customer advances	**315**	342

SSAP 9 defines 'foreseeable losses' as 'losses which are currently estimated to arise over the duration of the contract'.[32] This means that all future losses must be provided for in full as soon as they are known about, even though profits are taken over the duration of the contract. SSAP 9 is unclear about when it would be appropriate to classify the provision or accrual for foreseeable losses within creditors rather than provisions, and it is our view that under normal circumstances these amounts should be included in the balance sheet within provisions for liabilities and charges.

2.3.5 *Illustrative examples of the disclosure of long-term contracts*

The following example is based on Appendix 3 to SSAP 9, and serves to illustrate the financial statement disclosure requirements of SSAP 9 as they apply to the various circumstances which might arise concerning long-term contracts.

Example 16.1: Application of the principles of SSAP 9 to long-term contracts

The following assumptions apply to each of the contracts, and in each case the company's summarised profit and loss account for the year ended 31 October 2001 and a balance sheet as at that date is illustrated:

(1) This is the first year of the contract.

(2) The company has only one contract.

(3) All payments on account have actually been received in the form of cash.

(4) All costs incurred have been paid in cash.

(5) All the information is as at the balance sheet date, 31 October 2001.

(6) Share capital is minimal and is ignored.

(7) Any necessary finance is provided by bank overdraft.

Contract 1

	£'000
Turnover	145
Cost of sales	110
Payments on account	100
Costs incurred	110

Financial statement presentation of Contract 1 (SSAP 9, para. 30):

SUMMARISED PROFIT AND LOSS ACCOUNT for the year ended 31 October 2001

	£'000
Turnover	145
Cost of sales	110
Gross profit on long-term contracts	35

SUMMARISED BALANCE SHEET as at 31 October 2001

	£'000
Current assets	
Debtors	
Amounts recoverable on contracts [145 - 100]	45
Current liabilities	
Overdraft	10
Net current assets	35
Profit and loss account	35

Contract 2

	£'000
Turnover	520
Cost of sales	450
Payments on account	600
Costs incurred	510

Financial statement presentation of Contract 2 (SSAP 9, para. 30):

SUMMARISED PROFIT AND LOSS ACCOUNT for the year ended 31 October 2001

	£'000
Turnover	520
Cost of sales	450
Gross profit on long-term contracts	70

SUMMARISED BALANCE SHEET as at 31 October 2001

	£'000
Current assets	
Stocks (Note 1)	–
Cash	90
	90
Current liabilities	
Payments on account [600 - 520 - 60]	20
Net current assets	70
Profit and loss account	70

Note 1

Long-term contract balances	
Net cost [510 - 450]	60
less: payments on account	(60)
	–

Contract 3

	£'000
Turnover	380
Cost of sales	350
Payments on account	400
Costs incurred	450

Financial statement presentation of Contract 3 (SSAP 9, para. 30):

SUMMARISED PROFIT AND LOSS ACCOUNT for the year ended 31 October 2001

	£'000
Turnover	380
Cost of sales	350
Gross profit on long-term contracts	30

SUMMARISED BALANCE SHEET as at 31 October 2001

	£'000
Current assets	
Stocks	
Long-term contract balances (Note 1)	80
Current liabilities	
Overdraft	50
	30
Profit and loss account	30

Note 1

Long-term contract balances	
Net cost [450 - 350]	100
less: payments on account [400 - 380]	20
	80

Contract 4

	£'000	
Turnover	200	
Cost of sales	250	
Payments on account	150	
Costs incurred	250	
Provision for foreseeable losses	40	(not included in cost of sales above)

Financial statement presentation of Contract 4 (SSAP 9, para. 30):

SUMMARISED PROFIT AND LOSS ACCOUNT for the year ended 31 October 2001

	£'000
Turnover	200
Cost of sales [250 + 40]	290
Gross (loss) on long-term contracts	(90)

SUMMARISED BALANCE SHEET as at 31 October 2001

	£'000
Current assets	
Debtors	
Amounts recoverable on contracts [200 - 150]	50
Current liabilities	
Overdraft	100
Net current (liabilities)	(50)
Provisions for liabilities and charges	
Provision for foreseeable losses on contracts	(40)
	(90)
Profit and loss account	(90)

(Note that the provision for foreseeable losses of 40 is not offset against the debit balance of 50 included in debtors.)

Contract 5

	£'000	
Turnover	55	
Cost of sales	55	
Payments on account	80	
Costs incurred	100	
Provision for foreseeable losses	30	(not included in cost of sales above)

Financial statement presentation of Contract 5 (SSAP 9, para. 30):

SUMMARISED PROFIT AND LOSS ACCOUNT for the year ended 31 October 2001

	£'000
Turnover	55
Cost of sales [55 + 30]	85
Gross (loss) on long-term contracts	(30)

SUMMARISED BALANCE SHEET as at 31 October 2001

	£'000
Current assets	
Stocks	
Long-term contract balances (Note 1)	–
Current liabilities	
Overdraft	20
Payments on account [80 - 55 - 15]	10
Net current (liabilities)	(30)
Profit and loss account	(30)

Note 1

Long-term contract balances	
Net cost (after deducting foreseeable losses) [100 - 55 – 30]	15
Less: payments on account	(15)
	–

3 UK PRACTICAL ISSUES

3.1 Practical issues with stocks

3.1.1 Constituents of cost

Both SSAP 9 and the Companies Act 1985 require that stocks should be stated in the balance sheet at the lower of cost and net realisable value. Both SSAP 9 and the Companies Act 1985 also require that the purchase price of stocks shall be determined by adding to the actual purchase price paid any incidental expenses of acquisition, together with both directly and indirectly attributable overheads.[33] SSAP 9 states that:

> '… costs of stocks should comprise that expenditure which has been incurred in the normal course of business in bringing the product or service to its present location and condition. Such costs will include all related production overheads, even though these may accrue on a time basis.'
>
> 'The methods used in allocating costs to stocks need to be selected with a view to providing the fairest possible approximation to the expenditure actually incurred in bringing the product to its present location and condition.'[34]

Paragraph 17 goes on to say that 'this expenditure should include, in addition to cost of purchase, such costs of conversion as are appropriate to that location and condition'. Cost of purchase comprises 'purchase price' and 'any other directly attributable costs', and 'cost of conversion' includes 'other overheads, if any, attributable in the particular circumstances of the business to bringing the product or service to its present location and condition'.[35]

The term 'present location and condition' is not defined or explained in SSAP 9 and is therefore a matter of interpretation and judgement depending on the particular facts and circumstances surrounding the business in question. For example, in the context of a retail company, the particular circumstances of the business are that 'present location and condition' may be interpreted to mean positioned on the stores' shelves and ready for sale.

Appendix 1 to SSAP 9 incorporates ten paragraphs that deal with further practical considerations in respect of the allocation of overheads. Paragraph 10 of the Appendix reinforces the point that the allocation of all attributable overheads to the valuation of stock is a mandatory requirement of SSAP 9, and that even the prudence argument cannot be used as a reason for omitting selected overheads from such allocation. Paragraph 10 reads as follows:

> 'The adoption of a conservative approach to the valuation of stocks and long-term contracts has sometimes been used as one of the reasons for omitting selected production overheads. In so far as the circumstances of the business require an element of prudence in determining the amount at which stocks and long-term contracts are stated, this needs to be taken into account in the determination of net realisable value and not by the exclusion from cost of selected overheads.'

This means that overheads should be allocated to the cost of stock on a consistent basis from year to year, and should not be omitted in anticipation of a net realisable value difficulty. Once overheads have been allocated, the carrying value of stock should then be reviewed in order to ensure that it is stated at the lower of cost and net realisable value.

For the most part there are few problems over the inclusion of direct costs in stocks. However, problems may arise over the inclusion of certain types of overheads, and over the allocation of overheads into the stock valuation.

A Distribution costs

By law, distribution costs may not be included in the cost of stocks (see 2.1.2 above). However, SSAP 9 defines cost as 'that expenditure which has been incurred in the normal course of business in bringing the product or service to its present location and condition'.[36] As a result, a company which includes in stock the cost of transporting goods from its factory to its warehouse in accordance with the standard might, in theory, not be complying with the law. In practice, however, the costs of such transport are not likely to be material and the company can take advantage of paragraph 86 of Schedule 4 to the Companies Act 1985, which provides that immaterial amounts may be disregarded for the purposes of any provision of Schedule 4. An alternative and perhaps more reasonable view might be that the 'distribution costs' referred to in paragraph 26 of Schedule 4 are costs of distribution to customers, and that therefore the costs of transporting goods to a warehouse or retail outlet would not fall within the meaning of the prohibition.

B Selling costs

SSAP 9 states that normally only purchase and production costs should be included in the cost of stocks. However, in certain specific circumstances the standard recognises that it might be appropriate to include other types of cost in stock:

> 'Where firm sales contracts have been entered into for the provision of goods or services to customer's specification, overheads relating to design, and marketing and selling costs incurred before manufacture may be included in arriving at cost.'[37]

Although ordinarily such costs should be expensed in the period in which they are incurred, in the above circumstances they may be deferred and matched against their related revenues. This seems is a reasonable line for SSAP 9 to take, but one that may be in conflict with the asset definition based recognition criteria now adopted by the ASB in its *Statement of Principles* (see Chapter 2 at 5). Although probably not a major issue, it is possible that in the event of a revision to SSAP 9, such dispensation would be removed, as this type of deferred cost may not meet the ASB's definition of an asset.

It is noteworthy that IAS 2 (see 4.2.2 below) specifically excludes selling costs from the cost of inventories and requires them to be recognised as expenses in the period in which they are incurred.[38]

C Storage costs

Storage costs are not costs which would normally be incurred in bringing a product to its present location and condition. However, where it is necessary to store raw materials or work in progress prior to a further processing or manufacturing stage, the costs of such storage should be included in production overheads. In addition, the costs of storing maturing stocks, such as whisky, should be included in the cost of production.

Storage costs were specifically addressed by the IASC in its revision of IAS 2, which states that such costs should be excluded from the cost of stocks, unless they are necessary in the production process prior to a further production stage.[39]

D General/administrative overheads

SSAP 9 makes it clear that the costs of general, as opposed to functional, management are not normally costs of production and should therefore be excluded from the value of stock.[40] However, the standard recognises that in smaller organisations there may not be a clear distinction of management functions and that 'in such organisations the cost of management may fairly be allocated on suitable bases to the functions of production, marketing, selling and administration'.[41] Overheads relating to service departments, such as accounts and personnel departments, should be allocated to the main functions of production, marketing, selling and administration on a basis which reflects the amount of support supplied by the service department to the particular main function. SSAP 9 states that 'problems may also arise in allocating the costs of central service departments, the allocation of which should depend on the function or functions that the department is serving. For example, the accounts department will normally support the following functions:

(a) production – by paying direct and indirect production wages and salaries, by controlling purchases and by preparing periodic financial statements for the production units;

(b) marketing and distribution – by analysing sales and by controlling the sales ledger;

(c) general administration – by preparing management accounts and annual financial statements and budgets, by controlling cash resources and by planning investments.

Only those costs of the accounts department that can be allocated to the production function fall to be included in the cost of conversion.'[42]

E Allocation of overheads

SSAP 9 states that the overheads to be included in stock must be allocated on the basis of a company's normal level of activity.[43] While 'normal' is not defined, the standard does give some guidance about the factors to be considered:

> '(a) the volume of production which the production facilities are intended by their designers and by management to produce under the working conditions (e.g. single or double shift) prevailing during the year;
>
> (b) the budgeted level of activity for the year under review and for the ensuing year;
>
> (c) the level of activity achieved both in the year under review and in previous years'.[44]

No matter how overheads are being allocated to stock, it is necessary to ensure that only 'normal' costs are being included and that 'abnormal' costs, e.g. excess scrap and the cost of excess facilities, are being expensed as period costs. It may be necessary for an exercise to be carried out to ensure that no such abnormal costs have been included in closing stock. It is important to bear in mind that this exercise should be carried out on all cost categories, including direct costs.

The overheads to be included based on the normal level of activity should be applied by reference to the most significant direct cost. Thus if a process is particularly capital intensive the overheads should be applied to stock by an overhead recovery rate based on direct machine hours, while if labour costs are more significant the recovery rate should be based on direct labour hours. In computing the costs to be allocated via the overhead recovery rate, costs such as distribution and selling must be excluded, together with cost of storing raw materials and work in progress, unless it is necessary that these latter costs be incurred prior to further processing.

IAS 2 (see 4.2.2 below) is more specific on this issue and states that the allocation of fixed production overheads should be based on the normal capacity of the production facilities, although the actual level of production may be used if it approximates normal capacity.[45]

3.1.2 *Net realisable value*

As already discussed, it is the basic rule of accounting for stocks that they are stated at the lower of their cost and net realisable value. Net realisable value, as it applies in the UK, depends on the ultimate selling price of a completed product. Thus, a whisky distiller would not write down his stock of grain because of a fall in the grain price, so long as he expected still to sell the whisky at a profit.

The comparison of cost and net realisable value of finished goods is normally straightforward where there are established selling prices for the finished goods. Where a provision is required in respect of finished goods, the carrying value of any related raw materials, work in progress and spares must also be reviewed to see if any further provision is required.

Where the selling price of finished goods varies with the price of raw materials and there has been a fall in the price of the raw materials, then some provision may be required in respect of any stock of the finished goods (as well as possibly being required in respect of stocks of the raw materials and any forward purchase contracts).

Often raw materials are used to make a number of different products. In these cases it is normally not possible to arrive at a particular net realisable value for each item of raw material based on selling price. Therefore, current replacement cost might be the best guide to net realisable value in such circumstances. If current replacement cost is less than historical cost, however, a provision is only required to be made if the finished goods into which they will be made are expected to be sold at a loss. No provision should be made just because the anticipated profit will be less than normal.

3.1.3 *The valuation of high volumes of similar items of stock*

Practical problems in the valuation of stock arise in the case of businesses which have high volumes of various line items of stock. This situation occurs almost exclusively in the retail trade where similar mark-ups are applied to all stock items or groups of items, and the selling price is marked on each individual item of stock (e.g. in the case of a supermarket). In such a situation, it may be time-consuming to determine the cost of the period-end stock on a more conventional basis. Consequently, the most practical method of determining period end stock may be to record stock on hand at selling prices and then convert it to cost by removing the normal mark-up. Not surprisingly, this method of stock valuation is known as the 'retail method'.

However, a complication in applying the retail method is in determining the margin to be applied to the stock at selling price to convert it back to cost. Since different lines and different departments may have widely different margins, it is normally necessary to subdivide stock and apply the appropriate margins to each subdivision. Furthermore, where stocks have been marked down to below original selling price, adjustments have to be made to eliminate the effect of these markdowns so as to prevent any item of stock being valued at less than both its cost and its net realisable value. In practice, however, companies which use the retail method, tend to apply a gross profit margin computed on an average basis, rather than apply specific mark-up percentages. This practice is, in fact, acknowledged by IAS 2 which states that 'an average percentage for each retail department is often used'.[46]

Tesco is a company that applies the retail method, as shown in Extract 16.9.

> *Extract 16.9: Tesco PLC (2000)*
>
> **Accounting policies** [extract]
> **Stocks**
>
> Stocks comprise goods held for resale and development properties, and are valued at the lower of cost and net realisable value. Stocks in stores are calculated at retail prices and reduced by appropriate margins to the lower of cost and net realisable value.

It is noteworthy that Appendix 1 to SSAP 9 states that this method 'is acceptable only if it can be demonstrated that the method gives a reasonable approximation to the actual cost'.[47]

3.1.4 *Marking to market*

The practice has developed, principally among commodity dealing companies, of stating stock at market value and also taking into account profits and losses arising on the valuation of forward contracts ('marking to market'). This represents a departure from the statutory valuation rules in that stocks are being stated at more than cost, but this is generally justified as being necessary in order to show a true and fair view. SSAP 9 does not specifically deal with this issue; in fact it is difficult to come to any conclusion other than that the requirement in the standard that stocks should be included at the lower of cost and net realisable value has, in this instance, been dispensed with.

Advocates of marking to market would argue, however, that this is a specialised development to which the generality of SSAP 9 should not apply and which was not envisaged when SSAP 9 was being originally developed or addressed when it was revised. It is our opinion that under UK GAAP, despite the departure from the standard, marking to market is acceptable in certain circumstances. We would suggest that appropriate criteria might be that:

(a) the company's principal activity is the trading of commodities and/or marketable securities;

(b) the nature of the business is such that the commodities traded do not alter significantly in character between purchase and sale;

(c) the commodities are or can be traded on an organised terminal or futures market; and

(d) the market is sufficiently liquid to allow the company to realise its stock and forward contracts at prices close to those used in their valuation.

3.2 Practical issues with long-term contracts

3.2.1 *How much profit?*

Although SSAP 9 requires the accrual of attributable profit into long-term contract balances, it does not give detailed guidance on how the amount is actually to be computed. The following example illustrates difficulties which may arise under certain circumstances:

Example 16.2: Calculation of attributable profit

Halfway through its 2001 financial year a company starts work on a contract that will last for 24 months. The total sales value is £1,200 and this is to be invoiced in total on completion of the contract. The total expected costs are £600 and these will be incurred evenly throughout the contract. Everything goes according to plan for the rest of the financial year. During the following financial year, 2002, the company runs into problems on this contract and incurs additional costs of £100 which will not be recovered from the customer. At the end of that year the company is reasonably certain that costs to complete will still be the planned £150. Future experience bears this out.

Using the definition of attributable profit in paragraph 23 of SSAP 9, the profit taken could be calculated as follows:

	2001	2002	2003
	£	£	£
Total expected profit on contract	600	500	500
Percentage of contract completed	25%	75%	100%
∴ total profit to be attributed	150	375	500
Less: profit already taken	–	150	375
Attributable profit for the period	150	225	125

Some might hold the view that the above does not reflect the results of 2002 and 2003 fairly as it effectively defers inefficiencies of 2002 into 2003. The additional costs in 2002 are an unfortunate incident occurring in that year which, while impacting on the overall profitability of the contract, do not affect the costs to complete at the end of that year and should consequently be expensed in 2002. A fairer allocation of profits might be as follows:

	2001	2002	2003
	£	£	£
Turnover (being sales value of work done)	300	600	300
Cost of sales	150	*400	150
Attributable profit	150	200	150

* Comprises anticipated cost of sales of £300 and the additional costs of £100.

Paragraph 9 of SSAP 9 states that 'any known inequalities of profitability in the various stages of a contract' should be taken into account in calculating the attributable profit. It then goes on to confirm the latter treatment illustrated in the above example, by detailing the procedures which should be followed in order to take the inequalities into account. The procedures are 'to include an appropriate proportion of total contract value as turnover in the profit and loss account as the contract activity progresses. The costs incurred in reaching that stage of completion are matched with this turnover, resulting in the reporting of results that can be attributed to the proportion of work completed.'[48] As the above example shows, it is in fact desirable that such inequalities be taken into account, as otherwise there may not be a proper matching of costs and revenues.

In the above example the inequality was an inefficiency which had to be taken into account by being written off as a period expense. Some inequalities have to be taken into account in a different way, however. For example, where a contract is split into various stages with each stage having a separate price established, it may be necessary to allocate the total contract price over all the stages so as to reflect the 'real' profit on each stage. Obviously, where each stage's price reflects the relative value of that particular stage, this is not a problem and no adjustment is required. However, where there has been a payment in advance (or 'front-end loading') some adjustment will be necessary or profit will be taken in advance and not over the duration of the contract as it is earned.

3.2.2 *How much turnover?*

SSAP 9 states that it deliberately does not define turnover because of the different methods used in practice to determine it.[49] It does require, however, that the means by which turnover is ascertained be disclosed. Although there are a wide variety of methods used, whichever is selected the amount should represent an appropriate proportion of total contract value.[50] The following example illustrates some of the more common methods of computing turnover:

Example 16.3: Determination of turnover

A company is engaged in a long-term contract with an expected sales value of £10,000. It is the end of the accounting period during which the company commenced work on this contract and it needs to compute the amount of turnover to be reflected in the profit and loss account for this contract.

Scenario (i) An independent surveyor has certified that at the period-end the contract is 55% complete and that the company is entitled to apply for cumulative progress payments of £5,225 (after a 5% retention). In this case the company would record turnover of £5,500 being the sales value of the work done. (If it is anticipated that rectification work will have to be carried out to secure the release of the retention money then this should be taken into account in computing the attributable profit – it should have no bearing on the amount of turnover to be recorded.)

Scenario (ii) No valuation has been done by an independent surveyor as it is not required under the terms of the contract. The company's best estimate is that the contract is 60% complete. There is no real difference here from the first scenario. The value of the work done and, therefore, the turnover to be recognised is £6,000.

Scenario (iii) The company has incurred and applied costs of £4,000. £3,000 is the best estimate of costs to complete. The company should therefore recognise turnover of £5,714, being the appropriate proportion of total contract value, and computed thus:

$$\frac{4,000}{7,000} \text{ x } 10,000 = 5,714$$

If the costs incurred to date included, say, £500 in respect of unapplied raw materials, then the turnover to be recognised falls to £5,000 being:

$$\frac{\text{costs incurred and applied}}{\text{total costs}} \quad \frac{(4{,}000 - 500)}{7{,}000} \times 10{,}000 = 5{,}000$$

There are, however, other ways than cost of measuring work done, e.g. labour hours, which depending upon the exact circumstances might lead to a more realistic basis for computing turnover.

Note that in each of the above scenarios the computation of the amount of turnover is quite independent of the question of how much (if any) profit should be taken. This is as it should be, because even if a contract is loss-making the sales price will be earned and this should be reflected by recording turnover. In the final analysis, any loss arises because costs are greater than revenue, and costs should be reflected through cost of sales. In view of the different results that can arise from the use of different methods, the importance of disclosing the particular method used is highlighted.

The above example applies only to fixed-price contracts. Where a contract is on a cost-plus basis, it is necessary to examine the costs incurred to ensure they are of the type and size envisaged in the terms of the contract. Only once this is done and the recoverable costs identified can the figure be grossed up to arrive at the appropriate turnover figure.

3.2.3 *Approved variations and claims*

Appendix 1 to SSAP 9 states that 'where approved variations have been made to a contract in the course of it and the amount to be received in respect of these variations has not yet been settled and is likely to be a material factor in the outcome, it is necessary to make a conservative estimate of the amount likely to be received and this is then treated as part of the total sales value. On the other hand, allowance needs to be made for foreseen claims or penalties payable arising out of delays in completion or from other causes.'[51]

Owing to the extended periods over which contracts are carried out and to the circumstances prevailing when the work is in progress, it is quite normal for a contractor to submit claims for additional sums to a customer. Such claims arise 'from circumstances not envisaged in the contract' or 'as an indirect consequence of approved variations'[52] and their outcome can be crucial in determining whether the related contract will be profitable. Because their settlement is by negotiation (which can in practice be very protracted), they are subject to a very high level of uncertainty; consequently, no credit should be taken for them until they have been agreed at least in principle. In the absence of an agreed sum, the amount to be accrued should be prudently assessed.

In practice, few companies give any indication about how variations and claims are dealt with in their accounts. However, those companies which do deal with this matter in their accounting policies generally state that revenues derived from claims and variations on contracts are recognised only when they have been either received in cash or certified for payment.

3.2.4 *Should profits be accrued on short-term contracts?*

A question can arise over the accrual of profit on short-term contracts. This is as a result of the last sentence of the definition of a long-term contract, which states that

> 'some contracts with a shorter duration than one year should be accounted for as long-term contracts if they are sufficiently material to the activity of the period that not to record turnover and attributable profit would lead to a distortion of the period's turnover and results such that the financial statements would not give a true and fair view, provided that the policy is applied consistently within the reporting entity and from year to year'.[53]

The implication of this requirement is that even if a company is purely involved in short-term contracting work and has adopted the completed contract method, if it has a material amount of uncompleted short-term contracts at the year-end, they should be accounted for as long-term contracts – i.e. turnover should be recorded and profit accrued. Since many contracting companies are likely to be in this position, it seems that, on the face of it, most short-term contracts will have to be accounted for as long term – irrespective of the accounting policy adopted. Our view, however, is that this could hardly have been the standard's intention. Consequently, we believe that the crucial factor in applying this definition is to ensure that whatever policy is applied, it is used on a consistent basis. If contracts with a shorter duration than one year are accounted for as long-term contracts, this should be a stated accounting policy, and not applied only when it is expedient to do so.

3.2.5 *Inclusion of interest*

Paragraph 26(3)(b) of Schedule 4 to the Companies Act 1985 states that 'there may be included in the production cost of an asset interest on capital borrowed to finance the production of that asset, to the extent that it accrues in respect of the period of production'.[54] Appendix 1 to SSAP 9 deals with this issue in the context of long-term contracts, and states that 'in ascertaining costs of long-term contracts it is not normally appropriate to include interest payable on borrowed money. However, in circumstances where sums borrowed can be identified as financing specific long-term contracts, it may be appropriate to include such related interest in cost, in which circumstances the inclusion of interest and the amount of interest so included should be disclosed in a note to the financial statements.'[55]

It is our view that, provided all the criteria for capitalisation of interest costs are met (e.g. qualifying assets, period of production, etc.), it is perfectly acceptable to include interest costs; this is also the position adopted by IAS 11 – *Construction contracts*, see 4.3.2 below. Also see Chapter 15 for a detailed discussion of the circumstances under which interest may be capitalised.

4 IAS REQUIREMENTS

4.1 Introduction

Under IAS the customary UK terms 'stocks' and 'long-term contracts' are replaced by the respective equivalent terms 'inventories' and 'construction contracts'. There are two IASs that deal with these items: IAS 2 – *Inventories* – and IAS 11 – *Construction contracts.* The overall provisions of IAS 2 and IAS 11 are clearly within the same accounting convention as those of their UK equivalent SSAP 9; but there are important differences between their detailed provisions. The main provisions of each international standard are set out in detail below.

4.2 IAS 2 – Inventories

4.2.1 *Scope and definitions*

IAS 2 applies to inventories in all financial statements *except* work-in-progress on construction contracts (dealt with by IAS 11, see 4.3 below); financial instruments; agricultural and forest products, agricultural livestock; and certain mineral ores.[56]

Inventories are defined by IAS 2 as assets:

'(a) held for sale in the ordinary course of business;

(b) in the process of production for such sale; or

(c) in the form of materials or supplies to be consumed in the production process or in the rendering of services.'[57]

The standard has the basic rule that 'Inventories should be measured at the lower of cost and net realisable value.'[58] Net realisable value is defined as:

> 'the estimated selling price in the ordinary course of business less the estimated costs of completion and the estimated costs necessary to make the sale.'[59]

4.2.2 *Measurement*

A What may be included in cost

The cost attributed to inventories under IAS 2 'should comprise all costs of purchase, costs of conversion and other costs incurred in bringing the inventories to their present location and condition.'[60] These costs include import duties and other unrecoverable taxes, transport and other costs directly attributable to the inventories; but trade discounts and similar rebates should be deducted from the costs attributed.[61]

Under certain rare circumstances permitted in IAS 21, exchange differences arising directly from recent acquisitions of inventory may be included in their cost. However these differences must result from a severe devaluation or depreciation of a currency against which there is no practical means of hedging and that affects liabilities which cannot be settled.[62]

Costs of conversion include direct costs such as direct labour, and also a 'systematic allocation of fixed and variable production overheads that are incurred in converting materials into finished goods'.[63] The allocation of fixed production overheads is to be based on the normal capacity of the facilities. Normal capacity is defined as 'the production expected to be achieved on average over a number of periods or seasons under normal circumstances, taking into account the loss of capacity resulting from planned maintenance.' While actual capacity may be used if it approximates to normal capacity, increased overheads may not be allocated to production as a result of low output or idle capacity. In these cases the unrecovered overhead must be expensed.[64]

IAS 2 mentions the treatment to be adopted when a production process results in more than one product being produced, such as a by-product. In this instance if the costs of converting each product are not separately identifiable, they should be allocated between the products on a rational and consistent basis. This might be the relative sales value of each of the products. If the value of the by-product is immaterial, it may be measured at net realisable value and this value deducted from the cost of the main product.[65]

Other costs are to be included in inventories only to the extent that they bring them into their present location and condition. An example is given in IAS 2 of design costs for a special order for a particular customer as being allowable, and other non-production overheads may possibly be appropriately included. However a number of examples are given of costs that are specifically disallowed:

'(a) abnormal amounts of wasted materials, labour, or other production costs;

(b) storage costs, unless those costs are necessary in the production process prior to a further production stage;

(c) administrative overheads that do not contribute to bringing inventories to their present location and condition; and

(d) selling costs.'[66]

Extract 16.10 shows an example of the accounting policy for inventories adopted by Voest-Alpine Stahl, which illustrates many of these requirements for determining the cost of manufactured inventories.

Extract 16.10: Voest–Alpine Stahl (2001)

Inventories comprise **raw materials, supplies and consumables** as well as merchandise valued at acquisition cost and products valued at manufacturing cost.

Should the values be lower on the balance sheet date, due a decrease in prices on the stock exchange or the market, those lower values are presented.

Cost calculation is generally based on the standard schedule cost method based on the capacity in the next period.

Manufacturing cost comprise exclusively directly associated cost (manufacturing material, manufacturing wages) and pro rated general materials and manufacturing cost based on capacity utilization. General administrative expenses and expenses for voluntary social contributions and contributions to the company's retirement provisions and interest on borrowed capital are not reported as assets.

Acquisition and manufacturing costs are determined for similar assets based on the method of weighted average prices or similar methods. For risks to the inventory, appropriate discounts due to storage time or reduced usability are calculated.

IAS 2 states that 'in limited circumstances' borrowing costs may be included in the costs of inventories.[67] These circumstances are identified in the allowed alternative treatment in IAS 23 – *Borrowing Costs* – see Chapter 15 at 5.1.1.

Unlike its UK counterpart, IAS 2 deals specifically with the inventories of service providers – effectively their work-in-progress. For this type of business, IAS allows the labour and other costs of personnel directly engaged in providing the service, including supervisory personnel and attributable overheads, to be included in the cost of inventories. However, labour and other costs relating to sales and general administrative personnel must be expensed as incurred.[68]

Agricultural produce that has been harvested by the enterprise from its biological assets, is initially recognised at its fair value, less estimated point of sale costs at the point of harvest, as set out in IAS 41 – *Agriculture*. This figure becomes the cost of inventories at that date for the purposes of IAS 2.[69]

B Cost measurement methods

IAS 2 specifically allows the use of standard costing methods, or of the retail method (see 3.1.3 above) providing the method gives a result which approximates to cost. Standard costs should take into account normal levels of materials and supplies, labour, efficiency and capacity utilisation. They must be regularly reviewed and revised where necessary.[70] Where the retail method is used, an appropriate gross margin may be applied, though adjustments must be made to take into account any inventory marked down for sale below its cost, if material amounts are involved.[71] Items which are not interchangeable, and goods or services produced for specific projects, should have their costs specifically identified.[72]

Where it is necessary to use a cost-flow assumption, the 'benchmark treatment' in IAS 2 is for using either FIFO or weighted average. LIFO is the allowed alternative treatment, other than for those inventories that are not ordinarily interchangeable.[73] The question arose, as IAS 2 permits the use of both FIFO, LIFO and average cost methods of stock valuation, whether it was necessary for a business to use one method only for all its inventories. The Standing Interpretations Committee considered this matter and provided the following consensus in SIC–1 which was dated July 1997:

> 'An enterprise should use the same cost formula for all inventories having similar nature and use to the enterprise. For inventories with different nature or use (for example, certain commodities used in one business segment and the same type of commodities used in another business segment), different cost formulas may be justified. A difference in geographical location of inventories (and in the respective tax rules), by itself, is not sufficient to justify the use of different cost formulas.'[74]

This was further amplified in paragraph 5 of the consensus as follows:

> '… inventories with similar characteristics as to their nature and use should be measured using the same cost formula. The determination of groups of inventories with similar nature and use by a particular enterprise depends on the specific facts and circumstances. However, different cost formulas may be used for groups of inventories that have different characteristics. The treatment once chosen is applied consistently and is disclosed in accordance with the requirements of IAS.'

C Net realisable value

IAS 2 in paragraphs 25 to 30 carries substantial guidance on the identification of net realisable value, where this is below cost and therefore requires inventory to be written down. Such writes-down should be done on an item by item basis, normally; but it may be necessary to write down an entire product line or group of inventories in a given geographical area that cannot be practicably evaluated separately. IAS 2 specifically states that it is not appropriate to write down an entire class of inventory, such as finished goods, or all the inventory of a particular industry.[75]

Estimates of net realisable value must be based on the most reliable evidence available and also take into account the purpose for which the inventory is held. So that inventory held for a particular contract has its net realisable value based on the contract price, and only any excess inventory held would be based on general selling prices.[76] Specifically concerning materials for production IAS 2 states that:

> 'Materials and other supplies held for use in the production of inventories are not written down below cost if the finished products in which they will be incorporated are expected to be sold at or above cost. However, when a decline in the price of materials indicates that the cost of the finished products will exceed net realisable value, the materials are written down to net realisable value. In such circumstances, the replacement cost of the materials may be the best available measure of their net realisable value.'[77]

A new assessment of net realisable value must be made at each period end. When the circumstances that caused the write down no longer exist, the write down is reversed so that the revised carry value is the lower of cost and the revised net realisable value.[78]

4.2.3 *Recognition in the income statement*

IAS 2 specifies that when inventory is sold the carrying amount of the inventory must be recognised as an expense in the period the revenue is recognised. Although not stated, it is clear that a failure to recognise revenue would not justify the non-recognition as an expense of inventory that had been sold and over which the entity no longer had control. Any writes-down or losses of inventory must be recognised as an expense when the write-down or loss occurs. Reversals of previous writes-down should be recognised as a reduction in the inventory expense recognised in the period in which the reversal occurs.[79]

Inventory that goes into the creation of another asset, for instance into a self constructed item of property, plant or equipment, is expensed through the depreciation of that item during its useful life.[80]

4.2.4 *Disclosure requirements of IAS 2*

The financial statements should disclose:

(a) the accounting policies adopted in measuring inventories, including the cost formula used;

(b) the total carrying amount of inventories and the carrying amount in classifications appropriate to the enterprise;

(c) the carrying amount of inventories carried at net realisable value;

(d) the amount of any reversal of any write-down that is recognised as income in the period;

(e) the circumstances or events that led to the reversal of a write-down of inventories; and

(f) the carrying amount of inventories pledged as security for liabilities.[81]

IAS 2 does not specify the precise classifications that must be used to comply with (b) above. However it states that 'information about the carrying amounts held in different classifications of inventories and the extent of the changes in these assets is useful to financial statement users', and suggests suitable examples of common classifications such as: merchandise, production supplies, materials, work-in-progress, and finished goods.[82] These disclosures go further than those required under UK GAAP, since SSAP 9 only requires the equivalents of (a) and (b) above. Extract 16.11 shows a suitable example of how inventories may be classified and disclosed under IAS 2.

Extract 16.11: Roche Holding Ltd (2000)

Inventories in millions of CHF	2000	1999
Raw materials and supplies	963	1,298
Work in process	545	575
Finished goods	4,525	4,942
Less: provision for slow moving and obsolete inventory	(279)	(269)
Total inventories	5,754	6,546

Inventories held at net realisable value have a carrying value of 26 million Swiss francs (1999: 25 million Swiss francs).

Where the allowed alternative LIFO cost formula is used, the entity must disclose the difference between the amount of the stocks as disclosed in the balance sheet and either:

(a) the lower of the amount arrived at in accordance with either the FIFO or weighted average methods and net realisable value, or

(b) the lower of current cost at the balance sheet date and net realisable value.[83]

Finally the financial statements must disclose either:

(a) the cost of inventories recognised as an expense during the period; or

(b) the operating costs, applicable to revenues, recognised as an expense during the period, classified by their nature.[84]

4.3 The accounting and disclosure requirements of IAS 11 – Construction contracts

4.3.1 *Scope and definitions*

IAS 11 applies to accounting for construction contracts in the financial statements of the contractor.[85] It defines a construction contract, and two particular types of construction contract, as follows:

> 'A *construction contract* is a contract specifically negotiated for the construction of an asset or a combination of assets that are closely interrelated or interdependent in terms of their design, technology and function or their ultimate purpose or use.
>
> A *fixed price contract* is a construction contract in which the contractor agrees to a fixed contract price, or a fixed rate per unit of output, which in some cases is subject to cost escalation clauses.
>
> A *cost plus contract* is a construction contract in which the contractor is reimbursed for allowable or otherwise defined costs, plus a percentage of these costs or a fixed fee'.[86]

IAS 11 gives examples of construction contracts and these include single constructions such as a bridge, a building, a dam, a pipeline, a road, a ship or a tunnel. Examples also include a group of inter-related assets such as an oil refinery or complex pieces of plant and equipment. Construction contracts also include the provision of services directly related to the construction of an asset, such as project management and contracts for demolition and restoration of assets and restoration of the environment after an asset is demolished.[87]

A Combination and segmentation of contracts

IAS 11 should be applied separately to each construction contract.[88] However the 'substance over form' convention (as set out in the IASC's conceptual framework paragraph 35) may require a contract to be sub-divided, or a group of contracts to be treated as one. If this is the position, IAS 11 provides guidance in three separate cases. The first is where a single contract covers the construction of a number of separate assets. In this case the construction of each individual asset should be treated as a separate contract where:

> '(a) separate proposals have been submitted for each asset;
>
> (b) each asset has been subject to separate negotiation and the contractor and customer have been able to accept or reject that part of the contract relating to each asset; and
>
> (c) the costs and revenues of each asset can be identified'.[89]

The second case is where there are a group of contracts that may be with a single customer, or a group of customers. This group of contracts should be treated as a single contract where:

'(a) the group of contracts is negotiated as a single package;

(b) the contracts are so closely interrelated that they are, in effect, part of a single project with an overall profit margin; and

(c) the contracts are performed concurrently or in a continuous sequence.'[90]

Finally it is possible that a contract may envisage the construction of a further asset at the customer's discretion. This additional construction should be treated as a separate contract where:

'(a) the asset differs significantly in design, technology or function from the asset or assets covered by the original contract; or

(b) the price of the asset is negotiated without regard to the original contract price.'[91]

4.3.2 *The identification and measurement of contract revenue and costs*

A *Contract revenue*

IAS 11 states that contract revenue comprises the initially agreed contract revenue plus any variations, claims and incentive payments as long as these variations can be reliably measured and it is probable that they will result in revenue.[92] The standard makes it clear that such revenue is to be measured at fair value and any estimates must be regularly reviewed and adjusted for as the uncertainties are resolved.[93]

Variations, i.e. an instruction by the customer to change the work to be done under the contract, may only be included in revenue when it is probable that the customer will approve the variation and the amount to be charged for it, and the amount can be reliably measured. Similarly claims for costs not included in the original contract may only be included in revenue when negotiations are so advanced that it is probable that the customer will accept the claim, and this amount can be measured reliably.[94]

Any incentive payments, for example for early completion or superior performance, may only be included in contract revenue when the contract is at such a stage that it is probable the required performance will be achieved and the amount can be measured reliably.[95]

B *Contract costs*

IAS 11 sets out the costs that should be included in contract costs as follows:

'(a) costs that relate directly to the specific contract;

(b) costs that are attributable to contract activity in general and can be allocated to the contract; and

(c) such other costs as are specifically chargeable to the customer under the terms of the contract.'[96]

It gives a useful list of typical examples of each category, the examples it gives of directly related costs are as follows:

> '(a) site labour costs, including site supervision;
>
> (b) costs of materials used in construction;
>
> (c) depreciation of plant and equipment used on the contract;
>
> (d) costs of moving plant, equipment and materials to and from the contract site;
>
> (e) costs of hiring plant and equipment;
>
> (f) costs of design and technical assistance that is directly related to the contract;
>
> (g) the estimated costs of rectification and guarantee work, including expected warranty costs; and
>
> (h) claims from third parties.'[97]

These costs may be reduced by any incidental income not included in contract revenue, such as sales of surplus materials and disposal of equipment at the end of the contract.[98]

The second category of costs, being those attributable to contract activity generally, that therefore require allocation to a particular contract, are such things as design and technical assistance not directly related to an individual contract, insurance, and construction overheads such as the costs of preparing and processing the payroll for the personnel actually working on the contract. These must be allocated using systematic and rational methods and consistently applied to all costs having similar characteristics. Allocation must be based on the normal level of construction activity.[99]

IAS 11 also states that costs that may be attributable to contract activity in general and can be allocated to specific contracts include borrowing costs when the contractor adopts the IAS 23 allowed alternative treatment of capitalising interest costs.[100] See Chapter 15 for a detailed discussion of capitalisation of interest.

Paragraph 19 of IAS 11 acknowledges that general administration and development costs may be chargeable to a customer and specifically reimbursable under the terms of the contract. However, perhaps more importantly, IAS 11 gives a list of costs which it specifically disallows from being included in costs of a construction contract, as follows:

> '(a) general administration costs for which reimbursement is not specified in the contract;
>
> (b) selling costs;
>
> (c) research and development costs for which reimbursement is not specified in the contract; and
>
> (d) depreciation of idle plant and equipment that is not used on a particular contract.'[101]

IAS 11 states that 'contract costs include the costs attributable to a contract for the period from the date of securing the contract to the final completion of the contract.' Additionally, costs relating directly to the contract which have been incurred in gaining the business, may be included in contract costs providing they can be measured reliably and separately identified, and providing it is probable the contract will be won. However, once recognised as an expense in a previous period, such costs cannot subsequently be included in contract costs.[102] Obviously there is an element of judgement to be exercised here, as selling costs and costs incurred in securing a contract may be hard to distinguish. We consider that the latter mean such things as the building of models for demonstration purposes, travelling costs of technicians to survey sites, technical tendering costs, and similar expenses relating specifically to a given contract.

4.3.3 *The recognition of contract revenue and expenses*

IAS 11 requires that when the outcome of a construction contract can be reliably estimated, revenue and expenses associated with the construction contract should be recognised by reference to the stage of completion of the contract activity at the balance sheet date.[103]

When it is probable that the contract will result in an expected loss, the total loss expected should be recognised as an expense immediately, irrespective of:

(a) whether or not work has commenced on the contract;

(b) the stage of completion of contract activity; or

(c) the amount of profits expected to arise on other contracts with the same customer which are not treated as a single construction contract with the loss making one.[104]

The stage of completion of a contract may be determined in a variety of ways, including: the proportion that contract costs incurred for work performed to date bear to the estimated total contract costs; surveys of work performed; or completion of a physical proportion of the contract work.[105] However, IAS 11 states that when the stage of completion is determined by reference to the contract costs incurred to date, only those contract costs that reflect work performed are included in costs incurred to date. Examples of contract costs which are excluded are: contract costs that relate to future activity on the contract, such as costs of materials that have been delivered to a contract site or set aside for use in a contract but not yet installed, used or applied during contract performance, unless the materials have been made specially for the contract; and payments made to subcontractors in advance of work performed under the subcontract.[106]

Where a contractor has incurred contract costs that relate to future activity on the contract, which will often be the case in practice, these costs are recognised as an asset provided it is probable that they will be recovered, and included in the balance sheet as contract work in progress.[107]

Paragraph 38 of IAS 11 specifically lays down the treatment to be used when there are changes in estimate of contract revenues and costs. The percentage of completion method is applied on a cumulative basis in each accounting period to the current estimates of contract revenues and costs. Therefore the effect of any changes in estimates of revenue and costs, or the effect of any change in the estimate of the outcome of a contract, must be treated as a change in accounting estimate, as governed by IAS 8. The changed estimates must be used in determining the amount of revenue and expenses recognised in the income statement in the period in which the change is made, and in subsequent periods.

IAS 11 specifically defines what is meant by 'when the outcome of a construction contract can be reliably estimated' in relation to fixed price and cost plus contracts. In the case of a fixed price contract, the outcome of a construction contract can be estimated reliably when all the following conditions are satisfied:

'(a) total contract revenue can be measured reliably;

(b) it is probable that the economic benefits associated with the contract will flow to the enterprise;

(c) both the contract costs to complete the contract and the stage of contract completion at the balance sheet date can be measured reliably; and

(d) the contract costs attributable to the contract can be clearly identified and measured reliably so that actual contract costs incurred can be compared with prior estimates.'[108]

In the case of a cost plus contract, the outcome of a construction contract can be estimated reliably when the following conditions are satisfied:

'(a) it is probable that the economic benefits associated with the contract will flow to the enterprise; and

(b) the contract costs attributable to the contract, whether or not specifically reimbursable, can be clearly identified and measured reliably.'[109]

When the outcome of a construction contract cannot be estimated reliably, revenue should be recognised only to the extent of those costs incurred that it is probable will be recovered. Contract costs incurred under these circumstances should be recognised as an expense in the period in which they are incurred.[110]

This will often be the case during the early stages of a contract where the outcome may frequently not be capable of reliable estimation, but it will be probable that contract costs incurred will be recovered. Under these circumstances revenue is recognised only to the extent of the costs incurred that are expected to be recoverable, and no profit is recognised as the outcome cannot be estimated reliably. If alternatively, the situation exists where it is probable that total costs will exceed total revenues, even if the outcome of the contract cannot be estimated reliably, any expected contract overall loss must be expensed immediately.[111]

Under any circumstances, contract cost that are incurred which it is probable will not be recovered must be recognised as an expense immediately. 'Examples of circumstances in which the recoverability of contract costs incurred may not be probable and in which contract costs may need to be recognised as an expense immediately include contracts:

(a) which are not fully enforceable, that is, their validity is seriously in question;

(b) the completion of which is subject to the outcome of pending litigation or legislation;

(c) relating to properties that are likely to be condemned or expropriated;

(d) where the customer is unable to meet its obligations; or

(e) where the contractor is unable to complete the contract or otherwise meet its obligations under the contract.'[112]

Once uncertainties that prevent the outcome of the contract being estimated reliably no longer exist, revenue and expenses are recognised by the stage of completion method.[113]

4.3.4 *Disclosure requirements of IAS 11*

IAS 11 requires the following disclosures to be given by enterprises in respect of construction contracts:

(a) the amount of contract revenue recognised as revenue in the period;

(b) the methods used to determine the contract revenue recognised in the period; and

(c) the methods used to determine the stage of completion of contracts in progress.[114]

In the case of contracts in progress at the balance sheet date, an enterprise should disclose each of the following:

(a) the aggregate amount of costs incurred and recognised profits (less recognised losses) to date;

(b) the amount of advances received; and

(c) the amount of retentions.[115]

Retentions, progress billings and advances are defined as follows:

> 'Retentions are amounts of progress billings which are not paid until the satisfaction of conditions specified in the contract for the payment of such amounts or until defects have been rectified. Progress billings are amounts billed for work performed on a contract whether or not they have been paid by the customer. Advances are amounts received by the contractor before the related work is performed.'[116]

In addition, an enterprise should present:

(a) the gross amount due from customers for contract work as an asset for all contracts in progress for which costs incurred plus recognised profits (less recognised losses) exceed progress billings (i.e. the net amount of costs incurred plus recognised profits, less the sum of recognised losses and progress billings); and

(b) the gross amount due to customers for contract work as a liability for all contracts in progress for which progress billings exceed costs incurred plus recognised profits (i.e. the net amount of costs incurred plus recognised profits, less the sum of recognised losses and progress billings).[117]

4.3.5 *Accounting policies and other guidance*

It is envisaged in the Appendix to IAS 11 that there would be an accounting policy included in the financial statements which explained the methods by which contract revenues and costs were determined, for example:

> 'Revenue from fixed price construction contracts is recognised on the percentage of completion method, measured by reference to the percentage of labour hours incurred to date to estimated total labour hours for each contract.'

IAS 11 also contains a substantial appendix in which are included comprehensive examples illustrating a suitable method for determining the stage of completion of a contract and the timing and recognition of contract expenses. In addition a fully worked example of the required disclosures is provided.

Certain practical considerations in dealing with long-term contracts under UK GAAP are discussed at 3.2 above. The topics discussed may be helpful in relation to the application of IAS 11.

5 CONCLUSION

This is one area of financial reporting that remains fairly uncontroversial both in the UK and internationally.

One question that will inevitably be asked sooner or later is whether the gradual move towards a system of accounting that recognises an ever-broadening range of assets and liabilities in the balance sheet at their fair values, will ultimately see the measurement of stocks at fair value as well? It may seem unbelievable to any experienced accountant or businessperson, but given the following occurrences the valuation of stocks in financial reports at fair value (in effect in many cases selling prices) appears to be a real possibility.

(a) The ASB has replaced SSAP 2 with FRS 18 (discussed in Chapter 2 at 7) and downgraded of the prudence principle. In SSAP 2 prudence was defined by reference to realisation of profits with the specific requirement that profit should not be anticipated. The ASB's view inherent in FRS 18, and set out in Appendix IV to the standard, is that realisation is a less effective way to deliver reliability than focusing on reasonable certainty that a gain exists.

(b) The Board's recent revenue recognition paper advocates recognition criteria that would appear to allow the recognition of stocks at fair value (discussed in Chapter 3).

(c) The ASB's *Statement of Principles* enshrines recognition criteria which imply that unperformed contracts should be recognised (discussed in Chapter 2 at 5.6).

(d) The ASB has effectively abandoned the realisation principle, previously a key part of SSAP 2. The *Statement of Principles* does not consider it important, while FRS 18 includes the requirement to report realised profits only because the Companies Act requires it (discussed in Chapter 2 at 5 and 7).

(e) FRED 22 envisages reporting realised and unrealised profits together in a single statement of financial performance (discussed in Chapter 2 at 6).

(f) IAS 41 – *Agriculture* – requires that the carrying amount of crops being grown should gradually accrete up to the time the crop is harvested. At harvest the crop is not valued at its cost, but at its fair value at the point of harvest, which becomes its carrying value thereafter.

It is our earnest hope that this list is not indicative of the real agenda of the standard setters. Making the sale is the most difficult and unpredictable part of being in business, as anyone with commercial experience knows, and whether or not the sale is made represents the fundamental essence of business risk. If it is part of the agenda of the standard setters to value inventories at selling prices rather than cost (which is usually the effect of valuing inventories at fair value), it is our view that the reliability of financial statements would be noticeably diminished. We consider that to assume sales will occur and consequently to recognise a profit just because inventory is available, would be a serious departure from the business and commercial reality that, fundamentally, financial reporting exists to describe.

References

1 See, for example, SSAP 9, para. 1; ARB 43, Chapter 4, Statement 2; and Eldon S. Hendriksen, *Accounting Theory*, p. 299.
2 SSAP 9 (revised), *Stocks and long-term contracts*, ASC, 1988, para. 3.
3 This basic rule is entrenched in the UK, US and IASC pronouncements on stock: SSAP 9, para. 26; ARB 43, Chapter 4, Statement 5; IAS 2, para. 6.
4 SSAP 9 para. 4.
5 *Ibid.*, Appendix 1, para. 12.
6 CA 85, Sch. 4, para. 27(2)(b).
7 IAS 2, *Inventories* , Revised December 1993, IASC, para. 21.
8 *Ibid.*, para. 23.
9 CA 85, Sch. 4, Balance Sheet Formats.
10 *Ibid.*, Sch. 4, para. 3(3).
11 SSAP 9, para. 16.
12 *Ibid.*, para. 17.
13 *Ibid.*
14 *Ibid.*, para. 18.
15 *Ibid.*, para. 19.
16 *Ibid.*, para. 22.
17 *Ibid.*, para. 26.
18 *Ibid.*, para. 21.
19 *Ibid.*, Appendix 1, para. 20.
20 *Ibid.*, para. 26.
21 *Ibid.*, para. 27.
22 CA 85, Sch. 4, Balance Sheet Formats.
23 *Ibid.*, Sch. 4, para. 3(3).

24 SSAP 9, para. 22.
25 *Ibid.*, para. 28.
26 *Ibid.*
27 *Ibid.*, para. 29.
28 *Ibid.*, para. 23.
29 *Ibid.*, para. 32.
30 *Ibid.*, para. 30.
31 *Ibid.*, Appendix 3, para. 5.
32 *Ibid.*, para. 24.
33 CA 85, Sch. 4, para. 26; SSAP 9, paras. 17 to 19.
34 SSAP 9, paras. 1, 3 and 4.
35 *Ibid.*, paras. 18 and 19(c).
36 *Ibid.*, para. 17.
37 SSAP 9, Appendix 1, para. 2.
38 IAS 2, para. 14.
39 *Ibid.*
40 SSAP 9, Appendix 1, para. 5.
41 *Ibid.*, para. 6.
42 *Ibid.*, para. 7.
43 *Ibid.*, Appendix 1, para. 8.
44 *Ibid.*
45 IAS 2, para. 11.
46 *Ibid.*, para. 18.
47 SSAP 9, Appendix 1, para. 14.
48 *Ibid.*, para. 9.
49 *Ibid.*, Appendix 1, para. 23.
50 *Ibid.*, para. 9.
51 *Ibid.*, Appendix 1, para. 26.
52 *Ibid.*, Appendix 1, para. 27.
53 *Ibid.*, para. 22.
54 CA 85, Sch. 4, para. 26(3)(b).
55 SSAP 9, Appendix 1, para. 21.
56 IAS 2, *Inventories*, IASC, Revised December 1993, para. 1.
57 *Ibid.*, para. 4.
58 *Ibid.*, para. 6.
59 *Ibid.*, para. 4.
60 *Ibid.*, para. 7.
61 *Ibid.*, para. 8.
62 *Ibid.*, para. 9.
63 *Ibid.*, para. 10.
64 *Ibid.*, para. 11.
65 *Ibid.*, para. 12.
66 *Ibid.*, paras. 13 and 14.
67 *Ibid.*, para. 15.
68 *Ibid.*, para. 16.
69 *Ibid.*, para. 16A.
70 *Ibid.*, paras. 17.
71 *Ibid.*, paras. 18.
72 *Ibid.*, paras. 19.
73 *Ibid.*, paras. 21–24.
74 SIC-1 para. 3.
75 IAS 2, para. 26.
76 *Ibid.*, para. 28.
77 *Ibid.*, para. 29.
78 *Ibid.*, para. 30.
79 *Ibid.*, para. 31.
80 *Ibid.*, para. 33.
81 *Ibid.*, para. 34.
82 *Ibid.*, para. 35.
83 *Ibid.*, para. 36.
84 *Ibid.*, para. 37.
85 IAS 11, *Construction Contracts*, IASC, Revised December 1993, para. 1.
86 *Ibid.*, para. 3.
87 *Ibid.*, paras. 4 and 5.
88 *Ibid.*, para. 7.
89 *Ibid.*, para. 8.
90 *Ibid.*, para. 9.
91 *Ibid.*, para. 10.
92 *Ibid.*, para. 11.
93 *Ibid.*, para. 12.
94 *Ibid.*, para. 13 and 14.
95 *Ibid.*, paras. 13 to 15.
96 *Ibid.*, para. 16.
97 *Ibid.*, para. 17.
98 *Ibid.*, para. 17.
99 *Ibid.*, para. 18.
100 IAS 11, para. 18.
101 *Ibid.*, para. 20.
102 *Ibid.*, para. 21.
103 *Ibid.*, para. 22.
104 *Ibid.*, paras. 36 and 37.
105 *Ibid.*, para. 30.
106 *Ibid.*, para. 31.
107 *Ibid.*, para. 27.
108 *Ibid.*, para. 23.
109 *Ibid.*, para. 24.
110 *Ibid.*, para. 32.
111 *Ibid.*, para. 33.
112 *Ibid.*, para. 34.
113 *Ibid.*, para. 35.
114 *Ibid.*, para. 39.
115 *Ibid.*, para. 40.
116 *Ibid.*, para. 41.
117 *Ibid.*, paras. 42 to 44.

Chapter 17 Capital instruments

1 INTRODUCTION

1.1 Background

The accounting treatment of capital instruments – shares and debt securities – by their issuer was not historically regarded as presenting significant problems. However, the substantial development of innovative forms of finance during the 1980s made the accounting profession ask whether the conventional framework for distinguishing share and loan capital remained adequate. With the further development of financial derivatives in recent years this aspect of financial reporting has become increasingly complex.

The traditional distinction between shares and debt is clear. The issue of shares creates an ownership interest in a company, remunerated by dividends, which are accounted for as a distribution of profits, not a charge made in arriving at it. Loan finance, on the other hand, is remunerated by interest, which is charged in the profit and loss account as an expense. In general, lenders will rank before shareholders in priority of claims over the assets of the company, although in practice there may also be differential rights between different categories of lenders and classes of shareholders. The two forms of finance also have different tax implications, both for the investor and the investee.

In economic terms, however, the distinction between share and loan capital can be less clear-cut than the legal categorisation would suggest. For example, a redeemable preference share could be considered to be, in substance, much more like debt than equity, while on the other hand many would argue that a bond which will be converted into ordinary shares deserves to be thought of as being more in the nature of equity than of debt, even before conversion has occurred.

The fact that instruments which are otherwise similar in substance can have different tax and accounting consequences, because of their form, has encouraged the development of a number of complex forms of finance which exhibit characteristics of both equity and debt. The accounting profession has not always found it easy to decide how to balance competing considerations of substance and form in accounting for these instruments, especially since the fundamental distinction between debt and equity is rooted in form to begin with.

1.2 UK position

In the UK, many of these questions have been answered by FRS 4 – *Accounting for Capital Instruments* – which was issued in December 1993. This standard lays down a framework, albeit one constrained by the requirements of UK and EU companies legislation, for distinguishing between shares and debt, and also between sub-categories of each. In addition, it prescribes how these instruments and their associated finance costs are to be measured, and lays down detailed requirements for the disclosure of their terms. This chapter analyses the standard and explains how it is applied in practice at 2 and 4 below.

1.3 IAS position

Under IAS, capital instruments have been considered within the broader context of accounting for financial instruments in general, which is dealt with in IAS 32 *Financial Instruments: Disclosure and Presentation* and IAS 39 *Financial Instruments: Recognition and Measurement*. The general approach of IAS is more sophisticated than that of UK GAAP, partly because the IASC was able to develop its standards from first principles without regard to any potential legal obstacles. The requirements of IAS 32 and IAS 39 that are relevant to capital instruments are discussed at 5 below, their other requirements being dealt with in Chapters 10 and 18.

1.4 Possible future developments

As explained in Chapter 10, the ASB, together with other standard setters, has embarked upon a more fundamental re-examination of this subject under the broader umbrella of accounting for financial instruments (which looks at assets as well as liabilities). This has led to the publication by the ASB in December 2000 of a consultation document – *Financial Instruments and Similar Items*, prepared by the Joint Working Group of Standard-Setters. The document, which is discussed in more detail in Chapter 10, proposes a full fair value model for all financial assets and liabilities including the reporting company's own debt, and also espouses 'split accounting' (as described in 2.2.2 C and 5.6 below) for hybrid instruments such as convertible bonds. It also proposes abolition of hedge accounting. However, such proposals are highly controversial, and it remains to be seen whether they will command acceptance, either in the international context or in individual countries.

There is also a separate project on accounting for equity, which will reconsider where to draw the dividing line between liabilities and equity interests. These may eventually transform the whole approach to accounting for share and loan capital, but any such changes lie some way ahead. Some hint of the direction that this project may take has been given by the G4+1 group's discussion paper on accounting for share-based payment, which, as it relates primarily to employee share awards, is discussed in Chapter 22 at 4.

This chapter refers to some of these longer-term proposals in passing, but otherwise confines itself to the accounting rules for capital instruments as they stand at present.

2 FRS 4

2.1 The development of FRS 4

2.1.1 *TR 677*

In 1987 the Technical Committee of the ICAEW published TR 677 – *Accounting for complex capital issues.* This carried no mandatory status, but was issued as a discussion paper on which comment was invited. It was not subsequently developed into any more authoritative statement and has now been superseded by FRS 4. However, many of the principles underlying FRS 4 (e.g. that the finance cost of a loan should be recognised such that the charge to the profit and loss account in any year is based on the effective annual rate throughout the whole period of the loan) had their origins in TR 677.

2.1.2 *UITF 1*

The UITF published its first Abstract in July 1991.[1] This dealt with a relatively narrow topic: the accounting treatment of 'supplemental interest' on a convertible bond. Where a convertible bond was issued on terms which entitled the holder to receive an additional amount of backdated interest if he redeemed the bond, the UITF ruled that this supplemental interest had to be accrued from the outset. This outlawed the practice of ignoring the supplemental interest on the argument that conversion was likely to occur and hence that the supplemental interest would not become payable. The requirement was subsequently incorporated in FRS 4 and UITF 1 has been withdrawn.

2.1.3 *The ASB Discussion Paper*

In December 1991, the ASB published a Discussion Paper on capital instruments as the forerunner of the exposure draft of an accounting standard.[2] The paper addressed a wide range of issues, including the distinction between debt and equity and the measurement principles governing each category, together with their classification and disclosure in the balance sheet and profit and loss account.

2.1.4 *FRED 3*

A year later, in December 1992, the Board published the exposure draft of a standard on capital instruments, FRED 3.[3] This was based on the main proposals which had been set out in the earlier Discussion Paper, redrawn in the form of a draft standard, and it was subsequently converted into FRS 4 without substantial amendment.

2.1.5 *UITF 8*

In March 1993, the UITF published its eighth Abstract, dealing with the repurchase of debt.[4] This provided that, where a company has purchased its own debt at a price which differed from the carrying amount of the liability on its balance sheet, it should account for the difference as a profit or loss in the year of repurchase. As with UITF 1, this requirement was incorporated in FRS 4 and the Abstract has been withdrawn.

2.1.6 *FRS 4*

FRS 4 was issued in December 1993. As mentioned above, it contained only minor changes from the exposure draft and incorporated the requirements of UITFs 1 and 8, as a result of which these two Abstracts were withdrawn. The main features of the standard are summarised in the next section, while its application to particular types of capital instrument is dealt with in 4 below. The standard itself contains a set of Application Notes which illustrate how the rules are to be applied in practice. FRS 4 came into effect for accounting periods ending on or after 22 June 1994. Its requirements are discussed in 2.2 below.

As more fully discussed in Chapter 10, in July 1996 the ASB published a wide-ranging discussion paper on *Derivatives and other financial instruments*, proposing a radical new approach to the recognition and measurement of share and loan capital (as well as other financial items) and also suggesting substantial new disclosure requirements. This was to be progressed in two stages, with disclosure taking precedence, and in September 1998 the Board duly published FRS 13 as the standard that requires these disclosures. The recognition and measurement proposals are less immediate, and in any event have been largely superseded by the consultation paper on financial instruments issued by the Joint Working Group of Standard-Setters in December 2000 (see Chapter 10). This means that the approach in FRS 4 seems likely to remain in force until the UK adopts IAS under the European Commission's proposals for adoption of IAS throughout the EU (see Chapter 1 at 3.5).

2.2 The requirements of FRS 4

2.2.1 *The definition of capital instruments*

The standard defines capital instruments as 'all instruments that are issued by reporting entities as a means of raising finance, including shares, debentures, loans and debt instruments, options and warrants that give the holder the right to subscribe for or obtain capital instruments. In the case of consolidated financial statements the term includes capital instruments issued by subsidiaries except those that are held by another member of the group included in the consolidation.'[5]

FRS 4 discusses the accounting treatment of capital instruments only from the issuer's point of view; it does not say how investors should account for such instruments. In addition, three particular classes of capital instrument are excluded from the scope of the standard:

(a) warrants issued to employees under employee share schemes;

(b) leases;

(c) equity shares issued as part of a business combination that is accounted for as a merger.[6]

The first of these involves complex matters which the Board did not wish to address in this standard, although the UITF has since addressed certain issues concerning employee share schemes, which are discussed in Chapter 22. The remaining two were already the subject of rules from other sources – see Chapters 17 and 6. FRS 4 also has a minor exemption for investment companies allowing them to charge finance costs to capital in certain circumstances,[7] the details of which are beyond the scope of this book.

2.2.2 *The distinction between debt and share capital*

The first main issue which the standard discusses is how to distinguish an instrument between debt and share capital (or minority interests in the case of instruments issued by a subsidiary). The ASB bases the distinction on the definition of a liability in its *Statement of Principles for Financial Reporting* (see Chapter 2 at 5.5.2). This says that 'liabilities are obligations of an entity to transfer economic benefits as a result of past transactions or events',[8] so the Board's criterion is to classify all instruments which contain an obligation to transfer economic benefits as debt.[9] This applies equally whether the obligation is unconditional or merely contingent. This means that (for example) convertible debt has to be shown as a liability, rather than classifying it as shares on the argument that it is likely to be converted into shares in the future. It also applies to subordinated debt; even if debt is subordinated to the claims of all other creditors, that is not sufficient to make it equivalent to share capital, and it should therefore continue to be classified as debt.

On the other hand, under this approach, any obligation that the reporting entity can elect to satisfy by issuing the requisite number of new shares is regarded as an equity item rather than as debt. This is discussed further at 4.5 below.

A Equity and non-equity shareholders' funds

Applying the above approach might also be expected to result in redeemable preference shares being shown as debt. However, the standard does not go this far; any instrument which is part of the company's share capital must remain in the share capital section of the balance sheet. This may seem to be preferring form to substance, but the Board argues that shares should always be treated differently, because payments made under them are subject to legal restrictions and (more to the point) to classify them as liabilities would be in breach of the format requirements of the Companies Act.[10] There are, however, circumstances where shares issued by subsidiaries are treated as liabilities in the consolidated accounts (see B below).

Nevertheless, FRS 4 does require shareholders' funds to be subdivided into equity and non-equity components, so that shares which have more of the character of debt are distinguished from pure equity shares. For this purpose, the standard has had to distinguish between these two categories and has done so by defining non-equity shares and making equity shares the residual category. The definition of non-equity shares is somewhat complex; they are defined as shares possessing any of the following characteristics:

(a) any of the rights of the shares to receive payments (whether in respect of dividends, in respect of redemption or otherwise) are for a limited amount that is not calculated by reference to the company's assets or profits or the dividends on any class of equity share;

(b) any of their rights to participate in a surplus in a winding up are limited to a specific amount that is not calculated by reference to the company's assets or profits and such limitation had a commercial effect in practice at the time the shares were issued or, if later, at the time the limitation was introduced; or

(c) the shares are redeemable either according to their terms, or because the holder, or any party other than the issuer, can require their redemption.[11]

Some aspects of the definition are not particularly intuitive. A participating preference share, whose holder receives a dividend which is both partly fixed and partly variable, might be thought to be an equity share because the overall amount of the dividend is not limited; however, the relevant Application Note to FRS 4 says that they are non-equity shares, on the argument that the fixed element of the dividend is for a limited amount. This result suggests another way of looking at non-equity shares, as those whose holders enjoy a degree of priority over the equity shareholders, in the sense that they are entitled to receive certain amounts (provided they are available) without regard to the results of the company.

The rules for classification of shares as equity or non-equity under FRS 4 are not entirely consistent with those in companies legislation (see 3.1.2 below). Moreover, for the purposes of FRS 4, the disclosed amount of non-equity shareholders' funds may include items that are not explicitly shown in the statutory analysis of shareholders' funds, such as dividends in arrears. This is discussed further at 2.2.10 and 4.4.1 below.

B *Shares issued by subsidiaries*

The standard similarly calls for shares issued by subsidiaries, and shown as minority interests in the consolidated balance sheet, to be analysed into equity and non-equity categories. Cadbury Schweppes provides an example of this disclosure:

Extract 17.1: Cadbury Schweppes plc (2000)

Group balance sheet [extract]

Capital and Reserves		
Called up share capital	**255**	253
Share premium account	**991**	942
Capital redemption reserve	**90**	90
Revaluation reserve	**62**	61
Profit and loss account	**1,235**	894
Shareholders' Funds	**2,633**	2,240
Minority Interests		
Equity minority interests	**28**	139
Non-equity minority interests	**266**	245
	294	384
Total Capital Employed	**2,927**	2,624

22 Minority Interests

		Equity		Non-Equity
	2000	1999	**2000**	1999
	£m	£m	**£m**	£m
At beginning of year	**139**	61	**245**	236
Exchange rate adjustments	**(14)**	(1)	**20**	8
Share of profit after tax	**12**	79	**24**	22
Dividends declared	**(6)**	(3)	**(23)**	(21)
Purchase of share from minorities	**(103)**	–	**–**	–
Other	**–**	3	**–**	–
At end of year	**28**	139	**266**	245

The non-equity minority interest represents US$400m of 8.625% Cumulative Guaranteed Quarterly Income Preferred Securities issued by a subsidiary undertaking.

FRS 4 goes further than it was able to do with shares of the reporting entity by saying that shares held by minorities are sometimes equivalent to debt from the group's point of view and should therefore be shown as such. This applies if any member of the group has an obligation to transfer economic benefits to the minority shareholder, for example if the parent company guarantees the redemption of these shares.[12] An example of a company in this position is Billiton:

Extract 17.2: Billiton plc (2000)

18 Creditors [extract]	Group 2000 US$m	1999 US$m
Amounts falling due after more than one year:		
Debentures and other loans	**358**	292
Bank loans and overdrafts	**1,032**	673
Obligations under finance leases	**26**	40
Subsidiary company preference shares	**102**	99
Other creditors	**125**	126
	1,643	1,230

...

The subsidiary company preference shares have been issued by Billiton SA Limited and are redeemable between two and five years from issue. Company law in South Africa and the contractual arrangements relating to these shares are such that under generally accepted accounting principles in the United Kingdom, these shares are included in creditors with the dividends being included in interest and similar items. The preference shares pay a dividend at the rate of 72% of prime overdraft rate, are denominated in South African rand, and the holders' rights are subordinated to those of debt holders in Billiton SA Limited.

Sometimes, however, such a guarantee will be subordinated to such a degree that the rights of the holder of the shares in the subsidiary are no greater than those of a preference shareholder of the parent. If this is the case, FRS 4 allows the shares to remain in minority interests.[13] GlaxoSmithKline has issued auction market preferred stock (AMPs) that qualify for this treatment, as can be seen in Extract 17.23 at 4.4.1 A below.

C *Hybrid instruments*

One potentially controversial matter is the classification of 'hybrid' instruments – i.e., those which have characteristics of both debt and equity, such as convertible debt. As discussed in 4.2.4 below, in the years before the standard was issued some companies had developed the practice of showing certain convertible debt instruments in their balance sheet under share capital, on the argument that conversion into equity was highly probable. The standard takes a contrary view. Although it concedes that it is not certain that such instruments will result in the transfer of economic benefits, and therefore fall within the definition of a liability, it takes the view that any future conversion should not be anticipated, and accordingly that hybrid instruments should be classified according to their present form, although disclosed separately from other liabilities on the face of the balance sheet.[14]

An alternative approach would have been to split hybrid instruments into their debt and equity components. The ASB's earlier Discussion Paper invited comments on two variants of this, described in an Appendix to the Discussion Paper as 'split accounting' and the 'imputed interest approach'.[15] These attempt to recognise the substance of the convertible bond as a hybrid instrument with debt and equity elements – a combination of straight debt and an option or warrant – and account separately for each of the two components.

The steps involved in split accounting are as follows:

1. The net proceeds received from the issue of convertible debt are analysed between the amount that represents the liability and the amount in respect of the conversion rights. These two components are thereafter accounted for entirely separately.
2. The liability is accounted for as any other debt. As the amount repayable on redemption will normally exceed the amount allocated to the debt at the time of issue, a finance cost, additional to the coupon actually paid, will be accrued in each accounting period.
3. The amount of the proceeds which relates to the conversion rights is accounted for as a warrant (see 2.2.8 below).
4. In the event of conversion the liability is extinguished. The carrying amount of the liability is credited to called up share capital and share premium account.

The 'imputed interest' approach is similar in concept, but the accounting treatment is slightly different in its effect. It was originally proposed in TR 677, which suggested that 'an adjustment may need to be made to charge a fair interest cost in the profit and loss account and to treat the difference as a payment received for an option'.[16] In other words the proceeds of issue of the bond should be accounted for in the normal way, but thereafter the profit and loss account should be charged with a market rate of interest, with the excess charge over the actual coupon paid being credited to a capital reserve which is built up over the life of the bond to represent the equivalent of option proceeds discussed at 2.2.8 below.

An example of these two approaches is shown below:

Example 17.1: Split accounting and imputed interest

A company issues a bond for £50 million with an interest rate of 8% per annum, at a time when general interest rates indicate a rate of 12% per annum for straight borrowing. The bond is convertible into shares of the company after five years, and is otherwise redeemable at par. (Issue costs are ignored in this example.)

The 'split accounting' approach would analyse the proceeds of issue of the bond between two elements: one amount taken immediately to capital reserve to represent the value of the 'warrant' inherent in the bond, and the remainder shown as the liability under the straight borrowing element, in relation to which the coupon paid would represent a market rate of interest. The split would be made by discounting the interest payments of £4,000,000 per annum and the amount payable on redemption of £50,000,000 at 12%, to give a net present value of £42,790,000. The £7,210,000 difference between that and the proceeds of the issue is regarded as the amount attributable to the warrant and taken to reserves: in addition the £42,790,000 is built up to the redemption value of £50,000,000 by an additional finance cost charged in the profit and loss account. The mechanics would be as follows (all figures in £000s):

Year	Total finance cost	Interest paid	Amortisation of discount	Capital reserve
1	5,135	4,000	1,135	7,210
2	5,271	4,000	1,271	7,210
3	5,424	4,000	1,424	7,210
4	5,594	4,000	1,594	7,210
5	5,786	4,000	1,786	7,210
Total	27,210	20,000	7,210	

The 'imputed interest' method would calculate a finance cost of £6,000,000 per annum, being £50,000,000 at 12%. The £2,000,000 difference between that and the interest payment of £4,000,000 is credited to capital reserve each year. The mechanics would be as follows (all figures in £000s):

Year	Total finance cost	Interest paid	'Warrant element'	Capital reserve
1	6,000	4,000	2,000	2,000
2	6,000	4,000	2,000	4,000
3	6,000	4,000	2,000	6,000
4	6,000	4,000	2,000	8,000
5	6,000	4,000	2,000	10,000
Total	30,000	20,000	10,000	

The essential difference between the two approaches is that split accounting accounts for the warrant element at the time of the issue of the bonds rather than building it up over their life, and takes account of the time value of money in making the split, in effect by discounting the value applied to the option element.

Such an analysis has obvious merit in reflecting the economic substance of the arrangement, but the ASB regarded it as rather too radical for the time being, and FRS 4 rules out such an approach. It says that capital instruments should be accounted for separately only if they are capable of being transferred, cancelled or redeemed independently of each other.[17] Thus, for example, loan stock issued with detachable warrants would be accounted for as two instruments and the proceeds of the issue split between the two for accounting purposes, whereas convertible loan stock (which is very similar in substance) would be accounted for as one.

One problem with FRS 4's approach is that it continues to take hybrid instruments at face value, with the result that the finance cost is manipulable based on the terms of the instrument. In an extreme case, it could even be negative, as shown in this example:

Example 17.2: Convertible bonds with negative finance cost

A company issues convertible debt for £1,000,000 which is repayable at £900,000. The debt carries no coupon; to compensate for this, the conversion terms are extremely favourable. However, FRS 4 does not permit conversion to be assumed, and says that the finance cost must be measured on the assumption that conversion will not take place. The finance cost is negative as a result and the company can therefore *credit* £100,000 to its profit and loss account over the life of the instrument. When the conversion option is exercised at the end of that period, the apparent consideration for the shares would be £900,000. (When shares are issued by conversion of debt, FRS 4 says that the consideration for the issue is the carrying amount of the debt immediately before conversion.)[18] However, it is obviously questionable whether this could be regarded as giving a true and fair view.

In substance, this is more like a warrant than a convertible debt, because the likelihood of redemption must be very small. The example could be taken to a greater extreme by reducing the putative redemption amount yet further – even down to a negligible amount. FRS 4 would continue to imply that the whole of the difference between the amount subscribed and the amount available if the bond were not converted would be credited to the profit and loss account over the life of the instrument.

Clearly, a negative overall finance cost from such an arrangement would be regarded as too ridiculous to accept. However, a very low positive cost – perhaps even down to zero – might not. This is the essential weakness of accounting for hybrid instruments as if they were straight debt, which a split accounting approach would have gone some way to remedy.

Practice in this area is mixed. In its accounts for 1998 Granada showed a negative component of finance cost in relation to convertible preference shares with a redemption option at a price below their issue price, as shown in this extract:

Extract 17.3: Granada Group PLC (1998)

9 Dividends	**1998 £m**	1997 £m
Equity shares:		
Interim Dividend of 5.14p (1997: 4.66p) per share, paid 28 September 1998	**46**	40
Proposed final dividend of 11.56p (1997: 9.84p) per share, payable 1 April 1999	**105**	87
	151	127
Non-equity shares:		
Dividend of 7.5p per share, paid in two instalments on 31 January and 31 July 1998	**11**	13
Finance credit (FRS 4)	**(1)**	(1)
	10	12
	161	139

In contrast, Williams Holdings had the same kind of instrument but did not take credit for this negative component. This may have reflected a view that redemption was unlikely to occur so that the potential profit on redemption would never materialise, or it may simply have been on grounds of materiality (the total premium is about £8 million, to be spread over the term of the instrument).

Extract 17.4: Williams Holdings PLC (1998)

8 Dividends	**1998 £m**	1997 £m
Ordinary – interim paid 6.25p per share (1997 6.05p)	**46.1**	47.4
final proposed 10.04p per share (1997 9.75p)	**73.2**	76.3
Total equity dividends	**119.3**	123.7
10¾% cumulative preference shares	**0.2**	0.2
8½% cumulative redeemable preference shares	**1.1**	2.1
8.0p cumulative convertible redeemable preference shares	**20.5**	21.5
Non-cumulative convertible redeemable preference B shares	**0.2**	–
Total non-equity	**22.0**	23.8
Total dividends	**141.3**	147.5

20 Share capital [extract]

Conversion and redemption details

(a) The 8.0p preference shares, which were issued at 103p, a premium over redemption value of 3p, are convertible to ordinary shares at the shareholders' option on the basis of 0.31746 ordinary shares for each 8.0p preference share, up to a maximum of 77.4m ordinary shares, in May of each year to 2008 inclusive. If not converted, the shares may be redeemed at the company's option within the period from 30th June 2008 to 30th December 2018. If not converted or redeemed by 30th December 2018, all outstanding shares will be redeemed at 100p on 31st December 2018.

Another example of a hybrid instrument where the approach in FRS 4 does not always give a particularly satisfactory answer is a debt giving the holder the right to extend or shorten the term, which is in reality a debt plus a written option. This is discussed further at 4.1.6 below.

2.2.3 *The accounting treatment of debt instruments*

Under FRS 4, debt should initially be recorded in the balance sheet at the 'net proceeds', defined as 'the fair value of the consideration received upon the issue of a capital instrument after deduction of issue costs'.[19] Usually, the consideration received is cash, and there is thus no difficulty in determining its value. Thereafter, the difference between that amount and the total payments required to be made under the debt (interest and repayment of principal together with any premium) represents the total finance cost,[20] which is accounted for over the term of the debt. Except to the extent that it may be capitalised (see Chapter 15), this finance cost should be charged to the profit and loss account over the term at a constant rate of interest on the outstanding amount of the debt.[21] The carrying value of the debt is increased annually by the amount of the finance cost relating to that period, and reduced by the amount of payments made.[22]

The measurement of the finance cost is discussed in more detail in 2.2.5 below, and the mechanics of the process are illustrated in the examples shown in 4.1 below.

If debt is repurchased or settled before its maturity, the difference between the amount repaid and the carrying value should be recognised immediately in the profit and loss account.[23] The repurchase of debt is discussed further in 2.2.6 A below.

2.2.4 *The accounting treatment of share capital*

With the exception of shares issued in a business combination which is accounted for as a merger, share issues should be recorded at the net proceeds received. These net proceeds are taken direct to shareholders' funds and reported in the reconciliation of movements in shareholders' funds.[24] As in the case of debt, 'net proceeds' is defined as the fair value of the consideration received less costs that are incurred directly in connection with the issue.[25]

In the majority of cases, shares are issued for cash and therefore the fair value of the consideration received will be easy to determine. In some circumstances, however (e.g. where shares are issued for property), the fair value of the consideration received may not be so easily determined and external valuations may be required. Although the standard focuses on the value of the consideration for the shares, sometimes it may be expedient to consider the market value of the shares issued, to provide indirect evidence of the fair value of non-cash consideration received for them.

The standard does not give guidance on how to allocate 'net proceeds' to the various elements of total shareholders' funds. However, this is dictated by company law; the amount at which share capital is recorded is determined by the nominal value of the shares issued. If the net proceeds from the issue exceed that amount, the excess is to be recorded as share premium. This is discussed further at 3.1.1 A below.

Issue costs are regarded as inseparable from the consideration received, and are therefore taken straight to reserves; they should not be disclosed in either the statement of total recognised gains and losses or the profit and loss account. In fact this treatment is questionable in terms of the ASB's *Statement of Principles* since the costs of a share issue, while integral to the share issue, are clearly not transactions with shareholders but with lawyers, merchant bankers and other third parties. Indeed the treatment contrasts with that of tax relating to transactions with shareholders, which, although integral to those transactions, is required by FRS 16 and FRS 19 to be accounted for in the profit and loss account (see Chapter 24 at 3.1.1 and 5.9.1). Provided that the Companies Act conditions are satisfied (see 3.1.1 A below), issue costs may be set off against any share premium account.

The mechanics of a simple equity share issue are shown in the following example:

Example 17.3: Equity share issue

A company issues 1 million £1 ordinary shares at par. Issue costs of £20,000 are incurred.

If there is a share premium account in existence, the share issue may be recorded by increasing share capital by £1,000,000 and setting off the issue costs against share premium account. In the analysis of total shareholders' funds, the equity interests will have increased by £980,000.

If there is no share premium account, share capital will be increased by £1,000,000 but the issue costs would be deducted from another reserve (usually profit and loss account reserve) subject to the provisions of the company's articles. Prior to FRS 4, companies in this situation had to charge the issue costs to the profit and loss account for the year.

The accounting for non-equity shares is slightly different, because finance costs are to be measured in the same way as for debt instruments,[26] except that they are shown as an appropriation in the profit and loss account rather than as an expense. The effect of this is that, for non-equity shares with a finite term, issue costs are initially taken to reserves in the same way as for equity shares, but are subsequently recycled through the profit and loss account as an appropriation and charged in arriving at earnings per share.

Example 17.4: Non-equity share issue

A company issues 1 million £1 redeemable preference shares at par. Issue costs of £20,000 are incurred. The shares carry a coupon of 7% and are redeemable at par in five years.

In the same way as for the equity share issue in Example 17.3 above, the non-equity interests will increase by £980,000 in the analysis of total shareholders' funds. However, thereafter the appropriation in the profit and loss account will include not only the £70,000 dividend but also an annual instalment to write off the issue costs, allocated so as to produce a constant rate of finance charge on the outstanding carrying amount of non-equity shareholders' funds (see 2.2.5 below), which can be derived using discounting software as being approximately 7.5%. (In practice a simpler basis, such as straight-line amortisation, might be acceptable on the grounds of materiality.)

This treatment has the effect of transferring £20,000 from equity shareholders' funds to non-equity shareholders' funds over the five year life of the preference shares, at the end of which the non-equity shareholders' funds will be stated at the redemption amount of £1 million. To clarify, the profit and loss charges would be as follows (all figures in £000).

Year	Non-equity shareholders' funds b/f	Profit and loss charge	Cash paid	Non-equity shareholders' funds c/f
1	980	73	(70)	983
2	983	74	(70)	987
3	987	74	(70)	991
4	991	74	(70)	995
5	995	75	(1,070)	–

The increase in the amount of shareholders' funds would be a matter of disclosure only (see 2.2.10 below. The actual accounting entries that would be made (taking year 1 as an example) would be:

	£000	£000
Issue of shares		
Cash	980	
Share premium*	20	
Share capital		1,000
Finance cost		
Profit and loss account	73	
Profit and loss reserve		3
Cash		70

* If there were no share premium account, this would be charged to the profit and loss reserve

It can be seen that the accrual of the issue costs is a circular entry between the profit and loss account and the profit and loss reserve. However, under FRS 4 it conceptually represents a transfer from equity to non-equity shareholders' funds, which can be analysed in terms of the statutory reserves in the accounts as follows:

At issue	£000
Share capital	1,000
Share premium	(20)
Total	980

At redemption	£000
Share capital	1,000
Share premium	(20)
Profit and loss reserve	20
Total	1,000

However, where the non-equity share has no finite term, for example if it is an irredeemable preference share, it will not be appropriate to make this transfer and the issue costs will thus be dealt with in the same way as for equity shares (i.e. they will be charged to reserves at the time of issue).

2.2.5 *Finance costs*

Finance costs are defined by FRS 4 as 'the difference between the net proceeds of an instrument and the total amount of the payments (or other transfers of economic benefits) that the issuer may be required to make in respect of the instrument'.[27]

As mentioned at 2.2.3 above, the standard requires that finance costs should be accounted for over the term of the instrument at a constant rate on the carrying amount – in other words, at the effective rate implicit in all the cash flows which are to be made.[28] This may sound complex, but it is in fact what happens automatically in the case of a simple loan on which the interest is paid over the term of the loan. However, the requirement also accommodates more complex forms of borrowing, such as where a premium is payable on redemption, or the interest is not paid evenly over the life of the loan.

Applying these requirements hinges on the interpretation of the phrases 'net proceeds', 'payments that the issuer may be required to make' and 'term', which are discussed in turn below.

As noted in 2.2.4 above, FRS 4 requires the finance costs of non-equity shares to be allocated in the same way as those of debt. This can lead to a potential conflict between the requirements of FRS 4 and those of the Companies Act regarding distributable profits. This is discussed further at 4.4.1 below.

A Net proceeds

As noted in 2.2.3 above, FRS 4 defines 'net proceeds' as the 'fair value of the consideration received on the issue of a capital instrument after deduction of issue costs'. The effect of including this net amount in the calculation of finance costs is that the costs of issuing the instrument are spread over the life of the instrument as part of the finance cost. Issue costs are defined as 'the costs that are incurred directly in connection with the issue of a capital instrument, that is, those costs that would not have been incurred had the specific instrument in question not been issued'.[29] This definition is deliberately restrictive; it extends only to incremental costs, not to allocations of fixed costs, and they must be specific to the instrument in question.

It would be possible to interpret these words very narrowly indeed, by considering which of the costs would have been avoided on the hypothesis that an alternative instrument had been substituted for the actual instrument issued, and deciding that only these costs are specific to the actual instrument issued. However, we doubt if such a narrow interpretation is intended. The costs of the actual issue will generally fall within the definition, even if they are not peculiar to the particular instrument chosen.

Examples of costs that qualify as issue costs include underwriting fees, or arrangement fees to cover the administrative work involved in assessing and setting up the loan. Examples of costs that would not qualify include:

- costs of ascertaining the suitability or feasibility of particular instruments;
- costs of researching different sources of finance;
- allocations of internal costs that would still have been incurred if the instrument had not been issued (e.g. management remuneration);
- costs of viability studies commissioned by the lender which are borne by the issuer;
- costs of a financial restructuring or renegotiation (as they are incurred primarily to establish whether the whole exercise is worthwhile rather than related to the issue of replacement finance which occurs later).[30]

The principles apply not only to debt but also to non-equity shares,[31] except that dividends and transfers to reserves are to be dealt with as appropriations of profit, whereas the costs of debt will be charged in arriving at profit before taxation. Where the instrument is classified as a minority interest, the finance cost will again be calculated in the same way, but included in minority interests in the profit and loss account.[32]

B 'Payments (or other transfers of economic benefit) that the issuer may be required to make'

This phrase must be read carefully in order to determine both the existence and the amount of any finance cost under FRS 4. It clearly covers the usual costs of servicing a loan such as payments of interest and principal (or dividends and capital in the case of shares required to be accounted for as debt by FRS 4) and any premium payable on redemption of a loan or shares. However, there are cases where it may seem intuitively that such payments or other transfers of economic benefit are being made, but which on closer analysis turns out not to be the case.

Firstly, there must be a potential 'payment or other transfer of economic benefit'. Thus for example, if a listed company issues a bond, the interest on which is to be paid by the issue of shares in the company, there is clearly as a matter of fact no 'payment'. Moreover, under the ASB's *Statement of Principles*, an issue of shares does not constitute a 'transfer of economic benefit' as it does not decrease the net shareholders' funds of the company. This means that the interest on the bond does not constitute a 'finance cost' under FRS 4, even though it might well be perfectly appropriate to charge it to the profit and loss account. The treatment of capital instruments serviced using the issuer's own equity is discussed further at 4.5 below.

Similarly, if a company issues a convertible bond for £85 which converts into shares with a nominal value of £100, but the holder is never entitled to be repaid more than £85 in cash, the £15 difference does not constitute a 'finance cost' under FRS 4, and, indeed, might be most appropriately accounted for as a bonus issue by an appropriation of reserves.

Secondly, the payment (or other transfer of economic benefit) must be one that the issuer '*may* be *required* to make' (emphasis added). The key point is that the payment must be one over which the issuer has no control, irrespective of how likely or unlikely it is that it will be called upon to make it. It is the application of this rule that can lead to apparent absurdities such as the negative finance costs discussed in Example 17.2 at 2.2.2 C above.

An exception to this general rule is that obligations to transfer economic benefit that arise only on the insolvency of the issuer should not be taken into account in determining the finance cost of an instrument.[33] However, even this relaxation can lead to a very form-driven approach. Suppose that the bond in Example 17.2 above was mandatorily convertible, but that the holder had the right to receive £900,000 on a liquidation of the company. In that case, there would be no circumstances other than an insolvency in which the issuer could be compelled to pay £900,000, so there would be no finance credit. However, because on the facts of

Example 17.2 the holder has the right to require redemption at £900,000 in *all* circumstances (even though it might be totally irrational to do so other than on the insolvency of the issuer), there is a finance credit.

Another exception to this general rule is a payment that would arise as a result of an issuer call option being exercised is not taken into account until the option is exercised (see Example 17.5 in C below).

C Term

The term of an instrument is defined as follows:

'The period from the date of issue of the capital instrument to the date at which it will expire, be redeemed, or be cancelled. If either party has the option to require the instrument to be redeemed or cancelled and, under the terms of the instrument, it is uncertain whether such an option will be exercised, the term should be taken to end on the earliest date at which the instrument would be redeemed or cancelled on exercise of such an option. If either party has the right to extend the period of an instrument, the term should not include the period of the extension if there is a genuine commercial possibility that the period will not be extended.'[34]

Under FRS 4, the term of a debt instrument has a direct impact on the calculation and allocation of the finance costs of the instrument. Oddly enough, it does not determine the classification of debt between short term and long term nor any other analysis of the maturity of debt, which is governed by separate rules – see 2.2.7 below.

This therefore means that the term is taken to be the minimum which either party could insist upon, and since this dictates the period over which issue costs have to be written off, the definition has a conservative bias. This cautious approach to evaluating options to reduce or extend the term of debt instruments disregards the actual intentions of the option holder. The effect of this is often to produce a shorter 'term' for accounting purposes than that which will materialise in practice. Where the borrower has the ability to repay the debt at any time, as will often be the case, a literal interpretation of the standard would suggest that the issue costs should be written off immediately, because the term of the debt (as defined) is zero.

Some instruments contain terms which allow the borrower to repay early, but at a price. A strict application of FRS 4 could produce some unexpected results:

Example 17.5: Loan with issuer call option

A company issues a five year debt instrument carrying a fixed interest rate of 7%. The terms of the instrument include an 'issuer call option', permitting the company to redeem the debt early on payment of a premium.

On the face of it, the term of the instrument, as defined by FRS 4, is restricted to the period up to the first date at which the option could be exercised, as discussed at 2.2.5 C above. This means that issue costs have to be written off over that period. It might also be thought to mean that the premium payable under the option would have to be accrued as part of the finance costs, whether or not the company intends to exercise the option. The effect of this would be that the company would be accounting for the redemption of the instrument regardless of whether or not it actually intended to redeem it.

In order to avoid this result, in 1994 the UITF issued UITF 11 which made it clear that any payments required on the exercise of such options do not form part of the finance costs which have to be accounted for.[35] This is because they cannot be described as 'payments that the issuer may be required to make in respect of the instrument', since exercising the option, and therefore incurring the requirement to make the payment, is voluntary. However, UITF 11 does not affect the determination of the term of the instrument, which remains governed by FRS 4. The result of this is that the issue costs still have to be written off over the period up to the date on which the call option could be exercised, even though it is otherwise being assumed that the option will not be exercised. The treatment of finance costs is therefore based on two mutually exclusive assumptions, which seems rather anomalous.

There are other situations where a strict application of the rules in FRS 4 can give rise to perplexing results, as illustrated by Example 17.6.

Example 17.6: Discounted convertible bond with two repayment dates

A company issues a bond on 1 January 2001 for £1 million. It pays no interest. The holder has the following options:

- On 31 December 2002 to either (a) require redemption of the bond at £1 million or (b) require conversion into non-equity shares with a nominal value £1 million paying a dividend at a coupon above market rates at date of issue (to compensate for the lack of income in the first two years).
- On 31 December 2010 to require redemption of the bond at £2.4 million.

The finance cost of the bond is £1.4 million (i.e. difference between £1 million issue proceeds and amount potentially payable on redemption in 2010). However, the 'term' is the two years ended 31 December 2002. If read literally, FRS 4 therefore requires the £1.4 million to be charged over this period, notwithstanding that, were the bond to be redeemed in 2002, the finance cost would not be paid. In such a case, we believe that the only sensible approach is to accrue the cost over the full 10-year term. If the bond were converted at the end of 2002, its then carrying amount would be transferred to share capital and if applicable share premium account. If it were redeemed at that date the excess of the carrying value over the £1 million paid on redemption would be recognised as a profit on repayment of debt (see 2.2.6 A below).

2.2.6 Repurchase of capital instruments

A Repurchase of debt

Where a company buys in its own debt (or repays it early) at a price which differs from the liability carried in the balance sheet, the difference between the two amounts is taken to the profit and loss account as an additional finance cost or credit.[36] This applies even if the debt is not cancelled. For example, a company which bought some of its own listed debentures in the market would be at liberty to sell them again at some time in the future, but would still record a gain or loss in the meantime; if it resold them, that would be treated as a new debt issue, recorded at the proceeds of that sale.

As explained at 2.1.5 above, this issue was originally addressed by UITF 8, which was replaced by FRS 4 soon after. The UITF had taken up the issue to resolve the question of whether or not companies which refinanced their fixed-rate debt should spread the resulting gain or loss over the life of the replacement debt, and it concluded that they should not, except in circumstances where either:

(a) the replacement borrowing gives the same effective economic result as the original borrowing and thus there has been no change of substance in the debt. For this to be the case, as a minimum the following conditions should be met:

- The replacement borrowing and the original borrowing are both fixed rate;
- The replacement borrowing is of a comparable amount to the original borrowing;
- The maturity of the replacement borrowing is not materially different from the remaining maturity of the original borrowing;
- The covenants of the replacement borrowing are not materially different from those of the original borrowing.

A refinancing may fall within this exception whether or not the lender of the replacement debt is the same as the lender of the original debt; or

(b) the overall finance costs of the replacement borrowing are significantly different from market rates.[37]

These exceptions were not repeated in FRS 4. Notwithstanding this, some companies clearly believe that they still apply. Tate and Lyle disclosed this note in its 2000 accounts:

Extract 17.5: Tate & Lyle Public Limited Company (2000)

15 Borrowings – due after more than one year [extract]

On 10 June 1996, £191 million 5¾% Guaranteed Bonds were redeemed for £164 million and replaced by borrowings with substantially the same terms. The premium on redemption of £23 million is being amortised over the life of the replacement debt and is treated as a payment of interest in the statement of cash flows. The £164 million 7.863% unsecured borrowings due 2001, which replaced the Guaranteed Bonds, were fully drawn by a UK subsidiary undertaking and are guaranteed on a subordinated basis by Tate and Lyle PLC. The effective rate of interest (including both coupon and accrued issue discount) on the 5¾% Guaranteed Bonds, was 13.3%.

Although FRS 4 dictates how to account for the gain or loss on the repayment of debt, it does not address the equivalent issue when swaps are terminated, and some companies carry forward gains or losses that arise in these circumstances. Tesco is an example, as shown in this extract:

Extract 17.6: Tesco PLC (2001)

17 Creditors falling due within one year [extract]

A gain of £45m, realised in a prior year, on terminated interest rate swaps is being spread over the life of replacement swaps entered into at the same time for similar periods. Accruals and deferred income include £5m (2000 – £6m) attributable to these realised gains with £2m (2000 – £6m) being included in other creditors falling due after more than one year (note 18).

At first sight, this may seem inconsistent with the rules on the termination of loans, but in fact the arguments are rather different, as shown in this example:

Example 17.7: Termination of a swap

A company takes out a five-year floating rate loan of £10m and then swaps it to a fixed rate of 6% by entering into an interest rate swap whereby it pays £600,000 for 5 years in exchange for receiving a floating rate on £10m. It therefore presents the loan in its accounts as a fixed rate loan at 6%. A year later, interest rates have risen and the swap has a positive value of £500,000. The company terminates the swap. Should it take the £500,000 to its profit and loss account?

In our view it should not. The original hedging decision had the economic effect of fixing the rate at 6%, and the cancellation of the swap has not changed that. The £500,000 that the company receives is simply the present value of the future cash flows expected to be received under the swap, and whether or not the swap is cashed in, the protection that it has given to the interest payable under the loan is still there. Accordingly, the most appropriate treatment would be to spread the apparent gain over the life of the loan, which will mean that it will continue to show an interest rate of 6% (apart from the effect of subsequent movements in interest rates that were not foreseen when the swap was terminated).

A different result follows if the underlying loan itself is repaid. Again the accounting result is the same whether or not the swap is also terminated, because any such termination is only an acceleration of the expected cash flows. Since there is nothing left to hedge, if the swap is retained it should now be treated as a speculative instrument and marked to market, giving rise to a reported profit of £500,000.

Sometimes, rather than repurchasing or repaying their debt, companies enter into arrangements which have a similar economic effect. For example, they might irrevocably deposit funds with a third party which are to be applied solely in settlement of the debt, and agree with the creditor that he can look only to those funds for repayment of the debt. Such arrangements are sometimes referred to as resulting in 'defeasance' (meaning extinguishment) of the debt and are discussed in more detail in Chapter 18 at 3.7.

B Repurchase of shares

The standard refers only fleetingly to the repurchase of *shares.* This subject is discussed in the context of the Companies Act requirements at 3.3 below.

2.2.7 *The disclosure of debt maturities*

As discussed in 3.2 below, both the Companies Act and the *Listing Rules* require debt to be analysed in the accounts by reference to when the creditor is entitled to require repayment. The standard repeats that requirement.[38] However, in interpreting this rule, companies are to take account of committed facilities in existence at the year end that would permit short-term debt to be refinanced for a longer period, provided some exacting conditions are met. These conditions are as follows:

(a) the debt and the facility are under a single agreement or course of dealing with the same lender or group of lenders;

(b) the finance costs for the new debt are on a basis which is not significantly higher than that of the existing debt;

(c) the obligations of the lender (or group of lenders) are firm: the lender is not able legally to refrain from providing funds except in circumstances the possibility of which can be demonstrated to be remote; and

(d) the lender (or group of lenders) is expected to be able to fulfil its obligations under the facility.[39]

It is important to note that the borrower's own intentions and financial plans do not affect this reclassification; the rules require the position to be assessed from the lender's perspective only.

An example of this classification is shown by EMI:

> *Extract 17.7: EMI Group plc (2000)*
>
> **18 Net Borrowings** [extract]
>
> Long-term borrowings include £62.6m (1999: £41.0m) of borrowings repayable within one year, which are drawings under long-term committed facilities and, therefore, have been classified as such.

Before FRS 4 was issued, many companies which issued commercial paper reported it as long term, by reference to back-up facilities. Commercial paper is generally a cheaper alternative to short-term direct bank borrowing for many large companies, and the maturity periods are very short – usually between 5 and 45 days. Most programmes are backed up by lines of credit from banks, but as the back-up facility is not provided by the lenders (i.e. the investors who buy the paper), condition (a) quoted above cannot be met, suggesting that commercial paper borrowings will always be reported as short term.

Blue Circle provides an example of this analysis:

> *Extract 17.8: Blue Circle Industries plc (2000)*
>
> **18 Borrowings** [extract]
>
> In April 2000, the Company entered into a £1.6 billion credit facility which was partially used to finance the return of capital to shareholders in May 2000. At the year end, the facility had been reduced to £1.185m, of which £674.6m had been drawn. The unutilised amount of £510.4m with a remaining maturity of 4 years was backing up commercial paper debt of £344.9m (1999: £204.2m) included within the above as maturing within one year.

Nevertheless, some companies include commercial paper within amounts due in more than one year, an example being Pearson (see Extract 17.13 at 2.2.10 below). Presumably the 'refinancing contracts' referred to in that extract are with the current lenders of commercial paper; otherwise, the requirements of FRS 4 summarised above might not be satisfied.

Many companies also borrow on a short-term basis under multiple option funding facility agreements (MOFs). Short-term drawdowns under MOFs may be classified as long term by reference to the maturity date of the MOF provided all the four conditions above are met. Condition (a) will be satisfied even if it is not always the same banks who participate in individual financings under the MOF – they are regarded as being part of the same 'group of lenders' provided they are parties to the same agreement or course of dealing. Although the standard does not define the term 'course of dealing' which is used in condition (a), the choice of words suggests more latitude than the alternative – 'a single agreement'.

Condition (b) quoted above limits the choice of facilities even further. The drafting suggests that borrowings under the facility should be of the same type as those of the existing debt. So, for example, if the basis for determining the finance costs of the existing debt is a fixed margin over 1 month LIBOR, only facilities that allow borrowings that are priced on a similar basis should be considered. Hence it would not be possible to use a floating-rate medium-term facility to reclassify maturing fixed rate debt or vice versa.

In addition, the basis for determining the finance costs of borrowings under the facility should not be 'significantly higher'. The standard does not explain when one basis is significantly higher than another. However, in its discussion on the development of FRS 4, the ASB implicitly provides an indication of how this condition should be interpreted. It discusses why commercial paper should be shown as short term notwithstanding the back-up facilities and explains that conditions (a) and (b) above are not usually met. The prices of commercial paper back-up facilities are thus considered to be 'significantly higher' than commercial paper rates.[40]

Conditions (c) and (d) have a common goal. They seek to establish whether or not it is safe to rely on the borrowings under the facility. The conditions cover obvious escape routes that the provider of the facility (the lender) may have negotiated. Condition (d) is fairly straightforward; condition (c) focuses on the facility agreement and requires it to be both legally binding and genuinely committed. In this regard, FRS 4 requires that any circumstances specified in the facility agreement which permit the lender to refrain from providing new borrowings should be demonstrated to be remote, both at the balance sheet date and at the time the accounts are approved.

It will not be possible to confirm that the 'obligations of the lender are firm' if any of the circumstances in which the lender can refrain from providing new borrowings can only be interpreted subjectively. The example provided in the explanatory section of FRS 4 is that of a 'material adverse change' clause (i.e. a condition in the facility agreement allowing the lender to withhold funding in the event of a material adverse change in the borrower's financial position) where the term 'material adverse change' has not been defined.[41] This is probably a stricter test than is applied for existing long-term borrowings, where the existence of a term which would entitle the lender to early repayment is disregarded, provided that it is reasonable to believe that the circumstances that would allow the term to be invoked will not arise.

If maturity of debt analysis has been compiled by reference to committed facilities in existence at the balance sheet date, FRS 4 also requires disclosure of the amounts of the debt involved, analysed by the earliest date on which the lender could demand repayment in the absence of the facilities.[42]

2.2.8 *Warrants*

A warrant is defined in FRS 4 as 'an instrument that requires the issuer to issue shares (whether contingently or not) and contains no obligation for the issuer to transfer economic benefits'.[43] When a warrant is issued, the standard requires the net proceeds to be credited direct to shareholders' funds;[44] the implication appears to be that it should be reported only in the reconciliation of shareholders' funds, not in the statement of total recognised gains and losses, presumably on the argument that it is a transaction with (potential) shareholders.

Thereafter the accounting depends on whether the warrant is exercised or is allowed to lapse. If it is exercised, the proceeds on the original issue of the warrant are included in the net proceeds of the shares issued;[45] if it lapses, they are included instead in the statement of total recognised gains and losses,[46] since the original issue has turned out not to have been a transaction with shareholders after all, but a gain.

These conclusions are questionable. Given that the warrant may lapse, in which case the proceeds will be shown never to have been a transaction with shareholders, there is a case for saying that it should be shown as deferred income until the outcome is known, not credited to shareholders' funds. However, the ASB's definitions of the elements of financial statements (see Chapter 2 at 5.5) do not admit the possibility of deferred income, so presumably the ASB felt that this was not a course open to them. Furthermore, if the warrant does lapse the proceeds will constitute a realised profit which arguably belongs in the profit and loss account, not the statement of total recognised gains and losses. The rule in FRS 4 seems to be based on the fact that the transaction has a 'capital' flavour.

It should be noted that an option over shares falls within the definition of a warrant, although any premium payable for the exercise of the option may fall due at the date of exercise rather than the date of grant.

2.2.9 *Scrip dividends*

Scrip dividends arise when shareholders are given the opportunity to receive further fully paid up shares in their company as an alternative to cash dividends. The standard deals with only some of the accounting issues which arise in relation to such transactions, and in a rather ambiguous way. It says that the value of the shares should be deemed to be the amount receivable under the cash alternative.[47] However, this is probably addressing only the initial recording of the dividend in the profit and loss account before the shareholders have chosen whether to take cash or shares, not the subsequent recording of the issue itself, in respect of which a later passage in the standard suggests that a different treatment might be appropriate.[48] The standard also says that the whole cash amount should be set up as a liability until the number of shareholders who will elect to receive the scrip dividend is known.[49] These various topics are discussed further at 4.7 below.

2.2.10 *Disclosure requirements*

A large number of disclosures are required by FRS 4. These are as follows:

(a) The following analyses of balance sheet items:

- (i) An analysis of shareholders' funds between equity and non-equity interests.[50] The non-equity interests should be further analysed into each class of non-equity shares and series of warrants for non-equity shares;[51]
- (ii) An analysis of minority interests between equity and non-equity interests in subsidiaries;[52]
- (iii) An analysis of liabilities between amounts in respect of convertible debt and other amounts.[53]

Where these analyses are given in the notes rather than on the face of the balance sheet, the balance sheet caption should indicate that non-equity interests or convertible debt is included in the amount shown.[54] The balance sheet should also disclose the amount of shareholders' funds in total.[55]

Carlton's balance sheet shows the following analysis:

Extract 17.9: Carlton Communications plc (2000)

Consolidated Balance Sheet [extract]

Capital and Reserves	**2000 £m**	1999 £m
Called up share capital	**41.8**	47.9
Share premium	**148.8**	129.5
Other reserves	**12.5**	7.5
Profit and loss account	**248.3**	320.4
Shareholders' funds	**451.4**	505.3
Minority interests – equity	**0.9**	0.4
	452.3	505.7
Attributable to:		
Equity shareholders' funds (before goodwill)	**1,855.2**	2,031.5
Cumulative goodwill written off directly to reserves	**(1,567.6)**	(1,867.6)
Equity shareholders' funds	**287.6**	163.9
Non-equity shareholders' funds	**163.8**	341.4
Total shareholders' funds	**451.4**	505.3

A number of companies have fallen foul of the requirement to analyse shareholders' funds between equity and non-equity categories and have had to restate their accounts after intervention by the Financial Reporting Review Panel. One was Ransomes, as shown in Extract 17.10 below. The point at issue was that some time previously Ransomes had issued some non-equity shares at a premium and subsequently applied to the Court for cancellation of the share premium account arising on the issue in order to create a reserve against which to set off goodwill (as then permitted under SSAP 22). Ransomes had taken the view that this effectively reduced non-equity shareholders' funds. The Review Panel, however, took the view that as the offset of goodwill was not a transaction with the non-equity shareholders and therefore did not affect the amount to be disclosed for non-equity shareholders' funds. Carlton has also taken this view in Extract 17.9 above, where goodwill is presented as a deduction from *equity* shareholders' funds.

Extract 17.10: Ransomes plc (1996)

22. Shareholders' Funds [extract]

After discussion with the Financial Reporting Review Panel, the analysis of shareholders' funds between equity and non-equity interests at 30th September 1995 has been restated to conform with Financial Reporting Standard 4. The restatement for the Group has resulted in a £47.9m decrease in equity interests and a £47.9m increase in non-equity interests. The change relates to the inclusion of the premium arising on the issue of the 8.25p preference shares in 1989. This amount had previously been regarded as having been set-off by the write off of goodwill of £47.9m. The restatement in the Company books is £15.1m and is lower as the goodwill set-off only related to the intangible assets purchased on the acquisition of the Cushman Group in 1989. The 8.25p cumulative convertible preference shares are not redeemable. Total shareholders' funds remain unchanged. The restated analysis of shareholders' funds as at 30th September 1995 is given in the table below:

Group

	1995 £'000	Restated 1995 £'000	Change £'000
Equity interests	6,793	(41,075)	(47,868)
Non-equity interests	9,307	57,175	47,868
Shareholders' funds	16,100	16,100	–

Company

	1995 £'000	Restated 1995 £'000	Change £'000
Equity interests	45,663	30,590	(15,073)
Non-equity interests	42,102	57,175	15,073
Shareholders' funds	87,765	87,765	–

Alexon made a similar change, but also changed its treatment of dividends on non-equity shares, as shown in this note:

Extract 17.11: Alexon plc (1996)

24 Non equity shareholders' funds

Group and Company

	1996 £000	1995 £000
Non-equity shareholders' funds may be analysed as follows:		
Share capital	2,137	2,137
Share premium	18,219	18,220
Unamortised issue costs	(232)	(250)
Undeclared preference dividends	1,692	423
	21,816	20,530
Representing:		
6.25p (net) convertible cumulative redeemable preference shares of 10p each	21,698	20,416
5% (now 3.5% plus tax credit) cumulative preference shares of £1 each	105	101
Non-voting deferred shares of 10p each	13	13
	21,816	20,530

> Following developments in the application of Financial Reporting Standard No. 4 (FRS 4) and an enquiry by the Financial Reporting Review Panel, the directors have reviewed the disclosure for equity and non-equity shareholders' funds and have restated the analysis at 28 January 1995 to accord with the method specified by FRS 4. The effect has been to reduce equity shareholders' funds by £17,970,000 and to increase non-equity shareholders' funds by the same amount, and to include the accrued preference dividends within non-equity shareholders' funds. This has resulted in an increase in total shareholders' funds by the amount of the accrued preference dividends, previously included within creditors.

As can be seen from this extract, Alexon revised its accounts so as to include the accrued dividends on its preference shares (which were in arrears) within shareholders' funds rather than (as previously) showing them as a liability, even though they also showed them as an appropriation in the profit and loss account as required by FRS 4. This means that the appropriation entry was a circular one (i.e. DR Profit and loss account for the period CR Profit and loss reserve). The standard is not entirely clear about the balance sheet classification of accrued dividends; it can be read as requiring that *all* proposed dividends (not simply those in arrears, or those relating to non-equity shares) remain in shareholders' funds, because they do not become liabilities until they are declared, but we do not believe this was intended by the ASB and it is certainly not an interpretation that is applied in practice other than in circumstances similar to those of Alexon (see also 4.4.1 below).

An example of the required analysis of minority interests between equity and non-equity categories is given by Cadbury Schweppes in Extract 17.1 at 2.2.2 B above.

(b) A brief summary of the rights of each class of shares, including

  (i) the rights to dividends;

  (ii) the dates at which they are redeemable and the amounts payable in respect of redemption;

  (iii) their priority and the amounts receivable on a winding up; and

  (iv) their voting rights.

  If the rights vary according to circumstances, the details should be explained. The summary of rights should also be sufficient to explain why the class of shares has been classified as equity or non-equity shares.[56] The same disclosure also has to be given in respect of any shares of a new class which may have to be issued because of any existing warrants or convertible debt.[57]

  The description of rights specified above need not be given for routine equity shares with all of the following features:

  (i) no rights to dividends other than those that may be recommended by the directors;

  (ii) no redemption rights;

  (iii) unlimited right to share in the surplus remaining on a winding up after all liabilities and participation rights of other classes of shares have been satisfied; and

  (iv) one vote per share.[58]

BBA provides a good example of the disclosure of the rights of shares:

Extract 17.12: BBA Group plc (2000)

19 Capital and reserves [extract]

Rights of non-equity interests

5% Cumulative preference £1 shares:

i. entitle holders, in priority to holders of all other classes of shares, to a fixed cumulative preferential dividend at a rate of 5.0% per annum per share payable half yearly in equal amounts on 1 February and 1 August.

ii. on a return of capital on a winding up, or otherwise, will carry the right to repayment of capital together with a premium of 12.5p per share and a sum equal to any arrears or deficiency of dividend; this right is in priority to the rights of the convertible preference and ordinary shareholders;

iii. carry the right to attend and vote at a general meeting of the Company only if, at the date of the notice convening the meeting, payment of the dividend to which they are entitled is six months or more in arrears, or if a resolution is to be considered at the meeting for winding-up the company or reducing its share capital or sanctioning the sale of the undertakings of the Company or varying or abrogating any of the special rights attaching to them.

6.75% Cumulative redeemable convertible preference £1 shares

i. entitle holders (subject to the prior rights of the 5% cumulative £1 preference shares) to a fixed cumulative preferential dividend at a rate of 6.75% per annum per share, payable half yearly in equal amounts on 31 May and 30 November;

ii. carry the right to be converted into ordinary shares at the option of the holder on 31 May in any of the years 2001 to 2005 inclusive at the rate of 54.64 ordinary shares for every £100 nominal of convertible preference shares;

iii. will be redeemed by the Company on 31 May 2006 at par (if not previously converted or redeemed) and any arrears of dividend will be paid;

iv. on a return of capital on a winding up, or otherwise, will carry the right to repayment of capital and payment of accrued dividends in priority to ordinary shares but after the 5% cumulative £1 preference shares;

v. carry the right to attend and vote at a general meeting of the Company only if, at the date of the notice convening the meeting, payment of the dividend to which they are entitled is six months or more in arrears, or if a resolution is to be considered at the meeting for winding-up the Company, or for modifying or abrogating any special rights attaching to them.

(c) In respect of non-equity minority interests, a description of any rights of the holders against other group companies.[59]

(d) An analysis of the maturity of debt showing amounts falling due:

(i) in one year or less, or on demand;

(ii) in more than one year but not more than two years;

(iii) in more than two but not more than five years; and

(iv) in five years or more.[60]

Where short-term debt has been reclassified as long term because the lender has granted a longer term facility, the amount of the debt which has been reclassified should be disclosed, analysed by its maturity before such reclassification.[61]

Pearson's accounts contain an example of this disclosure:

Extract 17.13: Pearson plc (2000)

21 Financial Instruments [extract]

a. **Maturity of borrowings and other financial liabilities**

The maturity profile of the Group's borrowings and other financial liabilities is shown below.

all figures in £ millions	2000 Group	2000 company	1999 Group	1999 company
Maturity of borrowings				
Short-term				
Bank loans and overdrafts	112	225	47	130
Total due within one year	112	225	47	130
Medium and long-term				
Loans or instalments thereof repayable:				
From one to two years	100	–	155	155
From two to five years	1,626	905	1,617	906
After five years not by instalments	979	813	504	351
Total due after more than one year	2,705	1,718	2,276	1,412
Total borrowings	2,817	1,943	2,323	1,542

note: At 31 December 2000 £1,134m (1999: £547m) of debt, including commercial paper, currently classified from two to five years would be repayable within one year if refinancing contracts were not in place. The short-term bank loans and overdrafts of the Group are lower than those of the company because of bank offset arrangements.

(e) For convertible debt:

(i) the dates of redemption and the amounts payable on redemption;

(ii) the number and class of shares into which the debt may be converted, and the dates at or periods within which conversion may take place; and

(iii) whether conversion is at the option of the issuer or the holder.[62]

Cookson provides an example of this disclosure:

Extract 17.14: Cookson Group plc (2000)

15 Convertible bonds

In 1994, the Company issued £80.0m 7% convertible bonds. Interest on the bonds is payable semi-annually on 2 November and 2 May. Redemption of the bonds will take place on 2 November 2004, unless the bonds have previously been purchased, redeemed or converted. Redemption may now take place at any time at par at the option of the Company. All bonds purchased by the Company or any Group company must be cancelled. Holders of the bonds may convert them into ordinary shares of the Company at a price of 288p, as adjusted for the rights issue made in March 1995, representing a premium at the date of issue of 17.55% at any time prior to 26 October 2004.

(f) For debt in general:

   (i) anything unusual about the legal nature of the debt, for example that it is subordinated or that the obligation to repay it is conditional; and

   (ii) the amount payable, or which could be claimed on a winding up, if it is significantly different from the carrying amount.

   These disclosures may be summarised and need not be given for each individual instrument.[63]

(g) Where the summary of the terms of an instrument (required by (b), (c), (e) and (f) above) cannot adequately convey its full commercial effect, that fact has to be stated and particulars given of where the relevant information can be obtained. The principal features of the instruments still have to be stated.[64]

(h) Any gain or loss arising on the repurchase or early settlement of debt.[65]

(i) The aggregate dividends for each class of shares, disclosing separately the total amounts in respect of the following:

   (i) dividends on equity shares;

   (ii) participating dividends on non-equity shares (those dividends which, under the memorandum and articles, are always equivalent to a fixed multiple of the dividend payable on an equity share);[66] and

   (iii) other dividends on non-equity shares.

   Any additional appropriations in respect of non-equity shares should also be disclosed.

   This information may be shown in the dividends note rather than on the face of the profit and loss account so long as the profit and loss account caption indicates that the distributions include amounts in respect of non-equity shares if that is the case.[67]

(j) An analysis of the amount of the minority interest charge in the profit and loss account between equity and non-equity interests.[68]

(k) For investment companies, the amount of any finance costs which have been allocated to capital rather than revenue (as a separately disclosed item in the statement of total recognised gains and losses), and the accounting policy on which this allocation has been based.[69]

One further disclosure was proposed in FRED 3 but did not survive as a requirement in the standard: this is the market value of the company's debt and non-equity shares.[70] However, the explanatory section of FRS 4 did suggest that this disclosure be considered where 'information on market values would assist users',[71] and it is now required for major companies by FRS 13 (see Chapter 10 at 2.9).

FRS 13 prescribes several further disclosures for financial instruments in the notes to the accounts, several of which apply to share and loan capital. These are detailed in Chapter 10 at 2 and 3).

3 COMPANIES ACT REQUIREMENTS

3.1 Share capital

3.1.1 Measurement

A Share premium account

Under the Companies Act, the amount at which share capital is recorded is dictated by the nominal value of the shares issued, and if the value of the consideration received for the issue of shares exceeds that amount, the excess is recorded in the share premium account.[72] The share premium account is regarded as permanent capital of the company and only certain expenses of a capital nature may be set off against it, namely:

(a) the company's preliminary expenses;

(b) the expenses of, or the commission paid or discount allowed on, any issue of shares or debentures of the company; or

(c) the premium payable on redemption of debentures of the company.[73]

Under FRS 4, the costs of issuing debentures or non-equity shares have to be accounted for as a finance cost or an appropriation in the profit and loss account over the life of the instrument. The same is also true of any discounts on the issue of debentures and any premiums on their repayment. This treatment does not prevent such costs ultimately from being deducted from the share premium account, but they will have to get there by transfer from the profit and loss account reserve after having first been taken to the profit and loss account in accordance with the standard. The ability to offset finance costs related to debt against the share premium account is a rather anachronistic relic of nineteenth century companies legislation, which is almost certain to be abolished by the new Companies Act currently being planned by the Department of Trade and Industry.

It is not entirely clear how the requirement of the Companies Act to credit the 'value' of any premium received to the share premium account is to be interpreted, and in particular whether it means the same as the 'fair value' of net proceeds that is required to be recorded by FRS 4 (see 2.2.4 above). For example, if a company issues 1 million 5p shares for £1 million payable in five years time, the fair value of the consideration received would for accounting purposes generally now be regarded as the net present value of £1 million receivable in five years' time – assuming a discount rate of 5%, £783,526. This would, for example, be the approach to assigning a fair value to such a debtor under FRS 7 (see Chapter 6 at 2.4.3 B).

This would imply that the share capital account should be credited with £50,000 (1 million shares at the nominal value of 5p) and the share premium account with £733,526, rather than the balance of the full amount ultimately payable, £950,000. Some counsel have concurred this view, but have held that the balance of £216,474 should nevertheless be credited to a non-distributable reserve.

If this approach were adopted, the accounting treatment under FRS 4 would be to record a debtor of £783,526 at issue date together with share capital of £50,000 and share premium of £733,526. The debtor would then be accreted to £1 million over five years on a constant rate of return basis. There are arguments for taking the corresponding credit either:

- direct to a non-distributable reserve within shareholders' funds (on the basis that it represents a transaction with shareholders, and the amount received is not, on the legal view above, distributable); or
- to the profit and loss account (on the basis that it represents cash interest on a debtor (which although a shareholder is not now transacting with the company as such) and is therefore a realised, if not a distributable, profit), with a subsequent transfer to an undistributable reserve.

Matters are slightly complicated by the fact that, if instead the company had issued 1 million £1 shares for £1 million payable in five years' time, it would have been required to record share capital of £1 million by section 737 of the Companies Act, which defines called-up share capital as including 'any share capital to be paid on a specified future date'. In this case FRS 4 would strictly require the company to debit shareholders' funds with the discount of £216,474 and write this off over the period of the transaction.

There is no totally satisfactory answer to issues such as these, for the simple reason that the Victorian legislators drafted the Companies Act requirements to deal with straightforward issues of shares for cash rather than with more complex transactions.

B *Merger relief and group reconstruction relief*

The Companies Act gives relief from the requirement to set up a share premium account in certain circumstances where shares are being issued in exchange for shares in another company, and to limit the amount of the share premium account when shares are being issued to effect a group reconstruction (see 2.1.2 of Chapter 6).[74] This might have been affected to some degree by FRS 4, which requires shares to be recorded on the basis of the fair value of the consideration received,[75] exempting only instances where merger *accounting* is applied,[76] not where merger relief is taken. However, it seems that this change, if indeed it was one, was inadvertent; accounting standards do not usually seek to withdraw reliefs specifically granted by legislation. The ASB subsequently made it clear in FRS 6 that its rules on acquisition accounting were not intended to have any effect on the parent company's own accounts and in particular to the availability of merger relief and group reconstruction relief,[77] and we suggest that that interpretation be extended to FRS 4 as well.

C *Foreign currency share capital*

The share capital of UK companies is generally denominated in sterling, but there is no requirement for this to be the case, except that a public company must have a minimum share capital of £50,000.[78] Neither FRS 4 nor SSAP 20 addresses the treatment of translation of share capital denominated in a currency other than the reporting currency. This issue is discussed in more detail in Chapter 8 at 3.1.6.

3.1.2 *Classification of equity and non-equity shares*

Like FRS 4 (see 2.2.2 A above), the Companies Act 1985 effectively defines non-equity shares with equity shares being the residual category. However, whereas the classification of shares as equity or non-equity under FRS 4 has accounting implications, the classification under the Companies Act is primarily relevant for company law purposes. The Act defines equity share capital as 'issued share capital excluding any part of that capital which, neither as respects dividends nor as respects capital, carries any right to participate beyond a specified amount in a distribution'.[79] Whilst this definition will mean that in most cases the classification of a share will be the same under both the Act and FRS 4, this will not always be the case.

All redeemable shares are non-equity shares under FRS 4, whereas under the Companies Act they could be equity shares. For example, a fully participating redeemable preference share would be an equity share under the Act since there is no restriction on its right to participate in profit. Also, under FRS 4 a share with restrictions on the right to participate in dividends *or* on a winding up is a non-equity share, whereas under the Act there needs to be a restriction on the right to participate in dividends *and* on a winding up.

3.1.3 *Disclosure*

The main disclosure requirements in the Companies Act begin with the format in which the balance sheet is to be laid out. The formats require capital and reserves to be analysed as shown in the box.[80] In terms of this analysis, the following are 'Other reserves' (item IV.4):

> Capital and reserves
>
> I Called up share capital
>
> II Share premium account
>
> III Revaluation reserve
>
> IV Other reserves
>
> 1. Capital redemption reserve
> 2. Reserve for own shares
> 3. Reserves provided for by the articles of association
> 4. Other reserves
>
> V Profit and loss account

- a reserve arising when relief is taken under section 131 (merger relief) or section 132 (group reconstruction relief), but the company chooses to record a reserve equivalent to the share premium that would have been recorded, but for the relief;
- a reserve arising from cancellation of capital by the Court pursuant to section 135, except where the Court has indicated that such a reserve may be treated as a distributable profit, in which case it would be added to the Profit and loss account (item V).

The Act also requires the following note disclosures in respect of share capital:

(a) the authorised share capital;

(b) where there is more than one class of shares, the number and aggregate nominal value of each class of share allotted;[81]

(c) these details about redeemable shares which have been allotted:

  (i) their earliest and latest redemption dates;

  (ii) whether redemption is automatic, or is at the option of either the company or the shareholder; and

  (iii) the amount of any redemption premium;[82]

(d) in relation to the allotment of shares during the year:

  (i) the classes of shares allotted; and

  (ii) the number allotted, their aggregate nominal value and the consideration received, in respect of each class of shares;[83]

(e) in respect of contingent rights to the allotment of further shares (such as options to subscribe), the following information:

  (i) the number, description and amount of the shares involved;

  (ii) the period during which the right is exercisable; and

  (iii) the price to be paid for the shares allotted;[84] and

(f) the amount of any arrears of fixed cumulative dividends on any class of the company's shares, and the period for which they are in arrears.[85]

In respect of dividends, the Act requires that the total dividends paid and proposed in respect of the year are to be disclosed on the face of the profit and loss account, and the amount of proposed dividends has to be shown separately either on the face of the profit and loss account or in a note.[86] However, FRS 4 requires dividends on non-equity shares to be accounted for on an accruals basis if the entitlement to them is time-based,[87] and this may complicate the legal disclosure requirement if the accrued amount is not the same as that proposed for payment. The problem is similar to that arising when a company has to accrue for a premium or discount on redemption of preference shares as well as the dividend for the period, an example of which can be seen in Extract 17.3 at 2.2.2 above.

The Companies Act also contains various requirements for matters to be disclosed in the Directors' Report in respect of share capital. Those relating to directors' interests in shares are discussed in Chapter 30 at 3.1.1, while those in respect of the purchase by a company of its own shares are dealt with at 3.3 below. The *Listing Rules* also require listed companies to disclose details of holdings in the company's shares of 3% or more which have been notified to the company.[88]

3.2 Loan capital

In terms of the Companies Act, loan capital will fall under the general heading of creditors, which has to be analysed under the formats as shown here.[89]

Creditors

1. Debenture loans
2. Bank loans and overdrafts
3. Payments received on account
4. Trade creditors
5. Bills of exchange payable
6. Amounts owed to group undertakings
7. Amounts owed to undertakings in which the company has a participating interest
8. Other creditors including taxation and social security
9. Accruals and deferred income.

Most UK companies follow Format 1 of the two formats available in the Act, and this means that they have to give two separate analyses under these headings, one for amounts falling due within one year and the other for amounts falling due after more than one year.

In distinguishing amounts between these two categories, the deciding factor is the earliest date at which the creditor could demand repayment.[90] As discussed in 2.2.7 above, FRS 4 interprets this restrictively.

In addition to the formats, the Act requires the following disclosures in respect of each item shown under creditors in the balance sheet:

(a) the amount that is not repayable within five years of the balance sheet date and the terms of repayment and interest for such items;[91] and

(b) the total amount in respect of which any security has been given, and an indication of the nature of the security.[92]

The Act also requires the following information to be given in relation to the issue of debentures:

(a) the classes of debentures issued; and

(b) the amount issued and the consideration received in respect of each class.[93]

Details must also be given of any debentures held by a nominee or a trustee for the company.[94]

A debenture is not defined in the Companies Act, except that it is said to *include* 'debenture stock, bonds and other securities of a company, whether constituting a charge on the assets of the company or not'.[95] In general legal use, it is a term applying to any document evidencing a loan, and in the context of company law it means a debt instrument issued by the company and usually giving some form of security or charge over its assets, although this is not an essential feature.

The Companies Act requires interest payable to be analysed into two categories:

(a) that relating to bank loans and overdrafts; and

(b) interest on all other loans.[96]

3.3 Redemption and purchase of a company's own shares

3.3.1 *Redemption of shares*

At one time, UK companies were prohibited from purchasing their own shares and could redeem only preference shares. These restrictions were eased by the Companies Act 1981, and a new regime introduced which permitted both the purchase and redemption of shares on a wider basis, subject to various conditions and safeguards.[97] The most important of these are as follows:

(a) the capital of the company must be maintained, either by freezing up an equivalent amount of distributable profits in a 'capital redemption reserve' or by making it good from the proceeds of a fresh issue of shares made for the purposes of the redemption. However, there is a relaxation of this principle for private companies, discussed at A below;

(b) the shares which are redeemed or purchased must be cancelled and may not be reissued;

(c) the transaction must be permitted under the company's articles, and in certain cases must also be authorised by shareholder resolution; and

(d) a transaction may not be undertaken if its effect will be that no shares remain in issue, or that the only shares in issue will be redeemable shares.

Some examples of the accounting treatment of such transactions are shown below:

Example 17.8: Redemption of own shares

A company has the following balance sheet:	£
Cash	20,000
Ordinary £1 shares	8,000
Redeemable preference £1 shares	5,000
Profit and loss account	7,000
	20,000

It decides to redeem half of its preference shares at par. The entries to effect the redemption and to maintain the original capital are as follows:

	£	£
Redeemable preference shares	2,500	
Cash		2,500
to redeem the shares		
Profit and loss account reserve	2,500	
Capital redemption reserve		2,500
to maintain the capital at its original amount.		

As a result, the balance sheet will now be:

	£
Cash	17,500
Ordinary £1 shares	8,000
Redeemable preference £1 shares	2,500
Capital redemption reserve	2,500
Profit and loss account	4,500
	17,500

If there had been a fresh issue of shares, the second journal entry would not be needed except to the extent that the proceeds of the fresh issue fell short of £2,500.

If the redemption had been at a premium of (say) 20 pence per share, the entries and the balance sheet would have been as follows:

	£	£
Redeemable preference shares	2,500	
Profit and loss account reserve	500	
Cash		3,000
to redeem the shares		
Profit and loss account reserve	2,500	
Capital redemption reserve		2,500
to maintain the capital at its original amount.		

As a result, the balance sheet will now be:

	£
Cash	17,000
Ordinary £1 shares	8,000
Redeemable preference £1 shares	2,500
Capital redemption reserve	2,500
Profit and loss account	4,000
	17,000

The redemption premium of £500 must be met out of distributable profits; it cannot be met out of the proceeds of a fresh issue.

If the redeemable shares had originally been issued at a premium, and there is a fresh issue for the purposes of the redemption, then the premium on redemption can be met out of the proceeds of the fresh issue up to the limit of the lesser of:

(a) the premium received by the company on the issue of the shares now being redeemed, or

(b) the current balance on the share premium account including any premium on issue of the new shares.[98]

This is shown in the following example:

Example 17.9: Redemption of own shares at a premium

A company has the following balance sheet:

	£
Cash	40,000
Ordinary £1 shares	20,000
Redeemable preference £1 shares	5,000
Share premium account	3,000
Profit and loss account	12,000
	40,000

The preference shares were originally issued at a premium of 10 pence per share. The company now decides to redeem all of its preference shares, which carry a redemption premium of 30 pence per share, and at the same time have a fresh issue of 2,000 ordinary shares at an issue price of £2 per share. The entries are as follows:

	£	£
Cash	4,000	
Ordinary £1 shares		2,000
Share premium account		2,000
to record the proceeds of the new issue		
Redeemable preference shares	5,000	
Share premium account	500	
Profit and loss account reserve	1,000	
Cash		6,500
to effect the redemption, and		
Profit and loss account reserve	1,500	
Capital redemption reserve		1,500
to make good the capital.		

The amount initially credited to share premium account in respect of the preference shares (£500) is the limiting factor on what can be released to offset the premium payable on redemption of the shares – the rest has to be met from distributable profits. The capital has to be made good because the proceeds from the new issue (£4,000) less the amount already applied towards the redemption premium (£500) fell short of the nominal value of the shares redeemed (£5,000). The amount of £2,500 charged to the profit and loss account represents the difference between the redemption cost of £6,500 and the proceeds of the fresh issue of £4,000.

As a result, the balance sheet will now be:

	£
Cash	37,500
Ordinary £1 shares	22,000
Redeemable preference £1 shares	–
Share premium account	4,500
Capital redemption reserve	1,500
Profit and loss account	9,500
	37,500

It can be seen that the aggregate of the share capital and undistributable reserves remains the same before and after the transaction, which is the objective of the rules which lie behind these journal entries.

	Before £	After £
Ordinary £1 shares	20,000	22,000
Redeemable preference £1 shares	5,000	–
Share premium account	3,000	4,500
Capital redemption reserve	–	1,500
	28,000	28,000

A *Private companies*

As mentioned above, these capital maintenance rules are relaxed for private companies which are unable to meet the cost of redemption either out of their distributable profits or from the proceeds of a fresh issue.[99] In order to be permitted to do this, various procedures have to be followed which are designed to protect the creditors of the company from the consequences of eroding its capital base. In particular, the directors must make a statutory declaration that they are of the opinion that there will be no grounds on which the company could be found to be unable to pay its debts, both immediately following the transaction and for a year thereafter, and the auditors must confirm, after enquiry, that they are not aware of anything which would indicate that the directors' opinion was unreasonable. An example of the accounting treatment in such a case is set out below.

Example 17.10: Redemption of own shares out of capital

A private company has the following balance sheet:

	£
Cash	20,000
Ordinary £1 shares	10,000
Redeemable preference £1 shares	5,000
Share premium account	3,000
Profit and loss account	2,000
	20,000

The directors decide that they wish to redeem all the preference shares at par. The distributable profits of the company are not adequate to allow this without reduction of its capital and accordingly the requirements of the Act must be followed to permit the transaction to proceed. When this has been done, the necessary entries will be as follows:

	£	£
Redeemable preference shares	5,000	
Cash		5,000
to effect the redemption		
To effect the redemption, and		
Profit and loss account reserve	2,000	
Capital redemption reserve		2,000
to make good the capital so far as the company is able to do so from its distributable profits.		

As a result, the balance sheet will now be:

	£
Cash	15,000
Ordinary £1 shares	10,000
Redeemable preference £1 shares	–
Share premium account	3,000
Capital redemption reserve	2,000
Profit and loss account	–
	15,000

This time, the aggregate of the share capital and undistributable reserves is not the same before and after the transaction, because of the shortfall. The amount of the shortfall (£3,000 in this example) is referred to in the Act as the 'permissible capital payment'.

	Before £	After £
Ordinary £1 shares	10,000	10,000
Redeemable preference £1 shares	5,000	–
Share premium account	3,000	3,000
Capital redemption reserve	–	2,000
	18,000	15,000

At present, a public company wishing to reduce its capital other than by a redemption or purchase of shares out of distributable profits must apply to the Court for permission to do so. However, it is very likely that the new Companies Act currently being planned by the DTI will extend the regime for private companies to public companies.

B Foreign currency shares

When shares denominated in foreign currency are redeemed or purchased, the issue arises as to what amount should be transferred to the capital redemption reserve (i.e. the sterling equivalent of the shares at the date of issue or the date of redemption or purchase), and whether the answer to this question depends on whether or not the shares have been continuously retranslated for accounting purposes (see Chapter 8 at 3.1.6).

This is ultimately a legal question, and companies in this position should seek legal advice. Our view, however, would be that it is the sterling equivalent of the shares at the date of redemption or purchase that is relevant, irrespective of what accounting policy has been adopted. This is because if a company issues share capital of, say, 1 million US dollars, its obligation is to maintain capital of $1 million, not of the original sterling equivalent of $1 million at issue. An example of a company adopting this approach is Enterprise Oil, although it had not retranslated the share capital in its financial statements while it remained in issue.

Extract 17.15: Enterprise Oil plc (2000)

21. SHARE CAPITAL [extract]

On 10 October 2000 all of the 5,100,000 Series B Cumulative Dollar Preference Shares were redeemed at a premium of US$0.50 per share, resulting in an appropriation of £1.8 million. The Preference Shares were recorded at historical cost exchange rates within called-up share capital and the foreign exchange difference of £13.6 million which arose on redemption has been charged to reserves since the shares provided a partial hedge against currency movements of group's overseas investments. In accordance with UK legal requirements an amount equal to the nominal value of the redeemed shares has been credited to a Capital Redemption Reserve.

22. SHAREHOLDERS' FUNDS [extract]

(ii) Analysis of movements in share capital and reserves

	Share capital	Share premium	Capital redemption reserve	Other reserves	Profit and loss account	Total
	£m	£m	£m	£m	£m	£m
Group						
At 1 January 2000	198.9	100.5	103.8	179.7	494.9	1,077.8
Issues of new shares	0.1	2.5	–	–	–	2.6
Redemption of Series B preference shares	–	–	–	–	(89.7)	(89.7)
Capital redemption reserve transfer	(74.3)	–	87.9	–	(13.6)	–
Profit for the year before preference share redemption costs					443.9	443.9
Currency translation differences	–	–	–	–	18.2	18.2
At 31 December 2000	124.7	103.0	191.7	179.7	853.7	1452.8

3.3.2 *Purchase of shares*

The mechanics for accounting for purchases of shares are the same as those for redemptions as shown above. Where a company has purchased some of its shares, it has to make various disclosures in the directors' report. These include the number and nominal value of the shares purchased, together with the amount of the consideration paid and the reasons for the purchase, and the percentage of the called-up share capital which it represents. These and other similar disclosures are also required in other similar circumstances, such as where a company takes a lien or charge over its shares, or provides financial assistance for the purchase of its shares and has a beneficial interest in such shares.[100]

Barclays is an example of a company which regularly purchases its own shares. The relevant disclosures from its accounts are shown below:

Extract 17.16: Barclays plc (2000)

Directors' report

Share capital [extract]

During the year, Barclays plc purchased in the market for cancellation 19,562,682 of its ordinary shares of £1 each at a total cost of £311m as part of its programme of returning excess capital to shareholders. These transactions represented some 1% of the issued ordinary share capital at 31st December 2000. As at 7th February 2001, the Company has an unexpired authority to repurchase further shares up to a maximum of 204,437,318 ordinary shares.

Notes to the accounts

37 Called up share capital [extract]

	2000 £m	1999 £m
Called up share capital, allotted and fully paid		
Ordinary shares:		
At beginning of year	**1,494**	1,510
Issued to staff under the SAYE Share Option Scheme	**11**	11
Issuer under Executive Share Option Scheme	**–**	1
Issued to acquire The Woolwich	**176**	–
Repurchase of shares	**(20)**	(28)
At end of year	**1,661**	1,494
Staff shares	**1**	1
	1,662	1,495

In 2000, the Company repurchased ordinary shares with a nominal value of £20m at a total cost of £311m. In 1999, ordinary shares with a nominal value of £28m were repurchased at a total cost of £504m.

Consolidated statement of changes in reserves [extract]

	2000 £m	1999 £m
Capital redemption reserve		
At beginning of year	**207**	179
Repurchase of ordinary shares	**20**	28
At end of year	**227**	207
Profit and loss account [extract]		
Repurchase of ordinary shares	**(291)**	(476)
Transfer to capital redemption reserve	**(20)**	(28)

Listed companies have to give the following disclosure requirements in relation to the purchase of their own shares:

(a) any shareholders' authority which existed at the year end for the company to purchase its own shares (in Extract 17.16 above, Barclays give the more up-to-date information as at the date of approval of the accounts);

(b) the names of the sellers of any shares purchased or proposed to be purchased by the company during the year otherwise than through the market or by tender or partial offer to all shareholders; and

(c) where purchases, or options or contracts to make such purchases, have been entered into since the year end, the number, nominal value and percentage of the called up shares of the class purchased, the consideration paid and the reasons for the purchase.[101]

3.3.3 *Treasury stock*

In some jurisdictions, such as the United States, companies are permitted to purchase their own shares and reissue them later. Shares temporarily retired in this way are commonly referred to as 'treasury stock', and are typically accounted for by deducting the cost of repurchase from, and adding the proceeds of reissue to, shareholders' funds.

UK companies legislation currently does not permit a company to hold its own shares – any shares purchased must be cancelled as described in 3.3.1 and 3.3.2 above. It is likely that legislation will be introduced in the relatively near future to provide some relaxation of this rule, either as part of the proposed new Companies Act or as a separate matter. In practice, however, some *de facto* holdings of treasury stock are permitted, the most common being the holding by an employee share trust or similar vehicle of shares in the sponsoring company. However, such holdings are accounted for as assets rather than as deductions from shareholders' funds (even though the ASB's *Statement of Principles* requires the latter treatment), largely because the Companies Acts formats include an asset caption 'Own shares', implicitly requiring such shares to be treated as assets. The accounting treatment of employee share schemes is discussed more fully in Chapter 22.

Occasionally, however, a UK company may set up an entity that is not a subsidiary, but which is nevertheless effectively under its control, in order to undertake strategic repurchases of its own shares. Such structures avoid both the requirement for cancellation of shares repurchased by the company and the prohibition on the purchase of a company's shares by a subsidiary of the company. An example of a company that appears to have set up such an entity is Billiton. Interestingly, Billiton has not treated shares repurchased by this entity as assets but has, correctly in our view, invoked the 'true and fair override' in order to account for them as a deduction from shareholders' funds.

Extract 17.17: Billiton plc (2000)

Group balance sheet [extract]

	Note	Group 2000 US$m	1999 US$m
Capital and reserves			
Called up share capital	21	**1,069**	1,069
Share premium account	22	**27**	27
Profit and loss account	22	**3,996**	3,658
Interest in shares of Billiton Plc	23	**(118)**	(116)
Equity shareholders' funds	23	**4,974**	4,638

23 Reconciliation of movements in shareholders' funds	Group 2000 US$m	1999 US$m
Profit for the financial period	**577**	383
Other recognised gains and losses	**(7)**	(14)
Total recognised gains	**570**	369
Dividends	**(232)**	(218)
Share repurchase scheme	**(2)**	(116)
Net movement in shareholders' funds	**336**	35
Shareholders' funds at start of period as restated	**4,638**	4,603
Shareholders' funds at end of period	**4,974**	4,638

The Company has entered into an arrangement under which it has contingently agreed to purchase its own shares from a special purpose vehicle (Strand Investment Holdings Limited) established for that purpose. 53,884,402 ordinary shares have been purchased (1999: 53,298,029 ordinary shares) at an aggregate purchase price of US$118 million (1999: US$116 million), which has been funded by the Group. The cost of purchasing these shares has been deducted from shareholders' funds. There is no intention to trade these shares and no dividends are paid in respect of them outside the Group. Normally, the Companies Act 1985 requires the interests in own shares be included in the balance sheet as an asset. However, in this case the Directors consider that the arrangements are such that the shares owned by Strand Investment Holdings Limited have effectively been repurchased by the Group and so do not constitute an asset of the Group and that to show them as such would fail to show a true and fair view.

4 ACCOUNTING FOR PARTICULAR TYPES OF INSTRUMENT

4.1 Bonds with no rights to conversion

4.1.1 Fixed interest rate bonds

This is the most straightforward kind of borrowing to account for and the only mild complication is that the issue costs have to be deducted from the amount borrowed so as to be spread over the life of the loan.

Example 17.11: Fixed interest rate bonds

A company issues a £20 million bond for 5 years in respect of which the interest rate is 7%. The costs of the issue amount to £400,000.

FRS 4 requires the issue costs to be deducted from the proceeds of the borrowing to produce an initial net liability of £19.6 million. This is then accreted back up to the amount payable, in the following way (all figures in £000s):

Year	Total finance cost	Interest paid	Amortisation of issue costs	Balance sheet liability
0				19,600
1	1,469	1,400	69	19,669
2	1,474	1,400	74	19,743
3	1,480	1,400	80	19,823
4	1,485	1,400	85	19,908
5	1,492	1,400	92	20,000
Total	7,400	7,000	400	

The calculation of the total finance cost shown above is based on the rate inherent in all the cash flows (7.49% in this case), but in practice the amount of issue costs will usually not be material enough to require such rigour to be applied. Simplified methods of allocating the issue costs, such as straight line amortisation or even immediate write-off will often be acceptable on materiality grounds.

4.1.2 Variable interest rate bonds

These are again simple borrowing arrangements, the only difference being that the interest cost varies in accordance with some external rate, such as LIBOR. FRS 4 does not require the finance cost to be 'equalised'; the interest is simply charged at whatever rate is in force for the period. The only mild complication is again created by any other components of finance cost (such as issue costs or premiums payable on redemption). This treatment is essentially the same as that for index-linked bonds (see 4.1.5 below), in the sense that there is no attempt to predict future movements in an external variable (i.e. LIBOR, the retail price index or whatever). Instead, the issuer simply accounts for the bonds on the basis that interest rates at the time that the financial statements are prepared will remain unchanged for the remainder of the term of the instrument.

Example 17.12: Variable interest rate bonds

A company issues a £20 million bond for 5 years in respect of which the interest rate is LIBOR plus 1%. The cost of the issue is again £400,000. LIBOR is 6% at the outset but changes to 8% after 2 years.

Initially, this example is identical to the previous one and if LIBOR did not change, the accounting result would be exactly the same. The only variation comes when LIBOR changes. At that time, FRS 4 strictly requires a fresh calculation of the interest rate implicit in the arrangement – in other words, what is the rate needed to discount the future payments of interest (now £1.8m per annum) and principal to a present value of £19,743,000 (the amount carried in the balance sheet at the end of year 2). In this example, the rate changes from 7.49% to 9.51% and produces the following result (all figures in £000s):

Year	Total finance cost	Interest paid	Amortisation of issue costs	Balance sheet liability
0				19,600
1	1,469	1,400	69	19,669
2	1,474	1,400	74	19,743
3	1,878	1,800	78	19,821
4	1,886	1,800	86	19,907
5	1,893	1,800	93	20,000
Total	8,600	8,200	400	

Clearly in this example, the change makes a negligible difference to the pattern of amortising the non-interest component of finance costs, and the calculation need not therefore be performed in the rigorous way required by the standard. However, in some cases (for example, where the instrument is a deep discounted bond with a long life), the effect might be sufficiently material to justify making the calculation.

4.1.3 *Stepped bonds*

Stepped bonds are borrowing instruments whose interest rate escalates over the life of the bond in a predetermined way. This is illustrated in the following example:

Example 17.13: Stepped bonds

A company issues a £10 million bond for 10 years in respect of which the interest rate is 8% for the first three years, 10% for the next three and 13% for the final four. The annual interest payable therefore escalates from £800,000 to £1,300,000. (Issue costs are ignored in this example.)

If the company accounted for this on a cash basis it would record an artificially low finance cost in the early years and an artificially high cost towards the end of the life of the bond. FRS 4 requires that the total finance cost over the life of the bond should be calculated and charged to the profit and loss account at a constant rate on the outstanding amount rather than taking the cash payments at face value. This produces the following result (all figures in £000s):

Year	Finance cost	Interest paid	Difference	Accrued interest
1	1,006	800	206	206
2	1,027	800	227	433
3	1,050	800	250	683
4	1,075	1,000	75	758
5	1,082	1,000	82	840
6	1,091	1,000	91	931
7	1,100	1,300	(200)	731
8	1,080	1,300	(220)	511
9	1,057	1,300	(243)	268
10	1,032	1,300	(268)	0
Total	10,600	10,600		

The calculation of the interest charge shown above is again based on the rate inherent in all the cash flows, rather than simply the total interest charge (£10,600,000) divided by the period of the loan (10 years) which would give a flat annual charge of £1,060,000. Nevertheless in practice the straight line method is simpler and can often be used since it will seldom produce a material distortion.

4.1.4 *Deep discounted bonds*

A deep discounted bond is a bond which is issued at a discount to its par value and redemption value, and it is described as a deep discount because the proceeds on issue are considerably smaller than the par value. The instrument will normally pay either no interest (generally referred to as a zero coupon bond) or a very low annual rate of interest, so that the discount and any interest payable together represent a commercial rate of interest.

Under FRS 4, the discount forms part of the finance cost and is provided for through the profit and loss account over the life of the bond. The bond is therefore included as a liability at its issue price and thereafter accretes to the redemption value over its life, as shown in the example below:

Example 17.14: Deep discounted bonds

A company issues a bond for £47 million which is redeemable at its par value of £100 million at the end of 10 years. The interest rate is 3% per annum, and the annual interest payable is thus £3 million. The costs of issuing the bond are £2 million. Spreading the discount and the issue costs over the life of the bond in addition to the interest charge produces the following result (all figures in £000s):

Year	Finance cost	Interest paid	Amortisation of discount and issue costs	Balance sheet liability
0				45,000
1	5,953	3,000	2,953	47,953
2	6,344	3,000	3,344	51,297
3	6,785	3,000	3,785	55,082
4	7,287	3,000	4,287	59,369
5	7,854	3,000	4,854	64,223
6	8,496	3,000	5,496	69,719
7	9,223	3,000	6,223	75,942
8	10,046	3,000	7,046	82,988
9	10,978	3,000	7,978	90,966
10	12,034	3,000	9,034	100,000
Total	85,000	30,000	55,000	

Once again, the calculation of the total finance charge shown above is based on the rate inherent in all the cash flows (in this case 13.23%), rather than simply the total charge (£85,000,000) divided by the period of the loan (10 years) which would give a flat annual charge of £8,500,000. In this case, the more rigorous calculation is materially different from that which would be produced by amortising the total discount on a straight line basis, and the latter is therefore unlikely to produce an acceptable answer.

Since the balance sheet figure in the final column of the table falls substantially short of the liability ultimately payable (by the amount of finance costs to be recognised in the future, other than interest), it is necessary to disclose the full liability by way of note.[102]

4.1.5 Index-linked bonds

FRS 4 requires that, where the payments to be made under a debt instrument are contingent on future events, these events should be taken into account in the calculation of finance cost only when they have occurred.[103] This applies to variable interest loans (discussed at 4.1.2 above) but also to those whose interest or redemption values vary in accordance with a price index, such as the RPI.

A bond which is index-linked is analogous to one which is denominated in a foreign currency, and the accounting follows a similar pattern. The effect on the principal of the movement in the index is treated similarly to a translation difference; in other words the whole amount of the movement in the period is dealt with in the profit and loss account, while the interest payable in the period continues to be charged at whatever amount results from applying the index adjustment to it.

Example 17.15: Index-linked bonds (1)

A company issues a £10 million bond for 5 years in respect of which the interest rate is 2%, but both interest and principal payments are linked to the RPI at the end of the year. Issue costs are ignored in this example. This will be accounted for in the following way (all figures in £000s):

Year	Index	Interest paid	Indexation adjustment	Total finance cost	Balance sheet liability
0	100				10,000
1	103	206	300	506	10,300
2	104	208	100	308	10,400
3	106	212	200	412	10,600
4	109	218	300	518	10,900
5	111	222	200	422	11,100
Total		1,066	1,100	2,166	

The example above assumes that the index is constantly rising, as would be expected for an index such as RPI. Sometimes, however, bonds can be linked to more volatile indices, such as a general stock market index, which are quite likely to generate finance credits rather than debits in a particular period.

Sometimes, bonds that are linked to indices which move in a predictable way may really only be stepped loans in disguise. These should be accounted for in accordance with their substance – by forecasting the total finance cost payable over the term of the instrument and allocating it so as to achieve a constant rate on the outstanding balance. Accordingly it is necessary to distinguish between arrangements with a genuine economic purpose and those which are contrived solely to have a particular accounting effect. However, the dividing line between such arrangements is not always clear-cut, as the following example illustrates.

Example 17.16: Index-linked bonds (2)

On 1 July 2001 a company issues 100 million zero coupon five-year loan notes for £75m, redeemable at a premium linked to the market value of a particular UK government bond on the date of redemption. The government bond has a market value on 1 July 2001 of 75p per £1 nominal value, and is redeemable at par on the same day as the zero coupon loan notes. There can be no doubt that the market value of £100m nominal of the government bond at 1 July 2006 will be £100m, so that, in our view, the correct treatment would be simply to accrete the £75m carrying value of the loan notes up to

£100m using the normal 'constant effective rate' methodology of FRS 4, and ignore any fluctuations in the market value of the government bond in the intervening period.

Suppose instead, however, that the government bond concerned was redeemable at par one year later on 1 July 2007. In this case, it could be argued that the market value of £100m nominal of the bond a year before redemption could be materially (and unpredictably) different from £100m, as it would reflect the difference between the rate on the bond and prevailing interest rates at the time. This would suggest that the methodology for index-linked bonds would be more appropriate.

Where the precise cut-off point between the 'constant effective rate' method and the 'index-linked method' lies must ultimately be a matter of judgment in each particular case.

4.1.6 *Investor put bonds*

A investor put bond will generally be a fixed-rate bond that allows the investor to require the issuer to redeem the bond at one or more dates before it has run to term. The investor will usually pay a premium above par for this right. Application of FRS 4 to such bonds does not produce a totally satisfactory result as the following example shows.

Example 17.17: Investor put bonds

A company issues a ten-year bond with a par value of £100m for £103m. The bond bears interest at 8% per year and is redeemable at par. The investor may require redemption (at par) on the fifth anniversary of issue.

The 'term' of the bond is clearly five years (i.e. the shortest period until the investor can require redemption – see 2.2.5 C above), which means that issuer must recognise a finance credit of £3m (i.e. the difference between the £103m net proceeds and the £100m repayable on redemption) over the first five years of the bond's life. However, if the investor does not exercise his right to put the bond after five years (i.e. because 8% is a higher rate than that that could normally be obtained on 5-year debt issued at that date), the credit is arguably more properly attributable to the second period. This is because the issuer has been obliged to keep the bond in issue for a further five years at an above market rate, and the £3m premium on issue can be seen as being in substance the premium received for a call option giving this investor this right.

In reality, a bond such as this is a hybrid instrument (i.e. a bond plus a written option) the accounting for which, as noted at 2.2.2 C above, does not always fit very well into the overall model of FRS 4, and is more satisfactorily dealt with under IAS (see 5.3.6 below and Chapter 10 at 4.3.3).

4.2 Convertible bonds

4.2.1 *Traditional convertible bonds*

A convertible bond is a hybrid instrument which initially has the character of a loan, bearing interest, but also entitles the bondholder to exchange the bond for shares in the company at some date in the future in accordance with specified conditions. Because of the conversion right, the coupon on the bond is set at a lower level than would be appropriate for straight borrowing. The effect from the equity shareholders' point of view is that they gain the benefits of cheap borrowing for a period but ultimately are likely to suffer a dilution in their holding in the company when the bonds are converted.

FRS 4 requires these to be accounted for as debt rather than equity and the finance cost to be measured on the assumption that the debt will never be converted. If conversion does take place, the carrying value of the instrument at that time is regarded as the consideration for the issue of the shares; no gain or loss is recorded on the conversion.[104]

4.2.2 *Bonds with share warrants attached*

In this case, a deep discount bond is issued together with a detachable warrant; such instruments are sometimes known as 'synthetic convertibles'. The warrant entitles the holder to obtain ordinary shares, and the further price that has to be paid for those shares on exercise of the warrant is paid out of the redemption of the bond at the end of its life.

In this case FRS 4 does take the view that the two elements should be accounted for separately, and the treatment required is therefore based on the example of 'split accounting' described at 2.2.2 C above. It distinguishes the two cases on the basis that convertible debt is a single financial instrument whose various rights cannot be exercised independently, whereas bonds with warrants are really two separable instruments which should be accounted for individually. An example of this treatment can be found in the 1994 accounts of Pilkington, as shown below:

Extract 17.18: Pilkington plc (1994)

28. Called Up Share Capital [extract]

In April 1993 the company issued £80 million 7.5% bonds at an issue price of £95 million to finance the acquisition of the United Kingdom glass processing and merchanting business of Heywood Williams Group PLC. The bonds were issued with 78.2 million warrants, each warrant entitling the holder to procure up to 4 May 1998 the allotment of one share in Pilkington plc at a price of 120p.

The capital amount attributable to the warrants is £16.4 million and is included in other reserves.

4.2.3 *Convertible bonds with premium puts or enhanced interest*

A further elaboration on the convertible bond theme is to give the bondholder the option of putting his bond back to the company at a premium as an alternative to exercising his right to convert it into shares in the company. This raises a further question for the issuing company – whether to make provision for the premium over the life of the bond despite the fact that it may never become payable because the conversion option is exercised instead. A similar question arises when the interest rate on the bond is enhanced in later years if it remains unconverted; should the increased finance cost be accounted for from the outset, even though it may never be suffered?

FRS 4 requires that provision be made for such premiums or enhanced interest, and this is discussed in the Application Notes to the standard. This is consistent with an earlier ruling by the UITF[105] as well as the recommendation of TR 677. The standard requires that the finance cost on convertible debt should be calculated on the assumption that it will never be converted,[106] on the argument that this is the minimum return to which the holder is entitled, and is what he will be surrendering if he elects to convert. On the same argument, when conversion occurs, the consideration for the issue of the shares is the carrying amount of the debt, including the accrued premium.[107]

4.2.4 *Convertible capital bonds*

In the late 1980s, a number of groups issued convertible capital bonds, which are another form of hybrid instrument with features of both debt and equity. FRS 4 describes a typical example as being along the following lines: 'Convertible capital bonds are debt instruments on which interest is paid periodically, issued by a special purpose subsidiary incorporated outside the UK. Prior to maturity they may be exchanged for shares of the subsidiary which, at the option of the bondholder, are either immediately redeemed or immediately exchanged for ordinary shares of the parent. The bonds and payments in respect of the shares of the subsidiary are guaranteed by the parent. The parent has the right to issue convertible redeemable preference shares of its own in substitution for the bonds should it wish to do so.'[108]

A practice developed of showing such bonds at the end of the equity section of the balance sheet rather than within the liabilities section, on the argument that they were likely to form permanent capital of the company and that it was more realistic to include them with equity for such purposes as assessing the company's gearing. Because conversion into shares was mandatory except in a situation of default, it was argued that the liability to repay the debt was a remote contingency and could be disregarded. On this basis it was asserted that it was appropriate to treat the instrument as if it were a convertible preference share, the accounting for which is described at 4.4.2 below.

FRS 4 dismisses these arguments, because it does not permit conversion to be assumed under any circumstances. Accordingly, the relevant Application Note says that convertible capital bonds now have to be disclosed as debt in all cases.[109] However, the rationale in the Application Note is based on the key assumption that interest is payable on the bond.

If, however, a mandatorily convertible bond were to be issued on which no interest was payable, it would not be a liability as defined by FRS 4 and therefore outside the scope of the requirement not to anticipate conversion of convertible debt (i.e. because it is not 'debt' for FRS 4 purposes). A number of instruments have appeared in recent months that seek to by-pass FRS 4's requirements for convertible bonds in this way (see 4.5 below).

4.2.5 *Perpetual debt*

Debt is sometimes issued on such terms that it is irredeemable, but that a coupon payment is to be made indefinitely. FRS 4 dismisses any suggestion that this means that no liability need be shown on the balance sheet, because the standard's guiding principle is to look at all the payments which the company is contractually bound to make, whether they are characterised as being capital or revenue. Where there is an obligation to pay a perpetual interest payment, the carrying value of the debt will by definition always be the original issue proceeds, because that is the figure derived from discounting the future payments at the rate implicit in the loan.

Sometimes a more artificial arrangement is devised, generally with a tax motive, whereby substantially all of the interest payments are made in the early part of the life of the debt, and the payments thereafter are negligible or even nil. The substance of such an arrangement is that the 'interest' payments are in reality a mixture of interest and capital repayments, and following the principles of FRS 4, this is how they should be accounted for. A variation on the same theme is to use very long-dated rather than perpetual debt. Often, any obligation to make payments of interest and capital beyond the initial term is transferred to another party for a small consideration, or another group company buys the right to receive such amounts from the original lender, with the result in either case that the group is left with only the liability for the significant payments during the initial term.

Examples of such instruments are disclosed in the accounts of Cadbury Schweppes:

Extract 17.19: Cadbury Schweppes plc (2000)

19 Borrowings [extract]

	2000			1999
	Amounts due within one year £m	**Amounts due after one year £m**	Amounts due within one year £m	Amounts due after one year £m
Group Secured				
Bank overdrafts	**1**	**–**	2	–
Other loans	**–**	**–**	1	–
European Bank for Reconstruction and Development Loan	**5**	**30**	7	32
Unsecured				
Zero Coupon Convertible Debentures	**–**	**81**	–	–
Medium Term Notes	**171**	**245**	147	119
Obligations under perpetual loan (FFr560m)	**10**	**44**	9	53
Obligations under fixed rate notes	**5**	**–**	21	5
Commercial paper	**1,024**	**–**	173	–
Bank loans in foreign currencies	**23**	**6**	22	9
Bank overdrafts	**73**	**–**	32	–
Other loans	**3**	**–**	12	78
Obligations under finance leases (see Note 24)	**5**	**11**	6	15
	1,320	**417**	432	311

...

The obligation under the perpetual loan represents the present value of the future interest payments on the principal amount of FFr 1,600m which terminate in 2005; the interest rate is variable based on the Paris Inter-Bank Offered Rate. The obligations under the fixed rate notes represent the present value of future interest payments on £200 million of 12.55% Eurobonds up to 2001; the principal of the bonds and subsequent interest coupons have been acquired by a Group company. ...

4.3 Share options and warrants

As explained in 2.2.8, the standard requires the net proceeds of a warrant to be credited direct to shareholders' funds, and thereafter the accounting depends on whether the warrant is exercised or is allowed to lapse. If it is exercised, the proceeds on the original issue of the warrant are included in the net proceeds of the shares issued;[110] if it lapses, they are included instead in the statement of total recognised gains and losses.[111]

The question of what should be credited to share premium account is ultimately one of law.[112] It is not beyond legal doubt that warrant proceeds should be regarded subsequently as part of the consideration for the issue of shares if the warrant is exercised, which is the premise on which FRS 4's requirement is based. If this is the law, the same might be thought to apply to convertible instruments which are issued as an intermediate stage in a share issue, but this view does not always appear to be adopted in practice.

4.4 Preference shares

4.4.1 Redeemable preference shares

Redeemable preference shares can be regarded as quite similar in substance to fixed interest borrowings. There are, however, some important legal differences; for example, when they are redeemed, there is a requirement to make good the capital by a transfer to a capital redemption reserve; dividends can only be paid if there are sufficient distributable reserves; also, there are some significant differences between the treatment for both tax and accounting purposes of the dividends paid on shares compared to the interest paid on debt.

Dividends are regarded as a distribution of profits to the owners of the business rather than as an expense charged in measuring that profit. As such, prior to FRS 4 they were not generally accounted for on an accruals basis; this meant, for example, that when cumulative preference dividends were in arrears, they were not accrued in the accounts but simply noted as being in arrears. Similarly, if redeemable preference shares carried an escalating dividend rate, conventional accounting practice in the UK did not seek to 'equalise' the dividends in the way required for stepped bonds as discussed in 4.1.3 above. However, FRS 4 changed this practice, so that appropriations are now made on an accruals basis, measured in the same way as for a debt instrument, unless ultimate payment is remote.[113] This is required even if the company currently has no distributable profits. The only normal circumstances in which dividends are not accrued are where they are non-cumulative, so that the holder permanently loses his right to a return on the shares for that period. However, in its 1999 accounts Brunel Holdings decided not to accrue for dividends on preference shares within minority interests on slightly different grounds, as shown in this extract.

Extract 17.20: Brunel Holdings plc (1999)

26. Contingent liabilities [extract]

Brunel Holdings plc or the Group have the following contingent liabilities which have not been provided in the balance sheet since no actual liability is expected to arise:

(i) *Unpaid preference dividends*

As set out in note 23, Blackwood Hodge plc has two classes of cumulative preference shares in issue. There are arrears of dividends totalling £581,000 (1997: £506,000) in respect of these shares. In the opinion of the Directors payment of the arrears and future dividends is remote in view of the substantial deficit on the distributable reserves of Blackwood Hodge plc.

Where cumulative preference dividends which are in arrears are accrued under FRS 4, it has to be considered whether the credit entry should be shown as a liability or as an element of non-equity shareholders' funds. Since they have not been declared, they do not represent a liability of the company as defined in FRS 4 and there is therefore quite a persuasive argument that they should be shown in the shareholders' funds section; the only difficulty with this argument is that it applies to *all* accrued dividends which have not yet been declared, whereas conventional UK accounting practice is to show such dividends in the liabilities section. In the light of these conflicting arguments, we believe that either classification can be justified for preference dividends in arrears.

In 1997, Signet Group showed arrears of dividends within shareholders' funds rather than within liabilities, and described the appropriation in the profit and loss account as an additional finance cost, not as a dividend, as shown in this extract:

Extract 17.21: Signet Group plc (1997)

Consolidated profit and loss account
for the 52 weeks ended 1 February 1997 [extract]

	52 weeks ended 1 February 1997 £000	53 weeks ended 3 February 1996 £000
Profit for the financial period	**33,855**	17,517
Dividends	–	–
Additional finance costs of non-equity shares	**(26,398)**	(42,075)
Retained profit/(loss) attributable to equity shareholders	**7,457**	(24,558)

23 Non-equity shareholders' funds

On 20 January 1992 the directors announced that payment of dividends on all of the Company's various classes of preference shares would cease until further notice. No dividends have been paid since that date. Dividends on all classes of preference shares are cumulative and payment of arrears of preference dividends would be due to be made before payments of dividends on ordinary shares recommenced. Cumulative arrears of preference dividends as at 1 February 1997 amounted to £155,281,000 (1996: £128,517,000).

In addition to the dividend arrears above, £6,221,000 (1996: £6,587,000) of preference dividends were accumulated on a time basis at 1 February 1997, but not in arrears. The increase in unpaid preference dividends in the period is stated net of £5,012,000 exchange loss (1996: £3,867,000 loss). In accordance with FRS 4, the following analysis sets out net issue proceeds plus the cumulative amount of accrued finance costs in respect of each class of the Company's preference shares.

	1997			1996
Analysis of non-equity shareholders' funds	Net issue proceeds £000	Unpaid preference dividends £000	Total non-equity shareholders' funds £000	Total non-equity shareholders' funds £000
6.875p convertible preference shares of 20p each	33,841	13,093	46,934	44,565
Cumulative redeemable preference shares 1997 of £10 each	30,000	16,633	46,633	43,519
Variable term preference shares of US$1 each	149,537	87,832	237,369	222,956
Convertible preference shares of US$0.01 each	104,223	43,944	148,167	141,665
Total non-equity shareholders' funds	**317,601**	**161,502**	**479,103**	452,705

Equity shareholders' funds, representing the difference between total shareholders' funds and non-equity shareholders' funds, showed a deficit of £178,358,000 (1996: £181,378,000 deficit) for the Group. In the Company's balance sheet equity shareholders' funds at 1 February 1997 amounted to £117,437,000 (1996:£152,710,000).

FRS 4 requires the full finance cost of non-equity shares to be shown as appropriated from profits, even if the Company does not have sufficient distributable reserves to pay a dividend at that time. As it is not legally possible to show dividends payable if the Company has insufficient distributable reserves to support a dividend, the appropriation has been classified as an additional finance cost in respect of non-equity shares.

Upon the capital restructuring, which was approved by shareholders on 26 June 1997, becoming effective (expected to be on 21 July 1997), all of the preference shares will be converted into new ordinary shares and all arrears and accruals of preference dividends will be cancelled.

As mentioned at the end of the above extract, the group subsequently underwent a capital reduction to eliminate these arrears, as described in the following extract from its 1999 accounts.

Extract 17.22: Signet Group plc (1999)

22 Cancellation of dividend accruals and arrears

Before the capital restructuring became effective on 21 July 1997, there were in issue various classes of preference shares. Dividends on all the classes of preference shares were cumulative and payment of arrears of preference dividends would have been due to be made before payments of dividends on ordinary shares. Since no dividends had been paid since 20 January 1992, cumulative arrears and accruals of preference dividends as at 1 February 1997 amounted to £161,502,000. As part of the capital restructuring, all preference shares were redesignated as deferred shares and all arrears and accruals of preference dividends were cancelled.

FRS 4 required the full finance cost of non-equity shares to be shown as appropriated from profits, even if the Company did not have sufficient distributable reserves to pay a dividend at that time.

As it is not legally possible to show dividends payable if the Company has insufficient distributable profits to support a dividend, the appropriation was classed as an additional finance cost in respect of non-equity shares.

The cancellation of the accumulated arrears and accruals of dividends on preference shares was credited in the profit and loss account as follows:

	1999 £000	1998 £000	1997 £000
Appropriation to preference shareholders in the period	–	(3,840)	(26,398)
Appropriation from preference shareholders arising from cancellation of dividend arrears and accruals	–	165,342	–
	–	161,502	(26,398)
Costs of share capital reorganisation	–	(6,971)	–
	–	154,531	(26,398)

The appropriations to preference shareholders in 1998 and 1997 are stated net of £6,634,000 and £5,012,000 exchange gains respectively.

A *Auction Market Preferred Shares ('AMPS')*

Preference shares are sometimes structured so that they have a variable dividend level which depends on prevailing interest rates, which may be set at auction; the investors who make the lowest bid each month hold the instrument. The cost of this form of finance is thus similar to that of commercial paper, and it might be regarded as in substance a debt issue, but under FRS 4 they are nonetheless classified as non-equity shares.

GlaxoSmithKline has subsidiaries that have issued some shares of this kind, whose terms are fully described in this extract from its financial statements:

Extract 17.23: GlaxoSmithKline plc (2000)

29. Non-equity minority interest [extract]

SB Holdings Corporation (SBH Corp), a subsidiary incorporated in Delaware, USA, has in issue $500 million of Flexible Auction Market Preferred Stock (Flex AMPS), comprising 5,000 shares of $100,000 each, issued in two series, the dividend on which was fixed on issuance in 1996 over a five and seven year period respectively for each series. SBH Corp also has in issue $400 million of Auction Rate Preference Stock (ARPS), comprising 4,000 shares of $100,000 each, issued in five series, the dividend on which varies (predominately with prevailing interest rates) and is set every seven weeks at an auction at which the shares are also traded.

SmithKline Beecham Corporation (SB Corp), a subsidiary incorporated in Pennsylvania, USA, had in issue at 31st December 2000 $650 million of ARPS, comprising 1,300 shares of $500,000 each, issued in eight series. The dividend rate on each series varied (predominately with prevailing interest rates) and was set every seven weeks at an auction at which the shares were also traded.

Together, the ARPS and the Flex AMPS constitute the preference shares which represent the non-equity minority interest.

SmithKline Beecham plc in certain circumstances guarantees payment of dividends declared on the preference shares. SmithKline Beecham plc has also agreed with SB Corp and SBH Corp that in certain circumstances it will provide support to SB Corp and SBH Corp in relation to the principal. However, any guarantee or support is limited so that in no circumstances could the holder of preference shares be in a more favourable position than had they been a holder of a preference share in GlaxoSmithKline plc. The preference shares represent a long-term non-equity minority interest in the Group balance sheet in accordance with FRS 4 'Capital Instruments'.

The SB Corp ARPS were repaid in full in February and March 2001.

4.4.2 *Convertible preference shares*

Such instruments are simply disclosed as a separate class of non-equity share capital, with details of their terms. Where the preference shares have been issued by the parent, the only available treatment is to show them as a component of shareholders' funds, but frequently such shares are issued by a subsidiary company for tax reasons. In this case they will either fall under the category of minority interest on consolidation or, if guaranteed by the parent or another group company, they will be shown as liabilities in the consolidated balance sheet.

Convertible preference share issues may be issued with a premium put, so that, in effect, if the redemption option is chosen, an enhanced dividend will be paid. As with convertible debt, FRS 4 requires this to be taken into account in measuring the finance cost of the instrument. This requires an additional annual appropriation of profits to be made, so that the total amount appropriated in respect of the shares is at a constant proportion to the total amount recognised for the shares in the balance sheet.[114]

4.5 Capital instruments serviceable by issuing shares

As noted in 4.2.4 above, a recent trend has been the development of capital instruments which at the issuer's sole option can be repaid, as to both interest and principal, entirely through the issue of new shares in the issuer. The purpose of such structures is to allow an instrument that may have many characteristics of debt to be accounted for within shareholders' funds, but still be treated as debt for tax purposes.

Such an accounting treatment is in principle achievable under FRS 4, since the standard is quite clear that an instrument that does not contain an obligation to transfer economic benefits should be reported in shareholders' funds. Under the ASB's *Statement of Principles* an issue of shares, although giving rise to an asset in the hands of the recipient, does not give rise to a 'transfer of economic benefit' from the perspective of the issuer, since the interests of shareholders as a whole (including those receiving the new shares) are not reduced.

As an example of the application of this general principle, FRS 7 says that 'where contingent consideration is to be satisfied by the issue of shares, there is no obligation to transfer economic benefits and, accordingly, amounts recognised would be reported as part of shareholders' funds, for example as a separate caption representing shares to be issued'.[115] This applies even where the number of shares issued has to be varied to provide sufficient value to meet a fixed amount of consideration. Thus a capital instrument which can serviced using either by paying cash or by issuing fresh shares (at the issuer's sole discretion) is in principle included within shareholders' funds under FRS 4, even if the issuer in fact chooses to pay cash. An example of a company that has issued such an instrument and accounted for it as non-equity shareholders' funds is Northern Rock.

Extract 17.24: Northern Rock plc (2000)

Consolidated balance sheet [extract]

	Note	**2000**	1999
		£m	£m
Shareholders' funds			
Equity			
Called up share capital	30	**123.9**	130.6
Share premium account	31	**6.8**	–
Capital redemption reserve	31	**7.3**	–
Profit and loss account	31	**777.5**	752.9
		915.5	883.5
Non-equity			
Reserve capital instruments	32	**200.0**	-
Shareholders' funds	33	**1,115.5**	883.5

32. Reserve capital instruments [extract]

The reserve capital instruments were issued for a value of £200m on 21 September 2000 and are undated. They carry a coupon of 8.399% payable annually in arrears on 21 September each year. At each payment date Northern Rock will decide whether to declare or defer the coupon. If Northern Rock decides to declare the coupon, the holder will receive a cash payment equivalent to the coupon which, at Northern Rock's option, will be achieved either by the payment of cash directly, or by the issue of Ordinary Shares in Northern Rock which, when sold by a trustee in the market, will produce an amount equal to the cash payment. If Northern

> Rock elects to defer the coupon, it may not declare or pay a dividend on any share until the deferred coupons are satisfied. Deferred coupons and any interest accruing thereon can only be satisfied through the issue of shares. The coupon has been swapped into a variable rate payment. Northern Rock has a call option after 15 years, which it can only exercise with the consent of the Financial Services Authority. If the issue is not called, the coupon resets to yield 4.725% above the prevailing 5-year benchmark Gilt rate.
>
> The appropriation attributable to non-equity shareholders is stated net of tax and after the effect of the interest rate swap noted above.
>
> The maximum amount of reserve capital instruments permitted to be included in tier 1 capital is 15% of overall tier 1 capital. Any excess is allocated to upper tier 2 capital.

However, considerable care may be needed in order to ensure that such an instrument can actually be accounted for within shareholders' funds in a particular case. For example, in our view it is necessary to ensure that the issuer has not only no legal obligation, but also no commercial obligation, to pay cash. It would also be necessary to ensure that the terms of the instrument make provision for all situations in which the company might be prevented from issuing its own shares (e.g. because of a collapse in the share price or a suspension of trading in the shares), so as to ensure that a cash payment would not be, constructively if not legally, required in such cases.

The question arises as to how the interest cost of such instruments should be accounted for. One view would be that, since the instrument is included as part of shareholders' funds, the costs of servicing it should be treated as an appropriation of, rather than a charge on, profits. Another view would be that the cost should be treated as interest, since, as matter of law, it is only the costs of shares that can be treated as an appropriation of profit, and these instruments are not shares. A third view might be that where the cost is actually satisfied by an issue of shares rather than a cash payment, it could simply be accounted for as a bonus issue, as is often done in the case of dividends paid in shares (see 4.7 below). In our view, any of these approaches is acceptable, provided that it is adopted consistently. It may also be appropriate for companies to seek legal advice.

Some argue that the general principles of FRS 5 (see Chapter 18 at 2.1) require such instruments to be accounted for as debt. However, it is hard to reconcile such a view with the explicit requirement of FRS 5 that its remit does not extend to areas already dealt with by a more specific accounting standard. Moreover, if FRS 5's principle of giving substance precedence over form were applied to capital instruments generally, many instruments that FRS 4 requires to be accounted for as debt would be accounted for as equity. For example, if a company issues an interest-free mandatorily convertible bond for £1 million, FRS 4 requires it to be accounted for within shareholders' funds. If, however, it issues the same bond with an annual interest coupon of 0.0001%, FRS 4 requires it to be accounted for as a liability. In our view, FRS 5 would reject such a clearly form-based approach.

4.6 Interest rate swaps

An interest rate swap is an agreement between two counterparties that they will exchange fixed rate interest for floating rate interest on a notional amount of principal. The principal is notional in the sense that it itself is not exchanged, only the amounts of interest determined by reference to it.

The objective of entering into an interest rate swap is effectively to convert existing finance from a fixed interest basis to a floating rate basis or vice versa. The treatment recommended by TR 677 was therefore to incorporate the terms of the swap into those of the existing finance; for example, if a company has a floating rate loan but enters into an interest rate swap because it prefers not to have exposure to floating rates, then the accounts would portray the loan as if it were at fixed rates. The Technical Release went on to say that 'there should be full disclosure of the arrangement in the notes to the financial statements, so that the true commercial effect on the whole transaction, including any possible risk of exposure in the event of the failure of the swap-party, is clearly explained'.[116] The subject of interest rate swaps or other similar hedges is not addressed in FRS 4, but is now being addressed in the wider international project on financial instruments (see Chapter 10).

4.7 Scrip dividends

Scrip dividends arise when a company offers its shareholders the choice of receiving further fully paid up shares in the company as an alternative to receiving a cash dividend.

FRS 4 requires that a scrip dividend should initially be recorded at its cash amount as an appropriation in the profit and loss account. As it is unclear at that time how many shareholders will elect to receive shares, the whole amount of the dividend should be recorded as a liability in the balance sheet. This obviously applies to final dividends, since the take-up of the scrip will not be known until after the accounts have been prepared. However, where the interim dividend has taken the form of a scrip dividend during the year it will be possible to reflect exactly what has been paid in cash and what has been issued in the form of shares. We believe, however, that FRS 4 still intends that the dividend be shown as an appropriation in the profit and loss account at its full cash amount.[117]

Once shareholders have chosen to receive shares instead of cash, two possible approaches exist, described respectively as the reinvestment approach and the bonus share approach. As the name suggests, the former takes the view that a dividend has been paid, but then reinvested in shares; accordingly, the consideration for the issue of the shares is the amount of the dividend and is divided as appropriate between share capital (to the extent of their nominal value) and share premium account. The alternative view is that the shares are issued *instead* of a dividend; accordingly, no consideration has been received and the issue is a simple bonus issue, which results in the capitalisation of a suitable reserve to the extent of the nominal value of the shares issued.

FRS 4 is rather ambiguous about the choice between these approaches. On the one hand, paragraph 48 suggests that it favours the reinvestment approach, because it says that 'the value of such shares should be deemed to be the amount receivable if the alternative of cash had been chosen', but it may be that this is discussing only the initial treatment in the profit and loss account as mentioned above. Paragraph 99, on the other hand, says that if the 'scrip dividend takes the legal form of a bonus issue of shares, the appropriation should be written back as a reserve movement, and appropriate amounts transferred between reserves and share capital to reflect the capitalisation of reserves', which is the bonus share approach.

Some lawyers maintain that no choice is available between these two methods; the right method is dictated by the form of the transaction. They would say that the question of whether the shares are issued for consideration or not is one of legal fact, not of interpretation. Accordingly, where a shareholder signs a mandate form which says that he elects to receive an allotment of shares instead of the dividend (as is typically the case), he will thereafter receive a bonus issue, which should be accounted for as such. If one accepts this view, the normal accounting treatment would be as illustrated in this example:

Example 17.18: Scrip dividend

A company declares a final dividend for the year ended 31 December 1999 of 20 pence per share, but offers shareholders the alternative of accepting 1 share for every 10 held. The issued share capital of the company is 10 million £1 shares, and their current market price is £2 per share.

When it draws up its accounts for 1999 it does not know how many shareholders will opt for the scrip dividend. Under FRS 4, it records £2 million (being the cash amount) as an appropriation in the profit and loss account and provides the same amount within creditors as 'dividends payable'.

Subsequently, the shareholders accept the cash dividend in respect of 8 million shares but opt for the further shares in respect of the remaining 2 million.

Assuming that the legal form of the scrip dividend was a bonus issue, the issue of shares to those who have opted for them is viewed as a bonus issue and accounted for at nominal value. Thus the further journal entries which have to be made are as follows:

	£000	£000
Dividends payable	2,000	
Cash		1,600
Profit and loss account reserve		400

To reverse the previous entry to the extent of the scrip dividend and recognise the payment of the remainder, and

	£000	£000
Reserves	200	
Share capital		200

To record the bonus issue. The reserve to be used would depend on what was available, but could be, for example, a share premium account or a revaluation reserve as well as the profit and loss account reserve.

If, on the other hand, the scrip dividend did not take the legal form of a bonus issue, the share issue would have to be accounted for differently. This situation may arise if, under the mandate form, the shareholder elects to receive a cash dividend but irrevocably authorises the company to apply the cash on his behalf in subscribing for the appropriate number of new shares. As this is tantamount to an issue of shares for cash, FRS 4 would require the shares to be recorded by reference to the cash equivalent of the dividend foregone.

The guidance on scrip dividends in FRS 4 therefore remains rather ambiguous. It would seem likely that both the reinvestment approach and the bonus issue approach can continue to be used, subject to any legal advice which companies obtain as to the proper interpretation of the terms of the transaction and the particular requirements of the company's articles. However, it appears that the bonus issue approach has become the predominant method in practice; HSBC uses this approach.

Extract 17.25: HSBC Holdings plc (2000)

9 Dividends

	2000		1999		1998	
	US$ per share	**US$m**	US$ per share	US$m	US$ per share	US$m
First interim	**0.150**	**1,383**	0.133	1,118	0.123	996
Second interim	**0.285**	**2,627**	0.207	1,754	0.185	1,499
	0.435	**4,010**	0.340	2,872	0.308	2,495

Of the first interim dividend for 2000, US$476 million (1999: US$229 million; 1998: US$107 million) was settled by the issue of shares. Of the second interim dividend for 1999, US$468 million (1998: US$450 million; 1997: US$477 million) was settled by the issue of shares in 2000.

35 Reserves [extract]	*HSBC*	*HSBC Holdings*	*Associates*
	US$m	**US$m**	**US$m**
Share premium account:			
At 1 January 2000	**2,882**	**2,882**	**–**
Shares issued to QUEST	**372**	**372**	**–**
Shares issued under other option schemes	**89**	**89**	**–**
Shares issued in lieu of dividends	**(38)**	**(38)**	**–**
At 31 December 2000	**3,305**	**3,305**	**–**
Profit and loss account:			
At 1 January 2000	**23,954**	**4,422**	**225**
Retained profit for the year	**2,618**	**441**	**5**
Revaluation reserve realised on disposal of properties	**40**	**–**	**–**
Arising on shares issued in lieu of dividends	**944**	**944**	**–**
Capitalised on issue of shares to QUEST	**(324)**	**(324)**	**–**
Transfer of depreciation of revaluation reserve	**21**	**–**	**–**
Exchange and other movements	**(1,019)**	**–**	**(41)**
At 31 December 2000	**26,234**	**5,483**	**189**

As the above extract shows, HSBC has added back US$944m to the profit and loss account within its reserves note, being the amount of dividends (US$476m and US$468m) taken in shares rather than cash. The US$38m charged to share premium is the nominal value of the shares issued by way of the bonus issue.

An example of the reinvestment approach can be found in the 1996 accounts of Hillsdown Holdings:

Extract 17.26: Hillsdown Holdings plc (1996)

	1996	1995
	£m	£m
7 Dividends		
Per 10p ordinary share		
Interim – 2.2p (1995: 2.2p)	**15.5**	15.3
Final – 7.8p (1995: 7.3p)	**55.7**	51.1
	71.2	66.4
Canadian C$1,000 preference shares	**–**	0.7
	71.2	67.1

18 Reserves [extract]

	Share premium £m	Revaluation reserve £m	Profit and loss account £m	Total reserves £m
Group				
At 1st January 1996	63.3	51.4	453.0	567.7
Movements in year				
Profit retained	–	–	24.2	24.2
Revaluation reserve realised	–	(9.6)	9.6	–
Revaluations	–	(3.1)	–	(3.1)
Issue of ordinary shares:				
Scrip dividend election	3.8	–	–	3.8
Share option schemes	8.5	–	–	8.5
Goodwill arising from acquisitions	–	–	(115.5)	(115.5)
Exchange adjustments	–	–	(6.2)	(6.2)
At 31st December 1996	**75.6**	**38.7**	**365.1**	**479.4**

This time there is a credit rather than a debit to share premium, because the new shares are regarded as having been issued in exchange for reinvested dividends, not as a bonus issue. There is no adjustment to the dividends that have been declared, nor any add-back to retained earnings.

4.8 Capital contributions by owners

FRS 4 addresses the treatment of capital contributions by owners, which is discussed in more detail in Chapter 6 at 4.6.

4.9 Employee share schemes

FRS 4 does not address questions relating to transactions in the reporting entity's own shares for the purposes of employee share schemes. However, the Urgent Issues Task Force has issued a number of Abstracts dealing with different problems that have arisen in relation to such schemes. These are discussed in Chapter 22.

5 IAS REQUIREMENTS

5.1 Background

As noted at 1.3 above, IAS does not address capital instruments as a discrete topic in a single standard, but under the overall umbrella of accounting for financial instruments generally. The most directly applicable standards are the IAS conceptual framework, together with parts of IAS 32 – *Financial Instruments: Disclosure and Presentation* and IAS 39 – *Financial Instruments: Recognition and Measurement* and certain of the IAS 39 *Implementation Guidance Questions and Answers* ('Q&As') issued by the IAS 39 Implementation Guidance Committee.[118]

IAS 32 was amended by IAS 39 in 1998, the amendments being effective for any accounting period in which an enterprise adopts IAS 39. Since IAS 39 is mandatory for periods beginning on or after 1 January 2001,[119] the following discussion deals with IAS 32 as amended by IAS 39.

There have been three SIC Interpretations of IAS 32 affecting capital instruments:

- SIC-5 – *Classification of Financial Instruments – Contingent Settlement Provisions*;
- SIC-16 – *Share Capital – Reacquired Own Equity Instruments (Treasury Shares)*; and
- SIC-17 – *Equity – Costs of an Equity Transaction.*

IAS 1 – *Presentation of Financial Statements* – and IAS 10 – *Events After the Balance Sheet Date* – are also relevant.

5.2 Definitions

IAS 32 and IAS 39 define 'financial instrument' and related terms as follows.

A 'financial instrument' is any contract that gives rise to both a financial asset of one enterprise and a financial liability or equity instrument of another enterprise.[120]

A 'financial asset' is any asset that is:

- cash;
- a contractual right to receive cash or another financial asset from another enterprise;
- a contractual right to exchange financial instruments with another enterprise under conditions that are potentially favourable; or
- an equity instrument of another enterprise.[121]

A 'financial liability' is any liability that is a contractual obligation:

- to deliver cash or another financial asset to another enterprise; or
- to exchange financial instruments with another enterprise under conditions that are potentially unfavourable.[122]

IAS 39 amended IAS 32 as originally published so as to expand the definition of 'financial liability' to include a contractual obligation that the reporting enterprise can settle either by payment of financial assets or payment in the form of its own equity securities, if the number of equity securities required to settle the obligation varies with changes in their fair value so that the total fair value of the equity securities paid always equals the amount of the contractual obligation.[123]

An 'equity instrument' is any contract that evidences a residual interest in the assets of an enterprise after deducting all of its liabilities.[124]

The definition of 'financial liability' encompasses certain items that are nevertheless not accounted for as such under IAS 32 or IAS 39 either because they are dealt with by a more specific standard or have not yet been fully addressed. These include obligations in respect of:

- leases (accounted for under IAS 17 – see Chapter 19);
- pensions and other post-employment benefits (accounted for under IAS 19 – see Chapter 23);
- employee stock option and stock purchase plans (subject to some disclosure requirements under IAS 19 – see Chapter 22); and
- insurance contracts (not yet covered by IAS and generally beyond the scope of this book).

5.3 Distinction between debt and equity

The broad effect of the definitions set out in 5.2 above is that a capital instrument that requires the issuer to make payments in cash or other financial assets, or in shares of a fixed value (rather than a fixed number of shares), is a financial liability. Other capital instruments will be classified as equity. Any cost incurred by an enterprise to purchase a right to re-acquire its own equity instruments from another party is a deduction from its equity, not a financial asset.[125] The application of these definitions to specific instruments is discussed in more detail at 5.3.1 to 5.3.8 below.

The definitions of 'financial liability' and 'equity instrument' in 5.2 above are to be applied without regard to the legal form or manner of settlement of the instrument concerned. Any financial instrument that calls for the issuer to deliver cash or another financial asset, or to exchange another financial instrument on potentially unfavourable terms, is a liability. IAS 32 further clarifies that a restriction on the ability of the issuer to satisfy an obligation, such as lack of access to foreign currency or the need to obtain approval for payment from a regulatory authority, does not negate the issuer's obligation or the holder's right under the instrument.[126] Accordingly, an enterprise cannot classify an instrument subject to such restrictions as equity.

IAS 32 acknowledges that application of these principles may well mean that items that are legally equity are accounted for as debt.[127] While there is obvious conceptual merit in such an approach, it currently runs into conflict with the law in the UK (and other EU countries), where the balance sheet formats in the Companies Act require instruments that are legally shares to be included within capital and reserves (i.e. equity) of the issuer, whatever the rights of the holders. However, this is only a temporary difficulty, given the amendments and planned amendments of the EC accounting directives to remove conflicts with IAS (see Chapter 1 at 3.4 and following).

Moreover, it is not clear in some parts of IAS 32 that the legal status of a capital instrument is quite as irrelevant as is implied in others. For example, paragraph 21 of the standard, in explaining why an equity instrument does not constitute a financial liability states (emphasis added):

> 'Although the holder of an equity instrument may be entitled to receive a pro rata share of any dividends or other distributions out of equity, the issuer does not have a *contractual obligation* to make such distributions.'

This implies that the absence of a contractual obligation to transfer financial assets is critical to the classification of a capital instrument as equity, which brings a distinction based entirely on legal form to the fore.

The classification of an instrument as debt or equity is made when the instrument is first recognised and is not subsequently changed until the instrument is finally removed from the balance sheet.[128] It is not entirely clear how this is to be interpreted. If read literally, for example, it would require the liability 'element' (see 5.3.5 below) of convertible debt to be classified as debt on original recognition and not subsequently reclassified as equity on conversion, which cannot have been the IASC's intention. It may be that IAS 32 sees changes such as this in the fundamental nature of an instrument during its term as the derecognition of one capital instrument and the recognition of another, rather than the reclassification of a single instrument.

It is also important to note that an item is classified as debt or equity not just for the purposes of the balance sheet, but also those of the income statement. That means, for example, that a dividend paid on a preference share classified as a liability by IAS 32 will be shown in the income statement as a finance cost, not as a deduction from equity (see 5.4.1 below).

5.3.1 *Capital instruments with an issuer option to settle by transfer of equity*

Some instruments allow the issuer to settle a contractual obligation either by payment of financial assets or by payment in the form of own equity securities. As noted at 5.2 above, if the number of equity securities required to settle the obligation varies with changes in their fair value so that the total fair value of the equity securities paid always equals the amount of the contractual obligation, IAS 32 and IAS 39 require the instrument to be accounted for as a financial liability of the enterprise.

The argument for treating as a liability a capital instrument that can be settled using shares of a fixed value (rather than a fixed number of shares) is that, in such a case, the holder of the instrument is not exposed to fluctuations in the value of the issuer's equity.[129] However, there is no real explanation as to why the issuer of a capital instrument should be required to account for it from the perspective of a holder of the instrument. This approach is, however, reinforced by paragraph 12 of IAS 39 which states (albeit in the context of derivatives) that a financial instrument, the fair value of which is unrelated to changes in the price of an enterprise's equity securities, but which the enterprise can settle using its own shares, is not an equity instrument. However, this reasoning seems to rely on an implicit definition of 'liability' somewhat different from that actually contained in IAS 32 and IAS 39 (and the IAS framework).

Where an instrument requires the issuer to issue shares not of a given value, it is an equity instrument,[130] absent, of course, any other features that would require it to be classified as a liability.

Unfortunately, it appears that when IAS 32 was amended by IAS 39 so as to include within the definition of 'financial liability' an obligation to make payment in shares of a given value, a number of other paragraphs of IAS 32 should have been subject to consequential amendment, but were not. This means that IAS 32 puts out some rather mixed messages regarding the classification of instruments as debt or equity.

For example, paragraph 16 of IAS 32 states, without qualification, that:

> 'An obligation of an enterprise to issue or deliver its own equity instruments, such as a share option or warrant, is itself an equity instrument, not a financial liability, since the enterprise is not obliged to deliver cash or another financial asset.'

The wording of this paragraph is inconsistent with the definition of 'financial liability' set out in 5.2 above, since it makes no distinction for an obligation to deliver shares of a given value. We are inclined to regard these and similar passages in IAS 32 as 'rogue' paragraphs that should have been amended as a consequence of other amendments to IAS 32 made by IAS 39 in December 1998. In our view, the clear intention of IAS 32 is that any instrument, the obligations under which are settled using shares of a given value, is a liability, not an equity instrument.

5.3.2 *Perpetual debt*

'Perpetual debt' instruments are those that provide the holder with the contractual right to receive payments on account of interest at fixed dates extending into the indefinite future, either with no right to receive a return of principal or a right to a return of principal under terms that make it very unlikely or very far in the future. However, this does not mean that 'perpetual debt' is to be classified as equity, since the issue proceeds will typically represent the net present value of the liability for interest payments.

For example, an enterprise may issue a financial instrument requiring it to make annual payments in perpetuity equal to a stated interest rate of 8% applied to a stated par or principal amount of €1 million. Assuming 8% to be the market rate of interest for the instrument when issued, the issuer assumes a contractual obligation to make a stream of future interest payments having a fair value (present value) of €1 million.[131]

5.3.3 *Preferred shares*

A *Redeemable shares*

When a preferred share provides for mandatory redemption by the issuer for a fixed or determinable amount at a fixed or determinable future date, or gives the holder the right to require the issuer to redeem the share at or after a particular date for a fixed or determinable amount, the instrument meets the definition of a financial liability and is classified as such.[132] It does not cease to be a liability if the issuer is unable, whether through lack of funds or legal restrictions, to redeem the shares when contractually required to do so.[133]

Sometimes preferred shares may give rise to no explicit legal obligation for the issuer to redeem them, but nevertheless establish such an obligation indirectly through their terms and conditions. For example, a preferred share may not provide for mandatory redemption or redemption at the option of the holder, but require the issuer to pay an accelerating dividend such that, within the foreseeable future, the dividend yield is scheduled to be so high that the issuer will be economically compelled to redeem the instrument in order to avoid a penal finance cost. Likewise a preferred share may be redeemable on the occurrence of a future event that is in reality very likely to occur (see also 5.3.4 below). In these circumstances, IAS 32 takes the view that classification as a financial liability is appropriate on the grounds that the issuer has little, if any, real discretion to avoid redeeming the instrument.[134]

However, where preferred shares are redeemable solely at the option of the issuer (and have no terms effectively requiring redemption), they are equity instruments (provided that they have no other features requiring their classification as liabilities), but would become liabilities when the issuer notifies shareholders that it intends to redeem the shares.[135]

B *Non-redeemable shares*

When preferred shares are non-redeemable, IAS 32 states that the appropriate classification is determined by the other rights that may attach to them. When distributions to holders of the preferred shares (whether cumulative or non-cumulative) are at the discretion of the issuer, the shares are equity instruments.[136] Conversely, where distribution is mandatory (as will typically be the case, subject to the availability of distributable profits), the shares will be treated as liabilities.

C *Comparison of the treatment of redeemable and non-redeemable shares*

It appears from the analysis in A and B above that:

- if a preferred share is issued that is redeemable at the issuer's option, that alone is sufficient to make it an equity instrument, i.e. irrespective of the existence and nature of any dividend rights (IAS 32 paragraph A20), but
- if an non-redeemable preferred share is issued, it is an equity instrument only if dividends are paid at the issuer's sole discretion (IAS 32 paragraph A21).

This appears to indicate that dividend rights should be taken into account in determining whether a *non-redeemable* preference share is debt or equity, but generally ignored in classifying a *redeemable* preference share as debt or equity, where the share is redeemable (legally and commercially) at the issuer's option only.

Matters are slightly complicated by paragraph 22 of the standard (referred to in A above). This gives, as an example of a capital instrument to be treated a financial liability, a preference share that is not mandatorily redeemable or redeemable at the holder's option, but which pays escalating dividends if not redeemed. This implies that, if the dividend had been at a perpetual fixed rate, the share would not have been a liability. However, this view implicitly draws a distinction between:

- a preference share 'not mandatorily redeemable or redeemable at the holder's option'; and
- a 'non-redeemable' share.

It is debatable how real a distinction this is given that, in the UK at least, a company can purchase any of its shares, even those that are not redeemable. The distinction may be even less real in other jurisdictions with less stringent capital maintenance rules.

5.3.4 *Instruments with settlement contingent on uncertain future events*

IAS 32 provides that, if a financial instrument labelled as a share gives the holder an option to require redemption upon the occurrence of a future event that is highly likely to occur, classification as a financial liability on initial recognition reflects the substance of the instrument.[137] SIC-5 goes further than this by requiring any instrument to be classified as a liability if the issuer may be required to settle it in cash or another financial asset on the occurrence of an uncertain future event beyond the control of both the issuer and the holder, unless the occurrence of that event is remote at the time that the instrument is issued.[138]

SIC-5 gives as examples of such uncertain future events:

- the enterprise achieving (or failing to achieve) a particular level of revenues, net income or loss, or total assets or liabilities; and
- market conditions such as a stock market index, consumer price index or interest rates.[139]

Examples of circumstances where the likelihood of cash settlement of an instrument would normally be considered remote are where the issue of shares is contingent merely on formal approval by the authorities, or where cash settlement is triggered by an index reaching an 'extreme' level relative to its level at the time of initial recognition of the instrument.[140]

5.3.5 *Compound financial instruments*

Where an instrument contains both a liability element and an equity element, the two parts should be separately recognised and accounted for. This is commonly known as 'split accounting'. IAS 32 argues that it is more a matter of form than substance that both liabilities and equity interests are created by a single financial instrument rather than two or more separate instruments. Accordingly, an issuer's financial position is more faithfully represented by separate presentation of the liability and equity components contained in a single instrument.[141] The most common example of such an instrument is a convertible bond, which effectively comprises, from the issuer's perspective:

- a liability, being the contractual obligation to deliver cash or other financial instruments until conversion occurs; and
- an equity instrument, being a written option granting the holder the right, for a given period of time, to require the issuer to issue shares.

IAS 32 asserts that the economic effect of issuing such an instrument is substantially the same as issuing simultaneously a debt instrument with an early settlement provision and warrants to purchase common shares, or issuing a debt instrument with detachable share purchase warrants.[142] However, whether the effect is 'substantially the same' is a matter of some debate, since exercise of the 'early settlement option' would render the 'warrants' void, which would be unlikely to be the case if the two were independently traded instruments.

The original classification of the liability and equity of the liability and equity components of a convertible instrument is not revised to reflect changes in circumstances, such as the likelihood of conversion, after the instrument has been issued. IAS 32 argues that adjustment would not be appropriate, even when exercise of the option may appear to have become economically advantageous to some holders. Holders may not always act in the manner that might be expected because, for example, the tax consequences resulting from conversion may differ among holders. Furthermore, the likelihood of conversion will change from time to time. The issuer's obligation to make future payments remains outstanding until it is extinguished through conversion, the maturity of the instrument or some other transaction.[143]

IAS 32 notes that a financial instrument may contain components that are neither financial liabilities nor equity instruments of the issuer. For example, an instrument may give the holder the right to receive a non-financial asset such as a commodity and an option to exchange that right for shares of the issuer. In such a case, the issuer should recognise and present the equity instrument (the exchange option) separately from the liability components of the compound instrument, whether those liabilities are financial or non-financial.[144] In fact, however, as discussed further in Chapter 10 at 4.2.5, many commodity contracts will fall to be accounted for as financial instruments under IAS 39.

The mechanics of separating a compound instrument into its debt and equity components is discussed further at 5.6 below. This treatment is similar to the more general requirement of IAS 39 that, where an instrument contains an 'embedded derivative' not closely related to the underlying, or 'host' contract, the host contract and embedded derivative should be accounted for separately. The accounting treatment of financial instruments containing 'embedded derivatives' is discussed in more detail in Chapter 10 at 4.3.3.

5.3.6 *Instruments issued by subsidiaries*

Financial instruments issued by subsidiaries (other than intra-group instruments eliminated on consolidation) should be classified as liabilities or minority interests in the group accounts according to their classification in the subsidiary's financial statements. Those which are classified as liabilities by the subsidiary will be treated as liabilities in the consolidated accounts. Those which are classified as equity by the subsidiary will be treated in the consolidated accounts as minority interests, which are neither financial liabilities nor equity of the group.[145]

Interestingly, IAS 32 does not appear to require a reporting enterprise that is a group to consider the obligations of the group as a whole in respect of a capital instrument issued by a subsidiary, as would be the case, for example, under UK GAAP (see 2.2.2 B above). Thus if a subsidiary of the group issues an instrument that it classifies as an equity instrument, that instrument is apparently classified as minority interests on consolidation, even if another member of the group gives the holder of the instrument rights (such as a guarantee) which, if given by the issuing company itself, would have required the issuing company to classify the instrument as a liability. It might be that other member of the group would have to record the guarantee as a liability at fair value, but this could well be negligible or zero if the issuing company were solvent and, moreover, could presumably be structured as an intra-group guarantee, rather than a guarantee to the instrument holders, thereby ensuring its elimination on consolidation.

It may have been considerations such as this that have enabled Zurich Financial Services to treat certain preference shares issued by a subsidiary but with a parental support agreement as minority interests as described in the extract below.

Extract 17.27: Zurich Financial Services Group (2000)

18. Minority interests [extract]

Third-party equity interests and preference shares and similar instruments issued by consolidated subsidiaries of the Group are included in minority interests.

On 16 December 1999, Zurich Financial Services (Jersey) Limited, a wholly-owned subsidiary of Zurich Financial Services, issued 12,000,000 perpetual non-voting, non-cumulative Series A Preference Shares on the Euromarket with a par value of EUR 25 (EUR 300,000,000). The securities, which are rated Aa2 and A+ by Moody's and Standard and Poor's, respectively, benefit from a subordinated support agreement of Zurich Financial Services and carry a fixed coupon of 7.125%, payable quarterly. the securities are, subject to certain conditions, redeemable at the option of the issuer in whole, but not in part, from time to time on or after five years from the issue date. …

It is implicit in this treatment that there are no circumstances in which the company could be commercially compelled to redeem these shares. Otherwise, they would have had to be classified as liabilities (see 5.3.3 above).

5.3.7 *Written options over own shares*

The IAS 39 implementation guidance clarifies that, where a company writes a put option over its own equity, the proceeds should be credited to equity where the company is required, if the option is exercised, to deliver a fixed number of shares. Where, however, the option is required to be settled in cash, or the holder has the right to cash settlement, the proceeds should be treated as a liability.[146]

5.3.8 *Capital contributions by owners*

Consistent with the IASC Framework, IAS 1 requires contributions by owners to be accounted for as equity.[147]

5.4 Accounting for debt instruments

5.4.1 *General*

A debt instrument should initially be recognised at cost, defined by IAS 39 as the fair value of the consideration received for it, net of any transaction costs associated with its issue, but excluding those that would arise on any transfer or disposal of the instrument.[148] If the fair value is not reliably determinable, it should be estimated as the sum of all future cash payments or receipts, discounted, if the effect of doing so would be material, using the prevailing market rate(s) of interest for a similar instrument (similar as to currency, term, type of interest rate, and other factors) of an issuer with a similar credit rating.[149]

Subsequent to initial recognition, a debt instrument should be shown at 'amortised cost'.[150] The 'amortised cost' of a liability is the amount at which the financial asset or liability was measured at initial recognition minus principal repayments, plus or minus the cumulative amortisation of any difference between that initial amount and the maturity amount.[151]

All interest, dividends gains and losses relating to instruments classified as liabilities are reported in the income statement as expense or income.[152] Where amounts that are legally dividends are charged as an expense in this way, they may be shown either with interest on other liabilities or as a separate item.[153]

5.4.2 *Allocation of finance costs*

IAS 39 specifies that where a financial *asset* is measured at 'amortised cost', it should be accounted for using the 'effective interest rate' method,[154] defined somewhat circularly as a method of calculating amortisation using the effective interest rate of a financial asset or financial liability.[155]

The 'effective interest rate' is the rate that exactly discounts the expected stream of future cash payments through maturity or the next market-based repricing date to the current net carrying amount of the financial asset or financial liability. That computation should include all fees and points paid or received between parties to the contract. The effective interest rate is sometimes termed the level yield to maturity or to the next repricing date, and is the internal rate of return of the financial asset or financial liability for that period.[156]

Whilst IAS 39 does not explicitly state that the same approach should be adopted for *liabilities* measured at 'amortised cost', this is clearly intended, as is confirmed by the IAS implementation guidance.[157] Accordingly any discount or premium on issue, origination or redemption of liabilities should be amortised over the life of the liability; this would include a discount arising from the offset of transaction costs on issue (see 5.4.1 above).

Similarly, the cash flows on a stepped interest bond should be allocated to accounting periods so as to produce a constant rate of return.[158]

It is implicit in the definition of 'effective interest rate' (see above) that an instrument is always assumed to run to full term, as compared to (say) UK GAAP, which requires finance costs to be amortised over the 'term' of an instrument, defined as the period ending on the earliest date at which the holder of the instrument could require redemption (see 2.2.5 C above).

5.4.3 *Extinguishment of debt*

A General

IAS 39 requires an enterprise to derecognise (i.e. remove from its balance sheet) a financial liability (or a part of a financial liability) when, and only when, it is 'extinguished', that is, when the obligation specified in the contract is discharged, cancelled, or expires.[159] This will be achieved by the debtor either paying the creditor or being legally released from primary responsibility for the liability, either by action of law or by the creditor.[160] Extinguishment by legal release is discussed further at B below.

Where an enterprise repurchases a bond issued by itself with the intention of reissuing it, the enterprise should derecognise the bond. The intention to reissue does not in itself create a liability.[161]

'In substance defeasance' arrangements, e.g. payments to a third party such as a trust, are ineffective under IAS in the absence of legal release by the creditor.[162] Such arrangements, together with other aspects of extinguishment of debt that are more in the nature of off-balance sheet financing arrangements, are discussed in more detail in Chapter 18 at 4.

B Extinguishment by legal release by creditor

As noted above, a liability can be derecognised by a debtor if the creditor legally releases the debtor from the liability. It is clear both from IAS 39 itself and the implementation guidance that legal release is regarded as crucial, with the effect that very similar situations may lead to different results purely because of the legal form.

For example, IAS 39 provides that, where a debtor is legally released from a liability, derecognition is not precluded by the fact that the debtor has given a guarantee in respect of the liability. In such a case, however, it would be necessary to recognise the fair value of the guarantee (see E below).[163] However, the implementation guidance discusses the following situation.

Example 17.19: Transfer of obligations under debt without legal release

Enterprise A issues bonds that have a carrying amount and fair value of $1,000,000. Enterprise A pays $1,000,000 to Enterprise B for Enterprise B to assume responsibility for paying interest and principal on the bonds to the bondholders. The bondholders are informed that Enterprise B has assumed responsibility for the debt. However, Enterprise A is not legally released from the obligation to pay interest and principal by the bondholders. Accordingly, if Enterprise B does not make payments when due, the bondholders may seek payment from Enterprise A. Should Enterprise A derecognise the financial liability for the bonds and recognise a guarantee to pay if Enterprise B does not pay?

The guidance concludes that Enterprise A should not derecognise the bonds, on the basis that the bondholders have not legally released it from its obligations under the bonds.[164] However there is little, if any, substantial economic difference between:

(a) the bondholders releasing Enterprise A from its obligations, but having the benefit of a guarantee from Enterprise A in the event of default by Enterprise B; and

(b) the bondholders not releasing Enterprise A from its obligations, but having recourse to Enterprise A in the event of default by Enterprise B.

It is therefore anomalous, in our view, that under IAS 39 scenario (a) should apparently lead to derecognition of the bonds (together with a profit or loss of the difference between the carrying value of the bonds and the fair value of any guarantee given – see E below), but scenario (b) should result in no derecognition or profit.

C Extinguishment in exchange for transfer of assets not meeting the criteria for derecognition

IAS 39 notes that in some cases legal release may be achieved by transferring assets to the creditor which do not meet the criteria for derecognition (see Chapter 18 at 4.2). In such a case, the debtor will derecognise the liability from which it has been released, but recognise a new liability relating to the transferred assets that may be equal to the derecognised liability.[165] It is not entirely clear what was intended by this rather gnomic statement, but it may be some such scenario as the following.

Example 17.20: Extinguishment of debt in exchange for transfer of assets not meeting derecognition criteria.

An enterprise has a bank loan of €1 million. The bank agrees to accept in full payment of the loan the transfer to it by the company of a portfolio of shares with a market value of €1 million. The enterprise and the company then enter into a put and call option over the shares, the effect of which will be that the enterprise will repurchase the shares in three years' time at a price that gives the bank a lender's return on €1 million. As discussed further in Chapter 18 at 4.2, this would have the effect that the enterprise is unable to derecognise the shares.

Under the general rule in IAS 39, the enterprise would be able to derecognise the original bank loan, as it has been legally released from it. However, the provisions under discussion here have the overall result that the loan effectively continues to be recognised. Strictly, however, the analysis is that the original loan has been derecognised and a new one recognised. In effect the accounting is representing that the enterprise has repaid the original loan and replaced it with a new one secured on a share portfolio.

D *Exchanges of debt and modifications of terms of existing debt*

An exchange between an existing borrower and lender of debt instruments with 'substantially different' terms is an extinguishment of the old debt that should be accounted for as derecognition of that debt and recognition of a new debt instrument. Similarly, a substantial modification of the terms of an existing debt instrument (whether or not due to the financial difficulty of the debtor) should be accounted for as an extinguishment of the old debt.[166] IAS 39 defines the terms of exchanged debt as 'substantially different' if the discounted present value of the cash flows under the new terms, including any fees paid net of any fees received, is at least 10% different from the discounted present value of the remaining cash flows of the original debt instrument. Whilst a 'substantial modification' is not specifically defined, it is clear that the same criteria are intended to be applied.[167]

Interestingly, IAS 39 requires the net present values, not the fair values, of the old and new (or modified) debt to be compared for this purpose. An enterprise may calculate those net present values using the effective interest rate of either the old or the new debt, so long as it adopts a consistent approach to all modifications and exchanges of debt.[168] We are not entirely clear that the option of using the effective interest rate of the new debt has been fully thought through, since it seems to lead to a 'vicious circle.' This interest rate would be a function of the carrying value of the new debt (see 5.4.2 above), which will not be known until it has been determined whether or not the transaction is to be accounted for as a derecognition or not, which in turn depends on the interest rate. Even assuming that this difficulty can be overcome, we are also not convinced that the requirement to adopt a consistent approach is readily enforceable given that most companies will probably undertake a transaction such as this once or twice a decade at most.

If an exchange of debt instruments or modification of terms is accounted for as an extinguishment of the old debt, any costs or fees incurred are recognised as part of the gain or loss on the extinguishment (see E below). However, if the exchange or modification is not accounted for as an extinguishment, any costs or fees incurred are an adjustment to the carrying amount of the liability and are amortised over the remaining term of the modified loan,[169] together with the difference between the net present values of the debt under the old and new terms.[170]

E *Gains and losses on extinguishment of debt*

When a financial liability (or part of a liability) is extinguished or transferred to another party, a gain or loss is recognised in the net profit or loss for the period, calculated as the difference between (a) its carrying amount, including related unamortised costs, and (b) the amount paid for it.[171]

In some cases, a creditor may release a debtor from its present obligation to make payments, but the debtor assumes an obligation to pay if the party assuming primary responsibility defaults. In such a case, the debtor recognises a new liability based on the fair value for the obligation for the guarantee, together with a gain or loss based on the difference between (a) any proceeds and (b) the carrying amount of the original liability (including any related unamortised costs) less the fair value of the new liability.[172]

5.5 Accounting for equity instruments

5.5.1 *General*

All amounts relating to a financial instrument classified as equity by the issuer should, in the issuer's accounts, be accounted for directly in equity. These amounts will include issue proceeds, costs of redemption or refinancing, and distributions.[173] IAS 10 – *Events After the Balance Sheet Date* – prohibits dividends being provided for at the balance sheet date if they were approved or declared only after that date.[174]

5.5.2 *Costs of an equity transaction*

SIC-17 – *Equity – Costs of an Equity Transaction* – requires certain costs of an 'equity transaction' to be accounted for directly in equity, net of any tax relief. The costs of aborted transactions should be charged to the profit and loss account.[175] The costs, and any related tax relief, that are recognised directly in equity should be separately disclosed.[176]

For the purposes of SIC-17, an 'equity transaction' is the issue or acquisition by an enterprise of its own financial instruments classified by the enterprise as equity that results in a net increase or decrease to equity. This has the effect that the costs of equity-related transactions that do not result in an increase or decrease to equity are not costs of equity transactions, and must therefore by charged to the profit and loss account. These will include the costs of listing shares on a stock exchange, a secondary offering of shares, a share split or a stock dividend.[177]

SIC-17 restricts the costs of an equity transaction to those incremental external costs directly attributable to the transaction which would otherwise have been avoided.[178] Transactions relating to a compound instrument containing a liability element and an equity element should be allocated *pro rata* to the allocation of the net proceeds[179] (see 5.6 below). Transaction costs that relate jointly to more than one transaction (e.g. the costs of a concurrent offering of some shares and a stock exchange listing of other shares) should be allocated to those transactions using a basis of allocation which is rational and consistent with that used for similar transactions.[180]

SIC–17 does not apply to costs relating to:

- the issue of an equity instrument in connection with the acquisition of a business (which are dealt with in IAS 22 – see Chapter 6 at 5.4.2 B); or
- equity transactions associated with share-based compensation plans (which are as yet subject to no measurement or recognition requirements under IAS).

5.5.3 *Treasury shares*

IAS 32 states that any change in equity resulting from the purchase and cancellation of shares does not represent a gain or loss, as it represents a transfer between those holders of equity instruments who have given up their equity interest and those who continue to hold an equity interest, rather than a gain or loss by the enterprise.[181] The treatment of reacquired shares which are not cancelled, but held as treasury shares, is dealt with in SIC-16 – *Share Capital – Reacquired Own Equity Instruments (Treasury Shares).*

For the purposes of SIC-16, treasury shares are those instruments of the issuing enterprise which are:

- classified as equity under IAS 32;
- acquired and held by the issuing enterprise itself or by its consolidated subsidiaries; and
- legally available for re-issue or re-sale, even if the enterprise intends to cancel them,

other than those related to employee stock option and stock purchase plans.[182]

Treasury shares should be presented in the issuer's balance sheet as a deduction from equity, which should be disclosed separately on the face of the balance sheet or in the notes.[183] No gain or loss should be recognised in the income statement on the sale, issuance, or cancellation of treasury shares. In other words, the acquisition and resale of treasury shares should be presented in the financial statements as changes in equity.[184]

Where the reporting enterprise, or any of its subsidiaries, re-acquires its own shares from parties able to control or exercise significant influence over the enterprise, it should provide the disclosures required by IAS 24 – *Related Party Disclosures* (see Chapter 30 at 4.1.2).

5.6 Accounting for compound financial instruments

As noted in 5.3.6 above, where an instrument contains both a liability element and an equity element, the two elements should be separately recognised and accounted for, with the liability element being dealt with as summarised at 5.4 above, and the equity element as summarised at 5.5 above.

Whilst IAS 32 does not prescribe how a the carrying amount of a compound instrument is to be separated into its parts, it suggests two methodologies:

(a) assigning to the less easily measurable component (often an equity instrument), the residual amount after deducting from the instrument as a whole the amount separately determined for the more easily measurable component; and

(b) measuring the liability and equity components separately and, to the extent necessary, adjusting these amounts on a pro rata basis so that the sum of the components equals the amount of the instrument as a whole.[185]

This contrasts with the requirement for allocating initial carrying amounts to the component parts of a financial instrument with an embedded derivative, where IAS 39 requires the embedded derivative to be recorded at fair value with the host contract at the residual amount (see Chapter 10 at 4.3.3).

The Appendix to IAS 32 illustrates the two methods as follows.[186]

Example 17.21: Separating compound instruments

An enterprise issues 2,000 convertible bonds at the start of Year 1. The bonds have a three year term, and are issued at par with a face value of 1,000 per bond, giving total proceeds of 2,000,000. Interest is payable annually in arrears at a nominal annual interest rate of 6%. Each bond is convertible at any time up to maturity into 250 common shares.

When the bonds are issued, the prevailing market interest rate for similar debt without conversion options is 9%. At the issue date, the market price of one common share is 3. The dividends expected over the three year term of the bonds amount to 0.14 per share at the end of each year. The risk-free annual interest rate for a three year term is 5%.

Approach 1: Residual valuation of equity component

Under this approach, the liability component is valued first, and the difference between the proceeds of the bond issue and the fair value of the liability is assigned to the equity component. The present value of the liability component is calculated using a discount rate of 9%, the market interest rate for similar bonds having no conversion rights, as shown.

Present value of the principal - 2,000,000 payable at the end of three years[1]	1,544,367
Present value of the interest - 120,000 payable annually in arrears for three years[2]	303,755
Total liability component	1,848,122
Equity component (by deduction)	151,878
Proceeds of the bond issue	2,000,000

1 $2{,}000{,}000/1.09^3$

2 $120{,}000 \times (1/1.09 + 1/1.09^2 + 1/1.09^3)$

Approach 2: Option pricing model valuation of equity component

Option pricing models may be used to determine the fair value of conversion options directly rather than by deduction as illustrated above. Option pricing models are often used by financial institutions for pricing day-to-day transactions. There are a number of models available, of which the Black-Scholes model is one of the most well-known, and each has a number of variants. The following example illustrates the application of a version of the Black-Scholes model that utilises tables available in finance textbooks and other sources. The steps in applying this version of the model are set out below.

This model first requires the calculation of two amounts that are used in the option valuation tables:

(i) Standard deviation of proportionate changes in the fair value of the asset underlying the option multiplied by the square root of the time to expiry of the option.

This amount relates to the potential for favourable (and unfavourable) changes in the price of the asset underlying the option, in this case the common shares of the enterprise issuing the convertible bonds. The volatility of the returns on the underlying asset are estimated by the standard deviation of the returns. The higher the standard deviation, the greater the fair value of the option. In this example, the standard deviation of the annual returns on the shares is assumed to be 30%. The time to expiry of the conversion rights is three years. The standard deviation of proportionate changes in fair value of the shares multiplied by the square root of the time to expiry of the option is thus determined as:

$0.3 \times \sqrt{3} = 0.5196$

(ii) Ratio of the fair value of the asset underlying the option to the present value of the option exercise price.

This amount relates the present value of the asset underlying the option to the cost that the option holder must pay to obtain that asset, and is associated with the intrinsic value of the option. The higher this amount, the greater the fair value of a call option. In this example, the market value of each share on issuance of the bonds is 3. The present value of the expected dividends over the term of the option is deducted from the market price, since the payment of dividends reduces the fair value of the shares and thus the fair value of the option. The present value of a dividend of 0.14 per share at the end of each year, discounted at the risk-free rate of 5%, is 0.3813. The present value of the asset underlying the option is therefore:

3 - 0.3813 = 2.6187 per share

The present value of the exercise price is 4 per share discounted at the risk-free rate of 5% over three years, assuming that the bonds are converted at maturity, or 3.4554. The ratio is thus determined as:

2.6187 ÷ 3.4554 = 0.7579

The bond conversion option is a form of call option. The call option valuation table indicates that, for the two amounts calculated above (i.e. 0.5196 and 0.7579), the fair value of the option is approximately 11.05% of the fair value of the underlying asset.

The valuation of the conversion options can therefore be calculated as:

0.1105 x 2.6187 per share x 250 shares per bond x 2,000 bonds = 144,683

The fair value of the debt component of the compound instrument calculated above by the present value method plus the fair value of the option calculated by the Black-Scholes option pricing model does not equal the 2,000,000 proceeds from issuance of the convertible bonds (i.e. 1,848,122 + 144,683 = 1,992,805). The small difference can be prorated over the fair values of the two components to produce a fair value for the liability of 1,854,794 and a fair value for the option of 145,206.

In our view, this need to allocate the difference exposes a conceptual flaw in Approach 2 (at least as illustrated above), namely that it is adding 'apples and oranges' by using a fair value approach for the equity element (that takes into account the probability of conversion), but a discounted cash flow approach to the liability element (that ignores the possibility of conversion). The difference happens to be 'small' in the example in IAS 32, but might well not be.

5.7 Proposed accounting for puttable instruments

In September 2001 the SIC issued a draft interpretation SIC–D34 – *Financial Instruments – Instruments or Rights Redeemable by the Holder.* It addresses the accounting treatment of a 'puttable instrument' defined as a financial instrument or a right that gives the holder the right to put the instrument or right back to the issuer for cash or another financial asset where the amount payable on redemption is based on an index or other item that has the potential to increase or decrease. This includes instruments or rights (such as units in an open-ended fund or investment trust) that give their holders the right to redeem their interests for cash equal to their share of the underlying net assets of the enterprise.[187]

The draft interpretation proposes that a puttable instrument (other than one issued to a holder by that controls or jointly controls the issuer) should be treated as a hybrid instrument comprising a host contract, equivalent to a repayable deposit (which should be accounted for at amortised cost) and an embedded non-option derivative representing a principal payment indexed to an underlying variable (which should be accounted for at fair value).[188] The treatment of embedded derivatives under IAS 39 is discussed in more detail in Chapter 10 at 4.3.3.

In the case of a puttable instrument that can be put back at any time, the effect would be to measure the instrument at the amount that the issuer would have had to pay at the balance sheet date if the holder had exercised its right.[189] The two components of the instrument would be shown net in the balance sheet, as would any profit or loss on them in the income statement.[190]

This interpretation is perfectly consistent with the underlying principles of IAS 32 and IAS 39 but will, if approved by the SIC, have the somewhat radical consequence that open-ended investment funds and similar vehicles will all show net assets and profits of nil when reporting under IAS. It is not altogether clear how this will assist comparison between the performance of different funds.

5.8 Disclosure

The disclosure requirements for financial instruments in IAS 32 (including the capital instruments discussed in this Chapter) are discussed in Chapter 10 at 5. In addition IAS 1 requires the following disclosures.

There should be separate disclosure on the face of the balance sheet of:

- trade and other receivables;
- non-current interest bearing liabilities;
- minority interest; and
- issued capital and reserves.[191]

Under IAS 1 an enterprise may choose in presenting its balance sheet to either:

- distinguish current and non-current assets and liabilities; or
- present assets and liabilities broadly in order of liquidity.[192]

In either case, the enterprise should disclose, for each asset and liability item that combines amounts expected to be recovered or settled both before and after twelve months from the balance sheet date, the amount expected to be recovered or settled after more than twelve months.[193]

If the enterprise chooses to distinguish current and non-current items, a current item for this purpose is one that is expected to be settled within the normal course of the enterprise's operating cycle or within twelve months of the balance sheet date.[194] However, an enterprise should continue to classify its long-term interest-bearing liabilities as non-current, even when they are due to be settled within twelve months of the balance sheet date if:

(a) the original term was for a period of more than twelve months;

(b) the enterprise intends to refinance the obligation on a long-term basis; and

(c) that intention is supported by an agreement to refinance, or to reschedule payments, which is completed before the financial statements are authorised for issue.[195]

An enterprise should disclose, either on the face of the balance sheet or in the notes:

(a) for each class of share capital:
   (i) the number of shares authorised;
   (ii) the number of shares issued and fully paid, and issued but not fully paid;
   (iii) par value per share, or that the shares have no par value;
   (iv) a reconciliation of the number of shares outstanding at the beginning and at the end of the year;
   (v) the rights, preferences and restrictions attaching to that class including restrictions on the distribution of dividends and the repayment of capital;
   (vi) shares in the enterprise held by the enterprise itself or by subsidiaries or associates of the enterprise; and
   (vii) shares reserved for issuance under options and sales contracts, including the terms and amounts;

(b) a description of the nature and purpose of each reserve within owners' equity;

(c) when dividends have been proposed but not formally approved for payment, the amount included (or not included) in liabilities; and

(d) the amount of any cumulative preference dividends not recognised.

An enterprise without share capital, such as a partnership, should disclose information equivalent to that required above, showing movements during the period in each category of equity interest and the rights, preferences and restrictions attaching to each category of equity interest.[196]

The face of the income statement should disclose finance costs.[197] Dividends per share, declared or proposed, for the period covered by the financial statements should be shown on the face of the income statement or in the notes.[198]

5.9 Comparison with UK GAAP – summary

The often significant differences between UK GAAP and IAS in this area arise not so much from the accounting treatment of debt and equity (which are broadly similar), as from the criteria used to determine whether a particular instrument is a debt or equity instrument.

Some differences arise from the fact that the IASB is not constrained by any national legal requirements, whereas UK GAAP must have regard to the requirements of UK and EC company law. This allows IAS to take a much more 'purist' approach, distinguishing between debt and equity on the basis of economic substance rather than legal form. Thus, IAS would classify many, but not all, preference shares as debt, whereas under UK GAAP they are often included within shareholders' funds (albeit classified as non-equity rather than equity shares). Furthermore, UK GAAP normally adopts a rather crude 'all or nothing' approach to the classification of capital instruments – i.e. a capital instrument is included in full within either debt or shareholders' funds, even if it has characteristics of both debt and shares. IAS requires the separation not only of the debt and equity 'elements' of a hybrid instrument but also of any derivatives embedded in a capital instrument.

6 CONCLUSION

6.1 UK GAAP

In the UK, FRS 4 was useful in developing a framework of rules on capital instruments, since by the late 1980s the requirements of the Companies Act alone were no longer adequate to deal with innovative forms of finance. The standard created much more consistency in the classification and disclosure of companies' share and loan capital than had been displayed in the years before it was issued.

A major weakness in FRS 4, albeit not one of the ASB's making, is that its classification of capital instruments as debt or equity owes more to their legal form than their economic substance. As such, FRS 4 sits uneasily alongside the principle of substance over form enshrined in FRS 5 – unless one takes the view that a capital instrument primarily establishes a legal rather than an economic relationship, such that its real substance is indicated by the legal rights and obligations that it imposes.

Also the prohibition in FRS 4 of split accounting for complex instruments, whilst doubtless a sensible pragmatic approach when FRS 4 was originally issued, now appears rather unsophisticated, and, as the discussion above indicates, can lead to very strange results. It must not be forgotten that these issues have a profit and loss account dimension as well as a balance sheet one; for example, the use of split accounting in relation to convertible bonds seeks to charge earnings with a proper finance cost, which arguably is understated under the accounting approach which FRS 4 requires.

However, it seems unlikely that the ASB will make any major changes to FRS 4 in the short term, but will simply wait for it to be superseded by IAS in 2005.

6.2 IAS

IAS is conceptually more advanced in this area than UK GAAP. However, it remains to be seen just how practical and well understood the requirements of IAS actually are. The 2001-2 reporting season, when companies reporting under IAS are required to apply IAS 39 for the first time, will provide a real testing ground.

A major issue, as the discussion at 5 above illustrates, is that the fundamental question of what is debt and what is equity has not yet been fully resolved – a problem to some extent created by the changes made to IAS 32 by IAS 39. Reservations about IAS 39 are something of a recurring theme in this book – see for example, the discussion on derecognition of financial liabilities at 5.4.3 above and our comments at the end of Chapters 10 and 18. We believe that IAS 39 requires the IASB's urgent attention and therefore welcome the fact that the IASB has announced projects on the definition of the elements of financial statements (which would include the classification of items as debt or equity) and on derecognition in general.

References

1 UITF Abstract 1, *Convertible bonds – Supplemental interest/premium*, UITF, July 1991.
2 ASB Discussion Paper, *Accounting for capital instruments*, ASB, December 1991.
3 FRED 3, *Accounting for Capital Instruments*, ASB, December 1992.
4 UITF 8, *Repurchase of own debt*, UITF, March 1993.
5 FRS 4, *Capital Instruments*, ASB, December 1993, para. 2.
6 *Ibid.*, para. 21.
7 *Ibid.*, para. 52.
8 *Statement of Principles for Financial Reporting*, ASB, December 1999, para. 4.23.
9 FRS 4, para. 24.
10 CA 85, Sch. 4, para. 8.
11 FRS 4, para. 12.
12 *Ibid.*, para. 49.
13 *Ibid.*, para. 90.
14 *Ibid.*, para. 25.
15 ASB Discussion Paper, *Accounting for Capital Instruments*, Appendix 3.
16 TR 677, Appendix para. 5(a).
17 FRS 4, para. 22.
18 *Ibid.*, para. 26.
19 *Ibid.*, paras. 27 and 11.
20 *Ibid.*, para. 8.
21 *Ibid.*, para. 28.
22 *Ibid.*, para. 29.
23 *Ibid.*, para. 32.
24 *Ibid.*, para. 37.
25 *Ibid.*, para. 11.
26 *Ibid.*, para. 42.
27 *Ibid.*, para. 8.
28 *Ibid.*, para. 28.
29 *Ibid.*, para. 10.
30 *Ibid.*, para. 96.
31 *Ibid.*, para. 42.
32 *Ibid.*, para. 51.
33 *Ibid.*, para. 72.
34 *Ibid.*, para. 16.
35 UITF 11, *Accounting for Issuer Call Options*, UITF, September 1994.
36 FRS 4, para. 32.
37 UITF 8, para. 7.
38 FRS 4, para. 34.
39 *Ibid.*, para. 35.
40 *Ibid.*, Appendix III, paras. 34 and 35.
41 FRS 4., para. 81.
42 *Ibid.*, para. 36.
43 *Ibid.*, para. 17.
44 *Ibid.*, para. 45.
45 *Ibid.*, para. 46.
46 *Ibid.*, para. 47.
47 *Ibid.*, para. 48.
48 *Ibid.*, para. 99.
49 *Ibid.*, para. 48.
50 *Ibid.*, para. 40.
51 *Ibid.*, para. 55.
52 *Ibid.*, para. 50.
53 *Ibid.*, para. 25.
54 *Ibid.*, para. 54.
55 *Ibid.*, para. 38.
56 *Ibid.*, para. 56.
57 *Ibid.*, para. 58.
58 *Ibid.*, para. 57.
59 *Ibid.*, para. 61.
60 *Ibid.*, para. 33, as amended by FRS 13 *Derivatives and Other Financial Instruments: Disclosures*, ASB, September 1998, para. 77. Strictly, the amendment applies only to companies within the scope of FRS 13 but, as it corrects a drafting error in the original FRS 4, should clearly be applied by all entities reporting under FRS 4.
61 *Ibid.*, para. 36.
62 *Ibid.*, para. 62.
63 *Ibid.*, para. 63.
64 *Ibid.*, para. 65.
65 *Ibid.*, para. 64.
66 *Ibid.*, para. 13.
67 *Ibid.*, para. 59.
68 *Ibid.*, para. 60.
69 *Ibid.*, para. 52.
70 FRED 3, para. 59.
71 FRS 4, para. 102.
72 CA 85, s 130(1).
73 *Ibid.*, s 130(2).
74 *Ibid.*, ss. 131 and 132.
75 FRS 4, paras. 45 and 11.
76 *Ibid.*, para. 21c.
77 FRS 6, *Accounting for Business Combinations*, ASB, September 1994, Appendix I, para. 15.
78 CA 85, ss. 117 and 118.
79 *Ibid.*, s. 744.
80 *Ibid.*, Sch. 4, para. 8.
81 *Ibid.*, para. 38(1).
82 *Ibid.*, para. 38(2).
83 *Ibid.*, para. 39.
84 *Ibid.*, para. 40.
85 *Ibid.*, para. 49.
86 *Ibid.*, para. 3(7)(b) and (c).
87 FRS 4, para. 43.
88 *The Listing Rules*, Financial Services Authority, Chapter 12, para. 12.43(l).
89 CA 85, Sch. 4, para. 8.
90 *Ibid.*, para. 85.
91 *Ibid.*, para. 48(1) and (2).
92 *Ibid.*, para. 48(4).
93 *Ibid.*, para. 41(1).
94 *Ibid.*, para. 41(3).

95 *Ibid.*, s 744.
96 *Ibid.*, Sch. 4, para. 53(2).
97 CA 85, ss. 159–181.
98 *Ibid.*, s 170.
99 *Ibid.*, s 171 *et seq.*
100 *Ibid.*, Sch. 7, paras. 8 and 9.
101 *The Listing Rules*, Chapter 12, para. 12.43(n).
102 FRS 4, para. 63.
103 *Ibid.*, para. 31.
104 *Ibid.*, para. 26.
105 UITF 1, para. 5.
106 FRS 4, para. 25.
107 *Ibid.*, para. 26.
108 *Ibid.* – Application Notes.
109 *Ibid.*
110 FRS 4, para. 46.
111 *Ibid.*, para. 47.
112 CA 85, s 130.
113 FRS 4, para. 43.
114 *Ibid.*, paras. 42 and 28.
115 FRS 7, *Fair Values in Acquisition Accounting*, ASB, September 1994, para. 82.
116 TR 677, Appendix, para. 7.
117 FRS 4, para. 99.
118 The purpose and status of the Q&As is discussed in more detail in Chapter 10 at 4.1
119 IAS 39 *Financial Instruments: Recognition and Measurement*, IASC, December 1998 (revised October 2000) para. 71.
120 IAS 32 *Financial Instruments: Disclosure and Presentation*, IASC, March 1995 (revised December 1998 and October 2000), para. 5, and IAS 39 (revised October 2000), para. 8.
121 *Ibid.*
122 *Ibid.*
123 IAS 32, para. 5, IAS 39 para. 11.
124 IAS 32, para. 5; IAS 39, para. 8.
125 *Ibid.*, para. 16
126 IAS 32, para. 20.
127 *Ibid.*, para. 19.
128 *Ibid.*, para. 19.
129 IAS 32 para. 5; IAS 39 para. 11.
130 *Ibid.*, para. A8.
131 *Ibid.*, para. A19.
132 *Ibid.*, para. 22. Whilst much of the discussion of this issue in IAS 32 refers to 'preferred shares', these requirements would apply to any shares with similar terms.
133 *Ibid.*, para. A20.
134 *Ibid.*, para 22.
135 *Ibid.*, para. A20.
136 *Ibid.*, para. A21.
137 *Ibid.*, para. 22.
138 SIC-5, *Classification of Financial Instruments – Contingent Settlement Provisions*, SIC, October 1997, paras. 5-6.
139 *Ibid.*, Appendix.
140 *Ibid.*, para. 9.
141 IAS 32, paras. 23-24.
142 *Ibid.*, para. 25.
143 *Ibid.*, para. 26.
144 *Ibid.*, para. 27.
145 *Ibid.*, para. 17.
146 IAS 39, Q&A 11-1.
147 IAS 1, *Presentation of Financial Statements*, IASC, 1997, paras. 86-87.
148 IAS 39. para. 66, Q&A 66-1 and 66-2.
149 *Ibid.*, para. 67. Also IAS 18 (revised 1993) *Revenue*, IASC, December 1993 (amended December 1998, May 1999 and January 2001), para. 11.
150 IAS 39, para. 93.
151 *Ibid.*, para. 10.
152 IAS 32, para. 31.
153 *Ibid.*, para. 32.
154 IAS 39, para 73.
155 *Ibid.*, para. 10.
156 *Ibid.* and IAS 32, para. 61.
157 IAS 39, Q&A 93-1.
158 *Ibid.*, Q&A 10-12.
159 *Ibid.*, para. 57.
160 *Ibid.*, para. 58.
161 *Ibid.*, Q&A 57-2
162 *Ibid.*, para. 59.
163 *Ibid.*, para. 58(b).
164 *Ibid.*, Q&A 57-3.
165 *Ibid.*, para. 60.
166 *Ibid.*, para. 61.
167 *Ibid.*, para. 62.
168 *Ibid.*, Q&A 62-1.
169 *Ibid.*, para. 62.
170 *Ibid.*, Q&A 62-1.
171 *Ibid.*, para. 63.
172 *Ibid.*, para. 64
173 IAS 32, paras. 30-31; IAS 1, paras. 86(d), 87; and *Framework for the Preparation and Presentation of Financial Statements*, IASC, July 1989, paras. 65-68 and 70.
174 IAS 10 – *Events After the Balance Sheet Date*, IASC, May 1999, para. 11.
175 SIC-17, *Equity – Costs of an Equity Transaction*, SIC, May 1999, para. 6.
176 *Ibid.*, para. 9.
177 *Ibid.*, para. 3.
178 *Ibid*, para. 5.
179 *Ibid.*, para. 7.
180 *Ibid.*, para. 8.
181 IAS 32, para. A8.
182 SIC-16, *Share Capital – Reacquired Own Equity Instruments (Treasury Shares)*, SIC, June 1998, para. 3.
183 *Ibid.*, paras. 4 and 6.
184 *Ibid.*, paras. 4-5.
185 IAS 32, para. 28.
186 *Ibid.*, para. A23.

187 SIC D-34 *Financial Instruments – Instruments or Rights Redeemable by the Holder*, SIC, September 2001, paras. 1-2.
188 *Ibid.*, paras. 5 and 7-8.
189 *Ibid.*
190 *Ibid.*, paras. 9-10.
191 IAS 1, para. 66.
192 *Ibid.*, para. 53.
193 *Ibid.*, para. 54.
194 *Ibid.*, para. 60.
195 *Ibid.*, para. 63.
196 *Ibid.*, para. 74.
197 *Ibid.*, para. 75.
198 *Ibid.*, para. 85.

Chapter 18 Off balance sheet transactions

1 INTRODUCTION

1.1 Background

'Off balance sheet' transactions can be difficult to define, and this poses the first problem in discussing the subject. The term implies that certain things belong on the balance sheet and that those which escape the net are deviations from this norm.

The practical effect of off balance sheet transactions is that they do not result in full presentation of the underlying activity in the accounts of the reporting company. This is generally for one of two reasons. The items in question may be included in the balance sheet but presented 'net' rather than 'gross'; examples would include one-line presentation of an unconsolidated subsidiary rather than line by line consolidation, or netting off loans received against the assets they finance. Alternatively, the items might be excluded from the balance sheet altogether on the basis that they represent future commitments rather than present assets and liabilities. Examples would include operating lease commitments, obligations under take-or-pay contracts or consignment stock agreements, contingent liabilities under options, and so on. Another (generally less successful) technique is to attempt to house transactions in an entity that is not legally controlled by the reporting entity, but which is either controlled by a party responsive to the reporting entity's wishes or run according to a predetermined plan.

The result in all cases will be that the balance sheet suggests less exposure to assets and liabilities than really exists, with a consequential flattering effect on certain ratios, such as gearing and return on assets employed. There is usually also a profit and loss account dimension to be considered as well, perhaps because assets taken off balance sheet purport to have been sold (with a possible profit effect), and also more generally because the presentation of off balance sheet activity influences the timing or disclosure of associated revenue items. In particular, the presence or absence of items in the balance sheet usually affects whether the finance cost implicit in a transaction is reported as such or rolled up within another item of income or expense.

Depending on their roles, different people tend to react differently to the use of the term 'off balance sheet finance'. To an accounting standard setter, the expression carries the connotation of devious accounting, intended to mislead the reader of financial statements. Off balance sheet transactions are those which are designed to allow a company to avoid reflecting certain aspects of its activities in its accounts. The term is therefore a pejorative one, and the inference is that those who indulge in such transactions are up to no good and need to be stopped.

However, there is also room for a more honourable use of the term 'off balance sheet finance'. Companies may wish, for sound commercial reasons, to engage in transactions which share with other parties the risks and benefits associated with certain assets and liabilities. Increasingly sophisticated financial markets allow businesses to protect themselves from selected risks, or to take limited ownership interests which carry the entitlement to restricted rewards of particular assets. Also, off balance sheet transactions are often undertaken as an element of a company's tax planning strategy. Such transactions are not undertaken to mislead readers of their accounts, but because they are judged to be in the best commercial interests of the companies undertaking them.

In principle, it should be possible to determine what items belong in the balance sheet by reference to general principles such as those set out in the ASB's *Statement of Principles* or the IASB's *Framework for the Preparation and Presentation of Financial Statements*. In practice, however, such principles on their own would be a totally inadequate response to the increasingly ingenious and aggressive structures being developed for what would generally be regarded as the less honourable forms off balance sheet finance. Accordingly standard-setters throughout the world have developed increasingly detailed rules to deal with the issue.

1.2 UK position

In the UK, there is a fairly comprehensive standard dealing with off balance sheet transactions, FRS 5 – *Reporting the Substance of Transactions*, which was issued in April 1994, although it was in fact the culmination of nearly ten years' debate. FRS 5 draws heavily on what was then the ASB's draft *Statement of Principles* and seeks to deal with transactions whose form is at variance with their economic substance. The thrust of the standard is to identify what the substance is in reality and represent the transactions in that light. As will be seen from the discussion below, however, it sometimes leaves no room for any subjective judgment as to what the substance of a transaction is, and its approach to certain issues is in fact very form-driven. For example, the circumstances in which amounts due and from the same party can be presented net depends on the application of a strict set of rules rather than the application of any judgement.

FRS 5, although complex, has generally greatly improved financial reporting in the UK. However, where it is flawed, it is in our view deeply flawed and would benefit from urgent attention from the ASB in several areas, to which we draw attention in the discussion in 2 and 3 below.

1.3 IAS position

There is no comprehensive standard dealing with off-balance sheet finance under IAS, which is sometimes cited as a serious deficiency in IAS as compared to UK GAAP. However, this is a distortion of the real position, since many of the areas covered by FRS 5 (such as offset, derecognition, and special purpose entities), are covered by parts of different international standards. Indeed some of the detailed rules under IAS take a harsher view of certain types of transaction than FRS 5. Conversely, however, the absence of detailed guidance on particular transactions in IAS as compared to UK GAAP could well lead to a more benign treatment of those transactions under IAS than under UK GAAP. It would not therefore be surprising if the chairman of the IASB, Sir David Tweedie (who, as chairman of the ASB, presided over the issue of FRS 5 in the UK) wished to see a comprehensive IAS on off balance sheet transactions along the lines of FRS 5 sooner rather than later. For example, at the time of writing, the IASC's website indicates a comprehensive new project on derecognition to include non-financial assets (an area dealt with by FRS 5, but not currently by IAS).

2 REQUIREMENTS OF FRS 5

2.1 Scope and general requirements

FRS 5 – *Reporting the substance of transactions* – was published in April 1994. It applies to all entities whose accounts are intended to give a true and fair view, but it excludes a number of transactions from its scope, unless they form part of a larger series of transactions that does fall within the scope of the standard. These exclusions are:

(a) forward contracts and futures (such as those for foreign currencies or commodities);

(b) foreign exchange and interest rate swaps;

(c) contracts where a net amount will be paid or received based on the movement in a price or an index (sometimes referred to as 'contracts for differences');

(d) expenditure commitments (such as purchase commitments) and orders placed, until the earlier of delivery or payment; and

(e) employment contracts.[1]

Of these, (a) to (c) relate to financial derivatives and were presumably excluded because they were to be addressed in the ASB's financial instruments project. An important practical effect of their exclusion is that hedge accounting continues to be permitted for a wide range of transactions that would otherwise fall foul of the offset criteria (see 2.7 below).

Items (d) and (e) above are more problematic. They seem to have been excluded only because the application of the recognition criteria in the standard would otherwise have some undesirable effects. Literal application of these criteria could require companies to include assets and liabilities in their accounts in respect of contracts for future performance (see 2.4 below). The central premise of FRS 5 is that the substance and economic reality of an entity's transactions should be reported in its financial statements, and this substance should be identified by considering all the aspects and implications of a transaction, with the emphasis on those likely to have a commercial effect in practice. In determining the substance, it is necessary to consider whether the transaction has given rise to new assets and liabilities for the entity, and whether it has changed any of its existing assets and liabilities.[2]

2.1.1 *Linked transactions*

Sometimes there will be a series of connected transactions to be evaluated, not just a single transaction. The overall substance of these transactions must be determined as a whole and accounted for, rather than accounting for each individual transaction. Sometimes this can be relatively easy to identify, as the following example illustrates.

Example 18.1: Linked transactions

On 1 July 2001 a company borrows €1 million from a bank. On the same day it enters into a swap with the bank whereby it pays €1 million and receives £600,000. On 31 December 2001 the swap is settled by the company paying the bank £620,000 and the bank paying the company €1 million, which the company then uses to repay the €1 million loan.

When the cash flows in this transaction are analysed, the euro flows are in fact an irrelevance as they involve the bank and the company exchanging cash of the same amount on the same days. What has really happened is that the company has borrowed £600,000 for six months and paid £20,000 interest on it.

The standard quotes some examples of more complex arrangements to which its provisions will be particularly relevant. These involve the following features:

(a) the separation of legal title to an item from rights or other access to the principal future economic benefits associated with it and exposure to the principal risks inherent in these benefits;

(b) the linking of a transaction with others in such a way that the commercial effect can be understood only by considering the series as a whole; and

(c) the inclusion of options or conditions on terms that make it highly likely that the option will be exercised or the condition fulfilled.[3]

Where transactions include options which may or may not be exercised or conditions which may or may not apply, it is necessary to form a view as to their likely outcome, by considering the motivations of all the parties to the transaction and the possible scenarios which they have contemplated in negotiating the terms of the deal. Only in this way can the commercial substance of the arrangement be identified.

2.1.2 Interaction with other standards

The interaction of FRS 5 with other standards and statutory requirements is also something which must be considered. Transactions which are directly addressed by other pronouncements will sometimes also fall within the remit of FRS 5, which requires the more specific rules to be applied.[4] A particular example quoted is the leasing standard, SSAP 21, which addresses a particular aspect of off balance sheet finance but in a more narrowly prescribed way. Straightforward leases which fall squarely within the terms of SSAP 21 should continue to be accounted for without reference to FRS 5, but where their terms are more complex, or the lease is only one element in a larger series of transactions, then FRS 5 comes into play. More generally, the standard says that its overall principle of substance over form should apply to the operation of other existing rules.[5]

2.1.3 Specific applications of FRS 5

FRS 5 deals with certain specific aspects of off balance sheet finance through the medium of detailed Application Notes. These cover the following topics:

- Consignment stock
- Sale and repurchase agreements
- Factoring of debts
- Securitised assets
- Loan transfers
- The Private Finance Initiative and similar contracts.

The first five of these Application Notes were published as part of the original standard, while the last was added in 1998. They are intended to clarify and develop the methods of applying the standard to the particular transactions which they describe and to provide guidance on how to interpret it in relation to other similar transactions. They also contain specific disclosure requirements in relation to these transactions. The Application Notes are not exhaustive and they do not override the general principles of the standard itself, but they are regarded as part of the standard (i.e. they are authoritative) insofar as they assist in interpreting it.[6] Each of these topics is discussed in 3 below.

2.2 Definition of assets and liabilities

For the purpose of the standard, assets and liabilities are defined as follows:

Assets are rights or other access to future economic benefits controlled by an entity as a result of past transactions or events.[7] *Control*, in the context of an asset, is the ability to obtain the future economic benefits relating to an asset and to restrict the access of others to those benefits.[8]

Liabilities are an entity's obligations to transfer economic benefits as a result of past transactions or events.[9]

These definitions are the same as those in the ASB's *Statement of Principles,*[10] as discussed in Chapter 2.

2.3 Analysis of risks and rewards

The standard goes on to say that identifying the party that is exposed to variations in the benefits relating to an asset will generally indicate who has the asset itself.[11] It also says that if an entity is in certain circumstances unable to avoid an outflow of benefits, this will provide evidence that it has a liability.[12] The various risks and rewards relating to particular assets and liabilities are discussed in Application Notes which deal with different forms of off balance sheet finance.

In any consideration of where the risks and rewards lie as a result of a transaction, it is useful to remember that each of the risks and rewards relating to a particular asset or liability must lie *somewhere*. Although they may be partitioned and transferred as a result of the transactions, they cannot be increased or diminished in total. In addition, an analysis of the commercial effect of the deal can be expedited by looking at it from the point of view of each of the parties involved. By considering what risks and rewards they have acquired or disposed of, and their motivation for doing so, the substance of the transaction can be discerned more clearly than by considering the position of one of the parties alone.

2.4 Recognition

Once items which satisfy the definition of assets and liabilities have been identified, the next key question is whether they should be recognised in the balance sheet. This question, of course, is what the whole subject of off balance sheet finance is about. The standard says that 'where a transaction results in an item which meets the definition of an asset or liability, that item should be recognised in the balance sheet if:

(a) there is sufficient evidence of the existence of the item (including, where appropriate, evidence that a future inflow or outflow of benefit will occur); and

(b) the item can be measured at a monetary amount with sufficient reliability.'[13]

These principles are similar to those set out in the ASB's *Statement of Principles.*[14] They are rather abstract criteria, and are not particularly easy to understand in isolation; in particular, item (a) appears to add little but a reinforcement of the definition of an asset or liability. Critically, it does not really specify the defining event which dictates when to bring an item on to the balance sheet.

The difficulty is therefore in identifying exactly when an asset or liability is created in the terms in which they have been defined. Conventional accounting practice is to recognise most transactions only when they are performed, for example when goods are received under a purchase contract. However, an enthusiastic interpretation of the recognition criteria would say that merely entering into the contract has resulted in the creation of an asset (the right to the goods) and a liability (the amount due under the purchase contract). This is similar to the IASC's standard on financial instruments, which says that 'An enterprise should recognise a financial asset or financial liability on its balance sheet when, and only when, it becomes a party to the contractual provisions of the instrument.'[15] However this would be a radical change of practice.

This idea that the creation, rather than the execution, of a contract should be the event which triggers the recognition of assets and liabilities has an obvious theoretical appeal. However, quite apart from the difficulty of capturing the relevant information in a company's accounting system, it is debatable whether this forms a sensible basis for the preparation of a balance sheet. The difficulty with it is that every commitment under contract would become a liability; examples might include all leasing commitments (not just those for finance leases, as at present),[16] long-term supply contracts for raw materials, and even future salary payments under employment contracts (at least for the required period of notice). There could also be some difficulty in defining and describing the nature of the corresponding asset in such cases ('goods to be purchased', 'employees' services to be rendered'?). It is presumably to avoid this result that expenditure commitments and employment contracts have been scoped out of the standard, as discussed under 2.1 above, but this does not resolve the principle behind the recognition test.

The ASB's *Statement of Principles* attempts to address with this issue with concept of an executory contract. 'Executory contracts' – those where neither party has performed any of its obligations, or each has performed its obligations to an equal extent[17] – are discussed in more detail in Chapter 28 at 2.1.2. The argument is that an unperformed executory contract represents a net (nil) position comprising a combined right and obligation either to participate in the exchange or alternatively to be compensated (or to compensate) for the consequences of the exchange not taking place. However, as the contract progresses, if both parties have not performed their obligations equally, it may be necessary for each party to recognise a (net) asset or liability representing the unperformed part of the contract.[18] This rather arcane wording would, for example, require a company that pays its employees in arrears to accrue for the cost of services provided but not yet paid for (see Chapter 22 at 2.1 A).

2.5 Derecognition

2.5.1 *General principles*

As the word suggests, derecognition is the opposite of recognition. It concerns the question of when to remove from the balance sheet the assets and liabilities which have previously been recognised. FRS 5 addresses this issue only in relation to assets, not liabilities. In effect, FRS 5 approaches liability derecognition as an issue of derecognition of a related asset. For example if a third party advances funds to a company in connection with the transfer of an asset to the third party, FRS 5 requires the company to assess whether or not it can derecognise the asset. If it can, the transaction is a sale; if it cannot, the transaction is some form of financing secured on the asset transferred. Likewise, if a company uses an asset to settle of a liability, FRS 5 requires the company to assess whether or not it can derecognise the asset concerned. If it can, the liability has can be derecognised; if it cannot, both the asset and liability remain on balance sheet. There are, however, transactions involving a liability, but no corresponding asset (such as the forgiveness of debt by a creditor) that are not directly covered by FRS 5.

The rules for the derecognition of assets are designed to determine one of three outcomes – complete derecognition, partial derecognition and no derecognition, together with a fourth possibility, the linked presentation, which is discussed at 2.6 below. These are summarised in the following diagram:

Summary of derecognition test

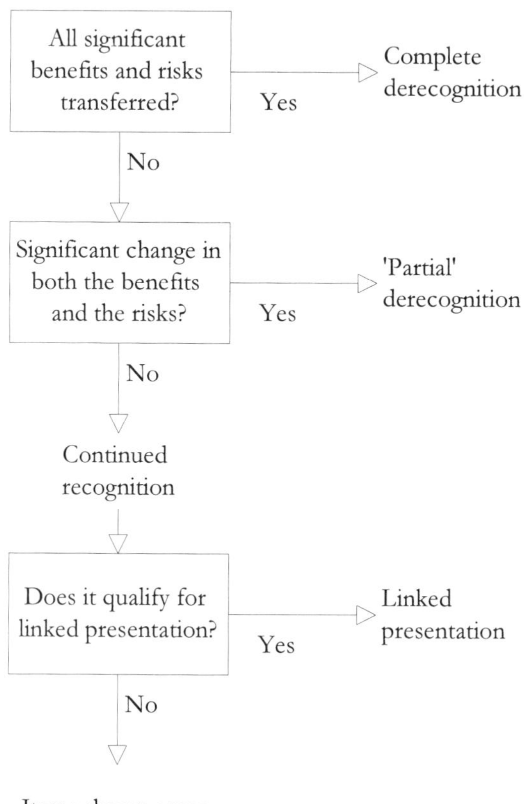

2.5.2 *Complete derecognition*

In the simplest case, where a transaction transfers to another party all the significant benefits and risks relating to an asset, the standard confirms that the entire asset should cease to be recognised.[19] In this context, the word 'significant' is explained further: it should not be judged in relation to all the conceivable benefits and risks that could exist, but only in relation to those which are likely to occur in practice.[20] This means that the importance of the risk retained must be assessed in the context of the total realistic risk which existed in the first place.

Understanding the significance of this requirement is key to a proper application of FRS 5, since it can lead to results which are not altogether expected. In particular, transactions that leave a significant amount of risk (in absolute terms) with a company can lead to complete derecognition of an asset, while others that leave (again in absolute terms) very little risk with the company may fail to achieve derecognition. This is best illustrated by way of example.

Example 18.2: Derecognition (1)

A company sells an asset and agrees to compensate the buyer for any subsequent loss in its value up to a maximum of 2% of the selling price., The significance of that retention of risk depends on how realistic it is that a fall in value of more than 2% will occur. If the asset is a portfolio of high quality receivables where the bad debt risk is very small (say ½p in the £), retaining a 2% risk means that the company has retained all the realistic risk that attaches to that asset, in which case the transaction would not qualify as a sale. However, if the asset is a much more volatile one, whose value could easily fall by 20% or 30%, then the degree of risk retained is relatively small and the transaction could be treated as a sale. The seller would simply provide for any expected loss under the guarantee in measuring the profit on sale.

Example 18.3: Derecognition (2)

A UK company has an obligation under a finance lease of £200 million. The lessor agrees to the company prepaying the entire liability by depositing AAA-rated government bonds in a bankruptcy-remote trust company incorporated in a politically stable country and managed by reputable trustees. If, however, the bonds fail to perform for any reason, the UK company must make good the shortfall for the lessor. From the perspective of the UK company, this is a virtually risk-free transaction. The only risks are default by the government, fraud or incompetence of the trustees and loss arising from war or government action. However, as all these risks are fully borne by the company, it is unable to derecognise the bonds as an asset. Nor does the transaction qualify for linked presentation (see 2.6 below), by virtue of the lessor's recourse to the UK company.

A consequence of the derecognition rules in FRS 5 is that, with some rather limited exceptions covered by the partial derecognition criteria (see 2.5.5 below) assets tend to be either on- or off-balance sheet in their entirety. This can be a rather blunt approach, leading to apparent anomalies such as those highlighted by the examples above. By contrast, IAS (see 4 below) and US GAAP adopt more of a 'component' based approach allowing for partial derecognition in more situations than is permitted by FRS 5.

2.5.3 Continued recognition

At the other end of the spectrum, where a transaction results in no significant change to the benefits *or* to the risks relating to the asset in question, no sale can be recorded and the entire asset should continue to be recognised.[21] It should be noted that retention of *either* the benefits *or* the risks is sufficient to keep the asset on the balance sheet. This means that the elimination of risk by financing the asset on a non-recourse basis will not remove it from the balance sheet; it would be necessary to dispose of the potential benefits as well, to justify recording a sale. (A further variant, the special case of a 'linked presentation', is discussed at 2.6 below).

The standard also says that any transaction that is 'in substance a financing' will not qualify for derecognition, with the item therefore staying on balance sheet, and the finance received being introduced as a liability. There is no explicit definition of transactions that are 'in substance a financing', but some of the discussion elsewhere in FRS 5 indicates that they are those where the reporting entity retains the significant benefits and risks of the asset while the other party earns only a lender's return on the deal. Examples of such transactions are shown in Extracts 18.17 and 18.18 at 3.2.2 below from the respective accounts of Barratt and Gleeson.

The Financial Reporting Review Panel considered an issue of this nature in its investigation of the accounts of Wiggins for the years 1996 to 2000 inclusive. One of the matters considered by the Panel was whether certain transactions involving various plots of land held by the company could be accounted for as sales. Most of the Panel's concerns focussed on the timing of the exchange of contracts for the sales – this is discussed further in Chapter 3 at 5.1. In one case, however, the Panel considered that no sale should have been recognised even after contracts had been exchanged. In its view, the substance of the transaction reflected a development being financed by the purchaser with the company paying an interest cost on monies received from the purchaser and retaining certain risks and rewards for the time being. Accordingly, in compliance with FRS 5, the transaction should have been treated as a financing arrangement until the interest payments ceased.[22]

2.5.4 *Partial derecognition*

As can be seen, the derecognition criteria above are relatively restrictive. At a late stage in the development of the standard, a third possibility was introduced, to deal with circumstances where, although not all of the benefits and risks have been transferred, the transaction is more than a mere financing and has transferred enough of the benefits and risks to warrant at least some derecognition of the asset. The standard addresses three such cases:

(a) where an asset has been subdivided;

(b) where an item is sold for less than its full life; and

(c) where an item is transferred for its full life, but some risk or benefit is retained.

These are discussed in turn below.

A *Asset subdivided*

Where an identifiable part of an asset is separated and sold off, with the remainder being retained, the asset should be split and a partial sale recorded. The examples quoted in the standard are those of the sale of a proportionate part of a loan receivable, where all future receipts are shared equally between the parties, or the stripping of interest payments from the principal of a debt instrument; other obvious examples would be the subdivision of a freehold property with part being sold off, the sale of a share in a racehorse, and so on.

For this to be permitted, the two parts must be distinct in the sense that the benefits and risks associated with the separate parts do not impact upon each other. Thus, the sale of a share of a loan qualifies for partial derecognition so long as the share sold is a proportionate one, but not if the effect of the separation results in the retention of the significant risks or rewards attaching to the whole asset. An example will illustrate this distinction:

Example 18.4: Partial sale of a receivable

Company A has a receivable, comprising the right to receive four amounts of £25,000 each from a third party over a period, totalling £100,000 in all. It wishes to sell half of its asset to Company B. This could be broadly done in one of two ways:

- sale of 50% of each instalment; or
- sale of first £50,000 to be received.

If Company A sold a 50% proportionate share in each of the receipts to Company B, the two parties would thereafter be equally exposed to the risk of the third party's default, and this would qualify as a partial sale. Accordingly, Company A would divide the carrying value of the asset in two, leaving one half on the balance sheet and taking the other half to the profit and loss account to match it with the proceeds received from Company B.

If, however, Company B bought the right to receive the first £50,000 of whatever amounts were received, the position could be different, because the bad debt risk would be unevenly shared between the parties. The answer under FRS 5 seems to depend on whether or not the total realistic bad debt risk falls within A's retained share, in other words whether there was only a remote possibility that more than half of the original receivable would prove bad. If this is the case, then from A's point of view there has been no significant change in the risks attaching to the (whole) asset, and accordingly the whole receivable has to stay on its balance sheet while the proceeds received from Company B would be shown as a liability. However, if there was a realistic risk of loss beyond the first 50%, then there has been a significant change in A's risk and it is entitled to treat the part transferred to B as a sale and remove it from the balance sheet.

In order to account for any partial sale, it is necessary to be able to apportion the previous carrying value of the asset between the part sold and the part which is retained so as to measure both the gain or loss on sale and the carrying value of the residual asset. The following example shows how this could be done in relation to an interest strip.

Example 18.5: Interest strip

Bank A has made a £10 million loan to Company C for 5 years. The loan carries a fixed interest rate of 8%. After one year, it sells the right to receive the interest payments for the remaining four years to Bank B for £2,700,000, but retains the right to the repayment of the principal.

In order to account for this, it is necessary for Bank A to apportion the £10 million asset in its balance sheet between the amount sold and the amount retained. It does this by discounting the future payments due under the loan at the interest rate implicit in the arrangement – 8% in this case. This shows that the present value of £10 million receivable in four years' time is £7,350,300, which stays in its balance sheet, whereas the similarly discounted value of four annual payments of £800,000 is £2,649,700. Comparing this to the proceeds of £2,700,000 produces a profit of £50,300.

B Item sold for less than its full life

This exception arises where the seller retains a residual value risk by agreeing to buy the asset back (if the buyer wishes to sell it back) at a predetermined price at a later stage in the asset's life. Such an arrangement is sometimes offered in relation to commercial vehicles, aircraft, and so on. The standard says that in such cases the original asset will have been replaced by a residual interest in the asset together with a liability for its obligation to pay the repurchase price. Again, it will be necessary to put a value on this in order to measure the profit or loss on the initial sale.

The standard does not make it entirely clear whether such residual assets and liabilities should be accounted for gross or net. This may depend on how likely it is that the repurchase will take place. If it is reasonably certain that it will, then it would be appropriate to reflect both the liability expected to be paid and the residual interest in the asset as separate items on opposite sides of the balance sheet. However, if it is more in the nature of a guarantee which may never be called upon, then it could be appropriate to provide only for the net exposure under the guarantee.

As can be seen from Extract 18.12 at 3.1 below, Lookers recognises an obligation to repurchase motor vehicles under a Motability arrangement, and has a corresponding asset representing its interest in the vehicles.

FRS 5 does not explicitly say how much of the life of the asset has to be disposed of in order to justify recording a sale and derecognising the asset. It does, however, say that both the benefits and the risks retained must be significantly different from those which were held before the transaction took place, and the examples discussed in the standard envisage that the asset will be transferred for most of its life, and will be repurchased in a substantially depreciated state.[23] This means that selling an asset and buying it back after only a short time would not allow any part of the asset to be removed from the balance sheet. This may be compared with accounting by lessors, where substantially all the risks and rewards of ownership must be disposed of under the lease in order for the lessor to be able to regard it as a finance lease and therefore record a sale.

C *Item transferred for its full life but some risk or benefit retained*

The standard discusses various examples of this.[24] Some risk may be retained because a company gives a warranty or residual value guarantee in relation to the product being sold, but this should not preclude the recording of the sale so long as the exposure under the warranty or guarantee can be assessed and provided for if necessary. Companies may also sometimes retain the possibility of an upward adjustment to the sale price of an asset based on its future performance – for example, when a business is sold subject to an earn-out clause – but again this should not preclude the recognition of the sale.

In its 1998 accounts, Countryside Properties disclosed the following information about guarantees given in relation to some of the houses that it had sold, but this did not prevent derecognition of the assets:

Extract 18.1: Countryside Properties PLC (1998)

23 Contingent liabilities

Sales of housing units amounting in aggregate to £12m benefit from the Group's Assured Value Guarantee under which any reduction in the resale prices of the units is guaranteed by the Group within predetermined time limits.

Rolls Royce and BAE Systems disclose some rather more complicated arrangements in relation to some of their sales:

Extract 18.2: Rolls-Royce plc (2000)

27 Contingent liabilities [extract]

In connection with the sale of its products, on some occasions the Group and Company enter into individually and collectively significant long-term contingent obligations. These can involve, inter alia, guaranteeing financing for customers, guaranteeing a proportion of the values of both engine and airframe, entering into leasing transactions, commitments to purchase aircraft and in certain circumstances could involve the Group and Company assuming certain of its customers' entitlements and related borrowing or cash flow obligations until the value of the security can be realised.

At December 31, 2000, having regard to the estimated net realisable value of the relevant security, the net contingent liabilities in respect of financing arrangements on all delivered aircraft amounted to **£184m** (1999 £118m). Sensitivity calculations are complex, but, for example, if the value of the relevant security was reduced by 20%, a net contingent liability of approximately **£347m** (1999 £272m) would result. There are also net contingent liabilities in respect of undelivered aircraft but it is not considered practicable to estimate these as deliveries can be many years in the future and the related financing will only be put in place at the appropriate time.

At the date these accounts are approved, the directors regard the possibility that there will be any significant loss arising from these contingencies, which cover a number of customers over a long period of time, as remote. In determining this, and the values above, the directors have taken account of advice, principally from Airclaims Limited, professional aircraft appraisers, who base their calculations on a current and future fair market value basis assuming an arms-length transaction between a willing seller and a willing buyer.

Extract 18.3: BAE SYSTEMS plc (2000)

1 Accounting policies

Aircraft financing

The group is exposed to actual and contingent liabilities arising from commercial aircraft financing, both from financing arranged directly by the group and from that arranged by third parties where the group has provided guarantees or has other recourse obligations. Provision for these risks is made on a systematic basis, having regard to the ability to re-lease or re-sell the underlying aircraft.

20 Commercial aircraft financing

Commercial aircraft are frequently sold for cash with the manufacturer retaining some financial exposure. Aircraft financing commitments of the group can be categorised as either direct or indirect. Direct commitments arise where the group has sold the aircraft to a third party lessor and then leased it back under an operating lease (or occasionally a finance lease) prior to an onward lease to an operator. Indirect commitments (contingent liabilities) may arise where the group has sold aircraft to third parties who either operate the aircraft themselves or lease the aircraft on to operators. In these cases the group may give guarantees in respect of the residual values of the related aircraft or certain head lease and finance payments to be made by either the third parties or the operators. The group's exposure to these commitments is offset by future lease rentals and the residual value of the related aircraft.

The group has entered into arrangements which reduce its exposure from commercial aircraft financing by obtaining insurance cover from a syndicate of leading insurance companies over a significant proportion of the contracted and expected income stream from the aircraft portfolio including those aircraft where the group has provided residual value guarantees..

The net exposure of the group to aircraft financing as at 31 December 2000 was:

	2000 £m	1999 £m
Direct operating lease commitments	**600**	722
Direct finance lease commitments	**4**	5
Indirect exposure through aircraft contingent liabilities	**1,414**	1,589
Exposure to residual value guarantees	**693**	524
Income guaranteed through insurance arrangements	**(1,727)**	(1,885)
Net exposure	**984**	973
Expected income not covered by insurance arrangements	**(43)**	(43)
Expected income on aircraft delivered post insurance arrangements	**(388)**	(330)
Adjustment to net present value	**(154)**	(158)
Recourse provision	**399**	536

Income guaranteed through insurance arrangements represents the future income stream from the aircraft assets guaranteed under the insurance arrangements after deducting the policy excess.

Expected income not covered by insurance arrangements represents the amount of additional income assumed by management for the purpose of provisioning.

Expected income on aircraft delivered post insurance arrangements represents the level of future income anticipated on aircraft delivered since the start of the insurance arrangements.

Given the long term nature of the liabilities, the Directors believe it is appropriate to state the recourse provision at its net present value. The provision covers costs to be incurred over a forecast period of 12 years from the balance sheet date. The *adjustment to net present value* reduces the expected liabilities from their outturn amounts to their anticipated net present value.

As can be seen from the above extracts, in the case of partial disposals, there may be uncertainty as to the measurement of the initial profit or loss. FRS 5 says that the normal rules of prudence should be applied, but also that the uncertainty should be explained if it could have a material effect on the accounts.[25]

It has to be said, however, that this remains a vague area of the standard, because it is not at all clear where to draw the line between recording a sale with substantial provision for attendant uncertainties and not regarding it as achieving a sale at all because of the extent of the risks retained. In contrast, SSAP 21 has a much clearer distinction (albeit one that still requires judgement) between leasing transactions that transfer substantially all the risks and rewards of the asset concerned and those that do not, and the latter do not qualify for sale recognition by the lessor. Applying such a perspective to some of the transactions illustrated above would give rise to very different accounting results.

2.6 The linked presentation

FRS 5 requires non-recourse finance to be shown on the face of the balance sheet as a deduction from the asset to which it relates (rather than in the liabilities section of the balance sheet), provided that certain stringent criteria are met.[26] The treatment, referred to a 'linked presentation' was devised by the ASB in response to strong representations from the banks in relation to certain transactions involving the securitisation of long-term loans (which were treated as off-balance sheet prior to FRS 5, but which the derecognition and offset criteria in FRS 5 would otherwise have required to be shown on a gross basis). Although the linked presentation is still most commonly adopted for transactions involving the securitisation of mortgages and consumer debt (which are discussed at 3.4 below), its use is not confined to transactions involving any particular kind of asset.

In a typical transaction accounted for using a linked presentation, the entity whose assets are the subject of the transactions retains the right to any surplus arising from the assets after the claims of the lenders have been met. The assets do not therefore qualify for full or partial derecognition under the criteria in 2.5 above, since the entity retains significant benefits of the assets. The object of the linked presentation is to show that the entity retains significant benefits and risks associated with the asset, and that the claim of the provider of finance is limited solely to the funds generated by it. It is therefore something of a halfway house, because it discloses the gross amount of the asset which remains a source of benefit to the entity, while simultaneously achieving a net presentation in the balance sheet totals.

There are two possible interpretations of what the linked presentation is seeking to achieve:

(a) A sale of the original asset has taken place, giving rise to a residual (net) asset, but because the entity continues to benefit from its interest in this net asset it should be grossed up within the assets section of the balance sheet to give additional information about its underlying components.

(b) No sale of the original asset has taken place. Instead, non-recourse finance has been advanced to the entity in respect of the asset. However, because of its close relationship with the asset, the finance should be deducted from it within the assets section of the balance sheet.

We suspect that (b) better reflects the ASB's thinking about the linked presentation. However, it creates a potential conflict with the law because moving a liability to the assets side of the balance sheet contravenes the format rules of the Companies Act (see also the further discussion of this issue at 3.4.3 A below). Accordingly, the ASB saw it necessary to present the argument in terms of (a) above, so that FRS 5 states that linked presentation is to be used when 'the commercial effect … is that the item is being sold but the sale process is not yet complete'.[27]

2.6.1 *Conditions for linked presentation*

FRS 5 says that the linked presentation should be used when an asset is financed in such a way that:

(a) the finance will be paid only from proceeds generated by the specific item it finances (or by transfer of the item itself) and there is no possibility whatsoever of a claim on the entity being established other than against funds generated by that item (or the item itself); and

(b) there is no provision whatsoever whereby the entity may either keep the item on repayment of the finance or reacquire it at any time.[28]

There are also some more specific conditions discussed below.

Part (b) above makes it clear that the non-recourse nature of the borrowing is not sufficient to justify the linked presentation; the entity must also relinquish its grip on the asset by dedicating it to repay the loan. The requirement to include both non-recourse finance and the related asset in a balance sheet illustrates an important feature of the standard's philosophy. Financiers tend to think of the isolation of risk as being the primary consideration in relation to questions of whether items should be included in the balance sheet or not. To them, the question as to which assets are available as security for which borrowings is of great significance and they would like the accounts to focus on this criterion. However, FRS 5 approaches the matter from a different angle: it wants to identify those assets and activities which are within the control of the reporting company and are a source of benefits and risks to it, because these are the things which are relevant to an assessment of the company's performance. In this context, the question of who has claims over which asset is of lesser importance, although perhaps it is one which lends itself to note disclosure.

The detailed qualifying criteria which have to be satisfied in order to justify a linked presentation are explained in the following terms:

(a) the finance relates to a specific item (or portfolio of similar items) and, in the case of a loan, is secured on that item but not on any other asset of the entity;

(b) the provider of the finance has no recourse whatsoever, either explicit or implicit, to the other assets of the entity for losses and the entity has no obligation whatsoever to repay the provider of finance;

(c) the directors of the entity state explicitly in each set of financial statements where a linked presentation is used that the entity is not obliged to support any losses, nor does it intend to do so;

(d) the provider of the finance has agreed in writing (in the finance documentation or otherwise) that it will seek repayment of the finance, as to both principal and interest, only to the extent that sufficient funds are generated by the specific item it has financed and that it will not seek recourse in any other form, and such agreement is noted in each set of financial statements where a linked presentation is used;

(e) if the funds generated by the item are insufficient to pay off the provider of the finance, this does not constitute an event of default for the entity; and

(f) there is no provision whatsoever, either in the financing arrangement or otherwise, whereby the entity has a right or an obligation either to keep the item upon repayment of the finance or (where title to the item has been transferred) to reacquire it at any time. Accordingly:

   (i) where the item is one (such as a monetary receivable) that directly generates cash, the provider of finance will be repaid out of the resulting cash receipts (to the extent these are sufficient); or

   (ii) where the item is one (such as a physical asset) that does not directly generate cash, there is a definite point at which either the item will be sold to a third party and the provider of the finance repaid from the proceeds (to the extent these are sufficient) or the item will be transferred to the provider of the finance in full and final settlement.[29]

2.6.2 *Application of the criteria*

The ASB has made it clear that these highly detailed criteria are indeed meant to be interpreted restrictively and that, as a result, only a narrow category of assets is likely to qualify for linked presentation. The more important aspects of the criteria are discussed below. Further clarification of these requirements in the context of securitisations is provided in Application Note D to FRS 5, which is discussed at 3.4.2 below.

A Nature of assets financed – Condition (a)

The explanation section of FRS 5 enlarges on (a) above as follows: 'A linked presentation should not be used where the finance relates to two or more items that are not part of a portfolio, or to a portfolio containing items that would otherwise be shown under different balance sheet captions. Similarly, a linked presentation should not be used where the finance relates to any kind of business unit, or for items that generate the funds required to repay the finance only by being used in conjunction with other assets of the entity. The item must generate the funds required to repay the finance either by unwinding directly into cash (as in the case of a debt), or by its sale to a third party.'[30]

B Who is the 'provider of finance'? – Conditions (b) and (d)

An essential condition for achieving linked presentation is that the provider of finance has no recourse other than to specific assets. It is obvious that the party that advances the non-recourse finance is a 'provider of finance'. However, in our view, where the nature of a non-recourse borrowing is altered by the use of one or more financial instruments, it may well be that any counterparty to those instruments must also be regarded as a 'provider of finance' for the purposes of FRS 5, and therefore have limited recourse to the specific assets concerned. This is illustrated by the following example.

Example 18.6: Linked presentation (modification of main borrowing through derivatives)

A company wishes to securitise some of its long-term sterling receivables. It does so by issuing a euro loan note secured on the receivables, on terms such that the transaction satisfies the criteria for linked presentation. To remove its exposure to the sterling/euro exchange rate, the company enters into a pay euro/receive sterling currency swap with a third party.

Where a company enters into a swap in this way, it would normally account for the swap and the euro borrowing together as a single synthetic sterling borrowing. If the company wishes to do this in the present case, and then to show the resulting synthetic sterling borrowing as linked finance, it is, in our view, essential that the conditions for linked presentation are satisfied not only in respect of payments due to the euro noteholders, but also in respect of payments due to the swap counterparty.

In a normal swap arrangement, this would not be the case, since the agreement would simply provide for a series of payments (or net payments) on particular dates, without regard to the performance of other assets of the entity. To achieve linked presentation, it will therefore be necessary to modify the terms of the swap such that the company is obliged to make payments under it only to the extent that funds are available from the realisation of the securitised assets. In many cases, some such provision would be made in the swap agreement, as much as means of controlling the company's credit exposure on the swap as of achieving a particular accounting outcome.

If the conditions for linked presentation were not met in respect of the company's obligations under the swap, the company would have two accounting options:

- to treat the borrowing and the swap as a synthetic sterling borrowing, but without using linked presentation;
- to use linked presentation in respect of the euro borrowing only, with the debtor or creditor arising from the swap shown separately. In our view, this solution, while permissible, is very unsatisfactory, as it divorces a hedging instrument from the transaction that it is seeking to hedge.

As discussed further at 3.4 below, the Application Note in FRS 5 on securitisations allows, in certain very limited circumstances, linked presentation to be adopted in respect of borrowings hedged with certain interest rate swaps, even though the obligations under the swaps do not themselves meet the criteria for linked presentation. Some might argue that this 'concession' should be extended to other hedging instruments. In our view, however, the rules in the Application Note are so tightly drawn, that they are to be read as applying exclusively to the precise circumstances that they describe.

C No recourse to entity – Conditions (b) and (e)

A number of the other conditions concern the need for the entity to be protected from losses in respect of the item transferred. FRS 5 notes that the forms of recourse which could breach these conditions are the following:

- an agreement to repurchase non-performing items or to substitute good items for bad ones;
- a guarantee given to the provider of the finance or any other party (of performance, proceeds or other support);
- a put option under which items can be transferred back to the entity;
- a swap of some or all of the amounts generated by the item for a separately determined payment; or
- a penalty on cancelling an ongoing arrangement such that the entity bears the cost of any items that turn out to be bad.[31]

Where conditions such as these apply to a funding arrangement, it is not possible for a company to achieve linked presentation by insuring against them if, in the event that the insurer were to fail, the company would still have to fulfil its obligations under the insured risks out of its own resources. Whilst the insolvency of the insurer might be remote, its effect would be that condition (b) in 2.6.1 above would not be satisfied, since this requires the provider of finance to have 'no recourse whatsoever' to the company, and the company to have 'no obligation whatsoever' to repay the provider of finance. It would, however, be quite acceptable (as is often the case) for the company to enhance the quality of the assets to be financed by purchasing insurance against risks such as slow payment or default for the benefit of the provider of finance, so long as the provider of finance, and not the company, bears the risk of any default by the insurer.

D Disclosure requirements – Conditions (c) and (d)

Under the standard, the use of the linked presentation is expressed as being mandatory whenever all the conditions listed above are met. However, because compliance with some of the conditions is itself voluntary, the treatment is in reality optional. For example, both conditions (c) and (d) above mean that the use of the linked presentation is conditional on certain disclosures being made in the accounts; it is therefore open to anyone who does not wish to use it to avoid doing so simply by failing to make the required disclosures and thus being disqualified from using the linked presentation.

An example of the use of the linked presentation is shown below:

Example 18.7: Linked presentation (disclosure)

Company A has a portfolio of receivables totalling £500,000. Past experience suggests that bad debts will not exceed 3%. It transfers title to the receivables to Company B in exchange for proceeds of £460,000 plus a further amount which varies according to when or whether the receivables are realised. In addition, Company B has recourse to Company A for the first £50,000 of any losses. Assuming all the conditions for a linked presentation are met, Company A's balance sheet would contain the following items:

	£000
Receivables subject to financing arrangements	
Gross receivables (after bad debt provision of £15,000)	485
Less: non-returnable proceeds	(410)
	75

The other £50,000 of the proceeds from Company B (i.e. the returnable portion) would be shown within creditors.

Inchcape has used a linked presentation in relation to discounted debts, as shown below:

Extract 18.4: Inchcape plc (2000)

14 Debtors [extract]

	2000	Group 1999
	£m	£m
Amounts due within one year:		
Trade debtors subject to limited recourse financing	**2.2**	3.1
Less: non-returnable amounts received	**(2.0)**	(2.8)
	0.2	0.3
...		
Amounts due after more than one year:		
Trade debtors subject to limited recourse financing	**20.2**	28.1
Less: non-returnable amounts received	**(18.0)**	(25.1)
	2.2	3.0
...		

Trade debtors subject to limited recourse financing represent hire purchase debtors discounted with banks, so that the majority of cash received by the Group on discounting is not returnable, that carry interest at variable rates. The returnable element of the proceeds is recorded as bank loans and overdrafts due within and after one year as appropriate. It has been agreed with the banks that the Group is not required to make good any losses over and above the agreed recourse limit.

As can be seen above, Inchcape has set out its note so as to segregate the debtors that are subject to limited course financing from those that are not, and the standard can be read as requiring this. However, this is not the only possible interpretation, and some other companies simply deduct the non-recourse finance from the total of the relevant category, and disclose the amount involved by way of footnote. Cookson provides an example of this.

Extract 18.5: Cookson Group plc (2000)

14 Debtors [extract]

	2000	Group 1999
	£m	£m
Amounts falling due within one year:		
Gross trade debtors	**496.9**	427.9
less: non-returnable proceeds	**(22.1)**	(14.3)
	447.5	413.6

...

The Group operates an asset securitisation programme in respect of certain of its US trade debtors. Under the terms of this programme, an interest in a pool of trade debtors is sold to a bank in exchange for cash, on which interest is payable to the bank. A security interest has been granted to the bank over this pool, which at 31 December 2000, comprised £75.3m (1999: £46.1m) of trade debtors, of which the cash received to date was £22.1m (1999: £14.3m).

The Group is not obliged (and does not intend) to support any losses arising from the assigned debts against which cash has been advanced. The providers of the finance have confirmed in writing that in the event of default in payment by a debtor, they will seek repayment of cash advanced only from the remainder of the pool of debts in which they hold an interest, and that repayment will not be required from the Group in any other way.

E No provision for retention or reacquisition of asset – Condition (f)

Consistent with the analysis of a linked presentation transaction as an incomplete sale (see 2.6 above), FRS 5 requires there to be no provision whatsoever whereby the originator (i.e. the original owner of the assets that are the subject of the transaction) can reacquire, or be compelled to reacquire, the assets concerned.

2.6.3 *Profit and loss account treatment*

Although the standard insists that gross amounts are disclosed for balance sheet purposes, it allows the corresponding revenues and costs to be dealt with net on the face of the profit and loss account and grossed up only in the notes, except if presentation of the gross figures on the face of the profit and loss account is thought necessary in order to give a true and fair view.[32] This is a rather glib statement, which does not really consider where in the profit and loss account such items may belong – for example, they may be a mixture of operating and financing items, in which case it would be inappropriate to present them on a single line. The standard offers no suggestion as to how items are to be presented in the cash flow statement.

FRS 5 says that, insofar as the non-returnable proceeds received exceed the amount of the asset being financed, the entity should regard the excess as a profit, but that otherwise profits and losses should continue to be recognised in the periods in which they arise. However, this exposes the essential ambiguity of the linked presentation as discussed at 2.6.1 above – i.e. does it reflect an incomplete sale or a strong linkage between non-recourse debt and the asset on which it is secured?

The problem is that the rules as to profit recognition quoted above are not really consistent with either of these interpretations. If the transaction *is* a sale then it would be appropriate to measure the profit *or loss* based on the difference between the proceeds and that proportion of the previous carrying value which is regarded as being sold – in other words it falls directly within the rules for partial derecognition discussed in 2.5 above. On the other hand, if it is *not* a sale, then it would not be appropriate to recognise any profit at that stage, whether or not the non-returnable proceeds exceeded the carrying value of the asset.

2.6.4 *Interaction with regulatory requirements*

As noted above, the linked presentation was initially devised by the ASB in response to strong representations from UK banks in relation to certain securitisation transactions, but use of the treatment is not confined to any particular kind of asset.

Entities that enter into transactions qualifying for linked presentation tend to have slightly different motives for doing so. Banks and similar regulated entities achieve both an acceleration of cash inflows and an enhancement of their capital base for regulatory purposes (because debt subject to linked presentation is treated more favourably than other debt in determining their required levels of capital). Other entities achieve only an acceleration of cash inflows, since it appears that credit rating agencies regard finance subject to linked presentation as no different from any other liability.

In the case of banks and similar entities, the UK regulators have hitherto tended to take the view that non-recourse borrowing achieves a reduction in debt for regulatory capital purposes only if it meets the criteria for linked presentation under FRS 5. However, our recent experience is that the UK Financial Services Authority may accept a transaction that does not fully meet the criteria for linked presentation in FRS 5 (but does meet its own detailed requirements and is approved by it) as effective in reducing debt for regulatory purposes. In our view, this is an extremely welcome development, since it recognises the fact that, for regulated entities, the issue is simply one of whether the entity has irrevocably reduced its overall exposure. FRS 5, on the other hand, regards such transactions more as an incomplete sale, and therefore imposes conditions which are arguably irrelevant to a simple determination of the entity's debt exposures.

If the regulatory requirements can be divorced from the accounting treatment (as is the case in most other major countries), the way would open for the abolition of the linked presentation for accounting purposes. In our view this would greatly improve financial reporting in the UK, since linked presentation is a highly ambiguous accounting treatment with shaky conceptual foundations that is not adopted anywhere else in the world. Whatever its pragmatic advantages, its introduction did not add to the elegance of the standard, particularly given the obsessively complex qualifying conditions which accompany it. Moreover, the legal complexity of most securitisation transactions is such that there must also be a concern that in practice linked presentation is being applied (in good faith) to transactions which do not strictly meet all the criteria for it.

2.7 Offset

FRS 5 makes it clear that assets and liabilities which qualify for recognition should be accounted for individually, rather than netted off. It is a general tenet of accounting practice that assets and liabilities should be dealt with separately in the absence of reasons for offsetting them, and this principle is also recognised in the Companies Act.[33] Netting off is allowed by the standard only where the debit and credit balances are not really separate assets and liabilities,[34] for example where they are amounts due to and from the same third party and where there is a legal right of set-off.

2.7.1 *Offset rules*

The detailed criteria which permit offset are set out in FRS 5 as follows:

(a) The reporting entity and another party owe each other determinable monetary amounts, denominated either in the same currency, or in different but freely convertible currencies. For this purpose a freely convertible currency is one for which quoted exchange rates are available in an active market that can rapidly absorb the amount to be offset without significantly affecting the exchange rate.

(b) The reporting entity has the ability to insist on a net settlement. In determining this, any right to insist on a net settlement that is contingent should be taken into account only if the reporting entity is able to enforce net settlement in all situations of default by the other party.

(c) The reporting entity's ability to insist on a net settlement is assured beyond doubt. It is essential that there is no possibility that the entity could be required to transfer economic benefits to another party whilst being unable to enforce its own access to economic benefits. For this to be the case it is necessary that the debit balance matures no later than the credit balance. It is also necessary that the reporting entity's ability to insist on a net settlement would survive the insolvency of the other party.[35]

The crux of the test is that the entity can enforce a right of set off so that there is no possibility of having to pay the creditor balance without recovering the debtor amount. Conditions (b) and (c) above seem only to be different elaborations of the same point.

2.7.2 *Application of the offset rules*

Some detailed aspects of the criteria are discussed below.

A Limitation of offset to two parties

Condition (a) above refers to offset of amounts owed between the reporting entity and 'another party'. This implies that offset is not permitted where more than two parties are involved, even where the reporting entity has enforceable rights which allow an amount due from one party to negate or reduce a liability to another (as could be allowed under IAS – see 4.3.2 A below). The rationale for this seems to be that FRS 5 is not really concerned with the likelihood of the liability being settled separately. Rather, as explained above, the argument is that what is being represented is not strictly the 'offset' of a discrete asset and liability, since in reality there is only a single net asset or liability. Indeed, for this reason, FRS 5 describes offset as 'necessary'[36] rather that merely permissible.

On this view, it is hard to see how a single net asset or liability could ever arise between more than two parties, a view strongly reinforced by the fact that the FRS 5 considers it necessary to clarify the position for groups of companies as set out in B below.

B *Offset between groups*

The explanation section of FRS 5 clarifies that, where the reporting entity or the other party is a group, offset of balances between the two groups is in principle permitted, even though more than two legal entities are involved. For example, if the A group has two subsidiaries A1 and A2, and the B group also has two subsidiaries B1 and B2, it may be possible to offset an amount due from A1 to B2 against an amount owed by B1 to A2. In such cases, FRS 5 notes that it is particularly important to ensure that the law of insolvency applicable to each party to the offset balances would allow the conditions set out above to be satisfied.[37] This may be particularly difficult where the legal entities involved are in different jurisdictions (see also C below).

One of the most common issues that arises in relation to these offset rules is the extent to which the various bank balances and overdrafts of various companies within a group that involve the same bank can be netted down in the consolidated accounts. Although the conditions of the banking arrangements will generally allow for a degree of offsetting, they do not always meet the demanding tests of FRS 5, and it is necessary to consider the precise contractual terms in each case. Tesco discloses the following note in relation to its banking arrangements:

Extract 18.6: Tesco PLC (2001)

Note 17 Creditors falling due within one year [extract]

	Group		Company	
	2001	2000	**2001**	2000
	£m	£m	**£m**	£m
Bank loans and overdrafts (a)	**1,389**	832	**1,312**	1,327

a) Bank deposits at subsidiary undertakings of £847m (1998 – £746m) have been offset against borrowings in the parent company under a legal right of set-off.

C *Certainty of ability to settle net*

Conditions (b) and (c) above require the reporting entity's ability to settle net to be 'beyond doubt' and to 'survive the insolvency' of the other party. Whether these conditions are satisfied or not is essentially a matter of law, but it is clear that FRS 5 requires absolute, rather than reasonable, assurance that the arrangements will succeed in all cases. Where amounts are owed between a UK group and members of another group incorporated overseas, it may simply not be possible to obtain the level of legal comfort necessary to satisfy the offset conditions in FRS 5. This is especially the case where the insolvency law of the overseas jurisdiction concerned is based on case-law rather than statute (making it less easy to predict the outcome in a particular situation), as is the case in some states in the US.

It is also important that, unlike IAS (see 4.3.2 B below), FRS 5 requires only that the reporting entity is able to settle net, rather than that it intends, or is even likely, to do so. Indeed, in referring to the possibility of the credit balance maturing before the debit balance (see paragraph (c) in 2.7.1 above), FRS 5 suggests that it does not anticipate actual net settlement as the norm.

D Offset of non-monetary amounts

Condition (a) above refers to the parties owing each other determinable monetary amounts in freely convertible currencies. However, we do not see any reason why, in principle, a non-monetary asset and liability should not be offset (subject to the other criteria in FRS 5 being satisfied), provided that the asset and liability are identical or fungible, such as where:

- one member of a UK group is required to deliver a non-monetary asset (such as shares) to a third party which is then required to deliver them to another member of the group;
- the reporting entity and another party are required to deliver a commodity (e.g. gold) to each other, with physical settlement.

However, there could, in our view, be no question of extending the offset criteria in this way to a non-monetary asset and liability that were not identical or fungible, such as where the reporting entity was required to deliver a machine to another party that was required to deliver cocoa in return.

E Deferred tax assets and liabilities

Deferred tax assets and liabilities accounted for under FRS 19 – *Deferred Tax* – are subject to specific offset rules using criteria somewhat different from those in FRS 5. These are discussed in Chapter 24 at 5.9.3 A.

2.8 Consolidation of other entities

The question of whether or not to consolidate the accounts of another entity can also be thought of as involving an off balance sheet finance issue. If an investee company is included in consolidated accounts, its assets and liabilities are shown on a line by line basis with those of the investor, whereas if it is only equity accounted, or carried at cost, it will be shown on one line, simply as an investment.

As discussed in Chapter 5, the definition of a 'subsidiary undertaking' introduced by the Companies Act 1989 means that consolidation of other entities is now based largely on de facto control. This change curtailed one of the major areas of abuse which had been possible under the old legislation, since it was previously very easy to conduct business through another company while keeping it outside the Companies Act definition of a subsidiary. However, FRS 5 takes the view that even the present definition is not conclusive in determining what entities are to be included in consolidated accounts. For example, the definition of 'subsidiary undertaking' would not include a trust established under UK law.[38] FRS 5 therefore envisages that there will be occasions where the need to give a true and fair view will require the inclusion of 'quasi subsidiaries'. This means that, even if a subservient entity escapes the legal definition of a subsidiary undertaking, it will still have to be consolidated as a quasi subsidiary if that is what the substance of the relationship dictates.

2.8.1 *Quasi-subsidiaries*

FRS 5 defines a quasi subsidiary in these terms:

'A quasi subsidiary of a reporting entity is a company, trust, partnership or other vehicle that, though not fulfilling the definition of a subsidiary, is directly or indirectly controlled by the reporting entity and gives rise to benefits for that entity that are in substance no different from those that would arise were the vehicle a subsidiary.'[39]

The key feature of the above definition is control, which in the context of a quasi subsidiary means the ability to direct its financial and operating policies with a view to gaining economic benefit from its activities.[40] Control is also indicated by the ability to prevent others from exercising those policies or from enjoying the benefits of the vehicle's net assets.[41] The Explanation section of FRS 5 emphasises that it is important to focus on the benefit flows from the *net* assets of the quasi subsidiary rather than on access to the whole of the benefit inflows arising from its gross assets and responsibility for the whole of the benefit outflows associated with its liabilities. This is because, from the point of view of the group, many subsidiaries do not give rise to a possible benefit outflow equal to their gross liabilities. Indeed, the limiting of benefit outflows in the event of losses occurring may have been a factor for the parent in establishing a subsidiary. In addition, as the liabilities of a subsidiary have a prior claim on its assets, the parent will not have access to benefit inflows of an amount equal to those gross assets.[42]

Control can be derived from a variety of sources and may be exercised in a number of different ways, some of which may be more evident than others. The standard acknowledges that it can sometimes be very hard to ascertain who is exercising control. Sometimes there will be little overt sign that control is being exercised, yet it may still exist, even if invisibly. For example, the mere threat of the exercise of control may persuade the quasi subsidiary to behave in accordance with the dominant party's perceived wishes, so that the actual exercise of control never becomes necessary. Conversely, the mere fact that a particular party has a right of veto over the operations of an entity may not necessarily indicate that that party has control, unless the effect is that major policy decisions are taken in accordance with the wishes of that party. Thus, it would not be possible, for example for a company to ensure that an entity was not its quasi-subsidiary simply by giving a 'friendly' third party a right of veto that in reality would never be exercised.

If the ostensible owner of the enterprise has accepted (real) severe constraints on its normal powers of ownership, it must be apparent that the real benefits of ownership lie elsewhere. For example, its share in the profits earned by the enterprise might be limited to a nominal sum or to an amount which really represents only a lending return on its investment, or a fee for making the vehicle available to the 'real' owner.

Often all of the remaining profits will be perpetually diverted to another party in the form, say, of a payment under a contract (e.g. to manage the assets of the company). In such circumstances, it may be evident that the recipient of the payment is the equity owner in substance, while the ostensible owner is more in the nature of a lender or simply an intermediary with no real interest in the enterprise.

As with many complex relationships, it is often helpful to consider the position of each of the parties in turn as a means of analysing the overall substance of the arrangement. By understanding what has motivated each party to accept its own particular rights and obligations under the deal, it becomes easier to see the commercial reality of the structure as a whole.

An example of an arrangement involving the use of a quasi subsidiary is as follows:

Example 18.8: Quasi subsidiary

A hotel company, Company H, sells some of its hotels to Company B, the subsidiary of a bank. B is financed by loans from the bank at normal interest rates. H and B enter into a management contract whereby H undertakes the complete management of the hotels. It is remunerated for this service by a management charge which is set at a level which absorbs all the profits of B after paying the interest on its loan finance. There are also arrangements which give H control over the sale of any of the hotels by B, and any gain or loss on such sales also reverts to it through adjustment of the management charge.

In these circumstances, it is clear that the bank's legal ownership of B is of little relevance. All the profits of B go to H, and the bank's return is limited to that of a secured lender. In substance, H holds the equity interest in both B and the hotels that it owns. B will therefore be regarded as a quasi subsidiary of H and will be consolidated by it. As a result, all transactions between the two companies will be eliminated from the group accounts of H, and the group balance sheet will show the hotels as an asset and the bank loans as a liability. The group profit and loss account will show the full trading results of the hotels and the interest charged by the bank on its loans, while the inter-company management charge will be eliminated on consolidation.

A 'deadlock' 50:50 joint venture will still be off balance sheet for both parties, but only if the two parties concerned are genuine equals in terms of both their ability to control the venture and their interests in its underlying assets. Such a relationship will seldom exist where one of the parties is a trading company and the other is a bank, because banks are primarily in the business of financing their customers, not entering into real joint ventures with them on an equal basis.

Example 18.9: Deadlock joint venture

A retailer, Company R, transfers a number of its shops to a newly created company, Company N, which is owned 50:50 by R itself and a third party, Company T. The shops are leased back to R on operating leases on normal commercial terms.

Provided that N is a genuine 50:50 company and that the risks and rewards of ownership of the shops are henceforth to be shared equally between its two shareholders, then R will simply have an investment in a joint venture which will be accounted for under the gross equity method in its balance sheet. This means that, although N's gross assets and liabilities will be displayed as an analysis of R's net investment in the joint venture, the underlying assets (the shops) and liabilities (the finance for the shops) will no longer be shown within the tangible assets and the debt sections of R's balance sheet. However, there are many possible pitfalls, any of which might put the assets and liabilities back into these balance sheet categories.

The first of these is that if R exercises a dominant influence over N, then it will be a subsidiary undertaking rather than an associate and will have to be fully consolidated. To avoid this, control over N must be balanced evenly between R and T.

Second, the sale of the shops must have succeeded in transferring the risks and rewards of ownership to N, and there must be no mechanism whereby they are transferred back to R. This means that the lease must genuinely be an operating lease, but also that R must not participate in future gains and losses on the shops except in its capacity as a 50% investor in N. For example, it must not have the opportunity to buy the shops back other than at their then market value, nor can it provide a guarantee which protects either N or T against future falls in the value of the shops, except to the extent that it is required to do so as a tenant under a normal repairing lease.

Other factors that would cause the deal to be looked upon with suspicion would be any arrangement whereby the profits and losses of N were not borne equally by R and T. Such an arrangement might take the form of differential rights to dividends, but could include also other factors, such as management charges which had the effect of stripping out profits, or guarantees of N's borrowings which were given by R alone.

The key factor which really dictates the substance of the arrangement is the identity of the two investors in N and their objectives in entering into the arrangement. If T is another retailer, a property company or some other party which is also selling its own properties to N, and if the two investors are content to accept half of the risks and rewards of each other's properties, then off balance sheet treatment is appropriate. However, if T is a financial institution and is seeking to achieve a lender's return on the deal, then it is unlikely that the conditions for off balance sheet treatment will be met.

A 'Autopilot' companies

In some cases, a quasi subsidiary may be formed as a so-called 'autopilot' company. As its name implies, an 'autopilot' company is one whose activities (and the allocation of the benefits and risks) are, either wholly or to a material degree, predetermined and immutable, so that the ostensible owner of the quasi subsidiary has surrendered its normal rights of ownership, and with them, control. In these cases the standard suggests that the best way of identifying the party in control might be to determine who is receiving the benefits of the quasi subsidiary's activities, since it can normally be presumed that the party entitled to the benefits will have made sure that it retains control. FRS 5 states that evidence of where these benefits lie is often given by which party stands to suffer or gain from the financial performance of the entity (i.e. which party has the risks inherent in the benefits).[43]

An example of such an entity might be a bankruptcy-remote company such as that described in Example 18.3 at 2.5.2 above, which would tend to be set up with a memorandum and articles (or local equivalent) effectively permitting it to undertake a single transaction and others directly ancillary to it.

2.8.2 Interaction with legal requirements for consolidated accounts

Since the law requires consolidated accounts to be drawn up to include subsidiary undertakings, and FRS 5 says that quasi subsidiaries (which by definition are not subsidiary undertakings) should also be so included, it is necessary to reconcile these two requirements. This is done by reference to the 'true and fair override', the provisions of the Companies Act which say that, where compliance with the detailed rules of the Act would not be sufficient to give a true and fair view, then the company should either give additional information in the accounts or (in special circumstances) depart from the detailed rules in order to give a true and fair view.[44] Including a quasi subsidiary in the consolidation is regarded as giving additional information in terms of this requirement. Accordingly, compliance with the standard will not result in a breach of the law even though it involves extending the definition of what has to be consolidated. FRS 5 requires that when quasi subsidiaries are included in consolidated accounts, the fact of their inclusion should be disclosed, together with a summary of their own financial statements. Where there are a number of quasi subsidiaries which fulfil a similar purpose, their accounts can be combined for the purposes of this summary.[45] The 1999 accounts of Associated Nursing Services provided an example of this disclosure:

Extract 18.7: Associated Nursing Services plc (1999)

12. Investments held as Fixed Assets
b) Shares in quasi-subsidiaries [extract]

For the reasons given in note 1(b) the following companies are accounted for as quasi-subsidiaries at 31 March 1999.

Name of company	Description of shares held	Percentage shareholding	Nature of business
Ebbgate Nursing Homes Limited	Ordinary	50%	Nursing Homes
Ebbgate Nursing Homes (London) Limited	Ordinary	50%	Nursing Homes
Hornchurch VCT Limited	Ordinary	50%	Nursing Homes

A summary of the combined quasi-subsidiary financial statements is shown [in note 29 below]. These companies are all registered and operate in England and Wales.

29. Summary of Combined Quasi-subsidiaries' Financial Statements included in the Consolidated Financial Statements

a) Profit and Loss Account

For the year to 31 March	**1999** **£000's**	Restated 1998 £000's
Turnover	**7,236**	11,861
Cost of services	**(4,715)**	(7,475)
Gross profit	**2,521**	4,386
Operating expenses	**(1,386)**	(2,754)
Operating profit	**1,123**	1,632
Exceptional items – profit on sale of Nursing Homes	**205**	–
Net interest payable	**(1,286)**	(2,119)
Interest receivable	**168**	637
Net profit before taxation	**210**	150
Taxation	**(370)**	(39)
Net profit after taxation	**(160)**	111
Dividends	**–**	(225)
Retained loss for the financial year	**(160)**	(114)

There are no recognised gains or losses other than those shown in the profit and loss account shown above.

b) Balance sheet

As at 31 March	1999 £000's	Restated 1998 £000's
Fixed assets		
Tangible assets	**10,740**	20,302
Long term bank deposit	**–**	–
	10,740	20,302
Current assets		
Debtors	**281**	2,291
Bank deposits	**–**	5,300
Cash at bank and in hand	**129**	464
	410	8,055
Creditors: amounts falling due within one year	**(2,979)**	(16,510)
Net current assets	**(2,569)**	(8,455)
Total assets less current liabilities	**8,171**	11,847
Creditors: amounts falling due after more than one year	**(8,051)**	(11,861)
Provisions for liabilities and charges	**(32)**	(367)
Net assets	88	(201)
Capital and reserves		
Called up share capital	16	12
Share premium account	736	542
Profit and loss account	(664)	(755)
	88	(201)

c) Cash flow statement As at 31 March	1999 £000's	1999 £000's	1998 £000's	1998 £000's
Net cash inflow from operating activities		**447**		2,283
Returns on investments and servicing of finance				
Interest paid	**(975)**		(1,650)	
Dividends paid to non-equity shareholders	**–**		389	
Interest received	**2,214**		21	
Net cash outflow from returns on investments		**1,239**		(2,018)
Advanced Corporation Taxation	**–**		(72)	
Corporation tax	**(135)**		(88)	
Tax paid		**(135)**		(160)
Capital expenditure and financial investment				
Payments to acquire tangible fixed assets	**(235)**		(3,882)	
Receipts from sale of fixed assets	**8,039**		2,599	
Net cash outflow from capital expenditure and financial investment		**7,804**		(1,283)
Net cash outflow before financing		**(9,355)**		(1,178)

Management of liquid resources				
Receipt from cash placed on deposit				249
Financing				
Proceeds from share issue	**367**		283	
Shares redeemed	**–**		(400)	
Bank loan repayments	**(8,558)**		(3,029)	
Bank loan received	**6,161**		3,325	
Other loans received	**490**		700	
Other loans repaid	**(13,610)**		–	
Net cash inflow from financing		**(15,150)**		879
Decrease in cash in the financial year		**(5,795)**		(50)

In fact, these companies are treated as quasi-subsidiaries as a result of an earlier challenge from the Financial Reporting Review Panel which developed into a lengthy dispute. In its 1996 accounts the company had said this:

Extract 18.8: Associated Nursing Services plc (1996)

1 Accounting Policies

Basis of consolidation [extract]

... The Panel has queried the Company's treatment in its 1995 consolidated financial statements of three companies as Associated Undertakings and of two sale and leaseback transactions. The Panel has expressed the view that, under the terms of Financial Reporting Standard No 5, the Associated Undertakings should have been consolidated as quasi-subsidiaries and the properties sold under sale and leaseback arrangements should have remained on the Balance Sheet at cost or valuation with the sales proceeds being included in borrowings.

The same treatments have been adopted in the 1996 consolidated financial statements. The Company does not and cannot alone control the Associated Undertakings and the purchaser of the properties has no access to the sales proceeds. Following consultation with its Auditors the Board does not agree with the current views of the Panel. It should be noted that if the Panel's views were implemented they would have no material impact on the profit before taxation for the year ended 31 March 1996. Having regard to these matters and following consultation with its Auditors, the Board considers that it would be inappropriate at this time to change the Company's accounting policies but it is in continuing discussions with the Panel.

As a result of these continuing discussions, however, the company was eventually persuaded to change its mind. The Panel issued a Press Notice explaining the issue and its reasoning in the following terms:

'ANS had entered into joint ventures with two partners and had treated the joint ventures as associated undertakings in the 1995 and 1996 Financial Statements.

'In one case, which involved a joint venture with a bank, the board of the joint venture company was 'deadlocked'. In the Panel's view however the financial and operating policies of that company were substantially predetermined by underlying agreements; and through its interest in the joint venture ANS gained benefits arising from the net assets of the company such that it had control. In the other case a venture capital arrangement with five venture capital funds had been set up through an intermediary. In the Panel's view the financial and operating policies of that company were again substantially predetermined by underlying agreements. Although in this case ANS held only a minority of the ordinary share capital, the investor's interests were effectively limited and the Panel took the view that ANS gained benefits arising from the net assets of the company such that it had control.

'In the Panel's view therefore the substance of the arrangements was such that the companies were quasi-subsidiaries as defined by FRS 5. Consequently they should not have been accounted for by the equity method but treated, as FRS 5 requires, as though they were subsidiaries.

'Under the accounting treatment adopted by the company and challenged by the Panel only the company's share of the net assets of the companies in question were reflected in the consolidated balance sheet. In the Panel's view, which the directors have now accepted, the substance of the transactions is such as to require that, in accordance with FRS 5, the full amount of their assets and liabilities should be included in the consolidated balance sheet with appropriate changes to the consolidated profit and loss account.'[46]

The Panel's analysis was interesting in that the description of the arrangements set out above, and in particular the fact that ANS had equity ownership in the companies concerned, might have more obviously led to the conclusion that these entities were subsidiary undertakings under Companies Act,[47] rather than quasi subsidiaries under FRS 5. However, it is clearly impossible to form a full view of the true situation without sight of all the underlying documentation that was available to the Panel.

A *Companies with no subsidiary undertakings*

Most companies that have quasi-subsidiaries will also have actual subsidiary undertakings and be presenting consolidated accounts. However, a company that has no subsidiary undertakings as defined in the Act will ordinarily produce only entity accounts. FRS 5 deals with this issue by saying that if such a company has a quasi subsidiary then it has to present consolidated accounts incorporating the quasi subsidiary with the same prominence as is given to its unconsolidated accounts.[48]

B *Exclusion from consolidation of quasi subsidiaries*

As discussed in Chapter 5 at 5, the Companies Act permits subsidiary undertakings to be excluded from the consolidation under various circumstances. Only one of these grounds for exclusion applies to quasi subsidiaries under FRS 5 – the case where the quasi subsidiary has not previously been included in the consolidation and is held exclusively for resale.[49]

2.8.3 *'Quasi subsidiary' as an alternative to offset*

Many structured finance solutions involve the reporting entity borrowing a significant amount (say £100 million) from a special purpose vehicle (SPV) owned by a bank and immediately depositing the bulk of the borrowings (say £90 million) with the SPV, the economic effect being that only the net £10 million has been borrowed. However, for tax and other reasons, it may be the case that the gross borrowing and deposit do not meet FRS 5's offset criteria (see 2.7 above). In such cases, it is tempting to argue that that the SPV is a quasi subsidiary of the reporting entity (in order to achieve offset of the gross asset and liability through consolidation adjustments), rather than a subsidiary of the bank.

However, the arrangement needs to be examined carefully, in order to ensure that the reporting entity is not, in order to achieve a 'convenient' result, treating as a quasi subsidiary a vehicle which it would not treat as such in other circumstances. It is particularly important to distinguish between true quasi subsidiaries that are under the economic control of the reporting entity as defined in FRS 5, and an SPV such as that described above, which has been established as a conduit for a transaction by the reporting entity, but which is in fact controlled by the bank. In the case above, it is the bank that is exposed to loss of the £10 million net assets of the SPV, indicating that it is the 'economic', as well as the legal, owner of the SPV.

2.8.4 *'Quasi associates' and 'quasi joint ventures'*

FRS 5 only requires consolidation of quasi subsidiaries. It does not require equity accounting of 'quasi associates' or 'quasi joint ventures' – i.e. entities in which the reporting entity has no ownership interest, but over which it exercises significant influence or joint control. However, where such arrangements do apparently occur, it is often the case that a more detailed analysis reveals them to be a joint arrangement that it not an entity (JANE) or a structure with the form but not the substance of a joint venture. This would lead to the requirement, under FRS 9, for the reporting entity to account for its share of the assets, liabilities, income and expenditure of the arrangement in full. This is discussed further in Chapter 7 at 2.3.

2.9 Disclosure

FRS 5 has a general requirement to disclose transactions in sufficient detail to enable the reader to understand their commercial effect, whether or not they have given rise to the recognition of assets and liabilities.[50] This means that where transactions or schemes give rise to assets and liabilities which are *not* recognised in the accounts, disclosure of their nature and effects still has to be considered in order to ensure that the accounts give a true and fair view. One company that fell foul of this requirement was Burn Stewart Distillers. In its 1996 accounts, the chairman made these remarks:

Extract 18.9: Burn Stewart Distillers PLC (1996)

Chairman's Statement [extract]

… I am dismayed to have to report sharply reduced profits for the year ended 30 June 1996. The principal reason for this decline is the application of accounting standard FRS 5, introduced in 1994. The strict application of this standard, which is technical and subjective, has had a modest effect on our turnover, cost of sales and distribution costs, but has impacted heavily and disproportionately on profit before tax. In simple terms, what has happened is that profit which was expected to feature in the year under review was deferred until a subsequent period. The effect on profit before tax is accentuated because the required adjustments leave overheads and finance costs substantially unchanged. The standard has been applied to business with one of our customers. Because of the relationship which has evolved with that customer, our auditors have judged it to be, in effect, not independent. The directors do not share this view. The business with this customer was not unusual in either scale or profitability, nor was the relationship with the customer particularly unusual in our industry. However, the combination of circumstances which led our auditors to take this view were somewhat unique and we do not foresee this problem arising again.

The chairman therefore seemed to regard this transaction as of great significance but, curiously, the accounts did not really explain what it was all about. This led to intervention by the Review Panel, who reminded the company of the requirement mentioned above and persuaded it to issue a supplementary note to its accounts which explained the transaction in the following terms:

Extract 18.10: Burn Stewart Distillers PLC (1996)

SUPPLEMENTARY NOTE TO FINANCIAL STATEMENTS FOR THE YEAR ENDED 30 JUNE 1996 [extract]

1996 Material Transaction

Under the terms of a sale in December 1995, the company sold whiskies at an invoice value of £5.1m, the customer made an immediate part payment of £3.0m and the balance is receivable no later than 31 December 1996. Settlement in kind of all or part of the balance is provided for at the company's discretion. The directors have concluded in compliance with FRS 5 that this sale cannot properly be recognised in the results for 1996 since settlement of the outstanding balance is considered to be conditional upon a sale of the whiskies by the customer or by a refinancing of the customer's entire undertaking. The exclusion of the sale is further supported by the fact that the customer is regarded as financially dependent on the company since its principal source of income at the date of sale arose from a marketing consultancy agreement with the company effective from 1993. The profit and loss account therefore excludes the invoiced sale of £5.1m and the related profit of £2.3m. The balance sheets of the company and the group include (i) in stocks £2.8m (although legal title to the whiskies has transferred to the customer) – see revised note 10; and (ii) in creditors and accruals the part payment of £3.0m.

It appears from this supplementary note that the directors had come to share the auditors' views on the accounting treatment of this transaction, despite the wording of the chairman's statement, which was still attached to the same accounts. To put the transaction in context, the Review Panel noted that the purported profit on this transaction of £2.3m was to be compared with the group's total profit for the year (which excluded the effect of transaction) of £1.01m. As it turned out, this £2.3m profit was never fully realised, as explained in this note from the following year's accounts, which vindicated the decision not to recognise it in 1996.

Extract 18.11: Burn Stewart Distillers PLC (1997)

3 PROFIT ON ORDINARY ACTIVITIES BEFORE TAXATION [extract]

Profit on ordinary activities before taxation is stated after charging

	1997	1996
	£000	£000
Provision against stocks acquired from related party (note i)	775	-

(i) HURLINGHAM INTERNATIONAL LIMITED (HIL)

HIL is a small organisation with whom the company has had a business relationship since 1993. At no time has the company had any interest in the shares of HIL. HIL is independently managed and advised.

Under an agreement entered into between the company and HIL in February 1993 and terminated in December 1996, HIL provided a marketing consultancy service to the company, principally in relation to overseas markets. HIL provided valuable assistance to the company in connection with a number of important initiatives in the Far East. The company also contracted with HIL to support HIL in the development of a range of spirit brands, with these amounts recoverable against commissions and other revenues earned by HIL from its trading activities. Over the whole course of the agreement the company has made payments totalling £419,000 and in addition funded brand development expenditure totalling £95,000. As at 30 June 1996 the company had provided £336,000 against such costs and the balance has been provided against in full during the current year.

Under a subsequent agreement entered into between the company and HIL in March 1997 the company has been appointed exclusive supplier to HIL in respect of the range of spirit products which HIL sells in a number of overseas markets. During the year ended 30 June 1997, the company supplied products under this agreement to a value of £22,000, all of which remained outstanding at the year end.

In December 1995 the company contracted with HIL to sell specific maturing whiskies at a total price of £5,091,000 with a book value of £2,754,000, the terms of which required HIL to pay £3,000,000 cash upon delivery in December 1995, with the balance to be paid no later than December 1996. HIL borrowed the cash paid upon delivery from its bankers and granted them a security over the whiskies purchased. The contract provided that the objective of the sale was to put HIL into a position to sell its whole undertaking, including its brands, and allowed for early payment of the balance of the price if this objective was achieved before December 1996. The contract also provided for settlement in kind of all or part of the balance of the price at the company's discretion. In addition, the company warranted to the bank which had provided funds to HIL that on 27 December 1995 the stocks were fairly valued at £5,091,000 and that the net realisable value of the stocks was not less than £3,600,000. The directors concluded, following discussion with the auditors, that this transaction should not be recorded in last year's accounts because settlement of the outstanding balance of the purchase price was considered to be dependent upon a sale of the whiskies by HIL or by a refinancing or sale of HIL's undertaking.

The company allowed HIL an extension of time until 30 June 1997 to settle the balance of the purchase price. In March 1997, following the sale by HIL of all the stocks, the company elected under the terms of the contract to take settlement in kind by purchasing from HIL certain specified whisky stocks. In June 1997 the company negotiated and agreed with HIL the purchase of whisky stocks in an amount of £1,906,000. The company has therefore recorded £5,091,000 in turnover for the year in respect of the December 1995 transaction. A provision of £185,000 has been made in respect of the remaining balance due and still owing by HIL as at 30 June 1997. Since the company and HIL are deemed to be related parties, the company has also made a provision of £775,000 against the invoiced value of the stocks acquired so as to record them at a pro rata share of the book cost of the stock originally sold to HIL. The profit recognised in the year on the December 1995 sale amounts to £1,377,000.

A further general disclosure requirement of FRS 5 is to give an explanation where there are any assets or liabilities whose nature is different from that which the reader might expect of assets or liabilities appearing in the accounts under that description.[51] For example, disclosure might be made where an asset appears in the balance sheet but is not available for use as security for liabilities of the entity. The standard also calls for specific disclosures in relation to the use of the linked presentation and the inclusion of quasi subsidiaries in the accounts, both of which have been described above, and the various transactions dealt with in the Application Notes discussed below.

3 COMMON FORMS OF OFF BALANCE SHEET FINANCE

This section discusses some of the most common forms of off balance sheet transactions and illustrates how FRS 5 tries to deal with them. The topics discussed in 3.1 to 3.6 below are the subjects of specific Application Notes in FRS 5.

3.1 Consignment stock (Application Note A)

Stocks held on a consignment basis are common in certain trades, particularly in motor vehicle dealerships. Essentially, this usually involves the manufacturer retaining title to stock despatched to dealers. Whether such arrangements come within the realm of off balance sheet transactions will depend on the terms of the relevant agreement, which have to be considered in their entirety so that the overall substance of the arrangement can be judged. The basic question is whether the risks and rewards of the stock have passed to the dealer in substance, even though legal title has not been transferred; has the dealer already bought the stock, on extended credit terms, or is he merely 'borrowing' it from the manufacturer? This is discussed in Application Note A to FRS 5.

3.1.1 Principal factors

The principal terms of the contract which bear on this question will be:

- the rights of each party to the arrangement to have the stock returned to the manufacturer;
- the price at which the sale is set when ownership eventually passes to the dealer;
- the existence, and terms, of any deposit that the dealer is required to make with the manufacturer when the stock is supplied; and
- whether or not the dealer has the right to use the stock.

These matters are discussed in turn below.

A Right to return stock

If either party has an absolute right to have the stock returned, then it would be difficult to argue that ownership had passed in substance to the dealer. However, even then there might be room for debate if (as is frequently the case) this right is never exercised in practice and is therefore not seen as an important term of the contract. In practice, neither party will usually have complete freedom to have the stock returned, but will be bound by certain contractual obligations or subject to certain penalties and it will be necessary to evaluate whether these terms are more consistent with the stock being the property of the manufacturer or the dealer. In particular, the party enforcing the return of the stock may have to compensate the other party in some way which neutralises the benefit of having the right of return.

B Price charged for stock when ownership passes

If the price is based on the manufacturer's factory price at the date of that eventual sale, it will tend to indicate that the manufacturer has never relinquished the risks and rewards of ownership of the stock during the time that it has been in the dealer's possession. Conversely, if the price is based on that ruling at the date of the initial supply plus interest it will tend to indicate that ownership of the stock has passed in substance and that the dealer has received a loan from the manufacturer to finance it. The date at which title will eventually pass to the dealer is also relevant. If it will inevitably pass after a certain time period, such as 90 days, even if the dealer has not sold or used it, the transaction will have more of the character of a sale on deferred payment terms. If, however, title does not pass until some other critical event takes place, such as the onward sale by the dealer to the end user, then it will suggest that the dealer has not yet assumed the risks and rewards of ownership. The interrelationship of the duration of the arrangement and the price will also be significant, because it will indicate who is financing the stock and is bearing the risk of slow movement.

C Dealer deposits

A requirement for the dealer to make a deposit with the manufacturer when the stock is supplied may indicate the parties' expectations as to the eventual outcome of the transaction. The terms of any such deposit, taken together with the terms as to the sale price, will indicate who is bearing the cost of financing the stock while it is in the dealer's possession.

D Dealer's right to use stock

The exercise of the right to use the stock, e.g. for demonstration purposes, is likely to trigger transfer of the title to the dealer, but the mere existence of that right does not by itself mean that it is an asset of the dealer before the right is exercised.

3.1.2 Required analysis

Application Note A discusses these factors, but concludes only that the stock should be included on the dealer's balance sheet if it has access to the principal benefits and risks of the stock, emphasising that the relative importance of the various terms will depend on the circumstances of each arrangement. In practice, the benefits and risks of ownership will tend to be shared between the two parties rather more evenly than in some of the other arrangements discussed in this chapter. These other arrangements often involve transactions between a commercial enterprise and a financier where their motivations are quite distinct. In the case of consignment stock, the manufacturer and the dealer have the mutual objective of selling cars to the ultimate customer, and this can make it difficult to categorise the arrangement in the manner required by FRS 5.

The following example illustrates the thought process which FRS 5 calls for:

Example 18.10: Consignment stock

A car manufacturer, M plc, supplies cars to a dealer, D Ltd, on a consignment basis. The terms of the deal permit either party to have the cars returned or (at the option of M) transferred to another dealer. D has to pay a monthly rental charge of 1% of the cost of the car for the privilege of displaying it in its showroom and it also has to arrange its own insurance for the cars. When the car is eventually sold to a customer, D has to pay M the lower of:

(i) the factory price of the car when it was first supplied, or

(ii) the current factory price of the car, less all the monthly charges paid to date.

D also has to pay for the cars (on the same terms) if they remain unsold after three months.

This example shows that it can be difficult to interpret the substance of the deal. The available accounting choices rest on whether D is considered to have already bought the car in substance or whether it is merely borrowing it from M. In practice, these arrangements generally have some features of both, and their overall substance falls between the two; this example is a case in point, because the risks and rewards of ownership are shared between the parties to some extent. This is not a helpful answer, however; the deal can only be accounted for in one way or the other. It is not possible to show the cars 'half-on' the balance sheet.

The factors which point towards treating the cars as stock of D are:

- its obligation to pay for the cars after three months, and to pay a monthly rental in the interim, which might be regarded as a finance charge on the amount outstanding. (However, if it has an unfettered right of return, it can (theoretically) avoid the obligation to pay for the cars by returning them before three months have elapsed; also, unless the factory price has gone up by 1% per month, it is able to recoup some of the rental/finance charge.)
- the fact that it cannot be compelled to pay more for the cars than the original factory price at the date of supply
- its obligation to insure the cars. (However, it would be a simple matter to transfer that obligation to M and pay a slightly increased monthly rental without altering the substance of the deal, so this element is not very persuasive.)

The main factors which point towards treating the cars as stock of M are its ability to demand return or transfer of the cars, D's right to return them to it, and the fact that it is deriving rental income from the cars in the meantime. However, this rental income will have to be refunded to the extent that the factory price increases fall short of 1% per month.

On balance, it is likely that this deal would be regarded as a sale and the cars would therefore appear in the balance sheet of D. However, before reaching that conclusion it would be necessary to see how the deal in fact worked in practice and to identify which of the terms were of real, rather than theoretical, significance.

The balance would be fundamentally affected if the settlement price was changed to become the *higher* of the two elements. D would then have to pay at least the current factory price for the cars when they were eventually purchased. This means that it would not yet have secured the main benefits of ownership and it would therefore be inappropriate to record the cars on its balance sheet.

Since the substantive ownership of the stock is frequently difficult to agree upon, a more fruitful approach is sometimes to look at the other side of the balance sheet instead. In other words, rather than focusing on whether or not the dealer has an asset, with a corresponding obligation to pay for it, it can be more useful to consider whether it has a liability, with a corresponding right to obtain the asset.

This approach might also be more in tune with the typical form of consignment stock arrangements than the approach discussed in the application note. Deposits are often paid to manufacturers, not by the dealer, but by a finance company which then charges interest to the dealer in one form or another. Since the dealer has paid no deposit itself, it may initially consider that it has no asset to account for (leaving aside for the moment the question of whether it is the substantive owner of the cars) but if it has a clear obligation to the finance company then it will have to recognise a liability under FRS 5, and an equal and opposite asset to match it. The corresponding asset is not necessarily stock – it might be equally appropriate to regard it as a deposit.

Lookers includes deposits paid to manufacturers in its stock note, in addition to consignment stock and its interest in Motability buy-back vehicles:

Extract 18.12: Lookers plc (2000)

12 STOCKS

	Group	
	31st December 2000 £000	31st December 1999 £000
Goods for resale	**47,553**	42,932
Bulk deposit paid for vehicles on consignment	**1,234**	1,556
Interest bearing consignment vehicles	**3,689**	5,862
Motability buy-back vehicles	**8,168**	13,686
	60,644	64,036

Principal Accounting Policies

6 STOCKS [extract]

... Deposits paid for vehicles on consignment represent bulk deposits paid to manufacturers. Interest bearing consignment vehicles and motability buy-back vehicles are included in stocks. The related liabilities are included in trade and other creditors respectively.

Henlys shows consignment stock within its stocks note, and as with Lookers above its description seems to imply that the interest-bearing nature of the arrangement may have been a major factor that determined that it should be brought on balance sheet. The group used to disclose by way of footnote a further category of off balance sheet consignment stock whose risks and benefits remained with the supplier, but no longer does so.

Extract 18.13: Henlys Group plc (2000)

13 Stocks [extract]

	Group 2000 £000	Group 1999 £000
Raw materials	**31,358**	28,750
Work in progress	**37,888**	36,619
Finished goods	**49,598**	43,052
Consignment stocks	**2,276**	6,605
Properties held for sale	**538**	1,756
	121,658	116,782

Consignment stocks include interest bearing consignment vehicles and the corresponding liability has been included in creditors.

Where it is concluded that the dealer owns the stock in substance, it will appear on its balance sheet with a corresponding liability to the manufacturer (offset to the extent of any deposit). Where the liability escalates through time as a result of the application of interest, such interest will be charged to the profit and loss account as it accrues. Where it is concluded that the stock remains in the ownership of the manufacturer, the only item which the dealer will have to account for is any deposit paid, which will be shown as a debtor in its accounts. Whether or not the stock is on the balance sheet, the notes to the accounts should disclose the nature of the arrangement, the amount of consignment stock held and the main terms on which it is held, including the terms of any deposit.[52]

Signet, Wolseley and Cookson all disclose that they hold material amounts of consignment stock but that it remains off balance sheet, as shown in these extracts:

Extract 18.14: Signet Group plc (2001)

12 Stocks [extract]

Subsidiary undertakings held £78.1 million of consignment stock as at 27 January 2001 (2000: £51.5 million) which is not recorded on the balance sheet. The principal terms of the consignment agreements, which can generally be terminated by either side, are such that the Group can return any or all of the stock to the relevant suppliers without financial or commercial penalties and the supplier can vary stock prices.

Extract 18.15: Wolseley plc (2000)

12. STOCKS [extract]

Certain subsidiary undertakings have consignment stock arrangements with suppliers in the ordinary course of business. Items drawn from consignment stock are generally invoiced to the companies concerned at the price ruling at the date of drawdown. The value of such stock, at cost, which has been excluded from the balance sheet in accordance with the application notes included in FRS 5, amounted to £4.8m (1999 £3.7m).

Extract 18.16: Cookson Group plc (2000)

13 Stocks [extract]

In addition to the stocks recorded in the balance sheet, the Group held precious metals on consignment terms with a total value at 31 December 2000 of £287.6m (1999: £202.6m) including the additional consignment arrangements entered into in connection with the acquisition, during the year, of the jewellery products division of Engelhard-CLAL. The Group also held precious metals of behalf of customers for processing, the total value of which at 31 December 2000 was £24.2m (1999: £23.3m).

The Group's precious metal fabrication operations utilise significant amounts of precious metals, primarily gold. These metals are held on consignment under arrangements the terms of which provide inter alia that the consignor retains title to the metal and both parties have a right of return over the metal without penalty. In the majority of cases, the metal the Group fabricates for its customers is consigned or sold directly from the consignor to the Group's customers, the Group charging customers for the fabrication process. Alternatively, the Group purchases metal from the consignor and sells it concurrently to the customer, thereby eliminating the Group's exposure to market fluctuations in metal prices. In view of the nature of these arrangements, the metal stocks so held are not recorded in the Group balance sheet. Consignment fees are charged by the consignor and totalled £6.8m in 2000 (1999: £5.2m).

Application Note A does not discuss the appropriate treatment in the accounts of the manufacturer, but under general rules of revenue recognition (see Chapter 3) the manufacturer could not treat the stock as sold in most cases. It is therefore quite possible that the stock will end up being shown on the balance sheets of both parties.

3.2 Sale and repurchase agreements (Application Note B)

Transactions of this kind can take many forms, but the essential feature which unites them is that the company which purports to have sold the asset in question has not relinquished all the risks and rewards associated with the asset in the manner which would have been expected of a normal sale. If there is no significant change in the company's access to the benefits of the asset and exposures to its risks, FRS 5 requires that the sale should not be recorded and the asset in question should remain on the company's balance sheet. A straightforward illustration of the rules is given by this example:

Example 18.11: Sale with contract to repurchase

A whisky blending company, W plc, has several years' worth of maturing whisky in stock. It contracts to sell a certain quantity of the whisky to a bank for £5 million, and agrees to buy it back one year later for £5.5 million. The whisky remains on its own premises.

Under FRS 5, this series of transactions would be accounted for as a financing deal. W has not transferred the risks and rewards of ownership of the whisky to the bank; instead, it has merely borrowed money on the security of the whisky. The accounts will continue to include the whisky stock in the balance sheet and show the £5 million received as the proceeds of a loan, extinguished one year later by the repayment of £5.5 million (which includes an interest charge of £0.5 million which would be accrued through the year).

This is a clear-cut arrangement with no uncertainty as to its outcome. However, it would not be difficult to imagine a more complex arrangement, such as this:

Example 18.12: Sale with options to repurchase/resell

W plc sells the same quantity of whisky as before in Example 16.7 to X Limited (another whisky company) for £5 million. The whisky is stored in a third party warehouse and responsibility for the storage costs thus passes to X. W arranges put and call options with X to purchase the same quantity of the same or equivalent whisky in one year's time for £6 million. (The factor which makes the repurchase price higher in this case is that X has to bear the cost of storing the whisky for a year.)

If one assumes that the existence of both the put and the call options makes it inevitable that one or other party will exercise the option, then there seems little difference between this case and the previous one. Even though the precise identity of the whisky might be different when it gets it back, W seems to be disposing of its whisky stock only temporarily, and on that argument, FRS 5 requires it to remain on the balance sheet, with the £1 million differential in the price being accrued as warehouse rent and interest.

The example could be complicated further by removing the put option, so that W had the right to reacquire the whisky, but not the obligation to do so. Presumably, if it could buy the equivalent whisky cheaper from another source in a year's time it would do so (assuming it wanted the whisky back at all). Effectively, W would have retained the right to increases but disposed of the risks of decreases in value of the whisky. The appropriate accounting would depend on all the circumstances of the transaction; unless it was clear that the option was very likely to be exercised, then there would be a good argument that the sale should be taken at face value and the stock removed from the balance sheet; W's only remaining asset would be its option to purchase the whisky. However, this depends on all the terms of the arrangement, as discussed below.

The principal question to be answered in all such arrangements is whether the reporting company has made a sale in substance, or whether the deal is a financing one. In approaching this question, it is instructive to consider which of the parties involved will enjoy the benefits, and be exposed to the risks, of the property in question during the period between the sale and the repurchase transactions. In the most straightforward kind of arrangement, this will generally be indicated by the prices at which the two transactions are struck; for example, if they are both at the market values current at the date of each transaction, then the risks and rewards of ownership are passed to the purchaser for this period; however, if the second selling price is linked to the first by an interest element, then these risks and rewards remain with the original owner throughout the period and the purchaser has the position only of a lender in the deal.

3.2.1 Commitments or options to repurchase

Another key factor in evaluating such an arrangement is the part of the agreement which permits or requires the repurchase to take place. As already illustrated, this may take the form of a contractual commitment which is binding on both parties, but it may also take the form of a put option allowing the buyer to resell the asset to the vendor, a call option allowing the vendor to repurchase the asset from the buyer, or a combination of such options.

A Binding sale agreement, or put and call options

Where there is a binding commitment, it is clear that the asset will revert to the vendor and the only remaining factor which will determine the accounting treatment of the overall deal is the price at which the transactions are struck, as discussed above. The same is likely to be true where there is both a put and a call option in force on equivalent terms; unless the option is to be exercised at the then market price of the asset in question, it must be in the interests of one or other of the parties to exercise its option so as to secure a profit or avoid a loss, and therefore the likelihood of the asset remaining the property of the buyer rather than reverting to the vendor must be remote. However, the position is less clear where there is only a put option or a call option in force rather than a combination of the two.

B Buyer's put option

Where there is only a buyer's put option, the effect will be (in the absence of other factors) that the vendor has disposed of the rewards of ownership to the buyer but retained the risks. This is because the buyer will only exercise its option to put the asset back to the vendor if its value at the time is less than the repurchase price payable under the option. This means that if the asset continues to rise in value the buyer will keep it and reap the benefits of that enhanced value; conversely if the value of the asset falls, the option will be exercised and the downside on the asset will be borne by the vendor.

This analysis does not of itself answer the question of whether the deal should be treated as a sale or as a financing transaction. The overall commercial effect will still have to be evaluated, by taking account of all the terms of the arrangement and by considering the motivations of both of the parties in agreeing to the various terms of the deal; in particular it will need to be considered why they have each agreed to have this one-sided option. It may be, for example, that the downside risks of the asset value compared to the option price can be seen to be negligible, in which case the fact that they remain with the vendor is not very important to the evaluation of the whole arrangement. However, in other cases the fact that the vendor retains these risks might be very significant, and sufficient to prevent the deal being treated as a sale; if the buyer has the right to put the asset back to the vendor, and if it appears reasonably likely that this option might be exercised, then it would be difficult for the vendor to say that it had made a sale, and realised any profit, on a transaction which the other party was at liberty to reverse. In other cases again, the transaction might qualify for partial derecognition as discussed at 2.5 above – for example, where a commercial vehicle manufacturer has sold a truck and given the customer an option to put it back at a guaranteed price in 5 years' time.

C Seller's call option

Where there is only a seller's call option, the position will be reversed. In this case, the seller has disposed of the risks, but retained the rewards to be attained if the value of the asset exceeds the repurchase price specified in the option. Once again, the overall commercial effect of the arrangement has to be evaluated in deciding how to account for the deal. Emphasis has to be given to what is likely to happen in practice, and it is instructive to look at the arrangement from the point of view of both parties to see what their expectations are and what has induced them to accept the deal on the terms which have been agreed.

It may be obvious from the overall terms of the arrangement that the call option will be exercised, in which case the deal will again be a financing arrangement and should be accounted for as such – for example, the seller may continue to use the asset, and it could be obvious that its commercial need for it would compel it to exercise the option. Similarly, the financial effects of *not* exercising the option (such as continued exposure to escalating costs) may sometimes make it obvious that the option will be exercised. But in other cases, it could be quite likely that the option will not be exercised and if this is the case the transaction could be treated as a sale. The seller need not include a liability in its balance sheet for the exercise price of the option if it is quite conceivable that it would not exercise it; correspondingly, the asset in its balance sheet would simply be the call option itself, not the underlying property that is the subject of the option.

Another example is shown below:

Example 18.13: Sale at below market value with call option

A building company, B plc, sells part of its land bank to a property investment company, P plc, for £40 million at a time when its market value is £50 million. It has the right under the agreement to buy it back for the same price plus interest at any time in the next three years. Conversely, however, P has no corresponding put option to require B to buy it back.

The effect of this deal is that B is protected from a collapse in the value of the land below 80% of its former price, because it cannot be compelled to buy it back. It has therefore passed that risk to P (which has presumably charged for it accordingly in the interest rate implicit in the deal). But it has retained the rewards of ownership, because it can always benefit from an increase in value of the land by exercising its option. Moreover, at the time of entering into the deal, it must have expected that it would exercise the option – otherwise it would have sold the property for full value, not for £10 million less. FRS 5 would be likely to interpret this as a financing deal, rather than a sale.

D Call option at market value

Sometimes a sale agreement will provide for the seller with an option to reacquire the asset at a future date for its then current market value. This situation is not directly addressed by Application Note B. In principle, however, we believe that such an arrangement should result in the derecognition of the asset concerned, on the grounds that the effect of the arrangement is that the buyer bears all the risks and rewards of ownership of the asset from the date of original sale to the date of repurchase (or until the buyer otherwise disposes of the asset).

There is however some tension on this issue in the Application Note, which suggests that it should be assumed that an option will be exercised, unless it is 'on terms that no genuine commercial possibility that the option will fail to be exercised', which include the possibility that the seller needs the asset on an ongoing basis in its business.[53] However, if the repurchase option is at a verifiable open market price, all the risks and rewards of the asset are transferred on original sale. There is no particular need to recognise the sale proceeds arising on the asset as (in effect) a liability to repurchase it, any more that if the company had sold one building, but was commercially required to reinvest the proceeds in another in order to conduct its business. In practice, however, the difficulty may be that it is difficult to ensure that there is a readily ascertainable market price for the asset concerned, so as to ensure that the option is truly at market value.

3.2.2 *Accounting treatment*

A Substance is a loan

Where the overall substance is that of a financing deal rather than a sale, neither a sale nor a profit will be recorded. Instead, the ostensible sales proceeds will be recorded as a loan, and any charges which are in substance interest on that loan will be accrued and disclosed as interest costs. (This means that they may qualify for capitalisation in appropriate circumstances – see Chapter 15.) A brief description of the arrangement and the status of the asset and the relationship between the asset and the liability should be disclosed in the notes to the financial statements.[54]

B Substance is a sale

Where the seller has made a sale and has a new asset and/or liability (such as an option) it should recognise or disclose such residual items as appropriate. Any unconditional commitment to repurchase needs to be recognised in the balance sheet, not merely disclosed. Profits and losses should be recognised on a prudent basis. The notes to the accounts should disclose the main features of the arrangement including the status of the asset, the relationship between the asset and the liability and the terms of any provision for repurchase (including any options) and of any guarantees.[55]

The 1998 accounts of Barratt Developments included a note showing that they had kept on the balance sheet houses sold to BES companies subject to a guarantee:

Extract 18.17: Barratt Developments PLC (1998)

13. STOCKS

Group	1998	1997
	£m	£m
Work in progress	551.3	415.4
Showhouse complexes and houses awaiting legal completion	111.3	107.5
Properties in Business Expansion Schemes	7.5	17.0
	670.1	539.9

In 1993 the group supported four Business Expansion Scheme companies to provide assured tenancy housing, all of which were fully subscribed at a total of £20.0m. A major portion of this amount was used to purchase properties at market value from various Barratt subsidiaries. The group gave guarantees that there would be sufficient cash resources available for distribution from the four BES companies in 1998 and 1999 to provide the BES investors with a guaranteed return per share. The sale of properties covered by the guarantees still in place has not been recognised in these accounts. The properties are held in the balance sheet at their original cost of £7.5m (1997 £17.0m). The sale proceeds of £8.3m (1997 £18.9m) are held in creditors and the profit attributable to the properties of £0.8m (1997 £1.9m) has not been recognised in these accounts.

Similarly, Gleeson made these disclosures in respect of properties sold to Business Expansion Scheme (BES) companies with an option to have them put back to it after five years:

Extract 18.18: M J Gleeson Group plc (1998)

1. Accounting policies [extract]
Stock and work in progress

iv) Properties sold to Cavendish Gleeson Cash Backed PLC are included in Stock and work in progress at their original cost and their sale proceeds are added to Deferred income.

22. Business Expansion Scheme Companies [extract]

The Company had previously entered into commitments in the form of put and call options with three BES companies. These commitments required the Company, on exercise of the Options, to purchase residential properties from these companies at such prices as to enable the shareholders to receive a set return on their investment. The substance of these transactions was that of secured loans and, in accordance with FRS 5, the cost of financing these debts (being the difference between the issue proceeds and the ultimate cost of exercising the options) was allocated over the periods of the loans at fixed rates. On February 19th 1998 and April 2nd 1998 the Company acquired the issued share capital of Cavendish Gleeson Guaranteed PLC and Cavendish Gleeson Second PLC respectively, two of the BES companies in settlement of the financing obligations in respect of these companies.

As at 30th June 1998 the remaining contingent liability in respect of the final BES company, Cavendish Gleeson Cash Backed PLC is £6,000,000 with an option to exercise date of 31st December 1998.

Although the policy refers to the proceeds as deferred income, the outstanding amount was included within creditors in the balance sheet, which is where it belongs.

3.2.3 *Sale and repurchase transactions in financial assets (repos)*

A common form of sale and repurchase agreement involves the 'sale' of an income-generating financial asset (very often a fixed income preference share) to a bank or other financial institution with an obligation to repurchase it for the same amount at some future date. There is clearly no question that FRS 5 requires the 'seller' to account for the transaction (often referred to as a repo) as a loan, with no derecognition of the asset.

The terms of the transaction will typically provide that during the period during which it is the legal owner of the shares, the bank keeps the dividends it receives. The commercial effect is that is that the bank receives interest on the 'loan' equal to the dividend income from the shares. However, the repurchase price will typically be adjusted by a formula designed to reimburse the bank, with interest, for any loss of income arising from non-performance of the asset. This raises the question as to whether, in its profit and loss account, the seller should:

(a) gross up its profit and loss account to show income from the shares and an interest expense; or

(b) simply provide for any excess of the interest due over the dividends actually paid on the shares while in the legal ownership of the bank.

The grounds for the treatment in (a) above are that if, for the purposes of the accounts, the seller is still held out to be the owner of the assets, it must still be earning the income on them. It is appropriate to record the interest on the loan as a separate item, as the seller is obliged to pay an amount equal to the dividend due on the shares as interest, whether or not the dividend is actually paid. The grounds for the treatment in (b) above would be that this reflects the reality of the underlying cash flows. This treatment also has some support from FRS 12 – *Provisions, Contingent Liabilities and Contingent Assets*. This requires that, where a liability is to be reimbursed by another party, the liability and the amount reimbursed should be shown gross in the balance sheet, but may be shown net in the profit and loss account (see Chapter 28 at 4.4).

In our view, method (a) is the more consistent with FRS 5's overall analysis of the transaction. However, as FRS 5 does not specifically address the profit and loss account treatment of such transactions, it cannot be said definitively to permit or prohibit one method or the other. In the seller's cash flow statement, however, nothing would be reflected apart from the receipt at the beginning, and the payment at the end, of the transaction.

3.2.4 *'Warehousing' arrangements*

FRS 5 states that Application Note B should be applied to arrangements under which one party holds an asset on behalf of another (sometimes called warehousing arrangements). Although such arrangements are not sale and repurchase agreements, they may have a similar commercial effect, so that a similar analysis is appropriate.[56]

An example of such an arrangement might be as follows.

Example 18.14: Warehousing arrangement

A bank buys a portfolio of shares on behalf of one of its clients A plc with a value of £10 million. A plc agrees to purchase the shares for their market value in one year's time. During the year A plc and the bank enter into a total return swap whereby A plc pays the bank interest on the amount paid by the bank for the shares and the bank pays A plc any increase (or receives from A plc any decrease) in the market value of the shares, on the assumption that any dividends received were immediately reinvested in further shares. Thus ensures that A plc receives a shareholder's return on the shares, whereas the bank receives a lender's return on the original cost of the shares.

The purchase commitment on its own would have no accounting consequences (either on a historical cost or a market value basis of accounting) for A plc, since it is a commitment to purchase at the prevailing market value (such that its fair value will always be nil and the contract could never become an onerous contract for the purposes of FRS 12 – see Chapter 28 at 2.1.2). Combined with the total return swap, however, the effect is the same as if:

- the bank had lent A plc £10 million, which had then been used to purchase the shares; or
- A plc had purchased the shares with its own resources and then entered into a repo (see 3.2.3 above) over the shares with the bank.

This suggests that Application Note B requires the shares to be recorded as an asset of A plc, and the £10 million as a liability to the bank, from the outset of the transaction. Payments on the interest 'leg' of the swap would be charged to the profit and loss account as an interest expense and receipts or payments on the equity 'leg' would be debited or credited to the carrying value of the liability in the balance sheet, so that this would equal the amount due at maturity. The accounting treatment of the shares would depend on A plc's accounting policy for similar investments (see Chapter 14).

3.3 Factoring of debts (Application Note C)

Factoring is a long-established means of obtaining finance by selling trade debtors so as to accelerate the receipt of cash following a sale on credit. The essence of the question posed by FRS 5 is again whether the transaction is really a sale in substance or whether it is simply a borrowing transaction with the trade debtors being used as collateral. Once again, the overall terms of the arrangement have to be considered in aggregate, and there may be a number of different services that the factor provides which will feature in this evaluation. Since there is no likelihood of any upside benefit in relation to debtors (except perhaps through reduced finance cost as a result of early payment) the focus in this case is on the risks of ownership rather than the rewards.

Application Note C says there are three possible treatments: derecognition, a linked presentation and a separate presentation. It does not mention 'partial' derecognition, although this could also be appropriate in some circumstances.

3.3.1 *Derecognition*

Derecognition will be appropriate if all the significant benefits and risks relating to the debts in question have been transferred to the factor. The standard indicates that this will normally be the case only if:

(a) the transaction takes place at an arms' length price for an outright sale;

(b) the transaction is for a fixed amount of consideration and there is no recourse whatsoever, either implicit or explicit, to the seller for losses from either slow payment or non-payment; and

(c) the seller will not benefit or suffer in any way if the debts perform better or worse than expected.[57]

If the conditions for derecognition are met, the debtors transferred will be set against the proceeds received from the factor with the difference being taken to the profit and loss account. Insofar as this represents discount on the sale of the debts it would seem appropriate to treat this as a finance cost, while other factoring costs should be included in administrative expenses.

3.3.2 *Linked presentation*

A linked presentation will be appropriate if the requirements of paragraphs 26 and 27 of FRS 5 are satisfied, as discussed in 2.6 above. In the context of debt factoring, this means that the trader may retain significant benefits and risks in relation to the factored debts, but there must be no arrangement permitting or requiring the trader to reacquire any of the debts and the trader must have limited its downside exposure to loss to a fixed monetary amount.[58]

Where a linked presentation is applied, the debtors will stay on the balance sheet but the amount of any non-returnable advance from the factor will be deducted from them rather than being shown as a separate liability. The factor's charges will be accrued, with the interest element being accounted for as interest expense, and other costs within administrative expenses, both of which are to be disclosed. The notes should also disclose the main terms of the arrangement and the gross amount of factored debts outstanding at the year end as well as the disclosures which are required by paragraph 27 of the FRS (see 2.6) whenever the linked presentation is used.[59]

3.3.3 *Separate presentation*

If neither of these sets of conditions is satisfied, a separate presentation is required. This means that the debtors will remain on the trader's balance sheet and amounts advanced by the factor will be shown as a loan within current liabilities. As with the linked presentation, the factor's charges should be accrued and appropriately analysed between interest and administrative expenses, but in this case the standard does not require these to be separately disclosed. The only required disclosure is the amount of factored debts outstanding at the year end.[60]

3.3.4 *Illustrative examples*

The Application Note contains two examples which illustrate different scenarios which could lead to different accounting treatments. These are as follows:

Example 18.15: Debt factoring with recourse

A company (S) enters into a factoring arrangement with a factor (F) with the following principal terms:

- S will transfer all its trade debts to F, subject only to credit approval by F and a limit placed on the proportion of the total that may be due from any one debtor;
- F administers S's sales ledger and handles all aspects of collection of the debts in return for an administration charge at an annual rate of 1% payable monthly, based on the total debts factored at each month end;
- S may draw up to 70% of the gross amount of debts factored and outstanding at any time, such drawings being debited in the books of F to a factoring account operated by F for S;
- F credits collections from debtors to the factoring account, and debits the account monthly with interest calculated on the basis of the daily balances on the account using a rate of base rate plus 2%. Thus this interest charge varies with the amount of finance drawn by S under the finance facility from F, the speed of payment of the debtors and base rate;
- any debts not recovered after 90 days are resold to S for an immediate cash payment which is credited to the factoring account;
- F pays for all other debts, less any advances and interest charges made, 90 days after the date of their assignment to F, and debits the payment to the factoring account; and
- on termination of the agreement the balance on the factoring account is settled in cash.

FRS 5 concludes that in substance the effect of these terms is that the deal is a financing one rather than an outright sale of the debts, and a separate presentation should be adopted. S continues to bear both the slow payment risk (the interest charged by F varies with the speed of payment by the debtors) and the bad debt risk (it must pay F for any debts not recovered after 90 days), and its exposure to loss is therefore unlimited.

Example 18.16: Debt factoring without recourse

A company (S) sells debts to a factor (F) on the following terms:

- S will transfer to F such trade debts as S shall determine, subject only to credit approval by F and a limit placed on the proportion of the total that may be due from any one debtor. F levies a charge of 0.15% of turnover, payable monthly, for this facility;
- S continues to administer the sales ledger and handle all aspects of collection of the debts;
- S may draw up to 80% of the gross amount of debts assigned at any time, such drawings being debited in the books of F to a factoring account operated by F for S;
- weekly, S assigns and sends copy invoices to F as they are raised;
- S is required to bank the gross amounts of all payments received from debts assigned to F direct into an account in the name of F. Credit transfers made by debtors direct into S's own bank account must immediately be paid to F;
- F credits such collections from debtors to the factoring account, and debits the account monthly with interest calculated on the basis of the daily balances on the account using a rate of base rate plus 2.5%. Thus this interest charge varies with the amount of finance drawn by S under the finance facility from F, the speed of payment of the debtors and base rate;
- F provides protection from bad debts. Any debts not recovered after 90 days are credited to the factoring account, and responsibility for their collection is passed to F. A charge of 1% of the gross value of all debts factored is levied by F for this service and debited to the factoring account;
- F pays for the debts, less any advances, interest charges and credit protection charges, 90 days after the date of purchase, and debits the payment to the factoring account; and
- on either party giving 90 days' notice to the other, the arrangement will be terminated. In such an event, S will transfer no further debts to F, and the balance remaining on the factoring account at the end of the notice period will be settled in cash in the normal way.

FRS 5 concludes that the effect of these terms is that S continues to bear the slow payment risk for 90 days (the interest charged by F varies with the speed of payment by the debtors) but thereafter all risks pass to F. Since it has not disposed of all significant risks, derecognition is not appropriate, but since its exposure is limited, a linked presentation is available. This allows the non-returnable proceeds from F to be shown on S's balance sheet as a deduction from the debts factored. The amount to be deducted will be the lower of the proceeds received and the gross amount of the debts less all charges to the factor in respect of them.

3.4 Securitised assets (Application Note D)

Securitisation is a process whereby finance can be raised from external investors by enabling them to invest in parcels of specific financial assets. Domestic mortgage loans were the first main type of assets to be securitised in the UK, but in principle the technique can readily be extended to other assets, such as credit card receivables, other consumer loans, lease receivables and so on.

A typical securitisation transaction involving a portfolio of mortgage loans would operate as follows:

The company which has initially advanced the loans in question (the originator) will sell them to another company set up for the purpose (the issuer). The issuer may be a subsidiary or associate of the originator, or it may be owned by a charitable trust or some other party friendly to the originator; in either case, its equity share capital will be small. The issuer will finance its purchase of these loans by issuing loan notes on interest terms which will be related to the rate of interest receivable on the mortgages. The originator will continue to administer the loans as before, for which it will receive a service fee.

The structure will therefore be as shown in this diagram:

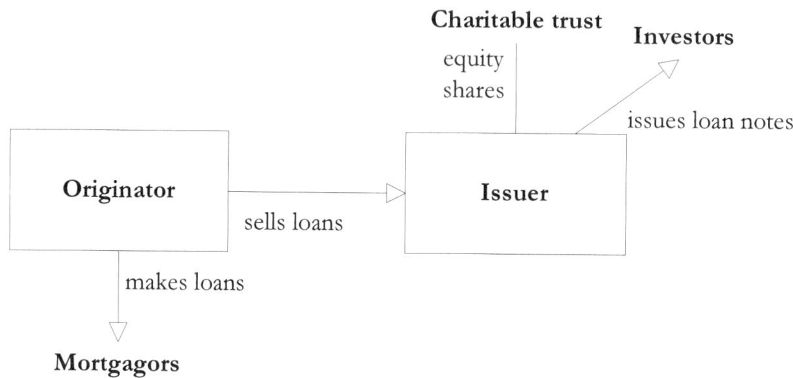

Potential investors in the mortgage-backed loan notes will want to be assured that their investment is relatively risk-free, and the issue will normally be supported by obtaining a high rating from a credit rating agency. This may be achieved by use of a range of credit enhancement techniques which will add to the security already inherent in the quality of the mortgage portfolio. Such techniques can include the following:

- limited recourse to the originator in the event that the income from the mortgages falls short of the interest payable to the investors under the loan notes and other expenses. This may be made available in a number of ways; for example, by the provision of subordinated loan finance from the originator to the issuer; by the deferral of part of the consideration for the sale of the mortgages; or by the provision of a guarantee;
- the provision of loan facilities from third parties to meet temporary shortfalls as a result of slow payments of mortgage interest; or
- insurance against default on the mortgages.

The overall effect of the arrangement is that outside investors have been brought in to finance a particular portion of the originator's activities. These investors have first call on the income from the mortgages which back their investment. The originator is left with only the residual interest in the differential between the rates paid on the notes and earned on the mortgages, net of expenses; generally, this profit element is extracted by adjustments to the service fee or through the mechanism of interest rate swaps. It has thus limited its upside interest in the mortgages, while its remaining downside risk on the whole arrangement will depend on the extent to which it has assumed obligations under the credit enhancement measures.

The question of whether or not the mortgage loans and the loan notes should appear on the balance sheet of the originator can be subdivided into two main issues:

(a) Whether the sale of the mortgages succeeded in transferring the risks and rewards of ownership from the originator to the issuer. Depending on the answer to this question, the accounting treatment will be either:

- derecognition, whereby the securitised assets are regarded as sold and therefore removed from the balance sheet;
- linked presentation, whereby the proceeds of the note issue are shown as a deduction from the securitised assets as a net figure within the assets section of the balance sheet; or
- separate presentation, whereby the gross securitised assets appear on the asset side of the balance sheet, with the proceeds of the issue within creditors.

In practice, most securitisations seek to achieve linked presentation. Derecognition is typically not possible since, as described above, the objective of most securitisations is for the originator to limit its exposure to losses, but still retain the benefit of any surplus arising from the securitised assets after the finance has been paid off. The retention of such benefits precludes derecognition.

Application Note D does not mention the possibility of 'partial' derecognition. This would only be appropriate if some of the significant benefits and some of the significant risks relating to the securitised assets were transferred to other parties as a result of the transaction while others were retained by the originator.

(b) Whether the issuer a subsidiary or quasi subsidiary of the originator. If it is, then the issuer's accounts will have to be consolidated with those of the originator, with the result that transactions between them will be eliminated on consolidation and the assets and liabilities which appear on the issuer's balance sheet will appear on the consolidated balance sheet of the originator.

3.4.1 *Originator's individual accounts*

A *Derecognition*

As with other forms of finance, FRS 5 says that derecognition is appropriate only if all the significant benefits and risks relating to the debts in question have been disposed of, which is likely to require that:

(a) the transaction takes place at an arms' length price for an outright sale;

(b) the transaction is for a fixed amount of consideration and there is no recourse whatsoever, either implicit or explicit, to the originator for losses from whatever cause. Normal warranties given in respect of the condition of the assets at the time of transfer would not breach this condition, but any warranties concerning their value or performance in the future would do so; and

(c) the originator will not benefit or suffer if the securitised assets perform better or worse than expected. This condition will not be satisfied where the originator has a right to further sums from the vehicle which vary according to the eventual value realised for the securitised assets.[61]

If all these conditions are met, the securitised assets are likely to be regarded as sold and will be removed from the balance sheet. They will be set against the proceeds received from the issue, with the difference being taken to the profit and loss account. If the conditions are not met, then either a linked presentation or a separate presentation is required.

B Linked presentation

A linked presentation will be appropriate if the requirements of paragraphs 26 and 27 of FRS 5 are satisfied, as discussed in 2.6 above. In the context of securitisation, this means that the originator may retain significant benefits and risks in relation to the securitised assets, but must have limited its downside exposure to loss to a fixed monetary amount. There must also be no arrangement under which the originator can reacquire any of the securitised assets in the future. These conditions are discussed further in paragraphs D10 to D13 of the Application Note, which make it clear that they are to be applied restrictively, as discussed below.

I Nature of assets securitised – paragraph 27(a)

A linked presentation should not be used where the assets that have been securitised cannot be separately identified. Nor should a linked presentation be used for assets that generate the funds required to repay the finance only by being used in conjunction with other assets of the originator.[62]

II Non-recourse agreement in writing – paragraph 27(d)

The requirement of FRS 5 for the provider of finance to agree in writing that it has no recourse to other assets of the originator will be satisfied where (as is typically the case) the noteholders have subscribed to a prospectus or offering circular that clearly states that the originator will not support any losses of either the issuer or the noteholders. Moreover linked presentation may be used where the noteholders have recourse to third party credit enhancement of the securitised assets (e.g. insurance). Where, however, credit enhancement is provided by the originator (e.g. through a guarantee), linked presentation is not appropriate.[63]

III No provision for originator to repurchase assets – paragraph 27(f)

Where there is provision for the originator to repurchase only part of the securitised assets (or otherwise to fund the redemption of loan notes by the issuer), the maximum payment that the originator could make pursuant to such a provision should be excluded from the amount deducted on the face of the balance sheet. Where there is provision for the issuer (but not the originator) to redeem loan notes before an equivalent amount has been realised in cash from the securitised assets (e.g. by borrowing additional funds from a third party), a linked presentation may still be appropriate. However, for this to be the case, there must be no obligation (legal, commercial or other) for the originator to fund the redemption (e.g. by repurchasing the securitised assets).[64]

IV Interest rate swaps and caps between originator and issuer

Suppose that an originator has a portfolio of floating rate mortgages which it wishes to securitise through the issue of fixed rate debt. Assuming the basic structure set out in the diagram above, the originator might sell the mortgages to the issuer and then enter into a pay fixed/receive floating interest rate swap with the issuer, thus ensuring that the issuer always has an appropriate amount of fixed rate interest income to satisfy its obligations to the noteholders. At first sight, the existence of such a swap would appear to preclude the use of linked presentation. This is because, if the originator is required under the swap to make fixed interest payments greater than the floating rate receipts, the overall effect will be that the issuer has recourse to assets of the originator in addition to the securitised mortgages, thus contravening paragraph 27(b) of FRS 5.

However, FRS 5 recognises that it may well be that, before transferring the mortgages to the issuer, the originator has already entered into a pay floating/receive fixed interest rate swap with a third party in order to hedge its interest rate risk. When the mortgages are transferred to the issuer, this swap ceases to be a hedge, and becomes a speculative contract. By entering into a similar swap with the issuer, the originator can, broadly speaking, neutralise its (now speculative) swap with the third party, and transfer to the issuer the assets as hedged by the originator prior to the transfer. FRS 5 therefore allows the use of linked presentation where an interest rate swap is entered into between the originator and issuer provided that all the following conditions are met:

- the swap is on arm's length market-related terms and the obligations of the issuer under the swap are not subordinated to any of its obligations under the loan notes;
- the variable interest rate(s) that are swapped are determined by reference to publicly quoted rates that are not under the control of the originator; and
- at the time of transfer of the assets to the issuer, the originator had hedged exposures relating to these assets (either individually or as part of a larger portfolio) and entering into the swap effectively restores the hedge position left open by their transfer. Thereafter, where the hedging of the originator's exposure under the swap requires continuing management, any necessary adjustments to the hedging position are made on an ongoing basis. This latter requirement will be particularly relevant where any prepayment risk involved cannot be hedged exactly.[65]

In what is more of a pure 'grandfathering' concession, FRS 5 provides that linked presentation can be adopted where there is an interest rate cap arrangement between the originator and the issuer provided that the conditions above are met, and the securitisation concerned was entered into before 22 September 1994 (the effective date of FRS 5).[66]

As discussed further at 2.6.2 above, this 'concession' cannot, in our view, be extended to other financial instruments that modify the profile of the securitised assets or borrowings such as foreign currency swaps.

V Revolving assets and 'top up' arrangements

As noted at 3.4 above, it is common to securitise credit card receivables. The assets concerned are essentially short term (being in most cases settled in full within 4 to 8 weeks), whereas the term of the borrowings secured on them is much longer. In practice, what often happens is that at the start of the securitisation a 'pool' of balances is transferred to the issuer. The borrowings will be repaid out of collections from this 'pool' of balances over a pre-agreed period. The proceeds received in the period will typically comprise both repayments of securitised balances existing at the start of the period and repayments of balances arising subsequently (for example arising from new borrowings in the period on the credit card accounts securitised). Thus, the borrowings will finally be repaid out of cash flows arising from credit card balances that did not exist at the start of the period. It is intuitively difficult to see how such an arrangement could qualify for linked presentation, given the requirement FRS 5 that linked presentation can only be used where the borrowing is repaid only out of the asset on which it was originally secured.

Application Note D, however, states that linked presentation may be used, provided that the borrowings are repaid only to the extent that there have been, in total, cash collections from securitised balances existing at the start of the repayment period equal to the amount repaid on the borrowings. This is necessary in order to ensure that the issuer is allocated its proper share of any losses.[67] The ASB's thinking may have been, as in explicitly stated in connection with 'top up' arrangements (see next paragraph), that, provided that this condition is strictly satisfied, the effect is the same as if the noteholders were fully repaid in cash every month and the cash immediately reinvested in new assets.

Similar considerations arise where a pool of receivables is securitised and certain of the assets are repaid sooner than was expected (as might be the case where a pool of 25-year domestic mortgages is securitised and some mortgagors elect to repay early). Application Note D states that, where there is a provision for the originator to add new assets to replace those that have been repaid earlier than expected (and thus to 'top up' the pool in order to extend the life of the securitisation), the conditions for a linked presentation may still be met. For a linked presentation to be used, it is necessary that the addition of new assets does not result either in the originator being exposed to losses on the new or the old assets, or in the originator re-acquiring assets. Provided these features are present, the effect is the same as if the noteholders were repaid in cash and they immediately reinvested that cash in new assets, so that a linked presentation may be appropriate.[68]

Where, however, the originator is required to replace poorly performing assets with better ones, this is equivalent to recourse to the originator, so that the conditions for linked presentation are not met.[69]

VI Multi-originator programmes

There are some arrangements where one issuer serves several originators. The arrangement may be structured such that each originator receives future benefits based on the performance of a defined portfolio of assets (typically those it has transferred to the issuer and continues to service or use). The effect is that each originator bears significant benefits and risks of a defined pool of mortgages, whilst being insulated from the benefits and risks of other mortgages held by the issuer. Each originator should show that pool of mortgages for which it has significant benefits and risks on the face of its balance sheet, using either a linked presentation (if the conditions for its use are met) or a separate presentation.[70]

VII Accounting and disclosure

Where a linked presentation is applied, the securitised assets remain on the balance sheet but the proceeds of the issue will be shown as deducted from them on the assets side of the balance sheet rather than as a liability. Extensive disclosure requirements are called for, namely:

- a description of the assets securitised;
- the amount of any income or expense recognised in the period, analysed as appropriate;
- the terms of any options for the originator to repurchase assets or to transfer additional assets to the issuer;
- the terms of any interest rate swap or interest rate cap agreements between the issuer and the originator that meet the conditions set out in paragraph D11 of the Application Note (see IV above);
- a description of the priority and amount of claims on the proceeds generated by the assets, including any rights of the originator to proceeds from the assets in addition to the non-recourse amounts already received;
- the ownership of the issuer; and
- the disclosures required by paragraph 27(c) and (d) of FRS 5 (see 2.6.1 above).[71]

The standard also says that where there are several securitisation arrangements they may be shown in aggregate if they relate to a single type of asset, but should otherwise be presented separately. Similarly, the note disclosures should only deal with the arrangements in aggregate to the extent that they relate to the same type of asset and are on similar terms.[72]

An example of the disclosures arising from typical securitisation transactions involving domestic mortgages is given by the Bank of Ireland.

Extract 18.19: Bank of Ireland (2001)

Group balance sheet [extract]

	THE GROUP	
	2001	2000
	€m	€m
ASSETS		
…		
Securitisation and loan transfers	**1,414**	708
Less: non returnable amounts	**1,273**	578
	141	130
…		

(b) Securities and loan transfers

The Group has sold the following pools of mortgages.

Year	Securitisations	Notes	Mortgages	Presentation in accounts	Value €m
1992	Private placements with UK financial Institutions	(ii),(vi)	Residential	Linked	234
1993	Private placements with UK financial Institutions	(ii),(vi)	Residential	Consolidated	161
1993	Residential Property Securities No. 3 plc (RPS3)	(i),(ii)	Residential	Linked	404
1994	Residential Property Securities No. 4 plc (RPS4)	(i),(iii)	Residential	Linked	807
1994	Commercial Loans on Investment Property Securitisation (No.1) plc (CLIPS)	(iv), (v)	Commercial	Linked	242
1997	Residential Property Securities No.5 plc (RPS5)	(i),(iii)	Residential	Linked	484
2000	Liberator Securities No. 1 plc	(v)	Residential	Linked	500
2000	Shipshape Residential Mortgages No.1 plc (SS1)	(vii)	Residential	Linked	485

All the issued shares in the above companies, excluding the private placements, are held by Trusts. The Group does not own directly or indirectly any of the share capital of these companies or their parent companies.

Under the terms of separate agreements, the Group continues to administer the mortgages, for which it receives fees and income. In addition, the Group is required to cover credit losses arising subject to specified limits as set out below. Specific provisions are maintained by the Group on a case by case basis for all loans where there is a likelihood of a loss arising and general provisions are maintained as a percentage of all remaining loans.

Notes

(i) These companies issued Mortgage Backed Floating Rate Notes ("Notes") to finance the purchase of the mortgage pools. Loan facilities have been made available by the group to finance certain issue related expenses and loan losses arising on the pools of mortgages sold. The loans are repayable when all Notes have been redeemed subject to the issuer having sufficient funds available.
The companies have hedged their interest rate exposure to fixed rate mortgages using interest exchange agreements with financial institutions including Bank of Ireland and Bank of Ireland Home Mortgages Limited.
The companies are incorporated under the Companies Acts 1985 and are registered and operating in the UK.

(ii) Under the terms of the mortgage sale agreements, the Group has an option to repurchase the mortgages at par when the aggregate balances of the mortgages fall below 10% of the original sale proceeds.

(iii) Under the terms of the mortgage sale agreements, the Group has an option to repurchase the mortgages at par when the aggregate balances of the mortgages fall below 5% of the original sale proceeds.

(iv) The company funded this purchase by the issued of floating rate mortgage backed securities, the lowest ranking of which have been purchased by the Group. Under the terms of this issue, the Group is not obliged to repurchase any of the assets, or to transfer in any additional assets. The issue terms of the notes include provisions that neither the company not the noteholders have recourse to the Group and no Group company is obliged or intends to support any losses of the company. The proceeds generated by the mortgage assets will be issued to pay the interest and capital on the notes and any other administrative expenses and taxation. Any residue is payable to the Group as deferred consideration.

(v) The company is incorporated under the Irish Companies Acts 1963 to 1999 and is registered and operating in the Republic of Ireland.

(vi) Under the terms of the agreements relating to the private placements, the Group has agreed to support losses to a maximum of Stg£1.2m. The providers of finance have agreed that they will seek no further recourse to the Company above this amount.

(vii) Under the terms of this issue, the Group is not obliged to repurchase any of the assets or to transfer in any additional assets, except in respect of individual mortgages in breach of warranty.
A summarised profit and loss account for the period to 31 March 2001 for CLIPS RPS3, RPS4, RPS5, the private placement of €234m, Liberator Securities No. 1 and SS1 No. 1 is set out below:

	2001	2000
	€m	€m
Interest receivable	**99**	55
Interest payable	**(89)**	(50)
Fee income	**2**	4
Deposit income	**4**	3
Operating expenses	**(9)**	(4)
Profit for the financial period	**7**	8

This discloses that linked presentation has been adopted for the securitisation of certain assets which the bank has the right to reacquire in certain circumstances, although FRS 5 states that linked presentation can be used only where there is 'no provision whatsoever' for the originator to reacquire the assets concerned (see 2.6.1 above). Presumably the effect of any such repurchase is considered immaterial.

Kingfisher has used the linked presentation in respect of securitised receivable arising from consumer credit transactions, as shown in this extract.

Extract 18.20: Kingfisher plc (2001)

Group balance sheet [extract]

£ millions	**2000**	**2000**	As restated 1999	As restated 1999
Current assets				
Development work in progress		**89.2**		96.7
Stocks		**2,095.5**		1669.4
Debtors due within one year		**973.5**		662.2
Debtors due after more than one year		**22.2**		146.8
Securitised consumer receivables	**261.1**		303.8	
Less: non-recourse secured notes	**(211.8)**	**49.3**	(234.5)	69.3
Investments		**168.6**		352.3
Cash at bank and in hand		**120.1**		156.6
		3,518.4		3153.3

Notes to the accounts

18 Securitised consumer receivables

In January 1996, the Group entered into an agreement to securitise consumer receivables (which derive principally from the provision of credit facilities by Time Retail Finance Ltd (TRF) to customers of the Group) through Time Finance Ltd (TFL). TRF sells the consumer receivables, with no impact on the profit and loss account, to TFL, who issues Notes secured on those assets. The issue terms of the Notes include provisions that their holders have no recourse to TRF or any other member of the Group. Neither TRF nor any other Group company is obliged to support any losses, nor does it intend to. Principal and interest is repayable from, and secured solely on, the consumer receivables. At 3 February 2001 the amount of consumer receivables securitised was £261.1m (2000: £303.8m) raising funds of £211.8m (2000: £234.5m) and this is shown on the balance sheet using linked presentation.

C *Separate presentation*

If the conditions for derecognition or a linked presentation are not satisfied, a separate presentation is required, which means that the securitised assets will remain on balance sheet and the proceeds of the issue will be shown as a loan within creditors. The gross amount of assets securitised at the year end is to be disclosed.[73]

3.4.2 *Issuer's individual accounts*

The considerations discussed in 3.4.1 above were in relation to the originator's accounts, but the same factors apply to the issuer's accounts as well. However, in the latter case the answer is generally clear – a separate presentation is required. In a securitisation, the issuer usually has access to all future benefits from the securitised assets (in the case of mortgages, to all cash collected from mortgagors) and is exposed to all their inherent risks. Hence, derecognition will not be appropriate. In addition, the noteholders usually have recourse to all the assets of the issuer (these may include the securitised assets themselves, the benefit of any related insurance policies or credit enhancement, and a small amount of cash). In this situation, the issuer's exposure to loss is not limited, and use of a linked presentation will not be appropriate.[74]

A question which can then arise is whether the issuer has to be consolidated by the originator, and if so, how that will affect the presentation.

3.4.3 *Originator's consolidated accounts*

Where the issuer is a subsidiary of the originator, it will be consolidated in the usual way (subject, however, to the comments on linked presentation in A below). Where the issuer is a quasi subsidiary of the originator (which will generally be the case where it is not a subsidiary),[75] the standard allows the assets and liabilities of the issuer to be included in the originator's group accounts in a linked presentation (provided the qualifying conditions are met from the point of view of the group) even if a separate presentation is required in the accounts of the issuer itself.[76]

A *Linked presentation in originator's consolidated accounts where issuer is subsidiary*

As noted above, most transactions accounted for using linked presentation involve the transfer of assets to a securitisation vehicle which is a quasi-subsidiary of the reporting entity. More recently, however, companies have begun to use subsidiaries for this purpose for tax and other reasons. This raises a potential difficulty, in that paragraph 102 of FRS 5 makes the following comment:

'Where an item and its finance are effectively ring-fenced in a quasi-subsidiary, a true and fair view of the position of the group is given by presenting them under a linked presentation. In this situation, the group does not have an asset equal to the gross amount of the item, nor a liability for the full amount of the finance. However, where the item and its finance are similarly ring-fenced in a subsidiary, a linked presentation may not be used. This is because the subsidiary is part of the group as legally defined – hence the item and its finance, being an asset and a liability of the subsidiary, are respectively an asset and liability of the group. The subsidiary would be consolidated in the normal way in accordance with companies legislation and a linked presentation would not be used (unless a linked presentation were appropriate in the subsidiary's individual financial statements).'

Some explanation of this conclusion would have been welcome since the reasoning behind it is by no means self-evident.[77] As noted at 2.6 above, FRS 5 asserts at least three times[78] that, in a transaction where linked presentation is applicable, the reporting entity does not have a gross asset and liability, but a new asset of the net amount. On this analysis, no offset is occurring, so that the offset rules in the Companies Act are irrelevant.

If, on the other hand, it is accepted for the sake of argument that the offset rules in the Companies Act prevent linked presentation, it could then never be permissible to use linked presentation even within the accounts of a single entity. This is because the offset rules for single entity accounts and group accounts are identical.[79] Thus, as a matter of law, linked presentation must, in our view, be either legal or illegal in both single entity and group accounts – it cannot be legal in one and illegal in the other.

However, in view of the comments in FRS 5, we urge companies wishing to adopt linked presentation in their consolidated accounts for transactions undertaken through a subsidiary to obtain their own legal advice before doing so.

3.5 Loan transfers (Application Note E)

Loan transfers is the collective term used to describe various methods by which banks and other lenders seek to transfer an advance to a different lender. Such transactions often involve a gain or loss because of movements in interest rates since the original loan was taken out, so they can have a profit and loss account dimension as well as giving rise to questions of balance sheet recognition and disclosure.

3.5.1 Types of loan transfer

Since the original loan is a contract which is personal to the parties involved, its transfer is not straightforward. It is necessary to effect the transfer of benefits and risks less directly, by one of the three following arrangements:

A Novation

In a novation, a new contract, with a new lender, is drawn up to replace the original one, which is cancelled. This therefore extinguishes the original loan altogether from the accounts of the lender as well as removing any residual obligations it had to the borrower (such as to make further advances under a committed facility). Unless there are any side agreements, no further questions of off balance sheet finance arise once this process has been completed.

B Assignment

This involves the assignment of some or all of the original lender's rights (but not obligations) to another lender, and may be done on either a statutory or an equitable basis, which have different legal requirements and effects. They are both subject to equitable reliefs; in particular, the borrower's rights under its contract with the original lender are not to be prejudiced.

In accounting terms, the effect of an assignment is less clear cut than that of a novation, because the original lender may have some residual rights and obligations to the other parties involved.

C Sub-participation

This does not involve the formal transfer of the legal rights and obligations involved in the loan, but the creation of a non-recourse back-to-back agreement with another lender (the sub-participant) whereby the sub-participant deposits with the original lender an amount in respect of the whole or part of the loan in exchange for the right to receive a share of the cash flows arising from the loan from the original lender. The accounting question that arises from such a transaction is whether the deposit and the loan can be offset to show only the net position.

3.5.2 *Accounting requirements*

As for other forms of finance, the three options which Application Note E offers are derecognition, a linked presentation and a separate presentation. However, it also refers to the possibility of splitting a loan so that some of it is transferred while the rest is retained, which constitutes 'partial' derecognition.

A Derecognition

Derecognition is appropriate when all the significant risks and rewards pertaining to the loans have been passed from the original lender to the transferee. In the absence of side agreements, this will generally be the case where the loan has been novated, but might also apply where there has been an assignment or a sub-participation.[80] The essential test is whether there are any circumstances in which the original lender retains the possibility of any benefit from the loans (or from the part transferred),[81] or might be called upon to repay the new lender so as to bear any losses or meet any obligations; if not, derecognition is appropriate and the loan is therefore taken off the balance sheet. The tests which generally have to be satisfied in order to achieve this are that:

(a) the transaction takes place at an arms' length price for an outright sale;

(b) the transaction is for a fixed amount of consideration and there is no recourse whatsoever, either implicit or explicit, to the lender for losses from whatever cause. Normal warranties given in respect of the condition of the loans at the time of transfer would not breach this condition, but any warranties concerning their condition or performance in the future would do so; and

(c) the lender will not benefit or suffer in any way if the loans perform better or worse than expected. This condition will not be satisfied where the lender has a right to further sums which vary according to the future performance of the loans (i.e. according to whether, when or how much the borrowers pay).[82]

Derecognition also gives rise to a profit and loss account effect, because the loans are regarded as 'sold', and accordingly the difference between their carrying amount and the proceeds received is taken to the profit and loss account. Insofar as all the proceeds have been received in cash, this poses no difficulty, but otherwise the profit should be restricted to the amount realised if there is uncertainty as to its eventual amount. Losses should, however, be provided in full.[83]

B Linked presentation

As with the other examples discussed earlier in this chapter, a linked presentation is appropriate where some of the risks and rewards relating to the loans have been retained (thus rendering derecognition unavailable) but the original lender's downside risk is nonetheless definitely limited to a fixed monetary amount. This combination of circumstances is less likely to apply in the case of loan transfers; it is more likely that the risks and rewards will have been wholly disposed of or wholly retained. However, there are various possible transactions which involve a partial transfer of the loans and result in the original lender's maximum exposure being capped, and these may give rise to the use of the linked presentation.[84]

Where the conditions are met, the non-returnable proceeds received will be shown as a deduction from the loans to which they relate within the assets section of the balance sheet. Insofar as these proceeds exceed the amount of the loans, FRS 5 says that the difference should be taken to the profit and loss account, but the standard does not explicitly require the recognition of equivalent losses even if a loss is implicit in the transaction. We believe that it is appropriate to apply the same principle to both profits and losses.

Application Note E calls for the following disclosures when a linked presentation is used:

(a) the main terms of the arrangement;

(b) the gross amount of loans transferred and outstanding at the balance sheet date;

(c) the profit or loss recognised in the period, analysed as appropriate; and

(d) the disclosures required by paragraph 27(c) and (d) (see 2.6 above).[85]

C Separate presentation

Where the conditions for neither derecognition nor a linked presentation are satisfied, a separate presentation is required; in other words, the original loan stays on balance sheet as an asset and the amount received from the transferee appears on the other side of the balance sheet as a loan payable. Application Note E calls for disclosure of the amount of loans outstanding at the year end which are subject to loan transfer arrangements.[86]

3.6 Transactions under the Private Finance Initiative (Application Note F)

The Private Finance Initiative (PFI) is designed to provide a new mechanism for procuring public services. The basic idea is that, rather than having bodies in the public sector take on the whole responsibility for funding and building roads, bridges, railways, hospitals, prisons and other infrastructure assets, some of these should be contracted out to private sector operators from whom the public sector bodies would buy services. The overriding goal is to maximise value for money from the taxpayers' perspective by passing such risks to the private sector as that sector is best able to manage.

A typical PFI transaction, therefore, is a long term contract whereby a private sector entity agrees to provide services to a public sector entity in exchange for a stream of payments. The contract is likely to specify that these payments will vary according to complex formulae, involving such factors as the volume of services delivered, the level of adherence to defined quality standards, and so on.

The accounting challenge is to reflect the substance of these payments fairly in the accounts of both the contracting parties. It would be possible simply to take the contract at face value and account for the amounts paid and received as service payments; however, closer analysis may sometimes reveal that this is in reality a composite transaction whereby the public sector body is buying assets as well as services. In such a case, it will be appropriate to subdivide the contract into its components and account for the asset-related part as if it were a finance lease.

From the point of view of the public body, the main issue is whether or not to recognise an asset together with an associated borrowing, by treating some of the future contractual payments as being akin to finance lease rentals. From the private entity's point of view, a similar analysis applies in reverse. A further complication is that the private sector entity is often a joint venture whose participants may include service providers, facilities managers, financial institutions, constructors or other bodies, so questions of joint venture accounting can also arise (see Chapter 7 at 4).

In September 1998 the ASB published a further Application Note (F) to FRS 5[87] to address the treatment of such transactions, which closely followed the terms of an exposure draft that had been issued nine months earlier. This requires a thorough analysis of the contract so as to determine its substance, focusing in particular on the formula for varying the contractual payments in order to identify the reasons for these variations, so as to see whether they relate to risks associated with the ownership of the asset, or to the risks of operating it to deliver services. The purpose of this is to see whether the variations are more consistent with a hypothesis that the asset belongs in substance to the public sector body and not to its ostensible owner, the private sector entity. As far as the parties involved are concerned, the distinctions that have to be made involve determining whether:

(a) the purchaser in a PFI contract (the public sector body) has an asset of the property used to provide the contracted services together with a corresponding liability to pay the operator for it or, alternatively, has a contract only for services; and

(b) the operator has an asset of the property used to provide the contracted services or, alternatively, a financial asset being a debt due from the purchaser.[88]

In practice (b) is not such a difficult issue as (a). It is clear that the operator has *some* kind of asset on its balance sheet, whereas the choice in relation to the purchaser's accounts is whether or not anything at all is recognised on its balance sheet.

Application Note F goes on to say that 'In some cases the contract may be separable, i.e. the commercial effect will be that elements of the PFI payments operate independently of each other. 'Operate independently' means that the elements behave differently and can therefore be separately identified. Where this is the case, and where some elements relate only to services (such as cleaning, laundry, catering etc.) rather than to the property, any such service elements are not relevant to determining whether each party has an asset of the property and should be ignored.'[89] It will not be relevant that the contract designates the payments as 'unitary' or, indeed, what labels they are given.

The next step under Application Note F, after excluding any separable service elements, is to distinguish PFI contracts between:

'(a) those where the only remaining elements are payments for the property. These will be akin to a lease and SSAP 21 (interpreted in the light of the FRS) should be applied.

(b) other contracts (i.e. where the remaining elements include some services). These contracts will fall directly within the FRS rather than SSAP 21.'[90]

Most PFI contracts will fall under (b) as the 'availability' element of the payment may vary if services are not performed to the agreed standard. For such contracts, determining which party has an asset of the property involves examining the extent to which each of them would bear any variations in property profits (or losses). Application Note F identifies three important principles that are relevant to this examination:

(a) a range of factors will be relevant and it will be necessary to look at the overall effect of these factors when taken together;

(b) any potential variations in profits (or losses) that relate purely to services should be excluded as they are not relevant to determining whether each party has an asset of the property; and

(c) greater weight should be given to those features that are more likely to have a commercial effect in practice. Where there is no genuine commercial possibility of a particular scenario or cash flow occurring, this scenario/cash flow should be ignored.[91]

The principle is to distinguish potential variations in costs and revenues that flow from features of the property which are relevant to determining whose asset it is. The main factors that are relevant are likely to be:

- who carries the demand risk;
- the presence, if any, of third-party revenues;
- who determines the nature of the property;
- penalties for underperformance or non-availability;
- potential changes in relevant costs;
- obsolescence, including the effects of changes in technology; and
- the arrangements at the end of the contract, which will indicate who bears the residual value risk.[92]

These are discussed in further detail in Application Note F. Needless to say, such an analysis may still not produce a clear-cut answer, not least because the contract may have been deliberately designed to produce an ambiguous accounting result. However, it is helpful to try to see it through the eyes of the contracting parties, and understand what has been in their minds in negotiating these particular terms.

PFI projects necessarily enjoy a high political profile and their accounting treatment can be highly sensitive as a result, since it affects the public perception of the economic substance of these transactions. This has led the Treasury to take a particular interest in the development of this guidance, that has not always appeared to be benign. This culminated in June 1999 in the issue of the Treasury's own guidance[93] on how the public sector should interpret the Application Note, and although the ASB has not demurred, the two documents do not really seem to be in complete harmony. The consequence is that this remains an area of some confusion, but we believe that Application Note F is the more reliable source of reference and that PFI transactions should be carefully analysed according to its approach.

A Accounting by the operator

The Application Note says relatively little about accounting by the private sector. The operator should treat its asset as a fixed asset or, if it is concluded that the property is an asset of the public sector, as a financial asset. In the latter case this financial asset is a debt due from the purchaser for the fair value of the property. Subsequently the operator will recognise in its profit and loss account only finance income relating to this debtor. The remainder of the PFI payments (ie, the total unitary payment less the amount allocated as repayment of, and interest on, the debt) will be shown in full in the profit and loss account.[94]

Carillion makes the following disclosures in respect of its PFI contracts

Extract 18.21: Carillion plc (2000)

Operating and Financial review [extract]

Accounting policies

The effect of FRS 5 – Application Note F – Private Finance Initiative and Similar Contracts on the accounting for several of our Private Finance projects should be noted. The application of this note has resulted in several of our Private Finance project companies recognising their projects as debtors, rather than fixed assets within in their own accounts. Under this treatment, during the operational phase, the debtor is treated as a finance debtor with the revenue arising in respect of the project being allocated between repayments of the finance debtor, interest receivable in respect of the finance debtor and payments in respect of the remaining services provided. The overall effect, compared to the treatment if the project was treated as a fixed asset in the accounts of the joint venture company, is a reduction in operating profit with interest receivable benefitting by a similar amount. Over the project life there is no effect on profit before tax as a result of this accounting policy.

Our secure establishment concession companies have reflected this approach for a number of years and the effect of applying it to our hospital companies is now beginning to be seen. Our first hospital, Darent Valley, became operational in September 2000. The effect if the application of this note, compared to an accounting treatment as a fixed asset has been a decrease in our share of joint ventures operating profit of £1.2 million. This is offset by an increase in our share of the interest receivable by the joint venture of a similar amount. This effect will become larger in future years, both to reflect a full year of Darent Valley and as a result of our other hospitals at Swindon, Glasgow and North Staffordshire becoming operational.

Moreover, since the Application Note was issued in 1998, however, the scope of PFI contracts has widened. There are now contracts that are primarily for the repair and maintenance of assets, with fixed assets being an insignificant part. These arrangements may not readily fall within the Application Note's analysis of accounting by the operator (for example there is no physical asset that could be 'sold' to the public sector) and may be more appropriately treated in another way, for example as long-term contracts under SSAP 9 (see Chapter 16 at 2.3).

3.6.1 *Similar arrangements in the private sector*

Arrangements that are similar in nature to PFI contracts are increasingly being formed between entities in the private sector as well. For example, a retailer may outsource its warehousing and distribution activities to a specialist distribution company, and questions might arise as to which party owns the warehouses in substance. Application Note F is also designed to be the appropriate source of guidance for interpreting such contracts.[95]

3.7 Debt defeasance

Sometimes, rather than repurchasing or repaying debt, companies enter into arrangements with a similar economic effect. For example, they might irrevocably deposit funds with a third party that are to be applied solely in settlement of the debt, and agree with the creditor that he can look only to those funds for repayment of the debt. Such arrangements are sometimes referred to as resulting in 'defeasance' (meaning extinguishment) of the debt.

As noted in 2.5.1 above, and in Chapter 17 at 2.2.6 B, neither FRS 4 nor FRS 5 contains rules for the derecognition of liabilities. In our view, however, the general principles of FRS 5 would lead to the view an arrangement such as that described above could at best lead to linked presentation, rather than complete recognition, of the asset and liability involved. This is because it involves the reporting entity depositing an asset with one party to be used to settle an amount due to another. As discussed in 2.7 above, the offset criteria in FRS 5 are apparently drafted so as not to permit an entity to offset an asset due from one party and a liability due from another.

However, offset may sometimes be achievable. For example, Pennon's 1999 accounts showed that at the beginning of the year it had reduced the disclosed amount of lease payables by £75m because it had deposited that amount with the lessor's bank group, as shown in this extract:

Extract 18.22: Pennon Group Plc (1999)

28 Loans and other borrowings [extract]

... at 31 March 1998, obligations under finance leases of £75.0 million had been offset against cash of an equal amount had been deposited with the lessor's bank group (collateralisation); South West Water Limited could insist this cash be utilised to meet the finance lease obligations as they fell due. During the year South West Water Limited withdrew the cash deposits placed with the lessor's bank group. Accordingly, a finance lease obligation of £75.0 million is included above.

It appears from the above description that Pennon was able to insist on a net settlement, even though the deposits were not with the lessor companies themselves but with other members of their group. Presumably this would still have applied in the event of the insolvency of any of the parties, otherwise the FRS 5 offset conditions would not have been satisfied.

Another kind of arrangement which has a similar economic effect to the repurchase of debt is illustrated in this extract from the 1994 accounts of Sears. In this case, however, the liability and the asset used to 'defease' it continued to be shown on a gross basis:

Extract 18.23: Sears plc (1994)

13. Debtors [extract]

Included within prepayments due after more than one year is a call option, which was purchased for £41.8 million on normal commercial terms and which gives the Company the right to acquire £50 million of Sears plc Bonds 1996. It is exercisable at certain dates up to January 1996 at an exercise price that is linked to the net present value of the remaining interest payable on the Bonds. Accordingly, the exercise price reduces during the period up to January 1996, resulting in an increase in the value of the call option. This increase in value is credited to interest receivable on an actuarial basis and is reflected in the carrying amount of the asset, which was £43.5 million at 31st January 1994.

£43.5 million equated to the present value of the principal of the debt (£50 million) if discounted at approximately 7.2%. From this it can be surmised that the exercise price under the option was little different from the present value of the outstanding interest payments. Subsequently, the 1996 accounts showed that the option had been sold for £50m on the same day as the debt was repaid. Interestingly, the purchase of the option was described in the 1994 accounts as 'Prepayment of 12½% bonds 1996' in the financing section of the cash flow statement, not as the purchase of an option in the investing section. It might therefore be argued that Sears had already repurchased its debt in substance, but in such a way that it did not have to write off the premium payable – instead, it was recognised over the remaining two years of the instrument as the difference between the interest payable on the debt, at 12½% and the accretion of interest on the prepayment, at 7.2%.

It is again debatable whether this should be regarded as the repurchase of debt or not. On the one hand, it achieves a similar result in economic terms, and therefore could be said to be a repurchase in substance. On the other, it would be possible to simulate a repurchase of debt in a variety of other ways, for example using derivatives without getting close to repurchasing the debt. Moreover, unless there is right of offset between the option and the debt, FRS 5 would again say that the two items should continue to be carried gross on opposite sides of the balance sheet.

As discussed in Chapter 17 at 5.4.3, IAS does address this issue, concluding that a transaction results in derecognition of the liability from the balance sheet only if the creditor legally releases the company from its obligation to settle the debt. Otherwise the arrangement is described as only 'in-substance defeasance', which IAS 39 says is ineffective in removing the debt from the balance sheet.

3.8 Take-or-pay contracts and throughput agreements

Take-or-pay contracts and throughput agreements are unconditional commitments to buy goods or services from a supplier in the future, generally from a new operational facility created by the supplier. From the supplier's point of view, such contracts guarantee a certain level of sales which gives assurance that the facility will be viable, and expedite the financing; from the purchaser's point of view, it secures a medium or long-term source of supply, probably at favourable prices. Sometimes the supplier is set up by a consortium of customers who wish to share a particular facility, such as a pipeline to service the needs of a number of oil companies.

Take-or-pay contracts and throughput agreements are essentially the same in concept. The only distinction between the two terms is that throughput agreements relate to the use of a supplier's transportation facility (such as a ship or a pipeline) or processing plant, whereas take-or-pay contracts relate to the supply of goods or other services.

Under these contracts, the purchaser is obliged to pay a certain minimum amount even if, in the event, it does not take delivery of the goods or make use of the services it has contracted for. The accounting question which therefore arises is whether the purchaser has to account for a liability (its commitment under the contract) together with a corresponding asset (its right to use the facilities it has contracted for).

FRS 5 does not address these transactions specifically. Under its general principles the rights and obligations under such contracts would seem to require to be recognised in the balance sheet, which would be a radical departure from present practice. Indeed, a literal application of the principles might require *all* purchase obligations to be recognised on the balance sheet whenever a purchase order is accepted, rather than when the contract is fulfilled, which would be an even more radical departure. However, the ASB has avoided this consequence by scoping all such transactions out of the standard; one of the exclusions from the scope of FRS 5 is 'expenditure commitments',[96] as a result of which it would appear that take-or-pay contracts are permitted to remain off balance sheet.

This, however, is not necessarily the end of the story. Such contracts might fall within the extended definition of a lease in SSAP 21, and therefore be bound by the terms of that standard. This definition says that 'the term "lease" as used in this statement also applies to other arrangements in which one party retains ownership of an asset but conveys the right to the use of the asset to another party for an agreed period of time in return for specified payments'.[97] Where this applies, it is necessary to consider whether the contract has the character of a finance lease, in which case the asset should be recognised in the balance sheet of the user. This will be the case where substantially all the risks and rewards of ownership of the asset are transferred to the user under the contract – typically where there is only ever going to be one user for the asset.

Scottish Power discloses this extensive range of commitments:

Extract 18.24: Scottish Power plc (2001)

30 Financial commitments
(c) Other contractual commitments

Under contractual commitments, the group has rights and obligations in relation to the undernoted contracts. The annual value of the purchases and sales arising from these contracts is provided below:

	Note	Commitment entered into	Commitment expires	Purchases/sales in year under group commitments 2001 £m	2000 £m	1999 £m
The purchase of electricity from British Energy Generation (UK) Limited		1990	2005	**265.8**	370.1	367.7
The purchase of electricity from Scottish and Southern Energy plc	(i)	1990	see below	**49.7**	72.4	78.8
The supply of electricity to Scottish and Southern Energy plc		1990	2005	**17.6**	17.6	18.2
Revenue from the operation of the company's transmission system and access by Scottish and Southern Energy plc to the Anglo-Scottish connector		1990	No fixed date of expiry	**32.4**	31.0	27.7
Purchase of coal from the Scottish Coal Company Limited		1998	2003	**41.0**	19.0	22.0
Purchase of coal from the Scottish Coal (Deep Mine) Company Limited		1998	2004	**44.8**	49.2	50.5
Purchase of gas from various fields in the North Sea		1994	2017	**172.0**	125.8	123.6

(i) There are two agreements relating to the purchase of electricity from Scottish and Southern Energy plc. These expire in 2012 and 2039.

In the US, the group manages its energy resource requirements by integrating long-term firm, short-term and spot market purchases with its own generating resources to economically operate the system (within the boundaries of Federal Energy Regulatory Commission requirements) and meet commitments for wholesale sales and retail load growth. The long-term wholesale sales commitments include contracts with minimum sales requirements of £331.9 million, £310.8 million, £196.2 million, £163.2 million and £139.9 million for the years 2002 to 2006 respectively. As part of its energy resource portfolio, PacifiCorp acquires a portion of its power through long-term purchases and/or exchange agreements which require minimum fixed payments of £296.1 million, £282.7 million, £237.7 million, £226.4 million and £224.3 million for the years 2002 to 2006 respectively. The purchase contracts include agreements with the Bonneville Power Administration, the Hermiston Plant and a number of cogenerating facilities.

4 IAS REQUIREMENTS

4.1 General

As noted in 1.3 above, there is no single international standard dealing specifically with off balance sheet transactions. However, IAS 1 – *Presentation of Financial Statements* – requires that '… management should develop policies to ensure that the financial statements provide information that is … reliable in that they … reflect the economic substance of events and transactions and not merely their legal form'.[98]

More detailed guidance is provided on:

- recognition and derecognition of financial assets and financial liabilities in *IAS 39 – Financial Instruments: Recognition and Measurement*, together with the *IAS 39 Implementation Guidance Questions and Answers* (see 4.2 below);
- offset of financial assets and financial liabilities, in IAS 1 – *Presentation of Financial Statements* and IAS 32 – *Financial Instruments: Disclosure and Presentation* (see 4.3 below); and
- consolidation of special purpose entities, in SIC-12 – *Consolidation – Special Purpose Entities* (see 4.4 below).

4.2 Derecognition of financial assets

IAS 39 contains rules for the recognition and derecognition of financial assets and financial liabilities. By contrast, FRS 5 addresses the recognition of all types of asset and liability and the derecognition of all types of asset (i.e. not just those of a financial nature), but does not address the derecognition of liabilities directly (see 2.5.1 above). IAS 39's criteria for derecognition of financial assets are discussed below. Those for recognition of financial assets and financial liabilities are discussed in Chapter 10 at 4.4.1, and those for derecognition of financial liabilities are dealt with in Chapter 17 at 5.4.3.

As will become apparent from the discussion below, the derecognition criteria for financial assets in IAS 39 are not particularly easy to read and, as a result, do not appear altogether consistent. This is probably because they seem to have been based partly on UK GAAP and partly on US GAAP, the approaches of which to derecognition are fundamentally different.[99] This has led to a considerable number of questions and answers on asset derecognition in the implementation guidance. These have added some clarification, but at the price of further confusion, since they appear on occasions to contradict IAS 39 and/or each other.

4.2.1 *Definitions*

The following definitions are relevant for the rules for derecognition of financial assets (and also the offset of financial assets and financial liabilities discussed in 4.3 below).

A 'financial asset' is any asset that is:

- cash;
- a contractual right to receive cash or another financial asset from another enterprise;
- a contractual right to exchange financial instruments with another enterprise under conditions that are potentially favourable; or
- an equity instrument of another enterprise.[100]

A 'financial liability' is any liability that is a contractual obligation:

- to deliver cash or another financial asset to another enterprise; or
- to exchange financial instruments with another enterprise under conditions that are potentially unfavourable.[101]

A 'financial liability' also includes a contractual obligation that the reporting enterprise can settle either by payment of financial assets or payment in the form of its own equity securities, if the number of equity securities required to settle the obligation varies with changes in their fair value so that the total fair value of the equity securities paid always equals the amount of the contractual obligation.[102]

The definition of 'financial liability' encompasses certain items that are not accounted for as such under IAS 32 or IAS 39 either because they are dealt with by other more specific IAS or have not yet been fully addressed. These include obligations in respect of:

- leases (accounted for under IAS 17 – see Chapter 19);
- pensions and other post-employment benefits (accounted for under IAS 19 – see Chapter 23);
- employee stock option and stock purchase plans (subject to some disclosure requirements under IAS 19 – see Chapter 22); and
- insurance contracts (not yet covered by IAS and generally beyond the scope of this book).

4.2.2 *General asset derecognition criteria*

An enterprise should derecognise a financial asset or a portion of a financial asset when, and only when, the enterprise loses control of the contractual rights that comprise the financial asset (or a portion of the financial asset). An enterprise loses such control if it realises the rights to benefits specified in the contract, or the rights expire, or the enterprise surrenders those rights.[103] 'Control' of an asset means the power to obtain the future economic benefits that flow from the asset.[104]

In determining whether or not it has lost control of a financial asset, the reporting enterprise should consider both its own position and that of the transferee.

Consequently, if the position of either enterprise indicates that the transferor has retained control, the transferor should not remove the asset from its balance sheet.[105]

Thus, on the face of it, under IAS, derecognition of an asset broadly occurs when an entity has transferred only the benefits of the asset. Under FRS 5, derecognition requires transfer of both the benefits and the risks of the asset (see 2.5.2 above). However, as will be apparent from the discussion in 4.2.3 below, the degree to which an enterprise has transferred the risks associated with an asset is also relevant under IAS.

A Accounting treatment

Where a financial asset (or portion of an asset) is derecognised, a net profit or loss should be recognised being the difference between:

(a) the carrying amount of an asset (or portion of an asset) transferred to another party; and

(b) the sum of:

   (i) the proceeds received or receivable, and

   (ii) any prior adjustment to reflect the fair value of that asset that had been reported in equity (see Chapter 10 at 4.6).[106]

Where a financial asset is transferred to another enterprise without derecognition being achieved, the transferor accounts for any consideration received as a collateralised borrowing (as would be the case under FRS 5). In such a case, any right to reacquire the asset is not accounted for as a derivative at fair value, as would normally be the case under IAS 39 (see Chapter 10 at 4.3.2), since to do so would effectively result in the same asset being recorded twice.[107]

4.2.3 *Application of general asset derecognition principles*

IAS 39 and the *Interpretation Guidance* expand on these general rules at some length, as discussed below. The headings used below do not correspond to any in IAS 39, but, in our view, are a useful means of categorising the complex, and sometimes apparently conflicting, requirements.

A Outright sale

Transfer of an asset by way of outright sale (i.e. without any right or obligation to repurchase the asset), is *prima facie* evidence that the asset should be derecognised.[108] The implementation guidance also addresses the situation where an asset is purchased immediately before or soon after the sale of the same asset, which the guidance refers to by the US term 'wash sale' – in the UK this would often be called a 'bed and breakfast' transaction. In such a case, the sale and purchase should be treated as two separate transactions; the fact that the transferor expects to reacquire an asset that it has recently sold does not preclude derecognition of the asset provided that there is no contractual commitment to repurchase the asset.[109] The treatment of any right (as opposed to contractual obligation) to repurchase the asset would follow the rules summarised in B below.

B Transfer with right to repurchase

A transferred financial asset should not be derecognised where the transferor has the right to reacquire the transferred asset unless either:

(a) the asset is readily obtainable in the market; or

(b) the reacquisition price is fair value at the time of reacquisition.[110]

IAS 39 explains that derecognition is not appropriate where the transferor has the right to repurchase the asset at a fixed price and the asset is not readily obtainable in the market, because the fixed price is not necessarily fair value at the time of reacquisition. For example, a transfer of a group of mortgage loans that gives the transferor the right to reacquire those same loans at a fixed price would not result in derecognition.[111] However, a sale of an asset subject to a right of first refusal to reacquire it at its fair value at the time of reacquisition would result in derecognition.[112]

It should be noted that criteria (a) and (b) above are joined by 'or' rather than 'and'. This has the effect that, where an asset that is readily obtainable in the market has been sold subject to a right to repurchase it, the asset should always be derecognised (unless the effect of the transaction is to give the transferee a lender's return – see C below), irrespective of whether the repurchase price is fair value at the time of reacquisition. In such a case, the transferor would adopt the accounting treatment summarised at 4.2.5 below (i.e. derecognition of the asset transferred coupled with recognition of a new financial asset or liability in respect of the right to repurchase the asset). The implementation guidance confirms that this approach should also be adopted in respect of a readily obtainable asset where the transferor has an obligation (as opposed to a right) to repurchase the asset through a put option held by the transferee (see D below).

IAS 39 itself does not explain on what basis it draws this distinction between assets that are readily obtainable in the market and those that are not. From a conceptual point of view, an entity either controls an asset or it does not and the relevance for making that judgement of the depth of the market for that asset is not immediately obvious. Some explanation is, however, provided in a draft of additional implementation guidance issued for comment by the IASC in June 2001. This argues that, in the case of an asset readily obtainable in the market, the transferee is able to dispose of the asset and, if necessary, reacquire it later. This suggests that the asset must be under the control of the transferee and (by implication, therefore) not the transferor.[113]

The implementation guidance also addresses the treatment of assets transferred with a right to repurchase in the somewhat esoteric context of a 'clean-up' call option. A bank may sell a portion of some of its loans to a third party, but retain the obligation to administer those loans. It may well be that, at some future date, the level of the loans falls to an extent that it is uneconomic for the bank to administer them. For this reason, the sale agreement may give the bank a call option to repurchase the loans. The guidance concludes that derecognition is not necessarily precluded by such an option 'because [it] is conditional on the cost of servicing' the loans, but that the existence of the option may suggest that a portion of the transferred assets does not qualify for derecognition (see 4.2.4 below).[114]

C Transfer with right and obligation to repurchase

A transferred financial asset should not be derecognised if the transferor is both entitled and obligated to repurchase or redeem the transferred asset on terms that effectively provide the transferee with a lender's return on the assets received in exchange for the transferred asset. A lender's return is one that is not materially different from that which could be obtained on a loan to the transferor that is fully secured by the transferred asset.[115]

However, an entitlement or obligation (whether arising from a forward purchase contract, or a combination of put and call options at approximately the same strike price, or otherwise) to repurchase the asset at fair value at the time of repurchase does not preclude derecognition of the asset,[116] because this does not provide the transferee with a lender's return.

The implementation guidance addresses this requirement in the context of a repurchase agreement ('repo') or stock lending transaction over an asset readily obtainable in the market on terms that, at settlement, the transferee may substitute assets similar, and of equal fair value, to those originally transferred. It concludes that, because such a transaction will effectively provide the transferee with a lender's return, the transferor should not derecognise of the original asset, unless and until the transferee returns a substitute asset.[117] This conclusion also seems to indicate that an asset sold subject to a right and obligation to repurchase that gives the transferee a lender's return should never be derecognised, irrespective of whether or not the asset is readily marketable (which is relevant in other circumstances – see B above and D below). This interpretation is explicitly confirmed in the draft of additional implementation guidance issued for comment by the IASC in June 2001.[118]

IAS 39 and the implementation guidance do not explicitly address the third possibility of a sale subject to a right and obligation to repurchase at a price other than fair value, which also does not give the transferee a lender's return. Presumably, in such cases the principles in B above and D below should be applied.

D Transfer subject to total return swap or transferee's put option

A transferred financial asset should not be derecognised where the asset transferred is not readily obtainable in the market and the transferor has either:

(a) retained substantially all of the risks and returns of ownership through a total return swap with the transferee (a total return swap provides the market returns and credit risks to one of the parties in return for an interest index to the other party, such as a LIBOR payment); or

(b) retained substantially all of the risks of ownership through an unconditional put option on the transferred asset held by the transferee.[119]

It will be seen here that the key issue appears to be whether or not the transferor has passed the risk of the asset to the transferee. However, as noted in 4.2.2 above, the basic (bold paragraph) criterion for derecognition of an asset is simply whether or not the benefits have been transferred. The significance of risk transfer is also discussed further at E below.

Paragraph (b) above refers to an 'unconditional' put option, begging the question of the treatment of a sale subject to a transferee's *conditional* put option. This is addressed by the implementation guidance, which states that where a sale is subject to a deep-in-the-money transferee's put option, the option should be treated as an unconditional option, and the asset should therefore not be derecognised. The example given in the implementation guidance is of an option exercisable if interest rates are over 5% when interest rates are 12%. This still leaves open the question of the treatment of an option that is in-the-money, but not *deep*-in-the-money (e.g., to adapt the example above, an option exercisable if interest rates are over 5% when interest rates are 6%).

It may be that the reference to the option in this example being 'deep in the money' is in fact something of a distraction, and that the real point is that, by its very nature, any option is conditional in the sense that no rational holder of an option will exercise it unless certain economic conditions apply. In other words, to revert to the example, there is no real difference between:

- a 'conditional' option that can be exercised only when interest rates are over 5%; and
- an 'unconditional' option that the holder would not rationally exercise unless interest rates were above 5%.

On this view, it might be more meaningful to regard as 'conditional' an option subject to conditions that would not influence the holder's decision as to whether to exercise it. An example might be an option under an employee share scheme that can be exercised only if the employee remains with the company for a certain period. The fact that the employee has remained in the company's employment does not affect his decision to exercise the option (although this condition will clearly affect the overall likelihood of the option being exercised). The other possibility is that by an 'unconditional' option the drafters of IAS 39 meant something that is in fact a forward purchase agreement, but which has been constructed as an option as a matter of legal form only.

The guidance reiterates that, where an asset readily obtainable in the market is sold subject to a put option, it is derecognised, and the put option measured at fair value, regardless of whether it is in the money, at the money or out of the money[120] (see also 4.2.5 below). This is because the rules for transfers subject to total return swaps and put options, like those for transfers of assets with a right to repurchase (see B above), apply only to assets that are not readily obtainable in the market. This leads to an apparent inconsistency with the rules applicable to transfers subject to a right and obligation to repurchase (see C above), where the asset (whether readily obtainable in the market or not) is not derecognised and the transaction is accounted for as a collateralised loan.

If an asset is transferred subject to a total return swap whereby the transferor pays LIBOR and the transferee pays or receives an amount depending on the performance of the asset, the transferee is clearly getting a lender's return. In this case, however, the asset must be derecognised if it is readily obtainable in the market. Thus it appears that a borrowing collateralised on an asset readily obtainable in the market is to be accounted for differently depending on whether it is structured using put and call options (treated as collateralised loan) or using a total return swap (treated as sale with provision for fair value of obligation to repurchase), even though the economic effect may be identical.

E Transfer subject to performance guarantees

This is addressed, in the context of a sale of receivables combined with various forms of guarantee by the seller, by IAS 39 and by three questions and answers ('Q&A's) in the implementation guidance, the overall message of which is unfortunately less than clear.

IAS 39 itself indicates that where receivables are sold subject to a credit guarantee by the seller, they should normally be derecognised and a financial liability recognised for the guarantee (see 4.2.5 below).

Q&A 35-2 addresses the treatment of a transaction in which the transferor transfers a portion of a loan to a third party. This states that 'if the transferor provides a guarantee to the investors for both credit risk and interest rate risk and there are no other substantive risks, the portion of the transferred financial assets that would otherwise qualify for derecognition is reduced to the extent that both of these risks are not transferred. The reduction is the lower of the maximum amount of the credit guarantee and the percentage of the transferred financial asset that is guaranteed by the transferor against interest rate risk'. This conclusion is rather curious, because the form of partial derecognition that it appears to be advocating, and in particular the formula for calculating it in the final sentence, have no obvious basis in IAS 39.

By contrast Q&A 38-2 discusses a situation where an entity sells some debts with a right of full recourse, under which the transferee can seek compensation from the transferor for non-payment by the debtors, and put the receivables back to the transferor in the event of unfavourable changes in interest rates or the credit ratings of the underlying debtors. This clearly also has the effect that (as in the situation discussed by Q&A 35-2) the transferor retains all the substantive risks of the receivables. However, here the conclusion is that derecognition is not possible.

The grounds for this conclusion are that the situation is 'similar to that governed by IAS 39.38(c)' – i.e. the rules discussed in D above. However, this seems questionable, since the cited paragraph of IAS 39 deals with an asset transfer where the transferee has an 'unconditional' put option (extended by the implementation guidance to include a deep-in-the-money conditional put option), not, as in the situation discussed in Question 38-2, a conditional put option. If the debts transferred were all high quality, and the likelihood of a material adverse change in interest rates was low (which, given that the transaction described in Question 38-2 lasts for only six months, is not an unreasonable assumption), it would be unlikely that the transferee's put option would be exercised. On this view, it might seem more reasonable for the transferor to derecognise the assets and recognise the put option as a liability. Ultimately, this discussion exposes the issue of whether there is any real basis for attempting to distinguish between 'conditional' and 'unconditional' options, as discussed at D above.

Q&A 37-1 discusses a situation in which an enterprise sells receivables subject to a guarantee to compensate the buyer for late payment by the debtors, but with other risks, such as interest rate risk, retained by the buyer. The conclusion in this case is that the enterprise should derecognise the receivables, and recognise the guarantee as a separate financial instrument. The distinction between the conclusion here and those discussed above appears to be that, in this case, only one risk (i.e. credit risk) has been retained. However, it is unfortunate that there is no discussion of what proportion of the total risk is represented by late payment risk. In other words, is the conclusion based on the *number* of risks, or the *level* of risk, retained? We would like to hope that the latter was intended. However, this seems doubtful since, in most debt factoring transactions, slow payment and bad debt risk, while possibly a minority of the number of total possible risks, comprise the great majority of the total risk.

To summarise, IAS 39 and the implementation guidance discuss four situations which, economically speaking are not in our view significantly different. The conclusion is that in two cases the appropriate treatment is full derecognition, in another no derecognition and in the third a form of partial derecognition with no apparent basis in IAS 39. This indicates, in our view, that the IASB needs to readdress the derecognition criteria, and in particular the significance of risk transfer, as a matter of some priority.

F Indications that control has passed to transferee

While the transferor and transferee are not required to consider the accounting treatment adopted by the other party, it is clear that, as a matter of principle, one or other party (but not both) must control the asset transferred.[121]

IAS 39 states that the transferor generally has lost control of a transferred financial asset only if the transferee has the ability to obtain the benefits of the transferred asset. That ability is demonstrated, for example, if the transferee:

- is free either to sell or to pledge approximately the full fair value of the transferred asset; or
- is a special-purpose entity whose permissible activities are limited, and either the special purpose entity itself or the holders of beneficial interests in that entity have the ability to obtain substantially all of the benefits of the transferred asset.[122]

However, IAS 39 warns that this guidance must not be read in isolation from that discussed at B to D above. For example, a bank may transfer a loan to another bank, on terms that, in order to preserve the relationship of the transferor bank with its customer, the acquiring bank is not allowed to sell or pledge the loan. Although this would suggest that the transferee has not obtained control of the loan, in this instance the transfer is a sale provided that the transferor does not have the right or ability to reacquire the transferred asset.[123] There may be cases (such as the transfer of part of a loan) where neither the transferor nor the transferee can sell or pledge the loan, as it is jointly owned. However, it may well be the case that the parties can sell or pledge their rights in the asset, if not their share of the actual asset itself. In such cases the transaction must be analysed using the general criteria discussed in B to D above.[124]

G Transfers of assets to special purpose entities

Derecognition of assets is neither precluded nor assured simply because they are transferred to a special purpose entity (SPE) rather than directly to investors. If the SPE falls within the scope of SIC-12 and is therefore consolidated by the reporting entity (see 4.4 below), derecognition in the reporting entity's consolidated financial statements will not occur on transfer of the assets from the reporting entity to the SPE, but only on any subsequent onward transfer of the assets by the SPE that meets the criteria for derecognition under IAS 39.[125]

4.2.4 *Partial derecognition of a financial asset*

If an enterprise transfers a part of a financial asset to others while retaining a part, the part transferred should be derecognised. This would be appropriate, for example, where the enterprise:

(a) separates the principal and interest cash flows of a bond and sells some of them to another party while retaining the rest; or

(b) sells a portfolio of receivables while retaining the right to service the receivables profitably for a fee, resulting in an asset for the servicing right.

When such a transaction occurs, the carrying amount of the financial asset should be allocated between the part retained and the part sold based on their relative fair values on the date of sale.[126] The fair value of the part remaining could be calculated either as the net present value of the cash flows associated with the part retained, or as a portion of the market value of the whole.[127] The part retained may well undergo a change of nature and become, for example, an intangible asset, as in (b) above.

A gain or loss should be recognised 'based on the proceeds for the portion sold',[128] which is presumably intended to mean that it is calculated as the proceeds less the carrying value allocated to the part sold, together with any adjustments to the fair value of the part sold previously reported in equity.[129]

An example of such a calculation is given in IAS 39 as follows:[130]

Example 18.17: Partial derecognition under IAS 39 (1)

An enterprise originates €1,000 of loans that yield 10% interest for their estimated lives of 9 years. The enterprise sells the €1,000 principal plus the right to receive interest income of 8% to another enterprise for €1,000. The transferor will continue to service the loans, and the contract stipulates that its compensation for performing the servicing is the right to receive half of the interest income not sold (i.e. 1% on the original principal). The remaining half of the interest income not sold is therefore considered an interest-only strip receivable.

At the date of the transfer, the fair value of the loans, including servicing, is €1,100, of which the fair value of the servicing asset (i.e. 100 basis points of the interest retained less the expected costs of servicing) is €40 and the fair value of the interest-only strip receivable is €60. Allocation of the €1,000 carrying amount of the loan is computed as follows:

	Fair Value (€)	Percentage of Total Fair Value	Allocated Carrying Amount (€)
Loans sold	1,000	91.0	910
Servicing asset	40	3.6	36
Interest-only strip receivable	60	5.4	54
Total	1,100	100.0	1,000

The transferor will recognise a gain of €90 on the sale of the loan – the difference between the net proceeds of 1,000 and the allocated carrying amount of €910. Its balance sheet will also report a servicing asset of €36 and an interest-only strip receivable of €54. The servicing asset is an intangible asset subject to the provisions of IAS 38 – *Intangible Assets.*

The conclusion in the last sentence that the servicing asset is an intangible asset under IAS 38 is convenient but somewhat problematic. Firstly, we are not clear that the servicing asset in fact forms part of the original loan held by the transferor, since the right to service a loan only has real meaning in the context of a loan held by a third party. On this view, the servicing asset arises as a result of the transfer.

If the servicing asset is part of the existing loan (as represented by Example 18.17 above), then it is an internally generated intangible that does not obviously meet IAS 38's demanding criteria for the recognition of such assets (see Chapter 11 at 5.3.1). If, instead, the servicing asset a newly purchased intangible asset, there is the issue that IAS 38 provides that, where an intangible is acquired through an exchange of assets, its cost should be measured as the fair value of any assets given up adjusted for any cash or cash equivalents transferred.[131] If this treatment is adopted, the table in Example 18.17 above would suggest that the carrying amount of the servicing asset should be its fair value (i.e. €40), not €36.

IAS 39 goes on to say that, in the rare circumstance that the fair value of the part of the asset retained (which may well be an intangible asset) cannot be measured reliably, then that asset should be recorded at zero. The entire carrying amount of the financial asset should be attributed to the portion sold, and a gain or loss should be recognised equal to the difference between (a) the proceeds and (b) the previous carrying amount of the financial asset plus or minus any prior adjustment that had been reported in equity to reflect the fair value of that asset[132] (see Chapter 10 at 4.6), as shown in the following example.

Example 18.18: Partial derecognition under IAS 39 (2)

An enterprise sells receivables with a carrying amount of $100 for $90. The selling enterprise retains the right to service those receivables for a fee that is expected to exceed the cost of servicing, but the fair value of the servicing right (an intangible asset) cannot be measured reliably. In that case, a loss of 10 would be recognised and the servicing right would be recorded at zero.[133]

This creates further potential tension between IAS 39 and IAS 38 since IAS 38 states that an intangible asset should be recognised only if its cost can be 'measured reliably',[134] a term that IAS 38 does not define, but which it clearly intends to be interpreted as implying a reasonably high degree of certainty. IAS 39, by contrast, for the purposes of its requirements to record certain items at fair value effectively deems almost anything other than certain unquoted equities, and derivatives of such equities, to be capable of being 'reliably determined'[135] (see Chapter 10 at 4.8). It appears that the drafters of IAS 39 may have assumed that 'reliably determined' in IAS 39 means the same as 'reliably measurable' in IAS 38, but it is not clear that this is the case. It is therefore not impossible that a partial derecognition of a financial asset could give rise to an intangible asset that is assumed by IAS 39 to be capable of being recognised, but which does not in fact meet the recognition criteria of IAS 38!

4.2.5 *Derecognition of financial asset coupled with a new financial asset or liability*

If an enterprise transfers control of an entire financial asset but, in doing so, creates a new financial asset or assumes a new financial liability, the enterprise should recognise the new financial asset or financial liability at fair value and should recognise a gain or loss on the transaction based on the difference between:

(a) the proceeds; and

(b) the carrying amount of the financial asset sold plus the fair value of any new financial liability assumed, minus the fair value of any new financial asset acquired, and plus or minus any adjustment that had previously been reported in equity to reflect the fair value of that asset (see Chapter 10 at 4.6).[136]

IAS 39 gives as examples of such a transaction:

- selling a portfolio of receivables while assuming an obligation to compensate the purchaser of the receivables if collections are below a specified level; and
- selling a portfolio of receivables while retaining the right to service the receivables for a fee, when the fee to be received is less than the costs of servicing, thereby resulting in a liability for the servicing obligation.[137]

However, as the discussion in 4.2.3 E above indicates, this should not be taken as implying that all debt factoring arrangements will be 'off-balance sheet' under IAS.

The treatment is illustrated in the example below.

Example 18.19: Derecognition of financial asset coupled with new financial asset or liability

A transfers certain receivables to B for a single, fixed cash payment. A is not required to make future payments of interest on the cash it has received from B. However, A guarantees B against default loss on the receivables up to a specified amount. Actual losses in excess of the amount guaranteed will be borne by B. As a result of the transaction, A has lost control over the receivables and B has obtained control. B now has the contractual right to receive cash inherent in the receivables as well as a guarantee from A. Under the requirements summarised above:

- A removes the receivables from its balance sheet because they were sold to B, and B recognises the receivables on its balance sheet; and
- the guarantee is treated as a separate financial instrument, created as a result of the transfer, to be recognised as a financial liability by A and a financial asset by B. For practical purposes, B might include the guarantee asset with the receivables.[138]

In the rare circumstance that the fair value of the new financial asset or new financial liability cannot be measured reliably, then:

(a) If a new financial asset is created but cannot be measured reliably, its initial carrying amount should be zero, and a gain or loss should be recognised equal to the difference between:

   (i) the proceeds; and

   (ii) the previous carrying amount of the derecognised financial asset plus or minus any prior adjustment that had been reported in equity to reflect the fair value of that asset (see Chapter 10 at 4.4.1) .

(b) If a new financial liability is assumed but cannot be measured reliably, its initial carrying amount should be such that no gain is recognised on the transaction (i.e. the excess of proceeds over carrying value is treated as the liability). In addition, if IAS 37 – *Provisions, Contingent Liabilities and Contingent Assets*, requires recognition of a provision (see Chapter 28 at 7.2), a loss should be recognised.

In determining whether or not the fair value of any new financial asset created or financial liability assumed is reliably measurable, a reporting enterprise should follow the general principles of IAS 39.[139] In broad terms, IAS 39 regards all financial assets and liabilities as reliably measurable except certain unquoted equities or instruments linked to them (see Chapter 10 at 4.8).

If application of these requirements results in a guarantee being recognised as a liability, it continues to be recognised as a liability of the guarantor, measured at its fair value (or at the greater of its original recorded amount and any provision required by IAS 37, if fair value cannot be reliably measured), until it expires. If the guarantee involves a large population of items, the guarantee should be measured by weighting all possible outcomes by their associated probabilities.[140]

4.3 Offset

4.3.1 *General (IAS 1)*

IAS 1 sets out the general principle that assets and liabilities should not be offset except where such offset is permitted or required by another accounting standard. However, it clarifies that the presentation of, for example, stock less a provision for obsolescence, or debtors net of a provision for bad and doubtful debts is not offsetting.[141]

4.3.2 *Offset of financial assets and financial liabilities (IAS 32)*

IAS 32 provides that a financial asset and a financial liability should be offset and the net amount reported in the balance sheet when an enterprise:

(a) has a legally enforceable right to set off the recognised amounts; and

(b) intends either to settle on a net basis, or to realise the asset and settle the liability simultaneously.[142]

Offset is appropriate in such circumstances, because the enterprise has in effect only a single cash flow and, hence, a single financial asset or financial liability.[143] Offset is not equivalent to derecognition, since no gain or loss can ever arise on offset, but may arise on derecognition.[144]

IAS 32 elaborates further on the detail of the conditions (which differ in many key respects from the offset criteria in FRS 5 – see 2.7 above) as follows.

A Offset between more than two parties

IAS 32 describes a right of set-off as 'a debtor's legal right, by contract or otherwise, to settle or otherwise eliminate all or a portion of an amount due to a creditor by applying against that amount an amount due from the creditor.' The effectiveness of the right of set-off is thus essentially a legal matter, so that the specific conditions supporting the right may vary from one legal jurisdiction to another. Care must therefore be taken to establish which laws apply to the relationships between the parties.[145]

In unusual circumstances, a debtor may have a legal right to apply an amount due from a third party against the amount due to a creditor provided that there is an agreement among the three parties that clearly establishes the debtor's right of set-off.[146] This contrasts with FRS 5, which appears to allow offset only between two parties (see 2.7.2 A above).

B *Intention to settle net*

IAS 32 emphasises that, in order to achieve offset of a financial asset and financial liability, it is necessary not only that the reporting enterprise is able to settle them net but also that it actually intends to do so. It is argued that offset is appropriate only when the reporting enterprise has no exposure to the gross cash flows associated with the asset and liability and that, in the absence of an intention to settle net, there is no change to that gross exposure.[147] This contrasts with the position under FRS 5, under which, consistent with the ASB's general rejection of management intention as a basis for financial reporting, offset requires only the ability to settle net (see 2.7.2 C above).

IAS 32 notes that an enterprise's intentions with respect to settlement of particular assets and liabilities may be influenced by its normal business practices, the requirements of the financial markets and other circumstances that may limit the ability to settle net or simultaneously. When an enterprise has a right of set-off but does not intend to settle net or to realise the asset and settle the liability simultaneously, the effect of the right on the enterprise's credit risk exposure is disclosed by giving the general credit risk disclosures required by IAS 32[148] (see Chapter 10 at 5.5).

C *Simultaneous settlement*

IAS 32 clarifies that the reference to 'simultaneous' settlement in the conditions for offset set out above is to be interpreted literally, as applying only to the realisation of a financial asset and settlement of a financial liability at the same moment. The standard gives as an example the type of overall market settlement that occurs in a clearing house or in a face-to-face exchange. In other circumstances, an enterprise may settle two instruments by receiving and paying separate amounts, becoming exposed to credit risk for the full amount of the asset or liquidity risk for the full amount of the liability. Such risk exposures, though relatively brief, may be significant, so that offset is not therefore appropriate.[149]

D *Situations where offset is not normally be appropriate*

IAS 32 comments that its offset criteria are not normally satisfied when:

(a) several different financial instruments are used to emulate the features of a single financial instrument (i.e. a 'synthetic instrument'). For example, if an enterprise issues floating rate debt and then enters into a pay fixed/receive floating interest rate swap, the combined economic effect is that the enterprise has issued fixed rate debt. However, other than in exceptional circumstances, the enterprise's rights and obligations in respect of the swap exist independently of its obligations with respect to the debt. Therefore, offset is not appropriate;

(b) financial assets and financial liabilities arise from financial instruments having the same primary risk exposure (e.g. assets and liabilities within a portfolio of forward contracts or other derivative instruments) but involve different counterparties;

(c) financial or other assets are pledged as collateral for non-recourse financial liabilities;

(d) financial assets are set aside in trust by a debtor for the purpose of discharging an obligation without those assets having been accepted by the creditor in settlement of the obligation (e.g. a sinking fund arrangement); or

(e) obligations incurred as a result of events giving rise to losses are expected to be recovered from a third party by virtue of a claim made under an insurance policy.[150]

See also E below.

E Master netting agreements

It is common practice for an enterprise that undertakes a number of financial instrument transactions with a single counterparty to enter into a 'master netting arrangement' with that counterparty. These arrangements are typically used by financial institutions to provide protection against loss in the event of bankruptcy or other events that result in a counterparty being unable to meet its obligations. Such an agreement provides for a single net settlement of all financial instruments covered by the agreement in the event of default on, or termination of, any one contract. Where a master netting arrangement creates a right of set-off that becomes enforceable only following a specified event of default, or in other circumstances not expected to arise in the normal course of business (as is usually the case), it does not constitute grounds for offset under IAS 32.[151] Under FRS 5, however, a master netting agreement does generally create conditions under which offset is required (see 2.7.2 C above).

F Offset of items other than financial assets and liabilities

As noted in 2.7.2 D above, FRS 5 strictly requires offset between only monetary assets and liabilities. The scope of IAS 32 is wider in that it allows the offset of financial assets and liabilities, which include (for example) equity shares, which are not monetary items. However, there could be contracts providing for the exchange of identical or fungible assets that are not financial assets and liabilities.

The general prohibition in IAS 1 on offset other than as permitted or required by another IAS (see 4.3.1 above) would appear to prevent offset being used in this case. However, this requirement must, in our opinion, be read in the context of the over-riding requirement of IAS 1 that the financial statements provide information reflecting the economic substance of events and transactions and not merely their legal form (see 4.1 above).

4.3.3 *Income tax assets and liabilities*

Current and deferred tax assets and liabilities accounted for under IAS 12 – *Income Taxes* – are subject to specific offset criteria somewhat different, particularly in the case of deferred tax, from those in FRS 5. These are discussed in Chapter 24 at 7.2.5 A.

4.4 Consolidation of Special Purpose Entities (SPEs)

Like the ASB in the UK, the IASC has had to address the issue of an enterprise conducting its affairs through a vehicle that, though not meeting the definition of a subsidiary, is still controlled by the enterprise. The relevant pronouncement under IAS is SIC-12 – *Consolidation – Special Purpose Entities.* This requires an enterprise to consolidate a 'special purpose entity' ('SPE') when the substance of the relationship between them indicates that the enterprise controls the SPE.[152]

4.4.1 Definition of SPE

SIC-12 is in fact careful not to define an SPE, so as to minimise the possibility of avoiding its requirements through exploitation of a loophole in the drafting. Instead an SPE is described as an entity 'created to accomplish a narrow and well-defined objective (e.g. to effect a lease, research and development activities or a securitisation of financial assets)'. An SPE may take the form of a corporation, trust, partnership or unincorporated entity. SPEs are often created with legal arrangements that impose strict and sometimes permanent limits on the decision-making powers of their governing board, trustee or management over the operations of the SPE that cannot be modified, other than perhaps by its creator or sponsor (i.e. they operate on 'autopilot').[153]

This description is extremely wide and would, in our view, encompass not only a separate legal entity, but also an economic entity represented by a parcel of 'ring fenced' assets and liabilities within a larger legal entity, such as a cell in a protected cell company (see Chapter 7 at 2.3)

The sponsor (or enterprise on whose behalf the SPE was created) frequently transfers assets to the SPE, obtains the right to use assets held by the SPE or performs services for the SPE, while other parties may provide the funding to the SPE. An enterprise that engages in transactions with an SPE (frequently the creator or sponsor) may in substance control the SPE.[154] A beneficial interest in an SPE may, for example, take the form of a debt instrument, an equity instrument, a participation right, a residual interest or a lease. Some beneficial interests may simply provide the holder with a fixed or stated rate of return, while others give the holder rights or access to other future economic benefits of the SPE's activities. In most cases, the creator or sponsor (or the enterprise on whose behalf the SPE was created) retains a significant beneficial interest in the SPE's activities, even though it may own little or none of the SPE's equity.[155]

Neither a post-employment benefit plan nor an equity compensation plan is an SPE for the purposes of SIC-12.[156] The accounting for such entities is dealt with in Chapters 22 and 23 respectively.

4.4.2 *Determining whether an entity is an SPE*

SIC-12 is an interpretation of IAS 27 – *Consolidated Financial Statements and Accounting for Investments in Subsidiaries* (see Chapter 5 at 6), and emphasises those provisions of IAS 27 that indicate that an enterprise has control over an entity, even though it owns one half or less (or even none) of the voting power in that entity.[157] In particular, it points out that, under IAS 27, control of an entity comprises the ability to control the entity's decision making with a view to obtaining benefits from the entity. The ability to control decision making alone is not sufficient to establish control for accounting purposes, but must be accompanied by the objective of obtaining benefits from the entity's activities.[158]

These reminders are doubtless made in the context that the first line of defence for those seeking to establish an off balance sheet entity tends to be to argue that some third party (such as a charitable trust) owns all the voting rights. However, if the trust (as is typically the case) does not obtain any real benefit from the entity, this indicates that it is not the entity's parent for accounting purposes.

SIC-12 states that determining whether or not an enterprise controls an SPE is a matter of judgement on the facts of each case. However, one or more of the circumstances set out in (a) to (d) below may indicate that an enterprise controls an SPE:[159]

(a) In substance, the activities of the SPE are being conducted on behalf of the enterprise according to its specific business needs so that the enterprise obtains benefits from the SPE's operation. This is particularly likely to be the case where the SPE was directly or indirectly created by the reporting enterprise. Examples are: where the SPE:

- is principally engaged in providing a source of long-term capital to an enterprise or funding to support an enterprise's ongoing major or central operations; or
- provides a supply of goods or services that is consistent with an enterprise's ongoing major or central operations which, without the existence of the SPE, would have to be provided by the enterprise itself.

However, economic dependence of an entity on the reporting enterprise (such as relations of suppliers to a significant customer) does not, by itself, lead to control.

(b) In substance, the enterprise has the decision-making powers (including those coming into existence after the formation of the SPE) to obtain the majority of the benefits of the activities of the SPE or, by setting up an 'autopilot' mechanism, the enterprise has delegated these decision-making powers. Examples of such powers are:

- power unilaterally to dissolve an SPE; or
- power to change, or veto proposed changes to, the SPE's charter or bylaws.

(c) In substance, the enterprise has rights to obtain the majority of the benefits of the SPE and therefore may be exposed to risks incident to the activities of the SPE. These rights may arise through a statute, contract, agreement, or trust deed, or any other scheme, arrangement or device. Such rights to benefits in the SPE may be indicators of control when they are specified in favour of an enterprise that is engaged in transactions with an SPE and that enterprise stands to gain those benefits from the financial performance of the SPE. Examples are:
   - rights to a majority of any economic benefits distributed by an entity in the form of future net cash flows, earnings, net assets, or other economic benefits; or
   - rights to majority residual interests in scheduled residual distributions or in a liquidation of the SPE.

(d) In substance, the enterprise retains the majority of the residual or ownership risks related to the SPE or its assets in order to obtain benefits from its activities. Frequently, the reporting enterprise guarantees a return or credit protection directly or indirectly through the SPE to outside investors who provide substantially all of the capital to the SPE. As a result of the guarantee, the enterprise retains residual or ownership risks and the investors are, in substance, only lenders because their exposure to gains and losses is limited. Examples are:
   - the capital providers do not have a significant interest in the underlying net assets of the SPE;
   - the capital providers do not have rights to the future economic benefits of the SPE;
   - the capital providers are not substantively exposed to the inherent risks of the underlying net assets or operations of the SPE; or
   - in substance, the capital providers receive mainly consideration equivalent to a lender's return through a debt or equity interest.

SIC-12 clarifies that the fact that an SPE is an 'autopilot' company does not of itself disqualify it from being consolidated on the grounds that it operates under severe long-term restrictions, since the reporting entity will have typically either established those restrictions itself, or been party to agreeing them.[160]

5 CONCLUSION

In the UK, FRS 5 has been fairly, although inevitably not completely, successful in curbing the wilder excesses of creative accountants. In particular, the requirement to consolidate quasi subsidiaries, together with the general injunction to account for the substance of transactions rather than being diverted by their narrow legal form, have provided useful ammunition against contrived schemes that rely on artificial structures or improbable interpretations of events.

Nonetheless, we believe that FRS 5 requires substantial revision. Its drafting is in places impenetrable and some of its key principles are questionable. Its recognition rules are difficult to understand and do not really underpin established practice. The derecognition rules are also insufficiently developed, relying for the most part on a rather crude approach whereby items are on- or off-balance sheet in their entirety, with the idea of partial derecognition appearing in the standard as something of an afterthought, and not consistently applied even in the Application Notes. Finally, the linked presentation is neither fish nor fowl, and would have been better strangled at birth.

Under IAS, the lack of a comprehensive standard on off-balance sheet transactions is undoubtedly something of a weakness, but one which should not be exaggerated, given the extensive coverage of some key areas in individual standards. Indeed, we think that the underlying 'components' approach of IAS (and US GAAP) to derecognition issues is in principle superior to that of FRS 5. In practice, however, there is no doubt that the implementation of this approach in IAS 39 is less than wholly successful. As the discussion at 4.2.3 above indicates, the IASB itself is struggling, on the evidence of its published implementation guidance, to interpret IAS 39's derecognition rules in a manner that gives convincing, or even consistent, results in very similar situations. We therefore hope that the IASB will reconsider these provisions as a matter of some priority, and we welcome the fact it has announced a project to address derecognition in general.

References

1 FRS 5, *Reporting the substance of transactions*, ASB, April 1994, para. 12.
2 *Ibid.*, para. 16.
3 *Ibid.*, para. 47.
4 *Ibid.*, para. 13.
5 *Ibid.*, para. 43.
6 *Ibid.*, Rubric to Application Notes. However, for reasons that are not clear this also states that the diagrams and tables in the Application Notes do not form part of the Statement of Standard Accounting Practice.
7 *Ibid.*, para. 2.
8 *Ibid.*, para. 3.
9 *Ibid.*, para. 4.
10 *Statement of Principles for Financial Reporting*, ASB, December 1999 ('SoP') paras 4.6-4.32.
11 FRS 5, para. 17.
12 *Ibid.*, para. 18.
13 *Ibid.*, para. 20.
14 SoP, Chapter 5, Principles. In fact the wording of FRS 5 is more like that used in the 1995 draft of the *Statement of Principles*.

15 IAS 39, *Financial Instruments: Recognition and Measurement*, IASC, December 1998, para. 27.
16 This, however, is a possible future development; see Chapter 19.
17 SoP, para. 4.33-4.36.
18 *Ibid.*
19 FRS 5, para. 22.
20 *Ibid.*, para. 25.
21 *Ibid.*, para. 21.
22 Press Notice FRRP PN 65, Financial Reporting Review Panel, March 2001.
23 FRS 5, para. 72.
24 *Ibid.*, para. 73.
25 *Ibid.*, para. 24.
26 *Ibid.*, paras. 26 and 27.
27 *Ibid.*, para. 81.
28 *Ibid.*, para. 26.
29 *Ibid.*, para. 27.
30 *Ibid.*, para. 82.
31 *Ibid.*, para. 83.
32 *Ibid.*, paras. 28 and 88.
33 CA 85, Sch. 4, para. 5.
34 FRS 5, para. 29.
35 *Ibid.*
36 *Ibid*, para. 90.
37 *Ibid*
38 This is because CA 85, s259 defines an 'undertaking' as being a body corporate or partnership or an unincorporated association carrying on a trade or business with or without a view to profit. A UK trust does not fall within any of these categories.
39 FRS 5, para. 7.
40 *Ibid.*, para. 8.
41 *Ibid.*, para. 33.
42 *Ibid*, para. 96.
43 *Ibid*, paras. 96-97.
44 CA 85, s 227(5) and (6).
45 FRS 5, para. 38.
46 FRRP PN 44, *Findings of the Financial Reporting Review Panel in respects of the accounts of Associated Nursing Services plc for the year ended 31 March 1995 and 31 March 1996*, FRRP, 17 February 1997.
47 Under section 258(4) (participating interest and either dominant influence or management on a unified basis – see Chapter 5 at 1.2.2 E.
48 FRS 5, para. 35.
49 *Ibid.*, para. 36.
50 *Ibid.*, para. 30.
51 *Ibid.*, para. 31.
52 *Ibid.*, Application Note A, paras. A11 and A12.
53 *Ibid*, Application Note B, para. B11.
54 *Ibid.*, para. B19.
55 *Ibid.*, para. B21.
56 *Ibid*, para. B1.
57 FRS 5, Application Note C, para. C12.
58 These conditions are discussed further in paras. C15 and C16 of the Application Note.
59 FRS 5, Application Note C, para. C19.
60 *Ibid.*, para. C20.
61 FRS 5, Application Note D, para. D8.
62 *Ibid.*, para. D10.
63 *Ibid.*
64 *Ibid.*
65 *Ibid.*, para. D11.
66 *Ibid.*
67 *Ibid.*, para. D12.
68 *Ibid.*, para. D13.
69 *Ibid.*
70 *Ibid.*, para. D15.
71 *Ibid.*, para. D22.
72 *Ibid.*, para. D23.
73 *Ibid.*, para. D24.
74 *Ibid.*, para. D16.
75 *Ibid.*, paras. D18-D19.
76 FRS 5, Application Note D, para. D20.
77 It is addressed in paragraph 28 of Appendix III, but this simply repeats the substance of paragraph 102 of the standard.
78 FRS 5, paras. 78, 80 and 91.
79 The rule is in CA 85, Sch 4, para. 5, which is applied to group accounts by CA 85, Sch 4A, para. 1.
80 This is explained more fully in para. E14 of Application Note E.
81 As discussed in para. 71 of FRS 5, where the proportionate share of benefits and risks of part of an asset has been transferred, that part can be treated as a separate asset.
82 FRS 5, Application Note E, para. E15.
83 *Ibid.*, para. E22.
84 *Ibid.*, paras. E19 and E20.
85 *Ibid.*, para. E23.
86 *Ibid.*, para. E24.
87 *Application Note F – Private Finance Initiative and Similar Contracts*, ASB, September 1998.
88 *Ibid.*, para. F4.
89 *Ibid.*, para. F6.
90 *Ibid.*, para. F7.
91 *Ibid.*, para. F8.
92 *Ibid.*, para. F22.
93 Technical Note No. 1 (Revised), *How to Account for PFI Transactions*, H M Treasury, June 1999.
94 *Application Note F*, paras. F59 and F60.
95 *Ibid.*, para. F3.
96 FRS 5, para. 12(d).
97 SSAP 21, *Accounting for leases and hire purchase contracts*, ASC, August 1984, para. 14.
98 IAS 1, *Presentation of Financial Statements*, IASC, Revised July 1977, para. 20(b)(ii).
99 In very crude terms, UK GAAP tends to adopt an 'all or nothing' approach (i.e. an item is either on balance sheet or it is not), whereas US GAAP tends to adopt more of a 'component' approach

(i.e. dividing assets and liabilities into various parts and derecognising only some of those parts).
100 IAS 32 *Financial Instruments: Disclosure and Presentation*, IASC, March 1995 (revised December 1998 and October 2000). IAS 39, *Financial Instruments: Recognition and Measurement*, IASC, December 1998 (revised October 2000), para. 8.
101 *Ibid.*
102 IAS 32, para. 5, IAS 39 para. 11.
103 IAS 39, para. 35.
104 *Ibid.*, para. 10.
105 *Ibid.*, para. 37.
106 *Ibid.*, para. 43.
107 *Ibid.*, para. 36, Q&A 36-1.
108 *Ibid.*, Q&A 35-2 (first bullet).
109 *Ibid.*, Q&A 35-5. It is not entirely clear why the Q&A refers to a sale of an asset *after* its purchase, as this would appear to be a normal sale requiring no special guidance!
110 *Ibid.*, para. 38(a), Q&A 35-2.
111 *Ibid.*, para. 39.
112 *Ibid.*, Q&A 38-1.
113 IAS 39 draft Q&A 38-6, IASB, June 2001. A similar rationale underlies some of the proposals in the financial instruments discussion paper of the Joint Working Group of Standard-Setters (see Chapter 10).
114 IAS 39, Q&A 38-5.
115 *Ibid.*, para. 38(b), Q&A 35-2
116 *Ibid.*, para. 40.
117 *Ibid.*, Q&A 38-3.
118 *Ibid.*, draft Q&A 38-6, IASB, June 2001.
119 *Ibid.*, para. 38(c), Q&A 35-2 and 38-2.
120 *Ibid.*, Q&A 38-4.
121 *Ibid.*, Q&A 35-4.
122 *Ibid.*, para. 41.
123 *Ibid.*, para. 42.
124 *Ibid.*, Q&A 35-1 and 35-2.
125 *Ibid.*, para. 41, Q&A 35-3 and 41-1
126 *Ibid.*, paras. 47-48.
127 *Ibid.*, Q&A 47-1.
128 *Ibid.*, paras. 47-48.
129 This is the basic formula used for similar situations elsewhere in IAS 39 (e.g. para. 47 last sentence, para. 51, para. 54), and appears to have been omitted here only as a drafting error.
130 IAS 39, para. 50, Q&A 50-1.
131 IAS 38, *Intangible Assets*, IASC, July 1998, para. 34.
132 IAS 39, paras. 47 and 49
133 *Ibid.*, para. 49.
134 IAS 38, para. 19(b).
135 IAS 39, para. 70.
136 *Ibid.*, para. 51.
137 *Ibid.*, para. 52.
138 *Ibid.*, para. 53.
139 *Ibid.*, paras. 54-55.
140 *Ibid.*, para. 56.
141 IAS 1, paras. 33 and 35.
142 IAS 32, para. 33.
143 *Ibid.*, para. 34.
144 *Ibid.*, para. 35.
145 *Ibid.*, para. 36.
146 *Ibid.*
147 *Ibid.*, para. 37.
148 *Ibid.*, para. 38.
149 *Ibid.*, para. 39.
150 *Ibid.*, paras. 40, A25.
151 *Ibid.*, para. 41.
152 *Ibid.*, para. 8.
153 SIC-12, *Consolidation – Special Purpose Entities*, SIC, November 1998, para. 1.
154 *Ibid.*, para. 2.
155 *Ibid.*, para. 3.
156 *Ibid.*, para. 6.
157 *Ibid.*, para. 9.
158 *Ibid.*, para. 13.
159 *Ibid.*, para. 10 and Appendix.
160 *Ibid.*, paras. 11, 14-15.

Chapter 19 Leases and hire purchase contracts

1 INTRODUCTION

SSAP 21 – *Leases and hire purchase contracts* – broke new ground in UK financial reporting in two ways: it was the first accounting standard to apply the concept of substance over form, and it was the first to incorporate the present value basis of measurement into the historical cost model.[1] These two innovations allowed the standard to introduce the requirement for companies to capitalise assets in their balance sheets (together with the corresponding obligations) in prescribed circumstances – irrespective of the fact that legal title to those assets vested in another party.

The substance over form approach was based on the view that a lease that transfers substantially all of the risks and benefits incident to the ownership of an asset to the lessee should be accounted for as the acquisition of the asset and the assumption of an obligation by the lessee, and as a sale or financing by the lessor. Such leases were termed 'finance leases' and are equivalent to what are known as 'capital leases' in the US. In the case of leases which did not transfer substantially all the risks and rewards of ownership of an asset to the lessee, the accounting was relatively unchanged. These leases became known as 'operating leases' and do not require capitalisation in the balance sheet. Instead, operating lease rentals are charged to the profit and loss account of the lessee on a straight line basis over the lease term.

The second SSAP 21 innovation, the incorporation of the present value basis of measurement within the historical cost model, related to the amount at which the lease finance obligation and the capitalised lease itself was to be stated in the lessee's balance sheet. This is because it is the present value of the minimum lease payments that is recognised in the balance sheet as the liability under the lease, whilst the corresponding asset that is capitalised (at the same amount) represents the right to the use of the physical asset over the lease term. This means that the 'asset' capitalised under a finance lease is not the leased asset itself – although clearly the amount capitalised should approximate to the fair value of the asset.

SSAP 21 – together with IAS 17, SFAS 13 and its other equivalent standards around the world – has been in place for many years.[2] Consequently, the distinction between finance and operating leases and the related accounting consequences are now widely accepted internationally. Moreover, little has changed in the requirements of lease accounting for more than a decade, with the result that the accounting requirements are generally well understood and appropriately applied in practice.

At the same time, though, conventional accounting in this area is being challenged, and some major standard-setters around the world have strongly held views that the finance/operating distinction should be removed and that all rights and obligations arising under lease contracts should be recognised as assets and liabilities in the financial statements of lessees at fair value. This proposed new approach is discussed at 1.4 below.

1.1 What are leases and hire purchase contracts?

A lease is defined in UK GAAP as 'a contract between a lessor and a lessee for the hire of a specific asset. The lessor retains ownership of the asset but conveys the right to the use of the asset to the lessee for an agreed period of time in return for the payment of specified rentals.'[3] The term 'lease' is also used to refer to any arrangement with a similar result.

'A *hire purchase contract* is a contract for the hire of an asset which contains a provision giving the hirer an option to acquire legal title to the asset upon the fulfilment of certain conditions stated in the contract';[4] usually, this merely involves the payment of a specified final rental.

Under International GAAP, IAS 17 defines a lease in similar terms to SSAP 21 as being 'an agreement whereby the lessor conveys to the lessee in return for a payment or series of payments the right to use an asset for an agreed period of time.'[5] The standard goes on to state that 'the definition of a lease includes contracts for the hire of an asset which contain a provision giving the hirer an option to acquire title to the asset upon the fulfilment of agreed conditions. These contracts are sometimes known as hire purchase contracts.'[6]

1.2 UK GAAP: Overview of SSAP 21

SSAP 21 was issued in August 1984 after a lengthy and active exposure/discussion period. ED 29,[7] which led to SSAP 21, was issued in October 1981 after approximately five years of debate. It was argued that comparability between companies would require capitalisation of finance leases by lessees; in particular, the effects of non-capitalisation on companies' gearing and rates of return on assets were said to affect comparability. It was further argued that readers of financial statements could not determine the economic substance of asset financing transactions from the financial statements. This was because, in effect, a leased fixed asset represented an asset financed by a borrowing in an identical fashion to an asset purchased with a bank loan. However, in the case of a lease, neither the asset nor the borrowing would have been recognised in the balance sheet.

One case highlighting this was that of Court Line Limited, a public company which collapsed in 1974. The group used leased aircraft to operate a package holiday business, and at 30 September 1973 had undisclosed leasing obligations relating to assets costing £40m.[8] The shareholders' funds shown in the group balance sheet at that date amounted to approximately £18m.[9] As the Inspectors stated, 'the amounts involved were material and should have been disclosed'.[10] Although this suggested that full disclosure might suffice (rather than new accounting treatments), it certainly highlighted the need for changes in financial statement presentation in order that readers could fully appreciate the financial position of a company involved in leasing.

At the time that it was issued, SSAP 21 was one of the most controversial accounting standards, as it effectively invoked a substance over form approach to give an accounting treatment possibly different from the legal ownership position. As discussed below, this is not done explicitly, however, as the lessee is required to capitalise the right to the use of an asset – not the asset itself – that corresponds to the present value of the minimum lease payments under a finance lease that constitutes the balance sheet liability. In practice, the fair value of the asset will approximate to the right that has been capitalised, and the inclusion of the latter as an asset achieves the accounting result of substance over form.

SSAP 21 essentially involves a decision as to whether or not a lease meets the given definition of a finance lease; if not, then an operating lease exists. Such decisions will be made independently by both the lessee and lessor to determine the appropriate accounting treatment and disclosures. Broad guidelines and requirements are given in SSAP 21, but many areas are not specifically covered or are discussed only in the Guidance Notes issued with it.[11]

Under SSAP 21, hire purchase contracts which are of a financing nature should be treated similarly to finance leases, whilst the others should be treated similarly to operating leases. The vast majority will be of a financing nature and were already being accounted for similarly to the finance lease treatment required by SSAP 21. This is because it is usually intended that the hirer will obtain title to the asset concerned at the end of the hire period. All references in this chapter to leases include hire purchase contracts of the appropriate type, unless the context requires otherwise.

SSAP 21 does not apply to lease contracts concerning the rights to explore for or to exploit natural resources such as oil, gas, timber, metals and other minerals. Nor does it apply to licensing agreements for items such as motion picture films, video recordings, plays, manuscripts, patents and copyrights.[12] This, however, does not preclude SSAP 21 from being referred to for general guidance where it is considered appropriate.

1.2.1 The accounting requirements of SSAP 21

Lessees should capitalise finance leases and recognise a corresponding obligation in creditors. The capitalised asset should then be depreciated over the shorter of the leased asset's useful life or the lease term (see 2.1.5 below); capitalised hire purchase contracts should be depreciated over the hired asset's useful life. The obligation will be reduced by the element of rental payments, which is calculated to relate to its repayment, as distinct from the payment of interest. Lessee accounting is discussed in detail at 3 below.

Lessors should treat finance leases to their customers as amounts receivable included in debtors, i.e. the assets which are so leased will not be included as fixed assets. The amount receivable will be reduced by the element of rental receipts which is calculated to relate to the repayment of the receivable. This involves a complex calculation of allocating the rental receipt between capital and revenue. Lessor accounting is discussed in detail at 5 below.

SSAP 21 involves no special accounting treatment of operating leases unless the rentals are payable/receivable by the lessee/lessor other than on a straight-line basis. In such a case, the rentals should be taken to profit and loss account on a straight-line basis unless a more systematic basis is more appropriate. This is discussed at 3.6 and 5.2 below for lessees and lessors respectively.

SSAP 21 specifies certain disclosures to be made by lessees and lessors in addition to the adoption of the required accounting treatments above. The disclosures are outlined and examples given at 4 (lessee) and 6 (lessor) below.

1.2.2 The ICAEW review of SSAP 21

In the Autumn of 1991 the ASB requested the technical and research committees of the various CCAB bodies to review a number of existing SSAPs with a view to submitting a report on problems that are being encountered with them in practice. One of the SSAPs which the ICAEW was given to review was SSAP 21, and the resulting report was issued in March 1992 as a Technical Release of the Institute's Financial Reporting & Auditing Group, titled FRAG 9/92 – *Review, for major practical problems, of SSAP 21.*

FRAG 9/92 discussed a number of practical difficulties which had been experienced with SSAP 21, and in particular it focused on the distinction between finance and operating leases, accounting for sale and leaseback transactions and accounting for residual values. The recommendations of this report are referred to as the relevant topics are discussed throughout this chapter.

1.3 International GAAP: IAS 17

IAS 17's general approach to both lessee and lessor accounting is the same as that of SSAP 21. However, there are some important differences in the detail. For example, on the matter of lease classification, SSAP 21 has a rebuttable presumption that the transfer of substantially all the risks and rewards occurs if, at the inception of the lease, the present value of the minimum lease payments including any initial payment, amounts to substantially all (normally 90 per cent or more) of the fair value of the leased asset.

By contrast, IAS 17 does not include this '90% test', but instead includes a number of examples of situations that would normally lead to a lease being classified as a finance lease:[13]

- the lease transfers ownership of the asset to the lessee by the end of the lease term;
- the lessee has the option to purchase the asset at a price which is expected to be sufficiently lower than the fair value at the date the option becomes exercisable such that, at the inception of the lease, it is reasonably certain that the option will be exercised;
- the lease term is for the major part of the economic life of the asset even if title is not transferred;
- at the inception of the lease the present value of the minimum lease payments amounts to at least substantially all of the fair value of the leased asset; and
- the leased assets are of a specialised nature such that only the lessee can use them without major modifications being made.

In addition, IAS 17 lists the following indicators of situations that, individually or in combination, could also lead to a lease being classified as a finance lease:[14]

- if the lessee can cancel the lease, the lessor's losses associated with the cancellation are borne by the lessee;
- gains or losses from the fluctuation in the fair value of the residual fall to the lessee (for example, in the form of a rent rebate equalling most of the sales proceeds at the end of the lease); and
- the lessee has the ability to continue the lease for a secondary period at a rent which is substantially lower than market rent.

In the case of lessor accounting, there exists also an important difference between UK and International GAAP. IAS 17 requires finance income to be calculated using the (pre-tax) *net investment* method, whereas SSAP 21 requires that a lessor's income on a finance lease should normally be calculated using the (post-tax) *net cash investment* method.

There is also an important difference in the disclosure requirements of the two systems: IAS 17 requires disclosure of the *total* outstanding commitments under operating leases, whereas SSAP 21 requires disclosure only of the payments that the lessee is committed to make during the next year.

The requirements of IAS 17 are discussed in detail at 8 below.

1.4 The G4+1's proposed new approach to lease accounting

The development of conceptual frameworks for financial reporting by the ASB, the IASC and other standard setting bodies around the world could fundamentally change the way in which financial contracts such as leases are accounted for. Each of these conceptual frameworks identifies the elements of financial statements, including assets, liabilities, equity, gains and losses as the basic elements, and sets down recognition rules for their incorporation in financial statements. In the case of lease accounting, assets and liabilities are the most relevant elements, and the ASB's *Statement of Principles* defines these particular elements as follows: assets are 'rights or other access to future economic benefits controlled by an entity as a result of past transactions or events',[15] whilst liabilities are 'obligations of an entity to transfer economic benefits as a result of past transactions or events'.[16]

Looking at these two definitions, it seems likely that most leases, including non-cancellable operating leases, will qualify for recognition as assets and liabilities. This is because, irrespective of whether the lease is finance or operating in nature, the lessee is likely to enjoy the future economic benefits embodied in the leased asset, and will have an unavoidable legal obligation to transfer economic benefits to the lessor.

1.4.1 *The G4+1's 1996 Discussion Paper*

This is the conclusion that was reached by a Working Group consisting of staff members of the standard-setting bodies of Australia, Canada, New Zealand, UK, the USA and the IASC (known as the G4+1 group of accounting standard-setters). In 1996 the Working Group published a discussion paper entitled *Accounting for leases: a new approach*, which discussed the limitations of current lease accounting standards and set out a new approach to lease accounting.[17] Although the paper was not officially approved by the boards of the various standard-setters involved in its preparation, it was seen to be influential.

The Working Group claimed that 'current lease accounting standards are now agreed by many observers to be unsatisfactory, at least with respect to accounting by lessees'.[18] It asserted that the 'most frequently noted concern relates to the fact that the standards do not require rights and obligations arising under operating leases to be recognised as assets and liabilities in the lessee's financial statements'.[19] According to the paper, the result has been that the standards have inadvertently promoted the structuring of financial arrangements so as to meet the conditions for classification as an operating lease, thereby avoiding recognition in lessees' balance sheets of material assets and liabilities arising from operating lease contracts. Consequently, the paper advocated a new approach to accounting for lease contracts that was aimed at overcoming these perceived concerns about the effectiveness of current lease accounting.

The Working Group's new approach to accounting for lease contracts was based on the definitions of assets and liabilities contained in the various conceptual frameworks. Under the IASC's *Framework*, an asset is defined as 'a resource controlled by the enterprise as a result of past events and from which future economic benefits are expected to flow to the enterprise', whilst a liability is defined as 'a present obligation of the enterprise arising from past events, the settlement of which is expected to result in an outflow from the enterprise of resources embodying economic benefits'.[20] According to the Working Group, the clear implication of applying the IASC *Framework* to accounting for lease contracts 'is that it can be reasoned that all finance leases and most, if not all, operating leases qualify for recognition as assets and liabilities'.[21]

The Working Group's reasoning seems to have been based on the belief that the rights and obligations established by operating leases are no different in nature to those established by finance leases. This conclusion was reached through the application of the asset and liability definitions of the IASC's *Framework*: under both finance and operating leases, the lessee acquires a contractual right to enjoy the future economic benefits embodied in the leased property and incurs a contractual obligation to compensate the lessor for the use of the leased property over the lease term.[22] However, the question which should be asked is whether the conclusion reached reflects a shortcoming in existing lease accounting or whether it exposes a flaw in the *Framework*.

Overall, the Working Group's paper was well written and thought provoking. On the other hand, though, whilst it raised a number of legitimate issues, it did not provide many solutions. For example, the paper was critical of the existing criteria laid down in accounting standards to distinguish between finance and operating leases (describing them as being 'arbitrary') and suggested a distinction based on cancellable and non-cancellable leases in its place. However, it did not resolve the problem of how to distinguish between cancellable and non-cancellable leases. Furthermore, the paper did not distinguish between non-cancellable leases and other commitments or executory contracts, such as electricity supply agreements, service contracts and contracted capital commitments. This was a major shortcoming of the paper, that was later addressed by the G4+1.

In any event, the G4+1 continued its discussions of these and other technical issues that emerged from the 1996 discussion paper, and in December 1999 issued a new Position Paper on the same subject.

1.4.2 The G4+1's 1999 Position Paper

This Position Paper, entitled *Leases: Implementation of a new approach*, explored further the principles that should determine the extent of the assets and liabilities that lessees and lessors would recognise under leases, and how they might be applied to account for many of the features that are found in lease contracts.

Following the criticism received on the 1996 paper's failure to deal with executory contracts, the Position Paper addressed this issue and concluded that leases can be distinguished from executory contracts by the fact that leases cease to be executory when the lessor has provided the lessee with access to the leased property for the lease term. Based on this distinction, the G4+1 was able to assert that the proposals set out in the new Position Paper would, therefore, not apply to executory contracts, including take-or-pay contracts or service contracts.

In dealing with accounting by lessees, the paper proposed that the objective should be to record, at the beginning of the lease term, the fair value of the rights and obligations that are conveyed by the lease. Under this approach, fair value is measured by the fair value of the consideration given by the lessee, including the liabilities incurred, except where the fair value of the asset received is more clearly evident.[23] This means that, where a renewal or purchase option has a significant value (and assuming its value can be ascertained with sufficient reliability), the option should be accounted for separately from the rights to use the property for the non-cancellable period of the lease, and a portion of the minimum lease payments would be deemed to relate to the purchase of the option.

Although leases normally specify minimum rentals that must be paid over the lease term, some leases require the lessee to pay additional amounts that are not fixed in advance. Instead, the actual amounts that the lessee will be required to pay are contingent on the outcome of uncertain future events. Such rentals are commonly referred to as contingent rentals. Common examples are motor vehicle leases containing clauses where rentals are increased to reflect the actual mileage driven above an initially agreed mileage; property leases in the retail industry where rentals are related to the turnover in the lessee's business; and property leases where rents are periodically reset to current market values to take account of inflation. Arrangements involving leases of intangible assets, such as licences of trade marks, patents or other intellectual property, also commonly require payments that are linked to the licensee's exploitation of the rights acquired (such as royalties on sales derived from the use of the property). Under present standards contingent rentals are not included in the minimum lease payments for the purpose of determining whether a lease is a finance lease or an operating lease. Nor are they included in the minimum lease payments that are recognised as assets and liabilities in the event that the lease is treated as a finance lease. Nevertheless, the treatment of contingent rentals is important under the approach advocated in this paper, because it directly affects the amount of assets and liabilities that would be recognised for many leases.

The paper asserts that leases that contain renewal and purchase options give rise to similar issues to leases that contain contingent rentals, especially those that vary with usage. The similarity is that both kinds of leases give the lessee the option to 'purchase more' of the asset; the difference is simply whether the lessee purchases more time or more usage. In view of this similarity, the paper suggests that the same principles ought to apply to both circumstances. From this follows the suggestion that if the minimum payments required by the lease (such as the minimum payments specified in leases with contingent rentals) are clearly unrepresentative of the value of the property rights conveyed by the lease, an amount reflecting the fair value of such rights should be recognised as assets and liabilities. The fair value of the property rights conveyed by a lease might be determined by having regard to the payments required by a similar lease that had no provision for contingent rentals.

Where a lease conveys the right to use the leased item for part of its economic life only and the lessee provides a guarantee of its residual value at the end of the lease, the paper suggests that an asset and liability should be recognised at the beginning of the lease term measured at the present value of the payments the lessee is required to make during the lease term and the fair value of the guarantee (if it is practical to quantify it). The asset initially recognised represents the fair value of the right to use the item for the lease term.

After initial recognition, whenever an increase or decrease in the value of the residual value guarantee obligation above or below its carrying amount in the lease liability is foreseen, the lease liability should be remeasured to reflect the current estimate of the expenditure expected to be required to settle the obligation. The G4+1's preferred view is that the carrying amount of both the lease liability and the lease asset should be increased or decreased (subject to the carrying amount of the asset not being increased above a value that would cause an impairment loss), and the asset's revised carrying amount should be depreciated over the remainder of the lease term.

The following table provides an overview of the items that would be included in the liabilities of a lessee (and reported as such, with an asset at the beginning of the lease of a corresponding amount) and those that would not.

Items included in initial assets and liabilities	*Items excluded from initial assets and liabilities*
Minimum payments required by lease	
Amounts payable in respect of obtaining renewal options	Rentals relating to optional renewal periods
Contingent rentals that represent consideration for the fair value of rights conveyed to lessee	Contingent rentals relating to optional additional usage
Fair value of residual value guarantees	Residual values guaranteed where transfer of economic benefits in settlement is not probable

Leases that are at present characterised as operating leases (and therefore not included on the balance sheet) would give rise to assets and liabilities – but only to the extent of the fair values of the rights and obligations that are conveyed by the lease.

The general effect of the approach proposed by the G4+1 is that the amounts recognised as an asset and a liability by a lessee in respect of a lease of a given item would vary in amount depending on the nature of the lease. The financial statements would thus reflect the extent to which different leasing arrangements result in financial obligations and provide financial flexibility.

The Paper also proposed significant changes to lessor accounting practices.[24] Lessors would report financial assets (representing amounts receivable from the lessee) and residual interests as separate assets. In the G4+1's view, this would be a marked improvement in lessor accounting, on the basis that a lessor's investment in a leased asset has two distinct elements, receivables and residual interests, which are subject to quite different risks. The amounts reported as financial assets by lessors would, in general, be the converse of the amounts reported by lessees as liabilities.

1.4.3 Comment on the G4+1 Position Paper

It has long been inevitable that lease accounting would be brought into line with more recent standards and the various conceptual frameworks of the G4+1 members, because these pronouncements clearly have a different underlying basis. However, whatever theoretical underpinnings are used to support the accounting treatment, we believe that it is fundamental that the approach taken in a revised leasing standard should be consistent with that taken in other standards, for example, those dealing with provisions such as FRSs 7 and 12, IASs 22 and 37 and the IASC's recently issued standard on *Investment Property*, IAS 40.

It is a matter of some debate how the changes in the balance sheet structure of reporting entities that would result from the proposals would be viewed by the markets. Logic dictates that, because the proposed accounting has no impact on the prediction of future cashflows, users of accounts should not be unduly concerned by changes in the way in which leases are accounted for. Nevertheless, although changes in accounting in themselves change nothing, they may focus attention on existing ancillary problems by making the resulting inconsistencies more obvious.

We believe that the Paper is confused in its approach to the initial measurement of assets and liabilities of lessees. This confusion lies in the manner in which the Paper rationalises its accounting for rights and obligations under lease contracts as being the simple application of 'the normal principle of recognising assets and liabilities'. The Paper states quite correctly that 'assuming arm's length parties, the cost of an acquired asset is normally measured by the fair value of the consideration given'.[25] This is the principle that is followed throughout IAS, including for the initial recognition of intangible assets under IAS 38 and investment property under IAS 40. However, what follows in the Discussion Paper is, in our view, a distortion of this principle. The distortion comes through in the Paper's ensuing discussion of the precise nature of the recognised asset.

The issue is that the Paper focuses in conceptual terms on the recognition of the acquired asset (right) 'obtained by the lease', whilst the mechanics of the accounting are driven entirely by the recognition of the corresponding liability. The Paper focuses on the lessee recognising at 'fair value' a tangible asset and corresponding liability, whilst the economic substance is that the lessee has incurred a liability (equal to the present value of the expected payments under the lease contract), and acquired an *intangible* asset in the form of the right to use the asset. The fair value of the liability represents the cost of an intangible asset, not the fair value of a tangible asset. We believe that this is a distinction that is important to the disclosure of the asset in the accounts as well as to its initial and subsequent measurement. We believe that it would be misleading to describe, for example, a short-term non-assignable property lease in the balance sheet as tangible fixed asset land and buildings; in our view, both in terms of economic substance and legal form, this is an intangible right to use an asset for a specified period and we believe that it should be described and presented as such in the accounts.

The problem is then exacerbated in the discussion of subsequent remeasurement,[26] where in our view the Paper misses the symmetry argument. The only time there is symmetry between the asset and liability is on initial recognition when the liability is recognised at present value of the expected payments under the contract, and the asset is measured at its corresponding cost. Subsequent accounting of the liability and asset should be governed by principles equivalent to those set out in IAS 37 and IAS 38 respectively.

1.4.4 *The next step*

It has long been the announced intention of the ASB, IASC and other major standard setters to remove the distinction between operating and finance leases such that all leases are reflected on the balance sheet on the basis of the fair value of their components. The two G4+1 papers on the subject have prepared the ground for such a move, and it now seems to be the intention of the IASB to follow this through. Although accounting for leases is not listed amongst the nine technical projects on the initial agenda of the IASB, it is listed amongst the sixteen other issues that are being worked on in collaboration with one or more of the IASB's national standard setting partners.

2 UK GAAP: DETERMINING THE LEASE TYPE

2.1 The 90% test

A finance lease is defined as 'a lease that transfers substantially all the risks and rewards of ownership of an asset to the lessee',[27] whilst an operating lease 'is a lease other than a finance lease'.[28]

SSAP 21 gives guidelines for deciding whether 'substantially all the risks and rewards' have passed to a lessee. It is stated that 'it should be presumed that such a transfer of risks and rewards occurs if at the inception of a lease the present value of the minimum lease payments, including any initial payment, amounts to substantially all (normally 90 per cent or more) of the fair value of the leased asset. The present value should be calculated by using the interest rate implicit in the lease ... . Notwithstanding the fact that a lease meets [these] conditions ... , the presumption that it should be classified as a finance lease may in exceptional circumstances be rebutted if it can be clearly demonstrated that the lease in question does not transfer substantially all the risks and rewards of ownership (other than legal title) to the lessee. Correspondingly, the presumption that a lease which fails to meet [these] conditions ... is not a finance lease may in exceptional circumstances be rebutted.'[29] The more important terms used in performing the 90% test in SSAP 21 are explained below.

2.1.1 *The fair value*

This 'is the price at which an asset could be exchanged in an arm's length transaction less, where applicable, any grants receivable towards the purchase or use of the asset'.[30] If this fair value cannot be determined for the purposes of the 90% test, then an estimate thereof should be used. This will not usually be required for lessors, but may be for lessees who are unaware of the cost of the leased asset.

2.1.2 *The implicit interest rate*

This 'is the discount rate that at the inception of a lease, when applied to the amounts which the lessor expects to receive and retain, produces an amount (the present value) equal to the fair value of the leased asset'.[31]

The amounts the lessor expects to receive and retain comprise the following:

(a) the minimum lease payments to the lessor (all elements (a) to (c) at 2.1.3 below); plus

(b) any unguaranteed residual value; less

(c) any part of (a) and (b) above for which the lessor will be accountable to the lessee.

If the implicit interest rate cannot be calculated due to inadequate information then an estimate may be used. This will not usually apply to the lessor, who will be likely to have all relevant information available. However, a lessee may not have access to this information and may be unable to make estimates thereof. If the interest rate implicit in the lease is not determinable, it should be estimated by reference to the rate which a lessee would be expected to pay on a similar lease.

Nevertheless, it was pointed out by the ICAEW working party that reviewed SSAP 21 that situations may arise where the lessee might also not know the rate payable on a similar lease. The working party recommended that in these circumstances the lessee's incremental borrowing rate should be used.[32]

2.1.3 *The minimum lease payments*[33]

There are three possible elements of this:

(a) the minimum payments over the remaining part of the lease term;

(b) any residual amount guaranteed by the lessee or a party related to the lessee; and

(c) any residual amounts guaranteed by any other party.

The elements to be included depend on the intended use of the minimum lease payments calculation as follows:

(i) all elements are used in the calculation of the implicit interest rate (for use in the 90% test);

(ii) all elements are used in the 90% test performed by the lessor. The total of these elements plus any unguaranteed residual value will represent the lessor's gross investment in the lease (see 5.3 below);

(iii) elements (a) and (b) are used in the 90% test performed by the lessee. The present value of this minimum lease payments figure will represent both the capitalised fixed asset and the initial finance lease obligation for the lessee (see 3.2 and 3.3 below respectively).

The minimum lease payments should not include any contingent rentals, for example those dependent on the level of use of the equipment. However if, for example, the lessee guaranteed to use the equipment to a certain level, then that level of rental would be included.

2.1.4 *An unguaranteed residual value*

This is 'that portion of the residual value of the leased asset (estimated at the inception of the lease), the realisation of which by the lessor is not assured or is guaranteed solely by a party related to the lessor'.[34]

2.1.5 *The lease term*

This is 'the period for which the lessee has contracted to lease the asset and any further terms for which the lessee has the option to continue to lease the asset, with or without further payment, which option it is reasonably certain at the inception of the lease that the lessee will exercise'.[35] Usually a lease can be easily divided into the primary term, during which the lessee is committed to make certain rental payments (with a termination rental payable upon termination before the end of the primary term) and a secondary term, for which the lessee can extend the lease if desired. It is general practice that any secondary term is only included in the lease term for 90% test calculations if it is highly probable that the term will be so extended, i.e. the 'reasonably certain' criterion is generally strictly interpreted. If a peppercorn (nominal) rental is payable in the secondary lease term period, the lease term should normally include the secondary term although the rentals can probably be ignored on materiality grounds in performing the 90% test.

2.2 90% test example

The following example illustrates the application of the 90% test:

Example 19.1

Details of a non-cancellable lease are as follows:

(i) Fair value (per 2.1.1 above) = £10,000

(ii) Five annual rentals payable in advance of £2,000

(iii) Total estimated residual value at end of five years = £3,000 of which £2,000 is guaranteed by the lessee.

The implicit interest rate in the lease (per 2.1.2 above) is that which gives a present value of £10,000 for the five rentals plus the total estimated residual value at the end of year 5. This rate can be calculated as 10.93%.

This rate is then used to calculate the present value of the minimum lease payments. As explained in 2.1.3 above, this example gives rise to identical minimum lease payments from both the lessee's and lessor's points of view. This is because there is no guarantee of any part of the residual by a party other than the lessee and the minimum lease payments will be the five annual rentals plus the residual guaranteed by the lessee of £2,000. The present value of these minimum lease payments is calculated as £9,405.

This present value figure is 94.05% of the asset's fair value and a finance lease is therefore indicated.

All of the above information will be known to the lessor as it will have been used in the pricing decision for the lease. However, the lessee may not know either the fair value or the unguaranteed residual value and, therefore, the implicit interest rate. If either of the first two of these is not known, the lessee is permitted by SSAP 21 to estimate what they are and so calculate the implicit interest rate. Alternatively, the lessee may feel that such an estimation is better made of the implicit interest rate directly, rather than of a parameter which will then allow that rate to be calculated.

It is important to note that the 90% test can result in different answers being given for the lessor and lessee, for example it may indicate a finance lease from the lessor but an operating lease to the lessee. There are two possible reasons for this. First, and most commonly, the lessor may receive a guarantee of the estimated (significant) residual of the leased asset by a party other than the lessee and accordingly, using the 90% test, an operating lease may be indicated for the lessee whereas a finance lease is indicated for the lessor. Second, as shown above, the lessee may not have the full information available to the lessor and his estimates of fair value or residual value may be so different from the correct figures (known to the lessor) that his classification of the lease is incorrect.

2.3 Determining the lease type – other factors

In 1987 the ICAEW published TR 664 – *Implementation of SSAP 21 'Accounting for leases and hire purchase contracts'* – in an attempt to influence the practice of interpreting the 90% test as a firm rule. It stated that any evaluation of a lease agreement should involve an overall examination of substantial risks and rewards as follows: 'Lease agreements give rise to a set of rights, rewards, risks and obligations and can be complex. The package must be analysed with greater weight given to aspects of the agreement which are likely to have a commercial effect in practice. In this way the substance of the transaction can be identified and then reflected in the financial statements in order to give a true and fair view. ... [The 90% test] does not provide a strict mathematical definition of a finance lease. Such a narrow interpretation would be contrary to the spirit of SSAP 21 and SSAPs generally.'[36]

Consequently, although the 90% test outlined above is important, there are a number of other factors which need to be considered in deciding whether or not substantially all the risks and rewards of ownership have passed. The crucial question is whether the terms of the transaction, taken as a whole, are such that the lessor can expect to be fully compensated for his investment in the leased asset without having to enter into further transactions with other parties. Affirmative answers to the following questions would tend to indicate that a finance lease exists:

(a) If the lessee can cancel the lease, will he bear any losses associated with the cancellation?

(b) Will the lessee gain or lose from any fluctuations in the market value of the residual? (For example, he may receive a rental rebate equalling most of the sales proceeds at the end of the lease.)

(c) Does the lessee have the ability to continue the lease for a secondary period at a nominal rental?

(d) Is the expected lease term equal to substantially all of the asset's expected useful life?

(e) Are the leased assets of a specialised nature such that only the lessee (or a limited number of other parties) can use them without major modifications being made?

One factor which is sometimes considered to be relevant in determining the lease type is whether or not the lessee is responsible for insurance, maintenance, etc. However, we do not believe that this should necessarily be a conclusive factor in determining the lease type. This is because, even if under the lease the lessor (or another party) accepts responsibility for these items, the lessee through making increased rental payments to the lessor (or the other party) is in fact bearing the responsibility for them. Consequently, the position is no different from that where the lessee owns an asset which is insured and is covered by a maintenance agreement.

In evaluating the risks and rewards, one should consider which factors are most likely to have an economic effect on the parties to the lease. The various factors are interdependent to some extent, for example if the lease term is for substantially all of the asset's expected useful economic life, or the asset is of a specialised nature, then the residual value is likely to be very low.

In fact, this was the approach favoured by the ICAEW working party which reviewed SSAP 21 for practical problems. In its report (see ICAEW Technical Release FRAG 9/92), the working party recommended a move away from the 90% test which, in its view, had become a mechanistically applied rule, towards an approach based on qualitative tests.

The report stated that 'any percentage test is arbitrary in that a 90% test for one asset may generate significant risks for a lessor and an 80% test for another asset may produce lower levels of risk for a lessor. … Some [of the working party] believe that a percentage test should be retained but relegated to one of several tests. However, the majority view is that a percentage test should be abandoned; if it remains there is a fear that its status will be elevated in the same way that SSAP 21's 90% guide has become a rule. We therefore suggest that if the "substantially all risks and rewards" route is to be taken the ASB considers replacing a numerical approach, whether guide or strict rule, with an approach based on qualitative tests.'[37]

The report then listed the following six examples of qualitative tests which might be considered in deciding whether or not substantially all the risks and rewards of ownership of an asset have been transferred:[38]

- are the lease rentals based on a market rate for use of the asset or a financing rate for use of the funds?
- what is the nature of the lessor's business?
- is the existence of put and call options a feature of the lease? If so, are they exercisable at a predetermined price or formula or are they exercisable at the market price at the time the option is exercised?

- which party carries the risk of a fall in value of the asset and which party benefits from any capital appreciation?
- does the lessee have the use of the asset for a period broadly equating to the likely useful economic life of the asset?
- does the lessor intend to earn his total return on this transaction alone or does he intend to rely on subsequent sales or lease revenue?

However, the working party points out that in applying these qualitative tests in practice, the answers to the above questions would have to be interpreted in the context of the risks that lessors will be prepared to take. In this context, the report noted that the leasing industry had changed considerably over the last ten years and that lessors will now take on very different risks. For this reason, it is suggested that a lessor should not, on the face of it, be equated to a bank; similarly, a lessor in a banking group is not *necessarily* a finance lessor.[39]

We fully support the ICAEW working party's recommendation for the abolition of the 90% test in favour of an approach based on qualitative tests. In fact, it is our view that a qualitative approach as outlined above is inherent in SSAP 21 as currently drafted and is, to a certain extent, already followed in practice. More importantly though, such an approach is endorsed by the general principles contained in FRS 5 for reporting the substance of transactions. However, as discussed at 1.4.4 above, it seems that the IASB will soon be putting forward proposals for the abolition of the operating/finance lease distinction; consequently, it seems highly unlikely that the ASB will embark on an exercise to refine SSAP 21.

2.4 Determining the lease type – the impact of FRS 5

Since the overriding principle of FRS 5 – *Reporting the Substance of Transactions* – is that transactions should be accounted for according to their economic substance rather than their legal form, some might suggest that FRS 5 has superseded SSAP 21 in the area of lease classification. However, FRS 5 states clearly that where the substance of a transaction or the treatment of any resulting asset or liability falls not only within the scope of FRS 5 but also directly within the scope of another FRS, SSAP or a specific statutory requirement governing the recognition of assets or liabilities, the standard or statute that contains the more specific provisions should be applied.[40]

Presumably, the purpose of this requirement is to ensure that FRS 5 does not inadvertently undermine the authority of existing standards and legislation. For example, obligations under non-cancellable operating leases which are currently off balance sheet under SSAP 21, would otherwise be caught by the FRS 5 definition of liabilities and would have to be brought on balance sheet, were it not for the requirement that the more specific provisions of (in this case) SSAP 21 should be applied.

Consequently, since SSAP 21 contains the more specific provisions governing lease accounting, one would look to that standard as the primary source of authoritative guidance in this area – despite the fact that it is stated in the explanation section of

FRS 5 that 'the general principles of the FRS will also be relevant in ensuring that leases are classified as finance or operating leases in accordance with their substance'.[41] The practical reality is that unless and until SSAP 21 is superseded and the 90% test abolished, preparers should continue to look to that standard when accounting for stand-alone leases that fall wholly within its parameters. However, where FRS 5 will come more into play in the classification of leases will be in situations such as sale and leaseback transactions involving options, where FRS 5 contains more specific guidance than SSAP 21. This is discussed in more detail at 7.4 below.

3 ACCOUNTING BY LESSEES

3.1 Introduction

When it is determined that material finance leases exist for a lessee on the basis of 2 above, there are two elements of the accounting entries which must be considered – the capitalised fixed asset and the related rental obligations. Each of these is dealt with in turn below.

3.2 Capitalised fixed asset

A finance lease should be capitalised at the present value of the minimum lease payments (MLP). The MLP have already been discussed at 2.1.3 above. The elements of MLP to be included for this purpose are:

(a) the minimum payments over the remaining part of the lease term; and

(b) any residual amounts guaranteed by the lessee or a party related to him.

This present value will be calculated using the implicit interest rate in the lease (the calculation of which is detailed at 2.1.2 above). In most cases the fair value of the leased asset at the inception of the lease will approximate to this amount. This is because we are calculating a present value of the relevant MLP using all MLP elements also used in the calculation of implicit interest rate, other than:

(a) any residual amounts guaranteed by a party other than the lessee (or parties related to him); and

(b) any part of either the total MLP to the lessor or unguaranteed residual value for which the lessor will be accountable to the lessee.

In most cases, these items will be insignificant, and the fair value of leased assets will, therefore, usually approximate to the present value of the relevant MLP. Example 19.1 at 2.2 above involved a situation where the present value of minimum lease payments was 94% of the fair value. This is lower than 100% because a part of the total estimated residual value is unguaranteed, i.e. the present value of the unguaranteed residual value (of £1,000) is 6% of the fair value of the asset. In such a situation a lessee would probably be entitled to take the fair value (of £10,000) as an approximation of the present value of MLP (of £9,405).

The capitalised fixed asset is then depreciated on a similar basis to owned assets (i.e. over the asset's useful economic life). For finance leases (but not hire purchase contracts) the depreciation should be calculated over the lease term, if this is shorter than the asset's useful economic life. The lease term should include any secondary periods over which it is reasonably certain that the lessee will exercise his extension option.

3.3 Finance lease obligation

Accounting for this can be split into three stages, as follows:

(a) the allocation of total rental payments over the lease term between finance charges and repayment of lease obligation;

(b) the allocation of the total finance charges to accounting periods; and

(c) the reduction of the obligation by the element of total rentals payable not allocated at (b).

In allocating total rental payments between finance charges and the repayment of lease obligation the total finance charge is calculated as the difference between the undiscounted total of MLP as per 3.2 above (i.e. including any residual amount guaranteed by the lessee), and the amount at which the lessee records the asset at the inception of the lease. This latter amount will, of course, be the discounted value of the relevant MLP (with the fair value of the leased asset usually being a close approximation to this). The discount element will, therefore, equal the total finance charges over the lease term.

The obligation under finance leases will be set up at an amount equal to the present value of relevant MLP with the other side of this accounting entry being the capitalised fixed asset described above.

3.4 Methods of allocating finance charges to accounting periods

In allocating the total finance charges over the lease term to accounting periods, SSAP 21 requires that this is done 'so as to produce a constant periodic rate of charge on the remaining balance of the obligation for each accounting period, or a reasonable approximation thereto'.[42]

The guidance notes to SSAP 21 detail three methods: actuarial, 'sum of the digits' ('rule of 78') or straight-line.[43] These are progressively easier to apply but also give progressively less accurate answers. There is, therefore, a trade-off to be made between the costs versus benefits of achieving complete accuracy. In making this trade-off, the question of materiality is important because differences between allocated finance charges under the three methods may be immaterial, such that the simplest method may be used for convenience. The following example illustrates the actuarial and sum of the digits methods of allocating finance charges to accounting periods:

Example 19.2

A five year lease of an asset commences on 1 January 2001. The rental is £2,600 p.a. payable in advance. The fair value of the asset at lease inception is £10,000 and it is expected to have a residual at the end of the lease of £2,372 (being its tax written down value at that time) which will be passed to the lessee as a refund of rentals. In addition, the lessee is responsible for all maintenance and insurance costs.

The minimum lease payments are 5 x £2,600 = £13,000 which gives finance charges of £13,000 – £10,000 = £3,000. The actuarial method attempts to calculate the finance charge in each period to give a constant periodic rate of charge on the remaining balance of the obligation for each period. This is done as follows:

Year	Capital sum at start of period	Rental paid	Capital sum during period	Finance charge (15.15% per annum)	Capital sum at end of period
	£	£	£	£	£
2001	10,000	2,600	7,400	1,121	8,521
2002	8,521	2,600	5,921	897	6,818
2003	6,818	2,600	4,218	639	4,857
2004	4,857	2,600	2,257	343	2,600
2005	2,600	2,600	–	–	–
		13,000		3,000	

The finance charge of 15.15% is that which results in a capital sum at the end of 2005 of zero and can be found by trial and error, using a financial calculator, computer program, mathematical formula or present value tables.

This lease involves fairly straightforward figures but it is still not easy to calculate manually. It is, therefore, possible to use the sum of the digits method to give an allocation of finance charge which is a close approximation to that given by the actuarial method.

The sum of the digits method calculations, for example, are as follows:

$$\text{number of rentals not yet due} \times \frac{\text{total finance charge}}{\text{sum of number of rentals}} = \text{Finance charge per annum}$$

Year	number of rentals not yet due			Finance charge per annum
				£
2001	4	x	£3,000 / 10 =	1,200
2002	3	x	£3,000 / 10 =	900
2003	2	x	£3,000 / 10 =	600
2004	1	x	£3,000 / 10 =	300
2005	–	x	£3,000 / 10 =	–
	10			3,000

We can now compare the finance charges in each of the five years under the actuarial and sum of the digits methods:

	Finance charge as % of total		Finance charge	
	Actuarial	Sum of the digits	Actuarial	Sum of the digits
Year	%	%	£	£
2001	37	40	1,121	1,200
2002	30	30	897	900
2003	21	20	639	600
2004	12	10	343	300
2005	–	–	–	–
	100	100	3,000	3,000

In situations where the lease term is not very long (typically not more than seven years) and interest rates are not very high, the sum of the digits method gives an allocation of finance charges which is close enough to that under the actuarial method to allow the simpler approach to be used.

It should be noted that the expected residual of £2,372 (which will be paid to the lessee) does not affect any of the above calculations. This expected residual will merely influence the depreciation policy of the lessee as regards the capitalised asset. He will depreciate to an expected residual of £2,372 and any difference between this net book value figure and the amount received by the lessee will give rise to a gain or loss on disposal of the asset.

3.5 Carrying values

At any point during the lease term the depreciated book value of a capitalised leased fixed asset and the remaining finance lease obligation under that lease will not usually be equal. Normally, this is because the method of depreciation bears no relation to that for allocating finance charges to accounting periods, as can be seen in the following example:

Example 19.3

If the lessee in the previous example depreciates the asset to its residual value of £2,372 on a straight-line basis over its life of five years, then the net book value compared with the outstanding lease obligation (using the actuarial method) at the end of each year will be as follows:

	Net book value	Outstanding lease obligation
Year	£	£
2001	8,474	8,521
2002	6,948	6,818
2003	5,422	4,857
2004	3,897	2,600
2005	2,372	–

3.6 Operating leases

3.6.1 *Lease rentals*

SSAP 21 requires that operating lease rentals are charged to the profit and loss account on a straight-line basis over the lease term irrespective of when payments are due.[44] This is logical as, for example, a large up-front payment made by the lessee should be allocated to the period over which a benefit is gained. Conversely, leases of land and buildings sometimes have a rent-free period in the early part of the lease, followed by a relatively higher rental over the remainder. Alternatively, leases are sometimes structured on the basis of stepped rentals, whereby lease rentals start at a below market rate, but are subject to pre-determined stepped increases, sometimes ending at above market rates to compensate for the lower rentals in the earlier years. In such cases, the rentals should again be charged to profit and loss account on a straight-line basis over the lease term. However, if a more systematic and rational basis is more appropriate, then that basis may be used; for example if the level of the use of the asset determines the level of rentals, then it would be appropriate to charge rentals when incurred.

3.6.2 *Reverse premiums and similar incentives*

An operating lease may include incentives for the lessee to enter into the lease. These incentives can take various forms, such as an up front cash payment to the lessee (a reverse premium), a rent-free period or a contribution to lessee costs. The question as to how such incentives should be accounted for in the accounts of lessees came to the fore following a decision of the Financial Reporting Review Panel in February 1994. The Panel was concerned about the adequacy of the information provided by Pentos plc in its 1992 accounts about the company's accounting treatment of reverse premiums received in respect of property leases. The relevant disclosures in Pentos' accounts were as follows:

Extract 19.1: Pentos plc (1992)

Accounting Policies

Reverse Premiums

Net income from reverse premiums is taken to profit over two accounting periods in order to match income received and start up costs incurred for new shops.

The amount taken to the profit and loss account in the year was included in 'Other Operating Expenses (Net)' and was not separately disclosed. The matter was resolved by the company agreeing to explain its accounting policy more fully in its 1993 accounts, and to disclose the amounts of reverse premiums received in 1993 and 1992. As a result, Pentos' 1993 accounts disclosed the following:

> *Extract 19.2: Pentos plc (1993)*
>
> **Accounting Policies**
>
> **Reverse Premia**
>
> Reverse premia arising in the period are matched with the costs of negotiating property leases and premia, and the costs of holding and maintaining unused property. The remaining balance of reverse premia is taken to profit over two accounting periods to match the initially low performance of new shops in the start up period.
>
> **Notes to the Accounts**
>
> **3 Expenses** [extract]
>
> Included in other operating expenses are property costs which are reduced by gross reverse premia in the amount of £3.4m (1992 – £6.3m).

However, despite the findings of the Panel, it is not entirely clear as to exactly what it was that the Panel was querying. Perhaps Pentos' referral to the Panel was driven by the school of thought which says that lessees should account for incentive payments received on a straight line basis over the period of the lease (as is the requirement under US GAAP)[45] and should not therefore be taken to income over the first two years of the lease. Evidence for the fact that the Panel was pursuing more than a mere disclosure issue may be found in the following paragraph in the Press Notice which publicised the Panel's decision: 'The Panel noted that existing requirements in the law and accounting standards did not provide unequivocal guidance as to the correct accounting treatment of reverse premiums and is drawing this matter to the attention of the Accounting Standards Board.'

In any event, the matter ended up on the agenda of the UITF which, in December 1994, issued Abstract 12 – *Lessee accounting for reverse premiums and similar incentives* – dealing with the issue.[46] However, since UITF 12 dealt only with lease incentives from the perspective of the lessee, the Abstract was subsequently superseded in February 2001 by UITF 28 – *Operating lease incentives* – which deals with the issue of how an incentive for an operating lease should be recognised in the financial statements of the lessee and the lessor.[47] The wording of UITF 28 has been taken largely from SIC–15, *Operating Leases – Incentives,* which was issued by The Standing Interpretations Committee (SIC) of the IASC in July 1999. (SIC–15 is discussed at 8.1.4 below.)

UITF 28 states that payment (or other transfer of value) from a lessor to (or for the benefit of) a lessee should be regarded as a lease incentive when that fairly reflects its substance. A payment to reimburse a lessee for fitting-out costs should be regarded as a lease incentive where the fittings are suitable only for the lessee and accordingly do not add to the value of the property to the lessor. On the other hand, insofar as a reimbursement of expenditure enhances a property generally and causes commensurate benefit to flow to the lessor, it should be treated as reimbursement of expenditure on the property. For example, where the lifts in a building are to be renewed and a lease has only five years to run, a payment made by the lessor may not be an inducement to enter into a lease but payment for an improvement to the lessor's property.[48]

The Abstract does not deal with incentives to surrender leases. However, it states that such incentives should be examined to determine whether in substance the incentive relates to the new lease, particularly where the offer of the incentive is linked to an arrangement to vacate a property under lease from a different lessor. Such consideration should take into account the market rentals applicable to the old and new leases. If it is determined that the incentive, or part of it, relates in substance to the new lease, the provisions of the Abstract apply.[49]

The UITF's consensus requires that all incentives for the agreement of a new or renewed operating lease shouldbe recognised as an integral part of the net payment agreed for the use of the leased sset irrespective of he incentive's nature or form or the timing of payments.[50] A esse should recoqnise the aggregate benefit of incentives as a reduction of rental epense. The benfit should be allocated over the shorter of the lease term and a perio ending on a de from which it is expected the prevailing market rental will be pable. The allocaon should be on a straight-line basis unless another systematic bas more represeative of the time pattern of the lessee's benefit from the use of the ed asset.[51]

3.6.3 *Onerous contract*

Although FRS 12 – *Provisions, cogent liabilities d contingent assets* – prohibits the recognition of provisions future operat losses,[52] the standard does specifically address the issue of ons contracts. It quires that if an enterprise has a contract that is onerous, the ent obligation under the contract should be recognised and measured as a pron.[53]

The standard defines an onerontract as 'a coract in which the unavoidable costs of meeting the obligationser it exceed theconomic benefits expected to be received under it'.[54] This seto require thathe contract is onerous to the point of being directly loss-maknot simply unenomic by reference to current prices. A common example o onerous contct seen in practice relates to operating leases for the rent of perty, and the andard includes the following example in Appendix III:

ract

An onay operates profitably from factory tht it has leaed under an operating lease. During December 2000 the entity relocates its operations to a new factory. The lease on the old factory continues for the next four years, it annot be cancelled and the factory cannot be re-let to another user.

Present obligation as a result of a past obligating event – The obligating event is the signing of the lease contract, which gives rise to a legal obligation.

Transfer of economic benefits in settlement – When the lease becomes onerous, a transfer of economic benefits is probable. (Until the lease becomes onerous, the entity accounts for the lease by applying SSAP 21 – *Accounting for leases and hire purchase agreements.*)

Conclusion – A provision is recognised for the best estimate of the unavoidable lease payments (see FRS 12, paragraphs 14 and 71).

The accounting for onerous contracts is discussed in more detail at 5.3 of Chapter 28.

4 DISCLOSURE BY LESSEES

4.1 SSAP 21 requirements

The following lessee disclosures are required by SSAP 21:

(a) policies adopted in accounting for operating and finance leases;[55]

(b) total operating lease rentals charged, analysed between those payable in respect of hire of plant and machinery and other operating leases.[56] All hire charges should be treated as operating lease rentals including very short-term rentals and rental of property;

(c) aggregate finance charges allocated for the period in respect of finance leases;[57]

(d) aggregate depreciation charged in the period on assets held under finance leases and hire purchase contracts;[58]

(e) totals of gross amount and accumulated depreciation for each major class of asset held under finance leases and hire purchase contracts. If this information is combined with owned assets then the net amount included in the overall total should be disclosed;[59]

(f) net obligations under finance leases and hire purchase contracts split between amounts payable in the next year, in two to five years inclusive and after five years. Alternatively, they may be shown as gross obligations with future finance charges being deducted from the total. The net obligations analysis may be combined with other obligations and liabilities;[60]

(g) payments committed to be made *in the next year* under operating leases for (1) leases of land and buildings, and (2) other leases; both amounts split between those expiring:

(i) within one year;

(ii) in the second to fifth years inclusive;

(iii) in over five years.

This disclosure, which is illustrated in Extracts 19.3 and below, is a rather incomplete requirement, since companies do not have to disclose the more useful total amount of minimum lease payments outstanding as of the balance sheet date (as is required for finance leases). In contrast, International GAAP requires that lessees with operating leases should disclose the total of future minimum lease payments under non-cancellable operating leases, analysed between the periods of up to one year, between one and five years, and in aggregate thereafter;[62] and

(h) commitments in respect of finance leases and hire purchase contracts existing at the balance sheet date when at that date neither has the asset been brought into use nor have rentals started to accrue.[63]

4.2 Related Companies Act requirements

The main disclosure requirements of the Companies Act which affect lessees are as follows:

(a) the balance sheet formats require creditors falling due within one year to be shown separately from creditors falling due after more than one year.[64] The net obligations under finance leases and hire purchase contracts will have to be split accordingly;

(b) particulars of financial commitments which:

  (i) have not been provided for; and

  (ii) are relevant to assessing the company's state of affairs.[65]

  Since finance leases are capitalised and the obligations are provided, this will normally only be relevant for operating leases. Usually, the disclosures required in (g) in 4.1 above will meet this requirement. Where, however, there are contingent rentals which have not been provided for, extra disclosure may be required.

There are a number of other disclosures required by the Companies Act which may affect lessees and these should also be considered; for example, details of movements in fixed assets[66] and details in relation to creditors.[67]

4.3 Disclosures in practice

The following are examples of disclosures given in practice by lessees:

Extract 19.3: Infast Group plc (2000)

Notes to the Accounts [extract]

1. **Accounting policies** [extract]

e. **Leasing**

Assets held under finance leases and hire purchase contracts are capitalised at the fair value of the asset at the inception of the lease, with an equivalent liability categorised as appropriate under creditors due within and after more than one year.

The interest element of the rental obligations is charged to the profit and loss account over the period of the lease and represents a constant proportion of the balance of the capital repayments outstanding.

Rentals under operating leases are charged to the profit and loss account on a straight-line basis over the lease term.

3. **Operating costs** [extract]

	2000 **£m**	1999 £m
Operating charges comprise the following charges/(credits):		
Depreciation of tangible fixed assets		
owned	**3.1**	6.6
held under finance leases	**0.8**	1.1
Operating lease rentals		
land and buildings	**1.8**	3.5
other	**1.1**	2.1

6. Net interest [extract]

	2000	1999
	£m	£m
Interest payable on:		
Finance leases	**0.2**	0.3

11. Tangible fixed assets [extract]

a. Group

	Land and buildings		Plant,	
		Long	equipment	
	Freehold	leasehold	and vehicles	Total
	£m	£m	£m	£m
Net book value:				
As at 31st December 2000	**5.9**	**1.2**	**11.6**	**18.7**
As at 1st January 2000	9.1	2.0	15.3	26.4
Net book value of assets held under finance leases included above:				
As at 31st December 2000	**–**	**1.2**	**2.7**	**3.9**
As at 1st January 2000	–	2.0	5.4	7.4

15. Creditors: amounts falling due within one year [extract]

	The Group		**Parent Company**	
	2000	1999	**2000**	1999
	£m	£m	**£m**	£m
Obligations under finance leases	**1.2**	2.0	**–**	0.1

16. Creditors: amounts falling due after more than one year [extract]

	The Group		**Parent Company**	
	2000	1999	**2000**	1999
	£m	£m	**£m**	£m
Obligations under finance leases	**0.8**	2.1	**–**	–

22. Analysis of net debt [extract]

The gross debt falls due as shown in the table below:

	Within one year	Within one to two years	Within two to five years	Over five years	Total
	£m	£m	£m	£m	£m
Finance leases	1.2	0.7	0.1	–	**2.0**

28. Capital commitments

The Group leases a number of properties and certain items of plant and equipment under operating leases. The minimum annual rentals under these leases are as follows:

	2000		1999	
	Land and buildings	**Other**	Land and buildings	Other
	£m	**£m**	£m	£m
Operating leases which expire:				
Within one year	**0.3**	**0.2**	0.1	0.3
In two to five years	**0.7**	**0.5**	0.3	0.6
Over five years	**1.2**	**–**	1.3	0.8
	2.2	**0.7**	1.7	1.7

It can be seen from the above extract that Infast Group discloses the information relating to its finance lease obligations within a note dealing with net debt. Another way is to give the information in a separate note, as illustrated below:

Extract 19.4: Arcadia Group plc (2000)

Notes to the Accounts [extract]

18. Lease obligations [extract]

	Group		Company	
	2000	1999	**2000**	1999
	£m	£m	**£m**	£m
Finance lease obligations falling due:				
Within one year	**1.0**	1.5	**1.0**	–
Between one and two years	**0.9**	–	**0.9**	–
Between two and five years	**0.6**	–	**0.6**	–
	2.5	1.5	**2.5**	–

As noted at 4.1(f) above, there is an alternative permitted method of disclosure of finance lease obligations. Rather than splitting the obligations by date of payment net of the future interest charges as illustrated in Extracts 19.3 and 19.4 above, some companies show the gross obligations with the future finance charges being deducted from the total. Cadbury Schweppes adopts this form of disclosure, as illustrated below:

Extract 19.5: Cadbury Schweppes plc (2000)

Notes to the Financial Statements [extract]

24 Leasing Commitments [extract]

The future minimum lease payments (excluding advances pending formal comments of leases) to which the Group is committed as at the year end were as follows:

	Finance leases		Operating leases
	2000	1999	**2000**
	£m	£m	**£m**
Within one year	**6**	8	**34**
Between one and two years	**5**	6	**25**
Between two and three years	**3**	5	**23**
Between three and four years	**2**	3	**15**
Between four and five years	**2**	2	**12**
After five years	**1**	2	**82**
	19	26	**191**
Less: Finance charges allocated to future periods	**(3)**	(5)	**–**
	16	21	**191**

As noted at 4.1(g) above, the requirement to disclose payments committed to be made in the next year under operating leases is, in our view, somewhat deficient. Far more useful disclosure would be that which is, for example, required under

US GAAP – namely the future minimum rental payments payable over each of the next five years and in aggregate thereafter. As can be seen from Extract 19.5 above, this disclosure has been provided by Cadbury Schweppes, although this is probably due to the fact that the company is an SEC registrant and prepares its UK annual report and Form 20-F as a combined document. In any event, several other UK companies that are registered with the SEC provide this sort of information on a voluntary basis in their UK annual reports. Included amongst these is BT:

Extract 19.6: British Telecommunications plc (2001)

Notes to the financial statements [extract]

29. Financial commitments, contingent liabilities and subsequent events

	Group		Company	
	2001	2000	**2001**	2000
	£m	£m	**£m**	£m
Operating lease payments payable within one year of the balance sheet date were in respect of leases expiring:				
Within one year	**7**	9	**3**	1
Between one and five years	**32**	37	**23**	26
After five years	**110**	140	**82**	85
Total payable within one year	**149**	186	**108**	112

Future minimum operating lease payments for the group at 31 March 2001 were as follows:

	2001
	£m
Payable in the year ending 31 March:	
2002	149
2003	139
2004	131
2005	121
2006	113
Thereafter	816
Total future minimum operating lease payments	1,469

Operating lease commitments were mainly in respect of leases of land and buildings

As illustrated in the above extract, SSAP 21 applies to leases of land and buildings as for any other assets. However, where property companies act as lessees of long leasehold investment properties, the commitments for ground rents under these operating leases are not usually shown.

One element of the disclosure requirements of SSAP 21 which is rarely seen in practice is that in respect of finance lease and hire purchase contract commitments existing at the balance sheet date when at that date neither has the asset been brought into use nor have rentals started to accrue.[68] Presumably companies are aggregating these commitments (where they exist) with their general disclosure of capital commitments contracted but not provided for.

5 ACCOUNTING BY LESSORS

5.1 Introduction

Essentially, a lessor is required to show amounts due from lessees under finance leases as amounts receivable in debtors, and assets leased out under operating leases as tangible fixed assets. The mechanics of lessor accounting for finance leases are more complex than those for a lessee, although, of course, the criteria which determine the classification of leases as either finance or operating are identical for both lessors and lessees.

5.2 Operating leases

Rentals receivable under an operating lease should be recognised on a straight-line basis (irrespective of when rentals are actually receivable) unless another systematic and rational basis is more representative of the time pattern in which the benefit from the leased asset is receivable.[69] This requirement of SSAP 21 is an attempt to ensure a proper matching of revenues with associated costs. A non-straight-line basis may be appropriate where, for example, operating lease rentals are dependent on the level of use of the leased asset. In this case, rentals should be recognised in the periods they become receivable.

Examples of situations where a lessor should recognise operating lease rentals on a straight-line basis, even if they are not so received, are where there is a rent-free period at the beginning of a lease of land or buildings, or where a balloon payment is to be made at the beginning or end of the lease period.

The issue of how an incentive for an operating lease should be recognised in the financial statements of a lessor has recently been addressed by the UITF in Abstract 28 – *Operating lease incentives*, which effectively provides an elaboration of paragraph 43 of SSAP 21. The UITF's consensus requires that all incentives for the agreement of a new or renewed operating lease should be recognised as an integral part of the net payment agreed for the use of the leased asset, irrespective of the incentive's nature or form or the timing of payments.[70] A lessor should recognise the aggregate cost of incentives as a reduction of rental income. The cost of the incentives should be allocated over the lease term or a shorter period ending on a date from which it is expected the prevailing market rental will be payable. The allocation should be on a straight-line basis unless another systematic basis is more representative of the time pattern in which the benefit from the leased asset is receivable. Where a building is accounted for as an investment property, the value at which it is stated in the balance sheet should not include any amount that is reported as a separate asset, for example, as accrued rent receivable. And finally, the Abstract states that, in accordance with normal accounting practice, an amount recognised as a debtor in respect of an operating lease incentive should be written down to the extent that it is not expected to be recovered.[71]

5.3 Finance leases

Broadly, there are two stages in accounting for finance lease receivables; first, the calculation of the gross earnings (finance lease income) element of total lease rentals receivable and, second, the allocation of gross earnings to accounting periods over the lease term. Gross earnings represent:[72]

(a) the lessor's gross investment in the lease which is the total of the minimum lease payments and any unguaranteed residual value estimated as accruing to the lessor; *less*

(b) the cost of the leased asset less any grants receivable towards purchase or use of the asset.

Gross earnings should then be allocated to accounting periods to give a constant periodic rate of return on the lessor's net cash investment.[73] The net cash investment is the amount of funds invested in a lease by the lessor and comprises the cost of the asset plus or minus certain related payments or receipts.[74] Tax-free grants that are available to the lessor against the purchase price of assets acquired for leasing should be spread over the period of the lease and dealt with by treating the grant as non-taxable income.[75]

The allocation of gross earnings to accounting periods is detailed at 5.4 (finance leases) and 5.5 (hire purchase contracts) below.

Having calculated the allocation of gross earnings to accounting periods, the lessor must then consider the amount at which the receivable should be shown in its balance sheet. The finance lease receivable should equal the lessor's net investment in the lease. This net investment will initially equal the cost of the asset less any grants receivable (i.e. the fair value) and will then be reduced by a portion of total rentals received. This portion will be the element of rentals receivable in a period which is not taken as gross earnings in the calculations described above.

5.4 Allocation of gross earnings – finance leases

5.4.1 *Introduction*

Owing to differences in tax treatments, different methods are used to allocate gross earnings to accounting periods under finance leases and hire purchase contracts. The latter is dealt with at 5.5 below, and the justification for the different treatments of finance leases and hire purchase contracts is considered at 5.4.5 below.

For finance leases, the gross earnings allocation should be made to give a constant periodic rate of return on the lessor's net cash investment. This involves the use of an 'after tax' method of allocation; the two most common are the actuarial after tax method and the investment period method.[76]

5.4.2 *Methodology*

The actuarial after tax and investment period methods allocate gross earnings on a basis which takes the tax effect on cash flows into account. This approach is used because we are attempting to match the revenue recognised under the lease with the expenses incurred (which may be partly notional) in funding the lessor's investment in the lease.

At any time during the lease, the lessor's net cash investment will represent:

(a) the original cost of the asset; less

(b) cumulative cash flow receipts to date (rental income, grants received, tax relieved through both capital allowances and payment of interest, together with interest receivable during any period of negative net cash investment); plus

(c) cumulative cash flow payments to date (interest payments and tax payable on both rental receipts and any interest receivable). This should also include an adjustment in respect of the profit the lessor takes out of the lease, because part of the rental receipts represents profit to the lessor over and above any interest he is estimated to be paying.

The interest payable/receivable is likely to be a notional figure, using appropriate rates for the lessor as at lease inception, to reflect an opportunity cost of funds raised or invested. Both interest payable/receivable and profit taken out should be calculated on the average net cash investment in any period. The profit taken out will be calçulated at the percentage rate which results in a net cash investment of zero at the end of the lease term.

The actuarial after tax method and the investment period method differ in their use of the calculated net cash investment at each period end to allocate gross earnings. Under the actuarial after tax method, the estimated profit taken out in each period is grossed up for tax and estimated interest costs, to give a derived apportionment of gross earnings in each period.

In contrast, under the investment period method the estimated net cash investment at each period end is divided by the total of such figures over the lease term to give the fraction of total gross earnings allocated to each period. Whereas the actuarial after tax method is more accurate, the investment period method may be preferred (if resulting differences are immaterial) since it is arithmetically simpler.

The application of the actuarial after tax and investment period methods is illustrated in the following example:

Example 19.4

The terms of a lease are as in Example 19.2 above, i.e. a five year lease of an asset commences on 1 January 2001. The rental is £2,600 p.a. payable in advance. The fair value of the asset at lease inception is £10,000 and it is expected to have a residual at the end of the lease of £2,372 (being its tax written down value at the time) which will be passed to the lessee. In addition, the lessee is responsible for all maintenance and insurance costs.

The lessor obtains writing down allowances on the leased asset at the rate of 25%. The rate of corporation tax is 35%. The lessor's accounting year-end is 31 December and he pays or recovers tax in the following year. Interest on funds borrowed is assumed to be 10% p.a., payable on 31 December.

The lessor's net cash investment in this lease can be analysed as follows:

Year	(a) Net cash investment at start of year	(b) Cash flows in year cost/tax	(c) Cash flows in year rentals	(d) Average net cash investment in year	(e) Interest paid	(f) Profit taken out of lease	(g) Net cash investment at end of year
	£	£	£	£	£	£	£
2001	–	(10,000)	2,600	(7,400)	(740)	(277)	(8,417)
2002	(8,417)	224	2,600	(5,593)	(559)	(210)	(6,362)
2003	(6,362)	(58)	2,600	(3,820)	(382)	(144)	(4,346)
2004	(4,346)	(284)	2,600	(2,030)	(203)	(76)	(2,309)
2005	(2,309)	(470)	2,600	(179)	(18)	(7)	(204)
2006	(204)	204	–	–	–	–	–
		(10,000)	13,000		(1,902)	(714)	
		(384)					

Notes to table:

(a) net cash investment at start of year: this is simply zero at the beginning of the lease and the previous year-end figure in later years;

(b) cash flows in year – cost and tax: the £10,000 outflow in 2001 is the purchase of the asset which is, for simplicity, assumed to take place on the day the lease commences. All other amounts relate to tax payable/repayable.

The basis of taxation of the lessor was detailed above and tax payable/repayable relates to the previous year's rentals receivable, interest paid and writing down allowance. The tax repayable in 2006 relates to 2005's rental receivable, interest paid, writing down allowance and the deduction relating to the passing of the asset's sales proceeds of £2,372 to the lessee. This deduction should actually enter the table in 2007, as that is when the tax repayment would arise from the sale in 2006, but is included in 2006 for simplicity. The sales proceeds and payment to the lessee are not shown as their net effect on the cash flows is nil;

(c) cash flows in year – rentals: the annual rentals received at the beginning of each year;

(d) average net cash investment in year: this is the sum of columns (a) to (c). For the purposes of this example, all cash flows are assumed to arise on 1 January of each year;

(e) interest paid: calculated at 10% of the average net cash investment in year shown in column (d);

(f) profit taken out of lease: this represents the amount required by the lessor to give a return on the lease over and above tax and interest costs. It is the percentage of the average net cash investment in year shown in column (d) which results in a net cash investment at the end of the whole transaction of zero. It can be found by trial and error but computer programs are usually used to do this. In this example the annual rate is 3.75%;

(g) net cash investment at end of year: this is the sum of columns (d) to (f). It can be seen that this is zero at the end of the whole transaction.

The above analysis is performed under both the actuarial after tax and investment period methods. However, these methods then differ in their use of the table to give gross earnings allocated to the years of the lease.

The actuarial after tax method merely grosses up the profit taken out of lease figure for each year by the tax rate of 35% and adds interest paid to give gross earnings allocated to each year as follows:

Year	Profit taken out of lease £	Tax (35/65ths) £	Profit grossed up for tax £	Interest paid £	Allocated gross earnings £
2001	277	149	426	740	1,166
2002	210	113	323	559	882
2003	144	77	221	382	603
2004	76	41	117	203	320
2005	7	4	11	18	29
	714	384	1,098	1,902	3,000

In contrast the investment period method allocates a portion of total gross earnings (of £13,000 – £10,000) to each year in the proportion of the net cash investment at the relevant year-end to the total of such net cash investments as follows:

Year	Net cash investment at end of year £	x	Total gross earnings / Sum of net cash investments =	Allocated gross earnings £
2001	8,417	x	3,000 / 21,638 =	1,167
2002	6,362	x	3,000 / 21,638 =	882
2003	4,346	x	3,000 / 21,638 =	603
2004	2,309	x	3,000 / 21,638 =	320
2005	204	x	3,000 / 21,638 =	28
	21,638			3,000

It can be seen that the differences between the gross earnings allocated to each year by each method in this example are negligible. Under the assumption of 35% tax and 25% writing down allowances, both methods give similar results. The reason for this is that the lease never goes into surplus. If different assumptions are made about rates of tax and allowances, cash surpluses may arise in certain periods, and in these circumstances the actuarial after tax method and the investment period method yield different results. Using the former method, the interest received on the cash surplus (the reinvestment income) is brought back and recognised in the periods when the lessor has funds invested in the lease, rather than taken to income when it arises. Thus no profit is recognised in the period when the lease is in surplus. Because of this effect, the lessor may be in an exposed position in this period in the event, for example, of early termination of the lease by the lessee. If this method is used, it may therefore be necessary to make an appropriate provision for early termination losses so that the net investment in the lease does not exceed the termination value at any time. Under the investment period method, any reinvestment income is recognised when it arises; that is, it is not brought back and recognised in the periods in which the lessor has funds invested in the lease. Thus, where cash surpluses arise, the investment period method is more conservative than the actuarial after tax method.[77]

The above example is a simplified one, in that all cash payments and receipts have been assumed to have occurred on either the first or last day of the year. In practice, the calculations would have to reflect the actual timing of the cash payments and receipts; for example, if the rentals were received monthly then the calculations would be performed at monthly rests.

5.4.3 *Assumptions*

Although they differ in the way gross earnings are allocated, both the actuarial after tax and investment period methods use the same assumptions and process to calculate the net cash investment at the end of each relevant period (quarter/year etc.).

The major assumptions used in this calculation of net cash investment are as follows:

(a) sufficient taxable capacity will exist to relieve any tax deductible expenses and capital allowances in the forecast period;

(b) borrowing and reinvestment interest rates and levels of taxation will be as predicted;

(c) defaults or termination of the lease will not occur;

(d) administrative costs will be negligible.

If any of these assumptions ceases to hold, and the effect on the calculated allocation of gross earnings to accounting periods is material, then the calculations should be re-performed from the date when the change in assumptions takes place.

5.4.4 *Other methods*

Many variations of the actuarial after tax and investment period methods are found in practice owing to differences in treatment of certain elements, for example reinvestment income. Further, other methods exist of allocating gross earnings, for example the net earnings sum of the digits method allocates gross earnings to each period using the usual sum of the digits arithmetic (i.e. the balance is allocated to a period in proportion to the number of periods remaining).

5.4.5 *Net investment or net cash investment*

A lessor is concerned with both his net cash investment in a lease for allocating gross earnings to accounting periods and, also, his net investment for calculating the finance lease receivable in his balance sheet. These amounts are quite different in their calculation and use. As is explained at 5.5 below, owners under hire purchase contracts use the net investment in the contract for both of the above purposes.

The difference between net cash investment and net investment can be illustrated by way of the actuarial after tax figures in Example 19.4 above. The gross earnings given are deducted from total rentals in the year to give the reduction in net investment in that year. The opening net investment is simply the cost of the asset. This is shown as follows:

Example 19.5

Year	Total rentals £	Gross earnings £	Reduction in net investment £	Net investment at year end £
2000	–	–	–	10,000
2001	2,600	1,166	1,434	8,566
2002	2,600	882	1,718	6,848
2003	2,600	603	1,997	4,851
2004	2,600	320	2,280	2,571
2005	2,600	29	2,571	–
	13,000	3,000	10,000	

The net investment at each year-end will be the finance lease debtor amount shown by the lessor in the balance sheet.

The use in SSAP 21 of both net investment and net cash investment for finance leases, but not hire purchase contracts, was explained by the less important tax effects of hire purchase contracts compared to finance leases for lessors; essentially because finance lessors receive capital allowances, but owners under hire purchase contracts do not. The Finance Act 1984 reduced the importance of these tax effects by lowering capital allowance and corporation tax rates. It is now questionable whether the extra complexity of the net cash investment approach of allocating gross earnings by finance lessors is warranted.

5.5 Allocation of gross earnings – hire purchase contracts

5.5.1 *Introduction*

As discussed above, the difference between the net investment and net cash investment in a lease relates to taxation and interest payable/receivable. SSAP 21 allows the use of a net investment method to allocate total gross earnings to accounting periods under those hire purchase contracts which are treated similarly to finance leases under SSAP 21 (the vast majority of them).[78] This is justified by the fact that capital allowances on an asset subject to a hire purchase contract usually accrue to the hirer. When SSAP 21 was introduced this meant that taxation was not such a major factor in the owner's evaluation of cash flows under a hire purchase contract as it was in the lessor's evaluation under a finance lease.

5.5.2 *Methodology*

There are two usual net investment methods of allocating gross earnings – the actuarial before tax method, and the sum of the digits ('rule of 78') method.[79]

The actuarial before tax method involves an analysis of the net investment in a contract for each period. The gross earnings percentage is then calculated such that when it is applied to the net investment figure in each period (to give a gross earnings allocation for each period) the net investment at the end of the lease/hire term is zero.

The sum of the digits method simply involves an apportionment of gross earnings over the hire purchase period in proportion to the number of future rentals receivable.

These methods usually ignore notional interest payments/receipts, with the result that the calculations are performed in exactly the same way as in Example 19 2 at 3.4 above in calculating the allocation of the finance charge for a lessee.

When considering hire purchase contracts it can be seen that the net investment in the lease/hire is used for both the allocation of gross earnings to accounting periods and the calculation of the lease/hire receivable in the owner's balance sheet. This contrasts with the position for finance leases (see 5.4.5 above).

5.5.3 *Choice of method*

The actuarial before tax method is the most accurate net investment method. Alternatives (the sum of the digits method or a simpler one, for example straight-line over the contract term) can be used where the differences in allocated gross earnings are immaterial.

6 DISCLOSURE BY LESSORS

6.1 SSAP 21 requirements

The following lessor disclosures are required by SSAP 21:

(a) policies adopted for accounting for operating and finance leases and, in detail, the policy for accounting for finance lease income;[80]

(b) aggregate rentals receivable in respect of the relevant accounting period from (i) finance leases and (ii) operating leases;[81]

(c) if the provisions of SSAP 21 have not been applied retroactively to all leases existing at 1 July 1984, disclosure of the gross earnings from the finance leases and hire purchase contracts which have arisen under each of the methods used;[82]

(d) net investment in (i) finance leases and (ii) hire purchase contracts;[83]

(e) costs of assets acquired for the purpose of letting under finance leases and hire purchase contracts;[84]

(f) gross amount of fixed assets held for use under operating leases, together with the related accumulated depreciation.[85]

6.2 Related Companies Act requirements

It is suggested in the Guidance Notes on SSAP 21 that the net investment in finance leases and hire purchase contracts should be included in current assets under the heading of debtors.[86] Accordingly, lessors who have to comply with Schedule 4 of the Companies Act, will have to comply with the requirement that 'the amount falling due after more than one year shall be shown separately for each item included under debtors'.[87]

There are a number of other disclosures required by the Companies Act which may affect lessors, and these should also be considered; for example details of fixed assets.[88] (This is relevant to assets leased under operating leases.)

6.3 Disclosure in practice

The following are examples of disclosures given in practice by lessors:

Extract 19.7: RMC Group p.l.c. (2000)

Accounting Policies [extract]

Finance lease receivables

Income from finance leasing contracts, being the excess of total rentals received over the cost of the net investment in finance leasing contracts, is taken to profit in accordance with the investment period method of accounting in direct relationship to the reducing capital invested during the primary leasing period.

Amounts written off the net investment in such leases are calculated to write off the cost over the primary periods of the contracts.

Extract 19.8: HSBC Holdings plc (2000)

Notes on The Financial Statements [extract]

2. **Principal Accounting Policies** [extract]

(f) *Finance and operating leases*

(i) Assets leased to customers under agreements which transfer substantially all the risks and rewards associated with ownership, other than legal title, are classified as finance leases. Where HSBC is a lessor under finance leases the amounts due under the leases, after deduction of unearned charges, are included in 'Loans and advances to banks' or 'Loans and advances to customers'. Finance charges receivable are recognised over the periods of the leases in proportion to the funds invested.

(ii) Where HSBC is a lessee under finance leases the leased assets are capitalised and included in 'Equipment, fixtures and fittings' and the corresponding liability to the lessor is included in 'Other liabilities'. Finance charges payable are recognised over the periods of the leases based on the interest rates implicit in the leases.

(iii) All other leases are classified as operating leases and, where HSBC is the lessor, are included in 'Tangible fixed assets'. Rentals payable and receivable under operating leases are accounted for on the straight-line basis over the periods of the leases and are included in 'Administrative expenses' and 'Other operating income' respectively.

Extract 19.9: Rolls-Royce plc (2000)

Notes to the financial statements [extract]

1 **Accounting policies** [extract]

Accounting for leases [extract]

ii) As Lessor

Amounts receivable under finance leases are included under debtors and represent the total amount outstanding under lease agreements less unearned income. Finance lease income, having been allocated to accounting periods to give a constant periodic rate of return on the net cash investment, is included in turnover.

Rentals receivable under operating leases are included in turnover on an accruals basis.

Extract 19.10: Cable and Wireless plc (2001)

Notes to the Accounts [extract]
19 Debtors [extract]

	Group		Company	
	2001	2000	**2001**	2000
	£m	£m	**£m**	£m
Amounts falling due within one year				
Net investment in finance leases	**6**	27	**–**	–
...				
Amounts falling due after more than one year				
Net investment in finance leases	**19**	39	**–**	–
...				
Net investment in finance leases				
Total lease payments receivable	**85**	80	**–**	–
Total rentals received during the year in respect of finance leases	**(60)**	(14)	**–**	–

7 PRACTICAL ISSUES

7.1 Classification of leases

7.1.1 Current practice

The 90% test detailed in SSAP 21 (discussed at 2.1 above) appears to have, in the past, been used in practice by some companies as a fairly definitive test instead of being only one factor in deciding whether substantially all of the risks and rewards of ownership have been transferred to the lessee under a lease. However, it would seem that more recently companies have tended to follow an approach based on qualitative tests rather than merely rely on the 90% test. Perhaps this is as a result of FRS 5 providing guidance on factors to be considered in establishing the economic substance of a transaction and influencing current thinking and practice towards adopting a more substance based approach to accounting.

7.1.2 Leasing as an off balance sheet transaction

It goes without saying that some lessees may prefer not to capitalise leased assets. This is because capitalisation adversely affects the lessee's gearing and return on assets. As a result, instances exist where leases are structured such that an operating lease treatment is permitted by SSAP 21 but, at least on certain interpretations, the substance of the lease is to provide a source of finance to the lessee.

Methods of achieving this typically involve use of the expected residual value of the leased asset because (based on our earlier outline of lease classification criteria) if this residual is significant and is not guaranteed by the lessee or a party related to him, then the lease is likely to be classified as an operating lease. Further, a lease may be structured such that the most likely outcome of events relating to the residual value indicates that no significant risk will attach to the lessee.

Example 19.6: A lease structured such that the most likely outcome is that the lessee has no significant residual risk

Brief details of a motor vehicle lease are:

Fair value – £10,000
Rentals – 20 monthly @ £275, followed by final of £2,000

At end of lease, lessee sells vehicle as agent for lessor, and if sold for

(i) more than £3,000, 99% of excess is repaid to lessee; or

(ii) less than £3,000, lessee pays deficit to lessor up to maximum of 0.4 pence per mile above 25,000 miles p.a. on average that the leased vehicle has done.

Therefore, as a result of (ii) above, this lease involves a guarantee of the residual value of the leased vehicle by the lessee of £3,000. However, the guarantee will only be called upon if both:

(a) the vehicle's actual residual value is less than £3,000; and

(b) the vehicle has travelled more than 25,000 miles per year on average over the lease term.

Further, the lessee is only liable to pay a certain level of the residual; namely, £100 for each 2,500 miles above 25,000 miles that the vehicle has done. It is arguable whether SSAP 21 intended that this guarantee should be treated similarly to a guarantee of £3,000 with no restrictions on when it will apply. One could argue that the guarantee should be assumed not to apply if experience or expectations of the sales price and/or the mileage that vehicles have done (and the inter-relationship between these) indicate that a residual payment by the lessee will not be made. On the other hand it could be said that the guarantee exists and therefore should be taken into account.

The treatment of the guarantee would obviously affect the 90% test and the overall consideration of factors which impinge on the risks and rewards of ownership.

7.2 Termination of leases

7.2.1 *Lease classification*

The expectations of lessors and lessees regarding the timing of termination of a lease may affect the classification of a lease as either operating or finance. This is because it will affect the expected lease term, level of payments under the lease and expected residual value of the lease assets.

Termination during the primary lease term will generally not be anticipated at the lease inception because the lessee can be assumed to be using the asset for at least that period. In addition, such an early termination will be unlikely because a termination payment is usually required which will give the lessor an amount equivalent to most or all of the rental receipts which would have been received if no such termination had taken place.

7.2.2 *Operating leases*

If a lease has been classified as an operating lease at its inception, then no major difficulty arises on a termination. Any termination payment due under the lease agreement will be accounted for as income when receivable by the lessor and as an expense when due by the lessee.

7.2.3 *Finance leases – lessee*

Early termination of a finance lease results in a disposal of the capitalised asset by the lessee. Any payment made by the lessee will reduce the lease obligation which is being carried in the balance sheet. If either a part of this obligation is not eliminated or the termination payment exceeds the previously existing obligation, then the remainder or excess will be included as a gain or loss (respectively) in calculating the total gain or loss arising on the disposal of the asset. Alternatively, if the termination is more in the nature of a refinancing, the gain or loss arising could be equated to the gain or loss arising on the redemption of debt under FRS 4 – *Capital instruments.*

A similar accounting treatment is required where the lease terminates at the expected date and there is a residual at least partly guaranteed by the lessee. For the lessee, a payment made under such a guarantee will reduce the obligation to the lessor under the lease as the guaranteed residual would obviously be included in the lessee's finance lease obligation. If any part of the guaranteed residual is not called upon, then the lessee would eliminate it by transferring it to the calculation of gain/loss on disposal of the leased asset. The effect on the overall gain or loss will depend on the extent to which the lessee expected to make the residual payment as this will have affected the level to which the capitalised asset has been depreciated. For example, if the total guaranteed residual was not expected to become payable by the lessee, then he would have calculated the depreciation charge to give a net book value at the end of the lease term equal to the residual element not expected to become payable. If this estimate was correct then the remaining obligation will equal (and contra out) the net book value of the relevant asset.

Example 19.7

We can consider this in the context of Example 19.6 in 7.1.2 above, where there is effectively a guarantee of a residual of £3,000 dependent on the mileage done by the leased vehicle. Assuming that the lease is capitalised as a finance lease, if the lessee considers at the lease inception that the guarantee will not be called upon, then he will depreciate the vehicle to an estimated residual value of £3,000 over the lease term. In the event that his estimate is found to be correct, then the asset written down value will simply contra out with the lease obligation of £3,000. However, if, for example, £1,000 of the guarantee was called upon, whereas the lessee had estimated that it would not be, then the net book value of £3,000 and the unused guarantee of £2,000 will both be eliminated and a loss of £1,000 will be shown on disposal of the vehicle.

7.2.4 *Finance leases – lessor*

Any termination payment received by a lessor upon an early termination will reduce the lessor's net investment in the lease shown as a receivable. If the termination payment is greater than the previously shown net investment, then a profit on termination of the lease will be shown by the lessee. On the other hand, if the termination payment is smaller than the net investment, a loss will be shown. Such a loss is usually deducted from finance lease income unless exceptionally large, in which case it is separately disclosed.

Any loss on termination is unlikely to arise in most situations because a finance lease is likely to have termination terms such that the lessor is compensated fully for early termination and the lessor has legal title to the asset. Because he has title, the lessor can continue to include the asset in current assets as a receivable to the extent that sales proceeds or new finance lease receivables are expected to arise. If the asset is then re-leased under an operating lease, the asset may be transferred to fixed assets and depreciated over its remaining useful life.

To some extent, these two reasons for losses on termination of a finance lease not arising (full compensation and legal title remaining with the lessor) are complementary. If the termination payment is intended to give full compensation, then the asset may be retained by the lessee and sold with any proceeds going to him. On the other hand, if the termination payment is not structured in this way then the lessor will repossess the asset and sell or re-lease it.

7.3 Tax variation clauses

7.3.1 *Introduction*

The level of rentals in a lease is determined using the tax regime which exists at the time the lease terms are agreed. Tax variation clauses are common in finance leases and are designed to protect the lessor from any adverse changes in the capital allowance or corporation tax rates which the lessor has assumed will exist when the level of rentals is agreed. These may also apply where any tax changes operate to the lessor's benefit.

7.3.2 *Adjustments*

Where a tax variation clause takes effect the rental adjustment may be made via:

(a) lump sum payments as and when the lessor pays the new higher/lower tax charge for any period; or

(b) the future rentals including stepped increases or decreases to reflect the changes; or

(c) a new fixed rental being calculated to be paid over the remainder of the primary lease term.

7.3.3 *Lessee*

As regards the lessee, any change in total rentals payable represents an alteration to his remaining finance charges under a lease. These alterations should be accounted for by spreading the revised finance charges over the remaining lease term using the methods detailed at 3.4 above. However, in the possibly unusual circumstances of 7.3.2 (a) above, where the calculations of lump sum payments are not made until the relevant tax calculation is made by the lessor, then the altered rentals should be accounted for in the periods in which they arise. Although a constant rate of charge on the lessee's remaining liability will not result, this approach is justified because the lessee does not know what the future rentals will actually be.

Under either approach, if any reduction in rentals exceeds the finance charges which were expected to accrue, then the excess should be deducted from the capitalised cost such that future depreciation charges are lower than they would have been.[89] Negative finance charges are not permitted.[90]

7.3.4 *Lessor*

Any variations in taxation and rentals (due to a tax variation clause) which materially alter the lessor's analysis of net cash investment in the lease over its remaining term will alter the total of future gross earnings and also their allocation to accounting periods. This will therefore affect the reduction in net investment in the lease (shown as a receivable in the lessor's balance sheet) over its remaining term. The specifics of such an exercise are outside the scope of this chapter.

7.4 Sale and leaseback transactions

7.4.1 *Introduction*

Such transactions involve the original owner of an asset selling it (usually to a finance house or a merchant bank) and immediately leasing it back. These parties will be termed the seller/lessee and buyer/lessor respectively. Sometimes, instead of selling the asset outright, the original owner will lease the asset to the other party under a finance lease and then lease it back. Such a transaction is known as a 'lease and leaseback' and has similar effects. The term 'sale and leaseback' is taken to include such a transaction.

Sale and leaseback transactions are a fairly common feature of an number of industries (such as the retail and hotel industries), where it is as accepted a form of financing as taking out a mortgage or a bank overdraft. However, from a commercial point of view, the important point of differentiation lies between an entity which decides that it is cheaper to rent than to own – and is willing to pass on the property risk to the landlord – and an entity which decides to use the property as a means of raising finance – and will therefore retain the property risk.

7.4.2 *Finance or operating lease?*

The buyer/lessor will treat the lease in the same way as he would any other lease which was not part of a sale and leaseback transaction.[91]

For the seller/lessee there are further considerations which may apply if the transaction has certain characteristics. He must first decide whether the leaseback transaction gives rise to an operating or finance lease in the normal way, i.e. the fact that he has sold the asset to the lessor is irrelevant for this purpose. The accounting consequences depend on this categorisation.

We discussed at 2 above the issues to be considered and the factors involved in determining the classification of a lease, including the fact that the general principles of FRS 5 are relevant in ensuring that a lease is classified as either finance or operating in accordance with its substance. These factors and considerations apply equally in the case of a sale and leaseback transaction. This means that, in order to enable the seller/lessee to derecognise the asset, recognise a profit (or loss) in his profit and loss account and account for the lease as an operating lease, he needs to ensure that substantially all the risks and rewards of ownership of the asset have passed to the buyer/lessor.

The ICAEW working party which reviewed SSAP 21 highlighted sale and leaseback as one of the areas where practical problems are encountered. In its report, the working party suggested that the problems manifest themselves in the fact that an owner of an asset may realise a profit on sale and continue to use the asset without retaining it on the balance sheet.[92] The report goes on to say that 'currently the conditions for removal of an existing owned asset from the balance sheet appear to differ in practice from those applying to capitalisation of an asset not previously owned by the lessee. A company wishing to acquire, say, an oil tanker may get a different answer depending upon whether it bought the oil tanker and then entered into a sale and leaseback transaction or whether it entered into a lease agreement in the first place. We believe this is wrong; we do not believe that there should be a difference between the conditions for recognition and for derecognition.'[93]

Consequently, the working party suggests that in order to determine whether or not the transaction should be recorded as a sale, six qualitative tests should be used as a guide in order to determine whether or not substantially all the risks and rewards of ownership have passed.[94] The six tests include the same tests as discussed at 2.3 above, and are as follows:

1. is the sale at market value?
2. are the lease rentals based on a market rate for use of the asset or a financing rate for use of the funds?
3. what is the nature of the lessor's business?
4. is the existence of put and call options a feature of the lease? If so, are they exercisable at a predetermined price or formula or are they exercisable at the market price at the time the option is exercised?
5. which party carries the risk of a fall in value of the asset and which party benefits from any capital appreciation?
6. does the lessee have the use of the asset for a period broadly equating to the likely useful economic life of the asset?

It is not altogether clear which 'general principles' of FRS 5 should be applied in ensuring that leases are classified as finance or operating leases in accordance with their substance, although presumably they will include both the principle of a lender's return and the requirement to consider the position of all the parties to a transaction, including their apparent expectations and motives for agreeing to its various terms. In any event, though, the above six tests may be helpful as a starting point in the process of identifying all the aspects and implications of a transaction.

Sale and leasebacks involving options are discussed at 7.4.4 below.

7.4.3 *Leaseback under a finance lease*

It follows from the discussion at 7.4.2 above that where the leaseback is of a financing nature and the sales value is greater than the written down value, then this apparent profit should not be taken to profit and loss account at the time of the sale and leaseback.[95] This is because it would be inappropriate to show a profit on disposal of an asset which has then, in substance, been reacquired under a finance lease.

However, SSAP 21 is somewhat ambivalent about the way in which the sale and leaseback transaction should be presented in the balance sheet; two alternative presentations are suggested in the standard and guidance notes:

(a) the asset is treated as sold in the normal way except that the apparent profit should be deferred and taken to the profit and loss account over the lease term. The asset and the obligation under the lease are recorded at the sales value; or

(b) the asset remains in the seller/lessee's balance sheet at its previous book value and the sales proceeds are shown as a creditor. This creditor balance represents the finance lease liability under the leaseback. When lease payments are then made, they are treated partly as a repayment of that creditor, and partly as a finance charge to the profit and loss account (in the usual way for a finance lease).

Nevertheless, FRS 5 now states that the carrying value of the asset should not be adjusted in such a transaction and, accordingly, (a) above should no longer be regarded as an option.[96] This is because treatment (b) reflects the substance of the transaction, namely the raising of finance secured on an asset that continues to be held and is not disposed of.

If the sales value is less than the written down value, the apparent loss arising on the sale should again not be taken to the profit and loss account at the time of the sale and leaseback; the transaction should be accounted for in the same way as described in (b) above. However, if the low sales value demonstrates that a permanent diminution in value has occurred, this will result in an immediate write down in the profit and loss account.

If an asset which is carried at a revalued amount is sold and leased back under a finance lease, then the relevant revaluation reserve should continue to be treated in the way it was prior to the sale and leaseback. If the revaluation reserve is being transferred to profit and loss reserve, this should now be over the shorter of the lease term and the asset's remaining useful life in order that the period of transfer matches the depreciation term of the leased asset.

7.4.4 Sale and leasebacks involving options

The point has already been made that since SSAP 21 contains the more specific provisions governing lease accounting, one would look to that standard as the primary source of authoritative guidance concerning lease accounting – although the general principles of FRS 5 will also be relevant in ensuring that leases are classified as finance or operating leases in accordance with their substance. However, in the case of a sale and leaseback arrangement where there is also an option for the seller/lessee to repurchase the asset, the provisions of Application Note B of FRS 5 are more specific than those of SSAP 21 and should therefore be applied in determining the appropriate accounting for such a transaction.

Sale and leaseback deals can take a variety of forms, but the essential feature which is common to all of them is that the company which purports to have sold the asset in question has not disposed of all the risks and rewards associated with the asset in the manner expected of a normal sale. If there is no significant change in the company's access to the benefits of the asset and exposures to the risks inherent in those benefits, then the substance of the deal is that of a secured loan. In such circumstances, FRS 5 requires that the sale should not be recorded and the asset in question should remain on the company's balance sheet.

Thus the principal question to be answered is whether the reporting company has made a sale in substance, or whether the deal represents the raising of finance secured on an asset. In approaching this question, FRS 5 tells us to consider the positions of both the buyer and seller, together with their apparent expectations and motives for agreeing to the various terms of the arrangement. In particular, where the substance is that of a secured loan, the buyer will require that it is assured of a lender's return on its investment and the seller will require that the buyer earns no more than this return. Conversely, if the buyer is not assured of a lender's return, this indicates that some benefit and some risk have been passed to the buyer such that the seller has not retained the original asset. Therefore, whether or not the buyer earns such a return is an important indicator of the substance of the transaction.[97]

The second key factor in determining the substance of a sale and leaseback transaction relates to an evaluation of the commercial effect of the option(s). This may take the form of a put option allowing the buyer to resell the asset to the seller, a call option allowing the seller to repurchase the asset from the buyer, or a combination of these.

Where there is both a put and a call option in force on equivalent terms, it is clear that the asset will revert to the seller. Unless the option is to be exercised at the then market price of the asset in question, it must be in the interests of one or other of the parties to exercise his option so as to secure a profit or avoid a loss, and therefore the likelihood of the asset remaining the property of the buyer rather than reverting to the seller must be remote. However, the position is less clear where there is only a put option or a call option in force rather than a combination of the two.

Where there is only a put option, the effect will be (in the absence of other factors) that the seller/lessee has disposed of the rewards of ownership to the buyer/lessor but retained the risks. This is because the buyer will only exercise his option to put the asset back to the seller if its value at the time is less than the repurchase price payable under the option. This means that if the asset continues to rise in value the buyer will keep it and reap the benefits of that enhanced value; conversely if the value of the asset falls, the option will be exercised and the downside on the asset will be borne by the seller.

This analysis does not of itself answer the question of whether the deal should be treated as a sale or as a financing transaction. The overall commercial effect will still have to be evaluated, taking account of all the terms of the arrangement and by considering the motivations of both of the parties in agreeing to the various terms of the deal; in particular it will need to be considered why they have each agreed to have this one-sided option.

Where there is only a call option, the position will be reversed. In this case, the seller has disposed of the risks, but retained the rewards to be attained if the value of the asset exceeds the repurchase price specified in the option. Once again, though, the overall commercial effect of the arrangement has to be evaluated in deciding how to account for the deal. Emphasis has to be given to what is likely to happen in practice, and it is instructive to look at the arrangement from the point of view of both parties to see what their expectations are and what has induced them to accept the deal on the terms which have been agreed. It may be obvious from the overall terms of the arrangement that the call option will be exercised, in which case the deal will again be a financing arrangement and should be accounted for as such. For example, the exercise price of the call option may be set at a significant discount to expected market value, the seller may need the asset to use on an ongoing basis in its business, or the asset may provide in effect the only source of the seller's future income.[98] Similarly, the financial effects of *not* exercising the option (such as continued exposure to escalating costs) may sometimes make it obvious that the option will be exercised. But in other cases, it could be quite likely that the option will not be exercised and if this is the case the transaction could be treated as a sale.

The following is an example of a sale and leaseback deal where the seller has a call option to repurchase the asset but has no commitment to do so:

Example 19.8: Sale and leaseback transaction involving escalating rentals and call options

Company S sells a property to Company B for £100,000,000 and leases it back on the following terms:

Rental for years 1 to 5	£3,900,000 per annum
Rental for years 6 to 10	£5,875,000 per annum
Rental for years 11 to 15	£8,830,000 per annum
Rental for years 16 to 20	£13,280,000 per annum
Rental for years 21 to 25	£19,970,000 per annum
Rental for years 26 to 30	£30,025,000 per annum
Rental for years 31 to 35	£45,150,000 per annum
Rental thereafter	open market rent

Rentals are payable annually in advance.

Company S has the right to buy back the property at the following dates and prices:

At the end of year 5	£125,000,000
At the end of year 10	£150,000,000
At the end of year 15	£168,000,000
At the end of year 20	£160,000,000
At the end of year 25	£100,000,000

Company B has no right to put the property back to Company S.

An analysis of the economics of this deal suggests that whilst Company S has no legal obligation to repurchase the property, there is no genuine commercial possibility that the option will not be exercised. This is because the rentals and option prices are structured in such a way as to give the buyer of the property a lender's return whilst, at the same time, there is no commercial logic for the seller not to exercise the option at year 25, if not earlier. Exercising the option at the end of year 25 will mean that Company S will regain ownership of the property and will have had the use of the £100,000,000 at an effective rate of approximately 8.2% per annum; failure to exercise the option will mean additional lease obligations of £375,875,000 over the ten years from years 25 to 35, followed by the obligation to pay market rents thereafter.

The 1994 accounts of Forte revealed that the group had in the past entered into sale and leaseback transactions involving escalating rentals and call options. As can be seen from the following extract, these transactions were accounted for by Forte as operating leases:

Extract 19.11: Forte Plc (1994)

Financial Review [extract]
Sale, leaseback and repurchase agreements

Details of the sale, leaseback and repurchase arrangements the Company has entered into are set out in note 29 to the Accounts. These arrangements affect a limited proportion of the properties operated by the Company. The leases are for between 20 and 30 years and may be renewed by the Company at prevailing market rates. The lessors have no rights to require repurchase.

The rentals paid under these leases currently amount to £37m per year and are approximately covered by the current earnings from the leased properties. Over the remaining periods of the leases the rental costs will not rise significantly in real terms and it can reasonably be expected that they will continue to be financed by the income from the properties concerned.

Notes to the Accounts
29 Commitments [extract]
Sale and leaseback agreements

In the normal course of its activities, the Group has entered into a number of sale and leaseback agreements, which include options for the Group to repurchase the leased properties. The current agreements were entered into during the period between 1986 and 1992 and gave rise to sale proceeds amounting to £480m. The leases have durations of between 20 and 30 years but may be renewed at the Group's option. The lessors have no rights to require repurchase by the Group. Under current accounting practice, these leases are treated as operating leases and the profit and loss account is charged with the rental payments made in each accounting period.

During the year ended 31 January 1994 the profit before rent from the properties concerned amounted to £34m and the total rental payments amounted to £37m. The present value of the average future rental payments under these leases amounts to £39m per annum (assuming the continuation of current interest rates for leases with variable rental clauses).

Although these sale and leaseback agreements were entered into prior to the implementation of FRS 5, there are one or two observations that can be made about them. First, it is noteworthy that whilst these leases were being accounted for as operating leases, the lease rentals were being charged to the profit and loss account as incurred and not, as is required by SSAP 21, on a straight-line basis. Second, taking the fact that the rental payments exceed the profit before rent from the properties together with Forte's assumption relating to current interest rates, it seems that rentals were linked to market interest rates and did not necessarily reflect market rentals. This might suggest that the leases had been structured in such a way that the lessors received no more than a lender's return, indicating that the substance of the transactions may have been that of a financing.

This, in fact, did prove to be the case as, following the implementation of FRS 5, a substantial proportion of these assets were brought back on balance sheet – as explained in Forte's 1995 accounts:

Extract 19.12: Forte Plc (1995)

Financial Review [extract]

Lease and sale and leaseback arrangements

We reported last year that the accounting authorities were introducing new procedures for accounting for sale and leaseback agreements – which have been a traditional form of financing in the hotel industry. During the year a new accounting standard, called Financial Reporting Standard No. 5 ('FRS5'), was issued which changed the basis on which leased properties are accounted for. Certain leasing arrangements which were previously accounted for as operating leases are now required to be treated as finance leases – with the lease obligations treated as a type of debt and the leased properties treated as assets in our own accounts. Following a detailed review of these accounting requirements, and the Company's leasing agreements, we have decided that certain lease and sale and leaseback agreements will now be accounted for on this basis.

The relevant assets (amounting to £415m) and the associated future obligations (amounting to £475m) have been included on the balance sheet. As required under the accounting rules, this has been done by way of a prior year adjustment and last year's figures have been restated on the new basis.

In the profit and loss account, an additional non-cash charge of £10m (1994 – £10m) has also been provided, representing the difference between rents payable under these agreements (previously accounted for as rentals charged against operating profits) and the financing cost under FRS5, accounted for as interest payable evenly over the period of the leases. The rents payable and the additional charge, amounting to £44m are now also treated as a financing cost.

This accounting will not give rise to any changes in the Company's cash flow. The leases involved generally have substantial periods to run before they expire and in practice the issue of possible repurchase will not generally arise for an average of at least fifteen years.

Notes to the Accounts

18 Lease and sale and leaseback agreements [extract]

In the normal course of its activities, in the period 1986 to 1992 the Group entered into a number of lease agreements and sale and leaseback agreements, which include options for the Group to acquire or repurchase the relevant properties.

FRS5 became effective during the current financial year and changes the basis on which leases are accounted for so that certain leases which were previously regarded as being operating leases are now required to be treated as finance leases.

Following a detailed review of the accounting requirements under FRS5 and the Group's leasing arrangements, it has been decided that certain sale and leaseback agreements will now be accounted for as finance leases. The original proceeds under these agreements were £407m. The agreements are secured on specific hotels and restaurants with a primary duration of 30 years and are renewable thereafter. The Group has options to repurchase the properties at varying intervals with the lessors having no rights to require repurchase. The relevant fixed assets, together with the associated future obligations have been included on the balance sheet by way of a prior year adjustment.

The hotel and restaurant properties under these agreements have been stated in the Group balance sheet as at 31 January 1994 at £430m, being fair market value.

It is interesting to note from these disclosures that the original proceeds which Forte received under these sale and leaseback agreements which were brought back on balance sheet were £407m – yet future lease obligations of £475m were required to be recognised on the balance sheet. This must raise at least some doubt as to whether Forte had disposed of all the risks associated with the assets at the time the original transactions were entered into.

The accounting for sale and leaseback transactions is an area where the Financial Reporting Review Panel has shown some interest. In February 1997, the Review Panel issued a Press Notice which explained that the 1995 and 1996 accounts of Associated Nursing Services plc (ANS) had been under consideration in respect of two matters – one of which related to the accounting treatment of a sale and leaseback transaction. The transaction at issue involved a 25-year lease, renewable for a further 25 years, and a call option held by ANS. The Review Panel's view (which the directors finally accepted after extended discussions with the Panel) was that the nature of the sale and leaseback transaction was such that not all the significant rights or other access to benefits relating to the asset in question and not all the significant exposure to the risk inherent in those benefits had been transferred to the purchaser. Consequently, in accordance with FRS 5, the asset should have remained on the balance sheet and the sale proceeds should have been included in borrowings. As a result of this Review Panel decision, the directors of ANS issued revised accounts. Interestingly enough, the 2000 accounts of ANS show an accounting policy for sale and leaseback arrangements:

Extract 19.13: ANS plc (2000)

Notes to the Financial Statements [extract]
Accounting Policies [extract]

j) **Sale and Leaseback Arrangements**

The Group has entered into certain sale and leaseback transactions whereby the risks and rewards of ownership of the assets concerned have not been substantially transferred to the lessor. In accordance with SSAP 21 and FRS 5 the assets subject to these sale and leaseback transactions have been retained on the Group's balance sheet and the proceeds of sale are included within creditors as liabilities under sale and leaseback arrangements. The rent payable by the Group throughout the term of the lease is apportioned first as a partial repayment of the related liabilities and, secondly, as interest charged to profits.

Any increase in rent under the terms of the lease will be charged to profit.

The fixed assets subject to the sale and leaseback arrangements are depreciated on a straight line basis over the period of the initial lease term.

7.4.5 *Leaseback under an operating lease*

Where a lessee enters into a sale and leaseback transaction which results in an operating lease then (1) the original asset should be treated as having been sold, and (2) the operating lease should be accounted for under the provisions of the standard (see 3.6 above).

Where the transaction is established at the fair value of the asset concerned, then any profit or loss on the sale of the asset should be recognised immediately.[99] Where the transaction is not based on the fair value of the asset, then the accounting treatment is best explained by the schedule, as shown below, which uses the following three amounts:

(a) WDV : the written down value of the asset prior to its sale by the seller/lessee;

(b) SV : the sales value at which the asset is sold to the buyer/lessor; and

(c) FV : the fair value of the asset, i.e. the price it would fetch if sold in an arm's length transaction to a third party (not as part of a sale and leaseback transaction).

Schedule of possibilities:[100]

1. SV<WDV<FV Loss (WDV–SV) recognised immediately unless lease rentals are below normal levels when it should be deferred and amortised.
2. SV<FV<WDV Loss based on fair value (WDV–FV) recognised immediately. Balance (FV–SV) should also be recognised immediately unless lease rentals are below normal levels when it should be deferred and amortised.
3. WDV<SV<FV Profit (SV–WDV) recognised immediately.
4. WDV<FV<SV Profit based on fair value (FV–WDV) recognised immediately. Balance (SV–FV) deferred and amortised.
5. FV<WDV<SV Loss based on fair value (WDV–FV) recognised immediately. Profit (SV–FV) deferred and amortised.
6. FV<SV<WDV Loss based on fair value (WDV–FV) recognised immediately. Profit (SV–FV) deferred and amortised.

Where any amounts are to be deferred and amortised, this should be done evenly over the shorter of the lease term and the period to the next lease rental review.

Transactions in categories 5 and 6 above are, essentially, dealt with in two stages. The asset is first written down to fair value because the asset is treated as having been sold for that amount; second, the excess of sales value over the fair value is treated as only an apparent profit, which is deferred and amortised.

The rationale behind the above treatments is that if the sales value is not based on fair values, then it is likely that the normal market rents will have been adjusted to compensate. Accordingly, the transaction should be recorded as if it had been based on fair values. However, this will not always be the case:

(a) where the fair value is above the written down value of the asset it is possible for the seller/lessee to arrange for the sales value to be anywhere within that range and report a gain in the year of sale based on that sales value. Any compensation which the seller/lessee obtains by way of reduced rentals will be reflected in later years; and

(b) where the sales value is less than fair value there may be legitimate reasons for this to be so, for example where the seller has had to raise cash quickly. In such situations, as the rentals under the lease have not been reduced to compensate, the profit or loss should be based on the sales value.

7.5 Income recognition by lessors

The ICAEW working party that reviewed SSAP 21 expressed particular concern about the standard's general lack of guidance concerning income recognition by lessors.[101] However, the working party believed that the basic rules for inter-period profit allocation, using the net cash investment as the key parameter, to be sound and that they were not the cause of the variety of accounting by lessors which may be found in practice. Instead, the working party believed that the problems related primarily to the definition and treatment of 'initial direct costs' which may effectively be deferred (that is, costs may be deferred or profit may be accelerated) and to the assessment and accounting treatment of residual values.[102]

7.5.1 Initial direct costs

Initial direct costs are defined in SSAP 21 as being 'those costs incurred by the lessor that are directly associated with negotiating and consummating leasing transactions, such as commissions, legal fees, costs of credit investigations and costs of preparing and processing documents for new leases acquired'.[103] The Guidance Notes on SSAP 21 make the point that this definition is not intended to exclude salespersons' costs.[104]

This means that in practice, initial direct costs may be variously interpreted as being limited to brokers' commissions or extended to encompass overhead costs sometimes tenuously attributed to the sales and new business departments of the leasing operation. The working party suggested that the definition should be drawn more restrictively so that costs that do not automatically reduce on a fall in levels of new business are excluded from the category of costs which may be effectively deferred.[105]

As far as the accounting for the initial direct costs is concerned, the Guidance Notes state that initial direct costs may be apportioned over the lease term on a systematic basis (or may be written off immediately). The same effect as apportioning the costs over the lease term may be achieved by either (a) treating the costs as a deduction from the total gross earnings before the latter are allocated to accounting periods or (b) recognising sufficient gross earnings in the first year to cover the costs. In the case of an operating lease initial direct costs may also either be written off immediately or be deferred and amortised over the lease term.[106]

7.5.2 *Residual values*

The collapse in April 1990 of Atlantic Computers highlighted the fact that there are major practical problems in relation to the estimation of residual values. Whether or not these problems are entirely due to an absence of definitive guidance in accounting standards is a moot point. An alternative view might be that a number of problems have arisen as a result of lessors being less than prudent in setting residual values by not paying sufficient regard to all the commercial risks involved. Nevertheless, the ICAEW working party recommended that a revised leasing standard 'should define residual value and provide guidance on the practical issues in accounting for residual values. It should provide guidance on the re-evaluation of residuals and how upward and downward adjustments should be respectively treated in the profit and loss account.'[107]

Whilst such guidance will be undoubtedly helpful, it may also be necessary to require lessors to provide considerably more disclosure in their accounts relating to residual values. These might include disclosures concerning assumptions, sensitivities, comparisons between aggregate residuals by category of asset compared with independently compiled statistics, etc.

7.6 Manufacturers/dealers

7.6.1 *Introduction*

A manufacturer or dealer (M/D) in assets may offer customers the option of either outright purchase or rental of the assets. Where a rental agreement is such that it comes within the definition of an operating lease, then the M/D should not recognise a selling profit.[108] Where, on the other hand, a rental agreement is such that it comes within the definition of a finance lease (as substantially all the risks and rewards of ownership have passed), then there can be seen to be two elements of the M/D's overall profit or loss on the transaction. These are:

(a) the selling profit or loss at the inception of the lease which is equivalent to the profit or loss that would arise on an outright sale made under an arm's length transaction; and

(b) the gross earnings received by the M/D as lessor under the finance lease.

7.6.2 *Allocating the total profit of the manufacturer/dealer*

If the M/D is in the (relatively unlikely) position of incurring an overall loss because the total rentals receivable under the finance lease are less than the cost of the asset to the M/D, then the prudence concept dictates that this loss should be taken to the profit and loss account at the inception of the lease. If an overall profit is made, then an allocation between the selling profit and lessor's gross earnings must be made.

In those situations where the customer is offered the choice of paying the cash price for the asset immediately or paying for it on deferred credit terms then, as long as the credit terms are the M/D's normal terms, the cash price can be used for determining the selling profit. However, in many cases such an approach should not be followed as the terms of the lease are often influenced by the M/D's marketing considerations. For example, a car dealer may offer 0% finance deals instead of reducing the normal selling price of his cars. It would be wrong in this instance for the dealer to record a profit on the sale of the car and no finance income under the lease.

It is not appropriate to take a 'normal' level of selling profit if the gross earnings under the finance lease would then be lower than normally expected. This is because the selling profit is taken to the profit and loss account at the lease inception and, if it is partly offset by lower than normal gross earnings under the lease, prudence dictates that this be taken into account. The correct practice is, therefore, to calculate gross earnings under the finance lease at the normal level, with any remaining element of the overall profit being taken as selling profit at the lease inception.

How then should the appropriate level of gross earnings under the finance lease be estimated? This clearly depends on the estimated interest rate implicit in the lease. In some situations the M/D will have a normal implicit interest rate based on his other leasing activity. However, in other situations where the M/D does not conduct other leasing business, an estimate will have to be made of the implicit rate for such leasing activity.

7.7 Sub-leases and back-to-back leases

7.7.1 *Introduction*

Situations arise where there are more parties to a lease arrangement than simply one lessor and one lessee. The discussion below relates to situations involving an original lessor, an intermediate party and an ultimate lessee. The intermediate party may be acting either as both a lessee and lessor of the asset concerned or, alternatively, as an agent of the lessor in the transaction.

Both sub-leases and back-to-back leases involve the intermediate party acting as both lessor and lessee of the asset. The difference between the two arrangements is that, for a back-to-back lease, the terms of the two lease agreements match to a greater extent than would be the case for a sub-lease arrangement. This difference is really only one of degree, and the important decision to be made concerns whether the arrangement is one of agency or, rather, the intermediate party is acting as both lessee and lessor in two related but independent transactions.

7.7.2 *The original lessor and the ultimate lessee*

The accounting treatment adopted by these parties will not be affected by the existence of sub-leases or back-to-back leases. The original lessor has an agreement with the intermediate party which is not affected by any further leasing of the assets by the intermediate party unless the original lease agreement is thereby replaced.

Similarly, the ultimate lessee has a lease agreement with the intermediate party. He will have use of the asset under that agreement and must make a decision, in the usual way, as to whether the lease is of a finance or operating type per SSAP 21.

7.7.3 *The intermediate party*

The appropriate accounting treatment by the intermediate party depends on the substance of the series of transactions. This turns on whether the intermediate party is acting either as an agent/broker for the original lessor or as a principal in both transactions. In the latter case, the intermediate party will act as lessee to the original lessor and lessor to the ultimate lessee.

In determining the role of the intermediate party, the question of recourse is important. If the ultimate lessee defaults on his lease obligations (for whatever reason), does the original lessor have recourse against the intermediate party for the outstanding payments under the lease?

Another important factor in the decision of how the intermediate party should account for the transaction is what happens if the original lessor defaults, for example through his insolvency. If the intermediate party is merely a broker/agent, then he will suffer no loss upon such default, and the ultimate lessee would only have a claim against the original lessor.

If these factors indicate that the intermediate party is acting merely as a broker or agent for the original lessor, he should not include any asset or obligation relating to the leased asset in his balance sheet. The income received by such an intermediary should be taken to profit and loss account on a systematic and rational basis.[109]

If, on the other hand, the intermediate party is taken to be acting as both lessee and lessor in two independent although related transactions, he should recognise his assets and obligations under finance leases in the normal way.

The recognition of income as lessor will be affected by the lease from the original lessor. Clearly, if the intermediate party had purchased the asset concerned outright, then his income recognition as a lessor would be on the usual net cash investment basis explained in 5.3 above. However, as he has obtained use of the asset under a finance lease, his income recognition will be based on the net investment in the lease. This is because the intermediate party's investment in the leased asset will be shown as the present value of the minimum lease payments, as reduced throughout the lease by the capital portion of total rental payable to the original lessor. In other words, there are no major tax consequences of the lease from the original lessor. The net investment approach to income recognition used for hire purchase contracts will therefore be appropriate (see 5.5 above).

It should not be inferred from the above discussion that all situations encountered can be relatively easily allocated as one of either a broker/agent or lessee/lessor in nature. In practice this is unlikely to be the case, as the risks and rewards will probably be spread between the parties involved. This is especially likely where more than the three parties discussed above are involved. In all cases, it is a question of judgement as to whether substantially all the risks and rewards from an asset attach to any party under the leases.

An illustration of the difficulties associated with transactions involving sub-leases can be found in the 1993 accounts of British Aerospace (BAe), which revealed for the first time the full extent of the seemingly significant financial risks that the group had been taking in order to sustain its civil aircraft manufacturing operations, including those associated with its participation in Airbus Industrie.

It has now become apparent that the bulk of BAe's commercial aircraft sales made in the 1980s were to banks and not airlines. It is understood that the banks then leased the aircraft back to BAe under 15 to 20 year agreements, and BAe leased the aircraft to airlines under sub-leases of between three and five years. The result was that the group was exposing itself to the risk of substantial losses if those sub-leases were not renewed. However, with the backdrop of a highly buoyant market in second-hand aircraft in the 1980s, this risk was presumably considered to be low, and deals of this nature were apparently common practice amongst commercial aircraft manufacturers. Furthermore, even when BAe did sell aircraft directly to airlines, the group often provided guarantees on leases which the airlines themselves entered into with banks.

Consequently, when the recession hit the travel industry following the Gulf War, the demand for second-hand commercial aircraft collapsed and the risks became a reality. The result was that BAe was faced with significant exposure to third party guarantees and other recourse obligations, as was evidenced in its 1996 accounts:

Extract 19.14: British Aerospace Public Limited Company (1996)

Notes to the Accounts

1 Accounting policies [extract]

Aircraft financing

The Group is exposed to actual and contingent liabilities arising from commercial aircraft financing, both from financing arranged directly by the Group and from that arranged by third parties where the Group has provided guarantees or has other recourse obligations. Provision for these risks is made on a systematic basis at the time of sale, having regard to the ability to re-lease or re-sell the underlying aircraft.

20 Commercial aircraft financing

Commercial aircraft are frequently sold for cash with the manufacturer retaining some financial exposure either by guaranteeing a minimum residual value of the aircraft at some date in the future or through the arrangement of lease finance on extended terms

Commercial aircraft are frequently sold for cash with the manufacturer retaining some financial exposure either by guaranteeing a minimum residual value of the aircraft at some date in the future or through the arrangement of lease finance on extended terms, which may include guarantees back to the manufacturer in the event of default by the lessee (the operator).

The following paragraphs summarise the actual and contingent liabilities of the Group in relation to Regional Jets, Turboprops and Airbus aircraft which arise from 1996 and prior year sales involving the types of financing arrangements described above.

Regional Jets and Turboprop aircraft

Aircraft financing commitments

Aircraft finance arranged by the Group may involve selling the aircraft to a third party lessor and leasing it back under an operating lease, the head lease. The aircraft are then leased under a sub-lease to an operator (the lessee) and it is not uncommon for an aircraft to be leased to several lessees during the period of the head lease. The commitment of the Group in respect of these head lease rental payments, which relate to sales in prior years, is set out below:

	1996	1995
	£m	£m
Head lease commitments on operating leases		
At 1st January	**1,373**	1,543
New commitments entered into	–	10
Commitments paid off	**(147)**	(171)
Foreign exchange and interest movements	–	(9)
At 31st December	1,190	1,373
Payments due under head leases		
In one year or less	**143**	143
Between one and five years	**521**	517
In later years	526	713
	1,190	1,373

Aircraft contingent liabilities

Aircraft finance arranged by the Group may also involve selling the aircraft to third parties who lease the aircraft to operators; again this may be to several operators during the life of the aircraft. The risks and benefits associated with the operator lease payments and the residual values of the aircraft rest with the third parties. However, the Group may give guarantees in respect of certain head lease and finance payments to be made by those third parties. Sales are also made directly to operators and this may involve the Group guaranteeing certain head lease and finance payments on behalf of those operators.

In the event of the guarantees to third parties or operators described above being called, the Group's exposure would be offset by future sub-lease rentals and the residual values of the related aircraft.

Provision for financing commitments and contingent liabilities

The following table sets out the Group's exposure to the above head lease financing commitments and contingent liabilities. Provision for these risks has been made in the accounts on a net present value basis.

	1996	1995
	£m	£m
Head lease commitments, as above	**1,190**	1,373
Finance leases on balance sheet	**20**	86
Aircraft contingent liabilities	1,726	1,766
	2,936	3,225
Contracted sub-lease income	**(1,051)**	(1,091)
Obligations less contracted income	**1,885**	2,134
Expected sub-lease income and residual aircraft values	**(1,203)**	(1,376)
Net risk	**682**	758
Adjustment to reduce to net present value	**(163)**	(173)
Recourse provision (note 19)	**519**	585

Head lease commitments (£1,190 million) arise from sale and operating leaseback transactions, which were entered into in prior years, and continue to reduce as existing obligations are paid off. As described above, these represent the amounts payable by the Group under head leases in future years.

Finance leases on balance sheet (£20 million) are the liability the Group has for aircraft held under finance leases. The decrease from 1995 arises from the restructuring of certain aircraft leases.

Aircraft contingent liabilities (£1,726 million) represent the exposure arising from transactions where the head lease obligations and finance payments of third parties have been guaranteed by the Group.

Contracted sub-lease income (£1,051 million) represents the outturn value of contracted lease income and takes into account the income due on these contracts to the first contractual right of an operator to return an aircraft. In many instances customers do not exercise such rights and will continue to lease aircraft to the full contractual term. Where anticipated, this additional income has been classified within expected sub-lease income.

Expected sub-lease income and residual aircraft values (£1,203 million) represent the amounts anticipated from extensions to existing contracted sub-leases and assumed future aircraft sub-leases on aircraft where the Group has a recourse exposure, and the anticipated market values of aircraft at the expiry of their head lease term based upon independent professional advice. The level of expected income has been calculated on a systematic basis, taking into account current and expected future market conditions, remarketing and other costs.

Given the long term nature of the liabilities, the Directors believe it is appropriate to state the recourse provision at its net present value. The *adjustment to reduce to net present value (£163 million)* reduces the expected liabilities described above from their outturn amounts to their anticipated net present value.

Residual value guarantees

In addition to the above, in some cases aircraft have been sold for cash with the transaction supported by a residual value guarantee. The majority of sales in 1996 were for cash with residual values guarantees given by the Group for values at specific dates in the future. At 31st December, 1996 the Group had given residual value guarantees for 52 aircraft totalling some £360 million (1995 20 aircraft, £160 million).

Based upon independent professional advice, the Directors believe that the Group's exposure to these guarantees is covered by the residual values of the related aircraft.

Airbus

The Group is involved in similar transactions through its participation in Airbus Industrie. Provision for the net exposure is included in the accounts of Airbus Industrie and included within the Group's share of the results of Airbus Industrie.

Although not part of UK GAAP at that time, it is noteworthy that the BAe Directors considered it appropriate to state the recourse provision at its net present value. Of course, both the ASB and IASC have issued standards (FRS 12 and IAS 37 respectively) that now require provisions to be measured at the present value of the expenditures expected to be required to settle the obligation.[110]

The 2000 accounts of the group (now renamed as BAE SYSTEMS plc) still show significant financial exposures as a result of its commercial aircraft financing arrangements; however, these are greatly lessened by the group having insured against a large proportion of the risk:

Extract 19.15: BAE SYSTEMS plc (2000)

Notes to the accounts [extract]

20 Commercial aircraft financing

Commercial aircraft are frequently sold for cash with the manufacturer retaining some financial exposure. Aircraft financing commitments of the group can be categorised as either direct or indirect. Direct commitments arise where the group has sold the aircraft to a third party lessor and then leased it back under an operating lease (or occasionally a finance lease) prior to an onward lease to an operator. Indirect commitments (contingent liabilities) may arise where the group has sold aircraft to third parties who either operate the aircraft themselves or lease the aircraft on to operators. In these cases the group may give guarantees in respect of the residual values of the related aircraft or certain head lease and finance payments to be made by either the third parties or the operators. The group's exposure to these commitments is offset by future lease rentals and the residual value of the related aircraft.

The group has entered into arrangements which reduce its exposure from commercial aircraft financing by obtaining insurance cover from a syndicate of leading insurance companies over a significant proportion of the contracted and expected income stream from the aircraft portfolio including those aircraft where the group has provided residual value guarantees.

The net exposure of the group to aircraft financing as at 31 December was:

	2000	1999
	£m	£m
Direct operating lease commitments	**600**	722
Direct finance lease commitments	**4**	5
Indirect exposure through aircraft contingent liabilities	**1,414**	1,589
Exposure to residual value guarantees	**693**	542
Income guaranteed through insurance arrangements	**(1,727)**	(1,885)
Net exposure	**984**	973
Expected income not covered by insurance arrangements	**(43)**	(43)
Expected income on aircraft delivered post insurance arrangements	**(388)**	(330)
Adjustment to net present value	**(154)**	(158)
Recourse provision	**399**	442

Income guaranteed through insurance arrangements represents the future income stream from the aircraft assets guaranteed under the insurance arrangements after deducting the policy excess.

Expected income not covered by insurance arrangements represents the amount of additional income assumed by management for the purpose of provisioning.

Expected income on aircraft delivered post insurance arrangements represents the level of future income anticipated on aircraft delivered since the start of the insurance arrangements.

Given the long term nature of the liabilities, the directors believe it is appropriate to state the recourse provisions at its net present value. The provision covers costs to be incurred over a forecast period of 12 years from the balance sheet date. The *adjustment to net present value* reduces the expected liabilities from their outturn amounts to their anticipated net present value.

Saab AB

The group is involved in similar transactions through its shareholding in Saab AB including aircraft financing commitments and contingent liabilities arising from guarantees in connection with aircraft sales.

Where Saab AB is exposed to financial risk from the above transactions, it makes provision against the expected net exposure on a net present value basis, after taking into account the expected future sub-lease income and residual values of the aircraft. The group's exposure is limited to its 35% shareholding in Saab AB. Further, in November 2000, Saab AB entered into a Financial Risk Insurance Programme similar in nature to that implemented by BAE SYSTEMS. This programme covers the majority of the Saab aircraft portfolio and in consequence significantly reduces the risk of potential future liabilities in that company.

Airbus

At 31 December 2000 the group was involved in similar transactions through its participation in Airbus Industrie GIE (AI) including aircraft financing commitments and contingent liabilities arising from credit guarantees and financing receivables under customer financing programmes.

Where AI is exposed to financial risk from the above transactions, it makes provision against the expected net exposure, after taking into account future sub-lease rentals and residual values of related aircraft where appropriate. Provision for the net exposure is included within the group's share of the results of AI. As at 31 December 2000 the group's obligations under the financing arrangements of AI were joint and several with its partner EADS.

8 IAS REQUIREMENTS

8.1 The development of IAS 17 (revised 1997)

IAS 17 – *Accounting for Leases* –was issued in September 1982 for accounting periods beginning on or after 1 January 1984.[111] Its basic requirements were similar to those of SSAP 21, with a finance lease being defined as one that 'transfers substantially all the risks and rewards incident to ownership of an asset'.[112] The standard then came under review as part of the IASC's improvements/comparability project undertaken during the late 1980s, and in July 1990 the IASC published a Statement of Intent[113] which set out its decisions following its review of the comments received on its proposals under this project. One of the issues on which the IASC deferred consideration pending further work related to IAS 17. At the time, the IASC stated that it believed that further study was required 'on the recognition of finance income on those leases on which the lessor's net investment outstanding is materially affected by income tax factors.'[114] This comment was made in the context of the fact that the standard allowed lessors accounting for finance leases to recognise finance income so as to reflect a constant periodic rate of return on either the net investment or net cash investment in the lease.

The IASC eventually gave the subject its attention in 1997, when it published Exposure Draft E56 – *Leases*. E56 proposed a very limited review of IAS 17, focusing only on those issues that the International Organization of Securities Commissions (IOSCO) considered essential for the purpose of fulfilling the IASC/IOSCO plan to complete a comprehensive set of core accounting standards that would be acceptable to all major stock exchanges for cross-border listings.

In December 1997, E56 was converted to IAS 17 (revised 1997) – *Leases* – which superseded the original IAS 17 with effect from 1 January 1999. The standards main features are summarised below:

8.2 Scope of IAS 17

The standard applies in accounting for all leases other than:

- lease agreements to explore for or use minerals, oil, natural gas and similar non-regenerative resources; and
- licensing agreements for such items as motion picture films, video recordings, plays, manuscripts, patents and copyrights.

Furthermore, the standard should not be applied to the measurement by:

- lessees of investment property held under finance leases; or
- lessors of investment property leased out under operating leases,

as in these cases IAS 40 – *Investment Property* – applies; (see IAS 40, Investment Property); or

- lessees of biological assets held under finance leases; or
- lessors of biological assets leased out under operating lease,

as in these cases IAS 41 – *Agriculture* – applies.[115]

The standard applies to agreements that transfer the right to use assets even though substantial services by the lessor may be called for in connection with the operation or maintenance of such assets. On the other hand, it does not apply to agreements that are contracts for services that do not transfer the right to use assets from one contracting party to the other.[116]

8.3 Lease classification

The standard defines a lease as 'an agreement whereby the lessor conveys to the lessee in return for a payment or series of payments the right to use an asset for an agreed period of time.' A finance lease is a 'lease that transfers substantially all the risks and rewards incident to ownership of an asset', and an operating lease is 'a lease other than a finance lease'.[117] The definition of a lease includes contracts for the hire of an asset which contain a provision giving the hirer an option to acquire title to the asset upon the fulfilment of agreed conditions (i.e., hire purchase contracts).[118]

The classification of leases adopted in the standard is, therefore, based on the extent to which risks and rewards incident to ownership of a leased asset lie with the lessor or the lessee. Risks include the possibilities of losses from idle capacity or technological obsolescence and of variations in return due to changing economic conditions. Rewards may be represented by the expectation of profitable operation over the asset's economic life and of gain from appreciation in value or realisation of a residual value.[119] However, unlike SSAP 21 under UK GAAP (which includes the rebuttable presumption that the transfer of substantially all the risks and rewards occurs if, at the inception of the lease, the present value of the minimum lease payments including any initial payment, amounts to substantially all (normally 90 per cent or more) of the fair value of the leased asset), IAS 17 provides no numerical guidelines to be applied in classifying a lease as either finance or operating. It seems that it was a conscious decision of the IASC Board not to refer to a percentage such as 90% in the standard, as it wanted to avoid the possibility of lease classification being reduced to a single pass or fail test.

Instead, the standard makes the general statement that the classification of a lease depends on the substance of the transaction rather than the form of the contract, and lists a number of examples of situations that would normally lead to a lease being classified as a finance lease:[120]

- the lease transfers ownership of the asset to the lessee by the end of the lease term (although it is clear from the standard that title does not have to be transferred to the lessee for a lease to be classified as a finance lease);[121]
- the lessee has the option to purchase the asset at a price which is expected to be sufficiently lower than the fair value at the date the option becomes exercisable such that, at the inception of the lease, it is reasonably certain that the option will be exercised;
- the lease term is for the major part of the economic life of the asset even if title is not transferred;
- at the inception of the lease the present value of the minimum lease payments amounts to at least substantially all of the fair value of the leased asset; and

- the leased assets are of a specialised nature such that only the lessee can use them without major modifications being made.

The standard then goes on to list the following indicators of situations that, individually or in combination, could also lead to a lease being classified as a finance lease:[122]

- if the lessee can cancel the lease, the lessor's losses associated with the cancellation are borne by the lessee;
- gains or losses from the fluctuation in the fair value of the residual fall to the lessee (for example, in the form of a rent rebate equalling most of the sales proceeds at the end of the lease); and
- the lessee has the ability to continue the lease for a secondary period at a rent which is substantially lower than market rent.

Whilst the fourth 'situation' in the first list above refers to the present value of the minimum lease payments being at least substantially all of the fair value of the asset (thereby adopting part of the UK GAAP definition of a finance lease), the standard does not go as far as putting a percentage to it. We have already speculated above as to why this may be; nevertheless, we see the lack of numerical guidance to be somewhat unhelpful. We therefore see no harm in practice in at least applying the '90% test' as a rule of thumb benchmark as part of the overall process in reaching a judgement as to the classification of a lease. Clearly, though, it should not be applied as a hard and fast rule.

Lease classification is made at the inception of the lease,[123] which is the earlier of the date of the lease agreement or of a commitment by the parties to the principal provisions of the lease.[124] However, if at any time the lessee and the lessor agree to change the provisions of the lease, other than by renewing the lease, in a manner that would have resulted in a different classification of the lease under the above criteria had the changed terms been in effect at the inception of the lease, the revised agreement is considered as a new agreement over its term. On the other hand, changes in estimates (for example, changes in estimates of the economic life or of the residual value of the leased item) or changes in circumstances (for example, default by the lessee) do not give rise to a new classification of a lease for accounting purposes.[125]

Leases of land and buildings are classified as operating or finance leases in the same way as leases of other assets. However, the standard makes an important point regarding the classification of a lease involving land. It notes that a characteristic of land is that it normally has an indefinite economic life and, if title is not expected to pass to the lessee by the end of the lease term, the lessee does not receive substantially all of the risks and rewards incident to ownership. A premium paid for such a leasehold represents pre-paid lease payments which are amortised over the lease term in accordance with the pattern of benefits provided.[126] This will have quite an important impact in the UK when companies adopt IAS, since current practice is to treat such leasehold premiums as tangible fixed assets rather than as operating lease prepayments.

8.4 Lessee accounting

8.4.1 Finance leases

The standard requires lessees to recognise finance leases as assets and liabilities in their balance sheets at amounts equal at the inception of the lease to the fair value of the leased item or, if lower, at the present value of the minimum lease payments. In calculating the present value of the minimum lease payments the discount factor is the interest rate implicit in the lease, if this is practicable to determine; if not, the lessee's incremental borrowing rate should be used.[127]

The interest rate implicit in the lease is the discount rate that, at the inception of the lease, causes the aggregate present value of (a) the minimum lease payments and (b) the unguaranteed residual value to be equal to the fair value of the leased asset. The lessee's incremental borrowing rate of interest is the rate of interest the lessee would have to pay on a similar lease or, if that is not determinable, the rate that, at the inception of the lease, the lessee would incur to borrow over a similar term, and with a similar security, the funds necessary to purchase the asset.[128]

Fair value is defined as the amount for which an asset could be exchanged or a liability settled, between knowledgeable, willing parties in an arm's length transaction.[129] In the case of a lessee, the minimum lease payments are the payments over the lease term that the lessee is, or can be required, to make excluding contingent rent, costs for services and taxes to be paid by and reimbursed to the lessor, together with any amounts guaranteed by the lessee or by a party related to the lessee. However, if the lessee has an option to purchase the asset at a price which is expected to be sufficiently lower than the fair value at the date the option becomes exercisable that, at the inception of the lease, it is reasonably certain to be exercised, the minimum lease payments comprise the minimum payments payable over the lease term and the payment required to exercise this purchase option.[130]

The lease term is the non-cancellable period for which the lessee has contracted to lease the asset together with any further terms for which the lessee has the option to continue to lease the asset, with or without further payment, which option at the inception of the lease it is reasonably certain that the lessee will exercise.[131]

Contingent rents (which are excluded from minimum lease payments) are defined in the standard as that portion of the lease payments that are not fixed in amount but are based on a factor other than just the passage of time (for example, percentage of sales, amount of usage, price indices, market rates of interest.).[132]

Where initial direct costs are incurred in connection with specific leasing activities (as in negotiating and securing leasing arrangements), the standard states that costs identified as directly attributable to activities performed by the lessee for a finance lease are included as part of the amount recognised as an asset under the lease.[133]

The standard requires that lease payments should be apportioned between the finance charge and the reduction of the outstanding liability. It goes on to state that the finance charge should be allocated to periods during the lease term so as to produce a constant periodic rate of interest on the remaining balance of the liability for each period.[134] However, although the standard notes that, in practice, in allocating the finance charge to periods during the lease term some form of approximation may be used to simplify the calculation,[135] it provides no guidance as to the methodology that should be applied in allocating finance charges to accounting periods.

Readers might therefore find it helpful to refer to Example 19.2 at 3.4 above, for guidance on how to determine the amounts to be allocated to each accounting period.

On the issue of depreciation, the standard notes that a finance lease gives rise to a depreciation expense for depreciable assets as well as a finance expense for each accounting period. It goes on to require that the depreciation policy for depreciable leased assets should be consistent with that for depreciable assets which are owned, and the depreciation recognised should be calculated on the basis set out in IAS 16 – *Property, Plant and Equipment* – and IAS 38 – *Intangible Assets*. If there is reasonable certainty that the lessee will obtain ownership by the end of the lease term, the period of expected use is the useful life of the asset. If there is no reasonable certainty that the lessee will obtain ownership by the end of the lease term, the asset should be fully depreciated over the shorter of the lease term or its useful life.[136]

8.4.2 *Operating Leases*

IAS 17 requires that lease payments under an operating lease (excluding costs for services such as insurance and maintenance) should be recognised as an expense in the income statement on a straight line basis over the lease term unless another systematic basis is representative of the time pattern of the user's benefit, even if the payments are not on that basis.[137]

On the matter of operating lease incentives, the SIC was asked to consider the accounting implications of a lessor providing incentives for a lessee to enter into a new or renewed operating lease agreement. Examples of such incentives are an up-front cash payment to the lessee or the reimbursement or assumption by the lessor of costs of the lessee (such as relocation costs, leasehold improvements and costs associated with a pre-existing lease commitment of the lessee). Alternatively, initial periods of the lease term may be agreed to be rent-free or at a reduced rent.

The consensus reached by the SIC in Interpretation SIC–15 – *Operating Leases – Incentives* – was that all incentives for the agreement of a new or renewed operating lease should be recognised as an integral part of the net consideration agreed for the use of the leased asset, irrespective of the incentive's nature or form or the timing of payments.[138]

It was agreed further the lessee should recognise the aggregate benefit of incentives as a reduction of rental expense over the lease term, on a straight-line basis unless another systematic basis is representative of the time pattern of the lessee's benefit from the use of the leased asset.[139]

And finally, SIC–15 requires that costs incurred by the lessee, including costs in connection with a pre-existing lease (for example, costs for termination, relocation or leasehold improvements), should be accounted for by the lessee in accordance with the IAS applicable to those costs, including costs which are effectively reimbursed through an incentive arrangement.[140]

In an Appendix to SIC–15, the SIC has set out the following two examples that illustrate the application of the Interpretation:

Example 1

An enterprise agrees to enter into a new lease arrangement with a new lessor. The lessor agrees to pay the lessee's relocation costs as an incentive to the lessee for entering into the new lease. The lessee's moving costs are 1,000. The new lease has a term of 10 years, at a fixed rate of 2,000 per year.

The accounting is:

The lessee recognises relocation costs of 1,000 as an expense in Year 1. Net consideration of 19,000 consists of 2,000 for each of the 10 years in the lease term, less a 1,000 incentive for relocation costs. Both the lessor and lessee would recognise the net rental consideration of 19,000 over the 10 year lease term using a single amortisation method in accordance with paragraphs 4 and 5 of SIC–15.

Example 2

An enterprise agrees to enter into a new lease arrangement with a new lessor. The lessor agrees to a rent-free period for the first three years as incentive to the lessee for entering into the new lease. The new lease has a term of 20 years, at a fixed rate of 5,000 per annum for years 4 through 20.

The accounting is:

Net consideration of 85,000 consists of 5,000 for each of 17 years in the lease term. Both the lessor and lessee would recognise the net consideration of 85,000 over the 20 year lease term using a single amortisation method in accordance with paragraphs 4 and 5 of this Interpretation.

8.4.3 Lessee disclosures

A Finance Leases

IAS 17 requires that lessees should, in addition to the financial instruments-related requirements of IAS 32 – *Financial Instruments: Disclosure and Presentation* – make the following disclosures for finance leases:[141]

(a) for each class of asset, the net carrying amount at the balance sheet date;

(b) a reconciliation between the total of minimum lease payments at the balance sheet date, and their present value. In addition, an enterprise should disclose the total of minimum lease payments at the balance sheet date, and their present value, for each of the following periods:

    (i) not later than one year;

    (ii) later than one year and not later than five years;

    (iii) later than five years;

(c) contingent rents recognised in income for the period;

(d) the total of future minimum sublease payments expected to be received under non-cancellable subleases at the balance sheet date; and

(e) a general description of the lessee's significant leasing arrangements including, but not limited to, the following:

 (i) the basis on which contingent rent payments are determined;

 (ii) the existence and terms of renewal or purchase options and escalation clauses; and

 (iii) restrictions imposed by lease arrangements, such as those concerning dividends, additional debt, and further leasing.

In addition, the requirements on disclosure under IAS 16 – *Property, Plant and Equipment*, IAS 36 – *Impairment of Assets*, IAS 38 – *Intangible Assets*, and IAS 40 – *Investment Property*, apply to the amounts of leased assets under finance leases that are accounted for by the lessee as acquisitions of assets.

B Operating leases

IAS 17 requires that lessees should, in addition to the financial instruments-related requirements of IAS 32 make the following disclosures for operating leases:[142]

(a) the total of future minimum lease payments under non-cancellable operating leases for each of the following periods:

 (i) not later than one year;

 (ii) later than one year and not later than five years;

 (iii) later than five years;

(b) the total of future minimum sublease payments expected to be received under non-cancellable subleases at the balance sheet date;

(c) lease and sublease payments recognised in income for the period, with separate amounts for minimum lease payments, contingent rents, and sublease payments;

(d) a general description of the lessee's significant leasing arrangements including, but not limited to, the following:

 (i) the basis on which contingent rent payments are determined;

 (ii) the existence and terms of renewal or purchase options and escalation clauses; and

 (iii) restrictions imposed by lease arrangements, such as those concerning dividends, additional debt, and further leasing.

C Examples of disclosures

Nestlé provides an excellent illustration of the required lessee disclosures in respect of both finance and operating leases:

Extract 19.16: Nestlé S.A. (2000)

ACCOUNTING POLICIES [extract]
Leased assets

Assets acquired under long term finance leases are capitalised and depreciated in accordance with the Group's policy on tangible fixed assets. The associated obligations are included in financial liabilities.

Rentals payable under operating leases are charged to the income statement as incurred.

NOTES [extract]
4. Expenses by nature

The following items are allocated to the appropriate headings of expenses by function in the income statement

In millions of CHF	**2000**	1999
...		
Depreciation of tangible fixed assets	**2,737**	2,597
Salaries and welfare expenses	**12,774**	12,224
Remuneration of the executive management and of the Directors	**19**	16
Auditors' remuneration	**26**	28
Operating lease charges	**362**	113
Exchange differences	**(55)**	(22)

11. Tangible fixed assets [extract]

At 31st December 2000, net tangible fixed assets include CHF 158 million (1999: CHF 123 million) of assets under construction. Net tangible fixed assets held under finance leases at 31st December 2000 amount to CHF 255 million (1999: CHF 80 million). Net tangible fixed assets of CHF 147 million (1999: CHF 192 million) are pledged as security for financial liabilities.

The fire risks, reasonably estimated, are insured in accordance with domestic requirements.

18. Medium and long term financial liabilities

In millions of CHF	**2000**	1999
...		
Loans from financial institutions	**1,442**	1,661
Bonds	**3,783**	3,994
Obligations under finance leases	**241**	81
	5,466	5,736
Current portion of medium and long term financial liabilities	**(698)**	(831)
	4,768	4,905

34. Lease commitments [extract]

The following charges arise from these commitments:

Operating leases

In millions of CHF	**2000**	1999
	Minimum lease payments Future value	
within one year	**346**	280
in the second year	**291**	246
in the third to fifth year inclusive	**648**	521
after the fifth year	**1,196**	1,215
	2,481	2,262

Finance leases

In million of CHF	**2000**		1999	
	Minimum lease payments			
	Present value	Future value	Present value	Future value
within one year	**22**	**24**	33	35
in the second year	**29**	**33**	14	17
in the third to fifth year inclusive	**157**	**177**	11	13
after the fifth year	**33**	**43**	23	29
	241	**277**	81	94

The difference between the future value of the minimum lease payments and their present value represents the discount on the lease obligations.

The following extract from the accounts of Lufthansa illustrates the financial instrument-related disclosures required in respect of finance leases:

Extract 19.17: Deutsche Lufthansa AG (1998)

Notes to the Consolidated Balance Sheet Annual Report 2000 [extract]

Other liabilities (finance lease agreements)

Weighted average interest rate	Fixed interest rate until	Carrying amount 31.12.2000 €m	Market value 31.12.2000 €m	Carrying amount 31.12.1999 €m	Carrying amount 31.12.1999 €m
7.5	2000	–	–	368.3	386.7
6-month DM-LIBOR	2000	–	–	12.8	12.8
6.8	2001	34.9	35.3	38.2	39.8
6-month DM-LIBOR	2001	33.2	33.2	176.3	176.3
5.5	2002	220.2	223.5	234.0	240.7
6-month DM-LIBOR	2002	56.6	56.6	62.2	62.2
1.8 (Yen)	2002	124.5	127.6	126.5	132.5
6.6	2003	112.0	116.3	127.8	134.5
6-month DM-LIBOR	2003	78.6	78.6	86.8	86.8
7.3	2004	84.0	90.3	89.0	97.1
6-month DM-LIBOR	2004	145.4	145.4	–	–
6-month DM-LIBOR	2005	255.2	255.2	278.7	278.7
6-month DM-LIBOR	2006	130.0	130.0	135.8	135.8
7.8	2014	28.6	33.2	29.2	34.0
		1303.2	1325.2	1765.6	1817.9

35 Deferred income [extract]

Deferred income includes mainly accrued book profits from finance lease transactions released affecting the income statement over the term of the respective lease agreement in accordance with IAS 17. …

The following extract from the accounts of VTech Holdings provides a good example of lessee operating lease disclosures, including detailed narrative disclosures concerning the leases.

Extract 19.18: VTech Holdings Ltd (2001)

Accounting Policies [extract]
K. Leases

Leases of property, plant and equipment that substantially transfer to the Group all the benefits and risks of ownership of assets, other than legal title, are accounted for as finance leases. At the inception of a finance lease, the fair value of the asset is recorded together with the obligation, excluding the interest element, to pay future rentals. Finance charges are debited to the income statement in proportion to the capital balances outstanding.

Leases of assets under which all the benefits and risks of ownership are effectively retained by the lessor are classified as operating leases. Payments made under leases are charged to the income statement on a straight line basis over the period of the lease.

When an operating lease is terminated before the lease period has expired, any payment required to be made to the lessor by way of penalty is recognized as an expense in the period in which the termination takes place.

Notes [extract]
24. COMMITMENTS [extract]

		2000	1999
		US$ million	US$ million
(ii)	Operating lease commitments		
	At 31st March the group has total commitments under operating leases payable as follows		
	Land and buildings		
	In one year or less	**11.7**	8.9
	Between one and two years	**11.6**	8.5
	Between two and five years	**21.4**	19.6
	In more than five years	**74.6**	74.0
		165,184	136,235

The Group has entered into agreements with an independent third party in the People's Republic of China ("PRC") to lease factory premises in Houjie, Dongguan comprising several factory buildings. There are totally four separate leases which expire in 2003, 2004, 2022, and 2029 respectively. The lease expiring in 2029 has a non-cancellable period of eight years which expires in 2007. At the end of this non-cancellable period, the lease can only be cancelled on six months' notice with a penalty equivalent to three months' rentals. All other buildings have lease terms which can be cancelled upon three to six months' notice with penalties equivalent to three to twelve months' rentals. The operating lease commitments above include total commitments over the entire lease terms.

In December 1995, the Group entered into an agreement with an independent third party in the People's Republic of China ("PRC") whereby the PRC party will construct in phases and lease to the Group a new production facility in Liaobu, Dongguan. Under a fifty year lease agreement, the Group will rent the first and second phases of the facility for non-cancellable periods of six and eight years after completion respectively. The total estimated rental commitment to the end of the non-cancellable periods, after offsetting the interest bearing amount advanced for construction is US$6.4 million (2000: US$1.1 million). This amount is included in operating lease commitments above. The Group also has an option to purchase each phase of the production facility at any time within four and a half years after the completion of each phase. The first phase became fully operational in April 1998 and the second phase is expected to be operational in October 2001.

8.5 Lessor accounting

8.5.1 *Finance leases*

The standard require lessors to recognise assets held under a finance lease in their balance sheets and present them as a receivable at an amount equal to the net investment in the lease.[143] The recognition of finance income should be based on a pattern reflecting a constant periodic rate of return on the lessor's net investment outstanding in respect of the finance lease.[144]

The original IAS 17 provided a free choice of method in the allocation of finance income by a lessor, namely the recognition of income basing on a pattern reflecting a constant periodic rate of return based on either:

- the lessor's net investment outstanding in respect of the finance lease; or
- the lessor's net cash investment outstanding in respect of the finance lease.

It is less than clear why it was that, in revising IAS 17, the IASC eliminated as an option the net cash investment method of recognising finance lease income. It is understood that IOSCO had asked the IASC to clarify the position as to when each of the two methods was appropriate – however this does not necessarily mean the elimination of one of them. What is clear is that in certain circumstances the net investment method is not appropriate (for example, when there are significant tax cash flows which affect the lessor) and that it does not make sense to require the net investment method to be applied in all circumstances. US GAAP requires the net investment method to be applied except in the case of leveraged leases as defined in SFAS 13, for which the net cash investment method is required. It would seem sensible for the IASC to have adopted a similar approach.

8.5.2 *Operating leases*

Lessors should present assets subject to operating leases in their balance sheets according to the nature of the asset. Lease income from operating leases should be recognised in income on a straight line basis over the lease term, unless another systematic basis is more representative of the time pattern in which use benefit derived from the leased asset is diminished.[145]

Costs, including depreciation, incurred in earning the lease income are recognised as an expense. Lease income (excluding receipts for services provided such as insurance and maintenance) is recognised in income on a straight line basis over the lease term even if the receipts are not on such a basis, unless another systematic basis is more representative of the time pattern in which use benefit derived from the leased asset is diminished. Initial direct costs incurred specifically to earn revenues from an operating lease are either deferred and allocated to income over the lease term in proportion to the recognition of rent income, or are recognised as an expense in the income statement in the period in which they are incurred.[146]

In negotiating a new or renewed operating lease, a lessor may provide incentives for the lessee to enter into the arrangement. This issue was addressed by the SIC in Interpretation SIC–15, which states that the lessor should recognise the aggregate cost of incentives as a reduction of rental income over the lease term, on a straight-line basis unless another systematic basis is representative of the time pattern over which the benefit of the leased asset is diminished.[147]

The depreciation of depreciable leased assets should be on a basis consistent with the lessor's normal depreciation policy for similar assets, and the depreciation charge should be calculated on the basis set out in IAS 16 and IAS 38.[148]

IAS 17 refers to IAS 36 in providing guidance on the need to assess the possibility of an impairment of assets.[149]

8.5.3 *Manufacturer/dealer lessors*

Manufacturers or dealers often offer customers the choice of either buying or leasing an asset. A finance lease of an asset by a manufacturer or dealer lessor gives rise to two types of income:

(a) the profit or loss equivalent to the profit or loss resulting from an outright sale of the asset being leased, at normal selling prices, reflecting any applicable volume or trade discounts; and

(b) the finance income over the lease term.[150]

Furthermore, manufacturer or dealer lessors sometimes quote artificially low rates of interest in order to attract customers. The use of such a rate would result in an excessive portion of the total income from the transaction being recognised at the time of sale. If artificially low rates of interest are quoted, selling profit would be restricted to that which would apply if a commercial rate of interest were charged.[151]

Consequently, IAS 17 requires that manufacturer or dealer lessors should recognise selling profit or loss in income for the period, in accordance with the policy followed by the enterprise for outright sales. If artificially low rates of interest are quoted, selling profit should be restricted to that which would apply if a commercial rate of interest were charged. Initial direct costs should be recognised as an expense in the income statement at the inception of the lease.[152]

A manufacturer or dealer lessor does not recognise any selling profit on entering into an operating lease because it is not the equivalent of a sale.[153]

Reference should be made to 7.6 above for further discussion of the allocation of profit for manufacturer/dealer lessors.

8.5.4 *Lessor disclosures*

A *Finance leases*

Lessors should, in addition to the financial instruments-related requirements of IAS 32 make the following disclosures for finance leases:[154]

(a) a reconciliation between the total gross investment in the lease at the balance sheet date, and the present value of minimum lease payments receivable at the balance sheet date. In addition, an enterprise should disclose the total gross investment in the lease and the present value of minimum lease payments receivable at the balance sheet date, for each of the following periods:

 (i) not later than one year;

 (ii) later than one year and not later than five years;

 (iii) later than five years;

(b) unearned finance income;

(c) the unguaranteed residual values accruing to the benefit of the lessor;

(d) the accumulated allowance for uncollectible minimum lease payments receivable;

(e) contingent rents recognised in income; and

(f) a general description of the lessor's significant leasing arrangements.

The standard suggests further that, as an indicator of growth, it is often useful also to disclose the gross investment less unearned income in new business added during the accounting period, after deducting the relevant amounts for cancelled leases.[155] However, this is a recommended, as opposed to mandatory, disclosure.

B Operating leases

In addition to the disclosures required under IAS 32, the standard requires the following disclosures to be made in respect of assets leased out under operating leases:[156]

(a) the future minimum lease payments under non-cancellable operating leases in the aggregate and for each of the following periods;
   (i) not later than one year;
   (ii) later than one year and not later than five years;
   (iii) later than five years;

(b) total contingent rents recognised in income; and

(c) a general description of the lessor's significant leasing arrangements.

The standard contains a reminder that the disclosure requirements of IAS 16, IAS 38, IAS 40 and IAS 41 also apply to assets leased out under operating leases.[157]

8.6 Sale and leaseback transactions

If a sale and leaseback transaction results in a finance lease, any excess of sales proceeds over the carrying amount should not be immediately recognised as income in the financial statements of a seller-lessee. Instead, it should be deferred and amortised over the lease term.[158]

If a sale and leaseback transaction results in an operating lease, and it is clear that the transaction is established at fair value, any profit or loss should be recognised immediately. If the sale price is below fair value, any profit or loss should be recognised immediately except that, if the loss is compensated by future lease payments at below market price, it should be deferred and amortised in proportion to the lease payments over the period for which the asset is expected to be used. If the sale price is above fair value, the excess over fair value should be deferred and amortised over the period for which the asset is expected to be used.[159]

For operating leases, if the fair value at the time of a sale and leaseback transaction is less than the carrying amount of the asset, a loss equal to the amount of the difference between the carrying amount and fair value should be recognised immediately,[160] whilst for finance leases, no such adjustment is necessary unless there has been an impairment in value, in which case the carrying amount is reduced to recoverable amount in accordance with IAS dealing with impairment of assets.[161]

The standard includes an Appendix, which comprises the following tabulation of the standard's requirements concerning sale and leaseback transactions, and is aimed at providing guidance in interpreting the various permutations of facts and circumstances that are set out in the requirements.

Sale price established at fair value (paragraph 52)	*Carrying amount equal to fair value*	*Carrying amount less than fair value*	*Carrying amount above fair value*
Profit	no profit	recognise profit immediately	not applicable
Loss	no loss	not applicable	recognise loss immediately

Sale price below fair value (paragraph 52)			
Profit	no profit	recognise profit immediately	no profit (note 1)
Loss not compensated by future lease payments at below market price	recognise loss immediately	recognise loss immediately	(note 1)
Loss compensated by future lease payments at below market price	defer and amortise loss	defer and amortise loss	(note 1)

Sale price above fair value (paragraph 52)			
Profit	defer and amortise profit	defer and amortise profit	defer and amortise profit (note 2)
Loss	no loss	no loss	(note 1)

Note 1 These parts of the table represent circumstances that would have been dealt with under paragraph 54 of the Standard. Paragraph 54 requires the carrying amount of an asset to be written down to fair value where it is subject to a sale and leaseback.

Note 2 The profit would be the difference between fair value and sale price as the carrying amount would have been written down to fair value in accordance with paragraph 54.

IAS 17's disclosure requirements for lessees and lessors apply equally to sale and leaseback transactions. The requirement in paragraph 23(e) of the standard for lessees to give a general description of their significant leasing arrangements (see 8.4.3 A above) will lead to the disclosure of unique or unusual provisions of the agreement or terms of the sale and leaseback transactions.[162] Furthermore, sale and leaseback transactions may meet the separate disclosure criteria for 'exceptional items' set out in IAS 8 (see Chapter 25 at 3.3).[163]

8.7 Transactions in the legal form of a lease and leaseback

At the time of writing (September 2001), the SIC had in issue a Draft Interpretation, SIC–D27 – *Transactions in the Legal Form of a Lease and Leaseback*. The Draft Interpretation has been exposed for public comment, and the SIC has completed its consideration of the matter, including comments received from the IASB. The SIC reaffirmed its consensus and is redrafting the Interpretation to focus on the principles involved. Essentially, the Interpretation deals with the issue of how to evaluate the substance of transactions, or a series of linked transactions, in the legal form of a lease. It seems that the main purpose of the Interpretation is to reinforce the principle of substance over form, and to ensure that, where appropriate, a series of linked transactions should be accounted for as one transaction.

It is likely that SIC–D27 will be issued as a final document towards the end of 2001.

9 CONCLUSION

Both SSAP 21 and IAS 17 have been in force for a long time. The two standards are similar, and practice under them both is well established. In the UK, although FRS 5 does not override SSAP 21, but it does provide additional guidance on the factors to be considered in ensuring that leases are classified as finance or operating leases in accordance with their substance. This would seem to provide further evidence of the reduced significance of the 90% test in favour of an approach based on qualitative considerations, which is more the philosophy underlying IAS 17.

In any event, though, both SSAP 21 and IAS 17 should be regarded as standards with a relatively short remaining shelf life. It is clear that the initiatives started by the G4+1 to change fundamentally the approach to lease accounting will now be pursued further by the IASB, in conjunction with one or more of the national standard setters. It is therefore likely to be the case that, by the time EU listed companies are required to apply IAS, the distinction between finance and operating leases will have been removed, and the rights and obligations of all leases will be recorded in the balance sheet at their fair values.

References

1 SSAP 21, *Accounting for leases and hire purchase contracts*, ASC, August 1984, paras. 15 and 32.
2 IAS 17, Leases, IASC, Revised 1997. SFAS 13, *Accounting for Leases*, FASB, November 1976. For the detailed US requirements relating to leases, see Financial Accounting Standards Board, *Accounting Standards as of June 1, 2000, Current Text 2000/2001 Edition, Volume I*, General Standards, FASB, 2000, Section L10, pp. 29141–29259.
3 SSAP 21, para. 14.
4 *Ibid.*, para. 18.
5 IAS 17, para. 3.
6 *Ibid*, para. 4.
7 ED 29, *Accounting for leases and hire purchase contracts*, ASC, October 1981.
8 Department of Trade, *Inspectors' Final Report on Court Line Limited*, p. 153.
9 *Ibid.*, Appendix J, p. 141.
10 *Ibid.*, p. 153.
11 ASC, *Guidance Notes on SSAP 21: Accounting for Leases and Hire Purchase Contracts*, August 1984.
12 SSAP 21, Introductory paragraph.
13 IAS 17, para. 8.
14 *Ibid.*, para. 9.
15 ASB Statement, *Statement of Principles for Financial Reporting*, ASB, December 1999, para. 4.6.
16 *Ibid.*, para. 4.23.
17 Warren McGregor, *Accounting for leases: a new approach: Recognition by Lessees of Assets and Liabilities Arising under Lease Contracts*, FASB, 1996.
18 *Ibid.*, p. 3.
19 *Ibid.*
20 *Framework for the Preparation and Presentation of Financial Statements*, IASC, September 1989, paras. 49(a) and (b).
21 W McGregor, *op. cit.*, p. 16.
22 *Ibid.*, p. 17.
23 G4+1 Group of Accounting Standard Setters, Position Paper, *Leases: Implementation of a new approach*, December 1999, Part II, *passim*.
24 *Ibid.*, Part III, *passim*.
25 *Ibid.*, para. 3.13.
26 *Ibid.*, para. 4.86 *et seq.*
27 SSAP 21, para. 15.
28 *Ibid.*, para. 17.
29 *Ibid.*, paras. 15 and 16.
30 *Ibid.*, para. 25.
31 *Ibid.*, para. 24.
32 ICAEW, *Financial Reporting & Auditing Group, Technical Release FRAG 9/92*, March 1992, para. 33.
33 SSAP 21, para. 20.
34 *Ibid.*, para. 26.
35 *Ibid.*, para. 19.
36 ICAEW, Technical Release 664, *Implementation of SSAP 21 'Accounting for leases and hire purchase contracts'*, July 1987, paras. 4 and 5.
37 ICAEW, FRAG 9/92, para. 35.
38 *Ibid.*
39 *Ibid.*, para. 36.
40 FRS 5, *Reporting the Substance of Transactions*, ASB, 1994, para. 13.
41 *Ibid.*, para. 45.
42 SSAP 21, para. 35.
43 Guidance Notes on SSAP 21, para. 20.
44 SSAP 21, para. 37.
45 FASB Technical Bulletin No. 85-3, *Accounting for Operating Leases with Scheduled Rent Increases*, FASB, November 14, 1985.
46 UITF 12, *Lessee accounting for reverse premiums and similar incentives*, ASB, 5 December 1994.
47 UITF 28, *Operating lease incentives*, ASB, 22 February 2001. UITF 28 became effective for financial statements relating to accounting periods ending on or after 22 September 2001 (including corresponding amounts for the immediately preceding period) in respect of lease agreements commencing in the current or the preceding accounting period.
48 *Ibid.*, para. 3.
49 *Ibid.*, para. 4.
50 *Ibid.*, para. 13.
51 *Ibid.*, para. 14.
52 FRS 12, *Provisions, contingent liabilities and contingent assets*, ASB, September 1998, para. 68.
53 *Ibid.*, para. 71.
54 *Ibid.*, para. 2.
55 SSAP 21, para. 57.
56 *Ibid.*, para. 55.
57 *Ibid.*, para. 53.
58 *Ibid.*, para. 50.
59 *Ibid.*
60 *Ibid.*, paras. 51 and 52.
61 *Ibid.*, para. 56.
62 IAS 17, para. 27.
63 SSAP 21, para. 54.
64 CA 85, Sch. 4, para. 8.
65 *Ibid.*, para. 50(5).
66 *Ibid.*, paras. 42 to 44.
67 *Ibid.*, para. 48.
68 SSAP 21, para. 54.
69 *Ibid.*, para. 43.
70 UITF 28, para. 13.
71 *Ibid.*, paras. 15–17.
72 SSAP 21, para. 28.

73 *Ibid.*, para. 39.
74 *Ibid.*, para. 23.
75 *Ibid.*, para. 41.
76 Guidance Notes on SSAP 21, para. 92.
77 *Ibid.*, para. 121. See *Guidance Notes on ED 29: Accounting for Leases and Hire Purchase Contracts*, ASC, October 1981, paras. 81–86 for an illustration of the difference that can arise in such circumstances.
78 SSAP 21, para. 39.
79 Guidance Notes on SSAP 21, para. 116.
80 SSAP 21, para. 60.
81 *Ibid.*
82 *Ibid.*, para. 61.
83 *Ibid.*, para. 58.
84 *Ibid.*, para. 61.
85 *Ibid.*, para. 59.
86 Guidance Notes on SSAP 21, para. 124.
87 CA 85, Sch. 4, para. 8.
88 *Ibid.*, paras. 42–44.
89 Guidance Notes on SSAP 21, para. 38.
90 SSAP 21, para. 34.
91 *Ibid.*, para. 48.
92 ICAEW, FRAG 9/92, para. 15.
93 *Ibid.*
94 *Ibid.*, para. 44.
95 SSAP 21, para. 46.
96 FRS 5, Application Note B, para. B20.
97 *Ibid.*, Application Note B, para. B6.
98 *Ibid.*, Application Note B, para. B11.
99 SSAP 21, para. 47.
100 Adapted from para. 122 of Guidance Notes on ED 29.
101 ICAEW, FRAG 9/92, para. 16.
102 *Ibid.*, para. 46.
103 SSAP 21, para. 30.
104 Guidance Notes on SSAP 21, para. 82.
105 ICAEW, FRAG 9/92, para. 47.
106 Guidance Notes on SSAP 21, para. 82.
107 *Ibid.*, para. 58.
108 SSAP 21, para. 45.
109 Guidance Notes on SSAP 21, para. 165.
110 FRS 12, *Provisions, Contingent Liabilities and Contingent Assets*, ASB, September 1998, para. 45; IAS 37, *Provisions, Contingent Liabilities and Contingent Assets*, IASC, September 1998, para. 45.
111 IAS 17, *Accounting for Leases*, IASC, September 1982 (reformatted 1994).
112 *Ibid.*, para. 3.
113 Statement of Intent, *Comparability of Financial Statements*, IASC, July 1990.
114 *Ibid.*, Appendix 3.
115 IAS 17 (revised 1997), para. 1.
116 *Ibid.*, para. 2.
117 *Ibid.*, para. 3.
118 *Ibid.*, para. 4.
119 *Ibid.*, para. 5.
120 *Ibid.*, para. 8.
121 *Ibid.*, para. 3.
122 *Ibid.*, para. 9.
123 *Ibid.*, para. 10.
124 *Ibid.*, para. 3.
125 *Ibid.*, para. 10.
126 *Ibid.*, para. 11.
127 *Ibid.*, para. 12.
128 *Ibid.*, para. 3.
129 *Ibid.*
130 *Ibid.*
131 *Ibid.*
132 *Ibid.*
133 *Ibid.*, para. 16.
134 *Ibid.*, para. 17.
135 *Ibid.*, para. 18.
136 *Ibid.*, paras. 19 and 20.
137 *Ibid.*, paras. 25 and 26.
138 SIC-15, *Operating Leases - Incentives*, Standing Interpretations Committee of the IASC, June 1998, para. 3.
139 *Ibid.*, para. 5.
140 *Ibid.*, para. 6.
141 IAS 17, para. 23.
142 *Ibid.*, para. 27.
143 *Ibid.*, paras. 28 and 29.
144 *Ibid.*, para. 30.
145 *Ibid.*, paras. 41 and 42.
146 *Ibid.*, paras. 43 and 44.
147 SIC–15, para. 4.
148 IAS 17, para. 45.
149 Ibid., para. 46.
150 *Ibid.*, para. 35.
151 *Ibid.*, para. 37.
152 *Ibid.*, para. 34.
153 *Ibid.*, para. 47.
154 *Ibid.*, para. 39.
155 *Ibid.*, para. 40.
156 *Ibid.*, para. 48.
157 *Ibid.*, para. 48A.
158 *Ibid.*, para. 50.
159 *Ibid.*, para. 52.
160 *Ibid.*, para. 54.
161 *Ibid.*, para. 55.
162 *Ibid.*, para. 56.
163 *Ibid.*, para. 57.

Chapter 20 Government grants

1 INTRODUCTION

Government grants are defined in SSAP 4 – *Accounting for government grants*, the relevant accounting standard in the UK on the subject, as 'assistance by government in the form of cash or transfers of assets to an enterprise in return for past or future compliance with certain conditions relating to the operating activities of the enterprise'.[1] Such assistance has been available to commercial enterprises for many years, although its form and extent have undergone various changes according to the shifting economic philosophies of the government of the day. The equivalent international standard, IAS 20 – *Accounting for Government Grants and Disclosure of Government Assistance* – defines government grants in similar terms.[2] Both standards regard the term 'government' to include governmental agencies and similar bodies whether local, national or international.[3]

The main accounting issue which arises is how to deal with the income which the grant represents. Both standards adopt a matching approach as their guiding principle, whereby grants of a capital nature, which are intended to subsidise the purchase of fixed assets, are credited to revenue over the life of the assets involved.

Both standards recognise that an enterprise may receive other forms of government assistance, such as advice, subsidised loans or guarantees. However, rather than prescribe how these should be accounted for, both standards require disclosure about such assistance.

The requirements of SSAP 4 are discussed at 2 to 4 below and those of IAS 20 at 5 below. However, it should be noted that in December 1999 the G4+1 group issued a Discussion Paper – *Accounting by Recipients for Non-Reciprocal Transfers, Excluding Contributions by Owners: Their Definition, Recognition and Measurement.*[4] The potential implications of this paper on the accounting treatment of grants is discussed further at 6 below.

2 THE DEVELOPMENT OF SSAP 4 IN THE UK

The original version of SSAP 4 was issued in April 1974 and it concentrated solely on capital grants, stating that revenue grants 'do not produce accounting problems as they clearly should be credited to revenue in the same period in which the revenue expenditure to which they relate is charged'.[5] It stated that grants which related to fixed assets were to be credited to revenue over the expected useful life of the asset concerned.[6] This was to be accomplished either:

(a) by setting the grant directly against the cost of the asset in the balance sheet, so that depreciation was charged on the net figure; or

(b) by carrying the grant in the balance sheet as a deferred credit, and releasing it to income over the life of the related asset to offset the depreciation charge.[7]

However, it became increasingly evident over the years that the standard did not give adequate guidance on how to account for the widely varying forms of government assistance which later became available. Furthermore, the terms on which certain grants were by then being made did not precisely identify the expenditure to which they related; as a result, accountants were often faced with the problem of how to ascribe grants to specific expenditure. In addition, the ASC noted that various requirements of IAS 20 which was issued in 1983 were not reflected in the UK standard, and that this should therefore be considered in a revision of it.

Consequently, the ASC issued a proposed revision to the standard, ED 43, in June 1988. This followed the same matching principle as SSAP 4, namely that grants of all kinds (both capital and revenue) should be recognised in income at the same time as the expenditure which they subsidise.[8] In respect of grants towards fixed assets, however, the exposure draft sought to eliminate option (a) above, requiring instead that the deferred credit approach be adopted. It advanced a number of reasons for this proposed change, one of which was that the netting approach might be in conflict with the Companies Act rules that fixed assets should be carried at their purchase price or production cost.[9]

However, a large number of commentators questioned the need for this change, stressing that the netting approach was a convenient practical method, and expressing doubt that a conflict with company law necessarily existed.

The revised version of the standard closely followed the proposals in ED 43, but left the option to use either form of balance sheet presentation, since the ASC considered that both treatments were acceptable and capable of giving a true and fair view. The new standard became effective for accounting periods beginning on or after 1 July 1990.

3 THE REQUIREMENTS OF SSAP 4

3.1 Accounting

3.1.1 *Treatment of capital grants*

Capital grants are to be recognised over the expected useful economic lives of the related assets.[10] As indicated above, SSAP 4 allows the use of either form of balance sheet presentation. However the Committee went on to say that it had obtained Counsel's opinion that the 'netting' approach would be illegal for enterprises governed by Schedule 4 to the Companies Act 1985, since grant-aided assets would as a result not be stated at their purchase price or production cost.[11] The Companies Act requirement comes from the EU Fourth Directive, but it is interesting to note that it is not interpreted in this way in other countries governed by the Directive. In Germany, for example, it is normal to net capital grants off against the cost of fixed assets and this is not seen as a legal problem.

Under SSAP 4, therefore, enterprises not governed by Schedule 4 are free to use either treatment, but the remainder should adopt the 'deferred credit' approach if they wish to avoid the risk of contravening the law. The great majority of companies now use the latter form of presentation.

Under the netting method, depreciation on fixed assets is charged net of government grants, thereby releasing the grant to income over the lives of the related assets in the form of a reduced depreciation charge. As discussed in 4.2 below, this form of presentation is also popular among companies which receive grants on assets that are not subject to depreciation.

One company which adopted neither presentation for its capital grants (and contributions from third parties in respect of capital expenditure) was London Underground, as illustrated in its 1999 accounts shown below.

Extract 20.1: London Underground Limited (1999)

BALANCE SHEETS [extract]

		Group		Company	
		1999	1998	**1999**	1998
at 31st March 1999	*Note*	**£m**	£m	**£m**	£m
Net assets		**7,627.6**	7,413.1	**7,627.6**	7,413.1
Capital and reserves					
Called-up share capital		**430.0**	430.0	**430.0**	430.0
Share premium account		**36.1**	36.1	**36.1**	36.1
Capital grant and reserves	*19*	**7,161.5**	6,947.0	**7,161.5**	6,947.0
Total capital employed		**7,627.6**	7,413.1	**7,627.6**	7,413.1

1 ACCOUNTING POLICIES [extract]

d) Grants

All grants are receivable from London Transport and consist of:

- Grants in respect of the renewal of infrastructure which are credited to the Profit and loss account.
- Capital grants and contributions from third parties in respect of capital expenditure which are credited to Capital grants and Capital reserve respectively. Capital grants and other forms of assistance are amortised to the Profit and loss account to match the depreciation charge on assets in service.

– Grants in respect of any loss, after allowing for any Renewals and PPP restructuring grants and the release of Capital grants to meet the depreciation charge, are credited to the Profit and loss account. The net surplus, after grants, is transferred to London Transport to the extent of its net loss and any remainder is transferred to Capital Reserve.

19 CAPITAL GRANT AND RESERVES (GROUP AND COMPANY)

	Capital reserve £m	Capital grant £m	Revaluation reserve £m	Total £m
Balance at 1 April 1998	303.1	4,556.6	2,087.3	6,947.0
Capital grant received during the year	–	301.3	–	301.3
Released to Profit and loss account:				
– to meet the depreciation charge	–	(79.2)	(44.3)	(123.5)
– on disposal of tangible fixed assets	–	(18.1)	(1.1)	(19.2)
Third-party contributions to fund tangible fixed assets	19.8	–	–	19.8
Transfer from Profit and loss account	5.4	–	–	5.4
Revaluation of tangible fixed assets	–	–	30.7	30.7
Balance at 31 March 1999	**328.3**	**4,760.6**	**2,072.6**	**7,161.5**

Although the capital grants (and the capital contributions) were being amortised to match the related depreciation charge, it can be seen that the balance was included within capital and reserves. However, this treatment was challenged by the Review Panel who said that SSAP 4 requires 'grants and other forms of assistance made as a contribution towards expenditure on fixed assets be treated as deferred income, and accordingly be taken into account in determining net assets'. (As indicated above, this is not what SSAP 4 actually says, since it also permits the grants to be netted against the fixed assets.) The Panel did not accept that the lack of a depreciation charge in respect of infrastructure assets precluded the company from treating the grants in accordance with the standard. Neither did the Panel accept that it was appropriate to credit grants in respect of depreciable assets to a capital account on the basis of consistency, either with the treatment of grants on the non-depreciable assets or with the parent company's accounting policy for such grants (where the treatment adopted was that required by the Secretary of State).[12] Accordingly, London Underground in its 2000 accounts has now reclassified all grants received as deferred income and restated the 1999 comparatives. It should also be noted that following the implementation of FRS 15 – *Tangible Fixed Assets*, the company has also revised its depreciation policy for its infrastructure assets such that they are now depreciated over their estimated useful lives.[13]

Grants in respect of non-depreciable assets are discussed further at 4.2 below.

3.1.2 *Treatment of revenue-based grants*

The general rule, that grants should be recognised in the profit and loss account so as to match them with the expenditure towards which they are intended to contribute, applies equally to revenue-based grants as it does to capital grants. In some situations, the revenue costs towards which a grant is given may already have been incurred, in which case the grant would be included in the profit and loss account as soon as it is capable of being recognised under the rules discussed in 3.1.3 below. However, where a grant has been received, but not all of the revenue costs have been incurred, it will be necessary to defer a proportion of the grant so as to match it with those costs. Railtrack is an example of a company whose accounting policy specifically refers to revenue grants:

> *Extract 20.2: Railtrack Group PLC (2001)*
>
> 1 **Principal accounting policies** [extract]
>
> (g) **Grants**
>
> Grants and other contributions received towards the cost of tangible fixed assets are included in creditors as deferred income and credited to the profit and loss account over the life of the asset. Revenue grants are credited to the profit and loss account so as to match them with the expenditure to which they relate.

One of the difficulties which companies face is that grants are sometimes given to provide assistance for projects which involve both revenue and capital costs; the question then arises as to which costs the grant should be matched against. This is considered further in 4.1 below.

3.1.3 *Accounting for receipt and repayment of grants*

SSAP 4 requires that grants should not be recognised in the profit and loss account until the conditions for their receipt have been complied with and there is reasonable assurance that the grant will be received.[14] This rule sets the earliest limit for the recognition of the grant, but does not address the question of how it is to be matched against related expenditure; this is discussed at 3.1.4 below.

Grants are frequently received on terms which could result in their repayment if certain conditions are not met throughout a subsequent qualifying period. The standard says that provision should be made for such repayment only to the extent that it is probable.[15] Again, the existence of these conditions does not directly enter into the question of when the grants should be recognised in income.

Where a grant does become repayable, the standard requires that the repayment should be accounted for by setting it off against any unamortised deferred credit relating to the grant, with any excess being charged to the profit and loss account.[16] This has the effect of minimising the impact on the profit and loss account; it means that any part of the grant which has not been retained will have been matched against depreciation of the earlier years of the asset's life (if a capital grant). An alternative approach would have been to recompute the release of grant to income as if the amount repaid had never been received, with the result that the reduced amount of the grant (if any) would be spread over the whole life of the asset involved, rather than allocated to the earlier years.

A literal interpretation of the above requirement could mean that, where the company uses the 'netting' method of presentation in the balance sheet (method (a) at 2 above), the whole amount of the repayment would have to be charged immediately to the profit and loss account because there is no deferred credit to absorb it. However, it is difficult to see the logic of this and we do not believe that such an interpretation was intended. We believe that the balance sheet treatment chosen should not influence the effect of a repayment on the profit and loss account, and that the reference to 'unamortised deferred credit' was intended to include the amount set off against the book value of the asset when the 'netting' approach is used.

3.1.4 *Matching grants against related expenditure*

In practice, this is the most significant accounting issue which arises in respect of government grants. The required approach is summarised by SSAP 4 as follows:

(a) provided the conditions for its receipt have been complied with and there is reasonable assurance that it will be received, a grant should be recognised in the profit and loss account so as to match it with the expenditure to which it is to contribute;

(b) the grant should be assumed to contribute to whatever expenditure is the basis for its receipt, unless there is persuasive evidence to the contrary;

(c) where the grant is a contribution to specific expenditure on fixed assets, it should be recognised over the expected useful economic lives of the related assets;

(d) if the grant is made in order to give immediate financial support or assistance or to reimburse costs previously incurred, it should be recognised in the profit and loss account of the period in which it becomes receivable; and

(e) if the grant is made to finance the general activities of an enterprise over a specific period or to compensate for a loss of current or future income it should be recognised in the profit and loss account of the period in which it is paid.[17]

The application of these rules still requires a significant amount of interpretation, and this is discussed in 4.1 below.

3.2 Disclosure

In terms of the Companies Act formats, the amount of any deferred credit in respect of grants will normally be shown under the heading of 'Accruals and deferred income' in one of two optional positions in the balance sheet.[18]

The Weir Group's accounts provide an example of this disclosure:

Extract 20.3: The Weir Group PLC (2000)

Balance Sheets [extract]

at 29th December 2000	Group		Company	
	2000	1999	**2000**	1999
	£'000	£'000	**£'000**	£'000
Creditors falling due after more than one year				
Loans	**165,826**	147,489	**107,419**	60,534
Obligations under finance leases	**1,564**	696	**–**	–
Provisions for Liabilities and Charges	**42,314**	37,641	**18,366**	13,053
Deferred Income				
Grants not yet credited to profit	**494**	506	**–**	–

SSAP 4 requires the following disclosures to be made:

(a) the accounting policy adopted for government grants[19] (this is in any case required in general terms by SSAP 2 (and now FRS 18);

An example is shown in Extract 20.2 at 3.1.2 above.

(b) the effect of government grants on the results of the period and/or the financial position of the enterprise;[20]

The Weir Group discloses the effect on the results as follows:

Extract 20.4: The Weir Group PLC (2000)

2.	**Profit on Ordinary Activities Before Tax** [extract]	**2000** **£000**	1999 £000
(c)	Profit on ordinary activities before tax is after charging/(crediting):		
	Depreciation	**22,333**	18,048
	Goodwill amortisation	**6,705**	3,330
	Government grant credits	**(140)**	(105)
	...		

As far as the disclosure of government grants on the financial position of the enterprise is concerned, the explanatory note to the standard makes it clear that this is to be done where the results of future periods are expected to be affected materially by the recognition in the profit and loss account of grants already received.[21] It would appear that the most straightforward way of doing this would simply be to disclose the amount of the deferred credit which is still to be released to income. Therefore the amount of deferred grants included within the heading of 'Accruals and deferred income' should be disclosed. (See Extract 20.3 above.)

Leeds Group has an elaborate disclosure, which is in effect a mirror image of its fixed assets note. It shows the following:

Extract 20.5: Leeds Group plc (2000)

20 Accruals and deferred income – Government grants

Group	Buildings £000	Plant and machinery £000	Total £000
Received:			
At 1 October 1999	149	124	273
Received in year	–	43	43
At 30 September 2000	**149**	**167**	**316**
Amortisation:			
At 1 October 1999	129	124	253
Credited in year	5	2	7
At 30 September 2000	**134**	**126**	**260**
Net book amount:			
At 30 September 2000	**15**	**41**	**56**
At 30 September 1999	20	–	20

However, Leeds Group is very much an exception; few companies give such detailed analysis of the deferred credit.

(c) any potential liability to repay grants in specified circumstances which needs to be disclosed, if necessary, in accordance with FRS 12[22] (which means that no disclosure is necessary if the possibility is remote, although consideration would have to be given to the requirements of the Companies Act).[23] Once again, this disclosure is clearly already required in terms of FRS 12 (and the Companies Act) – see Chapter 28 at 6.2;

(d) where the results of the period are affected materially by the receipt of government assistance in a form other than grants, the nature of that assistance and an estimate of its effects on the financial statements, to the extent that these effects can be measured.[24]

In the explanatory note section of the standard, a further disclosure requirement is suggested. This is that the period or periods over which grants are released to the profit and loss account should be disclosed, insofar as it is practicable given the number and variety of grants that are being received; it is suggested that normally a broad indication of the future periods in which grants already received will be recognised in the profit and loss account will be sufficient.[25] However, this apparent requirement does not appear in the standard section of SSAP 4, so its status is unclear, and it is virtually never seen in practice. It would seem likely that most companies will regard the disclosure of fixed asset lives which they will be giving as part of their depreciation policy note as a sufficient provision of this information, assuming that the grant relates to capital expenditure. However, there may be exceptional cases where a more explicit disclosure would be helpful to an understanding of the accounts.

4 PRACTICAL ISSUES

4.1 Achieving the most appropriate matching

Most problems of accounting for grants fall into a single category: that of interpreting the requirement to match the grant against the expenditure towards which they are expected to contribute. This apparently simple principle can be extremely difficult to apply, because it is sometimes far from clear what the essence of the grant was, and in practice grants are sometimes given for a particular kind of expenditure which forms an element of a larger project, making the allocation a highly subjective matter. For example, government assistance which is in the form of a training grant might be:

(a) matched against direct training costs; or

(b) taken over a period of time against the salary costs of the employees being trained, for example over the estimated duration of the project; or

(c) taken over the estimated period for which the company or the employees are expected to benefit from the training; or

(d) not distinguished from other project grants received and therefore matched against total project costs; or

(e) taken to income systematically over the life of the project, for example the total grant receivable may be allocated to revenue on a straight-line basis; or

(f) as in (d) or (e) above, but using, instead of project life, the period over which the grant is paid; or

(g) taken to income when received in cash.

Depending on the circumstances, any of these approaches might produce an acceptable result. However, we would comment on them individually as follows:

Under method (a), the grant could be recognised as income considerably in advance of its receipt, since often the major part of the direct training costs will be incurred at the beginning of a project and payment is usually made retrospectively. As the total grant receivable may be subject to adjustment, this may not be prudent or may lead to mismatching.

Methods (b) to (e) all rely on different interpretations of the expenditure to which the grant is expected to contribute, and could all represent an appropriate form of matching.

Method (f) has less to commend it, but the period of payment of the grant might in fact give an indication (in the absence of better evidence) of the duration of the project for which the expenditure is to be subsidised.

Similarly, method (g) is unlikely to be the most appropriate method per se, but may approximate to one of the other methods, or may, in the absence of any conclusive indication as to the expenditure intended to be subsidised by the grant, be the only practicable method which can be adopted.

Many grants are taxed as income on receipt; consequently, this is often the argument advanced for taking grants to income when received in cash. However, SSAP 4 specifically states that 'the treatment of an item for tax purposes does not necessarily determine its treatment for accounting purposes, and immediate recognition in the profit and loss account may result in an unacceptable departure from the principle that government grants should be matched with the expenditure towards which they are intended to contribute'.[26] Consequently, the recognition of a grant in the profit and loss account in a period different to that when it is taxed gives rise to a timing difference, and should be accounted for in accordance with relevant standard on deferred tax (see Chapter 24).

In the face of the problems (described above) of attributing a grant to related expenditure, it is difficult to offer definitive guidance; companies will have to make their own judgements as to how the matching principle is to be applied. The only overriding considerations are that the method should be systematically and consistently applied, and that the policy adopted (in respect of both capital and revenue grants, if material) should be adequately disclosed. However, it is possible to offer the following points for consideration:

4.1.1 *Should the grant be split into its elements?*

The grant received may be part of a package, the elements of which have different costs/conditions. It may be appropriate to treat these different elements on different bases rather than accounting for the entire grant in one way.

4.1.2 *What was the purpose of the grant?*

As discussed in 3.1.4 above, SSAP 4 says that in the absence of persuasive evidence to the contrary, government grants should be assumed to contribute towards the expenditure which is the basis for their payment.[27] However, the method by which the amount of grant receivable is calculated does not conclusively determine its accounting treatment. For example, the amount of the grant may be based on the creation of jobs but it may be intended to contribute towards capital expenditure or other costs as well. It will be necessary to examine the full circumstances of the grant in order to determine its purpose.

4.1.3 *What is the period to be benefited by the grant?*

The qualifying conditions which have to be satisfied are not necessarily conclusive evidence of the period to be benefited by the grant. For example, certain grants may become repayable if assets cease to be used for a qualifying purpose within a certain period; notwithstanding this condition, the grant should be recognised over the whole life of the asset, not over the qualifying period.

4.1.4 *Is a grant capital or revenue?*

In general, we recommend that grants should be regarded as linked to capital expenditure where this is a possible interpretation and there is no clear indication to the contrary, particularly where the payment of the grant is based on capital expenditure. However, we believe that the most important consideration where there are significant questions over how the grant is to be recognised, and where the effect is material, is that the accounts should explicitly state what treatment has been chosen and disclose the financial effect of adopting that treatment.

4.2 Capital grants on non-depreciating assets

Grants are sometimes given as a contribution to assets which are not depreciated on the grounds that they do not have a finite life. In these circumstances, following the basic rule of SSAP 4, the release of the grant to the profit and loss account is also indefinitely postponed. The question which then arises is whether it makes sense to show the amount received as deferred income, given that it is likely to be there permanently.

Public utility companies, such as those in the water or electricity industries, frequently face this issue. They often receive contributions to the costs of their infrastructure assets, and although they now charge some depreciation under the convoluted 'renewals accounting' expedient devised by FRS 15 (see Chapter 12 at 2.3.3 H), they do not regard these assets as having a finite life. Their usual response to the problem is to revert to the 'netting' approach, crediting the contributions against the cost of the asset concerned. An example of this approach is to be found in the accounts of Severn Trent:

Extract 20.6: Severn Trent Plc (2001)

1 **Accounting policies** [extract]

a Basis of accounting [extract]

The financial statements have been prepared under the historical cost convention in accordance with applicable Accounting Standards and, except for the treatment of certain grants and contributions, comply with the requirements of the United Kingdom Companies Act 1985 ('the Act'). An explanation of this departure from the requirements of the Act is given in the policy on grants and contributions below.

...

f Grants and contributions

Grants and contributions received in respect of non infrastructure assets are treated as deferred income and are recognised in the profit and loss account over the useful economic life of those assets.

Grants and contributions relating to infrastructure assets have been deducted from the cost of fixed assets. This is not in accordance with Schedule 4 to the Act, which requires assets to be shown at their purchase price or production cost and hence grants and contributions to be presented as deferred income. This departure from the requirements of the Act is, in the opinion of the Directors, necessary to give a true and fair view as, while a provision is made for depreciation of infrastructure assets, these assets do not have determinable finite lives and therefore no basis exists on which to recognise grants and contributions as deferred income. The effect of this departure is that the cost of fixed assets is £267.6 million lower than it would otherwise have been (2000: £236.1 million).

Those grants and contributions relating solely to maintaining the operating capability of the infrastructure network are taken into account in determining the depreciation charged for infrastructure assets.

The last three sentences of the middle paragraph in note 1f give the information required by UITF 7 when the 'true and fair override' is used to depart from the detailed requirements of the Companies Act and note 1a gives the required cross reference to the disclosures.[28] UITF 7 has now been superseded by FRS 18 – *Accounting Policies* – and its requirements embodied in that standard (see Chapter 2 at 7.9). However, many companies that use this approach do not agree that it is a departure from the Act, and thus do not make the disclosure.

It is interesting to note that, as discussed at 3.1.1 above, the Review Panel did not accept that the lack of a depreciation charge in respect of infrastructure assets precluded London Underground from treating the grants in accordance with the standard. The Press Notice went on to say 'The standard requires the grants made as a contribution towards expenditure on fixed assets should be recognised over the expected useful lives of the related assets (paragraph 23). As the infrastructure assets to which the grants relate all have useful economic lives it would be possible to comply with the standard notwithstanding the policy of non-depreciation.'[29] This seems to suggest that London Underground should have been crediting the grants to profit and loss account, even although it was not depreciating the assets. However, this ignores the first sentence of paragraph 23 of SSAP 4 which says '... government grants should be recognised in the profit and loss account so as to match them with the expenditure towards which they are intended to contribute.'

4.3 Non-government grants and assistance

As indicated at 1 above, SSAP 4 deals with government grants and assistance. However, it may be that a company receives grants and assistance from other sources. Paragraph 1 of SSAP 4 states that the standard 'is also indicative of best practice for accounting for grants and assistance from other sources'. Indeed, most companies that receive contributions from third parties to fund capital expenditure treat such income as if they were grants – see, for example, Severn Trent in Extract 20.6 above. Also, it should be noted that, based on its ruling on London Underground (see 3.1.1 above), the Review Panel regards SSAP 4 as applying to such contributions.

5 IAS REQUIREMENTS

The principal international standard which deals with this topic is IAS 20 – *Accounting for Government Grants and Disclosure of Government Assistance.* This was issued in 1983, and reformatted in 1994 without substantive amendment. In January 1998, the SIC issued an interpretation dealing with certain forms of government assistance, SIC-10, *Government Assistance – No Specific Relation to Operating Activities.* Government grants related to biological assets are excluded from the scope of IAS 20 and are dealt with in IAS 41 – *Agriculture* (see 5.4 below).

5.1 Nature of government grants and government assistance

Under IAS 20, government grants represent assistance by government in the form of transfers of resources to an entity in return for past or future compliance with certain conditions relating to the operating activities of the entity.[30] However, they exclude:

(a) assistance to which no value can reasonably be assigned, e.g. free technical or marketing advice, provisions of guarantees or the receipt of loan at below market interest rates;[31] and

(b) transactions with government which cannot be distinguished from the normal trading transactions of the entity, e.g. where the entity is being favoured by a government's procurement policy.[32]

Such excluded items are to be treated as falling within the standard's disclosure requirements for government assistance, which is defined as 'action by government designed to provide an economic benefit to an enterprise or range of enterprises qualifying under certain criteria'. However, such assistance does not include benefits provided only indirectly through action affecting general trading conditions, such as the provision of infrastructure in development areas or the imposition of trading constraints on competitors.[33]

This distinction between government grants and other forms of government assistance is important because the standard's accounting requirements only apply to the former.

However, one issue which has been considered by the SIC is the situation in some countries where government assistance is aimed at entities in certain regions or industry sectors, but without there being any conditions specifically relating to the operating activities of the entity concerned. In January 1998, the SIC determined that such forms of government assistance are to be treated as government grants.[34] This ruling was to avoid any implication that such forms of assistance were not governed by the standard and could be credited directly to equity.

Excluded from the scope of IAS 20 entirely are:[35]

(a) government assistance in the form of tax benefits, such as income tax holidays, investment tax credits, accelerated depreciation allowances and reduced income tax rates;

(b) government participation in the ownership of the entity; and

(c) government grants covered by IAS 41 – *Agriculture*.

The reason for exclusion (c) is that the IASC considered that the presentation permitted by IAS 20 of deducting government grants from the carrying amount of the asset (see 5.2.3 below), was inconsistent with a fair value model in which an asset is measured at its fair value. The requirements of IAS 41 in relation to government grants are dealt with at 5.4 below.

Interestingly, in issuing IAS 40, which adopts a similar fair value model for investment properties (see Chapter 12 at 5.3), the IASC did not introduce any requirements for government grants in that standard, nor did it revise IAS 20 to deal with the matter.

5.2 Accounting for government grants

5.2.1 *Recognition*

IAS 20 requires that government grants should be recognised only when there is reasonable assurance that:

(a) the entity will comply with the conditions attaching to them; and

(b) the grants will be received.[36]

The standard notes that just because a grant has been received does not of itself provide conclusive evidence that the conditions attaching to the grant have been or will be fulfilled.[37]

The accounting for government grants is not affected by the manner in which they are received, i.e. grants received in cash, as a non-monetary amount, or forgiveness of a government loan, are all accounted for in the same manner.[38] A forgivable loan from government is to be treated as a government grant when there is reasonable assurance that the entity will meet the terms for forgiveness of the loan.[39] One company which refers to forgivable loans in its accounting policy is GN Great Nordic as can be seen from Extract 20.8 at 5.2.3 below, although it would seem that it only recognises them as a grant at a later stage than envisaged by the standard.

A government grant in the form of a transfer of a non-monetary asset, which is intended for use of the entity, is usually recognised at the fair value of that asset. However, the alternative of recognising such assets, and the related grant, at a nominal amount is not prohibited.[40]

5.2.2 Matching grants against related expenditure

Grants should be recognised in income on a systematic basis that matches them with the related costs that they are intended to compensate. They should not be credited directly to shareholders' funds.[41] Income recognition on a receipts basis would only be acceptable if no basis existed for allocating a grant to periods other than the one in which it was received.[42]

IAS 20 envisages that in most cases, the periods over which an entity recognises the costs or expenses related to the government grant are readily ascertainable and thus grants in recognition of specific expenses are recognised as income in the same period as the relevant expense.[43]

Grants related to depreciable assets are usually recognised as income over the periods and in the proportions in which depreciation on those assets is charged.[44]

IAS 20 acknowledges that grants may be received as part of a package of financial or fiscal aids to which a number of conditions are attached. In such cases, the standard indicates that care is needed in identifying the conditions giving rise to the costs and expenses which determine the periods over which the grant will be earned. It may also be appropriate to allocate part of the grant on one basis and part on another.[45]

Where a grant relates to expenses or losses already incurred, or for the purpose of giving immediate financial support to the entity with no future related costs, the grant should be recognised in income when it becomes receivable (possibly as an extraordinary item, if appropriate).[46]

As in the UK, most problems of accounting for government grants relate to that of interpreting the requirement to match the grant with the related expenditure. The discussion of this issue in 4.1 above in relation to SSAP 4 in the UK is likely to be of some relevance to IAS 20. However, the problems are likely to be greater because of the international context in which IAS 20 is written, since it does not address specific questions which relate to particular types of grant that are available in individual countries.

5.2.3 Presentation of grants

Grants that are related to assets (i.e. those whose primary condition is that an entity qualifying for them should purchase, construct or otherwise acquire long-term assets) should be presented in the balance sheet either:

(a) by setting up the grant as deferred income; or

(b) by deducting the grant in arriving at the carrying amount of the asset, in which case the grant is recognised in income as a reduction of depreciation.[47]

An example of a company adopting the former treatment is Serono as shown below.

Extract 20.7: Serono International S.A. (2000)

1. General [extract]

1.9 Government grants

Government grants received are netted against the corresponding items in the income statement, except for those amounts received for the purchase of property, plant and equipment, which are recorded as deferred income in the balance sheet, in other current liabilities and other long-term liabilities as appropriate, and amortized over the useful life of the asset. Government grants become non-refundable upon the achievement of designated milestones.

3. Research and development

	Year ended December 31		
	2000	1999	1998
	US$000	US$000	US$000
Research and development expense, gross	**263,381**	222,116	200,540
Less government grants	**(229)**	(487)	(741)
Research and development expense, net	**263,152**	221,629	199,799

19. Other current liabilities [extract]

	As of December 31	
	2000	1999
	US$000	US$000
Deferred income	**2,279**	1,604

21. Other long-term liabilities [extract]

	As of December 31	
	2000	1999
	US$000	US$000
Deferred income	**2,686**	3,909

An example of a company adopting a policy of deducting capital grants against the cost of the assets is GN Great Nordic as illustrated below.

Extract 20.8: GN Great Nordic (2000)

Public Grants

Public grants relate to grants and funding for R&D activities, investment grants, etc.

Grants for R&D activities which are expensed directly to the income statement are booked as income in the income statement under development costs so that they correspond to the costs for which they compensate.

Grants for the acquisition of assets and development activities that are capitalized are set off against the cost price of the assets for which grants are awarded.

Forgivable loans provided by public bodies for funding development activities are treated as loans until the terms for remission of the loan have been met.

Note 30: Public Grants

In connection with research and development activities the GN Great Nordic Group received tax credits of DKK 11 million in 2000 (1999: DKK 10 million). GN Great Nordic did not receive any further public grants in 2000 or 1999.

Grants that are related to items in income (i.e. grants other than those related to assets) are to be presented as a credit in the income statement, either separately or as a reduction of the related expense.[48]

5.2.4 *Repayment of government grants*

A government grant that becomes repayable should be accounted for as a revision to an accounting estimate. Repayment of a grant related to income should be charged against the related unamortised deferred credit and any excess should be recognised as an expense immediately.[49]

Repayment of a grant related to an asset should be recognised by increasing the carrying amount of the related asset or reducing the related unamortised deferred credit. The cumulative additional depreciation that would have been recognised to date as an expense in the absence of the grant should be charged immediately to income.[50] It appears that the impact of a repayment differs depending on the balance sheet treatment of the grant. If an entity has an existing deferred credit balance of £50,000 and has to repay £40,000 of grants then all of the repayment can be charged against the deferred credit; no charge to the income account is necessary. However, if the entity had netted the original grant against the asset, then the repayment would be added to the asset. If the asset is halfway through its useful life, then £20,000 additional depreciation would need to be charged.

IAS 20 emphasises that the circumstances giving rise to the repayment of a grant related to an asset may require consideration to be given to the possible impairment of the asset.[51]

It should be noted that the treatment of the repayment of grants relating to assets in IAS 20 differs from that in SSAP 4 in the UK (see 3.1.3 above).

5.3 Disclosures

IAS 20 requires that entities should disclose the following information regarding government grants:

(a) the accounting policy, including the method of presentation adopted in the financial statements;

(b) a description of the nature and extent of the grants recognised and an indication of other forms of government assistance from which the entity has directly benefited; and

(c) unfulfilled conditions or contingencies attaching to government assistance that has been recognised.[52]

An example of a brief accounting policy is given by Novartis as shown below.

Extract 20.9: Novartis AG (2000)

1. Accounting policies [extract]

Government grants Government grants are deferred and recognized in the income statement over the period necessary to match them with the related costs which they are intended to compensate for.

22. Other short-term liabilities [extract]

	2000 CHF millions	**1999 CHF millions**
Deferred income relating to government grants	25	30

A fuller accounting policy is provided by Melexis as illustrated in the following extract.

Extract 20.10: Melexis NV (2000)

6.5.2. Summary of Significant Accounting Policies [extract]

GOVERNMENT GRANTS Government grants are deferred and amortised into income over the period necessary to match them with the related costs that they are intended to compensate. Grants received are treated as deferred income in the accompanying consolidated financial statements. Income relating to government grants is recognised as a deduction from the appropriate expense.

The company recognizes government grants if they have reasonable assurance that the grants will be received. They are recognized as income on a systematic and rational basis over the periods necessary to match them with the related costs. The grant related revenue is recorded net of the related expense in the income statement and as deferred income on the balance sheet.

6.5.4. Notes [extract]

J | DEFERRED INCOME

		31st December	
	2000 EUR	1999 EUR	1998 EUR
Capital grants	2.248.212	1.563.479	0
Total	2.248.212	1.563.479	0

N | GOVERNMENT GRANTS

The revenue government grants recognized in 2000 comprises:

	2000 EUR
Investment grants in building and machinery	1.365.171
Grants for research and development	–
	1.365.171

In addition to the disclosures noted above, for those forms of government assistance which are excluded from the definition of government grants (see 5.1 above), the significance of such benefits may be such that the disclosure of the nature, extent and duration of the assistance is necessary to prevent the financial statements from being misleading.[53]

One company which gives a detailed description of its government grants and other government assistance is Koç as shown below.

Extract 20.11: Koç Holding A.Ş. (2000)

Note 4 – SUMMARY OF SIGNIFICANT ACCOUNTING POLICIES [extract]

z) Government grants

Turkish government investment grants in the form of Resource Utilisation Support Premium ("RUSP") are accounted for on an accrual basis for estimated amounts expected to be realised under grant claims filed by the Group. These grants are accounted for as deferred income and amortised over the depreciation period of the relevant assets on a straight-line basis (Note 33).

Note 33 – GOVERNMENT GRANTS

Certain subsidiaries have obtained investment incentive certificates from the Turkish government authorities in connection with certain major capital expenditures which entitle the companies, among other things, to:

i) a 100% exemption from customs duty on machinery and equipment to be imported,

ii) investment allowance of 100% and 200% on approved capital expenditures,

iii) incentive premiums varying between 12% and 25% on the cost of the local content of the facilities,

iv) resource utilisation support premium (RUSP – an investment grant in the form of cost reimbursement) varying from 15% to 40% on a portion of the total approved capital expenditures.

The investment allowance indicated in (ii) above is deductible from current or future taxable profit for the purposes of corporation tax, is exempt from both corporation and minimum tax, but is subject to income tax.

As permitted by Turkish tax legislation, RUSP is recognised in the statutory accounts as income upon its receipt. The consolidated financial statements are adjusted and restated to account for RUSP on an accrual basis for estimated amounts to be received under grant claims filed, and to reflect it as deferred income to be amortised over the depreciation period of the related assets on a straight-line basis.

The accrued RUSP receivables are included in other receivables and current assets in the consolidated balance sheets, while the recognised portions of deferred income are included in other income in the consolidated statements of income.

The movement of deferred income for the years ended 31 December, expressed in terms of the purchasing power of the Turkish lira at 31 December 2000 is as follows:

	2000	**1999**
Balance, beginning of year	2,776	3,845
Deferred income recognised	(1,070)	(1,069)
Balance, end of year (Note 25)	**1,706**	**2,776**

5.4 Government grants related to biological assets

As noted at 5.1 above, IAS 20 excludes from its scope government grants dealt with in IAS 41 – *Agriculture*. That standard allows certain biological assets to be measured their fair value and for changes in such value to be reflected in income. The general requirements of IAS 41, which is mandatory for annual financial statements covering periods beginning on or after 1 January 2003, are discussed briefly in Chapter 3 at 3.2.3.

The IASC considered that the presentation permitted by IAS 20 of deducting government grants from the carrying amount of the asset (see 5.2.3 above), was inconsistent with a fair value model in which an asset is measured at its fair value. Using such an approach, would mean that in effect an enterprise would recognise a government grant immediately, even for a conditional grant.[54]

Accordingly, IAS 41 requires that an unconditional government grant related to a biological asset measured at its fair value less point-of-sale costs should be recognised as income, when and only when, the government grant becomes receivable.[55]

However, if a grant is conditional, including where a government grant requires an enterprise not to engage in specified agricultural activity, an enterprise should recognise the grant as income when, and only when, the conditions to the grant are met.[56]

The standard recognises that the terms and conditions of government grants may vary. By way of explanation as to how its requirements may be applied in practice, the standard discusses an example of a grant which requires an enterprise to farm in a particular location for 5 years. If the enterprise has to return all of the grant if it farms for less than that period, then the grant should not be recognised in income until the 5 years have passed. However, if part of the grant can be retained based on the passage of time, the enterprise should recognise the grant as income on a time proportion basis.[57]

If an enterprise does not account for biological assets using the fair value model, but instead accounts for them at cost, less any depreciation or impairment cost, then any government grants should not be accounted for on the basis set out in IAS 41, but under the requirements of IAS 20 discussed at 5.1 to 5.3 above.[58]

With respect to grants related to agricultural activity covered by IAS 41, an enterprise should disclose the following:

(a) the nature and extent of government grants recognised in the financial statements;

(b) unfulfilled conditions and other contingencies attaching to government grants; and

(c) significant decreases expected in the level of government grants.[59]

6 POSSIBLE FUTURE DEVELOPMENTS

As indicated at 1 above, in December 1999 the G4+1 group issued a Discussion Paper – *Accounting by Recipients for Non-Reciprocal Transfers, Excluding Contributions by Owners: Their Definition, Recognition and Measurement.*[60] This examines how items such as government grants and charitable donations should be accounted for by those who receive them. The paper reviews the appropriate accounting treatment in the light of the IASC's conceptual framework (see Chapter 2 at 8.1).

The paper's principal conclusion is that such items should be recognised as assets (or reductions in liabilities) and credited to income when the framework's definitions and criteria are met, rather than being based on the matching of related revenues and expenses as is done presently by SSAP 20 and IAS 20.

As far as government grants are concerned, the main impact of these proposals will clearly be on grants related to fixed assets as indicated in the following extract from the ASB's press notice when it published the discussion paper in the UK:

'Under the paper's proposals, a grant of £10,000 received for the purchase of a fixed asset of £15,000 (without further conditions) should not be accounted for as a reduction in the cost of the asset (with a corresponding reduction in the depreciation charged over the asset's life) or treated as deferred income. Instead the grant should be recognised as income in the period it is made and the carrying amount of the asset (and subsequent depreciation) should be based on the asset's cost of £15,000.'[61]

The press notice went on to quote Sir David Tweedie, then Chairman of the ASB and now chairman of the IASB, as saying:

'The paper makes a convincing case for an approach that is quite different from that set out in the present UK standard, the fundamental requirements of which go back more than a quarter of a century. We shall consider in the light of the comments received on this paper whether a review of that standard should be undertaken'.

However, it is unlikely that the IASB sees this as high on its agenda, although it is possible that it is covered as part of its 'improvements' project.

References

1 SSAP 4, *Accounting for government grants*, ASC, Revised July 1990, para. 22.
2 IAS 20, *Accounting for Government Grants and Disclosure of Government Assistance*, IASC, April 1983 (reformatted 1994), para. 3.
3 SSAP 4, para. 21; IAS 20, para. 3.
4 *Accounting by Recipients for Non-Reciprocal Transfers, Excluding Contributions by Owners: Their Definition, Recognition and Measurement*, Westwood and Mackenzie, December 1999.
5 SSAP 4 (Original), *The accounting treatment of government grants*, ASC, April 1974, para. 2.
6 *Ibid.*, para. 9.
7 *Ibid.*
8 ED 43, para. 27.
9 CA 85, Sch. 4, para. 17.
10 SSAP 4, para. 23.
11 *Ibid.*, para. 15.
12 FRRP PN 63, 18 October 2000.
13 London Underground Limited, Annual Report 2000, p. 12.
14 SSAP 4, para. 24.
15 *Ibid.*, para. 27.
16 *Ibid.*
17 *Ibid.*, paras. 23 and 24.
18 CA 85, Sch. 4, para. 8.
19 SSAP 4, para. 28(a).
20 *Ibid.*, para. 28(b).
21 *Ibid.*, para. 18.
22 *Ibid.*, para. 29. The standard in fact still refers to SSAP 18, which has been superseded by FRS 12.
23 CA 85, Sch. 4, para. 50(2).
24 SSAP 4, para. 28(c).
25 *Ibid.*, para. 17.
26 *Ibid.*, para. 7.
27 *Ibid.*, para. 23.
28 UITF 7, *True and fair view override disclosures*, UITF, December 1992, para. 4.
29 FRRP PN 63.
30 IAS 20, para. 3.
31 *Ibid.*, paras. 3, 35 and 37.
32 *Ibid.*, paras. 3 and 35.
33 *Ibid.*, para. 3.
34 SIC-10, *Government Assistance – No Specific Relation to Operating Activities*, IASC, January 1998, para. 3.
35 IAS 20, para. 2.
36 *Ibid.*, para. 7.
37 *Ibid.*, para. 8.
38 *Ibid.*, para. 9.
39 *Ibid.*, para. 10.
40 *Ibid.*, para. 23.
41 *Ibid.*, para. 12.
42 *Ibid.*, para. 16.
43 *Ibid.*, para. 17.
44 *Ibid.*
45 *Ibid.*, para. 19.
46 *Ibid.*, para. 20.
47 *Ibid.*, paras. 3, 24 and 27.
48 *Ibid.*, paras. 3 and 29.
49 *Ibid.*, para. 32.
50 *Ibid.*, para. 32.
51 *Ibid.*, para. 33.
52 *Ibid.*, para. 39.
53 *Ibid.*, para. 36.
54 IAS 41, *Agriculture*, IASC, January 2001, IASC, Appendix B, para. B66
55 IAS 41, para. 34.
56 *Ibid.*, para. 35.
57 *Ibid.*, para. 36.
58 *Ibid.*, para. 37.
59 *Ibid.*, para. 57.
60 *Accounting by Recipients for Non-Reciprocal Transfers, Excluding Contributions by Owners: Their Definition, Recognition and Measurement*, Westwood and Mackenzie, December 1999.
61 ASB PN 155, 13 January 2000.

Chapter 21 Segmental reporting

1 INTRODUCTION

Segmental reporting has been debated since the early 1960s, that period being significant for the rapid emergence and growth, especially in the US, of the multinational conglomerate business entity. As enterprises became involved in a large number of distinct products and markets, even industries, the readers of their accounts found it increasingly difficult to analyse the effect of different segments' results on past performance and the likely effect on future performance. Clearly, there could be a wide range of levels of profitability, levels of growth and risk factors concealed within the consolidated accounts of a diversified multinational business enterprise. Pressures grew, mainly from the investment analyst community, for disclosure of the results and resources of the different segments which comprised the whole business.

In the UK, the Companies Act 1967 introduced the requirement that where a company carried on business of two or more classes which 'in the opinion of the directors, differ substantially from each other', turnover and profit before tax split into those classes should be disclosed. The 1967 Act also required the directors' report to include a statement of the value of goods exported from the UK (unless turnover did not exceed £50,000). These requirements, as amended, continue to be a feature of companies legislation today.

The first international accounting standard on the issue of segmental reporting, IAS 14, was published in August 1981[1] and reformatted in 1994. It was revised again in 1997. In the UK, an accounting standard, SSAP 25, was issued in June 1990 and took effect for accounting periods beginning on or after 1 July 1990.[2] The standard has continued without amendment until the present day. The ASB did consider revisions to SSAP 25 in the light of the new standards that were developed by the IASC and by the FASB in the US. In May 1996 it published a discussion paper[3] explaining what was being proposed internationally and seeking comment. The responses showed little enthusiasm for change, and the Board subsequently took the matter off its agenda.

2 THE UK POSITION

2.1 Legislative requirements

The segmental disclosures first introduced by the Companies Act 1967 have been amended since then but the basic approach remains intact. If in the course of the financial year, a company has carried on business of two or more classes that, in the opinion of the directors, differ substantially from each other, disclosure is now required only of the amount of the turnover attributable to each class.[4] In addition, if the company has supplied markets that, in the opinion of the directors, differ substantially from each other, the amount of the turnover attributable to each such market should be stated.[5] Exemption is permitted 'where in the opinion of the directors, the disclosure ... would be seriously prejudicial to the interests of the company'. However, the fact that the information has not been disclosed is required to be stated.[6]

2.2 SSAP 25

2.2.1 *General approach*

SSAP 25 is based on the principle that, unless the financial statements of an entity contain segmental information, they do not enable the reader to make judgements about the nature of the different activities or of their contribution to its overall financial result.[7]

It aims to contribute to improved segmental reporting in two ways: first, by providing guidance as to how the reportable segments should be determined and, second, by specifying the information to be disclosed.

2.2.2 *Scope*

The standard contains two levels of disclosure requirements: those relating to the statutory requirements contained in the UK companies legislation apply to all companies (and to other entities to whom the standard applies),[8] and a number of additional provisions relating to segmental disclosures which are not required by companies legislation. These additional provisions only apply to:[9]

(a) public limited companies (as defined in section 1 of the Companies Act 1985) or holding companies that have one or more public companies as a subsidiary;

(b) banking and insurance companies or groups as defined in section 744 of the Companies Act, and preparing accounts in accordance with Schedules 9 or 9A thereto; and

(c) private companies (and other entities) which exceed the criteria, multiplied in each case by ten, for defining a medium-sized company under section 247 of the Companies Act, unless they are a subsidiary of a parent providing segmental disclosures under SSAP 25.

At present, this means that entities with any two of the following will have to give the extra information:

(i) turnover exceeding £112m,

(ii) total assets exceeding £56m, and

(iii) average number of employees exceeding 2,500.[10]

Entities that are not within the above categories are not subject to the full requirements of the standard, as explained in 2.2.4 below.

Where both parent entity and consolidated accounts are presented, segmental information is to be presented on the basis of the consolidated accounts.[11] Comparative figures for the previous accounting period are to be given.

The exemption remains that where, in the opinion of the directors, the disclosure of any information required would be seriously prejudicial to the interests of the company that information need not be disclosed, but the fact that any such information has not been disclosed must be stated.[12] In practice fairly few companies choose to take advantage of this exemption. One which does is Yorkshire Chemicals, as shown in this extract:

Extract 21.1: Yorkshire Chemicals plc (2000)

2. **TURNOVER** [extract]

Yorkshire Chemicals plc competes internationally with specialist divisions of the world's chemical majors. Because detailed information relating to this competitor activity is not published, the directors are of the opinion that to comply fully with the requirements of SSAP 25 'Segmental Reporting' would be seriously prejudicial to the interests of the group. Hence net assets by geographical area are not shown.

2.2.3 *What is a reportable segment?*

Information can be segmented in two main ways – by class of business and geographically. SSAP 25 supports the provisions of the Companies Act 1985 which state that it is the directors' responsibility to determine the analysis of the segments.[13] The standard does not seek to override these provisions; instead it aims to provide guidance on factors which should influence the definition of segments.

The basic guidance of the standard is that directors should have regard to the overall purpose of presenting segmental information and the need for the readers of the financial statements to be informed if a company carries on operations in different classes of business or in different geographical areas that:

(a) earn returns on investment that are out of line with the remainder of the business; or

(b) are subject to different degrees of risk; or

(c) have experienced different rates of growth; or

(d) have different potentials for future development.[14]

In establishing segments for both classes of business and geographical areas, there is no single set of factors which is universally applicable, nor is any single factor predominant in all cases. However, the standard suggests that in order to determine whether or not a company operates in different classes of business the directors should take into account the following:

(a) the nature of the products or services;
(b) the nature of the production processes;
(c) the markets in which the products or services are sold;
(d) the distribution channels for the products;
(e) the manner in which the entity's activities are organised; and
(f) any separate legislative framework relating to part of the business.[15]

Similarly, in determining whether or not a company operates in different geographical segments the directors should take into account the following:

(a) expansionist or restrictive economic climates;
(b) stable or unstable political regimes;
(c) exchange control regulations; and
(d) exchange rate fluctuations.[16]

Particularly in some parts of the world, adjacent countries may not share similar characteristics of these kinds and it may be appropriate to analyse them separately. The standard emphasises that 'although geographical proximity may indicate similar economic trends and risks, this will not always be the case'.[17]

Having established that a segment is distinguishable on the basis of features such as these, it is also necessary to consider whether it is significant enough to warrant separate disclosure. A segment will normally be regarded as significant if:

(a) its third party turnover is 10% or more of the total third party turnover of the entity; or
(b) its segment result, whether profit or loss, is 10% or more of the combined result of all segments in profit or of all segments in loss, whichever combined result is the greater; or
(c) its net assets are 10% or more of the total net assets of the entity.[18]

It should be noted that the segment need satisfy only one of these three criteria in order to be regarded as significant.

2.2.4 *What is to be reported?*

The company should define each of its reported classes of business and geographical segments.[19] For each separate class of business and geographical segment, those companies which are subject to the full requirements of the standard (broadly all public and large private companies, and those involved in banking or insurance – see 2.2.2 above) are required to disclose:

(a) turnover;
(b) results; and
(c) net assets.[20]

The discussion which follows is of the full requirements. The exemptions for smaller private companies are shown at the end of this section.

Turnover should be analysed between sales to external customers and sales between segments.[21]

The geographical analysis of turnover is to be given, in the first instance, with reference to its source (i.e. the geographical location from which products or services are supplied). This is consistent with the most likely basis for disclosure of geographical analyses of results and net assets. However, it is recognised that it would also be useful to readers of accounts to be provided with information on the markets which the company serves, which is the basis of the Companies Act requirement. There is, therefore, the additional requirement that turnover (but not results or net assets) be analysed between geographical segments with reference to its destination (i.e. the geographical area to which products or services are supplied). Where this amount is not materially different from turnover to third parties with reference to its source, disclosure is not required but a statement that this is the case should be made.[22]

The standard says that entities that are not required by statute to disclose turnover are not required to analyse such turnover segmentally, but this fact should be stated.[23] This referred at the time to banks, but the subsequently revised Schedule 9 to the Companies Act makes this exemption largely irrelevant. The schedule contains various segmental disclosure requirements,[24] and the banks have also published their own SORP on the subject.[25] However, the rules for specialised industries are beyond the scope of this book.

'Results' means the profit or loss before tax, minority interests and extraordinary items.[26] Profit or loss is normally taken before accounting for interest also. However, the profit or loss after interest is likely to be used in those companies where the earning of interest income or the incurring of interest expense is fundamental to the nature of the business; for example, companies in the financial sector.[27] In giving the geographical analysis of results it is considered that it will be more appropriate if it is based on the areas from which goods or services are supplied.[28] To gather the information based on destination would usually be very difficult in any event.

'Net assets' is not defined in the standard. Generally it is taken as non-interest bearing operating assets less non-interest bearing operating liabilities. However, where interest income/expense has been included in arriving at the segmental results the related interest bearing assets/liabilities should be taken into account in determining the net assets.[29] The aim should be to relate the definition of net assets to the definition of results so that a 'return on investment' type calculation can be performed. Operating assets and liabilities which are shared by more than one segment are to be allocated, as appropriate, to those segments.[30]

Because of the wide differences in their circumstances, it is inevitable that companies interpret net assets in various ways. The best that can be achieved is for companies to settle on one definition of net assets that is meaningful for themselves, and apply it consistently. This means that the value of comparison between companies of returns on assets employed may be limited, even apart from the effects of other differences of accounting policy.

The total of the information disclosed by segmental analysis should agree with the related totals in the financial statements. If they do not agree, a reconciliation between the two figures is required, with reconciling items properly identified and explained.[31]

As indicated in 2.2.2 above, certain of the disclosure requirements of SSAP 25 only apply to public companies (and groups with a public company as subsidiary), banking and insurance companies or groups and very large private companies (and other entities). Companies which are not within these categories need not disclose the following (although disclosure is still encouraged):[32]

(a) split of turnover between external customers and other segments;

(b) segmental analysis of results;

(c) net assets;

(d) share of results and net assets of significant associated undertakings; and

(e) geographical analysis of turnover by reference to its source (analysis by destination is still required by the Companies Act).

2.2.5 *Associated undertakings*

The standard requires groups to give segmental disclosure, in their consolidated accounts, of the following information in respect of their associated undertakings:

(a) their share of the profits or losses of associated undertakings before accounting for taxation, minority interests and extraordinary items; and

(b) their share of the net assets of associated undertakings (including goodwill to the extent it has not been written off) stated, where possible, after attributing fair values to the net assets at the date of the acquisition of the interest in each associated undertaking.

This disclosure should be of the aggregate information for all associated undertakings and should be shown separately in the segmental report.[33] For this purpose, associated undertakings are as defined in the Companies Act, and embrace both associates and joint ventures as they are defined in FRS 9 (see Chapter 7 at 2).

The disclosure is only required if the results or assets of associated undertakings form a material part of the group's results or assets. For this purpose, associated undertakings form a material part of the reporting company's results if, in total, they account for at least 20% of the total results or at least 20% of the total net assets of the reporting group (including the group's share of the results and net assets of the associated undertakings).[34]

Associated undertakings themselves often do not come within the scope of the standard and therefore do not disclose segmental information in their own accounts. Where this is the case the investing company may be unable to obtain the necessary information to meet the requirement of the standard as it does not control the associated undertaking. Similarly, publication of the information may be thought to be prejudicial to the business of the associate where, for example, its competitors are not owned by an entity to which all of the provisions of SSAP 25 apply. SSAP 25 recognises these problems by providing an exemption to the effect that the segmental information requirements do not apply where the company is unable to obtain the information or where publication of the information would be prejudicial to the business of the associate. However, in these circumstances, the reason for the non-disclosure should be stated by way of note, together with a brief description of the omitted business or businesses.[35]

2.2.6 *Common costs*

Common costs are costs relating to more than one segment.[36] The standard merely requires that they are treated in the way that the directors deem most appropriate with regard to the objectives of segmental reporting. If the apportionment of common costs would be misleading, then they should not be apportioned but the total should be deducted from the total of the segment results.[37]

2.2.7 *Disclosure in practice*

Most companies present their segmental information in a separate note to the accounts while a few show it in a separate statement alongside the primary statements. A good example of segmental disclosures is set out below:

Extract 21.2: Imperial Chemical Industries PLC (2000)

5 **Segment information** [extract]

Classes of business

	Turnover			**Profit before taxation, goodwill amortisation and exceptional items**			**Profit before interest and taxation after exceptional items***		
	2000	1999	1998	**2000**	1999	1998	**2000**	1999	1998†
	£m	£m	£m	**£m**	£m	£m	**£m**	£m	£m
Continuing operations									
International businesses									
National Starch	**1,894**	1,792	1,646	**245**	248	231	**238**	193	219
Quest	**687**	676	656	**103**	92	82	**103**	78	58
Performance Specialties	**837**	864	901	**75**	74	73	**76**	70	67
Paints	**2,152**	2,180	2,167	**177**	159	143	**164**	284	57
	5,570	5,512	5,370	**600**	573	529	**581**	625	401
Regional and Industrial	**892**	705	517	**17**	(39)	(9)	**13**	(83)	(9)
Inter-class eliminations	**(26)**	(24)	(27)						
	6,436	6,193	5,860	**617**	534	520	**594**	542	392
Sales to discontinued operations	**(21)**	(14)	(17)						
	6,415	6,179	5,843	**617**	534	520	**594**	542	392

Discontinued operations									
Total	**1,339**	2,333	3,556	**(5)**	72	130	**(535)**	245	104
Sales to continuing operations	**(6)**	(63)	(113)						
	1,333	2,270	3,443	**(5)**	72	130	**(535)**	245	104
Associates									
Share of profits less losses				**100**	61	3	**100**	61	3
Interest payable				**(60)**	(29)	–			
Group net interest charge				**(202)**	(262)	(332)			
Amounts written off investments							–	–	(34)
	7,748	8,449	9,286	**450**	376	321	**159**	848	465

	2000 £m	1999 £m	1998 £m
*Goodwill amortisation charged in arriving at the results			
National Starch	**18**	18	12
Performance Specialties	**1**	1	–
Paints	**16**	16	11
	35	35	23

† As restated – note 1.

Inter-class turnover affected several businesses the largest being sales from Regional and Industrial to Discontinued operations of £17m (1999 Discontinued operations to Paints £35m; 1998 £64m).

	Depreciation			Capital expenditure		
	2000 £m	1999 £m	1998 £m	**2000 £m**	1999 £m	1998 £m
Continuing operations						
International businesses						
National Starch	**64**	79	51	**96**	111	115
Quest	**18**	18	19	**28**	27	27
Performance Specialties	**28**	29	29	**39**	38	52
Paints	**54**	60	53	**54**	70	78
	164	186	152	**217**	246	272
Regional and Industrial	**37**	34	22	**18**	21	63
	201	220	174	**235**	267	335
Discontinued operations	**167**	95	189	**54**	143	219
	368	315	363	**289**	410	554

Geographic areas

The information [above] is re-analysed in the table below by geographic area. The figures for each geographic area show the turnover and profit made by, and the net operating assets owned by, companies located in that area; export sales and related profits are included in the areas from which those sales were made.

	Turnover			Profit before taxation, goodwill amortisation and exceptional items			Profit before interest and taxation after exceptional items		
	2000	1999	1998	**2000**	1999	1998	**2000**	1999	1998†
	£m	£m	£m	**£m**	£m	£m	**£m**	£m	£m
Continuing operations									
United Kingdom									
Sales in the UK									
External	**994**	856	608						
Intra-Group	**84**	114	34						
	1,078	970	642						
Sales overseas									
External	**338**	353	461						
Intra-Group	**193**	223	182						
	531	576	643						
	1,609	1,546	1,285	**71**	30	94	**64**	48	80
Continental Europe									
External	**1,087**	1,187	1,227						
Intra-Group	**323**	318	201						
	1,410	1,505	1,428	**126**	147	125	**120**	142	93
USA									
External	**2,094**	2,008	1,879						
Intra-Group	**156**	146	153						
	2,250	2,154	2,032	**192**	211	169	**183**	178	102
Other Americas									
External	**678**	619	672						
Intra-Group	**74**	54	48						
	752	673	720	**54**	38	60	**51**	36	59
Asia Pacific									
External	**1,171**	1,095	919						
Intra-Group	**122**	115	93						
	1,293	1,210	1,012	**169**	103	65	**171**	132	51
Other countries									
External	**53**	60	77						
Intra-Group	–	–	–						
	53	60	77	**5**	5	7	**5**	6	7
	7,367	7,148	6,554	**617**	534	520	**594**	542	392
Inter-area eliminations	**(931)**	(955)	(694)						
Sales to discontinued operations	**(21)**	(14)	(17)						
	6,415	6,179	5,843	**617**	534	520	**594**	542	392
Discontinued operations	**1,333**	2,270	3,443	**(5)**	72	130	**(535)**	245	104
Associates									
Shares of profits less losses				**100**	61	3	**100**	61	3
Interest payable				**(60)**	(29)	–			
Group interest payable				**(202)**	(262)	(332)			
Amounts written off investments							**–**	–	(34)
	7,748	8,449	9,286	**450**	376	321	**159**	848	465
After amortisation of goodwill							**35**	35	23

† As restated – note 1.
Turnover by Discontinued operations is primarily in the following geographic areas:

United Kingdom £1,113m, USA £92m, and Continental Europe £52m (1999 United Kingdom £1,131m, USA £564m and Continental Europe £406m; 1998 United Kingdom £1,535m, USA £936m, Continental Europe £689m).

Classes of business

	Total assets less current liabilities		
	2000	1999	1998
	£m	£m	£m
Net operating assets			
Continuing operations			
International businesses			
National Starch	**1,590**	1,531	1,451
Quest	**360**	342	336
Performance Specialties	**552**	545	558
Paints	**945**	948	1,114
	3,447	3,366	3,459
Regional and Industrial	**475**	518	601
	3,922	3,884	4,060
Discontinued operations	**251**	408	1,974
Total net operating assets	**4,173**	4,292	6,034
Net non-operating liabilities	**(590)**	(219)	(1,387)
	3,583	4,073	4,647

	Goodwill included above		
	2000	1999	1998
	£m	£m	£m
Goodwill			
National Starch	**309**	311	311
Performance Specialties	**21**	22	17
Paints	**276**	293	324
Regional and Industrial	**3**	–	–
	609	626	652

	Net non-operating liabilities		
	2000	1999	1998
	£m	£m	£m
Net non-operating liabilities			
Non-operating assets			
Fixed asset investments	**327**	292	170
Non-operating debtors	**299**	150	137
Investments and short-term deposits	**415**	394	455
Cash at bank	**255**	270	367
	1,296	1,106	1,129
Non-operating liabilities			
Short-term borrowings	**(765)**	(102)	(1,445)
Current instalments of loans	**(466)**	(647)	(585)
Non-operating creditors	**(655)**	(576)	(486)
	(1,886)	(1,325)	(2,516)
	(590)	(219)	(1,387)

Geographic areas

	Tangible fixed assets			Total assets less current liabilities		
	2000	1999	1998	**2000**	1999	1998
	£m	£m	£m	**£m**	£m	£m
Tangible fixed assets/Net operating assets						
Continuing operations						
United Kingdom	**300**	301	275	**983**	958	1,019
Continental Europe	**383**	360	411	**630**	679	720
USA	**801**	758	743	**1,312**	1,121	1,251
Other Americas	**184**	168	173	**290**	301	287
Asia Pacific	**544**	596	586	**694**	809	764
Other countries	**8**	9	9	**13**	16	19
	2,220	2,192	2,197	**3,922**	3,884	4,060
Discontinued operations	**178**	282	1,619	**251**	408	1,974
Total net operating assets				**4,173**	4,292	6,034
Net non-operating liabilities				**(590)**	(219)	(1,387)
	2,398	2,474	3,816	**3,583**	4,073	4,647

Total assets less current liabilities of Discontinued operations are primarily in the following geographic areas:

United Kingdom £83m, Continental Europe £33m, USA £130m (1999 United Kingdom £209m, Continental Europe £46m, USA £153m; 1998 United Kingdom £700m, Continental Europe £513m, USA £630m).

Turnover by customer location

	2000	1999	1998
	£m	£m	£m
Continuing operations			
United Kingdom	**952**	834	712
Continental Europe	**1,291**	1,372	1,350
USA	**2,012**	1,948	1,911
Other Americas	**727**	656	678
Asia Pacific	**1,312**	1,234	970
Other countries	**121**	135	222
	6,415	6,179	5,843
Discontinued operations	**1,333**	2,270	3,443
	7,748	8,449	9,286

Turnover by customer locations for Discontinued operations are primarily in the following geographic areas:

United Kingdom £864m, Continental Europe £201m and USA £97m (1999 United Kingdom £783m, Continental Europe £578m and USA £557m; 1998 United Kingdom £1,051m, Continental Europe £992m, and USA £848m).

Guidance on the form of presentation which may be followed in disclosing all of the information required by the standard is provided in the appendix to SSAP 25. During the development of the standard it was, at one point, suggested that a matrix format be encouraged. This gives additional information, because it means that each geographical segment is also analysed by activity and vice versa. However, while many commentators felt that a matrix approach had some merit, others contended that a complex matrix of segmental information may confuse readers as well as giving competitors valuable commercial advantage. Nevertheless certain companies present elements of their segmental information in this manner.[38]

2.2.8 *Voluntary segmental disclosures*

A number of companies give segmental information which goes beyond present requirements. In Extract 21.2 above, ICI has analysed depreciation and capital expenditure by class of business and in Extract 21.8 below BP Amoco has provided segmental analyses of capital expenditure and acquisitions.

3 PROBLEM AREAS

3.1 How to define the segments

SSAP 25 specifies that the definition of segments should be made by the management of the reporting company. Guidance on how such segments are defined can be given but only in very general terms (see 2.2.4 above).

The factors which provide guidance in determining an industry segment are often those which lead a company's management to organise its enterprise into divisions, branches or subsidiaries. In turn, this means that the company's own management accounts may well be prepared in this form and the information required for segmental reporting will be more readily available.

The standard recommends that the directors should review their definitions annually and redefine them when appropriate,[39] and this is now common in an environment where companies continually have to adapt to changing market conditions. Where this is done, the comparative figures should be restated to reflect the change; disclosure of the nature of, the reasons for, and the effect of the change should also be made.[40] United Business Media provides an example of such disclosures:

Extract 21.3: United Business Media plc (2000)

1. **BUSINESS ANALYSIS** [extract]

As a result of the disposals during 2000 the segmental analysis has been amended, and comparative amounts have been restated, to reflect the continuing business-to-business focus of United. The business services segment has been broken out into more detail, and now comprises the offline business of professional media, news distribution and market research. It has also been renamed business-to-business media. The offline business within the former broadcasting and entertainment and consumer publishing segments are now disclosed within consumer media. All online businesses are now shown separately in the online businesses segment. The impact of redefining the business segments previously reported in 1999 is as follows:

Business to business media – a decrease of £23.6 million in group turnover, an increase of £34.6 million in operating profit and a decrease of £122.2 million in operating net assets.

Consumer media – a decrease of £6.7 million in group turnover, an increase of £5.3 million in operating profit and £nil in operating net assets.

Companies who operate in global markets can have particular difficulty in analysing their operations geographically. The following extract shows the approach of Barclays to this problem:

> *Extract 21.4: Barclays PLC (2000)*
>
> **Accounting presentation** [extract]
> **Analyses by geographical segments and classes of business**
>
> The analyses by geographical segment are generally based on the location of the office recording the transaction.
>
> In note 60, the global swaps business is included within the UK segment. Foreign UK-based comprises activities in the UK with overseas customers, including sovereign lendings, and the main foreign exchange trading business arising in the UK. Of the £22.0bn of assets reported under this heading in 2000, it is estimated that £7.9bn relates to customers domiciled in Other European Union countries and £5.0bn relates to customers domiciled in the United States.
>
> UK includes business transacted through the Channel Islands and Isle of Man. United States includes business conducted through the Bahamas and the Cayman Islands.
>
> The world-wide activities of Barclays are highly integrated and, accordingly, it is not possible to present geographical segment information without making internal allocations, some of which are necessarily subjective. Where appropriate, amounts for each geographical segment and class of business reflect the benefit of earnings on a proportion of shareholders' funds, allocated generally by reference to weighted risk assets.

One or two companies assert that they have only one business operation, but then go on to give some further analysis of it. Since they do not regard the sub-units as separate segments, they avoid having to give the full range of disclosures required by SSAP 25.[41]

3.2 Inter-segment sales

The standard requires that the turnover disclosed for each segment be split between sales to external customers and sales to other segments. Prior to the introduction of SSAP 25 few companies disclosed all such information; they either disclosed the total turnover for each segment and deducted one figure for inter-segment sales or disclosed sales to external customers only.

Some companies voluntarily state the basis on which inter-segment sales are conducted. One example is Unilever, which gives this description in its accounting policies:

> *Extract 21.5: Unilever PLC (2000)*
>
> **Accounting information and policies** [extract]
> **Transfer pricing**
>
> The preferred method for determining transfer prices for own manufactured goods is to take the market price. Where there is no market price, the companies concerned follow established transfer pricing guidelines, where available, or else engage in arm's length negotiations.
>
> Trademarks owned by the parent companies and used by operating companies are, where appropriate, licensed in return for royalties or a fee.
>
> General services provided by central advisory departments, Business Groups and research laboratories are charged to operating companies on the basis of fees.

3.3 Common costs

Common costs will normally take the form of central administration overheads, but in practice there could be a wide range of categories of common costs. However, the standard emphasises that 'costs that are directly attributable to individual reportable segments are not common costs for the purposes of this accounting standard and therefore should be allocated to those segments, irrespective of the fact that they may have been borne by a different segment or by Head Office'.[42]

SSAP 25 allows common costs to be allocated to different segments on what the company's management believes is a reasonable basis (see 2.2.6 above) but where the apportionment of common costs would be misleading, the standard requires that they should not be apportioned but the total should be deducted from the total of the segment results. Notwithstanding this, one or two companies disclose that they have apportioned such costs. An example is shown below:

Extract 21.6: Cookson Group plc (2000)

3 Segmental analyses [extract]

In each of the following analyses, the costs and net assets of the Group's corporate activities have been allocated according to the relative sales contribution of each ongoing operation segment to the total.

Such a practice is consistent with the ASB's rules on the assessment of impairment of assets, whereby central assets such as head offices have to be apportioned across income-generating units for the purposes of the test (see Chapter 10 at 4.4). Nevertheless, we do not believe this to be a helpful approach, because it implies a relationship where none exists and is unlikely to add to the usefulness of the segmental information disclosed.

3.4 Allocation of interest income and interest expense

SSAP 25 suggests that in the majority of companies the individual segments will be financed by interest-bearing debt and equity in varying proportions. The interest earned or incurred by the individual segments is, therefore, a result of the holding company's overall policy rather than a proper reflection of the results of the various segments. For this reason, the standard requires that in these circumstances the results should exclude interest as 'comparisons of profit between segments or between different years for the same segment are likely to be meaningless if interest is included in arriving at the result'.[43]

However, where interest is fundamental to the nature of the business, the standard suggests that interest should be included in arriving at the segment result. Such an approach would be relevant to those companies involved in the financial sector, but it can also apply to diverse groups where some divisions are cash-generative and finance the others.

3.5 Exceptional items

The results which are to be analysed in terms of SSAP 25 are those 'before accounting for taxation, minority interests and extraordinary items', and usually also before interest.[44] The standard predated FRS 3 (see Chapter 25), which has virtually abolished extraordinary items but expanded the categories of exceptional items to be disclosed instead, and it is necessary to consider how these should be dealt with for segmental reporting purposes.

Exceptional items are not specifically addressed in SSAP 25, and by implication are to be included in the analysed results. In practice, some companies analyse their results before exceptional items, and do not always fully disclose to which segments the exceptional items belong.

In its 1993 accounts, BET excluded exceptional items from its operating profit and also its segmental analysis, but after the intervention of the Financial Reporting Review Panel, it restated the figures in its 1994 accounts, as shown below:

Extract 21.7: BET Public Limited Company (1994)

Accounting policies [extract]

The 1993 comparatives have been restated to show operating exceptional items of £76.0 million within the statutory format headings to which they relate (£60.2 million in cost of sales and £15.8 million in administrative expenses) in recognition of developing practice in the application of FRS 3 and after a recent discussion with the Financial Reporting Review Panel. The restatement of the previously disclosed operating exceptional items is highlighted in Note 1(c) on page 39.

Notes to the consolidated accounts
Note 1 Analysis of profit and loss account [extract]
(c) Adjustment to 1993 comparatives

	1993 Published £m	Adjustment £m	1993 Restated £m
BY BUSINESS SECTOR			
Business services	25.6	(11.5)	14.1
Distribution services	20.8	(11.5)	9.3
Plant services	26.5	(10.7)	15.8
Textile services	28.1	(22.5)	5.6
Trading activities	101.0	(56.2)	44.8
Associated undertakings	7.3	–	7.3
Corporate and other	(24.6)	(10.7)	(35.3)
Loss on disposal of property	(4.0)	–	(4.0)
Continuing operations	79.7	(66.9)	12.8
Discontinued operations	(5.5)	(9.1)	(14.6)
	74.2	(76.0)	(1.8)
Costs previously disclosed as operating exceptional items	(76.0)	76.0	–
Operating loss	(1.8)	–	(1.8)

BY GEOGRAPHICAL LOCATION			
Europe – UK	33.3	(51.7)	(18.4)
– Continent	20.3	(14.3)	6.0
North America	13.5	(9.4)	4.1
Rest of the World	7.1	(0.6)	6.5
	74.2	(76.0)	(1.8)
Costs previously disclosed as operating exceptional items	(76.0)	76.0	–
Operating loss	(1.8)	–	(1.8)

In our view the best approach is to analyse the profit after exceptional items, while also making it clear how much each segment has been affected by such items.

3.6 Changes in composition of the group

FRS 3 requires that 'where an acquisition, or a sale or termination, has a material impact on a major business segment this should be disclosed and explained'.[45]

Two of the companies shown earlier in this chapter have shown discontinued operations separately in their segmental analyses, namely ICI (Extract 21.2) and BET (Extract 21.7). The most common form of disclosure is simply to show discontinued operations as a residual category, analysing only the continuing operations into segments (which is not strictly what FRS 3 requires). Again, however, it is often evident from the discussion elsewhere in the accounts what the discontinued businesses related to.

The requirement in FRS 3 is a rather glib one, and deserves reconsideration when the standard is revised. In fact, a more rewarding approach might be to readdress the issue in any future revision of SSAP 25, because it would be more natural to incorporate such requirements into the framework of existing segmental disclosures. Indeed, the whole topic of disclosing the effects of acquisitions and discontinuances arguably fits more comfortably in the context of segmental reporting than in a general standard on the format of the profit and loss account.

3.7 How to define net assets

Net assets are not defined in the standard although it does indicate that, in most cases, these will be the non-interest bearing operating assets less the non-interest bearing operating liabilities. Where, and to the extent that, the segment result is calculated after accounting for interest, for example by companies in the financial sector, then the corresponding interest bearing assets and liabilities should be included in the calculation of net assets.[46]

Operating assets of a segment should not normally include loans or advances to, or investments in, another segment unless interest therefrom has been included in arriving at the segment result.[47]

Operating liabilities will normally include creditors which are included in working capital but will exclude liabilities in respect of proposed dividends and corporation tax as well as interest bearing liabilities such as loans, overdrafts and debentures. In the case of a consolidated balance sheet with a minority interest, the calculation of net assets should not involve the deduction of that interest.

Non-operating assets and liabilities, as well as unallocated assets and liabilities, should therefore be shown in the segmental analysis as reconciling items between the total of the individual segments' net assets and the figure for net assets appearing in the balance sheet.

As shown in Extract 21.2 above, ICI has shown a total of net non-operating liabilities which reconciles the segmentally analysed net assets to the balance sheet, and has listed the items included therein. BP Amoco has the following reconciliation to tie up the segmental figures with the balance sheet:

Extract 21.8: BP Amoco p.l.c. (2000)

17 Group balance sheet analysis [extract]

				$ million
	Capital expenditure and acquisitions		Operating capital employed	
	2000	1999	**2000**	1999
By business				
Exploration and Production	**6,383**	4,194	**56,500**	36,229
Gas and Power	**279**	18	**1,735**	1,093
Refining and Marketing	**8,750**	1,634	**29,066**	14,358
Chemicals	**1,585**	1,215	**11,008**	10,048
Other businesses and corporate (a)	**30,616**	284	**1,486**	1,192
	47,613	7,345	**99,795**	62,920
By geographical area				
UK (b)	**7,438**	1,518	**20,093**	14,298
Rest of Europe	**2,041**	831	**7,087**	4,884
USA (a)	**34,037**	2,963	**43,758**	27,426
Rest of World	**4,097**	2,033	**28,857**	16,312
	47,613	7,345	**99,795**	62,920
Includes the following amounts for the BP/Mobil joint venture	**170**	624		
Operating capital employed			**99,795**	62,920
Liabilities for current and deferred taxation			**(4,604)**	(4,034)
Capital employed			**95,191**	58,886
Financed by:				
Finance debt			**21,190**	14,544
Minority shareholders' interest			**585**	1,061
BP shareholders' interest			**73,416**	43,281
			95,191	58,886

(a) Capital expenditure and acquisitions for 2000 includes $27,506 million for the acquisition of ARCO.
(b) UK area includes the UK-based international activities of Refining and Marketing.

4 INTERNATIONAL REQUIREMENTS

4.1 IAS 14

The international standard on the issue of segmental reporting is IAS 14 – *Segment Reporting*. The original version was published by the IASC in August 1981[48] and reformatted in 1994, but was revised again in 1997. The main features of the current version are set out below:

4.1.1 *Scope*

IAS 14 applies to all enterprises whose equity or debt securities are publicly traded, or are about to be.[49] The latter reference would include companies preparing a prospectus for the issuance of equity or debt securities in the public securities markets. Segment information only needs to be reported on a consolidated level if the entity publishes both parent and consolidated financial statements.[50] Similarly, if the financial statements of an entity's equity method investments or joint ventures are attached to its financial statements, segment information only needs to be reported on the basis of the entity's own financial statements.[51] Entities that voluntarily report segment information need to prepare that information in accordance with the standard.[52] Unlike SSAP 25, there is no exemption in IAS 14 to allow companies not to disclose segmental information on the grounds that disclosure would be seriously prejudicial to the interests of the company.

4.1.2 *Identification of segments*

Like SSAP 25, IAS 14 requires information to be reported for both business segments and geographical segments, but one of these is to be regarded as the primary basis and the other as the secondary basis (requiring less information to be disclosed), depending on which is regarded as providing the more meaningful analysis of the predominant source and nature of risks and returns.[53] The segments are to be identified on the basis of the internal organisational structure and reporting systems, because they are presumed to be aligned to the same objectives. However, if the systems place equal emphasis on these two dimensions, the business segmentation is to be regarded as the primary basis for analysis and the geographical segmentation as the secondary one. Where management does not receive any segment information, a choice must be made whether business segmentation or geographical segmentation is most appropriate as the primary segment reporting format.[54]

A business segment is defined as 'a distinguishable component of an entity that is engaged in providing an individual product or service or a group of related products or services and that is subject to risks and returns that are different from those of other business segments.'[55] Business segments may be based on the nature of the products or services, production processes, customers, distribution methods or regulatory environment.[56] A geographical segment is a distinguishable component of an entity that is based on geographical considerations such as the similarity of economic and political conditions, relationships between geographical areas, proximity of operations, special risks associated with operations in an area, exchange control regulations and underlying currency risks.[57] Unlike SSAP 25, geographical segments can be based either on the location of the entity's operations or on the location of its markets or customers.[58]

As indicated above, IAS 14 requires a 'management approach' in identifying reportable segments, i.e. the segments used for external reporting purposes should be those segments for which information is reported to the board of directors and the chief operating officer.[59] Segments used in internal reporting that meet the definition of a business or geographical segment may be reportable segments. Where the segments for internal reporting do not meet those definitions, the entity should look to the next lower level of internal segmentation and determine whether those segments meet the definitions.[60]

Two or more internally reported segments that are substantially similar should be combined when they exhibit similar long-term financial performance and they do not qualify as separate external reporting segments.[61]

A business segment or geographical segment should be identified as a reportable segment when it derives the majority of its revenue from sales to external customers and:

(a) its internal and external revenue exceeds 10% of total revenue; or

(b) its segment result – as an absolute percentage – exceeds 10% of (1) the combined results of all profitable segments or (2) the combined results of all segments in loss, whichever is the greater in absolute amount; or

(c) its assets are in excess of 10% of the total assets of all segments.[62]

Unlike SSAP 25, if the reportable segments' revenue is less than 75% of total revenue, the entity should identify additional segments until at least 75% of total revenue is included in reportable segments – even if the segments do not meet the 10% thresholds described above. Internally reported segments may be designated as reportable segments despite their size or may be combined with other similar internal segments. Segments that are not separately reported or combined must be included as an unallocated reconciling item.[63]

An entity's internal reporting system may treat vertically integrated activities as separate selling and buying segments. If the entity does not consider such internal segments to be reportable segments it should combine the selling and buying segments, unless it is unreasonable to do so – in which case the selling segment must be included as an unallocated reconciling item.[64]

If a segment identified as a reportable segment in one period no longer meets the size criteria in the next period, management must judge whether the segment is of sufficient continuing importance to warrant separate presentation. When a segment is identified as a reportable segment for the first time, the prior period segment data should be restated to reflect the newly reportable segment separately.[65]

4.1.3 *Measurement*

Accounting policies applied in preparing the consolidated financial statements should also be applied in preparing segment information.[66] Nevertheless, it is permitted to disclose additional information that is prepared on a different basis when that information is used by the entity's key decision-makers and the alternative basis of measurement is clearly described.[67]

Assets that are used by more than one segment should be allocated to segments only if related revenues and expenses are also allocated to those segments.[68]

Inter-segment transfers should be measured and reported on the basis that was actually used by the entity to price those transfers. Unlike SSAP 25, the basis of inter-segment pricing and any change therein should be disclosed in the financial statements.[69]

IAS 14 contains the following detailed definitions of terms that affect the measurement and presentation of segment information:[70]

(a) *segment revenue* is that part of consolidated revenue that is attributable to a segment, but excludes extraordinary items and – unless the segments operations are primarily of a financial nature – interest or dividend income, gains on sales of investments or gains on extinguishments of debt;

(b) *segment expense* is that part of consolidated expense that is attributable to a segment, but excludes extraordinary items, the entity's share in equity method investments, income tax expense, unallocated general administrative expenses, unallocated corporate expenses and – unless the segments operations are primarily of a financial nature – interest, losses on sales of investments or losses on extinguishments of debt;

(c) *segment result* is segment revenue less segment expense, before any minority interest adjustments;

(d) *segment assets* are those consolidated assets that are attributable to the segment excluding income tax assets. Where segment result includes interest or dividend income, segment assets include the related receivables, loans, investments or other income-producing assets;

(e) *segment liabilities* are those consolidated liabilities that are attributable to the segment excluding income tax liabilities. Where segment result includes interest expense, segment liabilities include the related interest-bearing liabilities.

Segment assets, liabilities, revenue and expenses are determined before elimination of intra-group balances and transactions.[71]

4.1.4 *Information to be disclosed*

A Primary segment information

In respect of the primary segmental analysis, IAS 14 requires the following to be disclosed:

(a) segment revenue (both external and intra-segment);

(b) segment result;

(c) segment assets;

(d) segment liabilities;

(e) investment in assets that are expected to be used in more than one period (property, plant, equipment, and intangible assets);

(f) depreciation and amortisation expense; and

(g) other significant non-cash expense.[72]

An entity is encouraged to disclose separately, items of such size, nature or incidence, that their disclosure is relevant to explain segment performance.[73]

The aggregate amount of the entity's share in the net profit or loss of an equity method investment should be disclosed by segment, if substantially all of the investee's operations are within a single segment. Where this disclosure is made, the aggregate carrying amount of those equity method investments should be disclosed by segment also.[74]

B Secondary segment information

If an entity's primary reporting format is based on business segments, it should also disclose the following segment information:

(a) segment revenue from external customers for geographical segments – based on customer location – that exceed 10% of total revenue from sales to all external customers;

(b) segment assets for geographical segments that exceed 10% of the total assets of all geographical segments; and

(c) the total cost incurred to acquire segment assets that are expected to be used during more than one period by geographical location of assets, for geographical segments that exceed 10% of the total assets of all geographical segments.[75]

If an entity's primary reporting format is based on geographical segments, it should also disclose the following segment information for business segments whose revenue from sales to external customers exceeds 10% of total sales or whose assets exceed 10% of total assets:

(a) segment revenue from external customers;

(b) the total carrying amount of segment assets; and

(c) the total cost incurred during the period to acquire segment assets that are expected to be used during more than one period.[76]

Where an entity's primary reporting format is based on geographical location of assets, which differs from the location of its customers, the entity should disclose sales to external customers for geographical segments that exceed 10% of total revenue from sales to all external customers.[77]

Where an entity's primary reporting format is based on geographical location of customers, which differs from the location of its assets, it should also disclose the following segment information for geographical segments whose revenue from sales to external customers exceeds 10% of total sales or whose assets exceed 10% of total assets:

(a) the total carrying amount of segment assets; and

(b) the total cost incurred during the period to acquire segment assets that are expected to be used during more than one period.[78]

C Other disclosure matters

If a business or geographical segment that is reported to the entity's key management is not a reportable segment – on the basis that the majority of its revenue is derived from sales to other segments – but its sales to external customers exceed 10% of revenue from sales to all external customers, the entity should disclose:

(a) the aforementioned fact;

(b) sales to external customers; and

(c) internal sales to other segments.[79]

An entity should report which types of products and services are included in each reported business segment and indicate the composition of each reported geographical segment.[80]

IAS 14 encourages the voluntary disclosure of:

(a) vertically integrated activities as separate segments, with appropriate descriptions including disclosure of the basis of pricing inter-segment transfers;[81]

(b) the primary segment disclosures (see A above) for each reportable secondary segment;[82]

(c) the nature and amount of any items of segment revenue and segment expense that are of such size, nature, or incidence that their disclosure is relevant to explain the performance of each reportable segment for the period;[83] and

(d) the amount of the cash flows arising from the operating, investing and financing activities of each reported industry and geographical segment.[84] This disclosure is also encouraged by IAS 7 – see Chapter 29 at 4.1.14.

4.1.5 *Reconciliations*

An entity should present a reconciliation between the information disclosed for reportable segments and the entity's financial statements in the following manner:[85]

(a) segment revenue should be reconciled to revenue from external customers. Revenue from external customers not included in any segment revenue should be disclosed separately;

(b) segment result should be reconciled to a comparable measure of entity operating profit or loss as well as to entity net profit or loss;

(c) segment assets and liabilities should be reconciled to the entity's assets and liabilities, respectively.

4.1.6 *Restatement of previously reported information*

Changes in the accounting policies for segment reporting that have a material effect on segment information require disclosure of:[86]

(a) a description of the nature of the change;

(b) the reasons for the change;

(c) the financial effect of the change, if it is reasonably determinable;

(d) restated comparative information; and

(e) a statement that comparative information has been restated or that it was impracticable to do so.

When a segment is identified as a reportable segment for the first time, the prior period segment data should be restated to reflect the newly reportable segment separately, unless it is impracticable to do this.[87]

Where an entity changes the identification of reportable segments and does not restate prior period segment information, it should present segment information based on the old and the new bases of segmentation for the current period.[88]

4.1.7 *Examples of disclosures*

Nestlé provides an example of a primary reporting format based on geographical segments:

Extract 21.9: Nestlé S.A. (2000)

1 Segmental information

By management responsibility and geographic area

In millions of CHF	**2000**	1999	**2000**	1999
	Sales		Results	
Zone Europe	**26,285**	27,098	**2,753**	2,671
Zone Americas	**25,524**	22,045	**3,503**	2,799
Zone Asia, Oceania and Africa	**15,710**	13,611	**2,673**	2,185
Other activities (a)	**13,903**	11,906	**2,015**	1,675
	81,422	74,660	**10,944**	9,330
Unallocated items (b)			**(1,758)**	(1,416)
Trading profit			**9,186**	7,914

(a) Mainly Pharmaceutical products and Water, managed on a worldwide basis.
(b) Mainly corporate expenses, research and development costs as well as amortisation of goodwill.

The analysis of sales by geographic area is stated by customer destination. Intersegment sales are not significant.

In millions of CHF	2000	1999	2000	1999
	Assets		Liabilities	
Zone Europe	**12,913**	14,333	**5,279**	5,398
Zone Americas	**10,503**	10,332	**3,460**	3,187
Zone Asia, Oceania and Africa	**6,897**	6,919	**2,591**	1,936
Other activities (a)	**7,860**	7,316	**2,896**	2,855
	38,173	38,900	**14,226**	13,376
Unallocated items (c)	**10,635**	7,454	**386**	491
Eliminations	**(849)**	(637)	**(849)**	(637)
	47,959	45,717	**13,763**	13,230

(c) Corporate and research and development assets/liabilities, including goodwill.

In millions of CHF	2000	1999	2000	1999
	Capital expenditure		Depreciation of tangible fixed assets	
Zone Europe	**946**	923	**890**	928
Zone Americas	**766**	718	**767**	697
Zone Asia, Oceania and Africa	**550**	381	**481**	421
Other activities (a)	**949**	665	**519**	477
	3,211	2,687	**2,657**	2,523
Unallocated items (d)	**94**	119	**80**	74
	3,305	2,806	**2,737**	2,597

(d) Corporate and research and development fixed assets.

By product group

In millions of CHF	2000	1999	2000	1999
	Sales		Results	
Beverages	**23,044**	20,859	**4,318**	3,764
Milk products, nutrition and ice cream	**21,974**	19,411	**2,620**	2,168
Prepared dishes, cooking aids and petcare	**20,632**	20,185	**1,948**	1,850
Chocolate, confectionery and biscuits	**10,974**	10,195	**1,166**	882
Pharmaceutical products	**4,798**	4,010	**1,212**	1,077
	81,422	74,660	**11,264**	9,741
Unallocated items (a)			**(2,078)**	(1,827)
Trading profit			**9,186**	7,914

(a) Mainly corporate expenses, research and development costs, amortisation of goodwill as well as restructuring costs.

In millions of CHF	2000	1999
	Assets	
Beverages	**10,654**	10,104
Milk products, nutrition and ice cream	**11,215**	10,722
Prepared dishes, cooking aids and petcare	**8,980**	9,940
Chocolate, confectionery and biscuits	**6,685**	6,007
Pharmaceutical products	**2,589**	2,198
	40,123	38,971

In millions of CHF	**2000**	1999
	Capital expenditure	
Beverages	**936**	618
Milk products, nutrition and ice cream	**530**	366
Prepared dishes, cooking aids and petcare	**390**	464
Chocolate, confectionery and biscuits	**250**	280
Pharmaceutical products	**113**	91
	2,219	1,819
Administration, distribution, research and development	**1,086**	987
	3,305	2,806

5 CONCLUSION

It is clear that the general standard of segmental reporting in the UK has improved in the years since SSAP 25 was introduced. Large companies typically now devote a substantial amount of space in their annual reports to the description and analysis of their divisional activities. Provided it is applied constructively and with common sense, the present reporting framework gives companies the opportunity to present a good deal of useful information for the readers of their accounts.

The ASB has found little enthusiasm in the UK for any amendment that would bring the requirements under SSAP 25 closer to those of the international standard. It also seems that there is little appetite among users for any significant expansion in the extent of segmentally reported information. It may be that the analyst community already receives enough information on this from sources outside the financial statements.

References

1 IAS 14 (original), *Reporting Financial Information by Segment*, IASC, 1981.
2 SSAP 25, *Segmental reporting*, ASC, June 1990.
3 Discussion Paper – *Segmental Reporting*, ASB, May 1996.
4 CA 85, Sch. 4, para. 55(1).
5 *Ibid.*, para 55(2).
6 *Ibid.*, para. 55(5).
7 SSAP 25, para. 1.
8 *Ibid.*, paras. 3 and 40.
9 *Ibid.*, paras. 4 and 41.
10 These limits are reviewed from time to time.
11 SSAP 25, para. 35.
12 *Ibid.*, para. 43.
13 *Ibid.*, paras. 7-8.
14 *Ibid.*, para. 8.
15 *Ibid.*, para. 12.
16 *Ibid.*, para. 15.
17 *Ibid.*, para. 16.
18 *Ibid.*, para. 9.
19 *Ibid.*, para. 34.
20 *Ibid.*
21 *Ibid.*, para. 34(a).
22 *Ibid.*, para. 34.
23 *Ibid.*, para. 44.
24 See CA 85, Sch. 9, Part I, para. 76.
25 *Segmental Reporting*, British Bankers' Association and Irish Bankers' Federation, January 1993.
26 SSAP 25, para. 34.
27 *Ibid.*, para. 22.
28 *Ibid.*, para. 21.
29 *Ibid.*, para. 24.
30 *Ibid.*, para. 25.
31 *Ibid.*, para. 37.

32 *Ibid.*, paras. 4 and 41.
33 *Ibid.*, para. 36.
34 *Ibid.*
35 *Ibid.*
36 *Ibid.*, para. 23.
37 *Ibid.*
38 See The BOC Group plc, Report and accounts 2000, p. 74.
39 SSAP 25, para. 10.
40 *Ibid.*, para. 39.
41 See, for example, Safeway plc, Annual Report and Accounts 2001, p. 44.
42 SSAP 25, para. 23.
43 *Ibid.*, para. 22.
44 *Ibid.*, para. 34.
45 FRS 3, *Reporting Financial Performance*, ASB, December 1992, para. 15.
46 SSAP 25, para. 24.
47 *Ibid.*, para. 25.
48 IAS 14 (original), *Reporting Financial Information by Segment*, IASC, 1981.
49 IAS 14 (revised), *Segment reporting*, IASC, 1997, para. 3.
50 *Ibid.*, para. 6.
51 *Ibid.*, para. 7.
52 *Ibid.*, para. 5.
53 *Ibid.*, para. 26.
54 *Ibid.*, para. 27.
55 *Ibid.*, para. 9.
56 *Ibid.*
57 *Ibid.*
58 *Ibid.*, para. 13.
59 *Ibid.*, para. 31.
60 *Ibid.*, para. 32.
61 *Ibid.*, para. 34.
62 *Ibid.*, para. 35.
63 *Ibid.*, paras. 35-7.
64 *Ibid.*, para. 41.
65 *Ibid.*, paras. 42-3.
66 *Ibid.*, para. 44.
67 *Ibid.*, para. 46.
68 *Ibid.*, paras. 47-8.
69 *Ibid.*, para. 75.
70 *Ibid.*, para. 16.
71 *Ibid.*, para. 24.
72 *Ibid.*, paras. 50-8.
73 *Ibid.*, para. 59.
74 *Ibid.*, paras. 64-6.
75 *Ibid.*, para. 69.
76 *Ibid.*, para. 70.
77 *Ibid.*, para. 71.
78 *Ibid.*, para. 72.
79 *Ibid.*, para. 74.
80 *Ibid.*, para. 81.
81 *Ibid.*, para. 40.
82 *Ibid.*, para. 49.
83 *Ibid.*, para. 59.
84 *Ibid.*, para. 62.
85 *Ibid.*, para. 67.
86 *Ibid.*, para. 76.
87 *Ibid.*, para. 43.
88 *Ibid.*, para. 76.

Chapter 22 Employee benefits

1 INTRODUCTION

Employee benefits form such a significant part of any enterprise's costs that it may seem rather surprising that there is no comprehensive accounting standard dealing with them in the UK and that even the much more comprehensive international standard IAS 19 – *Employee Benefits*[1] – still does not address some issues fully. This is largely because the issues raised in accounting for employee benefits are, somewhat paradoxically, either so simple that an accounting standard is hardly necessary (such as the allocation of wages paid to an accounting period), or so complex that it is difficult to achieve a consensus (such as the treatment of defined benefit pension costs or share-based compensation).

In fact, a broad consensus on the treatment of pension costs has now been reached both in the UK and under IAS. The accounting for pension costs, and other employee benefits typically accounted for using actuarial measurement techniques, is discussed in Chapter 23. This Chapter deals with other employee benefits, such as short-term employee benefits, profit-sharing and bonus schemes (including share-based payment schemes), and termination benefits.

The major area where the picture is still far from complete is the accounting treatment of share-based compensation. In the UK, some issues have been addressed on a piecemeal basis by Abstracts of the Urgent Issues Task Force, but not by an accounting standard. The requirements of the Abstracts, which are discussed at 2.5 to 2.7 below, are sometimes difficult to reconcile with those of other UK accounting standards and companies legislation and even, on occasion, with each other. As a result, a considerable body of unwritten GAAP has been developed to fill the void.

IAS currently requires extensive disclosures of share-based payment schemes, but as yet lacks any rules for measuring their cost (see 3.4 below). However, in July 2000 the G4+1 group published a discussion paper – *Accounting for share based payment*[2] – proposing a full fair value approach to accounting for share-based compensation, which is discussed at 4 below. Whilst this undoubtedly represents the IASB's long-term goal, it remains to be seen how difficult it will be to secure the necessary support among the worldwide business community.

2 UK

As noted in 1 above, there is no comprehensive UK standard dealing with employee benefits comparable to IAS 19, so that much 'unwritten' GAAP has come into existence, often drawing directly or by analogy on other pronouncements. As a result of this, and also the 'piecemeal' nature of the written requirements, one often finds inconsistent approaches being taken to what seem to be very similar problems in different areas.

In order to facilitate comparison with IAS, summarised in 3 below, we have, so far as possible, discussed UK GAAP by reference to the specific types of benefit addressed by IAS 19. However, a completely parallel approach is not possible, since there is a major area of difference between the classification of benefits by IAS 19 and that currently adopted in UK GAAP. IAS 19 distinguishes between 'short-term' and 'long term' benefits (short-term benefits being those falling due within one year and long-term those falling due after more than one year), and requires 'long term' benefits to be accounted for on a discounted basis. Under UK GAAP the main distinction is between cash-based compensation (where there is little specific written guidance), share-based compensation (where there is more, though far from complete, guidance) and pension and other post-retirement benefits (which are covered by specific accounting standards). Moreover, under UK GAAP a discounting approach is adopted only for certain post-employment costs (see Chapter 23), and not for other benefits falling due after more than one year.

2.1 Short-term benefits

For the purposes of this discussion, these include such items as:

- wages, salaries and social security contributions;
- benefits in kind, such as cars, housing, medical benefits and free or subsidised goods or services;
- holiday pay and short-term sick pay.

None of these items is seen as a particularly contentious issue in the UK. Under normal accruals accounting, the broad objective of the accounting treatment is to recognise the cost of obtaining the services of an employee during an accounting period in that accounting period. Such costs are be charged to the profit and loss account for the period, although there are some cases in which it may be recognised as part of the cost of a tangible fixed asset (see Chapter 12 at 2.3.2 A), research and development expenditure (see Chapter 11 at 2.4) or stock and work in progress (see Chapter 16 at 2).

A Interaction with UK accounting standards

As noted in 1 above, the treatment of basic employment costs is not directly addressed in UK accounting standards. They would, however, lead to the conclusion above, albeit by a somewhat tortuous route, suggesting, as we comment elsewhere in this Chapter, that a balance sheet oriented conceptual framework such as the ASB's Statement of Principles can make heavy going of what should be simple issues of expense recognition and matching.

In our view, the difficulties start with the definition of liability in the ASB's *Statement of Principles*, i.e. an obligation to transfer economic benefit as the result of a past transaction or event.[3] If this definition were strictly applied to a typical employment contract providing for a standard notice period (say one month) by both employer and employee, it would suggest that, as soon as a new employment contract is signed, the company has a liability to pay one month's wages to the employee. It was possibly to avoid this unwelcome result that FRS 5 – *Reporting the Substance of Transactions*, which defines liabilities in the same terms as the *Statement of Principles*, specifically excludes employment contracts from its scope[4]. This issue is discussed further in Chapter 18 at 2.1 and 2.4.

To deal this difficulty, *Statement of Principles* and FRS 12 – *Provisions, Contingent Liabilities and Contingent Assets* developed the concept of an executory contract. 'Executory contracts' – those where neither party has performed any of its obligations, or each has performed its obligations to an equal extent[5] – are discussed in more detail in Chapter 28 at 2.1.2. FRS 12 requires no provision to be made for an executory contract (unless it is onerous) such that, no provision would be made on the signing of a new employment contract, since at that time the company owes the employee one month's pay, but the employee owes the company a month's work of equal value in return.

As the employee begins work, the contract ceases to be executory since one party (i.e. the employee) has performed more than the other, by providing services without immediate payment (assuming that the contract provides for payment in arrears), and the company should therefore make provision for its obligations under the contract. This would lead to the accounting treatment as described above, that a company should provide for the cost of an employee's services as the services are rendered.

The company would also have to provide for the contract if it were to become onerous to the company. This would be the case for example where, as a result of gross misconduct, an employee is summarily dismissed and escorted from the company's premises, but the company is still obliged to pay him one month's salary in lieu of notice. The contract is then onerous as the company has to pay the employee without receiving the benefit of any services in return.

2.1.1 Benefits in kind

A minor issue with regard to the treatment of benefits in kind is that, under current GAAP, the cost to be recognised is the actual cost to the company, which may be different to the value to the employee, and/or to the value assumed by the Inland Revenue (or equivalent overseas authority) in determining the employee's tax liability. For example, if a company manufactures a washing machine and allows an employee to buy it at cost price, the cost to the company is simply the cost of the machine. No account is taken of the opportunity cost to the company of the lost profit on a normal sale, which represents the value of the transaction to the employee. For this reason, it is often the case that a transaction is included in the disclosure of directors' emoluments at an amount different from that charged in the financial statements (see Chapter 32 at 2.3.2 A).

2.1.2 *Holiday pay*

Where a company grants an employee paid leave, it is typically the case that the maximum number of days' leave that can be taken in any one year depends *inter alia* on the number of days that the employee actually works in that year. It is also often the case that, if the employee leaves during a period before taking the full maximum entitlement to leave for that period, the company is obliged to make a payment in lieu of any days' leave not taken.

The question therefore arises as to whether holiday pay should be accounted for on a 'pay as you go' basis, or whether an accrual should be made at each reporting date for the accumulated cost of leave earned but not taken. Historically in the UK, companies have adopted both approaches,[6] often on the argument that in most cases there would be no material difference to the charge to the profit and loss account for the period.

Following the publication of FRS 12, it is arguable whether the 'pay as you go' method is strictly acceptable any longer. On the face of things, a provision for holiday pay would fall within the definition of a provision in FRS 12, i.e. 'a liability of uncertain timing and amount' and satisfy the criteria for recognition under that standard. Rather curiously, however, FRS 12 mentions holiday pay only to give it as an example of an 'accrual' as opposed to a 'provision' (and therefore outside the scope of FRS 12).[7] Whilst the reference to holiday pay as an accrual could be said to imply that the ASB believes that holiday pay should be accrued, this view is certainly not always followed in practice. Interestingly IAS 19 requires an accruals approach to holiday pay (see 3.1.2 below), although acknowledging that in most cases the liability will not be material.[8]

2.2 Cash-based incentive payments

Companies often pay employees amounts over and above their basic salary and benefits. Such amounts may be contractually payable to employees on meeting certain predetermined targets. These may be personal targets (e.g. commission paid for negotiation of a sale, or a given level of sales), or corporate or divisional targets (e.g. a particular level of profitability or productivity, achievement of a stock market flotation). Alternatively, companies may make non-contractual payments to reward exceptional performance or maintain motivation.

For the purposes of this discussion we refer collectively to such payments as 'incentive payments', although many of the comments below would apply to any payment other than of contractual basic salary and benefits.

Where such an incentive payment is paid in cash (including for the purposes of this discussion any other asset except shares in the reporting entity), there is not typically any doubt as to the total expense to be recognised in the financial statements. There is, however, a choice to be made as to the timing of the expense. Particular issues include:

- when a liability for incentive payment arises (see 2.2.1 below); and
- whether there are different accounting implications depending on whether the payment is made directly by the reporting entity or through an intermediate vehicle, such as an employee benefit trust (see 2.2.2 below).

2.2.1 *When does a liability for an incentive payment arise?*

The most relevant guidance is contained in FRS 12, which states that a provision should be recognised when:

- an entity has a present obligation (legal or constructive) as a result of a past event;
- it is probable that a transfer of economic benefits will be required to settle the obligation; and
- a reliable estimate can be made of the amount of the obligation.[9]

These criteria are discussed in more detail in Chapter 28 at 3.1. Their application to various types of incentive payment is discussed below.

A Payments relating to a single accounting period

In the case of an incentive scheme that is related solely to criteria that can be measured in a single accounting period, there can be little debate as to the accounting treatment. In other words, if the relevant criteria for payment of the incentive have been met in that period, the expense should be recognised in that period; if they have not, it should not.

A complication could arise in the case of an award that depends on the achievement of performance criteria during a period, but which is paid only to those employees still in employment at some date after the end of that period. The question then arises as to whether the cost should be recognised in full in the accounting period in which the performance criteria are met, or spread over that period and the subsequent period of required continuous employment. Consistency with the required treatment for share-based payments would suggest that the cost should normally be recognised in full in the accounting period in which the performance criteria are met. This is discussed in more detail at 2.5.3 E and 2.5.4 B below.

B Payments relating to more than one accounting period

In the case of a scheme that is related to performance over more than one period, there is more room for discussion. The issue is best illustrated by means of a simple example.

Example 22.1: Incentive payment covering more than one period (1)

ABC Limited has 1,000 employees. On 1 January 2001 it agrees to pay £2,000 each in cash to each employee if profit before tax in each of the three years ended 31 December 2003 increases by at least 6% over RPI for that particular year and the employee is still in employment at the end of that period. At the end of the years ended 31 December 2001 and 2002, the company's profit before tax has increased by more than 6% over RPI as compared to the previous period. There are (very broadly) three methods of accounting for this.

Method 1

No cost would be recognised until 31 December 2003, since it is only at that point that (a) it is confirmed that there is a liability at all and (b) the liability can be quantified as it is only at that point that the number of employees eligible for the award is known. This Method is based on the view that, in terms of FRS 12 the critical 'past event' for recognition of a liability for the award is the fulfilment of all the performance criteria.

Method 2

The cost would be recognised in full (subject possibly to discounting if material) at the end of 2001 on the basis that, since ABC is 'on target' to meet the performance criteria, it is more likely than not that the award will be paid. This Method is based on the view that, in terms of FRS 12 and the *Statement of Principles* the critical 'past event' for recognition of a liability for the award is the initial establishment of the scheme.

Method 3

The cost of the award is spread in some way over the three year performance period.

We recommend that companies should adopt Method 3, on the basis that it is most consistent with the manner in which the costs of share-based awards are required to be measured under the various UITF Abstracts discussed at 2.5 below. UITF 25, in particular, takes the view that this spreading approach is consistent with FRS 12 (see 2.5.5 below). From a conceptual viewpoint, however, we consider that the only credible candidates under FRS 12 for the critical 'past event' giving rise to the liability for the award are either the satisfaction of all performance criteria (as in Method 1) or the set-up of the scheme (as in Method 2). It is hard to see how, under this accounting model, it can ever be right to recognise a partial liability for the award (as under Method 3), since the award is an 'all or nothing' scheme.

To take an analogy from another area of accounting, when a company makes an acquisition with an element of deferred or contingent cash consideration dependent on the post-acquisition profits of the acquired entity, FRS 7 requires the company to recognise a liability for the amount of that consideration (see Chapter 6 at 2.3.4 and 2.3.5). The amount recognised is the full amount estimated to be payable, taking into account expected future profits; there is no question of recognising it in stages as those profits are earned, although the estimate of the amount provided would be refined as the actual level profits became clear. Of course, in the case of deferred consideration the corresponding debit for the liability is to cost of investment/goodwill. If the full liability were to be recognised for the bonus in Example 22.1, it would be necessary either to expense the whole amount immediately or create some form of spurious asset ('services to be rendered', perhaps?). Neither answer is very satisfactory, which, in our view, indicates the inadequacy of a balance sheet framework in addressing what should be (and were hitherto) straightforward issues of expense recognition and matching.

On the assumption, however, that Method 3 is adopted, we would suggest the approach in Example 22.2 below, which is consistent with the worked examples in UITF 17 (see 2.5.4 below).

Example 22.2: Incentive payment covering more than one period (2)

At the end of 2001, ABC takes the view that it is 'on target' to meet the performance criteria and that it expects (say) 750 of the original 1,000 employees to be in employment at 31 December 2003. The final cost of the award would therefore be £1,500,000 (750 employees at £2,000 each). ABC would therefore provide £500,000 (£1,500,000 x 1/3) in 2001.

At the end of 2002, ABC is still be on target but takes the view that it now expected 800 of the original employees to still be in employment at 31 December 2003. The total cost would now be expected to be £1,600,000 (800 employees at £2,000 each). ABC would therefore record a total provision of £1,066,666 (£1,600,000 x 2/3), giving rise to a profit and loss account charge of the increase in the provision of £566,666, which can be analysed as:

	£
Effect of revision to opening estimate of number of employees (£500,000 x [800-750]/750)	33,333
Additional entitlement earned in 2002 (1/3 x £1,600,000)	533,333
	566,666

In 2003 the final position would be known and a profit and loss account charge would be made so as to increase the provision at the end of 2002 to the final total cost.

Further complications could arise in Examples 22.1 and 22.2 above. For example, the award might be made to all employees in employment at 31 December 2003, provided that they remained with ABC for a further year. In that case, should the cost of the award be spread over three years, as above, or four years? Consistency with the required treatment for share-based payments would suggest that the three-year performance period should normally continue to be used. This is discussed in more detail at 2.5.3 E and 2.4.5 B below.

C *Schemes with criteria other than financial performance*

As noted above, incentive payments may be made to reward performance other than purely financial performance, such as the achievement of an initial public offering (IPO) or the opening of a new retail outlet. In such cases, in our view, it will typically be the case that it is not until the performance criteria have actually been met that there is sufficient certainty as to the final outcome for the liability for such awards to meet the criterion for recognition under FRS 12 (see above) that an outflow of economic benefit is 'probable'. For example, it is not unknown for an IPO to be postponed or abandoned at a very late stage. It may well be the case, however, that there is a requirement to disclose a contingent liability under FRS 12 (see Chapter 28 at 6.2.2). Guidance on the issues arising from share awards contingent on flotation is given by UITF 30 (see 2.5.6 B below).

D *Discretionary awards*

A number of companies make discretionary awards to employees, typically through an intermediate vehicle such as a trust, the accounting implications of which are discussed in 2.2.2 below. The question arises at what point the cost of such an award should be recognised. On the basis that it is a necessary condition for a provision to be recognised under FRS 12 (see above) that the company has a 'present obligation (legal or constructive)', it might be said that, if a scheme is truly discretionary, no liability can possibly arise until an award is actually made. However, this is not necessarily the case.

For example, it might be the case that the company is using a discretionary award scheme, for tax reasons, to deliver an obligation under a contractual bonus scheme. In that case, the company would clearly have a legal obligation which would be recognised under FRS 12. But there may be cases where a constructive obligation is created, as illustrated by Example 22.3.

Example 22.3: Discretionary awards (1)

DEF plc has for a number of years operated a contractual cash bonus scheme. At 1 April 2001 it decides that for the year ended 31 March 2002 it will operate a discretionary scheme. During the year it communicates this change to employees who were previously in the cash bonus scheme, but informally indicates to them that discretionary awards will take into account criteria similar to those applicable to the cash scheme. Those criteria were met during the year to 31 March 2002. Actual awards made under the new scheme are notified to individual employees on 1 June 2002. Should DEF recognise a liability for the cost of the award in the financial statements for the year ended 31 March 2002?

In our view, DEF should provide for the award, since it constitutes a constructive obligation of DEF. FRS 12 states that a constructive obligation exists where an 'event (which may be an action of the entity) creates valid expectations in other parties that the entity will discharge the obligation'.[10] In terms of this definition, the informal communication of the new scheme to the employees was a past event that created valid expectations of bonus payments among the employees of DEF. The fact that the payments to particular individuals had not been notified at 31 March 2002 does not preclude recognition of the liability, since FRS 12 notes that 'it is not necessary to know the identity of the party to whom the obligation is owed – indeed the obligation may be to the public at large'[11] (and therefore by implication to eligible employees at large). It is noteworthy that this is the position taken in IAS 19 (see 3.1.3 A below), since IAS 37 on provisions (see Chapter 28 at 7.2.1) is, in this respect, identical to FRS 12.

Indeed, a constructive obligation might well be created in less precise circumstances than those in Example 22.3, as illustrated by Example 22.4 below.

Example 22.4: Discretionary awards (2)

GHI plc has consistently given discretionary annual bonuses to its staff. This has created a virtual expectation among staff that bonuses will be paid (although how much and to whom remains a matter of conjecture), such that failure to pay them could lead to strained relations with employees or the departure of key staff. In these circumstances, GHI arguably has a constructive obligation to continue paying bonuses. This analysis is supported by Example 4 in Appendix III to FRS 12 which states that where a retailer has adopted a consistent policy of refunding customers without any legal obligation to do so, it nevertheless has a constructive obligation for such refunds so as to preserve customer goodwill.

However, there will be cases where it is clear that no obligation, either legal or constructive, is created, such as those in Example 22.5 below.

Example 22.5: Discretionary awards (3)

JKL plc prepares accounts for the year ended 31 December 2001 and by mid-December it is clear that JKL has had an exceptionally good year. The directors therefore resolve at a board meeting on 20 December 2001 to pay staff bonuses totalling £3 million, and on the same day the company transfers this sum to an employee benefit trust (EBT) set up on behalf of the company. There has been no established pattern of paying bonuses in the past. The staff receive the good news in letters from the trustees of the EBT on 15 January 2002.

In our view, JKL has neither a legal nor constructive obligation to pay bonuses as at 31 December 2000. FRS 12 states that 'a management or board decision does not give rise to a constructive obligation at the balance sheet date unless the decision has been communicated before the balance sheet date to those affected by it in a sufficiently specific manner to raise a valid expectation in them that the entity will discharge its responsibilities.'[12]

The fact that the company has transferred cash to the EBT before the 31 December 2001 year end is not relevant to this issue, since the EBT will typically be regarded as an extension of the reporting entity for financial reporting purposes. This is discussed further in 2.2.2 below.

2.2.2 *Intermediate payment vehicles*

As noted above, some employee costs (particularly bonus payments) are often routed through intermediate vehicles such as trusts rather than paid directly by the company. In the vast majority of cases, such vehicles are to required by UITF 13 to be accounted for as if they were part of the reporting entity. The rationale for, and implications of, this treatment are discussed in detail at 2.5.3 below. In July 2001 the UITF published for comment a draft Abstract on employee benefit trusts and other intermediate payment vehicles (see 2.5.3 L below), which reinforces this general approach.

An important consequence of this accounting treatment is that transferring an asset, such as cash, to an intermediate vehicle does not in itself give rise to an expense in the reporting entity. Indeed, it will not even give rise to a visible accounting entry for financial reporting purposes, as the effect is simply to transfer cash from one part of the reporting entity to another. An expense arises only when the reporting entity (or the intermediate vehicle) incurs a legal or constructive obligation to make payments to its employees, at which point a provision is recognised for the cost of the award.

Any such provision must be shown gross. It is not possible to offset it against the cash (or other assets) held by the intermediate vehicle, since the provision and the cash do not satisfy the criteria for offset or linked presentation set out in FRS 5 – *Reporting the Substance of Transactions* (see Chapter 18 at 2.6 and 2.7). This is because the reporting entity's obligation to its employees would remain, constructively if not legally, if the intermediate vehicle failed to discharge it (e.g. because the trustees of the vehicle failed to exercise their discretion in accordance with the employer's expectations, or misappropriated the assets of the vehicle).

This contrasts with the treatment required by UITF 13 for an award made using the company's shares, whereby the cost is recognised by amortising the carrying value of the shares to reduce it to the amount recoverable from the employee. This is discussed further at 2.5.3, and in particular 2.5.3 C III, below.

Companies are often anxious to recognise the cost of discretionary awards as early as possible in order to accelerate the corporation tax relief on them. It is therefore clearly important for a company wishing to claim tax relief to ensure that, at the relevant balance sheet date, there exists at least a constructive obligation to pay the award to its employees. It is unlikely that a payment by the company to an intermediate vehicle will be sufficient, on its own, to demonstrate this. It may well be in most cases that the date on which the obligation is incurred is the same as that on which a payment is made to the vehicle, but it is important to remember that it is the incurring of the obligation, not the payment of cash, which gives rise to an expense in the profit and loss account.

2.3 Other long-term benefits

IAS 19 defines long-term benefits as including (in addition to items discussed elsewhere in this Chapter or in Chapter 23) long term compensated absences such as long-service or sabbatical leave, together with jubilee or other long-service benefits (see 3.2 below). There is no pronouncement in UK GAAP dealing specifically with these issues, largely because, in the UK, such benefits are very rare and would typically be awarded on a purely discretionary basis. Where this is the case, it would be appropriate to account for such benefits at the time of the award (i.e. a 'pay as you go' basis).

However, a UK company with subsidiaries incorporated in overseas countries where such benefits are available may need to consider another basis of accounting for them in cases where their cost is material to the group. In our view, the general principles of FRS 12 would require a provision to be made for the cost of such benefits. If a sufficiently large number of employees was involved (as would probably be the case if the amounts were material to the group as whole), this might be done on an 'expected value' basis, possibly using actuarial techniques (see Chapter 28 at 4.1).

2.4 Termination benefits

There is no direct guidance in UK GAAP on redundancy and similar payments. However, the general principles of FRS 12 (see 2.2.1 above) would require a company to recognise a provision for redundancy payments when it has incurred a legal or constructive obligation to pay them. This would clearly be the case, at the latest, when particular individuals are notified that they are to be made redundant. Where redundancies occur in the context of a broader reorganisation or restructuring, it would be normal practice to make provision for the redundancy costs as part of the overall costs of the reorganisation, even though individual employees have not been notified at that point that they are to be made redundant. The accounting treatment of reorganisation costs is discussed in more detail at Chapter 28 at 5.1 and Chapter 25 at 2.6.3.

2.5 Share-based incentive schemes: summary of requirements

2.5.1 *Background*

Share-based awards can be made in a number of forms – typically a gift of shares, or options to acquire existing shares or subscribe for new shares. The accounting treatment of all share based-awards is broadly similar, whatever their precise legal form, and is currently one of the more difficult areas in UK GAAP.

The difficulties largely arise from a number of factors. Firstly, the written guidance is limited to a handful of UITF Abstracts, the underlying principles of which are not always clear. The UITF's approach often seems to have been not so much to apply the relevant accounting standards to the problem in question (which is strictly the limit of its powers) as to approach the issues from first principles, arrive at a 'desirable' answer, and only then attempt, with varying degrees of success, to reconcile that 'desirable' answer to the actual requirements of the standards and companies legislation.

Moreover, the Abstracts have tended to be issued in response to rather narrow, specific issues and seem to deal with some sort of renaissance ideal of a share scheme much more straightforward than any to be found in the real world. They therefore do not always address the wide range of share schemes implemented by companies in the UK. In particular:

- Share schemes involving the issue of new shares by the employing company or group also fall within the scope of certain accounting and capital maintenance provisions of the Companies Act, the objectives of which are not entirely compatible with the accounting requirements of the Abstracts, but which nevertheless have to be addressed.

- Where, as is typically the case, a share scheme involves an employing subsidiary, the parent company and some form of external trust, the accounting treatment in the financial statements of the subsidiary, the parent and the group may be so significantly different that adjustments going beyond the normal elimination of intra-group transactions may be required on consolidation.

We deal with the basic requirements of the UITF Abstracts below and their application to the more complex situations encountered in practice at 2.6 and 2.7 below.

It is also worth noting at this point that a remuneration consultant tends to categorise share-based schemes somewhat differently to a financial accountant. The remuneration consultant will focus on things such as the scope of the scheme (e.g. whether it is for all staff or certain staff only, or for UK employees or expatriates), its motivational purpose (e.g. to reward specific performance or to retain staff, or both), its tax advantages and so on. The accountant on the other hand sees all schemes as broadly very similar from a purely transactional perspective, and is more concerned with such matters as how and when the scheme is funded, and whether the employee is to receive existing shares or freshly issued shares.

In this Chapter, we clearly take an 'accountant's perspective', and do not attempt to describe and evaluate the various types of scheme available, for which reference should be made to a specialist publication. A consequence of taking an accountant's perspective is that we focus on those accounting issues that arise most commonly in practice, even though these issues may in reality affect relatively few share schemes, and it should not be assumed that features of share schemes described in the examples below are typical of all, or even a majority of, schemes.

2.5.2 *UITF 10*

UITF Abstract 10 – *Disclosure of Directors' Share Options* – was issued in September 1994. As its name implies it deals purely with disclosure issues and is discussed in Chapter 32 at 4.2.9 A.

2.5.3 *UITF 13*

UITF Abstract 13 – *Accounting for ESOP Trusts* – was issued in June 1995. It addresses the accounting treatment of employee share ownership plans ('ESOP trusts'), although, as discussed at L below, it should also be applied to similar vehicles such as all-employee share ownership plans ('AESOP trusts') and qualifying employee share trusts ('QUESTs') and employee benefit trusts ('EBTs') other than ESOP trusts, such as those holding assets other than shares.

Companies frequently establish ESOP trusts, which are generally legally constituted as trusts, for their employees, whereby the employees are given the opportunity to buy shares in the company on favourable terms, or to receive them free. For this purpose the ESOP trust may hold shares that have been issued to it by the company or shares that have been bought on the open market. One of the reasons for using a trust for this purpose is that the company itself and its subsidiaries are prohibited by the Companies Act 1985 from holding shares in the company.[13]

Where existing shares are used, they are often purchased by the ESOP trust financed by a loan from either the company itself or from a bank. In the latter case, the bank loan will usually be guaranteed by the company. The loan could be repaid out of the proceeds of the exercise of options by employees, with any shortfalls being made good by the employer.

The accounting issue that arises is how to deal with the trust in the employing company's accounts. This issue came to the UITF as an off-balance sheet finance question, requiring interpretation under FRS 5 – *Reporting the Substance of Transactions*. In our view, this was unfortunate for two reasons. Firstly, it is arguable that the more important issue is the recognition and measurement of the cost of such arrangements, and they would have been better addressed from that perspective. Secondly, it is questionable whether the Abstract is in fact entirely consistent with FRS 5.

A *Summary of accounting requirements*

UITF 13 requires that certain assets and liabilities of the trust should be accounted for as those of the employer company itself where the company 'has de facto control of the shares held by the ESOP trust and bears their benefits or risks'.[14] More specifically, UITF 13 requires that:

(a) Until such time as the shares held by the ESOP trust vest unconditionally in employees, they should be recognised as assets of the sponsoring company. Where shares have been gifted unconditionally to specific employees, they should no longer be recognised as assets of the sponsoring company, even if they are still held by the ESOP trust.

(b) Where the shares are held for the continuing benefit of the sponsoring company's business they should be classified as 'own shares' within fixed assets; otherwise they should be classified as 'own shares' within current assets.

(c) Where the shares are classified as fixed assets, any permanent diminution in their value should be recognised immediately.

(d) Where shares are conditionally gifted or put under option to employees at below the book value determined in (c) above, (i.e. for fixed assets, after taking account of any permanent diminution in value), the difference between book value and residual value should be charged as an operating cost over the period of service of the employees in respect of which the gifts or options are granted.

(e) The sponsoring company should record as its own liability any borrowings of the ESOP trust that are guaranteed, formally or informally, by the sponsoring company.

(f) Finance costs and any administrative expenses should be charged as they accrue and not as funding payments are made to the ESOP trust.

(g) Any dividend income arising on the shares should be excluded in arriving at profit before tax and deducted from the aggregate of dividends paid and proposed. The deduction should be disclosed on the face of the profit and loss account, if material, or in a note. Until such time as the shares vest unconditionally in employees, the shares should also be excluded from earnings per share calculations as, under FRS 14 – *Earnings per Share* – they are treated as if they were cancelled.[15]

A simple illustration of how this accounting treatment works in practice is given in Example 22.6 below.

Example 22.6: Allocation of cost of share award under UITF 13

On 1 June 2001 a company's shares are trading at £1 a share. The company grants an employee an option to acquire 1,000 shares in the company at 85p per share in three years' time subject to certain performance criteria being met. On the same day it transfers £1,000 to the ESOP trust to purchase the 1,000 shares that will be needed to satisfy the option if exercised. The company will record the shares as an asset of £1,000 and amortise this down to £850 (the exercise price) over the three year performance period at £50 per year. The £850 option proceeds received by the company on exercise by the employee of the option are set off against the carrying value of the shares. This arrives at the same profit and loss account charge as would have been obtained if the problem had been approached as a question of allocating an expense of £150 over three years.

We discuss the implications of the more difficult of these requirements in detail below.

B ESOP under de facto control of employer

Until the issue of UITF 13, companies had tended for financial reporting purposes to respect the legal form of ESOP trusts as separate entities under the control of independent trustees who were required to act in the interests of the beneficiaries of the trust (i.e. the employees) rather than those of the company. The accounting treatment was therefore to write off donations from the company to the ESOP trust as an expense (i.e. a 'pay as you go' basis) or, where the ESOP trust was funded by external borrowings, to treat those borrowings as 'off-balance sheet'.

The UITF, however, took the view that shares held by the ESOP trust are an asset of the employer under FRS 5 since it is the employer that bears most of the risks and many of the benefits of ownership of the shares. The employer bears the risk that the value of the shares will fall below their option price. In such circumstances, employees would be irrational to exercise their options, leaving the employer with the choice of either granting new options at a lower price (and thus realising a loss immediately) or of holding on to the shares in the hope of a recovery in the share price (and thus bearing the holding costs). The UITF also argued that the benefit of any increase in the value of the shares above their option price, although ultimately passed on to the employees on exercise of their options, rests with the employer during the period that the shares are held by the ESOP trust, as they effectively hedge the employer's obligations under the share scheme.[16] In other words, if the company did not buy shares to satisfy an option until the date of exercise, it would incur a loss equal to the increase in market value of the shares between the date of grant and date of exercise of the option.

The general thrust of the above is that companies should account for the transactions of their ESOP trusts as if they had conducted them themselves; the trust is portrayed as merely an extension of the company. A possible alternative (and, in our view, preferable) approach would have been to regard the trust as a quasi-subsidiary of the company, which would therefore have been consolidated in its group accounts only. It is not entirely clear why this approach was not adopted. It may have been on the grounds that, as an ESOP trust could enter into transactions that would be illegal if entered into by a subsidiary, it could not be said that an ESOP trust 'gives rise to benefits ... not different from those that would arise were [it] a subsidiary',[17] the definition of a quasi-subsidiary.

It is more likely, however, that the reason was the purely pragmatic one that, if the company had had to treat the ESOP trust as a quasi-subsidiary, it would have had to make the disclosures required by FRS 5 in respect of quasi-subsidiaries (see Chapter 18 at 2.8), which the treatment in UITF 13 does not require. If this was indeed the reason for the UITF's approach, its generosity was misplaced, as it creates more problems than it solves. The effect that is UITF 13 must be applied at the entity, as well as the group, level (even though this is not explicitly stated in the Abstract and may not even have been fully appreciated by the UITF at the time).

I Group schemes

It is thus not entirely clear what to do in the common situation where a number of operating subsidiaries each make contributions to the trust under a group scheme. Can it be said that each of them 'has de facto control of the shares held by the ESOP trust and bears their benefits or risks'? This wording rather assumes that the employer will be a single entity which both controls the trust and is exposed to the benefits or risks of the shares held. In a group situation the parent company is likely to be the only entity that can claim to exercise any control over the ESOP trust, although the exposure to benefits and risks typically lies with each of the operating companies (since the operating companies often subsidise the cost of the scheme to the group in relation to their particular employees).

In such cases, we recommend that the ESOP trust should normally be accounted for in the accounts of the group and the parent company. The operating subsidiaries should recognise as an expense, on an accruals basis, any contributions they are required to make to the ESOP trust. The accounting treatment to be adopted by the parent company for the receipts in such cases will vary according their precise timing, and is discussed more fully in context of the examples at 2.6 below.

II Transactions within the scope of the Abstract

Another consequence of UITF 13's 'extension of the company' approach is that it requires companies to account for transactions undertaken by the ESOP trust that were probably not within the sights of the Abstract when it was first issued, as the following simple example shows.

Example 22.7: Sale of shares by ESOP trust

A company makes a gift of £1 million to its ESOP trust, which uses the cash to purchase 200,000 shares at their current market price of £5.00, which will be awarded free of charge to employees if certain performance criteria are met over the next three years. By the end of the first year it is clear that the ESOP trust has bought about 50,000 too many shares and the company's share price is £6.00. The ESOP trustees therefore take the opportunity to sell 50,000 shares for £300,000, making a profit of £50,000.

An accounting approach which focused simply on the cost to the company of the ESOP trust might well take the view that all that is required is to allocate the original payment of £1 million to appropriate periods, and that what the ESOP trust subsequently does with that £1 million is no concern of the company. However, UITF 13 requires the company to take account of the sale of the shares by the ESOP trust, even though it is almost certain that the possibility of the ESOP trust entering into such transactions was never considered by the UITF at the time that UITF 13 was issued. The accounting treatment of such transactions is discussed at H below.

III Comparison with defined pension schemes

The economics of ESOP trusts are similar to those of a defined benefits pension scheme. The employer generally has to meet any shortfall in value of the shares in the trust in the same way as it would have to meet the balance of cost necessary to provide final salary pensions, and it thus has a direct economic interest in the fund even though the scheme is operated by independent trustees. However, FRS 5 does not require the assets and liabilities of pension funds to be brought on to the balance sheets of employers, saying that: 'As SSAP 24 contains the more specific provisions on accounting for pension obligations and does not require consolidation of pension funds, such funds should not be consolidated as quasi-subsidiaries.'[18]

An Appendix to the Abstract tries to reconcile its requirements with those applying to pension schemes, saying that 'the substance of ESOP trusts is different from that of pension schemes … in that pension schemes have a longer time-frame and are wider in scope with the result that the obligations imposed by trust law and statute have a much greater commercial effect in practice'.[19] However this distinction is unconvincing and some ESOP trustees have even seen this comparison as impugning their integrity in a rather offensive way. Moreover, any such distinction between pension funds and ESOP trusts has been largely removed by the issue of FRS 17, whose broad approach to accounting for defined benefit pension schemes is similar to that of UITF 13 (see Chapter 23).

C Treatment of shares held by ESOP as assets

The normal accounting treatment of shares held by an ESOP trust in order to satisfy a share-based award is to record them as fixed assets and amortise them over them over the period in respect of which the award is being made to a residual value of zero or, if higher, the option price, as illustrated by Example 22.6 at A above.

Common practical issues are:

- determining the cost of the shares (see D below);
- determining the period over which the shares should be amortised (see E below);
- the treatment of new shares issued to the ESOP trust (see G below); and
- accounting for sales of shares by the ESOP trust (see H below).

In addition to the purely practical problems, this accounting treatment raises some difficult conceptual issues, which UITF 13 does not discuss in detail, such as:

- are shares held by an ESOP trust assets?
- if they are, are they fixed assets?
- why does the company not recognise a liability for its obligation under the award, rather than write down the cost of the shares?

These are discussed below.

I Are shares held by an ESOP trust assets?

Under FRS 4 – *Capital Instruments* – and the ASB's *Statement of Principles* a purchase of a company's own shares is a transaction with shareholders not giving rise to an increase in the assets of the company. This would suggest that the correct accounting treatment would be the so-called 'treasury stock' method, whereby the cost of the shares would be deducted from, and the option proceeds credited to, shareholders' funds. Indeed, it could be argued that the transaction in Example 22.6 above is economically the same as if the company had redeemed 1,000 shares for £1,000 partially out of the proceeds of a fresh issue of shares for £850. In such a transaction, the £150 shortfall would be charged not to the profit and loss account for the year, but to retained reserves (see Chapter 17 at 3.3.1).

However, the Companies Act balance sheet formats contain a caption 'Own shares' in both fixed and current asset investments. This means that a company wishing to adopt the approach set out in the previous paragraph in respect of shares not legally redeemed or cancelled would probably have to invoke the 'true and fair over-ride' (see Chapter 1 at 2), as has been done by Billiton in respect of shares held by a non-ESOP trust (see Extract 17.17 in Chapter 17 at 3.3.3).

After the publication of UITF 17 (see 2.5.4 below), it became apparent that UITF 13 and UITF 17 sometimes required a different cost to be recognised for what was arguably the same transaction. Accordingly, in March 1999, the UITF issued a proposal to require the cost of all share awards to be measured under the rules in UITF 17, with all market purchases of shares being accounted for under the 'treasury stock' method.[20] However, respondents showed limited enthusiasm for this proposal, and the UITF subsequently dropped the issue, leaving it to be picked up by the ASB as part of its project on accounting for equity.[21]

II Are shares held by an ESOP trust fixed assets?

UITF 13 asserts that shares held by an ESOP trust should typically be classified as fixed assets.[22] However, the Companies Act defines fixed assets as those assets 'which are intended for use on a continuing basis in the company's activities'[23]. It is hard to see how this definition can include shares which are held for the sole purpose of being transferred to employees within a short period. If, for example, a company advanced cash to an employee benefit trust in respect of the likely cost of a bonus payable in three years' time, no-one would suggest that the cash thereby becomes a fixed, rather than a current, asset. The reality is that UITF 13 has to maintain the fiction that ESOP shares are fixed assets simply in order to allow the accounting treatment set out in Example 22.6. If they were treated as current assets, they would have to be recorded at the lower of cost and net realisable value, with much more volatile recognition of their cost in the profit and loss account. For example, any difference between cost and exercise price would have to be expensed immediately, rather than over the performance period.

III Why is no liability recognised in respect of the award?

As set out above, UITF 13 recognises the cost of a share scheme by amortising the cost of the shares purchased to satisfy the award. However, a proper application of FRS 5 would arguably have led to the expense being recognised by the company accruing a liability for its obligations under the award. At the exercise of the option, the liability would have been set off against the balance of the cost of the shares not recovered from the employee under the terms of the award. This would have reflected the, in our view correct, analysis under FRS 5 that the company's obligation to the employee under the option agreement exists independently of whether or not the ESOP trust holds shares to satisfy it, and that, as a result, the liability and the shares do not satisfy the criteria for either offset or linked presentation (see Chapter 18 at 2.6 and 2.7).

The treatment under UITF 13 leads to the anomaly that, if a company makes an award of shares to employees, the liability for that award is off-balance sheet (in the sense that is reflected as a reduction in an asset), whereas if it makes an award in cash, the full liability is on balance sheet until the cash is transferred to the employee (see 2.2.2 above). In effect the accounting model under UITF 13 is a hybrid – the absence of a liability is consistent with a 'treasury stock' method, but the treatment of own shares as assets is not.

D Determining the cost of shares

The worked examples in Appendix I to UITF 13 assume a rather perfect world in which a company has its ESOP trust purchase 100 shares and then proceeds to award employees options over those shares. In practice, ESOP trusts tend to make opportunistic purchases of shares in response to market price movements, which means that there is not necessarily a perfect match between the number of shares held by the ESOP trust and the number of shares under option. The ESOP may also participate in rights issues or bonus issues. This raises the question of whether the cost of unallocated shares held by the ESOP trust should be determined on a pooled basis or some other basis, such as 'first in, first out' (FIFO). In our view, given that the shares are fungible assets, either method is acceptable.

E Period for recognising cost of share award

A particularly confusing aspect of UITF 13 is the determination of the period over which shares held by an ESOP trust should be amortised, largely because UITF 13's guidance is ambiguous.

Paragraph 8(d) of the Abstract states that the cost should be amortised 'over the period of service of the employees in respect of which the gifts or options are granted'. In some share schemes, particularly long-term incentive plans (LTIPs), an employee becomes entitled to an award only after certain performance criteria have been satisfied (generally over a three year period) and some further period (a 'loyalty period') of employment has been completed. Quite often the award lapses in whole or in part if the loyalty period (generally at least two years) is not completed. As a matter of natural construction, therefore, the period of service would seem to be the total of the performance period and the loyalty period.

However, paragraph 6 of UITF 13 states that the period of service 'will generally be the earlier of

- the end of the period of service of the employee to which the gift or discount relates; and
- the first date that the gift becomes unconditional or the option can be exercised',

implying that the cost should be written off over the initial performance period only. That this is the real intention of UITF 13 is confirmed by Example 5 in Appendix II, which describes a scenario where shares are transferred to a profit-sharing trust to be distributed to employees in satisfaction of a profit-sharing scheme award for the current year.[24] It concludes that the cost of the shares should be recognised immediately, in particular noting:

> 'If the entitlement will lapse in the event that the employees do not remain with the company for a specified period, the shares do not yet belong to the employees but the residual value of the shares should be taken as nil. It is likely that the resulting charge should be recognised immediately rather than being spread over the period to vesting, since the bonus is a share of profit for the year ... .'

The argument essentially seems to be that the shares are awarded to reward the extra efforts needed for achievement of the performance criteria in the initial performance period, rather than (in effect) simply turning up for work in the loyalty period. The cost of the award should, on this basis, be matched with the profits earned in the performance period. We support this analysis, but suggest that it further highlights our general criticism of UITF 13 – that is addressing what is really an issue of expense allocation as a question of asset recognition.

Some clarification of the position is given in UITF 17, which also applies to shares awards satisfied using shares held by ESOP trusts. UITF 17 is much more explicit that the cost of a share award should normally be recognised over the performance period, rather than the loyalty period (see 2.5.4 B below). The method of allocating the cost of shares to individual accounting periods is also dealt with in UITF 17 (see 2.5.4 C below).

It is important, however, to note that paragraph 8(a) of UITF 13 (see A above) requires shares held by the ESOP trust to be recognised as assets of the company 'until such time as ... [they] vest *unconditionally* in employees' (emphasis added). This means that, even though shares held by an ESOP trust are generally to be amortised over the performance period only, they remain on the balance sheet until employees have become fully entitled to them. For example, where shares are to be gifted to employees, and have therefore been amortized to zero, the notes to the accounts will still continue to show the cost and cumulative amortisation for the shares until they have been vested unconditionally in employees. This is apparently illustrated by the following extract from the accounts of Express Dairies, which shows the derecognition of fully amortised own shares.

Extract 22.1: Express Diaries plc (2001)

13. Investments [extract]

Group	Listed £m	Unlisted £m	Total £m
Cost:			
At 1 April 2000	2.6	0.3	2.9
Additions	–	3.0	3.0
Disposals	(0.3)	–	(0.3)
At 31 March 2001	2.3	3.3	5.6
Amortisation:			
At 1 April 2000	1.6	–	1.6
Charge for the year	0.3	–	0.3
Disposals	(0.3)	–	(0.3)
At 31 March 2001	1.6	–	1.6
Net book amounts:			
At 31 March 2001	0.7	3.3	4.0
At 1 April 2000	1.0	0.3	1.3

The listed investment represents 1,393,444 (2000: 1,640,011) own shares with a normal value of 2p each held by Ogier Trustees Limited. The market value of the investment at 31 March 2001 was £0.6m (2000: £1.4m). The shares are held on behalf of the group LTIP, details of which are disclosed in the remuneration report. Dividends on the shares are waived. All expenses incurred by the trust are settled directly by the group and charged in the accounts as they arise. The directors consider that the book value of the unlisted investments approximates to market value.

In practice, however, the treatment of loyalty periods is becoming slightly less of an issue than it was when UITF 13 was first published, as fewer schemes now include such a period.

F *Permanent diminutions in value of shares held ESOP trust*

UITF 13 requires any permanent diminution in value of the company's shares to be recognised immediately, which, in our view, exposes yet another flaw in the treatment of ESOP shares as fixed assets. If the shares are considered purely as fixed assets, they suffer a permanent diminution in value the moment that they are put under option at a price lower than cost, no less than if the share price falls. Yet a permanent diminution arising from the granting of options is spread, and one arising from market price changes is recognised immediately. If the whole issue were treated as one of expense recognition there might be no particular reason to write down the unallocated shares immediately.

G *New shares issued to the ESOP trust*

UITF 13 is written in the implied context that the shares held by the ESOP trust are obtained through market purchase. However, it is very common for companies to satisfy share awards by the issue of fresh shares. For tax reasons, these might be issued to the ESOP trust (or QUEST or similar vehicle) some time in advance of their being required. The funds for the shares will typically be provided by a contribution from the employing subsidiary or a loan from the parent company or both. There are differing views as to how such shares should be accounted for, as illustrated in the example below.

Example 22.8: Newly issued shares held by ESOP trust

A company grants an employee an option to purchase 100 5p shares in the company at £2 each in three years' time. On the same day it lends £200 to its ESOP trust which uses the funds to subscribe for 100 new shares at £2 each. How should the company account for this share issue?

Some believe that the shares should be shown as an asset carried at £2 (i.e. the option strike price) with provision being made against that carrying amount if necessary (e.g. if the company's share price fell such that it was unlikely that an option at £2 would be exercised).

However, if, as is asserted by UITF 13, the ESOP trust is for accounting purposes part of the company, this transaction is internal to the company and results in no increase in its net assets or shareholders' funds. Accordingly we believe that net assets and shareholders' funds should not be increased as the result of such a transaction. As a matter of law, however, new shares have been issued and there is therefore a need to credit share capital and the share premium account with £200. As the overall increase in shareholders' funds is nil, the corresponding debit must be to another reserve within shareholders' funds, such as the profit and loss reserve.

On this view, when the employee exercises his option, the proceeds of £200 should be credited to shareholders' funds, since it is at that point that the shares have been issued from a true economic perspective. However, since, as noted above, the legal issue of shares has already been recorded, the proceeds should be credited not to share capital and the share premium account, but to another reserve within shareholders' funds, such as the profit and loss reserve. This treatment is illustrated in Examples 22.14 and 22.15 at 2.5.4 D below.

In practice, however, both treatments can be seen. An example of a company treating issues of shares to share trusts as not giving rise to an increase in net assets is Vodafone.

Extract 22.2: Vodafone Group Plc (2000)

19 Called up share capital [extract]

In February 1998, the Company established a Qualifying Employee Share Ownership Trust ('QUEST') to operate in connection with the Company's Savings Related Share Option Scheme. The trustee of the QUEST is Vodafone Group Share Trustee Limited, a wholly owned subsidiary of the Company. At 31 March 2001 the trustee held 5,861,959 Vodafone Group ordinary shares. No shares had been issued to the trustee during the year. The market value at 31 March 2001 for the total shareholding of the trustee was £11m. The dividend rights in respect of these shares have been waived. During the year 6,670,405 shares had been transferred to option holders exercising options under the Savings Related Share Option Scheme.

In July 1998, the Company established an Employee Benefit Trust ('EBT') to operate in connection with the Company's Savings Related Share Option Scheme and the executive share schemes. The trustee of the EBT is Vodafone Group Share Schemes Trustee Limited, a wholly owned subsidiary of the Company. A total of 874,656 new ordinary shares have been allotted for use by the EBT during the year, all of which have been transferred to employees exercising options under the relevant share option schemes,

The proceeds of share issues which have not been issued to parties outside the Group have been shown as deductions from the Group profit and loss account reserves.

An example of a company treating newly issued shares as fixed assets Tesco.[25]

> *Extract 22.3: Tesco PLC (2001)*
>
> **NOTE 13 Fixed asset investments** [extract]
>
> c The investment in own shares represents 70 million 5p ordinary shares in Tesco PLC with a weighted average value of £1.44 each. These shares are held by a qualifying employee share trust (QUEST) in order to satisfy options under savings-related share option schemes which become exercisable over the next few years. The carrying value of £101m (market value £190m) represents the exercise amount receivable in respect of these share subscribed for by the QUEST at market value. Funding is provided to the QUEST by Tesco Stores Limited the company's principal operating subsidiary. The QUEST has waived its rights to dividends on these shares.

This treatment does, however, come at a price since any subsequent write-down in shares treated as assets must be made through the profit and loss account, whereas no such charge to earnings would occur if, as under the treatment adopted by Vodafone, the shares had never been recorded as an asset in the first place.

H Sales of shares by ESOP trust

As noted above, it is not uncommon for ESOP trusts to sell shares in the sponsoring company and other assets held by them, and the question arises as to how such transactions should be reflected in the accounts of the sponsoring company. Similar issues arise when the option proceeds for particular shares exceed their original cost.

Where assets of the ESOP trust are accounted for as assets of the sponsoring company, any profit or loss on their disposal (whether through market sale, or on exercise of employee options) should, in our view, be accounted for like that on disposal of any other asset of the company. There may be some understandable reluctance to allow a company to recognise a profit from (in effect) trading in its own shares. We have considerable sympathy with this view, but it would be inconsistent with the treatment of the shares as assets required by UITF 13 not to recognise a profit. If, instead, they were treated as treasury stock, all disposal proceeds (whether arising through market sale or exercise of options) would be credited to shareholders' funds, an arguably more satisfactory result.

The UITF clearly has concerns about this issue since, in announcing its intention to abandon its proposal to move to a 'treasury stock' method (see 2.5.3 C I above), it noted that the treatment as an asset of an investment in a company's own share implies that a sale of the shares other than at book value gives rise to a profit or loss. Because of the 'special nature' of such profits or losses, they should be clearly disclosed if material, as required by FRS 3.[26]

However, where the shares concerned are shares freshly issued to the ESOP trust, we think it is inappropriate to record the difference between the amount subscribed by the ESOP trust and the amount at which they are sold as a profit. This is based on the view that, under FRS 4, such a difference represents – economically, though not legally – additional share proceeds, which should therefore be credited direct to shareholders' funds. This further supports the argument, we suggest, that such shares should not be treated as assets at all (see Example 22.8 above).

There may also be some concern as to whether it is appropriate to regard as a realised profit a gain represented by assets held by an ESOP trust which cannot be readily accessed by the company. However, provided that those assets are fully recoverable (i.e. through a reduction in the future cost of share options), there is no reason in our view not to regard such a profit as realised.

I ESOP trust funded by external borrowings

As an alternative to being funded by the sponsoring company, an ESOP trust may borrow externally. UITF 13 notes that in such cases the company will generally guarantee the external borrowings,[27] such that the company is in the same position as if it had borrowed the funds directly. In such cases, the company should, in accordance with FRS 5, account for the ESOP trust's borrowings (and the related assets) as its own.

J Dividends on ESOP shares

In practice, the trustees of an ESOP trust will often waive their right to dividends of shares held by the ESOP trust. Where such dividends are paid, UITF 13 requires the income received by the ESOP trust to be excluded from pre-tax profit and accounted for as a deduction from the aggregate of dividends paid and proposed. The deduction should be disclosed on the face of the profit and loss account, if material, or in a note.

This treatment could be seen as analogous to a the elimination of intra-group transactions in consolidated accounts on the basis that, as the ESOP trust is considered an extension of the company, any dividend paid on shares held by an ESOP is internal to the company. However, it seems rather inconsistent with UITF 13's requirement to treat shares held by an ESOP trust as fixed assets. If they are indeed fixed assets, income received from them should be arguably treated no differently than that from other fixed asset investments. The inconsistency probably arises from the fact that this requirement was inserted by FRS 14 – *Earnings per Share*, which treats shares held by an ESOP trust as 'treasury stock' rather than fixed assets. FRS 14 is in all material respects a copy of IAS and US GAAP, under which an investment in own shares would be accounted for under the 'treasury stock' method, and it would be consistent with that method to treat dividends on those shares as a deduction from total dividends. The more general requirements of FRS 14 for the treatment of shares held by ESOP trusts in calculating earnings per share are discussed further in Chapter 26 at 3 and 6.5.4.

K Disclosure

UITF 13 requires disclosure of sufficient information to enable readers of the accounts to understand the significance of the ESOP trust in the context of the sponsoring company, and in particular:

(a) a description of the main features of the ESOP trust including the arrangements for distributing shares to employees;

(b) the manner in which the costs are dealt with in the profit and loss account;

(c) the number and market value of shares held by the ESOP trust and whether dividends on those shares have been waived; and

(d) the extent to which these shares are under option to employees, or have been conditionally gifted to them.[28]

The accounts of BOC disclose the following information about the shares that are held in its ESOP trust:

Extract 22.4: The BOC Group plc (2000)

9. Fixed assets – investments [extract]

a) Group	Own shares at cost £million
At 1 October 1999	30.8
Acquisitions/additions	30.4
Disposals	(0.7)
At 30 September 2000	**60.5**

ii) Own shares

For share-based incentive schemes which do not use new issue shares, options are satisfied by the transfer of shares held in trust for the purpose. At 30 September 2000, options over 6.4 million shares were outstanding under these schemes, for which 6.5 million shares in the Company were held pending exercise.

Loans and advances for the purchase of shares in trust have been made either by the company or its subsidiaries. If the value of shares in trust is insufficient to cover the loans, the company and subsidiaries will bear any loss. The company also bears administrative costs on an accruals basis.

Based on the Company's share price on 30 September 2000 of 895p, the market value of own shares held in trust was £58.4 million. This compares with the acquisition cost shown above.

Own shares are shown as fixed asset investments for accounting purposes, in accordance with FRS 5 and UITF Abstract 13.

L *Application of UITF 13 principles to other entities*

It became apparent relatively soon after the issue of UITF 13 that companies were taking the view that it did not apply to ESOP trusts (or similar entities) that did not operate exactly in accordance with the generic description of an ESOP trust in UITF 13, even though the differences might in some cases be relatively minor. Accordingly in June 1998 the UITF clarified that UITF 13 was intended to be applied not only to ESOP trusts as described in UITF 13, but in 'analogous circumstances'.[29]

This position was broadly maintained for some time. However, during 2001 it came to the UITF's attention that some companies were not applying UITF 13 to certain discretionary trusts, in which the trustees are given unfettered powers to dispose of the assets as they see fit (although there is generally an 'understanding' that they will in fact use them to make payments to employees based on recommendations by the company). The argument was apparently that, whereas the assets of an ESOP trust or employee benefit trust can as a matter of law be used only to defray employee costs that would otherwise be borne by the company (and are, to that extent, assets of the company), the assets of a discretionary trust can be used for any purpose the trustees might choose. On this view, a discretionary trust is not under the 'de facto control' of the donor company and therefore outside the scope of UITF 13. The main practical effect of this view would be that any amount paid to a discretionary trust would be an expense, not an asset, of the company, thus potentially allowing tax relief to be obtained on any payment to the trust.

This argument is clearly somewhat disingenuous. If the directors of a company give £1 million to a trust in the genuine belief that they have no influence over what happens to that money, they are arguably in breach of their fiduciary duties no less than if they draw £1 million out of the bank in used notes and leave them in the street with a sign saying 'Please take one'. In reality, the directors make such donations in the near certain belief that the trustees will dispose of the assets according to the company's wishes.

In response to this, in July 2001 the UITF issued for comment a draft Abstract *Employee benefit trusts and other intermediate payment arrangements* to address this issue. It essentially states that where a company makes a payment for goods or services through an intermediate payment vehicle 'IPV' (such as an EBT) the company should account for the assets and liabilities of the IPV as its own where it has de facto control over it. It states that, even where the IPV is a discretionary trust, the company may still have de facto control if there is minimal risk in practice that the IPV will act otherwise than in accordance with the company's wishes. It notes that, in the case of an already established IPV, the fact that the trustees have thus far exercised their discretionary powers only in accordance with the company's wishes would be evidence that this is the case.[30] It follows from this approach that a company would not necessarily account for the transfer of cash or other assets to the IPV as an expense. An expense would be recognised only on the earlier of the company incurring a liability (e.g. by announcing a bonus to employees) or the IPV itself incurring a liability, or making a payment, to employees.

2.5.4 *UITF 17*

UITF 17 – *Employee share schemes* was issued in May 1997 and revised in October 2000. It deals with awards of shares or rights to shares (whether conditional or otherwise and whether provided directly or through convertible or other exchangeable instruments).[31] Typically such 'rights to shares' will be in the form of options. Save As You Earn ('SAYE') schemes and similar overseas schemes are exempt from the requirements of UITF 17 (see E below). The initial impetus for the issue of UITF 17 was to deal with the fact that UITF 13 was implicitly written on the assumption that share-based awards are made using shares purchased in the market whereas in many cases a fresh issue of shares is used. Moreover, a number of schemes had been devised which were seen as an abuse of UITF 13, as illustrated by the following example.

Example 22.9: 'Abuse' of UITF 13 using fresh issue of shares

A company grants options to a director to purchase 100 shares at £2 each, the current market price being £3. The company advances £200 to its EBT which the EBT uses to subscribe for 100 shares at £2. The company recognises those shares as an asset at £200. When the director exercises his options, the company offsets the £200 proceeds against the carrying value of the shares. If instead the company had bought the shares in the market on the date of grant it would have made a loss of £100 (£200 option proceeds less cost of shares £300).

The detailed requirements of UITF 17 are discussed below, but it essentially says that the total amount charged to the profit and loss account in such circumstances should calculated by reference to the fair value of the shares at the time the right to the shares is granted to the employee (less any amount payable by the employee).[32] Thus, in the example above, the profit and loss account charge would be £100, irrespective of whether the award is made using existing shares or a fresh issue.

Unfortunately, it is far from clear on the basis of what accounting standard this conclusion was reached. It seems to have originated from a knee-jerk presumption that the two transactions in Example 22.9 must give rise to the same cost, notwithstanding that, at least in cash flow terms, they are totally different. A market purchase of shares entails a real cash outflow of £100 to the company; a fresh issue of shares does not (since cash goes in a predetermined circle from the company to the share trust and back again). A fresh issue of shares at a discount to prevailing market price obviously entails a cost to the existing shareholders (since the holder of the new shares will participate equally with other shareholders in future earnings despite having contributed relatively less to the company's assets), but there seems no particular reason to reflect this in the accounts of the *company*, any more than one would try to capture in the accounts of the company the transfer of value from one group of shareholders to another that occurs in certain rights issues.

In our view, the most convincing case for the accounting treatment required by UITF 17 is made by FRS 4 – *Capital Instruments* (which is discussed in detail in Chapter 17), even though this is, somewhat ironically, not cited as a relevant source in UITF 17 itself. A possible analysis under FRS 4 would be that the employing company has issued a capital instrument (shares or options over shares). This must be recorded at the fair value of its issue proceeds, being the value of the services to be provided by the employee (which, to the extent that they do not meet the criteria for recognition as an asset, are expensed) together with any cash payments. This is broadly the analysis in the G4+1 group's discussion paper on share-based payments (see 4 below). However, this is a far from perfect analogy, since for example:

- a strict application of FRS 4 would require the total credit to shareholders' funds to be recognised at the date of award, together with corresponding asset (services to be rendered), which would be expensed over the performance period, whereas UITF 17 in fact requires the credit to shareholders' funds to be built up as services are rendered (see B to D below);
- in cases where the employee is not required to make any contribution, the award is arguably not a capital instrument as defined by FRS 4 (since it is not a 'means of raising finance' – see Chapter 17 at 2.2.1),[33] and therefore outside the scope of FRS 4.

A Calculation of the cost of a share award

The basic rule in UITF 17 is that cost of an award of shares or rights to shares (including options) should be recognised at the fair value of the shares at the date of award. This is to be taken, as a minimum, to be the difference between:

(i) either:

  (1) the fair value of the shares at the date the award is made to participants in the scheme; or

  (2) where purchases of shares have been made by an ESOP trust at fair value and reflected in the company's balance sheet in accordance with UITF 13 or have been revalued, the book value of shares that are available for the award; and

(ii) the amount of the consideration, if any, that participants may be required to pay for the shares.[34]

A simple example of the treatment required is given below.

Example 22.10: Cost of award under UITF 17

As in Example 22.9 above, a company grants options to a director to purchase 100 shares at £2 each, the current market price being £3.

If the award is to be satisfied by the use of a fresh issue of shares to the ESOP, the company will charge its profit and loss account with £100, being the difference between the fair value of the shares at the date of the award (£300) and the amount to be paid by the director in exercise of the option (£200).

If the award is to be satisfied by shares already held by the ESOP that were purchased in the market at fair value, the cost would be based on the difference between the cost of those shares and £200, which could be greater or less than £100.

If the award is to be satisfied by shares already held by the ESOP, but not purchased at fair value (e.g. by subscription for a fresh issue of shares at nominal value), a charge of £100 would be made.

In all cases, the period over which the relevant charge is made will depend on the various criteria discussed in B and C below. The detailed accounting entries are discussed in more detail at D below.

The charge required by UITF 17 is based on the so-called 'intrinsic value' of an option (i.e. the difference between the market value and option price at the date of grant). This means that there is no charge under UITF 17 in respect of options granted at market price at the date of grant (unless the award is satisfied using shares bought in the market at a higher price).

UITF 17 describes this charge as a 'minimum amount', as it does not reflect the time value of the options or any potential changes in its value arising from share price movements after the date of initial award, which would be taken into account under the proposals for accounting for share-based payments in the G4+1 discussion paper (see 4 below). The intention of UITF 17 is to allow companies to charge a fair value greater than intrinsic value if they so wish, although in our experience companies never do so.

It will be seen that UITF 17 applies also to the amortisation of shares held by ESOP trusts accounted for under UITF13 (see 2.5.3 above). The effect of the rule in UITF 17 is that there will be no difference between the profit and loss charge for a share based award using existing shares and one using a fresh issue of shares, provided that, where existing shares are used, they are purchased on the day that the award is made. If they are not purchased until a later date, the profit and loss account will bear (through a higher or lower UITF 13 amortisation charge) the increase or decrease in the market value of the shares between the date of the award and the date of purchase. By contrast, where a fresh issue of shares is made at market value using funds provided from the company, the increase is charged to reserves (see Example 22.8 at 2.5.3 G above, Examples 22.14 and 22.15 at D below and Example 22.21 at 2.6.3 below).

Some see this as penalising companies that wish to make awards using existing shares. The argument is that, although using existing shares is often in the best interests of current shareholders (because it involves no dilution of their interests), companies are deterred from doing so by the fact that they either have to bear the cost of holding shares and share price risk from the date of award, or suffer a higher charge in the profit and loss account as described above. Boots voices these concerns in the following extract, although the specific accounting difference referred to is more due to the arguably arbitrary exemption for SAYE schemes in UITF 17 (see E below) than to the overall approach of UITF 17 versus that of UITF 13.

Extract 22.5: The Boots Company PLC (2000)

Financial Review [extract]

QUEST The QUEST was established by the company in 1999 in connection with its existing SAYE share scheme, which is open to all UK employees. The QUEST enables the company to use existing shares to satisfy options. This is more tax efficient than issuing new shares, and avoids diluting existing shareholdings.

However, using existing shares requires the cost of the SAYE scheme to be charged against profits. If new shares are used a charge against profits is avoided. Most other companies therefore issue new shares. Accounting standards are gradually moving towards ending this anomaly.

The QUEST has bought in the market 5.7m shares (1999 16.9m) at an average price of 783p (1999 909p) to satisfy options granted during the year (the 1999 purchase covered options granted that year and all the outstanding options relating to prior years). The purchase of shares resulted in a charge to operating profit of £9.8m that has been charged to the businesses (1999 £59.7m to establish the QUEST was treated as an exceptional item at the group level). These costs are the difference between the market value of the shares bought by the QUEST and the option price payable by employees. In addition interest of £6.8m on borrowings to finance the shares in the QUEST has also been charged to the business.

B Period over which cost of award is recognised

Under UITF 17 the normal treatment is to spread the cost of share awards over the performance period only, and not any subsequent loyalty period (see 2.5.3 E above for further discussion of loyalty periods). The Abstract states:

> 'Long-term incentive schemes are intended to reward participants for their services over the period to which the performance criteria relate. In order to reflect this, the amount recognised should be spread over this period. Where a further period of continued employment is required before the participants become unconditionally entitled to the shares, the period over which the cost is recognised should not normally include that period unless it is clear that the effect of the scheme is to reward services over the longer period.'[35]

A simple illustration of the accounting treatment required is given in the example below:

Example 22.11: Period for recognition of cost of share scheme (1)

As in Example 22.9 above, a company grants options to a director to purchase 100 shares at £2 each, the current market price being £3. The award will be satisfied by new shares subscribed for by the ESOP trust, and will therefore give rise to a total charge under UITF 17 of £100 (see Example 22.10 at A above).

The terms of the award are that certain profit targets must be met for each of the current and the two following periods. If these criteria are met, the director will be entitled to exercise the options if he remains in employment for a further two years.

Assuming that the performance criteria are satisfied, UITF 17 requires the total cost of £100 to be amortised at £33.33 per year over the three years of the performance period. The detailed accounting entries are discussed in more detail at C and D below.

UITF 13 and UITF 17 state that this is the treatment that should 'generally' or 'normally' be adopted, implying that there are some exceptions. Notwithstanding these clarifications, however, it is not always clear how these rules should be applied in practice, as Example 22.12 below illustrates.

Example 22.12: Period for recognition of cost of share scheme (2)

A company grants employees options over 1,000 shares subject to certain performance criteria being met over the next three years. Before exercising their options, employees must remain with the company for an additional two years. If they do stay and exercise their options, however, the company will give them one share free for every share bought under option. Such an incentive is often referred to as a BOGOF, an acronym for 'buy one, get one free'. On the assumption that all 2,000 shares are eventually awarded to employees, over what period should their cost be recognised?

One approach would be to say that, notwithstanding the form of the offer to employees, the substance is that the company has really granted options over 2,000, not 1,000, shares and that the cost of all 2,000 shares should therefore be recognised in the same way. This would lead to the conclusion that the cost of all 2,000 shares should be recognised over the initial 3-year performance period, as in Example 22.11 above.

However, it could also be argued that that the BOGOF shares are an additional 'sweetener', beyond what would be offered in a normal share scheme, specifically designed to give employees an incentive to remain with the company beyond the end of the 3-year performance period. This could lead to the view that, in the words of UITF 17, 'it is clear that the effect of the scheme is to reward services over the longer period', which would allow recognition of the cost over the full 5-year period. The problem with this approach, however, is that it recognises the total cost of the scheme over a longer period than would have been the case if no BOGOF shares had been offered. Arguably, it is only the incremental cost as a result of the BOGOF scheme (i.e. the cost of shares awarded to employees who would have left during the 2-year loyalty period but for the existence of the BOGOF scheme) that should be recognised over that longer period, although this might be very difficult to quantify in practice.

An approximation of such an approach, however, would be to say that the 'basic' 1,000 shares and the 1,000 BOGOF shares should be considered separately, on the basis that the 'basic' shares are to reward performance over the 3 year period and the BOGOF shares to encourage employee retention. On this view, the cost of the 'basic' shares would be recognised over the 3-year performance period and that of the BOGOF shares over the full 5-year period. Some might argue that the cost of the BOGOF shares should be recognised over the 2-year loyalty period, but in our view this is not appropriate since it implies that the award of these shares is totally unrelated to the 3-year performance period, which is clearly not the case.

Sometimes share-based awards are made with no performance criteria (e.g. on flotation of a company). Paragraph 15 of UITF 17 states that, where an award is made subject to no performance criteria and the award is clearly unrelated to past performance, the cost should be recognised over the period from the date of the award to the date at which the employee becomes unconditionally entitled to the shares.[36] It is not entirely obvious how this is to be interpreted in practice, and the examples in UITF 13 and UITF 17 are not always clear.

For instance, Example 6 in Appendix II to UITF 13 describes a situation in which shares are awarded to key employees in connection with a flotation, which will vest provided that the employees remain with the company for three years after the flotation, and concludes that the cost of those shares should be recognised over the three year period. In our view, this is the appropriate treatment, but it is not altogether clear that it conforms to UITF 17, which requires this treatment only for an award that is 'clearly unrelated to past performance'. In the example under discussion, the award is made to lock in 'key employees', a description that implies that their past performance has at least some bearing on the award. This could be construed as meaning that this situation does not fall within paragraph 15 of UITF 17 and that the cost of the shares should be therefore recognised immediately.

Unfortunately, UITF 13 is somewhat vague in describing the award, saying that it is made 'in connection with' a flotation, leaving it open as a matter of interpretation as to whether this means that:

- in the run-up to the flotation, the employees were granted options exercisable if flotation was achieved (which might suggest immediate recognition of the cost on flotation, since the performance criterion – i.e. flotation – has been achieved); or
- on flotation, the company made an ex-gratia award to employees (which would more naturally lead to the conclusion in Example 6).

Further guidance on the treatment of a share award made in anticipation of a flotation or trade sale is given in UITF 30 (see 2.5.6 below). Determination of 'the date of award' (i.e. the start of the amortisation period) can also sometimes give rise to questions of interpretation, which are also addressed in UITF 30.

C *Allocation of cost of share award to individual accounting periods*

As well as determining the total period over which the cost of a share-based award is to be allocated, there is also the issue of allocating that total cost to individual accounting periods, the basic principle of which is illustrated in Example 22.6 at 2.5.3 A above and Example 22.11 at B above. In reality, however, things are more complicated since a company will not typically know the cost of a share-based award until the shares have been finally delivered to employees. This is because the final cost depends on a number of variable factors, such as the extent to which any variable performance criteria have been satisfied and the number of employees ultimately eligible for an award.

UITF 17 requires that the amount initially recognised should be based on a reasonable expectation of the extent that performance criteria will be met. That amount should be charged in the profit and loss account on a straight line basis (or another basis that more fairly reflects the services received) over the performance period, subject to subsequent adjustments as necessary to deal with changes in the probability of performance criteria being met, conditional awards lapsing or purchases of shares at different prices.[37] The mechanics of such adjustments are illustrated by Example 22.13 below. The accounting entries required are discussed at D below.

Example 22.13: Annual cost of share award

On 1 January 2001 a company grants options to 1,500 employees to acquire shares for £4 a share. The number of shares over which options may be exercised varies according to the company's position in a ranking of 100 companies, including the company, according to the growth in their total shareholder return (TSR) over the next three years, as follows.

Position in ranking	Number of options
1-25	1,000
26-50	750
51-75	0
76-100	0

Options may be exercised only if employees remain with the company for two years after the end of the performance period. On 1 January 2001 the ESOP trust buys £1,000,000 shares at £5 each, which the company recognises as a fixed asset of £5,000,000. For each share over which an option is exercised there will be a cost of £1 (i.e. £5 purchase price less £4 option exercise price).

The company has a 31 December year end. When preparing accounts for the years ended 31 December 2001 to 2003 it takes the view that it is likely that it will ultimately have to satisfy options over shares as follows.

	Options per employee	Number of employees	Total shares
2001	1,000	800	800,000
2002	750	700	525,000
2003	1,000	750	750,000

In 2001 the company assumes a total final cost of £800,000. As the cost of the scheme is to be recognised over the 3-year performance period, there is a profit and loss account charge of £800,000/3, i.e. £266,667.

In 2002 the company assumes a total final cost of £525,000. As the cost of the scheme is to be recognised over a 3-year performance period, the cumulative amount that should have been charged to the profit and loss account is £525,000 x 2/3, i.e. £350,000. £266,667 has already been charged in 2001, so the additional charge required in 2002 is £83,333.

In 2003 the company assumes a total final cost of £750,000. £350,000 has already been charged in 2001 and 2002, so the additional charge required in 2002 is £400,000.

This methodology is recommended, but not mandated, by the Appendix to UITF 17.

One issue not dealt with in Example 22.13 above is the treatment of changes to the final cost of the scheme arising from employees leaving during the loyalty period. Suppose for instance that 100 employees eligible for options left the company during 2005, with the result that the company would have to deliver only 650,000 shares. Practice in this area is difficult to deduce from published accounts and is probably varied.

One approach might be to say that an adjustment should be made to credit the profit and loss account, and increase the carrying value of the ESOP shares, by £100,000. Another approach might be to make no adjustment on the basis that the ESOP shares are fixed assets and FRS 15 requires (albeit in the context of tangible fixed assets rather than investments) that adjustments to depreciation should be recognised prospectively and that no adjustment should be made to what turns out with hindsight to have been over-enthusiastic depreciation. A counter-argument to this, however, would be that this is not an adjustment to amortisation, but more analogous to the reversal of a provision for permanent diminution in value that is no longer required. For all these reasons, we believe that no one of these approaches is either forbidden or required. However, a company should apply a consistent policy in such circumstances.

D Accounting entries required by UITF 17

The discussion so far has focused on the debit entry (i.e. the profit and loss account charge) required by UITF 17. The credit entry will depend on how the award is to be satisfied. If the award is to be made using shares purchased in the market by an ESOP trust (as was the case in Example 22.13 above), the credit will be to the carrying amount of investments in own shares.

If shares issued to the ESOP trust by the company are to be used, UITF 17 argues that, as the reporting entity has issued an equity instrument (a share option), the credit entry is to shareholders' funds and is not reported in the statement of total recognised gains and losses.[38] The basis for this accounting entry is in fact slightly questionable. Both FRS 4 and the Companies Act require the proceeds of an issue of shares to be recorded at the fair value of the consideration received[39]. In principle, this means that the value of the services rendered by the employee should be determined and that value attributed to the shares issued, rather than the converse position required by UITF 17, whereby the services are effectively valued by reference to the shares given for them. The controversy surrounding a number of share awards suggests that the two are not necessarily the same.

The UITF was advised that, for the purposes of determining the amount of any premium arising on issue of the shares under section 130 of the Companies Act 1985, the consideration for the issue of the shares could normally be taken as being only the amount of cash subscribed for the shares (whether by the employee at exercise date or by the company's ESOP, or similar entity, at an earlier date). This means that the credit corresponding to the UITF 17 charge is credited not to share capital and share premium but to another reserve, generally the profit and loss reserve.

The accounting treatment for the share issue itself will depend on whether the option proceeds are legally part of the consideration for the issue of the shares awarded or, as is more often the case, simply exchanged for shares already issued to the ESOP trust (or similar entity) by the company. The required accounting treatments required in each case are illustrated in Examples 22.14 and 21.15 below.

Example 22.14: Share award using freshly issued shares issued at exercise date

During 2001 a company grants a new key employee an option (on unusually favourable terms) exercisable on 31 March 2002 at £1.60 over 1,000 50p shares as part of an annual bonus for performance during 2001. The market price on the date of grant is £2.00. The performance criteria are achieved, and the option is exercised. The option proceeds are used to subscribe for newly issued shares.

The UITF 17 charge is £400 (1,000 shares x £[2.00-1.60]), and the accounting entry (in the 2001 accounts) is:

	£	£
Profit and loss account (employee costs)	400	
Profit and loss reserve (shareholders' funds)		400

The issue of shares is shown in the 2002 accounts as:

	£	£
Cash (option proceeds from employee)	1,600	
Share capital		500
Share premium		1,100

Example 22.15: Share award using freshly issued shares issued before exercise date

The facts are the same as in Example 22.14 above, except that on 1 June 2001 the company lends £500 to its ESOP trust, which uses it to subscribe for 1,000 shares in the company at par. On exercise of the option in March 2002, the employee pays £1,600 to the ESOP trust which delivers the shares to the employee. The UITF 17 charge in 2001 remains £400 as in Example 22.14 above. However, the 2001 accounts must deal with the issue of shares, which using the basis of accounting described in Example 22.8 at 2.5.3 G above, would be reflected as:

	£	£
Profit and loss reserve (shareholders' funds)	500	
Share capital		500

When the option proceeds are received from the employee in 2002, the accounting entry is:

Cash	1,600	
Profit and loss reserve (shareholders' funds)		1,600

Further complications may arise if a company grants an option or awards shares to an employee with the initial expectation that it will be satisfied by a fresh issue of shares, but later decides to use shares purchased in the market. This is touched on by the Appendix to UITF 17, which does not, however, deal with the specific accounting entries required. These are discussed in Example 22.16 (which is based on the Appendix to UITF 17).

Example 22.16: Switch from fresh issue to market purchase

A company awards its employees a conditional LTIP award of up to 1,000 shares (with a nominal value of 10p each) on 1 January 2001, when the market price of the shares is £5. The maximum number of shares will be transferred to participants after three years, provided that various performance targets are fully met. A lesser number of shares will be transferred if the targets are only partially met. Participants make no contribution for any shares transferred to them.

When the accounts for the year ended 31 December 2001 are being finalised it is considered that 50% of the maximum number of shares is likely to be awarded and that a fresh issue of shares will be used for the purpose. This estimate is re-assessed at 80% for the 2002 accounts. In June 2002 the company's ESOP has an opportunity to purchase of 1,000 shares at £4.50 per share, and it is decided to use these shares to satisfy the award.

For the purposes of the 2001 accounts, the UITF 17 charge is based on £5 per share (the market price at the date of the award less the employees' contribution of nil). The total expected charge is therefore £5 x 1,000 x 50% = £2,500 of which one third i.e. £833 is charged in the 2001 accounts, the entry being DR Profit and loss account, CR Profit and loss reserve (as above).

In June 2002, the ESOP trust purchases 1,000 shares for £4,500. The purchase is accounted for under UITF 13 as simply:

	£	£
Investment in own shares	4,500	
Cash		4,500

When the accounts for 2002 are prepared, this carrying value of the shares poses something of a conundrum. The cumulative charge to the profit and loss account by the end of 2002 should clearly be £4.50 x 1,000 x 80% x 2/3 = £2,400, implying a charge for the year of £1,567 (£2,400 less the £833 charged in 2001). However, the investment in own shares needs to be written down by the full £2,400, to reflect the fact 800 of the shares have been two-thirds amortised. Mechanically speaking, this has to be achieved with the following accounting entry:

	£	£
Profit and loss account (employee costs)	1,567	
Profit and loss reserve	833	
Investment in own shares		2,400

However, how can this entry be justified, as it seems to involve 'amortising' a fixed asset direct to reserves, contrary to the Companies Act and (although not directly applicable) FRS 10 and FRS 15?

A possible rationalisation is that the total credit of £2,400 to own shares comprises the £1,567 profit and loss account charge, together with £833 representing a reduction through the offset of a liability of £833 (arising from the fact that the £833 previously credited to shareholders' funds has now become a liability following the company's decision to satisfy the award through a market purchase). On this view, the debit to shareholders' funds is a transfer of an amount from shareholders' funds to liabilities, rather than the charging of a cost direct to reserves.

Further complications can arise in the application of UITF 17 to group share schemes. These are discussed further at 2.6 below.

E *Exemption for SAYE schemes*

As explained in Example 22.9 above, the initial impetus for the issue of UITF 17 was to curtail a perceived abuse by some companies awarding options to their directors at a discount to market price. However, by the time that the Abstract was ready for issue it ironically had no impact on such schemes, following a change to the Listing Rules to prevent companies granting options to directors at a discount without shareholder approval,[40] which effectively stopped the practice. Unfortunately, as originally drafted, the Abstract would have applied to SAYE schemes, under which employees could, subject to various conditions, be offered shares at a discount to market price of up to 20% free of income tax. At this point the UITF found itself at the centre of a political storm for being about to issue an Abstract that would not affect the so-called 'fat cat' share schemes that were its supposed target but would adversely impact the much more modest schemes aimed at employees in general.

In the face of overwhelming protest, the UITF agreed to make an exemption for SAYE schemes, but, perhaps over-sensitive to the charge of having simply caved in to vested interests, referred in the original Abstract to the exemption being for 'any employees' share scheme under which participation is offered on similar terms to all employees'.[41] With the benefit of hindsight this was a mistake, as companies justifiably argued that, expressed in these terms, the exemption did not apply only to SAYE schemes (even though that was the UITF's intention). This provoked Sir David Tweedie to publish an open letter to explain the UITF's position, in which he bluntly said 'The UK accounting community has a choice; does it want the UITF and the ASB to produce a detailed cookbook of rules for every possible situation or, as I hope, can we rely on preparers and auditors to act in the spirit of pronouncements?'[42]

The issue would not go away, however, and came to a head once more with the introduction of All-Employee Share Ownership Plans (AESOP trusts) in April 2000, which fitted the generically worded exemption in the original UITF 17 exactly. Accordingly in October 2000 the UITF issued the current revised version of UITF 17 which makes it plain that the exemption is only for SAYE schemes and similar overseas schemes, and does not apply to AESOP trusts or approved profit sharing schemes. A company that takes advantage of the exemption must disclose that it has done so.[43]

F Share options on an acquisition

A common situation, not directly addressed by UITF 17, is that a company acquires another company that has granted its employees share options that are outstanding at the date of acquisition, and which are sometimes automatically exercisable on a change of ownership of the company. The acquiring company will generally wish to avoid the minority shareholdings that would be created by the target's employees exercising their options, and may therefore:

- make a payment to the employees in return for surrender of the rights under their options;
- allow the employees to exercise their options and then purchase the shares from them; or
- offer options over its own shares in exchange for the employees surrendering their rights over their existing options.

If the latter course of action is chosen, it raises the question of the appropriate accounting treatment in such cases, as illustrated by the following example.

Example 22.17: Options issued in exchange for options of acquired entity

On 1 January 2001 T plc granted options over 2 million shares at the market price of £2.00 per share to a group of key employees, exercisable from 1 January 2004 subject to their remaining in employment with T plc throughout the three year period. A plc acquires T plc on 1 October 2001 by issuing 2 A plc shares, then with a market value of £8.00, for every 5 shares in T plc. As the terms of the original options issued by T plc contained no provision for payment by T plc in the event of a takeover, the employees of T plc agree to exchange their options in T plc for options in A plc with an equivalent intrinsic value.

The purchase consideration implies that the market value of a T plc share on acquisition was £3.20 (£8.00 x 2/5). The intrinsic value of the options at the date of acquisition is therefore £2.4 million (2,000,000 x £[3.20-2.00]), so that A plc awards the employees options over 800,000 (2,000,000 x 2/5) of its own shares at £5.00 per share (800,000 x £[8.00-5.00] = £2.4 million). How should A plc account for this?

One view[44] is that it should be accounted for in the same way that T plc would have done if it had issued replacement options with an equivalent intrinsic value on the date of acquisition. On this view, T plc would, under UITF 17, have attributed 9/36 of the cost (£600,000) to the past and expensed it immediately, and spread the balance of £1,800,000 over the remaining 2¾ years of the loyalty period. This would suggest that A plc should treat £600,000 as part of its cost of investment/goodwill with a credit to shareholders' funds, and the balance of £1,800,000 as a post-acquisition UITF 17 charge. In the absence of any formal guidance, this seems a perfectly reasonable approach. Implicitly, it is treating the £600,000 as the issue of a capital instrument to the employees in their capacity as potential shareholders (having already performed the services to entitle them to be such), and the £1,800,000 as an amount paid to them as employees.

An objection to this approach would be that the employees do not become shareholders until all conditions have been satisfied. This would lead to the conclusion that all that has happened is that A plc has issued options in return for the employees remaining within the group for a further 2¾ years, and that the entire £2.4 million should therefore be treated as a post-acquisition UITF 17 charge.

We believe that either treatment is acceptable, so long as it applied consistently.

2.5.5 *UITF 25*

UITF 25 *National Insurance contributions on share option gains* was published in July 2000. It deals with the accounting treatment of the employer's liability to national insurance on certain 'unapproved' share options (i.e. unapproved by the Inland Revenue) granted after 5 April 1999, and other analogous situations giving rise to a liability for employer's national insurance.[45] The Abstract does not deal with the recently enacted 'capping' provisions for such national insurance (see E below).

A The basic methodology

The 'capping' provisions aside, national insurance is payable on the difference between the exercise price of the option and the market price of a share on the date of exercise. The UITF took the view that, for the purposes of FRS 12, an obligation to pay national insurance is created by the grant, rather than the exercise, of the option, on the basis that, by granting the option that company has exposed itself to an obligation that it has no power to avoid. The UITF considers that the market price provides at the balance sheet date a reliable basis for estimating the final liability, which should be continually revised as the market price of the shares changes over the period from grant to exercise. The liability is required to be spread over the performance period (see B below) rather than recognised immediately,[46] the basic methodology being illustrated in Example 22.18 below.

The cost should be charged to the profit and loss account, except to the extent that it forms part of staff costs capitalised under companies legislation and accounting standards.[47] Specifically, the UITF has received legal advice that national insurance on share options is not a cost of issuing shares, such that it cannot be written off against the share premium account.[48]

Example 22.18: Basic methodology of UITF 25

The company's year-end is 31 December. A maximum of 10,000 share options are granted on 1 January 2001, when the market value is £1, at an exercise price of £1, dependent upon performance in the 3-year period from 1 January 2001 to 31 December 2003. The options are exercisable from 1 January 2004 to 31 December 2005. Employer's National Insurance contributions, currently at 11.9%, are payable on exercise of the options.

At 31 December 2001 the market value of a share is share is £1.80 and it is estimated that the maximum entitlement of options will be exercised. The cumulative liability, and the charge for the 2001, is 11.9% x 10,000 x (£1.80 - £1) x 1/3 = £317.

At 31 December 2002 the market value of a share is £2.80. It is now expected that only 8,000 share options will exercised. The cumulative liability is 11.9% x 8,000 x (£2.80-£1.00) x 2/3 = £1,142. The charge for the year is the movement in the liability (£1,142-£317) = £825.

At 31 December 2003 the market value of a share is £3.00. 6,000 options have vested, but none have been exercised. The cumulative liability is 11.9% x 6,000 x (£3.00 - £1.00) = £1,428. The charge for the year is the movement in the liability (£1,428-£1,142) = £286.

During 2004, options over 2,000 shares are exercised when the share price is £3.20, giving rise to a liability of 11.9% x 2,000 x (£3.20-£1) = £524. At 31 December 2004 the share price is £2.80. The total liability for the remaining options is restated to 11.9% x 4,000 x (£2.80-£1) = £856. The profit and loss account is credited with £48 (i.e. release of provision £572 (£1,428-£856) less national insurance paid £524).

During 2005, options over the remaining 4,000 shares are exercised when the share price is £3.10, giving rise to a final liability of 11.9% x 4,000 x (£3.10-£1) = £1,000, giving rise to an additional profit and loss account charge of £144 (£1,000-£856).

As discussed in connection with cash bonuses in 2.2.1 B above, it is not clear how this sort of methodology actually conforms to FRS 12. If the national insurance liability is created by the grant of the option, FRS 12 would require immediate recognition of the full liability. The debit entry would be an instant charge against profits. Establishing an asset to be amortised, as is the case with the future costs of decommissioning an oil rig (see Chapter 28 at 5.5), would not be appropriate in this case. A further issue is why the liability is measured by reference to the market value of the company's shares at the balance sheet date and not at the date of approval of the accounts. Any post-year end change in market value which would give a more up-to-date assessment of the liability at the balance sheet date, and would be regarded as an adjusting post-balance sheet event under SSAP 17 (see Chapter 27 at 2).

UITF 25 argues that its method of accounting recognises 'the extent that the employees have performed their side of the arrangement',[49] which is perhaps intended to imply that the services to be performed in future periods are, in terms of FRS 12 an 'executory contract', the costs of which should not be provided for in advance (see 2.1 A above and Chapter 28 at 2.1.2). We do not find this at all convincing, and suggest that, as in other aspects of accounting for employee costs, the UITF has been forced to shoehorn a perfectly reasonable accounting treatment, based on principles of expense recognition and matching, into a balance sheet framework that, if applied zealously, cannot really accommodate it.

B *Period over which costs are to be allocated*

UITF 25 requires the national insurance cost to be provided in full where there is no performance period, and otherwise be allocated over the 'performance period', which it defines as:

> 'the period during which the employee performs the services necessary to become unconditionally entitled to the options, which may entail satisfying specified performance criteria or remaining in the company's employment for a specified period of time.'[50]

This introduces some confusion since, as noted in 2.5.3 E above, the period over which an employee becomes 'unconditionally entitled' to a share award includes both the performance period and any subsequent loyalty period, implying that the national insurance on options should be amortised over the period until they vest unconditionally. However, the cost of share awards is normally written off over the performance period only (see 2.5.4 B above), and it would seem strange to amortise the UITF 17 charge for an unapproved option scheme over the performance period only, but any associated national insurance cost over the total period to vesting. Moreover, the wording above states that unconditional entitlement may entail performance criteria 'or' (as opposed to 'and' or 'and/or') remaining in employment for a specified period of time, suggesting perhaps that normally only one of these periods is relevant. In our view, either interpretation is possible, but we strongly recommend that, where a share award gives rise to a UITF 17 charge, the national insurance should be recognised over the same period as the UITF 17 charge.

It is interesting that spreading costs over the period to vesting would be required by the G4+1 Discussion Paper on share-based payment (see 4 below), which was published in the same month as UITF 25, and may have distracted the UITF's thinking on this issue.

C Reimbursements from employees

Any amounts to be reimbursed by employees should be accounted for in accordance with the provisions for reimbursements in FRS 12[51]. This is essentially that they should be shown as assets, not netted against the liability, although a net charge may be shown in the profit and loss account (see Chapter 28 at 4.4)

D Disclosure

FRS 12 requires, for each class of provision, disclosure of an indication of the uncertainties about the amount or timing of the eventual transfer of economic benefits and, where necessary to provide adequate information, the major assumptions made concerning future events (see Chapter 28 at 6.1.2). In the case of a provision for national insurance on share options, UITF 25 states that disclosure of the share price and of the effect of a significant movement in that price may be necessary to provide a full understanding of these factors.[52]

E Capping of national insurance liability

Shortly after the requirement to account for national insurance on unapproved options took effect, it became apparent that the potential liability for companies with rapidly escalating share prices was very high. Accordingly, new legislation was introduced in 2000 to allow companies to transfer the liability to the employees. However, companies were concerned that it could be very difficult to pass such a liability on to an employee after options had been granted.

Accordingly, a concession was made by the Social Security Contributions (Share Options) Act 2001 allowing companies to elect, between 11 May and 10 August 2001 inclusive, to cap the liability on any unapproved options granted between 6 April 1999 and 19 May 2000 inclusive, and remaining unexercised at 7 November 2000, by reference to what the liability would have been if the option had been exercised on 7 November 2000. If the option was 'out of the money' at that date, no national insurance will ever be payable, even if the option is subsequently exercised.

Where a company has elected to cap its national insurance liability in this way, the only significant accounting issue, given the time limits involved, is likely to be the period over which the cost is recognised. In other words, should the full cost be recognised immediately (net of any amount already accrued), or continue to be spread over the same period as would have been used if the liability had not been capped?

UITF 25's implicit argument for spreading the (uncapped) cost seems to be that it matches the cost with employees' efforts in raising the share price. If this is indeed the argument, in our view the capped cost exists independently of any future services provided by employees and must therefore be recognised immediately. An alternative view would be that it seems inconsistent to be required to recognise the cost of capped national insurance over a different period than would have been used for the uncapped liability. In our view, however, this second approach is even more difficult to reconcile with FRS 12 than the basic requirements of UITF 25.

An interesting illustration of the implementation of UITF 25, and also the share price volatility that gave rise to the perceived need for the capping arrangements, is given by QXL ricardo.

Extract 22.6: QXL ricardo plc (2001)

3 Exceptional items [extract]

	Notes	**31 March 2001 £'000**	31 March Restated 2000 £'000
Distribution costs			
Goodwill impairment provision		**72,948**	22,418
Administration expenses			
Goodwill impairment provision		**4,993**	–
Development of 'World of Antiques'		**–**	10,794
National Insurance provision	(ii)	**(2,378)**	2,432
Restructuring costs		**924**	–
		3,539	13,226

. . .

(ii) National Insurance provision

The provision for the year ended 31 March 2000 has been restated in accordance with UITF 25 to account for the potential liability arising on the exercise of share options based upon the market value of options at the balance sheet date and spread over the vesting period of the options as opposed to a single charge at the time of grant. For the year ended 31 March 2001 the provision for any potential National Insurance liability has decreased in line with the movement in the Company's share price.

. . .

23 Provisions for liabilities and charges [extract]

National Insurance on share options	**Group and Company 2001 £'000**	Group and Company 31 March 2000 £'000
At 1 April 2000 (restated following prior year adjustment of £9,125,000)	**2,432**	–
(Released)/charged during the year	**(2,378)**	2,432
Utilised on exercise of options	**(54)**	–
At 31 March 2001	**–**	2,432

QXL ricardo, having provided £2.4 million for national insurance at the end of the prior period (as a prior year adjustment to reserves), has had to release nearly all the provision (as a credit to current year earnings) as a result of the movement in its share price.

2.5.6 *UITF 30*

UITF 30 *Date of award to employees of shares or rights to shares* was published in March 2001, and is mandatory for accounting periods ending on or after 22 June 2001, with earlier adoption encouraged. It deals with two main issues: the determination of the date of an award of shares for the purposes of UITF 17, and the treatment of share-based awards made conditional on the company having its shares traded on any, or a specified stock exchange or on a trade sale of the company being achieved.[53]

A Date of award

During 2000 there were a number of cases where a company had undertaken to award share options to a director, usually as an inducement for the director to join the company, at a time when the company was actually not able to award options because it did not have the necessary authorisation from shareholders required by the Companies Act 1985 and the UK Listing Authority rules. Authorisation was to be sought at the next annual general meeting, and was generally fully expected to be obtained.

The issue that came to the UITF was whether such awards should be regarded as having been made on the date on which the company made the original undertaking to the director, or the subsequent date of approval. Some companies, typically those whose share price had remained relatively stable, argued that the later date should be used, thereby delaying the recognition of any charge for the cost of the award under UITF 17 (see 2.5.4 above) or any associated national insurance costs under UITF 25 (see 2.5.5 above) until the following accounting period. Other companies, typically those whose share price had risen markedly during the intervening period, argued equally strongly that the earlier date should be used, thereby restricting the UITF 17 charge to the amount calculated by reference to the lower share price.

The UITF ruled that an award of shares or rights to shares that requires shareholder approval is not made until the approval is obtained.[54] However it may be that a company, in promising a share-based award to an employee without the necessary shareholder approval, may have incurred a liability to that employee until the approval has been obtained. This liability may be explicit (e.g. where the employee is contractually entitled to an equivalent cash payment if authority is not obtained), or implicit (e.g. where the employee may have a right of action against the company if authority is not obtained).[55]

In such cases, the company should recognise a liability on the date on which the initial promise of an award is made, measured by reference to the share price at that date, which is charged to the profit and loss account. This estimate should be constantly reviewed by reference to the then prevailing share price until the date on which the award is authorised by shareholders. This treatment is broadly similar to that required by UITF 25 (see 2.5.5 above).[56] Once the award has been approved, the carrying amount of the liability is transferred to shareholders' funds, since it represents consideration for the issue of a capital instrument. In addition, any UITF 17 charge arising from the award should be reduced by any charge already to the profit and loss account.[57] This treatment is illustrated in Example 22.19 below.

Example 22.19: Conditional share award approved at later date

On 1 September 2001 a company agrees with a new director that it will award him 100,000 share options at £3 (the share price at that date), with no performance criteria, exercisable from 1 September 2004. There is no shareholder authorisation in place to grant the options and the agreement with the director is such as to create an obligation to him to pay him the intrinsic value of the options if they are not awarded. At the balance sheet date of 31 December 2001 the share price is £4. The award is approved at the company's annual general meeting on 25 May 2002, when the share price is £6.

At the balance sheet date of 31 December 2001 there is a liability to the director of £100,000 (100,000 shares x intrinsic value [£4-£3]), which would be provided for, with a corresponding charge to the profit and loss account.

By 25 May 2002 the provision will have increased to £300,000 (£100,000 x [£6-£3]), all of which will have been charged to the profit and loss account. When the award is made on 25 May 2002 the cost required to be recognised under UITF 17 is the intrinsic value of £300,000. As this has already been charged in the profit and loss account, no further charge is made.

The provision of £300,000 will cease to be recognised because it has been satisfied by making the award of options. It therefore represents consideration for granting the options and will therefore be credited to shareholders' funds, most naturally to the profit and loss reserve.

In reality, there might be some difficulty in establishing whether an obligation is in fact created on the initial promise of an award. Another issue is that, in the example above, a balance date comes between the date on which the award is promised and the date it is finally made. It might be that these dates occur in the same accounting period. This raises the question of whether companies should raise a provision and release it during the same period (which would be a 'visible' entry due to the disclosure requirements for provisions in FRS 12 and the Companies Act – see Chapter 28 at 6.1.2). Whilst this rather obsessive bookkeeping is strictly required, it will probably not be a significant issue in practice, since the publication of UITF 30 may well deter companies from making awards without obtaining shareholder approval in advance.

B Awards in connection with flotation or sale

The Abstract also deals with the treatment of share awards made in anticipation of, and conditional upon, the flotation or sale of a company. UITF 30 states that, in such cases the flotation or sale is a performance condition for the purposes of UITF 17. Where the award is made in the form of share options, its cost for the purposes of UITF 17 is to be taken as the intrinsic value of the option at the date the award is granted, rather than that based on the (potentially much higher) share price achieved on listing. Anticipating the obvious scope for abuse – i.e. that the intrinsic value of the option at the date of grant is negligible as there is no open market for the shares – the UITF states that a fair value should be determined taking into account the probability of flotation. However, where the award is made in the form of a right to subscribe for shares on flotation at preferential rates or an outright gift of shares, the cost for UITF 17 purposes is the intrinsic value at the date of flotation, i.e. based on the market price at flotation.[58]

These provisions deal with only part of the story, as they do not give any indication of the period over which the cost is to be recognised. One view would be that, just as the cost of an award for the achievement of a given profit is spread over the period from grant to achievement of the profit based on the probability of the profit being earned, so the cost of an award contingent on flotation should be spread over the period from date of grant to achievement of flotation, based on the probability of flotation occurring. The other, and in our opinion, preferable view is that experience shows that achievement, and the timing, of a flotation is so uncertain until it has actually occurred that it should not be anticipated and the cost of award should be recognised only once flotation has occurred.

It is also not entirely clear why an award of options should be treated differently from an award of discounted or free shares. Suppose that a company is aiming to float in nine months' time and there is a reasonable expectation that the flotation share price will be in the region of £5 per share. In these circumstances, there is arguably little difference between an option exercisable at £4 on flotation and the right to participate in the flotation at a discount of 20% to the flotation price. However, the latter will inevitably lead to a UITF 17 charge, whereas, in the case of the former, it will may be possible for a company to construct an argument that its share price at the date of grant was no more than £4, and thereby avoid a UITF 17 charge.

2.6 Group share option schemes

The analysis above has concentrated on the detailed requirements of the Abstracts in the context of a single company. In the great majority of cases, however, they have to be applied to share option schemes operated by groups of companies, raising further accounting questions not directly addressed by the Abstracts, which are explored in the discussion below. Whilst the focus of this discussion is on group share option schemes, many issues of principle will also be relevant to single company schemes, and to share awards other than by way of option (e.g. gifts of shares, rights to subscribe in new issues at a discount).

2.6.1 *Typical features of a group share option scheme*

The precise terms and structures of share option schemes operated by groups are so varied as to be almost infinite. From an accounting perspective, however, they can generally be boiled down to a basic prototype, as described below, which will serve as the basis of the discussion.

A group scheme typically involves three legal entities:

- the trust that administers the scheme, such an ESOP trust or QUEST;
- the subsidiary employing an employee who has been granted options ('the employing subsidiary'); and
- the parent company, over whose shares options are granted.

An option to acquire shares is generally granted to an employee by the parent company, which will in turn have an option exercisable against the trust for the shares that it may be required to deliver to the employee. Less commonly, the trustees of the trust grant options to the employees and enter into reciprocal arrangements with the parent.

If the parent takes the view that it will satisfy any options granted using existing shares it will often seek to fix the cost of the award by arranging for the trust to purchase shares in the market sufficient to satisfy all or part of the award on the day that the award is made. This purchase will be funded by external borrowings, a loan from the parent, or some combination. The cash received from the employee on exercise of the option can be used by the trust to repay any borrowings.

If the parent takes the view that it will satisfy the options with a fresh issue of shares, these will be issued to the trust, either:

(a) at the date on which the employee exercises his option (in which case the trust will subscribe for the new shares using the cash received from the employee together with any non-refundable contribution made by the employing subsidiary);

(b) at some earlier date (in which case the trust will subscribe for the new shares using external borrowings, a loan from the parent or a contribution from the employing subsidiary, or some combination. The cash received from the employee on exercise of the option may then be used be the trust to repay any borrowings); or

(c) some shares will be issued before the exercise date as in (b) above, and the balance on the exercise date as in (a) above.

As noted in (a) above, the employing subsidiary often makes a non-refundable contribution to the trust in connection with the scheme, through which the group obtains tax relief for the cost of the scheme.

From a financial reporting perspective, it is generally necessary to consider the accounting treatment in:

- the group accounts;
- the parent company's entity accounts; and
- the employing subsidiary accounts.

2.6.2 *Share options satisfied by market purchase of shares*

On the whole, these are relatively straightforward from an accounting perspective, as illustrated by the following example.

Example 22.20: Group share scheme (market purchase)

On 1 July 2001 S Limited, a subsidiary of the H plc group, awards one of its employees an option over 3,000 shares in H plc at £1.50 each, exercisable between 1 July 2006 and 1 July 2007, subject to certain performance criteria being met in the three years ending 30 June 2004. On 1 July 2001, in connection with the award, the H plc group share trust purchases 3,000 shares at the prevailing market price of £2.00 each, funded by a loan from H plc. On exercise of the option, S Limited is required to pay the differential between the purchase price of the shares and the exercise price of the option (50p per share) to the trust.

The option remains 'in the money' throughout its life, such that when preparing accounts H plc and S Limited assume that it will be exercised. The option is finally exercised on 1 September 2006, at which point the trust uses the option proceeds and the payment by S Limited to repay the loan from H plc. H plc and its subsidiaries have a 31 December year end.

A Group accounts

So far as the group accounts are concerned, the only transactions to be accounted for are the purchase of the shares by the trust and their subsequent amortisation and disposal by the trust to the employee. Transactions between H plc or S Limited and the trust are ignored since, under UITF 13, the trust is treated as an extension of the group. UITF 13 requires the shares to be treated as an asset of the group and the difference between the purchase price of the shares and the exercise price to be amortised over the performance period. The accounting entries required are (see also 2.5.3 and 2.5.4 above):

		£	£
1.7.2001	Investment in own shares	6,000	
	Cash		6,000
y/e 31.12.2001	Profit and loss (employee costs)[1]	250	
	Investment in own shares		250
y/e 31.12.2002	Profit and loss (employee costs)	500	
	Investment in own shares		500
y/e 31.12.2003	Profit and loss (employee costs)	500	
	Investment in own shares		500
y/e 31.12.2004	Profit and loss (employee costs)	250	
	Investment in own shares		250
1.9.2006	Cash (option proceeds)[2]	4,500	
	Investment in own shares		4,500

1 Total cost £1,500 (3000 shares x £[2.00-1.50]) spread over 36 months. Charge to period to December 2001 6/36 x £1,500 = £250, and so on. In practice, where options were granted to a group of individuals, or with variable performance criteria, the annual charge would be based on a continually revised cumulative charge (see further discussion at 2.5.4 B and C above).

2 3,000 shares at £1.50 per share.

Where tax relief is available for the profit and loss charge (via the equivalent charge made in the employing subsidiary – see C below), it will be recognised either as deferred tax as the charges are made or as current tax when a tax-deductible payment is made by the employing subsidiary. The precise timing of the recognition of such relief, and whether it is current or deferred tax, will depend on the circumstances of the group's tax affairs and whether it is complying with SSAP 15 or FRS 19 (see Chapter 24 at 3 and 5).

B Parent company

In a group share scheme, the share trust will normally be treated as an extension of the parent company (see 2.5.3 B I above). On this basis the advance and repayment of the loan to the trust are ignored for financial reporting purposes. The only transactions are the purchase of the shares and their subsequent disposal on exercise of the option. No amortisation charge is required in the parent company accounts under UITF 13 or UITF 17 because, from the company's perspective, the cost of the shares will be fully recovered out of the option exercise proceeds and the contribution from the employing subsidiary. The accounting entries are simply:

		£	£
1.7.2001	Investment in own shares	6,000	
	Cash		6,000
1.9.2006	Cash	6,000[1]	
	Investment in own shares		6,000

1 £4,500 option exercise proceeds from employee plus £1,500 contribution from S Limited

In practice companies might wish to show the same carrying value of the shares in both the parent company and the group accounts, which could be achieved by transferring an amount equivalent to the group amortisation charge each year to debtors. In principle, however, we do not think that this is appropriate, since the parent company (including for this purpose the trust) does not have any right to receive the option proceeds or the contribution from the subsidiary until the option is exercised, as would be implied by treating the amount as a debtor.

C *Employing subsidiary*

The employing subsidiary simply has a cost of the cash contribution made to the trust on exercise of the option. This should be accounted for on an accruals basis over the 3-year performance period from 1 July 2001, giving rise to charges to the profit and loss account equivalent to those in the group accounts see A above). However, if, as will usually be the case, the subsidiary is required to fund the discount on the shares over which options are actually exercised (rather than that on the total number of shares over which options are originally granted), it will be necessary to adjust the accrual to reflect the effect of leavers and other factors affecting the final number of shares, even though there may be no adjustment in the group accounts (see 2.5.4 C above).

The other side of the profit and loss account entries will be to provisions, which will be cleared by the cash payment of £1,500 on 1 September 2006. On consolidation these entries will be reversed and the entries set out in A above substituted.

Where tax relief is available for the payment to the trust, it will be recognised as deferred tax as the accruals are made or as current tax when payment is made. The precise timing of the recognition of such relief, and whether it is current or deferred tax, will depend on the circumstances of the company's tax affairs and whether it is complying with SSAP 15 or FRS 19 (see Chapter 24 at 3 and 5).

D *Parent company as employing company*

If options are granted to employees of the parent company, and the parent is regarded as the controlling party of the share trust for accounting purposes, the accounting treatment in the parent company's own accounts will be the same as that set out for the group in A above.

2.6.3 *Share options satisfied by fresh issue of shares*

Such schemes raise somewhat more complex accounting issues. Again, these are most easily illustrated by way of an example.

Example 22.21: Group share scheme (fresh issue)

On 1 July 2001 S Limited, a subsidiary of the H plc group, awards one of its employees options over 3,000 shares at £2.00 per share, exercisable between 1 July 2006 and 1 July 2007, subject to certain performance criteria being met in the three years ending 30 June 2004. The market value of H plc shares at 1 July 2001 is £2.00.

The option remains 'in the money' throughout its life, such when preparing accounts H plc and its subsidiaries assume that will be exercised. The option is finally exercised on 1 September 2006, at which point H plc issues 3,000 new shares to the trust at the then current market price of £3.50. The trust funds the purchase using the £4,500 option proceeds received from the employee together with £6,000 contributed by S Limited. H plc and its subsidiaries have a 31 December year end.

A Group accounts

The group accounts need to deal with:

- the charge required by UITF 17 in respect of the award;
- the issue of shares; and
- any tax relief available on the contribution by S Limited to the trust.

Transactions between H plc or S Limited and the trust are ignored since, under UITF 13, the trust is treated as an extension of the group.

I UITF 17 charge

As the option is granted at market price at the date of grant there is no UITF 17 charge in the group accounts.

II Issue of shares

At exercise date, the parent company issues shares to the trust for £10,500 (£4,500 option proceeds from the employee and £6,000 contribution from the employing subsidiary), which in accordance with the Companies Act must be credited to share capital and share premium in the parent company, and therefore in the group. However, the resources of the group are increased by only £4,500 (since the £6,000 from the employing subsidiary is an intra-group transaction). FRS 4 requires the group to record the issue of shares at the 'fair value of … proceeds received', i.e. £4,500, and FRS 2 and the Companies Act require intra-group transactions to be eliminated on consolidation. This is achieved by charging the £6,000 contributed by the employing subsidiary to reserves, as follows.

		£	£
1.9.2006	Cash	4,500	
	Profit and loss reserve	6,000	
	Share capital/premium		10,500

This reflects the fact that, from a group perspective, £6,000 of reserves has effectively been capitalised (mirroring the reduction in distributable reserves in the employing subsidiary – see C below). This £6,000 is not a loss and is therefore not included in the statement of total recognised gains and losses. It should, however, be included in the reconciliation of shareholders' funds, either as a separate item or netted off the proceeds of issue of shares. An example of this treatment in practice can be seen in the 2000 accounts of BPB.

Extract 22.7: BPB plc (2000)

23 Share capital [extract]
Option schemes

Allotments of shares by the parent company and options granted during the year under the company's employee share option schemes were as follows:

	Allotments		Options granted			
	Shares	Consideration	Number	Shares	Exercise period	Price
SAYE:						
	826,530	£1.9m	708	506,825	1.3.03 – 31.8.03	272p
			495	562,744	1.3.05 – 31.08.05	272p
Senior Executive:	1,463,922	£3.9m	55	1,025,700	15.7.02 – 14.7.09	395p

At the annual general meeting in 1999 shareholders approved the adoption of a further SAYE employee share option scheme (the 1999 scheme) to replace the existing 1989 SAYE scheme; no options have been granted under the 1989 scheme during the year, although outstanding rights under that scheme remain unaffected.

At 31 March 2000, 4,566 options over 8,501,961 shares were outstanding under the company's SAYE share option schemes, exercisable during various periods up to 31 August 2005 at prices between 171p and 278p per share. A further 274 options over 4,902,291 share were outstanding under the senior executive schemes, exercisable during various periods up to 14 July 2009 at prices between 161p and 395p per share.

In September 1999, the company established a qualifying employee share ownership trust (QUEST) to acquire BPB ordinary shares for transfer to employees exercising options under BPB's two UK SAYE share option schemes. The trustee of the QUEST is BPB QUEST Trustees Ltd, a wholly-owned subsidiary of the company. During the year, the QUEST acquired 2,828,001 shares at a cost of £10.2 million and transferred a total of 646,980 shares to employees on the exercise of options for a consideration of £1.7 million (excluded from the figures for shares allotted under the company's SAYE share option schemes given in the table above). All employees of UK group subsidiary companies, including executive directors of the company, are potential beneficiaries under the QUEST. The QUEST has waived the dividends payable on all the 2,181,021 (1999 nil) shares that it owned at 31 March 2000.

24 Reserves [extract]

Movement in reserves	Total £m	Share premium £m	Capital redemption reserve £m	Profit and loss account £m
Group				
At 1 April 1999	511.2	114.7	21.8	374.7
Currency adjustments				
Overseas net assets	(62.5)	–	–	(62.5)
Borrowings	21.2	–	–	21.2
Premium on shares issued	13.4	13.4	–	–
Share buy-backs	(59.1)	–	10.8	(69.9)
Movements relating to the Quest	(8.5)	–	–	(8.5)
Profit retained	91.7	–	–	91.7
At 31 March 2000	**507.4**	**128.1**	**32.6**	**346.7**

Company				
At 1 April 1999	186.6	114.7	21.8	50.1
Premium on shares issued	13.4	13.4	–	–
Share buy-backs	(59.1)	–	10.8	(69.9)
Movements relating to the QUEST	(0.4)	–	–	(0.4)
Profit retained	41.5	–	–	41.5
At 31 March 2000	**182.0**	**128.1**	**32.6**	**21.3**

Certain subsidiary and associated companies would be liable for additional tax if their reserves were distributed.

...

The movement in reserves relating to the qualifying employee share ownership trust (QUEST) represents payments made by group companies to the QUEST to allow it to purchase shares in BPB plc for the purpose of satisfying SAYE options on exercise, less amounts received by the QUEST from option holders.

Movements in shareholders' funds	2000 £m	1999 £m
At 1 April	748.5	777.1
Total recognised gains and losses for the year	107.5	108.5
Dividends	(57.1)	(56.8)
Movements relating to the QUEST	(8.5)	–
Share buy-backs	(69.9)	(84.4)
New shares issued	16.0	4.1
At 31 March	736.5	748.5

Note 23 in the extract above discloses that the company has issued shares to the QUEST for £10.2 million, and received £1.7 million from employees, with Note 24 confirming that the difference (£8.5 million) – equivalent to the £6,000 in the journal above – was supplied by the group itself. Note 24 discloses this £8.5 million as a charge to the group profit and loss reserve, and as a movement in shareholders' funds. The charge of £0.4 million to the company profit and loss reserve represents the difference between the legal issue proceeds of shares allotted to, and option proceeds received from, employees of the parent company (see also D below).

III Tax relief

In many cases the employing subsidiary obtains corporation tax relief on the contribution to the trust, which will be reflected as a credit in the tax charge in the profit and loss account. In this particular example, because there is no UITF 17 charge in the group accounts (and the profit and loss charge in the subsidiary will be reversed on consolidation – see C below), any tax relief is, from the perspective of the group a permanent difference, for which credit should be taken when it becomes receivable.

B Parent company

The only transaction to be recorded is the issue of shares for £10,500:

		£	£
1.9.2006	Cash	10,500	
	Share capital/premium		10,500

C Employing subsidiary

The employing subsidiary ultimately incurs a cost of £6,000. However, this cost will not be finally known until the date the option is exercised, as the amount that it is required to contribute to the trust is calculated by reference to be market value of H plc shares on the date of exercise. In our view, this cost should be recognised on an accruals basis and, in the absence of definitive guidance, we suggest that companies use the methodology in UITF 25 (see 2.5.5 A above), as illustrated below.

Assume that the price of an H plc share at each year end is as follows.

31 December	Price (£)
2001	2.40
2002	2.90
2003	3.10
2004	3.30
2005	3.20

The cost will be spread over the 36 month performance period, and then adjusted in the loyalty period. The total provision required at each balance sheet date is as set out below. In practice, where options were granted to a group of individuals, or with variable performance criteria, these factors would also be taken into account in the calculations.

31 December	Total provision (£)	
2001	450	(6/36 x 3,000 x £[2.40-1.50])
2002	2,100	(18/36 x 3,000 x £[2.90-1.50])
2003	4,000	(30/36 x 3,000 x £[3.10-1.50])
2004	5,400	(3,000 x £[3.30-1.50])
2005	5,100	(3,000 x £[3.20-1.50])

The profit and loss charges are simply the difference between the opening and closing provisions, as follows.

		£	£
y/e 31.12.2001	Profit and loss (employee costs)	450	
	Provisions		450
y/e 31.12.2002	Profit and loss (employee costs)	1,650	
	Provisions		1,650
y/e 31.12.2003	Profit and loss (employee costs)	1,900	
	Provisions		1,900
y/e 31.12.2004	Profit and loss (employee costs)	1,400	
	Provisions		1,400
y/e 31.12.2005	Provisions	300	
	Profit and loss (employee costs)		300
1.9.2006	Profit and loss (employee costs)	900	
	Provisions	5,100	
	Cash		6,000

This treatment is predicated on the assumption that the subsidiary has been notified in advance of its obligation to make a payment equal to the 'spread' between the exercise price and the market price at the date of exercise. There might be situations where there would be no grounds for recognising a provision in the subsidiary in the intervening years, in which case it would simply account for the cash payment in September 2006 as an expense at that point.

All accounting entries in the subsidiary (other than the receipt of tax relief) would be reversed on consolidation. Where tax relief is available for the payment to the trust, it will be recognised as deferred tax as the provision is made or as current tax when payment is made. The precise timing of the recognition of such relief, and whether it is current or deferred tax, will depend on the circumstances of the company's tax affairs and whether it is complying with SSAP 15 or FRS 19 (see Chapter 24 at 3 and 5).

D Parent company as employer

Where the parent company is the employing company, and is regarded as the controlling party of the share trust for accounting purposes, the accounting treatment will be the same as that in the group (see A above). In other words, the £6,000 contribution to the trust is not treated as an expense (as in the subsidiary's accounts – see C above) as there is no loss to the company. This means that, where tax relief is sought for such a contribution, it must be obtained by way of a specific statutory deduction rather than through the contribution being treated as an operating expense for accounting purposes. An example of this treatment where the parent company is the employer can be seen in the accounts of Weir Group.

Extract 22.8: The Weir Group plc (2000)

18 Reserves [extract]

	Profit and Loss Account £'000
Group	
At 1st January 2000	223,095
Premium on share issues	–
Cost of issuing shares through ESOT	(122)
Goodwill reinstated	8,839
Profit retained in year	19,397
Exchange differences	66
Tax on exchange	(1,512)
At 29th December 2000	**249,763**
Company	
At 1st January 2000	231,168
Premium on share issues	–
Cost of issuing shares through ESOT	(122)
Surplus on revaluation of investments	–
Surplus for year	17,551
At 29th December 2000	**248,597**

During the year the company issued 612,588 ordinary shares to an employee share ownership trust (ESOT) in respect of the exercise of options under the Savings Related Share Option Scheme 1991. The company made a contribution to the ESOT equal to the difference between the market price at date of issue and the option price at a cost to the company of £122,000.

2.6.4 *Pre-funding of a scheme*

For the sake of simplicity, the examples in 2.6.2 and 2.6.3 above assume that all cash flows (except the purchase of shares in a scheme using existing shares) occur at exercise date. In practice, however, a few schemes require the employee to make a nominal payment to the share trust at the date of grant. More commonly, in the case of QUESTs, the employing group makes payments to the trust to enable it to subscribe for new shares before exercise date (typically in order to accelerate the receipt of tax relief).

A Pre-funding by the employee

In our view, amounts prepaid in advance by the employee should be accounted for in accordance with FRS 4, as being amounts paid in connection with the issue of a capital instrument. On this basis, the treatment will depend on the precise conditions surrounding any such pre-funding. In the unlikely event that there are circumstances in which the payment could be refunded by the employee (e.g. if he leaves before vesting date), it should be shown as a liability until:

- it is repaid to the employee; or
- shares are issued to the employee, at which point the amount should be credited to shareholders' funds. It is credited to share capital and, if applicable, share premium if it forms part of the consideration for the issue of the shares for the purposes of section 130 of the Companies Act 1985, and otherwise to some other reserve (see Examples 22.14 and 22.15 at 2.5.4 D above);
- it ceases to be refundable for some other reason in which case it should be credited to shareholders' funds if shares could still be issued, or otherwise credited to the profit and loss account.

If, as is more often the case, the amount is not refundable in any circumstances, it should be credited direct to shareholders' funds. If it is to form, for the purposes of section 130 of the Companies Act 1985, part of the proceeds of issue of the shares to be used to satisfy the award, a suitable caption might be 'shares to be issued'. Such a receipt is broadly equivalent to the proceeds for the issue of a warrant under FRS 4 (see Chapter 17 at 4.3). On this analogy, if employees leave before shares are issued to them or the relevant performance criteria are not achieved, the advance payment would be shown as a gain in the statement of total recognised gains and losses. The amount of any capital reserve could be transferred to the profit and loss reserve, even though the cash will actually be held by the share trust.

B Pre-funding by the employer

As in 2.6.2 and 2.6.3 above, the accounting treatment needs to be considered from the perspective of the group, the parent company and the employing subsidiary.

I Group

Where cash is paid to a share trust and is held by the trust, we believe that no accounting entry should be made for financial reporting purposes on the basis that, if the trust is treated as part of the group for accounting purposes, the effect is simply to transfer cash from one part of the group to another.

When the cash is used to subscribe for shares in the parent company, share capital, and if applicable, share premium account, should be credited with the proceeds as determined for the purposes of the Companies Act 1985 with a corresponding debit to the profit and loss reserve (or other appropriate reserve) in shareholders' funds. The shares should, not, in our view, be shown as an asset of the group, although several major UK companies do in fact do so (see Example 22.8 at 2.5.3 G and Example 22.14 at 2.5.4 D above)

II Parent company

As above, it is assumed that the parent company is regarded as the controlling party of the share trust for financial reporting purposes. Where the parent makes payments to the trust, or issues shares to the trust for cash provided by the parent itself, the accounting treatment will the same as that for the group as set out in I above. Where the parent issues shares to the trust for cash provided by other members of the group, it will accounted for as a normal issue of shares for cash.

Where other members of the group contribute cash to the share trust, and the trust simply holds it, a strict application of the 'extension of the parent company' principle of UITF 13 would require the parent company to recognise that cash in its balance sheet with a corresponding creditor, so as to reflect that fact that the cash is effectively being held on behalf of other group members. In practice, however, this is not generally done, and such cash is recognised only when there is a transaction directly involving the parent company, such as an issue of shares.

III Employing subsidiary

In our view, the cost of a share scheme to the employing subsidiary should in principle be accounted for an accruals basis, using a methodology such as those set out in 2.6.2 C and 2.6.3 C above. Any cash payment made should therefore be treated as a reduction in provisions, or a prepayment. In practice, however, it might be possible to expense cash payments where the effect was not materially different from that resulting from a true accruals basis.

There might also be exceptional circumstances in which the subsidiary should not regard any advance payment made as an asset – for example if some options lapsed and the cash already contributed were used to subsidise awards to employees of other companies in the group rather than further awards of the employing subsidiary.

2.7 Phantom share schemes

A phantom share scheme is one in which an employee, instead of being given an award in the form of shares, is given the equivalent value in cash or other assets. For example, on 1 January 2001 employees might be given a phantom option over 100 shares at £1.00 a share, 'exercisable' from 1 January 2004, subject to certain performance criteria. If on 1 January 2004 the performance criteria have been met and the market price of a share is, say, £2.50, the employees will be paid £150 each in cash, being the gain that they would have made if they had exercised options over 100 shares at £1.00 at that date (i.e. 100 x [£2.50-£1.00]). In some cases a company will hedge any increase in the cost of such an award between the dates of 'grant' and 'exercise' by using either shares bought in the market or a fresh issue of shares.

It is rather questionable whether such arrangements should be regarded as hedging, since the only true hedge for such a phantom scheme would be a call option over the company's own shares. A market purchase of shares at date of 'grant' provides a hedge against an upward movement in the share price only, leaving the company exposed to a fall in price, and a fresh issue of shares is simply no more than a means of raising cash to pay some employment costs as required, rather than a hedge of the liability as it accrues.

For these reasons it is, in our view, important to consider what the accounting treatment for the award would have been if it had not been 'hedged'. Considered on its own, it is simply a cash liability calculated by a formula that happens to be based on the share price. It would therefore be accrued over the performance period, so as to recognise a provision at each balance sheet date based on the intrinsic value of the option at that date, perhaps using a methodology similar to that required by UITF 25 (see 2.5.5 A above). The basic question to be considered when the transaction is 'hedged' is the extent, if any, to which this accounting treatment should be altered.

2.7.1 *Phantom scheme hedged by market purchase of shares*

Consider the following.

Example 22.22: Phantom scheme hedged by market purchase

On 1 January 2001, a company awards an employee a phantom option over 1,000 shares at £1.00 per share, 'exercisable' from 1 January 2004, subject to certain performance criteria. The criteria are satisfied and on 1 January 2004 a payment of £4,000 is made to the employee, based on the market price of £5.00 at that date.

On 1 January 2001 the company's ESOP bought 1,000 shares in the market at the then current market price of £1.50 a share for £1,500. These are sold on 1 January 2004 for £5,000 and the £3,500 profit used to part pay the amount due to the employee. In cash terms, the company has made an overall loss of £500, equivalent to the (unhedged) intrinsic value of the award at the date of grant. Mechanically this could be reflected in the financial statements in several ways, none of which is altogether satisfactory.

Method 1

UITF 13 is applied to the shares, which are recorded at their cost of £1,500 with no further entries being made until they are sold. The cost of £500 is accrued as a liability. At 'exercise' date the £3,500 profit on sale is added to the liability, giving a total liability of £4,000 which is then settled in cash. The problem with this method is that it keeps £3,500 of the liability to the employee off-balance sheet during the life of the transaction, even though it does not meet the criteria for either offset or linked presentation under FRS 5 (since the liability exists quite independently of whether or not it has been hedged). However, it could be argued that it is no more a 'violation' of FRS 5 than that already sanctioned by UITF 13 (see 2.5.3 C III above).

Method 2

As Method 1, except that the cost is recognised by amortising the cost of the shares from £1,500 to £1,000 over the life of the transaction. It is difficult to rationalise this approach, as the shares are always recoverable at at least their purchase price throughout the life of the transaction. A possible explanation might be that the overall transaction is the same as if the company had granted an option over shares but agreed to sell them on behalf of the employee.

Method 3

A liability for the full £4,000 is accrued over the life of the transaction, using the methodology in UITF 25. At the same time the shares are continually revalued to market value with the gain being off set against the charge created by the accrual of the liability. The effect will be to recognise a net loss of £500 over the life of the transaction. This Method avoids the FRS 5 problem inherent in Methods 1 and 2, but it involves taking unrealised gains on the revaluation of the shares to the profit and loss account, which requires the use of the 'true and fair over-ride' (see Chapter 14). In this case, however, we consider this perfectly justified since the gain on the shares is no less realised than the charge for the hedged portion of the liability.

In our view, Method 3 is perhaps the most strictly correct, but Method 1 is acceptable and probably the most common treatment in current practice. However, we do not consider Method 2 acceptable since it results in the shares being amortised when there is no reason, under the normal principles of fixed asset accounting, to do so (since their cost will be fully recovered on sale).

There is in fact a fourth view, which is that it is wrong to apply UITF 13 to the shares at all, on the basis that UITF 13 is addressing the accounting treatment for investments in own shares held in anticipation of their being awarded to employees, not, as here, to shares held to hedge other transactions. This could suggest that the 'treasury stock' method of accounting (see 2.5.3 C III above) should be used. This would have the effect that the full £4,000 cost was charged to the profit and loss account, with the purchase and sale of the shares being accounted for in reserves.

However, this view seems rather harsh, particularly given that, as noted under 'Method 2' above there is no difference between a phantom award and a real award where the employee disposes of the shares immediately, or has the trustees of the share trust dispose of them for him (as is often the case). In such case UITF 17 would require a cost of only £500 to be accrued. However, the G4+1 group's discussion paper on share-based payment (see 4 below), if given effect in a future standard, would remove this anomaly by requiring a charge of £4,000 to be made in both cases.

2.7.2 *Phantom scheme 'hedged' by fresh issue of shares*

As noted above, such an arrangement does not constitute a hedge in the generally accepted sense of the word.

Example 22.23: Phantom scheme hedged by fresh issue of shares

On 1 January 2001, a company awards an employee a phantom option over 1,000 shares at £1.00 per share (the market value then being £1.50), 'exercisable' from 1 January 2004, subject to certain performance criteria. The criteria are satisfied and on 1 January 2004 a payment of £4,000 is made to the employee, based on the market price of £5.00 at that date.

On 1 January 2004 the company lends £1,000 to the ESOP trust which uses it to subscribe for 1,000 new shares at £1.00 a share. The ESOP then sells these shares for their market price of £5,000, using £4,000 to pay the employee and £1,000 to repay the loan from the company. In cash terms, this has cost the company nothing, leading some to argue that no cost should be recognised, the implied accounting entry being:

	£	£
Cash (from market sale)	5,000	
Cash (to employee)		4,000
Share capital/premium		1,000

This effectively treats the difference between the market price of the shares and their issue proceeds for Companies Act purposes as a profit.

We do not believe that it complies with FRS 4 for the reasons set out in Example 22.8 at 2.5.3 G above. If it were taken to its logical conclusion, the company could issue 1,000 shares with a nominal value of 1p, credit shareholders' funds with £10 and recognise a profit of £990, which is clearly inappropriate. In our view the substance of the transaction is that the company has issued new shares for £5.00 and used some of the issue proceeds to satisfy its liability under the phantom option. There is no instance in UK GAAP where the proceeds of an issue of shares for cash can be offset against an expense or the cost of an asset, even where the shares were specifically issued to meet the cost in question. On this analysis the accounting entries are:

		£	£
1.1.2001-31.12.2003	Profit and loss (employee costs)	4,000	
	Provisions		4,000
1.1.2004	Cash	5,000	
	Share capital/premium		1,000
	Profit and loss (or other) reserve (shareholders' funds)		4,000
	Provisions	4,000	
	Cash		4,000

This may seem a rather harsh result. For example, if the company had granted the employee a real option over the shares, the profit and loss charge under UITF 17 would have been only £500, the intrinsic value at date of grant. However, as noted at 2.5.4 A above, the UITF 17 charge is a 'minimum' charge, implying that it is more a question of UITF 17 understating the cost than the suggested treatment above overstating it.

2.8 Disclosure requirements of the Companies Act

In addition to the disclosures noted above, the Companies Act 1985 requires a number of disclosures in respect of employee costs. Disclosures required in respect of employee costs in general are:[59]

(a) the average monthly number of employees (including directors) employed under contracts of service in the period, analysed into such categories as the directors may determine; and

(b) in respect of the employees taken into account in calculating (a) above, the aggregate amount of:

  (i) wages and salaries payable in respect of the period;

  (ii) social security costs; and

  (iii) pension costs.

The average monthly number of employees for the purposes of (a) above is determined by (i) calculating, for each month in the financial year, the number of people employed under contracts of service for any part of that month; (ii) adding together the monthly totals calculated in (i); and (iii) dividing the total obtained in (ii) by the number of months in the financial year. Employees will include those directors (typically executive directors) who have contracts of employment with the company, but not those directors (typically non-executive directors) who receive fees from the company, but do not have contracts of employment. However, the emoluments of all directors will be included in the information disclosed in respect of directors' remuneration, which is discussed in Chapter 32 .

For the purposes of the amounts to be disclosed under (b), any employer's national insurance contributions should be included as part of social security costs (that is, any contributions by the company to any state social security or pension scheme, fund or arrangement).[60]

The treatment of benefits in kind, however, is less clear. While these may be provided under contracts of employment they do not fall under any of (b)(i) to (iii) above. If, however, a company rents a flat for the use of a director, it might seem appropriate to include the rental in this disclosure. In all cases, however, the amount included should reflect only the cost to the company, rather than the benefit to the director, which may well be different (see Chapter 32 at 2.3.2 A).

Another issue that may arise is the treatment of redundancy payments. One view might be that they fall outside all the headings above. Another might be that, contractual redundancy payments fall within this disclosure, but that ex gratia payments do not. In practice, however, wherever material redundancy payments are made they will tend to be fully disclosed anyway as part of a provision for closure costs (see Chapters 25 and 28).

The disclosures must be given in the notes to the accounts except, in the case of the disclosures required by (b) above, to the extent that they are given on the face of the profit and loss account.[61] A comprehensive example of the disclosures required is given by John Mowlem.

Extract 22.9: John Mowlem & Company plc (2000)

7 **Employees**	**2000 Number**	1999 Number
The average weekly number of persons employed by the Group including Directors during the year was:		
Construction Services	**7,469**	6,959
Facilities Services	**1,034**	840
Environmental Services	**788**	737
Insurance Services	**635**	862
Project Investment and Property and Corporate activities	**204**	205
Discontinued activities (2000: period to 16 June)	**2,085**	4,390
	12,215	13,993
	2000 £m	1999 £m
The aggregate payroll cost was:		
Wages and salaries	**255.3**	288.4
Social security costs	**18.5**	24.7
Other pension costs	**12.4**	13.8
	286.2	326.9

The balance sheet formats contain a caption 'Other creditors including taxation and social security'. The amount relating to taxation and social security must be disclosed separately from other creditors either on the face of the accounts or (as is almost universal practice) in the notes.[62]

Extensive disclosures are required in respect of pension costs by SSAP 24, FRS 17 and the Companies Act 1985 (see Chapter 23).

The disclosures required by the Companies Act in respect of share capital and contingent rights to the allotment of shares (see Chapter 17 at 3.1.2) are also relevant to share option schemes.

In addition there are extensive requirements that relate only to directors and officers of the company, which are discussed in detail in Chapters 31 and 32.

3 IAS REQUIREMENTS

The relevant standard is IAS 19 – *Employee Benefits*, the current version of which was issued in 1998, and subject to relatively minor amendments in 1999 and 2000. It deals with all employee benefits, defined as 'all forms of consideration given by an enterprise in exchange for services rendered by an employee'.[63] IAS 19 identifies the following main categories of benefit:

- short-term employee benefits (see 3.1 below);
- post-employment benefits (discussed in Chapter 23);
- other long-term employee benefits (see 3.2 below)
- termination benefits (see 3.3 below); and
- equity compensation benefits (see 3.4 below).

3.1 Short-term employee benefits

Short-term employee benefits are employee benefits (other than termination benefits and equity compensation benefits) which fall due wholly within twelve months after the end of the period in which the employees render the related service.[64] They include:

- wages, salaries and social security contributions;
- short-term compensated absences (such as paid annual leave and paid sick leave) where the absences are expected to occur within twelve months after the end of the period in which the employees render the related service;
- profit sharing and bonuses payable within twelve months after the end of the period in which the employees render the related service; and
- non-monetary benefits (such as medical care, housing, cars and free or subsidised goods or services) for current employees.[65]

3.1.1 General recognition criteria for short-term employee benefits

An enterprise should recognise the undiscounted amount of short-term benefits attributable to services that have been rendered in the period as an expense, unless another IAS requires or permits the benefits to be included in the cost of an asset. This may particularly be the case under IAS 2 – *Inventories* (see Chapter 16 at 4.2.2) and IAS 16 – *Property, Plant and Equipment* (see Chapter 12 at 5.2.1 A). Any difference between the amount of cost recognised and cash payments made should be treated as a liability or prepayment as appropriate.[66] There are further requirements in respect of short-term compensated absences and profit sharing and bonus plans.

3.1.2 Short-term compensated absences

These include absences for vacation (holiday), sickness and short-term disability, maternity or paternity leave, jury service and military service. These can either be accumulating and non-accumulating absences. Accumulating absences are those that can be carried forward and used in future periods if the entitlement in the current period is not used in full. They can be either vesting entitlements (which entitle employees to a cash payment in lieu of absences not taken on leaving the enterprise) or non-vesting entitlement (where no cash compensation is payable). Non-accumulating absences are those where there is no entitlement to carry forward unused days.[67]

A Accumulating absences

The cost of accumulating absences should be recognised when employees render the service that increases their entitlement to future compensated absences. No distinction should be made between vesting and non-vesting entitlements (see above), on the basis that the liability arises as services are rendered in both cases. However, in measuring non-vesting entitlements, the possibility of employees leaving before receiving them should be taken into account.[68]

The cost of accumulating absences should be measured as the additional amount that the enterprise expects to pay as a result of the unused entitlement that has accumulated at the balance sheet date. In the case of unused paid sick leave, provision should be made only to the extent that it is expected that employees will use the sick leave in subsequent periods, unless there is a formal or informal understanding that such unused sick leave can be taken as paid holiday.[69]

B Non-accumulating absences

The cost of non-accumulating absences should be recognised as and when they arise, on the basis that the entitlement is not directly linked to the service rendered by employees in the period. This is commonly the case for sick pay (to the extent that unused past entitlement cannot be carried forward), maternity or paternity leave and compensated absences for jury service or military service.[70]

3.1.3 *Profit sharing and bonus plans*

An enterprise should recognise the expected cost of profit sharing and bonus payments when, and only when:

- the enterprise has a present legal or constructive obligation to make such payments as a result of past events; and
- a reliable estimate of the obligation can be made.[71]

A Present legal or constructive obligation

A present obligation exists when, and only when, the enterprise has no realistic alternative but to make the payments.[72] IAS 19 clarifies that where a profit-sharing plan is subject to a loyalty period (i.e. a period during which employees must remain with the enterprise in order to receive their share), a constructive obligation is created during the period in which the relevant profit is earned. However, the possibility of employees leaving during the loyalty period should be taken into account in measuring the cost of the plan.[73] It also states that where an enterprise has a practice of paying bonuses, it has a constructive obligation to pay a bonus, even though there may be no legal obligation for it to do so. Again, however, in measuring the cost, the possibility of employees leaving before receiving a bonus should be taken into account.[74]

B Reliable estimate of provision

A reliable estimate of its legal or constructive obligation under a profit sharing or bonus plan can be made when, and only when:

- the formal terms of the plan contain a formula for determining the amount of the benefit;
- the enterprise determines the amounts to be paid before the financial statements are approved for issue; or
- past practice gives clear evidence of the amount of the enterprise's constructive obligation.[75]

IAS 19 states that an obligation under a profit sharing or bonus plan must be accounted for as expense and not a distribution of profit, since it results from employee service and not from a transaction with owners.[76] Where profit sharing and bonus payments are not due wholly within twelve months of the end of the period in which the employees render the relevant service, they should be accounted for as other long-term employee benefits (see 3.2 below). Where they meet the definition of equity compensation plans, they should be accounted for as summarised in 3.4 below.[77]

3.1.4 *Disclosure*

IAS 19 has no specific disclosure requirements in respect of short-term employee benefits, but contains reminders that:

- IAS 24 – *Related Party Disclosures* requires disclosure of employee benefits for key management personnel (see Chapter 30 at 4); and
- IAS 1 – *Presentation of Financial Statements* requires disclosure of staff costs.[78]

3.2 Long-term employee benefits other than post-employment benefits

These are employee benefits (other than post-employment benefits, termination benefits and equity compensation benefits) which do not fall due wholly within twelve months after the end of the period in which the employees render the related service.[79] They include:

- long-term compensated absences such as long-service or sabbatical leave;
- jubilee or other long-service benefits;
- long-term disability benefits;
- profit sharing and bonuses payable twelve months or more after the end of the period in which the employees render the related service; and
- deferred compensation paid twelve months or more after the end of the period in which it is earned.[80]

3.2.1 *Recognition and measurement*

For such benefits IAS 19 requires a simplified version of the accounting treatment required in respect of defined benefit pensions (which is discussed in detail in Chapter 23 at 6.8). The amount recognised as a liability for other long-term employee benefits should be the net total, at the balance sheet date, of the present value of the defined benefit obligation and the fair value of plan assets (if any) out of which the obligations are to be settled directly. The net total of the following amounts should be recognised as expense or income, except to the extent that another IAS requires or permits their inclusion in the cost of an asset:

(a) current service cost;

(b) interest cost;

(c) the expected return on any plan assets and on any reimbursement right recognised as an asset;

(d) actuarial gains and losses, which should all be recognised immediately;

(e) past service cost, which should all be recognised immediately; and

(f) the effect of any curtailments or settlements.

All assets, liabilities, income and expenditure relating to such benefits should be accounted for in the same way, and subject to the same restrictions on the recognition of assets, as those relating to a defined benefit pension plan (see Chapter 23 at 6.8), except that:

- actuarial gains and losses are recognised immediately (i.e. they are not limited to a 'corridor' – see Chapter 23 at 6.8.3 A); and
- all past service costs are recognised immediately (i.e. they not spread over the period to vesting – see Chapter 23 at 6.8.4 E).[81]

A Long-term disability benefit

Where long-term disability benefit depends on the length of service of the employee, an obligation arises as the employee renders service, which is to be measured according to the probability that payment will be required and the length of time for which payment is expected to be made. If, however, the level of benefit is the same for all employees, the cost is recognised only when an event causing disability occurs.[82]

It is not clear why the IASC makes this distinction, since in principle both types of benefit are equally susceptible to actuarial measurement. If anything the cost of benefits applicable to all employees regardless of service is probably easier to quantify actuarially.

3.2.2 Disclosure

IAS 19 requires no specific disclosures in respect of other long-term benefits but notes that other IAS may require disclosure, for example where:

- the expense resulting from such benefits is of such size, nature or incidence that its disclosure is relevant to explain the performance of the enterprise for the period (as required by IAS 8 – *Net Profit or Loss for the Period, Fundamental Errors and Changes in Accounting Policies* – see Chapter 25 at 3.3); or
- the expense relates to key management personnel (as required by IAS 24 – *Related Party Disclosures* (see Chapter 30 at 4.1).

3.3 Termination benefits

Termination benefits are employee benefits payable as a result of either:

- an enterprise's decision to terminate an employee's employment before the normal retirement date; or
- an employee's decision to accept voluntary redundancy in exchange for those benefits.[83]

They are accounted for differently from other employee benefits because the event that gives rise an obligation for them is the termination rather than the rendering of service by the employee.[84]

3.3.1 Recognition

An enterprise should recognise termination benefits as a liability and an expense when, and only when, the enterprise is demonstrably committed (see below) to either:

- terminate the employment of an employee or group of employees before the normal retirement date; or
- provide termination benefits as a result of an offer made in order to encourage voluntary redundancy.[85]

An enterprise is demonstrably committed to a termination when, and only when, the enterprise has a detailed formal plan for the termination and is without realistic possibility of withdrawal. The detailed plan should include, as a minimum:

- the location, function, and approximate number of employees whose services are to be terminated;
- the termination benefits for each job classification or function; and
- the time at which the plan will be implemented. Implementation should begin as soon as possible and the period of time to complete implementation should be such that material changes to the plan are not likely.[86]

IAS 19 distinguishes between those benefits that are payable as a result of the termination of employment by the enterprise and those payable to employees on leaving, regardless of the reason for their departure.

Benefits resulting from a termination by the enterprise are 'termination benefits' as defined by the standard, whether the obligation is imposed by law, contractual agreement with employees or their representatives, custom, or a desire to act equitably. They are generally given as lump-sum payments, but may include enhancement of retirement benefits or of other post-employment benefits (either indirectly through an employee benefit plan or directly) and salary until the end of a specified notice period if the employee renders no further service that provides economic benefits to the enterprise.[87]

By contrast benefits payable to employees on leaving (subject possibly to minimum service or vesting requirements) in all circumstances are not 'termination benefits' as defined in IAS 19, notwithstanding that they may be referred to as such in some jurisdictions. Benefits of this nature should be accounted for as post-employment benefits (see 3.2 above). It may also be that a type of hybrid arrangement operates, whereby employees receive a lower benefit for a voluntary termination at their request than for an involuntary one, and a higher benefit for an involuntary termination at the request of the enterprise. In such cases, only the difference between the lower and higher levels of benefit should be treated as a termination benefit.[88]

The cost of termination benefits should be recognised immediately on the grounds that they do not provide an enterprise with future economic benefits.[89] IAS 19 also points out that the recognition of termination benefits will often give rise to the need to account for a curtailment of retirement benefits or other employee benefits (see Chapter 23 at 6.8.4 F).[90]

3.3.2 *Measurement*

Where termination benefits fall due more than twelve months after the balance sheet date, they should be discounted by reference to market yields at the balance sheet date on high quality corporate bonds. In countries where there is no deep market in such bonds, the market yields (at the balance sheet date) on government bonds should be used. The currency and term of the corporate bonds or government bonds should be consistent with the currency and estimated term of the post-employment benefit obligations. This is the same discount rate as is required to be used in respect of defined benefit pension plans (see Chapter 23 at 6.8.2 B).[91]

Where an offer has been made to encourage voluntary redundancy, the termination benefits should be measured by reference to the number of employee expected to accept the offer.[92]

3.3.3 *Disclosure*

As in the case of the other forms of benefit discussed above, IAS 19 contains no specific disclosure requirements for termination benefits, but notes that the following requirements of other IAS will be relevant:

- where an offer of termination benefits is made to employees and the number of employees who will accept it is uncertain, a contingent liability exists, details of which must be disclosed under IAS 37 – *Provisions, Contingent Liabilities and Contingent Assets* (see Chapter 28 at 7.5.2), unless the possibility of an outflow in settlement is remote;
- termination benefits may be an expense of such size, nature or incidence that its disclosure is relevant to explain the performance of the enterprise for the period, as required by IAS 8 – *Net Profit or Loss for the Period, Fundamental Errors and Changes in Accounting Policies* (see Chapter 25 at 3.3); and
- termination benefits payable to key management personnel will be disclosed under IAS 24 – *Related Party Disclosures* (see Chapter 30 at 4.1)[93]

3.4 Equity compensation benefits

Equity compensation benefits are employee benefits under which either:

- employees are entitled to receive equity financial instruments issued by the enterprise (or its parent); or
- the amount of the enterprise's obligation to employees depends on the future price of equity financial instruments issued by the enterprise.[94]

They include such benefits as shares, share options and other equity instruments issued to employees at a discount to fair value at which they would be issued to a third party, together with cash payments, the amount of which depends on the future market price of the reporting enterprise's shares.[95]

3.4.1 *Recognition and measurement*

IAS 19 contains no rules for the recognition and measurement of such benefits. However, where a company operates a share scheme trust or similar employee trust, it could be argued that such a trust should in principle be consolidated as a 'special purpose entity' under SIC-12 – *Consolidation – Special Purpose Entities.* However, equity compensation plans do not fall within the scope of SIC-12 (see Chapter 18 at 4.4). Where an enterprise holds its own shares for the purposes of satisfying equity compensation benefits (either directly or through a consolidated entity), these could be accounted for as a deduction from equity (i.e. the 'treasury stock' method) in accordance with SIC-16 *Share Capital – Reacquired Own Equity Instruments*, even though shares held in connection with employee share schemes are outside the scope of SIC-16 (see Chapter 17 at 5.5.3). This is the treatment adopted by Jardine Matheson (see Extract 22.11 at 3.4.2 below).

3.4.2 Disclosure

To compensate for the lack of any accounting requirements, IAS 19 requires extensive disclosures in respect of equity compensation plans, defined as 'formal or informal arrangements under which an enterprise provides equity compensation benefits for one or more employees'.[96]

The disclosures are intended to enable users of financial statements to asses the effect of equity compensation benefits on an enterprise's financial position, performance and cash flows. Equity compensation benefits may affect the financial position by requiring the enterprise to issue equity financial instruments or convert financial instruments, and may affect performance and cash flows by reducing the amount of cash or other employee benefits that the enterprise provides to employees in exchange for their services.[97]

An enterprise should disclose:

(a) the nature and terms (including any vesting provisions) of equity compensation plans;

(b) the accounting policy for equity compensation plans;

(c) the amounts recognised in the financial statements for equity compensation plans;

(d) the number and terms (including, where applicable, dividend and voting rights, conversion rights, exercise dates, exercise prices and expiry dates) of the enterprise's own equity financial instruments which are held by equity compensation plans (and, in the case of share options, by employees) at the beginning and end of the period. The extent to which employees' entitlements to those instruments are vested at the beginning and end of the period should be specified;

(e) the number and terms (including, where applicable, dividend and voting rights, conversion rights, exercise dates, exercise prices and expiry dates) of equity financial instruments issued by the enterprise to equity compensation plans or to employees (or of the enterprise's own equity financial instruments distributed by equity compensation plans to employees) during the period and the fair value of any consideration received from the equity compensation plans or the employees;

(f) the number, exercise dates and exercise prices of share options exercised under equity compensation plans during the period;

(g) the number of share options held by equity compensation plans, or held by employees under such plans, that lapsed during the period; and

(h) the amount, and principal terms, of any loans or guarantees granted by the reporting enterprise to, or on behalf of, equity compensation plans.[98]

These disclosures may be made in total, or separately for each plan, or in such groups as are considered most useful in assessing the enterprise's obligation to issue equity financial instruments. They might for example distinguish between the location and seniority of the various employee groups covered.[99]

An enterprise should also disclose:

(a) the fair value, at the beginning and end of the period, of the enterprise's own equity financial instruments (other than share options) held by equity compensation plans; and

(b) the fair value, at the date of issue, of the enterprise's own equity financial instruments (other than share options) issued by the enterprise to equity compensation plans or to employees, or by equity compensation plans to employees, during the period.

If it is not practicable to determine the fair value of the equity financial instruments (other than share options), that fact should be disclosed.[100] The exemption from disclosing the fair value of share options is given on the basis that there is no consensus as to how their fair value is to be measured.[101]

The disclosures regarding options may be given in total, separately for each plan, or in such groups as are considered most useful for assessing the number of shares that may be issued, the timing of their issue and the cash that may be received as a result. For example, it may be useful to distinguish 'in the money' and 'out of the money' options, and not to combine options with a wide range of exercise prices or exercise dates.[102]

IAS 19 notes that IAS 24 – *Related Party Disclosures* (see Chapter 30 at 4) may require additional disclosures if an enterprise:

- provides equity compensation benefits to key management personnel;
- provides equity compensation benefits in the form of instruments issued by the enterprise's parent; or
- enters into related party transactions with equity compensation plans.[103]

Examples of the some of the disclosures required by IAS 19 are given by Deutsche Bank and Jardine Matheson.

Extract 22.10: Deutsche Bank AG (2000)

Equity-based compensation elements

With our entire range of compensation policy instruments we want to create an incentive to increase the value of our share and offer a competitive compensation package to talented people and specialists, for whom demand is strong.

Global Equity Plan

Year of issue	**2000**	**1999**	**1998**
Expires in	2003	2002	2001
Nominal interest rate	4.75%	3%	3%
Conversion price*	€29.83	€38.30	€62.81
Originally granted rights (nominal)	TDM 34,481	TDM 28,424	TDM 28,411
Take-up in %	76.90%	78.70%	83.10%
Balance at start of year		5,587,800	5,389,000
Forfeited in 2000	56,400	272,000	220,800
Allocations in 2000	–	–	–
Balance at end of year	6,911,800	5,315,800	5,168,200
Thereof: non-cancellable rights	0	31,000	105,400

* Assumption: APIPS constant, Deutsche Bank share price at end of 2000

In 2000, we gave roughly 3,250 of our executives the possibility of taking part in the Global Equity Plan (GEP). Roughly 77% of the entitled executives took up the offer and acquired convertible bonds. Participation in this plan is voluntary. The possibility of conversion depends directly on the bank's Adjusted Pretax Income Per Share (APIPS). Only if this figure exceeds the predetermined threshold in the respective reference period can the convertible bonds be converted into Deutsche Bank shares. 200 shares are granted per bond of DM 1,000 nominal value. If the conversion right is exercised, an additional cash payment must be made per share in the amount by which the conversion price exceeds the respective nominal amount of the bond to be converted. The conversion price is calculated accordingly to criteria already established today and taking into account the profits for the financial years 1998 to 2002.

No expenses arose in 2000 for the Global Equity Plan owing to the link with conditional capital.

db Share Plan

Issued in	**2000**	**1999**
Number of staff shares subscribed	2,171,526	1,900,074
Thereof: by retired employees	281,519	263,292
Take-up rate	65.3%	65.2%
Expense for staff shares	€ 81 m.	€ 54 m.
Market value of staff shares at date of issue	T€ 215,850	T€ 131,960
Options – exercisable in	**2003**	**2002**
Original number of option rights granted	1,889,237	1,636,782
Thereof: subscribed by Divisional Board members	0.02%	0.02%
Participation rate of Divisional Board members	66.7%	75.0%
Balance at start of year	-	1,633,288
Forfeited in 2000	4,771	29,783
Balance at end of year	1,884,466	1,603,505
Thereof: non-cancellable rights	1,240	9,856
Mark-down as at 31.12.2000*	66.67%	57.21%

* Assumption: APIPS constant, Deutsche Bank share price at end of 2000

We continue to support the shared responsibility of our employees through staff participation. We again offered staff shares to our employees in 2000; participation is voluntary. As in the year before, employees received one free option for each share bought (maximum 60 shares). This option can be exercised after three years. Here, too, the possibility of exercise depends directly on Adjusted Pretax Income Per Share (APIPS). Only if this figure exceeds the established threshold in the respective reference period can the options be exercised. No expense has arisen in this connection, as the free options are tied to conditional capital.

db Share Scheme

Grants in	**2000**	**1999**	**1998**
Originally granted rights	10,162,112	4,874,106	3,489,296
Balance at start of year	-	3,425,999	1,441,368
Forfeited in 2000	299,272	130,400	44,729
Allocations in 2000	1,975,126	1,269,146	998,368
Balance at end of year	7887,714	2,026,453	398,271
Thereof: allocation in			
2001	2,670,378	1,482,569	398,271
2002	4,429,812	543,884	–
2003	749,785	–	–
2004	37,739	–	–
Bank's average expense per right	€ 86,02	€ 60.17	€ 69.12

Within the framework of the annual bonus payments, members of staff in Global Corporates and Institutions, Asset Management, Private Banking and Global Technology and Services divisions receive part of their performance-related compensation (bonus) in the form of equity rights. Employees participating in this plan are entitled to subscribe to a certain number of shares or may, under certain conditions, receive a corresponding cash payment upon maturity. Allocation is usually in three equal parts. The expenses attributable to the respective financial year for the db Share Scheme are included in the Income Statement. This instrument underlines the special importance of value-based compensation in our bank.

Stock Appreciation Rights (SAR)

Grant in	**2000**
Original number of granted SAR	6,214,992
Forfeited in 2000	165,851
Balance at end of year	6,049,141
Exercise price of SAR	€ 70.00
Original number of granted SAR in Private Banking	458,500
Forfeited in 2000	0
Balance at end of year	458,500
Exercise price of SAR in Private Banking	€ 86.50

In February 2000, selected executives of the Group were granted Stock Appreciation Rights (SAR) for the first time, with a special programme being launched for Private Banking. The SAR are tied until January 2003 and as from that time can be exercised during the following three years. The executives receive the right to a cash payment equal to the difference between the exercise price and the share price on the day of exercise. This instrument, too, is an element of the value-based compensation for our bank's management.

The expense for the Stock Appreciation Rights is deferred over the maturity of the instrument and adjusted for share price changes. In 2000, € 46 million were charged to P&L.

Own shares

By resolution of the General Meeting on June 9, 2000, Deutsche Bank AG was authorised to purchase its own shares representing up to five per cent of its current share capital on or before September 30, 2001. The shares may be purchased via the stock market or by means of a public purchase offer to all shareholders. The countervalue for the purchase of the shares must not be more than 5% above or below the shares' average daily quotation on the Frankfurt Stock Exchange on the last three trading days prior to their purchase via the stock market. If a public purchase offer is made, the countervalue must not be more than 5% below or more than 15% above the shares' average daily quotation on the Frankfurt Stock Exchange on the last three trading days prior to the day on which the offer is published.

The Board of Managing Directors of Deutsche Bank AG was authorised, with the consent of the Supervisory Board, to dispose of the purchased shares other than via the stock market or by means of an offer to all shareholders, provided this is done against non-cash capital contribution for the purpose of acquiring companies or holdings in companies.

Furthermore, the Board of Managing Directors of Deutsche Bank AG was authorised, when disposing of its purchased own shares by means of an offer to all shareholders, to grant the holders of warrants, convertible bonds and convertible participatory rights issued by the bank pre-emptive rights to the shares to the extent to which they would be entitled after having exercised the option or conversion right. Shareholders' pre-emptive rights are excluded for these cases and to this extent.

Extract 22.11: Jardine Matheson Holdings Limited (2000)

25 Senior Executive Share Incentive Schemes [extract]

The Senior Executive Share Incentive Schemes were set up in order to provide selected executives with options to purchase ordinary shares in the Company. Under the Schemes ordinary shares are issued to the Trustee of the Schemes, Clare Investment and Trustee Company Limited, a wholly-owned subsidiary undertaking, which holds the ordinary shares until the options are exercised. Ordinary shares are issued at prices based on the average market price for the five trading days immediately preceding the date of grant of the options, which are exercisable for up to ten years following the date of grant.

As the shares issued under the Schemes are held on trust by a wholly-owned subsidiary undertaking, for presentation purposes they are netted off the Company's share capital in the consolidated balance sheet *(refer note 24)* and the premium attached to them is netted off the share premium account *(refer note 26)*.

Movements for the year:

	Ordinary shares in millions			
	2000	1999	**2000 US$m**	1999 US$m
At 1st January	**10.7**	8.4	**61.0**	53.4
Granted	**2.8**	2.7	**10.5**	8.7
Exercised	**(0.4)**	(0.4)	**(1.3)**	(1.1)
At 31st December	**13.1**	10.7	**70.2**	61.0

The exercise price of share options exercised during the year were in the range of US$3.2 to US$4.3 (*1999: US$2.3 to US$3.2*) per share.

Outstanding at 31st December:

	Exercise price	Ordinary shares in millions	
Expiry date	US$	**2000**	1999
2000	3.2 – 10.1	–	0.9
2001	3.2 – 8.0	**0.3**	0.7
2002	6.9 – 7.9	**0.2**	0.2
2003	7.7	**0.3**	0.3
2004	6.6 – 10.1	**1.0**	1.1
2005	7.5 – 8.0	**0.4**	0.5
2006	7.2	**0.3**	0.3
2007	6.1 7.7	**1.0**	1.1
2008	2.0 – 4.5	**0.6**	0.7
2009	3.2 – 3.3	**1.9**	2.3
2010	3.7 – 5.0	**2.7**	–
Unallocated	1.2 – 10.1	**4.4**	2.6
		13.1	10.7

4 POSSIBLE FUTURE DEVELOPMENTS

In July 2000 the 'G4+1 group' issued a joint discussion paper – *Share-based payment*, which was published in the UK by the ASB. Whilst its proposals were primarily developed with share-based employee remuneration in mind, they would, if carried forward into a future standard, apply to all transactions where an entity obtains goods or services from other parties in exchange for shares or options over shares, with the important exception of the issue of shares or share options in connection with a business combination.[104]

The main proposals in the paper are:

(a) A transaction whereby an entity obtains goods and services from other parties, including suppliers and employees, with payment taking the form of shares or share options issued by the entity to those other parties, should be recognised in the financial statements, with a corresponding charge to the income statement when those goods or services are consumed.

(b) The transaction should be measured at the fair value of the shares or options issued. In most cases, an option pricing model should be applied to establish the fair value of an option.

(c) The transaction should be measured at vesting date. Vesting date is the date upon which the other party (the employee or supplier), having performed all of the services or provided all of the goods necessary, becomes unconditionally entitled to the options or shares.

(d) Where performance by the other party occurs between grant date, being the date upon which the contract between the entity and the other party (the employee or supplier) is entered into, and vesting date, an estimate of the transaction amount should be accrued over the performance period.

These proposals are more radical than current GAAP anywhere in the world. They differ from current UK GAAP in the proposals to calculate the cost of an award as the fair value of shares or options at date of vesting (rather their intrinsic value at the date of grant), and to spread the cost of an award over the total period from grant to vesting (rather than over the initial performance period, but not normally any subsequent loyalty period). Whilst the paper is a useful contribution to the debate on this area, and summarises the issues well, we do not believe that it forms a credible basis for a future accounting standard. In particular, in our view, it merely asserts, rather than argues, that the issue of shares at a discount to the prevailing market price is a cost to the company, rather than (as we suggest) a cost to the current shareholders, which should not be dealt with in the company's financial statements. It also does not address the paradox that its proposed treatment effectively requires a company to record fluctuations in the value of its own equity as gains or losses, contrary to the IASC's conceptual framework.

Apart from the conceptual issues, there is the very practical issue of how the fair value of share options should be measured. Option valuation models are far from an exact science, and have not yet been developed to take account of the particular features of performance-related options. There is also a question of cost – specialists in our firm suggest that a bespoke valuation of the kind necessary to implement the proposals in the paper could cost in the region of £50,000 per share scheme. The paper does acknowledge the difficulties of valuation, but dismissively suggests that these will be rare exceptions rather than, as will in fact be the case, the norm. Indeed, it suggests, somewhat self-righteously, that if directors issue options without being able to determine their value they may be in breach of their fiduciary duties![105]

The accounting treatment in the G4+1 paper has its roots in similar proposals that the FASB in the United States tried to introduce some years ago,[106] only to be forced to back down in the face of concerted opposition from US business interests. Perhaps the IASB feels that, once its goal of international harmonisation is achieved, it will be easier to impose this accounting treatment, since companies will no longer be able to oppose it on the grounds of competitive disadvantage (as would be the case if it were required in certain jurisdictions only). However, we suspect that the IASB will find that this is the least of the objections of the business community, and that the discussion paper provides a basis for continuing debate rather than a blueprint for change.

References

1 IAS 19 *Employee Benefits* (Revised 2000), IASC, February 1998, revised October 2000.
2 Published in the UK as Discussion Paper, *Share-based payment*, ASB, July 2000.
3 *Statement of Principles for Financial Reporting* (SoP), ASB, December 1999, para. 4.23.
4 FRS 5 *Reporting the Substance of Transactions*, ASB, April 1994, para. 12(e).
5 SoP, para. 4.33-4.36, FRS 12 *Provisions, Contingent Liabilities and Contingent Assets*, ASB September 1998, para. 5.
6 See for example Extract 6.16 in Chapter 6 at 2.4.3, where holiday pay is listed as a fair value adjustment, implying that the acquiror does accrue for it and the acquiree did not. Extract 28.31 at 6.1.2 in Chapter 28 also refers to a provision for cumulative leave obligations.
7 FRS 12, para. 11.
8 IAS 19, Appendix C, paras. 86-88.
9 FRS 12, para. 14.
10 *Ibid.*, para. 17.
11 *Ibid.*, para. 20.
12 *Ibid.*
13 CA 85, s.23.
14 UITF 13, *Accounting for ESOP Trusts*, UITF, June 1995, para. 8.
15 *Ibid.* Sub-paragraph (g) is as amended by FRS 14, *Earnings per share*, ASB, September 1998, para. 16.
16 *Ibid.*, Appendix I.
17 FRS 5, *Reporting the substance of transactions*, ASB, April 1994, para. 7.
18 *Ibid.*, para. 44.
19 UITF 13, Appendix I.
20 UITF Information Sheet No 32, March 1999.
21 UITF Information Sheet No 33, June 1999.
22 UITF 13, para. 4.
23 Companies Act 1985, s262(1).
24 This example is cited to illustrate the general point of principle. In reality profit sharing schemes such as that described here are no longer very common. Moreover, in such a scheme the employee is often the beneficial owner of the shares as soon as they are transferred to the ESOP trust, which would not be the case in a typical LTIP.
25 That these are freshly issued shares is indicated by the reference in the note to their being 'subscribed for' by the QUEST.
26 UITF Information Sheet No. 33.
27 *Ibid.*, para. 2(b).
28 *Ibid.*, para. 9.
29 UITF Information Sheet No. 29, June 1998.
30 Draft UITF Abstract, *Employee benefit trusts and other intermediate payment arrangements*, UITF, July 2001.
31 UITF 17, para. 14(a)
32 *Ibid.*, para. 14(c).
33 *Share-based payment* (para. 3.18) would argue that the company has effectively issued a capital

instrument since the overall result is the same as issuing shares for cash and then paying that cash to employees.

34 *Ibid.*, paras. 14(c) and 16.

35 *Ibid.*, para. 11.

36 *Ibid.*, para. 15.

37 *Ibid.*, para. 14(d)

38 *Ibid.*, para. 17

39 FRS 4, *Capital Instruments*, ASB December 1993, paras. 11, 45 and Companies Act 1985, s130.

40 *The Listing Rules*, Financial Services Authority, April 2000, para. 13.30.

41 Original UITF 17, para. 17.

42 UITF Information Sheet no. 23, September 1997.

43 UITF 17, paras. 12 and 18.

44 See for example Accounting Solutions, Holgate and Ghosh, *Accountancy*, September 1999.

45 UITF 25, *National Insurance contributions on share option gains*, UITF, July 2000, paras. 1 and 8.

46 *Ibid.*, paras. 2-3.

47 *Ibid.*, para. 11.

48 *Ibid.*, References and legal considerations.

49 *Ibid.*, para. 5.

50 *Ibid.*

51 *Ibid.*, paras. 6 and 11.

52 *Ibid.*, para. 7.

53 UITF 30, *Date of award to employees of shares or rights to shares*, UITF, March 2001, paras. 2-3.

54 *Ibid.*, paras. 4 and 9.

55 *Ibid.*, para. 5.

56 *Ibid.*, paras. 5 and 10.

57 *Ibid.*, para. 6.

58 *Ibid.*, paras. 7 and 11.

59 CA 85, Sch. 4 para. 56. (Also Sch. 9, para. 77 and Sch 9A, para. 79).

60 *Ibid.*, para. 94(1). (Also Sch 9, para. 87(a) and Sch 9A, para. 86(a)).

61 *Ibid.*, para. 56. (Also Sch. 9, para. 77 and Sch 9A, para. 79).

62 *Ibid.*, para. 3(4), balance sheet formats and note 9 thereto.

63 IAS 19, para. 7.

64 *Ibid.*

65 *Ibid.*, para. 8.

66 *Ibid.*, para. 10.

67 *Ibid.*, paras. 12-13.

68 *Ibid.*, paras. 11(a) and 13.

69 *Ibid.*, paras. 14-15.

70 *Ibid.*, paras. 11(b) and 16.

71 *Ibid.*, para. 17.

72 *Ibid.*

73 *Ibid.*, para. 18.

74 *Ibid.*, para. 19.

75 *Ibid.*, para. 20.

76 *Ibid.*, para. 21.

77 *Ibid.*, para. 22.

78 *Ibid.*, para. 23.

79 *Ibid.*, para. 7.

80 *Ibid.*, para. 126.

81 *Ibid.*, paras. 127-129.

82 *Ibid.*, para. 130.

83 *Ibid.*, para. 7.

84 *Ibid.*, para. 132.

85 *Ibid.*, para. 133.

86 *Ibid.*, para. 134.

87 *Ibid.*, para. 135.

88 *Ibid.*, para. 136.

89 *Ibid.*, para. 137.

90 *Ibid.*, para. 138.

91 *Ibid.*, paras. 78 and 139.

92 *Ibid.*, para. 140.

93 *Ibid.*, paras. 141-143.

94 *Ibid.*, para. 7

95 *Ibid.*, para. 144.

96 *Ibid.* para. 7.

97 *Ibid.* para. 146.

98 *Ibid.*, para. 147.

99 *Ibid.*, para. 149.

100 *Ibid.*, para. 148.

101 *Ibid.*, para. 152.

102 *Ibid.*, para. 150.

103 *Ibid.*, para. 151.

104 *Share-based payment*, paras. 1.1-1.4.

105 *Ibid.*, para. 4.38.

106 As finally issued, FAS 123 *Accounting for stock based compensation* requires shares or options granted to suppliers other than employees to be recorded at fair value and recommends (but does not require) shares or options issued to employees to be recorded at the fair value at the date of grant.

Chapter 23 Retirement benefits

1 INTRODUCTION

1.1 UK

Accounting for the costs of retirement benefits in the accounts of employer companies presents one of the most difficult challenges in the whole field of financial reporting. The amounts involved are large, the timescale is long, the estimation process is complex and involves many areas of uncertainty which have to be made the subject of assumptions; in addition the actuarial mechanisms used for matching the costs to years of employment are complicated and their selection open to debate.

Before the introduction of SSAP 24 – *Accounting for pension costs*, generally accepted practice in the UK had been to charge pension costs in the profit and loss account on the basis of funding payments made to the pension scheme, which obviously meant that the reported profit of the employer company was susceptible to fluctuations because of changes in the contributions made. In addition, most companies gave only very limited information in their accounts about the obligations to pay the pensions to which they were committed, and the assets which had been built up in their pension funds to meet these obligations.

The effect of SSAP 24 was to look through the veil that lies between the employer company and its pension fund. The measure of pension cost ceased to be simply the amount of contributions paid to the fund; instead it became necessary to examine the condition of the fund itself to see what the long-term cost of providing pensions really was. Thus, pension expense was derived directly from actuarial valuations of the scheme, although the standard required that changes in these valuations be recognised only gradually, by amortising them over a number of years, so as to reduce the volatility which would otherwise result.

One further pronouncement of particular significance was issued after SSAP 24 came into force in 1988. In 1992, the Urgent Issues Task Force issued its sixth Abstract – *Accounting for post-retirement benefits other than pensions* – that extended the principles of SSAP 24 to health care and other similar post-retirement benefits.

The philosophy of SSAP 24 rested on the premise that the pension fund is in substance a vehicle of the employer company and that any surplus held by the fund should be regarded as a company asset, even if it is not directly shown as such on the company's balance sheet. This followed from the argument that, in a final salary scheme, the employer has to bear whatever cost is needed to provide the pensions promised to the workforce after taking account of their own (fixed) contributions; any excess of assets which emerges in the form of a pension scheme surplus therefore belongs to the employer. However, this stance is not free from controversy. Employees and their representatives frequently assert that a pension fund surplus morally belongs to the members, and the legal position will depend on the precise terms of the scheme and the trust deed under which the fund is administered.

However, the surplus may give the company the opportunity to reduce its future contributions to the fund below what they would otherwise be, and in these terms it may be appropriate to think of it as an asset; this was probably the main rationale for the approach adopted by the SSAP 24.

The meaning and treatment of the balance sheet figure was perhaps the main area of controversy in the application of SSAP 24, although the scope for flexibility in measurement and paucity of disclosure were also common criticisms of the standard. The ASB began the process of revising the standard with the publication in June 1995 of a Discussion Paper – *Pension Costs in the Employer's Financial Statements*. This set out two possible approaches to accounting for defined benefit schemes. The approach preferred by the majority of the board was to retain SSAP 24's overall philosophy, but to limit some of the options available to preparers when applying the standard and improve the disclosure requirements. In contrast, a minority favoured an alternative approach which required the 'market value' of the scheme to be recognised on the balance sheet each year. This was an estimate of the amount that a hypothetical third party would pay or receive in exchange for taking the future pension obligation away from the reporting entity. However, since the pension ultimately paid will be based on a future, as yet undetermined, salary, such a value is not readily available, and a calculation to approximate to this value was proposed. To limit the annual volatility to the profit and loss account it was also proposed that some movements would be taken to the statement of total recognised gains and losses (STRGL).

Respondents to this Discussion Paper strongly favoured the majority view and were dismissive of the alternative. Since then, however, the IASC revised its standard in a way that was much more in line with the approach favoured by the minority on the ASB (see 1.2 below). The ASB followed this in July 1998 with a further Discussion Paper – *Aspects of accounting for pension costs*. This was limited to the discussion of only four issues:

- the basis of valuation of the assets for a pension scheme – concluding that market value was the most appropriate measure on the grounds of reliability, objectivity and international harmonisation;
- the discount rate at which pension liabilities are discounted – favouring a rate of return from a hypothetical portfolio of assets which matched the liabilities.

It is interesting that this was not the approach taken in IAS 19, somewhat undermining the ASB's attempt to justify its proposals on the grounds of harmonisation;

- the method of dealing in the accounts with actuarial gains and losses.

  The paper considered four possible options for the treatment of actuarial gains and losses and discussed the pros and cons of each:

  - amortisation in the profit and loss account over the average service lives of employees, the required treatment under SSAP 24;
  - charge in full to the profit and loss account, as a non-operating exceptional item;
  - charge in full to the STRGL; and
  - charge in full to the STRGL and amortise from there to the profit and loss account over the average remaining service lives;
- treatment of past service costs – concluding that the majority of the ASB favoured charging the costs immediately when the improved benefits are awarded.

It was clear from this Discussion Paper that the Board now favoured an approach that would incorporate an annual valuation of the pension fund in the employer's balance sheet. It therefore seemed likely that the ASB would seek to introduce a new standard that adopted this approach, and in December 1999 the ASB issued an exposure draft on this topic, FRED 20 – *Retirement Benefits*. Notwithstanding a somewhat mixed reaction from commentators, FRED 20 was converted into a final standard – FRS 17 – with very few changes of substance. As discussed at 3 below, the new standard, requires a radical change to the treatment of the costs of pensions and other retirement benefits in the accounts of employers.

Somewhat unusually, the ASB has given FRS 17 a long implementation period, with phased disclosure requirements. The standard comes fully into force for accounting periods ending on or after 22 June 2003; early adoption is encouraged but not required. For periods ending on or after 22 June 2001 various disclosures relating to the balance sheet are required. These disclosures are supplemented, for periods ending on or after 22 June 2002, with information about the profit and loss account and STRGL.

The disclosure requirements for defined benefit schemes are discussed further at 3.9 below. It should be noted that until the new standard is implemented in full SSAP 24 (and UITF 6) remain in force, not just for accounting for defined benefit schemes but also for the various disclosures they require. This means that in the transitional period before full implementation of FRS 17 accounts will have to provide the disclosures set out at 3.9.2 below *in addition to* those already required by SSAP 24 (see 4.8 below).

When the standard is implemented in full, a prior period adjustment will be required to bring any necessary asset or liability onto the balance sheet in accordance with FRS 3 – *Reporting financial performance*. It will not be necessary to re-open goodwill calculations of earlier years because any pension surplus or deficit of an acquired company would (or should) have been accounted for by the acquirer at fair value in accordance with FRS 7 – *Fair values in acquisition accounting*. Any difference between the methodology used to estimate fair values in previous acquisitions and that prescribed by FRS 17 is to be treated as a post acquisition actuarial gain or loss, and hence recorded in the STRGL (the treatment of actuarial gains and losses is discussed at 3.8.1 D below).

1.2 IAS

In January 1983, the IASC issued IAS 19 – *Accounting for Retirement Benefits in the Financial Statements of Employers* – which was revised ten years later in November 1993 with the shortened title of *Retirement Benefit Costs*. It was broadly similar in its approach to SSAP 24, although there were quite a number of differences of detail.

In October 1996, however, the IASC published an exposure draft proposing to make fundamental changes to IAS 19.[1] In particular, the whole focus of the standard was to be shifted from the profit and loss account to the balance sheet. This led to the issue of a further revised version of IAS 19 in February 1998, to take effect for accounting periods beginning on or after 1 January 1999.

The requirements of IAS 19 regarding retirement benefits are similar in many respects to those of FRS 17. The principal difference lies in the treatment of actuarial gains and losses. In what at first glance appears to be a balance sheet approach, IAS 19 allows actuarial gains and losses up to 10% of the higher of gross assets or liabilities in the fund to simply be ignored (the 'width' of this corridor was set at 10% so as to be consistent with US GAAP). Any systematic method that results in faster recognition of actuarial gains and losses is allowed by IAS 19, provided that the same basis is applied to both gains and losses and that the basis is applied consistently from period to period.

The requirements of IAS 19 in relation to retirement benefits (and other long-term employee benefits typically accounted for using actuarial techniques) are discussed further at 6 below. IAS 19 also deals with other aspects of employee benefits; these are dealt with in Chapter 22.

2 THE ACTUARIAL ASPECTS OF ACCOUNTING FOR RETIREMENT BENEFITS

2.1 Actuarial valuation methods

2.1.1 Background

Retirement benefits of a defined benefit nature (for example, pensions linked to final salary or retirement healthcare) present particular difficulties of measurement in accounts. Whatever accounting model is adopted, the long time scales and numerous uncertainties involved require estimates to be made and accountants have long been accustomed to borrowing the techniques developed by the actuarial profession.

Actuarial methods have been developed, not with the objective of generating figures for the measurement of pension cost for accounting purposes, but with a view to valuing the fund and determining appropriate contribution rates. The focus of funding recommendations is to ensure that assets are set aside in a prudent and orderly way so as to meet the obligations of the scheme when they become due for payment; it is to do with cash flows, not with profit measurement.

Nevertheless, although the methods have been developed for funding purposes, they can provide a good basis for attributing cost to the years in which the employees render their services to the employer company. The difficulty is that, even if the actual amount of pensions which would eventually be paid to existing employees were known with precision, there is no particular method of attributing the cost of that pension to individual years of employment which is unarguably the best way of applying the matching concept. Different actuarial methods would approach this task in different ways.

SSAP 24 does not prescribe a particular valuation method, and leaves it to the employer, with actuarial advice, to ensure that the method chosen is appropriate. Conversely, FRS 17 and IAS 19 both require that the projected unit method (called the projected unit credit method in IAS 19) be used to measure defined benefit liabilities. Accordingly, the discussion of different actuarial methods which follows will be of most relevance to companies applying SSAP 24.

To explain these differences it is helpful to draw the distinction between the two main families of methods used by actuaries – 'accrued benefits methods' and 'projected benefits methods' (or 'level contribution methods' as they are sometimes called). These terms are defined in SSAP 24 as shown in 4.2 below, but the essential difference between the two can be explained, slightly simplistically, as follows:

- the accrued benefits approach measures the cost of providing the pension by putting a value directly on each incremental year's service so that it builds up towards the final liability which will arise on retirement;
- the projected benefits approach looks directly at the expected eventual liability and seeks to provide for it evenly over the whole period of service.

The first method will tend to show a rising trend of cost over the employee's working life, while the second will tend to show a flatter charge. The methods, and some of their different versions, are described more fully in 2.1.3 and 2.1.4 below.

There are different possible accounting arguments as to why either of these might be the more desirable way of matching cost and benefits. For example, the accrued benefits method could be portrayed as an approach which tries more precisely to measure the cost of the pension which has accrued in any specific year, and therefore is a more faithful application of the matching concept than the projected benefits method, which seems to adopt more of a 'smoothing' approach. Conversely, it may be argued that the benefits from employees' services accrue over their whole working lives and that the total cost of their pensions should be recognised evenly over those lives, as is achieved by the projected benefits approach, rather than weighting it towards the later years of their employment, as happens under the accrued benefits approach. A variety of further arguments could be summoned to support either side of the debate; but suffice it to say that there is no unanswerable point which seems to make either method conclusively the best.

The distinctions between the methods are in practice blurred when one moves from considering the cost of the pension of an individual employee to looking at the cost of a scheme comprising many employees, with a range of ages. For mature schemes where the age profile of the scheme remains steady through time, there will be comparatively little difference between the total cost calculated under either approach.

2.1.2 *The approach taken by accounting standards*

As noted earlier, FRS 17 requires the use of the projected unit method and requires that this be applied to 'scheme liabilities' which the standard defines. The projected unit method is discussed at 2.1.3 A below. FRS 17's requirements in this regard are discussed further at 3.7.2 below. IAS 19 takes a very similar approach to FRS 17, as discussed at 6 below.

SSAP 24 does not prescribe a particular valuation method, and leaves it to the employer, with the benefit of actuarial advice, to ensure that the method chosen can fulfil the accounting objective set out in the standard, that the cost should be recognised on a systematic and rational basis over the working lives of the employees in the scheme. Both of the broad categories of actuarial method described above could generally be said to meet that objective, although some of their variants may not, as discussed in the two sections which follow.

SSAP 24 says comparatively little about particular actuarial methods, but discusses them briefly in the following terms: 'In practice, it is common for actuaries to aim at a level contribution rate, as a proportion of pensionable pay in respect of current service. The contribution rate thus determined depends on the particular actuarial method used and the assumptions made regarding new entrants to the scheme. In broad terms, in projecting a stable contribution rate, accrued benefits methods rely on the assumption that the flow of new entrants will be such as to preserve the existing average age of the workforce; prospective benefits methods, on the other hand, normally look only to the existing workforce and seek a contribution rate that will remain stable for that group despite its increasing age profile until the last member retires or leaves. In a mature scheme both types of method may in practice achieve stable contribution rates, but the size of the fund under a prospective benefits method will tend to be larger than under an accrued benefits method because it is intended to cover the ageing of the existing workforce.'[2]

A group of companies will often have a number of different pension schemes in operation for different subsidiaries and the question often arises as to whether they must be valued using the same actuarial methods and assumptions. On the basis that the various methods attribute pension costs to years of service in a different way, there is an argument that a single method should be used throughout the group, just as it would be desirable to use the same depreciation method consistently throughout the group. However, provided the methods chosen all achieve the standard's aim of charging pension cost as a relatively consistent percentage of payroll, then it is acceptable to use different methods. It can be seen from Extract 23.18 at 4.8.2 below that uniform valuation methods are not necessarily used in practice.

It can also be seen from several of the extracts quoted in this chapter that different actuarial assumptions are commonly used for different schemes. Again this is quite legitimate provided the assumptions are appropriate for the schemes to which they are applied, and since the schemes themselves will not be uniform, there is no reason why the assumptions should be. In particular the economic assumptions used for the schemes of an international group will need to reflect the circumstances of each country, although a greater degree of consistency would be expected between schemes within the same country.

2.1.3 *Possible actuarial methods – accrued benefits methods*

As mentioned above, the accrued benefit approach focuses directly on the incremental liability which builds up year by year as pensionable service is recorded by the employee. It sees each year as giving rise to a further unit of pension entitlement, and values each unit separately to build up the total accrued liability.

Although the emphasis is on the benefits that have been earned to date, this does not mean that the method is incapable of looking to the future, and in particular it is not necessarily the case that it does not anticipate future pay rate inflation (which is a vital factor in a final salary scheme). Admittedly some variants of the accrued benefits approach do not take such factors into account, but the most significant version, the projected unit method, is based on estimates of final salary rather than on present rates of pay. (Confusingly, the projected unit method is in the 'accrued benefit' family of valuations, not the 'projected benefit' family.)

A Projected unit method

A definition of the projected unit method is given in FRS 17, as follows:

'An accrued benefits valuation method in which the scheme liabilities make allowance for projected earnings. An accrued benefits valuation method is a valuation method in which the scheme liabilities at the valuation date relate to:

(a) the benefits for pensioners and deferred pensioners (ie individuals who have ceased to be active members but are entitled to benefits payable at a later date) and their dependants, allowing where appropriate for future increases, and

(b) the accrued benefits for members in service on the valuation date.

The accrued benefits are the benefits for service up to a given point in time, whether vested rights or not.'[3]

A description, by the actuarial profession, of the main features of this method runs as follows:

'Under the projected unit method, a standard contribution rate expressed as a percentage of earnings is obtained by dividing the present value of all benefits which will accrue in the year following the valuation date (by reference to service in that year and projected final earnings) by the present value of members' earnings in that year. An actuarial liability is calculated by summing the present value of all benefits accrued at the valuation date (based on projected final earnings for members in service). The recommended contribution rate expressed as a percentage of earnings is obtained by modifying the standard contribution rate to reflect the difference between the value placed on the scheme assets for valuation purposes and this actuarial liability.'[4]

This method can result in a stable level of contributions provided the age profile of the workforce remains steady. In these circumstances it will generally form a suitable basis for the measurement of cost under SSAP 24. However, its use might have to be more critically considered if the characteristics of the scheme are likely to result in a more volatile contribution rate, and actuarial advice on this point may be necessary. Guidance Note 17 (GN 17) issued by the actuarial profession comments that (for SSAP 24 purposes) the method 'is unlikely to be satisfactory if it is evident from the circumstances that the standard contribution rate is likely to change in future years. A change might for example be foreseeable because (a) the scheme is or will be closed to new entrants, or (b) new entrants are admitted on a pension scale which is materially different in cost from the scale applicable to current members.'[5]

This method has emerged as the one which commands majority support among large companies applying SSAP 24. FRS 17 observes that, because of the time value of money, the economic reality is that the cost of providing a defined benefit increases nearer retirement.[6] Accordingly, it requires the use of the projected unit method as this particular method incorporates an estimate of future salary increases, which is considered necessary in order to achieve the fair value objective of the standard. Guidance on the projected unit method is given in the Guidance Note 26 (GN26) issued by the Faculty and Institute of Actuaries.'[7]

B Current unit method

This method is essentially similar to the projected unit method, with the vital distinction that it looks at current, rather than projected pay rates. As a result, the effects of salary inflation have to be picked up in future years in an accelerating pattern, which means that the cost is likely to be heavily skewed towards the later years of employment. For this reason such a method does not meet the accounting objective of SSAP 24. GN 17 comes to a similar conclusion, saying that the method 'is unsatisfactory if used without a control period [see C below] of adequate length, or if it is evident from the circumstances that the standard contribution rate is likely to change materially in future years. A change might for example be foreseeable (a) if the scheme is or will be closed to new entrants or if new entrants are admitted on a pension scale which is materially different in cost from the scale applicable to current members, or (b) as an effect of future pay increases upon accrued pension rights.'[8]

C Discontinuance method

This method, which is described in SSAP 24 as a 'current funding level' basis, is, as its name suggests, founded on the premise that the scheme is to be wound up immediately and the assets applied to meet the existing entitlements of the members. It therefore does not form an appropriate method for valuing the scheme on a forward-looking, going concern basis. Because of the objectives of the method, contribution rates are not calculated, and for all these reasons the use of a discontinuance approach could not provide an appropriate measure of cost under SSAP 24.

A variant of the discontinuance method, which is sometimes referred to as the 'discontinuance target method', is occasionally used to determine funding rates, and is quite commonly used by insurance companies. This involves funding for the discontinuance liability which would arise if the scheme were to be wound up at some specified time, say 20 years, in the future. The period chosen is referred to as the 'control period' in actuarial parlance. In principle this method would still not follow the accounting objective of SSAP 24, because it does not look through to the final salaries on which the pensions are expected to be paid. However, the greater the length of the control period, the nearer the method will become to one which is acceptable under the standard. Where the method is used, it will be necessary to obtain actuarial advice on whether it produces results which are materially different from one which is based on projected final salaries.

GN 17 says that 'a control period can be regarded as of adequate length if (a) the resulting standard contribution rate, which is to be used as the regular cost, is not altered materially by extending the control period and (b) the calculation of the pension cost makes specific provision for future increases in earnings not materially different from a full provision for all future increases in earnings, including merit increases, and not solely those occurring up to the end of the control period'.[9]

2.1.4 Possible actuarial methods – projected benefits methods

As discussed previously, these methods try to look at the eventual amount of pensions which are expected to be paid, and establish contribution rates which are designed to remain stable over the period of the employees' service. Usually, this means that they are designed to represent a level percentage of payroll costs, not a level figure in pounds, but the latter is also theoretically possible (although not an appropriate method for SSAP 24 purposes).

A Aggregate method

The actuaries' description of this method reads as follows:

'Under the aggregate method, a recommended contribution rate expressed as a percentage of earnings is obtained by dividing the excess of the present value of all benefits which have accrued and will accrue (based on total service and projected final earnings for members in service) over the value placed on the scheme assets for valuation purposes by the present value of total projected earnings for all members throughout their expected future membership.'[10]

This method does not in fact identify either the surplus or deficit on the fund or the element of contributions which relates to variations from regular cost. As a result it does not provide the analysis which the standard requires and is seldom likely to be a usable method without modification. It is regarded by some as rather a simplistic method of valuation, and while it has been quite extensively used in the past in the UK, it is now much less common.

GN 17 takes a similar view, but notes that it may be seen as a variant of the Attained Age Method or the Entry Age Method (both described below). It comments that it may be suitable where the scheme is closed to new entrants, but that otherwise one of these other two methods should be used so as to distinguish regular cost from variations.[11]

B *Attained age method*

This method is described by the actuaries thus:

'Under the attained age method, a standard contribution rate expressed as a percentage of earnings is obtained by dividing the present value of all benefits which will accrue to present members after the valuation date (by reference to service after the valuation date and projected final earnings) by the present value of total projected earnings for all members throughout their expected future membership. An actuarial liability is calculated by summing the present value of all benefits accrued at the valuation date (based on projected final earnings for members in service). The recommended contribution rate expressed as a percentage of earnings is obtained by modifying the standard contribution rate to reflect the difference between the value placed on the scheme assets for valuation purposes and the accrued actuarial liability.'[12]

GN 17 comments that the method is unlikely to be satisfactory '(a) where a scheme has a regular and significant flow of new entrants and if the payment of the standard contribution rate in respect of the new entrants is expected to create material surpluses or deficits, or (b) where a scheme is or will be closed to new entrants and the standard contribution rate is expected to increase materially at each succeeding valuation. (However the method can be satisfactory for a closed scheme where the regular cost is based throughout upon the standard contribution rate calculated in respect of the membership present at the time when the scheme was closed.)'[13]

C *Entry age method*

This method is comparatively rare in the UK, but has been more commonly used in North America. It is described as follows:

'Under the entry age method, a normal entry age is chosen which may be estimated from the actual membership records. A standard contribution rate expressed as a percentage of earnings is obtained by dividing the present value of all future benefits by reference to projected final earnings for a member entering at the normal entry age by the present value of total projected earnings throughout his expected future membership. An actuarial liability is calculated by deducting from the present value of total benefits (based on projected final earnings for members in service) the value of the standard contribution rate multiplied by the present value of total projected earnings for all members throughout their expected future membership. The recommended contribution rate expressed as a percentage of earnings is obtained by modifying the standard contribution rate to reflect the difference between the value placed on the scheme assets for valuation purposes and this actuarial liability.'[14]

According to GN 17, this method 'is unlikely to be satisfactory if the standard contribution rate is based on a weighted average of rates applicable to existing members of the scheme and the weights are likely to change in respect of future new entrants. A change might for example be foreseeable because (a) new entrants join at ages which are on average either higher or lower than the ages at which existing members joined, or (b) new entrants are admitted on a pension scale which is materially different in cost from the scale applicable to current members.'[15]

2.1.5 Actuarial valuation of assets

Under any of the above methods chosen for valuing the accrued benefits of the fund, the actuary will also have put a value on the fund's investments. Under SSAP 24 practice in this area differs, but generally the investments will not be valued directly at their quoted market prices on the relevant day but rather at a value which takes a longer term perspective. A common method will be to value the investments on the basis of their projected dividend income.

When this approach is applied, it provides an effective cushion against short-term fluctuations in the securities markets. Thus, the market crash which occurred in October 1987 did not have the devastating effect on the valuation of pension funds which would have resulted if the valuation had been based directly on market values. Conversely, the Budget change in July 1997 whereby pension funds lost the benefit of the tax credit on UK dividend income had a significant effect on the actuarial value of their investments, whereas there was no adverse movement in quoted share prices.[16]

As discussed at 3.7.1 below, FRS 17 requires scheme assets to be revalued annually to market value. Accordingly, there is no need for any actuarial advice in determining asset values for FRS 17 purposes. Actuarial advice will be required, however, for the much more subjective task of estimated expected returns on assets, this requirement of FRS 17 is discussed at 3.8.1 C below.

2.1.6 Conclusion

As noted above, SSAP 24 does not specify that a particular actuarial valuation method be used, so long as the effect is to allocate the cost rationally and systematically over the period of the employees' services. This means that the calculations must be based on the final salaries which are expected to be paid. It would seem, therefore, that the only methods discussed above which could *not* achieve this objective are those which do not try to take into account the value of the pension which will be paid on the basis of final salary – the current unit method and the discontinuance basis. As noted above, there may also be a difficulty, where the entry age method is used, in obtaining a sensible split between regular cost and variations.

For mature schemes, the remaining valuation methods seem likely in practice to produce broadly similar costs for recognition in the profit and loss account, and on that basis they are likely to be equally acceptable for SSAP 24 purposes. In fact it is often the case that the effect of using different methods is much less significant than the effect of varying the amounts of the key actuarial assumptions. However, for schemes which are likely not to remain stable in terms of their age profile, companies should discuss the circumstances in more detail with their actuaries. We recommend that they should base their choice of method on that which can be predicted to show greatest stability of pension cost as a percentage of pensionable payroll in the future.

As companies move from SSAP 24 to FRS 17, the choice of actuarial methods is removed as the projected unit method must be applied.

2.2 Actuarial assumptions and best estimates

Both SSAP 24 and FRS 17 discuss actuarial assumptions at a general level in similar, but not identical terms and these are discussed below. FRS 17 also provides more detailed guidance on certain issues, in particular the rate used to discount the scheme liabilities which is discussed at 2.2.2 below.

Both standards make reference to the use of 'best estimates' and in the context of such uncertain and long term liabilities this is worthy of comment.

It is quite difficult to talk about 'best estimates' in the context of actuarial assumptions, because the matters which are the subject of estimation can be extremely uncertain and a wide range of possible estimates could be made. Nevertheless it is appropriate that, so far as possible, the choice is made sensibly around the middle of the possible range rather than at the extreme. Regarding SSAP 24 valuations, GN 17 offers guidance to the effect that 'it is not inappropriate to adopt assumptions which, taken together, are somewhat more likely to lead to surplus rather than to deficiency at future valuations, this being in accordance with the accounting convention of prudence. However, it is not satisfactory to include significant margins which are likely to lead to future surpluses or deficits which are material … .'[17]

2.2.1 SSAP 24

SSAP 24 requires that the actuarial assumptions and method, taken as a whole, should be compatible and should lead to the actuary's best estimate of the cost of providing the pension benefits promised.[18] Frequently, the assumptions made by the actuary for funding purposes cannot be described as 'best estimates', because, for example, the company has consciously decided to fund the scheme strongly and has therefore asked that assumptions be made on a deliberately conservative basis. While this is entirely legitimate as the basis of funding decisions, it is necessary to reconsider the assumptions when they are to be used to measure cost for accounting purposes; if necessary it may lead to the use of two different sets of assumptions, one for accounting purposes and the other for the purposes of funding.

The standard talks about the assumptions 'taken as a whole': because of the way in which the various factors interrelate, it is possible to arrive at a similar overall result by flexing individual estimates in opposite directions so as to compensate for an optimistic estimate in one area by making a conservative assumption in another. In this way, it is also mathematically possible to make implicit allowance for factors which on the face of it are not provided for, such as increases in pensions.

In our view it is preferable that implicit offsetting allowances of this nature are not made, and that each assumption in isolation should seek to reflect a realistic view of what will happen in the future. We take this view partly because it makes the valuation process more explicit to those within the company who are involved in it, but also because the standard requires the key assumptions to be disclosed in the accounts and, unless they are meaningful on a stand-alone basis, the reader of the accounts may be misled as to the strength of the valuation on which the figures are based.

2.2.2 FRS 17

FRS 17 sets out a number of rules that need to be followed when making actuarial assumptions, as follows:

- they should be mutually compatible, and lead to the best estimate of future cash flows that will arise under the scheme liabilities;
- they should take account of expected future events that will affect the cost of the benefits promised (for example, cost of living increases, salary increases, and rates of early retirement where members of the scheme are entitled under the scheme to take early retirement); and
- financial assumptions (being those that are affected by economic conditions, such as the discount rate) should reflect market expectations at the balance sheet date.[19]

FRS 17 observes that some assumptions are affected by the same economic factors, and explains that such assumptions will be mutually compatible if they reflect the same underlying economic factors consistently. Furthermore, to be consistent with the measurement of scheme assets at fair value, assumptions should also reflect market expectations at the balance sheet date.[20] The standard illustrates the idea of mutual compatibility by noting that the assumed rate of salary increases and the discount rate must reflect the same rate of general inflation, and suggests that an indication of the general rate of inflation will be given by the yield on long-dated inflation-linked bonds (where a liquid market in such exists) relative to those on fixed rate bonds.[21]

The third bullet point above is perhaps the most significant. There was a great deal of debate during the development of FRS 17 regarding the most appropriate rate at which to discount the scheme liabilities, with the ASB initially indicating (in its second discussion paper) that it favoured a rate equal to the return on a hypothetical portfolio of assets that exactly matched the liabilities. Subsequent to further research conducted by the Faculty and Institute of Actuaries, the ASB changed its view and FRS 17 stipulates that the discount rate should be the current rate of return on a high quality corporate bond of equivalent currency and term to the scheme liabilities.[22] High quality bonds means those rated AA or equivalent status. However if there is no liquid market in appropriate bonds, a reasonable proxy should be used – the standard suggests that this could be the rate on a government bond plus a margin for assumed credit risk derived from global bond markets.[23]

There is an element of contradiction (or, perhaps more precisely, of redundant explanatory material) in the standard regarding the impact of inflation on measuring the present value of a future liability. There are two distinct approaches that may be taken. On the one hand, the future cash flows are expressed in current prices, in which case a discount rate which excludes the effects of general inflation should be used. Alternatively, the future cash flows are expressed in expected future prices, in which case a discount rate which includes a return to cover expected inflation should be used. Given that markets will price expected inflation in determining bond values (and hence yields), the current rate of return on a corporate bond is appropriate to the latter methodology.

As noted earlier, FRS 17 requires that the assumptions used in applying the projected unit method should be mutually compatible and lead to the best estimate of the future cash flows that will arise under the scheme liabilities.[24] This seems to mean quite clearly that inflation must be built into the cash flow projections, and hence the discount rate used should not be adjusted for inflation. In light of this, it is somewhat surprising that an explanatory paragraph of the standard discussing the discount rate appears to allow (in certain circumstances) a choice between the two methods. The standard observes that many pension schemes provide benefits at least partially linked to inflation, and that this feature could be reflected by using the rate of return on an index-linked bond.[25] In other words, account for inflation through the discount rate and therefore express cash flows in current prices. This approach seems to be in conflict with the earlier requirement, although the standard does note that in practice few index-linked bonds exist and that a more reliable approach would be to take account of inflation via the cash flows.[26]

The present value of a discounted liability will be the same whether inflation is taken account of in the cash flow projections or in the discount rate, as higher cash flows (increased by projected inflation) will be discounted at a higher discount rate. However, the unwinding of the discount through the profit and loss account (discussed at 6.8.1 B below) will not be the same. This was an issue the ASB seemed to have overlooked in its accounting standard dealing with provisions (see 4.2.4 of Chapter 28) and the confusion partially remains in FRS 17. Whilst the confusing and contradictory discussion of this issue in FRS 17 is clearly unhelpful, we believe that the most appropriate interpretation is to take account of inflation by increasing the projected future cash flows, then selecting a discount rate currently available on corporate bonds.

Making the various assumptions about the future that are necessary in applying the projected unit method, so as to arrive at a best estimate of the future cash flows of the scheme, is undoubtedly a subjective process requiring the exercise of judgement. FRS 17 notes that this is particularly difficult when estimating the future cost of providing retirement healthcare. In particular, the standard notes that such costs often increase at a faster rate than either the retail price index or national earnings rate. In light of this, the standard notes that relevant considerations in determining the assumptions used to arrive at the retirement healthcare obligation include:

- advances in medical skills and technologies, often involving more expensive treatment;
- the rise in the expectations of prospective patients; and
- the effect of the above on companies, governments and insurance schemes in cutting back benefits, or making the patient pay a proportion.[27]

2.3 The role of the actuary

By virtue of the wording of the trust document, many actuaries are appointed by, and are responsible only to, the trustees of the pension scheme and not to the employer company. Consideration should be given in these cases to extending the actuary's duties under the trust deed to report also to the company. However, this may not always be appropriate, and in these cases the company may wish to appoint a separate and independent actuary.

The accountancy bodies have produced an Audit Brief entitled 'The work of a pension scheme actuary'[28] which auditors, and other interested parties, may find useful when reviewing the results of actuaries' work. More recently, the Auditing Practices Board released a consultation draft of a proposed practice note on the auditors' consideration of the cost of retirement benefits under FRS 17 which may also prove of interest.[29]

2.3.1 SSAP 24

In carrying out his work in relation to SSAP 24, the actuary will need to ensure that the methods and assumptions which have been chosen fulfil the following requirements:

- they meet the accounting objective of recognising the expected cost of providing the benefits on a systematic and rational basis over the period during which the employer derives benefit from the employees' services;
- they make full provision for the expected benefits over the anticipated service lives of the employees;
- they take account of the circumstances of the specific employer and his workforce – for example, it would not be appropriate to use a method which assumes a steady flow of new entrants if the employer has pension arrangements which are available only to existing employees;
- they recognise the effect of expected future increases in earnings, including merit increases, up to the assumed retirement date or earlier date of leaving or dying in service;
- they take account of future increases in deferred pensions and pensions payment where the employer has expressed or implied a commitment to grant such increases;

- they enable benefit levels to be calculated based on situations most likely to be experienced and not on contingent events unlikely to occur. For example, if there has been a regular practice of enhancing pensions on early severance and this is likely to be a feature of the employer's employment policies, it would not be acceptable to assume no enhancement on early retirements;
- they are used consistently over all similar pension arrangements within the employer's business and consistently between different accounting periods except where different circumstances justify a different approach; and
- taken as a whole, they are mutually compatible and lead to the actuary's best estimate of the cost of providing the benefits.

2.3.2 *FRS 17*

As a matter of law, directors are responsible for preparing accounts, and accordingly, for making any judgements and estimates that are necessary. FRS 17 emphasises this by making it clear that the actuarial assumptions are ultimately the responsibility of the directors, however it goes on to require that the assumptions should be set upon the advice of a qualified actuary.[30] The emphasis of FRS 17 on the actuarial *assumptions* reflects the fact that many of the possible choices (open to actuarial judgement) available under SSAP 24 have been removed in the more prescriptive new standard.

3 REQUIREMENTS OF FRS 17

3.1 Objective

FRS 17 sets out its objective as follows:

'... to ensure that:

(a) financial statements reflect at fair value the assets and liabilities arising from an employer's retirement benefit obligations and any related funding;

(b) the operating costs of providing retirement benefits to employees are recognised in the accounting period(s) in which the benefits are earned by the employees, and the related finance costs and any other changes in value of the assets and liabilities are recognised in the accounting periods in which they arise; and

(c) the financial statements contain adequate disclosure of the cost of providing retirement benefits and the related gains, losses, assets and liabilities.'[31]

As can be seen, the key objective is to record in the balance sheet any pension asset or liability at fair value. From this starting point the standard then goes on to specify in detail how this amount should be calculated, and how changes in the value from one balance sheet to the next should be reflected in the profit and loss account and the STRGL.

3.2 Scope

FRS 17 applies to all accounts intended to give a true and fair view of a reporting employer's financial position and profit or loss (or income and expenditure), the only exception is the now customary exemption for the very smallest of companies who have adopted the *Financial Reporting Standard For Smaller Entities.*[32]

The rules in the standard apply to all retirement benefits, which are defined as 'all forms of consideration given by an employer in exchange for services rendered by employees that are payable after the completion of employment'.[33] By far the most common form of retirement benefit in the UK is a pension, and many of the issues discussed in this chapter are discussed in terms of pension schemes. It should be noted however that all the measurement and disclosure rules of FRS 17 apply equally to other retirement benefits (for example the provision of retirement healthcare), and also to overseas schemes.[34] FRS 17 stresses that it covers both funded and unfunded schemes and that it requires a liability to be recognised when benefits are earned by employees, and not when they are due to be paid. Furthermore, the fact that the employer is funded by central government, or any other body, is not a reason for the employer not to recognise its own liabilities arising under FRS 17.[35]

Retirement benefits do not include termination benefits payable as a result of either (i) an employer's decision to terminate an employee's employment before the normal retirement date or (ii) an employee's decision to accept voluntary redundancy in exchange for those benefits. This is because they will not meet the definition of a retirement benefit as they are not given 'in exchange for services rendered by employees'.[36]

3.3 Defined contribution schemes and defined benefit schemes

In common with its predecessor (SSAP 24) and its international equivalent (IAS 19), FRS 17 draws a distinction between defined contribution schemes and defined benefit schemes. The approach it takes is to define the former, with the latter being the default category, as follows:

'*Defined contribution scheme:-*

A pension or other retirement benefit scheme into which an employer pays regular contributions fixed as an amount or as a percentage of pay and will have no legal or constructive obligation to pay further contributions if the scheme does not have sufficient assets to pay all employee benefits relating to employee service in the current and prior periods.

An individual member's benefits are determined by reference to contributions paid into the scheme in respect of that member, usually increased by an amount based on the investment return on those contributions.

Defined contribution schemes may also provide death-in-service benefits. For the purposes of this definition, death-in-service benefits are not deemed to relate to employee service in the current and prior periods.

Defined benefit scheme:-

A pension or other retirement benefit scheme other than a defined contribution scheme.

Usually, the scheme rules define the benefits independently of the contributions payable, and the benefits are not directly related to the investments of the scheme. The scheme may be funded or unfunded.'[37]

The reference to a defined contribution scheme providing death in service benefits is a change from FRED 20. Whilst the wording is somewhat convoluted, what it appears to be saying is that a scheme will not be transformed from a defined contribution scheme into a defined benefit scheme just by the addition of life cover. Death in service benefits are discussed separately later in FRS 17, but only in a section of the standard dealing with defined benefit schemes, and it is far from clear if they are intended to apply to the death in service benefit element of defined contribution schemes as well. In our view they should be. This is because the alternative is that they would fall to be dealt with by FRS 12 which would produce (especially for any liabilities not insured with third parties) a significantly different treatment of a similar transaction depending on the nature of *other* benefits awarded by the scheme. The rules for death in service benefits under a defined benefit scheme are discussed at 3.7.2 B below.

3.4 Multi-employer schemes

Although FRS 17 applies to all accounts giving a true and fair view, there are some special provisions for multi-employer defined benefit schemes. Examples of such schemes would include those set up to provide pensions across an entire industry, and also (and more commonly) a corporate group where various subsidiaries participate in a joint scheme. The standard requires that a reporting entity participating in a multi-employer defined benefit scheme should follow the normal rules, subject to two important exceptions.

The first exception is where contributions are set only in relation to the current service period, and are not affected by any surplus or deficit in the scheme relating to the past service of employees of the reporting entity or any other participating employer.[38] In this scenario, whilst the scheme provides defined benefits to the employee, the employer is only committed to defined contributions. The standard notes that for this to be the case there must be clear evidence of a third party who will be liable to make up any shortfall in the fund.[39] As such schemes are, from the perspective of the employer, defined contribution schemes they should be accounted for as such.[40]

The second exception is potentially much more important. The standard acknowledges that an employer may participate in a multi-employer defined benefit scheme, with contributions affected by a surplus or deficit in the scheme, yet be unable to identify its share of the underlying assets and liabilities in the scheme on a consistent and reasonable basis.[41] The standard does not discuss what might constitute a 'consistent and reasonable basis' in this context. Accordingly it is not entirely clear what the circumstances need to be for an employer to determine that it is unable to identify its share of the underlying scheme assets and liabilities on such a basis. For instance, if the employer's contributions are affected by a surplus or deficit in the scheme, would an allocation of the scheme surplus or deficit on the basis of number of employees or payroll costs be a 'reasonable and consistent basis'? The explanatory text in the standard suggests it normally would not, as it cites as an example an arrangement where contributions are set at a common level without reference to the characteristics of the workforces of individual employer.[42] In such a case the reporting employer would be exposed to actuarial risks relating to the employees of other employers. In these circumstances FRS 17 allows the scheme to be accounted for as a defined contribution scheme, with enhanced disclosure[43] (see item (l) at 3.9.1 F below). The standard observes that many group schemes may be run on this basis.[44] When this is the case it may be possible that every individual company in the group (including the parent) will account for the scheme as a defined contribution scheme, with defined benefit accounting only applied in the group accounts.

3.5 Implementation date and transitional arrangements

As indicated at 1.1 above, the ASB has given FRS 17 a long implementation period, with phased disclosure requirements. The standard comes fully into force for accounting periods ending on or after 22 June 2003; early adoption is encouraged but not required. For periods ending on or after 22 June 2001 various disclosures relating to the balance sheet are required. These disclosures are supplemented, for periods ending on or after 22 June 2002, with information about the profit and loss account and STRGL. The ASB cites three reasons for requiring two years of increasing disclosure before the measurement rules come into force, as follows:

(a) to avoid companies having to revisit previous actuarial valuations;

(b) to give the Board a chance to persuade IASC to follow the UK approach on the immediate recognition of actuarial gains and losses; and

(c) to give preparers and users of accounts the opportunity to become accustomed to the figures arising under the FRS before they are recognised in the primary statements.[45]

The disclosure requirements for defined contribution schemes are discussed at 3.6.1 and those for defined benefit schemes at 3.9.

3.6 Defined contribution schemes

3.6.1 *Accounting*

Accounting for defined contribution (sometimes referred to as money purchase) schemes is straightforward under FRS 17. Since the employer has no obligation beyond payment of the contributions which it has agreed to make, there is no difficulty in measuring the cost of providing pensions; it is simply the amount of those contributions payable in respect of the accounting period.[46] If the amount actually paid in the period is more or less than the amount payable, a prepayment or accrual will appear in the balance sheet in accordance with normal accounting practice, but otherwise the payments made will simply be charged in the profit and loss account when made.

FRS 17 requires, without exception, that the cost relating to a defined contribution scheme should be recognised within operating profit in the profit and loss account.[47] In what appears to be a drafting oversight, the standard does not explicitly allow for cases when costs of defined contribution schemes are included in the cost of an asset, for example stock (although this treatment, required in certain circumstances by other accounting standards, is explicitly allowed by FRS 17 for defined benefit schemes). It seems unlikely that the ASB intended to disturb existing practice in this area.

Some defined contribution schemes may also provide death in service benefits. As discussed at 3.3 above, the definition of a defined contribution scheme in the standard means that it will not fail to be one by the addition of this particular type of defined benefit. However, any such death in service cover will still need to be accounted for, and this is discussed at 3.7.2 B below.

3.6.2 *Disclosure*

The disclosure requirements of the standard for defined contribution schemes are also very simple. They are:

(a) the nature of the scheme (i.e. defined contribution);

(b) the cost for the period; and

(c) any outstanding or prepaid contributions at the balance sheet date.[48]

3.7 Defined benefit schemes – balance sheet valuation and presentation

As noted at 3.1 above, the first accounting objective of FRS 17 is to estimate the fair value of any asset or liability arising from defined benefit schemes. The standard acknowledges that pension funds will not typically be subsidiaries of the sponsoring employer, and accordingly that consolidation would not be appropriate.[49] However, the assertion is that any net surplus or deficit in a scheme represents a net asset (to the extent that it is recoverable) or net liability (to the extent that there is a legal or constructive obligation to make good a deficit) of the employer. FRS 17 explains this assertion as follows:

'A surplus in the scheme gives rise to an asset of the employer to the extent that:

(a) the employer controls its use, ie has the ability to use the surplus to generate future economic benefits for itself, either in the form of a reduction in future contributions or a refund from the scheme; and

(b) that control is a result of past events (contributions paid by the employer and investment growth in excess of rights earned by the employees).

'Usually the employer's obligation under the trust deed is to pay such contributions as the actuary believes to be necessary to keep the scheme fully funded but without building up a surplus. When a surplus arises, it is unlikely that the employer can be required to make contributions to maintain the surplus. In addition, the award of benefit improvements is also usually in the hands of the employer. Thus, in general, the employer controls the use of a surplus in the scheme.

'Conversely, the employer has a liability if it has a legal or constructive obligation to make good a deficit in the defined benefit scheme. In general, the employer will either have a legal obligation under the terms of the scheme trust deed or will have by its past actions and statements created a constructive obligation as defined in FRS 12 'Provisions, Contingent Liabilities and Contingent Assets'. The legal or constructive obligation to fund the deficit should be assumed to apply to the deficit based on assumptions used under the FRS.'[50]

It is this net asset or liability that will be reflected in the balance sheet of the employer.[51] In order to calculate the balance sheet figure it is necessary to look through the trust structure of a typical pension scheme and consider the underlying assets and liabilities.

The standard sets out detailed rules for the measurement of the balance sheet figure which may be categorised as follows:

- valuation of the assets in the scheme;
- valuation of the defined benefit obligation;
- frequency of valuations;
- presentation of the resultant surplus or deficit in the balance sheet; and
- adjustments to the surplus or deficit for balance sheet purposes.

These aspects are discussed in turn below. The actuarial aspects of accounting for pensions are further discussed at 2 above.

3.7.1 *Valuation of the assets in the scheme*

Unlike IAS 19, FRS 17 does not define scheme assets. It does, however, state that 'Notional funding of a pension scheme does not give rise to assets in a scheme for the purposes of the FRS.'[52] Presumably this means that only assets transferred to an independent trust (as is usually the case for UK schemes) are covered by the rules in the standard, and that any other assets merely represent 'notional funding' and are treated in accordance with the normal rules for the assets in question. The assets of the scheme are to include current assets as well as investments, and should be reduced by any liabilities such as accrued expenses.[53]

Assets of the scheme should be measured at fair value as at the balance sheet date.[54] 'Fair value' is not defined for the purposes of FRS 17, although the term is used extensively in accounting standards, and is generally ascribed the meaning given in FRS 7 as follows: 'The amount at which an asset or liability could be exchanged in an arm's length transaction between informed and willing parties, other than in a forced or liquidation sale'.[55]

The standard sets down the following requirements for particular types of assets:

- quoted securities should be measured at mid-market value (or the average of bid and offer prices for unitised securities);

- for unquoted securities an estimate of fair value must be made. FRS 17 gives no guidance on how this estimation should be performed. The appropriate estimation methods will need to be determined by directors, although it would seem unlikely that trustees would allow a significant proportion of scheme assets to be invested in such securities;
- property should be measured at open market value, or another more appropriate basis in accordance with the Appraisal and Valuation Manual of the Royal Institution of Chartered Surveyors and the Practice Statements contained therein; and
- insurance policies should be valued by a method which gives the best approximation of fair value. A policy that exactly matches the amount and timing of some scheme liabilities should be measured at the same amount as those liabilities.[56]

It is worth noting that these valuation rules are very similar to those set out in the Statement of Recommended Practice – *Financial Reports of Pension Schemes* – (the SORP) published by the Pensions Research Accounting Group which will be adopted by most UK pension schemes in their own accounts. There is, however, one notable exception relating to insurance policies. In certain circumstances, for example when the purchase of a matching insurance policy means the trustees have in effect discharged their full liability to particular members or beneficiaries, the SORP recommends that the policies be included at a nil value.[57] In such circumstances adjustments will be necessary to asset values determined by a pension scheme in accordance with the SORP before they can be used for FRS 17 purposes by the employer.

3.7.2 *Valuation of the defined benefit obligation*

The obligations of a defined benefit scheme are the liabilities to pay pensions and other benefits to scheme members in the future. FRS 17 refers to these obligations as scheme liabilities, and defines them as follows:

'The liabilities of a defined benefit scheme for outgoings due after the valuation date.

Scheme liabilities measured using the projected unit method reflect the benefits that the employer is committed to provide for service up to the valuation date.'[58]

In the ASB's view, defined benefit obligations would ideally be measured at market value.[59] However, the liabilities of defined benefit schemes are not bought and sold on a market, which means that the balance sheet objective of the standard requires an estimate of fair value to be made. The long time-scale and numerous uncertainties involved mean that actuarial techniques are needed in estimating the fair value of scheme liabilities. This involves estimating the future cash flows arising under the scheme liabilities based on various actuarial assumptions (such as future salary growth and rates of mortality and staff turnover) then discounting the cash flows at an appropriate rate.[60] To this end, the standard specifies the actuarial method to be applied and gives guidance on the various assumptions used, including a requirement that they be set upon advice of an actuary.

A Actuarial method for estimating scheme liabilities

As observed at 2.1 above, there are various actuarial techniques for valuing defined benefit liabilities, which fall into two main categories – accrued benefits methods and prospective benefits methods. The main difference between them lies in their treatment of the time value of money. The ASB summarises these two categories in FRS 17 as follows:

'Under an accrued benefits method each period is allocated its share of the eventual undiscounted cost, the liability arising from the costs to date is discounted and the discount unwinds in the normal manner over the employee's service life. This results in a higher cost at the end of an employee's service life than at the beginning because the effect of discounting the cost lessens as the employee approaches retirement. Under a prospective benefits method, the total cost including all the interest that will accrue is spread evenly over the employee's service life.'[61]

FRS 17 observes that, because of the time value of money, the economic reality is that the cost of providing a defined benefit increases nearer retirement.[62] Accordingly, it requires the use of an accrued benefits method, and that the liabilities are discounted at a rate that reflects the time value of money and the characteristics of the liability.[63] In particular, FRS 17 specifies the projected unit method (see 2.1.3 A above) as this particular method incorporates an estimate of future salary increases, which is considered necessary in order to achieve the fair value objective of the standard.

This is to be applied not just to the benefits formally promised under the scheme but also to any constructive obligations for further benefits. A constructive obligation for further benefits arises where the employer has, by a public statement or past practice, created a valid expectation in the employees that such benefits will be granted.[64] An example could be giving inflationary increases to pensions beyond those guaranteed by the scheme rules.

As noted at 3.2 above, termination benefits payable as a result of either an employer's decision to terminate an employee's employment before the normal retirement date, or an employee's decision to accept voluntary redundancy in exchange for those benefits are not covered by FRS 17. It is likely, however, that terminations will have an impact on the assets and liabilities of a defined benefit scheme, and this is addressed by the standard. FRS 17 observes that an employer is not committed to make such terminations and that it is not appropriate to assume a reduction in scheme benefits on the grounds of a future curtailment.[65] Any impact of terminations on the defined benefit scheme will be accounted for as a settlement or curtailment, but only once the employer becomes committed to making them (these are discussed at 3.8.2 A below). However, if the scheme gives employees the right (either legally or through a constructive obligation) to take early retirement the expected rate of early retirement should be included in the actuarial assumptions.[66]

The normal application of the projected unit method is to allocate benefits to periods of service in accordance with the scheme rules. For example, a typical scheme may entitle employees to a pension of 2% of their final salary for each year of service to the employer – in other words benefits are earned on a straight-line basis. In what appears to be a pre-emptive anti-avoidance measure (or possibly a departure from the objective of balance sheet purity on the grounds of prudence), FRS 17 addresses the situation where the scheme formula 'attributes a disproportionate share of the total benefits to later years of service'. In such cases FRS 17 requires straight-line attribution to be used instead of the actual benefit formula.[67]

One further liability is acknowledged by FRS 17, over and above the routine obligations to pay defined benefits, and this relates to the often legally complex issue of who owns any surplus in a pension scheme. In cases where there is an obligation (either through the scheme rules or constructively) to share a surplus with employees, the standard requires that the amount that will be passed to members to be treated as increasing the scheme liabilities.[68] The standard does not give any indication of how the debit entry should be treated. One approach would be to allocate the debit entry to the profit and loss account and STRGL in a similar manner to that required for restricting a surplus to its recoverable amount (see 3.8.3 below). Another approach would be to treat it as an adjustment to the actuarial gains and losses and reflect it in the STRGL.

The standard also discusses the reverse of an obligation to share a surplus with employees – an obligation on members to help make good a deficit. Whilst it is normally to be assumed that a deficit will be borne by the employer, this is not the case if the scheme rules require members' contributions to be increased to help fund a deficit. In such cases the present value of the required additional contributions should be treated as reducing the deficit recognised by the employer.[69] FRS 17 is similarly silent on how this reduction of the deficit should be presented in the profit and loss account and STRGL.

B Death in service and incapacity benefits

In a change from FRED 20, FRS 17 contains a separate discussion of death in service and incapacity benefits. This is included in a section of the standard dealing only with defined benefit schemes although, as noted at 3.3 above, in our view it could also apply to life cover provided along with a defined contribution scheme. What FRS 17 says is this:

'A charge should be made to operating profit to reflect the expected cost of providing any death-in-service or incapacity benefits for the period. Any difference between that expected cost and amounts actually incurred should be treated as an actuarial gain or loss.

Where a scheme insures the death-in-service costs, the expected cost for the accounting period is simply the premium payable for the period. Where the costs are not insured, the expected cost reflects the probability of any employees dying in the period and the benefit that would then be paid out.'[70]

It is likely that this change was introduced to reflect the expectation that most schemes will put in place insurance cover for death in service benefits. When this is the case, it seems that rather than using actuarial techniques to estimate the expected liability, an insurance premium is taken to be a practical measure of the cost.

3.7.3 *Frequency of valuations*

FRS 17 only requires a full actuarial valuation by a qualified actuary at least every three years. However, the fair value objective of the standard requires that the actuary update the latest valuation at each balance sheet date, so as to reflect current conditions.[71] In particular, the assets in the scheme need to be updated to fair value and the scheme liabilities need to be updated for changes in financial assumptions such as current bond rates.[72]

The standard notes that other assumptions, such as mortality rates or the expected leaving rate, *may* not need to be updated annually.[73] The use of the word 'may' clearly indicates that the standard envisages circumstances when demographic assumptions *will* need to be reconsidered more frequently than every three years, although no further explanation is given. Examples might include significant changes to the membership profile of the scheme, for example following business acquisitions and disposals. Judgement will be required in individual cases to determine the extent to which actuarial valuations need to be reconsidered each year, and companies will need to discuss this with their actuaries. The ASB notes, in Appendix IV to the FRS, that the actuarial profession is preparing guidance on what the annual update should involve.[74]

3.7.4 *Presentation in the balance sheet*

Under FRS 17 a defined benefit surplus or deficit is to be presented separately on the face of the balance sheet.[75] Any unpaid contributions to the scheme will be shown within creditors in the normal way. The standard requires the creation of a new balance sheet caption for the scheme surplus or deficit, to be shown after all other assets and liabilities. If a reporting entity has more than one defined benefit scheme, a separate total should be given on the face of the balance sheet for defined benefit assets and for defined benefit liabilities.[76] For companies governed by the Companies Act 1985 (the Act) FRS 17 specifies the presentation by reference to the statutory formats set out in Schedule 4 to the Act, as follows:

'Companies adopting format 1 (which is the vast majority of UK companies) must present the pension balance between format item J (accruals and deferred income) and format item K (capital and reserves). This presentation is the same whether the balance is as asset or a liability.

Companies adopting format 2 will show any defined benefit asset after asset item D (prepayments and accrued income) and any liability after liability item D (accruals and deferred income).'

Whatever the location of the pension balance, it is to be stated net of any associated deferred tax.[77]

The standard does not explain why a defined benefit item in the balance sheet should be treated so differently from other assets and liabilities. In particular, there is no explanation as to why a pension asset should not be located with the other assets of the company, why a liability should not be included in the specific statutory caption (format 1 item I. 1. pensions and similar obligations) nor why the balance should be stated net of deferred tax.

Some company directors may have reservations over adapting the statutory formats in this way. Although the Act does allow adaptation of the arrangement, headings and sub-headings required by the formats, this only extends to those assigned an Arabic number and even then only when the special nature of the company's business requires such adaptation. Appendix II to the FRS dealing with legal requirements does not address this specific issue, however it does state that the ASB has received legal advice that the requirements of FRS 17 do not contravene the Act.[78]

3.7.5 *Adjustments to the surplus or deficit for balance sheet purposes*

The basic requirement of FRS 17 is that any scheme surplus or deficit is reflected (net of deferred tax) directly in the balance sheet. There are two circumstances, however, where the balance sheet figure will not simply be the surplus or deficit calculated as described above. The first relates to the recoverability of a surplus, and as such is consistent with the objective of recording any asset at fair value. The second, in what seems a departure from the balance sheet purity of the standard, relates to past service costs.

A Asset recoverability

FRS 17 observes that an employer may not control or be able to benefit from the whole of a surplus – it may be so large that the employer cannot absorb it all through reduced contributions, and refunds may be difficult to obtain.[79] Accordingly, FRS 17 sets a ceiling on any asset to be recognised by stipulating that a surplus may only be recognised as an asset to the extent that the employer is able to recover it either through reduced contributions in the future or through refunds from the scheme.[80] For the purposes of this recoverability test:

- any refunds must have been agreed by the trustees of the pension fund by the balance sheet date;[81] and
- the amount that can be recovered through reduced future contributions is the present value of the liability expected to arise from future service by current and future employees, less the present value of any future employee contributions. It should be based on the assumptions used under FRS 17 (not the funding assumptions) and should be discounted using the same discount rate applied to measure the scheme liabilities. In performing this calculation, a declining membership should be reflected if appropriate. If not it should be assumed that new joiners will replace leavers in perpetuity, but no growth in membership may be assumed.[82]

The standard does not explain what is meant by the phrase 'a declining membership should be reflected if appropriate' in this context. In particular, it does not discuss whether expected future redundancies should be taken into account in computing the recoverable surplus.

In practice, employers may use a surplus in the pension scheme to fund improvements to the benefits available to the members. FRS 17 stresses that if a surplus *could* be recoverable (in its terms) by reduced future contributions, then it must be reflected on the balance sheet – the amount recoverable reflects the *maximum* possible to be recovered without assuming an increase in the number of employees covered by the scheme.[83] An intention to use a surplus to enhance benefits does not alter this – any benefit improvements must instead be treated as a past service cost (see below) when, and only when, the employer is committed to this course of action.

Any restriction of a pension scheme surplus is accounted for by reducing the balance sheet asset, with separate disclosure in the note reconciling the surplus to the balance sheet figure (see 3.9 below). The treatment of this reduction in the profit and loss account and STRGL is discussed at 3.8.3 below.

B Past service costs

A past service cost is defined in FRS 17 as 'The increase in the present value of the scheme liabilities related to employee service in prior periods arising in the current period as a result of the introduction of, or improvement to, retirement benefits'.[84] In other words, members of the scheme become entitled to greater defined benefits than they were previously, and credit is given for years of service rendered before the award of the improvement. Accordingly, past service costs will not include increases that the employer is already committed to make (either formally or through a constructive obligation); these will have been accounted for already in the actuarial assessment of scheme liabilities. Examples of benefit improvements that would constitute past service costs include the introduction of spouse benefits or the grant of early retirement with added-on years of service.[85]

In an unexplained departure from the balance sheet objective of the standard, the increase in the actuarial liability as a result of such an award is recognised on a straight-line basis over the period during which the benefit vests.[86] Often, benefit improvements are fully vested on grant, which means the whole of the increase in the liability will be recognised immediately in the balance sheet. However, if an improvement vests over a longer period, accruing the increased liability on a straight-line basis will mean that the liability in the balance sheet is not equal to that calculated under the projected unit method. This is because the projected unit method involves an estimate of the total benefits expected to be paid in the future, including those that have been granted but have not yet vested. Any unrecognised past service costs should be deducted from the scheme liabilities for the purpose of calculating the balance sheet item.[87]

3.8 Defined benefit schemes – recognition in the performance statements

Although any net surplus or deficit in a defined benefit scheme is considered a single asset or liability for balance sheet purposes, the annual movement in this balance is not considered a single item of cost or income. Rather, the movement from the opening to closing balance (other than that arising from contributions to the scheme) must be analysed into a number of components which are then reported in different parts of the profit and loss account or in the STRGL.

The standard identifies four components which will be relevant to every reporting period (described as periodic costs) and two which will only be relevant when certain one-off transactions have been entered into (non-periodic costs).[88] Although not used elsewhere in the standard, the distinction between periodic and non-periodic costs is a convenient one, and has been adopted in the discussion below. Periodic costs and the required accounting treatment for them are considered at 3.8.1 below and non-periodic costs are considered at 3.8.2. In a welcome addition to FRED 20, FRS 17 also gives some guidance on how to reflect any restriction of a surplus to its recoverable amount (discussed at 3.7.5 above) in the two performance statements; this is discussed at 3.8.3 below.

3.8.1 Periodic costs

A Current service cost

This is defined as 'the increase in the present value of the scheme liabilities expected to arise from employee service in the current period.'[89] It will be actuarially determined as part of the projected unit methodology and is broadly similar to the regular cost under SSAP 24. One crucial difference between FRS 17's current service cost and SSAP 24's regular cost is the discount rate used in the computation. The current service cost is to be based on the interest rate used in measuring the scheme liabilities at the beginning of the period.[90] As discussed at 2.2.2 above, that rate is the current rate of return on a high quality corporate bond at that time, which means the current service cost will vary year-on-year with movements in the discount rate. It will no longer be possible to know several years in advance what proportion of total payroll will be charged as pension costs in the profit and loss account.

The current service cost, net of any employee contributions, should be included within operating profit except to the extent that it may be included within the cost of an asset in accordance with another accounting standard.[91]

B Interest cost

The interest cost is the expected increase during the period in the present value of the scheme liabilities because the benefits are one period closer to settlement. Similar to current service cost, it is based on the discount rate as at the beginning of the period.[92]

FRED 20 originally proposed that the unwinding discount should simply be based on the scheme liabilities at the start of the period and the discount rate at that date. However, FRS 17 has taken the computation a step further by now requiring, without further explanation, that the interest cost should in addition, reflect changes in the scheme liabilities during the year.[93] The standard does not set out to what level of detail the scheme liabilities need to be tracked for this purpose, and judgement will be required in individual cases. As the standard requires the computation of the interest cost to be based on the discount rate at the beginning of the period it seems reasonable to conclude that no adjustment is necessary to reflect changes in the scheme liabilities arising from changes in the discount rate during the period.

At the extreme, it could be read to require a re-computation on, say, a monthly basis and to take account of all changes in scheme liabilities (payments of pensions by the fund, accrual of further benefits by members, adjustments for leavers and joiners, changes in demographic assumptions etc). However, it seems unlikely that such an onerous requirement was intended by the ASB, particularly as it was introduced at a late stage and without public consultation. Given that, as discussed at 3.7.3 above, it is only necessary for a full actuarial valuation of the scheme liabilities to be carried out every three years and also that the expected return on assets (discussed below) is to take account of contributions to and payments of benefits from the fund, a less detailed calculation of the unwinding of the discount may be appropriate. Companies might, for example, take the view that adjustments need to be made only for significant one-off changes in the scheme, such as settlements and curtailments, benefit improvements and updated actuarial valuations.

It is possible that the illustrative disclosures given in Appendix I to FRS 17 shed some light on the intentions of the ASB in introducing the requirement to adjust the interest cost to reflect changes in the scheme liabilities during the year. Included in the very extensive disclosure requirements of the standard (see 3.9 below) are the requirements to disclose scheme liabilities and the rate used to discount them at the beginning of the accounting period, and also the interest cost for the period. Multiplying the value of opening scheme liabilities by the discount rate gives the interest cost *before* any such adjustments. Performing this calculation on the balances given in the illustrative example in Appendix I to FRS 17 produces the following:

Example 23.1: Analysis of interest cost disclosed in FRS 17's illustrative disclosures

Year	20X2	20X1
	£million	£million
Scheme liabilities at the beginning of the year	758	668
Discount rate at the beginning of the year	7.0%	8.5%
Computed interest cost	53.06	56.78
Interest cost as disclosed	53	57

It appears from the above that the ASB has made no adjustment to the interest cost to reflect changes in scheme liabilities during the year, even though there has been an increase in scheme liabilities in 20X2 of over £200m due to experience gains and losses and changes in actuarial assumptions. It is open to debate as to how much relevance to attribute to this; Appendix I is, after all, only an illustrative example. However, it could be seen as lending support to the view that adjustments need to be made only for significant one-off changes in the scheme, for example settlements and curtailments, benefit improvements and updated actuarial valuations.

For presentation in the profit and loss account, FRS 17 requires the creation of a new caption adjacent to interest, called other finance costs (or income).[94] The interest cost, net of the expected return on assets (see below) will be included with this caption. Appendix II to the standard notes that the reason for this approach is because the ASB received legal advice to that effect.[95] FRS 17 has made an amendment to FRS 12 Provisions, contingent liabilities and contingent assets to require the unwinding discount on provisions governed by that standard to also be included in this new caption.[96]

C Expected return on assets

The majority of UK defined benefit schemes are funded, with assets put aside in an orderly fashion so as to be available to pay the pension liabilities when they fall due. When this is the case, FRS 17 requires credit to be taken in the profit and loss account for an element of investment return. Given that many pension fund portfolios are heavily weighted in equities, the inclusion of the actual investment return (including changes in market value) in the profit and loss account would very likely produce enormous volatility in earnings. In order to avoid such volatility, yet retain a mark-to-market approach in the balance sheet, the ASB had to devise a mechanism to ensure that (at least some) of the volatile swings in asset values bypassed the profit and loss account. The standard requires that an estimate of the long-term expected return on the actual assets held by the scheme is made, and that this amount is credited to the profit and loss account.[97] It should be presented as a deduction from the interest cost (discussed above) in the newly created caption 'other finance costs'.[98] The difference between the actual return on the asset portfolio and the expected return is an actuarial gain or loss and, as discussed below, is accounted for in the statement of total recognised gains and losses.

This expected return on assets is arrived at by applying the rate of return the assets are *expected* to generate over the long term, as at the beginning of the period, to the value of the assets at that date. For these purposes, the expected rate of return on assets is defined as 'the average rate of return, including both income and changes in fair value but net of scheme expenses, expected over the remaining life of the related obligation on the actual assets held by the scheme'.[99]

For quoted government or corporate bonds, the expected rate of return is specified as being the current redemption yield at the start of the accounting period.[100]

For other assets, such as equities and investment properties, the expected rate of return will need to be estimated and the standard requires that the rate used is 'the rate expected over the long term at the beginning of the period (given the value of the assets at that date)'.[101]

The rather enigmatic phrase in brackets has been added since FRED 20 was exposed for public comment, and is presumably meant to mean that the long-term expected rate is not determined in a vacuum, and hence fairly stable over time, but rather varies inversely with movements in market value. In other words, if market values have risen sharply, then the return expected on them in the future is expected to be lower; conversely a sharp fall in market values would justify assuming a higher yield going forward. Whatever the merits of this argument, this seems to be the view of the ASB because FRS 17 asserts, without citing any evidence or explanation, that the expected return on assets to be included in the profit and loss account is expected to be reasonably stable.[102] Clearly, the product of a *stable* expected rate of return with a volatile market value would not result in a stable profit and loss item, so it seems reasonable to assume that the rate required by FRS 17 should vary to (at least partially) hedge the earnings volatility. Naturally, this is an area which will require the careful exercise of judgement by the preparers of accounts, in conjunction with advice from their actuaries.

In a similar change from FRED 20 to that relating to the interest cost, FRS 17 requires that the expected return on assets should, in addition, reflect changes in the assets of the scheme during the period as a result of contributions to and benefits paid out of the fund.[103] This requirement seems clearer than the equivalent requirement to adjust the interest cost, as it is limited to these two specific changes in the assets of the scheme. However, no guidance is given on the required level of detail of these adjustments, and judgement will be required in individual cases.

As was the case for the interest cost discussed above, it is interesting to consider the ASB's illustrative example contained in Appendix I to the standard. Included in the very extensive disclosure requirements of the standard (see 3.9 below) are the requirements to disclose:

- the value of scheme assets at the beginning of the accounting period (analysed by class of asset);
- the expected rate of return for the current and subsequent period for each asset class; and
- the expected return on assets credited to the profit and loss account for the period.

Multiplying the value of opening scheme assets by the expected rate of return (class by class) gives the expected return on assets *before* any adjustments to reflect changes in the assets of the scheme during the period. Performing this calculation on the balances given in the illustrative example produces the following:

Example 23.2: Analysis of expected return on assets disclosed in FRS 17's illustrative disclosures

Year	20X2			20X1		
	Opening asset value £million	Expected rate of return	Computed expected return £million	Opening asset value £million	Expected rate of return	Computed expected return £million
Equities	721	8.0%	57.68	570	9.3%	53.01
Bonds	192	6.0%	11.52	152	8.0%	12.16
Property	49	6.1%	2.99	38	7.9%	3.00
Total	962		72.19	760		68.17
Expected return on assets as disclosed			73			68

As was the case for interest cost above, it appears (subject to rounding) that the illustrative example in FRS 17 makes no adjustment to the expected return on assets credited to the profit and loss account. One explanation would be that payments from the scheme were sufficiently close in value to contributions to the scheme to render any adjustment immaterial.

D *Actuarial gains and losses*

These are changes in actuarial deficits or surpluses that arise because:

(a) events have not coincided with the actuarial assumptions made for the last valuation (experience gains and losses); or

(b) the actuarial assumptions have changed.[104]

They will be determined each time an actuarial valuation of the fund is carried out, both full valuations required at least every three years and each annual update of the full valuation (the requirements of the standard regarding frequency of valuations are discussed at 3.7.3 above). The most significant gains and losses, occurring annually, are likely to be:

- differences between the expected return on assets credited to profit and the actual performance of the portfolio; and
- adjustments to scheme liabilities to reflect changes in the discount rate.[105]

All actuarial gains and losses are to bypass permanently the profit and loss account by being charged or credited to the statement of total recognised gains and losses.[106] The subsequent recycling of actuarial gains and losses through the profit and loss account is prohibited.[107] This is perhaps the strangest feature of FRS 17, as it means that *all* the entries in the profit and loss account relating to defined benefit pension schemes are estimates – variances between these estimates and actual cash flows are consigned to the STRGL.

The ASB seeks to justify this approach, rather unconvincingly in our view, by analogy to fixed asset accounting. Regarding scheme assets, the ASB explains that 'The Board regards actuarial gains and losses as similar in nature to revaluation gains and losses on fixed assets' and that 'They are therefore best reported within the statement of total recognised gains and losses'.[108] What this does not explain is why, if fixed asset accounting is an appropriate analogy, the profit and loss account should be credited with investment income and gains as budgeted at the start of the year, with all variances taken through the STRGL.

The discussion of movements in scheme liabilities is similarly unconvincing. The ASB's explanation of the requirements includes the following: 'Subsequent changes in the value of the liabilities are generally related to financial assumptions and are caused by general changes in economic conditions. These fluctuations of the liabilities to reflect current market conditions are, like the market value fluctuations of the assets, incidental to the main operating business of the employer'.[109] No meaningful justification is given as to why changes in the estimate of ultimate costs of providing pensions should be treated in such a different manner from refinements to estimates of any other long-term liabilities. For example, it would not be appropriate under

FRS 12 to allow changes in the estimate of a decommissioning cost (such as those arising from a change in the discount rate) to bypass the profit and loss account.

3.8.2 *Non-periodic costs*

FRS 17 identifies two types of events that will have a one-off impact on the surplus or deficit in a scheme as calculated using the projected unit method, and these are discussed below.

A Settlements and curtailments

These terms are defined in the standard as follows:

'*Settlement:-*

An irrevocable action that relieves the employer (or the defined benefit scheme) of the primary responsibility for a pension obligation and eliminates significant risks relating to the obligation and the assets used to effect the settlement. Settlements include:

(a) a lump-sum cash payment to scheme members in exchange for their rights to receive specified pension benefits;

(b) the purchase of an irrevocable annuity contract sufficient to cover vested benefits; and

(c) the transfer of scheme assets and liabilities relating to a group of employees leaving the scheme.

Curtailment:-

An event that reduces the expected years of future service of present employees or reduces for a number of employees the accrual of defined benefits for some or all of their future service. Curtailments include:

(a) termination of employees' services earlier than expected, for example as a result of closing a factory or discontinuing a segment of a business, and

(b) termination of, or amendment to the terms of, a defined benefit scheme so that some or all future service by current employees will no longer qualify for benefits or will qualify only for reduced benefits.'[110]

As can be seen, settlements and curtailments are events that give rise to one-off changes in the estimated fair value of the scheme and, if they have not been allowed for in the actuarial assumptions (which is likely to be the case),[111] they should be accounted for as follows:

- losses should be computed and charged to the profit and loss account at the date on which the employer becomes demonstrably committed to the transaction; and
- gains should be computed and credited to the profit and loss account at the date on which all parties whose consent is required are irrevocably committed to the transaction.[112]

All amounts should be included within operating profit unless they relate to an item shown after operating profit, for example a profit or loss on the sale or termination of an operation shown as a post-operating exceptional item in accordance with FRS 3 – *Reporting financial performance* (see Chapter 25 at 2.6.3).

B Past service costs

A past service cost is 'the increase in the present value of the scheme liabilities related to employee service in prior periods arising in the current period as a result of the introduction of, or improvement to, retirement benefits'.[113] Examples given by FRS 17 are the creation of a pension benefit for a spouse where such a benefit did not exist before or a grant of early retirement with added-on years of service.[114] The standard notes that past service costs do not include increases in the expected cost of benefits which the employer is already committed to make (whether statutorily, contractually or implicitly) as such increases will be covered by the actuarial assumptions.[115]

As discussed at 3.7.5 B above, an increase in scheme liabilities resulting from such benefit improvements will only be recognised in full in the balance sheet if the benefit is fully vested at that time. If the benefit vests over a period, the increased liability will be recognised in the balance sheet on a straight-line basis over the vesting period.

Whatever the period over which the liability is recognised, the corresponding debit entry (or entries) will be accounted for within operating profit in the profit and loss account.[116] This approach could result in very significant one-off charges to the profit and loss account in the period when a benefit improvement is awarded, and the charge is still required even if the additional liability is covered by a surplus in the scheme.[117]

The only circumstance in which the charge in the profit and loss account is mitigated (apart from when the cost is capitalised as part of the cost of an asset) is when the scheme surplus had previously been restricted, for balance sheet purposes, to its recoverable amount (see 3.7.5 A above). In this case the unrecognised surplus may be applied to extinguish the past service cost. The accounting entries required when a surplus is restricted are discussed at 3.8.3 below.

3.8.3 *Impact of restricting an asset to its recoverable amount*

As discussed at 3.7.5 above, a scheme surplus may only be recorded as an asset of the employer to the extent that it is recoverable through refunds or through reduced future contributions.

In the first period in which part of a surplus becomes irrecoverable, once the 'normal' entries have been made in the profit and loss account and STRGL as described at 3.8.1 and 3.8.2 above (i.e. current service cost, interest cost, expected return on assets, gains and losses on settlements and curtailments and actuarial gains and losses) then a credit entry is required to reduce the asset to its recoverable amount. The question arises as to where the debit entry is posted, and in particular what amount should be charged against profit and what amount shown in the STRGL.

In subsequent periods, the surplus may need to be restricted further, or some of the surplus previously excluded as irrecoverable may become recoverable (and hence capable of being recognised), for example where trustees agree to a refund.

FRED 20 was entirely silent on this issue. However, four detailed paragraphs have been included in FRS 17 aimed at explaining how the restriction (or its reversal) is presented in the performance statements.[118]

It is fair to say that the provisions of the FRS on these issues are impenetrable, and the application of the rules in practice will require careful consideration. This may be because of the last-minute drafting of this part of the FRS. It is more likely, in our view, that the difficulties spring from the lack of any clear guiding principle as to why some elements of an annual movement in the balance sheet asset or liability should be recognised in the profit and loss account and others in the STRGL. Indeed, the ASB's own discussion of the issue seems to indicate that the allocation between the performance statements is somewhat arbitrary, as paragraph 54 of Appendix IV to FRS 17 says:

'The effect of the balance sheet limit might be allocated to the various pension components in the performance statements in a number of ways. The allocation required by the FRS is one that preserves the structure of the ongoing items (ie the current service cost, interest cost and expected return on assets) as far as possible but allows one-off costs (eg past service costs) to be offset against the unrecognised surplus.'

In any event, the result has been that the standard seeks to prescribe different accounting treatments depending on the reason why a decrease or increase in recoverable surplus has arisen, and this is the fundamental difficulty.

Any change in the amount of the surplus regarded by FRS 17 as recoverable is always a compound of all the changes in circumstances of the scheme. It seems meaningless to us to try and single out any particular cause (such as a fall in active membership).

The standard identifies six different scenarios which would require adjustments to the amounts recognised in the performance statements. Four are dealt with in one paragraph, which sets out the order in which each should be considered. The final two are addressed in a separate paragraph each.

Of the four possible adjustments which are to be considered sequentially the standard first addresses, somewhat counter-intuitively, two scenarios whereby an increase in the balance sheet amount is required over and above the 'routine' entries posted to the profit and loss account and STRGL.

First, if the trustees of the scheme agree to a refund covered by the unrecognised surplus, this should be credited to other finance income in the profit and loss account.[119] The FRS is silent regarding any tax consequences that may arise from a refund. This presumably means that the credit to other finance income should be gross with any tax shown as normal in the tax line of the profit and loss account. A credit to the profit and loss account is only appropriate where an unrecognised surplus is returned to the employer, any refund of a surplus already recognised on the balance sheet is simply a reclassification between pension surplus and cash. Secondly, an unrecognised surplus can be applied to extinguish past service costs or losses on settlements or curtailments that would otherwise be charged in the profit and loss account.[120]

The next adjustment to be considered is where a credit entry is required to restrict the balance sheet asset, and hence an equal debit is required in the profit and loss account, or STRGL, or both. Where this is the case, the expected return on assets in the profit and loss account is restricted first. It should be reduced so that it does not exceed the total of the current service cost, interest cost (and any past service costs and losses on settlements and curtailments not covered by the unrecognised surplus) and any increase in the recoverable surplus.[121] Finally, any further adjustment should be treated as an actuarial gain or loss.[122]

In our view, the standard could have spelt out more clearly the mechanics of these requirements, and the absence of any numerical examples strikes us as a significant failing. However, the general tenor of the rules on how a surplus should first be restricted seems to be based on the assumption that surpluses are built up as a result of prudent funding, with asset returns, over time, exceeding those assumed for funding purposes. The restriction required to reduce the surplus is then accounted for by reducing asset returns in each of the performance statements. First, by reducing the profit and loss item to a defined amount; the intention here seems to be that the profit and loss account should only show an overall net credit to the extent that it is recoverable. Secondly, any further restriction is taken through the STRGL. The varied circumstances which employers will face are hard to predict, and especial care will be required in applying the above provisions in practice. An example of what these requirements might entail, based on the illustrative example in the FRS, is set out below.

Example 23.3: Impact of the limit on a balance sheet asset

The following illustrations are based on the example in Appendix I to the FRS. Illustration 1 restricts the recoverable surplus at 20X2 from £479m to £300m, with all other facts unchanged. Illustration 2 similarly restricts the surplus to £300m, but assumes that £250m of the actual 20X2 asset return of £553m (£480m + £73m) was 'expected' at the beginning of the year (and hence included in the profit and loss account).

	Illustration 1 £million	**Illustration 2 £million**
Surplus in scheme at beginning of the year	204	204
Movement in year:		
Current service cost	(34)	(34)
Contributions	25	25
Past service cost	(12)	(12)
Net interest	(53)	(53)
Expected return on assets	73	250
Actuarial gain	276	99
Surplus in scheme at end of the year	479	479
Recoverable surplus	300	300

Restriction required	179	179
Limit on aggregate profit and loss account credit (£300m -£204m)	96	96
Profit and loss account items excluding asset return (£34m + £12m + £53m)	99	99
Maximum asset return	195	195
Unrestricted asset return	73	250
Impact of restriction on asset return in the profit and loss account	NONE	55
Accounting entries:		
Credit pension surplus	(179)	(179)
Debit expected return on assets	–	55
Debit actuarial gain in STRGL	179	124

The two scenarios considered in isolation by FRS 17 both relate to a change in the level of active membership of the fund resulting in a change in the amount of a surplus considered as recoverable. As noted above, the amount of surplus treated as recoverable (in the absence of trustee agreed refunds) is the present value of the liability expected to arise from future service by current and future scheme members but without assuming any growth in the number of members. Accordingly, an increase or decrease in the number of active scheme members will impact directly on the quantum of surplus treated as recoverable.

Any increase in recoverable surplus arising from increased membership is treated as an operating gain.[123] This is the case both for general recruitment and for membership increases following an acquisition. In particular, an increase resulting from employee transfers following an acquisition is still to be treated as a post acquisition operating gain, and not an adjustment to goodwill.[124]

The treatment of a decrease in recoverable surplus arising from a reduction in the membership of the scheme is treated differently depending on whether or not the reduction had been included in the actuarial assumptions underlying the amount previously considered recoverable. The decrease should be treated as an actuarial loss (i.e. debited to the STRGL) unless it arises from an event not covered by those assumptions, for example a settlement or curtailment. In those cases it should be treated as part of the loss arising on that event.[125]

3.8.4 *Tax*

Tax relief is usually available to UK employers for contributions made to a pension fund. In addition to any current tax relief available, deferred tax must be provided for on the timing difference represented by the balance sheet asset or liability in accordance with FRS 19 – *Deferred tax* – (discussed at 5 in Chapter 24). The question arises as to how current and deferred tax charges or credits should be reflected in the profit and loss account and STRGL.

The general rule in FRS 16 – *Current tax* – and FRS 19 is that tax should 'follow' the item giving rise to it, and be reported in the same performance statement as that item.[126] The problem with applying this approach is that a contribution to the scheme is accounted for under FRS 17 as a transfer between balance sheet items and has, in isolation, no impact on either statement. As indicated at 3.8.3 above, there is no clear principle determining what element of the movement in a pension asset or liability is recorded in the profit and loss account and what element in the STRGL, and this applies equally to any tax charge or credit.

A Current tax

The line taken by FRS 17 in relation to current tax relief seems a pragmatic solution to this issue: when relief arises on contributions to a pension scheme it is deemed to relate first to the items reported in the profit and loss account, and then any actuarial *losses* reported in the STRGL unless it is clear that some other basis of allocation is more appropriate. To the extent that the contribution exceeds these items, the excess relief should be allocated to the profit and loss account, with the same proviso that it should be allocated to the STRGL if it is clearly more appropriate to do so.[127]

The standard observes that it may sometimes be clear that a contribution relates to a specific event, and gives as an example a special contribution made to fund a deficit arising from a particular cause, for example an actuarial loss. In such a case it requires the current tax relief associated with the special contribution to be recorded in the STRGL along with the actuarial loss.[128] In our view, given the disconnect between the funding of a scheme and the fair value accounting model required by FRS 17, it will be rare that such a correlation will be identified; consequently, the default position of attributing current tax first to the profit and loss account and then to any losses in the STRGL will probably be more usual.

B Deferred tax

Rather surprisingly, neither FRS 17 nor FRS 19 specifically addresses the deferred tax relating to pensions. However, it is evident from the illustrative example appended to FRS 17 that full provision in relation to a pension scheme surplus or deficit seems to mean recognising a deferred tax liability or asset equal to the product of the balance sheet asset or liability and the appropriate tax rate.

As noted at 3.8.1 above, the ASB regards actuarial gains and losses as 'similar in nature to revaluation gains and losses on fixed assets'. On that basis there is potentially a tension between the approach set out in the illustrative example in FRS 17 and the rules for revalued assets in FRS 19. This is because the latter only allows deferred tax to be provided for on revaluation gains either once an entity becomes committed to selling the revalued asset in a manner that gives rise to tax, or when the asset in question is continuously revalued to fair value with changes in fair value being recognised in the profit and loss account (see Chapter 24 at 5.3). Neither of these scenarios seems to describe the balance sheet treatment of scheme surpluses required by FRS 17. Perhaps the ASB has considered this and taken the view that, where a company has invested in a pension fund for the express purpose of meeting an existing liability it is *de facto* committed to realising the fund, such that deferred tax should be provided for under FRS 19. Another argument might be that the balance sheet presentation of the defined benefit pension asset or liability under FRS 17 focuses on a net amount rather than explicitly recognising the underlying investments as such. Given the absence of detailed guidance in either standard, it seems likely that most companies will adopt the approach set out in FRS 17's illustration.

Once the amount of deferred tax to be shown in the balance sheet has been determined, the question then arises of where the other side of this accounting entry belongs – the profit and loss account or the STRGL or some in each. No further insight is given by the illustrative example contained in Appendix I to FRS 17, as this fails to set out the tax entries in the performance statements.

The basic rule in FRS 19 is that where a gain or loss is recognised in the STRGL, deferred tax attributable to that gain or loss should also be recognised in that statement. Otherwise deferred tax should be recognised in the profit and loss account.[129] This is echoed in FRS 17 by the requirement that 'tax on the actuarial gains and losses will be recognised in the statement of total recognised gains and losses'.[130] Given the complete divorce between how defined benefit schemes are accounted for under FRS 17 and how tax relief (be it deferred or current) is computed, this phrase is somewhat difficult to interpret. One possible interpretation is to apply the current enacted rate of tax to amounts recorded in the STRGL and to report that amount of deferred tax there, with the balance of deferred tax going to the profit and loss account.

However, whilst this seems most closely to apply the requirements as they are worded in FRS 19, it could result in a somewhat counter-intuitive allocation between the profit and loss account and the STRGL in circumstances where current tax relief is reported in both statements.

This is because the total deferred tax charge or credit must be the relevant tax rate multiplied by the aggregate movement in the pre-tax balance sheet amount. This aggregate movement will itself comprise the items taken to each performance statement and any cash contributed to the scheme, with the latter also attracting current tax relief. The current tax relief will be allocated between the performance statements in line with FRS 17's rules as described above, which may not be the same as the allocation of the equal and opposite deferred tax under FRS 19. This would result in the effective rate of total tax relating to pension items being different in each of the two statements.

One approach to deal with this mismatch would be to allocate deferred tax between the profit and loss account and STRGL so as to produce the same effective tax rate in each. This would be achieved by allocating that proportion of the overall deferred tax charge notionally arising on the contribution to the scheme in the same way as the corresponding current tax. FRS 19 can be read to support this as it says 'In exceptional circumstances it may be difficult to determine the amount of deferred tax that is attributable to gains or losses that have been recognised directly in the statement of total recognised gains and losses. In such circumstances, the attributable deferred tax is based on a reasonable pro rata allocation, or another allocation that is more appropriate in the circumstances.'[131] It seems reasonable similarly to apply 'another allocation that is more appropriate' to a scenario where deferred tax arises on a transaction (the transfer from a cash balance to a pension scheme asset) that is reported in *neither* the profit and loss account nor the STRGL.

The arithmetical consequence of this approach is that, whilst the effective rate of *total* tax is the same in each statement, any deferred tax will often be charged or credited in full to either the profit and loss account or the STRGL depending on the whether the cash contribution is more or less than the total of all other movements in the gross pension balance. This is explained in the following example.

Example 23.4: Allocation of tax to the performance statements

The opening and closing pension asset (before deferred tax) of a company, and the movements in that asset during the year, are as follows:

	£million
Opening pension asset	900
Total profit and loss account charge	(60)
Total actuarial loss	(30)
Cash contribution	80
Closing pension asset	890

Current tax

Assuming a 30% tax rate, the company receives current tax relief of £24m (30% of £80m), and this is allocated between the profit and loss account and STRGL in accordance with FRS 17 as follows:

	Profit and loss account £million	STRGL £million
Amount to 'cover' profit and loss account charge (30% of £60m)	18	–
Amount to 'cover' actuarial losses (total tax relief of £24m less £18m shown in the profit and loss account)	–	6
	18	6

In this example there is no 'excess' relief to be credited to the profit and loss account because the cash contribution (£80m) is less than the total of amounts charged to the profit and loss account and STRGL (£90m).

Deferred tax

Taking the deferred tax liability to be 30% of the balance sheet amount means that a total deferred tax credit of £3m is required (30% of £10m (£900m - £890m)). To achieve the same effective rate of *total* tax in each of the profit and loss account and STRGL requires that all of this deferred tax credit be included in the STRGL as follows:

	Profit and loss account £million	STRGL £million
Deferred tax	–	(3)
Current tax	(18)	(6)
Total tax	(18)	(9)
Gross pension charge	60	30
Effective rate of total tax	30%	30%

As noted above, an alternative interpretation of FRS 19 would be to provide deferred tax at 30% on the total pension charge in the STRGL with any balance of deferred tax being reported in the profit and loss account. This approach is demonstrated below, and illustrates the counter-intuitive effective tax rates that it produces.

	Profit and loss account £million	STRGL £million
Deferred tax	6 (c)	(9) (b)
Current tax (a)	(18)	(6)
Total tax	(12)	(15)
Gross pension charge	60	30
Effective rate of total tax	20%	50%

(a) Current tax allocated in accordance with FRS 17 as above.
(b) Deferred tax credit equal to 30% of actuarial loss of £30m.
(c) Balancing figure to give total deferred tax credit of £3m.

The allocation of *all* of the deferred tax credit to the STRGL in this example can be explained by viewing the total deferred tax movement as comprising three elements – being a notional deferred tax effect of each of the three categories of movement in the gross pension scheme asset (profit and loss account movement, STRGL movement and cash contribution). The following table sets out the impact on each of the performance statements and the balance sheet of considering each movement in the gross pension asset and a notional deferred tax effect in turn:

	Profit and loss account £million	STRGL £million	Gross pension asset £million	Deferred tax £million	Net pension asset £million
Opening balance			900	(270)	630
Pension cost	60		(60)		(60)
Deferred tax	(18)			18	18
Actuarial loss		30	(30)		(30)
Deferred tax		(9)		9	9
Cash contribution (a)			80		80
Current tax relief (b)	(18)	(6)			
Deferred tax	18	6		(24)	(24)
	42	21	890	(267)	623

	Profit and loss account £million	STRGL £million
Current tax	(18)	(6)
Deferred tax	–	(3)
Total tax	(18)	(9)

(a) the credit side of this debit entry to scheme assets is to cash,
(b) the debit side of these credit entries is to the tax debtor/creditor.

In this example, the cash contribution to the scheme of £80m was less than the total of the pension amounts charged in the performance statements of £90m. In such a case, to make the effective rate of tax the same in each statement requires allocating all the deferred tax movement to the STRGL. This is because the deferred tax notionally relating to the charge in the profit and loss account is equal and opposite to that notionally relating to the cash contribution, hence netting to nil.

If, on the other hand, the cash contributed to the scheme exceeded the total of the amounts charged in the performance statements all of the deferred tax would fall to be reported in the profit and loss account.

One further scenario is worthy of consideration; this is when a net charge is shown in the profit and loss account and a net credit shown in the STRGL (as is the case in the illustrative example in Appendix I to FRS 17). In such circumstances, FRS 17 requires all current tax relief to be shown in the profit and loss account (as it is only allocated to the STRGL to the extent that it covers actuarial *losses* in the STRGL). When this is the case, the overall deferred tax charge or credit will need to be allocated partly to the profit and loss account and partly to the STRGL if the same effective rate of total tax is to be shown in each statement. This is demonstrated in the following example which takes the figures from the illustrative example in FRS 17 for the year to 31 December 20X2 and allocates the deferred tax so as to produce the same effective rate of total tax in each performance statement.

Example 23.5: Allocation of deferred tax in the situation of a net loss in the profit and loss account and a net gain in the STRGL

	Profit and loss account £million	STRGL £million	Total £million	
Deferred tax	(0.3)	82.8	82.5	(a)
Current tax	(7.5)	–	(7.5)	(b)
Total tax	(7.8)	82.8	75.0	
Gross pension charge/(credit)	26.0	(276.0)	250.0	
Effective rate of total tax	30%	30%	30%	

(a) 30% of total increase in gross pension asset of £275m (£479m-£204m).
(b) 30% of cash contribution to scheme of £25m.

3.9 DEFINED BENEFIT SCHEMES – DISCLOSURE REQUIREMENTS

One of the criticisms made of SSAP 24 was that the disclosure requirements did not necessarily ensure that the pension cost and related amounts in the balance sheet were properly explained in the accounts.[132] FRS 17 has set out to correct this by requiring very extensive disclosure. As noted at 3.5 above, FRS 17 has a fairly lengthy implementation period, with escalating disclosure. The disclosures required in the transitional period are set out at 3.9.2 below. It should be noted that until the new standard is implemented in full SSAP 24 remains in force, not just for accounting for defined benefit schemes but also for the various disclosures it requires. This means that in the transitional period before full implementation of

FRS 17 accounts will have to provide the disclosures set out at 3.9.2 below *in addition to* those already required by SSAP 24 (see 4.8 below). The FRS 17 disclosures in relation to defined contribution schemes are set out at 3.6.2 above.

3.9.1 *Disclosure requirements*

FRS 17 requires very extensive disclosures in relation to defined benefit schemes. There is some flexibility allowed in aggregating disclosure where an employer has more than one scheme. In these circumstances, the disclosures set out below may be made separately for each scheme, in total or in such groupings as are considered most useful.[133] Examples of possible groupings which may be considered useful include: geographical location (e.g. distinguishing between UK and overseas schemes) and schemes with significantly different risk profiles (e.g. distinguishing between pensions and healthcare schemes).[134]

A further possible grouping not mentioned in the standard relates to whether each scheme represents a net asset or a net liability. As the total of defined benefit net assets and the total of defined benefit net liabilities need to be presented separately on the face of the balance sheet, it would seem logical for the note disclosures to also reflect this split. Where combined disclosures are given for a number of schemes, the assumptions (see (f) below) should be given as weighted averages or relatively narrow ranges (with any outside the range shown separately).[135] The disclosures required by the standard are as follows:

A *General*

(a) the nature of the scheme (i.e. that it is a defined benefit scheme);

(b) the date of the most recent full actuarial valuation on which the amounts in the accounts are based;

(c) if the actuary is an employee or officer of the reporting entity, or of the group of which it is a member, that fact;

(d) the contribution made in respect of the accounting period and any agreed contribution rates for future years;

(e) for closed schemes and those in which the age profile of the active membership is rising significantly, the fact that under the projected unit method the current service cost will increase as the members of the scheme approach retirement;[136]

B *Assumptions*

(f) each of the main financial assumptions used at the beginning of the period and at the balance sheet date. They should be disclosed as separate individual figures, not combined or netted. The standard notes that the normal requirement to give comparative figures applies equally to these disclosures of assumptions at the beginning of the period. The main financial assumptions include:

(i) the inflation assumption;

(ii) the rate of increase in salaries;

(iii) the rate of increase for pensions in payment and deferred pensions; and

(iv) the rate used to discount scheme liabilities;[137]

C Fair value and expected return on assets

(g) the fair value of the assets held by the pension scheme at the beginning and end of the period analysed into the following classes together with the expected rate of return assumed for each class for the period and the subsequent period (the standard notes that the normal requirement to give comparative figures applies equally to these disclosures at the *beginning* of the period):

(i) equities;

(ii) bonds; and

(iii) other (sub-analysed if material);[138]

D Reconciliation to the balance sheet

(h) the fair value of the scheme assets, the present value of the scheme liabilities based on the accounting assumptions and the resulting surplus or deficit;

(i) where the asset or liability in the balance sheet differs from the surplus or deficit in the scheme, an explanation of the difference. Such differences would include deferred tax, unvested past service costs and any restriction of a pension asset to its recoverable amount;

(j) an analysis of the movements during the period in the surplus or deficit in the scheme;[139]

E Analysis of reserves

(k) the analysis of reserves in the notes to the financial statements should distinguish the amount relating to the defined benefit asset or liability net of the related deferred tax;[140]

F Defined benefit schemes accounted for as defined contribution schemes

(l) when a defined benefit scheme is accounted for as if it were a defined contribution scheme on the grounds that the employer is unable to identify its share of the underlying assets and liabilities in the scheme on a consistent and reasonable basis:

(i) the fact that the scheme is a defined benefit scheme but that the employer is unable to identify its share of the underlying assets and liabilities; and

(ii) any available information about the existence of the surplus or deficit in the scheme and the implications of that surplus or deficit for the employer;[141]

G *Components of the defined benefit cost*

(m) the following amounts included within operating profit (or capitalised with the relevant employee remuneration):

  (i) the current service cost;

  (ii) any past service costs;

  (iii) any previously unrecognised surplus deducted from the past service costs;

  (iv) gains and losses on any settlements or curtailments; and

  (v) any previously unrecognised surplus deducted from the settlement or curtailment losses;[142]

(n) any gains and losses on settlements or curtailments (and any previously unrecognised surplus deducted from the losses) included within a separate item after operating profit;[143]

(o) the following amounts included as other finance costs (or income):

  (i) the interest cost;

  (ii) the expected return on assets in the scheme;[144] and

  (iii) any previously unrecognised surplus recognised when a refund to the employer is agreed;[145]

(p) the following amounts included within the statement of total recognised gains and losses:

  (i) the difference between the expected and actual return on assets;

  (ii) experience gains and losses arising on the scheme liabilities; and

  (iii) the effects of changes in the demographic and financial assumptions underlying the present value of the scheme liabilities;[146]

H *History of amounts recognised in the STRGL*

(q) for the accounting period and previous four periods:

  (i) the difference between the expected and actual return on assets expressed as an amount and as a percentage of the scheme assets at the balance sheet date;

  (ii) the experience gains and losses arising on the scheme liabilities expressed as an amount and as a percentage of the present value of the scheme liabilities at the balance sheet date; and

  (iii) the total actuarial gain or loss expressed as an amount and as a percentage of the present value of the scheme liabilities at the balance sheet date.[147]

Although these disclosure requirements are clearly very lengthy, most should not prove too problematical. Several, however, are worthy of note.

First is the requirement that the reserves note separately identifies 'the amount relating to the defined benefit asset or liability net of deferred tax'[148] (item (k) above). The standard does not define this term, nor does it explain why the disclosure is required and, accordingly, its interpretation is open to debate. In our view there is no obvious interpretation because, with the exception of certain statutory reserves (for example a revaluation reserve), reserves do not generally 'relate' to particular assets or liabilities at all – they are the cumulative result of recognising all assets and liabilities.

Two possible interpretations are that this amount of reserves means either:

- the cumulative total of all amounts that would have been charged or credited to the profit and loss account and STRGL under FRS 17; or
- simply an amount of reserves equal to the asset or liability recognised under the standard.

The two will be different because a surplus is increased or a deficit decreased by a contribution to the fund which is not reported in either the profit and loss account or the STRGL, and hence having no impact on reserves (payments from the fund will not be relevant as they reduce scheme assets and liabilities by the same amount). Regarding the first of these two possibilities, it is far from clear that the resultant amount of reserves 'relates to' the pension asset or liability, or that it provides any meaningful information.

A simplified example would be as follows. A company sets up a defined benefit scheme in the year, the total charge in the profit and loss account is £100 which is funded in cash, and there are no actuarial gains or losses. In this example the company would record a net pension asset of nil (as the assets exactly match the liabilities) yet reserves would have been charged with £100. It seems questionable to view a loss in reserves of £100 as relating to a net asset of nil. Furthermore, companies may well struggle in practice to obtain the information necessary to give this disclosure. It seems unlikely that any company will be able to retrospectively recreate accounting entries on an FRS 17 basis from the origination of a defined benefit scheme to the present. One approach may be to take the surplus or deficit at the balance sheet date and then deduct from it all cash contributions made to the scheme since its formation.

As regards the second possibility above, it seems to add nothing meaningful to the requirement to disclose the surplus or deficit itself. The illustrative disclosure example appended to the standard presents the amount of reserves relating to the defined benefit asset as simply the balance sheet amount (net of deferred tax). In the absence of a clear requirement, and reason for it, it seems likely that many companies will in practice apply the second suggestion above, although it is possible that other interpretations will be made.

Second is the disclosure required when a defined benefit scheme is accounted for as a defined contribution scheme on the grounds that the employer is unable to identify its share on a consistent and reasonable basis (item (l) above). In these circumstances the disclosures required include 'any available information about the existence of the surplus or deficit in the scheme and the implications of that surplus or deficit for the employer'.[149] Given that the ASB expects this to apply to many individual companies that are part of a group (see 3.4 above), it is surprising that no further guidance is given in the standard as to exactly what information is required. In the absence of an explanation of what is required, it may be reasonable to assume that:

- 'any available information about the existence of a surplus or deficit' should include all the information normally required for defined benefit schemes not subject to this special treatment (components of the surplus or deficit, actuarial assumptions etc); and
- 'the implications of that surplus or deficit for the employer' should include not just the effect on contributions charged in the profit and loss account but also a discussion of the effect on future contributions.

As discussed at 4.3.3 below, SSAP 24 allowed subsidiaries of UK and Irish companies participating in group schemes to give much reduced disclosures, and to cross refer to the accounts of the parent company which contained particulars of the actuarial valuation of the group scheme. A similar exemption has not been given in FRS 17, so it would seem that (whatever interpretation is put on them) these disclosure requirements are required in the individual accounts of each subsidiary.

The final disclosure worth commenting on is the five-year history of amounts taken to the STRGL (item (q) above). This is the only example of an historical summary required by an accounting standard, and seems to have come about through a fear that companies may manipulate the profit and loss account by the choice of assumptions. The standard asserts that a consistent trend of losses or gains in the STRGL may indicate that the assumptions used have been over-optimistic or under-optimistic, and that careful consideration then needs to be given to the choice of future assumptions.

We are not convinced that this is necessarily so as, for example, it seems perfectly possible that a consistent trend of falling interest rates could produce a trend of losses reported in the STRGL. Accordingly, we would advise users of accounts to exercise caution before assuming undue optimism or pessimism in the actuarial assumptions without first obtaining a full understanding of the circumstances.

The three required disclosures are to be given, for each of the five periods, as both an absolute amount and as a percentage of the scheme assets or liabilities (as appropriate) 'at *the* balance sheet date' (emphasis added). This could be read to mean that the percentages for each of the five years should all be based on the same balance sheet amounts – i.e. the current period's. However, it is evident from the illustrative example in Appendix I to the FRS that these percentage disclosures should be based on the *relevant* closing balance sheet of each period concerned.

3.9.2 *Disclosures in the transitional period*

FRS 17 comes fully into force for accounting periods ending on or after 22 June 2003 and only from then will entries need to be posted in the primary statements. Steadily increasing disclosures are required in the periods running up to full implementation, as set out below:

A Accounting periods ending on or after 22 June 2001

The disclosures set out in items (a) to (l) above should be presented, but only for the closing balance sheet (without comparatives).[150]

B Accounting periods ending on or after 22 June 2002

The disclosures set out in items (a) to (l) above should also be presented for the opening balance sheet (without comparatives). In addition, the disclosures relating to the performance statements set out in items (m) to (p) above should be given, but only for the current period.[151] The details to be given in the historical summary (item (q) above) should also be presented, but again only for the current period.[152]

C Accounting periods ending on or after 22 June 2003

All provisions of the standard come into force for periods ending on or after 22 June 2003, with one exception.[153] The historical summary of items reported in the STRGL (item (q) above) need not be created retrospectively beyond the disclosure discussed above.[154] This means only current period and comparative amounts will be required in the first year of full implementation.

3.10 PRACTICAL IMPACT AND IMPLEMENTATION ISSUES

FRS 17 represents a radical extension of the ASB's balance sheet focused model, and also the use of the STRGL as a performance statement. The numbers involved may well be very significant and volatile, collecting the required information in a timely manner will be burdensome for many companies and interpreting the legal restrictions on distributions may prove problematical. Some of these issues are considered in more detail below.

Whatever one's view of the merits of the requirements of FRS 17 they clearly involve the financial status of pension schemes (and indeed the wider economy) having a much greater impact on the accounts of employers. Articulating to the users of accounts what these new numbers mean for the prospects of the company will be, in our opinion, the key challenge for companies to meet.

3.10.1 *Early implementation*

As noted at 1.1 above, FRS 17 has a long implementation period with full adoption required only for periods ending on or after 22 June 2003. For periods ending on or after 22 June 2001 there is steadily increasing disclosure required by the standard, which is discussed at 3.9.2. One important question for companies to address is, therefore, whether to implement the standard early. To our knowledge only one listed company having a defined benefit scheme, Costain, adopted FRS 17 in full in the year to 31 December 2000. Relevant extracts from those accounts, which illustrate most of the routine requirements of the standard, are as follows:

Extract 23.1: Costain Group plc (2000)

Consolidated Profit and Loss Account [extract]

Year ended 31 December	Notes	**2000 Continuing £m**	1999 (restated) Continuing £m
Profit on ordinary activities before interest		**0.4**	2.4
Net interest receivable/(payable) and similar income/(charges)			
Group undertakings	4	**2.2**	1.2
Joint ventures		**(0.3)**	(0.4)
Other finance income – Group undertakings	5	**4.2**	3.2
Profit on ordinary activities before taxation	2,3	**6.5**	6.4

Statement of Total Consolidated Recognised Gains and Losses

	2000 £m	1999 (restated) £m
Profit for the financial year from Group undertakings	**4.1**	6.2
Profit/(loss) for the financial year from joint ventures	**1.0**	(1.3)
	5.1	4.9
Currency translation differences	**(0.9)**	(1.3)
Actuarial (loss)/gain recognised in the pension scheme	**(10.7)**	33.4
Deferred tax arising thereon	**3.2**	(10.0)
Total recognised (losses)/gains relating to the year	**(3.3)**	27.0
Prior year adjustments	**9.6**	
Total recognised gains/(losses) recognised since last annual report	**6.3**	

Consolidated Balance Sheet [extract]

	Notes	**2000 £m**	1999 (restated) £m
Net liabilities excluding pension asset		**(8.8)**	(10.6)
Pension asset	19	**34.6**	39.7
Net assets including pension asset		**25.8**	29.1

5 **Other finance income of Group undertakings**	**2000 £m**	1999 £m
Expected return on pension scheme assets	**22.6**	19.7
Interest on pension scheme liabilities	**(18.4)**	(16.5)
Net return	**4.2**	3.2

19 Pensions

The Group operates a number of pension schemes principally of the defined benefit type in the United Kingdom and overseas, under which contributions are paid by Group understandings and employees. The pension cost charge of the United Kingdom pension schemes amounted to £4.0m (1999: £4.1m).

A full actuarial valuation of the United Kingdom scheme was carried out at 31 March 1999 and was updated to 31 December 1999 and 31 December 2000 by a qualified independent actuary. The major assumptions used by the actuary were (in nominal terms):

	31.12.2000	31.12.1999	31.12.1998
Rate of increase in pensionable salaries	4.0%	4.4%	3.9%
Rate of increase in pensions in payment	2.5%	2.9%	2.4%
Discount rate	5.9%	6.2%	5.7%
Inflation assumption	2.5%	2.9%	2.4%

The assets in the scheme and the expected rate of return (net of administrative expenses) were:

	31.12.2000	31.12.2000 £m	31.12.1999	31.12.1999 £m	31.12.1998	31.12.1998 £m
Equities	7.4%	231.5	7.2%	240.2	7.3%	211.9
Bonds	4.6%	128.7	4.9%	117.2	4.5%	103.1
Total market value of assets		360.2		357.4		315.0
Actuarial value of liability		(310.8)		(300.7)		(293.8)
Surplus in the scheme		49.4		56.7		21.1
Related deferred tax liability		(14.8)		(17.0)		(6.5)
Net pension asset		34.6		39.7		14.7

Movement in surplus during the year

	2000 £m	1999 £m
Surplus in scheme at beginning of year	**56.7**	21.2
Movement in year (current service cost)	**(4.0)**	(4.1)
Contributions	**3.2**	3.0
Net return on assets/(interest cost)	**4.2**	3.2
Actuarial (loss)/gain	**(10.7)**	33.4
Surplus in scheme at end of year	**49.4**	56.7

The estimated actuarial valuation at 31 December 1999 showed a surplus of £56.7 million. The full actuarial valuation as at 31 March 1999 recommended that the employer contribution rate be increased from 9.25% to 9.6% of pensionable salaries with effect from 1 April 2000. Employer contributions were paid at these rates in 2000. It has been agreed with the trustees that employer contributions will remain at 9.6% of pensionable salaries until the completion of the next full actuarial valuation to be carried out as at 31 March 2001, subject to actuarial review during this period.

21 Reserves – Group [extract]

The prior year adjustment relates to the implementation of FRS 17 'Retirement Benefits'. No prior year adjustment has resulted from the implementation of FRS 19 'Deferred Tax'. The adoption of FRS 17 has resulted in an increase in the reported profit before taxation for 1999 of £4.3m. In 2000, the profit before taxation is £5.3m higher than would have been the case had FRS 17 not been adopted.

Other companies have, without adopting the standard early, chosen to give some information about the impact of FRS 17 in advance of the mandatory disclosures discussed at 3.9.2 above. These include BAA and Boots as shown in the following extracts:

Extract 23.2: BAA plc (2001)

32 **Pensions** [extract]
(b) **FRS 17 Retirement Benefits**

The valuation used for FRS 17 disclosures has been based on the most recent actuarial valuation at 30 September 1999 and updated by Bacon & Woodrow to take account of the requirements of FRS 17 in order to assess the liabilities of the scheme at 31 March 2001. Scheme assets are stated at their market value at 31 March 2001.

The financial assumptions used to calculate scheme liabilities under FRS 17 are:

Valuation method		**Project unit**
Discount rate		5.8%
Inflation rate		2.3%
Increase to deferred benefits during deferment		2.3%
Increases to pensions in payment	– Open Section	2.4%
	– Closed Section	2.5%
Salary increases		3.8%

The assets in the scheme and the expected rate of return were:

	Long-term rate of return expected at 31 March 2001	Value at 31 March 2001 £m
Equities	7.0%	1,430
Bonds	5.8%	228
Other	5.4%	61
Total market value of assets		1,719
Present value of scheme liabilities		(1,171)
Surplus in the scheme		548
Related deferred tax liability		(165)
Net pension asset		383

	2001 Group £m
Net assets	
Net assets excluding pension asset	4,839
Pension asset	383
Net assets including pension asset	5,222

	2001 Group £m
Reserves	
Profit and loss reserve excluding pension asset	1,987
Pension asset	383
Profit and loss reserve	2,370

BAA's approach seems to have been to accelerate the disclosure that FRS 17 would require for the accounts to 31 March 2002 by presenting them in the 2001 accounts. It is interesting to note that the figures given by BAA for 'Net assets excluding pension asset' and 'Profit and loss reserve excluding pension asset' are taken directly from the balance sheet, and hence are based on SSAP 24 (the 2001 balance sheet contains a provision under SSAP 24 of £8 million). In our view it would be more appropriate to adjust these figures to exclude any SSAP 24 asset or liability (other than accrual or prepayments of contributions), as we believe the intention of the transitional disclosure required by FRS 17 is to show what the accounts would include for retirement benefits under the new rules.

Boots has taken a different approach, by presenting in its financial review selected information on the impact of the new standard as follows:

Extract 23.3: The Boots Company PLC (2000)

20 Financial review [extract]

Pensions We welcome the publication of Financial Reporting Standard (FRS 17), the new accounting standard for pensions, which introduces valuable consistency and transparency into a complex area of financial reporting.

FRS 17 gives a present value of pension liabilities by discounting pension commitments, including salary growth, at an AA bond yield. The FRS 17 value of liabilities at the year end is £2.05bn and the market value of assets is £2.3bn, giving a pension scheme surplus of £250m.

The service or operating cost for the full year under FRS 17 would have been about 14% of pensionable salaries, or about £70m. The cost after net investment returns would be about 10% of pensionable salaries, or about £50m.

New members of the pension scheme now join a Defined Contribution scheme for five years, before having the opportunity to join the Defined Benefit scheme. Over the next five years this will reduce the service cost to about 12%.

We support the Government's proposals on Security for Occupational Pensions, published during the year. These envisage stricter conditions on wind-up of any pension scheme sponsor, which will improve security for all pension scheme members and lead to more direct involvement by sponsors in the activities of their pension schemes

3.10.2 Potentially large and volatile balances

A Balance sheet

The assets and liabilities of defined benefit schemes can, for many companies, be very significant. Indeed, during the development of FRS 17 one firm of actuaries observed that the assets of a mature pension scheme could exceed the market value of the sponsoring company. Needless to say, it is the net surplus or deficit that is reflected in an employer's balance sheet, not the gross assets in the fund. However, the volatility of the market values of assets typically held by pension schemes is unlikely to be mirrored by changes in the valuation of scheme liabilities, so if the assets in question are valued at more than the employing company the impact of this volatility could be highly material.

It is impossible to predict exactly what impact FRS 17 will have, given the varied circumstances of company pension schemes, although it is clear from the three extracts in 3.10.1 above that the effect can be significant. In the case of Costain (Extract 23.1 above) the net pension asset has, as shown in note 19 to the accounts, increased from £14.7 million to £39.7 million during 1999, falling back to £34.6 million by the end of 2000.

Although few companies have chosen to implement FRS 17 early, disclosures made under the current rules can give some insight into the possible scale of the impact of the new standard. An interesting example is Marks and Spencer, whose pension disclosures under SSAP 24 for its accounts to 31 March 2001 were as follows:

Extract 23.4: Marks and Spencer p.l.c. (2001)

10. EMPLOYEES [extract]

A Pension costs

The total pension cost for the Group was £120.1m (last year £124.5m) of which £110.6m relates to the UK Scheme (last year £112.1m), £nil relates to the Early Retirement Plan (last year £2.6m) and £9.5m relates to overseas schemes (last year £9.8m).

The Group operates a number of funded defined benefit schemes throughout the world.

The latest actuarial valuation of the UK Scheme was carried out at 1 April 1998 by an independent actuary using the projected unit method. The key assumptions adopted were:

Price inflation	3.5%
Rate of increase in salaries	5.25%
Rate of increase in pensions in payment	3.5%
Rate of return on investments	8.25%
Rate of increase in dividend income	4.5%
Rate of interest applied to discount liabilities	8.25%

The latest actuarial valuation revealed a shortfall of £74m in the actuarial value of the assets of the UK Scheme of £2,047m compared to the actuarial liability for pension benefits. (The market value of assets at 1 April 1998 was £2,709m.) This represents a funding level of 97%.

As can be seen the actuarial value of scheme assets of £2,047m fell short of the scheme liabilities (on a projected unit method) by £74m. This gives an actuarial value of scheme liabilities of £2,121m. Comparing this actuarial liability with the market value of the scheme assets implies, at first glance, an FRS 17 surplus of £558m – some 11% of total shareholders' funds. This analysis is probably not the whole story however. It is likely that the interest rate of 8.25% used to calculate the liability for SSAP 24 purposes was not the market rate on high quality corporate bonds (as required by FRS 17). It is entirely possible that the FRS 17 would require a lower discount rate, hence increasing the liability and reducing the surplus to be shown on the balance sheet. In any event, once a surplus (or deficit) has been brought on balance sheet it will then be subject to volatility in the market value of an asset portfolio of £2.7 billion, and it is far from certain that these potentially very large fluctuations will be hedged by changes in the liability.

B Earnings volatility

The ASB has attempted, in our view more out of expediency that any convincing underlying principle, to limit the profit and loss account volatility that the market value approach could produce. The mechanism for this is to credit the profit and loss account with an expected return on the scheme assets, with variations from this shown in the STRGL (permanently bypassing the profit and loss account) as an actuarial gain or loss.

Whilst it is hard to predict exactly how future market conditions will affect reported earnings, it does seem intuitively correct that the mechanism of essentially reporting budgeted figures in the profit and loss account with variances taken to the STRGL will mitigate earnings volatility. However, some volatility will remain. The current service cost will now be based on year-end corporate bond rates, and hence must vary along with those rates. Furthermore, the new item of other finance costs (or income) is a compound of unwinding discount and the expected return on assets. As noted at 3.8.1 C above, the ASB asserts that the expected return on assets will be reasonably stable. Assuming that this assertion is based on an expectation that a rise in fair value of assets will be accompanied by a fall in the expected return on them, that logic would seem to equally support an expectation of stability in the interest cost. However, no such assertion is made regarding the interest cost in FRS 17.

The variability of the total profit and loss account impact of FRS 17 is illustrated by the accounts of Costain (Extract 23.1 above). The overall profit and loss account effect of the defined benefit scheme is a net cost of £0.9 million in 1999 (current service cost of £4.1 million less net return on assets of £3.2 million), compared to net income of £0.2 million in 2000 (current service cost of £4 million less net return on assets of £4.2 million). Whilst these figures seem fairly significant in the context of pre-tax profits of £6.4 million and £6.5 million for 1999 and 2000, it is the STRGL which contains the much larger actuarial variances – a gain of £33.4 million in 1999 compared to a loss of £10.7 million in 2000 (before deferred tax).

In any event, though, given the ASB's intention to merge the STRGL and the profit and loss account into a single statement of financial performance (see FRED 22 – *Revision of FRS 3 'Reporting Financial Performance'*), any volatility that does exist will have a direct impact on reported earnings.

In conclusion, while the level of earnings volatility that FRS 17 will introduce remains to be seen, it is safe to say that it will no longer be possible to know up to three years in advance what percentage of payroll costs will be expensed as a pension charge. Indeed, as illustrated by Costain above, defined benefit schemes could result, under FRS 17, in a net cost one year and net income the next.

In addition to possible volatility, there is the issue of profit and loss account classification. In applying SSAP 24, most companies show all of the pension cost as an operating expense (although some account separately for notional interest on any balance sheet amount). For companies with schemes in surplus, this cost will have been net of a credit in respect of the amortisation of variations. Under FRS 17 however, operating profit is charged with the current service cost with a new caption below operating profit containing the unwinding discount on scheme liabilities less the expected return on scheme assets. Although the quantitative impact on operating profit remains to be seen, for companies with schemes in surplus it is likely that FRS 17's current service cost will exceed the equivalent pension cost under SSAP 24.

3.10.3 *Realised profits*

One practical issue that will be of great interest to company directors is the impact, if any, of FRS 17 on the ability of the company to pay dividends. The legality of a dividend made by a company, like that of any other of its actions, is ultimately a matter of law which can only be interpreted definitively by the courts. It is possibly for this reason that the ASB has included no guidance on the subject in FRS 17 and any detailed examination of the law is beyond the scope of this publication. However, set out below are some general observations which we hope will prove useful to directors as they begin to address the issue with their legal advisors, but they are not intended to represent an comprehensive analysis.

The ASB was aware, when developing FRS 17, of the issue that any balance sheet liability introduced by a new accounting standard could be considered a reduction in profits available for distribution for a UK company. To address these concerns, the subject was discussed (or at least partially so) in FRED 20, and a somewhat remarkable approach was proposed.[155]

What was suggested was that the whole of a deficit measured under the rules of the proposed standard need not be considered a liability at all for statutory purposes. Instead, for Companies Act purposes, a lower liability (calculated on a discontinuance basis) could be used with the excess liability on a projected unit basis shown as some kind of memorandum disclosure. There was no discussion at all of how this reduction in the liability should be reflected in the profit and loss account and STRGL. Due to responses made to FRED 20 pointing out the unsatisfactory nature of this approach, the ASB (quite rightly in our view) decided not to include it in the final standard. However, rather than substitute it with a reasoned discussion of how their proposals might affect distributable profits (perhaps including opinion from Counsel), FRS 17 contains no guidance at all on the subject. The reason put forward for this is that, in the ASB's view, a distribution problem is unlikely to arise often and that it is better for those few companies affected to find appropriate solutions with the help of their legal advisors. The explanation of this belief is to be found in a footnote to paragraph 58 of Appendix IV to the standard, as follows:

'A distribution problem will arise only when individual company accounts show a defined benefit liability so large that it reduces distributable reserves to below that needed to cover any intended distribution. In this context, it should be noted that the FRS allows an exemption in some circumstances from the recognition of a defined benefit liability in the accounts of individual companies that are members of a group defined benefit scheme.'

This observation by the ASB indicates that, in their view, when a net balance sheet liability is recognised under FRS 17, the corresponding fall in reserves constitutes a diminution in profits available for distribution.

It is somewhat unfortunate that an appendix to the standard refers to an exemption for group companies when what the standard actually says is:

'Subsidiaries are not exempt from the FRS and, where possible, will account for defined benefit schemes in accordance with its requirements.'[156]

Although in fairness the standard goes on to observe that many group schemes are run on a basis that means individual companies, crucially including the parent company, are unable to identify their share of underlying scheme assets and liabilities. As discussed at 3.4 above, this would appear to mean that any pension surplus or deficit could be accounted for only in consolidated accounts, and hence (as the legality of distributions is only an issue for individual companies) any problem avoided.

This apparently neat dismissal of the problem has, in our opinion, two possible flaws. First, whilst the larger and listed groups of companies in the UK may well be in this situation, it will not necessarily apply to all companies. Secondly, it is a rather strange notion that the liabilities of the group as a whole can be presented (aside of intra-group items) as being materially different from the sum of the liabilities of the members of the group. On that basis, many directors may have reservations that no individual company (or companies) in the group report this liability – particularly if the legality of their actions may rest upon it.

Accordingly, we believe that the question remains: what is the impact, if any, of FRS 17 on the ability of the company to pay dividends? Unfortunately, there is no obvious answer. The main problem arises from the fact that the concept of cash realisation in general, and distributions in particular, is considered an irrelevance by the ASB; and given likely future developments (for example in the area of financial instruments) this is set to become increasingly problematical. The problem is compounded in FRS 17 by the somewhat conflicting view of pensions taken in the balance sheet as compared to the performance statements.

As far as the balance sheet is concerned, a pension surplus or deficit represents one single asset or liability. On that basis, it might be reasonable to simply consider whether, if an asset is recognised under FRS 17, an equivalent amount of reserves can be considered a realised profit available for distribution. Given that any asset has not been realised by the company in cash or an asset close to cash, it could be argued that it represents an unrealised profit, and hence is not available for distribution. Should FRS 17 result in a net liability in the balance sheet, however, it is likely to be considered a reduction in distributable reserves. As noted above, this seems to be the view of the ASB.

Conversely, in the performance statements, the change from one balance sheet date to the next in this single asset or liability is considered to comprise a number of different components, some recorded in the profit and loss account and others bypassing it. This could perhaps support an argument that each individual item recorded in the profit and loss account and STRGL should be considered in isolation to decide whether it represents a realised profit. It may be reasonable to consider any credit items in the profit and loss account realised and those in the STRGL unrealised. This approach is illustrated in the following simplified example.

Example 23.6: Computing realised profits by reference to inclusion in the profit and loss account

A company forms a defined benefit scheme during the year, and contributes cash to it of 100. The profit and loss account and STRGL include the following items:

	Profit and loss account	STRGL
Current service cost	190	
Interest cost	20	
Expected return on assets	(10)	
Actuarial gain on scheme assets		(100)
Total	200	(100)

The pension deficit in the scheme shown on the balance sheet is, therefore, nil, calculated as follows:

Scheme assets	
Cash contributed	100
Actual return (10+100)	110
	210
Scheme liabilities	
Current service costs	190
Interest cost	20
	210

As a result of the above, shareholders' funds have fallen by 100 – with a loss of 200 reported in the profit and loss account, and a gain of 100 reported in the STRGL. Assuming gains and losses reported in the STRGL are included in the profit and loss account reserve (the standard is silent on this but the illustrative example in Appendix I to the standard appears to report STRGL items in the profit and loss account reserve), then that reserve will similarly have been reduced by 100. This means that if the whole of the balance on the profit and loss reserve is viewed as distributable it will take into account gains reported in the STRGL, which might otherwise have been considered unrealised.

If it is considered that items reported in the profit and loss account are realised and those in the STRGL unrealised, then in the above example distributable reserves will have been reduced by 200. Whilst this may have some conceptual merit as an avenue to explore, it seems highly unlikely that any companies will be able to recreate retrospectively the FRS 17 split between profit and loss account and STRGL entries from the launch of their defined benefit scheme to the present. Furthermore, if this approach were applied prospectively, it would require the separate tracking (and arguably the separate presentation in the accounts) of amounts reported in the STRGL.

3.10.4 *Information requirements*

Obtaining all the information required by FRS 17 will require careful consideration. In particular, detailed information requiring advice from actuaries will be needed annually and as at the employer's balance sheet date (which may not be that of the scheme). Employers will need to ensure that systems are in place to capture and process this data for each defined benefit scheme (worldwide) within their reporting timetable, starting with periods ending on or after 22 June 2001.

3.10.5 *Past service costs*

One possible planning opportunity may merit the consideration of employers before FRS 17 comes fully into force, and this relates to past service costs. As discussed at 3.8.2 above, the award of benefit improvements (even if funded out of a scheme surplus) may result in a significant one-off charge in the profit and loss account. Employers currently considering such improvements to scheme benefits out of an existing scheme surplus may wish to bring forward the award so as to avoid such a charge in future years.

4 REQUIREMENTS OF SSAP 24

4.1 Accounting objective

The basic accounting objective which SSAP 24 sets is that the employer should recognise the cost of providing pensions on a systematic and rational basis over the period during which he receives benefit from the employees' services.[157] The standard explicitly distinguishes this from the funding objective, which is described as being to build up assets in a prudent and controlled manner in advance of the retirement of the members of the scheme, in order that the obligations of the scheme may be met without undue distortion of the employer's cash flow.[158] It is emphasised that the funding plan will not necessarily provide a satisfactory basis for the allocation of pension cost to accounting periods.

The standard is expressed in terms of the profit and loss account, and no explicit objective is set in relation to the balance sheet. However, it can be demonstrated that the balance sheet will reflect the underlying surplus or deficit in the pension scheme, although this figure will be combined with the amount of variations in pension cost which are being carried forward for recognition in the profit and loss account of future years. The balance sheet dimension of SSAP 24 is explored further in 4.7.1 below.

4.2 Definition of terms

There are several technical terms relating to pensions which have specific meanings laid down by the standard. These are shown below.

Accrued benefits are the benefits for service up to a given point in time, whether the rights to the benefits are vested or not. They may be calculated in relation to current earnings or projected final earnings.

An *accrued benefits method* of actuarial valuation is a valuation method in which the actuarial value of liabilities relates at a given date to:

(a) the benefits, including future increases promised by the rules, for the current and deferred pensioners and their dependants; and

(b) the benefits which the members assumed to be in service on the given date will receive for service up to that date only.

Allowance may be made for expected increases in earnings after the given date, and/or for additional pension increases not promised by the rules. The given date may be a current or future date. The further into the future the adopted date lies, the closer the results will be to those of a prospective benefits valuation method (which is defined below).

The *average remaining service life* is a weighted average of the expected future service of the current members of the scheme up to their normal retirement dates or expected dates of earlier withdrawal or death in service. The weightings can have regard to periods of service, salary levels of scheme members and future anticipated salary growth in a manner which the actuary considers appropriate having regard to the actuarial method and assumptions used.

A *current funding level valuation* considers whether the assets would have been sufficient at the valuation date to cover liabilities arising in respect of pensions in payment, preserved benefits for members whose pensionable service has ceased and accrued benefits for members in pensionable service, based on pensionable service to and pensionable earnings at, the date of valuation including revaluation on the statutory basis or such higher basis as has been promised. (This is sometimes called a 'discontinuance' basis, because it evaluates the scheme's ability to meet its obligations if it were to be discontinued.)

A *discretionary or ex gratia increase* in a pension or an *ex gratia pension* is one which the employer has no legal, contractual or implied commitment to provide.

A *defined benefit scheme* is a pension scheme in which the rules specify the benefits to be paid and the scheme is financed accordingly. (These are commonly referred to as 'final salary' schemes. This means that the employer promises to pay the member a pension which is related to (usually) his final salary at or near the date of retirement; a typical example might give the employee a pension which was calculated at one sixtieth of his final salary for each year in which he was an employee and a member of the scheme. Because various factors, notably the amount of the final salary, will not be known until many years have elapsed, the eventual cost of providing the pension will have to be estimated.)

A *defined contribution scheme* is a pension scheme in which the benefits are directly determined by the value of contributions paid in respect of each member. Normally the rate of contribution is specified in the rules of the scheme. (These are commonly referred to as 'money purchase' schemes. In contrast to defined benefit (final salary) schemes, the employer has no obligation to provide a pension beyond that which is earned by the contributions which are payable under the scheme, so the cost of providing the pension is fixed and known from the outset.)

An *experience surplus or deficiency* is that part of the excess or deficiency of the actuarial value of assets over the actuarial value of liabilities, on the basis of the valuation method used, which arises because events have not coincided with the actuarial assumptions made for the last valuation.

A *funding plan* is the timing of payments in an orderly fashion to meet the future cost of a given set of benefits.

A *funded scheme* is a pension scheme where the future liabilities for benefits are provided for by the accumulation of assets held externally to the employing company's business.

The *level of funding* is the proportion at a given date of the actuarial value of liabilities for pensioners' and deferred pensioners' benefits and for members' accrued benefits that is covered by the actuarial value of assets. For this purpose, the actuarial value of future contributions is excluded from the value of assets.

An *ongoing actuarial valuation* is a valuation in which it is assumed that the pension scheme will continue in existence and (where appropriate) that new members will be admitted. The liabilities allow for expected increases in earnings.

Past service is used in SSAP 24 to denote service before a given date. It is often used, however, to denote service before entry into the pension scheme.

Pensionable payroll/earnings are the earnings on which benefits and/or contributions are calculated. One or more elements of earnings (e.g. overtime) may be excluded, and/or there may be a reduction to take account of all or part of the state scheme benefits which the member is deemed to receive.

A *pension scheme* is an arrangement (other than accident insurance) to provide pension and/or other benefits for members on leaving service or retiring and, after a member's death, for his/her dependants.

A *prospective benefits method* of valuation is a valuation method in which the actuarial value of liabilities relates to:

(a) the benefits for current and deferred pensioners and their dependants, allowing where appropriate for future pension increases; and

(b) the benefits which active members will receive in respect of both past and future service, allowing for future increases in earnings up to their assumed exit dates, and where appropriate for pension increases thereafter.

Regular cost is the consistent ongoing cost recognised under the actuarial method used.

4.3 Scope

SSAP 24 is very broad in its scope. It applies to all pension arrangements, whether they arise from an explicit contractual commitment, or from custom and practice, or even if they are of an ex gratia nature; it applies to both funded and unfunded schemes; it applies to defined benefit schemes, defined contribution schemes and to those which are a hybrid mixture of the two; it applies to all schemes, whether insured or self-administered; it applies both to UK schemes and to foreign schemes (although when it is difficult to apply it to the latter, there is a hint of de facto relaxation of the requirements in the standard); and it applies to schemes of all sizes. The only specific exclusions from the scope of the standard are in respect of state social security contributions and redundancy payments.

The application of the standard to other post-retirement benefits, such as private health care, was an area of some confusion. The standard itself says that its principles may be applicable to such benefits,[159] but the ASC subsequently indicated that this was not intended to be mandatory.[160] However, in November 1992 the UITF published an Abstract requiring SSAP 24 principles to be applied to all such benefits, although with an extended period for implementation.[161] This is discussed in more detail in 4.3.6 below.

4.3.1 *Hybrid schemes*

Although the standard lays down separate rules for defined contribution schemes and defined benefit schemes, in some cases the scheme will not fall so neatly into one or other of these classifications. There is a growing practice within pension schemes of offering elements of both kinds of arrangement; for example, a final pay scheme may give its members the option to take benefits based on an alternative money purchase-based formula, to allow them to participate to some extent in the investment performance of the fund if it proves successful. It will therefore be necessary to decide how to account for such arrangements.

The standard acknowledges that this difficulty exists. Although no easy solution can be offered, the only possible response is to try to identify the true underlying nature of the scheme as accurately as possible. Is it in essence a final pay scheme, but with some money purchase features as a theoretical extra? Alternatively, is it principally a money purchase scheme, but with some benefits linked to final pay to provide a safety net against bad fund performance? Only by assessing the basis under which benefits are likely to be paid in practice will it be possible to determine to which category the scheme can be regarded as belonging in substance. It will also be necessary to re-evaluate this regularly, since changes in economic conditions (such as inflation rates) could alter the probability that benefits will be payable on one basis rather than another. In most cases, this evaluation should be conducted with the benefit of advice from the actuary, who will advise on the most appropriate accounting treatment to be adopted.

Since the distinction between the two accounting treatments depends on whether or not the employer's obligation is limited to the contributions payable, the amount of those contributions will generally represent the minimum measure of the pension cost to be charged, and it will be necessary to consider whether the existence of the defined benefit formula means that additional costs have to be provided for in addition to those contributions. It may also be appropriate to disclose a more comprehensive description of the scheme than usual, in order to allow the reader of the accounts to appreciate the nature of the obligations to which the employer is committed.

4.3.2 Foreign schemes

A group which operates internationally may well have a number of local pension schemes, in some cases imposed by legal requirements of the host country, which are of quite a different nature from those of the parent company. In principle all the rules of the standard still apply, and the group accounts should contain consolidated information on these schemes which has been prepared using consistent policies and methods. However, in certain cases this may prove impracticable, and it could be considered unrealistic to expect quite disparate arrangements to be treated in a uniform way.

The standard acknowledges this difficulty, and broadly says that while the measurement rules should be applied so far as possible, in certain instances it will be necessary simply to take the cost as determined for local purposes as the basis of the charge. Whether or not this provides an acceptable answer will obviously also depend on the materiality of the amounts involved. Where it is not possible to apply the rules of the standard completely, it will be necessary to explain the circumstances involved, stating the amount of the charge which is affected by this difficulty, and the basis on which it has been determined.[162]

4.3.3 Group schemes

Where a number of group companies participate in a common group scheme, it will be necessary to allocate the regular cost among the individual companies in order to permit them to make the necessary entries in their own accounts. In principle, there are a number of ways in which this might be done. The most rigorous approach would be to analyse the membership of the scheme into those of each of the participating companies and to make the allocations on this basis. However, this could be an onerous task and a more practical approach could be to apportion the cost to individual companies at the same percentage of pensionable pay which the total charge represents for the group as a whole.

As well as allocating the regular cost, it will be necessary to allocate variations as they arise. Where the variation arises from the enhancement of rights of members of the scheme it may in theory be possible to allocate the cost to the companies for whom they work; however, where the variation relates to the performance of the fund, no such specific allocation would be possible, and in practice some simpler form of apportionment will have to be applied such as the uniform percentage of payroll referred to in the previous paragraph.

However, the starting point for allocating both the regular cost and variations is to consider how the group intends to recover the cost from the individual subsidiary companies. The accounting in each company should then follow whatever commercial decision is made as to the allocation of the charge. For example, some groups may prefer to deal with all variations at holding company level, and therefore charge individual companies with the regular cost, in which case the accounting should reflect that decision. Whatever the basis used, it is important that the notes to the accounts of the subsidiaries should indicate that the company is a member of a group scheme and explain the basis of the charge made.

4.3.4 *Multi-employer schemes*

Where a company participates in a scheme which has been established for a number of employers (perhaps a whole industry) it is necessary to adapt the measurement and disclosure rules of the standard appropriately. Sometimes the nature of the arrangement is such that, in essence, it constitutes a defined contribution scheme and should be accounted for as such. However, where it is in the nature of a defined benefit scheme it will be necessary to determinc what portion of the total fund is attributable to the reporting company.

Lookers provides an example of such an arrangement, as shown in the following extract:

Extract 23.5: Lookers plc (2000)

Principal Accounting Policies
9. Pension costs [extract]

The Group participates in the Retail Motor Industry Pension Plan which is a defined benefit scheme providing benefits based on final pensionable salary. The scheme has been registered with the Registrar of Pensions.

The assets of the scheme are held separately from those of the Group, being held in separate funds by the Trustees of the RMI plan.

Contributions to the scheme are charged to the Profit and Loss Account so as to spread the cost of pensions over employees' working lives with the Group. The contribution rate is recommended by a qualified actuary on the basis of triennial valuations, using the projected unit method.

Notes to the Financial Statements
9. INFORMATION REGARDING DIRECTORS AND EMPLOYEES [extract]

The Group participates in the Retail Motor Industry Pension Plan and the most recent valuation was at 6th April 1999 using the Projected Unit Method. The assumptions which have the most significant effect on the results of the valuation are those relating to the rate of return on investments and the rate of increase in salaries. It was assumed that the investment return would be 2% p.a. higher than the increase in salaries in the period up to retirement. No allowance was made for any future discretionary increases in benefits.

The latest available actuarial valuation showed that the market value of the scheme's assets attributable to the Lookers Group was £48,000,000 and that the actuarial value of the assets represented 122% of the liabilities at the valuation date, after allowing for expected future increases in earnings. The employer's future service contribution rate has been adjusted to take into account the surplus disclosed by the valuation, spread over the average remaining service lives of the members of the scheme.

4.3.5 *Unfunded schemes*

Unfunded schemes have been relatively uncommon among private sector companies in the UK, although they have become more popular as a result of tax changes introduced in the Finance Act 1989; they may also arise in respect of foreign subsidiaries which are included within the consolidated accounts of a UK parent. In addition, where a company offers post-retirement benefits other than pensions, they are likely to be unfunded. The standard says relatively little about unfunded schemes, but the same basic accounting rules apply. In essence, an unfunded scheme can be looked upon as equivalent to a funded scheme under which no contributions have yet been paid and which accordingly has no assets.

GKN has significant unfunded obligations in respect of pensions, as shown in this extract:

Extract 23.6: GKN plc (2000)

22. Provisions for liabilities and charges [extract]

	Deferred taxation	Post-retirement	Other	Total
	£m	£m	£m	£m
At 1 January 2000	1	198	73	272
Charge for the year	–	21	8	29
Credit for the year	(5)	–	–	(5)
Currency variations	–	4	4	8
Subsidiaries acquired and sold	5	(12)	–	(7)
Adjustment to fair value (note 25)	–	–	16	16
Paid or accrued during the year	–	(16)	(6)	(22)
At 31 December 2000	**1**	**195**	**95**	**291**

...

Post-retirement

Post-retirement provisions includes provisions relating to pension benefits of £161 million (1999 – £163 million) and provisions for other post-retirement benefits of £34 million (1999 – £35 million).

26 Post-retirement benefits [extract]

... In certain overseas companies funds are retained within the business to provide for retirement obligations. The annual charge to provide for these obligations, which is determined in accordance with actuarial advice or local statutory requirements, amounted to £18 million (1999 – £26 million).

One issue which is of particular relevance to unfunded schemes is the need to recognise interest in the measurement of the cost of providing the pension. The provision which is set up in the balance sheet will be assessed on a discounted basis. This means that the amount to be added to the provision in each year can be looked upon as having two components: an interest charge on the unfunded liability (or amortisation of the discount) together with a charge for the year which would be equivalent to the contribution which would be made if the scheme were funded. It is not clear, however, from the above extract whether GKN's pension cost includes a specific interest component.

4.3.6 *Post-retirement benefits other than pensions*

In addition to pensions, some employment contracts also provide post-retirement health care or other benefits. Arrangements of this sort are not particularly significant in the UK, but they are quite frequently found in some other countries, notably the United States. UK companies with US subsidiaries may therefore have to consider how to account for them on consolidation even if they have no material obligations to account for in the UK.

SSAP 24 says that, 'although this Statement primarily addresses pensions, its principles may be equally applicable to the cost of providing other post-retirement benefits'. However, the ASC subsequently issued Technical Release 756, which said that for the time being it was not necessary to apply SSAP 24 in relation to such benefits, although companies might consider it appropriate to do so.

In November 1992 the UITF published an Abstract on the subject.[163] This said that post-retirement benefits other than pensions were liabilities, which in accordance with the accruals and prudence concepts of SSAP 2 and the Companies Act should be recognised in accounts. Since such benefits share many of the characteristics of pensions, the principles of SSAP 24 were to be applied to their measurement and disclosure. However, in recognition that these obligations were particularly difficult to measure, the requirement to apply SSAP 24 principles was not to become mandatory until periods ending on or after 23 December 1994. In the first year of implementation, the previously unrecognised obligation relating to past service was to be provided for either by means of a prior year adjustment or by spreading it forward over a period. This period was to be either the expected service lives of current employees[164] or, following the US standard SFAS 106, a period of 20 years.[165] The transitional method chosen had to be disclosed.

HSBC is spreading the obligation over 20 years, as shown in this extract:

Extract 23.7: HSBC Holdings plc (2000)

2 Principal accounting policies

(h) Pension and other post-retirement benefits [extract]

Since 1 January 1993, the cost of providing post-retirement health-care benefits, which is assessed in accordance with the advice of qualified actuaries, has been recognised on a systematic basis over employees' service lives. At 1 January 1993, there was an accumulated obligation in respect of these benefits relating to current and retired employees which is being charged to the profit and loss account in equal instalments over 20 years.

5 Administrative expenses

(b) Retirement benefits [extract]

HSBC also provides post-retirement health-care benefits under schemes, mainly in the United Kingdom and also in the United States, Canada and Brazil. The charge relating to these schemes, which are unfunded, is US$42 million for the year (1999: US$37 million; 1998: US$30 million). The latest actuarial review estimated the present value of the accumulated post-retirement benefit obligation at US$411 million (1999: US$379 million; 1998: US$357 million), of which US$2453 million (1999: US$232 million; 1998: US$240 million) has been provided. The actuarial assumptions used to estimate this obligation vary according to the claims experience and economic conditions of the countries in which the schemes are situated. For the UK schemes, the main financial assumptions used at 31 December 1999 are price inflation at 2.5% per annum, health-care claims cost escalation of 7.5% per annum and a discount rate of 6% per annum.

In principle, the methods used by a company for measuring post-retirement benefits other than pensions should be the same as those already applied to pensions, but the Abstract refers to SFAS 106, as a source of guidance on the measurement bases which might be applied and says that they will be deemed to satisfy SSAP 24 principles.[166]

The Abstract also requires companies that have adopted a SSAP 24 basis of accounting for post-retirement benefits to make disclosures in relation to them equivalent to those required for pension schemes under SSAP 24, including details of any important assumptions which are specific to the measurement of such benefits, such as the assumed rate of inflation in the cost of providing the benefits. If it is material, the provision for post-retirement benefits has to be disclosed separately from other provisions in the notes to the accounts.[167]

4.4 Defined contribution schemes

4.4.1 *Accounting*

Accounting for defined contribution ('money purchase') schemes remains straightforward under SSAP 24. Since the employer has no obligation beyond payment of the contributions which he has agreed to make, there is no difficulty in measuring the cost of providing pensions; it is simply the amount of those contributions payable in respect of the accounting period.[168] If the amount actually paid in the period is more or less than the amount payable, a prepayment or accrual will appear in the balance sheet in accordance with normal accounting practice, but otherwise the payments made will simply be charged in the profit and loss account when made.

4.4.2 *Disclosure*

A Requirements

The disclosure requirements of the standard for defined contribution schemes are also very simple, and add little to the requirements of FRS 18 and the Companies Act. They are:

(a) the nature of the scheme (i.e. the fact that it is a defined contribution scheme);

(b) the accounting policy (arguably required already by FRS 18);

(c) the pension cost charge for the period (already required by the Companies Act – see 5.2 below);

(d) any outstanding or prepaid contributions at the balance sheet date.[169]

All these details could be given in a single note, but it is more common to deal with the different elements of the disclosure in different places. The policy and the nature of the scheme can be dealt with together as part of the statement of accounting policies, the expense for the year will be included in the statutory staff costs note, and any prepayment or accrual can readily be shown on the balance sheet or in a note analysing the relevant balance sheet figure. Unilever operates a number of defined contribution schemes, and makes these disclosures.

Extract 23.8: Unilever PLC (2000)

Accounting policies
Retirement benefits [extract]
Contributions to defined contribution pension plans are charged to the profit and loss account as incurred.

Notes to the consolidated accounts
3 Staff costs and employees [extract]

			€ million
	2000	1999	1998
Pensions costs:			
Defined contribution schemes	**(8)**	(4)	(16)

33 Pension and other benefit plans [extract]

The Group also operates a number of defined contribution plans. The assets of all the Group's defined contribution plans are held in independently administered funds. The pension costs charged to the profit and loss account represent contributions payable by the Group to the funds. The market value of the assets of externally funded defined contribution plans as at 31 December 2000 was €271 million (1999: €262 million).

4.5 Defined benefit schemes – regular pension cost

The accounting requirements for defined benefit ('final salary') schemes are very much more complicated. In this case the employer's commitment is open-ended, and in order to achieve the accounting objective mentioned at 4.1 above it is necessary to apply actuarial valuation techniques and use a large number of assumptions. The standard seeks to achieve this by drawing a distinction between regular (ongoing) pension cost and variations from that cost. The essence of the standard's measurement rules is that the basic charge for pension cost in the profit and loss account should be the regular cost, but with adjustments for the effects of the variations from that cost which arise from time to time (see 4.6 below). In addition, there is a third element of pension cost to be recognised, although regrettably SSAP 24 does not make this sufficiently clear. This is interest,[170] and is discussed in more detail in 4.6.8 below.

As can be seen from the list of definitions in 4.2 above, regular cost is the consistent ongoing cost recognised under the actuarial method used. The standard goes on to say that 'where a stable contribution rate for regular contributions, expressed as a percentage of pensionable earnings, has been determined, that rate will provide an acceptable basis for calculating the regular cost under the stated accounting objective so long as it makes full provision for the expected benefits over the anticipated service lives of employees'.[171] The actuary will be able to inform the company of the amount of the total cost which is to be regarded as the regular cost component.

Essentially, the regular cost is that amount which the actuary would regard as a sufficient contribution to the scheme to provide the eventual pensions to be paid in respect of future service, provided present actuarial assumptions about the future were borne out in practice and there were no future changes to the terms of the scheme. Even then, this amount will depend on the particular method which the actuary is using to attribute cost to individual years. (SSAP 24 does not stipulate that a particular actuarial method be used, provided that it meets the accounting objective of recognising the cost of pensions on a systematic and rational basis over the employees' working lives. However, as discussed at 3.7.2 above, FRS 17 will, once implemented, require the use of the projected unit method.)

4.6 Defined benefit schemes – variations from regular cost

4.6.1 *Examples of variations*

The standard identifies four categories of variations from regular cost.[172] The first two are to do with the actuarial process and the methods and assumptions which it entails, while the second two are to do with changes in the scope or the terms of the scheme itself. The four categories are:

(a) experience surpluses or deficiencies. These are surpluses or deficiencies which are identified in the course of an actuarial valuation of the scheme which have arisen because the assumptions which were made at the time of the previous valuation have not been fully borne out by subsequent experience. For example, an assumption will have been made as to the rate of return to be earned on the scheme's investments. If this rate was in fact exceeded in practice, this will give rise to a surplus at the time of the next valuation, and this will be an experience surplus as the term is used in the standard. Similar variations may arise in relation to all the other main assumptions, such as those relating to salary inflation, the pattern of people joining and leaving the scheme, and so on;

(b) the effects on the actuarial value of accrued benefits of changes in assumptions or method. Insofar as they relate to assumptions, these are similar to the previous category, except that they relate to the period beyond the date of the present valuation, rather than to the period since the previous valuation. Thus, a change in the assumption to increase the rate of predicted salary inflation in a final salary scheme would have the effect of increasing the total pension cost to be recognised and give rise to a variation. A change in actuarial method will have similar effects, in that it will give rise to a different present valuation of the scheme because of the particular way of attributing cost to particular years of service.

    The wording of the standard is perhaps deficient in referring only to the effects on the value of the accrued *benefits*, which might be regarded, by implication, as excluding effects on the valuation of assets available to meet these benefits. We do not believe that any such distinction was intended, and we believe that the proper way to apply the standard is to regard changes affecting any part of the actuarial valuation of the scheme as variations and account for them as such;

(c) retroactive changes in benefits or in conditions for membership. These might arise, for example, when the scope of a scheme is changed to include a class of employee which was previously excluded, and some credit is given for their past service with the company; alternatively, it might be an enhancement of the rights of existing members, say to give them an improvement in the terms of the formula under which their eventual pension will be calculated. These will generally entail an increase in the overall cost of pensions to the employer, and the past service element will give rise to a variation from regular cost; and

(d) increases to pensions in payment or to deferred pensions for which provision has not previously been made. The standard takes the position that all such increases, including those of a discretionary or an ex gratia nature, should preferably be embraced within the scope of the actuarial assumptions. Where this has been the position, but the actual increases granted are not in line with those previously assumed, the difference will give rise to a variation. However, where the increases are of a discretionary or ex gratia nature and no allowance has previously been made for them in the actuarial assumptions, then they fall outside the scope of the valuation of the scheme; they are not treated as variations under the standard but are dealt with separately (see 4.6.10 below).

4.6.2 *Amortisation of variations*

A Normally allocated over the remaining service lives of current employees

The basic rule set by the standard for all such variations from regular cost is that they should not be recognised immediately, but rather spread forward over the expected remaining service lives of employees in the scheme. The standard says that variations should normally be spread over the remaining service lives of employees currently in the scheme after making suitable allowances for future withdrawals, and that it is possible to apply this principle by using an average period relevant to the current membership if desired.[173] Where the average approach is taken, this will be determined by the actuary on the basis of the age profile of the workforce and the assumptions made about mortality, retirements and withdrawals. The period is usually likely to be shorter than might intuitively be assumed, and a range of 10 to 15 years might be typical.

SSAP 24 does not require the period of amortisation to be disclosed, but in practice a number of companies do so and we regard this as a helpful disclosure. An example is shown in Extract 23.18 at 4.8.2 below.

There are, however, a number of exceptions to this basic rule, some of which in our view detract from the conceptual cohesion of the standard. These are discussed at 4.6.3 to 4.6.7 below.

The rationale for this basic rule merits some discussion. First of all it has to be looked at in the context of the standard's overall approach, which is directed towards achieving a steady charge in the profit and loss account rather than valuing the fund in the balance sheet. If actuarial surpluses and deficiencies were included directly in the balance sheet as soon as they were recognised, there would be enormous volatility in the amounts reported and, assuming the differences between the balance sheet figures were charged or credited directly in the profit and loss account, there could be a very significant effect on earnings in the years of actuarial valuation. The standard has instead opted for a smoothing approach, so that these effects are recognised in the profit and loss account gradually rather than immediately following a valuation.

Insofar as these variations arise from changes to do with the actuarial process (categories (a) and (b) above), this treatment can be justified because of the high degree of uncertainty and subjectivity inherent in actuarial valuations; it would be wholly inappropriate to give immediate recognition to such changes, which are of a very long-term nature and may easily be reversed at the time of the next valuation. However, at first sight it may seem more justifiable to give immediate recognition to the other broad class of variations – those reflecting changes in the scheme itself, described above under headings (c) and (d).

Broadly, the reason for not doing so is that such changes, even if they are expressed in terms which give credit for periods relating to the past, are made with a view to providing benefits for the future, not to meet any latent obligation which already exists. An improvement to the pension terms of an employee is only one of a range of possible improvements to his remuneration package; it may be decided on, for example, as an alternative to (or in conjunction with) a future salary increase. Accordingly, it is thought appropriate, under SSAP 24, to spread such increases forward over the employee's working life.

SSAP 24 does not specify exactly how variations are to be amortised, and there are various possible ways of doing so. This is discussed in more detail at B below. Although factors such as interest and salary inflation should be built into the amortisation pattern in practice, these have been excluded from some of the worked examples shown in the remainder of this chapter for the purposes of simplicity. These examples also use an average period to represent the working lives of members in the scheme.

SSAP 24 does not provide any worked examples of the spreading treatment, but the forerunner of the standard, ED 39, contained two such examples, the second of which[174] is reproduced below to illustrate the mechanics of the accounting process:

Example 23.7: Spreading variations from regular cost

The actuarial valuation at 31 December 1998 of the pension scheme of company B showed a surplus of £260m. The actuary recommended that B eliminate the surplus by taking a contribution holiday in 1999 and 2000 and then paying contributions of £30m p.a. for 8 years. After that the standard contribution would be £50m p.a. The average remaining service life of employees in the scheme at 31 December 1998 was 10 years. B's year end is 31 December.

Assuming no change in circumstances, the annual charge in the profit and loss account for the years 1999 to 2008 will be:

$$\text{Regular cost} - \frac{\text{surplus}}{\text{average remaining service life}} = £50\text{m} - \frac{£260\text{m}}{10} = £24\text{m}$$

The funding in these periods will be:

1999–2000	Nil
2001–2008	£30m p.a.

The difference between the amounts funded and the amounts charged in the profit and loss account will be recognised as a provision, as follows:

Year	Funded	Charged	(Provision)
	£m	£m	£m
1999	–	24	(24)
2000	–	24	(48)
2001	30	24	(42)
2002	30	24	(36)
2003	30	24	(30)
2004	30	24	(24)
2005	30	24	(18)
2006	30	24	(12)
2007	30	24	(6)
2008	30	24	–

The effect can be shown in graphical form, as follows:

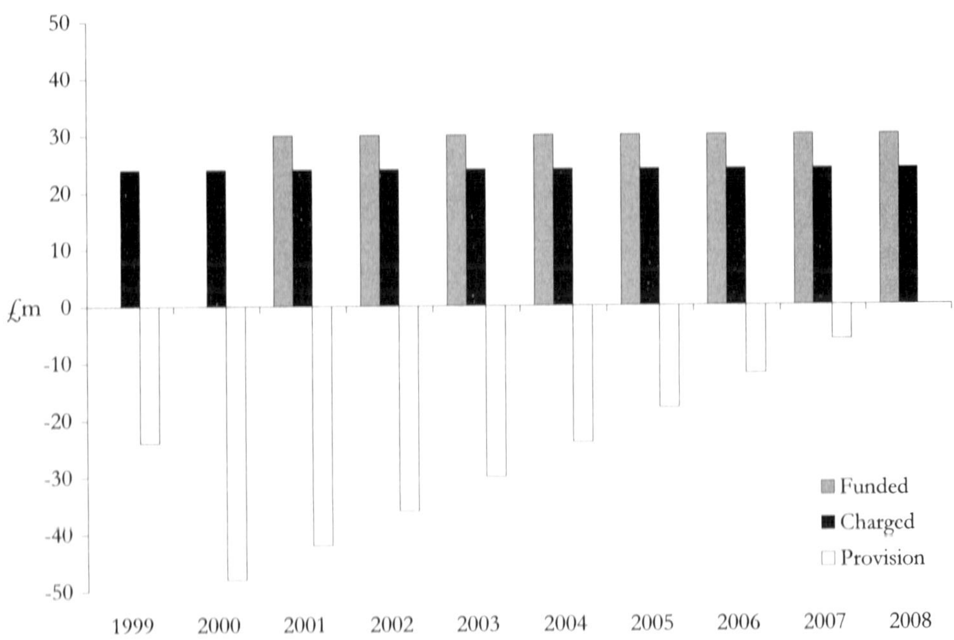

The example notes that in practice further actuarial valuations will occur, usually triennially, during the 10 year amortisation period and that these may reveal a surplus or deficiency which will require an adjustment to the charge and prepayment/provision in succeeding periods. However, it does not specify how this might be calculated. This point is considered at 4.6.2 C below.

SSAP 24 sets out some specific exceptions to the normal rule that variations from regular cost should not be recognised immediately, which are discussed at 4.6.3 and 4.6.4 below. Immediate recognition of actuarial variations would also be necessary if it was determined that the remaining service lives of employees was zero. This could be the case, for example, in a closed scheme where no employees accrue further benefits in return for services to the employer. A company in this position is Wiggins Group, which revised its accounting treatment after the intervention of the Financial Reporting Review Panel.[175] The supplementary note to the accounts delivered to the Stock Exchange in March 2001 explained the matter as follows: 'The Panel also questioned the treatment of the Wiggins Group plc Retirement Life Assurance and Disability Scheme (the "Scheme"). The Scheme was closed to new members following the reorganisation of the Group in 1993 but had, apart from pensioners and deferred pensioners, one active member who was on long term disability and whose employers contributions were paid by the insurers to the disability scheme. The actuary to the Scheme regarded it as a live Scheme because of this one member. The directors have now agreed that it should be treated as a closed Scheme in conformity with SSAP 24 and therefore any deficit should be charged to the profit and loss account. At 5 April 1999 the valuation of the Scheme showed a deficit of £1,307,000 of which £115,000 was provided in previous years. ... therefore a further provision of £1,192,000 has been included in these accounts.'

B Amortisation method

As mentioned above, the standard does not specify the particular method by which variations should be amortised, saying only that they should be amortised over the expected remaining service lives of the employees in the scheme, and that an average period may be used if desired.[176] Three main methods have emerged in practice, although others may also be permissible if they meet the objective described above. These three are known as (a) the straight line method (b) the mortgage method and (c) the percentage of pay method, and they are illustrated in the following three extracts:

Extract 23.9: Rio Tinto plc and Rio Tinto Limited (2000)

1 Principal accounting policies
m Post retirement benefits

The expected costs of post retirement benefits under defined benefit arrangements are charged to the profit and loss account so as to spread the costs over the service lives of employees entitled to those benefits. Variations from the regular cost are spread on a straight line basis over the expected average remaining service lives of relevant current employees. Costs are assessed in accordance with the advice of qualified actuaries.

36 Post retirement benefits [extract]

... The expected average remaining service life in the major schemes ranges from 10 to 23 years with an overall average of 12 years. ...

Extract 23.10: Reed Elsevier plc (2000)

4 Pension schemes [extract]

... Actuarial surpluses are spread as a level amount over the average remaining service lives of current employees. ...

Extract 23.11: Whitbread PLC (2000)

Accounting policies

K Pension funding

Pension costs are charged to the profit and loss account over the average expected service life of current employees. Actuarial surpluses are amortised over the expected remaining service lives of current employees, using the percentage of pensionable salaries method. Differences between the amount charged in the profit and loss account and payments made to the schemes are treated as assets or liabilities in the balance sheet.

There is no explicit requirement in SSAP 24 to disclose the method used, and most companies do not do so. However, the different methods can produce answers which are materially different, and we encourage disclosure of the method chosen: this has also been recommended by the ICAEW.[177] The majority of those companies who do make this disclosure use the percentage of pay method.

The mechanics of the three methods are illustrated by the following example, which is based on the same situation as discussed in Example 23.13 at 4.6.8 below.

Example 23.8: Methods of amortisation of variations

An actuarial valuation of a company's pension scheme identifies a variation of £1,400,000 to be spread over the working lives of the employees, which is assessed to be 8 years. The company's payroll cost is expected to increase at a rate of 7% per annum and the return earned on the fund's investments will be 9%. The figures derived from the three most common methods of spreading the variation are set out below.

Year	Straight line method £000	Mortgage method £000	Percentage of pay method £000
1	277	232	186
2	262	232	200
3	247	232	213
4	233	232	229
5	218	232	244
6	204	232	262
7	189	232	280
8	175	232	300
Total	1,805	1,856	1,914

The straight line method is computed by dividing the amount to be spread (£1,400,000) by the number of years (8) to achieve a level capital amount of £175,000. Interest is added to the balance which remains unamortised in each year to give the total charge.

The mortgage method involves calculating the annuity for 8 years which equates, at an interest rate of 9%, to a capital value of £1,400,000. The resulting annual figure can be regarded, as with the repayments under a mortgage, as comprising a relatively small capital element and a large interest element at the outset with the proportions reversing in later years.

The percentage of pay method is calculated by determining the stream of payments, escalating at the rate of annual payroll inflation (7% in this example) which has a present value of the amount to be amortised (£1,400,000).

It can be seen that each of these methods results in the amortisation of a total figure which exceeds the apparent amount (£1,400,000 in this example) which was to be amortised. This is because an actuarial surplus is not an absolute amount, but rather a discounted figure because of the calculations implicit in the valuation method. It is therefore necessary to include an interest element in the amortisation calculation, as is described in each of these methods. It is also necessary to charge or credit interest on the balance sheet figure in order to reflect fully the time value of money which is inherent in the calculation, as discussed at 4.6.8 below.

The three methods produce quite different profiles. The mortgage method produces a level amount, the straight line method results in a declining amount, while the percentage of pay method has the reverse effect. The effect of using these methods in the calculation of pension costs in the circumstances of Example 23.13 will be as shown in this graph:

Total pension cost under three different amortisation methods

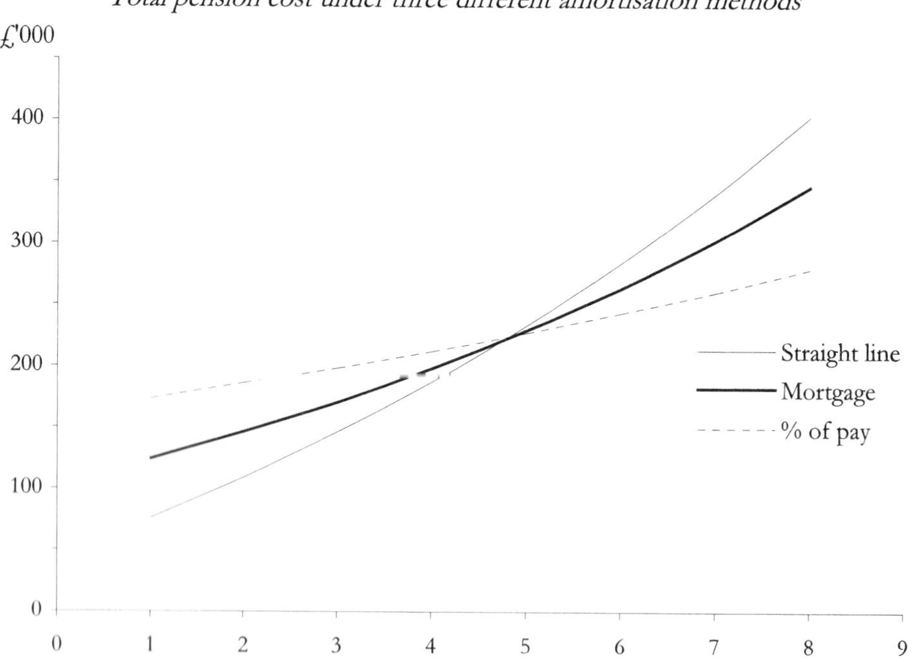

The percentage of pay method will tend to be used when the actuary expresses the variation in terms of the required change to the contribution rate rather than as a lump sum figure. It could also be argued that this is the most appropriate method because it means that the variation as well as the regular cost will be a stable proportion of the pensionable payroll. However, if the pension cost is analysed into the components shown in 4.6.8 below (regular cost, interest earned on the surplus in the fund and the release of variations *excluding* interest), different arguments could be summoned to support either of the other methods. The calculations of these amounts are illustrated below:

			Straight line method		Mortgage method		%age of pay method	
Year	Regular cost £000	Interest in fund £000	Release of variations £000	Total £000	Release of variations £000	Total £000	Release of variations £000	Total £000
1	360	109	175	76	127	124	78	173
2	385	101	175	109	138	146	98	186
3	412	91	175	146	151	170	123	198
4	441	79	175	187	165	198	150	212
5	472	64	175	233	179	229	181	227
6	505	46	175	284	195	263	216	243
7	540	25	175	340	213	302	255	260
8	578	0	175	403	232	346	299	279
	3,693	515	1,400	1,778	1,400	1,778	1,400	1,778

The first four columns of the table repeat the analysis shown in 4.6.8 below, while the remaining two pairs of columns show the effect of using the mortgage and the percentage of pay methods of spreading variations rather than the straight line method. As can be seen, the total cost shown in the last column is the same as the amount of contributions paid in Example 23.13, because the actuary had set the total contribution at the percentage of payroll which would have the effect of eliminating the surplus over eight years. The regular cost and the interest earned in the fund obviously do not change whatever amortisation method is used.

Under this analysis, it can be seen that the release of variations under the percentage of pay method is in fact heavily weighted to the end of the amortisation period, rising from only £78,000 in the first year to £299,000 in the last. The release is flexed in this way so as to offset the declining interest income earned by the fund as the surplus is reduced as a result of the lower level of contributions. However, it may be argued that pension cost *should* be proportionately lower when there is a surplus in the fund than when it has been run off, and therefore that the release of variations should not be designed to eliminate this effect. On this argument, there is more to be said for the straight line method, which releases the interest evenly over the amortisation period, or the mortgage method, which increases it only by the rate of interest used in the discounting calculation. Nevertheless, since the standard does not specify the use of any particular method, it would appear that any of the above would be acceptable, and indeed there are other methods which could also be applied.

C *How to account for the unamortised difference remaining in the year of the next actuarial valuation*

As mentioned at the end of 4.6.2 A above, no guidance has been given on how to account for the remaining part of previously identified variations, when a subsequent valuation is made and reveals fresh variations. Consider the situation, using the figures from Example 23.7, where a further actuarial valuation is conducted at 31 December 2001, and reveals a different surplus.

Example 23.9: Effect on unrecognised variations of subsequent valuations

The previous actuarial valuation at 31 December 1998 of the pension scheme of company B showed a surplus of £260m. The actuary recommended that B eliminate the surplus by taking a contribution holiday in 1999and 2000 and then paying contributions of £30m p.a. for 8 years. After that the standard contribution would be £50m p.a. The average remaining service life of employees in the scheme at 31 December 1998 was 10 years. As a result of the above, the accounts for the next three years showed the following:

Year	Funded	Charged	(Provision)
	£m	£m	£m
1999	–	24	(24)
2000	–	24	(48)
2001	30	24	(42)

The next actuarial valuation at 31 December 2001 showed a surplus of £80m. The actuary this time recommended that B should maintain the contribution rate at £30m p.a. until 2005 and then raise it to £50m thereafter. The average remaining service life of employees in the scheme was still 10 years. The company intends to take account of this valuation in its accounts for the year to 31 December 2002.

On the face of it, it might appear that there is a further £80m of surplus which will go to reduce the pension cost still further. However, on closer examination it is clear that there has in fact been a deterioration since the 1998 valuation, because a larger surplus would have been predicted based on that valuation. The valuation at that time showed a surplus of £260m, but contributions of only £30m have been made since then, compared with a regular cost requirement of £150m; the combination of these figures would have given rise to a predicted surplus of £140m (260+30-150), yet the surplus is now only £80m, which in fact represents a deterioration of £60m, not an improvement of £80m. There is therefore the equivalent of a new *deficit* of £60m to be accounted for over the future service lives of the employees. (NOTE: For the sake of simplicity, all these figures are presented ignoring the effects of interest and the time value of money. In practice these will form significant elements in the calculation.)

The question that then arises is how to combine the effect of this newly identified variation with the unamortised amount of the previously identified variation. Of the previously identified surplus of £260m, only 3 instalments totalling £78m have so far been recognised and the remaining £182m is still to be recognised as an adjustment of future pension costs. Either it could be combined with the newly identified variation of £60m, and the net amount of £122m could be written off over 10 years, or the original amortisation period (a further 7 years) could be retained for the original variation, and the new variation written off separately over a new period of 10 years starting from 2002. The effects of these two possibilities are shown below. Option 1 combines the elements to produce a constant charge of £37.8m (the regular cost of £50m less the amortisation of £122m over 10 years (£12.2m)), while option 2 keeps the components separate (regular cost of £50m less the amortisation of £182m over seven years (£26m) plus the amortisation of £60m over ten years (£6m)).

		Option 1		Option 2	
	Funded	Charged	(Provision)	Charged	(Provision)
Year	£m	£m	£m	£m	£m
Opening provision			(42.0)		(42)
2002	30	37.8	(49.8)	30	(42)
2003	30	37.8	(57.6)	30	(42)
2004	30	37.8	(65.4)	30	(42)
2005	30	37.8	(73.2)	30	(42)
2006	50	37.8	(61.0)	30	(22)
2007	50	37.8	(48.8)	30	2
2008	50	37.8	(36.6)	30	18
2009	50	37.8	(24.4)	56	12
2010	50	37.8	(12.2)	56	6
2011	50	37.8	–	56	–

Option 2 follows the literal requirement of the standard that variations should be spread over the remaining service lives of the employees in the scheme (i.e. without subsequent extension of that period) and may be regarded as the more appropriate method for that reason. However, option 1 can also be seen as being in line with the general philosophy of the standard that the effects of variations should be smoothed forward on a rolling basis. Nevertheless, it means that any individual variations will never be completely amortised, because the amortisation period will be continually extended, even if no significant variations arise from subsequent valuations.

In practice we believe that both methods are acceptable. Option 1 has the additional merit that it requires fewer detailed records and calculations; indeed the amount to be amortised can be identified directly following each valuation because it is the amount of the difference between the actuarial surplus or deficiency in the fund and whatever figure is in the employer's balance sheet; in the above case this works out as £122m (£80m + £42m).

Boots discloses that it applies Option 2, as shown in this extract:

Extract 23.12: The Boots Company PLC (2001)

26 Pensions [extract]

The pension charge for the year was £5m (2000 £5m). This arises as a result of the regular cost of pensions being offset by amortisation of the surpluses disclosed by the 1989, 1992 and 1998 valuations and increased by the amortisation of the deficit in respect of the 1995 valuation. The surplus disclosed at the 1998 valuation is being recognised over approximately 13 years, the expected average remaining service life of members. The remaining amortisation period of the surpluses/deficits disclosed at the 1989, 1992 and 1995 valuations are approximately one, five and eight years respectively.

4.6.3 *Reduction in the number of employees relating to the sale or termination of an operation*

The original version of the standard said that where the variation was associated with an event which gave rise to an extraordinary item, such as the closure of a business segment, the spreading rule was overridden by the requirements of SSAP 6.[178] When FRS 3 replaced SSAP 6, extraordinary items were defined almost out of existence, and consequential amendments were made to SSAP 24. As a result, the relevant paragraph of SSAP 24 now says that where a 'significant reduction in the number of employees is related to the sale or termination of an operation, the associated pension cost or credit should be recognised immediately to the extent necessary to comply with paragraph 18 of FRS 3'.[179] It is explained that 'this is because FRS 3 requires provisions consequent on the sale or termination of an operation to be made after taking account of future profits of the operation or the disposal of its assets'.[180]

The drafting of these paragraphs is unfortunate. They link the rule to paragraph 18 of FRS 3, which deals with provisions made in anticipation of a sale or termination rather than with the sale or termination itself. The literal result is that any pension credit arising on the sale or termination should be recognised immediately only to the extent that it offsets a provision for other aspects of the sale or termination, and that any excess credit therefore falls instead into the exception discussed at 4.6.4 below. However, we doubt if this was intended and we do not think it produces a sensible result. We believe that a company which closes or sells a segment of its business should account for all the financial effects of that event at the same time, including the full pension cost or credit that results. Where this gives rise to an overall credit, this means that it will be reported in the year in which the sale or closure takes place; on the other hand, if it is a net debit there may be circumstances in which it will be provided for in advance, provided the rules of paragraph 18 of FRS 3 (as modified by FRS 12 – see Chapter 28 at 4.5) regarding such provisions are satisfied. In neither case, however, does it make sense to dislocate any part of the pension effect from the other consequences of the sale or closure.

The operation of this exception can be illustrated by the following example, which is based on the figures used in Example 23.7:

Example 23.10: Variations arising from the sale or closure of an operation

The actuary advises that £50m out of the £260m surplus is attributable to the redundancy programme associated with the closure of a business segment in 1999. The accounting treatment in this instance will be to deal with this variation from regular cost immediately, as a credit to the cost of the closure, and to deal with the remaining £210m by amortising it over the working lives of the employees in the scheme. The effect of this amortisation on the amount charged will be as follows:

$$\text{Regular cost} - \frac{\text{surplus}}{\text{average remaining service life}} = £50\text{m} - \frac{£210\text{m}}{10} = £29\text{m}$$

The effect on the accounts will therefore be:

Year		Funded £m	Charged (Credited) £m	Prepayment (Provision) £m
1999	ordinary charge	–	29	
	exceptional credit		(50)	
			(21)	21
2000		–	29	(8)
2001		30	29	(7)
2002		30	29	(6)
2003		30	29	(5)
2004		30	29	(4)
2005		30	29	(3)
2006		30	29	(2)
2007		30	29	(1)
2008		30	29	–

4.6.4 *Other significant reductions in the number of employees*

The next exception from the general 'spreading' rule occurs where there is a significant change in the normal level of contributions in order to eliminate a surplus or a deficiency which results from a significant reduction in the number of employees in the scheme that does not arise from the sale or termination of an operation. The standard says that where these circumstances apply, the effect of the variation in cost should not be spread over the average working lives of the remaining employees, but rather recognised when the reduction in contributions occurs.[181] An example of this rule being invoked is to be found in the following extract from the 1991 accounts of ECC Group:

> *Extract 20.13: ECC Group plc (1991)*
>
> **3 EXCEPTIONAL ITEMS**
>
> In the fifteen months to 31st December 1990, the programme of reorganisation and cost reduction resulted in a provision of £32.0M being made which was shown as an exceptional item. As a result of this restructuring the Actuary has advised that at least £5M of the surplus within the Group's UK pension schemes is attributable to the reduction in manpower. Accordingly, the Group has reduced its contributions by £2.2M in 1991 (also shown as an exceptional item) and will take credit for a similar amount in 1992.

The rationale for this exception is probably that it makes little sense to spread this effect over the working lives of those who remain, when it arises from those who have left. An illustration of the effect of the exception is set out below, again using the same figures as for Example 20.7 above:

Example 23.11: Variations arising from a significant reduction in employees

The actuary advises that £50m out of the £260m surplus is attributable to a major redundancy programme occurring since the date of the last valuation. Accordingly the accounting treatment will be to deal with this variation from regular cost in line with the adjustments made to the funding programme, and deal with the remaining £210m by amortising it over the working lives of the employees in the scheme.

The effect of this amortisation on the amount charged will again be as follows:

$$\text{Regular cost} - \frac{\text{surplus}}{\text{average remaining service life}} = £50\text{m} - \frac{£210\text{m}}{10} = £29\text{m}$$

However it is still necessary to decide when to recognise the effect of the £50m which is attributable to the reduction of employees, because in reality the contributions have been adjusted to eliminate the whole of the £260m surplus, not just the £50m. If the whole of the contribution holiday in the first year were designated as intended to deal with this part of the surplus, the effect would be as follows:

Year	Funded	Charged (Credited)	Prepayment (Provision)
	£m	£m	£m
1999	–	(21)	21
2000	–	29	(8)
2001	30	29	(7)
2002	30	29	(6)
2003	30	29	(5)
2004	30	29	(4)
2005	30	29	(3)
2006	30	29	(2)
2007	30	29	(1)
2008	30	29	–
1999	–	(21)	21
2000	–	29	(8)

The credit in 1999 is calculated in the same way as in Example 23.10, although the whole effect is shown as part of the ordinary pension cost in this case. In fact, the result is the same as in that example only because the contribution holiday in 1999 is large enough to deal with the whole amount of the surplus arising from withdrawals.

Clearly, this produces a rather extreme and, some may say, unfair result. It would be possible to arrive at different results by attributing the changes in the contribution rates to their underlying reasons in a different way. For example if the allocation were made in proportion to the changes in the contribution rate, the effect would be as follows:

Year	Funded	Charged (Credited)	Prepayment (Provision)
	£m	£m	£m
1999	–	19.2	(19.2)
2000	–	19.2	(38.4)
2001	30	25.2	(33.6)
2002	30	25.2	(28.8)
2003	30	25.2	(24.0)
2004	30	25.2	(19.2)
2005	30	25.2	(14.4)
2006	30	25.2	(9.6)
2007	30	25.2	(4.8)
2008	30	25.2	–
1999	–	19.2	(19.2)
2000	–	19.2	(38.4)

(The effect on the funding rate has been to reduce it by £50m in each of the first two years and by £20m in the remaining eight. Accordingly, the total surplus of £50m attributable to the redundancy programme has been apportioned over that period in the same way, to reduce the £29m charge (calculated as shown above) by £9.8m in the first two years and by £3.8m in the remaining eight years.)

This appears to produce a more sensible and consistent charge, and may be regarded as preferable for that reason. Nevertheless either allocation, or indeed any other reasoned allocation, would appear to be acceptable under the terms of the standard. After the first year, the difference between the two approaches is not very significant in terms of the profit and loss account, but the effect on the balance sheet remains quite different for some time.

Although this exception is expressed as being mandatory, it only becomes so once it has been determined that the reduction in employees should be regarded as significant, and this term is not further defined.

The term could be thought of as meaning 'significant enough to make a measurable impact on the actuary's recommendations on funding rates', since the exception requires the accounting to follow whatever change in contributions results from the fall in the number of employees; if there is no measurable impact then clearly the provisions of this exception cannot be applied. In any event, we believe that the exception was intended to be applied relatively rarely, and should be used only where there has been a major scaling down of operations, rather than for every minor trimming exercise.

It should, however, be noted that the reduction need not result from one single closure – it could be the result of a series of redundancies over the period since the last valuation of the fund. Where it does relate to the sale or termination of an operation, the treatment will again be different, as described in 4.6.3 above.

Overall, we do not believe that this exception to the general spreading rule stands up very well to closer examination. The standard requires that recognition be given to the effects of significant reductions in the number of employees in line with the consequential change in contributions, which is an uneasy compromise between the basic spreading rule described at 4.6.2 A above and the immediate recognition required in the circumstances discussed at 4.6.3. Moreover, this leaves the timing of recognition to the whim of management, who may take it in the form of a contribution holiday, by a longer term reduction of the contribution rate, or they may even decide to make no change in the contribution rate at all. As illustrated above, even when they have amended the contribution rate they will still have to decide how to allocate the change in rate against the various factors which have given rise to it. As a result, we do not believe that this exception improves comparability and consistency in financial reporting.

In any event, the general thrust of the standard is to treat variations of all kinds in the same manner, and to look at the workforce as a whole, rather than to focus attention on particular groups of employees. We therefore think it odd to make an exception for these particular circumstances.

4.6.5 *Refunds subject to tax*

Another exception to the normal spreading rule which is allowed by the standard is where the company receives a refund from the scheme that is subject to the deduction of tax. The standard provides that, where such refunds are taken, the company is allowed (but not required) to credit the refund to income in the year of receipt, rather than spreading forward the effects of the variations which have given rise to the surplus.[182] In other words, it allows a cash basis to be used for this transaction if desired. It is very difficult to see any conceptual merit in this exception to the basic spreading rule. The only concession to comparability made by the standard is to require full disclosure of the treatment where a refund is taken.

As is discussed at 4.7.1 below, it can be shown that the surplus or deficit in the fund is represented in the balance sheet figure, although it will usually be combined with an amount which represents deferred variations which are being released to the profit and loss account. For this reason, it seems clear that the appropriate accounting treatment should be to credit the amount of any refund to the balance sheet figure and not to the profit and loss account, otherwise a double counting effect could result. This is most obvious in the case of a company which had a surplus in its scheme at the time of first implementing SSAP 24 and chose to incorporate the surplus in its balance sheet as a pension prepayment; if it subsequently took a refund from the scheme and accounted for it in the profit and loss account, the asset would remain intact in the balance sheet even though it had been converted into cash to the extent of the refund. But the same is true even if the company did not incorporate the surplus in its balance sheet on transition, because as demonstrated in 4.7.1, the surplus is still indirectly represented in the balance sheet figure and this is where the credit should go; at the very least, if the refund is taken to the profit and loss account, the subsequent release of variations to the profit and loss account must be reduced by an equivalent amount.

We regret that the option to credit refunds direct to the profit and loss account is available, because we believe that there is no logical case for it within the framework of SSAP 24. Unilever provides an example of a group that has received a refund from one of its pension schemes, and has taken the appropriate step of deducting it from the balance sheet prepayment rather than crediting it to the profit and loss account:

> *Extract 23.14: Unilever PLC (2000)*
>
> **30 Pension schemes** [extract]
>
> In 2000 the Group received a gross cash refund of €442 million from a Netherlands fund in a surplus position and expects to receive a further refund of the same amount in 2001. This was made in conjunction with a package of benefit improvements, the total value of which is €140 million. Further refunds have been received in 2000 of €40 million from a Finnish fund and €32 million from an Irish fund, both in surplus. These cash refunds do not directly impact the pension charge for 2000 as the surplus is amortised in accordance with the Group's accounting policies.

4.6.6 *Allocation of experience differences to funding consequences*

Any surplus or deficit identified by an actuarial valuation will result from a number of different causes, and it will be necessary to ask the actuary to provide an analysis in order to allow the appropriate accounting to be applied. Since there are exceptions to the normal 'spreading' rule for variations, some choices may emerge, depending on how the individual experience differences are linked with the funding consequences. An example will illustrate this:

Example 23.12: Allocation of experience differences to funding consequences

As a result of an actuarial valuation, a surplus of £5m has been identified. The actuary reports that this is mainly due to experience differences concerning investment performance of the fund, but that £1.2m of the surplus resulted from the withdrawal of a significant proportion of the workforce in the course of a redundancy programme over the last two years. The company decides that it will reduce the surplus both by suspending contributions to the fund for the next two years and also by taking a refund from the scheme of £1m, which will be subject to tax at 40%.

The standard permits taxed refunds to be taken to the profit and loss account when received, regardless of the reason for the surplus arising. It also requires variations resulting from significant reductions in the number of employees to be accounted for in line with their effect on the funding of the scheme. Accordingly the company would appear to have the following options open to it:

(a) to link the refund notionally to the reduction in the number of the employees rather than to the other experience differences. The effect of this would make it compulsory, rather than optional, to credit the refund to the profit and loss account immediately. That part of the contribution holiday which could be attributed to the remaining £0.2m surplus could also be recognised as affecting income in the year or years in which the holiday is taken. (There would appear to be a further choice between spreading it over the two years in which contributions were to be suspended and attributing it wholly to one or other of the years, although the latter would seem somewhat artificial.)

(b) to link the refund notionally to the other experience differences rather than to the reduction in the number of the employees. The effect of this would be to leave the company with the option of recognising the refund in the profit and loss account immediately, but also to require it to give full recognition to the effects of the reduction in the workforce in the year or years of the related contribution holiday. The combined effect of this notional allocation would allow the company to report higher profits in the short term than if the alternative allocation under (a) had been chosen.

No guidance can be offered on how to choose between these different approaches; either would be acceptable. This illustrates some of the anomalies which can arise because the various exceptions to the basic rule for spreading variations forward lack an adequate conceptual thread.

4.6.7 *Material deficits recognised over a shorter period*

The standard provides that, in very limited circumstances, prudence may require that recognition should be given to the costs of making good a material deficit over a period shorter than the normal amortisation period. This exception applies only where significant additional contributions have been required, and where the deficiency has been occasioned by a major event or transaction which has not been allowed for in the actuarial assumptions and is outside their normal scope.[183] An example which is quoted in the standard is that of a major mismanagement of the scheme's assets (presumably resulting in their loss for reasons other than the normal risks of investment). Although this may be a justifiable exception in certain cases, it is expected to be only very rarely applicable; however, it was applied by Mirror Group Newspapers in 1991 following the misappropriation of a large part of its pension fund.

4.6.8 *The treatment of interest*

Where an asset or liability emerges in the balance sheet because the cost charged in the profit and loss account is not the same as the funding payments made, we recommend that notional interest should be added to this amount thereafter as a third component of pension cost. Many companies explicitly do this (see for example the BOC Group at Extract 23.19 below), but others do not, and SSAP 24 is far from clear on the matter.[184] The standard touches on the issue in paragraph 40, but leaves it ambiguous, saying that the question of discounting is not unique to pensions but requires to be answered more generally for many different accounting issues. It says that the interest effects of short-term differences between the payment of contributions and the recognition of cost are likely to be immaterial and can therefore be ignored, but suggests that they should be recognised in relation to longer term differences, and in particular on unfunded liabilities. However, this does not really explore the meaning of the balance sheet figure, or address the purpose of applying interest to it. The issues are best illustrated by use of an example:

Example 23.13: Application of interest to balance sheet figures

A company has a pension fund with an actuarial surplus of £1.4 million at the time of the implementation of SSAP 24. The actuary has assumed that an interest rate of 9% will be earned by the surplus in the fund, and the average remaining service lives of the employees is 8 years. The regular cost of providing for pensions is 10% of pensionable payroll – this gives rise to a present figure of £360,000, which is expected to increase at an annual rate of 7%.

The table set out overleaf shows both the movements in the fund itself over the next eight years and the related accounting entries under the two different methods of implementing the standard in the first year of application. To simplify the interest calculations, it is assumed that the movements in the fund (i.e. contributions and regular cost) occur at the beginning of each year.

As a result of the surplus the actuary has recommended that the contributions for the next eight years be reduced to 4.82% of pensionable pay, which will mean that £173,000 will be contributed in year 1. As is shown in column 1 of the table, this has the effect of eliminating the surplus by the end of the eight year period, assuming everything else works out in line with the actuarial assumptions.

Where the company has chosen to implement SSAP 24 by incorporating the surplus directly in the balance sheet (rather than spreading it forward as a quasi-variation), columns 1 and 2 show the figures that will appear in its balance sheet and profit and loss account, provided that it recognises interest on the balance sheet figure. On implementing the standard, the company will set up the £1.4 million asset in its balance sheet, and in the profit and loss account for year 1 it will show a pension cost of £251,000, which represents the regular cost of £360,000 less interest of £109,000 (9% of (£1,400,000 + £173,000 - £360,000) – to simplify the calculation it is assumed that all movements in the fund are reflected at the beginning of the year) deemed to be earned on the balance sheet figure. The excess of this cost over the contributions paid of £173,000 will be applied to reduce the balance sheet figure by £78,000 to leave the closing balance sheet with an asset of £1,322,000. The same process is repeated in each year, and it can be seen that the balance sheet figure tracks the amount of the surplus in the fund throughout the period.

It is worth considering what would happen if interest on the balance sheet figure were not recognised. In this case the profit and loss account charge would simply be the regular cost of £360,000, and the balance sheet asset would be reduced by £187,000 (the difference between the profit and loss account charge and the £173,000 contribution). By the end of the eight year period this would result in the balance sheet showing a liability of £515,000, which would have no equivalent in the fund; it would simply be the amount of the interest earned in the fund over that period which the accounts had failed to recognise. Any new actuarial valuation carried out during the period would show an apparent variation (being the amount of unrecognised interest) which, in terms of SSAP 24, would be recognised prospectively, as an offset to the pension cost of the next 8 years. It would seem much more sensible to recognise this interest in the years in which it accrues rather than over a protracted future period.

Columns 3 and 4 show the figures which would appear in the balance sheet and the profit and loss account if the company adopted the other possible way of implementing the standard – treating the surplus as a quasi-variation and spreading it forward over the remaining service lives of the employees. The calculation of the pension cost is based on the regular cost of £360,000 less the release of an instalment of the £1.4 million quasi-variation which is spread in this example using the 'straight line method', and plus interest on the opening balance sheet figure in each year. There are two interest elements in this calculation. As well as the interest added on the balance sheet figure, the amortisation of the quasi-variation is done by releasing amounts which include interest so that their *present value* totals £1.4 million (see 4.6.2 B above for a more detailed discussion of spreading methods). The balance sheet figure is simply the cumulative difference between the profit and loss account charge and the contributions paid.

It can be seen that, over the eight years, the total charge to the profit and loss account under the 'prospective' method (column 4) is £1.4 million less than that under the 'PYA' method (column 2). This simply reflects the fact that the surplus is being channelled through the profit and loss account under the former method but taken straight to reserves under the latter. Column 5 shows how this total difference is allocated to each of the years involved; in this example it is a level amount of one-eighth of the total surplus, because the straight line method of amortisation was used. Column 6 shows the amount of the surplus remaining to be recognised at the end of each year, in other words the amount of the initial surplus successively reduced by the figures in column 5. Column 6 also represents the difference between the balance sheet figures under each of the two methods at the end of each year. (As explained at 4.7.1 below, the balance sheet figure under SSAP 24 can be defined as the net of the surplus or deficit in the fund and the amount of unamortised variations awaiting recognition in the profit and loss account.)

Year	Movements in pension fund	1 PYA method Balance sheet £000	2 PYA method P&L account £000	3 Prospective method Balance sheet £000	4 Prospective method P&L account £000	5 Difference £000	6 Unamortised variations £000
1	Surplus	1,400					
	Contribution	173					
	Regular cost	(360)					
	Interest	109					
	P&L charge		251		76	175	
2	Balance	1,322		97			1,225
	Contribution	186					
	Regular cost	(385)					
	Interest	101					
	P&L charge		284		109	175	
3	Balance	1,224		174			1,050
	Contribution	198					
	Regular cost	(412)					
	Interest	91					
	P&L charge		321		146	175	
4	Balance	1,101		226			875
	Contribution	212					
	Regular cost	(441)					
	Interest	79					
	P&L charge		362		187	175	
5	Balance	951		251			700
	Contribution	227					
	Regular cost	(472)					
	Interest	64					
	P&L charge		408		233	175	
6	Balance	770		245			525
	Contribution	243					
	Regular cost	(505)					
	Interest	46					
	P&L charge		459		284	175	
7	Balance	554		204			350
	Contribution	260					
	Regular cost	(540)					
	Interest	25					
	P&L charge		515		340	175	
8	Balance	299		124			175
	Contribution	279					
	Regular cost	(578)					
	Interest	0					
	P&L charge		578		403	175	
9	Balance	0		0			0
	Totals		3,178		1,778	1,400	

To illustrate the application of the calculations further, another example is shown in the table on the next page which assumes the same basic facts, except that the company has chosen to eliminate the surplus more quickly by taking a contribution holiday rather than reducing its rate of contribution over a longer period.

Example 23.14: Application of interest to balance sheet figure

This example alters the facts in Example 23.13 slightly, and shows the figures which would arise if the company eliminated the surplus by taking a contribution holiday for nearly four years rather than by reducing its contributions for eight years. Once again, column 1 in the following table shows the movements in the fund itself; the surplus is run off over four years as a result of the contribution holiday, and thereafter the fund is kept in equilibrium because the contributions are restored to an amount equal to the regular cost.

As before, columns 1 and 2 show the figures that will appear in the company's balance sheet and profit and loss account, provided that interest is recognised on the balance sheet figure. In this case the pension cost will be higher than in the previous example because the surplus in the fund is being reduced more sharply and as a result is earning less interest. From year 5 on, there is no surplus in the fund and the charge in the profit and loss account is simply the regular cost. Once again, the balance sheet figure tracks the amount of the surplus in the fund throughout the period, provided interest is recognised on the balance sheet figure.

Columns 3 and 4 again show the figures which appear in the balance sheet and the profit and loss account under the prospective approach. It can again be demonstrated that, over the eight years, the total charge to the profit and loss account under the prospective method is £1.4 million less than that under the PYA method.

Year	Movements in pension fund	1 PYA method Balance sheet £000	2 PYA method P&L account £000	3 Prospective method Balance sheet £000	4 Prospective method P&L account £000	5 Difference £000	6 Unamortised variations £000
1	Surplus	1,400					
	Contribution	0					
	Regular cost	(360)					
	Interest	94					
	P&L charge		266		91	175	
2	Balance	1,134		(91)			1,225
	Contribution	0					
	Regular cost	(385)					
	Interest	67					
	P&L charge		318		143	175	
3	Balance	816		(234)			1,050
	Contribution	0					
	Regular cost	(412)					
	Interest	36					
	P&L charge		376		201	175	
4	Balance	440		(435)			875
	Contribution	1					
	Regular cost	(441)					
	Interest	0					
	P&L charge		441		266	175	
5	Balance	0		(700)			700
	Contribution	472					
	Regular cost	(472)					
	Interest	0					
	P&L charge		472		297	175	
6	Balance	0		(525)			525
	Contribution	505					
	Regular cost	(505)					
	Interest	0					
	P&L charge		505		330	175	
7	Balance	0		(350)			350
	Contribution	540					
	Regular cost	(540)					
	Interest	0					
	P&L charge		540		365	175	
8	Balance	0		(175)			175
	Contribution	578					
	Regular cost	(578)					
	Interest	0					
	P&L charge		578		403	175	
9	Balance	0		0			0
	Totals		3,496		2,096	1,400	

Having given these illustrations, it is now possible to consider why the figures work out in the way that they do. Where the balance sheet figure simply represents the surplus in the fund (as it will to begin with under the PYA approach) then it is easy to see that it is necessary to recognise the interest which the fund is earning in the company accounts in order to preserve that relationship. However, where the prospective method is applied, it is harder to understand why interest should be applied to the balance sheet figure, and indeed, as in Example 23.14, it may be difficult to explain why an extra interest *charge* should be made on a balance sheet liability when the fund is still *earning* interest on a surplus.

To explain this, it is necessary to see the balance sheet figure in the light discussed in 4.7.1 below, as a composite figure which is the net of the surplus in the fund and the amount of unamortised variations awaiting recognition in the profit and loss account. Thus, the liability of £91,000 at the end of year 1 under the prospective method (column 3 in Example 23.14) is the net of the surplus in the fund of £1,134,000 and the unamortised variations of £1,225,000 (columns 1 and 6). Applying interest to the £91,000 can similarly be interpreted as a credit for interest on the surplus in the fund which is more than offset by a charge on the amount of the unamortised variations.

This analysis offers a different way of looking at the make-up of the pension cost charge, which may be more readily understood. The total pension cost can be explained as being made up of the regular cost less the interest on the surplus (even though it is not included in the balance sheet) and less the release of the quasi-variation into the profit and loss account. This can be illustrated as follows using the figures from Example 23.13:

Year	Regular cost	Interest in fund	Release of variations	Total
	£000	£000	£000	£000
1	360	109	175	76
2	385	101	175	109
3	412	91	175	146
4	441	79	175	187
5	472	64	175	233
6	505	46	175	284
7	540	25	175	340
8	578	0	175	403
	3,693	515	1,400	1,778

The method shown in Example 23.13 differs from this in two ways, which cancel each other out:

(a) interest is applied to the whole balance sheet figure, not just the surplus (i.e. it is also applied to the component which represents the deferred variations awaiting recognition in the profit and loss account);

(b) the variations are taken into the profit and loss account at amounts whose *net present value* adds up to £1.4m, not their absolute amount.

This analysis may be easier to understand in concept, but that which is given in Example 23.13 may be easier to apply in practice because it simply involves applying interest to the balance sheet figure, whatever it may be, rather than looking through it to see what the actual surplus in the fund is.

When interest is recognised in the profit and loss account, it is necessary to consider whether to include it as a component of pension cost, or as an amount of interest payable or receivable within the general classification of finance costs. Respectable arguments can be mounted for either treatment where the interest is simply that which is being earned in the fund itself (where the balance sheet figure directly represents the balance in the fund). However, where the interest is charged on a composite figure which includes an amount of unamortised variations, the interest charge or credit has no real significance by itself because it is inseparably linked to the release of these variations. For this reason, it is suggested that the preferable treatment in all cases is to include the interest as a component of pension cost. This was the tentative conclusion of the ASB in its 1995 Discussion Paper,[185] although the contrary suggestion was made in the Board's later paper on Discounting.[186]

In conclusion, it can be seen from the illustrations given above that interest considerations pervade the calculations which underlie pension accounting, and that unless they are consistently accounted for, the accounts will not allocate them to the periods to which they belong. Despite the apparent complexity of these examples, the rules to be applied are relatively straightforward; companies should both account for imputed interest on the balance sheet figure and also spread any variations into the profit and loss account on a basis which includes the effects of interest. If they do not do so, apparent variations will arise in subsequent actuarial valuations which are simply the result of the company's failure to recognise interest in the periods in which it has accrued.

4.6.9 *Negative pension cost*

Where the amount of interest and/or variations credited to pension cost exceeds the regular cost, then a net negative pension cost figure will arise. Typically this will be because the surplus in the scheme is so large that it would not be eliminated even by a pension holiday for the whole of the average working lives of the employees in the scheme. However, it could also be the result of using a 'front-end' loaded amortisation method of releasing variations to the profit and loss account.

The question that then arises is whether it is legitimate in principle to recognise negative expense in respect of pensions. To some extent, this depends on a matter of perception of what SSAP 24 involves. One view would be that it is designed simply to allocate the total cost of providing pensions to the years of employment of the eventual pensioners, and since that total cost will be positive, it does not make any sense for the amount allocated to any individual year to be negative. On this interpretation, the credit arising from interest or variations should be restricted to the amount of the regular cost, so that the minimum cost is zero and no credit is taken for any negative amount. Meyer International is an example of a company that explicitly restricts credit components of pension cost so that it does not report net credits to the profit and loss account:

> *Extract 23.15: Meyer International PLC (2000)*
>
> **1 ACCOUNTING POLICIES**
>
> **(i) Pensions**
>
> The expected costs of pensions are provided on systematic and rational bases over the estimated average service lives of members of the schemes. Variations arising from actuarial surpluses are spread over the average remaining service lives of members to the extent that the resulting credit does not exceed the regular cost.

The alternative interpretation looks more deeply into the pension scheme and sees it as a store of wealth which is a source of risks and benefits to the employer. Accordingly it seeks to apply the 'half-hearted' form of equity accounting described in 4.7.1 below. On this analysis, there is no reason in principle why negative pension cost should not be recognised, and indeed this would represent a limitation on recognition of interest and variations which would in many ways be arbitrary. BOC, in Extract 23.19 at 4.8.2 below, discloses negative cost for its principal schemes in 2000. We believe that this is an acceptable interpretation of the standard and therefore see no reason why negative pension cost should not be recognised. The ASB's 1995 Discussion Paper endorsed this view, although it qualified its approval by emphasising that the recognition of negative pension cost should not give rise to an asset which does not represent a source of benefits to the employer.[187]

4.6.10 Discretionary and ex gratia pension increases and ex gratia pensions

As mentioned in (d) at 4.6.1 above, the standard suggests that allowance should be made in the actuarial assumptions for pension increases of all kinds, even where these are not the result of any contractual obligation. Where this applies, any increases in pensions which are different from those previously assumed will be dealt with as giving rise to variations, to be treated as discussed in 4.6.2 above.

However, where no allowance has been made for such increases, different rules apply. The standard requires that the full capitalised value of these is provided for in the year in which they are made, except to the extent that they are covered by an existing surplus. This would appear to mean that if there is a surplus in the scheme at the time the increases are granted then the cost can, in effect, be spread forward (as a reduction of a variation which would otherwise have reduced future pension cost), but if there is no such surplus, or an insufficient surplus, then the cost must be charged against current profits.

It is not clear whether this applies only where it is possible in fact to use the surplus in the fund to meet this expense. This may be impossible if the provisions of the scheme do not permit the trustees to apply the funds for this purpose. It is arguable that even then the treatment may still be justifiable because the unrecognised gain in the fund provides sufficient reason to justify non-recognition of the unfunded liability for the discretionary or ex gratia award. However, we believe that the standard intended the narrower interpretation, that the offset can be applied only when the surplus in the scheme is in fact applied to meet the cost of the new award. Furthermore, we assume that the treatment is only available to the extent that the surplus has not already been recognised in the balance sheet; in other words the offset is permitted only against an *unrecognised* surplus, and even then it will be necessary to reduce the future variations being released to the profit and loss account by an equivalent amount.

The accounting policy of Wolseley makes specific reference to ex gratia payments:

Extract 23.16: Wolseley plc (2000)

ACCOUNTING POLICIES

Pensions [extract]

... The cost of ex gratia pensions is provided in full in the year in which they are awarded.

4.7 Defined benefit schemes - balance sheet

4.7.1 *Meaning of the balance sheet figure*

As explained earlier, the standard is expressed mainly in terms of the profit and loss account, and the asset or liability which appears in the balance sheet is literally the balancing figure. It is the cumulative difference between the amount which has been charged in the profit and loss account and the amount which has been paid in the form of contributions, and under SSAP 24 it is to be shown as a prepayment or an accrual, representing the extent to which contributions have been paid either ahead of or behind the recognition of cost. Since companies will generally continue to have contributions allowed for tax when they are paid, this figure will also represent the cumulative timing difference which has to be taken into account for the purposes of deferred tax.

It might be thought that this balance has no definable meaning, particularly as there are circumstances where it appears to 'go the wrong way'. For example, as is shown in Example 23.7 at 4.6.2 above, a company which takes a contribution holiday because there is an underlying surplus in the fund may end up showing a liability in its accounts, which may seem incongruous. However, in reality the balance can be explained as being the combination of two figures; the most recently reported actuarial surplus or deficiency in the fund (as adjusted for subsequent contributions and regular costs), combined with the cumulative amount of unamortised variations awaiting recognition in the profit and loss account. This can be shown using the figures in that example. The balance is analysed in this chart, and explained below:

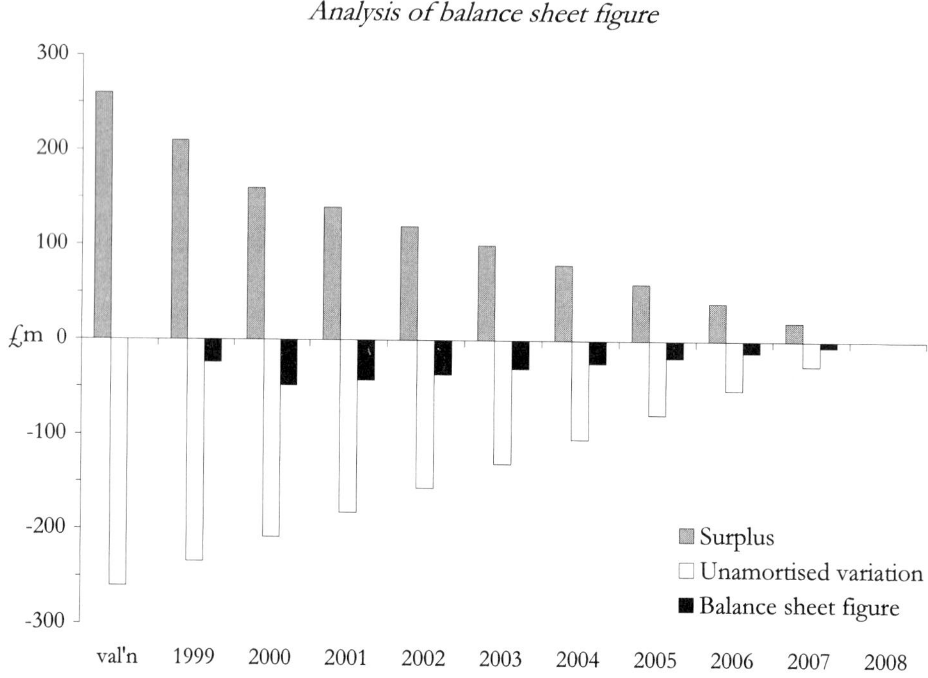

Example 23.15: Explanation of balance sheet figure

	Fund			*Financial statements*	
	1	2	3	4	5
Year	Contribution £m	Regular cost £m	Surplus £m	Unamortised variation £m	Balance £m
Actuarial surplus/variation			260	(260)	–
1999	–	50	210	(234)	(24)
2000	–	50	160	(208)	(48)
2001	30	50	140	(182)	(42)
2002	30	50	120	(156)	(36)
2003	30	50	100	(130)	(30)
2004	30	50	80	(104)	(24)
2005	30	50	60	(78)	(18)
2006	30	50	40	(52)	(12)
2007	30	50	20	(26)	(6)
2008	30	50	–	–	–

Columns 1 to 3 show the theoretical movements in the fund after the valuation resulting from the effects of contributions and regular costs; for the sake of simplicity the effects of interest and the time value of money have been ignored. Column 4 is the amount of the unrecognised variation, being the variation identified in the 1998 valuation, successively reduced by annual amortisation of £26m p.a. to reduce the pension cost charged in the profit and loss account. Column 5 is the net of columns 3 and 4 and is the amount shown as a provision in the balance sheet. Although it may seem odd that a liability is shown when an underlying surplus exists, it simply reflects the fact that the effects of the surplus have been recognised more quickly in cash terms (by the contribution holiday) than for accounting purposes.

When the prepayment or accrual is explained in this way, it can be seen that the standard is more balance sheet orientated than is often recognised. In effect, it is possible to regard SSAP 24 as requiring companies to adopt a half-hearted form of equity accounting for their pension funds, particularly if they adopted the 'prior year adjustment' method of implementing the standard and recognise interest on the surplus (as discussed at 4.6.8 above). The treatment is 'half-hearted' in the sense that the effect of variations is recognised gradually rather than immediately, and because there is no requirement to undertake an annual actuarial valuation of the pension fund to be reflected in the accounts.

This perception of the standard has a bearing on a number of other questions of interpretation which arise, such as the treatment of interest and its relationship with the amortisation of variations, and whether it is legitimate to recognise a negative pension cost (where regular cost is outweighed by variations or interest credited to the profit and loss account). These matters are discussed at 4.6.8 and 4.6.9 above.

As mentioned above, the standard requires any excess of contributions paid over the amount of cumulative pension cost charged to be shown as a prepayment (or provision if it is a shortfall) in the balance sheet. When the balance is described in these terms, its classification as a current asset or liability seems entirely reasonable; however, when its underlying nature is examined under the analysis set out above, it can be seen that it is really a composite figure made up of two long-term items: the surplus in the fund and the amount of unamortised variations. The first of these is itself a net figure, being the excess of the investments held by the pension scheme over its obligations to pay pensions (both long-term items), while the second is a deferred credit awaiting transfer to the profit and loss account over a number of years.

To include this composite figure as a prepayment has a major effect on some conventional balance sheet ratios. Initially, the position was accentuated for the minority of companies who originally chose to implement the standard by incorporating the surplus in the balance sheet, rather than by spreading it forward to reduce pension cost over the service lives of the members, because in these circumstances there would have been no offsetting deferred credit to reduce the composite figure to manageable proportions. But even companies who did not do so have often found that a material figure can quickly build up, since the balance sheet figure will always tend towards the amount of the surplus or deficit in the scheme as the deferred element is gradually released (although, of course, new valuations will create further variations to be deferred and released in this way). As shown in this extract, the prepayment in BP Amoco's accounts at the end of 2000 stood at $3.6 billion:

Extract 23.17: BP Amoco p.l.c. (2000)

22 Debtors [extract]

				$ million
		2000		**Group**
	Within 1 year	After 1 year	Within 1 year	After 1 year
Trade	**17,813**	**–**	9,417	–
Joint ventures	**582**	**–**	725	–
Associated undertakings	**98**	**46**	60	45
Prepayments and accrued income	**2,137**	**486**	1,229	549
Taxation recoverable	**412**	**–**	263	83
Pension prepayment	**–**	**3,609**	–	2,541
Other	**2,766**	**469**	1,653	327
	23,808	**4,610**	13,347	3,545

There is no easy solution to this problem. One approach would be to 'explode' the balance into its underlying components, so as to show the surplus within fixed asset investments and the unamortised variations within deferred income (preferably outside the current liabilities total). Alternatively, the prepayment classification could be maintained, but backed up by a note which 'explodes' it in the same way. In effect, this would provide a reconciliation between the balance sheet figure and the funded status of the scheme, which is a requirement of SFAS 87, the equivalent standard in the USA, and will be required in the UK on implementation of FRS 17 (see 3.9.1 above). Whatever approach is adopted, however, it would appear to be incumbent on the directors to provide a sufficient explanation of the balance to avoid giving a misleading impression of the liquidity of the company. As shown above, BP Amoco has correctly identified it as an amount not receivable within one year and many other companies do the same.

In July 1992, the UITF published an Abstract dealing with the general question of long-term debtors in current assets, mentioning pension assets as a possible example of such an item. This ruled that where amounts due after more than one year are very material, they should be shown separately on the face of the balance sheet (but still within current assets).[188]

4.7.2 *How to treat a balance sheet asset which is shown to have been eroded by a subsequent valuation*

In the circumstances described in Example 23.9 at 4.6.2 C above, the company was showing a liability in respect of pensions in its balance sheet. However, if it had previously incorporated the surplus as an asset in its balance sheet (on adoption of the standard for the first time), then it would be facing a different situation, as described in the following example:

Example 23.16: Effect on balance sheet figures of subsequent valuations

Company B acquires a subsidiary and in the course of the fair value exercise obtains an actuarial valuation of its pension fund which showed a surplus of £260m. Accordingly, B incorporates that amount in its consolidated balance sheet. The actuary subsequently recommends that the surplus is eliminated by a contribution holiday for the next two years and then reduced contributions of £30m p.a. for 8 years. After that the standard contribution would be £50m p.a. As a result of the above, the group accounts for the next three years included the following in respect of the acquired subsidiary:

Year	Funded £m	Charged £m	Prepayment £m
on implementation			260
1999	–	50	210
2000	–	50	160
2001	30	50	140

The next actuarial valuation at 31 December 2001 showed a surplus of £80m. The actuary this time recommended that the contribution rate at £30m p.a. should be maintained for four more years and then raised to £50m thereafter. The average working lives of the employees is ten years.

There has therefore been a deterioration of £60m (i.e. £140m - £80m) since the previous valuation and this represents the variation which has to be accounted for. Applying SSAP 24's normal approach of eliminating the variation over the average working lives of the members would add £6m to the regular cost of £50m and would produce the following results (ignoring interest etc. in order to simplify the illustration).

Year	Funded £m	Charged £m	Prepayment £m
brought forward			140
2002	30	56	114
2003	30	56	88
2004	30	56	62
2005	30	56	36
2006	50	56	30
2007	50	56	24
2008	50	56	18
2009	50	56	12
2010	50	56	6
2011	50	56	0

The only possible problem with this is that the asset in the balance sheet exceeds the surplus in the fund for the whole of the period 2002 to 2011, as shown below:

Year	Funded £m	Charged £m	Prepayment £m	Surplus £m	Difference £m
brought forward			140	80	60
2002	30	56	114	60	54
2003	30	56	88	40	48
2004	30	56	62	20	42
2005	30	56	36	0	36
2006	50	56	30	0	30
2007	50	56	24	0	24
2008	50	56	18	0	18
2009	50	56	12	0	12
2010	50	56	6	0	6
2011	50	56	0	0	0

The surplus of £80m is reduced by £20m for the first four years because the contribution is set at £30m while the regular cost remains at £50m. The difference, shown in the last column, represents the unamortised variations still to be recognised in the profit and loss account.

Normal accounting principles would dictate that, when it can be seen that an asset in the balance sheet will not be fully recoverable, it should be written down to reflect the impairment in value which has occurred. However, this would be contrary to the basic approach of the standard, which requires gradual rather than immediate recognition of experience differences, and does not discriminate between gains and losses for this purpose. Similarly, it does not require immediate recognition in the balance sheet of pension scheme deficits, whether on first application of the standard or as a result of subsequent valuations.

We suggest, however, that if significant adverse variations do arise, companies should at least consider analysing the balance sheet figure so as to distinguish the amount which represents the surplus in the scheme from that which is simply the total of unamortised variations to be charged in the profit and loss account of subsequent years.

4.7.3 *Deferred tax*

As mentioned at 4.7.1 above, the pension prepayment or accrual appearing in the balance sheet will generally represent the cumulative timing difference in respect of pension costs which should be taken into account in the company's assessment of its deferred tax position. (Since the company will receive tax deductions in respect of contributions paid to the scheme, and since the balance sheet figure represents the amount by which the recognition of pension cost in the profit and loss account has been cumulatively more or less than the contributions paid to date, it also represents the amount of this timing difference.) It follows that any movements in the balance sheet figure, including those arising from the application of interest (see 4.6.8 above) should also be regarded as giving rise to timing differences.

The treatment of deferred tax as regards SSAP 24 balances is discussed in Chapter 24 at 4.3.1 and 5.8.

4.8 Defined benefit schemes - disclosure

4.8.1 *Requirements*

Although SSAP 24 does deal with the calculation of pension cost, there is still a large degree of flexibility as to the measurement of the amounts to be recognised, partly because of the exceptions to the basic spreading rule mentioned above but also because there is a large degree of subjectivity inherent in the actuarial process, and because no single actuarial method has been specified. In this light, it is still possible to characterise the standard as being primarily a disclosure standard, because the disclosure requirements which it introduced are very extensive. These are as follows:[189]

(a) the nature of the scheme (i.e. the fact that it is a defined benefit scheme);

(b) whether it is funded or unfunded;

(c) the accounting policy and, if different, the funding policy;

(d) whether the pension cost and provision (or asset) are assessed in accordance with the advice of a professionally qualified actuary and, if so, the date of the most recent formal actuarial valuation or later formal review used for this purpose. If the actuary is an employee or officer of the reporting company, this fact should be disclosed;

(e) the pension cost charge for the period together with explanations of significant changes in the charge compared to that in the previous accounting period;

(f) any provisions or prepayments in the balance sheet resulting from a difference between the amounts recognised as cost and the amounts funded or paid directly;

(g) the amount of any deficiency on a current funding level basis (a 'discontinuance' basis) indicating the action, if any, being taken to deal with it in the current and future accounting periods. Where there is more than one pension scheme, the standard emphasises that it is not permitted to set off a surplus of this type arising on one scheme against a deficiency on another;

(h) an outline of the results of the most recent formal actuarial valuation or later formal review of the scheme on an ongoing basis. This should include disclosure of:

    (i) the actuarial method used and a brief description of the main assumptions (for SSAP 24 purposes, not for funding purposes, where the two are different).[190] This should include the assumption made regarding new entrants unless it is apparent from the description of the method used.[191] If there has been a change in the method, this fact should be disclosed and the effect quantified;[192]

    (ii) the market value of scheme assets at the date of their valuation or review. (Note that this means the actual market value of the assets, which will not generally be the same as the value on the basis used by the actuary for valuing the scheme – see 2.1.5 above);

    (iii) the level of funding expressed in percentage terms.[193] (This, taken with the previous requirement, will allow a reasonable estimate of the actuarial surplus or deficiency to be derived. It will be only an estimate because the previous requirement calls for the market value of the assets to be shown, rather than the value put on them for the purposes of the actuarial valuation);

    (iv) comments on any material actuarial surplus or deficiency indicated by (iii) above;[194] and

    (v) the effects of any significant post-valuation events;[195]

(i) any commitment to make additional payments over a limited number of years;

(j) the accounting treatment adopted in respect of a refund made under deduction of tax (see 4.6.6 above), where a credit appears in the financial statements in relation to it. (We presume that this means a credit in the profit and loss account rather than in the balance sheet, otherwise the last few words of the previous sentence add nothing to the requirement); and

(k) details of the expected effects on future costs of any material changes in the company's pension arrangements.[196]

4.8.2 *Extracts illustrating disclosure requirements*

Examples of comprehensive notes, taken from the accounts of Smiths Industries, BOC and SmithKline Beecham are set out below:

Extract 23.18: Smiths Industries plc (2000)

11 Post-retirement benefits

Smiths Industries operates a number of pension schemes throughout the world. The major schemes are located in the UK and the USA and are of the defined benefit type, with assets held in separate trustee administered funds.

Contributions to pension schemes are made on the advice of independent qualified actuaries, using in the UK the Projected Unit method and in the USA the Entry Age Normal method. The aim is for the benefits to be fully funded during the scheme members' working lives.

For both schemes the regular pension cost is assessed using the Projected Unit method. The latest actuarial assessments were as at 31 March 1998 for the UK scheme and 1 August 1999 for the USA scheme.

At these dates the market value of the schemes' assets was £729m for the UK and $284m for the USA, and the aggregate funding levels of the principal schemes were 125% and 127% respectively. The funding levels were determined by comparing the market value of the funds' assets with the value of benefits accrued to date. Allowance was made for future annual salary increases at approximately 5% and, for the UK schemes, for pension increases of approximately 3%. The future investment return assumed in assessing the present value of future benefits was 6% p.a. for UK pensioner liabilities and 7% p.a. for UK active member liabilities and a discount rate of 7.75% p.a. was used for the USA. These rates were derived from prevailing yields on government stocks and high quality fixed interest investments.

The regular pension cost is assessed at each actuarial valuation and applied until the next valuation. The variation from regular pension cost, which recognises the excess of assets over liabilities of the pension schemes, is spread over the average remaining working life of relevant employees, generally between 10 and 15 years.

A prepayment of £40.4m is included in debtors, this being the excess of the amount funded over the accumulated pension cost.

The pension costs of other schemes operated by the Company were assessed in accordance with local practice. The Company operates a defined contribution (401K) plan for its USA employees, and operates post retirement healthcare benefit plans, principally at Grand Rapids in the USA. The cost of the post retirement healthcare benefits is assessed by independent qualified actuaries and is fully accrued (see note 23). The major assumptions used are interest rate 7.25% p.a., and medical cost inflation 7% p.a., ultimately reducing to 5% p.a.

Extract 23.19: The BOC Group plc (2000)

6. Employees
e) Retirement benefits
i) Pensions – UK GAAP

The Group operates a number of pension schemes throughout the world. The majority of the schemes are self-administered and the schemes' assets are held independently of the Group's finances. Pension costs are assessed in accordance with the advice of independent, professionally qualified actuaries. In accordance with UK GAAP, disclosures concerning post-retirement costs other that pensions are satisfied by the US GAAP disclosures on pages 92 and 93.

The principal schemes are of the defined benefit type. The UK and South African schemes are based on final salary and the US on annual salary. With effect from 1 January 1998 the Australian scheme changed to operate primarily as a defined contribution scheme, although it retains some defined benefit guarantees. The accounting basis used is the same as the prior year. On the advice of respective actuaries, Group funding in most of the principal schemes is suspended and is unlikely to be required during the next financial year.

The cost for the year was:

	2000 £ million	1999 £ million	1998 £ million
Principal schemes			
Regular pension cost	**49.4**	46.9	44.8
Variations from regular cost	**(63.0)**	(48.3)	(39.9)
Interest	**(1.7)**	(1.3)	(1.8)
Other schemes	**8.0**	9.2	4.8
Net pension (credit)/cost	**(7.3)**	6.5	7.9

The results of the most recent UK GAAP valuations of the principal schemes, and the assumptions used for these valuations are set out below. The disclosures relate to valuations undertaken specifically for accounting purposes. Separate valuations were undertaken for funding purposes. In each principal scheme the projected unit credit method of valuation was used. Assets were taken at market value (smoothed market value in the UK and the US) and any surplus or deficit is amortised over the remaining working lifetimes of employee members as a uniform percentage of their pensionable pay.

The change in the net pension (credit)/cost between 2000 and 1999 arises as a result of new valuations for the UK and US schemes which disclosed higher surpluses than in previous years.

	UK[1]	US	Australia	South Africa
Date of latest UK GAAP valuation	31 March 2000	30 June 1999	31 December 1997	30 June 1998
Main assumptions for UK accounting purposes				
Rate of price inflation	2.7%	3.8%	3.0%	12.5%
Rate of return on assets[2]	3.6%	3.4%	3.5%	2.2%
Real increase in earnings[2]	2.0%	1.7%	1.5%	1.1%
Interest credit on members' balances[2]	–	2.4%	–	–
UK GAAP valuation data				
Assessed asset value (% of market value)	96%	94%	100%	82%
Market value of investments (£ million)	1,439	489	107	90
Level of funding[3]	131%	222%	125%	121%

1. Pension increases are assumed to be in line with the rate of price inflation.
2. Above price inflation
3. The actuarial value of assets expressed as a percentage of the accrued liabilities.

As the above extract shows, in 2000 BOC experienced a negative pension cost in relation to its principal schemes. The question of negative pension cost is discussed at 4.6.9 above.

Extract 23.20: SmithKline Beecham plc (1999)

28 RETIREMENT BENEFITS

The Group operates plans throughout the world covering the majority of employees. These plans are devised in accordance with local conditions and practices in the countries concerned and include defined contribution and benefit schemes. The assets of the plans are generally held in separately administered trusts or are insured, although in Germany the plans are not externally funded. Pension plan assets are managed by independent professional investment managers. It is the Group's policy that none of the assets of the funds are invested directly or indirectly in any Group company. The contributions to the plans are assessed in accordance with independent actuarial advice mainly using the projected unit credit method.

The total pension cost was £88 million (1998 – £87 million; 1997 – £94 million) of which £32 million (1998 – £38 million; 1997 – £44 million) relates to defined benefit plans in the U.K., U.S. and Germany which cover some 43% of total employees, and for which further disclosures are set out below.

	UK	US	Germany
Main assumptions:			
Investment return	10%	9.5%	7%
Salary increases p.a.	6.5%	5.5%	4.5%
Pension increases p.a.	3.5%	–	3%
Last valuation date	30.6.97	31.12.97	31.12.97
Level of funding, being the actuarial value of assets expressed as percentage of the accrued service liabilities	114%	100%	n/a
	£m	£m	£m
Market valuation of investment at last valuation date	735	1,035	n/a
Regular pension cost	13	21	2
Variations from regular cost	(8)	–	4
Total pension costs for 1999	5	27	6

Variations from regular cost are spread over the remaining service lives of current employees in the plans. A provision of £199 million (1998 – £216 million) is included in provisions for liabilities and charges, representing the excess of the accumulated pension cost over the amount funded (see note 17) including £51 million (1998 – £54 million) relating to Germany.

In addition to pension benefits, approximately 10,000 of SB's employees in the U.S. at the end of 1999 became eligible for certain healthcare and life insurance benefits upon retirement. The amount charged to the profit and loss account in the year for these items was £25 million (1998 – £26 million; 1997 – £23 million). The main assumptions used in determining the required provision are an investment return of 9.5% and medical cost inflation of 6% reducing to 5% by the year 2003. The last valuation date was 1 January 1999.

Some of the most varied forms of disclosure have been those relating to the actuarial assumptions used. In addition to the extracts shown above, some further examples of such disclosures from accounts are set out below. A straightforward form of this disclosure is given by Cadbury Schweppes:

Extract 23.21: Cadbury Schweppes plc (2000)

18 Pension Arrangements and other Post-Retirement Benefits [extract]

(a) UK GAAP

The major scheme is the Cadbury Schweppes Pension Fund in the UK for which the last full valuation was made as at 5 April 1999 on the projected unit method when the market value of the assets was £1,277m. The level of funding on the assumptions shown below was 114%.

The principal long term assumptions used for the purposes of the actuarial valuation were as follows:

Rate of return on new investments	7.25%
Earnings increases	5.00%
Pensions increases	3.00%
Growth of dividends	4.25%

Another approach to disclosing aggregated information about a large number of different schemes is illustrated by the accounts of ICI. The company has disclosed the main assumptions by means of weighted averages, rather than simply giving ranges of assumptions used:

Extract 23.22: Imperial Chemical Industries PLC (2000)

38 Pensions and other post-retirement benefits [extract]

Group

The Company and most of its subsidiaries operate retirement plans which cover the majority of employees (including directors) in the Group. These plans are generally of the defined benefit type under which benefits are based on employees' years of service and average final remuneration and are funded through separate trustee-administered funds. Formal independent actuarial valuations of the Group's main plans are undertaken regularly, normally at least triennially and adopting the projected unit method.

The actuarial assumptions used to calculate the projected benefit obligation of the Group's pension plans vary according to the economic conditions of the country in which they are situated. The weighted average discount rate used in determining the actuarial present values of the benefit obligations was 6.0% (1999 8.0%). The weighted average expected long-term rate of return on investments was 6.1% (1999 8.3%). The weighted average rate of increase of future earnings was 4.4% (1999 5.3%).

The actuarial value of the fund assets of these plans at the date of the latest actuarial valuations was sufficient to cover 99% (1999 93%) of the benefits that had accrued to members after allowing for expected future increases in earnings; their market value was £8,240m (1999 £8,166m).

The total pension cost for the Group for 2000 was £85m (1999 £132m). Accrued pension costs amounted to £13m (1999 £11m) and are included in other creditors (note 20); provisions for the benefit obligation of a small number of unfunded plans amounted to £205m (1999 £216m) and are included in provisions for liabilities and charges – unfunded pension (note 22). Prepaid pension costs amounting to £487m (1999 £382m) are included in debtors (note 17).

ICI Pension Fund

The ICI Pension Fund accounts for approximately 86% of the Group's plans in asset valuation and projected benefit terms.

From the date of the actuarial valuation of the ICI Pension Fund as at 31 March 1994 the Company has been making payments into the Fund to reflect the extra liabilities arising from early retirement as retirements occur. Based on a Funding Review as at 31 March 1997, the Company agreed to make six annual payments into the Fund of £100m pa from 1998 through 2003, subject to a review in 2000. The latest actuarial valuation of the fund, as at 31 March 2000, disclosed a solvency ratio of 98% and the company has agreed to make a further six annual payments of £30m per annum from 2001 to 2006, subject to review in 2003. The deficit, together with the prepayment, is taken into account in arriving at the employers' pension costs charged in the accounts by being amortised as a percentage of pensionable emoluments over the expected working lifetime of existing members. In 2000 this gave rise to a charge of £10m.

Sometimes, companies are less forthcoming about the absolute amounts of the assumptions used, perhaps because they believe that the disclosure of the salary assumption might compromise their negotiating position with the unions, although this information is in any event generally given in the actuarial statement which accompanies the fund accounts. One form of disclosure which is sometimes used is to give the information by reference to an (undisclosed) inflation assumption:

Extract 23.23: Balfour Beatty plc (2000)

22 Pensions [extract]

At the date of the latest valuations of the principal defined benefit schemes, the market value of the assets of those schemes amounted to £1,888m. The actuarial value of those assets exceeded the benefits which had accrued to members after allowing for expected future increases in earnings. The latest actuarial valuation of the Balfour Beatty Pension Fund (formerly the BICC Group Pension Fund) was carried out by independent actuaries at 31 March 1999 using the projected unit method and disclosed an excess of assets over past service liabilities of 11%, which is being used to reduce Company contributions over a period of ten years. The principal actuarial assumptions of the Balfour Beatty Pension Fund are for investment returns to exceed inflation by 4% per annum and for increases in dividends to exceed inflation by 0.5% per annum.

Although in principle this might be a permissible way of complying with the standard, Balfour Beatty does not seem to have disclosed the salary inflation assumption at all, which is important information for an assessment of the strength of the actuarial valuation.

Another way of disclosing these assumptions which is often seen in practice is simply to give their relationship to each other, without actually disclosing the absolute figures. One company which has adopted this approach is Aga Foodservice Group:

Extract 23.24: Aga Foodservice Group plc (2000)

5 Employee information [extract]

The latest full valuation of the main United Kingdom scheme was carried out by Watson Wyatt Partners, independent consulting actuaries, as at 31st March 1998 using the projected unit credit method. The principal assumptions on which the valuation was based for the purposes of establishing the Group's pension cost were that the investment return would be 2.75% greater than general salary increases, 4.25% greater than increases in future pension payments and 3.5% greater than the assumed rate of growth on United Kingdom equity dividends. The results of the valuation showed that the scheme had an aggregate market value of £746.5m and was 109% funded.

It is true that the relationship between the figures is generally more significant than the figures themselves, particularly the gap between the assumed investment return and the salary inflation assumption. Nevertheless the presentation of the absolute figures, as has been done in most of the extracts illustrated here, would provide the reader with this information in a more straightforward and understandable way.

General Accident is an example of a company which changed its actuarial valuation method in its 1993 accounts. The effect of the change is disclosed, as shown in the following extract:

Extract 23.25: General Accident plc (1993)

5 Pension and Other Post Retirement Benefits
(a) Staff Pension Costs

The principal pension schemes operate in the UK and North America. These schemes are of the defined benefit type and their assets are held in separate trustee administered funds. Each of the schemes has been subject to actuarial valuation or review in the last twelve months using the 'Projected Unit Credit' method. In previous years the 'Entry Age' method of actuarial valuation was applied in respect of the UK schemes. The effect of this change in method has been to reduce the annual pension cost by approximately £3.6 million. The actuarial valuation of the defined benefit scheme was carried out by a qualified actuary who is an employee of the Group.

5 RELATED COMPANIES ACT REQUIREMENTS

5.1 Pension commitments

The Companies Act 1985 requires that particulars should be disclosed of:

(a) any pension commitments included under any provision shown in the company's balance sheet; and

(b) any such commitments for which no such provision has been made.[197]

The requirement goes on to say that separate disclosure should be given to any part of these commitments which relate to pensions payable to former directors of the company.

The Act offers no further interpretation of what constitutes a pension commitment for the purposes of this disclosure requirement. It could be interpreted very broadly, so that disclosure of the commitment would require a full description of the obligation which the company had accepted in making pension promises to its employees; this would involve giving details of the terms of the pension scheme, together with a description of the arrangements which had been made to meet that obligation.

In practice, however, the general interpretation of the requirement has been much narrower. Many companies appear to have taken the view that as long as the pension scheme is adequately funded, there is no further commitment on the part of the company itself which has to be disclosed. Companies have generally confined their disclosure to a relatively brief description of the pension arrangements in force and the fact that the schemes were fully funded. Since the introduction of SSAP 24, the disclosures given by employer companies have been much more extensive (see 4.4.2 and 4.8 above), and we believe that this satisfies the Companies Act requirement to disclose pension commitments.

When companies implement FRS 17, more extensive disclosures will be required as discussed at 3.6.2 and 3.9 above. It is our view that compliance with FRS 17's disclosure requirements will also satisfy the statutory requirements above.

5.2 Pension costs

The Act also requires disclosure of pension costs charged in the profit and loss account. This is one of three elements of staff costs which have to be disclosed, the other two being wages and salaries and social security costs.[198] The Act goes on to say that for this purpose pension costs 'includes any costs incurred by the company in respect of any pension scheme established for the purpose of providing pensions for persons currently or formerly employed by the company, any sums set aside for the future payment of pensions directly by the company to current or former employees and any pensions paid directly to such persons without having first been set aside'.[199]

5.3 Directors' emoluments

There are detailed requirements in the Companies Act for the disclosure of directors' emoluments, including pensions. These are discussed in detail in Chapter 32.

6 IAS REQUIREMENTS

In January 1983, the International Accounting Standards Committee issued IAS 19 – *Accounting for Retirement Benefits in the Financial Statements of Employers* – which was revised ten years later in November 1993 with the shortened title of *Retirement Benefit Costs*. It was broadly similar in its approach to SSAP 24, although there were quite a number of differences of detail.

In October 1996, however, the IASC published an exposure draft proposing to make fundamental changes to IAS 19.[200] In particular, the whole focus of the standard was to be shifted from the profit and loss account to the balance sheet. This led to the issue of a further revised version of IAS 19 in February 1998, to take effect for accounting periods beginning on or after 1 January 1999. In October 2000 some further minor adjustments were made to IAS 19 relating to the treatment of assets in the form of insurance policies. These refinements come into force for periods beginning on or after 1 January 2001. The main features of this standard are summarised below. The practical application of the standard is illustrated by comprehensive extracts from the accounts of three companies applying IAS (see 6.10 below).

6.1 Objective

As mentioned above, the general approach of IAS 19 is focused on the balance sheet and accordingly is very similar in most respects to FRS 17. IAS 19 sets out its objective as follows:

'... to prescribe the accounting and disclosure for employee benefits. The Standard requires an enterprise to recognise:

(a) a liability when an employee has provided service in exchange for employee benefits to be paid in the future; and

(b) an expense when the entity consumes the economic benefit arising from service provided by an employee in exchange for employee benefits.'[201]

6.2 Scope

The new version of IAS 19 is entitled 'Employee Benefits', and as this name suggests it is not confined to pensions and other post-retirement benefits, but rather addresses all other forms of remuneration as well, including:[202]

(a) 'short-term' benefits, including wages and salaries, holiday pay, bonuses, benefits in kind, etc. The accounting treatment of these is discussed in Chapter 22 at 3.1;

(b) long term benefits, such as long service leave, long term disability benefits, long-term bonuses, etc. These are to be accounted for in a similar way to post-retirement benefits by using actuarial techniques and are discussed at 6.9 below;

(c) termination benefits. These are to be provided for and expensed when the employer becomes committed to the redundancy plan, on a similar basis to UK GAAP, and are discussed in Chapter 22 at 3.3); and

(d) equity compensation benefits, such as share option schemes, share purchase schemes at a discount, phantom share schemes etc. Here the standard ducks the difficult recognition and measurement issues that have continued to trouble other standard setters and only prescribes a set of disclosures about these arrangements, which are discussed in Chapter 22 at 3.4.

6.3 Defined contribution plans and defined benefit plans

6.3.1 *The distinction between defined contribution and defined benefit plans*

Similarly to FRS 17, IAS 19 draws the important distinction between defined contribution and defined benefit plans by defining the former, with the latter being the default category. The relevant terms defined by the standard are as follows:

'*Post-employment benefits* are employee benefits (other than termination benefits and equity compensation benefits) which are payable after the completion of employment.'

'*Post-employment benefit plans* are formal or informal arrangements under which an enterprise provides post-employment benefits for one or more employees.'

'*Defined contribution plans* are post-employment benefit plans under which an enterprise pays fixed contributions into a separate entity (a fund) and will have no legal or constructive obligation to pay further contributions if the fund does not hold sufficient assets to pay all employee benefits relating to employee service in the current and prior periods.'

'*Defined benefit plans* are post-employment benefit plans other than defined contribution plans'[203]

IAS 19 applies to all post-employment benefits (whether or not they involve the establishment of a separate entity to receive contributions and pay benefits) which include, for example, pensions, post-retirement life assurance or medical care.[204] Under defined benefit plans the employer's obligation is not limited the amount that it agrees to contribute to the fund. Rather, the employer is obliged (legally or constructively) to provide the agreed benefits to current and former employees. Examples of defined benefit schemes given by IAS 19 are:

(a) plans where the benefit formula is not linked solely to the amount of contributions;

(b) guarantees, either directly or indirectly through a plan, of a specified return on contributions; and

(c) those informal practices that give rise to a constructive obligation. For example, a history of increasing benefits for former employees to keep pace with inflation even where there is no legal obligation to do so.[205]

The most significant difference between defined contribution and defined benefit plans is that, under defined benefit plans, both actuarial risk and investment risk fall on the employer. This means that if actuarial or investment experience are worse than expected, the employer's obligation may be increased.[206] Consequently, because the employer is underwriting the actuarial and investment risks associated with the plan, the expense recognised for a defined benefit plan is not necessarily the amount of the contribution due for the period. Conversely, under defined contribution plans the benefits received by the employee are determined by the amount of contributions paid (either by the employer, or both the employer and the employee) together with investment returns, and hence actuarial and investment risk a borne by the employee.[207]

6.3.2 *Insured benefits*

IAS 19 recognises that some employers may fund their post-employment benefit plans by paying insurance premiums. Where this is the case, a company should treat such a plan as a defined contribution plan unless the entity has a legal or constructive obligation to:

(a) pay the employee benefits directly when they fall due; or

(b) pay further amounts if the insurer does not pay all future employee benefits relating to employee service in the current and prior periods.[208]

If the entity has retained such a legal or constructive obligation it should treat the plan as a defined benefit plan. In that case, the entity recognises its rights under a 'qualifying insurance policy' as a plan asset and recognises other insurance policies as reimbursement rights.[209] Plan assets are discussed at 6.8.2 below.

6.4 Multi-employer plans

Multi-employer plans, other than state plans (see 6.5 below), under IAS 19 are defined contribution plans or defined benefit plans that:

(a) pool assets contributed by various entities that are not under common control; and

(b) use those assets to provide benefits to employees of more than one entity, on the basis that contribution and benefit levels are determined without regard to the identity of the entity that employs the employees concerned.[210]

A multi-employer plan should be classified as either a defined contribution plan or a defined benefit plan in accordance with its terms in the normal way (see 6.3.3 above). If a multi-employer plan is classified as a defined benefit plan, IAS 19 requires that the employer should account for its proportionate share of the defined benefit obligation, plan assets and costs associated with the plan in the same way as for any other defined benefit plan (see 6.8 below). The employer should also disclose the same information as is required for any other defined benefit plan.[211]

The standard does, however, contain an exemption very similar to that in FRS 17 (see 3.4 above) as follows. If insufficient information is available to use defined benefit accounting for a multi-employer plan that is a defined benefit plan, an entity should:[212]

(a) account for the plan as if it were a defined contribution plan;

(b) disclose that the plan is a defined benefit plan and the reason why insufficient information is available to account for the plan as a defined benefit plan; and

(c) to the extent that a surplus or deficit in the plan may affect future contributions, disclose:

 (i) any available information about that surplus or deficit;

 (ii) the basis used to determine the surplus or deficit; and

 (iii) any implications for the entity.

Unlike FRS 17, however, IAS 19 further provides that defined benefit plans that pool the assets contributed by various enterprises under common control, for example a parent and its subsidiaries, are not multi-employer plans and that, therefore, an enterprise treats all such plans as defined benefit plans.[213] The wording in IAS 19 is not entirely clear and this could be read to mean that the exemption does not apply to the individual accounts of subsidiaries. It seems more likely, however, that this provision is simply intended to ensure that the group as a whole treats its defined benefit schemes as such.

IAS 19 also contains a reminder that IAS 37 – *Provisions, Contingent Liabilities and Contingent Assets* – requires an enterprise to recognise, or disclosure information in relation to, certain contingent liabilities, and notes that such contingencies may arise (in the context of a multi-employer plan) from:

(a) actuarial losses relating to the other participating enterprises because each enterprise that participates in a multi-employer plan shares in the actuarial risks of every other participating employer; or

(b) any responsibility under the terms of a plan to finance any shortfall in the plan if other enterprises cease to participate.[214] IAS 37 is discussed in Chapter 28 at 7.

6.5 State plans

IAS 19 observes that state plans are established by legislation to cover all enterprises (or all enterprises in a particular category, for example a specific industry) and are operated by national or local government or by another body (for example an autonomous agency created specifically for this purpose) which is not subject to control or influence by the reporting enterprise.[215] The standard requires that state plans be accounted for in the same way as for a multi-employer plan (see 6.4 above),[216] although it goes on to note that state plans will normally be of a defined contribution nature.[217]

6.6 Implementation date and transitional provisions

IAS 19 applied to financial statements covering periods beginning on or after 1 January 1999, though early adoption was encouraged.[218] For reporting periods beginning after 1 January 2001 further revisions have been made to this Standard relating to the treatment of qualifying insurance policies and any other insurance policies (see 6.8.2 and 6.8.5 below)[219].

On first adopting IAS 19 it is necessary for an enterprise to determine the 'transitional liability' for defined benefit plans as:

(a) the present value of the obligation at the date of adoption;

(b) minus the fair value of plan assets at the date of adoption;

(c) minus any past service cost that should be recognised in later periods.[220]

IAS 19 illustrates the computation of this transitional liability by way of a numerical worked example.[221] If the transitional liability exceeds the liability under the employer's previous accounting policy, then it should make an irrevocable choice to recognise that increase:

(a) immediately in accordance with the provisions of IAS 8 – *Net Profit or Loss for the Period, Fundamental Errors and Changes in Accounting Policies* (discussed in Chapter 25 at 3.5); or

(b) as an expense on a straight-line basis over a maximum of five years from the date of adoption. In this case the enterprise should:

   (i) apply the limit set by IAS 19 (see 6.8.7 below) in measuring any asset recognised in the balance sheet;

   (ii) disclose at each balance sheet date the amount of the increase that remains unrecognised and the amount recognised in the current period;

   (iii) limit the recognition of subsequent actuarial gains to unrecognised actuarial gains in excess of the unrecognised transitional obligation liability; and

   (iv) include the related part of the unrecognised transitional liability in determining any subsequent gain or loss on settlement or curtailment.

If the transitional liability is less that the liability under the previous accounting policy, the employer should recognise that decrease immediately under IAS 8.[222]

A typical example is ABB, which implemented IAS 19 in its accounts for the year to 31 December 1999 and set out the impact on opening reserves as follows:

Extract 23.26: ABB Ltd (1999)

Statement of changes in equity

Year ended December 31 (US$ in millions)	notes	1999	1998
Equity as at December 31, previous year (1998 and 1997 respectively)	17	**5,959**	**5,283**
Inclusion of ABB Ltd, ABB AB and ABB AG [a)]		34	–
Changes in accounting principles and other items [b)]		-935	-74
Dividend payments		-503	-460
Translation differences		-561	-95
Net income		1,614	1,305
Equity as at December 31		**5,608**	**5,959**

a) Net assets of ABB AB and ABB AG other than their holdings in the ABB Group contributed to ABB Ltd at June 28, 1999, ie, after pay-out of ordinary dividends to respective shareholders related to 1998 and a special dividend to ABB AG shareholders on June 25, 1999.

b) Introduction in 1999 of revised IAS 19 on Employee Benefits (refer to note 22) and in 1998 of revised IAS 12 on Income Taxes.

As can be seen, the implementation of IAS 19 resulted in the recognition of a further pension liability of nearly US$ 1 billion, or some 17% of closing equity. The notes to the accounts reveal that this comprises a deficit of US$ 1,030million net of deferred tax of US$ 120million, and that the fair value of plan assets is US$ 4,411million.

6.7 Defined contribution plans

6.7.1 Accounting requirements

Accounting for defined contribution plans is straightforward under IAS 19 because, as the standard observes, the reporting enterprise's obligation for each period is determined by the amounts to be contributed for that period. Consequently, no actuarial assumptions are required to measure the obligation or the expense and there is no possibility of any actuarial gain or loss to the reporting entity. Moreover, the obligations are measured on an undiscounted basis, except where they do not fall due wholly within twelve months after the end of the period in which the employees render the related service.[223]

IAS 19 requires that, when an employee has rendered services during a period, the employer should recognise the contribution payable to a defined contribution plan in exchange for that service:

(a) as a liability, after deducting any contribution already paid. If the contribution already paid exceeds the contribution due for service before the balance sheet date, the excess should be recognised as an asset when such prepayment will lead to a reduction in future payments or a cash refund; and

(b) as an expense, unless another International Accounting Standard requires or permits capitalisation of such expense.[224]

IAS 19 requires that contributions due to a defined contribution plan should be discounted when they are not due within twelve months after the end of the period in which the service was rendered,[225] whereas FRS 17 is silent on this issue. One possible reason for this is that the ASB considered the scenario unlikely in the UK.

The discount rate should be the yield on high quality corporate bonds of appropriate currency and term. In countries where there is no deep market in such bonds, the yield on government bonds should be used.[226]

6.7.2 *Disclosure requirements*

IAS 19 requires the disclose of the expense recognised for defined contribution plans.[227] Where required by IAS 24 – *Related Party Disclosures*, information should also be disclosed about contributions to defined contribution plans for key management personnel.[228] IAS 24 is discussed in Chapter 30.

6.8 Defined benefit plans

6.8.1 *General*

IAS 19's approach to defined benefit schemes is very similar to that of FRS 17, the principle difference is the treatment of actuarial gains and losses which is discussed at 6.8.3 below.

The standard notes that accounting for defined benefit plans is complex because actuarial assumptions are required to measure both the obligation and the expense, and there is a possibility of actuarial gains and losses. Moreover, the obligations are measured on a discounted basis because they may be settled many years after the employees render the related service.[229]

In addition to specifying accounting and disclosure requirements, IAS 19 provides a work programme of the steps necessary to apply its rules, as follows:

(a) using actuarial techniques, make a reliable estimate of the amount of benefit that employees have earned in return for their service in the current and prior periods. This requires an entity to determine how much benefit is attributable to the current and prior periods and to make estimates (actuarial assumptions) about demographic variables (such as employee turnover and mortality) and financial variables (such as future increases in salaries and medical costs) that will influence the cost of the benefit;

(b) discount that benefit using the projected unit credit method in order to determine the present value of the defined benefit obligation and the current service cost;

(c) determine the fair value of any plan assets;

(d) determine the total amount of actuarial gains and losses and the amount of those actuarial gains and losses that should be recognised;

(e) where a plan has been introduced or changed, determine the resulting past service cost; and

(f) where a plan has been curtailed or settled, determine the resulting gain or loss.[230]

All of the above steps are equally necessary each year for FRS 17 purposes, with the exception of the second item under (d). This is because IAS 19 does not require the immediate recognition of all actuarial gains and losses as is required by FRS 17. This is discussed at 6.8.3 below.

Where an employer has more than one defined benefit plan, it should apply the steps above for each material plan separately.[231]

6.8.2 Valuation of defined benefit plans

The measurement of any plan surplus or deficit under IAS 19 is essentially identical to that required by FRS 17 – it is the balance sheet recognition that differs.

A Plan assets

Unlike FRS 17, IAS 19 provides a definition of plan assets (which exclude unpaid contributions due from the employer to the fund, and any non-transferable financial instruments issued by the employer[232]) as follows:

'*Plan assets* comprise:

(a) assets held by a long-term employee benefit fund; and

(b) qualifying insurance policies.

Assets held by a long-term employee benefit fund are assets (other than non-transferable financial instruments issued by the reporting enterprise) that:

(a) are held by an entity (a fund) that is legally separate from the reporting enterprise and exists solely to pay or fund employee benefits; and

(b) are available to be used only to pay or fund employee benefits, are not available to the reporting enterprise's own creditors (even in bankruptcy), and cannot be returned to the reporting enterprise, unless either:

  (i) the remaining assets of the fund are sufficient to meet all the related employee benefit obligations of the plan or the reporting enterprise; or

  (ii) the assets are returned to the reporting enterprise to reimburse it for employee benefits already paid.

A qualifying insurance policy is an insurance policy issued by an insurer that is not a related party (as defined in IAS 24, Related Party Disclosures) of the reporting enterprise, if the proceeds of the policy:

(a) can be used only to pay or fund employee benefits under a defined benefit plan;

(b) are not available to the reporting enterprise's own creditors (even in bankruptcy) and cannot be paid to the reporting enterprise, unless either:

  (i) the proceeds represent surplus assets that are not needed for the policy to meet all the related employee benefit obligations; or

  (ii) the proceeds are returned to the reporting enterprise to reimburse it for employee benefits already paid.'[233]

In a UK context, the trust structure typical of most defined benefit schemes will mean that the assets of the scheme qualify as plan assets under IAS 19; and it is, perhaps, for this reason that the ASB considered it unnecessary to define scheme assets in FRS 17.

IAS 19 requires plan assets to be measured at their fair value,[234] which is defined as the amount for which an asset could be exchanged between knowledgeable, willing parties in an arm's length transaction.[235] When no market price is available, the fair value needs to be estimated, for example by discounting expected future cash flows at a discount rate reflecting both the risk and maturity date (or expected disposal date) of the asset.[236] Where plan assets include qualifying insurance policies that exactly match the amount and timing of some or all of the benefits payable under the plan, the fair value of those insurance policies is deemed to be the present value of the related obligations, subject to any reductions required if the amounts receivable under the insurance policies are not recoverable in full.[237]

Some employers may invest in insurance policies to fund defined benefit obligations which do not meet the definition of qualifying insurance policies above. In such a case, the expected payments under the policy are not *classified* as plan assets under IAS 19 (and hence they are not presented as part of a net pension asset/liability – see 6.8.3 below). Instead, the employer should recognise its right to reimbursement as a separate asset, but only when it is virtually certain that another party will reimburse some or all of the expenditure required to settle a defined benefit obligation. The asset should be measured at fair value. In all other respects it should be treated in the same way as plan assets. In the income statement, the expense relating to a defined benefit plan may be presented net of the amount recognised for a reimbursement.[238]

B Plan liabilities

IAS 19 refers to the liabilities of defined benefit plans as the present value of defined benefit obligations, which it defines as '… the present value, without deducting any plan assets, of expected future payments required to settle the obligation resulting from employee service in the current and prior periods'.[239]

The obligations should include not only the benefits set out in the plan, but also any constructive obligations which go beyond the formal plan terms, and should include an estimate of expected future salary increases.[240] A constructive obligation exists where a change in the employer's informal practices would cause unacceptable damage to its relationship with employees and which therefore leaves the employer with no realistic alternative but to pay those employee benefits.[241] IAS 19 also deals with the situation where the level of defined benefits payable by a scheme vary with the level of state benefits. When this is the case any changes in state benefit may only be factored into the actuarial computations if they are enacted by the balance sheet date or are predictable based on past history or other evidence (FRS 17 is silent on this issue).[242]

As is the case under FRS 17, plan obligations are to be measured using the projected unit credit method,[243] and IAS 19 provides a simple example of what this entails.[244] The obligations are discounted at a rate determined by reference to the yield (at the balance sheet date) on high quality corporate bonds of currency and term consistent with the liabilities. In countries where there is no deep market in such bonds, the yields on government bonds should be used instead.[245] As noted at 2.2.2 above, when selecting a discount rate in circumstances where there is no deep market in appropriate corporate bonds, FRS 17 requires the use of the rate on government bonds as adjusted for assumed credit risk spreads. IAS 19 does not require such an adjustment in these circumstances.

In applying the projected unit credit method, IAS 19 normally requires benefits to be attributed to periods of service under the plan's benefit formula. If, however, an employee's service in later years will lead to a materially higher level of benefit, the benefit should be attributed on a straight-line basis from:

(a) the date when service by the employee first leads to benefits under the plan; until

(b) the date when further service by the employee will lead to no material amount of further benefits under the plan, other than from further salary increases.[246]

IAS 19 illustrates the attribution of benefits to service periods with a number of worked examples.[247]

Actuarial assumptions should be unbiased, mutually compatible and represent the entity's best estimates of the variables that will determine the ultimate cost of providing post-employment benefits. Financial assumptions must be based on market expectations at the balance sheet date.[248]

Assumptions about medical costs should take account of inflation as well as specific changes in medical costs (including technological advances, changes in health care utilisation or delivery patterns, and changes in the health status of plan participants).[249] The standard provides a quite detailed discussion of the factors that should be taken into account in making actuarial assumptions about medical costs, in particular it notes:

(a) measuring post-employment medical benefits requires assumptions about the level and frequency of future claims, and the cost of meeting them. An employer should make such estimates based on its own experience, supplemented where necessary by historical data from other sources (such as other enterprises, insurance companies and medical providers);[250]

(b) the level and frequency of claims is particularly sensitive to the age, health status and sex of the claimants, and may also be sensitive to their geographical location. This means that any historical data used for estimating future claims needs to be adjusted to the extent that the demographic mix of the plan participants differs from that of the population used as the basis for the historical data. Historical data should also be adjusted if there is reliable evidence that historical trends will not continue;[251] and

(c) estimates of future medical costs should take account of any contributions that claimants are required to make based on the terms (whether formal or constructive) of the plan at the balance sheet date. Changes in such terms will constitute past service costs or, where applicable, curtailments (discussed at 6.8.4).[252]

Clearly, the application of actuarial techniques to compute plan obligations is a complex task, and it seems likely that few companies would seek to prepare valuations without the advice of qualified actuaries. However, unlike FRS 17, IAS 19 does not require that directors take actuarial advice.

Regarding the frequency of valuations, IAS 19 gives less prescriptive guidance on the FRS 17, simply requiring that the present value of defined benefit obligations, and the fair value of plan assets, should be determined frequently enough to ensure that the amounts recognised in the financial statements do not differ materially from the amounts that would be determined at the balance sheet date. If amounts determined before the balance sheet date are used, they should be updated to take account of any significant transactions or changes in circumstances up to the balance sheet date.[253] We believe the substance of the rules should produce the same results under each standard.

6.8.3 *Balance sheet presentation of defined benefit schemes*

A Measurement of the balance sheet asset or liability

The starting point under IAS 19 is that (subject to the special transitional provisions discussed at 6.6 above) a plan surplus or deficit is reflected directly in the employers balance sheet. However, in a significant difference from FRS 17, not all of the subsequent movements in the fair value of a surplus or deficit need be reflected in the balance sheet.

IAS 19 requires the balance sheet figure relating to a defined benefit plan to be the net total of:

(a) the present value of the defined benefit obligation at the balance sheet date;

(b) plus actuarial gains and less actuarial losses not yet recognised;

(c) less past service cost not yet recognised; and

(d) less the fair value of plan assets, at balance sheet date, out of which the obligations are to be settled directly [254]

This requirement is the same as that of FRS 17, with the exception of (b) above. Both the IASC and the ASB encountered the same fundamental problem in developing their standards on pension accounting. The zeal for balance sheet fair values which their respective conceptual frameworks demand leads inevitably to unacceptable volatility. As discussed at 3.8.1 above, the approach taken by the ASB to overcome earnings volatility was, in essence, to account for budgeted figures in the profit and loss account with variances consigned (permanently) to the STRGL as actuarial gains and losses.

The IAS took a different tack, and decided to adopt a 'corridor' mechanism. In what at first glance appears to be a balance sheet approach, IAS 19 does not require immediate recognition of actuarial gains and losses. Instead an employer need only recognise a portion the actuarial gains and losses to the extent that the net cumulative unrecognised actuarial gains and losses at the end of the previous reporting period exceeded the greater of:

(a) 10% of the present value of the defined benefit obligation; and

(b) 10% of the fair value of any plan assets.

The above 'corridor test' needs to be applied separately for each defined benefit plan. The excess actuarial gain or loss should be recognised over the expected average remaining working lives of employees participating in the plan. However, an entity may recognise actuarial gains and losses more quickly – as long as the same basis is applied to both gains and losses – even if they fall within the limits of the corridor.[255]

It is entirely possible that 10% of gross assets or liabilities will exceed the net balance sheet figure. This means that the balance sheet figure under IAS 19 could easily be 'wrong' by 100% or more, and even those actuarial movements that are recognised may be spread forward over a number of years. Given this, it is clear that, even though there are few major differences between IAS 19 and FRS 17, the accounting entries required by each will be very significantly different.

It remains to be seen whether the current work of the IASB on performance reporting will result in the immediate recognition of actuarial gains and losses in a similar manner to FRS 17.

The resulting balance sheet figure may be an asset, in which case it is subject to a ceiling test; the balance sheet asset should not exceed the net total of:

(a) any unrecognised actuarial losses and past service cost; and

(b) the present value of any economic benefit available in the form of refunds from the plan or reductions in future contributions to the plan.[256]

This ceiling test overrides the transitional option to recognise any reduction in net assets over a period of up to five years (see 6.6 above). It does not, however, override the delayed recognition of certain actuarial losses under the corridor approach described above. IAS 19 provides a worked example illustrating the interaction between this ceiling test and the 'normal' delayed recognition allowed by the corridor approach.[257]

This limitation is in fact quite problematic. First of all, it seems to limit the recognition of the benefit of any surplus to its cash flow benefit. This would appear to mean that if the employer intends to use a surplus to improve the benefits under the plan without further contributions having to be paid, it may not recognise the surplus as an asset. Secondly, it is not clear whether 'reductions in future contributions' refers to actual or hypothetical future cash flow benefits. If the former, the standard would only allow a surplus to be recognised to the extent that the employer intended to run it off, and this may seldom apply. Furthermore, any refunds or reductions in contributions would usually be based on a different actuarial valuation, producing a different surplus, than the one being used for accounting purposes. In the UK, the valuation for funding purposes is typically more conservative than that used for accounting purposes, so any limitation that is founded on actual or putative funding adjustments may be quite a severe one. It will therefore be interesting to see how practice develops in the interpretation of this restriction. FRS 17 sets out it's ceiling test in more precise terms (see 3.7.5 above). In particular, it makes clear that reduced future contributions for these purposes are hypothetical contributions, based on the measurement model in the standard, and not expected funding contributions.

B Presentation of balance sheet amounts

As noted at 3.7.4 above, FRS 17 requires the creation of a new balance sheet caption for pension surpluses/deficits, and also requires that they be presented net of deferred tax. IAS 19 does not contain similar rules and, accordingly, assets and liabilities under IAS 19 should be presented (gross) in the 'normal' balance sheet captions.

Employers with more than one fund may find that some are in surplus while others are in deficit. An asset relating to one plan may only be offset against a liability relating to another plan when there is a legally enforceable right to use a surplus in one plan to settle obligations under the other plan, and the employer intends to settle the obligations on a net basis or simultaneously.[258]

6.8.4 Income statement presentation

IAS 19 identifies the same six components of annual pension cost as FRS 17, as follows:

(a) current service cost;
(b) interest cost;
(c) the expected return on any plan assets (and any reimbursement rights);
(d) actuarial gains and losses (to the extent they are recognised);
(e) past service cost (to the extent they are recognised); and
(f) the effect of any curtailments or settlements.[259]

All these terms have the same meaning as they do under FRS 17 (see 3.8 above). In summary:

A Current service cost

The current service cost, which should be determined using the projected unit credit method, is the increase in the present value of the defined benefit obligation resulting from employee service in the current period.[260]

B Interest cost

Interest cost is the increase during a period in the present value of a defined benefit obligation which arises because the benefits are one period closer to settlement.[261] Interest cost is calculated by multiplying the discount rate at the beginning of the period by the present value of the defined benefit obligation throughout that period, taking account of any material changes in the obligation.[262]

C Expected return on plan assets (and any reimbursement rights)

The expected return on plan assets is based on market expectations at the beginning of the period for returns over the entire life of the related obligation, and reflects changes in the fair value of plan assets during the period arising from contributions to and benefits paid out of the fund.[263] The difference between the expected return and actual return on plan assets is an actuarial gain or loss.[264] IAS 19 illustrates the computation of the expected and actual return on plan assets with a simple worked example.[265]

D Actuarial gains and losses

Actuarial gains and losses comprise experience adjustments – the effects of differences between the previous actuarial assumptions and what has actually occurred – and the effects of changes in actuarial assumptions. These changes can result, for example, from:

(a) unexpectedly high or low rates of: employee turnover, early retirement, mortality, increases in salaries or benefits, or medical costs;

(b) the effect of changes in estimates of: future employee turnover, early retirement, mortality, increases in salaries or benefits, or medical costs;

(c) the effect of changes in the discount rate; and

(d) differences between the actual return on plan assets and the expected return on plan assets.[266]

The treatment of actuarial gains and losses is discussed at 6.8.2 above.

E Past service costs

Past service cost is the increase in the present value of the defined benefit obligation for employee service in prior periods, which occurs in the current period from the introduction of, or changes to, post-employment benefits or other long-term employee benefits. Past service cost may be either positive (where benefits are introduced or improved) or negative (where existing benefits are reduced).[267] Similarly to FRS 17, IAS 19 requires that in measuring its defined benefit liability, an employer should recognise past service cost as an expense on a straight-line basis over the average period until the benefits become vested, and illustrates this with a worked example.[268] If benefits are vested immediately following the changes to a defined benefit plan, the past service cost should be recognised immediately.[269]

F Settlements and curtailments

A settlement occurs when an employer enters into a transaction that eliminates all further legal or constructive obligations for part or all of the benefits provided under a defined benefit plan, for example, when a lump-sum cash payment is made to, or on behalf of, plan participants in exchange for their rights to receive specified post-employment benefits.[270] IAS 19 observes that an employer may acquire an insurance policy to fund some or all of the employee benefits relating to employee service in the current and prior periods. The acquisition of such a policy is not a settlement if the employer retains a legal or constructive obligation to pay further amounts if the insurer does not pay the employee benefits specified in the insurance policy.[271]

A curtailment occurs when an employer (1) is demonstrably committed to make a material reduction in the number of employees covered by a plan or (2) amends the terms of a defined benefit plan such that a material element of future service by current employees will no longer qualify for benefits or will qualify only for reduced benefits. The standard makes the somewhat circular observation that an event is material enough to qualify as a curtailment if the recognition of a curtailment gain or loss would have a material effect on the financial statements. A curtailment may arise from an isolated event, such as the closing of a plant, discontinuance of an operation or termination or suspension of a plan. IAS 19 notes that curtailments are often linked to a restructuring, in which case the curtailment gain or loss should be accounted for at the same time as the related restructuring.[272] The standard also illustrates the computation of and accounting for a curtailment by way of a worked example.[273]

Gains or losses on the curtailment or settlement of a defined benefit plan should be recognised when the curtailment or settlement occurs. The gain or loss should comprise:

(a) any resulting change in the present value of the defined benefit obligation;

(b) any resulting change in the fair value of the plan assets;

(c) any related actuarial gains and losses and past service cost that had not previously been recognised.[274]

Before determining the effect of a curtailment or settlement, the standard requires that the obligation and any related plan assets be remeasured using current actuarial assumptions.[275]

Where a curtailment relates to only some employees covered by a plan or only part of an obligation is settled, the gain or loss should include a proportionate share of the previously unrecognised past service costs and actuarial gains and losses.[276] IAS 19 notes that a settlement occurs together with a curtailment when a plan is terminated such that the obligation is settled and the plan ceases to exist. However, if the plan is replaced by a new plan offering benefits that are, in substance, identical to the old one, the event is not a settlement or a curtailment.[277]

G *Principal differences between FRS 17 and IAS 19 regarding income statement presentation*

The key differences between IAS 19's requirements and those of FRS 17 are:

(a) whilst, as discussed at 6.8.3 above, not all actuarial gains and losses need to be recognised under IAS 19, those that do are included in the income statement; and

(b) IAS 19 requires the above to be presented as a single net item in the income statement, other than to the extent that another IAS allows their inclusion in an asset.[278]

6.8.5 *Disclosure requirements*

IAS 19 requires the following information about defined benefit plans to be disclosed:

(a) the accounting policy for recognising actuarial gains and losses;

(b) a general description of the type of plan;

(c) a reconciliation of the assets and liabilities recognised in the balance sheet, showing at least:

  (i) the present value at the balance sheet date of defined benefit obligations that are wholly unfunded;

  (ii) the present value (before deducting the fair value of plan assets) at the balance sheet date of defined benefit obligations that are wholly or partly funded;

  (iii) the fair value of any plan assets at the balance sheet date;

  (iv) the net actuarial gains or losses not recognised in the balance sheet;

  (v) the past service cost not yet recognised in the balance sheet;

  (vi) any amount not recognised as an asset because of the limit (to recoverable amount) set by IAS 19;

  (vii) the fair value at the balance sheet date of any reimbursement right recognised as a separate asset – together with a brief description of the link between the reimbursement right and the related obligation; and

  (viii) the other amounts recognised in the balance sheet;

(d) the amounts included in the fair value of plan assets for:

  (i) each category of the reporting entity's own financial instruments; and

  (ii) any property occupied by, or other assets used by, the reporting entity;

(e) a reconciliation showing the movements during the period in the net liability (or asset) recognised in the balance sheet;

(f) the total expense recognised in the income statement for each of the following, and the line items of the income statement in which they are included:

  (i) current service cost;

  (ii) interest cost;

  (iii) expected return on plan assets;

  (iv) expected return on any reimbursement right recognised as a separate asset;

  (v) actuarial gains and losses;

  (vi) past service cost; and

  (vii) the effect of any curtailment or settlement;

(g) the actual return on plan assets and the actual return on any reimbursement right recognised as an asset; and

(h) the principal actuarial assumptions used as at the balance sheet date, including, where applicable:

  (i) the discount rates;

  (ii) the expected rates of return on any plan assets for the periods presented in the financial statements;

  (iii) the expected rates of return for the periods presented in the financial statements on any reimbursement right recognised as an asset;

  (iv) the expected rates of salary increases and of changes in an index or other variable specified in the formal or constructive terms of a plan as the basis for future benefit increase;

  (v) medical cost trend rates; and

  (vi) any other material actuarial assumptions used.

The actuarial assumptions should be disclosed in absolute terms and not just as a margin between different percentages or other variables.[279]

Items (c) (vii), (f) (iv), and (g) in relation to reimbursement rights and (h) (iii) are only applicable for periods beginning on or after 1 January 2001.

Like FRS 17, IAS 19 requires very extensive disclosures in relation to defined benefit schemes. There is some flexibility allowed in aggregating disclosure where an employer has more than one scheme. In these circumstances, the required disclosures may be made separately for each scheme, in total or in such groupings as are considered most useful. Examples of possible groupings which may be considered useful include: geographical location (e.g. distinguishing between domestic and foreign plans) and plans which are subject to materially different risks (e.g. distinguishing flat salary pension plans from final salary pension plans and from post-retirement medical plans).[280]

6.9 Other long-term employee benefits

6.9.1 Meaning of other long-term employee benefits

Other long-term employee benefits are those benefits – other than post-employment benefits, termination benefits and equity compensation benefits – that do not fall due within twelve months after the end of the period in which the employees render the related service.[281] Examples of such benefits given by IAS 19 are:

(a) long-term compensated absences such as long-service or sabbatical leave;

(b) jubilee or other long-service benefits;

(c) long-term disability benefits;

(d) profit sharing and bonuses payable twelve months or more after the end of the period in which the employees render the related service; and

(e) deferred compensation paid twelve months or more after the end of the period in which it is earned.[282]

The measurement of other long-term employee benefits is usually subject to less uncertainty than post-employment benefits, therefore a simplified method of accounting is required by IAS 19. This method requires immediate recognition of actuarial gains and losses and past service costs.[283]

6.9.2 *Recognition and measurement*

IAS 19 requires the recognition as a liability for other long-term employee benefits equal to (1) the present value of the defined benefit obligation at the balance sheet date minus (2) the fair value at the balance sheet date of plan assets out of which the obligations are to be settled directly. In measuring the liability the guidance in IAS 19 on post-employment benefits, which is described at 6.8 above, should be applied.[284]

The expense for other long-term employee benefits that should be recognised in income, to the extent these costs are not capitalisable, is the net of:

(a) current service cost;

(b) interest cost;

(c) the expected return on any plan assets and on any reimbursement right recognised as an asset;

(d) actuarial gains and losses;

(e) past service cost; and

(f) the effect of any curtailments or settlements.[285]

These terms have the same meaning as discussed at 6.8.4 above.

6.9.3 *Disclosure of other long-term employee benefits*

IAS 19 – *Employee Benefits* – does not require specific disclosures about other long-term employee benefits, but disclosures may be necessary under the requirements of other Standards, such as IAS 8 – *Net Profit or Loss for the Period, Fundamental Errors and Changes in Accounting Policies* – or IAS 24 – *Related Party Disclosures*.[286]

6.10 IAS 19 in practice

Set out below are extracts from the accounts of three companies which apply IAS, illustrating a number of different requirements under the standard.

Extract 26.27: Roche Holding Ltd (2000)

Notes to the Consolidated Financial Statements [extract]

1. Summary of significant accounting policies [extract]

Employee Benefits

Wages, salaries, social security contributions, paid annual leave and sick leave, bonuses, options and non-monetary benefits are accrued in the year in which the associated services are rendered by employees of the Group. Where the Group provides long-term employee benefits, the cost is accrued to match the rendering of the services by the employees concerned.

The Group operates a number of defined benefit and defined contribution plans throughout the world. The cost for the year for the defined benefit plans is determined using the projected unit credit method.

This reflects service rendered by employees to the dates of valuation and incorporates actuarial assumptions primarily regarding discount rates used in determining the present value of benefits, projected rates of remuneration growth, and long-term expected rates of return for plan assets. Discount rates are based on the market yields of high-quality corporate bonds in the country concerned. Differences between assumptions and actual experiences, and effects of changes in actuarial assumptions are allocated over the estimated average remaining working lives of employees, where these differences exceed a defined corridor. Past service costs are allocated over the average period until the benefits become vested. Pension assets and liabilities in different defined benefit schemes are not offset unless the Group has a legally enforceable right to use the surplus in one plan to settle obligations in the other plan.

The Group's contributions to the defined contribution plans are charged to the income statement in the year to which they relate.

8. Employee benefits in millions of CHF

Amounts recognised in arriving at operating profit are as follows:

	2000	1999
Wages and salaries	6,156	5,613
Social security costs	746	719
Post-employment benefits: defined benefit plans	298	322
Post-employment benefits: defined contribution plans	58	41
Other employee benefits	325	236
Total employees remuneration	7,583	6,931

The number of employees at the year-end was 64,758 (1999: 67,695).

Post-employment benefits

Most employees are covered by retirement benefit plans sponsored by Group companies. The nature of such plans varies according to legal regulations, fiscal requirements and economic conditions of the countries in which employees are employed. Other post-employment benefits consist mostly of post-retirement healthcare and life insurance schemes, principally in the USA. Plans are usually funded by payments from the Group and by employees to trusts independent of the Group's finances. Where a plan is unfunded, a liability for the whole obligation is recorded in the Group's balance sheet.

The amounts recognised in arriving at operating profit for post-employment defined benefit plans are as follows:

	2000	1999
Current service cost	333	311
Interest cost	675	677
Expected return on plan assets	(714)	(645)
Net actuarial (gains) losses recognised	2	–
Past service cost	3	7
(Gains) losses on curtailment	(1)	(28)
Total included in employees' remuneration	298	322

The actual return on plan assets was 1,175 million Swiss francs (1999: 932 Swiss francs).

The movements in the net asset (liability) recognised in the balance sheet for post-employment defined benefit plans are as follows:

	2000	1999
At the beginning of the year		
– as previously reported	(2,078)	(2,107)
– effect of implementing the revised International Accounting Standard for Employee Benefits in 1999	–	39
– as restated	(2,078)	(2,068)

Changes in Group organisation and Givaudan spin-off[3,7]	84	(4)
Total expenses included in employees' remuneration (as above)	(298)	(322)
Contributions paid	174	165
Benefits paid (unfunded plans)	135	125
Currency translation effects and other	134	26
At end of year (as below)	(1,849)	(2,078)

Amounts recognised in the balance sheet for post-employment defined benefits plans are as follows:

	2000	1999
Unfunded plans		
Recognised asset (liability) for actuarial present value of unfunded obligations due to past and present employees	(2,423)	(2,648)
Funded plans		
Actuarial present value of funded obligations due to past and present employees	(9,043)	(9,028)
Plan assets held in trusts at fair value	10,448	10,046
Plan assets in excess of actuarial present value of funded obligations	1,414	1,018
Less		
– Unrecognised actuarial (gains) losses	(862)	(467)
– Unrecognised past service costs	22	19
Recognised asset (liability) for funded obligations due to past and present employees	574	570
Assets (liability) recognised		
Deficit recognised as part of liabilities for post-employment benefits	(2,502)	(2,764)
Surplus recognised as part of other long-term assets [15]	653	686
Total net asset (liability) recognised	(1,849)	(2,078)

The above amounts include non-pension post-employment benefit schemes, principally medical plans, with an actuarial present value of obligations of 690 million Swiss francs (1999: 703 million Swiss francs) and plan assets of 649 million Swiss francs (1999: 576 million Swiss francs). The related net liability recognised is 147 million Swiss francs (1999: 190 million Swiss francs). Actuarial gains of 106 million Swiss francs (1999: 63 million Swiss francs) were unrecognised.

Amounts recognised in the balance sheet for post-employment defined benefit plans are predominately non-current and are reported as long-term assets and non-current liabilities.

Included within the fair value of the assets of the funded plans are 30 (1999: 1,700) of the Group's non-voting equity securities with a fair value of 0.5 million Swiss francs (1999: 32 million Swiss francs).

The Group operates defined benefit schemes in many countries and the actuarial assumptions vary based upon local economic and social conditions. The range of assumptions used in the actuarial valuations of the most significant defined benefit plans, which are in countries with stable currencies and interest rates, is as follows:

Discount rates	3 to 8%	(1999: 3 to 8%)
Projected rates of remuneration growth	2 to 9%	(1999: 2.5 to 9%)
Expected rates of return on plan assets	3 to 10%	1999: 3.5 to 10%)
Healthcare cost trend rate	4 to 10%	(1999: 4 to 9%)

Extract 26.28: Merck KGaA (1999)

(10) Provisions for pensions and other post-employment benefits

Depending on the legal, economic and fiscal circumstances prevailing in each country, different retirement benefit systems are provided for the employees of the Merck Group. As a rule, these systems are based on length of service and salary of the employees. Pension obligations in the Merck Group relate to both defined benefit and defined contribution plans.

In the Merck Group, defined benefit plans are funded and unfunded. The bulk of obligations from current pensions and accrued benefits for pensions payable in the future is covered by the (unfunded) provisions disclosed here. These provisions also contain other post-employment benefits, such as accrued future healthcare costs for pensioners (USA) and accrued severance payments. The obligations of our domestic German companies, which account for around 84% of total pension provisions, are measured using the projected unit credit method in compliance with IAS 19 (revised 1998). Annual actuarial opinions are prepared for this purpose. The calculation is based on assumed trends for salary growth of 2.5% or 3.0%, for pension increases of 1.5%, for fluctuation of 2.0% as well as a discount rate of 6.0%. Actuarial gains and losses are recognized using the 10% corridor rule. In the case of our foreign companies, obligations covered by provisions for pensions are calculated using comparable procedures.

Defined benefit plans resulted in a total expense of EUR 75.0 million during the year under review (previous year: EUR 66.9 million), composed of the following components:

		1999	1998
EUR million			
	Current service cost	37.8	25.7
+	Past service cost	–	–
+	Interest component	44.3	45.5
–	Expected return on plan assets	-7.3	-5.8
+/–	Net amortized actuarial gains/losses	0.2	1.5
+/–	Effects of curtailment or settlements	–	–
=	Total amounts recognized	75.0	66.9

The actual return on plan assets amounted to EUR 32.8 million in the year under review (previous year: EUR 14.3 million).

In the consolidated balance sheet, obligations from defined benefit plans are recorded in 'Provisions for pensions and other post-employment benefits'. Where pension funds are over-funded, the corresponding assets are recorded in 'Other receivables and other assets'. The net value of these balance sheet items is derived as follows:

		1999	1998
EUR million			
	Present value of unfunded benefit obligations	911.9	870.9
+	Present value of funded benefit obligations	210.8	129.7
=	Present value of benefit obligations	1,122.7	1,000.6
–	Fair value of plan assets	-215.5	-141.9
=	Present value of benefit obligations (after deduction of plan assets)	871.2	858.7
+/–	Net unrecognized actuarial gains/losses	13.3	5.3
+	Unrecognized past service cost	–	–
=	Net amounts recognized in balance sheets as of Dec. 31	884.5	864.0

During the period under review, the net amounts recognized in the balance sheet at Group level changed as follows:

		Dec 31, 1999	Dec 31, 1998
EUR million			
	Net amounts recognized in balance sheet as of Jan. 1	864.0	831.9
+/–	Change in companies consolidation	-16.8	–
+	Total amounts recognized	75.0	66.9
–	Pension payments during the period	-38.7	-34.8
+/–	Transfer	1.0	–
=	Net amounts recognized in balance sheet as of Dec. 31	884.5	864.0

The cost of current contribution payments during the year under review for defined contribution plans that are funded exclusively by external funds amounted to EUR 2.3 million (previous year: EUR 3.3 million). Apart from the interest component and the gains from plan assets, which are disclosed in the financial result, the relevant costs of defined benefit and defined contribution plans are contained in the profit from operations of the business sectors.

Extract 26.29: Wella AG (2000)

[29] Provisions for pensions and similar obligations

Provisions for Pensions and Similar Obligations (□ thousand)	1999	**2000**
Balance at Jan 1, 2000	243,753	**256,449**
Exchange rate changes	5,799	**-582**
Benefits paid	13,704	**11,832**
Release	1,947	**494**
Addition	22,548	**22,744**
Balance at Dec 31, 2000	256,449	**266,285**

Of the total amount reflecting these provisions €7.0 million (previous year: €5.9 million) are accounted for by similar obligations.

The employees of the Wella Group are entitled to a variety of retirement benefits in accordance with the legal, tax and economic rules in force in the countries in which the Group operates. In general, basis for the payment of benefits are years of service and the compensation paid to the employees. In addition, benefit obligations include salary portions accrued for future employee benefits.

The provisions for pensions and similar obligations were determined in accordance with IAS 19 (revised in 1998) using the Projected Unit Credit Method, which takes into account all foreseeable future developments, especially projections of future salary and pension increases. As in the previous year, the actuarial assumptions used to determine the benefit obligations are as follows:

Parameter	**In Germany**	**Outside Germany**
Discount rate	6.0%	3-8%
Salary progression rate	2.5%	1-5%
Retirement benefit increases	1.0%	1-8%
Employee turnover rate	4-5%	Varies acc. to country

Benefit obligations in Germany consist mainly of defined benefit plans for which pension provisions are set up. The actuarial computations are based on the 1998 mortality tables of Dr Heubeck.

Foreign subsidiaries that provide pension benefits to employees use similar methods (defined benefit plans) to build their pension provisions, with the actuarial assumptions being based on their specific local conditions

Actuarial gains or losses are not recognized as income or expense, until they exceed the greater of 10% of the present value of the benefit obligations and 10% of the fair value of any plan assets. The portion exceeding his 10% corridor is amortized over the expected average remaining working lives of the employees. The interest portion contained in the pension costs is shown as interest cost in the financial result. All other expenses are allocated to the costs of functional areas.
The cost of pension plans can be analysed as follows:

Pension Plans (€ thousand)	1999	**2000**
Current service cost	10,002	**8,477**
Interest cost on projected benefit obligations	12,546	**14,267**
Total	22,548	**22,744**

The following table shows the computation of pension provisions:

Pension Provisions (€ thousand)	Dec 31, 1999	**Dec 31, 2000**
Present value of funded benefit obligations	70,650	**151,867**
Fair market value of plan assets	50,786	**143,831**
Short cover	19,863	**8,036**
Present value of unfunded benefit obligations	233,352	**243,538**
Actuarial gains/(losses) not affecting income	3,234	**14,711**
Pension provisions in accordance with IAS 19	256,449	**266,285**

Foreign subsidiaries also include severance and redundancy payments under pension provisions; local laws in a number of countries require companies to pay extra compensation to employees who leave the company.

7 CONCLUSION

When SSAP 24 was introduced it represented a major stride forward in the presentation of meaningful information about pension costs in the accounts of UK companies. It took the subject from a low base, where the measurement of cost could only be described as unsophisticated, to a level where serious attempts have to be made to account for that cost on a systematic basis. Companies have now gained over ten years' experience of using the standard, and have a significantly greater understanding of the subject than at the outset. We are, however, not convinced that its successor, FRS 17, based in large part on international developments, will represent an overall improvement.

We broadly agreed with the changes proposed by the majority of the Board in the ASB's 1995 Discussion Paper; indeed they largely reflected the views we expressed in the 1994 edition of this book. However, the balance of opinion among standard-setters has swung towards the balance sheet approach that was said to be favoured by the minority of the ASB in that Discussion Paper, even though it gained little support from respondents at that time. As a result, FRS 17 and IAS 19 now adopt a balance sheet focused mark-to-market approach to pension schemes, even though there is rarely any intention or necessity for companies to liquidate such schemes in the short or medium term. This approach makes sense in terms of the IASC Framework and the ASB's *Statement of Principles*, but in our view this simply illustrates the inappropriateness of these concepts.

References

1 E54, *Employee Benefits*, IASC, October 1996.
2 SSAP 24, *Accounting for pension costs*, ASC, May 1988, para. 14.
3 FRS 17, Retirement benefits, ASB, November 2000, para. 2.
4 Pension Fund Terminology – Specimen descriptions of commonly used valuation methods, The Institute of Actuaries and The Faculty of Actuaries, May 1986.
5 GN 17: *Accounting for pension costs under SSAP 24*, Institute and Faculty of Actuaries, April 1991, para. 17.
6 FRS 17, *Retirement benefits*, ASB, November 2000, Appendix IV, para. 11.
7 FRS 17, para. 2.
8 GN 17, para. 18.
9 *Ibid.*, para. 20.
10 Pension Fund Terminology – Specimen descriptions of commonly used valuation methods.
11 GN 17, para. 19.
12 Pension Fund Terminology – Specimen descriptions of commonly used valuation methods.
13 GN 17, para. 16.
14 Pension Fund Terminology – Specimen descriptions of commonly used valuation methods.
15 GN 17, para. 15.
16 The UITF clarified, however, that this was not to be given any special treatment in profit and loss account recognition terms, although it might merit additional disclosure. It was simply a variation to be accounted for like any other under the standard. (UITF 18, *Pension costs following the 1997 tax changes in respect of dividend income*, UITF, 2 December 1997, para. 7.)
17 GN 17, para. 24.
18 SSAP 24, para. 79.
19 FRS 17, paras. 23, 27 and 28.
20 *Ibid.*, para. 25.
21 *Ibid.*, para. 26.
22 *Ibid.*, para. 32.
23 *Ibid.*, para. 33.
24 *Ibid.*, para. 23.
25 *Ibid.*, para. 34.
26 *Ibid.*

27 *Ibid.*, para. 30.
28 Auditing Practices Committee, August 1987.
29 Consultation Draft Of A Proposed Practice Note – *The Auditors' Consideration of FRS 17 'Retirement Benefits' - Defined Benefit Schemes*, Auditing Practices Board, July 2001.
30 FRS 17, para. 23.
31 *Ibid.*, para. 1.
32 *Ibid.*, paras. 3 and 6
33 *Ibid.*, para. 2.
34 *Ibid.*, para. 4.
35 *Ibid.*, para. 5.
36 *Ibid.*, para. 2.
37 *Ibid.*
38 *Ibid.*, para. 9(a).
39 *Ibid.*, para. 10.
40 *Ibid.*, para. 9(a).
41 *Ibid.*, para. 11.
42 *Ibid.*
43 *Ibid.*, para. 9(b).
44 *Ibid.*, para. 12.
45 *Ibid.*, Appendix IV, para. 57.
46 FRS 17, para. 7.
47 *Ibid.*
48 *Ibid.*, para. 75.
49 *Ibid.*, Appendix IV, para. 24.
50 FRS 17, paras. 38 and 39.
51 *Ibid.*, para. 37.
52 *Ibid.*, para. 19.
53 *Ibid.*, para. 15.
54 *Ibid.*, para. 14.
55 FRS 7, *Fair values in acquisition accounting*, ASB, September 1994, para. 2.
56 FRS 17, paras. 16-18.
57 *Financial Reports of Pension Schemes – A Statement of Recommended Practice*, Pensions Research Accountants Group, 1996, paras. 2.45-2.48.
58 FRS 17, para. 2.
59 *Ibid.*, Appendix IV, para. 11.
60 FRS 17, para. 24.
61 *Ibid.*, Appendix IV, para. 11.
62 *Ibid.*, para. 11
63 FRS 17, para. 32.
64 *Ibid.*, para. 20.
65 *Ibid.*, paras. 29 and 31.
66 *Ibid.*, para. 28(a).
67 *Ibid.*, para. 22.
68 *Ibid.*, para. 21.
69 *Ibid.*, para. 40.
70 *Ibid.*, paras. 73 and 74
71 *Ibid.*, para. 35.
72 *Ibid.*, para. 36.
73 *Ibid.*
74 *Ibid.*, Appendix IV, para. 23(b).
75 FRS 17, para. 47.
76 *Ibid.*
77 *Ibid.*, para. 49.
78 *Ibid.*, Appendix II, para. 6.
79 FRS 17, para. 43.
80 *Ibid.*, para. 37.
81 *Ibid.*, para. 42.
82 *Ibid.*, para. 41.
83 *Ibid.*, paras. 44 and 45.
84 *Ibid.*, para. 2.
85 *Ibid.*, para. 61.
86 *Ibid.*, para. 60.
87 *Ibid.*
88 *Ibid.*, para. 50.
89 *Ibid.*, para. 2.
90 *Ibid.*, para. 52.
91 *Ibid.*, para. 51.
92 *Ibid.*, para. 2.
93 *Ibid.*, para. 53.
94 *Ibid.*, para. 56.
95 *Ibid.*, Appendix II, para. 6.
96 FRS 17, para. 102.
97 *Ibid.*, para. 54.
98 *Ibid.*, para. 56.
99 *Ibid.*, para. 2.
100 *Ibid.*, para. 54.
101 *Ibid.*
102 *Ibid.*, para. 55.
103 *Ibid.*, para. 54.
104 *Ibid.*, para. 2.
105 *Ibid.*, para 58.
106 *Ibid.*, para. 57.
107 *Ibid.*, para. 59.
108 *Ibid.*, Appendix IV, para. 37.
109 *Ibid.*, para. 38.
110 FRS 17, para. 2.
111 *Ibid.*, paras. 65 and 66.
112 *Ibid.*, para. 64.
113 *Ibid.*, para. 2.
114 *Ibid.*, para. 61.
115 *Ibid.*, para. 62.
116 *Ibid.*, para. 60.
117 *Ibid.*, para. 63.
118 *Ibid.*, paras. 67-70.
119 *Ibid.*, para. 67(a).
120 *Ibid.*, para. 67(b).
121 *Ibid.*, para. 67(c).
122 *Ibid.*, para. 67(d).
123 *Ibid.*, para. 68.
124 *Ibid.*, para. 69.
125 *Ibid.*, para. 70.
126 FRS 16, *Current tax*, ASB, December 1999, paras. 5 and 6.
127 FRS 17, para. 71
128 *Ibid.*, para. 72.
129 FRS 19, *Deferred* tax, ASB, December 2000, paras. 34 and 35.
130 FRS 17, para. 72.
131 FRS 19, para. 36.
132 FRS 17, Appendix IV, para. 2.
133 FRS 17, para. 92.

134 *Ibid.*, para. 93.
135 *Ibid.*, para. 92.
136 *Ibid.*, para. 76.
137 *Ibid.*, para. 78.
138 *Ibid.*, para. 80.
139 *Ibid.*, para. 88.
140 *Ibid.*, para. 90.
141 *Ibid.*, para. 9(b).
142 *Ibid.*, para. 82.
143 *Ibid.*, para. 83.
144 *Ibid.*, para. 84.
145 *Ibid.*, para. 67.
146 *Ibid.*, para. 85.
147 *Ibid.*, para. 86.
148 *Ibid.*, para. 90.
149 *Ibid.*, para. 9.
150 *Ibid.*, para. 94(a).
151 *Ibid.*, para. 94(b).
152 *Ibid.*, para. 96.
153 *Ibid.*, para. 95.
154 *Ibid.*, para. 96.
155 FRED 20, *Retirement benefits*, ASB, November 1999, Appendix III, paras. 6-11.
156 FRS 17, para. 12.
157 SSAP 24, para. 16.
158 *Ibid.*, para. 12.
159 *Ibid.*, para. 75.
160 TR 756, *Statement by the Accounting Standards Committee on the application of the principles of SSAP 24 'Accounting for pension costs' to other post-retirement benefits*, July 1989.
161 UITF 6, November 1992.
162 SSAP 24, para. 91.
163 UITF 6, *Accounting for post-retirement benefits other than pensions*, UITF, November 1992.
164 *Ibid.*, para. 8.
165 *Ibid.*, para. 7.
166 *Ibid.*
167 *Ibid.*, para. 9.
168 SSAP 24, para. 78.
169 *Ibid.*, para. 87.
170 Applied either on the balance sheet figure or on the underlying surplus in the scheme, depending on how the variations are calculated — see 4.6.8.
171 SSAP 24, para. 20.
172 *Ibid.*, para. 21.
173 *Ibid.*, para. 23.
174 ED 39, *Accounting for pension costs*, ASC, May 1986, Appendix 2, Example 2.
175 FRRP PN 65, 8 March 2001.
176 SSAP 24, para. 80.
177 FRAG 10/92, *Review, for major practical problems, of SSAP* 24, ICAEW, 1992, para. 42.
178 SSAP 24, para. 81 (original version).
179 SSAP 24, (as revised by FRS 3, para. 33(m)).
180 *Ibid.*, para. 26 (as revised by FRS 3, para. 33(k)). In fact, the words 'or the disposal of its assets' have since been deleted from FRS 3 by FRS 12, para. 100.
181 *Ibid.*, para. 81.
182 *Ibid.*, para. 83.
183 *Ibid.*, para. 82.
184 It is, however, explicitly recognised as being the third component of cost in GN 17, para. 12. and by the ICAEW in FRAG 10/92, paras. 26 *et seq.*
185 *Pension Costs in the Employer's Financial Statements*, para. 5.3.4.
186 *Discounting in Financial Reporting*, ASB, April 1997, para. 7.3.
187 *Pension Costs in the Employer's Financial Statements* , para. 5.5.
188 UITF Abstract 4, *Presentation of long-term debtors in current assets*, July 1992.
189 SSAP 24, para. 88.
190 GN 17, para. 28.
191 SSAP 24, para. 48.
192 SSAP 24, para. 18.
193 The guidance issued by the actuarial profession indicates that this should be calculated using the Projected Accrued Benefit Method (GN 17, para. 30).
194 GN 17, para. 31 explains that part of this surplus or deficiency will be attributable to the use of the Projected Accrued Benefit Method for the previous disclosure unless the method used for funding is the Projected Unit method or the Attained Age method, and this fact should be explained.
195 SSAP 24, para. 49.
196 *Ibid.*, para. 92.
197 CA 85, Sch. 4, para. 50(4).
198 *Ibid.*, para. 56(4).
199 *Ibid.*, para. 94(2).
200 E54, *Employee Benefits,* IASC, October 1996.
201 IAS 19 (Revised 1998), *Employee benefits*, IASC, February 1998, Objective.
202 *Ibid.*, para. 4.
203 *Ibid.*, para. 7.
204 *Ibid.*, para. 24.
205 *Ibid.*, para. 26.
206 *Ibid.*, para. 27.
207 *Ibid.*, para. 25.
208 *Ibid.*, para. 39.
209 *Ibid.*, para. 41.
210 *Ibid.*, para. 7.
211 *Ibid.*, para. 29.
212 *Ibid.*, para. 30.
213 *Ibid.*, para. 34.
214 *Ibid.*
215 *Ibid.*, para. 37.
216 *Ibid.*, para. 36.
217 *Ibid.*, para. 38.
218 *Ibid.*, para. 157.
219 *Ibid.*, para. 159.

220 *Ibid.*, para. 154.
221 *Ibid.*, para. 156.
222 *Ibid.*, para. 155.
223 *Ibid.*, para. 43.
224 *Ibid.*, para. 44.
225 *Ibid.*, para. 45.
226 *Ibid.*, para. 78.
227 *Ibid.*, para. 46.
228 *Ibid.*, para. 47.
229 *Ibid.*, para. 50.
230 *Ibid.*
231 *Ibid.*
232 *Ibid.*, para. 103.
233 *Ibid.*, para. 7.
234 *Ibid.*, para. 54.
235 *Ibid.*, para. 7.
236 *Ibid.*, para. 102.
237 *Ibid.*, para. 104.
238 *Ibid.*, para. 104A.
239 *Ibid.*, para. 7.
240 *Ibid.*, para. 83.
241 *Ibid.*, para. 52.
242 *Ibid.*, para. 83.
243 *Ibid.*, para. 64.
244 *Ibid.*, para. 66.
245 *Ibid.*, para. 78.
246 *Ibid.*, para. 67.
247 *Ibid.*, paras. 68-71.
248 *Ibid.*, paras. 72, 73 and 77.
249 *Ibid.*, paras. 88 and 89.
250 *Ibid.*, para. 89.
251 *Ibid.*, para. 90.
252 *Ibid.*, para. 91.
253 *Ibid.*, paras. 56 and 57.
254 *Ibid.*, para. 54.
255 *Ibid.*, paras. 92 and 93.
256 *Ibid.*, para. 58.
257 *Ibid.*, para. 60.
258 *Ibid.*, para. 116.
259 *Ibid.*, para. 61.
260 *Ibid.*, paras. 7 and 64.
261 *Ibid.*, para. 7.
262 *Ibid.*, para. 82.
263 *Ibid.*, para. 106.
264 *Ibid.*, paras. 105.
265 *Ibid.*, para. 107.
266 *Ibid.*, paras. 7 and 94.
267 *Ibid.*, para. 7.
268 *Ibid.*, para. 97.
269 *Ibid.*, para. 96.
270 *Ibid.*, para. 112.
271 *Ibid.*, para. 113.
272 *Ibid.*, para. 111.
273 *Ibid.*, para. 115.
274 *Ibid.*, para. 109.
275 *Ibid.*, para. 110.
276 *Ibid.*, para. 115.
277 *Ibid.*, para. 114.
278 *Ibid.*, para. 61.
279 *Ibid.*, para. 120.
280 *Ibid.*, para. 122.
281 *Ibid.*, para. 7.
282 *Ibid.*, para. 126.
283 *Ibid.*, para. 127.
284 *Ibid.*, para. 128.
285 *Ibid.*, para. 129.
286 *Ibid.*, para. 131.

Chapter 24 Taxation

1 INTRODUCTION

1.1 Summary of UK and IAS position

1.1.1 UK

In the UK, accounting for tax is going through a period of significant change, with the issue of two new standards since the previous edition of this book, FRS 16 – *Current Tax*[1] – and FRS 19 – *Deferred Tax*[2]. FRS 16 was published in December 1999 and has been in force since March 2000, replacing SSAP 8 – *The treatment of taxation under the imputation system in the accounts of companies.*[3] FRS 19 was published a year later as a replacement to SSAP 15 – *Accounting for Deferred Tax*[4] – and, although it is not mandatory until January 2002, a number of companies have already adopted it and more seem likely to do so in respect of their December 2001 year ends.

Whilst FRS 16 was primarily a response to changes in the UK tax system, FRS 19 was issued mainly to bring the UK into line with international accounting practice. SSAP 15 had left the UK and Ireland almost totally isolated in retaining the partial provision approach to accounting for deferred tax, whereas IAS and US GAAP require full provision.

However, FRS 19's version of 'full provision' is entirely different to that of the equivalent IAS and US standards. Under these standards full provision is based on the balance sheet and 'temporary differences' (see 1.3.3 A below), whereas FRS 19 still requires deferred tax to be based on the income statement and 'timing differences' (see 1.3.2 below). Furthermore FRS 19 makes such substantial exceptions to its full provision approach that it is questionable whether it is a true full provision approach at all.

1.1.2 IAS

Under IAS, accounting for tax is 'bedding down', having come through a period of significant change following the implementation of IAS 12 (Revised) – *Income Taxes*[5] from 1998 onwards. As noted above, the approach under IAS 12, which is derived directly from US GAAP, focuses on the balance sheet rather than the income statement. IAS 12 has the advantage over FRS 19 of being relatively easy to apply, but it can be difficult to interpret and lead to perplexing results. Moreover, its conceptual basis is by no means universally accepted, and indeed has been explicitly rejected by the ASB in FRS 19. The real issue in the medium term will be whether UK GAAP is brought fully into line with IAS, or whether instead IAS 12 is modified to the less extreme version of full provision in FRS 19, particularly since Sir David Tweedie, who was chairman of the ASB when it published FRS 19, is now chairman of the IASB.

1.2 The nature of taxation

A discussion of how to deal with taxation in financial statements must begin with some consideration of what it is that is to be accounted for. Although it might be supposed that this is a simple question, and that taxation is a business expense to be dealt with in the same manner as any other cost, it has certain characteristics which set it apart from other costs and which might justify a different treatment. These characteristics include the fact that tax payments are not made in exchange for any goods or services and the fact that the business has no say in whether or not the payments are to be made. It is held by some that these elements mean that taxation is more in the nature of a distribution than an expense; in essence that the government is a stakeholder in the success of the business and participates in its results (generally in priority to other stakeholders).

The validity of this suggestion rather depends on what view is taken as to the purpose of financial statements and the nature of the reporting entity. It is consistent with a perspective which is sometimes adopted that business entities have an existence which is independent from that of their shareholders, and should account not simply to their legal owners but to all those with an economic interest in their activities.

Adoption of the 'distribution' view of taxation would render irrelevant most of the accounting questions which follow; these are generally to do with how to allocate taxation expense to accounting periods. If taxation were regarded as a distribution, however, the question of allocation would not arise, since distributions are generally not allocated to accounting periods in the same way as is done for items of expense.

It is fair to say, however, that the 'distribution' view of taxation is not adopted in practice, although some of the accounting approaches that are sometimes proposed to deal with certain issues have their roots within it. For all practical purposes, taxation is dealt with as an expense of the business, and the accounting rules which have been developed are based on that premise.

1.3 Allocation between periods

1.3.1 Background

The most significant accounting question which arises in relation to taxation is how to allocate the tax expense between accounting periods. The recognition of trading transactions in the financial statements relating to a particular year is governed primarily by the application of generally accepted accounting practice, and to a certain extent by the impact of company law. However, the timing of recognition of transactions for the purposes of measuring the taxable profit is governed by the application of tax law, which in some cases follows different rules from those under which the financial statements are drawn up. It is necessary to seek some reconciliation between these different sets of rules, which is where the concept of deferred taxation is brought into use.

Over time, there have evolved two broad methods (or, more correctly, groups of methods) for accounting for deferred tax. The older methods focussed only on the differences that arise between the amount of income and expenditure that has been reported for accounting purposes and the amount that has been subject to tax. These may be described as 'performance statement' methods, and are the basis of the approach currently taken in the UK in both SSAP 15 and FRS 19 and, until quite recently, by IAS and US GAAP. The more recent methods focus on all differences (whether arising from timing differences or otherwise) between the carrying amount of assets and liabilities and the amount attributed to them for tax purposes. These may be described as 'balance sheet' methods, and are the approach now required by IAS and US GAAP.

Summaries of the main 'performance statement' and 'balance sheet' methods are given in 1.3.2 and 1.3.3 below.

A Conformity of UK tax legislation with accounting rules

As an aside, a recent trend in tax legislation in the UK has been to bring the tax rules more into line with accounting standards, in areas such as leasing, foreign currencies and financial instruments. This may have the benefit of removing some of the differences that cause accounting problems in accounting for tax, but the trend is not entirely welcome in other ways. Particular areas of difficulty that arise in practice are:

- notwithstanding group relief and similar provisions, tax in the UK is basically levied on individual companies rather than groups. By contrast accounting standards are primarily addressed, at least implicitly, at consolidated financial statements;
- accounting standards implicitly assume that all transactions are entered into between independent parties on an arm's length basis and as such do not necessarily give appropriate results when applied to related party transactions (e.g. those between members of a group of companies);
- companies may enter into transactions of a type that were simply not contemplated by the standard setters, but which the tax legislation nevertheless requires, somewhat glibly from an accountant's perspective, to be taxed by reference to 'normal accountancy practice'; and
- accounting standards increasingly focus on the balance sheet and market values, whereas tax is (broadly) levied on realised profits.[6]

All this tends to put a greater strain on some of the accounting rules, which were not primarily designed to provide a basis for the measurement of tax.

1.3.2 *'Performance statement' methods of accounting for deferred tax*

All 'performance statement' methods of accounting for tax analyse differences between accounting profit and taxable profit into two categories – 'permanent differences' and 'timing differences'.

A 'Permanent' differences

Permanent differences arise from an item being taken into account for tax purposes but not for accounting purposes and vice versa.

A permanent difference can arise in three main ways under the UK tax system:

- where non-taxable income is included in the accounting profit, for example if certain government grant income is received;
- where certain types of expenditure are charged against accounting profit but not allowed as an expense against taxable profit, for example, certain entertainment expenditure and fines;
- indexation relief reduces many gains for tax purposes but has no effect on the gains reported in the financial statements.

It is generally accepted that there is no need to adjust the financial statements for permanent differences. The transaction giving rise to the permanent difference has no tax effect. Although the tax charge for the year in which the item is reported in the financial statements will deviate from the charge which would have been expected if the normal tax rate had been applied to the reported profits, this is not a distortion of the charge that needs to be corrected in any way; indeed, any 'correction' would introduce such a distortion.

B 'Timing' differences

Timing differences represent items of income or expenditure which are taxable or deductible, but in periods different from those in which they are dealt with in the financial statements. They therefore arise when items of income and expenditure enter into the measurement of profit for both accounting and taxation purposes, but in different accounting periods. They are said to 'originate' in the first of these periods and 'reverse' in one or more subsequent periods. Deferred taxation is the taxation which relates to timing differences.[7]

A timing difference can arise in a number of ways:

- income may be included in the financial statements but recognised in taxable profit in later years. For example, an increase in the value of a property might be recognised in the financial statements but taxed only in the period in which it was realised by disposal of the property;
- income may be included in taxable profit in a year earlier than it is recognised in the financial statements. For example, tax might be payable on the sale of stock from one member of a group to another at a profit, but that profit would be recognised in the consolidated financial statements only when the stock was sold outside the group;

- expenditure or losses in the financial statements may not be deductible in arriving at taxable profit until a later period. For example, a general bad debt provision could be charged in the financial statements, but a tax deduction given only when the specific bad debt charge was known; or
- expenditure or losses may be deducted from taxable income prior to their being charged against accounting profit. For example, research and development expenditure might be allowed as an immediate deduction against tax, but capitalised in the financial statements and amortised over its useful life.

The tax benefit or cost associated with timing differences usually reverses in future periods. There are, however, situations where there might not be a complete reversal of timing differences, such as the disposal of an industrial building after the expiry of its 25-year tax life.

The original version of SSAP 15 (issued in October 1977) distinguished between 'short-term' and 'other' timing differences. It defined a short-term timing difference as one which arises because an item is treated on a cash basis for tax purposes whereas the accruals concept is used in the accounts. When the term was first coined, it mainly involved such things as interest accruals, which usually reversed within a year of their origination (hence the name). More recently, however, the major timing differences of this sort have arisen on items such as pension costs, which are allowed for tax on the basis of cash contributions but accounted for on an accruals basis. Such timing differences are anything but short term, particularly for unfunded schemes, and this has shown that the category is not a very meaningful one, and the distinction was dropped in the current version of SSAP 15 (issued in May 1985). Nevertheless, several companies continue to refer to 'short term' timing differences in their financial statements.

A common form of timing difference is that created by the effect of capital allowances and the charge for depreciation. Capital allowances are the amounts by which fixed assets may be written down to arrive at taxable profit, and are therefore the tax equivalent of the charge for depreciation in the financial statements. The amount charged in the financial statements for depreciation is therefore normally disallowed in the tax computation, except in the case of some assets held under finance leases. Usually, because capital allowances might be given to provide some economic incentive for businesses to invest, the tax allowance will be given at a faster rate than the rate at which depreciation is charged in the financial statements, and the timing differences created are thus sometimes referred to as '*accelerated* capital allowances'. Occasionally, however, the asset is depreciated faster than the tax allowance is given, giving rise to '*decelerated* capital allowances'.

A timing difference arises since both the charge for depreciation and the capital allowance (after an adjustment for a balancing charge or allowance) will reduce the cost of the asset to its recoverable amount at the end of its useful life, but the sums charged against accounting profit and against taxable profit, although the same in total, are likely to differ in each year. An example will illustrate the impact:

Example 24.1: Illustration of timing differences

An item of plant and machinery is purchased in 2001 for £48,000 and is estimated to have a seven year useful life, at the end of which it is estimated that it will be sold for £6,000. The depreciation charge will therefore be £6,000 p.a. (£48,000 – £6,000 over seven years).

For the purpose of this example, the rate of capital allowance for plant and machinery is assumed to be 25% p.a. on a reducing balance basis. The timing differences will arise as follows (all figures in £000s):

	2001	**2002**	**2003**	**2004**	**2005**	**2006**	**2007**
Financial statements							
Carrying value of asset	48	42	36	30	24	18	12
Depreciation charge	6	6	6	6	6	6	6
Written down value	42	36	30	24	18	12	6
Tax computation							
Carrying value of asset	48	36	27	20	15	11	8
Capital allowance	12	9	7	5	4	3	2
Tax written down value	36	27	20	15	11	8	6
Timing difference arising							
Charge in accounts	6	6	6	6	6	6	6
Allowed in tax computation	12	9	7	5	4	3	2
Originating/(reversing)	6	3	1	(1)	(2)	(3)	(4)
Cumulative timing difference	6	9	10	9	7	4	0

The table shows that there are originating differences of £10,000 in the first three years, but this progressively diminishes and eventually reverses in subsequent years. For each of the first three years of the asset's life, the tax currently assessed (and hence the amount provided in the accounts as the current year tax charge for those years) is lower than the tax that will eventually fall to be paid on the profit reported in the financial statements. The difference reverses from year four onwards, when the tax allowances have fallen below the level of the depreciation charge. The tax assessed (and hence the amount provided in the accounts as the current year tax charge for those years) will be higher than the sum due on the profit reported in the financial statements.

The timing difference arising in any year represents the difference between the depreciation provided in the financial statement and the capital allowance given in the tax computation, as shown above. In practice, however, it is often calculated as the difference between the cumulative timing difference at the beginning and end of the period, computed by comparing the net book value of the asset in the financial statements with its written down value in the capital allowance computation (again all figures in £000s):

	2001	**2002**
Net book value per accounts	42	36
Written down value per tax computation	36	27
Cumulative timing difference	6	9
Timing difference arising in period (as above)	6	3

The computation of the total timing differences at any point in time is essentially a mathematical exercise. It is after this point that the picture becomes less clear, and different points of view arise as to:

(a) at what rate of tax the timing difference should be provided; and

(b) whether a company should account for deferred tax that it does not expect to convert into an actual liability to tax, because it can foresee that timing differences will not reverse in the future.

These questions lead us initially into the consideration of various methods of providing for deferred tax and then into the area of the 'partial provision' approach to deferred tax, all of which are discussed in C to G below.

C The deferral method

The deferral method was for many years the required method in North America. It places emphasis on the profit and loss account, and seeks to quantify the extent to which it has been affected by tax deferrals arising through the incidence of timing differences. When timing differences reverse, the deferral method takes the view that it is the former tax deferral which has become payable, and accordingly the deferred tax account is maintained in terms of the rates of tax which were in force when the various timing differences originated. On reversal, the amount taken out of the deferred tax account is the amount that was accrued there when the timing difference was provided for. The profit and loss account is therefore charged with a reversal which is unaffected by changes in the rates of tax in the years between origination and reversal.

Some would argue that this method is the most conceptually pure, on the grounds that the fundamental purpose of deferred tax accounting is the inter-period allocation of tax expense with taxable profits. However, others will argue that the balance sheet figure should be seen as an important figure in its own right and that the deferral method is deficient because it can produce meaningless balance sheet amounts when tax rates change (see Example 24.3 in D below). Adherents to this view would favour one of the variants of the liability method of accounting for deferred tax, which are described in the following sections.

Moreover, the integrity of the deferral method was undermined in practice by the fact that reversals were allowed to be made at the tax rate prevailing at the time of reversal rather than at the rate of origination.[8] This option was no doubt due to the sheer impracticality of maintaining the records necessary to track the rates at which individual timing differences originated.

D The liability method (with full provision/comprehensive allocation)

In contrast to the deferral method, the liability method places emphasis on the carrying amount of deferred tax in the balance sheet rather than the profit and loss account, and focuses on the future rather than on the past. However, it is still a member of the 'performance statement' family of methods because the amounts on which tax is provided are generated by timing differences, which arise from the performance statements.

The liability method treats the tax effects of timing differences as liabilities for taxes payable in the future (or as assets recoverable in the future), and the practical effect of this is that it responds to changes of tax rate by recalculating the asset or liability in the balance sheet on the basis of the new rate. This means that the charge for deferred tax in the profit and loss account will include the effects of any such change in rate which is applied to the opening balance of cumulative timing differences.

The principal objective of the liability method is to quantify the amount of tax that will become payable or receivable in the future. It follows, therefore, that the deferred tax balance is maintained at the current rate of tax since this rate is the best estimate of the rate that is likely to apply in the future when the timing differences reverse. Of course, if the future rates of tax are already set, it is necessary to examine the periods in which the timing differences will reverse, and then provide the amount of tax that is foreseen to arise as each year's reversal occurs.

A basic illustration of how the liability method works in practice, using the figures used by Example 24.1 above is given by Example 24.2.

Example 24.2: Calculation of deferred tax

A company makes annual profits before tax of £80,000 and is taxed at 30%. It experiences the following timing differences (all figures in £s):

	2001	**2002**	**2003**	**2004**	**2005**	**2006**	**2007**
Originating/(reversing)	6,000	3,000	1,000	(1,000)	(2,000)	(3,000)	(4,000)

Its tax computations for each year therefore show the following:

	2001	**2002**	**2003**	**2004**	**2005**	**2006**	**2007**
Accounting profit	80,000	80,000	80,000	80,000	80,000	80,000	80,000
Timing differences	(6,000)	(3,000)	(1,000)	1,000	2,000	3,000	4,000
Taxable profit	74,000	77,000	79,000	81,000	82,000	83,000	84,000
Tax payable @ 30%	22,200	23,100	23,700	24,300	24,600	24,900	25,200

Its accounts will show the following:

	2001	**2002**	**2003**	**2004**	**2005**	**2006**	**2007**
Profit before tax	80,000	80,000	80,000	80,000	80,000	80,000	80,000
Current tax @ 30%	22,200	23,100	23,700	24,300	24,600	24,900	25,200
Deferred tax	1,800	900	300	(300)	(600)	(900)	(1,200)
Profit after tax	56,000	56,000	56,000	56,000	56,000	56,000	56,000

The amount shown for deferred tax in the balance sheet will be:

1,800	2,700	3,000	2,700	2,100	1,200	0

This example gives the impression that the liability method is simply a form of 'tax equalisation' accounting. Indeed, the same result would be given by the deferral method, because there is no change in tax rate in the periods concerned. Where a difference in tax rate does occur, however, the differences between the two methods rapidly become apparent.

Example 24.3: Illustration of the difference between the deferral and liability methods

A company invests £48,000 in a fixed asset at the beginning of 2001, and depreciates it at £6,000 p.a. The asset attracts capital allowances of £12,000 in 2001 and £9,000 in 2002. In 2001, the tax rate is 30% and in 2002 it falls to 25%, the fall in rate not having been expected when the financial statements for 2001 were prepared.

Under the deferral method, the calculation would be made by reference to the timing differences arising in each year in the profit and loss account, thus:

Computation of the timing difference	**2001**	**2002**
	£	£
Depreciation per accounts	6,000	6,000
Capital allowances	12,000	9,000
Originating timing difference	6,000	3,000
Deferred tax provided, at 30%/25%	1,800	750
Deferred tax balance carried forward	1,800	2,550

(Under the deferral method, it is a matter of no concern that the balance carried forward, of £2,550, has no meaning in terms of the cumulative timing difference of £9,000 and the present tax rate of 25%.)

Under the liability method, the deferred tax account would be calculated by reference to the cumulative timing difference (computed by comparing the net book value of the asset in the accounts with its written down value in the capital allowance computation, thus):

Computation of the cumulative timing difference	**2001**	**2002**
	£	£
Depreciation per accounts	6,000	6,000
Capital allowances	12,000	9,000
Originating timing difference	6,000	3,000
Cumulative timing difference	6,000	9,000
Deferred tax balance, at 30%/25%	1,800	2,250
Deferred tax provided	1,800	450

The amount of deferred tax in the profit and loss account is simply the movement between the two balance sheet figures. In this example the £450 charge in 2002 is reconciled thus:

	£
Originating timing difference in 2001 – £3,000 @ 25%	750
Effect of change in rate on opening balance of cumulative timing differences – £6,000 x (30% - 25%)	(300)
	450

Where the whole amount of the cumulative timing difference is reflected in the amount provided in the balance sheet, the approach can be described as 'full provision', or 'comprehensive allocation'. This is to distinguish the method from a variant of the liability approach, 'partial provision', which is described below.

E *The liability method (with partial provision)*

Partial provision was the required UK method of accounting for deferred tax under SSAP 15. Under this approach, the full amount of the deferred tax liability is calculated, but only a portion of that full liability might actually be provided in the accounts. The amount provided is based on an estimate of the liability that is expected to arise in the future, based on a projection of the extent to which the cumulative timing differences are expected to reverse in net terms. A proportion of the timing differences can be viewed as non-reversing and thus equivalent to permanent differences (on which deferred tax is not provided).

Individual timing differences (by definition) will always reverse. However, the partial provision approach permits these reversals to be offset by such new originating timing differences as can be predicted with sufficient certainty to arise in the future. This can be illustrated by an example:

Example 24.4: Illustration of partial provision

Consider a company which commenced trade in 2001 by purchasing fixed assets for £1,000,000. It has an annual capital expenditure budget for the next four years of £400,000, £500,000, £600,000 and £700,000 respectively. Assets are depreciated over their useful lives of ten years and are expected to have a nil recoverable amount at that time. Capital allowances are 25% p.a. on a reducing balance basis, and tax is charged at a rate of 30%.

Fixed assets in accounts	**2001**	**2002**	**2003**	**2004**	**2005**
	£'000	£'000	£'000	£'000	£'000
Opening balance	–	900	1,160	1,470	1,820
Additions	1,000	400	500	600	700
Depreciation	(100)	(140)	(190)	(250)	(320)
Closing balance	900	1,160	1,470	1,820	2,200

Tax computation	**2001**	**2002**	**2003**	**2004**	**2005**
	£'000	£'000	£'000	£'000	£'000
Opening balance	–	750	862	1,022	1,216
Additions	1,000	400	500	600	700
Writing down allowance	(250)	(288)	(340)	(406)	(479)
Closing balance	750	862	1,022	1,216	1,437
Timing difference	150	298	448	604	763
Increase therein	150	148	150	156	159

This can be shown in the form of a graph, thus:

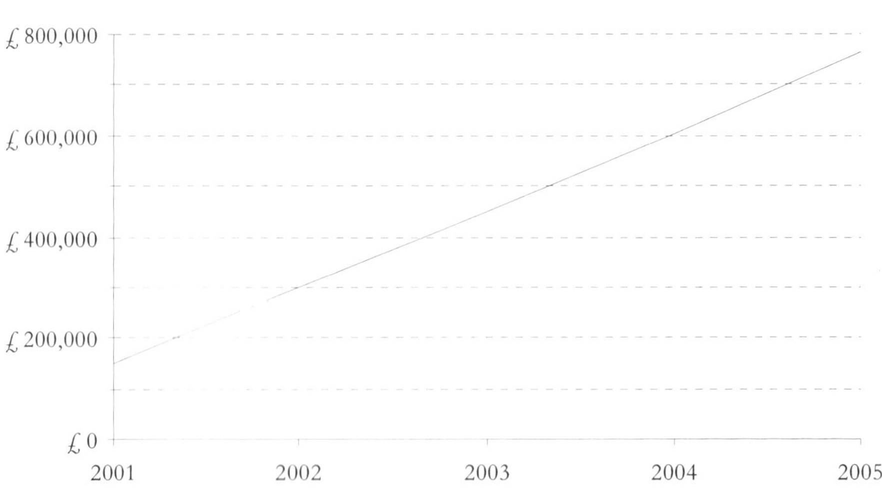

Under the full provision approach, the company would provide deferred tax at the end of 2001 of £45,000, being 30% of the timing difference of £150,000 at that time. However, the partial provision approach would consider whether any net reversal of the timing difference could be foreseen to arise in the future, and since the cumulative amount of timing differences is expected to rise, would make no provision at all in this case.

If timing differences were in fact expected to decline below the present level in the future, then provision would be made for the extent to which the timing differences were expected to reverse. Thus if the figures were the same as those above, except that the cumulative timing differences at the end of 2001 amounted to £400,000 rather than £150,000, then provision would be made for the net reversal which could be foreseen to arise when they fell to £298,000. The amount provided would be £30,600 ((£400,000 - £298,000) @ 30%). This pattern is shown in the following graph:

Timing differences

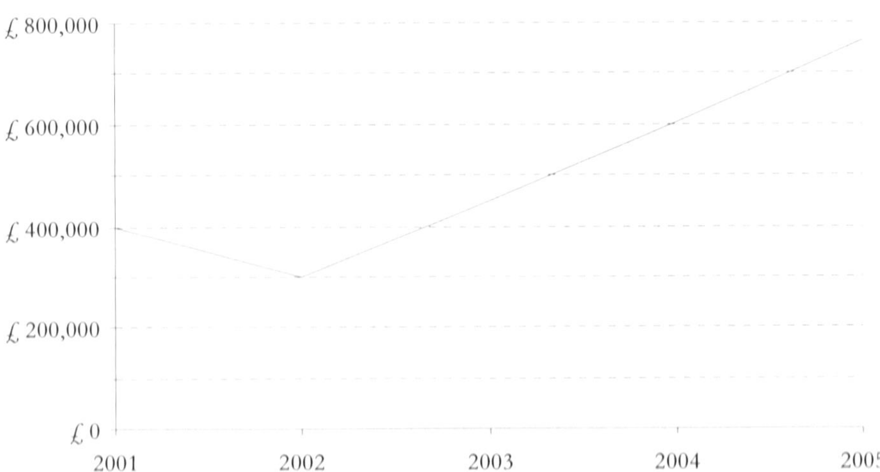

It should be noted that provision has to be made for this reversal, even though the reversal itself is expected to be temporary (in the sense that the timing differences expected to arise beyond 2002 will again lift the cumulative level above the present level). The basic rule is that provision should be made for tax on the excess of the present level of timing differences over the lowest level to which it is expected to fall at any year end in the future.

Where a converse pattern is foreseen (as shown in the next graph), the same basic rule still applies; in the following example, therefore, no provision would be needed because, although net reversals can be foreseen in years 2004 and 2005, they do not bring the cumulative level at the end of that period below its present level. However, if it were expected that this declining pattern would continue beyond 2005, it would be necessary to see to what level the timing differences could be expected to fall in the longer term, and if at any time it was expected that they would be less than the present level of £400,000, then provision would have to be made for the effect of that net reversal.

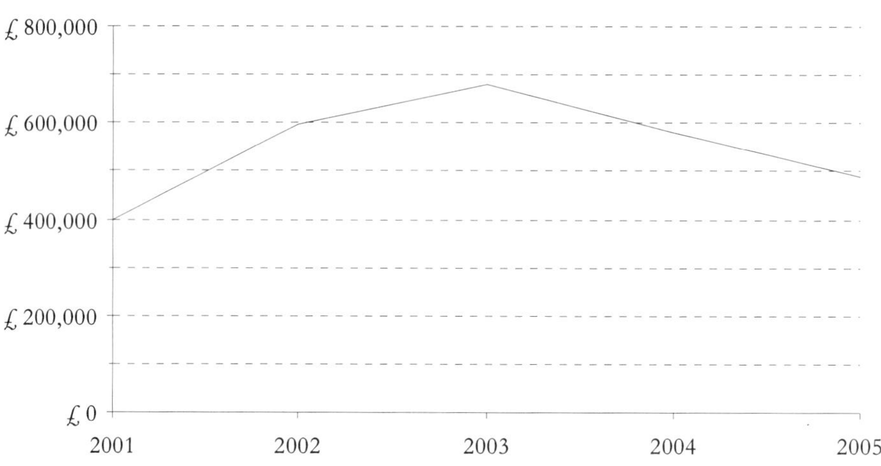

Because timing differences can be either positive or negative (representing the deferment or acceleration of tax), it is possible that the projection of future timing differences will show that they will cross the zero axis, as shown on this graph:

Timing differences

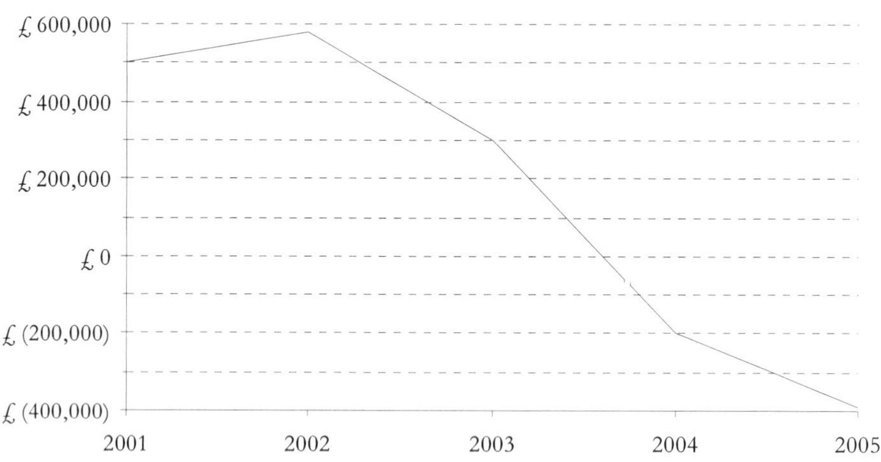

In these circumstances, the whole amount of the potential liability would be provided (£150,000 in the example – £500,000 @ 30%), but no provision would be made for the further effect of the future timing differences which went beyond the axis. The partial provision basis does not involve accounting for timing differences based on their future level; it simply seeks to identify whether a 'hard core' of timing differences exists, and if so, to avoid making provision for that amount because in substance it represents a permanent deferment of tax.

The partial provision approach arouses strong passions, both from those who support it and from those who condemn it. Most of the arguments in favour are in fact criticisms of the full provision approach on the grounds that it can lead to the provision of large sums for deferred tax which have only a remote likelihood of becoming payable. It is worth remembering that the partial provision method was introduced at a time when very substantial tax deductions were available in the form of stock appreciation relief and 100% first year allowances for capital investment, and it was much more appropriate in that context than it is now that these features have been removed from the tax system.

To provide for deferred tax on timing differences which are unlikely on reversal to give rise to a tax liability is said by advocates of the partial provision method to be pursuing form rather than substance and to mislead the users of accounts through the understatement of profit and capital employed. It can thereby portray companies as being more highly geared than they are in reality and give a false impression of poor creditworthiness. Further, it could affect a company's distributable reserves and borrowing powers (if they were computed by reference to reserves) because those reserves were understated because of a provision for deferred tax which might be regarded as unnecessary.

In contrast, partial provision is argued to give rise to liabilities that can be regarded as more realistic. Perhaps more importantly, the method produces an effective tax rate in the profit and loss account that reflects the company's tax planning strategies, whereas full provision simply reports a statutory tax rate which is impervious to its degree of success in managing its tax affairs more efficiently.

Critics of the partial provision approach generally say that the failure to provide for an expected reversal on the grounds that replacement will take place wrongly anticipates a future event (such as that a certain level of capital expenditure will take place). This is thought to be inappropriate partly because it may be at variance with the prudence concept, but partly also because it departs from normal accounting rules which account for the effects of transactions individually, rather than in combination with the effects of transactions which have not yet occurred. It is also argued that the method brings volatility and distortion into the profit and loss account, because earnings are affected by the incidence of transactions unrelated to trading performance, such as the acquisition of fixed assets which attract allowances for which no deferred tax provision is made.

The conceptual weakness of the partial provision approach was highlighted in 1992 by the issue of UITF 6 – *Accounting for post-retirement benefits other than pensions*, relating to post-retirement health care costs (see Chapter 23 at 4.3.6). This requires a company to charge such costs in its profit and loss account over the working lives of its employees and set up the corresponding liability in the balance sheet; however, it does not receive any tax deduction in respect of the health care costs until the payments are eventually made. Under a comprehensive allocation approach, this would give rise to a deferred tax asset, but because such an asset will continue to grow indefinitely (because the provision for health care costs will be doing so) the partial provision approach would require that no recognition be given to the asset.

This highlighted the main conceptual inconsistency between SSAP 15 and accounting practice in all other areas; partial provision applies a principle which has no parallel in other areas of accounting, namely that assets and liabilities should not be recognised when they are expected to be replaced by equivalents in the future. If the same principle were applied to the health care costs themselves, then no provision would have to be set up so long as the existing workforce continued to earn entitlement to health care as fast as their predecessors became eligible to receive them; a 'pay-as-you-go' basis would be applied, which would not be permitted under UITF 6. Critics pointed out that the deferred tax asset was as real an asset as the pension provision was a liability.

As a result of this, in December 1992 the ASB amended SSAP 15 so as to allow (but not require) deferred tax relating to all post-retirement costs (including pensions themselves) to be accounted for on a comprehensive allocation basis, despite the fact that all other timing differences remained on a partial provision basis.[9] Smiths Industries adopts this approach, as shown in the following extract:

Extract 24.1: Smiths Industries plc (2000)

Accounting policies [extract]
Taxation

Tax deferred or accelerated by the effect of timing differences is accounted for to the extent that it is considered probable that a liability or asset will crystallise in the foreseeable future. The only exception to this is in respect of deferred tax assets relating to provisions for post-retirement benefits which are recognised in full.

	Consolidated			
	Full provision basis		Provided	
	2000	1999	**2000**	1999
	£m	£m	**£m**	£m
19 Deferred taxation [extract]				
Deferred taxation:				
Accelerated capital allowances	**(11.5)**	(10.1)	**(11.5)**	(10.1)
Post-retirement benefits	**10.1**	9.3	**10.1**	9.3
Short-term and other timing differences	**19.7**	25.3	**7.7**	14.2
	18.3	24.5	**6.3**	13.4

This amendment to SSAP 15 really only compounded the inconsistencies inherent in the standard. The problem was not unique to post-retirement costs, but related to all timing differences which arise from different recognition bases as between the financial statements and the tax computation.

Moreover, the treatment required by SSAP 15 before the Amendment was perfectly consistent with the overall rationale of partial provision. If it is held that a long-term liability that is never settled in cash on a going concern basis (because it is being continually replaced with an equivalent liability) is not a real liability, it must follow that a long-term asset that is never recovered in cash for the same reason is not a real asset.

The ASB's 1995 Discussion Paper *Accounting for Tax*[10] (see 2 below) also criticised the partial provision approach on several more conceptual grounds by reference to its own (then) proposed framework: it used criteria for recognition that were not found elsewhere in GAAP; it inappropriately recognised the effects of future transactions; it relied on management intent; and it was internally inconsistent. The Board therefore suggested that the method should be abandoned in favour of full provision.

This has been done in FRS 19 (see 5 below), which cites as a further main reason for change the fact that the international consensus has now moved distinctly in favour of full provision. However, when one gets to the detail of FRS 19, one finds that it does not require true full provision either, since it incorporates numerous exemptions that go beyond the international consensus.

F The 'incremental liability' method

This is the conceptual method that is asserted to underpin FRS 19, which is discussed in more detail at 5 below. Essentially, the method seeks to distinguish between different types of timing difference according to whether or not they give rise to an additional (incremental) tax asset or liability at the balance sheet date, and to recognise deferred tax only in respect those timing differences that do give rise to an incremental asset or liability.

For example, it is argued that, if a company recognises a debtor for accrued interest that will be taxed on receipt, it cannot avoid the obligation to pay tax on that interest when it is received and a deferred tax liability should therefore be recognised. By contrast, if a company revalues an asset, it has discretion over whether or not to sell the asset in such a way as to crystallise the tax liability on the gain; deferred tax should therefore not be recognised until the point at which the company no longer has such discretion (i.e. where it has entered into a binding agreement to sell the asset).

As we discuss in more detail at 5.1.2 below, we do not believe that the 'incremental liability' approach stands up to much scrutiny, so that, in our view, it is much easier to treat FRS 19 as a series of more or less discrete rules than to seek to identify a common principle at work.

G The hybrid method

This method seeks to combine features of the deferral method and the liability method, by selecting the most appropriate method for the particular type of timing difference which has arisen, such that the deferred tax balance consists of elements derived under the deferral method and other elements derived under the liability method.

As discussed at B above, there are four basic classes of timing difference:

(a) income recognised in the accounts before being taxed;

(b) income taxed before being recognised in the accounts;

(c) expenditure recognised in the accounts before being allowed for tax;

(d) expenditure allowed for tax before being recognised in the accounts.

The hybrid method draws a distinction between those where the first leg of the timing difference passes through the accounts ('book before tax' differences – (a) and (c) above) and those where it passes through the tax computation ('tax before book' differences – (b) and (d) above).

In the case of 'book before tax' differences, the deferred tax liability cannot be quantified with absolute certainty. It is not possible to determine the tax consequences of these transactions as they will only be apparent in the future, and the ultimate liability will be determined by the rate of tax in effect at the time of the reversal. Accordingly the best estimate of the future liability is made and tax is provided at the latest known rate, and deferred tax on these types of timing differences is provided using the liability method. However, in the case of 'tax before book' differences, the tax effect of those transactions is known, and the tax expense or benefit is fixed. Accordingly, deferred tax on these types of timing differences is provided using the deferral method.

If the hybrid method is used the effect of a change in the rate of tax will affect only that part of the balance computed using the principles of the liability method. That part of the deferred tax balance computed using the deferral method is not adjusted since the tax effects of these timing differences is already known.

This method has the merit of some intellectual elegance, but the disadvantage of total impracticality, due to the need to track 'tax before book' and book before tax' differences separately. For example, under the current UK system, the timing differences relating to depreciation and capital allowances on a fixed asset typically change from 'tax before book' to 'book before tax' during the life of the asset.[11] It has never been adopted in any of the major developed countries of the world and is not considered further in this chapter.

1.3.3 *'Balance sheet' methods of accounting for deferred tax*

A *The 'temporary difference' approach*

This approach was developed by the FASB in the United States in SFAS 109 *Accounting for Income Taxes*[12], and has been incorporated with only minor modifications in IAS 12.

The essential difference between the 'timing' and 'temporary' difference approaches is that the timing difference approach focuses on the (comprehensive) income statement and the temporary difference approach on the balance sheet. The timing difference approach calculates the amount of tax payable on income that has been accounted for to date. The temporary difference approach therefore essentially calculates the tax that would be paid if the net assets of the reporting entity were realised at book value. A temporary difference is the difference between the carrying amount of an asset or liability and its 'tax base' (broadly, the amount at which the item concerned is recognised for tax purposes).

In many cases, this results in no arithmetical difference between the approaches, as the following simple example illustrates.

Example 24.5: 'Timing' versus 'temporary' differences (1)

A company buys a fixed asset for £1 million, which is to be depreciated over 4 years. It attracts a 40% first year allowance for tax purposes. At the end of the year of purchase, the 'timing difference' relating to the asset would be calculated as:

	£000
Tax allowances claimed	400
Depreciation charged	250
	150

The 'temporary difference' would be calculated as follows.

	£000
Net book value of asset	750
Tax base (i.e. tax written-down value) of asset	(600)
	150

The difference between the approaches can be particularly blurred by examples such as this, since, as illustrated in Example 24.1 above, it is usual in practice, when calculating accelerated capital allowances, even under the timing difference approaches, to use the difference between net book value and tax written value as a 'short cut' to the true calculation (i.e. the difference between cumulative deprecation and capital allowances).

In fact, it is generally true that all timing differences are also temporary differences. However, there are important instances of temporary differences that are not timing differences. An example that is not a timing difference is the purchase of an asset the cost of which is not fully deductible for tax purposes, as illustrated by Example 24.6.

Example 24.6: 'Timing' versus 'temporary' differences (2)

A company buys stock for £120, of which only £90 is deductible for tax purposes when the stock is sold. Under the timing difference approach, purchase of the stock creates no taxable or accounting income, and therefore no timing difference. The non-deductible £30 would be treated as a permanent difference that would be reflected in the financial statements by an effective tax rate higher than the statutory rate when the stock is sold.

Under the temporary difference approach, however, a temporary difference of £30 arises on purchase of the stock, being the difference between its carrying amount and the amount deductible for tax, on which a deferred tax liability must be recognised immediately.

In practice, however, IAS 12 requires provision to be made for tax on a temporary difference arising on initial recognition of an asset or liability only where it arises as the result of a business combination (see 7.2.2 below).

Supporters of the temporary difference approach maintain that it is the natural consequence of a conceptual framework (such as that of the IASC, ASB and FASB) that focuses on the balance sheet. The argument (which, it must be admitted, is explained much more clearly in SFAS 109 than in IAS 12) is broadly as follows. If an asset is currently carried in the balance sheet at, say, £1,000 there is an implicit assumption in the accounts that the asset will ultimately be recovered or realised by a cash inflow of at least £1,000. If that inflow will enter into the determination of future taxable income, the tax (if any) on realisation of the £1,000 carrying amount of the asset should be provided for. The 'basis for conclusions' section in SFAS 109[13] puts it as follows:

'A government levies taxes on net taxable income. Temporary differences will become taxable amounts in future years, thereby increasing taxable income and taxes payable, upon recovery or settlement of the recognised and reported amounts of an enterprise's assets or liabilities .... .

'A contention that those temporary differences will never result in taxable amounts ... would contradict the accounting assumption inherent in the statement of financial position that the reported amounts of assets and liabilities will be recovered and settled, respectively; thereby making that statement internally inconsistent.'

We find this argument unconvincing and suggest that it is at best a brave attempt to rationalise the *status quo*. The reality is that, if deferred tax had not already been a generally accepted accounting practice in the early 1990s, no-one would have been suddenly inspired with the insight that it was required by the FASB's or IASC's conceptual framework on the argument set out above. On any natural construction of the English words in the IASC framework's definition of 'liability' (i.e. a present obligation arising from past events), the only tax 'liability' is the amount actually due to the tax authorities – i.e. current tax, suggesting that the true 'balance sheet' method is in fact the flow-through method (see C below).

In developing FRS 19, the ASB rejected the temporary difference approach on the basis that it could not accept the fundamental assumption underlying the approach that the carrying value of an asset represents the minimum *pre-tax* cash flows that the asset would generate.[14] There can be circumstances in which tax cash flows might also be reflected in the carrying value. For example, if an entity paying tax at 30% bought a non-deductible asset for £100 and carried it at its historical cost of £100, this would not be because it expected to generate pre-tax cash flows of £100, on which it would pay tax of £30. Rather it would expect to generate pre-tax cash flows of at least £143, on which it would pay tax of £43. The carrying value of £100 would therefore have already taken account of future tax cash flows, such that any further provision for deferred tax (as required by the temporary difference approach) would be a form of double counting.[15]

Supporters of IAS 12 would doubtless argue that this is not a real issue because, as noted in Example 24.6 above, IAS 12 does not in fact require provision for deferred tax in such circumstances (other than in the context of a business combination). However, in our view, and presumably that of ASB, the very fact that IAS 12 finds it necessary to make such an exception merely highlights the validity of the ASB's concerns.

Ideally, we would like to see the IASB re-debate accounting for tax from first principles. In practice, however, we suspect that a number of factors make the prospect of any significant change to IAS 12 in the near future extremely unlikely.

B *The 'valuation adjustment' approach*

This theoretical approach was apparently supported by a number of the ASB in preference to the 'incremental liability' method discussed at 1.3.2 F above.[16] It is based on the idea that deferred tax might need to be provided for in order to ensure that other assets were not valued at more than their economic (i.e. post-tax) values to the business.

For example, it is argued, a fixed asset for which full capital allowances are not available (e.g. a revalued tax-exhausted asset) is less valuable than one for which full allowances may be claimed and provision for deferred tax is required to reflect this difference. The net effect of this approach would, in most cases, be the same as the temporary difference approach discussed in A above.

However, the argument underlying this approach is essentially that underlying the net-of-tax method (see 1.3.5 below), and it is difficult to reconcile with the presentation of deferred tax as a separate asset or liability.

C *The flow-through method*

This approach, while clearly a balance sheet approach, is not really a method of accounting for deferred tax at all, but rather a justification for not accounting for it. Under the flow-through method, the tax charge is simply the amount payable based on the profits of that year, with no attempt to reallocate it between periods by reference to timing differences. The method therefore deals with tax as if it were either a period cost or a distribution (see 1.1 above).

Whilst flow-through is not presently generally regarded as an acceptable approach, it is clear that it is gradually receiving more recognition from influential sources. Most notably, FRS 19 makes it plain that it is the method preferred by 'a number' of the ASB, who accepted FRS 19's full provision approach only in the interests of international harmonisation.[17]

Those ASB members who support flow-through do so for one of two reasons. One argument is that tax is assessed annually on profits as determined for tax purposes, not on accounting profits. The tax authorities impose a single tax assessment on the entity and that is its only liability to tax for that period. Any tax assessed in future years will depend on future events and hence is not a present liability as defined in the ASB's *Statement of Principles* or the IAS conceptual framework.

Others argue that even if, in principle, timing differences do give rise to tax liabilities, in practice such liabilities cannot always be measured reliably. The future tax consequences of current transactions depend upon a complex interaction of future events, such as the profitability, investment and financing transactions of the entity, and changes in tax rates and laws. Only those that could be measured reliably (typically very short-term discrete timing differences) should be provided for. The problem with this 'modified flow-through' approach, however, is that it is notoriously difficult to distinguish 'short-term' differences (see 1.3.2 B above).

The main conceptual argument against the flow-through method is that it is essentially cash accounting at odds with the accruals basis on which financial statements are normally prepared. Also the army of tax planners and advisers employed by any major company suggests a general belief in the underlying stability of the tax system, which lies uneasily with the assumptions underlying the flow-through approach.

As noted in A above, it is our view that the ASB's and IASC's conceptual frameworks most obviously support the flow-through method of accounting for tax, as it is the only method that records a true 'obligation'. However, we see this more indicative of weakness in the frameworks than of the merits of flow-through.

1.3.4 Discounting the liability

Over the years the suggestion has been made that deferred tax should be provided on a discounted basis, and it is now a permitted option in UK GAAP under FRS 19 (see 5.11 below), although prohibited by IAS 12 (see 7.2.4 below).

This has an obvious intuitive appeal, because by definition deferred tax involves the postponement of the tax liability, and it is therefore possible to regard the deferred liability as equivalent to an interest-free loan from the tax authorities. An appropriate way to reflect the benefit of this postponement could be to discount the liability by reference to the period of the deferment, and accordingly to record a lower tax charge by reason of that discount. The discount would then be amortised over the period of the deferment.

However, this poses some considerable conceptual challenges. For example, is the objective of discounting deferred tax to reflect the fair value of deferred tax (for which discounting can be seen as a surrogate) or to reflect the time value of money? If it is the latter, there arises the basic problem that for most other liabilities subject to discounting it is relatively easy to determine the future cash flows to be discounted (or, at least, what cash flows should in principle be discounted) and the discount rate to be used. Where deferred tax is concerned, however, there is little agreement on either issue.

A Cash flows to be discounted

With regard to the cash flows to be discounted, for example, some argue that it is unrealistic simply to discount the deferred tax inherent in timing differences at the balance sheet date, as it may well be that they have no effect on tax cash flows in the year that they reverse. For example, capital allowances on future investment or other tax losses may further postpone the cash settlement of the deferred tax liability.

Others believe that it is appropriate to discount deferred tax arising on timing differences originating in the accounts ('book before tax' differences), but not those originating in the tax computation ('tax before book' differences). The argument, which is essentially the same as that underpinning the hybrid method (see 1.3.2 G above), is that the tax on a 'book before tax' difference is a future cash flow, which can be discounted, whereas the tax on a 'tax before book' difference is a past cash flow, which cannot. The counter-argument to this is that, where a 'tax before book' difference is discounted, what is being discounted is not in fact the past tax cash flow but rather the variation in future cash flows that has become inevitable as a result of the past cash flow.[18]

Another issue is whether discounting gives rise to a form of double counting. For example, some argue that the purchase price of an asset already reflects the net present value of future income earned from the asset, and is thus, from an economic perspective, an already discounted amount. If depreciation is already discounted, it is not appropriate to discount further the deferred tax arising from it.

B Choice of discount rate

There is as much debate on the discount rate to be used. The basic issue is whether the rate should be specific to the entity or to the liability.

If an entity-specific rate is thought the more appropriate, further debate ensues as to whether a debt rate or an equity rate should be used. Some argue that deferred tax is more akin to equity, as it can be paid only out of future profits. In either case, there is the real paradox that, if the entity gets into financial difficulty, its cost of borrowing will increase and any liability discounted at that rate will therefore decrease. This would have the effect of reducing the reported deferred tax liability at the very time when its crystallisation was most likely to be accelerated (because the company would lack the resources to undertake sufficient capital expenditure to maintain its 'hard core' of timing differences).

If a liability-specific rate is favoured, there is an intuitive logic to using a government bond rate, on the grounds that deferred tax is in effect a loan from the government. However, unlike a government bond, deferred tax bears no interest, leading some to argue that the appropriate discount rate is zero, and others that it must be right to discount because an interest-free liability must be less onerous than an interest-bearing one.

FRS 19's solutions to these issues are discussed in more detail at 5.11 below.

1.3.5 *The net-of-tax method*

The net-of-tax approach is not a discrete method of measuring the tax effects of timing differences, but is concerned with the manner of its presentation in the accounts. The method recognises the tax effects of timing differences as an integral part of the asset or liability that caused the timing difference to arise. Before applying the net-of-tax approach the deferred tax liability is computed via one of the methods set out above, but then included in the carrying value of the item to which the difference relates. Thus, a deferred tax liability arising from accelerated capital allowances would be deducted from the balance sheet carrying value of the asset concerned, or the amount of a disallowable provision (such as a general bad debt provision) would be stated net of the tax effect which would arise when the provision was utilised and became tax deductible.

This method has seldom been used in practice, although there are occasions where it has been applied, particularly in relation to large provisions. Indeed, FRS 17 – *Retirement Benefits* – requires the asset or liability for defined benefit pensions accounted for under FRS 17 to be accounted for on what amounts to a net-of-tax basis (see Chapter 23 at 3.7.4 and 5.10.3 below. It is also clear (see 1.3.3 B above) that some members of the ASB support the 'valuation adjustment' approach to accounting for deferred tax, the rationale for which is essentially the same as that for the net-of-tax method.

SSAP 15 dismisses the net-of-tax method by saying that 'it fails to distinguish between a transaction and its tax consequences and therefore should not be used in financial statements'.[19]

1.4 Allocation within periods

As well as allocating tax to particular accounting periods, it is also sometimes necessary to allocate it within an accounting period for presentation purposes. Normally, it will be shown in the profit and loss account under the caption of tax on profit on ordinary activities, but it may have to be allocated to the statement of total recognised gains and losses or the reconciliation of movements in shareholders' funds.

With the publication of FRS 16 and FRS 19, this issue has been largely settled. The basic principle is that tax should be accounted for in the profit and loss account unless it relates to an item accounted for in the statement of total recognised gains and losses. This is discussed in more detail at 3.1 and 5.10 below.

Occasionally, unusual taxes give rise to some debate as to how they should be presented. An example was the windfall tax levied on privatised utilities in the July 1997 Budget. Because it is based on a formula which relies on the capitalised value of profits over a period of up to four years, it is arguably inappropriate to include it in the normal tax line in the profit and loss account, which under the Companies Act formats is captioned 'tax on profit or loss on ordinary activities'. A more appropriate alternative under these formats might be the penultimate line, 'Other taxes not shown under the above items'. The approach adopted by Thames Water in the extract below has elements of both these possible treatments, since the windfall tax is shown adjacent to, but not as part of, tax on profit on ordinary activities.

Extract 24.2: Thames Water Plc (1998)

Consolidated profit and loss account [extract]

	Note	**1998** **Total** **£m**	1997 Total £m
Profit on ordinary activities before taxation		**418.6**	371.8
Taxation on profit on ordinary activities		**(62.2)**	(51.4)
Windfall tax	9	**(230.7)**	–
Profit for the financial year		**125.7**	320.4

. . .

9. Windfall tax

In accordance with the Finance (No 2) Act 1997 enacted on 31 July 1997, £230.7m has been charged to the profit and loss account in respect of the windfall tax of which £115.4m was paid on 1 December 1997. The balance of £115.3m will be paid on 1 December 1998.

1.4.1 *FRED 22*

The intra-period allocation of the total tax charge will become a much more dynamic accounting issue in the UK if the proposals in FRED 22 – *Revision of FRS 3 – Reporting Financial Performance* are converted into an accounting standard. FRED 22, which is discussed in more detail in Chapter 2 at 6.1.2 and Chapter 25 at 4.3.2, proposes a comprehensive income statement in three main sections: operating, financing and treasury, and other gains and losses and requires two separate tax charges (or credits) to be shown for (a) the total of operating and financing and treasury items and (b) other items.[20]

In our view, FRED 22 rather underestimates the difficulty of making such an allocation, at least meaningfully, particularly in the light of the challenges posed by the (much more straightforward) current requirement to allocate the tax for a period between the profit and loss account and statement of total recognised gains and losses (see 3.1.1 and 5.9.1 below). If, as seems probable, FRED 22 does become a standard in substantially its current form, we anticipate having to address the issue in some detail in future editions of this book.

2 THE DEVELOPMENT OF ACCOUNTING FOR TAXATION IN THE UK[21]

2.1 Current tax

The timing and content of UK accounting standards on current tax has been largely dictated by changes in the tax system relating to advance corporation tax (ACT). ACT was introduced with effect from April 1973 and abolished with effect from April 1999. Both the introduction and abolition of the tax raised significant, but relatively straightforward, accounting issues relating to current tax, which had to be addressed at short notice. This led to the issue by the ASC of SSAP 8 – *The treatment of taxation under the imputation system in the accounts of companies* in 1974, and its withdrawal and replacement by FRS 16, published by the ASB in late 1999. FRS 16 is discussed at 3 below. Like SSAP 8 before it, FRS 16 is not a particularly controversial standard.

2.2 Deferred tax

By contrast, it has always proved much more difficult to achieve a UK consensus on accounting for deferred tax, which may be another reason why both the ASC and ASB preferred to deal with it in isolation from current tax.

As noted in 1 above, at the time that FRS 19 was issued last year, the UK and Ireland were the only major countries in the world still to require partial, rather than full, provision for deferred tax. The reason for this was in no small measure a matter of history. A key feature of the UK corporation tax system during the 1970s and early 1980s was a high tax rate (50-52%) tempered by generous allowances for investing in plant and holding stock. The effect of this system, combined with the high inflation then being experienced in the UK, was that few companies in fact paid corporation tax at anything like the full 52% nominal rate. Indeed, some paid no mainstream corporation tax at all, paying only ACT on dividends.

Against this background, in 1975 the ASC issued its first deferred tax standard, SSAP 11 – *Accounting for Deferred Taxation*, requiring full provision for deferred tax, only to be forced by overwhelming opposition to withdraw it before its effective date and to issue SSAP 15, requiring partial provision, in its place. Quite simply, the general view at the time was that it was wrong for all companies to be required to show a constant effective tax rate of 52% in the profit and loss account (as would broadly have been the case under the full provision method), when most companies were actually paying tax at well below that rate.

However, since the issue of SSAP 15, a number of things have occurred to make the original case for its partial provision approach far less convincing. First, the basic economics are different. Inflation is low, allowances for plant are much less front-loaded and there is no allowance for holding gains on stock, meaning that most companies pay tax at or near the statutory rate. Moreover, business is much more multinational, such that UK groups may in fact pay much of their tax overseas, calling into question the extent to which the accounting treatment of tax should be driven by features unique to the UK tax system.

Secondly, SSAP 15, which was designed to deal with the perceived problems of long-term deferred tax *liabilities*, seemed less adept at dealing with long-term deferred tax *assets*. This emerged following the implementation in the early 1990s of SSAP 24 and UITF 6, which deal with accounting for the cost of pensions and other post-retirement benefits. This led to the 1992 amendment to SSAP 15 that permitted, but did not require, companies to provide for deferred tax in full on timing differences relating to pensions and other post-retirement benefits, while continuing to provide on a partial provision basis for all other items. Whilst this was a widely supported change, it clearly left SSAP 15 lacking any conceptual credibility. This is discussed in more detail at 1.3.2 E above.

Finally, and most importantly, the inexorable trend in international accounting thought has been towards the full provision method. In 1992 the FASB in the US issued SFAS 109, requiring full provision based on the so called 'temporary difference' approach (see 1.3.3 A above). SFAS 109 became the blueprint for the international standard, IAS 12, which was issued in 1996 and revised in 2000 (see 7 below).

In the light of these developments, in 1995 the ASB published a comprehensive Discussion Paper – *Accounting for tax* – which addressed the subject from first principles and concluded that SSAP 15 was untenable and that it should be replaced with a standard requiring some variant of full provision on a discounted basis. The Discussion Paper received a rather frosty reception from respondents, who largely felt that partial provision, whatever its faults, was well established and understood and, in a UK context, gave intuitively right answers.

In reality, however, the days of partial provision had been numbered from the moment that the UK committed itself to participation in the IASC's project to harmonise accounting practices internationally. The question was not whether the

ASB would propose full provision but when it would judge such a proposal politically acceptable, or at least not unacceptable, among its constituency.

During 1998 and 1999 the ASB gave a number of increasingly clear hints that it was preparing an exposure draft of a standard proposing full provision for tax, albeit with some modifications in respect of revaluation gains.[22] This is indeed the broad approach proposed in FRED 19 – *Deferred tax*, published in August 1999, the proposed requirements of which were carried through with relatively little change into FRS 19, published in December 2000. The requirements of FRS 19 are summarised at 5 below.

A notable feature of FRS 19 is its unusually comprehensive discussion (in Appendix V to the standard) of the development of, and conceptual basis for, the standard, although this leaves the reader with the unexpected overall impression that the ASB's enthusiasm for FRS 19 was less than wholehearted, and indeed that it may have been a compromise that was not the first choice of accounting method for a majority of the Board. Appendix V suggests that the main influences on the final shape of FRS 19 were:

- the need for the ASB to demonstrate commitment to the international harmonisation programme by moving the UK onto full provision;
- the serious reservations of the ASB as a whole about the 'temporary difference' approach in IAS 12 (see 1.3.3 A above); and
- the view of a significant minority of the Board that in fact the flow-through method was the correct approach under its *Statement of Principles* (see 1.3.3 C above).

FRS 19 bravely tried to give some accommodation to all these views but, in our opinion, failed to do so for the simple reason that they are ultimately irreconcilable. Whilst we fully support the ASB in rejecting the international approach, there is no escaping a double irony. First, in the name of international harmonisation, the ASB has issued an FRS which, as demonstrated by the analysis in 7 below, still leaves accounting for tax in the UK and the Republic of Ireland significantly different from that in the rest of the world. Second, FRS 19, while nominally a full provision standard, has many features that are more consistent with the flow through method.

3 CURRENT TAX

3.1 FRS 16

The objective of FRS 16 – *Current Tax* is 'to ensure that reporting entities recognise current taxes in a consistent and transparent manner'.[23] Current tax is defined as:

'The amount of tax estimated to be payable or recoverable in respect of the taxable profit or loss for a period, along with adjustments to estimates in respect of previous periods.'[24]

FRS 16 covers all financial statements intended to give a true and fair view, except those prepared by small entities applying the *Financial Reporting Standard for Smaller Entities* (FRSSE).[25] Because FRS 16 (like all FRSs) applies in both the

United Kingdom and the Republic of Ireland, it necessarily contains a number of detailed provisions that are relevant only to the Irish tax system. These are not dealt with in this chapter.

The main accounting provisions of FRS 16 deal with:

- the allocation of the total current tax charge between the profit and loss account and the statement of total recognised gains and losses;
- the treatment of tax credits and withholding taxes;
- items subject to tax at non-standard rates;
- measurement of the current tax charge; and
- recoverable ACT.

These aspects are discussed in turn below.

FRS 16 was issued in December 1999 and has been mandatory for accounting periods ending on or after 23 March 2000.[26]

3.1.1 *Allocation of the current tax charge between the profit and loss account and STRGL*

FRS 16 requires that current tax should be recognised in the profit and loss account, except to the extent that it relates to an item that is or has been recognised in the statement of total recognised gains and losses (STRGL), where the tax relating to such an item should also be recognised in the STRGL.[27]

The most common example of items falling into this latter category are:

- gains on disposals of fixed assets that have been revalued through the STRGL prior to disposal; and
- exchange profits and losses on borrowings used to hedge overseas investments. These are discussed in more detail at 6.3 below.

The effect of FRS 16 is to require tax relating to items that are recognised neither in the profit and loss account nor in the STRGL, but only in the reconciliation of movements in shareholders' funds, to be recognised in the profit and loss account rather than in the reconciliation of movements in shareholders' funds.

Such items do occur, albeit rarely. Examples include:

- tax relief in some jurisdictions for goodwill which has been set off against reserves in accordance with SSAP 22 – *Accounting for goodwill* – and the transitional arrangements in FRS 10 – *Goodwill and Intangible Assets* (see Chapter 11 at 2.3.6);
- tax relief for qualifying employee share trusts (QUESTs), the charge for which is normally dealt with in the reconciliation of shareholders' funds (see Chapter 22 at 2.6).

This differs from IAS 12, which requires the tax effects of *all* items charged or credited directly to equity also to be taken directly to equity (see 7.2.5 B below). However, we believe that the position in FRS 16 is more consistent with the ASB's *Statement of Principles* (and the IAS framework). Under the *Statement of Principles*, tax is not a transaction with shareholders and must therefore be reported in the profit and loss account unless it relates to an item recognised in the STRGL.

In fact general practice before the issue of FRS 16 was to report tax relief on items accounted charged to shareholders' funds in the profit and loss account. However, an example of company that changed its previous practice of crediting the tax relief to shareholders' funds in response to FRS 16 was Whitbread.

Extract 24.3: Whitbread PLC (2000)

1 **Changes to accounting policies** [extract]

FRS 16 (Current Tax) has been adopted, which has led to tax relief on the discount on shares issued to employees under share option schemes being accounted for in the profit and loss account rather than reserves as previously. The amount of the relief is £0.5m (1998/9 - £1.9m). Comparative amounts have been adjusted.

FRS 16 notes that in exceptional circumstances it may be impossible to determine the tax relating to items in the STRGL, in which case the total tax should be allocated on either a 'reasonable pro-rata basis', or using 'another allocation that is more appropriate in the circumstances'.[28] It is perhaps unfortunate that (unlike the ASB's 1995 discussion paper) the standard is not more specific as to the basis of allocation, since, even in relatively straightforward cases, more than one valid method suggests itself, as the following example illustrates.

Example 24.7: Allocation of current tax between the profit and loss account and STRGL

A company bought a plot of land in 1986 for £2 million. In 1995 it revalued the land to £4 million, but provided no deferred tax on the gain on the basis that no disposal was anticipated in the foreseeable future. On implementing FRS 15, the company adopted the transitional arrangements and 'froze' this revaluation, subject to a review for impairment. In 2001 an opportunity for disposal suddenly arises and the land is sold for £5 million. Tax payable is £500,000, after allowing for indexation relief of £1.3m (these are purely notional figures and are not intended to represent the actual UK tax position).

In pre-tax terms the company will have recognised total gains of £3 million (£2 million in the STRGL in 1995 and £1 million in the profit and loss account in 2001). The options would seem to be to allocate the tax between the profit and loss account and STRGL:

(a) pro-rata to the pre-tax gains, such that £166,667 (£500,000 x £1,000,000/£3,000,000) is dealt with in the profit and loss account and the balance of £333,333 in the STRGL; or

(b) on some basis that reflects the fact that the indexation relief (being a relief for inflation) relates more to the first £2 million of the gain recognised in the STRGL in 1995 than to the £1 million recognised in the profit and loss account in 2001. This could be done by calculating the tax that would have arisen on a disposal in 1995 and allocating this to the STRGL, with the balance of the amount actually paid being shown in the profit and loss account.

Method (b) has the advantage of being arguably the more accurate method, but the disadvantage of being somewhat esoteric and complicated. It also relies on the tax system having remained substantially unchanged throughout the period of ownership of the asset. In our view, therefore, (a) is the better approach to adopt in practice.

FRS 16 requires the STRGL to include tax on an item that 'is *or has been*' recognised in the STRGL. We take this to mean that, where an item has been recognised in the STRGL of a previous period but is taxed only in the current period, the tax should still be accounted for in the STRGL of the current period, even though this does not include the related pre-tax gain or loss. A typical example might be the realisation (and taxation) in the current period of a revaluation gain on a fixed asset recognised in the STRGL of a prior period. An example of a company in this situation is Land Securities.

Extract 24.4: Land Securities PLC (2000)

3 **Statement of total recognised gains and losses** [extract]

STATEMENT OF TOTAL RECOGNISED GAINS AND LOSSES	Notes	**2000 £m**	1999 £m
Profit on ordinary activities after taxation (page 42)		**252.0**	216.4
Unrealised surplus on valuation of properties	21	**454.0**	332.9
Taxation on valuation surpluses realised on sales of properties	21	**(5.2)**	–
Total gains and losses recognised since last financial statements		**700.8**	549.3

3.1.2 *Tax credits and withholding taxes*

FRS 16 defines a 'tax credit' as:

> 'The tax credit given under UK legislation to the recipient of a dividend from a UK company'[29]

and 'withholding tax' as:

> 'Tax on dividends or other income that is deducted by the payer of the income and paid to the tax authorities wholly on behalf of the recipient'.[30]

In these definitions, it is seen as a key distinction between withholding taxes and tax credits that withholding tax is explicitly paid on behalf of the recipient (such that the recipient suffers tax on the income, but is given relief for the withholding tax paid), whereas a tax credit recognises that the income has already been subject to tax (such that it becomes tax-free in the hands of the recipient).[31]

A Profit and loss account

On the basis of this distinction FRS 16 requires that outgoing dividends, interest and similar items should be recognised in the profit and loss account at an amount that includes withholding taxes, but excludes any other taxes, such as attributable tax credits, not payable wholly on behalf of the recipient.[32] The requirement to include withholding taxes is not directly relevant to UK companies, as the UK has no withholding tax. However, it will be relevant when recording dividends to minority shareholders, or interest, paid by overseas subsidiaries of a UK group incorporated in jurisdictions with withholding taxes.

Similarly, incoming dividends, interest or other income should be recognised at an amount that includes withholding taxes (with any withholding tax suffered being included in the tax charge), but excludes any other taxes, such as attributable tax credits, not payable wholly on behalf of the recipient.[33]

I Underlying tax

FRS 16 clarifies that dividends, interest and similar items should not be grossed up for underlying tax (i.e. the tax paid by the paying company on the profits from which the dividend or other income has been paid).[34] This clarification was necessary because relief for underlying tax (where available) is given in a way that is very similar to relief for withholding tax – i.e. the UK taxpayer's taxable income is grossed up by the amount of underlying tax, with relief being given for the underlying tax suffered in the tax computation.

FRS 16 cites as the reasons for this approach:

(a) withholding tax is paid on behalf of the recipient of the income, whereas underlying tax is suffered by the paying entity on its profits and is not 'payable wholly' on behalf of another person; and

(b) withholding tax is readily quantifiable, whereas underlying tax can be difficult to calculate and agree with the Inland Revenue.[35]

In our view, the appeal in (a) above to the literal wording of the standard fails to address the real issue (i.e. that, in the hands of a UK tax-paying company, underlying tax and withholding tax are economically very similar), and it is hard to resist the conclusion that the true reason for the ASB's conclusion may have been the practical difficulties noted in (b).

II UK income tax

FRS 16 does not specifically address items from which UK income tax has been deducted at source. However, such income tax would appear to fall within the definition of 'withholding tax' above. Accordingly, in our view, income and expenses subject to UK income tax at source should be shown gross in the profit and loss account.

III Avoir fiscal and similar reclaimable tax credits

The UK's tax treaty with France provides that, when a French company pays dividends to a UK-resident 'portfolio' investor (one holding not less than 10% of the French company), credit for the underlying tax of the French company is given by the French, rather than the UK, tax authorities. This credit, known as 'avoir fiscal', is paid to the UK investor and is subject to UK tax. Similar arrangements exist with Italy, where the credit is referred to as 'credito imposta'.

Shortly after the issue of FRS 16, the question was raised as to whether avoir fiscal and similar credits should be treated, for the purposes of FRS 16, as a tax credit (such that the dividends to which they related should be shown net) or a withholding tax (leading to a gross presentation). Whilst the ASB has never issued any formal public ruling on this matter, it has privately made it clear that it regards such credits as tax credits, and not withholding tax, for the purposes of FRS 16, on the grounds they are more in the nature of a refund of underlying tax, which is not shown gross (see I above).

IV Non-taxpaying entities eligible for transitional relief

Some non-taxpaying entities, mainly charities, are entitled until April 2004 to a tapering transitional relief under the tax legislation whereby they may reclaim from the tax authorities an amount to compensate them for the loss of the tax credit that they were able to reclaim before the abolition of ACT (see 3.1.5 below). Such entities may continue to gross up income subject to such transitional relief if they so choose.

B Cash flow statement

FRS 16 does not specifically address the treatment of items subject to withholding tax in the cash flow statement. FRS 1 (Revised 1996) – *Cash flow statements* – requires that the main heading 'Returns on investment and servicing of finance' should include:

- interest received on which tax has been recovered on a gross basis;
- interest paid from which tax has been deducted on a gross basis; and
- dividends received net of tax credits, on a net basis.[36]

However, FRS 1 has no specific rules on the treatment of incoming dividends subject to recoverable withholding tax. However, they are so similar to interest from which tax is deducted at source that it would seem reasonable to include them on a gross basis.

3.1.3 *Items subject to non-standard rates of tax*

Income and expenses taxed at non-standard rates should be included in the pre-tax results at the actual amounts receivable and payable and not grossed up to reflect the notional amount of additional tax that would have arisen if the transaction had been taxed, or allowed for tax, on a different basis.[37] This will also to non-taxable income or non-deductible expenditure.[38]

This simply repeated the requirements of UITF Abstract 16 *Income and expenses subject to non-standard rates of tax*, issued in 1997, which was withdrawn by FRS 16.

The issue is solely one of presentation. Prior to the issue of UITF 16, the practice had developed, particularly in the financial services sector, of grossing up the post-tax results of certain transactions in the profit and loss account so as to show a standardised tax rate and pre-tax result whereas the actual economics of the transaction depended on non-standard tax effects for their profitability.

A common example was so-called 'preference share lending', whereby banks, rather than making a straightforward loan, subscribed for preference shares in the borrowing company. Because dividend income was franked investment income, but interest income was taxed at the higher corporation tax rate, the banks required a lower pre-tax return on preference shares than on a loan to earn the same post-tax profit, and could therefore lend more cheaply.

However, if Bank A made a straightforward loan, but Bank B 'lent' using preference shares and both reported the actual cash flows, Bank A would appear much more profitable at the pre-tax level than Bank B, whilst the underlying economics were the same. It was argued that the best way of adjusting for this apparent difference was to gross up Bank B's profit and loss account. The UITF's consensus, now incorporated in FRS 16, was that such practices were inappropriate, and that the profit and loss account should show the actual pre-tax and tax numbers without any such adjustment.

The 1996 accounts of Lloyds TSB showed the effect of this change:

> *Extract 24.5: Lloyds TSB Group plc (1996)*
>
> NOTES TO THE ACCOUNTS
>
> 2 Accounting policies
>
> Accounting policies are unchanged from 1995. Abstract 16 issued by the Urgent Issues Task Force of the Accounting Standards Board, requires the gross-up calculations on certain transactions, the overall profitability of which is determined on a post-tax basis, to be made at the underlying rate of tax. In previous years, for the purposes of presentation in the profit and loss account, the income from these transactions has been grossed-up using the standard rate of tax. The 1996 accounts have been adjusted to take account of the new requirement, which has the effect of reducing total income and profit before tax by £22 million (net interest income by £12 million and other income by £10 million). The tax charge is also reduced by the same amount, so the resulting after tax figure is unaffected. No adjustment has been made to the comparative 1995 figures on the grounds of immateriality.

FRS 16 clarifies that this requirement applies only to notional tax. It is not intended to disturb the long-standing practice in certain industries, such as leasing and life assurance, of allocating profits to accounting periods on a post-tax basis and then grossing up those post-tax profits by the actual effective rate of tax suffered on the profits in question.[39]

3.1.4 *Measurement of the current tax charge*

FRS 16 requires current tax to be measured at the amounts expected to be paid or recovered using the tax rates and laws that have been enacted or 'substantively enacted' by the balance sheet date. A UK tax rate is to be taken as 'substantively enacted' if it is included in either:

- a Bill that has been passed by the House of Commons and is awaiting only passage through the House of Lords and Royal Assent; or
- a resolution having statutory effect that has been passed under the Provisional Collection of Taxes Act 1968.[40]

Although the above criteria refer only to the 'tax *rate*', we assume that they are also intended to apply to other aspects of the tax law (as is required by FRS 19 and IAS 12).

Prior to FRS 16, there has been almost no guidance on this issue in UK GAAP, but practice had tended to be for tax provisions to take account of proposals announced in the latest Budget before the accounts were approved, as well as the law as 'substantially enacted' at the balance sheet date. Indeed this treatment is indirectly supported by SSAP 17 – *Accounting for post balance sheet events*, the Appendix to which gives as an example of an adjusting post-balance sheet event 'the receipt of information regarding rates of taxation'. The reference to tax rates in SSAP 17 was curiously left unamended by FRS 16, although it has now been removed by FRS 19 (see 5.9.2 below).

We do not believe that this was a change for the better. We accept that in the majority of cases it may have little impact but it has the potential for creating almost absurd results. For example, in a typical year the Finance Act is enacted shortly before the summer Parliamentary recess. Thus, a company with a year end between 31 March and the enactment of the Finance Act will have to base its accounts tax charge on the rate in the law at the balance sheet date, even though a different rate may have been subsequently enacted in the Finance Act before the accounts are approved. Any difference would presumably have to be dealt with in the following period as an 'adjustment to prior years'.

The real reason for introducing this requirement was to conform with the IAS 12. However, it should be remembered that IAS 12's requirement to use only enacted legislation derives from the US standard SFAS 109. In the context of the United States, where in recent memory political differences between the legislature and executive led to difficulties in approving the federal budget, such a rule makes eminent sense. Whether it is so relevant in the context of the UK constitution where the government normally controls the legislature is less certain.

Moreover FRS 16's 'harmonisation' with IAS 12 is incomplete, since FRS 16 reproduces only the main bold paragraph requirement of IAS 12. In fact, the 'small print' of the IAS 12 (see 7.2.4 below) allows use of an as yet unenacted rate 'in jurisdictions where announcements of tax rates and laws have the substantive effect of actual enactment' – a form of words which describes the UK position fairly well. In other words, a true harmonisation with IAS 12 would arguably have allowed previous UK practice to continue.

3.1.5 Recoverable ACT

A Background

From April 1973 to April 1999 the UK operated an 'imputation' system of taxation. An imputation system aims to ensure that a company's profits are taxed only once (as opposed to a 'classical' system, whereby a company pays dividends out of taxed profits, and those dividends are fully subject to tax in the hands of the shareholder). This was achieved through advance corporation tax (ACT).

ACT was a complicated tax and well beyond the scope of a book such as this to discuss in detail.[41] The basic mechanics, however, were that a UK company would pay ACT in respect of dividends paid, and UK shareholders would receive credit for the ACT paid in determining their tax liability. The rate at which ACT was payable varied over time, but was linked to the basic or lower rate of income tax.

From the perspective of the paying company, any ACT paid in an accounting period was treated as an advance payment of corporation tax (hence the name) for that period, and was offset against the mainstream liability for that period. However, there were restrictions on the amount of ACT that could be offset in any one period. Any ACT that could not be relieved in a particular period could be relieved against earlier and later periods, again subject to restrictions.

The offset restrictions meant that it was quite common for companies to be unable to relieve all the ACT they paid against mainstream corporation tax, so that, by the time that ACT ceased to operate in 1999, many companies had accumulated significant amounts of unrelieved ('surplus') ACT. It was considered inequitable that such companies should have no further opportunity to recover surplus ACT and accordingly an arrangement known as the 'shadow ACT' regime has been put in place to allow companies to recover surplus ACT paid in previous periods.

The broad intention of the shadow ACT regime is to allow companies with surplus ACT from previous periods to recover it as if there had been no change in the law. In other words surplus ACT may still be offset against future liabilities to corporation tax, but only to the extent that it would have been recoverable if ACT had continued to be accounted for on dividends paid in those later periods. As a result of these rules, recoverable ACT is likely to remain an accounting issue for some years, despite the abolition of ACT.

B Requirements of FRS 16

FRS 16 provides that any unrelieved ACT carried forward for relief against future taxable profits should be recognised on the balance sheet only to the extent that it is regarded as recoverable.[42] Some detailed guidance on making this assessment is given in Appendix II to the standard, which defines ACT as recoverable where it can be:

(a) set off against a corporation tax liability on the profits of the period under review or of previous periods; or

(b) properly set off against a credit balance on the deferred tax account; or

(c) expected to be recoverable taking into account expected profits and dividends – normally those of the next accounting period only.[43]

With respect to (b) above, FRS 16 states that, where there is a deferred tax account, ACT should be offset against it only to the extent that, in the period in which the underlying timing differences are expected to reverse, the reversal will create sufficient taxable profits to enable ACT to be recovered under the shadow ACT system.[44]

With respect to (c) above, FRS 16 reiterates that, in the absence of a deferred tax account, ACT should not normally be treated as recoverable unless its recovery in the next accounting period can be reasonably foreseen.[45] However, the word 'normally' leaves some apparent room for manoeuvre. In certain cases, there may be a reasonable argument for carrying the ACT forward if the company foresees with reasonable certainty that its expected profits and planned dividends will allow the ACT to be relieved outside the strict one year timescale laid down by the standard. The question of carrying forward ACT as an asset is also dealt with in SSAP 15, as discussed in 4.4.3 below.

Where recoverable ACT can be offset against the deferred tax account, it should be shown deducted from it. An example of a company adopting this treatment is Rolls Royce.

Extract 24.6: Rolls-Royce plc (2000)

22 Provisions for liabilities and charges [extract]

	Group		Company	
	2000	1999	**2000**	1999
Deferred taxation	**£m**	£m	**£m**	£m
Provided in accounts:				
Fixed asset timing differences	**8**	5	**–**	–
Other timing differences	**60**	70	**–**	–
Advance corporation tax	**(19)**	(15)	**–**	–
	49	60	**–**	–
Full potential liability/(asset):				
Fixed asset timing differences	**136**	127	**112**	99
Other timing differences	**57**	52	**(2)**	(14)
	193	179	**110**	85
Advance corporation tax	**(19)**	(75)	**–**	(56)
	174	104	**110**	29

In other cases, it should be shown as a deferred tax asset.[46] This is slightly inconsistent with the requirement above that ACT should be set off against the deferred tax balance only to the extent that it represents taxable profits against which the ACT can be relieved, which implies that ACT is a receivable rather than deferred tax. If ACT is deferred tax (as implied by this requirement), there seems no reason to restrict its offset against a credit deferred tax balance, given that:

- SSAP 15 does not otherwise restrict the offset of debit and credit deferred tax balances for presentation purposes; and
- FRS 19, whilst it does restrict them does not do by reference to whether the assets and liabilities at the balance sheet date can be offset directly (see 5.10.3 A below).

Where ACT previously regarded as recoverable becomes irrecoverable (and vice-versa), the effect should be disclosed as a separate component of the tax charge.[47]

3.1.6 *Disclosure*

FRS 16 requires an analysis of the current tax charge (or credit) in both the profit and loss account and the statement of total recognised gains and losses (STRGL). This should show UK tax and foreign tax, each of which should be sub-analysed to distinguish tax for the current period and adjustments recognised in respect of prior periods. The total UK tax charge (or credit) should also be shown before and after double taxation relief. A suggested, but non-mandatory, format of the note for the current tax charge on the profit and loss account is given in Appendix I to the standard as follows.

	£000	£000
UK corporation tax		
Current tax on income for the period	a	
Adjustments in respect of prior periods	b	
	c	
Double taxation relief	(d)	
		e
Foreign tax		
Current tax on income for the period	f	
Adjustments in respect of prior periods	g	
		h
Tax on profit in ordinary activities		i

This broad layout, with the primary analysis being between UK and overseas tax, was also suggested in SSAP 8. In practice, most companies make the primary analysis of the tax charge between current and deferred tax, with a sub-analysis of each of these between UK and overseas tax, as will be seen from several extracts in this chapter. Such a presentation still gives all the information required by FRS 16, and is, in our view, more useful to users of financial statements. Moreover, it is the presentation suggested by FRS 19 (see 5.12 below).

The analysis of the tax charge made by Barclays gives examples of most of the disclosures required by FRS 16.

Extract 24.7: Barclays PLC (2000)

11 Tax [extract]

The charge for tax assumes an effective UK corporation tax rate of 30% (1999 30.25%, 1998 31%) and comprises:

	2000	1999	1998
	£m	£m	£m
Current tax:			
UK	**719**	427	374
Overseas	**219**	271	162
Total current tax	**938**	698	536
Deferred tax charge/(credit):			
UK	**14**	(19)	(24)
Overseas	**(7)**	(33)	4
Total deferred tax	7	(52)	(20)
Associated undertakings and joint ventures, including overseas tax of £2m (1999 £2m, 1998 £3m)	**(1)**	(2)	4
Total charge	**944**	644	520

In common with many companies, Barclays discloses the tax rate. This used to be required by the Companies Act in all cases and by SSAP 8 in cases where the rate was not known for all or part of the period. The reason for there being no equivalent requirement in FRS 16 is presumably that FRS 16 requires tax to be computed using enacted legislation, so that the rate will be known.

As can be seen from the following extract, BOC discloses the effective corporation tax rate not only for the UK but also for the other main jurisdictions in which the group has operations.

Extract 24.8: The BOC Group plc (2000)

4. **Tax** [extract] a) **Tax on profit on ordinary activities**	**2000** **£ million**	1999 £ million	1998 £ million
Payable in the UK			
Corporation tax at 30% (1999: 31%/30%, 1998: 31%)	**54.8**	51.7	79.3
Advance corporation tax (ACT)	**–**	(0.3)	(15.6)
Double tax relief	**(16.3)**	(17.7)	(21.6)
	38.5	33.7	42.1
Payable overseas			
US – Federal tax at 35% (1999: 35%, 1998: 35%)	**2.1**	4.4	1.1
– State and local taxes	**1.6**	2.9	1.4
– Prior year tax	**(1.1)**	(4.9)	–
Australia at 36% (1999: 36%, 1998: 36%)	**18.2**	14.3	14.4
South Africa at 30% (1999: 30%, 1998: 35%)	**14.5**	8.7	9.2
Japan at 48% (1999: 48%, 1998: 51%)	**11.2**	9.1	6.9
Other countries	**12.8**	13.1	41.8
	59.3	47.6	74.8
Provision for deferred tax – UK	**–**	–	4.3
Provision for deferred tax – overseas	**(1.6)**	(3.0)	(7.1)
Share of tax charge arising in joint ventures	**5.4**	6.7	8.9
Share of tax charge arising in associates	**2.1**	0.3	0.6
	103.7	85.3	123.6

The tax charge includes a credit of £8.6 million for the operating exceptional charges (1999: £10.6 million, 1998: £21.2 million). No tax arises from the profit on disposal of businesses in the current year (1999: £nil, 1998: £(30.0) million). The effective rate of tax excluding exceptional items was 25 per cent (1999: 24 per cent, 1998: 29 per cent).

The share of the tax charge of joint ventures and associates is given in compliance with FRS 9 – *Associates and joint ventures* – see Chapter 7 at 3.1.1 A (see also Extract 24.7 above). The footnote information is given in compliance with the Companies Act and FRS 3 requirements to give information on 'special circumstances' affecting the tax charge (see 6.1 below).

FRS 16 does not give a suggested format (comparable to that for the profit and loss account set out above) for the required analysis of the tax charge or credit in the STRGL. An issue here may be that, as discussed in 3.1.1 above, the STRGL for the current period may well include tax relating to an item accounted for in the STRGL of a previous period. In our view, such tax should still be included in the disclosures supporting the tax figure in the STRGL under the heading 'Current tax for the period'. The caption 'Adjustments in respect of prior periods' should be used only for corrections of errors or estimates in previous tax computations.

Some disclosures are also required in respect of recoverable ACT (see 3.1.5 above).

In addition, a non-tax paying entity eligible for transitional relief that chooses to gross up its income by the amount of any relief claimed (see 3.2.1 A IV above) must disclose the nature and amount of the relief.[48]

3.2 Tax losses and group relief

3.2.1 General

Where a tax loss has been incurred that can be relieved by a refund of tax previously paid, it will be accounted for as a current tax credit and recorded in the balance sheet as a debtor (which may be a non-current debtor depending on the precise circumstances of the tax-paying company). Where losses can be relieved only by carry-forward against future profits, these represent timing differences and are accordingly accounted for as deferred tax assets under SSAP 15 (see 4.4.2 below) or FRS 19 (see 5.5 below).

3.2.2 Group relief

A Background

Where a member of a group has tax losses it may surrender them to another group member to be set off against their taxable profits of the same period, subject to a number of detailed provisions of the tax legislation. Such a transfer may be made with or without payment by the company receiving the group relief; this is a matter of policy for the group to decide. Where payment is made it is usually at the applicable tax rate in force, so that the profitable company is in effect paying as group relief what it would otherwise have paid in tax, and the loss-making company is having its losses relieved at the same rate.

B The accounts of the profitable company

Group relief gives rise to no significant accounting implications so far as the profitable company is concerned, so long as it is being paid for at the effective rate of tax as described above; whether it pays tax to the Revenue or a payment for group relief to another company, the financial impact on it will be the same. The only difference will be that it will disclose the payments made as 'group relief' within its note analysing the tax charge, rather than as corporation tax payable.

However, where it is receiving relief without payment, different considerations apply. Where the incidence of the relief gives rise to an unusually low tax charge, it will generally be appropriate to disclose the reason for this because it constitutes 'special circumstances which affect liability in respect of taxation of profits … for the financial year'.[49]

C The accounts of the loss-making company

From the point of view of the loss-making company, any losses surrendered without payment to other group companies clearly have no value to it. However, where the losses are being surrendered for consideration, the effect will be to allow the company to recoup some value from these losses sooner, and with greater certainty, than it otherwise might. In most cases, credit will be taken in the year in which the taxable loss arises, as the holding company will generally have determined the group relief situation within the group. Nevertheless, in some situations, on grounds of prudence, it may be appropriate to take no credit for this until it is certain that it will be received, which may not be until the group election has been made. Where a credit for these losses appears within the tax charge note it should be described as 'group relief receivable'.

4 DEFERRED TAX – SSAP 15

As noted in 1 above, SSAP 15 is in the process of being superseded by FRS 19, which is mandatory for accounting periods ending on or after 23 January 2002, and is discussed at 5 below. Whilst early adoption of FRS 19 is encouraged, its complexity, and potentially adverse accounting consequences, will deter many companies from complying with it until they are required to do so. This means that SSAP 15 remains very much in force for December 2001 year ends in practice as well as in theory.

4.1 General approach

SSAP 15 indicates that it is concerned with accounting for tax on profits and surpluses which are recognised in the accounts in one period but assessed in another. It thus relates primarily to deferred corporation tax and income tax in the United Kingdom and in the Republic of Ireland and, insofar as the principles are similar, to overseas taxes on profits payable by UK and Irish enterprises or their subsidiaries.[50]

Interestingly, the standard considers other taxes also, by providing that 'a number of other taxes, including value added tax, petroleum revenue tax and some overseas taxes, are not assessed directly on profits for an accounting period and are therefore not addressed specifically in this statement. For such taxes, enterprises should generally follow the principle underlying this statement, that deferred tax should be provided to the extent that it is probable that a liability or asset will crystallise but not to the extent that it is probable that a liability or asset will not crystallise.'[51]

The standard chooses the partial provision method as its general approach, and summarises it as follows:

'Deferred tax should be accounted for in respect of the net amount by which it is probable that any payment of tax will be temporarily deferred or accelerated by the operation of timing differences which will reverse in the foreseeable future without being replaced. Partial provision recognises that, if an enterprise is not expected to reduce the scale of its operations significantly, it will often have what amounts to a hard core of timing differences so that the payment of some tax will be permanently deferred. On this basis, deferred tax has to be provided only where it is probable that tax will become payable as a result of the reversal of timing differences.'[52]

The standard considers that there are two main methods of computation, the liability method and the deferral method. It then points out that the liability method is the method consistent with the aim of partial provision, which is to provide the deferred tax which it is probable will be payable or recoverable.[53]

4.2 Definitions

Part 2 of the standard contains the definitions of the terms that are used throughout its text.

Deferred tax is the tax attributable to timing differences.[54]

Timing differences are differences between profits or losses as computed for tax purposes and results as stated in financial statements, which arise from the inclusion of items of income and expenditure in tax computations in periods different from those in which they are included in financial statements. Timing differences originate in one period and are capable of reversal in one or more subsequent periods.[55]

The following definitions are given for specific timing differences:

(a) a loss for tax purposes which is available to relieve future profits from tax constitutes a timing difference;[56]

(b) the revaluation of an asset (including an investment in an associated or subsidiary company) will create a timing difference when it is incorporated into the balance sheet, insofar as the profit or loss that would result from realisation at the revalued amount is taxable, unless disposal of the revalued asset and of any subsequent replacement assets would not result in a tax liability, after taking account of any expected rollover relief;[57]

(c) the retention of earnings overseas will create a timing difference only if:

    (i) there is an intention or obligation to remit them; and

    (ii) remittance would result in a tax liability after taking account of any related double tax relief.[58]

The *liability method* is a method of computing deferred tax whereby it is calculated at the rate of tax that it is estimated will be applicable when the timing differences reverse. Under the liability method deferred tax not provided is calculated at the expected long-term tax rate.[59]

4.3 Computing deferred tax

4.3.1 *Basic method of computation*

Deferred tax should be computed under the liability method. Tax deferred or accelerated by the effect of timing differences should be accounted for to the extent that it is probable that a liability or asset will crystallise. Tax deferred or accelerated by the effect of timing differences should not be accounted for to the extent that it is probable that a liability or asset will not crystallise.[60] For this purpose, the combined effect of all timing differences should be considered rather than looking at individual categories in isolation,[61] except that timing differences relating to post-retirement benefits may be considered separately and provided for in full as a result of the amendment to SSAP 15 referred to in 1.3.2 E and 2.2 above.

A number of examples illustrating the basic principles of SSAP 15 are given at 1.3.2 E above.

4.3.2 *Combining different categories of timing difference*

SSAP 15 requires timing differences to be looked at in aggregate for the purposes of determining what net reversal need be provided for, rather than individually.[62] This is illustrated by the following example:

Example 24.8: Combination of timing differences

Assume that a company has the following projected cumulative timing differences for the next five years, and it is preparing accounts at the end of 2001:

	2001	2002	2003	2004	2005
	£'000	£'000	£'000	£'000	£'000
Accelerated capital allowances	500	600	450	800	900
Other timing differences	(300)	(350)	(400)	(450)	(500)
Net position	200	250	50	350	400

The important line to focus on is the one which shows the net position, rather than either of the two which represent its components. Accordingly, the amount to be provided is determined by the extent to which the net deferral of £200,000 will fall – it can be seen that there will be a fall of £150,000 to £50,000 at the end of 2003, and accordingly the amount to be provided, at 30%, is £45,000.

Although the terms of the standard clearly state that the timing differences are to be looked at in aggregate rather than individually, it is sometimes argued that those timing differences which would give rise to debit balances may not be used to offset other timing differences if they are expected to be perpetuated. Accountants Digest No. 174 contains the following passage:

'It is important to note that, just as deferred tax liabilities should not be created unless it is probable that a liability will crystallise, so deferred tax liabilities should not be reduced by deferred tax debit balances which will not crystallise because recovery of the tax is continually deferred. For example, deferred tax liabilities should not be reduced by deferred tax debit balances arising from timing differences on recurring general bad debt provisions.'[63]

It can be argued that this approach produces anomalous results, as demonstrated by the following example:

Example 24.9: Combination of timing differences involving continuing debit balances

Assume that the same company had different expectations as to the accelerated capital allowance element of its projected cumulative timing differences, so as to give rise to the following figures for the next five years. It is still preparing accounts at the end of 2001:

	2001	2002	2003	2004	2005
	£'000	£'000	£'000	£'000	£'000
Accelerated capital allowances	300	200	100	100	100
Other timing differences	(300)	(350)	(400)	(450)	(500)
Net position	–	(150)	(300)	(350)	(400)

Under the approach suggested in the Accountants Digest, the company would provide £60,000 (30% of £200,000, being the difference between the £300,000 deferred tax liabilities at 2001 less the lowest anticipated future balance, £100,000) for deferred tax in 2001, even though the incidence of timing differences experienced by it has been completely neutral in its effect, resulting in neither a postponement nor an acceleration of tax suffered. The provision would be, in effect, a provision for the effects of the acceleration of tax which was expected to occur in the future but had not yet taken place. This does not seem to produce a sensible result; it would be more appropriate to look at the effect of the timing differences in aggregate rather than individually, than to anticipate effects that will be experienced in 2002 and beyond.

4.3.3 Future projections

The assessment of whether deferred tax liabilities or assets will or will not crystallise should be based upon reasonable assumptions. The assumptions should take into account all relevant information available up to the date on which the accounts are approved by the board of directors, and also the intentions of management. Ideally this information will include financial plans or projections covering a period of years sufficient to enable an assessment to be made of the likely pattern of future tax liabilities. A prudent view should be taken in the assessment of whether a tax liability will crystallise, particularly where the financial plans or projections are susceptible to a high degree of uncertainty or are not fully developed for the appropriate period.[64]

Under the original SSAP 15, it was easy for an enterprise to ignore the partial provision approach and to remain fully provided, simply by failing to produce, or pleading an inability to produce, future plans or projections. Under the revised requirements, it is theoretically not permissible to do this, as there are two separate requirements: to provide for the tax that is expected to crystallise, and not to provide for tax that is not expected to crystallise. However, an inability to foresee the future with enough clarity may still lead to full provision in practice. Moreover, changes in the tax system since SSAP 15 was introduced mean that many companies do effectively make provision for deferred tax except in respect of such contingent liabilities as the remittance of overseas earnings and the realisation of revaluation gains. An example is Laporte (see Extract 24.15 at 4.7 below).

There is no longer a minimum time period which should be covered by the projections, which is a change from SSAP 15 in its original form, where 'normally three years' was quoted, although the Appendix to the standard now mentions a period of three to five years as an example of a relatively short period which might be appropriate where the pattern of timing differences is expected to be regular.[65] In practice the projection will obviously become less reliable the further into the future it goes, and the period which may be forecast with a reasonable degree of accuracy is perhaps no more than two years. Much depends on whether a pattern of originating or reversing timing differences can be discerned, which will depend on such factors as whether expansion is envisaged, and whether capital expenditure has a cyclical nature.

Each year the pattern of expected timing differences should be compared against the reversal of timing differences experienced in the past. Plans and projections require regular review; they can be influenced by many indirectly related factors, for example the reassessment of asset lives, a decision to close part of the business which renders certain assets no longer needed, or the provision of a sum in respect of the permanent diminution of an asset.

It is important that the plans and projections are based on reasonable and realistic assumptions. In particular, a planned expansion programme may allow timing differences to be projected as continuing to originate well into the future, but the working capital resources to finance the expansion need to be available to the enterprise for that expansion programme to take place.

4.3.4 *Tax rates to be used*

At each year end a company will provide for the appropriate level of deferred tax and will use the best estimate of the rate that will be payable on the taxable profits when the timing differences reverse. This is the fundamental approach of the liability method. Timing differences by their very nature will reverse over many years and the rate of tax will not normally be known in advance for these years. Of course, if rates were set some years in advance then those rates would be applied to the element of timing differences expected to reverse in each of the future years, and the liability computed accordingly.

Generally, the best estimate of the rate of tax that will be applied to reversing differences is the standard rate of tax currently in force, and accordingly deferred tax provisions are made on this basis. Any under or over accrual arising from a rate change will pass through the company's profit and loss account as (a separately disclosed) part of the deferred tax charge for the year, in the year in which the rate changes.

If a change of rate is announced after the year end but before the accounts are prepared, the principles of SSAP 15 would suggest that its effect should be reflected in the year which has already ended. Moreover, this is given in the Appendix to SSAP 17 as an example of an adjusting event.[66] However, it should be noted that FRS 16 already requires current tax to be calculated by reference only to enacted or substantively enacted legislation (see 3.4 above), and FRS 19 will require this in respect of deferred tax and delete the reference to changing tax rates from SSAP 17 (see 5.9.2 below). Companies may wish to consider whether, in these circumstances, it is really appropriate to continue to calculate deferred tax on the basis of best estimates rather than enacted legislation.

A *Companies taxed at small company or marginal rate*

Companies which suffer tax at the small companies rate should generally provide for deferred tax at that rate unless they foresee that the taxable profits in the forthcoming years will rise above the small company threshold. Such taxable profits are not just the timing differences that are expected to reverse in a particular year, but must include an estimate of the taxable trading profit that will arise, since this will form part of the total taxable profits of the company. A similar estimate should be made to determine if the marginal relief provisions will apply to any of the forthcoming years, but this can be even more difficult to assess. It may in certain circumstances be impossible to determine if the marginal reliefs will apply, and in such cases the prudent view should prevail and the standard rate of tax should be used to calculate the provision.

4.4 Debit balances

4.4.1 *General*

The provision for deferred tax liabilities should be reduced by any deferred tax debit balances arising from separate categories of timing differences and any advance corporation tax which is available for offset against those liabilities.[67] This provides for the situation where there is advance corporation tax recoverable, which will effectively rank as a payment on account for the tax due on the future reversal of any timing differences. Further, it allows unrelieved tax losses to be netted off against deferred tax liabilities.

Deferred tax net debit balances should not be carried forward as assets, except to the extent that they are expected to be recoverable without replacement by equivalent debit balances.[68] This is simply the obverse of the same rule for liabilities. Under SSAP 15, a liability is not provided where there is a 'hard core' of timing differences which represent a perpetual postponement of tax; correspondingly, a hard core of timing differences which represents a permanent acceleration of the tax liability should not be regarded as an asset.

4.4.2 *Tax losses*

A General

A tax loss may be carried forward to be utilised against taxable profits which arise in the future. In such circumstances the tax loss can only be recognised in the accounts if enough taxable profit is likely to emerge in the future. It is probable that a taxable profit will emerge in the future if the company has a balance on its deferred tax account, since under the rules of partial provision, the company will have provided for deferred tax only if there is the probability of a tax liability crystallising. As the timing differences which have been identified (and provided for) reverse in future accounting periods, they will automatically give rise to taxable income against which the tax losses can be set.

Accordingly, the deferred tax account is the first point of set off for tax losses which are carried forward. An example is to be found in the accounts of Brunel Holdings (see Extract 21.13 at 4.7 below). The amount of deferred tax provided in the accounts should be reduced to the extent of the tax effect of the available losses. However, complications arise if the enterprise carries on a number of different trades, because a credit balance arising from one trade may not be capable of offset against a debit balance of another trade, or if the loss arises in a company which is in a different tax jurisdiction from the profitable companies, so that again no offset would be possible in practice. It will only be legitimate to make the kind of offset discussed above if the loss could in fact be applied to prevent the payment of tax having to be made if the timing differences reversed so as to crystallise a liability.

B Losses carried forward against future profits

Particular guidance is given in the Appendix to the standard on when it is permitted to regard tax losses as recoverable assets (which is distinguishable from when they may be set off against deferred tax liabilities). The conditions to be satisfied are as follows:

(i) the loss has resulted from an identifiable and non-recurring cause; and

(ii) the enterprise, or predecessor enterprise, has been consistently profitable over a considerable period, with any past losses being more than offset by income in subsequent periods; and

(iii) it is assured beyond reasonable doubt that future taxable profits will be sufficient to offset the current loss during the carry-forward period prescribed by tax legislation.[69]

These rules are framed in an attempt to ensure that an asset is recognised only when its recoverability is assured with a very high degree of certainty and, in practice, these conditions can seldom be met.

C Capital losses

There are specific rules relating to capital losses, which prescribe the following conditions for such losses to be treated as recoverable assets:

(i) a potential chargeable gain not expected to be covered by rollover relief is present in assets which have not been revalued in the financial statements to reflect that gain and which are not essential to the future operations of the enterprise; and

(ii) the enterprise has decided to dispose of these assets and thus realise the potential chargeable gain; and

(iii) the unrealised chargeable gain (after allowing for any possible loss in value before disposal) is sufficient to offset the loss in question, such that it is assured beyond reasonable doubt that a tax liability on the relevant portion of the chargeable gain will not crystallise.[70]

Again, the rules require such a high degree of certainty that, in practice, these conditions can seldom be met.

D Future tax losses

This is an area which causes a great deal of debate. A fundamental question emerges when looking at the foreseeable future for the purposes of assessing the deferred tax provision – if a trading loss is foreseen in the future, may it be taken into account when assessing the level of deferred tax to be provided? Take the following example:

Example 24.10: Future tax losses

A company is preparing its accounts for the year ended 31 December 2001, during which it earned a taxable profit of £100,000, on which tax of £30,000 is payable.

In considering the deferred tax provision that should be set up in its 2001 accounts, the company foresees a reversal of timing differences amounting to £150,000 in 2002, but has identified a trend from 2003 onwards of a level of capital expenditure that should give rise to originating timing differences when compared to the amount of depreciation which will be charged in the profit and loss account.

However, the company forecasts that a trading loss of £100,000 will be made in 2002 and therefore expects that the tax effect of these losses will at least partly mitigate the timing difference reversal.

The amount on which the company should base its provision is either £150,000 or £50,000, but which?

Those in favour of reducing the deferred tax liability would argue that the loss when incurred will reduce the amount of tax payable, and under the partial provision rules (which require that tax should be accounted for to the extent that it is probable that a liability will crystallise, and should not be accounted for to the extent that it is probable that a liability will not crystallise) would say that, since tax on only £50,000 will be payable, then that is all that should be provided.

The counter argument to this is that the deferred tax liability cannot be reduced by a trading loss which has not yet been incurred and which has not been accounted for. The proponents of this argument would maintain that it is only correct to recognise the tax consequences of an event when the accounting consequences have been recognised, and not before. There is no suggestion that the deferred tax provision would be *increased* if a trading *profit* were foreseen in the following year (so that in effect the originating timing differences would not offset the reversals arising in that year). It is not the function of deferred tax to anticipate the effects of future trading results, only to account for the impact of timing differences which have affected trading results reported to date.

Supporters of this view would argue that it is only possible to take account of future timing differences in assessing the deferred tax liability which is to be provided. This explains why it is considered to be legitimate to anticipate the effects of future capital expenditure but not to anticipate future trading results. Part of the confusion in this area is related to the question of whether trading losses do in fact give rise to timing differences. As mentioned at 4.2 above, SSAP 15 states that a loss for tax purposes which is available to relieve future profits from tax constitutes a timing difference. This is true in respect of current and past trading losses; they have been dealt with in the accounts, but not yet in arriving at the liability to tax as assessed in the tax computation. However, it is not true in respect of future trading losses, which so far have been dealt with in *neither* statement. Indeed, to recognise the tax effects of future losses, but not otherwise to provide for them in the accounts would have the effect of *creating* a timing difference where none had previously existed.

We prefer the second of these two arguments, and accordingly believe that the forecast loss should not figure in the assessment of the reversing timing differences and the deferred tax provision should be based on timing differences of £150,000 in this example. In general terms the effects of a tax loss may only be recognised if the loss has been incurred and accounted for in the accounts. Anticipated tax losses may not be used to reduce, or to avoid, a provision for deferred taxation.

4.4.3 ACT

There are quite extensive provisions in SSAP 15 on the treatment of ACT. However, most of these are no longer relevant in the context of the shadow ACT regime and, of the provisions that are still relevant, some are not entirely consistent with the rules in FRS 16 (see 3.5 above). The discussion below is restricted to those paragraphs of SSAP 15 that, in our view, remain relevant.

SSAP 15 requires that debit balances arising in respect of ACT other than on dividends payable or proposed at the balance sheet date should be written off unless their recovery is assured beyond reasonable doubt. It further provides that such recovery will normally be assured only where the debit balances are recoverable out of corporation tax arising on profits or income of the succeeding accounting period.[71] This is broadly consistent with FRS 16.

In discussing the offset of ACT against the deferred tax balance, SSAP 15 states that: 'It *may* be incorrect to carry forward an amount of ACT to offset an equal credit amount of deferred tax'[72] (emphasis added). However, as noted in 3.1.5 above, FRS 16 is clear that ACT should be offset against deferred tax only to the extent that, in the period in which the underlying timing differences are expected to reverse, the reversal will create sufficient taxable profits to enable ACT to be recovered under the shadow ACT system. We recommend that companies should follow FRS 16. Not only is FRS 16 the clearer and more recent standard, but it also seems that the ASB regards it as saying all that needs to be said on ACT, since there is no reference to ACT in FRS 19.

4.5 Group accounts

Group accounts raise particular issues with regard to deferred tax, on which there is little direct guidance in SSAP 15. While some of these issues have been addressed by FRS 19, it is unlikely, in our view, to be appropriate for companies still following SSAP 15 selectively to apply those requirements of FRS 19 that relate to group accounts, even though they may not strictly be in conflict with SSAP 15.

4.5.1 *Offsetting consolidated tax balances*

The accounts of the group are prepared as if it were a single entity, and the question of how to portray the tax affairs of the whole group has to be considered in that light; it will not simply be a matter of aggregating the accounts of all the group companies, which have to consider their own tax position in isolation, but rather one of reassessing the position of the group as a whole. However, individual group companies may operate in different tax jurisdictions, or be subject to other constraints which keep their tax affairs separate, so it will be necessary to have regard to these factors in deciding what can be netted off for the purposes of the group accounts.

The distinction between the approach which has to be taken at group and company level is explained in this extract from the 1998 accounts of Glynwed:

> *Extract 24.9: Glynwed International plc (1998)*
>
> **1. ACCOUNTING POLICIES**
> **Deferred taxation**
>
> Deferred taxation is taken into account to the extent that a liability will probably arise in the foreseeable future and is calculated at taxation rates expected to apply at that time. In the holding company and its subsidiaries the liability is assessed with reference to the individual company. On consolidation the liability is assessed with reference to the Group as a whole.

Some groups simplify things by arranging that the holding company will indemnify subsidiaries against any reversal of timing differences. The effect is that the subsidiaries do not have to make any provision for deferred tax; it can all be dealt with in the accounts of the holding company. EMI is an example of such a group, as shown in this extract:

> *Extract 24.10: EMI Group plc (2000)*
>
> **23. DEFERRED TAXATION** [extract]
>
> The Company has undertaken to discharge the liability to corporation tax of the majority of its wholly-owned UK subsidiaries; their deferred tax liabilities are therefore dealt with in the accounts of the Company.

Where one company expects to have reversals of timing differences in the future, and another expects to have originating timing differences, these may in principle be looked at in aggregate to see whether any overall reversal need be provided for, subject to certain caveats. Even if one company ends up paying more tax because of the reversal, the other will pay less because of its originating differences, and the overall effect on the group will therefore be as if the timing differences had been in one company. However, this approach will have to be modified if the companies are paying tax at different rates, or if the company with originating timing differences is put into a tax loss situation which cannot be relieved, so that the group suffers a net cash outflow: in these circumstances it will be necessary to provide for the effects of that inability to treat the companies as one for tax purposes. An example will illustrate these points.

Example 24.11: Assessing the deferred tax position in a group

Company S is a wholly owned subsidiary of company H. At the end of 2001, the companies assess that their future patterns of cumulative timing differences will be as follows:

	2001	**2002**	**2003**	**2004**	**2005**
	£'000	£'000	£'000	£'000	£'000
Company H	400	500	600	650	700
Company S	500	300	250	200	200
Aggregate	900	800	850	850	900

It is expected that no reversal of timing differences will take place beyond 2003 in either company.

Taking the companies in isolation, company H would make no provision for deferred tax because it foresaw no reversal of timing differences; however, it would not be permitted to anticipate the benefit of future originating timing differences, so its balance sheet would carry neither a deferred tax asset nor a liability. Company S, on the other hand, would have to provide for tax on its anticipated reversals of £300,000 (£500,000 - £200,000).

When the group is considered as a whole, it can be seen that net reversals of only £100,000 are expected to occur (£900,000 - £800,000) so in the normal course of events, the group's deferred tax liability need be calculated only on that figure; that is the amount which would have been the basis of the provision if all the timing differences had been in a single company, and that will represent the effect of timing differences on the group as a whole.

Complications arise, however, if the companies are situated in different tax jurisdictions. If, for example, company S is in a country where tax is payable at a rate of 50%, while company H is paying tax at 35%, it is necessary to recompute the above calculation to take account of the tax rates involved. This results in the following picture:

	2001	**2002**	**2003**	**2004**	**2005**
	£'000	£'000	£'000	£'000	£'000
Company H – tax effects at 35%	140	175	210	227	245
Company S – tax effects at 50%	250	150	125	100	100
Aggregate	390	325	335	327	345

On this basis it can be seen that deferred tax of £65,000 should be provided (£390,000 - £325,000) in respect of the reversal of gross aggregate timing differences of £100,000. This is simply because the reversal in company S is taxed at a higher rate than the relief obtained in company H from its originating timing differences.

A further complication may arise if the originating timing differences anticipated by company H are likely to result in taxable losses in that company. If the two companies were in the UK, that would not make any difference, because the effect of these losses could then be transferred to S in the form of group relief. However, where the countries are in different jurisdictions, this will not be possible and the group will experience the adverse effects of company S's reversal without the benefit of any tax saving in respect of company H. In these circumstances, provision should be made in the group accounts for the deferred tax liability which relates to company S.

The implications of the above are that it is necessary to assess the deferred tax position of the group carefully to see what will be the real result, in tax terms, of future movements in timing differences. As a practical matter, it may be helpful to approach this by examining the overall position for all the group companies in each tax jurisdiction as an interim stage in the process. In general terms, the deferred tax effects of companies in different jurisdictions should not be netted off where there is a significant possibility that increased tax charges in one country might not be offset by tax savings in others.

4.5.2 *Tax effects of consolidation adjustments*

Members of a group are generally assessed to tax on an individual basis, so the total amount of tax borne by the group is not affected by consolidation adjustments. Examples of such adjustments would be where inter-company profit on stock was eliminated on consolidation and recognised only when the stock was eventually sold to a third party; or where borrowing costs incurred to finance the creation of an asset were expensed by a subsidiary but capitalised on consolidation. In the first of these cases, the profit on the inter-company sale would be taxed in advance of being reported in the group accounts, while in the second case, the group would benefit from a tax deduction without having reported the associated expense in the consolidated accounts; that expense would only be reported as part of the subsequent depreciation or disposal of the asset being created.

A purist view might be that consolidation adjustments are not timing differences since they appear in the financial statements, but not the tax computation. However, they do result in the acceleration or postponement of tax in relation to the consolidated results of the group, and on that basis it is customary to recognise such effects within the deferred tax account. Moreover, the Appendix to SSAP 15 gives a consolidation adjustment in respect of an intra-group profit on sale of stock as an example of a timing difference.[73] An example of a company adopting this approach is GlaxoSmithKline (see Extract 24.11 at 4.5.4 A below).

4.5.3 *Fair value adjustments in acquisition accounting*

Like consolidation adjustments, fair value adjustments made on the acquisition of a business are not strictly timing differences, since they never into the determination of group income, although the goodwill arising from them may do so. However, there are cases in which it seems appropriate to treat such adjustments as timing differences and this is a fairly common practice (see Chapter 6 at 2.4.3 E).

4.5.4 *Retained overseas earnings*

When a UK group incorporates the earnings of a foreign subsidiary or associate in its consolidated accounts, a timing difference will arise if the earnings are to be remitted to the UK in a later period and will give rise to incremental tax payments when they are remitted. SSAP 15 requires that these timing differences should be taken into account in the calculation of deferred tax unless it is intended to retain the earnings in the foreign country indefinitely so that no further tax liability will arise.

In practice it can be extremely difficult to determine how much to provide, since this will be subject to many uncertainties; the amount of any liability will depend on factors such as the relative tax rates of the UK and the foreign country concerned, the provisions of any tax treaty between the countries, and the level of UK taxable profits at the time of the remittance. Furthermore, groups may find methods of restructuring their groups so as to minimise their tax liabilities if a major repatriation of dividends becomes necessary. Nonetheless, it is necessary that companies which expect that a liability will emerge should make the best estimate that they can in the circumstances.

SSAP 15 requires companies to disclose the fact that provision has not been made, where this is the case.[74] However, the reasoning behind this rule is somewhat confused. Even where earnings *will* be remitted, and where tax *will* become payable as a result, it might be concluded that no provision is needed because other originating timing differences are forecast to arise in the year of remittance. Accordingly, it is not really possible to read very much into this disclosure when it is made.

A FRS 2

In July 1992, the ASB published FRS 2 – *Accounting for subsidiary undertakings* – which added a further layer of complication to the rules on the disclosure of the potential tax liability on the distribution of retained earnings of overseas subsidiaries. It requires disclosure of:

(a) the extent to which deferred tax has been accounted for in respect of future remittances of the accumulated reserves of overseas subsidiary undertakings; and

(b) the reason for not making full provision (unless provision has been made in full).[75]

Item (a) seems redundant, because SSAP 15 already requires the deferred tax balance to be analysed into its main components (see 4.7 below). Moreover, item (b) appears to be based on the premise that full remittance of profits is the norm from which deviations must be explained, and also that there would not usually be any offsetting effects which would limit the tax payable in such an eventuality. This does not seem to be a realistic foundation on which to base the rule, and it does not seem to have resulted in the provision of much useful information. This requirement of FRS 2 is withdrawn for companies complying with FRS 19.[76]

An example of a company giving the disclosures required by FRS 2 is GlaxoSmithKline.

Extract 24.11: GlaxoSmithKline plc (2000)

13 Taxation [extract]

Save as shown in these accounts, no provision has been made for taxation which would arise on the distribution of profits retained by overseas subsidiary and associated undertakings, on the grounds that no remittance of profit retained at 31st December 2000 is required in such a way incremental tax will arise.

	Full potential		**Provided**	
	At 31.12.00	At 31.12.99	**At 31.12.00**	At 31.12.99
Deferred taxation asset/(liability)	**£m**	£m	**£m**	£m
Accelerated capital allowances	**(619)**	(604)	**(11)**	(14)
Unremitted foreign investment income	**–**	(3)	**–**	(3)
Stock valuation adjustment	**(64)**	(70)	**(64)**	(70)
Intra-Group profit	**314**	376	**44**	35
Diversified Pharmaceutical Services disposal	**10**	29	**10**	29
Pensions and other post-retirement benefits	**300**	311	**300**	311
Manufacturing restructuring	**55**	31	**55**	31
Tax losses	**209**	211	**209**	211
Other timing differences	**563**	388	**346**	212
	768	669	**889**	742

4.5.5 *Group relief*

The basic operation of group relief is described at 3.2.2 above.

Group relief may have a significant effect on deferred tax, because a company in a group may be told by the holding company that there is no need to provide for the tax arising on the expected reversal of timing differences because it will be relieved without cost by losses made available to it by other group companies.

The availability of group relief without charge might strictly be thought to represent a permanent difference, because it features in the company's tax computation, and not in its accounts. In general, we believe that it is inappropriate to anticipate the effect of future permanent differences as a reason for not providing for an expected reversal of timing differences. However, even if this is true as a general rule, it is specifically contradicted in relation to group relief by SSAP 15, which states that, 'where a company is a member of a group, it should, in accounting for deferred tax, take account of any group relief which, on reasonable evidence, is expected to be available and any charge which will be made for such relief'.[77]

The standard does not explain the reasoning behind this ruling. However, it could be justified on the view that the profitable company *is* in fact providing for deferred tax, but at the rate at which it will pay for the group relief rather than at the tax rate in force. Where the group relief rate has been set at 0%, therefore, the amount of the provision will properly be calculated as being nil.

This has no overall effect on the amount of deferred tax provided by the group as a whole, because the position of the group has to be looked at as a separate exercise in any event (see 4.5.1 to 4.5.3 above).

4.6 Revaluations of fixed assets

SSAP 15 discusses the revaluation of fixed assets in relation to the tax consequences which would arise if they were disposed of at their revalued amounts. However, it contains no discussion of the effects of revaluation on the calculation of deferred tax relating to timing differences between the amounts of depreciation charged in the accounts and of capital allowances in the tax computation. Furthermore, the standard does not contain a clear statement of the concept on which it is based, from which it might be possible to infer what the treatment should be. Indeed, a large part of the problem is that the conceptual reasons for including revaluations in historical cost accounts are themselves elusive. The rules on this issue are therefore obscure; the two main possibilities are described below.

For the purposes of this discussion, it is assumed that the assets in question are depreciated and attract capital allowances, so that they will be written off over a period for both accounting and tax purposes.

The first way of looking at the revaluation of a depreciable asset is that it creates a further timing difference, because in effect it is an adjustment of depreciation, which is itself an element of a timing difference. Where, for example, an asset is purchased for £10,000, subsequently depreciated to £6,000 and then revalued to £9,000, the £3,000 revaluation surplus could be regarded as reinstating the depreciation which was previously charged, and therefore reversing the deferred tax effect of charging that depreciation. On this basis, the £9,000 would be compared with the tax written down value of the asset in order to determine the amount of the timing difference which gives a potential liability to deferred tax. This is the view taken by the Accountants Digest on SSAP 15.[78]

The alternative viewpoint sees the revaluation as giving rise to a permanent difference. This is on the basis that the revaluation, and its subsequent reversal through depreciation, has no equivalent within the tax computation and hence does not give rise to a timing difference. The revaluation is not a reversal of previous depreciation, which properly reflected the consumption of part of the asset based on its then carrying value; it simply means that the remaining part of the asset has a different value and its consumption will be measured at a different amount. The future depreciation charge will have two components; the original charge based on cost, and the further amount based on the revaluation surplus. That further amount has no tax equivalent and it would be wrong to make any tax adjustment in respect of it.

We believe that both of these arguments are coherent, and in the absence of more definitive guidance from the standard itself, we consider that they are both acceptable, so long as the approach taken is consistently applied.

Where the revaluation takes the value of the asset above its original cost, it takes the matter out of the realm of accelerated capital allowances and into that of chargeable gains. As mentioned above, SSAP 15 does deal with this issue and says that a timing difference will be created 'insofar as the profit or loss that would result from realisation at the revalued amount is taxable, unless disposal of the revalued asset and of any subsequent replacement assets would not result in a tax liability, after taking account of any expected rollover relief'.[79] Provision for this should then be considered if it is intended to dispose of the asset, unless the tax effect would be mitigated by the effects of other originating timing differences.

The reference to rollover relief in the passage quoted above adds a further element of confusion to an already confused topic. Since the effect of rollover relief is to postpone the crystallisation of a tax liability rather than to cancel it altogether, it is difficult to see whether its availability has a bearing on whether or not a timing difference has been created, although it does of course have a bearing on whether provision has to be made in respect of it. No change to a company's tax exposure is made by rolling a gain on to a replacement asset rather than keeping the old asset, and it is therefore hard to see why this should be thought to reduce any timing difference considered to have arisen as a result of the revaluation.

Rollover relief is not only relevant in the context of revalued assets. Where an asset has been sold at a profit, and tax has been deferred by the operation of rollover relief, a latent tax liability will exist quite independently of whether or not the old asset had been revalued, and arguably this should be disclosed as a potential liability. The Appendix to SSAP 15 mentions this, but in an unsatisfactory way; it says: 'Where rollover relief has been obtained on the sale of an asset, with the "base cost" of the replacement asset for tax purposes thereby being reduced, and the potential tax liability has not been disclosed, the standard requires disclosure of the fact that the revaluation does not constitute a timing difference and that tax has therefore not been quantified, as it will not otherwise be evident from the accounts.'[80] However, this mixes up two unrelated matters; as mentioned above, the tax exposure can arise without any revaluation ever having occurred, and we recommend that it should be disclosed as a potential liability.

4.7 Disclosure

SSAP 15 requires disclosure of the following:

(a) The amount of deferred tax charged or credited in the profit and loss account for the period, split between that relating to ordinary activities and that relating to any extraordinary items.[81]

There is also a requirement within FRS 3 to disclose the amount of taxation (i.e. not just deferred taxation) attributable to extraordinary items, as well as that relating to certain exceptional items.[82]

(b) The amount of any unprovided deferred tax in respect of the period, analysed into its major components.[83] The following extract shows this disclosure:

Extract 24.12: John Lewis Partnership plc (2001)

6 Tax on Profit on Ordinary Activities

	2001	2000
	£m	£m
Corporation tax based on the profit for the year	**23.1**	33.5
Corporation tax – previous years	**0.4**	0.3
Deferred tax	**0.4**	(0.4)
	23.9	33.4

The tax charge is based on a corporation tax rate of 30% (30%) and has been reduced by £4.9m (£7.3m) as a result of capital allowances in excess of depreciation.

Total taxation deferred and unprovided in respect of all capital allowances in excess of depreciation amounts to £103.1m (£98.2m) based on corporation tax at 30% (30%).

No provision has been made in these accounts for the liability to taxation of £47.7m (£41.8m) on capital gains, which would arise if properties were to be sold at the amounts at which they were revalued and included in these accounts.

The wording of the requirement in the standard presupposes that the effect to be disclosed is of new originating differences for which no provision is made. However, sometimes companies have to disclose the opposite effect – that the tax charge for the year has been increased by unanticipated reversals.

(c) Any adjustments to deferred tax passing through the profit and loss account which relate to changes in tax rates or in tax allowances. The effect of any fundamental change in the tax system should be separately disclosed within the tax charge on the face of the profit and loss account.[84] Before FRS 3 was issued, the effect of such a change was treated as an extraordinary item if it was sufficiently material,[85] but this is no longer possible.

(d) The deferred tax balance, analysed into its major components, and the amount of unprovided deferred tax, similarly analysed.[86] Where no information on unprovided deferred tax in respect of a revalued asset is given on the grounds that it is argued not to be a timing difference (because it will never crystallise), the fact that the potential liability has not been quantified should be stated.[87] Brunel Holdings' accounts contain the following example of this analysis:

Extract 24.13: Brunel Holdings plc (2000)

20. Provisions for liabilities and charges [extract]

Deferred tax	Provided		Unprovided	
	2000	1999	**2000**	1999
	£000	£000	**£000**	£000
Capital allowances in excess of depreciation	**142**	471	**(6)**	(18)
Other timing differences	**108**	97	**(221)**	(388)
Losses available for offset	**(93)**	(366)	**(6,030)**	(4,345)
Pension prepayment	**–**	–	**6,526**	6,439
	157	202	269	1,688

No deferred tax liability is expected to arise in the foreseeable future on realisation of revalued properties held as fixed assets, and accordingly this is not provided or quantified.

Another example of a company not quantifying the tax deferred by roll-over relief is Laporte (see Extract 24.15 below).

Rather than analysing the *unprovided* amount as required by the standard, many companies continue to follow the requirement of the original SSAP 15 (before it was amended in 1985) to show the full potential liability and the amount which has been provided, analysed by category.[88] Of course, this information allows the reader to derive the analysis of the unprovided amount, by a simple process of subtraction. An example of this form of disclosure is to be found in the accounts of The Davis Service Group:

Extract 24.14: The Davis Service Group Plc (2000)

21 Provisions for liabilities and charges

	Group 2000 £000	Group 1999 £000	**Company 2000 £000**	Company 1999 £000
(a) The provisions for liabilities and charges comprise deferred taxation which is attributable to:				
Excess of tax allowances over depreciation	**9,246**	7,118	**–**	–
Other timing differences	**100**	53	**5**	5
	9,346	7,171	**5**	5
The movement during the year in the provision for deferred tax was:				
Beginning of the year	**7,171**	5,224	**5**	4
Acquisition of subsidiaries	**–**	51	**–**	–
Currency translation differences	**3**	(40)	**–**	–
Movement in respect of current and prior years	**2,172**	1,936	**–**	1
End of year	**9,346**	7,171	**5**	5
(b) The full potential amount of deferred taxation on all timing differences, including amounts provided, is as follows:				
Excess of tax allowances over depreciation	**14,310**	10,838	**(37)**	(37)
Other timing differences	**(803)**	(1,223)	**5**	5
Attributable to trading activities	**13,507**	9,615	**(32)**	(32)
Corporation tax on capital gains arising on the disposal of properties that have been deferred under the roll-over provisions	**1,368**	1,368	**–**	–
Taxes that would arise if properties were to be disposed of at their revalued amounts	**342**	532	**–**	–

It is arguable that the analysis of the full potential liability in fact gives much more meaningful information than can be obtained by analysing the amount which has been provided or the amount which has not been provided. Since SSAP 15 specifies that all categories of timing difference are to be considered in aggregate rather than individually for the purposes of deciding the overall net reversal which is to be provided for, it often makes little sense to try to say which particular category has been included in the provision and which has not.

(e) Transfers to and from the deferred tax balance.[89]

An example of this disclosure was given in the 1999 accounts of Laporte:

Extract 24.15: Laporte plc (1999)

19 Provisions for liabilities and charges [extract]

	Deferred tax (see below) £m
Balance at start of year	**44.4**
Profit and loss account	
Before exceptional items	**3.1**
Exceptional items – Charge	**–**
– Release	**(3.8)**
Acquisition of subsidiary undertakings	
Fair value adjustments	**–**
Disposal of subsidiary undertakings	**–**
Utilised in year	**–**
Currency translation differences	**(2.6)**
Balance at end of year	**41.1**

	1999 £m	1998 £m
Deferred tax is represented by		
Excess of book values of fixed assets over those for taxation purposes	**29.7**	35.9
Other timing differences	**11.4**	8.5
	41.1	44.4

Deferred tax

Deferred taxation is provided in full with the exception of any further tax which would be payable on the remittance of the retained profits of overseas companies where there is currently no intention to remit to the UK. Current tax is provided, if appropriate, when it is known that profits will be remitted to the UK. Deferred taxation has not been quantified on roll-over relief claims on the basis that they are not expected to arise in the foreseeable future.

(f) Movements in reserves which relate to deferred tax.[90]

(g) Where the value of an asset is disclosed by way of note and differs from its book value, the tax effect of disposing of it at that value.[91]

(h) Any assumptions regarding the availability of group relief and the payment therefor which are relevant to an understanding of the company's deferred tax position.[92]

(i) The fact (if applicable) that provision has not been made for tax which would become payable if retained earnings of foreign subsidiaries were remitted to the UK.[93]

EMI includes the following footnote in its accounts to explain this point:

> *Extract 24.16: EMI Group plc (2000)*
>
> **22. DEFERRED TAXATION** [extract]
>
> No provision has been made for further taxes which could arise if subsidiary or associated undertakings are disposed of or if overseas companies were to remit dividends to the UK in excess of those anticipated in these accounts: it is considered impracticable to estimate the amount of such taxes.

Cable & Wireless similarly makes no provision, but quantifies the unprovided amount:

> *Extract 24.17: Cable and Wireless plc (2000)*
>
> **21(i) Deferred taxation** [extract]
>
> The potential deferred tax liability does not include an amount of £891m (1999 – £862m) of contingent tax liability arising on the reserves of overseas subsidiaries, associates and joint ventures which the Group does not expect to remit to the United Kingdom.

Companies sometimes disclose positively that they make provision for this liability where appropriate, an example being Laporte (see Extract 4.15 above). FRS 2 requires further disclosures with respect to deferred tax on retained overseas earnings (see 4.5.4 A above).

5 DEFERRED TAX – FRS 19

FRS 19 was published by the ASB in December 2000 and is mandatory for accounting periods ending or after 23 January 2002, although earlier adoption is encouraged. FRS 19 has two stated objectives.

The first, drawing heavily on the language of the ASB's *Statement of Principles*, is to ensure that 'future tax consequences of past transactions and events are recognised as assets or liabilities in the financial statements'.[94] This objective is quite different from the historical purpose of deferred tax accounting, which was to match items of income and expenditure with their tax consequences. The second objective, based on a disclosure requirement in the Companies Act 1985 (see 6.1 below), is to ensure that 'the financial statements disclose any other special circumstances that may have an effect on future tax charges'.[95]

FRS 19 applies to all financial statements intended to give a true and fair view, except those prepared by small entities applying the *Financial Reporting Standard for Smaller Entities* (FRSSE).[96] However, it covers only taxes calculated on the basis of taxable profits, including withholding taxes paid on behalf of the reporting entity. Thus it does not cover taxes that are not assessed directly on profits for an accounting period, such as value added tax and petroleum revenue tax.[97]

Because FRS 19 (like all FRSs) applies in both the United Kingdom and the Republic of Ireland, it contains a number of detailed provisions of more relevance to the Irish tax system. These are not dealt with in this chapter.

5.1 Overall approach of FRS 19

5.1.1 *Definition of 'deferred tax'*

FRS 19 defines deferred tax as:

'Estimated future tax consequences of transactions and events recognised in the financial statements of the current and previous periods'.[98]

This represents a change of emphasis from SSAP 15, which defines deferred tax as the tax relating to timing differences (see 4.2 above). The approach in FRS 19 is to define all future tax consequences of past events as 'deferred tax', but then to restrict the provision for deferred tax to certain classes of timing difference, as set out in 5.2 and following below.

Indeed, the definition of deferred tax encompasses some permanent differences. For example, a purchase of a non-deductible asset is a past transaction recognised in the financial statements that will have 'future tax consequences', i.e. a higher effective tax rate, as the asset is depreciated. This appears to be confirmed by paragraph 7 of FRS 19, which requires deferred tax to be recognised only in respect of 'timing differences' (subject to various clarifications and exceptions discussed in 5.2 and following below) and not to be recognised in respect of 'permanent differences'.

5.1.2 *Definitions of 'timing differences' and 'permanent differences'*

'Timing differences' are defined as:

'Differences between an entity's taxable profits and its results as stated in the financial statements that arise from the inclusion of gains and losses in tax assessments in periods different from those in which they are recognised in financial statements. Timing differences originate in one period and are capable of reversal in one or more subsequent periods'.[99]

'Permanent differences' are defined as:

'Differences between an entity's taxable profits and its results as stated in the financial statements that arise because certain types of income and expenditure are non-taxable or disallowable, or because certain tax charges or allowances have no corresponding amount in the financial statements'.[100]

FRS 19 gives the following (non-exhaustive) examples of timing differences:[101]

- tax deductions for the cost of a fixed asset (including deductions for expenditure on infrastructure assets capitalised and depreciated using renewals accounting[102]) are accelerated or decelerated, i.e. received before or after the cost of the fixed asset is recognised in the profit and loss account;
- pension liabilities are accrued in the financial statements but are allowed for tax purposes only when paid or contributed at a later date;
- interest charges or development costs are capitalised on the balance sheet but are treated as revenue expenditure and allowed as incurred for tax purposes;[103]
- intragroup profits in stock, unrealised at group level, are reversed on consolidation;

- an asset is revalued in the financial statements but the revaluation gain becomes taxable only if and when the asset is sold;
- a tax loss is not relieved against past or present taxable profits but can be carried forward to reduce future taxable profits; and
- the unremitted earnings of subsidiary and associated undertakings and joint ventures are recognised in the group results but will be subject to further taxation only if and when remitted to the parent undertaking.

Some of these examples represent a slight change of emphasis from SSAP 15. For example, under FRS 19 all revaluations are designated as 'timing differences', although, as explained in 5.3 below, in most cases no deferred tax is recognised in respect of them. Under SSAP 15, revaluations are (rather dubiously, from a conceptual point of view) regarded as timing differences only to the extent that any tax payable on disposal of the revalued asset could not be mitigated by rollover relief (see 4.2 above). However, the accounting effect may be much the same under both standards (i.e. no provision for deferred tax).

5.1.3 *Application of the overall approach*

As noted in 5.1.1 above, the general rule in FRS 19 is that deferred tax should be recognised on timing differences but not on permanent differences.

FRS 19 notes that this general rule is not meant to disturb the long-standing practice among lessors of allocating profits on a post-tax basis and determining the tax charge by applying the effective tax rate to the post-tax profit.[104] There is a similar comment in FRS 16, which refers to lessors and life insurers (see 3.3 above). It is not clear why life insurers are not specifically mentioned in FRS 19, given that for them deferred tax may well be much more material than current tax.

This general rule is subject to a number of important exceptions and clarifications, which FRS 19 explains as following from the ASB's approach to deferred tax accounting, described in Appendix V to the FRS as the 'incremental liability approach'.[105] This approach is discussed in A below, and specifically affects:

- capital allowances (see 5.2 below);
- revaluations of non-monetary assets (see 5.3 below);
- unremitted earnings of subsidiaries, associates and joint ventures (see 5.4 below);
- deferred tax assets (see 5.5 below); and
- fair value adjustments in acquisition accounting (see 5.6 below).

We also briefly discuss the deferred tax treatment of:

- adjustments to align accounting policies in merger accounting (see 5.7 below); and
- defined benefit pension schemes (see 5.8 below),

neither of which is specifically addressed in FRS 19.

One consequence of this approach is that it is difficult for a company to summarise its accounting policy for deferred tax in one concise sentence, as was possible under SSAP 15. Specifically, it is not possible to assert that 'provision is made for all timing differences'. This has led companies that have implemented FRS 19 to give quite detailed summaries of their accounting policy for tax, an example being Kingston Communications.

Extract 24.18: Kingston Communications (HULL) PLC (2001)

1. Accounting Policies [extract]
Taxation

The charge for taxation is based on the profit for the year and takes into account taxation deferred because of timing differences between the treatment of certain items for taxation and accounting purposes.

FRS 19 'Deferred Taxation' was issued on 7 December 2000 and is mandatory for years ending on or after 23 January 2002. The Group has decided to adopt FRS 19 early.

Deferred tax is recognised in respect of all timing differences that have originated but not reversed at the balance sheet date where transactions or events that result in an obligation to pay more, or a right to pay less, tax in the future have occurred at the balance sheet date, with the following exceptions:

> provision is made for gains on disposal of fixed assets that have been rolled over into replacement assets only where, at the balance sheet date, there is a commitment to dispose of the replacement assets

> provision is made for the tax that would arise on remittance of the retained earnings of overseas subsidiaries only to the extent that, at the balance sheet date, dividends have been accrued as receivable

> deferred tax assets are recognised only to the extent that the Directors consider that it is more likely than not that there will be suitable taxable profits from which the future reversal of the underlying timing differences can be deducted

Deferred tax is measured on a non-discounted basis at the tax rates that are expected to apply in the periods in which timing differences reverse, based on tax rates and laws enacted or substantively enacted at the balance sheet date.

A *The 'incremental liability' approach*

In the ASB's view, some timing differences give rise to an asset or liability as defined in its *Statement of Principles* (i.e. a right to receive tax relief, or obligation to pay tax, in the future) and some do not. FRS 19 aims to distinguish between timing differences on this basis, by requiring that deferred tax should be recognised only in respect of those timing differences that give rise to an asset or liability at the balance sheet date.

For example, it is argued that, if a company recognises a debtor for accrued interest that will be taxed on receipt, it cannot avoid the obligation to pay tax on that interest when it is received and a deferred tax liability should therefore be recognised. By contrast, if a company revalues an asset, it has discretion over whether or not to sell the asset in such a way as to crystallise the tax liability on the gain; deferred tax should therefore not be recognised until the point at which the company no longer has such discretion (i.e. where it has entered into a binding agreement to sell the asset). Similarly, there is no liability in respect of the tax that would arise on the remittance of the retained earnings of investments so long as the investing company or group is able to avoid remittance of those earnings.[106]

Unfortunately, in our view, the 'incremental liability' approach does not bear much scrutiny, so that, from a purely practical standpoint, it may be easier to treat FRS 19 as a series of more or less discrete rules than to seek to identify a common principle at work.

The ASB's choice of a timing difference arising from accrued interest receivable to illustrate its approach is actually very selective,[107] since there are instances of deferred tax assets and liabilities, for which FRS 19 requires provision, but which cannot be rationalised in this way. Suppose for example that an item is taxed on receipt but credited for accounting purposes over one or more future periods. FRS 19 would require a deferred tax asset to be set up for the tax paid, even though it cannot be recovered from the tax authorities.

In our view, cases such as this demonstrate that deferred tax does not truly constitute an asset or liability as defined in the ASB's *Statement of Principles* and that the real rationale for it is the matching concept. In other words, since recognition of the income has been deferred, recognition of the tax paid on it should be deferred also.

With regard to the treatment of deferred tax on revaluation gains, the argument for not recognising deferred tax is essentially that the reporting entity has no plan or obligation to realise the gain through sale of the asset. In our view, however, this is an equally compelling argument for not recognising the gain in the first place, or at least for not regarding it as forming part of the reporting entity's overall financial performance, as is required by FRS 3 – *Reporting Financial Performance*, and even more explicitly in the comprehensive income statement proposed in FRED 22 – *Revision of FRS 3 Reporting Financial Performance* (see Chapter 2 at 6.1.2)

Although FRS 19 is based on this 'incremental liability' approach, Appendix V to the FRS notes that a minority of the ASB favour the 'valuation adjustment' method (see 1.3.3 B above).[108]

5.2 Capital allowances

5.2.1 *General*

Deferred tax should be recognised in full on capital allowances for an asset received before or after the cost of the asset is recognised in the profit and loss account. However, 'if and when all conditions for retaining the allowances have been met', the deferred tax should be released.[109] To understand how this rule is to applied in certain specific situations, it is necessary to understand the ASB's rationale for the need to provide for deferred tax on accelerated allowances.

This is set out in Appendix V to FRS 19. The argument is that, where a company receives capital allowances for an asset, it does so on condition that the service potential of the asset is consumed in the business. The company therefore has a potential obligation to refund the allowances received until the corresponding amount of the service potential of the asset has been consumed. For example, if an asset on which accelerated capital allowances (ACAs) have been received is sold at book value, there arises (through a balancing charge or adjustment to the asset pool) a liability equivalent to the ACAs. This consumption of service potential is demonstrated for financial reporting purposes by depreciation (including a write-down for impairment) or disposal of the asset.[110]

Illustrations of the some of the practical effects of FRS 19 on timing differences arising from capital allowances can be found in Examples 24.12 and 24.13 in discussion of the treatment of revaluations and gains on disposal of non-monetary assets at 5.3.2 below.

5.2.2 *Non-depreciated and partially depreciated assets*

FRS 19 requires deferred tax to be recognised in full on all capital allowances received for an asset that is not being depreciated.[111] This represents a change from a current practice under SSAP 15 of crediting such allowances to income as they are received, on the argument that, since the asset is not being depreciated, the tax relief represents a permanent difference.

Where a non-depreciated asset is eligible for an industrial buildings allowance (IBA), any such deferred tax may be released 25 years after the purchase of the asset, since there is no obligation under the tax legislation to refund any IBAs received on a sale of the asset after that time (i.e. 'all conditions for retaining the allowances have been met').[112] Where, however, a non-depreciated asset attracts capital allowances with no time limit on their potential clawback, deferred tax must be provided until the asset is subject to a write-down for impairment (see below). This may mean that some deferred tax provisions are more or less permanent.

Where an asset is not *currently* being depreciated but has 'otherwise been written down to a carrying value less than cost', the normal rule applies (i.e. deferred tax is recognised only to the extent that allowances have been received in excess of the amount written down). This will be the case where an asset has been depreciated to a residual value in excess of zero, or has been subject to an impairment write-down under FRS 11 – *Impairment of Fixed Assets and Goodwill*, but not depreciated further.

5.2.3 *Infrastructure assets*

During the exposure period of FRED 19, some commentators raised concerns on the position of companies (such as water and other utility companies) with a network of infrastructure assets accounted for under the renewals accounting method permitted by FRS 15 – *Tangible Fixed Assets* (see Chapter 12 at 2.3.3). Under this method, fixed assets are not explicitly depreciated. Instead the actual cost of annual repairs is capitalised, while the profit and loss account for the year is charged with an estimate of the average annual expenditure required to maintain the network. The resulting provision is deducted from the carrying amount of fixed assets as if it were depreciation.

The concern was that, if such assets were regarded as 'not depreciated' for the purposes of FRS 19, companies would never, under the rules set out above, be able to take credit for the tax relief received for their capitalised repairs expenditure. It is arguable that FRS 15 had already made clear the ASB's view that such assets are being depreciated, as it describes the annual charge as 'a method of estimating depreciation'.[113] Nevertheless, FRS 19 clarifies, albeit in a rather roundabout way, that such assets are in fact being depreciated.[114] This means such that deferred tax is to be recognised on allowances received for such assets only to the extent that the cumulative capital allowances exceed, or fall short of, cumulative renewals charges to the profit and loss account.[115]

5.3 Non-monetary assets – revaluations and gains on disposal

FRS 19 distinguishes two main classes of asset under this heading:

- assets continuously revalued to fair value with changes in fair value recognised in the profit and loss account; and
- other non-monetary assets.

However, the 'small print' of the part of the standard dealing with revaluations of 'other non-monetary assets' shows that those requirements are also relevant to fair value adjustments to non-monetary assets in acquisition accounting, which are discussed separately at 5.6 below.

5.3.1 *Assets continuously revalued to fair value through the profit and loss account*

FRS 19 requires deferred tax to be recognised in full on any timing differences created by revaluation of non-monetary assets where the valuation adjustments are recognised in the profit and loss account.[116] Typically, these will be shares and securities held by financial institutions.

These rules refer to assets that are 'continuously' revalued through the profit and loss account. They therefore do not apply to an asset subject to a 'one-off' valuation adjustment through the profit and loss account (e.g. a write-down for impairment under FRS 11, or provision for permanent diminution in value under the Companies Act 1985).

The treatment of deferred tax on assets continuously revalued to fair value is quite different from that of deferred tax on other revaluations (see 5.3.2 below), which is essentially that no deferred tax should be recognised unless the reporting entity is committed to realise the gain through sale. Appendix V to the FRS argues that gains and losses taken to the profit and loss account, although not necessarily realised, are readily realisable. It is therefore necessary, in order to show a true and fair view, to recognise the tax consequences of such gains and losses.[117]

This is not, in our view, a particularly convincing argument. The critical point seems to be the ease with which the revaluation gain could be realised. It is therefore not clear why this was not explicitly used as the criterion for determining whether deferred tax should be recognised, rather than (in effect) deeming all valuation adjustments in the profit and loss account to be readily realisable and all those in the statement of total recognised gains and losses (STRGL) as not. The fact is that a gain on a portfolio of quoted shares can be realised as easily by a manufacturer that revalues them through the STRGL as by a stockbroker that revalues them through the profit and loss account.

A further inconsistency is introduced by the fact that FRS 17 – *Retirement Benefits* apparently envisages that full provision should be made for deferred tax on timing differences relating to defined benefit pension schemes, even though a significant portion of such differences arise from marking the underlying pension fund investments to market through the STRGL rather than the profit and loss account. This is discussed further at 5.8 below.

There is some ambiguity as to whether FRS 19 requires provision for deferred tax simply on the gross timing difference, or whether it is possible to take account of any potential rollover or holdover relief. On the one hand, the recognition rules in FRS 19 deal with such reliefs only in the context of 'Other non-monetary assets' (see 5.3.2 below). On the other, the rules for discounting (see 5.10.3 D below) provide that, in discounting deferred tax on continuously revalued assets, account can be taken of 'any available reliefs'. It would seem inconsistent to take account of such reliefs in calculating a discounted, but not an undiscounted, provision.

Fortunately, as FRS 19 itself acknowledges, these difficulties may not create significant practical issues, since most companies that account for investments on a 'mark to market' basis are also taxed on that basis, such that there is only current tax on any revaluation gains and losses accounted for in the profit and loss account.[118]

5.3.2 *Other non-monetary assets*

Where a non-monetary asset is revalued other than through the profit and account, deferred tax should not be recognised on the resulting timing difference unless, by the balance sheet date, the reporting entity has:

(a) entered into a binding agreement to sell the revalued assets; and

(b) recognised the gains and losses expected to arise on sale.[119]

The more significant condition is (a). Condition (b) is simply saying that, where an asset has been revalued to an amount less than the agreed sale price, deferred tax should be recognised only on the gain that has already been recognised in the financial statements.

Deferred tax should also not be recognised on a gain arising on revaluation or sale if, on the basis of all available evidence, it is more likely than not that the taxable gain will be eligible for rollover relief, being charged to tax only if and when the assets into which the gain has been rolled over are sold, or deemed to have been sold for tax purposes.[120] Any deferred tax not recognised, either because there is no commitment to sale at the balance sheet date or because rollover relief is anticipated, must be disclosed (see 5.11.3 below).

There are undoubtedly some problems with FRS 19's rules for the deferred tax consequences of revaluations, which are explored in the discussion in A to F below. However, it is thankfully doubtful whether they will create much practical difficulty in the longer term, given that the great majority of companies have ceased to revalue assets on adopting FRS 15 – *Tangible Fixed Assets*.

A *What is a 'revaluation' under FRS 19?*

The accounting treatment for deferred tax on a 'revaluation' is quite different from that on most other timing differences. In broad terms, the norm is that no provision is made for deferred tax on revaluations, but that full provision is made on most other timing differences. Given the importance of this distinction, it is regrettable that FRS 19 does not define or clarify what exactly it means by a 'revaluation'.

In our view, the standard needs to be interpreted using the common accounting usage of 'revaluation' – i.e. a change in the carrying value of an asset representing a value movement, which is accounted for in the STRGL. This seems to be what was in the mind of the drafters of FRS 19 because the rules are couched in terms of taxable gains arising on a sale.

By contrast the following are *not*, in our view, 'revaluations':

- a write-down in the carrying value of a fixed asset to reflect impairment of the asset;
- a write-down to net realisable value of the carrying value of stock and work in progress; or
- any subsequent reversal of such write-downs,

all of which are typically accounted for in the profit and loss account.

If our interpretation is correct, FRS 19 appears to have slightly different implications for those fixed assets that are eligible for capital allowances and those that are not (including the revalued element of any revalued asset, only the cost of which is tax-deductible), particularly where the interaction with FRS 11 – *Impairment of Fixed Assets and Goodwill* – is considered, as illustrated by Examples 24.12 and 24.13 below.

Example 24.12: Fixed assets not eligible for capital allowances

A company buys a property for £1 million that is not eligible for capital allowances. Any depreciation or impairment write-down under FRS 11 will create a permanent difference, which has no deferred tax consequences under FRS 19. The latent deferred tax asset (arising from the fact that the property's tax base cost is higher than its carrying amount) would be recognised, subject to its recoverability (see 5.5 below), only when the company entered into a binding agreement to sell the property.

Likewise any subsequent reversal of an impairment write-down is a permanent difference with no deferred tax consequences, except where it arises in the context of a binding agreement to sell the property.

If the company revalues the property upwards or downwards, a timing difference is created under FRS 19, but, in accordance with the rules above, a deferred tax asset or liability is not recognised until the company enters into a binding contract to sell the asset.

Example 24.13: Fixed assets eligible for capital allowances

A company buys a factory for £1 million that is eligible for industrial buildings allowances of 4% per year and is depreciated over 40 years. The company pays tax at 30%. A timing difference arises from the accelerated industrial buildings allowances, which should be recognised in accordance with the rules for such timing differences discussed in 5.3 above. On this basis, 4 years after the asset was bought, its carrying value would be £900,000, giving rise to a deferred tax liability of £18,000 calculated as:

	£000
Cumulative IBAs (4 x £40,000)	160
Cumulative depreciation (4 x £25,000)	(100)
Timing difference	60
Deferred tax at 30%	18

By the end of Year 5, the market for the product manufactured in the factory has collapsed. In accordance with FRS 11, the company records an impairment write-down to reduce the property to its recoverable amount of £600,000. In our view, such an impairment write down is simply accelerated depreciation, giving rise to a deferred tax asset of £60,000, calculated as:

	£000
Cumulative IBAs (5 x £40,000)	200
Cumulative depreciation	(400)
Timing difference	(200)
Deferred tax at 30%	(60)

The new carrying value of £600,000 would then be depreciated over its remaining useful life of 35 years, giving rise to a deprecation charge of £17,143 per year. At the end of Year 10, the property would therefore be carried at £514,285.

At this point, it is revalued to £800,000, as a result of a change in the expected use of the property. In accordance with FRS 11, £235,715 of the uplift is taken to the profit and loss account and £50,000 to the statement of total recognised gains and losses (STRGL). This is because FRS 11 restricts the reversal of the impairment in the profit and loss account to the amount that raises the carrying amount of the asset up to the amount that it would have been had the original impairment at the end of Year 5 not occurred (i.e. £750,000, being 30/40 of the original cost of £1 million). In our view, since the £235,715 accounted for in the profit and loss account represents an adjustment to depreciation, it creates a timing difference, giving rise to a deferred tax liability of £45,000 calculated as:

	£000
Cumulative IBAs (10 x £40,000)	400
Cumulative depreciation*	(250)
Timing difference	150
Deferred tax at 30%	45

* Difference between original cost £1 million and carrying amount £800,000, less £50,000 revaluation gain accounted for in the STRGL.

From this point onwards the common short-cut method of calculating accelerated capital allowances (i.e. net book value less tax written down value) would not generate the correct deferred tax liability because the net book value would include the £50,000 gain credited to the STRGL. Deferred tax would be recognised on the £50,000 credited to the STRGL only if and when the company entered into a binding agreement to dispose of the property for its carrying amount.

B Limited relevance in the UK?

FRS 19 may have the effect that deferred tax is hardly ever recognised on revaluations of property in the UK, since property sales in the UK are generally taxed on exchange of 'unconditional' contracts. It is hard to see much distinction between an 'unconditional' contract and the 'binding' sale agreement demanded by FRS 19. In other words, at the point at which FRS 19 requires recognition of tax on a revaluation gain, such tax will generally in fact either be current tax, or deferred tax not recognised by virtue of the anticipated availability of rollover relief.

C Significance of conditions at the balance sheet date

A slightly confusing feature of the recognition provisions is the relevance of the balance sheet date. The basic principle seems to be that post-balance sheet events and management plans *must not* be taken into account in determining recognition (i.e. whether a deferred tax liability exists at the balance sheet date), but *must* be taken into account in determining measurement (i.e. whether any such liability is eligible for rollover relief).

The requirement for there to be a binding sale agreement by the balance sheet date before deferred tax can be recognised represents a significant change to current practice under SSAP 15, which is essentially that deferred tax should be recognised on revaluation gains to the extent that it is probable that it will crystallise, after taking account of rollover relief (see 4.6 above). Thus it has been possible, when a company decides to seek a buyer for a surplus property, for it to revalue the property to expected selling price,[121] and also to provide for any tax payable on a sale at that price. Any such provision will have to be released on implementation of FRS 19, except in cases where a binding sale agreement has been reached.

The requirement for there to be a binding sale agreement by the balance sheet date is inconsistent with FRS 3 – *Reporting Financial Performance*, which states that 'a binding contract entered into after the balance sheet date may provide additional evidence of … commitments at the balance sheet date'. However, there is a precedent for this inconsistency in FRS 12 – *Provisions, Contingent Liabilities and Contingent Assets*, which states that 'no obligation arises for the sale of an operation until the entity is committed to the sale, ie there is a binding agreement'. This inconsistency is discussed further in Chapter 28 at 5.1.2.

We have a concern that FRS 19's requirement for there to be a binding sale agreement before a deferred tax liability can be recognised could lead to a distortion of reported liabilities, as the following simple example shows.

Example 24.14: Recognition of deferred tax on revaluation gains

A UK group has a year end of 31 December. On 1 October 2001 an overseas subsidiary identifies a property as surplus to requirements and begins to seek a buyer. On 15 November an offer of £4 million is accepted. If the property is sold at that amount, tax of £500,000 will be paid by the subsidiary on completion of the sale.

The property is revalued to £4 million in the financial statements for the year ended 31 December 2001. If unconditional contracts for the sale of the property are exchanged on 31 December, the tax would be recognised (as deferred tax) in the accounts for the year ended 31 December 2001. If, however, contracts are exchanged on 1 January 2002, the tax would be recognised (as current tax) for the year ended 31 December 2002.

It seems rather counter-intuitive that the reporting group in Example 24.14 should, in effect, be able to choose whether or not to provide for deferred tax on the revaluation gain in the 2001 accounts. Although FRS 19 purports to focus on whether or not the company has an obligation at the balance sheet date, in reality the company may have almost complete discretion over the exact timing of the exchange of contracts and, therefore, the creation of the obligation.

There is also the broader issue that, when these rules are put side by side with those for assets revalued through the profit and loss account and for capital allowances on fixed assets (discussed at 5.2 above), some strange inconsistencies emerge, as the following example illustrates.

Example 24.15: Interaction of FRS 19 rules for fixed assets and revaluations

Assume that the overseas subsidiary of the UK group in Example 24.14 above actually exchanges contracts for the sale of the surplus property on 15 January 2002, with completion on the same day. At 31 December 2001 a UK subsidiary of the group holds a portfolio of shares that it revalues through the profit and loss account and a building for which industrial buildings allowances (IBAs) have been claimed, but which has not been depreciated on the grounds that any such depreciation would be immaterial. The subsidiary has no plans to realise its whole portfolio of shares, and any obligation to refund the IBAs will expire on 1 March 2002.

The financial statements for the year ended 31 December 2001 are approved on 1 April 2002.

FRS 19 requires provision to be made for deferred tax[122] on the revaluation of the shares (which is unlikely to crystallise) and on the accelerated IBAs (which it is known by the time the financial statements are approved will never crystallise), but prohibits provision for deferred tax on the revaluation of the sold property (which has crystallised by the time the accounts are approved). Many will see this as requiring recognition of a totally unreal liability, while at the same time preventing recognition of a real one.

There is a further apparent inconsistency between the rules for recognition of deferred tax on revaluations and those for recognition of capital losses (see 5.5 below).

D Rollover relief

In measuring the liability, account must be taken of rollover relief that is 'more likely than not' to be available.[123] It is not therefore necessary to demonstrate that rollover relief is virtually certain to be available. The ASB takes the view that deferred tax subject to potential reduction by rollover relief is a contingent liability, which, in accordance with the principles of FRS 12 – *Provisions, Contingent Assets and Contingent Liabilities*, should be recognised only when it is more likely than not to crystallise (see Chapter 28 at 3.2).[124]

In assessing whether rollover relief is more likely than not to be available, FRS 19 requires the reporting entity to have regard to all available evidence, including that provided by events occurring after the balance sheet date. Whilst FRS 19 does not elaborate on this, it presumably means that, by the time that the accounts are approved, management must have in place investment plans sufficient for an informed assessment to be made. The standard contains a reminder that the qualifying investment must occur within three years of sale of the original asset.[125]

FRS 19 notes that the evidence supporting the availability of rollover relief may change with time, such that it may be necessary to recognise, derecognise or remeasure a deferred tax liability. If such an adjustment is required, it represents a change in estimate and accordingly is recognised in the results for the period in which circumstances change.[126]

E Holdover relief

Where a taxable gain that meets the recognition criteria of FRS 19 qualifies for holdover relief rather than rollover relief, deferred tax should normally be recognised on the basis that the tax is merely deferred for a finite period. If, however, there is the possibility of converting holdover relief into rollover relief by investment in qualifying assets, an assessment should be made of whether rollover relief is more likely than not to be available using the rules discussed above. FRS 19 states that 'it may be more difficult to arrive at the conclusion that it is more likely than not that the gain will be rolled over'.[127]

This comment is made in the context that the period for converting holdover relief into rollover relief is ten years. Presumably the ASB's view is that companies will not normally be able to predict asset purchases with sufficient certainty much beyond the three year period relevant for rollover relief (see D above).

F Indexation allowance

Rather curiously, there is no explicit mention of indexation allowances in FRS 19. The accounting issue here is whether an estimate can be made of future allowance or whether credit can be taken only for the allowance that has accrued at the balance sheet date.

The argument against taking account of a future indexation allowance would be that it is contingent on a future event (i.e. an increase in the retail price index) outside the reporting entity's control, unlike rollover relief, which is contingent on future asset purchases, which are within its control. The counter-argument would be that all past experience suggests that it is certain that the retail price index will increase. Therefore so long as the reporting entity is able to defer realisation of a gain for as long as it may take for the indexation allowance to reach a particular level, there is no reason not to take account of indexation allowances in the same way as rollover relief and holdover relief.

This is of limited importance in the context of deferred tax on revaluations, since the requirement for there to be a binding sale agreement by the balance sheet date means that such gains will typically crystallise so soon after the balance sheet date that the effect of any additional indexation allowance will be immaterial. However, it may raise more significant issues in other areas, such as transactions where accounting income is taxed as capital and the reporting entity has discretion over when to realise that income in a manner that will give rise to a tax liability.

In our view, the better analysis is that no account should be taken of any mitigating effect of indexation on a deferred tax liability until the indexation has actually accrued. As noted above, tax indexation is contingent on a future event (inflation) that, although likely to occur, is totally outside the reporting entity's control. Moreover, it would, in our view, be completely inconsistent for an entity to recognise a gain giving rise to a deferred tax liability in the profit and loss account (implying that the gain is readily realisable), but then to argue that no deferred tax should be provided on the grounds that realisation of the gain will be delayed by as long as is necessary to extinguish it through indexation allowance.

5.4 Unremitted earnings of subsidiaries, associates and joint ventures

No provision should be made for the potential tax liability arising on remittance of the retained earnings of subsidiaries, associates and joint ventures except to the extent that, at the balance sheet date:

- dividends have been accrued as receivable; or
- a binding agreement to distribute the past earnings in future has been entered into by the subsidiary, associate or joint venture.

Any provision should be stated after taking account of double tax relief.[128]

In something of an understatement, FRS 19 notes that there will rarely be a binding agreement of the type referred to above, such that in practice the rule will be that distribution taxes are recognised once the dividend is accrued as receivable in the accounts of the relevant parent company.[129]

FRS 19 does not apparently require the dividend to be accrued in both the paying and receiving company, but in the receiving company only. This is presumably intended to deal with the fact that in some overseas jurisdictions (and under IAS) dividends declared after the balance sheet date may not be recognised as liabilities, although under UK GAAP it is normal to accrue a final dividend for a particular period in the accounts for that period, whenever it is declared (see Chapter 17 at 2.2.10, 4.4.1 and 5.5.1).

The threshold for provision for the tax consequences of distributions is set somewhat higher in FRS 19 than in SSAP 15 which requires provision if there is 'an intention or obligation to remit them' (see 4.2 above). SSAP 15 therefore allows companies to provide for tax on retained earnings once it decides to remit them, which, in a group with ongoing tax planning strategies may be some time before the dividend is actually declared and remitted. SSAP 15 would also require (or, at least, allow) provision for a 'commercial' obligation to remit retained earnings (e.g. where, in a recession, it is clear that next year's profit will be insufficient to sustain a dividend, requiring a drawdown of retained reserves).

In neither case would FRS 19 allow a provision, unless the dividend has been accrued in the receiving company. It is not clear that this is a change for the better, as it seems to make the accounting for such tax dependent more on a book entry (and, moreover, in group accounts, a book entry that may not appear as it has been eliminated on consolidation) than on the underlying economic reality. It also seems rather inconsistent with the rationale given in Appendix V of FRS 19 for the rules for recognition of deferred tax on revaluations that the mere act of revaluation does not give rise to a tax liability.

In a more subtle change from SSAP 15, FRS 19 refers to all retained earnings, whereas SSAP 15 referred to earnings retained overseas. This change has probably been made for consistency with IAS 12 but is, in any event, more correct in principle. We do not foresee it as having any real practical impact. Unlike IAS 12 (see 7.2.8 below), FRS 19 does not refer specifically to the treatment of the retained reserves of branches. In our view, however, the rules applicable to subsidiaries, associates and joint ventures should also be applied to branches.

5.5 Deferred tax assets (including losses)

5.5.1 *General*

FRS 19 requires deferred tax assets (including those arising from tax losses) to be recognised to the extent that they are regarded as recoverable. They are regarded as recoverable to the extent that, on the basis of all available evidence, it can be regarded as more likely than not that there will be 'suitable taxable profits' from which the future reversal of the underlying timing differences can be deducted.[130]

'Suitable taxable profits' are defined as those that are:

(a) generated in the same taxable entity (or in an entity whose profits would be available via group relief) and assessed by the same taxation authority as the income or expenditure giving rise to the deferred tax asset;

(b) generated in the same period as that in which the deferred tax asset is expected to reverse, or in a period to which a tax loss arising from the reversal of the deferred tax asset may be carried back or forward; and

(c) of a type (such as capital or trading) from which the taxation authority allows the reversal of the timing difference to be deducted.[131]

FRS 19 allows any assessment of the likelihood of there being suitable taxable profits to take account of tax planning opportunities, such as:

- accelerating taxable amounts or deferring claims for writing down allowances to recover losses being carried forward (perhaps before they expire);
- changing the character of taxable or deductible amounts from trading gains or losses to capital gains or losses or vice versa; or
- switching from tax-free to taxable investments.[132]

It also clarifies that a deferred tax liability recognised under FRS 19 can be presumed to give rise to a future taxable profit. However, it will be necessary to apply the criteria in (a) to (c) above to determine whether it is a 'suitable taxable profit'.[133]

In more simple terms, these rules are effectively saying that a deferred tax asset can *always* be recognised (assuming that the criteria in (a) to (c) above are satisfied) if it can be offset against:

- a deferred tax liability recognised in the accounts; or
- a current tax liability of the current or a previous period.

However, to the extent that a deferred tax asset can be recovered only out of future taxable profits (i.e. other than those represented by a recognised deferred tax liability), an assessment of the likelihood of its recovery must be made (see 5.5.2 below).

FRS 19 states that where any tax loss is not expected to be recovered for some time, its recovery is likely to be relatively uncertain, and it may therefore not be appropriate to recognise the deferred tax asset at all.[134] This is a slightly dangerous generalisation, as there may well be entities, such as single project companies, where the recovery of deferred tax assets in 20 or 30 years' time is (barring changes in tax legislation) almost certain. However, the clear underlying message is that the onus is on the reporting entity to justify the recognition as assets of losses the recovery of which is not expected within a fairly short period, perhaps the next two or three years.

The evidence supporting the recoverability of deferred tax assets may change with time, such that it may be necessary to recognise, derecognise or remeasure an asset. If such an adjustment is required, it represents a change in estimate and is accordingly recognised in the results for the period in which circumstances change.[135]

5.5.2 *Deferred tax assets recoverable out of future taxable profits other than deferred tax liabilities*

FRS 19 provides some guidance for making an assessment of the recoverability of such assets. Its overall effect is to impose restrictions of the recognition of such assets considerably more stringent than the basic rule for recognition of deferred tax assets (i.e. that they should be 'more likely than not' to be recoverable) would imply.

The reason for this is that the 'more likely than not' test is based on IAS 12, which in turn derives from the US standard SFAS 109.[136] In the United States, for which these words were first drafted, losses can be carried forward for a finite period only – a critical factor in assessing whether or not a deferred tax asset is 'more likely than not' to be recovered.

In the UK, however, losses can generally be carried forward indefinitely, so that the hurdle for their recognition as assets under SSAP 15 is set very high – their recovery must be 'assured beyond reasonable doubt' (see 4.4.2 B above). In our view, the ASB was clearly concerned that simply to introduce the more neutral test of IAS 12 into the UK tax environment would allow the argument that all UK tax losses should be recognised as assets, on the grounds that, as they can be carried forward indefinitely, any company that is a going concern and expected to be profitable in future must eventually recover them.

We therefore see the detailed guidance on this issue in FRS 19 as an attempt to steer a requirement that is on the face of it consistent with IAS 12 back towards something closer to the current position in SSAP 15. However, Appendix V to FRS 19 makes it clear that the ASB is not simply trying to maintain the *status quo*. In particular, it makes the valid point that there is no particular reason to set a higher recognition threshold for a tax loss than for any other deferred tax asset that can be recovered only out of future taxable profits.[137]

FRS 19 suggests that all evidence as to the existence of future 'suitable taxable profits' must be considered, but that the most objective evidence is likely to be that provided by historical financial performance, unless this is unavailable or of limited relevance because of recent or forthcoming changes in circumstances. In particular, the existence of unrelieved tax losses at the balance sheet date is normally strong evidence that there will not be future 'suitable taxable profits', unless there is 'persuasive and reliable evidence' to the contrary.[138]

This is reinforced by a requirement for companies with a record of losses that have nevertheless recognised deferred tax assets recoverable only out of future profits to disclose why they have done so (see 5.11 below).

A Trading losses

In the case of trading losses, such 'persuasive and reliable evidence' may exist if the loss resulted from an identifiable and non-recurring cause and the reporting entity has otherwise been consistently profitable over a long period, with any past losses being more than offset by income in later periods.[139] It is noteworthy that these words are almost exactly the same as those dealing with losses in the Appendix to SSAP 15 (see 4.4.2 B above). This suggests to us that, in the ASB's mind, there may be no significant difference between the requirement of SSAP 15 that the recovery of losses should be 'assured beyond reasonable doubt' and the semantically less strict requirement of FRS 19 for 'persuasive and reliable evidence'.

B Capital losses

In the case of a capital loss that can be relieved only against future capital gains, 'persuasive and reliable evidence' of its recovery will normally exist only where:

(a) a potential chargeable gain not expected to be covered by rollover relief is present in assets but has not been recognised as a deferred tax liability;

(b) plans are in place for the sale of these assets; and

(c) the carried-forward loss will be offset against the resulting chargeable gain for tax purposes.[140]

These criteria are rather counter-intuitive for a number of reasons. First, they allow recognition of a capital loss as an asset without any account being taken of the taxable gain on which its recovery depends, as the following example illustrates.

Example 24.16: Capital losses

As in Example 24.14 at 5.3.2 C above, a UK group has a year end of 31 December. On 1 October 2001 it identifies a property as surplus to requirements and begins to seek a buyer. On 15 November an offer of £4 million is accepted. On 15 January 2002 contracts are exchanged for the sale, which gives rise to tax of £500,000.

Earlier in 2001, the group had sold another property, giving rise to a tax loss worth £300,000.

FRS 19 permits ABC to take credit for the £300,000 in 2001, but prohibits any recognition of the £500,000 tax liability out of which it will be recovered until 2002 (since there was no binding sale agreement in place on 31 December 2001).

The logic appears to be similar to that for measuring deferred tax on revaluation gains, discussed in 5.3.2 B above. In other words, assets and liabilities can be *recognised* by reference only to conditions at the balance sheet date but, once recognised, can be *measured* by reference to subsequent events.

Also, the criteria above do not require the assets, the sale of which will yield the tax liability against which the capital loss will be recovered, actually to have been sold, or even that a buyer is being sought. It is sufficient that there are merely 'plans in place' to sell them, which seems little different to permitting a company to recognise a trading tax loss if it has 'plans in place' to make a profit! Perhaps this provision is intended to be symmetrical with the rules for rollover relief discussed under 5.3.2 D above, which allow future reinvestment plans to be taken into account in measuring a deferred tax liability.

5.5.3 *Surplus ACT and double tax relief*

Surplus advance corporation tax (ACT) eligible for recovery under the 'shadow ACT' regime is not dealt with in FRS 19 as it is covered by FRS 16 (see 3.5 above). There is no specific provision in either FRS 16 or FRS 19 for the treatment of any double tax relief (or similar overseas relief) that is recoverable other than through offset against the current year's tax charge. In our view, however, the general principles for recognition of tax assets in FRS 19 should be applied.

5.6 Acquisition accounting

FRS 19 amends the previously rather ambiguous requirements of FRS 7 – *Fair Values in Acquisition Accounting* with regard to deferred tax in a fair value exercise in two main areas:

- fair value adjustments; and
- tax assets recognised as the result of the acquisition.

These are discussed in turn at 5.6.1 and 5.6.2 below.

A further issue, discussed at 5.6.3 below, is the need to restate the deferred tax liability of any acquired entity onto a basis consistent with FRS 19.

5.6.1 *Fair value adjustments*

As amended, FRS 7 states that deferred tax should be recognised on fair value adjustments in accordance with FRS 19.[141] Taken on its own, this would imply that deferred tax should not be recognised on fair value adjustments, which are permanent differences, as they do not enter into the determination of group income. Even where the fair value adjustments are 'pushed down' into the accounts of the acquired entity (such that they are reported in the profit and loss account or STRGL of that entity) they do not enter into the group profit and loss account or STRGL.

However, the explanation section of FRS 7, as amended, states that deferred tax should be recognised on fair value adjustments 'as if they were timing differences in the [acquired] entity's own accounts'.[142] That this is the real intention of FRS 19 is further reinforced by the summary of FRS 19 given in Appendix IV to the standard, where it is contrasted with IAS 12.[143] Appendix IV, however, expresses the treatment required by FRS 19 in a slightly different way, saying that fair value adjustments should be treated 'as if [they] had been gains or losses recognised before the acquisition'.

Somewhat unhelpfully, FRS 7 as amended and FRS 19 each give an example of a fair value adjustment where deferred tax should *not* be recognised – upward adjustments to fixed assets and stock – but no example of when provision would be appropriate which, as the following discussion shows, is not always clear.

A Fixed assets

The explanation section of FRS 7 as amended gives the example of a building revalued to fair value on an acquisition. If the acquired entity were to reflect this value in its own financial statements, it would do so as a revaluation, which would therefore fall within the rules for revaluation of a non-monetary assets (see 5.3.2 above). Therefore no deferred tax would be recognised by the acquired entity until it was committed to dispose of the building. Since no deferred tax would have been recognised by the acquired entity, no deferred tax is recognised in the fair value exercise.[144] A curious effect of this is that an acquirer will often simply 'inherit' the acquired entity's deferred tax balance, the relevance of which to the acquirer is not immediately clear, particularly as it may have been inherited by the acquired entity from one its own previous acquisitions. Example 24.17 below illustrates this point.

Example 24.17: Deferred tax on non-deductible fixed assets acquired as part of a larger acquisition

ABC Group acquires XYZ Ltd. In the books of XYZ, plant and machinery is carried at £60 million, and has a tax written down value of £40 million, giving rise to a timing difference of £20 million, on which deferred tax of £6 million was recognised. A fair value of £70 million is attributed to the plant and machinery. No deferred tax is recognised on the fair value adjustment, in accordance with the provisions of FRS 19 outlined above.

Under FRS 7, XYZ's £6 million deferred tax balance is a liability of the acquired entity, which will go forward into the group balance sheet of ABC, subject to any fair value adjustments. However, from the point of view of ABC, it has acquired some fixed assets with (so far as its own group accounts are concerned) no past history of either depreciation or capital allowances.

If ABC had bought assets for £70 million attracting tax relief of only £40 million as a discrete transaction, it would have recorded no deferred tax on acquisition. It would start to arise only as the asset began to be depreciated and capital allowances to be received. This begs the question of why a different accounting treatment should apply to the purchase of the same asset in the context of a larger acquisition.

As noted in 5.1.3 A above, some board members would have supported the 'valuation adjustment' method, which would take the view that a provision for deferred tax is necessary to reflect the fact that an asset costing £70 million with tax deductions of only £40 million available must be worth less than one that is fully tax-deductible. On this view, however, deferred tax would be recognised by reference to ABC's cost of £70 million (as is done under IAS 12 and SFAS 109), rather than XYZ's net book value which is totally irrelevant to this issue.

Similarly, no deferred tax would be recognised on a fair value adjustment that is made to reflect a reassessment of asset lives or residual values. This is because the acquired entity could reflect such an adjustment in its own accounts only as a revaluation (since FRS 15 requires changes in asset lives and residual values to be dealt with prospectively in the profit and loss account – see Chapter 12 at 2.3.4).

A downward revaluation of a fixed asset in the fair value exercise that represents an impairment required to be recognised under FRS 11 would have to be reflected in the acquired entity's own financial statements if these were prepared under UK GAAP. Whether or not such a write-down would give rise to a timing difference at the entity level will depend on whether or not the impaired asset is eligible for capital allowances (see Examples 24.12 and 24.13 at 5.3.2 above). If the adjustment would give rise to a timing difference, deferred tax should be recognised on the fair value adjustment; if it would not, it should not. It would appear that this is the approach that has been adopted by Scottish Power (see Extract 24.19 at 5.6.3 below).

Fair value adjustments to fixed assets reflecting differences between the accounting policies of the acquirer and the acquiree will often give rise to deferred tax on consolidation. For example, it might be that the acquiring entity's accounting policy was to capitalise interest directly attributable to the construction of fixed assets, but the acquired entity's policy was to expense it as incurred. The acquirer will usually make an accounting policy adjustment in the fair value exercise so as to reflect this difference.

If the acquired entity had accounted for this itself, it would have done so as a change of accounting policy at the date of acquisition. It would therefore have recognised a deferred tax liability on the cumulative timing difference between depreciation on the element of the property represented by capitalised interest and tax relief for the interest. Accordingly, deferred tax would be recognised on the fair value adjustment.

A further quirk of FRS 7 as amended by FRS 19 is that it appears to require no provision for deferred tax on fixed assets where an acquisition is structured as a purchase of a business, rather than of a company, even though the underlying economics may be much the same. Suppose that in Example 24.17 above ABC Group had purchased the trade and net assets, excluding any tax liabilities, of XYZ Ltd, and that the sale and purchase agreement had attributed a sale price to the fixed assets at £40m (their tax written down value). For accounting purposes, ABC would ignore the legal purchase price and record the assets at fair value of £70 million as before, but would generally be able to claim capital allowances only on the legal purchase price of £40 million.[145] However, as XYZ's tax liabilities are not transferred to ABC, they are not reflected in the fair value exercise.

One could argue that this different accounting treatment correctly reflects the underlying economics, in that where ABC purchases the shares of XYZ it inherits XYZ's tax history (and therefore the potential obligation to refund capital allowances already claimed). By contrast, in a net asset purchase ABC starts with a 'clean slate'. On the other hand it could be said that, given the remote possibility of allowances on working assets already claimed by XYZ having to be repaid, the accounting focuses on an unreal difference rather than the real similarity, which is that in both cases ABC is buying assets worth £70 million that attract capital allowances of only £40 million. It therefore seems rather surprising that the accounting is different in each case.

There are some transfers of assets (for example certain intra-group transfers) where the acquiring company does inherit the selling company's tax 'history' with respect to the assets transferred, and therefore the potential obligation to refund accelerated capital allowances received. In such cases, we believe that, in accordance with the principle underlying the general rules for capital allowances discussed in 5.2 above. FRS 19 requires the acquiring company to set up a deferred tax provision in respect of accelerated allowances already claimed on the assets by the seller.

B Stock

FRS 19 refers to a fair value adjustment of stock on an acquisition as an example of a revaluation. Accordingly, no provision should be made for deferred tax unless there is a binding sale agreement for the stock. FRS 19 states that the fact that stock is, as a matter of fact, manufactured solely for the purpose of resale does not mean that the acquired entity has a binding agreement to sell it. Indeed, it goes on to say that, even if there is in fact a binding contract for the sale, perhaps because the stock has been made to a specific order, such a contract is an executory contract, which would not normally be recognised until performance (i.e. despatch or delivery of the goods to the customer). The practical effect of this is that deferred tax will not be recognised on upward fair value adjustments to stock reflecting their market value.[146]

In our view, this aspect of FRS 19 is flawed, since upward fair value adjustments to stock, although classified as 'revaluations' in a fair value table prepared under

FRS 7, are not truly analogous to revaluations in an ongoing entity. Such 'true' revaluation gains and losses enter into the determination of comprehensive income; fair value adjustments do not, although the goodwill generated by them will do if capitalised and amortised. The effect of not providing for deferred tax is illustrated by Example 24.18.

Example 24.18: Deferred tax on fair value adjustments to stock

ABC Group acquires XYZ Ltd. In the books of XYZ stock is carried at £5 million, but a fair value of £6 million is assigned to it. When the stock is sold for (say) £8 million, the group accounts will show a gross profit of £2 million, but XYZ will pay tax on the profit as stated in its own books (i.e. £3 million) – i.e., assuming a tax rate of 30%, £900,000.

If deferred tax were recognised on the fair value adjustment of £1 million, a provision of £300,000 would be set up on acquisition and released when the stock was sold. If no deferred tax were set up, the post-acquisition group profit and loss account would be charged with the full £900,000 tax paid by the subsidiary. This may be summarised as follows:

	Deferred tax £000	No deferred tax (FRS 19) £000
Gross profit	2,000	2,000
Current tax	900	900
Deferred tax	(300)	–
Total tax	600	900
Profit after tax	1,400	1,100
Effective tax rate	30%	45%

Even allowing for the fact that Example 24.18 does not quite give the complete picture, because it ignores the differing amounts of (non-deductible) goodwill that would be amortised in either case, it is hard to accept the result required by FRS 19. The argument for making provision is quite simply one of consistency. In the real world XYZ, while a subsidiary of the ABC group, makes and is taxed on a profit of £3 million. Under the conventions of acquisition accounting, however, the group accounts represent that £1 million of that profit was in fact paid for by ABC at the time of acquisition and is therefore not regarded as part of the group profit and loss account for the post-acquisition period. If part of the real taxable profit of XYZ is to be excluded from the group accounts, a corresponding part of the real tax should be similarly excluded.

As in the case of fixed assets, we do not consider that the effect of FRS 19 is to preclude provision for deferred tax on all fair value adjustments to stock. For example, stock might be written up in an adjustment to align accounting policies (e.g. where the acquirer has a policy of including certain types of overhead in stock and the acquiree does not). If the acquiree had reflected this adjustment as change of policy in its own books at the date of acquisition (i.e. as a prior year adjustment), a timing difference would arise, which would therefore be recognised as deferred tax in the fair value exercise in the consolidated accounts.

Again, to use a possibly more realistic example, the acquiring entity might take a more conservative view of the net realisable value of the acquiree's stock than the acquiree did itself, and make the requisite write down as a fair value adjustment. If the acquiree reflected this adjustment in its own books at the date of acquisition, it would (in the UK) normally attract tax relief in the current year's tax computation. It would therefore be appropriate to recognise deferred tax on the fair value adjustment in the consolidated accounts.

C Other assets and liabilities

As noted above, there are no examples in either FRS 7 and FRS 19 of fair value adjustments on which deferred tax must be provided. The following is a brief discussion of our views as to the application of FRS 7 to other common types of fair value adjustment.

I Debtors

The carrying value of trade debtors is commonly adjusted to reflect the acquired entity's accounting policy for bad and doubtful debts. If this adjustment were made by the acquired entity, it would be charged or credited to its profit and loss account (as a change in measurement), giving rise to a timing difference and deferred tax in that entity's financial statements. Accordingly, deferred tax should be recognised on the fair value adjustment on consolidation.

II Liabilities

FRS 7 requires liabilities to be stated at fair value. Whilst the book and fair value of liabilities will often be the same, adjustments are sometimes required. These adjustments may be either in the nature of changes of estimate or in the nature of a revaluation.

In the case of an adjustment reflecting a change of estimate (e.g. a revision of a provision to reflect the acquirer's accounting policy for such items), it will typically be the case that, if such an adjustment were reflected in the financial statements of the acquired subsidiary, it would give rise to a timing difference on which deferred tax would be provided under FRS 19. Accordingly, deferred tax should be recognised on the fair value adjustment on consolidation.

In the case of an adjustment reflecting a revaluation of a liability (e.g. to reflect the fact that the acquired entity has borrowings at a fixed interest rate that is significantly different to the market rate at the time of acquisition) the position is far less clear, since FRS 19 does not address the revaluation of liabilities directly. This may well be because, under current UK GAAP, it is not generally possible to revalue liabilities other than in the context of acquisition accounting. This in itself could support an argument that, since the fair value adjustment could not be reflected in the financial statements of the acquired subsidiary, no timing difference, and therefore no deferred tax, could possibly arise at the entity level, and should not therefore be recognised on consolidation. Moreover, even if it is accepted for the sake of argument that such an adjustment could be made in the acquired entity's books, it would give rise to a permanent difference, since it represents an adjustment to the principal of the liability, which is not normally tax-deductible.

A possible argument for providing for deferred tax is that the amount of the fair value adjustment represents the amount that the acquired entity would have been obliged to pay, or entitled to receive, if it had terminated its existing borrowings early and taken out new borrowings on 'on-market' terms. Such a payment or receipt would normally be subject to tax in the UK, suggesting that deferred tax should be provided. However, this seems contrary to the general rule in FRS 19, with respect to revalued *assets*, that deferred tax should not be provided for the tax that would arise on realisation of any gain until the entity is committed to realisation.

We therefore consider that deferred tax should generally not be provided for on fair value adjustments to liabilities in the nature of revaluations.

III Contingent assets and liabilities

A contingent liability that crystallises as a result of an acquisition (e.g. a remuneration payment that becomes due on a change of ownership of the company), will be recognised both in the acquired entity's financial statements and as a fair value adjustment on consolidation. To the extent that such liabilities will attract tax relief when settled, they represent timing differences at the entity level, and accordingly deferred tax should be recognised on the fair value adjustment.

It may be the case that contingent assets that could not be recognised in the financial statements of the acquired entity under FRS 12 are recognised as fair value adjustments under FRS 7 (see Chapter 6 at 2.4.3 C). As discussed under II above, this could support an argument that, since the fair value adjustment could not be reflected in the financial statements of the acquired subsidiary, no timing difference, and therefore no deferred tax, could possibly arise at the entity level, and should not therefore be recognised on consolidation.

However, the adjustment to the carrying value of a liability such as that referred to in II above is essentially a difference between the basis of *valuation* of an item in the accounts of the acquired entity and those of the group. In the case of a contingent asset recognised in the fair value exercise, however, the issue is one of there being a different basis of *recognition* of an asset as between the accounts of the underlying entity and those of the group. We therefore think that this situation is more analogous to the recognition in a fair value exercise of a surplus or deficit on a defined benefit pension scheme, on which (as discussed in IV below) we believe that deferred tax should be recognised.

IV Defined benefit pension schemes

A fair adjustment may be made to recognise a defined benefit pension scheme asset or liability not previously recognised in the accounts of the acquired entity. Again, the requirements of FRS 19 are not beyond doubt. It could be argued that, as the acquired entity could not recognise such an asset or liability in its own financial statements under current UK GAAP (since SSAP 24 requires actuarial surpluses or deficits to be amortised over the remaining service lives of employees in almost all circumstances), a timing difference could not therefore arise in those accounts, such that deferred tax should not be recognised on consolidation. On the other hand, if the acquired entity were not a UK company that had had previously provided for pensions on a 'pay as you go' basis under local GAAP, it could be conversely argued that the catch-up adjustment *could* be reflected in the acquired subsidiary's financial statements as a prior year adjustment, under the transitional arrangements for initial implementation of SSAP 24 as set out in that standard.

We very much doubt, however, that the ASB anticipated such a 'legalistic' reading of FRS 19 in this case, but intended that deferred tax should be recognised on fair value adjustments to pension assets and liabilities. Moreover, when FRS 17 is implemented, full provision will be required on a defined pension scheme asset or liability (see 5.8 below), so that any deferred tax not recognised on a pension surplus or deficit will be required to be recognised at that point anyway.

D Goodwill

Consolidation goodwill arising on an acquisition in the UK is not tax-deductible, and therefore has no current or deferred tax consequences. In some other jurisdictions, however, goodwill is tax-deductible. FRS 19 makes no specific provision in respect of goodwill, and therefore the general rules of the standard will apply. In our view, goodwill does not fall within the general rules for fair value adjustments discussed above, since goodwill is not itself a fair value adjustment, but rather a residual that arises as a result of fair value adjustments to other assets and liabilities.

Where goodwill has been capitalised, it will therefore be treated like any other fixed asset. In other words, if it is not tax-deductible, any amortisation will constitute a permanent difference.[147] Where it is tax-deductible, timing differences will arise if the cumulative amount amortised differs from cumulative tax allowances. Deferred tax should be recognised on such timing differences in accordance with the rules discussed in 5.2 above.

In the case of goodwill set off against reserves under SSAP 22, as continued by the transitional rules in FRS 10 ('SSAP 22 goodwill'), the position is perhaps less clear-cut. Prior to FRS 19, any tax relief for SSAP 22 goodwill has normally been credited to the profit and loss account as it arises, with no provision being made for deferred tax. This is because FRS 16 requires current tax to be accounted for in the profit and loss account unless it relates to an item accounted for in the STRGL (see 3.1 above), and FRS 3 states that a set-off of goodwill under SSAP 22 is not a loss and should therefore accounted for in the reconciliation of movements in shareholders' funds, but not in the STRGL.[148] Whether this treatment has been adopted because such tax relief is considered a permanent difference, or a timing difference that is unlikely to crystallise in the foreseeable future, is a matter of academic interest only, given that the end result is the same. Under FRS 19, however, this analysis is clearly important.

In our view, where tax relief is claimed for SSAP 22 goodwill, a timing difference is created because (in accordance with FRS 2 and FRS 10) the goodwill will be charged to the profit and loss account on any subsequent disposal (see Chapter 11 at 2.3.6). Under FRS 19, deferred tax should therefore be recognised on that timing difference in the same way as any other capital allowance – i.e. until all conditions for retaining it have been met (see 5.2 above). Thus, if such tax relief would be clawed back on disposal of the business concerned, we believe that it should all be treated as deferred tax rather than credited to income.

Some might maintain that the capital allowances provisions of FRS 19 do not apply because paragraph 9 of the FRS refers to 'allowances for the cost of a fixed asset', the argument being that SSAP 22 goodwill is not included within fixed assets in the balance sheet. However, we consider that SSAP 22 goodwill is a fixed asset, notwithstanding that it is set off against reserves rather than included within fixed assets. Moreover, many companies argue (correctly in our view) that SSAP 22 goodwill should be considered as an asset when applying the cover method of accounting for foreign currency net assets hedged by foreign currency borrowings as set out in SSAP 20 *Foreign Currency Translation* (see Chapter 8 at 3.5.4). We cannot see any credibility in the view that SSAP 22 goodwill is an asset for the purposes of SSAP 20, but not for those of FRS 19.

E Summary

In our view, FRS 19's approach to fair value adjustments is a recipe for confusion. The problem lies in its cumbersome approach of basing the group deferred tax provision on an imaginary accounting entry in the books of the acquired entity. This leaves too much to chance, as it raises the question, as the discussion under C above shows, of whether or not the acquired entity is to be envisaged as *strictly* complying with UK GAAP. Indeed, similar issues arise even in the context of revaluation adjustments to non-monetary assets, since an acquired entity that has not adopted an accounting policy of continuous revaluation under FRS 15 would not in fact be able to reflect any such revaluation in its own accounts.

Whilst it would be rash to claim to be able to extract any hard-and-fast rules from the requirements of FRS 19, we believe that deferred tax should be provided on fair value adjustments that represent differences in the recognition or measurement of assets or liabilities as between the accounts of the acquired entity and those of the group, but not on those adjustments that represent differences in the valuation basis of the items concerned.

5.6.2 Tax assets

FRS 19 also amends FRS 7 to clarify the accounting treatment for previously unrecognised tax assets (typically tax losses) of the acquirer or acquiree that become recoverable as the result of an acquisition. Assets of the acquirer should be accounted for as a credit to the post-acquisition tax charge. Those of the acquiree should be recognised in the fair value exercise, as they are regarded as contingent assets that have crystallised as a result of the acquisition. FRS 7 could be construed as requiring this already, but as amended it is much clearer.[149]

There is no specific guidance on the converse situation where, as the result of an acquisition, a previously recognised tax asset of the acquirer or acquiree becomes irrecoverable. In our view, the general principles of FRS 7 suggest that, in either case, the adjustment should normally form part of the post-acquisition tax charge, since it results from the actions or plans of the acquiring entity.

There is also no detailed specific guidance, comparable to that in IAS (see 7.2.7 below), for the treatment of a tax asset of an acquired entity existing at the time of acquisition, but not recognised until after the acquisition. However, the general principles of FRS 7 suggest that, if such an asset were recognised during the hindsight period for measurement of goodwill (i.e. the period ending on the date of the second set of financial statements issued after the acquisition), it would be treated as an adjustment to goodwill, if the recognition simply clarified the true state of affairs of the acquired entity at acquisition. If, however, it could be demonstrated that the asset had become recoverable as a result of the actions or plans of the acquirer, it would be credited to the post-acquisition tax charge, as would any tax asset recognised after the end of the hindsight period.

A ACT

ACT does not fall within the scope of FRS 19, and FRS 16 makes no specific provision in respect of ACT in the context of acquisition accounting. In our view, however, we believe that the general rules for deferred tax assets summarised above should also apply both to ACT of the acquiring or acquired entity that is recognised at the time of the acquisition, and to ACT of the acquired entity that is recognised subsequently.

5.6.3 *Initial implementation of FRS 19*

When FRS 19 is implemented for the first time, it is the treatment of acquisitions in previous periods, rather than those of the current period, that is likely to prove the real issue. There are no specific transitional provisions in FRS 19. This means that, in principle, every acquisition that the reporting entity has made must be reopened and accounted for as if FRS 19 had applied to it – there are no 'grandfathering' provisions for old acquisitions comparable to those that applied on implementation of the Companies Act 1989, or FRSs 6, 7 and 10. In practice, however, companies will need to balance the potentially significant cost of undertaking such an exercise against the likely materiality, and value to users, of the consequential adjustments.

The main areas to be considered will be:

- what the deferred tax of the acquiree would have been under FRS 19 at the date of acquisition (including the effect of the acquiree's own acquisitions);
- whether deferred tax would have been recognised on any fair value adjustments made;
- the tax treatment of any tax losses recognised as the result of an acquisition Given the lack of clarity in FRS 7 as currently drafted, it is possible that, contrary to FRS 19, either losses of an acquired entity were not recognised as fair value adjustments, or losses of the acquiring entity were recognised; and
- any consequential adjustments to goodwill. If there is a change to the deferred tax balance recognised on an acquisition, the goodwill (as the balancing figure) must also change. Where such goodwill is being capitalised and amortised in accordance with FRS 10, there will be an adjustment to the amortisation charge in prior periods.

An example of a company adjusting the fair value exercise for a previous acquisition on implementation of FRS 19 is Scottish Power.

Extract 24.19: Scottish Power PLC (2001)

30 Revision to provisional fair values of PacifiCorp

On 29 November 1999 the group acquired PacifiCorp for a total consideration of £4,111.3 million. As set out in the March 2000 Accounts the fair values of the assets and liabilities of PacifiCorp, established for the purposes of those Accounts, were provisional due to the size and complexity of the acquisition. In the year ended 31 March 2001 these fair values have been finalised as permitted by FRS 7. The details of the adjustments to the provisional fair values are set out below.

Fair value of PacifiCorp consideration	Provisional fair values as previously stated £m	Prior year adjustment (Note a) £m	Provisional fair values as restated £m	Revisions to provisional fair values attributable to businesses held for disposal £m	Revisions to other provisional fair values (Note b) £m	Final fair values £m
Tangible fixed assets	4,882.6	–	4,882.6	–	(222.6)	4,660.0
Investments	123.8	–	123.8	–	–	123.8
Businesses held for disposal	551.0	–	551.0	1.4	–	552.4
Current assets	1,030.3	–	1,030.3	–	(155.7)	874.6
Creditors: amounts falling due within one year						
– Loans and other borrowings	(199.1)	–	(199.1)	–	–	(199.1)
– Other creditors	(844.0)	92.6	(751.4)	–	(150.8)	(902.2)
Creditors: amounts falling due after more than one year						
– Loans and other borrowings	(2,366.5)	–	(2,366.5)	–	–	(2,366.5)
Provisions for liabilities and charges	(533.1)	(668.7)	(1,201.8)	–	113.7	(1,088.1)
Minority interest	(135.0)	–	(135.0)	–	–	(135.0)
Net assets	2,510.0	(576.1)	1,933.9	1.4	(415.4)	1,519.9
Goodwill arising on acquisition of PacifiCorp	1,601.3	576.1	2,177.4	(1.4)	415.4	2,591.4
Purchase consideration	4,111.3		4,111.3			4,111.3

(a) Prior year adjustment

The provisional fair values attributed to the net assets of PacifiCorp have been restated for the effects of the implementation of the group's new accounting policy for deferred tax in accordance with FRS 19 (see Note 6).

(b) Revisions to provisional fair values of PacifiCorp

Revisions have been made during the year ended 31March 2001 to the provisional fair values originally attributed to the net assets of PacifiCorp in the March 2000 Accounts. The principal revisions are:

(i) at the time of the PacifiCorp acquisition, various regulatory rates cases and depreciation studies were outstanding. All of these have now been concluded and tangible fixed assets have been written down by £222.6 million following the outcome.

(ii) US regulatory assets, included within debtors, have been reduced by £137.8 million following reassessment of their recoverability in the context of the US regulatory regime.

(iii) provision of £150.8 million has been made for liabilities for taxation, including related interest, arising out of US tax authorities' audits of PacifiCorp's pre-acquisition tax computations and other liabilities including legal costs.

(iv) the deferred tax effect of the above.

It will be noted in this case that the acquisition was still within the hindsight period for adjustment of fair values permitted by FRS 7 (see Chapter 6 at 2.4.2), so that the fair value exercise would have been reopened in any event in order to revise the fair values attributed to the net assets acquired.

As can be seen, Scottish Power made an adjustment to restate the fair value of the deferred tax provision in the previous year's provisional fair value exercise from a SSAP 15 basis to an FRS 19 basis, resulting in a substantial increase in the provision as would be expected when a capital-intensive company moves from a partial to a full provision for deferred tax. It has also provided for deferred tax on the additional fair value adjustments made in the period. Although the basis of the provision is not specifically stated, we infer that provision has been made in respect of (some of) the provision against fixed assets and the write-down of the regulatory assets, but (as would be expected) not in respect of the additional provision for disputed tax liabilities.[150]

5.7 Merger accounting – alignment of accounting policies

Where a business combination is accounted for as a merger, the assets and liabilities of the legally acquired entity are not recorded at fair value in the consolidated accounts. However, the carrying amount of assets and liabilities of one or both entities may be adjusted in order to align the accounting policies of both entities. The question arises as to whether deferred tax should be recognised on such accounting policy alignments.

FRS 19 is silent on this issue. It is our view, however, that deferred tax should be recognised on such items according to the principles for fair value adjustments, as discussed in 5.6 above. In other words deferred tax should be recognised on those policy alignments which, if recognised in the individual financial statements of the relevant combining entity, would have led to a provision for deferred tax in that entity.

5.8 Defined benefit pension scheme assets and liabilities

5.8.1 *Defined benefit pension schemes accounted for under FRS 17*

FRS 19 requires the deferred tax relating to an asset or liability for a defined benefit pension scheme accounted for in accordance with FRS 17 – *Retirement Benefits* – to be presented separately from other deferred tax (see 5.10.3 below). However, there is little further guidance, in either FRS 17 or FRS 19, as to how the deferred tax on defined benefit pensions should be calculated.

Appendix 1 to FRS 17 gives an example of the disclosures required by that standard, in which the deferred tax is calculated as 30% of the gross amount recognised in the balance sheet. This implies that deferred tax should be recognised in full on the timing difference represented by the gross amount. However, a material part of any net asset or liability arising on a funded defined benefit scheme accounted for under FRS 17 will in fact be the assets of the fund at market value. FRS 17 requires most movements in the market value of the fund to be accounted for in the STRGL.

It is clear from the rules discussed in 5.3 above that, if a company directly holds a portfolio of shares that it revalues annually through the STRGL, FRS 19 requires that, in the absence of any binding agreement to sell the portfolio, no deferred tax be recognised on the revaluation gains and losses. If, however, the same shares are held indirectly through the pension fund, and revalued annually through the STRGL, FRS 17 implies that deferred tax should be recognised in full. This seems inconsistent.

Perhaps the ASB has considered this and taken the view that, where a company has invested in a pension fund for the express purpose of meeting an existing liability it is *de facto* committed to realising the fund, such that deferred tax should be recognised under FRS 19. Another argument might be that the balance sheet presentation of the defined pension asset or liability under FRS 17 focuses on a net amount rather than explicitly recognising the underlying investments as such.

A further issue that FRS 17 has had to deal with is the allocation of the overall tax charge or credit relating to defined benefit pension schemes. This discussed further in Chapter 23 at 3.8.4.

5.8.2 *Defined benefit pension schemes accounted for under SSAP 24*

Where a defined pension benefit scheme is accounted for under SSAP 24, any asset or liability arising simply represents the cumulative difference between amounts recognised in the profit and loss account and contributions to the fund, rather than explicitly representing the assets and liabilities of the scheme, so that the conceptual issues raised by FRS 17 do not arise.

Where tax relief is given for such schemes accounted for under SSAP 24 on the basis of contributions paid, any asset or liability will represent a timing difference on which deferred tax should be recognised under the normal provisions of FRS 19. Since the full amount of any charge or credit under SSAP 24 is recognised in the profit and loss account, any deferred tax should also be recognised in full in the profit and loss account, under the general principles of FRS 16 and FRS 19 (see 3.1 above and 5.9.1 below).

5.9 Presentation and measurement of deferred tax

5.9.1 *Allocation of deferred tax between the profit and loss account and the STRGL*

FRS 19 requires all deferred tax to be recognised in the profit and loss account, except to the extent that it relates to an item that is or has been recognised in the STRGL, where the tax relating to such an item should also be recognised in the STRGL.[151] This is identical to the requirements in FRS 16 for current tax (see 3.1 above).

Any deferred tax relating to items that are recognised neither in the profit and loss account nor in the STRGL, but only in the reconciliation of movements in shareholders' funds, would be recognised in the profit and loss account rather than in the reconciliation of movements in shareholders' funds. Such items occur only rarely and any tax on them will more typically be current tax rather than deferred tax.

FRS 19 requires the STRGL to include deferred tax on an item that 'is or has been' recognised in the STRGL. In other words, where an item has been recognised in the STRGL of a previous period but deferred tax on it is recognised only in the current period, the tax should still be accounted for in the STRGL of the current period, even though this does not include the related pre-tax gain or loss. An example might be that in the current period a company enters into a binding agreement to sell a property which had been revalued to expected sale proceeds in a previous period.

FRS 19 notes that in exceptional circumstances it may be impossible to determine the tax relating to items in the STRGL, in which case the total tax should be allocated on either a 'reasonable pro-rata basis', or using 'another allocation that is more appropriate in the circumstances'.[152] In practice, it will probably be very rare that a provision for deferred tax will have to be allocated in this way, except in the context of accounting for defined benefit pension schemes under FRS 17, which is discussed in Chapter 23 at 3.8.4.

5.9.2 *Tax rates and laws used to measure deferred tax*

Mirroring FRS 16's requirements for current tax (see 3.4 above), FRS 19 requires deferred tax to be measured at the tax rates expected to apply in the periods in which the timing differences are expected to reverse, using the tax rates and laws that have been enacted or 'substantively enacted' by the balance sheet date.[153] A UK tax rate is to be taken as 'substantively enacted' if it is included in either:

- a Bill that has been passed by the House of Commons and is awaiting only passage through the House of Lords and Royal Assent; or
- a resolution having statutory effect that has been passed under the Provisional Collection of Taxes Act 1968.[154]

We have doubts as to the wisdom of this rule in a UK context for the reasons set out in 3.1.4 above. Consequent on these changes, SSAP 17 *Accounting for post balance sheet events* has been amended so that a change in tax rates after the balance sheet date is no longer listed as an adjusting event.[155]

Like FRS 16, FRS 19 gives no criteria for determining whether matters of tax law other than the tax rate (e.g. capital allowances, rollover relief, treatment of losses) have been enacted or substantively enacted. This seems to be a simple drafting slip, and we assume that these criteria are indeed intended to refer to all aspects of tax legislation.

Where the enacted or substantively enacted rates for future periods are graduated (i.e. different rates apply to different levels of taxable income), the reporting entity should provide for deferred tax at an average rate for those periods, rather than at the marginal rate that would apply if the reversing timing differences were the only taxable items in that period. The average rate is to be calculated by estimating the taxable profits, and thus the total tax payable, for those future periods.[156] However, FRS 19 also states that averaging should not be used where different types of profit (e.g. trading income and capital gains) are taxed at different rates, or where the reporting entity is taxed in different jurisdictions at different rates. In such cases the actual rate applicable to the type of profits concerned should be used.[157]

A Income and expenditure taxed at non-standard rates

For reasons that are not entirely clear, there is no provision in FRS 19 equivalent to that in FRS 16 requiring income and expenses taxed at non-standard rates to be included in the pre-tax results at the actual amounts receivable and payable and not grossed up to reflect the notional amount of additional tax that would have arisen if the transaction had been taxed, or allowed for tax, on a different basis (see 3.3 above). In our view, this principle should be applied whether the items concerned are subject to current or to deferred tax.

B Intra-group transactions eliminated on consolidation

There is no discussion in the main body of FRS 19 of the deferred tax treatment, in the consolidated financial statements, of profits and losses on intra-group transactions that have been eliminated on consolidation. However, Appendix IV to the standard, in comparing FRS 19 to IAS 12, states that IAS 12 requires deferred tax to be recognised using the buying company's tax rate, whereas FRS 19 requires the selling company's tax rate to be used.[158]

We are not convinced that this interpretation of FRS 19 is actually correct, as we do not see why FRS 19 would require the selling company's tax rate to be used. The basic requirement, as set out above, is to measure deferred tax at the tax rates '… in the periods in which the timing differences are expected to reverse'. On reversal (i.e. onward sale by the buying company to a third party) the timing differences will be taxed at the *buying* company's tax rate.

The treatment asserted by Appendix IV to be required by FRS 19 would be required under the deferral method of accounting for deferred tax (see 1.3.3 C above), but seems inconsistent with the liability method of FRS 19. Significantly, the full deferral approach is required by US GAAP, but only as an explicit exception from the normal liability method of SFAS 109.[159]

The effect of the two methods is illustrated by Example 24.19 below.

Example 24.19: Deferred tax on intra-group transactions eliminated on consolidation

PQR Limited, a company taxed at 30%, has a US subsidiary TUV, a company taxed at 34%. On 15 December 2001 TUV sells goods with cost of £100,000 to PQR for £120,000, giving rise to a taxable profit of £20,000 and tax of £6,800. On 31 January 2002, PQR sells the stock on to a third party for £150,000, giving rise to a taxable profit (at the entity level) of £30,000 and tax of £9,000. If PQR were preparing group accounts for the year ended 31 December 2001, the profit made by TUV on the sale to PQR would be eliminated.

Under US GAAP, the £6,800 tax paid by TUV would be deferred and recognised as an expense when the stock was finally sold on by PQR. Under this approach, the group accounts for the year ended 31 December 2002 would include a profit on sale of the stock of £50,000 (i.e. sale proceeds of £150,000 less original cost to the group £100,000) and tax of £15,800. This accounts for all the tax relating to the stock in 2002. The rationale for this approach is that as the profit on sale has, from a group perspective, been deferred, the tax should also be deferred.

Under IAS, a deferred tax asset would be recognised on the unrealised profit of £20,000, based not on TUV's tax rate, but on PQR's 30% tax rate, i.e. £6,000. The additional £800 tax actually paid by TUV would be recognised in the profit and loss account for the period ended 31 December 2001. The rationale for this approach is that, by transferring the stock from one tax jurisdiction to another with a lower tax rate, the group has denied itself tax deductions of £800 (i.e. £20,000 at the tax rate differential of 4%) for the cost of the stock, which should be recognised immediately.

The difference between the US GAAP and IAS treatment is equivalent to the different treatment, under the deferral and liability methods, of the situation where a timing difference reverses at a tax rate different from that at which it originated (see Example 24.3 at 1.3.2 D above). In the context of an intra-group transaction, we prefer the deferral approach of US GAAP. UK companies that wish to adopt it must be entitled to rely on the ASB's own view, set out in FRS 19, that this treatment is also required by FRS 19, even though, for the reasons set out above, we are not clear as to the basis for this interpretation.

5.9.3 *Balance sheet presentation of deferred tax*

Deferred tax relating to a defined benefit pension scheme asset or liability is offset against that asset or liability in accordance with FRS 17 – *Retirement Benefits*. Other than this, net deferred tax liabilities are included within provisions for liabilities and charges, and net deferred tax assets within debtors, as a separate subheading of debtors if material.[160]

A *Offset of deferred tax assets and liabilities*

Under SSAP 15 all deferred tax balances are generally aggregated and shown as a provision if a net credit balance and as a debtor if a net debit balance. This is no longer permitted by FRS 19, which requires the offset of deferred tax credit and debit balances only to the extent, that they:

(a) relate to taxes levied by the same tax authority; and

(b) arise in the same taxable entity or in a group of taxable entities where the tax losses of one entity can reduce the taxable profits of another.[161]

This has its origins in an almost identical requirement in IAS 12 (see 7.2.5 A below). The practical effect seems to be that it is not possible to offset:

- deferred tax liabilities arising in one tax jurisdiction against deferred tax assets in another; or
- deferred tax liabilities and assets arising in the same tax jurisdiction between members of the group that are not members of the same tax group, or are not otherwise able to relieve losses of one company against profits of another.

It is, however, possible to offset:

- deferred tax assets and liabilities that relate to the same tax jurisdiction arising in the same company; and
- deferred tax assets and liabilities arising among different members of a tax group in a single tax jurisdiction.[162]

Condition (b) merely requires that the offset assets and liabilities arise either in a taxable single entity or in a group of taxable entities that are able to offset profits and losses for tax purposes. In other words, it does not require that the actual balances recognised in the accounts are offsettable for tax purposes.

Thus, it seems that, for example:

- in a UK individual company, an asset arising from a capital loss should be offset against a liability arising from accelerated capital allowances (which will unwind as taxable trading profits), even though the two cannot actually be offset in any tax computation;
- an asset arising from a prior period loss in one member of a UK tax group should be offset against a liability arising from accelerated capital allowances in another, even though it is not possible to group relieve losses of one period against profits in another;
- in an individual company or a group, an asset crystallising next year should be offset against a liability crystallising in five years' time in the same tax jurisdiction, even though, again, never the twain shall meet in the same tax computation.

The FRS 19 offset requirements should not be too onerous a burden for preparers. As a matter of practicality, in the majority of cases compliance with the standard will be achieved simply by analysing the deferred tax balances of the members of a group by tax jurisdiction and then sub-analysing the companies in each tax jurisdiction into tax groups – analyses that will probably have been undertaken in order to calculate current and deferred tax.

It is, however, important to remember that these criteria relate only to the presentation of deferred tax. In particular, the fact that a deferred tax asset is eligible for offset against a liability under these provisions is not *prima facie* evidence that it is recoverable, which must be determined in accordance with the much more stringent provisions summarised in 5.5 above.

As noted above, the real reason for this approach is undoubtedly to achieve harmonisation with IAS 12. However, it creates some confusion in the context of UK GAAP since it introduces offset criteria for deferred tax assets and liabilities that are significantly different to those in FRS 5 – *Reporting the Substance of Transactions* for assets and liabilities generally (see Chapter 18 at 2.7). Also, there is still some divergence from IAS 12, which also contains rules for the offset of current tax balances (see 7.2.5 A below) which have no equivalent in FRS 19 or FRS 16.

In Appendix V to FRS 19, the ASB argues that deferred tax balances are adjustments to future tax assets and liabilities rather than assets and liabilities in their own right and therefore (by implication) outside the scope of the offset rules in FRS 5. More realistically, the ASB also suggests that to have required strict application of the normal FRS 5 offset criteria would have been too onerous.[163]

B Separate disclosure of material deferred tax balances

FRS 19 requires deferred tax assets and liabilities to be shown separately on the face of the balance sheet if the amounts are so material within the context of net current assets or net assets that, in the absence of such disclosure, readers may misinterpret the financial statements.[164] This is more likely to be relevant to deferred tax assets than liabilities and is arguably already required by UITF 4 – *Presentation of long-term debtors in current assets.*[165]

5.9.4 *Profit and loss account presentation of deferred tax*

FRS 19 requires all deferred tax recognised in the profit and loss account to be included within the heading 'tax on profit or loss on ordinary activities'. This is intended to clarify that, where deferred tax has been discounted, the unwinding of the discount forms part of the tax charge and not, as under FRS 12 and FRS 17 for example, a finance cost (see respectively Chapter 28 at 4.2.4 and Chapter 23 at 3.8). This is discussed further at 5.10.5 below.

5.10 Discounting deferred tax

5.10.1 *General*

A general discussion of the issues raised in discounting deferred tax may be found at 1.3.4 above. In the face of all these difficulties, one might wonder why the ASB decided in the 1995 Discussion Paper to put forward discounting as an option at all. The motive was probably a mixture of principle and politics. Some members of the ASB genuinely felt that discounting was the right approach. Others may have not been so convinced, but considered that it would be easier to 'sell' full provision to the UK corporate sector on a discounted rather than an undiscounted basis.

FRS 19 allows reporting entities to choose whether or not to discount deferred tax. However, where an entity chooses to discount deferred tax it must do so under the methodology set out in FRS 19.[166] Appendix 1 to the standard gives a worked example of how the methodology is to be applied in practice, which is discussed further in 5.10.2 to 5.10.5 below. As a precedent to its decision to allow companies a choice in this matter, the ASB cites the choice given in FRS 15 as to whether or not to capitalise interest attributable to the construction of fixed assets.[167] This is, however, a little disingenuous, as the effect of discounting deferred tax will generally be much more material than that of capitalising interest. Moreover, the real reason for the choice given in FRS 15 was arguably in order to harmonise UK GAAP with IAS, which allow a similar choice with respect to capitalisation of interest, whereas the option to discount under FRS 19 introduces a difference between UK GAAP and IAS.

The real reason for the Board's decision to make discounting an option was almost certainly that it had received such strong representations from different sectors of industry both in favour and against discounting, that allowing a choice was probably the only way of achieving sufficient consensus to allow the timely issue of FRS 19. Whilst we sympathise with the pressures on the ASB, there is no ducking the fact that the option to discount creates the potential for a far greater lack of comparability between the deferred tax provisions of different entities than was ever the case under SSAP 15.[168]

5.10.2 *Criteria for discounting*

In deciding whether or not to discount deferred tax, an entity should be guided by the requirements and guidance set out in FRS 18 *Accounting Policies* (see Chapter 2 at 7). FRS 19 suggests that the following factors are likely to be particularly relevant to any choice of policy:

- the materiality of the effect of discounting;
- whether the benefit to users of discounting outweighs the costs of data collection and calculation; and
- whether discounting deferred tax is the established practice in the industry concerned.[169]

In practice, we imagine that industry practice will be the main determining factor. So far as the other factors are concerned, it is our view that in general the effect of discounting will be material, but not worth the cost to preparers for the limited additional benefit to users given proper disclosure.

FRS 19 also requires that, where a policy of discounting is adopted, it must be consistently applied to all deferred tax assets and liabilities, except those relating to items that are already discounted at the pre-tax level.[170] As examples of such items, FRS 19 gives provisions for pensions and other long-term liabilities and a lessor's investment in finance leases.[171] Another example might be the carrying amount of a discounted or stepped interest bond accounted for under FRS 4 *Capital Instruments* (see Chapter 17 at 2.2.3).

The standard explains that as the deferred tax on such items is calculated as the tax effect of an already discounted amount, it is itself already discounted and should not therefore be discounted further. Whilst this is true in principle, it does have the effect that the entity's total deferred tax balance may be discounted at a number of different rates, which raises questions as to the internal consistency of the financial statements.

FRS 19 clarifies that the following categories of timing difference are eligible for discounting:

- accelerated capital allowances;
- revaluation gains and losses;
- carried forward tax losses.

With regard to the latter, however, the standard reiterates that, where there is expected to be some delay before a loss is expected to be relieved, it may not be appropriate to recognise it at all.[172]

The inclusion of revaluation gains and losses in the list of items the deferred tax effects of which may be discounted is not without controversy. In the case of a marketable investment (or investment property) for example, there is a strong argument that its market price represents the discounted net present value of expected future cash flows from it. If this view is accepted, it follows that any valuation movement in respect of such an investment is itself a discounted amount, such that deferred tax on it should not be discounted under the rule discussed above.

5.10.3 *Scheduling the 'cash flows' to be discounted*

FRS 19 requires reversing timing differences to be used as a surrogate for tax cash flows. Deferred tax is then discounted by the period(s) from the balance sheet date to the date(s) on which it is expected that the underlying timing differences at the balance sheet date will reverse.[173] Accordingly, the first step in any deferred tax discounting calculation is to schedule all timing differences at the balance sheet date by their year of reversal.

The scheduling exercise must take account of the remaining tax effects of transactions that have already been reflected in the financial statements, but must not take account of timing differences on future transactions, or of future tax losses.[174] For clarification, the standard stresses that, in discounting accelerated capital allowances, no account should be taken of any potential further postponement of the deferred tax liability by timing differences that might arise from future capital expenditure.[175] It would, of course, be inconsistent with the full provision approach to deferred tax accounting to take account of such future investment, which would be appropriate only under the partial provision approach.

This scheduling exercise must also use assumptions consistent with those made elsewhere in the financial statements.[176] For example, if plant and machinery is depreciated over ten years in the accounts, the same life must be used for the purpose of this exercise. Similarly, the sales proceeds of fixed assets should be assumed to equal their residual value for depreciation purposes.

FRS 19 permits the use of 'approximations and averages' when scheduling the reversal of deferred tax arising from accelerated or decelerated capital allowances.[177]

Whilst the requirements of the main body of FRS 19, as summarised above, provide a broad outline of the methodology, some important details have to be inferred from two examples in the standard. Example 24.20 below is closely based on that in Appendix 1 to FRS 19.

Example 24.20: Scheduling reversing timing differences (1)

A company that operates solely in the UK depreciates its plant and machinery on a straight-line basis over 10 years. Residual value is estimated to be 1/11th of cost. The company receives capital allowances at a rate of 25 per cent per year on a reducing balance basis. It is taxed on its profits at 30 per cent. The company has three groups of assets costing £1,100 each, purchased six years, three years and one year ago (in each case at the end of the financial year). The net book value of plant and machinery at the balance sheet date (year 0) is:

	£
Original cost	3,300
Cumulative depreciation	(1,000)
Net book value	2,300

The tax written-down values of the plant and machinery pool, and the consequential timing difference, at the balance sheet date are:

	£
Net book value	2,300
Tax written-down value	(1,114)
Timing difference at end of year 0	1,186

The future reversals of the liability are scheduled below. The future depreciation of the existing pool of fixed assets (column b) is compared with the future writing-down allowances available on the pool (column c) to determine the years of reversal of the capital allowances (column d). When forecasting capital allowances for future periods, it is assumed that allowances will be claimed as early as possible and that the residual values of the assets will equal those forecast for depreciation purposes.

Years from now	Depreciation (Note 1)	Capital allowances (Note 2)	Reversal of timing difference
	£	£	£
a	b	c	d (=b-c)
1	300	278	22
2	300	209	91
3	300	157	143
4	300	93	207
5	200	69	131
6	200	52	148
7	200	14	186
8	100	11	89
9	100	(17)	117
10+	–	(52)	52
Total	2,000	814	1,186

1 For each 'block' of plant, the annual depreciation is cost less estimated sales proceeds amortised over ten years, i.e. (£1,100 - £100)/10 = £100. The three 'blocks' of plant have, respectively, nine, four and seven years' depreciation to come.

2 Allowance represents 25% brought forward balance on the 'pool' of assets for tax purposes, e.g. for year 1, 25% x £1,114 (given above) = £278. The pool is also reduced by any sales proceeds. Thus, at start of year 3, the pool balance is £1,114 – £(278+209+157) = £470. This is then reduced by £100 sales proceeds in year 4 to £370, on which a 25% allowance of £93 is claimed.

A Period of discounting

As noted in the summary above, FRS 19 requires deferred tax to be discounted by reference to 'the date on which it is estimated that the underlying timing differences will reverse'. This is not, at least in the UK, the date on which tax will actually be paid or relief received. Whilst this is an error of principle, it is probably a necessity, since the mechanics of dealing with payments under, say, the UK corporation tax self assessment system (CTSA) would have been too horrendous to contemplate.

Another point of detail not dealt with explicitly in the standard is that, in principle, some timing differences (e.g. those relating to capital allowances) gradually reverse on a daily basis whereas others (e.g. provisions for costs for which tax relief is given on a cash basis) reverse in more discrete steps. Clearly, to schedule reversing timing differences according to their real dates of reversal would be next to impossible in any but the simplest situations. This is where 'approximations and averages' as described above must come into play. Example 24.20 above indicates that the ASB's approach to this problem is to assume that all timing differences reversing in a particular period reverse on the last day of that period.

The Example also uses of the following further 'approximations and averages':

- making assumptions as to the average useful life of assets; and
- treating all years from year 10 onwards as a single period. In our view, 10 years was chosen in Example 24.20 above because all the assets currently held by the company in the example will have been fully depreciated or sold by this time. It is not intended to imply that it is always appropriate to treat 'year 10' and later periods as a single period.

B Effect of future transactions

As noted above, FRS 19 provides that the scheduling of reversing timing differences must not take account of timing differences on future transactions. However, Example 24.20 above indicates that, while no account can be taken of the timing differences arising on future capital expenditure, it is possible to make an assumption that such expenditure will occur.

The schedule of reversing differences is calculated on the basis that the proceeds of sale of the assets in year 9 give rise to a reduction in available allowances of £17 in year 9 and £52 in subsequent periods. This treatment implicitly assumes that the company will buy sufficient new fixed assets to ensure that the balance on the pool for tax purposes does not fall below zero. If instead the calculation had assumed that there would be no further capital expenditure after the balance sheet date, the £300 sale proceeds in year 9 would have exceeded the brought forward balance on the pool of £231, giving rise to a balancing charge of £69 in that year.

C Future originating differences on existing assets

FRS 19 requires the scheduling of reversals to take account of 'the remaining tax effects of transactions that have already been reflected in the financial statements'. An illustrative example between paragraphs 49 and 50 of FRS 19 clearly interprets 'the remaining tax effects' as including future originating differences on assets held at the balance sheet date, which we understand to have been the ASB's intention. On this view, it is the *purchase of the asset* that is the transaction 'already … reflected in the financial statements', the 'remaining tax effects' of which include the right to receive future capital allowances, so that account should be taken of future originating differences arising from them.

An alternative – and, in our opinion, more correct – view would have been that the transaction 'already … reflected in the financial statements' is the *claiming of accelerated tax allowances*, the 'remaining tax effects' of which are the obligation to refund those allowances until the amount of the asset for which allowances have been claimed has been consumed in the business. On this analysis, no account would be taken of net originating differences in future periods.

These two approaches give very different results, best illustrated using the situation set out in Example 24.21 below.

Example 24.21: Scheduling reversing timing differences (2)

A company prepares accounts to 31 March. On 1 April 2001 it acquires an investment property costing £1 million eligible for annual tax allowances of 4% of cost. Any allowances claimed are recoverable on any sale of the asset for more than its tax written down value.

In accordance with SSAP 19, the company does not depreciate the property, which it expects to sell for at least £1 million on 31 March 2011. On this basis, if JKL claims tax allowances in full, the timing differences arising in each period and the cumulative timing differences at each balance sheet date are as follows:

Year ended 31 March	Timing difference £000	Cumulative timing difference £000
2002	40	40
2003	40	80
2004	40	120
2005	40	160
2006	40	200
2007	40	240
2008	40	280
2009	40	320
2010	40	360
2011	(360)	–

The company decides to discount deferred tax. When preparing its accounts for the period ended 31 March 2002, it determines that the appropriate discount rate (calculated as described in 5.10.4 below) is 4%. On an undiscounted basis, at 31 March 2002 the company would show a deferred tax *liability* calculated on timing differences of £40,000. Applying the methodology in FRS 19, however, will give rise to a deferred tax *asset* calculated on a timing difference of £(16,380). This is arrived by scheduling all the anticipated originating and reversing differences set out in the table above and discounting them, as follows.

Years from 31.3.2002 *(n)*	Undiscounted *(£)*	Discount factor *($1/1.04^n$)*	Discounted *(£)*
1	(40,000)	0.961538	(38,462)
2	(40,000)	0.924556	(36,982)
3	(40,000)	0.888996	(35,560)
4	(40,000)	0.854804	(34,192)
5	(40,000)	0.821927	(32,877)
6	(40,000)	0.790315	(31,613)
7	(40,000)	0.759918	(30,397)
8	(40,000)	0.730690	(29,228)
9	360,000	0.702587	252,931
Total timing difference	40,000		(16,380)

This rather counter-intuitive result arises from the fact that the liability at the balance sheet date, when analysed in this way, represents the net of increases in the liability in the earlier years and reversals in the later ones. Thus, when each year of the overall balance is discounted, the increases in earlier years (which are, in effect, cash inflows) are weighted more heavily than the reversal at year 9 (which is, in effect, a cash outflow).[178]

We believe that the approach set out in FRS 19 is wrong in principle. Essentially, what it does is to produce an investment appraisal of the future tax cash flows of an asset using discounted cash flow techniques, rather than to discount the actual deferred tax liability recognised in the accounts at the balance sheet date. If FRS 19 is followed through to its logical conclusion, it seems to mean that, even if the company had chosen not to claim allowances in 2001/2, it could still have recognised a deferred tax asset on a discounted basis. This is because its undiscounted deferred tax (i.e. zero) could be analysed as representing allowances to be claimed in years 2 to 9 less the clawback on disposal.

Our preferred approach in Example 24.21 above would be to say that the gross timing difference of £40,000 at 31 March 2002 reverses on 31 March 2011 (when the asset is sold), and should therefore be discounted by 9 years. On this basis the company would recognise a deferred tax liability based on a discounted timing difference of £28,103 (i.e. £40,000 x $1/1.04^9$). Having said all this, however, we accept that there is a serious practical difficulty with this approach. This is that, in the more typical case of a large pool of depreciating assets, the reversals plotted for future periods will almost invariably be a mixture of originating differences on recently purchased assets and reversing differences on older ones. It would simply not be possible to separate these originating and reversing differences, so that the only workable methodology is probably that set out in FRS 19.

D *Continuously revalued non-monetary assets*

The approach outlined in C above presents some difficulty when applied to the deferred tax on gains and losses on non-monetary items continually revalued to fair value through the profit and loss account (see 5.3.1 above). The problem is that deferred tax is required to be recognised on such gains and losses, whether or not there is any binding agreement in place to dispose of the assets in question. In the absence of any such agreement, or indeed intention, to dispose of the assets, there is no certain date on which the deferred tax will crystallise.

FRS 19 anticipates this difficulty and, in such cases, simply requires a best estimate to be made of the date on which the 'tax [on disposal] will become payable'.[179] This is different from the approach adopted in respect of other discounted deferred tax, which, as noted above, is discounted by reference to the date(s) on which the timing differences at the balance sheet date reverse, rather than the date on which the tax to which the reversal gives rise is actually payable.

The timing difference is then discounted from that date taking account of any available reliefs (presumably meaning rollover relief, holdover relief and, possibly, indexation allowance – see further discussion on this issue at 5.3.2 F above).[180] As noted in 5.3.1 above, it is not clear why FRS 19 makes this point. If such reliefs had already been taken account of in calculating the gross (i.e. undiscounted) provision, there would be no need to take account of them again. If, on the other hand, the implication is that the reliefs should have been ignored in calculating the gross provision, this is hard to understand in the absence of any explanation.

Where the underlying assets concerned are an investment portfolio (as will typically be the case), the reporting entity should draw on historical data regarding average turnover periods, and the average effective tax rate on previous disposals. However, it should also consider the extent to which that historical data will remain reliable in the future.[181]

E Non-depreciated assets eligible for capital allowances

As noted in 5.2.2 above, FRS 19 requires full provision for deferred tax on accelerated capital allowances claimed on assets that are either not depreciated or depreciated to a residual value greater than zero, until all conditions for retaining the allowances have been met.

In discounting such deferred tax relating to an asset that is depreciated to a residual value greater than zero, it would be consistent with the assumptions underlying the accounts to assume that the asset concerned is disposed of for its residual value at the end of its life.

Where the asset concerned is not depreciated (or is depreciated, but no depreciation is actually charged on the grounds that it would be immaterial), the position is less clear. The difficulty is in determining the date on which the timing differences arising from capital allowances will reverse. Where there is a history of disposals of such assets, it may be possible to determine an average period for holding such assets, and to assume that all timing differences will reverse at the end of that period. Where there is no such period, there may be little choice but to make a relatively arbitrary assumption (20 years, 30 years, or whatever) as to the period for which the asset will be held.

5.10.4 Discount rates

FRS 19 requires deferred tax to be discounted at the post-tax yield to maturity that could be obtained, at the balance sheet date, on government bonds with maturity dates and in currencies similar to those of the deferred tax assets and liabilities.[182] The yield to maturity of a bond is the internal rate of total return (i.e. interest and principal) on an investment in the bond at market value. Yield rates for UK Treasury gilts are quoted in the Financial Times, but can be calculated with discounting software, or by 'trial and error' methods, if need be.

The FRS requires the calculated yield to be adjusted to reflect the tax rate paid by 'an entity' holding the bond, rather than by the reporting entity.[183] It is quite obvious, however, that the rate applicable to the reporting entity should be used, as is made somewhat clearer in the worked example in Appendix 1 to the standard.

Appendix V to FRS 19 justifies the use of a government bond rate by arguing that, as the future cash flow represented by the deferred tax liability is relatively certain, it would be appropriate to fund it out of low-risk assets of similar maturity and currency. The same rate can be used for deferred tax assets because, although these are intrinsically more risky than deferred tax liabilities, the restrictions on their recognition (see 5.2 above) mean that any amount recognised has already been risk-adjusted. The post-tax rate should be used because deferred tax liabilities are not themselves tax deductible and would, if funded by a bond, have to be met out of post-tax income.[184]

In practical terms, this requires a company with a year end of 31 December 2001 to discount a UK deferred tax liability that reverses over ten years by applying the post-tax yield rate, at 31 December 2001, of a UK government bond maturing on 31 December 2002 to the amount reversing in year 1, the rate, at 31 December 2001, on a bond maturing on 31 December 2003 to the amount reversing in year 2 and so on. The same process should be applied to deferred tax assets and liabilities in each jurisdiction.

Clearly this could be a very time-consuming exercise and the extent to which companies will actually do it, or are even expected by FRS 19 to do it, is a moot point. For example, as noted above, even the 'bold paragraph' requirement of the standard is to use the rate on bonds of 'similar' (rather than 'the same') maturity and currency. It is not clear whether this is intended to refer only to explicitly linked currencies (such as those in the euro zone), or whether it extends to different currencies in the same economic area (such as the USA and Canada).

The standard then goes on to say that, while the approach outlined in the previous paragraph is required 'in theory', it may be possible to use 'approximations and averages' to simplify the calculations without introducing material errors.[185] In fact, some 'approximations and averages' will almost invariably be required anyway, since it is likely that for at least some of the dates when timing differences reverse, there will no relevant government bonds of similar maturity. For those dates, the discount rate will have to be calculated by an interpolation method, such as that shown in Example 24.22 below, which is based on the example in Appendix 1 to the standard.

Example 24.22: Discount rate calculated by interpolation

An entity wishes to discount deferred tax by four years. Published post-tax yields for a relevant government bonds maturing in 3 and 5 years respectively are 4.2% and 3.9%. The rate for year 4 could be taken as the mean of [(4.2-3.9)/2]%, i.e. 4.0%.

The requirement to discount deferred tax at a government bond rate means that the rates used will, currently, tend to be low single figure rates. This in itself may well deter companies from discounting as the effect may be relatively immaterial. Moreover, FRS 19 requires discounting to be done using not the constant nominal rate of a bond, but the variable yield rate, which will be affected by changes in general market rates. In other words, it may be that the yield rate on the same bond is 6% at one balance sheet date and 4% at the next. Such a movement will be accounted for in full in the year of change 5.10.5, leading to a decrease in the discount and therefore an increase in the deferred tax provision and the tax charge. This creates the real, and rather counter-intuitive, possibility of discounting leading to an effective tax rate *higher* than the statutory rate.

5.10.5 *Accounting for movements in the discount*

Where deferred tax is discounted the movement between the discount on the opening and closing deferred tax balances can be analysed into three components:

- the 'unwinding' of the discount (i.e. one year's interest on the opening discounted deferred tax balance at the opening discount rate);
- changes in the underlying timing differences and tax rates; and
- discount rate changes (i.e. the difference between the opening deferred tax balance discounted at the opening and closing rates).

In FRED 19 it was proposed that the unwinding of the discount, like that on other provisions accounted for under FRS 12 or FRS 17 (see, respectively, Chapter 28 at 4.2.4 and Chapter 23 at 3.8.1 B) would be accounted for as a financing item with the other two components forming part of the tax charge. Under FRS 19, however, all movements in the discount should be accounted for as part of the tax charge.[186]

The ASB apparently still believes that, in principle, the unwinding of the discount should be dealt with as a financing item. However, in view of the accounting provisions of the Companies Act 1985 to show profit before tax as a separate item on the face of the profit and loss account, the Board decided that the whole movement on the discount should be accounted for as part of the tax charge. The argument is that the discount on deferred tax, however it is viewed conceptually, is clearly tax and not part of pre-tax profit.[187] This is slightly puzzling, since it could equally be argued that the unwinding of any discount on a provision made under FRS 12 or FRS 17 clearly falls within one of the operating cost headings in the Companies Act formats, rather than other finance costs adjacent to interest.

Whatever the basis of the ASB's decision, however, it is very welcome since accounting for the discount as interest can lead to strange results. For example, the accounts may show an effective tax rate higher than the statutory rate, because the pre-tax profit is being charged with a discount which, being in reality tax, is not tax-deductible.

5.10.6 *Use of discounting in practice*

Given the relatively small number of companies that have implemented FRS 19 up to the date of writing this book, it would unwise to draw any firm conclusions on the extent to which UK companies will opt to discount deferred tax. Of those companies that have implemented FRS 19, and whose accounts are cited in this chapter, Kingston Communications has elected not to discount, as has Scottish Power (despite being in a sector that apparently lobbied for discounting as an option). Railtrack has discounted deferred tax, the effects being shown in Extract 24.21 at 5.11.3 H below.

5.11 Disclosure

FRS 19 contains extensive disclosure requirements. Some of these are simply continuations of requirements of SSAP 15, but many are new. Like much of FRS 19, several of the new disclosures are derived from IAS 12, but in a modified form. The existing requirements of SSAP 15 that were relevant only in the context of its partial provision approach are withdrawn. Examples of all the disclosures, and their interaction with those in FRS 16, are given in Appendix II to the standard.

5.11.1 *Disclosures supplementing the performance statements*

The notes to the accounts should disclose the amount of deferred tax charged or credited within tax on ordinary activities in the profit and loss account and the amount charged or credited directly in the STRGL. Both these amounts should be analysed further, so as to give separate disclosure of the material components of the charge or credit, including those attributable to:

(a) changes in deferred tax balances (before discounting, where applicable) arising from:

  (i) the origination and reversal of timing differences;

(ii) changes in tax rates and laws; and

(iii) adjustments to the estimated recoverable amount of deferred tax assets arising in previous periods; and

(b) where applicable, changes in the amounts of discount deducted in arriving at the deferred tax balance.[188]

Like SSAP 15, FRS 19 requires no analysis of deferred tax between UK tax and foreign tax, as required by FRS 16 in respect of current tax. Similarly, there is no requirement, comparable to that in FRS 16 for current tax, to analyse the current year's deferred tax charge between the amount relating to profits for the period and adjustments in respect of prior periods. There would be nothing to preclude companies giving this further analysis.[189]

Of the items above, (a)(ii) was already required by SSAP 15 (see 4.9 above), but the others are new, as is the requirement to analyse any deferred tax accounted for in the STRGL.

5.11.2 *Disclosures supplementing the balance sheet*

FRS 19 requires an analysis of the deferred tax balance and further information regarding the recoverability of deferred tax assets, as summarised below.

A Analysis of deferred tax balance

FRS 19 requires disclosure of:

(a) the total deferred tax balance (before discounting, where applicable), showing the amount recognised for each significant type of timing difference separately;

(b) the impact of discounting on, and the discounted amount of, the deferred tax balance; and

(c) the movement between the opening and closing net deferred tax balance, analysing separately:

(i) the amount charged or credited in the profit and loss account for the period;

(ii) the amount charged or credited directly in the statement of total recognised gains and losses for the period; and

(iii) movements arising from the acquisition or disposal of businesses.[190]

It will be seen the analysis above is required in respect of the deferred tax 'balance' (singular), whereas under the presentation requirements of FRS 19 (see 5.9.3 above) there may be up to three separate deferred tax balances:

- the amount relating to defined benefit pensions accounted for under FRS 17 *Retirement Benefits*, offset against the asset or liability for such pensions;
- other deferred tax liabilities included within provisions for liabilities and charges; and
- other deferred tax assets included within debtors.

We presume that the ASB intends the analysis above to be undertaken for the net total of these three balances rather than for each balance separately, which would be neither practical nor meaningful. This is because it is quite possible for a particular category of timing difference to give rise to an asset in one period and a liability the next and *vice versa*. It may also be the case that a particular category of timing difference gives rise to a deferred tax asset, but that, for presentation purposes, that asset is included within deferred tax liabilities by virtue of FRS 19's offset provisions.

B Recoverability of deferred tax assets

The financial statements should disclose the amount of a deferred tax asset and the nature of the evidence supporting its recognition if:

(a) the recoverability of the deferred tax asset is dependent on future taxable profits in excess of those arising from the reversal of deferred tax liabilities; and

(b) the reporting entity has suffered a loss in either the current or preceding period in the tax jurisdiction to which the deferred tax asset relates.[191]

The 'evidence supporting [the] recognition' of a deferred tax asset is the specific circumstances that allowed its recognition under FRS 19 (see 5.5 above).[192] This requirement is derived from IAS 12 and is clearly intended to ensure that companies respect the restrictions on the recognition of such assets.

5.11.3 Circumstances affecting current and future tax charges

There is a general requirement that the notes to the accounts should highlight circumstances that affect the current and total tax charges or credits for the current period or that may affect the current and total tax charges in future periods.[193] FRS 19 specifies that this should include the following specific disclosures.

A Reconciliation of the tax charge or credit

A reporting entity should present a reconciliation of the actual current tax charge or credit on ordinary activities for the period reported in the profit and loss account to the 'expected' current tax charge (i.e. that which would result from applying a relevant standard rate of tax to the profit on ordinary activities before tax.) Either the monetary amounts or the rates (as a percentage of profits on ordinary activities before tax) may be reconciled. Where material, positive amounts should not be offset against negative amounts or *vice versa*: they should be shown as separate reconciling items. The basis on which the standard rate of tax has been determined should be disclosed.[194]

This is a major new disclosure requirement for UK companies, although a tax reconciliation is already required by US GAAP for listed companies and by IAS 12 for all companies. However, whereas US GAAP and IAS require a reconciliation of the 'expected' tax charge to the *total* tax charge in the financial statements, FRS 19 requires a reconciliation of the 'expected' tax charge to the *current* tax charge.[195] Appendix V to the FRS argues, justifiably in our view, that this information is actually more useful to users. A current tax reconciliation enables users to form a view as to whether reconciling items such as accelerated capital allowances are of a level that is likely to recur and, thus, whether the entity's current tax charge is sustainable.[196]

By contrast, a total tax reconciliation does not highlight the components of the deferred tax charge, and so tends not to include very much beyond tax rate differences and permanent differences. It is also probably not without significance that a current tax reconciliation would be the natural disclosure to complement the flow-through method of accounting (see 1.3.3 C above), which is known to be supported by a significant number of the ASB.

Disclosure of the basis on which the 'expected' tax charge (or rate) has been calculated is required because FRS 19 does not prescribe how this is to be calculated, beyond indicating that a 'relevant' standard tax rate should be used. The standard points out, that where a reporting entity is taxed in several jurisdictions at different rates (as will be the case for most UK groups), the UK tax rate may be of limited relevance, and it may be more appropriate to calculate an average tax rate, weighted according to the relative amount of accounting profit taxed at each rate. This could be done by aggregating reconciliations prepared for each major tax jurisdiction.[197]

It is clear the ASB and users of accounts have high hopes for this disclosure. Ultimately, however, there is a risk that, in the absence of any specific requirements as to its contents, a tax reconciliation may be only as effective as preparers want it to be. FRS 19 notes that it is not an onerous requirement as the information needed to prepare it is already available from tax computations.[198] However, this slightly misses the point. It is one thing to be forthcoming about the effect of accelerated capital allowances and another to reveal details of proprietary tax planning strategies.

B Unprovided deferred tax on revalued assets

Where an entity has revalued assets in the financial statements without deferred tax being recognised on the gain or loss, it should disclose:

- an estimate of tax that could be payable or recoverable if the assets were sold at the values shown;
- the circumstances in which the tax would be payable or recoverable; and
- and an indication of the amount that may become payable or recoverable in the foreseeable future.

As under SSAP 15, the same disclosures should be made where the market value of assets is disclosed, but not recognised, in the financial statements.[199]

The requirements in respect of potential deferred tax on assets revalued in the financial statements represent a significant change from SSAP 15. Under SSAP 15 (see 4.9 above), the position was essentially that, if deferred tax on a revaluation gain was considered unlikely to crystallise because of rollover relief (and was therefore not considered a timing difference), this fact should be disclosed, but there is no need to quantify the potential liability (although many companies in fact did so). By contrast, FRS 19 requires quantification of the potential liability, irrespective of the likelihood of crystallisation. The relevant paragraph of FRS 19 refers to the amount of tax that '*could be* payable or recoverable'. We understand this to mean that the disclosure of the unprovided deferred tax should be of the full potential liability (i.e. ignoring the possibility of rollover and other reliefs).

In another change from SSAP 15, FRS 19 does not simply require disclosure of the unprovided deferred tax, but also the amount of unprovided deferred tax that is likely to crystallise in the foreseeable future. The objective of this seems to be to disclose the additional amount of deferred tax that would have been recognised if SSAP 15 had still been in force. We consider that any amount disclosed as likely to crystallise in the foreseeable future should take account of likely available reliefs such as rollover relief.

This supplementary disclosure of amounts likely to crystallise in the foreseeable future is, to some extent, a natural consequence of the fact that the hurdle for recognition of deferred tax on revaluations is set much higher in FRS 19 than in SSAP 15. In other words, is quite possible that under FRS 19 there will be material amounts of unprovided deferred tax that are very likely to crystallise (and, indeed may already have crystallised before the financial statements are approved – see Examples 24.14 and 24.15 at 5.3.2 B above).

However, it does seem rather strange to have this 'mezzanine' category of deferred tax which is apparently considered neither real enough to be recognised in the financial statements nor remote enough to be disclosed in aggregation with other unprovided amounts. In our view, the perceived need for such disclosure should have prompted the ASB to reconsider the rather purist recognition criteria in FRS 19.

On implementation of FRS 15 most companies have ceased to revalue assets. Where companies have 'frozen' the carrying amount of previously revalued assets under the transitional arrangements in FRS 15, such 'frozen' amounts are effectively treated as cost (see Chapter 12 at 2.5.2). For the purposes of FRS 19, however, we believe that such assets should be considered as revalued. There may be a potential tax liability associated with any asset that is carried above its original cost, irrespective of whether or not that carrying amount is treated as a 'revaluation' for accounting purposes.

It seems that this disclosure requirement also applies to any non-monetary asset that has been subject to a fair value adjustment on acquisition. This is because FRS 7, as amended by FRS 19, requires fair value adjustments to be treated as if they were timing differences in the acquired entity's accounts (see 5.6 above). In the absence of any provision to the contrary, we believe that this requires such adjustments to be treated as revaluations for all purposes of FRS 19 (i.e. including disclosure), and not just the recognition and measurement criteria. Moreover, if these disclosure requirements were not treated as applying to assets subject to fair value adjustments, there would be an inconsistency in the accounts disclosures. The potential tax liability arising on a directly acquired property that is carried in the accounts at a revalued amount greater than its tax value is the same as that on an equivalent property acquired as part of a larger acquisition. It would be strange to disclose only one of these potential liabilities.

As noted above, these disclosure requirements apply not only to assets that are carried at a valuation in the financial statements, but also to assets the market value of which has been disclosed. It is not entirely clear how wide the scope of this requirement is intended to be. For example it could, on the face of it, include assets the fair value of which is disclosed under FRS 13 – *Derivatives and Financial Instruments: Disclosures* (see Chapter 10 at 2.9).

We are not, however, convinced that the ASB intended this requirement of FRS 19 to embrace such items, since it refers only to 'assets' the 'market value' of which is disclosed. As drafted, this would require disclosure of the potential deferred tax payable on realisation of assets disclosed at market value, but not of assets disclosed at a fair value other than market value, or of liabilities. Moreover, this requirement is not new, but carried forward from SSAP 15. General practice so far indicates that preparers of accounts do not see the corresponding disclosure requirement of SSAP 15 as extending to items the fair value of which is disclosed pursuant to FRS 13. It has also been indicated to us informally that this was not the ASB's intention.

C Availability of rollover relief

If the reporting entity has sold (or entered into a binding agreement to sell) an asset but has not recognised deferred tax on a taxable gain because the gain has been or is expected to be rolled over into replacement assets, it should disclose:

- the conditions that will have to be met to obtain the rollover relief; and
- an estimate of the tax that would become payable if those conditions were not met.[200]

We assume that the intention is to disclose any latent liability to tax on all previous disposals and committed future disposals of assets. In other words, we read the words 'has sold … an asset' as referring to any previous sale rather than simply a sale in the current accounting period (as their more natural English construction might imply).

D Unrecognised deferred tax assets

If a deferred tax asset has not been recognised on the grounds that there is insufficient evidence that the asset will be recoverable, the reporting entity should disclose:

- the amount that has not been recognised; and
- the circumstances in which the asset would be recovered.[201]

This is fairly self-explanatory. The one possible issue is that there may well be more than one way in which some assets might potentially be recovered. In such cases, the entity should presumably indicate the various possible means of recovery.

E Other unrecognised deferred tax

In respect of any unrecognised deferred tax not covered by one of the disclosures above, the reporting entity should disclose:

- the nature of the amounts not recognised;
- the circumstances in which the tax would become payable or recoverable; and
- an indication of the amount that may become payable or recoverable in the foreseeable future.[202]

This is a 'sweep-up' disclosure requirement, which again seems fairly self-explanatory. In contrast to the disclosure requirements for unprovided deferred tax on revalued assets (discussed above), FRS 19 does not require quantification of all unprovided deferred tax, but only of the amount that is likely to crystallise in the foreseeable future. The 'nature' of all unprovided amounts must, however, be given.

As drafted, this arguably requires disclosure of the impact of any material permanent differences, such as those arising from non-deductible assets. This is because, as noted in 5.1.1 above, FRS 19 defines deferred tax as the 'future tax consequences' of 'transactions and events' already recognised in the financial statements. It is clear from the methodology prescribed for discounting (see 5.10.3 C above) that the ASB regards the purchase of an asset (as opposed to simply the subsequent depreciation and claiming of tax allowances) as a transaction with future tax consequences. The purchase of a non-deductible asset is a 'transaction … already recognised in the financial statements' that will have 'future tax consequences', i.e. a higher effective tax rate, as it is depreciated. We are not, however, convinced that this disclosure requirement was intended to be so all-embracing.

It may also require disclosure of such matters as disputes with taxation authorities, which is currently more within the scope of FRS 12 (see 6.2 below).

F Retained earnings

FRS 19 amends FRS 2 so as to abolish its requirement to disclose the reason why tax has not been recognised on retained overseas earnings of subsidiaries. This is a welcome change, since the purpose of this disclosure has never been clear, as the reason for any non-provision was that it was the treatment required by SSAP 15 (see 4.5.4 A above).

Appendix V to FRS 19 states that the standard requires disclosure of the amounts of deferred tax not recognised on the unremitted earnings of subsidiaries, associates and joint ventures only to the extent that the earnings are expected to be remitted in the foreseeable future.[203] However, there is no requirement to this effect in the main body of the standard. It is not clear whether this is a drafting slip, or whether the ASB took the view that this is an example of a situation covered by the requirements under 'Other unrecognised deferred tax' in E above.

As noted in the discussion of the recognition provisions for retained earnings at 5.4 above, FRS 19, unlike IAS 12, does not refer specifically to branches. In our view, however, these disclosures should also be made in respect of the retained earnings of any branches.

G Deferred tax recognised but unlikely to crystallise?

A final thought is that companies may want to give, in addition to the required disclosures in respect of unprovided deferred tax that is likely to crystallise, voluntary disclosure of deferred tax that has been recognised, but which is unlikely to crystallise in the foreseeable future. We have in mind such items as the deferred tax on non-depreciated assets (see 5.2.2 above) and on assets continually revalued through the profit and loss account (see 5.3.1 above).

H *Examples of disclosures*

Kingston Communications and Railtrack implemented FRS 19 in their March 2001 accounts and provided the following disclosures.

Extract 24.20: Kingston Communications (HULL) PLC (2001)

Notes to the accounts [extract]

8 Taxation

a) Analysis of tax charge in the year

The charge based on the loss for the year comprises:	**2001** **£'000**	2000 (as restated) £'000
UK corporation tax:		
– (loss)/profit of the period	**–**	–
– Adjustment in respect of the previous period	**–**	(797)
Foreign tax:		
– Profit of the period	**–**	(44)
– Adjustment in respect of the previous period	**(6)**	–
Associate tax	**(39)**	107
Total current tax	**(45)**	(734)
UK deferred tax:		
Origination and reversal of timing differences in respect of:		
– (loss)/profit in the period (excluding exceptional items)	**(381)**	2,892
– Non recurring operating items	**(1,306)**	–
– Exceptional items	**2,611**	187
Total deferred tax (note 22)	**924**	3,079
Tax on (loss)/profit on ordinary activities	**879**	2,345

b) Factors affecting tax charge for the period

	2001 **£'000**	2000 (as restated) £'000
Group (loss)/profit on ordinary activities before tax	**(9,647)**	8,090
Group (loss)/profit on ordinary activities before tax at 30%	**(2,894)**	2,427
Effects of:		
Expenses not deductible for tax purposes	**1,138**	737
Accounting depreciation not eligible for tax purposes	**202**	198
Goodwill amortised	**161**	137
Non taxable grant income	**(43)**	(45)
Accounting depreciation in excess of tax depreciation	**(1,746)**	(2,362)
Current tax losses not utilised	**2,243**	537
Adjustments relating to prior years corporation tax	**(6)**	(797)
Allowable deduction not debited to profit and loss account	**–**	(1,566)
Chargeable gains not recognised in current year profit and loss account	**900**	–
Total current tax	**(45)**	(734)

c) Factors that may affect future tax charges

No provision has been made for deferred tax where potentially taxable gains have been rolled over into replacement assets. Such gains would become taxable only if the assets were sold without it being possible to claim rollover relief. The amount not provided is £0.7 million. At present, it is not envisaged that any tax will become payable in the foreseeable future.

No deferred tax is recognised on the unremitted earnings of overseas subsidiaries. As the earnings are continually reinvested by the Group, no tax is expected to be payable in the foreseeable future.

22 Provisions for liabilities and charges

	Consolidated		Parent Company	
	2001	2000	**2001**	2000 (as restated)
	£'000	£'000	**£'000**	£'000
Deferred taxation				
At 31 March 2000	**17,906**	14,827	**903**	(129)
Transfer to profit and loss account	**924**	3,079	**(903)**	1,032
At 31 March 2001	**18,830**	17,906	**–**	903
Total provisions for liabilities and charges	**18,830**	17,906	**–**	903

The major components of the provision for deferred taxation and the amounts not provided are as follows:

	Provided		Not provided	
	2001	2000 (as restated)	**2001**	2000 (as restated)
	£'000	£'000	**£'000**	£'000
Consolidated				
Unutilisable tax losses	**(460)**	(538)	**(1,083)**	(211)
Accelerated capital allowances	**19,290**	17,544	**–**	–
Other timing differences	**–**	900	**–**	–
	18,830	17,906	**(1,083)**	(211)
Parent Company				
Accelerated capital allowances	**–**	3	**–**	–
Other timing differences	**–**	900	**–**	–
	–	903	**–**	–

Extract 24.21: Railtrack Group PLC (2001)

23 Deferred taxation

	£m
Group	
At 1 April 2000 (originally £23 million before adjusting for the prior year adjustments of £440 million)	463
Deferred tax credited to the profit and loss account	(207)
At 31 March 2001	**256**

	At 31 March 2001	At 31 March 2000 (Restated)
	£m	£m
Accelerated capital allowances	**1,140**	1,061
Short term timing differences	**(20)**	(72)
Tax losses carried forward	**(272)**	–
Undiscounted provision for deferred tax	**848**	989
Discount	**(592)**	(526)
Discounted provision for deferred tax	**256**	463

The current rate of corporation tax of 30% (1999/2000: 30%) has been used to calculate the amount of deferred taxation. Provision has been made for all deferred taxation assets and liabilities in respect of accelerated capital allowances, short term timing differences and tax losses carried forward, arising from transactions and events recognised in the financial statements of the current year and previous years. These deferred taxation assets and liabilities, have been discounted because timing differences giving rise to them will reverse after a number of years.

The recoverability of tax losses carried forward has been estimated having regard to forecast taxable profits arising over the following three years. No account has been taken of timing differences arising on future transactions or of future tax losses.

The amounts of deferred taxation not provided in the accounts are as follows:	**At 31 March 2001 £m**	At 31 March 2000 (Restated) £m
Rolled over gains	**170**	160
Revaluation of fixed assets	**15**	23
Deferred taxation not provided at 30% (1999/2000: 30%)	**185**	183

The £170 million (31 March 2000: £160 million) of tax in respect of rolled over gains relates primarily to the estimated amount of gains realised by the British Railways board which have been deferred through the application of capital gains rollover relief into assets vested in Railtrack PLC. No provision has been made in respect of deferred taxation in relation to these gains as no liability is expected to arise. No provision has been made for £15 million (31 March 2000: £23 million) of tax in respect of gains arising from the revaluation of fixed assets.

As disposal is not contemplated, provision has not been made for the tax that would arise if the company sold its shares in Railtrack PLC for the revalued amount. The amount of deferred tax not provided is £627 million (31 March 2000: £763 million).

10 Tax (credit)/charge on profit/(loss) on ordinary activities [extract]

(i) **Analysis of charge in year**	**2001 £m**	2000 £m
Current UK corporation tax at 30%		
Credit for the year	**(3)**	(13)
Over provision in respect of prior years	**(17)**	–
Total current tax	**(20)**	(13)
Deferred tax at 30%		
(Credit)/charge for timing differences arising in the year	**(141)**	140
Increase in discount	**(66)**	(62)
Total deferred tax	**(207)**	78
Tax (credit)/charge on (loss)/profit on ordinary activities	**(227)**	65

£174 million of the deferred tax credit relates to the exceptional item.

(ii) Current factors affecting the tax charge for the year

The tax assessed for the year is lower than the standard rate of corporation tax in the UK (30%). The differences are explained below:

	2001 £m	2000 £m
(Loss)/profit on ordinary activities before tax	**(534)**	360
(Loss)/profit on ordinary activities multiplied by the standard rate of corporation tax in the UK of 30%		
(1999/2000: 30%)	**(160)**	108
Accelerated capital allowance	**(79)**	(94)
Tax losses carried forward	**272**	–
Utilisation of provisions	**(52)**	(46)
Adjustments in respect of prior years	**(17)**	–
Permanent differences	**19**	37
Current tax losses offset against profits charged to reserves	**(3)**	(18)
Total current tax credit	**(20)**	(13)

(iii) Factors that may affect future tax charges and credits

Based on current expenditure plans, the Group expects to be able to claim capital allowances substantially in excess of related depreciation for a number of years. The combined effect of these accelerated capital allowances and the availability of tax losses carried forward is expected to eliminate any significant current corporation tax liabilities for a number of years.

The total tax charge or credit in future years will include discounted deferred taxation. Consequently, changes in the medium and long term interest rates used to discount deferred taxation assets and liabilities will affect the amount of deferred taxation charged or credited in the profit and loss account.

5.12 FRS 19 and distributable reserves

For most companies the likely net effect of FRS 19 is to increase the deferred tax provision above that required by SSAP 15, raising the very real question of what impact this has on distributable reserves. Appendix III to FRS 19 addresses this issue briefly, and not altogether convincingly, in the limited context of deferred tax on assets that are continually revalued to fair value through the profit and loss account, but gives no guidance on the broader issues.

Distributable reserves are determined by reference to the profits of individual companies, rather than those of groups. This means that deferred tax recognised on consolidation only (e.g. on fair value adjustments and other items accounted for differently at the group and entity level) may generally be ignored for this purpose.

In our view, the legal position is that a provision for deferred tax does reduce a company's distributable reserves. The basic requirement, in section 263 of the Companies Act 1985, is that a distribution can be made only out of 'accumulated, realised profits … less accumulated, realised losses'. The issue is therefore whether a provision for deferred tax is a 'realised loss' for the purposes of this section. This question, often a matter for some discussion, is in this particular case put beyond debate by section 275 of the Act which states that 'a provision of any kind mentioned in paragraphs 88 and 89 of Schedule 4'[204] (which includes a provision for deferred tax) is to be treated as a realised loss. A further issue for public companies is that section 264 of the Act, in effect, treats any debit to the retained profit and loss reserve as a realised loss.

Whilst the Act does not provide such direct guidance as to whether deferred tax assets are realised profits, we see no reason why a deferred tax asset properly recognised under FRS 19 should not be treated as a realised profit. Nevertheless, companies may well wish for prudential reasons not to distribute profits represented largely by tax assets recoverable only out of future profits.

It is possible that the prior year adjustment made on implementation of FRS 19 will create a deficit on distributable reserves. If this happens, it does not mean that dividends previously paid were illegal, since this depends on the level of distributable profits at the time that the dividend is paid, determined by reference to accounting principles at that time. It may therefore be possible for companies that anticipate the elimination of distributable reserves on implementation of FRS 19 to make a full distribution of those reserves in advance. We would, however, sound two notes of caution.

First, where such a distribution is made to another group company but not to the ultimate shareholders, the eventual provision for deferred tax in the paying company may create a deficit on net assets in that company, which may in turn require the receiving company to write down the carrying amount of its investment in the paying company. This could eliminate, or at least reduce, the amount of the original dividend that could be passed on to the ultimate shareholders. Second, directors may wish to seek legal advice to ensure that a dividend paid in anticipation of a known accounting change of this nature is not unlawful.

As noted above, FRS 19 briefly addresses the question of deferred tax on gains (and losses) on assets continually revalued through the profit and loss account. FRS 19 argues that, since such gains are unrealised, any deferred tax on them should be treated as a reduction in the unrealised gain, rather than as a realised loss.[205] In our view, this is more what the law ought to say than what it does say.

In any event, we are not sure that the argument is particularly relevant, since current accounting thought would tend to categorise gains arising on continuous revaluation of marketable securities as realised, a view reinforced by the fact that they are generally taxed on this basis. If the gross gain is treated as realised, any deferred tax on it must be realised also.

6 OTHER UK PRONOUNCEMENTS

6.1 Companies Act 1985

The Companies Act also imposes various disclosure requirements in relation to taxation. These can be summarised as follows:

(a) any special circumstances affecting the liability to tax on profits, income or capital gains for the current or future years.[206] (There is a similar requirement in FRS 3, which also requires the individual effects to be quantified.)[207]

Companies complying with FRS 19 effectively give this information through the tax reconciliation (see 5.11.3 A above). Those not yet complying with

FRS 19 deal with this requirement by way of narrative disclosures, examples of which can be seen in Extracts 24.8 and 24.12 at, respectively, 3.6 and 4.7 above.

Dawson International and GlaxoSmithKline, although not complying with FRS 19 give more detailed reconciliations, to explain the difference between the actual tax charge and notional charge which would have been derived from applying the statutory tax rate to the reported profit for the year. Dawson International reconciles the notional to the actual tax *charge*.

Extract 24.22: Dawson International PLC (2000)

9 Taxation [extract]

	2000 **£m**	1999 £m
Reconciliation of the tax charge:		
Notional charge/(credit) on profit/(loss) on ordinary activities before exceptional charges at UK corporation tax rate of 30% (1999: 30%)	**1.5**	(2.8)
Differences in effective overseas taxation rates	**(0.1)**	0.1
Tax losses not utilised	**–**	1.9
Other items	**(0.4)**	0.3
	1.0	(0.5)
Exceptional charges	**(1.0)**	–
	–	(0.5)

There are significant tax losses available for carry forward in both the UK and USA for which no benefit has been recognised.

By contrast, GlaxoSmithKline reconciles the notional to the actual tax *rate*.

Extract 24.23: GlaxoSmithKline plc (2000)

13. Taxation [extract]

Reconciliation of the taxation rate:	**2000** **%**	1999 %	1998 %
UK statutory rate taxation	**30.0**	30.3	31.0
Deferred taxation not provided on fixed assets	**(0.3)**	(0.1)	0.1
Effect of special taxation status in manufacturing locations	**(3.6)**	(3.4)	(1.8)
Net cost of different rates of taxation in overseas undertakings	**2.4**	2.3	2.1
Share option deductions in the USA	**(0.9)**	(0.7)	(1.5)
Tax losses and R&D credits not previously recognised	**(1.2)**	(2.7)	(0.4)
Prior year items	**–**	(0.6)	0.4
ACT written back	**–**	–	(1.5)
Other differences	**0.9**	3.1	0.8
Taxation rate on business performance	**27.3**	28.2	29.2
Merger and restructuring costs	**0.9**	0.6	(1.8)
Taxation rate on total group results	**28.2**	28.8	27.4

Profits arising from manufacturing operations in Singapore, Puerto Rico and Ireland are taxed at reduced rates. The effect of this reduction in the taxation charge increased earnings per Ordinary Share by 3.6p in 2000, by 2.3p in 1999 and by 1.0p in 1998.

Tax reconciliations are required under US GAAP and IAS 12. Often those UK companies that currently give a reconciliation have some form of US listing and are therefore required to report this information for US purposes anyway. As discussed in 5.11.3 A above, FRS 19 requires all UK companies to give a tax reconciliation, but only of the current tax charge, and in a format different to that required by US GAAP.

(b) the amount of the tax charge on ordinary activities and on extraordinary items, respectively analysed into:
   (i) UK corporation tax, and the amount by which it has been reduced by the application of double tax relief,
   (ii) UK income tax,
   (iii) overseas tax;[208]

(c) the amount of the taxation creditor balance.[209] Where there is an amount receivable in respect of tax, the Schedule 4 formats do not specify that it should be shown separately, although it is likely that it will be disclosed if material as a separate item within debtors;

(d) movements during the year on any provision in respect of tax;[210] and

(e) the amount of any provision for deferred taxation, shown separately from any other taxation provision.[211]

As can be seen from the above, there is substantial overlap between the disclosure requirements of accounting standards and those of the Companies Act. Illustrations of most of these disclosures have already been given (see in particular Extracts 24.7 and 24.8 at 3.6 above).

6.2 FRS 12

FRS 12 – *Provisions, Contingent Liabilities and Contingent Assets* – is discussed fully in Chapter 28. By virtue of the fact that FRS 12 does not apply to items dealt with in other standards (see Chapter 28 at 2.1.4), it does not apply to deferred tax, which is covered by SSAP 15 or FRS 19, as applicable. However, it does apply to other tax provisions.

Companies often include provisions for tax liabilities in the corporation tax creditor in the accounts, including those to cover potential liabilities which either are not yet the subject of an enquiry by tax authorities or are under dispute with tax authorities but where the eventual liability is uncertain. FRS 12 applies to such provisions, although companies obviously have to tread a wary course between compliance with the relevant disclosure requirements and prejudicing their tax position.

GlaxoSmithKline gives the following disclosure in respect of tax provisions.

> *Extract 24.24: GlaxoSmithKline plc (2000)*
>
> **13. Taxation** [extract]
>
> The integrated nature of the Group's worldwide operations, with cross-border supply routes into numerous end-markets, gives rise to complexity and delay in negotiations with revenue authorities as to the profits that fall to be taxed in individual territories: resolution of such transfer pricing issues is an inevitable and continuing fact of life for the Group. For a number of years Glaxo Wellcome has had significant open issues relating to transfer pricing in the USA. The issues, principally relating to the success of Zantac, relate to all years from 1989 to the present and there remains a wide variation between the claims of the Internal Revenue Service and the Group's estimation of its taxation liabilities. These issues are now the subject of discussions between the US and UK tax authorities under the terms of the double tax convention between the two countries. Having taken appropriate professional advice in seeking to manage these issues to a satisfactory conclusion, the Directors continue to believe that the Group has made adequate provision for the liabilities likely to arise from open assessments.

Such provisions are clearly not deferred tax as defined in SSAP 15 as they are not related to timing differences. However, there is in fact an issue as to whether such disclosures fall within the remit of FRS 12 for a company complying with FRS 19. This is because, as discussed at 5.1.1 above, the definition of deferred tax under FRS 19 is not simply the tax relating to timing differences, but the 'future tax consequences of transactions and events recognised in the financial statements of the current and previous periods.' This suggests that FRS 19 directly requires disclosure such as that in Extract 24.24 above under its general 'sweep-up' disclosure requirements discussed at 5.11.3 E above.

6.3 UITF 19

In 1995/6 new tax rules on the taxation of foreign exchange differences were introduced in the UK. These have the effect that in certain cases the exchange movements on borrowings taken out to hedge overseas investments are taxable. The (pre-tax) exchange gains and losses on such borrowings are taken direct to reserves in accordance with SSAP 20 and reported in the statement of total recognised gains and losses (STRGL) – see Chapter 8 at 2.3.7, 2.4.5 and 3.5. The question therefore arose as to where the tax should be shown, an issue which was discussed by the UITF in 1997.

The UITF ruled, in UITF 19, that the tax on foreign exchange differences reported in the STRGL should also be reported in the STRGL. This requirement has now been incorporated in FRSs 16 and 19 (see 3.1 and 5.10.1 above). However, UITF 19 has not been withdrawn because it contains the following further requirements:

(a) the gross exchange difference and the related tax should be separately disclosed. An example of a company giving this disclosure is Tate & Lyle

Extract 24.25: Tate & Lyle Public Limited Company (2000)

Statement of Recognised Gains and Losses	**78 weeks To March 2000 £ million**	52 weeks To September 1998 £ million
Profit for the period	**184**	124
Currency difference on foreign currency net investments	**38**	(97)
Taxation on currency difference on foreign currency net investments	**3**	2
Total recognised gains for the period	**225**	29

(b) the restriction on the amount of the exchange movements on the borrowing that can be taken to reserves under SSAP 20 (see Chapter 8 at 2.3.7 and 2.4.5) should be applied on an after-tax basis.

The clarification in (b) above has led to an increase in companies hedging overseas investments on a 'grossed up for tax' basis. For example, a company with a 30% tax rate wishing to hedge (say) $100 of net assets will borrow $143 – i.e. $100 x (100/[100-30]), and elect to be subject to tax on any exchange movement on the borrowing. The after-tax exchange movement on $143 is equivalent to an untaxed exchange movement on $100, thus providing a perfect hedge against exchange movements on the net assets. It is important, however, that companies entering into such arrangements are able to predict their effective tax rate with reasonable certainty. If the company had insufficient tax capacity to absorb the tax on the full exchange movement on the borrowing, the after-tax exchange difference on the borrowings would be greater than that on the net assets, and the excess would have to be accounted for in the profit and loss account.[212]

6.4 SSAP 5 – VAT

The ASC published SSAP 5 – *Accounting for value added tax* – in 1974,[213] based on an exposure draft which had been published in the previous year. The standard is a very brief one, simply requiring that:

(a) turnover should be shown net of VAT on taxable outputs (or shown as a deduction if the gross amount is also shown);[214] and

(b) irrecoverable VAT should be included in the cost of fixed assets and any other disclosed items in the financial statements to which it relates, where it is practicable to do so and material.[215]

6.5 Petroleum Revenue Tax (PRT)

In 1981, the ASC issued an exposure draft of a statement on Accounting for Petroleum Revenue Tax.[216] The subject was not proceeded with and the exposure draft was subsequently withdrawn. The Oil Industry Accounting Committee also studied the topic with the aim of producing a SORP, but did not continue the project. The tax is complex and presents difficult accounting problems, but its specialised nature places it beyond the scope of this chapter.

7 IAS REQUIREMENTS

7.1 Development of accounting for tax under IAS

The original version of International Accounting Standard No. 12 – *Accounting for Taxes on Income* – was published in 1979. This was so accommodating as to hardly merit the name 'standard', since it allowed either the deferral method or the liability method to be used, and permitted both comprehensive allocation and partial provision. This was inevitable given the divergence of treatment in the countries that constituted the main members of the IASC at the time.

In January 1989, the IASC published a new exposure draft E33 – *Accounting for Taxes on Income* – which proposed that only the liability method should be permitted, and that comprehensive allocation should be the preferred method, although partial provision would remain a permitted alternative. However, this exposure draft was not taken further, largely because it was overtaken by the issue of the US standard SFAS 109.

A new exposure draft E49 – *Income Taxes* – was issued in 1994, proposing an approach to deferred tax that drew on the approach to accounting for deferred tax prescribed by SFAS 109. This was subsequently converted into a revised version of IAS 12 in October 1996 which came into force for accounting periods beginning on or after 1 January 1998. Some relatively minor changes were made to IAS 12 in April and October 2000. In addition, the SIC has issued two interpretations of IAS 12, SIC-21 – *Income Taxes – Recovery of Revalued Non-Depreciable Assets*[217] – and SIC-25 – *Income Taxes – Changes in the Tax Status of an Enterprise or its Shareholders.*[218]

7.2 IAS 12

In contrast to the position in the UK, IAS 12 deals with both current and deferred tax in a single standard.

7.2.1 *Definitions*

For the purposes of IAS 12, and the discussion in this section of the Chapter, 'accounting profit' is net profit or loss for a period before deducting tax expense.

'Tax expense (tax income)' is the aggregate amount included in the determination of net profit or loss for the period in respect of current tax and deferred tax.

'Current tax' is the amount of income taxes payable (recoverable) in respect of the 'taxable profit (tax loss)' for a period, i.e. the profit (loss) for a period determined in accordance with the rules established by the taxation authorities, upon which income taxes are payable (recoverable).

With respect to deferred tax, IAS 12 adopts the temporary difference approach, which is described in general terms at 1.3.3 A. Subject to some important exceptions, discussed in 7.2.2 below, IAS 12 requires deferred tax to be provided for on all temporary differences. 'Temporary differences' are differences between the carrying amount of an asset or liability in the balance sheet and its tax base. Temporary differences may be either:

(a) 'taxable temporary differences', which are temporary differences that will result in taxable amounts in determining taxable profit (tax loss) of future periods when the carrying amount of the asset or liability is recovered or settled; or

(b) 'deductible temporary differences', which are temporary differences that will result in amounts that are deductible in determining taxable profit (tax loss) of future periods when the carrying amount of the asset or liability is recovered or settled.

'Deferred tax liabilities' are the amounts of income taxes payable in future periods in respect of taxable temporary differences. 'Deferred tax assets' are the amounts of income taxes recoverable in future periods in respect of deductible temporary differences, together with the carryforward of unused losses and tax credits.

The 'tax base' of an asset or liability is 'the amount attributed to that asset or liability for tax purposes'.[219] As this is the definition on which all the others relating to deferred tax ultimately depend, understanding it is key to a proper interpretation of IAS 12.

A Tax base

In some cases, the 'tax base' of an asset or liability is relatively obvious. In the case of a tax-deductible fixed asset, for instance, the 'amount attributed to [it] for tax purposes' is (to use UK terminology) its tax written-down value (see Example 24.5 at 1.3.3 A above).

Other items, however, require more careful analysis. For example, a company may have accrued interest receivable of £1,000 that will be taxed only on receipt. The 'amount attributed ... for tax purposes' to that £1,000 (and therefore its tax base) could appear, on a natural reading of the English words, to be £1,000, since this is the amount that will be taxed on receipt. However, a tax base of £1,000 would imply a temporary difference of nil and therefore that no deferred tax should be recognised on the accrued income, which would clearly be wrong. The correct analysis is that the 'amount attributed ... for tax purposes' *at the balance sheet date* is nil. This is because, at that date, the interest is a 'nothing' from the point of view of the tax authorities, as it will be taxed only on receipt. This would give rise to a temporary difference of £1,000 (i.e. £1,000 carrying amount less tax base nil), in respect of which a deferred tax liability would be recognised

A similar example might be a provision of, say, £1 million for unfunded pension costs, for which tax relief is given on settlement of the liability. Like the accrued interest in the previous paragraph, this would appear in the accounts, but until it was actually funded it would not be of any relevance for tax purposes, so that the 'amount attributed to [it] for tax purposes' at the balance sheet date is nil. This would give rise to a temporary difference of £1 million (i.e. carrying amount of £1 million less tax base of nil) in respect of which a deferred tax asset would be recognised, as would be expected.

Unfortunately, this analysis does not appear to hold true in the case of an item neither the origination nor settlement of which has any tax consequences. Take, for example, a bank loan of £1,000. Since there are as a rule no tax deductions for principal, this is just as much a 'nothing' for tax purposes at the balance sheet date as the unfunded pension provision just discussed. This would suggest that the 'tax base' of the loan as defined by IAS 12 should also be nil. However, that would give the absurd result that a deferred tax asset would be provided for on the carrying amount of the loan. The temporary difference relating to the loan must be nil which implies that its tax base must therefore be its carrying amount of £1,000.

IAS 12 addresses this problem by providing that in the case of:

(a) an asset the recovery of which does not give rise to taxable income; and

(b) a liability the settlement of which is not deductible for tax purposes,

the tax base is to be taken as being the carrying amount;[220] in other words, there is no temporary difference, and therefore no deferred tax. On this basis no deferred tax would be provided in respect of the loan (because its settlement will not be tax-deductible).

This is clearly the right result, but it does leave the basic definition of 'tax base' looking rather inadequate. If an item does not exist for tax purposes, the 'amount attributable to it for tax purposes' would be more obviously nil than its carrying amount! A harsher view might be that in these paragraphs IAS 12 does not so much clarify the definition of tax base as rewrite it.

In fact IAS 12 tacitly admits as much, since it goes on to state that 'where the tax base of an asset or liability is not immediately apparent, it is helpful to consider the fundamental principle on which this Standard is based: that an enterprise should, with certain limited exceptions, recognise a deferred tax liability (asset) wherever recovery or settlement of the carrying amount of an asset or liability would make future tax payments larger (smaller) than they would be if such recovery or settlement were to have no tax consequences'.[221] In other words: provide for the tax that would be payable if the balance sheet were to be liquidated at book value.

As this is indeed the underlying principle of IAS 12, it would be more correct to say that the tax base of an item is whatever it needs to be to generate the right deferred tax number in accordance with that principle! To put it more formally, the basic equation is:

carrying amount – tax base = temporary difference,

but there is some ambiguity as to whether the true unknown is the temporary difference (as stated in paragraph 5 of the IAS) or the tax base (as implied by paragraph 10 quoted above). In our view, it is unsatisfactory, as a matter of drafting, that the 'bold paragraph' definition of 'tax base' is effectively over-ridden by an explanatory paragraph in this way.

In our view, this confusion arises from the fact that the temporary difference approach focuses on settlement of assets and liabilities, whereas in the real world tax is levied on gains and losses. The fundamental difference, in this context, between a bank loan and the other items discussed above is that the recognition of the other items gives rise to gains and losses whereas recognition of the loan does not.

7.2.2 *Recognition of tax assets and liabilities*

A Current tax

Current tax for current and prior periods should, to the extent unpaid, be recognised as a liability. If the amount already paid in respect of current and prior periods exceeds the amount due for those periods, the excess should be recognised as an asset.[222]

The benefit relating to a tax loss that can be carried back to recover current tax of a previous period should be recognised as an asset. When a tax loss is used to recover current tax of a previous period, an enterprise recognises the benefit as an asset in the period in which the tax loss occurs because it is probable that the benefit will flow to the enterprise and the benefit can be reliably measured.[223]

B Deferred tax

IAS 12 broadly requires deferred tax to be recognised in respect of all temporary differences except those arising from:

(a) goodwill that is not deductible for tax purposes or negative goodwill which is treated as deferred income in accordance with IAS 22 – *Business Combinations*; or

(b) the initial recognition of an asset or liability in a transaction which:

   (i) is not a business combination; and

   (ii) at the time of the transaction, affects neither accounting profit nor taxable profit (tax loss).[224]

This, at first sight somewhat arbitrary, set of rules is difficult to understand without some explanation as to the reason for them.

I Non-deductible goodwill and negative goodwill

The exemption for non-deductible goodwill and negative goodwill is simply in order to avoid the 'vicious circle' that would otherwise be set in motion. Goodwill is a function of all the net assets of the acquired business, including deferred tax. It follows that, if deferred tax is provided on goodwill, the goodwill itself changes, which means that the deferred tax on the goodwill changes, which means that the goodwill changes again, and so on.

II Initial recognition of assets and liabilities

This is simply a pragmatic exception to the general rule designed to deal with the problem highlighted by Example 24.6 in 1.3.3 A above, i.e. the fact that the temporary difference approach, if applied strictly, would require provision to be made for deferred tax on the acquisition of a non tax-deductible asset.

However, if there were no modification to this exemption, it would also preclude recognition of deferred tax arising from fair value adjustments in acquisition accounting, since these result in temporary differences which arise 'from the initial recognition of an asset or liability in a transaction which …, at the time of the transaction, affects neither accounting profit nor taxable profit'. This would have been an unfortunate result, since one of the perceived strengths of the temporary difference approach when it was originally developed in the United States was that, unlike the timing difference approach (see 5.6.1 above), it allowed recognition of deferred tax on fair value adjustments.

IAS 12's response to this is simply to provide an exception to the exception above so as to require recognition of deferred tax on fair value adjustments. The requirements of IAS 12 in respect of business combinations are discussed more fully at 7.2.7 below.

It is hard to suppress the wry observation that the overall practical result of these rules, exceptions and exceptions to exceptions is not very different from requiring deferred tax to be provided for on timing differences and fair value adjustments – a rule which would be much easier to both understand and apply!

There are clearly significant differences between IAS 12 and SSAP 15 simply because SSAP 15 provides for deferred tax on a partial provision approach and IAS 12 a full provision approach, although these differences are a relatively short-term issue due to the introduction of FRS 19 in the UK. We therefore do not address differences between SSAP 15 and IAS 12 in detail.

There are, however, also real differences between FRS 19 and IAS 12, which largely arise from two main conceptual differences. Firstly, FRS 19 requires deferred tax to be recognised on timing differences, and IAS 12 on temporary differences. Secondly, although under the conceptual frameworks of both the ASB and the IASC assets and liabilities are defined as future rights or obligations arising from past events, FRS 19 sometimes takes a different view from IAS 12 as to what is the critical 'past event' that gives rise to a deferred tax asset or liability. For example, when an asset is revalued, the critical past event under IAS 12 is the recognition of the gain or loss on revaluation in the financial statements, whereas under FRS 19 it is the creation of a binding obligation to sell the asset. These inconsistent approaches lead to a number of recognition differences, to which we draw attention at appropriate points below.

7.2.3 *Revaluations and tax rebasing of assets*

The effect of the basic rule set out in 7.2.2 above is that deferred tax must be provided on all revaluation surpluses in a tax system, such as that in the UK, where tax deductions in respect of an asset in use are based on its historical cost. This is because the gain is considered to represent an amount that will be recovered through future taxable income that will be fully taxed, as no offsetting tax allowances will be available. For the same reason, where a fixed asset is not depreciated (e.g. on the grounds that the annual charge would be immaterial), but capital allowances are claimed in respect of the asset, IAS 12 would require a deferred tax liability to be established.

There are also cases in the UK where the tax base of an asset may be higher than its carrying amount. For example, if a company bought freehold land for £1 million in 1970 and has not revalued it, its base cost for tax purposes will be well in excess of £1 million due to 1982 rebasing and cumulative indexation allowances. IAS 12 would require a deferred tax asset to be recognised in respect of the land, but subject to its restrictions on the recognition of assets (see 7.2.6 below).

Under UK GAAP, the overall position is significantly different (see 5.3 above). FRS 19 requires provision on revaluations only where:

- the assets concerned are continually revalued through the profit and loss account, or
- by the balance sheet date, the entity has entered into a binding contract to sell the asset at its revalued amount, and is not more likely than not to obtain rollover relief.

Even here, FRS 19 requires provision only if rollover relief has not been, and is not expected to be, obtained. Also, under FRS 19 an increase in tax cost has no deferred tax consequences, except to the extent that it requires an already recognised asset or liability to be remeasured.

7.2.4 *Measurement*

Current tax should be measured by reference to tax rates and laws that have been enacted or substantively enacted by the balance sheet date.[225] Deferred tax should be measured by reference to the tax rates and laws, as enacted or substantively enacted by the balance sheet date, that are expected to apply in the periods in which the assets and liabilities to which the deferred tax relates are realised or settled.[226] However, IAS 12 comments that in some jurisdictions, announcements of tax rates (and tax laws) by the government have the substantive effect of actual enactment, which may follow the announcement by a period of several months. In these circumstances, tax assets and liabilities are measured using the announced tax rate (and tax laws).[227] In the UK, FRS 16 and FRS 19 require provision to be made only on the basis of legislation that is either already enacted or awaiting only Royal Assent (see 3.1.4 and 5.9.2 above).

Deferred tax should be measured by reference to the tax consequences that would follow from the manner in which the enterprise expects, at the balance sheet date, to recover or settle the asset or liability to which it relates.[228] This is best illustrated with a simple example.

Example 24.23: Calculation of deferred tax depending on method of realisation of gain

A building, for which full capital allowances are available, originally cost £1 million. At the balance sheet date it is carried at £750,000, but tax allowances of £400,000 have been claimed in respect of it. If the building were sold, these allowances would be clawed back, but the tax indexed cost of the building would be £1.5 million. The company revalues the building to its current market value of £1.75 million. What deferred tax liability is required to be established under IAS 12, assuming a tax rate of 30%?

If the intention is to retain the asset in the business, it will be recovered out of future income of £1.75 million, on which tax of £345,000 will be paid, calculated as:

	£000
Gross income	1,750
Future tax allowances for asset (£1m less £400,000 claimed to date)	600
	1,150
Tax at 30%	345

If, however, the intention is to sell the asset, the required deferred tax liability is only £195,000, calculated as:

	£000
Sales proceeds	1,750
Tax base cost	(1,500)
	250
Clawback of tax allowances claimed	400
	650
Tax at 30%	195

The amounts of £345,000 and £195,000 above are the total required liability. The amount charged to equity would be the difference between these amounts and the existing provision of £45,000, being 30% of (£750,000 - £600,000).

SIC-21 clarifies that where a non-depreciable asset is revalued, any deferred tax on the revaluation should be calculated by reference to the tax consequences that would arise if the asset were sold at book value (on the basis that, in accounting terms the asset is never recovered through use, irrespective of the basis on which it is valued).[229] However, SIC-21 is clearly written in the context of a fully non-depreciable asset, such as land, and does not address the treatment of an asset that is depreciated to a residual value greater than zero. For UK GAAP, there is no comparable guidance on this issue in FRS 19, since provision for deferred tax on a revaluation gain will normally be made only where the reporting enterprise is committed to dispose of the asset concerned, so that there will be no doubt as to the method of realisation of the gain.

In some jurisdictions, the rate at which is tax is paid depends on whether profits are distributed or retained. In other jurisdictions, distribution may lead to an additional liability to tax, or a refund of tax already paid. IAS 12 requires current and deferred taxes to be measured using the rate applicable to undistributed profits until a liability to pay a dividend is recognised, at which point the tax consequences of that dividend should also be recognised[230] (see also 7.2.5 below). Under UK GAAP, this is not an issue for UK-registered companies, since such differential tax rates do not apply in the UK. To the extent that that differential rates apply to an overseas  investment of a UK group, FRS 19's rules for the treatment of the retained earnings of such investments (see 5.4 above) will achieve a result broadly comparable to that required under IAS.

Under IAS 12 deferred tax may not be discounted, except to the extent that it relates to a pre-tax amount that is itself discounted (such as an unfunded pension liability).[231] Under UK GAAP, FRS 19 permits discounting (see 5.10 above).

Where unrealised intra-group profits are eliminated on consolidation, IAS 12 requires deferred tax to be recognised using the buying company's tax rate, whereas FRS 19 apparently requires the selling company's tax rate to be used (see the further discussion on this issue at 5.9.2 B above).

7.2.5 Presentation

A Balance sheet

Tax assets and liabilities should be shown separately from other assets and liabilities and current tax should be shown separately from deferred tax. Deferred tax should not be shown as part of current assets or liabilities.[232] UK GAAP does not require current tax to be shown on the face of the balance sheet, and FRS 19 requires deferred tax to be shown on the face of the balance sheet only where readers might otherwise misinterpret the financial statements (see 5.9.3 B above).

Current tax assets and liabilities should be offset if, and only if, the enterprise has a legally enforceable right to set off the recognised amounts and intends either to settle them net or simultaneously.[233]

Deferred tax assets and liabilities should be offset if, and only if:

(a) the enterprise has a legally enforceable right to set off current tax assets and liabilities; and

(b) the deferred tax assets and liabilities concerned relate to income taxes raised by the same taxation authority on either:

   (i) the same taxable entity; or

   (ii) different taxable entities which intend, in each future period in which significant amounts of deferred tax are expected to be settled or recovered, to settle their current tax assets and liabilities either on a net basis or simultaneously.[234]

The restrictions for current tax are based on the offset criteria in IAS 32 (see Chapter 18 at 4.3.2), and have no parallel in UK GAAP. Those for deferred tax are based on the somewhat dubious principle that where current tax can be offset, deferred tax can also (even if the deferred tax balances actually recognised in the balance sheet would not satisfy the criteria for the offset of current tax). This is discussed further in the context of the virtually identical requirement of FRS 19 at 5.9.3 A above.

B Income statement and equity

Tax is normally recognised in the income statement, except to the extent that it relates to an item that has been recognised directly in equity (see below) or a business combination that is an acquisition (see 7.2.7 below).[235] Where a tax liability is remeasured subsequent to its initial recognition (e.g. because of a change in tax law), the change should be accounted for in the income statement, unless it relates to an item originally recognised in equity, in which case the change should also be accounted for in equity.[236]

Any deferred tax on items recognised directly in equity, is also recognised directly in equity. Such items include:

- revaluations of property;
- prior year adjustments;
- exchange differences arising on translation of the financial statements of a foreign entity;
- amounts taken to equity on initial recognition of a compound financial instrument (so called 'split accounting' – see Chapter 17 at 5.3.5).[237]

However, where taxes are remeasured as a result of a the recognition of a liability to pay a dividend (see 7.2.4 above), the difference should normally be recognised in the income statement rather than in equity, even though the dividend itself is recognised in equity under IAS. IAS 12 takes the view that the additional (or lower) tax liability is more directly linked to the original transaction subject to tax than to the distribution to shareholders. Where, however, the original transaction was an item, such as those above, that was recognised in equity, the adjustment to the tax liability should also be recognised in equity.[238]

IAS 12 acknowledges that, in exceptional circumstances, it may be difficult to determine the amount of tax that relates to items recognised in equity. In these cases a reasonable pro-rata method, or another method that achieves a more appropriate allocation in the circumstances, may be used.[239]

Where an enterprise depreciates a revalued asset, it may choose to transfer the depreciation in excess of that that would have arisen on a historical cost basis from revaluation surplus to retained earnings. In such cases, the relevant portion of any deferred tax liability recognised on the revaluation should be transferred to retained earnings also.[240]

Where an asset is revalued for tax purposes, and the tax revaluation is related to a past or expected future accounting valuation, the effect of the tax valuation is recognised in equity in the same period as the related accounting valuation. If, however, the tax valuation is not related to an accounting valuation, its effect should be recognised in the income statement for period.[241] It is not entirely clear how this would be applied to, say, the indexation of certain assets for UK tax purposes. At one level, since indexation is based on increases in the retail price index and arises irrespective of the treatment of the asset for accounting purposes, it would seem that it is not related to any accounting valuation. On the other hand, any accounting valuation will take account *inter alia* of the same inflationary increase for which the indexation is given, so that, to that extent, they are 'related'.

Where dividends are paid subject to withholding tax, the withholding tax should be included as part of the dividend charged to equity.[242] Unlike FRS 16 in the UK (see 3.1.2 above), IAS 12 gives no specific guidance on the treatment of incoming dividends and other distributions.

Sometimes there is a change in an enterprise's tax assets and liabilities as a result of a change in the tax status of the enterprise itself or that of its shareholders. SIC-25 clarifies that the effect of such change should be recognised in the income statement, except to the extent that it involves a remeasurement of tax originally accounted for in equity, in which case the change should also be dealt with in equity.[243]

Under UK GAAP, FRS 16 and FRS 19 both require the current and deferred tax relating to items charged or credited directly to equity, but not accounted for in the statement of total recognised gains and losses, to be charged or credited to the profit and loss account (see 3.1.1 and 5.9.1 above)

7.2.6 *Deferred tax assets*

A Deductible temporary differences

All deferred tax assets arising from deductible temporary differences should (subject to the general recognition rules discussed in 7.2.2 above) be recognised to the extent that it is probable that taxable profit will be available against which the deductible temporary differences can be utilised.[244] It is 'probable' that there will be sufficient taxable profit if a deferred tax asset can be offset against a deferred tax liability relating to the same tax authority which will reverse in the same period as the asset, or in a period into which a loss arising from the asset may be carried back or forwards.[245]

Where there are insufficient deferred tax liabilities to offset the asset, it should be recognised only to the extent that it is probable that in future periods there will be either:

- sufficient taxable profits relating to the same tax authority in the same period as the asset, or in a period into which a loss arising from the asset may be carried back or forwards; or
- tax planning opportunities that will create taxable profit in appropriate periods.[246]

'Tax planning opportunities' are actions that the enterprise would take in order to create or increase taxable income in a particular period before the expiry of a tax loss or tax credit carryforward. For example, in some jurisdictions, taxable profit may be created or increased by:

- electing to have interest income taxed on either a received or receivable basis;
- deferring the claim for certain deductions from taxable profit;
- selling, and perhaps leasing back, assets that have appreciated but for which the tax base has not been adjusted to reflect such appreciation; and
- selling an asset that generates non-taxable income (such as, in some jurisdictions, a government bond) in order to purchase another investment that generates taxable income.

Where tax planning opportunities advance taxable profit from a later period to an earlier period, the utilisation of a tax loss or tax credit carryforward still depends on the existence of future taxable profit from sources other than future originating temporary differences.[247]

B Tax losses and tax credits

A deferred tax asset should be recognised for the carryforward of unused tax losses and credits to the extent that it is probable that future taxable profit will be available against which the unused tax losses and unused tax credits can be utilised.[248] The criteria for recognition are essentially the same as those for deductible temporary differences, as set out in A above. However, IAS 12 emphasises that the existence of unused tax losses is strong evidence that taxable profits (other than those represented by deferred tax liabilities) may not be available. For this reason, IAS 12 requires disclosure of the recognition of losses in such circumstances (see 7.2.9 below).[249] Additionally, the following matters should be considered:

- the probability of sufficient taxable profits (whether from the reversal of deferred tax liabilities or otherwise) arising before the tax losses or credits expire;
- whether the unused tax losses result from identifiable causes that are unlikely to recur; and
- the availability of tax planning opportunities (see A above).[250]

C Subsequent remeasurement of deferred tax assets

The carrying amount of deferred tax assets should be reviewed at each balance sheet date. An enterprise should reduce the carrying amount of a deferred tax asset to the extent that it is no longer probable that sufficient taxable profit will be available to enable the asset to be recovered in full. Any reduction so made should be reversed if it subsequently becomes probable that sufficient taxable profit will be available.[251]

The basic requirements of UK GAAP in respect of deferred tax assets are fairly similar to those of IAS. However, the 'small print' of FRS 19 seems intended to ensure that in practice the hurdle for recognition of tax assets under FRS 19 is set higher than under IAS (see the further discussion at 5.5 above).

7.2.7 Acquisition accounting

In accordance with the basic rule in 7.2.2 above, deferred tax should be established in respect of the difference between the fair values assigned to acquired assets and liabilities and their tax bases.[252] If, as a result of the acquisition, the acquiring entity is able to recognise a previously unrecognised tax asset of its own (e.g. unused tax losses), the amount of the asset should be credited to goodwill, not to income.[253]

If a deferred tax asset of the acquiree which was not recognised at the time of the acquisition is subsequently recognised, the resulting credit is taken to the profit for the period. However, the carrying amount of goodwill is reduced to the amount (net of amortisation) at which it would have been carried if the deferred tax asset had been recognised at the time of the acquisition, and the resulting write-off is charged to profit in the same period. No adjustment is made to the extent it would create or add to negative goodwill.[254]

Under UK GAAP, FRS 7 (as amended by FRS 19), requires provision is made for deferred tax only on those fair value adjustments which, if reflected in the accounts of the acquired entity, would give rise to deferred tax in that entity under the principles in FRS 19. Also, losses arising in the acquired entity are treated as fair value adjustments, but those arising in the acquiring entity as post-acquisition income. There are no specific requirements under UK GAAP on the treatment of a deferred tax asset of an acquired entity which was not recognised at the time of acquisition is subsequently recognised in the consolidated financial statements. However, the general principles of FRS 7 should be applied. In most cases this will result in the asset being accounted for as a credit to the profit and loss account for the period (see further discussion at 5.6 above).

7.2.8 Subsidiaries, branches, associates and joint ventures

Temporary differences will almost inevitably arise, in both the single entity and group accounts of an investor, between the carrying value of its investment in, or net assets of, a subsidiary, branch associate or joint venture and its tax base. The most common cause will be undistributed profits of such entities, where distribution to the investor would trigger a tax liability. Temporary differences might also arise from exchange movements and provisions against, or revaluations of, the carrying value of investments.[255]

IAS 12 requires the deferred tax effects of such temporary differences to be recognised:

(a) in the case of taxable temporary differences (i.e. deferred tax liabilities), unless:
   (i) the parent, investor or venturer is able to control the timing of the reversal of the temporary difference; and
   (ii) it is probable that the temporary difference will not reverse in the foreseeable future; or

(b) in the case of deductible temporary differences (i.e. deferred tax assets), only to the extent that:
   (i) the temporary difference will reverse in the foreseeable future; and
   (ii) taxable profit will be available against which the temporary difference can be utilised.[256]

What this means in practice is best illustrated by reference to its application to the retained earnings of subsidiaries, branches and joint ventures on the one hand, and associates on the other. In the case of a subsidiary or a branch, the parent is able to control when and whether the retained earnings are distributed. Therefore, no provision need be made for the tax consequences of distribution of profits that the parent has determined will not be distributed in the foreseeable future.[257] In the case of a joint venture, provided that the investor can control the distribution policy, similar considerations apply.[258] In the case of an associate, however, the investor cannot control distribution policy. Therefore provision should be made for the tax consequences of the distribution of the retained earnings of an associate, except to the extent that there is a shareholders' agreement that those earnings will not be distributed.[259]

We consider this an almost perverse result. In reality, it is extremely unusual for any enterprise (other than one set up for a specific project) to pursue a policy of full distribution. To the extent that it occurs at all, it is much more likely in a wholly-owned subsidiary than in an associate; and yet IAS 12 effectively treats full distribution by associates as the norm and that by subsidiaries as the exception! Moreover, it seems to ignore the fact that the development of equity accounting in the 1960s had its origins in the perceived ability of investors in associates to exert some degree of control over the amount and timing of dividends from them. This is discussed further in the introduction to Chapter 7.

Under UK GAAP, FRS 19 requires provision to be made only to the extent that, at the balance sheet date, a dividend has been accrued or there is a binding agreement to make distributions in future. It also contains no specific guidance in relation to branches (see 5.4 above).

7.2.9 *Disclosures*

IAS 12 imposes quite extensive disclosure requirements as follows.

The major components of tax expense (income) should be disclosed separately. These may include:

(a) current tax expense (income);

(b) any adjustments recognised in the period for current tax of prior periods;

(c) the amount of deferred tax expense (income) relating to the origination and reversal of temporary differences;

(d) the amount of deferred tax expense (income) relating to changes in tax rates or the imposition of new taxes;

(e) the amount of the benefit arising from a previously unrecognised tax loss, tax credit or temporary difference of a prior period that is used to reduce current tax expense;

(f) the amount of the benefit from a previously unrecognised tax loss, tax credit or temporary difference of a prior period that is used to reduce deferred tax expense;

(g) deferred tax expense arising from the write-down, or reversal of a previous write-down, of a deferred tax asset; and

(h) the amount of tax expense (income) relating to those changes in accounting policies and fundamental errors which are included in the determination of net profit or loss for the period in accordance with the allowed alternative treatment in IAS 8 – *Net Profit or Loss for the Period, Fundamental Errors and Changes in Accounting Policies* (see Chapter 25 at 3.5 and 3.7).[260]

The following should also be disclosed separately:

(a) the aggregate current and deferred tax relating to items that are charged or credited to equity;

(b) tax expense (income) relating to extraordinary items recognised during the period;

(c) an explanation of the relationship between tax expense (income) and accounting profit in either or both of the following forms:

  (i) a numerical reconciliation between tax expense (income) and the product of accounting profit multiplied by the applicable tax rate(s), disclosing also the basis on which the applicable tax rate(s) is (are) computed; or

  (ii) a numerical reconciliation between the average effective tax rate and the applicable tax rate, disclosing also the basis on which the applicable tax rate is computed;

(d) an explanation of changes in the applicable tax rate(s) compared to the previous accounting period;

(e) the amount (and expiry date, if any) of deductible temporary differences, unused tax losses, and unused tax credits for which no deferred tax asset is recognised in the balance sheet;

(f) the aggregate amount of temporary differences associated with investments in subsidiaries, branches and associates and interests in joint ventures, for which deferred tax liabilities have not been recognised;

(g) in respect of each type of temporary difference, and in respect of each type of unused tax losses and unused tax credits:

  (i) the amount of the deferred tax assets and liabilities recognised in the balance sheet for each period presented;

  (ii) the amount of the deferred tax income or expense recognised in the income statement, if this is not apparent from the changes in the amounts recognised in the balance sheet; and

(h) in respect of discontinued operations, the tax expense relating to:

  (i) the gain or loss on discontinuance; and

  (ii) the profit or loss from the ordinary activities of the discontinued operation for the period, together with the corresponding amounts for each prior period presented; and

(i) the amount of income tax consequences of dividends to shareholders of the enterprise that were proposed or declared before the financial statements were authorised for issue, but are not recognised as a liability in the financial statements.[261]

Where there are different tax consequences for an enterprise depending on whether profits are retained or distributed (see 7.2.4 above), the enterprise should disclose the nature of the potential income tax consequences that would arise from a payment of dividends to shareholders. It should quantify the amount of potential income tax consequences that it practicably determinable and whether there are any potential income tax consequences that are not practicable determinable. The reason for this rather complicated requirement is that, as IAS 12 acknowledges, it can often be very difficult to quantify the tax consequences of a full distribution of profits (e.g. where there are a large number of overseas subsidiaries). However, to the extent that they can be quantified, they should be disclosed.[262]

Separate disclosure is required of the amount of any deferred tax asset that is recognised, and the nature of the evidence supporting its recognition, when:

(a) utilisation of the deferred tax asset is dependent on future profits in excess of those arising from the reversal of deferred tax liabilities; and

(b) the enterprise has suffered a loss in the current or preceding period in the tax jurisdiction to which the asset relates.[263]

A Example of disclosures

An example of some of the disclosures required under IAS 12 is given by Nokia.

Extract 24.26: Nokia Corporation (2000)

1. Accounting policies [extract]

Income taxes

Current taxes are based on the results of the Group companies and are calculated according to local tax rules.

Deferred tax assets and liabilities are determined, using the liability method, for all temporary differences arising between the tax basis of assets and liabilities and their carrying values for financial reporting purposes. Currently enacted tax rates are used in the determination of deferred income tax.

Under this method the Group is required, in relation to an acquisition, to make provision for deferred taxes on the difference between the fair values of the net assets acquired and their tax base.

The principal temporary differences arise from intercompany profit in inventory, depreciation on property, plant and equipment, untaxed reserves and tax losses carried forward. Deferred tax assets relating to the carryforward of unused tax losses are recognized to the extent that it is probable that future taxable profit will be available against which the unused tax losses can be utilized.

9. Income taxes	**2000 EURm**	1999 EURm
Current tax	**-1 852**	-1 250
Deferred tax	**68**	61
Total	**-1 784**	-1 189
Finland	**-1 173**	-740
Other countries	**-611**	-449
Total	**-1 784**	-1 189

The differences between income tax expense computed at statutory rates (29% in Finland in 2000 and 28% in 1999) and income tax expense provided on earnings are as follows at December 31:

	2000 EURm	1999 EURm
Income tax expense at statutory rate	**1 689**	1 078
Deduction for write-down of investments in subsidiaries	**-28**	–
Amortization of goodwill	**40**	17
Provisions without income tax benefit/expense	**53**	35
Taxes for prior years	**53**	8
Tax on foreign subsidiaries' net income in excess of income taxes at statutory rates	**-29**	32
Operating losses with no current tax benefits	**25**	22
Group adjustments	**–**	4
Other	**-19**	1
Income tax expense	**1 784**	1 189

Certain of the Group companies' income tax returns for periods ranging from 1995 through 1999 are under examination by tax authorities. The Group does not believe that any significant additional taxes in excess of those already provided for will arise as a result of the examinations.

19. Deferred taxes

	2000 EURm	1999 EURm
In companies' balance sheet		
Tax losses carried forward	**73**	40
Temporary differences	**147**	91
	220	131
On consolidation		
Intercompany profit in inventory	**87**	88
Property, plant and equipment	**6**	6
Other	**17**	1
	110	95
Appropriations		
Untaxed reserves	**2**	-49
	2	-49
Net deferred tax asset	**332**	177

of which in 2000 deferred tax assets amounted to EUR 401 million (EUR 257 million in 1999) and deferred tax liabilities to EUR 69 million (EUR 80 million in 1999).

In 2000 the Group recognized a provision for social security costs on unexercised stock options. The cumulative prior year net effect of the change has been recorded as an adjustment to the opening balance of retained earnings. Deferred tax asset for the provision, EUR 84 million, has been recorded as an adjustment to the opening balance of deferred taxes.

Deferred income tax liabilities have not been established for withholding tax and other taxes that would be payable on the unremitted earnings of certain subsidiaries, as such earnings are permanently reinvested.

At December 31, 2000 the Group had loss carryforwards of EUR 28 million (EUR 84 million in 1999) for which no deferred tax asset was recognized due to uncertainty of utilization of these losses. These losses will expire in the years 2003 to 2005.

B Comparison with UK disclosure requirements

IAS 12 requires a reconciliation of the 'expected' total tax to the actual tax charge in the accounts. FRS 19 requires a reconciliation of the actual current tax charge to the 'expected' tax charge.

IAS 12 requires the tax relating to discontinued operations to be shown separately. FRS 19 does not.

IAS 12 requires disclosure of the total unprovided deferred tax relating to undistributed earnings of subsidiaries, branches, associates and joint ventures (to the extent it is quantifiable). FRS 19 requires disclosure only of the amount that is expected to become payable in the foreseeable future. It also contains no specific provisions relating to branches.

FRS 19 requires disclosure of the general circumstances affecting the current and total tax charge for the current and future periods. IAS 12 does not. FRS 19 also requires disclosures regarding discounting and rollover relief that would be of no relevance under the accounting approach of IAS 12, which accordingly does not require them.

The UK requirements are discussed in more detail at 5.11 above.

8 CONCLUSION

The withdrawal of SSAP 15 in the UK and Ireland means that the partial provision approach is no longer applied by any major player in the financial reporting world. However, it remains to be seen whether the version of full provision that gains general acceptance is the temporary difference approach of US GAAP and IAS 12, or the incremental timing difference approach of FRS 19.

In the Press Release issued on publication of FRS 19,[264] the ASB implied that it hopes to persuade the International Accounting Standards Committee (IASC) to abandon its rather extreme version of full provision in IAS 12 in favour of that set out in FRS 19. However, we think it unlikely, since it will be easy for members of the IASB who support the temporary difference approach to point to FRS 19's apparent ambiguities and internal inconsistencies. IAS 12 may, in the view both of the ASB and of ourselves, be founded on fatally flawed logic, but it at least applies that logic (reasonably) consistently and clearly, and the anecdotal evidence is that, other than at the margins, it is reasonably easy to apply in practice.

Ideally, we believe that the international debate on accounting for tax should be reopened from first principles. IAS 12, FRS 19 and the flow through method adopt very different approaches to accounting for tax, yet are all claimed by their supporters to be consistent with the same conceptual framework. This suggests either that at least two of these bodies of opinion are mistaken, or that the framework itself requires revision as being too imprecise to be an appropriate foundation for accounting standards. It would, however, be unrealistic to expect such a fundamental re-examination of either IAS 12 or the framework at this stage.

For these reasons, we suspect that FRS 19 will prove to be a 'holding standard' to be applied only for two or three reporting seasons before UK GAAP is superseded by IAS, in line with the proposals announced by the European Commission in June 2000. Given this scenario, it is unfortunate that, in addition to the major differences of principle, which in fact might not lead to much difference in the reported numbers, there are many apparently unnecessary minor differences between FRS 19 and IAS 12.

References

1 FRS 16, *Current Tax*, ASB, December 1999.
2 FRS 19, *Deferred Tax*, ASB, December 2000.
3 SSAP 8 – *The treatment of taxation under the imputation system in the accounts of companies*, ASC, August 1974.
4 SSAP 15, *Accounting for deferred tax*, ASC, Revised May 1985.
5 IAS 12 (Revised), *Income Taxes*, IASC, October 1996, amended April and October 2000.
6 For further discussion of this point, see *Tax and Accounts: Romance and Divorce*, Roger Muray, The Tax Journal 5 February 2001 and *Treasury taxation and the accounting revolution* by the same author, Financial Instruments Tax & Accounting Review, February 2001.
7 This is the 'traditional' definition of deferred tax used in SSAP 15. The definition in FRS 19, however, is somewhat wider (see 5.1.1 below)
8 APB 11, *Accounting for Income Taxes*, AICPA, December 1967.
9 *Amendment to SSAP 15, Accounting for deferred tax*, ASB, December 1992, para. 1.
10 Discussion Paper *Accounting for Tax*, ASB, March 1995.
11 See *Accounting for Tax*, section 6.7, for a more detailed discussion.
12 SFAS 109, *Accounting for Income Taxes*, FASB, 1992
13 *Ibid.*, paras. 77-78.
14 FRS 19, Appendix V, para. 32.
15 It seems that the drafters of IAS 12 also recognised this issue, since IAS 12 para. 22(c) states that, if deferred tax were recognised in these circumstances, the other side of the entry would be an adjustment to the cost of the asset, rather than as a charge to income or equity.
16 FRS 19., Appendix V, paras. 45-49.
17 *Ibid.*, paras. 20-22.
18 For example, where accelerated capital allowances (ACAs) are claimed, future tax assessments are greater by the amount of those ACAs than they would have been if the ACAs had not been claimed.
19 SSAP 15, para. 16.
20 FRED 22, *Revision of FRS 3 – Reporting Financial Performance*, ASB, December 2000, paras.70-76.
21 A more detailed discussion of the contents of the various exposure drafts and standards in issue before SSAP 15 and FRSs 16 and 19 can be found in the sixth edition of this book.
22 In particular, *Inside Track*, ASB, April 1999.
23 FRS 16, para. 1.
24 *Ibid.*, para. 2.
25 *Ibid*, paras. 3-4.
26 *Ibid.*, para. 18.
27 *Ibid.*, paras. 5-6.
28 *Ibid.*, para. 7.
29 *Ibid.*, para. 2.
30 *Ibid.*
31 *Ibid.* (and Appendix V, para. 12).
32 FRS 16, para. 8.
33 *Ibid.*, para. 9
34 *Ibid.*, para. 10.
35 *Ibid.*, Appendix V, para. 18.
36 FRS 1 (Revised 1996), *Cash flow statements*, ASB, October 1996, paras. 14-15.
37 FRS 16, para. 11.
38 *Ibid.*, para. 12.
39 *Ibid.*, para. 13. Strictly the calculation is to apply the fraction $t/(1-t)$, where t is the tax rate, to the post-tax profit, and not the effective tax rate as stated in FRS 16.
40 *Ibid.*, paras. 14-15.
41 More detailed discussion, and worked examples, may be found in the sixth edition of this book.
42 FRS 16, para. 20.
43 *Ibid.*, Appendix II, para. 1.
44 *Ibid.*, para. 4.
45 *Ibid.*, para. 3.
46 *Ibid.*, para. 5.
47 *Ibid.*, para. 20 and Appendix II, paras. 6-7.
48 *Ibid.*, para. 19.
49 CA 85, Sch. 4, para. 54(2) and FRS 3, para. 23.
50 SSAP 15, para. 1.
51 *Ibid.*, para. 2.
52 *Ibid.*, para. 12.
53 *Ibid.*, para. 14.
54 *Ibid.*, para. 17.
55 *Ibid.*, para. 18.
56 *Ibid.*, para. 19.
57 *Ibid.*, para. 20.
58 *Ibid.*, para. 21.
59 *Ibid.*, para. 23.
60 *Ibid.*, paras. 24–26.
61 *Ibid.*, Appendix, para. 4.
62 *Ibid.*
63 Accountants Digest No. 174, ICAEW, *A Guide to Accounting Standards — Deferred Tax*, Summer 1985.
64 SSAP 15, paras. 27 and 28.
65 *Ibid.*, Appendix, para. 4.
66 SSAP 17, *Accounting for post balance sheet events*, ASC, August 1980, Appendix, item (g) of examples of adjusting events.
67 *Ibid.*, para. 29.
68 *Ibid.*, para. 30.
69 *Ibid.*, Appendix, para. 14.

70 *Ibid.*, para. 15.
71 SSAP 15, para. 32.
72 *Ibid*, Appendix, para. 17.
73 SSAP 15., para. 5(c).
74 *Ibid.*, para. 44.
75 FRS 2, *Accounting for subsidiary undertakings*, ASB, July 1992, para. 54.
76 FRS 19, para. 70.
77 SSAP 15, para. 43.
78 Accountants Digest No. 174, p. 12.
79 SSAP 15, para. 20.
80 *Ibid.*, Appendix, para. 11.
81 SSAP 15, paras. 33 and 34.
82 FRS 3, paras. 20 and 22.
83 SSAP 15, para. 35.
84 FRS 3, para. 23.
85 SSAP 15, para. 36.
86 *Ibid.*, paras. 37 and 40.
87 *Ibid.*, para. 41.
88 Original SSAP 15, para. 33.
89 SSAP 15, para. 38.
90 *Ibid.*, para. 39.
91 *Ibid.*, para. 42.
92 *Ibid.*, para. 43.
93 *Ibid.*, para. 44.
94 FRS 19, para 1(a).
95 *Ibid.*, para. 1(b).
96 *Ibid.*, paras. 3 and 6.
97 *Ibid.*, paras. 4-5.
98 *Ibid.*, para. 2.
99 *Ibid.*
100 *Ibid.*
101 *Ibid.*
102 This method is explained in Chapter 12 at 2.3.3 H. See also the further discussion at 5.3.3 of this chapter.
103 In a UK context, this usually arises from a policy of expensing such items in single entity accounts and capitalising them on consolidation.
104 FRS 19 para. 8. Strictly the calculation is to apply the fraction $t/(1-t)$, where t is the tax rate, to the post-tax profit, and not the effective tax rate as stated in FRS 19.
105 *Ibid.*, Appendix V, para. 23 *et seq.*
106 *Ibid.*, paras. 40-44.
107 It is also slightly strange in view of the fact that in the UK, following the Finance Act 1996, interest is almost invariably taxed on an accruals basis.
108 FRS 19, Appendix V, paras. 45-49.
109 FRS 19, para. 9.
110 *Ibid.*, Appendix V, paras 53 *et seq*
111 FRS 19, para. 10.
112 *Ibid.*, para. 11.
113 FRS 15, Tangible Fixed Assets, ASB, February 1999, para. 97.
114 FRS 19, para. 2 footnote and Appendix V, para. 62
115 Where tax relief is given for the charges to the profit and loss account rather than for the actual expenditure, book and tax depreciation will be the same, so that no deferred tax will arise.
116 FRS 19, para. 12.
117 *Ibid.*, Appendix V, paras. 65-66.
118 FRS 19, para. 13.
119 *Ibid.*, para. 14.
120 *Ibid.*, para. 15.
121 This treatment will be far less common following implementation of FRS 15 *Tangible Fixed Assets*, which prohibits selective valuation, and has led most companies to stop revaluing properties.
122 This is on the assumption that these gains and losses are not assessed to tax as they arise.
123 FRS 19, para. 19.
124 *Ibid.*, Appendix V, para. 75.
125 FRS 19, para. 20.
126 *Ibid.*
127 *Ibid.*, para. 19.
128 *Ibid.*, para. 21.
129 *Ibid.*, para. 22.
130 *Ibid.*, para. 23.
131 *Ibid.*, para. 24.
132 *Ibid.*, para. 25.
133 *Ibid.*, para. 26.
134 *Ibid.*, para. 32.
135 *Ibid.*, para. 33.
136 The wording in IAS 12 is 'probable', and in SFAS 109 'more likely than not'.
137 FRS 19, Appendix V, paras. 78-79.
138 FRS 19, paras. 28-29.
139 *Ibid.*, para. 30.
140 *Ibid.*, para. 31.
141 FRS 7, *Fair values in acquisition accounting*, ASB, September 1994, para. 21, as inserted by FRS 19 para. 71(a) December 2000.
142 *Ibid.*, para. 74, as inserted by FRS 19, para. 71(b).
143 FRS 19, Appendix IV, para. 2 (table).
144 FRS 7, para. 74, as inserted by FRS 19, para. 71(b).
145 In practice, the Inland Revenue may query large differences between the accounting fair value of assets and their legal purchase price, particularly where the latter is the greater amount.
146 FRS 19, paras. 17-18.
147 There is an argument that amortisation creates a timing difference in cases where the cost of the investment in the business to which the goodwill relates would be deductible on any subsequent disposal. However, the resulting deferred tax asset would be very unlikely to meet the criteria for recognition under FRS 19 until such time as the entity was committed to disposal of the relevant investment.
148 FRS 3, *Reporting Financial Performance*, ASB, October 1992, para. 27 (footnote).

149 FRS 7, paras. 22 and 75, as inserted by FRS 19, para. 71.
150 The provision of £113.7 million represents 30% of the total of the adjustments to fixed assets and debtors, which is lower than current US federal tax rates, implying that some of these adjustments are not tax-effected.
151 FRS 19, paras. 34-35.
152 *Ibid.*, para. 36.
153 *Ibid.*, para. 37.
154 *Ibid.*, para 40.
155 *Ibid.*, para 69.
156 *Ibid.*, para. 38.
157 *Ibid.*, para 39.
158 *Ibid.*, Appendix IV, para. 2 (table, item 6).
159 SFAS 109, para. 9e.
160 FRS 19, para. 55.
161 *Ibid.*, para 56.
162 *Ibid.*, para 57.
163 *Ibid.*, Appendix V, paras. 124-127.
164 FRS 19, para. 58.
165 UITF 4 *Presentation of long-term debtors in current assets*, UITF, July 1992.
166 FRS 19, para. 42.
167 *Ibid.*, Appendix V, para. 105.
168 This is particularly the case bearing in mind that, in practice, the great majority of companies other than listed companies probably provided on a full provision basis under SSAP 15.
169 FRS 19, para. 43.
170 *Ibid.*, para. 44.
171 *Ibid.*, para. 45.
172 *Ibid.*, para. 46.
173 *Ibid.*, para. 47.
174 *Ibid.*
175 *Ibid.*, para. 48.
176 *Ibid.*
177 *Ibid.*, para. 49.
178 This assumes that a constant tax rate is applied to all years. It is possible that if (for example) a low tax rate were applied to the 'asset' years and a high rate to the 'liability' years, the accounts would still include an overall liability.
179 FRS 19, para. 50.
180 *Ibid.*
181 *Ibid.*, para. 51.
182 *Ibid.*, para. 52.
183 *Ibid.*, para. 53.
184 *Ibid.*, Appendix V, paras. 113-119.
185 FRS 19, para. 54.
186 *Ibid.*, para. 59.
187 *Ibid.*, Appendix V, paras. 120-123.
188 FRS 19, para. 60.
189 The amount of current (and deferred) tax relating to prior periods will be highlighted by the tax reconciliation required by FRS 19 (see [5.3] below), suggesting that the requirement in FRS 16 is redundant once FRS 19 becomes effective.
190 FRS 19, para. 61.
191 *Ibid.*, para. 62.
192 *Ibid.*, para. 63.
193 *Ibid.*, para. 64.
194 *Ibid.*, para. 64(a).
195 In addition, a US GAAP tax reconciliation requires the expected tax charge to be based on the reporting entity's domestic tax rate, whereas FRS 19 encourages the use of a weighted average rate for a multinational group. This means that it is extremely unlikely that the same tax reconciliation can be used for both UK and US GAAP purposes.
196 *Ibid.*, Appendix V, paras. 132-135.
197 FRS 19, para. 65.
198 *Ibid.*, Appendix V, para. 135.
199 FRS 19, para. 64(b).
200 *Ibid.*, para. 64(c).
201 *Ibid.*, para. 64(d).
202 *Ibid.*, para. 64(e).
203 *Ibid.*, Appendix V, para. 131.
204 By virtue of Schedule 11 to the Act, provisions made under the equivalent paragraphs of Schedules 9 (banks) and 9A (insurance companies) are also deemed to be realised losses.
205 FRS 19, Appendix III, paras. 13-14.
206 CA 85, Sch. 4, para. 54(2).
207 FRS 3, para. 23.
208 CA 85, Sch. 4, para. 8 Profit and loss account formats and para. 54(3).
209 *Ibid.*, para. 8 Balance sheet formats.
210 *Ibid.*, para. 46.
211 *Ibid.*, para. 47.
212 In July 2001 the Inland Revenue issued a consultative document proposing legislative changes that could effectively prevent hedging on a grossed-up basis.
213 SSAP 5, *Accounting for value added tax*, ASC, April 1974
214 SSAP 5, para. 8.
215 *Ibid.*, para. 9.
216 ED 28, *Accounting for Petroleum Revenue Tax*, ASC, March 1981.
217 SIC-21 *Income Taxes – Recovery of Revalued Non-Depreciable Assets*, SIC, August 1999.
218 SIC-25 *Income Taxes – Changes in the Tax Status of an Enterprise or its Shareholders*, SIC, August 1999.
219 IAS 12, para. 5.
220 *Ibid.*, paras. 7-8.
221 *Ibid.*, para. 10.
222 *Ibid.*, para. 12.
223 *Ibid.*, paras. 13-14.
224 *Ibid.*, para. 15.
225 *Ibid.*, para. 46.
226 *Ibid.*, para. 47.

227 *Ibid.*, para. 48.
228 *Ibid.*, para. 51.
229 SIC-21, paras. 6-7.
230 IAS 12, paras. 52A-52B.
231 *Ibid.*, paras. 53-5.
232 *Ibid.*, paras. 69 and 70.
233 *Ibid.*, para. 71.
234 *Ibid.*, para. 74.
235 *Ibid.*, para. 58.
236 *Ibid.*, para. 60.
237 *Ibid.*, paras. 61-62.
238 *Ibid.*, para. 52B.
239 *Ibid.*, para. 63.
240 *Ibid.*, para. 64.
241 *Ibid.*, para. 65.
242 *Ibid.*, para. 65A.
243 SIC-25, para. 4.
244 IAS 12, para. 24.
245 *Ibid.*, para. 28.
246 *Ibid.*, para. 29.
247 *Ibid.*, para. 30.
248 *Ibid.*, para. 34.
249 *Ibid.*, para. 35.
250 *Ibid.*, para. 36.
251 *Ibid.*, para. 56.
252 *Ibid.*, para. 19.
253 *Ibid.*, para. 67.
254 *Ibid.*, para. 68.
255 *Ibid.*, para. 38.
256 *Ibid.*, paras. 39 and 44.
257 *Ibid.*, para. 40.
258 *Ibid.*, para. 43.
259 *Ibid.*, para. 42.
260 *Ibid.*, paras. 79-80.
261 *Ibid.*, para. 81.
262 *Ibid.*, paras. 82A and 87A-87C.
263 *Ibid.*, para. 82.
264 ASB Press Notice PN 177, ASB, December 2000.

Chapter 25 Reporting financial performance

1 THE NEED FOR A STANDARD

1.1 Income measurement

The concept of income and the emphasis placed on the transactions approach to income measurement in the development of historical cost accounting theory is discussed in Chapter 2 of this book. In summary, financial accounting under the historical cost system essentially involves allocating the effects of transactions between reporting periods, with the result that the balance sheet consists of the residuals of the income measurement process. Despite the conflict discussed in Chapter 2 between the asset and liability approach on the one hand, and the revenue and expense approach on the other, the importance attributed to income measurement is highlighted by the FASB's Concepts Statement No. 1. This states that 'the primary focus of financial reporting is information about an enterprise's performance provided by measures of earnings and its components. Investors, creditors, and others who are concerned with assessing the prospects for enterprise net cash inflows are especially interested in that information.'[1] In addition, the emphasis that analysts place on companies' reported earnings as a measure of performance further illustrates the importance of income measurement.

Although the term 'income' is used to describe a concept, rather than something that is specific or precise, specific rules and procedures have been developed by accountants to measure income. These rules have been based on the concept of financial capital maintenance, which has been subscribed to by the FASB in SFAC No. 6 in terms of 'comprehensive income'. Comprehensive income is defined as 'the change in equity of a business enterprise during a period from transactions and other events and circumstances from nonowner sources'.[2] Therefore, the comprehensive income of a business enterprise over its entire lifetime will be the net of its cash receipts and cash outlays.[3]

In any event, the need for businesses to measure their income annually for financial reporting purposes highlighted two major accounting issues. First, there was the issue of how to allocate the effects of transactions between accounting periods for reporting purposes, instead of merely allowing them to fall in the periods in which the transactions took place. This issue has traditionally been dealt with through the development of allocation rules based on the fundamental accounting concepts of matching and prudence. The second issue that arose was whether or not all recorded transactions should be included in the calculation of the figure for 'net profit/loss for the period'. Some accountants have held the view that net profit/loss should reflect the effects of all recorded transactions, whilst others have contended that net profit/loss should not be distorted by abnormal, unusual and non-recurring events and transactions. These differing viewpoints have led to two basic concepts of income: the all-inclusive concept and the current operating performance concept.[4]

1.1.1 *The all-inclusive (comprehensive income) concept*

Under this concept, net profit/loss would include all transactions (except dividends and capital transactions) that affect the net change in equity. Proponents of the all-inclusive concept put forward the following arguments in favour of this basis of income measurement:

(a) the annual reported net profits/losses, when aggregated over the life of the business enterprise, should be equal to the comprehensive income of the enterprise. Therefore, since charges and credits arising from extraordinary events and from corrections of prior periods are part of an enterprise's earnings history, the omission of such items from periodic income statements will result in the misstatement of the net profit/loss for a series of years;

(b) the omission of certain charges and credits from the computation of the net profit/loss for a period opens the door to possible manipulation or smoothing of results over a period;

(c) a profit and loss account which includes the effects of all transactions is more easily understood and less subject to variations resulting from the application of subjective judgements; and

(d) full disclosure in the profit and loss account of the nature of all transactions will enable users to make their own assessments of the importance of the items and derive an appropriate measurement of income based on their own specific needs.

1.1.2 *The current operating performance concept*

Under this concept, the emphasis is on the ordinary, normal, recurring operations of the enterprise during the accounting period. If extraordinary or prior period transactions have occurred, their inclusion in the current period's profit and loss account 'might impair the significance of net income to such an extent that misleading inferences might be drawn from the amount so designated'.[5] Advocates of the current operating performance concept put forward the following arguments in its favour:[6]

(a) users attach a particular business significance to the profit and loss account and the net profit/loss reported therein. While some users are able to analyse a profit and loss account and to eliminate from it those extraordinary and prior period transactions that may tend to impair its usefulness for their purposes, many users are not trained to do this. They believe that management (subject to the attestation of the independent auditors) is in a better position to do this and eliminate the effect of such items from the amount designated as net profit/loss for the period; and

(b) extraordinary and prior period transactions should be disclosed as direct adjustments of retained earnings, since this eliminates any distortion of reported earnings for the period, resulting in a more meaningful figure for inter-period and inter-firm comparison.

1.1.3 *Which concept?*

The fundamental difference in the two concepts of income discussed above lies in the perceived objectives of reporting net operating income for a particular period. The ASB's *Statement of Principles* asserts that 'the objective of financial statements is to provide information about the reporting entity's financial performance and financial position that is useful to a wide range of users for assessing the stewardship of management and for making economic decisions.'[7] It goes on to explain the ASB's views on the predictive role of reporting financial performance as follows:

'Investors require information on financial performance because such information:

(a) provides an account of the stewardship of management and is useful in assessing the past and anticipated performance of the entity;

(b) is useful in assessing the entity's capacity to generate cash flows from its existing resource base and in forming judgements about the effectiveness with which the entity has employed its resources and might employ additional resources; and

(c) provides feedback on previous assessments of financial performance and can therefore assist users in modifying their assessments for, or in developing expectations about, future periods.'[8]

In FRED 22 – *Revision of FRS 3 'Reporting Financial Performance'* – which proposes radical change to the system of performance reporting under UK GAAP, the ASB has made it clear that it is proposing to adopt the 'all-inclusive' concept of income.[9] This will be achieved through the introduction of a single statement of financial performance that will effectively combine the existing the profit and loss account and statement of total recognised gains and losses into a single statement of financial performance. (FRED 22 is discussed in 4.3.2 below.)

Although the ASB does not use the term 'comprehensive income' in its *Statement of Principles*, comprehensive income would equate to 'gains' minus 'losses'. Gains are increases in ownership interest not resulting from contributions from owners, whilst losses are decreases in ownership interest not resulting from distributions to owners.[10] FRED 22 then equates 'comprehensive income' with 'total financial performance', which is defined as encompassing all recognised gains and losses, that is 'the change in net assets from the end of the previous period to the end of the present period, excluding distributions to and contributions from owners'.[11]

1.2 The position under UK GAAP

1.2.1 The original SSAP 6

The first standard in the UK dealing with the issue was SSAP 6 – *Extraordinary items and prior year adjustments* – which was issued in 1974. The principal objective of the standard was to ensure that all extraordinary or prior year items, with certain specified exceptions, would be accounted for through the profit and loss account for the period and not through reserves. In order to achieve this without losing information on the performance of the ongoing operations, SSAP 6 required the separate disclosure of profits and losses on extraordinary items after the profit or loss on ordinary activities, defining which items could be regarded as extraordinary. The standard also prescribed the only two instances where items could be retrospectively adjusted through reserves by means of a prior year adjustment.

Although SSAP 6 reduced the extent of reserve accounting, it inadvertently caused the development of a multiplicity of items classified as 'extraordinary', which would consequently be excluded from profit or loss on ordinary activities after taxation, and earnings per share. There was evidence of significant inconsistencies between the way different companies disclosed the effect of apparently similar events in their profit and loss accounts.

1.2.2 The revision of SSAP 6

The new accounts formats introduced in the Companies Act 1981[12] required separate disclosure in the profit and loss account of extraordinary items and the associated tax thereon after the profit or loss on ordinary activities, and thus both standardised, and gave statutory backing to, the disclosure requirements of SSAP 6. This added impetus to the growing disquiet about the effectiveness of the standard, and in 1983 the ASC issued a discussion paper that identified some of the problems that had arisen since the introduction of SSAP 6 and proposed some solutions.[13] In 1985, as a result of responses to this discussion paper, the ASC issued ED 36,[14] which embodied some of the solutions originally proposed in the 1983 discussion paper. ED 36 was eventually converted to SSAP 6 (Revised) in 1986.

1.2.3 FRED 1

The ASB issued FRED 1 – *The Structure of Financial Statements – Reporting of Financial Performance* – in December 1991 at the same time as Chapter 6 of the first piecemeal Discussion Draft version of its Draft *Statement of Principles – Presentation of financial information*. The two documents gave the accounting world its first view of the ASB's plans to revolutionise the reporting of financial performance in general, and the profit and loss account in particular. They introduced the idea of an additional primary financial statement of performance and, although not confirmed until the publication of the third and fourth Discussion Draft chapters of the Draft *Statement of Principles* in July 1992, gave the first indication of the ASB's preference for a balance sheet approach to the recognition of comprehensive income.

1.2.4 *FRS 3*

Despite receiving extensive comments on FRED 1, the ASB issued FRS 3 in October 1992 with few changes in substance. The requirements of FRS 3 are dealt with in 2 below.

1.2.5 *FRED 22*

In December 2000 the ASB published FRED 22 – *Revision of FRS 3 'Reporting Financial Performance'.* FRED 22 is the product of an international initiative undertaken by the G4+1 Group of standard setters, and is based heavily on a G4+1 Position Paper – *Reporting Financial Performance* – that had been issued in June 1999.

If converted to a standard, the FRED would require reporting entities to present a single statement of financial performance, combining the current profit and loss account and statement of total recognised gains and losses. All changes in net assets that occur between the opening and closing balance sheet dates (other than those involving transactions with shareholders) would be reflected in this statement of total performance.

This new statement would be divided into three sections: operating, financing and treasury, and other gains and losses. The format would be adapted for banking and insurance entities. The proposed standard would then specify which items should be reported as 'financing and treasury' and 'other gains and losses', with the result that the 'operating' section would be the default. Classification of items would depend on their nature, without any distinction being made between realised and unrealised gains and losses.

The proposals in FRED 22 are discussed in detail in 4.3.2 below.

1.3 The IAS position

As yet, there is no single IASC standard that deals with the reporting of financial performance in its entirety. However, there are several standards that, to a greater or lesser extent, impinge on the issue. These include: IAS 1 – *Presentation of Financial Statement*, IAS 8 – *Net Profit and Loss for the Period, Fundamental Errors and Changes in Accounting Policies*, and IAS 35 – *Discontinuing Operations.* These standards are dealt with in detail in 3 below.

The most notable feature of performance reporting under IAS is that it is somewhat less rigid than UK GAAP. IAS are not restricted by the legal formats that exist in EU law and, as a result, companies reporting under IAS have considerably more freedom in the presentation of their performance than do companies reporting under UK GAAP. This freedom is extended by the fact that there is no definition in IAS of the results of operating activities, a lack of clarity concerning the reporting of exceptional items as either operating or non-operating, and an apparent sanctioning of the reporting of extraordinary items. As a result, the comparability of income statement performance measures as between companies reporting under IAS is somewhat reduced.

1.4 The move internationally towards a single performance statement

The issue of performance reporting is a major challenge facing the IASB and specifically and national standard setters generally. This is because many of the projects currently on the IASB's agenda – such as financial instruments, leases, share-based payments and asset revaluations – raise important questions regarding performance reporting. All of these projects involve the application of fair value measurements, with the result that the question of how changes in fair value should be reported is frequently being asked.

Meanwhile, the G4+1 Group of standard setters has published two papers advocating that the traditional income statement and statement of changes in equity (or statement of total recognised gains and losses, in the case of the UK) should be replaced by a single statement of total performance. As mentioned above, this has now been taken on board by the ASB, and is reflected in the proposals contained in FRED 22. More importantly, though, the IASB has announced that performance reporting will be one of four priority projects intended to provide leadership and promote convergence. The former IASC Performance Reporting Steering Committee has now been converted into an Advisory Committee to the IASB, and the project is under ongoing discussion at the IASB.

The move internationally towards a single statement of financial performance is discussed in detail in 4 below.

2 THE REQUIREMENTS OF FRS 3

2.1 The principal features of FRS 3

'Making Corporate Reports Valuable', a project undertaken by the Research Committee of ICAS, identified four basic shortcomings of present-day financial reporting: the adherence to legal form rather than economic substance, the use of cost rather than value, the concentration on the past rather than the future and the interest in 'profit' rather than 'wealth'.[15] Bearing in mind that Sir David Tweedie, former Chairman of the ASB, was a member of the Committee that prepared the MCRV document, it is not difficult to identify many of the ASB's initiatives as attempts to address these shortcomings. For example, the objective of FRS 5 – *Reporting the substance of transactions* – is to ensure that the substance of an entity's transactions is reported in its financial statements; the ASB's *Statement of Principles* advocates greater use of current values in financial reporting, and the Statement on the Operating and Financial Review is designed to encourage reporting entities to discuss issues that are relevant to an assessment of their future prospects.

It is not surprising, therefore, that FRS 3 was also aimed at ameliorating some of these perceived shortcomings. This was borne out by the standard's objective, which was stated as being 'to require reporting entities falling within its scope to highlight a range of important components of financial performance to aid users in understanding the performance achieved by a reporting entity in a period and to assist them in forming a basis for their assessment of future results and cash flows'.[16] Furthermore, as is more fully explained below, the new statement of financial performance introduced by FRS 3 – the statement of total recognised gains and losses – represented the ASB's first step towards requiring the reporting of changes in wealth as opposed to traditional historical cost profit and loss.

In summary, the changes to the reporting of financial performance brought about by FRS 3 were as follows:

- the profit and loss account was reshaped into a so-called 'layered format' so as to highlight a number of important components of performance:
  - the results of continuing operations (including the results of acquisitions);
  - the results of discontinued operations;
  - profits and losses on the sale or termination of an operation, costs of a fundamental reorganisation or restructuring and profits or losses on the disposal of fixed assets; and
  - extraordinary items;
- the analysis between continuing operations, acquisitions (as a component of continuing operations) and discontinued operations should be disclosed to the level of operating profit. As a minimum, the analysis of turnover and operating profit must be given on the face of the profit and loss account, with the analysis of the remaining headings allowed to be relegated to the notes.

  The question of whether the analysis of results between continuing and discontinued operations should include interest and taxation was debated extensively by the ASB. However, the ASB concluded that the analysis should only be required to the pre-interest level because interest payable is often a reflection of a reporting entity's overall financing policy, involving both equity and debt funding considerations on a group-wide basis, rather than an aggregation of the particular types of finance allocated to individual segments of the entity's operations. Consequently, any allocation of interest would involve a considerable degree of subjectivity; irrespective of the method used, assumptions would have to be made regarding such factors as the use of disposal proceeds, the appropriate interest rate to use and the reporting entity's cost of capital. However, the standard did not preclude the allocation of interest or taxation between continuing and discontinued operations, but if it is allocated, the method and underlying assumptions used in making the allocations should be disclosed;[17]
- the standard laid down strict criteria for distinguishing between continuing and discontinued operations;
- extraordinary items were effectively eliminated, although EPS is, in any event, to be calculated *after* extraordinary items. Most (if not all) items which were previously classified as extraordinary under SSAP 6 should now be treated as exceptional items;
- all exceptional items (other than the three listed below) should be included in the profit and loss account under the statutory format headings to which they relate. They should be disclosed separately by way of note or, where it is

necessary in order that the financial statements give a true and fair view, on the face of the profit and loss account. The following items, including provisions in respect of such items, should be shown separately on the face of the profit and loss account after operating profit and before interest, analysed between continuing and discontinued operations:

  - profits or losses on the sale or termination of an operation;
  - costs of a fundamental reorganisation or restructuring; and
  - profits or losses on the disposal of fixed assets;

- the standard introduced a new primary financial statement in the form of a 'Statement of total recognised gains and losses'. The statement would reflect the ways in which the reporting entity's net assets have increased or decreased from all sources other than investment by its owners, and represented the ASB's first step towards the reporting of changes in wealth;
- the standard introduced a requirement to disclose a memorandum note of historical cost profits and losses immediately following the profit and loss account or statement of total recognised gains and losses. This is an abbreviated restatement of the profit and loss account which adjusts the reported profit to show that figure excluding the effects of any asset revaluations;
- the standard required a reconciliation of the opening and closing totals of shareholders' funds for the period. The reconciliation may be presented either as a note to the financial statements or as a fifth primary statement. Where it is presented as a primary statement the FRS requires it to be shown separately from the statement of total recognised gains and losses; and
- prior period adjustments must be accounted for by restating the comparative figures for the preceding period in the primary statements and notes and by adjusting the opening balance of reserves in the current and previous periods for the cumulative effect. The cumulative effect of the adjustments should also be noted at the foot of the statement of total recognised gains and losses of the current period.

Each of these aspects of FRS 3 is discussed in more detail in the sections that follow. Illustrative examples of the requirements of the standard are set out in an Appendix to the standard, part of which is reproduced below, showing the two alternative formats of the restyled profit and loss account:

Profit and loss account example 1

	1993	**1993**	**1992** as restated
	£ million	*£ million*	*£ million*
Turnover			
Continuing operations	550		500
Acquisitions	50		
	600		
Discontinued operations	175		190
		775	690
Cost of sales		(620)	(555)
Gross profit		155	135
Net operating expenses		(104)	(83)
Operating profit			
Continuing operations	50		40
Acquisitions	6		
	56		
Discontinued operations	(15)		12
Less 1992 provision	10		
		51	52
Profit on sale of properties in continuing operations		9	6
Provision for loss on operations to be discontinued			(30)
Loss on disposal of discontinued operations	(17)		
Less 1992 provision	20		
		3	
Profit on ordinary activities before interest		63	28
Interest payable		(18)	(15)
Profit on ordinary activities before taxation		45	13
Tax on profit on ordinary activities		(14)	(4)
Profit on ordinary activities after taxation		31	9
Minority interests		(2)	(2)
[Profit before extraordinary items]		29	7
[Extraordinary items] (included only to show positioning)		–	–
Profit for the financial year		29	7
Dividends		(8)	(1)
Retained profit for the financial year		21	6
Earnings per share		39p	10p
Adjustments		*xp*	*xp*
[to be itemised and an adequate description to be given]			
Adjusted earnings per share		*yp*	*yp*

[Reason for calculating the adjusted earnings per share to be given]

Profit and loss account example 2

	Continuing operations 1993	Acquisitions 1993	Discontinued operations 1993	Total 1993	Total 1992 as restated
	£ million	*£ million*	*£ million*	*£ million*	*£ million*
Turnover	550	50	175	775	690
Cost of sales	(415)	(40)	(165)	(620)	(555)
Gross profit	135	10	10	155	135
Net operating expenses	(85)	(4)	(25)	(114)	(83)
Less 1992 provision			10	10	
Operating profit	50	6	(5)	51	52
Profit on sale of properties	9			9	6
Provision for loss on operations to be discontinued					(30)
Loss on disposal of discontinued operations			(17)	(17)	
Less 1992 provision			20	20	
Profit on ordinary activities before interest	59	6	(2)	63	28
Interest payable				(18)	(15)
Profit on ordinary activities before taxation				45	13
Tax on profit on ordinary activities				(14)	(4)
Profit on ordinary activities after taxation				31	9
Minority interests				(2)	(2)
[Profit before extraordinary items]				29	7
[Extraordinary items] (included only to show positioning)				–	–
Profit for the financial year				29	7
Dividends				(8)	(1)
Retained profit for the financial year				21	6
Earnings per share				**39p**	**10p**
Adjustments					
[to be itemised and an adequate description to be given]				xp	xp
Adjusted earnings per share				yp	yp

[Reason for calculating the adjusted earnings per share to be given]

Notes to the financial statements

Note required in respect of profit and loss account example 1

	1993			1992 (as restated)		
	Continuing	Discontinued	Total	Continuing	Discontinued	Total
	£ million	*£ million*	*£ million*	*£ million*	*£ million*	*£ million*
Cost of sales	455	165	620	385	170	555
Net operating expenses						
Distribution costs	56	13	69	46	5	51
Administrative expenses	41	12	53	34	3	37
Other operating income	(8)	0	(8)	(5)	0	(5)
	89	25	114	75	8	83
Less 1992 provision	0	(10)	(10)			
	89	15	104			

The total figures for continuing operations in 1993 include the following amounts relating to acquisitions: cost of sales £40 million and net operating expenses £4 million (namely distribution costs £3 million, administrative expenses £3 million and other operating income £2 million).

Note required in respect of profit and loss account example 2

	1993			1992 (as restated)		
	Continuing	Discontinued	Total	Continuing	Discontinued	Total
	£ million	*£ million*	*£ million*	*£ million*	*£ million*	*£ million*
Turnover				500	190	690
Cost of sales				385	170	555
Net operating expenses						
Distribution costs	56	13	69	46	5	51
Administrative expenses	41	12	53	34	3	37
Other operating income	(8)	0	(8)	(5)	0	(5)
	89	25	114	75	8	83
Operating profit				40	12	52

The total figure of net operating expenses for continuing operations in 1993 includes £4 million in respect of acquisitions (namely distribution costs £3 million, administrative expenses £3 million and other operating income £2 million).

2.2 The scope of FRS 3

FRS 3 applies to all financial statements intended to give a true and fair view of the financial position and results of the reporting entity. The standard states that such entities 'should apply the requirements of the FRS except to the extent that these requirements are not permitted by the statutory framework (if any) under which the entity reports'.[18]

The implication of this is that where specific industry legislation merely permits an entity not to disclose certain information, this clause within the scope section of the FRS will not be sufficient to allow the entities to depart from the requirements of the FRS. However, this is contrary to the ASB's *Foreword to Accounting Standards, which* would allow a departure from the requirements of a standard in such circumstances.[19]

2.3 Continuing and discontinued operations

FRS 3 requires each of the statutory profit and loss account headings between turnover and operating profit to be analysed between continuing operations, acquisitions (as a component of continuing operations) and discontinued operations. Although the term 'operating profit' is not used in the Companies Act formats, it is not defined in FRS 3 either. However, the standard does state that 'for non-financial reporting entities operating profit is normally profit before income from shares in group undertakings'.[20]

This is a somewhat curious interpretation of operating profit, since it seems to draw a distinction between operating and non-operating profit on the basis of the legal form of the income-earning vehicle, rather than on the basis of the nature of the income itself. However, this approach has now been confirmed by FRS 9 – *Associates and joint ventures* – which (a) differentiates between associates and joint ventures and (b) specifies where the income from them is to be shown in relation to operating profit in the profit and loss account.

FRS 9 states that the share of associates' operating results should be included after the group operating result and, where applicable, after and separately from the share of the operating results of joint ventures[21] (see Extract 25.1 below). We presume that this approach is to be followed at each level of the profit and loss account where the share of associates' and joint ventures' results is to be included. This is implied by the illustrative examples in Appendix IV to FRS 9, but not explicitly stated.

Extract 25.1: Cable and Wireless plc (2001)

CONSOLIDATED PROFIT AND LOSS ACCOUNT [extract]
FOR THE YEAR ENDED 31 MARCH

	Continuing operations £m	Discontinued operations £m	2001 £m
Turnover of the Group including its share of joint ventures and associates	7,498	995	**8,493**
Share of turnover of – joint ventures	(333)	–	**(333)**
– associates	(60)	(1)	**(61)**
Group turnover	7,105	994	**8,099**
Operating costs before depreciation, amortisation and exceptional items	(5,737)	(580)	**(6,317)**
Exceptional operating costs	–	–	**–**
Operating costs before depreciation and amortisation	(5,737)	(580)	**(6,317)**
EBITDA	1,368	414	**1,782**
Depreciation before exceptional items	(1,006)	(129)	**(1,135)**
Exceptional depreciation	(444)	–	**(444)**
Depreciation	(1,450)	(129)	**(1,579)**
Amortisation of capitalised goodwill	(466)	(3)	**(469)**
Group operating (loss)/profit	(548)	282	**(266)**
Share of operating profits in joint ventures	97	–	**97**
Share of operating profits in associates	17	–	**17**
Total operating (loss)/ profit	(434)	282	**(152)**
Exceptional profits less (losses) on sale and termination of operations	5	4,067	**4,072**
Exceptional costs of fundamental reorganisation	(530)	–	**(530)**
Profits less (losses on disposal of fixed assets before exceptional items)	4	–	**4**
Exceptional items	42	–	**42**
Profits less (losses) on disposal of fixed assets	46	–	**46**
Exceptional write down of investments	(43)	–	**(43)**
(Loss)/profit on ordinary activities before interest	(956)	4,349	**3,393**
Net interest and other similar income/(charges)			
– Group (including exceptional finance charges of £110m, 2000 - £nil)			**–**
– joint ventures and associates			**–**
Total net interest and other similar income/(charges)			**–**
Profit on ordinary activities before taxation			**3,393**
Tax on profit on ordinary activities			**(503)**
Profit on ordinary activities after taxation			**2,890**
Equity minority interests			**(258)**
Profit for the financial year			**2,632**
Dividends – interim			**(138)**
– final (proposed)			**(324)**
Profit for the year retained			**2,170**

* Discontinued operations comprise Cable & Wireless HKT Limited and the consumer operations of Cable & Wireless Communications plc.

2.3.1 *The definition of discontinued operations*

Under FRS 3, discontinued operations are operations of the reporting entity that are sold or terminated and that satisfy all of the following conditions:[22]

(a) the sale or termination is completed either in the period or before the earlier of three months after the commencement of the subsequent period and the date on which the financial statements are approved;

(b) if a termination, the former activities have ceased permanently;

(c) the sale or termination has a material effect on the nature and focus of the reporting entity's operations and represents a material reduction in its operating facilities resulting either from its withdrawal from a particular market (whether class of business or geographical) or from a material reduction in turnover in the reporting entity's continuing markets; and

(d) the assets, liabilities, results of operations and activities are clearly distinguishable, physically, operationally and for financial reporting purposes.

Operations not satisfying all these conditions are classified as continuing.

Perhaps the most notable feature of this definition is the fact that 'discontinued' means what it says. The operations must have been discontinued (i.e. either sold or ceased permanently) within the financial year or shortly after the year end. Clearly, the ASB's underlying rationale for this approach was to improve the predictive value of the profit and loss account by providing users with a basis for the assessment of future income. Users now have the assurance that operations reported as discontinued in the profit and loss account will have no impact on future performance.

Another clear feature of this definition is that it is not limited to business or geographical segments that are reportable under SSAP 25, which means that operations that are sold or terminated can be classified as discontinued for FRS 3 reporting purposes, even if the operations were not separately identified for segmental reporting purposes. In fact, FRS 3 specifically requires that where a sale or termination has a material impact on a major business segment this should be disclosed and explained.[23]

The standard also makes it clear that only income and costs directly related to discontinued operations should appear under the heading of discontinued operations. This means that reorganisation or restructuring of continuing operations resulting from a sale or termination should be treated as a part of continuing operations.[24]

2.3.2 *The meaning of 'ceased permanently'*

In the case of a termination, the operation cannot be classified as discontinued unless the 'former activities have ceased permanently'. However, FRS 3 provides no guidance about how this requirement should be applied in practice and leaves open a number of questions about when an operation can be regarded as having ceased permanently. This is because the waters are somewhat muddied by a passing reference to 'downsizing' in the explanation section of the standard, which seems to recognise that where a company takes a strategic decision 'to curtail materially its presence in a continuing market', the affected operation may be classified as discontinued.[25] Nevertheless, downsizing is not referred to at all in the standard itself and this isolated reference to the concept does not sit very comfortably with the standard's definition of discontinued operations. One possible interpretation might be that the principle of downsizing can be applied to a business which is made up of a number of distinct parts; if a significant number of the parts of the business have closed and have ceased permanently, but the other parts continue then, taken together, the business as a whole has been downsized.

In any event, whatever the term means, the standard seems to recognise downsized operations as qualifying for the discontinued classification, with the result that the phrase 'ceased permanently' presents some interpretational difficulties.

These difficulties arise most commonly in run-off situations. For example, a group might have an insurance underwriting subsidiary that has ceased business permanently, although it is possible that material unprovided claims might arise in the future. When would this business be regarded as discontinued under FRS 3? Is it when it ceases writing new business, or is it when it stops paying out claims (which might be several decades in the future)? In our view, FRS 3 does not provide a clear-cut answer to this sort of issue. However, we would suggest that since the subsidiary is in the business of underwriting, the day it ceases writing new business is the day on which the business can be regarded as discontinued. Provision would be made for future claims, which would be reassessed on an annual basis and adjusted if necessary.

Similar issues would arise in the case of a group with a leasing subsidiary that ceased writing new leases, or a group with an investment property division that had announced its withdrawal from the investment property business and had sold all but an immaterial amount of its investment property portfolio.

2.3.3 *The meaning of 'material effect on the nature and focus'*

To be included in the category of discontinued operations, a sale or termination must have a material effect on the nature and focus of the reporting entity's operations and represent a material reduction in its operating facilities resulting either from its withdrawal from a particular market (whether class of business or geographical) or from a material reduction in turnover in the reporting entity's continuing markets. In the explanation section of FRS 3, the ASB states that the phrase 'nature and focus of the reporting entity's operations' refers to the positioning of its products or services in their markets including the aspects of both quality and location. It then cites the example of a hotel company selling a chain of hotels in the lower end of the market and replacing it with a chain in the luxury end of the market; whilst remaining in the business of operating hotels, the group would be changing the nature and focus of its operations. Similarly, if the company sold its hotels in the US and bought hotels in Europe, that sale would also be classified as discontinued. Conversely, the sale of hotels and the purchase of others within the same market sector and similar locations would be treated as wholly within continuing operations.[26]

However, these examples are simplistic and the situations that arise in practice are far less clear-cut, requiring the application of a considerable amount of subjective judgement in order to determine whether or not a sale or termination should be classified as discontinued. The matter is further obscured by the requirement that the material reduction in operating facilities must have resulted either from the withdrawal from a particular market or from a material reduction in turnover in the reporting entity's continuing markets.[27] It is in the context of this latter case that the notion of 'downsizing' is introduced in the explanation section of the standard. Downsizing is explained as being a strategic decision by the reporting entity to curtail materially its presence in a continuing market.[28]

However, the standard provides no further help about how this concept is to be applied in practice, with the result that its use merely adds to the difficulty of applying the discontinued operations definition in practice, thereby opening the door to fairly wide interpretation. In fact, the only point that is clarified is that the sale or termination of a component of a reporting entity's operations which is undertaken primarily in order to achieve productivity improvements or other cost savings is a part of the entity's continuing operations and the effects of the sale or termination should be included under that heading.[29]

Nevertheless, in practice it might be difficult to determine whether or not a downsizing has been carried out with the primary objective of achieving productivity improvements and/or cost savings. What is important, though, is that a downsizing can only be classified under discontinued operations where the sale or termination also has a material effect on the nature and focus of the reporting entity's operations. So, for example, if a supermarket chain decides to close a third of its stores because they are unprofitable, then this downsizing cannot be regarded as a discontinuance as the nature and focus of the entity's operations will be unchanged. Conversely, if the supermarket chain closes the stores because it is repositioning itself in the market, and the closed stores no longer fit the chain's new market profile, then the downsizing might well fall into the discontinued category.

Amstrad presents a good example of this distinction being applied in practice. As can be seen from the following extract from its 1996 accounts, the Group's consumer electronics business (ACE) was downsized as part of a cost reduction exercise. Consequently, whilst the resulting restructuring costs were regarded as being fundamental to the Group's operations (and therefore classified in the profit and loss account as non-operating), they were nevertheless considered to be part of the Group's continuing operations:

Extract 25.2: Amstrad plc (1996)

OPERATING REVIEW [extract]

ACE has continued to experience very tough market conditions, especially in Germany, and trading losses have been incurred. The arrangements with Betacom will result in significant headcount reduction and downsizing of UK and overseas operations that will greatly reduce costs and are expected to eliminate loss making activities.

Notes to the Accounts

3 Restructuring costs

In addition to the above on 1 July 1996 the company announced a fundamental restructuring and downsizing of the Amstrad Consumer Electronics business. The costs of this restructuring (£6.7 million) have been disclosed as a non-operating exceptional item.

2.3.4 *The meaning of 'clearly distinguishable'*

The fourth condition that must be fulfilled for a sale or termination to be classified as discontinued is that the assets, liabilities, results of operations and activities of the operations that are sold or terminated must be clearly distinguishable, physically, operationally and for financial reporting purposes. This means that if the financial results of a sold or terminated operation are not identifiable separately from the accounting records or to a material extent can only be derived through making allocations of income or expenses, then the operation cannot be classified as a discontinued operation.

However, the example that is given in the explanation section of the standard to illustrate the practical application of this condition seems to bear little relationship to the condition itself. The example which is cited is that of a manufacturing facility that is closed down but which lacks an external market price for its output. According to the example, this closure cannot be classified as a discontinued operation.[30] It is unclear what the link is between an operation having an external market price for its output and the requirement for the operation's assets, liabilities, results of operations and activities to be clearly distinguishable. Consequently, it again seems that the application of this condition in practice is open to considerable subjective judgement. On the other hand, it is difficult to imagine the situation of a sale or termination meeting the first three conditions for a discontinued classification but not meeting the fourth.

2.3.5 *Application of the discontinued operations definition in practice*

Although we agree that the rules on discontinued operations were in need of reform, we have reservations about the way in which the disclosure of discontinued operations has been dealt with in FRS 3. We would have preferred it if discontinued operations had been addressed as an aspect of segmental reporting, not by amendment to the presentation of the profit and loss account, for this reason: FRS 3 only considers the profit and loss account, whereas the approach to discontinued operations should be consistent throughout the accounts. Dealing with it as a segmental issue would have required the net assets of the discontinued operations to be disclosed as well (provided, of course, that they are still there), and might also have provided an opportunity to introduce segmental disclosure of cash flows (for both continuing and discontinued operations).

P&O's demerger of its cruise business provides a good example of the disclosure in the profit and loss account and notes of a discontinued operation:

Extract 25.3: The Peninsular and Oriental Steam Navigation Company (2000)

Report of the directors [extract]

Principal changes in the Group [extract]

On 23 October 2000, the Group demerged its cruise business to form P&O Princess Cruises plc, a separate listed company.

Group profit and loss account
for the year ended 31 December 2000 [extract]

		Note	2000 £m	2000 £m	1999 £m	1999 £m
Turnover: Group and share of joint ventures				5,774.7		7,648.2
Less: share of joint ventures' turnover				(1,830.5)		(1,511.6)
Continuing operations			2,563.0		2,366.7	
Discontinued operations			1,381.2		3,769.9	
Group turnover		2		3,944.2		6,136.6
Net operating costs		3		(3,462.1)		(5,593.1)
Group operating profit				482.1		543.5
Share of operating results of:	joint ventures			110.4		51.5
	associates			10.6		14.2
Continuing operations			365.3		326.8	
Discontinued operations			237.8		282.4	
Total operating profit		2		603.1		609.2
Continuing operations						
(Loss)/profit on sale of properties held as fixed assets				(17.1)		5.1
Loss on sale of investments, ships and other fixed assets				(4.2)		(7.0)
Loss on sale and termination of businesses				(85.1)		(65.4)
Discontinued operations						
Loss on sale of investments, ships and other fixed assets				(0.5)		(2.9)
(Loss)/profit on sale and termination of businesses				(207.8)		120.9
Profit on ordinary activities before interest				288.4		659.9

Notes to the accounts

2 Analysis of results and net operating assets [extract]

Turnover [extract] By division: Continuing operations	Group 2000 £m	Joint ventures 2000 £m	Total 2000 £m
Ports	531.6	49.4	581.0
Logistics	1,096.8	–	1,096.8
Ferries	433.4	240.0	673.4
P&O Nedlloyd	–	1,498.4	1,498.4
Bulk shipping	103.5	13.8	117.3
Property	397.7	28.9	426.6
Discontinued operations			
Cruises	1,381.2	–	1381.2
	3,944.2	1,830.5	5,774.7

Operating profit [extract] By division: Continuing operations	Group 2000 £m	Joint ventures 2000 £m	Associates 2000 £m	Total 2000 £m
Ports	80.2	14.5	7.8	102.5
Logistics	24.8	–	–	24.8
Ferries	(4.5)	24.6	–	20.1
P&O Nedlloyd	(2.5)	68.7	–	66.2
Bulk shipping	18.3	(0.5)	–	17.8
Property	128.3	3.1	2.5	133.9
Discontinued operations				
Cruises	237.5	–	0.3	237.5
	482.1	110.4	10.6	603.1

Loss on sale of investments, ships and other fixed assets [extract]				
Discontinued operations				
Cruises	(0.5)	–	(0.5)	(2.9)
	(0.5)	–	(0.5)	(2.9)

(Loss)/profit on sale and termination of businesses [extract]				
Discontinued operations				
Cruises	(208.0)	0.2	(207.8)	–

3 Net operating costs

	Continuing operations 2000 £m	Discontinued operations 2000 £m	Total 2000 £m
Cost of sales	(2,035.1)	(977.1)	(3,012.2)
Distribution costs	(7.4)	–	(7.4)
Administrative expenses	(294.4)	(168.3)	(462.7)
Other operating income	18.5	1.7	20.2
	(2,318.4)	(1,143.7)	(3,462.1)

Hanson's demerger in 1996 of its chemicals and other businesses provides another clear-cut example of a discontinued operation under FRS 3. The discontinuance was described in the group's accounts as follows:

Extract 25.4: Hanson PLC (1996)

NOTES TO THE ACCOUNTS

21 Acquisitions, demergers and disposals [extract]

Demergers

On October 1, 1996 Hanson demerged its chemicals businesses together with its investment in Suburban Propane through Millennium and its tobacco businesses through Imperial. As a result of the demerger, approved by shareholders of Hanson at an extraordinary general meeting on September 25, 1996, each Hanson shareholder received by way of a dividend in specie one share of Millennium common stock for every 70 Hanson ordinary shares owned and one ordinary share of Imperial for every 10 Hanson ordinary shares owned. ...

The results of both Millennium and Imperial are reported within discontinued operations in the consolidated profit and loss account. The assets and liabilities of Millennium are not included in the balance sheet at October 1, 1996 whereas they are included in the balance sheet at September 30, 1995. The consolidated cash flow statement includes the cash flows of both Millennium and Imperial for the period to the date of the demergers.

As part of the demerger transactions parts of Cornerstone and Grove were demerged with Millennium on October 1, 1996 and repurchased six days after that demerger. These parts have been treated as continuing businesses in the results to October 1, 1996.

In order for a discontinuance to meet FRS 3's definition of a discontinued operation, the operation either must have been sold or have ceased permanently within the financial year or the earlier of three months after the year end and when the accounts are approved. As a result, some companies find themselves in the position of having made a decision to discontinue an operation, but then not being able to disclose it as discontinued in the profit and loss account because the operation had not ceased permanently by the time the accounts are approved.

Therefore, it is increasingly becoming the practice when this situation occurs for companies to highlight the operations to be discontinued by showing them as a separate component of continuing operations. De Vere is an example of a company that has followed this approach, distinguishing between continuing operations that are ongoing, continuing operations that are to be discontinued and discontinued operations:

Extract 25.5: De Vere Group plc (2000)

Chairman's Statement [extract]

During the year under review further significant changes took place within our Group, reflecting the Board's commitment to enhancing shareholder value. The sale of the Pubs & Restaurants business in December 1999 for £1.1 billion was a leading industry strategic move which, with the consequent restructuring to the renamed De Vere Group plc, has completed the successful transition to a focused hotels and health and fitness group.

Chief Executive's Operating Review [extract]

Trading over the second half at Tavern has suffered from a continued decline in on-trade volumes, compounded by a poor Summer, resulting in a loss for the year of £6.1 million (1999: loss of £3.2 million) on turnover of £175.4 million (1999: £213.1 million). The rationalisation programme has continued with the closure of 19 depots during the year, resulting in an exceptional charge of £6.9 million. Since our trading statement in October 2000, we have sold the database for World Wines Direct (WWD) and consequently closed the business. WWD contributed a loss of £1.3 million during the year and the cost of closure was £0.8 million. As previously reported, Tavern has experienced difficult trading conditions and we are pursuing a number of options regarding its future; the Tavern business will be discontinued within the Group before the end of March 2001.

Consolidated Profit and Loss Account
for the 53 weeks ended 1 October 2000 [extract]

	Notes	**2000 £000 (53 weeks)**	1999 £000 (52 weeks) restated
TURNOVER			
Continuing operations - continuing	1	**232,543**	204,863
Continuing operations – to be discontinued	1	**175,378**	213,143
		407,921	418,006
Discontinued operations	1	**70,465**	480,946
		478,386	898,952
COST OF SALES	2	**(208,417)**	(353,175)
GROSS PROFIT		**269,969**	545,777
Other operating expenses (net)	2/3	**(230,264)**	(421,654)
OPERATING PROFIT			
Continuing operations – continuing	1	**46,453**	45,558
– to be discontinued	1	**(6,061)**	(3,185)
Exceptional items	4	**(7,697)**	(12,200)
		32,695	30,173
Discontinued operations	1	**7,010**	93,950
		39,705	124,123
Loss on disposal of businesses	4	**–**	(149,793)
Reorganisation costs	4	**–**	(217,300)
Surplus on disposal of properties	4	**446**	(527)
		40,151	(243,497)

Notes to the Accounts
1 Segmental Analysis [extract]
Turnover, profit and net assets

	2000			1999		
Analysis of turnover, profit and net assets by class of business	**Turnover £000**	**Operating Profit £000**	**Net assets £000**	**Turnover £000**	Operating Profit £000 restated*	Net assets £000 restated*
To be discontinued – Tavern	**175,378**	**(6,061)**	**20,951**	**213,143**	(3,185)	37,053

Interestingly enough, the particular disclosure route that De Vere has chosen reflects the approach that is followed under International GAAP. IAS 35 – *Discontinuing Operations* – addresses the presentation and disclosures relating to discontinuing (as opposed to discontinued) operations. The objectives of IAS 35 are to establish a basis for segregating information about a major operation that an enterprise is discontinuing from information about its continuing operations and to specify minimum disclosures about a discontinuing operation.

Under IAS 35, a discontinuing operation is a relatively large component of an enterprise (such as a business or geographical segment under IAS 14 – *Segment Reporting*) that the enterprise, pursuant to a single plan, either is disposing of substantially in its entirety or is terminating through abandonment or piecemeal sale.[31] The Standard uses the term 'discontinuing operation' rather than the traditional 'discontinued operation' because 'discontinued operation' implies that recognition of a discontinuance is necessary only at or near the end of the process of discontinuing the operation (as is the case under FRS 3). Instead, IAS 35 requires that disclosures about a discontinuing operation begin earlier than that, namely when a detailed formal plan for disposal has been adopted and announced or when the enterprise has already contracted for the disposal. (IAS 35 is discussed in detail in 3.8 below.)

Consequently, there is a fairly significant difference in philosophy between the ASB's approach on 'discontinued' operations and that of the IASC on 'discontinuing' operations. Whilst FRS 3 focuses in on operations that have ceased permanently in the current financial year or shortly thereafter, the IASC calls for disclosure at an earlier point in time, namely, as soon as there is a board decision, a detailed plan and public announcement.[32] Relating this to the situation of De Vere as illustrated in the above extract, the businesses that are in the process of divestment do not qualify as discontinued operations under FRS 3, yet it appears that they would be classified as discontinuing operations under IAS 35.

A question that sometimes arises is whether the partial disposal of a business (for example, the sale of a 70% interest in a previously wholly-owned subsidiary) meets FRS 3's definition of a discontinued operation. There is a school of thought that argues that a subsidiary becoming an associated undertaking is, ipso facto, a discontinuance. However, we consider, on balance, that for a sale to be classified as a discontinued operation it must still satisfy all the necessary conditions contained in paragraph 4 of FRS 3, set out in 2.3.1 above.

It is perhaps noteworthy that this situation has been addressed in the US in a SEC Staff Accounting Bulletin. The situation considered by the SEC staff was that of a company which disposes of a controlling interest in a business segment and either retains a minority voting interest directly in the segment or holds a minority voting interest in the buyer of the segment. This minority interest enables the company to exert significant influence over the operating and financial policies of the segment thereby requiring it to account for its residual investment using the equity method. In the view of the SEC staff, the retention of an interest sufficient to enable the company to exert significant influence was inconsistent with a discontinued operations classification.[33]

2.4 Accounting for the consequences of a decision to sell or terminate an operation

Although FRS 3 is primarily a disclosure standard, it also deals with some recognition and measurement issues. Perhaps the most controversial amongst these relates to the principle underlying the establishment of provisions as a consequence of a decision to sell or terminate an operation. This is because the principle underlying the use of provisions in FRS 3 stemmed originally from the definition of a liability in the ASB's (then Draft) *Statement of Principles* – namely, that a provision is only raised when an obligation to transfer economic benefits arises. This principle has now been entrenched in UK GAAP by FRS 12 – *Provisions, Contingent Liabilities and Contingent Assets* – which first defines liabilities as 'obligations of an entity to transfer economic benefits as a result of past transactions or events', and then defines a provision as 'a liability of uncertain timing or amount'.[34]

FRS 3 requires that if a decision has been made to sell or terminate an operation, any consequential provisions should reflect the extent to which obligations have been incurred that are not expected to be covered by the future profits of the operation.[35] Prior to FRS 12, this requirement in FRS 3 also extended to considering the extent to which the obligations were expected to be covered by profits on the disposal of the operation's assets. However, FRS 12 made a consequential amendment to paragraph 18 of FRS 3 to the extent that expected gains from the disposal of assets should not be taken into account in determining the amount of the provision for the sale or termination of an operation. The ASB's rationale being that it believes that liabilities should be measured independently of the recognition and measurement rules for assets.

BAA provides an illustration of provisions for discontinuance, comprising a provision for closure costs and fixed asset impairment:

Extract 25.6: BAA plc (2000)

Chief Executive's Review [extract]

In September 1999 we wrote down goodwill by £147 million in respect of the World Duty Free Americas' airport division and inflight division. Subsequently, we have taken the decision to exit from the inflight business because the very slow recovery in the trans-Pacific market after the Asian economic crisis has been compounded by the loss of intra-EU duty-free in the transatlantic and short-haul markets. This left a complex business with costly overheads in a structurally unattractive market.

Notes to the Accounts [extract]
2 Exceptional items [extract]
Operating items [extract]

	2000 £m	1999 £m
Non-operating items		
World Duty Free's inflight division to be discontinued		
– Provision for costs of closure (see note 21)	(21)	–
– Fixed asset impairment charge (see note 12 (a))	(8)	–

Low & Bonar provides an example of a provision for the closure of an operation, although the closure did not meet the definition of a discontinued operation. The company refers also to the anticipated proceeds from the disposal of fixed assets, which, under FRS 3, could not be taken account of in the determination of the amount of the provision:

Extract 25.7: Low & Bonar PLC (1998)

FINANCIAL REVIEW [extract]

… we have made a provision of £7.5 million to cover the costs of closure. This figure excludes an estimated gain of approximately £2 million which we anticipate on the disposal of the land, buildings and certain equipment which, due to changing accounting standards, cannot be accounted for until the assets are sold. The cash costs associated with the Irlam closure net of disposal proceeds when the land, buildings and equipment are sold, are anticipated to be between £2 million and £3 million. …

Further, FRS 3 requires that a provision is not set up until the reporting entity is demonstrably committed to the sale or termination, arguing that it is only at this point that the obligation arises. This should be evidenced, in the case of a sale, by a binding sale agreement and, in the case of a termination, by a detailed formal plan for termination from which the reporting entity cannot realistically withdraw.[36] In the explanation section of the standard, the ASB states that evidence of such a commitment might be the public announcement of specific plans, the commencement of implementation, or other circumstances effectively obliging the reporting entity to complete the sale or termination. It then goes on to say that 'a binding contract entered into after the balance sheet date may provide additional evidence of asset values and commitments at the balance sheet date.'[37] The significance of this is that the requirement in paragraph 18 of FRS 3 for there to be a binding sale agreement does not stipulate that the binding sale agreement has to be in place at the year end. This means that, as long as the company is demonstrably committed to the sale of an operation at the year end (through, for example, public announcement or other circumstances effectively obliging the reporting entity to complete the sale, such as a sale agreement that is subject only to shareholder approval), and the sale contract becomes binding before the accounts are signed, then paragraph 18's conditions for establishing a provision to reflect the consequences of the decision to sell the operation will be met.

In the case of an intended sale for which no legally binding sale agreement exists, no obligation has been entered into by the reporting entity and accordingly no provision for the direct costs of the decision to sell and for the future operating losses should be made. However, any impairment of fixed assets should be recognised in the financial statements in accordance with FRS 11.[38] Nevertheless, although FRS 11 states that an impairment loss recognised in the profit and loss account should be included within operating profit under the appropriate statutory heading, and disclosed as an exceptional item if appropriate,[39] it seems that in practice companies are disclosing impairments in respect of contemplated discontinuances as non-operating exceptional items. This is illustrated in Extract 25.8 below:

Extract 25.8: Tomkins PLC (2001)

Consolidated profit and loss account [extract]

For the year ended 30 April 2001	**Before goodwill amortisation and exceptional items £ million**	**Goodwill amort-isation £ million**	**Exceptional items £ million**	**Total £ million**	Before goodwill amortisation and exceptional items £ million	Goodwill Amort-isation £ million	Exceptional items £ million	Total £ million
Operating profit including associates	**320.0**	**(9.9)**	**–**	**310.1**	526.0	(5.0)	–	521.0
Loss on disposal of operations	–	–	**(280.9)**	**(280.9)**	–	–	(6.3)	(6.3)
Reversal of provision for loss on disposal of business	–	–	**215.0**	**215.0**	–	–	–	–
Provision for loss on disposal of business to be discontinued:								
Impairment of goodwill	–	–	**(42.2)**	**(42.2)**	–	–	(171.4)	(171.4)
Impairment of assets	–	–	**(23.0)**	**(23.8)**			–	–
Payments directly related to the disposal	–	–	–	–	–	–	(43.6)	(43.6)
Profit before interest	**320.0**	**(9.9)**	**(131.9)**	**178.2**	526.0	(5.0)	(221.3)	299.7

28 Acquisitions and disposals [extract]

Disposals:

Engineered & Construction Products:

Homer of Redditch Limited, Twiflex Limited and T. A. Knight Limited were sold on 18 May 2000, 23 June 2000 and 16 February 2001 respectively for a total cash consideration, net of costs, of £3.1 million. £1.0 million of goodwill previously written off to reserves was written off to the profit and loss account resulting in a loss on sale of £1.8 million.

> *Food Manufacturing:*
>
> The Red Wing Company Inc was sold on 14 July 2000 for a cash consideration, net of costs, of $140.9 million (£93.8 million). The sale of the remaining Food Manufacturing business segment was completed on 31 August 2000 for a total cash consideration of £1,138.0 million. £171.4 million of the £828.7 million of goodwill previously written off to reserves on acquisition of the business was included in the write-off of the impaired goodwill in the year ended 29 April 2000 and the remaining £657.3 million was charged to the profit and loss account. Costs of the sale were offset by the reversal of the £43.6 million provision established at 29 April 2000 for payments directly related to the disposal, which included a provision of £25.0 million for pension payments arising as a result of the transaction. The net loss on sale charged to the profit and loss account for the year ended 30 April 2001 was £1.8 million.
>
> *Professional, Garden & Leisure Products:*
>
> Murray Inc and Hayter Limited were sold on the 5 October 2000 for a provisional consideration of $219.3 million (£148.3 million). Of the proceeds, $206.3 million (£139.5 million) has been received in cash and $13.0 million (£8.8 million) in a secured subordinated loan note, repayable in 2006. There was a loss on sale of £62.3 million after charging £73.9 million of goodwill, previously written off to reserves and £2.1 million of costs of disposal.
>
> As a result of the agreement signed subsequent to the year end relating to the disposal of Smith & Wesson (see note 29), a provision of £66.0 million for the loss on sale, which includes £42.2 million for the impairment of goodwill, has been charged to the profit and loss account.

The provision for the sale or termination of an operation should cover only:

(i) the direct costs of the sale or termination; and

(ii) any operating losses up to the date of the sale or termination.

In both cases, the provision should be calculated after taking into account the aggregate profit, if any, to be recognised in the profit and loss account from the future profits of the operation. Again, prior to FRS 12, FRS 3 required that the provision amount should take into account profits to be recognised from the disposal of the assets of the operation, but a consequential change brought about by FRS 12 has removed this requirement.

Where the operation is classified as continuing in the period under review, the write down of assets and the provision for operating losses and for the loss on sale or termination will be included in the continuing operations category. In the subsequent period the provisions will be used to offset the results of the operations. The related disclosure in that subsequent period will be to show the trading results of the operation under each of the statutory format headings with the utilisation of the provisions being separately highlighted on the face of the profit and loss account under the operating loss and, if appropriate, the loss on sale or termination of the operation. The results will be included in whichever category is appropriate, either discontinued or still under continuing. The following extract from one of FRS 3's profit and loss account examples illustrates the presentation:

	1993	1993	1992
			as restated
	£ million	*£ million*	*£ million*
Operating profit			
Continuing operations	50		40
Acquisitions	6		
	56		
Discontinued operations	(15)		12
Less 1992 provision	10		
		51	52
Profit on sale of properties in continuing operations		9	6
Provision for loss on operations to be discontinued			(30)
Loss on disposal of discontinued operations	(17)		
Less 1992 provision	20		
		3	
Profit on ordinary activities before interest		63	28

FRS 3's rules on the establishment of provisions as a consequence of a decision to sell or terminate an operation reflected the ASB's underlying philosophy that costs and losses should be charged in the profit and loss account in the periods to which they relate and that future income should not be enhanced by 'buckets' of provisions being established in the current year. This was a practice which had grown from SSAP 6's somewhat liberal approach to accounting for terminated activities. Under SSAP 6, as soon as a decision had been made to discontinue a business segment, provision would be made for all anticipated future costs and losses which were expected to arise in connection with the discontinuance – even if the discontinuance was expected to take several years to complete. Since these provisions were generally charged as extraordinary items, the current and future earnings per share were protected against loss-making operations which were in the process of termination.

FRS 3 clearly took a much stricter line on the way in which discontinuing operations were to be accounted for and disclosed. Not only must the sale or termination be completed in the period to qualify for a discontinued classification in the profit and loss account, but there is also much less facility for exuberant provisioning. This is because there needs to be more than just a decision to sell or terminate: in the case of a sale, there needs to be a binding sale agreement and, in the case of a termination, a detailed formal plan for termination from which the reporting entity cannot realistically withdraw.

2.5 The effect of acquisitions

FRS 3 requires that any material contribution to the results of a group from acquisitions made during the year should also be disclosed on the face of the profit and loss account, as a separate component of the results of continuing operations. The term 'acquisitions' is defined in the standard (somewhat circularly) as being 'operations of the reporting entity that are acquired in the period'.[40] However, the standard acknowledges that it will sometimes be impracticable to provide this disclosure – for example, if the acquired business is integrated with existing businesses in such a way that this full analysis is unobtainable. In such cases, an indication should be given in the notes to the accounts of the contribution of the acquisition to the turnover and operating profit of the continuing operations, or a statement, with reasons, that not even this information can be determined.[41]

The standard does not explain the reasoning behind this disclosure requirement, although it is presumably designed to distinguish organic growth from purchased growth and is therefore regarded as the mirror image of the requirements on discontinued operations. However, it is clear that the definition of acquisitions does not mirror that for a discontinued operation; with the latter being a lot more restrictive. For example, an operation could be classified as an acquisition even though it does not affect the nature and focus of the entity's operations, whereas the disposal of that same operation would not be classified as a discontinued operation.

The usefulness of the information presented will often be questionable. The length of the period for which the results will be analysed separately in this way will depend entirely on when the acquisition happens to fall in the financial year. For example, a company with a 31 December year end might buy a subsidiary on 2 January; if so, it would show virtually the whole of the next year's results of the subsidiary in the acquisitions column, but if it had made the acquisition two days earlier, all of the results of that same year would be presented as stemming from continuing activities. The effect of the acquisition would not be highlighted at all, and any hope of facilitating a comparison with the previous year would be frustrated. For these reasons, we believe that these disclosures are of limited value.

In addition to the above disclosure, the standard also requires that, where an acquisition has a material impact on a major business segment, this should be disclosed and explained.[42] The following extract from the accounts of Bass (now Six Continents) provides detailed disclosure of the impact of acquisitions and discontinued operations on the group's segmental analysis by class of business:

Extract 25.9: Bass PLC (2000)

Notes to the Financial Statements [extract]

	2000			1999		
2 TURNOVER*	**External £m**	**Inter-divisional £m**	**Total £m**	External £m	Inter-divisional £m	Total £m
Bass Hotel & Resorts:						
Ongoing operations	**1,281**	–	**1,281**	1,162	–	1,162
Acquisitions	**300**	–	**300**	–	–	–
	1,581	–	**1,581**	1,162	–	1,162
Bass Leisure Retail:						
Ongoing operations	**1,406**	–	**1,406**	1,428	–	1,428
Acquisitions	**268**	–	**268**	–	–	–
	1,674	–	**1,674**	1,428	–	1,428
Britvic Soft Drinks	**507**	**32**	**539**	507	36	543
Other activities	**13**	**11**	**24**	13	14	27
Continuing operations	**3,775**	**43**	**3,818**	3,110	50	3,160
Discontinued**	**1,383**	**237**	**1,620**	1,576	264	1,840
	5,158	**280**	**5,438**	4,686	314	5,000

* Reflects 52 weeks (1999 53 weeks) trading, with the exception of Bass Hotels & Resorts which reflects 12 months (1999 12 months) trading.

** Represents Bass Brewers.

3 COSTS AND OVERHEADS LESS OTHER INCOME [extract]	2000 Acquisitions £m	2000 Continuing operations £m	2000 Discontinued operations** £m	2000 Total £m	1999 Continuing operations £m	1999 Discontinued operations £m	1999 Total £m
Raw materials and consumables	89	759	222	981	654	274	928
Changes in stocks of finished goods and work in progress	–	(11)	1	(10)	3	(2)	1
Staff costs (see note 6)	164	1,024	126	1,150	838	138	976
Depreciation of tangible fixed assets	12	208	75	283	150	87	237
Hire of plant and machinery	–	54	6	60	46	7	53
Property rentals	98	181	2	183	95	2	97
Income from fixed asset investments	–	(15)	(7)	(22)	(15)	(7)	(22)
Other external charges	120	800	839	1,639	681	927	1,608
	483	3,000	1,264	4,264	2,452	1,426	3,878

* Includes acquisitions
** Represents Bass Brewers

4 PROFIT	2000 Total operating profit** post–FRS 15 £m	2000 Non-operating exceptional items post-FRS 15 £m	2000 Profit on ordinary activities before interest post-FRS 15 £m	1999 Total pro forma operating profit** post-FRS 15*** £m	1999 Total operating exceptional items pre-FRS 15 £m	1999 Non-operating exceptional items pre-FRS 15 £m	1999 Profit on ordinary activities before interest pre-FRS 15 £m
Bass Hotels & Resorts: (see note 5)							
Ongoing operations	364	(4)	360	304	321	(107)	214
Acquisitions	12	–	12	–	–	–	–
	376	(4)	372	304	321	(107)	214
Bass Leisure Retail:							
Ongoing operations	273	–	273	281	298	–	298
Acquisitions	73	–	73	–	–	–	–
	346	–	346	281	298	–	298
Britvic Soft Drinks	46	1	47	44	44	–	44
Other activities	8	5	13	1	1	2	3
Continuing operations	776	2	778	630	664	(105)	559
Discontinued operations ****	129	1,232	1,361	160	160	(7)	153
	905	1,234	2,139	790	824	(112)	712

**** Represents Bass Brewers

It should be noted that the disclosure required by the standard in respect of acquisitions is in addition to those already required by (i) the Companies Act 1985, (for example, the requirement in paragraph 13 of Schedule 4A to disclose the profit or loss of an acquired subsidiary for the period prior to its acquisition by the group and for the previous year), and (ii) other accounting standards (for example, the FRS 6 requirements to disclose information about the results of new subsidiaries).[43]

2.6 Extraordinary and exceptional items

2.6.1 *Extraordinary items*

Extraordinary items are defined in FRS 3 as 'material items *possessing a high degree of abnormality* which arise from events or transactions that fall outside the ordinary activities of the reporting entity and which are not expected to recur. They do not include exceptional items nor do they include prior period items merely because they relate to a prior period.'[44] (The words in italics are our emphasis, to highlight an important difference between this definition and the corresponding definition under IAS. Extraordinary items under IAS are discussed below in 3.4.) FRS 3 regards extraordinary items as being 'extremely rare', so rare indeed that no examples are provided. Items which under SSAP 6 were traditionally treated as extraordinary (for example, profits or losses on the sale of fixed assets and profits or losses on the sale or termination of an operation) are now specifically listed in FRS 3 as exceptional items.[45]

In fact, Sir David Tweedie (former ASB Chairman) is on record as saying that the ASB has effectively succeeded in outlawing extraordinary items – despite the fact that FRS 3 provides the theoretical facility for such items to arise. Nevertheless, taking the standard's definition of extraordinary items at face value, it is still relatively easy to suggest items which fall within the extraordinary items definition (for example, costs incurred in defending a hostile take-over bid). However, the sting in the tail lies not in the standard's definition of extraordinary items, but in its definition of ordinary activities, which are stated as being 'any activities which are undertaken by a reporting entity as part of its business and such related activities in which the reporting entity engages in furtherance of, incidental to, or arising from, these activities. Ordinary activities include the effects on the reporting entity of any event in the various environments in which it operates, including the political, regulatory, economic and geographical environments, irrespective of the frequency or unusual nature of the events.'[46]

The consequence of such an all-embracing definition is that it is difficult to imagine any 'events or transactions that fall outside the ordinary activities of the reporting entity'. For example, it is difficult to argue that a hostile take-over bid is not an event of the various environments in which most, if not all, entities operate.

Nevertheless, Fairway Group presented an example of a company which clearly did not believe that extraordinary items had been outlawed by FRS 3. In implementing FRS 3 for the first time in 1993, the company persevered with showing 'costs of aborted acquisition' as an extraordinary item in the comparative figures, and did not reclassify the item as exceptional as was done by other companies:

Extract 25.10: Fairway Group Plc (1993)

Notes to the Accounts

	1993	1992
	£'000	£'000
Costs of aborted acquisition	–	(162)

The above item fell outside the ordinary activities of the Company and is not expected to recur.

It is a moot point whether the costs of an aborted acquisition incurred by an entity that has made acquisitions in the past can fall outside its ordinary activities as defined by FRS 3. Clearly, though, the directors and auditors of Fairway considered this to be the case at the time. However, this is a rare example, and the lack of any recent evidence of companies reporting extraordinary items would seem to indicate that the ASB has been successful in effectively outlawing them.

This is evidenced, for example, in a recent finding of the Financial Reporting Review Panel in the case of Princedale Group plc. In the company's profit and loss account for the 16 month period ended 30 April 2000, a £3.7 million loss arising from the sale of a subsidiary (made up of £1.8 million loss on disposal and £1.9 million goodwill write-back) was disclosed on the face of the profit and loss account after profit after tax and before dividends. Although the company did not describe this as an extraordinary item, the charge had been positioned in the profit and loss account in the line where extraordinary items would normally be shown. The effect was that the company reported a profit before tax of £694,000, rather than a loss before tax of £3.1 million.

The Panel ruled that the company had not complied with paragraph 20 of FRS 3 (i.e. it should have disclosed this as a non-operating exceptional item after operating profit – see 2.6.3 below), and the directors have agreed to correct this in the company's 2001 accounts. In its ruling, the Panel did not accept the company's argument that, because the disposal related to a non-core activity, the presentation adopted highlighted the real profitability an underlying value of the ongoing business. In the Panel's view, the effect of the non-compliance was compounded by certain of the comments in the Chairman's Report and Operating and Financial Review that interpreted the trend of results.[47]

2.6.2 *Exceptional items*

Exceptional items are defined in FRS 3 as being 'material items which derive from events or transactions that fall within the ordinary activities of the reporting entity and which individually or, if of a similar type, in aggregate, need to be disclosed by virtue of their size or incidence if the financial statements are to give a true and fair view'.[48] Although this definition is substantially unchanged from that in SSAP 6, there has been a significant change in the way that exceptional items are disclosed in the profit and loss account and notes. Under SSAP 6 exceptional items used to be aggregated on the face of the profit and loss account under one heading; not so under FRS 3, which states that all exceptional items, other than those included in the items listed in paragraph 20 of the standard, should be credited or charged in arriving at the profit or loss on ordinary activities by inclusion under the statutory format headings to which they relate. They should be attributed to continuing or discontinued operations as appropriate. The amount of each exceptional item, either individually or as an aggregate of items of a similar type, should be disclosed separately by way of note, or on the face of the profit and loss account if that degree of prominence is necessary in order to give a true and fair view.[49]

As a definitional matter, therefore, FRS 3 recognises that there are two categories of exceptional item:

- those listed in paragraph 20 of the standard (which must be shown on the face of the profit and loss account after operating profit and before interest); and
- all others, which should be credited or charged in arriving at the profit or loss on ordinary activities by inclusion under the statutory format headings to which they relate, and which should be disclosed separately either by way of note, or on the face of the profit and loss account.

The disclosure of the first category of exceptional item would appear to be clear-cut: if one of the items listed in paragraph 20 arises it must be shown separately in a specific position on the face of the profit and loss account. For ease of reference we refer to this category of items as non-operating exceptional items. These are discussed at 2.6.3 below.

As far as the second category of exceptional item is concerned, attributing exceptional items to the relevant statutory format headings will, in most cases, be a straightforward exercise. However, circumstances do arise when the directors of a reporting entity reach the view that specific exceptional items are not accommodated easily within specific format headings. This eventuality is specifically provided for in Paragraph 3(2) of Schedule 4 to the Companies Act which states that a company's profit and loss account may include an item representing or covering the amount of any income or expenditure not otherwise covered by any of the items listed in the format adopted. It goes on to state in Paragraph 3(3) that, in preparing a company's profit and loss account, the directors of the company shall adapt the arrangement and headings and sub-headings otherwise required by paragraph 1 in respect of items to which an Arabic number is assigned in the format adopted.

This means that situations will arise where a new line item will have to be added to the face of the profit and loss item to accommodate an exceptional item which does not relate to any specific statutory format heading. Examples of these might include bid defence costs and abortive acquisition costs. The precise position in the profit and loss account of these items depends on the directors' view of what they consider to be most appropriate. Whether the items appear before or after the operating profit line depends entirely on the directors' definition of operating profit, since the term is not used in the statutory formats and is not formally defined in FRS 3.

We are aware that there exists a school of thought that FRS 3 precludes the disclosure of exceptional items, other than those listed in paragraph 20, after operating profit. We believe, however, that this view is mistaken and arises from the assumption that the profit or loss on ordinary activities, which is a defined term in the Companies Act, is the same thing as operating profit or loss. Of course it is not, since the term 'operating profit or loss' is defined in neither the statutory formats nor FRS 3. Indeed, the different wording highlights the anomaly of any assumption that the two terms have the same meaning. It is therefore clear that FRS 3 does permit the inclusion in the profit and loss account of non-operating exceptional items over and above those listed in paragraph 20.

2.6.3 *Non-operating exceptional items*

The only exception to the rule that exceptional items must be included under the statutory format headings to which they relate, applies in the case of three specific items which, if they arise, must (irrespective of the statutory formats) be shown separately on the face of the profit and loss account after operating profit and before interest, and be included under the appropriate heading of continuing or discontinued operations. The three items (including provisions in respect of such items) are as follows:

(a) profits or losses on the sale or termination of an operation;

(b) costs of a fundamental reorganisation or restructuring having a material effect on the nature and focus of the reporting entity's operations; and

(c) profits or losses on the disposal of fixed assets.[50]

Only the revenue and costs directly related to the items should be taken into account in calculating the profit or loss for each of the items. This means, for example, that if a factory is sold and all the workers are made redundant, then the related redundancy costs should not be included in the profit/loss on disposal of the factory. The explanation section of FRS 3 also states that the profits or losses on the disposal of fixed assets in (c) above are not intended to include profits and losses that are in effect no more than marginal adjustments to depreciation previously charged.[51] It is not altogether clear what this means in practice, but we interpret it as meaning only that immaterial profits or losses on the disposal of depreciable fixed assets would not be disclosed as a non-operating exceptional item. Materiality should be applied to the aggregate net profits and losses for each category of fixed asset, and not to each individual asset.

The implication of this requirement is that all profits and losses on the disposal of fixed assets are excluded from the calculation of operating profit. This means that companies which are in the business of 'fixed assets trading' (i.e. have a high level of activity in buying and selling assets which are classified as fixed assets – for example, oil acreage in the case of an oil and gas company and pubs in the case of a brewer) are precluded from including the profits/losses arising on the disposal of such items within operating profit.

It should also be noted that provisions in respect of the three non-operating items must also be shown separately on the face of the profit and loss account after operating profit and before interest. This means, for example, that the provision for loss on disposal of a fixed asset which is expected to be sold in the future should be included in this category.

The standard requires further that the relevant headings for items (a) and (c) should appear on the face of the profit and loss account even where the exceptional profits and the exceptional losses within the headings net down to an immaterial amount. In such a case the standard requires that there should be a reference to a related note analysing the constituent profits and losses.

The notes to the financial statements should disclose, as a minimum, the effect on tax and on minority interest of items (a) to (c) in aggregate. However, the standard further requires that if the effect on tax and minority interests differs for the three categories further information should be given, where practicable, to assist users to assess the impact of the different items on the net profit or loss attributable to shareholders. It is not clear what the ASB had in mind in setting down this requirement. We suggest that in such a case the effect on tax and minority interests should be given for each of the categories.

Whilst the recognition and measurement of non-operating exceptional items falling within categories (a) and (c) above are reasonably clear-cut, the situation concerning item (b) is less so. This is because FRS 3 contains no additional guidance or explanation about the criteria which differentiate 'fundamental' reorganisations and restructurings from other (non-fundamental) ones – apart from the fact that they must have a material effect on the nature and focus of the reporting entity's operations. The only clue to what this means is to be found in the explanation section of the standard, which deals with discontinued operations.

To be included in the category of discontinued operations, a sale or termination must, inter alia, have a material effect on the nature and focus of the reporting entity's operations. The standard explains that the phrase 'nature and focus of the reporting entity's operations' refers to the positioning of its products or services in their markets including the aspects of both quality and location.[52] However, even on the assumption that this interpretation can be applied to fundamental restructurings, it is of little additional practical value. As a result, the distinction between fundamental and non-fundamental restructurings and reorganisations becomes a highly subjective and judgmental exercise. Clearly, companies would normally prefer these provisions to be classified as non-operating, thereby protecting the operating profits line in the profit and loss account.

Even FRS 12 does not shed any further light on the distinction between fundamental and non-fundamental reorganisations and restructurings. FRS 12 defines a restructuring as 'a programme that is planned and controlled by management and materially changes either:

(a) the scope of a business undertaken by an entity; or

(b) the manner in which that business is conducted.'[53]

This is said to include:

(a) sale or termination of a line of business;

(b) the closure of business locations in a country or region or the relocation of business activities from one country or region to another;

(c) changes in management structure, for example, eliminating a layer of management; and

(d) fundamental reorganisations that have a material effect on the nature and focus of the entity's operations.[54]

In the absence of any requirement for companies to give details of the ways in which the nature and focus of their operations have been materially affected by the reorganisation or restructuring, the disclosure of items in this category has become fairly widespread. However, it should be noted that, just because the provision is for a large amount, it does not necessarily mean that it is a non-operating fundamental provision. It must also have a material effect on the nature and focus of the entity's operations.

It would be reasonable to expect companies that have established such provisions to give an explanation in their Operating and Financial Reviews about the fundamental nature of the reorganisation or restructuring.

The following extract from the 2000 accounts of AstraZeneca illustrates the disclosure of all three categories of the paragraph 20 non-operating exceptional items. Although AstraZeneca uses the description 'merger costs', this is presumably intended to fall within the category of 'fundamental reorganisation or restructuring'.

Extract 25.11: AstraZeneca PLC (2000)

Group Profit and Loss Account [extract]

	2000 Total $m	1999 Total $m	1998 Total $m
Turnover: Group and share of joint ventures	**18,298**	18,653	16,482
Less: Share of joint venture turnover	**(195)**	(208)	(1,080)
Group turnover	**18,103**	18,445	15,402
Operating costs	**(14,361)**	(15,888)	(12,613)
Other operating income	**266**	189	353
Group operating profit	**4,008**	2,746	3,142
Share of operating (loss)/profit of joint ventures and associates	**(149)**	(7)	539
Profits less losses on sale, closure, or demerger of operations	**(150)**	237	(46)
Merger costs	**–**	(1,013)	–
Profits on sale of fixed assets	**–**	–	17
Dividend income	**3**	–	–
Profit on ordinary activities before interest	**3,712**	1,963	3,652

2.6.4 *Disclosure of exceptional items in practice*

Perhaps not unexpectedly, the disclosures in practice of exceptional items have become varied somewhat between companies. For example, one company might show abortive acquisition costs as a non-operating exceptional item, whilst another might choose to show the same costs as an exceptional item under the format heading 'Administrative expenses'. This is perhaps not surprising, given that operating profit is not defined in FRS 3, with the result that directors are required to select a definition which is most appropriate to the circumstances of their business. Consequently, the profit and loss account positioning of individual exceptional items will depend on the nature of the item, the nature of the entity's operations and the judgement of the directors.

This has become necessary largely as a result of an ill-conceived rule in FRS 3 which is based on the premise that the statutory format headings cater for all eventualities and that the objectives of FRS 3 can be achieved within the strait-jacket of the Companies Act formats. Not only do the various formats contain different headings, but a company which had adopted either Format 3 or 4 would find it virtually impossible to comply with FRS 3. Furthermore, because FRS 3 contains no additional guidance or explanation about the criteria which differentiate 'fundamental' reorganisations and restructuring from other (non-fundamental) ones, it is difficult to see any pattern of consistency in the presentation of these items.

2.6.5 *The impact of the effective abolition of extraordinary items*

We agree that it was appropriate for the ASB to limit the use of extraordinary items to very rare circumstances, but we consider that the standard should have explained exactly what these circumstances are, and give examples. On the other hand, if FRS 3's abstruse drafting in this area reflected the ASB's intention to ensure that companies do not report extraordinary items under any circumstances, it seems to have succeeded. However, since most items which were once shown as extraordinary are now shown as exceptional, we are concerned about the growing perception that the 'important' figure to look at in the profit and loss account is the profit from continuing operations before exceptional items, particularly as FRS 3 requires prominence to be given to certain exceptional items as a separate category on the face of the profit and loss account. Such a presentation will encourage the same misconception which was previously applied to extraordinary items under SSAP 6 – namely, that these items are something apart from the trading operations of the business and may be set on one side in any consideration of its performance. At the same time, FRS 3's definition of exceptional items is weaker even than SSAP 6's definition of extraordinary items, which can make it very easy to 'manage' the pre-exceptional figure. Apart from the three non-operating exceptional items discussed above, the exceptional item classification may now include:

- highly unusual items which would previously have been classified as extraordinary under SSAP 6;
- items which quite often arise, but not in every year, which might previously have been classified as exceptional under SSAP 6; and
- items which arise annually, but happen to be unusually large in the current year.

In the last of these three items, the exceptional effect on the results is not the whole amount of the item, but only the excess over a 'normal' amount. Similarly, it could be misleading to show the whole amount of a charge for bad and doubtful debts as exceptional. In any event, we think it is unnecessary that exceptional items be overemphasised on the face of the profit and loss account. We would have preferred FRS 3 to have given emphasis to the overall result for the year and to have regarded the analysis of it as a secondary disclosure. As demonstrated by the current fixation on earnings per share, simplistic classifications on the face of the primary statements merely tend to encourage superficial analysis.

Carlton Communications is an example of a company that has highlighted its results and earnings per share before both exceptional items and the results of its loss-making investment in digital television. As can be seen from the following extract, the company refers to this as 'Headline':

Extract 25.12: Carlton Communications plc (2000)

CONSOLIDATED PROFIT AND LOSS ACCOUNT
For the year ended 30 September 2000

				2000			
	Notes	Headline £m	Exceptional items (note 5) £m	Digital Media (note 2) £m	Continuing operations £m	Discontinued operations (note 6) £m	Total £m
Turnover		2,047.7	–	67.4	2,115.1	28.6	2,143.7
Less: share of joint ventures		(10.4)	–	(53.3)	(63.7)	–	(63.7)
Group turnover	1	2,037.3	–	14.1	–	28.6	2,080.0
Operating costs before exceptionals		(1,700.4)	–	(56.3)	(1,756.7)	(52.4)	(1,809.1)
Exceptional operating charges	5	–	(18.5)	(20.5)	(39.0)	–	(39.0)
Total operating costs		(1,700.4)	(18.5)	(76.8)	(1,795.7)	(52.4)	(1,848.1)
EBITDA		409.7	(18.5)	(60.7)	330.5	(21.5)	309.0
Depreciation		(66.1)	–	(2.0)	(68.1)	(2.3)	(70.4)
Amortisation		(6.7)	–	–	(6.7)	–	(6.7)
Group operating profit/(loss)	1, 3	336.9	(18.5)	(62.7)	255.7	(23.8)	231.9
Share of operating results of joint ventures		1.1	–	(143.2)	(142.1)	–	(142.1)
Share of operating results of associated companies		10.1	–	(9.1)	1.0	–	1.0
		348.1	(18.5)	(215.0)	114.6	(23.8)	90.8
Loss on sale of business							
Deficit on net assets		–	–	–	–	(4.3)	(4.3)
Goodwill written back		–	–	–	–	(300.0)	(300.0)
Total loss on sale of businesses		–	–	–	–	(304.3)	(304.3)
Profit/(loss) on ordinary activities before interest		348.1	(18.5)	(215.0)	114.6	(328.1)	(213.5)
Net interest payable	7	(5.9)	–	(22.5)	(28.4)	–	(28.4)
Profit/(loss) on ordinary activities before taxation		342.2	(18.5)	(237.5)	86.2	(328.1)	(241.9)
Taxation	8	(104.4)	1.6	69.9	(32.9)	7.2	(25.7)
Minority interest		–	–	–	–	–	–
Profit/(loss) on ordinary activities after taxation		237.8	(16.9)	(167.6)	53.3	(320.9)	(267.6)
Dividends equity and non-equity	9	(123.5)	–	–	(123.5)	–	(123.5)
Retained profit/(loss)		114.3	(16.9)	(167.6)	(70.2)	(320.9)	(391.1)
Earnings per share (pence)	10						
Basic		35.0	(2.6)	(25.9)	6.5	(49.5)	(43.0)
Diluted		33.6	(2.5)	(24.8)	6.3	(47.5)	(41.2)

Cable and Wireless have adopted an approach that has become quite widespread of disclosing an earnings per share number based on earnings before exceptional items and goodwill amortisation. This is a measure that many companies consider to represent 'maintainable earnings':

Extract 25.13: Cable and Wireless plc (2001)

CONSOLIDATED PROFIT AND LOSS ACCOUNT
for the year ended 31 March [extract]

	Note	2001	2000
Basic earnings per share	13	**96.4p**	153.6p
Basic earnings per share before exceptional items and goodwill amortisation	13	**16.0p**	19.4p
Diluted earnings per share	13	**95.4p**	150.9p
Dividends per share		**16.5p**	15.0p

ICI provides a fairly typical example of a multi-column profit and loss account that splits its results from continuing operations into two columns ('before exceptional items' and 'exceptional items'), with 'discontinued operations' being shown in a further column. When it comes to comparative figures, ICI goes further than most by presenting its profit and loss account over two facing pages in its annual report, giving comparative figures for the previous two years, set out in four columns for each year. However, this is probably due to the fact that the company is a US SEC registrant and prepares its UK annual report and Form 20-F as a combined document. Only the figures for 2000 are included below:

Extract 25.14: Imperial Chemical Industries PLC (2000)

Group profit and loss account for the year ended 31 December 2000

		2000			
		Continuing operations		Discontinued operations	
	Notes	Before exceptional items £m	Exceptional items £m	£m	Total £m
Turnover	5, 6	6,415		1,333	7,748
Operating costs	4, 6	(5,876)	–	(1,350)	(7,226)
Other operating income	6	43	–	12	55
Trading profit (loss)	4, 5, 6	582	–	(5)	577
After deducting goodwill amortisation	5	*(35)*			*(35)*
Share of operating profit less losses of associates	7	91	–	9	100
		673	–	4	677
Fundamental reorganisation costs	4		(14)	–	(14)
Profits less losses on sale or closure of operations	4		16	(531)	(515)
Profits less losses on disposals of fixed assets	4		10	1	11
Amounts written off investments	4		–		–
Profit (loss) on ordinary activities before interest	5	673	12	(526)	159
Net interest payable	4, 8				
Group		(201)	16	(1)	(186)
Associates		(60)	–	–	(60)
		(261)	16	(1)	(246)
Profit (loss) on ordinary activities before taxation		412	28	(527)	(87)
Taxation on profit (loss) on ordinary activities	9	(112)	(6)	1	(117)
Profit (loss) on ordinary activities after taxation		300	22	(526)	(204)
Attributable to minorities		(24)	–	–	(24)
Net profit (loss) for the financial year		276	22	(526)	(228)
Dividends	10				(232)
Profit (loss) retained for the year	25				(460)
Earnings (loss) per £1 Ordinary Share	11				
Basic		38.2p	3.0p	(72.8)p	(31.6)p
Diluted		38.2p	3.0p	(72.8)p	(31.6)p

It would seem that companies that present their profit and loss accounts in this form are perhaps wishing to focus the readers' attention on the first column, which reflects profit and earnings per share for the financial year before exceptional items and discontinued operations. It is a moot point whether or not pre-exceptional profit is the most appropriate measure of a company's underlying earning capacity; on the other hand, there is the argument that a profit and loss account presented in this way enhances the predictive value of the information. In any event, in order for the shareholders of a company to assess management performance and stewardship, they need to look at its *total* performance.

2.7 Profit or loss on the disposal of an asset

Prior to FRS 3, when an entity disposed of an asset carried at valuation, the directors had the choice of calculating the profit or loss on disposal by reference either to the depreciated historical cost or to the amount at which the asset was carried in the balance sheet. If the latter option was selected, that portion of the revaluation reserve which related to the asset would usually be transferred, as a reserve movement, to realised reserves.

FRS 3 removed this choice, requiring that the profit or loss on the disposal of an asset must be calculated as the difference between the net sale proceeds and the net carrying amount, whether carried at historical cost (less any provisions made) or at valuation.[55] A subsequent amendment to FRS 3 allowed insurance businesses limited relief from this particular requirement as it applied to the gains and losses arising on the disposal of investments. The amendment applied to insurance companies and insurance groups, both in relation to their own accounts and where these are incorporated in the consolidated accounts of a group whose main business is not insurance. These entities were thus granted an exemption from the requirement to calculate gains and losses on disposal of investments by reference to their carrying amount rather than original cost.[56] However, a further amendment to FRS 3 made in June 1999 effectively negated this exemption, by requiring insurance companies and groups to include in the profit and loss account both realised and unrealised gains and losses on investments held as part of their investment portfolios. The effect of this will be to ensure that the same amount will be accounted for on disposal of an investment held as part of the investment portfolio as would be accounted for whether or not the original exemption applied.

The reason for FRS 3's revised approach to determining the profit or loss on the disposal of an asset lies in the ASB's balance sheet approach to the recognition of gains and losses. Under its *Statement of Principles*, the ASB defines gains and losses as being increases and decreases in ownership interest, other than those relating to contributions from and distributions to owners. Recognition is triggered where a past transaction or other event indicates that there has been a measurable change in the assets and liabilities of the entity. Thus, where a change in assets is not offset by an equal change in liabilities, a gain or a loss will result (unless the change relates to a transaction with the entity's owners, in which case a contribution from owners or distribution to owners will be recognised). Consequently, once an asset has been revalued in an entity's balance sheet, any subsequent transactions must be based on the balance sheet carrying amount of that asset.

It is therefore clear why the ASB has removed the option of calculating the profit or loss on disposal of a revalued asset by reference to the asset's historical cost. Nevertheless, its removal did receive a rather mixed reaction from the business community, including the following amusing comment from the chairman of Ilex Limited, a property investment company:

Extract 25.15: Ilex Limited (1993)

CHAIRMAN'S STATEMENT

Profits after tax have risen from £564,000 to £1,698,000. These figures have been drawn up in accordance with the latest Accounting Standards and last year's figure is adjusted to make it comparable. The main change is to the manner in which capital items are taken through the Profit and Loss Account with a resulting volatility in earnings per share. We consider this a mistaken method for property investment companies which will only serve to confuse shareholders. Since it is mandatory, we accept it somewhat grumpily: the accounting profession seems to have an endemic tendency towards committees recommending changes which add to its workload and its clients' fees.

Some might argue that, so long as UK accounting is underpinned by a system of company law that recognises capital maintenance and distributable profits on an historical cost basis, companies should be able to report profits in the profit and loss account on an historical cost basis. However, there is the alternative view that income statements should be primarily concerned with the measurement of performance, and that when reported figures are not related to current values there may be over- or understatement of performance as measured by profits and return on assets. Consequently, the ASB has taken the view that, in the light of the present modified historical cost system and all its associated problems, companies that revalue assets should be required to measure future transactions by reference to the revalued amount.

2.8 Note of historical cost profits and losses

Because the profit or loss on the disposal of an asset is now to be calculated by reference to the asset's balance sheet carrying amount, FRS 3 introduced the requirement that, where there is a material difference between the result as disclosed in the profit and loss account and the result on an unmodified historical cost basis, a note of the historical cost profit or loss for the period should be presented.[57] This is a memorandum item that is an abbreviated restatement of the profit and loss account, adjusting the reported profit or loss so as to show it as if no asset revaluations had been made. Where full historical cost information is unavailable or cannot be obtained without unreasonable expense or delay, the earliest available values should be used. The note should include a reconciliation of the reported profit on ordinary activities before taxation to the equivalent historical cost amount and should also show the retained profit for the financial year reported on the historical cost basis.

Essentially, the note will incorporate adjustments for (i) the difference between the profit on the disposal of an asset calculated on depreciated historical cost and that calculated on a revalued amount, and (ii) the difference between an historical cost depreciation charge and the depreciation charge calculated on the revalued amount included in the profit and loss account of the period. The following extract from the example contained in the Appendix to FRS 3 illustrates the presentation of the note:

Note of historical cost profits and losses

	1993	**1992**
		as restated
	£ million	*£ million*
Reported profit on ordinary activities before taxation	45	13
Realisation of property revaluation gains of previous years	9	10
Difference between a historical cost depreciation charge and the actual depreciation charge of the year calculated on the revalued amount	5	4
Historical cost profit on ordinary activities before taxation	59	27
Historical cost profit for the year retained after taxation, minority interests, extraordinary items and dividends	35	20

The note should be presented immediately following the profit and loss account or the statement of total recognised gains and losses. In consolidated financial statements, the profit and loss account figure for minority interests should be amended for the purposes of this note to reflect the adjustments made where they affect subsidiary companies with a minority interest.

The standard does not contain a definition of an unmodified historical cost basis. However, it is stated in the explanation section of the standard that the following are not deemed to be departures from the historical cost convention: (a) adjustments necessarily made to cope with the impact of hyper-inflation on foreign operations and (b) the practice of market makers and other dealers in investments of marking to market where this is an established industry practice.[58]

This still leaves open the position of entities marking to market where it is not industry practice. The implication from the FRS is that these other entities are deemed to have departed from the unmodified historical cost basis. However, there is an alternative view, which we support, that marking to market is not a departure from the historical cost convention, but is a method to ensure appropriate revenue recognition and as such it applies irrespective of the industry in which the entity operates. We would not therefore expect any adjustments to be included in the note of historical cost profits and losses in respect of marking current asset investments to market.

Nevertheless, in its *Statement of Principles*, the ASB does refer to the 'mixed measurement system' where 'some categories of assets or liabilities could be measured on a historical cost basis and some on a current value basis'.[59] The ASB goes on to state that the term modified historical cost 'is something of a misnomer because it is a mixed measurement system'.[60] This seems to suggest that all gains and loses that are recognised on the basis of current values will need to be reflected in the note of historical cost profits and losses.

It is, therefore, perhaps not surprising that when the ASB amended FRS 3 to require insurance companies to include in the profit and loss account both realised and unrealised gains and losses on investments held as part of their investment portfolios, it also exempted them from having to prepare a note of historical cost profit and losses for gains and losses arising on the holding or disposal of investments.[61]

2.9 Statement of total recognised gains and losses

2.9.1 Primary financial statement

FRS 3 introduced into UK GAAP a fourth primary financial statement: the statement of total recognised gains and losses. The statement has to be presented with the same prominence as the other primary statements and must show the components as well as the total of recognised gains and losses. Although there was not necessarily general agreement on the point, the statement was regarded by the ASB at least as being a statement of performance or 'comprehensive income'. It represented the ASB's first step towards requiring the reporting of changes in wealth as opposed to traditional historical cost profit and loss. The ethos of the statement lies in the ASB's *Statement of Principles* and, in particular, in its balance sheet approach to the recognition of assets, liabilities, gains and losses.

According to the *Statement of Principles*, recognition is triggered where a past transaction or event indicates that there has been a measurable change in the assets and liabilities of an entity, and where a change in assets is not offset by an equal change in liabilities a gain or loss will result (unless the change relates to a transaction with the entity's owners, in which case a contribution from owners or distribution to owners will be recognised). At the time that FRS 3 was issued, the ASB's thinking was that gains or losses should be recognised either in the profit and loss account or in the statement of total recognised gains and losses. However, as already stated, the latest proposals that the ASB has on the table are that all gains and losses should be recognised in a single statement of total financial performance. These proposals are discussed at 4.3.2 below.

Because of the company law framework that underpins UK financial reporting, it might be logical to assume that gains that are earned and realised are recognised in the profit and loss account, whilst gains that are earned (but not realised) are recognised in the statement of total recognised gains and losses – and this is more or less how things work at the moment. However, it is evident from the ASB's *Statement of Principles* generally, and FRED 22 specifically, that it is seeking to change this approach.

Nevertheless, at the moment FRS 3 prevails, and UK GAAP still requires companies to present both a profit and loss account and a statement of total recognised gains and losses. The following extract from the example contained in the Appendix to FRS 3 illustrates the presentation of the statement:

Statement of total recognised gains and losses

	1993	1992
		as restated
	£ million	£ million
Profit for the financial year	29	7
Unrealised surplus on revaluation of properties	4	6
Unrealised (loss)/gain on trade investment	(3)	7
	30	20
Currency translation differences on foreign currency net investments	(2)	5
Total recognised gains and losses relating to the year	28	25
Prior year adjustment (as explained in note x)	(10)	
Total gains and losses recognised since last annual report	18	

The £18 million net total gains represents the increase in net assets which occurred between the opening and closing balance sheet dates, and which were brought about by all transactions that the entity had entered into, other than those involving shareholders. Since the statement comprises total realised and unrealised gains and losses, the realised profit for the financial year (before dividends) is brought in as the first line of the statement. This means that the profit and loss account now provides the detailed analysis of the single line in the statement of total recognised gains and losses, whilst the unrealised gains and losses are itemised in the statement.

Where a reporting entity has no recognised gains or losses other than the profit or loss for the period, a statement to this effect immediately below the profit and loss account will suffice.

2.9.2 *Share issue costs*

The treatment of issue costs of both debt and equity instruments presented the ASB with an accounting dilemma. In developing FRS 4, the ASB wished to defer such costs but realised that they are not assets as defined in the *Statement of Principles*. As a result, FRS 4 laid down the requirement that issue costs be accounted for as a reduction in the proceeds of a capital instrument. In the case of shares, FRS 4 states that 'issue costs are integral to a transaction with owners and for this reason the FRS requires them to be taken into account in determining the net proceeds that are reported in the reconciliation of movements in shareholders' funds. They should not be disclosed in the statement of total recognised gains and losses.'[62] However, whilst issue costs might be integral to a transaction with owners, the expenditure itself does not constitute a transaction with owners and should, therefore, be charged in the profit and loss account. Nevertheless, FRS 4 precludes this from happening.

2.10 Taxation

If a company reports exceptional items which fall under paragraph 20 of FRS 3, the standard requires their effect on the tax charge to be disclosed in a note to the profit and loss account.[63] In addition, where (rarely) there is an extraordinary item, it is necessary to state the extraordinary item net of the tax effect, and any adjustments to the tax on extraordinary items in subsequent years also has to be shown as extraordinary.[64]

To calculate the amount to be allocated to these items, FRS 3 requires the 'with-and-without' method to be applied.[65] This means that the tax charge should be calculated as if the item(s) had not existed, then recalculated with the inclusion of the item(s); the difference between the two calculations should be attributed to the item(s) in question. Where there is more than one such item, it will be necessary to apportion the tax figure derived by this process, either pro rata or by a more appropriate method if one is available. The standard goes on to say that 'it is recognised that analysing an entity's total taxation charge between component parts of its result for a period can involve arbitrary allocations that tend to become less meaningful the more components there are. However, in respect of items such as disposal profits or losses, the tax can often be identified with the exceptional item concerned and the relationship between the profit or loss and the attributable tax may be significantly different from that in respect of operating profits or losses. In such circumstances it is relevant to identify the tax charge or credit more specifically.'[66]

There is no corresponding requirement to analyse tax between the results of continuing and discontinued operations, but where companies choose to do so they are required to explain the method and assumptions underlying the allocation.[67]

FRS 3 does not discuss the treatment of tax relating to items reported in the statement of total recognised gains and losses, but this is addressed by FRS 16 – *Current Tax* – and FRS 19 – *Deferred Tax* (see Chapter 24 at, respectively, 3.1.1 and 5.9.1). The general principle is that all tax is recognised in the profit and loss account, unless it relates to an item recognised in the statement of total recognised gains and losses, in which case the tax should also be recognised in that statement. Where a prior year adjustment is made involving an adjustment to the opening balance on shareholders' funds, any tax effect attributable to the adjustment should be dealt with in the same way.

2.11 Measures of performance

2.11.1 EPS redefined

The ASB has long maintained that undue emphasis is placed on EPS numbers and that this leads to simplistic interpretations of financial performance.[68] In the explanation section of FRS 3, the ASB presented the view that 'it is not possible to distil the performance of a complex organisation into a single measure'. It went on to say that 'undue significance, therefore, should not be placed on any one such measure which may purport to achieve this aim. To assess the performance of a reporting entity during a period all components of its activities must be considered.'[69]

As a result, the Board attempted to de-emphasise EPS and, in so doing, laid down the requirement that EPS be calculated *after* extraordinary items. This was later reaffirmed by FRS 14 – *Earnings per share* – which stated that 'basic earnings per share should be calculated by dividing the net profit or loss for the period attributable to ordinary shareholders by the weighted average number of ordinary shares outstanding during the period.'[70] The standard went on to say that 'all items of income and expense that are recognised in a period, including tax expense, exceptional and extraordinary items and minority interests, are included in the determination of the net profit or loss for the period'.[71] The requirements of FRS 14 are dealt with in Chapter 26.

FRS 3 provided further that if an additional EPS calculated at any other level of profit is disclosed it should be presented on a consistent basis over time and, wherever disclosed, reconciled to the amount required by the FRS. Such a reconciliation should list the items for which an adjustment is being made and disclose their individual effect on the calculation. The EPS required by FRS 3 should be at least as prominent as any additional version presented and the reason for calculating the additional version should be explained. The reconciliation and explanation should appear adjacent to the EPS disclosure, or a reference should be given to where they can be found.[72]

All of this led the Institute of Investment Management and Research to issue its Statement of Investment Practice No. 1 – *The Definition of IIMR Headline Earnings* – which seeks to find an earnings figure that will reflect a company's trading performance but that will also limit the need to exercise judgement in its calculation, so that it can be used as an unambiguous reference point between users, the press and statistical companies. The IIMR headline earnings measure is discussed in 5.5.1 of Chapter 26.

2.11.2 EBITDA

Following the introduction of new accounting standards such as FRS 10 and FRS 15, which require fairly large depreciation and amortisation charges to be recorded in the profit and loss account, there has been a noticeable trend of companies highlighting EBITDA (i.e. earnings before interest, taxation, depreciation and amortisation) as a key performance measure (see, for example, the profit and loss accounts of Cable and Wireless and Carlton Communications set out respectively in Extracts 25.1 and 25.12

above). In practice, pure EBITDA is sometimes stretched to exclude other non-recurring costs and profits, as well as non-cash earnings. For example, the definition used by Cable and Wireless in Extract 25.1 above is earnings before interest, taxation, depreciation and amortisation, the costs of a fundamental reorganisation, profits and losses on the disposal of operations and fixed assets, the impairment of certain assets and the equity accounted earnings of joint ventures and associates. EBITDA is promoted as a rule-of-thumb measure of a company's maintainable cash generating capability and, by implication, its ability to service its debt. The argument is that, because depreciation and amortisation are non-cash charges, they should be excluded from any forward-looking measure of a company's ability to generate cash and service its debt. In fact, there is a certain similarity between EBITDA and the ASB's methodology for determining the value in use of an income generating unit, as set out in FRS 11 (see Chapter 13 at 2.2.5). Both focus on the business in its current condition and ignore the need for future capital expenditure if cash flows are to be generated in perpetuity.

However, despite its growing popularity amongst preparers of accounts and promotion by investment banks, EBITDA will never be more than a blunt instrument to be used with caution. Its shortcomings include the following:

- any cash flow required to re-invest in capital assets is ignored, which could spell danger for some companies that are required to replace capital assets on a regular basis. Moreover, EBITDA will be boosted if refurbishment expenditure necessary to maintain the existing condition of fixed assets is capitalised rather than expensed;
- EBITDA assumes that all revenues are earned in cash, which again is a risky assumption, particularly in instances of aggressive revenue recognition and working capital growth; and
- EBITDA tells the user of accounts nothing about the quality of earnings, and does not enable users to make inter-company comparisons where different accounting policies are applied. This is particularly relevant in the context of the global capital markets, where different systems of GAAP are applied.

A further trend emerging is for companies to base the measure of interest cover on EBITDA rather than on the traditional benchmark of EBIT. This again is potentially hazardous measure for users to follow without at least taking into account necessary capital expenditure.

We therefore believe that whilst EBITDA has its place amongst a number of performance indicators, but it should be used with caution and then only with a full understanding of its limitations.

2.12 Reconciliation of movements in shareholders' funds

The standard requires that a note be presented reconciling the opening and closing totals of shareholders' funds of the period.[73] The rationale for this requirement was that whilst the profit and loss account and statement of total recognised gains and losses reflected the performance of a reporting entity in a period, there were other changes in shareholders' funds that could also be important in understanding the change in the financial position of the entity. The purpose of the reconciliation was to highlight those other changes.[74]

The explanation section of the standard permits the reconciliation to be presented as a 'primary statement', rather than as a note to the financial statements. However, if included as a primary statement, the reconciliation should be shown separately from the statement of total recognised gains and losses. This seems remarkable. The reconciliation is either a primary statement of financial performance, or it is not; it should not be left to the whim of preparers of accounts to make that decision.

The appendix to FRS 3 includes the following example of the reconciliation presented as a note:

Reconciliation of movements in shareholders' funds

	1993	**1992**
		as restated
	£ million	*£ million*
Profit for the financial year	29	7
Dividends	(8)	(1)
	21	6
Other recognised gains and losses relating to the year (net)	(1)	18
New share capital subscribed	20	1
Goodwill written-off	(25)	
Net addition to shareholders' funds	15	25
Opening shareholders' funds (originally £375 million before deducting prior year adjustment of £10 million)	365	340
Closing shareholders' funds	380	365

The reconciliation will include the profit or loss for the period as recorded in the profit and loss account, all other recognised gains and losses for the period and all other movements to shareholders' funds. The other movements will be:

- dividends for the period; and
- capital contributed by or repaid to shareholders during the period, for example, the amount subscribed for new shares during the period.

Since FRS 10 no longer permits the direct write off of goodwill against reserves, the elimination of goodwill no longer features in the reconciliation. However, the transitional provisions of FRS 10 did not require companies to reinstate previously written off goodwill, with the result that many companies will still have cumulative amounts of goodwill previously eliminated against reserves that FRS 10 requires to be charged in the profit and loss account if and when the businesses to which it related are disposed of or closed down.[75]

When goodwill is reinstated and taken into account in calculating the profit or loss arising on disposal or closure it does not affect total shareholders' funds since it will be credited to reserves to reinstate it, and debited in the profit and loss account for the period. Since it does not affect total shareholders' funds it might be thought that it should not be included in the reconciliation. However, the profit for the period is included in the reconciliation and will be stated after the debit in respect of the goodwill. Accordingly, the reversal of the previous elimination of goodwill against reserves should also appear in the reconciliation; this will then cancel the debit that has been charged in the reconciliation through its inclusion in the profit for the year; for example:

Extract 25.16: AstraZeneca PLC (2000)

Notes relating to the financial statements [extract]

22 Reconciliation of movements in Shareholders' funds

	2000 $m	1999 $m	1998 $m
Shareholders' funds at beginning of year	**10,302**	10,929	9,552
Net profit for the financial year	**2,538**	1,143	2,611
Dividends			
Cash	**(1,236)**	(1,242)	(1,061)
Dividend in specie	**(1,669)**	–	–
	(367)	(99)	1,550
Issues of AstraZeneca PLC Ordinary Shares	**19**	19	12
Repurchase of AstraZeneca PLC Ordinary Shares	**(353)**	(183)	–
Astra AB minority interest buyout	**(8)**	(142)	–
Goodwill written back	**862**	410	–
Exchange adjustments on net assets	**(1,038)**	(740)	(178)
Translation differences on foreign currency borrowings	**154**	132	(7)
Tax on translation differences on foreign currency borrowings	**(42)**	(22)	2
Movement in unrealised holding gains and losses on short-term investments	**–**	–	2
Other movements	**(8)**	(2)	(4)
Net (reduction in)/addition to Shareholders' funds	**(781)**	(627)	1,377
Shareholders' funds at end of year	**9,521**	10,302	10,929

Unlike its guidance on the statement of total recognised gains and losses, FRS 3 does not contain any guidance as to whether or not the note is required where the only movements in shareholders' funds are the profit for the year, other recognised gains and losses and dividends (which are required to be disclosed in the profit and loss account). The FRS similarly does not discuss whether or not the reconciliation of movements in shareholders' funds can be combined with the note, required by Schedule 4 to the Companies Act, showing the movement on reserves. The implication from the appendix to the FRS is that the two notes should be presented separately. The justification for this lies in the assertion in the explanatory section of the FRS that the purpose of the reconciliation is to highlight the changes in shareholders' funds other than the recognised gains and losses. The ASB possibly took the view that the other changes would not be sufficiently highlighted if the two notes were to be combined. Furthermore, whilst there is no requirement to give comparatives for the reserves note, the FRS requires comparatives for the reconciliation.

Nevertheless, the requirements of the standard add to the ever-increasing catalogue of unnecessary and duplicated disclosures in company accounts.

2.13 Statement of movements on reserves

It is clear that FRS 3's requirements in respect of the statement of total recognised gains and losses and the reconciliation of movements in shareholders' funds have superseded SSAP 6's former requirement that accounts should include a statement of movements on reserves. Nevertheless, the Companies Act imposes the following requirements in respect of reserve movements:

(a) any amount set aside or proposed to be set aside, or withdrawn, or proposed to be withdrawn from reserves must be separately disclosed;[76]

(b) where any amount is transferred to or from reserves, the amounts of the reserves at the beginning and end of the financial year, the amounts transferred to or from the reserves and the sources and application of these amounts must be disclosed.[77]

This means that companies will still have to prepare a conventional reserves movements note. The Appendix to FRS 3 included the following example of such a note:

Reserves

	Share premium account	Revaluation reserve	Profit and loss account	Total
	£ million	*£ million*	*£ million*	*£ million*
At beginning of year as previously stated	44	200	120	364
Prior year adjustment			(10)	(10)
At beginning of year as restated	44	200	110	354
Premium on issue of shares (nominal value £7 million)	13			13
Goodwill written-off			(25)	(25)
Transfer from profit and loss account of the year			21	21
Transfer of realised profits		(14)	14	0
Decrease in value of trade investment		(3)		(3)
Currency translation differences on foreign currency net investments			(2)	(2)
Surplus on property valuations		4		4
At end of year	57	187	118	362

Note: Nominal share capital at end of year £18 million (1992 £11 million).

2.14 Prior period adjustments

2.14.1 Definition

FRS 3 defines prior period adjustments as 'material adjustments applicable to prior periods arising from changes in accounting policies or from the correction of fundamental errors. They do not include normal recurring adjustments or corrections of accounting estimates made in prior periods.'[78]

2.14.2 Identification of prior year adjustments

The explanation section of the standard emphasises that 'the majority of items relating to prior periods arise mainly from the corrections and adjustments which are the natural result of estimates inherent in accounting and more particularly in the periodic preparation of financial statements'.[79] Such items are dealt with in the profit and loss account of the period in which they are identified and their effect is stated where material. They are not exceptional or extraordinary merely because they relate to a prior period; their nature will determine their classification. Prior period adjustments – that is, prior period items which should be adjusted against the opening balance of retained profits or reserves – are rare and limited to items arising from changes in accounting policies or from the correction of fundamental errors.[80]

The standard goes on to say that 'estimating future events and their effects requires the exercise of judgement and will require reappraisal as new events occur, as more experience is acquired or as additional information is obtained. Because a change in estimate arises from new information or developments, it should not be given retrospective effect by a restatement of prior periods. Sometimes a change in estimate may have the appearance of a change in accounting policy and care is necessary to avoid confusing the two.'[81]

2.14.3 Changes in accounting policy

An accounting policy should only be changed if the new policy is preferable to the policy it replaces because it will give a fairer presentation of the results and of the financial position of the business. A characteristic of a change in policy is that it is the result of a change between two accounting bases.

As stated above, a change in estimate may have the appearance of a change in accounting policy and care is necessary in order to avoid confusing the two; for example, a company may change the rate at which it depreciates a particular class of fixed asset. Such a change is not a change in accounting policy but a change in estimate of either the useful life or depreciable amount of the assets and, therefore, the effect of the change should be reflected prospectively and not as a prior year adjustment.

It is noteworthy also that a change in accounting policy which is necessitated by the adoption of a new accounting pronouncement may not necessarily result in a prior year adjustment, since the transitional or implementation provisions of the new pronouncement may override FRS 3. This was highlighted by, for example, FRS 10 – *Goodwill and intangible assets* – which gave companies the choice of either reinstating goodwill that had previously been written off to reserves by means of a prior year adjustment, or of not reinstating it and leaving it eliminated against reserves. Similar, on adopting FRS 15 – *Tangible fixed assets*, companies that did not adopt a policy of revaluation, but the carrying amount of their tangible fixed assets reflected previous revaluations, were given the choice of either retaining the book amounts or of restating the carrying amount of the tangible fixed assets to historical cost, as a change in accounting policy.

2.14.4 *Correction of fundamental errors*

The standard stresses that a fundamental error is only likely to occur in exceptional circumstances. The term 'fundamental' is implicitly defined as being of such significance as to destroy the presentation of a true and fair view and hence the validity of those financial statements.[82] The corrections of such fundamental errors and the cumulative adjustments applicable to prior periods have no bearing on the results of the current period and they are therefore not included in arriving at the profit or loss for the current period.

However, it is worth noting that when this term was introduced originally in SSAP 6 there was no available procedure that allowed companies to correct and reissue accounts which are considered to be defective. Such provisions now exist in the law,[83] which means that the facility to correct fundamental errors by means of a prior year adjustment must be of less significance as a result; if the directors consider their accounts to be defective then they should avail themselves of the provisions under the Companies Act which enable them to revise the accounts; they do not have to wait to make the amendment in the accounts of the following year by means of a prior year adjustment. Nevertheless, circumstances will arise where a fundamental error is either discovered shortly before the following year's accounts are due to be issued or does not, in the opinion of the directors, warrant the preparation of revised accounts. In both instances, therefore, it would be appropriate to follow FRS 3's procedures for the correction of the error.

It is tempting to think of any adjustment which relates to an event or circumstance which arose in a prior year as a prior year item; however, if the adjustment derives from new information about that event, then it simply represents a change in the estimate of the effect of that event and is therefore a current period item. For example, if a company has to write off a debt which it previously considered to be recoverable, then the charge should be reflected in the current year's profit or loss and not accounted for by way of prior year adjustment. It is therefore appropriate to consider whether the information which indicates that a fundamental error has arisen was actually available at the time that the financial statements for the prior period were approved.

2.14.5 *Accounting treatment*

FRS 3 requires that prior period adjustments be accounted for by restating the comparative figures for the preceding period in the primary statements and notes and adjusting the opening balance of reserves for the cumulative effect. The cumulative effect of the adjustments should also be noted at the foot of the statement of total recognised gains and losses of the current period.[84]

This means that in the case of a change in accounting policy, the amounts for the current and corresponding periods should be restated on the basis of the new policy. The cumulative adjustments should also be noted at the foot of the statement of total recognised gains and losses of the current period and included in the reconciliation of movements in shareholders' funds of the corresponding period in order to highlight for users the effect of the adjustments. The following example illustrates the mechanics of such a process:

Example 25.1: Illustration of a change in accounting policy

Up until 31 December 2001, a company has adopted a policy of writing off its development expenditure in the year in which it was incurred. The company's financial statements for the year ended 31 December 2001 disclosed the following:

Profit and loss account	2001 £'000	2000 £'000
Profit on ordinary activities before taxation	4,200	3,800
Taxation	(1,575)	(1,400)
Profit on ordinary activities after taxation	2,625	2,400
Dividends	(600)	(500)
Retained profit for year	2,025	1,900
Balance sheet		
Tangible fixed assets	8,000	7,100
Net current assets	2,025	800
	10,025	7,900
Deferred taxation	(1,000)	(900)
	9,025	7,000
Share capital	1,000	1,000
Profit and loss account	8,025	6,000
	9,025	7,000

In preparing its financial statements for the year ended 31 December 2002 it considers that a policy of capitalising the development expenditure and amortising it over a period of four years from the date of commencing production would give a fairer presentation of the results and financial position of the company. Accordingly, it will be necessary to restate the figures for 2001 on the basis of the new policy. This initially involves computing:

(i) the net book value of the development expenditure at 31 December 2001;

(ii) the amortisation charge for the year ended 31 December 2001; and

(iii) the net book value of the development expenditure at 31 December 2000.

The development expenditure incurred in each of the five years ended 31 December 2001 and the calculation of the above figures are as follows (for the purposes of this example the date of commencing production is taken to be 1 January following the year in which the development expenditure was incurred):

Year	Development expenditure incurred £'000	(i) £'000	(ii) £'000	(iii) £'000
1997	260	–	65	65
1998	100	25	25	50
1999	240	120	60	180
2000	400	300	100	400
2001	40	40	–	–
		485	250	695

Development expenditure in 2002 amounted to £800,000.

The adjustment to the pre-tax profit for 2001 will, therefore, be a reduction of £210,000 being the amortisation of £250,000 less the development expenditure of £40,000 previously charged to the profit and loss account.

Having computed these figures it is then necessary to ascertain whether any other figures in the financial statements will be affected by the change in policy; in particular, deferred taxation and stocks. For the purposes of this example the only other figures, apart from retained profits, affected by the change in policy are those relating to deferred taxation. Assuming that the development expenditure has been fully allowed as a deductible expense in arriving at the corporation tax payable in respect of the year in which it was incurred, then the new policy will give rise to timing differences for which deferred tax may have to be provided. The company considers that full provision has to be made for deferred tax and accordingly the provision at 31 December 2001, the charge for the year then ended, and the provision at 31 December 2000 have to be adjusted as follows:

	Gross timing difference £'000	Provision at 35% £'000
31 December 2001	485	170
31 December 2000	695	243
Tax charge for year		(73)

As a result of these calculations the financial statements for the year ended 31 December 2002 will therefore show the following figures in the profit and loss account, the statement of total recognised gains and losses, the balance sheet and reconciliation of movements in shareholders' funds (the 2002 figures having been prepared on the basis of the new accounting policy):

Profit and loss account

	2002 £'000	Restated 2001 £'000
Profit on ordinary activities before taxation	5,000	3,990
Taxation	(1,820)	(1,502)
Profit on ordinary activities after taxation	3,180	2,488
Dividends	(700)	(600)
Retained profit for year	2,480	1,888

Statement of total recognised gains and losses

	2002 £'000	Restated 2001 £'000
Profit for the financial year	3,180	2,488
Total recognised gains and losses relating to the year	3,180	2,488
Prior year adjustment	315	
Total gains and losses recognised since last annual report	3,495	

Balance sheet

	2002 £'000	Restated 2001 £'000
Fixed assets		
Intangible	1,090	485
Tangible fixed assets	10,000	8,000
	11,090	8,485
Net current assets	2,212	2,025
	13,302	10,510
Deferred taxation	(1,482)	(1,170)
	11,820	9,340
Share capital	1,000	1,000
Profit and loss account	10,820	8,340
	11,820	9,340

Reconciliation of movements in shareholders' funds

	2002 £'000	Restated 2001 £'000
Profit for the financial year	3,180	2,488
Dividends	(700)	(600)
Net addition to shareholders' funds	2,480	1,888
Opening shareholders' funds (originally £9,025,000 before adding prior year adjustment of £315,000)	9,340	7,452
Closing shareholders' funds	11,820	9,340

Reserves note
Profit and loss account

	£'000
At 1 January 2002	
— as previously reported	8,025
Prior year adjustment	315
— as restated	8,340
Retained profit for the year	2,480
At 31 December 2002	10,820

Where prior year figures are restated it will generally be necessary (unless the effect would be immaterial) to restate the balance sheet and profit and loss account, but it should be unnecessary to amend the cash flow statement because, of course, the cash flows have not changed. However, some of the reconciling notes to the cash flow statement may be affected, particularly the calculation of operating cash flow where the indirect method has been used to generate this figure. Care should also be taken to ensure that all figures in the accounts which are affected by the change in policy are adjusted, in particular, deferred taxation.

2.14.6 *Disclosing the effect of a change in accounting policy*

One further requirement of FRS 3 in respect of prior period adjustments is that 'the effect of prior period adjustments on the results for the preceding period should be disclosed where practicable'.[85] This overlaps with the Companies Act disclosures that are required when there is a departure from the fundamental accounting principles laid down in the Act.[86] In the case of a change in accounting policy, it will be necessary for the directors to depart from the fundamental principle of consistency, in which case they are required to disclose in a note to the accounts the particulars of and reasons for the departure 'and its effect'.[87]

This gave rise to an issue of interpretation as to whether the Companies Act requirement to disclose 'its effect' related to the current period, the prior period or both. In tracing the requirement back to the EU Fourth Directive, it seems clear that the intention of the legislation was for companies to disclose the effect of the departure on the current year's financial statements as a whole, and not just on the results. The wording of the relevant Article in the Fourth Directive is as follows: 'Any such departures must be disclosed in the notes on the accounts and the reasons for them given together with an assessment of their effect on the assets, liabilities, financial position and profit or loss.'[88]

However, irrespective of what might have been the original intention of the legislation, the practice which had developed was to provide only details of the effect on the prior period's results (i.e. the information which is required by FRS 3). Apart from anything else, the principal reason for this was that it is often impracticable to provide the information in respect of the current period. For example, a company preparing its first set of accounts in compliance with FRS 4 and FRS 5 would, in order to illustrate fully the effect of the relevant changes, effectively have to present alongside the current year's accounts, a second set of accounts prepared under the old rules. Not only is this impracticable, but it is of little value to the user.

Nevertheless, this is an issue which was referred to the UITF – apparently at the insistence of the Review Panel. The UITF's deliberations resulted in UITF Abstract 14 – *Disclosure of changes in accounting policy* – which was issued in November 1995. The consensus reached by the UITF was that the disclosures necessary when a change of accounting policy is made should include, in addition to the disclosure of the effect required by FRS 3, an indication of the effect on the current year's results. In those cases where the effect on the current year was either immaterial or similar to the quantified effect on the prior year 'a simple statement saying this would suffice'. The Abstract provided further that where it was not practicable to give the effect on the current year, that fact, together with the reasons, should be stated.[89]

UITF 14 has since been superseded by FRS 18 – *Accounting Policies* – which has incorporated similar disclosures. FRS 18 requires that companies should disclose in their financial statements details of any changes to the accounting policies that were followed in preparing financial statements for the preceding period, including:[90]

(i) a brief explanation of why each new accounting policy is thought more appropriate;

(ii) where practicable, the effect of a prior period adjustment on the results for the preceding period, in accordance with FRS 3 – *Reporting Financial Performance*; and

(iii) where practicable, an indication of the effect of a change in accounting policy on the results for the current period.

Where it is not practicable to make the disclosures described in (ii) or (iii) above, that fact, together with the reasons, should be stated.[91]

As stated above, we believe that these are sometimes meaningless and impracticable disclosures, and companies will in such cases make use of FRS 18's get-out to avoid having to provide them.

2.15 Comparative figures

Comparative figures are required both for the figures in the primary statements and such notes thereto as are required by the standard. The comparatives in respect of the profit and loss account have to be analysed into continuing operations, acquisitions and discontinued operations to the same level as the current year's results. However, the analysis of the comparatives does not have to be on the face of the profit and loss account, but can be given in the notes.

The comparative figures will, in total, be the same as the figures reported in the previous year's profit and loss account. However, the analysis will be different; the continuing category in the comparatives should only include results of activities that are classified as continuing in the current year. Consequently the discontinued column in the comparatives will include the results of the activities that were discontinued in both the current and the previous year. The results of the operations that were classified as acquisitions in the previous year's profit and loss account will not be presented as acquisitions in the comparative figures for the current period; they will be included in continuing activities. This is because the analysis of the comparative figures must be based on the status of an operation in the current year's profit and loss account.

The standard provides that in some circumstances it may also be useful to disclose the results of acquisitions for the first full financial year for which they are a part of the reporting entity's activities. In this case, the standard suggests that it may be helpful also to provide the comparative figures for the acquisitions.

3 IAS REQUIREMENTS

As yet, there is no single IASC standard that deals with the reporting of financial performance in its entirety. However, there are several standards that, to a greater or lesser extent, impinge on the issue. These include: IAS 1 – *Presentation of Financial Statement*, IAS 8 – *Net Profit and Loss for the Period, Fundamental Errors and Changes in Accounting Policies*, and IAS 35 – *Discontinuing Operations.*

3.1 Overview of the form and content of the income statement

3.1.1 IAS 1 (revised)

In August 1997, the IASC issued IAS 1 (revised) – *Presentation of Financial Statements* – which consolidated and replaced IAS 1 – *Disclosure of Accounting Policies*, IAS 5 – *Information to be Disclosed in Financial Statements*, and IAS 13 – *Presentation of Current Assets and Current Liabilities.* IAS 1 can best be described as the IASC's version of the EU Fourth Directive. It deals with the components of financial statements, fair presentation, fundamental accounting concepts, disclosure of accounting policies, the structure and content of financial statements and the statement of changes in equity. The standard can only really be termed controversial in two respects: (1) it introduced the possibility for companies reporting under IAS to apply a fair presentation override,[92] and (2) it adds the requirement for companies to present a statement of changes in equity as a fourth primary financial statement.[93]

In approving the Standard, the IASC Board agreed that, in extremely rare circumstances, enterprises may depart from a requirement if to do so is necessary in order to achieve fair presentation. (The issues of fair presentation in accordance with International Accounting Standards and the use of the override are discussed in detail in Chapter 1 at 2.7.2.)

IAS do not prescribe a standard layout for the income statement. However, IAS 1 does require that the following information be presented as a minimum:

The face of the income statement should include line items which present the following amounts:[94]

- revenue;
- the results of operating activities;
- finance costs;
- share of profits and losses of associates and joint ventures accounted for using the equity method;
- tax expense;
- profit or loss from ordinary activities;
- extraordinary items;
- minority interest; and
- net profit or loss for the period.

The standard is silent as to the order in which these items should appear on the face of the income statement. However, the items are listed in a logical order – except perhaps for the share of profits and losses of associates and joint ventures accounted for using the equity method, which could arguably more appropriately be disclosed as being included in the total for the results of operating activities (see 3.2 below).

In any event, the standard requires that additional line items, headings and sub-totals should be presented on the face of the income statement when required by an IAS, or when such presentation is necessary to present fairly the enterprise's financial performance.[95]

IAS 1 also sets down strict requirements regarding offsetting. It states that assets and liabilities should not be offset except when offsetting is required or permitted by another IAS. Similarly, items of income and expense should be offset only when an IAS requires or permits it, or when gains, losses and related expenses arising from the same or similar transactions and events are not material. Immaterial amounts should be aggregated with amounts of a similar nature or function.[96]

An entity should present, either on the face of the income statement or in the notes to the income statement, an analysis of expenses using a classification based on either the nature of expenses or their function within the enterprise.[97] The choice of method depends on both historical and industry factors and the nature of the organisation. Both methods provide an indication of those costs that might be expected to vary, directly or indirectly, with the level of sales or production of the enterprise. Because each method of presentation has merit for different types of entity, IAS 1 requires a choice to be made between classifications based on that which most fairly presents the elements of the entity's performance. However, because information on the nature of expenses is useful in predicting future cash flows, entities classifying expenses by function should disclose additional information on the nature of expenses, including depreciation and amortisation expense and staff costs.[98] (The appendix to IAS 1 provides non-mandatory illustrative examples of the layout of the income statement.)

An example of a classification using the nature of expense method is as follows:[99]

Revenue		X
Other operating income		X
Changes in inventories of finished goods and work in progress	X	
Raw materials and consumables used	X	
Staff costs	X	
Depreciation and amortisation expense	X	
Other operating expenses	X	
Total operating expenses		(X)
Profit from operating activities		X

The change in finished goods and work in progress during the period represents an adjustment to production expenses to reflect the fact that either production has increased inventory levels or that sales in excess of production have reduced inventory levels.[100]

An example of a classification using the function of expense method is as follows:[101]

Revenue	X
Cost of sales	(X)
Gross profit	X
Other operating income	X
Distribution costs	(X)
Administrative expenses	(X)
Other operating expenses	(X)
Profit from operating activities	X

This presentation often provides more relevant information to users than the classification of expenses by nature, but the allocation of costs to functions can be arbitrary and involves considerable judgement. In addition, the standard requires that enterprises classifying expenses by function should disclose additional information on the nature of expenses, including depreciation and amortisation expense and staff costs.[102] And finally, companies are required to disclose, either on the face of the income statement or in the notes, the amount of dividends per share, declared or proposed, for the period covered by the financial statements.[103]

Although IAS 1 encourages reporting enterprises to present the analysis of expenses either by nature or function on the face of the income statement, this is not a mandatory requirement and the analysis may be given in the notes. As a result, and because of the increasing desire by companies to be able to present EBITDA on the face of the income statement (see 2.11.2 above), many companies use a hybrid approach in the income statement classification of expenses. The Danish group FLS Industries provides an example of this, as follows:

Extract 25.17: FLS Industries A/S (2000)

Consolidated profit and loss account

DKKm		**1999**	**2000**
Notes			
2	Net turnover	20,993	19,205
3	Production costs	16,180	14,734
	Gross profit	**4,813**	**4,471**
3	Sales and distribution costs	1,303	1,647
3	Administrative expenses and other expenses	2,324	2,411
4	Other operating income	208	132
	Earnings before interest, tax, depreciation and amortisation (EBITDA)	**1,394**	**545**
15	Amortisation and write-down of intangible fixed assets	801	876
14	Depreciation and write-down of tangible fixed assets	118	127
	Earnings before interest and tax (EBIT)	**475**	**(458)**

17	Share of pre-tax profit of associated undertakings	1,053	1,603
5	Profit and loss on the disposal of undertakings	1,350	60
6	Financial income	1,068	1,446
6	Financial expenses	1,190	1,922
	Earnings before tax (EBT)	**2,756**	**729**
7	Tax for the year	216	(114)
	Profit for the year	**2,540**	**843**
	Minority interests' share of the profit for the year	452	578
	FLS Industries A/S' share of the profit for the year	**2,088**	**265**
29	Earnings per share	44.9	5.7
29	Earnings per share, diluted	45.6	5.8

It seems clear that FLS Industries wishes to focus the users' attention on EBITDA and EBIT, but in so doing has provided an analysis of expenses above the EBITDA sub-total by function, and those below EBITDA by nature. It is only by studying the notes to the accounts is the reader able to obtain a full picture of the expenses analysed by nature. An alternative approach would be to provide a full analysis of expenses on the face of the income statement by function, and then to disclose EBITDA by way of a pro forma sub-total. An example of how this might be done is provided by Carlton Communications in Extract 25.12 at 2.6.5 above.

3.1.2 *IAS 8*

The objective of IAS 8 – *Net Profit or Loss for the Period, Fundamental Errors and Changes in Accounting Policies* – is to prescribe the classification, disclosure and accounting treatment of certain items in the income statement so that all enterprises prepare and present an income statement on a consistent basis.[104]

Its main features are as follows:

- All items of income or expense recognised in the income statement should be included in the determination of profit or loss unless an IAS permits or requires otherwise.[105]
- The profit or loss for the period is to be split between (a) the profit and loss from ordinary activities and (b) extraordinary items, both of which are to be disclosed on the face of the income statement,[106] with the nature and amount of each extraordinary item disclosed in a note.[107] The definitions of extraordinary items and ordinary activities are less than rigorous, although IAS 8 states that 'only on rare occasions does an event or transaction give rise to an extraordinary item'.[108]
- When items of income and expense within profit or loss from ordinary activities are of such size, nature or incidence as to be relevant to an explanation of the performance for the period, the nature and amount of such items are to be disclosed separately (the term 'exceptional items' is not used).[109]
- The effect of a change in an accounting estimate should be included in the determination of net profit or loss in the period of the change (if the change affects the period only), or in the period of the change and future periods (if the change affects both).[110] The effect of a change in an accounting estimate should

be included in the same income statement classification as was used previously for the estimate.[111] In addition, the nature and amount of a change in an accounting estimate that has a material effect in the current period or which is expected to have a material effect in subsequent periods should be disclosed. If it is impracticable to quantify the amount, this fact should be disclosed.[112]

- Fundamental errors and changes in accounting policy are to be dealt with either as a prior year adjustment (the 'benchmark treatment') or as a separate item in the current year's profit or loss (the 'allowed alternative treatment').[113] In both cases, disclosures are required – see 3.5.2 and 3.7 below.

3.2 The results of operating activities

Although paragraph 75 of IAS 1 requires 'the results of operating activities' to be shown as a line item on the face of the income statement, neither IAS 1 nor IAS 8 provides a definition or explanation of 'operating activities'. The difficulty is exacerbated by paragraphs 80 and 82 of IAS 1, which refer to 'other operating income' and 'other operating expenses' without providing any guidance as to what these items include. IAS 7 – *Cash Flow Statements* – does provide a definition for operating activities, but this relates specifically to the cash flow statement, and cannot be applied in any meaningful way to the income statement.

Current practice seems to suggest that companies have substantial freedom in determining which items are and are not included within the operating activities line of the income statement. As a result, many companies reporting under IAS are now reporting material non-recurring items (such as reorganisation and restructuring costs) outside of their results from operating activities. In the case of FLS Industries (see Extract 25.17 above) it is not entirely clear which total the company considers represents its results from operating activities.

The operating profit is an important figure for users of accounts, as the utility of financial reports is reduced if it is not comparable between businesses. Consequently, in our view, companies should formulate a rigorous definition of their results of operating activities, disclose the definition in their accounts and apply it consistently. For example, companies will need to decide whether or not the share of profits and losses of associates and joint ventures accounted for using the equity method are included within operating activities. Our preference would be to include such profits and losses within operating activities, but it is not entirely clear from the literature what the correct approach should be. Paragraph 75 of IAS 1 perhaps suggests that they should be shown 'finance cost' and 'tax expense'. IAS 28 requires that the results of associates included in the income statement should be separately disclosed, but does not specify the 'level' of the income statement at which they should be included.

As can be seen from Extract 25.18 below, Nokia includes the results of its associates as part of investment income on the face of the profit and loss account, below operating profit:

Extract 25.18: Nokia Corporation (2000)

Consolidated profit and loss account, IAS [extract]

Financial year ended December 31	2000 EURm	1999 EURm
Net sales	**30 376**	19 772
Cost of goods sold	**-19 072**	-12 227
Research and development expenses	**-2 584**	-1 755
Selling, general and administrative expenses	**-2 804**	-1 811
Amortization of goodwill	**-140**	-71
Operating profit	**5 776**	3 908
Share of results of associated companies	**-16**	-5
Financial income and expenses	**102**	-58
Profit before tax and minority interests	**5 862**	3 845
Tax	**-1 784**	-1 189
Minority interests	**-140**	-79
Net profit	**3 938**	2 577

Although Nokia does not specify whether these amounts are its share of the pre- or post-tax results of its associates, it appears from the notes to the accounts to be almost certain that they are the post-tax results.

Nestlé, however, includes the post-tax results of its associates as the last item in its group profit and loss account, as illustrated below:

Extract 25.19: Nestlé S.A. (2000)

Consolidated income statement for the year ended 31st December 2000 [extract]

In millions of CHF	Notes	2000	1999
...			
Profit before taxes	4	**8 341**	6,859
Taxes	5	**(2 761)**	(2 314)
Net profit of consolidated companies		**5 580**	4 545
Share of profit attributable to minority interests		**(212)**	(160)
Share of results of associated companies	6	**395**	339
Net profit for the year		**5 763**	4 724

Notes

6. Share of results of associated companies

In millions of CHF	2000	1999
Share of profit before taxes	**605**	521
Less share of taxes	**(210)**	(182)
Share of profit after taxes	**395**	339

The difference between the two perfectly acceptable approaches of Nokia and Nestlé illustrated above highlights the importance of the IASB developing an approach that leads to greater consistency.

The same applies to items such as gains and losses on the disposal of fixed assets, the amortisation of goodwill, and restructuring costs. In the case of the amortisation of goodwill, IAS 22 merely requires companies to disclose the line item(s) in the income statement in which the amortisation charge is included, and does not deal with the issue of whether or not the charge should be included within the results of operating activities.[114] Our view is that goodwill amortisation should be charged in arriving at operating profit, which is the approach followed, for example, by Nokia (see Extract 25.18 above). Nevertheless, IAS are unspecific on this issue, and it is therefore hoped that the IASB's current improvements project will be able to provide some clarity in the whole area of defining which items fall within and which items fall outside 'the results of operating activities'.

3.3 Exceptional items

IAS do not address exceptional items directly. Nevertheless, there are certain references in the literature that would indicate that the separate disclosure of individually material items is sometimes appropriate. For example, the IASC's *Framework* states that the ability to make predictions from financial statements is enhanced 'by the manner in which information on past transactions and events is displayed. For example, the predictive value of the income statement is enhanced if unusual, abnormal and infrequent items of income or expense are separately disclosed.'[115] This is taken up by IAS 8, which states that 'when items of income and expense within profit or loss from ordinary activities are of such size, nature or incidence that their disclosure is relevant to explain the performance of the enterprise for the period, the nature and amount of such items should be disclosed separately.'[116]

IAS 8 goes on to state that, although these are not extraordinary items, 'the nature and amount of such items may be relevant to users of financial statements in understanding the financial position and performance of an enterprise and in making projections about financial position and performance.'[117] Although there is nothing to prevent companies disclosing these items on the face of the income statement, IAS 8 states that the 'disclosure of such information is usually made in the notes to the financial statements'.[118]

The standard then lists the following circumstances that may give rise to the separate disclosure of these items of income and expense:[119]

(a) the write-down of inventories to net realisable value or property, plant and equipment to recoverable amount, as well as the reversal of such write-downs;

(b) a restructuring of the activities of an enterprise and the reversal of any provisions for the costs of restructuring;

(c) disposals of items of property, plant and equipment;

(d) disposals of long-term investments;

(e) discontinued operations;

(f) litigation settlements; and

(g) other reversals of provisions.

Thus, it seems that IAS 8 is recognising the need to disclose what are commonly known as 'exceptional items', without either defining them or providing any guidance as to whether or not they should be charged within the results of operating activities.

3.4 Extraordinary items

Under IAS 8, extraordinary items are defined as 'income or expenses that arise from events or transactions that are clearly distinct from the ordinary activities of the enterprise and therefore are not expected to recur frequently or regularly'.[120] The standard defines 'ordinary activities' extremely widely, presumably in an attempt to limit the incidence of items being disclosed as extraordinary. Ordinary activities are defined as 'any activities which are undertaken by an enterprise as part of its business and such related activities in which the enterprise engages in furtherance of, incidental to, or arising from these activities'.[121] The standard goes on to explain that virtually all items of income and expense included in the determination of net profit or loss for the period arise in the course of the ordinary activities of the enterprise and that, therefore, only on rare occasions does an event or transaction give rise to an extraordinary item.[122]

The standard emphasises the fact that whether an event or transaction is clearly distinct from the ordinary activities of the enterprise is determined by the nature of the event or transaction in relation to the business ordinarily carried on by the enterprise, rather than by the frequency with which such events are expected to occur.[123] Therefore, an event or transaction may be extraordinary for one enterprise but not extraordinary for another because of the differences between their respective ordinary activities. The standard cites 'the expropriation of assets' and 'an earthquake or other natural disaster' as events that generally give rise to extraordinary items for most enterprises.[124]

Consequently, on the face of it, it seems that the incidence of companies reporting extraordinary items will be rare; however, it seems that in practice they are not quite so rare as the standard implies, as evidenced by the following extract from the accounts of Siemens:

Extract 25.20: Siemens AG (2000)

Statements of income [extract]

Years ended September 30 *(in millions of euros)*

		Siemens worldwide	
	Notes	2000	1999
...			
Income from ordinary activities before income taxes		**5,289**	**2,870**
Taxes on income from ordinary activities	7	(1,908)	(1,005)
Net income before extraordinary items		**3,381**	**1,865**
Extraordinary items after taxes	9	4,520	
Net income		**7,901**	**1,865**
...			

Notes [extract]

9 Extraordinary items after taxes [extract]

(in millions of euros)	2000
Extraordinary gains	7,809
Extraordinary losses	(3,661)
Extraordinary items before income taxes	4,148
Income tax on extraordinary items	372
Extraordinary items after taxes	4,520

Extraordinary items include proceeds from the sale of businesses as described in detail in Management's discussion and analysis and in the Notes under "Companies included in consolidation." In addition, extraordinary items include gains resulting from the public offering of Infineon Technologies AG, which has remained part of the Siemens organization, as well as nonrecurring expenses.

Extraordinary expense of €1,268 million has been recorded to account for the one-time adjustment of the domestic pension accruals to the internationally accepted projected unit credit method which has been adopted to prepare for the changeover to U.S. GAAP accounting in fiscal year 2001.

Extraordinary expenses also relate to corporate issues in a total amount of approximately €900 million. These issues include, among other things, an increase in environmental remediation accruals in connection with the cleanup of the closed fuel element facility in Hanau, Germany; an allowance to provide for a loan granted to Fujitsu Siemens Computers (Holding) B.V., a subsidiary accounted for under the equity method; and an accrual for loss contingencies set up to account for the liquidation of two centrally managed projects.

On account of the Company's excellent results, employees will receive a special bonus which led to a one-time charge of €600 million.

The Company recorded a nonrecurring charge of approximately €140 million for purchased in-process research and development expenses associated with the takeover of Shared Medical Systems Corporation and the mobile communications development operations of Robert Bosch GmbH.

The remaining extraordinary expenses include a charge for goodwill impairment of €136 million related to Argon Networks, Inc., Wilmington, DE, U.S.A., and the Siemens contribution to the German Economy Foundation Initiative "Remembrance, Responsibility and the Future."

It is not for us to comment on whether or not the items listed above are appropriately classified as extraordinary. However, suffice it to say that the sheer number and size of items disclosed by Siemens as extraordinary does raise the issue as to whether IAS 8 provides sufficient clarity in this whole area. Nevertheless, it is perhaps interesting to note that IAS 8's definition of ordinary activities is virtually identical to the ordinary activities definition in FRS 3. Yet, as discussed in 2.6.1 above, it is the all-embracing nature of the FRS 3 definition of ordinary activities that has been instrumental in effectively outlawing the reporting of extraordinary items under UK GAAP.

3.5 Change in accounting policy

The principles underlying the accounting treatment of changes in accounting policies under IAS focus on the need for entities to achieve consistency and comparability in reporting their financial position and performance.[125]

In the period when IAS are applied in full for the first time as the primary accounting basis, the financial statements of an entity should be prepared and presented as if the financial statements had always been prepared in accordance with the Standards and Interpretations effective for the period of first-time application. That is, first time application of IAS may not be treated as a change in accounting policies, and the Standards and Interpretations effective for the period of first-time application should be applied retrospectively, except when:

- individual Standards or Interpretations require or permit a different transitional treatment; or
- the amount of the adjustment relating to prior periods cannot reasonably be determined.[126]

3.5.1 *When can a change in accounting policy occur?*

Accounting policies are the principles, bases, conventions, rules and practices that an entity uses in preparing and presenting its financial statements.[127] Changes in accounting policies should be made only if required by statute, by an accounting standard setting body or if the change will result in a more relevant or reliable presentation of financial information.[128] If IAS allow alternative accounting policies for similar events or transactions, the entity must choose and consistently apply one of those policies unless it is specifically permitted or required to apply different policies to different categories of items.[129]

The following are not changes in accounting policies:[130]

- the adoption of an accounting policy for events or transactions that differ in substance from previously occurring events or transactions; and
- the adoption of a new accounting policy for events or transactions which did not occur previously or that were immaterial.

A change in accounting policy in order to comply with a new IAS must be accounted for in accordance with the transitional provisions of that Standard. Only in the absence of transitional provisions may the change be accounted for in accordance with the general rules of IAS 8.[131]

3.5.2 *Reporting a change in accounting policy*

IAS 8 permits two alternative approaches to accounting for changes in accounting policies – the benchmark treatment and allowed alternative treatment described below. However, the application if SIC-18 to these options requires a single approach to be selected and applied consistently, unless a specific Standard or Interpretation requires a different approach to be followed.[132]

A Benchmark treatment

The benchmark treatment requires changes in accounting policies to be accounted for retrospectively. Therefore, comparative information is restated and the amount of the adjustment relating to periods prior to those included in the financial statements is adjusted against the opening balance of retained earnings of the earliest period presented. If the resulting adjustment that relates to prior periods is not reasonably determinable, the change in accounting policy is to be applied prospectively.[133]

An entity should disclose the following information:[134]

- the reasons for the change;
- the amount of the adjustment for each of the periods presented and the total for those periods not presented; and
- the fact that comparative information has been restated or that it was impracticable to do so.

B Allowed alternative treatment

The allowed alternative treatment requires the change in accounting policy to be accounted for retrospectively by recognising the effect relating to prior periods in income for the period. When this method is applied, comparative financial information should be presented as reported in the financial statements of the prior period. However, additional pro forma information prepared in accordance with the benchmark treatment should be presented, unless it is impracticable to do so. If the resulting adjustment that relates to prior periods is not reasonably determinable, the change in accounting policy is to be applied prospectively.[135]

An entity should disclose the following information:[136]

- the reasons for the change;
- the amount of the adjustment recognised in the current period; and
- pro forma information prepared in accordance with the benchmark treatment and the amount of the adjustment for each of the periods presented and the total for those periods not presented. If it is impracticable to present pro forma information, this fact must be disclosed.

The Russian group OAO Rostelecom has effectively adopted the allowed alternative treatment under IAS for the change in their dividend policy – in this example, however, there is no cumulative effect to recognise in income in the current year, but the prior year amounts have not been restated.

Extract 25.21: OAO Rostelecom (1999)

5. PRINCIPAL ACCOUNTING POLICIES [extract]

o) Change in accounting policy

In 1999, the Group changed, starting with the current year, its accounting policy with respect to the recognition of the liability for dividends declared. Dividends are recognized as a liability in the year in which they are proposed and declared. However, the statement of changes in shareholders' equity has not been restated for dividends of Rbl 482 million, which were declared in 1998 and accrued in 1997. If the current accounting policy had been applied in the past, the opening retained earnings as of January 1, 1997 and January 1, 1998 would have been increased by Rbl 314 million and Rbl 482 million respectively.

Entities that apply IAS for the first time may not apply the allowed alternative treatment to account for the effect of the changes in accounting policies resulting from the transition from national GAAP.[137] Therefore, any adjustments arising from the transition to IAS should be treated as adjustments to the opening balance of retained earnings of the earliest period presented in accordance with IAS. In the period when IAS are applied for the first time, the accounts should be prepared and presented as if the accounts had always been prepared in accordance with IAS.

3.6 Change in accounting estimate

As a result of the uncertainties inherent in business activities, many financial statement items cannot be measured with precision but can only be estimated. The estimation process involves judgements based on the latest information available. Estimates may be required, for example, of bad debts, inventory obsolescence or the useful lives or expected pattern of consumption of economic benefits of depreciable assets. The use of reasonable estimates is an essential part of the preparation of financial statements and does not undermine their reliability.[138]

Nevertheless, an estimate may have to be revised if changes occur regarding the circumstances on which the estimate was based or as a result of new information, more experience or subsequent developments. By its nature, the revision of the estimate does not bring the adjustment within the definitions of an extraordinary item or a fundamental error (see 3.7 below).[139]

The effect of a change in an accounting estimate should not be given retrospective effect by restating prior periods. The effect has to be included in the determination of the result for the period of the change and, where appropriate, future periods. The effect of a change in accounting estimate should be included in the income statement caption that was previously used for the estimate.[140]

Where it is difficult to distinguish between a change in accounting policy and a change in an accounting estimate, the change is treated as a change in an accounting estimate, with 'appropriate disclosure'.[141] Presumably, the disclosure that is required is a full description of the circumstances of the change such that the reader of the accounts is able to make his own judgement.

The nature and amount of a change in accounting estimate that has a material effect on the current period or subsequent periods should be disclosed. If it is impracticable to quantify the amount, this fact should be disclosed.[142]

3.7 Correction of a fundamental error

Fundamental errors are defined in IAS 8 as 'errors discovered in the current period that are of such significance that the financial statements of one or more prior periods can no longer be considered to have been reliable at the date of their issue'.[143]

Errors may occur as a result of mathematical mistakes, mistakes in applying accounting policies, misinterpretation of facts, fraud or oversights. The correction of these errors is normally included in the determination of net profit or loss for the current period. However, on rare occasions, an error has such a significant effect on the financial statements of one or more prior periods that those financial statements can no longer be considered to have been reliable at the date of their issue. These errors are referred to as fundamental errors. An example of a fundamental error is the inclusion in the financial statements of a previous period of material amounts of work in progress and receivables in respect of fraudulent contracts that cannot be enforced

Under IAS, two methods are permitted in accounting for fundamental errors.[144] However, the application of SIC-18 to these two methods requires a single approach to be selected and applied consistently.[145]

3.7.1 *Benchmark treatment*

The benchmark treatment requires the adjustment of the opening balance of retained earnings and the restatement of comparative information to account for fundamental errors that relate to prior periods, unless it is impracticable to do so.[146] An entity should disclose the following information:[147]

- the nature of the fundamental error;
- the amount of the correction for each of the periods presented and the total for those periods not presented; and
- the fact that comparative information has been restated or that it was impracticable to do so.

3.7.2 *Allowed alternative treatment*

The allowed alternative treatment requires the effect of fundamental errors to be included in the determination of the income for the current period and prohibits restatement of prior periods. However, additional pro forma information prepared in accordance with the benchmark treatment should be presented, unless it is impracticable to do so.[148] An entity should disclose the following information:[149]

- the nature of the fundamental error;
- the amount of the correction recognised in income in the current period; and
- pro forma information prepared in accordance with the benchmark treatment, the amount of the correction for each of the periods presented, and the total for those periods not presented. If it is impracticable to present pro forma information, this fact should be disclosed.

3.8 Discontinuing operations

The IASC issued IAS 35 – *Discontinuing Operations* – in June 1998. The standard is concerned only with the presentation and disclosures relating to discontinuing operations. It contains no recognition or measurement rules of its own, although it does require that provisions for discontinuing operations should be calculated in accordance with IAS 36 – *Impairment of assets* – and IAS 37 – *Provisions, Contingent Liabilities and Contingent Assets*. It also notes that IAS 19 – *Employee Benefits* – and IAS 16 – *Property, Plant and Equipment* – may also be relevant.[150]

The objective of IAS 35 is to establish principles for reporting information about discontinuing operations, thereby enhancing the ability of users of financial statements to make projections of an enterprise's cash flows, earnings-generating capacity, and financial position by segregating information about discontinuing operations from information about continuing operations.

A discontinuing operation is a relatively large component of an enterprise, such as a business or geographical segment under IAS 14 – *Segment Reporting*, that the enterprise, pursuant to a single plan, either is disposing of substantially in its entirety or is terminating through abandonment or piecemeal sale. The standard defines a discontinuing operation as 'a component of an enterprise:

(a) that the enterprise, pursuant to a single plan, is:
    (i) disposing of substantially in its entirety, such as by selling the component in a single transaction, by demerger or spin-off of ownership of the component to the enterprise's shareholders;
    (ii) disposing of piecemeal, such as by selling off the component's assets and settling its liabilities individually; or
    (iii) terminating through abandonment;
(b) that represents a separate major line of business or geographical area of operations; and
(c) that can be distinguished operationally and for financial reporting purposes.'[151]

The standard places a restriction on the use of the term 'discontinuing operation' by stating that a restructuring, transaction, or event that does not meet the standard's definition of a discontinuing operation should not be called a discontinuing operation.[152]

Under criterion (a) of the above definition, a discontinuing operation may be disposed of in its entirety or piecemeal, but always pursuant to an overall plan to discontinue the entire component. If an enterprise sells a component substantially in its entirety, the result can be a net gain or net loss. For such a discontinuance, there is a single date at which a binding sale agreement is entered into, although the actual transfer of possession and control of the discontinuing operation may occur at a later date. In addition, payments to the seller may occur at the time of the agreement, at the time of the transfer, or over an extended future period.[153]

Instead of disposing of a major component in its entirety, an enterprise may discontinue and dispose of the component by selling its assets and settling its liabilities piecemeal (individually or in small groups). For piecemeal disposals, while the overall result may be a net gain or a net loss, the sale of an individual asset or settlement of an individual liability may have the opposite effect. Moreover, there is no single date at which an overall binding sale agreement is entered into. Rather, the sales of assets and settlements of liabilities may occur over a period of months or perhaps even longer, and the end of a financial reporting period may occur part way through the disposal period. To qualify as a discontinuing operation, the disposal must be pursuant to a single co-ordinated plan.[154]

An enterprise may terminate an operation by abandonment without substantial sales of assets. An abandoned operation would be a discontinuing operation if it satisfies the criteria in the definition. However, changing the scope of an operation or the manner in which it is conducted is not an abandonment because that operation, although changed, is continuing.[155]

Business enterprises frequently close facilities, abandon products or even product lines, and change the size of their work force in response to market forces. While those kinds of terminations generally are not, in and of themselves, discontinuing operations as that term is used in the standard, they can occur in connection with a discontinuing operation.[156]

The Standard uses the term 'discontinuing operation' rather than the traditional 'discontinued operation' because 'discontinued operation' implies that recognition of a discontinuance is necessary only at or near the end of the process of discontinuing the operation (as is the case under FRS 3). Instead, IAS 35 requires that disclosures about a discontinuing operation begin earlier than that, namely when a detailed formal plan for disposal has been adopted and announced or when the enterprise has already contracted for the disposal. This is described in the standard as the 'initial disclosure event', which is defined as being 'the occurrence of one of the following, whichever occurs earlier:

(a) the enterprise has entered into a binding sale agreement for substantially all of the assets attributable to the discontinuing operation; or

(b) the enterprise's board of directors or similar governing body has both (i) approved a detailed, formal plan for the discontinuance and (ii) made an announcement of the plan.'[157]

The disclosures required by the standard (which should be presented separately for each discontinuing operation)[158] may be presented either in the notes to the financial statements or on the face of the financial statements, except that the disclosure of the amount of the pre-tax gain or loss recognised on the disposal of assets or settlement of liabilities attributable to the discontinuing operation (paragraph 31(a)) should be shown on the face of the income statement.[159] It should be noted that the standard states explicitly that a discontinuing operation should not be presented as an extraordinary item.[160]

An enterprise should include the following information relating to a discontinuing operation in its financial statements beginning with the financial statements for the period in which the initial disclosure event (as defined above) occurs:

(a) a description of the discontinuing operation;

(b) the business or geographical segment(s) in which it is reported in accordance with IAS 14;

(c) the date and nature of the initial disclosure event;

(d) the date or period in which the discontinuance is expected to be completed if known or determinable;

(e) the carrying amounts, as of the balance sheet date, of the total assets and the total liabilities to be disposed of;

(f) the amounts of revenue, expenses, and pre-tax profit or loss from ordinary activities attributable to the discontinuing operation during the current financial reporting period, and the income tax expense relating thereto as required by paragraph 81(h) of IAS 12; and

(g) the amounts of net cash flows attributable to the operating, investing, and financing activities of the discontinuing operation during the current financial reporting period.[161]

In measuring the assets, liabilities, revenues, expenses, gains, losses, and cash flows of a discontinuing operation for the purpose of the disclosures required by the standard, such items can be attributed to a discontinuing operation if they will be disposed of, settled, reduced, or eliminated when the discontinuance is completed. To the extent that such items continue after completion of the discontinuance, they should not be allocated to the discontinuing operation.[162]

The above disclosures should also be made if a plan for disposal is approved and publicly announced after the end of an enterprise's financial reporting period but before the financial statements for that period are approved.[163]

When an enterprise disposes of assets or settles liabilities attributable to a discontinuing operation or enters into binding agreements for the sale of such assets or the settlement of such liabilities, it should include in its financial statements the following information when the events occur:[164]

(a) for any gain or loss that is recognised on the disposal of assets or settlement of liabilities attributable to the discontinuing operation, (i) the amount of the pre-tax gain or loss and (ii) income tax expense relating to the gain or loss, as required by paragraph 81(h) of IAS 12 – *Income Taxes*; and

(b) the net selling price or range of prices (which is after deducting the expected disposal costs) of those net assets for which the enterprise has entered into one or more binding sale agreements, the expected timing of receipt of those cash flows, and the carrying amount of those net assets.

In addition to the disclosures described above, an enterprise should include in its financial statements for periods subsequent to the one in which the initial disclosure event occurs a description of any significant changes in the amount or timing of cash flows relating to the assets and liabilities to be disposed of or settled and the events causing those changes.[165] Examples of events and activities that would be disclosed include the nature and terms of binding sale agreements for the assets, a demerger of the assets via spin-off of a separate equity security to the enterprise's shareholders, and legal or regulatory approvals.[166]

The disclosures required by the standard should continue in financial statements for periods up to and including the period in which the discontinuance is completed. A discontinuance is completed when the plan is substantially completed or abandoned, though payments from the buyer(s) to the seller may not yet be completed.[167] If an enterprise abandons or withdraws from a plan that was previously reported as a discontinuing operation, that fact and its effect should be disclosed.[168] This would include the reversal of any prior impairment loss or provision that was recognised with respect to the discontinuing operation.[169]

Appendix A to IAS 35 provides examples of the presentation and disclosures required by the standard. Comparative information for prior periods that is presented in financial statements prepared after the initial disclosure event should be restated to segregate continuing and discontinuing assets, liabilities, income, expenses, and cash flows in a manner similar to that required by the disclosure requirement of the standard.[170] Appendix B to the standard illustrates the application of this requirement.

3.9 The statement of changes in equity

In amending IAS 1, the IASC Board agreed that financial statements prepared in accordance with IAS should include, as a separate component, a statement showing:[171]

- the net profit or loss for the period;
- each item of income and expense, gain or loss which, as required by other Standards, is recognised directly in equity, and the total of these items; and
- the cumulative effect of changes in accounting policy, and correction of fundamental errors, dealt with under the Benchmark treatment in IAS 8.

In addition, an enterprise should also present, either within this statement or in the notes:[172]

- capital transactions with owners and distributions to owners;
- the balance of accumulated profit or loss at the beginning of the period and at the balance sheet date, and the movements for the period; and
- a reconciliation between the carrying amount of each class of equity capital, share premium and each reserve at the beginning and the end of the period, separately disclosing each movement.

This is, of course, a compromise solution which is aimed at satisfying a number of different constituencies. For example, from a UK perspective, the first three parts correspond to FRS 3's statement of total recognised gains and losses, with the result that the remaining three items can be disclosed in the notes thereby leaving the statement of total recognised gains and losses intact. The proposals are also compatible with the US standard, SFAS 130, as a result of the flexibility on both sides. The IASC does not view the statement as a statement of performance, but it can be made into one if people so desire.

However, as can be seen from 4 below, the IASC sees IAS 1's statement of changes in equity as an interim measure, pending the appearance of a single statement of performance that will effectively combine the profit and loss account and the first three parts of the statement of changes in equity.

4 REPORTING COMPREHENSIVE INCOME: THE MOVE TOWARDS A SINGLE STATEMENT OF TOTAL FINANCIAL PERFORMANCE

4.1 A fundamental issue facing the IASB

Performance reporting is a problem that has vexed standard setters for many years and is still not resolved in any way that has received international acceptance. However, with the increasing use of fair values in financial reporting, the definition of financial performance and the manner in which performance is reported have now become *the* fundamental issues currently facing the IASB. This is because many of the projects currently on the IASB's agenda – such as financial instruments, leases, share-based payments and asset revaluations – raise important questions regarding performance reporting. All too often, standard setters have been unable to find satisfactory solutions to asset and liability measurement issues because agreement could not be reached on how measurement changes should be reflected in the financial statements. Examples include the free choice in IAS 39 – *Financial Instruments: Recognition and Measurement* – to recognise changes in the fair value of available for sale financial assets either in the income statement or directly in equity, and the rather unsatisfactory compromise in IAS 40 – *Investment Property* – that allows companies to choose to apply either an historical cost or fair value approach to the measurement of investment properties. The current IASB project on performance reporting is discussed at 4.4.below.

4.2 The US experience

The term 'comprehensive income' was first introduced in the official US literature via the FASB's conceptual framework (discussed in Chapter 2 at 3). SFAC No. 5 concluded that comprehensive income and its components should be reported as part of a full set of financial statements. This has now come to pass through the publication of SFAS 130 – *Reporting Comprehensive Income* – which was issued by the FASB in June 1997.[173] However, a close examination of the statement soon reveals that in name only does it resemble what was envisaged by the conceptual framework. This perhaps accounts for the fact that the statement was passed with two of the seven FASB members dissenting.

Some of the proposals contained in the Exposure Draft which preceded SFAS 130 met with quite strong resistance both in comment letters and at a public hearing. For example, the exposure draft proposed that comprehensive income should be seen as a performance measure and that entities should be required to disclose a per-share amount for comprehensive income. As a result of the not inconsiderable opposition to many of its proposals, the FASB decided to limit the project's scope to issues or presentation and disclosure 'so that it could complete the project in a timely manner'.[174] As a result, the statement does not address issues of recognition or measurement of comprehensive income and its components.

Consequently, the statement is unusually tentative for the FASB. It uses the SFAC No. 6 definition of comprehensive income, namely the change in equity of a business enterprise during a period from transactions and other events and circumstances from non-owner sources. It includes all changes in equity during a period except those resulting from investments by owners and distributions to owners. The statement uses the term 'comprehensive income' to describe the total of all components of comprehensive income, including net income. It then uses the term 'other comprehensive income' to refer to revenue, expenses, gains and losses that are included in comprehensive income but excluded from net income.

However, having set down these basic concepts, the statement then, in effect, gives preparers *carte blanche* to report comprehensive income in virtually whatever manner they choose, provided that all components of comprehensive income are reported in the financial statements in the period in which they are recognised, and the total amount of comprehensive income is disclosed in the financial statement where the components of other comprehensive income are reported.[175]

Appendix B to SFAS 130 contains four different formats for reporting comprehensive income. These comprise a single statement approach, a two statement approach, and two alternative ways of displaying comprehensive income as part of the statement of changes in equity. But even then, other formats are possible: the statement states that 'other formats or levels of detail may be appropriate for certain circumstances'.[176] An observer may be forgiven for thinking that this seems to be a bit of a free-for-all. In fact, this was the root of the concern of the two FASB members who voted against the statement. In their dissenting opinion, they expressed the concern that 'it is likely that most enterprises will meet the requirements of this Statement by providing the required information in a statement of changes in equity, and that displaying items of other comprehensive income solely in that statement as opposed to reporting them in a statement of financial performance will do little to enhance their visibility and will diminish their perceived importance'.[177]

Perhaps the most interesting aspect of the statement is that it contains requirements relating to 'reclassification adjustments' (otherwise known as recycling). The statement states that these adjustments need to be made in order to avoid double counting in comprehensive income items that are displayed as part of net income for a period that also had been displayed as part of other comprehensive income in that period or earlier periods.[178] The reclassification being required as a result of a previously reported unrealised gain being realised. This is where SFAS 130 is fundamentally different from FRS 3 in the UK. Under FRS 3, once an item has been reported in either the profit and loss account or the statement of total recognised gains and losses, it is not reported again in either of the statements. So for example, if an investment is revalued, the revaluation is reported in the statement of total recognised gains and losses, and if it is later sold for its revalued amount (i.e. the gain is realised), no further amount is reported in either statement. Not so with SFAS 130. In this example, the gain would again be reported, this time in the income statement and, to avoid double counting, a deduction would be made at the same time through other comprehensive income for the period. This requirement to record reclassification adjustments does, indeed, mean that the statement of comprehensive income is not a measure of performance. Consequently, the term 'comprehensive income' is somewhat of a misnomer.

4.3 The ASB's proposals for change to reporting financial performance

4.3.1 *G4+1 Discussion Papers*

In June 1999, the ASB published a discussion paper – *Reporting Financial Performance: Proposals for Change.* This had been developed in association with other members of the G4+1 group, and followed an earlier paper published by that group in 1998.[179] The crux of the G4+1's proposals was that the profit and loss account and the statement of total recognised gains and losses should be combined into a single performance statement divided into three sections: operating (or trading) activities; financing and other treasury activities; and other gains and losses (comprising some of those shown as non-operating exceptional items under FRS 3 together with those formerly shown in the statement of total recognised gains and losses). In total, this statement would include all movements between one balance sheet and the next, other than transactions with shareholders such as dividends or changes in share capital.

The ASB subsequently developed the G4+1 paper into an exposure draft, FRED 22, which it issued in December 2000. FRED 22 – *Revision of FRS 3 Reporting Financial Performance* – proposes significant amendments to FRS 3, through the proposed adoption of a single statement of financial performance in which realisation plays no significant part.

4.3.2 *FRED 22 – Revision of FRS 3: 'Reporting Financial Performance'*

FRED 22 defines financial performance as:

> 'The financial performance of an entity comprises the return it obtains on the resources it controls, the components of that return and the characteristics of those components, insofar as they can be captured by the accounting model.
>
> 'Financial performance of an entity for a period encompasses all recognised gains and losses. As such, in mathematical terms it is the change in net assets of the reporting entity from the end of the previous period to the end of the present period, excluding distributions to and contributions from owners.'[180]

This is a key passage that formally installs the recognition of all gains and losses as the definition financial performance. Thus, the reporting structure of financial performance will not in future have the earned profits focus it has had previously.

FRED 22 advocates a single statement of financial performance,[181] in place of the profit and loss account and a statement of recognised gains and losses. In line with the G4+1 paper that preceded it, FRED 22 adopts a three section approach:

> 'An entity should divide its performance statement into the following three sections:
>
> (a) operating;
>
> (b) financing and treasury; and
>
> (c) other gains and losses.
>
> All gains and losses recognised in the financial statements for the period should be included in a section of the single performance statement.'[182]

Dividends paid or declared will no longer be included, but be given in memorandum form at the foot of the statement, together with earnings per share figures and cumulative adjustments recognised in the period that arise from prior period adjustments.[183]

The FRED also advocates the addition of a new primary statement, the 'Reconciliation of ownership interests'. This statement is required because the single performance statement is limited solely to gains and losses which therefore exclude dealings with the owners. It will contain a reconciliation of the opening and closing totals of ownership interests of the period. The FRED mandates that certain reconciling items namely: the results of the period as reported in the performance statement; dividends for the period (broken down into equity and non-equity dividends as required by FRS 4 – *Capital Instruments*); and the cumulative effect of prior period adjustments; should be disclosed separately in the reconciliation.[184]

However, it is the single performance statement that is the most far-reaching alteration proposed by FRED 22. Appendix 1 gives two illustrative examples, the second of which is reproduced below:

STATEMENT OF FINANCIAL PERFORMANCE (Example 2)

	Continuing operations 2001 £m	Acquisitions 2001 £m	Discontinued operations 2001 £m	Total 2001 £m	Total 2000 Restated £m
Operating					
Turnover	600	50	175	825	690
Cost of sales	(445)	(40)	(165)	(650)	(555)
Gross profit	155	10	10	175	135
Other expenses	(95)	(4)	(25)	(124)	(83)
Operating income/profit	**60**	**6**	**(15)**	**51**	**52**
Financing and treasury					
Interest on debt				(26)	(15)
Financing relating to pension provision				20	11
Financing and treasury income/profit				**(6)**	**(4)**
Operating and financing income before taxation				**45**	**48**
Taxation on operating and financing income				(5)	(10)
Operating and financing income after taxation				40	38
Minority interests				(5)	(4)
Income from operating and financing activities for the period*				**35**	**34**
Other gains and losses					
Revaluation gain on disposal of properties in continuing operations				6	4
Revaluation of fixed assets				4	3
Actuarial gain on defined benefit pension scheme				276	91
Profit on disposal of discontinued operations				3	–
Exchange translation differences on foreign currency net investments				(2)	5
Other gains and losses before taxation				**287**	**103**
Taxation on other gains and losses				(87)	(33)
Other gains and losses after taxation				200	70
Minority interests				(30)	(10)
Other gains and losses of the period				**170**	**60**
Total gains and losses of the period				**205**	**94**
MEMORANDUM ITEMS					
Earnings per share				39p	41p
Adjustments [to be itemised and described]				Xp	Xp
Adjusted earnings per share				Yp	Yp
Diluted earnings per share				Zp	Zp
Dividend per share: equity				3.0p	1.8p
preference				0.6p	0.6p
Total dividend for the period: equity				£6.7m	£0.7m
preference				£1.3m	£1.3m
Prior period adjustment recognised during the period (see note X)				(£10m)	-

*Any extraordinary items would be shown after this line, with a subsequent subtotal for the statutory 'profit for the financial year' after extraordinary activities.

The FRS 3 requirement for the performance statement to be analysed between acquired, continuing and discontinued businesses is kept, but modified. FRED 22 is considering adopting the IAS approach of requiring information about *discontinuing* operations to be disclosed (see 3.8 above).

It is clear that the above is driven by the ASB's balance sheet based recognition of gains and losses, and its consequent dismissal of the importance of realisation. The 'financing and treasury' section in particular seems to exist in order to facilitate a possible intention of the standard setters to alter radically the manner in which liabilities are recorded. The FASB Statement of Financial Account Concepts on discounting (see Chapter 2 at 3.7) envisages the recognition of borrowings in the balance sheet at their net present value (NPV) taking into account differences between prevailing and contracted rates of interest, and the credit standing of the entity involved. A simple example of this would be a fixed rate loan of £1m at 8% for 5 years. At the end of the first year, interest rates fall to 4% and remain at that level for the rest of the term of the loan.

Following an historical cost approach, the balance sheet would show a liability of £1m throughout the term of the loan, while the profit and loss account would show a finance cost of £80,000 for each of the five years. Applying the approach outlined above, in place of historical costs, would produce a very different accounting treatment. In year 1 the interest payment of £80,000 would all be charged to the performance statement as before. However, the loan would then be revalued to £1,145,200 (reflecting the NPV of the future cash payments discounted at 4%). The increase so produced of £145,200 would be charged to the financing and treasury section of the performance statement. As this procedure gives a liability in the balance sheet at the end of year 1 substantially greater than the actual repayment of principal to be made at the end of the term, it presents a difficulty. This difficulty would be fixed by allocating the subsequent interest payments in two separate ways: that part of the payment that represents interest at the market rate of 4% is charged in the financing and treasury section as a finance cost. The remainder is debited to the loan account to begin the process of reducing it to the actual repayable principal by the end of the fifth year.

However counter-intuitive it would seem that a loss of £145,200 can result solely from borrowing £1m at a fixed interest rate, in reality things can become substantially more complex, for example where interest rates fluctuate in subsequent years. The overall result is a significant disconnect between the performance statement and the balance sheet on the one hand, and the cash payment reality on the other. This is because the performance statement will carry a charge of £145,200 in our example at the end of year 1, which is neither a year 1 cash payment nor a loss at all, while the balance sheet shows a liability overstated by the same amount. The consequences of this added complication for understandability, a key objective of financial reporting, are considerable.

This complication is brought a significant step nearer by FRED 22's promotion of a single performance statement with a section designed to accept just such adjustments. The procedure explained above is discussed in both the ASB's and the

FASB's discounting publications (both discussed in Chapter 2 of this book) and it remains quite clearly part of their agendas for changing financial reporting.

A difficulty inherent in a three part performance statement is what should go into each part. The FRED lays down the following rules:

- Gains and losses may be excluded from the operating section of the performance statement only if they are permitted or required to be taken to another section by the [draft] FRS, other accounting standards or UITF Abstracts.[185]
- The financing and treasury section should contain only:
  - (a) interest payable and receivable;
  - (b) the unwinding of the discount on long-term items, for example, pensions;
  - (c) income from investments held as part of treasury activities;
  - (d) gains and losses arising on the repurchase or early settlement of debt (as determined in accordance with FRS 4 – *Capital Instruments*); and
  - (e) any other recognised gain or loss identified for inclusion by another accounting standard or by a UITF Abstract.[186]
- The other gains and losses section should contain the following only:
  - (a) revaluation gains and losses on fixed assets (as determined in accordance with FRS 15 – *Tangible Fixed Assets*);
  - (b) gains and losses on disposal of properties in continuing operations (as determined in accordance with FRS 15);
  - (c) actuarial gains and losses arising on defined benefit schemes (as determined in accordance with FRS 17 – *Retirement Benefits*);
  - (d) profits and losses on disposal of discontinuing operations;
  - (e) exchange translation differences on foreign currency net investments (as determined in accordance with SSAP 20 – *Foreign currency translation*);
  - (f) revaluation gains and losses arising on investment properties (as determined in accordance with SSAP 19 – *Accounting for investment properties*)
  - (g) on the lapse of an unexercised warrant, the amount previously recognised in respect of that warrant (as determined in accordance with FRS 4 – *Capital Instruments*); and
  - (h) any other recognised gain or loss as determined in accordance with or identified by another accounting standard or a UITF Abstract.[187]

Thus, the 'operating' section becomes the default and the remaining two sections are specified.

In order to accommodate statutory requirements under UK law for profit on ordinary activities, the FRED states that a profit figure shall be struck after the financing and treasury section and these first two sections will comprise the statutory profit and loss account. As the proposal stands these two sections will not necessarily include all realised profits, but it will not include any unrealised ones, which an appendix to the FRED considers sufficient to comply with company law.[188] It is also necessary for a taxation figure to be calculated at this point.[189]

However there is a difficulty faced by this plan when it comes to the disposal of assets on which gains have been recorded but not realised. 'Recycling' – that is the re-reporting of an unrealised gain when it becomes realised – is not allowed under FRS 3 currently, or by the proposed standard. Normally, revaluations would go into the 'other' category, unless they are reversals of a loss previously recognised in the operating section. However what if a fixed asset is sold at a price different from its revalued or historical cost carrying amount, where does the profit or loss go at that point, as it will be a realised gain or loss not a revaluation? In this instance, the FRED requires all companies, even those compiling their accounts on a strict historical cost basis, to revalue the asset just before it is sold to its selling price.[190] Thus, the FRED requires that no distinction may be made in the performance statement between a revaluation and a sale of an asset.

Our view is that FRED 22 is quite badly flawed in a number of areas, including, for example, the fact that in removing the distinction between realised and unrealised profits it makes no attempt to align performance measurement with cash flow generation. In any event, though, we consider it unlikely that FRED 22 will be progressed any further, given the fact that the IASB has now formally adopted performance reporting on to its agenda as a leadership project.

4.4 The IASB project on performance reporting

During the time of the development of the Joint Working Group's Draft Standard on the recognition and measurement of financial instruments (discussed in Chapter 10 at 1.1), the IASC Board realised that the issue of performance reporting would be critical to the final outcome of the JWG project. As a result, the Board established a Steering Committee to address broadly the issues related to the display and presentation in the financial statements of all recognised changes in assets and liabilities from transactions or other events except those related to transactions with owners as owners (i.e., comprehensive income). The Steering Committee was asked to consider items that presently are reported in the income statement, cash flow statement, and statement of changes in equity. However, the Steering Committee's work was overtaken by the events of the restructuring of the IASC Board, and in the end it was not able to publish its thinking on the subject.

Nevertheless, the IASB has recognised the importance of performance reporting to its overall technical agenda, and has therefore announced, after consultation with the Standards Advisory Council, that performance reporting will be one of four priority projects intended to provide leadership and promote convergence. The former Steering Committee has now been converted into an Advisory Committee to the IASB, and the project is under ongoing discussion at the IASB.

The work-in-progress of the former Steering Committee will be converted into a report for presentation to the IASB. It is likely that the report will contain the following key recommendations:

- There should be a single statement of 'recognised income and expenses' which should report all increases or decreases in net assets of the enterprise, other than those increases or decreases arising from transactions with owners in their capacity as owners.
- Recycling between categories in the statement and between the statement and the statement of shareholders' equity would be prohibited (i.e., an item of income or expense is recognised only once).
- The principal category of the statement should be the 'residual' category. This will usually be the 'business activities' category. Other categories are 'financing activities' and 'investing activities' (or, under an alternative being explored, these activities would be combined a 'treasury activities'). As far as possible, these categories would align with those in the cash flow statement.
- There would be differentiation within the categories between items that are recognised under accrual accounting conventions and those that represent fair value adjustments.
- Certain items would be reported separately in the statement of recognised income and expenses: income taxes (as determined by IAS 12 – *Income Taxes*), discontinuing operations (IAS 35 – *Discontinuing Operations*) and the cumulative foreign exchange translation account.
- Capital transactions would be reported in a separate statement of shareholders' equity, which would be revised and made mandatory (that is, note disclosure of movements in lieu of a separate financial statement would not be permitted).
- IAS 7 – *Cash Flow Statements* – would be amended to align, where necessary, with the statement of recognised income and expenses. Capital transactions would be reported as a separate category. It is possible that the direct method of determining business activity cash flows would be mandatory.

It seems clear that the IASB's thinking in this area is considerably more developed than that of the ASB as set out in FRED 22, which did little more than rehearse the proposals of the 1999 G4+1 document on the subject. Consequently, it seems likely that the ASB will now stand back and allow the IASB to provide the leadership in the quest for a global solution to performance reporting.

5 CONCLUSION

When it was issued in 1992, FRS 3 represented a radical new approach to the reporting of financial performance. Contrary to first appearances, it was much more than a mere exercise in the reformatting of the profit and loss account and the introduction of additional analyses of reserve movements. It significantly changed the rules of recognition and measurement governing many aspects of a company's performance, including discontinued operations, extraordinary and exceptional items and provisions.

However, much has changed in last decade, and FRS 3's requirements are now looking rather dated. This is mainly because the piecemeal introduction of fair value measurement into UK and International GAAP has raised a number of important questions concerning performance reporting. Consequently, perhaps the most fundamental issue currently facing the IASB surrounds the definition of financial performance and the manner in which performance is reported. Although this issue was not addressed in any detail in the Joint Working Group's Draft Standard on the recognition and measurement of financial instruments, it is clear from that document that the JWG is convinced that all changes in fair value of all financial instruments should be recorded in the income statement. It is clear also that the JWG rejects any suggestion that unrealised gains and losses should be recognised anywhere in the financial statements other than the income statement.

Clearly, the JWG is concerned only with reporting gains and losses on financial instruments. However, this is an issue that cannot be viewed in isolation. The issues surrounding the display of gains and losses pervades many other key projects currently on the IASB's agenda, including leases, share based payments, employee benefits and asset revaluations. This is a problem that has vexed standard setters for many years and is still not resolved in any way that has received international acceptance. We are therefore pleased to note that performance reporting has now been adopted on the IASB's agenda as a high priority project. We hope that the IASB will be able to engage the national standard setters, preparers and users from around the world in a meaningful dialogue during the course of this project. If the national standard setters are able to reach agreement on the definition of financial performance and the manner in which performance is reported, then the future for global harmonisation will indeed look promising.

References

1 SFAC No. 1, *Objectives of Financial Reporting by Business Enterprises*, FASB, November 1978, para. 43.

2 SFAC No. 6, *Elements of Financial Statements*, FASB, December 1985, para. 70.

3 *Ibid.*, para. 73.

4 For a full discussion of these two concepts of income, see ARB No. 43, *Restatement and Revision of Accounting Research Bulletins*, AICPA, June 1953, Chapter 8, or APB 9, *Reporting the Results of Operations*, AICPA, December 1966, paras. 9–14.

5 APB 9, para. 10.

6 *Ibid.*, para. 11.

7 ASB Statement, *Statement of Principles for Financial Reporting*, ASB, December 1999, Chapter 1, Principles.

8 *Ibid.*, para. 1.14.

9 FRED 22, *Revision of FRS 3 'Reporting Financial Performance',* ASB, December 2000, Appendix IV, para. 12.
10 ASB Statement, *Statement of Principles for Financial Reporting*, para. 4.39.
11 FRED 22, para. 2.
12 CA 81, Sch. 1, Part. 1, Section B; now CA 85, Sch. 4, Part. 1, Section B.
13 ASC Discussion Paper, *A review of SSAP 6*, 1983
14 ED 36, *Extraordinary items and prior year adjustments*, January 1985.
15 The Institute of Chartered Accountants of Scotland, *Making Corporate Reports Valuable*, ICAS, 1988, para. 1.18.
16 FRS 3, *Reporting financial performance*, ASB, October 1992, para. 1.
17 *Ibid.*, para. 14.
18 *Ibid.*, para. 12.
19 *Foreword to Accounting Standards*, ASB, June 1993, para. 15.
20 FRS 3, para. 14.
21 FRS 9, *Associates and joint ventures*, ASB, November 1997, para. 27.
22 FRS 3, para. 4.
23 *Ibid.*, para. 15.
24 *Ibid.*, para. 17.
25 *Ibid.*, para. 43.
26 *Ibid.*, para. 42.
27 *Ibid.*, para. 4(c).
28 *Ibid.*, para. 43.
29 *Ibid.*, para. 43.
30 *Ibid.*, para. 44.
31 IAS 35, *Discontinuing Operations*, IASC, 1998, para. 2.
32 *Ibid.*, para., 16.
33 SAB No. 93, *Accounting and Disclosure Regarding Discontinued Operations*, SEC, 11-4-93, Question 4.
34 FRS 12, *Provisions, Contingent Liabilities and Contingent Assets*, ASB, September 1998, para. 2.
35 FRS 3, para. 18.
36 *Ibid.*
37 *Ibid.*, para. 45.
38 *Ibid.*
39 FRS 11, *Impairment of Fixed Assets and Goodwill*, ASB, July 1998, para. 67.
40 FRS 3, para. 3.
41 *Ibid.*, para. 16.
42 *Ibid.*, para. 15.
43 FRS 6, *Acquisitions and Mergers*, ASB, September 1994, para. 36.
44 FRS 3, para. 6.
45 *Ibid.*, para. 20.
46 *Ibid.*, para. 2.
47 The Financial Reporting Review Panel, *Press Notice: Findings of the Financial Reporting Review Panel in respect of the accounts of Princedale Group plc for the period ended 30 April 2000,* FRRP PN 69, 28 August 2001.
48 FRS 3, para. 5.
49 *Ibid.*, para. 19.
50 *Ibid.*, para. 20.
51 *Ibid.*, para. 46.
52 *Ibid.,* para. 42.
53 FRS 12, para. 2.
54 *Ibid.*, para. 75.
55 FRS 3, para. 21.
56 *Ibid.*, para. 31A.
57 *Ibid.*, para. 26.
58 *Ibid.*, para. 55.
59 ASB Statement, *Statement of Principles for Financial Reporting*, para. 6.2(b).
60 *Ibid.,* Appendix III, para. 52.
61 FRS 3, para. 31A.
62 FRS 4, *Capital Instruments*, para. 93.
63 FRS 3, para. 20.
64 *Ibid.*, para. 22.
65 *Ibid.*, para. 24.
66 *Ibid.*, para. 50.
67 *Ibid.*, para. 14.
68 See, for example, Preface to FRED 1, para. iv.
69 FRS 3, para. 52.
70 FRS 14, *Earnings per share*, ASB, October 1998, para. 9.
71 *Ibid.*, para. 11,
72 FRS 3. para. 25.
73 FRS 3, para. 28.
74 *Ibid.*, para. 59.
75 FRS 10, paras. 69 and 71(a)(iii).
76 CA 85, Sch. 4, para. 3(7).
77 *Ibid.*, para. 46.
78 FRS 3, para. 7.
79 *Ibid.*, para. 60.
80 *Ibid.*
81 *Ibid.*, para. 61.
82 FRS 3, para. 63.
83 CA 85, ss 245–245B.
84 FRS 3, para. 29.
85 *Ibid.*
86 CA 85, Sch. 4, para. 15.
87 *Ibid.*
88 EU Fourth Company Law Directive (78/660/EEC), Article 31(2).
89 UITF 14, *Disclosure of changes in accounting policy*, UITF, 21 November 1995, para. 3.
90 FRS 18, *Accounting Policies*, ASB, December 2000, para. 55(c).
91 *Ibid.*
92 IAS 1, *Presentation of Financial Statements*, IASC, August 1997, para. 13.
93 *Ibid.*, paras. 7 and 86-89.
94 *Ibid.,* para. 75.
95 *Ibid.*
96 *Ibid.,* paras. 33 to 37.
97 *Ibid.*, para. 77.

98 *Ibid.,* para. 84.
99 *Ibid.,* para. 80.
100 *Ibid.,* para. 81.
101 *Ibid.,* para. 82.
102 *Ibid.,* para. 83.
103 *Ibid.,* para. 85.
104 IAS 8 (revised 1993), *Net Profit or Loss for the Period, Fundamental Errors and Changes in Accounting Policies,* IASC, Revised December 1993, Objective.
105 *Ibid.,* para. 7.
106 *Ibid.,* para. 10.
107 *Ibid.,* para. 11.
108 *Ibid.,* para. 12.
109 *Ibid.,* para. 16.
110 *Ibid.,* para. 26.
111 *Ibid.,* para. 28.
112 *Ibid.,* para. 30.
113 *Ibid.,* paras. 34–57.
114 IAS 22 (revised 1998), *Business Combinations,* IASC, September 1998, para. 88(d).
115 IASC, *Framework,* para. 28.
116 IAS 8, para. 16.
117 *Ibid.,* para. 17.
118 *Ibid.*
119 *Ibid.,* para. 18.
120 *Ibid.,* para. 6.
121 *Ibid.*
122 *Ibid.,* para. 12.
123 *Ibid.,* para. 13.
124 *Ibid.,* para. 14.
125 *Ibid.,* para. 41.
126 SIC–8, *First-Time Application of IASs as the Primary Basis of Accounting,* IASC, January 1998, para. 3.
127 IAS 8, para. 6.
128 *Ibid.,* para. 42.
129 SIC–18, *Consistency – Alternative Methods,* IASC, May 1999. para. 3.
130 IAS 8, para. 44.
131 *Ibid.,* para. 46.
132 SIC–18, para. 3.
133 IAS 8, paras. 49-52.
134 *Ibid.,* para. 53.
135 *Ibid.,* paras. 54-56.
136 *Ibid.,* para. 57.
137 SIC–8, para. 11.
138 IAS 8, para. 23.
139 *Ibid.,* para. 24.
140 *Ibid.,* paras. 26 and 28.
141 *Ibid.,* para. 25.
142 *Ibid.,* para. 30.
143 *Ibid.,* para. 6.
144 *Ibid.,* paras. 31-32.
145 SIC–18, para. 3.
146 IAS 8, para. 34.
147 *Ibid.,* para. 37.
148 *Ibid.,* para. 38.
149 *Ibid.,* para. 40.
150 IAS 35, paras. 17 to 26.
151 *Ibid.,* para. 2.
152 *Ibid.,* para. 43.
153 *Ibid.,* paras. 3 and 4.
154 *Ibid.,* para. 5.
155 *Ibid.,* para. 6.
156 *Ibid.,* para. 7.
157 *Ibid.,* para. 16.
158 *Ibid.,* para. 38.
159 *Ibid.,* para. 39.
160 *Ibid.,* para. 41.
161 *Ibid.,* para. 27.
162 *Ibid.,* para. 28.
163 *Ibid.,* para. 29.
164 *Ibid.,* para. 31.
165 *Ibid.,* para. 33.
166 *Ibid.,* para. 34.
167 *Ibid.,* para. 35.
168 *Ibid.,* para. 36.
169 *Ibid.,* para. 37.
170 *Ibid.,* para. 45.
171 IAS 1, para. 86.
172 *Ibid.*
173 SFAS 130, *Reporting Comprehensive Income,* FASB, June 1997.
174 *Ibid.,* para. 53.
175 *Ibid.,* para. 14.
176 *Ibid.,* para. 129.
177 *Ibid.,* Messrs. Cope and Foster's dissenting opinion. Mr Cope is now a member of the IASB.
178 *Ibid.,* para. 18.
179 *Reporting Financial Performance: Current Practice and Future Developments,* G4+1, January 1998.
180 FRED 22, para. 2.
181 *Ibid.,* para. 6.
182 *Ibid.,* paras. 14-15.
183 *Ibid.,* paras. 93 to 97.
184 *Ibid.,* para. 91.
185 *Ibid.,* para. 18.
186 *Ibid.,* para. 22.
187 *Ibid.,* para. 26.
188 *Ibid.,* Appendix II para. 20.
189 *Ibid.,* para. 70.
190 *Ibid.,* Appendix II, paras. 13 and 14.

Chapter 26 Earnings per share

1 INTRODUCTION

Earnings per share (EPS) is one of the most widely quoted statistics in financial analysis. It came into great prominence in the US during the late 1950s and early 1960s due to the widespread use of the price earnings ratio (PE) as a yardstick for investment decisions. By the late 1960s, its popularity had switched across the Atlantic and for the purposes of consistency and comparability, it became important that an agreed method of computing EPS was established.

In March 1971, the Accounting Standards Steering Committee issued an exposure draft, ED 4 – *Earnings per share*. The exposure draft represented a departure by UK accounting bodies into the area of financial ratios and financial analysis. ED 4 was, in general, favourably received and in February 1972, SSAP 3 – *Earnings per share* – was issued with the objective of providing a minimum standard for disclosure of EPS in financial statements and the basis of its calculation.

EPS has also served as a means of assessing the stewardship and management role performed by company directors and managers; by linking remuneration packages to EPS growth performance, some companies deliberately increase the pressure on management to improve EPS. Not surprisingly, such powerful factors and incentives have all contributed to the growth of attempts to distort EPS.

The ASB has stated its belief that undue emphasis is placed on EPS numbers and that this leads to simplistic interpretations of financial performance. As a result in October 1992 when it issued FRS 3 – *Reporting of financial performance* – the ASB attempted to de-emphasise EPS by requiring it to be calculated *after* extraordinary items. In view of this change and the other requirements of FRS 3 (see Chapter 25) the EPS number which companies were required to disclose became much more volatile and was really only a starting point for further analysis. The ASB recognised that companies would therefore be likely to provide additional EPS numbers prepared on what they saw as a more meaningful basis and therefore introduced rules dealing with the disclosure of such additional numbers.

SSAP 3 had operated fairly satisfactorily for over 20 years and, without the impulse of international harmonisation, it is unlikely that the ASB would have sought to change it. Indeed, the Board has hinted that earnings per share is perhaps not an appropriate subject for an accounting standard at all, since it concerns financial analysis more than financial reporting. Nevertheless in May 1996 the ASB issued a Discussion Paper – *Earnings Per Share*, in order to solicit comments on proposals put forward by the IASC in its exposure draft (E52) on the topic. In the US, the FASB had also issued a similar exposure draft to E52. Both of these bodies subsequently published new standards based on those proposals. In the interests of international harmonisation the ASB therefore issued FRED 16 in June 1997 containing proposals for a revised standard which, with minimal exceptions, followed the international standard, IAS 33. In March 1998 the ASB issued a supplement to FRED 16, dealing with three issues: contingently issuable shares, employee share schemes and the coupling of a special dividend with a share consolidation. FRS 14 – *Earnings per share* was published on 1 October 1998 and superseded SSAP 3 for periods ending on or after 23 December 1998. FRS 14 is based on its international equivalent, and adopts a similar structure and wording. It also includes detailed interpretative guidance and illustrative examples which draw heavily on the US standard.

2 OBJECTIVE AND SCOPE OF FRS 14

2.1 Objective

The objective of the standard is:

'to improve the comparison of the performance of different entities in the same period and of the same entity in different accounting periods by prescribing methods for determining the number of shares to be included in the calculation of earnings per share and other amounts per share and by specifying their presentation.'[1]

The underlying logic here is that EPS, including diluted EPS, should be an historical performance measure. This impacts particularly on diluted EPS, in steering it away from an alternative purpose: to warn of potential future dilution. Indeed the tension between these differing objectives is evident in the standard. As discussed more fully at 6.5.5 below, FRS 14 sets out a very restrictive regime for including certain potentially dilutive shares in the diluted EPS calculation. Yet diluted EPS is only to take account of those potential shares that would dilute earnings from *continuing* operations which seems to have more of a forward looking 'warning signal' flavour.

Also noteworthy is the strong emphasis in the objective on the denominator of the calculation, effectively making it a 'per share' standard, whilst avoiding reference to the provisions the standard actually contains relating to the numerator.

2.2 Scope

FRS 14 applies to all entities whose ordinary shares (or potential ordinary shares) are publicly traded and to entities that are in the process of issuing ordinary shares (or potential ordinary shares) in public securities markets.[2] Thus companies whose shares are traded on the Alternative Investment Market (AIM) are required to follow the standard. SSAP 3 did not apply to AIM listed companies, but a number disclosed earnings per share figures. FRS 14 also applies to any other entity which discloses earnings per share. Where both the parent's and consolidated accounts are presented, the standard only requires consolidated earnings per share to be given.[3]

The detailed wording of the standard is phrased in terms of *earnings* per share, whether those specifically required or other elements of earnings. The scope section of the standard, in a change from FRED 16 and IAS 33, makes it clear that the rules in FRS 14 should be used in determining the number of shares to be used, as far as appropriate, in any per share disclosures, such as net assets per share.[4]

The customary exclusion for entities adopting the financial reporting standard for smaller entities (FRSSE) is not included in FRS 14, presumably on the grounds that no listed companies can adopt the FRSSE.

3 THE BASIC EPS

FRS 14 defines, or rather describes, basic earnings per share as follows:

'Basic earnings per share should be calculated by dividing the net profit attributable to ordinary shareholders by the weighted average number of ordinary shares outstanding during the period.'[5]

The earnings figure to be used in the basic EPS calculation is the net profit or loss for the period attributable to ordinary shareholders after deducting preference dividends and other appropriations in respect of non-equity shares.[6]

Ordinary shares are defined as 'an instrument falling within the definition of equity shares as defined in FRS 4' (see Chapter 17 at 2.2.2). Whilst it may seem strange that one defined term should be referred to by two different names in two different standards, the reason for this is that IAS 33 uses the term 'ordinary share' rather than 'equity share'. Where there is more than one class of ordinary shares, earnings should be apportioned between them based on their respective rights to dividends or other profit participation and separate EPS figures given for each class.[7]

Under FRS 14 all ordinary shares are to be included in the calculation of the weighted average number of shares, whereas under SSAP 3 it was only equity shares which ranked for dividend in the period which were included. How shares rank for dividend, however, still has some impact on the calculation. Under FRS 14, shares that are issued as partly paid are included in the weighted average as a fraction of a share based on dividend participation relative to fully paid shares.[8]

There is an exception to the above rule that all ordinary shares should be included in the calculation, which relates to shares held by a group member. Any non-cancelled ordinary shares held by an entity within the group should be excluded from the calculation. In particular, shares held by an employee share ownership (ESOP) trust shown as assets in the balance sheet should be treated as if they were cancelled for EPS purposes until they vest unconditionally in the employees.[9]

The standard contains some specific guidance on when newly issued ordinary shares should be brought into the calculation. In general shares are to be included from the date consideration is receivable, for example:[10]

- shares issued in exchange for cash are included when cash is receivable;
- shares issued on the voluntary reinvestment of dividends on ordinary or preference shares are included at the dividend payment date;
- shares issued as a result of the conversion of a debt instrument to ordinary shares are included as of the date interest ceases accruing;
- shares issued in place of interest or principal on other financial instruments are included as of the date interest ceases accruing;
- shares issued in exchange for the settlement of a liability of the entity are included as of the settlement date; and
- shares issued as consideration for the acquisition of an asset other than cash are included as of the date on which the acquisition is recognised.

More generally, the standard goes on to say that due consideration should be given to the substance of any contract associated with the issue.[11] No illustrations are given of such associated contracts, but one example could be convertible unsecured loan stock (CULS). Although less fashionable in recent years, these were a not uncommon mechanism allowing companies to finance potential acquisitions by the issue of shares, while retaining the flexibility to return funds not subsequently needed.

Tomkins, for example, issued CULS to finance an acquisition and converted it into shares a short time later. The loan stock carried no interest and was simply an intermediate step in the share issue. The practical impact was that 60% of the consideration for the shares was received over a month before they were actually issued.

Extract 26.1: Tomkins PLC (1993)

18 SHARE CAPITAL [extract]

The Company financed the purchase of RHM by way of a rights issue which took the form of 5p nominal non-interest bearing convertible unsecured loan stock (loan stock) which was payable in two instalments of 120p and 80p on 30 November 1992 and 4 January 1993 respectively. … The 335,784,658 units of loan stock, which were issued under the rights issue at 200p per unit, were converted into fully paid ordinary shares of 5p each, on a one for one basis, on 5 January 1993.

One question that arises is when should the new shares be brought into the calculation of the weighted average in such circumstances? Given the examples in the standard which focus on the date consideration is received, and the requirement to consider the substance of associated contracts, it seems such shares should be deemed to be issued in partly paid form on 30 November.

Ordinary shares that are issuable on the satisfaction of certain conditions (contingently issuable shares) are to be included in the calculation of basic EPS only from the date when all necessary conditions have been satisfied; in effect when they are no longer contingent.[12] This provision is interpreted strictly, as illustrated in Example 6 of the standard. In that example earnings in a period, by exceeding a given threshold, trigger the issue of shares. Because this condition was not satisfied until the end of the year the new shares are excluded from basic EPS until the following year.

The calculation of the basic EPS is often simple but a number of complications can arise; these may be considered under the following two headings:

(a) changes in equity share capital; and

(b) matters affecting the numerator.

These are discussed in the next two sections.

4 CHANGES IN EQUITY SHARE CAPITAL

Changes in equity share capital can occur under a variety of circumstances, the most common of which are dealt with below. Whenever such a change occurs during the accounting period, an adjustment is required to the number of shares in the EPS calculation for that period; furthermore, in certain situations the EPS for previous periods will also have to be recalculated.

4.1 Issue for cash at full market price

If new ordinary shares have been issued for cash at full market price the earnings should be divided by the average number of shares outstanding during the period weighted on a time basis.[13]

Example 26.1: Weighted average calculation

At 1 January, 3,000,000 ordinary shares were in issue. On 30 September, 1,000,000 further shares were issued for cash at full market price.

The number of shares to be used in the calculation of EPS will be:

	m
For 9/12 (of the year) x 3m (shares in issue)	2.25
For 3/12 (of the year) x 4m (shares in issue)	1.00
Number of shares to be used in the calculation	3.25

The use of a weighted average number of shares is necessary because the increase in the share capital would have affected earnings only for that portion of the year during which the issue proceeds were available to management for use in the business.

It is possible that shares could be allotted as a result of open offers, placings and other offerings of equity shares not made to existing shareholders, at a discount to the market price. In such cases it would be necessary to consider whether the issue contained a bonus element, akin to a rights issue (see 4.3.3 below), or rather simply reflected differing views on the fair value of the shares. In our opinion the latter seems a far more realistic alternative. Accordingly the shares should be dealt with on a weighted average basis without calculating any bonus element when computing the EPS.

4.2 Purchase and redemption of own shares

A company may, if it is authorised to do so by its articles and it complies with the related provisions of the Companies Act, purchase/redeem its own shares (see Chapter 17 at 3.3). Assuming this is done at fair value, then the earnings should be apportioned over the weighted average share capital in issue for the year. If, on the other hand, the repurchase is at significantly more than market value then FRS 14 requires adjustments to be made to EPS for periods before buy-back. This is discussed at 4.3.5 below.

4.3 Changes in ordinary shares without corresponding changes in resources

FRS 14 requires the number of shares used in the calculation to be adjusted (for all periods presented) for any transaction (other than the conversion of potential ordinary shares) which changes the number of shares outstanding without a corresponding change in resources.[14] This is also to apply where such changes have happened after the year end but before the approval of the accounts.[15]

Unlike its predecessor SSAP 3, FRS 14 requires that adjustments are made for *all* events which change the number of shares outstanding without a corresponding change in resources. In contrast, the equivalent SSAP 3 provisions were limited to specified types of transaction.

The standard gives the following as examples of such changes in the number of ordinary shares without a corresponding change in resources:

'(a) a bonus issue;

(b) a bonus element in any other issue or buy-back, for example a bonus element in a rights issue to existing shareholders or a put warrant, involving the repurchase of shares at significantly more than their fair value;

(c) a share split; and

(d) a share consolidation.'[16]

The adjustments required to EPS for each of these is discussed below.

The standard requires that other per share disclosures for earlier periods, notably dividends per share, are similarly adjusted for such changes.[17]

4.3.1 *Bonus issue, share split and share consolidation*

A bonus issue has the effect of increasing the number of shares in issue without any inflow of funds to the company. Consequently, no additional earnings will accrue as a result of the issue. The bonus shares should be treated as having been in issue for the whole year and also included in the previous year's EPS calculation to give a comparable result. The EPS for the earlier period should therefore be adjusted by the following fraction:

$$\frac{\text{Number of shares before the bonus issue}}{\text{Number of shares after the bonus issue}}$$

Similar considerations apply where equity shares are split into shares of smaller nominal value. Financial ratios for earlier periods, which are based on the number of equity shares at a year end (e.g. dividend per share) should also be adjusted by the above factor.[18]

The notes to the financial statements should refer to the adjustments made,[19] as illustrated in the following extract:

Extract 26.2: Datamonitor plc (2000)

10 LOSS PER SHARE

£000	**2000**	1999
Loss for the period attributable to shareholders	**(7,152)**	(2,626)
Weighted average number of shares in issue	**54,452,167**	52,473,200
Basic loss per ordinary share	**(13.13p)**	(5.00p)

The weighted number of shares in issue for 1999 has been adjusted to take into account a bonus issue of 19 ordinary shares for each ordinary share held on 13 April 2000 and a bonus issue of 3 ordinary shares for each ordinary share held on 6 October 2000. Diluted earnings per share is not disclosed as its computation results in an anti-dilutive effect.

Scrip dividends refer to the case where a company offers its shareholders the choice of receiving further fully paid up shares in the company as an alternative to receiving a cash dividend. The accounting entries for scrip dividends are discussed in Chapter 17 at 4.7. As regards EPS, practice in this area has varied in the past. Some companies have taken the view that shares issued are in substance bonus issues which require the EPS for the earlier period to be adjusted. Others have considered that the dividend foregone represents payment for the shares, usually at fair value, and hence no restatement is appropriate. In our view the more general approach in FRS 14 to corresponding changes in resources seems to support the latter view, as illustrated in the following extract:

Extract 26.3: Rolls-Royce plc (2000)

7 Earnings per ordinary share

Basic earnings per ordinary share are calculated by dividing the profit attributable to ordinary shareholders of **£83m** (1999 £284m) by **1,558 million** (1999 1,506 million) ordinary shares, being the average number of ordinary shares in issue during the year, excluding own shares held under trust (note 13) which have been treated as if they had been cancelled.

Underlying earnings per ordinary share have been calculated as follows.

		2000		1999
	Pence	**£m**	Pence	£m
Profit attributable to ordinary shareholders	**5.33**	**83**	18.86	284
Exclude				
Net loss on sale of business – materials handling	**4.69**	**73**	–	–
– other	**0.32**	**5**	0.93	14
Loss/(profit) on sale of fixed assets (excluding lease engines and aircraft sold by financial services companies)	**0.06**	**1**	(1.13)	(17)
Amortisation of goodwill	**2.95**	**46**	0.33	5
Restructuring of acquired businesses	**1.03**	**16**	0.40	6
Exceptional rationalisation	**0.58**	**9**	–	–
Energy – exceptional charge	**7.70**	**120**	–	–
Related tax effect	**(1.03)**	**(16)**	0.13	2
Underlying earnings per ordinary share	**21.63**	**337**	19.52	294

Diluted basic earnings per ordinary share are calculated by dividing the profit attributable to ordinary shareholders of **£83m** (1999 £284m) by **1,566 million** (1999 1,525 million) ordinary shares, being **1,558 million** (1999 1,506 million) as above adjusted by the bonus element of existing share options of 8 million (1999 19 million).

...

24 Share capital [extract]

	Non-equity special share of £1	**Equity ordinary shares of 20p each**	**Nominal value £m**
Authorised			
At January 1 and December 31, 2000	1	**2,000,000,000**	**400**
Issued and fully paid			
At January 1, 2000	1	**1,545,024,330**	**309**
Exercise of share options	-	**6,620,836**	**1**
In lieu of paying dividends in cash	-	**17,612,912**	**4**
At December 31, 2000	1	**1,569,258,078**	**314**

The weighted average number of ordinary shares for 1999 of 1,506 million remains unchanged from that used in the 1999 accounts, indicating that no adjustment has been made to earlier EPS figures to reflect a bonus issue.

This view is not, however, universally held. As illustrated in the following example BAA considers its scrip dividend as being a change in ordinary shares without corresponding changes in resources, and adjusts earlier EPS accordingly.

Extract 26.4: BAA plc (2000)

10 Earnings per share	**2000 £m**	1999 £m
Net profit for the financial year before exceptional items	**369**	389
Exceptional items	**(110)**	9
Profit attributable to shareholders	**259**	398
Interest on convertible bonds	**16**	17
Diluted profit	**275**	415
Average number of shares in issue	**1,067m**	1,063m
Share options	**6m**	7m
Conversion of 4.875% bonds due 2004	**30m**	30m
Conversion of 5.75% bonds due 2006	**41m**	45m
Diluted average number of shares in issued	**1,144m**	1,145m
Earnings per share before exceptional items	**34.5p**	36.6p
(Loss)earnings per share on exceptional items	**(10.3)p**	0.9p
Earnings per share	**24.2p**	37.5p
Diluted earnings per share	**24.0p**	36.3p

The number of shares in issue for 2000 and 1999 have been adjusted so as to treat the shares issued under the scrip dividend scheme as though they were a bonus issue. This resulted in the earnings per share for 1999 being restated at 37.5p per share from 37.6p per share.

Earnings per share before exceptional items has been disclosed to show the impact of the exceptional items on the underlying results of the business.

In practice the fair value of shares received as a scrip alternative may exceed the cash alternative; this is often referred to as an enhanced scrip dividend. In these cases FRS 14 will require a bonus element to be identified, and prior EPS figures restated accordingly. This is essentially the same as adjustments for the bonus element in a rights issue, discussed at 4.3.3 below.

Occasionally, companies will consolidate their equity share capital into a smaller number of shares of a greater nominal value. Again in such situations the EPS for the earlier period should be adjusted for by the following fraction:

$$\frac{\text{Number of shares before the share consolidation}}{\text{Number of shares after the share consolidation}}$$

An example of a company making such an adjustment is shown in the following extract:

Extract 26.5: Communisis plc (2000)

7. Earnings per share [extract]

Calculations of basic earnings per share are based on the average number of ordinary shares in issue during the year ranking for dividend of 121,720,114 (1999 – 11,180,578) after deducting shares held in trust of 309,628 (1999 – nil). Diluted earnings per share are calculated after the effect of dilutive share options of 701,062 shares (1999 – nil). Comparative earnings per share for 1999 have been re-calculated to reflect the share consolidation during the year (note 17).

4.3.2 Share consolidation with a special dividend

Share consolidations as discussed at 4.3.1 above normally do not involve any outflow of funds from the company. However, a number of companies have been returning surplus cash to their shareholders by paying special dividends accompanied by a share consolidation, the purpose of which is to maintain the value of each share following the payment of the dividend. This issue is specifically addressed by FRS 14, presumably as such schemes were quite common when it was first being drafted. The normal rule of restating all periods' EPS for a share consolidation is not applied when 'a share consolidation is combined with a special dividend where the overall commercial effect in terms of net assets, earnings and number of shares is of a repurchase at fair value'.[20] In such cases the weighted average number of shares is adjusted for the consolidation from the date the special dividend is paid. As discussed at 4.3 above, the initial need to restate EPS for a share consolidation stems from the requirement that prior periods' EPS should be adjusted for events which change the number of shares outstanding without a corresponding change in resources. So what the standard is saying here is that a special dividend can be such a corresponding change in resources. An example of a company carrying out a share consolidation in conjunction with a special dividend is Dawson International, as follows:

Extract 26.6: Dawson International PLC (2000)

11 Earnings per share [extract]

On 22 May 2000 the company carried out a two for one share consolidation in conjunction with the payment of a special dividend, which had a similar effect to a repurchase of shares at fair value. No adjustment is therefore made to previously reported earnings per share in this respect.

There is undoubtedly a conceptual attraction in trying to standardise adjustments made to prior years' EPS figures. However, in our view the approach taken by the standard is rather piecemeal, in that restatement is only ever triggered by a change in the number of shares, and it will not necessarily achieve the objective of standardising the restatement of EPS. Companies may return capital to their shareholders in various different ways, including demergers and group reconstructions, as well as share buybacks and special dividends. In many such cases the number of shares in issue is only reduced if the company opts to consolidate its shares. The natural consequence of returning capital is that earnings will fall, so it is debatable whether a fall in EPS in these circumstances should be regarded as a distortion that needs to be corrected at all. Of course, if a company buys back its shares, the number of shares will automatically be reduced and therefore affect the EPS calculation in a way that other returns of capital do not, but this does not necessarily mean that a special dividend should be treated as if it were a share buyback. However, the standard is now extant, so companies must apply these new provisions so that this specific type of return of capital will fall to be treated as a share repurchase, but only when the company also chooses to consolidate its shares.

4.3.3 Rights issue

A rights issue is a popular method through which public companies are able to access the stock market for further capital. Under the terms of such an issue, existing shareholders are given the opportunity to acquire further shares in the company on a pro-rata basis to their existing shareholdings.

The 'rights' shares will usually be offered either at the current market price or at a price below that. In the former case, the treatment of the issue for EPS purposes is as discussed in 4.1 above. However, where the rights price is at a discount to market it is not quite as straightforward, since the issue is equivalent to a bonus issue combined with an issue at full market price (see Example 26.2B below). In such cases, FRS 14 states that it is necessary to adjust the number of shares in issue before the rights issue to reflect the bonus element inherent in the issue.[21] The notes to the financial statements should state that such adjustments have been made.[22]

The bonus element of the rights issue is given by the following fraction, sometimes referred to as the bonus fraction:[23]

$$\frac{\text{Fair value per share immediately before the exercise of rights}}{\text{Theoretical ex - rights fair value per share}}$$

The fair value per share immediately before the exercise of rights is the *actual* price at which the shares are quoted inclusive of the right to take up the future shares under the rights issue. Where the rights are to be traded separately from the shares the fair value used is the closing price on the last day on which the shares are traded inclusive of the right.[24]

The 'ex-rights fair value' is the *theoretical* price at which the shares would be expected to be quoted, other stock market factors apart, after the rights issue shares have been issued.

Example 26.2: Illustration of calculation of EPS following a rights issue at less than full market price

Capital structure

Issued share capital at 31 December 1998
24m Ordinary shares of 50p each, fully paid.

Trading results	1999	1998
	£	£
Profit on ordinary activities after taxation	1.2m	1.0m

A rights issue took place on 31 August 1999 on a 1 for 4 basis at 80p. The fair value per share immediately before the exercise of rights was £1 per share.

The calculation of EPS can be tackled in the following manner:

A – What is the theoretical ex-rights fair value per share?

The theoretical ex-rights fair value per share is calculated as follows:

	No.		p
Initial holding of	4	shares, market value	400
Rights taken up	1	share, at a cost of	80
New holding	5	shares, theoretical value	480

$$\frac{\text{Theoretical ex - rights fair value}}{5} = \frac{480}{5} = 96 \text{ pence}$$

which is the average price per share of the final holding.

B – What is the bonus element inherent in this issue?

The *bonus element* of the rights issue is given by the fraction:

$$\frac{\text{Fair value per share immediately before the exercise of rights}}{\text{Theoretical ex - rights fair value per share}} = \frac{100}{96} = \frac{25}{24}$$

This corresponds to a bonus issue of 1 for 24. Circumstances may arise where fair value per share immediately before the exercise of rights is less than the theoretical ex-rights fair value per share giving a bonus fraction of less than 1, in which case the rights issue should be treated as an issue for cash at full market price for EPS purposes (see 4.1 above). This may be the case where, for example, the market has suffered a significant downturn during the rights period which was not anticipated when the rights issue was announced.

Hence, the rights issue can be split into a bonus issue of 1 for 24, which will reduce the theoretical price per share to 96 pence, combined with an issue of the residue of the shares at the new theoretical price per share of 96 pence. This can be illustrated by considering the position of a shareholder who holds 360 shares before the rights issue takes place.

	No.		£
Initial holding of	360	shares, valued at	360
Bonus issue (1 for 24)	15	shares,	–
	375	shares, (theoretical price per share : 96p)	360
Issue at full market	75	shares, at a cost of	72
New holding	450	shares, cost	432

The shareholder is indifferent as to whether he is offered a 1 for 4 rights issue at 80 pence a share *or* a combination of a 1 for 24 bonus issue (bringing the market price down from £1 to 96p) and a 1 for 5 rights issue at full market price (i.e. 96p). Consequently, it is appropriate to treat the rights issue as a combination of a bonus issue and a rights issue at full market price.

C – Weighted average share capital

In order to calculate the earnings per share for the year in which a rights issue is made, it will be necessary to calculate the weighted average share capital for the year after adjusting the capital in issue before the rights issue for that part which represents the bonus element. The number of shares in issue before the rights issue, adjusted for the bonus element would be:

$$24\text{m x } \frac{25}{24} = 25\text{m}$$

The number of shares after the rights issue would be:

$$24\text{m x } \frac{5}{4} = 30\text{m}$$

The share issue may be summarised as follows:

		m
1.1.X2	Opening number of shares	24
31.8.X2	Bonus issue (1 for 24)	1
	Adjusted opening number of shares	25
31.8.X2	Full market price issue (1 for 5)	5
31.12.X2	Closing number of shares	30

Therefore the weighted average number of shares during the year will be:

For 8/12 (of the year) x 25m	16,666,667
For 4/12 (of the year) x 30m	10,000,000
Weighted average number of shares	26,666,667

D – EPS calculation

To make the previous year's EPS comparable, the number of shares used in the recalculation has to increase to take into account the bonus element. Thus:

Current year's EPS:	*Previous year's EPS was:*	*Previous year's EPS now is:*
$\frac{£1.2\text{m}}{26.67\text{m}} = 4.50\text{p}$	$\frac{£1\text{m}}{24\text{m}} = 4.17\text{p}$	$\frac{£1\text{m}}{24\text{m x } 25/24} = 4.00\text{p}$

Rather than multiplying the denominator by 25/24ths, the previous year's EPS (and any EPS disclosures in a historical summary) could alternatively be arrived at by multiplying the original EPS by 24/25ths. One company which gave very full disclosure about the restatement of comparative EPS amounts as a result of a rights issue during the year was Rolls-Royce, as shown below; although it predates FRS 14 the adjustment under current guidance would be the same:

Extract 26.7: Rolls-Royce plc (1993)

11 Earnings/(loss) per share [extract]

Earnings/(loss) per ordinary share on the net basis are calculated by dividing the profit attributable to the shareholders of Rolls-Royce plc of £63m (1992 loss £202m) by 1,058 million (1992 966 million) ordinary shares, being the average number of shares in issue during the year.

Prior year restatement

On September 2, 1993 the Company announced a rights issue to raise approximately £307m, net of expenses. Under the terms of the rights issue 242,736,773 new ordinary shares were issued in September 1993 at 130p per share on the basis of one new ordinary share for every four existing ordinary shares.

The actual cum rights price on September 6, 1993, the last day of quotation cum rights, was 148.5p and the theoretical ex rights price for an ordinary share was therefore 144.8p per share. The comparative earnings per share are shown after applying the factor 144.8/148.5 to the published figures for 1992 in order to adjust for the bonus element in the rights issue.

Many companies, however, simply include a statement that the comparative EPS amounts have been restated as a result of a rights issue.

4.3.4 *B share schemes*

One method by which some companies have returned capital to shareholders is the so called B share scheme. These schemes involve issuing 'B shares' (usually undated preference shares with low or zero coupons) to existing shareholders, either as a bonus issue or via a share split. These are then repurchased for cash and cancelled, following which the ordinary shares are consolidated. The overall effect is intended to be the same as a repurchase of ordinary shares at fair value. A typical example is Severn Trent. Although this pre-dates FRS 14 it illustrates the required treatment.

Extract 26.8: Severn Trent Plc (1998)

Directors' report [extract]

Capital reorganisation

On 8 August 1997 the company effected a capital reorganisation under which each Ordinary Share of £1 was divided into one ordinary share of 62p and one B share of 38p. Following this sub-division every 20 ordinary shares of 62p each were consolidated into 19 Ordinary Shares of 65 5/19p each. Schroders acting as agents for the company offered to purchase from shareholders all their B Shares at their nominal value on 11 August 1997. A second repurchase offer was made in September 1997. …

8 Earnings per share [extract]

Earnings per share is calculated on the net basis on earnings of £14.7 million being profit for the financial year of £14.9 million (1997: £316.7 million), less £0.2 million B share dividend (1997: nil), divided by 343.6 million shares, being the weighted average number of Ordinary Shares in issue during the year (1997: 363.3 million), excluding those held in the Severn Trent Employee Share Ownership Trust on which dividends have been waived. ...

> **18 Called up share capital** [extract]
>
> b) Capital reorganisation
>
> As a result of the 19 for 20 consolidation and issue of B shares on 8 August 1997, 356,623,364 ordinary shares of £1 became 338,792,195 ordinary shares of 65 5/19p and 356,623,364 B Shares of 38p. ...
>
> c) Shares purchased during the year
>
> In August 1997 and September 1997, the company purchased for cancellation 297,054,463 and 35,723,317 B Shares of 38p ...

The number of shares used in the EPS calculation for the comparative year of 363.3 million is unchanged from the 1997 annual accounts. This indicates that the prior periods' EPS figures have not been restated for the share consolidation, which would have been required under a literal reading of SSAP 3. Instead Severn Trent, in common with other companies who had returned capital in this way, took the view that the substance of the combined transaction is a buy-back at fair value, and hence no restatement is needed. Before FRS 14, the only authoritative rationale for such a treatment would have been paragraph 14 of FRS 5 *Reporting the substance of transactions* which includes the requirement that 'A group or series of transactions that achieves or is designed to achieve an overall commercial effect should be viewed as a whole.'[25]

FRS 14 seems to remove the doubt over which treatment is appropriate by requiring companies to adjust prior periods' EPS only when the change in shares happens without a corresponding change in resources. However, some room for doubt remains, as it is not entirely clear in FRS 14 when a change in resources and a change in the number of shares should be viewed as corresponding to one another. On the one hand a quite wide interpretation of this correspondence is required; as discussed at 4.3.2 above, when a special dividend is combined with a share consolidation it *is* treated as a corresponding change in resource. This is the case notwithstanding the fact that the change in resources does not take the legal form of consideration for the reduction in shares. On the other hand, Appendix II to the standard, which sets out the development of the FRS, indicates that treating transactions that replicate repurchases, but do not take their legal form, *as* repurchases was intended to be limited to the case of special dividends.

One further subtlety relates to how closely the ratio of share consolidation succeeds in mirroring the commercial effect of a fair value repurchase. In the Severn Trent example above, of the potential repurchase of 356,623,364 B shares only 332,777,780 were in fact bought back. It seems likely that the consolidation of 19 for 20 would have been calculated so as to reproduce the effects of a fair value repurchase assuming *all* the B shares were redeemed. If so then the share consolidation is *more* than adjusting for the resources that have left the group. FRS 14 would strictly require that some element of the consolidation should be viewed as happening without a corresponding change in resource, and hence prior periods' EPS adjusted accordingly.

4.3.5 *Put warrants priced above market value*

The reference to put warrants at significantly more than fair value is a change from FRED 16 and its supplement, and it is not mentioned in Appendix II to the standard dealing with the development of the FRS. It may have been added because such a scheme came to the attention of the ASB whilst it was finalising the standard, for example the scheme proposed by GEC in its accounts to 31 March 1998.

Extract 26.9: The General Electric Company plc (1998)

Finance Director's review [extract]

To manage the balance sheet structure of the Group and ensure all shareholders participate equitably, the Board also proposes to make a bonus issue of Put Warrants to shareholders, pro rata to their shareholdings. The Put Warrants will entitle each shareholder to sell to the Company one share for every 50 shares they hold, at a price that is 150 pence higher than the market price, subject to a maximum of 650 pence per share. This enables shareholders either to maintain their percentage shareholding and receive a distribution of cash of up to 13 pence per share held on 4th September, 1998 which will provide a total cash distribution (including the dividend) of 24.43 pence per share; or shareholders can retain all their shares and will still benefit from these proposals by increasing their percentage ownership and selling the warrants for up to 150 pence each (3 pence per share).

If shareholders wish to sell their entitlement to Put Warrants they need take no action and will bear no expense; the Company will automatically organise the sale.

GEC's proposed scheme was effected in the year to 31 March 1999. The 1999 accounts disclose adjustments to prior period EPS as follows:

Extract 26.10: The General Electric Company plc (1999)

8 Earnings per share [extract]

Earnings per share are calculated by reference to a weighted average of 2,711.6 million ordinary shares (1998 restated 2,793.4 million ordinary shares) in issue during the year, which have been adjusted following the exercise of the put warrants on 6th October, 1998, as required by FRS 14.

Unfortunately the standard does not give an illustrative calculation for a put warrant at significantly more than fair value, but it does for the familiar rights issue[26] (rights issues are discussed at 4.3.3 above). In a rights issue new shares are issued at a discount to market value, whereas with put warrants shares are bought back at a premium to market value. In both cases the remaining shares are viewed as being devalued for the purposes of comparing EPS over time. Applying the logic of adjusting EPS when there is a change in the number of shares without a corresponding change in resources seems to require that put warrants are treated as a reverse rights issue. This would mean calculating a similar 'adjustment factor', and applying it to the number of shares outstanding before the transaction. The difference in the calculation would be that the number of shares issued and the consideration received for them would be replaced by negative amounts representing the number of shares put back to the company and the amount paid for them.

An illustration of what this might entail is as follows:

Example 26.3: Put warrants priced above market value

The following example takes the same scenario as Example 26.2 above (a rights issue), altered to illustrate a put warrant scheme. In that example the shares are issued at a discount of 20p to the £1 market price on a one for four basis 8 months into the year. Reversing this would give a put warrant to sell shares back to the company at a 20p premium, again on a one for four basis. All other details have been left the same for comparability, although in reality the rising earnings following a rights issue may well become falling earnings after a buy-back. The calculation would then become:

Computation of theoretical ex-warrant value per share

$$\frac{\text{fair value of all outstanding shares} - \text{total amount paid on exercise of warrants}}{\text{shares outstanding before exercise} - \text{shares cancelled in the exercise}}$$

$$\frac{(£1.00 \times 24{,}000{,}000) - (£1.20 \times 6{,}000{,}000)}{24{,}000{,}000 - 6{,}000{,}000} = £0.93$$

Computation of adjustment factor

$$\frac{\text{Fair value per share before exercise of warrants}}{\text{Theoretical ex - warrant value per share}} = \frac{£1.00}{£0.93} = 1.075$$

Computation of earnings per share

	1998	1999
1998 EPS as originally reported:	4.17p	
£1m / 24m shares		
1998 EPS restated for warrants:	3.88p	
£1 / (24m shares x 1.075)		
1999 EPS including effects of warrants:		5.17p

$$\frac{£1.2\text{m}}{(24\text{m} \times 1.075 \times 8/12) + (18\text{m} \times 4/12)}$$

Whilst the above seems a sensible interpretation of the requirements, as the procedure is not specified there may be scope for other interpretations. Furthermore the standard refers to put warrants at *significantly* more than their fair value. In practice a lot may turn on the interpretation of when 'more than fair' value becomes 'significantly more'.

4.4 Options exercised during the year

Shares allotted as a result of options being exercised should be dealt with on a weighted average basis in the basic EPS.[27] Furthermore, options which have been exercised during the year will also affect diluted EPS calculations. If the options in question would have had a diluting effect on the basic EPS had they been exercised at the beginning of the year, then they should be considered in the diluted EPS calculation as explained in 6.5.2 below, but on a weighted average basis for the period up to the date of exercise. The exercise of options is a 'conversion of potential ordinary shares'. The standard excludes such conversions from the general requirement (see 4.3 above) to adjust prior periods' EPS when a change in the number of shares happens without a corresponding change in resources.[28]

4.5 Post balance sheet changes in capital

The EPS shown in the profit and loss account should not reflect any change in the capital structure occurring after the accounting date, but before the accounts are approved, which was effected for fair value. This is because any proceeds received from the issue were not available for use during the period. However, EPS for all periods presented should be adjusted for any bonus element in post year end changes in the number of shares. When this is done that fact should be stated.[29]

An example of such disclosure is shown in the following extract from the accounts of Calluna for the year ended 31 March 1999:

Extract 26.11: Calluna plc (1999)

7 Loss per share [extract]

The above calculations of basic and diluted loss per share for both 1999 and 1998 have been retrospectively adjusted to take account of the bonus element of the April 1999, 33 for 100 rights issue at 12.5p per ordinary share.

4.6 Issue to acquire another business

As a result of a share issue to acquire another business, funds or other assets will flow into the business and extra profits will be generated. When calculating EPS, it should be assumed that the shares were issued on the first day that profits of the newly acquired business are recognised in the profit and loss account (even if the actual date of issue is later).[30] Under FRS 2, this will be the date on which control of a subsidiary undertaking passes to its new parent undertaking.[31]

If the business combination is accounted for as an acquisition, this means that when calculating EPS, the period for which earnings of the acquired company are consolidated should be the same as the period for which the shares are weighted, thus achieving comparability within the EPS calculation.

Where a business combination has been accounted for as a merger, the number of shares taken as being in issue for all periods should be the aggregate of the weighted average number of shares of the merged companies, adjusted to equivalent shares of the post merger holding company.[32] This treatment reflects the fact that earnings are combined for both years and is appropriate even where not all of the consideration given for the equity share capital in the 'offeree' company is in the form of equity share capital.

4.7 Group reconstructions

In the case where a new holding company is established by means of a share for share exchange and merger accounting principles have been adopted, the number of shares taken as being in issue for both the current and preceding periods should be the number of shares issued by the new holding company in the reconstruction. However, EPS calculations for previous periods in the new holding company's financial statements would have to reflect any issues for cash by the former holding company that may have occurred in those periods, as illustrated in the example below:

Example 26.4: Calculation of EPS where a new holding company is established

Company A has acquired Company B in a one for one share exchange on 30 June 1999. At that date, Company B has 1,000,000 £1 ordinary shares in issue. Previously, on 30 June 1998 Company B had issued 200,000 £1 ordinary shares for cash at full market price. Both companies have a 31 December year end and the trading results of Company B are as follows:

	1999	1998
	£	£
Profit for equity shareholders after taxation	500,000	300,000

The earnings per share calculation of Company A is shown below:

	1999		1998
Number of equity shares			
		$800,000 \times \frac{6}{12} =$	400,000
		$1,000,000 \times \frac{6}{12} =$	500,000
	1,000,000		900,000
EPS	$\frac{500,000}{1,000,000} = 50p$		$\frac{300,000}{900,000} = 33.33p$

If, in the above example, the share exchange did not take place on a one for one basis, but Company A issued three shares for every one share held in Company B, then the number of shares issued by Company B in 1998 would have to be apportioned accordingly before carrying out the weighted average calculation. The earnings per share calculation would, therefore, have been as follows:

	1999		1998
Number of equity shares			
		$2,400,000 \times \frac{6}{12} =$	1,200,000
		$3,000,000 \times \frac{6}{12} =$	1,500,000
	3,000,000		2,700,000
EPS	$\frac{500,000}{3,000,000} = 16.67p$		$\frac{300,000}{2,700,000} = 11.11p$

4.8 Adjustments to EPS in five year summaries

In order to ensure comparability of EPS figures quoted in a five year summary, the previously published EPS figures should be adjusted for subsequent changes in capital not involving full consideration at fair value in the manner described in 4.3 above; they should also be adjusted for merger accounting. The resultant figures should be described as restated and should be clearly distinguished from other financial data which is not so adjusted.[33] Where there is more than one such change, these factors will operate cumulatively.

5 MATTERS AFFECTING THE NUMERATOR

5.1 Earnings

The earnings figure on which the EPS calculation is based should be the consolidated net profit or loss for the year after tax, exceptional and extraordinary (if any) items, minority interests and after deducting preference dividends and other appropriations in respect of non-equity shares.[34]

5.2 Preference dividends

If a company has preference shares, the amount of preference dividends that is deducted from the net profit for the period is:

(a) the amount of any preference dividends on non-cumulative preference shares declared in respect of the period; and

(b) the full amount of the required preference dividends for cumulative preference shares for the period, whether or not the dividends have been declared, as the undeclared amount is still deductible as an appropriation. The amount of preference dividends for the period does not include the amount of any preference dividends for cumulative preference shares paid or declared during the current period in respect of previous periods.[35]

As indicated at 4.4.1 of Chapter 17, FRS 4 requires such dividends to be accounted for on an accruals basis, except in those circumstances where ultimate payment is remote. Accordingly, the amount to be taken into account will normally be that accounted for as the appropriation for the year.

As indicated at 5.1 above, any other appropriations in respect of the preference shares should also be deducted in arriving at the earnings figure.

5.3 Prior year adjustments

Where comparative figures have been restated (for example, to correct a fundamental error or as a result of a change in accounting policy), earnings per share for the corresponding previous period should also be restated.

5.4 Different classes of ordinary shares

If there is more than one class of ordinary shares, earnings should be apportioned over the different classes of shares in accordance with their dividend rights or other rights to participate in profits.[36]

5.5 Other bases

As indicated at 1 above, the ASB when issuing FRS 3 attempted to de-emphasise EPS by requiring it to be calculated *after* extraordinary items. In view of this change and the other requirements of FRS 3 (see Chapter 25) the EPS number which companies are required to disclose has become much more volatile, and really only a starting point for further analysis. The ASB recognised that companies would therefore be likely to provide additional EPS numbers prepared on what they saw as a more meaningful basis and therefore the ASB introduced rules dealing with such additional EPS disclosures.[37]

These disclosure requirements are repeated in FRS 14 as follows: 'Such additional earnings per share computations should be presented on a consistent basis over time and, wherever disclosed, reconciled to the amount required by the FRS. The reconciliation should list the items for which an adjustment is being made and disclose their individual effect on the calculation. The earnings per share required by the FRS should be at least as prominent as any additional version presented and the reason for calculating the additional version should be explained. The reconciliation and explanation should appear adjacent to the earnings per share disclosure, or a reference should be given to where they can be found. Where both additional basic and diluted amounts per share are presented, they should be disclosed with equal prominence.'[38]

The standard also makes clear that the number of shares used in the denominator for additional EPS disclosures should be the same as that used for the required EPS figures.[39]

Since the issue of FRS 3, many companies have been providing additional EPS numbers; however, it is clear that there is no universal view as to the basis of such a number. Indeed, as can be seen from some of the extracts below some companies give a number of additional EPS figures.

5.5.1 IIMR headline earnings

In view of the volatility of 'earnings' numbers of companies following the issue of FRS 3, the Institute of Investment Management and Research ('IIMR') sought to find an earnings figure that would reflect a company's trading performance but that would limit the need to exercise judgement in its calculation so that it could be used as an unambiguous reference point between users, the press and statistical companies. Accordingly, in September 1993 the IIMR issued Statement of Investment Practice No. 1 in which it sets out a definition of 'headline' earnings. The statement is not mandatory. However, the IIMR does suggest that companies themselves may wish to adopt the IIMR calculation of headline earnings in presenting an additional EPS in their accounts.

The IIMR discusses both maintainable and headline earnings. Maintainable earnings is the level of earnings that is expected to be earned in future years. The IIMR argues that, although it is maintainable earnings that should ideally be used in a price-earnings ratio computation, its calculation is too subjective to be calculated on a standardised basis. Headline earnings is a measure of the company's trading performance in the year and is calculated by adjusting a company's profit for certain specific items. The need for judgement in the calculation, while not completely eliminated, is reduced. The IIMR therefore concluded that headline earnings should be the benchmark measure.

Headline earnings is the trading results, after interest and taxation, for the year. It is the result actually achieved and contains no 'as if' adjustments; for example, where a subsidiary is acquired part way through a year it does not require adjustments to reflect the earnings that would have been achieved if the subsidiary had been part of the group all along.

To arrive at headline earnings, the profit for the financial year is adjusted for the after tax and minority interest effect of, amongst other things, the following:

(a) profits/losses on sale/termination of an operation. However, the trading results of the discontinued operation remain in the calculation;

(b) profits/losses on disposal of, and permanent diminutions in, fixed assets, irrespective of whether such amounts are included in arriving at operating profit or not;

(c) the reversal of provisions in respect of FRS 3's paragraph 20 items (see Chapter 25 at 2.6.3); and

(d) any goodwill charged in the profit and loss account.

Reorganisation provisions, fundamental or otherwise, are not excluded. Exceptional trading items are also to be included in the calculation of headline earnings.

A number of companies have disclosed an additional EPS number based on IIMR headline earnings, as illustrated in the following extract:

Extract 26.12: Marks and Spencer p.l.c. (2001)

Consolidated profit and loss account [extract]

	Notes	52 weeks ended 31 March 2001	53 weeks ended 1 April 2000
Basic earnings per share	9	0.0p	9.0p
Diluted basic earnings per share	9	0.0p	9.0p
Adjusted earnings per share	9	11.4p	13.2p
Diluted adjusted earnings per share	9	11.4p	13.2p
Dividend per share	8	9.0p	9.0p

9. Earnings per share

The calculation of earnings per ordinary share is based on earnings after tax and minority interests and the weighted average number of ordinary shares in issue during the year.

An adjusted earnings per share figure has been calculated in addition to the earnings per share per share required by FRS14, 'Earnings per Share' and is based on earnings excluding the effect of the exceptional charges. It has been calculated to allow shareholders to gain a clearer understanding of the trading performance of the Group. Details of the adjusted earnings per share are set out below:

	2001			2000		
	£m	Basic pence per share	Diluted pence per share	£m	Basic pence per share	Diluted pence per share
Basic earnings	1.3	0.0	0.0	258.7	9.0	9.0
Exceptional operating charges	19.3	0.7	0.7	53.0	1.8	1.8
Loss on sale of property and other fixed assets	83.2	2.9	2.9	22.3	0.8	0.8
Loss on sale/termination of operations	1.7	0.1	0.1	45.4	1.6	1.6
Provisions for loss on operations to be discontinued	222.7	7.7	7.7	–	–	–
Adjusted earnings	328.2	11.4	11.4	379.4	13.2	13.2

The IIMR earnings per share has also been calculated in addition to the basic earnings per share and is based on earnings adjusted to eliminate certain capital items as follows:

	£m	Basic pence per share	Diluted pence per share	£m	Basic pence per share	Diluted pence per share
Basic earnings	1.3	0.0	0.0	258.7	9.0	9.0
Loss on sale of property and other fixed assets	83.2	2.9	2.9	22.3	0.8	0.8
Loss on sale/termination of operations	1.7	0.1	0.1	45.4	1.6	1.6
Provisions for loss on operations to be discontinued	222.7	7.7	7.7	–	–	–
IIMR earnings	308.9	10.7	10.7	326.4	11.4	11.4

The weighted average number of ordinary shares used in the calculation of earnings per share are as follows:

	2001 m	2000 m
Weighted average ordinary shares in issue during the year ended 31 March	2,872.4	2,872.1
Potentially dilutive share options under the Group's share option schemes	9.8	13.6
Weighted average ordinary shares for diluted earnings per share	2,882.2	2,885.7

The above extract illustrates the requirement under FRS 14 to provide a reconciliation between the additional EPS and that required under the standard, showing the individual effect of each item.[40] Additionally, Marks and Spencer, in common with many other companies, has presented a reconciliation of total (as opposed to per-share) earnings. In our view this is helpful additional disclosure as it allows the adjustments to earnings to be more easily interpreted in the context of the other accounting disclosures.

5.5.2 *Excluding exceptional items*

As mentioned above, in calculating headline earnings all reorganisation costs and exceptional trading items are to be included. Clearly, some companies believe it is more meaningful to provide an alternative EPS excluding the effects of all exceptional items. This information was given by Marks and Spencer in addition to headline EPS, as shown in Extract 26.12 above. Another company providing additional disclosure of EPS excluding exceptional items is BAA, as shown in Extract 26.4 at 4.3.1 above.

Some companies, rather than disclosing an additional EPS which excludes the effects of all exceptional items, only exclude certain exceptional items in providing an alternative EPS number. For example, T&N only excluded its exceptional asbestos-related costs:

Extract 26.13: T&N plc (1997)

Group profit and loss account [extract]

	Notes	**1996**	1995
Earnings/(loss) per share	8	**22.9p**	(75.4)p
Earnings per share pre asbestos-related costs	8	**20.4p**	14.8 p

In addition to the exceptional asbestos-related costs, T&N also had some non-operating exceptional items.

5.5.3 *Excluding discontinued operations*

One of the main impacts of FRS 3 has been for companies to analyse their results between continuing and discontinued operations (see Chapter 25 at 2.3). Accordingly, a number of companies have provided an additional EPS by excluding the amounts relating to the discontinued operations, thereby disclosing a figure related purely to the continuing operations, as illustrated in the following extract:

Extract 26.14: Delta plc (2000)

Group Profit and Loss Account [extract]

	Notes	Continuing					**2000**
		Pre-exceptional, goodwill and operations to be discontinued £ million	Operations to be discontinued £ million	Exceptional items (note 5) and goodwill amortisation £ million	Sub total £ million	Discontinued operations £ million	Total £ million
Profit for the financial year		13.2	3.5	(76.5)	(59.8)	52.4	(7.4)
Dividends	9	(12.1)	–	–	(12.1)	–	(12.1)
Transfer (from) to reserves	25	1.1	3.5	(76.5)	(71.9)	52.4	(19.5)
Earnings per 25p ordinary share:							
Basic	10	8.8p	2.3p		(40.1)p		(5.0)p
Diluted	10	8.7p	2.3p		(39.8)p		(5.0)p

Earnings per 25p ordinary share before goodwill amortisation:							
Basic	10				(37.0)p		(1.9)p
Diluted	10				(36.8)p		(1.9)p
Earnings per 25p ordinary share before exceptional items and goodwill amortisation							
Basic	10				11.1p		15.5p
Diluted	10				11.0p		15.4p

	Notes						**1999**
		Continuing					
		Pre-exceptional, goodwill and operations to be discontinued £ million	Operations to be discontinued £ million	Exceptional items (note 5) and goodwill amortisation £ million	Sub total £ million	Discontinued operations £ million	Total £ million
Profit for the financial year		9.4	5.1	(8.7)	5.8	(0.4)	5.4
Dividends	9	(12.1)	–	–	(12.1)	–	(12.1)
Transfer (from) to reserves	25	(2.7)	5.1	(8.7)	(6.3)	(0.4)	(6.7)
Earnings per 25p ordinary share:							
Basic	10	6.2p	3.4p		3.8p		3.5p
Diluted	10	6.2p	3.4p		3.8p		3.5p
Earnings per 25p ordinary share before goodwill amortisation:							
Basic	10				6.8p		6.5p
Diluted	10				6.8p		6.5p
Earnings per 25p ordinary share before exceptional items and goodwill amortisation							
Basic	10				9.6p		12.4p
Diluted	10				9.6p		12.3p

10. Earnings per share

Basic earnings per share (EPS) is calculated in accordance with FRS 14, by dividing the earnings attributable to ordinary shareholders by the weighted average number of ordinary shares in issue during the year. For diluted earnings per share, the weighted average number of ordinary shares in issue is adjusted to assume conversion of all dilutive potential ordinary shares. The Group has only one category of dilutive potential ordinary shares: those options granted to employees where the exercise price is less than the average market price of the Company's ordinary shares during the year. Reconciliation of the earnings and weighted average number of shares used in the calculation are set out in the table below.

To give a better understanding of the underlying results of the year, additional earnings per share figures are given on the face of the profit and loss account for continuing activities (both are pre and post operations to be discontinued, exceptional items and amortisation of goodwill). The earnings are based on the attributable profit (pre and post-exceptional items) less preference dividends and goodwill amortisation (where applicable) as shown below. The weighted average number of shares used in the calculations are those shown in the table below.

	2000			1999		
	Total earnings £ million	**Weighted average no. of shares**	**Per-share amount total pence**	Total earnings £ million	Weighted average no. of shares	Per-share amount total pence
(Loss) profit attributable to shareholders	**(7.4)**	**149,526,229**		5.4	149,301,733	
Less preference dividends	**(0.1)**			(0.1)		
Basic EPS	**(7.5)**	**149,526,229**	**(5.0)**	5.3	149,301,733	3.5
Effect of dilutive securities: options		**890,622**	**–**		923,904	–
Diluted EPS	**(7.5)**	**150,416,851**	**(5.0)**	5.3	150,225,637	3.5
Basic EPS (as above)	**(7.5)**	**149,526,229**	**(5.0)**	5.3	149,301,733	3.5
Effect of goodwill amortisation	**4.6**		**3.1**	4.5		3.0
Basic EPS excluding goodwill amortisation	**(2.9)**	**149,526,229**	**(1.9)**	9.8	149,301,733	6.5
Diluted EPS excluding goodwill amortisation	**(2.9)**	**150,416,851**	**(1.9)**	9.8	150,225,637	6.5
Basic EPS excluding goodwill amortisation (as above)	**(2.9)**	**149,526,229**	**(1.9)**	9.8	149,301,733	6.5
Effect of operating exceptional items before taxation (note 5)	**6.6**		**4.4**	4.7		3.1
Effect of non-operating exceptional items before taxation (note 5)	**13.4**		**8.9**	4.5		3.0
Effect of taxation on exceptional items (note 5ii)	**6.1**		**4.1**	(0.4)		(0.2)
Minority share of post tax exceptional items	**–**		**–**	(0.1)		–
Basic EPS excluding exceptional items and goodwill amortisation	**23.2**	**149,526,229**	**15.5**	18.5	149,301,733	12.4
Diluted EPS excluding exceptional items and goodwill amortisation	**23.2**	**150,416,851**	**15.4**	18.5	150,225,637	12.3

Since the implementation of FRS 10 increasing numbers of companies have chosen to present an EPS figure excluding goodwill amortisation, as illustrated by Delta above.

5.5.4 *Other amounts per share*

For some companies, the conventional method of assessing performance by reference to reported earnings is not entirely satisfactory; for example, many property companies consider the 'net assets per ordinary share' to be a more appropriate performance indicator. In such circumstances, in addition to the requirements of FRS 14, we believe that it is desirable to present other statistics that are appropriate to assessing the company's performance, including an adequate explanation of the basis of calculation.

There is some ambiguity in FRS 14 as to what number of shares to include in the denominator for per share figures other than earnings. The scope section of the standard contains the following 'The provisions of the FRS are drafted principally in terms of amounts per share as components of net profit; however, the requirements also apply, as far as appropriate, to other amounts per share, eg net assets per share.'[41] Whilst the specific mention of net assets per share could be read as a requirement to base such disclosure on the weighted average number of shares, the inclusion of 'as far as appropriate' seems to leave room for other interpretations. One quite persuasive argument is that, as net assets represent a snap-shot of the entity at its balance sheet date, it is more appropriate to base net assets per share on the number of shares as at that date. This was the approach taken by Slough Estates, which also discloses a number of performance indicators, as illustrated below:

Extract 26.15: Slough Estates plc (2000)

9. Earnings, capital surplus and net assets per ordinary share

			Basic		Fully diluted	
			2000	1999	**2000**	1999
The earnings, capital surplus and net assets per ordinary share have been calculated as follows:						
Profit attributable to ordinary shareholders	(a)	£m	**106.5**	100.8	**118.1**	100.8
Profit attributable to ordinary shareholders excluding profits and losses on sale of investment properties	(b)	£m	**106.0**	89.1	**117.6**	89.1
Capital surplus	(c)	£m	**261.6**	253.7	**261.6**	253.7
Average of shares in issue during the year	(d)	shares m	**413.3**	409.8	**466.3**	410.6
Earnings per share (a) ÷ (d)		pence	**25.8**	24.6	**25.3**	24.6
Earnings per share excluding profits and losses on sale of investment properties (b) ÷ (d)		pence	**25.7**	21.7	**25.2**	21.7
Capital surplus per share		pence	**63.3**	61.9	**56.1**	54.8
Equity attributable to ordinary shareholders	(e)	£m	**2,286.8**	1,965.8	**2,427.1**	2,106.9
Shares in issue at the end of the year	(f)	shares m	**413.9**	412.8	**466.9**	465.9
Net assets per share (e) ÷ (f)		pence	**553**	476	**520**	452

	2000	1999
	m	m
Average of shares in issue during the year	**413.3**	409.8
Adjustment for the dilutive effect of employee share options, save as you earn schemes and preference shares	**53.0**	0.8
Average of shares in issue during the year diluted	**466.3**	410.6

In 1999 the anti-dilutive effect of the preference shares was excluded from the diluted earnings per share calculation. In 2000 the effect is dilutive and therefore the preference shares are included in the 2000 diluted calculation.

The earnings per share and fully diluted earnings per share excluding profits and losses (net of tax and minority) on the sale of investment properties have been calculated in addition to the disclosures required by FRS3, since in the opinion of the directors this gives shareholders a more meaningful measure of performance.

The question of whether the weighted average or year end number of shares is a more appropriate basis applies also to dividends per share, which companies sometimes present on the face of the profit and loss account. In our view the ambiguity in the standard allows companies the discretion to base such a figure on the basis they consider most appropriate.

6 DILUTED EARNINGS PER SHARE

6.1 The need for diluted EPS

The presentation of basic EPS seeks to show a performance measure, by computing how much profit a company has earned for each of the shares in issue for the period. Companies often enter into commitments to issue shares in the future which would result in a change in basic EPS. FRS 14 refers to such commitments as potential ordinary shares, which it defines as follows:

'A financial instrument or a right that may entitle its holder to ordinary shares.

Examples of potential ordinary shares are:

(a) debt or equity instruments, including preference shares, that are convertible into ordinary shares;

(b) share warrants and options;

(c) rights granted under employee share plans that may entitle employees to receive ordinary shares as part of their remuneration and similar rights granted under other share purchase plans; and

(d) rights to ordinary shares that are contingent upon the satisfaction of certain conditions resulting from contractual arrangements, such as the purchase of a business or other assets, i.e. contingently issuable shares.'[42]

When potential shares are actually issued, the impact on basic EPS will be two-fold. Firstly the number of shares in issue will change, secondly profits could be affected, for example by lower interest charges or the return made on cash inflows. This potential change in EPS is quantified by computing diluted EPS.

SSAP 3 only required the disclosure of fully diluted EPS in certain circumstances, so as to act as a warning signal for possible future falls in EPS. FRS 14, however, requires disclosure of diluted EPS in all circumstances as a more sophisticated measure of past performance.[43] Accordingly, it gives more specific guidance on the calculation than SSAP 3 did, including the sequence in which potential shares should be considered when calculating the diluted EPS.

The rationale that a *future* dilution is relevant for measuring *past* performance is this. Companies can use potential ordinary shares to achieve illusory growth in basic EPS. Consider, for example, a company that has used convertible loan stock or convertible preference shares to finance an acquisition or expansion. These securities usually carry a low fixed interest or dividend coupon due to the presence of a compensatory factor, the conversion privilege. It is therefore possible to boost basic EPS so long as the incremental post-tax finance cost is covered and current performance is sustained. However, examination of the underlying trend in the diluted EPS figures will reveal a more 'real' growth in earnings so far as concerns existing equity shareholders, since an attempt is made to reflect the ultimate 'cost' of using convertible securities to finance growth in earnings. Convertible securities are discussed in more detail at 4.2 in Chapter 17.

6.2 Calculation of diluted EPS

In calculating diluted EPS, the number of shares should be that used in calculating basic EPS, plus the weighted average number of shares that would be issued on the conversion of all the dilutive potential ordinary shares into ordinary shares. Potential ordinary shares should be deemed to have been converted into ordinary shares at the beginning of the period or, if not in existence at the beginning of the period, the date of the issue of the financial instrument or the granting of the rights by which they are generated.[44]

6.2.1 Earnings

The earnings figure should be adjusted to reflect any changes in profit that would arise when the potential shares outstanding in the period are actually issued. Adjustment is to be made for the post-tax effects of:

(a) any dividends on potential shares, for example on convertible preference shares, that have been deducted in calculating the earnings for basic EPS;

(b) interest recognised in the period on the potential shares such as convertible loan stock; and

(c) any other changes in income or expense that would result from the conversion of the potential shares.[45]

These adjustments will also include any amounts charged in the profit and loss account under FRS 4 as a result of allocating fees, premiums or discounts over the term of the instrument.

An example of an adjustment covered by (b) above is as follows:

Extract 26.16: BAA plc (2001)

10. Earnings per share [extract]	**2001**	2000
	£m	£m
Profit attributable to shareholders	**398**	259
Interest on convertible bonds	**16**	16
Diluted profit	**414**	275

The standard notes that certain earnings adjustments directly attributable to the instrument could have a knock on impact on other profit and loss items which will need to be accounted for. For example, the lower interest charge on conversion of convertible debt could lead to higher charges under profit sharing schemes.[46]

Unlike SSAP 3, however, no imputed earnings are taken into account in respect of share options or warrants. The effect of such potential ordinary shares on the diluted EPS is reflected in the computation of the denominator. This is discussed at 6.5.2 below.

In the vast majority of cases the earnings impact will be covered by the first two points above, or be nil.

6.2.2 *Number of shares*

FRS 14 discusses a number of specific types of potential ordinary shares, and how they should be brought into the calculation, which are discussed later. More generally, the standard first discusses, in two explanatory paragraphs,[47] the impact on the basic requirement that *all* dilutive potential ordinary shares are included of situations where an entity may be entitled or required to fulfil its obligations either in shares or cash. The general tenor of these two paragraphs seems to be that if the outcome is uncertain, then the more dilutive outcome should be assumed. However, the wording of these paragraphs and how they interact is far from clear, and is discussed in more detail below.

(a) The standard notes that the number of shares issued on the conversion of an instrument will be governed by the terms of the instrument, and concludes by saying 'The computation assumes the most advantageous conversion rate or exercise price from the stand point of the holder'.[48] Whilst the meaning of this is fairly obscure, the fact that it envisages more than one outcome presumably encompasses scenarios where the holder has a choice whether to accept cash or shares.

(b) Contracts which can be settled either in shares or cash are specifically covered. The standard indicates that where 'past experience or a stated policy provides a reasonable basis for concluding how the contract will be satisfied, that policy or experience is followed'. In the absence of any such past experience or stated policy it should be presumed that the contract will be settled by the more dilutive method.[49]

A possible question that arises is what happens if these two requirements are in conflict with each other? An example would be a contract providing for the issue of a fixed quantity of shares or a fixed monetary sum at the option of the holder. If the value of the shares were less than the cash option then (a) above seems to be saying that, for diluted EPS purposes, it should be assumed that cash will be paid (most advantageous for the holder). However, (b) above appears to require either 'past experience or a stated policy' or, in the absence of such, that the cash route were more dilutive. The standard does not elaborate on how to compare, in these circumstances, a cash payment with a share issue to decide which is more dilutive. At first sight a cash payment (say to buy an asset), would have no dilutive impact, whereas a share issue clearly would. It is possible that the standard is trying to allude to a wider interpretation of dilutive, and that some notional interest cost associated with a cash payment should be considered.

Given that the overall tenor of the FRS is to arrive at the most fully diluted EPS it seems the most likely interpretation would be to include such potential shares. However the lack of clarity surrounding the issue will require detailed consideration of each specific case.

6.3 Dilutive potential ordinary shares

Only those potential shares whose issue would have a dilutive effect on EPS are brought into the calculation. The standard gives detailed guidance for determining which potential shares are deemed to be dilutive, and hence brought into the diluted EPS calculation. This guidance covers: the sequence in which potential shares are tested to establish cumulative dilution, and the element of profit which needs to be diluted to trigger inclusion. Each is discussed below.

6.3.1 *Dilution judged by the cumulative impact of potential shares*

Where a company has a number of different potential ordinary shares, in deciding whether they are dilutive (and hence reflected in the calculation), each type is to be considered in sequence from the most to the least dilutive. Only those potential shares which produce a cumulative dilution are to be included.[50] This means that some potential shares which would dilute basic EPS if viewed on their own may need to be excluded. This results in a diluted EPS showing the maximum overall dilution of basic EPS. The way this is to be done is illustrated in the following example.

Example 26.5: Determining whether potential ordinary shares are dilutive or antidilutive

Capital structure

Issued share capital as at 31 December 1998 and 31 December 1999:
2,000,000 ordinary shares of 10p each
The average market price of the shares during the year was 75p.

Options have been granted to the directors and certain senior executives giving them the right to subscribe for 100,000 ordinary shares between 2003 and 2005 at 60 pence per share.

800,000 8% convertible cumulative preference shares of £1 each
Each preference share is convertible into 2 ordinary shares.

£1,000,000 of 5% Convertible bonds
Each bond is convertible into 2 ordinary shares.

Trading results

Net profit attributable to ordinary shareholders for the year ended 31 December 1999 is £100,000, all of which relates to continuing operations.

Assume corporation tax at 30%.

Increase in earnings attributable to ordinary shareholders on conversion of potential ordinary shares

	Increase in earnings £	Increase in number of ordinary shares No	Earnings per incremental share Pence
(a) Options	–	20,000	–
(b) Convertible cumulative preference shares	64,000	1,600,000	4.00
(c) 5% Convertible bonds	35,000	2,000,000	1.75

(a) As discussed at 6.5.2 below, under FRS 14 conversion of options is treated as not giving rise to any increase in earnings, but the dilution is calculated as if the proceeds on conversion had been received for issuing a certain number of shares at fair value and the excess for zero consideration. It is only the excess which is taken into account in calculating diluted EPS (see Example 26.9 below). In this example the number can be computed as being 100,000 x (75-60)/75.

(b) Increase in earnings represents the dividends on the shares being 8% x £800,000. The increase in shares resulting from conversion would be 800,000 x 2.

(c) Increase in earnings represents interest saved of £50,000 being 5% x £1,000,000 less taxation thereon at 30% (£15,000). The increase in shares resulting from conversion would be 1,000,000 x 2.

These are therefore taken into account in computing whether they are dilutive or antidilutive in the order of (a), (c) and (b) as follows:

Computation of whether potential ordinary shares are dilutive or antidilutive

	Net profit from continuing operations £	Ordinary shares No	Per share Pence	
Basic net profit from continuing operations per share	100,000	2,000,000	5.00	
Options	–	20,000		
	100,000	2,020,000	4.95	Dilutive
5% Convertible bonds	35,000	2,000,000		
	135,000	4,020,000	3.36	Dilutive
Convertible cumulative preference shares	64,000	1,600,000		
	199,000	5,620,000	3.54	Antidilutive

Notwithstanding the fact that the convertible cumulative preference shares would be dilutive on their own (basic EPS of 5.00p would be diluted to 4.56p), since the effect of the convertible cumulative preference shares increases the pence per share from 3.36p (after taking account of the more dilutive items) to 3.54p, then these are regarded as antidilutive and are to be ignored in the calculation of diluted earnings per share. Therefore, in this example, the diluted EPS to be disclosed would be 3.36p.

One company which discloses a diluted EPS, excluding items which have no dilutive effect, is Balfour Beatty, as illustrated below:

Extract 26.17: Balfour Beatty plc (2000)

7 Earnings per ordinary share

The calculation of earnings per ordinary share is based on the profit for the financial year, after charging preference dividends, divided by the weighted average number of ordinary shares in issue during the year of 419.3m (1999: 421.4m).

The calculation of diluted earnings per ordinary share is based on the profit for the financial year after charging preference dividends, divided by the weighted average number of ordinary shares in issue adjusted for the conversion of share options by 1m (1999: nil). As in 1999, no adjustment has been made in respect of the conversion of the cumulative redeemable preference shares which were antidiulutive throughout the year.

6.3.2 Dilution judged by effect on profits from continuing operations

Potential ordinary shares are only to be treated as dilutive if their conversion to ordinary shares would dilute net profit per share from *continuing* operations.[51] The 'control number' that this focuses on is therefore the net profit from continuing operations, which is the net profit from ordinary activities after deducting preference dividends and after excluding items relating to discontinued operations. This number will not always be evident from the profit and loss account as FRS 3 requires the profit from continuing and discontinued operations to be analysed before tax and interest. An allocation of interest and tax will therefore be necessary; this is permitted to be done on a pro-rata basis at the operating profit level in the absence of a 'practical, more reliable method'.[52] The standard states that such an allocation will often be possible for post operating exceptionals presented in accordance with FRS 3.[53]

This means that the EPS to be disclosed will not necessarily be the same as that computed in testing whether the potential ordinary shares were dilutive, because the starting point is the earnings used in computing the basic EPS. This can lead to some strange results. As illustrated in the following example (which is based on Example 26.5 above) it is possible to exclude instruments which would dilute basic EPS (but not continuing EPS), and even show a diluted EPS that exceeds basic EPS.

Example 26.6: Computation of diluted EPS where the control number for computing dilutive effects is different from profits used in computing basic EPS

In Example 26.5, the net profit attributable to ordinary shareholders used in the calculation of basic EPS all related to continuing operations. If, however, there were also profits of £150,000 attributable to discontinued operations then the diluted EPS to be disclosed would be 7.09p computed as follows:

	Net profit attributable to ordinary shareholders £	Ordinary shares No	Per share Pence
Basic EPS	250,000	2,000,000	12.50
Options	–	20,000	
5% Convertible bonds	35,000	2,000,000	
Diluted EPS	285,000	4,020,000	7.09

However, if the convertible cumulative preference shares were taken into account then the diluted EPS would have been 6.21p computed as follows:

	Net profit attributable to ordinary shareholders £	Ordinary shares No	Per share Pence
Basic net profit from continuing operations per share	250,000	2,000,000	12.50
Options	–	20,000	
5% Convertible bonds	35,000	2,000,000	
Convertible cumulative preference shares	64,000	1,600,000	
	349,000	5,620,000	6.21

If, however, instead of profits of £150,000 attributable to discontinued operations there were losses of £75,000 attributable to discontinued operations then the diluted EPS to be disclosed would be 1.49p computed as follows:

	Net profit attributable to ordinary shareholders £	Ordinary shares No	Per share Pence
Basic EPS	25,000	2,000,000	1.25
Options	–	20,000	
5% Convertible bonds	35,000	2,000,000	
Diluted EPS	60,000	4,020,000	1.49

In our view it is a mistake to use net profit per share from continuing ordinary operations as the control number for the purpose of determining the items to be included in the calculation of diluted EPS, when this is not the focus of the earnings per share disclosure nor a required disclosure in the accounts. There is clearly a tension between this requirement and the idea of EPS as a past performance measure rather than a warning signal for future dilution. This conflict is acknowledged in FRS 14,[54] and the treatment is justified because profit from continuing operation is expected to be more stable over time and 'stability was of primary importance to the function of the control number'.[55] However there is nothing to prevent companies from presenting additional figures which they believe to be more meaningful.

6.4 Dilution in the context of a loss per share

In a change from SSAP 3, FRS 14 requires basic and diluted EPS to be presented in all circumstances, even if the amounts disclosed are negative (i.e. a loss per share).[56]

In the vast majority of cases, if basic EPS is a loss, then diluted EPS will be exactly the same number. The reason for this is that potential shares are only considered dilutive, and hence included in the calculation, when their conversion would decrease a net profit or *increase a net loss per share*.[57] The impact on the calculation (if any) of all potential shares is to increase the denominator, hence (in the absence of any adverse earnings impact) making a loss per share smaller not larger, meaning that the instrument is antidilutive and therefore excluded. An example of a company specifically referring to this is Liberty, as follows:

Extract 26.18: Liberty Public Limited Company (2000)

10 Loss per ordinary share

The loss per ordinary share is calculated by reference to the loss attributable to ordinary shareholders, after deducting dividends on preference shares. This calculation was; in 1999/00 a loss of £4.4m (1998/99: loss of £2.1m) on a weighted average number of the ordinary shares in issue during the year of 22,665,421 (1998/99: 22,665,421).

The loss attributable to ordinary shareholders and weighted average number of ordinary shares for the purpose of calculating the diluted earnings per ordinary share are identical to those used for basic earnings per ordinary share. This is because the exercise of share options would have the effect of reducing the loss per ordinary share and is therefore not dilutive under the terms of Financial Reporting Standard 14 "Earnings per share".

In order to increase a loss per share there would need to be a *negative* earnings impact resulting from conversion sufficient to increase the loss by proportionately more than the rise in the number of shares. In our view such potential ordinary shares are unlikely to be seen in practice.

It would seem that the stress the standard lays on always presenting diluted EPS, even if the amounts are negative, has led some loss making companies to bring anti-dilutive instruments into the diluted EPS calculation. An example is PPL Therapeutics, as follows:

Extract 26.19: PPL Therapeutics plc (2000)

Consolidation Profit and Loss Account [extract]

	Note	**2000**	1999
Loss per share	10		
Basic		**(23p)**	(29p)
Diluted		**(22p)**	(29p)

10 Loss per share

The basic loss per ordinary share is based on the loss after taxation of £11,233,000 (1999: £14,441,000) and on the weighted average number of ordinary shares in issue during the year of 49,685,292 (1999: 49,626,510). The diluted loss per ordinary share is based on a diluted weighted average number of shares of 50,684,882 (1999: 49,685,542). The dilutive effect of the Company share option schemes was 684,184 (1999: 43,605) and the SAYE scheme was 315,405 (1999: 15,427).

The results of PPL Therapeutics arise entirely on continuing operations, and as can be seen the only dilutive instruments are options which leads to the diluted loss per share being a lower loss than the basic one.

There is, rather counter-intuitively, one situation when a diluted loss per share could be different from the basic loss per share. It arises from the requirement to test for the dilutive impact of potential shares by reference to their effect on profits from *continuing* operations. If an overall net loss (and hence loss per share) comprised a profit on continuing activities and a larger loss on discontinued activities then potential ordinary shares could be brought into the calculation, resulting in the actual diluted loss per share that is disclosed being a smaller loss than the basic one. An illustration of how this might happen is given as follows:

Example 26.7: Computation of diluted EPS where there are overall net losses, yet profits from continuing operations

Capital structure

Issued share capital as at 31 December 1998 and 31 December 1999:
2,000,000 ordinary shares of 10p each

£1,000,000 of 5% Convertible bonds
Each £1 nominal value of bond is convertible into 2 ordinary shares.

Trading results

Net loss attributable to ordinary shareholders for the year ended 31 December 1999 is £50,000, comprising £100,000 profit from continuing operations and a loss of £150,000 from discontinued activities.

Assume corporation tax at 30%.

Computation of whether potential ordinary shares are dilutive or antidilutive

	Net profit from continuing operations	Ordinary shares	Per share
	£	No	Pence
Profit from continuing operations	100,000	2,000,000	5.000
5% Convertible bonds (1)	35,000	2,000,000	
Diluted EPS	135,000	4,000,000	3.375

(1) Increase in earnings represents interest saved of £50,000 being 5% x £1,000,000 less taxation thereon at 30% (£15,000). The increase in shares resulting from conversion would be 1,000,000 x 2.

Hence the convertible bonds are dilutive, and are used in the diluted EPS calculation as follows.

Computation of basic and diluted EPS to be disclosed on the P&L account

	Net profit attributable to ordinary shareholders	Ordinary shares	Per share
	£	No	Pence
Basic loss per share	(50,000)	2,000,000	(2.5)
5% Convertible bonds	35,000	2,000,000	
Diluted loss per share	(15,000)	4,000,000	(0.4)

6.5 Particular types of dilutive instruments

6.5.1 Convertible securities

In order to secure a lower rate of interest, companies sometimes attach benefits to loan stock or debentures in the form of conversion rights. These permit the stockholder to convert his holding in whole or part into equity capital. The right is normally exercisable between specified dates. The ultimate conversion of the loan stock will have the following effects:

(a) there will be an increase in earnings by the amount of the loan stock interest no longer payable. Because this interest is allowable for corporation tax purposes, the effect on earnings will be net of corporation tax relief; and

(b) the number of ordinary shares in issue will increase. The diluted EPS should be calculated assuming that the loan stock is converted into the maximum possible number of shares.

Example 26.8: Treatment of convertible loan stock in diluted EPS calculations

Net profit	£1,000
Ordinary shares outstanding	10,000
Basic earnings per share	10p
Convertible 10% bonds	1,000

Each block of 10 bonds is convertible into 15 ordinary shares

Interest expense for the current year relating to the liability component of the convertible bond	£100
Current and deferred tax relating to that interest expense	£30
Adjusted net profit	£1,000 + £100 - £30 = £1,070
Number of ordinary shares resulting from conversion of bond	1,500
Number of ordinary shares used to compute diluted earnings per share	10,000 + 1,500 = 11,500
Diluted earnings per share	$\frac{£1,070}{11,500} = 9.3\text{p}$

The rules for convertible preference shares are very similar to those detailed above in the case of loan stock, i.e. the dividend is added back to earnings and the maximum number of ordinary shares that could be issued on conversion should be used in the calculation.

6.5.2 *Options or warrants to subscribe for ordinary shares*

Companies may grant options to directors and employees or issue warrants which give holders (not usually employees) the right to subscribe for shares at fixed prices on specified future dates. If the options or warrants are exercised then:

(a) the number of shares in issue will be increased; and

(b) funds will flow into the company and these will produce income.

Under FRS 14 no imputed income is taken into account in respect of share options or warrants; rather the effects of such potential ordinary shares on the diluted EPS are reflected in the computation of the denominator.

For this purpose, the weighted average number of shares used in calculating the basic EPS is still increased, but not by the full number of shares that would be issued on exercise of the instruments. To work out how many additional shares to include in the denominator, the assumed proceeds from these issues are to be treated as having been received in exchange for:

- a certain number of shares at fair value (i.e. no EPS impact); and
- the remainder for no consideration (i.e. full dilution with no earnings enhancement).[58]

This means that the excess of the total number of potential shares over the number that could be issued at fair value out of the issue proceeds is included within the denominator; the calculation is illustrated as follows:

Example 26.9: Effects of share options on diluted earnings per share

Capital structure

Issued share capital for both years ending 31 December 1998 and 1999:
400,000 ordinary shares of 25p each.

Options have been granted to the directors and certain senior executives giving them the right to subscribe for ordinary shares between 2003 and 2005 at 90 pence per share.

Options outstanding at	31 December 1998	40,000
	31 December 1999	50,000

(The additional 10,000 options were granted on 1 January 1999.)

Average market value of ordinary shares:

Year ending 31 December 1998	£1.50
Year ending 31 December 1999	£1.80

Trading results

Profit for equity shareholders after taxation:

Year ending 31 December 1998	£60,000
Year ending 31 December 1999	£70,000

Calculation of diluted EPS

	1999	1998
	£	£
Profit for basic EPS	70,000	60,000

The profit is not increased for any notional income on proceeds of options issuable.

Number of equity shares after exercise of options:

	1999	1998
	No.	No.
Number of equity shares for basic EPS	400,000	400,000
Number of shares under option	50,000	40,000
Number of shares that would have been issued at fair value:		
(50,000 x £0.90)/£1.80	(25,000)	
(40,000 x £0.90/£1.50		(24,000)
Adjusted capital	425,000	416,000

	1999	1998
Diluted EPS	$= \frac{£70,000}{425,000}$	$= \frac{£60,000}{416,000}$
	= 16.47p	= 14.42p

As can be seen the profit used in the calculation is not increased, but the number of shares has been increased by 25,000 (19X1 16,000) shares which are deemed to have been issued for no consideration.

Fair value for this purpose is calculated on the basis of the average price of the ordinary shares during the reporting period.[59] These would be deemed to have been issued at the beginning of the period or, if later, the date of issue of the warrants or options. Options which are exercised or lapse in the period are included for the portion of the period during which they were outstanding.[60]

It is not immediately obvious why the fair value used should be the average for the reporting period rather than, for example, the value at balance sheet date or that on the date the instruments were issued, or the average for the period they were outstanding (if issued or lapsed in the period). The reason given is contained in paragraph 15 of Appendix II to FRS 14 – the development of the standard. This says, without further elaboration, that a period average best fits the objective of EPS as a past performance measure. That explanation seems quite clearly to rule out a year end or issue date price. However, in our view, a credible case could be made that an average price over the life of the instrument would be more relevant for instruments issued or lapsed in the year.

One practical problem of this requirement is that the average market price of ordinary shares for the reporting period may not be available. Examples would include a company only listed for part of the period, or an unlisted company giving voluntary disclosures. In such cases estimates of the market price would need to be made.

A further possible anomaly resulting from this approach surrounds partly paid shares, and is discussed below.

6.5.3 Partly paid shares

As noted at 3 above, shares issued in partly paid form are to be included in the *basic* EPS as a fraction of a share, based on dividend participation. As regards *diluted* EPS they are to be treated, to the extent that they are not entitled to participate in dividends, as the equivalent of options or warrants.[61] The mechanics of this treatment are not spelt out in the standard, but curiously the phrase 'treated as a fraction of an ordinary share' is not repeated. Whilst this could be read to mean that the remaining unpaid consideration is to be treated as the exercise price for options over *all* of the shares, the results would make little sense. The more sensible interpretation is that the unpaid capital should be viewed as the exercise price for options over the proportion of the shares *not* reflected in the basic EPS. This would mean that if the average share price for the period was the same as the total issue price, then no dilution would be reported. This gives rise to the somewhat counter-intuitive result that the additional number of shares (if any) to be included for diluted EPS will not just be a function of dividend participation, but also of the average share price for the period. An illustration of what the calculation would look like is as follows:

Example 26.10: Partly paid shares

Capital structure

Issued share capital as at 31 December 1998:
2,000,000 ordinary shares of 10p each

Issued on 1 January 1999:
500,000 part paid ordinary shares of 10p each. Full consideration of 50p per share (being fair value at 1 January 1999) paid up 50% on issue. Dividend participation 50% until fully paid. New shares remain part paid at 31 December 1999.

Average fair value of one ordinary share for the period 60p.

Trading results

Net profit attributable to ordinary shareholders for the year ended 31 December 1999: £100,000.

Computation of basic and diluted EPS

	Net profit attributable to ordinary shareholders £	Ordinary shares No	Per share Pence
Fully paid shares	100,000	2,000,000	
Partly paid shares (1)		250,000	
Basic EPS	100,000	2,250,000	4.44
Dilutive effect of partly paid shares (2)		41,667	
Diluted EPS	100,000	2,291,667	4.36

(1) 50% dividend rights for 500,000 shares.

(2) Outstanding consideration of £125,000 (500,000 x 25p), using fair value of 60p this equates to 208,333 shares, hence the number of dilutive shares deemed issued for free is 41,667 (250,000-208,333).

The example assumes the fair value of the shares over the year is higher than the issue price, which explains why some extra shares fall to be included in the diluted EPS. If the average fair value remained at the issue price of 50p then no additional shares would be included for diluted EPS.

6.5.4 *Employee share incentive plans*

The standard comments that share option and other incentive schemes are an increasingly common feature of employee remuneration, and acknowledges that they come in many forms.[62] However, for diluted EPS purposes employee share schemes are divided into two categories:

- long-term incentive schemes – where awards are based on performance criteria; and
- any other schemes.

Schemes in the first category are to be treated as contingently issuable shares (see 6.5.5 below). This gives rise to an apparent paradox relating to shares held by an employee share ownership plan (ESOP) trust. The rules for, and indeed the title, 'contingently issuable shares' clearly refers to shares which do not exist at the balance sheet date, but may be issued subsequently.[63] Shares held by an ESOP to satisfy employee options are obviously already in issue, so a literal reading of the standard would imply that these have no dilutive impact. In our view this makes little sense, and does not seem to be what the standard setters intended. A sensible interpretation would be to consider the vesting of ESOP shares (and hence ceasing to be treated as cancelled for EPS purposes[64]) as an issue for calculating diluted EPS.

Those in the second category are to be treated as options (see 6.5.2 above). They should be regarded as outstanding from the grant date, even if they vest, and hence can be realised by the employees, at some later date.[65] An example would be an unexpired loyalty period. This means that some shares may be included in diluted EPS which never, in fact, get issued to employees because they fail to remain with the company for this period. Whilst this requirement is clear, it sits rather awkwardly with the rules for contingently issuable shares which, as discussed at 6.5.5 below, tend to restrict the number of potential shares accounted for. Furthermore the proceeds figure to be used in calculating the dilution under such schemes should be increased by any UITF 17 cost which has yet to be charged to the profit and loss account. The standard provides an example of this latter point (Example 5), as follows:

Example 26.11: Share option scheme not related to performance

Company A has in place an employee share option scheme that awards share options to employees and their dependants on the basis of period of service with the company.

The provisions of the scheme are as follows at the 20X0 year-end.

Date of grant	1 January 20X0
Market price at grant date	£4.00
Exercise price of option	£2.50
Date of vesting	31 December 20X2
Number of shares under option	1 million

Applying UITF 17, the profit and loss account is charged with 50p per option in each of the three years 20X0-20X2.

Net profit for year 20X0	£1,200,000
Weighted average number of ordinary shares outstanding	5 million
Average fair value of an ordinary share during the year	£5.00
Assumed proceeds per option	£3.50 (exercise price of £2.50 and compensation cost attributable to future service, not yet recognised, of £1.00).
	Next year £3.00 (ie £2.50 plus 50p).

Computation of earnings per share

	per share	earnings	shares
Net profit for year 20X0		£1,200,000	
Weighted average shares outstanding for 20X0			5m
Basic earnings per share	24p		
Number of shares under option			1m
Number of shares that would have been issued at fair value: (1 million x £3.50) / £5.00			(0.7m)
Diluted earnings per share	22.6p	£1,200,000	5.3m

This example alludes to the fact that the dilutive effect of the options increases over the three years as the deemed proceeds on exercise of the options reduces. The computational impact of this increasing dilution can be illustrated as follows. Assuming the average share price remained constant for the remaining two years, the number of shares used in the diluted EPS calculation would increase as follows:

	20X1	20X2
Weighted average shares outstanding	5m	5m
Number of shares under option	1m	1m
Number of shares that would have been issued at fair value:		
20X1: (1 million x £3.00) / £5.00	(0.6m)	
20X2: (1 million x £2.50) / £5.00		(0.5m)
Number of shares for diluted EPS	5.4m	5.5m

Assuming constant net profit of £1.2m for these years, diluted EPS would fall to 22.2p in 20X1 and 21.8p in 20X2.

FRS 14 rationalises this escalating dilution as follows: 'Initially, dilution is less because part of the consideration consists of future services not yet received. It becomes greater, over time, as the entity's earnings reflect the benefits of having received those services.'[66] Given that this provision only applies to non-performance based share schemes, then any UITF 17 cost that is spread forward (rather than expensed immediately) must presumably relate to a loyalty period. In our view such a treatment under UITF 17 would be rare, as that abstract says, 'Where a further period of continued employment is required before the participants become unconditionally entitled to the shares, the period over which the cost is recognised should not normally include that period unless it is clear that the effect of the scheme is to reward services over the longer period.'[67]

6.5.5 Contingently issuable shares

Whereas SSAP 3 gave no guidance on contingently issuable shares, FRS 14 contains eight detailed paragraphs and a numerical worked example. The basic rule is that the number of contingently issuable shares to be included in the diluted EPS calculation is 'based on the number of shares that would be issuable if the end of the reporting period was the end of the contingency period'.[68] This requirement to look at the status of the contingency at the balance sheet date, rather than to consider the most likely outcome, seems to have the overall result of *reducing* the amount of dilution disclosed. Furthermore, these detailed rules on contingently issuable shares (which are contained in explanatory sections of the standard) are at odds with the more general requirement to 'give effect to *all* dilutive potential ordinary shares outstanding during the period'.[69]

Having introduced the basic rule for contingently issuable shares the standard goes on to explore it in more detail, and includes some briefly sketched narrative examples and one numerical worked example. The discussions cover three broad categories: earnings-based contingencies, share-price-based contingencies, and other contingencies. These are discussed in turn below.

A Earnings-based contingencies

When the number of shares that could be issued depends on earnings, the basic rule above (i.e. how many shares would be issued if the reporting date was the end of the contingency period) is applied very strictly. In deciding how many shares should be included it is assumed that no more profits will be earned after the balance sheet date. This is a reversal of the line taken in FRED 14, which required a steady state extrapolation of earnings.[70] The narrative example given is 'if the number of shares to be issued depends on whether profits average £100,000 over a three-year period, the condition is expressed as in terms of a cumulative target of £300,000 over the three-year period. If, at the end of the first year, profits are £150,000, no additional shares are brought into the calculation.'[71] This example illustrates the new principle that a contingency which is expressed in terms of an average over a number of reporting periods should be treated as if it were a cumulative target over the entire period.

We do not agree that such a methodology gives the most meaningful EPS figure. A better approach, in our view, would have been to base the dilution on a reasonable assessment of the outcome of the contingency; this would also be more consistent with the treatment of other contingent forms of finance. For example if contingent consideration under an earn-out clause is payable in cash, FRS 7 requires the best estimate of the amount payable to be provided at its present value, with the result that EPS will bear interest on this amount as the discount unwinds. It would seem appropriate for diluted EPS similarly to reflect the likely dilution when the consideration is in the form of shares. Notwithstanding this, the rule for contingencies determined solely by an entity's earnings is now clear. However, the treatment of contingencies which are partly determined by earnings and partly by other criteria is less clear.

The standard only discusses earnings criteria based on *absolute* measures; in the example above a cumulative profit of £300,000. In our experience such criteria are rare. In practice criteria are often phrased in terms of *relative* performance against an external benchmark. Examples would be earnings growth targets of RPI plus 2% or EPS growth being in the top quartile of a group of competitors. For contingencies such as these it is impossible to establish an absolute target in order to ask whether it is met at the year end. For example, consider the earnings contingency in FRS 14, discussed above, to average profits of £100,000 over a three-year period. If this instead required the profits to be £100,000 rising in line with RPI, it would be impossible to express it as a cumulative hurdle. Until the end of the three year period the absolute level of profit required would be unknown; it would be more or less than £300,000 depending on the level of inflation or deflation over the period.

There would seem to be (at least) two different ways of interpreting the requirements of FRS 14 in such a scenario, each resulting in a different diluted EPS figure. One approach would be to consider such criteria as being 'based on a condition other than earnings or market price'. That would mean (as discussed under C below) that the number of shares brought into diluted EPS would be based on the status of the condition at the balance sheet date.[72] So, if the target was earnings growth of RPI plus 2% over three years and at the end of year one earnings growth had been RPI plus 3%, then all the shares would be included for diluted EPS. An alternative approach would be to regard it as an earnings-based contingency and make an assumption as to future RPI movements over the contingency period. This would allow a cumulative hurdle to be calculated and compared with actual earnings to date. Given the lack of clarity in the standard, it seems likely that either of the above approaches may be selected in practice.

B Share-price-based contingencies

The provisions here are more straightforward. The share price used to compute how many, if any, shares to bring in to the calculation is 'the current market price at the end of the current reporting period or the average over a specified period, depending on the terms of the underlying contract'.[73] However, in cases where the quantity of shares is derived from a period average share price, it is not clear how 'the average over a specified period' should be interpreted. At any time within the contingency period the choice would be between average to date and final average if the share price remained at its current level. Consistency with the rules for earnings-based contingencies would imply that the former is required by the standard.

There is a specific rule for deferred consideration agreements, where a fixed monetary sum is to be satisfied by a variable quantity of shares. In such cases the market price at the balance sheet date is to be used.[74]

C Other contingencies

The requirement regarding contingencies not driven by earnings or share price is 'shares are included on the assumption that the current status of the condition at the end of the reporting period will remain unchanged until the end of the contingency period.'[75]

The standard illustrates the 'other contingency' rules as follows: 'if a further issue of shares is generated on the opening of the tenth new retail outlet and at the year end only five have been opened, no contingently issuable shares are included in the diluted earnings per share computation.'[76] As is specifically required for earnings-based contingencies discussed above, it would seem that such conditions are always deemed to be expressed as a cumulative hurdle which may or may not be met by the balance sheet date. Accordingly, the required treatment would be the same if the condition had been expressed in terms of achieving a certain average annual level of shop openings. Once again it seems inappropriate to us that management plans for a shop opening programme would be disregarded for EPS purposes when such estimates would be essential in other accounting areas, for example to determine the reasonable estimates required by FRS 7 or UITF 17, or to support any deferred tax computations.

7 PRESENTATION, RESTATEMENT AND DISCLOSURE

7.1 Presentation

Disclosure of basic and diluted EPS is required on the face of the profit and loss account, with equal prominence, for each class of ordinary shares that has a different right to share in the profit for the period.[77] In practice however, more than one class of ordinary share is rarely seen. Diluted EPS must always be disclosed, even when the basic EPS is a loss per share, although as discussed at 6.4 above in most cases these will be the same.[78] The specific exemption in SSAP 3 on grounds of materiality (dilution less than 5%) was dropped in FRS 14. Comparative figures are to be given in all cases. Appendix II to the standard reveals the reason for removing the 5% test, by reiterating that EPS under FRS 14 is a past performance measure rather than a warning signal for future dilution.[79] This logic also explains the requirement to give basic and diluted EPS for all periods presented, hence showing trends over time. A typical example of profit and loss account presentation is Marks and Spencer as shown in Extract 26.12 at 5.5.1 above. That example illustrates a literal reading of the standard by presenting a separate line for each of basic and diluted EPS, even though the amounts are identical (as rounded to one tenth of a penny). Another approach would be to present one line in the profit and loss account, and amend the title accordingly for example 'basic and diluted earnings per share'.

7.2 Restatement

FRS 14 contains requirements to restate prior periods' EPS for events that change the number of shares outstanding without a corresponding change in resources. Additionally it specifies circumstances when EPS should not be restated.

Basic and diluted EPS for all periods presented should be adjusted for:[80]

- events (other than the conversion of potential ordinary shares) which change the number of ordinary or potential ordinary shares without a corresponding change in resources (discussed at 4.3 above); and
- the effects of business combinations that are accounted for as a merger under FRS 6 (discussed at 4.6 above).

No adjustment should be made:

- to basic or diluted EPS when a share consolidation is combined with a special dividend where the overall commercial effect is that of a share repurchase at fair value[81] (discussed at 4.3.2 above);
- to prior period diluted EPS for changes in the assumptions used or for the conversion of potential ordinary shares into ordinary shares;[82] and
- to prior period diluted EPS as a result of a contingency period coming to an end without the conditions attaching to contingently issuable shares being met.[83]

FRS 14 also contains some rules for figures in any historical summary, which are the same as those previously contained in SSAP 3.

- any restatement required by the rules noted above should be applied retrospectively to all figures in the historical summary, with the cumulative effect on EPS taken into account;[84]
- restated figures are described as such and clearly distinguished from non-adjusted data;[85]
- the same requirements for restatement and description should be applied to any dividend per share figures included in the summary;[86] and
- any dividend cover figures presented should be based on the theoretical maximum dividend (i.e. after allowing for any further tax triggered by a distribution) rather than simply total earnings.[87]

It is not clear however, given that such summaries are voluntary and usually presented outside the accounts, what authority an accounting standard has regarding them.

7.3 Disclosure

7.3.1 *Components of the calculation*

For each class of ordinary share, disclosure is required, for both the basic and diluted EPS, of the numerators and denominators used in the calculations. The numerators are to be reconciled to the net profit or loss for the period and the denominators are to be reconciled to each other (see, for example, Extract 26.12 at 5.5.1 above).[88] Companies choosing to present additional EPS figures are required to reconcile these to those required by the standard and explain why the additional version is given. The reconciliation should list the items for which adjustment is being made, and disclose their individual effect on the calculation.[89] Presentation of additional EPS is discussed at 5.5 above.

7.3.2 *Post year end share transactions*

Changes in share capital which happen after the year end will fall into two categories, similar to adjusting and non-adjusting events under SSAP 17 *Accounting for post balance sheet events*. The first category comprises those transactions which change the number of shares outstanding without a corresponding change in resources (bonus issues, share consolidations etc). As described at 4.5 above such transactions occurring before the issue of the accounts will be incorporated in the EPS calculations for all periods presented. When the EPS calculations reflect such changes in the number of shares, that fact should be disclosed.[90] The second category will comprise any other transactions in ordinary shares or potential ordinary shares. Disclosure is required of a description of any such transactions when 'they are of such importance that non-disclosure would affect the ability of users of the financial statements to make proper evaluations and decisions.'[91] The standard gives the following examples of the types of transactions involved:[92]

(a) the issue of shares for cash;

(b) the issue of shares when the proceeds are used to repay debt or preference shares outstanding at the balance sheet date;

(c) the redemption of ordinary shares;

(d) the issue of potential ordinary shares;

(e) the buy back of ordinary shares outstanding;

(f) the conversion of potential ordinary shares, outstanding at the balance sheet date, into ordinary shares; and

(g) the achievement of conditions that would result in the issue of contingently issuable shares.

It is not clear how these latter disclosures, which were not included in the exposure draft, help achieve the objective of a consistently calculated EPS as a measure of past performance. Furthermore, we are not sure that this requirement adds any more disclosure to that which would be required under SSAP 17. It seems the ASB must have in contemplation some post balance sheet events which do not affect users' ability to 'reach a proper understanding of the financial position' (the test in

SSAP 17), but which do affect their ability to 'make proper evaluations and decisions'. Unfortunately the standard does not give any examples to illustrate the subtlety of this distinction.

7.3.3 *Share consolidation with a special dividend*

As discussed at 4.3.2 above, in certain circumstances no adjustment is made to prior periods' EPS when a share consolidation is combined with a special dividend. Where that is the case disclosure should be made of that fact.[93]

7.3.4 *Potential ordinary shares*

The standard notes that the terms and conditions of potential ordinary shares may determine whether they are dilutive, and if so the effect they will have on the figures used in the diluted EPS calculation. In such cases it encourages, but does not require, disclosure of those terms and conditions.[94]

8 IAS REQUIREMENTS

The relevant international standard is IAS 33 – *Earnings Per Share* – which was published in June 1997. IAS 33 is applicable for accounting periods beginning on or after 1 January 1998, with earlier application encouraged.

As noted earlier, FRS 14 is based on IAS 33, and adopts a similar structure and wording. Accordingly, the computation and presentation of EPS figures under IAS 33 will be familiar to both preparers and users of UK GAAP accounts, as illustrated in the following extract.

Extract 26.20: Mandarin Oriental International Limited (2000)

Consolidated profit and loss account [extract]

	Note	**2000 USc**	1999 USc
Earnings per share	*7*		
– basic		**2.21**	2.39
– diluted		**2.20**	2.38
Earnings per share excluding non-recurring items	*7*		
– basic		**1.74**	2.39
– diluted		**1.74**	2.38

7 EARNINGS PER SHARE

Basic earnings per share are calculated on the profit after tax and minority interests of US$18.11 million (1999: US$17.4 million) and on the weighted average number 820.4 million shares (1999: 726.7 million shares) in issue during the year. The weighted average number of shares excludes shares held by the Trustee of the Senior Executive Share Incentive Schemes (refer note 18).

Diluted earnings per share are calculated on the weighted average number of shares after adjusting for the number of shares which are deemed to be issued for no consideration under the Senior Executive Share Incentive Schemes based on the average share price during the year. The convertible bonds are anti-dilutive and therefore ignored in calculating diluted earnings per share.

	Ordinary shares in millions	
	2000	1999
Weighted average number of shares in issue	**820.4**	726.7
Adjustment for shares deemed to be issued for no consideration	**2.0**	1.7
Weighted average number of shares for diluted earnings per share	**822.4**	728.4

Earnings per share excluding non-recurring items for 2000 were calculated on the profit after tax and minority interests and after adjusting for the non-recurring items of US$3.8 million.

Set out below is a discussion of the requirements of IAS 33 which cross refers where necessary to the foregoing analysis of FRS 14 and also highlights the (relatively minor) differences between the two standards.

8.1 Scope of IAS 33

Like FRS 14, IAS 33 applies to all entities whose ordinary shares or potential ordinary shares are publicly traded, or are in the process of becoming so.[95] Earnings per share information only needs to be presented based on consolidated information if the entity publishes both parent and consolidated financial statements.[96]

As is the case under FRS 14, any voluntarily disclosed EPS information must be prepared in accordance with IAS 33.[97] As discussed at 2.2 above, FRS 14 explicitly requires that its rules be applied for computing any other per-share figures presented. IAS 33 does not extend its scope in this way.

8.2 Basic earnings per share

Basic earnings per share is calculated by dividing net profit or loss for the period attributable to ordinary shareholders by the weighted average number of ordinary shares outstanding during the period.[98]

The net profit or loss attributable to ordinary shareholders is the net profit or loss for the period minus preference dividends, which are calculated as the sum of dividends declared on non-cumulative preference shares plus the required dividends in respect of cumulative preference shares.[99] One issue which has been under consideration by the SIC relates to the redemption of preference shares. The SIC considered whether any difference between the value of consideration given and the carrying amount of a preference share classified as equity represents a preference dividend when the share is redeemed. At its meeting in May 2001, the SIC preliminarily concluded that a premium or discount does represent a preference dividend for EPS purposes. In July 2001, however, the SIC removed the topic from its agenda, noting that it expected the issue to be dealt with as part of the improvements project which the IASB had added to its agenda.

The weighted average number of ordinary shares outstanding takes into account the portion of the period that the ordinary shares were outstanding, by applying a time-weighting factor to the number of shares.[100] IAS 33 presents the same guidance on determining the issue date of new ordinary shares as FRS 14, discussed at 3 above, supplemented by one further example. Where shares are issued in consideration for the rendering of services, they should be included in the basic

EPS computation as the services are rendered.[101] Partially paid shares are treated, in determining the weighted average number of shares outstanding, as a fraction of an ordinary share based on their relative dividend entitlement.[102]

Changes in the number of ordinary shares outstanding during the period without a corresponding change in resources (other than the conversion of potential ordinary shares), such as a bonus issue, share split, share consolidation or the bonus element of a rights issue are treated by IAS 33 in the same way as FRS 14, as discussed at 4.3 above.[103] In summary, the number of shares used in calculating EPS for all periods presented should be adjusted as follows:

- for share splits, share consolidations and bonus issues, the number of ordinary shares outstanding before the event should be adjusted for the proportionate change in the number of shares as if the event occurred at the beginning of the earliest period presented;[104] and
- for a rights issue, the number of ordinary shares outstanding before the event should be multiplied by an adjustment factor, computed as the fair value per share immediately before the exercise of rights divided by the theoretical ex-rights fair value per share (illustrated at 4.3.3 above).[105]

As described at 4.3.2 above, FRS 14 requires that the usual restatement of EPS for a share consolidation is not applied when the consolidation is accompanied by a special dividend where the overall effect is a similar to a share buy-back at fair value. IAS 33 does not address such 'in substance' buy-backs, however a similar approach is seen in practice under IAS as illustrated in the following extract.

Extract 26.21: Dairy Farm International Holdings Limited (1999)

6. EARNINGS PER SHARE [extract]

Basic earnings per share are calculated on the profit attributable to ordinary shareholders of US$37.3 million (1998: US$157.3 million) and on the weighted average number of 1,795.7 million ordinary shares issued during the year (1998: 1,833.0 million). The weighted average number excludes the shares held by the Trustee under the Senior Executive Share Incentive Schemes (note 19).

18. SHARE CAPITAL [extract]

In October 1999, every ten ordinary shares of US¢5 each were consolidated into nine new ordinary shares of US¢5 5/9 each.

CORPORATE GOVERNANCE [extract]

Special Dividend and Share Capital Consolidation

At a Special General Meeting held on 30th September 1999, shareholders approved the payment of a special dividend of US¢9.65 per ordinary share and the consolidation of every ten ordinary shares of US¢5 each into nine new ordinary shares of US¢5 5/9 each. As a result, an aggregate of 1,886,481,512 were consolidated into 1,691,418,772 new ordinary shares of US¢5 5/9 each.

Although not expressly discussed by Dairy Farm, it seems the consolidation and special dividend have been treated, for EPS purposes, as a re-purchase of shares at fair value. This is because the quantity of shares disclosed in the 1999 accounts as used in the computation for the prior period (1,833 million shares) is the same as that used in the 1998 accounts. This indicates that the comparative EPS figure has not been adjusted to take account of the share consolidation.

As is the case under FRS 14, EPS figures should also be restated when such changes in capital structure occur after the balance sheet date but before issue of the financial statements. Where earnings per share information has been restated this fact should be disclosed.[106]

Unlike FRS 14, IAS 33 does not discuss the treatment of ordinary shares of the reporting entity that are held by a group member. Although not explicitly addressed by the requirements of the standard, it is clear from one of the illustrative examples in IAS 33 that treasury shares (own shares held by the issuing company) are presented as a deduction from the number of shares outstanding and hence not taken into account in calculating the weighted average number of shares outstanding.[107] Extracts 26.20 and 26.21 above both illustrate companies excluding shares held in trust under share incentive schemes.

IAS 33 recognises that an enterprise may have more than one class of ordinary shares,[108] and requires the presentation of separate EPS figures for each class that has a different right to share in the net profit for the period.[109]

Shares which are issuable upon the satisfaction of certain conditions (contingently issuable shares) should be considered outstanding, and included in the basic EPS calculation, from the date that all conditions for their issuance have been met. IAS 33 goes on to say that conditionally returnable shares are treated as contingently issuable shares.[110] Although this is not entirely clear, it presumably means that, just as contingently issuable shares are not brought into basic EPS until all conditions for their issue are met, so contingently returnable shares *remain* in the basic EPS calculation until all conditions for their return are met.

8.3 Diluted earnings per share

To calculate diluted EPS, IAS 33 requires similar adjustments to be made to the earnings figure and the number of shares used for basic EPS so as to reflect the effects of potential ordinary shares, as are required by FRS 14 and discussed at 6 above.[111]

The net profit or loss attributable to ordinary shareholders, as used in the calculation of basic earnings per share, must be adjusted for the after-tax effect of:

- any dividends on dilutive potential ordinary shares which have been deducted in arriving at the net profit attributable to ordinary shareholders;
- interest recognised in the period for the dilutive potential ordinary shares; and
- any other changes in income or expense that would result from the conversion of the dilutive potential ordinary shares.[112]

The standard goes on to explain that the requisite earnings adjustments would include:

- any consequential changes to the expense recognised for non-discretionary employee profit sharing plans;[113] and
- fees and discount or premium that are accounted for as yield adjustments.[114]

Potential ordinary shares have the same meaning under IAS 33 as under FRS 14 (discussed at 6.1 above).[115] In particular, potential ordinary shares issued by subsidiaries, associates or joint ventures which are convertible into either ordinary shares of the issuing entity or the reporting entity should be included in the computation (if the effect is dilutive).[116]

In calculating diluted EPS, IAS 33 requires that the weighted average number of ordinary shares outstanding, as used in the calculation of basic earnings per share, be adjusted for the weighted average number of ordinary shares that would be issued on the conversion of all dilutive potential ordinary shares. The number of shares which would be issued on conversion is determined from the terms of the instrument involved, assuming the most advantageous conversion rate or exercise price from the standpoint of the holder.[117] The conversion into ordinary shares is deemed to have taken place at the beginning of the reporting period or the later date of issue of the potential ordinary shares.[118] The diluted EPS for any prior period presented should not be restated for changes in the assumptions used or for the conversion of potential ordinary shares.[119]

Options and other share purchase arrangements are dilutive when they would result in the issue of shares for less than fair value.[120] The dilutive effect of options is reflected by increasing the number of shares in the denominator by the difference between the number of ordinary shares issued and the number of shares that would have been issued at fair value (the average price of ordinary shares during the period) in exchange for the same proceeds.[121] Fair value for these purposes is the average price of the shares during the year.[122] IAS 33 observes that the method it prescribes for calculating the dilutive effect of options produces the same result as the treasury stock method which is used in some countries. It goes on to note, however, that this does not imply that the enterprise has contracted to purchase its own shares, which may not be practicable in certain circumstances or legal in some jurisdictions.[123]

Partly paid shares that are not entitled to dividends must be treated as the equivalent of warrants or options.[124]

Potential ordinary shares should be treated as dilutive when, and only when, their conversion to ordinary shares would decrease net profit per share from continuing ordinary operations.[125] Net profit from continuing ordinary activities is the net profit from continuing activities (as defined by IAS 8, discussed at 3.2 in Chapter 25) after deducting preference dividends and after excluding items relating to discontinued operations. It therefore excludes extraordinary items and the effects of changes in accounting policies and corrections of fundamental errors.[126] Potential ordinary shares are anti-dilutive if their conversion would increase earnings, or decrease a loss, per share from continuing ordinary operations. Such instruments are ignored in calculating diluted earnings per share.[127]

To maximise the dilution of basic earnings per share, IAS 33 requires that each issue or series of potential share is considered in turn, with the most dilutive potential ordinary shares are taken into account first.[128] This is the same approach as that taken in FRS 14, discussed at 6.3.1 above.

Potential ordinary shares which were cancelled or which lapsed during the period should be included in the diluted EPS calculation for the period that they were outstanding. Potential ordinary shares that have been converted during the period should be included in the calculation of diluted EPS from the beginning of the period to the date of conversion, from that point on they will be included in both basic and diluted EPS.[129]

Employee share options meet the definition of potential ordinary shares and should be taken into account in calculating diluted earnings per share. However, IAS 33 does not provide any specific guidance in this area, which FRS 14 does (see 6.5.4 above).

As discussed at 6.2.2 above, FRS 14 provides that where a contract may be settled either in shares or in cash, and a stated policy or past experience provide a reasonable basis for concluding how the contract will be settled, then that policy or experience should be followed when calculating diluted EPS. IAS 33 does not specifically discuss these types of contracts, other that indirectly by defining a potential ordinary share as 'a financial instrument or other contract that *may* [emphasis added] entitle its holder to ordinary shares.'[130] The issue was considered by the SIC in February 2000, which concluded that 'All financial instruments or other contracts that may result in the issuance of ordinary shares of the reporting enterprise to the holder of the financial instrument or other contract, at the option of the issuer or the holder, are potential ordinary shares of the entity.'[131] The SIC explained their decision thus: 'An intended manner of settlement, or policy or past pattern of choosing a particular settlement method, does not overcome the possibility that the holder may be entitled to receive ordinary shares under the terms of the financial instrument or other contract.'[132]

IAS 33 contains the same basic rule for contingently issuable shares as FRS 14. They should treated as outstanding as of the beginning of the period (or date of the contingent share agreement if later) if the conditions for issuance have been met. If the conditions have not been met, the number of contingently issuable shares included in the diluted EPS calculation should be based on the number of shares that would be issuable if the end of the reporting period were the end of the contingency period and if the result would be dilutive.[133] These rules also apply to conditionally issuable potential shares. Restatement of earnings per share information is not permitted if the conditions are not met when the contingency period expires.[134] FRS 14 provides, in addition to these basic rules, further detailed guidance regarding particular types of contingently issuable shares (discussed at 6.5.5 above) which is not discussed by IAS 33. It is possible, therefore, that the same contingency could be treated differently (for EPS purposes) under the two standards.

8.4 Presentation and Disclosure

IAS 33 requires basic and diluted EPS to be presented on the face of the income statement with equal prominence for all periods presented, even if the amounts are negative (a loss per share). [135] This information must be given for each class of ordinary shares that has a different right to participate in the net profit for the period.[136] In addition, the following must be disclosed:

- the amounts used as the numerators in calculating basic and diluted earnings per share, and a reconciliation of those amounts to the net profit or loss for the period;
- the weighted average number of ordinary shares used as the denominator in calculating basic and diluted earnings per share, and a reconciliation of these denominators to each other; and [137]
- if an additional EPS figure is presented based on a component of net profit which is not reported as a line item in the income statement, a reconciliation must be provided between that component and a line item in the income statement.[138]

The standard also encourages disclosure of certain additional information as follows:

- the terms and conditions of financial instruments and other contracts generating potential ordinary shares, whether or not such disclosure is required by IAS 32 (discussed in Chapter 10 at 5);[139] and
- a description of transactions in shares or potential shares (other than capitalisation issues or share splits) which happen after the balance sheet date.[140]

9 CONCLUSION

In our view ratios for financial analysis, like EPS, do not properly fall within the remit of accounting standard setters. Companies use their annual report and accounts to communicate with shareholders on a variety of issues, many of which are supplementary to giving a true and fair view of profit for the period and the state of affairs at the balance sheet date. A widespread practice of giving information is not, of itself, sufficient grounds for regulators to start specifying computational methods. Many companies frequently disclose other financial analysis statistics, such as return on capital and gearing, yet (thankfully) there seems no impetus for accounting standards on these. Indeed the stated view of the ASB that 'it is not possible to distil the performance of a complex organisation into a single measure'[141] sits rather uneasily with an accounting standard requiring companies to do just that (or two such measures if one counts the diluted EPS).

The case for international harmonisation is similarly a nebulous one. It is true that FRS 14 and IAS 33 prescribe virtually identical denominators for the EPS calculation. However, given the potentially wide ranging GAAP differences affecting the numerator it is hard to see what is achieved by such harmonisation.

As regards the content of FRS 14, most of its provisions are not unreasonable and should prove workable for companies. It is a shame, however, that some of the more complex issues (particularly contingently issuable shares) were not more thoroughly field tested in a UK context, which may have helped remove some of the difficulties discussed earlier.

References

1 FRS 14, *Earnings per share*, ASB, October 1998, para. 1.
2 *Ibid.*, para. 3.
3 *Ibid.*, para. 4.
4 *Ibid.*, para. 8.
5 *Ibid.*, para. 9.
6 *Ibid.*, para. 10.
7 *Ibid.*, para. 13.
8 *Ibid.*, para. 19.
9 *Ibid.*, para. 16.
10 *Ibid.*, para. 17.
11 *Ibid.*, para. 17.
12 *Ibid.*, para. 20.
13 *Ibid.*, para. 14.
14 *Ibid.*, para. 21.
15 *Ibid.*, para. 63.
16 *Ibid.*, para. 22.
17 *Ibid.*, para. 77.
18 *Ibid.*, para. 76.
19 *Ibid.*, para. 63.
20 *Ibid.*, para. 26.
21 *Ibid.*, para. 24.
22 *Ibid.*, para. 63.
23 *Ibid.*, para. 24.
24 *Ibid.*, para. 24.
25 FRS 5, *Reporting the substance of transactions*, ASB, April 1994, para. 14.
26 FRS 14, para. 24.
27 *Ibid.*, para. 62.
28 *Ibid.*, para. 21.
29 *Ibid.*, para. 63.
30 *Ibid.*, para. 18.
31 FRS 2, *Accounting for subsidiary undertakings*, ASB, July 1992, para. 45.
32 FRS 14, para. 18.
33 *Ibid.*, para. 76.
34 *Ibid.*, paras. 10 and 11.
35 *Ibid.*, para. 12.
36 *Ibid.*, para. 13.
37 FRS 3, para. 25.
38 FRS 14, para. 74.
39 *Ibid.*, para. 73.
40 *Ibid.*, para. 74.
41 *Ibid.*, para. 8.
42 *Ibid.*, para. 2.
43 *Ibid.*, para. 69.
44 *Ibid.*, para. 29.
45 *Ibid.*, para. 53.
46 *Ibid.*, para. 55.
47 *Ibid.*, para. 31 and 32.
48 *Ibid.*, para. 31.
49 *Ibid.*, para. 32.
50 *Ibid.*, para. 61.
51 *Ibid.*, para. 56.
52 *Ibid.*, para. 60.
53 *Ibid.*, para. 59.
54 *Ibid.*, Appendix 1, para. 17.
55 *Ibid.*, Appendix 1, para. 19.
56 *Ibid.*, para. 70.
57 *Ibid.*, para. 56.
58 *Ibid.*, para. 35.
59 *Ibid.*, para. 36.
60 *Ibid.*, para. 62.
61 *Ibid.*, para. 34.
62 *Ibid.*, para. 39.
63 *Ibid.*, para. 46.
64 *Ibid.*, para. 16.
65 *Ibid.*, para. 41.
66 *Ibid.*, para. 42.
67 UITF 17, para. 13(d).
68 FRS 14, para. 46.
69 *Ibid.*, para. 29.
70 FRED 16 Supplement, para. 41D
71 FRS 14, para. 46.
72 *Ibid.*, para. 49.
73 *Ibid.*, para. 47.
74 *Ibid.*, para. 48.
75 *Ibid.*, para. 49.
76 *Ibid.*, para. 49.
77 *Ibid.*, para. 69.
78 *Ibid.*, para. 70.
79 *Ibid.*, Appendix 1, para. 24.
80 *Ibid.*, para. 63.
81 *Ibid.*, para. 64.
82 *Ibid.*, para. 65.
83 *Ibid.*, para. 52.
84 *Ibid.*, para. 76.
85 *Ibid.*, para. 76.
86 *Ibid.*, para. 77.
87 *Ibid.*, para. 78.
88 *Ibid.*, para. 71.
89 *Ibid.*, para. 74.
90 *Ibid.*, para. 63.
91 *Ibid.*, para. 66.
92 *Ibid.*, para. 67.
93 *Ibid.*, para. 64.
94 *Ibid.*, para. 72.
95 IAS 33, *Earnings Per Share*, IASC, February 1997, para. 1.
96 *Ibid.*, para. 2.
97 *Ibid.*, para. 4.
98 *Ibid.*, para. 10.
99 *Ibid.*, paras. 11-13.
100 *Ibid.*, paras. 14, 15 and 17.
101 *Ibid.*, para. 16.
102 *Ibid.*, para. 18.
103 *Ibid.*, paras. 20 and 21.
104 *Ibid.*, para. 22.
105 *Ibid.*, para. 23.
106 *Ibid.*, para. 43.

107 *Ibid.*, para. 15.
108 *Ibid.*, para. 7.
109 *Ibid.*, para. 47.
110 *Ibid.*, para. 19.
111 *Ibid.*, para. 24 and 25.
112 *Ibid.*, para. 26.
113 *Ibid.*, para. 28.
114 *Ibid.*, para. 27.
115 *Ibid.*, paras. 6 and 8.
116 *Ibid.*, para. 32.
117 *Ibid.*, para. 30.
118 *Ibid.*, para. 29.
119 *Ibid.*, para. 44.
120 *Ibid.*, para. 35.
121 *Ibid.*, para. 33.
122 *Ibid.*, para. 34.
123 *Ibid.*, para. 36.
124 *Ibid.*, para. 37.
125 *Ibid.*, para. 38.
126 *Ibid.*, para. 39.
127 *Ibid.*, para. 40.
128 *Ibid.*, para. 41.
129 *Ibid.*, para. 42.
130 *Ibid.*, para. 6.
131 SIC-24, *Earnings Per Share – Financial Instruments and Other Contracts that May Be Settled in Shares,* Standing Interpretations Committee, February 2000, para. 4.
132 *Ibid.*, para. 6.
133 IAS 33, para. 31.
134 *Ibid.*, para. 31.
135 *Ibid.*, paras. 47 and 48.
136 *Ibid.*, para. 47.
137 *Ibid.*, para. 49.
138 *Ibid.*, para. 51.
139 *Ibid.*, para. 50.
140 *Ibid.*, para. 45.
141 FRS 3, para. 52.

Chapter 27 Post balance sheet events

1 INTRODUCTION

The relevant standard in the UK is SSAP 17 – *Accounting for post balance sheet events*, which was issued by the ASC in August 1980. This adopted a similar approach to that adopted in the then equivalent international standard, IAS 10 – *Contingencies and Events Occurring After the Balance Sheet Date*, which was issued in October 1978. A revised version of the international standard was issued in May 1999 dealing only with this topic, IAS 10 – *Events After the Balance Sheet Date*, but this only made a number of limited changes to the standard.

'Post balance sheet events' are defined by SSAP 17 as 'those events, both favourable and unfavourable, which occur between the balance sheet date and the date on which the financial statements are approved by the board of directors'.[1] IAS 10 defines them in almost identical terms.[2] The definitions, therefore, incorporate all events occurring between those dates – irrespective of whether or not they relate to conditions which existed at the balance sheet date. Consequently, the principal issue to be resolved is which post balance sheet events should be reflected in the financial statements?

Since the financial statements of an entity purport to present, inter alia, its financial position at the balance sheet date, it is clear that the statements should be adjusted for all post balance sheet events which offer greater clarity of conditions that existed at the balance sheet date. Both standards therefore require that entities should adjust the amounts recognised in the financial statements for those 'adjusting events' that provide evidence of conditions that existed at the balance sheet date. As far as those post balance sheet events which concern conditions that only arose after the balance sheet date, these should not be recognised in the financial statements. However, where such non-adjusting events are significant both standards call for disclosures to be made.

However, the application of the prudence concept might take this further and suggest that *all* post balance sheet events which adversely affect the value of assets and liabilities should be reflected in financial statements – even if they relate to conditions which arise subsequent to the balance sheet date. Whether provisions should be made will depend on the particular circumstances and the requirements of more relevant accounting standards; in particular, the recently issued standards on impairment (FRS 11[3] and IAS 36[4]) and provisions (FRS 12[5] and IAS 37[6]). These standards are discussed in Chapters 13 and 28 respectively.

One exception to their general rule of not making adjustments for non-adjusting events made by the standards is where the going concern basis is no longer appropriate.

In addition to the above, SSAP 17 also attempts to deal with the practice of 'window dressing' – a practice of manipulating the balance sheet by going outside the normal trading pattern of the business on a short-term basis in order to display a more favourable financial position. This could be done by either delaying or bringing forward specific transactions or by entering into transactions which are reversed shortly after the balance sheet date.

The requirements of SSAP 17 and practical issues resulting therefrom are dealt with at 2 and 3 below. The international requirements are dealt with at 4 below.

2 REQUIREMENTS OF SSAP 17

2.1 Definitions

As stated above, SSAP 17 defines post balance sheet events as 'those events, both favourable and unfavourable, which occur between the balance sheet date and the date on which the financial statements are approved by the board of directors'.[7]

This therefore includes events that provide additional evidence as to conditions which existed at the balance sheet date and those that do not.

Adjusting events are 'post balance sheet events which provide additional evidence of conditions existing at the balance sheet date. They include events which because of statutory or conventional requirements are reflected in the financial statements.'[8]

Examples given of events normally classified as adjusting are as follows:[9]

(a) the subsequent determination of the purchase price or the sales proceeds of fixed assets purchased or sold before the year end;

(b) a valuation of property which indicates a permanent diminution in value of the asset at the balance sheet date;

(c) the receipt of information, such as financial statements of an unlisted company, which provides evidence of a permanent diminution in value of a long-term investment;

(d) the sale of stock after the balance sheet date showing that the estimate of net realisable value was incorrect;

(e) the discovery of evidence showing that estimates of accrued profit on a long-term contract were inaccurate;

(f) a trade debtor going into liquidation or receivership;

(g) the declaration of dividends by subsidiaries and associated companies for periods prior to the balance sheet date;

(h) a change in taxation rates applicable to periods before the balance sheet date (deleted for those entities applying FRS 19 – *Deferred Tax* – see Chapter 24 at 5.9.2);

(i) the receipt of insurance claims which were in the process of negotiation at the balance sheet date; and

(j) the discovery of significant errors or frauds which show that the financial statements were misstated.

The standard states that non-adjusting events are 'post balance sheet events which concern conditions which did not exist at the balance sheet date'.[10]

The appendix to the standard gives examples of items which would usually be classified as non-adjusting events.[11] These include:

(a) mergers and acquisitions;

(b) reconstructions and proposed reconstructions;

(c) the issue of shares and debentures;

(d) the purchase or disposal of fixed assets and investments;

(e) the loss of fixed assets or stocks due to a catastrophe such as a fire or a flood;

(f) the opening of new trading activities or extension of existing trading activities;

(g) the closing of a significant part of trading activities if this was not foreseen at the balance sheet date;

(h) a decrease in the value of property and investments held as fixed assets, if it can be shown that the decline took place subsequent to the balance sheet date;

(i) changes in foreign currency exchange rates;

(j) government action, such as nationalisation;

(k) strikes and other labour disputes; and

(l) the augmentation of pension benefits.

2.2 Events requiring adjustment

SSAP 17 requires that the financial statements be adjusted to take account of:

(a) an adjusting event; or

(b) a post balance sheet event which indicates that the application of the going concern concept to the whole or a material part of the company is no longer appropriate.[12] This could include a deterioration of trading results and the financial position, or the refusal of the bank to continue overdraft facilities.

2.3 Events not requiring adjustment but requiring disclosure

The standard states that an event of this type should be disclosed where:

'(a) it is a non-adjusting event of such materiality that its non-disclosure would affect the ability of the users of financial statements to reach a proper understanding of the financial position; or

(b) it is the reversal or maturity after the year end of a transaction entered into before the year end, the substance of which was primarily to alter the appearance of the company's balance sheet.'[13] Such alterations include those commonly known as 'window dressing' (see 3.5 below).

The ambiguity which renders SSAP 17 relatively meaningless in the case of (a) above is the *date* as at which the financial position is to be understood by the users. If it is the balance sheet date (which is what the law requires), then non-adjusting events need never be disclosed, since it is difficult to see how the financial statements could ever fail to give a true and fair view of the year end position because of the absence of such disclosure. What the standard's requirements in this area boil down to, therefore, is to highlight those major non-adjusting post balance sheet events which have resulted in the financial position at the date of approval being significantly different from that portrayed by the balance sheet.

The non-adjusting events which appear most regularly in financial statements are possibly the acquisition/disposal of a fixed asset, normally an investment in a subsidiary or a business, subsequent to the balance sheet date. Examples of disclosure in such situations are shown in the following extracts:

Extract 27.1: Cobham plc (2000)

37 Post Balance Sheet Events

In 2001, the acquisitions of South Africa-based Omnipless (Proprietary) Limited and its wholly-owned subsidiary Omnipless Antenna Systems (Proprietary) Limited, together with TEAM S.A. were completed. The business of Omnipless centres on the design, manufacture and sale of microwave flat-panel steerable antennas used in mobile satellite communications. Consideration for the purchase amounted to £38.0m, satisfied as to £30.7m in cash and £7.3m by the issue of 640,064 fully-paid ordinary shares in Cobham. A further maximum of £2.5m of deferred consideration is payable in cash upon the achievement of certain gross profit targets of the business over the next four years. Omnipless offers substantial new opportunities for growth in both global aeronautical and maritime markets. The fast-growing demand for mobile communications, internet connectivity and data transfer requires ever-increasing innovation in hi-gain antenna technology. Omnipless has developed a leading-edge position as supplier or partner with such leading prime manufacturers as Honeywell, Rockwell Collins, Thrane & Thrane and Universal Avionics. The French company TEAM S.A. was acquired for a cash consideration of FF80.3m (£7.7m) to secure 80.3% of that company's issued share capital. The offer is being extended so as to acquire the outstanding shares for a cash consideration of up to FF19.7m (£1.8m); and, at this time, 98.5% of the company's shareholders have accepted the offer. TEAM is the European leader in airborne audio and radio management systems, and is the current supplier of such systems to the Airbus family of aircraft.

Extract 27.2: Friends' Provident Life Office (2000)

34. Post balance sheet event

In February 2001 London & Manchester Group plc, a subsidiary undertaking, entered into a conditional agreement for the sale of its managed funds subsidiary, Friends Ivory & Sime Managed Pension Funds Limited, to Friends Ivory & Sime plc.

Also in February 2001 Friends Provident Investment Holdings Limited and FP Business Holdings Limited entered into a conditional agreement for the sale of Friends' Provident Unit Trust Managers Limited and Ivory & Sime Trustlink Limited, to Friends Ivory & Sime plc.

The transactions were approved at an Extraordinary General Meeting of the shareholders of Friends Ivory & Sime plc on 28 February 2001 and become unconditional on 2 March 2001 when the new shares issued as consideration were accepted for trading on the London Stock Exchange.

The consideration for the acquisition was approximately £128.9m, based on the middle market quotation of an Ordinary Share of 454p for 30 January 2001. The consideration payable for the acquisition comprised the issue to Friends Provident Investment Holdings Limited and London & Manchester plc, both subsidiaries of the Office, of an aggregate of 28,392,070 ordinary shares of Friends Ivory & Sime plc. Ivory & Sime Trustlink Limited was sold for nil consideration.

An immaterial loss on sale arises in the consolidated accounts of the Group as a result of these transactions. No charge to taxation arises.

In March 2001 the High Court approved the transfer of the Office's entire Industrial Business assets and liabilities to Royal Liver Assurance Limited for nil consideration. The transaction had an effective date of 31 March 2001, and £479m of assets were transferred at that date, based on a provisional valuation of Industrial Business liabilities. The final valuation will be carried out in due course and any balancing payment made in cash.

Assets transferred were in excess of transferred liabilities by an amount of £16m representing Royal Liver's estimated liability to taxation on the unrealised gains on the assets transferred. This will result in a loss of approximately £16m to the Office. No charge to taxation arises to the Office or in the consolidated accounts of the Group as a result of the transfer.

Extract 27.3: The Greenalls Group plc (1998)

25 PROPOSED SALE OF INN PARTNERSHIP

The Group has announced the proposed disposal of Inn Partnership, subject to Shareholders' approval, for a cash consideration of £370m. The approval of Shareholders will be sought at an Extraordinary General Meeting of the Company on 11 January 1999.

The profit on disposal, based on the net book amount of assets being sold as at 25 September 1998, is £48.5m after disposal costs and before adjusting for goodwill previously written off. The disposal will also give rise to a corresponding increase in Shareholders' funds before payment of the special dividend. The loss on disposal, net of goodwill previously written off, will be approximately £1.3m. This will be accounted for as an exceptional item. In addition, the Directors expect to make a provision for reorganisation costs directly attributable to the disposal of £11.0m net of tax.

It is intended that £100m would be distributed to Shareholders by way of special dividend payable after 6 April 1999, subject to completion of the proposed disposal. It is also proposed that in connection with the payment of the special dividend, a subdivision and consolidation of the Ordinary share capital will be carried out, primarily to maintain comparability of future and historical earnings per share, dividends per share and share price.

This transaction will be accounted for in the Accounts for the year ending 24 September 1999.

Extract 27.4: Cookson Group plc (1998)

34 Post balance sheet events

In February 1999, the Group disposed of Cookson Fibres, Inc. for a cash consideration of £93.0m ($153m). Cookson Fibres achieved operating profits of £10.3m in 1998. The disposal resulted in a loss of £61.3m, including £58.3m in respect of goodwill.

The sale of the Group's 45% interest in Zimco, a South African-based industrial group, was completed in February 1999 for a consideration of £3.4m. Zimco contributed £2.2m to the Group's operating profit in 1998. The transaction resulted in a loss of £9.0m, including £2.1m in respect of goodwill.

Information in respect of these disposals has been included in the notes to the accounts as discontinued operations both for 1998 and 1997. Information relating to 1997 for these two businesses, together with those sold or terminated in 1997 is shown as discontinued operations for that year.

It can be seen from the last two extracts that both companies expect to make a loss on disposal, after taking account of goodwill written off to reserves. An issue therefore arises as to whether provision should be made for such a loss. This is discussed at 3.4 below.

In disclosing information about such post balance sheet events some companies do so by providing pro forma information, as illustrated below:

Extract 27.5: Amersham International plc (1997)

34 Post balance sheet event

Merger of Amersham Life Science and Pharmacia Biotech Subsequent to the balance sheet date, Amersham has entered into a conditional agreement with Pharmacia & Upjohn Inc. ('P&U') to merge Amersham Life Science with Pharmacia Biotech, the biotechnology supply business of P&U, forming a new Company, proposed to be named Amersham Pharmacia Biotech Limited ('Amersham Pharmacia Biotech').

Under the terms of the merger, Amersham and P&U will transfer their respective life science businesses to Amersham Pharmacia Biotech, of which Amersham will own 56% of the issued ordinary share capital and P&U will hold the remaining 45%. In addition, Amersham and P&U will receive US$61m (£37m) and US$50m (£31m) respectively of preference shares. Amersham and P&U will also, in effect, contribute US$89m (£55m) and US$52m (£32m) respectively of debt to the combined entity.

The merger of the two businesses will, for accounting purposes, be treated by Amersham as a disposal of a 45% minority interest in Amersham Life Science and an acquisition of a 55% controlling interest in Pharmacia Biotech.

The following unaudited *pro forma* statement of net assets of the enlarged Amersham Group is provided for illustrative purposes only. Its purpose is to illustrate the effect on the net assets and equity shareholders' funds of the Amersham Group of the merger of the two life science businesses.

	Amersham Group as at 31 March 1997 (audited)	Pharmacia Biotech as at 31 December 1996 (unaudited)	Adjustments	Pro forma
	£m	£m	£m	£m
Fixed assets				
Intangible assets	1.3	–	–	1.3
Tangible assets	120.9	84.6	–	205.5
Investments	34.5	1.1	–	35.6
	156.7	85.7	–	242.4
Current assets				
Stocks	41.3	48.8	–	90.1
Debtors	100.5	75.3	–	175.8
Short term deposits and interest bearing investments	16.8	–	–	16.8
Cash at bank and in hand	9.5	12.4	(12.4)	9.5
	168.1	136.5	(12.4)	292.2
Creditors: amounts due within one year				
Loans	(16.4)	(61.7)	61.7	(16.4)
Other creditors	(83.5)	(86.8)	27.9	(142.4)
	(99.9)	(148.5)	89.6	(158.8)
Net current assets/(liabilities)	68.2	(12.0)	77.2	133.4
Total assets less current liabilities	224.9	73.7	77.2	375.8
Creditors: amounts falling due after more than one year				
Loans	(73.6)	(7.3)	(30.9)	(111.8)
Other creditors	(3.7)	(1.0)	–	(4.7)
	(77.3)	(8.3)	(30.9)	(116.5)
Provisions for liabilities and charges	(38.3)	(32.2)	–	(70.5)
Accruals and deferred income				
Investment grants	(4.8)	–	–	(4.8)
Total net assets	104.5	33.2	46.3	184.0
Minority interest	(1.8)	–	(42.6)	(44.4)
Equity shareholders' funds	102.7	33.2	3.7	139.6

Notes

1 The Pharmacia Biotech figures have been extracted from unaudited financial information for the year ended 31 December 1996 adjusted for UK GAAP and are stated before any fair value adjustments.

2 The adjustments represent certain assets and liabilities of Pharmacia Biotech retained by P&U, additional debt injected into Pharmacia Biotech prior to completion and the increase in minority interest.

3 Pharmacia Biotech's financial information has been translated into sterling at a rate of £1:SEK11.685, being the rate of exchange as at the close of business on 31 December 1996.

4 The *pro forma* balance sheet excludes any trading results or cash flows by Pharmacia Biotech after 31 December 1996 and Amersham Group after 31 March 1997 and is stated before transaction costs.

Extract 27.6: Aga Foodservice Group plc (2000)

30. Post balance sheet events

On 9th March 2001 the Group disposed of Pipe Systems for an initial consideration of £786m cash. The initial consideration will be adjusted, on a pound for pound basis, to the extent that the tangible net assets set out in the completion balance sheet exceed or fall short of £401.1m.

The anticipated loss on disposal of these businesses is calculated as follows:

	£m	£m
Sale proceeds	786.0	
Less professional fees	(7.0)	
		779.0
Tangible net assets disposed of	(401.1)	
Minority interest	1.0	
Capitalised goodwill at completion	(210.1)	
Total net assets sold		(610.2)
Provision for additional costs		(29.0)
Goodwill previously written off		(175.8)
Net loss on disposal		(36.0)
Tax on loss on disposal		1.7

As discussed on page 6 the cash proceeds will be used to pay down the Group's debt and to undertake a tender offer to return up to £386m to shareholders.

The Exchangeables were exchanged for ordinary shares in Aga Foodservice Group plc on 9th March 2001 (see note 20).

The effect of the above transactions had they occurred at 31st December 2000 would have been:

	Actual balance sheet 31st December £m	Disposal of assets £m note (i)	2000 disposal provision expensed £m note (ii)	Convert Exchange-ables £m note (iii)	Cash returned to shareholders £m note (iv)	Pro forma balance sheet £m
Fixed assets	288.2	(256.0)	–	–	–	**32.2**
Stocks	194.4	(173.4)	–	–	–	**21.0**
Operating debtors less creditors and provisions	(53.2)	28.3	36.0	–	–	**11.1**
Total net operating assets	429.4	(401.1)	36.0	–	–	**64.3**
Goodwill	275.8	(216.2)	–	–	–	**59.6**
Tax	3.3	2.4	–	–	–	**5.7**
Deferred tax	(2.0)	3.7	–	–	–	**1.7**
Dividends	(21.3)	–	–	–	–	**(21.3)**
Cash/(borrowings)	(304.3)	786.0	(36.0)	33.5	(386.0)	**93.2**
Total net assets employed	**380.9**	**174.8**	**–**	**33.5**	**(386.0)**	**203.2**
Share capital and reserves	379.6	175.8	–	33.5	(386.0)	**202.9**
Minority interests	1.3	(1.0)	–	–	–	**0.3**
Total funds	**380.9**	**174.8**	**–**	**33.5**	**(386.0)**	**203.2**

Notes

The above pro forma balance sheet has been prepared on the following basis:

(i) Assets and liabilities relating to Pipe Systems as at 31st December 2000 disposed of in exchange for initial consideration of £786m.

(ii) Transaction cost and additional costs arising on the disposal are assumed to have been settled in cash.

(iii) Exchangeables converted to shares in Aga Foodservice Group plc (see note 20).

(iv) Proposed return of capital to shareholders excluding associated transaction costs.

Examples of disclosures in respect of other types of non-adjusting events are shown in the following extracts:

Extract 27.7: British Polythene Industries plc (2000)

29. Post Balance Sheet Event

At an Extraordinary General Meeting of the Company held on 19 January 2001 resolutions were passed to give the Company authority to purchase up to 11,074,818 ordinary shares (representing 30% of the Company's issued ordinary share capital) and giving the Company the necessary borrowing powers to enable the purchase of these shares. The Company then exercised this authority to purchase 11,074,818 shares on 29 January 2001 at a total cost including expenses of £35.9 million.

Extract 27.8: Reuters Group PLC (2000)

33. POST BALANCE SHEET EVENTS

On 8 February 2001, Reuters announced that Instinet, its wholly owned electronic brokerage subsidiary, had filed a Registration Statement with the SEC for a proposed initial public offering (IPO). Instinet intends to apply for quotation of its common stock on the Nasdaq Stock Market. It is expected that the IPO will be completed by the middle of 2001. This will be a primary offering of common stock all of which will be issued by Instinet. Following the IPO, Reuters will continue to own a substantial majority of Instinet's common stock.

Extract 27.9: United Business Media plc (2000)

34. POST BALANCE SHEET EVENTS

On 9 February 2001 the company announced its proposal to return to shareholders £1.25 billion arising from the sale of its ITV businesses to Granada Media by means of a capital reorganisation and consolidation. This is expected to be completed by the end of April 2001.

Extract 27.10: Celltech Group plc (2000)

29 Post balance sheet events

CDP 870
On 5 March 2001 a co-development and co-promotion agreement for CDP 870 with Pharmacia Corporation was announced. Pharmacia will provide upfront payments totalling $50m and will make additional payments to Celltech of up to $230m based on the achievement of certain development and sales milestones.

Sale of Armstrong to Andrx
On the 12 February 2001, the Group announced the disposal of the Armstrong business ("Armstrong") to Andrx Corporation for $18m (£12m). This sale completed the programme to divest non-core businesses following the merger with Medeva.

Abgenix technology and co-development agreement
On the 6 February 2001, the Group announced that it had entered into an agreement with Abgenix Inc, which provides the Group with rights to use Abgenix's proprietary Selected Lymphocyte Antibody Method (SLAM) technology, for rapid selection in vitro of high affinity antibodies including the direct selection of fully human antibodies. The financial terms of the agreement include a payment by the Group of $17m to Abgenix, in new Celltech ordinary shares. Celltech will pay a royalty to Abgenix on sales of products which arise from the agreement.

Extract 27.11: Marks and Spencer p.l.c. (1999)

31. Post balance sheet events

On 28 April, the Group announced the closure of its Canadian operations. As a consequence, its subsidiary, Marks & Spencer Canada Inc, will cease to operate during the financial year ending 31 March 2000. The total cost of closure is estimated to be £25m, excluding goodwill of £24.4m previously written off to reserves.

On 10 May, the Group announced the rationalisation of its UK store management. The cost of this rationalisation is estimated to be £14m.

Extract 27.12: Pilkington plc (1999)

43 Post-balance sheet event

On 26th May 1999 the Group announced its plans to reorganise and streamline its automotive manufacturing operations in North America. This will involve the closure of a plant and the transfer of its production to two other existing facilities in North America. The programme is expected to involve exceptional restructuring costs of approximately £30 million, of which half are expected to be cash costs. No adjustment for this has been made in the financial statements

The last two extracts illustrate examples of situations prior to the issue of FRS 12 would normally have been dealt with as adjusting events on the basis that the directors had taken the decisions before the balance sheet date. However, as a result of the recognition rules contained in FRS 12, provision can no longer be made for such costs where the announcements are made post year-end. This issue is discussed in 5.1.2 of Chapter 28.

All of the above extracts disclose the information about the post balance sheet event in a note to the financial statements. Other companies have gone further by including a pro-forma column on the face of the balance sheet to illustrate the impact of the post balance sheet event as shown in the extracts below:

Extract 27.13: Geest PLC (1995)

Balance sheets
As at 30 December 1995

		Group		Company	
£millions	**Pro forma (note 25) 1995**	**1995**	**1994**	**1995**	**1994**
Fixed assets					
Tangible assets	**69.9**	**179.6**	183.5	**1.2**	1.5
Investments	**3.3**	**3.5**	2.4	**72.0**	41.0
	73.2	**183.1**	185.9	**73.2**	42.5
Current assets					
Stocks	**10.3**	**14.5**	16.6	**0.1**	0.1
Debtors	**45.5**	**69.9**	72.4	**49.2**	62.7
Cash at bank and short term deposits	**42.0**	**25.0**	33.5	**28.0**	29.6
	97.8	**109.4**	122.5	**77.3**	92.4

Creditors: due within one year					
Borrowings	–	**(18.8)**	(22.8)	**(15.7)**	(27.3)
Other creditors	**(75.7)**	**(98.7)**	(114.6)	**(30.9)**	(27.7)
Net current assets/(liabilities)	**22.1**	**(8.1)**	(14.9)	**30.7**	37.4
Total assets less current liabilities	**95.3**	**175.0**	171.0	**103.9**	79.9
Creditors: due after one year					
Borrowings	–	**(96.6)**	(87.7)	**(42.4)**	(12.8)
Other creditors	–	**(1.8)**	–	–	–
Provisions for liabilities and charges	**(9.2)**	**(9.5)**	(11.5)	**(0.1)**	(0.1)
Net assets	**86.1**	**67.1**	71.8	**61.4**	67.0
Capital and reserves					
Called up share capital	**3.6**	**3.6**	3.6	**3.6**	3.6
Share premium account	**12.6**	**12.6**	12.6	**12.6**	12.6
Revaluation reserve	**0.2**	**0.2**	0.2	–	–
Merger reserve	–	–	–	**14.5**	14.5
Profit and loss account	**68.9**	**49.9**	54.3	**30.7**	36.3
Equity shareholders' funds	**85.3**	**66.3**	70.7	**61.4**	67.0
Equity minority interests	**0.8**	**0.8**	1.1	–	–
	86.1	**67.1**	71.8	**61.4**	67.0

Statement of accounting policies [extract]

2 **Pro forma information** – On 9 January 1996 the disposal of the Group's Banana Sector was completed. In order to provide shareholders with additional information as to the financial impact of the disposal, the directors have included a pro forma consolidated balance sheet as at 30 December 1995. This has been prepared on the basis that both proceeds and costs were paid out on 30 December 1995. More information on the disposal is given in the financial review on page 14.

25 **Post balance sheet events**

On 9 January 1996, the sale of the Banana Sector was completed for a cash consideration of £92.3 million and the assumption of financing obligations attaching to Geest's two Island Class vessels, which amounted to £54.8 million as at 30 December 1995. In addition the consideration is to be increased (or decreased) by the amount of the adjusted net working capital of the Banana Sector at completion. The disposal is estimated to give rise to a £19.0 million increase in the Group's pro forma net assets as at 30 December 1995 to £86.1 million and is shown on page 26. After estimated disposal costs of £7.7 million, including those related to overhead reduction, this generates a pro forma exceptional profit of £18.2 million, the remaining £0.8 million being attributable to goodwill. The basis of preparation is detailed in the accounting policies note 2 on page 23.

Of the purchase consideration £5.0 million has been paid into an escrow account, amounts will only be released, to Geest, on registration of certain Costa Rican property.

Geest will continue to be the guarantor of the obligations under the two Island Class Charters whilst this guarantee remains outstanding. The Buyer has agreed to indemnify Geest against any liabilities in respect of the guarantee.

Extract 27.14: Costain Group plc (1995)

CONSOLIDATED BALANCE SHEET
As at 31 December

	Notes	1995 £m	1994 £m	Pro forma 1995 (unaudited) (note 30) £m
Fixed assets				
Tangible assets	13	94.0	192.4	94.0
Investments	14	30.1	74.6	30.1
		124.1	267.0	124.1
Current assets				
Stocks	15	34.7	42.7	34.7
Debtors				
– pension fund prepayment	16	55.5	60.0	55.5
– other	16	202.1	235.6	202.1
Cash at bank, monies on deposit and in hand	17	58.7	63.0	96.1
		351.0	401.3	388.4
Less Creditors:				
amounts falling due within one year				
Borrowings	18	124.3	36.4	30.1
Other creditors	19	265.9	300.3	265.9
		390.2	336.7	296.0
Net current (liabilities)/assets				
Due within one year		(108.9)	(14.3)	22.7
Due after one year		69.7	78.9	69.7
		(39.2)	64.6	92.4
Total assets less current liabilities		84.9	331.6	216.5
Less Creditors:				
amounts falling due after more than one year				
Borrowings	18	10.8	123.5	68.8
Other creditors	19	34.4	51.7	34.4
		45.2	175.2	103.2
Less provisions for liabilities and charges	20	70.5	54.7	70.5
Net (liabilities)/assets		(30.8)	101.7	42.8
Share capital and reserves				
Called up ordinary share capital	21	5.2	129.5	20.7
Share premium account	22	27.3	141.0	85.4
Revaluation reserve	22	–	22.7	–
Profit and loss account	22	(62.4)	(193.0)	(62.4)
Ordinary shareholders' funds		(29.9)	100.2	43.7
Equity minority interests		(0.9)	1.5	(0.9)
		(30.8)	101.7	42.8

30 Note to pro forma unaudited consolidated balance sheet

The proforma balance sheet of the Group is based on the audited consolidated balance sheet of the Group as at 31 December, 1995 adjusted in accordance with the notes set out below.

Since the balance sheet date, as detailed in note 27, the Group has completed an open offer to raise £73.6m (net of expenses). The directors consider the commercial impact significant enough to justify separate identification on a proforma basis as at 31 December 1995.

NOTE	Costain Group as at 31 December, 1995 £m	Net proceeds of the open offer £m (i)	New banking arrange-ments £m (ii)	Proforma Group (unaudited) £m
Fixed assets				
Tangible assets	94.0			94.0
Investments	30.1			30.1
	124.1			124.1
Current assets				
Stocks	34.7			34.7
Debtors				
– pension fund prepayment	55.5			55.5
– other	202.1			202.1
Cash at bank, monies on deposit and in hand	58.7	37.4		96.1
	351.0	37.4		388.4
Less Creditors: amounts falling due within one year				
Borrowings	124.3	(36.2)	(58.0)	30.1
Other creditors	265.9			265.9
	390.2	(36.2)	(58.0)	296.0
Net current (liabilities)/assets				
Due within one year	(108.9)	73.6	58.0	22.7
Due after one year	69.7			69.7
	(39.2)	73.6	58.0	92.4
Total assets less current liabilities	84.9	73.6	58.0	216.5
Less Creditors: amounts falling due after more than one year				
Borrowings	10.8		58.0	68.8
Other creditors	34.4			34.4
	45.2		58.0	103.2
Less provisions for liabilities and charges	70.5			70.5
Net (liabilities)/assets	(30.8)	73.6		42.8
Ordinary shareholders' funds	(29.9)	73.6		43.7
Equity minority interests	(0.9)			(0.9)
	(30.8)	73.6		42.8

NOTES

(i) The proceeds of the open offer are derived from gross proceeds of £77.6m less £4.0m of expenses.

(ii) £58.0m of short term borrowings have been converted into long term borrowings as part of the new banking arrangements.

(iii) The proforma takes no account of trading results since 1 January 1996.

27 Post balance sheet events

On 4 July 1996 the Group announced an underwritten open offer of ordinary shares, on the basis of 3 new shares for each existing share, to raise £73.6m (net of expenses). The open offer was approved by shareholders on 22 July 1996 and was completed on 31 July 1996.

On 1 July 1996, the Group completed the sale of Costain Industrial Services for £2.0m, paid in cash.

2.4 Disclosure requirements

As SSAP 17 requires consideration to be given to events which occur up to the date on which the financial statements are approved by the board of directors, then the standard requires that date to be disclosed.[14] This is normally done by dating the signature of the directors signing the balance sheet.

SSAP 17 states that for each post balance sheet event for which disclosure is required as per 2.3 above, the nature of the event and an estimate of its financial effect should be stated by way of note in financial statements. Where it is not practicable to estimate the financial effect, then a statement should be made explaining this fact.[15] The estimate of the financial effect should be disclosed before taking account of taxation, and the taxation implications should be explained where necessary for a proper understanding of the financial position.[16]

In addition, the Companies Act 1985 states that the directors' report must include 'particulars of any important events affecting the company or any of its subsidiary undertakings which have occurred since the end of the financial year'.[17] This links in with another Companies Act requirement to give an indication of likely future developments in the business of the company and of its subsidiary undertakings, i.e. the requirement to discuss the period after the balance sheet date falls under two headings. It is not primarily intended as an equivalent to the requirement of SSAP 17. The Companies Act requirement would seem to imply that both adjusting and non-adjusting events should be disclosed; however, in practice, only non-adjusting events will normally be included.

There is considerable diversity in the financial statement disclosure of post balance sheet events. Some companies disclose these events in both the directors' report and notes to the financial statements, whilst others provide disclosure in either the directors' report or notes.

The following extracts are examples of companies which have discussed post balance sheet events in the directors' report, but not in the notes to the financial statements:

Extract 27.15: Headlam Group plc (1998)

Report of the directors [extract]
Post balance sheet events

On 27 February 1999, the company acquired Tayrich Limited and its wholly owned subsidiary company, Joseph, Hamilton & Seaton Limited, from Interface Europe Limited for a cash consideration of £7.0 million funded from internal resources. Tayrich Limited, through its subsidiary, Joseph, Hamilton & Seaton Limited, is a contract floorcovering supplier based in Tamworth, Staffordshire. As at 3 January 1999, these companies had net assets of £1.9 million and, for the twelve month-period ended 3 January 1999, recorded a profit before taxation of £1.1 million on sales of £12.0 million.

Extract 27.16: De La Rue plc (2001)

Directors' Report [extract]
Post balance sheet events

On 2 April 2001, De La Rue completed the acquisition from Ascom Autelca AG of the business of Ascom Business Unit Cash Handling (Ascom BUCH), the Swiss cash handling sales and service network for a consideration of CHF 20.9m. The business of Ascom BUCH Belgium, the sales and support network covering both Belgium and Luxembourg was also completed on 2 April 2001 for a consideration of Euro 622,000. Contracts were exchanged on 21 March 2001 for the sale of 13.35 acres of land at Overton to a residential property developer. Completion took place on 18 April 2001 for a gross consideration of £4m.

It would appear that these companies have taken the view that SSAP 17 does not require disclosure of these events as 'non-adjusting events', but that the Companies Act does. This highlights an important difference between a non-adjusting post balance sheet event under SSAP 17 (requiring disclosure in the notes), and a post balance sheet event under the Companies Act (requiring disclosure in the directors' report). Whilst SSAP 17 requires disclosure of non-adjusting events which are of such materiality that their non-disclosure 'would affect the ability of the users of financial statements to reach a proper understanding of the financial position'[18] of the company, the Companies Act has the much wider requirement for disclosure of 'any important events affecting the company or any of its subsidiaries which have occurred since the end of the financial year'.[19] One unusual example of such disclosure is shown in the following extract:

Extract 27.17: De La Rue plc (1999)

Directors' Report [extract]
Post balance sheet events

Mr Michael Pugh, managing director, Security Paper and Printing Division, retired from the Board on 6 April 1999. The Company announced on 13 April 1999 that Mr Richard Laing, finance director, had decided to leave the Company. Mr Laing will continue in his role until the end of August when he will resign as a director.

Although most companies would note changes to the directorate after the year end, this would not normally be done under the heading of 'post balance sheet events' but as part of the section of the directors' report dealing with directors and their interests.

Where it is considered that a post balance sheet event requires disclosure under both SSAP 17 and the Companies Act, then theoretically disclosure should be made both in the notes to the financial statements and in the directors' report. However, in our view it would suffice if disclosure is made in either the notes or the directors' report, with an appropriate cross reference in the other as illustrated in the following extract:

Extract 27.18: Daily Mail and General Trust plc (2000)

Directors' Report [extract]
Post Balance Sheet Events

In November 2000, the dmg world media paid US $70 million for an initial 25% stake in George Little Management, the United States' largest privately-held tradeshow management company. It also announced that it is taking a 44.75% interest in Whereoware, an e-commerce platform set up to serve the North American gift and home industry.

In December 2000, a 75% owned subsidiary of the Group paid Aus$70 million (£26 million) to acquire an FM radio licence for Melbourne, Australia.

Changes to the number of 'A' ordinary Non-Voting shares, held by DMGT Trustees Limited, the Trustee of the DMGT Share Trust, are set out in the Remuneration Report on page 35.

Since the year end, the Group has raised £88 million through the issue of further 2021 10% bonds with a nominal value of £65 million.

42 Post Balance Sheet Events

Details of material post balance sheet events are given in the Directors' Report on page 29.

3 PRACTICAL ISSUES

3.1 Reclassification of a non-adjusting event as adjusting in exceptional circumstances

The general guidance given in the Appendix to SSAP 17, states that 'in exceptional circumstances, to accord with the prudence concept, an adverse event which would normally be classified as non-adjusting may need to be reclassified as adjusting. In such circumstances, full disclosure of the adjustment would be required.'[20]

Whilst this may appear to be a concession by the ASC, following the comments raised during the exposure period of ED 22 (the exposure draft that preceded SSAP 17) that the definition of adjusting events was too narrow, it should be emphasised that the issue has been dealt with in the Appendix to SSAP 17, rather than in the main body of the standard. Consequently, three issues arise in the application of this provision: first, it has limited status, and therefore may result in inconsistency in its application; second, its application will negate the fundamental distinction between an adjusting and non-adjusting event; and, third, what is meant by the phrase 'in exceptional circumstances', as the Appendix fails to provide any guidance as to the circumstances under which the provision should be applied?

The argument always exists that if full details of the non-adjusting event are disclosed in the directors' report and/or notes to the financial statements, users will be able to make their own adjustments and evaluate the impact of the event for themselves. However, it is our view that this application of the prudence override should only be used when the loss due to the post balance sheet event is of such magnitude that its exclusion from the financial statements would render them completely misleading.

In the US, it has been long established practice that events which provide evidence with respect to conditions that did not exist at the balance sheet date, but arose subsequent to that date, should not result in adjustment of the financial statements. This is referred to in the above terms in SAS 1 – *Codification of Auditing Standards and Procedures*.[21] However, SAS 1 goes on to say that some of these events 'may be of such a nature that disclosure of them is required to keep the financial statements from being misleading. Occasionally such an event may be so significant that disclosure can best be made by supplementing the historical financial statements with pro forma financial data giving effect to the event as if it had occurred on the date of the balance sheet. It may be desirable to present pro forma statements, usually a balance sheet only, in columnar form on the face of the historical statements.'[22]

In the UK, companies seem to prefer to follow the US approach of presenting pro-forma financial statements, rather than adopt the more drastic step of reflecting the non-adjusting event in the financial statements. Extracts 27.5, 27.6, 27.13 and 27.14 at 2.3 above illustrate examples of companies which have produced pro-forma information.

3.2 The valuation of stock realised after the balance sheet date

The sale of stock after the balance sheet date is normally a good indicator of the realisable value at that date. However, there will be circumstances where there is evidence which suggests that a fall in realisable value has taken place because of conditions which did not exist at the balance sheet date.

The problem, therefore, is determining when the fall in realisable value occurred; did the fall in value occur as a result of circumstances which existed at the balance sheet date, or did it occur as a result of circumstances which arose subsequently? A decrease in price is merely a response to changing conditions, and so it is important that the reasons behind these changes are fully assessed.

This can be seen by reviewing some examples of changing conditions:

(a) Price reductions due to a sudden increase in cheap imports

Whilst it could be argued that the 'dumping' of cheap imports after the balance sheet date is a condition that has arisen subsequent to that date, it is more likely to be the case that this will be a reaction to a condition which already existed, such as overproduction in other parts of the world. Thus, it might be appropriate in such a situation to be prudent and adjust the value of stock to its subsequent net realisable value.

(b) Price reductions due to increased competition

It is common for companies to adjust the valuation of stocks when their fall in value is due to price reductions of competitors. This is because the reasons for price reductions will not have arisen overnight, but will normally have occurred over a period of time. For example, a competitor may have built up a comparative advantage because of investment in more efficient machinery in the past. Thus, it is usually appropriate for a company to adjust its valuation in stocks, as its past investment in technology will have been inferior to its competitors, and will not have arisen subsequent to the balance sheet date.

(c) Price reductions due to the introduction of an improved competitive product

As an improved product introduced by competitors is unlikely to have been developed overnight it is correct to adjust the valuation of stock to its net realisable value following that introduction. This is because it reflects the company's failure to maintain its position in relation to technological improvements.

It can be seen in these cases that when a company is forced to reduce its prices after the balance sheet date, the fall provides additional evidence of conditions which existed at the balance sheet date. The reason for this is that, in general, the post balance sheet reduction in the realisable value of stock represents the culmination of conditions which existed over a relatively long period of time, with the result that their effects would normally require adjustment in the financial statements. However, there will be certain types of stock for which there is clear evidence of a higher price available at the year end, when it would be inappropriate to write down the stock to reflect a subsequent decline. An example of this would be stocks for which there was a price on the international commodities market.

3.3 Long-term contracts

It is not uncommon for events to take place after the balance sheet date which provide further evidence as to the profitability of long-term work in progress. It is our view that *all* further evidence of eventual profit should be taken into account in determining the valuation of long-term contract balances.

3.4 Acquisitions and disposals of fixed assets

If at the balance sheet date there are fixed assets in the process of being bought or sold, where there has been a contract signed before the year end, but there is uncertainty as to the amounts involved, the subsequent realisation of those amounts should be treated as an adjusting event.

Clearly, it is appropriate to make provision for known losses on the disposal of fixed assets which were in the process of being sold at the year end; and this will normally be the case whether or not a contract had been signed before the balance sheet date. However, a difficulty arises in the case where the assets are sold at a profit. Should the gain on disposal be recognised in the profit and loss account as an adjusting event? The answer lies in determining whether or not the sale had been completed at the year end. It is unlikely that a sale would be complete if the sale price had yet to be determined; however, if this were the case then the sale should be recognised in the financial statements.

Disposals of fixed assets after the balance sheet date, but which were not contemplated at that date, are generally non-adjusting events. However, if a large loss results this might provide evidence of impairment, and so an adjustment to the net book value may be appropriate. Whether an impairment loss is recognised will depend on the application of the impairment review under FRS 11. Such reviews are generally carried out at the level of income-generating units, rather than individual assets. It may therefore be the case that no impairment loss needs to be recognised because the recoverable amount of the income generating unit is greater than the carrying value of the overall net assets attributable to the income generating unit. However, FRS 11 also states that 'the income stream of a fixed asset to be disposed of will be largely independent of the income stream of other assets. Such an asset therefore forms an income-generating unit of its own and does not belong to any other income-generating unit.'[23] As most of the income that the asset will be generating is its disposal proceeds, then this would suggest that if such proceeds are lower than the net book value then an impairment loss should be recognised. This issue is discussed more fully at 2.2 of Chapter 13.

Similar issues also arise where subsidiaries or businesses are in the course of being sold or terminated and companies expect to make a loss on disposal or termination. Whether or not companies should provide for such losses will depend on the particular circumstances and the requirements of other accounting standards.

As discussed further at 2.4 of Chapter 25, FRS 3 – *Reporting Financial Performance* – requires that if a decision has been made to sell an operation, any consequential provisions should reflect the extent to which obligations have been incurred that are not expected to be covered by the future profits of the operation. Such a provision is not to be set up until the reporting entity is demonstrably committed to the sale; this should be evidenced by a binding sale agreement. This suggests that unless the binding sale agreement has been entered into by the balance sheet date no provision can be made. However, FRS 3 contains an additional suggestion in its explanatory section that a binding contract entered into after the balance sheet date may provide additional evidence of commitments at the balance sheet date. This implies that the binding sale agreement does not have to be in place at the balance sheet date, as long as there is demonstrable commitment to sell by the balance sheet date, and the binding sale agreement is entered into before the accounts are signed. Where there is only an intention to sell, but there is no legally binding contract, FRS 3 does not allow a provision to be made for the consequences of the sale; however, it does emphasise that asset values need to be considered.

FRS 12 is now also relevant. This standard allows provisions to be made only where an entity has a present obligation (i.e. at the balance sheet date) as a result of a past event and it states that no obligation arises for the sale of an operation until the entity is committed to the sale, i.e. there is a binding sale agreement.[24] Although this is similar to FRS 3, FRS 12 does not repeat the explanatory wording that is contained in FRS 3. As discussed further at 5.1.2 of Chapter 28, it could be argued that if the explanatory paragraph in FRS 3 has previously been used to justify setting up provision for the disposal of an operation where the binding sale agreement was entered into after the balance sheet date but before the accounts were signed, this interpretation is no longer allowable under FRS 12. However, this is unclear, given that the relevant paragraph in FRS 3 itself has not been deleted or amended. If the sale of an operation is envisaged as part of a larger restructuring, FRS 12 notes that the assets of the operation must be reviewed for impairment under FRS 11 (see 2.2 of Chapter 13).

Extracts 27.3, 27.4 and 27.6 at 2.3 above illustrate examples of companies in the process of selling off businesses and which are expected to make a loss on disposal, after taking account of goodwill written off to reserves. Cookson Group (Extract 27.4) and Aga Foodservice Group (Extract 27.6) provided for the losses on disposal. In both these cases the companies had binding sale agreements after the year end so it appears that provision has been made using the explanatory paragraph of FRS 3. On the other hand, Greenalls (Extract 27.3) still had to obtain shareholders' approval to the sale. It therefore did not have a binding sale agreement and accordingly could not provide for the expected loss on sale. It would have had to consider whether the assets had been impaired, but such an exercise need not be extended to include goodwill written off to reserves.

3.5 Window dressing

SSAP 17 requires the disclosure of the reversal or maturity after the year end of transactions entered into before the year end, the substance of which was primarily to alter the appearance of the company's balance sheet.[25] Such alterations include those commonly referred to as 'window dressing'.

The difficulty that arises is that there is no clear view of what 'window dressing' is; this fact was conceded by the ASC in their Technical Release issued on the publication of SSAP 17.[26] The term can encompass both:

(a) the fraudulent falsification of accounts to make things look better than they really are; and

(b) the lawful arrangement of affairs over the year end to make things look different from the way they usually are.[27]

Nevertheless, the ASC indicated that as the 'fraudulent falsification of accounts is clearly unacceptable and unlawful and is not a subject for an accounting standard',[28] the term 'window dressing' as used in SSAP 17 is confined to the meaning in (b) above.[29] However, this interpretation raises the question as to whether or not it is the function of the balance sheet to reflect the company's typical financial position throughout the year. For example, should the balance sheet illustrate the typical gearing throughout the year, or only at the year end? Companies quite legitimately select the year end as being the time when stocks are lowest, their monthly creditors have been paid etc. Therefore, in order to develop any rule which requires disclosure or restatement of disclosure from the norm, we need to understand what the norm actually is. Furthermore, if what are regarded as artificial transactions are discovered, should they not be restated, rather than merely disclosed?

The end result is that the SSAP 17 definition of these so called window dressing transactions is inadequate. Consequently, SSAP 17 is inevitably ineffectual in this regard, and this is possibly supported by the fact that there is no significant evidence of such disclosure in practice.

3.6 Valuations of property

If an asset is revalued after the balance sheet date and a significant fall in the value of that asset is revealed, there are two matters which need to be considered.

The first matter to be considered is the determination of the period in which the decline in value took place. If there is sufficient evidence to show that the asset had fallen in value after the year end, then no adjustment should be made but full disclosure should be made of the subsequent fall in value. However, in many situations this will not be the case; the valuation is likely to indicate that the decline in value had already taken place prior to the balance sheet date.

If that is the case, then the second matter to be considered is whether an adjustment should be made to the carrying value of the asset. If the fall in value is deemed to have taken place before the balance sheet date then, as such a fall in value is one of the examples contained within FRS 11 which indicate the possible impairment of the asset, an impairment review will need to be carried out. If, having carried out the review, the recoverable amount is less than the carrying amount, an adjustment would have to be made because FRS 11 requires the impairment loss to be recognised. The treatment of impairment losses is discussed more fully at 2.2 of Chapter 13.

3.7 Insolvency of a debtor

The insolvency of a debtor and his inability to pay his debts usually builds up over a period of time which would commence long before the balance sheet date. Consequently, if a debtor has an amount outstanding at the year end, and this amount has to be written off due to information received subsequent to the period end, it is normal to classify the event as adjusting. If, however, there is evidence to suggest that the insolvency of the debtor has been determined solely by an event occurring after the balance sheet date, then the event should be treated as non-adjusting.

4 IAS REQUIREMENTS

The relevant international standard is IAS 10 – *Events After the Balance Sheet Date*. The original IAS 10 – *Contingencies and Events Occurring After the Balance Sheet Date* – was issued in October 1978. However, in 1998 the portion of that standard dealing with contingencies was replaced by IAS 37 – *Provisions, Contingent Liabilities and Contingent Assets* – and IAS 10 was revised in May 1999 so as to deal only with events after the balance sheet date.

4.1 Definitions

Like SSAP 17 in the UK, IAS 10 defines events after the balance sheet date as 'those events, both favourable and unfavourable, that occur between the balance sheet date and the date when the financial statements are authorised for issue' and notes that there are two types of events, adjusting and non-adjusting.[30] Where an enterprise is required to submit its accounts to its shareholders, or a supervisory board, for approval, IAS 10 regards the financial statements as having been authorised for issue on the date of original issuance, not when approved by the shareholders or the supervisory board.[31]

4.2 Adjusting events

An enterprise should adjust the amounts recognised in its financial statements to reflect adjusting events after the balance sheet date,[32] i.e. those that provide evidence of conditions that existed at the balance sheet date.[33]

Examples given of such adjusting events are as follows:[34]

(a) the resolution after the balance sheet date of a court case which, because it confirms that an entity already had a present obligation at the balance sheet date, requires the entity to adjust a provision already recognised, or to recognise a provision instead of merely disclosing a contingent liability;

(b) the receipt of information after the balance sheet date indicating that an asset was impaired at the balance sheet date, or that the amount of a previously recognised impairment loss for that asset needs to be adjusted. For example:

    (i) the bankruptcy of a customer which occurs after the balance sheet date usually confirms that a loss already existed at the balance sheet date on a trade receivable account and that the entity needs to adjust the carrying amount of the trade receivable account; and

    (ii) the sale of inventories after the balance sheet date may give evidence about their net realisable value at the balance sheet date;

(c) the determination after the balance sheet date of the cost of assets purchased, or the proceeds from assets sold, before the balance sheet date;

(d) the determination after the balance sheet date of the amount of profit sharing or bonus payments, if the entity had a present legal or constructive obligation at the balance sheet date to make such payments as a result of events before that date (see Chapter 22 at 3.1.3); and

(e) the discovery of fraud or errors that show that the financial statements were incorrect.

Some of these examples are the same as those given in SSAP 17 in the UK (see 2.1 above) and therefore the discussion in 3.2, 3.4 and 3.7 above will be relevant in interpreting the IAS requirement.

4.3 Non-adjusting events

An enterprise should not adjust the amounts recognised in its financial statements to reflect non-adjusting events after the balance sheet date,[35] i.e. those that are indicative of conditions that arose after the balance sheet date,[36] although it may need to make additional disclosures (see 4.5 below).[37]

In explaining this requirement, IAS 10 cites a decline in market values of investments between the balance sheet date and the date when the financial statements are authorised for issue as an example of a non-adjusting event. This is because the fall in value does not normally relate to the condition of the investments at the balance sheet date, but reflects circumstances that have arisen in the following period.[38] As discussed at 4.5 below, the standard cites a number of other examples of non-adjusting events.

IAS 10 therefore does not allow adjustments for non-adjusting events, whereas the Appendix to SSAP 17 theoretically allows for the reclassification of a non-adjusting event as adjusting in exceptional circumstances (see 3.1 above).

The main area of difference between IAS 10 and the UK is in the accounting treatment of dividends. IAS 10 requires that 'if dividends to holders of equity instruments … are proposed or declared after the balance sheet date, an enterprise should not recognise those dividends as a liability at the balance sheet date.'[39] They are thus treated as a non-adjusting event. The disclosure of such dividends is required by IAS 1 – *Presentation of Financial Statements*. IAS 1 permits an enterprise to make this disclosure either:[40]

(a) on the face of the balance sheet as a separate component of equity; or

(b) in the notes to the financial statements.

In the UK such dividends are treated as adjusting events and are accounted for in the period to which they relate.

An example of a company having to change its treatment as a result of adopting IAS 10 is AngloGold as shown in Extract 27.22 at 4.6 below.

Similarly, as noted at 2.1 above, the declaration of dividends by subsidiaries and associated companies for periods prior to the balance sheet date are treated as adjusting events in the UK. Although IAS 10 does not specifically address such items, IAS 18 – *Revenue* – requires that dividends are recognised when the shareholder's right to receive payment is established.[41] Accordingly, such dividends would be recognised when the dividend is declared and therefore are non-adjusting events.

4.4 Going concern

Where management determines after the balance sheet date either that it intends to liquidate the enterprise or to cease trading, or that it has no realistic alternative but to do so, an enterprise should not prepare its financial statements on a going concern basis.[42] Deterioration in operating results and financial position after the balance sheet date may indicate a need to consider whether the going concern assumption is still appropriate. Although this seems like adjusting for a non-adjusting event, because the effect is pervasive the IASC sees this as a fundamental change in the basis of accounting, rather than an adjustment to the amounts recognised within the original basis of accounting.[43] Although this requirement is similar to SSAP 17, it does not allow adjustment where the going concern basis is not appropriate for only part of the enterprise.

4.5 Disclosures

Where non-adjusting events are of such importance that non-disclosure would affect the ability of the users of the financial statements to make proper evaluations and decisions, an enterprise should disclose the following information for each significant category of non-adjusting event after the balance sheet date:

(a) the nature of the event; and

(b) an estimate of its financial effect, or a statement that such an estimate cannot be made.[44]

Examples given of such non-adjusting events which may require disclosure are:[45]

(a) a major business combination after the balance sheet date (IAS 22 – *Business Combinations*, requires specific disclosures in such cases – see Chapter 6 at 5.5.3) or disposing of a major subsidiary;

(b) announcing a plan to discontinue an operation, disposing of assets or settling liabilities attributable to a discontinuing operation or entering into binding agreements to sell such assets or settle such liabilities (IAS 35 – *Discontinuing Operations*, requires specific disclosures in these cases – see Chapter 25 at 3.8);

(c) major purchases and disposals of assets, or expropriation of major assets by government;

(d) the destruction of a major production plant by a fire after the balance sheet date;

(e) announcing, or commencing the implementation of, a major restructuring;

(f) major ordinary share transactions and potential ordinary share transactions after the balance sheet date;

(g) abnormally large changes after the balance sheet date in asset prices or foreign exchange rates;

(h) changes in tax rates or tax laws enacted or announced after the balance sheet date that have a significant effect on current and deferred tax assets and liabilities;

(i) entering into significant commitments or contingent liabilities, for example, by issuing significant guarantees; and

(j) commencing major litigation arising solely out of events that occurred after the balance sheet date.

These disclosure requirements are equivalent to those in SSAP 17 in the UK (see 2.4 above), but IAS 10 requires the disclosures to be given only for each category, whereas SSAP 17 requires the disclosures to be given for each event. Also, SSAP 17 requires the financial effect to be disclosed pre-tax with an explanation of the tax implications where necessary. Like SSAP 17, IAS 10 requires disclosure of the date when the financial statements were authorised for issue. However, it also requires disclosure of who gave that authorisation, and if the enterprise's owners or other parties have the power to amend the financial statements after issuance, the enterprise should disclose that fact.[46]

If an enterprise receives information after the balance sheet date about conditions that existed at the balance sheet date, IAS 10 requires the enterprise to update the disclosures that relate to these conditions, in the light of the new information.[47] This applies even when the information does not affect the amount that the enterprise recognises in its financial statements. An example given by the standard of such a need to update disclosures is when evidence becomes available after the balance sheet date about a contingent liability that existed at the balance sheet date.[48] There is no such equivalent requirement in SSAP 17, but in practice this will generally be done.

4.6 Examples of disclosures

Extract 27.19: Nestlé S.A. (2000)

36. Events after the balance sheet date

Creation of a Major International Petcare Business

On 16th January 2001 Nestlé S.A. and Ralston Purina Company announced that they had entered into a merger agreement. Nestlé will acquire all of the outstanding shares of Ralston Purina for USD 10.3 billion. The transaction is expected to be completed at the latest by the end of 2001. The agreement is subject to Ralston Purina shareholders' and to regulatory approval.

At 22nd February 2001, date of the approval of the consolidated accounts by the Board of Directors, the Group had no subsequent adjusting events that warrant a modification of the values of assets and liabilities.

Extract 27.20: Novartis AG (2000)

30. Subsequent events

In December 2000 the Generics sector announced that it was in the process of concluding the following three acquisitions subject to obtaining the required regulatory approval:

- The acquisition of 100% of Apothecon Inc., USA from Bristol-Myers Squibb for approximately USD 50 million.
- The acquisition from BASF AG, Germany of its generics business in six European countries for CHF 175 million (Euro 115 million).
- The 100% acquisition of Labinca SA, Buenos Aires, Argentina for approximately CHF 123 million.

The acquisitions will be accounted for under the purchase method of accounting and the related goodwill, if any, will be amortized on a straight-line basis over a period not exceeding 20 years.

Extract 27.21: Münchener Rückversicherungs-Gesellschaft AG (2000)

(40) Events after the balance sheet date

On 1st April 2001 Munich Re and Allianz AG announced their intention to continue the restructuring of their shareholdings. Munich Re will sell its directly and indirectly held stakes in Dresdner Bank to Allianz and also make available around 4% of Allianz shares. Besides this, Munich Re intends to sell its 40.6% interest in Allianz Life to Allianz. In return, Munich Re will acquire from Allianz and Dresdner Bank all of their shares in HypoVereinsbank, thus increasing Munich Re's stake in HypoVereinsbank to 25.7%. In addition, Munich Re is planning to increase its holding in ERGO Versiherungsgruppe AG from the current level of 62.9% to up to 95%. Further details can be found under "Prospects for 2001" in the management report (Section 05).

The measures will result in a large tax-free gain on the disposal of investments in the business year 2002 and in a significant increase in the consolidated shareholders' equity.

No other events have occurred since the balance sheet date which would have a material effect on the financial position of the Group as presented in the financial statements.

Extract 27.22: AngloGold Limited (2000)

37 Comparative figures

Where appropriate, comparative figures have been restated to facilitate improved disclosure.

Dividends to shareholders are now accounted for on the date of declaration as a result of the adoption of IAS10. As a result, the retained earnings have been restated as disclosed in the statement of changes in shareholders' equity.

38 Events after balance sheet date

AngloGold Limited has announced that it has reached agreement in principle on the sale of two of its South African gold mines, Elandsrand and Deelkraal, to Harmony Gold Mining Company Limited for R1 billion ($132 million) in cash.

The transaction is subject to the fulfilment of the following suspensive conditions.

- obtaining the necessary regulatory approvals for the transfer of the mineral rights and the cession of the mining leases from the Minister of Minerals and Energy;
- granting the necessary mining authorisations to Harmony;
- obtaining approval of the transaction by the shareholders of Harmony in general meeting;
- obtaining approval of the transaction from the Competitions Tribunal and the Minister of Trade and Industry in terms of the Competition Act (Act 89 of 1998).

The above will have a positive impact on the group's earnings.

Extract 27.23: Serono International S.A. (2000)

36. Subsequent events

The primary financial statements were approved by the Board of Directors on February 14, 2001. On April 9, 2001, the full consolidated financial statements were approved by the Board of Directors for presentation to the General Meeting of Shareholders. The proposed dividends are detailed in the holding company financial statements on page 99.

24. Distribution of earnings [extract]

At the Annual Shareholders' Meeting on May 15, 2001, the Board of Directors will propose a cash dividend in respect of 2000 of CHF2.40 gross (1999: CHF0.80) per registered share, CHF6.00 gross (1999: CHF2.00) per bearer share or CHF0.15 per American depositary share, amounting to a total of CHF96.4 million (1999: CHF30.0 million). These financial statements do not reflect the dividends payable, which will be accounted for in shareholders' equity as an appropriation of retained earnings in the year ending December 31, 2001.

Extract 27.24: Roche Holding Ltd (2000)

29. Subsequent events

At the Annual General Meeting on 3 April 2001, the shareholders will be asked to approve a 100 for 1 stock split of the shares and non-voting equity securities of Roche Holding Ltd. If approved the split will take place after changes in the relevant Swiss company law will have entered into force.

References

1 SSAP 17, *Accounting for post balance sheet events*, ASC, August 1980, para. 18.
2 IAS 10, *Events After the Balance Sheet Date*, IASC, May 1999, para. 2.
3 FRS 11, *Impairment of Fixed Assets and Goodwill*, ASB, July 1998.
4 IAS 36, *Impairment of Assets*, IASC, June 1998.
5 FRS 12, *Provisions, Contingent Liabilities and Contingent Assets*, ASB, September 1998.
6 IAS 37, *Provisions, Contingent Liabilities and Contingent Assets*, IASC, September 1998.
7 SSAP 17, para. 18.
8 *Ibid.*, para. 19.
9 *Ibid.*, Appendix.
10 *Ibid.*, para. 20.
11 *Ibid.*, Appendix.
12 *Ibid.*, para. 22.
13 *Ibid.*, para. 23.
14 *Ibid.*, para. 26.
15 *Ibid.*, para. 24.
16 *Ibid.*, para. 25.
17 CA 85, Sch. 7, para. 6(a).
18 SSAP 17, para. 23(a).
19 CA 85, Sch. 7, para. 6(a).
20 SSAP 17, Appendix.
21 AICPA, *Codification of Statements on Auditing Standards*, AU § 560.05.
22 *Ibid.*, AU § 560.05.
23 FRS 11, para. 31.
24 FRS 12, para. 83.
25 SSAP 17, para. 23(b).
26 TR 398, *Statement by the Accounting Standards Committee on the publication of SSAP 17: Accounting for post balance sheet events*, para. 14.
27 *Ibid.*
28 *Ibid.*
29 *Ibid.*
30 IAS 10, para. 2.
31 *Ibid.*, paras. 4 and 5.
32 *Ibid.*, para. 7.
33 *Ibid.*, para. 2.
34 *Ibid.*, para. 8.
35 *Ibid.*, para. 9.
36 *Ibid.*, para. 2.
37 *Ibid.*, para. 10.
38 *Ibid.*
39 *Ibid.*, para. 11.
40 IAS 1, *Presentation of Financial Statements*, IASC, Revised 1997, para. 74.
41 IAS 18, *Revenue*, IASC, Revised 1993, para. 30.
42 IAS 10, para. 13.
43 *Ibid.*, para. 14.
44 *Ibid.*, para. 20.
45 *Ibid.*, para. 21.
46 *Ibid.*, para. 16.
47 *Ibid.*, para. 18.
48 *Ibid.*, para. 19.

Chapter 28 Provisions and contingencies

1 INTRODUCTION

1.1 Background

In the UK, a provision is defined in the Companies Act as 'any amount retained as reasonably necessary for the purposes of providing for any liability or loss which is either likely to be incurred, or certain to be incurred but uncertain as to amount or as to the date on which it will arise.'[1] This definition applies only to 'provisions for liabilities or charges', in other words those that appear in the liabilities section of the balance sheet, and not to provisions for depreciation or diminution in value of assets, which are separately defined in the Act.[2] Similarly, this chapter focuses only on provisions that are shown as liabilities, and does not deal with amounts written off against assets.

The relevant standard in the UK, FRS 12 – *Provisions, Contingent Liabilities and Contingent Assets*, likewise only deals with provisions which are liabilities.[3] The definition of a provision in FRS 12 is much shorter than that in the Act merely stating that it is 'a liability of uncertain timing or amount'.[4] The ASB says that it believes that 'although the Act and the FRS define provisions in different terms, when taken in their respective contexts, FRS 12 is consistent with the requirements of the Schedule 4.'[5] This form of words is subtle, because it is clear that the ASB's wording has deliberately excluded some aspects of the Act's definition that it has found troublesome. In particular, the reference in the Act to *retaining* amounts carries connotations of appropriations, and sounds altogether too discretionary for the ASB's taste. Consistent with its *Statement of Principles*, the ASB is anxious to ensure that only those amounts that meet its definition of liabilities end up being reported as such in the balance sheet. Liabilities are defined as 'obligations of an entity to transfer economic benefits as a result of past transactions or events'.[6]

A similar line is taken by the IASC in its standard IAS 37 – *Provisions, Contingent Liabilities and Contingent Assets*.[7] IAS 37 was developed in parallel with FRS 12 under a joint project between the ASB and the IASC and the two standards were published on the same day. Both FRS 12 and IAS 37 appear to contradict the requirements of European Accounting Directives: the Fourth Directive Article 31.1(c)(bb) requires businesses to take account of 'all foreseeable liabilities and potential losses arising in the course of the financial year concerned or of a previous one even if such liabilities or losses become apparent only between the date of the balance sheet and the date on which it is drawn up'. This conflict has been noted by the European Commission in a document published by the Contact Committee on the Accounting Directives, stating that 'IAS 37's definition of a provision as it is applied to the specific case of restructuring provisions is inconsistent with the Fourth Directive because it will prevent provision being made for items for which provision is required by Articles 31.1(c)(bb) and 31(d) of the Directive.'[8]

The Act's reference to 'providing for any … loss that is … likely to be incurred' also seems to open up a possibility that the ASB wished to close down; it was anxious to prevent companies from providing for future operating losses, because they properly belong in the future. However, as discussed later in this chapter, this distinction is sometimes less easy to make than it might appear.

There is clearly an area of overlap between provisions and contingent liabilities; although contingent liabilities are clearly not certain to give rise to outflows, provision may nonetheless be required for them if they are sufficiently likely to do so. Accordingly, both the ASB and the IASC have addressed provisions and contingent liabilities in the same standard, and thrown in contingent assets for good measure. Previously, contingent assets and liabilities were governed by SSAP 18[9] (see 1.2.1 below) in the UK and internationally by IAS 10.[10] In the UK, the Companies Act also imposes rules for the disclosure of contingent liabilities (see 6.2.1 below).

A further demarcation line has to be drawn between provisions and other liabilities, such as trade creditors and accruals. Both the ASB and the IASC differentiate provisions on the basis that the uncertainty about the timing or amount of the future expenditure required in settlement is greater than that relating to trade creditors and accruals.[11]

This is true, but by concentrating on trade creditors and their associated accruals only the most straightforward case has been cited. In practice the difference between provisions and liabilities is often far from clear-cut, and reclassification from one category to the other is not uncommon. (This is discussed further at 2.2 below.)

One reason why this distinction matters is that provisions are subject to disclosure requirements that do not apply to other creditors, as discussed at 6.1 and 7.5.1 below. In fact, although questions of recognition and measurement are important, transparency of disclosure is also a very significant issue in relation to accounting for provisions. The problem is that, once a provision has been established, expenditure that is charged to it bypasses the profit and loss account and to some extent therefore disappears from view. The original charge may well have been dealt with as an exceptional item and glossed over by management in any discussion of their performance, and the subsequent application of the provision has no further impact on earnings – giving rise to a kind of 'off profit and loss account' treatment. And in recent years, some of the provisions that have been set up have been extremely large and wide-ranging. An example is to be found in the 1993 accounts of what was then British Gas:

Extract 28.1: British Gas plc (1993)

Review of operating results [extract]
Operating costs [extract]

The results for 1993 include an exceptional charge of £1,650 million for the major restructuring of the UK Gas Business. This restructuring into five separate business streams will ensure that the Company's UK Gas Business will be leaner, more competitive and more commercially focused at a time when the gas market in Great Britain is undergoing radical change. The exceptional charge comprises severance and pension costs associated with the reduction in approximately 25,000 people and the related costs of restructuring the integrated UK Gas Business. The cash effect of this restructuring will be borne largely over the next three years.

The corresponding note to the profit and loss account contained substantially the same information but added that the amount also included 'other incremental costs that will be required to implement the restructuring, such as training, property related costs and information technology costs'. The effect of this charge was to convert a pre-tax profit of approximately £1 billion into a loss of £613 million.

The need to restrict the creation of such 'big bath' provisions provided much of the impetus for the ASB's (and the IASC's) projects on provisions, although some other important issues have been addressed as well, notably on how provisions should be measured.

1.2 UK position

1.2.1 SSAP 18

The first standard to address matters now covered by FRS 12 was SSAP 18 – *Accounting for contingencies* – issued by the ASC in August 1980.

The requirements of SSAP 18 were very similar in effect to those now in FRS 12, even though the approach and the definitions used by FRS 12 are rather different. In particular, FRS 12 approaches the subject from a balance sheet perspective, setting rules for the recognition of assets and liabilities, whereas SSAP 18 focused on the recognition of gains and losses.

1.2.2 The ASB Discussion Paper

The ASB published a Discussion Paper – *Provisions* – in November 1995. This proposed the general principles that should govern the recognition, measurement and disclosure of provisions; these were derived from the Board's *Statement of Principles*, which was published in draft on the same day. It devoted much of its content to the consideration of three particular kinds of provision: those for future operating losses, reorganisation costs and environmental liabilities, and these topics continued to feature prominently in the project as it progressed towards an accounting standard. However, the paper did not deal with contingencies at all, and at that stage it was intended that SSAP 18 should be left in force.

1.2.3 *FRED 14*

FRED 14 was issued in June 1997. The exposure draft closely followed the philosophy of the Discussion Paper, but it had now been expanded to embrace contingencies as well as provisions and accordingly was intended to supersede SSAP 18.

1.2.4 *FRS 12*

The ASB published FRS 12 in September 1998. Its stated objective is 'to ensure that appropriate recognition criteria and measurement bases are applied to provisions, contingent liabilities and contingent assets and that sufficient information is disclosed in the notes to the financial statements to enable users to understand their nature, timing and amount'.[12]

FRS 12 came into effect for financial statements relating to accounting periods ending on or after 23 March 1999. Since it embraces contingencies, SSAP 18 was withdrawn. FRS 3 – *Reporting Financial Performance* was also amended to bring it in line with the FRS 12 measurement rules for gains on disposals of assets, as explained in 4.5 below.

The requirements of FRS 12 are discussed at 2 to 6 below.

1.2.5 *Companies Act*

As noted at 1.1 above, the Companies Act has a definition of 'provisions'. The Act contains disclosure requirements with respect to such provisions and also in respect of contingent liabilities. These are dealt with respectively at 6.1.1 and 6.2.1 below.

1.3 International position

The first IASC standard in this field was IAS 10 – *Contingencies and Events Occurring After the Balance Sheet Date*, and its requirements on contingencies were in essence the same as those of SSAP 18. In November 1996, the IASC issued a Draft Statement of Principles – *Provisions and Contingencies*, proposing to take contingencies out of IAS 10 and to deal with them in the same standard as provisions, using the same recognition and measurement rules.[13] In July 1997, the IASC published an exposure draft on this basis, which was converted into a standard – IAS 37 – in September 1998. This standard applies to accounting periods beginning on or after 1 July 1999.

As indicated at 1.1 above, IAS 37 was developed in parallel with FRS 12 under a joint project between the ASB and the IASC and the two standards were published on the same day. There are no differences of substance between the requirements of the two standards – indeed the text is mostly identical – but FRS 12 touches on two additional areas:

- recognition of an asset when a provision is recognised (see 3.3 below), and
- slightly more guidance on the discount rate to be used in the net present value calculation (see 4.2 below).

The requirements of IAS 37 are dealt with at 7 below.

2 SCOPE OF FRS 12

The only entities specifically exempt from FRS 12 are those applying the ASB's Financial Reporting Standard for Smaller Entities (FRSSE).[14] As indicated at 1.1 above, FRS 12 only deals with provisions which are liabilities. Provisions for depreciation, impairment of assets and doubtful debts are not addressed in the standard, since these are adjustments to the carrying amounts of assets.[15] In addition, certain specific provisions, contingent liabilities and contingent assets are exempt.[16]

2.1 Exemptions

2.1.1 Financial instruments carried at fair value

Although the standard makes an exemption for such financial instruments, it emphasises, on the other hand, that it does apply to financial instruments (including guarantees) that are *not* carried at fair value.[17] This is somewhat confusing. It is understandable that items such as guarantees, which give rise to contingent liabilities, fall within the scope of the standard. However, if the scope of the standard were extended to other financial instruments, some surprising results would be achieved.

For example, consider a forward foreign currency contract taken out to hedge future contracted purchases of goods from an overseas supplier, which is to be settled after the balance sheet date. Such derivatives would currently be accounted for as hedges, fixing the rate at which the purchases are recorded next year. However, applying FRS 12 could give rise to the requirement for a provision to be made for any loss subsisting on the contract at the balance sheet date.

We do not believe that the ASB intended this standard to change current accounting for financial instruments such as derivatives, given that it is currently reviewing the accounting for financial instruments in a separate project. This view is supported by the fact that FRS 13 – *Derivatives and Other Financial Instruments: Disclosures* – came into effect at the same time as FRS 12 and contains disclosure requirements for financial instruments which are consistent with the view that the accounting requirements have not changed. (See Chapter 10 at 2 for a discussion of these requirements.)

2.1.2 Executory contracts, except where the contract is onerous

The standard uses the term executory contracts to mean 'contracts under which neither party has performed any of its obligations or both parties have partially performed their obligations to an equal extent'.[18] This means that contracts such as supplier purchase contracts and capital commitments, which would otherwise fall within the scope of the standard, are exempt.

This exemption prevents the balance sheet from being grossed up by all sorts of commitments that an entity has entered into, and is to be welcomed as a pragmatic measure. However, there is little theoretical justification for the exemption, in that such items meet the definition of liabilities used by the standard. The need for this exemption arises because the liability framework on which this standard is based would otherwise give rise to unwelcome effects.

An executory contract will still require provision if the contract becomes onerous. Onerous contracts are dealt with in 5.3 below.

2.1.3 *Contracts with policy-holders in insurance entities*

The ASB refers to the special regulatory position of insurance companies and the review of the accounting framework for insurance companies as reasons for this exemption. However, the standard requires insurance entities to apply the standard to other (non-insurance) provisions and contingencies.[19]

2.1.4 *Provisions or contingencies covered by another FRS or a SSAP*

Where there is a more relevant standard, it should be applied to the provision or contingency it addresses instead of FRS 12. Examples given in the standard are:[20]

- long term contracts (dealt with in SSAP 9 – *Stocks and long-term contracts*)
- deferred tax (dealt with in SSAP 15 – *Accounting for deferred tax* or FRS 19 – *Deferred Tax*).
- leases (dealt with in SSAP 21 – *Accounting for leases and hire purchase contracts*). However, the standard argues that if operating leases become onerous, there are no specific requirements within SSAP 21 to address the issue and thus FRS 12 applies to such leases.
- pension costs (dealt with in SSAP 24 – *Accounting for pension costs* or FRS 17 – *Retirement Benefits*). Although not specifically mentioned, it would be reasonable to assume that the exemption also extends to other post retirement benefits, which are addressed in UITF 6 – *Accounting for post-retirement benefits other than pensions.*

The standard does not give provisions for discontinued operations (which are dealt with in FRS 3 – *Reporting Financial Performance*) as an example of an item which is exempt from FRS 12. Instead, it specifically requires that where a restructuring meets the definition of a discontinued operation, the additional FRS 3 disclosures are given in addition to complying with FRS 12.[21] Presumably, this is because the standard does not consider that such provisions are more specifically dealt with in FRS 3.

2.2 Provisions and other liabilities

As noted at 1.1 above, FRS 12 draws a demarcation line between provisions and other liabilities, such as trade creditors and accruals. The ASB differentiates provisions on the basis that 'there is uncertainty about the timing or amount of the future expenditure required in settlement. By contrast:

(a) trade creditors are liabilities to pay for goods or services that have been received or supplied and have been invoiced or formally agreed with the supplier; and

(b) accruals are liabilities to pay for goods or services that have been received or supplied but have not been paid, invoiced or formally agreed with the supplier, including amounts due to employees (for example amounts relating to accrued holiday pay). Although it is sometimes necessary to estimate the amount or timing of accruals, the uncertainty is generally much less than is the case for provisions.

Accruals are often reported as part of trade and other creditors whereas provisions are reported separately.'[22]

This is true, but by concentrating on trade creditors and their associated accruals the Board has cited only the most straightforward case. In practice the difference between provisions and other liabilities is often far from clear-cut, and reclassification from one category to the other is not uncommon. TI Group provides an example of a company making such a change on implementation of FRS 12:

Extract 28.2: TI Group plc (1998)

22 PROVISIONS FOR LIABILITIES AND CHARGES [extract]

	Pensions and Other Post-Retirement Obligations	Product Warranty And Onerous Contracts	Deferred Taxation	Other Liabilities	Group Total
	£m	£m	£m	£m	£m
At 31st December 1997	112.2	–	30.4	–	142.6
Exchange rate adjustments	1.0	0.3	0.1	–	1.4
Transferred from creditors	6.7	11.6	–	0.9	19.2
Transferred to debtors falling due within one year	–	–	21.9	–	21.9
New subsidiaries	27.7	14.6	(6.7)	15.7	51.3
Utilised	(6.9)	(3.5)	–	(7.9)	(18.3)
Profit and loss account	9.6	3.5	(3.3)	5.5	15.3
At 31st December 1998	**150.3**	**26.5**	**42.4**	**14.2**	**233.4**

Provisions for liabilities and charges include provisions for

- Unfunded post-retirement medical and welfare benefit schemes, unfunded pension arrangements, principally overseas, and the actuarially estimated deficit in the EIS Group UK pension schemes (see note 32);
- Future product warranty costs arising in the normal course of business from prior period sales, and onerous contract liabilities;
- Deferred taxation;
- Other liabilities, which include actual and potential legal claims where resolution is anticipated during 1999 and committed reorganisation expenditure.

Following the adoption of FRS 12 'Provisions, Contingent Liabilities and Contingent Assets', certain balances relating to the above items, previously reported within Creditors, have been reclassified as Provisions with effect from 1st January 1998. 1997 comparatives have not been restated.

One reason why this distinction matters is that provisions are subject to disclosure requirements that do not apply to other creditors, as discussed at 6.1 below.

2.3 Provisions and contingent liabilities

As noted at 1.1 above, there is clearly an overlap between provisions and contingent liabilities and FRS 12 deals with both of them.

The standard notes that in a general sense, all provisions are contingent because they are uncertain in timing or amount. However, in FRS 12 the term 'contingent' is used for liabilities and assets that are not recognised because their existence will be confirmed only by the occurrence of one or more uncertain future events not wholly within the entity's control. In addition, the term 'contingent liability' is used for liabilities that do not meet the recognition criteria.[23]

Accordingly, the standard distinguishes between:

(a) provisions – which are recognised as liabilities (assuming that a reliable estimate can be made) because they are present obligations where it is probable that a transfer of economic benefits will be required to settle the obligations; and

(b) contingent liabilities – which are not recognised as liabilities because they are either:

  (i) possible obligations, as it has yet to be confirmed whether the entity has an obligation that could lead to a transfer of economic benefits; or

  (ii) present obligations that do not meet the recognition criteria in the standard because either it is not probable that a transfer of economic benefits will be required to settle the obligation, or a sufficiently reliable estimate of the amount of the obligation cannot be made.[24]

The recognition criteria are dealt with below.

3 RECOGNITION

3.1 Provisions

FRS 12 requires that a provision should be recognised when, and only when, three conditions are all satisfied:

(a) an entity has a present obligation (legal or constructive) as a result of a past event;

(b) it is probable that a transfer of economic benefits will be required to settle the obligation; and

(c) a reliable estimate can be made of the amount of the obligation.[25]

Each of these three conditions is discussed separately below.

3.1.1 *'An entity has a present obligation (legal or constructive) as a result of a past event.'*

The standard defines both legal and constructive obligations. The definition of a legal obligation is fairly straightforward and uncontroversial; it refers to an obligation that derives from a contract (through its explicit or implicit terms), legislation or other operation of law.[26]

Constructive obligations, on the other hand, may give rise to more problems of interpretation. A constructive obligation is defined as 'an obligation that derives from an entity's actions where:

(a) by an established pattern of past practice, published policies or a sufficiently specific current statement, the entity has indicated to other parties that it will accept certain responsibilities; and

(b) as a result, the entity has created a valid expectation on the part of those other parties that it will discharge those responsibilities.'[27]

The essence of the idea is that the entity may be committed to certain expenditure because any alternative would be too unattractive to contemplate. The standard cites habitual refunds made to customers, and contamination clean-ups as examples of this.[28]

The standard states that in almost all cases it will be clear whether a past event has given rise to a present obligation. However, it notes that there will be some rare cases, such as a lawsuit against an entity, where this will not be so. In these cases, a past event is deemed to give rise to a present obligation if, taking account of all available evidence (including, for example, the opinion of experts), it is more likely than not that a present obligation exists at the balance sheet date. The evidence to be considered includes any additional evidence occurring after the balance sheet date. Accordingly, if on the basis of the evidence it is concluded that a present obligation is more likely than not to exist, a provision will be required (assuming that the other recognition criteria are met).[29] Unfortunately, this is a direct contradiction of the standard's condition (a) for the recognition of a provision, which requires there to be a definite obligation, not just a probable one!

The second half of this condition uses the phrase 'as a result of a past event'. This is based on the concept of an obligating event, which the standard defines as 'an event that creates a legal or constructive obligation and that results in an entity having no realistic alternative to settling that obligation.'[30] The standard says that this will be the case only:

(a) where the settlement of the obligation can be enforced by law; or

(b) in the case of a constructive obligation, where the event (which may be an action of the entity) creates valid expectations in other parties that the entity will discharge the obligation.[31]

This concept of obligating event is used in the standard when discussing specific examples of recognition, which we discuss further in 5 below. However, it is worth mentioning here that this concept, like that of a constructive obligation, is open to interpretation, as the obligating event is not always easy to identify.

The standard notes that the financial statements deal with the financial position of an entity at the end of its reporting period, not of its possible position in the future. Accordingly, no provision is to be recognised for costs that need to be incurred to operate in the future. The only liabilities to be recognised are those that exist at the balance sheet date.[32]

FRS 12 disallows certain provisions that might otherwise qualify to be recognised by stating that 'It is only those obligations arising from past events existing independently of an entity's future actions (i.e. the future conduct of its business) that are recognised as provisions'.[33] It illustrates this restriction with an example of an entity required, because of commercial pressures or legal requirements, to fit smoke filters in a factory. It argues that the entity can avoid the expenditure by its future actions, for example by changing its method of operation, so there is no present obligation for the future expenditure.[34] Other kinds of provisions disallowed because the entity can avoid the future expenditure are repairs and maintenance of assets, and future staff training, both of which are illustrated in the examples.[35]

There is no requirement for an entity to know to whom an obligation is owed. The obligation may be to the public at large. It follows that the obligation could be to one party, but the amount ultimately payable will be to another party. For example, in the case of a constructive obligation for an environmental clean-up, the obligation is to the public, but the liability will be settled by making payment to the contractors engaged to carry out the clean-up. However, the principle is that there must be another party for the obligation to exist. It follows from this that a board decision will not give rise to a constructive obligation unless it is communicated in sufficient detail to those affected by it before the balance sheet date.[36] The most significant application of this requirement relates to restructuring provisions, which is discussed further in 5.1 below.

The standard discusses the possibility that an event that does not give rise to an obligation immediately may do so at a later date, because of changes in the law or an act by the entity which gives rise to a constructive obligation.[37] Changes in the law will be relatively straightforward to identify. The only issue that arises will be exactly when that change in the law should be recognised. FRS 12 states that an obligation arises only when the legislation is virtually certain to be enacted as drafted, and suggests that in many cases, this will not be until it is enacted.[38]

The more subjective area is the possibility that an act by the entity will give rise to a constructive obligation. The example given is of an entity publicly accepting responsibility for rectification of previous environmental damage in a way that creates a constructive obligation.[39] This seems to introduce a certain amount of flexibility to management in reporting results. By bringing forward or delaying a public announcement of a commitment that management had always intended to honour, it can affect the period in which a provision is charged.

As the FASB has also commented,[40] the critical event that creates a constructive obligation tends to be elusive, and this is demonstrated by the discussion of some of the examples in 5 below. That is not to say that we believe that only legal obligations deserve to be in the balance sheet, but we doubt if this particular approach is the best way of determining which additional items deserve to be there. As with other aspects of the ASB's framework and its recognition criteria in particular, we think that the question is in reality one of expense recognition – in what period should the cost be charged to the profit and loss account – not liability recognition at all.

3.1.2 *'It is probable that a transfer of economic benefits will be required to settle the obligation.'*

This requirement has been included as a result of the standard's attempt to incorporate contingent liabilities within the definition of provisions. This is discussed in detail in 3.2 below.

The interpretation of *probable* in these circumstances is that the transfer of economic benefits is more likely than not to occur; that is, it has a probability greater than 50%. The standard also makes it clear that where there are a number of similar obligations, the probability that a transfer will occur is based on the class of obligations as a whole. This is because in the case of certain obligations such as warranties, the possibility of a transfer for an individual item is very small (likely to be much less than 50%) whereas the possibility of at least some transfer of economic benefits for the population as a whole will be much greater (almost certainly greater than 50%).[41]

3.1.3 *'A reliable estimate can be made of the amount of the obligation.'*

The standard takes the view that a reasonable estimate can always be made for a provision where an entity can determine a range of possible outcomes. Hence, it will only be in extremely rare cases that a range of outcomes cannot be determined and so no provision is recognised. In these circumstances, the liability should be disclosed as a contingent liability (see disclosure requirements in 6.2 below).[42]

3.2 Contingencies

FRS 12 says that contingent assets and liabilities should not be recognised, but only disclosed.[43]

3.2.1 *Contingent liabilities*

At least for contingent liabilities, this may seem a surprising position to take and one which is different from the previous regime under SSAP 18. However, the explanation lies in the peculiar way in which a contingent liability has been defined. It is:

(a) a possible obligation that arises from past events and whose existence will be confirmed only by the occurrence of one or more uncertain future events not wholly within the entity's control; or

(b) a present obligation that arises from past events but is not recognised because:

   (i) it is not probable that a transfer of economic benefits will be required to settle the obligation; or

   (ii) the amount of the obligation cannot be measured with sufficient reliability.[44]

This approach is very different from that used in SSAP 18. What the ASB has done is to define the category in a back to front way that depends on the recognition rule that it wants to apply. Contingent liabilities as defined are now meant to be those that the ASB does not think deserve recognition.

Even with that explanation, the above definition is not easy to understand. One problem with (a) is that the term 'possible' is not defined. Literally, it could mean any probability greater than 0% and less than 100%. However, in the context of the standard, a more sensible assumption is that since 'probable' is used within the standard as meaning 'more likely than not to occur' (see 3.1.2 above), i.e. a probability of greater than 50%, then 'possible' means a probability of 50% or less. Assuming that this is what is meant, the definition restricts contingent liabilities to those where either the existence of the liability or the transfer of economic benefits arising is less than 50+% probable (or where the obligation cannot be measured at all, but as noted in 3.1.3 above, this would be very rare).

The ASB's definition of a contingent liability is therefore tortuous and counter-intuitive. To say that a contingent liability is no longer contingent if it becomes more than 50% probable is likely to cause a great deal of confusion. It is contrary to the natural meaning of the words, whereby a contingent liability is a liability that is contingent on a future event.

If the meaning of contingent liabilities is restricted in this way, the question obviously arises as to what happens to those items where the existence of the liability and the resulting transfer of economic benefits are greater than 50% probable. The answer is that the standard has attempted to catch these within provisions. As noted in 3.1 above, the recognition criteria for provisions include the requirement that it is probable that a transfer of economic benefits will be required to settle the obligation. Hence an item that would previously have been regarded as a contingent liability under SSAP 18, for which a cash outflow is probable, is classified as a provision under FRS 12.

However, the uncertainty surrounding a liability is not always related only to whether a cash outflow will arise, but may also relate to whether the liability exists at all. For example, take the case of litigation against a company. The facts may suggest that the company will probably be found negligent and required to pay appropriate damages, but it is still contesting the action and may win the case. In these circumstances, as well as uncertainty over any level of damages, there is currently uncertainty over whether the company has a liability at all.

Nevertheless, as discussed at 3.1.1 above, the standard has attempted to deal with these circumstances by stating that there will be some rare cases, such as a lawsuit against an entity, where it will not be clear that there is a 'present obligation'. In these cases, a past event is deemed to give rise to a present obligation if, taking account of all available evidence (including, for example, the opinion of experts), it is more likely than not that a present obligation exists at the balance sheet date'. The evidence to be considered includes any additional evidence occurring after the balance sheet date. Accordingly, if on the basis of the evidence it is concluded that a present obligation is more likely than not to exist, a provision will be required (assuming that the other recognition criteria are met). If it is considered that it is more likely that no present obligation exists, then the entity discloses a contingent liability (unless the possibility of a transfer of economic resources is remote).[45] The disclosure requirements are detailed at 6.2 below.

The standard requires that contingent liabilities are assessed continually to determine whether a transfer of economic benefits has become probable. Where this becomes the case, then provision should be made in the period in which the change in probability occurs (except in the rare circumstances where no reliable estimate can be made).[46] To illustrate this, the Appendix to FRS 12 includes an example of an entity guaranteeing the borrowings of another entity, the financial condition of which deteriorates from one year to the next such that provision then needs to be made for the obligation, rather than continuing to just disclose the contingent liability.[47]

3.2.2 *Contingent assets*

A contingent asset is defined in a more normal way. It is 'a possible asset that arises from past events and whose existence will be confirmed only by the occurrence of one or more uncertain future events not wholly within the entity's control'.[48] In this case, the word 'possible' is *not* confined to a level of probability of 50% or less, which may further increase the confusion over the different meaning of the word in the definition of contingent liabilities.

Contingent assets usually arise from unplanned or other unexpected events that give rise to the possibility of an inflow of economic benefits to the entity. An example is a claim that an entity is pursuing through legal process, where the outcome is uncertain.[49]

The standard states that a contingent asset should not be recognised, as this could give rise to recognition of profit that may never be realised. However, when the realisation of profit is virtually certain, then the related asset is no longer regarded as contingent and recognition is appropriate.[50] SSAP 18 had a similar criterion, but used the phrase 'reasonably certain' rather than 'virtually certain'. It is not clear whether the ASB intended there to be a different level of certainty required by using the phrase 'virtually certain', but in practice the level of certainty required was already high (a suggested interpretation being between 95% and 100% probable).

The standard requires disclosure of the contingent asset when the inflow of economic benefits is probable.[51] As noted earlier, 'probable' is used within the standard as meaning 'more likely than not to occur' (see 3.1.2 above). The disclosure requirements are detailed in 6.3 below.

As with contingent liabilities, any contingent assets should be assessed continually. If it has become virtually certain that an inflow of economic benefits will arise, the asset and the related profit should be recognised in the period in which the change occurs. If an inflow becomes probable, then the contingent asset should then be disclosed.[52]

3.2.3 *Summary*

Despite the changes in terminology that FRS 12 introduced, therefore, in practice contingencies continue to be dealt with on a similar basis to the regime established by SSAP 18.

The following matrix summarises the treatment of contingencies under FRS 12:

Likelihood of outcome	*Accounting treatment: contingent liability*	*Accounting treatment: contingent asset*
Virtually certain (say, >95% probable)	Not a contingent liability, therefore provide	Not a contingent asset, therefore accrue
Probable (say, 50+ – 95% probable)	Not a contingent liability, therefore provide	Disclose
Possible but not probable (say, 5 – 50% probable)	Disclose	No disclosure permitted
Remote (say, <5% probable)	No disclosure required under FRS 12, but consider disclosure under CA 85, Sch. 4, para. 50	No disclosure permitted

The standard does not put a numerical measure of probability on either 'virtually certain' or 'remote', which lie at the outer ends of the range, but we think it reasonable to regard them as falling above the 95th percentile and below the fifth percentile respectively. However, these are not definitive guides and each case must be decided on its merits. In any event, it is usually possible to assess the probability of the outcome of a particular event only very approximately.

3.3 Recognising an asset when recognising a provision

In most cases, the recognition of a provision results in an immediate charge to the profit and loss account. Nevertheless, in some cases it may be appropriate to recognise an asset. However, under FRS 12 this should only be done when, and only when, the incurring of the present obligation recognised as a provision gives access to future economic benefits, that are to be enjoyed over more than one period. The reason for this requirement is to deal with provisions which are set up under the standard for decommissioning costs. Since an obligation for such costs is incurred by commissioning, say, an oil rig, the standard therefore requires recognition of the liability at that time. However, since the oil rig provides access to oil reserves over the years of its operations, an asset is recognised at the same time.[53] This issue is discussed further at 5.5 below.

4 MEASUREMENT

4.1 Best estimate of provision

A provision is to be measured before tax, as the tax consequences of the provision, and changes to it, are dealt with under the relevant standard for tax (see Chapter 24).[54]

FRS 12 says that the amount provided should be the best estimate of the expenditure required to settle the present obligation at the balance sheet date.[55] The standard equates this estimate with 'the amount that an entity would rationally pay to settle the obligation at the balance sheet date or to transfer it to a third party at that time'.[56] It is interesting that a hypothetical transaction of this kind should be proposed as the conceptual basis of the measurement required, rather than putting the main emphasis upon the actual expenditure that is expected to be incurred in the future. This represents 'relief value' as described in the ASB's *Statement of Principles*,[57] and belongs in a current value system rather than one founded on historical cost.

The standard does acknowledge that it would often be impossible or prohibitively expensive to settle or transfer the obligation at the balance sheet date. However, it goes on to state that 'the estimate of the amount that an entity would rationally pay to settle or transfer the obligation gives the best estimate of the expenditure required to settle the present obligation at the balance sheet date'.[58]

The estimates of outcome and financial effect are determined by the judgement of the entity's management, supplemented by experience of similar transactions and, in some cases, reports from independent experts. The evidence considered will include any additional evidence provided by events after the balance sheet date.[59]

Different methods of dealing with the uncertainties surrounding the amount to be recognised as a provision are detailed in the standard. Where a large population of items is being measured, such as warranty costs, the standard advances the use of 'expected values'. This is a statistical computation which weights the cost of all the various possible outcomes according to their probabilities, as illustrated in the following example taken from FRS 12.[60]

Example 28.1: Calculation of expected value

An entity sells goods with a warranty under which customers are covered for the cost of repairs of any manufacturing defects that become apparent within the first six months after purchase. If minor defects were detected in all products sold, repair costs of £1 million would result. If major defects were detected in all products sold, repair costs of £4 million would result. The entity's past experience and future expectations indicate that, for the coming year, 75 per cent of the goods sold will have no defects, 20 per cent of the goods sold will have minor defects and 5 per cent of the goods sold will have major defects. In accordance with paragraph 24 of FRS 12 (see 3.1.2 above) an entity assesses the probability of a transfer for the warranty obligations as a whole.

The expected value of the cost of repairs is:

(75% of nil) + (20% of £1m) + (5% of £4m) = £400,000.

Another measurement approach described in the standard covers the situation where there is a continuous range of possible outcomes and each point in that range is as likely as any other. FRS 12 requires that, in this case, the mid-point of the range should be used.[61] This is not a particularly helpful example. It does not make it clear what the principle is meant to be, since the mid-point in this case represents the median as well as the expected value. The latter may have been what the ASB had in mind, but the median could be equally well justified on the basis that it is 50% probable that at least this amount will be payable, while anything in excess of that constitutes a possible but not a probable liability, that should be disclosed rather than accrued. Interestingly, US GAAP has a different approach to this issue in relation to contingencies. FASB Interpretation No. 14 states that where a contingent loss could fall within a range of amounts then, if there is a best estimate within the range, it should be accrued, with the remainder noted as a contingent liability. However, if there is no best estimate then the *lowest* figure within the range should be accrued, with the remainder up to the maximum potential loss noted as a contingent liability.[62]

Where the obligation being measured relates to a single item, the standard suggests that the best estimate of the liability may be the individual most likely outcome.[63] However, it notes that regard should be had to other possible outcomes. It gives an example of an entity that has to rectify a fault in a major plant that it has constructed. The most likely outcome is that the repair will succeed at the first attempt. However, a provision should be made for a larger amount if there is a significant chance that further attempts will be necessary.[64] This again sounds like a vague leaning towards an expected value approach.

This example illustrates an inconsistency between these measurement rules and the recognition rules for contingent liabilities. Compare the above example with a case where the most likely outcome is that no repair will be required at all, but there is still a significant chance that a repair will be needed. In this scenario, there is a less than 50% probability that a cash outflow will arise, and so the item will fall within the definition of a contingent liability and no provision will be required. No account will have been taken of any other possible outcomes, unlike the first scenario.

It is also interesting to consider how the measurement rules detailed above should reflect prudence. It is worth noting that FRED 14 required the provision to be a 'realistic and prudent estimate',[65] but this was altered to refer to 'best estimate' in the final standard, with references to prudence being dropped.

The standard does however discuss the concept of risk. It refers to risk as being variability of outcome, and states that 'the risks and uncertainties that inevitably surround many events and circumstances should be taken into account in reaching the best estimate of a provision'. It suggests that a risk adjustment may increase the amount at which a liability is measured, but gives no indication of how this may be done. It indicates that caution is needed in making judgements under conditions of uncertainty, so that expenses or liabilities are not understated. However, it says that uncertainty does not justify the creation of excessive provisions or a deliberate overstatement of liabilities. The paragraph goes on to warn against duplicating adjustments for risk, for example by estimating costs of an adverse outcome on a prudent basis and then overestimating its probability.[66] Any uncertainties surrounding the amount of the expenditure are to be disclosed (see 6.1.2 below).[67]

The overall result of all this is somewhat confusing. The measurement rules no longer appear to take account of prudence. Certainly, using a best estimate based on the expected value concept or the mid-point of a range cannot be building in prudence to the estimate. However, the discussion on risk gives the impression that some sort of adjustment should be made which builds prudence into the estimate, but quite how this might be done is unclear. This rather vague drafting leaves a certain amount of scope in the estimation of provisions.

4.2 Discounting

The standard requires that where the effect of the time value of money is material, the provision should be discounted to its net present value.[68] The discount rate (or rates) used should be 'a pre-tax rate (or rates) that reflect(s) current market assessments of the time value of money and the risks specific to the liability. The discount rate(s) should not reflect risks for which the future cash flow estimates have been adjusted.'[69] However, it is worth noting that for many provisions, no discounting will be required as the cash flows will not be far enough into the future for discounting to have a material impact.[70] A number of problems arise on the issue of discounting which are discussed below.

4.2.1 *Real v. nominal rate*

The discount rate used depends on whether:

(a) the future cash flows are expressed in current prices, in which case a real discount rate (which excludes the effects of general inflation) should be used; or

(b) the future cash flows are expressed in expected future prices, in which case a nominal discount rate (which includes a return to cover expected inflation) should be used.[71]

The standard allows either method to be used, and both these methods may produce the same figure for the initial present value of the provision. However, the effect of the unwinding of the discount will be different in each case.

4.2.2 *Adjusting for risk*

As noted at 4.1 above, FRS 12 also requires that risk is taken into account in the calculation of a provision, but gives little guidance as to how this should be done. Within the discounting section, it goes on to suggest that using a discount rate that reflects the risk associated with the liability (a risk-adjusted rate) may be the easiest method of reflecting risk.[72] It gives no indication of how to calculate such a risk adjusted rate, but a little more information can be obtained from the ASB's earlier Working Paper – *Discounting in Financial Reporting*,[73] which included this example.

Example 28.2: Calculation of a risk-adjusted rate

A company has a provision for which the expected value of the cash outflow in three years' time is £150, and the risk-free rate is 5%. The company is risk averse and would settle instead for a certain payment of £160 in three years' time. The effect of risk in calculating the present value is that either:

(a) the 'certainty equivalent' of £160 is discounted at the risk-free rate of 5%, giving a present value of £138; or

(b) the expected cash flow of £150 is discounted at a risk-adjusted rate that will give the present value of £138, i.e. a rate of 2.8%.

As can be seen from this example, the risk-adjusted rate is a *lower* rate than the risk-free rate. The problem with this approach is that this risk-adjusted rate is a theoretical rate (which may even be negative) and has no obvious meaning in real life. It is also difficult to see how a risk-adjusted rate could be obtained in practice. In this example, it was obtained only by working backwards; it was already known that the net present value that we wanted to obtain was £138, so the risk-adjusted rate was just the discount rate applied to £150 to give that result.

The standard does offer an alternative approach – instead of using a risk-adjusted discount rate, the cash flows themselves can be adjusted for risk and then discounted using a risk-free rate.[74] This does of course give the problem of how to adjust the cash flows for risk. However, this may be easier than attempting to risk-adjust the discount rate.

The standard suggests that an example of a risk-free rate would be a government bond rate.[75] Presumably, this government bond rate should strictly have a similar remaining term to the liability, although this is not specified in the standard.

Whichever method of reflecting risk is adopted, the standard emphasises that care must be taken that the effect of risk is not double-counted by inclusion in both the cash flows and the discount rate.[76]

4.2.3 Pre-tax discount rate

Since FRS 12 requires provisions to be measured before tax, it follows that cash flows should be discounted at a pre-tax discount rate. No further explanation of this is given in the body of the standard. However, paragraph 27 in the Appendix on the *Development of the FRS* states that 'the discount rate should be the rate of return that will, after tax has been deducted, give the required post-tax rate of return'. The paragraph goes on to explain that because the tax consequence of different cash flows may be different, the pre-tax rate of return is not always the post-tax rate of return grossed up by the standard rate of tax.

In practice, it is unlikely that companies need be too concerned about this paragraph. This is because, in reality, the discount rate will be calculated directly as a pre-tax discount rate, as the required post-tax rate of return will not be known. Supposing, for example, that the risk-free rate of return is being used, then the discount rate used will be a government bond rate. This rate will be obtained gross. Thus, the idea of obtaining a required post-tax rate of return and adjusting it for the tax consequences of different cash flows will seldom be relevant.

The calculation is illustrated in the following example.

Example 28.3: Use of discounting and tax effect

It is estimated that the settlement of an environmental provision will give rise to a gross cash outflow of £500,000 in three years time. The gross interest rate on a government bond maturing in three years time is 6%. The tax rate is 30%.

The net present value of the provision is £419,810 (£500,000 x $1/(1.06)^3$). Hence, a provision of £419,810 should be booked in the balance sheet. A corresponding deferred tax asset of £125,943 (30% of £419,810) would be set up if it met the criteria for recognition in the relevant standard on deferred tax. (See Chapter 24 at 4.4 and 5.5.)

4.2.4 *Unwinding of the discount*

The standard as originally drafted requires that 'the unwinding of the discount should be included as a financial item adjacent to interest, but should be shown separately from other interest either on the face of the profit and loss account or in a note'.[77] However, in developing its standard on retirement benefits, FRS 17, the ASB received legal advice that the interest cost (which represents the unwinding of a discount rate) and expected return on assets should be presented in a new format heading separate from 'interest and similar charges'.[78] Accordingly, FRS 12 was amended to require that 'the unwinding of the discount should be included as other finance costs adjacent to interest'.[79]

This is the only guidance that the standard gives on the unwinding of the discount. There is no discussion of the impact that the original selection of discount rate can have on its unwinding, that is the selection of real versus nominal rates, and risk-free versus risk-adjusted rates. The ASB appears to have overlooked the fact that these different discount rates will unwind differently. This is best illustrated by way of an example.

Example 28.4: Effect of different bases of interest

A provision is required to be set up for an estimated cash outflow of £100,000 (estimated at current prices), payable in three years' time. The real discount rate is 2.5%, and inflation is estimated at 5%.

The net present value of £100,000, discounted at 2.5%, is £92,860. This is the provision that should be booked in the balance sheet in year 0. The same balance sheet provision would also be arrived at if the cash outflow was adjusted to reflect future prices, and then discounted at 7.5%.

In year 1, if a real discount rate is used and all assumptions remain valid, the effect of unwinding the discount gives rise to a finance charge of £2,322.

However, if a nominal rate is used, the result in year 1 is a finance charge of £6,965.

Obviously, using the real discount rate will give rise to a much lower finance charge. This leads to the question of whether it also leads to a lower provision in the balance sheet at the end of year 1. Provisions have to be revised annually to reflect the current best estimate of the obligation (see 4.6 below). Thus, the provision in the above example will be adjusted to reflect current prices at the end of year 1 and any other adjustments that arise from changes in estimate of the provision, as well as being adjusted for the unwinding of the discount. If prices do increase at the rate of inflation assumed (5% in this example), then the balance sheet provision at the end of year 1 will be £99,825 under both methods. What will be different under the two methods, however, is the allocation of the change in provision between operating costs and finance charges. If the real discount rate is used, the finance charge each year will be lower and the operating costs higher than if the nominal rate is used.

A similar issue arises with the option of using the risk-free or the risk-adjusted discount rate. However, this is a more complex problem, because it is not clear what to do with the risk-adjustment built into the provision. This is illustrated in the following example, using the same facts as in Example 28.2 at 4.2.2 above:

Example 28.5: Use of risk-free and risk-adjusted figures

As before, a company is required to make a provision for which the expected value of the cash outflow in three years' time is £150, when the risk-free rate is 5%. The reporting entity is risk averse and would settle instead for a certain payment of £160 in three years' time. The discounting options are:

(a) the 'certainty equivalent' of £160 is discounted at the risk-free rate of 5%, giving a present value of £138; or

(b) the expected cash flow of £150 is discounted at a risk-adjusted rate that will give the present value of £138, i.e. a rate of 2.8%.

Assuming that there are no changes in estimate required to be made to the provision during the three year period, alternative (a) will unwind to give an overall finance charge of £22 and a final provision of £160. Alternative (b) will unwind to give an overall finance charge of £12 and a final provision of £150.

In this example, the unwinding of different discount rates gives rise to different provisions. The difference of £10 relates to the risk adjustment that has been made to the provision. The standard gives no guidance as to how to treat this £10 if the provision is unwound at the risk-free rate. Given that the expected cash outflow is only £150, this additional £10 is likely to have to be released at some point, but it is unclear how to do this. Two alternatives are that it could be done gradually over the period in which the provision is unwound (perhaps as a reassessment of the required provision as it becomes less risky), or could be taken in total once the provision has been settled. The lack of guidance in the standard appears to give companies flexibility on this point.

4.2.5 *Change in interest rates*

The standard requires the discount rate to reflect current market assessments of the time value of money.[80] This appears to mean that where interest rates change, the provision should be recalculated on the basis of revised interest rates. This interpretation is reinforced by the disclosure requirement in the standard that entities should disclose the effect of any change in discount rate.[81] As with the equivalent proposals in relation to financial instruments and the requirements of FRS 11 in respect of impaired assets (see Chapters 10 and 13 respectively) this implicitly introduces a new capital maintenance concept into accounting, based on the ability of the entity to earn a current market rate of return.

This will give rise to an adjustment, but the standard does not explicitly say how this should be treated. Arguably, it should be treated in the same way as the unwinding of the discount and therefore charged within the other finance costs line in the year of change, which may be either a debit or a credit depending on which way interest rates move. Alternatively, it could be treated as a change in estimate of the provision. Indeed, this latter approach is the one recommended in the recent SORP issued by the Oil Industry Accounting Committee in relation to provisions for decommissioning (see 5.5 below). However, in that case the adjustment is not taken to the profit and loss account but treated as an adjustment to the carrying value of the corresponding asset. For other provisions, the adjustment would have to be taken to the profit and loss account.

Calculating this adjustment is not straightforward either, because the standard gives no guidance on how it should be done. For example, it is unclear whether the new interest rate should be applied during the year or just at year end, and whether the rate should be applied to the new estimate of the provision or the old estimate. This again appears to give companies flexibility in the approach that they adopt, although once a particular approach is adopted, it should be applied consistently.

4.2.6 *Conclusions on discounting*

The ASB has introduced the concept of discounting into FRS 12, with almost no guidance on the related implementation issues that arise, resulting in all sorts of ambiguities in the requirements.

However, the considerations detailed above lead us to suggest that for practical purposes, cash flows are assessed prudently and then discounted using the gross rate on a government bond (taking either a real rate or a nominal rate depending on whether the future cash flows are being estimated using current or future prices). On unwinding the discount, a number of options appear to be acceptable, so long as they are consistently applied.

4.3 Future events

The standard states that 'future events that may affect the amount required to settle an obligation should be reflected in the amount of a provision where there is sufficient objective evidence that they will occur'.[82] The types of future events that the standard has in mind are advances in technology and changes in legislation.

This is intended to mean that a provision cannot be reduced simply on the basis that new technology may be developed in the intervening period before the liability is settled. There will need to be sufficient objective evidence of this new technology. For example, an entity may believe that the cost of cleaning up a site at the end of its life will be reduced by future changes in technology. The amount recognised has to reflect a reasonable expectation of technically qualified, objective observers, taking account of all available evidence as to the technology that will be available at the time of the clean-up. Thus it is appropriate to include, for example, expected cost reductions associated with increased experience in applying existing technology or the expected cost of applying existing technology to a larger or more complex clean-up operation than has previously been carried out. However, an entity does not anticipate the development of a completely new technology for cleaning up unless it is supported by sufficient objective evidence.[83]

Similarly, if new legislation is to be anticipated, there will need to be evidence of what the legislation will demand, and whether it is virtually certain to be enacted and implemented in due course. In many cases sufficient objective evidence will not exist until the new legislation is enacted.[84]

These requirements are most likely to impact provisions for liabilities that will be settled some distance in the future, such as decommissioning costs (see 5.5 below).

4.4 Recoveries from third parties

In some circumstances an entity is able to look to a third party to reimburse part of the costs required to settle a provision or to pay the amounts directly. Examples are insurance contracts, indemnity clauses and suppliers' warranties.[85] In the majority of cases where a recovery is expected, the entity would remain liable for the whole costs if the third party failed to pay for any reason, for example as a result of the third party's insolvency.

If the entity would not be liable for these costs even if the third party failed to pay, the amount should not be included within the provision.[86] However, if the entity remains liable for the whole amount, the provision should be made gross and any such reimbursement should be treated as a separate asset (provided it is virtually certain that the reimbursement will be received if the entity settles the obligation). The amount recognised for the reimbursement should not exceed the amount of the provision.[87] This is different from the previous rule under SSAP 18, where such provisions were made net of expected recoveries, although FRS 12 still allows the amounts to be netted off in the profit and loss account.[88]

This change caused Hanson to reinstate insured environmental liabilities on its balance sheet, as shown in this extract from its 1999 accounts.

Extract 28.3: Hanson PLC (1999)

Provisions

The adoption of Financial Reporting Standard 12 'Provisions, Contingent Liabilities and Contingent Assets' (FRS 12) has necessitated an adjustment to certain provisions made in prior years. FRS 12 has required changes in the method of accounting for reclamation costs, health care obligations in respect of US employees, environmental obligations, decommissioning costs and other liabilities. Provisions have been discounted at a rate of 2.5% on current prices, except where more appropriate discounting rates have been used having regard to information provided by actuaries or other independent advisers.

In the case of Koppers environmental liabilities the obligation is recognised in provisions with a corresponding asset representing the amounts receivable under the insurance arrangements entered into in 1998. Under these arrangements the funding and risk of the environmental liabilities relating to the former Koppers company operations of Beazer PLC have been transferred to and underwritten by subsidiaries of two of the world's largest reinsurance companies, Centre Solutions (a member of the Zurich Group) and Swiss Re.

balance sheets [extract]
At December 31, 1999

	Notes	Consolidated 1999 £m	1998 £m
Prepayments and accrued income			
Amounts due from insurers for Koppers liabilities (see below)	17	**175.0**	164.3
Provisions for liabilities and charges	17		
Koppers liabilities transferred to insurers (see above)		**175.0**	164.3
Provisions for other liabilities		**523.5**	630.7
		698.5	795.0

29 Restatement of comparatives [extract]

The adoption of Financial Reporting Standard 12 'Provisions, Contingent Liabilities and Contingent Assets' (FRS 12) has required changes in the method of accounting for reclamation costs, health care obligations in respect of US employees, environmental obligations, decommissioning costs and other liabilities.

As a result of these changes in accounting policy the comparatives have been restated as follows:
a) Consolidated balance sheet

	Tangible fixed assets £m	Prepayments £m	Koppers liabilities transferred to insurers £m	Provision for liabilities and changes £m	Shareholders' Funds £m
1998 as previously reported	2,000.3	–	–	(684.6)	(1,539.4)
Adoption of FRS 12 at January 1, 1998	(1.0)	164.3	(164.3)	70.3	(69.3)
During 1998 (see below)	–	–	–	(16.4)	16.4
Adoption of FRS 12 at December 31, 1998	(1.0)	164.3	(164.3)	53.9	(52.9)
1998 restated	**1,999.3**	**164.3**	**(164.3)**	**(630.7)**	**(1,592.3)**

The principal changes arise from the elimination, increase and reclassification of provisions for liabilities and charges. In the case of Koppers environmental liabilities the obligation is recognised in provisions with a corresponding asset representing the amounts receivable under the insurance arrangements entered into in 1998. Under these arrangements the funding and risk of the environmental liabilities relating to the former Koppers company operations of Beazer PLC have been transferred to and underwritten by subsidiaries of two of the world's largest reinsurance companies, Centre Solutions (a member of the Zurich Group) and Swiss Re.

We are not convinced that the standard's requirement to gross up in such circumstances is an improvement on the previous rules. Again, it is a consequence of approaching the subject from a balance sheet perspective rather than as an expense recognition issue, but it has the effect of including assets in the balance sheet that do not meet the usual recognition criteria. Furthermore, it is inconsistent with existing practice under a number of other standards. For example, under FRS 3, provisions for the sale or termination of an operation have to be calculated 'after taking into account the aggregate profit … from the future profits of the operation'.[89] Under SSAP 9 provision has to be made for long-term contracts which are projected to make a loss, but there is no suggestion that the remaining revenue and costs would have to be recorded in the balance sheet in full even though the contract had not been completed.[90]

In an attempt to rationalise the inconsistency, FRED 14 acknowledged the FRS 3 case cited above but said that 'the Board is of the view that it is appropriate to calculate closure provisions on a net basis because a unit that is not a going concern is most usefully represented to users in one line, separately from continuing operations'.[91] Interestingly, this justification is now considered inappropriate with respect to gains on expected disposal of assets in measuring such provisions (see 4.5 below).

One area where it might be thought appropriate to gross up for expected recoveries is vacant leasehold property provisions. This is discussed further at 5.3 below where it can be seen from Extracts 28.14 and 28.15 that Thorntons had originally grossed up its balance sheet on implementation of FRS 12 for the first time, but then restated on a net basis the following year in line with the practice that had developed for such onerous contracts.

The issue that may give more concern is whether the strict criteria that need to be applied to the corresponding asset might mean that some reimbursements will not be able to be recognised at all. For items such as insurance contracts, this may not be a concern, as entities will probably be able to argue that a recovery on an insurance contract is virtually certain if the entity is required to settle the obligation. For other types of reimbursement, however, recovery may be less certain.

It is interesting to contrast this approach with the case where an entity is jointly and severally liable for an obligation. In that case, the company provides only for its own share and the remainder that is expected to be met by other parties is treated only as a contingent liability.[92] This means that a similar economic position is not always portrayed in the same way. If it were, then a liability would have to be set up for the whole amount for which the entity is jointly and severally liable, with a corresponding asset being recognised for the amount expected to be met by other parties.

4.5 Gains on disposals of related assets

One refinement to the measurement rules was only introduced after the exposure draft stage – that gains from the expected disposal of assets should not be taken into account in measuring a provision, even if the expected disposal is closely linked to the event giving rise to the provision.[93] The rationale behind this is that the ASB believes that liabilities should be measured independently of the recognition and measurement rules for assets.[94] The area where this requirement is likely to have most impact is in the measurement of restructuring provisions. Low & Bonar refers to this in relation to a provision in its 1998 accounts:

Extract 28.4: Low & Bonar PLC (1998)

FINANCIAL REVIEW [extract]

... we have made a provision of £7.5 million to cover the costs of closure. This figure excludes an estimated gain of approximately £2 million which we anticipate on the disposal of the land, buildings and certain equipment which, due to changing accounting standards, cannot be accounted for until the assets are sold. The cash costs associated with the Irlam closure net of disposal proceeds when the land, buildings and equipment are sold, are anticipated to be between £2 million and £3 million. ...

Rather more spectacularly, this change led British Aerospace to write off the remarkable sum of £267 million, as shown in this extract:

Extract 28.5: British Aerospace Public Limited Company (1998)

24 Reserves [extract]

FRS 12 – Provisions, contingent liabilities and contingent assets

In previous years, expenditure on rationalisation schemes initiated before 1991 was included within development properties to the extent that it was recoverable from the estimated disposal proceeds. FRS 12 does not permit such expected gains to be taken into account when assessing the level of provision relating to such schemes. These rationalisation costs which amounted to £267 million at 31 December 1997 are now no longer included.

FRS 3 – *Reporting Financial Performance* – was amended to bring it in line with this requirement in FRS 12. A provision made for the sale or termination of an operation under FRS 3 is no longer able to take into account gains from expected disposals of assets, although it is still able to take into account future profits of the operation (see Chapter 25 at 2.4).

4.6 Changes and uses of provisions

The standard requires provisions to be revised annually to reflect the current best estimate of the obligation. If it is no longer probable that the obligation will be settled, the provision should be reversed.[95] Where discounting is used, the carrying amount of the provision increases to reflect the passage of time, and this is recognised as a finance cost.[96] This seems uncontroversial, other than in relation to changes in discount rates, which are discussed in 4.2.5 above.

The standard emphasises that provisions should be used only for expenditures for which the provision was originally recognised, as to do otherwise would conceal the impact of two different events.[97] This means that the questionable practice of charging costs against a provision that was set up for a different purpose is specifically prohibited and the profit and loss account will have to charge the new expenses separately from any release of an unused provision.

5 EXAMPLES OF PROVISIONS IN PRACTICE

5.1 Restructuring provisions

5.1.1 Definition

FRS 12 defines a restructuring as 'a programme that is planned and controlled by management, and materially changes either:

(a) the scope of a business undertaken by an entity; or

(b) the manner in which that business is conducted.'[98]

This is said to include:

(a) sale or termination of a line of business;

(b) the closure of business locations in a country or region or the relocation of business activities from one country or region to another;

(c) changes in management structure, for example, eliminating a layer of management; and

(d) fundamental reorganisations that have a material effect on the nature and focus of the entity's operations.[99]

This definition is very wide, and could encourage companies to classify all kinds of operating costs as restructuring costs, and thereby invite the reader to perceive them in a different light from the 'normal' costs of operating in a dynamic business environment. Even though FRS 12 prevents such costs being expensed too early (see recognition rules below), and FRS 3 might stop them being charged outside the operating profit section of the profit and loss account, their separate disclosure as restructuring costs may nonetheless cause users of accounts to misinterpret the business's performance. 'Restructuring' is a term of art which can be, and is, used to cover a multitude of sins, and there is a risk that the standard will perpetuate this. The reality is that change has become a perennial feature of business and it is potentially misleading to afford it any special status in accounting terms.

5.1.2 Recognition

FRS 12 requires that restructuring costs are recognised only when the general recognition criteria in the standard are met.[100] The interpretation of these criteria give rise to further specific requirements that 'a constructive obligation to restructure arises only when an entity:

(a) has a detailed formal plan for the restructuring identifying at least:

  (i) the business or part of a business concerned;

  (ii) the principal locations affected;

  (iii) the location, function, and approximate number of employees who will be compensated for terminating their services;

  (iv) the expenditures that will be undertaken; and

  (v) when the plan will be implemented; and

(b) has raised a valid expectation in those affected that it will carry out the restructuring by starting to implement that plan or announcing its main features to those affected by it.'[101]

The standard gives examples of the entity's actions that may provide evidence that the entity has started to implement a plan, quoting the dismantling of plant or selling of assets, or the public announcement of the main features of the plan. However, it also emphasises that the public announcement of a detailed plan to restructure will not automatically create an obligation; the important principle is that the entity's actions give rise to valid expectations in other parties such as customers, suppliers and employees.[102]

The standard also suggests that for a plan to give rise to a constructive obligation, its implementation needs to be planned to begin as soon as possible and to be completed in a timeframe that makes significant changes to the plan unlikely. Any extended period before commencement of implementation, or if the restructuring will take an unreasonably long time, will mean that a provision is premature, because the entity is still likely to have a chance of changing the plan.[103]

In summary, these conditions require the plan to be detailed and specific, to have gone beyond the directors' powers of recall and to be put into operation without delay or significant alteration.

The criteria set out above for the recognition of provisions mean that a board decision, if it is the only relevant event arising before the balance sheet date, is no longer sufficient. This message is reinforced specifically in the standard, the argument being made that a constructive obligation is not created by a management decision. There will only be a constructive obligation where the entity has, before the balance sheet date:

(a) started to implement the restructuring plan; or

(b) announced the main features of the restructuring plan to those affected by it in a sufficiently specific manner to raise a valid expectation in them that the entity will carry out the restructuring.[104]

Examples are given in the Appendix to FRS 12 illustrating the impact of these conditions.[105]

The standard acknowledges that there will be examples where a board decision does trigger recognition, but this would only be if earlier events such as negotiations with employee representatives for termination payments, or with purchasers for the sale of an operation, have been concluded subject only to board approval. In such circumstances, it is reasoned that when board approval has been obtained and communicated to the other parties, the entity is committed to restructure, assuming all other conditions are met.[106]

There is also discussion in the standard of the situation that may arise in some countries where, for example, employee representatives may sit on the board, so that a board decision effectively communicates the decision to them, which may result in a constructive obligation to restructure.[107]

These recognition rules are substantially different from those that most companies applied in the past. De La Rue provides an example of a group that on implementation of FRS 12 had to restate the accounts of earlier years to alter the timing of recognition of such costs.

Extract 28.6: De La Rue plc (1999)

29 Prior year adjustments [extract]

The implementation of new accounting standards has resulted in a number of prior year adjustments. These can be summarised as follows:

(a) The reorganisation cost of £14.8m in respect of Security Paper and Print which was previously charged in 1996/97 has been recharged in 1997/98.

(b) Camelot has also restated its results on the implementation of FRS 12, the net impact of which has been to increase our equity accounted share of its profits by £1.2m in 1997/98 and £1.2m prior to 1997/98.

...

The dismissal of the significance of board decisions was not well supported when the ASB proposed it in FRED 14. A large number of commentators suggested that board decisions should act as a trigger for recognition of provisions, particularly if supported by subsequent events between the year end and approval of the accounts which indicate that the board decision was a meaningful one. However, the ASB made no concessions to this view, and has merely added a paragraph in the final standard which suggests that where events after the balance sheet date indicate the existence of a constructive obligation to restructure that did not exist at the balance sheet date, this may require disclosure as a non-adjusting event under SSAP 17[108] (see Chapter 27 at 2.3).

The 1999 accounts of both Pilkington and Marks and Spencer disclosed the costs of restructurings that were announced after the year end and hence were not provided for.

Extract 28.7: Pilkington plc (1999)

43 Post-balance sheet event

On 26th May 1999 the Group announced its plans to reorganise and streamline its automotive manufacturing operations in North America. This will involve the closure of a plant and the transfer of its production to two other existing facilities in North America. The programme is expected to involve exceptional restructuring costs of approximately £30 million, of which half are expected to be cash costs. No adjustment has been made for this in the financial statements.

Extract 28.8: Marks and Spencer p.l.c. (1999)

31 Post-balance sheet events

On 28 April, the Group announced the closure of its Canadian operations. As a consequence, its subsidiary Marks & Spencer Canada Inc. will cease to operate during the financial year ending 31 March 2000. The total cost of closure is estimated to be £25m, excluding goodwill of £24.4m previously written off to reserves.

On 10 May, the Group announced the rationalisation of its UK store management. The total cost of this rationalisation is estimated to be £14m.

De La Rue gave supplementary disclosure in its financial review of its future expected reorganisation costs, which contrast with the provisions it was able to make under FRS 12, as shown in this extract.

Extract 28.9: De La Rue plc (1999)

Financial Review [extract]
Analysis of reorganisation costs

During the last year, we have announced major reorganisations within Cash Systems and Security Paper and Print, together with the relocation of our head office. In line with current accounting practice, costs are written off against profits as committed. A significant element of these costs will not be committed until our financial year ending in March 2000. Set out in Table 1 is a summary which shows the charge in 1999 and the expected charge in our current year's accounts and corresponding cash outflows.

Table 1 – Reorganisation costs

		Expected	
	1999	**2000**	**2001**
	£m	**£m**	**£m**
Cash Systems	25.9	20.0	–
Security Paper and Print	18.7	5.0	–
Head Office relocation	3.9	–	–
Total profit and loss cost	48.5	25.0	–
Cash outflow	26.2	28.0	5.0

17 Provisions for liabilities and charges [extract]

The reorganisation within Security Paper and Print utilised £3.7m of the provision created in 1996/97, leaving a total of £0.2m carried forward within other provisions. Further reorganisation provisions were established during the current year of which £1.4m remains within other provisions.

With regard to the Cash Systems reorganisation, £2.9m is carried forward within other provisions.

A total of £2.8m is carried forward in other provisions in respect of the relocation of Head Office from London to Basingstoke.

Disclosure of this kind adds to the transparency of such costs and can be very helpful to the reader. Nevertheless, we are not convinced that the change in recognition of reorganisation costs that FRS 12 has brought about is a beneficial one. We believe that it is misguided to ignore the effect of management intentions in portraying the financial performance and position of an entity, as this can often be highly relevant to an understanding of the entity's affairs. Although board decisions are capable of being reversed, this does not happen as a general rule.

Furthermore, the exclusion of the effect of management decisions is not a principle that has been applied consistently by the ASB. Take the example of a restructuring which is announced shortly after the balance sheet date involving the closure of plants and large scale redundancies. The reporting entity will be precluded from recognising the direct costs of the restructuring, as it does not have a constructive obligation at the balance sheet date. However, the entity will be required to make provision for impairment in the carrying value of plant and other assets at the affected sites under FRS 11 (see Chapter 13 at 2.2). Hence, board decisions would appear to be relevant when assessing impairment of assets but not when determining the reporting entity's liabilities, with the result that only some of the costs that result from the closure decision are recognised.

It is also the case that the apparently robust tests of a constructive obligation set out in the standard are weaker than they seem. The interpretation of the concept of actions that 'raise a valid expectation in third parties' is extremely difficult and subjective. Even if a trigger point is easily identifiable, such as when an entity makes a detailed public announcement which meets all the specified criteria, it does not necessarily commit management to the 'restructuring' as such, but only to specific items of expenditure such as redundancy costs. Nevertheless, in practice, once a trigger point has been identified, an entity will presumably provide for all the costs of the reorganisation, assuming that they meet the measurement criteria set out in 5.1.3 below.

Furthermore, the test is at least as manipulable as board decisions. Companies anxious to accelerate or postpone recognition of a liability could readily do so by advancing or deferring an event that signals such a commitment, such as a public announcement, without any change to the substance of their position.

FRS 12 has some further specific rules governing when to recognise the loss arising on the sale of an operation. It is unclear why this should have been the case, since such provisions are really adjustments to the carrying amounts of the assets concerned, not provisions as defined by the standard. Nevertheless, many companies include such items within provisions. The standard states that no obligation arises for the sale of an operation until the entity is committed to the sale, i.e. there is a binding sale agreement.[109] This therefore suggests that a provision cannot be made for a loss on disposal unless a binding sale agreement is in place at the balance sheet date. The standard says that this applies even when an entity has taken a decision to sell an operation and announced that decision publicly, it cannot be committed to the sale until a purchaser has been identified and there is a binding sale agreement. Until there is such an agreement, the entity will be able to change its mind and indeed will have to take another course of action if a purchaser cannot be found on acceptable terms.[110] This requirement is similar to one already contained in FRS 3 (see Chapter 25 at 2.4). However, FRS 3 contains an additional suggestion in its explanatory section that a binding contract entered into after the balance sheet date may provide additional evidence of commitments at the balance sheet date.[111] The meaning of this explanatory paragraph has never been clarified, and similar wording is not included within FRS 12. Hence, it could be argued that if the explanatory paragraph in FRS 3 has previously been used to justify setting up provision for the disposal of an operation where the binding sale agreement was entered into after the balance sheet date but before the accounts were signed, this interpretation is no longer allowable under FRS 12. However, this is unclear, given that the relevant paragraph in FRS 3 itself has not been deleted or amended.

In practice, it appears that companies continue to make provisions for loss on disposal of operations where they do not have binding contracts at the year end as shown in the following extract.

Extract 28.10: Tomkins PLC (2001)

Consolidated profit and loss account [extract]

For the year ended 30 April 2001	**Before goodwill amortisation and exceptional items £ million**	**Goodwill amort-isation £ million**	**Exceptional items £ million**	**Total £ million**	Before goodwill amortisation and exceptional items £ million	Goodwill Amort-isation £ million	Exceptional items £ million	Total £ million
Operating profit including associates	**320.0**	**(9.9)**	**–**	**310.1**	526.0	(5.0)	–	521.0
Loss on disposal of operations	**–**	**–**	**(280.9)**	**(280.9)**	–	–	(6.3)	(6.3)
Reversal of provision for loss on disposal of business	**–**	**–**	**215.0**	**215.0**	–	–	–	–
Provision for loss on disposal of business to be discontinued:								
Impairment of goodwill	**–**	**–**	**(42.2)**	**(42.2)**	–	–	(171.4)	(171.4)
Impairment of assets	**–**	**–**	**(23.8)**	**(23.8)**	–	–	–	–
Payments directly related to the disposal	**–**	**–**	**–**	**–**	–	–	(43.6)	(43.6)
Profit before interest	**320.0**	**(9.9)**	**(131.9)**	**178.2**	526.0	(5.0)	(221.3)	299.7

28 Acquisitions and disposals [extract]

Disposals:

Engineered & Construction Products:

Homer of Redditch Limited, Twiflex Limited and T. A. Knight Limited were sold on 18 May 2000, 23 June 2000 and 16 February 2001 respectively for a total cash consideration, net of costs, of £3.1 million. £1.0 million of goodwill previously written off to reserves was written off to the profit and loss account resulting in a loss on sale of £1.8 million.

Food Manufacturing:

The Red Wing Company Inc was sold on 14 July 2000 for a cash consideration, net of costs, of $140.9 million (£93.8 million). The sale of the remaining Food Manufacturing business segment was completed on 31 August 2000 for a total cash consideration of £1,138.0 million. £171.4 million of the £828.7 million of goodwill previously written off to reserves on acquisition of the business was included in the write-off of the impaired goodwill in the year ended 29 April 2000 and the remaining £657.3 million was charged to the profit and loss account. Costs of the sale were offset by the reversal of the £43.6 million provision established at 29 April 2000 for payments directly related to the disposal, which included a provision of £25.0 million for pension payments arising as a result of the transaction. The net loss on sale charged to the profit and loss account for the year ended 30 April 2001 was £1.8 million.

Professional, Garden & Leisure Products:

Murray Inc and Hayter Limited were sold on the 5 October 2000 for a provisional consideration of $219.3 million (£148.3 million). Of the proceeds, $206.3 million (£139.5 million) has been received in cash and $13.0 million (£8.8 million) in a secured subordinated loan note, repayable in 2006. There was a loss on sale of £62.3 million after charging £73.9 million of goodwill, previously written off to reserves and £2.1 million of costs of disposal.

As a result of the agreement signed subsequent to the year end relating to the disposal of Smith & Wesson (see note 29), a provision of £66.0 million for the loss on sale, which includes £42.2 million for the impairment of goodwill, has been charged to the profit and loss account.

Another example of a company making provision for losses on disposals after the year end is Aga Foodservice Group as shown in Extract 27.6 in Chapter 27 at 2.3.

Where it is considered that a provision for the loss on disposal cannot be recognised, then the standard emphasises that where the sale of the operation is envisaged as part of a larger restructuring, the standard notes that the assets of the operation must be reviewed for impairment. This may therefore mean that the profit and loss account reflects effectively the same loss; it is just that the provision is presented as a reduction of the value of fixed assets rather than as a liability. The standard also recognises that where a sale is part of a larger restructuring, the entity could be committed to the other parts of restructuring before the binding sale agreement is in place.[112] Hence, the costs of the restructuring will be spread over different accounting periods.

5.1.3 *Costs that can be recognised within a restructuring provision*

The recognition tests for reorganisation costs that are set out above are designed to establish whether or not there is a liability at the balance sheet date, which is consistent with the conceptual approach of the standard and indeed with the ASB's *Statement of Principles*. It is therefore rather surprising to find an additional paragraph in the standard that further limits the costs that can be provided for and which is founded on quite a different conceptual approach. It states that 'provision should include only the direct expenditures arising from the restructuring, which are those that are both:

(a) necessarily entailed by a restructuring; and

(b) not associated with the ongoing activities of the entity'.[113]

While (a) is perhaps a further elaboration of the rules for defining the extent of the company's obligations, the rationale for (b) is not so straightforward. The justification given for it ties in with the more general requirement in the standard that 'it is only those obligations arising from past events existing independently of an entity's future actions that should be recognised'.[114] Hence, these costs are recognised on the same basis as if they arose independently of the restructuring.[115]

In reality, this is an approach based on expense recognition, in that the costs associated with ongoing activities will produce future benefits, and thus should not be anticipated, whether or not a liability for them exists. Expense recognition is a concept not adequately acknowledged by the ASB's *Statement of Principles*, but one which the Board seems unable to do without.

The standard gives specific examples of those costs that may not be included within the provision. Such costs include:

(a) retraining or relocating continuing staff;

(b) marketing; or

(c) investment in new systems and distribution networks.[116]

United Utilities disclosed a restructuring provision in its 1998 accounts:

Extract 28.11: United Utilities PLC (1998)

20 Provisions for liabilities and charges [extract]

						Group	Company
	Restructuring £m	Onerous contracts £m	Bangkok £m	Retail divestment £m	Other £m	Total £m	Other £m
At 31 March 1997	127.7	166.6	42.0	41.8	51.2	429.3	12.3
Utilised	(49.0)	(5.7)	(21.2)	(20.6)	(39.8)	(136.3)	(3.9)
Profit and loss account	(6.5)	–	–	–	(4.7)	(11.2)	–
At 31 March 1998	72.2	160.9	20.8	21.2	6.7	281.8	8.4

Restructuring

The restructuring provisions relate primarily to:

- the cost of completing the reorganisation of North West Water operations;
- the cost of completing the voluntary redundancy programme established by NORWEB plc prior to the acquisition; and
- the cost of reorganising the Group following the acquisition of NORWEB plc (including an expansion of the Norweb voluntary redundancy programme outlined above).

The above costs primarily relate to terminations, training, relocation of employees and systems improvements.

The description of the costs in the last sentence of this extract shows that some of the items provided for appear to be associated with ongoing activities, which meant that they would not be permitted in the future under FRS 12. Accordingly, in its 1999 accounts United Utilities amended its provisions as shown in this extract.

Extract 28.12: United Utilities PLC (1999)

1 **Accounting policies** [extract]

(a) **Basis of preparation of financial statements** [extract]

- restatement of provisions to comply with Financial Reporting Standard 12. The effect of this standard is to change the allocation of restructuring costs between previous reporting periods. Costs previously provided for did not meet the stringent criteria for recording a liability now embodied in Financial Reporting Standard 12. Consequently, the results of previous periods have been amended to reflect the requirements of the new standard and the results for the year ended 31 March 1998 have been reduced by £55.6 million and for the year ended 31 March 1997 have been reduced by £46.5 million. These adjustments reflect the profile of the utilisation of the original provisions. There has been no material impact on the results for the year ended 31 March 1999 in respect of these adjustments.

19 **Provisions for liabilities and charges** [extract]

						Group	Company
	Restructuring Restated £m	Onerous contracts Restated £m	Bangkok £m	Retail divestment £m	Other £m	Total Restated £m	Other £m
At 1 April 1998	38.8	192.9	20.8	21.2	6.7	280.4	8.4
Utilised	(23.5)	(8.0)	(2.2)	(0.7)	(3.9)	(38.3)	(1.8)
At 31 March 1998	**15.3**	**184.9**	**18.6**	**20.5**	**2.8**	**242.1**	**6.6**

> *Restructuring*
> The restructuring provisions relate primarily to:
> – the cost of completing the reorganisation of North West Water operations;
> – the cost of completing the voluntary redundancy programme established by NORWEB plc prior to the acquisition; and
> – the cost of reorganising the Group following the acquisition of NORWEB plc (including an expansion of the Norweb voluntary redundancy programme outlined above).

No examples of allowable costs are given within the standard. However, FRED 14 gave certain examples. These were the costs of:

(a) making employees redundant;

(b) terminating leases and other contracts whose termination results directly from the reorganisation; and

(c) expenditures to be made in the course of the reorganisation, such as employees' remuneration while they are engaged in such tasks as dismantling plant, disposing of surplus stocks and fulfilling contractual obligations.[117]

Examples (a) and (b) would certainly be permitted under the rules in FRS 12. Example (c) is slightly more contentious in relation to employee remuneration, in that unless an employee is being retained solely for the purpose of dismantling plant, etc, before being made redundant, it is questionable whether the remuneration costs meet the definition of being 'necessarily entailed by a restructuring'.

A further rule in FRS 12 is that the provision should not include identifiable future operating losses up to the date of the restructuring, unless they relate to an onerous contract.[118] This is consistent with the more general requirement in the standard that provision should not be made for future operating losses, discussed in 5.2 below. Since sales or termination of businesses fall within the definition of a restructuring in FRS 12 as discussed at 5.1.1 above, it might be thought that this means that no provision can be made for the future operating losses relating to such businesses. However, provisions in such circumstances are also dealt with in FRS 3 where they are required to include any operating losses of the operation up to the date of sale or termination.[119] Given that no amendment has been made to FRS 3, it seems reasonable to assume that entities are able to continue to make provision for future operating losses in these circumstances.

The general rule noted in 4.5 above that gains on the expected disposal of assets cannot be taken into account in the measurement of provisions is also particularly relevant to the measurement of restructuring provisions.[120] This has meant that larger restructuring provisions than before have been required as any corresponding expected gains on assets are no longer available for set off, as was the case with British Aerospace as shown in Extract 28.5 above. However, sometimes the impact of this rule will be mitigated by the fact that fewer costs will also be recognised within a provision, as some will not meet the criteria set out above.

5.2 Operating losses

The standard explicitly states that 'provisions should not be recognised for future operating losses'.[121] This is because such losses do not meet the definition of a liability and the general recognition criteria of the standard (see 3.1 above).[122] Such costs should be left to be reported in the future in the same way as future profits are.

However, it would be wrong to assume that this requirement has effectively prevented any future operating losses from being anticipated, because they are sometimes recognised as a result of requirements in another standard. For example:

- under SSAP 9, stocks are written down to the extent that they will not be recovered from future revenues, rather than leaving the non-recovery to show up as future operating losses (see Chapter 16 at 2.2.3);
- under FRS 11, fixed asset impairment is measured on the basis of the present value of future operating cash flows, meaning that provision will be made not simply for future operating losses but for sub-standard operating profits as well (see Chapter 13 at 2.2). FRS 12 specifically makes reference to the fact that an expectation of future operating losses may be an indication that certain assets are impaired;[123]
- provision is made for future operating losses of operations that are committed to be sold or terminated under FRS 3 (see Chapter 25 at 2.4); and
- provision is made for losses expected on long-term construction contracts under SSAP 9. Indeed, this sometimes extends even to provision for future administration costs where existing unprofitable contracts will absorb a large part of the company's future capacity.[124]

This is therefore a rather more complex issue than FRS 12 acknowledges.

5.3 Onerous contracts

Although future operating losses in general cannot be provided for, FRS 12 requires that 'If an entity has a contract that is onerous, the present obligation under the contract should be recognised and measured as a provision'.[125]

The standard notes that many contracts (for example, some routine purchase orders) can be cancelled without paying compensation to the other party, and therefore there is no obligation. However, other contracts establish both rights and obligations for each of the contracting parties. Where events make such a contract onerous, the contract falls within the scope of the standard and a liability exists which is recognised. As noted at 2.1.2 above, executory contracts that are not onerous fall outside the scope of the standard.[126]

FRS 12 defines an onerous contract as 'a contract in which the unavoidable costs of meeting the obligations under it exceed the economic benefits expected to be received under it'.[127] This seems to require that the contract is onerous to the point of being directly loss-making, not simply uneconomic by reference to current prices. In this respect the definition is narrower than should be applied in the context of acquisition accounting, where the task is to put a fair value on identifiable assets and liabilities (see Chapter 6 at 2.4.3 F III).

In the context of ongoing operations, however, FRS 12 considers that 'the unavoidable costs under a contract reflect the least net cost of exiting from the contract ie the lower of the cost of fulfilling it and any compensation or penalties arising from failure to fulfil it'.[128] An example of such a provision is BG's gas contract loss provisions, which stood at £215 million at 31 December 2000, and are described in this extract.

Extract 28.13: BG plc (2000)

22 PROVISIONS FOR LIABILITIES AND CHARGES [extract]
Long-term gas contract loss provisions

These represent forecast future losses under certain gas purchase and supply sales contracts assigned to BG on the demerger of Centrica plc in 1997. Some of the contracts terminated this year, with others due to terminate in 2009. The estimated net losses have been discounted at around 10% and are dependent upon factors such as prices, which vary with a basket of indices, and supply and demand volumes, BG also uses its own gas to supply these contracts. To account for BG's own gas sales and transportation of all gas at the contract prices, the difference between market and contract prices is included within Other activities.

The most common example of an onerous contract in practice probably relates to leasehold property. From time to time entities may hold vacant leasehold property (or property which is only partly occupied) which they have substantially ceased to use for the purpose of their business and where sub-letting is either unlikely, or would be at a significantly reduced rental from that being paid by the entity.

This issue had been addressed previously in 1993, when the UITF proposed to introduce an abstract to require provision to be made, but as a result of the large amount of opposition that it received to its draft did not proceed with the abstract.

However, the issue is now covered by the standard, and reinforced by the inclusion of a specific example of a provision for a vacant leasehold property.[129] Companies now have to make systematic provision when such properties become vacant, and on a discounted basis where the effect is sufficiently material. Indeed, it is not just when the properties become vacant that provision would be required; provision is required at the time the expected economic benefits of using the property fall short of the unavoidable costs under the lease.

Nevertheless, a number of difficulties remain. The first is how the provision should be calculated. It is unlikely that the provision will simply be the net present value of the future rental obligation, because if a substantial period of the lease remains, the entity will probably be able either to agree a negotiated sum with the landlord to terminate the lease early, or to sub-lease the building at some point in the future. Hence, the entity will have to make a best estimate of its future cash flows taking all these factors into account.

Another issue that arises from this is whether the provision should be shown net of any cash flows that may arise from sub-leasing the property, or whether the provision must be shown gross, with a corresponding asset set up for expected cash flows from sub-leasing only if they meet the recognition criteria of being 'virtually certain' to be received. The strict offset criteria in the standard (see 4.4 above) would suggest the latter to be required, as the entity would normally retain liability for the full lease payments if the sub-lessor defaulted. It is unlikely that this is really the result that the ASB intended, particularly as the ASB's earlier Discussion Paper said that provisions for vacant leasehold properties should be net of expected recoveries from subletting the property, and did not suggest that all future rental income and expenditure should be brought on to the balance sheet.[130] However, the standard makes no reference to this issue. One company which on adopting FRS 12 recognised such provision on a gross basis, with any expected recovery from sub-letting as a corresponding debtor was Thorntons as illustrated below.

Extract 28.14: Thorntons PLC (1999)

8 Prior period adjustment – onerous leases

FRS 12 'Provisions, Contingent Assets and Contingent Liabilities' was adopted with effect from 28 June 1998, and as a result, the comparatives for the period ended 27 June 1998 and the opening balances have been restated to reflect the new guidelines with respect to the recognition of onerous lease obligations.

The effects of adopting this new accounting standard are summarised below:

	1999 £'000	**1999 £'000**	1998 £'000	1998 £'000
Consolidated profit and loss account:				
Provision created for onerous lease obligations	**(982)**		(3,561)	
Asset created for onerous lease sublet receivables	**180**		105	
		(802)		(3,456)
Provision released on exit from onerous leases		**1,374**		887
Net onerous lease obligations credited/(charged) in the period		**572**		(2,569)
Release of UK restructuring provision		**–**		211
Increase/(decrease) to profit before tax in the financial period		**572**		(2,358)
Taxation		**(172)**		731
Increase/(decrease) to retained profit in the financial period		**400**		(1,627)
Consolidated balance sheet:				
Onerous lease sublet receivables debtor due after more than one year		**1,651**		1,677
Onerous lease sublet receivables debtor due within one year		**190**		140
Corporation tax recoverable on amounts provided		**1,071**		1,243
Onerous lease provision carried forward		**(4,955)**		(5,827)
Decrease to net assets in the financial period		**(2,043)**		(2,767)

24 Provisions for liabilities and charges [extract]

The provision for onerous leases is in respect of closed leasehold properties, from which the Group no longer trades, but is liable to fulfil rent and other property commitments up to the lease expiry date. If a property is sub-let below the head rent, a separate asset has been established and disclosed within debtors. Obligations are payable within a range of one to 18 years, the average being ten years. Amounts have been provided on current rentals which, following a rent review, could require additional provision.

However, the company had a change of heart the following year, adopting a net approach since this was 'best practice' and restating the 1999 accounts by of prior year adjustment as shown below.

Extract 28.15: Thorntons PLC (2000)

Changes in financial information [extract]

FRS 12 'Provisions, Contingent Assets and Contingent Liabilities' was adopted with effect from 28 June 1998, and reflected in the 1999 Annual Report as a prior period adjustment. Subsequent to those financial statements, in line with best practice we have disclosed the effect of onerous lease provisions as the net impact of the full provision and any sublet receivables provided. We have therefore restated the sublet receivables debtor within provisions as at 26 June 1999.

24 Provisions for liabilities and charges [extract]

	Group and Company Deferred tax	Group and Company Onerous leases	Group and Company UK restructure	Group and Company Total
	£'000	£'000	£'000	£'000
Summary of provisions				
At 26 June 1999 – as reported	–	4,955	1,480	6,435
Re-disclose onerous lease sublet receivables	–	(1,841)	–	(1,841)
At 26 June 1999 – as restated	–	3,114	1,480	4,594
Accelerated write-down of fixed assets (see note 15)	–	–	(639)	(639)
Expenditure in the period	–	(245)	(841)	(1,086)
Released to the consolidated profit and loss account	–	(1,428)	–	(1,428)
At 24 June 2000	**–**	**1,441**	**–**	**1,441**

The provision for onerous leases is in respect of closed leasehold properties, from which the Group no longer trades, but is liable to fulfil rent and other property commitments up to the lease expiry date. If a property is sublet below the head rent, or for a period shorter than the remaining lease term, an asset has been established for the total sublet receivables. Obligations are payable within a range of one to 17 years (1999: one to 18 years), the average being nine years (1999: ten years). Amounts have been provided on current rentals which, following a rent review, could require additional provision.

We believe that such a net approach is the most appropriate treatment for such onerous contracts. Indeed, it could be argued that the provision is only in respect of the onerous element of the contract and therefore there is no corresponding asset to be recognised.

In the past, some companies have maintained that no provision is required for vacant properties, because if the property leases are looked at on a portfolio basis, the overall economic benefits from properties exceed the overall costs. However, this argument does not appear to be sustainable under FRS 12, as the definition of an onerous contract refers specifically to costs and economic benefits *under the contract.*

It is more difficult to apply the definition of onerous contracts to the lease on a head office which is not generating revenue specifically. If the definition were applied too literally, one might end up concluding that all head office leases should be provided against because no specific economic benefits are expected under them. It would be more sensible to conclude that the entity as a whole obtains economic benefits from its head office, which was presumably the reason for entering in to the lease to start with. However, this does not alter the fact that if circumstances alter and the head office becomes vacant, a provision should then be made against the lease.

The standard also requires that any assets dedicated to an onerous contract should be written down before a provision is made.[131] For example, any leasehold improvements that have been capitalised should be written off before provision is made for excess future rental costs.

5.4 Environmental provisions

FRED 14 proposed specific recognition rules in relation to environmental liabilities. It said that 'provisions for environmental liabilities should be recognised at the time and to the extent that the entity becomes obliged, legally or constructively, to rectify environmental damage or to perform restorative work on the environment.'[132] The further discussion in the draft focused on the idea of 'constructive obligations', making it clear that provision was possible only if the company had no real option but to carry out the remedial work.[133]

These specific rules are not included in the final standard, but the general recognition rules which apply have the same impact. These requirements are not particularly controversial, apart from the general difficulty in knowing exactly when a constructive obligation comes into existence.

The standard illustrates two examples of circumstances where environmental provisions would be required. The first deals with the situation where it is virtually certain that legislation will be enacted which will require the clean up of land already contaminated.[134] In these circumstances, a provision would obviously be required. However, in its discussion about what constitutes an obligating event, the standard notes that 'differences in circumstances surrounding enactment make it impossible to specify a single event that would make the enactment of a law virtually certain. In many cases, it will be impossible to be virtually certain of the enactment of a law until it is enacted.[135] The second example deals with the situation where an entity has contaminated land, but is not legally required to clean it up.[136] In these circumstances, a provision is required if the entity has a constructive obligation to clean up the land. In the example given, a constructive obligation is said to exist because the entity has a widely publicised environmental policy undertaking to clean up all contamination that it causes, and has a record of honouring this policy.

ICI's policy on environmental liabilities is shown below.

Extract 28.16: Imperial Chemical Industries PLC (2000)

Accounting policies [extract]
Environmental liabilities

The Group is exposed to environmental liabilities relating to its past operations, principally in respect of soil and groundwater remediation costs. Provisions for these costs are made when expenditure on remedial work is probable and the cost can be estimated within a reasonable range of possible outcomes.

In fact, this is exactly the same as the policy that ICI adopted pre-FRS 12.

BP Amoco similarly had a policy of providing for such liabilities prior to FRS 12.

Extract 28.17: BP Amoco p.l.c. (1998)

Accounting policies [extract]
Environmental liabilities

Environmental expenditures that relate to current or future revenues are expensed or capitalized as appropriate. Expenditures that relate to an existing condition caused by past operations and that do not contribute to current or future earnings are expensed.

Liabilities for environmental costs are recognized when environmental assessments or clean-ups are probable and the associated costs can be reasonably estimated. Generally, the timing of these provisions coincides with the commitment to a formal plan of action or, if earlier, on divestment or on closure of inactive sites.

However, potentially the more significant effect of the standard is its requirement that provisions should be discounted, which will have a material impact if the expenditure is not expected to be incurred for some time. As a result of implementing FRS 12, BP Amoco has changed its policy to reflect this, which had the effect of reducing its environmental provision by £350 million because of the discount factor, and its current policy is as shown in the following extract.

Extract 28.18: BP Amoco p.l.c. (2000)

Accounting policies [extract]
Environmental liabilities

Environmental expenditures that relate to current or future revenues are expensed or capitalized as appropriate. Expenditures that relate to an existing condition caused by past operations and that do not contribute to current or future earnings are expensed.

Liabilities for environmental costs are recognized when environmental assessments or clean-ups are probable and the associated costs can be reasonably estimated. Generally, the timing of these provisions coincides with the commitment to a formal plan of action or, if earlier, on divestment or on closure of inactive sites. The amount recognized is the best estimate of the expenditure required. Where the liability will not be settled for a number of years the amount recognized is the present value of the estimated future expenditure.

		$ million
26 Other provisions [extract]		
	Decommissioning	**Environmental**
At 1 January 2000	2,785	917
Exchange adjustments	(133)	(10)
Acquisitions	484	1,222
New provisions	139	228
Unwinding of discount	110	55
Utilized/deleted	(384)	(281)
At 31 December 2000	**3,001**	**2,131**

At 31 December 2000 the provision for the costs of decommissioning the group's oil and natural gas production facilities and pipelines at the end of their economic lives was $3,001 million ($2,785 million). These costs are expected to be incurred over the next 30 years. The provision has been estimated using existing technology, at current prices and discounted using a real discount rate of 3.5% (3.5%).

The provision for environment liabilities at 31 December 2000 was $2,131 million ($917 million). This represents primarily the estimated environmental restoration and remediation costs for closed sites or facilities that have been sold. These costs are expected to be incurred over the next 10 years. The provision has been estimated using existing technology, at current prices, and discounted using a real discount rate of 3.5% (3.5%).

5.5 Decommissioning provisions

Decommissioning costs are those that arise, for example, when an oil rig or nuclear power station has to be dismantled at the end of its life. The impact of the standard on such costs is profound. Previous practice in line with the SORP of the Oil Industry Accounting Committee (OIAC) was to build up the required provision over the life of the facility by appropriate charges against revenues. BP Amoco described the process in this policy note:

Extract 28.19: BP Amoco p.l.c. (1998)

Accounting policies [extract]
Decommissioning

Provision is made for the decommissioning of production facilities in accordance with local conditions and requirements on the basis of costs estimated as at the balance sheet date. The provision is allocated over accounting periods using a unit-of-production method based on estimated proved reserves.

The scale of this obligation is evident from its provisions note at that time:

Extract 28.20: BP Amoco p.l.c. (1998)

23 Other provisions [extract]

	$ million
	Decommissioning
At 1 January 1998	3,201
Exchange adjustments	10
Charged to income	130
Utilized/deleted	(31)
At 31 December 1998	**3,310**

FRS 12, on the other hand, requires that the liability is recognised as soon as the obligation exists, which will normally be at commencement of operations. The example in the standard discusses the situation where ninety per cent of the damage is done by building the rig, and ten per cent through the extraction of oil.[137] In these circumstances, a provision for ninety per cent of the total costs will be set up when the rig has been constructed, with the balance being recognised as the oil is extracted.

FRS 12 also says that provisions should be capitalised if the expenditure provides access to future economic benefits.[138] Hence, in the case of decommissioning costs, the oil rig provides access to oil reserves over the years of its operation, so the balance sheet will be grossed up to show this corresponding asset representing access to future oil reserves.

Although we understand why the ASB's conceptual framework pushes it towards recognition of the full liability, it seems that this can only be achieved by including a spurious asset on the other side of the balance sheet. In any case, if the principle that a liability should be recognised once costs have become unavoidable were really to be applied on a consistent basis, various other commitments (for example, expenditure commitments under licence agreements) would also be caught and there would be considerable grossing up of balance sheets. We therefore question whether this change has much merit.

This form of presentation had been considered but rejected by the Oil Industry Accounting Committee when it produced its earlier SORP on the subject. Although acknowledging the conceptual arguments that now lie behind FRS 12, it said that 'the OIAC has no doubt that the gradual build-up of the provision is the appropriate method of recognising this obligation because of the fact that changes in the scope of work, technology and prices are likely to result in great subsequent changes, downwards as well as upwards, in the amounts originally recognised. Whilst changes in estimates of liabilities are an unavoidable and therefore accepted feature of historical cost accounting, these changes would also affect the recorded amounts of assets. The OIAC believes that the resulting changes to the structure of oil company balance sheets would be unlikely to enhance their usefulness.'[139]

The more significant change for most companies, however, involved the use of discounting for the measurement of the liability. Although it had been used for some time in the nuclear industry, discounting was not consistent with previous accounting practice for oil companies. The effect of discounting on the profit and loss account is to split the cost of the eventual decommissioning into two components: an operating cost based on the discounted amount of the provision; and a finance element representing the unwinding of the discount. The overall effect is to produce a rising pattern of cost over the life of the facility, often with most of the total cost of the decommissioning recognised as a finance cost. In contrast, previous practice for oil companies was to show the whole amount in arriving at their operating results, and to aim to charge a level amount for each barrel of oil extracted, although the effects of changing estimates of costs, particularly inflation (which was not factored into the original estimates made), meant that this was not precisely achieved.

As a result of FRS 12, BP Amoco has changed its policy, and its current policy is as shown below.

Extract 28.21: BP Amoco p.l.c. (2000)

Accounting policies [extract]

Decommissioning

Provision for decommissioning is recognized in full at the commencement of oil and natural gas production. The amount recognized is the present value of the estimated future expenditure determined in accordance with local conditions and requirements.

A corresponding tangible fixed asset of an amount equivalent to the provision is also created. This is subsequently depreciated as part of the capital costs of the production and transportation facilities. Any change in the present value of the estimated expenditure is reflected as an adjustment to the provision and the fixed asset.

The extent of BP Amoco's decommissioning provision can be seen in Extract 28.18 at 5.4 above.

As noted at 4.6 above, the standard requires provisions to be revised annually to reflect the current best estimate of the provision. Where the estimate of the expenditure changes from the amount originally provided for, the difference is to added to or deducted from the asset, and this is what BP Amoco has chosen to do, as shown in the policy quoted above. As discussed at 4.2.5 above, the standard does not explicitly say how the effects of changes in the interest rate used in discounting the provision should be treated. However, the recent SORP issued by the Oil Industry Accounting Committee regards changes in discount rates like any other change in estimate and therefore the effect should be adjusted against the asset.[140]

5.6 Cyclical repairs

Before FRS 12 came into force, it was common for some companies to account for the costs of major periodic repair to large assets by making regular provisions against which the repairs were then charged when incurred.[141]

Provisions of this kind are specifically disallowed under the standard. The examples it gives are of a furnace that has a lining that needs replacing every five years, and an aircraft that needs overhauling every three years.[142] Neither of these provisions is allowed to be set up on the basis that there is no obligation to carry out the expenditure independently of the company's future actions. This argument is used even in the circumstances where there is a legal requirement for the asset in question to be repaired, since it is asserted that, even then, the entity could avoid the expenditure by, for example, selling the asset. (It is unclear why a similar argument has not been used in respect of decommissioning costs, where presumably an entity could avoid such costs by selling its oil and gas assets!)

As a result, Pilkington amended its practice in its 1999 accounts as shown in this extract.

Extract 28.22: Pilkington plc (1999)

7 Changes in accounting policies [extract]
(c) FRS 12 (Provisions, Contingent Liabilities and Contingent Assets)

The previous policy of providing for the accrued proportion of the future estimated revenue costs of major glass tank repairs, carried out periodically, has changed in accordance with the new standard and the balance has been released to this year's profit and loss account ((note 30(e)). All such revenue costs are now charged in the period in which the float tanks are repaired.

30 Provisions for liabilities and charges [extract]

	1999 Group £m
(e) Other provisions [extract]	
At beginning of the year	80
Exchange rate adjustments	1
Charged to profit and loss account during the year	21
Released to profit and loss account during the year	(10)
Utilised during year	(22)
At end of the year	70

As a result of the introduction of FRS 12, the tank repair provision at 31st March 1998 has been released to the profit and loss account during the year.

This change was made as a current year credit to the profit and loss account rather than as a change of policy requiring a prior year adjustment, but perhaps the £10 million release was regarded as insufficiently material to warrant restatement.

It is interesting to note that Railtrack did not reverse its 'property maintenance backlog provision' on implementing FRS 12. This stood at £259 million at 31 March 1999 (£92 million having been utilised in the year) and was described in the following words in the accounts drawn up to that date.

Extract 28.23: Railtrack Group PLC (1999)

22 PROVISIONS FOR LIABILITIES AND CHARGES [extract]

The Group, as publicly stated in its Share Offer Prospectus dated 1 May 1996, has implemented a programme of repairs in respect of the property maintenance backlog at stations and depots which is due to be completed by 31 March 2001.

There can be no doubt about Railtrack's need to carry out this work; however, it is difficult to see exactly why this qualifies as a liability under FRS 12 whereas, for example, an airline company is considered not to have any obligation to continue to overhaul its planes. If there is a distinction, it is perhaps to do with the 'backlog' feature of the maintenance work – Railtrack had this inheritance when it was floated – but it is hard to see this as a relevant distinction. This again illustrates the rather nebulous nature of the concept of a 'constructive obligation'. In fact, as it transpires, not all of these repairs have been carried out and £117m has been released to the profit and loss account as can be seen from the extract from its 2001 accounts below.

Extract 28.24: Railtrack Group PLC (2001)

22 Provisions for liabilities and charges

	At 1 April 2000 (restated)	Provision over accrued	Provision released in respect of major stations	Utilised in year	**At 31 March 2001**
	£m	£m	£m	£m	**£m**
Deferred tax (note 23)	463	–	–	(207)	**256**
Environmental liabilities	53	–	–	(5)	**48**
Property maintenance backlog provision	167	(24)	(93)	(50)	**–**
Other	8	–	–	(1)	**7**
	691	(24)	(93)	(263)	**311**

The Group, as publicly stated in its share offer prospectus dated 1 May 1996, implemented a programme of repairs in respect of the property maintenance backlog at stations and depots. This was completed by 31 March 2001 with the exception of a small number of mainly major stations. The amount of surplus provision remaining (after deducting the element relating to those few stations that have not yet been regenerated) has been released to the profit and loss account. In addition, because of the uncertainty surrounding the commencement of the regeneration of the remaining stations, primarily being the likelihood of major stations master plans being delivered, the provision in respect of those stations has been released in the year and treated as an exceptional item.

The Group has provided for the anticipated costs of remedial works on land inherited from the British Railways board which has suffered contamination, and where contractual or other obligations require the company to clean up these sites. Following a review of the planned expenditure it is estimated that the provision will be entirely utilised within four years.

The effect of this prohibition on setting up provisions for repairs obviously impacts on balance sheet presentation. It may not always, however, have as much impact on the profit and loss account. This is because it is suggested that depreciation might be adjusted to take account of the repairs. For example, in the case of the furnace lining, the lining should be depreciated over five years in advance of its expected repair. Similarly, in the case of the aircraft overhaul, the example in the standard suggests that an amount equivalent to the expected maintenance costs is depreciated over three years. The result of this is that the overall charge to the profit and loss account that will now arise from depreciation may be equivalent to that which would previously have arisen from the combination of depreciation and provision for repair.

Water utility companies used to follow a similar policy of provisioning in relation to the maintenance of their infrastructure assets. In this case there were slightly different arguments because external regulation on both pricing structures and service standards had a bearing on the maintenance required. Maintenance expenditure in any particular year could vary significantly from the long term norm that had been agreed with the regulator, but the charge against profits was a normalised amount, with the difference taken up in a rolling provision (or a prepayment, if actual expenditure exceeded the norm). Despite the influence of the regulator, the ASB still does not believe that such a provision qualifies as an obligation under FRS 12, but the Board has again permitted the same profit and loss account effect to be preserved by flexing the asset accounting to fit, using 'renewals accounting' as it is described in FRS 15 (see Chapter 12 at 2.3.3 H).

Scottish Power's accounts for 1999 showed the effect of this change.

Extract 28.25: Scottish Power plc (1999)

Accounting Policies and Definitions [extract]

Infrastructure accounting

Water infrastructure assets, being mains and sewers, reservoirs, dams, sludge pipelines and sea outfalls comprise a network of systems. Expenditure on water infrastructure assets relating to increases in capacity or enhancement of the network and on maintaining the operating capability of the network in accordance with defined standards of service is treated as an addition to fixed assets.

The depreciation charge for water infrastructure assets is the estimated level of annualised expenditure required to maintain the operating capability of the network and is based on the asset management plan agreed with the water industry regulator as part of the price regulation process.

The asset management plan is developed from historical experience combined with a rolling programme of reviews of the condition of infrastructure assets.

The method of accounting for water infrastructure renewals has been revised following the introduction of FRS 12 'Provisions, contingent liabilities and contingent assets' and the infrastructure renewals accounting basis as set out in FRS 15 'Tangible fixed assets'. As a consequence the balance sheet has been restated to take account of the necessary changes since the date of acquisition of Southern Water in August 1996. Further information is given in Note 16. The change of accounting policy has no effect on the profit and loss account other than to reclassify the renewals charge on depreciation.

> **Notes to the Balance Sheets**
>
> **16 Tangible fixed assets** [extract]
>
> (iv) The opening balances in respect of cost or valuation and depreciation of water infrastructure assets have been restated as a result of implementing the infrastructure renewals accounting basis as set out in FRS 15 'Tangible fixed assets'. The effect of the adjustment has been to increase tangible fixed assets and reduce prepayments and accrued income by £15.7 million (1998 £5.4 million). There is no effect on the profit and loss account other than to reclassify the renewals charge as depreciation.

It is difficult to see this as a beneficial change. The previous approach had the benefit of transparency, whereas now the maintenance expenditure is mingled with genuine additions to fixed assets. The profit and loss account effect is unaltered, so it appears that the ASB's only reason for requiring the reclassification has been to preserve the supposed purity of its conception of a liability. And even that is somewhat debatable; many would think that agreeing a maintenance programme with the industry regulator would have been enough to create at least a constructive obligation.

5.7 Dilapidation and other provisions relating to leased assets

The requirements discussed above relate to repairs and maintenance of owned assets (including assets held under finance leases). Operating leases often contain clauses which specify that the tenant should incur periodic charges for maintenance or make good dilapidations or other damage occurring during the rental period. Hence, some entities in the past have built up a provision over the life of the lease for costs of repair and renovation of the property.

The question arises as to whether such a provision meets the recognition criteria in the standard. The issue, whilst not addressed in FRS 12 itself, is mentioned briefly in the appendix discussing the development of the standard. This notes that 'the principle illustrated in [the example on repairs] does not preclude the recognition of such liabilities once the event giving rise to the obligation under the lease has occurred'.[143]

This means that a provision for specific damage done to the property would meet the criteria, as the event giving rise to the obligation under the lease has certainly occurred. For example, if an entity has erected partitioning or internal walls and under the lease these have to be removed at the end of the lease, then provision should be made for this cost (on a discounted basis, if material) at the time of putting up the partitioning or the walls. In this case, an equivalent asset would be created and depreciated over the term of the lease. This is similar to a decommissioning provision discussed at 5.5 above.

What is less clear is whether a more general provision can be built up over time for maintenance charges and dilapidation costs. It could be argued that in this case, the event giving rise to the obligation under the lease is simply the passage of time, and so a provision can be built up over time. However, a stricter interpretation of the phrase 'the event giving rise to the obligation under the lease' may lead one to conclude that a more specific event has to occur; there has to be specific evidence of dilapidation etc before any provision can be made.

The fact that provision for repairs can be made at all in these circumstances might appear inconsistent with the circumstances where the asset is owned by the entity.

In these circumstances, as discussed in 5.6 above, no provision for repairs could be made. There is, however, a difference between the two cases. Where the entity owns the asset, it has the choice of selling it rather than repairing it, and so the obligation is not independent of the entity's future actions. However, in the case of an entity leasing the asset, it has a legal obligation to repair any damage from which it cannot walk away.

5.8 Warranty provisions

Warranty provisions are specifically addressed in one of the examples appended to FRS 12, which concludes that such provisions are appropriate.[144] The example deals with a manufacturer that gives warranties at the time of sale of its product. Under the terms of contract for sale the manufacturer undertakes to make good, by repair or replacement, manufacturing defects that become apparent within 3 years from the date of sale. On past experience, it is probable (i.e. more likely than not) that there will be some claims under the warranties. The obligating event giving rise to the legal obligation is the sale of the product on which the warranty is given. We concur with this view, although in practice considerations of materiality may sometimes permit such costs to be treated on a pay-as-you-go basis.

As noted in 4.1 above, the standard makes it clear that where there are a number of similar obligations, the probability that an economic outflow will occur is based on the class of obligations as a whole. Hence, the probability of an economic outflow occurring for warranties as a whole will need to be evaluated. If this probability exceeds 50% (which seems very likely), then the expected value of the estimated warranty costs should be calculated and provided for.

Vosper Thornycroft is an example of a company that provides for such costs, as described in this note.

Extract 28.26: Vosper Thornycroft Holdings plc (2000)

20 Provisions for liabilities and charges [extract]

Group	Contract and warranty provisions £000
At 1 April 2000	9,075
Acquisition of subsidiary undertaking	1,454
Exchange differences	90
Created during the year	5,781
Unused amounts reversed	(1,501)
Utilised	(2,382)
At 31 March 2001	**12,517**

Contract and warranty provisions

Provisions are made when contracts are put to sales to cover expected warranty claims. Provisions are based on an assessment of future claims with reference to past experience. Such costs are generally incurred within one to five years post delivery.

5.9 Self insurance

One of the examples in FRS 12 deals with the practice of self insurance,[145] which arises when an entity decides not to take out external insurance in respect of a certain category of risk because it would be uneconomic to do so. The same position may arise when a group insures its risks with a captive insurance subsidiary, the effects of which have to be eliminated on consolidation. The standard's example considers the question of whether provision can be made for the amount expected to arise in a normal year. The conclusion reached is that no such provision can be made, as the entity does not have a present obligation for this amount. Instead, it should recognise the reality of the situation – that it is uninsured – and report losses based on their actual incidence, rather than smoothing them from period to period by reference to a simulated insurance premium that it has not in fact paid. As a result, any provisions that appear in the balance sheet should reflect only the amounts expected to be paid in respect of those losses that have occurred by the balance sheet date.

In fact, however, the example is somewhat misleading, since it deals with a very basic case where it is known with certainty at the time of preparing the accounts that no losses have arisen in the period. In real life, a provision will often be needed not simply for known incidents, but also for those which insurance companies call IBNR – Incurred But Not Reported – representing an estimate of the latent liabilities at the year end that experience shows will come to the surface only gradually.

It can be seen from the following extract that Severn Trent takes account of such items in respect of its insurance provision:

Extract 28.27: Severn Trent Plc (2001)

1 Accounting policies [extract]

k Insurance — Provision is made for claims notified and for claims incurred but which have not yet been notified, based on advice from the group's external insurance advisers.

17 Provisions for liabilities and charges: [extract]

a Provisions comprise:

	Balance at 1 April 2000 £m	Acquired with subsidiaries £m	Charged to profit & loss account £m	Exchange adjustments £m	Utilised £m	**Balance at 31 March 2001 £m**
Insurance	13.5	–	7.5	–	(5.7)	**15.3**

Derwent Insurance Limited, a captive insurance company, is a wholly owned subsidiary of the group. Provisions for claims are made as set out in note 1k. The associated outflows are estimated to arise over a period of up to five years from the balance sheet date.

It is entirely appropriate that provision for such expected claims is made. However, it might be questioned whether this should properly be described as a provision for *insurance* claims; from a group perspective, there is no insurance, and the provision is simply for legal claims from third parties.

5.10 Litigation and other legal claims

FRS 12 includes an example of a court case in its Appendix to illustrate how its principles for recognising a provision should be applied in such situations.[146] However, the assessment of the particular case is clear-cut. In most situations, assessing the need to provide for legal claims is one of the most difficult tasks in the field of provisioning. This is due mainly to the inherent uncertainty in the judicial process itself, which may be very long and drawn out. Furthermore, this is an area where either provision or disclosure might risk prejudicing the outcome of the case, because they give an insight into the company's own view on the strength of its defence that can assist the claimant. Similar considerations apply in other related areas, such as tax disputes.

In principle, whether a provision should be made will depend on whether the 3 conditions for recognising a provision are met, i.e.

(a) there is a present obligation as a result of a past event;

(b) it is probable that a transfer of economic benefits will be required to settle the obligation; and

(c) a reliable estimate can be made of the amount of the obligation.[147]

As noted at 3.1.1 above, in situations such as these, a past event is deemed to give rise to a present obligation if, taking account of all available evidence (including, for example, the opinion of experts), it is more likely than not that a present obligation exists at the balance sheet date. The evidence to be considered includes any additional evidence occurring after the balance sheet date. Accordingly, if on the basis of the evidence it is concluded that a present obligation is more likely than not to exist, a provision will be required, assuming the other conditions are met.

Condition (b) will be met if the transfer of economic benefits is more likely than not to occur, that is, it has a probability greater than 50%. In making this assessment, it is likely that account should be taken of any expert advice.

As far as condition (c) is concerned, as noted at 3.1.3 above, the standard takes the view that a reasonable estimate can generally be made and it is only in extremely rare cases that this will not be the case.

Clearly, whether an entity should make provision for the costs of settling a case or to meet any award given by a court will depend on a reasoned assessment of the particular circumstances, based on appropriate legal advice.

Powerscreen disclosed that it had provided for certain litigation losses, as shown in this extract from its 1999 accounts.

> *Extract 28.28: Powerscreen International PLC (1999)*
>
> **25 Contingent liabilities**
> **a. Legal contingencies**
>
> A number of claims have been made against the group, the most significant of which related to:
>
> i) alleged patent infringements. The directors have received expert opinion that no infringement of valid patents has taken place.
> ii) product liability claims involving personal injuries allegedly sustained from the use of the products manufactured by certain group companies.
> iii) general commercial disputes.
>
> Notwithstanding the intention of the directors to defend vigorously these claims, some of which are substantial, a provision of £10,279,000 has been made in respect of these claims and associated costs. Having obtained legal advice and on the basis of the information available, the directors believe that the provision made represents their best estimate of the outcome of the claims and associated costs.

P&O, on the other hand, has made no provision for a fine that has been levied on one of its joint ventures, on the grounds that it believes that the fine will be reversed on appeal and thus still does not represent a probable liability. It has therefore just disclosed details about the contingent liability.

> *Extract 28.29: The Peninsular and Oriental Steam Navigation Company (2000)*
>
> **28 Contingent liabilities** [extract]
>
> Other contingent liabilities in the Group and the Company include £13.7m (1999 £13.6m), being the Group's share of fines imposed by the European Union on P&O Nedlloyd for anti-competitive practices on the North Atlantic trade. Together with other members of the Trans Atlantic Conference Agreement, P&O Nedlloyd has appealed against the fines and, on the basis of legal advice, is confident the appeal will succeed and the fines will in any event be severely reduced or quashed. Accordingly no provision has been made in these accounts.

5.11 Refunds policy

An example is given within FRS 12 of a retail store that has a policy of refunding goods returned by dissatisfied customers. There is no legal obligation to do so, but the company's policy of making refunds is generally known.[148]

The example argues that the conduct of the store has created a valid expectation on the part of its customers that the store will refund purchases. The obligating event is the original sale of the item, and the probability of some economic outflow is greater than 50%, as there will nearly always be some customers demanding refunds. Hence, a provision should be made, presumably calculated again on the 'expected value' basis (see 4.1 above).

This example is straightforward when the store has a very specific and highly publicised policy on refunds. However, some stores' policies on refunds might not be so clear cut. A store may offer refunds under certain circumstances, but not widely publicise its policy. In these circumstances, it is likely to be open to interpretation as to whether the store has created a valid expectation on the part of its customers that the store will refund purchases.

5.12 Staff training costs

FRS 12 gives an example of the government introducing changes to the income tax system, such that an entity in the financial services sector needs to retrain a large proportion of its administrative and sales workforce in order to ensure continued compliance with financial services regulation. At the balance sheet date no retraining has taken place.[149]

The standard argues that the obligating event is the staff retraining, and since at the year end no training has taken place, there is no obligating event, and so no provision should be made. We agree with this outcome, but the reasoning behind it seems fragile. This example again seems to illustrate the subjectivity of the concepts of 'constructive obligations' and 'obligating events'. Another interpretation of the position could be that the entity has a constructive obligation to retrain its sales force, as it has built up a valid expectation in its employees and customers that the sales force will be up to date on changes to the income tax system which affect the products it sells, to enable it to adequately meet the needs of its customers. If this approach were taken, a provision would be required. The argument could be strengthened if the entity had published some sort of policy statement reassuring employees and customers that the sales force would receive adequate training on the income tax changes.

A counter argument might be that the standard states that an entity can only provide for obligations which are independent of the entity's future actions. Hence, in this case, the entity can avoid the costs of staff training by changing its method of operation and no longer selling certain products to customers. However, this argument does not help in distinguishing staff training costs from provisions for refunds, which are required to be made. After all, the customer in the example on refunds has no legal right to a refund. The entity could refuse, but presumably would not because of the bad publicity and loss of goodwill that would be suffered. Similarly, in this example, the sales force could cease selling certain financial products, but would not do so because it would lose customers.

In reality, the distinction between the two examples comes down to when the benefits are obtained in each case, not whether the entity has a liability at the year end. In the case of the refund policy, the revenue from the sale has already been booked, so any reversal of it should be recognised. However, in the case of staff training, the benefits of the training will be the impact on future sales, so it is not appropriate to provide for the costs of training in advance. This dimension of revenue and expense recognition is not acknowledged in the standard, but it does seem to underlie a number of the conclusions that are reached.

5.13 Regulatory correction factors

In Appendix VII to FRS 12, which discusses the development of the standard, it is noted that by basing the recognition of a provision on the existence of a present obligation, the standard rules out the recognition of any provision made simply to allocate results over more than one period or otherwise to smooth the results reported. To illustrate this, it goes on to say 'For example, in a regulated industry the results achieved in the current period may cause the pricing structure in the next period to be adjusted, eg the higher the profits in this year the lower the prices permitted for next year. There is no justification under the FRS for a provision to be recognised in such circumstances. The purpose of such a provision would be to transfer some of the current year's profit to the following year, which would suffer from lower prices because of the current year's profits. However, there is no present obligation that requires the transfer of economic benefits to settle it and nothing to justify recognition of a provision.'[150]

No reference is made elsewhere within the standard to this type of situation, so its exact status was unclear. The UITF was asked to consider this and it confirmed that the principles of FRS 12 should be applied to regulated industries, as discussed in the paragraph cited above, and consequently no liability should be recognised for a price reduction or similar regulatory correction factors in subsequent accounting periods required by a regulator. The UITF agreed that liabilities for such items should not be included in financial statements unless the company had a binding obligation actually to repay amounts to customers at the balance sheet date rather than adjusting prices in the following year; the mere making of book entries would not result in such an obligation. The requirement for a binding obligation at the balance sheet date applies whether the liability is classified as a provision, creditor or other class of liability.[151]

As the UITF considered that the requirements of FRS 12 on this issue are clear, it concluded that no purpose would be served by issuing an abstract on this topic.

5.14 Employee benefits

As indicated at 2.1.4 above, FRS 12 excludes from its scope any provisions covered by a more relevant standard and quotes pension costs as an example. Also, in drawing a demarcation line between provisions and accruals, the standard refers to accruals 'including amounts due to employees (for example amounts relating to holiday pay' (see 2.2 above). However, apart from these, FRS 12 does not include any discussion as to whether or not, and if so, how its requirements apply to the costs of providing other employee benefits.

One issue which has been addressed by the UITF is the accounting for national insurance contributions on certain share option gains, where the principles in FRS 12 were applied in arriving at the consensus in the Abstract. This is discussed in Chapter 22 at 2.5.5. In the absence of a UK standard on employee benefits, we believe that the principles of FRS 12 should also be applied to cash-based incentive payments, other long-term benefits, termination benefits and phantom share schemes. These are discussed in Chapter 22 at 2.2, 2.3, 2.4 and 2.7 respectively.

6 DISCLOSURE REQUIREMENTS

6.1 Provisions

6.1.1 Companies Act

The Companies Act requires disclosure of the amount of provisions at the beginning and the end of the year and movements during the year saying where they have come from and gone to, except for those amounts which have been applied for the purpose for which the provision was established.[152]

6.1.2 FRS 12

The standard requires disclosure of the following information:

(a) For each class of provision:

   (i) the carrying amount at the beginning and end of the period;

   (ii) additional provisions made in the period, including increases to existing provisions;

   (iii) amounts used (i.e. incurred and charged against the provision) during the period;

   (iv) unused amounts reversed during the period; and

   (v) the increase during the period in the discounted amount arising from the passage of time and the effect of any change in the discount rate.

   Comparative information is not required.[153]

Disclosure (v) effectively requires the charge for discounting that is recognised in the profit and loss account to be split between the element that relates to the straightforward unwinding of the discount, and any further charge or credit that arises if discount rates have changed during the period. It is interesting that there is no specific requirement to disclose the discount rate used, although this information is given in one of the illustrative examples in Appendix IV to the standard, where discounting has been applied.

These disclosures build on the Companies Act requirements to show movements on provisions. One of the important disclosures which is reinforced here is the requirement to disclose the release of provisions found to be unnecessary. This disclosure, along with the requirement in the standard that provisions should be used only for the purpose for which the provision was originally recognised, is designed to prevent entities from concealing expenditure by charging it against a provision that was set up for another purpose.

(b) For each class of provision:

   (i) a brief description of the nature of the obligation, and the expected timing of any resulting transfers of economic benefits;

   (ii) an indication of the uncertainties about the amount or timing of those transfers of economic benefits. Where necessary to provide adequate information, an entity should disclose the major assumptions concerning future events, as addressed in paragraph 51 of FRS 12. This refers to future developments in technology and legislation and is of particular relevance to environmental liabilities.; and

(iii) the amount of any expected reimbursement, stating the amount of any asset that has been recognised for that expected reimbursement.[154]

Appendix IV to the standard provides examples of suitable disclosures in relation to warranties and decommissioning costs.

Examples of disclosures in respect of FRS 12's disclosure requirements are illustrated below.

Extract 28.30: Cable and Wireless plc (2001)

22 Provisions for liabilities and charges [extract]

	Note	At 1 April 2000 £m	Additions £m	Amounts used £m	Other Movements £m	At 31 March 2001 £m
Group						
Deferred tax – amount provided	(i)	193	92	–	114	**399**
Pensions	(ii)	52	56	(29)	–	**79**
Redundancy	(iii)	–	145	(8)	1	**138**
Onerous contracts	(iv)	–	68	–	–	**68**
Litigation claims	(v)	5	–	(1)	–	**4**
Other	(vi)	31	23	(4)	(12)	**38**
		281	**384**	**(42)**	**103**	**726**

...

(iii) Redundancy

On 13 March 2001, the Group announced a major redundancy programme. Provision has been made for the associated costs which are expected to be utilised within twelve months.

(iv) Onerous contracts

Implementation of the Group's strategy and the redundancies referred to above, has resulted in a number of properties becoming vacant. Provision has been made for the best estimate of the unavoidable lease payments on these properties being the difference between the rentals due and any income expected to be derived from their being sub-let. The provision is expected to be utilised between 6 and 15 months.

(v) Litigation claims

Relates to actual and threatened claims against a subsidiary for alleged breach of contract in respect of the provision of telecommunications services to a third party. These provisions are expected to be utilised within twelve months.

(vi) Other

Included within this provision is an amount of £2.0m (2000 – £1.8m) to cover the cost of former Directors' pension entitlements as shown on page 31. Other movements relate to a decrease in provisions on claims outstanding.

Extract 28.31: Pilkington plc (2001)

29 Provisions for liabilities and charges [extract]

		2001		2000	
		Group	**Company**	Group	Company
		£m	**£m**	£m	£m
(c)	**Warranty and litigation**				
	At beginning of the year	**49**	**1**	57	9
	Exchange rate adjustments	**1**	**–**	(4)	–
	Changes in composition of the Group	**–**	**–**	(1)	–
	Charged to profit and loss account during the year	**9**	**3**	10	1
	Released to profit and loss account during the year	**(6)**	**–**	(1)	–
	Utilised during the year	**(7)**	**–**	(12)	(9)
	At end of the year	**46**	**4**	49	1
	Maturity profile:				
	Within one year	**17**	**4**	21	1
	Between one and two years	**10**	**–**	8	–
	Between two and five years	**9**	**–**	8	–
	Over five years	**10**	**–**	12	–
		46	**4**	49	1

Warranty provisions are created where the Group has given a guarantee to cover the reliability and performance of products over an extended period.

		2001		2000	
		Group	**Company**	Group	Company
		£m	**£m**	£m	£m
(d)	**Redundancies and restructuring**				
	At beginning of the year	**76**	**–**	77	–
	Exchange rate adjustments	**3**	**–**	(3)	–
	Charged to profit and loss account during the year	**22**	**–**	98	–
	Released to profit and loss account during the year	**(1)**	**–**	(1)	–
	Utilised during the year	**(41)**	**–**	(95)	–
	At end of the year	**59**	**–**	76	–
	Maturity profile:				
	Within one year	**41**	**–**	48	–
	Between one and two years	**7**	**–**	12	–
	Between two and five years	**7**	**–**	13	–
	Over five years	**4**	**–**	3	–
		59	**–**	76	–

The redundancy and restructuring provisions relate to the ordinary and exceptional provisions set up in Building products (£24 million), Automotive products (£29 million) and Group operations and technology management (£6 million).

		2001		2000	
		Group	Company	Group	Company
		£m	£m	£m	£m
(e)	**Other provisions**				
	At beginning of the year	**56**	**1**	70	1
	Exchange rate adjustments	**4**	**–**	(1)	–
	Changes in composition of the Group	**–**	**–**	(1)	–
	Charged to profit and loss account during the year	**17**	**–**	12	–
	Released to profit and loss account during the year	**(1)**	**–**	(3)	–
	Utilised during the year	**(11)**	**–**	(21)	–
	At end of the year	**65**	**1**	56	1
	Maturity profile:				
	Within one year	**14**	**1**	8	–
	Between one and two years	**8**	**–**	5	–
	Between two and five years	**15**	**–**	18	1
	Over five years	**28**	**–**	25	–
		65	**1**	56	1

The closing balance on other provisions at 31st March 2001 principally includes cumulative leave and payroll obligations amounting to £31 million (2000 £32 million) and environmental provisions amounting to £18 million (2000 £14 million).

Unusually, Pilkington has given comparative movements. Most companies do not give such information since it is not required by FRS 12. Also, it has given a maturity analysis for each class of provision. This is presumably to meet the requirement under (b) (i) above about the expected timing of any transfer of benefits. Most companies, however, meet this requirement by giving disclosure along the lines of that given by Cable and Wireless.

The standard states that in determining which provisions may be aggregated to form a class, it is necessary to consider whether the nature of the items is sufficiently similar for a single statement about them to fulfil the requirements of (b)(i) and (ii) above.[155] An example is given of warranties: it is suggested that, while it may be appropriate to treat warranties of different products as a single class of provision, it would not be appropriate to aggregate normal warranties with amounts that are subject to legal proceedings. However, companies may quite often be reluctant to show litigation provisions separately because they fear that the information might be used against them by the other litigating parties. It can be seen from Extract 28.31 above that Pilkington has a 'warranty and litigation' provision, but since the rest of the disclosure only refers to warranties it may be that any litigation element is not material. This requirement could be interpreted to mean that in disclosing restructuring costs, the different components of the costs, such as redundancies, termination of leases, etc, should be disclosed separately. Indeed, in Extract 28.30 above, Cable and Wireless has disclosed its provisions for redundancies and onerous contracts separately, even although the latter has arisen as a result of the restructuring which has led to the redundancies. However, materiality will be an important consideration in judging how much analysis is required.

6.2 Contingent liabilities

6.2.1 *Companies Act*

The Companies Act requires disclosure of the following information in respect of any material contingent liability not provided for:

(a) the amount or estimated amount of the liability;

(b) its legal nature; and

(c) whether any valuable security has been provided by the company in connection with that liability and if so, what.[156]

6.2.2 *FRS 12*

FRS 12 requires the following disclosure for each class of contingent liability at the balance sheet date unless the possibility of any transfer in settlement is remote:

(a) a brief description of the nature of the contingent liability, and where practicable:

(b) an estimate of its financial effect, measured in accordance with paragraphs 36–55 of FRS 12;

(c) an indication of the uncertainties relating to the amount or timing of any outflow; and

(d) the possibility of any reimbursement.[157]

Where any of the information above is not disclosed because it is not practicable to do so, that fact should be stated.[158]

The guidance given in the standard on determining which provisions may be aggregated to form a class referred to in 6.1.2 above also applies to contingent liabilities.

A further point noted in the standard is that where a provision and a contingent liability arise from the same circumstances, an entity should ensure that the link between the provision and the contingent liability is clear.[159] This may arise, for instance, where there is a range of possible losses under a claim, for which part of the potential maximum has been provided. A further example of when this may arise would be where an entity is jointly and severally liable for an obligation. As noted in 4.4 above, in these circumstances the part that is expected to be met by other parties is treated as a contingent liability.

It is not absolutely clear what is meant by 'financial effect' in (b) above. Is it the *potential* amount of the loss or is it the *expected* amount of the loss? The explicit cross-reference to the measurement principles in paragraphs 36–55 might imply the latter, but in our view the former would be preferable. A number of companies adopt this approach and disclose the potential amounts involved, as illustrated in the following extract:

Extract 28.32: Brammer plc (2000)

21 Contingencies

In the ordinary course of business certain leasehold properties which the group no longer requires have been assigned to third parties. The ultimate responsibility for the lease payments relating to some of the properties remains with the group. In the event of the assignees defaulting, the maximum annual liability of the group (ignoring the effects of possible future rent reviews) is £118,000 (1999 £107,000).

However, some other companies tend not to disclose the potential amounts involved where claims have been made against them or they are involved in litigation, but rather comment that once resolved there is unlikely to be any significant effect, as illustrated in the following extracts:

Extract 28.33: Charter plc (2000)

22 Commitments and contingencies [extract]

Charter, together with certain of its wholly-owned subsidiaries, has been named as defendant in a number of asbestos-related actions in the United States on the basis that it is allegedly liable for the acts of a former subsidiary Cape PLC. Charter contests the existence of any such liability. The issue went to trial in three cases involving the Company's principal subsidiary, Charter Consolidated P.L.C., and other wholly-owned subsidiaries, between 1985 and 1987. In the first of these cases, tried in Pennsylvania, after an adverse lower court decision the appeal court gave judgement in the Charter defendants' favour. In the second case, in New Jersey, judgement was also given for the Charter defendants. The third case, in South Carolina, was dismissed for lack of subject matter jurisdiction, without a decision having been rendered on the issue. During recent years, Charter and/or certain of its subsidiaries have been served in a number of cases in Mississippi and a few other states. Charter is seeking dismissals in these pending cases. Upon advice of counsel, Charter has settled some of the cases brought in Mississippi and will continue to pursue dismissals in the remainder. The directors have received legal advice that Charter and its wholly-owned subsidiaries should be able to continue to defend successfully the actions brought against them, but that uncertainty must exist as to the eventual outcome of the trial of any particular action. It is not practicable to estimate in any particular case the amount of damages which might ensue if liability were imposed on Charter or any of its wholly-owned subsidiaries. The litigation is reviewed each year and, based on that review and legal advice, the directors believe that the aggregate of any such liability is unlikely to have a material effect on Charter's financial position. In these circumstances, the directors have concluded that it is not appropriate to make any provision in respect of such actions.

Extract 28.34: British American Tobacco p.l.c. (2000)

23 Contingent liabilities and financial commitments

There are contingent liabilities in respect of litigation, overseas taxes and guarantees in various countries.

Group companies, notably Brown & Williamson Tobacco Corporation ('B&W'). as well as other leading cigarette manufacturers, are defendants, principally in the United States, in a number of product liability cases, including a substantial number of new cases filed in 2000, although a number of cases were discontinued by claimants (without payment by any defendants) in the year. In a number of these cases, the amounts of compensatory and punitive damages sought are significant.

US litigation

The total number of US product liability cases pending at year end involving Group companies was approximately 4,740 (31 December 1999 537 cases). UK based group companies were named as co-defendants in some 1,345 of those cases (1999 161 cases). Only perhaps a couple of dozen cases or fewer are likely to come to trial in 2001. Since many of these pending cases seek unspecified damages, it is not possible to determine the total amount of claims pending, but the aggregate amounts involved in such litigation are significant. The cases fall into four broad categories:

(1) Medical reimbursement cases. These civil actions seek to recover amounts spent by government entities and other third party providers on health care and welfare costs claimed to result from illnesses associated with smoking.

Despite the almost uniform success of the industry's defence to these actions, to date, the United States Department of Justice has filed suit against the leading US cigarette manufacturers, certain affiliated companies (including parent companies), and others seeking reimbursement for Medicare and other health expenses incurred by the US federal government as well as various equitable remedies, including paying over of proceeds from alleged unlawful acts. The court has dismissed the reimbursement claims but is allowing the government to proceed with its claims for equitable relief. The court has tentatively scheduled trial for July 2003. At 31 December 2000, similar reimbursement suits were pending against B&W amongst others by seven Indian tribes and by five county or other political subdivisions of certain states. The settlement of the states' suits includes a credit for any amounts paid in suits brought by the states' political subdivisions; nevertheless, B&W intends to defend these cases vigorously.

Based on somewhat different theories of claim are some 34 non-government medical reimbursement cases and health insurers claims, the majority of which were filed by labour union health and welfare funds on behalf of their members. To date, seven federal appellate courts have issued decisions dismissing this type of case entirely and some but not all state courts have issued similar decisions. Only one union health fund case (Ohio Iron Workers) has been tried, resulting in a verdict for defendants, including B&W, in March 1999. Four third party reimbursement cases are currently scheduled for trial in 2001.

(2) Class actions. As at 31 December 2000, B&W was named as a defendant in some 35 (31 December 1999 38) separate actions attempting to assert claims on behalf of classes of persons allegedly injured by smoking. While most courts refused to do so, ten courts have certified classes of tobacco claimants in cases involving B&W but five of these classes have subsequently been decertified. Even if the classes remain certified and the possibility of class-based liability is eventually established, it is likely that individual trials will still be necessary to resolve any actual claims. If this happens, it is possible that many of the defences that have contributed to more than 600 individual cases being successfully disposed of over the years by B&W will be available.

In the first phase of the trifurcated trial in Engle (Florida), the jury returned a verdict that included general findings that smoking causes several specified diseases and other findings including that the defendants' conduct rose to a level that would permit a potential award of punitive damages. The second phase of the trial included two parts. The first portion of phase two was a trial of the three named class representatives' compensatory damages claims. In that portion, the jury awarded a total of $12.7 million to the three class representatives but found that one of the representatives' claims ($5.8 million of that total) was time-barred. In the second portion of phase two, the jury assessed $17.6 billion in punitive damages against B&W and $127 billion in total punitive damages against the other major companies in the US tobacco industry. Although the trial court has entered a final judgement on those verdicts, B&W contends that that judgement was improperly entered. In any event, B&W continues to believe confidently that the pending Engle decisions will eventually be reversed on appeal given the inappropriateness of class certification, the numerous errors committed during trial, and the significant constitutional issues involved in the case. Immediate payment of punitive damages pursuant to the verdict is unlikely for numerous reasons that will be presented to the trial and appellate courts, including, among others, that the punitive damages cannot be final until completion of a series of further individual trials for every member of the class (the so-called phase three of the Engle trial plan, which will take many years); that the jury's determination of punitive damages violates several provisions of Florida law; and that, pursuant to recently adopted legislation, in Florida any enforcement of punitive damages must be stayed upon the posting of a bond in an amount equal to the lower of 10 per cent of the defendant's net worth or $100 million. Although the Florida legislation is intended to apply to the Engle case, the outcome of any challenge to its application cannot be predicted. B&W has delivered a surety bond that meets the requirements of Florida's legislation to stay enforcement of punitive damages in class actions.

Trial of a class action in West Virginia (Blankenship), in which a class of smokers sought funding for medical monitoring of their health, ended in a mistrial. Another medical monitoring class action in Louisiana (Scott) is currently scheduled for trial in June 2001.

(3) Individual cases. Approximately 4,637 cases were pending against B&W at 31 December 2000 (31 December 1999 421) filed by or on behalf of individuals in which it is contended that diseases or deaths have been caused by cigarette smoking or by exposure to environmental tobacco smoke (ETS). Of these cases: (a) approximately two thirds are ETS cases brought by flight attendants who were members of a class action (Broin) that was settled on terms that allow compensatory but not punitive damage claims by class members; (b) approximately one quarter of the individual cases against B&W are cases brought in consolidated proceedings in West Virginia; and (c) less than eight per cent are cases filed by other individuals.

A jury verdict against B&W for $750,000 (Carter) was recently reinstated by the Florida Supreme Court. B&W is currently seeking review of that decision by the US Supreme Court.

(4) Other claims. At 31 December 2000, eight cases were pending on behalf of asbestos companies. Those companies seek reimbursement for costs and judgements paid in litigation brought by third parties against them. These companies claim that but for the smoking of the claimants against them, their damages would have been less.

A reimbursement case brought by a trust established to pay asbestos litigation claims (Falise) ended in mistrial in January 2001 because the jury was unable to reach a unanimous decision. According to press reports, 10 jurors favoured the tobacco company defendants while two would have found for plaintiffs.

At 31 December 2000, B&W was named as defendant in 18 US cases brought by foreign government entities seeking reimbursement of medical costs which they incurred for treatment for persons in their own countries who are alleged to have smoked imported cigarettes including those manufactured by B&W. Four foreign government cases had been dismissed at 31 December 2000. One foreign government case (Marshall Islands) is set for trial in 2001.

In addition, conduct-based claims, including antitrust and RICO claims, have been filed in the US. Among these are some 37 class action antitrust cases brought by wholesalers or retailers alleging that B&W and other major US cigarette manufacturers conspired to fix prices for cigarettes. Although plaintiffs in these class actions have not specified the damages they claim, the amounts could be significant. None of these conduct-based claims is considered to be meritorious.

B.A.T Industries has been named as a co-defendant in the US in most of the medical reimbursement cases, in a quarter or fewer of the class actions and even fewer of the individual cases. It is contesting the jurisdiction of the US courts since it is a 'holding' company not transacting business in the United States. In the 53 cases that have decided this issue to date, 30 courts have dismissed them prior to trial. In the balance of 23 cases, there has been no adverse ruling on the issue of jurisdiction affirmed on the merits through appeal. Some 135 plaintiffs have voluntarily agreed to drop the Company (or B.A.T Industries) or substitute the Company's indirectly held subsidiary British American Tobacco (Investments) Limited (formerly called British-American Tobacco Company Ltd.), as a co-defendant.

Legal matters outside the United States

At year end, there were no active claims against Group companies in respect of health-related claims outside Argentina, Australia, Brazil, Canada, Chile, Finland, France, Germany, Israel, the Netherlands, Pakistan, the Philippines, Republic of Ireland, Sri Lanka and Uganda.

Conclusion

While it is impossible to be certain of the outcome of any particular case or of the amount of any possible adverse verdict, the Company believes that the defences of the Group companies to all these various claims are meritorious both on the law and the facts, and a vigorous defence is being made everywhere. If an adverse judgement were entered against any of the Group companies in any case, an appeal would be made. Such appeals could require the posting of appeal bonds or substitute security by the appellants in amounts which could in some cases equal or exceed the amount of the judgement. At least in the aggregate and despite the quality of defences available to the Group, it is not impossible that the results of operations or cash flows of the Group in particular quarterly or annual periods could be materially affected by this and by the final outcome of any particular litigation.

Having regard to all these matters, the Directors (i) do not consider it appropriate to make any provision in respect of any pending litigation and (ii) do not believe that the ultimate outcome of all this litigation will significantly impair the financial condition of the Group.

As indicated above, where it is not practicable to make an estimate of the financial effect, FRS 12 requires a statement explaining this fact. Mirror Group provides an example of this disclosure, although it predates FRS 12:

Extract 28.35: Mirror Group PLC (1998)

23 Contingent liabilities [extract]

INVESTIGATION UNDER SECTIONS 432 AND 442 OF THE COMPANIES ACT 1985

On 8 June 1992 the President of the Board of Trade appointed inspectors under Sections 432 and 442 of the Companies Act 1985 to examine the affairs of the Group, particularly the circumstances surrounding its flotation in April 1991. The directors have been advised that it is possible that the circumstances surrounding the flotation, and the conduct of its affairs between its flotation in April 1991 and December 1991, may give rise to claims against the Company. However, it is not at this stage possible to identify specific claims against the Company nor to quantify either the prospect of success of such claims or the magnitude of any potential liability. Moreover, if such claims were successfully established the Company might have claims against certain of its professional advisers who acted at that time. After discussing all circumstances known to the Company with its legal advisers, no provision has been made in the financial statements for any such claims.

UNUSUAL RECEIPTS AND PAYMENTS DURING 1991

During 1991 the Group recorded substantial payments to and receipts from financial institutions and payments from Maxwell controlled companies outside the ordinary course of business. The directors are unaware of any unprovided claims against the Group arising from these transactions and, other than where the receipt of cash is certain, no benefit has been taken for potential recoveries.

FRS 12, like SSAP 18 before it, does not require the disclosure of remote contingencies, as discussed above. An Accountants Digest published soon after the issue of SSAP 18 stated that 'the application of this concession is, however, limited by the over-riding requirements of the 1948 and 1967 Companies Acts which require disclosure of the "general nature of any contingent liabilities not provided for and, where practicable, the aggregate amount or estimated amount of those liabilities, if it is material".'[160] (Since that time, the Companies Act provisions have been amended so as to require the disclosures described in 6.2.1 above.)

Possibly because of this apparent overriding Companies Act requirement to disclose *all* material contingent liabilities not provided for, companies sometimes include information in their financial statements on contingencies which could be considered to be remote. Some examples of such disclosures are shown below.

A Guarantees of subsidiary company liabilities

Where companies are disclosing the fact that they have guaranteed the liabilities of another party, consideration has to be given as to what amount should be disclosed in respect of the guarantee. The amount given is often merely the year end liability guaranteed, whilst in other cases it is not stated whether the amount given is the year end liability or the maximum liability guaranteed. It could be argued that both amounts require disclosure, as the maximum amount is part of the 'nature' of the guarantee and the year end amount is the 'estimate' of the financial effect. We therefore believe that best practice is to disclose both the year end liability and the maximum amount guaranteed, as shown in the following extract:

Extract 28.36: Inchcape plc (2000)

20 Guarantees and contingent liabilities [extract]

	Company	
	2000	1999
	£m	£m
Guarantees of various subsidiaries' borrowings (against which £77.9m has been drawn, 1999 – £112.0m)	**327.9**	362.0

In contrast, Silentnight Holdings discloses only the year end liability, as shown below:

Extract 28.37: Silentnight Holdings Plc (2001)

31. Contingent liabilities [extract]
Bank guarantees

The company has provided cross guarantees in respect of certain bank loans and overdrafts of its subsidiary undertakings. The amount outstanding at 3 February 2001 was £7,227,000 (2000: £10,479,000).

Where the amount of the liability at the year end varies significantly from the amount at the date on which the accounts are approved by the directors, consideration should be given to disclosing both amounts.

On the other hand, certain guarantees are sometimes disclosed without any amounts at all being given. For example:

Extract 28.38: Tesco PLC (2001)

NOTE 29 Contingent liabilities [extract]

The company has irrevocably guaranteed the liabilities as defined in Section 5(c) of the Republic of Ireland (Amendment Act) 1986 of various subsidiary undertakings incorporated in the Republic of Ireland.

B Bills discounted with recourse

Clearly, where a company discounts bills without recourse in the event of the bills being dishonoured on maturity, no contingent liability exists and, therefore, no disclosure is required. Also under FRS 5, where bills have been discounted with recourse, it will in most circumstances be necessary to account for such liabilities on the balance sheet, not simply as a disclosed contingency – see Chapter 18.

However, where bills are discounted with recourse and a liability does not need to be recognised under FRS 5, the question arises as to what amount should be disclosed in the financial statements as the contingent liability. Is it the amount which relates to all such bills discounted at the balance sheet date, or is it the amount which relates to those bills which have yet to mature at the date of approval of the financial statements? It could be argued that it is the latter and, therefore, if all the bills have matured by that date no disclosure is required. However, if the company is continually discounting bills of exchange then at the date of approval the company will have a contingent liability in respect of bills discounted since the year end. Consequently, we believe that in order to provide information relevant to the financial position of the company, the amount of bills outstanding at the balance sheet date should be disclosed.

C *Membership of VAT groups*

Companies may be part of a VAT group and as such have joint and several liability for the whole of the group VAT liability. Again, similar considerations apply as to the amount to be disclosed as were discussed above in relation to discounted bills. Consequently, we believe that the amount of this contingent liability at the balance sheet date should be disclosed in each group member's financial statements. For example:

Extract 28.39: British Polythene Industries plc (2000)

23. Contingent Liabilities [extract]

The Company also has an obligation under the Group VAT registration amounting at 31 December 2000 to £3.2 million (1999 – £3.6 million).

D *Performance bonds*

It is common practice in some industries for companies to procure that a third party guarantees to their customers that they will carry out their contracts to a specific standard. The question then arises as to whether the existence of such a performance bond means that the company has a contingent liability which has to be disclosed. The granting of the performance bond does not normally impose any greater liability on the company than does the contract itself. If a company regularly fulfils its obligations on time and up to the required standard and there is nothing to suggest that there are any unusual circumstances which might affect this, then there is justification in deciding that there is no contingency which needs to be disclosed.

In addition to performance bonds, companies may also arrange tender bonds (i.e. a guarantee against the company withdrawing from the contract after having submitted a tender for the contract which has been accepted) and advance payment bonds (i.e. a guarantee to reimburse advance payments made by the customer if the company cannot fulfil the contract).

In most cases the above bonds or guarantees will be given by the company's bankers and the company will indemnify the bank. Again, this does not normally impose any greater liability on the company than that under the contract with the customer.

Although it could be argued that in most cases above no contingent liability arises and therefore no disclosure is necessary, it would appear that many companies do give some disclosure in respect of such bonds. In practice, many companies merely note the existence of the bonds. For example:

Extract 28.40: Balfour Beatty plc (2000)

24 Contingent liabilities [extract]

The Company and certain subsidiary undertakings have, in the normal course of business, given guarantees and entered into counter-indemnities in respect of bonds relating to the Group's own contracts and given guarantees in respect of the Group's share of certain contractual obligations of joint ventures and associates.

Some other companies do, however, quantify the amount of the bonds or guarantees. For example:

Extract 28.41: Hepworth PLC (1998)

28. Contingent liabilities [extract]

As part of its normal trading, the Group had issued guarantees and performance bonds as at 31 December 1998 amounting to £1.6m (1997, £1.0m)

In our view, given the fact that the company in most cases will incur no extra liability as a result of the performance bond, it is sufficient just to disclose the existence of the bonds without quantification. Where, however, a parent company or other group company guarantees or counter-indemnifies a bank for the performance of another group company then it would be preferable if the amount were quantified as this would be consistent with the approach generally taken in respect of guarantees of group borrowings.

6.3 Contingent assets

FRS 12 requires disclosure of contingent assets where an inflow of economic benefits is probable. The disclosures required are:

(a) a brief description of the nature of the contingent assets at the balance sheet date; and

(b) where practicable, an estimate of their financial effect, measured using the principles set out for provisions in paragraphs 36–55 of FRS 12.[161]

Where any of the information above is not disclosed because it is not practicable to do so, that fact should be stated.[162] The standard goes on to emphasise that the disclosure must avoid giving misleading indications of the likelihood of a profit arising.[163]

In practice, disclosures of contingent assets are relatively rare. One example can be seen in the 1996 accounts of Graseby:

> *Extract 28.42: Graseby plc (1996)*
>
> **28 Contingent items** [extract]
>
> (d) The group has a claim for compensation against a customer for cancellation of long term contracts in 1995. Compensation received in 1996 of £384,000 (1995 £240,000) has been recognised in the profit and loss account as a contribution towards overheads incurred. The final outcome of the claim cannot be determined with any certainty at present. However, the directors continue to expect that further appropriate compensation will be received.

One problem that arises with FRS 12 is that it requires the disclosure of an estimate of the potential financial effect for contingent assets to be measured in accordance with the measurement principles in the standard. Unfortunately, the measurement principles in the standard are all set out in terms of the measurement of provisions, and these principles cannot readily be applied to the measurement of contingent assets. Hence, judgement will have to be used as to how rigorously these principles should be applied.

6.4 Exemption from disclosure when seriously prejudicial

FRS 12 contains an exemption from disclosure of information in the following circumstances. It says that, 'in extremely rare cases, disclosure of some or all of the information required by [the disclosure requirements in 6.1.2, 6.2.2 and 6.3 above] can be expected to prejudice seriously the position of the entity in a dispute with other parties on the subject matter of the provision, contingent liability or contingent asset.'[164]

In such circumstances, the information need not be disclosed unless it is required by law. However, disclosure will still need to be made of the general nature of the dispute, together with the fact that, and the reason why, the required information has not been disclosed.[165]

This exemption applies to provisions, contingent liabilities and contingent assets. It is unclear, however, as to whether it can actually be used in practice for contingent liabilities. This is because the Companies Act requires disclosure of contingent liabilities including the estimated amount of each contingent liability and contains no exemption for information that is seriously prejudicial to the entity. Therefore, a strict interpretation of this exemption would suggest that it will never be available for contingent liabilities. Unfortunately, no clarification of the position is given in the appendix to the standard that discusses the corresponding legal requirements.

One company which has used this exemption in respect of a provision for warranties, indemnities and other litigation issues in relation to certain of its business exits (which at 31 December 2000 amounted to £54m) is Inchcape as shown below.

Extract 28.43: Inchcape plc (2000)

19 Provisions for liabilities and charges [extract]

Non-Motors business exits – provision has been made for warranties, indemnities and other litigation issues in relation to these exits. Any detailed disclosure of these issues could seriously prejudice negotiations. Accordingly, no information is given in regard to the likely timing or cash impact as normally required under FRS 12. Attention is drawn to note 20, which refers to two of these issues. During 2000, £5.6m was paid out in settlement of such items.

20 Guarantees and contingent liabilities [extract]

Certain claims have been notified by Intertek Testing Services Limited ("ITS") against the Group under warranties given in connection with the sale of Inchcape Testing Services in 1996. The claims by ITS relate principally to discrepancies which have been discovered in testing data provided to clients by various laboratories in the United States. These matters are under investigation by the US Department of Justice and the US Environmental Protection Agency and ITS may incur civil and criminal liabilities as a result. ITS may seek to recover costs which are alleged to arise from the discovery of the discrepancies, including liabilities to third parties, in repeating work for, or refunding fees to, customers, in investigating the data discrepancies and in dealing with government authorities. As yet insufficient information has been provided to enable the merits of value or any claims to be assessed fully. In the meantime, Inchcape intends to resist the claims vigorously and any proceedings that may be brought.

Aon Corporation has made certain claims under an indemnity given in connection with the sale of Bain Hogg Limited in 1996 relating to liabilities in respect of advice given on the sale of pensions and related products, opt-outs and transfers by Bain Hogg Financial Services Limited and Gardner Mountain Financial Services Limited. Aon may seek to make further claims in respect of such advice and related costs. On the information currently available to the Company, it is not possible to assess fully the merits or value of claims under this indemnity. The Directors have taken legal advice and are pursuing all options open to them to defend or minimise the claims.

The Directors having reviewed the matters set out above and having made certain provisions consider, based on the information currently available, that they will not have a material impact on the financial position of the Group.

However, it can be seen from note 20 that Inchcape has not used the exemption in respect of its disclosure of the related contingent liabilities.

7 IAS REQUIREMENTS

As indicated at 1 above, the relevant international standard, IAS 37, was developed in parallel with the UK standard, FRS 12, under a joint project between the ASB and the IASC and the two standards were published on the same day. There are no differences of substance between the requirements of the two standards – indeed the text is mostly identical – but FRS 12 touches on two additional areas – recognition of an asset when a provision is recognised, and slightly more guidance on the discount rate to be used in the net present value calculation.

The requirements of IAS 37 are outlined below, together with extracts from accounts of companies that have had to implement the standard. However, since the text of IAS 37 is almost identical to FRS 12, reference is made to the corresponding discussions of the equivalent FRS 12 requirements earlier in this chapter rather than repeating them in the context of IAS 37.

7.1 Scope of IAS 37

As IAS 37 defines a provision as a 'liability of uncertain timing or amount',[166] it does not address other 'provisions' such as depreciation, impairment of assets and doubtful debts; these are adjustments to the carrying amounts of assets.[167]

The standard applies to all enterprises in accounting for provisions, contingent liabilities and contingent assets, except:

(a) those resulting from financial instruments that are carried at fair value;

(b) those resulting from executory contracts, except where the contract is onerous;

(c) those arising in insurance enterprises from contracts with policyholders; or

(d) those covered by another International Accounting Standard.[168]

These are similar to the exemptions in FRS 12 discussed at 2.1 above. Like FRS 12, IAS 37 emphasises that it applies to financial instruments (including guarantees) that are *not* carried at fair value,[169] although this is clearly more relevant in an IAS context given that IAS 39 requires most financial instruments to be included at fair value (see Chapter 10 at 4). It contains the same definition of executory contracts as in FRS 12[170] and it emphasises that the standard applies to non-insurance types of provisions and contingencies of insurance enterprises.[171] The examples of the types of provisions and contingencies covered by other standards are the same as those in FRS 12, i.e.

(a) construction contracts (IAS 11);

(b) income taxes (IAS 12);

(c) leases (IAS 17), although it indicates that the standard does apply to operating leases that have become onerous;

(d) employee benefits (IAS 19).[172]

It also notes that some amounts treated as provisions may relate to the recognition of revenue, for example where an enterprise gives guarantees in exchange for a fee, and states that the standard does not address the recognition of revenue. This is dealt with by IAS 18 and IAS 37 is not changing the requirements of that standard.[173]

IAS 37 draws the same demarcation line between provisions and other liabilities as in FRS 12 (see 2.2 above)[174] and it contains the same discussion about the relationship between provisions and contingent liabilities (see 2.3 above).[175]

An example of a company reclassifying provisions as other liabilities, presumably as a result of implementing IAS 37, is Nestlé as shown below.

Extract 28.44: Nestlé S.A. (2000)

22. Provisions

In millions of CHF					**2000**	1999
	Restructuring	Environment	Litigation	Other	Total	Total
At 1st January					**2 289**	2 415
Introduction of IAS 37					**(132)**	
Restated figures at 1st January	322	74	1 633	128	**2 157**	
Currency retranslation	(11)	2	3	5	**(1)**	
Provisions made in the period	166	2	211	66	**445**	
Modification of the scope of consolidation	–	–	135	33	**168**	
Amounts used	(277)	(2)	(121)	(56)	**(456)**	
Unused amounts reversed	(6)	(6)	(64)	(33)	**(109)**	
At 31st December	194	70	1 797	143	**2 204**	2 289

At 1st January 1999, this caption included provisions for impairment of assets as well as certain other liabilities for a total of CHF 491 million. In 1999, this amount has been reclassified as a reduction of the carrying value of the related assets or shown as accrued liabilities.

7.2 Recognition

7.2.1 *Provisions*

IAS 37 requires that a provision should be recognised when:

(a) an enterprise has a present obligation (legal or constructive) as a result of a past event;

(b) it is probable that an outflow of resources embodying economic benefits will be required to settle the obligation; and

(c) a reliable estimate can be made of the amount of the obligation.

If these conditions are not met, no provision should be recognised.[176]

The standard defines both legal and constructive obligations in exactly the same terms as FRS 12.[177] It contains the same discussion as FRS 12 of each of these conditions (see 3 above).[178] As with FRS 12, IAS 37 illustrates how these recognition requirements are to be applied by including a number of examples in an appendix to the standard,[179] some of which are discussed at 7.4 below.

7.2.2 Contingencies

Contingent liabilities should not be recognised, but should just be disclosed (unless remote).[180] It is only if it becomes probable (i.e. more likely than not) that an outflow of future economic benefits will be required that a provision is then required.[181] Similarly, contingent assets, such as a claim that an enterprise is pursuing through legal process, should not be recognised since this may result in the recognition of income that may never be realised. When the realisation of income is virtually certain, then the related asset is no longer contingent, and its recognition appropriate.[182] Until such time as they are recognised, contingent assets should only be disclosed where an inflow of benefits is probable.[183]

These requirements are the same as those on FRS 12 which are discussed further at 3.2 above.

7.2.3 Recognising an asset when recognising a provision

As noted at 7 above, this is one of the areas where IAS 37 differs from FRS 12. IAS 37 does not deal with this at all, other than to say 'Other International Standards specify whether expenditures are treated as assets or as expenses. These issues are not addressed in this Standard. Accordingly, this Standard neither prohibits nor requires capitalisation of the costs recognised when a provision is made.'[184] FRS 12, on the other hand, contains a specific requirement that when a provision or a change in a provision is recognised, an asset should also be recognised when, and only when, the incurring of the present obligation recognised as a provision gives access to future economic benefits; otherwise the setting up of the provision should be charged immediately to the profit and loss account. This issue is discussed further at 3.3 above.

Extract 28.49 at 7.4.4 B below illustrates an example of a company capitalising costs in respect of its provision for decommissioning costs.

7.3 Measurement

A provision is to be measured before tax, as the tax consequences of the provision, and any changes in it, are dealt with under IAS 12 (see Chapter 24 at 7).

7.3.1 Best estimate of provision

The amount recognised as a provision should be the best estimate of the expenditure required to settle the present obligation at the balance sheet date.[185] In assessing this best estimate, the risks and uncertainties that inevitably surround many events and circumstances should be taken into account.[186] IAS 37 expands on these requirements in the same way as FRS 12, which is discussed at 4.1 above.

7.3.2 Present value

Like FRS 12, IAS 37 requires that where the effect of the time value of money is material, the amount of a provision should be the present value of the expenditures expected to be required to settle the obligation.[187] The discount rate (or rates) should be a pre-tax rate (or rates) that reflect(s) current market assessments of the time value of money and the risks specific to the liability. The discount rate(s) should not reflect risks for which future cash flow estimates have been adjusted.[188]

As noted at 7 above, this is one of the areas where IAS 37 differs from FRS 12. IAS 37 gives no guidance as to how these requirements are to be applied. FRS 12, on the other hand, gives slightly more guidance on the discount rate to be used in the net present value calculation. Issues related to the use of discounting are discussed at 4.2 above.

7.3.3 *Future events*

Future events that may affect the amount required to settle an obligation should be reflected in the amount of a provision where there is sufficient objective evidence that they will occur.[189] Again, IAS 37 expands on this requirement in the same way as FRS 12, which is discussed at 4.3 above.[190]

7.3.4 *Reimbursements from third parties*

In some circumstances an enterprise is able to look to a third party to reimburse part of the costs required to settle a provision or to pay the amounts directly. Examples are insurance contracts, indemnity clauses and suppliers' warranties.[191]

Where some or all of the expenditure required to settle a provision is expected to be reimbursed by another party, the reimbursement should be recognised when, and only when, it is virtually certain that reimbursement will be received if the enterprise settles the obligation. The reimbursement should be treated as a separate asset. The amount recognised for the reimbursement should not exceed the amount of the provision.[192]

In the income statement, the expense relating to the provision may be presented net of the amount recognised for the reimbursement.[193]

The above requirements will apply in most such cases. However, where the enterprise will not be liable for the costs in question if the third party fails to pay, than in such a case the enterprise has no liability for those costs and they are not included in the provision.[194]

These requirements are discussed further in IAS 37 in the same way as in FRS 12 (see 4.4 above).[195]

Extract 28.47 at 7.4.4 A below illustrates an example of a company treating amounts recoverable from third parties as separate assets.

7.3.5 *Gains on disposals of related assets*

Like FRS 12, IAS 37 states that gains from the expected disposal of assets should not be taken into account in measuring a provision, even if the expected disposal is closely linked to the event giving rise to the provision. Such gains should be recognised at the time specified by the IAS dealing with the assets concerned.[196] This is likely to be of particular relevance in relation to restructuring provisions (see 7.4.1 below). However, it may also apply in other situations. Extract 28.49

at 7.4.4 B below illustrates an example of a company excluding gains from the expected disposal of assets in determining its provision for decommissioning costs.

7.3.6 *Changes and uses of provisions*

Provisions should be reviewed at each balance sheet date and adjusted to reflect the current best estimate. If it is no longer probable that an outflow of resources embodying economic benefits will be required to settle the obligation, the provision should be reversed.[197] Where discounting is used, the carrying amount of a provision increase in each period to reflect the passage of time. This increase is recognised as a borrowing cost.[198]

Like FRS 12, IAS 37 emphasises that a provision should be used only for expenditures for which the provision was originally recognised, as to do otherwise would conceal the impact of two different events.[199]

7.4 Application of the recognition and measurement rules

As is done in FRS 12, IAS 37 expands on the general recognition and measurement rules outlined at 7.2 and 7.3 above, by also including more specific requirements for particular situations, i.e. restructuring, future operating losses and onerous contracts. These are outlined below at 7.4.1 to 7.4.3 below. In addition, IAS 37 contains a number of examples in an appendix which illustrate how the general recognition and measurement rules apply to other types of items where enterprises may or may not have made provision in the past.

7.4.1 *Restructuring provisions*

IAS 37 defines a restructuring in the same terms as FRS 12, i.e. as 'a programme that is planned and controlled by management, and materially changes either:

(a) the scope of a business undertaken by an entity; or

(b) the manner in which that business is conducted.'[200]

This is said to include:

(a) sale or termination of a line of business;

(b) the closure of business locations in a country or region or the relocation of business activities from one country or region to another;

(c) changes in management structure, for example, eliminating a layer of management; and

(d) fundamental reorganisations that have a material effect on the nature and focus of the entity's operations.[201]

In addition to the general requirements for recognition of a provision, IAS 37 sets out the following requirements which also need to be met in recognising a provision in respect of restructurings.

Under IAS 37, a constructive obligation to restructure arises only when an entity:

(a) has a detailed formal plan for the restructuring identifying at least:
   (i) the business or part of a business concerned;
   (ii) the principal locations affected;
   (iii) the location, function, and approximate number of employees who will be compensated for terminating their services;
   (iv) the expenditures that will be undertaken; and
   (v) when the plan will be implemented; and

(b) has raised a valid expectation in those affected that it will carry out the restructuring by starting to implement that plan or announcing its main features to those affected by it.'[202]

This is the same as in FRS 12, and IAS 37 contains equivalent discussion as to how these requirements are to be applied, particularly with respect to condition (b).[203] These issues are discussed in the context of FRS 12 at 5.1 above.

IAS 37 also states that no obligation arises for the sale of an operation until the enterprise is committed to the sale, i.e. there is a binding sale agreement.[204] Thus a provision cannot be made for a loss on sale unless there is a binding sale agreement by the year end. The standard says that this applies even when an entity has taken a decision to sell an operation and announced that decision publicly, it cannot be committed to the sale until a purchaser has been identified and there is a binding sale agreement. Until there is such an agreement, the entity will be able to change its mind and indeed will have to take another course of action if a purchaser cannot be found on acceptable terms. IAS 37 goes on to indicate that when the sale of an operation is envisaged as part of a restructuring, the assets of the operation are reviewed for impairment, under IAS 36. Also, when a sale is only part of a restructuring, a constructive obligation can arise for the other parts of the restructuring before a binding sale agreement exists.[205] This is the same as in FRS 12 in the UK.

One difference with the UK is that neither IAS 37 nor the standard on discontinuing operations, IAS 35, contains an equivalent of the suggestion in FRS 3 that a binding contract entered into after the balance sheet date may provide additional evidence of commitments at the balance sheet date discussed at 5.1.2 above.

Like FRS 12, IAS 37 limits the costs that can be included within a restructuring provision. It states that 'a restructuring provision should include only the direct expenditures arising from the restructuring, which are those that are both:

(a) necessarily entailed by a restructuring; and
(b) not associated with the ongoing activities of the entity'.[206]

The standard quotes the same examples as FRS 12 of costs that cannot be included, i.e. retraining or relocating continuing staff, marketing, or investment in new systems and distribution networks.[207] Furthermore, it emphasises that identifiable future operating losses up to the date of restructuring cannot be included, unless they relate to an onerous contract, and that gains on the expected disposal of assets cannot be taken into account even if the disposal is envisaged as part of the restructuring.[208] This is discussed further in the context of FRS 12 at 5.1.3 above.

One company which makes provision for restructuring costs on the basis of IAS 37 is Syngenta as shown in its accounting policies in Extract 28.47 at 7.4.4 A below. The following extract from its accounts gives further information about its provision for such costs.

Extract 28.45: Syngenta AG (2000)

22 Restructuring charges [extract]

(US$ million)	Employee termination costs	Other third party costs	Total
31 December 1999	**33**	**20**	**53**
Cash payments	(13)	(193)	(206)
Acquisition of Zeneca agrochemicals business	45	168	213
Additions	128	201	329
Non-income property, plant and equipment write-offs	–	(23)	(23)
Releases	(12)	–	(12)
Translation gain/(loss), net	(3)	(1)	(4)
31 December 2000	**178**	**172**	**350**

Following the formation of Syngenta in November 2000, Syngenta embarked on a plan to integrate and restructure the combined businesses in order to achieve cost savings. Such plans involve termination of employees, integration of systems and the closure of duplicate head office, research and development and manufacturing facilities. The charge to income in 2000 of US$329 million comprised of US$128 million for employee termination, and US$201 million for other third party costs. Approximately 1,020 jobs will be eliminated in respect of plans announced by 31 December 2000. The asset impairments were measured by comparing future expected cash flows generated by the assets to the assets' carrying amount on the date of acquisition. The future benefit of these assets should expire within 2001 due to this acquisition.

…

The releases to income in each year were a result of settlements of liabilities at lower amounts than originally anticipated.

It can be seen from the extract that the plans were announced by the year end. Although the note refers to 'integration of systems' as being part of the plans, it may appear that such costs have been included in the provision. However, the company's accounting policy included in Extract 28.47 at 7.4.4 A below, states that 'Costs relating to the ongoing activities of Syngenta are not provided for.'

7.4.2 *Future operating losses*

IAS 37 clarifies that provisions should not be recognised for future operating losses, since these do meet the definition of a liability and the general recognition criteria of the standard.[209] Like FRS 12, it emphasises that an expectation of future losses is an indication that certain assets may be impaired.[210] However, as noted at 5.2 above in the context of FRS 12, the anticipation of operating losses may also be recognised as a result of the requirements of other standards, such as writing down the carrying value of inventories under IAS 2 (see Chapter 16 at 4.2) and making provision for expected losses on construction contracts under IAS 11 (see Chapter 16 at 4.3).

7.4.3 *Onerous contracts*

As with FRS 12, even although future operating losses in general cannot be provided for, IAS 37 requires that 'if an enterprise has a contract that is onerous, the present obligation under the contract should be recognised and measured as a provision.'[211] The standard contains the same discussion of this issue as FRS 12[212] and defines an onerous contract in the same terms, i.e. 'a contract in which the unavoidable costs of meeting the obligations under it exceed the economic benefits expected to be received under it'.[213] As noted at 5.3 above in the context of FRS 12, this seems to require that the contract is onerous to the point of being directly loss-making, not simply uneconomic by reference to current prices. One of the most common examples of an onerous contract in practice relates to leasehold property. This is reinforced by the inclusion of a specific example of a provision for a vacant leasehold property.[214]

Like FRS 12, IAS 37 requires that any impairment loss that has occurred in respect of assets dedicated to an onerous contract is recognised before establishing a provision for the onerous contract.[215]

Issues relating to the equivalent requirements in FRS 12 are discussed at 5.3 above.

One company which has provided for onerous leases is Jardine Matheson as indicated by the following extract.

Extract 28.46: Jardine Matheson Holdings Limited (2000)

Provisions

Provisions are recognised when the Group has present legal or constructive obligations as a result of past events, it is probable that an outflow of resources embodying economic benefits will be required to settle the obligations, and a reliable estimate of the amount of the obligations can be made.

21 Provisions

	Closure cost provisions US$	Obligations under onerous leases US$	Others US$	Total US$
At 1st January 2000	13.5	10.0	20.4	43.9
Exchange rate adjustments	(0.9)	(1.0)	(0.5)	(2.4)
Additional provisions	11.8	15.4	2.4	29.6
Unused amounts reversed	(1.4)	(3.1)	–	(4.5)
Utilised	(6.9)	(1.9)	(16.0)	(24.8)
At 31st December 2000	**16.1**	**19.4**	**6.3**	**41.8**

Closure costs are established when legal or constructive obligations arise on closure of businesses.

Provisions are made for obligations under onerous operating leases when the properties are not used by the Group and the net costs of exiting from the leases exceed the economic benefits expected to be received.

Other provisions comprise provisions in respect of indemnities on disposal of businesses, lease dilapidations and legal claims.

7.4.4 *Other types of provisions*

IAS 37 also deals with other types of situations where provisions may or may not have been made in the past. Although the standard does not include particular requirements about such items, it has either included an example in an appendix dealing with such situations or has mentioned them in passing while discussing the general recognition requirements of the standard. These are dealt with below.

A *Environmental provisions*

The standard illustrates two examples of circumstances where environmental provisions would be required. The first deals with the situation where it is virtually certain that legislation will be enacted which will require the clean up of land already contaminated.[216] In these circumstances, a provision would obviously be required. However, in its discussion about what constitutes an obligating event, the standard notes that 'differences in circumstances surrounding enactment make it impossible to specify a single event that would make the enactment of a law virtually certain. In many cases, it will be impossible to be virtually certain of the enactment of a law until it is enacted.'[217] The second example deals with the situation where an entity has contaminated land, but is not legally required to clean it up.[218] In these circumstances, a provision is required if the entity has a constructive obligation to clean up the land. In the example given, a constructive obligation is said to exist because the entity has a widely publicised environmental policy undertaking to clean up all contamination that it causes, and has a record of honouring this policy.

This issue is discussed further in the context of FRS 12 (which contains the same examples) at 5.4 above. As noted in that discussion, these requirements are not particularly controversial, apart from the general difficulty in knowing exactly when a constructive obligation comes into existence. However, potentially the more significant effect of the standard is its requirement that provisions should be discounted to their present value, which will have a material impact if the expenditure is not expected to be incurred for some time.

One company which makes provision for environmental costs is Syngenta as shown below.

Extract 28.47: Syngenta AG (2000)

Provisions

A provision is recognized in the balance sheet when Syngenta has a legal or constructive obligation as a result of a past event and it is probable that an outflow of economic benefits will be required to settle the obligation. If the effect of discounting is material, provisions are determined by discounting the expected value of future cash flows at a pre-tax rate that reflects current market assessments of the time value of money and, where appropriate, the risks specific to the liability. Where some or all of the expenditure required to settle a provision is expected to be reimbursed by another party, the reimbursement is recognized only when reimbursement is virtually certain. The amount to be reimbursed is recognized as a separate asset. Where Syngenta has a joint and several liabilities with one or more other parties, no provision is recognized to the extent that those other parties are expected to settle part or all of the obligation.

Environmental provisions

Syngenta is exposed to environmental liabilities relating to its past operations, principally in respect of remediation costs. Provisions for non-recurring remediation costs are made when there is a present obligation, it is probable that expense on remediation work will be required and the cost can be estimated within a reasonable range of possible outcomes. The costs are based on currently available facts, technology expected to be available at the time of the clean-up, laws and regulations presently or virtually certain to be enacted and prior experience in remediation of contaminated sites. Environmental liabilities are recorded at the present value of the expenditures expected to be required to settle the obligation, unless the time value of money is considered immaterial, in which case the liability is recorded on an undiscounted basis.

Restructuring provisions

A provision for restructuring is recognized when Syngenta has approved a detailed and formal restructuring plan and the restructuring has either commenced or been announced publicly. Costs relating to the ongoing activities of Syngenta are not provided for.

21 Provisions [extract]

(US$ million)	2000	1999	1998
Environmental provisions (Note 28)	275	170	176

The following table analyses the movements in provisions during 2000:

(US$ million)	Balance at 1 January 2000	Acquisition of Zeneca agro-chemicals business	Charged to income net of releases	Payments	Other movement, including translation (gains)/losses	Balance at 31 December 2000
Environmental provisions (Note 28)	170	101	22	(17)	(1)	275

28 Commitments and contingencies [extract]

Environmental matters

Syngenta has environmental liabilities at some currently or formerly owned, leased and third party sites throughout the world.

In the US, Syngenta, or its indemnities, has been named under federal legislation (the Comprehensive Environmental Response, Compensation and Liability Act of 1980, as amended) as a potentially responsible party ('PRP') in respect of several sites Syngenta expects to be indemnified against liabilities associated with a number of these sites by the seller of the businesses associated with such sites and, where appropriate, actively participates in or monitors the clean-up activities at the sites in respect of which it is a PRP.

During 2000 Syngenta was named as a PRP in respect of a manufacturing site in the US. A provision has been recorded at 31 December 2000 in respect of the estimated costs of remediation of US$27 million, which are due to be indemnified by the previous owner of the site under the relevant purchase agreement and therefore a corresponding receivable has been recorded.

In April 2000, Part IIA of the Environmental Protection Act 1999 (contaminated land provisions) was passed into legislation in the UK. The new legislation gives local environmental agencies significant powers to register contaminated sites and to require the owners of these sites to carry out environmental remediation. Environmental remediation costs associated with this legislation are included in provisions recorded on acquisition of the Zeneca agrochemicals business.

> Syngenta has provisions in respect of environmental remediation costs in accordance with the accounting policy described in Note 2. At 31 December 2000, 1999 and 1998, Syngenta had recorded in other current and non-current provisions a total of US$275 million, US$170 million and US$176 million respectively, to cover future environmental expenditures. Amounts recoverable of US$29 million at 31 December 2000 (1999 and 1998: US$0 million), from third parties for such costs have been recorded in current and non-current receivables. The environmental provision is principally related to potential liability at various locations. The estimated provision takes into consideration the number of other PRPs at each site and the identity and financial positions of such parties in light of the joint and several nature of the liability.
>
> The requirement in the future for Syngenta ultimately to take action to correct the effects on the environment of prior disposal or release of chemical substances by Syngenta or other parties, and its costs, pursuant to environment laws and regulations, is inherently difficult to estimate. The material components of the environmental provisions consist of a risk assessment based on investigation of the various sites. Syngenta's future remediation expenses are affected by a number of uncertainties which include, but are not limited to, the method and extent of remediation, the percentage of material attributable to Syngenta at the remediation sites relative to that attributable to other parties, and the financial capabilities of the other potentially responsible parties.
>
> Syngenta believes that its provisions are adequate based upon currently available information. However, given the inherent difficulties in estimating liabilities in this area, it cannot be guaranteed that additional costs will not be incurred beyond the amounts accrued. The effect of resolution of environmental matters on results of operations cannot be predicted due to uncertainty concerning both the amount and the timing of future expenditures and the results of future operations. Management believes that such additional amounts, if any, would not be material to Syngenta's financial condition but could be material to Syngenta's results of operations in a given period.

B Decommissioning provisions

Decommissioning costs are those that arise, for example, when an oil rig or nuclear power station has to be dismantled at the end of its life.[219] The impact of the standard on such costs is profound.

The accounting for decommissioning costs is dealt with in IAS 37 by way of an example in an appendix.[220] This example requires that an entity should recognise a liability as soon as the decommissioning obligation is created, which is normally when the facility is constructed and the damage that needs to be restored is done. The total decommissioning cost is estimated, discounted to its present value and it is this amount which forms the initial provision and is added to the corresponding asset's cost. Thereafter, the asset is depreciated over its useful life, while the discounted provision is progressively unwound, with the unwinding charge showing as a borrowing cost.

As noted at 7.3.6 above, the standard requires provisions to be revised annually to reflect the current best estimate of the provision. However, the standard gives no guidance on accounting for changes in the decommissioning provision. In our view, where the best estimate of the eventual decommissioning costs changes from the amount originally provided for, the difference should be added to or deducted from the asset and dealt with in the future as an adjustment to amortisation. This is consistent with the requirement of FRS 12 as noted in the discussion of decommissioning provisions at 5.5 above. However, as noted in that discussion one other matter is how the effects of changes in the interest rate used in discounting the provision should be treated. In the UK, a recent SORP issued by the Oil Industry

Accounting Committee regards changes in discount rates like any other change in estimate and therefore the effect should be adjusted against the asset.[221]

One company affected by these requirements was AngloGold, which explained the restatement of its prior year figures as a result of implementing IAS 37 in its 1999 accounts as follows:

Extract 28.48: AngloGold Limited (1999)

Restatement of prior year

The group has adopted International Accounting Standard No. 37 (IAS 37) "Provisions, contingent liabilities and contingent assets" with effect from 1 January 1998, prior to the effective date of this statement. In accordance with IAS 37, full provision has been made for the group's estimated future decommissioning costs. Previously the provision for environmental rehabilitation had been built up on a units of production basis over the life of a mine.

A decommissioning asset has now been recognised in respect of the net present value of future decommissioning costs and is amortised using the units of production method over the life of a mine.

The decommissioning obligation is unwound over the life of the mine and included in the income statement.

Estimated restoration costs are accrued and expensed over the operating life of a mine using the units-of-production method.

The implementation of IAS 37 had no unfavourable effect on the current year's income statement, when compared to the rehabilitation provision raised in accordance with the previous policy and the prior year adjustment is disclosed below:

SA Rands	Decom-missioning assets	Accumulated amortisation	Decom-missioning obligation	Restoration obligation	Environ-mental Rehabil-itation	Retained earnings
As at 31 December 1997 as previously reported inclusive of merger adjustment	–	–	–	–	551.4	1,279.6
Adjustment in respect of adoption of IAS 37	196.9	130.7	196.9	354.5	(551.4)	66.2
As restated at 31 December 1997	196.9	130.7	196.9	354.5	–	1,345.8

AngloGold's accounting policies and provisions note in respect of decommissioning obligations and restoration obligations are shown in the following extract from its 2000 accounts:

Extract 28.49: AngloGold Limited (2000)

Provisions [extract]

Provisions are recognised when the group has a present obligation, whether legal or constructive, as a result of a past event for which it is probable that an outflow of resources embodying economic benefits will be required to settle the obligation and a reliable estimate can be made of the amount of the obligation.

Environmental expenditure

Long-term environmental obligations comprising decommissioning and restoration are based on the group's environmental management plans, in compliance with the current environmental and regulatory requirements.

Decommissioning costs

The provision for decommissioning represents the cost that will arise from rectifying damage caused before production commenced.

Decommissioning costs are provided for at the present value of the expenditures expected to settle the obligation, using estimated cash flows based on current prices. When this provision gives access to future economic benefits, an asset is recognised and included within mining infrastructure. The unwinding of the decommissioning obligation is included in the income statement. The estimated future cost of decommissioning obligations are regularly reviewed and adjusted as appropriate for new circumstances or changes in law or technology. The estimates are discounted at a pre-tax rate that reflects current market assessments of the time value of money.

Gains from the expected disposal of assets are not taken into account when determining the provision.

Restoration costs

The provision for restoration represents the cost for restoration of site damage arising, after the commencement of production, from rectifying work whose cost was reported through the income statement.

Gross restoration costs are estimated at the present value of the expenditures expected to settle the obligation, using estimated cashflows based on current prices. The estimates are discounted at a pre-tax rate that reflects current market assessments of the time value of money.

Restoration costs are accrued and expensed over the operating life of each mine using the units-of-production method based on estimated proved and probable mineral reserves. Expenditure on ongoing restoration costs is brought to account when incurred.

Environmental Rehabilitation Trust

Annual contributions are made to the AngloGold Environmental Rehabilitation Trust, created in accordance with South African statutory requirements, to fund the estimated cost of rehabilitation during and at the end of the life of a mine. The funds that have been paid into the Trust fund plus the growth in the Trust fund is shown as an asset on the balance sheet.

		2000	1999
		SA rands	
27	**Provisions** [extract]		
	Environmental rehabilitation obligations		
	Provision for decommissioning		
	Balance at beginning of year	**383**	211
	Through acquisition of subsidiaries (note 32)	**–**	154
	Unwinding of decommissioning obligation (refer note 6)	**2**	18
	Prior year adjustment	**4**	–
	Translation adjustment	**12**	–
	Balance at end of year	**401**	383
	Provision for restoration		
	Balance at beginning of year	**814**	396
	Through acquisition of subsidiaries (note 32)	**4**	331
	Charge to income statement	**–**	87
	Translation adjustment	**37**	–
	Balance at end of year	**855**	814

It can be seen from the above extract that AngloGold has made a distinction between decommissioning costs and restoration costs. The former are provided in full at the point of creating the damage and a corresponding asset created, whereas the latter costs are being provided over the life of the mine using a unit-of-production method (which is the method that had been used for all of the environmental costs prior to IAS 37 as shown in Extract 28.48 above). This is presumably because the costs of restoring the damage caused by extracting the minerals from the mine at any balance sheet date is proportional to the overall restoration costs once the mine is at the end of its life.

C *Repairs and maintenance provisions*

This is another area which is dealt with by way of examples in an appendix, both dealing with cyclical refurbishment costs. The examples it gives are of a furnace that has a lining that needs replacing every five years, and an aircraft that needs overhauling every three years.[222] Neither of these provisions is allowed to be set up on the basis that there is no obligation to carry out the expenditure independently of the company's future actions. This argument is used even in the circumstances where there is a legal requirement for the asset in question to be repaired, since it is asserted that, even then, the entity could avoid the expenditure by, for example, selling the asset.

The effect of this prohibition on setting up provisions for repairs obviously impacts on balance sheet presentation. It may not always, however, have as much impact on the profit and loss account. This is because it is suggested that depreciation might be adjusted to take account of the repairs. For example, in the case of the furnace lining, the lining should be depreciated over five years in advance of its expected repair. Similarly, in the case of the aircraft overhaul, the example in the standard suggests that an amount equivalent to the expected maintenance costs is depreciated over three years. The result of this is that the overall charge to the profit and loss account that will now arise from depreciation may be equivalent to that which would previously have arisen from the combination of depreciation and provision for repair.

This issue is discussed further in the context of FRS 12 (which contains the same examples) at 5.6 above.

One company which had to change its policy as a result of this requirement is Kemira as shown by the following extract from its 1999 accounts when it implemented IAS 37.

Extract 28.50: Kemira Oyj (1999)

SUMMARY OF SIGNIFICANT ACCOUNTING POLICIES [extract]

Large, seldom performed maintenance works

Large, seldom performed maintenance works are treated as a capital expenditure as from 1999 and acquisition costs are depreciated over their useful lifetimes (IAS 37). Previously, provisions for expenses were booked for them in advance. The effect of the change on net income and shareholders' equity is stated in Note 16.

16. SHAREHOLDERS' EQUITY [extract]

The change in accounting principles includes a charge of EUR 9.2 million for the deferred tax liability on revaluations (IAS 12) in 1998, and an increase in equity of EUR 18.6 million after taxes for the change in accounting policy for major maintenance works (IAS 37). The change in accounting policy for maintenance works, after tax, was a charge of EUR 0.1 million in the income statement in 1999.

The above prohibition of repair provisions applies to repairs and maintenance of owned assets. However, operating leases often contain clauses which specify that the tenant should incur periodic charges for maintenance or make good dilapidations or other damage occurring during the rental period. Hence, some entities in the past have built up a provision over the life of the lease for costs of repair and renovation of the property.

The question arises as to whether such a provision meets the recognition criteria in the standard. This issue is not addressed in either IAS 37 or FRS 12. However, it is mentioned briefly in the appendix discussing the development of FRS 12. This notes that 'the principle illustrated in [the example on repairs] does not preclude the recognition of such liabilities once the event giving rise to the obligation under the lease has occurred'.[223] Since the repair examples in IAS 37 are the same as those in FRS 12, then we believe that the same comment should also apply to IAS 37. This issue is discussed further at 5.7 above.

Extract 28.46 at 7.4.3 above, shows an example of a company that has provided for dilapidation costs.

D Warranty provisions

Warranty provisions are specifically addressed in one of the examples appended to IAS 37, which concludes that such provisions are appropriate.[224] The example deals with a manufacturer that gives warranties at the time of sale of its product. Under the terms of contract for sale the manufacturer undertakes to make good, by repair or replacement, manufacturing defects that become apparent within 3 years from the date of sale. On past experience, it is probable (i.e. more likely than not) that there will be some claims under the warranties. The obligating event giving rise to the legal obligation is the sale of the product on which the warranty is given. We concur with this view, although in practice considerations of materiality may sometimes permit it to be treated on a pay-as-you-go basis.

The standard makes it clear that where there are a number of similar obligations, the probability that an economic outflow will occur is based on the class of obligations as a whole. Hence, the probability of an economic outflow occurring for warranties as a whole will need to be evaluated. If this probability exceeds 50% (which seems very likely), then the expected value of the estimated warranty costs should be calculated and provided for.[225] IAS 37 discusses this method of 'expected value' and illustrates how it is calculated in an example of a warranty provision.[226] The equivalent example in FRS 12 is discussed at 4.1 above.

An example of a company that makes a warranty provision is Nokia as shown below.

Extract 28.51: Nokia Corporation (2000)

Provisions

Provisions are recognized when the Group has a present legal or constructive obligation as a result of past events, it is probable that an outflow of resources will be required to settle the obligation, and a reliable estimate of the amount can be made. Where the Group expects a provision to be reimbursed, the reimbursement would be recognized as an asset but only when the reimbursement is virtually certain.

The Group recognizes the estimated liability to repair or replace products still under warranty at the balance sheet date. The provision is calculated based on historical experience of the level of repairs and replacements.

Another example is GN Great Nordic as shown in Extract 28.52 at 7.5.1 below.

E *Litigation and other legal claims*

IAS 37 includes an example of a court case in its Appendix to illustrate how its principles for recognising a provision should be applied in such situations.[227] However, the assessment of the particular case is clear-cut. In most situations, assessing the need to provide for legal claims is one of the most difficult tasks in the field of provisioning. This is due mainly to the inherent uncertainty in the judicial process itself, which may be very long and drawn out. Furthermore, this is an area where either provision or disclosure might risk prejudicing the outcome of the case, because they give an insight into the company's own view on the strength of its defence that can assist the claimant. Similar considerations apply in other related areas, such as tax disputes.

This issue is discussed further in the context of FRS 12 at 5.10 above.

F *Refunds policy*

An example is given in the appendix of IAS 37 of a retail store that has a policy of refunding goods returned by dissatisfied customers. There is no legal obligation to do so, but the company's policy of making refunds is generally known.[228]

The example argues that the conduct of the store has created a valid expectation on the part of its customers that the store will refund purchases. The obligating event is the original sale of the item, and the probability of some economic outflow is greater than 50%, as there will nearly always be some customers demanding refunds. Hence, a provision should be made, presumably calculated again on the 'expected value' basis.

This example is straightforward when the store has a very specific and highly publicised policy on refunds. However, some stores' policies on refunds might not be so clear cut. A store may offer refunds under certain circumstances, but not widely publicise its policy. In these circumstances, it is likely to be open to interpretation as to whether the store has created a valid expectation on the part of its customers that the store will refund purchases.

G *Staff training*

IAS 37 gives an example of the government introducing changes to the income tax system, such that an entity in the financial services sector needs to retrain a large proportion of its administrative and sales workforce in order to ensure continued compliance with financial services regulation. At the balance sheet date no retraining has taken place.[229]

The standard argues that the obligating event is the staff retraining, and since at the year end no training has taken place, there is no obligating event, and so no provision should be made. As discussed at 5.12 above, in the context of the same example in FRS 12, we agree with this outcome, but the reasoning behind it seems fragile.

H Self-insurance

Another situation where enterprises have sometimes made provisions is self insurance which arises when an entity decides not to take out external insurance in respect of a certain category of risk because it would be uneconomic to do so. The same position may arise when a group insures its risks with a captive insurance subsidiary, the effects of which have to be eliminated on consolidation. This is the only situation illustrated in the examples in FRS 12 where there is no equivalent example in IAS 37. The example in FRS 12 is discussed at 5.9 above. In that discussion, we note the example is somewhat misleading, since it deals with a very basic case where it is known with certainty at the time of preparing the accounts that no losses have arisen in the period. In real life, a provision will often be needed not simply for known incidents, but also for those which insurance companies call IBNR – Incurred But Not Reported – representing an estimate of the latent liabilities at the year end that experience shows will come to the surface only gradually. We believe that it is entirely appropriate that provision for such expected claims is made.

7.5 Disclosure requirements

7.5.1 Provisions

For each class of provision an enterprise should disclose a reconciliation of the carrying amount of the provision at the beginning and end of the period showing:

(a) additional provisions made in the period, including increases to existing provisions;

(b) amounts used, i.e. incurred and charged against the provision, during the period;

(c) unused amounts reversed during the period; and

(d) the increase during the period in the discounted amount arising from the passage of time and the effect of any change in the discount rate.

Comparative information is not required.[230]

In addition, for each class of provision an enterprise should disclose the following:

(a) a brief description of the nature of the obligation and the expected timing of any resulting outflows of economic benefits;

(b) an indication of the uncertainties about the amount or timing of those outflows. Where necessary to provide adequate information, an entity should disclose the major assumptions made concerning future events; and

(c) the amount of any expected reimbursement, stating the amount of any asset that has been recognised for that expected reimbursement.[231]

Appendix D to the standard provides examples of suitable disclosures in relation to warranties and decommissioning costs.

These disclosure requirements are the same as those in FRS 12 discussed at 6.1.2 above.

Most of the above disclosures are illustrated in the extract below.

Extract 28.52: GN Great Nordic (2000)

Note 21: Other Provisions

Consolidated (DKK millions)	Restructuring in Companies Acquired	Other Restructuring	Warranty Provisions	Other Provisions	Total
Provisions at January 1	143	–	102	53	298
Implications of changed accounting policies	–	–	(2)	–	(2)
Additions	7	2	60	197	266
Consumed	(105)	–	(22)	–	(127)
Reversed provision	–	–	(7)	–	(7)
Exchange differences	13	–	6	5	24
Provisions at year-end	58	2	137	255	452

Provisions for restructuring purposes only concerns the acquisition of ReSound Corporation. The estimated costs are based on a detailed plan prepared by Management, which has been discussed and announced to the affected employees. Restructuring is expected to be carried out before year-end 2001.

Warranty provisions concern products sold from NetTest, GN Netcom and GN ReSound, delivered with between one and three year warranties. The provision has been calculated on the basis of historical warranty costs of the Group's products. The provision is expected to be spent within the next three years.

The total conditional acquisition payment of DKK 47 million (FRF 41 million) in connection with the acquisition of Optran is included in other provisions. The total conditional payment of DKK 24 million (USD 3 million) in connection with the acquisition of AGC is also included. The acquisition payments have been included since it is considered most likely that the acquisition conditions will be met. The provisions are expected to be spent within one to four years. In other provisions the obligation to take back goods is included. The provision is expected to be spent within one to two years.

7.5.2 *Contingencies*

IAS 37 requires the following disclosure for each class of contingent liability at the balance sheet date unless the possibility of any outflow in settlement is remote:

(a) a brief description of the nature of the contingent liability, and where practicable:

(b) an estimate of its financial effect, measured in accordance with paragraphs 36-52 of IAS 37;

(c) an indication of the uncertainties relating to the amount or timing of any outflow; and

(d) the possibility of any reimbursement.[232]

Where any of the information above is not disclosed because it is not practicable to do so, that fact should be stated.[233]

A further point noted in the standard is that where a provision and a contingent liability arise from the same circumstances, an entity should ensure that the link between the provision and the contingent liability is clear.[234]

IAS 37 requires disclosure of contingent assets where an inflow of economic benefits is probable. The disclosures required are:

(a) a brief description of the nature of the contingent assets at the balance sheet date; and

(b) where practicable, an estimate of their financial effect, measured using the principles set out for provisions in paragraphs 36–52 of IAS 37.[235]

Where any of the information above is not disclosed because it is not practicable to do so, that fact should be stated.[236] The standard goes on to emphasise that the disclosure must avoid giving misleading indications of the likelihood of a profit arising.[237]

These disclosure requirements are the same as those in FRS 12 discussed at 6.2.2 and 6.3 above.

Examples of disclosures about contingent liabilities are illustrated below.

Extract 28.53: GN Great Nordic (2000)

Parent Company			Notes – Balance Sheet	Consolidated	
1999	**2000**	Note	(DKK millions)	**2000**	1999
		Note 26:	***Contingent Liabilities***		
5	5		Guarantees and other contingent liabilities	47	11

Outstanding Lawsuits and Arbitration Proceedings

GN Great Nordic Ltd. and its subsidiaries and associated companies are parties in various lawsuits and arbitration proceedings, the outcomes of which are not expected to be of importance to the evaluation of the Company's or the Group's financial position. The parent company does not expect any proceedings which could affect the financial position of the parent company or the Group. The local tax authorities have increased the Group's joint taxation income for the years 1993 – 1996 by a not unsubstantial amount concerning the right to deduct depreciation charges from investments in cable projects in Eastern Europe. GN Great Nordic considers the tax authorities' claims to be unfounded and has referred the case to the Danish National Tax Tribunal. Tax based on the tax authorities' allegations has not been included in the financial statements. In 2000, GN Great Nordic has paid the levy due to the increase imposed by the Copenhagen company taxation authorities. The tax paid is included in receivables in the amount of DKK 168 million.

Conditional payments in connection with acquisitions

According to concluded acquisition agreements the Group is under an obligation to pay a further DKK 950 million in acquisition payment in addition to the amounts concerning company acquisitions included in the balance sheet. The amount is not included in the balance sheet as it is not considered likely that the amount will fall due for payment.

Extract 28.54: Novartis AG (2000)

28. Commitments and contingencies [extract]

Contingencies Group companies have to observe the laws, government orders and regulations of the country in which they operate. A number of them are currently involved in administrative proceedings arising out of the normal conduct of their business.

The Group, along with numerous other prescription drug manufacturers, is a defendant in various actions brought by certain US retail pharmacies, alleging antitrust and pricing violations. The Group believes that these actions are without merit.

A number of Group companies are also the subject of litigation arising out of the normal conduct of their business, as a result of which claims could be made against them which, in whole or in part, might not be covered by insurance. In the opinion of Group management, however, the outcome of the actions referred to will not materially affect the Group's financial position, result of operations or cash flow.

The material components of the environmental liability consist of a risk assessment based on investigation of the various sites. The Group's future remediation expenses are affected by a number of uncertainties. These uncertainties include, but are not limited to, the method and extent of remediation, the percentage of material attributable to the Group at the remediation sites relative to that attributable to other parties, and the financial capabilities of the other potentially responsible parties. The Group does not expect the resolution of such uncertainties to have a material effect on the consolidated financial statements.

Extract 28.55: Roche Holding Ltd (2000)

27. Contingent liabilities

The operations and earnings of the Group continue, from time to time and in varying degrees, to be affected by political, legislative, fiscal and regulatory developments, including those relating to environmental protection, in the countries in which it operates. The industries in which the Group is engaged are also subject to physical risks of various kinds. The nature and frequency of these developments and events, not all of which are covered by insurance, as well as their effect on future operations and earnings are not predictable.

Provisions have been recorded in respect of the vitamin case, as disclosed in Note 5. These provisions are the Group's best current estimate of the total liability that may arise. As the various investigations outside the United States of America and private civil suits are still in progress it is possible that the ultimate liability may be different from this.

5. Vitamin case

Following the settlement agreement with the US Department of Justice on 20 May 1999 regarding pricing practices in the vitamin market, the Group recorded pre-tax expenses of 2,426 million Swiss francs in respect of the vitamin case in 1999. Cash outflows in 1999 were 1,282 million Swiss francs.

On 28 March 2000 a US federal judge approved the overall settlement agreement to a class action suit brought by the US buyers of bulk vitamins. Several customers in the class action have decided to opt out of the proposed settlement and pursue claims against the Group individually. As these individual suits are still in process it is not possible to determine the timing and amount of the ultimate settlement of these claims

On 10 October 2000 settlement agreements were executed with Attorneys General and private class counsels representing US indirect purchasers and consumers in 22 states and with Attorneys General in respect of governmental entities in 43 states. The class action settlements remain subject to court approval. If approved, Roche will pay up to 171 million US dollars, plus interest and legal fees. Certain suits in other states are still in process and it is not possible to determine the outcome of these claims.

> On 6 July 2000 the European Commission issued a Statement of Objections against 13 producers of bulk vitamins, including Roche. This is the beginning of the Commission's formal investigation into the vitamin case and it is not yet possible to determine the ultimate outcome of this investigation.
>
> The provisions that were recorded in respect of the vitamin case at 31 December 1999, less the amounts utilised during 2000, remain the Group's best current estimate of the total liability that may arise. Therefore no additional expenses have been charged in 2000. Net cash inflows in 2000 were 41 million Swiss francs. Following the opt-out of some of the US buyers of bulk vitamins from settlement agreement, the Group received a repayment of part of the amounts paid into a trust fund in 1999.

An example of a company disclosing contingent gains is Nestlé as shown below.

> *Extract 28.56: Nestlé S.A. (2000)*
>
> **35. Contingent assets and liabilities**
>
> The Group is exposed to contingent liabilities amounting to about CHF 400 million representing various potential litigation. An amount of about CHF 280 million could result in liabilities.
>
> Contingent assets for litigation claims in favour of the Group amount to about CHF 260 million.

7.5.3 *Exemption from disclosure when seriously prejudicial*

Like FRS 12, IAS 37 contains an exemption from disclosure of information in the following circumstances. It says that, 'in extremely rare cases, disclosure of some or all of the information required by [the disclosure requirements in 7.5.1 and 7.5.2 above] can be expected to prejudice seriously the position of the enterprise in a dispute with other parties on the subject matter of the provision, contingent liability or contingent asset.'[238]

In such circumstances, the information need not be disclosed. However, disclosure will still need to be made of the general nature of the dispute, together with the fact that, and the reason why, the required information has not been disclosed.[239]

8 CONCLUSION

The subject of provisions and contingencies is a wide ranging one, but at its heart lie fundamental questions concerning the recognition and measurement of items in the accounts. The ASB and the IASC see these issues straightforwardly in terms of balance sheet recognition, and has sought to apply their respective conceptual frameworks as a means of resolving them, but in many cases we think this does not work well and that it is more fruitful to address the question from the point of view of expense recognition. In particular, we think the concepts of 'obligating events' and 'constructive obligations' are rather more nebulous than they are represented to be, and not always useful in identifying reliably when to include certain items in the accounts. We would not be as dismissive as the standard setters about the relevance of management intent, since accounts necessarily represent the report of management and it is futile to try to divorce them from that context. We are also concerned that the approach of FRS 12 and IAS 37 means that the balance sheet will be inappropriately grossed up in some cases so as to include dubious assets.

The measurement requirements also have their difficulties. We are concerned that they seem to be seeking to derive some form of theoretical market value for the obligations reported whereas we would prefer to focus more directly on the actual expenditure that the company is likely to make. We also think that the rules on discounting should have been given much deeper consideration. The use of discounting also means that the operating results of an entity are often heavily flattered at the expense of finance costs.

As a result, we do not think that FRS 12 and IAS 37 are very satisfactory standards. While the answers they give rise to are usually acceptable, the reasoning that lies behind them is frequently suspect and is more likely to puzzle readers than enlighten them. We think that there are likely to be many problems of interpretation in practice as a result.

References

1 CA 85, Sch. 4, para. 89.
2 *Ibid.*, para. 88.
3 FRS 12, *Provisions, Contingent Liabilities and Contingent Assets*, ASB, September 1998, para. 9.
4 *Ibid.*, para. 2.
5 *Ibid.*, Appendix V, para. 5.
6 FRS 12, para. 2.
7 IAS 37, *Provisions, Contingent Liabilities and Contingent Assets*, IASC, September 1998, para. 10.
8 *Examination of the conformity between IAS 37 and the European Accounting Directives*, XV/6010/99 EN, Brussels, 27 April 1999.
9 SSAP 18, *Accounting for contingencies*, ASC, August 1980.
10 IAS 10, *Contingencies and Events Occurring After the Balance Sheet Date*, IASC, October 1978.
11 FRS 12, para. 11; IAS 37, para. 11.
12 FRS 12, para 1.
13 Draft Statement of Principles, *Provisions and Contingencies*, IASC, November 1996, paras. 89-95.
14 FRS 12, para. 4.
15 *Ibid.*, para. 9.
16 *Ibid.*, para. 3.
17 *Ibid.*, para. 5.
18 *Ibid.*, para. 6.
19 *Ibid.*, para. 7.
20 *Ibid.*, para. 8.
21 *Ibid.*, para. 10.
22 *Ibid.*, para. 11.
23 *Ibid.*, para. 12.
24 *Ibid.*, para. 13.
25 *Ibid.*, para. 14.
26 *Ibid.*, para. 2.
27 *Ibid.*
28 *Ibid.*, Appendix III, Examples 2B and 4.
29 FRS 12, paras 15 and 16.
30 *Ibid.*, para. 2.
31 *Ibid.*, para. 17.
32 *Ibid.*, para. 18.
33 *Ibid.*, para. 19.
34 *Ibid.*, Appendix III, Example 6.
35 *Ibid.*, Examples 11A and 7.
36 FRS 12, para. 20.
37 *Ibid.*, para. 21.
38 *Ibid.*, para. 22.
39 *Ibid.*, para. 21.
40 FASB Newsletter No. 310, 25 February 1999, p. 5.
41 FRS 12, paras. 23 and 24.
42 *Ibid.*, paras. 25 and 26.
43 *Ibid.*, paras. 27, 28, 31 and 34.
44 *Ibid.*, para. 2.
45 *Ibid.*, paras. 15 and 16.
46 *Ibid.*, para. 30.
47 *Ibid.*, Appendix III, Example 9.
48 FRS 12, para. 2.
49 *Ibid.*, para. 32.
50 *Ibid.*
51 *Ibid.*, paras. 34 and 94.
52 *Ibid.*, para. 35.
53 *Ibid.*, paras. 66 and 67.
54 *Ibid.*, para. 41.
55 *Ibid.*, para. 36.
56 *Ibid.*, para. 37.

57 *Statement of Principles for Financial Reporting*, ASB, December 1999, para. 6.9.
58 FRS 12, para. 37.
59 *Ibid.*, para. 38.
60 *Ibid.*
61 *Ibid.*
62 FASB Interpretation No. 14, *Reasonable Estimation of the Amount of a Loss*, FASB, September 1976, para. 3.
63 FRS 12, para. 40.
64 *Ibid.*
65 FRED 14, *Provisions and Contingencies*, ASB, June 1997, para. 7.
66 FRS 12, para. 42 and 43.
67 *Ibid.*, para. 44.
68 *Ibid.*, para. 45.
69 *Ibid.*, para. 47.
70 *Ibid.*, para. 46.
71 *Ibid.*, para. 50.
72 *Ibid.*, para. 49.
73 *Discounting in Financial Reporting*, ASB, April 1997.
74 FRS 12, para. 49.
75 *Ibid.*
76 *Ibid.*
77 *Ibid.*, para. 48.
78 FRS 17, *Retirement Benefits*, ASB, November 2000, Appendix II, para. 6.
79 *Ibid.*, para. 102(b).
80 FRS 12, para. 47.
81 *Ibid.*, para. 89(e).
82 *Ibid.*, para. 51.
83 *Ibid.*, para. 52.
84 *Ibid.*, para. 53.
85 *Ibid.*, para. 58.
86 *Ibid.*, para. 60.
87 *Ibid.*, paras. 56 and 59.
88 *Ibid.*, para. 57.
89 FRS 3, *Reporting financial performance*, ASB, October 1992, para. 18.
90 SSAP 9, *Stocks and long-term contracts*, ASC, revised September 1988, para. 11.
91 FRED 14, Appendix III, para. 21.
92 FRS 12, paras. 29 and 61.
93 *Ibid.*, paras. 54 and 55.
94 *Ibid.*, Appendix VII, para. 28.
95 FRS 12, para. 62.
96 *Ibid.*, para. 63.
97 *Ibid.*, para. 64 and 65.
98 *Ibid.*, para. 2.
99 *Ibid.*, para. 75.
100 *Ibid.*, para. 76.
101 *Ibid.*, para. 77.
102 *Ibid.*, para. 78.
103 *Ibid.*, para. 79.
104 *Ibid.*, para. 80.
105 *Ibid.*, Appendix III, Examples 5A and 5B.
106 FRS 12, para. 81.
107 *Ibid.*, para. 82.
108 *Ibid.*, para. 80.
109 *Ibid.*, para. 83.
110 *Ibid.*, para. 84.
111 FRS 3, para. 45.
112 FRS 12, para. 84.
113 *Ibid.*, para. 85.
114 *Ibid.*, para. 19.
115 *Ibid.*, para. 86.
116 *Ibid.*
117 FRED 14, para. 61.
118 FRS 12, para. 87.
119 FRS 3, para. 18.
120 FRS 12, para. 88.
121 *Ibid.*, para. 68.
122 *Ibid.*, para. 69.
123 *Ibid.*, para. 70.
124 SSAP 9, para. 11.
125 FRS 12, para. 71.
126 *Ibid.*, para. 72.
127 *Ibid.*, para. 2.
128 *Ibid.*, para. 73.
129 *Ibid.*, Appendix III, Example 8.
130 Discussion Paper – *Provisions*, ASB, November 1995, para. 2.6.
131 FRS 12, para. 74.
132 FRED 14, para. 5(c).
133 *Ibid.*, para. 48.
134 FRS 12, Appendix III, Example 2A.
135 FRS 12, para. 22.
136 *Ibid.*, Appendix III, Example 2B.
137 *Ibid.*, Example 3.
138 FRS 12, para. 66.
139 Statement of Recommended Practice, *Accounting for abandonment costs*, OIAC, June 1988, para. 10.
140 Statement of Recommended Practice, *Accounting for Oil and Gas Exploration, Development, Production and Decommissioning Activities*, OIAC, June 2001, paras. 96 and 97.
141 See, for example, the extracts from the 1998 accounts of St Ives, Rugby Group and Pilkington included at 4.6 in Chapter 25 of the Sixth Edition of this book.
142 FRS 12, Appendix III, Examples 11A and 11B.
143 *Ibid.*, Appendix VII, para. 39.
144 *Ibid.*, Appendix III, Example 1.
145 *Ibid.*, Example 12.
146 *Ibid.*, Example 10.
147 FRS 12, para. 14.
148 *Ibid.*, Appendix III, Example 4.
149 *Ibid.*, Example 7.
150 *Ibid.*, Appendix VII, para. 16.
151 Information Sheet 35, UITF, 24 February 2000.
152 CA 85, Sch. 4, para. 46(1) and (2).
153 FRS 12, para. 89.
154 *Ibid.*, para. 90.
155 *Ibid.*, para. 92.

156 CA 85, Sch. 4, para. 50(2).
157 FRS 12, para. 91.
158 *Ibid.*, para. 96.
159 *Ibid.*, para. 93.
160 Accountants Digest No. 113, *Accountants Digest Guide to Accounting Standards – Accounting for Contingencies*, Winter 1981/82, p. 5.
161 FRS 12, para. 94.
162 *Ibid.*, para. 96.
163 *Ibid.*, para. 95.
164 *Ibid.*, para. 97.
165 *Ibid.*
166 IAS 37, para. 10.
167 *Ibid.*, para. 7.
168 *Ibid.*, para. 1.
169 *Ibid.*, para. 2.
170 *Ibid.*, para. 3.
171 *Ibid.*, para. 4.
172 *Ibid.*, para. 5.
173 *Ibid.*, para. 6.
174 *Ibid.*, para. 11.
175 *Ibid.*, paras. 12 and 13.
176 *Ibid.*, para. 14.
177 *Ibid.*, para. 10.
178 *Ibid.*, paras. 15–26.
179 *Ibid.*, Appendix C.
180 IAS 37, paras. 27 and 28.
181 *Ibid.*, para. 30.
182 *Ibid.*, paras. 31–33.
183 *Ibid.*, para. 34.
184 *Ibid.*, para. 8.
185 *Ibid.*, para. 36.
186 *Ibid.*, para. 42.
187 *Ibid.*, para. 45.
188 *Ibid.*, para. 47.
189 *Ibid.*, para. 48.
190 *Ibid.*, para. 49 and 50.
191 *Ibid.*, para. 55.
192 *Ibid.*, para. 53.
193 *Ibid.*, para. 54.
194 *Ibid.*, para. 57.
195 *Ibid.*, paras. 55–58.
196 *Ibid.*, paras. 51 and 52.
197 *Ibid.*, para. 59.
198 *Ibid.*, para. 60.
199 *Ibid.*, paras. 61 and 62.
200 *Ibid.*, para. 10.
201 *Ibid.*, para. 70.
202 *Ibid.*, para. 72.
203 *Ibid.*, paras. 73–77.
204 *Ibid.*, para. 78.
205 *Ibid.*, para. 79
206 *Ibid.*, para. 80.
207 *Ibid.*, para. 81.
208 *Ibid.*, paras. 82 and 83.
209 *Ibid.*, paras. 63 and 64.
210 *Ibid.*, para. 65.
211 *Ibid.*, para. 66.
212 *Ibid.*, paras. 67–69.
213 *Ibid.*, para. 10.
214 *Ibid.*, Appendix C, Example 8.
215 IAS 37, para. 69.
216 *Ibid.*, Appendix C, Example 2A.
217 IAS 37, para. 22
218 *Ibid.*, Appendix C, Example 2B.
219 IAS 37, para. 19.
220 *Ibid.*, Appendix C, Example 3.
221 *Accounting for Oil and Gas Exploration, Development, Production and Decommissioning Activities*, paras. 96 and 97.
222 IAS 37, Appendix C, Examples 11A and 11B.
223 FRS 12, Appendix VII, para. 39.
224 IAS 37, Appendix C, Example 1.
225 IAS 37, para. 39.
226 *Ibid.*, para. 40.
227 *Ibid.*, Appendix C, Example 10.
228 *Ibid.*, Example 4.
229 *Ibid.*, Example 7.
230 IAS 37, para. 84.
231 *Ibid.*, paras. 84 and 85.
232 *Ibid.*, para. 86.
233 *Ibid.*, para. 91.
234 *Ibid.*, para. 88.
235 *Ibid.*, para. 89.
236 *Ibid.*, para. 91.
237 *Ibid.*, para. 90.
238 *Ibid.*, para. 92.
239 *Ibid.*

Chapter 29 Cash flow statements

1 INTRODUCTION

The importance of providing cash flow information was originally recognised in the US by the FASB through its concepts statements. SFAC No. 1 states that 'financial reporting should provide information to help present and potential investors and creditors and other users in assessing the amounts, timing, and uncertainty of prospective cash receipts from dividends or interest and the proceeds from the sale, redemption, or maturity of securities or loans. The prospects for those cash receipts are affected by an enterprise's ability to generate enough cash to meet its obligations when due and its other cash operating needs, to reinvest in operations, and to pay cash dividends ... Thus, financial reporting should provide information to help investors, creditors, and others assess the amounts, timing, and uncertainty of prospective net inflows to the related enterprise.'[1]

Further recognition of the need to provide cash flow information was given by SFAC No. 5, which states that 'a full set of financial statements for a period should show: ... cash flows during the period'.[2] It adds that 'a statement of cash flows directly or indirectly reflects an entity's cash receipts classified by major sources and its cash payments classified by major uses during a period. It provides useful information about an entity's activities in generating cash through operations to repay debt, distribute dividends, or reinvest to maintain or expand operating capacity; about its financing activities, both debt and equity; and about its investing or spending of cash. Important uses of information about an entity's current cash receipts and payments include helping to assess factors such as the entity's liquidity, financial flexibility, profitability, and risk.'[3]

As a result of the increasing recognition of the significance of cash flow information, the FASB issued SFAS 95 – *Statement of Cash Flows* – in November 1987. The US requirement to present a statement of cash flows started a worldwide trend in financial reporting. In September 1991, the ASB published FRS 1 – *Cash flow statements* – which required reporting entities to prepare a modified US-style cash flow statement. In 1992, the IASC revised IAS 7, which now requires enterprises to prepare a cash flow statement instead of a statement of changes in financial position.

FRS 1 generally worked well in practice and enhanced the quality of financial reporting considerably. However, it was felt that the standard fell short in a number of respects from what could be achieved.[4] Consequently, the decision by the ASB to call for comments on the functioning of the standard in March 1994 was well received. The most common complaint concerned the definition of cash equivalents ('short-term, highly liquid investments which are readily convertible into known amounts of cash without notice and which were within three months of maturity when acquired; less advances from banks repayable within three months from the date of the advance'[5]). In practice, companies' treasury operations did not draw the distinction between investment and cash management in the way that the original standard seemed to imply, since the three month cut-off for cash equivalents bore little relationship to companies' treasury maturity horizons. Normal treasury management meant investing in instruments which, as far as the company was concerned, were cash equivalents, but which were not treated as such for FRS 1 purposes. Cash flows related to these instruments had to be included under a heading of 'investing activities'. This aspect and others were addressed in the revised version of FRS 1 which was published in October 1996, and became mandatory for accounting periods ending on or after 23 March 1997.[6]

2 FRS 1

2.1 Scope and exemptions

Like its predecessor, the revised FRS 1 applies to accounts intended to give a true and fair view of the reporting entity's financial position and profit or loss (or income and expenditure).[7] Although the relevance of a statement of cash flows to the truth and fairness of the financial position or the profit or loss for the period has never been entirely clear, the press release which accompanied the original FRS 1 stressed that the cash flow statement formed 'an essential element of the information required for accounts to give a true and fair view of the state of affairs of [large] companies at the end of the financial year, and of the profit or loss for the year. Accordingly, non-compliance with the standard may be a matter to be taken into account by the Financial Reporting Review Panel or the court in any consideration of whether or not accounts comply with the Companies Act.'[8] The Auditing Practices Board seems to have adopted a similar line of reasoning because its example of a qualified audit report in circumstances where a cash flow statement has been omitted explains that 'information about the company's cash flows is necessary for a proper understanding of the company's state of affairs and profit [loss].'[9]

Notwithstanding the apparent importance of cash flow information to the truth and fairness of the accounts, the standard exempts certain entities from the requirement to prepare a cash flow statement:[10]

(a) Subsidiary undertakings where 90% or more of the voting rights are controlled within the group, provided that group accounts which include the subsidiary are publicly available

This exemption is similar to the one in FRS 8 (see Chapter 27 at 2.3.5 C) and it applies regardless of the country of incorporation of the parent. The choice of a

90% threshold would seem to be a pragmatic compromise designed to deal with subsidiaries with small amounts of voting preference shares, or small numbers of shares held by employees. Neither FRS gives any guidance as to what is meant by 'publicly available'. The rationale behind this stipulation is a little puzzling since there is no requirement for the publicly available group accounts to contain a cash flow statement, or for that matter to be in English.

The reason given by the ASB for exempting subsidiaries where 90% of the votes are held by the group is that the solvency, liquidity and financial adaptability of these entities will essentially depend on the group rather than their own cash flows.[11]

Because the exemption applies to subsidiaries where 90% or more of the votes are *held by the group*, the effective interest held by the parent whose group accounts are publicly available is irrelevant.

(b) *Mutual life assurance companies*

The ASB is of the view that insurance companies should include the cash flows of their long-term business only to the extent of cash transferred and available to meet the obligations of the company or group as a whole.[12] This is because the shareholders of an insurance company generally have restricted rights to the profits and associated cash surpluses made by their long-term business. Mutual life assurance companies, which are owned by policy holders, are accordingly exempt from the requirements of the FRS.

(c) *Pension funds*

Pension funds are exempt because a cash flow statement would add little information to that already available from the rest of the accounts.

(d) *Open-ended investment funds substantially all of whose investments are highly liquid and carried at market value, on condition that a statement of changes in net assets is provided*

This exemption is similar to that for pension funds, recognising that a cash flow statement would be of limited additional use. The definition of an 'investment fund' in the standard is based on that used in companies legislation, but with the notable exception that there is no restriction on the distribution of capital profits.[13]

(e) *Small (but not medium-sized) companies entitled to the filing exemptions under sections 246 and 247 of the Companies Act 1985*

As at August 2001, these are, broadly speaking, companies which satisfy two of the following criteria:

- turnover not more than £2.8 million;
- balance sheet total not more than £1.4 million; and
- not more than 50 employees.[14]

PLCs, banks, insurance companies and companies authorised under the Financial Services Act 1986 do not qualify for the exemption, nor do members of a group which contains any of these entities.

(f) *Small entities which would have qualified under the previous category had they been companies*

This exemption is a natural consequence of the exemption for small companies referred to above.

2.2 The definition of cash

Since the objective of a cash flow statement is to provide an analysis of the reporting entity's inflows and outflows of cash, the definition of cash is crucial to its presentation:

Cash – Cash in hand and deposits repayable on demand with any qualifying financial institution, less overdrafts from any qualifying financial institution repayable on demand. Deposits are repayable on demand if they can be withdrawn at any time without notice and without penalty or if a maturity or period of notice of not more than 24 hours or one working day has been agreed. Cash includes cash in hand and deposits denominated in foreign currencies.[15]

Overdrafts ('a borrowing facility repayable on demand that is used by drawing on a current account with a qualifying financial institution')[16] are often a source of finance that extends for a significant period of time. Nevertheless, the standard is clear that they should be treated as negative cash balances. Pragmatically, this is the only possible treatment, since otherwise all cheques written on an overdrawn account would have to be shown under the financing heading of the cash flow statement as new borrowings and payments in to the account would have to be separately shown as repayments of those borrowings.

It is sometimes argued that certain deposits with notice or maturity periods in excess of 24 hours should be treated as cash. This is because these funds will often be available on demand, albeit that interest is then recalculated as if the deposit were a current account. However, the standard makes it clear that deposits qualify as cash only if the money is available within 24 hours *without penalty*.

It is clear that the amount shown alongside 'cash at bank and in hand' in the balance sheet will rarely be a reliable guide to 'cash' for FRS 1 purposes. Apart from the need to include overdrafts for cash flow purposes, the balance sheet caption will often include bank deposits with notice or maturity periods in excess of 24 hours. However, because the standard requires the amount of cash and other components of net debt to be traced back to the equivalent captions in the balance sheet,[17] any difference between 'cash' for FRS 1 purposes and 'cash' for balance sheet purposes will be evident from the notes to the accounts.

2.3 Format of the cash flow statement

The format of the cash flow statement is tightly prescribed. Cash flows are required to be presented under a series of standard headings:[18]

- operating activities;
- dividends from joint ventures and associates;
- returns on investments and servicing of finance;

- taxation;
- capital expenditure and financial investment;
- acquisitions and disposals;
- equity dividends paid;
- management of liquid resources; and
- financing.

The first seven headings (but not necessarily the last two – see Extract 29.1 below) should follow the sequence shown above.[19] Cash flows relating to the management of liquid resources and financing can be combined under a single heading provided that the cash flows relating to each are shown separately and that separate sub-totals are given.[20]

Within each standard heading, the FRS identifies certain categories of cash inflows and outflows which are to be separately identified, where they are material. This can be done either on the face of the statement or in a note.[21]

The cash flow statement in the 2000 accounts of BP Amoco is of particular interest – see Extract 29.1 below. As permitted by the FRS, the last two headings have been reversed. Another feature is that the statement does not focus on the net decrease or increase in cash. Instead, the last two headings and the movement in cash have been combined to produce a sub-total which equates to the 'net cash inflow (outflow)' for the year:

Extract 29.1: BP Amoco p.l.c. (2000)

Group cash flow statement [extract]

		$ million
For the year ended 31 December	**2000**	1999
Net cash inflow from operating activities	**20,416**	10,290
Dividends from joint ventures	**645**	949
Dividends from associated undertakings	**394**	219
Servicing of finance and returns on investments		
Interest received	**444**	179
Interest paid	**(1,354)**	(1,065)
Dividends received	**42**	34
Dividends paid to minority shareholders	**(24)**	(151)
Net cash outflow from servicing of finance and returns on investments	**(892)**	(1,003)
Taxation		
UK corporation tax	**(869)**	(559)
Overseas tax	**(5,329)**	(701)
Tax paid	**(6,198)**	(1,260)
Capital expenditure and financial investment		
Payments for fixed assets	**(10,037)**	(6,457)
Purchase of shares for employee share schemes	**(64)**	(77)
Proceeds from the sale of fixed assets	**3,029**	1,149
Net cash outflow for capital expenditure and financial investment	**(7,072)**	(5,385)

Acquisitions and disposals		
Investments in associated undertakings	**(985)**	(197)
Acquisitions	**(6,265)**	(102)
Net investment in joint ventures	**(218)**	(750)
Proceeds from the sale of businesses	**8,333**	1,292
Net cash inflow for acquisitions and disposals	**865**	243
Equity dividends paid	**(4,415)**	(4,135)
Net cash inflow (outflow)	**3,743**	(82)
Financing	**3,413**	(954)
Management of liquid resources	**452**	(93)
Increase (decrease) in cash	**(122)**	965
	3,743	(82)

The ASB considered prescribing a format which results in the increase or decrease in cash being shown as the residual amount. This approach had a number of supporters but the respondents to the exposure draft did not want it to be mandatory. Preparers have accordingly been allowed to choose the format of their cash flow statements 'provided that these comply with the requirements for classification and order.'[22]

In Extract 29.1 above, the individual cash flows required to be shown under returns on investments and servicing of finance, taxation, capital expenditure and financial investment, and acquisitions and disposals are shown on the face of the cash flow statement. As permitted by the FRS, the individual cash flows under the financing and management of liquid resources headings appear in a separate note to the accounts, which is reproduced below:

Extract 29.2: BP Amoco p.l.c. (2000)

31 Group cash flow statement analysis [extract]

		$ million
Financing	**2000**	1999
Long-term borrowing	**(1,680)**	(2,140)
Repayments of long-term borrowing	**2,353**	2,268
Short-term borrowing	**(4,120)**	(3,136)
Repayments of short-term borrowing	**4,821**	2,299
	1,374	(709)
Issue of share capital	**(257)**	(245)
Share buyback	**2,001**	–
Stamp duty reserve tax	**295**	–
Net cash outflow (inflow)	**3,413**	(954)

Management of liquid resources

Liquid resources comprise current asset investments which are principally commercial paper issued by other companies. The net cash outflow from the management of liquid resources was $452 million ($93 million inflow).

Irrespective of whether the individual categories of inflows and outflows under the standard headings are shown on the face of the statement or in a note, they must be shown gross. This rule does not apply to cash flows relating to operating activities and certain cash flows under the management of liquid resources and financing headings.[23] To qualify for net presentation, the cash flows within management of liquid resources and financing must *either*:

- be related in substance to a single financing transaction as defined by FRS 4 (one where the debt and the facility are under a single agreement with the same lender, the finance costs for the new debt are not significantly higher than the existing debt, the obligations of the lender are firm and the lender is expected to be able to fulfil its obligations);[24] *or*
- be due to short maturities and high turnover occurring from rollover or reissue (for example, short-term deposits or a commercial paper programme).[25] Extract 29.2 above is an example of net presentation using this dispensation.

It should be noted that the financing cash flows arising under a commercial paper programme do not qualify as a single financing transaction as defined in FRS 4. This is because the debt and the back-up facility are not under a single agreement with the same lender.[26] Although net presentation is not sanctioned by the first dispensation referred to above, it is permitted under the second.

Notwithstanding the dispensations referred to above, gross presentation will still be required for many of the cash flows under the management of liquid resources heading. For example, the placing of surplus cash on short-term deposit from time to time followed by the subsequent withdrawal of these funds when needed gives rise to two cash flows, one out and the other in. However, in many instances it will not be possible to extract this information from the books and records without expending considerable time and effort. Whether this provides useful additional information must be doubtful.

2.4 Classification of cash flows by standard heading

2.4.1 *General principle*

The standard requires each cash flow to be classified according to the substance of the transaction or event giving rise to it.[27] Because the other primary statements are based on accounting standards which, in theory, use the same substance principle, the end result should be consistent treatment across all the primary statements. In essence, this means that capitalised development costs should appear under capital expenditure and financial investment. Finance lease rentals should be split into their interest and capital elements, with the former appearing under returns on investments and servicing of finance and the latter under financing. Operating lease rentals should appear under operating activities. Classification in the cash flow statement effectively becomes a function of the accounting policies adopted by the reporting entity. Some might regard this as counter-intuitive, but it is designed to achieve the ASB's objective of consistent treatment in all the primary statements.

An example of the requirement for consistent treatment across the primary statements was the impact of FRS 12 on the cash flow statements of certain public utilities. Prior to FRS 12, a provision for planned infrastructure maintenance expenditure was charged in arriving at operating profit. In accordance with paragraph 11 of FRS 1, the cash outflow for maintenance expenditure was shown as part of the cash flow from operating activities. Under FRS 12, such maintenance expenditure is being capitalised and subsequently depreciated, so the related cash outflow now falls to be included under capital expenditure and financial investment (see 2.4.6 below).

2.4.2 *Operating activities*

Somewhat tentatively, the standard explains that cash flows from operating activities are *in general* those related to operating or trading activities, *normally* shown in the profit and loss account in arriving at operating profit (emphases added).[28] 'Operating or trading activities' are not defined which leaves the definition dangerously close to being circular. However, the standard does contain some examples of operating or trading activities, namely receipts from customers, payments to suppliers and payments to employees, including redundancy.[29]

The presentation of cash flows related to the reorganisation and restructuring of acquired businesses has not always been consistent. Prior to FRS 7, the cost of restructuring acquired subsidiaries was often not charged in the profit and loss account at all. This was sometimes cited as a reason for excluding the related cash flows from the operating activities heading. A similar argument existed in connection with the costs of a fundamental restructuring which (if certain conditions are met) FRS 3 requires to be excluded from the operating profit total.[30] In order to standardise practice in this area, FRS 1 states that 'operating item cash outflows relating to provisions' should appear under operating activities *regardless* of whether the provision was deducted in arriving at operating profit.[31] As examples of such cash flows, the standard[32] cites operating item cash flows provided for on an acquisition and redundancy payments provided for on the termination of an operation or for a fundamental reorganisation or restructuring, the last two under paragraphs 20a and 20b of FRS 3.

FRS 1 allows a choice between the direct and indirect methods of presenting operating cash flows.[33] The direct method is essentially based on an analysis of the cash book. It shows operating cash receipts and payments, including cash receipts from customers, cash payments to suppliers and cash payments to and on behalf of employees which, when added to the other operating cash payments, aggregate to the net cash flow from operating activities.

A The indirect method

The indirect method arrives at the same net cash flow from operating activities, but does so by working back from operating profit in the form of a reconciliation.

To obtain the cash flow information, the balance sheet figures have to be analysed according to the various standard headings in the cash flow statement. Thus the reconciliation of operating profit to cash flow from operating activities will include, not the increase or decrease in all debtors or creditors, but only those elements which relate to operating activities, as highlighted in Extract 29.4 below. Accordingly, accrued interest or amounts payable in respect of the acquisition of fixed assets or investments will be excluded from the movement in creditors included in this reconciliation. Although this may not present practical difficulties in the preparation of single company cash flow statements, it is necessary to ensure that sufficient information is collected from subsidiaries for purposes of preparing the group cash flow statement. Where a group has made an acquisition of a subsidiary during the year, the change in working capital has to be split between the increase due to the acquisition and the element related to operating activities which will appear in the operating profit reconciliation.

The reconciliation of operating profit to cash inflow from operating activities is required to be disclosed, either adjoining the cash flow statement itself (provided it is clearly labelled), or as a note.[34] Two of the four illustrative examples in Appendix I to the standard show the cash flow statement wedged in between two reconciliations – one to operating profit and the other to net debt (or its equivalent). To comply with the labelling requirement, the heading 'Cash Flow Statement' has to be duplicated – an untidy outcome. Not surprisingly, the great majority of companies have elected to show the reconciliation of operating profit to cash inflow from operating activities in a note, as illustrated in the following extract:

Extract 29.3: United Business Media plc (2000)

Notes to the financial statements

28. Reconciliation of operating profit to cash inflow from operating activities [extract]	**Total Continuing 2000 £m**	**Dis-continued 2000 £m**	**Total 2000 £m**
Operating (loss)/profit	(71.9)	61.4	(10.5)
Depreciation charges	21.4	18.2	39.6
Amortisation of intangible assets – group	121.2	46.4	167.6
Share of results of joint ventures	9.9	(10.3)	(0.4)
Share of results of associates	20.3	(1.3)	19.0
Income from participating interests	(4.9)	–	(4.9)
Profit on sale of fixed asset investments	(2.4)	–	(2.4)
Profit on sale of tangible fixed assets	(6.1)	(0.1)	(6.2)
Payment against provisions	(1.1)	(0.3)	(1.4)
Increase in stocks	(0.5)	(34.5)	(35.0)
Increase in debtors	(27.4)	(27.2)	(54.6)
Increase/(decrease) in creditors	29.7	(27.3)	2.4
Other non-cash items including movements on provisions	10.2	(11.4)	(1.2)
Cash inflow from operating activities	98.4	13.6	112.0

The extract above illustrates the requirement to disclose separately the movements in stocks, debtors and creditors related to operating activities and other differences between cash flows and profits.[35] The inclusion of reconciling items for the share of results of joint ventures and associates is a consequence of the operating profit above being the total operating profit (inclusive of joint ventures and associates), not that of the group. Dividends received from joint ventures and associates appear under their own heading (see section 2.4.3 below).

United Business Media has analysed the cash inflow from operating activities between continuing and discontinued operations. Reporting entities are encouraged, but not required, to disclose additional information like this.[36] Other suggestions put forward by the ASB include the provision of segmental information[37] and the division of cash flows in a way that highlights different degrees of access to the underlying cash balances which might be of special relevance to regulated industries like insurance.[38]

B The direct method

The ASB encourages disclosure of the information provided by the direct method where it is not too costly to obtain.[39] However, the information provided by the indirect method is required even where the direct method has been adopted[40] so there is little incentive to adopt the direct method. This, coupled with the additional burden involved, means that it is rarely used in practice. It is sometimes found in the accounts of property companies, as shown in the next extract:

Extract 29.4: Frogmore Estates plc (2000)

Group cash flow statement [extract]

YEAR ENDED 30TH JUNE 2000

	2000	1999
	£000	£000
Operating activities		
Cash received from tenants	**17,907**	23,761
Other receipts	**11,488**	4,839
Property expenses paid	**(7,164)**	(11,019)
Sales of trading properties and developments	**328,209**	264,375
Purchases of and additions to trading properties and developments	**(229,108)**	(213,699)
Other payments	**(8,030)**	(7,083)
Net cash inflow from operating activities	**113,302**	61,174

Notes to the group cash flow statement [extract]

Net cash inflow from operating activities

	2000	1999
	£000	£000
Operating profit	**52,470**	48,134
Depreciation	**361**	379
Goodwill amortisation	**907**	1,093
Loss on sale of other fixed assets	**10**	31
Decrease/(increase) in trading properties and developments	**44,958**	(311)
(Increase)/decrease in debtors relating to operating activities	**(4,075)**	13,557
Increase/(decrease) in creditors relating to operating activities	**6,538**	(1,557)
Increase/(decrease) in provisions	**12,133**	(152)
Net cash inflow from operating activities	**113,302**	61,174

2.4.3 *Dividends from joint ventures and associates*

The requirement to show dividends received from joint ventures and associates under a separate heading below operating activities was brought about by the publication of FRS 9 in November 1997.[41] The change is a consequence of the requirement in FRS 9 to exclude the results of these entities from group operating profit. It reflects the ASB's view that dividends from joint ventures and associates are not on a comparable basis to the cash flows arising from the group's operating activities and have a different significance from its returns on investments.[42]

Although the drafting of the amendment to FRS 1 is not entirely clear, it would seem that 'Dividends from joint ventures and associates' is intended to be a single main heading[43] which is required to be analysed further.[44] Separate disclosure of the dividends from joint ventures and those from associates is consistent with the approach adopted throughout FRS 9. Other cash flows from associates and joint ventures – those arising from trading, or loan interest, for example – should be included under the appropriate heading.

2.4.4 *Returns on investments and servicing of finance*

Returns on investments and servicing of finance are receipts resulting from the ownership of investments and payments to providers of finance, non-equity shareholders and minority interests, excluding those items (like dividends from joint ventures and associates) which are specifically required by the standard to be classified under another heading.[45]

Because FRS 1 requires cash flows that are treated as finance costs under FRS 4 to be shown under returns on investments and servicing of finance,[46] debt and non-equity share issue costs appear under this heading. The same principle means that the redemption of deep discount bonds is required to be split between interest and principal, with the former being shown under returns on investments and servicing of finance and the latter under financing (see Extract 29.7 under 2.4.10 below).

Dividends paid on an entity's non-equity shares (as defined in FRS 4) appear under returns on investments and servicing of finance[47] whereas dividends paid on equity shares appear lower down the statement (see 2.4.8 below).

Although the cash flows to be included under returns on investments and servicing of finance are essentially interest and dividends received and paid, there are some complications in the identification of the relevant amounts. With respect to interest, deduction of tax at source means that amounts received may be net of tax. The amount of cash actually received should be shown as a cash inflow but if any tax withheld is subsequently recovered, this should also be included as part of interest received.[48] Similarly, where tax is withheld when interest is paid, the interest actually paid should be included as a cash outflow together with the tax paid to the relevant tax authority.[49] Dividends received and paid should be shown at the amount of cash actually received and paid.[50] However, FRS 1 has no specific rules on the treatment of incoming dividends subject to recoverable withholding tax.

Because they are so similar to interest from which tax is deducted at source, it would seem reasonable to include them on a gross basis.

In a departure from the general principle outlined under 2.4.1 above, the standard requires all interest paid (even if capitalised) to appear under this heading. This is because the ASB wants the cash flow statement to 'give a complete picture' of the interest cash flows.[51]

2.4.5 *Taxation*

Cash flows included under the taxation heading are those to or from taxation authorities in respect of the reporting entity's revenue and capital profits.[52] Inclusion of these cash flows under a separate section in the cash flow statement reflects the ASB's view that 'it is not useful to divide taxation cash flows into constituent parts relating to the activities that gave rise to them because the apportionment will, in many cases, have to be made on an arbitrary basis.'[53] A further complication is that taxation cash flows generally arise from activities in an earlier period. This makes it difficult to report taxation cash flows along with the transactions that gave rise to them.

VAT, other sales taxes, property taxes and any other taxes not assessed on the revenue and capital profits of the reporting entity should not be included under the taxation heading.

Cash flows associated with VAT and other sales taxes should normally be dealt with as a single net cash flow in the operating activities section of the statement.[54] Thus, all cash flows should be shown net of any attributable VAT or other sales tax. Although the actual cash flows will include VAT where appropriate, the taxation element has only a short-term effect on the entity's overall cash position. Although the practice of collapsing these tax flows into a net payment to or from the tax authorities should usually be adopted, a different treatment may be applied if it is more appropriate. In particular, where VAT or other sales tax paid by a business is irrecoverable, cash flows should include the associated tax. If this is impracticable, the irrecoverable tax should be included under the most appropriate standard heading.[55] This will be the case for businesses which are exempt or partially exempt, for example charities.

Taxation cash flows, other than those in respect of the reporting entity's profits and VAT or other sales taxes, should be included under the same standard heading as the cash flow that gave rise to the taxation cash flow, unless a different treatment is more appropriate.[56]

Although there is no requirement to split UK and overseas tax paid, this is sometimes done in practice:

Extract 29.5: Bass PLC (2000)

GROUP CASH FLOW STATEMENT
for the year ended 30 September 2000 [extract]

	2000	**2000**	1999	1999
	£m	**£m**	£m	£m
UK corporation tax paid	**(101)**		(138)	
Overseas corporate tax paid	**(57)**		(36)	
Taxation		**(158)**		(174)

The standard includes guidance for subsidiaries on cash flows relating to group relief. These should be included under 'taxation' even though they are not paid to a taxation authority.

2.4.6 *Capital expenditure and financial investment*

Cash flows required to be included under capital expenditure and financial investment are those related to the acquisition or disposal of fixed assets (including investments).[57] In addition, current asset investments that do not qualify as 'liquid resources' (see 2.4.9 below) effectively default to this section. Cash flows related to the acquisition or disposal of investments in associates and joint ventures should be excluded because they are required to be shown under acquisitions and disposals.[58]

The capital expenditure and financial investment heading will usually include the following cash flows, which should be separately disclosed:[59]

(a) receipts from sales of, and payments made to acquire, property, plant and equipment;

(b) receipts from the repayment of, and loans made to, other entities (other than payments forming part of an acquisition or disposal or a movement in liquid resources – see 2.4.7 and 2.4.9 below); and

(c) receipts from the sale of, and payments to acquire, debt instruments of other entities (other than payments forming part of an acquisition or disposal or a movement in liquid resources – see 2.4.7 and 2.4.9 below).

Where there are no cash flows relating to financial investment (i.e. those under (b) and (c) above), the section heading may be reduced to capital expenditure.[60]

The treatment of loans to associates (and the repayment thereof) is not entirely clear and has given rise to some inconsistency, stemming from whether they constitute an 'investment in' the associate concerned or whether they are loans made to another entity (which clearly belong under the capital expenditure and financial investment heading).

The outflow shown in the cash flow statement in respect of the acquisition of property, plant or equipment is unlikely to be the same as 'additions' as reported in the fixed assets note. Whilst this is usually a function of movements in creditors relating to fixed assets and the inception of finance leases, it may also be due to exchange rate differences on foreign currency liabilities incurred on the purchase of fixed assets. The amount paid might be different to that used to record the increase in fixed assets, with the difference taken to the profit and loss account as an exchange gain or loss.

The purchase of fixed assets on credit is a complicated area because the associated cash flows may sometimes not be capital expenditure. In the US, SFAS 95 takes the line that only advance payments, the down payment or other amounts paid at or near to the time of purchase of fixed assets are investing cash flows.[61] This treatment also appears to be implicit in FRS 1. The most common example of this (although the payments are strictly not made to purchase the asset) is where a reporting entity makes payments in respect of assets obtained under a finance lease. In this case, the payments of principal are classified as financing rather than capital expenditure. The interest element of the lease payments would be shown under returns on investments and servicing of finance. The acquisition of assets under hire purchase contracts would be dealt with in a similar way. On the other hand, short-term differences between acquisition and payment should not be interpreted as changing the nature of the cash flow from capital expenditure to financing.

2.4.7 *Acquisitions and disposals*

Included under this heading are cash flows related to the acquisition or disposal of any trade or business, or of an investment in an entity that is or, as a result of the transaction, becomes or ceases to be either an associate, a joint venture or a subsidiary.[62]

In addition to the payments made on the purchase of subsidiaries, FRS 1 requires any balances of cash and overdrafts acquired to be shown separately.[63] The same rule applies to any balances of cash and overdrafts transferred as part of the sale of subsidiaries.[64] It is not entirely clear whether the separate disclosure of these cash balances and overdrafts should be part of the cash flow statement itself or whether it could be relegated to another note. The former treatment is consistent with the illustrative example in Appendix I to the standard,[65] but both treatments are seen in practice.

The principle discussed at 2.4.6 above regarding the acquisition of fixed assets on credit also applies to deferred consideration on the acquisition of a subsidiary. No cash flows arise at the time that the liability is set up. When the deferred consideration is ultimately paid, the resulting cash flow should arguably be shown under financing, although this approach is generally not adopted in practice (see Extract 29.8 under 2.4.11 below), possibly because the related creditor is not included as part of net debt. Where the deferred consideration takes the form of loan notes, the cash outflows on redemption of the notes are more clearly in the nature of financing as they involve a reduction in the amount of net debt.

A question that sometimes arises is how to treat a payment made to the vendor of a new subsidiary to take over a loan that is owed to the vendor by that subsidiary. Payments made to acquire debt instruments of other entities are normally included under capital expenditure and financial investment. However, the FRS states that this is not appropriate for payments 'forming part of' an acquisition or disposal[66] because the cash flows 'related to' such transactions are required to be shown under acquisitions and disposals.[67] This presentation can be contrasted with the repayment of external debt in the new subsidiary, using funds provided by the parent, which falls to be included as an outflow under the financing heading.

A similarly fine distinction might apply on the demerger of subsidiaries. These sometimes involve the repayment of intra-group indebtedness out of external finance raised by the demerged subsidiary. If the money is raised immediately prior to the demerger, it is strictly a financing inflow in the parent company's consolidated cash flow statement. If raised and repaid after the demerger, there would be an argument for showing the inflow under capital expenditure and financial investment, being the repayment of a loan to another entity. Alternatively, it could conceivably be shown under acquisitions and disposals, being a cash inflow 'related to' to an entity that has ceased to be a subsidiary undertaking. Although FRS 1 does not seem to have been written with demergers in mind, practice has been to show the cash and overdrafts in the demerged entity under the acquisitions and disposals heading. This is on the basis that they are 'related to ... an investment in an entity that ... as a result of the transaction ... ceases to be ... a subsidiary undertaking.'[68]

2.4.8 *Equity dividends paid*

Included under this heading are dividends paid on the reporting entity's equity shares (as defined in FRS 4).[69] As noted at 2.4.4 above, the amount shown should exclude any related tax credit.

Dividends paid to preference shareholders and minorities are not shown under this heading but under returns on investments and servicing of finance (see 2.4.4 above).

2.4.9 *Management of liquid resources*

Cash flows required to be classified under management of liquid resources are those related to 'current asset investments held as readily disposable stores of value'.[70] The key to this definition is 'readily disposable', by which is meant that the investment 'is disposable by the reporting entity without curtailing or disrupting its business; and is *either*:

- readily convertible into known amounts of cash at or close to its carrying amount, or
- traded in an active market'.[71]

In the ASB's view, the first bullet point above would tend to exclude short-term deposits with a maturity of more than one year, measured from the date the deposit was made.[72] That aside, the definition deliberately allows the inclusion of a wide range of investments in order to recognise the different ways in which reporting entities manage their resources to ensure the availability of cash to carry on or expand the business. Reporting entities must explain their policy for determining liquid resources and any changes to it.[73]

Cash inflows from the management of liquid resources will include the following, which should be separately disclosed:

(a) withdrawals from short-term deposits not qualifying as cash; and

(b) inflows from the disposal or redemption of any other investments (such as government securities, loan stock, equities and derivatives) held as liquid resources.[74]

Cash outflows will include the following separately disclosable items:

(a) payments into short-term deposits not qualifying as cash; and

(b) outflows to acquire any other investments (such as government securities, loan stock, equities and derivatives) held as liquid resources.[75]

The following extract is an example of the cash flows required to be shown under this heading. It includes unlisted securities (which may not be readily convertible into known amounts of cash) which is a little unusual:

Extract 29.6: Reuters Group PLC (2000)

NOTES ON THE CONSOLIDATED CASH FLOW STATEMENT

10. ANALYSIS OF CASH FLOWS FOR HEADINGS NETTED IN THE CASH FLOW STATEMENT [extract]

	2000	1999	1998
	£M	£M	£M
Management of liquid resources			
Increase in term deposits	**(3,719)**	(3,920)	(7,145)
Decrease in term deposits	**3,842**	4,277	7,250
Purchase of certificates of deposit	**(108)**	(226)	(580)
Sale of certificates of deposit	**113**	352	597
Purchase of listed/unlisted securities	**(989)**	(360)	(465)
Sale of listed/unlisted securities	**859**	353	656
	(2)	476	313

As discussed in 2.3 above, net presentation is allowed under this heading where the cash inflows and outflows are due to short maturities and high turnover occurring from rollover or reissue. However, the placing of surplus cash on term deposit followed by the subsequent withdrawal of these funds gives rise to two cash flows, one out and the other in. These gross cash flows do not qualify for net presentation because there is no rollover or reissue.

2.4.10 *Financing*

Financing cash flows are receipts from, and repayments to, external providers of finance.[76] However, as discussed at 2.4.4 above and as illustrated in Extract 29.7 below, only cash flows relating to *principal* amounts of finance are dealt with here, since those relating to interest and other finance costs are dealt with under returns on investments and servicing of finance.

Financing cash flows include the following separately disclosable items:

(a) receipts from the issue of shares and other equity instruments;

(b) receipts from the issue of debentures, loans, notes and bonds and from other long-term and short-term borrowing (other than overdrafts);

(c) repayments of amounts borrowed (other than overdrafts);

(d) the capital element of finance lease rental repayments;

(e) payments to reacquire or redeem the entity's shares; and

(f) payments of expenses or commissions on any issue of equity shares.[77]

In addition, any financing cash flows received from or paid to equity accounted entities should be disclosed separately.[78]

The following example illustrates the items commonly found under this heading:

Extract 29.7: Arcadia Group plc (1998)

Consolidated cash flow statement [extract]

For the financial year ended 29th August 1998	**1998 £m**	**1998 £m**	1997 £m	1997 £m
Financing				
Issue of ordinary shares	**32.5**		6.0	
Redemption of loan stocks	**(0.1)**		(2.2)	
Repayment of Zero Coupon Secured Bonds	**–**		(61.0)	
Repayment of bank and term loans	**(8.0)**		(10.6)	
Repayment of property lease obligations	**(37.7)**		–	
New bank and term loans	**15.0**		16.5	
Capital element of finance lease rental payments	**(0.4)**		(0.4)	
		1.3		(51.7)

In June 1997, Arcadia Group redeemed the £100m Zero Coupon Secured Bonds originally issued at 60.98 per cent in June 1992. Because the premium paid on redemption (£39.0m) is treated as a finance cost under FRS 4, it appears under returns on investments and servicing of finance and not under financing.

2.4.11 *Exceptional and extraordinary items*

To allow users to understand the effect on cash flows of items shown as exceptional or extraordinary in the profit and loss account, there is a requirement to identify the related cash flows and to explain their relationship with the originating item in profit and loss account.[79] BAA dealt with this as follows:

Extract 29.8: BAA plc (2001)

Notes to the accounts

33 Notes to the cash flow statement [extract]

(d) **Cashflows in respect of exceptional items**	**2001** **£m**	2000 £m
Net cash inflow from operating activities		
Costs of terminating World Duty Free contracts	**(3)**	–
Costs of reorganisation of UK operations	**(12)**	(4)
Closure of World Duty Free's inflight division	**(6)**	–
Returns on investments and servicing of finance		
Costs associated with exchange of convertible bonds	**(3)**	–
Premium on early redemption of loan	–	(4)
Capital expenditure and financial investment		
Sale of fixed assets	**128**	337
Cash inflow from exceptional items	**104**	329

(f) **Cashflows in respect of acquisitions and disposals**

The purchase consideration for GESAC was deferred under the terms of the sale and purchase agreement dated August 1997. During the year this deferred consideration was paid. The consideration for the sale of the Group's 5% holding in GESAC in May 1999 was receivable under similar terms and hence payment was received during the year.

As shown above, cash flows related to exceptional items should appear under the format heading which best reflects the nature of the item.[80] Many exceptional items will not entail any cash flow – provisions for impairment of fixed assets and exceptional stock provisions clearly have no consequences for the cash flow statement. For exceptional items like the profit or loss on disposal of fixed assets, the inclusion of the cash proceeds from the sale under capital expenditure and financial investment is uncontroversial and hardly needs to be spelt out as exceptional.

The standard recognises that some cash flows might be exceptional of themselves and requires sufficient disclosure to be given to explain their cause and nature.[81] Users would undoubtedly like exceptional non-recurring cash flows to be highlighted but drafting guidance for preparers of accounts is far from straightforward. FRS 1 is not very forthcoming on this point, but says simply that 'for a cash flow to be exceptional on the grounds of its size alone, it must be exceptional in relation to cash flows of a similar nature'. An example provided by the ASB is a large prepayment against a pension liability.[82]

The publication of FRS 3, which effectively outlawed extraordinary items, made the requirement to disclose the cash flows related to these items redundant.

2.5 Reconciliations

In addition to the reconciliation to operating profit discussed at 2.4.2 above, FRS 1 requires two additional reconciliations to be given.

The first is a requirement to reconcile the increase or decrease in cash to the movement in net debt in the period.[83] The revised standard explains that movements in net debt are widely used as indicators of changes in liquidity and in assessing the financial strength of the reporting entity. The reconciliation to net debt is accordingly intended to provide information that assists in the assessment of liquidity, solvency and financial adaptability,[84] a key objective of the standard.[85]

'Net debt' is defined as borrowings (capital instruments that are classified as liabilities under FRS 4) together with related derivatives and obligations under finance leases, less cash and liquid resources.[86] As explained at 2.4.9 above, liquid resources are essentially current asset investments held as readily disposable stores of value. The reference to FRS 4 means that redeemable preference shares issued by the reporting entity are excluded from net debt whereas the same shares issued by a subsidiary, but guaranteed by the parent, would be included. Where cash and liquid resources exceed debt, the surplus should be described as 'net funds'.[87]

To reconcile the movement of cash in the period to the movement in net debt, it is necessary first to adjust the change in cash shown at the foot of the cash flow statement to arrive at the change in net debt resulting from cash flows. This entails adding back the cash flows related to borrowings and finance leases shown under financing as well as the cash flows shown under management of liquid resources. The second stage is to include the changes in net debt which have been excluded from the cash flow statement altogether, i.e. those that do not involve cash flows, such as:

- liquid resources and borrowings in entities acquired or disposed of during the period;
- debt instruments issued as consideration for acquisitions;
- new finance leases;
- the conversion of debt into equity;
- exchange adjustments to cash, borrowings and liquid resources; and
- other adjustments such as the amortisation of debt issue costs, the accretion of redemption premiums, changes in market value and the profit or loss on the sale of current asset investments qualifying as liquid resources.

Many of the reconciling items listed above are included in the following example:

Extract 29.9: Cable and Wireless plc (2001)

NOTES TO THE ACCOUNTS [extract]

29 Reconciliation of net cash flow to movement in net funds/(debt)

For the year ended 31 March	2001 £m	2000 £m
Increase in cash in the year	**423**	33
Cash outflow/(inflow) resulting from decrease/(increase) in debt and lease financing	**984**	(288)
Cash (inflow)/outflow resulting from (decrease)/increase in liquid resources	**(129)**	3,080
Decrease in net debt resulting from cash flows	**1,278**	2,825
Conversion of unsecured loan stock	**37**	34
Borrowings of businesses acquired and disposed	**2,044**	(189)
Inception of finance lease contracts	**–**	(7)
Translation and other differences	**190**	64
Movement in net debt in the year	**3,549**	2,727
Net debt at 1 April	**(1,257)**	(3,984)
Net funds/(debt) at 31 March	**2,292**	(1,257)

The reconciliation to net debt should be given either adjoining the cash flow statement or in a note.[88]

Because 'net debt' will not be readily apparent from the accounts, the standard requires a second reconciliation whereby the component parts are traced back to the equivalent captions in the opening and closing balance sheets. In addition, this reconciliation is required to show the changes in the component parts of net debt, analysed between:

(a) the cash flows of the entity;

(b) the acquisition or disposal of subsidiaries;

(c) other non-cash changes; and

(d) the recognition of changes in market value and exchange rate movements.[89]

A number of companies have elected to combine the two reconciliations required by the FRS into one enlarged note. In doing this, it should be borne in mind that comparative figures are required for the former (Extract 29.9 above) but not the latter[90] (Extract 29.10 below). Combining the two has the disadvantage of having to present comparative figures for the changes in the component parts of net debt.

Extract 29.10: Daily Mail and General Trust plc (2000)

Notes to the Cash Flow Statement [extract]

18 Analysis of Net Debt

	At beginning of year	Cash Flow	Acquisition (excluding cash and overdrafts)	Foreign exchange movements	Other non-cash changes	At end of year
	£m	£m	£m	£m	£m	£m
Cash	65.0	28.4	–	–	–	93.4
Bank overdrafts	(0.1)	(3.8)	–	–	–	(3.9)
	64.9	24.6	–	–	–	89.5
Debt due within one year	(87.4)	39.4	(7.6)	–	–	(55.6)
Debt due after one year						
Eurobonds	(261.4)	(215.3)	–	–	(2.3)	(479.0)
Loans	(292.2)	11.9	(5.0)	(12.0)	–	(297.3)
	(553.6)	(203.4)	(5.0)	(12.0)	(2.3)	(776.3)
Finance lease obligations	(50.0)	6.1	–	–	–	(43.9)
	(691.0)	(157.9)	(12.6)	(12.0)	(2.3)	(875.8)
Short-term investments	17.8	(20.2)	3.6	–	–	1.2
Net debt	(608.3)	(153.5)	(9.0)	(12.0)	(2.3)	(785.1)

(i) The increase in debt of £9.0 million (excluding cash and overdrafts) arising from acquisitions was due to the issue of loan notes of £7.6 million and to the assumption of loans of £5.0 million mainly in Bristol United Press, offset by short-term investments of £3.6 million.

(ii) Other non-cash movements of £2.3 million include the accretion to the principal of the 2.5% deep discount Eurobond of £1.8 million and the amortisation of issue costs of Eurobonds of £0.5 million.

(iii) Cash flows in respect of Eurobonds comprise the issue of the 7.5% Eurobond for net proceeds of £223.6 million, offset by the repurchase of bonds with a carrying value of £8.3 million.

2.6 Comparative figures

Comparative figures are required for all items in the cash flow statement and the related notes. The only exceptions are the note analysing changes in the balance sheet amounts making up net debt (Extract 29.10 above) and the note showing the material effects of acquisitions and disposals on the standard headings (Extract 29.12 below).[91]

2.7 Groups

The cash flow statement presented with group accounts should reflect the external cash flows of the group. Cash flows that are internal to the group (such as payments and receipts for intra-group sales, management charges, dividends, interest and financing arrangements) should be eliminated.[92] However, dividends paid to minority shareholders in subsidiaries represent an outflow of cash from the perspective of the shareholders in the parent company. They should accordingly be included under returns on investments and servicing of finance.[93]

2.7.1 *Acquisition and disposal of subsidiaries*

When a subsidiary joins or leaves the group, it should be included in the group cash flow statement for the same period as its results are reported in the group profit and loss account.[94]

As noted at 2.4.7 above, the consideration shown under acquisitions and disposals should be the cash paid or received, together with any cash balances (including overdrafts) obtained or surrendered as part of the purchase or sale.

Although the impact on the cash flow statement itself might be limited, a note is required of the effects of the acquisition or disposal, indicating how much of the consideration comprised cash:[95]

Extract 29.11: GKN plc (2000)

Notes on the cash flow statement [extract]

B Purchase and sale of subsidiaries

	Acquisitions		Sales	
	2000	1999	**2000**	1999
	£m	£m	**£m**	£m
Fixed assets	**(92)**	(176)	**34**	–
Working capital and provisions	**(9)**	20	**9**	–
Taxation payable	**6**	29	**(1)**	–
Cash	**1**	(1)	**3**	–
Loans and finance leases	**26**	200	**(2)**	–
Minority interests	**(13)**	10	**5**	–
	(81)	82	**48**	–
Change from joint venture status	**20**	–	**–**	–
Surplus on sales	**–**	–	**64**	–
Goodwill	**(160)**	(372)	**5**	–
Total consideration	**(221)**	(290)	**117**	–
Deferred consideration	**8**	(1)	**–**	–
Consideration (paid)/received	**(213)**	(291)	**117**	–
Less: cash	**(1)**	1	**(3)**	–
Net cash (outflow)/inflow	**(214)**	(290)	**114**	–

GKN has followed the illustrative example in the FRS and provided a full breakdown of the assets and liabilities acquired and disposed of, together with an analysis of the consideration paid and received. Comparative figures have also been given as required. However, it is not entirely clear whether 'a summary of the effects of acquisitions and disposals of subsidiary undertakings indicating how much of the consideration comprised cash'[96] requires this extent of detail. Some companies have read it as requiring only disclosure of the more limited information about the cash consideration paid and any cash balances acquired.

The FRS also requires disclosure of the effect (where material) on the standard headings in the cash flow statement of the cash flows of subsidiaries acquired or disposed of in the period.[97] Comparative figures are not required.[98] GKN dealt with this requirement in respect of its acquisitions, but not its disposals (possibly because they were not deemed to be sufficiently material), as follows:

Extract 29.12: GKN plc (2000)

Notes on the Accounts

25 Acquisitions [extract]

The post-acquisition contribution of subsidiary acquisitions to group cash flow was a net cash inflow of £12 million from operating activities, payments of £4 million in respect of interest, payments of £6 million in respect of taxation and payments of £14 million in respect of capital expenditure and financial investment.

2.7.2 *Preparation of the group cash flow statement*

In principle, the group cash flow statement should be built up from the cash flow statements prepared by individual subsidiaries with intra-group cash flows being eliminated as part of the aggregation process.

In practice, however, it may be possible to work at a more consolidated level, using the adjustments performed as part of the accounts consolidation process together with external cash flow information provided by individual subsidiaries. Thus, the group's cash flow from operating activities could be calculated using the indirect method based on operating profit in the consolidated profit and loss account. The cash flows under the other standard headings could similarly be derived from a reconciliation of profit and loss account entries to balance sheet movements. In all cases, however, subsidiaries would have to provide supplementary information to prevent gross cash flows from being netted off and to ensure that the cash flows are shown under the correct headings. In particular, detailed information about debtors and creditors is essential to ensure that the movements included in the reconciliation of operating profit to cash inflow from operating activities relate only to operating debtors and creditors.

The 'consolidated level' approach described above is more complicated when there are overseas subsidiaries accounted for under the closing rate/net investment method. The movement in stocks, debtors and creditors between the opening and closing group balance sheets will include changes in exchange rates. For example, an increase in stocks held by a US subsidiary from $240 to $270 during the year will be reported as an unchanged amount of £150 if the opening exchange rate of £1=$1.60 becomes £1=$1.80 by the year-end. In these circumstances it is usually easier to take the financial statements of the foreign subsidiary as the starting point. The $30 increase in stocks can then be translated using either the closing or average exchange rate, as discussed at 2.8.2 below.

2.7.3 *Associates, joint ventures and joint arrangements*

The cash flow statements of associates and joint ventures have a limited impact on the group cash flow statement, which will reflect only the cash actually transferred between the group and the associate or joint venture. Examples include cash dividends received and loans made or repaid. The amounts of any financing cash flows received from, or paid to, equity accounted entities should be disclosed separately (see 2.4.10 above), as should any cash dividends received (2.4.3 above).

Participants in a joint arrangement that is not an entity should account for their own cash flows, measured according to the terms of the agreement.[99] This is because each participant is deemed to be, in effect, operating its own business independently of the others.

2.8 Foreign currency

2.8.1 *Individual entities*

When an entity enters into a transaction denominated in a foreign currency, there are no consequences for the cash flow statement until payments are received or made. The receipts and payments will be recorded in the accounts at the exchange rate ruling at the date of payment (or at the contracted rate if applicable) and these amounts should be reflected in the cash flow statement.

Exchange differences will appear in the profit and loss account when the settled amount differs from the amount recorded at the date of the transaction. Alternatively, if the transaction remains unsettled, exchange differences will also be taken to the profit and loss account on the retranslation of the unsettled monetary balances at year-end rates.

Where the exchange differences relate to operating items such as sales or purchases of stock, no further adjustments need be made when the indirect method of calculating the cash flow from operating activities is used. Thus, if a sale transaction and cash settlement take place in the same period, the operating profit will include both the amount of the sale and the amount of the exchange difference, the combined effect being the amount of the cash flow. No reconciling item would therefore be needed in the reconciliation of operating profit to cash flow from operating activities. Similarly, where an exchange difference has been recognised on an unsettled balance no reconciling item is needed. This is because the movement in the related debtor or creditor included in the reconciliation to operating profit will incorporate the exchange gain or loss, effectively reversing the amount taken to the profit and loss account.

However, where an exchange difference on a non-operating item such as the purchase of plant has been accounted for in arriving at operating profit, this should appear as a reconciling item between operating profit and the cash flow from operating activities. The difference needs to be taken into account in calculating the cash flow to be shown under the relevant standard heading, in this case capital expenditure and financial investment, which would otherwise be recorded at the amount shown in the fixed assets note.

Exchange differences arising on foreign currency denominated cash balances, borrowings and liquid resources which have been taken to the profit and loss account should be extracted and shown as part of the reconciliation to net debt. These exchange differences do not represent cash flows and have no place in the cash flow statement.

2.8.2 *Groups*

Where the temporal method is used to account for an overseas operation, the issues that arise are no different to those for foreign currency denominated transactions discussed at 2.8.1 above. Use of the closing rate/net investment method, by contrast, requires the application of different principles which are discussed below.

The standard requires the cash flow statements of foreign subsidiaries to be translated on the same basis used for their profit and loss accounts (which under the closing rate method will be either the year-end exchange rate or an average for the reporting period).[100] Where the year-end exchange rate is used, this rate must be applied to *all* the foreign entity's cash flows, not just those from operating activities. Thus, a cash inflow from an external loan raised on the first day of the financial period would be translated into sterling at the closing rate rather than the rate prevailing at the date of the transaction.

When the indirect method is used to calculate the cash inflow from operating activities, the movement in stocks, debtors and creditors shown in the reconciliation to operating profit should be arrived at by converting the foreign currency movement into sterling at the same exchange rate used for the profit and loss account.[101] For example, an increase in stocks held by a US subsidiary from $240 to $270 during the year will be translated into sterling at either the year-end exchange rate or the average for the period, depending on which rate is used to translate the subsidiary's operating profit. The reconciliation of operating profit to operating cash inflow should show an increase in stocks regardless of the movement in the sterling balance sheet. The latter may, for example, show an unchanged amount of £150 if the opening exchange rate of £1 = $1.60 becomes £1 = $1.80 by the year-end. Using the same exchange rate to translate operating profit and the movement in stocks, debtors and creditors ensures that the cash inflow from operating activities under the indirect method is the same as the sterling equivalent of subsidiary's cash inflow from operating activities calculated under the direct method.

The anomaly highlighted in the previous paragraph of an increase in stocks for FRS 1 purposes when the balance sheet amount is unchanged, could apply equally to the items making up net debt. In the latter case, the impact needs to be quantified and disclosed in the reconciliation to net debt. Using the figures in the previous example, the change in cash reported in the cash flow statement would be the sterling equivalent of the increase from $240 to $270. This should be reconciled to the unchanged balance sheet movement in net funds of £150. Where the closing rate (£1 = $1.80) is used to translate the increase of $30 into £17, the only exchange difference will be that arising on the retranslation of the opening net funds of $240 from opening rate of £1 = $1.60 to the closing rate (a loss of £17). When the average rate is used, two elements have to be recorded. These are the retranslation of the opening balances from opening rate to closing rate and the difference arising on translating the cash flows in the period at an average rate rather than the closing rate.

Translating a foreign subsidiary's cash flows at the same exchange rate used for that entity's profit and loss account is problematic when there are intra-group cash flows. This is because there will invariably be a residual exchange difference. In these circumstances, the standard allows the actual rate of exchange at which the intra-group cash flows took place to be used. If this is not done, the exchange difference should be included in the exchange rate movements shown as part of the reconciliation to net debt.[102]

2.8.3 *Hedging transactions*

FRS 1 requires cash flows from futures contracts, forward contracts, option contracts or swap contracts that are accounted for as hedges to be shown under the same heading as the transaction that is the subject of the hedge.[103] An example is an interest rate swap. An entity wishing to convert an existing fixed rate borrowing into a floating rate equivalent could enter into an interest rate swap under which it receives fixed rates and pays floating rates. All the cash flows under the swap should be reported under returns on investments and servicing of finance because they are equivalent to interest or are hedges of interest payments.

2.9 Notes to the cash flow statement

There are several requirements for the cash flow statement to be supplemented by the disclosure of additional information in a note. Those discussed in earlier sections of this chapter are summarised below for ease of reference:

- a reconciliation of operating profit to cash flow from operating activities (see 2.4.2 above);
- the reporting entity's policy for determining liquid resources and any changes to it (2.4.9);
- cash flows related to exceptional or extraordinary items and cash flows that are exceptional in their own right because of their size or incidence (2.4.11);
- a reconciliation of the change in cash to the movement in net debt (2.5);
- an analysis of the changes in the opening and closing component amounts of net debt (2.5);
- a summary of the effects of acquisitions and disposals of subsidiary undertakings (2.7.1); and
- a note of the material effects of acquisitions and disposals of subsidiary undertakings on each of the standard headings (2.7.1).

In addition to the above, there are two other disclosure requirements. These are discussed below.

2.9.1 *Restrictions on remittability*

Where restrictions (like exchange control) prevent the transfer of cash from one part of the business to another, there should be disclosure of the amounts involved and an explanation of the circumstances.[104] It would seem that this requirement is referring to the balance sheet amounts, not the cash flows during the period.

The ASB is keen to stress that note disclosure is required only where external factors have a severe effect in practice, rather than where the sole constraint is a special purpose designated by the entity itself. Examples of the former could include cash balances in escrow, deposited with a regulator or held within an employee share ownership trust.[105] The implication is that, whilst these balances still fall within the definition of 'cash', additional disclosure is necessary to provide meaningful information about liquidity, solvency and financial adaptability. The following extract illustrates this requirement:

Extract 29.13: The Go-Ahead Group plc (2000)

Notes to the Cash Flow Statement [extract]

5 RESTRICTED CASH

Included in cash at bank and cash on short-term deposit are balances amounting to £34,712,000 (1999 – £30,070,000) held by the train companies which cannot be distributed by means of a dividend of which £16,546,000 (1999 – £16,188,000) is cash collateral for railway season ticket bonds.

2.9.2 *Material non-cash transactions*

In order to provide a better understanding of the underlying transactions and a full picture of the change in financial position, FRS 1 requires material non-cash transactions to be disclosed in the notes.[106] Examples include shares issued for the acquisition of a subsidiary, the exchange of major assets or the inception of finance lease contracts.

3 BANKS AND INSURANCE COMPANIES

FRS 1 contains a number of specific provisions affecting the preparation of cash flow statements by banks and insurance companies. These are covered in broad outline below.

3.1 Banks

It has been argued that a cash flow statement is not particularly relevant to a bank because cash is its stock in trade. Measures like regulatory capital ratios derived from statements of capital resources may therefore give a better indication of a bank's solvency and financial adaptability. Although the ASB shares this view, banks are not exempted from preparing cash flow statements because the ASB believes that the statement contains useful information about the generation and utilisation of cash.[107] However, the special nature of banking and its regulation are recognised in certain aspects of the detailed requirements. These apply to 'any entity whose business is to receive deposits or other repayable funds from the public and to grant credits for its own account':[108]

- definition of cash – because banks do not usually have borrowings with the characteristics of an overdraft, cash for their purposes should normally include only cash and balances at central banks, together with loans and advances to other banks repayable on demand;[109]
- presentation of interest – to the extent that interest received or paid (and dividends received) are included as part of operating profit, the related cash flows should appear under operating activities. Where interest clearly relates

to financing, the cash flows should be included under returns on investments and servicing of finance. Examples include loan capital and other subordinated liabilities;[110]

- investments held for trading – the related cash flows should be included under operating activities;[111]
- management of liquid resources – this heading is not required because meaningful identification of cash flows relating to the management of liquid resources is not possible;[112]
- reconciliation to net debt – this is not required because the change in net debt has very little (if any) meaning in the context of a bank;[113] and
- notes to the cash flow statement – in the absence of the reconciliation to net debt it would seem that the note which reconciles all items shown under financing to the opening and closing balance sheets (for both years) might still be required.[114] This interpretation is supported by current practice.[115]

3.2 Insurance companies

Since insurance premiums are received in advance of the related cash outflows, sometimes long in advance, it has been argued that an insurance company's cash flow statement provides little information about liquidity, viability and financial adaptability, a key objective of the FRS.

Presumably because the provision of information about liquidity, solvency and financial adaptability is not the sole objective of the FRS (the other is the standardised reporting of cash generation and absorption), insurance companies (other than mutual life assurers) have not been exempted from the requirement to prepare a cash flow statement. However, the special nature of their business is recognised in certain departures from the presentation used by other entities:

- cash flows relating to long-term business (long-term life, pensions and annuity businesses) should be included only to the extent of cash transferred and available to meet the obligations of the company or group as a whole.[116] This is because the shareholders of an insurance company generally have restricted rights to the profits and associated cash surpluses made by their long-term business. Mutual life assurance companies, which are owned by policy holders, are therefore exempt from the requirements of the FRS;[117]
- internal cash flows of the long-term business may be shown as supplementary information in a note to the cash flow statement;[118]
- an analysis of portfolio investment should replace management of liquid resources and explain how the cash inflow for the period has been invested (including the movement in cash holdings);[119]
- portfolio investment for the period (as shown in the cash flow statement) should be reconciled to the balance sheet movement in portfolio investments less financing;[120]
- the note analysing the balance sheet movements in portfolio investment less financing should show the component parts and highlight the movements in

long-term business to the extent that these are consolidated in the accounts;[121] and

- the reconciliation of operating profit to cash flow from operating activities should normally start with profit before tax because returns on investments form part of operating activities.[122]

The FRS encourages the use of segmentation to reflect the different degrees of access to cash balances.[123]

Appendix I to the FRS contains an example of a cash flow statement for an insurance company. This reveals a very different statement to that required of other entities in that it shows the net investment of cash flows rather than the net change in cash.

4 INTERNATIONAL REQUIREMENTS

4.1 IAS 7

4.1.1 Introduction

In October 1977, the IASC issued IAS 7 – *Statement of Changes in Financial Position* – which required the presentation of a statement of sources and uses of funds. A separate project on cash flow statements was started in April 1989. This culminated in the publication in 1992 of a revised version of IAS 7 – *Cash Flow Statements*.

4.1.2 Objective and scope

The stated objective of IAS 7 is 'to require the provision of information about the historical changes in cash and cash equivalents of an enterprise by means of a cash flow statement which classifies cash flows during the period from operating, investing and financing activities'.[124]

IAS 7 applies to all enterprises including banks, insurance companies and other financial institutions. The reason for this is explained as follows: 'Users of an enterprise's financial statements are interested in how the enterprise generates and uses cash and cash equivalents. This is the case regardless of the nature of the enterprise's activities and irrespective of whether cash can be viewed as the product of the enterprise, as may be the case with a financial institution. Enterprises need cash for essentially the same reasons however different their principal revenue-producing activities might be. They need cash to conduct their operations, to pay their obligations, and to provide returns to their investors. Accordingly, this Standard requires all enterprises to present a cash flow statement.'[125]

4.1.3 Cash equivalents

IAS 7 defines cash equivalents as short-term, highly liquid investments that are readily convertible to known amounts of cash and which are subject to an insignificant risk of changes in value.[126]

Normally, only an investment with an original maturity of three months or less qualifies under the above definition.[127] Equity shares are excluded unless they are cash equivalents in substance, an example being redeemable preference shares acquired within a short period of their maturity.[128]

Although bank borrowings are generally considered to be financing activities, bank overdrafts repayable on demand are included as a component of cash and cash equivalents. This is because, under this kind of banking arrangement, the bank balance often fluctuates from being positive to overdrawn.[129]

There is a requirement to disclose both the policy adopted in determining the composition of cash and cash equivalents and the component parts (which should be reconciled to the equivalent items reported in the balance sheet).[130]

Significant cash and cash equivalent balances that are not available for use by the group should be disclosed, together with a commentary by management.[131]

4.1.4 *Presentation of the cash flow statement*

IAS 7 requires cash flows (inflows and outflows of cash and cash equivalents) to be classified by operating, investing and financing activities, in a manner which is most appropriate to the business of the enterprise.[132] This is intended to allow users to assess the impact of these three types of activity on the financial position of the enterprise and the amount of its cash and cash equivalents.

Provided that a consistent approach is adopted and that they are disclosed separately, cash flows from interest and dividends received and paid can be classified as either operating, investing or financing activities.[133] Although a literal reading of IAS 7 might suggest that interest paid should be disclosed as a single figure under one of the three headings,[134] it would seem appropriate to follow the US approach of classifying the element of interest that has been capitalised as an investing activity.[135]

Cash flows arising from futures contracts, forward contracts, option contracts and swap contracts which are accounted for as hedges of an identifiable position should be classified in the same manner as the cash flows of the position being hedged.[136] The terminology used in IAS 7 has not been updated to reflect IAS 39 – *Financial Instruments: Recognition and Measurement* – but this should not change the treatment of these contracts in the cash flow statement when they are accounted for as fair value hedges or cash flow hedges under IAS 39.

The IAS 7 cash flow statement is illustrated in Extract 29.14 below. As permitted by the standard, Nestlé has included interest received and paid under operating activities, dividends received from associates under investing activities and dividends paid under financing activities. However, it is not clear why the cash flows related to marketable securities and other liquid assets as well as short term investments are included as part of financing rather than investing activities. Possibly, this is because the company regards investing in these assets as part of its normal treasury management.

Extract 29.14: Nestlé S.A. (2000)

Consolidated cash flow statement
for the year ended 31st December 2000 [extract]

In millions of CHF		**2000**		1999
Operating activities				
Net profit of consolidated companies	**5,580**		4,545	
Depreciation of tangible fixed assets	**2,737**		2,597	
Impairment of tangible fixed assets	**223**		373	
Amortisation of goodwill	**414**		384	
Depreciation of intangible assets	**179**		92	
Impairment of goodwill	**230**		212	
Increase/(decrease) in provisions and deferred taxes	**(4)**		101	
Decrease/(increase) in working capital	**(368)**		235	
Other movements	**(140)**		(352)	
Operating cash flow [(a)]		**8,851**		8,187
Investing activities				
Expenditure on tangible fixed assets	**(3,305)**		(2,806)	
Expenditure on intangible assets	**(188)**		(139)	
Sale of tangible fixed assets	**355**		363	
Acquisitions	**(2,846)**		(440)	
Disposals	**780**		253	
Income from associated companies	**107**		86	
Other movements	**39**		(76)	
Cash flow from investing activities		**(5,058)**		(2,759)
Financing activities				
Dividend for the previous year	**(1,657)**		(1,469)	
Purchase of treasury shares (net)	**1,072**		(2,311)	
Premium on warrants issued	**81**		–	
Movements with minority interests	**(221)**		(190)	
Bonds issued	**1,016**		328	
Bonds repaid	**(1,143)**		(400)	
Increase/(decrease) in other medium/ long term financial liabilities	**(155)**		500	
Increase/(decrease) in short term financial liabilities	**921**		(3,488)	
Decrease/(increase) in marketable securities and other liquid assets	**(2,788)**		(355)	
Decrease/(increase) in short term investments	**1,452**		12	
Cash flow from financing activities		**(1,422)**		(7,373)
Translation differences on flows		**(175)**		49
Increase/(decrease) in cash and cash equivalents		**2,196**		(1,896)

Cash and cash equivalents at beginning of year	**3,322**		4,984	
Effects of exchange rate changes on opening balance	**(67)**		234	
Cash and cash equivalents retranslated at beginning of year		**3,255**		5,218
Cash and cash equivalents at end of year		**5,451**		3,322

(a) Taxes paid amount to CHF 2,714 million (1999: CHF 2,304 million). Interest received/paid does not differ materially from interest shown under note 2 "Net financing cost".

4.1.5 *Operating activities*

Operating activities are defined as the principal revenue-producing activities of the enterprise and other activities that are not investing or financing activities.[137] Cash flows from operating activities generally result from transactions and other events that enter into the determination of net profit or loss.[138] Examples include:

(a) cash receipts from the sale of goods and the rendering of services;

(b) cash receipts from royalties, fees, commissions and other revenue;

(c) cash payments to suppliers for goods and services;

(d) cash payments to and on behalf of employees; and

(e) cash payments or refunds of income taxes unless they can be specifically identified with financing and investing activities.[139]

Cash flows arising from taxes on income should be separately disclosed and classified under this heading unless they can be specifically identified with financing and investing activities.[140]

Interest (paid and received) and dividends received may be classified as operating cash flows because they are included in arriving at net profit.[141] Dividends paid may be classified as a component of operating cash flow in order to assist users in determining the ability of the enterprise to pay dividends out of operating cash flows.[142]

Where securities and loans are held for dealing or trading purposes, the related cash flows are classified as operating activities.[143]

4.1.6 *Investing activities*

Investing activities are defined as the acquisition and disposal of long-term assets and other investments not included in cash equivalents.[144] Cash flows required to be shown under this heading include:

(a) payments to acquire, and receipts from the sale of, property, plant and equipment, intangibles and other long-term assets;

(b) payments to acquire, and receipts from the sale of, equity or debt instruments of other enterprises and interests in joint ventures (other than payments for those instruments considered to be cash equivalents or those held for dealing or trading purposes); and

(c) advances and loans made to, and repaid by, other parties (other than advances and loans made by a financial institution).[145]

As discussed under 2.4.6 above, the purchase of fixed assets on credit is potentially a complicated area because the associated cash flows may sometimes not be capital expenditure. In the US, SFAS 95 takes the line that only advance payments, the down payment or other amounts paid at or near to the time of purchase of fixed assets are investing cash flows.[146] This treatment also appears to be implicit in IAS 7. The most common example of this (although the payments are strictly not made to purchase the asset) is where a reporting entity makes payments in respect of assets obtained under a finance lease. In this case, the payments of principal are classified as a financing activity (see 4.1.7 below) rather than as an investing activity.[147]

Cash flows resulting from acquisitions and disposals of subsidiaries or business units must be presented separately net of cash and cash equivalents acquired or disposed of.[148]

Interest and dividends received may be classified as investing cash flows because they represent returns on investments.[149]

For acquisitions and disposals of subsidiaries and businesses, there is a requirement to disclose, in aggregate, the purchase or disposal consideration (including the portion thereof discharged by means of cash and cash equivalents) and a summary by major category of the assets and liabilities, including the cash and cash equivalents, in the unit acquired or sold.[150]

4.1.7 *Financing activities*

Financing activities are defined as those that result in changes in the size and composition of the equity capital and borrowings of the enterprise.[151] Cash flows from financing activities include:

(a) proceeds from issuing shares or other equity instruments;

(b) payments to owners to acquire or redeem the enterprise's shares;

(c) proceeds from issuing, and outflows to repay, debentures, loans, notes, bonds, mortgages and other short- or long-term borrowings; and

(d) payments by a lessee for the reduction of the outstanding liability relating to a finance lease.[152]

Interest and dividends paid may be treated as financing cash flows because they are a cost of obtaining financial resources.[153]

4.1.8 *Cash flows from investing and financing activities are presented gross*

Major classes of gross receipts and gross payments should be reported separately[154] unless the cash flows reflect the activities of the customer rather than those of the enterprise[155] or the cash flows relate to items in which the turnover is quick, the amounts are large, and the maturities are short.[156]

4.1.9 *Non-cash transactions*

Investing and financing transactions that do not involve cash or cash equivalents should be excluded from the cash flow statement but disclosed elsewhere in the accounts in order to provide all relevant information about these activities.

Examples listed include converting debt to equity, acquiring assets by assuming directly related liabilities or by means of a finance lease and the acquisition of another enterprise via an equity issue.[157]

4.1.10 *Use of the direct or indirect methods*

Although enterprises are encouraged to use the direct method whereby major classes of gross cash receipts and gross cash payments are disclosed, the indirect method of presentation is also available for reporting the net cash flow from operating activities.[158]

4.1.11 *Foreign currency cash flows*

Transactions in a foreign currency should be reported in the cash flow statement by applying the exchange rate ruling on the date of the cash flow.[159] Similarly, the cash flows of a foreign subsidiary should be converted using the exchange rates prevailing at the dates of the cash flows.[160] An approximation of the actual rates (like a weighted average for the period) is permitted.[161]

Although the effect of exchange rate movements on foreign currency cash and cash equivalents is not a cash flow, it is necessary to include these exchange differences at the foot of the statement in order to reconcile the movement in cash and cash equivalents to the equivalent amounts shown in the balance sheet at the beginning and end of the period.[162]

4.1.12 *Extraordinary items*

Cash flows from extraordinary items are classified according to their nature as either operating, investing or financing flows and are disclosed separately.[163]

4.1.13 *Investments in subsidiaries, associates and joint ventures*

Investments in entities accounted for under the equity or cost methods will impact on the cash flow statement only to the extent of the cash actually transferred between the group and the investee. Examples include cash dividends received and loans made or repaid.[164]

Where interests in jointly controlled entities are accounted for using proportionate consolidation, the cash flow statement will reflect the proportionate share of the jointly controlled entity's cash flows.[165]

4.1.14 *Voluntary disclosures*

IAS 7 encourages the disclosure of certain additional cash flow related information such as:[166]

(a) the amount of undrawn borrowing facilities that may be available for future operating activities and to settle capital commitments, indicating any restrictions on the use of these facilities;

(b) the aggregate amounts of the cash flows from each of operating, investing and financing activities related to interests in joint ventures reported using proportionate consolidation;

(c) the aggregate amount of cash flows that represent increases in operating capacity separately from those cash flows that are required to maintain operating capacity; and

(d) the amount of the cash flows arising from the operating, investing and financing activities of each reported industry and geographical segment.

In the UK, the ASB decided it was not feasible for an accounting standard 'to set out how to distinguish expenditure for expansion from expenditure for maintenance'[167] and IAS 7 does not contain any guidance in relation to the voluntary disclosure referred to under (c) above.

IAS 7 contains an example of the segmental disclosure advocated under (d) above but it might be difficult to allocate financing cash flows across the segments, given that this is not how treasury functions tend to operate in practice.[168]

4.1.15 *Summary of principal differences between FRS 1 and IAS 7*

The key differences between the international and UK standards are to be found in the definition of cash flows and their categorisation in the cash flow statement. Whereas IAS 7 is concerned with reporting inflows and outflows of cash and cash equivalents, FRS 1 concentrates on changes in cash. Cash flows related to cash equivalents are included under the management of liquid resources section in the UK.

Because IAS 7 does not have separate headings for dividends from joint ventures and associates, returns on investments and servicing of finance, taxation, capital expenditure and financial investment, acquisitions and disposals and equity dividends paid as is the case in the UK:

- interest and dividends can be classified as either operating, investing or financing activities provided this is done in a consistent manner from period to period;[169]
- cash flows arising from taxes on income are classified as operating activities unless they can be specifically identified with financing and investing activities;[170] and
- cash flows arising from the acquisition and disposal of long-term assets and other investments (other than those included in cash equivalents) as well as those arising from the acquisition and disposal of subsidiaries and business units should be classified as investing activities.[171]

Other significant differences between the two standards are that:

- IAS 7 permits both the direct and indirect methods to be used for reporting the net cash flow from operating activities but, unlike FRS 1, does not require the reconciliation to operating profit when the direct method is used. Also, when the indirect method is used, the reconciliation may be shown as part of the cash flow statement itself (see Extract 29.14 above);
- IAS 7 does not require the reconciliation to the movement in net debt stipulated by FRS 1; and

- IAS 7 requires foreign subsidiary cash flows to be translated at the exchange rates prevailing at the dates of the cash flows (or a suitable weighted average as an approximation[172]) whereas FRS 1 requires the same exchange rate as used for translating the results of those subsidiaries in the profit and loss account.

5 CONCLUSION

The original FRS 1 was undoubtedly a quantum leap in the ASB's financial reporting reform process. It generally worked well in practice and enhanced the quality of financial reporting considerably. It was clear, though, that certain aspects of the original standard needed re-examining and most of these were addressed in the 1996 revision.

However, in deciding to withdraw the original standard the ASB arguably used a sledgehammer to crack a nut. The three month cut-off in the old definition of cash equivalents was clearly unsatisfactory but it might have been possible to adopt a more flexible definition, similar to that used in IAS 7. International harmonisation was also not helped by converting the three standard headings into eight, subsequently increased to nine by the FRS 9 amendment.

Nevertheless there are areas where the UK standard is arguably superior. In particular, the reconciliation to net debt has worked well in practice and helped to place the cash flow statement in its proper context. Also, the requirement to identify and explain the cash flows related to exceptional items provides valuable additional information about the link between operating profit and the cash inflow from operating activities.

It would appear that the topic of cash flow statements is not high on the agenda of the IASB. Whether the international standard will ultimately be amended to incorporate some of the features of the UK equivalent remains to be seen.

References

1 SFAC No. 1, *Objectives of Financial Reporting by Business Enterprises*, FASB, November 1978, para. 37.
2 SFAC No. 5, *Recognition and Measurement in Financial Statements of Business Enterprises*, FASB, December 1984, para. 13.
3 *Ibid.*, para. 52.
4 FRS 1, *Cash Flow Statements*, ASB, October 1996, Appendix III, para. 6.
5 FRS 1 (Original), *Cash flow statements*, ASB, September 1991, para. 3.
6 FRS 1, para. 49.
7 *Ibid.*, para. 5.
8 ASB, Press Notice PN 6, 26 September 1991.
9 SAS 600, *Auditors' Reports on Financial Statements*, APB, May 1993, Appendix 2, Example 12.
10 FRS 1, para. 5.
11 *Ibid.*, Appendix III, para. 12.
12 FRS 1, para. 36.
13 *Ibid.*, Appendix III, para. 12.
14 These limits are reviewed from time to time.
15 FRS 1, para. 2.
16 *Ibid.*
17 *Ibid.*, para. 33.
18 *Ibid.*, para. 7.

19 *Ibid.*
20 *Ibid.*
21 *Ibid.*, para. 8.
22 *Ibid.*, Appendix III, para. 13.
23 FRS 1, para. 9
24 FRS 4, *Capital Instruments*, ASB, December 1993, para. 35.
25 FRS 1, para. 9.
26 FRS 4, para. 35.
27 FRS 1, para. 10.
28 *Ibid.*, para. 11.
29 *Ibid.*, para. 58.
30 FRS 3, *Reporting financial performance*, ASB, October 1992, para. 20.
31 FRS 1, para. 11.
32 *Ibid.*, para. 58.
33 *Ibid.*, para. 7.
34 *Ibid.*, para. 12.
35 *Ibid.*
36 *Ibid.*, para. 56.
37 *Ibid.*, para. 8.
38 *Ibid.*, para. 56.
39 *Ibid.*, Appendix III, para. 18.
40 FRS 1, para. 58.
41 FRS 9, *Associates and Joint Ventures*, ASB, November 1997, para. 61.
42 *Ibid.*, Appendix III, para. 22.
43 FRS 9, para. 61(a).
44 *Ibid.*, para. 61(d).
45 FRS 1, para. 13.
46 *Ibid.*, para. 15.
47 *Ibid.*
48 *Ibid.*, para. 14.
49 *Ibid.*, para. 15.
50 *Ibid.*, paras. 14 and 25.
51 *Ibid.*, Appendix III, para. 17.
52 FRS 1, para. 16.
53 *Ibid.*, para. 61.
54 *Ibid.*, para. 39.
55 *Ibid.*
56 *Ibid.*, para. 40.
57 *Ibid.*, para. 19.
58 *Ibid.*, para. 22.
59 *Ibid.*, paras. 8, 20, 21.
60 *Ibid.*, para. 19.
61 SFAS 95, *Statement of Cash Flows*, FASB, November 1987, para. 17.
62 FRS 1, para. 22.
63 *Ibid.*, para. 24.
64 *Ibid.*, para. 23.
65 *Ibid.*, Appendix I, Example 2.
66 FRS 1, para. 21(b).
67 *Ibid.*, para. 22.
68 *Ibid.*
69 *Ibid.*, para. 25.
70 *Ibid.*, para. 2.
71 *Ibid.*
72 *Ibid.*, para. 52.
73 *Ibid.*, para. 26.
74 *Ibid.*, paras. 8 and 27.
75 *Ibid.*, paras. 8 and 28.
76 *Ibid.*, para. 29.
77 *Ibid.*, paras. 8, 30, 31.
78 *Ibid.*, para. 32.
79 *Ibid.*, para. 37.
80 *Ibid.*
81 *Ibid.*, para. 38.
82 *Ibid.*, para. 63.
83 *Ibid.*, para. 33.
84 *Ibid.*, para. 53.
85 *Ibid.*, para. 1.
86 *Ibid.*, para. 2.
87 *Ibid.*
88 *Ibid.*, para. 33.
89 *Ibid.*
90 *Ibid.*, para. 48.
91 *Ibid.*
92 *Ibid.*, para. 43.
93 *Ibid.*, para. 15.
94 *Ibid.*, para. 43.
95 *Ibid.*, para. 45.
96 *Ibid.*
97 *Ibid.*
98 *Ibid.*, para. 48.
99 FRS 9, para. 18.
100 FRS 1, para. 41.
101 *Ibid.*
102 *Ibid.*
103 *Ibid.*, para. 42.
104 *Ibid.*, para. 47.
105 *Ibid.*, para. 68.
106 *Ibid.*, para. 46.
107 *Ibid.*, Appendix III, para. 20.
108 FRS 1, para. 2.
109 *Ibid.*, para. 34.
110 *Ibid.*, para. 60.
111 *Ibid.*, para. 34.
112 *Ibid.*, Appendix III, para. 21.
113 *Ibid.*
114 FRS 1, Appendix I, Example 3, Note 3.
115 See, for example, the Barclays PLC Annual Report 2000, p. 126 and the Bank of Scotland Report and Accounts 2001, p. 63.
116 FRS 1, para. 36.
117 *Ibid.*, para. 5.
118 *Ibid.*, Appendix III, para. 24.
119 FRS 1, para. 35.
120 *Ibid.*
121 *Ibid.*, para. 36.
122 *Ibid.*, para. 35.
123 *Ibid.*, Appendix III, para. 23.
124 IAS 7, *Cash Flow Statements*, IASC, Revised 1992, Objective.
125 *Ibid.*, para. 3.
126 *Ibid.*, para. 6.
127 *Ibid.*, para. 7.

128 *Ibid.*
129 *Ibid.,* para. 8.
130 *Ibid.,* paras. 45-6.
131 *Ibid.,* para. 48.
132 *Ibid.,* para. 11.
133 *Ibid.,* para. 31.
134 *Ibid.,* paras. 31-2.
135 SFAS 95, para. 17.
136 IAS 7, para. 16.
137 *Ibid.,* para. 6.
138 *Ibid.,* para. 14.
139 *Ibid.*
140 *Ibid.,* para. 35.
141 *Ibid.,* para. 33.
142 *Ibid.,* para. 34.
143 *Ibid.,* para. 15.
144 *Ibid.,* para. 6.
145 *Ibid.,* para. 16.
146 SFAS 95, para. 17.
147 IAS 7, para. 17.
148 *Ibid.,* paras. 39 and 42.
149 *Ibid.,* para. 33.
150 *Ibid.,* para. 40.
151 *Ibid.,* para. 6.
152 *Ibid.,* para. 17.
153 *Ibid.,* paras. 33-4.
154 *Ibid.,* para. 21.
155 *Ibid.,* para. 22(a).
156 *Ibid.,* para. 22(b).
157 *Ibid.,* paras. 43-4.
158 *Ibid.,* paras. 18-9.
159 *Ibid.,* para. 25.
160 *Ibid.,* para. 26.
161 *Ibid.,* para. 27.
162 *Ibid.,* para. 28.
163 *Ibid.,* para. 29.
164 *Ibid.,* para. 37.
165 *Ibid.,* para. 38.
166 *Ibid.,* para. 50.
167 FRS 1, Appendix III, para 14.
168 IAS 7, Appendix A.
169 IAS 7, para. 31.
170 *Ibid.,* para. 35.
171 *Ibid.,* paras. 6 and 39.
172 *Ibid.,* paras. 26–7.

Chapter 30 Related parties

1 INTRODUCTION

Related party relationships and transactions between related parties are a normal feature of business. Many enterprises carry on their business activities through subsidiaries and associates and there will inevitably be transactions between the parties comprising the group. It is also common for companies under common control, but not comprising a legal group, to transact with each other. However, experience shows that the existence of related party relationships brings with it the scope for abuse. This was illustrated in the UK in the early 1990s by the Robert Maxwell affair, where it was alleged that both the MGN Group and Maxwell Communications and their pension funds had suffered serious losses as a result of a number of related party transactions.

Whilst there has been an international standard on the topic, IAS 24 – *Related Party Disclosures* – since 1984, and a number of other countries (including the US, Canada, Australia and New Zealand) have had accounting standards for some time, the relevant UK standard, FRS 8 – *Related Party Disclosures*, was not issued until 1995. The ASC had issued ED 46 – *Disclosure of related party transactions* – in April 1989. Nothing ever came from ED 46, however, and the ASB regarded the topic as a relatively low priority when it inherited the ASC's work programme on its formation in 1990. However, in the light of the Maxwell affair, the ASB revived the related party project, issuing FRED 8 – *Related Party Disclosures* – in March 1994, which was converted into FRS 8 in October 1995.

1.1 The related party issue

The problem with related party relationships and transactions is expressed in FRS 8 as follows:

'In the absence of information to the contrary, it is assumed that a reporting entity has independent discretionary power over its resources and transactions and pursues its activities independently of the interests of its individual owners, managers and others. Transactions are presumed to have been undertaken on an arm's length basis, ie on terms such as could have been obtained in a transaction with an external party, in which each side bargained knowledgeably and freely, unaffected by any relationship between them.

'These assumptions may not be justified when related party relationships exist, because the requisite conditions for competitive, free market dealings may not be present. Whilst the parties may endeavour to achieve arm's length bargaining the very nature of the relationship may preclude this occurring. …

'Even when terms are at arm's length, the reporting of material related party transactions is useful information, because the terms of future transactions are more susceptible to alteration as a result of the nature of the relationship than they would be in transactions with an unrelated party.'[1]

A related party relationship can affect the financial position and operating results of an enterprise in a number of ways:

- Transactions may be entered into with a related party which would not occur if the relationship did not exist. For example, a company may sell a large proportion of its production to its parent company, where it might not have found an alternative customer if the parent company had not purchased the goods;
- Transactions may be entered into with a related party on terms different from those applicable to an unrelated party. For example, a subsidiary may lease equipment to a fellow subsidiary on terms imposed by the common parent entirely unrelated to market prices for similar leases; indeed, the terms may be such that no financial consideration passes between the parties; or
- Transactions with third parties may be affected by the existence of the relationship; for example, two enterprises in the same line of business may be controlled by a common party that has the ability to increase the volume of business done by each.

1.2 Possible solutions

1.2.1 Remeasurement of transactions at fair values

One solution would be to try to adjust the financial statements to reflect the transaction as if it had occurred with an independent third party and record the transaction at the corresponding arm's length price. However, as a study by the Accountants International Study Group stated, it often is impossible to establish what would have been the terms of any non-arm's length transaction had it been bargained on an arm's length basis, because no comparable transactions may have taken place and, in any event, the transaction might never have taken place at all if it had been bargained using different values.[2]

1.2.2 Disclosure of transactions

As a result of the above difficulty, accounting standards internationally have required disclosure of related party transactions and relationships, rather than adjustment of the financial statements. This is the approach adopted by the IASC in IAS 24 (see 4 below), and by the ASB in FRS 8 (see 2 below).

The main issues which have to be considered in determining the disclosures to be made are as follows:

- identification of related parties;
- types of transactions and arrangements; and
- information to be disclosed.

1.3 Additional considerations in the UK

Before the publication of FRS 8, companies legislation introduced disclosures on a piecemeal basis, which are largely restricted to transactions with directors and balances with group companies.

The legal disclosure requirements relating to loans and other transactions with directors, which are now incorporated in the Companies Act 1985, are discussed in Chapter 31. They were originally introduced in the Companies Act 1980, largely as a result of reports by DTI Inspectors on their investigations into the affairs of various companies, in which related party matters, particularly transactions with directors, featured prominently. Ironically, one of the earliest examples was the 1969 report on the affairs of Pergamon Press Limited, whose chairman was one Robert Maxwell.

The Companies Act also requires disclosure about directors' remuneration and the Financial Services Authority requires extensive disclosures by listed companies on directors' remuneration. These requirements are dealt with in Chapter 32.

In addition to the requirements of FRS 8 and the Companies Act, the Financial Services Authority and the London Stock Exchange impose additional disclosures on listed and AIM companies respectively which impinge on related party issues.

These other requirements are discussed at 3 below.

2 FRS 8

2.1 Objective

The objective of FRS 8 is 'to ensure that financial statements contain the disclosures necessary to draw attention to the possibility that the reported financial position and results may have been affected by the existence of related parties and by material transactions with them'.[3]

In FRS 8 the ASB opted for a more conventional approach than that originally advocated by the ASC in ED 46, which had proposed the disclosure of only 'abnormal' related party transactions, which it defined and illustrated. The logic behind the ASC's suggested approach was to attempt to avoid the plethora of disclosures that would inevitably arise if all transactions were to be disclosed. However, not only was this approach contrary to generally accepted international practice, but also it was seen by most commentators to be unworkable. Moreover, as noted above, there is a view that the existence of a related party relationship brings with it the possibility that future transactions may be undertaken on a non-arm's length basis and, accordingly, all material transactions with such parties should be disclosed, whatever their terms.

Accordingly, FRS 8 requires disclosure of all material related party transactions, although there are some exceptions (see 2.3.5 below), together with the names of any parties who can control the reporting entity (see 2.4 below).

FRS 8 is a short standard and its basic requirements are deceptively simple. However, it has often proved to be far from easy to apply in practice. We address the more common questions of interpretation in the following discussion.

2.2 Identification of related parties

FRS 8 sets out four general definitions of 'related party', two of which are based on the concept of 'control', and two on that of 'influence'; these are discussed in 2.2.1 below. These general definitions are supplemented by two lists of specific examples. One (in paragraph 2.5(b) of the standard) gives types of entities and individuals that are always to be regarded as related parties; the other (in paragraph 2.5(c)) lists entities and individuals that are normally, in the absence of evidence to the contrary, to be so regarded. As a shorthand, the following discussion refers to parties named in paragraph 2.5(b) as 'deemed related parties' and those in paragraph 2.5(c) as 'presumed related parties'.

In many instances it is possible to decide whether or not an entity or individual is a related party purely by reference to the lists of deemed and presumed related parties, which are discussed in 2.2.2 and 2.2.3 below. However, the standard indicates that these examples are not intended to be exhaustive.[4] It will therefore be necessary to refer to the general definitions in other cases.

The explanation section of the standard clarifies that, where relevant, the definitions are intended to include both natural and legal persons. For example, the party that 'controls' the reporting entity could be either a company (or other vehicle) or an individual. The standard also states that, while all the definitions and examples are framed in terms of single entities or individuals, they are to be read as including entities and/or individuals acting in concert.[5]

2.2.1 *General definitions of related party*

FRS 8 defines two or more parties as related parties when at any time during the financial period:

(a) one party has direct or indirect control of the other party; or

(b) the parties are subject to common control from the same source; or

(c) one party has influence over the financial and operating policies of the other party to an extent that that other party might be inhibited from pursuing at all times its own separate interests; or

(d) the parties, in entering a transaction, are subject to influence from the same source to such an extent that one of the parties to the transaction has subordinated its own separate interests.[6]

The wording of these general definitions clearly envisages reciprocity – in other words, if A is a related party of B, B is a related party of A. Somewhat inconsistently, however, this is not always the case with the more specific definitions of deemed and presumed related parties. Instances of this are noted in the discussion in 2.2.2 and 2.2.3 below.

A Definitions based on control

The definitions based on 'control' (Definition (a) and Definition (b) above) are relatively easy to understand. Control is defined as 'the ability to direct the financial and operating policies of an undertaking with a view to gaining economic benefits from its activities'.[7] The same definition is used in FRS 5 – *Reporting the substance of transactions* – in respect of 'control of another entity'.[8] It is thus not restricted to voting (i.e. ownership) control, but includes economic control as well.

Definition (a) will most obviously include the reporting entity's parent and subsidiary undertakings and any individuals controlling the entity or its ultimate parent undertaking. However, it can include other relationships, for example those between the reporting entity and its directors or other key management, or its shareholders. Indirect control is simply control exercised through another vehicle (e.g. an intermediate holding company).

Definition (b) has the effect that fellow subsidiary undertakings of the same parent are related parties of each other. It also means that members of so-called 'horizontal' groups (i.e. entities controlled by the same non-corporate shareholders such as individuals, partnerships or trusts) are related parties of each other, even though under UK company law they are not members of the same group.

The explanation section of the standard clarifies that common control is also deemed to exist where two or more parties are subject to control from boards having a 'controlling nucleus' of directors in common.[9] It is thus not open to a reporting entity to argue that common directorships can never give rise to related parties by virtue of the directors' common law duty (in the UK at least) to act in the best interests of each individual company. 'Controlling nucleus' is not defined, but the intention seems reasonably clear

B Definitions based on 'influence'

The definitions of related party based on 'influence' (Definition (c) and Definition (d) above) are far less straightforward than those based on 'control', partly because there is no specific definition of 'influence'. However, the explanation section of the standard contrasts influence with control on the criterion that the outcome (or potential outcome) of a relationship based on influence is less certain than one based on control.[10]

For example, a company can effectively compel a subsidiary to enter into a particular transaction (control). However, it cannot ensure that a 30%-owned associated undertaking enters into the same transaction, although it may well be able to persuade it to do so (influence). The practical implication of this is that, whereas the existence of a relationship based on control will generally be clear cut, the existence of one based on influence will be open to debate. This is most easily illustrated by considering the definitions themselves.

Definition (c) is similar, but not identical, to the concept of 'significant influence' used in the definition of 'associate' in FRS 9 – *Associates and Joint Ventures* – and the Companies Act. Thus, it will clearly capture the relationship between investors and their associates. However, it also covers situations where one entity influences another without having any ownership interest (e.g. through a 'friendly' director on the other entity's board).

Significantly, Definition (c) requires that the party subject to influence '*might* be' (rather than has *actually* been) inhibited from pursuing its own interests. It does not therefore seem possible to contend that Definition (c) does not apply in a particular case by arguing that, although one party (A) is subject to the influence of another (B), A *has not* failed to pursue its own interests. Rather, it would appear to be necessary to argue that A *could never* fail to pursue its own interests as the result of B's influence – a much heavier burden of proof. In this respect, the threshold at which influence is seen to exist by FRS 8 is somewhat lower than that for determining whether an investee is an associated undertaking under FRS 9, which requires the investor actually to exercise significant influence (see Chapter 7).

There is also the question of what is meant by a party's being 'inhibited from pursuing ... its separate interests'. A narrow view would be that it implies that the party has entered into a transaction on unfavourable terms. A broader view would be that it means simply that the party has entered into a transaction that it would not have undertaken otherwise, whatever its terms. This is not specifically addressed, although it seems clear that the broader view should be taken, since, as noted in 1.1 above, FRS 8 states that related party transactions can occur on arm's length terms. In other words, it is not a necessary condition of a related party transaction that one party has apparently been financially disadvantaged.

Definition (d) above is fundamentally different from all the others, in that its focus is the circumstances of individual transactions rather than the overall relationship between the parties. In contrast to Definition (c), which refers merely to the possibility that one party might influence the other, Definition (d) also requires the transacting parties actually to have been subject to common influence. Furthermore, a much stronger degree of influence is implied by Definition (d) (which requires that one party '*has subordinated* its own ... interests') than by Definition (c) (which merely requires that the party subject to influence '*might be inhibited* from pursuing ... its own ... interests'). Somewhat confusingly, Definition (d), which refers to the concept of 'influence' uses the same wording ('subordinated its separate interests') as is used in the explanation section of the standard to describe the concept of 'control' and contrast it with that of 'influence'![11]

In our view, the intention of Definition (d) can be explained only when one understands how it evolved. Originally, FRED 8 proposed that a party subject to control and another subject to influence from the same source would be related parties of each other.[12] This would have had the effect, for example, that a subsidiary and an associated undertaking of the same investor were treated as related parties. In developing FRS 8, the ASB took the view that this was both too wide and too narrow a definition of a related party. On the one hand, a subsidiary and associate of the same investor may happen to transact with each other without any interference from their common shareholder. On the other hand, a common shareholder is clearly in a position to engineer transactions not only between its subsidiaries and associates but also between different associates or joint ventures.

The final version of Definition (d) is intended to resolve this dilemma by requiring the circumstances of each case to be examined. The explanation section of the standard reinforces this point by stating that the effect of Definition (d) is that two parties are not 'necessarily' related purely because:

(a) they are both associates (or one is an associate and another a subsidiary) of the same investor; or

(b) they have a director in common.[13]

Nevertheless, and somewhat confusingly, the great majority of parties related by virtue of Definition (d) will probably fall into one or other of these categories.

Whilst we understand the difficulty facing the ASB in drafting Definition (d), we believe that the final wording is unsatisfactory, since it is clear that in practice it leads to different views being taken of similar situations, as the following example illustrates:

Example 30.1

Mr X is a director of A plc, a listed company, and the owner of B Limited. Both companies are supplied by S Limited. Mr X has negotiated a deal with S Limited to supply goods to B Limited at a discount that would not normally be available to a company of the size of B Limited.

In discussing a virtually identical situation, Wild and Creighton conclude that B Limited and S Limited are related parties under Definition (d) because they have transacted at the instigation of Mr X, who has influenced S Limited 'to subordinate its own separate interests and offer discounts that it would otherwise not have given.'[14] In our view, however, the opposite conclusion is equally valid, on the basis that S's purpose in offering discounts to B is presumably to retain and, possibly expand, its relationship with A. On this construction of the facts, S is promoting, rather than subordinating, its own interests, and therefore Definition (d) does not apply. We also question whether, given the history of Definition (d), it was ever really intended to apply to this type of situation at all.

As noted above, Definition (d) focuses on an individual transaction rather than an ongoing relationship. It would therefore seem logical that, where a party is related to the reporting entity by virtue of a transaction of a type described by Definition (d), it is only that transaction that is disclosable and not, for example, routine sales and purchases of goods. However, the standard makes it clear that two parties are related when the circumstances giving rise to the relationship exist 'at any time during the financial period'.[15] In other words, even if only one transaction of this type occurs during a financial period, all other transactions with the relevant party in that period are deemed to be related party transactions. This can lead to the slightly strange result that two parties are treated as related in one year but not the next, even though they have transacted a similar amount of business, as the following example shows:

Example 30.2

S is a subsidiary undertaking, and A an associated undertaking, of H. In both 1998 and 1999 S makes sales of £1 million of finished goods to A which, for the purposes of this example, do not fall within Definition (d). However, in 1998 A also bought a freehold property from S for £100,000 at the instigation of H, a transaction that therefore does fall within Definition (d). Thus S and A are related parties in 1998, but not in 1999. Their 1998 accounts (subject to the availability of any exemptions, discussed in 2.3.5 below) will therefore disclose related party transactions of £1.1 million (with a comparative of nil), whilst those for 1999 will show related party transactions of nil, with a comparative of £1.1 million. This verges on the misleading, since it confuses the true related party transaction with the ongoing trading relationship.

In our view, the above discussion indicates that reconsideration of Definition (d) should be a high priority for the ASB in any future review of FRS 8.

2.2.2 *Deemed related parties*

FRS 8 states that 'for the avoidance of doubt, the following are related parties of the reporting entity':

(a) its ultimate and intermediate parent undertakings, subsidiary undertakings, and fellow subsidiary undertakings;

(b) its associates and joint ventures;

(c) the investor or venturer in respect of which the reporting entity is an associate or a joint venture;

(d) directors of the reporting entity and the directors of its ultimate and intermediate parent undertakings; and

(e) pension funds for the benefit of employees of the reporting entity or of any entity that is a related party of the reporting entity.[16]

Entities falling within (a) above have not, in our experience, given rise to any difficulties of interpretation or identification in practice. Issues raised by the other categories are discussed below.

A Associates and joint ventures and their investors

As noted in 2.2.1 above, it is slightly curious that certain of the deemed and presumed related party relationships are not reciprocal. In other words, it may be the case that A and B are deemed or presumed to be related parties when A is the reporting entity, but not when B is the reporting entity. This contradicts the general definitions of related party, which explicitly assume that relationships are reciprocal in all cases. The deemed relationships between associates and their investors are a common case in point, as the following example illustrates:

Example 30.3

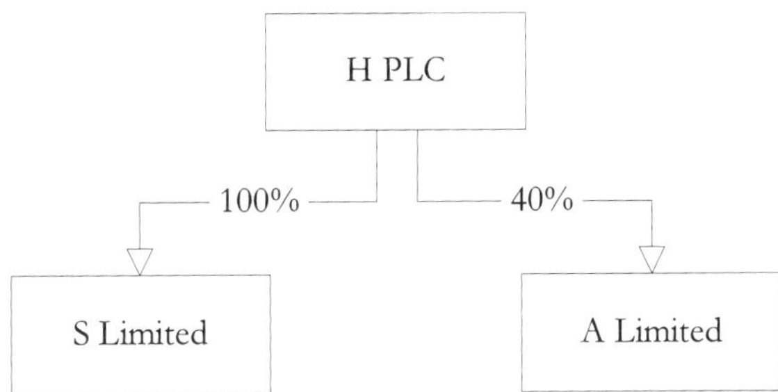

If H is the reporting entity, A is deemed to be a related party of both H and the H group (because it is an associate of both). Thus any transactions between A and either H or S will automatically be disclosed in H's accounts. If, however, A is the reporting entity, H is deemed to be a related party (because it is the investor of which A is an associated undertaking), but S is not. This has the effect that, if A transacts directly with H, those transactions will be disclosed in A's accounts, but, if it undertakes identical transactions with S, disclosure is not *automatically* required. It would be necessary to show that the relationship fell within one of the general definitions based on 'influence' discussed in 2.2.1 above, the more likely being Definition (d).

Another possible issue is that an investor and investee may have a different perception of the relationship between them. It has not been unknown for an investor to equity account for an investee which does not regard itself as being subject to significant influence from the investor, although this is now unlikely to happen following the implementation of FRS 9. In such cases, it would appear sensible to have regard to the perception of the reporting entity. However, there may still be a related party relationship by virtue of the presumption (discussed at 2.2.3 B below) that investors owning 20% or more of the reporting entity are related parties.

B Directors of the reporting entity and its parent undertakings

In treating directors of the reporting entity and its parent undertakings (but not those of its subsidiary undertakings) as related parties, FRS 8 has taken its lead from the Companies Act 1985, rather than the Financial Services Authority and the London Stock Exchange, which also treat directors of subsidiaries as related parties – see 3.3.3 below. Again echoing the Companies Act, FRS 8 states that 'directors' for this purpose include shadow directors as defined in the Act[17] (see Chapter 31 at 2.2). However, because the definition of 'materiality' used by FRS 8 is different from that used by the Companies Act, FRS 8 may well require disclosure of some transactions with directors that escape disclosure under the Companies Act. This is discussed more fully in 2.3.2 below.

A final point of detail is that, for many companies the only related party transactions are with directors and, accordingly, they are disclosed within the directors' report or the remuneration report. However, the Financial Reporting Review Panel has indicated, in its ruling on the 1997 accounts of H & C Furnishings (now Harveys Furnishings), that it interprets strictly the requirement of FRS 8 that the disclosures should be given in the 'financial statements'.[18] Thus it is not sufficient to give such disclosures in the directors' report or the remuneration report only and there should be at least a cross-reference thereto in the main accounts.

C Pension funds

Given the alleged transactions between companies controlled by Robert Maxwell and their pension funds, it was inevitable that FRS 8 would treat pension funds as deemed related parties. However, the ASB was clearly concerned that this might offend the sensitivities of some pension fund trustees. Accordingly, the standard emphasises that the fact that pension funds are treated as related parties 'is not intended to call into question the independence of trustees with regard to their fiduciary obligations to members of the scheme'. The standard goes on to say, although without explaining why, that 'transactions between the reporting entity and the pension fund may be in the interest of members but nevertheless need to be reported in the accounts of the reporting entity.'[19]

In any event, as discussed in 2.3.5 D, contributions paid to the scheme are exempt from disclosure. It is only other transactions with the reporting entity (e.g. loans, sales of fixed assets) that must be disclosed. A more common transaction in practice is the recharge of administrative costs by the sponsoring company, an example being Rank:

Extract 30.1: The Rank Group Plc (2000)

34 RELATED PARTY TRANSACTIONS [extract]

The Group recharges the Rank Group UK Pension Schemes with the costs of administration and independent pension advisers borne by the Group. The total amount recharged in the year ended 31 December 2000 was £1.8 m (1999 - £1.7m).

It is curious that a pension fund and the sponsoring employer are deemed to be related parties when the employer is the reporting entity, but not when the fund is the reporting entity. This is another example of the non-reciprocal nature of some of the deemed and presumed related party relationships referred to above. However, the SORP on accounting for pension schemes requires the sponsoring employer to be treated as a related party.[20]

2.2.3 *Presumed related parties*

FRS 8 requires that the following should be presumed to be related parties of the reporting entity:

(a) the key management of the reporting entity and the key management of its parent undertaking or undertakings;

(b) a person owning or able to exercise control over 20% or more of the voting rights of the reporting entity, whether directly or through nominees;

(c) each person acting in concert in such a way as to be able to exercise control or influence over the reporting entity; and

(d) an entity managing or managed by the reporting entity under a management contract.[21]

The presumption that the above are related parties of the reporting entity can be rebutted in a particular case only if 'it can be demonstrated that neither party has influenced the financial and operating policies of the other in such a way as to inhibit the pursuit of separate interests.'[22]

It is far from clear by virtue of which of the general definitions of related party (Definitions (a) to (d), discussed in 2.2.1 above) these parties are presumed to be related. In particular, the fact that it is possible to rebut the presumption that these parties are related if neither party '*has influenced*' the other contradicts Definition (c), which defines a relationship as created by the mere ability to exercise, rather than the actual exercise of, influence.

FRS 8 gives no guidance as to what is meant by the words 'inhibit the pursuit of separate interests'. One interpretation would be that one of the parties has been disadvantaged, financially or otherwise. However, this seems inconsistent with the ASB's view that a related party transaction can be undertaken on an arm's length basis. We therefore interpret this phrase as meaning that one of the parties has entered into a transaction that it would not have undertaken in the absence of the relationship, rather than that it has been disadvantaged. On this view, a heavy burden of proof is needed to rebut the presumption that the parties listed above are related parties if they have transacted with the reporting entity. Against that, however, as the following discussion shows, parties falling under most of these headings will be relatively rare.

A Key management

The standard defines 'key management' as 'those persons in senior positions having authority or responsibility for directing or controlling the major activities and resources of the reporting entity'.[23] This clearly cannot include directors or shadow directors, since these are treated as related parties in all circumstances, as set out in 2.2.2 above.

The main intention of the definition is presumably to ensure that transactions with persons with responsibilities similar to those of directors do not escape disclosure simply because they are not directors. This would otherwise have provided an obvious loophole in the standard. However, it is not clear whether many individuals will fall within this heading. It seems, for example, to be restricted to even fewer persons than the term 'officer' used by the Companies Act to refer to senior persons other than directors.

In the first place, the individual concerned must apparently be in a position to direct or control 'the major activities and resources' of the entity – i.e. all of them, not just one or some of them. It is doubtful whether most board directors would have such power, let alone other staff. It may be that this is a drafting slip and that the ASB's intention was that a member of key management should control '*a* major activity or resource'. This semantic quibble aside, it is still doubtful whether many persons will fall into this category. For example, a purchasing manager may have wide discretion to choose suppliers and negotiate prices, but he will generally be subject to various constraints imposed by the board, so that his authority falls short of an ability to 'direct and control' the purchasing function.

In our view, the type of person most likely to be a 'key manager' is a director of a subsidiary undertaking, but not of the holding company, who nevertheless participates in the management of the group. Companies may argue that, if the individual concerned were truly part of the 'key management' of the group, he would be on the parent company board. However, this would be inconsistent with the view taken by the ASB at the individual company level that 'key management' may be found outside the boardroom. Moreover, a review of the chairman's statement (and the photographs!) in the published accounts of certain groups makes it fairly clear that such individuals do exist.

While 'key management' would normally be employees of the reporting entity (or of a company in the same group), seconded staff and persons engaged under management or outsourcing contracts may well have a level of authority or responsibility such that they should be regarded as 'key management'. However, the wording of the definition of 'key management' appears to restrict its application to natural persons. It is hard to see how corporate entities could be regarded as 'persons in a senior position'.

Perhaps for the various reasons set out above, disclosures relating to key managers (at least, explicitly described as such) are relatively rare. An example is given by Friends' Provident, although the disclosure indicates that this effectively aggregates transactions with key management and those with directors:

Extract 30.2: Friends' Provident Life Office (2000)

33. Related party transactions [extract]

i) Key management, which includes their close family and undertakings controlled by them, had various transactions with the Group during the year. Key management consists of all directors and executive management of the Group.

In aggregate these were as set out below:	Group	
	2000	1999
	£000	£000
Payments during the year by key management in respect of policies and investments issued or managed by the Group:		
Periodic payments	**165**	110
Single payments	**811**	138
Payments during the year by the Group to key management in respect of such policies and investments	**35**	47

All these transactions were completed on terms which were no better than those available to staff.

B Shareholders owning 20% or more

There will not normally be any difficulty identifying such persons. The debate will be whether it is possible to rebut the presumption that such persons are related parties. Where the party holding 20% or more is itself a minority shareholder this may be relatively easy. In other cases, however, the issue will not be so clear cut, as the following example shows:

Example 30.4

Company A holds 25% of Company B as the result of a failed takeover bid. It has no representation on the board of Company B and does not account for it as an associated undertaking. On the face of it, it might seem possible to rebut the presumption that A exercises sufficient influence over B to require them to be treated as related parties. On the other hand, if A and B are transacting with each other, the question must be asked as to why those transactions are occurring, and this may lead to the conclusion that they are indeed related parties.

If the transactions are occurring at non-arm's length prices, the presumption must be that A and B are related parties. Even if B is purchasing goods from A on arm's length terms, it begs the question as to why B is choosing to put business in the direction of an unwelcome predator. It may be that B is anxious to maintain a good relationship with A, which could (for example) crash B's share price by suddenly offloading a large part of its shareholding on to the market. In this case B could clearly be construed as acting under the influence (albeit passive) of A. On the other hand if A were a long-standing trading partner, particularly if it were the only available supplier of a particular product, it could be reasonable to rebut the presumption that A and B are related. It would also be possible to rebut the presumption if the transactions arose from contracts entered into before the bid.

A rather curious, and we suspect unintended, side-effect of the presumption that major shareholders are related parties is that participation by those shareholders in share issues and dividends should technically be disclosed as related party transactions. In practice, however, this requirement does not generally appear to be followed strictly, presumably on the view that if both major shareholders and total transactions with shareholders are disclosed, the portion relating to individual shareholders can be readily derived. However, some companies do disclose this information, an example being Associated British Foods (see Extract 30.9 at 2.3.3 below).

C *Each person acting in concert so as to be able to control or influence the reporting entity*

'Control' and 'influence' mean the same here as in the context of the general definitions of related party discussed in 2.2.1 above.[24] Persons acting in concert 'comprise persons who, pursuant to an agreement or understanding (whether formal or informal), actively co-operate, whether through the ownership by any of them of shares in an undertaking or otherwise, to exercise control or influence over that undertaking'.[25]

The concept is clear enough. An individual who is not able to control or influence the reporting entity on his own may be able to do so by acting with others. The practical difficulty is how to identify concert parties, particularly as the standard creates a presumed related party relationship where a concert party 'is able to' (rather than actually does) control or influence the reporting entity.

It is very unlikely that a concert party would be constituted under a formal agreement, and in any event such an agreement would be a private matter between the members of the concert party. The fact that a group of shareholders consistently vote together at meetings of the company might be evidence of a concert party; on the other hand, it could simply be coincidental. As is often the case when applying FRS 8, it would be necessary to look behind the position 'on paper' to the actual circumstances of the case. For example, a group of shareholders who regularly force through controversial resolutions at extraordinary general meetings will probably comprise a concert party, whereas a group who simply vote the same way on routine matters will probably not.

D *Entities managing or managed by the reporting entity*

The relationship between an entity and one managed by it is not dissimilar to that between a company and its directors and key management. However, related parties falling under this heading may be less common than might appear at first sight, since the requirement, at least if read literally, is that one entity must manage another (i.e. as a whole). In practice, however, many management contracts cover specific assets and functions of an entity, not the entity as a whole.

Suppose that A is a property company that owns a block of flats. Under a management contract, company B manages the flats on a day-to-day basis. B is managing an asset (in fact the sole asset) of A, but is not managing A as a whole, and therefore does not apparently fall within this definition. One would therefore have to consider whether A and B fell within one of the general definitions of related party discussed above. In practice, it is very unlikely that there would be any transactions between A and B, other than the payment of the management fee. The issue would rather be whether B used its influence to initiate transactions between A and another party connected in some way with B.

A rare example of disclosure under this requirement is given by ANS:

Extract 30.3: ANS plc (2000)

29. Related Party Transactions [extract]

The following companies are deemed to be related parties by virtue of the fact that ANS plc manages their day to day operations and has influence over their financial and operating policies.

Assured Care Centres plc
ANS plc had a management contract to manage the Borehamwood Nursing Home and Close Care Units at two different sites. The management contract was terminated during the period.

Grosvenor Care plc
ANS plc had a management contract to manage The Haven Nursing Home. This home was sold by Grosvenor Care plc to ANS Homes Limited during the period.

Nightingale Nursing Homes plc
ANS plc had a management contract to manage the Nightingale Nursing Home. This contract was terminated during the period.

Summerville Nursing Homes plc
ANS plc has a management contract to manage the Summerville Nursing Home.

. . .

During the period the following amounts were charged to related parties for the following services:

Period ended 29 February 2000

	Management fees £000's	Other £000's	Total £000's
Assured Care Centres plc	11	–	11
Grosvenor Care plc	13	–	13
Nightingale Nursing Homes plc	12	–	12
Summerville Nursing Homes plc	–	–	5
	36	5	41

...

The following amounts were outstanding at:
Period ended 29 February 2000

	Management fees £000's	Construction fees £000's	Other £000's	Total £000's
Summerville Nursing Homes plc	131	14	1	146

...

2.2.4 *Close family and controlled entities*

Where an individual is identified as a related party of the reporting entity, there is a presumption that the following are also related parties:

(a) the 'close family' of that individual; and

(b) any partnerships, companies, trusts or other entities controlled by that individual or his 'close family'.[26]

A Close family

'Close family' of an individual is defined as 'those family members, or members of the same household, who may be expected to influence, or be influenced by, that person in their dealings with the reporting entity'.[27] FRED 8 referred to 'immediate' rather than 'close' family and listed the relatives who would normally fall under this heading. FRS 8 abandoned this approach, on the basis that the degree of influence arising from the relationship is more important than its immediacy. However, we assume that 'close family' in FRS 8 is normally intended to include at least those relatives identified as 'immediate family' in FRED 8, i.e. a spouse, parent, child (adult or minor), brother, sister and the spouses of any of these.[28]

The definition refers to the person's 'dealings' with the reporting entity, but it does not make it clear whether the standard is concerned with dealings in a business capacity only, or also those in a private capacity. We presume that the former only are intended. Otherwise it would, for example, be necessary (subject to considerations of materiality) for a food retailer to disclose details of each director's household shopping at its supermarkets!

An example of a disclosure made as a result of this requirement (and, to some extent, possibly Part II of Schedule 6 to the Companies Act as well) is given by Kwik-Fit (Sir Tom Farmer being at that time the chairman and chief executive):

Extract 30.4: Kwik-Fit Holdings plc (1999)

9. DIRECTORS' REMUNERATION AND INTERESTS [extract]
(d) Transactions [extract]

Sir Tom and Lady Farmer and family lease certain properties to the Group. The rentals payable on these properties were £348,837 (1998 – £341,000) and the balance owing by the Group at 28 February 1999 was Nil (1998 – Nil).

B Controlled entities

Although FRS 8 does not specify whether legal or de facto control is intended in this context, we believe that the broad definition of control used elsewhere in the standard is meant to apply. In other words, controlled entities are not restricted to those subject to legal control. Kwik-Fit provides examples of disclosure that may have been given in pursuance of this provision of the standard, although they could equally have been given in order to comply with one or more requirements of Schedule 6 to the Companies Act:

Extract 30.5: Kwik-Fit Holdings plc (1999)

9. DIRECTORS' REMUNERATION AND INTERESTS [extract]
(d) Transactions [extract]

E. Landau is a partner in Landau Nock who received professional fees and reimbursement of expenses of £476,933 (1998 – £479,578) in relation to services provided to the Group during the year. The balance owing to Landau Nock at 28 February 1999 was Nil (1998 – Nil).

J. Padget is a Principal of Padget Associates B.V. who received fees of £65,623 (1998 – £107,446) and reimbursement of expenses of £10,562 (1998 – £16,002) in relation to services provided to the Group during the year in addition to the Director's fees shown in (a) above. The balance owing to Padget Associates B.V. at 28 February 1999 was Nil (1998 – £53,439).

Entities controlled by an individual related party are a further example of a presumed related party relationship that is not reciprocal, as the following example illustrates. Suppose that Mr X is a director of A plc and the owner of B Limited. If A is the reporting entity, B is presumed to be a related party (because it is an entity controlled by Mr X, who, being a director of A, is a deemed related party of A). However, if B is the reporting entity, A is not presumed to be a related party (because FRS 8 does not presume that a company, a director of which controls the reporting entity, is a related party of the reporting entity).

This seems slightly counter intuitive, since, if A (a listed company) and B (a small private company) are transacting, the chances are that those transactions are in fact more significant to B than to A. However, this is not the end of the matter, since it could be that A and B are related parties by virtue of one of the general definitions discussed in 2.2.1 above.

C Rebutting the presumption

We assume that the presumption that close family and controlled entities are related parties is rebuttable, although the standard provides no guidance as to whether, or on what basis, it may be rebutted. In general, though, it seems very difficult to rebut the presumption where transactions are occurring.

Suppose, for example, that the reporting entity X buys widely available raw materials from Y, a company controlled by Mrs A, the sister of Mr B, a director of X. The transactions are on normal commercial terms, but as has been emphasised elsewhere, the standard takes the view that this is not relevant. Rather, the basic question that must be addressed is why, out of all of the suppliers in the country, the reporting entity chose Y. Is it really credible that it had nothing to do with the family connection between Mrs A and Mr B?

2.2.5 Parties presumed not to be related parties

FRS 8 does not require the following entities to be treated as related parties:

(a) providers of finance in the ordinary course of business;

(b) utility companies;

(c) government departments and their sponsored bodies; or

(d) parties with whom the reporting entity transacts a significant volume of business.[29]

The reason for this exemption is that, without it, many entities that would not normally be regarded as related parties could fall within the general definitions of related party. For example, a small clothing manufacturer selling 90% of its output to a high street chain could be under the effective control of that customer. The ASB has already (and more appropriately) addressed the issue in its Statement on the *Operating and Financial Review* (OFR), under the heading of 'Dynamics of the business'. Here it is suggested that the OFR should discuss the main factors and influences that may have a major effect on future results, whether or not they were significant in the period under review; for example, dependence on major suppliers or customers.[30]

The exemption is effective only where these parties would be considered as related to the reporting entity 'simply as a result of their role' as providers of finance etc. If there are other reasons why a party would be considered a related party, the exemption does not apply.[31] For example, the water company that supplies the reporting entity is not considered a related party if the only link between the two is the supply of water. If, however, the water company is also an associated undertaking of the reporting entity, the exemption does not apply and the two are considered related parties, in which case transactions relating to the supply of water must be disclosed if material.

2.3 Disclosure of related party transactions

FRS 8 requires disclosure of material related party transactions in the 'financial statements'.[32] Where disclosure is made in another part of the annual report (e.g. the directors' report, remuneration report, or OFR), it is important that there is a cross-reference to it in the main body of the accounts, particularly in view of the Review Panel's ruling on the 1997 accounts of H & C Furnishings (see 2.2.2 B above).

A transaction is defined as 'the transfer of assets or liabilities or the performance of services by, to or for a related party irrespective of whether a price is charged'.[33] Read literally, this definition requires many transactions to be disclosed more than once. For example, if a company buys goods on credit from a related party and pays for them 30 days later, both the original sale and the final payment represent a 'transfer of assets … by [or] to … a related party' and should therefore on the face of it be separately disclosed. However, we doubt that this was the ASB's intention, and the nature of the disclosures required by FRS 8 seems to support this view.

2.3.1 *Disclosable transactions*

FRS 8 provides a list, not intended to be exhaustive, of the types of transaction which should be disclosed:

(a) purchases or sales of goods (finished or unfinished);

(b) purchases or sales of property and other assets;

(c) rendering or receiving of services;

(d) agency arrangements;

(e) leasing arrangements;

(f) transfer of research and development;

(g) licence agreements;

(h) provision of finance (including loans and equity contributions in cash or in kind);

(i) guarantees and the provision of collateral security; and

(j) management contracts.[34]

The standard emphasises that disclosure is required irrespective of whether or not a price is charged.[35] This means that the standard applies to gifts of assets or services and to asset swaps. Common examples of such transactions include:

- administration by a company of the company pension scheme free of charge;
- transfer of group relief from one member of a group to another without payment;
- guarantees by directors of bank loans to the company.

2.3.2 *Materiality*

FRS 8, like all accounting standards, applies only to material items. However, the standard contains a definition of materiality that goes well beyond the undefined concept in general use, which focuses more on the financial effect on the company's accounts, and is often thought of as a percentage of turnover, profit or net assets.

For the purposes of FRS 8, 'transactions are material when their disclosure might reasonably be expected to influence decisions made by the users of general purpose financial statements'.[36] This has the effect that virtually any related party transaction whose disclosure is sensitive (for tax reasons perhaps) is by definition material, because it is expected by the reporting entity to influence a user of the accounts. It is therefore not possible to avoid disclosing such items on the grounds that they are financially immaterial.

FRS 8 does not clarify whether the materiality of transactions is to be considered individually or in aggregate. Whilst a literal reading of the standard suggests that they should be considered individually, such an interpretation cannot, in our view, be correct, since it would effectively frustrate the intentions of the standard, as the following example shows:

Example 30.5

H plc is a small listed company for which transactions of £1 million or more are regarded as material. Each month it makes sales of £90,000 to its associated undertaking A. If each transaction is considered in isolation no disclosure would be made. If, however, the total transactions for the year (i.e. £1,080,000) are considered together disclosure would be made. In this case, we believe that the latter interpretation is correct.

The situation becomes less clear, however, if for example H had made sales of £90,000 to each of twelve different associates, or to an assortment of associates, joint venture partners and its pension fund. In such cases, it seems more important to focus on the likelihood that disclosure of the transactions will influence a reader of the accounts than on their purely financial materiality.

In addition, where the related party is:

(a) a director, key manager, or other individual in a position to influence, or accountable for stewardship of, the reporting entity;

(b) a member of the close family of any individual within (a) above; or

(c) an entity controlled by any individual within (a) or (b) above,

the standard requires the materiality of related party transactions with such individuals and entities to be judged 'not only in terms of their significance to the reporting entity, but also in relation to the other related party'.[37] The intention is clearly to ensure that transactions that could be beneficial to individuals do not escape disclosure on the basis that they are immaterial to the reporting entity.

This requirement impacts mainly on disclosure of transactions with directors and persons or companies connected with them. Such transactions are prima facie disclosable under Part II of Schedule 6 to the Companies Act, except when the interest of the director concerned is not considered material. Prior to FRS 8, there was some debate as to whether materiality should be judged by reference to the circumstances of the company or those of the director (see Chapter 31 at 3.5). FRS 8 now requires materiality to be judged by reference to the circumstances of both parties. We have considerable doubts as to the wisdom of this aspect of FRS 8. As a matter of principle, it seems wrong that an accounting standard should require disclosure of transactions that are not material to the truth and fairness of the accounts. If it is thought desirable to make such disclosures for other reasons, the proper place to make them is in the report on corporate governance matters, not the financial statements. In addition, strict application of the requirement could lead to anomalies, as the following example shows:

Example 30.6

X PLC sells two company cars to two retiring directors, Mr A and Mr B, for £10,000 and £15,000 respectively, which are their fair market values. Neither transaction is material to the company. Mr A earns £40,000 and Mr B £400,000 a year. The effect of FRS 8 could be that the (lower) £10,000 transaction is disclosed (because it is material to Mr A, but not the company), but that the (higher) £15,000 transaction is not (because it is not material either to the company or to Mr B).

In practice, many companies, perhaps mindful of the spirit of the Combined Code and its predecessors, the Cadbury and Greenbury codes, seem to prefer to disclose details of all transactions with which a director is associated, whether they are material or not and even where the third party would not strictly be regarded as a related party by either FRS 8 or the Companies Act. An example of this was given in the 1996 accounts of Redland PLC (the 'Braas group companies' referred to then being subsidiaries of Redland):

Extract 30.6: Redland PLC (1996)

19 Related Party Transactions [extract]

Mrs H Bruhn-Braas, a non-executive director of Redland PLC, has a controlling interest in BTI. During the year ended 31st December 1996, Braas group companies paid to BTI a total of £16.2 million for transportation services on an arm's length basis. At 31st December 1996, the Braas group owed BTI £0.8 million.

Mr DRW Young, an executive director of Redland PLC, is Chairman and a director of Young Samuel Chambers (YSC) Limited, a management consultancy company, which provided Redland companies with services invoiced at a cost of £17,131 during the year ended 31st December 1996. The amount involved is not considered material to either party. Mr Young has no financial interest in, nor received any director's fees from, YSC in 1996.

Whilst we are obviously not privy to the full facts, it is our view that, on the basis of the above descriptions, the transaction involving Mrs Bruhn-Braas did require disclosure, but that involving Mr Young strictly did not and appears to have been given more for the sake of completeness.

Some companies disclose that immaterial transactions have taken place with directors, but do not quantify them. An example is Royal Sun Alliance:

> *Extract 30.7: Royal & Sun Alliance Insurance Group plc (2000)*
>
> 43 **TRANSACTIONS WITH RELATED PARTIES** [extract]
>
> A number of the directors, other key managers, their close families and entities under their control have general and/or long term insurance policies with subsidiary companies of the Group. Such policies are on normal commercial terms except that executive directors and key managers are entitled to special rates which are also available to other members of staff. The Board has considered the financial effect of such insurance policies and other transactions with Group companies and has concluded that they are not material to the Group or the individuals concerned and, if disclosed, would not influence decisions made by users of these financial statements.
>
> The Board has also concluded that there are no transactions with other directors or key managers that are material to their own financial affairs.

This represents quite extensive disclosure in respect of items that do not require disclosure! Perhaps this indicates that the company shares our doubts as to whether FRS 8 really intended to capture transactions such as this, but is concerned not to be seen as ignoring the prima facie requirement for disclosure.

An example of a company which actually quantified what it regarded as a material transaction for its directors was Norwich Union.

> *Extract 30.8: Norwich Union plc (1998)*
>
> **Remuneration report of the Board** [extract]
>
> 10. ...
>
> For the purpose of reporting related party transactions with directors, as required by FRS 8, materiality of transactions has to be considered in the context of the financial affairs of each director. The directors consider that transactions with individual directors which total less than £10,000 are immaterial. ...

In our view, there is a clear case in any future revision of FRS 8 to exempt from disclosure transactions undertaken on non-preferential terms by individuals in a private (as opposed to a business) capacity with companies whose normal business is trading directly with the general public (e.g. high street banks, certain insurance companies, and retailers).

2.3.3 *Disclosures required*

FRS 8 requires the following details to be given in respect of related party transactions:

(a) the names of the related parties;

(b) a description of the relationship between the parties;

(c) a description of the transactions;

(d) the amounts involved;

(e) any other elements of the transactions necessary for an understanding of the financial statements;

(f) the amounts due to or from related parties at the balance sheet date and provisions for doubtful debts due from such parties at that date; and

(g) amounts written off in the period in respect of debts due to or from related parties.[38]

A comprehensive example of the required disclosures, covering various categories of related party, is given by Associated British Foods.

Extract 30.9: Associated British Foods plc (2000)

31. Related party transactions

The group's related parties, as defined by Financial Reporting Standard 8, the nature of the relationship and the extent of the transactions with them are summarised below:

	Sub note	**2000 £'000**	1999 £'000
Management charge from Wittington Investments Limited, principally in respect of directors and secretarial staff of ABF paid by Wittington	1	**450**	450
Charges to Wittington Investments Limited in respect of services provided by the company and its subsidiary undertakings	1	**(57)**	(43)
Dividends paid by the company and received in a beneficial capacity by:			
(i) Trustees of The Garfield Weston Foundation	2	**3,118**	19,768
(ii) Directors of Wittington Investments Limited who are not Trustees of The Foundation		**563**	3,568
(iii) Directors of the company who are not Trustees of The Foundation and are not directors of Wittington Investments Limited	3	**9**	71
(iv) a member of the Weston family employed within the group	4	**313**	1,985
		£m	£m
Sales to fellow subsidiary on normal trading terms	5	**5**	7
Amounts due from fellow subsidiary undertaking	5	**–**	1
Sales to joint ventures and associates on normal trading terms	6	**46**	50
Purchases from joint ventures and associates on normal trading terms	6	**7**	6
Amounts due from joint ventures and associates	6	**6**	5
Amounts due to joint ventures and associates	6	**3**	1

Sub notes

1. At 16 September 2000 Wittington Investments Limited together with its subsidiary undertaking, Howard Investments Limited, held 431,515,108 ordinary shares (1999 – 416,955,671) representing in aggregate 54.5% (1999 – 52.7%) of the total issued ordinary share capital of the company.
2. The Garfield Weston Foundation ("The Foundation") is an English charitable trust, established in 1958 by the late W Garfield Weston. The foundation has no direct interest in the company, but as at 16 September 2000 held 683,073 shares in Wittington Investments Limited representing 79.2% of that company's issued share capital and is, therefore, the company's ultimate controlling party. At 16 September 2000, trustees of The Foundation comprised six of the late W Garfield Weston's children, including Garry H Weston, chairman of the board of trustees, and four of Garry H Weston's children.
3. Details of the directors are given on page 28. Their beneficial interests, including family interests, in the company and its subsidiary undertakings are given on page 34. Directors' remuneration, including share options, is disclosed on pages 31 to 33.
4. A member of the Weston family who is employed by the group and is not a director of the company or Wittington Investments Limited and is not a Trustee of the Foundation.
5. The fellow subsidiary undertaking is Fortnum and Mason plc.
6. Details of the group's principal joint ventures and associates are set out on page 68.

None of the disclosures appears to present much practical difficulty, other than, in some cases, sensitivity. In Extract 30.9 above, for instance, the name of the 'member of the Weston family employed within the ABF group' has not been given as strictly required by the standard (although, in our view, and presumably that of the company, it would add no useful additional information).

One possible problem area is the need to give 'any other elements of the transactions necessary for an understanding of the financial statements'. This is one of the less clear requirements of FRS 8. It was proposed in FRED 8, which noted in the explanatory section that 'an example falling within this requirement would be a material difference between the fair value and the transacted amount where material transfers of assets, liabilities or services have taken place'.[39] This provoked some adverse comment, largely because of the difficulties in calculating it.

There was also some concern that the proposals in FRED 8 would have required commercially sensitive transfer pricing information to be given. In fact, such concern was misplaced since nearly all such transactions would have been exempt from disclosure as being between members of the same group (see 2.3.5 below). Be that as it may, the ASB attempted to address these concerns by modifying the final wording in FRS 8 to say that an example of a disclosure falling within this requirement 'would be the need to give an indication that the transfer of a major asset had taken place at an amount materially different from that obtainable on normal commercial terms'.[40]

We consider this somewhat confusing. Either fair value disclosures are required or they are not; and if they are, the requirement should be in the main body of the proposed standard, rather than dealt with almost in passing in the explanation section. Our strong view is that FRS 8 should not require disclosure of the fair value of transactions, since it is often impossible to calculate them meaningfully. We suspect that the underlying objective is to indicate the entity's true economic performance, as if it were unaffected by the influence of related parties. But this may not reflect the reality of the reporting entity's position, since many transactions with related parties would simply not occur at all if the parties were unrelated and it would be misleading to disclose the terms on which they might have been undertaken with third parties.

Example 30.7

A company sells a surplus property whose fair value is said to be £2 million to a related party for £1.5 million. If the financial statements were to disclose the transaction in these bald terms, users would inevitably infer that the company's interests had been prejudiced to the tune of £500,000. However, it may be the case that, in the market conditions at the time, the chances of making any sale were unlikely, and the company is better off with £1.5 million now than the off-chance of £2 million in several months' time. In these circumstances, a case could be made that the property's fair value, on the basis of an immediate sale to a third party, was nearer zero than £2 million, although few would regard a disclosure to this effect as acceptable either.

Perhaps, given the history of this paragraph, there is room to argue that the example in the standard is a hint that fair value information is required for 'one-off' capital transactions but not for ongoing revenue items. However, this is a frankly unsatisfactory distinction, for which there can be no conceptual justification. On the other hand, from a pragmatic point of view, it would deal with preparers' concerns about giving sensitive pricing information, which is generally more of an issue when the transfer of goods or services is involved.

A further complication arises where assets, liabilities or services are transferred without charge. Where an asset or liability is transferred free of charge, its carrying amount prior to transfer gives at least a starting point for disclosing the value of the transaction. Problems may arise, however, with such items as ceded tax losses which may arguably have markedly different values to the transferor and transferee (e.g. because they can be used by the transferee sooner than by the transferor, or because there is a tax rate difference).

FRS 8 discourages companies from making 'boiler plate' disclosures to the effect that transactions have been undertaken on normal commercial terms. Such assertions should not be made 'unless the parties have conducted the transactions in an independent manner'. The standard clearly implies that the ASB believes this will rarely be the case, although it gives as a possible example the situation where two fellow subsidiary undertakings deal with each other without interference from their parent.[41] Notwithstanding this hint in the standard, however, disclosures that transactions have been undertaken on an arm's length basis are very common, as shown by the extracts from Redland (Extract 30.6 at 2.3.2 above), Royal Sun Alliance (Extract 30.7 at 2.3.2 above) and Associated British Foods (Extract 30.9 above).

2.3.4 *Aggregation*

Because of the voluminous disclosures that could result if each related party transaction were shown separately, FRS 8 permits aggregation of similar transactions with similar parties. However, this should not be done in a way that obscures the importance of significant transactions. For example, purchases or sales of goods with group companies could be aggregated, but any purchases or sales of fixed assets with such companies should be shown as a separate category. Equally, it would not be acceptable to aggregate sales of fixed assets to group companies with sales of fixed assets to key management.[42]

Most companies have taken advantage of the opportunity to aggregate disclosures in this way, very often in relation to transactions with associated undertakings. BPB adopts the aggregated approach in respect of trading transactions, but gives separate disclosure of what it presumably regards as a significant loan transaction with an individual joint venture.

Extract 30.10: BPB plc (2001)

28 Related party transactions [extract]

During the year the group purchased goods from, and sold goods to, its associated companies and joint ventures for £4.1 million and £2.2 million respectively *(2000 £0.9 million and £2.5 million).* The amounts outstanding at the year end on these purchases and sales were £0.8 million and £0.6 million respectively *(2000 £0.1 million and £0.3 million).*

The group received royalties from associated companies of £0.1 million *(2000 £0.4 million).* In addition, the group recharged £1.3 million (*2000 £1.6 million*) to its associated companies in respect of administrative costs incurred on their behalf; the amount outstanding at the year end was £0.1 million *(2000 £0.4 million).*

At the year end, loans outstanding from associated companies totalled £1.2 million *(2000 £0.2 million).* A loan from BPB United Kingdom Ltd to a joint venture, British Gypsum-Isover Ltd, of £9.0 million was outstanding *(2000 £10.5 million).*

However, BAE Systems discloses trading transactions with each of its main joint ventures separately, presumably because these transactions form such a significant part of its business:

Extract 30.11: BAE SYSTEMS plc (2000)

31 Related party transactions

The Group has an interest in a number of joint ventures as disclosed in note 12. Transactions occur with these joint ventures in the normal course of business. The more significant transactions are disclosed below.

Related party	Sales to related party £m	Purchases from related party £m	Amounts owed by related party £m	Amounts owed to related party £m
Airbus Industrie GIE	1,400	–	–	–
Eurofighter Jagdflugzeug GmbH	573	–	72	–
Matra BAe Dynamics SAS	56	7	36	140
Panavia Aircraft GmbH	97	78	18	–
Saab AB	10	6	1	–
Alenia Marconi Systems NV	39	47	15	7
Thomson Marconi Sonar NV	1	25	–	5

FRS 8 additionally requires that any material transactions with an individual should be shown separately and not aggregated with others.[43] Thus, if a company sells two assets to two different directors, and the transactions are both material, they cannot be grouped as 'Sales to directors' but must be disclosed individually.

A Transactions with directors and officers of banking companies

As discussed more fully in 4.1 of Chapter 31, the Companies Act permits banking companies to disclose in aggregate certain types of transactions with directors which other (non-banking) companies would be required to disclose for each individual director. Banking companies that take advantage of this exemption are also exempt from the requirement of FRS 8 to give individual disclosure of these transactions, by virtue of the *Foreword to Accounting Standards*; this states that 'where accounting standards prescribe information to be contained in financial statements, such requirements do not override exemptions from disclosure given by law to, and utilised by, certain types of entity'.[44]

2.3.5 *Exemptions from disclosure*

FRS 8 does not require disclosure:

(a) in consolidated financial statements, of any transactions or balances between group entities that have been eliminated on consolidation;

(b) in a parent's own financial statements when those statements are presented together with its consolidated financial statements;

(c) in financial statements of subsidiary undertakings, 90 per cent or more of whose voting rights are controlled within the group, of transactions with entities that are part of the group or investees of the group qualifying as related parties, provided that the consolidated financial statements in which that subsidiary is included are publicly available;

(d) of contributions paid to a pension fund; or

(e) of emoluments in respect of services as an employee of the reporting entity.

Reporting entities that take advantage of exemption (c) are required to state that fact.[45] Although these exemptions appear quite extensive, in many cases they are effectively over-ridden by other requirements, as explained in the following discussion.

A Transactions eliminated on consolidation

This is not so much an exemption as a statement of the obvious since, so far as the group accounts are concerned, such items do not exist. The effect is that no related party disclosures relating to subsidiary undertakings are required in group accounts. However, disclosure is still required in respect of transactions or balances with associates or joint ventures since these are not 'eliminated' on consolidation, although they may be subject to consolidation adjustments.

Where a subsidiary joins or leaves the group during the period, it is treated as a related party for the whole period, not just for the period when it is a subsidiary, because FRS 8 makes it clear that two parties are related when the circumstances giving rise to the relationship exist 'at any time during the financial period'.[46] Where the reporting entity has transacted with such a company during the part of the period when it was not a member of the group, the transactions during that time will not have been eliminated on consolidation and, accordingly, must be disclosed. An example of such disclosure was given in the 1996 accounts of Thomas Cook:

Extract 30.12: Thomas Cook Limited (1996)

27. Related party disclosures [extract]

On 28 June 1996, Sunworld Limited and its subsidiaries were acquired. Trading between this entity and the Thomas Cook Group post acquisition has been eliminated upon consolidation. However, from 1 January 1996 to the point of acquisition, it is classed as a related party under FRS 8. Sales to the Thomas Cook Group during this period were £23.2 million.

In 1999 Kwik-Fit disclosed transactions with a company that had been an associate for part of the accounting period, before becoming a wholly-owned subsidiary.

Extract 30.13: Kwik-Fit Holdings plc (1999)

32. GROUP UNDERTAKINGS [extract]
(c) Transactions with associated undertakings [extract]

Up to the date of its acquisition by the Company, Apples Limited had rent of £924,306 (1998 – £1,238,962) and invoice collection fees of £115,232 (1998 – £97,890) payable to the Group. During that period, the Group purchased servicing costs for resale of £1,150,480 (1998 – £1,215,795) from Apples Limited.

This extract highlights an inevitable anomaly arising from the disclosures required by FRS 8 in that the comparative figures represent amounts for the whole prior period, and the current year figures cover only the nine-month period when Apples Limited was an associate (since transactions after that period will have been eliminated on consolidation and are therefore exempt from disclosure). However, it may well have been the case that the actual transactions between the two entities in each period were not significantly different.

An example of disclosure of the converse situation of a company leaving a group was given in the 1998 accounts of Debenhams.

Extract 30.14: Debenhams plc (1998)

32 RELATED PARTY TRANSACTIONS [extract]

On 26 January 1998, Debenhams demerged from Burton Group (now known as Arcadia Group plc). Prior to that date Burton Group exercised control over all of the operations of Debenhams and provided a number of group services to those operations. All transactions since 26 January 1998 have been on an arms length basis on normal commercial terms.

In 1998, Arcadia raised management charges of £nil (1997: £32.2 million) in respect of the continuing operations and recharged Debenhams for central service costs of £nil in 1998 (1997: £15.6 million). It has not been practicable to quantify all other, and less material, services arising between the Arcadia Group and Debenhams.

B Parent company financial statements when group accounts presented

This exemption is largely a logical extension of the last. However, this is a case where the requirements of other pronouncements largely negate the FRS 8 exemption. For example:

- the statutory accounts formats in Schedules 4, 9 and 9A to the Companies Act require separate disclosure in the parent company balance sheet of balances with subsidiary and associated undertakings (see 3.1.3 G below); and
- Part II of Schedule 6 to the Companies Act requires disclosure of certain transactions between directors of the parent company and group companies (see Chapter 31 at 3.3).

Also, all related party transactions of the company (other than those eliminated on consolidation) will in any event be disclosed in the group accounts. Parent companies that do not prepare group accounts (e.g. those heading small or medium-sized groups, or subsidiaries of parents complying with the EU Seventh Directive) have to comply with FRS 8 in full in their own accounts, subject to the '90% subsidiary' exemption (see C below).

C *Transactions with group investees in accounts of 90% (or more) owned subsidiaries*

This exemption covers only transactions with members, or investees (such as associates and joint ventures), of the group. Transactions with other types of related party (e.g. directors or major shareholders) must still be disclosed. In our view, this exemption is unsatisfactory for a number of reasons and should be carefully re-examined by the ASB in any future review of FRS 8.

The choice of 90%-owned subsidiaries as a threshold is odd, since it is unclear whose interest it serves. If the general public is regarded as the main user, it is sufficient for them to be aware that the reporting entity is a subsidiary undertaking, whatever the level of ownership. If, however, the intention is to protect the interests of minority shareholders, a 100% threshold would have been more appropriate. The standard suggests that the choice of 90% is a pragmatic compromise to deal with subsidiaries with small amounts of voting preference shares, or small numbers of shares held by employees.[47]

Be that as it may, the following examples show how the exemption can lead to plainly anomalous results:

Example 30.8

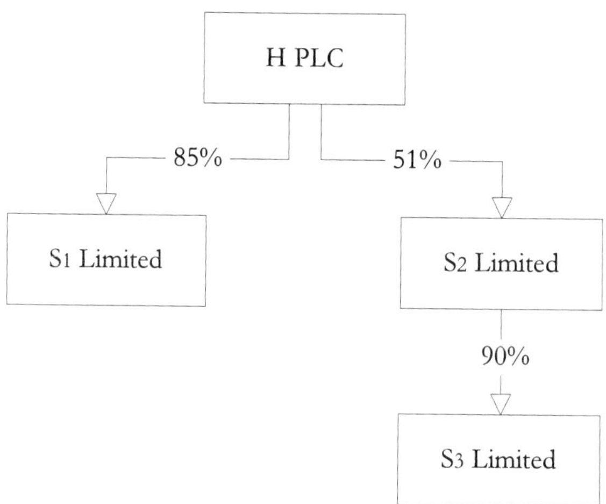

The minority shareholding in S1 Limited is owned by the controlling shareholder of H, whereas those of S2 and S3 are held by completely independent third parties. S1 is not eligible to claim the exemption because only 85% of its voting rights are controlled within the H group. However, S3 can claim the exemption because 90% of its voting rights are controlled by the H group, even though H's effective interest in S3 is only 46%. This means that, if S1 transacts with S3, details of the transactions must, somewhat perversely, be given in the accounts of S1 (whose minority shareholder is presumably fully aware of the transactions), but not those of S3 (whose minority shareholders may not be).

Example 30.9

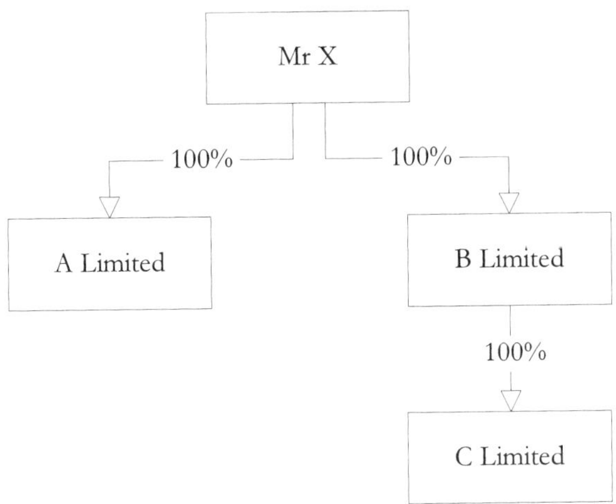

C derives 50% of its profit from transactions with A and 50% from transactions with B. Assuming that B Limited prepares group accounts, C will not have to disclose details of its transactions with B, but will have to disclose details of those with A, even though in substance there is little difference between them. This is because A is a related party of C (both are under the common control of Mr X), but not an investee of the B group.

It should be emphasised, however, that the over-riding requirement for accounts to give a true and fair view may still require disclosure of transactions covered by an exemption under FRS 8.

FRS 8 does not provide explicit guidance on the situation where the reporting entity seeking to claim the exemption is not a 90% (or more) owned subsidiary for the whole period. However, we interpret the phrase 'in the financial statements of subsidiary undertakings' as indicating that it is the status of the reporting entity at the balance sheet date that is relevant.

The exemption is simply conditional upon group accounts including the reporting entity being 'publicly available', without any further requirement for the group accounts concerned to give related party disclosures comparable to those required by FRS 8 (or, for that matter, to be in English or even the Western alphabet!). A further issue is that, even if the group accounts comply with FRS 8, many of the transactions exempt from disclosure at the subsidiary level will be eliminated on consolidation and will therefore not be disclosed at the group level either.

If the group accounts on which the exemption depends will not provide users with the information omitted from the subsidiary's accounts, it is in practice irrelevant whether or not they are publicly available. Perhaps it is for this reason that the standard requires companies taking advantage of this exemption to disclose that they have done so.

In our view, for the exemption to be available it is not necessary for the group accounts concerned to be deposited in some central bureau comparable to Companies House in the UK. They could equally be 'publicly available' on request, from the offices of an overseas parent for example. However, companies taking advantage of the exemption will be subject to the Companies Act requirement to disclose the address from which group accounts can be obtained (see 3.1.3 A below).[48]

In any event, this exemption is largely negated by other requirements. For example, the accounts formats in the Companies Act and FRS 9 – *Associates and Joint Ventures* – require some information, particularly year-end balances, to be given in respect of transactions with group companies and investees.

All in all, we consider this exemption ill-thought out and urge the ASB to reconsider it in any future review of FRS 8. We much prefer the approach of the equivalent exemption in the international standard IAS 24 (see 4.3 below).

D Pension contributions to a pension fund

This seems a reasonable exemption and, as noted above, may have been granted in order to mitigate the requirement to treat pension funds as related parties in all circumstances. However, the information may well be given more or less directly in the disclosures required by SSAP 24 – *Accounting for pension costs*, particularly in the case of defined contribution schemes. Nevertheless, once a company has to implement the necessary requirements of FRS 17 – *Retirement benefits*, the information will be given explicitly as part of the reconciliation of the movement in the balance sheet figure for pension costs.[49] The exemption covers only contributions paid to the scheme and not, for example, refunds of surpluses and other transactions with the scheme.

E Emoluments in respect of services as an employee of the reporting entity

In many cases, this will be over-ridden by the disclosure requirements in respect of directors' emoluments contained in Part I of Schedule 6 to the Companies Act and, for listed companies, the Financial Services Authority requirements. It does, however, mean that salaries of key management other than directors do not need to be disclosed. There is no requirement that such amounts must be paid under a contract of employment, so that ex gratia bonuses and similar payments are exempt from disclosure.

Fees paid to directors (particularly non-executive directors) in their capacity as such may not be exempt from disclosure under FRS 8, since they are not 'emoluments is respect of services as an *employee*'. However, this is unlikely to have much practical significance. So far as listed companies are concerned, fees for each director will be disclosed under the Financial Services Authority requirements. For other companies, if they have non-executive directors at all, the materiality of the amounts involved will mean that disclosure of fees by individual director will rarely be required.

2.3.6 *Transactions subject to a duty of confidentiality*

In addition to the types of transaction discussed in 2.3.5 above, FRS 8 does not require any related party transaction to be disclosed where this would involve the reporting entity's breaching a legal duty of confidentiality. It is clear from the explanatory section of the standard that this concession is aimed principally at banks and similar institutions and covers only those obligations imposed by a generally applicable statute or common law. It does not include the effects of terms in a private contract, for the obvious reason that compliance with the standard would otherwise be voluntary, because companies could insert a confidentiality clause in all related party contracts.[50]

2.4 Disclosure of control

FRS 8 asserts that where a reporting entity is controlled by another party, that fact is relevant information, irrespective of whether transactions have taken place with that party. This is because the control relationship prevents the reporting entity from having independent discretionary power over its resources and transactions. The standard goes on to suggest that the existence and identity of the controlling party may sometimes be at least as relevant in appraising an entity's prospects as are the performance and financial position presented in its accounts. The reason is that the controlling party may establish the entity's credit standing, determine the source and price of its raw materials, determine the products it sells, to whom and at what price, and may affect the source, calibre and allegiance of its management.[51]

Where the reporting entity is controlled by another party, FRS 8 requires it to disclose the identity of that controlling party and, if different, of the ultimate controlling party. This disclosure is required irrespective of whether or not the entity has entered into any transactions with the controlling party or parties. If the ultimate controlling party is not known, that fact should be disclosed.[52] The controlling party simply means, in the context of a company, the entity or individual that directly controls the company. The ultimate controlling party means the entity or individual at the top of any 'chain' that controls the immediate controlling party.

For many companies this requirement will be satisfied by disclosing the names of the immediate and ultimate parent companies, the latter being required already by the Companies Act. However, FRS 8 also requires the identification of non-corporate controlling persons such as trusts, partnerships or individuals. An example of disclosure of control by a trust is given by Associated British Foods (see Extract 30.9 in 2.3.3 above).

Control by directors is disclosed in the directors' report by virtue of the Companies Act requirement to give certain details of directors' interests in the shares of the company and other group companies.[53] However, FRS 8 requires disclosure of the controlling party to be made in the 'financial statements' (rather than the directors' report). In the light of the ruling of the Financial Reporting Review Panel on the 1997 accounts of H & C Furnishings referred to at 2.2.2 B above, it would be advisable for there to be at least a note within the accounts cross-referred to the directors' report.

The standard, obviously, does not supersede the Companies Act requirements to disclose the ultimate parent company and the parent undertaking(s) of the largest and, if different, smallest groups of which the company is a member and for which group accounts are prepared. This means that, potentially, a company may have to disclose as many as five parties further up the 'chain':

(a) the immediate parent undertaking;[54]

(b) the parent undertaking of the smallest group for which group accounts are prepared;[55]

(c) the parent undertaking of the largest group for which group accounts are prepared;[56]

(d) the ultimate parent company;[57] and;

(e) the ultimate controlling party (where this is not a company).[58]

Incidentally, this provides a vivid illustration of the somewhat absurd over-disclosure that can arise when rules are made piecemeal by different sources of regulation (in this case UK law, the EU Seventh Directive and UK accounting standards) without regard to their overall context and pre-existing requirements.

3 OTHER REQUIREMENTS IN THE UK

In addition to the requirements of FRS 8, the disclosure of some related party matters is dealt with in the Companies Act 1985, existing standards and, for listed and AIM companies, the respective Financial Services Authority and London Stock Exchange requirements.

3.1 Legislative requirements

The Companies Act 1985 requires the financial statements (or directors' report) to contain what might be considered as related party disclosures in relation to:

(a) directors;

(b) non-director officers or senior employees; and

(c) group companies (including associates and other major investments).

The disclosures for other related party matters are only regulated by the overriding requirement for the financial statements to give a true and fair view.

The disclosure requirements relating to each of the above categories of related parties are outlined below.

3.1.1 Directors

In general, the Companies Act requires the following information to be disclosed in respect of directors of a company:

(a) names of directors who have served during the year;[59]

(b) interests of each director in the share capital or debentures of the company or of any other group company;[60]

(c) information about directors' remuneration (see Chapter 32); and

(d) loans and other transactions with directors or persons connected with the directors (see Chapter 31).

3.1.2 Non-director officers

The Companies Act also requires disclosure of information relating to loans and other transactions with officers of the company other than directors; these requirements are discussed in Chapter 31 at 6.

3.1.3 Subsidiary, associated and other related undertakings

Schedules 4 and 5 to the Companies Act set out detailed disclosure requirements in respect of group companies (including undertakings in which the company has a participating interest),[61] many of which were added by the Companies Act 1989 when the EU Seventh Company Law Directive was incorporated into UK companies legislation. Certain of these disclosures apply to companies which are not required to prepare group accounts and subsidiary undertakings which have been excluded from the consolidated accounts.

A Ultimate parent company and parent undertaking(s) drawing up accounts for larger group

Where a company or parent company is itself a subsidiary undertaking, it must give the name and, if known to the directors, the country of incorporation (if outside Great Britain[62]) of the company (if any) regarded by the directors as the company's ultimate parent company. For this purpose, the term 'company' includes any body corporate (i.e. a UK corporate entity not registered under the Companies Act or an overseas corporate entity).[63]

The Companies Act also requires additional disclosures in relation to the parent undertaking(s) (which need not be a corporate entity) of the largest and smallest group of undertakings for which group accounts are drawn up and of which the reporting company is a member.

The information to be given about each such parent undertaking is:

(a) its name;

(b) its country of incorporation (if outside Great Britain)

(c) if unincorporated, the address of its principal place of business; and

(d) if copies of its group accounts are available to the public, the address from which they may be obtained.[64]

B Subsidiary undertakings

A parent company, whether or not it is preparing group accounts, must give the following information about each of its subsidiary undertakings:

(a) its name;

(b) its country of incorporation (if outside Great Britain);

(c) if it is unincorporated, the address of its principal place of business;[65] and

(d) the identity of each class of shares held and the proportion of the nominal value of the shares of that class represented by those shares. If applicable, the holdings should be split between those held directly by the parent company, and those held indirectly via other group companies.[66]

A parent company that does not prepare group accounts must disclose, for each subsidiary undertaking, its profit or loss for, and capital and reserves at the end of, its 'relevant financial year' – i.e. its latest financial year coterminous with, or ending before, that of the parent. In a case where a subsidiary's relevant financial year ends before that of the parent, the year-end date must given.

However, this information need not be given if the parent is exempt from preparing accounts under section 228 of the Companies Act 1985 (subsidiary of EEA parent – see Chapter 5 at 4.1), or if the group's investment in the undertaking is included in the accounts by way of the equity method of valuation, or if:

(a) the undertaking is not required by any provision of the Companies Act to deliver a copy of its balance sheet for its relevant financial year and does not otherwise publish its balance sheet in Great Britain or elsewhere; and

(b) the holding of the group is less than 50% of the nominal value of the shares in the undertaking.[67]

Where a parent company does prepare group accounts it must disclose why each subsidiary is a subsidiary undertaking, unless the reason is (as it typically will be) that the subsidiary's immediate parent holds a majority of voting rights, and the same proportion of the shares, in the subsidiary undertaking.[68] It must also state whether each subsidiary undertaking is included in the consolidation, and give the reason for non-consolidation in any particular case.[69]

In respect of each unconsolidated subsidiary, the parent must disclose its profit or loss for its 'relevant financial year' (see above) and its total capital and reserves at the end that year. However, this information need not be given in respect of any subsidiary undertaking if the group's investment in the undertaking is included in the accounts by way of the equity method of valuation or if:

(a) the undertaking is not required by any provision of the Companies Act to deliver a copy of its balance sheet for its relevant financial year and does not otherwise publish its balance sheet in Great Britain or elsewhere; and

(b) the holding of the group is less than 50% of the nominal value of the shares in the undertaking.[70]

For each subsidiary undertaking whose financial year did not end with that of the company, the parent must explain why the directors of the parent consider this appropriate, and give the date of its last year-end before that of the reporting company. Alternatively, where there are a number of subsidiary undertakings, the earliest and latest of those dates may be given.[71]

C Associated undertakings

The following information must be given in group accounts in respect of each associated undertaking:

(a) its name;

(b) its country of incorporation (if outside Great Britain);

(c) if it is unincorporated, the address of its principal place of business; and

(d) the identity of each class of shares held and the proportion of the nominal value of the shares of that class represented by those shares. If applicable, the holdings should be split between those held directly by the parent company, and those held indirectly via other group companies.[72]

D Joint ventures

Where an undertaking is accounted for in group accounts using proportional consolidation, the following information must be disclosed:

(a) its name;

(b) its principal place of business;

(c) the factors on which joint management is based;

(d) the proportion of the capital of the joint venture held by the group; and

(e) where the financial year end of the joint venture did not coincide with that of the parent company of the reporting group, the date of its last year-end ending before that of the parent.[73]

In practice, this requirement has been rendered redundant by the prohibition of proportional consolidation by FRS 9 – *Associates and Joint Ventures* (see Chapter 7).

E Investments in 'qualifying undertakings'

Where a company or group has an investment in a 'qualifying undertaking' (i.e. a partnership or unlimited company each of whose members is either a limited company or an unlimited company (or Scottish firm), each of whose members is a limited company),[74] it must state the name and legal form of the qualifying undertaking together with its address or that of its head office. This information need not be given if it is not material.

There must also be stated either:

(a) that a copy of the latest accounts of the undertaking has been, or is to be, appended to the copy of the company's accounts filed with the Registrar of Companies; or

(b) the name of at least one body corporate (which can be the reporting company) in whose consolidated accounts the qualifying undertaking has been included. This information need not be given if the qualifying undertaking is exempt from preparing accounts.[75] (Somewhat contrarily, the key condition for obtaining such an exemption is that the undertaking has been included in the consolidated accounts of one of its members!)[76]

F Other significant holdings of the parent company or group

Schedule 5 to the Companies Act also requires certain disclosures to be given where a parent company has a significant investment in an undertaking which is not a subsidiary or associated undertaking or joint venture.[77]

A holding is 'significant' for the purposes of these disclosures if either:

(a) it amounts to 20% or more of the nominal value of any class of shares in the undertaking; or

(b) the book value of the holding exceeds one-fifth of the company's (or group's) assets as stated in its accounts.

For companies required to prepare group accounts, the disclosures must be given both for investments of the parent company of the reporting group and investments of the group as a whole.

In relation to holdings which amount to 20% or more of the nominal value of the shares in the investee, companies must also disclose (if material):

(a) the aggregate amount of its capital and reserves of the undertaking at the end of its relevant financial year; and

(b) its profit or loss for that year.

However, this information need not be given if:

(a) the undertaking is not required by any provision of the Companies Act to deliver a copy of its balance sheet for its relevant financial year and does not otherwise publish its balance sheet in Great Britain or elsewhere, and the holding of the group is less than 50% of the nominal value of the shares in the undertaking; or

(b) the company is not required to prepare group accounts because it is an intermediate holding company, and the company's investment in all undertakings in which it has such a holding is shown, in aggregate, in the notes to the accounts by way of the equity method of valuation.

G Transactions with group undertakings and undertakings in which the company has a participating interest

In addition to requiring the amounts in respect of shares in group undertakings and participating interests to be separately disclosed, the balance sheet formats also require separate disclosure of the following inter-company balances involving (i) group undertakings and (ii) undertakings in which the company has a participating interest:

(a) loans to (under the heading of fixed asset investments);

(b) amounts owed by (under the heading of current assets, debtors);

(c) amounts owed to (under both headings for creditors).[78]

The profit and loss account formats contained in the Companies Act require separate disclosure of:

(a) income from shares in group undertakings;

(b) income from participating interests;

(c) income and interest derived from group undertakings; and

(d) interest and similar charges payable to group undertakings.[79]

In group accounts, amounts relating to participating interests must be analysed between those relating to associated undertakings and those relating to other participating interests.[80]

The Companies Act requires companies to disclose details of any guarantees and other financial commitments.[81] Where such guarantees or commitments are undertaken on behalf of or for the benefit of:

(a) any parent undertaking or fellow subsidiary undertaking; or

(b) any subsidiary undertaking of the company,

they are required to be disclosed separately from any other guarantees and financial commitments; furthermore, guarantees and commitments within (a) above should be disclosed separately from those within (b).[82]

3.2 UK accounting standards other than FRS 8

The main UK accounting standards other than FRS 8 which impinge on the issue of related parties are FRS 2 – *Accounting for Subsidiary Undertakings* and FRS 9 – *Associates and Joint Ventures*, which require certain disclosures to be made in the financial statements of the investing company in addition to those required by the Companies Act as described in 3.1 above. These are discussed in detail in Chapters 5 and 7 respectively.

3.3 Requirements of the Financial Services Authority and London Stock Exchange

The Financial Services Authority requires listed companies to disclose, in their annual reports and accounts, various information relevant to related parties, or which indicate the existence of related parties, in addition to that required by the Companies Act. The specific disclosures relevant to related parties concern either the directors or the shareholders of the company. These are dealt with in 3.3.1 to 3.3.3 below.

The London Stock Exchange has less onerous requirements for AIM companies and these are dealt with in 3.3.4 below.

3.3.1 Directors

A Emoluments and other benefits

There are extensive requirements for the disclosure of individual directors' emoluments and other benefits, introduced in response to the Cadbury and Greenbury codes. These are discussed in Chapter 32 at 3.

B Directors' interests in share capital

The requirements extend beyond those contained in the Companies Act 1985 in that they require disclosure of:

(a) beneficial and non-beneficial interests, separately distinguished. For this purpose a holding is non-beneficial only if neither the director, nor his spouse, nor any of his children under 18 has any beneficial interest; and

(b) changes in interests between the balance sheet date and a date not more than one month before the date of the notice of the annual general meeting. If there has been no change, then that fact should be disclosed.[83]

C Contracts of significance with directors

Particulars of any contract of significance subsisting during the financial year, to which the company or one of its subsidiary undertakings is a party, and in which a director of the company is or was materially interested are required to be disclosed by listed companies.[84]

A 'contract of significance' is defined as one which represents in amount or value, a sum equal to 1% or more, calculated on a group basis where relevant, of:

(a) in the case of a capital transaction or a transaction of which the principal purpose or effect is the granting of credit, the aggregate of the group's share capital and reserves; or

(b) in other cases, the total annual purchases, sales, payments or receipts, as the case may be, of the group.[85]

(See Chapter 31 at 5 for further discussion of these requirements.)

3.3.2 *Shareholders*

A Substantial holdings of the company's shares

A statement is required to be given showing, as at a date not more than one month prior to the date of the notice of the annual general meeting, the information which has been notified to the company in accordance with the Companies Act in respect of certain major interests in the share capital of the company. A notifiable interest is 3% or more of the nominal value of any class of share capital having full voting rights where the interest is a material interest (as defined in section 199(2A) of the Companies Act) and 10% or more of the nominal value of any class of share capital having full voting rights for an interest that is not a material interest. If there is no such interest, a statement of that fact is required to be made.[86]

B Contracts of significance

Particulars of any contract of significance between the company, or one of its subsidiaries, and a controlling shareholder are required to be disclosed by listed companies.[87]

A controlling shareholder is one who is entitled to exercise, or control the exercise of, 30% or more of the rights to vote at general meetings, or is able to control the appointment of directors who are able to exercise a majority of votes at board meetings.[88]

In addition, particulars of any contract for the provision of services to the company or any of its subsidiaries by a controlling shareholder are also required to be disclosed. Such a contract need not be disclosed, if it is a contract for the provision of services which it is the principal business of the shareholder to provide and it is not a contract of significance.[89]

C Waived dividends

Particulars of any arrangement under which a shareholder has waived or agreed to waive any dividends are required to be disclosed. Where a shareholder has agreed to waive future dividends, details should be given of such waiver together with those relating to dividends which are payable during the period under review. Waivers of less than 1% of the total value of any dividend may be disregarded provided that some payment has been made on each share of the relevant class during the relevant calendar year.[90]

In practice, waivers are likely to arise only where the shareholder is a director or has some influence over the company.

D Purchase by the company of its own shares

The Companies Act contains provisions requiring disclosures of certain information where a company has purchased some of its own shares.[91] The Stock Exchange extends these for listed companies by requiring disclosure of, in the case of purchases made otherwise than through the market or by tender or partial offer to all shareholders, the names of the sellers of such shares purchased.[92] Again, in most cases, this is likely to arise only where the shareholder is a director or has some influence over the company.

3.3.3 *Smaller related party transactions*

Under the Listing Rules of the Financial Services Authority, listed companies are normally required to issue a circular to shareholders where a related party transaction is contemplated.[93] In the case of some smaller transactions, however, companies are able instead, subject to various conditions, to disclose details of the transactions in their accounts. The transactions concerned are those where one or more of the following ratios is between 0.25% and 5%:

(a) gross assets the subject of the transaction, to those of the listed company;

(b) profits attributable to the assets the subject of the transaction, to those of the listed company;

(c) turnover attributable to the assets the subject of the transaction, to those of the listed company;

(d) consideration, to market capitalisation of the ordinary shares of the listed company; and

(e) where a company or business is being acquired, its gross capital, to that of the listed company.[94]

'Related party transactions' are defined for this purpose as transactions (other than revenue transactions in the ordinary course of business) between a related party and the company or any company in the same group.[95]

'Related parties' are defined for this purpose as:

(a) a 'substantial shareholder' (broadly a person able to control, now or at any time during the previous 12 months, 10% of the votes of the company or any other group company);

(b) any person who is (or was during the previous 12 months) a director or shadow director of the company or any other group company; or

(c) an associate of any person falling within (a) or (b). An 'associate' is broadly:

 (i) with respect to an individual: his immediate family; a trust for the benefit of him or his immediate family; or a company in which he and/or his immediate family can either control 30% of the votes or appoint a majority of the board; and

 (ii) with respect to a company: any company in the same group; any company whose directors are accustomed to act in accordance with its instructions; or any company in which it and/or its other associates can either control 30% of the votes or appoint a majority of the board.[96]

In order to qualify for this exemption a company must, prior to completing the transaction:

(a) inform the Financial Services Authority in writing of the details of the proposed transaction;

(b) provide the Financial Services Authority with written confirmation from an independent adviser acceptable to the Financial Services Authority that the terms of the proposed transaction with the related party are fair and reasonable so far as the shareholders of the company are concerned; and

(c) undertake in writing to the Financial Services Authority to include details of the transaction in the company's next published annual accounts, including the identity of the related party, the value of the consideration for the transaction and all other relevant circumstances.[97]

The requirement to include details of small related party transactions in the annual report and accounts of companies which have taken advantage of the facility of not having to issue a circular to shareholders is listed as one of the continuing obligations of the Listing Rules.[98] The following are examples of disclosures which appear to have been made in pursuance of this requirement:

Extract 30.15: EMI Group plc (1997)

32. RELATED PARTY TRANSACTIONS [extract]

EMI Music Publishing acquired the music publishing catalogues of The Entertainment Group of Companies on 31 March 1997 for a total consideration of US$7.8m (£4.8m). These companies were owned by Charles Koppelman and Martin Bandier, directors of certain Group companies.

Extract 30.16: TI Group plc (1996)

31. RELATED PARTY TRANSACTIONS [extract]

On 30th December 1996 Bundy Corporation sold its 20% investment in Usui Bundy Tubing Ltd ('Usui') to Usui Kokusai Sangyo Kaisha Ltd, which already held 60% of Usui, for ¥1,077m (£6m). TI Group retained the rights to use the name 'Bundy' in Japan.

3.3.4 *AIM companies*

AIM companies are required by the London Stock Exchange to disclose in their accounts details of any transaction with a related party (effectively defined as for listed companies in 3.3.3 above)[99] where any one of the following ratios exceeds 0.25%:

(a) gross assets the subject of the transaction, to those of the AIM company;

(b) profits attributable to the assets the subject of the transaction, to those of the AIM company;

(c) turnover attributable to the assets the subject of the transaction, to that of the AIM company;

(d) consideration, to market capitalisation of the ordinary shares of the AIM company; and

(e) where a company or business is being acquired, its gross capital, to that of the AIM company.

The details given must include the identity of the related party and the value of the consideration.[100]

4 IAS REQUIREMENTS

The relevant international standard which deals with the disclosure of related parties and transactions between a reporting enterprise and its related parties is IAS 24 – *Related Party Disclosures* – which was originally issued in July 1984 and issued in a revised format in 1994.

4.1 Definition of related party

IAS 24 considers two parties as related 'if one party has the ability to control the other party or to exercise significant influence over the other party in making financial and operating decisions'.[101] For the purposes of IAS 24, 'control' is defined as 'ownership, directly, or indirectly through subsidiaries, of more than one half of the voting power of an enterprise, or a substantial interest in voting power and the power to direct, by statute or agreement, the financial and operating policies of the management of the enterprise'.[102] This is somewhat wordier that the equivalent definition in FRS 8 (which is similar to the definition of 'control' used in IAS 27 – *Presentation of Consolidated Financial Statements* – see Chapter 5 at 6.1), but has much the same result.

'Significant influence' is defined as 'participation in the financial and operating policy decisions of an enterprise, but not control of those policies'. IAS 24 goes on to say that whilst significant influence will normally be exercised through board representation, it may also arise through 'participation in the policy making process, material intercompany transactions, interchange of managerial personnel or dependence on technical information.' Whether significant influence arises as a result of share ownership is to be determined in accordance with IAS 28 – *Accounting for Investments in Associates* (see Chapter 7 at 6.1).[103] Taken at face value, therefore, IAS 24's definition of 'significant influence' is more restrictive than that of 'influence' in FRS 8 (see 2.2.1 B above). In practice, however, we see their effect as essentially the same.

Notwithstanding the broad definition of related party, however, IAS 24 requires disclosure only in respect of the following types of related party that meet the general definition:

(a) enterprises controlling, controlled by, or under common control with, the reporting enterprise;

(b) associates;

(c) individuals owning, directly or indirectly, an interest in the voting power of the reporting enterprise that gives them significant influence over the enterprise, and close members of the family of any such individual;

(d) key management personnel, that is, those persons having authority and responsibility for planning, directing and controlling the activities of the reporting enterprise, including directors and officers of companies and close members of the families of such individuals; and

(e) enterprises in which a substantial interest in the voting power is owned, directly or indirectly, by any person described in (c) or (d) or over which such a person is able to exercise significant influence. This includes enterprises owned by directors or major shareholders of the reporting enterprise and enterprises that have a member of key management in common with the reporting enterprise.[104]

For the purposes of (c) and (d) above 'close members of the family' are defined as 'those that may be expected to influence, or be influenced by, that person in their dealings with the enterprise'.[105]

Moreover, the standard deems the following not to be related parties:

- two companies 'simply' because they have a director in common, although 'it is necessary to consider the possibility, and to assess the likelihood, that the director would be able to affect the policies of both companies in their mutual dealings';
- providers of finance, trade unions, public utilities and government departments and agencies, in each case in the course of their normal dealings with the enterprise by virtue only of those dealings (although they may circumscribe the freedom of action of an enterprise or participate in its decision-making process);
- a single customer, supplier, franchisor, distributor or general agent with whom the enterprise conducts a significant volume of business merely by virtue of the resulting economic dependence.[106]

This is broadly similar to, but somewhat more extensive than, the list of such parties in FRS 8 (see 2.2.5 above).

It is entirely possible that parties falling outside the scope of items (a) to (e) above, and therefore outside the scope of the disclosure requirements of IAS 24, would be included within the FRS 8 definition of a related party. In these circumstances disclosure would be required under UK GAAP but not under IAS. One example of this would be that of a venturer in a joint venture. Under FRS 8 both such parties are deemed to be related parties of each other, but such parties are not mentioned in IAS 24 as being of the type of related party relationship covered by the disclosure requirements of the standard. (This is notwithstanding the fact that they fall within the broad definition of 'related party' in IAS 24, since if the venturer has joint control over the joint venture, it must have the ability to exercise significant influence over the joint venture.)

4.2 Disclosures required

As under FRS 8, related party relationships where control exists should be disclosed irrespective of whether there have been transactions between the related parties.[107]

Where transactions have taken place between related parties, the reporting enterprise should disclose the nature of the related party relationships as well as the types of transactions and the elements of the transactions necessary for an understanding of the financial statements.[108] The elements of the transaction would normally include:

(a) an indication of the volume of the transactions, either as an amount or as an appropriate proportion;

(b) amounts or appropriate proportions of outstanding items; and

(c) pricing policies.[109]

Items of a similar nature may be disclosed in aggregate, except when separate disclosure is necessary for an understanding of the effects on the financial statements.[110] The standard points out that certain other IASs call for disclosures which may also be relevant in respect of related parties.[111]

IAS 24 gives an indicative list of transactions that 'may lead to disclosures' of related party transactions,[112] which is identical to that in FRS 8 (see 2.3.1 above).

The disclosure requirements of IAS 24 are, however, considerably less rigorous than those of FRS 8 discussed at 2.3.3 above. IAS 24 does not specifically require disclosure of either the name of the related party, the amounts involved in the transactions, the amounts of outstanding balances, provision for doubtful debts due from related parties or amounts written off in the period in respect of debts due to or from related parties. On the other hand, IAS 24 includes 'pricing policies' as part of the elements to be disclosed, whereas FRS 8 has a vague requirement to disclose 'any other elements of the transactions necessary for an understanding of the financial statements'.

4.3 Exemptions from disclosure

IAS 24 does not require disclosure of related party transactions:

(a) in consolidated financial statements in respect of intra-group transactions;

(b) in parent company financial statements when they are made available or published with the consolidated financial statements;

(c) in financial statements of a wholly-owned subsidiary if its parent is incorporated in the same country and provides consolidated financial statements in that country; and

(d) in financial statements of state-controlled enterprises of transactions with other state-controlled enterprises.[113]

(a) and (b) mirror the similar exemptions in FRS 8 (see 2.3.5 above). There is no equivalent of (d) in FRS 8, and conversely IAS 24 contains no exemptions for contributions to pension funds or employees' emoluments comparable to those in FRS 8. The lack of this exemption has the effect that IAS 24 requires disclosure of emoluments of key management personnel (including directors). Examples of such disclosure are illustrated in some of the extracts at 4.4 below (although it may that in some cases these have been given to meet local regulatory requirements). It will be seen that the information given is far less than would be required for a listed UK company, particularly with respect to directors (see Chapters 31 and 32). However, it is fair to say that many accounts purporting to comply with IASs do not give any disclosures about emoluments of, or transactions with, key management personnel.

The exemption for subsidiaries (item (c) above) is superficially similar to the equivalent in FRS 8, but differs in all key respects as the following matrix illustrates.

	IAS 24	*FRS 8*
Qualifying entities	wholly-owned subsidiaries	90% or more owned subsidiaries
Exempt transactions	all related party transactions	transactions with other members of the group, or investees of the group qualifying as related parties
Group accounts required to be prepared	by parent in same country and publicly available in that country	by parent in any country and publicly available anywhere
Disclosure required	none	that exemption has been taken, and where group accounts can be obtained

As noted in 2.3.5 C above, we consider the exemption in IAS 24 preferable to that in FRS 8. Interestingly, this is the only major difference between FRS 8 and IAS 24 highlighted in FRS 8 itself,[114] although, as the discussion above indicates, there are numerous other differences of detail.

4.4 Examples of disclosures

The following extracts illustrate related party disclosures in IAS accounts, although it may be that some of the information is given to comply with local regulatory requirements rather than IAS 24.

Extract 30.17: AngloGold Limited (2000)

34 Related parties

Related party transactions are concluded on an arm's length basis. Details of material transactions with those related parties not dealt with elsewhere in the financial statements are summarised below:

	2000		1999	
	Purchases from related parties	**Amounts owed to related parties**	Purchases from related parties	Amounts owed to related parties
SA Rands				
With fellow subsidiaries, associates and joint ventures of the Anglo American plc group				
Boart Longyear Limited – mining services	**55**	**9**	67	1
Haggie Limited – mining equipment	**32**	**3**	35	2
Mondi Limited – timber	**153**	**–**	138	–
Scaw Metals Limited – steel and engineering	**56**	**–**	50	–
Shaft Sinkers (Pty) Ltd – mining services	**93**	**–**	112	–
With associates				
Rand Refinery Limited – gold refinery	**27**	**–**	25	–
US Dollars				
With fellow subsidiaries, associates and joint ventures of the Anglo American plc group				
Boart Longyear Limited – mining services	**7**	**1**	11	–
Haggie Limited – mining equipment	**4**	**–**	6	–
Mondi Limited – timber	**20**	**–**	18	–
Scaw Metals Limited – steel and engineering	**7**	**–**	7	–
Shaft Sinkers (Pty) Ltd – mining services	**12**	**–**	18	–
With associates				
Rand Refinery Limited – gold refinery	**4**	**–**	4	–

Directors

Details relating to directors' emoluments and shareholdings in the company are disclosed in the directors' report.

Shareholders

The principal shareholders of the company are detailed on page 101.

Extract 30.18: Deutsche Lufthansa AG (2000)

40 Related party transactions

The business segments of the Lufthansa Group render numerous services to non-consolidated subsidiaries within the scope of their ordinary activities. In turn, the respective investments render services to the Lufthansa Group within the scope of their business objectives. These extensive delivery and service relationships are handled on the basis of market prices.

In addition, the Group and non-consolidated subsidiaries have concluded numerous settlement agreements regulating the mutual utilisation of services. The administration services rendered in such cases are charged as cost allocations.

The cash management of the Lufthansa Group is centralised, and regarding this the Lufthansa Group assumes a "banking function" also in respect of non-consolidated investments. The non-consolidated subsidiaries included in the Group's cash management invest their available cash in the Group or borrow funds from the Group and effect their derivative hedging transactions there. All transactions are processed under market conditions.

Because of the spatial proximity, a large number of sublease contracts have been concluded between the Lufthansa Group and related parties; in these cases, the Lufthansa Group re-debits rental costs and incidental costs to the respective companies on a pro rata basis.

The following table shows the volume of services rendered to or obtained from related parties:

Company	Volume of services rendered		Volume of services utilised	
	2000	1999	2000	1999
	€m	€m	€m	€m
Condor Flugdienst GmbH	139.5	127.7	23.1	15.0
Condor/Cargo Technik GmbH	27.4	27.7	19.1	15.3
Lufthansa Technik Logistik GmbH	11.2	25.9	87.5	74.2
Lufthansa Flight Training GmbH	22.1	21.5	64.3	70.8
Delvag Luftfahrtversicherungs-AG	31.4	16.3	10.9	8.1
Miles&More International Inc.	18.7	14.4	–	–
Lufthansa AirPlus Servicekarten GmbH	11.9	14.3	47.2	37.8
Lufthansa Revenue Services GmbH	5.3	11.2	89.1	55.2
Lufthansa Airmotive Ireland Ltd.	7.9	10.3	68.0	36.4
Airline Training Center GmbH	5.2	1.5	5.1	1.0
Lufthansa Catering Logistik GmbH	9.9	8.6	43.8	42.0
Lufthansa Consulting GmbH	4.0	4.6	14.0	4.8
Lufthansa A.E.R.O. GmbH	4.4	1.0	7.0	5.7
Lido GmbH Lufthansa Aeronautical Services	3.5	3.6	11.5	12.0
Lufthansa LOEWE Druck und Distribution GmbH	1.7	3.2	15.2	13.8
Lufthansa City Center Reisebüropartner GmbH	0.5	3.1	4.5	6.0
Lufthansa Technical Training GmbH	2.2	2.2	8.8	7.3
Lufthansa Process Management GmbH	1.9	1.9	8.1	7.3
Lufthansa Engineering and Operational Services GmbH	2.4	1.8	24.1	24.7
Lufthansa Systems AS GmbH	0.1	1.4	6.0	12.9
Lufthansa Shannon Turbine Technologies Limited	0.9	0.7	9.7	8.0
Shannon Aerospace Ltd.	0.2	0.3	27.1	18.4
Global Tele Sales Ltd.	0.1	0.3	8.1	7.8
Albatros Versicherungsdienste GmbH	1.4	–	10.1	9.9

41 Supervisory Board and Executive Board

The members of the Supervisory Board and the Executive Board are listed on pages 140/141. For discharging their duties in the parent company and in subsidiary companies, the members of the Executive Board received remuneration in the amount of €2.3m for 2000 and €0.1m for 1999 in financial year 2000, and €1.9m for 1999 and €0.2m for 1998 in financial year 1999. A claim arising from a loan arrangement in the amount of €16t to a member of the Executive Board exists as of 31 December 2000. €2t was paid back in the year 2000; the interest rate is 4 per cent, the residual term is five years.

The members of the Supervisory Board received €0.7m (prior year: €0.5m). These amounts include benefits from concessionary travel in line with the applicable IATA regulations.

Pensions obligations to former members of the Executive Board and their surviving dependants in the amount of €31.9m (prior year: €29.1m) exist. In financial year 2000, current remuneration amounted to €2.3m for 2000 and €3t for 1999. In financial year 1999, current remuneration amounted to €2.2m for 1999, including remuneration from subsidiaries.

Extract 30.19: Münchener Rückversicherungs-Gesellschaft AG (2000)

(33) Related enterprises

Munich Re has diverse and extensive relations with Allianz, one of the world's largest insurance and financial service groups.

Munich Re holds 24.9% of the voting capital of Allianz AG. Conversely, Allianz holds 24.9% of the voting capital of Munich Re. In addition, Allianz and Munish Re both have shareholdings in Frankfurter Versicherungs-AG, Bayerische Versicherungsbank AG, Allianz Lebensversicherungs-AG and Karlsruher Lebensversicherung AG.

Members of the Board of Management of Munich Re and Allianz hold seats on the Supervisory Boards of the above-mentioned companies and, in individual instances, on the Boards of other companies in each other's Groups. Dr.jur. Henning Schulte-Noelle, Chairman of the Board of Management of Allianz AG, is Deputy Chairman of the Munich Reinsurance Company's Supervisory Board.

With regard to the planned restructuring of shareholdings between Munich Re and Allianz, reference is made to note (40) and the remarks in Section 05 (Prospects for 2001).

The relations between Munish Re and Allianz are also given documented form in a general agreement. This agreement deals in particular with the question of reciprocal shareholdings, with details of shareholdings in jointly held insurance companies (see above) and with general arrangements regarding reinsurance relations. The earliest possible date of termination is 31st December 2005.

The Munich Re Group assumes and cedes reinsurance and retrocessions from and to the Allianz Group under a large number of reinsurance and retrocession agreements. The following table shows Munich Re's premiums assumed from and ceded to Allianz as at 31st December:

All figures in €m	**2000**	**1999**
Gross premiums assumed	**2,550**	2,600
Gross premiums ceded	**900**	810

In the year under review, Allianz's cessions to Munich Re amounted to 13.9% (16.9%) of our gross premiums in reinsurance or 8.2% (9.5%) of our overall consolidated premiums. Munich Re's cessions to Allianz amounted to 42.2% (42.7%) of our ceded premiums.

The reinsurance agreements between Munich Re and Allianz are concluded at market conditions.

Besides this, there are further contractual relations between Munich Re and Allianz in connection with the normal running of our business, such as the conclusion of insurance policies for own risks (e.g. buildings insurance policies).

Munich Re also discloses information about long-term incentive plans, emoluments and loans relating to board members in separate notes.

Extract 30.20: Serono International S.A. (2000)

31. Principal shareholder

At December 31, 2000, Bertarelli & Cie, a partnership limited by shares with its principal offices at Chéserex (Vaud), Switzerland, held 51.67% of the capital and 60.93% of the voting rights in Serono S.A. Ernesto Bertarelli controls Bertarelli & Cie. On the same date, Maria-Iris Bertarelli, Ernesto Bertarelli and Donata Bertarelli Späth owned in the aggregate 7.03% of the capital an 9.81% of the voting rights of Serono S.A.

32. Related parties

Transactions with related parties

In 2000, we leased from an unaffiliated company, under a lease that expires in 2006, a building then under construction adjacent to our headquarters building that we have used to expand our headquarters facilities. The lease provides for a market rate rent of approximately $800,000 per year. Subsequent to the negotiation of the lease, Ernesto Bertarelli, our Chief Executive Officer, acquired a controlling interest in the company that owns the building. In addition, we rent from a company controlled by Mr. Bertarelli a building that we use as an executive conference facility. The annual rent for this facility is approximately $100,000.

In 1999, we made a loan to an executive officer of approximately $195,000. The loan bears interest at LIBOR, adjusted annually. Half of the loan will be amortized monthly through May 2010, and the remainder will be payable at that time. During 2000, the largest principal amount outstanding on the loan was approximately $94,000.

The company holds an equity investment in Cansera International Inc. ("Cansera"), a Canadian company specializing in the supply of Fetal Bovine Serum. Purchases from Cansera are carried out on commercial terms and conditions and at market prices. Total company purchases from Cansera for the year-ended December 31, 2000 were $1.4 million (1999: $2.0 million). As at December 31, 2000, the payable due to Cansera was nil (1999: $0.2 million).

During the year, the loan due from Cansera (1999: $0.5 million) was received in full.

Remuneration of the Board of Directors and the Executive Committee

Details of the members of the Board of Directors and the Executive Committee are provided elsewhere in this annual report. In 2000, the combined remuneration of the members of the Board of Directors and the Executives Committee was $5.3 million (1999: $4.7 million).

Stock options granted to the Board of Directors and the Executive Committee

As part of the stock option plan described in note 25, 3,200 (1999: 3,640) share options were granted to the members of the Board of Directors and the Executive Committee during the year. The share options were granted on the same terms and conditions as those offered to other employees of the company. The outstanding number of share options granted to the members of the Board of Directors and the Executive Committee at the end of the year was 8,360 (1999: 7,320).

In addition to options granted to employees under the stock option plan (note 25), options to purchase bearer shares of Serono S.A. have been granted to each of the directors. 3,200 directors' options were granted in 2000 (1999: 6,400). The exercise price of CHF1,398 (1999: CHF512) has been determined as the market price of the Serono S.A. bearer shares at the date of the grant. Directors' options granted prior to 1998 have an exercise price of CHF 523. Directors' options generally vest on December 31 of each year over a period of five years, but they may not be exercised for a period of five years from the date of the grant. After the options become exercisable, directors may generally exercise their options for a period of five years. As at December 31, 2000, 10,920 (1999: 7,720) directors' options were outstanding and 4,520 (1999: 2,268) directors' options were vested. No directors' options were exercisable as at December 31, 2000and 1999.

Extract 30.21: Jardine Matheson Holdings Limited (2000)

35 Related Party Transactions

In the normal course of business the Group undertakes on an arms-length basis a wide variety of transactions with certain of its associates and joint ventures. The more significant of such transactions are described below.

Banking services
The Group provides banking services to Hongkong Land. The net deposits placed by Hongkong Land at 31st December 2000 amounted to US$47.2 million *(1999: US$48.1 million).*

Property services
The Group rents property from Hongkong Land. The gross annual rentals paid by the Group in 2000 to Hongkong Land were US$5.5 million *(1999: US$6.5 million).*

The Group provided property services to Hongkong Land in 2000 in aggregate amounting to US$21.4 million *(1999: US$21.5 million).*

4 Operating Profit [extract]

	2000	1999
	US$m	US$m
Directors' remuneration *(refer Directors' emoluments on page 91)*	**9.9**	6.5

Extract 30.22: GN Great Nordic (2000)

Note 29: Transactions between related parties

The Group's related parties comprise the Board of Directors and Management of the parent company as well as important stockholders in the parent company, GN Great Nordic.

No agreements or any other transactions have been entered into with the Company, in which the Board of Directors or Management of the parent company have had a financial interest besides transactions stemming from conditions of employment.

Trade between the parent company and the other companies of the GN Great Nordic Group is performed on market terms.

No agreements or other transactions have been entered into with GN Great Nordic, in which an important stockholder has had a financial interest.

Note 2: Employees and Personnel Costs [extract]

	Consolidated	
(DKK millions)	**2000**	1999
Remuneration to the parent company's Board of Directors	(2)	(2)
Remuneration to the parent company's Executive Management	(8)	(7)

The parent company's Executive Management receives separate bonus based on earnings before tax. Executive Management remuneration for the year includes DKK 2 million. (1999: DKK 2 million).

Stock options
In 2000, the parent company's Executive Management was awarded the option to buy 116,250 GN Great Nordic shares at a price of DKK 146.6 each from April 2003 to March 2005.
In the period from July to September Executive Management has exercised 438,000 stock options at an average price of 41.6.
At December 31, 2000, the Executive Management held stock options for a total of 150,250 shares.
The total price of the stock options is DKK 18 million. The commitment is covered by the Company's holding of treasury stock. The market price of these shares was DKK 21 million as at December 31, 2000.

Extract 30.23: Nokia Corporation (2000)

26. Related party transactions

Nokia Pension Foundation is a separate legal entity that manages and holds in trust the assets for the Group's Finnish employee benefit plans these assets include 0.3% of Nokia's shares. Nokia Pension Foundation is also the counterparty to an equity swap agreement with the Group. This transaction was executed on standard commercial terms and conditions. The notional amount of this swap is EUR 336 million and the fair value at December 31, 2000 is EUR -19 million.

There were no loans granted to top management at December 31, 2000 and 1999.

See Note 3, Personnel Expenses for officers and directors remunerations.

3. Personnel expenses [extract]

	2000	1999
	EURm	EURm
Remuneration of the Chairman and the other members of the Boards of Directors, Group Executive Board and Presidents and Managing Directors*	**17**	15
* Incentives included in remuneration	**4**	3

Pension commitments for the management:

The retirement age of the management of the Group companies is between 60–65 years. For the Chief Executive Officer of the Parent Company the retirement age is 60 years.

5 CONCLUSION

FRS 8, though brief, is a much more complex standard than it appears at a first reading. In the light of our experience in dealing with it in the last few reporting seasons, there are certain aspects of it which should be re-addressed in any future standard, in particular:

- the inconsistency between the treatment of the concept of 'significant influence' in FRS 8 on the one hand and in FRS 9 on the other (see 2.2.1 B above);
- the definition of related party in paragraph 2.5(a)(iv) of the standard based on entities transacting on terms such that one has subordinated its own interests (see 2.2.1 above);
- the requirement, in certain cases, to judge materiality by reference to the circumstances of the related party rather than those of the reporting entity (see 2.3.2 above); and
- the exemptions from disclosure for 90% (or more) owned subsidiaries (see 2.3.5 C above).

The main problem with IAS 24 is that it has not been updated significantly since it was first issued in 1984 and is probably due an overhaul. There are also clearly a number of differences between it and the more recent UK standard.

Whilst we would not advocate a return to a general 'abnormal transaction' approach such as that proposed in ED 46, we are concerned that FRS 8 (and IAS 24) unintentionally embraces certain types of transactions, disclosure of which distracts readers from those related party transactions that are more truly worthy of their attention. We believe that, where possible, such transactions should be removed from the scope of any future standard. Obvious examples include:

- participation by major shareholders in transactions with shareholders as a whole (e.g. dividends, rights issues); and
- where companies trade with the public (e.g. retailers, certain banks and insurance companies), transactions with directors and key managers (and their close family and entities controlled by them) as members of the public on non-preferential terms. However, transactions with such individuals (and persons and entities connected with them) in a business capacity should, in our view, always be disclosed whatever their terms.

However, it is unlikely that the IASB sees this as high on its agenda, although it is possible that it is covered as part of its 'improvements' project.

References

1 FRS 8, *Related Party Disclosures*, ASB, November 1995, paras. 8-10.
2 Accountants International Study Group, *Related Party Transactions*, para. 15.
3 FRS 8, para. 1.
4 *Ibid.*, para. 2.5.
5 *Ibid.*, para. 11.
6 *Ibid.*, para. 2.5(a).
7 *Ibid.*, para. 2.2.
8 FRS 5, *Reporting the substance of transactions*, ASB, April 1994, para. 8.
9 FRS 8, para. 13.
10 *Ibid.*, para. 14.
11 *Ibid.*
12 FRED 8, *Related party disclosures*, ASB, March 1994, para. 2(a)(iv).
13 FRS 8, para. 14.
14 *Implementing FRS 8: Some practical aspects*, Ken Wild and Brian Creighton, Accountancy, October 1996, page 128.
15 FRS 8, para. 2.5(a).
16 *Ibid.*, para. 2.5(b).
17 *Ibid.*, para. 2.5(b)(iv), footnote.
18 FRRP PN 53, August 1998.
19 FRS 8, para. 15.
20 Statement of Recommended Practice, *Financial Reports of Pension Schemes*, Pensions Research Accountants Group, July 1996, para. 2.65.
21 FRS 8, para. 2.5(c).
22 *Ibid.*
23 *Ibid.*, para. 2.3.
24 *Ibid.*, paras. 2.2 and 2.5(c)(iii) (footnote).
25 *Ibid.*, para. 2.4.
26 *Ibid.*, para. 2.5.
27 *Ibid.*, para. 2.1.
28 FRED 8, para. 2(d)(iii).
29 FRS 8, para. 4.
30 ASB Statement, *Operating and Financial Review*, ASB, July 1993, para. 12.
31 FRS 8, para. 4.
32 *Ibid.*, para. 6.
33 *Ibid.*, para. 2.6.
34 *Ibid.*, para. 19.
35 *Ibid.*, paras. 2.6 and 19.
36 *Ibid.*, para. 20.
37 *Ibid.*
38 *Ibid.*, para. 6.
39 FRED 8, paras. 8(f) and 23.
40 FRS 8, para. 22.
41 *Ibid.*, para. 10.
42 *Ibid.*, paras. 6 and 21.
43 *Ibid.*, para. 21.
44 *Foreword to Accounting Standards*, ASB, June 1993, para. 15.
45 FRS 8, para. 3.
46 *Ibid.*, para 2.5(a).

47 *Ibid.*, Appendix IV, para 12.
48 CA 85, Sch. 5, paras. 11 and 30.
49 FRS 17, *Retirement benefits*, ASB, November 2000, para. 88.
50 FRS 8, para.16.
51 *Ibid.*, para. 18.
52 *Ibid.*, para. 5.
53 CA 85, Sch. 7, paras. 2-2B.
54 FRS 8, para. 5.
55 CA 85, Sch. 5, paras. 11 and 30.
56 *Ibid.*
57 *Ibid.*, paras. 12 and 31.
58 FRS 8, para. 5.
59 CA 85, s 234(2).
60 *Ibid.*, Sch. 7, para. 2A.
61 Under the Companies Act and FRS 9, an undertaking in which a participating interest is held and over which significant influence is exercised is an 'associated undertaking'.
62 Throughout section 3.1, references to 'Great Britain' should, where the reporting entity is a company incorporated in Northern Ireland, be read as references to 'Northern Ireland'. The relevant legislation for such companies is the Companies (Northern Ireland) Order 1986, the provisions of which are in substance identical to those of the Companies Act 1985.
63 CA 85, Sch. 5, paras. 12 and 31, section 740.
64 *Ibid.*, paras. 11 and 30.
65 *Ibid.*, para. 15(2) and (3).
66 *Ibid.*, paras. 2(2) and 16(1).
67 *Ibid.*, para. 4.
68 *Ibid.*, para. 15(5).
69 *Ibid.*, para. 15(4).
70 *Ibid.*, para. 17.
71 *Ibid.*, para. 19.
72 *Ibid.*, para. 22.
73 *Ibid.*, para. 21.
74 SI 1993/1820, *The Partnerships and Unlimited Companies (Accounts) Regulations 1993*, Regulation 3.
75 CA 1985, Sch. 5, paras. 9A and 28A.
76 SI 1993/1820, Regulation 7.
77 CA 85, Sch. 5, paras. 7–9 and 23–28.
78 *Ibid.*, Schs. 4, 9 and 9A, balance sheet formats.
79 *Ibid.*, profit and loss account formats.
80 CA 85, Sch. 4A, para. 21.
81 *Ibid.*, Sch 4, para. 50.
82 *Ibid.*, para. 59A.
83 *The Listing Rules*, Financial Services Authority, Chapter 12, para. 12.43(k)
84 *Ibid.*, para. 12.43(q).
85 *Ibid.*, para. 12.44.
86 *Ibid.*, para. 12.43(l); CA 85, s 199(2).
87 *Ibid.*, para. 12.43(r).
88 *Ibid.*, Chapter 3, paras. 3.12 and 3.13.
89 *Ibid.*, Chapter 12, para. 12.43(s).
90 *Ibid.*, para. 12.43(e).
91 CA 85, Sch. 7, para. 8.
92 *The Listing Rules*, Chapter 12, para. 12.43(n).
93 *Ibid.*, Chapter 11.
94 *Ibid.*, Chapter 10, para. 10.5 and Chapter 11, para. 11.8.
95 *Ibid.*, Chapter 11, para. 11.1.
96 *Ibid.*
97 *Ibid.*, para. 11.8.
98 *Ibid.*, Chapter 12, para. 12.43(t).
99 *The Aim rules*, London Stock Exchange, Definitions.
100 *Ibid.*, rule 17 (for ratios, see Appendix Three).
101 IAS 24, *Related Party Disclosures*, IASC, 1984 (reformatted 1994), para. 5.
102 *Ibid.*
103 *Ibid.*
104 *Ibid.*, para. 3.
105 *Ibid.*, footnote.
106 *Ibid.*, para. 6.
107 *Ibid.*, para. 20.
108 *Ibid.*, para. 22.
109 *Ibid.*, para. 23.
110 *Ibid.*, para. 24.
111 *Ibid.*, para. 18.
112 *Ibid.*, para. 19.
113 *Ibid.*, para. 4.
114 *Ibid.*, Appendix III.

Chapter 31 Directors' and officers' loans and transactions

1 INTRODUCTION

In the UK, company directors are treated as fiduciaries[1] and as such must not permit their personal interests and their duty to the company to conflict. In order to avoid such conflicts or potential conflicts arising, transactions between a company and its directors are restricted. Such transactions are regulated in a number of ways, in particular, by means of statutory prohibition, corporate approval and disclosure in the statutory accounts. In this chapter, attention is focused on the Companies Act requirements within the UK for disclosure in a company's financial statements of transactions involving directors (except for those relating to directors' remuneration, including share options, which are dealt with in Chapter 32). The provisions determining the legality or otherwise of such transactions are discussed in outline in the Appendix to this chapter.

In considering the disclosures to be made in respect of transactions involving directors (and persons connected with them) it will also be necessary to consider the requirements of FRS 8 – *Related Party Disclosures*, an accounting standard issued by the ASB in November 1995. These are only referred to in passing in this chapter; they are dealt with in their entirety in Chapter 30.

1.1 Outline of historical development in the UK

The Companies Act 1948 provided that a public company could not make a loan to any of its directors or directors of its holding company.[2] Loans to directors of exempt private companies (in essence, companies where the number of members was restricted) were permitted.[3] However, it became apparent over the years that directors could circumvent the restrictions on loans by carefully structuring transactions with their company. Thus, a company could make payments in respect of a director's personal expenditure and seek reimbursement from him without contravening the statutory prohibitions. In such cases, the director would be in substantially the same position as if he had been lent funds to pay off his debts. In an effort to close these loopholes, more extensive requirements were enacted by the Companies Act 1980;[4] for example, the types of unlawful transaction were extended to encompass quasi-loans and credit transactions (see respectively 2.7 and 2.8 below). The relevant legislation is now consolidated in the Companies Act 1985.[5]

2 DEFINITIONS

In order to promote a fuller understanding of this chapter, the following definitions from the Companies Act have been included:

2.1 Director

This term includes any person occupying the position of director, by whatever name called;[6] i.e. it is a person's role and duties and not his title which determines whether or not he is a director. Thus, for example, a director's appointment may be defective because the procedure prescribed in the company's articles has not been followed; however, if he performs the functions associated with a person in such a position, he will be regarded as a director for the purposes of the legislation. Conversely, a person may be designated a director yet not be regarded as a director for statutory purposes; for example, it is common for companies to recognise senior managers by conferring titles such as divisional director[7] on them. These persons usually only exercise limited managerial power and hence are unlikely to be subject to the restrictions on directors' transactions, although the disclosure requirements relating to officers may be of relevance (see 2.5 and 6 below).

2.2 Shadow director

This is a person in accordance with whose directions or instructions the directors of the company as a whole (i.e. the board as a collective unit) are accustomed to act; it does not apply to a person in accordance with whose directions and instructions only one of the directors is accustomed to act. However, if the board's reason for following a person's advice is that it is given in a professional capacity, that person is not regarded as a shadow director.[8] Clearly, a professional adviser might fall to be treated as a shadow director if the advice which he gives to the board is not given in a professional capacity.

A holding company is not deemed to be a shadow director of a subsidiary even though the directors of the subsidiary act as the holding company directs.[9]

2.3 Alternate director

Broadly, an alternate director is a person who is nominated by another director to act in that director's place during his absence from the company.[10] Alternate directors may only be appointed if the company's articles expressly so provide; for example, Table A[11] provides that: 'any director (other than an alternate director) may appoint any other director or any other person approved by resolution of the directors and willing to act, to be an alternate director and may remove from office an alternate director so appointed by him'.

2.4 Connected person

If the restrictions on directors' transactions extended solely to directors, they could easily be circumvented by the company making, say, a loan to the director's spouse or a company controlled by him. The concept of the connected person seeks to close this loophole.

A person is connected with a director if (not being a director himself) he is:

(a) that director's spouse, child or step-child (legitimate or otherwise) under the age of 18; or

(b) a body corporate with which the director is associated.

Broadly speaking, a company is associated with a director if the director and persons connected with him are either interested in at least 20% of the company's equity share capital or are entitled to exercise or control more than 20% of the voting power in general meeting.

The director's interest may be direct (i.e. he personally owns the shares or controls the votes) or indirect (i.e. a company that he controls owns the shares or controls the votes). In this latter context, a director will have control of a company (X Co.) if:

(i) he and persons connected with him are interested in X Co.'s equity share capital or are entitled to exercise voting power at a general meeting of X Co.; and

(ii) he, persons connected with him, and fellow directors are together interested in more than 50% of X Co.'s share capital or are entitled to exercise more than 50% of the voting power in general meeting.

In order to determine whether or not a company is associated with or controlled by a director, another company with which the director is associated is only deemed to be connected with him if connected by virtue of (c) or (d) below; similarly for these purposes, a trustee of a trust, the beneficiaries of which include another company with which the director is associated, is not thereby deemed to be connected with the director;

(c) a person acting as trustee of any trust, the beneficiaries of which include the director or his family or a company with which the director is associated. In addition, where the director or his family or an associated company is the object of a discretionary trust, the trustee thereof is also deemed to be a connected person. Trustees of employee share or pension schemes are excluded;

(d) a partner of the director or any person connected with him by virtue of (a) to (c) above;

(e) a Scottish firm in which the director or a connected person is a partner, or in which a partner is a Scottish firm in which the director or a connected person is a partner.[12]

These provisions are complex and may be illustrated in the following example:

Example 31.1

Mr A owns 40% of the equity capital of Company X, and his wife and his daughter, aged 17, each hold 6% of the company's equity capital. Company X holds 12% of the equity capital of Company Y. Mr A's partner, Mr B, holds 13% of Company Y's equity capital.

Company X is clearly a connected person of Mr A; he and members of his family are interested in more than 20% of the company's equity capital.

The position of Company Y is more difficult. In order to determine whether Company Y is connected with Mr A, Company X's interest in Company Y's equity capital must initially be disregarded.[13] However, Mr A, by virtue of his family's holdings in Company X, is deemed to control the company (i.e. the total holding of Mr A and his connected persons is 52% of Company X's equity capital).[14] Company Y therefore, is connected with Mr A because he is deemed to have an interest in 25% of the company's equity capital (since Mr B's 13% stake in Company Y is added to Company X's holding of 12%).[15]

It should be noted that FRS 8 presumes that 'close family' members of a director are related parties for the purposes of that standard (see Chapter 30 at 2.2.4 A). The definition of 'close family' is likely to encompass more than just the family members mentioned in (a) above. Thus transactions which may escape disclosure under the Companies Act may need to be disclosed under FRS 8.

2.5 Officer

The statutory definition of officer encompasses directors, managers and company secretaries.[16] This definition is not, however, exhaustive and it would appear that the term extends to any person who exercises a significant degree of managerial power; for example, a financial controller of a company is likely to be an officer, whereas a branch manager of a bank is not.

2.6 Loan

There is no statutory definition of a loan for the purpose of the legislation. However, the term has been judicially defined as 'a sum of money lent for a time, to be returned in money or money's worth'.[17] It is crucial to this definition that the parties to the agreement intend that the amount will be repaid. Recurring problems in this context arise where a director draws remuneration on account or expense advances. Such drawings may constitute a loan depending on the particular circumstances. There is no litmus test which can be applied in determining whether, say, a salary advance is in fact a loan; it is necessary to examine each transaction to decide whether in light of all the facts the director is really receiving an interest free loan. The example below illustrates this problem:

Example 31.2

Mr A, a director of Company Y, draws an expense advance of £9,000, on 1 January 2001. By the end of the financial year (31 December 2001), the director has only incurred business expenditure of £2,500 and the outstanding sum is then repaid. Ordinary expense advances would not normally fall within the scope of the legislation because such advances are made on the understanding that the director will apply the funds in performance of his duties to the company. However, in these circumstances the funds have remained outstanding for an unusually long period and, prima facie, the advance appears to have taken on the nature of a loan.

2.7 Quasi-loan

This is a transaction under which one party (the creditor) pays a sum on behalf of another (the borrower) or reimburses expenditure incurred by a third party for the borrower, in circumstances:

(a) where the borrower (or a person on his behalf) will reimburse the creditor; or

(b) which gives rise to a liability on the borrower to reimburse the creditor.[18]

A quasi-loan will only arise where the borrower is under an obligation to reimburse the expenditure incurred by the company. Quasi-loans commonly arise where a director is permitted to use a company credit card to pay for private and business expenditure and he undertakes to reimburse the company in respect of personal expenses charged to the card. Likewise, if a company pays a director's household bills on the understanding that the expenses will be recouped by making a deduction from his monthly salary, a quasi-loan will arise.

The following example shows the distinction between a loan and a quasi-loan:

Example 31.3

A director of Company X wishes to buy a painting for £2,000 which is coming up for sale, but will not have the money at that time. If he draws a cheque for £2,000 from the company made payable to himself so that he can buy the painting then, assuming he intends to repay this sum, this will constitute a loan as it is 'a sum of money lent for a time, to be returned in money or money's worth'. If, however, he arranges for the company to pay for the painting on his behalf in the meantime, with the intention that he will repay the company at a later date, then this will be a quasi-loan.

2.8 Credit transaction

This is a transaction whereby a person either:

(a) supplies any goods or sells any land under a hire-purchase agreement or a conditional sale agreement; or

(b) leases or hires any land or goods in return for periodical payments; or

(c) otherwise disposes of land or supplies goods or services on the understanding that payment (whatever form it may take) is to be deferred; i.e. repayment need not be made by means of instalment but could be made by means of a single lump sum.[19]

In this context, services are defined as anything other than goods or land.[20]

The examples below indicate two of the many forms which a credit transaction may assume:

Example 31.4

A property company leases a residence to a director in return for monthly rental payments. This constitutes a credit transaction under (b) above, irrespective of whether the rental payments are made in advance or arrears. Consideration should also be given to whether this arrangement gives rise to a benefit-in-kind which requires disclosure (see 2.3.2 of Chapter 32).

If, however, the lease was rent-free then it would not be a credit transaction as there are no periodical payments. Alternatively, if the company had granted the director a one year lease but he had made a lump sum payment covering the term of the lease at the outset, then again the transaction would not have constituted a credit transaction, as there would have been no periodical payments.

Example 31.5

A director of a company which repairs motor vehicles has his motor car serviced by the company and payment is to be effected by a single deduction from his following month's salary. The company normally requires payment immediately after the work has been done. This constitutes a credit transaction under (c) above, as payment has been deferred.

However, what if the company's normal procedure was to invoice customers for work done and request payment 30 days after the date of invoice, and the date the amount is to be deducted from the director's salary falls before the date the invoice would be due for payment?

It is unclear whether or not this would constitute a credit transaction, since the legislation does not define what is meant by 'deferred'. It could be argued that this is not a credit transaction as payment is not deferred beyond normal credit terms. However, the legislation makes no reference to normal credit terms and the service would thus appear to require disclosure as a credit transaction.

There is, however, a degree of overlap between credit and material interest transactions and, therefore, those transactions referred to in the above examples which are not credit transactions might require disclosure as material interest transactions (see 3.5 below) or under the requirements of FRS 8 (see generally Chapter 30).

3 DISCLOSURE REQUIREMENTS

3.1 Introduction

A director (including a shadow director) of a company who is interested in a contract with the company must declare the nature of that interest to the board.[21] In this context, transactions include loans, quasi-loans and credit transactions[22] (see E of the Appendix below).

A considerable level of disclosure is required in the notes to both group and individual company financial statements in respect of transactions with directors (including shadow directors).[23] Even where the holding company is not required to produce group accounts by virtue of one of the statutory exemptions (for example, because it is itself a wholly owned subsidiary or the group qualifies as a small or medium-sized group), these requirements still apply in full,[24] and therefore, for example, require disclosure of transactions between the directors and subsidiaries.

If the notes to the financial statements do not disclose the required details of directors' transactions, it is the auditors' duty to include the relevant information in their audit report 'so far as they are reasonably able to do so'.[25]

3.2 Scope

A company's financial statements must disclose transactions between the following:[26]

(a) the company and its directors and their connected persons;

(b) the company's subsidiaries (including non-UK subsidiaries) and its directors and connected persons thereof;

(c) the company, its subsidiaries and the directors (and their connected persons) of any holding company of the company.

A company need not disclose details of transactions entered into between the company or its subsidiaries and directors (and their connected persons) of the subsidiaries (provided the director is not also a director of the company or its holding company).

It should be noted that the term 'subsidiary undertaking' (see Chapter 5 at 2.2) does not apply in this context and therefore transactions entered into by such entities, which are not also 'subsidiaries', with a director of the company or any holding company, will not require to be disclosed.

The multiplicity of disclosures which may ensue from a single transaction are detailed below:

Example 31.6

Assume the following group structure:

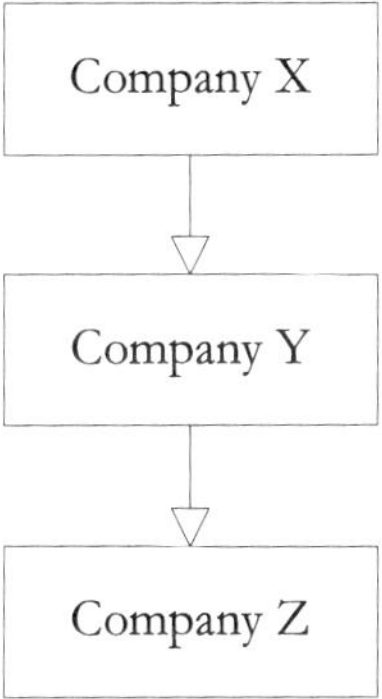

Companies Y and Z are both wholly owned subsidiaries of Company X. Company Z undertakes to guarantee a loan made by a bank to Mr A, a director of company X. The guarantee will be disclosed as follows:

(a) in the financial statements of Company Z as a guarantee of a loan to a director of its holding company;

(b) in the financial statements of Company Y as a guarantee of a loan by a subsidiary to a director of its holding company;

(c) in the financial statements of Company X as a guarantee of a loan by a subsidiary to a director.

These requirements do not apply to banking companies under the Banking Act 1987, which are subject to separate disclosure provisions (see 4 below).[27]

3.3 Transactions requiring disclosure

Broadly, the legislation[28] requires disclosure of two types of transaction involving directors, namely:

(a) loans, quasi-loans, credit transactions, related guarantees,[29] assignments and arrangements (section 330 type transactions); and

(b) transactions (other than section 330 type transactions) in which a director has a material interest.

The disclosure provisions apply irrespective of whether:

(a) the transaction was lawful;

(b) the person for whom the transaction was made was at the time of its execution a director or a connected person; or

(c) the company was a subsidiary at the time the transaction was executed.[30]

For example, details of the following transactions would need to be disclosed in a company's financial statements:

(a) a loan made to an employee who later becomes a director; for example:

> *Extract 31.1: BAA plc (1999)*
>
> 3 **Directors' remuneration** [extract]
> At 31 March 1999 the company had outstanding an £18,958 interest free loan to Mr Collie. The loan was made on 1 August 1992, prior to his appointment to the BAA board, for relocation purposes. At 1 April 1998 the loan was £21,458, its maximum for the year.

(b) a contract entered into with a director who retired during the financial year; for example:

> *Extract 31.2: Cable and Wireless plc (1999)*
>
> **DIRECTORS' REPORT** [extract]
>
> **Directors' remuneration**
> After his resignation as a Director [on 26 June 1998] payments of £122,500 were made to Sir Brian Smith for consultancy services and his continuing Non-executive Directorship of Hong Kong Telecommunications Limited.

(c) a credit transaction entered into with a director of another company which then becomes the reporting company's parent.

3.4 Section 330 transactions

3.4.1 Introduction

Details of these transactions must be disclosed in both group and individual company financial statements (subject to various exemptions: see 3.6 below).[31]

Thus, disclosure must be made where any company:

(a) makes a loan or a quasi-loan to, or enters into a credit transaction with, or enters into a guarantee or provides any security in connection therewith for one of its directors, a director of its holding company or a connected person thereof;

(b) arranges for the assignment to it, or the assumption by it, of any rights or obligations or liabilities under a transaction that would have contravened section 330 if the company had originally entered into it (see B.3 of the Appendix below);

(c) takes part in any arrangement such that another person enters into a transaction that would have contravened section 330 had the company entered into it (see B.4 of the Appendix below);

(d) agrees to enter into any of the above transactions or arrangements.

3.4.2 *Disclosure requirements*

The particulars to be disclosed are the principal terms of the transaction, arrangement or agreement.[32] The principal terms must include, as a minimum:[33]

(a) a statement of the fact that the transaction was made or existed during the financial year;

(b) the name of the person for whom it was made and, if this person is connected with a director, that director's name;

(c) for loans (including agreements and arrangements relating thereto):

  (i) the principal and interest at the beginning and the end of the financial year,

  (ii) the maximum amount outstanding during the year,

  (iii) the amount of any interest due but unpaid,

  (iv) the amount of any provision in respect of non-payment of the loan;

(d) for guarantees and security:

  (i) the potential liability of the company (or its subsidiary) at the beginning and the end of the financial year,

  (ii) the maximum potential liability of the company (or its subsidiary),

  (iii) any amount paid and any liability incurred by the company in fulfilling the security or discharging the security;

(e) for quasi-loans and credit transactions, it is necessary to disclose the value of the transaction. The value of a quasi-loan is defined as the maximum amount which the person to whom the quasi-loan is made is liable to reimburse the creditor. In the case of a credit transaction, value is defined as the price which it is reasonable to expect could be obtained for the goods, land or services to which the transaction or arrangement relates if they had been supplied in the ordinary course of business and on the same terms (apart from price) as they have been supplied, under the transaction or arrangement in question.[34] Although the legislation does not specify the extent of disclosures, given that details of any transaction subsisting during the year must be disclosed, it would be relevant for the disclosures to be similar to those for loans (see (c) above).

In addition to the above, it may be necessary to disclose other principal terms of the transaction; for example, the repayment term in the case of a loan or the credit limit for credit transactions and quasi-loans.

The following extracts illustrate a variety of section 330 type transactions:

A Loans

Extract 31.3: Friends' Provident Life Office (1996)

10. Loans to Directors [extract]

	Amount outstanding 1 January 1996	31 December 1996	Maximum outstanding during the year
	£	£	£
K. Satchell			
House purchase loan (repaid during year)	30,000	–	30,000

The loan was secured by mortgage on the property and by a life assurance policy on the life of the borrower. The rate of interest payable was 4% p.a. on the first £15,000 and 8% p.a. on the remainder. The loan was made by the Office on the same terms as were available to other employees.

Extract 31.4: Cordiant plc (1996)

Remuneration and Nominations Committee report [extract]

On appointment to the Board on 9 January 1995, Mr Bungey already had a loan from the Company which totalled US$261,699 including interest charged at US prime rate. At 31 December 1995, he owed US$79,400 (which included interest of US$4,400) which was repaid in full in April 1996. During 1996, the maximum amount outstanding was US$81,144. There are no outstanding loans granted by any member of the Group to any of the Directors or guarantees provided by any member of the Group for their benefit.

It can be seen from the above extracts that, even though there are no amounts outstanding at the year end, disclosure is required; this is because the transactions *existed* during the period. This would also be the case where there are no amounts outstanding at either the beginning or the end of the year. (An example of this is shown in Extract 31.8 below in respect of a quasi-loan.)

Similarly, even if the individual concerned is no longer a director at the year end, disclosure would be required; this is because the loan was in respect of someone who was a director at some time during the financial year.

B Guarantees and security

Extract 31.5: The Body Shop International PLC (1996)

7 Directors [extract]
Transactions involving Directors

Prior to her appointment as a Director on 25 July 1994, the Company provided a bank guarantee in respect of J Reid. This guarantee had been cleared to nil by 2 March 1996 (1995: £73,750).

C Credit transactions

Extract 31.6: First Leisure Corporation PLC (1998)

23 Transactions with related parties [extract]

(ii) Directors

Mr Bollom, through a company controlled by him, had an interest in a lease of property owned by the Group in Blackpool. Payments under this lease in the year ended 31st October 1998 amounted to £0.4m (1997: £0.4m). The property was disposed of in September 1998.

Extract 31.7: The Body Shop International PLC (1996)

7 Directors [extract]

Transactions involving Directors

M J Ross owns jointly with his wife all the shares in Craigross Holdings Limited ("Craigross"), subsidiaries of which hold six franchises with the Company.

...

In common with the arrangements with other UK franchisees, the Company has leased the premises relating to three of the franchised outlets to Craigross and has guaranteed the lease commitments on the three other shops. The annual rentals payable in respect of the premises leased to Craigross by the Company were £0.267 million (1995: £0.227 million). ...

D Quasi-loans

Extract 31.8: Chrysalis Group PLC (2000)

28 Related party transactions [extract]

b During the year a quasi loan was made to C N Wright. The highest amount outstanding during the year was £42,730. The amount outstanding at 31st August 200 was £nil (1999: £nil).

3.5 Material interest transactions

3.5.1 *Introduction*

The group and individual company financial statements must disclose details of transactions or arrangements in which any person who was a director of the company, its holding company or a connected person thereof had a material interest (subject to various exemptions: see 3.6 below).[35] Section 330 type transactions are excluded from this category.[36]

It is for the directors to determine whether a transaction is material.[37] For these purposes, a transaction is not material if the directors of the reporting company (or at least a majority of them), excluding the director whose interest is under review, decide that it is not.[38] However, if the directors do not consider the question of materiality, it cannot be presumed that the interest was immaterial.[39] In these circumstances, the question of the materiality of the transaction will be regarded as a matter of fact.

3.5.2 *Definition of material interest*

The definition of 'material' has proved to be one of the more problematic issues in this area of the law. There are two widely accepted interpretations; namely, that 'material':

(a) should be judged by what is relevant to the users of the financial statements (the relevant view). Rumbelow[40] suggests that the rationale for this disclosure requirement is to ensure that shareholders are better informed about their directors and better able to take any decisions they may have to take as shareholders (particularly as regards those directors). Consequently, he reasons that to decide what is material, one must look to see if the interest is such that its disclosure would be likely to influence a reasonable shareholder in making those decisions;

(b) means substantial in relation to the individual transaction in which the director is interested (the 'Mars Bar' view). Proponents of this view claim that the wording of the provision points to this interpretation.

However, as the following example illustrates, the 'Mars Bar' view may give rise to curious results:

Example 31.7

A director arranges a £50m contract on behalf of his company; the agreement provides for an arrangement fee of ½% of the value of the contract (i.e. commission of £250,000). The director will not need to disclose his interest if the 'Mars Bar' approach is adopted because his interest in the transaction is insignificant in relation to that transaction. However, if a director purchases a bar of chocolate for himself in the staff restaurant, the 'Mars Bar' view would demand disclosure of this transaction (subject to the de minimis exceptions: see 3.6.3 below); in this instance, he has a 100% interest in the transaction.

There is a third possible interpretation; namely, that material must be determined by reference to the director's financial position. Proponents of this view argue that if a transaction is not material vis-à-vis the director's personal position, there will be no conflict of duty and interest. However, the jurisprudence in this area makes it clear that the courts will not look into the merits of a transaction but adhere strictly to the rule that the possible conflict of interest and duty must not be allowed to arise, hence this rationale is somewhat spurious. On a practical note, if this view were adopted curious results could arise, as shown in the following example:

Example 31.8

Mr M, a director of ABC plc, has amassed a personal fortune of £10m. The latest audited accounts of ABC plc show net assets of £50,000 and turnover of £200,000. XYZ plc, a company of which Mr M is the majority shareholder, enters into a contract to buy goods worth £20,000 from ABC plc. Arguably, if the foregoing basis of assessing materiality is used, the transaction would not require disclosure.

On balance, we prefer the relevant view since its application is most likely to satisfy the needs of the users (or potential users) of the accounts, by keeping them informed of the types of dealing between a company and its directors which impact upon investment, credit and other decisions which they may be required to take. Clearly, this test involves the making of a qualitative judgement, that is, whether disclosure of the transaction might make a difference to a business decision. In practice, as Swinson argues,[41] this qualitative assessment may often be answered by establishing whether a director's interest is material in quantitative terms. If an interest is immaterial in quantitative terms, it may be irrelevant to the users of the accounts and vice-versa.

It should be emphasised that the above discussion of 'material' is only in the context of whether the transaction requires disclosure as a result of the Companies Act. However, this will not be the end of the matter in determining whether disclosure is necessary in the accounts because the requirements of FRS 8 also apply. As discussed at 2.3.2 in Chapter 30, FRS 8 requires that in considering whether transactions with individuals (such as directors) need to be disclosed, materiality has to be judged not only in terms of their significance to the reporting entity but also in relation to the other party, which in this case is the director.

The effect of FRS 8 has been that more transactions with directors are now disclosed than hitherto under the Companies Act requirements.

3.5.3 *Disclosure requirements*

The principal terms of material interest transactions must be disclosed;[42] in particular:

(a) the name of the director who has the material interest and the nature thereof;[43]

(b) the value of the transaction.[44]

The types of transaction in which a director may have an interest are diverse: the purchase or disposal of residential properties, other arrangements in respect of such property which arise due to the relocation of the directors, purchase or disposal of investments or businesses, provision of professional services and transactions in the ordinary course of business. Some of these are illustrated in the following extracts:

Extract 31.9: The Royal Bank of Scotland Group plc (2000)

51 Transactions with directors, officers and others [extract]

(b) Sir George Mathewson, an executive director of the company, the Bank and NatWest, has a right to repurchase from the Bank his former dwellinghouse which the Bank purchased from him and his wife in May 1988 at a price of £125,000. The right will become exercisable (1) in the event that Sir George ceases to be an executive director of the company or its subsidiaries; or (2) on 31 May 2008 in the event that he remains an executive director at that date; or (3) on such earlier date as the directors of the company may allow. Any repurchase is to be at the higher of the purchase price paid by the Bank or a price determined by independent professional valuation at the time of repurchase. The dwellinghouse is at present let by the Bank on a commercial basis, with any rental payments being received wholly by the Bank.

Extract 31.10: Coats Viyella Plc (2000)

Report by the Board on Directors' Remuneration [extract]

In 1992, the Company, through a subsidiary, acquired a joint interest in a property with Mr Flower on his taking permanent residence in England. The subsidiary's investment was £180,000. Under the agreement Mr Flower has the option to purchase the Group's interest at market value. The Group's investment was reduced to £75,000 in January 1994 following partial exercise of Mr Flower's option.

Extract 31.11: Alfred McAlpine PLC (1996)

14. Fixed Assets – Investments [extract]
During 1996, the Group completed the deferred consideration payments to the Grove family in respect of the acquisition of the minority holding of Alfred McAlpine Homes Holdings Limited (formerly Alfred McAlpine Developments Limited). Mr E W Grove is a former director of both the Company and Alfred McAlpine Homes Holdings Limited. The final element of the deferred consideration was agreed at £15,242,000 and was settled during the year by cash payments of £7,621,000, plus interest of £99,000, and the issue of ordinary shares in the Company to the Grove family to the value of £7,621,000.

(Mr Grove resigned as a non-executive director during the year, on 22 July 1996.)

Extract 31.12: Rio Tinto plc and Rio Tinto Limited (1998)

36 RELATED PARTY TRANSACTIONS [extract]

Mr L A Davis occupied, without payment of rent, accommodation in central London under a licence agreement granted by a subsidiary company. The value based on the estimated market rent was £201,504.

This extract highlights the fact that the value of the transaction is not necessarily the amount at which the transaction is transacted, but is the amount which could have been obtained in the ordinary course of business.[45]

Where the value of the transaction cannot be expressed as a specific amount of money, then it is deemed to exceed £100,000,[46] as the following extract shows:

Extract 31.13: British Gas plc (1991)

3. Directors and employees [extract]

Norman Blacker was required to relocate during the year ended 31 March 1990 and Cedric Brown during the year ended 31 March 1991. Norman Blacker participated in the Company's relocation scheme throughout the period to December 1991 and Cedric Brown until May 1991. The value of these arrangements cannot be expressed as a specific sum of money and in these circumstances the Companies Act 1985 provides that the value is individually deemed to exceed £100 000. During 1991 approximately 570 employees participated in this scheme, which complies with Inland Revenue guidelines.

Extract 31.14: Kwik-Fit Holdings plc (1999)

9. DIRECTOR'S REMUNERATION AND INTERESTS [extract]
(d) Transactions

Sir Tom and Lady Farmer and family lease certain properties to the Group. The rentals payable on these properties were £348,837 (1998 – £341,000) and the balance owing by the Group at 28 February 1999 was Nil (1998 – Nil).

E. Landau is a partner in Landau Nock who received professional fees and reimbursement of expenses of £476,933 (1998 – £479,578) in relation to services provided to the Group during the year. The balance owing to Landau Nock at 28 February 1999 was Nil (1998 – Nil).

J. Padget is a Principal of Padget Associates B.V. who received fees of £65,623 (1998 – £107,446) and reimbursement of expenses of £10,562 (1998 – £16,002) in relation to services provided to the Group during the year in addition to the Director's fees shown in (a) above. The balance owing to Padget Associates B.V. at 28 February was Nil (1998 – £53,439).

The above extract illustrates the situation where a professional firm, such as solicitors, in which one of the directors is a partner, provide services to the company in the ordinary course of business.

Disclosure of such transactions is not required where the firm, or company, providing the services is not a connected person as defined by the Act (see 2.4 above); for example, where the director concerned is not a partner in the firm providing the services, but is merely a consultant. Nevertheless some companies disclose information about such transactions within the directors' report, presumably to meet the requirements of the Financial Services Authority or the London Stock Exchange (see 5 below). One company which disclosed such a transaction, but within the notes to the accounts, as well as numerous other directors' interests in transactions is Chrysalis Group, as shown below:

Extract 31.15: Chrysalis Group PLC (2000)

28 Related party transactions [extract]

a Sir George Martin has an interest in certain subsidiary undertakings' agreements with Airborn Productions Limited and Airborn Productions (Overseas) Limited by virtue of his share interests in those companies. The producer royalties payable to these companies in respect of the year were £25,809 (1999: £33,089). The amount accrued (but not due) at the balance sheet date was £13,376 (1999: £1,153).

...

c S G Lewis has an interest in a subsidiary company The Echo Label Limited by virtue of his interest in the share capital of Armourvale Limited ('Armourvale') and Lapishaven Limited ('Lapishaven'), two companies which together hold 75% of the share capital of The Echo Label Limited. Mr Lewis' interest in The Echo Label Limited amounts to 18.75% of its capital. Certain put and call option agreements exist between the Group and Mr Lewis in respect of his shares in Armourvale and Lapishaven other than his B shares in Lapishaven, as referred to in note 27a [below].

d C J C Levison has, since 1st August 1994, been a consultant with one of the Group's solicitors, Harbottle & Lewis, and as such consultant Mr Levison received fees from Harbottle & Lewis through his company, Clarion Media Europe Limited. All fees paid to Harbottle & Lewis by the Group are on ordinary commercial terms incurred in the normal course of the Group's business. Neither Mr Levison nor Clarion Media Europe Limited participate in any fees or profits of Harbottle & Lewis relating to the Group, or any of its subsidiary or joint venture companies.

e From 1st September 1996 the services of C N Wright provided to Loftus Road plc (a company in which Mr Wright has a beneficial interest of 30% of the issued share capital and of which he, Mr Butterfield and Mr Levison are all non-executive directors), were being reimbursed to Chrysalis Group PLC at a rate of £8,000 per month. These arrangements terminated on 28th September 1999. The amount due from Loftus Road plc at 31st August 2000 was £nil (1999: £56,755). None of these directors receive any remuneration from Loftus Road plc.

...

There are no provisions for doubtful debts or amounts written off during the year in respect of any of the above transactions.

27 Capital commitments [extract]

a Under the terms of the Option Agreement dated 29th November 1993 between the Group and Mr S G Lewis, set out in the circular to shareholders dated 30th November 1993, the Group may be required to purchase certain of Mr Lewis' shares in Armourvale Limited and Lapishaven Limited (which holds the Group's interest in The Echo Label Limited. Mr Lewis may exercise this put option at any time after 1st September 1998 whilst he is still employed by the Company, or within 30 days of the subsequent termination of his employment, for a consideration based upon the fair market value of the shares, and capped at £10 million.

3.6 Exemptions from disclosure

The following transactions involving directors do not require disclosure:

3.6.1 *General*

(a) Transactions between companies in which a director is interested only by virtue of his being a director of both companies;[47]

(b) directors' service contracts.[48] However, details of service contracts of directors of listed companies may require disclosure (see 3.2.10 of Chapter 32);

(c) transactions which were not entered into or which did not subsist during the year.[49] However, transactions which were entered into after the year end will require disclosure if at the year end there was an agreement between the parties to enter into the transaction.[50] In addition, material transactions involving directors post year-end may fall to be disclosed as post balance sheet events in accordance with the provisions of SSAP 17 (see Chapter 27).

3.6.2 *Section 330 transactions*

(a) Credit transactions and related guarantees, arrangements and agreements where the aggregate amount outstanding for the director and his connected persons did not at any time during the financial year exceed £5,000;[51]

(b) there is a reduced level of disclosure for intra-group loans and quasi-loans,[52] although relief has not been granted for guarantees, credit transactions etc. The only details to be disclosed in respect of such transactions are:

  (i) a statement that the transaction etc. was made or subsisted during the financial year;

  (ii) the name of the person for whom it was made and in the case of a loan or quasi-loan to a connected person, the name of the director.

  This exemption only applies if there are no minority interests involved.

3.6.3 *Material interest transactions*

(a) Transactions in which the director's interest is not material (as decided by a majority of his fellow directors);[53]

(b) transactions in which a director has a material interest which are entered into at arm's length in the ordinary course of business. The exact wording of this exemption is:

  'Neither paragraph [15](c) nor paragraph [16](c) applies in relation to any transaction or arrangement if-

  (a) each party to the transaction or arrangement which is a member of the same group of companies (meaning a holding company and its subsidiaries) as the company entered into the transaction or arrangement in the ordinary course of business, and

  (b) the terms of the transaction or arrangement are not less favourable to any such party than it would be reasonable to expect if the interest mentioned in that sub-paragraph had not been an interest of a person who was a director of the company or of its holding company.'[54]

This has given rise to particular difficulty. It is sometimes argued that the exemption, as presently drafted, only applies if each party to the transaction is a member of the same group. The explanatory note to the statutory instrument[55] which introduced the exemption indicates that there is no need for the counterparties to the transaction to be group companies. Given that one of the aims of introducing the exemption was to reduce the level of disclosure, it seems logical to interpret the provision as exempting all arm's length material interest transactions involving directors. This view, however, is not universally held.[56]

(c) any material interest transaction between members of a group of companies which would have been disclosable only because of a director being associated (see 2.4 above) with the contracting companies, provided that no minority interests in the reporting company are affected.[57] A higher level of disclosure is required where there are minority interests since minorities can be affected by transfers of value within a group. The wording of this exemption is arcane and the drafting is considered to be defective;

(d) transactions in which a director had a material interest where the value of each transaction (with no reduction in the amount outstanding) in the financial year and the value of transactions in preceding financial years (less the amount by which the director's liabilities have been reduced) did not at any time during the financial year exceed £1,000 or, if more than £1,000, did not exceed £5,000 or 1% of the value of the net assets of the reporting company. Net assets is defined as the aggregate of the company's assets, less the aggregate of its liabilities.[58] It is not clear how this provision interacts with the other exemptions for material interest transactions (see (b) and (c) above). Unless these provisions are discrete, the exemptions are likely to be rendered ineffective.

Whether the effect of any of these exemptions will result in non-disclosure of the relevant transactions in the accounts will depend on whether or not FRS 8 requires disclosure of the transactions. As noted at 3.5.2 above, FRS 8 has a different concept of materiality; it also requires transactions to be disclosed even when the terms are at arm's length. Companies should therefore ensure that, before relying on any of the exemptions above, they have considered the requirements of FRS 8 (see generally Chapter 30).

4 BANKING COMPANIES UNDER THE BANKING ACT 1987

A banking company under the Banking Act 1987 is subject to different disclosure requirements in respect of section 330 type transactions to which the company is a party.[59] Material interest transactions involving directors of banking companies must be disclosed as for other companies (see 3.5 above).[60] Similar requirements apply to a company which is the holding company of a credit institution. References to banking companies below should be read as including such companies.

In brief,[61] banking companies must maintain a register of section 330 type transactions for the current and preceding ten financial years.[62] A statement of such transactions must be:[63]

(a) made available for members to inspect; and

(b) examined and reported on by the company's auditor.

4.1 Disclosure of transactions by banking companies

The financial statements must disclose:

(a) the aggregate amounts of loans, quasi-loans, credit transactions and related transactions outstanding at the end of the financial year; and

(b) the number of persons for whom the transactions were made.[64]

In this context,[65] amount outstanding means the outstanding liabilities of the person for whom the transaction was made and as respects a guarantee or security, the amount guaranteed or secured.

The following extract provides an illustration of the disclosures of transactions between a banking company and its directors:

Extract 31.16: National Westminster Bank Plc (1998)

49 Transactions with related parties [extract]

i The aggregate amounts outstanding at 31 December 1998 under transactions, arrangements and agreements made by institutions authorised under the Banking Act 1987 within the Group for persons who are, or were, directors of the Bank during the year and their connected persons, and with executive officers listed on page 60 and their connected persons comprised the following:–

	Number of directors/ officers	Number of connected persons	Aggregate amount £000
Directors and their connected persons			
Loans and credit card transactions	5	8	61
Other executive officers			
Loans and credit card transactions	19	5	904

It must be emphasised that these disclosures only apply to section 330 type transactions with the banking company. The disclosure requirements outlined in 3.4.2 above still apply to any such transaction with other companies within the group.

5 REQUIREMENTS OF THE FINANCIAL SERVICES AUTHORITY AND LONDON STOCK EXCHANGE

In addition to the disclosure provisions imposed by the Companies Act 1985 (and those of FRS 8 – see Chapter 30), the Financial Services Authority imposes additional requirements in respect of transactions involving directors of listed companies.[66]

Transactions (other than those of a revenue nature in the ordinary course of business) involving directors, shadow directors, past directors of the company (or other member of the group) and their associates (similar to connected persons) constitute transactions with related parties (formerly known as Class 4 transactions).[67] Generally, full particulars of the transaction must be given in a circular including the name of the related party concerned and of the nature and extent of the interest of such party in the transaction.[68]

Normally these particulars should be circulated to the company's shareholders prior to obtaining their approval[69] and the Financial Services Authority must also be notified of the proposed transaction.[70] A number of exceptions from the requirements are made, one of which is for small transactions provided that an independent adviser expresses the opinion that the terms of the transaction are fair and reasonable. Where this exception applies, the company must also disclose details of the transaction in the next published annual accounts, including the identity of the related party, the value of the consideration for the transaction and all other relevant circumstances.[71]

The annual report and accounts of listed companies must also disclose particulars of any contract of significance to which the company, or one of its subsidiary undertakings, is a party and in which a director of the company is or was materially interested.[72] A contract of significance is defined as one which represents in amount or value, a sum equal to 1% or more, calculated on a group basis where relevant, of:

(a) in the case of a capital transaction or a transaction the principal purpose of which is the granting of credit, the aggregate of the group's share capital and reserves; or

(b) in other cases, the total annual purchases, sales, payments or receipts, as the case may be, of the group.[73]

There is no need to make a statement if there has been no such contract.

The London Stock Exchange also imposes additional requirements on companies quoted on the Alternative Investment Market.

Where an AIM company proposes to enter into related party transactions (similar to those for listed companies) which result in specified percentage ratios being 5% or more then it must give particulars to the Stock Exchange and send a copy of the announcement to the shareholders.[74] Where any of the percentage ratios exceed 0.25%, then disclosure of the transaction must be made in the next set of published accounts, including the identity of the related party and the consideration for the transaction.[75]

6 TRANSACTIONS INVOLVING OFFICERS

6.1 Introduction

The Act requires certain details of transactions between a company and its officers to be disclosed.[76] To this end, group and individual company financial statements must contain particulars in the notes of transactions entered into by officers. A holding company's financial statements must take into account transactions between the company and its subsidiaries with officers of the company; however, transactions between the subsidiaries and their officers do not need to be included in the holding company's financial statements. If a company does not produce group financial statements by virtue of one of the statutory exemptions, these requirements still apply in full.[77]

6.2 Disclosure requirements

The financial statements must disclose the following details in respect of transactions with officers (which, for these purposes, in order to avoid duplication of disclosure excludes directors):[78]

(a) the aggregate amounts of loans, quasi-loans, credit transactions, guarantees and arrangements outstanding at the end of the financial year; and

(b) the number of officers for whom the transactions were made.[79]

For these purposes, the amount outstanding is defined as the outstanding liabilities of the person for whom the transaction was made and in the case of a guarantee or security, the amount guaranteed or secured.[80]

Disclosure of such transactions is not, however, necessary for a particular officer if the aggregate amount outstanding under the transactions at the end of the financial year for that officer does not exceed £2,500.[81]

The following extracts illustrate the disclosure of transactions involving officers:

Extract 31.17: BAE SYSTEMS plc (2000)

5 **Employees and directors** [extract]

Transactions

At 31 December 2000 there was an aggregate balance of £229,688 (1999 £71,477) outstanding on house purchase loans made to, or arranged for, five officers (1999 three officers) to assist with their relocation at the company's request.

Extract 31.18: Imperial Chemical Industries PLC (1998)

41 Statutory and other information [extract]

Included in debtors is an interest-free loan of £8,000 (1997 £30,000) to an officer (1997 two officers) of the Company.

6.3 Banking companies under the Banking Act 1987

Financial statements of banking companies (or companies which are holding companies of credit institutions) do not generally require disclosure of transactions between officers (who were not also directors) and the banking company. However, the information described at 6.2 above is required to be disclosed in respect of transactions between the banking company (or as the case may be the credit institution) and a chief executive or manager of the company or its holding company.[82]

A 'chief executive' means a person who, either alone or jointly with one or more other persons, is responsible under the immediate authority of the directors for the conduct of the business of the company and a 'manager' means a person (other than a chief executive) who, under the immediate authority of a director or chief executive of the financial institution, exercises managerial functions or is responsible for maintaining accounts or other records of the financial institution.[83]

7 IAS REQUIREMENTS

The relevant international standard which covers this area is IAS 24 – *Related Party Disclosures.* Key management personnel, including directors and officers of companies and close family members of such individuals, and enterprises in which such individuals have a substantial interest or over which they are able exercise significant influence, are regarded as related parties for the purpose of that standard. The requirements of IAS 24 are dealt with in Chapter 30 at 4.

It should also be borne in mind that other countries may also have legislation requiring disclosures about transactions with directors and officers.

8 CONCLUSION

The provisions of the Companies Act governing the disclosure of transactions between a company and its directors and officers are generally regarded as unsatisfactory. They do not appear to form a coherent whole whereby a director's contractual freedom can be meaningfully regulated; for example, there are de minimis exemptions from disclosure of credit and material interest transactions yet no parallel provisions for loans and quasi-loans. In addition, aspects of the legislation are difficult to comprehend, for example, the material interest transaction exemptions.

Over the years various professional bodies have made representations to the DTI suggesting that the legislation be clarified and simplified. The Companies Act 1989 did make some minor amendments relating to this area, although it was indicated while the Bill was going through the parliamentary process that further changes would be made by Statutory Instrument.[84]

The DTI had indicated that it was the intention to review the legislation in this area, but that it was a long-term task. It did publish in 1991 a consultative document in which it proposed to simplify the rules contained in Schedule 6 to the Act, dealing with the information required to be disclosed in companies' financial statements, but nothing has ever come of it.[85]

In September 1998, the Law Commission and the Scottish Law Commission published a joint Consultation/Discussion Paper – *Company Directors: Regulating Conflicts of Interest and Formulating a Statement of Duties* – which considered this whole area. However, earlier in 1998 the Government had announced the launch of a fundamental review of the framework of core company law, and the Law Commissions' work covers ground which is part of the area in which that review will be making integrated proposals, principally in relation to corporate governance. It is therefore likely to be quite a while before there is any change to the legislation.

APPENDIX: LEGAL REQUIREMENTS

A INTRODUCTION

Although the primary objective of this chapter is to discuss how transactions with directors should be disclosed in a company's financial statements, a brief exposition of the statutory provisions determining the legality of such transactions is considered necessary in order to place the disclosure requirements in context.

B PROHIBITED TRANSACTIONS

The Companies Act 1985 contains complex provisions[86] which prohibit or restrict many transactions involving directors (and shadow directors).[87] The legality of a transaction is determined at the time of its execution. Therefore, a loan to a person who subsequently becomes a director is legal because the recipient was not a director at the time of its making.

The basic prohibitions are dealt with in B.1 to B.4 below and the exemptions therefrom are dealt with in C below.

B.1 Loans

A company may not make a loan to its directors or those of its holding company.[88] In addition, a relevant company[89] (i.e. a public company or a company which is part of a group which includes a public company) may not make a loan to a connected person thereof.[90] Likewise, a company may not enter into a guarantee[91] or provide any security in connection with a loan made by another person to its directors or those of its holding company[92] and, in the case of a relevant company, a connected person thereof.[93]

B.2 Quasi-loans and credit transactions

A relevant company may not make a quasi loan nor enter into a credit transaction with its directors, the directors of its holding company or a connected person thereof. There is a similar restriction on the provision of guarantees or security in connection with such transactions.[94]

B.3 Assignment/assumption of rights, obligations or liabilities

A company may not arrange for the assignment to, or the assumption by it, of any rights, obligations or liabilities in respect of transactions which, if undertaken by the company in the first place, would have been unlawful;[95] for example:

Example 31.9

A bank makes a loan to a director of Company X and thereafter assigns its rights to Company X. The company will have entered into an unlawful assignment.

Example 31.10

The facts are as above, but the loan from the bank is guaranteed by a friend of the director. Subsequently, Company X becomes the guarantor of the loan releasing the director's friend from his obligations. The assumption of the guarantee by Company X is unlawful.

B.4 Arrangements

Schemes whereby a third party enters into an arrangement which if entered into by the company would have been unlawful, in circumstances where the company (or a fellow group company) provides a benefit to the third party, are not permitted;[96] for example:

Example 31.11

Company X arranges for a bank to make a loan to one of its directors on favourable terms in return for which the company places business with the bank. This series of transactions constitutes an unlawful arrangement whereby the bank enters into an arrangement forbidden to Company X and receives a benefit for so doing.

C EXEMPTED TRANSACTIONS

C.1 Loans of small amounts

A loan to a director of a company or its holding company is not illegal if the aggregate of the sums advanced to the director does not exceed £5,000; in computing the sum of £5,000, amounts already advanced to the director must be taken into account.[97] It should be noted that this exemption does not extend to loans of small amounts to connected persons of directors of a relevant company.

C.2 Short-term quasi-loans

Quasi-loans by a relevant company are permitted if made on the condition that the director reimburses the company within two months and where the aggregate of the sums outstanding under quasi-loans does not exceed £5,000.[98] Again, this exemption does not extend to quasi-loans made to connected persons of directors of a relevant company.

C.3 Minor or business credit transactions

A relevant company may enter in a credit transaction for a person if:

(a) the aggregate of such amounts does not exceed £10,000;[99] or

(b) the transaction is entered into by the company in the ordinary course of its business on terms which the company would have extended to a person of the same financial standing unconnected with the company.[100]

It should be noted that this exemption extends to credit transactions for connected persons of directors of a relevant company.

C.4 Inter-company transactions

A relevant company is not prohibited from making loans and quasi-loans to a group company where a director of one company is associated with another.[101] Likewise, a company may make a loan or quasi-loan to or enter into a credit transaction as creditor for its holding company.[102]

Furthermore, a holding company may make a loan to a director of its subsidiary or a connected person thereof; similarly, a subsidiary may make a loan to a director of a fellow subsidiary (provided in both cases that the director is not on the board of the company or the holding company and that the other group company does not thereby obtain some benefit: see B.4 above).

C.5 Directors' business expenditure

A director can be placed in funds to enable him properly to perform his duties as a corporate officer. However, funds may only be advanced:

(a) if prior approval of the company in general meeting has been obtained; or

(b) where approval is not obtained at or before the next annual general meeting, the loan is to be repaid within six months of the conclusion of that meeting.[103]

Furthermore, relevant companies may only advance an aggregate of £20,000 to the director for these purposes.[104]

C.6 Money-lending companies

A money-lending company (namely one whose ordinary business includes the making of loans or quasi-loans) may make loans or quasi-loans or enter into related guarantees to its directors, directors of its holding company and connected persons. However, such transactions are only permitted if made by the company in the ordinary course of its business on terms which are no more preferential than are available to persons who have no connection with the company. In addition, relevant companies (excluding banking companies: see 4 above) may make loans or quasi-loans only up to a £100,000 limit.[105]

Loans made for the purpose of facilitating the purchase of or improving a director's house may also be made by money-lending companies if the facility is ordinarily available to employees of the company on equally favourable terms; this exemption is again subject to a £100,000 limit for all companies.[106]

There is some doubt as to the interaction between the monetary limit on housing and 'other' loans to directors of relevant money-lending companies (which are not banking companies under the Banking Act 1987: see 4 above). This problem is compounded by what appears to be a drafting error[107] in references in section 339(1) which impacts upon how previous loans etc. made by money-lending companies are to be aggregated with amounts already advanced to directors and their connected persons. On balance, we believe that the intention of the legislation is that the aggregate value of all loans, whatever their nature, made by money-lending companies to any given director and his connected persons, must not exceed £100,000.

C.7 Companies registered overseas[108]

The following transactions entered into by an overseas company are not subject to the statutory restrictions; transactions entered into by an overseas incorporated subsidiary:

(a) with a director of its UK incorporated parent; and

(b) of a UK incorporated parent with a director of the UK parent's overseas incorporated holding company.

D SANCTIONS

D.1 Civil remedies

A prohibited transaction is voidable at the company's option unless:

(a) restitution is impossible, for example, where the proceeds of an illegal loan have been used to build an extension to the director's house; or

(b) the company has been indemnified for the loss suffered by it; or

(c) rights have been acquired by a bona fide purchaser for value who does not have notice of the contravention.[109]

The director, any connected person for whom the transaction was made and any director who authorised the transaction is liable:

(a) to account for any gain which he has made; and

(b) to make good any loss made by the company.[110]

However, where the transaction is made for a person connected with a director, then that director will not be liable if he can demonstrate that he took all reasonable steps to secure the company's compliance with the legislation.[111]

The person connected with the director and any other director who authorised the transaction will not be liable if he can demonstrate that at the time the transaction was entered into he did not know the circumstances constituting the contravention.[112]

D.2 Criminal penalties

A director of a relevant company who authorises or permits the company to enter into a transaction knowing or believing that the transaction was illegal is guilty of an offence and is liable to imprisonment and/or a fine. A relevant company entering into an illegal transaction is also guilty of an offence unless it did not know the circumstances at the time of the transaction. A person who knowingly procures the transaction or arrangement is also guilty of an offence.[113]

E INTERESTS IN CONTRACTS

A director must, upon pain of a fine,[114] declare any interest (direct or indirect) in a contract with the company at a board meeting.[115] In this context, an interest in a section 330 type transaction requires disclosure[116] (see generally 3 above). If the contract is merely proposed, the director must declare his interest at the board meeting at which the contract is under consideration.[117] The Court of Appeal held in *Guinness plc v Saunders & Ward* [118] that this duty cannot be fulfilled by disclosure to a sub-committee of the board; only disclosure to a properly convened meeting of the full board will suffice. If the director was not interested in the contract at the time it was made, disclosure should be made at the first board meeting after the director becomes interested.[119] For these purposes, a general notice of interest in specific types of contracts given to the board suffices.[120]

Example 31.12

Mr A, a director of Company X is the majority shareholder in Company Y. Company X purchases quantities of stock from Company Y. Mr A must disclose his interest in such contracts to the board of Company X.

These requirements also apply to shadow directors who are required to make disclosure of interests in contracts by means of a written notice addressed to the board.[121]

In addition to the statutory restrictions, the company's articles may amplify the director's ability to enter into contracts. Thus, Table A provides that: 'Subject to the provisions of the Act, and provided that he has disclosed to the directors the nature and extent of any material interest of his, a director notwithstanding his office:

(a) may be a party to, or otherwise interested in, any transaction or arrangement with the company or in which the company is otherwise interested;

(b) may be a director or other officer of, or employed by, a party to any transaction or arrangement with, or otherwise interested in, any body corporate promoted by the company or in which the company is otherwise interested; and

(c) shall not, by reason of his office, be accountable to the company for any benefit which he derives from any such office or employment or from any such transaction or arrangement or from any interest in any such body corporate and no such transaction or arrangement shall be liable to be avoided on the ground of any such interest or benefit.'[122]

F SUBSTANTIAL PROPERTY TRANSACTIONS

A director or connected person may not acquire from or sell to the company a non-cash asset, i.e. any asset other than cash (including foreign currency),[123] above the requisite value unless the transaction has been approved by the company in general meeting. If the transaction occurs between the company and a director or connected person of its holding company, the holding company's approval is also required.[124]

In this context, the requisite value of transactions is the lower of 10% of the company's net asset value or £100,000. This is subject to a de minimis threshold of £2,000, below which property transactions do not require approval.[125]

There are a number of exemptions from the requirement to obtain approval; for example, an acquisition of an asset of the requisite value:

(a) by a director from a company which is a wholly owned subsidiary of another company, or

(b) by a person from a company of which he is a member (i.e. a shareholder acting in his capacity as member), or

(c) by one group company from another, provided there are no minority interests involved,

does not require approval. In addition, no approval is required for transactions entered into through an independent broker.[126]

A transaction entered into without the necessary approval is voidable at the company's option unless:

(a) restitution of the property is impossible; or

(b) rights to the property have been acquired by a bona fide purchaser for value who does not know that approval has not been obtained; or

(c) the arrangement has been affirmed by the company (and if appropriate its holding company) in general meeting within a reasonable period.[127]

The director, any connected person for whom the transaction was made and any director who authorised the transaction is liable:

(a) to account for any gain which he has made; and

(b) to make good any loss made by the company.[128]

However, where the transaction is made for a person connected with a director, and that director can demonstrate that he took all reasonable steps to secure the company's compliance with these provisions,[129] he will escape liability.

The person connected with the director and any other director who authorised the transaction will not be liable if he can demonstrate that at the time the transaction was entered into he did not know the circumstances constituting the contravention.[130]

G TRANSACTIONS INVOLVING OFFICERS

Officers, other than directors, are not subject to any statutory restrictions on their ability to transact with their company. A company's articles may address the contractual position of its officers, although Table A[131] is silent on this issue.

References

1 A person who holds anything in trust. A fiduciary relationship arises where a person has rights and powers which he is bound to exercise for the benefit of another. Hence he is not allowed to derive any profit or advantage from the relationship between them, except with the knowledge and consent of the other person: J. Burke, *Jowitt's Dictionary of English Law, Volume I A–K*, p. 788. If a director breaches this duty, a range of remedies is available to the company. The company may, inter alia, seek an injunction, claim damages or compensation, require the director to account for profits made or rescind contracts entered into with him.
2 CA 48, s 190(1).
3 *Ibid.*, s 190(1)(a).
4 CA 80, ss 49–50.
5 CA 85, ss 330–346, Sch. 6, Parts II and III.
6 *Ibid.*, s 741(1).
7 Companies should ensure that they do not allow persons described as divisional directors to hold themselves out as being members of the board. Otherwise there is a danger that contracts entered into by such persons, in excess of their managerial authority, may be binding on the company.
8 CA 85, s 741(2).
9 *Ibid.*, s 741(3).
10 The position of the alternate director is discussed in more detail in R. Pennington, *Company Law*, p. 628, and C. M. Schmithoff (ed.), *Palmer's Company Law Volume I*, p. 879.
11 The Companies (Tables A–F) Regulations 1985 (SI 1985 No. 85), Table A, Article 65.
12 CA 85, s 346.
13 *Ibid.*, s 346(6)(a).
14 *Ibid.*, s 346(7) and Sch. 13, para. 5.
15 *Ibid.*, s 346(8)
16 *Ibid.*, s 744.
17 *Champagne Perrier–Jouet SA v H.H. Finch Ltd* [1982] 1 WLR 1359.
18 CA 85, s 331(3).
19 *Ibid.*, s 331(7).
20 *Ibid.*, 331(8).
21 *Ibid.*, ss 317(1), (8).
22 *Ibid.*, s 317(6).
23 *Ibid.*, ss 232(1)–(2) and Sch. 6, Part II.
24 *Ibid.*, Sch. 6, para. 15.
25 *Ibid.*, s 237(4).
26 *Ibid.*, s 232(1)–(2) and Sch. 6, paras. 15–16.
27 *Ibid.*, Sch. 9, Part IV.
28 *Ibid.*, s 232(1)–(2), and Sch. 6, paras. 15–16.
29 This includes indemnities: *Ibid.*, s 331(2).
30 *Ibid.*, Sch. 6, para. 19.
31 *Ibid.*, ss 232(1)–(2) and Sch. 6, paras. 15(a)–(b) and 16(a)–(b).
32 *Ibid.*, Sch. 6, para. 22(1).
33 *Ibid.*, para. 22(2).
34 *Ibid.*, para. 27(c).
35 *Ibid.*, ss 232(1)–(2) and Sch. 6, paras. 15(c) and 16(c).
36 *Ibid.*, Sch. 6, paras. 15(c) and 16(c) refer to any 'other transaction or arrangement'.
37 *Ibid.*, para. 17(2). Materiality for these purposes should not be confused with the materiality level calculated for the purposes of the audit of the financial statements.
38 *Ibid.* Assuming the directors' opinion is formed in good faith and is not perverse, their view should prevail. However, in extreme circumstances the directors' opinion may need to be overridden in order for the accounts to give a true and fair view.
39 *Ibid.*
40 C. Rumbelow, 'When Directors Must Tell', *The Law Society's Gazette*, Wednesday 3 November 1982, pp. 1390–1392.
41 C. Swinson, 'Director's "Material interest" – just how do you measure it', *Accountancy*, October 1983, p. 110.
42 CA 85, Sch. 6, para. 22(1).
43 *Ibid.*, para. 22(2)(c).
44 *Ibid.*, para 22(2)(f).
45 *Ibid.*, s 340(6).
46 *Ibid.*, s 340(7).
47 *Ibid.*, Sch. 6, para. 18(a).
48 *Ibid.*, para. 18(b).
49 *Ibid.*, para. 18(c).
50 *Ibid.*, paras. 15(b) and 16(b).
51 *Ibid.*, para. 24.
52 *Ibid.*, para. 23.
53 *Ibid.*, para. 17(2).
54 *Ibid.*, para. 20.
55 SI 1984 No. 1860.
56 B. Johnson and M. Patient, *Accounting Provisions of the Companies Act 1985*, p. 270.
57 CA 85, Sch. 6, para. 21.
58 *Ibid.*, para. 25.
59 *Ibid.*, Sch. 9, Part IV, para. 2.
60 *Ibid.*, para. 3.
61 See generally *Ibid.*, ss 343–344.
62 *Ibid.*, s 343(2).
63 *Ibid.*, ss 343(5)–(6).
64 *Ibid.*, Sch. 9, Part IV, para. 3 and Sch. 6, Part III.
65 *Ibid.*, Sch. 6, para. 30.
66 *The Listing Rules*, Financial Services Authority, Chapter 11.
67 *Ibid.*, para. 11.1.
68 *Ibid.*, para. 11.10(c).
69 *Ibid.*, para. 11.4(c).
70 *Ibid.*, para. 11.3.
71 *Ibid.*, paras. 11.7 and 11.8.

72 *Ibid.*, Chapter 12, para. 12.43(q).
73 *Ibid.*, para. 12.44.
74 *The AIM rules*, London Stock Exchange, rule 12 and Schedule Three. The percentage ratios are based on assets, profits, turnover, consideration to market capitalisation and gross capital.
75 *Ibid.*, rule 17 and Schedule Three.
76 CA 85, ss 232(1)–(2) and Sch. 6, Part III.
77 *Ibid.*, ss 232(1)–(2) and Sch. 6, para. 29.
78 *Ibid.*, Sch. 6, para. 29.
79 *Ibid.*, paras. 28 and 29(1).
80 *Ibid.*, para. 30.
81 *Ibid.*, para. 29(2).
82 *Ibid.*, Sch. 9, Part IV, para. 3(1).
83 Banking Act 1987, ss 105(6)–(7).
84 Hansard, *Parliamentary Debates*, 22 June 1989, Column 507.
85 DTI, *Consultative Document on Amendments to Schedule 6 to the Companies Act 1985: Disclosure by Companies of Dealings in favour of Directors*, October 1991.
86 CA 85, ss 317, 320, 330–346.
87 *Ibid.*, ss 317(8), 320(3), 330(5).
88 *Ibid.*, s 330(2).
89 *Ibid.*, s 331(6).
90 *Ibid.*, s 330(2)(b).
91 This includes indemnities: *Ibid.*, s 331(2).
92 *Ibid.*, s 330(2)(b).
93 *Ibid.*, s 330(3)(c).
94 *Ibid.*, ss 330(3)–(4).
95 *Ibid.*, s 330(6).
96 *Ibid.*, s 330(7).
97 *Ibid.*, s 334. S 339 determines how the threshold is to be calculated.
98 *Ibid.*, s 332.
99 *Ibid.*, s 335(1). See also s 339.
100 *Ibid.*, s 335(2).
101 *Ibid.*, s 333.
102 *Ibid.*, s 336.
103 *Ibid.*, ss 337(1)–(3).
104 *Ibid.*, s 337(3). See also s 339.
105 *Ibid.*, ss 338(1)–(4). See also s 339.
106 *Ibid.*, s 338(6).
107 If the pre-consolidation legislation is to be reproduced accurately, the reference in s 339(1) to s 338(4) should actually be a reference to s 338(1).
108 The legislation applies to companies; that is, an entity formed and registered under the various Companies Acts: *Ibid.*, s 735. This definition applies unless the contrary intention appears: *Ibid.*, s 735(4). Since no contrary intention is expressed, a body incorporated overseas is not a company for the purposes of the directors' transactions provisions.
109 *Ibid.*, s 341(1).
110 *Ibid.*, s 341(2).
111 *Ibid.*, s 341(4).
112 *Ibid.*, s 341(5).
113 *Ibid.*, s 342.
114 *Ibid.*, 317(7).
115 *Ibid.*, s 317(1).
116 *Ibid.*, s 317(6).
117 *Ibid.*, s 317(2).
118 [1988] 1 WLR 863.
119 CA 85, s 317(2).
120 *Ibid.*, s 317(3).
121 *Ibid.*, s 317(8).
122 The Companies (Tables A–F) Regulations 1985, *op. cit*, Article 85.
123 CA 85, s 739(1).
124 *Ibid.*, s 320(1).
125 *Ibid.*, s 320(2).
126 *Ibid.*, s 321.
127 *Ibid.*, ss 322(1)–(2).
128 *Ibid.*, s 322(2).
129 *Ibid.*, s 322(5).
130 *Ibid.*, s 322(6).
131 The Companies (Tables A–F) Regulations 1985, *op. cit.*

Chapter 32 Directors' remuneration

1 INTRODUCTION

This chapter focuses primarily on the disclosure requirements in the UK in respect of directors' remuneration. However, preparers of company financial statements should possess an awareness of the law governing the remuneration of directors and their service contracts. Accordingly, a brief exposition of these requirements has been included (see 1.1 to 1.4 below).[1]

Professor Gower reasoned that the need to disclose directors' remuneration was because 'it is too obvious that the system [of remunerating directors] lends itself to abuse, since directors will be encouraged to bleed the company by voting themselves excessive salaries and expense allowances. The latest Act [the Companies Act 1948] attempts to minimise these dangers by providing for full disclosure of the total emoluments received by directors ... '.[2] This requirement is simply a feature of the principle that a fiduciary should not allow his personal interests and duty to the company to conflict.[3]

These original requirements for aggregate information were added to in 1967 by the introduction of a requirement for individual information by the disclosure of the emoluments of the chairman, and of the highest paid director where this was not the chairman, together with the number of directors whose remuneration fell within specified bandings.[4] Although there had been a number of amendments over the years since then (principally revising the amounts of the bandings and when such individual information is required, as well as tightening up some of the potential loopholes), these basic requirements had until recently been in place for 30 years. As a result, they failed to keep up with recent developments in remuneration packages and accounting practice. This had been most evident in the case of listed companies.

In recent years executive remuneration has become a focus of public attention. Controversy surrounding the salaries and benefits of directors of British Gas and some other privatised utility companies in 1995 was simply the most well-publicised expression of public concern as to both the level and the structure of boardroom pay.

This concern was first addressed in 1992 by the Cadbury Committee, which was set up in May 1991 by the Financial Reporting Council, the London Stock Exchange and the accountancy profession, when it issued its report on 'corporate governance'.[5] At the heart of the Committee's recommendations was its Code of Best Practice for the boards of listed companies, paragraph 3.2 of which stated that 'there should be full and clear disclosure of directors' total emoluments and those of the chairman and highest paid UK director, including pension contributions and stock options. Separate figures should be given for salary and performance-related elements and the basis on which performance is measured to be explained.'

In view of increasing debate about share options granted to directors, in September 1994 the UITF issued Abstract 10 – *Disclosure of Directors' Share Options*. This recommends that further information concerning the option prices applicable to individual directors, together with market price information at the year end and at the date of exercise, should be disclosed (see 3.2.9 A below). However, the UITF had received legal advice that the recommended disclosures could not all be construed as being necessary to meet the legal requirements. Consequently, the disclosures are only recommendations and are not mandatory, although as a result of later developments discussed below they are effectively mandatory for listed companies.

The remit of the Cadbury Committee had been corporate governance as a whole, of which executive remuneration was only a part. The comprehensive review of directors' pay as a single issue fell to the Study Group on Directors' Remuneration, commonly known as the Greenbury Committee after its chairman Sir Richard Greenbury, chairman of Marks and Spencer. This Committee was established in January 1995 at the initiative of (but independent from) the CBI, with the remit of identifying good practice in determining directors' remuneration and preparing a Code of such practice for use by UK PLCs.

The Greenbury Committee issued its report in July 1995.[6] This included a Code of Best Practice containing a number of recommendations. In October 1995 and June 1996 the London Stock Exchange gave effect to certain of these recommendations by amending its *Listing Rules* and in May 1997 completed the jigsaw by introducing its requirements on the disclosure of directors' pension entitlements. These required listed companies to produce a report to the shareholders on behalf of the board by the remuneration committee (remuneration committee report), which included, inter alia, a statement of remuneration policy and for each director an analysis of remuneration, details of share options (in accordance with the recommendations of UITF 10), long-term incentive schemes and pension benefits.

In the light of these detailed disclosures required by listed companies, the Greenbury Committee recommended that the Companies Act requirements should be amended by removing the obligation to give banding information and to change the requirements in respect of disclosure of directors' pensions. Accordingly, the

DTI issued a consultative document in January 1996 which aimed to implement the recommendations of the Greenbury Committee, align the Companies Act with the revised *Listing Rules* and, where possible, reduce disclosure requirements for unlisted companies.

Thus in February 1997 the DTI issued The Company Accounts (Disclosure of Directors' Emoluments) Regulations 1997 (SI 1997/570), which changed the requirements for directors' emolument disclosures for accounting periods ending on or after 31 March 1997.

The Stock Exchange requirements were then further amended as a result of the work of the successor body to the Cadbury Committee, under the chairmanship of Sir Ronald Hampel, Chairman of ICI. In January 1998 the final report of the Committee on Corporate Governance (the Hampel Committee) was issued[7] and in June 1998, the Stock Exchange published the final version of the Principles of Good Governance and Code of Best Practice (the Combined Code), together with revised *Listing Rules*.

The Combined Code deals with corporate governance as a whole and has been derived from the Hampel Committee's final report and from the Cadbury and Greenbury Reports. It contains both principles and detailed Code provisions. Under the revised *Listing Rules*, companies are required to disclose how they have applied the principles and the extent to which they have complied with the detailed provisions of the Combined Code in their annual report (see 2 of Chapter 4). Part B of Section 1 of the Combined Code deals with directors' remuneration (see 3.1 below). However, the changes made to the *Listing Rules* in respect of directors' remuneration were relatively minor. The report to shareholders is now to be made by the board (rather than by the remuneration committee on its behalf) but the information to be included within the report is virtually the same as before.

1.1 Remuneration

Remuneration paid to directors may assume any form and its amount will depend on the terms of the directors' service contracts (if any) and the company's articles of association; for example, Table A[8] provides that 'the directors shall be entitled to such remuneration as the company may by ordinary resolution determine ... '. Accordingly, if the directors do not have service contracts and the articles are silent on this issue, the directors are not *entitled* to receive anything.[9]

Remuneration may not be paid to a director (in whatever capacity he acts) free of income tax nor may a company pay him remuneration of an amount such that, after paying income tax, it will leave a specified sum in his hands.[10] Any provision in a company's articles, or in any contract, or in any resolution for payment to a director of remuneration free of income tax takes effect as if it provided for payment of the gross amount subject to income tax payable by the director.[11]

1.2 Pensions

Pensions are only payable to former directors if the company is authorised to do so by its memorandum or articles of association. Table A[12] contains an express power to provide benefits to former directors and for any member of his family or any dependant and to make contributions to secure such benefits.

1.3 Compensation for loss of office

Payments to a director for loss of office, or as consideration for or in connection with his retirement from office, must be disclosed to and approved by the company in general meeting.[13] It is unclear whether payments to directors in respect of compensation for loss of other offices, for example, the company secretaryship, require approval. Pennington[14] believes that this rule applies irrespective of the office lost, although this view is not universally held. This requirement does not apply to 'any bona fide payment by way of damages for breach of contract or by way of pension in respect of past services'.[15] Thus, for approval purposes, a payment is only treated as compensation for loss of office if the company is under no legal obligation to make it.

1.4 Service contracts

In outline, the provisions of the Companies Act 1985 relating to service contracts are as follows:

(a) a copy or memorandum of the terms of directors' service contracts must be kept at an appropriate place, e.g. the company's registered office, and be available for inspection. The level of information required for directors who discharge their duties wholly or mainly outside the UK is reduced. These requirements do not apply where the unexpired portion of the contract is less than 12 months or where the company is able to terminate within the ensuing 12 months the director's contract without payment of compensation;[16]

(b) terms incorporated into a director's service contract for a period of more than five years during which time his employment either cannot be terminated or can only be terminated in special circumstances are void unless approved by the company in general meeting. The resolution is only valid if a written memorandum setting out the proposed agreement is available for inspection for 15 days before and at the meeting itself.[17]

The Financial Services Authority imposes additional requirements in relation to service contracts of directors of listed companies. These are discussed at 3.2.10 below.

2 DISCLOSURE OF REMUNERATION UNDER THE COMPANIES ACT 1985

2.1 Introduction

The Companies Act 1985 requires the following information in respect of directors to be disclosed in aggregate by way of note to the company's financial statements:[18]

(a) emoluments (see 2.2 to 2.4 below);

(b) gains made on exercise of share options (see 2.5 below);

(c) cash and/or value of other assets (excluding share options) receivable under long-term incentive schemes (see 2.6 below);

(d) pension contributions in respect of money purchase benefits (see 2.7 below);

(e) excess retirement benefits (see 2.8 below);

(f) compensation for loss of office (see 2.9 below); and

(g) sums paid to third parties in respect of directors' services (see 2.10 below).

There are exceptions to the requirements under (b) and (c) above for companies which are not listed on the Stock Exchange or quoted on the Alternative Investment Market. Information is also required in respect of the number of directors to whom retirement benefits are accruing (see 2.7 below). In certain circumstances, individual information is required to be given in respect of the highest paid director (see 2.11 below). Comparative figures are required for all disclosures.[19]

In group financial statements, the above requirements only extend to directors of the holding company. It is the duty of each director to give notice to the company of such matters relating to himself as may be necessary for the purposes of these disclosures.[20] If these disclosures are not made in the financial statements, it is the auditors' duty to include in their report, so far as they are 'reasonably able to do so', a statement giving the required particulars.[21]

In view of the fact that companies listed on the Stock Exchange will be giving information in respect of each director, the Companies Act has granted dispensation from providing some of the above information which is to be given on an aggregate basis. Accordingly, the Act states that 'any information, other than the aggregate amount of gains made by directors on the exercise of share options (b) above, shall be treated as shown if it is capable of being readily ascertained from other information which is shown'. Apart from (b) above, this dispensation applies to all of the other disclosures noted above, other than (e) and (g) above. It also extends to the disclosures in respect of the highest paid director (from the information given for each director, users will be able to determine who it is). Accordingly, aggregate information should always be given for gains made on exercise of share options, excess retirement benefits and sums paid to third parties in respect of directors' services. In using this dispensation, listed companies should ensure that all comparative figures can also be ascertained.

2.2 Disclosure of aggregate emoluments

2.2.1 *Legal requirements*

The aggregate amount of emoluments paid to or receivable by directors in respect of qualifying services must be disclosed.[22] Qualifying services mean services:

(a) as director of the company;

(b) as director of any of the company's subsidiary undertakings (whilst a director of the company);

(c) in connection with the management of the affairs of the company or any of its subsidiary undertakings (whilst a director of the company).[23]

In this context, the definition of a subsidiary undertaking is extended to include the situation where the director of the reporting company is nominated by that company to act as its representative on the board of another undertaking (whether or not it is actually a subsidiary undertaking of the reporting company).[24] This extended definition applies for the purposes of all the disclosures discussed in 2.3 to 2.9 below, and is illustrated in Examples 32.1 and 32.2 below:

Example 32.1

Company X has an investment in Company Y. Company X appoints one of its directors, Mr A, to the board of Company Y. Mr A receives fees of £10,000 in respect of this appointment. The financial statements of Company X must include the fees receivable by Mr A in respect of his services as director of Company Y, in the relevant disclosures.

Example 32.2

Company A is a debenture holder of a non-group company, Company B. The trust deed entitles Company A to appoint one of its directors to the board of Company B. The emoluments of the appointee from Company B must be included in the relevant disclosures in Company A's financial statements.

The definition of emoluments and the computation thereof are dealt with at 2.3 and 2.4 below. An example of disclosure of aggregate emoluments is shown in Extract 32.4 at 2.3.1 below.

2.2.2 *Problem areas*

A *Other services*

The disclosures in respect of directors' remuneration relate to a person's services as director of a company and management services (see 2.2.1 above). In some companies, particularly small private companies, directors may also perform services unrelated to the above and for which they receive remuneration. Such remuneration should be excluded from the directors' emoluments disclosures, as illustrated in the example below:

Example 32.3

A journalist director of a small provincial newspaper is paid a fee for writing a weekly column. Since this fee is quite distinct from his directors' fees or management remuneration, it should be excluded from the remuneration disclosures. However, consideration should be given to disclosing this arrangement as a transaction in which a director has a material interest (see 3.5 of Chapter 31) or as a related party transaction under FRS 8 (see generally Chapter 30).

In practice however, it is often difficult to determine whether or not such services are, in fact, unrelated, since directors are often appointed as a result of the other services which they perform. In such cases where doubt exists, the remuneration for other services is often included with directors' remuneration.

One company which has excluded fees received for services from the aggregate amount of emoluments is Volex Group, as shown below:

Extract 32.1: Volex Group p.l.c. (1999)

10 Directors' remuneration, interests and transactions [extract]

* Total aggregate emoluments for directors during the year comprised £785,531 (1998 – £740,729).

In addition to the emoluments shown above:

(i) Mr Kennedy received fees of £10,320 (1998 – £10,320) during the year in respect of services provided under a consultancy agreement.

These fees are in addition to fees received as a non-executive director. In many other cases 'consultancy fees' are paid in respect of the person's services as director and management services and are therefore included as part of the emoluments.

B 'Golden hellos'

A number of companies offer payments (of varying kinds) as incentives for particular staff to join them (so-called 'golden hellos'). These payments made to directors do not relate to a person's services as director of the company; nor do they pertain to management services. Thus it might be thought that they are not required to be disclosed as part of directors' remuneration. However, the Companies Act is clear that such 'golden hellos' paid to or receivable by a director are to be treated as 'emoluments paid or receivable ... in respect of his services as director'; consequently, such payments have to be included within emoluments disclosed in financial statements.[25]

Examples of golden hellos are shown below:

Extract 32.2: Marks and Spencer p.l.c. (2001)

Remuneration Report [extract]
1 **Directors' emoluments** [extract]

[1] Luc Vandevelde was the highest paid director both this year and last. His emoluments this year are £834,000. He was appointed to the Board on 28 February 2000 and his emoluments last year of £2,070,000 included compensation for loss of future benefits from his previous employer in the form of 'restricted shares' at a cost of £1,997,000.

[2] Roger Holmes was appointed to the Board on 1 January 2001. Included within his benefits is compensation for loss of future benefits and bonus from his previous employer in the form of 'restricted shares' at a cost of £554,000 and a payment of £100,000 (see section 2 – Recruitment of directors).

2 **Recruitment of directors**

During the year, Roger Holmes was recruited and appointed to the Board as Managing Director, UK Retail. In order to secure early release from his previous employer, he was recruited as an employee from 15 December to 31 December 2000, with salary and benefits totalling £22,000 for this period (included within section 1). He was appointed as a director on 1 January 2001 on the following terms:

- salary of £425,000 p.a.;
- payment of £100,000 as compensation for loss of bonus from his previous employer (included within benefits in section 1);
- compensation for loss of future benefits from his previous employer in the form of 282,326 'restricted shares' purchased on his behalf at a cost of £554,000. He is the beneficial owner of the shares but they will not be transferred to him until the 3rd anniversary of employment (included within benefits in section 1);
- interest free loan of £501,000 for a period of 17 days to facilitate the exercise of share options from his previous employer and avoid further compensation payments under the terms of his engagement. This was repaid in full prior to taking up his appointment to the Board on 1 January 2001 (see note 11 – Transactions with directors);
- supplement of 10% of the difference between the pension earnings cap and his base salary (see section 4 – Pensions) (included within benefits in section 1);
- award of shares under 2000 Executive Share Option Scheme with a market value at the date of employment of four times base salary (see section 6 – Long-term benefits).

Extract 32.3: United Utilities PLC (2001)

Remuneration Report [extract]
Notes: [extract]

On becoming directors, Simon Batey's and Les Dawson's annual salaries were £260,000 and £200,000 respectively. As part of their recruitment packages, to compensate them for loss of payments due to them under their previous companies' incentive award schemes, Les Dawson has received a payment of £32,000 and Simon Batey has received a payment of £75,000 and is due to receive a further payment of £50,000. As a consequence of these payments, Simon Batey was the highest paid director in the year ended 31 March 2001.

There is no specific requirement to disclose the fact that 'golden hellos' are included within the figures or to disclose any details. However, consideration may need to be given as to whether disclosure is still required as a transaction in which a director has a material interest (see 3.5 of Chapter 31). In any event, companies may wish to give disclosure in order to explain any distorting effect of including such payments within emoluments in view of their 'one-off' nature.

2.3 Definition of emoluments

2.3.1 Legal requirements

Emoluments are defined as including:[26]

- salary;
- fees;
- bonuses;
- any sums paid by way of expenses allowance (insofar as those sums are charged to UK income tax); and
- the estimated money value of any other benefits received by the director otherwise than in cash (this will include, in particular, company cars, cheap loans (including mortgage subsidies) and cheap accommodation).

However, emoluments are not to include any of the following:[27]

- the value of any share options granted to a director or the amount of any gains made on the exercise of such options;
- any contributions paid, or treated as paid, in respect of the director under any pension scheme or any benefits to which he is entitled under any such scheme. For these purposes, a pension scheme has the meaning assigned to 'retirement benefit scheme' by section 611 of the Income and Corporation Taxes Act 1988;[28] or
- any money or other assets paid to or received or receivable by a director under any long-term incentive scheme.

These have been excluded as there are separate requirements for such items.

The aggregate emoluments disclosure should exclude employers' national insurance contributions as such sums are not paid to or receivable by the director. However, these contributions will need to be disclosed in the wages and salaries note as part of social security costs (see 2.8 of Chapter 22).

Although there are various items to be included within aggregate emoluments, there is no need under the Companies Act to give separate disclosure in respect of them as the requirement is merely to disclose the aggregate amount.

Nevertheless a number of companies do give separate disclosure of the amounts included within aggregate emoluments, as shown below:

Extract 32.4: Caledonia Investments plc (2001)

33 DIRECTORS' REMUNERATION AND INTERESTS [extract]

Directors' remuneration

Total emoluments were as follows:

	2001	2000
	£'000	£'000
Fees	**57**	56
Salaries	**1,016**	965
Benefits	**82**	69
Performance related bonuses	**610**	198
	1,765	1,288
Gains on exercise of share options	**133**	–
	1,898	1,288

2.3.2 *Problem areas*

A Benefits-in-kind

(a) General

There is no universally accepted basis upon which the estimated money value of benefits received by directors is assessed; consequently, the valuation of such benefits is problematic. There are a number of possible methods whereby such benefits may be determined, in particular:

(i) market value of the facility provided for the private benefit of the director (less any personal contribution paid by him);

(ii) taxable values. Tax scale rates are often used as a yardstick whereby the values of benefits-in-kind can be readily determined. Indeed, in practice, this method is the most widely used thereby ensuring some degree of comparability between the relevant disclosure in the financial statements of different companies (see (f) below).

(iii) cost to the company. Proponents of this method argue that since the directors are appointed by the shareholders of a company to run the company on their behalf, they are entitled to be informed as to how much it is costing the company, and therefore ultimately themselves, for the directors to perform this stewardship function. However, this interpretation does not appear to be supported by the wording of the legislation, which refers to the *money value* of benefits received;

(iv) perceived benefit to the director. It is sometimes argued that companies expect their directors to maintain certain appearances and thus provide them with, say, a particular motor car which they would not drive if they had to finance the transaction personally. In this particular example, the benefit to the director would be the cost of the make of car which he himself would have purchased, had he not been provided with a company car. This argument assumes that the company restricts the director's freedom of choice by imposing the particular benefit on him which, in practice, is unlikely.

We believe that given the wording of the legislation, the most appropriate basis for determining the money value of benefits-in-kind received by the director is by reference to the market value of the facility provided for his benefit, (i) above, notwithstanding computational difficulties inherent in using this basis. Where it is not practicable to use the market value basis, taxable values, (ii) above, should be used.

Based on our preferred approach, the method of determining the more common benefits might be as follows:

(b) Motor cars

Where a company provides a director with a leased motor car, the market value of this facility could be calculated with reference to the lease payments and any additional running costs borne by the company. Likewise, if the company purchases a car for the use of the director, then the sum disclosed could be calculated by reference to the annual running costs, including depreciation, and associated interest costs. This may involve distinguishing between private and business mileage.

(c) Cheap loans

The benefit derived by a director on a cheap loan (including a subsidised mortgage) could be assessed as the difference between the interest payable on the loan and the market interest payable on a like loan, calculated in accordance with a weighted average rate for the financial year.

Companies should ensure that any loans made to directors do not contravene the prohibitions on transactions with directors (see generally Chapter 31).

(d) Cheap accommodation

Directors of companies are frequently permitted to reside in property owned or leased by the company. Where the company owns the property, the benefit derived by the director is the difference between the rent he pays and the estimated market rent for that property which the company would receive if it were to lease the premises on a commercial basis. If the company merely leases the property, the benefit could be assessed as the difference between the rent and other expenses paid by the company and that paid by the director.

Companies should ensure that any such arrangements do not contravene the restrictions on transactions with directors (see generally Chapter 31).

(e) Indemnity insurance

Companies may purchase and maintain for any officer, including directors, insurance against any liability he may incur for negligence, default, breach of duty, or breach of trust.[29] Where such insurance is purchased or maintained, it is arguable that the premiums incurred should be regarded as being the value of the benefit to be included within the figure for directors' emoluments.

(f) Disclosure in practice

Although our preferred treatment is to include benefits-in-kind based on their market value, it would seem that in practice a number of companies use taxable values, as indicated by the following extracts:

Extract 32.5: Carclo plc (2001)

Remuneration report [extract]
Directors' remuneration and pension entitlements [extract]

(iii) Benefits comprise taxable non cash emoluments, mainly in respect of the provision of a company car, medical insurance, and relocation expenses which are provided as part of the directors' service contract.

Extract 32.6: Land Securities PLC (2001)

7 Directors' Emoluments, Share Options and Interests in Ordinary Shares [extract]

Benefits include all assessable tax benefits arising from employment within the group comprising: the provision of a company car, private medical facilities, the value of shares allocated under the 1989 and 1999 Profit Sharing Schemes and a bonus of 18 per cent of salary payable under the senior executive annual bonus scheme apportioned equally in cash and shares.

It can be seen from the above extracts that the nature of the benefits has been disclosed. There is no requirement under the Companies Act for such disclosure but the Greenbury Report had recommended that the nature of benefits should be disclosed and it is now arguably required by listed companies under Schedule B to the Combined Code (see 3.2.3 below). The benefits identified in the above extracts are probably the more common types of benefits receivable by directors. Other examples are illustrated below:

Extract 32.7: Cable and Wireless plc (2001)

Directors' Report [extract]
Directors' remuneration [extract]

Allowances and benefits include such items as medical insurance. Linus W L Cheung's allowances and benefits include housing and related benefits, which it is common practice to pay on behalf of senior executive officers in Hong Kong.

Extract 32.8: Chloride Group plc (1998)

9 Directors' emoluments and pension entitlements [extract]

Certain directors and officers of the Group's subsidiary undertakings in the USA, including Mr Vass, were indemnified by US subsidiaries against personal liability which they might incur in their capacity as directors and/or officers of relevant subsidiary undertakings and remained covered by those indemnities in 1997/98. The value attributable to the indemnities granted to Mr Vass is unascertainable as at 23 July 1997, the date Mr Vass ceased to be a director, since the indemnities are of a contingent nature and no claims were outstanding in connection with them.

It can be seen that in this case no value has been placed on the benefit as the value is unascertainable.

2.4 Computing aggregate emoluments

2.4.1 *Legal requirements*

A Bonuses

The amounts to be disclosed are the sums receivable in respect of a financial year irrespective of when paid.[30] Thus, a director's service contract may provide that he is to receive a bonus for the financial year of X% of the company's profits as disclosed in the statutory financial statements duly presented to the members in general meeting. This bonus should be accrued and included in the financial statements for the relevant financial year, notwithstanding that it is not payable until the financial statements are laid in general meeting.

An example of a company including bonuses on this basis is Chloride Group, as indicated below:

Extract 32.9: Chloride Group plc (2001)

9 Directors' emoluments and pension entitlements [extract]

Performance-related bonuses are earned in respect of the year under which they are shown but are not paid until the following year.

Some bonuses given in respect of services or performance for the financial year may be subject to the condition that the director has to remain in employment until the bonus is paid. Should this be disclosed in the year to which it relates or in the year in which this further condition is satisfied?

Example 32.4

A company with a 30 June year end has a bonus scheme whereby bonuses will be payable based on the EPS performance for each financial year. Payments are to be made to participating employees on 31 March the following year, subject to them remaining in employment until then. For the year ended 30 June 1999 a director is due to receive £20,000 based on the performance for that year. Should this be disclosed as part of the director's emoluments in the 1999 or the 2000 accounts?

Although this bonus is clearly in respect of the year ended 30 June 1999, it is only to be disclosed in that year's accounts if it is *receivable* by the director. It could be argued that the director is entitled to the bonus at the year end, subject to the fulfilment of a condition which is not that onerous and therefore it should be regarded as being receivable and disclosed in the 1999 accounts. Alternatively, the fact that there is this condition means that the director is only entitled to the bonus if he is still employed by the company on 31 March 2000 and it is at that date the amount is receivable by the director. On this basis, disclosure would therefore be made in the 2000 accounts.

On balance, we believe that the bonus should be disclosed in the 1999 accounts as this is when it was earned by the director. This would align the disclosure with the accounting for the bonus (see Chapter 22 at 2.2.1 A).

For companies listed on the Stock Exchange, such a bonus falls within the definition of a 'deferred bonus' which has to be separately disclosed in the remuneration table for the period under review (see 3.2.5 below).

A number of companies listed on the Stock Exchange have introduced bonus schemes whereby the director may apply a proportion of his annual bonus for the purchase of shares in the company with an equivalent value which, generally, will be matched by an equivalent number of shares at nil cost. This raises further issues and these are discussed at 3.2.5 below.

As noted at 2.1 above, bonuses which are to be included within 'emoluments' do not include any bonuses which are receivable under a long-term incentive scheme.

B Amounts repayable by directors

If a director is liable to repay the company for any amount paid to him (for example, a season-ticket advance) such payments do not require disclosure as emoluments.[31] However, if the director is subsequently released from the liability or any expense allowance is charged to tax after the end of the financial year, these sums must be:[32]

(a) disclosed in the first financial statements in which it is practicable to show them; and

(b) distinguished from other remuneration.

In order to prevent companies making indefinite loans to directors, any such amount which a director is liable to repay which remains unpaid for two years or more after the due date, will require disclosure as above.[33]

C Payments by other persons

The sums disclosed must include all sums paid by or receivable from the company, its subsidiary undertakings or any other person.[34] Indeed, in group situations, where directors of the holding company also act as directors of subsidiary companies, it is common for the holding company to remunerate the directors in respect of their services to the subsidiary companies. The notes to the financial statements of those subsidiaries must include details of the emoluments paid by the holding company in respect of the directors' services. Where this is the case, we consider that the notes to the subsidiaries' financial statements should explain that the charge for directors' remuneration has been borne by the holding company. Similarly, a blanket management charge may be made by a holding company to its subsidiaries in respect of a variety of expenditure incurred by it on the subsidiaries' behalf including the emoluments of the subsidiaries' directors. The reporting company should seek to analyse the expenditure between types and thereby arrive at a figure for directors' emoluments. If such an exercise is not practicable, the notes to the reporting company's financial statements should state this fact; for example:

> 'A management charge of £100,000 in respect of administration costs has been made by Y Co. the company's holding company, which includes the directors' emoluments which it is not possible to identify separately.'

In some groups, all contracts of employment and/or directors' service contracts are vested in one company. The company will provide the personnel requirements (including directors) of other group companies and in return will levy a management charge. In these situations, the considerations outlined above are equally applicable.

If it is necessary to apportion the emoluments received by a director (for example, where he acted as director for a number of group companies and was remunerated by a single composite sum from the holding company which requires analysis between the group companies), the directors may apportion these payments in such manner as they deem appropriate.[35] However, where the directors consider that they are unable to make an appropriate apportionment, the note to the subsidiaries' financial statements should reflect this fact. For example:

> 'The directors of the company are also directors of the holding company and fellow subsidiaries. The directors received total remuneration for the year of £120,000 (1998: £105,000), all of which was paid by the holding company. The directors do not believe that it is practicable to apportion this amount between their services as directors of the company and their services as directors of the holding and fellow subsidiary companies.'

The aggregate emoluments for the directors of an intermediate holding company should include all amounts paid to or receivable by them for qualifying services, which as indicated at 2.2.1 above, includes services as director of any of its subsidiaries and services in connection with the management of the affairs of its subsidiaries. Accordingly, if the directors are remunerated by the subsidiaries concerned, disclosure is required of the emoluments for such services in the accounts of the intermediate holding company even if it is not preparing consolidated accounts (see Chapter 5 at 4.1). If the emoluments are paid by another group company (such as the ultimate parent company) then similar considerations to those outlined above are equally applicable.

D Payments to connected persons

Payments made to persons connected with the director or persons connected with a body corporate 'controlled' by a director are required to be included in the aggregate emoluments to be disclosed.[36] 'Connected persons' and 'controlled bodies corporate' are as defined for directors' loans and transactions (see Chapter 31 at 2.4). An example of such payments are shown below:

Extract 32.10: Kwik-Fit Holdings plc (1999)

9. DIRECTORS' REMUNERATION AND INTERESTS [extract]

Fees, including expenses, for N. Hood and I McIntosh are paid to Neil Hood Associates and Ian McIntosh Limited respectively. Fees, including expenses, for J. Padget are paid to Padget Associates B.V. in addition to consultancy payments and expenses disclosed in Note 9(d).

The fees were included within aggregate emoluments.

2.4.2 *Problem areas*

A Payments to consultancy firms

It is not uncommon for a director's emoluments to be paid to a consultancy firm of which the director and/or members of his family are shareholders or partners. In such situations the consultancy firm levies a charge to the company preparing the financial statements for the services of the director. Such payments are required to be included in aggregate emoluments if the consultancy firm is a person connected with the director. Clearly, if it is a consultancy partnership then this will be the case; however, if it is a consultancy company this may not always be so. If the consultancy company is not a person connected with the director then, even though payments need not be included in aggregate emoluments, separate disclosure will be required as a payment to a third party for the services of a director (see 2.10 below).

These arrangements may also require disclosure as transactions in which a director has a material interest (see 3.5 of Chapter 31) or as related party transactions under FRS 8 (see generally Chapter 30).

B Payments to other connected persons

In some companies, particularly in family held companies, payments and/or benefits in kind are paid to a director's spouse. Where the spouse is unconnected with the company, then any such payments made should be included as part of the director's emoluments. Difficulties may arise, however, where the spouse either is employed by, or provides a service to, the company. Where the amounts paid to the spouse are commensurate with the services rendered then these should not be included within the directors' emoluments disclosures. However, where the amounts paid are excessive, then it is likely that a proportion of the payment effectively relates to the director's services and therefore should be included in the director's emoluments. Again, these arrangements may also require disclosure as transactions in which a director has a material interest (see 3.5 of Chapter 31) or as related party transactions under FRS 8 (see generally Chapter 30).

C Services to holding company

Complications may also arise if the reporting company considers that emoluments paid by its holding company are purely in respect of a director's services to the holding company and not for services as director of the reporting company. It is sometimes argued that the emoluments do not need to be disclosed in the subsidiary's financial statements but should simply be disclosed in the financial statements of its holding company, assuming that:

(a) the director is also a director of that company; and

(b) the holding company is incorporated in the UK.

However, it is our view that if the director's services to the subsidiary company occupy a significant amount of time, an appropriate apportionment should be made and the relevant disclosures given. If the directors consider that they are unable to make an appropriate apportionment, the note to the subsidiary's financial statements should reflect this fact (see 2.4.1 C above). If the director's services to the subsidiary company do not occupy a significant amount of time, it may be concluded that the director is not remunerated for them and that, therefore, the subsidiary's financial statements should reflect the director as not having received any remuneration. It will be necessary to review the particular facts in each case to ascertain whether disclosure is necessary.

However, in the case of a foreign holding company where the director works full-time in managing its UK subsidiary, disclosure of the emoluments for such work should be made in the subsidiary's financial statements as the director is clearly providing full-time management services to that company.

2.5 Gains made on exercise of share options

As noted at 3.2.9 A below, the UITF believed that under the old legislation the grant of an option should be treated as giving rise to a benefit and should be included in the aggregate of directors' emoluments. However, the UITF recognised the practical difficulties of attributing a meaningful estimated money value to the option at the date of grant, particularly where the rights under the option are contingent on future performance or other factors, and also given the differing views on whether to apportion any benefit over time. Accordingly, the UITF concluded that it was not practicable at that time for it to specify an appropriate valuation method for options as a benefit in kind and therefore recommended detailed disclosures in respect of directors' options as a surrogate for any value.

The current legislation has dispensed with these problems of valuing any benefit at the time of granting the option by requiring the disclosure of the aggregate amount of gains made by directors on the exercise of share options,[37] an example of which is shown in Extract 32.4 at 2.3.1 above.

The amount of the gain is calculated as being the difference between:

(a) the market price of the shares on the day on which the option was exercised, and

(b) the price actually paid for the shares.[38]

The figure to be disclosed is therefore unaffected by whether a director immediately sells the shares after exercising the option or retains them. (This is highlighted in Extract 32.11 below.) Where they are retained then no disclosure is required of any subsequent gain (or loss) when the shares are eventually sold.

'Share option' means a right to acquire shares which in turn means shares (whether allotted or not) in the company, or any undertaking which is a group undertaking in relation to the company, and includes a share warrant as defined by section 188(1) of the Act.[39] This means that it will encompass options to subscribe for new shares and options to acquire shares from, say, an ESOP trust, not only in respect of shares of the reporting company, but also, say, in respect of shares of a subsidiary or a holding company.

By omitting the words 'in respect of qualifying services' in the requirement, this means that the amount of the gains will also include gains made on the exercise of options which had been granted prior to the director's appointment as a director. However, this has also meant that where a director has ceased to be a director during the year and has subsequently exercised options then it would appear that any gains made on the exercise of such options are not to be included in the aggregate amount to be disclosed. For companies listed on the Stock Exchange such amounts may be apparent from their disclosures under the requirements of the *Listing Rules* (see 3.2.9 A below). If in such circumstances the former director is allowed to exercise options earlier than would otherwise have been the case, then any gains should probably be disclosed as part of compensation for loss of office (see 2.9 below).

This requirement is only to apply to listed companies. However, this term is wider than its normal usage, because the Act defines a listed company as being 'a company –

(a) whose securities have been admitted to the Official List of the Stock Exchange in accordance with the provisions of Part IV of the Financial Services Act 1986; or

(b) dealings in whose securities are permitted on any exchange which is an approved exchange for the purposes of that Part'.[40]

The inclusion of (b) means that companies quoted on the Alternative Investment Market are to be treated as listed for this purpose and will therefore have to comply with this requirement.

As noted earlier, although companies listed on the Stock Exchange (and any other companies which choose to do so) give disclosure of individual directors' options, including information under UITF 10 which would allow the calculation of gains made on exercise of options, they need to give the aggregate information which is required by the Act (including comparatives). Indeed, Marks and Spencer has made such disclosure even although the amount of gains are quantified for each director, as shown below:

Extract 32.11: Marks and Spencer p.l.c. (1999)

REMUNERATION REPORT [extract]

2 GAINS MADE ON DIRECTORS' SHARE OPTIONS

	1999	1998		**1999**	1998
	£000	£000		**£000**	£000
Sir Richard Greenbury	–	242	J T Rowe	–	66
P L Salsbury	**4**	30	D K Hayes	**10**	0
P G McCracken	**7**	49	C Littmoden	–	9
Lord Stone of Blackheath	**11**	152	S J Sacher	–	201
R Aldridge	**7**	309	P P D Smith	**56**	188
J R Benfield	**7**	470	J K Oates (3)	–	747
R W C Colvill	–	375	D G Trangmar	**n/a**	172
Mrs C E M Freeman	**14**	240	The Hon David Sieff	**n/a**	84
B S Morris	–	68			

(1) The total gain made by the directors on their exercise of their share options was £116,000 (last year £3.4m).

(2) Details of options giving rise to these gains can be found on pages 13 to 15. The gains are calculated as at the date of exercise although the shares may have been retained. (Directors' interests in shares are shown on page 16.)

(3) J K Oates resigned from the Board and took early retirement on 31 January 1999. His details are calculated to this date.

This requirement to disclose the aggregate gains on share options exercised by the directors, notwithstanding the fact that information is disclosed which allows the amounts to be calculated, was highlighted in the Review Panel's ruling on the 1997 accounts of H & C Furnishings.[41]

The original Consultative Document issued by the DTI had proposed that the requirement should apply to all companies, but they recognised that for unlisted companies there may not be a readily available market value to use as a basis for calculating the gain when the option is taken up. Accordingly, companies which are not listed (as defined by the Act) are not required to give this disclosure. This will even apply in situations where the gains are easily quantified such as where a director of an unlisted subsidiary exercises options over shares in a listed parent. As a quid pro quo for not disclosing the amount of any gains made by directors on the exercise of options, unlisted companies are required to state the number of directors who exercised share options (including share options granted prior to a director's appointment as director).[42]

2.6 Long-term incentive schemes

In recent years there has been a move, principally by companies listed on the Stock Exchange, to provide a greater proportion of a director's remuneration by way of rewarding long-term performance. This was further encouraged by the Greenbury Committee recommending that in general there should be a move away from short-term cash-based schemes to longer-term share-based schemes. Disclosure about long-term incentive schemes has become more of a feature in the disclosures of directors' emoluments by listed companies (see 3.2.9 B below).

In the light of this, the Companies Act now requires disclosure of the aggregate of:

(a) the amount of money paid to or receivable by directors under long-term incentive schemes in respect of qualifying services; and

(b) the net value of assets (other than money and share options) received or receivable by directors under such schemes in respect of such services.[43]

A 'long-term incentive scheme' is defined as being 'any agreement or arrangement under which money or other assets may become receivable by a director and which includes one or more qualifying conditions with respect to service or performance which cannot be fulfilled within a single financial year; and for this purpose the following shall be disregarded:

(a) bonuses, the amount of which falls to be determined by reference to service or performance within a single financial year;

(b) compensation for loss of office, payments for breach of contract and other termination payments; and

(c) retirement benefits'.[44]

This is similar to the definition contained in the *Listing Rules* (see 3.2.9 B below).

In this context, 'net value' in relation to assets received or receivable by a director means value after deducting any money paid or other value given by the director in respect of those assets and 'value' in relation to shares received or receivable by a director on any day means the market price of the shares on that day.[45]

This requirement applies to all companies. However, for companies which are not listed (as defined in the Act – see 2.5 above), the net value of assets received or receivable excludes the value of shares received or receivable by directors.[46] However, in that case, the number of directors (if any) in respect of whose qualifying services shares were received or receivable has to be disclosed.[47]

As with gains made on share options (see 2.5 above), the original Consultative Document issued by the DTI had proposed that the requirement should apply to all companies, but the exclusion of share awards for unlisted companies was included for the same reasons as for share options. Again this will apply in situations where the share awards are easily quantified such as where a director of an unlisted subsidiary is awarded shares in a listed parent.

Unlike the requirement in respect of share options the words 'in respect of qualifying services' are included in this requirement. This would appear to mean that any amount which relates to the period prior to the director's appointment as a director is not to be included in the disclosure. However, it can be seen from Extract 32.12 below that such amounts are included. Where a director has ceased to be a director during the year, then any amount that he is entitled to under the scheme should be included in the amount to be disclosed. If in such circumstances the former director is given an amount to which he was not entitled then it should be disclosed as part of compensation for loss of office (see 2.9 below).

An example of a company disclosing the aggregate amount of cash receivable by directors is Boots, as illustrated below:

Extract 32.12: The Boots Company PLC (2000)

Board Remuneration Report [extract]

Long term bonus schemes The schemes provide a direct link between the pay of executive directors and the creation of value for shareholders. Company performance is measured over rolling four year cycles, in terms of total shareholder return (TSR) relative to a peer group of ten other leading companies.

During the cycle ended 31st March 2000 the chosen peer group was:

Great Universal Stores	Sears
Kingfisher	Smith & Nephew
Marks & Spencer	SmithKline Beecham
Reckitt Benckiser	Tesco
J Sainsbury	W H Smith

The peer group is reviewed before each performance cycle to maintain its relevance.

For the four year cycle which ended on 31st March 2000 the amount of bonus depended upon the company's comparative performance against its peer group on the following scale:

Comparative position in peer group league table	1	2	3	4	5	6	7	8	9	10	11
Bonus % of average annual salary	90	90	90	65	55	45	35	25	Nil	Nil	Nil

For the cycles which commenced in April 1997 and April 1998 there will be nil bonus if the position in the above league table is eighth of lower.

For the above scheme, one half of any bonus earned is paid in cash after the end of each performance cycle. The value of the remaining half is converted into an equivalent number of shares in the company in respect of which the executive director will have conditional rights. The number of shares is calculated by dividing half of the value of the long term bonus by the quotation for a share as derived from the Daily Official List of the London Stock Exchange on the date for payment of the cash proportion (in 2000, being 20th June).

For the four year cycles that commenced on or after April 1999 a new scheme has been approved. A maximum potential bonus award (MPBA) is calculated for executive directors by multiplying the basic annual salary at the beginning of the cycle by a factor of 125%. The MPBA is then expressed in share units using the average share price over the previous three months. At the end of the performance cycle a percentage of the MPBA is gained based on the TSR performance against a peer group of ten other leading companies. The scale applied is:

Comparative position in peer group league table	1	2	3	4	5	6	7	8	9	10	11
% of MPBA gained	100	80	64	48	36	24	Nil	Nil	Nil	Nil	Nil

The value of the award is based on share price movement over the four years. For this new scheme, one half of the award is paid in cash after the end of each performance cycle and one half in shares. The value of the cash bonus is calculated by multiplying one half of the number of earned share units by the average share price over the last three months of the performance cycle, as derived from the Daily Official List of the London Stock Exchange.

For the above schemes the executive director will normally become entitled to receive shares only after remaining employed for a further three years (two years for the new scheme commencing April 1999). If a director leaves the company during this period, except in the case of retirement, disability or death, his conditional entitlement to those shares will lapse.

In respect of the four year period to 31st March 2000, the company achieved position five in the league table referred to on page 34. Accordingly the long term bonus amounts earned in respect of that period by executive directors, including amounts relating to periods of service before appointment to the board, were as follows:

£000	**Cash**	**Value of vested shares**	**Total 2000**	Total 1999
Lord Blyth	**155**	–	**155**	170
B Clare	**38**	–	**38**	–
M F Ruddell	**68**		**68**	74
S G Russell	**87**	–	**87**	87
D A R Thompson	**88**	–	**88**	93
J J H Watson	**51**	–	**51**	49
	487	–	**487**	473

Each executive director will also be awarded conditional rights to receive ordinary shares in the company having a market value on 20th June 2000 equivalent to the cash bonus shown above. The director will normally become entitled to receive those shares in June 2003 if the conditions are satisfied. There were no shares that vested during the year.

Details of the numbers of shares which have been conditionally awarded during the year under the long term bonus scheme for the cycle which was completed at the end of the previous financial year and the cumulative conditional entitlement are shown below:

	Conditional entitlement 2000	Conditional entitlement 1999	Conditional entitlement 1998	Cumulative Total
Lord Blyth	**21,992**	15,956	22,263	60,211
B Clare	**4,621**	3,221	4,190	12,032 *
M F Ruddell	**9,552**	6,991	9,525	26,068
S G Russell	**11,200**	7,652	9,570	28,422
D A R Thompson	**12,072**	8,538	11,475	32,085
J J H Watson	**6,377**	4,242	4,876	15,495
	65,814	46,600	61,899	174,313

*B Clare's cumulative entitlement accrued before he was appointed to the board on 1st April 1999.

It can be seen from the above example Boots has gone further than the Companies Act requires, by disclosing the amounts for each director. However, this will have been given so as to meet the requirements of the *Listing Rules* (see 3.2.9 B below).

Such long-term bonuses are to be disclosed in the year in which they become receivable and therefore a similar question arises as with annual bonuses when some or all of the bonus is conditional on the director remaining in employment with the company for a future period (see Example 32.4 at 2.4.1 A above).

In Extract 32.12 above, Boots has clearly regarded the cash element as receivable. However, this only represents half of the bonus. The remainder is to be converted into a certain number of shares with an equivalent value and the director will normally become entitled to these shares only after remaining employed for a further three years. If a director leaves the company during that period then (except in specified circumstances), his conditional entitlement will lapse. Whether such amounts should be included or not will for companies listed on the Stock Exchange normally be of academic interest only, because sufficient information will generally be disclosed to meet the requirements of the *Listing Rules* (see 3.2.9 B below). If that is the case, then the Companies Act requirement (whatever it may be) will have been deemed to have been met under the dispensation that 'information shall be treated as shown if it is capable of being readily ascertained from other information which is shown' (see 2.1 above).

It should be emphasised that the disclosure of the amounts receivable under long-term incentive schemes is completely independent of the charge recognised in the profit and loss account for such schemes. In April 1997, the UITF published its seventeenth Abstract, *Employee share schemes*.[48] This addresses how companies should recognise and measure the charge in the profit and loss account in respect of any shares issued as part of an employee share scheme. This is discussed further at 2.5.4 of Chapter 22.

2.7 Pension contributions in respect of money purchase schemes

As discussed at 3.2.8 below, the Greenbury Report had recommended that the pension benefit receivable by a director should be measured as the present value of pension entitlement earned during the year resulting from additional length of service, increases in salary or changes in the terms of the scheme, less any contributions made by the director during the year. In the light of this, the DTI proposed in its Consultative Document that there should be disclosure of the aggregate value of directors' pension entitlements and that this would apply to all companies. However, following comments received on the Consultative Document, this proposal was dropped, although there is a requirement for such information in respect of the highest paid director (see 2.11 below).

Accordingly, all that the Companies Act requires is disclosure of the aggregate value of any company contributions paid, or treated as paid, to a pension scheme in respect of directors' qualifying services, being contributions by reference to which the rate or amount of any money purchase benefits that may become payable will be calculated.[49]

For this purpose, the following definitions apply:

- 'Company contributions' mean 'any payments (including insurance premiums) made, or treated to be made, to the scheme in respect of the director by a person other than the director'.[50] The words 'treated to be made' are to cater for disclosure of notional contributions under underpinned schemes (see below).
- 'Pension scheme' has the meaning assigned to 'retirement benefits scheme' by section 611 of the Income and Corporation Taxes Act 1988.[51] This latter definition is generally interpreted as extending to unfunded pension arrangements.
- 'Money purchase benefits' are defined as 'retirement benefits payable under a pension scheme the rate or amount of which is calculated by reference to payments made, or treated as made, by the director or by any other person in respect of the director and which are not average salary benefits'.[52]
- 'Retirement benefits' has the meaning assigned to 'relevant benefits' by section 612(1) of the Income and Corporation Taxes Act 1988.[53]

In most cases the amount to be disclosed will be the contributions to a money purchase scheme (defined contribution scheme) but it will also include contributions to a defined benefit scheme, to the extent that the contributions go to entitling directors to money purchase benefits under that scheme.

The legislation also provides for disclosure of information relating to a pension scheme with an underpin. Such a scheme, although primarily a defined benefit scheme or a money purchase scheme, has a shadow scheme underpinning it with notional contributions and rates. Accordingly the Act states that 'where a pension scheme provides for any benefits that may become payable to or in respect of any director to be whichever are the greater of:

(a) money purchased benefits as determined under the scheme; and

(b) defined benefits as so determined,

the company may assume that those benefits will be money purchased benefits, or defined benefits, according to whichever appears more likely at the end of the financial year'.[54]

It should be emphasised that comparative figures are required for such aggregate pension contributions. For companies listed on the Stock Exchange who rely on the dispensation allowed under the Companies Act referred to at 2.1 above, it is important that where such pension contributions are given for each individual director within the remuneration table, then unless comparative figures are also given for the pension contributions, disclosure of the comparative aggregate amount needs to be made.

As a quid pro quo for not requiring disclosures in respect of the value of pension entitlements under defined benefit schemes (other than in respect of the highest paid director, where applicable – see 2.11 below), the Act also requires disclosure of the number of directors (if any) to whom retirement benefits are accruing in respect of qualifying services under:

(a) money purchase schemes; and

(b) defined benefit schemes.[55]

A 'money purchase scheme' is defined as being a pension scheme under which *all* benefits that may become payable to a director are money purchase benefits.[56] The Act has not used the term 'defined contribution scheme' in order to align the terminology with the definition of money purchase benefits (see above).

A 'defined benefit scheme' means a pension scheme which is not a money purchase scheme.[57] The most obvious example is a final salary scheme. However, any scheme which is not classified as a money purchase scheme will fall to be regarded as defined benefit scheme. Therefore if a director is a member of a hybrid pension scheme under which both money purchase and defined benefits are payable then it is to be classified as a defined benefit scheme.

For the purpose of determining whether a pension scheme is a money purchase or defined benefit scheme, any death in service benefits provided for by the scheme are disregarded.[58] Thus a scheme in which the only defined benefit element relates to death in service benefits should be classified as a money purchase scheme.

In our view such information on the number of directors is virtually worthless and should never have been introduced. We would recommend that where companies listed on the Stock Exchange are disclosing information for individual directors (see 3.2.8 below), then they should use the dispensation allowed under the Companies Act referred to at 2.1 above.

2.8 Excess retirement benefits of directors and past directors

The Companies Act requires disclosure to be given of the aggregate amount of retirement benefits paid to or receivable by directors and past directors under pension schemes in excess of the retirement benefits to which they were respectively entitled on the date on which the benefits first became payable or 31 March 1997, whichever is the later.[59]

Amounts paid or receivable under the pension scheme need not be included in the aggregate amount if:

(a) the funding of the scheme was such that the amounts were or, as the case may be, could have been paid without recourse to additional contributions; and

(b) amounts were paid to or receivable by all pensioner members of the scheme on the same basis.[60]

For this purpose, 'pension scheme' and 'retirement benefits' have the same meaning as discussed at 2.7 above and 'pensioner member' means any person who is entitled to the present payment of retirement benefits under the scheme.[61]

The intention of this requirement is to ensure that companies disclose any discretionary increases in pensions of directors or former directors. However, if a former director receives, say, a discretionary 3% inflationary increase in his pension and this is given to all pensioner members then this amount, although in excess of his entitlement when benefits first became payable, is not to be disclosed under this provision.

The inclusion of the reference to 31 March 1997 in the requirement provides the baseline for disclosures in respect of pensions in payment at the commencement of the first financial year to which the legislation applied.

The amounts to be disclosed in respect of retirement benefits include any benefits in kind given in respect of retirement benefits at the estimated money value of the benefit. In such a case, the nature of the benefit is also required to be disclosed.[62]

For companies listed on the Stock Exchange it is important to note that the dispensation allowed under the Companies Act referred to at 2.1 above does not apply to excess retirement benefits. Accordingly, where information about such benefits is given for each individual director or past director, it will be necessary to disclose the aggregate amount for the current and the comparative period.

2.9 Compensation for loss of office

2.9.1 Legal requirements

The aggregate amount of any compensation payable to directors or past directors in respect of loss of office must be disclosed.[63]

In this context, compensation for loss of office includes compensation in consideration for, or in connection with, a person's retirement from office.[64]

The changes made to the legislation by SI 1997/570 also clarified that it is to include payments made by way of damages for breach of the person's contract with the company or with a subsidiary undertaking of the company or payments made by way of settlement or compromise of any claim in respect of the breach.[65]

These are illustrated in the following extracts:

Extract 32.13: Meyer International PLC (1999)

Report on Directors' remuneration [extract]

Following Mr J G R Perry's resignation as a Director of the Company on 27th May 1998, it was agreed that he would continue to receive basic salary and certain benefits until the earlier of 30th November 1999 or the date he commences comparable permanent full-time employment. In the event of the latter occurring, he would then be entitled to receive 50% of the balance of the emoluments which he would have received under these arrangements had he continued to be employed by the Company until 30th November 1999.

The payments made to Mr Perry in accordance with these arrangements are as follows:

	1999	1998
	£000	£000
Payment to former Director	129	–
Pension contributions for former Director	43	–

In accordance with the arrangements disclosed in the 1997/98 Report of the Compensation and Appointments Committee, payments made to Mr B Wright who resigned as a Director of the Company in January 1997 are as follows:

	1999	1998
	£000	£000
Payment to former Director	58	178
Pension contributions for former Director	19	57

Extract 32.14: Volex Group p.l.c. (1997)

9 Directors' remuneration, interests and transactions [extract]

§ Total aggregate emoluments for directors during the year comprised £921,072.

In addition to the emoluments shown above:

(i) Mr Chapple received payments under the terms of a compromise agreement made upon his resignation from the Board on 21 May 1996 comprising cash payments of £131,429 and contributions to a funded unapproved retirement benefit scheme of £12,850: a further contribution of £17,176 was outstanding at the end of the year. The compromise agreement provides for payments to Mr Chapple throughout the unexpired portion of his service agreement (i.e. to 20 May 1998) net of all income earned by Mr. Chapple from other sources during that period.

(ii) Mr. Davies received an ex gratia payment of £28,333 upon his retirement on 31 March 1997.

Contributions to a pension scheme made in connection with a director's loss of, or retirement from, office should be included within the aggregate amount of compensation to be disclosed, as illustrated below:

> *Extract 32.15: Norcros plc (1997)*
>
> **REPORT OF THE REMUNERATION COMMITTEE** [extract]
> *Compensation for loss of office and pension rights of Mr M E Doherty and Mr R H Alcock*
>
> Mr M E Doherty received compensation for his change of status in May 1996 from executive to non-executive Chairman, as a consequence of the termination with effect from 4 April 1996 of his previous executive employment agreement (which had a two year notice period). A sum of £234,000 was paid into the Norcros Security Plan to augment his pension by £21,781 per annum to give a total of £147,972 per annum payable from his normal retirement age of 60. In addition, an amount of £6,000 was paid to the Norcros Security Plan to provide a lump sum death benefit.
>
> A sum of £250,000 was paid to Mr R H Alcock as compensation for loss of office. In addition he received fees of £102,570 plus VAT under the terms of a consultancy agreement dated 6 May which expired on 31 October 1996.

Although no aggregate amount for compensation for loss of office is disclosed in the above extracts they are deemed to have been disclosed in view of the dispensation mentioned at 2.1 above.

Another company which has disclosed such pension contributions is Sainsbury, as shown below:

> *Extract 32.16: J Sainsbury plc (1997)*
>
> **Report of the Remuneration Committee** [extract]
>
> 4. Retired as a Director on 26th April 1996. 1997 pension contributions included £556,000 in respect of compensation for loss of office.

Elsewhere in the report, the amount of compensation for loss of office for 1997 is disclosed as £336,000. Although this method of presentation might not be ideal, it does comply with the requirement for the reason mentioned above in respect of the other extracts.

These requirements extend to the loss of any office or otherwise in connection with the management of the affairs of the company or any of its subsidiary undertakings[66] and apply whether or not the compensation requires company approval (see 1.3 above). For example, if the managing director of a subsidiary company ceases to act in that capacity but remains on the boards of both that company and its parent, any compensation paid by the subsidiary in respect of this loss of office should be disclosed in both the holding company's and subsidiary's financial statements.

The amounts to be disclosed in respect of compensation include any benefits received, or receivable, otherwise than in cash, at the estimated money value of the benefit.[67] In such a case, the nature of the benefit is also required to be disclosed.[68] One company which has made such disclosure is PIC, as shown below:

Extract 32.17: PIC International Group PLC (1998)

REPORT OF THE REMUNERATION COMMITTEE [extract]
DIRECTORS' REMUNERATION

R J Clothier resigned as a director on 12 September 1997 and left the Group's employment on 30 September 1997. He received compensation for loss of office of £505,345, subject to deduction of tax, which included non-cash compensation for the use of a motor car, and medical, personal accident and life assurance cover to 31 March 1999. He receives a pension of £145,848 per annum which commenced on 1 October 1997 and has retained rights to exercise his outstanding executive share options in the period up to 26 September 2000.

R N Harris retired as a director on 30 September 1997 and received compensation for loss of office of £105,135, subject to deduction of tax, and which included non-cash compensation for the provision of medical insurance cover to January 1999. He receives a pension of £120,000 per annum which commenced on 1 October 1997, and he retained the right to exercise his outstanding share options in the period up to 16 March 2001.

P Kirk, who resigned as a director on 1 May 1998, was paid £320,221 in compensation for loss of office and which included non-cash compensation for the loss of medical, personal accident and life insurance cover. He also received cash compensation of £67,821 in lieu of an annual bonus for the year, and entitlements under the Dalgety Long Term Incentive Plan. Mr Kirk receives a pension of £93,537 per annum which commenced 23 May 1998, and he retained the right to exercise his outstanding executive share options in the period up to 13 November 2001.

K G Hanna is to relinquish his position as Group Chief Executive on 30 September 1998. He will receive compensation for loss of office of £794,722, subject to deduction of tax, together with an additional deferred pension of £15,500 per annum payable at normal retirement age, in 2013. Mr Hanna remains entitled to a proportionate payment of any bonus payable in 1999 under the Long Term Incentive Plan, the amount of which will depend on the results achieved in the three years ending 30 June 1999. His compensation includes an amount payable for relinquishing his right under the Long Term Incentive Plan to a bonus prospectively payable in June 2000, and also includes compensation for the loss of use of a motor car, medical, personal accident and life insurance cover to 30 September 2000. Mr Hanna has retained rights to exercise his outstanding share options. The majority must be exercised by 30 September 1999 and 25,677 by 7 November 2000. Mr Hanna is to serve as a non-executive director of the Company from 1 October 1998.

A particular problem associated with non-cash compensation relates to the valuation of such benefits. Ordinarily, the market value of any asset transferred should be disclosed; however, if the book value of the asset is used, an explanatory note should indicate the asset's market value. For example:

Example 32.5

A director is given a motor car upon retirement from the company and the book value of the car is £2,000 and its market value is £3,000. The company should either disclose the market value of the car in the compensation for loss of office disclosure or use the book value of the asset and append an explanatory note to the directors' remuneration note to the following effect: 'the amount for compensation for loss of office includes the written down value of a [description of vehicle] the market value of which was £3,000'.

2.9.2 *Problem areas*

A *Ex-gratia payments*

Ex-gratia payments which do not constitute compensation for loss of office and which are not in connection with a person's retirement need not be disclosed. In order to decide whether a payment is ex-gratia, regard should be had to the nature of and all the circumstances surrounding the payment. The donor company's classification of the payment is irrelevant. The following examples distinguish a disguised retirement payment from an ex-gratia payment:

Example 32.6

Mr A retires from the board of Company X. The following week, Company X makes Mr A an ex-gratia payment of £25,000. In these circumstances, the payment, albeit described as ex-gratia, should be disclosed as compensation for loss of office for it would appear to be connected with the director's retirement from the board.

Example 32.7

Mr A is a former director of Company X. After leaving Company X, Mr A sets up his own business, which through no fault of his own, goes into liquidation. Company A learns of Mr A's plight and gifts him the sum of £20,000. In these circumstances, the payment is unrelated to Mr A's retirement from the board of Company X and need not be disclosed in its financial statements as compensation for loss of office.

Where an ex-gratia payment requires to be disclosed as a compensation payment, the note will generally indicate the 'ex-gratia' nature of the payment, as seen in Extract 32.14 at 2.9.1 above.

Companies listed on the Stock Exchange would require to disclose the payment in Example 32.7 if it was considered significant (see 3.2.7 below).

B *Augmentation of pension rights*

As discussed above, contributions to a pension scheme made in connection with a director's loss of, or retirement from, office should be included within the aggregate amount of compensation to be disclosed. However, it may be that in certain situations where there is a surplus on the company's pension scheme, it is agreed with the trustees of the scheme that the augmentation of the pension rights of the retiring director is to be met out of the surplus of the pension scheme, with no specific contribution being made by the company. In these circumstances, we believe that the capital cost of the augmentation of the pension rights should still be disclosed as part of the compensation for loss of office. This is because the amounts to be included within compensation for loss of office are to include non-cash benefits and are also to include payments made not only by the company and its subsidiary undertakings, but any other person (i.e. the pension scheme). One company which appears to have adopted this view was APV in its 1993 accounts, as illustrated below:

Extract 32.18: APV plc (1993)

4 **DIRECTORS** [extract]	**1993** **£'000**	1992 £'000
Compensation for loss of office	**332**	–

(iv) Compensation of £216,042 was paid in respect of loss of office of a former director, together with an additional deferred pension of £9,875 per annum payable at normal retirement date. The actuarial valuation of this deferred pension has been calculated as £116,400.

However, such an approach is not always followed, as illustrated in Gerrard Group's 1997 accounts below:

> *Extract 32.19: Gerrard Group plc (1997)*
>
> **Report of the Remuneration Committee** [extract]
>
> *d) Termination payments*
>
> Arrangements for the early termination of contracts are carefully considered by the Committee. When calculating termination payments, the Committee takes into account a variety of factors including age, years of service and the individual director's obligation to mitigate his own loss by seeking new employment.
>
> D A Brayshaw retired from the Board on 31st March 1996. At that date he had a two year rolling contract. The Committee agreed to make a termination payment of £139,000 and not to apply any additional actuarial discount to his pension when he draws it early at age 50 in 1998. R B Williamson retired as executive chairman in December 1996. He received a termination payment of £100,000 and was granted a full pension even although he had not reached the Normal Retirement Age. T W Fellows retired in November 1996 and was granted a full pension even although he had not reached the Normal Retirement Age.

C *Consultancy agreements*

Over the years, a number of ex-directors have entered into consultancy agreements with the companies on whose boards they have ceased to serve. Typically, these grant the ex-directors a guaranteed fee for a period of time. Whether payments to be made under such agreements should be disclosed as compensation for loss of office will depend on the particular circumstances and the extent to which it is envisaged that consultancy services will be provided by the former director. Where it is unlikely that the director will provide any consultancy service we believe that the amount should be disclosed as compensation for loss of office. However, where it is considered that the ex-director will provide services commensurate with the level of fees which are to be made then it may be appropriate not to include the fees as compensation for loss of office. Nevertheless, in such a situation consideration would need to be given as to whether such a consultancy agreement was a transaction in which the director had a material interest. An example of a company disclosing consultancy fees is Gerrard Group as shown below.

> *Extract 32.20: Gerrard Group plc (1999)*
>
> **Report of the Remuneration Committee** [extract]
>
> N F Andrews retired on 30th June 1998. The remuneration shown is that paid during the year. In addition, a consultancy payment of £75,000 was paid to N F Andrews. Greig Middleton has entered into an arrangement with N F Andrews for five years, during which the Company will be entitled to call upon his services for a specified number of days each year in return for a consultancy payment of £100,000.

Another example is that of Norcros (see Extract 32.15 at 2.9.1 above).

However, companies listed on the Stock Exchange would require to disclose the payments in respect of consultancy agreements if they were considered significant (see 3.2.7 below).

2.10 Payments to third parties

The Companies Act requires disclosure of the aggregate amounts payable to or receivable by third parties for making available the services of any person:

(a) as director of the company; or

(b) as director of any of the company's subsidiary undertakings (whilst a director of the company); or

(c) in connection with the management of the affairs of the company or any of its subsidiary undertakings (whilst a director of the company).[69]

'Third parties' means persons other than:

(a) the director himself; or

(b) persons connected with the director or connected with bodies corporate controlled by the director; or

(c) the company and any of its subsidiary undertakings.[70]

(These are not exemptions from disclosure; payments to such persons are covered by the other disclosure requirements.)

Consequently, payments made to an unconnected organisation, such as a bank, for persons on secondment as a director will have to be disclosed; payments made to a holding company, or fellow subsidiary, for the services of a director will also have to be disclosed. Examples of disclosures in these circumstances are shown in the following extracts:

Extract 32.21: Powell Duffryn plc (2000)

2 **Directors and employees** [extract]

The aggregate remuneration of all directors during the year was as follows:

	2000 **£000**	1999 £000
Emoluments	**1,450**	1,166
Gains on share option exercise	**–**	57
Amounts receivable under long-term incentive schemes	**327**	–
Company pension contributions to money purchase schemes	**–**	–
Sums paid to third parties for directors' services	**22**	19

£22,000 was paid to Smith & Nephew plc for the services of Mr Hooley as a non-executive director during the year. No sums were paid to former directors during the year or the previous year in respect of consultancy services. Retirement benefits are accruing to five directors under a defined benefit scheme.

The above disclosure in respect of payments to third parties is what is strictly required to comply with the requirement. However, other companies include such payments within aggregate remuneration, but as long as the aggregate amount paid to third parties is separately identified then they are deemed to meet the requirements for the disclosure of aggregate emoluments under the dispensation noted at 2.1 above. One company which adopts such a treatment is Pilkington, as illustrated below:

Extract 32.22: Pilkington plc (1999)

Report on directors' remuneration [extract]
Non-executive directors' remuneration

Sir Nigel Rudd's remuneration amounted to £200,000 (1998 £153,000), of which £nil (1998 £90,000) was paid to Williams PLC, his employer.

The amounts disclosed have to include any benefits in kind given to a third party for the services of a director at the estimated money value of the benefit. In such a case, the nature of the benefit is also required to be disclosed.[71]

For companies listed on the Stock Exchange it is important to note that the dispensation allowed under the Companies Act referred to at 2.1 above does not apply to the payments to third parties. Accordingly, where information about such payments is given for individual directors, it will be necessary to disclose the aggregate amount for the current and the comparative period.

2.11 Highest paid director

Where the aggregate amounts shown under 2.2 (emoluments), 2.5 (gains on exercise of share options, where applicable) and 2.6 (long-term incentive schemes) total £200,000 or more, the following shall be shown in respect of the highest paid director:

(a) the total of such aggregate amounts (there is no need to disclose the separate amounts);[72]

(b) the value of any pension contributions shown under 2.7 above;[73] and

(c) where he/she has performed qualifying services during the financial year by reference to which the rate or amount of any defined benefits that may become payable will be calculated;

  (i) the amount at the end of the year of his/her accrued pension; and

  (ii) where applicable, the amount at the end of the year of his/her accrued lump sum.[74]

Examples of such disclosures are shown below:

Extract 32.23: John Lewis Partnership plc (2001)

9 DIRECTORS' EMOLUMENTS [extract]

The emoluments of the Chairman, who was also the highest paid director, were £493,000 (£485,000), including Partnership bonus of £44,000 (£62,000). The Chairman's aggregate pension entitlement from the age of 60 accrued at the end of the year was £261,000 per annum (£230,000 per annum). The transfer value of the increase in accrued entitlement during the year was £437,000 (£418,000).

The transfer value is not required to be disclosed by the Companies Act, but companies listed on the Stock Exchange are required to disclose such information for all directors (see 3.2.8 below).

Extract 32.24: Scottish Power plc (2001)

Remuneration Report of the Directors [extract]
Table 28 – Directors' Emoluments 2000-01 [extract]

The emoluments of the highest paid director (Sir Ian Robinson) excluding pension contributions were £546,862 (2000 £688,611). In addition, gains on exercise of share options during the year by Sir Ian Robinson amounted to £17,301 (2000 £nil). Details of other share related incentives are contained in Tables 30 and 31. Pension contributions made by the company under approved pension arrangements for Sir Ian Robinson amounted to £nil (2000 £nil). Sir Ian Robinson also has an entitlement under the unapproved pension benefits described further in Table 29, note (iii) below. The total liabilities for the 15 executives and senior employees arising in relation to unapproved benefits for service for the year to 31 March 2001 was £500,000 (2000 £600,000). All benefits for the above are provided on a defined benefit basis.

Table 29 – Defined Benefits Pension Scheme 2000-01 [extract]

(i) The accrued entitlement of the highest paid director (Sir Ian Robinson) was £319,200 (2000 £226,904). The figures shown in the table above relate to Sir Ian's accrual of pension over the year on the basis of his contract in force at the start of the year. In addition, following a change to his contract, his pension earned in the year increased by a further £31,192 per annum with an added value of £854,263. The agreed change to his contract of employment was to allow Sir Ian to retire on his promised pension on 31 May 2001, being one year prior to his Normal Pension Date.

(iii) Executives who joined the company on or after 1 June 1989 are subject to the earnings cap introduced in the Finance Act 1989. Pension entitlements which cannot be provided through the company's approved schemes due to the earnings cap are provided through unapproved pension arrangements. Full details are included in the Remuneration Report. The pension benefits disclosed above include approved and unapproved pension arrangements.

As with many of the disclosure requirements, the Act will regard such information as having been disclosed if it can be determined from other information which is shown (see 2.1 above). As companies listed on the Stock Exchange are required to provide information for each director, then they will generally have complied with this requirement. It is important, however, if listed companies are to rely on this dispensation that sufficient information is given, particularly about gains on exercise of share options and accrued pension benefits, so that the details for the highest paid director in *both* years can be determined.

The determination of whether disclosure of information in respect of the highest paid director is required excludes the following amounts:

- pension contributions in respect of money purchase benefits (see 2.7 above);
- excess retirement benefits (see 2.8 above);
- compensation for loss of office (see 2.9 above); and
- sums paid to third parties in respect of directors' services (see 2.10 above).

However, 'Golden hellos' (see 2.2.2 B above) and payments made to persons connected with a director (see 2.4.1 D above) have to be taken into account.

Once it is determined that disclosure of information about the highest paid director is required, the next step is to identify which director this is.

The 'highest paid director' for this purpose means the director to whom is attributable the greatest part of the total of the aggregates under 2.2 (emoluments),

2.5 (gains on exercise of share options, where applicable) and 2.6 (long-term incentive schemes). This therefore excludes the value of any pension contributions shown under 2.7 above (even though such amounts are to be disclosed for whoever is determined to be the highest paid director).

In view of the fact that gains on exercise of share options and amounts receivable under long-term incentive schemes are included in this determination, some companies which are listed on the Stock Exchange may wish to identify the highest paid director and highlight such amounts that are applicable to that director, as it may appear from the remuneration table provided (see 3.2.3 below) that another director is the highest paid director. An example of such disclosure is given by BAA, as shown below:

Extract 32.25: BAA plc (1999)

3 Directors' emoluments [extract]

	Salary/fees		Bonus		Benefits		Total	
	1999	1998	**1999**	1998	**1999**	1998	**1999**	1998
(a) Emoluments	**£000**	£000	**£000**	£000	**£000**	£000	**£000**	£000
Executive directors								
Sir John Egan	**494**	475	**160**	92	**28**	25	**682**	592
J R F Walls	**285**	274	**91**	53	**22**	21	**398**	348

The highest paid director was Sir John Egan whose emoluments are shown above, but when emoluments and gains on the exercise of share options are aggregated, the highest paid director in 1999 was Mr Walls (emoluments: £398,000, gains on options: £322,000) and, in 1998, was Sir John Egan (emoluments: £592,000, gains on options: £697,000).

As indicated earlier, comparative information is required to be given for the highest paid director. However, this does not mean that the comparatives to be disclosed are for the individual director who is identified as being the highest paid director for the current year. The information to be disclosed is in respect of the individual who was identified in the previous year as being the highest paid director for that year. This is illustrated in the extract above.

For the purposes of the disclosure of (c) above, 'accrued pension' and 'accrued lump sum' mean respectively the amount of the annual pension, and the amount of the lump sum, which would be payable under the scheme on his/her attaining normal pension age if:

(a) he/she had left the company's service at the end of the financial year;

(b) there were no increase in the general level of prices in Great Britain during the period beginning with the end of that year and ending with his/her attaining that age;

(c) no question arose of any commutation of the pension or inverse commutation of the lump sum; and

(d) any amounts attributable to voluntary contributions paid by the director to the scheme, and any money purchase benefits which would be payable under the scheme, were disregarded.[75]

'Normal pension age' means the age at which the director will first become entitled to receive a full pension on retirement of an amount determined without reduction to take account of its payment before a later age (but disregarding any entitlement to pension upon retirement in the event of illness, incapacity or redundancy).[76]

Most defined benefit schemes entitle employees to a pension, some of which can be commuted for a lump sum. As a result of (c) above, there is therefore only a need to disclose the accrued pension as done by John Lewis and Scottish Power in Extracts 32.23 and 32.24 above. Both amounts should only be disclosed if the pension scheme benefits are such that the director receives a pension *and* a lump sum. Although the director may be able to commute either some of the pension for an extra lump sum or vice versa, the effect of paragraph (c) is that such a choice should be ignored.

Example 32.8 at 3.2.8 below illustrates how the accrued pension is calculated.

For unlisted companies (as defined – see 2.5 above) which have not disclosed amounts in respect of gains made on the exercise of options or share awards under long-term incentive schemes, then there is no requirement to disclose any such amounts in respect of the highest paid director. However, such companies are required to state whether the highest paid director exercised any share options and whether any shares were receivable by that director under a long-term incentive scheme.[77] If the highest paid director has not been involved in any such transactions then that fact need not be stated.[78]

3 REQUIREMENTS FOR LISTED COMPANIES

As discussed more fully at 1 above, in recent years executive remuneration of companies listed on the Stock Exchange has become a focus of public attention with regard to both the level and the structure of boardroom pay. This concern has been addressed by a number of committees over the years. As a result, the *Listing Rules* now require most listed companies to:

(a) disclose in their annual report how they have applied the principles and the extent to which they have complied with the detailed provisions of the Combined Code in their annual report. The principles and detailed provisions of the Code relating to directors' remuneration are outlined at 3.1 below; and

(b) include a remuneration report within their annual report containing a statement of the company's policy on executive remuneration together with detailed information about the remuneration of each director (see 3.2 below).

3.1 Combined Code

As indicated earlier, the Combined Code contains principles and detailed provisions of the Code relating to directors' remuneration. Companies therefore need to disclose how they have applied these principles and the extent to which they have complied with the detailed provisions. These deal with the level and make-up of remuneration, procedure and disclosure and are set out below.

3.1.1 Principle B.1 The Level and Make-up of Remuneration

Levels of remuneration should be sufficient to attract and retain the directors needed to run the company successfully, but companies should avoid paying more than is necessary for this purpose. A proportion of executive directors' remuneration should be structured so as to link rewards to corporate and individual performance.

Code Provisions - Remuneration policy

- The remuneration committee should provide the packages needed to attract, retain and motivate executive directors of the quality required but should avoid paying more than is necessary for this purpose. (B.1.1)
- Remuneration committees should judge where to position their company relative to other companies. They should be aware what comparable companies are paying and should take account of relative performance. But they should use such comparisons with caution, in view of the risk that they can result in an upward ratchet of remuneration levels with no corresponding improvement in performance. (B.1.2)
- Remuneration committees should be sensitive to the wider scene, including pay and employment conditions elsewhere in the group, especially when determining annual salary increases. (B.1.3)
- The performance-related elements of remuneration should form a significant proportion of the total remuneration package of executive directors and should be designed to align their interests with those of shareholders and to give these directors keen incentives to perform at the highest levels. (B.1.4)
- Executive share options should not be offered at a discount save as permitted by paragraphs 13.30 and 13.31 of the *Listing Rules*. (B.1.5)
- In designing schemes of performance related remuneration, remuneration committees should follow the provisions in Schedule A to this code. (B.1.6)

Code Provisions - Service Contracts and Compensation

- There is a strong case for setting notice or contract periods at, or reducing them to, one year or less. Boards should set this as an objective; but they should recognise that it may not be possible to achieve it immediately. (B.1.7)
- If it is necessary to offer longer notice or contract periods to new directors recruited from outside, such periods should reduce after the initial period. (B.1.8)
- Remuneration committees should consider what compensation commitments (including pension contributions) their directors' contracts of service, if any, would entail in the event of early termination. They should in particular consider the advantages of providing explicitly in the initial contract for such compensation commitments except in the case of removal for misconduct. (B.1.9)

- Where the initial contract does not explicitly provide for compensation commitments, remuneration committees should, within legal constraints, tailor their approach in individual early termination cases to the wide variety of circumstances. The broad aim should be to avoid rewarding poor performance while dealing fairly with cases where departure is not due to poor performance and to take a robust line on reducing compensation to reflect departing directors' obligations to mitigate loss. (B.1.10)

3.1.2 *Principle B.2 Procedure*

Companies should establish a formal and transparent procedure for developing policy on executive remuneration and for fixing the remuneration packages of individual directors. No director should be involved in deciding his or her own remuneration.

Code Provisions

- To avoid potential conflicts of interest, boards of directors should set up remuneration committees of independent non-executive directors to make recommendations to the Board, within agreed terms of reference, on the company's framework of executive remuneration and its cost; and to determine on their behalf specific remuneration packages for each of the executive directors, including pension rights and any compensation payments. (B.2.1)
- Remuneration committees should consist exclusively of non-executive directors who are independent of management and free from any business or other relationship which could materially interfere with the exercise of their independent judgement. (B.2.2)
- The members of the remuneration committee should be listed each year in the board's remuneration report to shareholders B.3.1 below. (B.2.3)
- The Board itself or, where required by the Articles of Association, the shareholders should determine the remuneration of the non-executive directors, including members of the remuneration committee, within the limits set in the Articles of Association. Where permitted by the Articles, the Board may however delegate this responsibility to a small sub-committee, which might include the chief executive officer. (B.2.4)
- Remuneration committees should consult the chairman and/or chief executive officer about their proposals relating to the remuneration of other executive directors and have access to professional advice inside and outside the company. (B.2.5)
- The chairman of the Board should ensure that the company maintains contact as required with its principal shareholders about remuneration in the same way as for other matters. (B.2.6)

3.1.3 *Principle B.3 Disclosure*

The company's annual report should contain a statement of remuneration policy and details of the remuneration of each director.

Code Provisions

- The board should report to the shareholders each year on remuneration. The report should form part of, or be annexed to, the company's annual report and accounts. It should be the main vehicle through which the company reports to shareholders on directors' remuneration. (B.3.1)
- The report should set out the company's policy on executive directors' remuneration. It should draw attention to factors specific to the company. (B.3.2)
- In preparing the remuneration report, the board should follow the provisions in Schedule B to this code. (B.3.3)
- Shareholders should be invited specifically to approve all new long term incentive schemes (as defined in the *Listing Rules*) save in the circumstances permitted by paragraph 13.13A of the *Listing Rules*. (B.3.4)
- The board's annual remuneration report to shareholders need not be a standard item of agenda for AGMs. But the board should consider each year whether the circumstances are such that the AGM should be invited to approve the policy set out in the report and should minute their conclusions. (B.3.5)

As far as the content of the remuneration report is concerned, Schedule B to the Combined Code requires the following to be included:

- Full details of all elements in the remuneration package of each individual director by name, such as basic salary, benefits in kind, annual bonuses and long term incentive schemes including share options.
- Information on share options, including SAYE options, should be given for each director in accordance with the recommendations of UITF 10.
- If grants under executive share option or other long-term incentive schemes are awarded in one large block rather than phased, the report should explain and justify.
- Also included in the report should be pension entitlements earned by each individual director during the year, disclosed on one of the alternative bases recommended by the Faculty of Actuaries and the Institute of Actuaries and included in the *Listing Rules*. Companies may wish to make clear that the transfer value represents a liability of the company, not a sum paid or due to the individual.
- If annual bonuses or benefits in kind are pensionable the report should explain and justify.
- Any service contracts which provide for, or imply, notice periods in excess of one year (or any provisions for predetermined compensation on termination which exceed one year's salary and benefits) should be disclosed and the reasons for the longer notice periods explained.

The amounts received by, and commitments made to, each director under the first, second and fourth bullet points above should be subject to audit.

These broadly repeat what had already been required by the Stock Exchange, following the Greenbury Code, although Schedule B incorporates the Hampel Committee's suggestion that companies might spell out that the transfer value of a director's increase in accrued pension is not a sum paid or due to the individual. Interestingly, it doesn't repeat the Committee's suggestion that it cannot meaningfully be added to annual remuneration.

3.2 Remuneration Report and other requirements of the Listing Rules

The *Listing Rules* require all listed companies (other than investment companies, investment trusts, investment property companies and venture capital trusts with no executive directors) to include within their annual report and accounts a report to the shareholders by the board (remuneration report) containing:[79]

(a) a statement of the company's policy on executive directors' remuneration;

(b) the amount of each element in the remuneration package for the period under review of each director by name, including, but not restricted to:

- basic salary and fees;
- the estimated money value of benefits in kind;
- annual bonuses;
- deferred bonuses;
- compensation for loss of office and payments for breach of contract or other termination payments;

together with the total for each director for the period under review and for the corresponding prior period, and any significant payments made to former directors during the period under review.

Such details are to be presented in tabular form, unless inappropriate, together with explanatory notes as necessary;

(c) information on share options, including SAYE options, for each director by name in accordance with the recommendations of UITF 10. Such information is to be presented in tabular form together with explanatory notes as necessary;

(d) details of any long-term incentive schemes, other than share options details of which have been disclosed under (c) above, including:

- the interests of each director by name in the long-term incentive schemes at the start of the period under review;
- entitlements or awards granted and commitments made to each director under such schemes during the period, showing which crystallise either in the same year or subsequent years;
- the money value and number of shares, cash payments or other benefits received by each director under such schemes during the period; and
- the interests of each director in the long-term incentive schemes at the end of the period;

(e) explanation and justification of any element of remuneration, other than basic salary, which is pensionable;

(f) details of any directors' service contract with a notice period in excess of one year or with provisions for predetermined compensation on termination which exceeds one year's salary and benefits in kind, giving the reasons for such notice period;

(g) the unexpired term of any directors' service contract of a director proposed for election or re-election at the forthcoming AGM and, if any director proposed for election or re-election does not have a service contract, a statement to that effect;

(h) a statement of the company's policy on the granting of options or awards under its employees' share schemes and other long-term incentive schemes, explaining and justifying any departure from that policy in the period under review and any change in the policy from the preceding year;

(i) for defined benefit schemes (as defined in the Companies Act – see 2.7 above):

- details of the amount of the increase during the period under review (excluding inflation) and of the accumulated total amount at the end of the period in respect of the accrued benefit to which each director would be entitled on leaving service or is entitled having left service during the period under review;
- and either:

  (i) the transfer value (less director's contributions) of the relevant increase in accrued benefit (to be calculated in accordance with Actuarial Guidance Note GN11 but making no deduction for any underfunding) as at the end of the period; or

  (ii) so much of the following information as is necessary to make a reasonable assessment of the transfer value in respect of each director:

    – current age;
    – normal retirement age;
    – the amount of any contributions paid or payable by the director under the terms of the scheme during the period under review;
    – details of spouse's and dependants' benefits;
    – early retirement rights and options, expectations of pension increases after retirement (whether guaranteed or discretionary); and
    – discretionary benefits for which allowance is made in transfer values on leaving and any other relevant information which will significantly affect the value of the benefits.

Voluntary contributions and benefits should not be disclosed; and

(j) for money purchase schemes (as defined in the Companies Act – see 2.7 above): details of the contribution or allowance payable or made by the company in respect of each director during the period of review.

Whilst these requirements are closely based on the Greenbury Code, there are some differences of emphasis and detail, which are noted in the relevant sections below.

In June 1996 the Stock Exchange also introduced a requirement that where a company (unusually) sets up a long-term incentive scheme for an individual director then certain detailed disclosures about such a scheme have to be disclosed in the next annual report.[80]

In addition to the above disclosure requirements the *Listing Rules* have a long-standing requirement relating to directors' remuneration which is to disclose particulars of arrangements under which a director has either waived or agreed to waive any current or future emoluments (this applies in respect of emoluments from the company or any of its subsidiaries).[81] This remains despite the fact that the Companies Act no longer requires information about emoluments which have been waived.

3.2.1 *Positioning of Remuneration Report*

Although the *Listing Rules* require the detailed disclosures to be given in 'a report to the shareholders by the Board', it is silent as to where this report should appear in the annual report and accounts. As might therefore be expected, there is some variety of treatment among companies. Most companies give all the required information in a separate remuneration report presented alongside (or as part of) the directors' report, the chairman's statement and similar sections of the annual report. Where this is done, many such companies do not include any of the information required by the Companies Act in the main body of the accounts, but merely make a statement along the lines of 'Details, for each director, of remuneration, compensation for loss of office, pension entitlements and interests in share options are set out on pages …'.

Another treatment is for the remuneration report to consist of the narrative disclosures only, with the figures being included in the main body of the accounts.

3.2.2 *Statement of remuneration policy*

Item (a) at 3.2 above requires the remuneration committee report to include 'a statement of the company's policy on executive directors' remuneration'. Combined Code Provision B.3.2 adds that 'it should draw attention to factors specific to the company'.

This is a considerably less detailed requirement than that of the corresponding paragraph (B2) of the Greenbury Code, which recommended disclosure of 'the company's policy on executive Directors' remuneration, including levels, comparator groups of companies, individual components, performance criteria and measurement, pension provision, contracts of service and compensation commitments on early termination'.

The Greenbury Report expanded on this recommendation by suggesting that the section on general policy should set out the company's policy on major issues such as:

- the total level of remuneration;
- the main components and the arrangements for determining them, including the division between basic and performance-related components;
- the comparator groups of companies considered;
- the main parameters and rationale for any annual bonus schemes, including caps;
- how performance is measured, how rewards are related to it, how the performance measures relate to longer-term objectives and how the company has performed over time relative to comparator companies;
- the company's policy on allowing executive directors to accept appointments and retain payments from sources outside the company;
- the company's policy on contracts of service and early termination;
- the pension and retirement benefit schemes for directors, including the main types of scheme, the main terms and parameters, what elements of remuneration are pensionable, how the Inland Revenue pensions cap has been accommodated and whether the scheme is part of, or separate from, the main company scheme.[82]

The Greenbury Report also recommended that the provisions should also apply to non-executive directors and that the report should state how, and by whom, the fees and other benefits of the non-executive directors are determined.[83]

General practice among companies is to give only factual details rather than policies in respect of all these items and to give only a general policy on remuneration, as required by the *Listing Rules*. Examples of statements made about particular elements, such as bonuses, share options and long-term incentive schemes, are illustrated in the extracts in the relevant sections below.

This was an issue considered by the Hampel Committee which stated that 'a number of companies have met the letter of [the Stock Exchange] requirement with anodyne references to the need to "recruit, retain and motivate" or to pay "market rates".' By including within Combined Code Provision B.3.2 that the report 'should draw attention to factors specific to the company' the Committee hopes that companies will provide more informative statements.[84]

3.2.3 *Individual directors' emoluments*

The remuneration report is to include the amount of each element in the remuneration package for the period under review of each director by name 'including, but not restricted to, basic salary and fees, the estimated money value of benefits in kind, annual bonuses, deferred bonuses, compensation for loss of office and payments for breach of contract or other termination payments, together with the total for each director for the period under review and for the corresponding prior period …'.

Disclosure of annual bonuses, deferred bonuses and compensation payments is discussed in more detail at 3.2.4, 3.2.5 and 3.2.6 below.

This requirement for a detailed breakdown of each director's remuneration is probably the most sensitive incremental disclosure arising from the implementation of the Greenbury Code. Previously, such analyses had been required (by virtue of the Cadbury Code) in respect only of the pay packages of the chairman and highest paid director (normally the chief executive); the other directors being anonymously included within the bandings formerly required by the Companies Act.

An illustration of the required disclosure is given in the following extract:

Extract 32.26: Christian Salvesen PLC (2001)

Remuneration Report [extract]

Directors' emoluments excluding pension contributions and payments in lieu thereof

	Note	Salary £'000	Fees £'000	Taxable benefits £'000	Cash bonus £'000	Other taxable pay £'000	**2001 Total £'000**	2000 Total £'000
Chairman								
J M Fry		73	25	–	–	–	**98**	90
Executive directors								
E J Roderick		331	–	17	–	3	**351**	345
P G Aspden		193	–	14	–	1	**208**	221
Former director								
P D Carvell	(i)	125	–	12	–	4	**141**	26
Non-executive directors								
P E B Cawdron		–	25	–	–	–	**25**	22
Dr A Edelman		–	25	–	–	–	**25**	22
R S Salvesen		–	25	–	–	–	**25**	22
Other former director								
A M Callaghan		–	–	–	–	–	**–**	94
		722	**100**	**43**	**–**	**8**	**873**	842

Note:

(i) Emoluments in respect of the period to 31 January 2001, the date of resignation. Other taxable pay includes outstanding holiday pay paid on termination of his employment

It can be seen from the above extract that not only is information given for the executive directors but information is also included in respect of the non-executive directors. However, this is what is required even although the policy statement discussed at 3.2.2 above is only required by the *Listing Rules* to be in respect of the executive directors.

It can also be seen that the table excludes pension contributions as disclosures about the pension benefits of directors are covered by a separate requirement (see 3.2.8 below). Nevertheless some companies include pension contributions as part of the remuneration table as illustrated below:

Extract 32.27: Land Securities PLC (2001)

7 Directors' Emoluments, Share Options and Interests in Ordinary Shares [extract]
EMOLUMENTS [extract]

The emoluments of the directors, including pension contributions and the value of shares in the company of **£190,800** (2000 £Nil) at 880p per share, awarded under the company's long term incentive plan ('LTIP') in respect of the year ended 31 March 1999 vested unconditionally on 30 March 2001, amounted to **£3,580,000** (2000 £1,899,000).

		Benefits							
£'000	**Basic Salary**	**Profit Sharing & Bonuses**	**LTIP Shares**	**Car & Medical**	**Fees**	Total emoluments excluding pensions **2001**	2000	Pension contributions **2001**	2000
EXECUTIVE:									
I J Henderson	**398**	**101**	**63**	**11**	–	**573**	395	**151**	141
M R Griffiths	**233**	**61**	**42**	**14**	–	**350**	274	**81**	79
K Redshaw (retired 20.3.2001)	**235**	**61**	**42**	**12**	–	**350**	303	**620**	79
J I K Murray	**250**	**227**	**44**	**12**	–	**533**	331	**87**	82
P Walicknowski (appointed 1.9.2000)	**297**	**143**	–	**6**	–	**446**	–	**8**	–
M Chande (appointed 29.11.2000)	**101**	**18**	–	**5**	–	**124**	–	**25**	–
NON-EXECUTIVE:									
P G Birch (Chairman)	–	–	–	–	**138**	**138**	137	–	–
John Hull (retired 14.7.1999)	–	–	–	–	–	–	14	–	–
P B Hardy	–	–	–	–	**31**	**31**	28	–	–
Sir Alistair Grant (to 22.1.2001)	–	–	–	–	**21**	**21**	25	–	–
Sir Winfried Bischoff	–	–	–	–	**29**	**29**	11	–	–
G I Henderson (appointed 2.10.2000)	–	–	–	–	**13**	**13**	–	–	–
Total 2001	**1,514**	**611**	**191**	**60**	**232**	**2,608**		**972**	
Total 2000	1,020	238	–	56	204		1,518		381

Although the pension contributions are included in the remuneration table, it can be seen from the above extract that a sub-total excluding the pension contributions is also given, not only for the current year but also for the comparative year. This will generally be necessary to comply with the requirement of the *Listing Rules* and enable sufficient information to be disclosed so that the aggregate amounts of emoluments and pension contributions in respect of money purchase schemes required by the Companies Act can be determined. Some companies include the pension contributions in arriving at a total figure for each director and give a comparative total. Although this allows the current emoluments excluding pension contributions to be computed for each director, it does not allow the comparative figures excluding pension contributions to be determined as required (see A below).

The Greenbury Report also recommended that the nature of benefits in kind should be disclosed.[85] Although not required by the *Listing Rules* many companies give such disclosure (see extracts at 2.3.2 A above). Arguably, Schedule B to the Combined Code could be interpreted to require such information as it says that 'full details of all elements in the remuneration package … such as … benefits in kind' should be included within the remuneration report.

A Comparative figures

The above extracts do not include comparatives for each element of the total remuneration package. However, this is all that is necessary as the requirement is just to provide comparatives in respect of the total emoluments for each director; this is the approach followed by many companies. However, other companies disclose comparative amounts for each element, as shown below:

Extract 32.28: United Utilities PLC (2001)

Remuneration Report [extract]
The directors' emoluments [extract]

Emoluments comprise salaries, fees, taxable benefits and the value of short-term incentive awards (2000) or annual bonus (2001). The directors' aggregate emoluments in the year ended 31 March 2001 were £2.120 million (2000 – £1.776 million). Individual emoluments for the financial year were:

	Salary/ Fees		Annual bonus/ Short-term incentive award		Taxable benefits		Total	
	2001 £'000	2000 £'000	**2001 £'000**	2000 £'000	**2001 £'000**	2000 £'000	**2001 £'000**	2000 £'000
John Roberts	**311.7**	175.0	**168.3**	69.8	**20.3**	12.7	**500.3**	257.5
Simon Batey	**260.0**	–	**140.4**	–	**15.8**	–	**416.2**	–
Les Dawson	**83.3**	–	**45.0**	–	**7.2**	–	**135.5**	–
Gordon Waters	**180.8**	175.8	**97.6**	40.1	**19.3**	13.9	**297.7**	229.8
John Beckitt	**64.3**	187.7	**210.5**	75.9	**5.7**	27.9	**280.5**	291.5
Sir Richard Evans	**67.5**	29.2	**–**	–	**–**	–	**67.5**	29.2
Norman Broadhurst	**35.0**	32.5	**–**	–	**–**	–	**35.0**	32.5
Sir Peter Middleton	**150.0**	49.3	**–**	–	**–**	–	**150.0**	49.3
Jane Newell	**45.0**	44.3	**–**	–	**–**	–	**45.0**	44.3
John Seed	**35.0**	34.3	**–**	–	**–**	–	**35.0**	34.3

A related issue is whether the disclosure of comparative amounts should identify the names of former directors who received remuneration in the previous year but did not receive any remuneration in the current year or indeed whether such payments need to be disclosed at all. The requirement seems to be only in respect of the directors in the period under review, i.e. the current year; this suggests that the amounts in respect of such former directors are not required. However, although the totals of such amounts are not required by the *Listing Rules* they will still have to be given, thereby providing sufficient information to enable the company to comply with the requirement of the Companies Act of disclosing comparative figures for aggregate emoluments (unless such an amount is separately disclosed for Companies Act purposes).

Notwithstanding the fact that it is unnecessary to name such former directors and quantify their individual emoluments in the previous year, as can be seen from the above extracts a number of companies do disclose such information.

B Companies Act information

As noted at 2.1 above, the Companies Act deems that the information that it specifies for disclosure is treated as having been given if it can be ascertained from information disclosed elsewhere. Many listed companies appear to take advantage of this dispensation as they do not disclose all of the Companies Act information together as a separately identifiable section of the remuneration report or within a note to the accounts.

3.2.4 *Annual bonuses*

A Performance criteria

Item (b) at 3.2 above requires the amount of the annual bonus payment made to each director to be disclosed. This falls a little short of what was apparently envisaged by the Greenbury Report, which also recommended that 'the extent to which any performance criteria have been met should be explained, as should any particular performance criteria on which individual Directors' entitlements depend and any special arrangements for them'.[86]

In practice, however, many companies attempt to comply with the spirit of Greenbury rather than just the letter of the *Listing Rules*. This is hardly surprising given that an explanation of the operation of bonus schemes had been recommended by the Cadbury Code in 1992. Such disclosure is generally given in the policy statement dealing with the annual bonus element of the remuneration package.

Where a bonus scheme is linked to a relatively straightforward accounting measure, it can be clearly summarised in a few lines, as illustrated below:

Extract 32.29: Carclo plc (2001)

Remuneration report [extract]
Remuneration policy [extract]

(ii) **Performance related bonus** – executive directors participate in an annual non pensionable performance related cash bonus scheme known as the Short Term Incentive ("STI") Scheme to encourage operating efficiency and earnings growth. The STI Scheme for executive directors is based on the growth in pre tax earnings per share before exceptional items ("pre tax earnings") above a minimum performance target, the basis of which is annually determined by the committee taking into account inflation and prevailing market conditions. The bonus is calculated as follows:

2000/2001 – The minimum performance target was set at a level of 5% above the previous year's pre tax earnings. For executive directors other than the chief executive an increase of 0.1% in pre tax earnings beyond the minimum performance target is rewarded by a bonus equivalent to 0.15% on salary up to a total maximum bonus equivalent to 37.5% of salary. For the chief executive an increase of 0.1% in pre tax earnings beyond the minimum performance target is rewarded by a bonus equivalent to 0.2% on salary up to a total maximum bonus equivalent to 50% of salary. The effect of these arrangements is for the maximum bonus to be earned if the pre tax earnings increase by 31.3% over the previous year.

No bonus is payable in respect of 2000/2001.

2001/2002 – The minimum performance target has been set at a level of 2.5% above the previous year's pre tax earnings. For executive directors other than the chief executive an increase of 0.1% in pre tax earnings beyond the minimum performance target will be rewarded by a bonus equivalent to 0.25% on salary up to a total maximum bonus equivalent to 37.5% of salary. For the chief executive an increase of 0.1% in pre tax earnings beyond the minimum performance target will be rewarded by a bonus equivalent to 0.33% on salary up to a total maximum bonus equivalent to 50% of salary. At least 50% of any bonus payable to the chief executive in respect of the 2001/2002 STI scheme must be invested in the Deferred Bonus Share Plan as described in paragraph iii) below. The effect of these arrangements is for the maximum bonus to be earned if the pre tax earnings increase by 17.9% over the previous year.

Extract 32.30: The Boots Company PLC (2001)

Board remuneration report [extract]
Components of emoluments [extract]

Short term executive bonus scheme This scheme rewards executive directs for achieving operating efficiencies and profitable growth in the relevant year by reference to challenging but achievable forecasts derived at the beginning of the year from strategic plans.

During 2000/01, the performance criterion was profit after tax. A bonus of 10% of base salary was payable for performance at 95% of profit after tax target rising to 25% of salary for performance at target level and to a maximum of 50% when profit after tax was 110% of target. Performance against target during the year was such that a bonus equal to 22% was earned by executive directors.

However, there remains the basic problem that very few companies state exactly what the relevant performance criteria are and even fewer explain how achievement of those criteria translates into payments to directors. This is not necessarily a criticism of the companies concerned, but in many cases simply reflects the fact that criteria for short-term bonus schemes tend to be more complicated than the more objective yardsticks (such as earnings per share or total shareholder return) used for longer-term schemes.

Performance may be linked to a number of financial measures, some of which may not be apparent from the published accounts (e.g. average daily cash balances), production targets, comparison with peer groups and personal performance; it is therefore more difficult to meet what Greenbury recommended.

In such situations, we would recommend that companies give a general description of the factors that are taken into account in determining the annual bonuses, the maximum bonus which may be payable and the extent to which a bonus has been paid. For example:

Extract 32.31: BAA plc (2001)

Report on directors' remuneration [extract]
Annual incentive scheme

The executive directors participate in the SMIS [senior management incentive scheme] which is designed to link reward to both corporate and individual performance, based upon the attainment of stretching performance target that are aligned with the achievement of BAA's business strategy. Bonus payments under the SMIS are discretionary and the performance measures currently used, which are agreed by the remuneration committee, include earnings per share improvement, key business performance indicators and individual performance against objectives. The maximum bonus potential under the SMIS is set at 50% of salary. The average payment made under the 2000/01 SMIS for executive directors is 42% (nil in 1999/2000).

B Caps

The Greenbury Report expressed the view that 'bonuses should not be allowed to become, in effect, another guaranteed element of remuneration. They should normally be subject to an upper limit or cap, such as a specified percentage of basic pay'.[87] Each of the extracts shown above discloses the existence of caps. As noted previously, we recommend that disclosure of any such caps should be given as part of the details in respect of the annual bonus scheme.

C Incentives to take shares

The Greenbury Report suggested that 'some proportion at least of any bonuses paid to Directors should take the form of shares to be held for a minimum period rather than cash'.[88] One company which had such a bonus scheme was TI Group, as shown below:

Extract 32.32: TI Group plc (1999)

Remuneration Report [extract]
Remuneration Package [extract]
ii Annual bonus

For headquarters staff executive Directors the annual bonus is based partly on Group performance against plan, and partly on achievement of individual objectives. The annual bonus for executive Directors with line responsibility for operations is based partly on a combination of Group performance and business area performance against annual plan and partly on achievement of individual objectives. The annual plan includes specific cash targets. In 1999 the maximum potential cash bonus for executive Directors was 60% or 80% of base salary, with the maximum amount normally achievable only if performance exceeds plan by a clear margin. Subject to the approval of the proposed Senior Executive Share Incentive Plan ("SESIP"), mentioned on page 41, a possible further element, deferred for three years, may be achievable. Details of the proposed SESIP, which will be submitted for shareholder approval at the Annual General Meeting on 11th May 2000, are contained in the Circular dated 7th April 2000 which shareholders will receive with this Report.

Payments in respect of 1999, comprising shares and/or cash, are shown in the table on page 49. The share element reflects Directors' individual elections to be paid annual bonus in TI shares at market value at time of transfer rather than cash.

Summary Remuneration Table [extract]
Executive Directors
– Salary, Annual Bonus and Benefits

As in prior years the annual performance-related bonus is an amount determined in cash. Executive Directors may elect to receive a proportion of this bonus in the form of TI shares. Details of such elections appear in the table below.

	1998 Base Salary £'000	**1999** Base Salary £'000	Benefits (Note 1) £'000	Annual Bonus Cash £'000	Annual Bonus Elected Share Allocation (Note 2) £'000	**1999 Total £'000**	1998 Total £'000
Sir Christopher Lewinton	725	730	50	0	580	**1,360**	1,348
William J Laule	431	531	136	0	382	**1,049**	925
Martin D Angle	350	400	38	113	112	**663**	677
John Langston (appointed 20th October 1998)	44	250	29	69	79	**427**	76
David P Lillycrop (appointed 24th June 1998)	103	253	28	78	111	**470**	171
James L Roe (retired 17th December 1999)	225	231	13	32	75	**351**	363
T Allan Welsh (appointed 1st January 1999)	–	300	16	0	180	**496**	–

Notes:

2 Where the Directors have elected to receive an element of annual bonus in TI shares from the TI Group Employee Share Trusts, the numbers of shares thus acquired are included in the holdings as at 2nd March 2000 shown in the summary of Directors' share interests on page 66.

Some companies have introduced schemes whereby a director may receive free shares if he uses some of his annual bonus to purchase shares. The receipt of the extra shares are normally conditional upon the director remaining in employment with the company. Such schemes are discussed at 3.2.5 below.

D Pensionable bonuses etc.

The Greenbury Report stated that 'Annual bonuses are a management instrument designed to promote and reward short-term performance. In general neither they nor payments under long-term incentive schemes nor benefits in kind should be pensionable. If such elements are pensionable, the remuneration committee report should explain and justify why.'[89] This has been implemented by the *Listing Rules* requirement set out at (e) at 3.2 above. Schedule B to the Combined Code also requires an explanation and justification to be given where annual bonuses or benefits in kind are pensionable (see 3.1.3 above).

3.2.5 *Deferred bonuses*

The *Listing Rules* define a deferred bonus as 'any arrangement pursuant to the terms of which the participant(s) may receive an award of any asset (including cash or any security) in respect of service and/or performance in a period not exceeding the length of the relevant financial year notwithstanding that any such asset may, subject only to the participant(s) remaining a director or employee of the group, be receivable by the participant(s) after the end of the period to which the award relates'.[90]

Such bonuses are identified as one of the elements to be included within the remuneration table under (b) at 3.2 above. However, it is fair to say that it is unusual to see a heading of 'deferred bonuses' as part of the table; it may be that companies consider it inappropriate to include them, particularly as they generally involve shares, and therefore provide explanatory notes as necessary.

It is unclear from the requirement as to whether the deferred bonuses to be included for the period under review are those bonuses in respect of the current period but which are deferred or whether it is bonuses which relate to previous years, the conditions of which have been fulfilled during the period under review and the award finally given to the director.

A number of companies have introduced bonus schemes whereby the director may apply a proportion of his annual bonus for the purchase of shares in the company with an equivalent value which, generally, will be matched by an equivalent number of shares at nil cost. Such schemes normally involve a condition whereby the director must remain in employment with the company and are therefore 'deferred bonuses'.

Perhaps as a result of differing views of the interpretation of the disclosure requirement, or it may be because of differences between the various schemes, the treatment of such 'deferred bonus plans' varies. One company which has such a scheme is Booker:

Extract 32.33: Booker plc (1996)

Report of the Remuneration Committee [extract]

- **Share based incentives**

In addition to the all-employee SAYE share option scheme, the company has a deferred bonus plan (open to all senior managers on invitation) in order to encourage over the longer term identification with the success of Booker. For those electing to participate in this plan, part (currently one-third) of any performance-related bonus is put into a discretionary employee benefit trust, together with a further payment by the company. The trustees of the plan use the funds to purchase Booker shares in the market. After three years the bonus shares plus an equal number of matching shares become distributable, alternatively participants (who remain in the company's employment) can elect to leave them in the plan for a further two years, after which they will receive twice the bonus shares. The company's current policy is to offer executive share options once only when executives join the company.

Directors' remuneration

	Salary (incl. Fees)	Benefits	Annual Bonus	1996 Total	1995 Total	Pension entitlement accrued in:	
						1996	1995
	£000	£000	£000	£000	£000	£000	£000
Chairman							
J F Taylor	122	7	–	129	213	–	2
Executive Directors							
C J Bowen	313	2	–	315	343	11	11
A J Busby	147	3	18 2	168	–	10	6
J E Kitson	158	11	–	169	187	2	3
J D Nelson	220	4	18	242	277	7	7
E C Robinson	151	10	11 2	172	171	10	12

Notes:

2 These executive directors have elected to participate in the deferred bonus plan described on page 30 whereby part (currently one-third) of the bonus is put into a discretionary trust. The bonus payments shown above therefore relate solely to the cash element.

It can be seen that Booker has only included the cash element of the bonus. Therefore the one-third of the bonus which the directors are putting into the plan is excluded as well as any of the matching shares to be provided by the company.

Another treatment that is adopted by some companies is to include all of the annual bonus (including that proportion that the director will effectively take in shares by putting them into the plan), but not the matching shares. For example:

Extract 32.34: Laporte plc (1998)

35 Directors remuneration [extract]
Table 1 Executive directors
Remuneration excluding pensions

	Basic Salary 1998 £'000	Basic Salary 1997 £'000	**Bonus 1998 £'000**	Bonus (a) 1997 £'000	**Benefits and other payments 1998 £'000**	Benefits and other payments 1997 £'000	**Total 1998 £'000**	Total 1997 £'000
J W Leng	**400**	385	**158**	223	**27**	38	**595(e)**	646(e)
P H Fearn	**211**	203	**83**	118	**15**	15	**309**	336
M A Kayser	**200**	187	**79**	108	**13**	13	**292**	308
M J Kenny (b)	**214**	209	**84**	121	**71**	16	**369**	346
R Parrot (c)	**211**	203	**83**	118	**13**	12	**307**	333

Notes

a Annual bonus amounts are stated at their cash amounts. In 1997, half of these awards were taken in cash and the balance in shares.

The following executive directors have been awarded shares under the Company's bonus and long-term incentive plans.

Director	Balance at 1.1.98	Shares awarded	Shares waived	Shares taken up Number	Shares taken up Market value	Balance at 31.12.98	Earliest vesting date
J W Leng							
Annual bonus plan							
1996 bonus shares	10,000					10,000	9.7.97
1996 incentive shares	5,000					5,000	9.7.98
1997 bonus shares	–	14,788				14,788	27.3.98
1997 incentive shares	–	14,788				14,788	28.3.01
Deferred bonus	–	39,939				39,939	31.12.99
Long-term incentive plan	66,042	31,870	66,042			31,870	28.3.01
P H Fearn							
Annual bonus plan							
1997 bonus shares	–	7,797				7,797	27.3.98
1997 incentive shares	–	7,797				7,797	28.3.01
Deferred bonus	–	21,058				21,058	31.12.99
Long-term incentive plan	35,142	16,804	35,142			16,804	28.3.01
M A Kayser							
Annual bonus plan							
1997 bonus shares		7,182				7,182	27.3.98
1997 incentive shares	–	7,182				7,182	28.3.01
Deferred bonus	–	19,399				19,399	31.12.99
Long-term incentive plan	32,370	15,480	32,370			15,480	28.3.01

M J Kenny					
Annual bonus plan					
1996 bonus shares	5,573			5,573	9.7.97
1996 incentive shares	2,786			2,786	9.7.98
1997 bonus shares	–	7,859		7,859	27.3.98
1997 incentive shares	–	7,859		7,859	28.3.01
Deferred bonus	–	21,767		21,767	31.12.99
Long-term incentive plan	35,940	17,089	35,940	17,089	28.3.01
R Parrot (c)					
Annual bonus plan					
1997 bonus shares	–	7,797		7,797	27.3.98
1997 incentive shares	–	7,797		7,797	1.1.99
Deferred bonus	–	21,058		21,058	1.1.99
Long-term incentive plan	35,142	16,804	35,142	16,804	1.1.99

Notes

a The 1996 and 1997 annual bonus plans provide for an initial award of bonus shares plus an entitlement to receive additional shares which vest at a later date, provided that the relevant bonus shares have not previously been sold.

b Shares awarded under the deferred bonus scheme were given in respect of the successful achievement of the Group's restructuring and will vest subject to continuous employment with the Group until the vesting date.

c The 1996 and 1997 awards under the long-term incentive plan were waived by all directors and lapsed on 8 January 1998. The shares awarded in 1998 will vest subject to the performance criteria set out on page 27.

d Awards are made in the form of market price options or nil paid options as appropriate.

e Mr Parrott retired on 31 December 1998. His annual bonus plan shares will lapse if not taken up by 30 June 1999 and his deferred bonus shares will lapse if not taken up by 31 December 1999. He will retain 11,203 of the 16,804 long-term incentive plan shares which must be taken up by 31 December 1999.

36 **Employee share schemes** [extract]

b **The 1997 Laporte Deferred Bonus Scheme**

The awards under this plan have been made to the executive directors and other key executives who were fundamental to the successful achievement of the Group's restructuring. The award of shares will vest on 1 January 2000 subject to continuous employment with the Group until that date.

c **The Laporte plc Annual Bonus Scheme**

Share awards under this plan consist of a bonus share option and an incentive share option. As an incentive to defer the receipt of the bonus shares for up to seven years from the date of grant, the executive is entitled to receive additional shares, the right to which lapses if the relevant bonus shares are taken up before a specified date. For the 1996 bonus, executives were able to take their award in cash or shares or a combination of both. Those who elected to receive their bonus as shares were entitled to receive additional incentive shares which vested in equal annual instalments, commencing on the first anniversary of the award. In 1997, half of the awards could be taken in the form of shares, deferral of which for at least three years would attract the right to receive additional incentive shares.

By disclosing that half of the 1997 bonus was taken in shares Laporte has effectively identified the share element of the 'deferred bonus'. Although the additional shares have been excluded, the footnote discloses the bonus and the incentive shares separately and therefore the value of the additional shares, at the date of the award, can be computed. It can be seen from the above extract that Laporte also has another deferred bonus scheme. The value of this bonus in 1997 has been excluded from the remuneration table, but the number of shares awarded to each director is disclosed.

One company which goes further and includes the additional shares in quantifying the bonus is Prudential, as shown below:

Extract 32.35: Prudential Corporation plc (1998)

Remuneration Report [extract]
Executive Directors' Remuneration
Annual bonus

This element of the directors' remuneration package is designed to encourage directors to achieve the highest levels of annual corporate performance.

During 1998, executive directors other than Derek Higgs qualified for awards under the Group's short-term deferred bonus plan, known as the Share Participation Plan. Awards were determined by the Remuneration Committee based on the performance of the Group against quantitative financial and business targets, as well as specific personal objectives, up to a maximum total award of 45 per cent of salary at the time of the award.

Under the Plan executive directors received an initial cash award. Either the net amount of this award had to be used to buy shares or an equivalent number of shares had to be lodged with the Trustees of the Plan. The Company then lodged additional shares with the Trustees equivalent to the gross value of the cash award. Both sets of shares are held in trust for five years. If a director leaves prior to this, the additional shares may be released in certain circumstances.

During 1998, Derek Higgs was eligible to be awarded a bonus, up to a maximum of 100 per cent of salary at the time of the award. Half of the net amount of the bonus was used to buy Prudential shares. The bonus was based on the overall performance of Prudential Portfolio Managers, his performance as an executive director of the Company and performance against personal objectives.

For 1999, both the above arrangements will be replaced by a short-term incentive plan in which awards will be made in cash with no deferral period. These awards will continue to be based on the performance of the Group against quantitative financial and business targets, and to take account of an element of personal performance. The maximum awards under this plan will remain as at present. Awards under this plan will not be pensionable.

Directors' Remuneration	Salary /Fees £000	Annual Bonus £000	Benefits £000	Total 1998 £000	Total 1997 £000
Executive directors					
Keith Bedell-Pearce	275	75	27	377	336
Jonathan Bloomer	347	99	30	476	457
Sir Peter Davis	513	148	28	689	655
Derek Higgs	347	172	19	538	486
Jim Sutcliffe (resigned 30/9/97, note 2)					359
Total executive directors	1,482	494	104	2,080	2,293

Notes:

4. The annual bonus reflects the total award under the Share Participation Plan, including the cost of the shares lodged by the Company with the Plan Trustees.

On balance we believe that where the only condition is that the director has to remain in employment for a future period, then as the bonus has been earned for the year in question the total value (including that relating to the additional shares) should be disclosed. However, other treatments such as that adopted by Laporte are acceptable. The important issue is that all of the relevant details are disclosed whereby the full value of the bonus can be determined. Such an approach will also meet the Companies Act requirements given that as long as information is disclosed it is deemed to have been disclosed under the Act (see 2.1 above).

To the extent that bonus schemes involve awards which are conditional upon future performance over a longer period than the financial year, then such a scheme is a long-term incentive scheme (see 3.2.9 B below).

3.2.6 *Compensation payments*

The Greenbury Committee took the view that 'compensation payments to Directors on loss of office have been a cause of public and shareholder concern in recent times'.[91] It is therefore rather surprising that the Greenbury Code contained no recommendation for disclosure of such payments. However, as noted in item (b) at 3.2 above, the *Listing Rules* require such payments to be disclosed for each director. The Companies Act requires only an aggregate figure for all directors (see 2.9.1 above).

It could be regarded that the inclusion of compensation figures within the remuneration table is the minimum to be disclosed because the relevant requirement also says that 'such details are to be presented in tabular form, unless inappropriate, together with explanatory notes as necessary'.

Possibly as a result of this, a number of companies go further than just disclosing the amounts by disclosing details of the compensation arrangement. Extracts 32.14, 32.15 and 32.17 at 2.9.1 above illustrate such extra disclosures. We believe it is good practice for such disclosures to be made and we would recommend that companies in this situation should provide this extra information.

3.2.7 *Payments to former directors*

The Greenbury Report recommended disclosure of 'any payments and benefits not previously disclosed, including any additional pension provisions, receivable by Directors who have retired during the accounting period or the previous accounting period'.[92] The intention of this recommendation was that amounts that are in substance compensation payments do not escape disclosure by being dressed up as something else. However, this has been translated into a *Listing Rules* requirement to disclose 'any significant payments made to former directors during the period under review', which is a little curious in two respects.

First, whereas the other amounts (e.g. basic salary, benefits, annual bonus etc.) disclosed under item (b) at 3.2 above must be given for each director by name, payments to former directors can apparently be given in aggregate and without naming the directors concerned (although each of the extracts noted below identifies the former directors concerned).

Second, unlike the original Greenbury recommendation, the *Listing Rules* requirement applies to all former directors, not just those who have retired in the current or previous period. The reason for this change is clear. Had the original Greenbury recommendation been retained, disclosure could easily have been avoided by deferring such payments until the second accounting period after retirement.

Examples of the type of payments which will need to be disclosed under this requirement will be payments under consultancy arrangements, as illustrated in the following extracts:

Extract 32.36: Scapa Group plc (1999)

Report of the Board on Directors' Remuneration [extract]
Directors' Emoluments [extract]

Payments were made to Mr A. J. Ainsworth, a former director in a consultancy capacity amounting to £148,413.

Extract 32.37: The Body Shop International PLC (2001)

Remuneration Report [extract]
Directors' Emoluments [extract]

The Company has a consultancy agreement with EF Helyer, a former Director, who received £89,600 (2000: £84,000) not included in the amounts above. This agreement expires at the end of May 2001.

Another example of the type of payment which could be caught by this requirement is the payment of pensions by the company to former directors. One company which has disclosed this information is Marks and Spencer, as shown below:

Extract 32.38: Marks and Spencer p.l.c. (2001)

Remuneration Report [extract]
5 Payments to former directors

Details of payments made under the Early Retirement Plan and other payments made to former directors during the year are:

	Date of retirement	Payable until	**Paid in Year £000**	Paid in 2000 £000
Early retirement pensions[1]				
James Benfield	31 December 1999	22 April 2009	**68**	17
Lord Stone of Blackheath	31 December 1999	7 September 2002	**91**	23
Derek Hayes	31 May 1999	19 November 2008	**63**	52
Chris Littmoden	31 May 1999	28 September 2003	**85**	70
Paul Smith	31 March 1999	20 December 2000	**49**	65
Keith Oates[2]	31 January 1999	3 July 2002	**170**	197
Unfunded pensions[3]				
Lord Sieff of Brimpton[4]	30 September 1985	Death	**61**	65
Clinton Silver	31 July 1994	Death	**86**	84

1 Under the Early Retirement Plan the Remuneration Committee could, at its discretion, offer an unfunded Early Retirement Pension, separate from the Company pension, which was payable from the date of retirement to age 60. With effect from 31 March 2000, the Early Retirement Plan was withdrawn but payments continue for awards made before this date.

2 The payment to Keith Oates for the year 2000 covered 14 months from the date of his retirement to 31 March 2000.

3 The pension scheme entitlement for Lord Sieff and Clinton Silver is supplemented by an additional, unfunded pension paid by the Company.

4 Payments to Lord Sieff ceased following his death on 23 February 2001.

Although such payments are strictly required to be disclosed when significant, we do not believe that such pension payments should be disclosed in all circumstances. Where such unfunded entitlements have been taken into account when giving the disclosures discussed at 3.2.8 below in respect of the former directors whilst they were directors then this would effectively be disclosing the benefit twice. Also, the Companies Act only requires disclosure of the pension payments which are in excess of their original entitlement (see 2.8 above).

Another situation which would be covered by this requirement is when a dispute over a former director's termination of employment is finally settled as illustrated below.

Extract 32.39: United Utilities PLC (1999)

Remuneration report [extract]
Directors' emoluments [extract]

During the year, the company settled its dispute with Brian Staples, the previous Chief Executive, whose employment with the company terminated on 31 July 1997. The company paid £60,000 (plus VAT) towards Mr Staples' legal fees. Mr Staples was allowed to exercise options granted on 18 September 1995 to subscribe for 124,435 ordinary shares at an exercise price of 530.12p per ordinary share. All other options to subscribe for ordinary shares granted to him subsequently under the executive share option scheme, and options granted to him under the employee sharesave scheme, lapsed. The mid market price of a share on the day of exercise was 895 pence. Mr Staples was reimbursed for previously incurred relocation expenses of £34,142 (inclusive of VAT) in accordance with the company's relocation policy. Pursuant to that policy, that amount was grossed up to take account of higher rate income tax payable by Mr Staples on receipt of that payment.

A possible unwelcome side-effect of the *Listing Rules* wording is that, if a person who ceases to be a main board director continues to work for the group, amounts paid to that person would appear, in principle, to be required to be disclosed until ceasing to be an employee.

A company which faced this dilemma was National Westminster Bank. In its 1995 accounts the company disclosed the following:

Extract 32.40: National Westminster Bank Plc (1995)

Remuneration committee's annual report to shareholders [extract]
Mr J Tugwell

Mr Tugwell resigned as a director of the Bank in December 1995, although he continues to be employed as Chairman and Chief Executive of Bancorp. He is resident in the US and does not receive benefits under the remuneration schemes applicable to UK-based directors. His contract of employment is with Bancorp. He has a rolling three-year service agreement and, in accordance with US practice, his agreement excludes mitigation in the event of early termination. His emoluments are reviewed annually by Bancorp's board, with assistance from independent consultants, and referred to the Committee.

...

There then followed a further 30 lines of detailed disclosure of Mr Tugwell's remuneration package. Arguably, a literal interpretation of the requirement would mean that any payments (including his emoluments as an employee) made to Mr Tugwell should be disclosed in the report every year until he retired from the group altogether. However, it would appear that National Westminster Bank thought otherwise as there was no disclosure in its 1996 remuneration committee report of any payments made to Mr Tugwell during 1996 up until the time Bancorp was sold.

3.2.8 Pension benefits

As noted at 1 above, this was the last remaining aspect of the Greenbury recommendations to be given effect by the Stock Exchange in the *Listing Rules* requirements.

The Greenbury Report had recommended that the cost of defined benefit pension schemes should be measured as 'the present value of pension entitlement earned during the year resulting from additional length of service, increases in salary or changes in the terms of the scheme, less any contributions made by the Director during the year'. However, it conceded that there was a 'technical issue' as to how such benefits should be valued and noted that the actuarial profession had agreed to advise on the issue.[93]

In response to this request, in January 1996 the Institute of Actuaries and the Faculty of Actuaries issued a joint consultation paper – *Disclosure of directors' pensions: Possible methods of calculation of entitlements.* They discussed, and sought comments on, five possible methods of calculating the pension benefit for disclosure purposes.

In April 1996, a second paper was published summarising the comments received. Broadly, these indicated no consensus in favour of a single method, but showed strong support for Method 2 (accrued benefit – the change in the director's accrued pension entitlement over the period) from industry and for Method 3 (transfer value – the change in the transfer value of the director's accrued pension entitlement over the period) from advisers and investors. In the absence of consensus, the paper recommended disclosure combining aspects of both Methods.

In May 1996 the Stock Exchange responded by issuing a consultative document seeking comments on its proposals to amend the *Listing Rules* so as to require disclosure of individual directors' pension benefits. As a result of responses received, a number of minor changes were made to clarify the requirements and also to reflect the fact that the Institute of Actuaries and the Faculty of Actuaries had revised their Guidance Note, *GN11 – Retirement Benefit Schemes – Transfer Values,* when the final requirements were published a year later in May 1997. Illustrative examples of the disclosures and how to calculate the year's increase in, and the accumulated total of, the accrued pension were given in an accompanying note.[94] These new requirements (see items (i) and (j) at 3.2 above) were mandatory for accounting periods ending in or after 1 July 1997.

The required disclosures for defined benefit schemes are illustrated in the following extract:

Extract 32.41: Caledonia Investments plc (2001)

33 DIRECTORS' REMUNERATION AND INTERESTS [extract]
Directors' pensions

Pension benefits earned by directors during the year and the accumulated total accrued pension at 31 March 2001 were as follows:

	Increase in accrued pension **£'000**	Transfer value of increase **£'000**	Total accrued pension at year end **£'000**
P N Buckley	**10**	**165**	**181**
M G Wyatt	**4**	**72**	**54**
Sir David Kinloch	**16**	**244**	**163**
J H Cartwright	**7**	**7**	**59**
Hon C W Cayzer	**4**	**37**	**49**

The pension entitlement shown is that which would be paid annually on retirement based on service to the end of the year. The increase is accrued pension during the year excludes any increase for inflation.

The transfer value has been calculated on the basis of actuarial advice, in accordance with Actuarial Guidance Note GN11, less directors' contributions. This value represents a liability of the company – not a sum paid or due to the individual director – and cannot therefore be added meaningfully to annual remuneration.

This disclosure follows closely the wording recommended by the Stock Exchange in its illustrative disclosures.

The calculation of the accrued pension benefit information is relatively straightforward, as illustrated in the following example:

Example 32.8

Mr A, a director, is a member of the company's defined benefit pension scheme which provides for a pension of one-sixtieth of final pensionable salary for each year of pensionable service. At the start of the year Mr A had 10 years' service and a salary of £120,000 p.a. During the year his salary was increased to £150,000 p.a. Inflation during the year was 5%.

The accumulated total and the increase in the year are as follows:

		£
Accumulated total at end of year: 11/60 x £150,000	=	27,500
Accumulated total at beginning of year: 10/60 x £120,000	=	20,000
Increase in accrued pension during the year	=	7,500
Less effect of inflation on total accrued pension: £20,000 x 5%	=	1,000
Increase in accrued pension during the year excluding inflation		6,500

The amounts to be disclosed under the *Listing Rules* requirements are the £6,500 and the £27,500.

It should be emphasised, however, that if Mr A is the highest paid director then under the Companies Act (see 2.11 above), the comparative figure of £20,000 would also need to be disclosed or else sufficient information to allow it to be calculated, for example, by disclosing either the inflation rate or the inflationary increase. The inflation rate to be used in the calculation should be that rate published by the Secretary of State for Social Security each year in accordance with Schedule 3 to the Pension Schemes Act 1993.[95]

The omission of such comparative information appears to be a common error in annual accounts. This may be due to the fact that when the requirement first came in, the Stock Exchange's illustrative example reflected the then current exemption in the Companies Act from such disclosure. Extract 32.24 at 2.11 above provides an example of a company disclosing the comparative information for the highest paid director. Other companies go further by disclosing the comparative accrued benefit for all of the directors (see Extract 32.44 below). Cable & Wireless not only discloses the comparative accrued pension but also gives a full analysis of the increase in the accrued benefit over the year as illustrated below.

Extract 32.42: Cable and Wireless plc (2001)

DIRECTORS' REPORT [extract]
Directors' pension entitlement per annum [extract]

Robert E Lerwill, Michael McTighe, Stephen R Pettit and Graham M Wallace are in defined benefit pension schemes. Details of their pensions are as follows:

	Robert E Lerwill £	Michael McTighe £	Stephen R Pettit £	Graham M Wallace £
Accrued pension at 1 April 2000 (or date of appointment if later)	31,015	22,495	49,781	64,963
Increase in accrued pension during year as a result of inflation	700	65	1,123	1,466
Adjustment to accrued pension as a result of salary increase, other than for inflation	6,394	733	6,674	22,184
Increase in accrued pension as a result of an additional period's service	11,726	11,213	9,465	27,983
Accrued pension at 31 March 2001	**49,835**	**34,506**	**67,043**	**116,596**
Employee contributions during the year	–	13,770	–	–
Age at 31 March 2001	49	47	49	52

Great Portland in addition to disclosing the accrued pension benefit as required also discloses the current pension entitlement of the directors at the year end as shown below.

Extract 32.43: Great Portland Estates plc (2001)

Report of the Directors [extract]

John Whiteley has a personal pension to which the Company contributes. Peter Shaw's contributions by the Company were split between his personal pension and the Group Pension Plan. Pension benefits earned by directors who are members of the Group Pension Plan set out below:

	Age at 31st March 2001	Years of Pensionable Service	Increase in Accrued Pension in the Year £000	Accumulated Total Accrued Pension at 31st March 2001 £000	Current Pension Entitlement at 31st March 2001 £000
Peter Shaw	54	2	1	3	2
Paul Gittens	54	30	10	86	59

The accumulated total accrued pension is that which would be paid annually to Paul Gittens and Peter Shaw from the age of 64 and 65 respectively, if they retired on 31st March 2001 and did not claim a pension until reaching that age, and is based on service to 31st March 2001. The current pension entitlement is the annual pension which the directors could have received from 1st April 2001 had they retired on 31st March. The increase in accrued pension during the year excludes any increase for inflation. The Group Pension Plan is non-contributory but members have the option to pay Additional Voluntary Contributions; neither such contributions not their resulting benefits are included in the above table.

Although the calculation of the accrued pension benefit information is relatively straightforward, this is not the case with respect to the calculation of the transfer value of the increase in the accrued benefit. This will require to be calculated by an actuary in accordance with the Actuarial Guidance Note GN11.

It can be seen that Caledonia chose the option of disclosing the transfer value of the increase in the accrued benefits. Another example is Marks and Spencer, as shown below:

Extract 32.44: Marks and Spencer p.l.c. (2001)

Remuneration report [extract]

4 Directors' pension information

The executive directors, management and employees (except for staff employed by Marks & Spencer Outlet Ltd) all participate in the Company's defined benefit Pension Scheme. The Scheme is non-contributory, fully funded and the subject of an Independent Trust. The normal retirement age under the Pension Scheme for senior management is 60 to harmonise with the Company contractual retirement age. For all other employees the normal retirement age is 65 (previously 60) but for those employees who joined the Scheme prior to 1 January 1996 their accrued rights were not affected by this change.

The Pension Scheme enables members to achieve the maximum pension of two-thirds of their salary in the twelve months ending at normal retirement date after 30 years' service. For employees (including senior management) who joined the Scheme prior to 1 January 1996 no actuarial reduction is applied to pensions payable from the age of 58. Employees who joined the Scheme on or after 1 January 1996 are subject to an actuarial reduction in their pension if payment starts prior to their normal retirement date.

In the case of earnings over £100,000 pa, the pensionable salary is usually based on an average of the earnings over the last three years to retirement.

Pension commutation to enable participants to received a lump sum on retirement is permitted within Inland Revenue limits.

For death before retirement, a capital sum equal to four times salary is payable, together with a spouse's pension of two-thirds of the member's prospective pension at the age of 65 (60 for senior management). For death in retirement, a spouse's pension is paid equal to two-thirds of the member's current pension. In the event of death after leaving service but prior to commencement of pension, a spouse's pension of two-thirds of the accrued preserved pension is payable. In all circumstances, children's allowances are also payable, usually up to the age of 16. Substantial protection is also offered in the event of serious ill health.

Post-retirement increases for pension earned from 6 April 1997 are awarded on a statutory basis. For pension earned prior to 6 April 1997 it was the Company's practice to award discretionary increases, usually in line with inflation. With effect from 26 July 2000, it was agreed that, in future, all pension earned for service prior to 6 April 1997 would be guaranteed to increase by the rise in inflation, up to a maximum of 3% per annum. Increases beyond this figure will continue to be reviewed on a discretionary basis.

	Age at 31 March 2001	Years of service at 31 March 2001 or date of retirement	Increase in transfer value in excess of inflation[1] during the year ended 31 March 2001 £000	Increase in pension earned in excess of inflation[1] during the year ended 31 March 2001 £000	**Accrued entitlement at 31 March 2001[2] £000**	Accrued entitlement at 31 March 2000 £000
Luc Vandevelde[3]	50	–	–	–	**–**	–
Robert Colvill	60	16	480	25	**140**	109
Roger Holmes[4]	41	n/a	8	1	**1**	n/a
Alan McWalter[4]	47	1	23	2	**3**	1
David Norgrove[7]	53	13	360	25	**71**	n/a
Retired directors						
Clara Freeman	48	25	(3)	–	**122**	120
Guy McCracken[5]	52	25	2,047	3	**213**	207
Peter Salsbury[5,6]	51	30	2,519	(27)	**270**	292
Roger Aldridge[5,6]	54	27	1,129	(2)	**162**	162
Barry Morris[8]	53	30	36	2	**85**	82
Joe Rowe[5]	53	25	1,398	10	**160**	148

[1] Inflation has been assumed to be equivalent to the actual rate of price inflation which was 3.3% for the year to 30 September 2000. This measurement date accords with the Listing Rules.

[2] The pension entitlement shown above is that which would be paid on retirement based on service to 31 March 2001 or date of retirement if earlier.

[3] Luc Vandevelde does not participate in the Company Pension Scheme (see section 1, footnote 10).

[4] Roger Holmes and Alan McWalter joined the scheme on 1 January 2001 and 1 January 2000 respectively. They are both, therefore, subject to the pension earnings 'cap' (£91,800 at 31 March 2001) which is reviewed annually by the Government. Their pensions are based on a uniform accrual of two-thirds of that 'cap' less the pension which they have accrued from membership of previous employers' pension schemes (see section 1, footnote 9).

[5] The greater part of the actuarial increase in transfer value in respect of these directors relates to the effect, on the year, of their full pension being paid immediately (following retirement) and/or the contractual requirement for their pension to be calculated as though their service had ceased one year later than their actual retirement date.

[6] The accrued entitlement for Roger Aldridge has not increased and for Peter Salsbury has fallen during the year. This reflects the fact that the reduction factor due to their early retirement offsets any increase in pension for service completed during the year.

[7] Pension figures are from 18 September 2000 when David Norgrove was appointed director.

[8] Pension figures are to 19 July 200 when Barry Morris ceased to be a director.

[9] The pension entitlement shown excludes any additional pension purchased by the member's Additional Voluntary Contributions and also the enhancements made by Guy McCracken and Joe Rowe detailed in section 3, footnote 3 of this report.

It can be seen that Marks and Spencer has shown more information in the table than is required by the *Listing Rules*. It has also felt it necessary to explain some of the figures.

As indicated at 3.1.3 above, Schedule B to the Combined Code suggests that companies may wish to make it clear that the transfer value represents a liability of the company, not a sum paid or due to the individual. Such a statement is illustrated in Extract 32.41 above.

Clearly not all companies will wish to disclose the transfer values, particularly as it can be a sizeable number compared to the increase in the accrued benefit for the year and it will be necessary for it to be calculated by an actuary. However, in that case it will be necessary to give the alternative information required by the *Listing Rules*. One company which does this is Boots, as shown below:

Extract 32.45: The Boots Company PLC (2001)

Board remuneration report [extract]

Pension Entitlement

All executive directors in office at 31st March 2001 receive pension entitlements from the company's principal UK defined benefit pension scheme, referred to in note 26, and supplementary pension arrangements which provide additional benefits aimed at producing a pension of two-thirds final base salary at normal retirement age. Non-executive directors are not members of the pension scheme. Pension entitlement is calculated only on the salary element of remuneration.

Details of pensions earned by the executive directors in office at 31st March 2001 or at date of retirement are shown below:

	Age at 31st March 2001	Directors' contributions during the year £000	Increase in accrued pension entitlement during the year £000	Total accrued pension entitlement at 31st March 2001 £000
Lord Blyth	–	10	5	392*
B Clare	48	13	22	81
K S Piggott	52	14	63	157
M F Ruddell	57	14	16	185*
S G Russell	56	21	74	294
D A R Thompson	58	21	48	286
J J H Watson	59	11	14	158

* at date of retirement

The total accrued pension entitlement for Mr S G Russell, the highest paid director, at 31st March 2000 was £213 thousand.

The pension entitlement shown is that which would be paid annually on retirement based on service to the end of the year. No account is taken of any retained benefits from previous employments which will act to reduce the benefits shown. The increase in accrued pension during the year is after deducting the increase due to inflation on the previous year's accrued pension. Members of the scheme have the option to pay additional voluntary contributions; neither the contributions nor the resulting benefits are included in the above table.

The normal retirement age is 60. Early retirement is available subject to Trustee consent and a reduction in the accrued pension. Under the early retirement terms the pension can be drawn from age 59 without reduction.

On death after retirement, spouses' pensions of two-thirds of members' pensions and children's pensions of two-ninths of members' pensions for up to three dependent children are payable (subject to Inland Revenue limits).

> Pensions in payment are guaranteed to be increased annually by 5% or the increase in the Index of Retail Prices (RPI) if less. Additional increases may be granted at the discretion of the Trustees and subject to the consent of the company.
>
> Any transfer value calculations would make allowance for discretionary benefits including pension increases and early retirement.

We have to say that such a compromise treatment is less than ideal. Although this alternative information is intended to be a surrogate for the transfer value, it is incomprehensible to the non-actuary and, even for an actuary, is likely to be less than sufficient to allow the transfer value to be calculated.

For companies with defined contribution schemes the requirements are less onerous. An example of such disclosure is illustrated below:

> *Extract 32.46: Halma plc (2001)*
>
> **Report on Remuneration** [extract]
> **Money purchase arrangements**
>
> Mr J C Conacher has a money purchase arrangement in an overseas pension plan established under a trust into which he paid 5% of his salary. The Company also paid into this plan an additional amount equal to 24.4% of salary each year. In the financial year this amount was £58,000 (2000: £50,000).

The Finance Act 1989 introduced a restriction for employees joining a company after 31 May 1989 on the amount of earnings that could be pensioned through an Inland Revenue approved pension scheme (earnings cap). Accordingly, many companies have put in place additional arrangements to compensate those directors affected by the earnings cap. The disclosures that need to be given for these additional arrangements will depend on their exact nature. It may be that companies will provide a top-up arrangement such that the directors are put in the same position as directors whose pensions are unaffected by the earnings cap. If that is the case then the defined benefit disclosures should be made taking account of the top-up arrangement. This is done by Scottish Power as illustrated in Extract 32.24 at 2.11 above. If the arrangement is akin to a defined contribution scheme then disclosure as such should be made as shown below:

> *Extract 32.47: Safeway plc (2001)*
>
> **Report of the Directors** [extract]
> **Pensions** [extract]
>
> All executive directors are members of the Safeway Pension Scheme which is a funded, Inland Revenue approved, final salary, occupational pension scheme (Note 23.3 on page 50).
>
> The Finance Act 1989 introduced a restriction ("Cap") for employees joining the Company after 31 May 1989, on earnings that could be pensioned through an Inland Revenue approved pension scheme. The limit is based on a maximum annual pensionable salary (currently £95,400). Accordingly, the Company has established a Funded Unapproved Retirement Benefits Plan ("FURB") for executive directors (currently three) subject to the Cap and pays a defined annual contribution to this Plan which is based on a percentage of their basic salary over the Cap. The Company also makes a discretionary annual pension related payment to executive directors subject to the Cap. This payment is sufficient to meet the income tax liability that executive directors suffer on the Company's contributions to the FURB, and is fixed such that the combination of the FURB contributions and this payment is 25% of pensionable salary over the Cap.

For the directors who held office during the year, the pension benefits earned in the Safeway Pension Scheme and the Company's contributions to the FURB (and related payments) were as follows:

			Safeway Pension Scheme			FURB
	Age at year end	Years of service	Directors' contributions in the year (Note 1) £'000	Increase in accrued pension during the year (Note 2) £'000	Accumulated total pension at year end (Note 3) £'000	Company contribution including related payment £'000
D G C Webster	56	24	33	26	348	–
C Criado-Perez	49	2	5	3	5	110
L R Christensen	57	27	13	9	129	–
S T Laffin	41	11	5	2	23	47
R G Williams	44	10	5	2	24	42
G Wotherspoon (Note 6)	53	30	1	1	155	–

It can be seen from the above extract that the top-up arrangements were provided by means of a Funded Unapproved Retirement Benefit Scheme (FURB). Another company that used this means was British Land, but as can be seen from the following extract, the benefits to be received by the directors are defined lump sums.

Extract 32.48: The British Land Company PLC (2001)

4 Directors' emoluments and staff costs [extract]
Directors' pension benefits for the year [extract]

Three executive directors, Mr N. S. J. Ritblat, Mr R. E. Bowden and Mr S. Adam until his death, earned pension benefits in the scheme during the year.

Mr Bowden's benefits from the tax approved scheme are restricted by the earnings cap and he is, therefore, entitled to benefit from the Company's Funded Unapproved Retirement Benefit Scheme (FURBS). Mr Adam was similarly restricted and entitled to benefit from the FURBS. The benefits provided by the FURBS are defined lump sums. Mr Bowden is liable to income tax, which the Company has agreed to pay on his behalf, (known as pension related payments) on Company contributions paid into the FURBS. The liability of the Company at 31 March 2001 is £157,000 (2000 – £Nil).

Non-executive directors do not participate in any Company sponsored pension arrangement.

The pension benefits earned during the year by Mr Ritblat, Mr. Bowden and Mr. Adam were as follows:

Name	Age at year end	Increase in accrued pension during the year £	Total accrued pension entitlement at year end £	Increase in accrued FURBS lump sum entitlement during the year £	Total accrued FURBS lump sum entitlement at year end £
N. S. J. Riblat	39	14,000	60,000		
R. E. Bowden	57	2,000	18,000	63,000	234,000
S. Adam	53	3,000	14,000	93,000	182,000

Notes:

1 The pension entitlement shown is that which would be paid annually on retirement at age 60 based on service to the end of the year. The total accrued FURBS lump sum entitlement shown is that which would be paid, on retirement at age 60 based on service to the end of the year.

FURBS

a Normal retirement age for arrangements is age 60.

b Retirement may take place at any age after 50 subject to the Company's consent. Benefits are reduced to allow for their early retirement.

c On death in service top up lump sums are provided so that, in aggregate, the payee receives broadly the same value of benefits (net of tax) as if the earnings cap did not apply. On death in deferment if a spouse's or dependant's pension is payable from the main scheme a lump sum of two-thirds of the member's accrued lump sum is also payable.

d In deferment accrued lump sums are increased in line with statutory increases on pensions in deferment.

Alternatively, companies may just make additional payments to the directors affected by the earnings cap. In this case, these could be disclosed as other benefits although it may be that companies would wish to disclose them separately as done by Christian Salvesen as shown below.

Extract 32.49: Christian Salvesen PLC (2001)

Remuneration report [extract]
Pensions [extract]

The pension arrangements of Mr Roderick, Mr Aspden, and Mr Carvell were based upon membership of the Scheme. However, they are all subject to the Earnings Cap and received payments based on the amount that it would otherwise have cost the company to fund their pension benefits. Death in service benefit cover was also provided, outside the Scheme arrangements, on salary above the cap. In addition to the emoluments shown above in respect of the period they were directors of the Company during the year they received the following payments/benefits:

	Payment in lieu of pension benefits		Cost of death in service cover	
	2001	2000	**2001**	2000
	£	£	**£**	£
E J Roderick	**83,473**	56,227	**2,240**	3,806
P G Aspden	**49,854**	34,815	**1,040**	1,659
P D Carvell	**20,423**	2,876	**510**	173

3.2.9 *Share options and other long-term schemes*

The Greenbury Report took the view that in general there should be a move away from short-term cash-based bonus schemes to longer-term share-based bonus schemes.[96] However, such schemes should be based on genuinely demanding criteria, rather than simply vesting after a given time period. For example, they should aim to measure the company's performance against that of comparator companies using measures such as total shareholder return. Share-based schemes should also be designed to encourage the holding of shares for the longer term rather than realising them for cash.

The disclosures required by the *Listing Rules* to reinforce these recommendations are, briefly:

- in respect of share options, the information required by UITF 10;
- various details of other long-term incentive schemes; and
- statement of policy in granting options or awards under such long-term incentive schemes.

A Share options – UITF 10

The Stock Exchange had for some years required companies to disclose in respect of each director the number of options outstanding at the beginning and end of the year, together with material changes since the year end.[97] The Companies Act 1989 added to this a requirement to disclose the number of options granted and exercised during the year. Companies typically dealt with these two requirements by giving a reconciliation between the numbers of options outstanding at the beginning and end of the financial year, together with any material changes after the end of the year.

In 1992, the Cadbury Committee recommended that 'relevant information about stock options [and] stock appreciation rights … should also be given'. In response, in September 1994 the UITF issued Abstract 10 – *Disclosure of Directors' Share Options.*

As noted at 2.5 above, the UITF believed that the grant of an option should be treated as giving rise to a benefit and should be included in the aggregate of directors' emoluments, but concluded that it was not practicable for it to specify an appropriate valuation method for options as a benefit in kind.

Nevertheless, the UITF considered that further information concerning the option prices applicable to individual directors, together with market price information at the year end and at the date of exercise, should be disclosed. In an appendix to the Abstract it also states that for each director, the following information for options exercisable at different prices and/or dates should be disclosed:

(a) the number of shares under option at the end of the year and at the beginning of the year (or date of appointment if later);

(b) the number of options (i) granted, (ii) exercised and (iii) lapsed unexercised during the year;

(c) the exercise prices;

(d) the dates from which the options may be exercised;

(e) the expiry dates;

(f) the costs of the options (if any);

(g) for any options exercised during the year, the market price of the shares at the date of exercise; and

(h) a concise summary of any performance criteria conditional upon which the options are exercisable.

In addition, the market price of the shares at the end of the year, together with the range during the year (high and low) is to be disclosed.

Where the information disclosed would be excessive in length, a more concise disclosure using weighted average exercise prices for each director may be given. Where this is done then:

(a) disclose total shares under option at the beginning and end of the year for each director, with appropriate weighted average prices applicable to shares under option at the end of the year;

(b) disclose full details of any movements during the year (covering options granted and lapsed during the year with disclosure of the exercise price and options exercised in the year disclosing the exercise price and the share price at date of exercise);

(c) 'out of the money' options should be distinguished from 'in the money' options;

(d) unusually large individual items may need to be noted to prevent misleading conclusions being drawn from an average; and

(e) a reference should be made to the fact that the company's register of directors' interests (which is open to inspection) contains full details of directors' shareholdings and options to subscribe.

Such disclosures did not have mandatory status because the UITF had received legal advice that the recommended disclosures, other than the number of options granted or exercised during the year which were specifically required by the Companies Act, could not be construed as being necessary to meet the legal requirements. Consequently, the disclosures were only recommendations and were not mandatory. Notwithstanding the fact that they were not mandatory most listed companies gave the disclosures suggested.

However, the impact of the *Listing Rules* requirement set out in item (c) at 3.2 above is that it has effectively made UITF 10 mandatory for listed companies.

The following extract illustrates one way of giving these disclosures:

Extract 32.50: Allied Domecq PLC (2000)

Report of the Remuneration Committee [extract]

The following movements in share options took place during the year.

		Number of options at 1 September 1999 or at date of appointment	Options granted during year	Options exercised during year	Options lapsed during year	Number of options at 31 August 2000	Exercise price	Market price at date of exercise	Gain made on exercise £'000	Date from which exercisable	Expiry date
P Bowman	(d)	–	3,697	–	–	3,697	262p	–	–	01.01.03	30.06.03
	(e)	–	608,187	–	–	608,187	342p	–	–	01.11.02	31.10.09
Total		**–**	**611,884**	**–**	**–**	**611,884**					
G C Hetherington	(a)	8,734	–	–	8,734	–	570p	–	–	19.12.97	06.09.99
	(a)	1,423	–	–	1,423	–	609p	–	–	19.12.97	06.09.99
	(a)	633	–	–	633	–	631p	–	–	19.12.97	06.09.99
	(d)	–	6,440	–	–	6,440	262p	–	–	01.01.05	30.06.05
	(e)	–	263,157	–	–	263,157	342p	–	–	01.11.02	31.10.09
Total		**10,790**	**269,597**	**–**	**10,790**	**269,597**					
T D Martin	(e)	184,210	–	–	–	184,210	342p	–	–	01.11.02	31.10.09
	(e)	–	147,435	–	–	147,435	331p	–	–	05.05.03	04.05.10
Total		**184,210**	**147,435**	**–**	**–**	**331,645**					
D Scotland	(a)	49,210	–	–	49,210	–	609p	–	–	08.01.96	06.09.99
	(a)	2,295	–	–	2,295	–	569p	–	–	17.06.97	06.09.99
	(c)	28,191	–	–	28,191	–	0.1p	–	–	27.07.99	06.09.99
	(e)	–	350,877	–	–	350,087	342p	–	–	01.11.02	31.10.99
Total		**79,696**	**350,877**	**–**	**79,696**	**350,087**					
R G Turner	(a)	24,809	–	–	24,809	–	570p	–	–	27.07.99	06.09.99
	(b)	1,885	–	–	1,885	–	609p	–	–	27.07.99	06.09.99
	(b)	11,829	–	–	11,829	–	631p	–	–	27.07.99	06.09.99
	(b)	5,881	–	–	5,881	–	569p	–	–	27.07.99	06.09.99
	(c)	16,914	–	–	16,914	–	0.1p	–	–	27.07.99	06.09.99
	(d)	–	3,697	–	–	3,697	262p	–	–	01.01.03	30.06.03
	(e)	–	304,093	–	–	304,093	342p	–	–	01.11.02	31.10.09
Total		**61,318**	**307,790**	**–**	**61,318**	**307,790**					

(a) 1991 Executive Share Option Scheme (b) 1991 International Executive Share Option Scheme (c) Long Term Incentive Scheme
(d) SAYE Scheme 1999 (e) Executive Share Option Scheme 1999

The aggregate value of the gain made on the exercise of share options by all directors during the year was £nil. The middle market price of the ordinary shares at 31 August 2000 was 320.0p and the range during the year to 31 August 2000 was 249.25p to 377.25p.

(Options granted under the long-term incentive scheme are disclosed elsewhere in the report.)

It can be seen from the above extract that such disclosure can be quite voluminous and indeed a common practical problem for companies in complying with UITF 10 is the need to condense details of several option schemes into a digestible note.

Accordingly a number of companies adopt the alternative treatment of providing the information on a weighted average basis, as illustrated below:

Extract 32.51: Smiths Industries plc (2000)

14 Directors' emoluments and interests [extract]

Directors' share options

	Scheme	Options held on 31 July 2000	Options held on 31 July 1999	Weighted average	Options exercised				Options granted			
		Number	Number	Exercise price	Date exercised	Number	Exercise price	Market price†	Date of grant	Number	Exercise price	Expiry date
K.O. Butler-Wheelhouse	B	291,107	274,301	832.45p					1/10/99	16,806	858.50p	1/10/2009
	C	2,578	2,578	669.00p								
	D	35,284	23,443	0.10p					3/11/99	11,841	0.10p	3/10/2006
N.V. Barber	B	29,659	29,659	823.00p								
(Note: retired 31 July 2000)	C	2,729	2,729	632.00p								
	D	5,926	11,837	0.10p	17/5/00	5,911	0.10p	861.50p				
J. Ferrie	B	55,424	0*	765.00p					11/4/00	55,424	765.00p	11/4/2010
	C											
	D											
G.M. Kennedy	B	54,501	54,501	875.70p								
(Note: retired 4 August 2000)	C	1,582	3,312	612.00p	5/7/00	3,312	430.20p	861.50p	11/5/00	1,582	612.00p	4/2/2001
	D	11,508	18,424	0.10p	6/4/00	6,916	0.10p	762.00p				
L.H.N. Kinet	B	59,733	0*	750.00p					31/3/00	59,733	750.00p	31/3/2010
	C											
	D											
E Lindh	A	16,851	16,851	451.00p								
	B	146,677	78,045	806.90p					1/10/99	32,001	858.50p	1/10/2009
									31/3/00	36,631	750.00p	31/3/2010
	C	3,409	3,409	572.00p								
	D	29,880	23,140	0.10p					3/11/99	6,740	0.10p	3/10/2006
A.M. Thompson	A	62,500	62,500	480.00p								
	B	121,920	97,130	802.44p					1/10/99	24,790	858.50p	1/10/2009
	C	3,015	3,015	572.00p								
	D	23,771	17,581	0.10p					3/11/99	6,190	0.10p	3/10/2006

Key:

A. The Smith Industries (1984) Executive Share Option Scheme
B. The Smith Industries 1995 Executive Share Option Scheme
C. The Smith Industries 1982 SAYE Share Option Scheme
D. The Smith Industries Senior Executive Deferred Share Option Scheme
* Options held at date of appointment (L.H.N. Kinet – 1 February 2000; J. Ferrie – 10 April 2000)
† Mid-market closing quotation from the London Stock Exchange Daily Official List or actual sale price if shares sold on date of acquisition.

Notes:

The high and low market prices of the ordinary shares during the period 1 August 1999 to 31 July 2000 were 642p and 1000.5p respectively. The mid-market price on 31 July 1999 was 869p and on 31 July 2000 was 915p.

All options held on 31 July 2000 were granted at exercise prices less than the market price on that date except for options granted under the Smiths Industries 1995 Executive Share Option Scheme on 17 October 1997 (Exercise price 934p/share). No options lapsed during the period 1 August 1999 to 31 July 2000. No options have been granted or exercised or have lapsed between 1 August and 26 September 2000.

There are no performance criteria for the Smiths Industries (1984) Executive Share Option Scheme or The Smith Industries Senior Executive Deferred Share Scheme apart from market price. The Smith Industries 1995 Executive Share Option Scheme is subject to performance criteria based on total shareholder return of the Company versus the total return of the General Industrials Sector of the FTSE All Shares Index.

Deferred Share Scheme options were granted on 3 November 1999 at an Exercise Price of 0.1p per share and match shares purchase in the market by the grantee on that day. At 31 July 2000 the Deferred Share Scheme held 232,607 shares for the benefit of senior executives (including the directors as disclosed above). The market value of these shares at that date was £2.128m and dividends of approximately £49,977 were waived in the year in respect of the shares.

Special provisions permit early exercise of SAYE Options in the event of retirement; redundancy; death; etc.

No other Director held any options over the Company's shares during the period 1 August 1999 to 31 July 2000.

Full details of the Directors' shareholdings and options are contained in the Register of Directors' Interests in Shares (which is open to inspection).

As discussed earlier, the Companies Act now requires the aggregate gains made by directors on the exercise of options to be disclosed by listed companies (see 2.5 above) and also such gains made by the highest paid director (see 2.11 above). This information must be disclosed notwithstanding the fact that the information enabling such amounts to be calculated is disclosed under UITF 10. Indeed, some companies in addition to giving the information required under UITF 10 are disclosing the gains made on the exercise of options by each director (see Extract 32.50 above).

One particular issue which is not clear in either the *Listing Rules* requirement, Schedule B to the Combined Code or UITF 10 is whether such information is required in respect of all persons who served as directors during the period or only in respect of directors at the year end (as is the case for interests in shares disclosed under the Companies Act). Some companies do not provide the information for those directors who retired or resigned during the year, presumably on the basis that the information is similar to that required for interests in shares. However, as this information is being given as part of directors' remuneration information, it would seem more in line with the rest of the requirements if the information was given for all directors who served during the year.

B Long-term incentive schemes

The *Listing Rules* define a 'long-term incentive scheme' as 'any arrangement (other than a retirement benefit plan, a deferred bonus or any other arrangement specified by paragraph 12.43A(c)(ii) as an element of a remuneration package) which may involve receipt of any asset (including cash or any security) by a director or employee of the group:

(a) which includes one or more conditions in respect of service and/or performance to be satisfied over more than one financial year; and

(b) pursuant to which the group may incur (other than in relation to the establishment and administration of the arrangement) either cost or a liability, whether actual or contingent'.

This is similar to the definition incorporated in the Companies Act (see 2.6 above). It can be seen that the definition excludes retirement benefit plans (for disclosure purposes these are subject to separate requirements – see 3.2.8 above). A distinction is also made between a long-term incentive scheme and a deferred bonus. The definition of this latter item is discussed at 3.2.5 above. The distinguishing feature of a long-term incentive scheme is that the conditions as to service and/or performance is to satisfied over more than one financial period.

The requirements for long-term incentive schemes are set out at (d) at 3.2 above. It can be seen that the details do not specifically include performance criteria – rather surprisingly perhaps, in view of the importance that the Greenbury Committee attached to them and the fact that such information is required by UITF 10 for option schemes within its scope. However, in most cases such information will generally be given in a discussion of the scheme as part of the remuneration policy disclosures.

Since the Greenbury Report a number of companies have been introducing long-term incentive schemes (or L-TIPs as they are commonly called), although the names and the form of the schemes may be different. Accordingly, many of the companies have only recently given conditional awards and have not had to consider the disclosures necessary once the awards have crystallised. One company which has introduced such a scheme whereby conditional allocations of shares have been awarded is United Assurance Group:

Extract 32.52: United Assurance Group plc (1998)

REPORT ON DIRECTORS' REMUNERATION [extract]

The committee believes that share ownership, particularly if it is deferred, facilitates the alignment of employee aspirations with those of the shareholders. Accordingly, the Company encourages staff to participate in the Company sharesave scheme.

Following shareholder approval at the last annual general meeting, a new performance share plan and a discretionary executive share option plan were introduced to replace the previous executive share option plan which had become time-expired. These plans were designed to enhance the link between the remuneration of executives and the Company's medium and long term performance by incorporating challenging performance targets, based on total shareholder return (TSR) represented by dividends paid and the change in the share price relative to, in the case of the performance share plan, specified United Kingdom quoted life assurance companies and, in the case of the discretionary executive share option plan, the FTSE 250 index (excluding investment trusts). Executive directors may only participate up to the Inland Revenue approved limit of £30,000 in respect of the discretionary executive share option plan.

Under the performance share plan, executive directors are conditionally allocated shares up to a maximum value of 80% of their basic salary. The shares are held in trust and the number that are eventually awarded to them depends on the extent to which the performance conditions are met. No awards will be made unless the Company's TSR performance is at least equal to the average TSR of the comparator group. (Threshold). If the Threshold is achieved, awards may be made over an amount of up to 30% of the value of the shares conditionally allocated. For the 1998 conditional share allocation, the number of shares over which awards may be made rises on a straight line basis from the Threshold to a TSR performance equal to or above the average TSR of the top two companies in the comparator group, when awards of the total value of allocations may be made. The remuneration committee retains a discretion to withhold or reduce awards under the plan to any extent it considers appropriate, having regard to the Company's underlying financial performance and irrespective of the level of attainment of the TSR performance targets.

Because of the importance of the performance share plan in facilitating senior executive focus on shareholder returns, the remuneration committee will monitor the results of the plan's operation, and the scheme's parameters, such as the comparator group, the performance targets and the size of the awards will be adjusted, if necessary, to ensure the scheme's efficacy.

Details of conditional share allocations and share option grants to directors are set out in the tables on pages 24 and 25.

PERFORMANCE SHARE PLAN

Details of the Company's ordinary shares provisionally allocated to directors under the performance share plan are as follows:

	Shares held under the plan at 1 January 1998	Rights granted during the year	Shares held under the plan at 31 December 1998
F A Crayton	–	19,607	19,607
A J Frost	–	35,014	35,014
W M McDonald	–	19,607	19,607
J J McLachlan	–	2,408	2,408

Shares provisionally allocated under the performance plan to A J Frost will be provided from the United Friendly Group plc Employee Share Trust. Shares provisionally allocated to the other directors will be brought to the market and be held by the United Assurance Group plc Employee Share Trust. At 31 December 1998, no acquisition of shares for this purpose had been made. The cost of conditional awards is being charged to the profit and loss account over the three-year performance period to which they relate. In 1998, an appropriate amount was charged to the profit and loss account.

Subject to performance and other criteria being satisfied, awards will be granted during the six-week period following the announcement of the preliminary financial results for the year ended 31 December 2000. The awards will be included in directors' emoluments in the year in which they are granted.

The aggregate maximum value of the provisional allocations shown above, based on the maximum number of shares which would be transferred to the directors if the Company's total shareholder return (TSR) is equal to or above the average TSR of the top two companies in the comparator group, and on the market price of the Company's shares at 31 December 1998 of £5.475 per share, would have been £529,082.

By virtue of being a potential beneficiary of the United Friendly Group plc Employee Share Trust (Trust), A J Frost is deemed, for the purpose of the Companies Act 1985, to have an interest in the shares held in the Trust. At 31 December 1998, the Trust held 3,244,431 ordinary shares (31 December 1997 – 4,347,474) for the benefit of certain Group employees.

A variant on such schemes is where a conditional allocation of shares is made, but the director will receive cash at the end of the day rather than receiving the shares. One company which has introduced such a scheme is Powerscreen International, as illustrated below:

Extract 32.53: Powerscreen International PLC (1999)

REMUNERATION REPORT [extract]
Executive long term incentive agreements

A. Share Value Plan As reported in our 1997 Annual Report and Accounts, on May 28, 1996 a new Share Value Plan ("the plan") was adopted by the Remuneration Committee. The plan is a cash bonus scheme based on increases in the value of shares in the Company. Under it, a participant in the plan may be awarded a right to receive a cash bonus calculated by reference to a specified number of ordinary shares multiplied by the result obtained by subtracting the initial market values of those shares from the market value per share as at the date the bonus is exercised. The committee believes a significant advantage of the plan therefore to be that it provides a similar incentive to that provided by share options without causing any dilution of existing holdings. All executive directors and employees are eligible to participate.

The initial market value of a share by reference to which an award is made may not be less than the market value per share on the date of award. The plan gives an absolute discretion in determining when to make awards under it although no award can be made in breach of the Model Code on Directors' Dealings in Securities.

The receipt of a bonus under the plan may be made conditional upon the achievement of an objective performance target determined by the committee when the original award is made. The minimum performance target which the committee intends to impose on the making of awards under the plan will be that in normal circumstances a bonus may only be paid if, during a period of three consecutive years (commencing no earlier than the year in which the award is made) the growth in earnings per share of the Company is at least 2% per annum in excess of the growth in the retail prices index (as published by the Central Statistical Office) over the same three year period.

Awards under the plan will not be transferable and bonuses may normally only be paid between the third and tenth anniversaries of the date of award to a person who remains a director or employee. Bonuses may, however, be paid during a limited period at other times in certain special circumstances including death, retirement, redundancy, ill-health, injury or disability of the award holder or where the award holder's employing company or business is disposed of outside the group, or upon a change in control of the Company, or, at the discretion of the committee, if the award holder ceases to be employed within the group in any other circumstances. Within these limits the timing of the calculation and payment of the bonus will be determined by the award holder. In the event of any rights issues, rights offers, capitalisation issues or other variation of or increase in the share capital of the Company, the number and/or nominal value of shares the subject of awards and/or the relevant share values may be adjusted by the committee in such manner as it deems appropriate.

The criteria on which performance related awards will be based under the Share Value Plan are determined by the Remuneration Committee from time to time with due regard to Association of British Insurers guidelines and industry practice.

The Remuneration Committee put into effect during the year its proposals set out in last year's Report and Accounts to make awards under the Share Value Plan. The awards made to the directors and company secretary are set out on page 28 and in addition, awards in respect of a further 575,000 shares were made to management and key employees during the year. The exercise criteria for these awards were that during a period of three consecutive years (commencing no earlier than the year in which the award was made) the growth in the Company's earnings per share exceed by at least 6% the growth in the retail prices index over the same three year period.

C. Cash bonus arrangement for Mr Kennerley

As permitted under the Listing Rules, Mr Kennerley is the sole participant in a cash bonus arrangement which was put in place in order to recruit him in July 1998. The full text of the arrangement is set out in Schedule 2 of Mr Kennerley's 23 July 1998 service agreement with the Company (a copy of which is available for inspection at the Company's registered office during normal business hours). Mr Kennerley's participation in the arrangements was effective on the date of his service agreement. The principal terms of the arrangement are as follows:

i) Mr Kennerley has been awarded the right to receive a cash bonus calculated by reference to the amount by which the market value of 250,000 shares in the Company, on the date the bonus is exercised, exceeds 100p per share and also the amount by which the market value of a further 250,000 shares in the Company on the date the bonus is exercised, exceeds 150p per share. These share prices are higher than the market value of a company share on the date at which the arrangement took effect.

ii) The receipt of the cash bonus is subject to the condition that during the three consecutive years prior to the date such award is exercised, the growth in the Company's earnings per share must have been at least 2% per annum in excess of the growth in the retail prices index over the same three year period.

iii) The right to receive the cash bonus is exercisable by Mr Kennerley in whole or in part during the period commencing after the third anniversary of the date of this service agreement and the day immediately before the tenth anniversary.

iv) The right is personal and not transferable. The bonus may, however, be paid during a limited period at other times in special circumstances including death, retirement, redundancy, ill health or disability, or a change in control of the Company.

v) In the event of any re-organisation for any reason of the Company's issued share capital, the remuneration committee can make the appropriate adjustment to Mr Kennerley's rights.

Table 4 – **Awards under the Share Value Plan for directors and company secretary**

	At 31.3.98 (or date of appointment if later)	**Granted**	**Exercised**	**Lapsed**	**At 31.3.99 (or date of departure if earlier)**	**Exercise price**	**Exercise period**
Director							
J E Craig	–	250,000	–	–	250,000	78.5p	2001/2008
W M Caldwell	–	–	–	–	–	–	–
A D Harris*	–	100,000	–	–	100,000	78.5p	2001/2008
P A Perry	–	–	–	–	–	–	–
H J Watson	–	250,000	–	–	250,000	78.5p	2001/2008
J F W Kennerley**	–	200,000	–	–	200,000	92.0p	2001/2008
B J Kearney	–	250,000	–	–	250,000	100.0p	2001/2008
	–	250,000	–	–	250,000	150.0p	2001/2008
	–	300,000	–	–	300,000	92.0p	2001/2008

* Upon his appointment to the Board on 1 April 1999, Mr Harris was granted a further award in respect of 150,000 shares at 112.4p exercisable 20002/2009.

** Mr Kennerley is also entitled to a bonus linked to increases in the company's share price as set out in more detail on page 30.

Some companies have introduced schemes which combine aspects of both deferred bonuses and long-term incentive schemes, an example of which is shown below:

Extract 32.54: Rebus Group plc (1997)

Report of the Remuneration Committee [extract]

The Rebus Group 1996 Restricted Share Plan (the Plan")

The principal objectives of the Plan, which was adopted by the Board on 20 March 1996, are to encourage a community of interest between the participants in the Plan and the shareholders and to establish a clear link between the rewards of the participants and the Group's performance. The Plan uses existing shares in the Company rather than newly issued shares.

The Plan was operated for the first time immediately following the demerger of the Company from its former parent company in April 1996. The current participants in the Plan are the four executive directors of the Company, although it may ultimately be extended to other senior executives of the Group. The principal terms of the Plan are summarised below.

For each year in which the Plan is operated, the Remuneration Committee, acting on recommendations of the Board, will decide which senior executives should be granted awards ("Awards") under the Plan for that year. The Committee will notify the participants selected that they have been granted Awards and will inform them of the value of the ordinary shares subject to their Awards, the periods over which the ordinary shares subject to the Awards are capable of vesting and the performance criteria applicable to the vesting of the ordinary shares.

As the Plan is currently operated, Awards have an initial five year life (extending to a maximum of eight years in the event that any ordinary shares subject to the Award remain unvested at the fifth anniversary). In addition, each Award is split into three equal parts and different performance criteria and periods of vesting are applicable to those parts.

The performance criteria applicable to the first part of the Award are linked to the Company's performance against annual budgets set each year by the Remuneration Committee. In each year, a maximum of one fifth of the ordinary shares subject to this part of the Award can vest and, therefore, ultimately be capable of transfer to the participant.

The performance criteria for the other two parts of the Award are the Company's performance measured against an index of the companies in the FTSE 350 as at the date of grant of the Award. One part of the Award is subject to the Company's comparative performance by reference to the increase in its share price over the five year life of the Award and the second part is subject to the Company's comparative performance by reference to the increase in its earnings per share over the same period. After the fifth anniversary of the grant of an Award, any ordinary shares remaining unvested can vest and be transferred to the participant at any time until the eighth anniversary of the grant of the Award, provided that the performance criteria are met.

The number of ordinary shares subject to parts two and three of the Award that vest and which will, therefore, be capable of transfer to the participant subject to the Plan rules and the time at which vesting will occur is determined by reference to the Company's ranking in the relevant index.

While shares can vest under the respective parts of the Award over the life of the Award, a participant will have no entitlement to receive any ordinary shares subject to his Award unless either he remains in employment until the fifth anniversary of the date when the Award was made to him or his employment is terminated prior to that time in certain circumstances. Vested ordinary shares may be transferred earlier in the event of the termination of the participant's employment by reason of injury, disability, illness or redundancy or for any other reason at the discretion of the Remuneration Committee prior to the date on which vested ordinary shares would otherwise have qualified for transfer.

In the event of a reorganisation of the share capital of the Company, the ordinary shares subject to Awards will be adjusted on a basis approved as appropriate by the Remuneration Committee.

Any dividends paid on any ordinary shares subject to Awards that have vested will accrue to the relevant participant and will be reinvested in further ordinary shares in the Company. Any such further ordinary shares will be held subject to such of the terms of the Plan as are applicable to the ordinary shares from which they derive.

The rules of the Plan may be amended by the Remuneration Committee, where necessary with the consent of the trustee of The Rebus Group Employee Share Trust. The Plan cannot be amended to the advantage of participants without the prior approval of shareholders in general meeting, except for minor amendments to benefit its administration or to take account of any changes in legislation or to obtain or maintain favourable taxation, exchange control or regulatory treatment for the Company or a participating company or an associated company of the Company or any participant in the Plan.

Details of directors' remuneration

Awards have been granted to the executive directors, and restricted shares have vested in respect of performance during the year, under the Plan described above as follows:

	Date of Award	Number of restricted to shares subject Award	Number of restricted shares vested	Number of restricted shares lapsed	Number of restricted shares still capable of vesting
D A Laking	17 April 1996	252,551	5,000	11,837	235,714
N J Loney	17 April 1996	229,591	3,500	11,806	214,285
P E Presland	17 April 1996	378,826	7,000	18,255	353,571
R D Summers	17 April 1996	252,551	5,000	11,837	235,714

The restricted shares that have vested will in due course be transferred to the directors only in accordance with the rules of the Plan described above. The amount charged against profits by the Group in the year ended 31 March 1997 in respect of the Plan was £173,000.

The restricted shares that have vested are presumably those shares relating to the first part of the award which is linked to annual performance and therefore represent the 'deferred bonus' element of the scheme.

One company which has had long-term incentive schemes for a number of years is Safeway. It has therefore had to consider the disclosures required when the awards crystallise:

Extract 32.55: Safeway plc (1997)

Report of the remuneration committee [extract]
Long term incentive plan

The Company has operated a long term incentive plan since 1988. The plan is designed to align the efforts of key executives with the Company's objective of creating shareholder value in the longer term. Executives are selected to participate on the basis that they are in a position to influence significantly the performance of the Company.

The plan is a performance share plan. Under the terms of the plan, executives receive a conditional award of shares at the beginning of a three year period. The actual number of shares to which executives obtain vested rights depends on the Company's performance over that same period. Executives have no rights or entitlements to an award of shares and no awards are made if a participant has left the Company's employment prior to the end of the performance period.

Shares for use in the plan are ordinary shares in the Company which are transferred out of the Safeway plc Employee Share Ownership Plan ("ESOP"), a discretionary trust, set up to administer the plan (Note 13.1 on page 52). In order to hedge the Company's liability to payments under the plan, the Company funds the anticipated payout over each three year cycle by ensuring that the Trustee has sufficient funds to purchase the Company's ordinary shares through the ESOP.

Cycles:

1992 cycle – The performance objectives under the 1992 cycle, which covered the three financial years ended 1 April 1995, were not achieved and accordingly no awards were made in the year or in previous financial years.

1994 cycle – Awards due under the 1994 cycle, covering the three financial years ended 29 March 1997, are determined by comparing the Company's Total Shareholder Return to that of a weighted, by market capitalisation, basket of competitor companies (comprising Asda, Budgens, Iceland, Kwik Save, Wm. Morrison, J. Sainsbury and Tesco) based on the average three month period up to both the 1994 and 1997 year ends. Actual awards to be made to executive directors and other senior executives under the 1994 cycle will vest in the two financial years immediately following the end of the performance period, ie. in the 1998 and 1999 financial years.

Over the three year period from April 1994 to March 1997, the Company's Total Shareholder Return increased on average by 17.77% per annum compared to the basket of competitor companies which increased by 9.41% per annum. Over the same period, the FTSE 100 Index increased by 13.5% per annum and the FTSE All Share Index by 12.3% per annum. Accordingly, the Company out-performed the index of competitor companies by 8.36% per annum which, dependent on the discretion of the Committee and the Trustee, could give rise to the following awards to executive directors:

	Vesting in 1998	Vesting in 1999	Total Shares (if awarded)
Sir Alistair Grant	382,860	127,620	510,480
D G C Webster	239,287	79,763	319,050
C D Smith	233,970	155,980	389,950
R G B Charters	53,175	17,725	70,900
S T Laffin	74,445	24,815	99,260
G Wotherspoon	132,937	44,313	177,250
Total	1,116,674	450,216	1,566,890

Mr D G C Webster and Mr C D Smith have confirmed that any shares vested in them in 1998 will be retained in full (net of any sales necessary to pay the income tax liability) for a minimum period of three years.

In addition, Mr R G B Charters and Mr S T Laffin have confirmed that they will retain all and Mr G Wotherspoon half, the number of shares that may be awarded to them in 1998 (net of any sales necessary to pay the income tax liability).

The charges made in the profit and loss account in respect of the 1994 cycle and included in staff costs (Note 8.2 on page 48) totalled £8.9 million (executive directors £4.9 million and senior executives £4.0 million). In addition, £1.1 million has been provided in respect of estimated National Insurance payable. Of this, £5.7 million (including National Insurance) was charged in the year ended 29 March 1997 (1996 – £1.4 million; earlier years – £2.9 million).

1996 and 1997 cycles – In July 1996, the Company sought and obtained the approval of shareholders to its long term incentive plan as explained more fully above. Cycles of the plan are now annual and the Remuneration Committee believes that the plan has served the Company well. Accordingly, the Remuneration Committee initiated a 1996 and a 1997 cycle with effect from the beginning of the 1997 and 1998 financial years.

The 1996 and 1997 cycles cover the three financial years ending in 1999 and in 2000. Awards will be determined after measuring the Company's performance according to:

(a) the Company's Total Shareholder Return compared to that of a basket of competitor companies; and
(b) the increase in the Earnings per share of the Company

Both measures are determined independently and each may provide up to 50% of an individual's personal maximum award. The maximum award that any executive director could receive under these cycles is:

	Maximum share award	
	1996 cycle	1997 cycle
D G C Webster	120,000	138,000
C D Smith	140,000	140,000
R G B Charters	80,000	78,000
S T Laffin	57,500	58,000
G Wotherspoon	65,000	63,000
	462,500	477,000

The actual position will not be known until the end of the 1999 and 2000 financial years and could, dependent upon performance, be a nil award or up to a maximum of the number of shares shown in the table above. Details of the actual awards will be reported in future Remuneration Committee Reports.

A provisional amount of £1.1 million (including £0.1 million of estimated National Insurance payable) has been charged this year in respect of the 1996 cycle and is included in staff costs (Note 8.2 on page 48).

In this case, disclosure has been given of the number of shares which are likely to be awarded to the directors based on the three-year performance up to the year end, with an indication of when they will ultimately vest, but no value has been disclosed.

This highlights one of the problems with the requirements. The third bullet point of the requirement set out in (d) at 3.2 above is that it is 'the money value and number of shares, cash payments or other benefits received by each director under such schemes during the period' which are to be disclosed. As in this case the shares have not yet been 'received' then arguably there is no need for any disclosure. A similar issue arises in respect of the Companies Act requirement in respect of long-term incentive schemes as to when such amounts are 'receivable'. This is discussed at 2.6 above.

However, as with the Boots example illustrated in Extract 32.12 at 2.6 above, sufficient information is likely to have been given to satisfy the interpretation that such an amount was receivable in the year the performance period ended as this will usually be the year end and the company's share price at that date will have been disclosed under UITF 10 (see A above).

It should be emphasised that the disclosures in respect of long-term incentive schemes are completely independent of the charge recognised in the profit and loss account for such schemes, although some companies disclose the annual charge and the cumulative provision (see Extracts 32.54 and 32.55 above). In April 1997, the UITF published its seventeenth Abstract, *Employee share schemes.*[98] This addresses how companies should recognise and measure the charge in the profit and loss account in respect of any shares issued as part of an employee share scheme. This is discussed further at 2.5.4 of Chapter 22.

Where a company (unusually) sets up a long-term incentive scheme for an individual director then certain detailed disclosures about such a scheme have to be disclosed in the next annual report (see 3.2 above).

C *Policy in granting options or awards under such long-term incentive schemes*

The Greenbury Report stated that 'to reduce freak results from share price fluctuations, grants of share options should normally be phased over time rather than made as one large block. Executive options should never be issued at a discount.'[99] Paragraph B6 of the Greenbury Code recommended that 'if grants under executive share option or other long-term incentive schemes are awarded in one large block rather than phased, the report should explain and justify'. This has been repeated in Schedule B to the Combined Code (see 3.1.3 above).

The requirement introduced by the Stock Exchange set out in (h) at 3.2 above to effect the latter recommendation, however, goes further than the Code because it requires a company to give a statement of the policy, whatever it might be, not just where such items are awarded in a large block. At the same time as introducing this disclosure requirement, the Stock Exchange also changed the *Listing Rules* such that options could not be issued at a discount to the prevailing market price without being first approved by the shareholders (although exceptions to this rule are allowed in specific circumstances, such as for employee share schemes which are available to substantially all the employees).[100]

Examples of such policies in respect of long-term incentive schemes are illustrated in the extracts shown at B above.

As far as policies in respect of the granting of options are concerned, many of them do no more than give a description of the option schemes that are in place. In our view a statement of policy should deal with whether options are phased or granted in blocks, whether there are annual or overall caps in the number of shares which can be under option and whether there are any performance criteria to be satisfied. This last item is required, in any case, in respect of options which have already been granted (see A above). Examples of policies in respect of options are illustrated below:

Extract 32.56: AstraZeneca PLC (2000)

Report of the Board on Remuneration of Directors [extract]
Components of the Remuneration Package [extract]

For Executive Directors, the individual components are:

...

– longer term bonus – Executive Directors are also rewarded for improvement in the share price performance of the Company over a period of years by the grant of share options; the grant of options under the AstraZeneca Share Option Plan is supervised by the Remuneration Committee which also determines whether any performance targets will apply to the grant and/or exercise of options; the exercise of options previously granted under the Zeneca 1994 Executive Share Option Scheme is currently subject to the performance condition that before any exercise, earnings per share must grow by at least the increase in the UK retail prices index plus 3% per annum over a continuous three year period following grant; ...

As stated above, the Remuneration Committee determines the grant of options under the AstraZeneca Share Option Plan and ensures that, on every occasion before the grant of any option, the performance of the Company and the performance and contribution of each participant is fully taken into account when determining the number of shares to be put under option and the number of options to be granted. In respect of the grant of options under the Plan in August 2000, the Committee considered the overall performance of the Company against a range of key performance indicators, including the prospects for growth, new product launches and synergy benefits, and decided that it was sufficient to justify a grant of options. The Committee also received assurances from each member of the Senior Executive Team that the participants for whom they were recommending a grant of options had achieved the appropriate level of performance.

Extract 32.57: Allied Domecq PLC (2000)

Report of the Remuneration Committee [extract]
8 Share options [extract]

During the year, the company established the following new option schemes, under which the directors are eligible to be granted options:

(a) SAYE Scheme 1999 – This scheme is based on a three or five year savings contract and is open to all UK employees. Options are granted at an exercise price of not less than 80 per cent of the market value.

(b) International SAYE Scheme 1999 – This scheme is based on an 18 month, three year or five year savings contract and is open to all employees in certain jurisdictions. Options are granted at an exercise price of not less than 80 per cent of the market value.

(c) United States Share Purchase Plan – This scheme is based on an 18 month savings contract and is open to all employees in the USA. Options are granted at an exercise price of not less than 85 per cent of the market value.

(d) Inland Revenue Approved Executive Share Option Scheme 1999 – Options up to a value of £30,000 per participant may be granted at an exercise price not less than market value and under normal circumstances remain exercisable between the third and tenth anniversaries of the date of grant.

(e) Executive Share Option Scheme 1999 – Options are granted at an exercise price not less than market value and under normal circumstances remain exercisable between the third and tenth anniversaries of the date of grant (though shorter life options may be granted).

As explained in the listing particulars issued in June 1999, an initial grant over shares with a value of four times salary was made under the executive schemes to executive directors during the year. Options will become exercisable only if the Total Shareholder Return (change in value of the shares plus gross dividends paid, treated as re-invested) on Allied Domecq shares equals or exceeds that of the median Total Shareholder Return achieved by the constituents of the FTSE 100 Index over any consecutive three-year period between the dates of grant and exercise.

In line with current market practice, and in order to enable the company to operate competitively across the world, the board is seeking shareholder approval to amend the rules of the Executive Share Option Scheme 1999 to enable future grants of options in excess of one times earnings where deemed appropriate with reference to relevant market practice, role and responsibility. The board remains committed to closely aligning executives' reward with business performance and the interests of shareholders. Hence the underpinning performance conditions of the scheme will be linked to sustainable earnings growth measured over three years. Performance may be re-measured over extended period of four and five years. If the performance condition is not then satisfied the option will lapse. Where larger grants are made, and where appropriate, it is the intention of the remuneration committee to attach supplemental performance conditions to such awards.

3.2.10 *Directors' service contracts*

The Greenbury Report took the view that 'there is a strong case for setting [directors'] notice or contract periods at, or reducing them to, one year or less'.[101] Accordingly paragraph B10 of the Greenbury Code recommended that companies should disclose contracts with notice periods in excess of one year, and explain why such periods are considered appropriate. This recommendation has been incorporated in the *Listing Rules* requirements (see (f) at 3.2 above). Schedule B to the Combined Code has a similar requirement (see 3.1.3 above).

The Stock Exchange already had an existing rule that the directors' report must state the unexpired portion of any service contract of any director proposed for re-election at the forthcoming AGM (where details are required to be available for inspection) or that there are no such contracts. Given the requirement for companies to have a remuneration report, the opportunity was taken to modify this rule by requiring the information to be given in the remuneration report (see (g) at 3.2 above). A 'directors' service contract' is defined by the *Listing Rules* as 'a service contract with a notice period of one year or more or with provisions for predetermined compensation on termination of an amount which equals or exceeds one year's salary and benefits in kind'.[102]

An example of such disclosures is given by Scottish Power, as shown below:

Extract 32.58: Scottish Power plc (2001)

Remuneration Report of the Directors [extract]
Service Contracts

Existing executive directors appointed before 1 April 1999, have service contracts terminable by the company on two years' notice (prior to September 1994 notice periods were three years) and by the individuals concerned on one year's notice. The Committee believes that it remains appropriate for these executive directors to continue to be on two-year rolling contracts. Executive directors, Charles Berry, David Nish and Alan Richardson, were appointed to the Board on or after 1 April 1999; these appointments have service contracts terminable on one year's notice from both parties.

The Committee's policy on early termination is to emphasise the duty to mitigate to the fullest extent practicable. Senior managers within the company have notice periods ranging from six months to one year.

In addition to the above disclosure requirements in respect of directors' service contracts, the Stock Exchange also requires that such contracts or written memoranda of the terms of all directors' service contracts must be available for inspection at the registered office during normal business hours on each business day and at the place of the annual general meeting for at least 15 minutes prior to and during the meeting.[103]

4 IAS REQUIREMENTS

The relevant international standard which covers this area is IAS 24 – *Related Party Disclosures*. Key management personnel, including directors and officers of companies and close family members of such individuals, and enterprises in which such individuals have a substantial interest or over which they are able exercise significant influence, are regarded as related parties for the purpose of that standard. The requirements of IAS 24 are dealt with at 4 in Chapter 30. As noted at 4.3 of that chapter, IAS 24 contains no exemptions for employees' emoluments comparable to those in FRS 8. The lack of this exemption has the effect that IAS 24 requires disclosure of emoluments of key management personnel (including directors), although many accounts purporting to comply with IASs do not give this information. Even where information is disclosed (see some of the extracts included at 4.4 of Chapter 30), the information given is far less than would be required for a listed UK company as seen in the rest of this chapter.

It should also be borne in mind that other countries may also have legislation requiring disclosures about directors' emoluments.

5 CONCLUSION

The disclosure of directors' remuneration in the UK remains a bit of a nightmare. Over the past few years there has been a dramatic increase in the volume of disclosure given by listed companies on directors' pay and benefits, as companies have implemented the disclosure requirements imposed by the *Listed Rules*. In some cases the sheer volume of information has become a barrier to effective communication.

The rationalisation of the Companies Act requirements is welcomed in this regard. This has gone some way to reduce the volume of disclosures given by listed companies and has also been beneficial to companies which are not governed by the *Listing Rules* requirements, but some of the requirements are still too complicated and confusing.

Although pleased when the Stock Exchange had finally decided upon its rules on pension disclosures, we were sorry that it felt it necessary not only to require both accrued benefit and transfer value information, but also to allow alternative information as a surrogate for transfer values, thereby adding further incomprehensible information to that already disclosed. Too much of a company's annual report has to be devoted to directors' emoluments nowadays, and we would like to see the rules substantially simplified.

References

1 A more detailed exposition of the law governing directors' remuneration can be found in R. Pennington, *Company Law*, pp. 634–641 and C.M. Schmitthoff (ed.), *Palmer's Company Law (Volume I)*, pp. 902–907.
2 L. C. B. Gower, *The Principles of Modern Company Law*, p. x.
3 See Chapter 28, footnote 1.
4 CA 67, s 6.
5 The Committee on the Financial Aspects of Corporate Governance, *The Financial Aspects of Corporate Governance*, (The Cadbury Report), December 1992.
6 The Study Group on Directors' Remuneration, *Directors' Remuneration: Report of a Study Group chaired by Sir Richard Greenbury*, (The Greenbury Report), July 1995.
7 Committee on Corporate Governance, *Final Report*, (The Hampel Report), January 1998.
8 The Companies (Tables A–F) Regulations 1985 (SI 1985 No. 805), Table A, Article 82.
9 *Hutton v West Cork Railway* (1883) 23 Ch.D. 654. For a discussion of the extent to which company law is able to control the level of directors' remuneration, see J. E. Parkinson, *Directors' Remuneration*, pp. 130–132, 142–143.
10 CA 85, s 311(1).
11 *Ibid.*, s 311(2).
12 The Companies (Tables A–F) Regulations 1985 (SI 1985 No. 805), Table A, Article 87.
13 CA 85, s 312.
14 Pennington, *op. cit.*, p. 639.
15 CA 85, s 316(3).
16 *Ibid.*, s 318.
17 *Ibid.*, s 319.
18 *Ibid.*, ss 232(1)–(2), Sch. 6, Part I. If the directors are entitled to deliver accounts to the registrar modified as for small companies, the modified accounts may omit these details. In the annual accounts for shareholders, small companies need only disclose the aggregate amount of directors' emoluments (being emoluments, amounts under long-term incentive schemes and pension contributions in respect of money purchase benefits), the numbers of directors who are members of money purchase and defined benefit schemes,

compensation for loss of office and sums paid to third parties in respect of directors' services.
19 CA 85, Sch. 4, para. 58.
20 *Ibid.*, s 232(3). This duty also extends to anyone who is, or has within the last five years been, an officer of the company.
21 *Ibid.*, s 237(4). A discussion of the procedures which the auditor should adopt in relation to directors' emoluments can be found in A. Brown and D. Foster, *Directors' loans, other transactions and remuneration*, pp. 25–27.
22 CA 85, Sch. 6, para. 1(1)(a).
23 *Ibid.*, para. 1(5).
24 *Ibid.*, para. 13(2)(a).
25 *Ibid.*, para. 1(6)(b).
26 *Ibid.*, para. 1(3)(a).
27 *Ibid.*, para. 1(3)(b).
28 *Ibid.*, para. 13(3)(a).
29 CA 85, s 310(3)(a).
30 *Ibid.*, Sch. 6, para. 11(1).
31 *Ibid.*, para. 10(2).
32 *Ibid.*, para. 11(2).
33 *Ibid.*
34 *Ibid.*, para. 10(2).
35 *Ibid.*, para. 12.
36 *Ibid.*, para. 10(4).
37 *Ibid.*, para. 1(1)(b).
38 *Ibid.*, para. 1(5).
39 *Ibid.*
40 *Ibid.*
41 FRRP PN 53, 7 August 1998.
42 CA 85, Sch. 6, para. 1(2).
43 *Ibid.*, para. 1(1)(c).
44 *Ibid.*, para. 1(4).
45 *Ibid.*, para. 1(5).
46 *Ibid.*, para. 2(a).
47 *Ibid.*, para. 2(b).
48 UITF 17, *Employee share schemes*, UITF, April 1997.
49 CA 85, Sch. 6, para. 1(1)(d).
50 *Ibid.*, para. 1(5).
51 *Ibid.*, para. 13(3).
52 *Ibid.*, para. 1(5).
53 *Ibid.*, para. 13(3).
54 *Ibid.*, para. 1(7).
55 *Ibid.*, para. 1(1)(e).
56 *Ibid.*, para. 1(5).
57 *Ibid.*
58 *Ibid.*, para. 1(8).
59 *Ibid.*, para. 7(1).
60 *Ibid.*, para. 7(2).
61 *Ibid.*
62 *Ibid.*, para. 7(4).
63 *Ibid.*, para. 8(1).
64 *Ibid.*, para. 8(4).
65 *Ibid.*
66 *Ibid.*, para. 8(2)(b).
67 *Ibid.*, para. 8(3).
68 *Ibid.*
69 *Ibid.*, para. 9(1).
70 *Ibid.*, para. 9(3).
71 *Ibid.*, para. 9(2).
72 *Ibid.*, para. 2(1)(a).
73 *Ibid.*, para. 2(1)(b).
74 *Ibid.*, para. 2(2).
75 *Ibid.*, para. 2(5).
76 *Ibid.*
77 *Ibid.*, para. 2(3).
78 *Ibid.*, para. 2(4).
79 *The Listing Rules*, Financial Services Authority, Chapter 12, para. 12.43A(c).
80 *Ibid.*, para. 12.43(u). The detailed requirements are set out in Chapter 13, paras. 13.13A and 13.14.
81 *Ibid.*, para. 12.43(d).
82 The Greenbury Report, para. 5.5.
83 *Ibid.*, para. 5.7.
84 The Hampel Report, para. 4.15.
85 The Greenbury Report, para. 5.8.
86 *Ibid.*, para. 5.9.
87 *Ibid.*, para. 6.21.
88 *Ibid.*, para. 6.22.
89 *Ibid.*, para. 6.44.
90 *The Listing Rules*, Definitions.
91 The Greenbury Report, para. 7.2
92 *Ibid.*, para. 5.10.
93 *Ibid.*, para. 5.19.
94 *Note to subscribers to the Listing Rules Amendment No. 10*, London Stock Exchange, May 1997.
95 *Ibid.*
96 The Greenbury Report, paras. 6.23–40.
97 This had been required by *The Listing Rules*, Chapter 12, para. 12.43(k).
98 UITF 17, *Employee share schemes*, UITF, April 1997.
99 The Greenbury Report, para. 6.29.
100 *The Listing Rules*, Chapter 13, paras. 13.30–31.
101 The Greenbury Report, para. 7.13.
102 *The Listing Rules*, Definitions.
103 *Ibid.*, Chapter 16, para. 16.9.

Chapter 33 Interim reports and preliminary announcements

1 INTRODUCTION

The publication of interim financial reports and preliminary announcements have been requirements for UK listed companies for many years, although the rules governing their form and content remain sketchy. However, in 1997 the ASB issued a non-mandatory Statement on interim reports,[1] based on work undertaken by the Financial Reporting Committee of the ICAEW, and in 1998 followed this up with a similar non-mandatory Statement on preliminary announcements.[2]

In January 2000, the Stock Exchange (which from May 2000 relinquished responsibility for the Listing Rules to the Financial Services Authority) extended the disclosures required for interim reports and preliminary announcements, reflecting in part the proposals in these ASB non-mandatory statements (see 2.1 and 5.2 below).

In contrast, the IASC has issued a standard on interim reporting, IAS 34 – *Interim Financial Reporting*,[3] for companies presenting their interim financial statements in accordance with IAS. However, companies may still prepare annual IAS financial statements even if their interim financial statements do not comply with IAS 34.[4]

The most frequently debated issue relating to interim financial reporting is whether the interim period should be regarded as a discrete period in its own right, or whether it should be seen primarily as a mere instalment of the financial year. Under the first perspective, it would be appropriate to apply the same accounting policies and principles as are used for the annual accounts, treating the interim period in just the same way as the full financial year. Under the second, some modifications to these policies and principles are made to allow the interim report to give a better guide to the outcome of the year as a whole. The former approach is generally referred to as the 'discrete' approach, and the latter as the 'integral' approach. In practice, however, these categories are less clear-cut than the above description might suggest, and companies generally follow an approach which is a hybrid of these two theoretical extremes.

The integral approach has no clear definition. It implies some pragmatic modification of the inter-period allocation of transactions, so as to match costs more evenly with revenues in the different halves (or quarters) of the year. Critics would say that this is not matching, but smoothing, and that it obscures the results of the interim period rather than presents them more fairly. On the other hand, supporters would say that such modifications are necessary to prevent meaningless distortions arising; an interim period is an even more artificial interval than a financial year, and that to report transactions without trying to relate them to the annual cycle of activity for which they have been incurred would not make sense.

The extent of disclosure in interim reports raises similar issues. If interim reporting is no different in concept from annual reporting, but is simply a more frequent version of the same thing, then one might suppose that the form and content of the report should also be the same. If, however, it is seen as a subsidiary form of reporting which only deals with an instalment of a longer period, then it is easier to justify a different reporting package. Present practice undoubtedly reflects the latter view, although probably more as an expedient compromise than as the result of an attempt to meet a carefully researched need.

In the UK, the normal frequency of reporting is biannual. Relatively few British companies follow the North American practice of reporting every quarter. However, companies listing under Chapter 25[5] rules for innovative high growth companies without a three year trading record (introduced to facilitate the development of techMARK within the main market) are required to report quarterly. In July 2001, the European Commission issued a Consultation Document[6] which proposes updated disclosure requirements for issuers of both equity and debt securities traded in regulated markets situated or operating in EU Member States. These include proposals for quarterly financial reporting, to comprise a condensed set of financial statements for each quarterly period, which would be subject to a limited review by the auditors of the company. Both annual and interim financial reports should be made available, in electronic form, within 60 days of the period end, a tighter deadline than the current situation in the UK. In addition, the Financial Services Authority is considering a requirement for listed companies to publish quarterly financial reports as part of a wider review of the Listing Rules to be undertaken in late 2001. In this chapter, reference is often made to 'half-yearly' reports, but the discussion applies to interim reports of any duration.

It should be explained that the term 'interim accounts' also appears in the Companies Act, but with quite a different meaning. This refers to the accounts which public companies have to draw up to justify paying a dividend if their last annual accounts show that their distributable reserves were insufficient for this purpose.[7] Such requirements are beyond the scope of this book and are not discussed further in this chapter.

Preliminary announcements are regarded as very important by the stock market because they are the first formal release of annual results and are highly price-sensitive. In contrast, when the full annual report is subsequently released it rarely triggers any share price reaction or receives much attention from analysts. It is therefore paradoxical that, until the ASB's Statement, so little guidance on preliminary announcements had been developed in the past compared to the extensive regulation of the full annual report.

The ASB, having finalised its Statement on preliminary announcements, asked its working party to review the year-end financial reporting structure as a whole, and to develop ideas and proposals for consideration by the Board. In February 2000, the Board published a Discussion Paper – *Year-End Financial Reports: improving communication*,[8] which addressed how companies could simplify their financial statements, making them more accessible to private shareholders, but without introducing a significant cost burden. Although preliminary announcements were not its main focus, it encouraged companies to publish these on websites, but did not suggest that these should be routinely sent to private shareholders.

The ASB's work coincided with the Department of Trade and Industry sponsored Company Law Review which has taken this debate forward. The initial proposals of the Company Law Review Steering Group's Consultation Paper – *Modern Company Law for a Competitive Economy: Developing the Framework*[9] – included preparation and publication of a statutory statement of preliminary results. This was to be prepared and published on a website within 70 days of the year end, and distributed within a further 10 days (or if earlier, with the AGM notice) to shareholders.

Its revised proposals, a Consultation Paper – *Modern Company Law for a Competitive Economy: Completing the Structure*[10] – rejected the idea of a statutory preliminary announcement for public quoted companies. The Paper recommended that the timing, form and content, and enforcement of preliminary announcements for listed companies should remain with market regulators. However, to ensure that shareholders have equal access to information released in the market place, it proposed immediate publication of the preliminary announcement on a website, with electronic notification of this fact to shareholders that register for this. This contrasts with the current situation where there is no obligation for companies to send copies of the preliminary announcement to shareholders (see 5.2 below). Although less stringent than that proposed in *Developing the Framework*, the revised proposals envisaged a significant acceleration in the year end reporting timetable for all companies. For public quoted companies, it proposed that the full annual report should be published on a website, as soon as practicable after approval, within 90 days of the year end (putting an effective time limit on publication of the preliminary announcement).

In July 2001, *Modern Company Law for a Competitive Economy: Final Report*[11] was published and its proposals will now be considered by the Government. Significantly, the *Final Report* confirms that regulation of preliminary announcements for quoted companies (comprising listed or publicly traded) companies should be a matter for market regulators. Also, where preliminary announcements are prepared, company law should require their immediate publication on a website with electronic notification for shareholders registering for this. In order to achieve flexibility, it recommends that the Secretary of State should designate which markets are relevant in determining whether companies are 'quoted' or not. The year end reporting timetable has been relaxed yet again such that the proposed requirement to publish the full statements within 120 days places an effective deadline for publication of a preliminary announcement, where prepared, but is no different from the current deadline for preliminary announcements under the Listing Rules (see 5.2 below).

2 UK REQUIREMENTS FOR INTERIM REPORTS

2.1 The Listing Rules

The UK Listing Authority (currently the Financial Services Authority) requires listed companies to publish a half-yearly report on their activities and financial information covering the first six months of their financial year. For companies listing under chapter 25 rules for innovative high growth companies, quarterly reports are required for the first three quarters giving cumulative year-to-date figures, and for the final quarter if it does not coincide with the year end. These companies must present, in addition to the financial information detailed below, figures for non-financial operating data included in their Listing Particulars as key measures of the development of the business, together with comparatives (unless the UK Listing Authority agrees otherwise).[12] The Listing Rules embody the requirements of the then EU Regular Reporting Directive,[13] which were enacted in UK law in 1984.[14]

The financial information which the UK Listing Authority requires is as follows:

(a) a profit and loss account comprising:
  - (i) net turnover;*
  - (ii) operating profit or loss;
  - (iii) interest payable less interest receivable (net);
  - (iv) profit or loss before taxation and extraordinary items;*
  - (v) taxation on profits (UK taxation and, if material, overseas and share of associated undertakings' taxation to be shown separately);
  - (vi) profit or loss on ordinary activities after tax;
  - (vii) minority interests;
  - (viii) profit or loss attributable to shareholders, before extraordinary items;
  - (ix) extraordinary items, net of taxation;
  - (x) profit or loss attributable to shareholders;
  - (xi) rates of dividend(s) paid and proposed and amount absorbed thereby;* and
  - (xii) earnings per share expressed as pence per share;

(b) a balance sheet; and

(c) a cash flow statement.[15]

Items (a)(ii), (a)(iii), (a)(vi), (b) and (c) were introduced in January 2000 and reflect some but not all of the recommendations of the non-mandatory ASB Statement on interim reports (see 2.2 below).

These figures should be on a consolidated basis and figures for the corresponding period in the prior year should also be given.[16] They should use the same policies and form of presentation as adopted in the previous annual accounts, unless (a) these are to be changed in the next set of annual accounts (e.g. to conform with a new standard or piece of legislation), in which case the new accounting policies and presentation should be followed and the changes and reasons for these must be explained, or (b) if the UK Listing Authority otherwise agrees.[17]

British American Tobacco recently implemented a change in accounting policy relating to FRS 19,[18] which under FRS 3[19] should be dealt with by prior period restatement, as illustrated below:

Extract 33.1: British American Tobacco p.l.c. (Q1, 31 March 2001)

ACCOUNTING POLICIES AND BASIS OF PREPARATION [extract]

The financial statements comprise the unaudited results for the three months ended 31 March 2001 and 31 March 2000 and the audited results for the twelve months ended 31 December 2000.

The unaudited Group results have been prepared under the historical cost convention and in accordance with applicable accounting standards using the accounting policies set out in the Report and Accounts for the year ended 31 December 2000, with the exception of deferred tax as described below.

From 1 January 2001 the Group is adopting the new accounting standard FRS19: Deferred Tax which requires full provision to be made for deferred tax arising from timing differences between the recognition of gains and losses in the financial statements and their recognition in the tax computation. In adopting FRS19, the Group has chosen not to discount deferred tax assets and liabilities.

The comparative figures for 2000 have been restated to reflect the impact of FRS19. Consequently the interest of British American Tobacco's shareholders at 1 January 2000 and 31 December 2000, as published last year, have been reduced by £95 million and £81 million respectively to reflect recognition of the additional net provision in respect of deferred tax. The impact of FRS19 is to decrease the tax charge as shown below:

3 months to		Year to
31.3.01	31.3.00	31.12.00
£m	£m	£m
7	22	23

The reduction in the tax charge in 2000 principally arises from the setting up of a deferred tax asset under FRS19 for the exceptional charge in respect of the cigarette stocks reacquired from S.C.A. Tobacco Corporation (SCAT) on 31 March 2000.

If it is not practicable to implement a known future change, the ASB Statement recommends that companies give an estimate of the effect of the change, or an explanation where this is not possible.[20] Greene King is an example of such a situation, and Bass was unable to complete the fair value exercise on the acquisition of Posthouse in time for the interim report. Companies in such a position should consult with their brokers.

Extract 33.2: Greene King plc (1999)

1. Basis of preparation [extract]

The new fixed asset accounting standard, FRS 15, has not been adopted in these interim accounts as there has been insufficient time since the acquisition of Morland to assemble the necessary data. The standard will be adopted in the results for the full year to 29 April 2000.

Extract 33.3: Bass PLC (2001)

13 INVESTMENT IN POSTHOUSE [extract]

On 4 April 2001, the Group completed the purchase of the Posthouse hotel business. The consideration, excluding costs, was £810m and comprised cash, the acceptance of debt and the issue of preference shares. The cash element of the consideration is subject to an adjustment in due course in respect of working capital. In addition, cash of £262m was acquired.

The Posthouse hotel business is included in the balance sheet at 14 April 2001 as a fixed asset investment as it has not been possible to establish fair values of the assets and liabilities acquired in the time available. Fair values will be included in the Annual Report 2001.

The asterisked items in the above list may be omitted if the UK Listing Authority agrees that their disclosure would be seriously detrimental to the company, so long as 'such omission would not be likely to mislead the public with regard to facts and circumstances, knowledge of which is essential for the assessment of the shares in question.'[21] This can only be described as a nonsensical proposition, but it comes straight from the European Directive. The UK Listing Authority can also authorise omission of these figures on public interest grounds,[22] and indeed has discretion to authorise any other omissions if it believes it necessary or appropriate to do so.[23] Companies should also modify the items disclosed if they are not suited to their particular activities.[24]

Although this version of the Listing Rules was published in 2000, it still reflects a rather out of date view of the profit and loss account. In particular, it clings to a pre-1981 Companies Act approach, which does not seek to explain the link between turnover and pre-tax profit, and it takes no account of the substantial changes made to the profit and loss account by FRS 3, which was issued in 1992. Following FRS 3, extraordinary items remain only a theoretical possibility but various new components of performance have to be identified, notably those relating to exceptional items and discontinued operations, as discussed in Chapter 25.

Other aspects of the requirements are strange as well, e.g. they require the tax charge to be analysed to show that which relates to associates, but do not require the associates' results themselves to be disclosed. The rules also say that in exceptional circumstances the UK Listing Authority may allow 'estimated figures for profit and loss' to be given so long as this is explained.[25] Again, this comes from the Directive and suggests a rather limited understanding of the nature of financial reporting; *all* profit figures should be seen as 'estimates' rather than as precise and objective statements of fact.

As well as the numerical information described above, the Listing Rules require the half-yearly report to contain the following:

- an explanatory statement including any significant information enabling investors to make an informed assessment of the trend of the group's activities and profit or loss;
- an indication of any special factor which has influenced those activities and the profit or loss during the period in question;
- enough information to enable a comparison to be made with the corresponding period of the preceding financial year; and
- so far as possible, a reference to the group's prospects in the current financial year.[26]

The Combined Code provision D.1.2[27] (see Chapter 4 at 2.3) makes clear that 'the board's responsibility to present a balanced and understandable assessment extends to interim and other price-sensitive public reports as well as to information required to be presented by statutory requirements'.

The report must be published within 90 days of the end of the half-year to which it relates.[28] It may be either sent to the shareholders, or inserted as an advertisement in a national newspaper,[29] and it must also be communicated to the Company Announcements Office.[30] If the company extends its accounting period to more than 14 months, it must publish a further interim report covering the period up to its old year end, or another period that ends not more than six months before the new year end.[31] Where the figures in the half-year report have been audited or reviewed by auditors pursuant to the APB Bulletin Review of Interim Financial Information,[32] the report of the auditors should be reproduced in full.[33]

2.2 The ASB's Statement

In September 1997, the ASB published a non-mandatory Statement – *Interim Reports*. The Statement discusses the form and content of interim reports, and measurement principles. It recommends publication of the interim report within 60 days of the end of the interim period[34] which is a more demanding timescale than the UK Listing Rules requirement of 90 days (see 2.1 above). The measurement principles are similar to those required by IAS 34 – *Interim Financial Reporting* – and are discussed in 4 below.

2.2.1 *Statements to be included*

The ASB calls for interim reports to include summarised versions of all the four primary statements that are required in annual accounts – a profit and loss account, balance sheet, cash flow statement and (where relevant) a statement of total recognised gains and losses – together with a narrative management commentary.[35] Two sets of comparative figures (for the corresponding interim period in the prior year, and the whole of the previous financial year) are recommended, although the Statement is rather tentative about the need for a comparative balance sheet for the previous interim period.[36] The Listing Rules, of course, require comparatives for the corresponding interim period in the prior year only.[37] Since the comparative figures for the full year will not constitute full statutory accounts, they will have to be accompanied by a statement explaining that these are not the statutory accounts for that year, and that the statutory accounts have been delivered to the Registrar of Companies and have been the subject of an auditors' report which was unqualified (assuming that to be the case).[38]

The Statement says that disclosures required by accounting standards, subject to the limited exceptions discussed below, are not generally required in interim reports.[39]

A Profit and loss account

The Statement seeks to improve the UK Listing Authority rules for the profit and loss account by adding various items and bringing it more in line with FRS 3. It suggests that the following items should be disclosed:

- turnover;
- operating profit or loss;
- exceptional items (individually), both those included in operating profit which should be included under the relevant statutory headings and disclosed and described in a note, and the three specified by paragraph 20 of FRS 3 to come after operating profit and before interest, namely
  - profits and losses on the sale or termination of an operation;
  - costs of a fundamental reorganisation or restructuring having a material effect on the nature and focus of the reporting entity's operations; and
  - profits and losses on the disposal of fixed assets;
- interest payable less interest receivable (net);
- profit or loss on ordinary activities before tax;
- tax on profit or loss on ordinary activities (with separate disclosure of the tax effects of exceptional items that have been shown on the face of the profit and loss account);
- profit or loss on ordinary activities after tax;
- minority interests;
- profit or loss for the period; and
- dividends paid and proposed.[40]

The Statement calls for separate disclosure of any of the above amounts that relate to associates and joint ventures, and also for the provision of segmental analyses of turnover and profit on the same basis as is used in the annual accounts.[41]

The Statement also asks that the turnover and operating profit relating to acquisitions and discontinued operations should be disclosed separately, i.e. those activities that were discontinued before the interim report was issued with an overall limit of three months after the end of the interim period.[42] Extra disclosure could be given, in a note or the management commentary, of activities that are in the process of being terminated or are likely to be shown as discontinued in the full year accounts.[43]

The Statement notes that the Listing Rules require earnings per share to be disclosed, and says that it should be calculated and disclosed in the same manner as is used in the annual accounts. This means that both basic and diluted figures should be given, and companies who give additional versions of earnings per share for the full year should also do so in their interim reports.[44]

B Balance sheet

The Statement says that the balance sheet should adopt a similar classification to that used in the full year accounts, and recommends that the following information should be presented:

- fixed assets;
- current assets;
  - stocks;
  - debtors;
  - cash at bank and in hand;
  - other current assets;
- creditors: amounts falling due within one year;
- net current assets/(liabilities);
- total assets less current liabilities;
- creditors: amounts falling due after more than one year;
- provisions for liabilities and charges;
- capital and reserves; and
- minority interests.[45]

The Statement says that the balance sheet should highlight significant movements in key indicators of the company's financial position,[46] and this may require some further analysis; a frequent example of this would be to show the components of net debt, which is not necessarily available from the above headings.

A reconciliation of shareholders' funds is only required where movements other than those in the statement of total recognised gains and losses (see D below) need to be explained.[47]

C Cash flow statement

The Statement suggests that companies should use the main headings specified for the cash flow statement by FRS 1,[48] namely:

- net cash inflow/outflow from operating activities;
- returns on investments and servicing of finance;
- taxation;
- capital expenditure and financial investment;
- acquisitions and disposals;
- equity dividends paid;
- management of liquid resources;
- financing;
- increase/decrease in cash.[49]

However, this list predates FRS 9,[50] which amended FRS 1 to require extra lines to be included on the face of the cash flow statement for dividends received from associates and joint ventures. We recommend that these should be given where they are material.

The two main reconciliations required by FRS 1 – a reconciliation of operating profit to operating cash flow, at least in outline, and of the movement in cash to the movement in net debt and its various components – should also be given.[51]

D Statement of total recognised gains and losses

The Statement calls for a statement of total recognised gains and losses to be presented where there have been any material gains and losses other than profit or loss for the interim period.[52] International groups will require such a statement if there are material foreign currency differences to be recognised, but there may be little else to report. The ASB acknowledges that companies will seldom revalue their properties in the middle of the year, although investment companies with a portfolio of quoted securities at market value will revalue them for interim reporting purposes.[53] In addition, where there have been changes in accounting policies or other prior period adjustments, these should be noted at the foot of the statement of total recognised gains and losses in accordance with FRS 3[54] (see Chapter 25).

E Management commentary

The Statement emphasises the importance of a narrative commentary in which management discusses and analyses the interim performance being reported. This may be regarded as a cut-down version of the operating and financial review (see Chapter 4 at 5), which aims to explain movements in key indicators and trends affecting the business, focusing on areas of change since the last annual report. Among the more specific matters that the Board recommends be discussed are:

- the effects of seasonality on the business, with an explanation of the principles that have been used to reflect seasonal results in the interim report;
- material changes in the business's capital structure or financing;
- changes in contingencies, commitments and off balance sheet financial instruments since the previous year end;
- the effect of major acquisitions and disposals of major fixed assets or investments during the period; and
- post balance sheet events (since the end of the interim period).[55]

3 IAS REQUIREMENTS

The IASC published a standard, IAS 34 – *Interim Financial Reporting* – in February 1998. The standard does not dictate who should prepare interim reports, although it encourages publicly traded companies to provide interim reports at least at the half-year, and make these available within 60 days of the end of the interim period. Instead, the standard sets rules for the form and content of such reports for enterprises that are required or elect to produce them in accordance with international accounting standards.[56] This contrasts with the ASB's approach in issuing a statement which is only a non-mandatory recommendation rather than a standard on interim reporting.

3.1 Statements to be included

Interim financial reports may contain either a complete set of financial statements, prepared in accordance with IAS 1[57] (which are not discussed further – see Chapter 1) or a set of condensed financial statements as described in IAS 34.[58] The recognition and measurement guidance in the standard, together with the specific note disclosures applicable to interim periods, required by the standard apply to both complete and condensed financial statements.[59]

The standard also requires interim reports to include, at a minimum, the following:

- a condensed balance sheet;
- a condensed income statement, including disclosure of basic and diluted earnings per share;
- a condensed statement showing either (a) all changes in equity or (b) changes in equity other than those arising from capital transactions with owners and distributions to owners (equivalent to the statement of total recognised gains and losses in the UK), in which case changes in equity arising from capital transactions with and distributions to owners should be disclosed in the notes;
- a condensed cash flow statement; and
- certain notes.[60]

The format of the condensed statements should include at least all of the headings and subtotals that were included in the equivalent primary statements in the enterprise's last annual financial statements. Additional line items or notes should be included where their omission would be misleading.[61] The presentation of changes in equity should follow the same format as in the annual financial statements.[62] If the last annual financial statements were consolidated financial statements, the interim financial report is also prepared on a consolidated basis, with no requirement to give the parent's separate financial statements.[63]

The approach to comparative figures is somewhat different from that taken in the UK. The balance sheet at the previous year end is required but no full year comparatives need be given for the other three statements. Instead, these other three statements must be for the cumulative position for the year to date, with comparatives for the corresponding periods in the previous year. The income statement should also show the current interim period (again with comparatives for the corresponding period in the prior year). Therefore, where the enterprise reports quarterly, the income statement must show the results of the most recent quarter as well as its cumulative results to date (both with comparatives). Also in contrast to UK practice, no balance sheet need be presented as at the end of the equivalent interim period last year.[64]

As in the UK, enterprises should apply the same accounting policies as applied in the annual financial statements except for accounting policy changes which are to be reflected in the next annual financial statements.[65] Under IAS 34, a change in accounting policy, for which no transitional arrangements are specified should be effected by either (a) retrospective restatement of all prior periods or (b) if the allowed alternative treatment under IAS 8[66] is followed (to include the entire cumulative retrospective adjustment in the determination of net profit or loss of the current period), restatement of prior interim periods of the current financial year only.[67]

A number of companies have given disclosures in 2001 for first implementation of IAS 39 – *Financial instruments: recognition and measurement*,[68] which is required to be implemented for periods beginning on or after 1 January 2001. The transitional rules do not permit retrospective application, and adjustments on implementation are reflected in opening reserves. Nokia is an example.

Extract 33.4: Nokia Corporation (Q1, 31 March 2001)

Change in Accounting Principles [extract]

The Group has adopted, beginning January 1, 2001, IAS 39, Financial instruments: recognition and measurement. The impact of the changes in policy on opening shareholders' equity is quantified as follows:

	[EUR million]
Total shareholders' equity at 31 December 2000 as previously reported	10 808
IAS 39 transition adjustments:	
Fair value adjustments to available-for-sale debt and equity investments 1)	58
Transfer of gains and losses on qualifying cash flow hedging derivatives 2)	- 114
Total shareholders' equity at 1 January 2001	10 752

1) Available-for-sale investments in debt and equity securities and investments in unlisted equity shares are measured at fair value unless investments are held for trading or originated loans or unlisted equities cannot be measured reliably.

2) Gains and losses on foreign exchange forward contracts that are properly designated and are highly effective as cash flow hedges of highly probable forecast foreign currency cash flows are deferred in a hedging reserve within equity. Previously, such gains and losses were reported as deferred income or expenses.

CONSOLIDATED STATEMENT OF CHANGES IN SHAREHOLDERS' EQUITY, EUR million (unaudited) [extract]

	Share capital	Share issue premium	Treasury shares	Translation differences	Fair value and other reserves	Retained earnings	Total
Balance at December 31, 2000	282	1 695	-157	347	–	8 641	10 808
Share issue		4					4
Disposal of treasury shares			3				3
Stock options issued on acquisitions		4					4
Stock options exercised related to acquisitions		-3					-3
Dividend						-1 314	-1 314
Translation differences				-56			-56
Effect of change in accounting principle (IAS 39)					-56		-56
Cash flow hedges and fair value adjustments					-76		-76
Other increase/ decrease, net						-10	-10
Net profit						975	975
Balance at March 31, 2001	282	1 700	-154	291	-132	8 292	10 279

Preussag implemented IAS for the first time in its 1998/9 annual financial statements, with retrospective application. Therefore, in the half-yearly report for 1999/2000 comparatives were restated in accordance with IAS.

Extract 33.5: Preussag AG (1st half year, 31 March 2000)

Accounting principles

Just as the consolidated financial statements for the financial year 1998/99, the interim financial statements as per 31 March 2000 were prepared in accordance with the accounting rules of the IASC – the International Accounting Standards (IAS) and the interpretations of the Standing Interpretations Committee (SIC) – on the basis of the historical cost principle.

As a matter of principle, the interim financial statements complied with the same accounting and valuation methods as those applied in the consolidated financial statements for the financial year 1998/99. Accordingly, the previous year's figures as per 31 March 1999 were adjusted to IAS accounting. The accounting and valuation methods applied were outlined in detail in the notes to the consolidated financial statements as per 30 September 1999. With the commencement of the financial year 1999/2000, reporting was converted to the Euro throughout the group.

Enterprises should disclose at least the following information, usually on a financial year to date basis but also provide details of any events or transactions which are material to an understanding of the current interim period:

- a statement that the accounting policies and methods of computation are the same as those followed in the most recent annual financial statements, or if these have changed, a description of the nature and effect of the change;
- explanatory comments about seasonality or cyclicality of interim operations;
- the nature and amount of items affecting assets, liabilities, equity, net income, or cash flows that are unusual because of their nature, size or incidence;
- the nature and amount of changes in estimates of amounts reported in prior interim periods of the current financial year or changes in estimates of amounts reported in prior financial years if those changes have a material effect in the current interim period;
- issuances, repurchases and repayments of debt and equity securities;
- dividends paid (aggregate or per share) separately for ordinary shares and other shares;
- if segmental reporting is required under IAS 14 – *Segment Reporting*[69] – in the annual financial statements, segment revenue and result for business or geographical segments, whichever is the primary basis of segmental reporting;
- material events subsequent to the interim period end, not reflected in the interim financial statements;
- the effect of changes in composition of the enterprise during the interim period, including business combinations, acquisition or disposal of subsidiaries and long-term investments, restructurings, and discontinuing operations; and
- changes in contingent liabilities or contingent assets since the last balance sheet date.[70]

If the interim financial report complies with IAS, meaning compliance with all applicable standards and interpretations of the Standing Interpretations Committee, this fact should be disclosed, as in the Preussag extract above.[71]

The standard then goes on to give examples of items required to be disclosed,[72] including details of impairments and reversals of impairments of assets, reversal of costs of restructuring, acquisitions and disposals of property, plant and equipment, commitments for the purchase of property, plant and equipment, litigation settlements, corrections of fundamental errors in previously reported financial statements, extraordinary items, any debt default or breach of debt covenant that has not been corrected subsequently, and related party transactions. Other disclosures required by IAS are not required where the interim financial report comprises condensed financial statements and selected explanatory notes.[73]

The notes specified for inclusion are thus more extensive than those required in the UK, although in practice UK companies will tend to deal with most of the issues covered either in notes to the interim accounts or in the accompanying narrative statement. One specific requirement of IAS 34 which is not common in the UK, however, is to disclose the nature and effect, where material, of changes made in the current interim period to estimates made in earlier periods.[74] Deutsche Bank in Extract 33.15 at 4.5 below illustrates this in relation to a release of restructuring provisions. There is also a requirement to make equivalent disclosure in the full year accounts of adjustments to estimates made in the final interim period, unless a separate financial report is published for the final interim period.[75]

4 MEASUREMENT ISSUES IN INTERIM REPORTING

4.1 Measurement principles

Except in relation to taxation, the ASB espouses the discrete approach.[76] It does not really explain its reasoning, beyond saying that the discrete approach has the advantage that the elements of financial statements are defined in the same way as for the annual accounts and achieves consistency and understandability.[77]

The Statement says that 'items of income and expense are measured and recognised on a basis consistent with that used in the preparation of annual financial statements (the discrete method). ... Depending on the item, this might be for example, on the basis of time expired, the benefit received, or the activity associated with the period.'[78] Interestingly, the wording of the last sentence is borrowed from the relevant US standard, APB 28,[79] but in fact that standard endorses the integral approach! This underlines the difficulty in distinguishing the two methods, and the ambiguity of the extract quoted above. Allocating costs on the basis of time expired suggests the discrete approach, whereas matching it with benefits received or activity associated with the period moves towards the integral method.

Like other standard setters, the IASC's approach reflects something of a hybrid between the discrete and the integral methods. However, it does explain the principles underlying interim reporting more clearly than the ASB Statement. The principles for recognising assets, liabilities, income and expenses for interim periods are the same as in the annual financial statements. However, there is an additional principle in IAS 34 to say that 'the frequency of an enterprise's reporting (annual, half-yearly or quarterly) should not affect the measurement of its annual results. To achieve that objective, measurements for interim reporting purposes should be made on a year-to-date basis.'[80] The effect of this is that certain measurement adjustments which would be regarded as irreversible if made at the year end can be revisited if they were made in the first interim period and circumstances justify a different answer by the end of the year (or by the end of a subsequent interim period).

For example, inventory write-downs, impairments or provisions for restructurings should be recognised and measured in the same way as if the interim period end was a financial year end. If the estimate changes in a subsequent interim period in the financial year, the original estimate may need to be changed, either by recognising additional accruals or reversals of the previously recognised amount in the subsequent interim period.[81]

IAS 34 states that 'a cost that does not meet a definition of an asset at the end of an interim period is not deferred on the balance sheet either to await future information as to whether it has met the definition of an asset or to smooth earnings over interim periods within a financial year'.[82] In accordance with IAS 38,[83] in respect of intangible assets, costs incurred before the recognition criteria are met are expensed. Only those incurred since the recognition criteria are met are capitalised; there is no reinstatement as an asset in a later period of costs previously expensed because the recognition criteria was not met at that time.

This is therefore a rather more subtle approach than the discrete method, because each quarter (say) is evaluated not as an isolated period but as part of a cumulative period that builds up to a full year whose results are not to be influenced by the operation of interim reporting practices. Amounts reported for previous interim periods are not retrospectively adjusted, and therefore year to date measurements may involve changes in estimates of amounts reported in previous interim periods of the current financial year. As discussed at 3.1 above, IAS 34 requires disclosure of the nature and amount of material changes in estimate, both in the interim financial statements and in the full year financial statements, if there are material changes in estimate since the latest interim financial statements.[84]

Both the ASB Statement[85] and IAS 34[86] state that materiality should be assessed in relation to the results and financial position for the interim period, while IAS 34 notes that in determining materiality, it should be recognised that interim measurements may rely on estimates to a greater extent than for the annual accounts.

4.2 Exchange rates

The ASB Statement says that the profit and loss account of foreign entities included using the net investment method should be translated at the average rate for the interim period or the closing rate at the end of that period, whichever is the normal policy.[87] Under IAS 34, the same accounting policy as adopted in the annual accounts should also be applied. IAS 21 requires income and expense items of a foreign entity not integral to the operations of the foreign enterprises to be translated at the date of the transaction; frequently for practical reasons, entities will use a rate approximating actual exchange rates, such as an average rate for the period and this approach is endorsed by the standard.[88] IAS 34 appears to assume that the latter case is the norm and in an Appendix it states that the actual average and closing rates for the interim period should be used for foreign entities not integral to the operations of the reporting enterprise.[89]

This approach can cause difficulties for companies who report quarterly rather than half-yearly, as discussed more fully in Chapter 8 at 3.4.11. The basic problem is that the results of later interim periods can be distorted by the catch-up effect of updating the exchange rates that were used to translate the results of earlier interim periods. Under IAS 34, as discussed above, this is dealt with by requiring disclosure on the effect of changes in estimates on the current interim period, or in the annual financial statements.

It is not uncommon for companies to use constant exchange rates when making inter-period comparisons in narrative statements such as the operating and financial review or even in the notes to the accounts (see Marks and Spencer below).

Extract 33.6: Marks and Spencer p.l.c. (2000)

7. Foreign Currencies [extract]

The results of overseas subsidiaries have been translated using average rates of exchange ruling during the period. The movements in exchange rates used for translation, compared to the same period last year, have increased international sales (excluding Canada) by £13.9m and reduced the operating loss by £1.7m. When expressed at constant rates for translation, turnover increases on last year become:

	TURNOVER INCREASE %	
	AS REPORTED	**AT CONSTANT RATES**
Europe	0.3	5.8
The Americas		
Brooks Brothers (incl. Japan)	16.6	7.6
Kings Super Markets	13.8	6.3
Far East	11.7	7.1
Total International Retail excluding Canada	8.8	6.5

However, it is unusual to see the primary statements reported on this basis. A rare example is Unilever,[90] which uses the exchange rates of the *previous* year for all the detailed analysis of its interim profit and loss accounts, restating only the bottom line on the basis of current exchange rates. However, whether the result is really meaningful seems questionable, as this extract from the group's interim statement for the third quarter of 1998 demonstrates:

Extract 33.7: Unilever PLC (1998)

UNILEVER RESULTS
Business performance [extract]

In Asia & Pacific, sales increased by 13%, largely reflecting price increases to recover higher costs in South East Asia following currency devaluations …

CONSOLIDATED PROFIT AND LOSS ACCOUNT
Constant exchange rates

In the profit and loss account given below, the results in both years have been translated at constant exchange rates, being the annual average exchange rates for 1997. This reporting convention facilitates comparisons since the impact of exchange fluctuations is eliminated.

GEOGRAPHICAL ANALYSIS [extract]

Third quarter		*£ millions*	Nine months	
1998	**1997**	**Operating profit – before exceptional items**	**1998**	**1997**
536	522	Europe	**1 242**	1 214
174	193	North America	**367**	341
57	43	Africa and Middle East	**141**	103
131	106	Asia and Pacific**	**363**	281
74	83	Latin America	**257**	227
972	947	Sub-total	**2 370**	2 166

**Note: At current rates of exchange for the first nine months, 1998 operating profit for those countries in South East Asia which have experienced significant currency devaluation, reduces by approximately £82 million.

The footnote appears to say that the entire reported growth of £82 million in the profit of Unilever's Asia & Pacific region (from £281 million in 1997 to £363 million in 1998), is due to its use of out-of-date exchange rates. As the commentary on Business performance quoted in the extract explains, the currency devaluation in that region made it necessary to increase prices, but if that is the case it does not seem appropriate to use *pre-devaluation* exchange rates to translate results that have benefited from the *post-devaluation* price increases; far from removing a distorting effect, this approach seems positively to introduce one.

An Appendix to IAS 34 also discusses interim financial reporting in hyperinflationary economies. As at the year end, the financial statements (including comparatives) of an enterprise reporting in the currency of a hyperinflationary economy should be presented in the measuring unit as of the end of the interim period. Recognition of the entire resulting gain or loss should be included in the interim period's net income. The recognition of the gain or loss, therefore, should not be annualised, nor should an estimated annual inflation rate be used in preparing an interim financial report in a hyperinflationary economy.[91] In the UK, the issue is not specifically addressed by the ASB Statement. UITF 9[92] describes two approved methods for dealing with enterprises in hyperinflationary economies (see Chapter 9) but where the accounting policy adopted is to remeasure the financial statements in current prices, similar considerations to above would apply.

4.3 Seasonal businesses

Some companies operate in businesses which are heavily seasonal, for example, agricultural businesses with seasonal crops, holiday companies, domestic fuel suppliers, retailers who depend on Christmas sales. Their financial year is often chosen to fit their annual operating cycle, but this may equally mean that their first six months gives little indication of their likely annual results. In some cases, they may have negligible sales in the first half of the year.

An extreme application of the integral approach in theory might suggest that they should try to predict their annual results and contrive to report half of that in the interim accounts. However, this would be a pointless exercise, and would bear little relation to the reality of their business in the first six months. In practice, seasonal companies report their actual sales (if any) for the first six months, and those which espouse the integral approach may then seek to flex their costs to some degree to match their sales.

So far as direct costs are concerned, this is entirely appropriate. The more controversial area concerns indirect costs which would normally be accounted for on a time basis. Recognising these in the normal way could easily result in a loss being reported in the first half of the year because there are insufficient revenues to cover them. This would be the result of applying the discrete approach in its pure form; it would reflect the reality of that period's performance, but it would also emphasise the limited usefulness of the interim report, because it would show that the results of that period really have little meaning in isolation. Allocating them in proportion to expected activity levels for the two halves of the year would be an attempt to show the results in their proper context, but it involves a higher degree of uncertainty and it becomes at least partly an exercise in forecasting rather than a report on the results of an expired period.

The ASB's Statement says that 'fluctuating revenues of seasonal businesses are generally understood by the marketplace and it is appropriate to report them as they arise'.[93] This rather misses the point, because it could not be seriously suggested that revenues should be transferred from one interim period to another. The real issue concerns the possible flexing of associated costs, but the Statement is silent on this matter apart from the general statement quoted at 4.1 above that expenses should be recognised on the basis of time expired, the benefit received, or the activity associated with the period. As already noted, this ambiguous statement might either support some flexing of costs to match seasonal revenues (on the basis of activity associated with the period) or forbid such a practice (on the basis of time expired).

The Statement's recommendations on the management commentary relating to seasonal businesses are more constructive. It says that 'the commentary should describe the nature of any seasonal activity and, together with other disclosures, provide adequate information for the performance of the business and its financial position at the end of the period to be understood in the context of the annual cycle. The principles by which seasonal results are reflected in the interim report should be stated, particularly where there are any expected changes in the effects of seasonality.'[94]

Such a discussion provides the essential context for the reader to interpret the information presented. In addition, of course, the relationship between first half and full year results can already be seen from the comparative figures when both of these are shown for the previous period. However, the reality is that interim reports are necessarily of lesser value for seasonal businesses because they focus on only part (and a potentially misleading part) of the story.

Scottish Power included this note in its interim report for the six months to 30 September 1998 to describe a change to its policy on seasonal adjustments.

Extract 33.8: Scottish Power plc (1998)

1 Basis of preparation [extract]

(c) To comply with the recommendation of the Accounting Standards Board's Statement on Interim Reports, comparative figures have been restated to eliminate seasonal adjustments in relation to accounting for the cost of electricity sales. This statement recommends that revenues and costs, wherever possible, should be recognised on a discrete basis for the purposes of the interim Accounts and not treated as a component of the full year's results, as was previously the policy adopted. The adjustments relate to the interim figures only and do not affect the full year results.

The effect on the comparative figures for the half-year ended 30 September 1997 is as follows:

	Cost of sales £m	Ordinary taxation £m	Loss retained £m	Net assets £m
As previously reported	(803.5)	(56.9)	(214.0)	1,537.5
Effect of implementing new accounting policy	4.7	(1.2)	3.5	3.5
As restated	**(798.8)**	**(58.1)**	**(210.5)**	**1,541.0**

IAS 34 prohibits the anticipation or deferral of revenues received seasonally or cyclically,[95] or of costs incurred unevenly throughout the financial year,[96] at the interim date if anticipation or deferral would be inappropriate at the year end. This harks back to the principle that assets and liabilities must be recognised and measured using the same criteria that would apply if the interim period was the financial year end.[97] This principle would seem to prevent flexing of costs in seasonal businesses, where to do so, would result in assets or liabilities that would not have been appropriate were the interim period to be the year end.

IAS 34 also requires enterprises to give explanatory comments about the seasonality or cyclicality of interim operations.[98] Where businesses are highly seasonal, IAS 34 encourages reporting of additional information for the twelve months ending on the interim period date and comparatives for the prior twelve month period.[99]

A number of companies give comments on seasonality, or absence thereof as illustrated by Nestlé.

Extract 33.9: Nestlé S.A. (2000)

1. Seasonality

The business of the Group does not present pronounced cyclical patterns, seasonal evolutions in some countries or product groups being compensated within the Group.

Preussag in its first quarter 2001 interim report discusses the seasonal nature of tourism in detail, including the following general comment illustrated below.

Extract 33.10: Preussag AG (Q1, 31 March 2001)

Economic Situation
Results by divisions [extract]

Results were primarily characterised by the seasonal nature of the tourism business which regularly closes in the red in the first quarter due to the significantly reduced business volume in the winter season compared with the summer season on the one hand and the advance expenditure to be effected for the summer season business on the other.

4.4 Taxation

Taxation is assessed on an annual basis, which makes the discrete approach particularly difficult to apply. This is especially so in the UK where, under SSAP 15's[100] partial provision approach to deferred tax and even under the specific full provision method advocated by FRS 19, tax is not accounted for on all timing differences (see Chapter 24). A rigorous application of the discrete approach would, therefore, require a detailed examination of the timing differences which arose in the six months under review, without regard to what might happen in the remainder of the year. This could give rise to some very strange results, particularly for companies whose capital investment programme was weighted towards one end of the year or the other.

For these reasons, the approach generally adopted in practice is to predict what the effective tax rate is likely to be for the year and then to apply it to whatever results are reported for the interim period. There will be an effective annual effective rate to apply to the interim result, even if the result for the year is expected to be breakeven. Where practicable, a separate estimated average annual effective tax rate is applied for each tax jurisdiction or category of income, but often use of weighted average tax rates may achieve a reasonable approximation.[101] While this appears to be an application of the integral approach, it is endorsed by the ASB's Statement, which asserts that it is consistent with the generally recommended discrete approach.[102] Coats Viyella provides an example of this approach:

Extract 33.11: Coats Viyella Plc (2000)

3. Taxation

The taxation charge for the six months ended 30 June 2000 is based on the estimated effective tax rate for the full year, including the effect of prior period tax adjustments together with the estimated taxation payable in respect of the disposal of the Indian Garments business of some £2.4 million.

The Statement says that 'events and expenditure that are expected to fall in the second part of the year and would affect the effective annual tax rate should be brought into the estimate on a prudent basis. Capital expenditure is usually planned in advance; it is, therefore, usually possible to take account of the expected capital allowances in calculating the effective tax rate for the year. It would not normally be appropriate, however, to take account of the tax effects of other significant events that, although expected to arise in the second part of the year, are subject to considerable uncertainty.'[103] Where such events are anticipated, the basis of the effective rate should be explained in the narrative commentary.[104] Similarly the tax effect of exceptional items, where material, should not be included in the effective annual rate applied to pre-exceptional results but should be recognised in the same period as the exceptional item, as illustrated by Coats Viyella above.[105]

The ASB Statement goes on: 'In determining the amount of tax losses and recoverable advance corporation tax to recognise in the interim period, an estimate should be made of the utilisation expected over the whole tax year. The amount recognised in the interim period should be proportional to the profit before tax of the interim period and the estimated annual profit before tax, but limited to the amount recoverable for the year as a whole.'[106] Deferred tax assets for interim losses, therefore, should only be recognised where recoverable in accordance with the accounting standard on deferred tax. The Statement illustrates the treatment of tax losses with the following example:

Example 33.1 Treatment of tax losses brought forward

Company A has losses brought forward of £75,000. It has earned taxable profits of £100,000 in the interim period, but expects to record taxable losses of £40,000 in the remaining part of the year. How should the effect of the opening tax losses be taken into account in the interim period, assuming an effective tax rate of 30%?

The Statement notes that in these circumstances the tax charge for the year will be nil, with £60,000 of the losses being utilised in the full year to relieve an equal amount of profits. But the passage quoted above also says that the amount of losses recognised in the interim period should be limited to the amount recoverable for the year as a whole (£60,000), which means that tax on profits of £40,000 have to be provided in the interim accounts, giving rise to a tax charge of £12,000 for the half year. In the second half of the year, the losses of £40,000 will be relieved by a tax credit of £12,000 that brings the tax charge for the year back to nil.

IAS 34 adopts a similar approach and requires that the income tax expense should be accrued using the estimated weighted average annual income tax rate applied to pre-tax income of the interim period[107] as illustrated by Zellweger Luwa below. This could include the effects of enacted or substantively enacted changes in income tax rates taking effect later in the financial year. Again separate rates for each tax jurisdiction or category of income should be used, but it is acceptable to use weighted average tax rates giving a reasonable approximation. Where the financial reporting and tax year differ, separate rates should be determined for each tax year and applied to the pre-tax income earned in those tax years.[108]

Extract 33.12: Zellweger Luwa AG (2000)

1. Principles of consolidation and valuation [extract]

Income tax expense is recognized based on the best estimate of the weighted average annual income tax rate expected for the full financial year.

An Appendix to IAS 34[109] addresses tax losses in more detail. The guidance is similar to that in the ASB Statement, but as it is expressed in a different way in both documents, it is possible that the recommended treatment of certain tax losses may differ under IAS.

The Appendix to IAS 34 repeats the guidance in IAS 12[110] and states that for carryforward of unused tax losses and tax credits, a deferred tax asset should be recognised 'to the extent that it is probable that future taxable profit will be available against which the unused tax losses and unused tax credits can be utilised.'[111] In assessing whether future taxable profit is available, the criteria described in IAS 12[112] should be applied at the interim date. Where these criteria are met, 'the effect of the tax loss carryforward is reflected in the computation of the estimated average annual effective income tax rate.'[113]

In contrast, 'the benefits of a tax loss carryback are reflected in the interim period in which the related tax loss occurs.'[114] The ASB Statement does not explicitly address carryback of tax losses. Consequently, differences in interpretation between IAS 34 and the ASB Statement may arise. For example, where a loss is reasonably expected in both interim periods and the total loss expected for the year exceeds the amount available for carryback, the Statement could be interpreted as recommending spreading of the benefit of the tax loss carryback throughout the year rather than recognition biased towards the first interim period.

The Appendix to IAS 34 also discusses in more detail the treatment of tax credits, which may for example be based on amounts of capital expenditures, exports, research and development expenditures. Such anticipated benefits are usually granted and calculated on an annual basis and therefore should be reflected in computing the effective annual tax rate. Where they relate to a one-time event, however, they should be excluded from the annual rate and dealt with separately. Occasionally, such tax credits are more akin to a government grant and should be recognised in the interim period in which they arise.[115]

As the interim tax charge is based on an estimate of the weighted average annual rate, the charge in a subsequent interim period may need to be adjusted if that estimate changes.[116] IAS 34 requires disclosure of material changes in estimate of amounts reported in an earlier period, or in the annual financial statements, material changes in estimate of amounts reported in the latest interim financial statements.[117]

4.5 Other items determined on an annual basis

Like tax, a number of other items are also determined only at the end of a year (which is not necessarily always the financial year) or sometimes even a longer period. These include staff bonuses or profit sharing, sales commissions, volume discounts on both purchases and sales, contingent lease payments and so on. The outcome for the whole year should be predicted in order to determine the effective rate to apply in measuring the results for the interim period. While this appears to apply an integral approach, in reality it is no different from the estimates which have to be made in annual accounts whenever the base period for measuring a variable amount of this kind is different from the financial year.

This issue is acknowledged by the ASB Statement, but it argues that provision should be made only where there is a recognisable obligation at the period end, using the same approach as FRS 12[118] on provisions (see Chapter 28). Thus, the Statement would support provision for an estimated liability under a contractual supplier's volume discount, or for a profit-related bonus where the staff's expectations give rise to a constructive obligation, but not for a 'genuinely discretionary one-off bonus given at the end of the year'.[119]

In 2000, Railtrack disclosed in its interim accounts that it has changed its policy for accounting for Performance Regime bonuses to a discrete basis:

> *Extract 33.13: Railtrack Group PLC (2000)*
>
> 1. **BASIS OF PREPARATION** [extract]
>
> The interim financial statements have been prepared using accounting policies set out in the Group's 2000 annual report and accounts.
>
> The Group has changed from accounting for Performance Regime bonuses and penalties on the basis of an estimate of the amounts receivable and payable for the financial year as a whole to a discrete basis. The adoption of discrete accounting for the Performance Regime has increased the Group's equity shareholders' funds at 30 September 1999 by £16m and the profit for the six months ended 30 September 1999 by £16m. The change to discrete accounting for the Performance Regime has had no effect on the results for the year ended 31 March 2000. It is not practical given the current circumstances surrounding performance to estimate the effect of not changing the policy to discrete accounting on the profit for the six months ended 30 September 2000.
>
> **CHAIRMAN'S STATEMENT** [extract]
>
> The interim results reflect a change in the accounting treatment for the performance regime. Performance bonuses and penalties are now reflected in full, within the period in which they are incurred, rather than being smoothed on an estimated basis across the full year.

Bank of Scotland's interim report includes a charge in respect of staff profit sharing schemes, which is explained in this note:

> *Extract 33.14: Bank of Scotland (2000)*
>
> 3. Provision has been made in the Interim Accounts towards the end of year allocation of profit to the Staff Profit Sharing Schemes. This provision is calculated on the results for the half year to 31 August 2000. The actual allocation will be calculated by reference to the results for the full year.

A similar approach is taken by IAS 34 which discusses many examples in an Appendix.[120] An enterprise should apply the same criteria in recognising and measuring a provision at an interim date, as at the end of the financial year. Therefore, as in the UK, contractual volume rebates or discounts, contingent lease payments and staff bonuses giving rise to a legal or constructive obligation at the interim date should be provided for if it is probable they will take effect (even if the required volume or other targets have not yet been met at the interim date) and the amounts can be measured reliably. Similarly, where employer payroll taxes and National Insurance contributions are assessed on an annual basis, the employers related expense should be recognised in interim periods using an estimated annual average effective rate, even if this does not reflect the timing of the payments made. Pension costs should be calculated on a year to date basis using the actuarially determined pension cost rate at the end of the prior year, adjusted for significant market fluctuations, curtailments, settlements, or other one-time events. IAS 34 also discusses the cost of accumulating short-term compensated absences which in accordance with IAS 19[121] should be measured at the amount the enterprise expects to pay as a result of unused entitlement accumulated at the interim date.

Deutsche Bank illustrates a provision for retention payments.

Extract 33.15: Deutsche Bank AG (September 2000)

Restructuring expenses [extract]

Bankers Trust retention payments	In connection with the acquisition of Bankers Trust a retention payment programme was agreed for certain employees. The proportionate share for January to September 2000 amounts to €119 million.
Income from the release of restructuring provisions	As certain restructuring measures will no longer be implemented, €116 million had to be released in particular from the restructuring provision set up in the 1999 financial year in connection with the integration of Bankers Trust and from restructuring provisions in Group Divisions Global Technology and Services as well as Corporates and Real Estate.

4.6 Non-recurring items

When major items of expenditure arise in the first half of the year which will not be repeated in the second (or vice versa), the question arises as to whether these should be spread over the whole year or dealt with in the period in which they fall. Such items may be genuinely one-off, such as reorganisation costs or a loss on repurchasing debt, or they may be cyclical expenditures such as major repairs during an annual shutdown of a plant.

The discrete approach would obviously let all such costs lie in whatever period they are incurred using the same principles as applied at year end and the ASB supports this view, specifically discussing exceptional items.[122] Proponents of the integral approach, on the other hand, might wish to spread them over the year, particularly if they are of a regular but cyclical nature.

IAS 34 requires that costs incurred unevenly during the year should be anticipated or deferred if and only if it would be appropriate to do so were the interim period the end of the financial year.[123] This policy is illustrated by Zellweger Luwa below, without being specific about what types of income and expenditure occur unevenly during the financial year. Consequently, it will generally be inappropriate to anticipate the cost of a major planned periodic maintenance or overhaul, or other planned (but usually discretionary) costs like employee training or charitable donations. Such costs will generally not give rise to an obligation at the interim date.[124]

Extract 33.16: Zellweger Luwa AG (2000)

1. **Principles of consolidation and valuation** [extract]

Items of income and expenditure which occur unevenly during the financial year are anticipated or deferred in the interim financial statements only if it would also be appropriate to anticipate or defer such items at the end of the financial year.

Again, this issue can be defused to some extent by disclosure. The desire to spread these costs springs from a concern that false conclusions will be drawn about the sustainable profitability of the business and in particular the likely result for the full year. But so long as such costs are disclosed and appropriately explained, the reader will not be likely to jump to the wrong conclusion about the company's underlying profitability.

4.7 Asset values and use of estimates

UK GAAP requires current assets to be carried at the lower of cost and net realisable value and fixed assets to be written down to their recoverable amount if they are impaired. The question which arises is whether such assessments have to be made at the date of the interim balance sheet in just the same way as they are made at the end of the year. The ASB's support for the discrete approach would suggest that they should.

We are not convinced that this will always make sense. In the case of stocks, for example, there may be a fall in value at the half-year which simply reflects the seasonality of the product, but which will be restored by the year end. Also, some accounting routines are governed by accounting standards which were written with annual accounts in mind. For example, SSAP 13[125] permits development expenditure to be capitalised only when the profitable outcome of the project can be foreseen (see Chapter 11 at 2.4.2). Having to make this assessment more frequently because of shorter reporting periods would result in less being capitalised, because it would curtail the time available for the expenditure to prove its worth. Again, we think this would be inappropriate, and that an annual perspective should be retained. In general, we do not believe that the needs of interim reporting should affect the application of accounting standards in this way.

An Appendix to IAS 34[126] discusses the application of its measurement rules to asset values, and certain approaches that may be permissible in the UK are, therefore, restricted. For example, as discussed in 4.1 above, IAS 34 requires the normal criteria for measurement and recognition of assets to be applied at the interim date. Costs should not be deferred in the hope that the recognition criteria will be met later in the year.[127] In terms of impairment, an entity should apply the same impairment criteria at an interim date as at the year end. It should review for indications of significant impairment in the interim period and determine whether a more detailed calculation is required.[128]

Similarly, the same measurement principles for inventories should be adopted as at year end, although greater use of estimates are frequently used at an interim date. Net realisable values should be determined using selling prices and costs to complete and dispose at the interim date; if appropriate, a write down should be reversed in a subsequent interim period. Manufacturing cost variances should be recognised in income at the interim date to the same extent that they would be at a year end (and therefore should not be deferred even if the variances are expected to be absorbed by year end), so that inventory is stated at its portion of the actual cost of manufacture. However, in an apparent but sensible departure from this principle, a temporary reduction (e.g. due to a one-off strike or seasonal fluctuations), which is expected to be restored by year end, in the quantity of LIFO inventories should not be reflected in an interim inventory valuation.[129] This is justified by reference to the principle that the frequency of measurement of an entity's results should not affect the measurement of its annual results, mainly because it could have a distortive effect on the interim results and also because LIFO measurements are often tax driven and therefore frequently made on an annual basis.

The ASB's Statement does modify its approach for certain assets. It says that it would be in order to leave revalued properties at the amounts shown at the previous year end where these are the most recent valuations (but it would like this fact disclosed and it encourages commentary on significant price movements since the last valuation),[130] and also that new actuarial valuations of the pension scheme would only be required if a significant event rendered the previous estimate misleading.[131] However, it says that where more recent valuations are available, they should be used in the interim financial statements and quoted stocks carried at market value should be updated to values ruling at the end of the interim period.[132]

Unusually, Liberty has a practice of valuing properties at the half-year, as disclosed in this extract.

Extract 33.17: Liberty International PLC (2000)

Investment properties Completed investment properties are professionally valued on an open market basis by external valuers at the balance sheet date.

IAS 34 also discusses the use of estimates and also illustrates this with specific examples in an Appendix.[133] The measurement procedures followed in an interim financial report should be designed to ensure appropriate disclosure of all relevant and reliable material financial information. However, the standard recognises that interim financial statements will generally require greater use of estimation methods than at the year end.[134] Consequently, in measuring assets and liabilities there may be less use of outside experts in determining amounts for items such as provisions, contingencies, revalued fixed assets or pensions. Reliable measurement of such amounts may simply involve updating the year end position.[135] Similarly, it may not be necessary to perform a full stock take at an interim date; estimates using sales margins or for LIFO stocks, using representative samples for each LIFO layer or pool and inflation indices may be sufficient.[136]

5 REQUIREMENTS FOR PRELIMINARY ANNOUNCEMENTS

5.1 Introduction

The preliminary announcement is an important factor in the market's evaluation of a company's performance. Under the Listing Rules of the UK Listing Authority, listed companies are required to notify the Company Announcements Office of their preliminary statement of annual results and dividends (known as the preliminary announcement) without delay after board approval. There is a widely held view that the preliminary announcement is more price-influential than the subsequent publication of a company's full annual report and accounts. Consequently there has been a tendency for companies to publish more information in their preliminary announcements than is strictly required by the UK Listing Authority. These developments clearly influenced the ASB to publish in July 1998 its non-mandatory Statement – *Preliminary Announcements* – which is intended to provide 'valuable guidance for directors wishing to embrace best practice when preparing their preliminary announcements.'[137] The Statement provides voluntary guidance which is intended to supplement the requirements of the UK Listing Authority.[138]

The Statement intends to 'improve the timeliness, quality, relevance and consistency of preliminary announcements within the constraints of reliability.'[139] The Statement refers to the similarity between interim reports and preliminary announcements and states that their contents are likely to be similar.[140] However, as forewarned in the introduction to the Statement,[141] the interaction of the preliminary announcement with the year end financial reporting structure has now been examined as part of a wide-ranging Company Law Review. The Company Law Review Steering Group have recently issued their *Final Report* and its proposals, which are briefly discussed in 1 above, are being considered by the Government.

IAS does not address preliminary announcements. The content of preliminary announcements for those companies adopting IAS is, therefore, governed by the regulatory requirements of the exchanges involved.

5.2 The Listing Rules

The Listing Rules require listed companies to make a preliminary announcement by notifying the Company Announcements Office of its annual results immediately after board approval has been obtained.[142] This information is then disseminated by electronic means by the Stock Exchange's Regulatory News Service. It is not mandatory for preliminary announcements to be sent to shareholders; in practice, often only financial analysts and institutional shareholders receive them. The Listing Rules mandate publication of the preliminary announcement within 120 days of the year end (unless in exceptional circumstances the UK Listing Authority grants an extension).[143]

The preliminary announcement must have been agreed with the auditors and must show at least the items required to be shown in a half-yearly report (see 2.1 above). These figures should be shown in the form of a table, consistent with the presentation to be adopted in the full annual accounts. The announcement must also show any significant additional information necessary for the purpose of assessing the results.[144]

The preliminary announcement must also contain details of any decision to pay or make any dividend or other distribution on the listed shares or to withhold any dividend or interest payment on listed securities, giving details of:

- the exact net amount payable per share;
- the payment date;
- the record date (where applicable); and
- any foreign income dividend election, together with any income tax treated as paid at the lower rate and not repayable.[145]

If the audit report is likely to be qualified, details of the nature of the qualification need to be given.[146]

Although the Listing Rules require the preliminary announcement to have been 'agreed' with the company's auditors, this term is not defined. There is clearly an expectation that the information will be consistent with that in the audited financial statements, which at that stage may not be complete. However, guidance for auditors was issued in July 1998 by the Auditing Practices Board in Bulletin 1998/7 – *The Auditors' Association with Preliminary Announcements*.[147] The Bulletin includes guidance on:

- audit procedures to be completed before agreeing an 'unaudited' announcement;
- communication of the auditors' agreement to the directors; and
- actions to be taken when directors make an announcement without agreement.

5.3 The ASB's Statement

5.3.1 *Overview of the Statement*

In July 1998, the Accounting Standards Board published a non-mandatory Statement – *Preliminary Announcements*. It follows the same approach adopted in the Statement on Interim Reports (see 2.2 above).

The Statement is non-mandatory and has been issued as a result of companies frequently producing far more comprehensive and detailed preliminary announcements than the then Listing Rules actually required. The ASB therefore took the view, as with its interim reporting statement, that guidance about best practice would be valuable, thereby promoting increased comparability between preliminary announcements and previously published accounts, while also being consistent with the subsequently published full annual report and accounts. The content and presentation recommended for preliminary announcements are in line with current reporting practice, but there is considerable scope for the individual company to exercise judgement over exactly what degree of detail is included. The Statement is full of phrases, relating to what should be disclosed, such as: 'significant movements', 'sufficient information should be given to understand', and 'should explain any other matter that the directors think would help users'. Therefore much of what is recommended is of a generalised rather than specific nature.

5.3.2 *Statements to be included*

As for interim reports, the ASB calls for preliminary announcements to contain:

- a narrative commentary, along similar lines to the operating and financial review, although not as lengthy and with greater focus on areas of change;[148]
- a summarised profit and loss account, based on the presentation used in the full accounts;[149]
- a statement of total recognised gains and losses;[150]
- a summarised balance sheet, using similar presentation to that in the full accounts;[151] and
- a summarised cash flow statement, using the headings stipulated in FRS 1.[152]

The Statement also recommends that segmental information should be given for turnover and profit on the same basis as in the full annual report[153] and that the turnover and operating profit relating to acquisitions and discontinued operations be presented on the face of the summarised profit and loss account.[154]

The Statement also notes that the Listing Rules require earnings per share to be disclosed, and says that it should be calculated and disclosed in the same manner as is used in the annual accounts. This means that both basic and diluted figures should be given, and companies who give additional versions of earnings per share in their annual accounts should also do so in their preliminary announcement.[155]

The information to be included is, therefore, essentially the same as that recommended for interim reports as discussed at 2.2.1 above.

The ASB notes that the 'market normally tends to react only to new information arising from the final interim period (i.e. the second half, or if quarterly reporting is adopted, the fourth quarter of the year) that has not been previously reported upon. However, the preliminary announcement and the annual results have traditionally focused on the results for the year, generally without presenting or discussing the results for the final interim period of the year. This means that the results for this period are subsumed within those for the year and not generally reported to shareholders.'[156] Accordingly, the Statement calls for the salient events and features of the final interim period to be referred to and explained as part of the management commentary.[157] It also encourages companies to give separate presentation of the final interim period figures, together with corresponding amounts, although in some cases it suggests that a reference to the key figures in the narrative commentary will suffice.[158]

5.3.3 *Accounting policies and prior year adjustments*

The accounting policies and presentation of figures in the preliminary announcement should be consistent with those in the full accounts, that have yet to be published.[159] The ASB recommends that the preliminary announcement should include a statement that they are prepared on the basis of the accounting policies as set out in the most recently published set of annual accounts. Accounting policies need to be stated and explained only where they differ from those adopted in the previous year.[160] Following a change in accounting policy, the amounts for the current and prior years should be restated on the basis of the new policy, consistent with the annual accounts. The cumulative effect on opening reserves should be disclosed at the foot of the statement of total recognised gains and losses of the year. Similar disclosures are recommended in respect of other prior year adjustments.[161]

5.3.4 *Distribution*

The Statement notes that although it is not mandatory for preliminary announcements to be sent to shareholders, all shareholders should be entitled, on request, to have access to the preliminary announcement as soon as it becomes available,[162] and provides the following examples of how this can be achieved:[163]

- press advertisements containing the essential details of the preliminary announcement;
- pre-registration schemes (e.g. with reply cards that could be sent out with interim reports);
- publicising an address or telephone number by which shareholders can obtain copies of the announcement; and
- notifying shareholders (e.g. with the last interim report of the period) of the exact date that the announcement is expected to be issued, so that they can take appropriate action.

It also recommends that companies explore the use of electronic means, e.g. the Internet, as a way of disseminating financial information, and in particular the preliminary announcement, to a wider audience.[164] As discussed in 1 above, the *Final Report* of the Company Law Review Steering Group proposes immediate publication of preliminary announcements on a website, with electronic notification of publication to those shareholders that register for this.

5.3.5 *Reliability*

As noted at 5.2 above, the Listing Rules require the preliminary announcement to be agreed by the auditors before publication. The Statement indicates that there is an expectation that the information in the preliminary announcement will be consistent with that in the audited accounts and to achieve this:

- the audit should be complete or at least at an advanced stage at the date of the preliminary announcement;
- all the figures in the preliminary announcement should agree with the figures in the audited accounts or in the draft accounts; and

- the other information and commentary in the preliminary announcement should be consistent with the figures in the preliminary announcement and with the audited or draft accounts.[165]

The ASB emphasises that the overriding consideration is that the information in the preliminary announcement should be reliable and not subject to later alterations. The risk of later changes to figures can only be extinguished if the preliminary announcement is issued at the same time as the full accounts are approved by the directors and the auditors have signed their opinion on them. However, against this, the ASB notes that there is the need for timely publication of price-sensitive information and that the Listing Rules require the preliminary announcement to be notified to the Exchange without delay after board approval.[166] The Statement goes on to say: 'It is accepted practice, therefore, that, where the reliability of the information in the announcement is not compromised, the main figures and highlights from the financial statements are issued as the preliminary announcement when the audit is at an advanced stage (i.e. when any outstanding audit matters are unlikely to have a material impact on the financial statements or disclosures in the preliminary announcement), but before the audit report on the financial statements has been signed.'[167]

5.3.6 *Timescale*

The Statement notes that the benefits of providing the market with early notification of the annual results needs to be balanced against the practical problems of producing the information at an acceptable cost, and with the same reliability as is required of the full annual accounts. With this in mind, the ASB suggests that companies should consider ways of accelerating their year end timetable, so that they can issue their preliminary announcement as soon as possible after the year end. Within the bounds of practicality, it encourages companies to issue their preliminary announcements within 60 days of the year end.[168] At the time, the Listing Rules effectively allowed six months for publication (being the deadline for the annual accounts); in January 2000, the Listing Rules were amended to require publication of the preliminary announcement within 120 days of the year end.[169]

5.3.7 *Companies Act*

The Companies Act does not contain any specific provisions relating to preliminary announcements. However, for the purpose of section 240 of the Act, preliminary announcements constitute non-statutory accounts and, therefore, they must include a statement indicating:

- that they are not the statutory accounts;
- whether statutory accounts dealing with any financial year covered by the announcement have been delivered to the Registrar of Companies;
- whether the auditors have reported on the statutory accounts for any such financial year; and

- if so, whether any auditors' report so made was qualified or contained a statement under section 237(2) or (3) (accounting records or returns inadequate, accounts not agreeing with records and returns or failure to obtain necessary information and explanations).[170]

As the preliminary announcement will normally include comparative figures, the statement will need to refer not only to the position for the current financial period, but also for the comparative period.

6 CONCLUSION

Interim reports and preliminary announcements were for many years neglected subjects in the UK. Practice had grown up around the minimal reporting requirements of the Listing Rules, although major companies tended to go considerably beyond that minimum. The ASB's Statements have codified these better practices by prescribing more comprehensive reporting packages and have also addressed the issues of accounting measurement that interim reporting throws up.

Companies that present their interim financial statements in accordance with IAS, must follow the IASC's standard on interim reporting, IAS 34. However, that standard states that companies may still adopt IAS in the annual financial statements but not in interim reports. In such cases, they must not state that the interim financial statements comply with IAS.[171] IAS does not address preliminary announcements.

It has to be said, however, that neither the ASB or IASC's discussion of measurement issues in interim reporting is not wholly convincing. The theoretical debate between the discrete approach and the integral approach remains a sterile one, because the distinctions between the methods are more than a little blurred in practice. Furthermore, the actual recommendations made by the ASB and other standard setters who have addressed these issues still involve a number of pragmatic compromises.

The underlying issue that has been inadequately discussed concerns the essential purpose of interim reporting. The ASB's Statement asserts that 'interim reports, like annual financial statements, are presented in respect of a distinct reporting period. A fair assessment of the progress of the business can be made only if the interim accounts are presented on a consistent and comparable basis taking one reporting period with another.'[172] Starting from that presumption, it is no surprise that the discrete approach is favoured, particularly as this is such a tidy answer for a standard setter to adopt. But is interim reporting *really* only a more frequent version of annual reporting, but with fewer disclosures? This is probably not how it is perceived by preparers and users, who see it much more as a signalling device as to the outcome of the real period they are interested in, the financial year. It would be fruitful to give deeper consideration to the essential purpose of the exercise before the next revision of the rules on interim reporting is undertaken.

The role of the preliminary announcement and its interaction with the year end reporting process has recently been considered as part of a wide-ranging Company Law Review (see 1 above). The Company Law Review Steering Group's *Final Report*[173] notably proposes leaving regulation of preliminary announcements to market regulators, but where a preliminary announcement is prepared, it proposes that it should be published immediately on a website, with electronic notification of this fact to shareholders who register for this.

References

1 Statement, *Interim Reports*, ASB, September 1997.
2 Statement, *Preliminary Announcements*, ASB, July 1998.
3 IAS 34, *Interim Financial Reporting*, IASC, February 1998.
4 *Ibid.*, para. 2.
5 *The Listing Rules*, Chapter 25, Financial Services Authority.
6 *Towards an EU regime on transparency obligations of issuers whose securities are admitted to trading on a regulated market*, Consultation Document of the Services of the Internal Market Directorate General, European Commission, July 2001.
7 CA 85, s 270(4).
8 Discussion Paper, *Year-End Financial Reports: improving communication*, ASB, February 2000.
9 *Modern Company Law for a Competitive Economy: Developing the Framework*, A consultation document from the Company Law Review Steering Group, Chapter 5, March 2000.
10 *Modern Company Law for a Competitive Economy: Completing the Structure*, A consultation document from the Company Law Review Steering Group, Chapter 6, November 2000.
11 *Modern Company Law for a Competitive Economy: Final Report*, Company Law Review Steering Group, Chapter 8, July 2001.
12 *The Listing Rules*, Chapter 25, paras. 25.13–25.16.
13 On 28 May 2001, the EU Regular Reporting Directive 82/121/EEC was repealed and its text was included in Directive 2001/34/EC on the admission of securities to official stock exchange listing and on information to be published on those securities, which consolidated the provisions of Directives 79/279/EEC, 82/121/EEC and 88/627/EEC.
14 SI 1984 No. 716.
15 *The Listing Rules*, Chapter 12, paras. 12.46 and 12.52.
16 *Ibid.*, para. 12.52.
17 *Ibid.*, para. 12.47.
18 FRS 19, *Deferred Tax*, ASB, December 2000.
19 FRS 3, *Reporting Financial Performance*, ASB, October 1992.
20 *Interim Reports*, para. 11.
21 *The Listing Rules*, para. 12.58.
22 *Ibid.*
23 *Ibid.*, para. 12.59.
24 *Ibid.*, para. 12.53.
25 *Ibid.*, para. 12.55.
26 *Ibid.*, para. 12.56.
27 *Ibid.*, The Combined Code Principles of Good Governance and Code of Best Practice, Committee on Corporate Governance, provision D.1.2 , June 1998.
28 *Ibid.*, para. 12.48.
29 *Ibid.*, para. 12.50.
30 *Ibid.*, para. 12.49.
31 *Ibid.*, para. 12.60.
32 Bulletin 1999/4, *Review of Interim Financial Information*, APB, July 1999. This has been in part superseded by Bulletin 2001/2 *Revisions to the wording of auditors' reports on financial statements and the interim review report*, APB, January 2001.
33 *The Listing Rules*, para. 12.54.
34 *Interim Reports*, para. 3.
35 *Ibid.*, para. 31.
36 *Ibid.*, paras. 55 and 56.
37 *The Listing Rules*, para. 12.52.
38 CA 85, s 240(3).
39 *Interim Reports*, para. 57.
40 *Ibid.*, paras. 40 and 45–47.
41 *Ibid.*, paras. 40 and 43–44.
42 *Ibid.*, para. 41.
43 *Ibid.*, para. 42.
44 *Ibid.*, para. 48.

45 *Ibid.*, para. 52.
46 *Ibid.*, para. 52 and Appendix I, para. 8.
47 *Ibid*, para. 51.
48 FRS 1, *Cash Flow statements*, ASB, Revised October 1996.
49 *Interim Reports*, para. 53.
50 FRS 9, *Associates and Joint Ventures*, ASB, March 1996, para. 61.
51 *Interim Reports,* para. 54.
52 *Ibid.*, para. 49.
53 *Ibid.*, paras. 26 and 50.
54 *Ibid.*, para. 12.
55 *Ibid.*, paras. 34–39.
56 IAS 34, paras. 1 and 2.
57 IAS 1, *Presentation of Financial Statements*, IASC, Revised July 1997.
58 IAS 34, paras. 5–7.
59 *Ibid*, para. 7.
60 *Ibid.*, paras. 8 and 13.
61 *Ibid.*, para. 10.
62 *Ibid.*, para. 13.
63 *Ibid.*, para. 14.
64 *Ibid.*, para. 20.
65 *Ibid*, paras. 28, 43 and 44.
66 IAS 8, *Net Profit or Loss for the Period, Fundamental Errors and Changes in Accounting Policies*, IASC, Revised December 1993, para. 54.
67 IAS 34, paras. 43 and 44.
68 IAS 39, *Financial instruments: recognition and measurement*, IASC, Revised October 2000.
69 IAS 14, *Segment Reporting*, IASC, Revised 1997, para. 3.
70 IAS 34, para. 16.
71 *Ibid.*, para. 19.
72 *Ibid.*, para. 17.
73 *Ibid.*, para. 18.
74 *Ibid.*, para. 16(d).
75 *Ibid.*, para. 26.
76 *Interim Reports*, para. 8.
77 *Ibid.*, para. 7 and Appendix I, para. 1.
78 *Ibid.*, para. 8.
79 APB 28, *Interim Financial Reporting*, Accounting Principles Board, May 1973.
80 IAS 34, paras. 28 and 29.
81 *Ibid.,* para. 30.
82 *Ibid.*
83 IAS 38, *Intangible Assets*, IASC, July 1998, para. 59.
84 IAS 34, paras. 16, 26, 35–36.
85 *Interim Reports*, para. 28.
86 IAS 34, paras. 23–25.
87 *Interim Reports*, para. 25.
88 IAS 21, *The Effects of Changes in Foreign Exchange Rates*, IASC, Revised 1993, paras. 30-31.
89 IAS 34, Appendix B, paras. 29–31.
90 Unilever now reports in Euros but still adopts a similar approach in translating the results in both years at constant exchange rates, being the annual average exchange rates for the previous year. British American Tobacco takes a slightly different approach. It translates the current period's results at the average rate for that period, but the comparatives for the quarter and the preceding full year are both translated using the average rates for the preceding full year.
91 IAS 34, Appendix B, paras. 32–34.
92 UITF 9, *Accounting for operations in hyper-inflationary economies*, para. 6.
93 *Interim Reports*, para. 16.
94 *Ibid.*, para. 37.
95 IAS 34, para. 37.
96 *Ibid.*, para. 39.
97 *Ibid.*, para. 29.
98 *Ibid.*, para. 16.
99 *Ibid.*, para. 21.
100 SSAP 15, *Accounting for deferred tax*, ASC, Revised May 1985.
101 *Interim Reports*, paras. 18–19.
102 *Ibid.*, para. 8.
103 *Ibid.*, para. 21.
104 *Ibid.*, para. 22.
105 *Ibid.*, para. 20.
106 *Ibid.*, para. 24.
107 IAS 34, para. 30 and Appendix B, para. 12.
108 *Ibid.*, Appendix B, paras. 13–18.
109 *Ibid.*, Appendix B.
110 IAS 12, *Income Taxes*, IASC, Revised October 2000.
111 *Ibid.*, para. 34.
112 *Ibid.*, para. 36.
113 IAS 34, Appendix B, para. 21.
114 *Ibid.*, para. 20.
115 *Ibid.*, para. 19.
116 IAS 34, para. 30.
117 *Ibid.*, paras. 16 and 26.
118 FRS 12, *Provisions, Contingent Liabilities and Contingent Assets*, ASB, September 1998.
119 *Interim Reports*, para. 15.
120 IAS 34, Appendix B, paras. 3–7, 9–11, 23.
121 IAS 19, *Employee Benefits*, IASC, Revised 2000, para. 14.
122 *Interim Reports*, paras. 8 and 45.
123 IAS 34, para. 39.
124 *Ibid.*, Appendix B, paras. 2 and 11.
125 SSAP 13, *Accounting for research and development*, ASC, Revised January 1989.
126 IAS 34, Appendix B.
127 *Ibid.*, para. 30 and Appendix B, para. 8.
128 *Ibid.*, Appendix B, paras. 35–36.
129 *Ibid.*, paras. 25–28.
130 *Interim Reports,* para. 26.
131 *Ibid.*, para. 27.
132 *Ibid.*, paras. 26 and 27.
133 IAS 34, para. 41 and Appendix C.
134 *Ibid.*, para. 41.

135 *Ibid.*, Appendix C, paras. 3, 4, 6–8.
136 *Ibid.*, para. 1.
137 Statement, *Preliminary Announcements*, ASB, July 1998, Foreword.
138 *Ibid.*, Introduction.
139 *Ibid.*
140 *Ibid.*
141 *Ibid.*
142 *The Listing Rules*, para. 12.40.
143 *Ibid.*
144 *Ibid.*, para. 12.40(a).
145 *Ibid.*, para. 12.40(c).
146 *Ibid.*, para. 12.40(a)(iii).
147 Bulletin 1998/7, *The Auditors' Association with Preliminary Announcements*, APB, July 1998.
148 *Preliminary announcements*, paras. 27–32.
149 *Ibid.*, paras. 36–41.
150 *Ibid.*, paras. 42 and 43.
151 *Ibid.*, para. 44.
152 *Ibid.*, paras. 45 and 46.
153 *Ibid.*, para. 38.
154 *Ibid.*, para. 37.
155 *Ibid.*, para. 41.
156 *Ibid.*, para. 33.
157 *Ibid.*, para. 34.
158 *Ibid.*, para. 35.
159 *Ibid.*, para. 16.
160 *Ibid.*, para. 17.
161 *Ibid.*, para. 18.
162 *Ibid.*, para. 6.
163 *Ibid.*, para. 8.
164 *Ibid.*, para. 7.
165 *Ibid.*, para. 12.
166 *Ibid.*, paras. 13 and 14.
167 *Ibid.*, para. 14.
168 *Ibid.*, para. 9.
169 *Listing Rules*, para. 12.40.
170 CA 85, s240(3).
171 IAS 34, paras. 2–3.
172 *Interim Reports*, para. 4.
173 *Modern Company Law for a Competitive Economy: Final Report.*

Index of extracts from UK GAAP accounts

Index of extracts from IAS accounts

NOTES

NOTES

NOTES

NOTES

NOTES

NOTES

NOTES

NOTES

THE UNIVERSITY OF BIRMINGHAM
INFORMATION SERVICES